PEARSON ALWAYS LEARNING

University Calculus

Third Custom Edition for University of Massachusetts Lowell

Taken from:

University Calculus: Early Transcendentals, Second Edition
by Joel Hass, Maurice D. Weir, and George B. Thomas, Jr.

Fundamentals of Precalculus, Second Edition
by Mark Dugopolski

Cover Art: Jean-Francois COLONNA (CMAP/ECOLE POLYTECHNIQUE, www.lactamme.polytechnique.fr)

Taken from:

University Calculus: Early Transcendentals, Second Edition
by Joel Hass, Maurice D. Weir, and George B. Thomas, Jr.

Published by Addison Wesley
Boston, Massachusetts 02116

Fundamentals of Precalculus, Second Edition
by Mark Dugopolski

Published by Addison Wesley

This special edition published in cooperation with Pearson Learning Solutions.

Pearson Learning Solutions, 501 Boylston Street, Suite 900, Boston, MA 02116
A Pearson Education Company
www.pearsoned.com

Printed in the United States of America

5 6 7 8 9 10 0BRV 16 15 14 13

000200010270775525

CY

PEARSON

ISBN 10: 1-256-29019-X
ISBN 13: 978-1-256-29019-3

Algebra

Subsets of the Real Numbers

Natural numbers = $\{1, 2, 3, \ldots\}$
Whole numbers = $\{0, 1, 2, 3, \ldots\}$
Integers = $\{\ldots -3, -2, -1, 0, 1, 2, 3, \ldots\}$
Rational = $\left\{\frac{a}{b} \middle| a \text{ and } b \text{ are integers with } b \neq 0\right\}$
Irrational = $\{x | x \text{ is not rational}\}$

Properties of the Real Numbers

For all real numbers a, b, and c

$a + b$ and ab are real numbers.	Closure
$a + b = b + a$; $a \cdot b = b \cdot a$	Commutative
$(a + b) + c = a + (b + c)$; $(ab)c = a(bc)$	Associative
$a(b + c) = ab + ac$; $a(b - c) = ab - ac$	Distributive
$a + 0 = a$; $1 \cdot a = a$	Identity
$a + (-a) = 0$; $a \cdot \frac{1}{a} = 1 \quad (a \neq 0)$	Inverse
$a \cdot 0 = 0$	Multiplication property of 0

Absolute Value

$$|a| = \begin{cases} a & \text{for } a \geq 0 \\ -a & \text{for } a < 0 \end{cases}$$

$\sqrt{x^2} = |x|$ for any real x

$|x| = k \Leftrightarrow x = k$ or $x = -k \quad (k > 0)$

$|x| < k \Leftrightarrow -k < x < k \quad (k > 0)$

$|x| > k \Leftrightarrow x < -k$ or $x > k \quad (k > 0)$

(The symbol $\Leftrightarrow$ means "if and only if.")

Interval Notation

$(a, b) = \{x \| a < x < b\}$	$[a, b] = \{x \| a \leq x \leq b\}$
$(a, b] = \{x \| a < x \leq b\}$	$[a, b) = \{x \| a \leq x < b\}$
$(-\infty, a) = \{x \| x < a\}$	$(a, \infty) = \{x \| x > a\}$
$(-\infty, a] = \{x \| x \leq a\}$	$[a, \infty) = \{x \| x \geq a\}$

Exponents

$a^n = a \cdot a \cdot \cdots \cdot a$ (n factors of a)

$a^0 = 1 \qquad a^{-n} = \frac{1}{a^n}$

$a^r a^s = a^{r+s} \qquad \frac{a^r}{a^s} = a^{r-s}$

$(a^r)^s = a^{rs} \qquad (ab)^r = a^r b^r$

$\left(\frac{a}{b}\right)^r = \frac{a^r}{b^r} \qquad \left(\frac{a}{b}\right)^{-r} = \left(\frac{b}{a}\right)^r$

Radicals

$a^{1/n} = \sqrt[n]{a} \qquad a^{m/n} = (\sqrt[n]{a})^m = \sqrt[n]{a^m}$

$\sqrt[n]{ab} = \sqrt[n]{a} \cdot \sqrt[n]{b} \qquad \sqrt[n]{\frac{a}{b}} = \frac{\sqrt[n]{a}}{\sqrt[n]{b}}$

Factoring

$a^2 + 2ab + b^2 = (a + b)^2$

$a^2 - 2ab + b^2 = (a - b)^2$

$a^2 - b^2 = (a + b)(a - b)$

$a^3 - b^3 = (a - b)(a^2 + ab + b^2)$

$a^3 + b^3 = (a + b)(a^2 - ab + b^2)$

Rational Expressions

$\frac{ac}{bc} = \frac{a}{b} \qquad \frac{a}{b} + \frac{c}{d} = \frac{ad + bc}{bd}$

$\frac{a}{b} \cdot \frac{c}{d} = \frac{ac}{bd} \qquad \frac{a}{b} \div \frac{c}{d} = \frac{a}{b} \cdot \frac{d}{c}$

Quadratic Formula

The solutions to $ax^2 + bx + c = 0$ with $a \neq 0$ are

$$x = \frac{-b \pm \sqrt{b^2 - 4ac}}{2a}.$$

Distance Formula

The distance from (x_1, y_1) to (x_2, y_2), is

$$\sqrt{(x_2 - x_1)^2 + (y_2 - y_1)^2}.$$

Algebra Formulas were taken from *Fundamentals of Precalculus,* Second Edition by Mark Dugopolski.

Algebra

Midpoint Formula

The midpoint of the line segment with endpoints (x_1, y_1) and (x_2, y_2) is

$$\left(\frac{x_1 + x_2}{2}, \frac{y_1 + y_2}{2}\right).$$

Slope Formula

The slope of the line through (x_1, y_1) and (x_2, y_2) is

$$\frac{y_2 - y_1}{x_2 - x_1} \quad (\text{for } x_1 \neq x_2).$$

Linear Function

$f(x) = mx + b$ with $m \neq 0$

Graph is a line with slope m.

Quadratic Function

$f(x) = ax^2 + bx + c$ with $a \neq 0$

Graph is a parabola.

Polynomial Function

$f(x) = a_n x^n + a_{n-1}x^{n-1} + \cdots + a_1 x + a_0$ for n a nonnegative integer

Rational Function

$f(x) = \dfrac{p(x)}{q(x)}$, where p and q are polynomial functions with $q(x) \neq 0$

Exponential and Logarithmic Functions

$f(x) = a^x$ for $a > 0$ and $a \neq 1$

$f(x) = \log_a(x)$ for $a > 0$ and $a \neq 1$

Properties of Logarithms

Base-a logarithm: $y = \log_a(x) \Leftrightarrow a^y = x$

Natural logarithm: $y = \ln(x) \Leftrightarrow e^y = x$

Common logarithm: $y = \log(x) \Leftrightarrow 10^y = x$

One-to-one: $a^{x_1} = a^{x_2} \Leftrightarrow x_1 = x_2$

$\log_a(x_1) = \log_a(x_2) \Leftrightarrow x_1 = x_2$

$\log_a(a) = 1$ $\quad$ $\log_a(1) = 0$

$\log_a(a^x) = x$ $\quad$ $a^{\log_a(N)} = N$

$\log_a(MN) = \log_a(M) + \log_a(N)$

$\log_a(M/N) = \log_a(M) - \log_a(N)$

$\log_a(M^x) = x \cdot \log_a(M)$

$\log_a(1/N) = -\log_a(N)$

$$\log_a(M) = \frac{\log_b(M)}{\log_b(a)} = \frac{\ln(M)}{\ln(a)} = \frac{\log(M)}{\log(a)}$$

Compound Interest

P = principal, t = time in years, r = annual interest rate, and A = amount:

$A = P\left(1 + \dfrac{r}{n}\right)^{nt}$ (compounded n times/year)

$A = Pe^{rt}$ (compounded continuously)

Variation

Direct: $y = kx$ $\quad (k \neq 0)$
Inverse: $y = k/x$ $\quad (k \neq 0)$
Joint: $y = kxz$ $\quad (k \neq 0)$

Straight Line

Slope-intercept form: $y = mx + b$
Slope: m $\quad$ y-intercept: $(0, b)$
Point-slope form: $y - y_1 = m(x - x_1)$
Standard form: $Ax + By = C$
Horizontal: $y = k$ $\quad$ Vertical: $x = k$

Algebra

Parabola

$y = a(x - h)^2 + k \qquad (a \neq 0)$
Vertex: (h, k)
Axis of symmetry: $x = h$

Focus: $(h, k + p)$, where $a = \dfrac{1}{4p}$

Directrix: $y = k - p$

Circle

$(x - h)^2 + (y - k)^2 = r^2 \qquad (r > 0)$
Center: (h, k) Radius: r
$x^2 + y^2 = r^2$
Center $(0, 0)$ Radius: r

Ellipse

$\dfrac{x^2}{a^2} + \dfrac{y^2}{b^2} = 1 \qquad (a > b > 0)$

Center: $(0, 0)$ Major axis: horizontal
Foci: $(\pm c, 0)$, where $c^2 = a^2 - b^2$

$\dfrac{x^2}{b^2} + \dfrac{y^2}{a^2} = 1 \qquad (a > b > 0)$

Center: $(0, 0)$ Major axis: vertical
Foci: $(0, \pm c)$, where $c^2 = a^2 - b^2$

Hyperbola

$\dfrac{x^2}{a^2} - \dfrac{y^2}{b^2} = 1$

Center: $(0, 0)$ Vertices: $(\pm a, 0)$
Foci: $(\pm c, 0)$, where $c^2 = a^2 + b^2$

Asymptotes: $y = \pm\dfrac{b}{a}x$

$\dfrac{y^2}{a^2} - \dfrac{x^2}{b^2} = 1$

Center: $(0, 0)$ Vertices: $(0, \pm a)$
Foci: $(0, \pm c)$, where $c^2 = a^2 + b^2$

Asymptotes: $y = \pm\dfrac{a}{b}x$

Arithmetic Sequence

$a_1, a_1 + d, a_1 + 2d, a_1 + 3d, \ldots$

Formula for nth term: $a_n = a_1 + (n - 1)d$

Sum of n terms:

$$S_n = \sum_{i=1}^{n} [a_1 + (i - 1)d] = \frac{n}{2}(a_1 + a_n)$$

Geometric Sequence

$a_1, a_1 r, a_1 r^2, a_1 r^3, \ldots$

Formula for nth term: $a_n = a_1 r^{n-1}$

Sum of n terms when $r \neq 1$:

$$S_n = \sum_{i=1}^{n} a_1 r^{i-1} = \frac{a_1 - a_1 r^n}{1 - r}$$

Sum of all terms when $|r| < 1$:

$$S = \sum_{i=1}^{\infty} a_1 r^{i-1} = \frac{a_1}{1 - r}$$

Counting Formulas

Factorial notation: $n! = 1 \cdot 2 \cdot 3 \cdot \cdots \cdot (n - 1) \cdot n$

Permutation: $P(n, r) = \dfrac{n!}{(n - r)!}$ for $0 \leq r \leq n$

Combination: $C(n, r) = \dbinom{n}{r} = \dfrac{n!}{(n - r)!r!}$ for $0 \leq r \leq n$

Binomial Expansion

$(a + b)^2 = a^2 + 2ab + b^2$

$(a + b)^3 = a^3 + 3a^2b + 3ab^2 + b^3$

$(a + b)^4 = a^4 + 4a^3b + 6a^2b^2 + 4ab^3 + b^4$

$(a + b)^n = \displaystyle\sum_{r=0}^{n} \binom{n}{r} a^{n-r} b^r$, where $\dbinom{n}{r} = \dfrac{n!}{(n - r)!r!}$

Geometry

Rectangle

Area = LW

Perimeter = $2L + 2W$

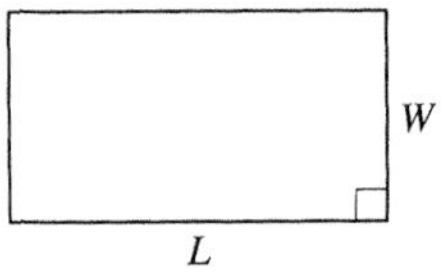

Square

Area = s^2

Perimeter = $4s$

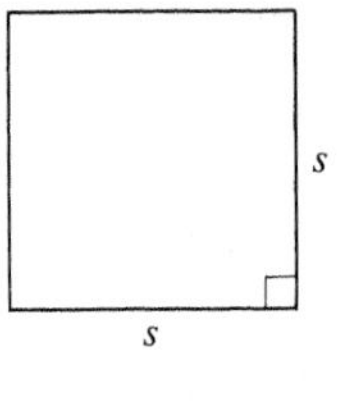

Triangle

Area = $\frac{1}{2}bh$

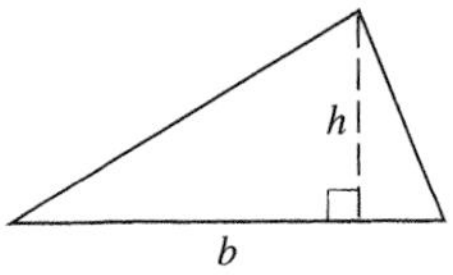

Right Triangle

Area = $\frac{1}{2}ab$

Pythagorean theorem:
$c^2 = a^2 + b^2$

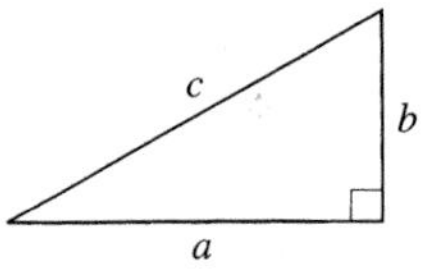

Parallelogram

Area = bh

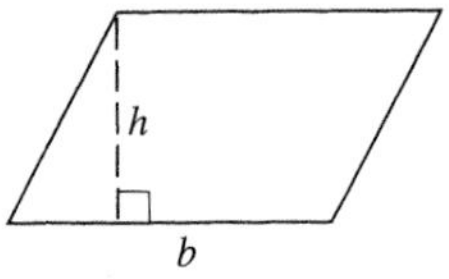

Trapezoid

Area = $\frac{1}{2}h(b_1 + b_2)$

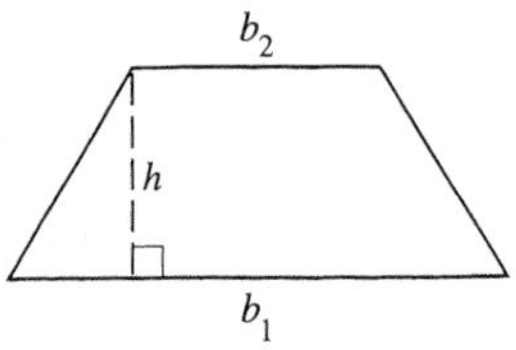

Circle

Area = πr^2

Circumference = $2\pi r$

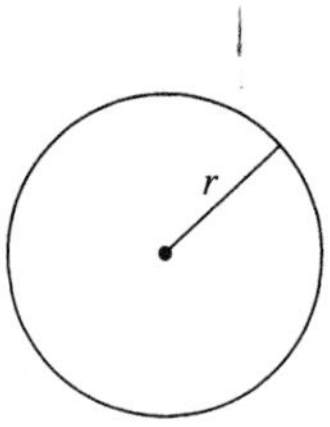

Right Circular Cone

Volume = $\frac{1}{3}\pi r^2 h$

Lateral surface area = $\pi r\sqrt{r^2 + h^2}$

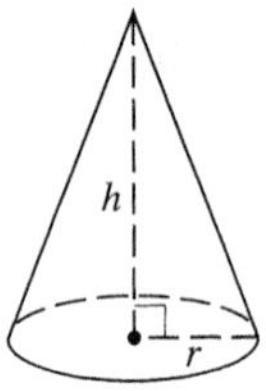

Right Circular Cylinder

Volume = $\pi r^2 h$

Lateral surface area = $2\pi rh$

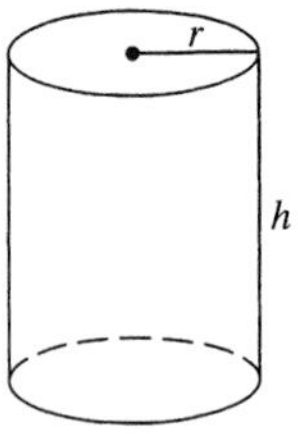

Sphere

Volume = $\frac{4}{3}\pi r^3$

Surface area = $4\pi r^2$

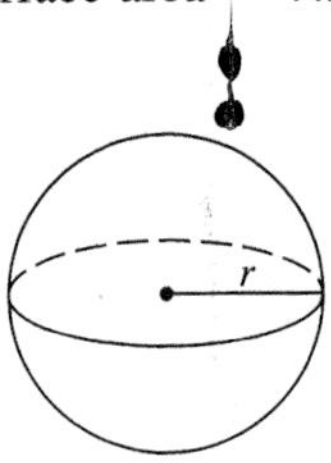

Metric Abbreviations

Length		Volume		Weight	
mm	millimeter	mL	milliliter	mg	milligram
cm	centimeter	cL	centiliter	cg	centigram
dm	decimeter	dL	deciliter	dg	decigram
m	meter	L	liter	g	gram
dam	dekameter	daL	dekaliter	dag	dekagram
hm	hectometer	hL	hectoliter	hg	hectogram
km	kilometer	kL	kiloliter	kg	kilogram

English-Metric Conversion

Length	Volume (U.S.)	Weight
1 in. = 2.540 cm	1 pt = 0.4732 L	1 oz = 28.35 g
1 ft = 30.48 cm	1 qt = 0.9464 L	1 lb = 453.6 g
1 yd = 0.9144 m	1 gal = 3.785 L	1 lb = 0.4536 kg
1 mi = 1.609 km		

Length	Volume (U.S.)	Weight
1 cm = 0.3937 in.	1 L = 2.2233 pt	1 g = 0.0353 oz
1 cm = 0.03281 ft	1 L = 1.0567 qt	1 g = 0.002205 lb
1 m = 1.0936 yd	1 L = 0.2642 gal	1 kg = 2.205 lb
1 km = 0.6215 mi		

Geometry Formulas were taken from *Fundamentals of Precalculus*, Second Edition by Mark Dugopolski.

Trigonometry

Trigonometric Functions

If the angle α (in standard position) intersects the unit circle at (x, y), then

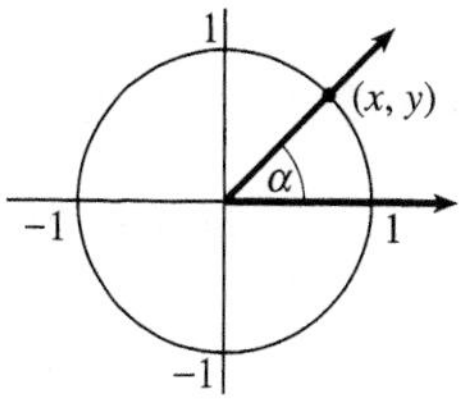

$\sin \alpha = y$ $\qquad \cos \alpha = x$ $\qquad \tan \alpha = \frac{y}{x}$

$\csc \alpha = \frac{1}{y}$ $\qquad \sec \alpha = \frac{1}{x}$ $\qquad \cot \alpha = \frac{x}{y}$

Trigonometric Ratios

If (x, y) is any point other than the origin on the terminal side of α and $r = \sqrt{x^2 + y^2}$, then

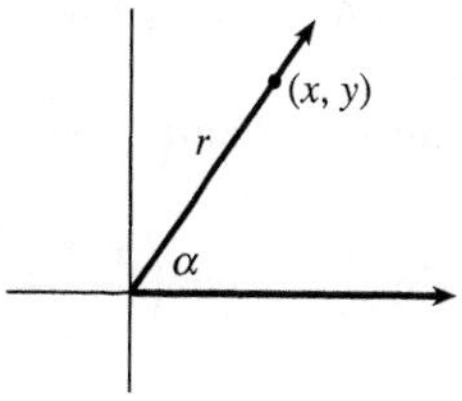

$\sin \alpha = \frac{y}{r}$ $\qquad \cos \alpha = \frac{x}{r}$ $\qquad \tan \alpha = \frac{y}{x}$

$\csc \alpha = \frac{r}{y}$ $\qquad \sec \alpha = \frac{r}{x}$ $\qquad \cot \alpha = \frac{x}{y}$

Right Triangle Trigonometry

If α is an acute angle of a right triangle, then

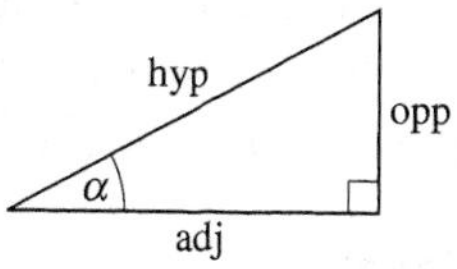

$\sin \alpha = \frac{\text{opp}}{\text{hyp}}$ $\qquad \cos \alpha = \frac{\text{adj}}{\text{hyp}}$ $\qquad \tan \alpha = \frac{\text{opp}}{\text{adj}}$

$\csc \alpha = \frac{\text{hyp}}{\text{opp}}$ $\qquad \sec \alpha = \frac{\text{hyp}}{\text{adj}}$ $\qquad \cot \alpha = \frac{\text{adj}}{\text{opp}}$

Special Right Triangles

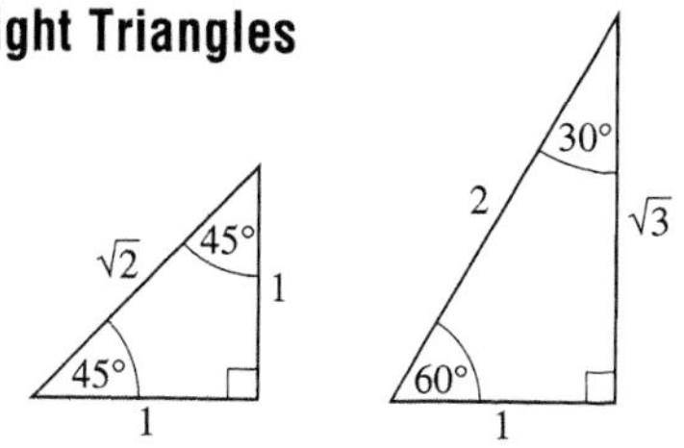

Exact Values of Trigonometric Functions

x degrees	x radians	$\sin x$	$\cos x$	$\tan x$
0°	0	0	1	0
30°	$\frac{\pi}{6}$	$\frac{1}{2}$	$\frac{\sqrt{3}}{2}$	$\frac{\sqrt{3}}{3}$
45°	$\frac{\pi}{4}$	$\frac{\sqrt{2}}{2}$	$\frac{\sqrt{2}}{2}$	1
60°	$\frac{\pi}{3}$	$\frac{\sqrt{3}}{2}$	$\frac{1}{2}$	$\sqrt{3}$
90°	$\frac{\pi}{2}$	1	0	—

Basic Identities

$$\tan x = \frac{\sin x}{\cos x} = \frac{1}{\cot x} \qquad \cot x = \frac{\cos x}{\sin x} = \frac{1}{\tan x}$$

$$\sin x = \frac{1}{\csc x} \qquad \csc x = \frac{1}{\sin x}$$

$$\cos x = \frac{1}{\sec x} \qquad \sec x = \frac{1}{\cos x}$$

Pythagorean Identities

$$\sin^2 x + \cos^2 x = 1 \qquad 1 + \cot^2 x = \csc^2 x$$

$$\tan^2 x + 1 = \sec^2 x$$

Odd Identities

$$\sin(-x) = -\sin(x) \qquad \csc(-x) = -\csc(x)$$

$$\tan(-x) = -\tan(x) \qquad \cot(-x) = -\cot(x)$$

Even Identities

$$\cos(-x) = \cos(x) \qquad \sec(-x) = \sec(x)$$

Trigonometry Formulas were taken from *Fundamentals of Precalculus,* Second Edition by Mark Dugopolski.

Trigonometry

Cofunction Identities

$$\sin\left(\frac{\pi}{2} - u\right) = \cos u \qquad \cos\left(\frac{\pi}{2} - u\right) = \sin u$$

$$\tan\left(\frac{\pi}{2} - u\right) = \cot u \qquad \cot\left(\frac{\pi}{2} - u\right) = \tan u$$

$$\sec\left(\frac{\pi}{2} - u\right) = \csc u \qquad \csc\left(\frac{\pi}{2} - u\right) = \sec u$$

Cosine of a Sum or Difference

$$\cos(\alpha + \beta) = \cos \alpha \cos \beta - \sin \alpha \sin \beta$$
$$\cos(\alpha - \beta) = \cos \alpha \cos \beta + \sin \alpha \sin \beta$$

Sine of a Sum or Difference

$$\sin(\alpha + \beta) = \sin \alpha \cos \beta + \cos \alpha \sin \beta$$
$$\sin(\alpha - \beta) = \sin \alpha \cos \beta - \cos \alpha \sin \beta$$

Tangent of a Sum or Difference

$$\tan(\alpha + \beta) = \frac{\tan \alpha + \tan \beta}{1 - \tan \alpha \tan \beta}$$
$$\tan(\alpha - \beta) = \frac{\tan \alpha - \tan \beta}{1 + \tan \alpha \tan \beta}$$

Double-Angle Identities

$$\sin 2x = 2 \sin x \cos x$$
$$\cos 2x = \cos^2 x - \sin^2 x = 2\cos^2 x - 1 = 1 - 2\sin^2 x$$
$$\tan 2x = \frac{2 \tan x}{1 - \tan^2 x}$$

Half-Angle Identities

$$\sin \frac{x}{2} = \pm\sqrt{\frac{1 - \cos x}{2}} \qquad \cos \frac{x}{2} = \pm\sqrt{\frac{1 + \cos x}{2}}$$

$$\tan \frac{x}{2} = \pm\sqrt{\frac{1 - \cos x}{1 + \cos x}} = \frac{\sin x}{1 + \cos x} = \frac{1 - \cos x}{\sin x}$$

Product-to-Sum Identities

$$\sin A \cos B = \frac{1}{2}[\sin(A + B) + \sin(A - B)]$$
$$\sin A \sin B = \frac{1}{2}[\cos(A - B) - \cos(A + B)]$$
$$\cos A \sin B = \frac{1}{2}[\sin(A + B) - \sin(A - B)]$$
$$\cos A \cos B = \frac{1}{2}[\cos(A - B) + \cos(A + B)]$$

Sum-to-Product Identities

$$\sin x + \sin y = 2 \sin\left(\frac{x + y}{2}\right)\cos\left(\frac{x - y}{2}\right)$$
$$\sin x - \sin y = 2 \cos\left(\frac{x + y}{2}\right)\sin\left(\frac{x - y}{2}\right)$$
$$\cos x + \cos y = 2 \cos\left(\frac{x + y}{2}\right)\cos\left(\frac{x - y}{2}\right)$$
$$\cos x - \cos y = -2 \sin\left(\frac{x + y}{2}\right)\sin\left(\frac{x - y}{2}\right)$$

Reduction Formula

If α is an angle in standard position whose terminal side contains (a, b), then for any real number x

$$a \sin x + b \cos x = \sqrt{a^2 + b^2} \sin(x + \alpha).$$

Oblique Triangle

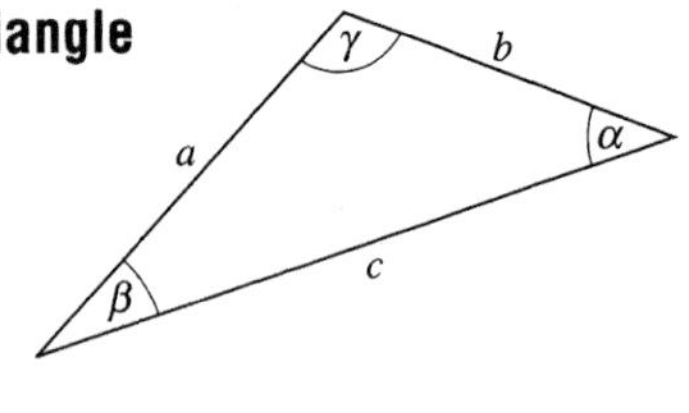

Law of Sines

In any triangle, $\dfrac{\sin \alpha}{a} = \dfrac{\sin \beta}{b} = \dfrac{\sin \gamma}{c}$.

Law of Cosines

$$a^2 = b^2 + c^2 - 2bc \cos \alpha$$
$$b^2 = a^2 + c^2 - 2ac \cos \beta$$
$$c^2 = a^2 + b^2 - 2ab \cos \gamma$$

Function Gallery: Some Basic Functions and Their Properties

Constant Function

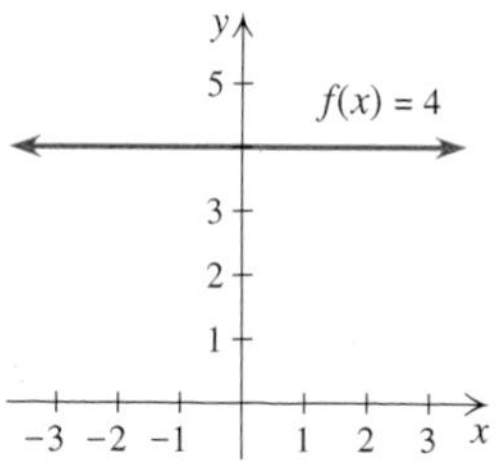

Domain $(-\infty, \infty)$
Range $\{4\}$
Constant on $(-\infty, \infty)$
Symmetric about y-axis

Identity Function

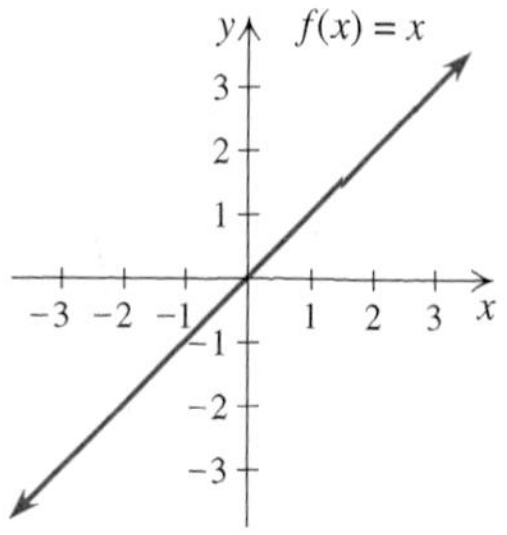

Domain $(-\infty, \infty)$
Range $(-\infty, \infty)$
Increasing on $(-\infty, \infty)$
Symmetric about origin

Linear Function

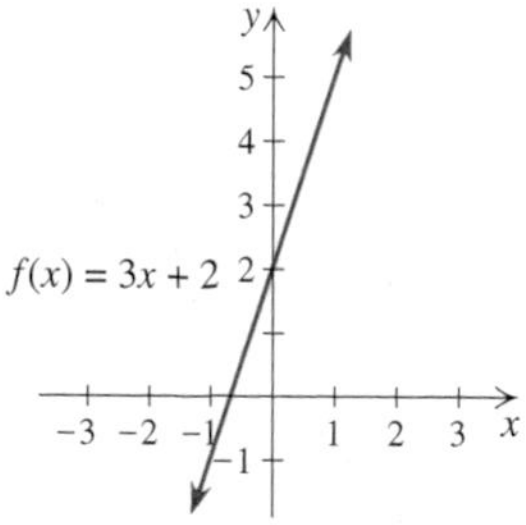

Domain $(-\infty, \infty)$
Range $(-\infty, \infty)$
Increasing on $(-\infty, \infty)$

Absolute-Value Function

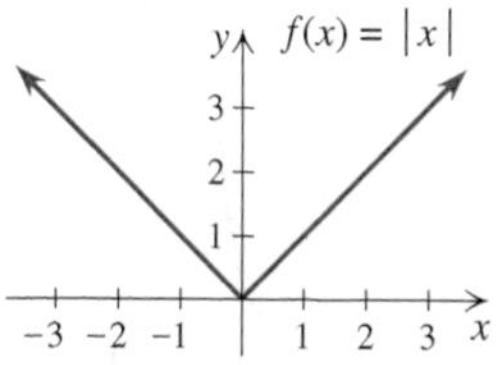

Domain $(-\infty, \infty)$
Range $[0, \infty)$
Increasing on $(0, \infty)$
Decreasing on $(-\infty, 0)$
Symmetric about y-axis

Square Function

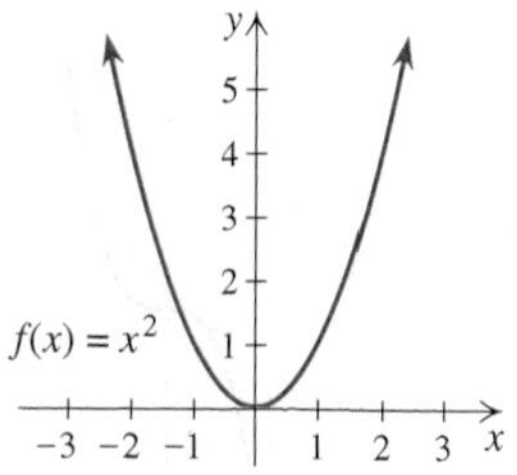

Domain $(-\infty, \infty)$
Range $[0, \infty)$
Increasing on $(0, \infty)$
Decreasing on $(-\infty, 0)$
Symmetric about y-axis

Square-Root Function

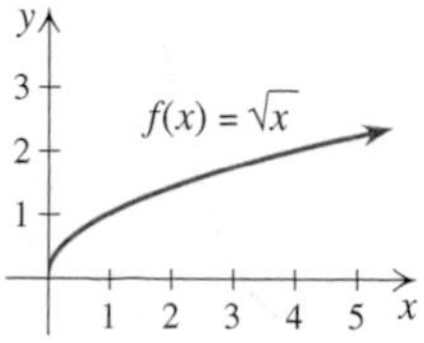

Domain $[0,\infty)$
Range $[0, \infty)$
Increasing on $(0,\infty)$

Cube Function

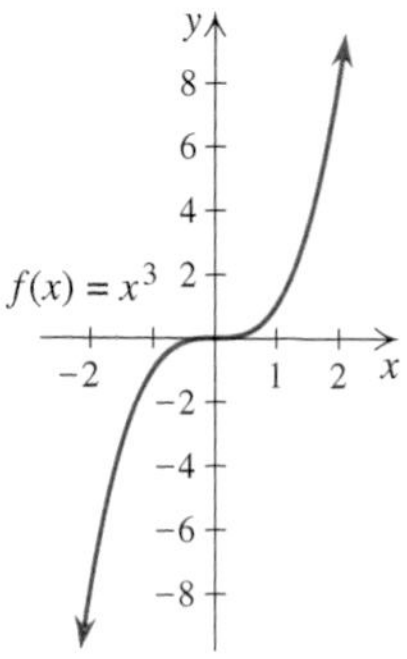

Domain $(-\infty, \infty)$
Range $(-\infty, \infty)$
Increasing on $(-\infty, \infty)$
Symmetric about origin

Cube-Root Function

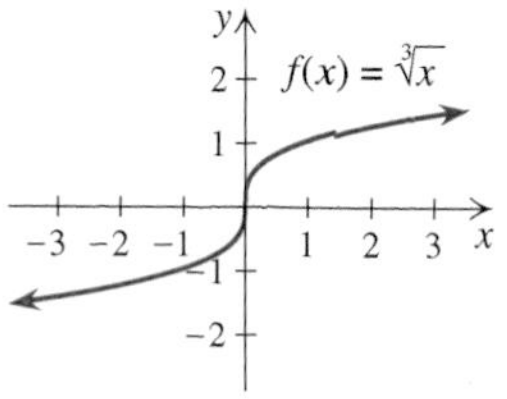

Domain $(-\infty, \infty)$
Range $(-\infty, \infty)$
Increasing on $(-\infty, \infty)$
Symmetric about origin

Greatest Integer Function

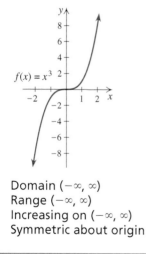

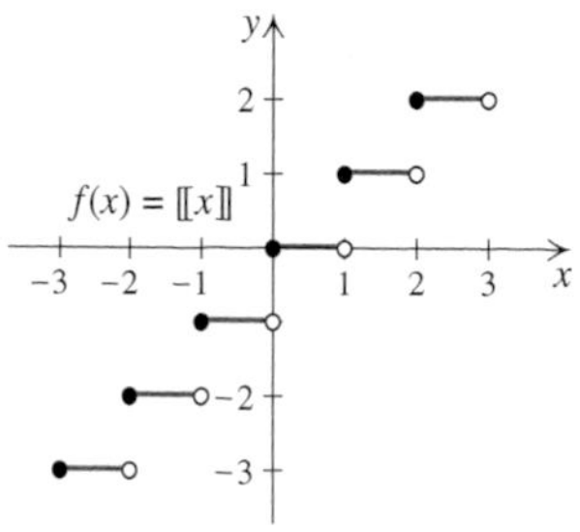

Domain $(-\infty, \infty)$
Range $\{n \mid n \text{ is an integer}\}$
Constant on $[n, n + 1)$
for every integer n

Function Gallery: Some Basic Functions and their properties was taken from *Fundamentals of Precalculus*, Second Edition by Mark Dugopolski.

Function Gallery: Some Inverse Functions

Linear

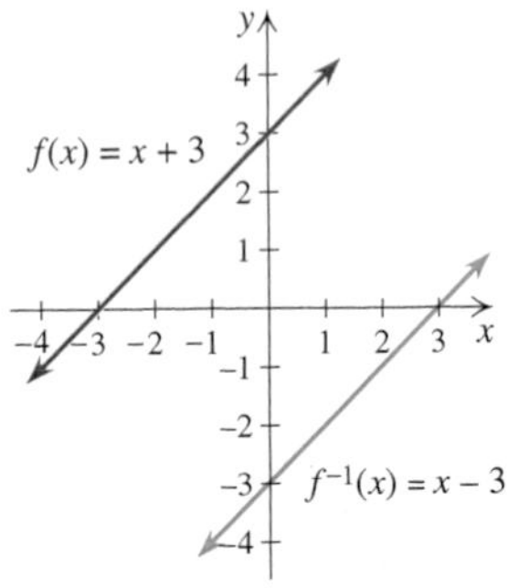

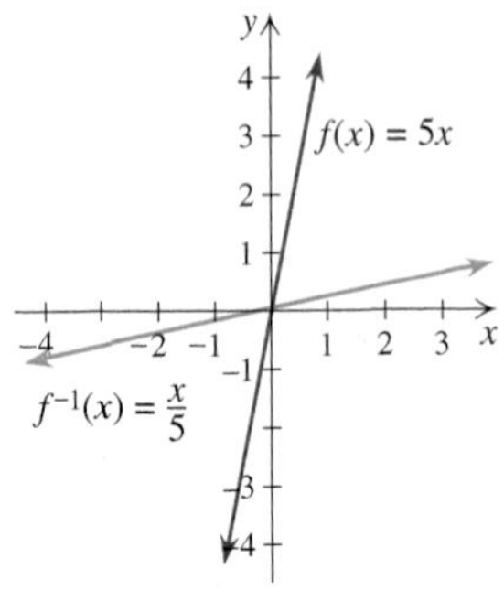

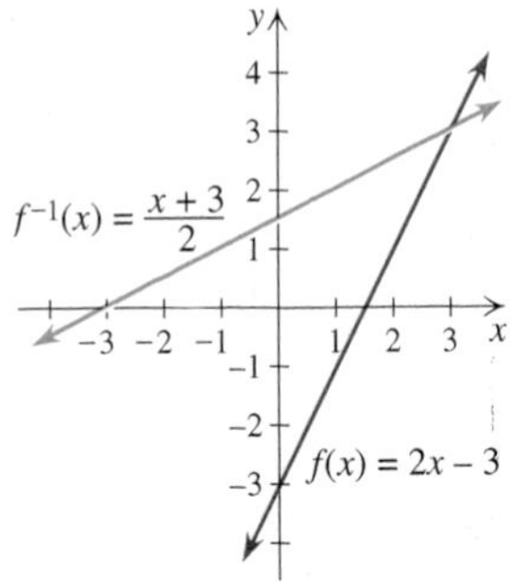

Power and Roots

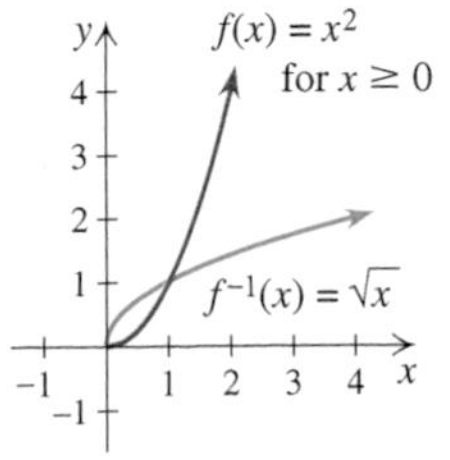

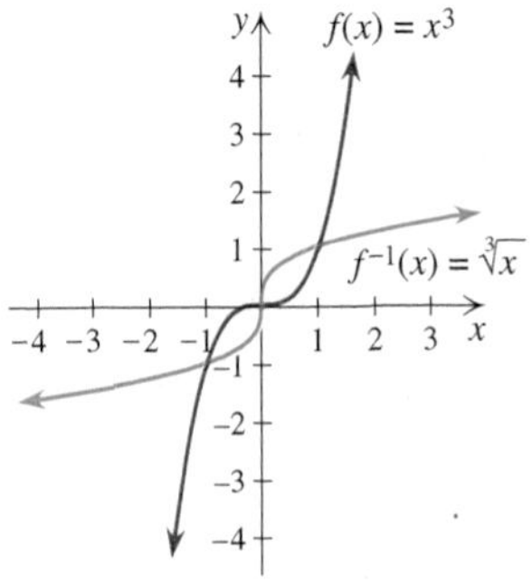

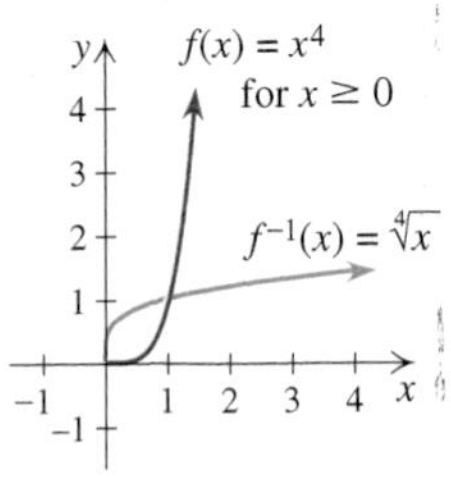

Function Gallery: Polynomial Functions

Linear: $f(x) = mx + b$, domain $(-\infty, \infty)$, range $(-\infty, \infty)$ if $m \neq 0$, slope m, y-intercept $(0, b)$

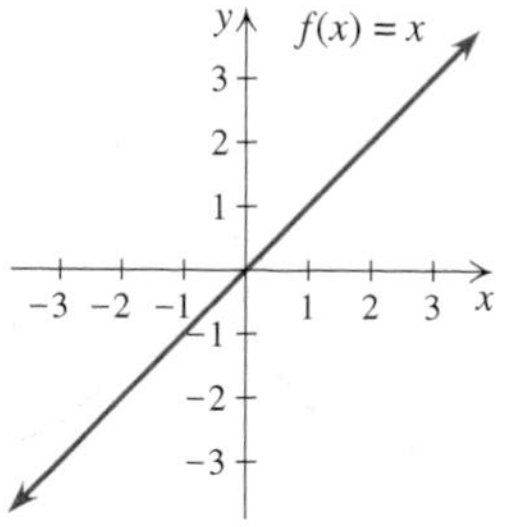

Slope 1, y-intercept $(0, 0)$

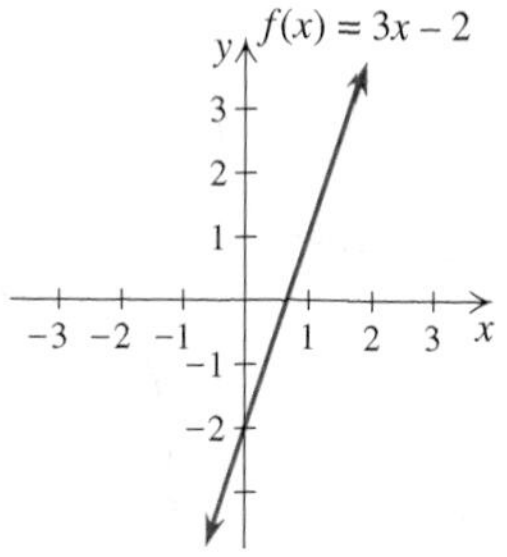

Slope 3, y-intercept $(0, -2)$

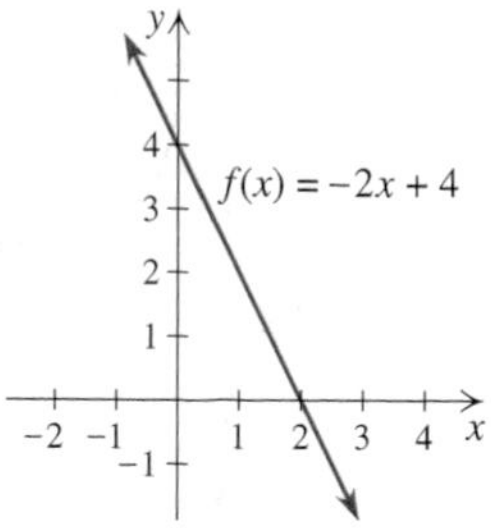

Slope -2, y-intercept $(0, 4)$

Quadratic: $f(x) = ax^2 + bx + c$ or $f(x) = a(x - h)^2 + k$, domain $(-\infty, \infty)$, vertex (h, k) or $x = -b/(2a)$

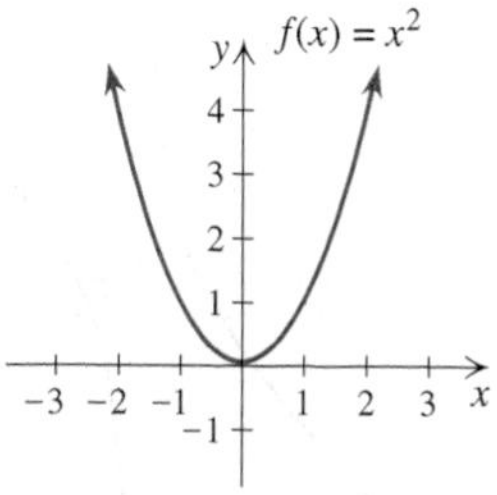

Vertex $(0, 0)$
Range $[0, \infty)$

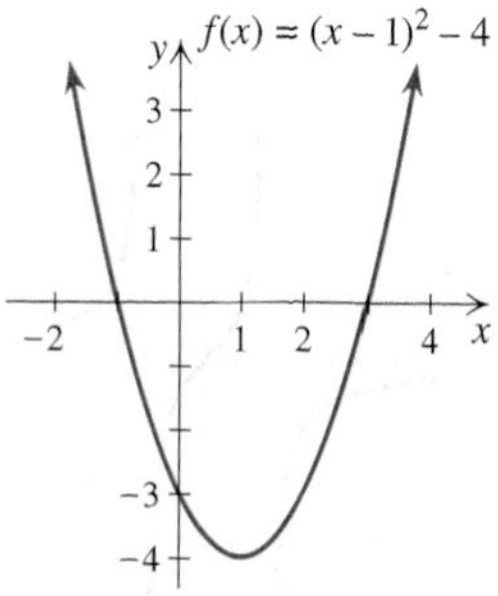

Vertex $(1, -4)$
Range $[-4, \infty)$

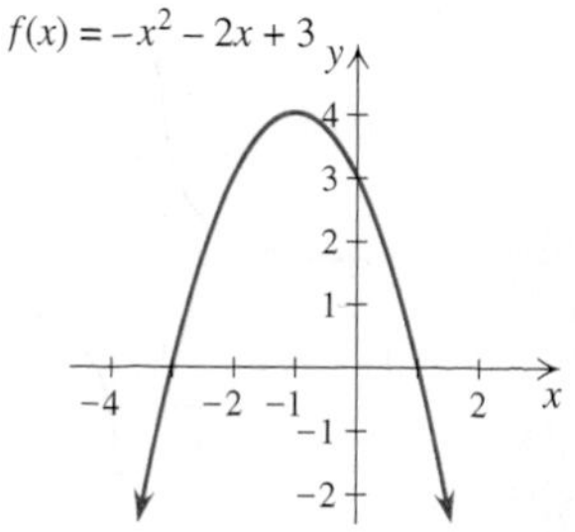

Vertex $(-1, 4)$
Range $(-\infty, 4]$

Cubic: $f(x) = ax^3 + bx^2 + cx + d$, domain $(-\infty, \infty)$, range $(-\infty, \infty)$

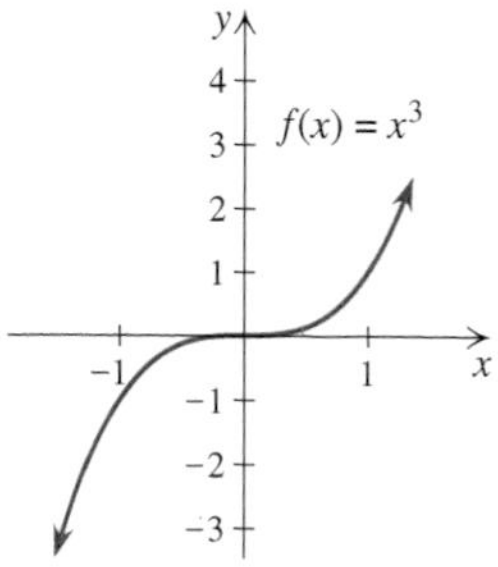

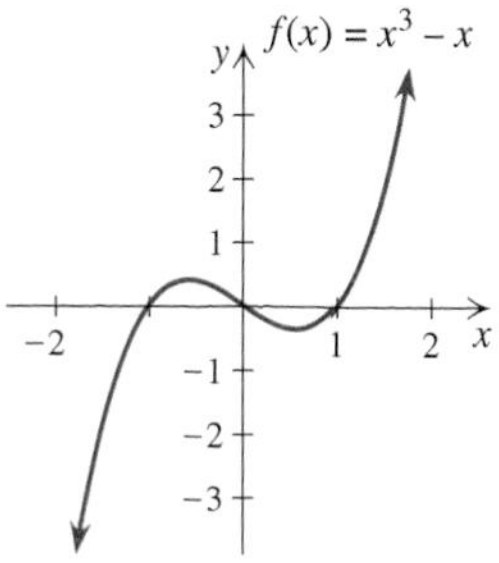

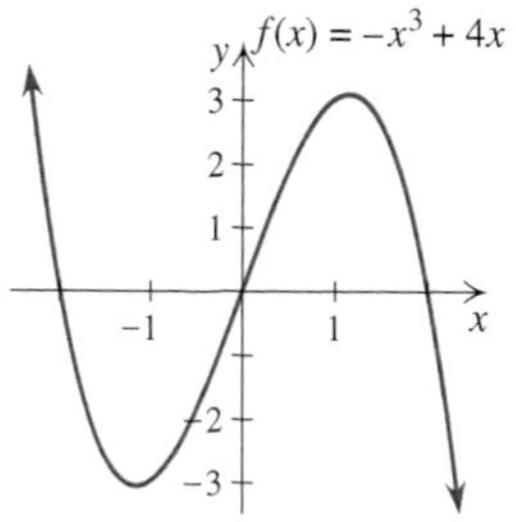

Quartic or Fourth-Degree: $f(x) = ax^4 + bx^3 + cx^2 + dx + e$, domain $(-\infty, \infty)$

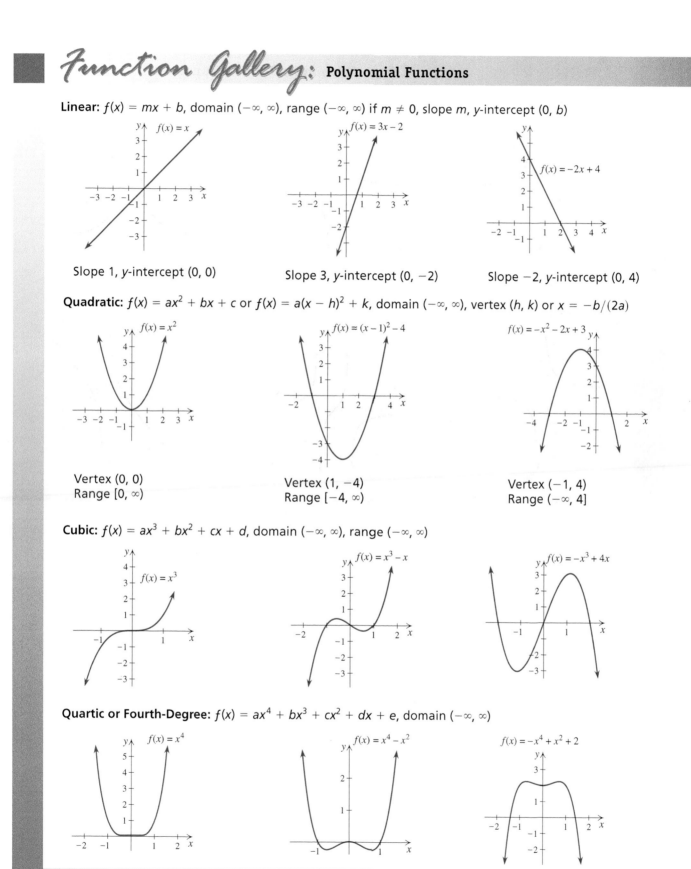

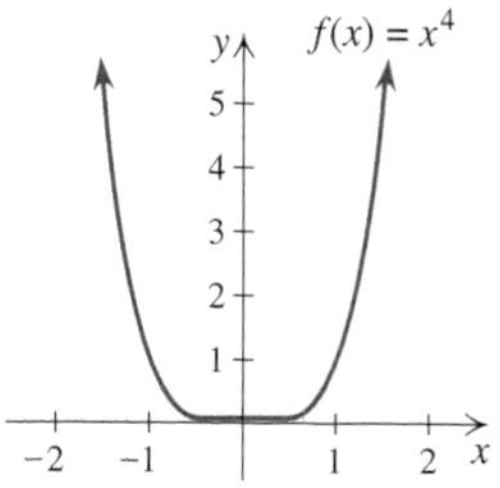

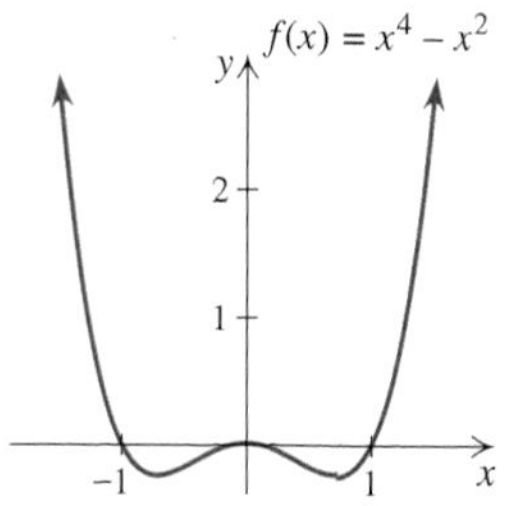

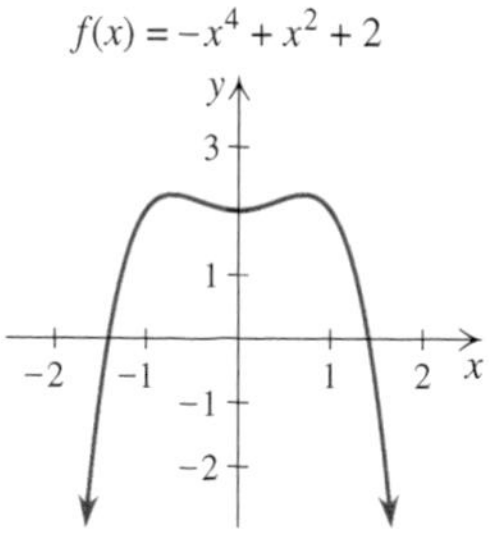

Function Gallery: Some Basic Rational Functions

Horizontal Asymptote x-axis and Vertical Asymptote y-axis

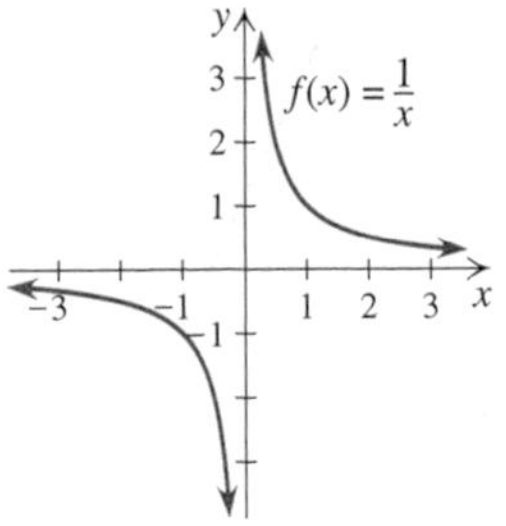

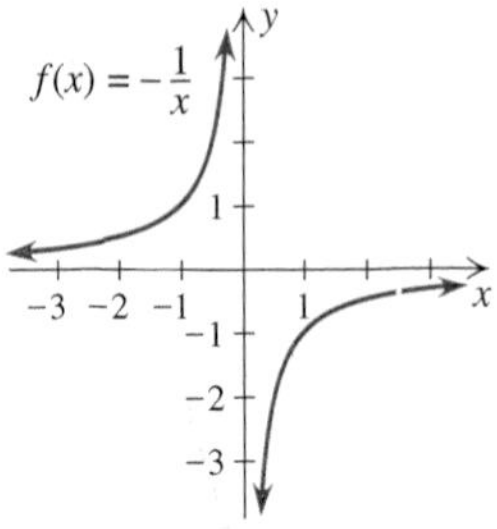

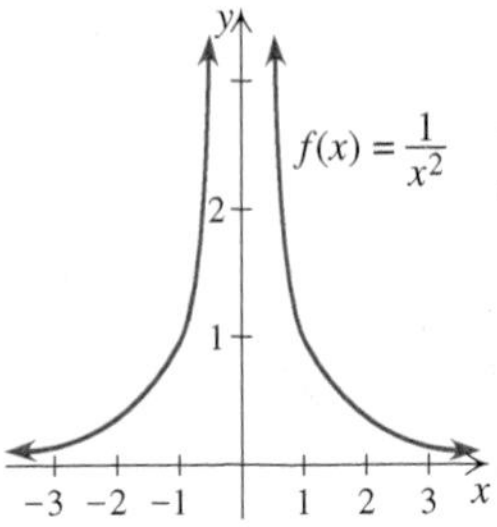

Various Asymptotes

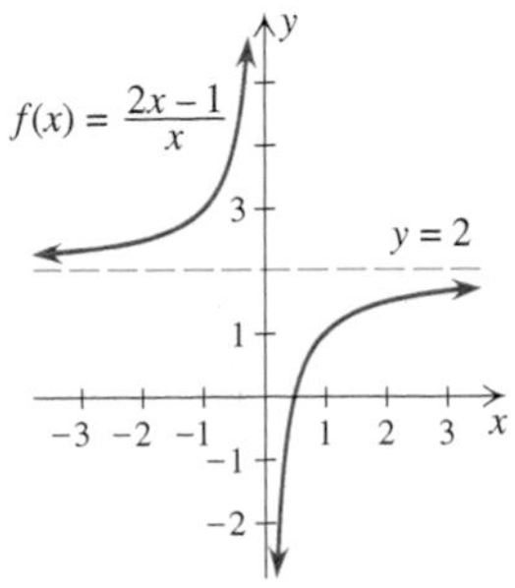

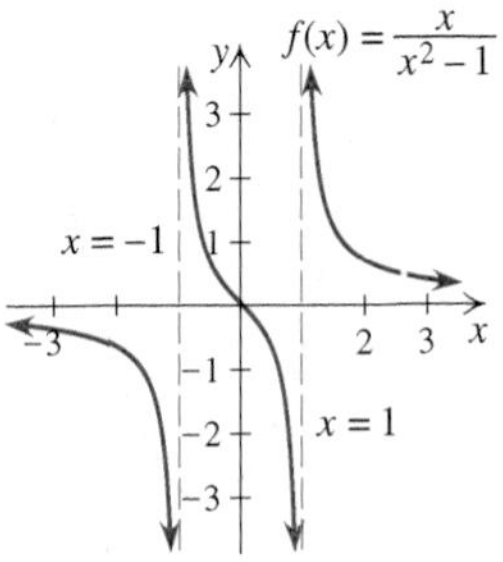

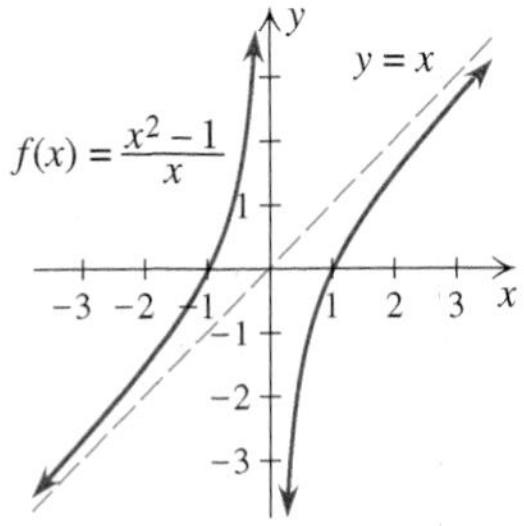

Function Gallery: Exponential and Logarithmic Functions

Exponential: $f(x) = a^x$, domain $(-\infty, \infty)$, range $(0, \infty)$

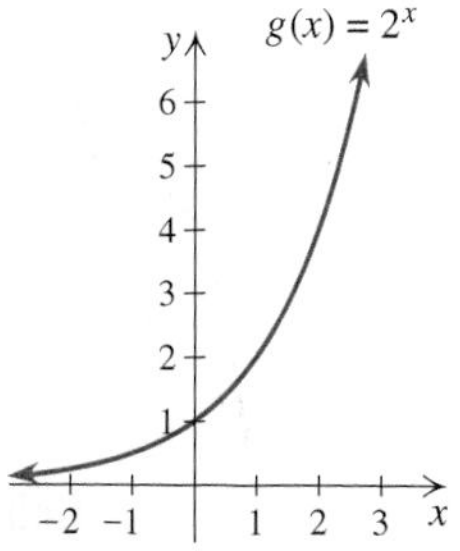

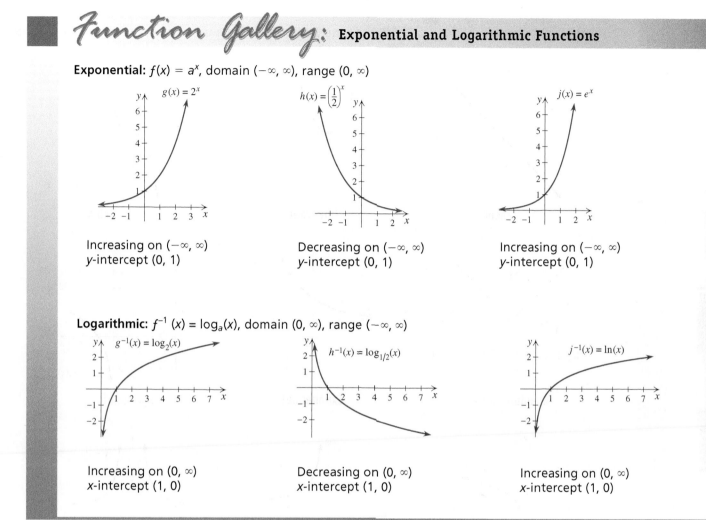

Increasing on $(-\infty, \infty)$
y-intercept $(0, 1)$

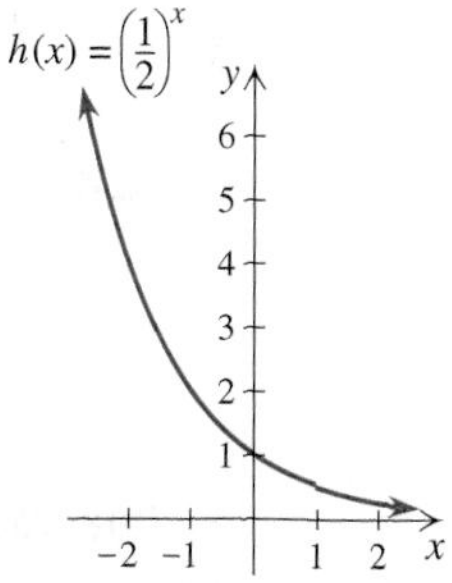

Decreasing on $(-\infty, \infty)$
y-intercept $(0, 1)$

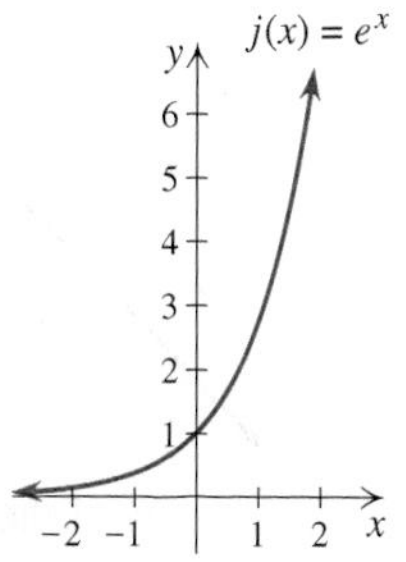

Increasing on $(-\infty, \infty)$
y-intercept $(0, 1)$

Logarithmic: $f^{-1}(x) = \log_a(x)$, domain $(0, \infty)$, range $(-\infty, \infty)$

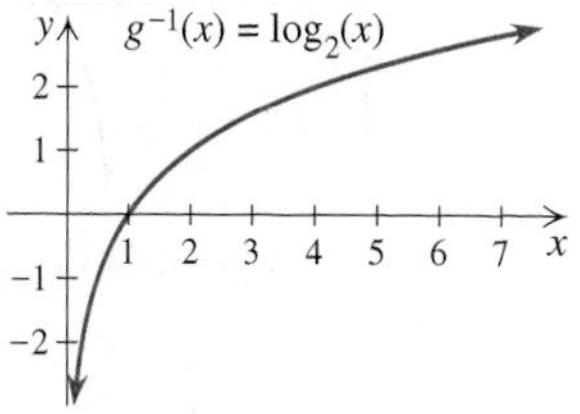

Increasing on $(0, \infty)$
x-intercept $(1, 0)$

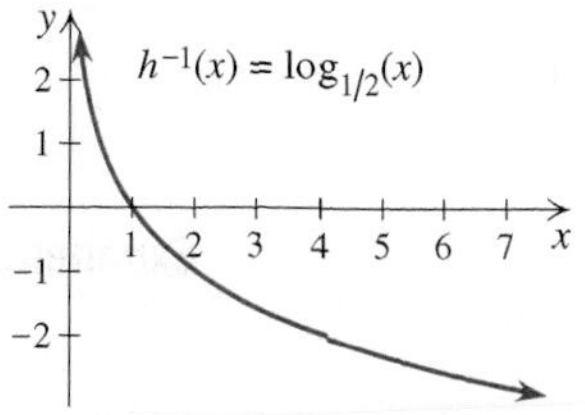

Decreasing on $(0, \infty)$
x-intercept $(1, 0)$

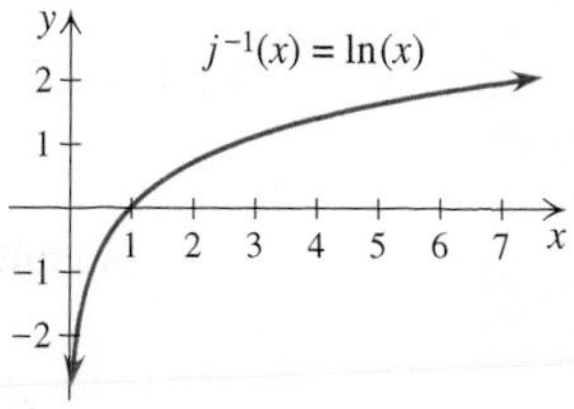

Increasing on $(0, \infty)$
x-intercept $(1, 0)$

Function Gallery: Some Basic Functions of Algebra with Transformations

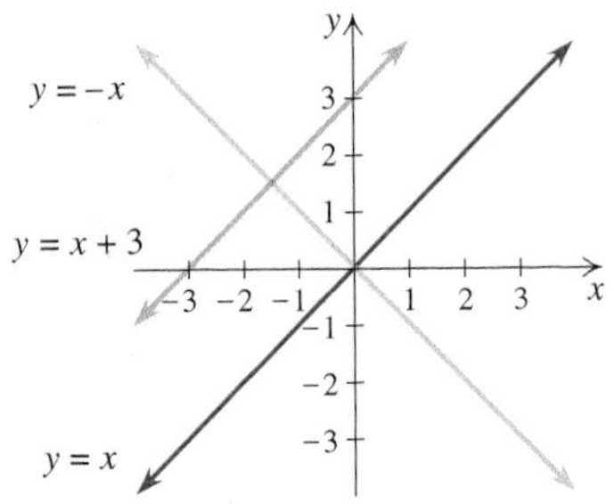

Linear

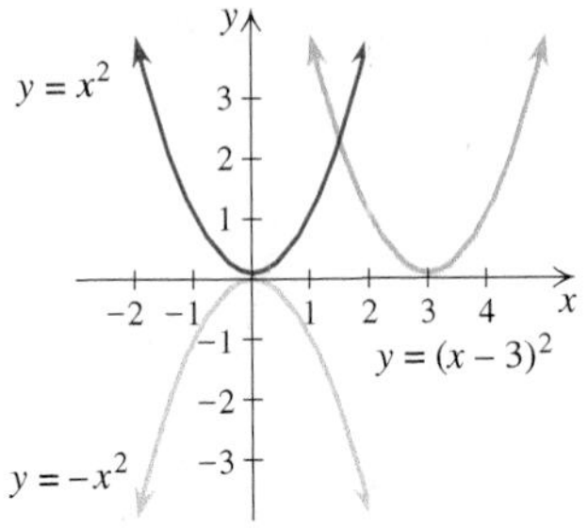

Quadratic

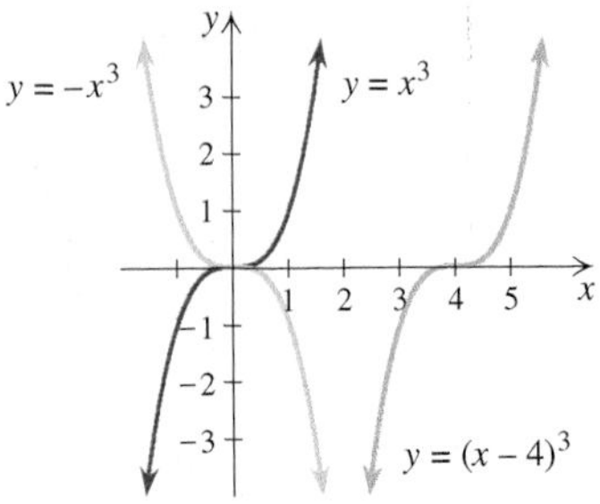

Cubic

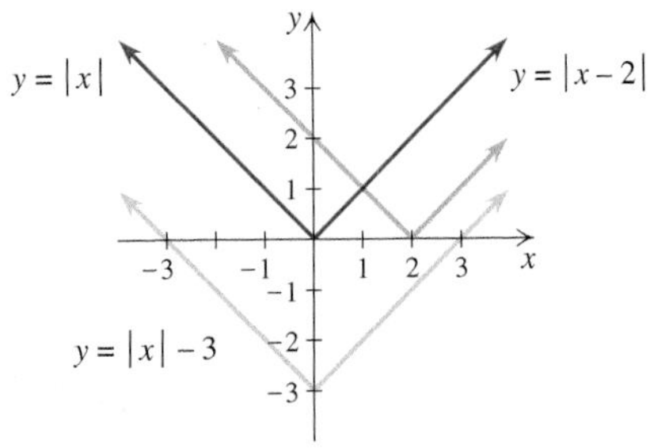

Absolute value

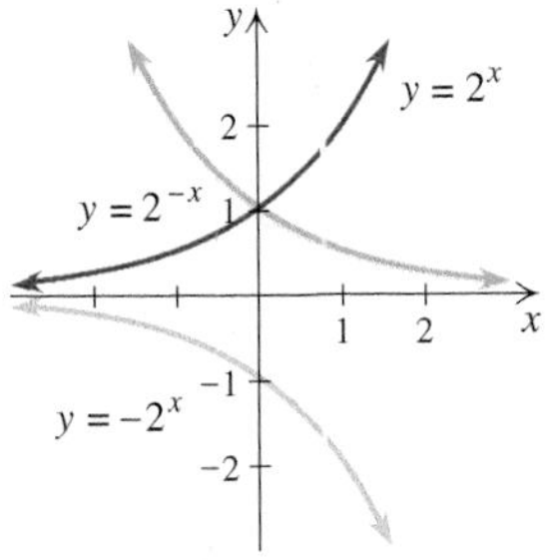

Exponential

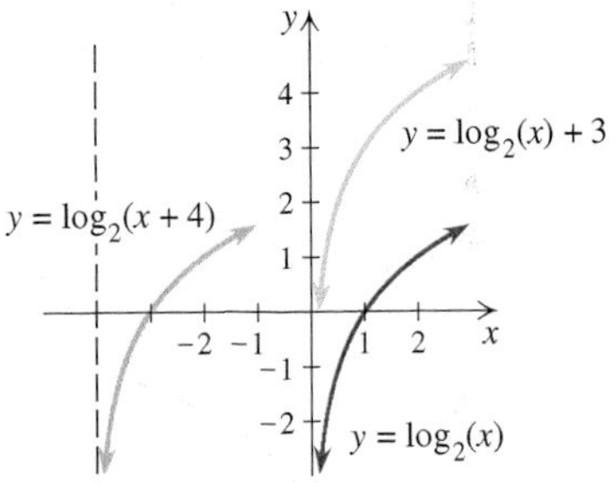

Logarithmic

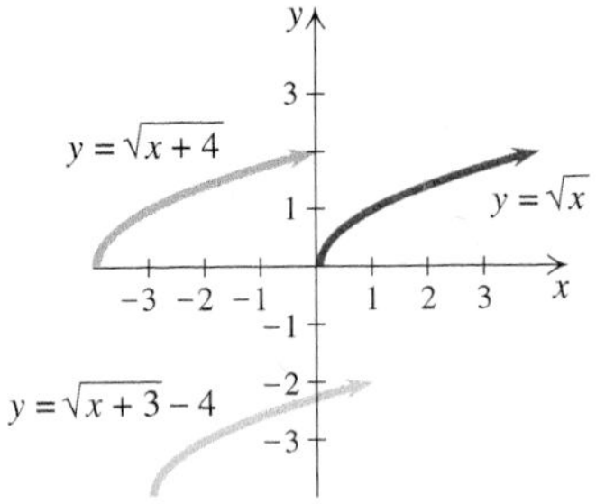

Square root

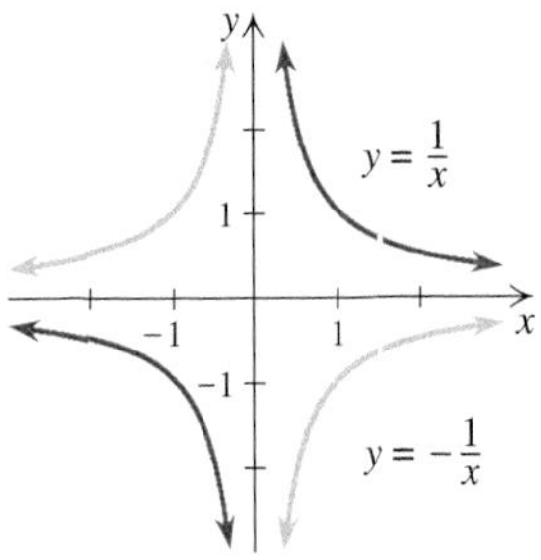

Reciprocal

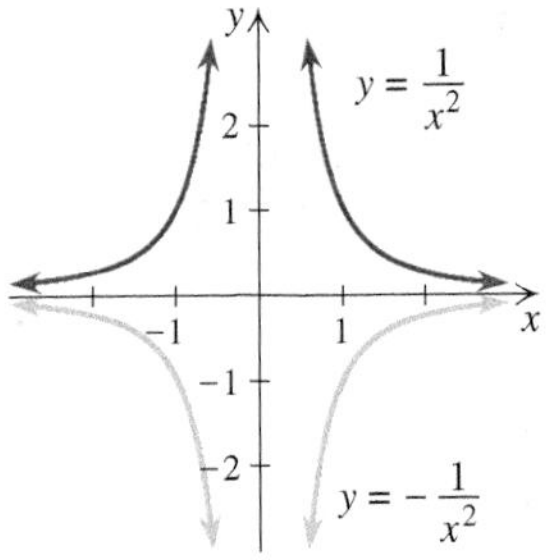

Rational

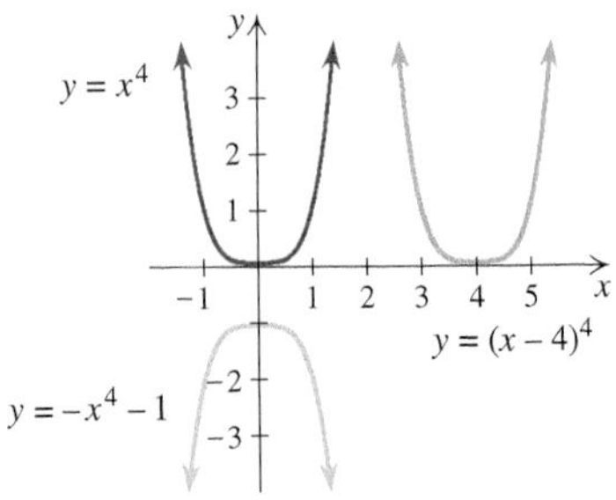

Fourth degree

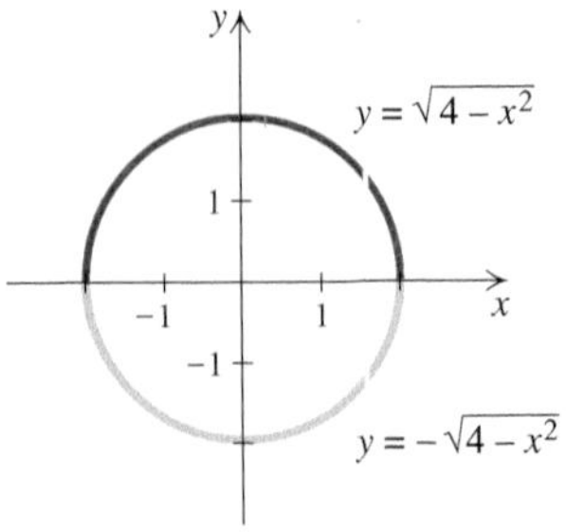

Semicircle

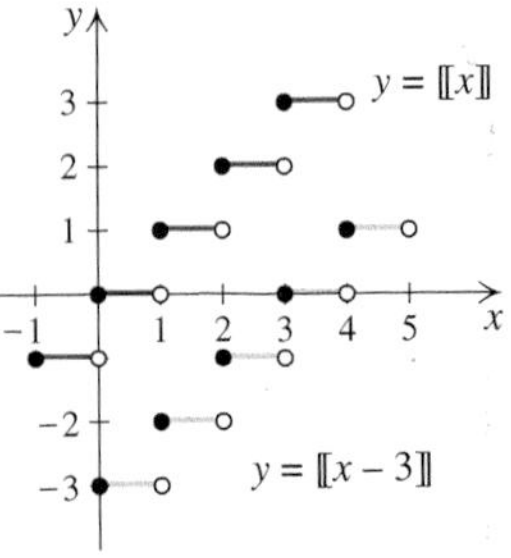

Greatest integer

Function Gallery: The Sine and Cosine Functions

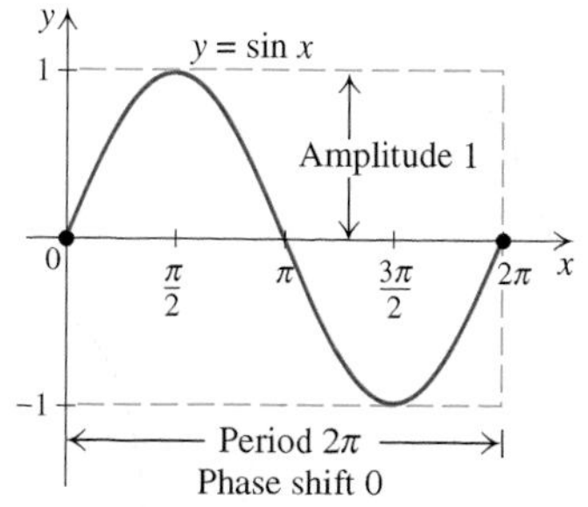

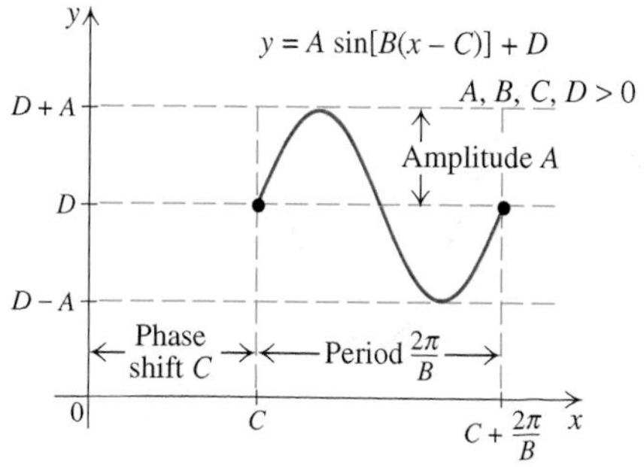

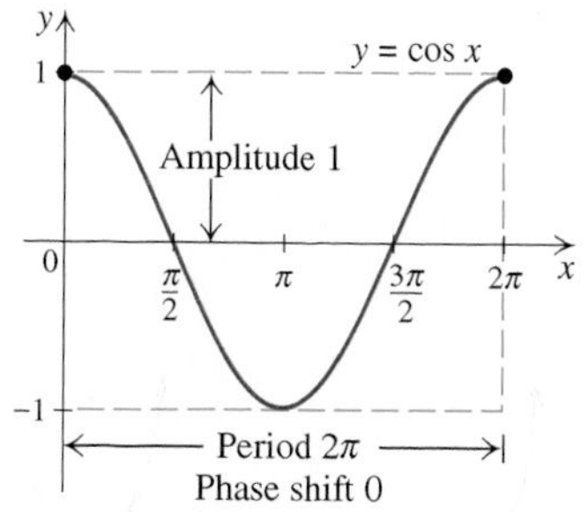

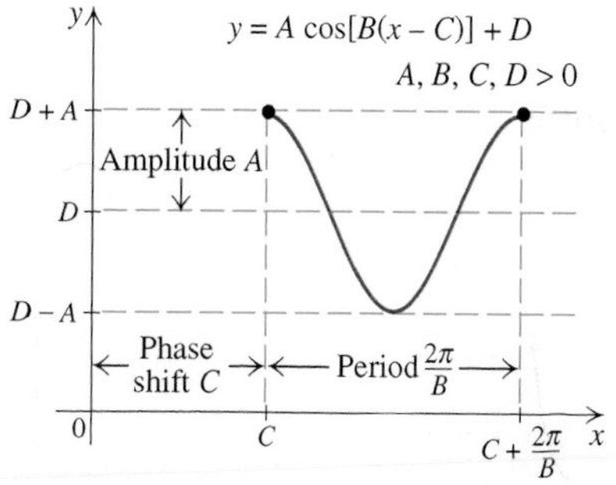

Function Gallery: Periods of Sine, Cosine and Tangent (B > 1)

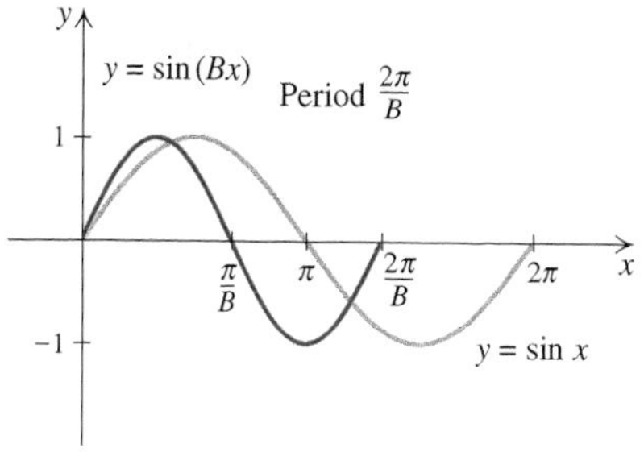

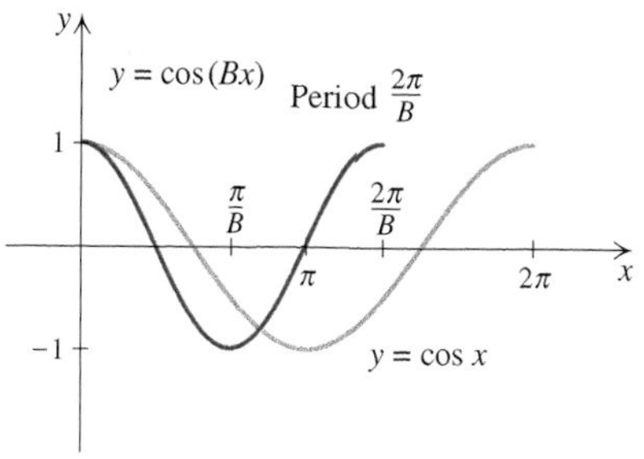

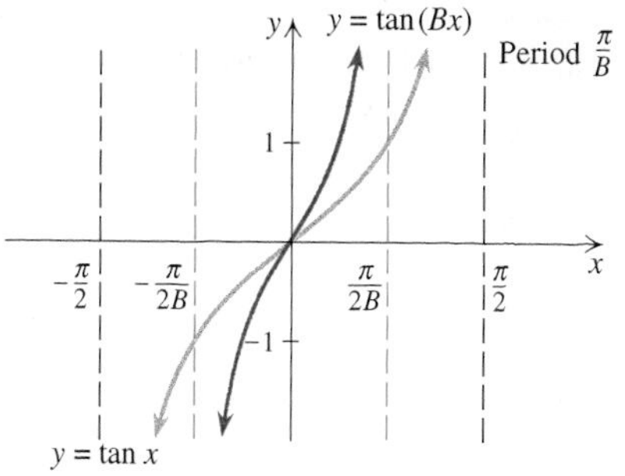

Function Gallery: Trigonometric Functions

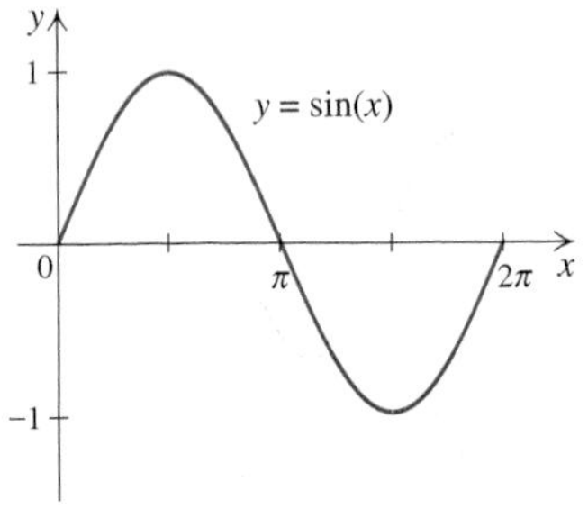

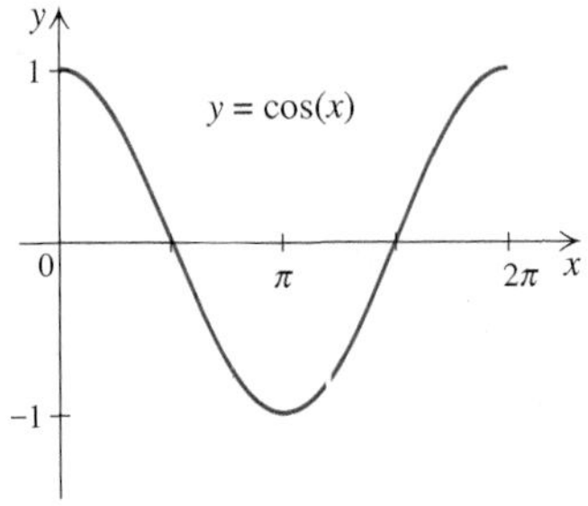

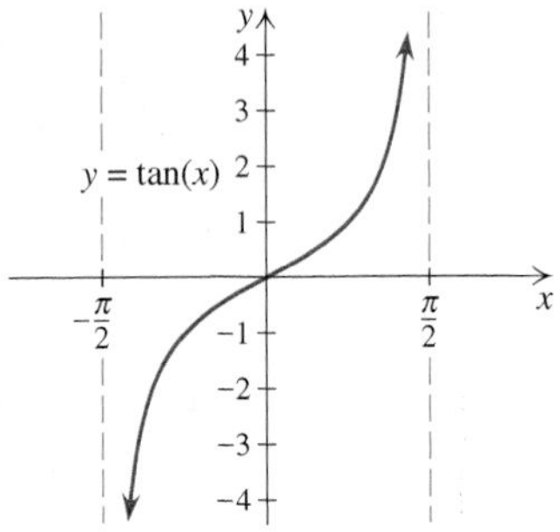

	$y = \sin(x)$	$y = \cos(x)$	$y = \tan(x)$
Domain (*k* any integer)	$(-\infty, \infty)$	$(-\infty, \infty)$	$x \neq \frac{\pi}{2} + k\pi$
Range	$[-1, 1]$	$[-1, 1]$	$(-\infty, \infty)$
Period	2π	2π	π
Fundamental cycle	$[0, 2\pi]$	$[0, 2\pi]$	$\left[-\frac{\pi}{2}, \frac{\pi}{2}\right]$

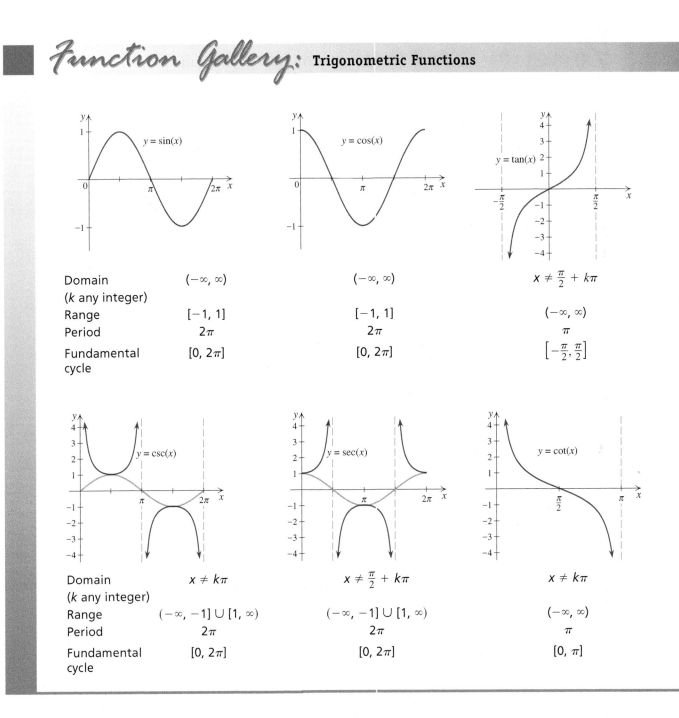

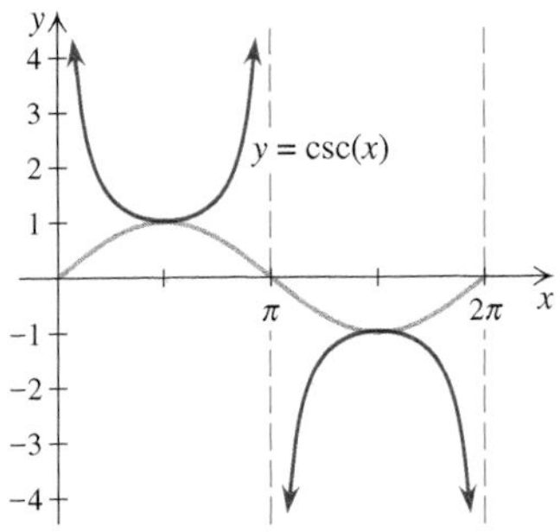

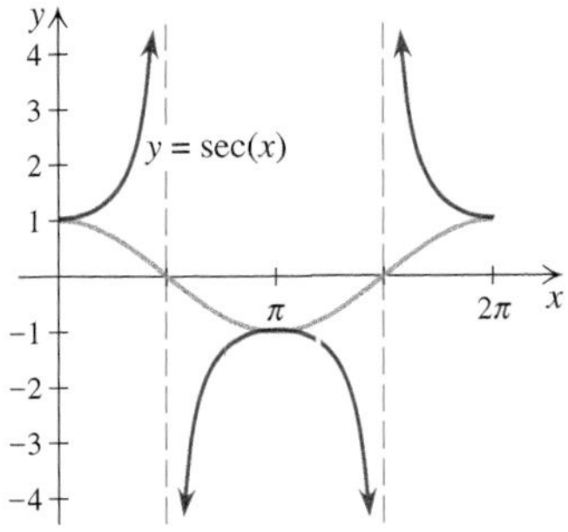

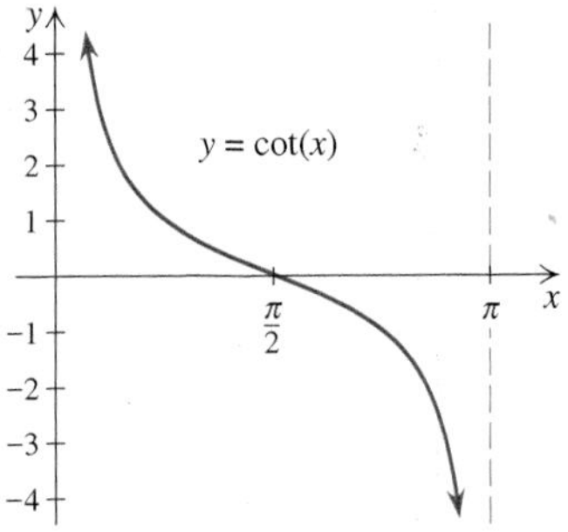

	$y = \csc(x)$	$y = \sec(x)$	$y = \cot(x)$
Domain (*k* any integer)	$x \neq k\pi$	$x \neq \frac{\pi}{2} + k\pi$	$x \neq k\pi$
Range	$(-\infty, -1] \cup [1, \infty)$	$(-\infty, -1] \cup [1, \infty)$	$(-\infty, \infty)$
Period	2π	2π	π
Fundamental cycle	$[0, 2\pi]$	$[0, 2\pi]$	$[0, \pi]$

Function Gallery: Inverse Trigonometric Functions

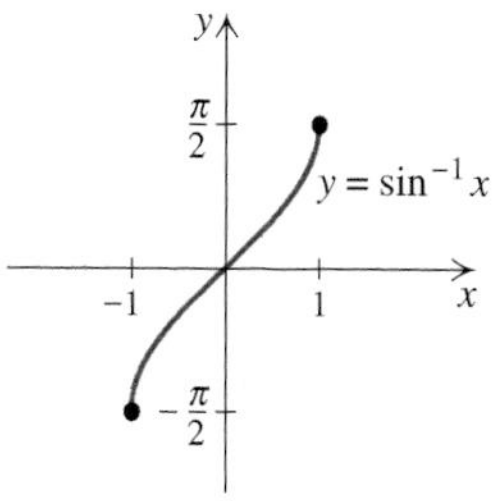

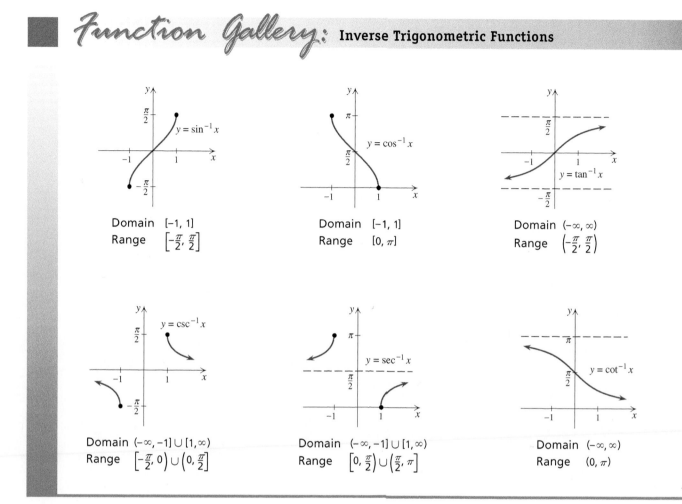

Domain $[-1, 1]$
Range $\left[-\frac{\pi}{2}, \frac{\pi}{2}\right]$

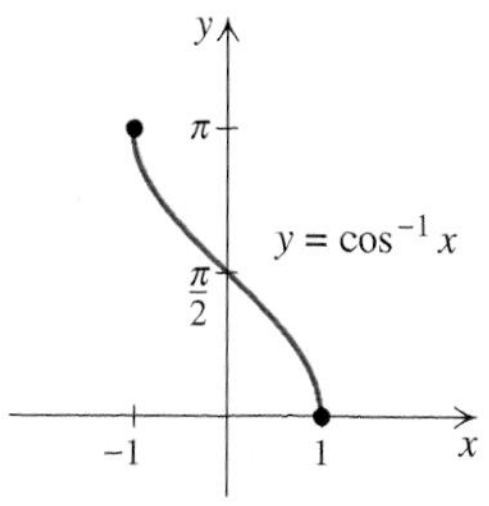

Domain $[-1, 1]$
Range $[0, \pi]$

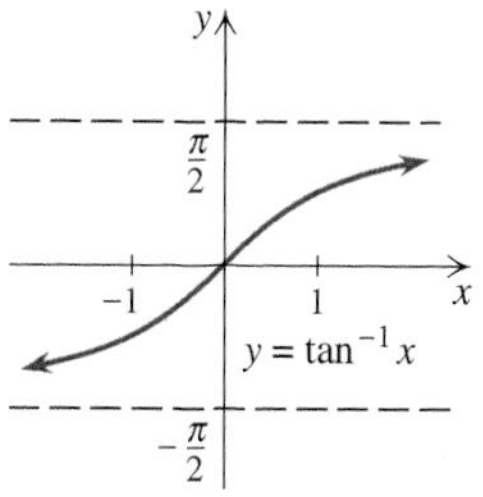

Domain $(-\infty, \infty)$
Range $\left(-\frac{\pi}{2}, \frac{\pi}{2}\right)$

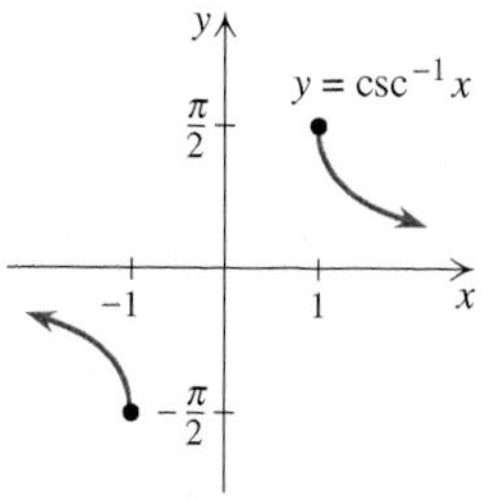

Domain $(-\infty, -1] \cup [1, \infty)$
Range $\left[-\frac{\pi}{2}, 0\right) \cup \left(0, \frac{\pi}{2}\right]$

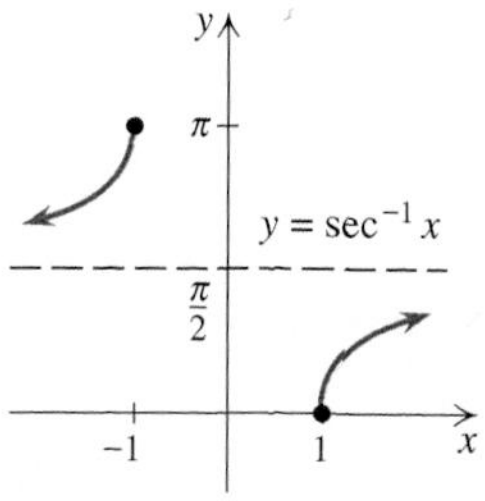

Domain $(-\infty, -1] \cup [1, \infty)$
Range $\left[0, \frac{\pi}{2}\right) \cup \left(\frac{\pi}{2}, \pi\right]$

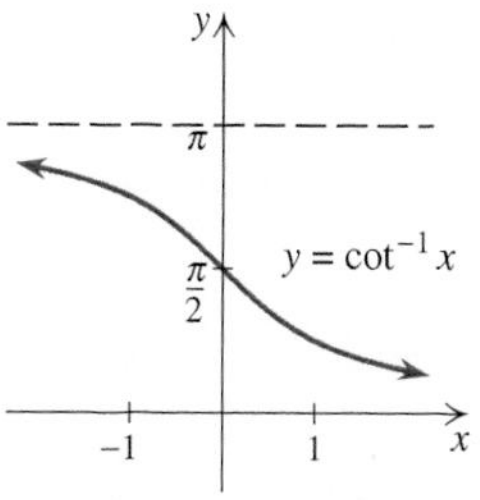

Domain $(-\infty, \infty)$
Range $(0, \pi)$

CONTENTS

The following content was taken from *University Calculus: Early Transcendentals*, Second Edition by Joel Hass, Maurice D. Weir, and George B. Thomas, Jr.

4 Applications of Derivatives 214

5 Integration 289

6 Applications of Definite Integrals 353

7 Integrals and Transcendental Functions 401

1 FUNCTIONS

OVERVIEW Functions are fundamental to the study of calculus. In this chapter we review what functions are and how they are pictured as graphs, how they are combined and transformed, and ways they can be classified. We review the trigonometric functions, and we discuss misrepresentations that can occur when using calculators and computers to obtain a function's graph. We also discuss inverse, exponential, and logarithmic functions. The real number system, Cartesian coordinates, straight lines, circles, parabolas, ellipses, and hyperbolas are reviewed in the Appendices.

1.1 Functions and Their Graphs

Functions are a tool for describing the real world in mathematical terms. A function can be represented by an equation, a graph, a numerical table, or a verbal description; we will use all four representations throughout this book. This section reviews these function ideas.

Functions; Domain and Range

The temperature at which water boils depends on the elevation above sea level (the boiling point drops as you ascend). The interest paid on a cash investment depends on the length of time the investment is held. The area of a circle depends on the radius of the circle. The distance an object travels at constant speed along a straight-line path depends on the elapsed time.

In each case, the value of one variable quantity, say y, depends on the value of another variable quantity, which we might call x. We say that "y is a function of x" and write this symbolically as

$$y = f(x) \qquad (\text{“}y \text{ equals } f \text{ of } x\text{”}).$$

In this notation, the symbol f represents the function, the letter x is the **independent variable** representing the input value of f, and y is the **dependent variable** or output value of f at x.

DEFINITION A **function** f from a set D to a set Y is a rule that assigns a *unique* (single) element $f(x) \in Y$ to each element $x \in D$.

The set D of all possible input values is called the **domain** of the function. The set of all values of $f(x)$ as x varies throughout D is called the **range** of the function. The range may not include every element in the set Y. The domain and range of a function can be any sets of objects, but often in calculus they are sets of real numbers interpreted as points of a coordinate line. (In Chapters 12–15, we will encounter functions for which the elements of the sets are points in the coordinate plane or in space.)

Often a function is given by a formula that describes how to calculate the output value from the input variable. For instance, the equation $A = \pi r^2$ is a rule that calculates the area A of a circle from its radius r (so r, interpreted as a length, can only be positive in this formula). When we define a function $y = f(x)$ with a formula and the domain is not stated explicitly or restricted by context, the domain is assumed to be the largest set of real x-values for which the formula gives real y-values, the so-called **natural domain**. If we want to restrict the domain in some way, we must say so. The domain of $y = x^2$ is the entire set of real numbers. To restrict the domain of the function to, say, positive values of x, we would write "$y = x^2, x > 0$."

FIGURE 1.1 A diagram showing a function as a kind of machine.

Changing the domain to which we apply a formula usually changes the range as well. The range of $y = x^2$ is $[0, \infty)$. The range of $y = x^2, x \geq 2$, is the set of all numbers obtained by squaring numbers greater than or equal to 2. In set notation (see Appendix 1), the range is $\{x^2 | x \geq 2\}$ or $\{y | y \geq 4\}$ or $[4, \infty)$.

When the range of a function is a set of real numbers, the function is said to be **real-valued**. The domains and ranges of many real-valued functions of a real variable are intervals or combinations of intervals. The intervals may be open, closed, or half open, and may be finite or infinite. The range of a function is not always easy to find.

A function f is like a machine that produces an output value $f(x)$ in its range whenever we feed it an input value x from its domain (Figure 1.1). The function keys on a calculator give an example of a function as a machine. For instance, the $\sqrt{x}$ key on a calculator gives an output value (the square root) whenever you enter a nonnegative number x and press the $\sqrt{x}$ key.

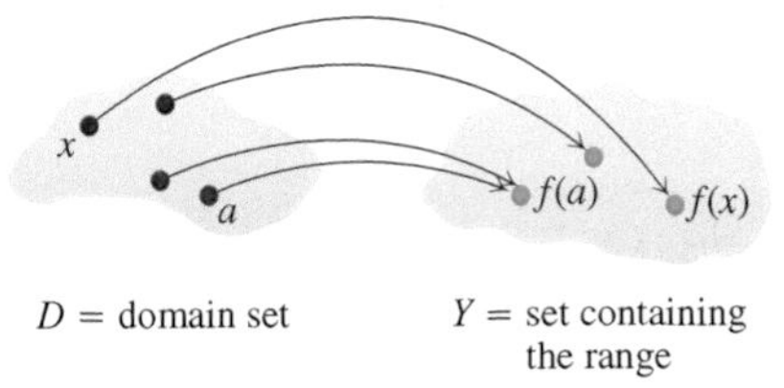

FIGURE 1.2 A function from a set D to a set Y assigns a unique element of Y to each element in D.

A function can also be pictured as an **arrow diagram** (Figure 1.2). Each arrow associates an element of the domain D with a unique or single element in the set Y. In Figure 1.2, the arrows indicate that $f(a)$ is associated with a, $f(x)$ is associated with x, and so on. Notice that a function can have the same *value* at two different input elements in the domain (as occurs with $f(a)$ in Figure 1.2), but each input element x is assigned a *single* output value $f(x)$.

EXAMPLE 1 Let's verify the natural domains and associated ranges of some simple functions. The domains in each case are the values of x for which the formula makes sense.

Function	**Domain (x)**	**Range (y)**
$y = x^2$	$(-\infty, \infty)$	$[0, \infty)$
$y = 1/x$	$(-\infty, 0) \cup (0, \infty)$	$(-\infty, 0) \cup (0, \infty)$
$y = \sqrt{x}$	$[0, \infty)$	$[0, \infty)$
$y = \sqrt{4 - x}$	$(-\infty, 4]$	$[0, \infty)$
$y = \sqrt{1 - x^2}$	$[-1, 1]$	$[0, 1]$

Solution The formula $y = x^2$ gives a real y-value for any real number x, so the domain is $(-\infty, \infty)$. The range of $y = x^2$ is $[0, \infty)$ because the square of any real number is nonnegative and every nonnegative number y is the square of its own square root, $y = (\sqrt{y})^2$ for $y \geq 0$.

The formula $y = 1/x$ gives a real y-value for every x except $x = 0$. For consistency in the rules of arithmetic, *we cannot divide any number by zero*. The range of $y = 1/x$, the set of reciprocals of all nonzero real numbers, is the set of all nonzero real numbers, since $y = 1/(1/y)$. That is, for $y \neq 0$ the number $x = 1/y$ is the input assigned to the output value y.

The formula $y = \sqrt{x}$ gives a real y-value only if $x \geq 0$. The range of $y = \sqrt{x}$ is $[0, \infty)$ because every nonnegative number is some number's square root (namely, it is the square root of its own square).

In $y = \sqrt{4 - x}$, the quantity $4 - x$ cannot be negative. That is, $4 - x \geq 0$, or $x \leq 4$. The formula gives real y-values for all $x \leq 4$. The range of $\sqrt{4 - x}$ is $[0, \infty)$, the set of all nonnegative numbers.

The formula $y = \sqrt{1 - x^2}$ gives a real y-value for every x in the closed interval from -1 to 1. Outside this domain, $1 - x^2$ is negative and its square root is not a real number. The values of $1 - x^2$ vary from 0 to 1 on the given domain, and the square roots of these values do the same. The range of $\sqrt{1 - x^2}$ is $[0, 1]$. ■

Graphs of Functions

If f is a function with domain D, its **graph** consists of the points in the Cartesian plane whose coordinates are the input-output pairs for f. In set notation, the graph is

$$\{(x, f(x)) \mid x \in D\}.$$

The graph of the function $f(x) = x + 2$ is the set of points with coordinates (x, y) for which $y = x + 2$. Its graph is the straight line sketched in Figure 1.3.

The graph of a function f is a useful picture of its behavior. If (x, y) is a point on the graph, then $y = f(x)$ is the height of the graph above the point x. The height may be positive or negative, depending on the sign of $f(x)$ (Figure 1.4).

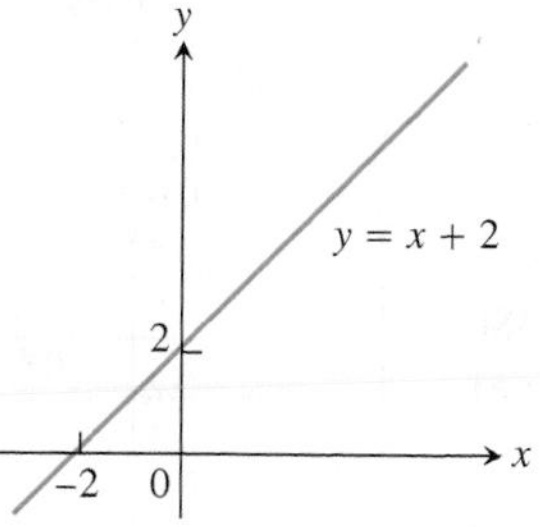

FIGURE 1.3 The graph of $f(x) = x + 2$ is the set of points (x, y) for which y has the value $x + 2$.

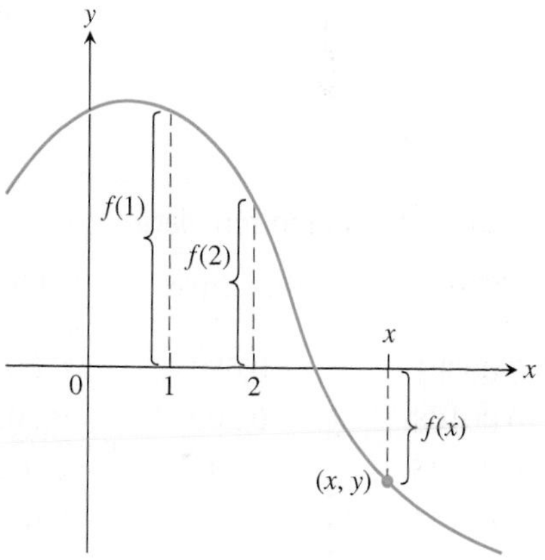

FIGURE 1.4 If (x, y) lies on the graph of f, then the value $y = f(x)$ is the height of the graph above the point x (or below x if $f(x)$ is negative).

x	$y = x^2$
-2	4
-1	1
0	0
1	1
$\frac{3}{2}$	$\frac{9}{4}$
2	4

EXAMPLE 2 Graph the function $y = x^2$ over the interval $[-2, 2]$.

Solution Make a table of xy-pairs that satisfy the equation $y = x^2$. Plot the points (x, y) whose coordinates appear in the table, and draw a *smooth* curve (labeled with its equation) through the plotted points (see Figure 1.5). ■

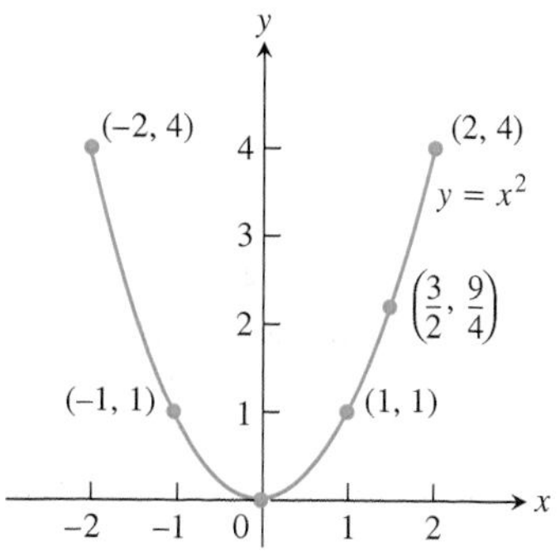

FIGURE 1.5 Graph of the function in Example 2.

How do we know that the graph of $y = x^2$ doesn't look like one of these curves?

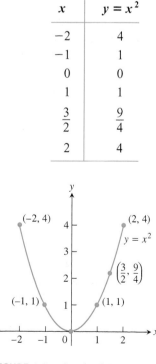

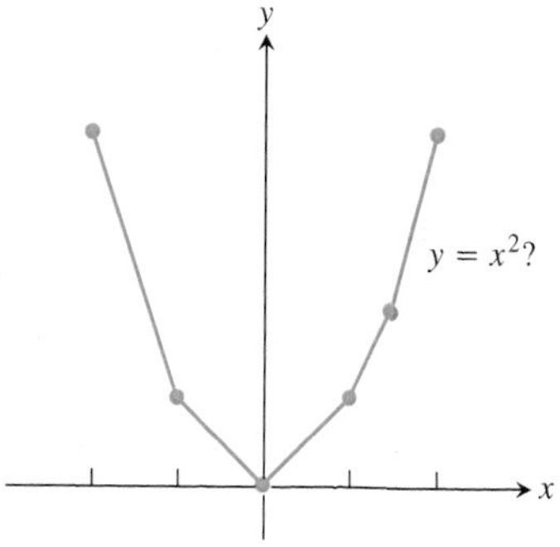

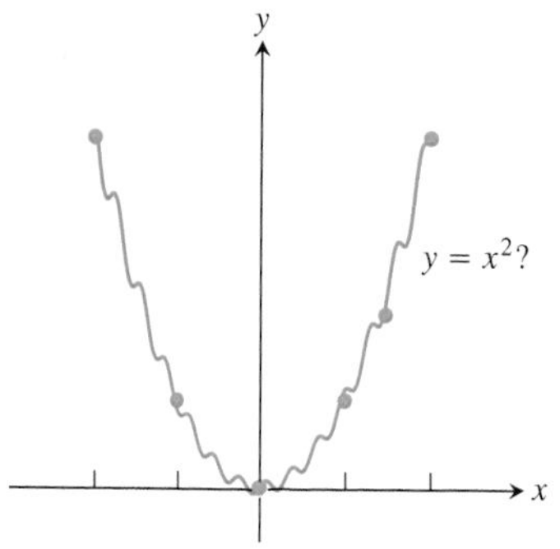

To find out, we could plot more points. But how would we then connect *them*? The basic question still remains: How do we know for sure what the graph looks like between the points we plot? Calculus answers this question, as we will see in Chapter 4. Meanwhile, we will have to settle for plotting points and connecting them as best we can.

Representing a Function Numerically

We have seen how a function may be represented algebraically by a formula (the area function) and visually by a graph (Example 2). Another way to represent a function is **numerically**, through a table of values. Numerical representations are often used by engineers and scientists. From an appropriate table of values, a graph of the function can be obtained using the method illustrated in Example 2, possibly with the aid of a computer. The graph consisting of only the points in the table is called a **scatterplot**.

EXAMPLE 3 Musical notes are pressure waves in the air. The data in Table 1.1 give recorded pressure displacement versus time in seconds of a musical note produced by a tuning fork. The table provides a representation of the pressure function over time. If we first make a scatterplot and then connect approximately the data points (t, p) from the table, we obtain the graph shown in Figure 1.6.

TABLE 1.1 Tuning fork data

Time	Pressure	Time	Pressure
0.00091	−0.080	0.00362	0.217
0.00108	0.200	0.00379	0.480
0.00125	0.480	0.00398	0.681
0.00144	0.693	0.00416	0.810
0.00162	0.816	0.00435	0.827
0.00180	0.844	0.00453	0.749
0.00198	0.771	0.00471	0.581
0.00216	0.603	0.00489	0.346
0.00234	0.368	0.00507	0.077
0.00253	0.099	0.00525	−0.164
0.00271	−0.141	0.00543	−0.320
0.00289	−0.309	0.00562	−0.354
0.00307	−0.348	0.00579	−0.248
0.00325	−0.248	0.00598	−0.035
0.00344	−0.041		

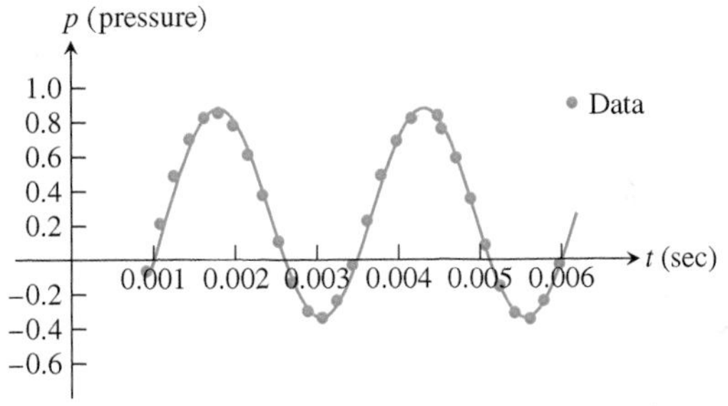

FIGURE 1.6 A smooth curve through the plotted points gives a graph of the pressure function represented by Table 1.1 (Example 3).

■

The Vertical Line Test for a Function

Not every curve in the coordinate plane can be the graph of a function. A function f can have only one value $f(x)$ for each x in its domain, so *no vertical* line can intersect the graph of a function more than once. If a is in the domain of the function f, then the vertical line $x = a$ will intersect the graph of f at the single point $(a, f(a))$.

A circle cannot be the graph of a function since some vertical lines intersect the circle twice. The circle in Figure 1.7a, however, does contain the graphs of *two* functions of x: the upper semicircle defined by the function $f(x) = \sqrt{1 - x^2}$ and the lower semicircle defined by the function $g(x) = -\sqrt{1 - x^2}$ (Figures 1.7b and 1.7c).

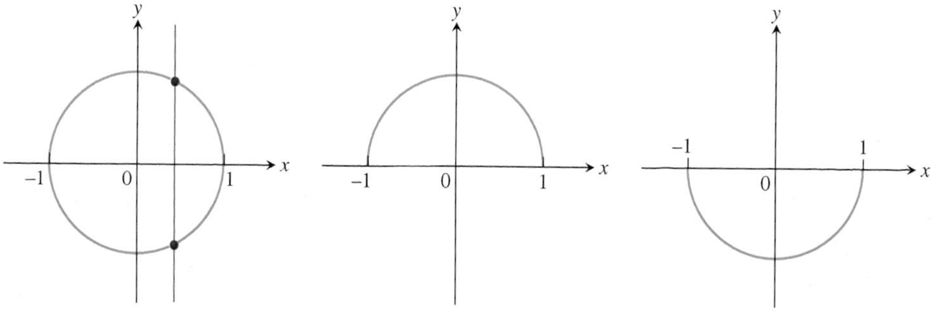

(a) $x^2 + y^2 = 1$ (b) $y = \sqrt{1 - x^2}$ (c) $y = -\sqrt{1 - x^2}$

FIGURE 1.7 (a) The circle is not the graph of a function; it fails the vertical line test. (b) The upper semicircle is the graph of a function $f(x) = \sqrt{1 - x^2}$. (c) The lower semicircle is the graph of a function $g(x) = -\sqrt{1 - x^2}$.

Piecewise-Defined Functions

Sometimes a function is described by using different formulas on different parts of its domain. One example is the **absolute value function**

$$|x| = \begin{cases} x, & x \geq 0 & \text{First formula} \\ -x, & x < 0, & \text{Second formula} \end{cases}$$

whose graph is given in Figure 1.8. The right-hand side of the equation means that the function equals x if $x \geq 0$, and equals $-x$ if $x < 0$. Piecewise-defined functions often arise when real-world data are modeled. Here are some other examples.

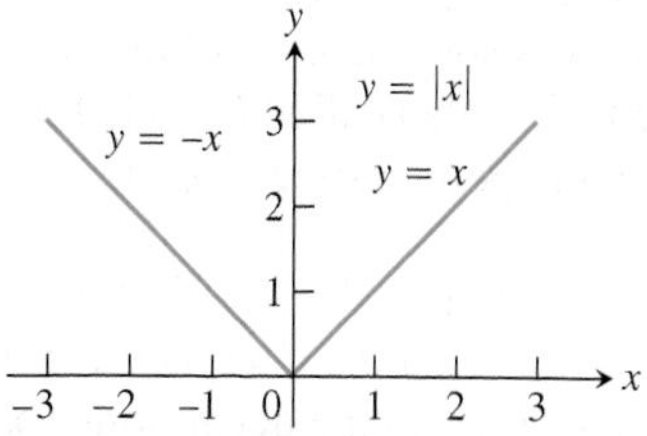

FIGURE 1.8 The absolute value function has domain $(-\infty, \infty)$ and range $[0, \infty)$.

EXAMPLE 4 The function

$$f(x) = \begin{cases} -x, & x < 0 & \text{First formula} \\ x^2, & 0 \leq x \leq 1 & \text{Second formula} \\ 1, & x > 1 & \text{Third formula} \end{cases}$$

is defined on the entire real line but has values given by different formulas, depending on the position of x. The values of f are given by $y = -x$ when $x < 0$, $y = x^2$ when $0 \leq x \leq 1$, and $y = 1$ when $x > 1$. The function, however, is *just one function* whose domain is the entire set of real numbers (Figure 1.9). ∎

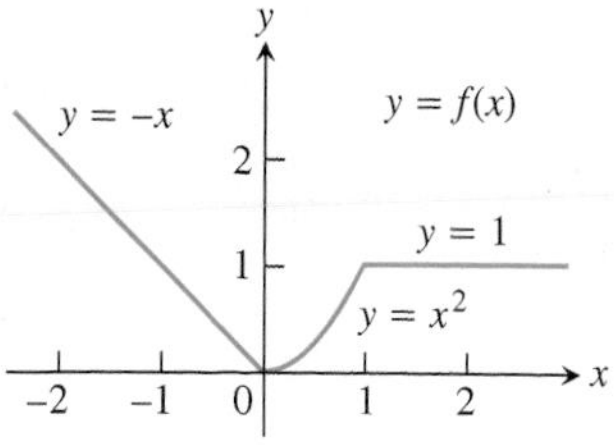

FIGURE 1.9 To graph the function $y = f(x)$ shown here, we apply different formulas to different parts of its domain (Example 4).

EXAMPLE 5 The function whose value at any number x is the *greatest integer less than or equal to x* is called the **greatest integer function** or the **integer floor function**. It is denoted $\lfloor x \rfloor$. Figure 1.10 shows the graph. Observe that

$$\lfloor 2.4 \rfloor = 2, \quad \lfloor 1.9 \rfloor = 1, \quad \lfloor 0 \rfloor = 0, \quad \lfloor -1.2 \rfloor = -2,$$
$$\lfloor 2 \rfloor = 2, \quad \lfloor 0.2 \rfloor = 0, \quad \lfloor -0.3 \rfloor = -1 \quad \lfloor -2 \rfloor = -2. \quad ∎$$

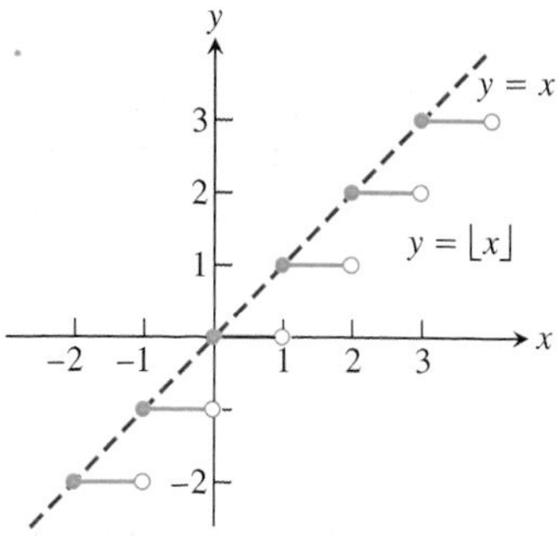

FIGURE 1.10 The graph of the greatest integer function $y = \lfloor x \rfloor$ lies on or below the line $y = x$, so it provides an integer floor for x (Example 5).

EXAMPLE 6 The function whose value at any number x is the *smallest integer greater than or equal to x* is called the **least integer function** or the **integer ceiling function**. It is denoted $\lceil x \rceil$. Figure 1.11 shows the graph. For positive values of x, this function might represent, for example, the cost of parking x hours in a parking lot which charges \$1 for each hour or part of an hour. ∎

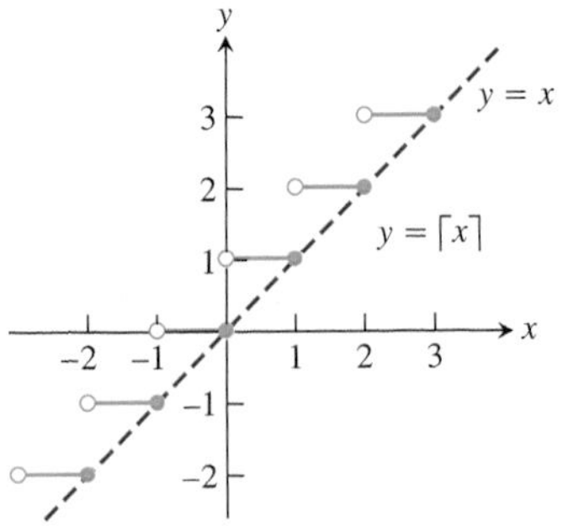

FIGURE 1.11 The graph of the least integer function $y = \lceil x \rceil$ lies on or above the line $y = x$, so it provides an integer ceiling for x (Example 6).

Increasing and Decreasing Functions

If the graph of a function *climbs* or *rises* as you move from left to right, we say that the function is *increasing*. If the graph *descends* or *falls* as you move from left to right, the function is *decreasing*.

> **DEFINITIONS** Let f be a function defined on an interval I and let x_1 and x_2 be any two points in I.
>
> 1. If $f(x_2) > f(x_1)$ whenever $x_1 < x_2$, then f is said to be **increasing** on I.
> 2. If $f(x_2) < f(x_1)$ whenever $x_1 < x_2$, then f is said to be **decreasing** on I.

It is important to realize that the definitions of increasing and decreasing functions must be satisfied for *every* pair of points x_1 and x_2 in I with $x_1 < x_2$. Because we use the inequality $<$ to compare the function values, instead of $\leq$, it is sometimes said that f is *strictly* increasing or decreasing on I. The interval I may be finite (also called bounded) or infinite (unbounded) and by definition never consists of a single point (Appendix 1).

EXAMPLE 7 The function graphed in Figure 1.9 is decreasing on $(-\infty, 0]$ and increasing on $[0, 1]$. The function is neither increasing nor decreasing on the interval $[1, \infty)$ because of the strict inequalities used to compare the function values in the definitions. ■

Even Functions and Odd Functions: Symmetry

The graphs of *even* and *odd* functions have characteristic symmetry properties.

> **DEFINITIONS** A function $y = f(x)$ is an
>
> **even function of x** if $f(-x) = f(x)$,
> **odd function of x** if $f(-x) = -f(x)$,
>
> for every x in the function's domain.

The names *even* and *odd* come from powers of x. If y is an even power of x, as in $y = x^2$ or $y = x^4$, it is an even function of x because $(-x)^2 = x^2$ and $(-x)^4 = x^4$. If y is an odd power of x, as in $y = x$ or $y = x^3$, it is an odd function of x because $(-x)^1 = -x$ and $(-x)^3 = -x^3$.

The graph of an even function is **symmetric about the y-axis**. Since $f(-x) = f(x)$, a point (x, y) lies on the graph if and only if the point $(-x, y)$ lies on the graph (Figure 1.12a). A reflection across the y-axis leaves the graph unchanged.

The graph of an odd function is **symmetric about the origin**. Since $f(-x) = -f(x)$, a point (x, y) lies on the graph if and only if the point $(-x, -y)$ lies on the graph (Figure 1.12b). Equivalently, a graph is symmetric about the origin if a rotation of 180° about the origin leaves the graph unchanged. Notice that the definitions imply that both x and $-x$ must be in the domain of f.

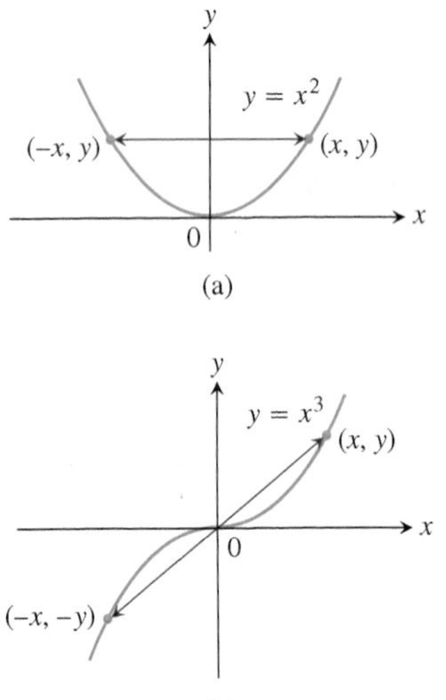

FIGURE 1.12 (a) The graph of $y = x^2$ (an even function) is symmetric about the y-axis. (b) The graph of $y = x^3$ (an odd function) is symmetric about the origin.

EXAMPLE 8

$f(x) = x^2$	Even function: $(-x)^2 = x^2$ for all x; symmetry about y-axis.
$f(x) = x^2 + 1$	Even function: $(-x)^2 + 1 = x^2 + 1$ for all x; symmetry about y-axis (Figure 1.13a).
$f(x) = x$	Odd function: $(-x) = -x$ for all x; symmetry about the origin.
$f(x) = x + 1$	Not odd: $f(-x) = -x + 1$, but $-f(x) = -x - 1$. The two are not equal. Not even: $(-x) + 1 \neq x + 1$ for all $x \neq 0$ (Figure 1.13b). ■

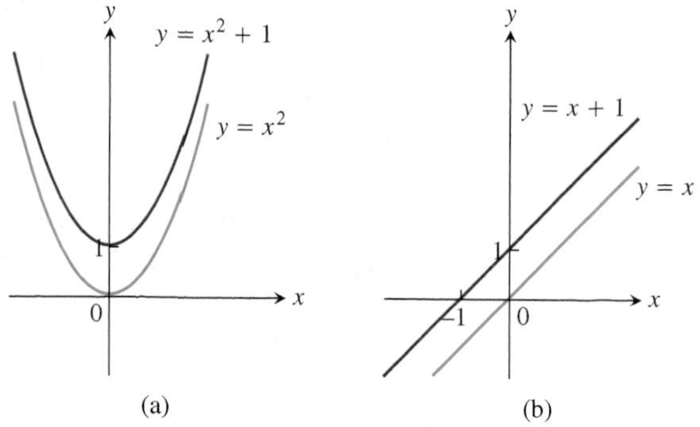

FIGURE 1.13 (a) When we add the constant term 1 to the function $y = x^2$, the resulting function $y = x^2 + 1$ is still even and its graph is still symmetric about the y-axis. (b) When we add the constant term 1 to the function $y = x$, the resulting function $y = x + 1$ is no longer odd. The symmetry about the origin is lost (Example 8).

Common Functions

A variety of important types of functions are frequently encountered in calculus. We identify and briefly describe them here.

Linear Functions A function of the form $f(x) = mx + b$, for constants m and b, is called a **linear function**. Figure 1.14a shows an array of lines $f(x) = mx$ where $b = 0$, so these lines pass through the origin. The function $f(x) = x$ where $m = 1$ and $b = 0$ is called the **identity function**. Constant functions result when the slope $m = 0$ (Figure 1.14b). A linear function with positive slope whose graph passes through the origin is called a *proportionality* relationship.

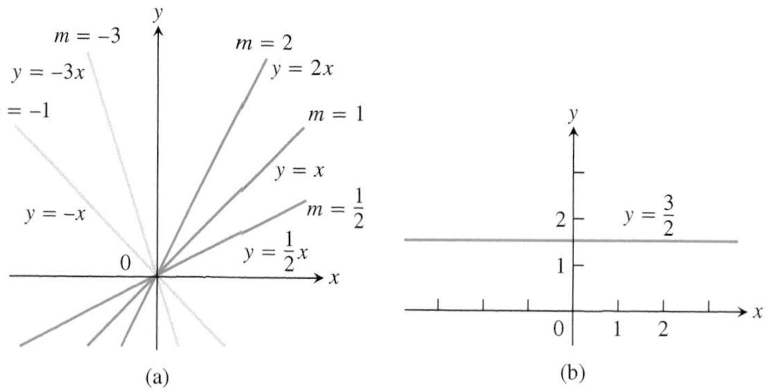

FIGURE 1.14 (a) Lines through the origin with slope m. (b) A constant function with slope $m = 0$.

> **DEFINITION** Two variables y and x are **proportional** (to one another) if one is always a constant multiple of the other; that is, if $y = kx$ for some nonzero constant k.

If the variable y is proportional to the reciprocal $1/x$, then sometimes it is said that y is **inversely proportional** to x (because $1/x$ is the multiplicative inverse of x).

Power Functions A function $f(x) = x^a$, where a is a constant, is called a **power function**. There are several important cases to consider.

(a) $a = n$, a positive integer.

The graphs of $f(x) = x^n$, for $n = 1, 2, 3, 4, 5$, are displayed in Figure 1.15. These functions are defined for all real values of x. Notice that as the power n gets larger, the curves tend to flatten toward the x-axis on the interval $(-1, 1)$, and to rise more steeply for $|x| > 1$. Each curve passes through the point $(1, 1)$ and through the origin. The graphs of functions with even powers are symmetric about the y-axis; those with odd powers are symmetric about the origin. The even-powered functions are decreasing on the interval $(-\infty, 0]$ and increasing on $[0, \infty)$; the odd-powered functions are increasing over the entire real line $(-\infty, \infty)$.

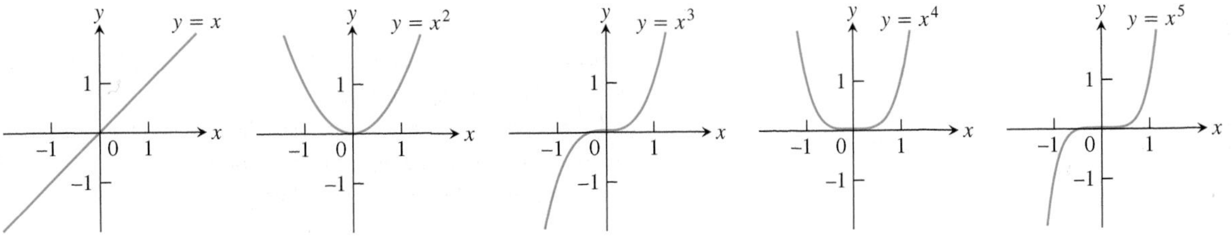

FIGURE 1.15 Graphs of $f(x) = x^n$, $n = 1, 2, 3, 4, 5$, defined for $-\infty < x < \infty$.

(b) $a = -1$ or $a = -2$.

The graphs of the functions $f(x) = x^{-1} = 1/x$ and $g(x) = x^{-2} = 1/x^2$ are shown in Figure 1.16. Both functions are defined for all $x \neq 0$ (you can never divide by zero). The graph of $y = 1/x$ is the hyperbola $xy = 1$, which approaches the coordinate axes far from the origin. The graph of $y = 1/x^2$ also approaches the coordinate axes. The graph of the function f is symmetric about the origin; f is decreasing on the intervals $(-\infty, 0)$ and $(0, \infty)$. The graph of the function g is symmetric about the y-axis; g is increasing on $(-\infty, 0)$ and decreasing on $(0, \infty)$.

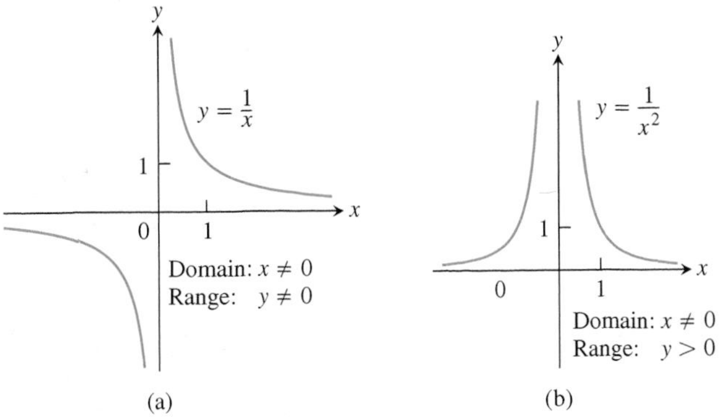

FIGURE 1.16 Graphs of the power functions $f(x) = x^a$ for part (a) $a = -1$ and for part (b) $a = -2$.

(c) $a = \frac{1}{2}, \frac{1}{3}, \frac{3}{2}$, and $\frac{2}{3}$.

The functions $f(x) = x^{1/2} = \sqrt{x}$ and $g(x) = x^{1/3} = \sqrt[3]{x}$ are the **square root** and **cube root** functions, respectively. The domain of the square root function is $[0, \infty)$, but the cube root function is defined for all real x. Their graphs are displayed in Figure 1.17, along with the graphs of $y = x^{3/2}$ and $y = x^{2/3}$. (Recall that $x^{3/2} = (x^{1/2})^3$ and $x^{2/3} = (x^{1/3})^2$.)

Polynomials A function p is a **polynomial** if

$$p(x) = a_n x^n + a_{n-1}x^{n-1} + \cdots + a_1 x + a_0$$

where n is a nonnegative integer and the numbers $a_0, a_1, a_2, \ldots, a_n$ are real constants (called the **coefficients** of the polynomial). All polynomials have domain $(-\infty, \infty)$. If the

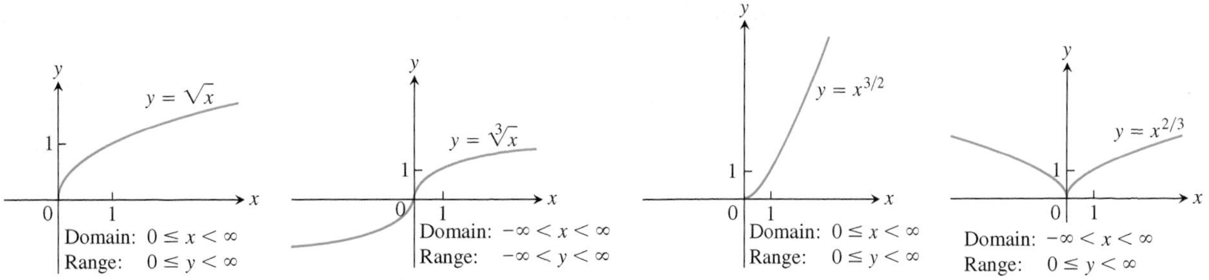

FIGURE 1.17 Graphs of the power functions $f(x) = x^a$ for $a = \frac{1}{2}, \frac{1}{3}, \frac{3}{2}$, and $\frac{2}{3}$.

leading coefficient $a_n \neq 0$ and $n > 0$, then n is called the **degree** of the polynomial. Linear functions with $m \neq 0$ are polynomials of degree 1. Polynomials of degree 2, usually written as $p(x) = ax^2 + bx + c$, are called **quadratic functions**. Likewise, **cubic functions** are polynomials $p(x) = ax^3 + bx^2 + cx + d$ of degree 3. Figure 1.18 shows the graphs of three polynomials. Techniques to graph polynomials are studied in Chapter 4.

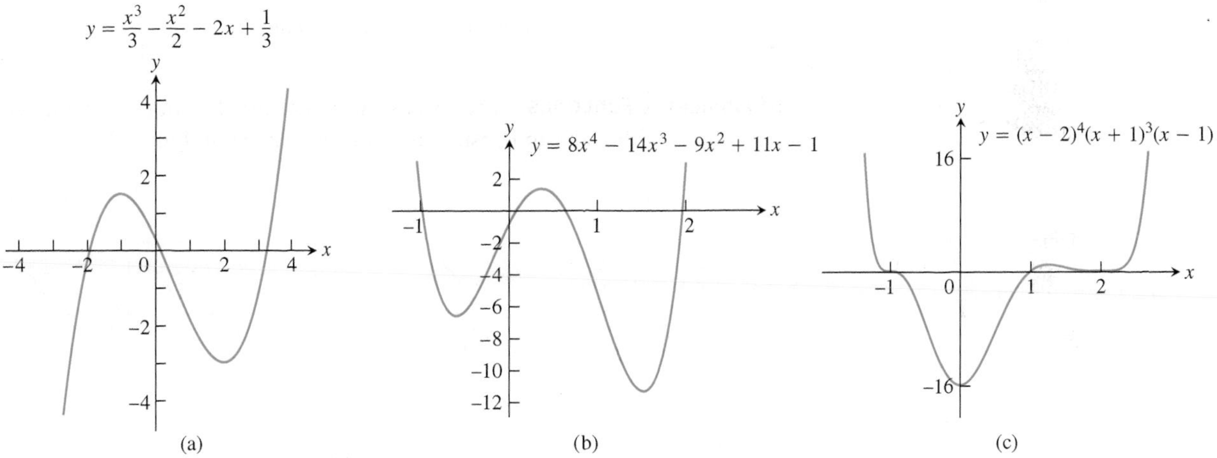

FIGURE 1.18 Graphs of three polynomial functions.

Rational Functions A **rational function** is a quotient or ratio $f(x) = p(x)/q(x)$, where p and q are polynomials. The domain of a rational function is the set of all real x for which $q(x) \neq 0$. The graphs of several rational functions are shown in Figure 1.19.

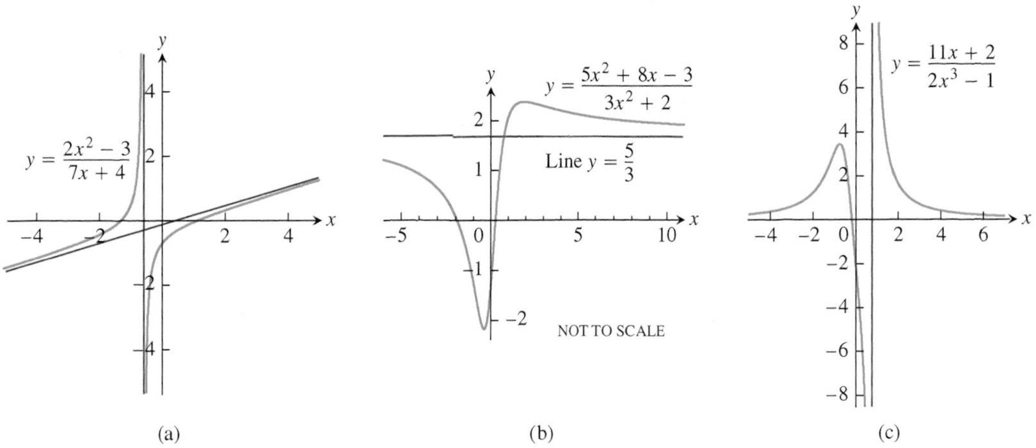

FIGURE 1.19 Graphs of three rational functions. The straight red lines are called *asymptotes* and are not part of the graph.

Algebraic Functions Any function constructed from polynomials using algebraic operations (addition, subtraction, multiplication, division, and taking roots) lies within the class of **algebraic functions**. All rational functions are algebraic, but also included are more complicated functions (such as those satisfying an equation like $y^3 - 9xy + x^3 = 0$, studied in Section 3.7). Figure 1.20 displays the graphs of three algebraic functions.

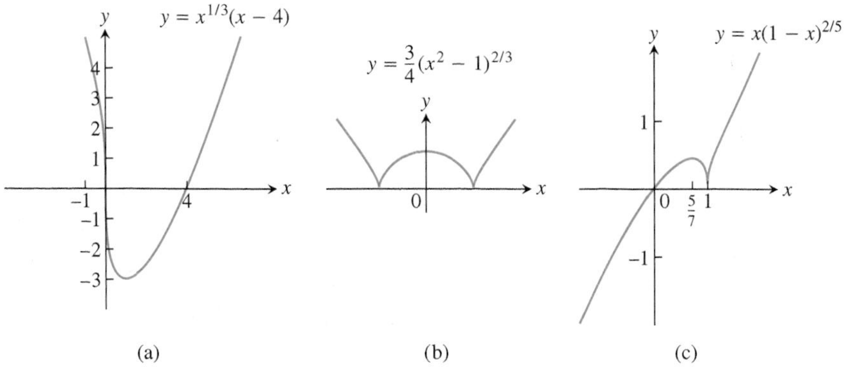

FIGURE 1.20 Graphs of three algebraic functions.

Trigonometric Functions The six basic trigonometric functions are reviewed in Section 1.3. The graphs of the sine and cosine functions are shown in Figure 1.21.

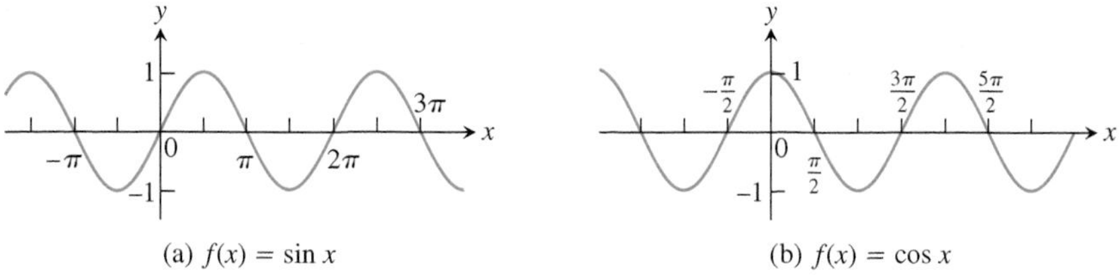

FIGURE 1.21 Graphs of the sine and cosine functions.

Exponential Functions Functions of the form $f(x) = a^x$, where the base $a > 0$ is a positive constant and $a \neq 1$, are called **exponential functions**. All exponential functions have domain $(-\infty, \infty)$ and range $(0, \infty)$, so an exponential function never assumes the value 0. We discuss exponential functions in Section 1.5. The graphs of some exponential functions are shown in Figure 1.22.

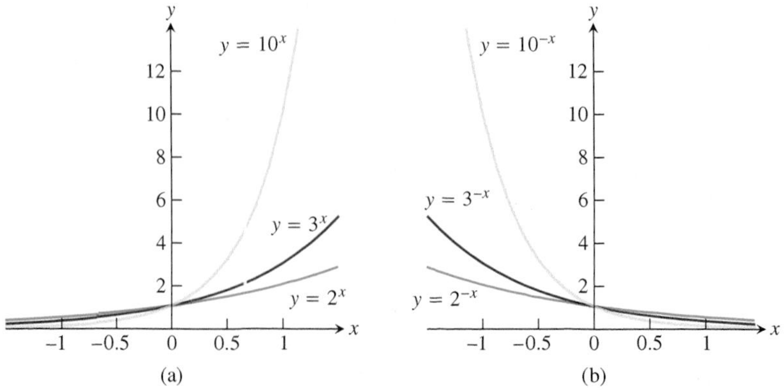

FIGURE 1.22 Graphs of exponential functions.

Logarithmic Functions These are the functions $f(x) = \log_a x$, where the base $a \neq 1$ is a positive constant. They are the *inverse functions* of the exponential functions, and we discuss these functions in Section 1.6. Figure 1.23 shows the graphs of four logarithmic functions with various bases. In each case the domain is $(0, \infty)$ and the range is $(-\infty, \infty)$.

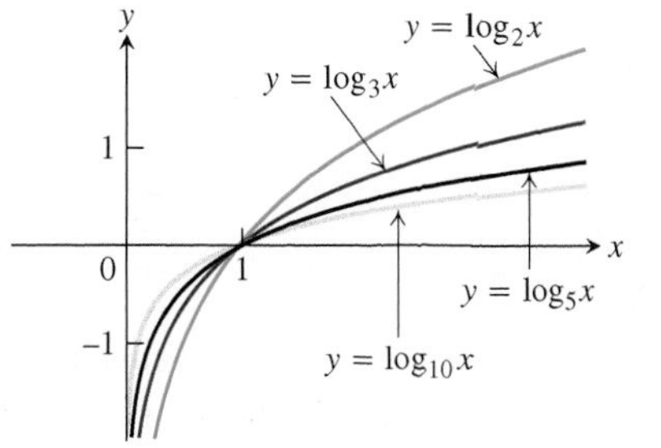

FIGURE 1.23 Graphs of four logarithmic functions.

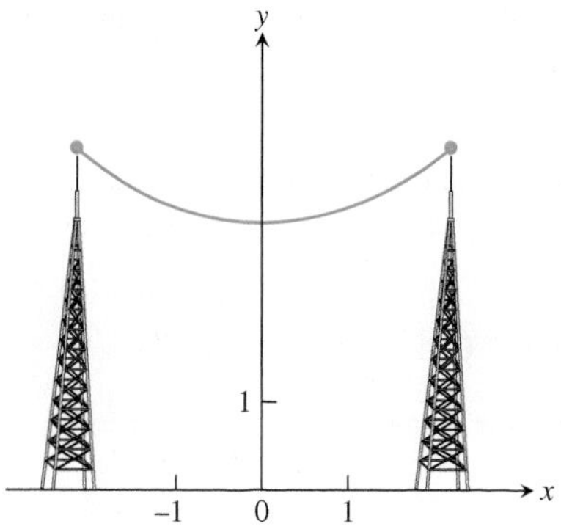

FIGURE 1.24 Graph of a catenary or hanging cable. (The Latin word *catena* means "chain.")

Transcendental Functions These are functions that are not algebraic. They include the trigonometric, inverse trigonometric, exponential, and logarithmic functions, and many other functions as well. A particular example of a transcendental function is a **catenary**. Its graph has the shape of a cable, like a telephone line or electric cable, strung from one support to another and hanging freely under its own weight (Figure 1.24). The function defining the graph is discussed in Section 7.3.

Exercises 1.1

Functions

In Exercises 1–6, find the domain and range of each function.

1. $f(x) = 1 + x^2$

2. $f(x) = 1 - \sqrt{x}$

3. $F(x) = \sqrt{5x + 10}$

4. $g(x) = \sqrt{x^2 - 3x}$

5. $f(t) = \dfrac{4}{3 - t}$

6. $G(t) = \dfrac{2}{t^2 - 16}$

In Exercises 7 and 8, which of the graphs are graphs of functions of x, and which are not? Give reasons for your answers.

7. a.

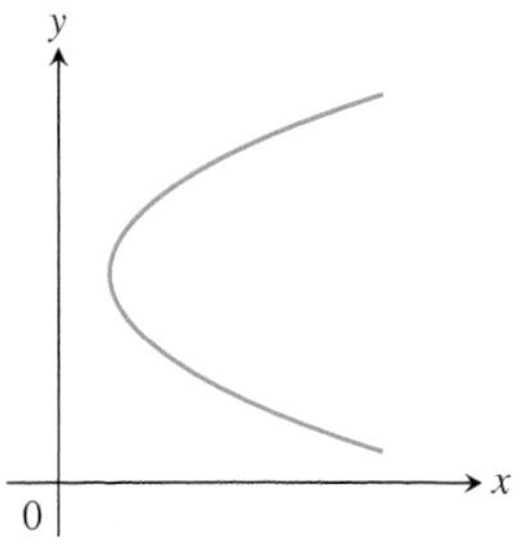

b.

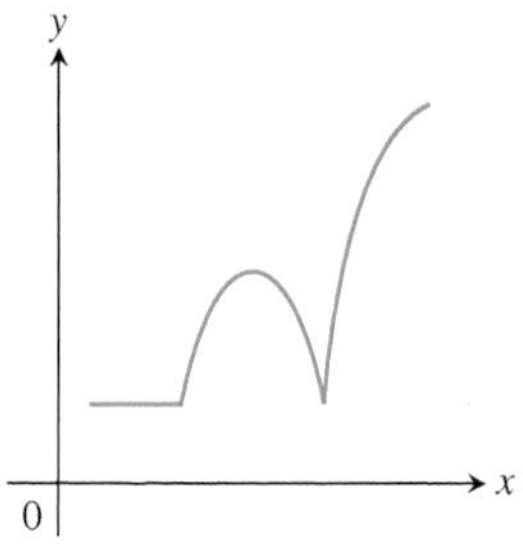

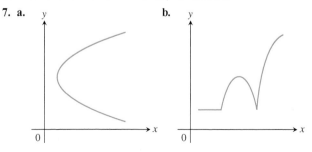

8. a.

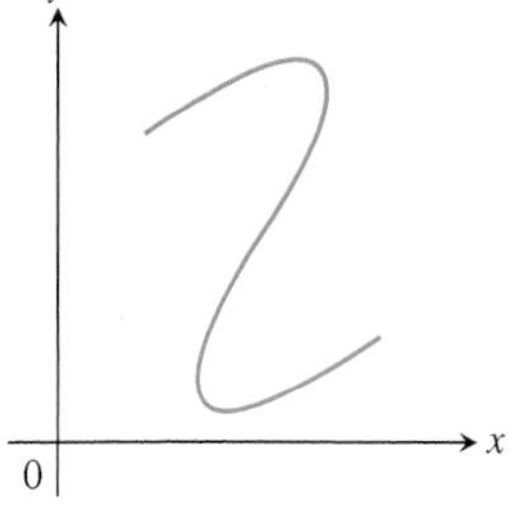

b.

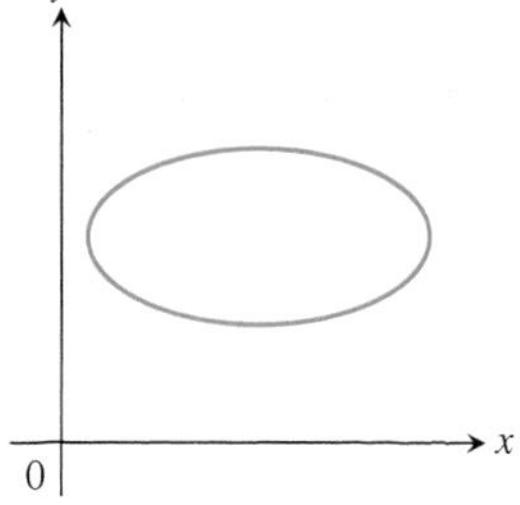

Finding Formulas for Functions

9. Express the area and perimeter of an equilateral triangle as a function of the triangle's side length x.

10. Express the side length of a square as a function of the length d of the square's diagonal. Then express the area as a function of the diagonal length.

11. Express the edge length of a cube as a function of the cube's diagonal length d. Then express the surface area and volume of the cube as a function of the diagonal length.

12. A point P in the first quadrant lies on the graph of the function $f(x) = \sqrt{x}$. Express the coordinates of P as functions of the slope of the line joining P to the origin.

13. Consider the point (x, y) lying on the graph of the line $2x + 4y = 5$. Let L be the distance from the point (x, y) to the origin $(0, 0)$. Write L as a function of x.

14. Consider the point (x, y) lying on the graph of $y = \sqrt{x - 3}$. Let L be the distance between the points (x, y) and $(4, 0)$. Write L as a function of y.

Functions and Graphs

Find the domain and graph the functions in Exercises 15–20.

15. $f(x) = 5 - 2x$ **16.** $f(x) = 1 - 2x - x^2$

17. $g(x) = \sqrt{|x|}$ **18.** $g(x) = \sqrt{-x}$

19. $F(t) = t/|t|$ **20.** $G(t) = 1/|t|$

21. Find the domain of $y = \dfrac{x + 3}{4 - \sqrt{x^2 - 9}}$.

22. Find the range of $y = 2 + \dfrac{x^2}{x^2 + 4}$.

23. Graph the following equations and explain why they are not graphs of functions of x.

a. $|y| = x$ **b.** $y^2 = x^2$

24. Graph the following equations and explain why they are not graphs of functions of x.

a. $|x| + |y| = 1$ **b.** $|x + y| = 1$

Piecewise-Defined Functions

Graph the functions in Exercises 25–28.

25. $f(x) = \begin{cases} x, & 0 \le x \le 1 \\ 2 - x, & 1 < x \le 2 \end{cases}$

26. $g(x) = \begin{cases} 1 - x, & 0 \le x \le 1 \\ 2 - x, & 1 < x \le 2 \end{cases}$

27. $F(x) = \begin{cases} 4 - x^2, & x \le 1 \\ x^2 + 2x, & x > 1 \end{cases}$

28. $G(x) = \begin{cases} 1/x, & x < 0 \\ x, & 0 \le x \end{cases}$

Find a formula for each function graphed in Exercises 29–32.

29. a.

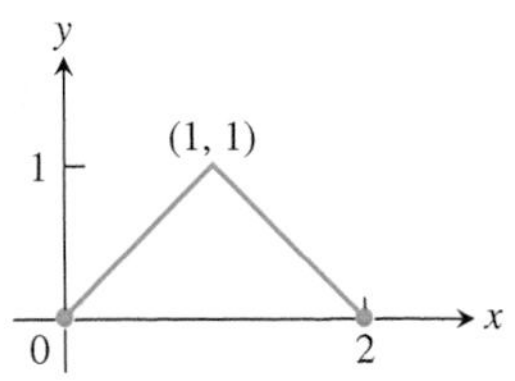

b.

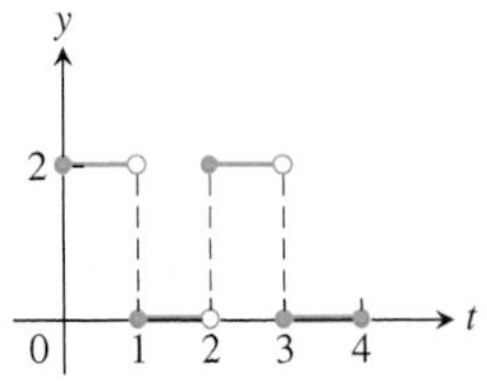

30. a.

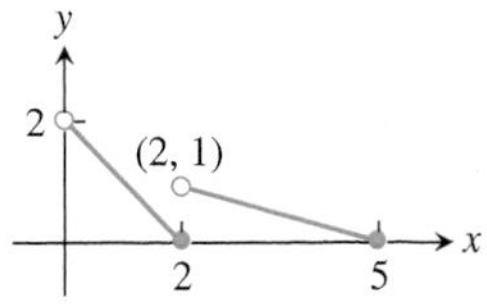

b.

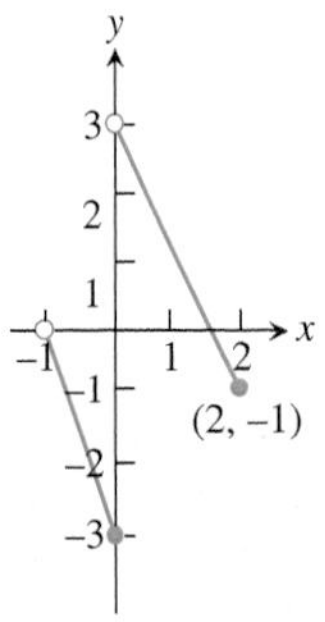

31. a.

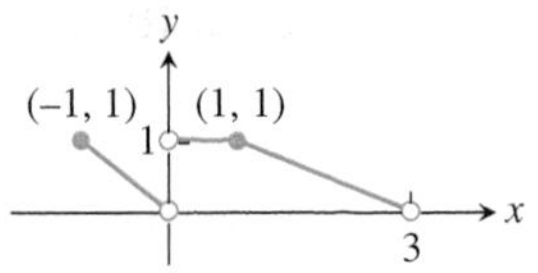

b.

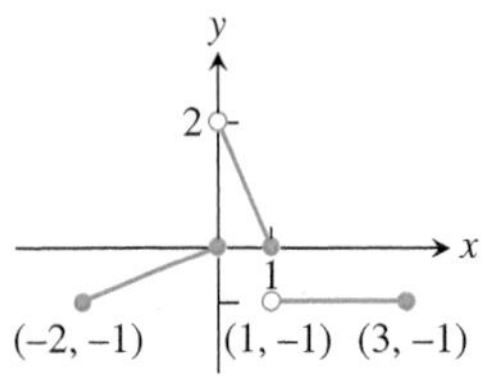

32. a.

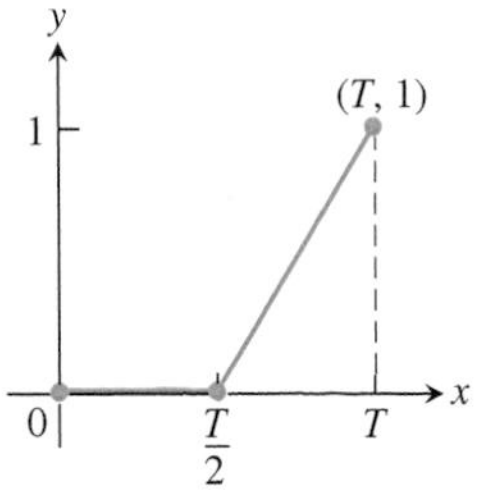

b.

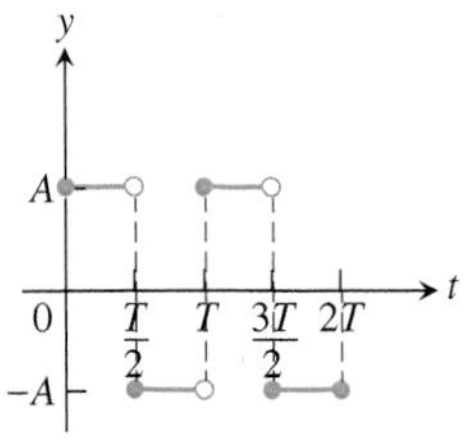

The Greatest and Least Integer Functions

33. For what values of x is

a. $\lfloor x \rfloor = 0$? **b.** $\lceil x \rceil = 0$?

34. What real numbers x satisfy the equation $\lfloor x \rfloor = \lceil x \rceil$?

35. Does $\lceil -x \rceil = -\lfloor x \rfloor$ for all real x? Give reasons for your answer.

36. Graph the function

$$f(x) = \begin{cases} \lfloor x \rfloor, & x \ge 0 \\ \lceil x \rceil, & x < 0. \end{cases}$$

Why is $f(x)$ called the *integer part* of x?

Increasing and Decreasing Functions

Graph the functions in Exercises 37–46. What symmetries, if any, do the graphs have? Specify the intervals over which the function is increasing and the intervals where it is decreasing.

37. $y = -x^3$ **38.** $y = -\dfrac{1}{x^2}$

39. $y = -\dfrac{1}{x}$ **40.** $y = \dfrac{1}{|x|}$

41. $y = \sqrt{|x|}$ **42.** $y = \sqrt{-x}$

43. $y = x^3/8$ **44.** $y = -4\sqrt{x}$

45. $y = -x^{3/2}$ **46.** $y = (-x)^{2/3}$

Even and Odd Functions

In Exercises 47–58, say whether the function is even, odd, or neither. Give reasons for your answer.

47. $f(x) = 3$ **48.** $f(x) = x^{-5}$

49. $f(x) = x^2 + 1$ **50.** $f(x) = x^2 + x$

51. $g(x) = x^3 + x$ **52.** $g(x) = x^4 + 3x^2 - 1$

53. $g(x) = \dfrac{1}{x^2 - 1}$ **54.** $g(x) = \dfrac{x}{x^2 - 1}$

55. $h(t) = \dfrac{1}{t - 1}$ **56.** $h(t) = |t^3|$

57. $h(t) = 2t + 1$ **58.** $h(t) = 2|t| + 1$

Theory and Examples

59. The variable s is proportional to t, and $s = 25$ when $t = 75$. Determine t when $s = 60$.

60. Kinetic energy The kinetic energy K of a mass is proportional to the square of its velocity v. If $K = 12{,}960$ joules when $v = 18$ m/sec, what is K when $v = 10$ m/sec?

61. The variables r and s are inversely proportional, and $r = 6$ when $s = 4$. Determine s when $r = 10$.

62. Boyle's Law Boyle's Law says that the volume V of a gas at constant temperature increases whenever the pressure P decreases, so that V and P are inversely proportional. If $P = 14.7$ lb/in^2 when $V = 1000$ in^3, then what is V when $P = 23.4$ lb/in^2?

63. A box with an open top is to be constructed from a rectangular piece of cardboard with dimensions 14 in. by 22 in. by cutting out equal squares of side x at each corner and then folding up the sides as in the figure. Express the volume V of the box as a function of x.

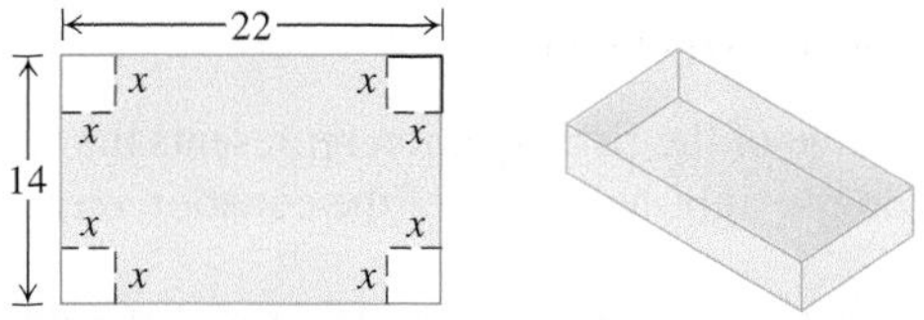

64. The accompanying figure shows a rectangle inscribed in an isosceles right triangle whose hypotenuse is 2 units long.

a. Express the y-coordinate of P in terms of x. (You might start by writing an equation for the line AB.)

b. Express the area of the rectangle in terms of x.

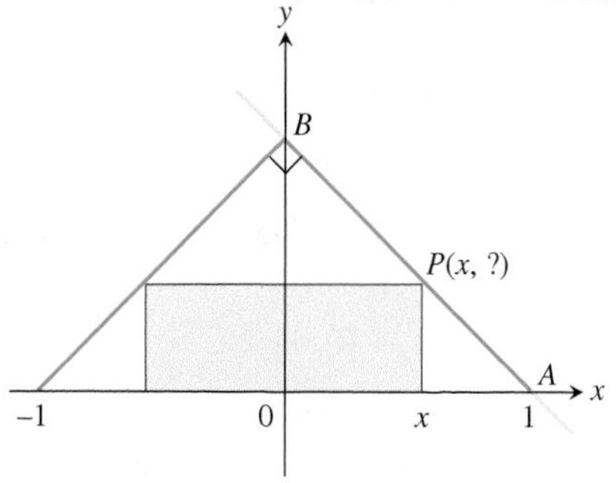

In Exercises 65 and 66, match each equation with its graph. Do not use a graphing device, and give reasons for your answer.

65. a. $y = x^4$ **b.** $y = x^7$ **c.** $y = x^{10}$

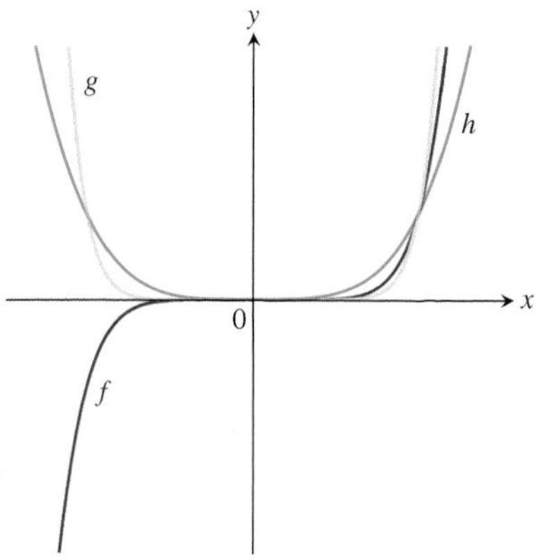

66. a. $y = 5x$ **b.** $y = 5^x$ **c.** $y = x^5$

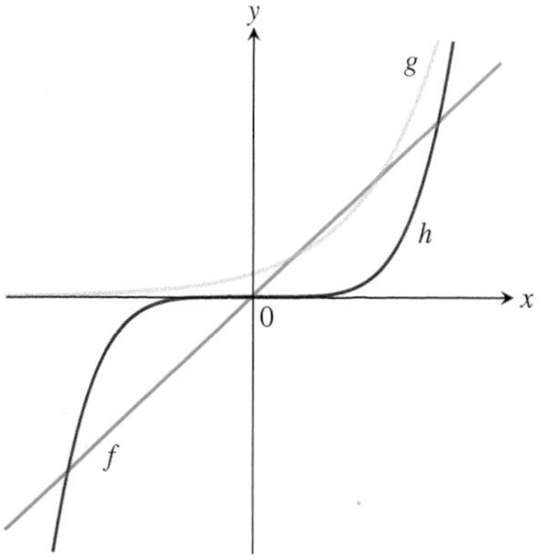

T **67. a.** Graph the functions $f(x) = x/2$ and $g(x) = 1 + (4/x)$ together to identify the values of x for which

$$\frac{x}{2} > 1 + \frac{4}{x}.$$

b. Confirm your findings in part (a) algebraically.

T **68. a.** Graph the functions $f(x) = 3/(x - 1)$ and $g(x) = 2/(x + 1)$ together to identify the values of x for which

$$\frac{3}{x - 1} < \frac{2}{x + 1}.$$

b. Confirm your findings in part (a) algebraically.

69. For a curve to be *symmetric about the x-axis*, the point (x, y) must lie on the curve if and only if the point $(x, -y)$ lies on the curve. Explain why a curve that is symmetric about the x-axis is not the graph of a function, unless the function is $y = 0$.

70. Three hundred books sell for \$40 each, resulting in a revenue of (300)(\$40) = \$12,000. For each \$5 increase in the price, 25 fewer books are sold. Write the revenue R as a function of the number x of \$5 increases.

71. A pen in the shape of an isosceles right triangle with legs of length x ft and hypotenuse of length h ft is to be built. If fencing costs \$5/ft for the legs and \$10/ft for the hypotenuse, write the total cost C of construction as a function of h.

72. Industrial costs A power plant sits next to a river where the river is 800 ft wide. To lay a new cable from the plant to a location in the city 2 mi downstream on the opposite side costs \$180 per foot across the river and \$100 per foot along the land.

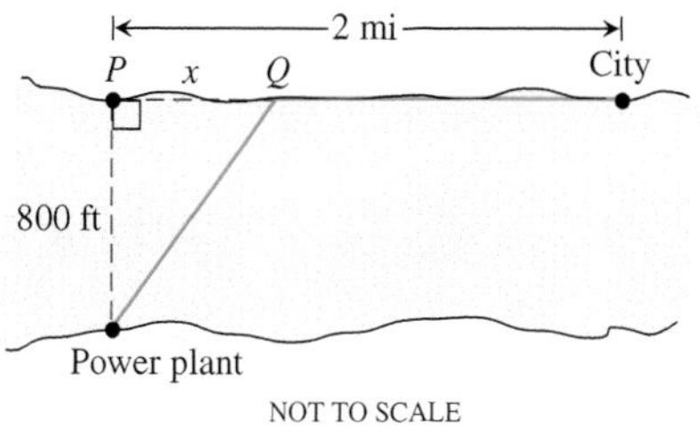

a. Suppose that the cable goes from the plant to a point Q on the opposite side that is x ft from the point P directly opposite the plant. Write a function $C(x)$ that gives the cost of laying the cable in terms of the distance x.

b. Generate a table of values to determine if the least expensive location for point Q is less than 2000 ft or greater than 2000 ft from point P.

1.2 Combining Functions; Shifting and Scaling Graphs

In this section we look at the main ways functions are combined or transformed to form new functions.

Sums, Differences, Products, and Quotients

Like numbers, functions can be added, subtracted, multiplied, and divided (except where the denominator is zero) to produce new functions. If f and g are functions, then for every x that belongs to the domains of both f and g (that is, for $x \in D(f) \cap D(g)$), we define functions $f + g$, $f - g$, and fg by the formulas

$$(f + g)(x) = f(x) + g(x).$$
$$(f - g)(x) = f(x) - g(x).$$
$$(fg)(x) = f(x)g(x).$$

Notice that the + sign on the left-hand side of the first equation represents the operation of addition of *functions*, whereas the + on the right-hand side of the equation means addition of the real numbers $f(x)$ and $g(x)$.

At any point of $D(f) \cap D(g)$ at which $g(x) \neq 0$, we can also define the function f/g by the formula

$$\left(\frac{f}{g}\right)(x) = \frac{f(x)}{g(x)} \qquad (\text{where } g(x) \neq 0).$$

Functions can also be multiplied by constants: If c is a real number, then the function cf is defined for all x in the domain of f by

$$(cf)(x) = cf(x).$$

EXAMPLE 1 The functions defined by the formulas

$$f(x) = \sqrt{x} \qquad \text{and} \qquad g(x) = \sqrt{1 - x}$$

have domains $D(f) = [0, \infty)$ and $D(g) = (-\infty, 1]$. The points common to these domains are the points

$$[0, \infty) \cap (-\infty, 1] = [0, 1].$$

The following table summarizes the formulas and domains for the various algebraic combinations of the two functions. We also write $f \cdot g$ for the product function fg.

Function	Formula	Domain
$f + g$	$(f + g)(x) = \sqrt{x} + \sqrt{1 - x}$	$[0, 1] = D(f) \cap D(g)$
$f - g$	$(f - g)(x) = \sqrt{x} - \sqrt{1 - x}$	$[0, 1]$
$g - f$	$(g - f)(x) = \sqrt{1 - x} - \sqrt{x}$	$[0, 1]$
$f \cdot g$	$(f \cdot g)(x) = f(x)g(x) = \sqrt{x(1 - x)}$	$[0, 1]$
f/g	$\frac{f}{g}(x) = \frac{f(x)}{g(x)} = \sqrt{\frac{x}{1 - x}}$	$[0, 1)$ ($x = 1$ excluded)
g/f	$\frac{g}{f}(x) = \frac{g(x)}{f(x)} = \sqrt{\frac{1 - x}{x}}$	$(0, 1]$ ($x = 0$ excluded)

■

The graph of the function $f + g$ is obtained from the graphs of f and g by adding the corresponding y-coordinates $f(x)$ and $g(x)$ at each point $x \in D(f) \cap D(g)$, as in Figure 1.25. The graphs of $f + g$ and $f \cdot g$ from Example 1 are shown in Figure 1.26.

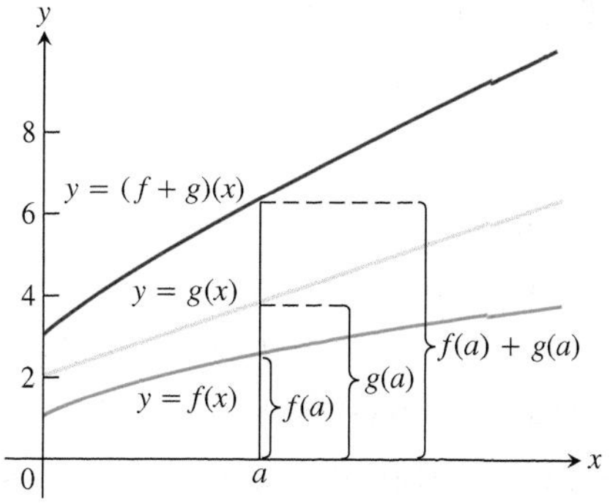

FIGURE 1.25 Graphical addition of two functions.

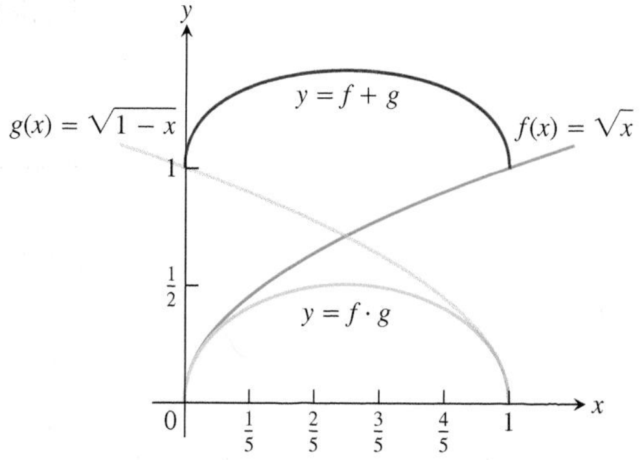

FIGURE 1.26 The domain of the function $f + g$ is the intersection of the domains of f and g, the interval $[0, 1]$ on the x-axis where these domains overlap. This interval is also the domain of the function $f \cdot g$ (Example 1).

Composite Functions

Composition is another method for combining functions.

> **DEFINITION** If f and g are functions, the **composite** function $f \circ g$ ("f composed with g") is defined by
>
> $$(f \circ g)(x) = f(g(x)).$$
>
> The domain of $f \circ g$ consists of the numbers x in the domain of g for which $g(x)$ lies in the domain of f.

The definition implies that $f \circ g$ can be formed when the range of g lies in the domain of f. To find $(f \circ g)(x)$, *first* find $g(x)$ and *second* find $f(g(x))$. Figure 1.27 pictures $f \circ g$ as a machine diagram and Figure 1.28 shows the composite as an arrow diagram.

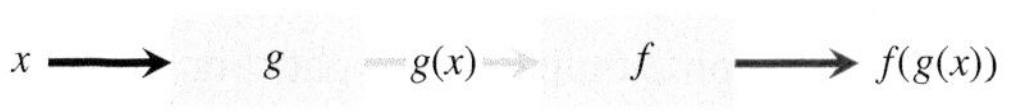

FIGURE 1.27 A composite function $f \circ g$ uses the output $g(x)$ of the first function g as the input for the second function f.

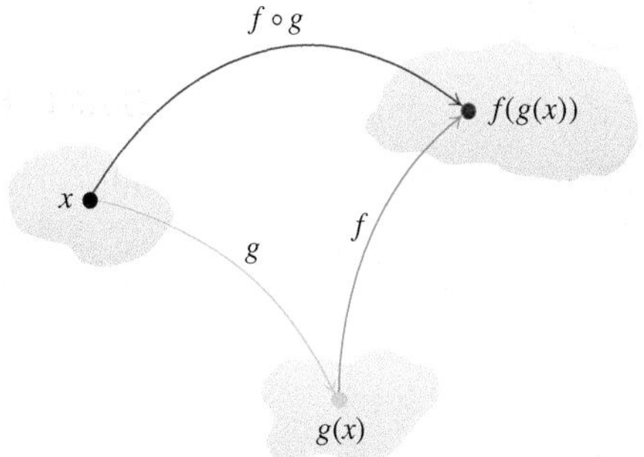

FIGURE 1.28 Arrow diagram for $f \circ g$. If x lies in the domain of g and $g(x)$ lies in the domain of f, then the functions f and g can be composed to form $(f \circ g)(x)$.

To evaluate the composite function $g \circ f$ (when defined), we find $f(x)$ first and then $g(f(x))$. The domain of $g \circ f$ is the set of numbers x in the domain of f such that $f(x)$ lies in the domain of g.

The functions $f \circ g$ and $g \circ f$ are usually quite different.

EXAMPLE 2 If $f(x) = \sqrt{x}$ and $g(x) = x + 1$, find

(a) $(f \circ g)(x)$ **(b)** $(g \circ f)(x)$ **(c)** $(f \circ f)(x)$ **(d)** $(g \circ g)(x)$.

Solution

Composite	Domain
(a) $(f \circ g)(x) = f(g(x)) = \sqrt{g(x)} = \sqrt{x+1}$	$[-1, \infty)$
(b) $(g \circ f)(x) = g(f(x)) = f(x) + 1 = \sqrt{x} + 1$	$[0, \infty)$
(c) $(f \circ f)(x) = f(f(x)) = \sqrt{f(x)} = \sqrt{\sqrt{x}} = x^{1/4}$	$[0, \infty)$
(d) $(g \circ g)(x) = g(g(x)) = g(x) + 1 = (x + 1) + 1 = x + 2$	$(-\infty, \infty)$

To see why the domain of $f \circ g$ is $[-1, \infty)$, notice that $g(x) = x + 1$ is defined for all real x but belongs to the domain of f only if $x + 1 \geq 0$, that is to say, when $x \geq -1$. ■

Notice that if $f(x) = x^2$ and $g(x) = \sqrt{x}$, then $(f \circ g)(x) = (\sqrt{x})^2 = x$. However, the domain of $f \circ g$ is $[0, \infty)$, not $(-\infty, \infty)$, since $\sqrt{x}$ requires $x \geq 0$.

Shifting a Graph of a Function

A common way to obtain a new function from an existing one is by adding a constant to each output of the existing function, or to its input variable. The graph of the new function is the graph of the original function shifted vertically or horizontally, as follows.

Shift Formulas

Vertical Shifts

$y = f(x) + k$ Shifts the graph of f *up* k units if $k > 0$
Shifts it *down* $|k|$ units if $k < 0$

Horizontal Shifts

$y = f(x + h)$ Shifts the graph of f *left* h units if $h > 0$
Shifts it *right* $|h|$ units if $h < 0$

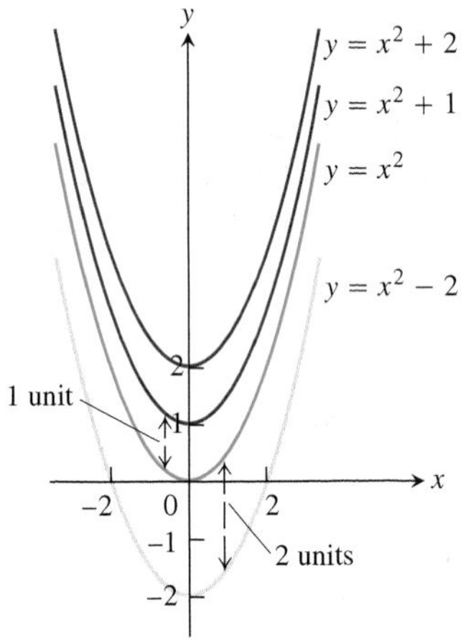

FIGURE 1.29 To shift the graph of $f(x) = x^2$ up (or down), we add positive (or negative) constants to the formula for f (Examples 3a and b).

EXAMPLE 3

(a) Adding 1 to the right-hand side of the formula $y = x^2$ to get $y = x^2 + 1$ shifts the graph up 1 unit (Figure 1.29).

(b) Adding -2 to the right-hand side of the formula $y = x^2$ to get $y = x^2 - 2$ shifts the graph down 2 units (Figure 1.29).

(c) Adding 3 to x in $y = x^2$ to get $y = (x + 3)^2$ shifts the graph 3 units to the left, while adding -2 shifts the graph 2 units to the right (Figure 1.30).

(d) Adding -2 to x in $y = |x|$, and then adding -1 to the result, gives $y = |x - 2| - 1$ and shifts the graph 2 units to the right and 1 unit down (Figure 1.31). ■

Scaling and Reflecting a Graph of a Function

To scale the graph of a function $y = f(x)$ is to stretch or compress it, vertically or horizontally. This is accomplished by multiplying the function f, or the independent variable x, by an appropriate constant c. Reflections across the coordinate axes are special cases where $c = -1$.

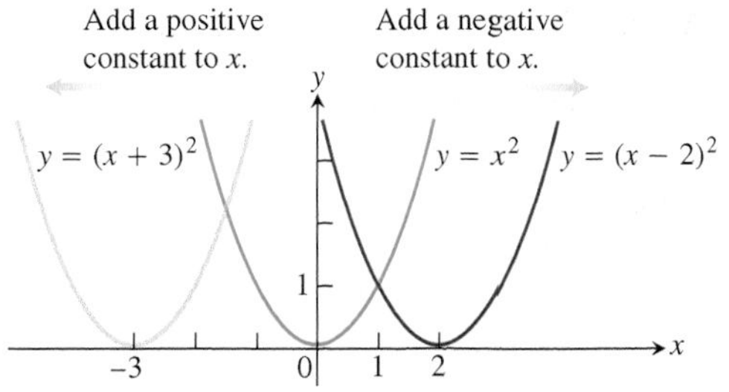

FIGURE 1.30 To shift the graph of $y = x^2$ to the left, we add a positive constant to x (Example 3c). To shift the graph to the right, we add a negative constant to x.

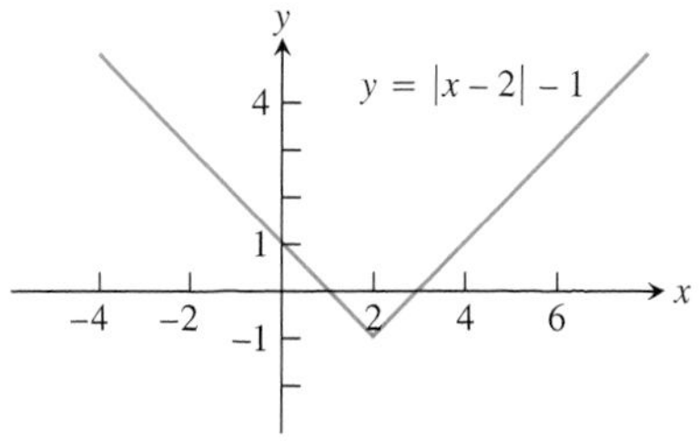

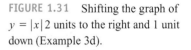

FIGURE 1.31 Shifting the graph of $y = |x|$ 2 units to the right and 1 unit down (Example 3d).

Vertical and Horizontal Scaling and Reflecting Formulas

For $c > 1$, the graph is scaled:

$y = cf(x)$	Stretches the graph of f vertically by a factor of c.
$y = \frac{1}{c}f(x)$	Compresses the graph of f vertically by a factor of c.
$y = f(cx)$	Compresses the graph of f horizontally by a factor of c.
$y = f(x/c)$	Stretches the graph of f horizontally by a factor of c.

For $c = -1$, the graph is reflected:

$y = -f(x)$	Reflects the graph of f across the x-axis.
$y = f(-x)$	Reflects the graph of f across the y-axis.

EXAMPLE 4 Here we scale and reflect the graph of $y = \sqrt{x}$.

(a) Vertical: Multiplying the right-hand side of $y = \sqrt{x}$ by 3 to get $y = 3\sqrt{x}$ stretches the graph vertically by a factor of 3, whereas multiplying by $1/3$ compresses the graph by a factor of 3 (Figure 1.32).

(b) Horizontal: The graph of $y = \sqrt{3x}$ is a horizontal compression of the graph of $y = \sqrt{x}$ by a factor of 3, and $y = \sqrt{x/3}$ is a horizontal stretching by a factor of 3 (Figure 1.33). Note that $y = \sqrt{3x} = \sqrt{3}\sqrt{x}$ so a horizontal compression *may* correspond to a vertical stretching by a different scaling factor. Likewise, a horizontal stretching may correspond to a vertical compression by a different scaling factor.

(c) Reflection: The graph of $y = -\sqrt{x}$ is a reflection of $y = \sqrt{x}$ across the x-axis, and $y = \sqrt{-x}$ is a reflection across the y-axis (Figure 1.34). ■

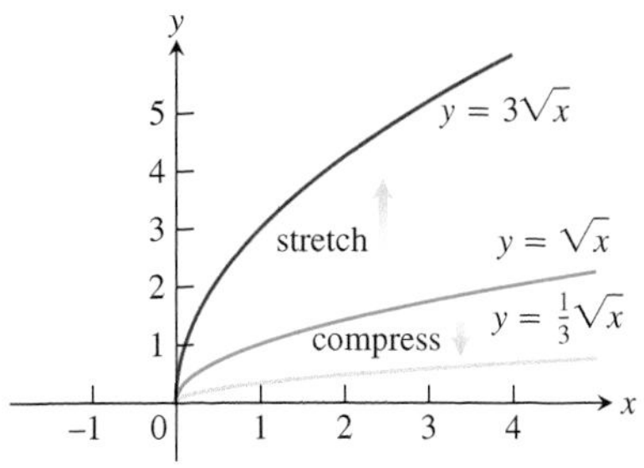

FIGURE 1.32 Vertically stretching and compressing the graph $y = \sqrt{x}$ by a factor of 3 (Example 4a).

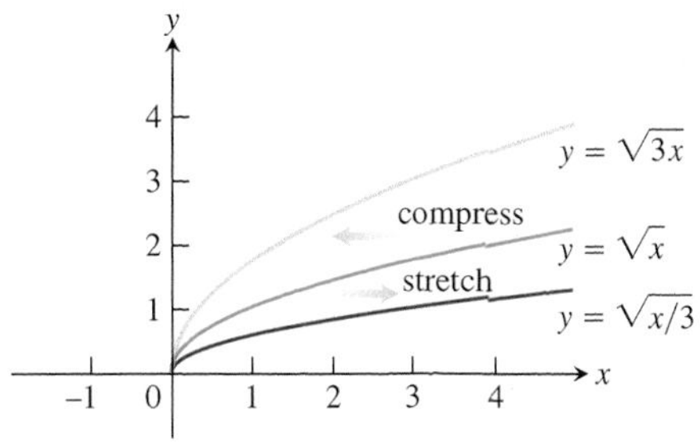

FIGURE 1.33 Horizontally stretching and compressing the graph $y = \sqrt{x}$ by a factor of 3 (Example 4b).

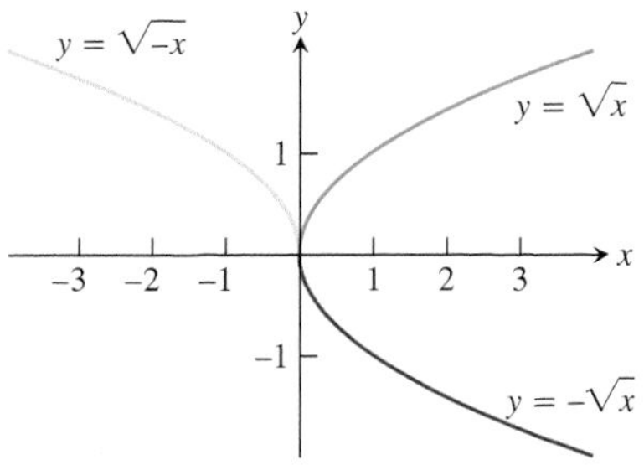

FIGURE 1.34 Reflections of the graph $y = \sqrt{x}$ across the coordinate axes (Example 4c).

EXAMPLE 5 Given the function $f(x) = x^4 - 4x^3 + 10$ (Figure 1.35a), find formulas to

(a) compress the graph horizontally by a factor of 2 followed by a reflection across the y-axis (Figure 1.35b).

(b) compress the graph vertically by a factor of 2 followed by a reflection across the x-axis (Figure 1.35c).

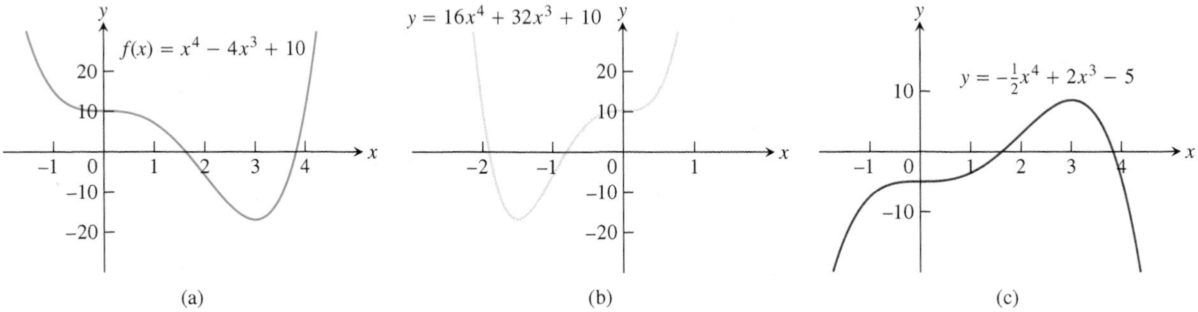

FIGURE 1.35 (a) The original graph of f. (b) The horizontal compression of $y = f(x)$ in part (a) by a factor of 2, followed by a reflection across the y-axis. (c) The vertical compression of $y = f(x)$ in part (a) by a factor of 2, followed by a reflection across the x-axis (Example 5).

Solution

(a) We multiply x by 2 to get the horizontal compression, and by -1 to give reflection across the y-axis. The formula is obtained by substituting $-2x$ for x in the right-hand side of the equation for f:

$$\begin{aligned} y &= f(-2x) = (-2x)^4 - 4(-2x)^3 + 10 \\ &= 16x^4 + 32x^3 + 10. \end{aligned}$$

(b) The formula is

$$y = -\frac{1}{2}f(x) = -\frac{1}{2}x^4 + 2x^3 - 5.$$ ■

Exercises 1.2

Algebraic Combinations

In Exercises 1 and 2, find the domains and ranges of f, g, $f + g$, and $f \cdot g$.

1. $f(x) = x, \quad g(x) = \sqrt{x - 1}$

2. $f(x) = \sqrt{x + 1}, \quad g(x) = \sqrt{x - 1}$

In Exercises 3 and 4, find the domains and ranges of f, g, f/g, and g/f.

3. $f(x) = 2, \quad g(x) = x^2 + 1$

4. $f(x) = 1, \quad g(x) = 1 + \sqrt{x}$

Composites of Functions

5. If $f(x) = x + 5$ and $g(x) = x^2 - 3$, find the following.

a. $f(g(0))$ **b.** $g(f(0))$
c. $f(g(x))$ **d.** $g(f(x))$
e. $f(f(-5))$ **f.** $g(g(2))$
g. $f(f(x))$ **h.** $g(g(x))$

6. If $f(x) = x - 1$ and $g(x) = 1/(x + 1)$, find the following.

a. $f(g(1/2))$ **b.** $g(f(1/2))$
c. $f(g(x))$ **d.** $g(f(x))$
e. $f(f(2))$ **f.** $g(g(2))$
g. $f(f(x))$ **h.** $g(g(x))$

In Exercises 7–10, write a formula for $f \circ g \circ h$.

7. $f(x) = x + 1, \quad g(x) = 3x, \quad h(x) = 4 - x$

8. $f(x) = 3x + 4, \quad g(x) = 2x - 1, \quad h(x) = x^2$

9. $f(x) = \sqrt{x + 1}, \quad g(x) = \dfrac{1}{x + 4}, \quad h(x) = \dfrac{1}{x}$

10. $f(x) = \dfrac{x + 2}{3 - x}, \quad g(x) = \dfrac{x^2}{x^2 + 1}, \quad h(x) = \sqrt{2 - x}$

Let $f(x) = x - 3$, $g(x) = \sqrt{x}$, $h(x) = x^3$, and $j(x) = 2x$. Express each of the functions in Exercises 11 and 12 as a composite involving one or more of f, g, h, and j.

11. a. $y = \sqrt{x} - 3$ **b.** $y = 2\sqrt{x}$
c. $y = x^{1/4}$ **d.** $y = 4x$
e. $y = \sqrt{(x-3)^3}$ **f.** $y = (2x - 6)^3$

12. a. $y = 2x - 3$ **b.** $y = x^{3/2}$
c. $y = x^9$ **d.** $y = x - 6$
e. $y = 2\sqrt{x - 3}$ **f.** $y = \sqrt{x^3 - 3}$

13. Copy and complete the following table.

	$g(x)$	$f(x)$	$(f \circ g)(x)$
a.	$x - 7$	$\sqrt{x}$	?
b.	$x + 2$	$3x$	?
c.	?	$\sqrt{x - 5}$	$\sqrt{x^2 - 5}$
d.	$\dfrac{x}{x - 1}$	$\dfrac{x}{x - 1}$	?
e.	?	$1 + \dfrac{1}{x}$	x
f.	$\dfrac{1}{x}$	?	x

14. Copy and complete the following table.

	$g(x)$	$f(x)$	$(f \circ g)(x)$
a.	$\dfrac{1}{x - 1}$	$\lvert x \rvert$	?
b.	?	$\dfrac{x - 1}{x}$	$\dfrac{x}{x + 1}$
c.	?	$\sqrt{x}$	$\lvert x \rvert$
d.	$\sqrt{x}$	?	$\lvert x \rvert$

15. Evaluate each expression using the given table of values:

x	-2	-1	0	1	2
$f(x)$	1	0	-2	1	2
$g(x)$	2	1	0	-1	0

a. $f(g(-1))$ **b.** $g(f(0))$ **c.** $f(f(-1))$
d. $g(g(2))$ **e.** $g(f(-2))$ **f.** $f(g(1))$

16. Evaluate each expression using the functions

$$f(x) = 2 - x, \quad g(x) = \begin{cases} -x, & -2 \le x < 0 \\ x - 1, & 0 \le x \le 2. \end{cases}$$

a. $f(g(0))$ **b.** $g(f(3))$ **c.** $g(g(-1))$
d. $f(f(2))$ **e.** $g(f(0))$ **f.** $f(g(1/2))$

In Exercises 17 and 18, **(a)** write formulas for $f \circ g$ and $g \circ f$ and find the **(b)** domain and **(c)** range of each.

17. $f(x) = \sqrt{x + 1}$, $g(x) = \dfrac{1}{x}$

18. $f(x) = x^2$, $g(x) = 1 - \sqrt{x}$

19. Let $f(x) = \dfrac{x}{x - 2}$. Find a function $y = g(x)$ so that $(f \circ g)(x) = x$.

20. Let $f(x) = 2x^3 - 4$. Find a function $y = g(x)$ so that $(f \circ g)(x) = x + 2$.

Shifting Graphs

21. The accompanying figure shows the graph of $y = -x^2$ shifted to two new positions. Write equations for the new graphs.

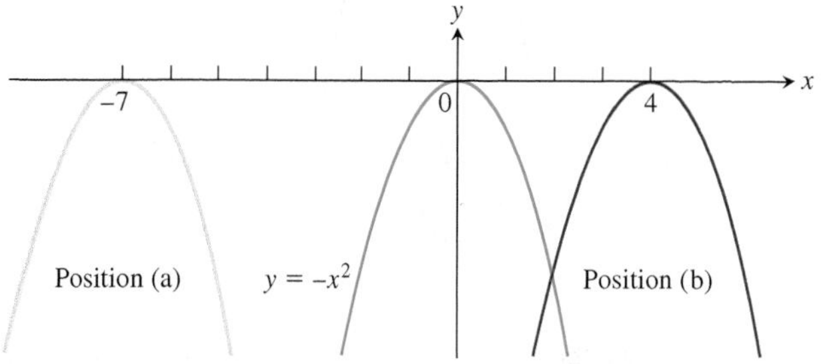

22. The accompanying figure shows the graph of $y = x^2$ shifted to two new positions. Write equations for the new graphs.

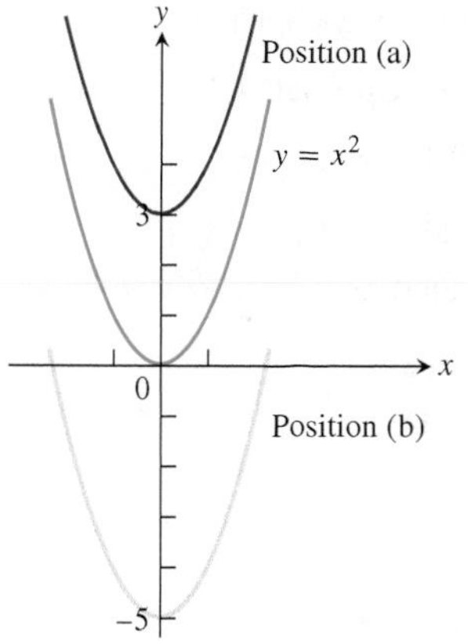

23. Match the equations listed in parts (a)–(d) to the graphs in the accompanying figure.

a. $y = (x - 1)^2 - 4$ **b.** $y = (x - 2)^2 + 2$
c. $y = (x + 2)^2 + 2$ **d.** $y = (x + 3)^2 - 2$

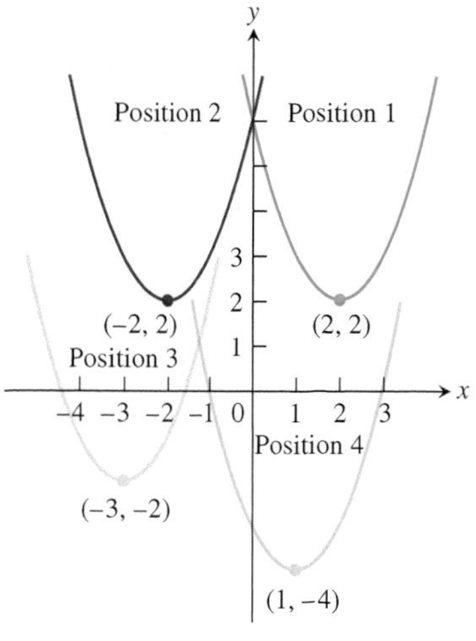

24. The accompanying figure shows the graph of $y = -x^2$ shifted to four new positions. Write an equation for each new graph.

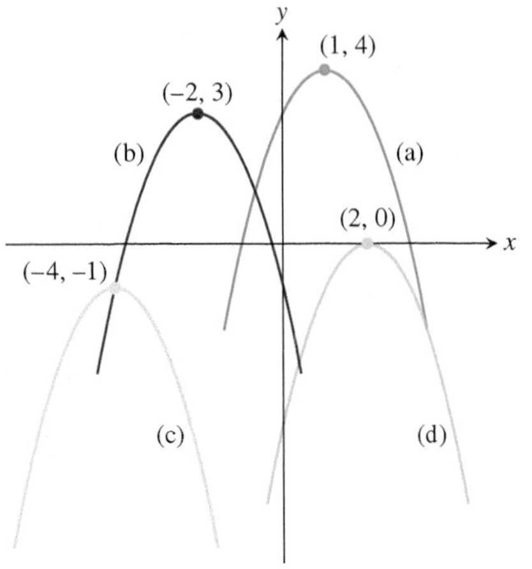

Exercises 25–34 tell how many units and in what directions the graphs of the given equations are to be shifted. Give an equation for the shifted graph. Then sketch the original and shifted graphs together, labeling each graph with its equation.

25. $x^2 + y^2 = 49$ Down 3, left 2

26. $x^2 + y^2 = 25$ Up 3, left 4

27. $y = x^3$ Left 1, down 1

28. $y = x^{2/3}$ Right 1, down 1

29. $y = \sqrt{x}$ Left 0.81

30. $y = -\sqrt{x}$ Right 3

31. $y = 2x - 7$ Up 7

32. $y = \frac{1}{2}(x + 1) + 5$ Down 5, right 1

33. $y = 1/x$ Up 1, right 1

34. $y = 1/x^2$ Left 2, down 1

Graph the functions in Exercises 35–54.

35. $y = \sqrt{x + 4}$

36. $y = \sqrt{9 - x}$

37. $y = |x - 2|$

38. $y = |1 - x| - 1$

39. $y = 1 + \sqrt{x - 1}$

40. $y = 1 - \sqrt{x}$

41. $y = (x + 1)^{2/3}$

42. $y = (x - 8)^{2/3}$

43. $y = 1 - x^{2/3}$

44. $y + 4 = x^{2/3}$

45. $y = \sqrt[3]{x - 1} - 1$

46. $y = (x + 2)^{3/2} + 1$

47. $y = \dfrac{1}{x - 2}$

48. $y = \dfrac{1}{x} - 2$

49. $y = \dfrac{1}{x} + 2$

50. $y = \dfrac{1}{x + 2}$

51. $y = \dfrac{1}{(x - 1)^2}$

52. $y = \dfrac{1}{x^2} - 1$

53. $y = \dfrac{1}{x^2} + 1$

54. $y = \dfrac{1}{(x + 1)^2}$

55. The accompanying figure shows the graph of a function $f(x)$ with domain $[0, 2]$ and range $[0, 1]$. Find the domains and ranges of the following functions, and sketch their graphs.

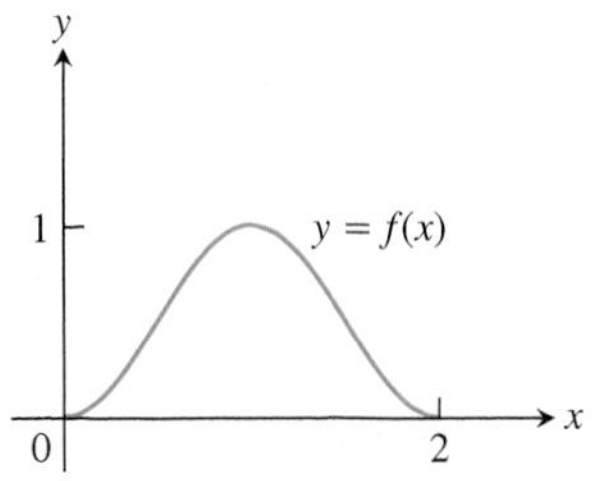

a. $f(x) + 2$ **b.** $f(x) - 1$

c. $2f(x)$ **d.** $-f(x)$

e. $f(x + 2)$ **f.** $f(x - 1)$

g. $f(-x)$ **h.** $-f(x + 1) + 1$

56. The accompanying figure shows the graph of a function $g(t)$ with domain $[-4, 0]$ and range $[-3, 0]$. Find the domains and ranges of the following functions, and sketch their graphs.

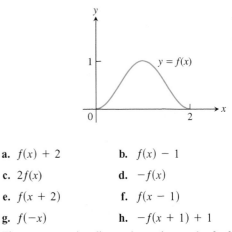

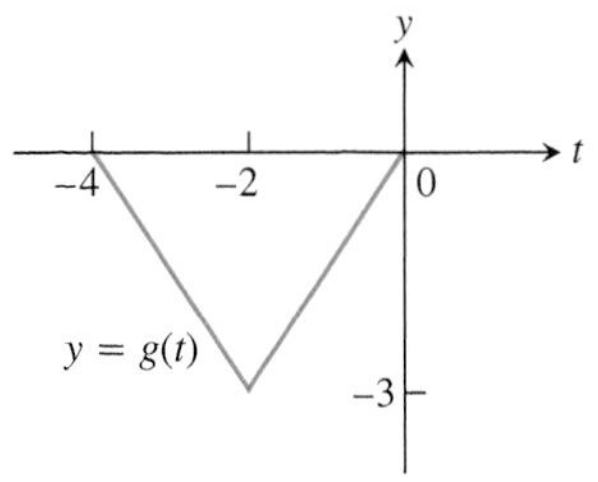

a. $g(-t)$ **b.** $-g(t)$

c. $g(t) + 3$ **d.** $1 - g(t)$

e. $g(-t + 2)$ **f.** $g(t - 2)$

g. $g(1 - t)$ **h.** $-g(t - 4)$

Vertical and Horizontal Scaling

Exercises 57–66 tell by what factor and direction the graphs of the given functions are to be stretched or compressed. Give an equation for the stretched or compressed graph.

57. $y = x^2 - 1$, stretched vertically by a factor of 3

58. $y = x^2 - 1$, compressed horizontally by a factor of 2

59. $y = 1 + \dfrac{1}{x^2}$, compressed vertically by a factor of 2

60. $y = 1 + \dfrac{1}{x^2}$, stretched horizontally by a factor of 3

61. $y = \sqrt{x + 1}$, compressed horizontally by a factor of 4

62. $y = \sqrt{x + 1}$, stretched vertically by a factor of 3

63. $y = \sqrt{4 - x^2}$, stretched horizontally by a factor of 2

64. $y = \sqrt{4 - x^2}$, compressed vertically by a factor of 3

65. $y = 1 - x^3$, compressed horizontally by a factor of 3

66. $y = 1 - x^3$, stretched horizontally by a factor of 2

Graphing

In Exercises 67–74, graph each function, not by plotting points, but by starting with the graph of one of the standard functions presented in Figures 1.14–1.17 and applying an appropriate transformation.

67. $y = -\sqrt{2x + 1}$

68. $y = \sqrt{1 - \dfrac{x}{2}}$

69. $y = (x - 1)^3 + 2$

70. $y = (1 - x)^3 + 2$

71. $y = \dfrac{1}{2x} - 1$

72. $y = \dfrac{2}{x^2} + 1$

73. $y = -\sqrt[3]{x}$

74. $y = (-2x)^{2/3}$

75. Graph the function $y = |x^2 - 1|$.

76. Graph the function $y = \sqrt{|x|}$.

Combining Functions

77. Assume that f is an even function, g is an odd function, and both f and g are defined on the entire real line $\mathbb{R}$. Which of the following (where defined) are even? odd?

a. fg **b.** f/g **c.** g/f

d. $f^2 = ff$ **e.** $g^2 = gg$ **f.** $f \circ g$

g. $g \circ f$ **h.** $f \circ f$ **i.** $g \circ g$

78. Can a function be both even and odd? Give reasons for your answer.

T **79.** (*Continuation of Example 1.*) Graph the functions $f(x) = \sqrt{x}$ and $g(x) = \sqrt{1 - x}$ together with their (a) sum, (b) product, (c) two differences, (d) two quotients.

T **80.** Let $f(x) = x - 7$ and $g(x) = x^2$. Graph f and g together with $f \circ g$ and $g \circ f$.

1.3 Trigonometric Functions

This section reviews radian measure and the basic trigonometric functions.

Angles

Angles are measured in degrees or radians. The number of **radians** in the central angle $A'CB'$ within a circle of radius r is defined as the number of "radius units" contained in the arc s subtended by that central angle. If we denote this central angle by θ when measured in radians, this means that $\theta = s/r$ (Figure 1.36), or

$$s = r\theta \qquad (\theta \text{ in radians}). \tag{1}$$

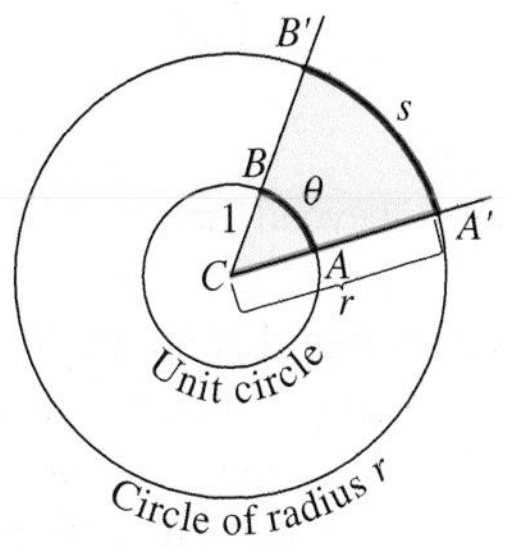

FIGURE 1.36 The radian measure of the central angle $A'CB'$ is the number $\theta = s/r$. For a unit circle of radius $r = 1$, θ is the length of arc AB that central angle ACB cuts from the unit circle.

If the circle is a unit circle having radius $r = 1$, then from Figure 1.36 and Equation (1), we see that the central angle θ measured in radians is just the length of the arc that the angle cuts from the unit circle. Since one complete revolution of the unit circle is 360° or 2π radians, we have

$$\pi \text{ radians} = 180° \tag{2}$$

and

$$1 \text{ radian} = \frac{180}{\pi} (\approx 57.3) \text{ degrees} \qquad \text{or} \qquad 1 \text{ degree} = \frac{\pi}{180} (\approx 0.017) \text{ radians}.$$

Table 1.2 shows the equivalence between degree and radian measures for some basic angles.

TABLE 1.2 Angles measured in degrees and radians

Degrees	−180	−135	−90	−45	0	30	45	60	90	120	135	150	180	270	360
θ (radians)	$-\pi$	$\frac{-3\pi}{4}$	$\frac{-\pi}{2}$	$\frac{-\pi}{4}$	0	$\frac{\pi}{6}$	$\frac{\pi}{4}$	$\frac{\pi}{3}$	$\frac{\pi}{2}$	$\frac{2\pi}{3}$	$\frac{3\pi}{4}$	$\frac{5\pi}{6}$	π	$\frac{3\pi}{2}$	2π

An angle in the xy-plane is said to be in **standard position** if its vertex lies at the origin and its initial ray lies along the positive x-axis (Figure 1.37). Angles measured counterclockwise from the positive x-axis are assigned positive measures; angles measured clockwise are assigned negative measures.

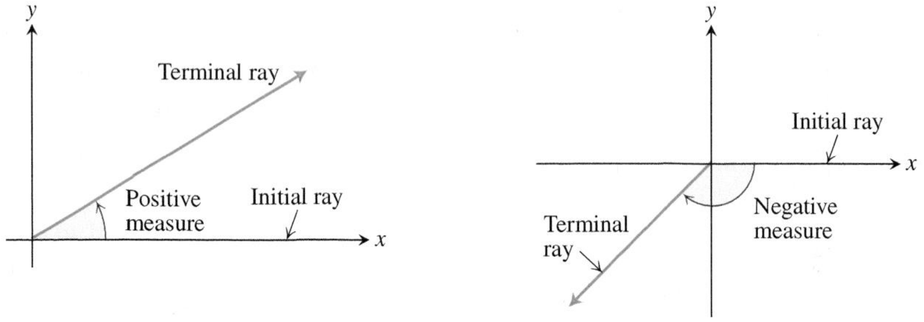

FIGURE 1.37 Angles in standard position in the xy-plane.

Angles describing counterclockwise rotations can go arbitrarily far beyond 2π radians or 360°. Similarly, angles describing clockwise rotations can have negative measures of all sizes (Figure 1.38).

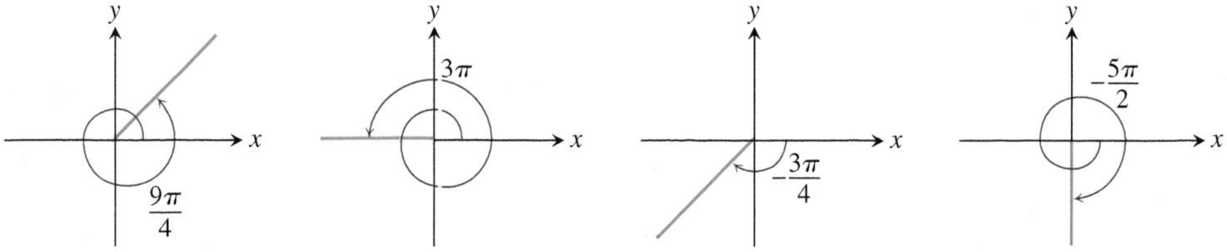

FIGURE 1.38 Nonzero radian measures can be positive or negative and can go beyond 2π.

Angle Convention: Use Radians From now on, in this book it is assumed that all angles are measured in radians unless degrees or some other unit is stated explicitly. When we talk about the angle $\pi/3$, we mean $\pi/3$ radians (which is 60°), not $\pi/3$ degrees. We use radians because it simplifies many of the operations in calculus, and some results we will obtain involving the trigonometric functions are not true when angles are measured in degrees.

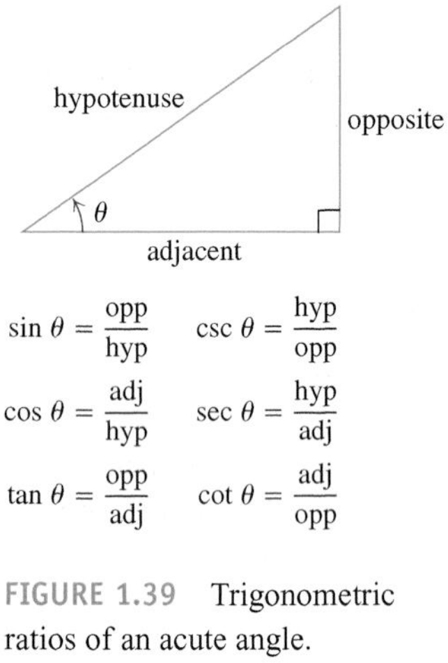

$$\sin\theta = \frac{\text{opp}}{\text{hyp}} \qquad \csc\theta = \frac{\text{hyp}}{\text{opp}}$$

$$\cos\theta = \frac{\text{adj}}{\text{hyp}} \qquad \sec\theta = \frac{\text{hyp}}{\text{adj}}$$

$$\tan\theta = \frac{\text{opp}}{\text{adj}} \qquad \cot\theta = \frac{\text{adj}}{\text{opp}}$$

FIGURE 1.39 Trigonometric ratios of an acute angle.

The Six Basic Trigonometric Functions

You are probably familiar with defining the trigonometric functions of an acute angle in terms of the sides of a right triangle (Figure 1.39). We extend this definition to obtuse and negative angles by first placing the angle in standard position in a circle of radius r. We then define the trigonometric functions in terms of the coordinates of the point $P(x, y)$ where the angle's terminal ray intersects the circle (Figure 1.40).

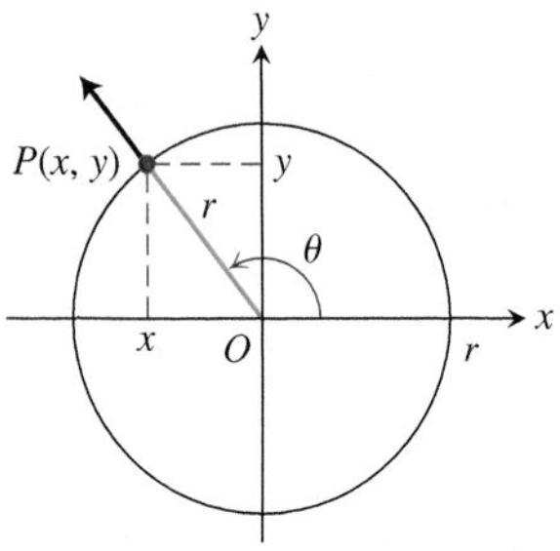

FIGURE 1.40 The trigonometric functions of a general angle θ are defined in terms of x, y, and r.

$$\textbf{sine:} \quad \sin\theta = \frac{y}{r} \qquad \textbf{cosecant:} \quad \csc\theta = \frac{r}{y}$$

$$\textbf{cosine:} \quad \cos\theta = \frac{x}{r} \qquad \textbf{secant:} \quad \sec\theta = \frac{r}{x}$$

$$\textbf{tangent:} \quad \tan\theta = \frac{y}{x} \qquad \textbf{cotangent:} \quad \cot\theta = \frac{x}{y}$$

These extended definitions agree with the right-triangle definitions when the angle is acute.

Notice also that whenever the quotients are defined,

$$\tan\theta = \frac{\sin\theta}{\cos\theta} \qquad \cot\theta = \frac{1}{\tan\theta}$$

$$\sec\theta = \frac{1}{\cos\theta} \qquad \csc\theta = \frac{1}{\sin\theta}$$

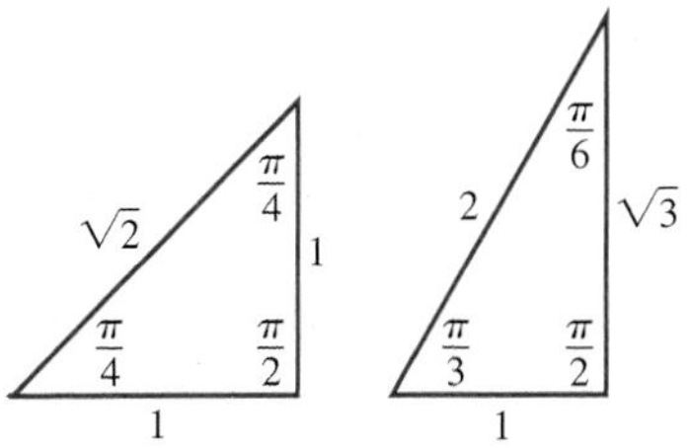

FIGURE 1.41 Radian angles and side lengths of two common triangles.

As you can see, $\tan\theta$ and $\sec\theta$ are not defined if $x = \cos\theta = 0$. This means they are not defined if θ is $\pm\pi/2, \pm 3\pi/2, \ldots$. Similarly, $\cot\theta$ and $\csc\theta$ are not defined for values of θ for which $y = 0$, namely $\theta = 0, \pm\pi, \pm 2\pi, \ldots$.

The exact values of these trigonometric ratios for some angles can be read from the triangles in Figure 1.41. For instance,

$$\sin\frac{\pi}{4} = \frac{1}{\sqrt{2}} \qquad \sin\frac{\pi}{6} = \frac{1}{2} \qquad \sin\frac{\pi}{3} = \frac{\sqrt{3}}{2}$$

$$\cos\frac{\pi}{4} = \frac{1}{\sqrt{2}} \qquad \cos\frac{\pi}{6} = \frac{\sqrt{3}}{2} \qquad \cos\frac{\pi}{3} = \frac{1}{2}$$

$$\tan\frac{\pi}{4} = 1 \qquad \tan\frac{\pi}{6} = \frac{1}{\sqrt{3}} \qquad \tan\frac{\pi}{3} = \sqrt{3}$$

The CAST rule (Figure 1.42) is useful for remembering when the basic trigonometric functions are positive or negative. For instance, from the triangle in Figure 1.43, we see that

$$\sin\frac{2\pi}{3} = \frac{\sqrt{3}}{2}, \qquad \cos\frac{2\pi}{3} = -\frac{1}{2}, \qquad \tan\frac{2\pi}{3} = -\sqrt{3}.$$

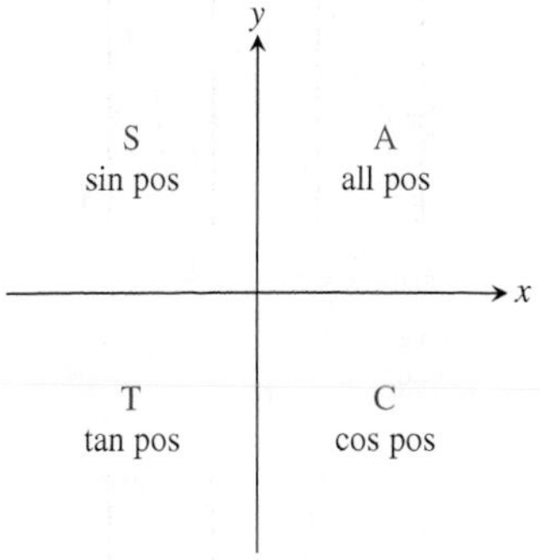

FIGURE 1.42 The CAST rule, remembered by the statement "Calculus Activates Student Thinking," tells which trigonometric functions are positive in each quadrant.

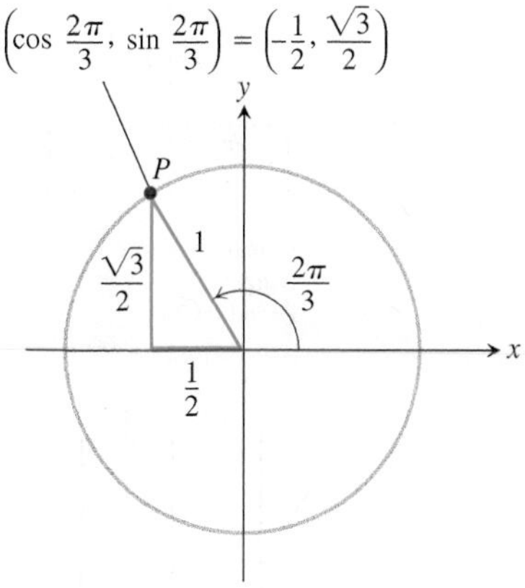

FIGURE 1.43 The triangle for calculating the sine and cosine of $2\pi/3$ radians. The side lengths come from the geometry of right triangles.

Using a similar method we determined the values of $\sin\theta$, $\cos\theta$, and $\tan\theta$ shown in Table 1.3.

TABLE 1.3 Values of $\sin\theta$, $\cos\theta$, and $\tan\theta$ for selected values of θ

Degrees	**−180**	**−135**	**−90**	**−45**	**0**	**30**	**45**	**60**	**90**	**120**	**135**	**150**	**180**	**270**	**360**
θ (radians)	$-\pi$	$\frac{-3\pi}{4}$	$\frac{-\pi}{2}$	$\frac{-\pi}{4}$	0	$\frac{\pi}{6}$	$\frac{\pi}{4}$	$\frac{\pi}{3}$	$\frac{\pi}{2}$	$\frac{2\pi}{3}$	$\frac{3\pi}{4}$	$\frac{5\pi}{6}$	π	$\frac{3\pi}{2}$	2π
$\sin\theta$	0	$\frac{-\sqrt{2}}{2}$	-1	$\frac{-\sqrt{2}}{2}$	0	$\frac{1}{2}$	$\frac{\sqrt{2}}{2}$	$\frac{\sqrt{3}}{2}$	1	$\frac{\sqrt{3}}{2}$	$\frac{\sqrt{2}}{2}$	$\frac{1}{2}$	0	-1	0
$\cos\theta$	-1	$\frac{-\sqrt{2}}{2}$	0	$\frac{\sqrt{2}}{2}$	1	$\frac{\sqrt{3}}{2}$	$\frac{\sqrt{2}}{2}$	$\frac{1}{2}$	0	$-\frac{1}{2}$	$\frac{-\sqrt{2}}{2}$	$\frac{-\sqrt{3}}{2}$	-1	0	1
$\tan\theta$	0	1		-1	0	$\frac{\sqrt{3}}{3}$	1	$\sqrt{3}$		$-\sqrt{3}$	-1	$\frac{-\sqrt{3}}{3}$	0		0

Periodicity and Graphs of the Trigonometric Functions

When an angle of measure θ and an angle of measure $\theta + 2\pi$ are in standard position, their terminal rays coincide. The two angles therefore have the same trigonometric function values: $\sin(\theta + 2\pi) = \sin\theta$, $\tan(\theta + 2\pi) = \tan\theta$, and so on. Similarly, $\cos(\theta - 2\pi) = \cos\theta$, $\sin(\theta - 2\pi) = \sin\theta$, and so on. We describe this repeating behavior by saying that the six basic trigonometric functions are *periodic*.

Periods of Trigonometric Functions

Period π: $\tan(x + \pi) = \tan x$
$\cot(x + \pi) = \cot x$

Period 2π: $\sin(x + 2\pi) = \sin x$
$\cos(x + 2\pi) = \cos x$
$\sec(x + 2\pi) = \sec x$
$\csc(x + 2\pi) = \csc x$

DEFINITION A function $f(x)$ is **periodic** if there is a positive number p such that $f(x + p) = f(x)$ for every value of x. The smallest such value of p is the **period** of f.

When we graph trigonometric functions in the coordinate plane, we usually denote the independent variable by x instead of θ. Figure 1.44 shows that the tangent and cotangent functions have period $p = \pi$, and the other four functions have period 2π. Also, the symmetries in these graphs reveal that the cosine and secant functions are even and the other four functions are odd (although this does not prove those results).

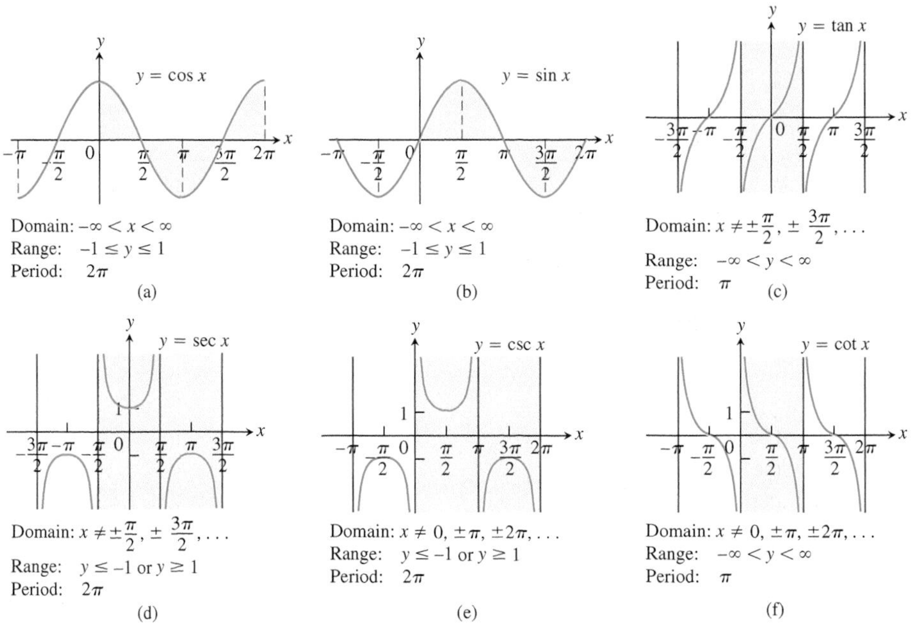

FIGURE 1.44 Graphs of the six basic trigonometric functions using radian measure. The shading for each trigonometric function indicates its periodicity.

Even

$\cos(-x) = \cos x$
$\sec(-x) = \sec x$

Odd

$\sin(-x) = -\sin x$
$\tan(-x) = -\tan x$
$\csc(-x) = -\csc x$
$\cot(-x) = -\cot x$

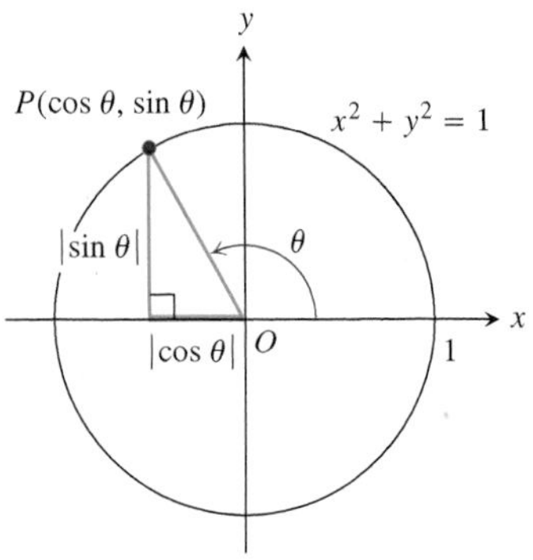

FIGURE 1.45 The reference triangle for a general angle θ.

Trigonometric Identities

The coordinates of any point $P(x, y)$ in the plane can be expressed in terms of the point's distance r from the origin and the angle θ that ray OP makes with the positive x-axis (Figure 1.40). Since $x/r = \cos\theta$ and $y/r = \sin\theta$, we have

$$x = r\cos\theta, \qquad y = r\sin\theta.$$

When $r = 1$ we can apply the Pythagorean theorem to the reference right triangle in Figure 1.45 and obtain the equation

$$\cos^2\theta + \sin^2\theta = 1. \tag{3}$$

This equation, true for all values of θ, is the most frequently used identity in trigonometry. Dividing this identity in turn by $\cos^2\theta$ and $\sin^2\theta$ gives

$$1 + \tan^2\theta = \sec^2\theta$$
$$1 + \cot^2\theta = \csc^2\theta$$

The following formulas hold for all angles A and B (Exercise 58).

Addition Formulas

$$\begin{aligned}\cos(A + B) &= \cos A\cos B - \sin A\sin B\\ \sin(A + B) &= \sin A\cos B + \cos A\sin B\end{aligned} \tag{4}$$

There are similar formulas for $\cos(A - B)$ and $\sin(A - B)$ (Exercises 35 and 36). All the trigonometric identities needed in this book derive from Equations (3) and (4). For example, substituting θ for both A and B in the addition formulas gives

Double-Angle Formulas

$$\begin{aligned}\cos 2\theta &= \cos^2\theta - \sin^2\theta\\ \sin 2\theta &= 2\sin\theta\cos\theta\end{aligned} \tag{5}$$

Additional formulas come from combining the equations

$$\cos^2\theta + \sin^2\theta = 1, \qquad \cos^2\theta - \sin^2\theta = \cos 2\theta.$$

We add the two equations to get $2\cos^2\theta = 1 + \cos 2\theta$ and subtract the second from the first to get $2\sin^2\theta = 1 - \cos 2\theta$. This results in the following identities, which are useful in integral calculus.

Half-Angle Formulas

$$\cos^2\theta = \frac{1 + \cos 2\theta}{2} \tag{6}$$

$$\sin^2\theta = \frac{1 - \cos 2\theta}{2} \tag{7}$$

The Law of Cosines

If a, b, and c are sides of a triangle ABC and if θ is the angle opposite c, then

$$c^2 = a^2 + b^2 - 2ab\cos\theta. \tag{8}$$

This equation is called the **law of cosines**.

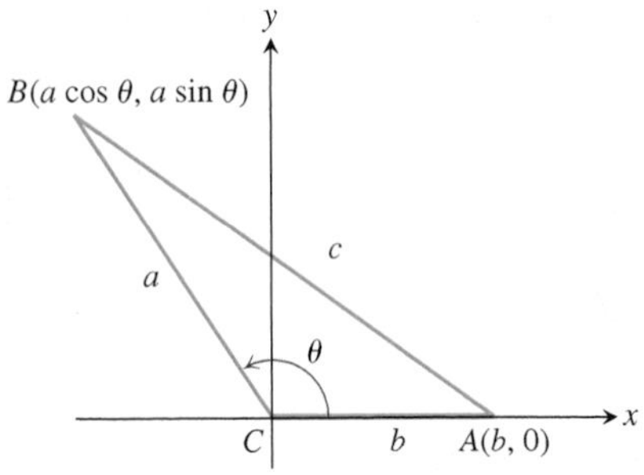

FIGURE 1.46 The square of the distance between A and B gives the law of cosines.

We can see why the law holds if we introduce coordinate axes with the origin at C and the positive x-axis along one side of the triangle, as in Figure 1.46. The coordinates of A are $(b, 0)$; the coordinates of B are $(a\cos\theta, a\sin\theta)$. The square of the distance between A and B is therefore

$$\begin{aligned} c^2 &= (a\cos\theta - b)^2 + (a\sin\theta)^2 \\ &= a^2\underbrace{(\cos^2\theta + \sin^2\theta)}_{1} + b^2 - 2ab\cos\theta \\ &= a^2 + b^2 - 2ab\cos\theta. \end{aligned}$$

The law of cosines generalizes the Pythagorean theorem. If $\theta = \pi/2$, then $\cos\theta = 0$ and $c^2 = a^2 + b^2$.

Transformations of Trigonometric Graphs

The rules for shifting, stretching, compressing, and reflecting the graph of a function summarized in the following diagram apply to the trigonometric functions we have discussed in this section.

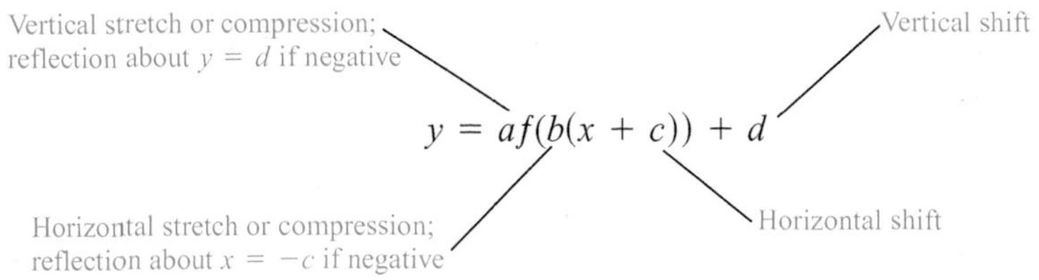

The transformation rules applied to the sine function give the **general sine function** or **sinusoid** formula

$$f(x) = A\sin\left(\frac{2\pi}{B}(x - C)\right) + D,$$

where $|A|$ is the *amplitude*, $|B|$ is the *period*, C is the *horizontal shift*, and D is the *vertical shift*. A graphical interpretation of the various terms is given below.

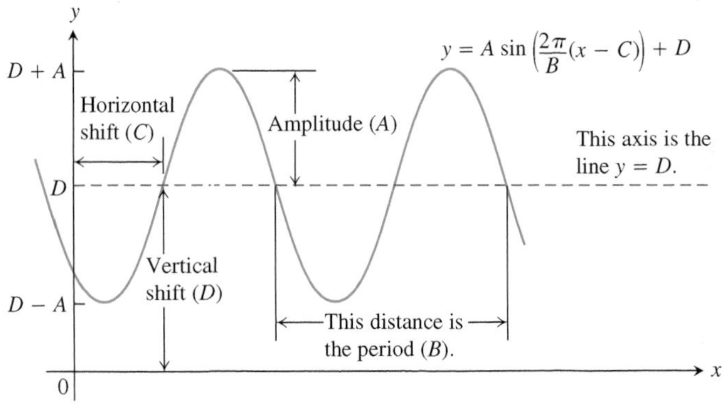

Two Special Inequalities

For any angle θ measured in radians,

$$-|\theta| \le \sin\theta \le |\theta| \quad \text{and} \quad -|\theta| \le 1 - \cos\theta \le |\theta|.$$

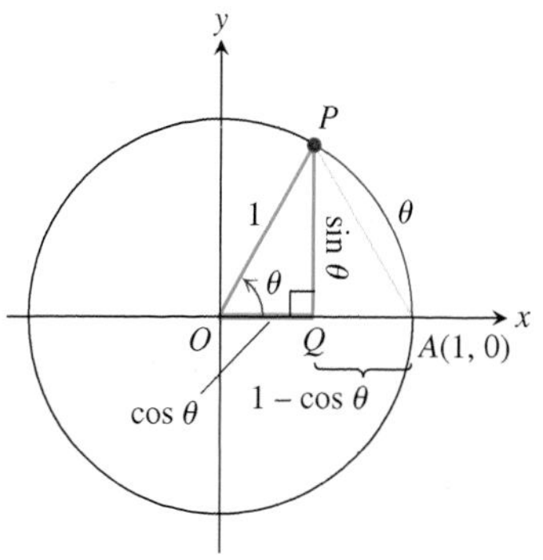

FIGURE 1.47 From the geometry of this figure, drawn for $\theta > 0$, we get the inequality $\sin^2 \theta + (1 - \cos\theta)^2 \le \theta^2$.

To establish these inequalities, we picture θ as a nonzero angle in standard position (Figure 1.47). The circle in the figure is a unit circle, so $|\theta|$ equals the length of the circular arc AP. The length of line segment AP is therefore less than $|\theta|$.

Triangle APQ is a right triangle with sides of length

$$QP = |\sin\theta|, \qquad AQ = 1 - \cos\theta.$$

From the Pythagorean theorem and the fact that $AP < |\theta|$, we get

$$\sin^2\theta + (1 - \cos\theta)^2 = (AP)^2 \le \theta^2. \tag{9}$$

The terms on the left-hand side of Equation (9) are both positive, so each is smaller than their sum and hence is less than or equal to θ^2:

$$\sin^2\theta \le \theta^2 \qquad \text{and} \qquad (1 - \cos\theta)^2 \le \theta^2.$$

By taking square roots, this is equivalent to saying that

$$|\sin\theta| \le |\theta| \qquad \text{and} \qquad |1 - \cos\theta| \le |\theta|,$$

so

$$-|\theta| \le \sin\theta \le |\theta| \qquad \text{and} \qquad -|\theta| \le 1 - \cos\theta \le |\theta|.$$

These inequalities will be useful in the next chapter.

Exercises 1.3

Radians and Degrees

1. On a circle of radius 10 m, how long is an arc that subtends a central angle of (**a**) $4\pi/5$ radians? (**b**) 110°?
2. A central angle in a circle of radius 8 is subtended by an arc of length 10π. Find the angle's radian and degree measures.
3. You want to make an 80° angle by marking an arc on the perimeter of a 12-in.-diameter disk and drawing lines from the ends of the arc to the disk's center. To the nearest tenth of an inch, how long should the arc be?
4. If you roll a 1-m-diameter wheel forward 30 cm over level ground, through what angle will the wheel turn? Answer in radians (to the nearest tenth) and degrees (to the nearest degree).

Evaluating Trigonometric Functions

5. Copy and complete the following table of function values. If the function is undefined at a given angle, enter "UND." Do not use a calculator or tables.

θ	$-\pi$	$-2\pi/3$	0	$\pi/2$	$3\pi/4$
$\sin\theta$					
$\cos\theta$					
$\tan\theta$					
$\cot\theta$					
$\sec\theta$					
$\csc\theta$					

6. Copy and complete the following table of function values. If the function is undefined at a given angle, enter "UND." Do not use a calculator or tables.

θ	$-3\pi/2$	$-\pi/3$	$-\pi/6$	$\pi/4$	$5\pi/6$
$\sin\theta$					
$\cos\theta$					
$\tan\theta$					
$\cot\theta$					
$\sec\theta$					
$\csc\theta$					

In Exercises 7–12, one of $\sin x$, $\cos x$, and $\tan x$ is given. Find the other two if x lies in the specified interval.

7. $\sin x = \dfrac{3}{5}, \quad x \in \left[\dfrac{\pi}{2}, \pi\right]$
8. $\tan x = 2, \quad x \in \left[0, \dfrac{\pi}{2}\right]$
9. $\cos x = \dfrac{1}{3}, \quad x \in \left[-\dfrac{\pi}{2}, 0\right]$
10. $\cos x = -\dfrac{5}{13}, \quad x \in \left[\dfrac{\pi}{2}, \pi\right]$
11. $\tan x = \dfrac{1}{2}, \quad x \in \left[\pi, \dfrac{3\pi}{2}\right]$
12. $\sin x = -\dfrac{1}{2}, \quad x \in \left[\pi, \dfrac{3\pi}{2}\right]$

Graphing Trigonometric Functions

Graph the functions in Exercises 13–22. What is the period of each function?

13. $\sin 2x$
14. $\sin(x/2)$
15. $\cos \pi x$
16. $\cos \dfrac{\pi x}{2}$
17. $-\sin \dfrac{\pi x}{3}$
18. $-\cos 2\pi x$
19. $\cos\left(x - \dfrac{\pi}{2}\right)$
20. $\sin\left(x + \dfrac{\pi}{6}\right)$

21. $\sin\left(x - \frac{\pi}{4}\right) + 1$ **22.** $\cos\left(x + \frac{2\pi}{3}\right) - 2$

Graph the functions in Exercises 23–26 in the *ts*-plane (*t*-axis horizontal, *s*-axis vertical). What is the period of each function? What symmetries do the graphs have?

23. $s = \cot 2t$ **24.** $s = -\tan \pi t$

25. $s = \sec\left(\frac{\pi t}{2}\right)$ **26.** $s = \csc\left(\frac{t}{2}\right)$

T **27. a.** Graph $y = \cos x$ and $y = \sec x$ together for $-3\pi/2 \le x \le 3\pi/2$. Comment on the behavior of $\sec x$ in relation to the signs and values of $\cos x$.

b. Graph $y = \sin x$ and $y = \csc x$ together for $-\pi \le x \le 2\pi$. Comment on the behavior of $\csc x$ in relation to the signs and values of $\sin x$.

T **28.** Graph $y = \tan x$ and $y = \cot x$ together for $-7 \le x \le 7$. Comment on the behavior of $\cot x$ in relation to the signs and values of $\tan x$.

29. Graph $y = \sin x$ and $y = \lfloor \sin x \rfloor$ together. What are the domain and range of $\lfloor \sin x \rfloor$?

30. Graph $y = \sin x$ and $y = \lceil \sin x \rceil$ together. What are the domain and range of $\lceil \sin x \rceil$?

Using the Addition Formulas

Use the addition formulas to derive the identities in Exercises 31–36.

31. $\cos\left(x - \frac{\pi}{2}\right) = \sin x$ **32.** $\cos\left(x + \frac{\pi}{2}\right) = -\sin x$

33. $\sin\left(x + \frac{\pi}{2}\right) = \cos x$ **34.** $\sin\left(x - \frac{\pi}{2}\right) = -\cos x$

35. $\cos(A - B) = \cos A \cos B + \sin A \sin B$ (Exercise 57 provides a different derivation.)

36. $\sin(A - B) = \sin A \cos B - \cos A \sin B$

37. What happens if you take $B = A$ in the trigonometric identity $\cos(A - B) = \cos A \cos B + \sin A \sin B$? Does the result agree with something you already know?

38. What happens if you take $B = 2\pi$ in the addition formulas? Do the results agree with something you already know?

In Exercises 39–42, express the given quantity in terms of $\sin x$ and $\cos x$.

39. $\cos(\pi + x)$ **40.** $\sin(2\pi - x)$

41. $\sin\left(\frac{3\pi}{2} - x\right)$ **42.** $\cos\left(\frac{3\pi}{2} + x\right)$

43. Evaluate $\sin\frac{7\pi}{12}$ as $\sin\left(\frac{\pi}{4} + \frac{\pi}{3}\right)$.

44. Evaluate $\cos\frac{11\pi}{12}$ as $\cos\left(\frac{\pi}{4} + \frac{2\pi}{3}\right)$.

45. Evaluate $\cos\frac{\pi}{12}$. **46.** Evaluate $\sin\frac{5\pi}{12}$.

Using the Double-Angle Formulas

Find the function values in Exercises 47–50.

47. $\cos^2\frac{\pi}{8}$ **48.** $\cos^2\frac{5\pi}{12}$

49. $\sin^2\frac{\pi}{12}$ **50.** $\sin^2\frac{3\pi}{8}$

Solving Trigonometric Equations

For Exercises 51–54, solve for the angle θ, where $0 \le \theta \le 2\pi$.

51. $\sin^2\theta = \frac{3}{4}$ **52.** $\sin^2\theta = \cos^2\theta$

53. $\sin 2\theta - \cos\theta = 0$ **54.** $\cos 2\theta + \cos\theta = 0$

Theory and Examples

55. The tangent sum formula The standard formula for the tangent of the sum of two angles is

$$\tan(A + B) = \frac{\tan A + \tan B}{1 - \tan A \tan B}.$$

Derive the formula.

56. (*Continuation of Exercise 55.*) Derive a formula for $\tan(A - B)$.

57. Apply the law of cosines to the triangle in the accompanying figure to derive the formula for $\cos(A - B)$.

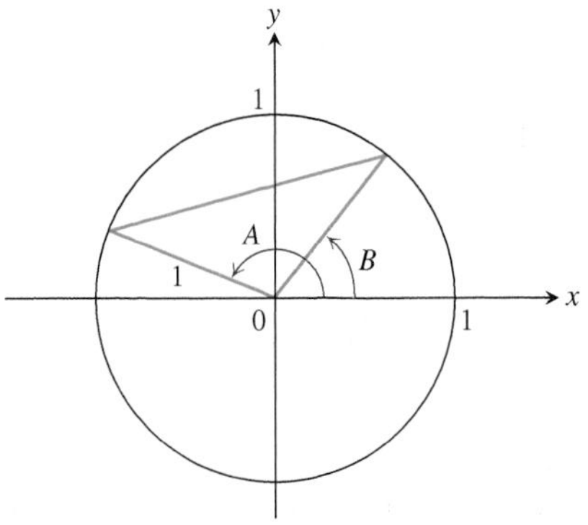

58. a. Apply the formula for $\cos(A - B)$ to the identity $\sin\theta = \cos\left(\frac{\pi}{2} - \theta\right)$ to obtain the addition formula for $\sin(A + B)$.

b. Derive the formula for $\cos(A + B)$ by substituting $-B$ for B in the formula for $\cos(A - B)$ from Exercise 35.

59. A triangle has sides $a = 2$ and $b = 3$ and angle $C = 60°$. Find the length of side c.

60. A triangle has sides $a = 2$ and $b = 3$ and angle $C = 40°$. Find the length of side c.

61. The law of sines *The law of sines* says that if a, b, and c are the sides opposite the angles A, B, and C in a triangle, then

$$\frac{\sin A}{a} = \frac{\sin B}{b} = \frac{\sin C}{c}.$$

Use the accompanying figures and the identity $\sin(\pi - \theta) = \sin\theta$, if required, to derive the law.

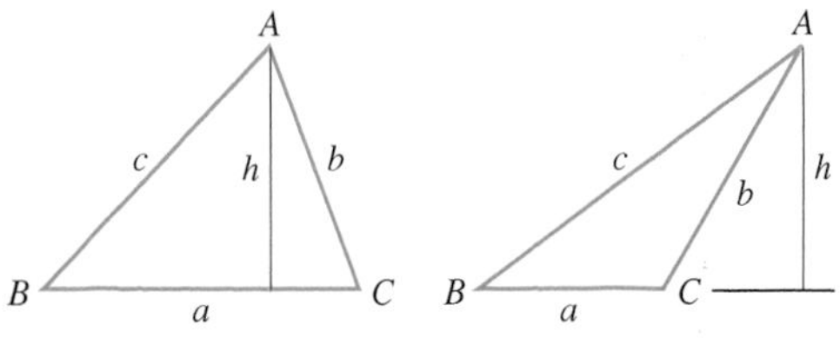

62. A triangle has sides $a = 2$ and $b = 3$ and angle $C = 60°$ (as in Exercise 59). Find the sine of angle B using the law of sines.

63. A triangle has side $c = 2$ and angles $A = \pi/4$ and $B = \pi/3$. Find the length a of the side opposite A.

T 64. **The approximation $\sin x \approx x$** It is often useful to know that, when x is measured in radians, $\sin x \approx x$ for numerically small values of x. In Section 3.11, we will see why the approximation holds. The approximation error is less than 1 in 5000 if $|x| < 0.1$.

a. With your grapher in radian mode, graph $y = \sin x$ and $y = x$ together in a viewing window about the origin. What do you see happening as x nears the origin?

b. With your grapher in degree mode, graph $y = \sin x$ and $y = x$ together about the origin again. How is the picture different from the one obtained with radian mode?

General Sine Curves

For

$$f(x) = A\sin\left(\frac{2\pi}{B}(x - C)\right) + D,$$

identify A, B, C, and D for the sine functions in Exercises 65–68 and sketch their graphs.

65. $y = 2\sin(x + \pi) - 1$

66. $y = \frac{1}{2}\sin(\pi x - \pi) + \frac{1}{2}$

67. $y = -\frac{2}{\pi}\sin\left(\frac{\pi}{2}t\right) + \frac{1}{\pi}$

68. $y = \frac{L}{2\pi}\sin\frac{2\pi t}{L}, \quad L > 0$

COMPUTER EXPLORATIONS

In Exercises 69–72, you will explore graphically the general sine function

$$f(x) = A\sin\left(\frac{2\pi}{B}(x - C)\right) + D$$

as you change the values of the constants A, B, C, and D. Use a CAS or computer grapher to perform the steps in the exercises.

69. **The period B** Set the constants $A = 3$, $C = D = 0$.

a. Plot $f(x)$ for the values $B = 1, 3, 2\pi, 5\pi$ over the interval $-4\pi \le x \le 4\pi$. Describe what happens to the graph of the general sine function as the period increases.

b. What happens to the graph for negative values of B? Try it with $B = -3$ and $B = -2\pi$.

70. **The horizontal shift C** Set the constants $A = 3$, $B = 6$, $D = 0$.

a. Plot $f(x)$ for the values $C = 0, 1$, and 2 over the interval $-4\pi \le x \le 4\pi$. Describe what happens to the graph of the general sine function as C increases through positive values.

b. What happens to the graph for negative values of C?

c. What smallest positive value should be assigned to C so the graph exhibits no horizontal shift? Confirm your answer with a plot.

71. **The vertical shift D** Set the constants $A = 3$, $B = 6$, $C = 0$.

a. Plot $f(x)$ for the values $D = 0, 1$, and 3 over the interval $-4\pi \le x \le 4\pi$. Describe what happens to the graph of the general sine function as D increases through positive values.

b. What happens to the graph for negative values of D?

72. **The amplitude A** Set the constants $B = 6$, $C = D = 0$.

a. Describe what happens to the graph of the general sine function as A increases through positive values. Confirm your answer by plotting $f(x)$ for the values $A = 1, 5$, and 9.

b. What happens to the graph for negative values of A?

1.4 Graphing with Calculators and Computers

A graphing calculator or a computer with graphing software enables us to graph very complicated functions with high precision. Many of these functions could not otherwise be easily graphed. However, care must be taken when using such devices for graphing purposes, and in this section we address some of the issues involved. In Chapter 4 we will see how calculus helps us determine that we are accurately viewing all the important features of a function's graph.

Graphing Windows

When using a graphing calculator or computer as a graphing tool, a portion of the graph is displayed in a rectangular **display** or **viewing window**. Often the default window gives an incomplete or misleading picture of the graph. We use the term *square window* when the units or scales on both axes are the same. This term does not mean that the display window itself is square (usually it is rectangular), but instead it means that the x-unit is the same as the y-unit.

When a graph is displayed in the default window, the x-unit may differ from the y-unit of scaling in order to fit the graph in the window. The viewing window is set by specifying an interval $[a, b]$ for the x-values and an interval $[c, d]$ for the y-values. The machine selects equally spaced x-values in $[a, b]$ and then plots the points $(x, f(x))$. A point is plotted if and only if x lies in the domain of the function and $f(x)$ lies within the interval $[c, d]$. A short line segment is then drawn between each plotted point and its next neighboring point. We now give illustrative examples of some common problems that may occur with this procedure.

EXAMPLE 1 Graph the function $f(x) = x^3 - 7x^2 + 28$ in each of the following display or viewing windows:

(a) $[-10, 10]$ by $[-10, 10]$ **(b)** $[-4, 4]$ by $[-50, 10]$ **(c)** $[-4, 10]$ by $[-60, 60]$

Solution

(a) We select $a = -10$, $b = 10$, $c = -10$, and $d = 10$ to specify the interval of x-values and the range of y-values for the window. The resulting graph is shown in Figure 1.48a. It appears that the window is cutting off the bottom part of the graph and that the interval of x-values is too large. Let's try the next window.

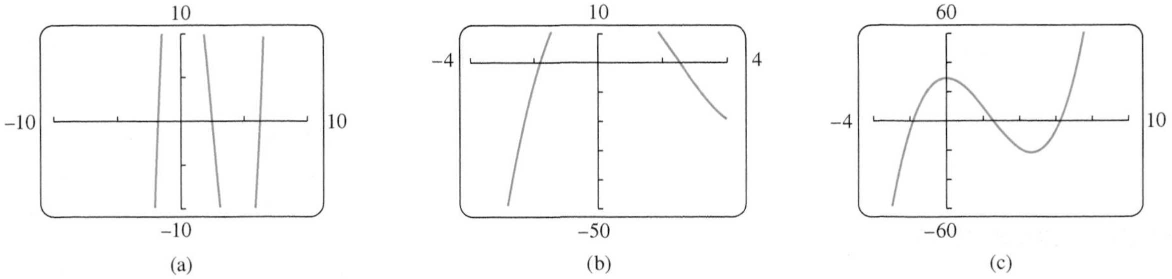

FIGURE 1.48 The graph of $f(x) = x^3 - 7x^2 + 28$ in different viewing windows. Selecting a window that gives a clear picture of a graph is often a trial-and-error process (Example 1).

(b) We see some new features of the graph (Figure 1.48b), but the top is missing and we need to view more to the right of $x = 4$ as well. The next window should help.

(c) Figure 1.48c shows the graph in this new viewing window. Observe that we get a more complete picture of the graph in this window, and it is a reasonable graph of a third-degree polynomial. ■

EXAMPLE 2 When a graph is displayed, the x-unit may differ from the y-unit, as in the graphs shown in Figures 1.48b and 1.48c. The result is distortion in the picture, which may be misleading. The display window can be made square by compressing or stretching the units on one axis to match the scale on the other, giving the true graph. Many systems have built-in functions to make the window "square." If yours does not, you will have to do some calculations and set the window size manually to get a square window, or bring to your viewing some foreknowledge of the true picture.

Figure 1.49a shows the graphs of the perpendicular lines $y = x$ and $y = -x + 3\sqrt{2}$, together with the semicircle $y = \sqrt{9 - x^2}$, in a nonsquare $[-4, 4]$ by $[-6, 8]$ display window. Notice the distortion. The lines do not appear to be perpendicular, and the semicircle appears to be elliptical in shape.

Figure 1.49b shows the graphs of the same functions in a square window in which the x-units are scaled to be the same as the y-units. Notice that the scaling on the x-axis for Figure 1.49a has been compressed in Figure 1.49b to make the window square. Figure 1.49c gives an enlarged view of Figure 1.49b with a square $[-3, 3]$ by $[0, 4]$ window. ■

If the denominator of a rational function is zero at some x-value within the viewing window, a calculator or graphing computer software may produce a steep near-vertical line segment from the top to the bottom of the window. Example 3 illustrates this situation.

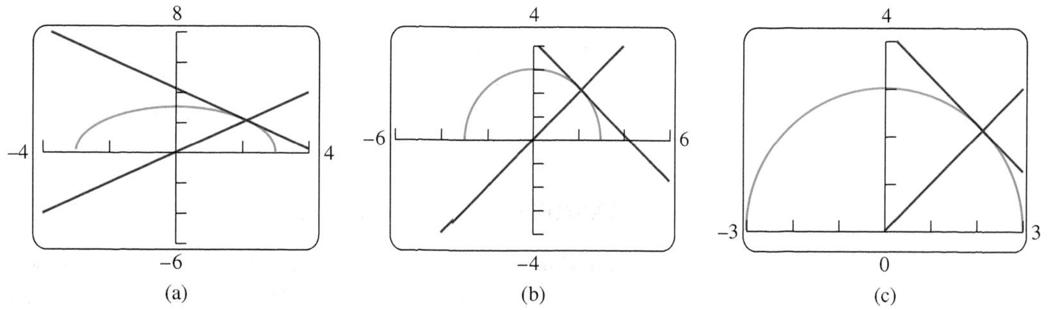

FIGURE 1.49 Graphs of the perpendicular lines $y = x$ and $y = -x + 3\sqrt{2}$, and the semicircle $y = \sqrt{9 - x^2}$ appear distorted (a) in a nonsquare window, but clear (b) and (c) in square windows (Example 2).

EXAMPLE 3 Graph the function $y = \dfrac{1}{2 - x}$.

Solution Figure 1.50a shows the graph in the $[-10, 10]$ by $[-10, 10]$ default square window with our computer graphing software. Notice the near-vertical line segment at $x = 2$. It is not truly a part of the graph and $x = 2$ does not belong to the domain of the function. By trial and error we can eliminate the line by changing the viewing window to the smaller $[-6, 6]$ by $[-4, 4]$ view, revealing a better graph (Figure 1.50b). ■

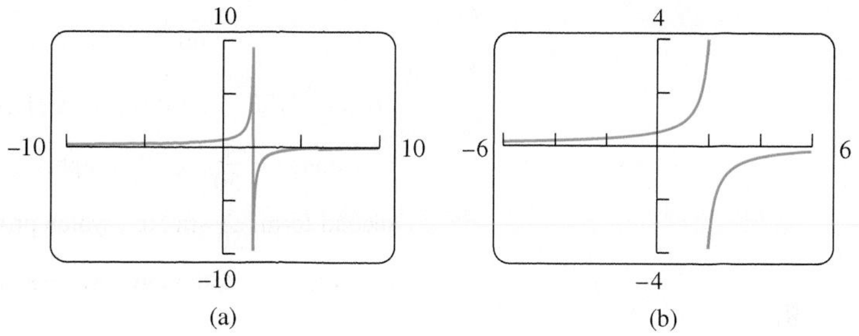

FIGURE 1.50 Graphs of the function $y = \dfrac{1}{2 - x}$. A vertical line may appear without a careful choice of the viewing window (Example 3).

Sometimes the graph of a trigonometric function oscillates very rapidly. When a calculator or computer software plots the points of the graph and connects them, many of the maximum and minimum points are actually missed. The resulting graph is then very misleading.

EXAMPLE 4 Graph the function $f(x) = \sin 100x$.

Solution Figure 1.51a shows the graph of f in the viewing window $[-12, 12]$ by $[-1, 1]$. We see that the graph looks very strange because the sine curve should oscillate periodically between -1 and 1. This behavior is not exhibited in Figure 1.51a. We might

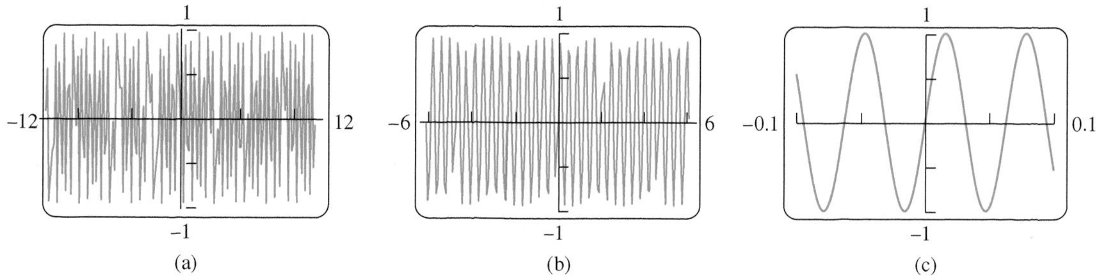

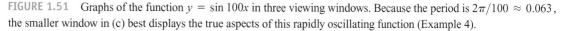

FIGURE 1.51 Graphs of the function $y = \sin 100x$ in three viewing windows. Because the period is $2\pi/100 \approx 0.063$, the smaller window in (c) best displays the true aspects of this rapidly oscillating function (Example 4).

experiment with a smaller viewing window, say $[-6, 6]$ by $[-1, 1]$, but the graph is not better (Figure 1.51b). The difficulty is that the period of the trigonometric function $y = \sin 100x$ is very small $(2\pi/100 \approx 0.063)$. If we choose the much smaller viewing window $[-0.1, 0.1]$ by $[-1, 1]$ we get the graph shown in Figure 1.51c. This graph reveals the expected oscillations of a sine curve. ■

EXAMPLE 5 Graph the function $y = \cos x + \frac{1}{50}\sin 50x$.

Solution In the viewing window $[-6, 6]$ by $[-1, 1]$ the graph appears much like the cosine function with some small sharp wiggles on it (Figure 1.52a). We get a better look when we significantly reduce the window to $[-0.6, 0.6]$ by $[0.8, 1.02]$, obtaining the graph in Figure 1.52b. We now see the small but rapid oscillations of the second term, $(1/50)\sin 50x$, added to the comparatively larger values of the cosine curve. ■

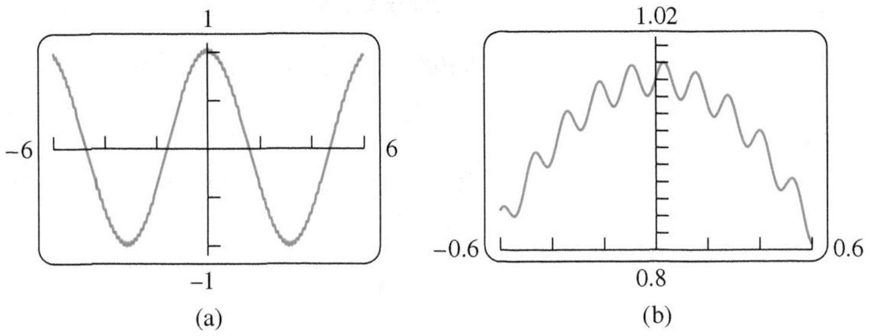

FIGURE 1.52 In (b) we see a close-up view of the function $y = \cos x + \frac{1}{50}\sin 50x$ graphed in (a). The term $\cos x$ clearly dominates the second term, $\frac{1}{50}\sin 50x$, which produces the rapid oscillations along the cosine curve. Both views are needed for a clear idea of the graph (Example 5).

Obtaining a Complete Graph

Some graphing devices will not display the portion of a graph for $f(x)$ when $x < 0$. Usually that happens because of the procedure the device is using to calculate the function values. Sometimes we can obtain the complete graph by defining the formula for the function in a different way.

EXAMPLE 6 Graph the function $y = x^{1/3}$.

Solution Some graphing devices display the graph shown in Figure 1.53a. When we compare it with the graph of $y = x^{1/3} = \sqrt[3]{x}$ in Figure 1.17, we see that the left branch for

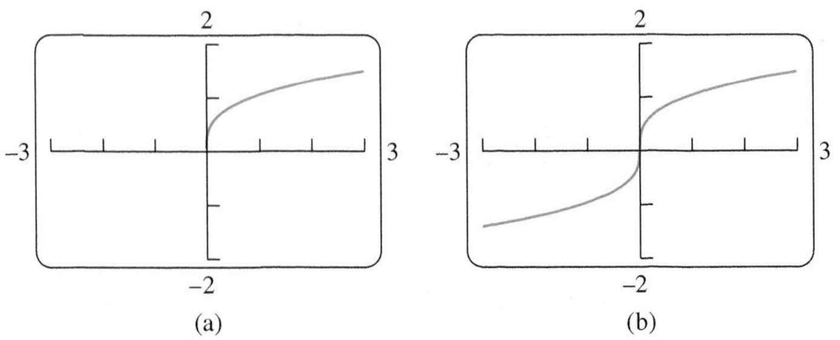

FIGURE 1.53 The graph of $y = x^{1/3}$ is missing the left branch in (a). In (b) we graph the function $f(x) = \frac{x}{|x|} \cdot |x|^{1/3}$, obtaining both branches. (See Example 6.)

$x < 0$ is missing. The reason the graphs differ is that many calculators and computer software programs calculate $x^{1/3}$ as $e^{(1/3)\ln x}$. Since the logarithmic function is not defined for negative values of x, the computing device can produce only the right branch, where $x > 0$. (Logarithmic and exponential functions are introduced in the next two sections.)

To obtain the full picture showing both branches, we can graph the function

$$f(x) = \frac{x}{|x|} \cdot |x|^{1/3}.$$

This function equals $x^{1/3}$ except at $x = 0$ (where f is undefined, although $0^{1/3} = 0$). The graph of f is shown in Figure 1.53b. ■

Exercises 1.4

Choosing a Viewing Window

T In Exercises 1–4, use a graphing calculator or computer to determine which of the given viewing windows displays the most appropriate graph of the specified function.

1. $f(x) = x^4 - 7x^2 + 6x$
   a. $[-1, 1]$ by $[-1, 1]$ b. $[-2, 2]$ by $[-5, 5]$
   c. $[-10, 10]$ by $[-10, 10]$ d. $[-5, 5]$ by $[-25, 15]$
2. $f(x) = x^3 - 4x^2 - 4x + 16$
   a. $[-1, 1]$ by $[-5, 5]$ b. $[-3, 3]$ by $[-10, 10]$
   c. $[-5, 5]$ by $[-10, 20]$ d. $[-20, 20]$ by $[-100, 100]$
3. $f(x) = 5 + 12x - x^3$
   a. $[-1, 1]$ by $[-1, 1]$ b. $[-5, 5]$ by $[-10, 10]$
   c. $[-4, 4]$ by $[-20, 20]$ d. $[-4, 5]$ by $[-15, 25]$
4. $f(x) = \sqrt{5 + 4x - x^2}$
   a. $[-2, 2]$ by $[-2, 2]$ b. $[-2, 6]$ by $[-1, 4]$
   c. $[-3, 7]$ by $[0, 10]$ d. $[-10, 10]$ by $[-10, 10]$

Finding a Viewing Window

T In Exercises 5–30, find an appropriate viewing window for the given function and use it to display its graph.

5. $f(x) = x^4 - 4x^3 + 15$
6. $f(x) = \frac{x^3}{3} - \frac{x^2}{2} - 2x + 1$
7. $f(x) = x^5 - 5x^4 + 10$
8. $f(x) = 4x^3 - x^4$
9. $f(x) = x\sqrt{9 - x^2}$
10. $f(x) = x^2(6 - x^3)$
11. $y = 2x - 3x^{2/3}$
12. $y = x^{1/3}(x^2 - 8)$
13. $y = 5x^{2/5} - 2x$
14. $y = x^{2/3}(5 - x)$
15. $y = |x^2 - 1|$
16. $y = |x^2 - x|$
17. $y = \frac{x + 3}{x + 2}$
18. $y = 1 - \frac{1}{x + 3}$
19. $f(x) = \frac{x^2 + 2}{x^2 + 1}$
20. $f(x) = \frac{x^2 - 1}{x^2 + 1}$
21. $f(x) = \frac{x - 1}{x^2 - x - 6}$
22. $f(x) = \frac{8}{x^2 - 9}$
23. $f(x) = \frac{6x^2 - 15x + 6}{4x^2 - 10x}$
24. $f(x) = \frac{x^2 - 3}{x - 2}$
25. $y = \sin 250x$
26. $y = 3 \cos 60x$
27. $y = \cos\left(\frac{x}{50}\right)$
28. $y = \frac{1}{10} \sin\left(\frac{x}{10}\right)$
29. $y = x + \frac{1}{10} \sin 30x$
30. $y = x^2 + \frac{1}{50} \cos 100x$
31. Graph the lower half of the circle defined by the equation $x^2 + 2x = 4 + 4y - y^2$.
32. Graph the upper branch of the hyperbola $y^2 - 16x^2 = 1$.
33. Graph four periods of the function $f(x) = -\tan 2x$.
34. Graph two periods of the function $f(x) = 3 \cot \frac{x}{2} + 1$.
35. Graph the function $f(x) = \sin 2x + \cos 3x$.
36. Graph the function $f(x) = \sin^3 x$.

Graphing in Dot Mode

T Another way to avoid incorrect connections when using a graphing device is through the use of a "dot mode," which plots only the points. If your graphing utility allows that mode, use it to plot the functions in Exercises 37–40.

37. $y = \frac{1}{x - 3}$
38. $y = \sin \frac{1}{x}$
39. $y = x\lfloor x \rfloor$
40. $y = \frac{x^3 - 1}{x^2 - 1}$

1.5 Exponential Functions

Exponential functions are among the most important in mathematics and occur in a wide variety of applications, including interest rates, radioactive decay, population growth, the spread of a disease, consumption of natural resources, the earth's atmospheric pressure, temperature change of a heated object placed in a cooler environment, and the dating of fossils. In this section we introduce these functions informally, using an intuitive approach. We give a rigorous development of them in Chapter 7, based on important calculus ideas and results.

Exponential Behavior

When a positive quantity P doubles, it increases by a factor of 2 and the quantity becomes $2P$. If it doubles again, it becomes $2(2P) = 2^2P$, and a third doubling gives $2(2^2P) = 2^3P$. Continuing to double in this fashion leads us to the consideration of the function $f(x) = 2^x$. We call this an *exponential* function because the variable x appears in the exponent of 2^x. Functions such as $g(x) = 10^x$ and $h(x) = (1/2)^x$ are other examples of exponential functions. In general, if $a \neq 1$ is a positive constant, the function

$$f(x) = a^x, \quad a > 0$$

is the **exponential function with base a.**

Don't confuse the exponential function 2^x with the power function x^2. In the exponential function, the variable x is in the exponent, whereas the variable x is the base in the power function.

EXAMPLE 1 In 2010, \$100 is invested in a savings account, where it grows by accruing interest that is compounded annually (once a year) at an interest rate of 5.5%. Assuming no additional funds are deposited to the account and no money is withdrawn, give a formula for a function describing the amount A in the account after x years have elapsed.

Solution If $P = 100$, at the end of the first year the amount in the account is the original amount plus the interest accrued, or

$$P + \left(\frac{5.5}{100}\right)P = (1 + 0.055)P = (1.055)P.$$

At the end of the second year the account earns interest again and grows to

$$(1 + 0.055) \cdot (1.055P) = (1.055)^2P = 100 \cdot (1.055)^2. \qquad P = 100$$

Continuing this process, after x years the value of the account is

$$A = 100 \cdot (1.055)^x.$$

This is a multiple of the exponential function with base 1.055. Table 1.4 shows the amounts accrued over the first four years. Notice that the amount in the account each year is always 1.055 times its value in the previous year.

TABLE 1.4 Savings account growth

Year	Amount (dollars)	Increase (dollars)
2010	100	
2011	$100(1.055) = 105.50$	5.50
2012	$100(1.055)^2 = 111.30$	5.80
2013	$100(1.055)^3 = 117.42$	6.12
2014	$100(1.055)^4 = 123.88$	6.46

In general, the amount after x years is given by $P(1 + r)^x$, where r is the interest rate (expressed as a decimal). ■

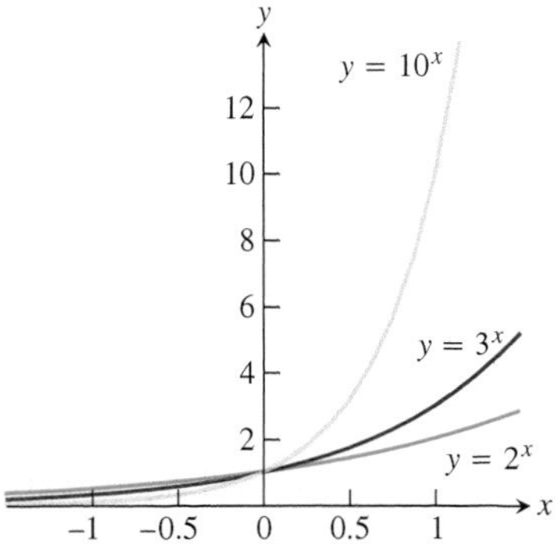

(a) $y = 2^x, y = 3^x, y = 10^x$

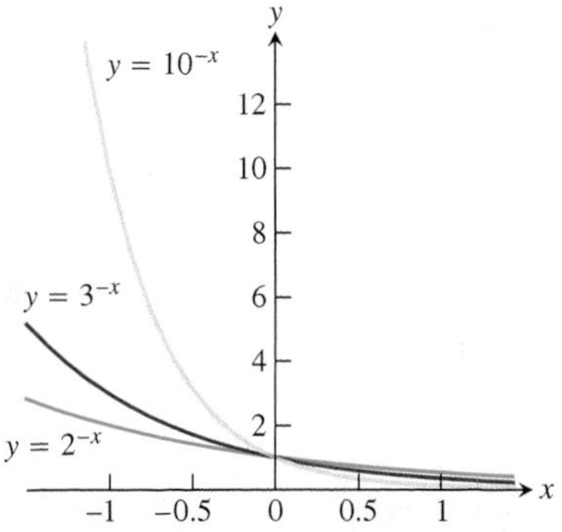

(b) $y = 2^{-x}, y = 3^{-x}, y = 10^{-x}$

FIGURE 1.54 Graphs of exponential functions.

For integer and rational exponents, the value of an exponential function $f(x) = a^x$ is obtained arithmetically as follows. If $x = n$ is a positive integer, the number a^n is given by multiplying a by itself n times:

$$a^n = \underbrace{a \cdot a \cdot \cdots \cdot a}_{n \text{ factors}}.$$

If $x = 0$, then $a^0 = 1$, and if $x = -n$ for some positive integer n, then

$$a^{-n} = \frac{1}{a^n} = \left(\frac{1}{a}\right)^n.$$

If $x = 1/n$ for some positive integer n, then

$$a^{1/n} = \sqrt[n]{a},$$

which is the positive number that when multiplied by itself n times gives a. If $x = p/q$ is any rational number, then

$$a^{p/q} = \sqrt[q]{a^p} = \left(\sqrt[q]{a}\right)^p.$$

If x is *irrational*, the meaning of a^x is not so clear, but its value can be defined by considering values for rational numbers that get closer and closer to x. This informal approach is based on the graph of the exponential function. In Chapter 7 we define the meaning in a rigorous way.

We displayed the graphs of several exponential functions in Section 1.1, and show them again here in Figure 1.54. These graphs describe the values of the exponential functions for all real inputs x. The value at an irrational number x is chosen so that the graph of a^x has no "holes" or "jumps." Of course, these words are not mathematical terms, but they do convey the informal idea. We mean that the value of a^x, when x is irrational, is chosen so that the function $f(x) = a^x$ is *continuous*, a notion that will be carefully explored in the next chapter. This choice ensures the graph retains its increasing behavior when $a > 1$, or decreasing behavior when $0 < a < 1$ (see Figure 1.54).

Arithmetically, the graphical idea can be described in the following way, using the exponential function $f(x) = 2^x$ as an illustration. Any particular irrational number, say $x = \sqrt{3}$, has a decimal expansion

$$\sqrt{3} = 1.732050808\ldots.$$

We then consider the list of numbers, given as follows in the order of taking more and more digits in the decimal expansion,

$$2^1, 2^{1.7}, 2^{1.73}, 2^{1.732}, 2^{1.7320}, 2^{1.73205}, \ldots. \tag{1}$$

We know the meaning of each number in list (1) because the successive decimal approximations to $\sqrt{3}$ given by 1, 1.7, 1.73, 1.732, and so on, are all *rational* numbers. As these decimal approximations get closer and closer to $\sqrt{3}$, it seems reasonable that the list of numbers in (1) gets closer and closer to some fixed number, which we specify to be $2^{\sqrt{3}}$.

Table 1.5 illustrates how taking better approximations to $\sqrt{3}$ gives better approximations to the number $2^{\sqrt{3}} \approx 3.321997086$. It is the *completeness property* of the real numbers (discussed briefly in Appendix 7) which guarantees that this procedure gives a single number we define to be $2^{\sqrt{3}}$ (although it is beyond the scope of this text to give a proof). In a similar way, we can identify the number 2^x (or a^x, $a > 0$) for any irrational x. By identifying the number a^x for both rational and irrational x, we eliminate any "holes" or "gaps" in the graph of a^x. In practice you can use a calculator to find the number a^x for irrational x, taking successive decimal approximations to x and creating a table similar to Table 1.5.

Exponential functions obey the familiar rules of exponents listed on the next page. It is easy to check these rules using algebra when the exponents are integers or rational numbers. We prove them for all real exponents in Chapters 4 and 7.

TABLE 1.5 Values of $2^{\sqrt{3}}$ for rational r closer and closer to $\sqrt{3}$

r	2^r
1.0	2.000000000
1.7	3.249009585
1.73	3.317278183
1.732	3.321880096
1.7320	3.321880096
1.73205	3.321995226
1.732050	3.321995226
1.7320508	3.321997068
1.73205080	3.321997068
1.732050808	3.321997086

Rules for Exponents

If $a > 0$ and $b > 0$, the following rules hold true for all real numbers x and y.

1. $a^x \cdot a^y = a^{x+y}$

2. $\dfrac{a^x}{a^y} = a^{x-y}$

3. $(a^x)^y = (a^y)^x = a^{xy}$

4. $a^x \cdot b^x = (ab)^x$

5. $\dfrac{a^x}{b^x} = \left(\dfrac{a}{b}\right)^x$

EXAMPLE 2 We illustrate using the rules for exponents to simplify numerical expressions.

1. $3^{1.1} \cdot 3^{0.7} = 3^{1.1+0.7} = 3^{1.8}$

2. $\dfrac{\left(\sqrt{10}\right)^3}{\sqrt{10}} = \left(\sqrt{10}\right)^{3-1} = \left(\sqrt{10}\right)^2 = 10$

3. $\left(5^{\sqrt{2}}\right)^{\sqrt{2}} = 5^{\sqrt{2} \cdot \sqrt{2}} = 5^2 = 25$

4. $7^\pi \cdot 8^\pi = (56)^\pi$

5. $\left(\dfrac{4}{9}\right)^{1/2} = \dfrac{4^{1/2}}{9^{1/2}} = \dfrac{2}{3}$ ■

The Natural Exponential Function e^x

The most important exponential function used for modeling natural, physical, and economic phenomena is the **natural exponential function**, whose base is the special number e. The number e is irrational, and its value is 2.718281828 to nine decimal places. (In Section 3.8 we will see a way to calculate the value of e.) It might seem strange that we would use this number for a base rather than a simple number like 2 or 10. The advantage in using e as a base is that it simplifies many of the calculations in calculus.

If you look at Figure 1.54a you can see that the graphs of the exponential functions $y = a^x$ get steeper as the base a gets larger. This idea of steepness is conveyed by the slope of the tangent line to the graph at a point. Tangent lines to graphs of functions are defined precisely in the next chapter, but intuitively the tangent line to the graph at a point is a line that just touches the graph at the point, like a tangent to a circle. Figure 1.55 shows the slope of the graph of $y = a^x$ as it crosses the y-axis for several values of a. Notice that the slope is exactly equal to 1 when a equals the number e. The slope is smaller than 1 if $a < e$, and larger than 1 if $a > e$. This is the property that makes the number e so useful in calculus: **The graph of $y = e^x$ has slope 1 when it crosses the y-axis.**

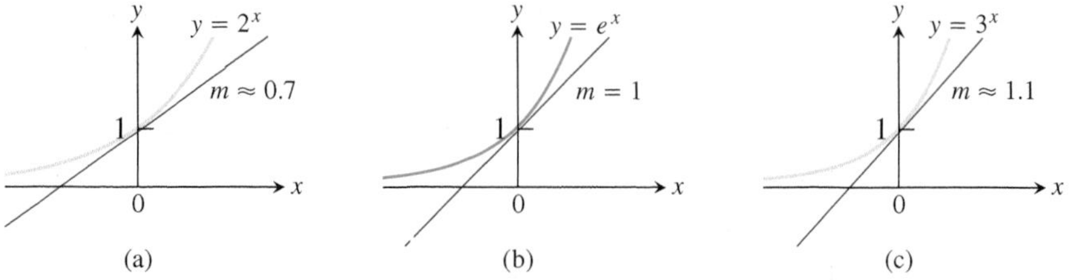

FIGURE 1.55 Among the exponential functions, the graph of $y = e^x$ has the property that the slope m of the tangent line to the graph is exactly 1 when it crosses the y-axis. The slope is smaller for a base less than e, such as 2^x, and larger for a base greater than e, such as 3^x.

Exponential Growth and Decay

The exponential functions $y = e^{kx}$, where k is a nonzero constant, are frequently used for modeling exponential growth or decay. The function $y = y_0 e^{kx}$ is a model for **exponential growth** if $k > 0$ and a model for **exponential decay** if $k < 0$. Here y_0 represents a constant. An example of exponential growth occurs when computing interest **compounded continuously** modeled by $y = P \cdot e^{rt}$, where P is the initial monetary investment, r is the interest rate as a decimal, and t is time in units consistent with r. An example of exponential decay is the model $y = A \cdot e^{-1.2 \times 10^{-4} t}$, which represents how the radioactive isotope carbon-14 decays over time. Here A is the original amount of carbon-14 and t is the time in years. Carbon-14 decay is used to date the remains of dead organisms such as shells, seeds, and wooden artifacts. Figure 1.56 shows graphs of exponential growth and exponential decay.

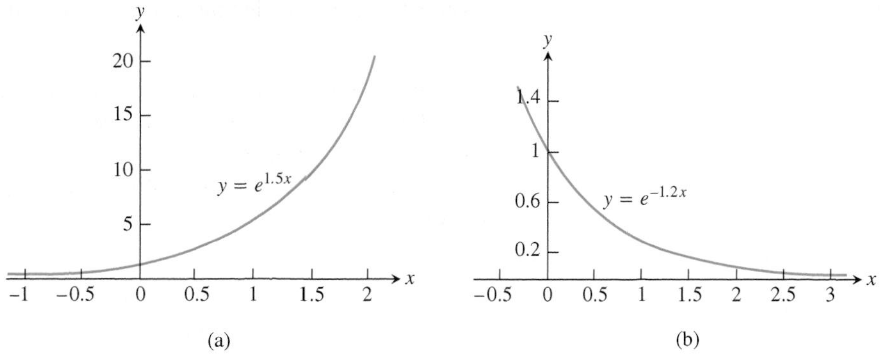

FIGURE 1.56 Graphs of (a) exponential growth, $k = 1.5 > 0$, and (b) exponential decay, $k = -1.2 < 0$.

EXAMPLE 3 Investment companies often use the model $y = Pe^{rt}$ in calculating the growth of an investment. Use this model to track the growth of \$100 invested in 2000 at an annual interest rate of 5.5%.

Solution Let $t = 0$ represent 2010, $t = 1$ represent 2011, and so on. Then the exponential growth model is $y(t) = Pe^{rt}$, where $P = 100$ (the initial investment), $r = 0.055$ (the annual interest rate expressed as a decimal), and t is time in years. To predict the amount in the account in 2014, after four years have elapsed, we take $t = 4$ and calculate

$$\begin{aligned} y(4) &= 100e^{0.055(4)} \\ &= 100e^{0.22} \\ &= 124.61. \qquad \text{Nearest cent using calculator} \end{aligned}$$

This compares with \$123.88 in the account when the interest is compounded annually from Example 1. ∎

EXAMPLE 4 Laboratory experiments indicate that some atoms emit a part of their mass as radiation, with the remainder of the atom re-forming to make an atom of some new element. For example, radioactive carbon-14 decays into nitrogen; radium eventually decays into lead. If y_0 is the number of radioactive nuclei present at time zero, the number still present at any later time t will be

$$y = y_0 e^{-rt}, \qquad r > 0.$$

The number r is called the **decay rate** of the radioactive substance. (We will see how this formula is obtained in Section 7.2.) For carbon-14, the decay rate has been determined experimentally to be about $r = 1.2 \times 10^{-4}$ when t is measured in years. Predict the percent of carbon-14 present after 866 years have elapsed.

Solution If we start with an amount y_0 of carbon-14 nuclei, after 866 years we are left with the amount

$$\begin{aligned} y(866) &= y_0\, e^{(-1.2\times10^{-4})(866)} \\ &\approx (0.901)y_0. \qquad \text{Calculator evaluation} \end{aligned}$$

That is, after 866 years, we are left with about 90% of the original amount of carbon-14, so about 10% of the original nuclei have decayed. In Example 7 in the next section, you will see how to find the number of years required for half of the radioactive nuclei present in a sample to decay (called the *half-life* of the substance). ■

You may wonder why we use the family of functions $y = e^{kx}$ for different values of the constant k instead of the general exponential functions $y = a^x$. In the next section, we show that the exponential function a^x is equal to e^{kx} for an appropriate value of k. So the formula $y = e^{kx}$ covers the entire range of possibilities, and we will see that it is easier to use.

Exercises 1.5

Sketching Exponential Curves

In Exercises 1–6, sketch the given curves together in the appropriate coordinate plane and label each curve with its equation.

1. $y = 2^x, y = 4^x, y = 3^{-x}, y = (1/5)^x$

2. $y = 3^x, y = 8^x, y = 2^{-x}, y = (1/4)^x$

3. $y = 2^{-t}$ and $y = -2^t$

4. $y = 3^{-t}$ and $y = -3^t$

5. $y = e^x$ and $y = 1/e^x$

6. $y = -e^x$ and $y = -e^{-x}$

In each of Exercises 7–10, sketch the shifted exponential curves.

7. $y = 2^x - 1$ and $y = 2^{-x} - 1$

8. $y = 3^x + 2$ and $y = 3^{-x} + 2$

9. $y = 1 - e^x$ and $y = 1 - e^{-x}$

10. $y = -1 - e^x$ and $y = -1 - e^{-x}$

Applying the Laws of Exponents

Use the laws of exponents to simplify the expressions in Exercises 11–20.

11. $16^2 \cdot 16^{-1.75}$

12. $9^{1/3} \cdot 9^{1/6}$

13. $\dfrac{4^{4.2}}{4^{3.7}}$

14. $\dfrac{3^{5/3}}{3^{2/3}}$

15. $\left(25^{1/8}\right)^4$

16. $\left(13^{\sqrt{2}}\right)^{\sqrt{2}/2}$

17. $2^{\sqrt{3}} \cdot 7^{\sqrt{3}}$

18. $\left(\sqrt{3}\right)^{1/2} \cdot \left(\sqrt{12}\right)^{1/2}$

19. $\left(\dfrac{2}{\sqrt{2}}\right)^4$

20. $\left(\dfrac{\sqrt{6}}{3}\right)^2$

Composites Involving Exponential Functions

Find the domain and range for each of the functions in Exercises 21–24.

21. $f(x) = \dfrac{1}{2 + e^x}$

22. $g(t) = \cos(e^{-t})$

23. $g(t) = \sqrt{1 + 3^{-t}}$

24. $f(x) = \dfrac{3}{1 - e^{2x}}$

Applications

T In Exercises 25–28, use graphs to find approximate solutions.

25. $2^x = 5$

26. $e^x = 4$

27. $3^x - 0.5 = 0$

28. $3 - 2^{-x} = 0$

T In Exercises 29–36, use an exponential model and a graphing calculator to estimate the answer in each problem.

29. Population growth The population of Knoxville is 500,000 and is increasing at the rate of 3.75% each year. Approximately when will the population reach 1 million?

30. Population growth The population of Silver Run in the year 1890 was 6250. Assume the population increased at a rate of 2.75% per year.

a. Estimate the population in 1915 and 1940.

b. Approximately when did the population reach 50,000?

31. Radioactive decay The half-life of phosphorus-32 is about 14 days. There are 6.6 grams present initially.

a. Express the amount of phosphorus-32 remaining as a function of time t.

b. When will there be 1 gram remaining?

32. If John invests \$2300 in a savings account with a 6% interest rate compounded annually, how long will it take until John's account has a balance of \$4150?

33. **Doubling your money** Determine how much time is required for an investment to double in value if interest is earned at the rate of 6.25% compounded annually.

34. **Tripling your money** Determine how much time is required for an investment to triple in value if interest is earned at the rate of 5.75% compounded continuously.

35. **Cholera bacteria** Suppose that a colony of bacteria starts with 1 bacterium and doubles in number every half hour. How many bacteria will the colony contain at the end of 24 hr?

36. **Eliminating a disease** Suppose that in any given year the number of cases of a disease is reduced by 20%. If there are 10,000 cases today, how many years will it take

a. to reduce the number of cases to 1000?

b. to eliminate the disease; that is, to reduce the number of cases to less than 1?

1.6 Inverse Functions and Logarithms

A function that undoes, or inverts, the effect of a function f is called the *inverse* of f. Many common functions, though not all, are paired with an inverse. In this section we present the natural logarithmic function $y = \ln x$ as the inverse of the exponential function $y = e^x$, and we also give examples of several inverse trigonometric functions.

One-to-One Functions

A function is a rule that assigns a value from its range to each element in its domain. Some functions assign the same range value to more than one element in the domain. The function $f(x) = x^2$ assigns the same value, 1, to both of the numbers -1 and $+1$; the sines of $\pi/3$ and $2\pi/3$ are both $\sqrt{3}/2$. Other functions assume each value in their range no more than once. The square roots and cubes of different numbers are always different. A function that has distinct values at distinct elements in its domain is called one-to-one. These functions take on any one value in their range exactly once.

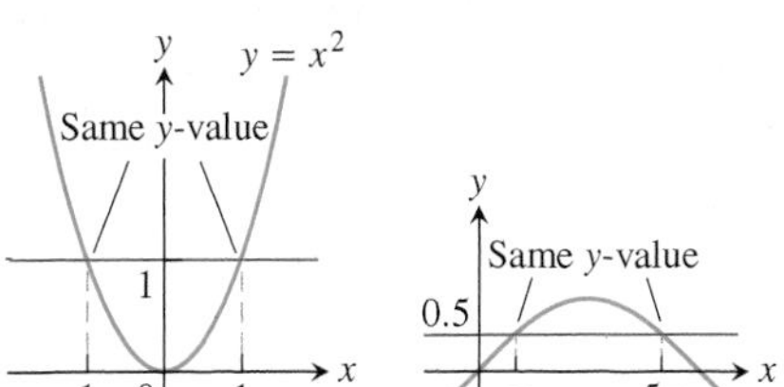

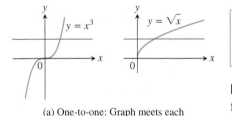

(a) One-to-one: Graph meets each horizontal line at most once.

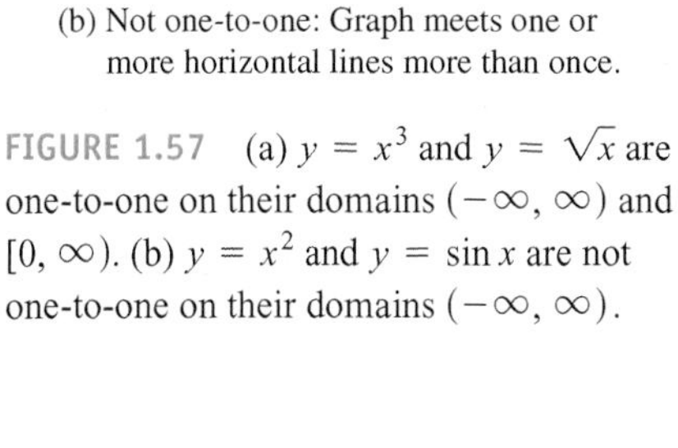

(b) Not one-to-one: Graph meets one or more horizontal lines more than once.

FIGURE 1.57 (a) $y = x^3$ and $y = \sqrt{x}$ are one-to-one on their domains $(-\infty, \infty)$ and $[0, \infty)$. (b) $y = x^2$ and $y = \sin x$ are not one-to-one on their domains $(-\infty, \infty)$.

DEFINITION A function $f(x)$ is **one-to-one** on a domain D if $f(x_1) \neq f(x_2)$ whenever $x_1 \neq x_2$ in D.

EXAMPLE 1 Some functions are one-to-one on their entire natural domain. Other functions are not one-to-one on their entire domain, but by restricting the function to a smaller domain we can create a function that is one-to-one. The original and restricted functions are not the same functions, because they have different domains. However, the two functions have the same values on the smaller domain, so the original function is an extension of the restricted function from its smaller domain to the larger domain.

(a) $f(x) = \sqrt{x}$ is one-to-one on any domain of nonnegative numbers because $\sqrt{x_1} \neq \sqrt{x_2}$ whenever $x_1 \neq x_2$.

(b) $g(x) = \sin x$ is *not* one-to-one on the interval $[0, \pi]$ because $\sin(\pi/6) = \sin(5\pi/6)$. In fact, for each element x_1 in the subinterval $[0, \pi/2)$ there is a corresponding element x_2 in the subinterval $(\pi/2, \pi]$ satisfying $\sin x_1 = \sin x_2$, so distinct elements in the domain are assigned to the same value in the range. The sine function *is* one-to-one on $[0, \pi/2]$, however, because it is an increasing function on $[0, \pi/2]$ giving distinct outputs for distinct inputs. ■

The graph of a one-to-one function $y = f(x)$ can intersect a given horizontal line at most once. If the function intersects the line more than once, it assumes the same y-value for at least two different x-values and is therefore not one-to-one (Figure 1.57).

The Horizontal Line Test for One-to-One Functions
A function $y = f(x)$ is one-to-one if and only if its graph intersects each horizontal line at most once.

Inverse Functions

Since each output of a one-to-one function comes from just one input, the effect of the function can be inverted to send an output back to the input from which it came.

DEFINITION Suppose that f is a one-to-one function on a domain D with range R. The **inverse function** f^{-1} is defined by

$$f^{-1}(b) = a \text{ if } f(a) = b.$$

The domain of f^{-1} is R and the range of f^{-1} is D.

The symbol f^{-1} for the inverse of f is read "f inverse." The "-1" in f^{-1} is *not* an exponent; $f^{-1}(x)$ does not mean $1/f(x)$. Notice that the domains and ranges of f and f^{-1} are interchanged.

EXAMPLE 2 Suppose a one-to-one function $y = f(x)$ is given by a table of values

x	1	2	3	4	5	6	7	8
$f(x)$	3	4.5	7	10.5	15	20.5	27	34.5

A table for the values of $x = f^{-1}(y)$ can then be obtained by simply interchanging the values in the columns (or rows) of the table for f:

y	3	4.5	7	10.5	15	20.5	27	34.5
$f^{-1}(y)$	1	2	3	4	5	6	7	8

■

If we apply f to send an input x to the output $f(x)$ and follow by applying f^{-1} to $f(x)$, we get right back to x, just where we started. Similarly, if we take some number y in the range of f, apply f^{-1} to it, and then apply f to the resulting value $f^{-1}(y)$, we get back the value y with which we began. Composing a function and its inverse has the same effect as doing nothing.

$$(f^{-1} \circ f)(x) = x, \qquad \text{for all } x \text{ in the domain of } f$$

$$(f \circ f^{-1})(y) = y, \qquad \text{for all } y \text{ in the domain of } f^{-1} \text{ (or range of } f)$$

Only a one-to-one function can have an inverse. The reason is that if $f(x_1) = y$ and $f(x_2) = y$ for two distinct inputs x_1 and x_2, then there is no way to assign a value to $f^{-1}(y)$ that satisfies both $f^{-1}(f(x_1)) = x_1$ and $f^{-1}(f(x_2)) = x_2$.

A function that is increasing on an interval so it satisfies the inequality $f(x_2) > f(x_1)$ when $x_2 > x_1$ is one-to-one and has an inverse. Decreasing functions also have an inverse. Functions that are neither increasing nor decreasing may still be one-to-one and have an inverse, as with the function $f(x) = 1/x$ for $x \neq 0$ and $f(0) = 0$, defined on $(-\infty, \infty)$ and passing the horizontal line test.

Finding Inverses

The graphs of a function and its inverse are closely related. To read the value of a function from its graph, we start at a point x on the x-axis, go vertically to the graph, and then move horizontally to the y-axis to read the value of y. The inverse function can be read from the graph by reversing this process. Start with a point y on the y-axis, go horizontally to the graph of $y = f(x)$, and then move vertically to the x-axis to read the value of $x = f^{-1}(y)$ (Figure 1.58).

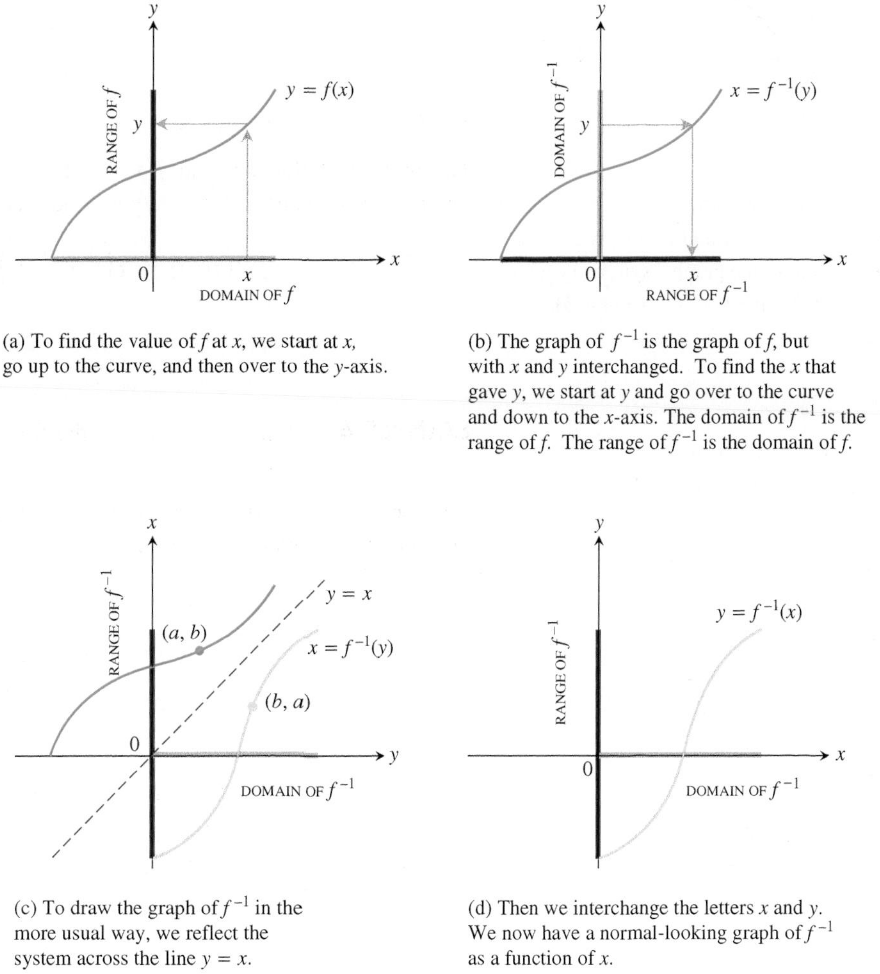

(a) To find the value of f at x, we start at x, go up to the curve, and then over to the y-axis.

(b) The graph of f^{-1} is the graph of f, but with x and y interchanged. To find the x that gave y, we start at y and go over to the curve and down to the x-axis. The domain of f^{-1} is the range of f. The range of f^{-1} is the domain of f.

(c) To draw the graph of f^{-1} in the more usual way, we reflect the system across the line $y = x$.

(d) Then we interchange the letters x and y. We now have a normal-looking graph of f^{-1} as a function of x.

FIGURE 1.58 The graph of $y = f^{-1}(x)$ is obtained by reflecting the graph of $y = f(x)$ about the line $y = x$.

We want to set up the graph of f^{-1} so that its input values lie along the x-axis, as is usually done for functions, rather than on the y-axis. To achieve this we interchange the x- and y-axes by reflecting across the 45° line $y = x$. After this reflection we have a new graph that represents f^{-1}. The value of $f^{-1}(x)$ can now be read from the graph in the usual way, by starting with a point x on the x-axis, going vertically to the graph, and then horizontally to the y-axis to get the value of $f^{-1}(x)$. Figure 1.58 indicates the relationship between the graphs of f and f^{-1}. The graphs are interchanged by reflection through the line $y = x$.

The process of passing from f to f^{-1} can be summarized as a two-step procedure.

1. Solve the equation $y = f(x)$ for x. This gives a formula $x = f^{-1}(y)$ where x is expressed as a function of y.
2. Interchange x and y, obtaining a formula $y = f^{-1}(x)$ where f^{-1} is expressed in the conventional format with x as the independent variable and y as the dependent variable.

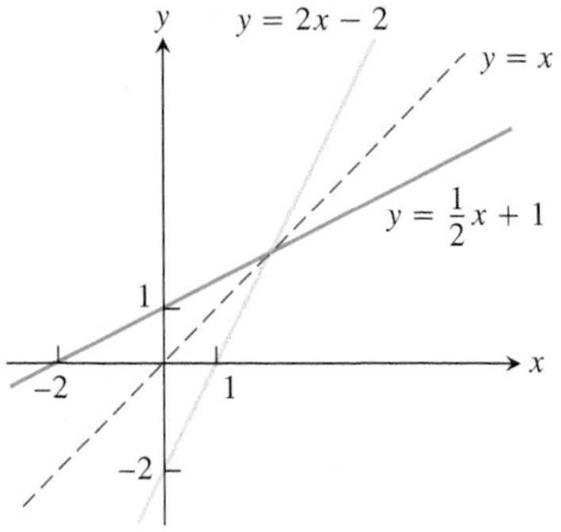

FIGURE 1.59 Graphing $f(x) = (1/2)x + 1$ and $f^{-1}(x) = 2x - 2$ together shows the graphs' symmetry with respect to the line $y = x$ (Example 3).

EXAMPLE 3 Find the inverse of $y = \frac{1}{2}x + 1$, expressed as a function of x.

Solution

1. *Solve for x in terms of y:*
$$y = \frac{1}{2}x + 1$$
The graph is a straight line satisfying the horizontal line test (Fig. 1.59).
$$2y = x + 2$$
$$x = 2y - 2.$$
2. *Interchange x and y:* $y = 2x - 2$.

The inverse of the function $f(x) = (1/2)x + 1$ is the function $f^{-1}(x) = 2x - 2$. (See Figure 1.59.) To check, we verify that both composites give the identity function:

$$f^{-1}(f(x)) = 2\left(\frac{1}{2}x + 1\right) - 2 = x + 2 - 2 = x$$

$$f(f^{-1}(x)) = \frac{1}{2}(2x - 2) + 1 = x - 1 + 1 = x.$$ ■

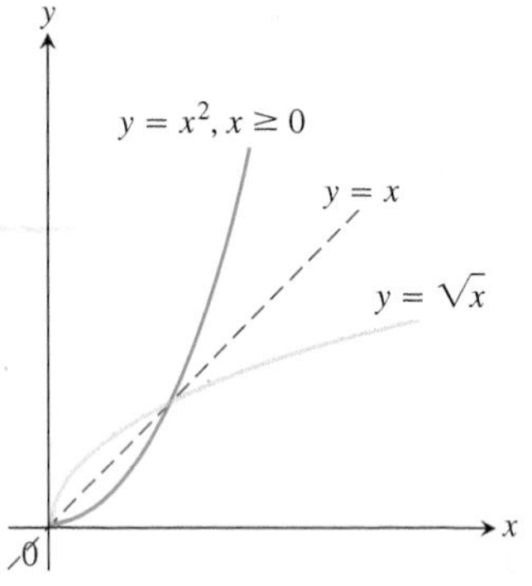

FIGURE 1.60 The functions $y = \sqrt{x}$ and $y = x^2, x \geq 0$, are inverses of one another (Example 4).

EXAMPLE 4 Find the inverse of the function $y = x^2, x \geq 0$, expressed as a function of x.

Solution For $x \geq 0$, the graph satisfies the horizontal line test, so the function is one-to-one and has an inverse. To find the inverse, we first solve for x in terms of y:

$$y = x^2$$
$$\sqrt{y} = \sqrt{x^2} = |x| = x$$
$|x| = x$ because $x \geq 0$

We then interchange x and y, obtaining

$$y = \sqrt{x}.$$

The inverse of the function $y = x^2, x \geq 0$, is the function $y = \sqrt{x}$ (Figure 1.60).

Notice that the function $y = x^2, x \geq 0$, with domain *restricted* to the nonnegative real numbers, *is* one-to-one (Figure 1.60) and has an inverse. On the other hand, the function $y = x^2$, with no domain restrictions, *is not* one-to-one (Figure 1.57b) and therefore has no inverse. ■

Logarithmic Functions

If a is any positive real number other than 1, the base a exponential function $f(x) = a^x$ is one-to-one. It therefore has an inverse. Its inverse is called the *logarithm function with base a*.

> **DEFINITION** The **logarithm function with base *a***, $y = \log_a x$, is the inverse of the base a exponential function $y = a^x$ $(a > 0, a \neq 1)$.

The domain of $\log_a x$ is $(0, \infty)$, the range of a^x. The range of $\log_a x$ is $(-\infty, \infty)$, the domain of a^x.

Figure 1.23 in Section 1.1 shows the graphs of four logarithmic functions with $a > 1$. Figure 1.61a shows the graph of $y = \log_2 x$. The graph of $y = a^x$, $a > 1$, increases rapidly for $x > 0$, so its inverse, $y = \log_a x$, increases slowly for $x > 1$.

Because we have no technique yet for solving the equation $y = a^x$ for x in terms of y, we do not have an explicit formula for computing the logarithm at a given value of x. Nevertheless, we can obtain the graph of $y = \log_a x$ by reflecting the graph of the exponential $y = a^x$ across the line $y = x$. Figure 1.61 shows the graphs for $a = 2$ and $a = e$.

Logarithms with base 2 are commonly used in computer science. Logarithms with base e and base 10 are so important in applications that calculators have special keys for them. They also have their own special notation and names:

$$\log_e x \quad \text{is written as} \quad \ln x.$$
$$\log_{10} x \quad \text{is written as} \quad \log x.$$

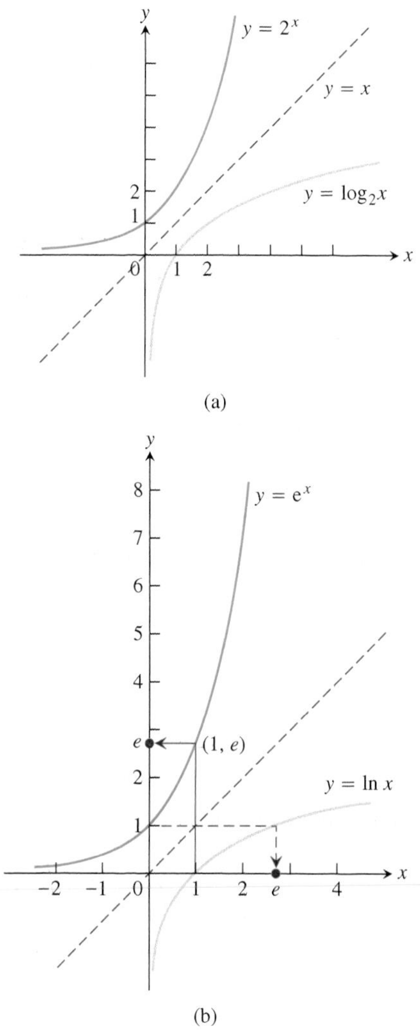

FIGURE 1.61 (a) The graph of 2^x and its inverse, $\log_2 x$. (b) The graph of e^x and its inverse, $\ln x$.

HISTORICAL BIOGRAPHY*

John Napier
(1550–1617)

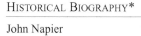

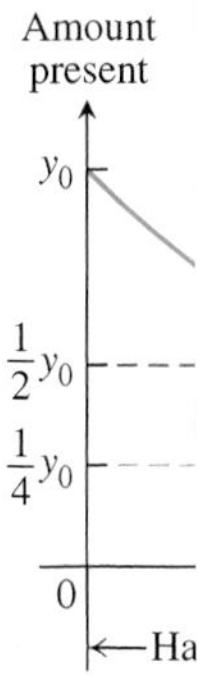

FIGURE 1
present at
number o
present (E

The function $y = \ln x$ is called the **natural logarithm function**, and $y = \log x$ is often called the **common logarithm function**. For the natural logarithm,

$$\ln x = y \iff e^y = x.$$

In particular, if we set $x = e$, we obtain

$$\ln e = 1$$

because $e^1 = e$.

Properties of Logarithms

Logarithms, invented by John Napier, were the single most important improvement in arithmetic calculation before the modern electronic computer. What made them so useful is that the properties of logarithms reduce multiplication of positive numbers to addition of their logarithms, division of positive numbers to subtraction of their logarithms, and exponentiation of a number to multiplying its logarithm by the exponent.

We summarize these properties for the natural logarithm as a series of rules that we prove in Chapter 3. Although here we state the Power Rule for all real powers r, the case when r is an irrational number cannot be dealt with properly until Chapter 4. We also establish the validity of the rules for logarithmic functions with any base a in Chapter 7.

THEOREM 1—Algebraic Properties of the Natural Logarithm For any numbers $b > 0$ and $x > 0$, the natural logarithm satisfies the following rules:

1. *Product Rule*: $\ln bx = \ln b + \ln x$
2. *Quotient Rule*: $\ln \frac{b}{x} = \ln b - \ln x$
3. *Reciprocal Rule*: $\ln \frac{1}{x} = -\ln x$ Rule 2 with $b = 1$
4. *Power Rule*: $\ln x^r = r \ln x$

*To learn more about the historical figures mentioned in the text and the development of many major elements and topics of calculus, visit **www.aw.com/thomas**.

If we set $t_0 = 1$ and then expand the numerator in Equation (1) and simplify, we find that

$$\frac{\Delta y}{\Delta t} = \frac{16(1 + h)^2 - 16(1)^2}{h} = \frac{16(1 + 2h + h^2) - 16}{h}$$

$$= \frac{32h + 16h^2}{h} = 32 + 16h.$$

For values of h different from 0, the expressions on the right and left are equivalent and the average speed is $32 + 16h$ ft/sec. We can now see why the average speed has the limiting value $32 + 16(0) = 32$ ft/sec as h approaches 0.

Similarly, setting $t_0 = 2$ in Equation (1), the procedure yields

$$\frac{\Delta y}{\Delta t} = 64 + 16h$$

for values of h different from 0. As h gets closer and closer to 0, the average speed has the limiting value 64 ft/sec when $t_0 = 2$ sec, as suggested by Table 2.1. ■

The average speed of a falling object is an example of a more general idea which we discuss next.

Average Rates of Change and Secant Lines

Given an arbitrary function $y = f(x)$, we calculate the average rate of change of y with respect to x over the interval $[x_1, x_2]$ by dividing the change in the value of y, $\Delta y = f(x_2) - f(x_1)$, by the length $\Delta x = x_2 - x_1 = h$ of the interval over which the change occurs. (We use the symbol h for Δx to simplify the notation here and later on.)

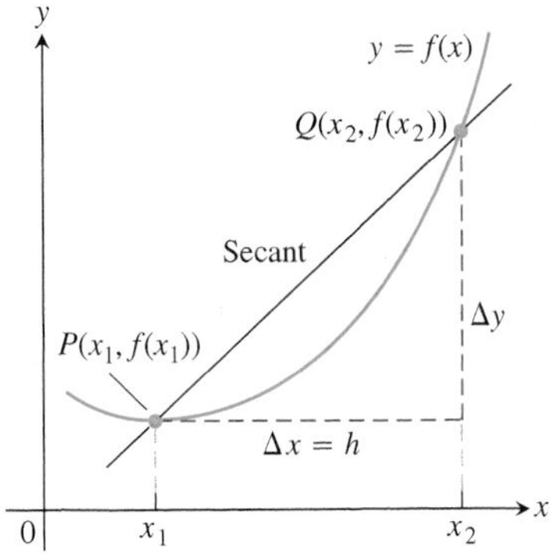

FIGURE 2.1 A secant to the graph $y = f(x)$. Its slope is $\Delta y/\Delta x$, the average rate of change of f over the interval $[x_1, x_2]$.

DEFINITION The **average rate of change** of $y = f(x)$ with respect to x over the interval $[x_1, x_2]$ is

$$\frac{\Delta y}{\Delta x} = \frac{f(x_2) - f(x_1)}{x_2 - x_1} = \frac{f(x_1 + h) - f(x_1)}{h}, \qquad h \neq 0.$$

Geometrically, the rate of change of f over $[x_1, x_2]$ is the slope of the line through the points $P(x_1, f(x_1))$ and $Q(x_2, f(x_2))$ (Figure 2.1). In geometry, a line joining two points of a curve is a **secant** to the curve. Thus, the average rate of change of f from x_1 to x_2 is identical with the slope of secant PQ. Let's consider what happens as the point Q approaches the point P along the curve, so the length h of the interval over which the change occurs approaches zero. We will see that this procedure leads to defining the slope of a curve at a point.

Defining the Slope of a Curve

We know what is meant by the slope of a straight line, which tells us the rate at which it rises or falls—its rate of change as a linear function. But what is meant by the *slope of a curve* at a point P on the curve? If there is a *tangent* line to the curve at P—a line that just touches the curve like the tangent to a circle—it would be reasonable to identify *the slope of the tangent* as the slope of the curve at P. So we need a precise meaning for the tangent at a point on a curve.

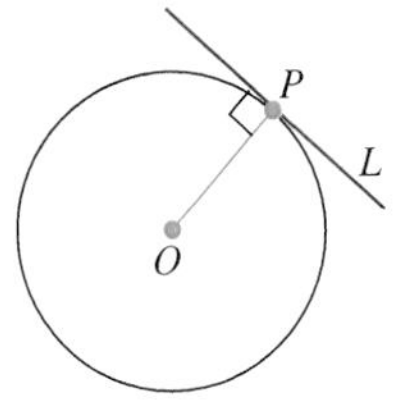

FIGURE 2.2 L is tangent to the circle at P if it passes through P perpendicular to radius OP.

For circles, tangency is straightforward. A line L is tangent to a circle at a point P if L passes through P perpendicular to the radius at P (Figure 2.2). Such a line just *touches* the circle. But what does it mean to say that a line L is tangent to some other curve C at a point P?

To define tangency for general curves, we need an approach that takes into account the behavior of the secants through P and nearby points Q as Q moves toward P along the curve (Figure 2.3). Here is the idea:

1. Start with what we *can* calculate, namely the slope of the secant PQ.
2. Investigate the limiting value of the secant slope as Q approaches P along the curve. (We clarify the *limit* idea in the next section.)
3. If the *limit* exists, take it to be the slope of the curve at P and *define* the tangent to the curve at P to be the line through P with this slope.

This procedure is what we were doing in the falling-rock problem discussed in Example 2. The next example illustrates the geometric idea for the tangent to a curve.

HISTORICAL BIOGRAPHY

Pierre de Fermat
(1601–1665)

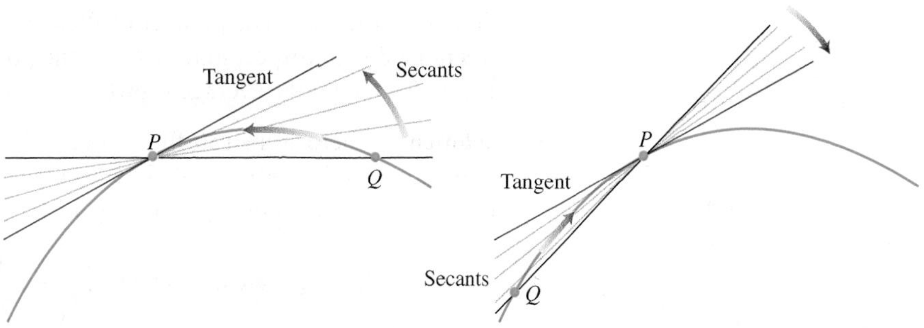

FIGURE 2.3 The tangent to the curve at P is the line through P whose slope is the limit of the secant slopes as $Q \to P$ from either side.

EXAMPLE 3 Find the slope of the parabola $y = x^2$ at the point $P(2, 4)$. Write an equation for the tangent to the parabola at this point.

Solution We begin with a secant line through $P(2, 4)$ and $Q(2 + h, (2 + h)^2)$ nearby. We then write an expression for the slope of the secant PQ and investigate what happens to the slope as Q approaches P along the curve:

$$\text{Secant slope} = \frac{\Delta y}{\Delta x} = \frac{(2+h)^2 - 2^2}{h} = \frac{h^2 + 4h + 4 - 4}{h}$$

$$= \frac{h^2 + 4h}{h} = h + 4.$$

If $h > 0$, then Q lies above and to the right of P, as in Figure 2.4. If $h < 0$, then Q lies to the left of P (not shown). In either case, as Q approaches P along the curve, h approaches zero and the secant slope $h + 4$ approaches 4. We take 4 to be the parabola's slope at P.

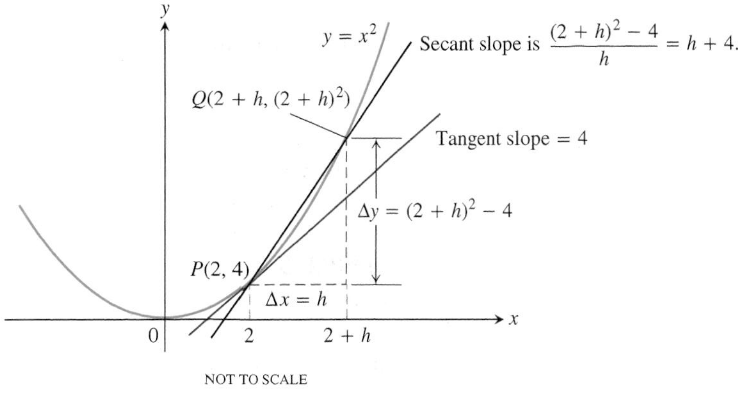

FIGURE 2.4 Finding the slope of the parabola $y = x^2$ at the point $P(2, 4)$ as the limit of secant slopes (Example 3).

The tangent to the parabola at P is the line through P with slope 4:

$$y = 4 + 4(x - 2) \qquad \text{Point-slope equation}$$

$$y = 4x - 4.$$

■

Instantaneous Rates of Change and Tangent Lines

The rates at which the rock in Example 2 was falling at the instants $t = 1$ and $t = 2$ are called *instantaneous rates of change*. Instantaneous rates and slopes of tangent lines are intimately connected, as we will now see in the following examples.

EXAMPLE 4 Figure 2.5 shows how a population p of fruit flies (*Drosophila*) grew in a 50-day experiment. The number of flies was counted at regular intervals, the counted values plotted with respect to time t, and the points joined by a smooth curve (colored blue in Figure 2.5). Find the average growth rate from day 23 to day 45.

Solution There were 150 flies on day 23 and 340 flies on day 45. Thus the number of flies increased by $340 - 150 = 190$ in $45 - 23 = 22$ days. The average rate of change of the population from day 23 to day 45 was

$$\text{Average rate of change: } \frac{\Delta p}{\Delta t} = \frac{340 - 150}{45 - 23} = \frac{190}{22} \approx 8.6 \text{ flies/day}.$$

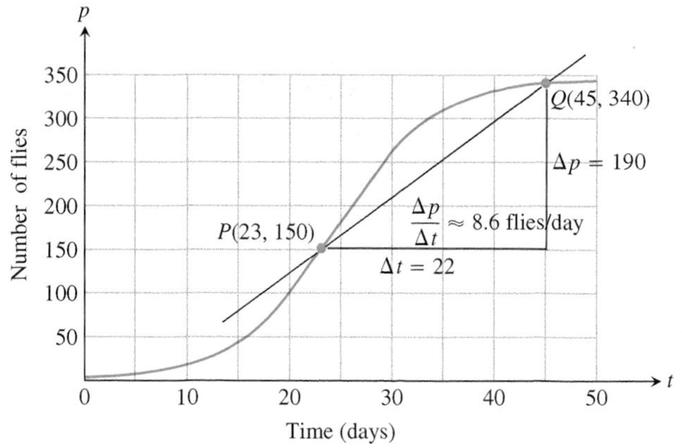

FIGURE 2.5 Growth of a fruit fly population in a controlled experiment. The average rate of change over 22 days is the slope $\Delta p/\Delta t$ of the secant line (Example 4).

This average is the slope of the secant through the points P and Q on the graph in Figure 2.5. ■

The average rate of change from day 23 to day 45 calculated in Example 4 does not tell us how fast the population was changing on day 23 itself. For that we need to examine time intervals closer to the day in question.

EXAMPLE 5 How fast was the number of flies in the population of Example 4 growing on day 23?

Solution To answer this question, we examine the average rates of change over increasingly short time intervals starting at day 23. In geometric terms, we find these rates by calculating the slopes of secants from P to Q, for a sequence of points Q approaching P along the curve (Figure 2.6).

Q	Slope of $PQ = \Delta p / \Delta t$ (flies/day)
(45, 340)	$\frac{340 - 150}{45 - 23} \approx 8.6$
(40, 330)	$\frac{330 - 150}{40 - 23} \approx 10.6$
(35, 310)	$\frac{310 - 150}{35 - 23} \approx 13.3$
(30, 265)	$\frac{265 - 150}{30 - 23} \approx 16.4$

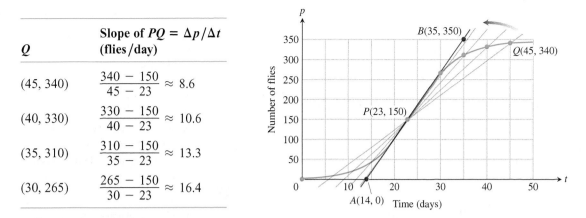

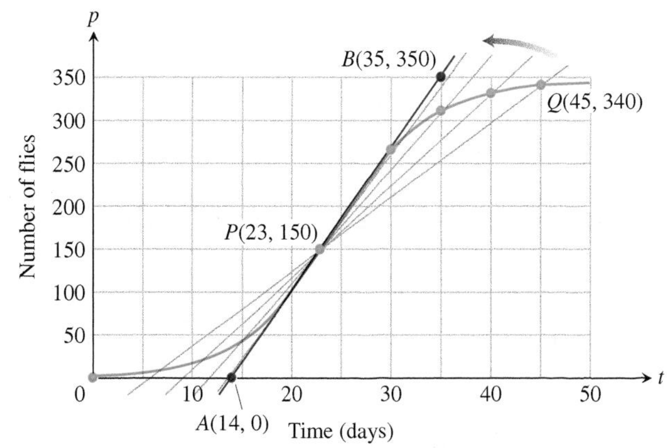

FIGURE 2.6 The positions and slopes of four secants through the point P on the fruit fly graph (Example 5).

The values in the table show that the secant slopes rise from 8.6 to 16.4 as the t-coordinate of Q decreases from 45 to 30, and we would expect the slopes to rise slightly higher as t continued on toward 23. Geometrically, the secants rotate about P and seem to approach the red tangent line in the figure. Since the line appears to pass through the points (14, 0) and (35, 350), it has slope

$$\frac{350 - 0}{35 - 14} = 16.7 \text{ flies/day (approximately).}$$

On day 23 the population was increasing at a rate of about 16.7 flies/day. ■

The instantaneous rates in Example 2 were found to be the values of the average speeds, or average rates of change, as the time interval of length h approached 0. That is, the instantaneous rate is the value the average rate approaches as the length h of the interval over which the change occurs approaches zero. The average rate of change corresponds to the slope of a secant line; the instantaneous rate corresponds to the slope of the tangent line as the independent variable approaches a fixed value. In Example 2, the independent variable t approached the values $t = 1$ and $t = 2$. In Example 3, the independent variable x approached the value $x = 2$. So we see that instantaneous rates and slopes of tangent lines are closely connected. We investigate this connection thoroughly in the next chapter, but to do so we need the concept of a *limit*.

Exercises 2.1

Average Rates of Change

In Exercises 1–6, find the average rate of change of the function over the given interval or intervals.

1. $f(x) = x^3 + 1$

a. $[2, 3]$ **b.** $[-1, 1]$

2. $g(x) = x^2$

a. $[-1, 1]$ **b.** $[-2, 0]$

3. $h(t) = \cot t$

a. $[\pi/4, 3\pi/4]$ **b.** $[\pi/6, \pi/2]$

4. $g(t) = 2 + \cos t$

a. $[0, \pi]$ **b.** $[-\pi, \pi]$

5. $R(\theta) = \sqrt{4\theta + 1};\quad [0, 2]$

6. $P(\theta) = \theta^3 - 4\theta^2 + 5\theta;\quad [1, 2]$

Slope of a Curve at a Point

In Exercises 7–14, use the method in Example 3 to find **(a)** the slope of the curve at the given point P, and **(b)** an equation of the tangent line at P.

7. $y = x^2 - 3, \quad P(2, 1)$

8. $y = 5 - x^2, \quad P(1, 4)$

9. $y = x^2 - 2x - 3, \quad P(2, -3)$

10. $y = x^2 - 4x, \quad P(1, -3)$

11. $y = x^3, \quad P(2, 8)$

12. $y = 2 - x^3, \quad P(1, 1)$

13. $y = x^3 - 12x, \quad P(1, -11)$

14. $y = x^3 - 3x^2 + 4, \quad P(2, 0)$

Instantaneous Rates of Change

15. **Speed of a car** The accompanying figure shows the time-to-distance graph for a sports car accelerating from a standstill.

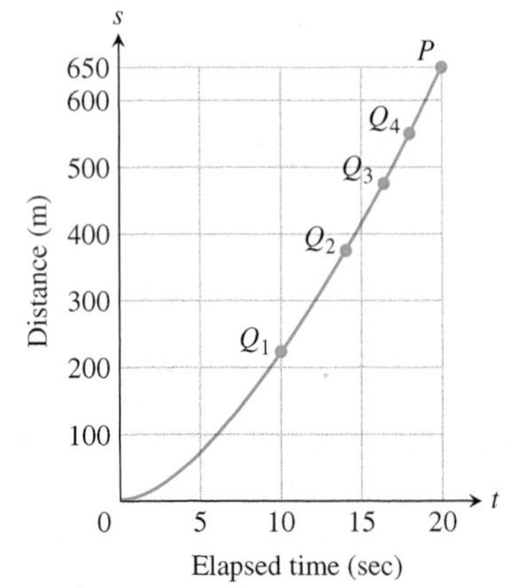

a. Estimate the slopes of secants PQ_1, PQ_2, PQ_3, and PQ_4, arranging them in order in a table like the one in Figure 2.6. What are the appropriate units for these slopes?

b. Then estimate the car's speed at time $t = 20$ sec.

16. The accompanying figure shows the plot of distance fallen versus time for an object that fell from the lunar landing module a distance 80 m to the surface of the moon.

a. Estimate the slopes of the secants PQ_1, PQ_2, PQ_3, and PQ_4, arranging them in a table like the one in Figure 2.6.

b. About how fast was the object going when it hit the surface?

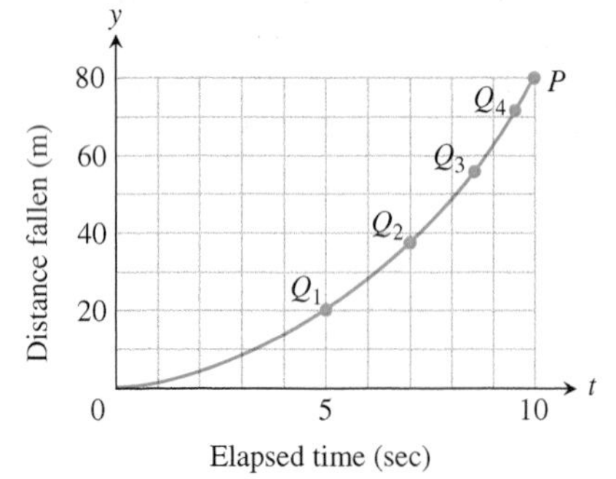

T 17. The profits of a small company for each of the first five years of its operation are given in the following table:

Year	Profit in $1000s
2000	6
2001	27
2002	62
2003	111
2004	174

a. Plot points representing the profit as a function of year, and join them by as smooth a curve as you can.

b. What is the average rate of increase of the profits between 2002 and 2004?

c. Use your graph to estimate the rate at which the profits were changing in 2002.

T 18. Make a table of values for the function $F(x) = (x + 2)/(x - 2)$ at the points $x = 1.2$, $x = 11/10$, $x = 101/100$, $x = 1001/1000$, $x = 10001/10000$, and $x = 1$.

a. Find the average rate of change of $F(x)$ over the intervals $[1, x]$ for each $x \neq 1$ in your table.

b. Extending the table if necessary, try to determine the rate of change of $F(x)$ at $x = 1$.

T 19. Let $g(x) = \sqrt{x}$ for $x \geq 0$.

a. Find the average rate of change of $g(x)$ with respect to x over the intervals $[1, 2]$, $[1, 1.5]$ and $[1, 1 + h]$.

b. Make a table of values of the average rate of change of g with respect to x over the interval $[1, 1 + h]$ for some values of h approaching zero, say $h = 0.1, 0.01, 0.001, 0.0001, 0.00001$, and 0.000001.

c. What does your table indicate is the rate of change of $g(x)$ with respect to x at $x = 1$?

d. Calculate the limit as h approaches zero of the average rate of change of $g(x)$ with respect to x over the interval $[1, 1 + h]$.

T 20. Let $f(t) = 1/t$ for $t \neq 0$.

a. Find the average rate of change of f with respect to t over the intervals (i) from $t = 2$ to $t = 3$, and (ii) from $t = 2$ to $t = T$.

b. Make a table of values of the average rate of change of f with respect to t over the interval $[2, T]$, for some values of T approaching 2, say $T = 2.1, 2.01, 2.001, 2.0001, 2.00001$, and 2.000001.

c. What does your table indicate is the rate of change of f with respect to t at $t = 2$?

d. Calculate the limit as T approaches 2 of the average rate of change of f with respect to t over the interval from 2 to T. You will have to do some algebra before you can substitute $T = 2$.

21. The accompanying graph shows the total distance s traveled by a bicyclist after t hours.

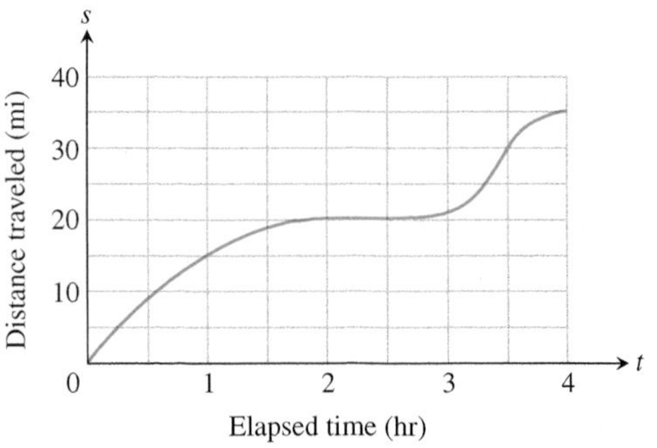

a. Estimate the bicyclist's average speed over the time intervals $[0, 1]$, $[1, 2.5]$, and $[2.5, 3.5]$.

b. Estimate the bicyclist's instantaneous speed at the times $t = \frac{1}{2}$, $t = 2$, and $t = 3$.

c. Estimate the bicyclist's maximum speed and the specific time at which it occurs.

22. The accompanying graph shows the total amount of gasoline A in the gas tank of an automobile after being driven for t days.

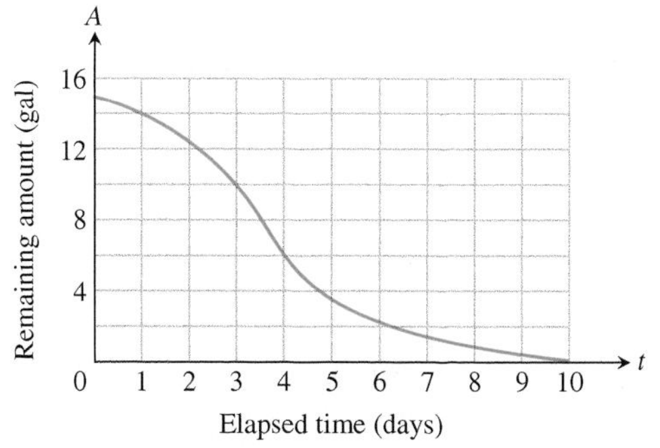

a. Estimate the average rate of gasoline consumption over the time intervals [0, 3], [0, 5], and [7, 10].

b. Estimate the instantaneous rate of gasoline consumption at the times $t = 1$, $t = 4$, and $t = 8$.

c. Estimate the maximum rate of gasoline consumption and the specific time at which it occurs.

2.2 Limit of a Function and Limit Laws

In Section 2.1 we saw that limits arise when finding the instantaneous rate of change of a function or the tangent to a curve. Here we begin with an informal definition of *limit* and show how we can calculate the values of limits. A precise definition is presented in the next section.

HISTORICAL ESSAY

Limits

Limits of Function Values

Frequently when studying a function $y = f(x)$, we find ourselves interested in the function's behavior *near* a particular point c, but not *at* c. This might be the case, for instance, if c is an irrational number, like π or $\sqrt{2}$, whose values can only be approximated by "close" rational numbers at which we actually evaluate the function instead. Another situation occurs when trying to evaluate a function at c leads to division by zero, which is undefined. We encountered this last circumstance when seeking the instantaneous rate of change in y by considering the quotient function $\Delta y/h$ for h closer and closer to zero. Here's a specific example where we explore numerically how a function behaves near a particular point at which we cannot directly evaluate the function.

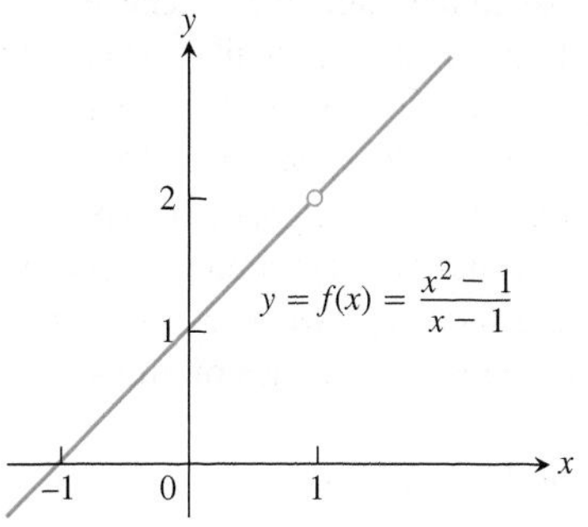

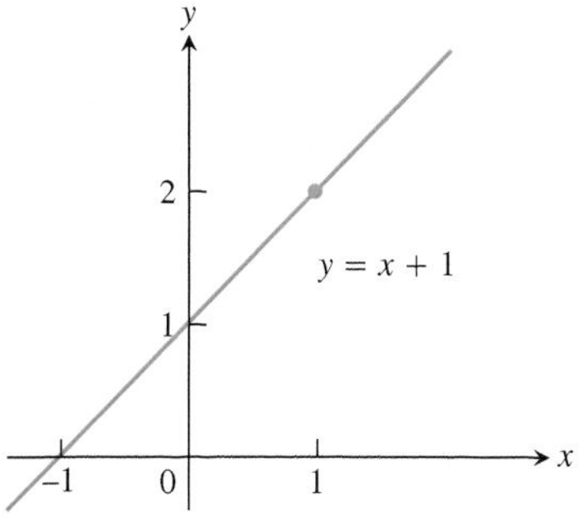

FIGURE 2.7 The graph of f is identical with the line $y = x + 1$ except at $x = 1$, where f is not defined (Example 1).

EXAMPLE 1 How does the function

$$f(x) = \frac{x^2 - 1}{x - 1}$$

behave near $x = 1$?

Solution The given formula defines f for all real numbers x except $x = 1$ (we cannot divide by zero). For any $x \neq 1$, we can simplify the formula by factoring the numerator and canceling common factors:

$$f(x) = \frac{(x - 1)(x + 1)}{x - 1} = x + 1 \qquad \text{for} \qquad x \neq 1.$$

The graph of f is the line $y = x + 1$ with the point (1, 2) *removed*. This removed point is shown as a "hole" in Figure 2.7. Even though $f(1)$ is not defined, it is clear that we can make the value of $f(x)$ *as close as we want* to 2 by choosing x *close enough* to 1 (Table 2.2). ∎

TABLE 2.2 The closer x gets to 1, the closer $f(x) = (x^2 - 1)/(x - 1)$ seems to get to 2

Values of x below and above 1	$f(x) = \frac{x^2 - 1}{x - 1} = x + 1, \quad x \neq 1$
0.9	1.9
1.1	2.1
0.99	1.99
1.01	2.01
0.999	1.999
1.001	2.001
0.999999	1.999999
1.000001	2.000001

Let's generalize the idea illustrated in Example 1.

Suppose $f(x)$ is defined on an open interval about c, *except possibly at c itself.* If $f(x)$ is arbitrarily close to L (as close to L as we like) for all x sufficiently close to c, we say that f approaches the **limit** L as x approaches c, and write

$$\lim_{x \to c} f(x) = L,$$

which is read "the limit of $f(x)$ as x approaches c is L." For instance, in Example 1 we would say that $f(x)$ approaches the *limit* 2 as x approaches 1, and write

$$\lim_{x \to 1} f(x) = 2, \qquad \text{or} \qquad \lim_{x \to 1} \frac{x^2 - 1}{x - 1} = 2.$$

Essentially, the definition says that the values of $f(x)$ are close to the number L whenever x is close to c (on either side of c). This definition is "informal" because phrases like *arbitrarily close* and *sufficiently close* are imprecise; their meaning depends on the context. (To a machinist manufacturing a piston, *close* may mean *within a few thousandths of an inch.* To an astronomer studying distant galaxies, *close* may mean *within a few thousand light-years.*) Nevertheless, the definition is clear enough to enable us to recognize and evaluate limits of specific functions. We will need the precise definition of Section 2.3, however, when we set out to prove theorems about limits. Here are several more examples exploring the idea of limits.

EXAMPLE 2 The limiting value of a function does not depend on how the function is defined at the point being approached. Consider the three functions in Figure 2.8. The function f has limit 2 as $x \to 1$ even though f is not defined at $x = 1$. The function g has

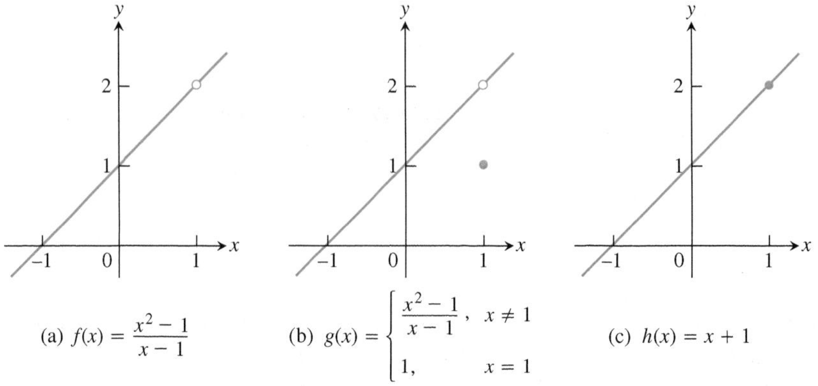

FIGURE 2.8 The limits of $f(x)$, $g(x)$, and $h(x)$ all equal 2 as x approaches 1. However, only $h(x)$ has the same function value as its limit at $x = 1$ (Example 2).

limit 2 as $x \to 1$ even though $2 \neq g(1)$. The function h is the only one of the three functions in Figure 2.8 whose limit as $x \to 1$ equals its value at $x = 1$. For h, we have $\lim_{x\to 1} h(x) = h(1)$. This equality of limit and function value is significant, and we return to it in Section 2.5. ■

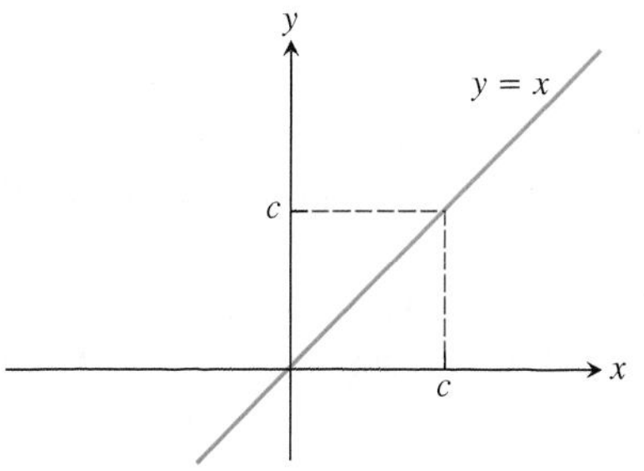

(a) Identity function

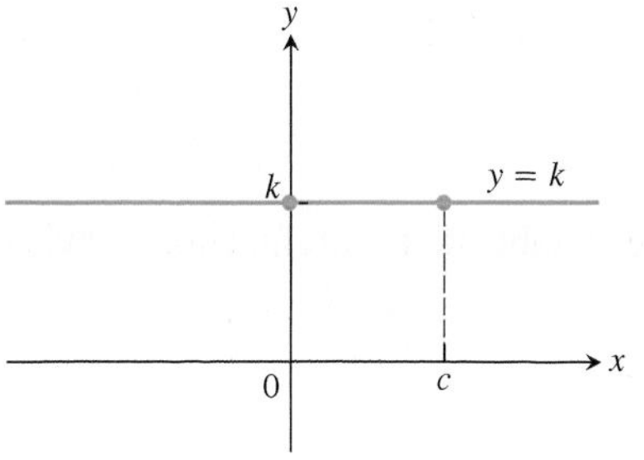

(b) Constant function

FIGURE 2.9 The functions in Example 3 have limits at all points c.

EXAMPLE 3

(a) If f is the **identity function** $f(x) = x$, then for any value of c (Figure 2.9a),

$$\lim_{x\to c} f(x) = \lim_{x\to c} x = c.$$

(b) If f is the **constant function** $f(x) = k$ (function with the constant value k), then for any value of c (Figure 2.9b),

$$\lim_{x\to c} f(x) = \lim_{x\to c} k = k.$$

For instances of each of these rules we have

$$\lim_{x\to 3} x = 3 \qquad \text{and} \qquad \lim_{x\to -7} (4) = \lim_{x\to 2} (4) = 4.$$

We prove these rules in Example 3 in Section 2.3. ■

Some ways that limits can fail to exist are illustrated in Figure 2.10 and described in the next example.

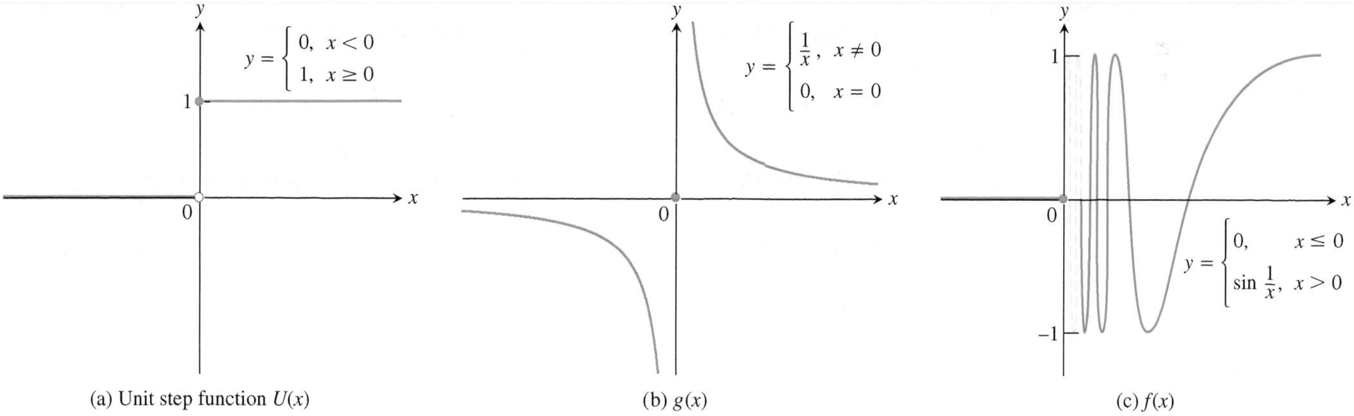

FIGURE 2.10 None of these functions has a limit as x approaches 0 (Example 4).

EXAMPLE 4 Discuss the behavior of the following functions as $x \to 0$.

(a) $U(x) = \begin{cases} 0, & x < 0 \\ 1, & x \geq 0 \end{cases}$

(b) $g(x) = \begin{cases} \dfrac{1}{x}, & x \neq 0 \\ 0, & x = 0 \end{cases}$

(c) $f(x) = \begin{cases} 0, & x \leq 0 \\ \sin\dfrac{1}{x}, & x > 0 \end{cases}$

Solution

(a) It *jumps*: The **unit step function** $U(x)$ has no limit as $x \to 0$ because its values jump at $x = 0$. For negative values of x arbitrarily close to zero, $U(x) = 0$. For positive values of x arbitrarily close to zero, $U(x) = 1$. There is no *single* value L approached by $U(x)$ as $x \to 0$ (Figure 2.10a).

(b) It *grows too "large" to have a limit*: $g(x)$ has no limit as $x \to 0$ because the values of g grow arbitrarily large in absolute value as $x \to 0$ and do not stay close to *any* fixed real number (Figure 2.10b).

(c) It *oscillates too much to have a limit*: $f(x)$ has no limit as $x \to 0$ because the function's values oscillate between $+1$ and -1 in every open interval containing 0. The values do not stay close to any one number as $x \to 0$ (Figure 2.10c). ■

The Limit Laws

To calculate limits of functions that are arithmetic combinations of functions having known limits, we can use several easy rules.

THEOREM 1—Limit Laws If L, M, c, and k are real numbers and

$$\lim_{x \to c} f(x) = L \quad \text{and} \quad \lim_{x \to c} g(x) = M, \quad \text{then}$$

1. *Sum Rule:* $\lim_{x \to c}(f(x) + g(x)) = L + M$
2. *Difference Rule:* $\lim_{x \to c}(f(x) - g(x)) = L - M$
3. *Constant Multiple Rule:* $\lim_{x \to c}(k \cdot f(x)) = k \cdot L$
4. *Product Rule:* $\lim_{x \to c}(f(x) \cdot g(x)) = L \cdot M$
5. *Quotient Rule:* $\lim_{x \to c} \dfrac{f(x)}{g(x)} = \dfrac{L}{M}, \quad M \neq 0$
6. *Power Rule:* $\lim_{x \to c}[f(x)]^n = L^n$, n a positive integer
7. *Root Rule:* $\lim_{x \to c} \sqrt[n]{f(x)} = \sqrt[n]{L} = L^{1/n}$, n a positive integer

(If n is even, we assume that $\lim_{x \to c} f(x) = L > 0$.)

In words, the Sum Rule says that the limit of a sum is the sum of the limits. Similarly, the next rules say that the limit of a difference is the difference of the limits; the limit of a constant times a function is the constant times the limit of the function; the limit of a product is the product of the limits; the limit of a quotient is the quotient of the limits (provided that the limit of the denominator is not 0); the limit of a positive integer power (or root) of a function is the integer power (or root) of the limit (provided that the root of the limit is a real number).

It is reasonable that the properties in Theorem 1 are true (although these intuitive arguments do not constitute proofs). If x is sufficiently close to c, then $f(x)$ is close to L and $g(x)$ is close to M, from our informal definition of a limit. It is then reasonable that $f(x) + g(x)$ is close to $L + M$; $f(x) - g(x)$ is close to $L - M$; $kf(x)$ is close to kL; $f(x)g(x)$ is close to LM; and $f(x)/g(x)$ is close to L/M if M is not zero. We prove the Sum Rule in Section 2.3, based on a precise definition of limit. Rules 2–5 are proved in Appendix 4. Rule 6 is obtained by applying Rule 4 repeatedly. Rule 7 is proved in more advanced texts. The sum, difference, and product rules can be extended to any number of functions, not just two.

EXAMPLE 5 Use the observations $\lim_{x\to c} k = k$ and $\lim_{x\to c} x = c$ (Example 3) and the properties of limits to find the following limits.

(a) $\lim\limits_{x\to c}(x^3 + 4x^2 - 3)$ **(b)** $\lim\limits_{x\to c}\dfrac{x^4 + x^2 - 1}{x^2 + 5}$ **(c)** $\lim\limits_{x\to -2}\sqrt{4x^2 - 3}$

Solution

(a)
$$\begin{aligned}\lim_{x\to c}(x^3 + 4x^2 - 3) &= \lim_{x\to c} x^3 + \lim_{x\to c} 4x^2 - \lim_{x\to c} 3 && \text{Sum and Difference Rules}\\ &= c^3 + 4c^2 - 3 && \text{Power and Multiple Rules}\end{aligned}$$

(b)
$$\begin{aligned}\lim_{x\to c}\frac{x^4 + x^2 - 1}{x^2 + 5} &= \frac{\lim_{x\to c}(x^4 + x^2 - 1)}{\lim_{x\to c}(x^2 + 5)} && \text{Quotient Rule}\\ &= \frac{\lim_{x\to c} x^4 + \lim_{x\to c} x^2 - \lim_{x\to c} 1}{\lim_{x\to c} x^2 + \lim_{x\to c} 5} && \text{Sum and Difference Rules}\\ &= \frac{c^4 + c^2 - 1}{c^2 + 5} && \text{Power or Product Rule}\end{aligned}$$

(c)
$$\begin{aligned}\lim_{x\to -2}\sqrt{4x^2 - 3} &= \sqrt{\lim_{x\to -2}(4x^2 - 3)} && \text{Root Rule with } n = 2\\ &= \sqrt{\lim_{x\to -2} 4x^2 - \lim_{x\to -2} 3} && \text{Difference Rule}\\ &= \sqrt{4(-2)^2 - 3} && \text{Product and Multiple Rules}\\ &= \sqrt{16 - 3}\\ &= \sqrt{13}\end{aligned}$$

■

Two consequences of Theorem 1 further simplify the task of calculating limits of polynomials and rational functions. To evaluate the limit of a polynomial function as x approaches c, merely substitute c for x in the formula for the function. To evaluate the limit of a rational function as x approaches a point c *at which the denominator is not zero*, substitute c for x in the formula for the function. (See Examples 5a and 5b.) We state these results formally as theorems.

THEOREM 2—Limits of Polynomials

If $P(x) = a_n x^n + a_{n-1}x^{n-1} + \cdots + a_0$, then

$$\lim_{x\to c} P(x) = P(c) = a_n c^n + a_{n-1}c^{n-1} + \cdots + a_0.$$

THEOREM 3—Limits of Rational Functions

If $P(x)$ and $Q(x)$ are polynomials and $Q(c) \neq 0$, then

$$\lim_{x\to c}\frac{P(x)}{Q(x)} = \frac{P(c)}{Q(c)}.$$

EXAMPLE 6 The following calculation illustrates Theorems 2 and 3:

$$\lim_{x \to -1} \frac{x^3 + 4x^2 - 3}{x^2 + 5} = \frac{(-1)^3 + 4(-1)^2 - 3}{(-1)^2 + 5} = \frac{0}{6} = 0$$ ■

Identifying Common Factors
It can be shown that if $Q(x)$ is a polynomial and $Q(c) = 0$, then $(x - c)$ is a factor of $Q(x)$. Thus, if the numerator and denominator of a rational function of x are both zero at $x = c$, they have $(x - c)$ as a common factor.

Eliminating Zero Denominators Algebraically

Theorem 3 applies only if the denominator of the rational function is not zero at the limit point c. If the denominator is zero, canceling common factors in the numerator and denominator may reduce the fraction to one whose denominator is no longer zero at c. If this happens, we can find the limit by substitution in the simplified fraction.

EXAMPLE 7 Evaluate

$$\lim_{x \to 1} \frac{x^2 + x - 2}{x^2 - x}.$$

Solution We cannot substitute $x = 1$ because it makes the denominator zero. We test the numerator to see if it, too, is zero at $x = 1$. It is, so it has a factor of $(x - 1)$ in common with the denominator. Canceling the $(x - 1)$'s gives a simpler fraction with the same values as the original for $x \neq 1$:

$$\frac{x^2 + x - 2}{x^2 - x} = \frac{(x - 1)(x + 2)}{x(x - 1)} = \frac{x + 2}{x}, \qquad \text{if } x \neq 1.$$

Using the simpler fraction, we find the limit of these values as $x \to 1$ by substitution:

$$\lim_{x \to 1} \frac{x^2 + x - 2}{x^2 - x} = \lim_{x \to 1} \frac{x + 2}{x} = \frac{1 + 2}{1} = 3.$$

See Figure 2.11. ■

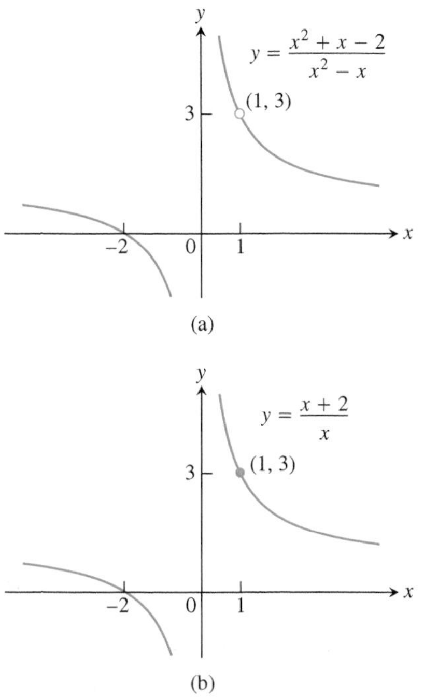

FIGURE 2.11 The graph of $f(x) = (x^2 + x - 2)/(x^2 - x)$ in part (a) is the same as the graph of $g(x) = (x + 2)/x$ in part (b) except at $x = 1$, where f is undefined. The functions have the same limit as $x \to 1$ (Example 7).

Using Calculators and Computers to Estimate Limits

When we cannot use the Quotient Rule in Theorem 1 because the limit of the denominator is zero, we can try using a calculator or computer to guess the limit numerically as x gets closer and closer to c. We used this approach in Example 1, but calculators and computers can sometimes give false values and misleading impressions for functions that are undefined at a point or fail to have a limit there, as we now illustrate.

EXAMPLE 8 Estimate the value of $\displaystyle\lim_{x \to 0} \frac{\sqrt{x^2 + 100} - 10}{x^2}$.

Solution Table 2.3 lists values of the function for several values near $x = 0$. As x approaches 0 through the values ± 1, ± 0.5, ± 0.10, and ± 0.01, the function seems to approach the number 0.05.

As we take even smaller values of x, ± 0.0005, ± 0.0001, ± 0.00001, and ± 0.000001, the function appears to approach the value 0.

Is the answer 0.05 or 0, or some other value? We resolve this question in the next example. ■

TABLE 2.3 Computer values of $f(x) = \dfrac{\sqrt{x^2+100}-10}{x^2}$ near $x = 0$

x	$f(x)$	
± 1	0.049876	approaches 0.05?
± 0.5	0.049969	
± 0.1	0.049999	
± 0.01	0.050000	
± 0.0005	0.050000	approaches 0?
± 0.0001	0.000000	
± 0.00001	0.000000	
± 0.000001	0.000000	

Using a computer or calculator may give ambiguous results, as in the last example. The calculator does not keep track of enough digits to avoid rounding errors in computing the values of $f(x)$ when x is very small. We cannot substitute $x = 0$ in the problem, and the numerator and denominator have no obvious common factors (as they did in Example 7). Sometimes, however, we can create a common factor algebraically.

EXAMPLE 9 Evaluate

$$\lim_{x\to 0} \frac{\sqrt{x^2+100}-10}{x^2}.$$

Solution This is the limit we considered in Example 8. We can create a common factor by multiplying both numerator and denominator by the conjugate radical expression $\sqrt{x^2+100}+10$ (obtained by changing the sign after the square root). The preliminary algebra rationalizes the numerator:

$$\begin{aligned}\frac{\sqrt{x^2+100}-10}{x^2} &= \frac{\sqrt{x^2+100}-10}{x^2}\cdot\frac{\sqrt{x^2+100}+10}{\sqrt{x^2+100}+10}\\ &= \frac{x^2+100-100}{x^2\left(\sqrt{x^2+100}+10\right)}\\ &= \frac{x^2}{x^2\left(\sqrt{x^2+100}+10\right)} && \text{Common factor } x^2\\ &= \frac{1}{\sqrt{x^2+100}+10}. && \text{Cancel } x^2 \text{ for } x \neq 0.\end{aligned}$$

Therefore,

$$\begin{aligned}\lim_{x\to 0}\frac{\sqrt{x^2+100}-10}{x^2} &= \lim_{x\to 0}\frac{1}{\sqrt{x^2+100}+10}\\ &= \frac{1}{\sqrt{0^2+100}+10} && \text{Denominator not 0 at } x = 0\text{; substitute.}\\ &= \frac{1}{20} = 0.05.\end{aligned}$$

This calculation provides the correct answer, in contrast to the ambiguous computer results in Example 8. ■

We cannot always algebraically resolve the problem of finding the limit of a quotient where the denominator becomes zero. In some cases the limit might then be found with the

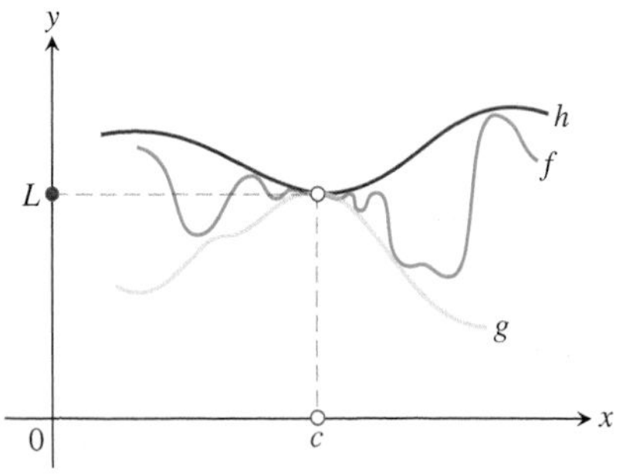

FIGURE 2.12 The graph of f is sandwiched between the graphs of g and h.

aid of some geometry applied to the problem (see the proof of Theorem 7 in Section 2.4), or through methods of calculus (illustrated in Section 4.5). The next theorem is also useful.

The Sandwich Theorem

The following theorem enables us to calculate a variety of limits. It is called the Sandwich Theorem because it refers to a function f whose values are sandwiched between the values of two other functions g and h that have the same limit L at a point c. Being trapped between the values of two functions that approach L, the values of f must also approach L (Figure 2.12). You will find a proof in Appendix 5.

THEOREM 4—The Sandwich Theorem Suppose that $g(x) \leq f(x) \leq h(x)$ for all x in some open interval containing c, except possibly at $x = c$ itself. Suppose also that

$$\lim_{x \to c} g(x) = \lim_{x \to c} h(x) = L.$$

Then $\lim_{x \to c} f(x) = L$.

The Sandwich Theorem is also called the Squeeze Theorem or the Pinching Theorem.

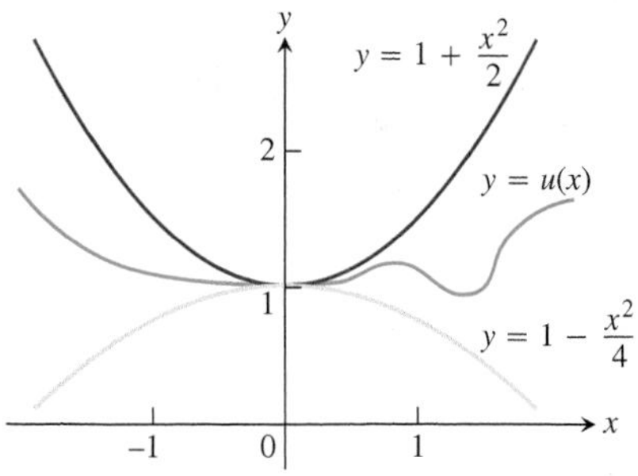

FIGURE 2.13 Any function $u(x)$ whose graph lies in the region between $y = 1 + (x^2/2)$ and $y = 1 - (x^2/4)$ has limit 1 as $x \to 0$ (Example 10).

EXAMPLE 10 Given that

$$1 - \frac{x^2}{4} \leq u(x) \leq 1 + \frac{x^2}{2} \quad \text{for all } x \neq 0,$$

find $\lim_{x \to 0} u(x)$, no matter how complicated u is.

Solution Since

$$\lim_{x \to 0} (1 - (x^2/4)) = 1 \quad \text{and} \quad \lim_{x \to 0} (1 + (x^2/2)) = 1,$$

the Sandwich Theorem implies that $\lim_{x \to 0} u(x) = 1$ (Figure 2.13). ■

EXAMPLE 11 The Sandwich Theorem helps us establish several important limit rules:

(a) $\lim_{\theta \to 0} \sin \theta = 0$ **(b)** $\lim_{\theta \to 0} \cos \theta = 1$

(c) For any function f, $\lim_{x \to c} |f(x)| = 0$ implies $\lim_{x \to c} f(x) = 0$.

Solution

(a) In Section 1.3 we established that $-|\theta| \leq \sin \theta \leq |\theta|$ for all θ (see Figure 2.14a). Since $\lim_{\theta \to 0} (-|\theta|) = \lim_{\theta \to 0} |\theta| = 0$, we have

$$\lim_{\theta \to 0} \sin \theta = 0.$$

(b) From Section 1.3, $0 \leq 1 - \cos \theta \leq |\theta|$ for all θ (see Figure 2.14b), and we have $\lim_{\theta \to 0} (1 - \cos \theta) = 0$ or

$$\lim_{\theta \to 0} \cos \theta = 1.$$

(c) Since $-|f(x)| \leq f(x) \leq |f(x)|$ and $-|f(x)|$ and $|f(x)|$ have limit 0 as $x \to c$, it follows that $\lim_{x \to c} f(x) = 0$. ■

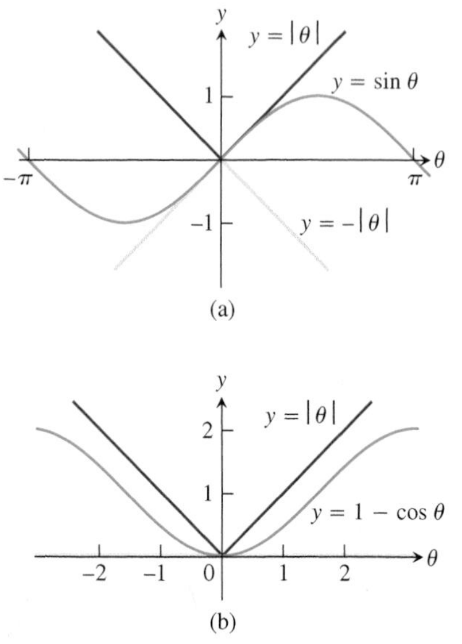

FIGURE 2.14 The Sandwich Theorem confirms the limits in Example 11.

Another important property of limits is given by the next theorem. A proof is given in the next section.

THEOREM 5 If $f(x) \leq g(x)$ for all x in some open interval containing c, except possibly at $x = c$ itself, and the limits of f and g both exist as x approaches c, then

$$\lim_{x \to c} f(x) \leq \lim_{x \to c} g(x).$$

The assertion resulting from replacing the less than or equal to ($\leq$) inequality by the strict less than ($<$) inequality in Theorem 5 is false. Figure 2.14a shows that for $\theta \neq 0$, $-|\theta| < \sin\theta < |\theta|$, but in the limit as $\theta \to 0$, equality holds.

Exercises 2.2

Limits from Graphs

1. For the function $g(x)$ graphed here, find the following limits or explain why they do not exist.

   a. $\lim_{x \to 1} g(x)$ b. $\lim_{x \to 2} g(x)$ c. $\lim_{x \to 3} g(x)$ d. $\lim_{x \to 2.5} g(x)$

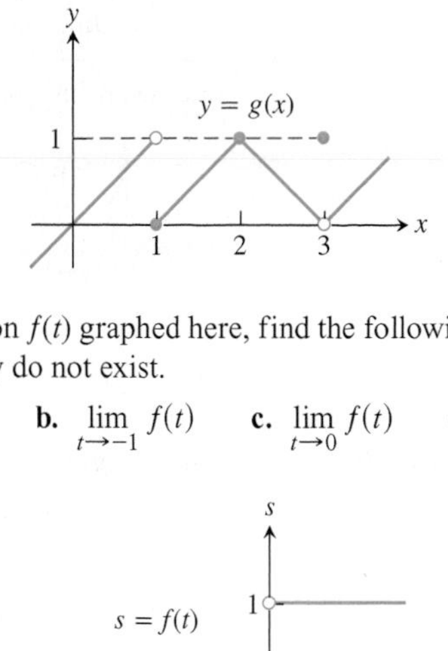

2. For the function $f(t)$ graphed here, find the following limits or explain why they do not exist.

   a. $\lim_{t \to -2} f(t)$ b. $\lim_{t \to -1} f(t)$ c. $\lim_{t \to 0} f(t)$ d. $\lim_{t \to -0.5} f(t)$

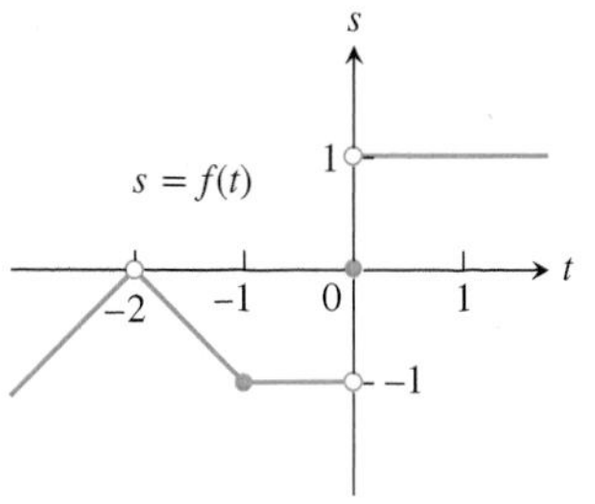

3. Which of the following statements about the function $y = f(x)$ graphed here are true, and which are false?

   a. $\lim_{x \to 0} f(x)$ exists.
   b. $\lim_{x \to 0} f(x) = 0$
   c. $\lim_{x \to 0} f(x) = 1$
   d. $\lim_{x \to 1} f(x) = 1$
   e. $\lim_{x \to 1} f(x) = 0$
   f. $\lim_{x \to c} f(x)$ exists at every point c in $(-1, 1)$.
   g. $\lim_{x \to 1} f(x)$ does not exist.

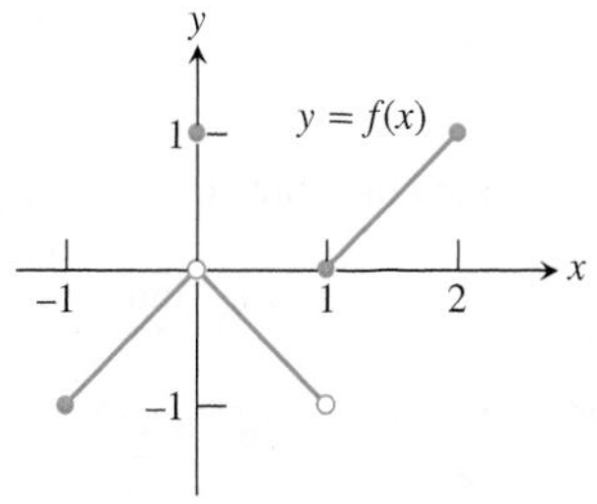

4. Which of the following statements about the function $y = f(x)$ graphed here are true, and which are false?

   a. $\lim_{x \to 2} f(x)$ does not exist.
   b. $\lim_{x \to 2} f(x) = 2$
   c. $\lim_{x \to 1} f(x)$ does not exist.
   d. $\lim_{x \to c} f(x)$ exists at every point c in $(-1, 1)$.
   e. $\lim_{x \to c} f(x)$ exists at every point c in $(1, 3)$.

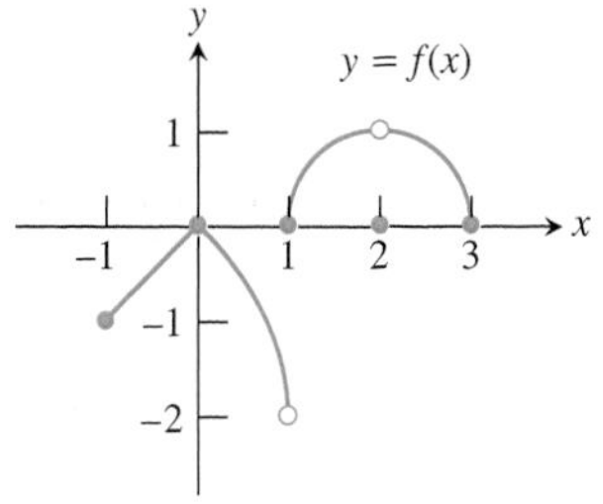

Existence of Limits

In Exercises 5 and 6, explain why the limits do not exist.

5. $\lim_{x \to 0} \dfrac{x}{|x|}$

6. $\lim_{x \to 1} \dfrac{1}{x - 1}$

7. Suppose that a function $f(x)$ is defined for all real values of x except $x = c$. Can anything be said about the existence of $\lim_{x \to c} f(x)$? Give reasons for your answer.

8. Suppose that a function $f(x)$ is defined for all x in $[-1, 1]$. Can anything be said about the existence of $\lim_{x \to 0} f(x)$? Give reasons for your answer.

9. If $\lim_{x\to 1} f(x) = 5$, must f be defined at $x = 1$? If it is, must $f(1) = 5$? Can we conclude *anything* about the values of f at $x = 1$? Explain.

10. If $f(1) = 5$, must $\lim_{x\to 1} f(x)$ exist? If it does, then must $\lim_{x\to 1} f(x) = 5$? Can we conclude *anything* about $\lim_{x\to 1} f(x)$? Explain.

Calculating Limits

Find the limits in Exercises 11–22.

11. $\lim_{x\to -7} (2x + 5)$

12. $\lim_{x\to 2} (-x^2 + 5x - 2)$

13. $\lim_{t\to 6} 8(t - 5)(t - 7)$

14. $\lim_{x\to -2} (x^3 - 2x^2 + 4x + 8)$

15. $\lim_{x\to 2} \dfrac{x + 3}{x + 6}$

16. $\lim_{s\to 2/3} 3s(2s - 1)$

17. $\lim_{x\to -1} 3(2x - 1)^2$

18. $\lim_{y\to 2} \dfrac{y + 2}{y^2 + 5y + 6}$

19. $\lim_{y\to -3} (5 - y)^{4/3}$

20. $\lim_{z\to 0} (2z - 8)^{1/3}$

21. $\lim_{h\to 0} \dfrac{3}{\sqrt{3h + 1} + 1}$

22. $\lim_{h\to 0} \dfrac{\sqrt{5h + 4} - 2}{h}$

Limits of quotients Find the limits in Exercises 23–42.

23. $\lim_{x\to 5} \dfrac{x - 5}{x^2 - 25}$

24. $\lim_{x\to -3} \dfrac{x + 3}{x^2 + 4x + 3}$

25. $\lim_{x\to -5} \dfrac{x^2 + 3x - 10}{x + 5}$

26. $\lim_{x\to 2} \dfrac{x^2 - 7x + 10}{x - 2}$

27. $\lim_{t\to 1} \dfrac{t^2 + t - 2}{t^2 - 1}$

28. $\lim_{t\to -1} \dfrac{t^2 + 3t + 2}{t^2 - t - 2}$

29. $\lim_{x\to -2} \dfrac{-2x - 4}{x^3 + 2x^2}$

30. $\lim_{y\to 0} \dfrac{5y^3 + 8y^2}{3y^4 - 16y^2}$

31. $\lim_{x\to 1} \dfrac{\frac{1}{x} - 1}{x - 1}$

32. $\lim_{x\to 0} \dfrac{\frac{1}{x - 1} + \frac{1}{x + 1}}{x}$

33. $\lim_{u\to 1} \dfrac{u^4 - 1}{u^3 - 1}$

34. $\lim_{v\to 2} \dfrac{v^3 - 8}{v^4 - 16}$

35. $\lim_{x\to 9} \dfrac{\sqrt{x} - 3}{x - 9}$

36. $\lim_{x\to 4} \dfrac{4x - x^2}{2 - \sqrt{x}}$

37. $\lim_{x\to 1} \dfrac{x - 1}{\sqrt{x + 3} - 2}$

38. $\lim_{x\to -1} \dfrac{\sqrt{x^2 + 8} - 3}{x + 1}$

39. $\lim_{x\to 2} \dfrac{\sqrt{x^2 + 12} - 4}{x - 2}$

40. $\lim_{x\to -2} \dfrac{x + 2}{\sqrt{x^2 + 5} - 3}$

41. $\lim_{x\to -3} \dfrac{2 - \sqrt{x^2 - 5}}{x + 3}$

42. $\lim_{x\to 4} \dfrac{4 - x}{5 - \sqrt{x^2 + 9}}$

Limits with trigonometric functions Find the limits in Exercises 43–50.

43. $\lim_{x\to 0} (2 \sin x - 1)$

44. $\lim_{x\to \pi/4} \sin^2 x$

45. $\lim_{x\to 0} \sec x$

46. $\lim_{x\to \pi/3} \tan x$

47. $\lim_{x\to 0} \dfrac{1 + x + \sin x}{3 \cos x}$

48. $\lim_{x\to 0} (x^2 - 1)(2 - \cos x)$

49. $\lim_{x\to -\pi} \sqrt{x + 4} \cos (x + \pi)$

50. $\lim_{x\to 0} \sqrt{7 + \sec^2 x}$

Using Limit Rules

51. Suppose $\lim_{x\to 0} f(x) = 1$ and $\lim_{x\to 0} g(x) = -5$. Name the rules in Theorem 1 that are used to accomplish steps (a), (b), and (c) of the following calculation.

$$\lim_{x\to 0} \frac{2f(x) - g(x)}{(f(x) + 7)^{2/3}} = \frac{\lim_{x\to 0} (2f(x) - g(x))}{\lim_{x\to 0} (f(x) + 7)^{2/3}} \quad \text{(a)}$$

$$= \frac{\lim_{x\to 0} 2f(x) - \lim_{x\to 0} g(x)}{\left(\lim_{x\to 0} (f(x) + 7)\right)^{2/3}} \quad \text{(b)}$$

$$= \frac{2 \lim_{x\to 0} f(x) - \lim_{x\to 0} g(x)}{\left(\lim_{x\to 0} f(x) + \lim_{x\to 0} 7\right)^{2/3}} \quad \text{(c)}$$

$$= \frac{(2)(1) - (-5)}{(1 + 7)^{2/3}} = \frac{7}{4}$$

52. Let $\lim_{x\to 1} h(x) = 5$, $\lim_{x\to 1} p(x) = 1$, and $\lim_{x\to 1} r(x) = 2$. Name the rules in Theorem 1 that are used to accomplish steps (a), (b), and (c) of the following calculation.

$$\lim_{x\to 1} \frac{\sqrt{5h(x)}}{p(x)(4 - r(x))} = \frac{\lim_{x\to 1} \sqrt{5h(x)}}{\lim_{x\to 1} (p(x)(4 - r(x)))} \quad \text{(a)}$$

$$= \frac{\sqrt{\lim_{x\to 1} 5h(x)}}{\left(\lim_{x\to 1} p(x)\right)\left(\lim_{x\to 1} (4 - r(x))\right)} \quad \text{(b)}$$

$$= \frac{\sqrt{5 \lim_{x\to 1} h(x)}}{\left(\lim_{x\to 1} p(x)\right)\left(\lim_{x\to 1} 4 - \lim_{x\to 1} r(x)\right)} \quad \text{(c)}$$

$$= \frac{\sqrt{(5)(5)}}{(1)(4 - 2)} = \frac{5}{2}$$

53. Suppose $\lim_{x\to c} f(x) = 5$ and $\lim_{x\to c} g(x) = -2$. Find

a. $\lim_{x\to c} f(x)g(x)$

b. $\lim_{x\to c} 2f(x)g(x)$

c. $\lim_{x\to c} (f(x) + 3g(x))$

d. $\lim_{x\to c} \dfrac{f(x)}{f(x) - g(x)}$

54. Suppose $\lim_{x\to 4} f(x) = 0$ and $\lim_{x\to 4} g(x) = -3$. Find

a. $\lim_{x\to 4} (g(x) + 3)$

b. $\lim_{x\to 4} xf(x)$

c. $\lim_{x\to 4} (g(x))^2$

d. $\lim_{x\to 4} \dfrac{g(x)}{f(x) - 1}$

55. Suppose $\lim_{x\to b} f(x) = 7$ and $\lim_{x\to b} g(x) = -3$. Find

a. $\lim_{x\to b} (f(x) + g(x))$

b. $\lim_{x\to b} f(x) \cdot g(x)$

c. $\lim_{x\to b} 4g(x)$

d. $\lim_{x\to b} f(x)/g(x)$

56. Suppose that $\lim_{x\to -2} p(x) = 4$, $\lim_{x\to -2} r(x) = 0$, and $\lim_{x\to -2} s(x) = -3$. Find

a. $\lim_{x\to -2} (p(x) + r(x) + s(x))$

b. $\lim_{x\to -2} p(x) \cdot r(x) \cdot s(x)$

c. $\lim_{x\to -2} (-4p(x) + 5r(x))/s(x)$

Limits of Average Rates of Change

Because of their connection with secant lines, tangents, and instantaneous rates, limits of the form

$$\lim_{h\to 0}\frac{f(x+h)-f(x)}{h}$$

occur frequently in calculus. In Exercises 57–62, evaluate this limit for the given value of x and function f.

57. $f(x) = x^2, \quad x = 1$

58. $f(x) = x^2, \quad x = -2$

59. $f(x) = 3x - 4, \quad x = 2$

60. $f(x) = 1/x, \quad x = -2$

61. $f(x) = \sqrt{x}, \quad x = 7$

62. $f(x) = \sqrt{3x+1}, \quad x = 0$

Using the Sandwich Theorem

63. If $\sqrt{5-2x^2} \le f(x) \le \sqrt{5-x^2}$ for $-1 \le x \le 1$, find $\lim_{x\to 0} f(x)$.

64. If $2 - x^2 \le g(x) \le 2\cos x$ for all x, find $\lim_{x\to 0} g(x)$.

65. a. It can be shown that the inequalities

$$1 - \frac{x^2}{6} < \frac{x\sin x}{2 - 2\cos x} < 1$$

hold for all values of x close to zero. What, if anything, does this tell you about

$$\lim_{x\to 0}\frac{x\sin x}{2-2\cos x}?$$

Give reasons for your answer.

T **b.** Graph $y = 1 - (x^2/6)$, $y = (x\sin x)/(2 - 2\cos x)$, and $y = 1$ together for $-2 \le x \le 2$. Comment on the behavior of the graphs as $x \to 0$.

66. a. Suppose that the inequalities

$$\frac{1}{2} - \frac{x^2}{24} < \frac{1-\cos x}{x^2} < \frac{1}{2}$$

hold for values of x close to zero. (They do, as you will see in Section 9.9.) What, if anything, does this tell you about

$$\lim_{x\to 0}\frac{1-\cos x}{x^2}?$$

Give reasons for your answer.

T **b.** Graph the equations $y = (1/2) - (x^2/24)$, $y = (1 - \cos x)/x^2$, and $y = 1/2$ together for $-2 \le x \le 2$. Comment on the behavior of the graphs as $x \to 0$.

Estimating Limits

T You will find a graphing calculator useful for Exercises 67–76.

67. Let $f(x) = (x^2 - 9)/(x + 3)$.

a. Make a table of the values of f at the points $x = -3.1$, -3.01, -3.001, and so on as far as your calculator can go. Then estimate $\lim_{x\to -3} f(x)$. What estimate do you arrive at if you evaluate f at $x = -2.9, -2.99, -2.999, \ldots$ instead?

b. Support your conclusions in part (a) by graphing f near $c = -3$ and using Zoom and Trace to estimate y-values on the graph as $x \to -3$.

c. Find $\lim_{x\to -3} f(x)$ algebraically, as in Example 7.

68. Let $g(x) = (x^2 - 2)/(x - \sqrt{2})$.

a. Make a table of the values of g at the points $x = 1.4, 1.41$, 1.414, and so on through successive decimal approximations of $\sqrt{2}$. Estimate $\lim_{x\to\sqrt{2}} g(x)$.

b. Support your conclusion in part (a) by graphing g near $c = \sqrt{2}$ and using Zoom and Trace to estimate y-values on the graph as $x \to \sqrt{2}$.

c. Find $\lim_{x\to\sqrt{2}} g(x)$ algebraically.

69. Let $G(x) = (x + 6)/(x^2 + 4x - 12)$.

a. Make a table of the values of G at $x = -5.9, -5.99, -5.999$, and so on. Then estimate $\lim_{x\to -6} G(x)$. What estimate do you arrive at if you evaluate G at $x = -6.1, -6.01$, $-6.001, \ldots$ instead?

b. Support your conclusions in part (a) by graphing G and using Zoom and Trace to estimate y-values on the graph as $x \to -6$.

c. Find $\lim_{x\to -6} G(x)$ algebraically.

70. Let $h(x) = (x^2 - 2x - 3)/(x^2 - 4x + 3)$.

a. Make a table of the values of h at $x = 2.9, 2.99, 2.999$, and so on. Then estimate $\lim_{x\to 3} h(x)$. What estimate do you arrive at if you evaluate h at $x = 3.1, 3.01, 3.001, \ldots$ instead?

b. Support your conclusions in part (a) by graphing h near $c = 3$ and using Zoom and Trace to estimate y-values on the graph as $x \to 3$.

c. Find $\lim_{x\to 3} h(x)$ algebraically.

71. Let $f(x) = (x^2 - 1)/(|x| - 1)$.

a. Make tables of the values of f at values of x that approach $c = -1$ from above and below. Then estimate $\lim_{x\to -1} f(x)$.

b. Support your conclusion in part (a) by graphing f near $c = -1$ and using Zoom and Trace to estimate y-values on the graph as $x \to -1$.

c. Find $\lim_{x\to -1} f(x)$ algebraically.

72. Let $F(x) = (x^2 + 3x + 2)/(2 - |x|)$.

a. Make tables of values of F at values of x that approach $c = -2$ from above and below. Then estimate $\lim_{x\to -2} F(x)$.

b. Support your conclusion in part (a) by graphing F near $c = -2$ and using Zoom and Trace to estimate y-values on the graph as $x \to -2$.

c. Find $\lim_{x\to -2} F(x)$ algebraically.

73. Let $g(\theta) = (\sin\theta)/\theta$.

a. Make a table of the values of g at values of θ that approach $\theta_0 = 0$ from above and below. Then estimate $\lim_{\theta\to 0} g(\theta)$.

b. Support your conclusion in part (a) by graphing g near $\theta_0 = 0$.

74. Let $G(t) = (1 - \cos t)/t^2$.

a. Make tables of values of G at values of t that approach $t_0 = 0$ from above and below. Then estimate $\lim_{t\to 0} G(t)$.

b. Support your conclusion in part (a) by graphing G near $t_0 = 0$.

75. Let $f(x) = x^{1/(1-x)}$.

a. Make tables of values of f at values of x that approach $c = 1$ from above and below. Does f appear to have a limit as $x \to 1$? If so, what is it? If not, why not?

b. Support your conclusions in part (a) by graphing f near $c = 1$.

76. Let $f(x) = (3^x - 1)/x$.

a. Make tables of values of f at values of x that approach $c = 0$ from above and below. Does f appear to have a limit as $x \to 0$? If so, what is it? If not, why not?

b. Support your conclusions in part (a) by graphing f near $c = 0$

Theory and Examples

77. If $x^4 \le f(x) \le x^2$ for x in $[-1, 1]$ and $x^2 \le f(x) \le x^4$ for $x < -1$ and $x > 1$, at what points c do you automatically know $\lim_{x \to c} f(x)$? What can you say about the value of the limit at these points?

78. Suppose that $g(x) \le f(x) \le h(x)$ for all $x \ne 2$ and suppose that

$$\lim_{x \to 2} g(x) = \lim_{x \to 2} h(x) = -5.$$

Can we conclude anything about the values of f, g, and h at $x = 2$? Could $f(2) = 0$? Could $\lim_{x \to 2} f(x) = 0$? Give reasons for your answers.

79. If $\lim_{x \to 4} \dfrac{f(x) - 5}{x - 2} = 1$, find $\lim_{x \to 4} f(x)$.

80. If $\lim_{x \to -2} \dfrac{f(x)}{x^2} = 1$, find

a. $\lim_{x \to -2} f(x)$ **b.** $\lim_{x \to -2} \dfrac{f(x)}{x}$

81. **a.** If $\lim_{x \to 2} \dfrac{f(x) - 5}{x - 2} = 3$, find $\lim_{x \to 2} f(x)$.

b. If $\lim_{x \to 2} \dfrac{f(x) - 5}{x - 2} = 4$, find $\lim_{x \to 2} f(x)$.

82. If $\lim_{x \to 0} \dfrac{f(x)}{x^2} = 1$, find

a. $\lim_{x \to 0} f(x)$ **b.** $\lim_{x \to 0} \dfrac{f(x)}{x}$

T **83.** **a.** Graph $g(x) = x \sin(1/x)$ to estimate $\lim_{x \to 0} g(x)$, zooming in on the origin as necessary.

b. Confirm your estimate in part (a) with a proof.

T **84.** **a.** Graph $h(x) = x^2 \cos(1/x^3)$ to estimate $\lim_{x \to 0} h(x)$, zooming in on the origin as necessary.

b. Confirm your estimate in part (a) with a proof.

COMPUTER EXPLORATIONS

Graphical Estimates of Limits

In Exercises 85–90, use a CAS to perform the following steps:

a. Plot the function near the point c being approached.

b. From your plot guess the value of the limit.

85. $\lim_{x \to 2} \dfrac{x^4 - 16}{x - 2}$ **86.** $\lim_{x \to -1} \dfrac{x^3 - x^2 - 5x - 3}{(x + 1)^2}$

87. $\lim_{x \to 0} \dfrac{\sqrt[3]{1 + x} - 1}{x}$ **88.** $\lim_{x \to 3} \dfrac{x^2 - 9}{\sqrt{x^2 + 7} - 4}$

89. $\lim_{x \to 0} \dfrac{1 - \cos x}{x \sin x}$ **90.** $\lim_{x \to 0} \dfrac{2x^2}{3 - 3\cos x}$

2.3 The Precise Definition of a Limit

We now turn our attention to the precise definition of a limit. We replace vague phrases like "gets arbitrarily close to" in the informal definition with specific conditions that can be applied to any particular example. With a precise definition, we can prove the limit properties given in the preceding section and establish many important limits.

To show that the limit of $f(x)$ as $x \to c$ equals the number L, we need to show that the gap between $f(x)$ and L can be made "as small as we choose" if x is kept "close enough" to c. Let us see what this would require if we specified the size of the gap between $f(x)$ and L.

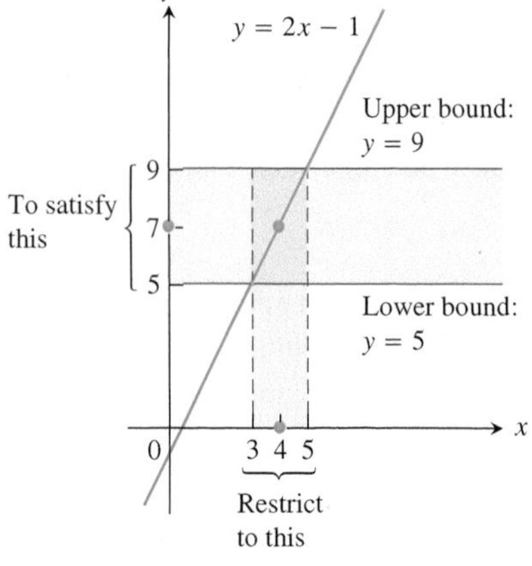

FIGURE 2.15 Keeping x within 1 unit of $x = 4$ will keep y within 2 units of $y = 7$ (Example 1).

EXAMPLE 1 Consider the function $y = 2x - 1$ near $x = 4$. Intuitively it appears that y is close to 7 when x is close to 4, so $\lim_{x \to 4}(2x - 1) = 7$. However, how close to $x = 4$ does x have to be so that $y = 2x - 1$ differs from 7 by, say, less than 2 units?

Solution We are asked: For what values of x is $|y - 7| < 2$? To find the answer we first express $|y - 7|$ in terms of x:

$$|y - 7| = |(2x - 1) - 7| = |2x - 8|.$$

The question then becomes: what values of x satisfy the inequality $|2x - 8| < 2$? To find out, we solve the inequality:

$$\begin{aligned} |2x - 8| &< 2 \\ -2 < 2x - 8 &< 2 \\ 6 < 2x &< 10 \\ 3 < x &< 5 && \text{Solve for } x. \\ -1 < x - 4 &< 1. && \text{Solve for } x - 4. \end{aligned}$$

Keeping x within 1 unit of $x = 4$ will keep y within 2 units of $y = 7$ (Figure 2.15). ■

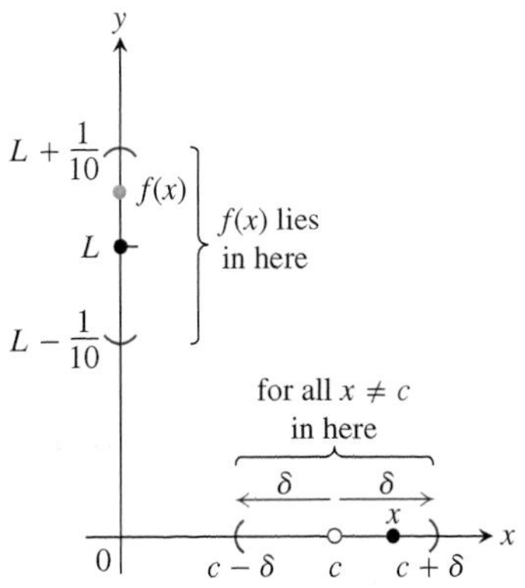

FIGURE 2.16 How should we define $\delta > 0$ so that keeping x within the interval $(c - \delta, c + \delta)$ will keep $f(x)$ within the interval $\left(L - \frac{1}{10}, L + \frac{1}{10}\right)$?

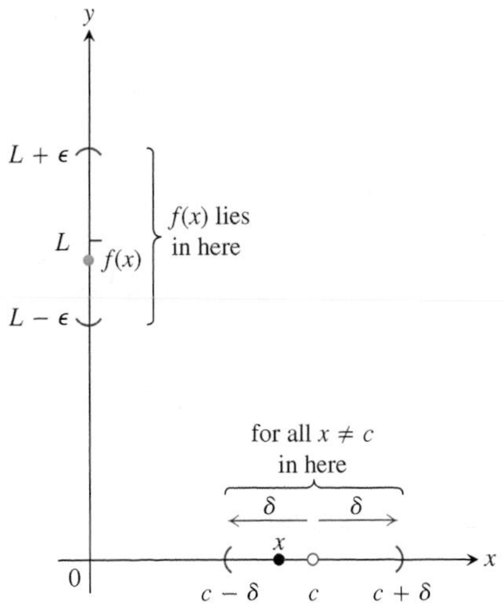

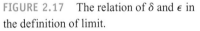

FIGURE 2.17 The relation of δ and ϵ in the definition of limit.

In the previous example we determined how close x must be to a particular value c to ensure that the outputs $f(x)$ of some function lie within a prescribed interval about a limit value L. To show that the limit of $f(x)$ as $x \to c$ actually equals L, we must be able to show that the gap between $f(x)$ and L can be made less than *any prescribed error*, no matter how small, by holding x close enough to c.

Definition of Limit

Suppose we are watching the values of a function $f(x)$ as x approaches c (without taking on the value of c itself). Certainly we want to be able to say that $f(x)$ stays within one-tenth of a unit from L as soon as x stays within some distance δ of c (Figure 2.16). But that in itself is not enough, because as x continues on its course toward c, what is to prevent $f(x)$ from jittering about within the interval from $L - (1/10)$ to $L + (1/10)$ without tending toward L?

We can be told that the error can be no more than $1/100$ or $1/1000$ or $1/100{,}000$. Each time, we find a new δ-interval about c so that keeping x within that interval satisfies the new error tolerance. And each time the possibility exists that $f(x)$ jitters away from L at some stage.

The figures on the next page illustrate the problem. You can think of this as a quarrel between a skeptic and a scholar. The skeptic presents ϵ-challenges to prove that the limit does not exist or, more precisely, that there is room for doubt. The scholar answers every challenge with a δ-interval around c that keeps the function values within ϵ of L.

How do we stop this seemingly endless series of challenges and responses? By proving that for every error tolerance ϵ that the challenger can produce, we can find, calculate, or conjure a matching distance δ that keeps x "close enough" to c to keep $f(x)$ within that tolerance of L (Figure 2.17). This leads us to the precise definition of a limit.

DEFINITION Let $f(x)$ be defined on an open interval about c, except possibly at c itself. We say that the **limit of $f(x)$ as x approaches c is the number L**, and write

$$\lim_{x \to c} f(x) = L,$$

if, for every number $\epsilon > 0$, there exists a corresponding number $\delta > 0$ such that for all x,

$$0 < |x - c| < \delta \quad \Rightarrow \quad |f(x) - L| < \epsilon.$$

One way to think about the definition is to suppose we are machining a generator shaft to a close tolerance. We may try for diameter L, but since nothing is perfect, we must be satisfied with a diameter $f(x)$ somewhere between $L - \epsilon$ and $L + \epsilon$. The δ is the measure of how accurate our control setting for x must be to guarantee this degree of accuracy in the diameter of the shaft. Notice that as the tolerance for error becomes stricter, we may have to adjust δ. That is, the value of δ, how tight our control setting must be, depends on the value of ϵ, the error tolerance.

Examples: Testing the Definition

The formal definition of limit does not tell how to find the limit of a function, but it enables us to verify that a suspected limit is correct. The following examples show how the definition can be used to verify limit statements for specific functions. However, the real purpose of the definition is not to do calculations like this, but rather to prove general theorems so that the calculation of specific limits can be simplified.

The challenge:
Make $\left| f(x) - L \right| < \epsilon = \frac{1}{10}$

Response:
$\left| x - c \right| < \delta_{1/10}$ (a number)

New challenge:
Make $\left| f(x) - L \right| < \epsilon = \frac{1}{100}$

Response:
$\left| x - c \right| < \delta_{1/100}$

New challenge:
$\epsilon = \frac{1}{1000}$

Response:
$\left| x - c \right| < \delta_{1/1000}$

New challenge:
$\epsilon = \frac{1}{100,000}$

Response:
$\left| x - c \right| < \delta_{1/100,000}$

New challenge:
$\epsilon = \cdots$

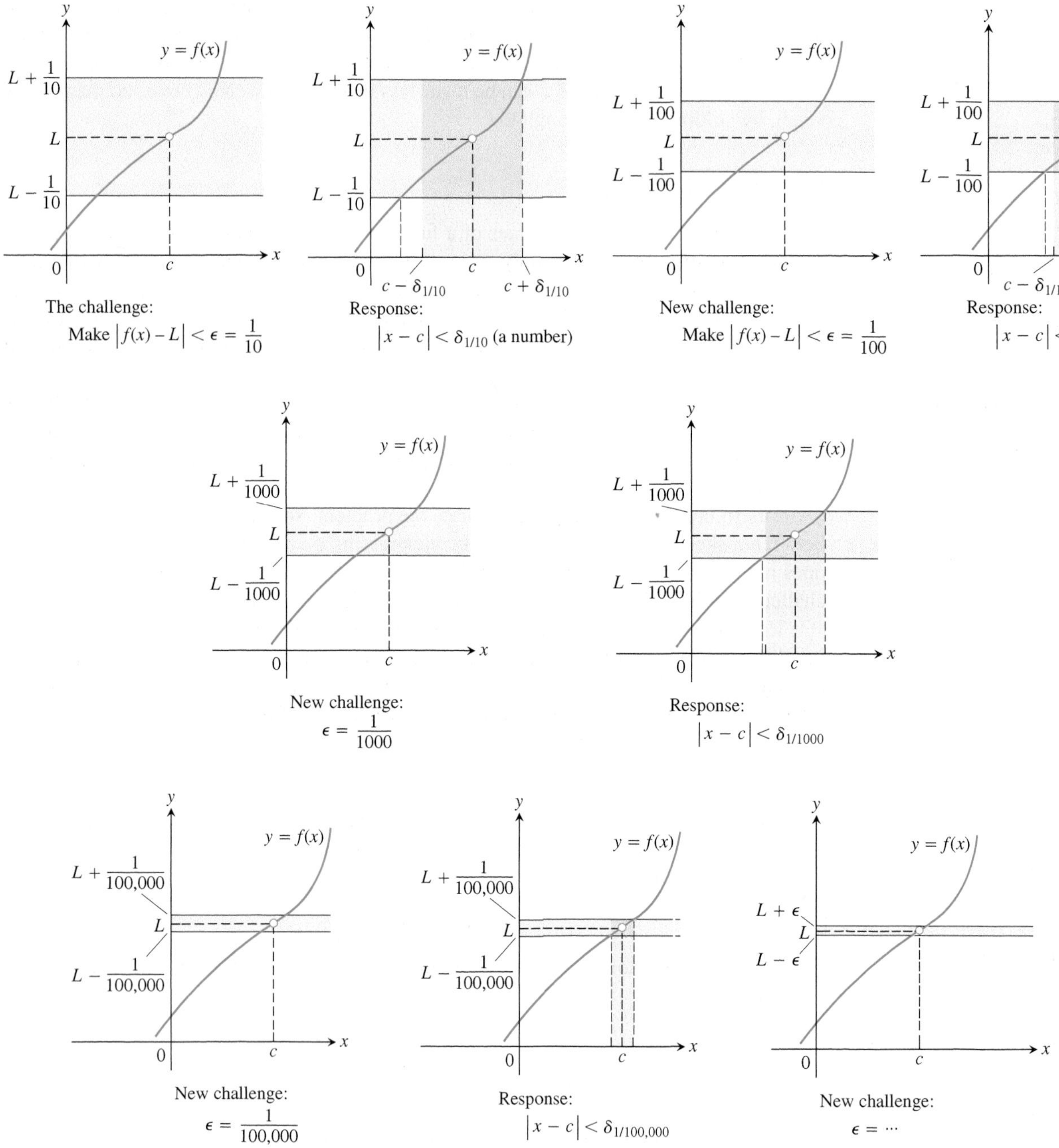

EXAMPLE 2 Show that

$$\lim_{x \to 1} (5x - 3) = 2.$$

Solution Set $c = 1$, $f(x) = 5x - 3$, and $L = 2$ in the definition of limit. For any given $\epsilon > 0$, we have to find a suitable $\delta > 0$ so that if $x \neq 1$ and x is within distance δ of $c = 1$, that is, whenever

$$0 < \left| x - 1 \right| < \delta,$$

it is true that $f(x)$ is within distance ϵ of $L = 2$, so

$$\left| f(x) - 2 \right| < \epsilon.$$

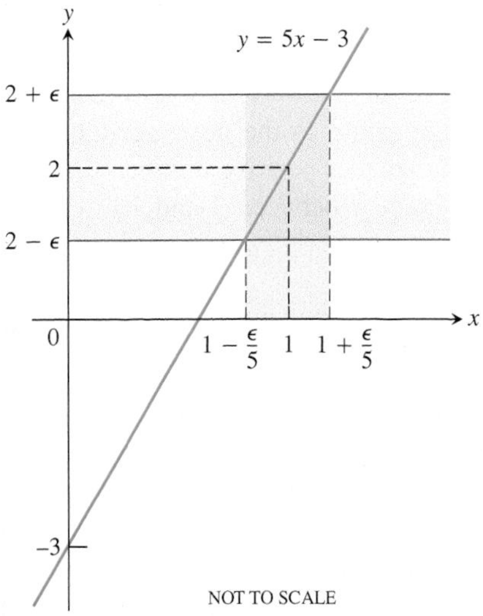

FIGURE 2.18 If $f(x) = 5x - 3$, then $0 < |x - 1| < \epsilon/5$ guarantees that $|f(x) - 2| < \epsilon$ (Example 2).

We find δ by working backward from the ϵ-inequality:

$$\begin{aligned} |(5x - 3) - 2| = |5x - 5| &< \epsilon \\ 5|x - 1| &< \epsilon \\ |x - 1| &< \epsilon/5. \end{aligned}$$

Thus, we can take $\delta = \epsilon/5$ (Figure 2.18). If $0 < |x - 1| < \delta = \epsilon/5$, then

$$|(5x - 3) - 2| = |5x - 5| = 5|x - 1| < 5(\epsilon/5) = \epsilon,$$

which proves that $\lim_{x\to 1}(5x - 3) = 2$.

The value of $\delta = \epsilon/5$ is not the only value that will make $0 < |x - 1| < \delta$ imply $|5x - 5| < \epsilon$. Any smaller positive δ will do as well. The definition does not ask for a "best" positive δ, just one that will work. ■

EXAMPLE 3 Prove the following results presented graphically in Section 2.2.

(a) $\lim_{x\to c} x = c$ **(b)** $\lim_{x\to c} k = k$ (k constant)

Solution

(a) Let $\epsilon > 0$ be given. We must find $\delta > 0$ such that for all x

$$0 < |x - c| < \delta \quad \text{implies} \quad |x - c| < \epsilon.$$

The implication will hold if δ equals ϵ or any smaller positive number (Figure 2.19). This proves that $\lim_{x\to c} x = c$.

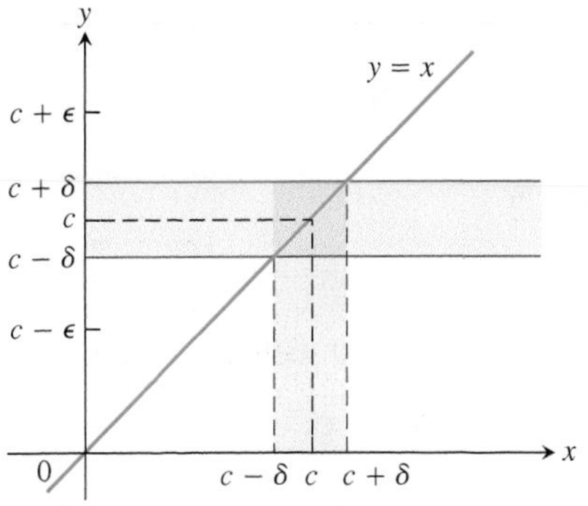

FIGURE 2.19 For the function $f(x) = x$, we find that $0 < |x - c| < \delta$ will guarantee $|f(x) - c| < \epsilon$ whenever $\delta \le \epsilon$ (Example 3a).

(b) Let $\epsilon > 0$ be given. We must find $\delta > 0$ such that for all x

$$0 < |x - c| < \delta \quad \text{implies} \quad |k - k| < \epsilon.$$

Since $k - k = 0$, we can use any positive number for δ and the implication will hold (Figure 2.20). This proves that $\lim_{x\to c} k = k$. ■

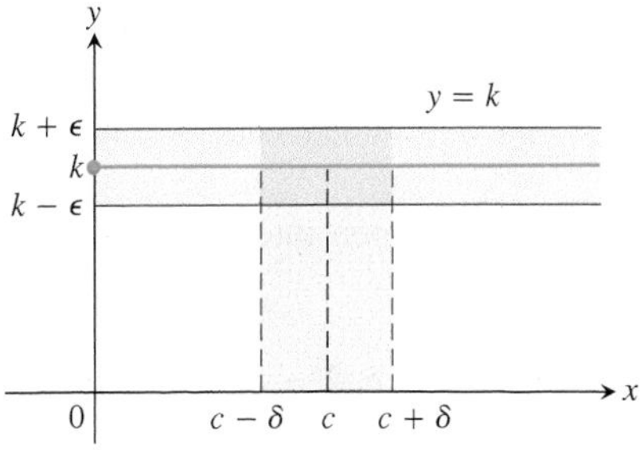

FIGURE 2.20 For the function $f(x) = k$, we find that $|f(x) - k| < \epsilon$ for any positive δ (Example 3b).

Finding Deltas Algebraically for Given Epsilons

In Examples 2 and 3, the interval of values about c for which $|f(x) - L|$ was less than ϵ was symmetric about c and we could take δ to be half the length of that interval. When such symmetry is absent, as it usually is, we can take δ to be the distance from c to the interval's *nearer* endpoint.

EXAMPLE 4 For the limit $\lim_{x\to 5}\sqrt{x - 1} = 2$, find a $\delta > 0$ that works for $\epsilon = 1$. That is, find a $\delta > 0$ such that for all x

$$0 < |x - 5| < \delta \quad \Rightarrow \quad |\sqrt{x - 1} - 2| < 1.$$

Solution We organize the search into two steps.

1. *Solve the inequality $|\sqrt{x - 1} - 2| < 1$ to find an interval containing $x = 5$ on which the inequality holds for all $x \neq 5$.*

$$\begin{aligned} |\sqrt{x - 1} - 2| &< 1 \\ -1 < \sqrt{x - 1} - 2 &< 1 \\ 1 < \sqrt{x - 1} &< 3 \\ 1 < x - 1 &< 9 \\ 2 < x &< 10 \end{aligned}$$

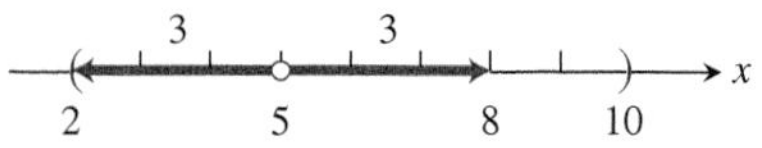

FIGURE 2.21 An open interval of radius 3 about $x = 5$ will lie inside the open interval (2, 10).

The inequality holds for all x in the open interval (2, 10), so it holds for all $x \neq 5$ in this interval as well.

2. *Find a value of* $\delta > 0$ *to place the centered interval* $5 - \delta < x < 5 + \delta$ (centered at $x = 5$) *inside the interval* (2, 10). The distance from 5 to the nearer endpoint of (2, 10) is 3 (Figure 2.21). If we take $\delta = 3$ or any smaller positive number, then the inequality $0 < |x - 5| < \delta$ will automatically place x between 2 and 10 to make $|\sqrt{x-1} - 2| < 1$ (Figure 2.22):

$$0 < |x - 5| < 3 \quad \Rightarrow \quad |\sqrt{x-1} - 2| < 1. \quad \blacksquare$$

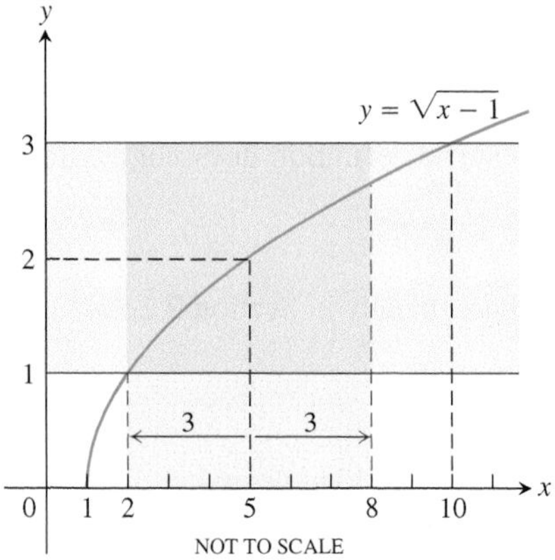

FIGURE 2.22 The function and intervals in Example 4.

How to Find Algebraically a δ for a Given f, L, c, and $\epsilon > 0$

The process of finding a $\delta > 0$ such that for all x

$$0 < |x - c| < \delta \quad \Rightarrow \quad |f(x) - L| < \epsilon$$

can be accomplished in two steps.

1. *Solve the inequality* $|f(x) - L| < \epsilon$ to find an open interval (a, b) containing c on which the inequality holds for all $x \neq c$.
2. *Find a value of* $\delta > 0$ that places the open interval $(c - \delta, c + \delta)$ centered at c inside the interval (a, b). The inequality $|f(x) - L| < \epsilon$ will hold for all $x \neq c$ in this δ-interval.

EXAMPLE 5 Prove that $\lim_{x \to 2} f(x) = 4$ if

$$f(x) = \begin{cases} x^2, & x \neq 2 \\ 1, & x = 2. \end{cases}$$

Solution Our task is to show that given $\epsilon > 0$ there exists a $\delta > 0$ such that for all x

$$0 < |x - 2| < \delta \quad \Rightarrow \quad |f(x) - 4| < \epsilon.$$

1. *Solve the inequality* $|f(x) - 4| < \epsilon$ *to find an open interval containing* $x = 2$ *on which the inequality holds for all* $x \neq 2$.

For $x \neq c = 2$, we have $f(x) = x^2$, and the inequality to solve is $|x^2 - 4| < \epsilon$:

$$|x^2 - 4| < \epsilon$$
$$-\epsilon < x^2 - 4 < \epsilon$$
$$4 - \epsilon < x^2 < 4 + \epsilon$$
$$\sqrt{4 - \epsilon} < |x| < \sqrt{4 + \epsilon} \qquad \text{Assumes } \epsilon < 4\text{; see below.}$$
$$\sqrt{4 - \epsilon} < x < \sqrt{4 + \epsilon}. \qquad \text{An open interval about } x = 2 \text{ that solves the inequality}$$

The inequality $|f(x) - 4| < \epsilon$ holds for all $x \neq 2$ in the open interval $\left(\sqrt{4 - \epsilon}, \sqrt{4 + \epsilon}\right)$ (Figure 2.23).

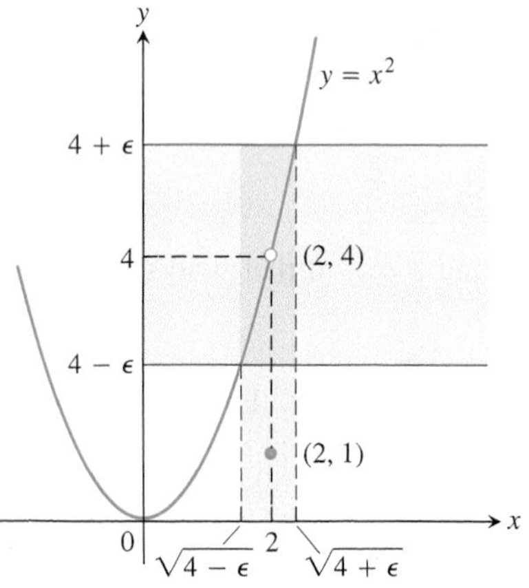

FIGURE 2.23 An interval containing $x = 2$ so that the function in Example 5 satisfies $|f(x) - 4| < \epsilon$.

2. *Find a value of* $\delta > 0$ *that places the centered interval* $(2 - \delta, 2 + \delta)$ *inside the interval* $\left(\sqrt{4 - \epsilon}, \sqrt{4 + \epsilon}\right)$.

Take δ to be the distance from $x = 2$ to the nearer endpoint of $\left(\sqrt{4 - \epsilon}, \sqrt{4 + \epsilon}\right)$. In other words, take $\delta = \min\left\{2 - \sqrt{4 - \epsilon}, \sqrt{4 + \epsilon} - 2\right\}$, the *minimum* (the smaller) of the two numbers $2 - \sqrt{4 - \epsilon}$ and $\sqrt{4 + \epsilon} - 2$. If δ has this or any smaller positive value, the inequality $0 < |x - 2| < \delta$ will automatically place x between $\sqrt{4 - \epsilon}$ and $\sqrt{4 + \epsilon}$ to make $|f(x) - 4| < \epsilon$. For all x,

$$0 < |x - 2| < \delta \quad \Rightarrow \quad |f(x) - 4| < \epsilon.$$

This completes the proof for $\epsilon < 4$.

If $\epsilon \geq 4$, then we take δ to be the distance from $x = 2$ to the nearer endpoint of the interval $\left(0, \sqrt{4 + \epsilon}\right)$. In other words, take $\delta = \min\left\{2, \sqrt{4 + \epsilon} - 2\right\}$. (See Figure 2.23.) ■

Using the Definition to Prove Theorems

We do not usually rely on the formal definition of limit to verify specific limits such as those in the preceding examples. Rather, we appeal to general theorems about limits, in particular the theorems of Section 2.2. The definition is used to prove these theorems (Appendix 5). As an example, we prove part 1 of Theorem 1, the Sum Rule.

EXAMPLE 6 Given that $\lim_{x \to c} f(x) = L$ and $\lim_{x \to c} g(x) = M$, prove that

$$\lim_{x \to c} (f(x) + g(x)) = L + M.$$

Solution Let $\epsilon > 0$ be given. We want to find a positive number δ such that for all x

$$0 < |x - c| < \delta \quad \Rightarrow \quad |f(x) + g(x) - (L + M)| < \epsilon.$$

Regrouping terms, we get

$$\begin{aligned} |f(x) + g(x) - (L + M)| &= |(f(x) - L) + (g(x) - M)| \\ &\leq |f(x) - L| + |g(x) - M|. \end{aligned}$$

Triangle Inequality: $|a + b| \leq |a| + |b|$

Since $\lim_{x \to c} f(x) = L$, there exists a number $\delta_1 > 0$ such that for all x

$$0 < |x - c| < \delta_1 \quad \Rightarrow \quad |f(x) - L| < \epsilon/2.$$

Similarly, since $\lim_{x \to c} g(x) = M$, there exists a number $\delta_2 > 0$ such that for all x

$$0 < |x - c| < \delta_2 \quad \Rightarrow \quad |g(x) - M| < \epsilon/2.$$

Let $\delta = \min\{\delta_1, \delta_2\}$, the smaller of δ_1 and δ_2. If $0 < |x - c| < \delta$ then $|x - c| < \delta_1$, so $|f(x) - L| < \epsilon/2$, and $|x - c| < \delta_2$, so $|g(x) - M| < \epsilon/2$. Therefore

$$|f(x) + g(x) - (L + M)| < \frac{\epsilon}{2} + \frac{\epsilon}{2} = \epsilon.$$

This shows that $\lim_{x \to c} (f(x) + g(x)) = L + M$. ■

Next we prove Theorem 5 of Section 2.2.

EXAMPLE 7 Given that $\lim_{x \to c} f(x) = L$ and $\lim_{x \to c} g(x) = M$, and that $f(x) \leq g(x)$ for all x in an open interval containing c (except possibly c itself), prove that $L \leq M$.

Solution We use the method of proof by contradiction. Suppose, on the contrary, that $L > M$. Then by the limit of a difference property in Theorem 1,

$$\lim_{x \to c} (g(x) - f(x)) = M - L.$$

Therefore, for any $\epsilon > 0$, there exists $\delta > 0$ such that

$$|(g(x) - f(x)) - (M - L)| < \epsilon \qquad \text{whenever} \quad 0 < |x - c| < \delta.$$

Since $L - M > 0$ by hypothesis, we take $\epsilon = L - M$ in particular and we have a number $\delta > 0$ such that

$$|(g(x) - f(x)) - (M - L)| < L - M \qquad \text{whenever} \quad 0 < |x - c| < \delta.$$

Since $a \leq |a|$ for any number a, we have

$$(g(x) - f(x)) - (M - L) < L - M \qquad \text{whenever} \quad 0 < |x - c| < \delta$$

which simplifies to

$$g(x) < f(x) \qquad \text{whenever} \quad 0 < |x - c| < \delta.$$

But this contradicts $f(x) \leq g(x)$. Thus the inequality $L > M$ must be false. Therefore $L \leq M$. ■

Exercises 2.3

Centering Intervals About a Point

In Exercises 1–6, sketch the interval (a, b) on the x-axis with the point c inside. Then find a value of $\delta > 0$ such that for all x, $0 < |x - c| < \delta \quad \Rightarrow \quad a < x < b$.

1. $a = 1, \quad b = 7, \quad c = 5$

2. $a = 1, \quad b = 7, \quad c = 2$

3. $a = -7/2, \quad b = -1/2, \quad c = -3$

4. $a = -7/2, \quad b = -1/2, \quad c = -3/2$

5. $a = 4/9, \quad b = 4/7, \quad c = 1/2$

6. $a = 2.7591, \quad b = 3.2391, \quad c = 3$

Finding Deltas Graphically

In Exercises 7–14, use the graphs to find a $\delta > 0$ such that for all x

$$0 < |x - c| < \delta \quad \Rightarrow \quad |f(x) - L| < \epsilon.$$

7.

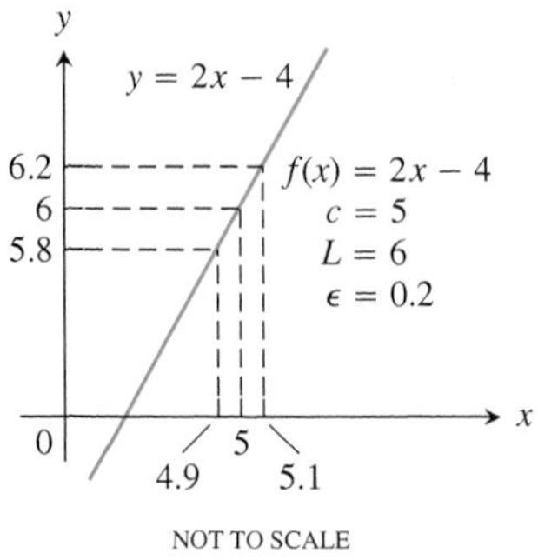

8.

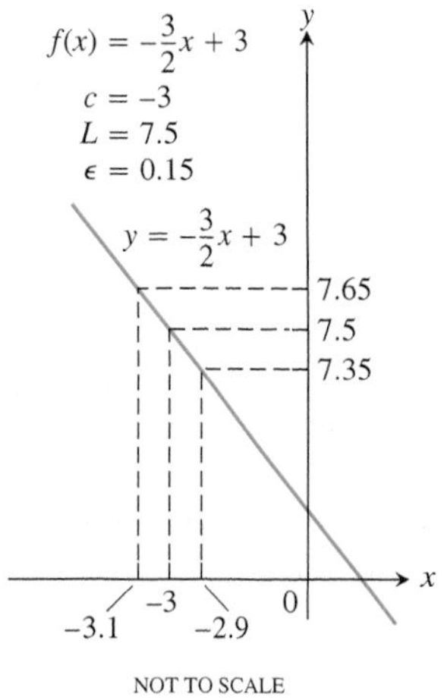

9.

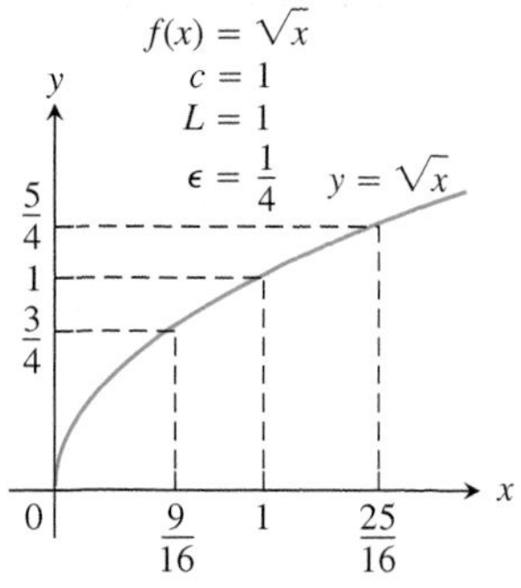

10.

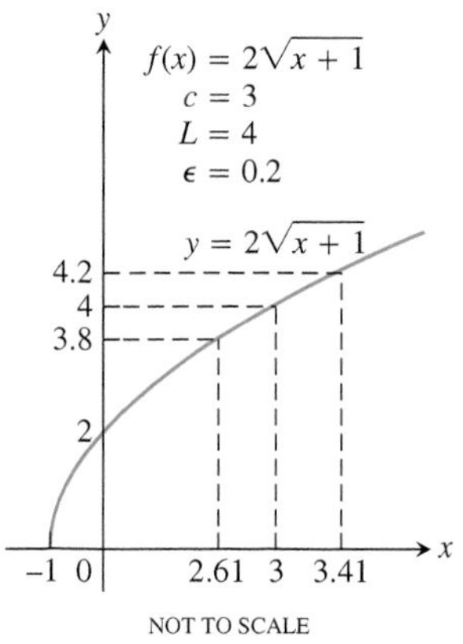

11.

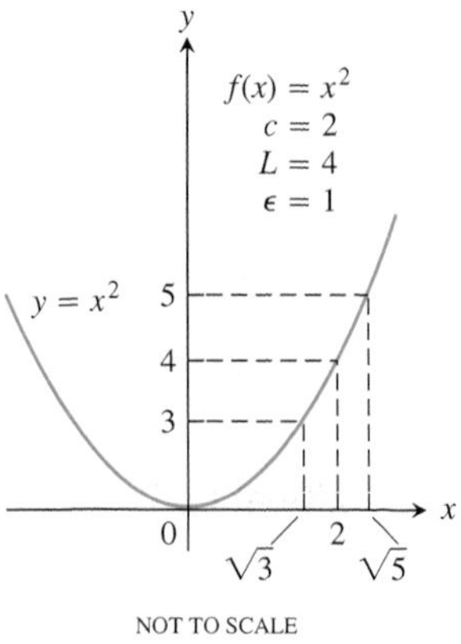

12.

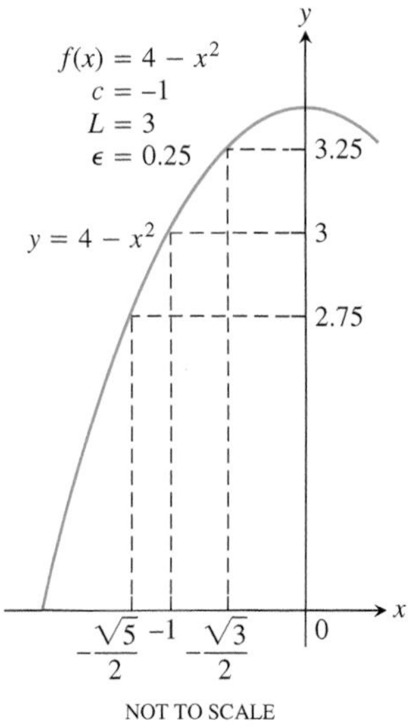

13.

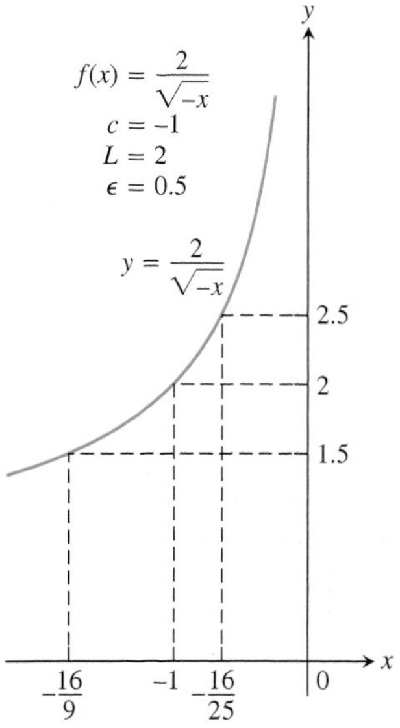

14.

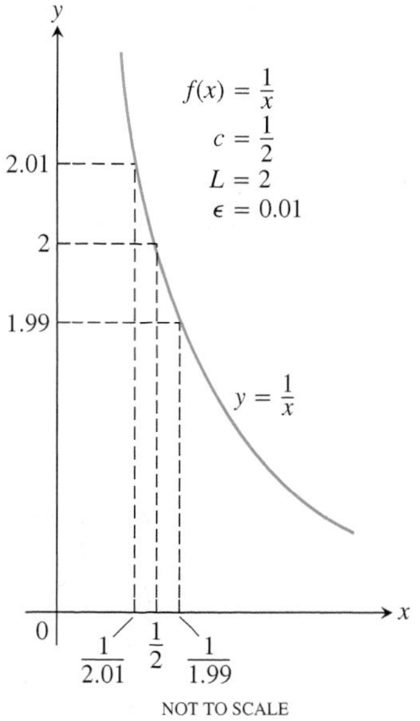

Finding Deltas Algebraically

Each of Exercises 15–30 gives a function $f(x)$ and numbers L, c, and $\epsilon > 0$. In each case, find an open interval about c on which the inequality $|f(x) - L| < \epsilon$ holds. Then give a value for $\delta > 0$ such that for all x satisfying $0 < |x - c| < \delta$ the inequality $|f(x) - L| < \epsilon$ holds.

15. $f(x) = x + 1, \quad L = 5, \quad c = 4, \quad \epsilon = 0.01$

16. $f(x) = 2x - 2, \quad L = -6, \quad c = -2, \quad \epsilon = 0.02$

17. $f(x) = \sqrt{x + 1}, \quad L = 1, \quad c = 0, \quad \epsilon = 0.1$

18. $f(x) = \sqrt{x}, \quad L = 1/2, \quad c = 1/4, \quad \epsilon = 0.1$

19. $f(x) = \sqrt{19 - x}, \quad L = 3, \quad c = 10, \quad \epsilon = 1$

20. $f(x) = \sqrt{x - 7}, \quad L = 4, \quad c = 23, \quad \epsilon = 1$

21. $f(x) = 1/x, \quad L = 1/4, \quad c = 4, \quad \epsilon = 0.05$

22. $f(x) = x^2, \quad L = 3, \quad c = \sqrt{3}, \quad \epsilon = 0.1$

23. $f(x) = x^2, \quad L = 4, \quad c = -2, \quad \epsilon = 0.5$

24. $f(x) = 1/x, \quad L = -1, \quad c = -1, \quad \epsilon = 0.1$

25. $f(x) = x^2 - 5, \quad L = 11, \quad c = 4, \quad \epsilon = 1$

26. $f(x) = 120/x, \quad L = 5, \quad c = 24, \quad \epsilon = 1$

27. $f(x) = mx, \quad m > 0, \quad L = 2m, \quad c = 2, \quad \epsilon = 0.03$

28. $f(x) = mx, \quad m > 0, \quad L = 3m, \quad c = 3, \quad \epsilon = c > 0$

29. $f(x) = mx + b, \quad m > 0, \quad L = (m/2) + b,$
$c = 1/2, \quad \epsilon = c > 0$

30. $f(x) = mx + b, \quad m > 0, \quad L = m + b, \quad c = 1,$
$\epsilon = 0.05$

Using the Formal Definition

Each of Exercises 31–36 gives a function $f(x)$, a point c, and a positive number ϵ. Find $L = \lim_{x \to c} f(x)$. Then find a number $\delta > 0$ such that for all x

$$0 < |x - c| < \delta \quad \Rightarrow \quad |f(x) - L| < \epsilon.$$

31. $f(x) = 3 - 2x, \quad c = 3, \quad \epsilon = 0.02$

32. $f(x) = -3x - 2, \quad c = -1, \quad \epsilon = 0.03$

33. $f(x) = \dfrac{x^2 - 4}{x - 2}, \quad c = 2, \quad \epsilon = 0.05$

34. $f(x) = \dfrac{x^2 + 6x + 5}{x + 5}, \quad c = -5, \quad \epsilon = 0.05$

35. $f(x) = \sqrt{1 - 5x}, \quad c = -3, \quad \epsilon = 0.5$

36. $f(x) = 4/x, \quad c = 2, \quad \epsilon = 0.4$

Prove the limit statements in Exercises 37–50.

37. $\lim_{x \to 4} (9 - x) = 5$

38. $\lim_{x \to 3} (3x - 7) = 2$

39. $\lim_{x \to 9} \sqrt{x - 5} = 2$

40. $\lim_{x \to 0} \sqrt{4 - x} = 2$

41. $\lim_{x \to 1} f(x) = 1 \quad \text{if} \quad f(x) = \begin{cases} x^2, & x \neq 1 \\ 2, & x = 1 \end{cases}$

42. $\lim_{x \to -2} f(x) = 4 \quad \text{if} \quad f(x) = \begin{cases} x^2, & x \neq -2 \\ 1, & x = -2 \end{cases}$

43. $\lim_{x \to 1} \dfrac{1}{x} = 1$

44. $\lim_{x \to \sqrt{3}} \dfrac{1}{x^2} = \dfrac{1}{3}$

45. $\lim_{x \to -3} \dfrac{x^2 - 9}{x + 3} = -6$

46. $\lim_{x \to 1} \dfrac{x^2 - 1}{x - 1} = 2$

47. $\lim_{x \to 1} f(x) = 2 \quad \text{if} \quad f(x) = \begin{cases} 4 - 2x, & x < 1 \\ 6x - 4, & x \geq 1 \end{cases}$

48. $\lim_{x \to 0} f(x) = 0 \quad \text{if} \quad f(x) = \begin{cases} 2x, & x < 0 \\ x/2, & x \geq 0 \end{cases}$

49. $\lim_{x \to 0} x \sin \dfrac{1}{x} = 0$

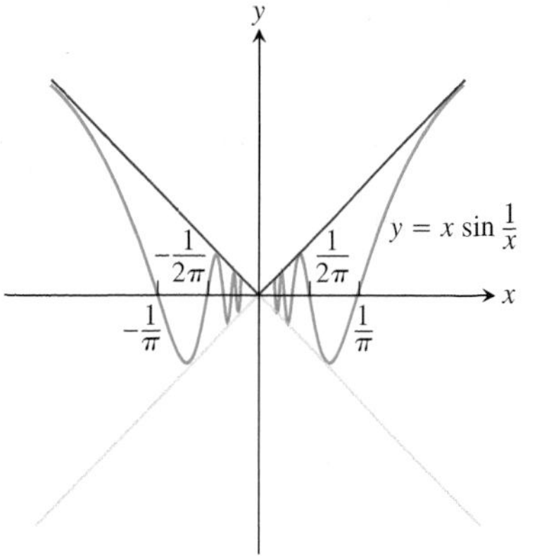

50. $\lim_{x \to 0} x^2 \sin \frac{1}{x} = 0$

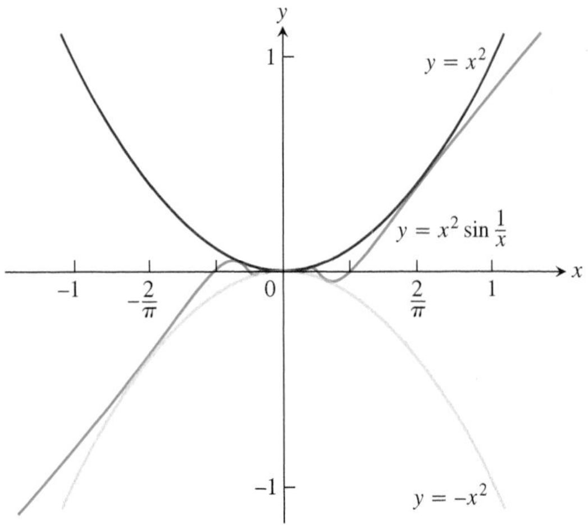

Theory and Examples

51. Define what it means to say that $\lim_{x \to 0} g(x) = k$.

52. Prove that $\lim_{x \to c} f(x) = L$ if and only if $\lim_{h \to 0} f(h + c) = L$.

53. A wrong statement about limits Show by example that the following statement is wrong.

> The number L is the limit of $f(x)$ as x approaches c if $f(x)$ gets closer to L as x approaches c.

Explain why the function in your example does not have the given value of L as a limit as $x \to c$.

54. Another wrong statement about limits Show by example that the following statement is wrong.

> The number L is the limit of $f(x)$ as x approaches c if, given any $\epsilon > 0$, there exists a value of x for which $|f(x) - L| < \epsilon$.

Explain why the function in your example does not have the given value of L as a limit as $x \to c$.

T **55. Grinding engine cylinders** Before contracting to grind engine cylinders to a cross-sectional area of 9 in^2, you need to know how much deviation from the ideal cylinder diameter of $c = 3.385$ in. you can allow and still have the area come within 0.01 in^2 of the required 9 in^2. To find out, you let $A = \pi(x/2)^2$ and look for the interval in which you must hold x to make $|A - 9| \le 0.01$. What interval do you find?

56. Manufacturing electrical resistors Ohm's law for electrical circuits like the one shown in the accompanying figure states that $V = RI$. In this equation, V is a constant voltage, I is the current in amperes, and R is the resistance in ohms. Your firm has been asked to supply the resistors for a circuit in which V will be 120 volts and I is to be 5 ± 0.1 amp. In what interval does R have to lie for I to be within 0.1 amp of the value $I_0 = 5$?

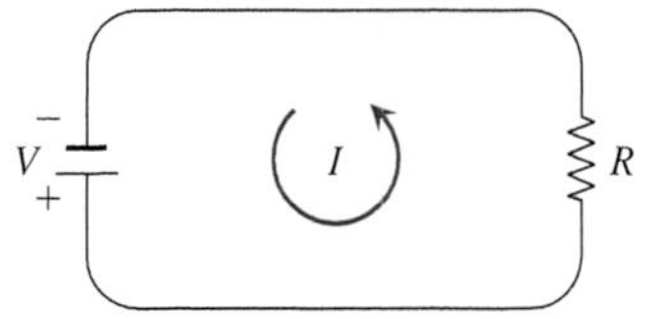

When Is a Number L Not the Limit of $f(x)$ as $x \to c$?

Showing L is not a limit We can prove that $\lim_{x \to c} f(x) \ne L$ by providing an $\epsilon > 0$ such that no possible $\delta > 0$ satisfies the condition

$$\text{for all } x, \quad 0 < |x - c| < \delta \quad \Rightarrow \quad |f(x) - L| < \epsilon.$$

We accomplish this for our candidate ϵ by showing that for each $\delta > 0$ there exists a value of x such that

$$0 < |x - c| < \delta \quad \text{and} \quad |f(x) - L| \ge \epsilon.$$

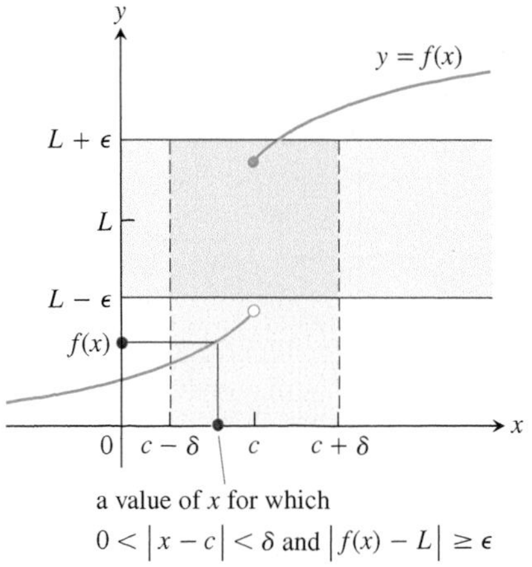

57. Let $f(x) = \begin{cases} x, & x < 1 \\ x + 1, & x > 1. \end{cases}$

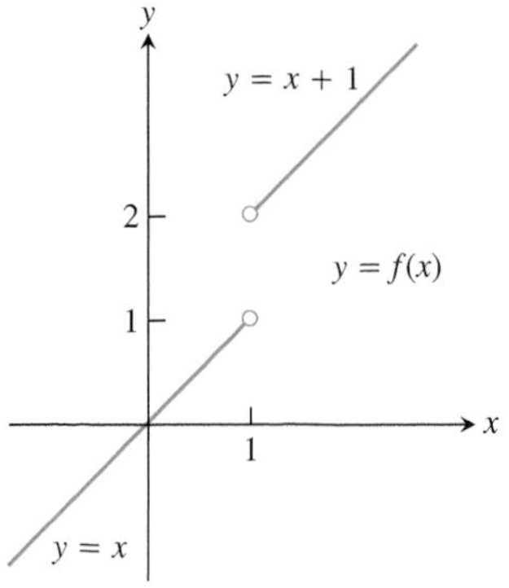

a. Let $\epsilon = 1/2$. Show that no possible $\delta > 0$ satisfies the following condition:

$$\text{For all } x, \quad 0 < |x - 1| < \delta \quad \Rightarrow \quad |f(x) - 2| < 1/2.$$

That is, for each $\delta > 0$ show that there is a value of x such that

$$0 < |x - 1| < \delta \quad \text{and} \quad |f(x) - 2| \ge 1/2.$$

This will show that $\lim_{x \to 1} f(x) \ne 2$.

b. Show that $\lim_{x \to 1} f(x) \ne 1$.

c. Show that $\lim_{x \to 1} f(x) \ne 1.5$.

58. Let $h(x) = \begin{cases} x^2, & x < 2 \\ 3, & x = 2 \\ 2, & x > 2. \end{cases}$

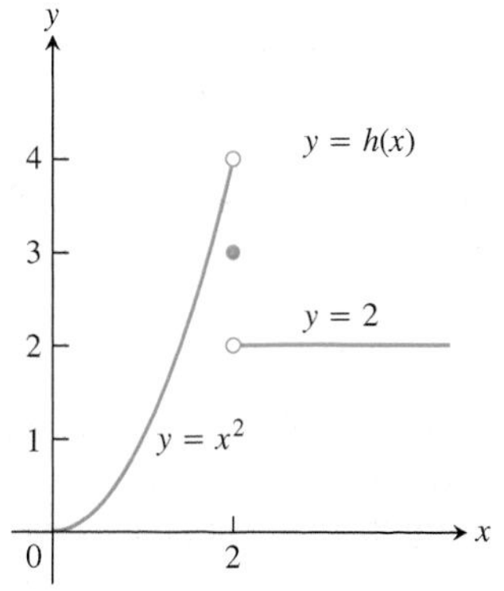

Show that

a. $\lim_{x \to 2} h(x) \neq 4$

b. $\lim_{x \to 2} h(x) \neq 3$

c. $\lim_{x \to 2} h(x) \neq 2$

59. For the function graphed here, explain why

a. $\lim_{x \to 3} f(x) \neq 4$

b. $\lim_{x \to 3} f(x) \neq 4.8$

c. $\lim_{x \to 3} f(x) \neq 3$

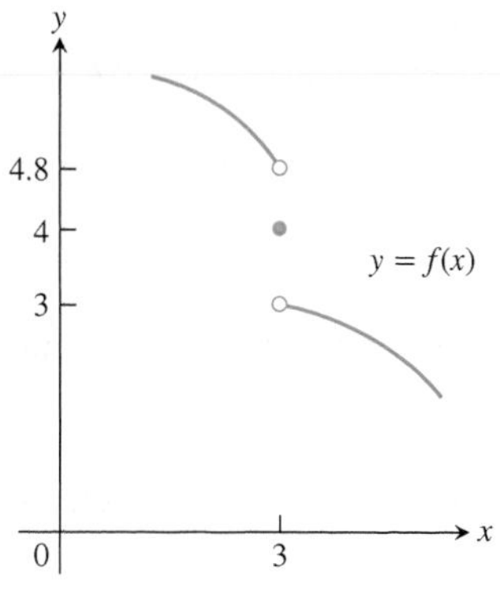

60. a. For the function graphed here, show that $\lim_{x \to -1} g(x) \neq 2$.

b. Does $\lim_{x \to -1} g(x)$ appear to exist? If so, what is the value of the limit? If not, why not?

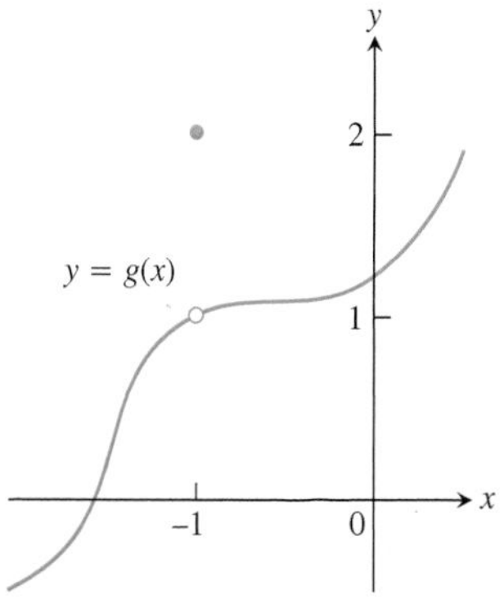

COMPUTER EXPLORATIONS

In Exercises 61–66, you will further explore finding deltas graphically. Use a CAS to perform the following steps:

a. Plot the function $y = f(x)$ near the point c being approached.

b. Guess the value of the limit L and then evaluate the limit symbolically to see if you guessed correctly.

c. Using the value $\epsilon = 0.2$, graph the banding lines $y_1 = L - \epsilon$ and $y_2 = L + \epsilon$ together with the function f near c.

d. From your graph in part (c), estimate a $\delta > 0$ such that for all x

$$0 < |x - c| < \delta \quad \Rightarrow \quad |f(x) - L| < \epsilon.$$

Test your estimate by plotting f, y_1, and y_2 over the interval $0 < |x - c| < \delta$. For your viewing window use $c - 2\delta \le x \le c + 2\delta$ and $L - 2\epsilon \le y \le L + 2\epsilon$. If any function values lie outside the interval $[L - \epsilon, L + \epsilon]$, your choice of δ was too large. Try again with a smaller estimate.

e. Repeat parts (c) and (d) successively for $\epsilon = 0.1, 0.05$, and 0.001.

61. $f(x) = \dfrac{x^4 - 81}{x - 3}, \quad c = 3$

62. $f(x) = \dfrac{5x^3 + 9x^2}{2x^5 + 3x^2}, \quad c = 0$

63. $f(x) = \dfrac{\sin 2x}{3x}, \quad c = 0$

64. $f(x) = \dfrac{x(1 - \cos x)}{x - \sin x}, \quad c = 0$

65. $f(x) = \dfrac{\sqrt[3]{x} - 1}{x - 1}, \quad c = 1$

66. $f(x) = \dfrac{3x^2 - (7x + 1)\sqrt{x} + 5}{x - 1}, \quad c = 1$

2.4 One-Sided Limits

In this section we extend the limit concept to *one-sided limits*, which are limits as x approaches the number c from the left-hand side (where $x < c$) or the right-hand side $(x > c)$ only.

Approaching a Limit from One Side

To have a limit L as x approaches c, a function f must be defined on *both sides* of c and its values $f(x)$ must approach L as x approaches c from either side. Because of this, ordinary limits are called **two-sided**.

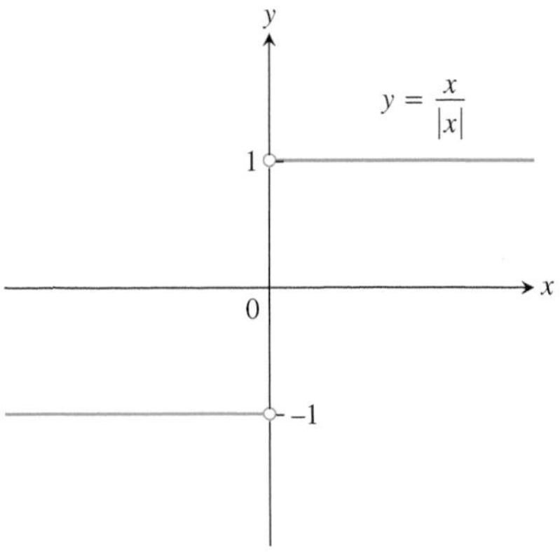

FIGURE 2.24 Different right-hand and left-hand limits at the origin.

If f fails to have a two-sided limit at c, it may still have a one-sided limit, that is, a limit if the approach is only from one side. If the approach is from the right, the limit is a **right-hand limit**. From the left, it is a **left-hand limit**.

The function $f(x) = x/|x|$ (Figure 2.24) has limit 1 as x approaches 0 from the right, and limit -1 as x approaches 0 from the left. Since these one-sided limit values are not the same, there is no single number that $f(x)$ approaches as x approaches 0. So $f(x)$ does not have a (two-sided) limit at 0.

Intuitively, if $f(x)$ is defined on an interval (c, b), where $c < b$, and approaches arbitrarily close to L as x approaches c from within that interval, then f has **right-hand limit** L at c. We write

$$\lim_{x \to c^+} f(x) = L.$$

The symbol "$x \to c^+$" means that we consider only values of x greater than c.

Similarly, if $f(x)$ is defined on an interval (a, c), where $a < c$ and approaches arbitrarily close to M as x approaches c from within that interval, then f has **left-hand limit** M at c. We write

$$\lim_{x \to c^-} f(x) = M.$$

The symbol "$x \to c^-$" means that we consider only x-values less than c.

These informal definitions of one-sided limits are illustrated in Figure 2.25. For the function $f(x) = x/|x|$ in Figure 2.24 we have

$$\lim_{x \to 0^+} f(x) = 1 \quad \text{and} \quad \lim_{x \to 0^-} f(x) = -1.$$

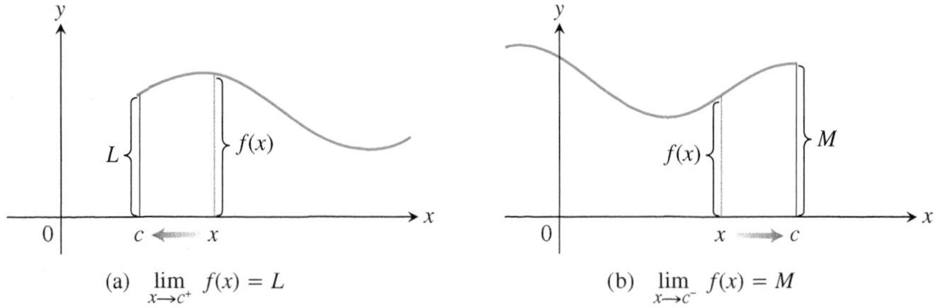

FIGURE 2.25 (a) Right-hand limit as x approaches c. (b) Left-hand limit as x approaches c.

EXAMPLE 1 The domain of $f(x) = \sqrt{4 - x^2}$ is $[-2, 2]$; its graph is the semicircle in Figure 2.26. We have

$$\lim_{x \to -2^+} \sqrt{4 - x^2} = 0 \quad \text{and} \quad \lim_{x \to 2^-} \sqrt{4 - x^2} = 0.$$

The function does not have a left-hand limit at $x = -2$ or a right-hand limit at $x = 2$. It does not have ordinary two-sided limits at either -2 or 2. ■

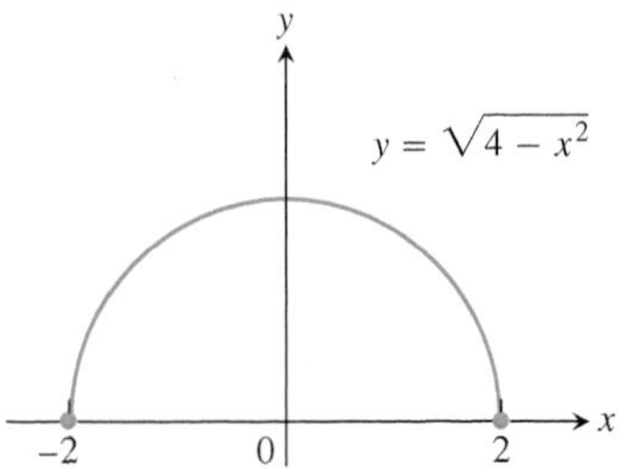

FIGURE 2.26 The function $f(x) = \sqrt{4 - x^2}$ has right-hand limit 0 at $x = -2$ and left-hand limit 0 at $x = 2$ (Example 1).

One-sided limits have all the properties listed in Theorem 1 in Section 2.2. The right-hand limit of the sum of two functions is the sum of their right-hand limits, and so on. The theorems for limits of polynomials and rational functions hold with one-sided limits, as do the Sandwich Theorem and Theorem 5. One-sided limits are related to limits in the following way.

THEOREM 6 A function $f(x)$ has a limit as x approaches c if and only if it has left-hand and right-hand limits there and these one-sided limits are equal:

$$\lim_{x \to c} f(x) = L \quad \Leftrightarrow \quad \lim_{x \to c^-} f(x) = L \quad \text{and} \quad \lim_{x \to c^+} f(x) = L.$$

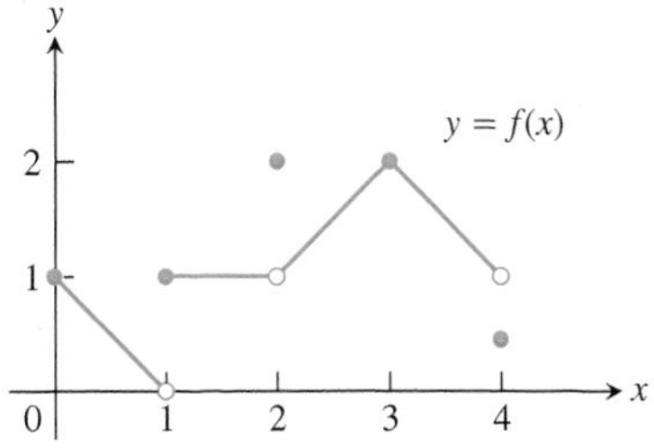

FIGURE 2.27 Graph of the function in Example 2.

EXAMPLE 2 For the function graphed in Figure 2.27,

At $x = 0$: $\lim_{x\to 0^+} f(x) = 1$,

$\lim_{x\to 0^-} f(x)$ and $\lim_{x\to 0} f(x)$ do not exist. The function is not defined to the left of $x = 0$.

At $x = 1$: $\lim_{x\to 1^-} f(x) = 0$ even though $f(1) = 1$,

$\lim_{x\to 1^+} f(x) = 1$,

$\lim_{x\to 1} f(x)$ does not exist. The right- and left-hand limits are not equal.

At $x = 2$: $\lim_{x\to 2^-} f(x) = 1$,

$\lim_{x\to 2^+} f(x) = 1$,

$\lim_{x\to 2} f(x) = 1$ even though $f(2) = 2$.

At $x = 3$: $\lim_{x\to 3^-} f(x) = \lim_{x\to 3^+} f(x) = \lim_{x\to 3} f(x) = f(3) = 2$.

At $x = 4$: $\lim_{x\to 4^-} f(x) = 1$ even though $f(4) \neq 1$,

$\lim_{x\to 4^+} f(x)$ and $\lim_{x\to 4} f(x)$ do not exist. The function is not defined to the right of $x = 4$.

At every other point c in $[0, 4]$, $f(x)$ has limit $f(c)$. ■

Precise Definitions of One-Sided Limits

The formal definition of the limit in Section 2.3 is readily modified for one-sided limits.

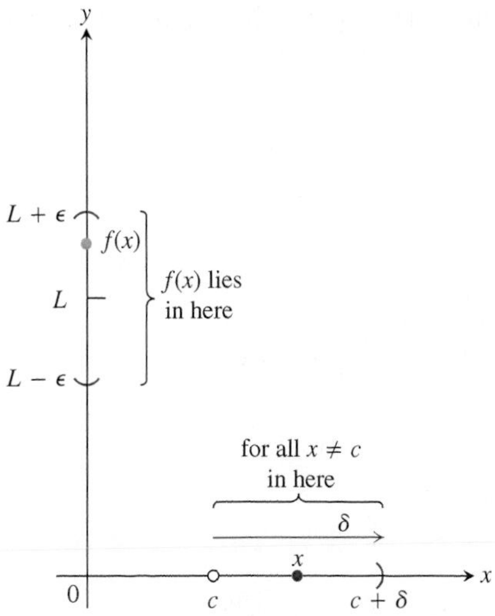

FIGURE 2.28 Intervals associated with the definition of right-hand limit.

DEFINITIONS We say that $f(x)$ has **right-hand limit L at c**, and write

$$\lim_{x\to c^+} f(x) = L \qquad \text{(see Figure 2.28)}$$

if for every number $\epsilon > 0$ there exists a corresponding number $\delta > 0$ such that for all x

$$c < x < c + \delta \quad \Rightarrow \quad |f(x) - L| < \epsilon.$$

We say that f has **left-hand limit L at c**, and write

$$\lim_{x\to c^-} f(x) = L \qquad \text{(see Figure 2.29)}$$

if for every number $\epsilon > 0$ there exists a corresponding number $\delta > 0$ such that for all x

$$c - \delta < x < c \quad \Rightarrow \quad |f(x) - L| < \epsilon.$$

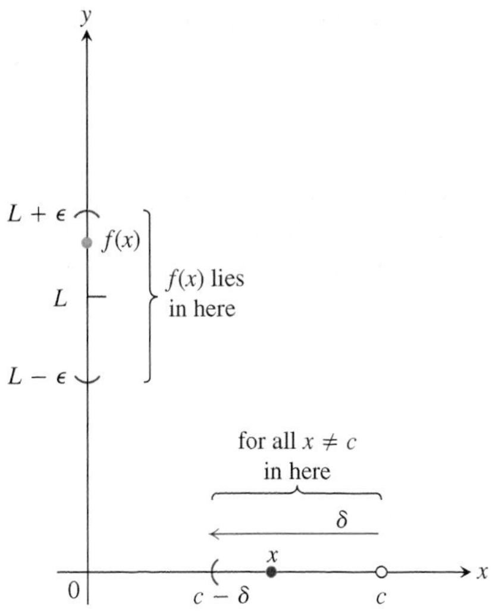

FIGURE 2.29 Intervals associated with the definition of left-hand limit.

EXAMPLE 3 Prove that

$$\lim_{x\to 0^+} \sqrt{x} = 0.$$

Solution Let $\epsilon > 0$ be given. Here $c = 0$ and $L = 0$, so we want to find a $\delta > 0$ such that for all x

$$0 < x < \delta \quad \Rightarrow \quad |\sqrt{x} - 0| < \epsilon,$$

or

$$0 < x < \delta \quad \Rightarrow \quad \sqrt{x} < \epsilon.$$

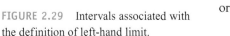

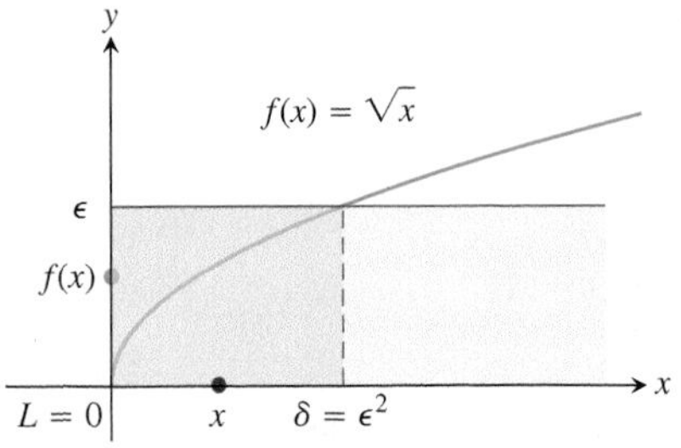

FIGURE 2.30 $\lim_{x \to 0^+} \sqrt{x} = 0$ in Example 3.

Squaring both sides of this last inequality gives

$$x < \epsilon^2 \quad \text{if} \quad 0 < x < \delta.$$

If we choose $\delta = \epsilon^2$ we have

$$0 < x < \delta = \epsilon^2 \quad \Rightarrow \quad \sqrt{x} < \epsilon,$$

or

$$0 < x < \epsilon^2 \quad \Rightarrow \quad |\sqrt{x} - 0| < \epsilon.$$

According to the definition, this shows that $\lim_{x \to 0^+} \sqrt{x} = 0$ (Figure 2.30). ■

The functions examined so far have had some kind of limit at each point of interest. In general, that need not be the case.

EXAMPLE 4 Show that $y = \sin(1/x)$ has no limit as x approaches zero from either side (Figure 2.31).

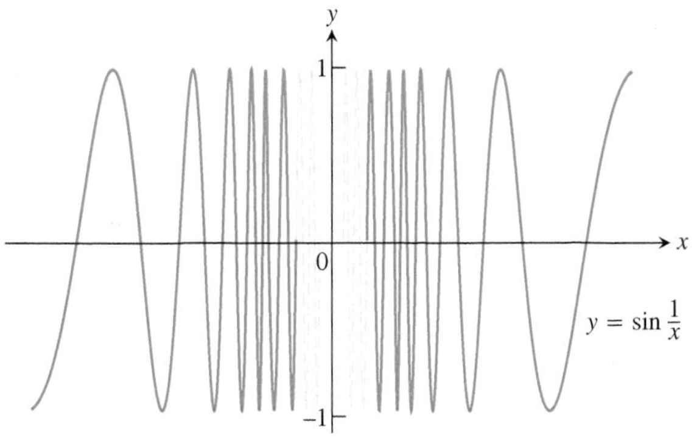

FIGURE 2.31 The function $y = \sin(1/x)$ has neither a right-hand nor a left-hand limit as x approaches zero (Example 4). The graph here omits values very near the y-axis.

Solution As x approaches zero, its reciprocal, $1/x$, grows without bound and the values of $\sin(1/x)$ cycle repeatedly from -1 to 1. There is no single number L that the function's values stay increasingly close to as x approaches zero. This is true even if we restrict x to positive values or to negative values. The function has neither a right-hand limit nor a left-hand limit at $x = 0$. ■

Limits Involving $(\sin \theta)/\theta$

A central fact about $(\sin \theta)/\theta$ is that in radian measure its limit as $\theta \to 0$ is 1. We can see this in Figure 2.32 and confirm it algebraically using the Sandwich Theorem. You will see the importance of this limit in Section 3.5, where instantaneous rates of change of the trigonometric functions are studied.

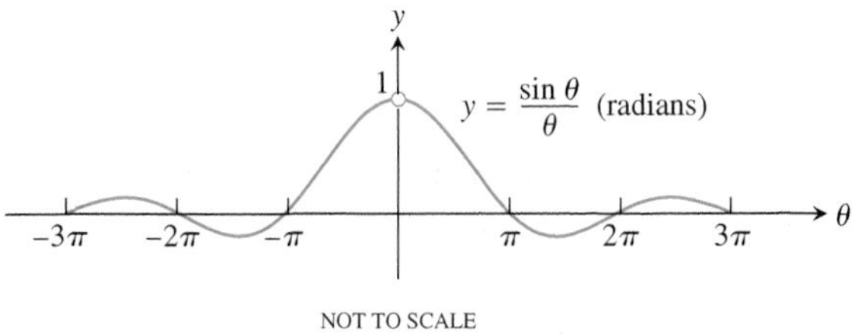

FIGURE 2.32 The graph of $f(\theta) = (\sin \theta)/\theta$ suggests that the right- and left-hand limits as θ approaches 0 are both 1.

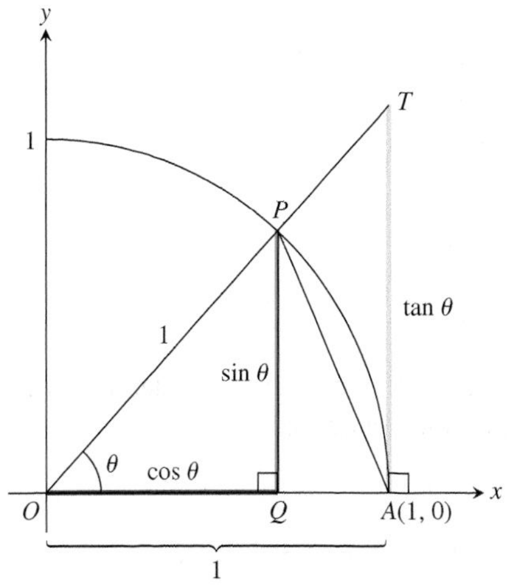

FIGURE 2.33 The figure for the proof of Theorem 7. By definition, $TA/OA = \tan\theta$, but $OA = 1$, so $TA = \tan\theta$.

THEOREM 7—Limit of the ratio $\sin\theta/\theta$ as $\theta \to 0$

$$\lim_{\theta\to 0} \frac{\sin\theta}{\theta} = 1 \qquad (\theta \text{ in radians}) \tag{1}$$

Proof The plan is to show that the right-hand and left-hand limits are both 1. Then we will know that the two-sided limit is 1 as well.

To show that the right-hand limit is 1, we begin with positive values of θ less than $\pi/2$ (Figure 2.33). Notice that

$$\text{Area } \Delta OAP < \text{ area sector } OAP < \text{ area } \Delta OAT.$$

We can express these areas in terms of θ as follows:

$$\begin{aligned} \text{Area } \Delta OAP &= \frac{1}{2}\text{base} \times \text{height} = \frac{1}{2}(1)(\sin\theta) = \frac{1}{2}\sin\theta \\ \text{Area sector } OAP &= \frac{1}{2}r^2\theta = \frac{1}{2}(1)^2\theta = \frac{\theta}{2} \\ \text{Area } \Delta OAT &= \frac{1}{2}\text{base} \times \text{height} = \frac{1}{2}(1)(\tan\theta) = \frac{1}{2}\tan\theta. \end{aligned} \tag{2}$$

Equation (2) is where radian measure comes in: The area of sector OAP is $\theta/2$ only if θ is measured in radians.

Thus,

$$\frac{1}{2}\sin\theta < \frac{1}{2}\theta < \frac{1}{2}\tan\theta.$$

This last inequality goes the same way if we divide all three terms by the number $(1/2)\sin\theta$, which is positive since $0 < \theta < \pi/2$:

$$1 < \frac{\theta}{\sin\theta} < \frac{1}{\cos\theta}.$$

Taking reciprocals reverses the inequalities:

$$1 > \frac{\sin\theta}{\theta} > \cos\theta.$$

Since $\lim_{\theta\to 0^+}\cos\theta = 1$ (Example 11b, Section 2.2), the Sandwich Theorem gives

$$\lim_{\theta\to 0^+} \frac{\sin\theta}{\theta} = 1.$$

Recall that $\sin\theta$ and θ are both *odd functions* (Section 1.1). Therefore, $f(\theta) = (\sin\theta)/\theta$ is an *even function*, with a graph symmetric about the y-axis (see Figure 2.32). This symmetry implies that the left-hand limit at 0 exists and has the same value as the right-hand limit:

$$\lim_{\theta\to 0^-} \frac{\sin\theta}{\theta} = 1 = \lim_{\theta\to 0^+} \frac{\sin\theta}{\theta},$$

so $\lim_{\theta\to 0}(\sin\theta)/\theta = 1$ by Theorem 6. ■

EXAMPLE 5 Show that **(a)** $\displaystyle\lim_{h\to 0} \frac{\cos h - 1}{h} = 0$ and **(b)** $\displaystyle\lim_{x\to 0} \frac{\sin 2x}{5x} = \frac{2}{5}$.

Solution

(a) Using the half-angle formula $\cos h = 1 - 2\sin^2(h/2)$, we calculate

$$\lim_{h\to 0}\frac{\cos h - 1}{h} = \lim_{h\to 0} -\frac{2\sin^2(h/2)}{h}$$

$$= -\lim_{\theta\to 0}\frac{\sin\theta}{\theta}\sin\theta \qquad \text{Let } \theta = h/2.$$

$$= -(1)(0) = 0. \qquad \text{Eq. (1) and Example 11a in Section 2.2}$$

(b) Equation (1) does not apply to the original fraction. We need a $2x$ in the denominator, not a $5x$. We produce it by multiplying numerator and denominator by $2/5$:

$$\lim_{x\to 0}\frac{\sin 2x}{5x} = \lim_{x\to 0}\frac{(2/5)\cdot\sin 2x}{(2/5)\cdot 5x}$$

$$= \frac{2}{5}\lim_{x\to 0}\frac{\sin 2x}{2x} \qquad \text{Now, Eq. (1) applies with } \theta = 2x.$$

$$= \frac{2}{5}(1) = \frac{2}{5}$$

■

EXAMPLE 6 Find $\lim_{t\to 0}\dfrac{\tan t\sec 2t}{3t}$.

Solution From the definition of $\tan t$ and $\sec 2t$, we have

$$\lim_{t\to 0}\frac{\tan t\sec 2t}{3t} = \frac{1}{3}\lim_{t\to 0}\frac{\sin t}{t}\cdot\frac{1}{\cos t}\cdot\frac{1}{\cos 2t}$$

$$= \frac{1}{3}(1)(1)(1) = \frac{1}{3}. \qquad \text{Eq. (1) and Example 11b in Section 2.2}$$

■

Exercises 2.4

Finding Limits Graphically

1. Which of the following statements about the function $y = f(x)$ graphed here are true, and which are false?

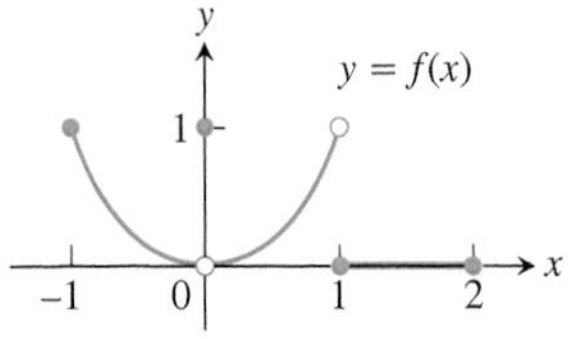

a. $\lim_{x\to -1^+} f(x) = 1$
b. $\lim_{x\to 0^-} f(x) = 0$
c. $\lim_{x\to 0^-} f(x) = 1$
d. $\lim_{x\to 0^-} f(x) = \lim_{x\to 0^+} f(x)$
e. $\lim_{x\to 0} f(x)$ exists.
f. $\lim_{x\to 0} f(x) = 0$
g. $\lim_{x\to 0} f(x) = 1$
h. $\lim_{x\to 1} f(x) = 1$
i. $\lim_{x\to 1} f(x) = 0$
j. $\lim_{x\to 2^-} f(x) = 2$
k. $\lim_{x\to -1^-} f(x)$ does not exist.
l. $\lim_{x\to 2^+} f(x) = 0$

2. Which of the following statements about the function $y = f(x)$ graphed here are true, and which are false?

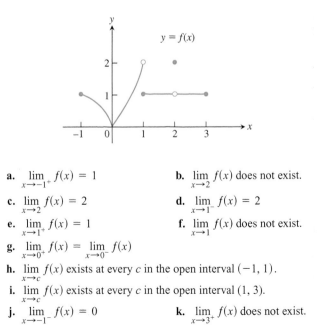

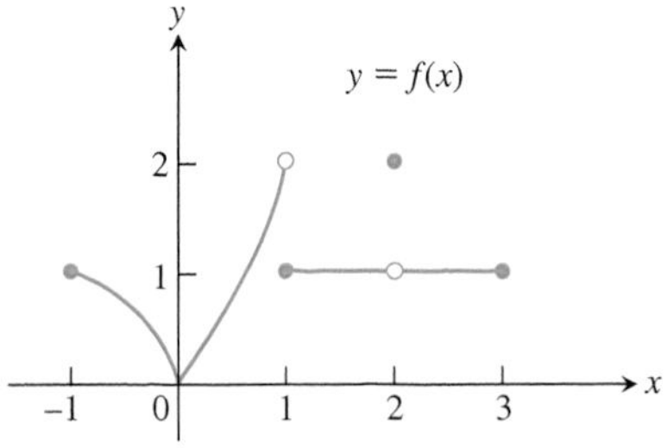

a. $\lim_{x\to -1^+} f(x) = 1$
b. $\lim_{x\to 2} f(x)$ does not exist.
c. $\lim_{x\to 2} f(x) = 2$
d. $\lim_{x\to 1^-} f(x) = 2$
e. $\lim_{x\to 1^+} f(x) = 1$
f. $\lim_{x\to 1} f(x)$ does not exist.
g. $\lim_{x\to 0^+} f(x) = \lim_{x\to 0^-} f(x)$
h. $\lim_{x\to c} f(x)$ exists at every c in the open interval $(-1, 1)$.
i. $\lim_{x\to c} f(x)$ exists at every c in the open interval $(1, 3)$.
j. $\lim_{x\to -1^-} f(x) = 0$
k. $\lim_{x\to 3^+} f(x)$ does not exist.

3. Let $f(x) = \begin{cases} 3 - x, & x < 2 \\ \dfrac{x}{2} + 1, & x > 2. \end{cases}$

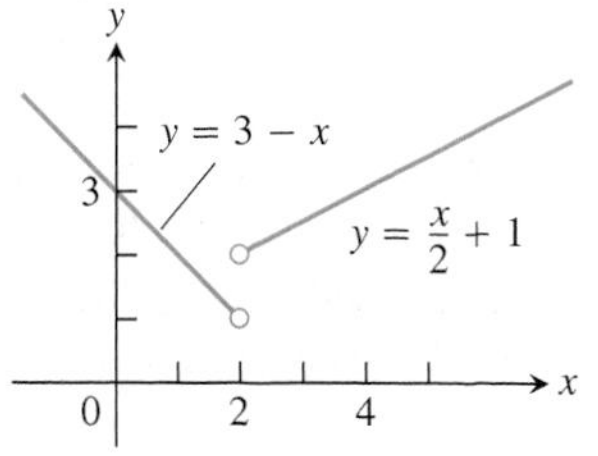

a. Find $\lim_{x \to 2^+} f(x)$ and $\lim_{x \to 2^-} f(x)$.

b. Does $\lim_{x \to 2} f(x)$ exist? If so, what is it? If not, why not?

c. Find $\lim_{x \to 4^-} f(x)$ and $\lim_{x \to 4^+} f(x)$.

d. Does $\lim_{x \to 4} f(x)$ exist? If so, what is it? If not, why not?

4. Let $f(x) = \begin{cases} 3 - x, & x < 2 \\ 2, & x = 2 \\ \dfrac{x}{2}, & x > 2. \end{cases}$

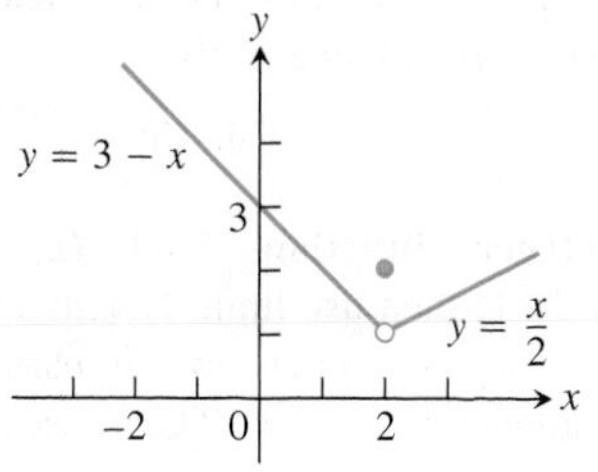

a. Find $\lim_{x \to 2^+} f(x)$, $\lim_{x \to 2^-} f(x)$, and $f(2)$.

b. Does $\lim_{x \to 2} f(x)$ exist? If so, what is it? If not, why not?

c. Find $\lim_{x \to -1^-} f(x)$ and $\lim_{x \to -1^+} f(x)$.

d. Does $\lim_{x \to -1} f(x)$ exist? If so, what is it? If not, why not?

5. Let $f(x) = \begin{cases} 0, & x \le 0 \\ \sin \dfrac{1}{x}, & x > 0. \end{cases}$

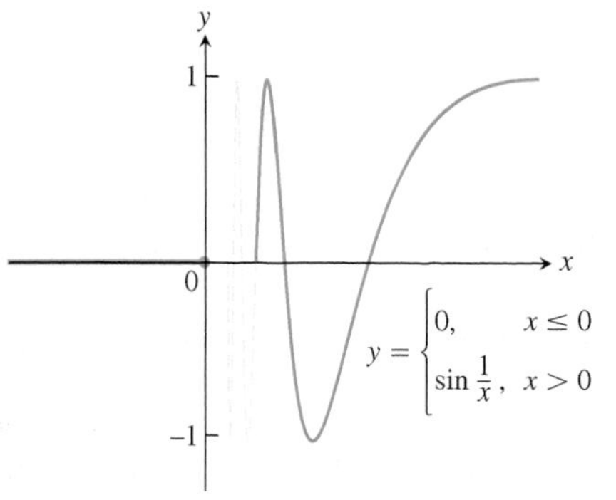

a. Does $\lim_{x \to 0^+} f(x)$ exist? If so, what is it? If not, why not?

b. Does $\lim_{x \to 0^-} f(x)$ exist? If so, what is it? If not, why not?

c. Does $\lim_{x \to 0} f(x)$ exist? If so, what is it? If not, why not?

6. Let $g(x) = \sqrt{x} \sin(1/x)$.

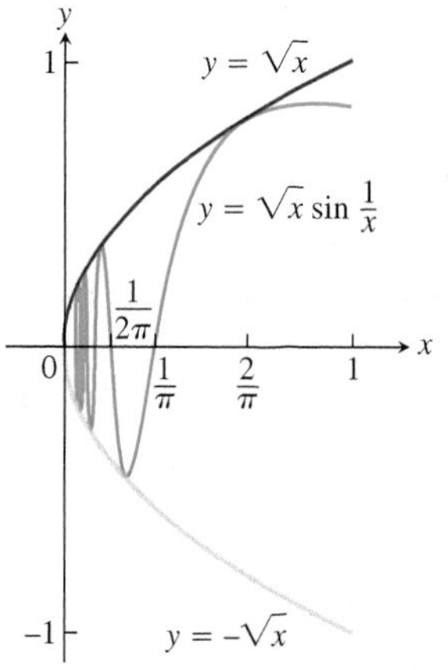

a. Does $\lim_{x \to 0^+} g(x)$ exist? If so, what is it? If not, why not?

b. Does $\lim_{x \to 0^-} g(x)$ exist? If so, what is it? If not, why not?

c. Does $\lim_{x \to 0} g(x)$ exist? If so, what is it? If not, why not?

7. **a.** Graph $f(x) = \begin{cases} x^3, & x \ne 1 \\ 0, & x = 1. \end{cases}$

b. Find $\lim_{x \to 1^-} f(x)$ and $\lim_{x \to 1^+} f(x)$.

c. Does $\lim_{x \to 1} f(x)$ exist? If so, what is it? If not, why not?

8. **a.** Graph $f(x) = \begin{cases} 1 - x^2, & x \ne 1 \\ 2, & x = 1. \end{cases}$

b. Find $\lim_{x \to 1^+} f(x)$ and $\lim_{x \to 1^-} f(x)$.

c. Does $\lim_{x \to 1} f(x)$ exist? If so, what is it? If not, why not?

Graph the functions in Exercises 9 and 10. Then answer these questions.

a. What are the domain and range of f?

b. At what points c, if any, does $\lim_{x \to c} f(x)$ exist?

c. At what points does only the left-hand limit exist?

d. At what points does only the right-hand limit exist?

9. $f(x) = \begin{cases} \sqrt{1 - x^2}, & 0 \le x < 1 \\ 1, & 1 \le x < 2 \\ 2, & x = 2 \end{cases}$

10. $f(x) = \begin{cases} x, & -1 \le x < 0, \text{ or } 0 < x \le 1 \\ 1, & x = 0 \\ 0, & x < -1 \text{ or } x > 1 \end{cases}$

Finding One-Sided Limits Algebraically

Find the limits in Exercises 11–18.

11. $\lim_{x \to -0.5^-} \sqrt{\dfrac{x + 2}{x + 1}}$

12. $\lim_{x \to 1^+} \sqrt{\dfrac{x - 1}{x + 2}}$

13. $\lim_{x \to -2^+} \left(\dfrac{x}{x + 1}\right)\left(\dfrac{2x + 5}{x^2 + x}\right)$

14. $\lim_{x \to 1^-} \left(\dfrac{1}{x + 1}\right)\left(\dfrac{x + 6}{x}\right)\left(\dfrac{3 - x}{7}\right)$

15. $\lim_{h \to 0^+} \dfrac{\sqrt{h^2 + 4h + 5} - \sqrt{5}}{h}$

16. $\lim_{h\to 0^-} \dfrac{\sqrt{6} - \sqrt{5h^2 + 11h + 6}}{h}$

17. a. $\lim_{x\to -2^+} (x + 3)\dfrac{|x + 2|}{x + 2}$ b. $\lim_{x\to -2^-} (x + 3)\dfrac{|x + 2|}{x + 2}$

18. a. $\lim_{x\to 1^+} \dfrac{\sqrt{2x}\,(x - 1)}{|x - 1|}$ b. $\lim_{x\to 1^-} \dfrac{\sqrt{2x}\,(x - 1)}{|x - 1|}$

Use the graph of the greatest integer function $y = \lfloor x \rfloor$, Figure 1.10 in Section 1.1, to help you find the limits in Exercises 19 and 20.

19. a. $\lim_{\theta\to 3^+} \dfrac{\lfloor \theta \rfloor}{\theta}$ b. $\lim_{\theta\to 3^-} \dfrac{\lfloor \theta \rfloor}{\theta}$

20. a. $\lim_{t\to 4^+} (t - \lfloor t \rfloor)$ b. $\lim_{t\to 4^-} (t - \lfloor t \rfloor)$

Using $\lim_{\theta\to 0} \dfrac{\sin \theta}{\theta} = 1$

Find the limits in Exercises 21–42.

21. $\lim_{\theta\to 0} \dfrac{\sin \sqrt{2}\theta}{\sqrt{2}\theta}$

22. $\lim_{t\to 0} \dfrac{\sin kt}{t}$ (k constant)

23. $\lim_{y\to 0} \dfrac{\sin 3y}{4y}$

24. $\lim_{h\to 0^-} \dfrac{h}{\sin 3h}$

25. $\lim_{x\to 0} \dfrac{\tan 2x}{x}$

26. $\lim_{t\to 0} \dfrac{2t}{\tan t}$

27. $\lim_{x\to 0} \dfrac{x \csc 2x}{\cos 5x}$

28. $\lim_{x\to 0} 6x^2(\cot x)(\csc 2x)$

29. $\lim_{x\to 0} \dfrac{x + x \cos x}{\sin x \cos x}$

30. $\lim_{x\to 0} \dfrac{x^2 - x + \sin x}{2x}$

31. $\lim_{\theta\to 0} \dfrac{1 - \cos \theta}{\sin 2\theta}$

32. $\lim_{x\to 0} \dfrac{x - x \cos x}{\sin^2 3x}$

33. $\lim_{t\to 0} \dfrac{\sin (1 - \cos t)}{1 - \cos t}$

34. $\lim_{h\to 0} \dfrac{\sin (\sin h)}{\sin h}$

35. $\lim_{\theta\to 0} \dfrac{\sin \theta}{\sin 2\theta}$

36. $\lim_{x\to 0} \dfrac{\sin 5x}{\sin 4x}$

37. $\lim_{\theta\to 0} \theta \cos \theta$

38. $\lim_{\theta\to 0} \sin \theta \cot 2\theta$

39. $\lim_{x\to 0} \dfrac{\tan 3x}{\sin 8x}$

40. $\lim_{y\to 0} \dfrac{\sin 3y \cot 5y}{y \cot 4y}$

41. $\lim_{\theta\to 0} \dfrac{\tan \theta}{\theta^2 \cot 3\theta}$

42. $\lim_{\theta\to 0} \dfrac{\theta \cot 4\theta}{\sin^2 \theta \cot^2 2\theta}$

Theory and Examples

43. Once you know $\lim_{x\to a^+} f(x)$ and $\lim_{x\to a^-} f(x)$ at an interior point of the domain of f, do you then know $\lim_{x\to a} f(x)$? Give reasons for your answer.

44. If you know that $\lim_{x\to c} f(x)$ exists, can you find its value by calculating $\lim_{x\to c^+} f(x)$? Give reasons for your answer.

45. Suppose that f is an odd function of x. Does knowing that $\lim_{x\to 0^+} f(x) = 3$ tell you anything about $\lim_{x\to 0^-} f(x)$? Give reasons for your answer.

46. Suppose that f is an even function of x. Does knowing that $\lim_{x\to 2^-} f(x) = 7$ tell you anything about either $\lim_{x\to -2^-} f(x)$ or $\lim_{x\to -2^+} f(x)$? Give reasons for your answer.

Formal Definitions of One-Sided Limits

47. Given $\epsilon > 0$, find an interval $I = (5, 5 + \delta)$, $\delta > 0$, such that if x lies in I, then $\sqrt{x - 5} < \epsilon$. What limit is being verified and what is its value?

48. Given $\epsilon > 0$, find an interval $I = (4 - \delta, 4)$, $\delta > 0$, such that if x lies in I, then $\sqrt{4 - x} < \epsilon$. What limit is being verified and what is its value?

Use the definitions of right-hand and left-hand limits to prove the limit statements in Exercises 49 and 50.

49. $\lim_{x\to 0^-} \dfrac{x}{|x|} = -1$

50. $\lim_{x\to 2^+} \dfrac{x - 2}{|x - 2|} = 1$

51. **Greatest integer function** Find **(a)** $\lim_{x\to 400^+} \lfloor x \rfloor$ and **(b)** $\lim_{x\to 400^-} \lfloor x \rfloor$; then use limit definitions to verify your findings. **(c)** Based on your conclusions in parts (a) and (b), can you say anything about $\lim_{x\to 400} \lfloor x \rfloor$? Give reasons for your answer.

52. **One-sided limits** Let $f(x) = \begin{cases} x^2 \sin (1/x), & x < 0 \\ \sqrt{x}, & x > 0. \end{cases}$

Find **(a)** $\lim_{x\to 0^+} f(x)$ and **(b)** $\lim_{x\to 0^-} f(x)$; then use limit definitions to verify your findings. **(c)** Based on your conclusions in parts (a) and (b), can you say anything about $\lim_{x\to 0} f(x)$? Give reasons for your answer.

2.5 Continuity

When we plot function values generated in a laboratory or collected in the field, we often connect the plotted points with an unbroken curve to show what the function's values are likely to have been at the times we did not measure (Figure 2.34). In doing so, we are assuming that we are working with a *continuous function*, so its outputs vary continuously with the inputs and do not jump from one value to another without taking on the values in between. The limit of a continuous function as x approaches c can be found simply by calculating the value of the function at c. (We found this to be true for polynomials in Theorem 2.)

Intuitively, any function $y = f(x)$ whose graph can be sketched over its domain in one continuous motion without lifting the pencil is an example of a continuous function. In this section we investigate more precisely what it means for a function to be continuous.

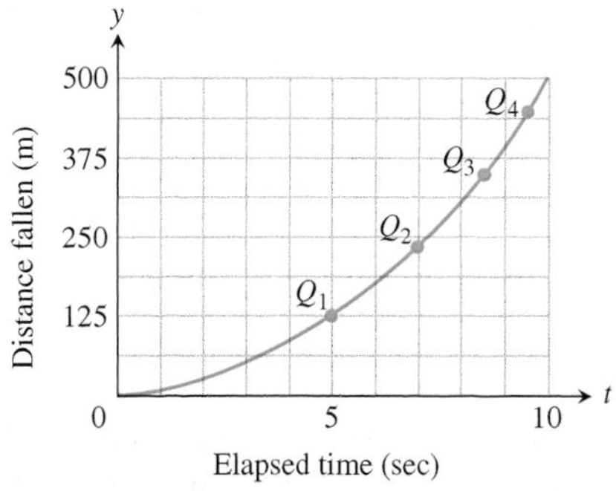

FIGURE 2.34 Connecting plotted points by an unbroken curve from experimental data $Q_1, Q_2, Q_3, \ldots$ for a falling object.

We also study the properties of continuous functions, and see that many of the function types presented in Section 1.1 are continuous.

Continuity at a Point

To understand continuity, it helps to consider a function like that in Figure 2.35, whose limits we investigated in Example 2 in the last section.

EXAMPLE 1 Find the points at which the function f in Figure 2.35 is continuous and the points at which f is not continuous.

Solution The function f is continuous at every point in its domain $[0, 4]$ except at $x = 1, x = 2$, and $x = 4$. At these points, there are breaks in the graph. Note the relationship between the limit of f and the value of f at each point of the function's domain.

Points at which f is continuous:

At $x = 0$, $\lim_{x \to 0^+} f(x) = f(0)$.

At $x = 3$, $\lim_{x \to 3} f(x) = f(3)$.

At $0 < c < 4, c \neq 1, 2$, $\lim_{x \to c} f(x) = f(c)$.

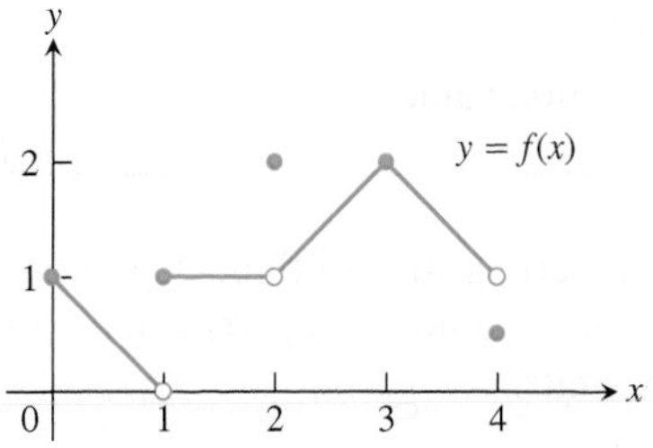

FIGURE 2.35 The function is continuous on $[0, 4]$ except at $x = 1, x = 2$, and $x = 4$ (Example 1).

Points at which f is not continuous:

At $x = 1$, $\lim_{x \to 1} f(x)$ does not exist.

At $x = 2$, $\lim_{x \to 2} f(x) = 1$, but $1 \neq f(2)$.

At $x = 4$, $\lim_{x \to 4^-} f(x) = 1$, but $1 \neq f(4)$.

At $c < 0, c > 4$, these points are not in the domain of f. ∎

To define continuity at a point in a function's domain, we need to define continuity at an interior point (which involves a two-sided limit) and continuity at an endpoint (which involves a one-sided limit) (Figure 2.36).

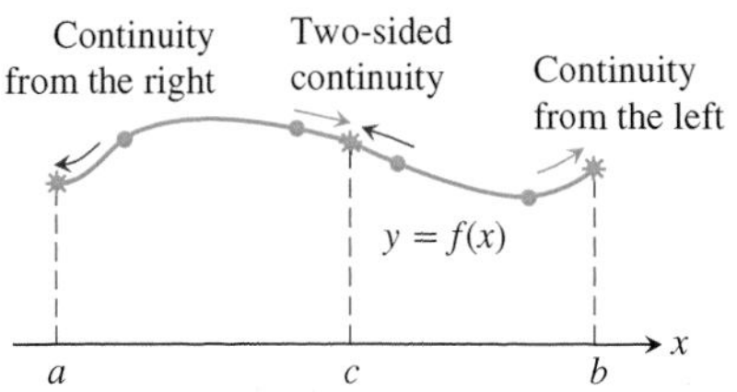

FIGURE 2.36 Continuity at points a, b, and c.

DEFINITION

Interior point: A function $y = f(x)$ is **continuous at an interior point c** of its domain if

$$\lim_{x \to c} f(x) = f(c).$$

Endpoint: A function $y = f(x)$ is **continuous at a left endpoint a** or is **continuous at a right endpoint b** of its domain if

$$\lim_{x \to a^+} f(x) = f(a) \quad \text{or} \quad \lim_{x \to b^-} f(x) = f(b), \quad \text{respectively.}$$

If a function f is not continuous at a point c, we say that f is **discontinuous** at c and that c is a **point of discontinuity** of f. Note that c need not be in the domain of f.

A function f is **right-continuous (continuous from the right)** at a point $x = c$ in its domain if $\lim_{x \to c^+} f(x) = f(c)$. It is **left-continuous (continuous from the left)** at c if $\lim_{x \to c^-} f(x) = f(c)$. Thus, a function is continuous at a left endpoint a of its domain if it is right-continuous at a and continuous at a right endpoint b of its domain if it is left-continuous at b. A function is continuous at an interior point c of its domain if and only if it is both right-continuous and left-continuous at c (Figure 2.36).

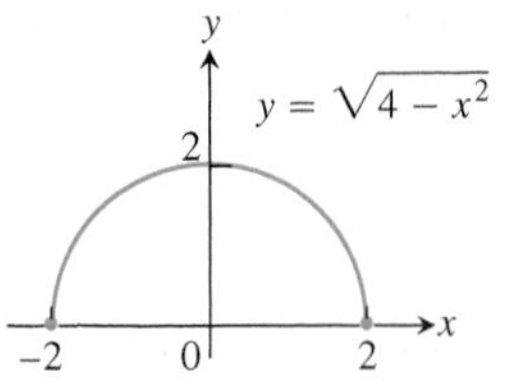

FIGURE 2.37 A function that is continuous at every domain point (Example 2).

EXAMPLE 2 The function $f(x) = \sqrt{4 - x^2}$ is continuous at every point of its domain $[-2, 2]$ (Figure 2.37), including $x = -2$, where f is right-continuous, and $x = 2$, where f is left-continuous. ■

EXAMPLE 3 The unit step function $U(x)$, graphed in Figure 2.38, is right-continuous at $x = 0$, but is neither left-continuous nor continuous there. It has a jump discontinuity at $x = 0$. ■

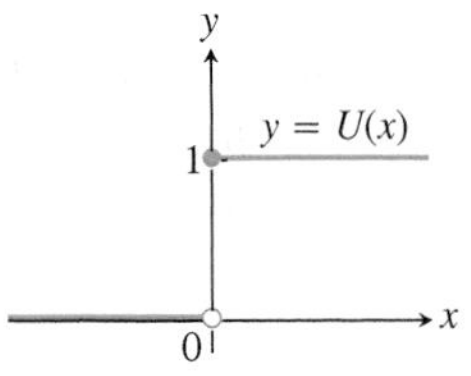

FIGURE 2.38 A function that has a jump discontinuity at the origin (Example 3).

We summarize continuity at a point in the form of a test.

Continuity Test

A function $f(x)$ is continuous at an interior point $x = c$ of its domain if and only if it meets the following three conditions.

1. $f(c)$ exists (c lies in the domain of f).
2. $\lim_{x \to c} f(x)$ exists (f has a limit as $x \to c$).
3. $\lim_{x \to c} f(x) = f(c)$ (the limit equals the function value).

When we say a function is continuous at c, we are asserting that all three conditions hold. For one-sided continuity and continuity at an endpoint, the limits in parts 2 and 3 of the test should be replaced by the appropriate one-sided limits.

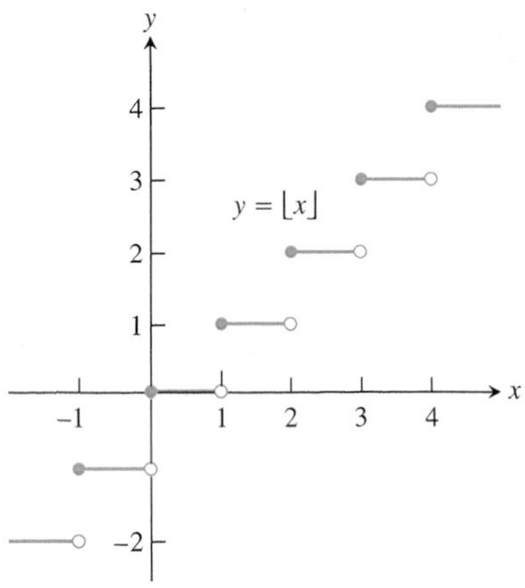

FIGURE 2.39 The greatest integer function is continuous at every noninteger point. It is right-continuous, but not left-continuous, at every integer point (Example 4).

EXAMPLE 4 The function $y = \lfloor x \rfloor$ introduced in Section 1.1 is graphed in Figure 2.39. It is discontinuous at every integer because the left-hand and right-hand limits are not equal as $x \to n$:

$$\lim_{x \to n^-} \lfloor x \rfloor = n - 1 \quad \text{and} \quad \lim_{x \to n^+} \lfloor x \rfloor = n.$$

Since $\lfloor n \rfloor = n$, the greatest integer function is right-continuous at every integer n (but not left-continuous).

The greatest integer function is continuous at every real number other than the integers. For example,

$$\lim_{x \to 1.5} \lfloor x \rfloor = 1 = \lfloor 1.5 \rfloor.$$

In general, if $n - 1 < c < n$, n an integer, then

$$\lim_{x \to c} \lfloor x \rfloor = n - 1 = \lfloor c \rfloor.$$ ■

Figure 2.40 displays several common types of discontinuities. The function in Figure 2.40a is continuous at $x = 0$. The function in Figure 2.40b would be continuous if it had $f(0) = 1$. The function in Figure 2.40c would be continuous if $f(0)$ were 1 instead of 2. The discontinuities in Figure 2.40b and c are **removable**. Each function has a limit as $x \to 0$, and we can remove the discontinuity by setting $f(0)$ equal to this limit.

The discontinuities in Figure 2.40d through f are more serious: $\lim_{x \to 0} f(x)$ does not exist, and there is no way to improve the situation by changing f at 0. The step function in Figure 2.40d has a **jump discontinuity**: The one-sided limits exist but have different values. The function $f(x) = 1/x^2$ in Figure 2.40e has an **infinite discontinuity**. The function in Figure 2.40f has an **oscillating discontinuity**: It oscillates too much to have a limit as $x \to 0$.

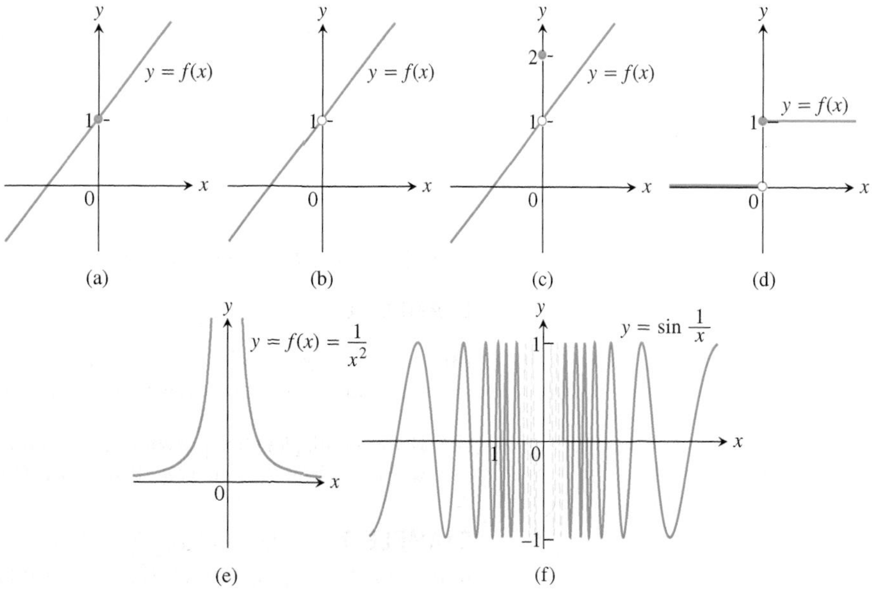

FIGURE 2.40 The function in (a) is continuous at $x = 0$; the functions in (b) through (f) are not.

Continuous Functions

A function is **continuous on an interval** if and only if it is continuous at every point of the interval. For example, the semicircle function graphed in Figure 2.37 is continuous on the interval $[-2, 2]$, which is its domain. A **continuous function** is one that is continuous at every point of its domain. A continuous function need not be continuous on every interval.

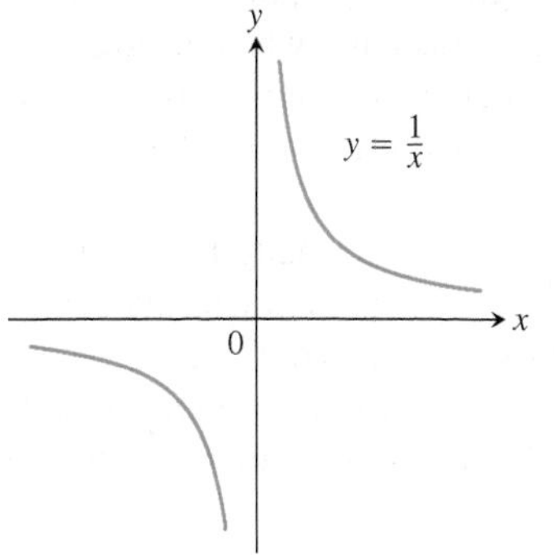

FIGURE 2.41 The function $y = 1/x$ is continuous at every value of x except $x = 0$. It has a point of discontinuity at $x = 0$ (Example 5).

EXAMPLE 5

(a) The function $y = 1/x$ (Figure 2.41) is a continuous function because it is continuous at every point of its domain. It has a point of discontinuity at $x = 0$, however, because it is not defined there; that is, it is discontinuous on any interval containing $x = 0$.

(b) The identity function $f(x) = x$ and constant functions are continuous everywhere by Example 3, Section 2.3. ■

Algebraic combinations of continuous functions are continuous wherever they are defined.

THEOREM 8—Properties of Continuous Functions If the functions f and g are continuous at $x = c$, then the following combinations are continuous at $x = c$.

1. *Sums:* $f + g$
2. *Differences:* $f - g$
3. *Constant multiples:* $k \cdot f$, for any number k
4. *Products:* $f \cdot g$
5. *Quotients:* f/g, provided $g(c) \neq 0$
6. *Powers:* f^n, n a positive integer
7. *Roots:* $\sqrt[n]{f}$, provided the root is defined on an open interval containing c, where n is a positive integer

Most of the results in Theorem 8 follow from the limit rules in Theorem 1, Section 2.2. For instance, to prove the sum property we have

$$\begin{aligned}\lim_{x\to c}(f+g)(x) &= \lim_{x\to c}(f(x)+g(x)) \\ &= \lim_{x\to c} f(x) + \lim_{x\to c} g(x), && \text{Sum Rule, Theorem 1} \\ &= f(c)+g(c) && \text{Continuity of } f, g \text{ at } c \\ &= (f+g)(c).\end{aligned}$$

This shows that $f + g$ is continuous.

EXAMPLE 6

(a) Every polynomial $P(x) = a_n x^n + a_{n-1}x^{n-1} + \cdots + a_0$ is continuous because $\lim_{x\to c} P(x) = P(c)$ by Theorem 2, Section 2.2.

(b) If $P(x)$ and $Q(x)$ are polynomials, then the rational function $P(x)/Q(x)$ is continuous wherever it is defined $(Q(c) \neq 0)$ by Theorem 3, Section 2.2. ■

EXAMPLE 7 The function $f(x) = |x|$ is continuous at every value of x. If $x > 0$, we have $f(x) = x$, a polynomial. If $x < 0$, we have $f(x) = -x$, another polynomial. Finally, at the origin, $\lim_{x\to 0}|x| = 0 = |0|$. ■

The functions $y = \sin x$ and $y = \cos x$ are continuous at $x = 0$ by Example 11 of Section 2.2. Both functions are, in fact, continuous everywhere (see Exercise 70). It follows from Theorem 8 that all six trigonometric functions are then continuous wherever they are defined. For example, $y = \tan x$ is continuous on $\cdots \cup (-\pi/2, \pi/2) \cup (\pi/2, 3\pi/2) \cup \cdots$.

Inverse Functions and Continuity

The inverse function of any function continuous on an interval is continuous over its domain. This result is suggested from the observation that the graph of f^{-1}, being the reflection of the graph of f across the line $y = x$, cannot have any breaks in it when the graph of f has no breaks. A rigorous proof that f^{-1} is continuous whenever f is continuous on an interval is given in more advanced texts. It follows that the inverse trigonometric functions are all continuous over their domains.

We defined the exponential function $y = a^x$ in Section 1.5 informally by its graph. Recall that the graph was obtained from the graph of $y = a^x$ for x a rational number by filling in the holes at the irrational points x, so the function $y = a^x$ was defined to be continuous over the entire real line. The inverse function $y = \log_a x$ is also continuous. In particular, the natural exponential function $y = e^x$ and the natural logarithm function $y = \ln x$ are both continuous over their domains.

Composites

All composites of continuous functions are continuous. The idea is that if $f(x)$ is continuous at $x = c$ and $g(x)$ is continuous at $x = f(c)$, then $g \circ f$ is continuous at $x = c$ (Figure 2.42). In this case, the limit as $x \to c$ is $g(f(c))$.

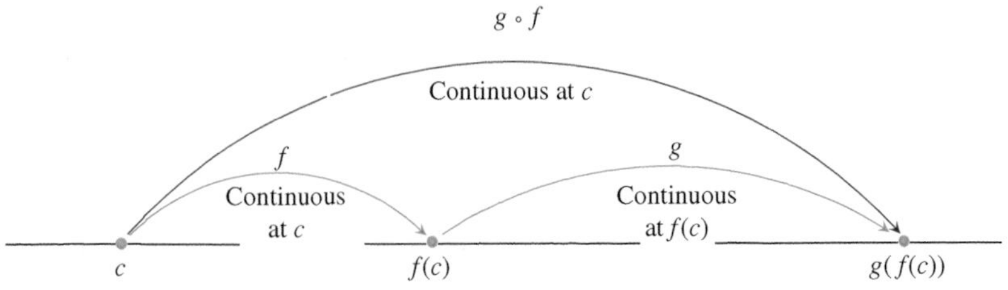

FIGURE 2.42 Composites of continuous functions are continuous.

THEOREM 9—Composite of Continuous Functions If f is continuous at c and g is continuous at $f(c)$, then the composite $g \circ f$ is continuous at c.

Intuitively, Theorem 9 is reasonable because if x is close to c, then $f(x)$ is close to $f(c)$, and since g is continuous at $f(c)$, it follows that $g(f(x))$ is close to $g(f(c))$.

The continuity of composites holds for any finite number of functions. The only requirement is that each function be continuous where it is applied. For an outline of a proof of Theorem 9, see Exercise 6 in Appendix 5.

EXAMPLE 8 Show that the following functions are continuous everywhere on their respective domains.

(a) $y = \sqrt{x^2 - 2x - 5}$ **(b)** $y = \dfrac{x^{2/3}}{1 + x^4}$

(c) $y = \left|\dfrac{x - 2}{x^2 - 2}\right|$ **(d)** $y = \left|\dfrac{x \sin x}{x^2 + 2}\right|$

Solution

(a) The square root function is continuous on $[0, \infty)$ because it is a root of the continuous identity function $f(x) = x$ (Part 7, Theorem 8). The given function is then the composite of the polynomial $f(x) = x^2 - 2x - 5$ with the square root function $g(t) = \sqrt{t}$, and is continuous on its domain.

(b) The numerator is the cube root of the identity function squared; the denominator is an everywhere-positive polynomial. Therefore, the quotient is continuous.

(c) The quotient $(x - 2)/(x^2 - 2)$ is continuous for all $x \neq \pm\sqrt{2}$, and the function is the composition of this quotient with the continuous absolute value function (Example 7).

(d) Because the sine function is everywhere-continuous (Exercise 70), the numerator term $x \sin x$ is the product of continuous functions, and the denominator term $x^2 + 2$ is an everywhere-positive polynomial. The given function is the composite of a quotient of continuous functions with the continuous absolute value function (Figure 2.43). ■

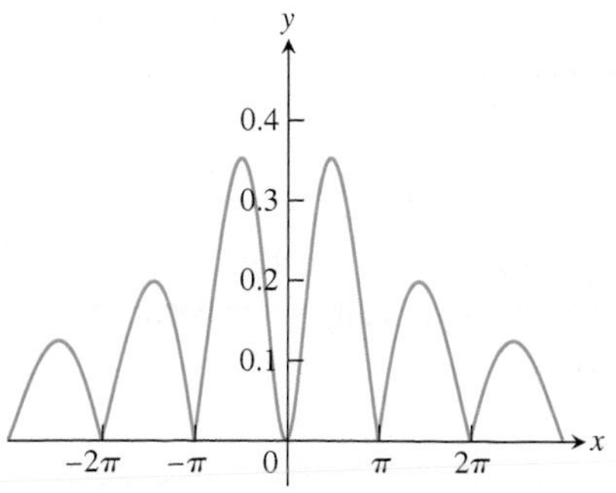

FIGURE 2.43 The graph suggests that $y = |(x \sin x)/(x^2 + 2)|$ is continuous (Example 8d).

Theorem 9 is actually a consequence of a more general result which we now state and prove.

THEOREM 10—Limits of Continuous Functions If g is continuous at the point b and $\lim_{x\to c} f(x) = b$, then

$$\lim_{x\to c} g(f(x)) = g(b) = g(\lim_{x\to c} f(x)).$$

Proof Let $\epsilon > 0$ be given. Since g is continuous at b, there exists a number $\delta_1 > 0$ such that

$$|g(y) - g(b)| < \epsilon \quad \text{whenever} \quad 0 < |y - b| < \delta_1.$$

Since $\lim_{x\to c} f(x) = b$, there exists a $\delta > 0$ such that

$$|f(x) - b| < \delta_1 \quad \text{whenever} \quad 0 < |x - c| < \delta.$$

If we let $y = f(x)$, we then have that

$$|y - b| < \delta_1 \quad \text{whenever} \quad 0 < |x - c| < \delta,$$

which implies from the first statement that $|g(y) - g(b)| = |g(f(x)) - g(b)| < \epsilon$ whenever $0 < |x - c| < \delta$. From the definition of limit, this proves that $\lim_{x\to c} g(f(x)) = g(b)$. ■

EXAMPLE 9 As an application of Theorem 10, we have the following calculations.

(a) $$\lim_{x\to\pi/2} \cos\left(2x + \sin\left(\frac{3\pi}{2} + x\right)\right) = \cos\left(\lim_{x\to\pi/2} 2x + \lim_{x\to\pi/2} \sin\left(\frac{3\pi}{2} + x\right)\right)$$
$$= \cos(\pi + \sin 2\pi) = \cos \pi = -1.$$

(b) $$\lim_{x\to1} \sin^{-1}\left(\frac{1-x}{1-x^2}\right) = \sin^{-1}\left(\lim_{x\to1} \frac{1-x}{1-x^2}\right)$$ Arcsine is continuous.
$$= \sin^{-1}\left(\lim_{x\to1} \frac{1}{1+x}\right)$$ Cancel common factor $(1 - x)$.
$$= \sin^{-1}\frac{1}{2} = \frac{\pi}{6}$$

We sometimes denote e^u by $\exp u$ when u is a complicated mathematical expression.

(c) $$\lim_{x\to0} \sqrt{x+1}\, e^{\tan x} = \lim_{x\to0} \sqrt{x+1} \cdot \exp\left(\lim_{x\to0} \tan x\right)$$ Exponential is continuous.
$$= 1 \cdot e^0 = 1$$ ■

Intermediate Value Theorem for Continuous Functions

Functions that are continuous on intervals have properties that make them particularly useful in mathematics and its applications. One of these is the *Intermediate Value Property*. A function is said to have the **Intermediate Value Property** if whenever it takes on two values, it also takes on all the values in between.

THEOREM 11—The Intermediate Value Theorem for Continuous Functions If f is a continuous function on a closed interval $[a, b]$, and if y_0 is any value between $f(a)$ and $f(b)$, then $y_0 = f(c)$ for some c in $[a, b]$.

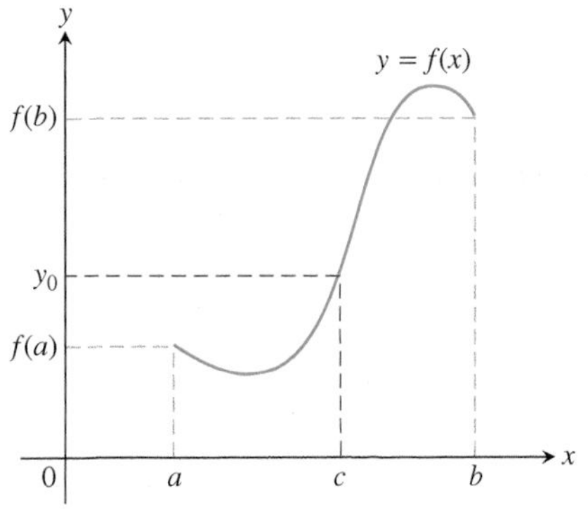

Theorem 11 says that continuous functions over *finite closed* intervals have the Intermediate Value Property. Geometrically, the Intermediate Value Theorem says that any horizontal line $y = y_0$ crossing the y-axis between the numbers $f(a)$ and $f(b)$ will cross the curve $y = f(x)$ at least once over the interval $[a, b]$.

The proof of the Intermediate Value Theorem depends on the completeness property of the real number system (Appendix 7) and can be found in more advanced texts.

The continuity of f on the interval is essential to Theorem 11. If f is discontinuous at even one point of the interval, the theorem's conclusion may fail, as it does for the function graphed in Figure 2.44 (choose y_0 as any number between 2 and 3).

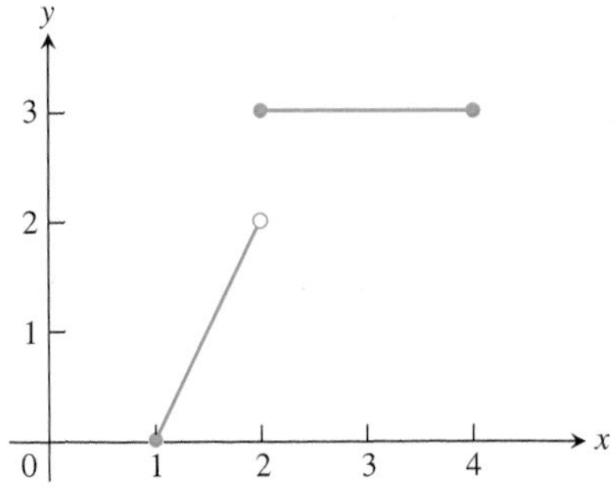

FIGURE 2.44 The function $f(x) = \begin{cases} 2x - 2, & 1 \le x < 2 \\ 3, & 2 \le x \le 4 \end{cases}$ does not take on all values between $f(1) = 0$ and $f(4) = 3$; it misses all the values between 2 and 3.

A Consequence for Graphing: Connectedness Theorem 11 implies that the graph of a function continuous on an interval cannot have any breaks over the interval. It will be **connected**—a single, unbroken curve. It will not have jumps like the graph of the greatest integer function (Figure 2.39), or separate branches like the graph of $1/x$ (Figure 2.41).

A Consequence for Root Finding We call a solution of the equation $f(x) = 0$ a **root** of the equation or **zero** of the function f. The Intermediate Value Theorem tells us that if f is continuous, then any interval on which f changes sign contains a zero of the function.

In practical terms, when we see the graph of a continuous function cross the horizontal axis on a computer screen, we know it is not stepping across. There really is a point where the function's value is zero.

EXAMPLE 10 Show that there is a root of the equation $x^3 - x - 1 = 0$ between 1 and 2.

Solution Let $f(x) = x^3 - x - 1$. Since $f(1) = 1 - 1 - 1 = -1 < 0$ and $f(2) = 2^3 - 2 - 1 = 5 > 0$, we see that $y_0 = 0$ is a value between $f(1)$ and $f(2)$. Since f is continuous, the Intermediate Value Theorem says there is a zero of f between 1 and 2. Figure 2.45 shows the result of zooming in to locate the root near $x = 1.32$. ■

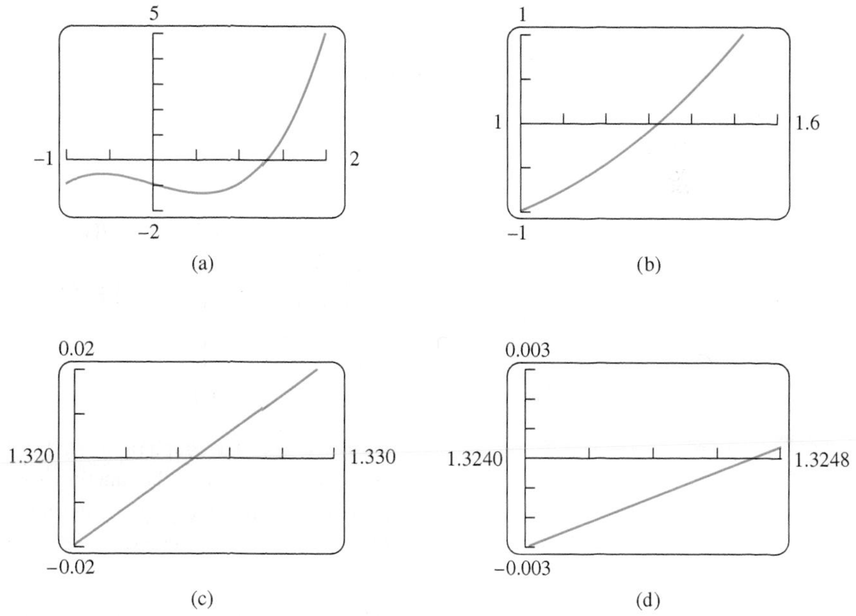

FIGURE 2.45 Zooming in on a zero of the function $f(x) = x^3 - x - 1$. The zero is near $x = 1.3247$ (Example 10).

EXAMPLE 11 Use the Intermediate Value Theorem to prove that the equation

$$\sqrt{2x + 5} = 4 - x^2$$

has a solution (Figure 2.46).

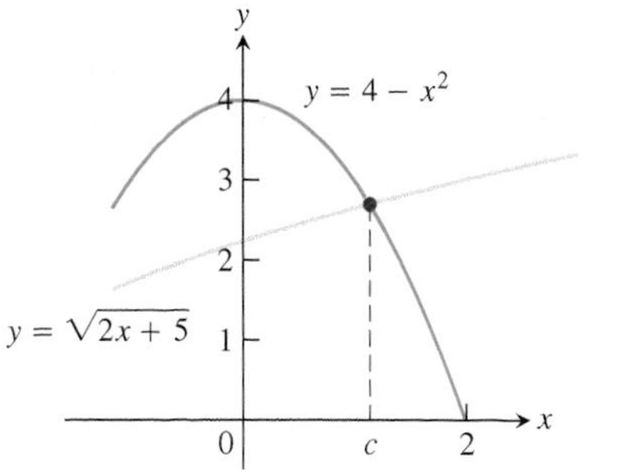

FIGURE 2.46 The curves $y = \sqrt{2x + 5}$ and $y = 4 - x^2$ have the same value at $x = c$ where $\sqrt{2x + 5} = 4 - x^2$ (Example 11).

Solution We rewrite the equation as

$$\sqrt{2x + 5} + x^2 = 4,$$

and set $f(x) = \sqrt{2x + 5} + x^2$. Now $g(x) = \sqrt{2x + 5}$ is continuous on the interval $[-5/2, \infty)$ since it is the composite of the square root function with the nonnegative linear function $y = 2x + 5$. Then f is the sum of the function g and the quadratic function $y = x^2$, and the quadratic function is continuous for all values of x. It follows that $f(x) = \sqrt{2x + 5} + x^2$ is continuous on the interval $[-5/2, \infty)$. By trial and error, we find the function values $f(0) = \sqrt{5} \approx 2.24$ and $f(2) = \sqrt{9} + 4 = 7$, and note that f is also continuous on the finite closed interval $[0, 2] \subset [-5/2, \infty)$. Since the value $y_0 = 4$ is between the numbers 2.24 and 7, by the Intermediate Value Theorem there is a number $c \in [0, 2]$ such that $f(c) = 4$. That is, the number c solves the original equation. ■

Continuous Extension to a Point

Sometimes the formula that describes a function f does not make sense at a point $x = c$. It might nevertheless be possible to extend the domain of f, to include $x = c$, creating a new function that is continuous at $x = c$. For example, the function $y = f(x) = (\sin x)/x$ is continuous at every point except $x = 0$. In this it is like the function $y = 1/x$. But $y = (\sin x)/x$ is different from $y = 1/x$ in that it has a finite limit as $x \to 0$ (Theorem 7). It is therefore possible to extend the function's domain to include the point $x = 0$ in such a way that the extended function is continuous at $x = 0$. We define a new function

$$F(x) = \begin{cases} \dfrac{\sin x}{x}, & x \neq 0 \\ 1, & x = 0. \end{cases}$$

The function $F(x)$ is continuous at $x = 0$ because

$$\lim_{x \to 0} \frac{\sin x}{x} = F(0)$$

(Figure 2.47).

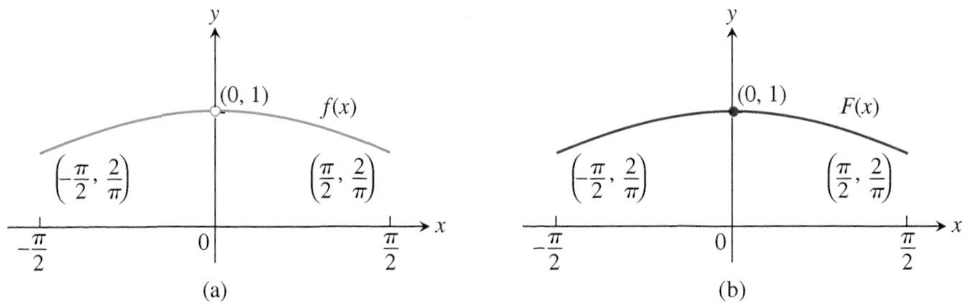

FIGURE 2.47 The graph (a) of $f(x) = (\sin x)/x$ for $-\pi/2 \leq x \leq \pi/2$ does not include the point (0, 1) because the function is not defined at $x = 0$. (b) We can remove the discontinuity from the graph by defining the new function $F(x)$ with $F(0) = 1$ and $F(x) = f(x)$ everywhere else. Note that $F(0) = \lim_{x \to 0} f(x)$.

More generally, a function (such as a rational function) may have a limit even at a point where it is not defined. If $f(c)$ is not defined, but $\lim_{x \to c} f(x) = L$ exists, we can define a new function $F(x)$ by the rule

$$F(x) = \begin{cases} f(x), & \text{if } x \text{ is in the domain of } f \\ L, & \text{if } x = c. \end{cases}$$

The function F is continuous at $x = c$. It is called the **continuous extension of f** to $x = c$. For rational functions f, continuous extensions are usually found by canceling common factors.

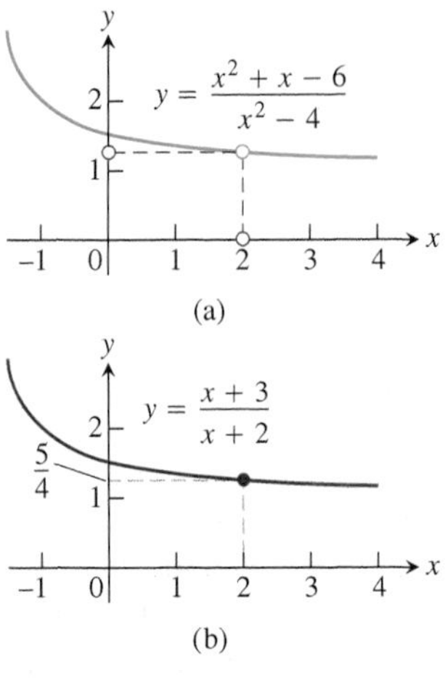

FIGURE 2.48 (a) The graph of $f(x)$ and (b) the graph of its continuous extension $F(x)$ (Example 12).

EXAMPLE 12 Show that

$$f(x) = \frac{x^2 + x - 6}{x^2 - 4}, \quad x \neq 2$$

has a continuous extension to $x = 2$, and find that extension.

Solution Although $f(2)$ is not defined, if $x \neq 2$ we have

$$f(x) = \frac{x^2 + x - 6}{x^2 - 4} = \frac{(x - 2)(x + 3)}{(x - 2)(x + 2)} = \frac{x + 3}{x + 2}.$$

The new function

$$F(x) = \frac{x + 3}{x + 2}$$

is equal to $f(x)$ for $x \neq 2$, but is continuous at $x = 2$, having there the value of $5/4$. Thus F is the continuous extension of f to $x = 2$, and

$$\lim_{x\to 2} \frac{x^2 + x - 6}{x^2 - 4} = \lim_{x \to 2} f(x) = \frac{5}{4}.$$

The graph of f is shown in Figure 2.48. The continuous extension F has the same graph except with no hole at $(2, 5/4)$. Effectively, F is the function f with its point of discontinuity at $x = 2$ removed. ■

Exercises 2.5

Continuity from Graphs

In Exercises 1–4, say whether the function graphed is continuous on $[-1, 3]$. If not, where does it fail to be continuous and why?

1.

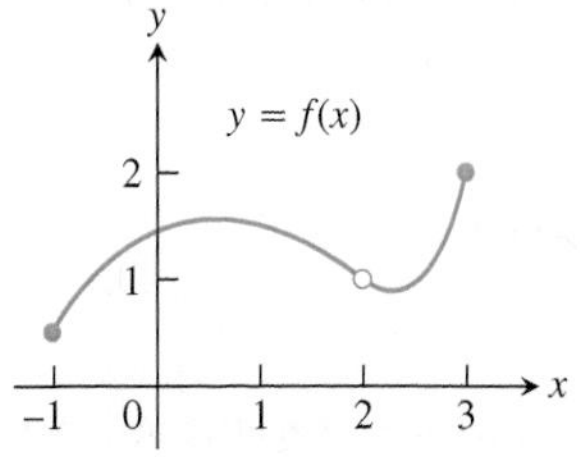

2.

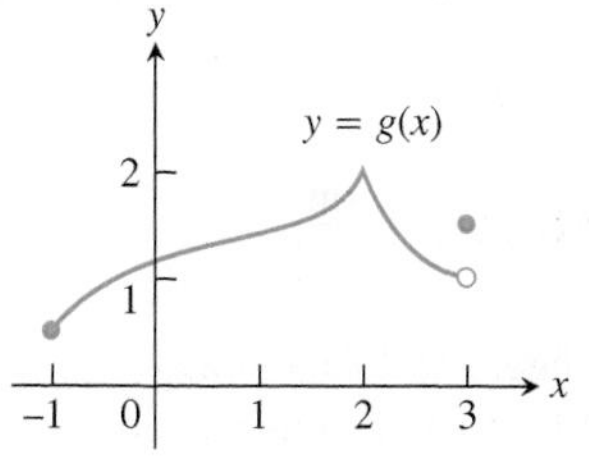

3.

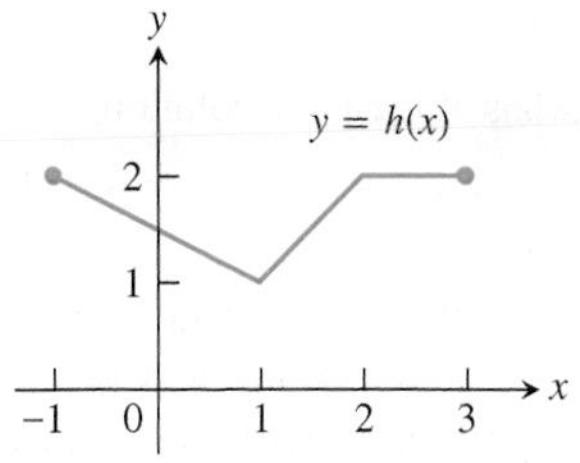

4.

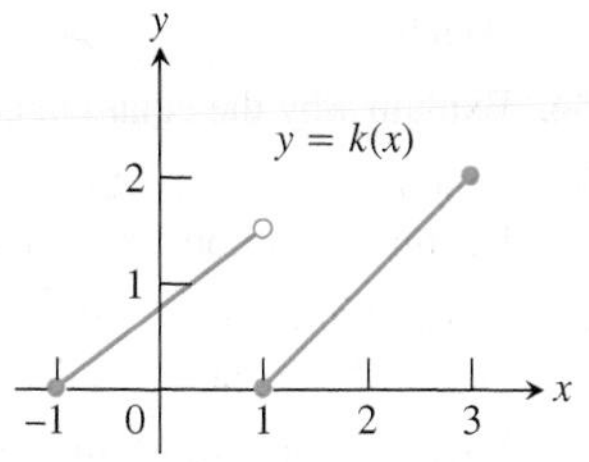

Exercises 5–10 refer to the function

$$f(x) = \begin{cases} x^2 - 1, & -1 \le x < 0 \\ 2x, & 0 < x < 1 \\ 1, & x = 1 \\ -2x + 4, & 1 < x < 2 \\ 0, & 2 < x < 3 \end{cases}$$

graphed in the accompanying figure.

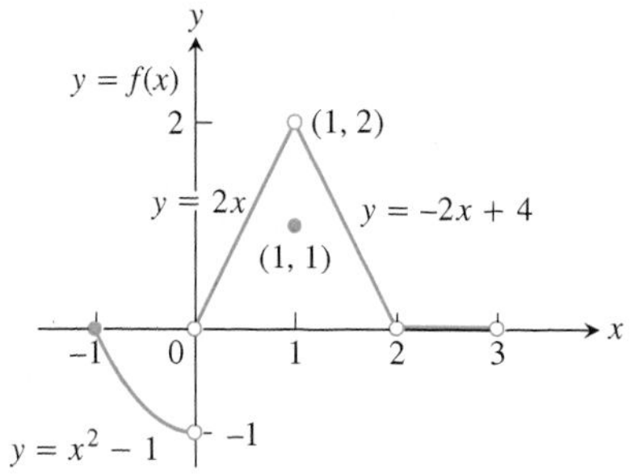

The graph for Exercises 5–10.

5. a. Does $f(-1)$ exist?

b. Does $\lim_{x\to -1^+} f(x)$ exist?

c. Does $\lim_{x\to -1^+} f(x) = f(-1)$?

d. Is f continuous at $x = -1$?

6. a. Does $f(1)$ exist?

b. Does $\lim_{x\to 1} f(x)$ exist?

c. Does $\lim_{x\to 1} f(x) = f(1)$?

d. Is f continuous at $x = 1$?

7. a. Is f defined at $x = 2$? (Look at the definition of f.)

b. Is f continuous at $x = 2$?

8. At what values of x is f continuous?

9. What value should be assigned to $f(2)$ to make the extended function continuous at $x = 2$?

10. To what new value should $f(1)$ be changed to remove the discontinuity?

Applying the Continuity Test

At which points do the functions in Exercises 11 and 12 fail to be continuous? At which points, if any, are the discontinuities removable? Not removable? Give reasons for your answers.

11. Exercise 1, Section 2.4

12. Exercise 2, Section 2.4

At what points are the functions in Exercises 13–30 continuous?

13. $y = \dfrac{1}{x - 2} - 3x$

14. $y = \dfrac{1}{(x + 2)^2} + 4$

15. $y = \dfrac{x + 1}{x^2 - 4x + 3}$

16. $y = \dfrac{x + 3}{x^2 - 3x - 10}$

17. $y = |x - 1| + \sin x$

18. $y = \dfrac{1}{|x| + 1} - \dfrac{x^2}{2}$

19. $y = \dfrac{\cos x}{x}$

20. $y = \dfrac{x + 2}{\cos x}$

21. $y = \csc 2x$

22. $y = \tan \dfrac{\pi x}{2}$

23. $y = \dfrac{x \tan x}{x^2 + 1}$

24. $y = \dfrac{\sqrt{x^4 + 1}}{1 + \sin^2 x}$

25. $y = \sqrt{2x + 3}$

26. $y = \sqrt[4]{3x - 1}$

27. $y = (2x - 1)^{1/3}$

28. $y = (2 - x)^{1/5}$

29. $g(x) = \begin{cases} \dfrac{x^2 - x - 6}{x - 3}, & x \neq 3 \\ 5, & x = 3 \end{cases}$

30. $f(x) = \begin{cases} \dfrac{x^3 - 8}{x^2 - 4}, & x \neq 2, x \neq -2 \\ 3, & x = 2 \\ 4, & x = -2 \end{cases}$

Limits Involving Trigonometric Functions

Find the limits in Exercises 31–38. Are the functions continuous at the point being approached?

31. $\lim_{x \to \pi} \sin(x - \sin x)$

32. $\lim_{t \to 0} \sin\left(\frac{\pi}{2} \cos(\tan t)\right)$

33. $\lim_{y \to 1} \sec(y \sec^2 y - \tan^2 y - 1)$

34. $\lim_{x \to 0} \tan\left(\frac{\pi}{4} \cos(\sin x^{1/3})\right)$

35. $\lim_{t \to 0} \cos\left(\frac{\pi}{\sqrt{19 - 3 \sec 2t}}\right)$

36. $\lim_{x \to \pi/6} \sqrt{\csc^2 x + 5\sqrt{3} \tan x}$

37. $\lim_{x \to 0^+} \sin\left(\frac{\pi}{2} e^{\sqrt{x}}\right)$

38. $\lim_{x \to 1} \cos^{-1}(\ln \sqrt{x})$

Continuous Extensions

39. Define $g(3)$ in a way that extends $g(x) = (x^2 - 9)/(x - 3)$ to be continuous at $x = 3$.

40. Define $h(2)$ in a way that extends $h(t) = (t^2 + 3t - 10)/(t - 2)$ to be continuous at $t = 2$.

41. Define $f(1)$ in a way that extends $f(s) = (s^3 - 1)/(s^2 - 1)$ to be continuous at $s = 1$.

42. Define $g(4)$ in a way that extends
$$g(x) = (x^2 - 16)/(x^2 - 3x - 4)$$
to be continuous at $x = 4$.

43. For what value of a is
$$f(x) = \begin{cases} x^2 - 1, & x < 3 \\ 2ax, & x \geq 3 \end{cases}$$
continuous at every x?

44. For what value of b is
$$g(x) = \begin{cases} x, & x < -2 \\ bx^2, & x \geq -2 \end{cases}$$
continuous at every x?

45. For what values of a is
$$f(x) = \begin{cases} a^2x - 2a, & x \geq 2 \\ 12, & x < 2 \end{cases}$$
continuous at every x?

46. For what value of b is
$$g(x) = \begin{cases} \dfrac{x - b}{b + 1}, & x < 0 \\ x^2 + b, & x > 0 \end{cases}$$
continuous at every x?

47. For what values of a and b is
$$f(x) = \begin{cases} -2, & x \leq -1 \\ ax - b, & -1 < x < 1 \\ 3, & x \geq 1 \end{cases}$$
continuous at every x?

48. For what values of a and b is
$$g(x) = \begin{cases} ax + 2b, & x \leq 0 \\ x^2 + 3a - b, & 0 < x \leq 2 \\ 3x - 5, & x > 2 \end{cases}$$
continuous at every x?

T In Exercises 49–52, graph the function f to see whether it appears to have a continuous extension to the origin. If it does, use Trace and Zoom to find a good candidate for the extended function's value at $x = 0$. If the function does not appear to have a continuous extension, can it be extended to be continuous at the origin from the right or from the left? If so, what do you think the extended function's value(s) should be?

49. $f(x) = \dfrac{10^x - 1}{x}$

50. $f(x) = \dfrac{10^{|x|} - 1}{x}$

51. $f(x) = \dfrac{\sin x}{|x|}$

52. $f(x) = (1 + 2x)^{1/x}$

Theory and Examples

53. A continuous function $y = f(x)$ is known to be negative at $x = 0$ and positive at $x = 1$. Why does the equation $f(x) = 0$ have at least one solution between $x = 0$ and $x = 1$? Illustrate with a sketch.

54. Explain why the equation $\cos x = x$ has at least one solution.

55. **Roots of a cubic** Show that the equation $x^3 - 15x + 1 = 0$ has three solutions in the interval $[-4, 4]$.

56. **A function value** Show that the function $F(x) = (x - a)^2 \cdot (x - b)^2 + x$ takes on the value $(a + b)/2$ for some value of x.

57. **Solving an equation** If $f(x) = x^3 - 8x + 10$, show that there are values c for which $f(c)$ equals **(a)** π; **(b)** $-\sqrt{3}$; **(c)** 5,000,000.

58. Explain why the following five statements ask for the same information.

   a. Find the roots of $f(x) = x^3 - 3x - 1$.

   b. Find the x-coordinates of the points where the curve $y = x^3$ crosses the line $y = 3x + 1$.

   c. Find all the values of x for which $x^3 - 3x = 1$.

   d. Find the x-coordinates of the points where the cubic curve $y = x^3 - 3x$ crosses the line $y = 1$.

   e. Solve the equation $x^3 - 3x - 1 = 0$.

59. **Removable discontinuity** Give an example of a function $f(x)$ that is continuous for all values of x except $x = 2$, where it has a removable discontinuity. Explain how you know that f is discontinuous at $x = 2$, and how you know the discontinuity is removable.

60. **Nonremovable discontinuity** Give an example of a function $g(x)$ that is continuous for all values of x except $x = -1$, where it has a nonremovable discontinuity. Explain how you know that g is discontinuous there and why the discontinuity is not removable.

61. **A function discontinuous at every point**
   a. Use the fact that every nonempty interval of real numbers contains both rational and irrational numbers to show that the function
$$f(x) = \begin{cases} 1, & \text{if } x \text{ is rational} \\ 0, & \text{if } x \text{ is irrational} \end{cases}$$
   is discontinuous at every point.
   b. Is f right-continuous or left-continuous at any point?

62. If functions $f(x)$ and $g(x)$ are continuous for $0 \le x \le 1$, could $f(x)/g(x)$ possibly be discontinuous at a point of $[0, 1]$? Give reasons for your answer.

63. If the product function $h(x) = f(x) \cdot g(x)$ is continuous at $x = 0$, must $f(x)$ and $g(x)$ be continuous at $x = 0$? Give reasons for your answer.

64. **Discontinuous composite of continuous functions** Give an example of functions f and g, both continuous at $x = 0$, for which the composite $f \circ g$ is discontinuous at $x = 0$. Does this contradict Theorem 9? Give reasons for your answer.

65. **Never-zero continuous functions** Is it true that a continuous function that is never zero on an interval never changes sign on that interval? Give reasons for your answer.

66. **Stretching a rubber band** Is it true that if you stretch a rubber band by moving one end to the right and the other to the left, some point of the band will end up in its original position? Give reasons for your answer.

67. **A fixed point theorem** Suppose that a function f is continuous on the closed interval $[0, 1]$ and that $0 \le f(x) \le 1$ for every x in $[0, 1]$. Show that there must exist a number c in $[0, 1]$ such that $f(c) = c$ (c is called a **fixed point** of f).

68. **The sign-preserving property of continuous functions** Let f be defined on an interval (a, b) and suppose that $f(c) \neq 0$ at some c where f is continuous. Show that there is an interval $(c - \delta, c + \delta)$ about c where f has the same sign as $f(c)$.

69. Prove that f is continuous at c if and only if
$$\lim_{h \to 0} f(c + h) = f(c).$$

70. Use Exercise 69 together with the identities
$$\sin(h + c) = \sin h \cos c + \cos h \sin c,$$
$$\cos(h + c) = \cos h \cos c - \sin h \sin c$$
to prove that both $f(x) = \sin x$ and $g(x) = \cos x$ are continuous at every point $x = c$.

Solving Equations Graphically

T Use the Intermediate Value Theorem in Exercises 71–78 to prove that each equation has a solution. Then use a graphing calculator or computer grapher to solve the equations.

71. $x^3 - 3x - 1 = 0$
72. $2x^3 - 2x^2 - 2x + 1 = 0$
73. $x(x - 1)^2 = 1$ (one root)
74. $x^x = 2$
75. $\sqrt{x} + \sqrt{1 + x} = 4$
76. $x^3 - 15x + 1 = 0$ (three roots)
77. $\cos x = x$ (one root). Make sure you are using radian mode.
78. $2 \sin x = x$ (three roots). Make sure you are using radian mode.

2.6 Limits Involving Infinity; Asymptotes of Graphs

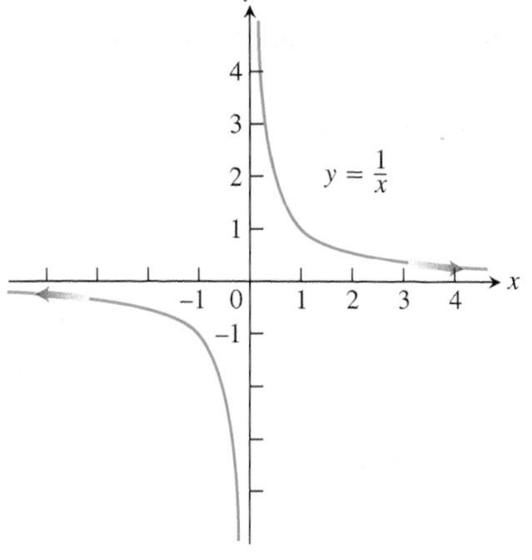

FIGURE 2.49 The graph of $y = 1/x$ approaches 0 as $x \to \infty$ or $x \to -\infty$.

In this section we investigate the behavior of a function when the magnitude of the independent variable x becomes increasingly large, or $x \to \pm\infty$. We further extend the concept of limit to *infinite limits*, which are not limits as before, but rather a new use of the term limit. Infinite limits provide useful symbols and language for describing the behavior of functions whose values become arbitrarily large in magnitude. We use these limit ideas to analyze the graphs of functions having *horizontal* or *vertical asymptotes*.

Finite Limits as $x \to \pm\infty$

The symbol for infinity (∞) does not represent a real number. We use ∞ to describe the behavior of a function when the values in its domain or range outgrow all finite bounds. For example, the function $f(x) = 1/x$ is defined for all $x \neq 0$ (Figure 2.49). When x is positive and becomes increasingly large, $1/x$ becomes increasingly small. When x is negative and its magnitude becomes increasingly large, $1/x$ again becomes small. We summarize these observations by saying that $f(x) = 1/x$ has limit 0 as $x \to \infty$ or $x \to -\infty$, or that 0 is a *limit of* $f(x) = 1/x$ *at infinity and negative infinity*. Here are precise definitions.

DEFINITIONS

1. We say that $f(x)$ has the **limit L as x approaches infinity** and write
$$\lim_{x\to\infty} f(x) = L$$
if, for every number $\epsilon > 0$, there exists a corresponding number M such that for all x
$$x > M \quad\Rightarrow\quad |f(x) - L| < \epsilon.$$

2. We say that $f(x)$ has the **limit L as x approaches minus infinity** and write
$$\lim_{x\to-\infty} f(x) = L$$
if, for every number $\epsilon > 0$, there exists a corresponding number N such that for all x
$$x < N \quad\Rightarrow\quad |f(x) - L| < \epsilon.$$

Intuitively, $\lim_{x\to\infty} f(x) = L$ if, as x moves increasingly far from the origin in the positive direction, $f(x)$ gets arbitrarily close to L. Similarly, $\lim_{x\to-\infty} f(x) = L$ if, as x moves increasingly far from the origin in the negative direction, $f(x)$ gets arbitrarily close to L.

The strategy for calculating limits of functions as $x \to \pm\infty$ is similar to the one for finite limits in Section 2.2. There we first found the limits of the constant and identity functions $y = k$ and $y = x$. We then extended these results to other functions by applying Theorem 1 on limits of algebraic combinations. Here we do the same thing, except that the starting functions are $y = k$ and $y = 1/x$ instead of $y = k$ and $y = x$.

The basic facts to be verified by applying the formal definition are

$$\lim_{x\to\pm\infty} k = k \quad \text{and} \quad \lim_{x\to\pm\infty} \frac{1}{x} = 0. \tag{1}$$

We prove the second result in Example 1, and leave the first to Exercises 87 and 88.

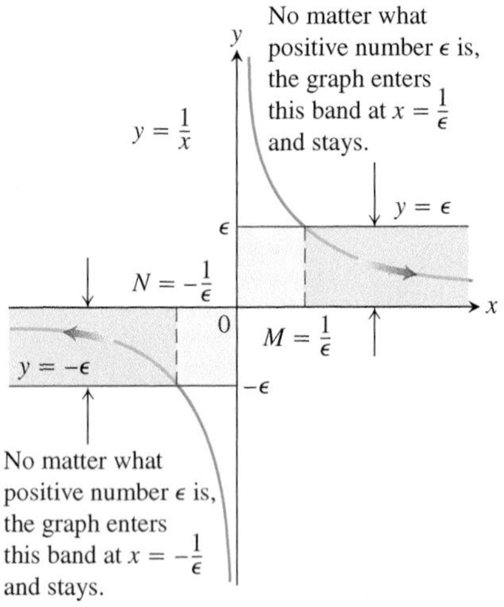

No matter what positive number ϵ is, the graph enters this band at $x = \frac{1}{\epsilon}$ and stays.
y
$y = \frac{1}{x}$
$y = \epsilon$
ϵ
$N = -\frac{1}{\epsilon}$
0
$M = \frac{1}{\epsilon}$
x
$y = -\epsilon$
$-\epsilon$
No matter what positive number ϵ is, the graph enters this band at $x = -\frac{1}{\epsilon}$ and stays.

FIGURE 2.50 The geometry behind the argument in Example 1.

EXAMPLE 1 Show that

(a) $\lim_{x\to\infty} \frac{1}{x} = 0$ **(b)** $\lim_{x\to-\infty} \frac{1}{x} = 0.$

Solution

(a) Let $\epsilon > 0$ be given. We must find a number M such that for all x
$$x > M \quad\Rightarrow\quad \left|\frac{1}{x} - 0\right| = \left|\frac{1}{x}\right| < \epsilon.$$
The implication will hold if $M = 1/\epsilon$ or any larger positive number (Figure 2.50). This proves $\lim_{x\to\infty}(1/x) = 0$.

(b) Let $\epsilon > 0$ be given. We must find a number N such that for all x
$$x < N \quad\Rightarrow\quad \left|\frac{1}{x} - 0\right| = \left|\frac{1}{x}\right| < \epsilon.$$
The implication will hold if $N = -1/\epsilon$ or any number less than $-1/\epsilon$ (Figure 2.50). This proves $\lim_{x\to-\infty}(1/x) = 0$. ■

Limits at infinity have properties similar to those of finite limits.

THEOREM 12 All the limit laws in Theorem 1 are true when we replace $\lim_{x\to c}$ by $\lim_{x\to\infty}$ or $\lim_{x\to-\infty}$. That is, the variable x may approach a finite number c or $\pm\infty$.

EXAMPLE 2 The properties in Theorem 12 are used to calculate limits in the same way as when x approaches a finite number c.

$$\text{(a)} \lim_{x\to\infty}\left(5+\frac{1}{x}\right) = \lim_{x\to\infty} 5 + \lim_{x\to\infty}\frac{1}{x} \qquad \text{Sum Rule}$$

$$= 5 + 0 = 5 \qquad \text{Known limits}$$

$$\text{(b)} \lim_{x\to-\infty}\frac{\pi\sqrt{3}}{x^2} = \lim_{x\to-\infty} \pi\sqrt{3}\cdot\frac{1}{x}\cdot\frac{1}{x}$$

$$= \lim_{x\to-\infty}\pi\sqrt{3}\cdot\lim_{x\to-\infty}\frac{1}{x}\cdot\lim_{x\to-\infty}\frac{1}{x} \qquad \text{Product Rule}$$

$$= \pi\sqrt{3}\cdot 0\cdot 0 = 0 \qquad \text{Known limits}$$

■

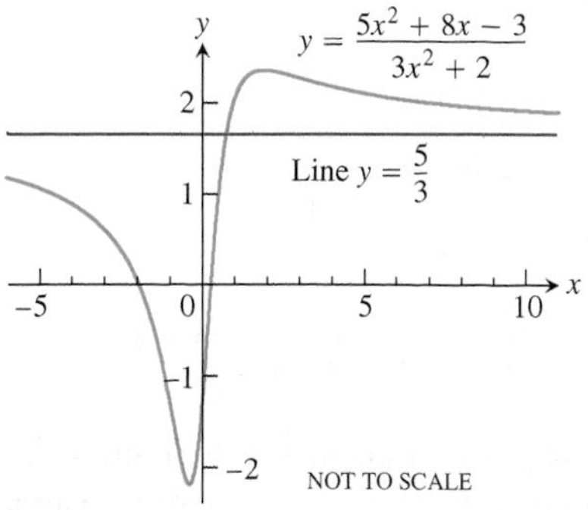

FIGURE 2.51 The graph of the function in Example 3a. The graph approaches the line $y = 5/3$ as $|x|$ increases.

Limits at Infinity of Rational Functions

To determine the limit of a rational function as $x \to \pm\infty$, we first divide the numerator and denominator by the highest power of x in the denominator. The result then depends on the degrees of the polynomials involved.

EXAMPLE 3 These examples illustrate what happens when the degree of the numerator is less than or equal to the degree of the denominator.

$$\text{(a)} \lim_{x\to\infty}\frac{5x^2+8x-3}{3x^2+2} = \lim_{x\to\infty}\frac{5+(8/x)-(3/x^2)}{3+(2/x^2)} \qquad \text{Divide numerator and denominator by } x^2.$$

$$= \frac{5+0-0}{3+0} = \frac{5}{3} \qquad \text{See Fig. 2.51.}$$

$$\text{(b)} \lim_{x\to-\infty}\frac{11x+2}{2x^3-1} = \lim_{x\to-\infty}\frac{(11/x^2)+(2/x^3)}{2-(1/x^3)} \qquad \text{Divide numerator and denominator by } x^3.$$

$$= \frac{0+0}{2-0} = 0 \qquad \text{See Fig. 2.52.}$$

■

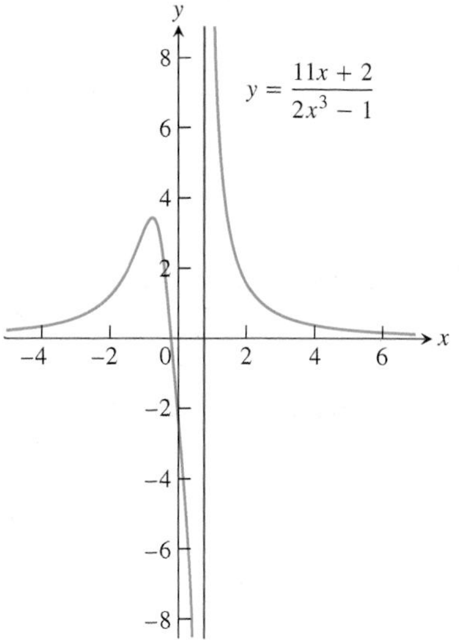

FIGURE 2.52 The graph of the function in Example 3b. The graph approaches the x-axis as $|x|$ increases.

A case for which the degree of the numerator is greater than the degree of the denominator is illustrated in Example 10.

Horizontal Asymptotes

If the distance between the graph of a function and some fixed line approaches zero as a point on the graph moves increasingly far from the origin, we say that the graph approaches the line asymptotically and that the line is an *asymptote* of the graph.

Looking at $f(x) = 1/x$ (see Figure 2.49), we observe that the x-axis is an asymptote of the curve on the right because

$$\lim_{x\to\infty}\frac{1}{x} = 0$$

and on the left because

$$\lim_{x\to-\infty}\frac{1}{x} = 0.$$

We say that the x-axis is a *horizontal asymptote* of the graph of $f(x) = 1/x$.

DEFINITION A line $y = b$ is a **horizontal asymptote** of the graph of a function $y = f(x)$ if either

$$\lim_{x\to\infty} f(x) = b \qquad \text{or} \qquad \lim_{x\to-\infty} f(x) = b.$$

The graph of the function

$$f(x) = \frac{5x^2 + 8x - 3}{3x^2 + 2}$$

sketched in Figure 2.51 (Example 3a) has the line $y = 5/3$ as a horizontal asymptote on both the right and the left because

$$\lim_{x\to\infty} f(x) = \frac{5}{3} \quad \text{and} \quad \lim_{x\to-\infty} f(x) = \frac{5}{3}.$$

EXAMPLE 4 Find the horizontal asymptotes of the graph of

$$f(x) = \frac{x^3 - 2}{|x|^3 + 1.}$$

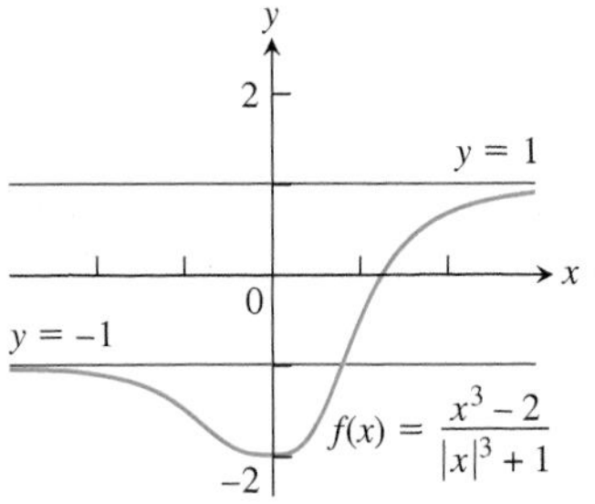

FIGURE 2.53 The graph of the function in Example 4 has two horizontal asymptotes.

Solution We calculate the limits as $x \to \pm\infty$.

For $x \geq 0$: $$\lim_{x\to\infty} \frac{x^3 - 2}{|x|^3 + 1} = \lim_{x\to\infty} \frac{x^3 - 2}{x^3 + 1} = \lim_{x\to\infty} \frac{1 - (2/x^3)}{1 + (1/x^3)} = 1.$$

For $x < 0$: $$\lim_{x\to-\infty} \frac{x^3 - 2}{|x|^3 + 1} = \lim_{x\to-\infty} \frac{x^3 - 2}{(-x)^3 + 1} = \lim_{x\to-\infty} \frac{1 - (2/x^3)}{-1 + (1/x^3)} = -1.$$

The horizontal asymptotes are $y = -1$ and $y = 1$. The graph is displayed in Figure 2.53. Notice that the graph crosses the horizontal asymptote $y = -1$ for a positive value of x. ■

EXAMPLE 5 The x-axis (the line $y = 0$) is a horizontal asymptote of the graph of $y = e^x$ because

$$\lim_{x\to-\infty} e^x = 0.$$

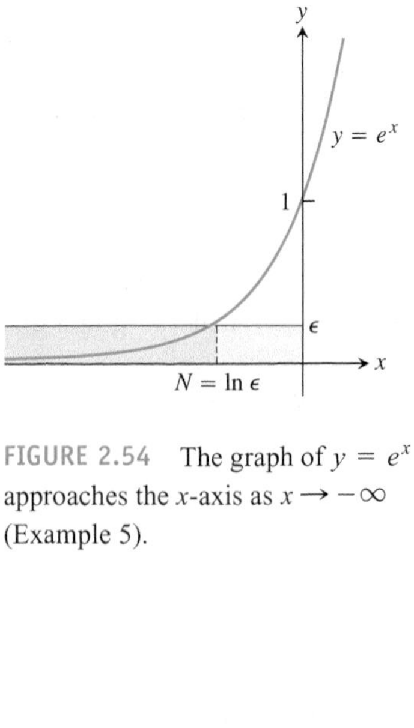

FIGURE 2.54 The graph of $y = e^x$ approaches the x-axis as $x \to -\infty$ (Example 5).

To see this, we use the definition of a limit as x approaches $-\infty$. So let $\epsilon > 0$ be given, but arbitrary. We must find a constant N such that for all x,

$$x < N \quad \Rightarrow \quad \left|e^x - 0\right| < \epsilon.$$

Now $\left|e^x - 0\right| = e^x$, so the condition that needs to be satisfied whenever $x < N$ is

$$e^x < \epsilon.$$

Let $x = N$ be the number where $e^x = \epsilon$. Since e^x is an increasing function, if $x < N$, then $e^x < \epsilon$. We find N by taking the natural logarithm of both sides of the equation $e^N = \epsilon$, so $N = \ln \epsilon$ (see Figure 2.54). With this value of N the condition is satisfied, and we conclude that $\lim_{x\to-\infty} e^x = 0$. ■

EXAMPLE 6 Find **(a)** $\lim_{x\to\infty} \sin(1/x)$ and **(b)** $\lim_{x\to\pm\infty} x \sin(1/x)$.

Solution

(a) We introduce the new variable $t = 1/x$. From Example 1, we know that $t \to 0^+$ as $x \to \infty$ (see Figure 2.49). Therefore,

$$\lim_{x\to\infty} \sin\frac{1}{x} = \lim_{t\to 0^+} \sin t = 0.$$

(b) We calculate the limits as $x \to \infty$ and $x \to -\infty$:

$$\lim_{x\to\infty} x \sin\frac{1}{x} = \lim_{t\to 0^+} \frac{\sin t}{t} = 1 \quad \text{and} \quad \lim_{x\to -\infty} x \sin\frac{1}{x} = \lim_{t\to 0^-} \frac{\sin t}{t} = 1.$$

The graph is shown in Figure 2.55, and we see that the line $y = 1$ is a horizontal asymptote. ■

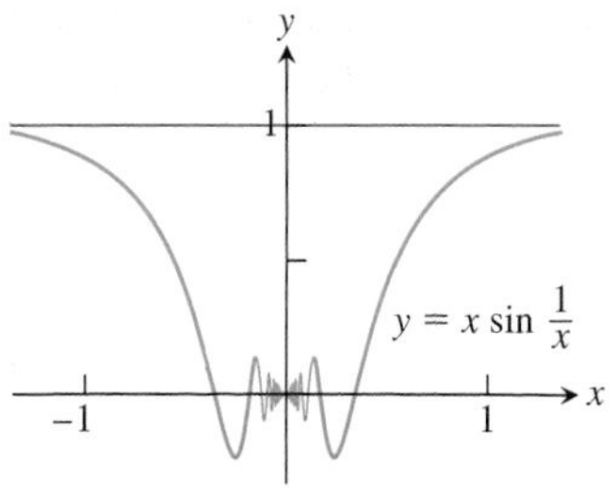

FIGURE 2.55 The line $y = 1$ is a horizontal asymptote of the function graphed here (Example 6b).

Likewise, we can investigate the behavior of $y = f(1/x)$ as $x \to 0$ by investigating $y = f(t)$ as $t \to \pm\infty$, where $t = 1/x$.

EXAMPLE 7 Find $\lim_{x\to 0^-} e^{1/x}$.

Solution We let $t = 1/x$. From Figure 2.49, we can see that $t \to -\infty$ as $x \to 0^-$. (We make this idea more precise further on.) Therefore,

$$\lim_{x\to 0^-} e^{1/x} = \lim_{t\to -\infty} e^t = 0 \quad \text{Example 5}$$

(Figure 2.56). ■

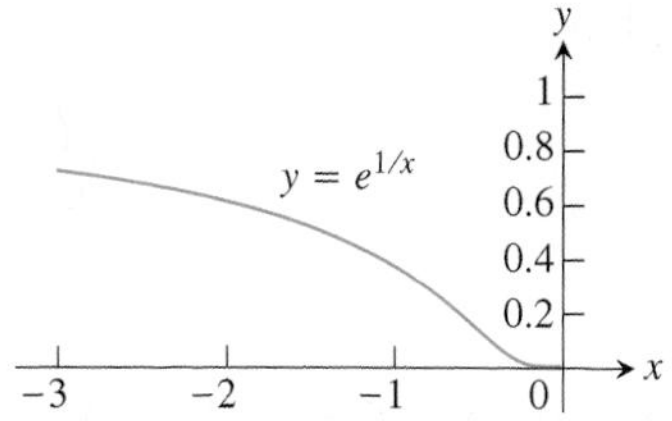

FIGURE 2.56 The graph of $y = e^{1/x}$ for $x < 0$ shows $\lim_{x\to 0^-} e^{1/x} = 0$ (Example 7).

The Sandwich Theorem also holds for limits as $x \to \pm\infty$. You must be sure, though, that the function whose limit you are trying to find stays between the bounding functions at very large values of x in magnitude consistent with whether $x \to \infty$ or $x \to -\infty$.

EXAMPLE 8 Using the Sandwich Theorem, find the horizontal asymptote of the curve

$$y = 2 + \frac{\sin x}{x}.$$

Solution We are interested in the behavior as $x \to \pm\infty$. Since

$$0 \le \left|\frac{\sin x}{x}\right| \le \left|\frac{1}{x}\right|$$

and $\lim_{x\to\pm\infty} |1/x| = 0$, we have $\lim_{x\to\pm\infty} (\sin x)/x = 0$ by the Sandwich Theorem. Hence,

$$\lim_{x\to\pm\infty}\left(2 + \frac{\sin x}{x}\right) = 2 + 0 = 2,$$

and the line $y = 2$ is a horizontal asymptote of the curve on both left and right (Figure 2.57).

This example illustrates that a curve may cross one of its horizontal asymptotes many times. ■

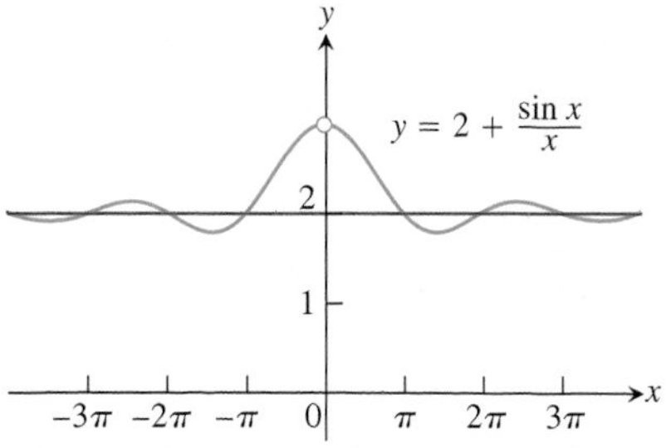

FIGURE 2.57 A curve may cross one of its asymptotes infinitely often (Example 8).

EXAMPLE 9 Find $\lim_{x\to\infty}\left(x - \sqrt{x^2 + 16}\right)$.

Solution Both of the terms x and $\sqrt{x^2 + 16}$ approach infinity as $x \to \infty$, so what happens to the difference in the limit is unclear (we cannot subtract ∞ from ∞ because the symbol does not represent a real number). In this situation we can multiply the numerator and the denominator by the conjugate radical expression to obtain an equivalent algebraic result:

$$\lim_{x\to\infty}\left(x - \sqrt{x^2 + 16}\right) = \lim_{x\to\infty}\left(x - \sqrt{x^2 + 16}\right)\frac{x + \sqrt{x^2 + 16}}{x + \sqrt{x^2 + 16}}$$

$$= \lim_{x\to\infty}\frac{x^2 - (x^2 + 16)}{x + \sqrt{x^2 + 16}} = \lim_{x\to\infty}\frac{-16}{x + \sqrt{x^2 + 16}}.$$

As $x \to \infty$, the denominator in this last expression becomes arbitrarily large, so we see that the limit is 0. We can also obtain this result by a direct calculation using the Limit Laws:

$$\lim_{x\to\infty} \frac{-16}{x + \sqrt{x^2 + 16}} = \lim_{x\to\infty} \frac{-\dfrac{16}{x}}{1 + \sqrt{\dfrac{x^2}{x^2} + \dfrac{16}{x^2}}} = \frac{0}{1 + \sqrt{1 + 0}} = 0.$$

■

Oblique Asymptotes

If the degree of the numerator of a rational function is 1 greater than the degree of the denominator, the graph has an **oblique** or **slant line asymptote**. We find an equation for the asymptote by dividing numerator by denominator to express f as a linear function plus a remainder that goes to zero as $x \to \pm\infty$.

EXAMPLE 10 Find the oblique asymptote of the graph of

$$f(x) = \frac{x^2 - 3}{2x - 4}$$

in Figure 2.58.

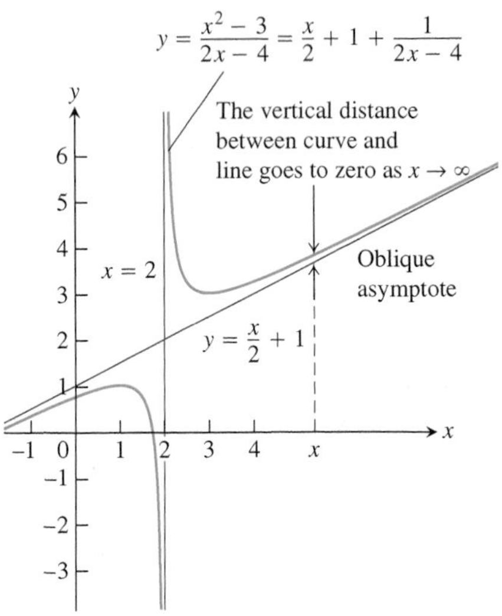

$y = \frac{x^2 - 3}{2x - 4} = \frac{x}{2} + 1 + \frac{1}{2x - 4}$
The vertical distance between curve and line goes to zero as $x \to \infty$
Oblique asymptote
$x = 2$
$y = \frac{x}{2} + 1$
y
x

FIGURE 2.58 The graph of the function in Example 10 has an oblique asymptote.

Solution We are interested in the behavior as $x \to \pm\infty$. We divide $(2x - 4)$ into $(x^2 - 3)$:

$$\begin{array}{r} \frac{x}{2} + 1 \\ 2x - 4 \overline{\big)\, x^2 - 3} \\ \underline{x^2 - 2x} \\ 2x - 3 \\ \underline{2x - 4} \\ 1 \end{array}$$

This tells us that

$$f(x) = \frac{x^2 - 3}{2x - 4} = \underbrace{\left(\frac{x}{2} + 1\right)}_{\text{linear } g(x)} + \underbrace{\left(\frac{1}{2x - 4}\right)}_{\text{remainder}}.$$

As $x \to \pm\infty$, the remainder, whose magnitude gives the vertical distance between the graphs of f and g, goes to zero, making the slanted line

$$g(x) = \frac{x}{2} + 1$$

an asymptote of the graph of f (Figure 2.58). The line $y = g(x)$ is an asymptote both to the right and to the left. The next subsection will confirm that the function $f(x)$ grows arbitrarily large in absolute value as $x \to 2$ (where the denominator is zero), as shown in the graph. ■

Notice in Example 10 that if the degree of the numerator in a rational function is greater than the degree of the denominator, then the limit as $|x|$ becomes large is $+\infty$ or $-\infty$, depending on the signs assumed by the numerator and denominator.

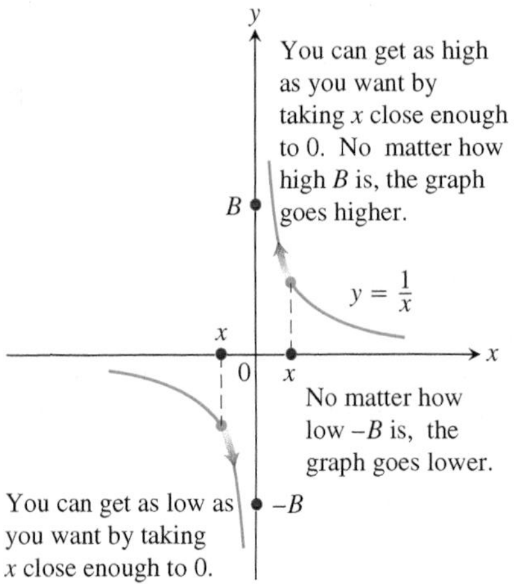

You can get as high as you want by taking x close enough to 0. No matter how high B is, the graph goes higher.
$y = \frac{1}{x}$
No matter how low −B is, the graph goes lower.
You can get as low as you want by taking x close enough to 0.
B
−B
0
x
y

FIGURE 2.59 One-sided infinite limits: $\lim_{x\to 0^+} \frac{1}{x} = \infty$ and $\lim_{x\to 0^-} \frac{1}{x} = -\infty$.

Infinite Limits

Let us look again at the function $f(x) = 1/x$. As $x \to 0^+$, the values of f grow without bound, eventually reaching and surpassing every positive real number. That is, given any positive real number B, however large, the values of f become larger still (Figure 2.59).

Thus, f has no limit as $x \to 0^+$. It is nevertheless convenient to describe the behavior of f by saying that $f(x)$ approaches ∞ as $x \to 0^+$. We write

$$\lim_{x\to 0^+} f(x) = \lim_{x\to 0^+} \frac{1}{x} = \infty.$$

In writing this equation, we are *not* saying that the limit exists. Nor are we saying that there is a real number ∞, for there is no such number. Rather, we are saying that $\lim_{x\to 0^+}(1/x)$ *does not exist because* $1/x$ *becomes arbitrarily large and positive as* $x \to 0^+$.

As $x \to 0^-$, the values of $f(x) = 1/x$ become arbitrarily large and negative. Given any negative real number $-B$, the values of f eventually lie below $-B$. (See Figure 2.59.) We write

$$\lim_{x\to 0^-} f(x) = \lim_{x\to 0^-} \frac{1}{x} = -\infty.$$

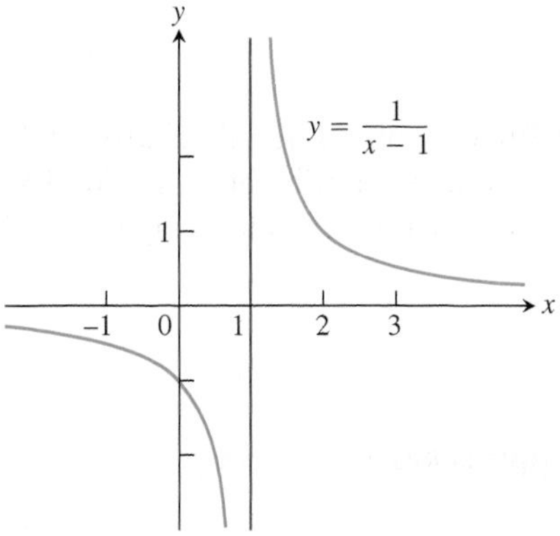

FIGURE 2.60 Near $x = 1$, the function $y = 1/(x-1)$ behaves the way the function $y = 1/x$ behaves near $x = 0$. Its graph is the graph of $y = 1/x$ shifted 1 unit to the right (Example 11).

Again, we are not saying that the limit exists and equals the number $-\infty$. There *is* no real number $-\infty$. We are describing the behavior of a function whose limit as $x \to 0^-$ *does not exist because its values become arbitrarily large and negative.*

EXAMPLE 11 Find $\lim_{x\to 1^+} \frac{1}{x-1}$ and $\lim_{x\to 1^-} \frac{1}{x-1}$.

Geometric Solution The graph of $y = 1/(x-1)$ is the graph of $y = 1/x$ shifted 1 unit to the right (Figure 2.60). Therefore, $y = 1/(x-1)$ behaves near 1 exactly the way $y = 1/x$ behaves near 0:

$$\lim_{x\to 1^+} \frac{1}{x-1} = \infty \quad \text{and} \quad \lim_{x\to 1^-} \frac{1}{x-1} = -\infty.$$

Analytic Solution Think about the number $x - 1$ and its reciprocal. As $x \to 1^+$, we have $(x-1) \to 0^+$ and $1/(x-1) \to \infty$. As $x \to 1^-$, we have $(x-1) \to 0^-$ and $1/(x-1) \to -\infty$. ■

EXAMPLE 12 Discuss the behavior of

$$f(x) = \frac{1}{x^2} \quad \text{as} \quad x \to 0.$$

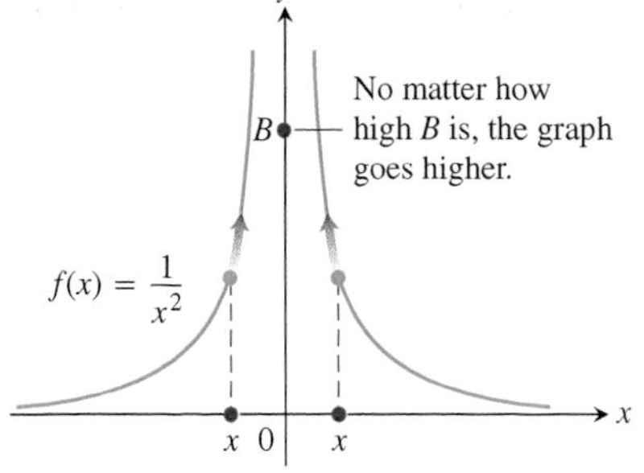

FIGURE 2.61 The graph of $f(x)$ in Example 12 approaches infinity as $x \to 0$.

Solution As x approaches zero from either side, the values of $1/x^2$ are positive and become arbitrarily large (Figure 2.61). This means that

$$\lim_{x\to 0} f(x) = \lim_{x\to 0} \frac{1}{x^2} = \infty.$$ ■

The function $y = 1/x$ shows no consistent behavior as $x \to 0$. We have $1/x \to \infty$ if $x \to 0^+$, but $1/x \to -\infty$ if $x \to 0^-$. All we can say about $\lim_{x\to 0}(1/x)$ is that it does not exist. The function $y = 1/x^2$ is different. Its values approach infinity as x approaches zero from either side, so we can say that $\lim_{x\to 0}(1/x^2) = \infty$.

EXAMPLE 13 These examples illustrate that rational functions can behave in various ways near zeros of the denominator.

(a) $$\lim_{x\to 2} \frac{(x-2)^2}{x^2-4} = \lim_{x\to 2} \frac{(x-2)^2}{(x-2)(x+2)} = \lim_{x\to 2} \frac{x-2}{x+2} = 0$$

(b) $$\lim_{x\to 2} \frac{x-2}{x^2-4} = \lim_{x\to 2} \frac{x-2}{(x-2)(x+2)} = \lim_{x\to 2} \frac{1}{x+2} = \frac{1}{4}$$

(c) $\lim_{x\to 2^+} \dfrac{x-3}{x^2-4} = \lim_{x\to 2^+} \dfrac{x-3}{(x-2)(x+2)} = -\infty$ The values are negative for $x > 2$, x near 2.

(d) $\lim_{x\to 2^-} \dfrac{x-3}{x^2-4} = \lim_{x\to 2^-} \dfrac{x-3}{(x-2)(x+2)} = \infty$ The values are positive for $x < 2$, x near 2.

(e) $\lim_{x\to 2} \dfrac{x-3}{x^2-4} = \lim_{x\to 2} \dfrac{x-3}{(x-2)(x+2)}$ does not exist. See parts (c) and (d).

(f) $\lim_{x\to 2} \dfrac{2-x}{(x-2)^3} = \lim_{x\to 2} \dfrac{-(x-2)}{(x-2)^3} = \lim_{x\to 2} \dfrac{-1}{(x-2)^2} = -\infty$

In parts (a) and (b) the effect of the zero in the denominator at $x = 2$ is canceled because the numerator is zero there also. Thus a finite limit exists. This is not true in part (f), where cancellation still leaves a zero factor in the denominator. ■

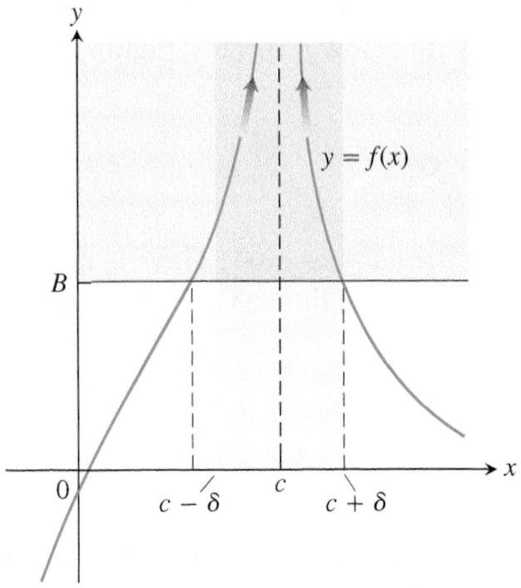

FIGURE 2.62 For $c - \delta < x < c + \delta$, the graph of $f(x)$ lies above the line $y = B$.

Precise Definitions of Infinite Limits

Instead of requiring $f(x)$ to lie arbitrarily close to a finite number L for all x sufficiently close to c, the definitions of infinite limits require $f(x)$ to lie arbitrarily far from zero. Except for this change, the language is very similar to what we have seen before. Figures 2.62 and 2.63 accompany these definitions.

DEFINITIONS

1. We say that ***f*(*x*) approaches infinity as *x* approaches *c***, and write
$$\lim_{x\to c} f(x) = \infty,$$
if for every positive real number B there exists a corresponding $\delta > 0$ such that for all x
$$0 < |x - c| < \delta \quad\Rightarrow\quad f(x) > B.$$
2. We say that ***f*(*x*) approaches minus infinity as *x* approaches *c***, and write
$$\lim_{x\to c} f(x) = -\infty,$$
if for every negative real number $-B$ there exists a corresponding $\delta > 0$ such that for all x
$$0 < |x - c| < \delta \quad\Rightarrow\quad f(x) < -B.$$

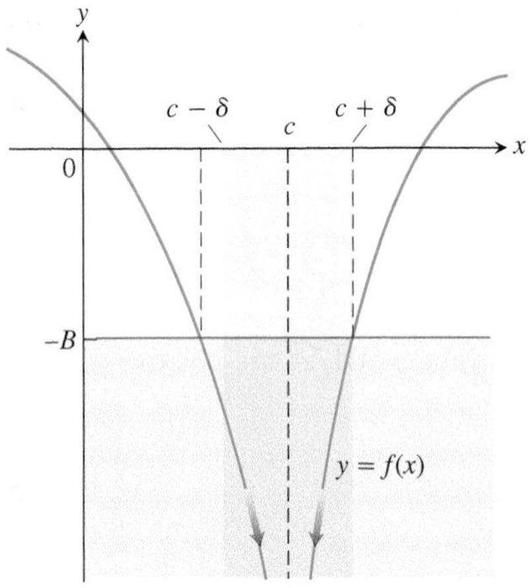

FIGURE 2.63 For $c - \delta < x < c + \delta$, the graph of $f(x)$ lies below the line $y = -B$.

The precise definitions of one-sided infinite limits at c are similar and are stated in the exercises.

EXAMPLE 14 Prove that $\lim_{x\to 0} \dfrac{1}{x^2} = \infty$.

Solution Given $B > 0$, we want to find $\delta > 0$ such that
$$0 < |x - 0| < \delta \quad \text{implies} \quad \frac{1}{x^2} > B.$$
Now,
$$\frac{1}{x^2} > B \qquad \text{if and only if } x^2 < \frac{1}{B}$$
or, equivalently,
$$|x| < \frac{1}{\sqrt{B}}.$$

Thus, choosing $\delta = 1/\sqrt{B}$ (or any smaller positive number), we see that

$$|x| < \delta \quad \text{implies} \quad \frac{1}{x^2} > \frac{1}{\delta^2} \geq B.$$

Therefore, by definition,

$$\lim_{x \to 0} \frac{1}{x^2} = \infty.$$

■

Vertical Asymptotes

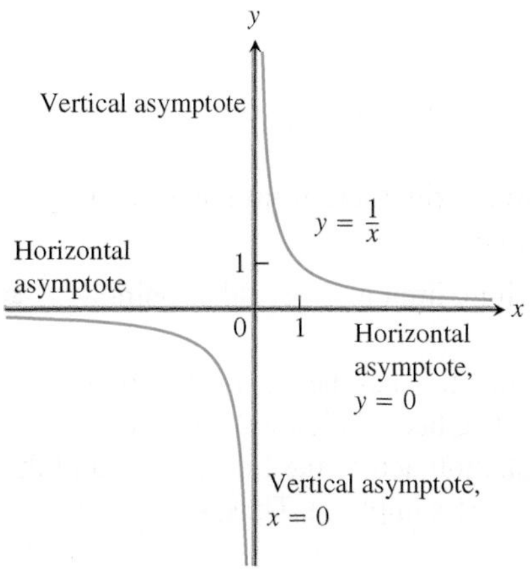

FIGURE 2.64 The coordinate axes are asymptotes of both branches of the hyperbola $y = 1/x$.

Notice that the distance between a point on the graph of $f(x) = 1/x$ and the y-axis approaches zero as the point moves vertically along the graph and away from the origin (Figure 2.64). The function $f(x) = 1/x$ is unbounded as x approaches 0 because

$$\lim_{x \to 0^+} \frac{1}{x} = \infty \quad \text{and} \quad \lim_{x \to 0^-} \frac{1}{x} = -\infty.$$

We say that the line $x = 0$ (the y-axis) is a *vertical asymptote* of the graph of $f(x) = 1/x$. Observe that the denominator is zero at $x = 0$ and the function is undefined there.

> **DEFINITION** A line $x = a$ is a **vertical asymptote** of the graph of a function $y = f(x)$ if either
>
> $$\lim_{x \to a^+} f(x) = \pm\infty \quad \text{or} \quad \lim_{x \to a^-} f(x) = \pm\infty.$$

EXAMPLE 15 Find the horizontal and vertical asymptotes of the curve

$$y = \frac{x + 3}{x + 2}.$$

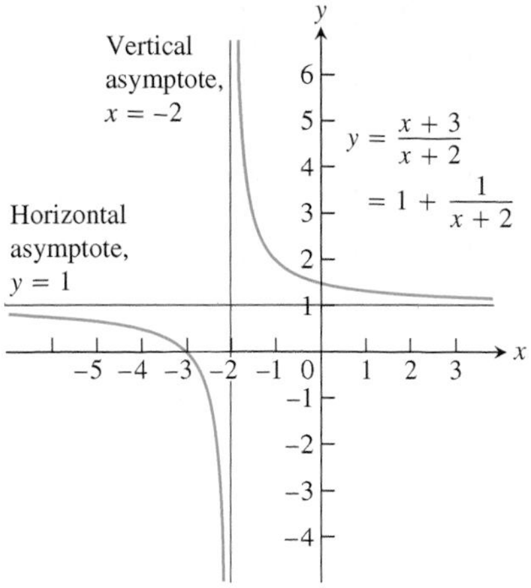

FIGURE 2.65 The lines $y = 1$ and $x = -2$ are asymptotes of the curve in Example 15.

Solution We are interested in the behavior as $x \to \pm\infty$ and the behavior as $x \to -2$, where the denominator is zero.

The asymptotes are quickly revealed if we recast the rational function as a polynomial with a remainder, by dividing $(x + 2)$ into $(x + 3)$:

$$\begin{array}{r} 1 \\ x + 2 \overline{) x + 3} \\ \underline{x + 2} \\ 1 \end{array}$$

This result enables us to rewrite y as:

$$y = 1 + \frac{1}{x + 2}.$$

As $x \to \pm\infty$, the curve approaches the horizontal asymptote $y = 1$; as $x \to -2$, the curve approaches the vertical asymptote $x = -2$. We see that the curve in question is the graph of $f(x) = 1/x$ shifted 1 unit up and 2 units left (Figure 2.65). The asymptotes, instead of being the coordinate axes, are now the lines $y = 1$ and $x = -2$. ■

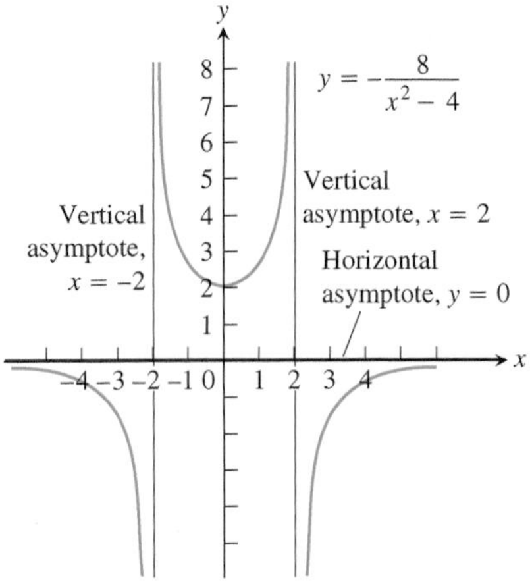

FIGURE 2.66 Graph of the function in Example 16. Notice that the curve approaches the x-axis from only one side. Asymptotes do not have to be two-sided.

EXAMPLE 16 Find the horizontal and vertical asymptotes of the graph of

$$f(x) = -\frac{8}{x^2 - 4}.$$

Solution We are interested in the behavior as $x \to \pm\infty$ and as $x \to \pm 2$, where the denominator is zero. Notice that f is an even function of x, so its graph is symmetric with respect to the y-axis.

(a) *The behavior as* $x \to \pm\infty$. Since $\lim_{x\to\infty} f(x) = 0$, the line $y = 0$ is a horizontal asymptote of the graph to the right. By symmetry it is an asymptote to the left as well (Figure 2.66). Notice that the curve approaches the x-axis from only the negative side (or from below). Also, $f(0) = 2$.

(b) *The behavior as* $x \to \pm 2$. Since

$$\lim_{x\to 2^+} f(x) = -\infty \qquad \text{and} \qquad \lim_{x\to 2^-} f(x) = \infty,$$

the line $x = 2$ is a vertical asymptote both from the right and from the left. By symmetry, the line $x = -2$ is also a vertical asymptote.

There are no other asymptotes because f has a finite limit at every other point. ∎

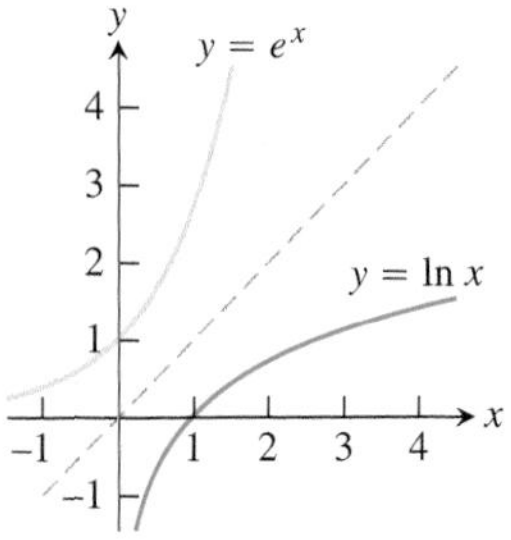

FIGURE 2.67 The line $x = 0$ is a vertical asymptote of the natural logarithm function (Example 17).

EXAMPLE 17 The graph of the natural logarithm function has the y-axis (the line $x = 0$) as a vertical asymptote. We see this from the graph sketched in Figure 2.67 (which is the reflection of the graph of the natural exponential function across the line $y = x$) and the fact that the x-axis is a horizontal asymptote of $y = e^x$ (Example 5). Thus,

$$\lim_{x\to 0^+} \ln x = -\infty.$$

The same result is true for $y = \log_a x$ whenever $a > 1$. ∎

EXAMPLE 18 The curves

$$y = \sec x = \frac{1}{\cos x} \qquad \text{and} \qquad y = \tan x = \frac{\sin x}{\cos x}$$

both have vertical asymptotes at odd-integer multiples of $\pi/2$, where $\cos x = 0$ (Figure 2.68).

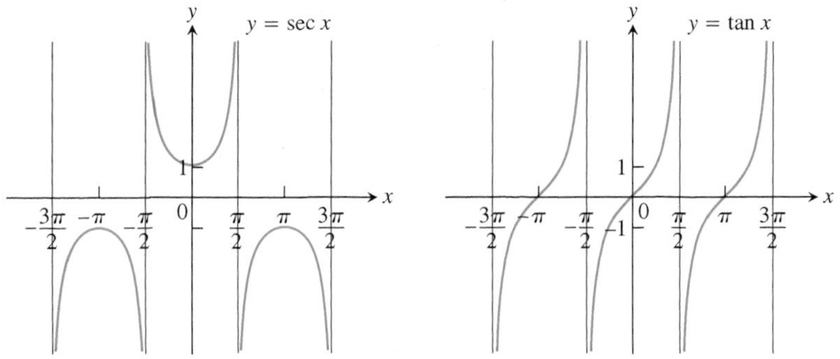

FIGURE 2.68 The graphs of $\sec x$ and $\tan x$ have infinitely many vertical asymptotes (Example 18). ∎

Dominant Terms

In Example 10 we saw that by long division we could rewrite the function

$$f(x) = \frac{x^2 - 3}{2x - 4}$$

as a linear function plus a remainder term:

$$f(x) = \left(\frac{x}{2} + 1\right) + \left(\frac{1}{2x - 4}\right).$$

This tells us immediately that

$$f(x) \approx \frac{x}{2} + 1 \qquad \text{For } |x| \text{ large, } \frac{1}{2x-4} \text{ is near 0.}$$

$$f(x) \approx \frac{1}{2x - 4} \qquad \text{For } x \text{ near 2, this term is very large.}$$

If we want to know how f behaves, this is the way to find out. It behaves like $y = (x/2) + 1$ when $|x|$ is large and the contribution of $1/(2x - 4)$ to the total value of f is insignificant. It behaves like $1/(2x - 4)$ when x is so close to 2 that $1/(2x - 4)$ makes the dominant contribution.

We say that $(x/2) + 1$ **dominates** when x is numerically large, and we say that $1/(2x - 4)$ dominates when x is near 2. **Dominant terms** like these help us predict a function's behavior.

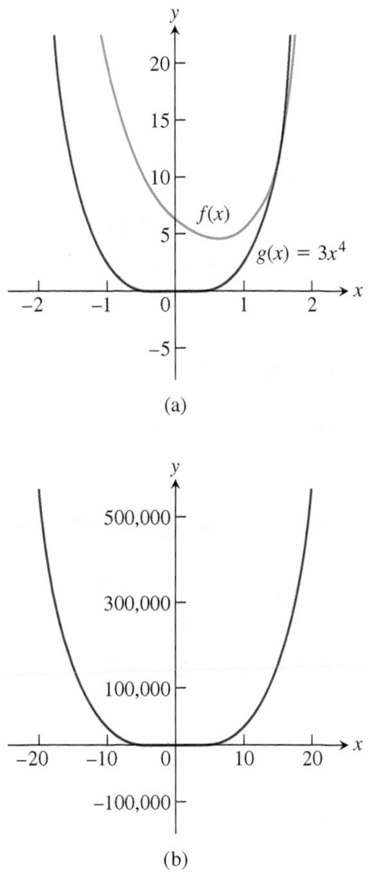

FIGURE 2.69 The graphs of f and g are (a) distinct for $|x|$ small, and (b) nearly identical for $|x|$ large (Example 19).

EXAMPLE 19 Let $f(x) = 3x^4 - 2x^3 + 3x^2 - 5x + 6$ and $g(x) = 3x^4$. Show that although f and g are quite different for numerically small values of x, they are virtually identical for $|x|$ very large, in the sense that their ratios approach 1 as $x \to \infty$ or $x \to -\infty$.

Solution The graphs of f and g behave quite differently near the origin (Figure 2.69a), but appear as virtually identical on a larger scale (Figure 2.69b).

We can test that the term $3x^4$ in f, represented graphically by g, dominates the polynomial f for numerically large values of x by examining the ratio of the two functions as $x \to \pm\infty$. We find that

$$\begin{aligned}\lim_{x\to\pm\infty} \frac{f(x)}{g(x)} &= \lim_{x\to\pm\infty} \frac{3x^4 - 2x^3 + 3x^2 - 5x + 6}{3x^4} \\ &= \lim_{x\to\pm\infty} \left(1 - \frac{2}{3x} + \frac{1}{x^2} - \frac{5}{3x^3} + \frac{2}{x^4}\right) \\ &= 1,\end{aligned}$$

which means that f and g appear nearly identical when $|x|$ is large. ■

Summary

In this chapter we presented several important calculus ideas that are made meaningful and precise by the concept of the limit. These include the three ideas of the exact rate of change of a function, the slope of the graph of a function at a point, and the continuity of a function. The primary methods used for calculating limits of many functions are captured in the algebraic limit laws of Theorem 1 and in the Sandwich Theorem, all of which are proved from the precise definition of the limit. We saw that these computational rules also apply to one-sided limits and to limits at infinity. Moreover, we can sometimes apply these rules when calculating limits of simple transcendental functions, as illustrated by our examples or in cases like the following:

$$\lim_{x\to 0} \frac{e^x - 1}{e^{2x} - 1} = \lim_{x\to 0} \frac{e^x - 1}{(e^x - 1)(e^x + 1)} = \lim_{x\to 0} \frac{1}{e^x + 1} = \frac{1}{1 + 1} = \frac{1}{2}.$$

However, calculating more complicated limits involving transcendental functions such as

$$\lim_{x\to 0}\frac{x}{e^{2x}-1},\qquad \lim_{x\to 0}\frac{\ln x}{x},\qquad \text{and}\qquad \lim_{x\to 0}\left(1+\frac{1}{x}\right)^x$$

requires more than simple algebraic techniques. The *derivative* is exactly the tool we need to calculate limits such as these (see Section 4.5), and this notion is the main subject of our next chapter.

Exercises 2.6

Finding Limits

1. For the function f whose graph is given, determine the following limits.

   a. $\lim_{x\to 2} f(x)$ b. $\lim_{x\to -3^+} f(x)$ c. $\lim_{x\to -3^-} f(x)$
   d. $\lim_{x\to -3} f(x)$ e. $\lim_{x\to 0^+} f(x)$ f. $\lim_{x\to 0^-} f(x)$
   g. $\lim_{x\to 0} f(x)$ h. $\lim_{x\to \infty} f(x)$ i. $\lim_{x\to -\infty} f(x)$

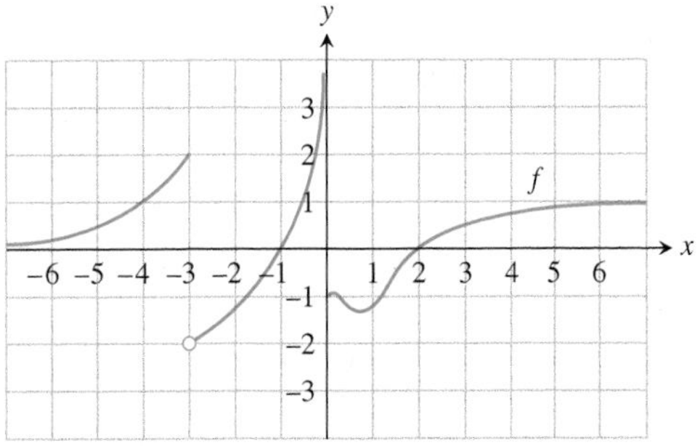

2. For the function f whose graph is given, determine the following limits.

   a. $\lim_{x\to 4} f(x)$ b. $\lim_{x\to 2^+} f(x)$ c. $\lim_{x\to 2^-} f(x)$
   d. $\lim_{x\to 2} f(x)$ e. $\lim_{x\to -3^+} f(x)$ f. $\lim_{x\to -3^-} f(x)$
   g. $\lim_{x\to -3} f(x)$ h. $\lim_{x\to 0^+} f(x)$ i. $\lim_{x\to 0^-} f(x)$
   j. $\lim_{x\to 0} f(x)$ k. $\lim_{x\to \infty} f(x)$ l. $\lim_{x\to -\infty} f(x)$

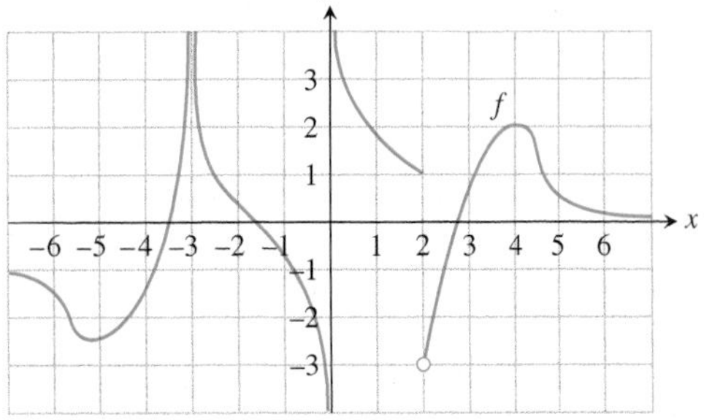

In Exercises 3–8, find the limit of each function **(a)** as $x\to\infty$ and **(b)** as $x\to-\infty$. (You may wish to visualize your answer with a graphing calculator or computer.)

3. $f(x)=\frac{2}{x}-3$

4. $f(x)=\pi-\frac{2}{x^2}$

5. $g(x)=\frac{1}{2+(1/x)}$

6. $g(x)=\frac{1}{8-(5/x^2)}$

7. $h(x)=\frac{-5+(7/x)}{3-(1/x^2)}$

8. $h(x)=\frac{3-(2/x)}{4+(\sqrt{2}/x^2)}$

Find the limits in Exercises 9–12.

9. $\lim_{x\to\infty}\frac{\sin 2x}{x}$

10. $\lim_{\theta\to-\infty}\frac{\cos\theta}{3\theta}$

11. $\lim_{t\to-\infty}\frac{2-t+\sin t}{t+\cos t}$

12. $\lim_{r\to\infty}\frac{r+\sin r}{2r+7-5\sin r}$

Limits of Rational Functions

In Exercises 13–22, find the limit of each rational function **(a)** as $x\to\infty$ and **(b)** as $x\to-\infty$.

13. $f(x)=\frac{2x+3}{5x+7}$

14. $f(x)=\frac{2x^3+7}{x^3-x^2+x+7}$

15. $f(x)=\frac{x+1}{x^2+3}$

16. $f(x)=\frac{3x+7}{x^2-2}$

17. $h(x)=\frac{7x^3}{x^3-3x^2+6x}$

18. $g(x)=\frac{1}{x^3-4x+1}$

19. $g(x)=\frac{10x^5+x^4+31}{x^6}$

20. $h(x)=\frac{9x^4+x}{2x^4+5x^2-x+6}$

21. $h(x)=\frac{-2x^3-2x+3}{3x^3+3x^2-5x}$

22. $h(x)=\frac{-x^4}{x^4-7x^3+7x^2+9}$

Limits as $x\to\infty$ or $x\to-\infty$

The process by which we determine limits of rational functions applies equally well to ratios containing noninteger or negative powers of x: divide numerator and denominator by the highest power of x in the denominator and proceed from there. Find the limits in Exercises 23–36.

23. $\lim_{x\to\infty}\sqrt{\frac{8x^2-3}{2x^2+x}}$

24. $\lim_{x\to-\infty}\left(\frac{x^2+x-1}{8x^2-3}\right)^{1/3}$

25. $\lim_{x\to-\infty}\left(\frac{1-x^3}{x^2+7x}\right)^5$

26. $\lim_{x\to\infty}\sqrt{\frac{x^2-5x}{x^3+x-2}}$

27. $\lim_{x\to\infty}\frac{2\sqrt{x}+x^{-1}}{3x-7}$

28. $\lim_{x\to\infty}\frac{2+\sqrt{x}}{2-\sqrt{x}}$

29. $\lim_{x\to-\infty}\frac{\sqrt[3]{x}-\sqrt[5]{x}}{\sqrt[3]{x}+\sqrt[5]{x}}$

30. $\lim_{x\to\infty}\frac{x^{-1}+x^{-4}}{x^{-2}-x^{-3}}$

31. $\lim_{x\to\infty}\frac{2x^{5/3}-x^{1/3}+7}{x^{8/5}+3x+\sqrt{x}}$

32. $\lim_{x\to-\infty}\frac{\sqrt[3]{x}-5x+3}{2x+x^{2/3}-4}$

33. $\lim_{x\to\infty} \frac{\sqrt{x^2+1}}{x+1}$

34. $\lim_{x\to-\infty} \frac{\sqrt{x^2+1}}{x+1}$

35. $\lim_{x\to\infty} \frac{x-3}{\sqrt{4x^2+25}}$

36. $\lim_{x\to-\infty} \frac{4-3x^3}{\sqrt{x^6+9}}$

Infinite Limits

Find the limits in Exercises 37–48.

37. $\lim_{x\to0^+} \frac{1}{3x}$

38. $\lim_{x\to0^-} \frac{5}{2x}$

39. $\lim_{x\to2^-} \frac{3}{x-2}$

40. $\lim_{x\to3^+} \frac{1}{x-3}$

41. $\lim_{x\to-8^+} \frac{2x}{x+8}$

42. $\lim_{x\to-5^-} \frac{3x}{2x+10}$

43. $\lim_{x\to7} \frac{4}{(x-7)^2}$

44. $\lim_{x\to0} \frac{-1}{x^2(x+1)}$

45. **a.** $\lim_{x\to0^+} \frac{2}{3x^{1/3}}$ **b.** $\lim_{x\to0^-} \frac{2}{3x^{1/3}}$

46. **a.** $\lim_{x\to0^+} \frac{2}{x^{1/5}}$ **b.** $\lim_{x\to0^-} \frac{2}{x^{1/5}}$

47. $\lim_{x\to0} \frac{4}{x^{2/5}}$

48. $\lim_{x\to0} \frac{1}{x^{2/3}}$

Find the limits in Exercises 49–52.

49. $\lim_{x\to(\pi/2)^-} \tan x$

50. $\lim_{x\to(-\pi/2)^+} \sec x$

51. $\lim_{\theta\to0^-} (1+\csc\theta)$

52. $\lim_{\theta\to0} (2-\cot\theta)$

Find the limits in Exercises 53–58.

53. $\lim \frac{1}{x^2-4}$ as

a. $x\to2^+$ **b.** $x\to2^-$

c. $x\to-2^+$ **d.** $x\to-2^-$

54. $\lim \frac{x}{x^2-1}$ as

a. $x\to1^+$ **b.** $x\to1^-$

c. $x\to-1^+$ **d.** $x\to-1^-$

55. $\lim \left(\frac{x^2}{2}-\frac{1}{x}\right)$ as

a. $x\to0^+$ **b.** $x\to0^-$

c. $x\to\sqrt[3]{2}$ **d.** $x\to-1$

56. $\lim \frac{x^2-1}{2x+4}$ as

a. $x\to-2^+$ **b.** $x\to-2^-$

c. $x\to1^+$ **d.** $x\to0^-$

57. $\lim \frac{x^2-3x+2}{x^3-2x^2}$ as

a. $x\to0^+$ **b.** $x\to2^+$

c. $x\to2^-$ **d.** $x\to2$

e. What, if anything, can be said about the limit as $x\to0$?

58. $\lim \frac{x^2-3x+2}{x^3-4x}$ as

a. $x\to2^+$ **b.** $x\to-2^+$

c. $x\to0^-$ **d.** $x\to1^+$

e. What, if anything, can be said about the limit as $x\to0$?

Find the limits in Exercises 59–62.

59. $\lim\left(2-\frac{3}{t^{1/3}}\right)$ as

a. $t\to0^+$ **b.** $t\to0^-$

60. $\lim\left(\frac{1}{t^{3/5}}+7\right)$ as

a. $t\to0^+$ **b.** $t\to0^-$

61. $\lim\left(\frac{1}{x^{2/3}}+\frac{2}{(x-1)^{2/3}}\right)$ as

a. $x\to0^+$ **b.** $x\to0^-$

c. $x\to1^+$ **d.** $x\to1^-$

62. $\lim\left(\frac{1}{x^{1/3}}-\frac{1}{(x-1)^{4/3}}\right)$ as

a. $x\to0^+$ **b.** $x\to0^-$

c. $x\to1^+$ **d.** $x\to1^-$

Graphing Simple Rational Functions

Graph the rational functions in Exercises 63–68. Include the graphs and equations of the asymptotes and dominant terms.

63. $y=\frac{1}{x-1}$

64. $y=\frac{1}{x+1}$

65. $y=\frac{1}{2x+4}$

66. $y=\frac{-3}{x-3}$

67. $y=\frac{x+3}{x+2}$

68. $y=\frac{2x}{x+1}$

Inventing Graphs and Functions

In Exercises 69–72, sketch the graph of a function $y=f(x)$ that satisfies the given conditions. No formulas are required—just label the coordinate axes and sketch an appropriate graph. (The answers are not unique, so your graphs may not be exactly like those in the answer section.)

69. $f(0)=0,\ f(1)=2,\ f(-1)=-2,\ \lim_{x\to-\infty} f(x)=-1$, and $\lim_{x\to\infty} f(x)=1$

70. $f(0)=0,\ \lim_{x\to\pm\infty} f(x)=0,\ \lim_{x\to0^+} f(x)=2$, and $\lim_{x\to0^-} f(x)=-2$

71. $f(0)=0,\ \lim_{x\to\pm\infty} f(x)=0,\ \lim_{x\to1^-} f(x)=\lim_{x\to-1^+} f(x)=\infty$, $\lim_{x\to1^+} f(x)=-\infty$, and $\lim_{x\to-1^-} f(x)=-\infty$

72. $f(2)=1,\ f(-1)=0,\ \lim_{x\to\infty} f(x)=0,\ \lim_{x\to0^+} f(x)=\infty$, $\lim_{x\to0^-} f(x)=-\infty$, and $\lim_{x\to-\infty} f(x)=1$

In Exercises 73–76, find a function that satisfies the given conditions and sketch its graph. (The answers here are not unique. Any function that satisfies the conditions is acceptable. Feel free to use formulas defined in pieces if that will help.)

73. $\lim_{x\to\pm\infty} f(x)=0,\ \lim_{x\to2^-} f(x)=\infty$, and $\lim_{x\to2^+} f(x)=\infty$

74. $\lim_{x\to\pm\infty} g(x)=0,\ \lim_{x\to3^-} g(x)=-\infty$, and $\lim_{x\to3^+} g(x)=\infty$

75. $\lim_{x\to-\infty} h(x)=-1,\ \lim_{x\to\infty} h(x)=1,\ \lim_{x\to0^-} h(x)=-1$, and $\lim_{x\to0^+} h(x)=1$

76. $\lim_{x\to\pm\infty} k(x)=1,\ \lim_{x\to1^-} k(x)=\infty$, and $\lim_{x\to1^+} k(x)=-\infty$

77. Suppose that $f(x)$ and $g(x)$ are polynomials in x and that $\lim_{x\to\infty}(f(x)/g(x)) = 2$. Can you conclude anything about $\lim_{x\to-\infty}(f(x)/g(x))$? Give reasons for your answer.

78. Suppose that $f(x)$ and $g(x)$ are polynomials in x. Can the graph of $f(x)/g(x)$ have an asymptote if $g(x)$ is never zero? Give reasons for your answer.

79. How many horizontal asymptotes can the graph of a given rational function have? Give reasons for your answer.

Finding Limits of Differences when $x \to \pm\infty$

Find the limits in Exercises 80–86.

80. $\lim_{x\to\infty}\left(\sqrt{x+9} - \sqrt{x+4}\right)$

81. $\lim_{x\to\infty}\left(\sqrt{x^2+25} - \sqrt{x^2-1}\right)$

82. $\lim_{x\to-\infty}\left(\sqrt{x^2+3} + x\right)$

83. $\lim_{x\to-\infty}\left(2x + \sqrt{4x^2+3x-2}\right)$

84. $\lim_{x\to\infty}\left(\sqrt{9x^2-x} - 3x\right)$

85. $\lim_{x\to\infty}\left(\sqrt{x^2+3x} - \sqrt{x^2-2x}\right)$

86. $\lim_{x\to\infty}\left(\sqrt{x^2+x} - \sqrt{x^2-x}\right)$

Using the Formal Definitions

Use the formal definitions of limits as $x \to \pm\infty$ to establish the limits in Exercises 87 and 88.

87. If f has the constant value $f(x) = k$, then $\lim_{x\to\infty} f(x) = k$.

88. If f has the constant value $f(x) = k$, then $\lim_{x\to-\infty} f(x) = k$.

Use formal definitions to prove the limit statements in Exercises 89–92.

89. $\lim_{x\to 0}\frac{-1}{x^2} = -\infty$

90. $\lim_{x\to 0}\frac{1}{|x|} = \infty$

91. $\lim_{x\to 3}\frac{-2}{(x-3)^2} = -\infty$

92. $\lim_{x\to -5}\frac{1}{(x+5)^2} = \infty$

93. Here is the definition of **infinite right-hand limit.**

> We say that $f(x)$ approaches infinity as x approaches c from the right, and write
>
> $$\lim_{x\to c^+} f(x) = \infty,$$
>
> if, for every positive real number B, there exists a corresponding number $\delta > 0$ such that for all x
>
> $$c < x < c + \delta \quad \Rightarrow \quad f(x) > B.$$

Modify the definition to cover the following cases.

a. $\lim_{x\to c^-} f(x) = \infty$

b. $\lim_{x\to c^+} f(x) = -\infty$

c. $\lim_{x\to c^-} f(x) = -\infty$

Use the formal definitions from Exercise 93 to prove the limit statements in Exercises 94–98.

94. $\lim_{x\to 0^+}\frac{1}{x} = \infty$

95. $\lim_{x\to 0^-}\frac{1}{x} = -\infty$

96. $\lim_{x\to 2^-}\frac{1}{x-2} = -\infty$

97. $\lim_{x\to 2^+}\frac{1}{x-2} = \infty$

98. $\lim_{x\to 1^-}\frac{1}{1-x^2} = \infty$

Oblique Asymptotes

Graph the rational functions in Exercises 99–104. Include the graphs and equations of the asymptotes.

99. $y = \frac{x^2}{x-1}$

100. $y = \frac{x^2+1}{x-1}$

101. $y = \frac{x^2-4}{x-1}$

102. $y = \frac{x^2-1}{2x+4}$

103. $y = \frac{x^2-1}{x}$

104. $y = \frac{x^3+1}{x^2}$

Additional Graphing Exercises

T Graph the curves in Exercises 105–108. Explain the relationship between the curve's formula and what you see.

105. $y = \frac{x}{\sqrt{4-x^2}}$

106. $y = \frac{-1}{\sqrt{4-x^2}}$

107. $y = x^{2/3} + \frac{1}{x^{1/3}}$

108. $y = \sin\left(\frac{\pi}{x^2+1}\right)$

T Graph the functions in Exercises 109 and 110. Then answer the following questions.

a. How does the graph behave as $x \to 0^+$?

b. How does the graph behave as $x \to \pm\infty$?

c. How does the graph behave near $x = 1$ and $x = -1$?

Give reasons for your answers.

109. $y = \frac{3}{2}\left(x - \frac{1}{x}\right)^{2/3}$

110. $y = \frac{3}{2}\left(\frac{x}{x-1}\right)^{2/3}$

Chapter Questions to Guide Your Review

1. What is the average rate of change of the function $g(t)$ over the interval from $t = a$ to $t = b$? How is it related to a secant line?

2. What limit must be calculated to find the rate of change of a function $g(t)$ at $t = t_0$?

3. Give an informal or intuitive definition of the limit

$$\lim_{x\to c} f(x) = L.$$

Why is the definition "informal"? Give examples.

4. Does the existence and value of the limit of a function $f(x)$ as x approaches c ever depend on what happens at $x = c$? Explain and give examples.

5. What function behaviors might occur for which the limit may fail to exist? Give examples.

6. What theorems are available for calculating limits? Give examples of how the theorems are used.

7. How are one-sided limits related to limits? How can this relationship sometimes be used to calculate a limit or prove it does not exist? Give examples.

8. What is the value of $\lim_{\theta\to 0}((\sin\theta)/\theta)$? Does it matter whether θ is measured in degrees or radians? Explain.

9. What exactly does $\lim_{x\to c} f(x) = L$ mean? Give an example in which you find a $\delta > 0$ for a given f, L, c, and $\epsilon > 0$ in the precise definition of limit.

10. Give precise definitions of the following statements.

    a. $\lim_{x\to 2^-} f(x) = 5$ b. $\lim_{x\to 2^+} f(x) = 5$

    c. $\lim_{x\to 2} f(x) = \infty$ d. $\lim_{x\to 2} f(x) = -\infty$

11. What conditions must be satisfied by a function if it is to be continuous at an interior point of its domain? At an endpoint?

12. How can looking at the graph of a function help you tell where the function is continuous?

13. What does it mean for a function to be right-continuous at a point? Left-continuous? How are continuity and one-sided continuity related?

14. What does it mean for a function to be continuous on an interval? Give examples to illustrate the fact that a function that is not continuous on its entire domain may still be continuous on selected intervals within the domain.

15. What are the basic types of discontinuity? Give an example of each. What is a removable discontinuity? Give an example.

16. What does it mean for a function to have the Intermediate Value Property? What conditions guarantee that a function has this property over an interval? What are the consequences for graphing and solving the equation $f(x) = 0$?

17. Under what circumstances can you extend a function $f(x)$ to be continuous at a point $x = c$? Give an example.

18. What exactly do $\lim_{x\to\infty} f(x) = L$ and $\lim_{x\to -\infty} f(x) = L$ mean? Give examples.

19. What are $\lim_{x\to\pm\infty} k$ (k a constant) and $\lim_{x\to\pm\infty}(1/x)$? How do you extend these results to other functions? Give examples.

20. How do you find the limit of a rational function as $x \to \pm\infty$? Give examples.

21. What are horizontal and vertical asymptotes? Give examples.

Chapter 2 Practice Exercises

Limits and Continuity

1. Graph the function

$$f(x) = \begin{cases} 1, & x \le -1 \\ -x, & -1 < x < 0 \\ 1, & x = 0 \\ -x, & 0 < x < 1 \\ 1, & x \ge 1. \end{cases}$$

Then discuss, in detail, limits, one-sided limits, continuity, and one-sided continuity of f at $x = -1, 0,$ and 1. Are any of the discontinuities removable? Explain.

2. Repeat the instructions of Exercise 1 for

$$f(x) = \begin{cases} 0, & x \le -1 \\ 1/x, & 0 < |x| < 1 \\ 0, & x = 1 \\ 1, & x > 1. \end{cases}$$

3. Suppose that $f(t)$ and $g(t)$ are defined for all t and that $\lim_{t\to t_0} f(t) = -7$ and $\lim_{t\to t_0} g(t) = 0$. Find the limit as $t \to t_0$ of the following functions.

    a. $3f(t)$ b. $(f(t))^2$

    c. $f(t)\cdot g(t)$ d. $\dfrac{f(t)}{g(t) - 7}$

    e. $\cos(g(t))$ f. $|f(t)|$

    g. $f(t) + g(t)$ h. $1/f(t)$

4. Suppose the functions $f(x)$ and $g(x)$ are defined for all x and that $\lim_{x\to 0} f(x) = 1/2$ and $\lim_{x\to 0} g(x) = \sqrt{2}$. Find the limits as $x \to 0$ of the following functions.

    a. $-g(x)$ b. $g(x)\cdot f(x)$

    c. $f(x) + g(x)$ d. $1/f(x)$

    e. $x + f(x)$ f. $\dfrac{f(x)\cdot\cos x}{x - 1}$

In Exercises 5 and 6, find the value that $\lim_{x\to 0} g(x)$ must have if the given limit statements hold.

5. $\lim_{x\to 0}\left(\dfrac{4 - g(x)}{x}\right) = 1$

6. $\lim_{x\to -4}\left(x\lim_{x\to 0} g(x)\right) = 2$

7. On what intervals are the following functions continuous?

    a. $f(x) = x^{1/3}$ b. $g(x) = x^{3/4}$

    c. $h(x) = x^{-2/3}$ d. $k(x) = x^{-1/6}$

8. On what intervals are the following functions continuous?

    a. $f(x) = \tan x$ b. $g(x) = \csc x$

    c. $h(x) = \dfrac{\cos x}{x - \pi}$ d. $k(x) = \dfrac{\sin x}{x}$

Finding Limits

In Exercises 9–28, find the limit or explain why it does not exist.

9. $\lim \dfrac{x^2 - 4x + 4}{x^3 + 5x^2 - 14x}$

a. as $x \to 0$ **b.** as $x \to 2$

10. $\lim \dfrac{x^2 + x}{x^5 + 2x^4 + x^3}$

a. as $x \to 0$ **b.** as $x \to -1$

11. $\lim\limits_{x \to 1} \dfrac{1 - \sqrt{x}}{1 - x}$

12. $\lim\limits_{x \to a} \dfrac{x^2 - a^2}{x^4 - a^4}$

13. $\lim\limits_{h \to 0} \dfrac{(x + h)^2 - x^2}{h}$

14. $\lim\limits_{x \to 0} \dfrac{(x + h)^2 - x^2}{h}$

15. $\lim\limits_{x \to 0} \dfrac{\dfrac{1}{2 + x} - \dfrac{1}{2}}{x}$

16. $\lim\limits_{x \to 0} \dfrac{(2 + x)^3 - 8}{x}$

17. $\lim\limits_{x \to 1} \dfrac{x^{1/3} - 1}{\sqrt{x} - 1}$

18. $\lim\limits_{x \to 64} \dfrac{x^{2/3} - 16}{\sqrt{x} - 8}$

19. $\lim\limits_{x \to 0} \dfrac{\tan(2x)}{\tan(\pi x)}$

20. $\lim\limits_{x \to \pi^-} \csc x$

21. $\lim\limits_{x \to \pi} \sin\left(\dfrac{x}{2} + \sin x\right)$

22. $\lim\limits_{x \to \pi} \cos^2(x - \tan x)$

23. $\lim\limits_{x \to 0} \dfrac{8x}{3 \sin x - x}$

24. $\lim\limits_{x \to 0} \dfrac{\cos 2x - 1}{\sin x}$

25. $\lim\limits_{t \to 3^+} \ln(t - 3)$

26. $\lim\limits_{t \to 1} t^2 \ln\left(2 - \sqrt{t}\right)$

27. $\lim\limits_{\theta \to 0^+} \sqrt{\theta}\, e^{\cos(\pi/\theta)}$

28. $\lim\limits_{z \to 0^+} \dfrac{2e^{1/z}}{e^{1/z} + 1}$

In Exercises 29–32, find the limit of $g(x)$ as x approaches the indicated value.

29. $\lim\limits_{x \to 0^+} (4g(x))^{1/3} = 2$

30. $\lim\limits_{x \to \sqrt{5}} \dfrac{1}{x + g(x)} = 2$

31. $\lim\limits_{x \to 1} \dfrac{3x^2 + 1}{g(x)} = \infty$

32. $\lim\limits_{x \to -2} \dfrac{5 - x^2}{\sqrt{g(x)}} = 0$

T Roots

33. Let $f(x) = x^3 - x - 1$.

a. Use the Intermediate Value Theorem to show that f has a zero between -1 and 2.

b. Solve the equation $f(x) = 0$ graphically with an error of magnitude at most 10^{-8}.

c. It can be shown that the exact value of the solution in part (b) is

$$\left(\frac{1}{2} + \frac{\sqrt{69}}{18}\right)^{1/3} + \left(\frac{1}{2} - \frac{\sqrt{69}}{18}\right)^{1/3}.$$

Evaluate this exact answer and compare it with the value you found in part (b).

T 34. Let $f(\theta) = \theta^3 - 2\theta + 2$.

a. Use the Intermediate Value Theorem to show that f has a zero between -2 and 0.

b. Solve the equation $f(\theta) = 0$ graphically with an error of magnitude at most 10^{-4}.

c. It can be shown that the exact value of the solution in part (b) is

$$\left(\sqrt{\frac{19}{27}} - 1\right)^{1/3} - \left(\sqrt{\frac{19}{27}} + 1\right)^{1/3}.$$

Evaluate this exact answer and compare it with the value you found in part (b).

Continuous Extension

35. Can $f(x) = x(x^2 - 1)/|x^2 - 1|$ be extended to be continuous at $x = 1$ or -1? Give reasons for your answers. (Graph the function—you will find the graph interesting.)

36. Explain why the function $f(x) = \sin(1/x)$ has no continuous extension to $x = 0$.

T In Exercises 37–40, graph the function to see whether it appears to have a continuous extension to the given point a. If it does, use Trace and Zoom to find a good candidate for the extended function's value at a. If the function does not appear to have a continuous extension, can it be extended to be continuous from the right or left? If so, what do you think the extended function's value should be?

37. $f(x) = \dfrac{x - 1}{x - \sqrt[4]{x}}, \quad a = 1$

38. $g(\theta) = \dfrac{5 \cos \theta}{4\theta - 2\pi}, \quad a = \pi/2$

39. $h(t) = (1 + |t|)^{1/t}, \quad a = 0$

40. $k(x) = \dfrac{x}{1 - 2^{|x|}}, \quad a = 0$

Limits at Infinity

Find the limits in Exercises 41–54.

41. $\lim\limits_{x \to \infty} \dfrac{2x + 3}{5x + 7}$

42. $\lim\limits_{x \to -\infty} \dfrac{2x^2 + 3}{5x^2 + 7}$

43. $\lim\limits_{x \to -\infty} \dfrac{x^2 - 4x + 8}{3x^3}$

44. $\lim\limits_{x \to \infty} \dfrac{1}{x^2 - 7x + 1}$

45. $\lim\limits_{x \to -\infty} \dfrac{x^2 - 7x}{x + 1}$

46. $\lim\limits_{x \to \infty} \dfrac{x^4 + x^3}{12x^3 + 128}$

47. $\lim\limits_{x \to \infty} \dfrac{\sin x}{\lfloor x \rfloor}$ (If you have a grapher, try graphing the function for $-5 \le x \le 5$.)

48. $\lim\limits_{\theta \to \infty} \dfrac{\cos \theta - 1}{\theta}$ (If you have a grapher, try graphing $f(x) = x(\cos(1/x) - 1)$ near the origin to "see" the limit at infinity.)

49. $\lim\limits_{x \to \infty} \dfrac{x + \sin x + 2\sqrt{x}}{x + \sin x}$

50. $\lim\limits_{x \to \infty} \dfrac{x^{2/3} + x^{-1}}{x^{2/3} + \cos^2 x}$

51. $\lim\limits_{x \to \infty} e^{1/x} \cos \dfrac{1}{x}$

52. $\lim\limits_{t \to \infty} \ln\left(1 + \dfrac{1}{t}\right)$

53. $\lim\limits_{x \to -\infty} \tan^{-1} x$

54. $\lim\limits_{t \to -\infty} e^{3t} \sin^{-1} \dfrac{1}{t}$

Horizontal and Vertical Asymptotes

55. Use limits to determine the equations for all vertical asymptotes.

a. $y = \dfrac{x^2 + 4}{x - 3}$ b. $f(x) = \dfrac{x^2 - x - 2}{x^2 - 2x + 1}$

c. $y = \dfrac{x^2 + x - 6}{x^2 + 2x - 8}$

56. Use limits to determine the equations for all horizontal asymptotes.

a. $y = \dfrac{1 - x^2}{x^2 + 1}$ b. $f(x) = \dfrac{\sqrt{x} + 4}{\sqrt{x + 4}}$

c. $g(x) = \dfrac{\sqrt{x^2 + 4}}{x}$ d. $y = \sqrt{\dfrac{x^2 + 9}{9x^2 + 1}}$

Chapter 2 Additional and Advanced Exercises

T 1. **Assigning a value to 0^0** The rules of exponents tell us that $a^0 = 1$ if a is any number different from zero. They also tell us that $0^n = 0$ if n is any positive number.

If we tried to extend these rules to include the case 0^0, we would get conflicting results. The first rule would say $0^0 = 1$, whereas the second would say $0^0 = 0$.

We are not dealing with a question of right or wrong here. Neither rule applies as it stands, so there is no contradiction. We could, in fact, define 0^0 to have any value we wanted as long as we could persuade others to agree.

What value would you like 0^0 to have? Here is an example that might help you to decide. (See Exercise 2 below for another example.)

a. Calculate x^x for $x = 0.1, 0.01, 0.001$, and so on as far as your calculator can go. Record the values you get. What pattern do you see?

b. Graph the function $y = x^x$ for $0 < x \le 1$. Even though the function is not defined for $x \le 0$, the graph will approach the y-axis from the right. Toward what y-value does it seem to be headed? Zoom in to further support your idea.

T 2. **A reason you might want 0^0 to be something other than 0 or 1** As the number x increases through positive values, the numbers $1/x$ and $1/(\ln x)$ both approach zero. What happens to the number

$$f(x) = \left(\frac{1}{x}\right)^{1/(\ln x)}$$

as x increases? Here are two ways to find out.

a. Evaluate f for $x = 10, 100, 1000$, and so on as far as your calculator can reasonably go. What pattern do you see?

b. Graph f in a variety of graphing windows, including windows that contain the origin. What do you see? Trace the y-values along the graph. What do you find?

3. **Lorentz contraction** In relativity theory, the length of an object, say a rocket, appears to an observer to depend on the speed at which the object is traveling with respect to the observer. If the observer measures the rocket's length as L_0 at rest, then at speed v the length will appear to be

$$L = L_0\sqrt{1 - \frac{v^2}{c^2}}.$$

This equation is the Lorentz contraction formula. Here, c is the speed of light in a vacuum, about 3×10^8 m/sec. What happens to L as v increases? Find $\lim_{v \to c^-} L$. Why was the left-hand limit needed?

4. **Controlling the flow from a draining tank** Torricelli's law says that if you drain a tank like the one in the figure shown, the rate y at which water runs out is a constant times the square root of the water's depth x. The constant depends on the size and shape of the exit valve.

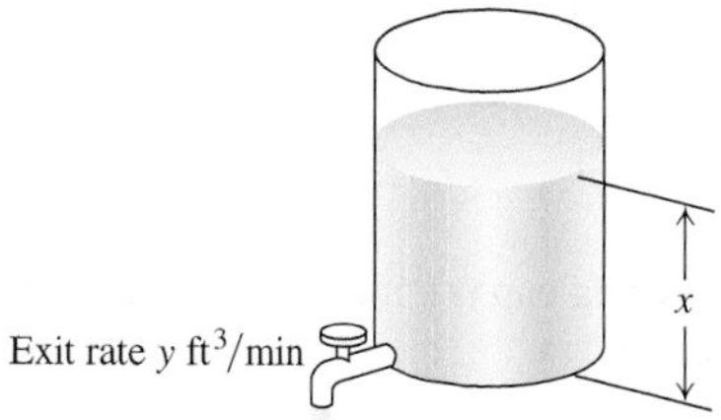

Suppose that $y = \sqrt{x}/2$ for a certain tank. You are trying to maintain a fairly constant exit rate by adding water to the tank with a hose from time to time. How deep must you keep the water if you want to maintain the exit rate

a. within 0.2 ft^3/min of the rate $y_0 = 1$ ft^3/min?

b. within 0.1 ft^3/min of the rate $y_0 = 1$ ft^3/min?

5. **Thermal expansion in precise equipment** As you may know, most metals expand when heated and contract when cooled. The dimensions of a piece of laboratory equipment are sometimes so critical that the shop where the equipment is made must be held at the same temperature as the laboratory where the equipment is to be used. A typical aluminum bar that is 10 cm wide at 70°F will be

$$y = 10 + (t - 70) \times 10^{-4}$$

centimeters wide at a nearby temperature t. Suppose that you are using a bar like this in a gravity wave detector, where its width must stay within 0.0005 cm of the ideal 10 cm. How close to $t_0 = 70$°F must you maintain the temperature to ensure that this tolerance is not exceeded?

6. **Stripes on a measuring cup** The interior of a typical 1-L measuring cup is a right circular cylinder of radius 6 cm (see accompanying figure). The volume of water we put in the cup is therefore a function of the level h to which the cup is filled, the formula being

$$V = \pi 6^2 h = 36\pi h.$$

How closely must we measure h to measure out 1 L of water (1000 cm^3) with an error of no more than 1% (10 cm^3)?

(a)

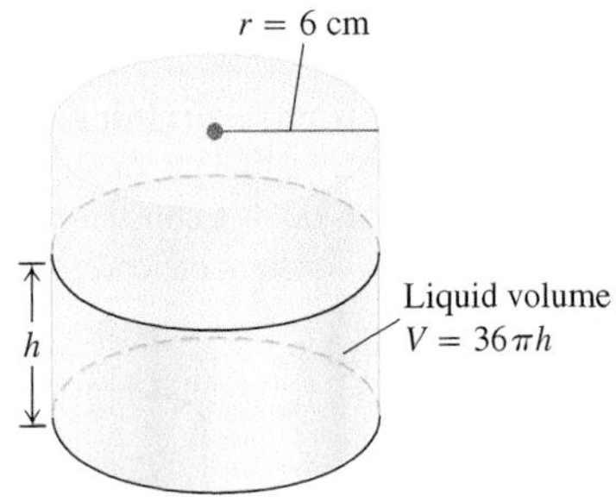

(b)

A 1-L measuring cup (a), modeled as a right circular cylinder (b) of radius $r = 6$ cm

Precise Definition of Limit

In Exercises 7–10, use the formal definition of limit to prove that the function is continuous at c.

7. $f(x) = x^2 - 7, \quad c = 1$ **8.** $g(x) = 1/(2x), \quad c = 1/4$

9. $h(x) = \sqrt{2x - 3}, \quad c = 2$ **10.** $F(x) = \sqrt{9 - x}, \quad c = 5$

11. Uniqueness of limits Show that a function cannot have two different limits at the same point. That is, if $\lim_{x \to c} f(x) = L_1$ and $\lim_{x \to c} f(x) = L_2$, then $L_1 = L_2$.

12. Prove the limit Constant Multiple Rule:

$$\lim_{x \to c} kf(x) = k \lim_{x \to c} f(x) \quad \text{for any constant } k.$$

13. One-sided limits If $\lim_{x \to 0^+} f(x) = A$ and $\lim_{x \to 0^-} f(x) = B$, find

a. $\lim_{x \to 0^+} f(x^3 - x)$ **b.** $\lim_{x \to 0^-} f(x^3 - x)$

c. $\lim_{x \to 0^+} f(x^2 - x^4)$ **d.** $\lim_{x \to 0^-} f(x^2 - x^4)$

14. Limits and continuity Which of the following statements are true, and which are false? If true, say why; if false, give a counterexample (that is, an example confirming the falsehood).

a. If $\lim_{x \to c} f(x)$ exists but $\lim_{x \to c} g(x)$ does not exist, then $\lim_{x \to c}(f(x) + g(x))$ does not exist.

b. If neither $\lim_{x \to c} f(x)$ nor $\lim_{x \to c} g(x)$ exists, then $\lim_{x \to c} (f(x) + g(x))$ does not exist.

c. If f is continuous at x, then so is $|f|$.

d. If $|f|$ is continuous at c, then so is f.

In Exercises 15 and 16, use the formal definition of limit to prove that the function has a continuous extension to the given value of x.

15. $f(x) = \dfrac{x^2 - 1}{x + 1}, \quad x = -1$ **16.** $g(x) = \dfrac{x^2 - 2x - 3}{2x - 6}, \quad x = 3$

17. A function continuous at only one point Let

$$f(x) = \begin{cases} x, & \text{if } x \text{ is rational} \\ 0, & \text{if } x \text{ is irrational.} \end{cases}$$

a. Show that f is continuous at $x = 0$.

b. Use the fact that every nonempty open interval of real numbers contains both rational and irrational numbers to show that f is not continuous at any nonzero value of x.

18. The Dirichlet ruler function If x is a rational number, then x can be written in a unique way as a quotient of integers m/n where $n > 0$ and m and n have no common factors greater than 1. (We say that such a fraction is in *lowest terms*. For example, 6/4 written in lowest terms is 3/2.) Let $f(x)$ be defined for all x in the interval [0, 1] by

$$f(x) = \begin{cases} 1/n, & \text{if } x = m/n \text{ is a rational number in lowest terms} \\ 0, & \text{if } x \text{ is irrational.} \end{cases}$$

For instance, $f(0) = f(1) = 1, f(1/2) = 1/2, f(1/3) = f(2/3) = 1/3, f(1/4) = f(3/4) = 1/4$, and so on.

a. Show that f is discontinuous at every rational number in [0, 1].

b. Show that f is continuous at every irrational number in [0, 1]. (*Hint*: If ϵ is a given positive number, show that there are only finitely many rational numbers r in [0, 1] such that $f(r) \geq \epsilon$.)

c. Sketch the graph of f. Why do you think f is called the "ruler function"?

19. Antipodal points Is there any reason to believe that there is always a pair of antipodal (diametrically opposite) points on Earth's equator where the temperatures are the same? Explain.

20. If $\lim_{x \to c} (f(x) + g(x)) = 3$ and $\lim_{x \to c} (f(x) - g(x)) = -1$, find $\lim_{x \to c} f(x)g(x)$.

21. Roots of a quadratic equation that is almost linear The equation $ax^2 + 2x - 1 = 0$, where a is a constant, has two roots if $a > -1$ and $a \neq 0$, one positive and one negative:

$$r_+(a) = \frac{-1 + \sqrt{1 + a}}{a}, \qquad r_-(a) = \frac{-1 - \sqrt{1 + a}}{a}.$$

a. What happens to $r_+(a)$ as $a \to 0$? As $a \to -1^+$?

b. What happens to $r_-(a)$ as $a \to 0$? As $a \to -1^+$?

c. Support your conclusions by graphing $r_+(a)$ and $r_-(a)$ as functions of a. Describe what you see.

d. For added support, graph $f(x) = ax^2 + 2x - 1$ simultaneously for $a = 1, 0.5, 0.2, 0.1$, and 0.05.

22. Root of an equation Show that the equation $x + 2\cos x = 0$ has at least one solution.

23. Bounded functions A real-valued function f is **bounded from above** on a set D if there exists a number N such that $f(x) \leq N$ for all x in D. We call N, when it exists, an **upper bound** for f on D and say that f is bounded from above by N. In a similar manner, we say that f is **bounded from below** on D if there exists a number M such that $f(x) \geq M$ for all x in D. We call M, when it exists, a **lower bound** for f on D and say that f is bounded from below by M. We say that f is **bounded** on D if it is bounded from both above and below.

a. Show that f is bounded on D if and only if there exists a number B such that $|f(x)| \leq B$ for all x in D.

b. Suppose that f is bounded from above by N. Show that if $\lim_{x\to c} f(x) = L$, then $L \le N$.

c. Suppose that f is bounded from below by M. Show that if $\lim_{x\to c} f(x) = L$, then $L \ge M$.

24. Max $\{a, b\}$ and min $\{a, b\}$

a. Show that the expression

$$\max\{a, b\} = \frac{a+b}{2} + \frac{|a-b|}{2}$$

equals a if $a \ge b$ and equals b if $b \ge a$. In other words, $\max\{a, b\}$ gives the larger of the two numbers a and b.

b. Find a similar expression for $\min\{a, b\}$, the smaller of a and b.

Generalized Limits Involving $\frac{\sin\theta}{\theta}$

The formula $\lim_{\theta\to 0}(\sin\theta)/\theta = 1$ can be generalized. If $\lim_{x\to c} f(x) = 0$ and $f(x)$ is never zero in an open interval containing the point $x = c$, except possibly c itself, then

$$\lim_{x\to c}\frac{\sin f(x)}{f(x)} = 1.$$

Here are several examples.

a. $\displaystyle\lim_{x\to 0}\frac{\sin x^2}{x^2} = 1$

b. $\displaystyle\lim_{x\to 0}\frac{\sin x^2}{x} = \lim_{x\to 0}\frac{\sin x^2}{x^2}\lim_{x\to 0}\frac{x^2}{x} = 1\cdot 0 = 0$

c. $\displaystyle\lim_{x\to -1}\frac{\sin(x^2-x-2)}{x+1} = \lim_{x\to -1}\frac{\sin(x^2-x-2)}{(x^2-x-2)}\cdot \lim_{x\to -1}\frac{(x^2-x-2)}{x+1} = 1\cdot\lim_{x\to -1}\frac{(x+1)(x-2)}{x+1} = -3$

d. $\displaystyle\lim_{x\to 1}\frac{\sin\left(1-\sqrt{x}\right)}{x-1} = \lim_{x\to 1}\frac{\sin\left(1-\sqrt{x}\right)}{1-\sqrt{x}}\frac{1-\sqrt{x}}{x-1} = 1\cdot\lim_{x\to 1}\frac{\left(1-\sqrt{x}\right)\left(1+\sqrt{x}\right)}{(x-1)\left(1+\sqrt{x}\right)} = \lim_{x\to 1}\frac{1-x}{(x-1)\left(1+\sqrt{x}\right)} = -\frac{1}{2}$

Find the limits in Exercises 25–30.

25. $\displaystyle\lim_{x\to 0}\frac{\sin(1-\cos x)}{x}$

26. $\displaystyle\lim_{x\to 0^+}\frac{\sin x}{\sin\sqrt{x}}$

27. $\displaystyle\lim_{x\to 0}\frac{\sin(\sin x)}{x}$

28. $\displaystyle\lim_{x\to 0}\frac{\sin(x^2+x)}{x}$

29. $\displaystyle\lim_{x\to 2}\frac{\sin(x^2-4)}{x-2}$

30. $\displaystyle\lim_{x\to 9}\frac{\sin\left(\sqrt{x}-3\right)}{x-9}$

Oblique Asymptotes

Find all possible oblique asymptotes in Exercises 31–34.

31. $y = \dfrac{2x^{3/2}+2x-3}{\sqrt{x}+1}$

32. $y = x + x\sin\dfrac{1}{x}$

33. $y = \sqrt{x^2+1}$

34. $y = \sqrt{x^2+2x}$

3

DIFFERENTIATION

OVERVIEW In the beginning of Chapter 2, we discussed how to determine the slope of a curve at a point and how to measure the rate at which a function changes. Now that we have studied limits, we can define these ideas precisely and see that both are interpretations of the *derivative* of a function at a point. We then extend this concept from a single point to the *derivative function*, and we develop rules for finding this derivative function easily, without having to calculate any limits directly. These rules are used to find derivatives of most of the common functions reviewed in Chapter 1, as well as various combinations of them. The derivative is one of the key ideas in calculus, and we use it to solve a wide range of problems involving tangents and rates of change.

3.1 Tangents and the Derivative at a Point

In this section we define the slope and tangent to a curve at a point, and the derivative of a function at a point. We will see that the derivative gives a way to find both the slope of a graph and the instantaneous rate of change of a function.

Finding a Tangent to the Graph of a Function

To find a tangent to an arbitrary curve $y = f(x)$ at a point $P(x_0, f(x_0))$, we use the procedure introduced in Section 2.1. We calculate the slope of the secant through P and a nearby point $Q(x_0 + h, f(x_0 + h))$. We then investigate the limit of the slope as $h \to 0$ (Figure 3.1). If the limit exists, we call it the slope of the curve at P and define the tangent at P to be the line through P having this slope.

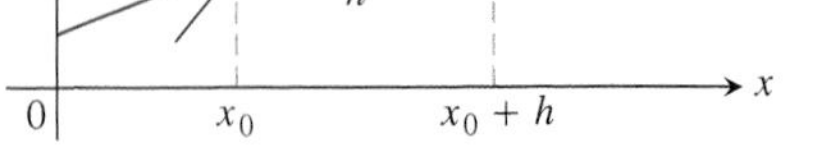

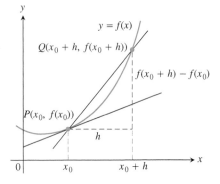

FIGURE 3.1 The slope of the tangent line at P is $\lim_{h\to 0} \dfrac{f(x_0 + h) - f(x_0)}{h}$.

DEFINITIONS The **slope of the curve** $y = f(x)$ at the point $P(x_0, f(x_0))$ is the number

$$m = \lim_{h\to 0} \frac{f(x_0 + h) - f(x_0)}{h} \quad \text{(provided the limit exists).}$$

The **tangent line** to the curve at P is the line through P with this slope.

In Section 2.1, Example 3, we applied these definitions to find the slope of the parabola $f(x) = x^2$ at the point $P(2, 4)$ and the tangent line to the parabola at P. Let's look at another example.

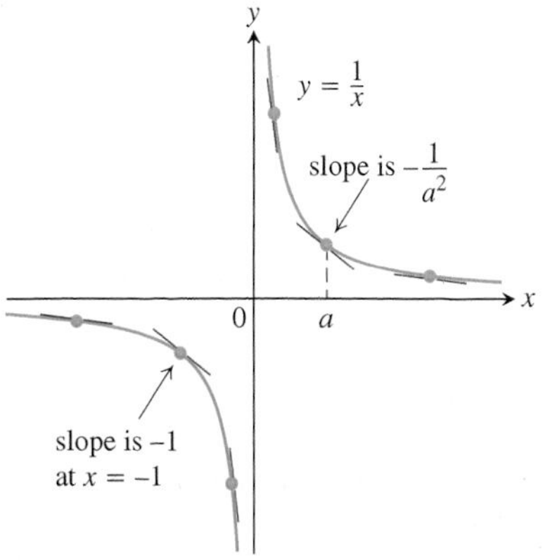

FIGURE 3.2 The tangent slopes, steep near the origin, become more gradual as the point of tangency moves away (Example 1).

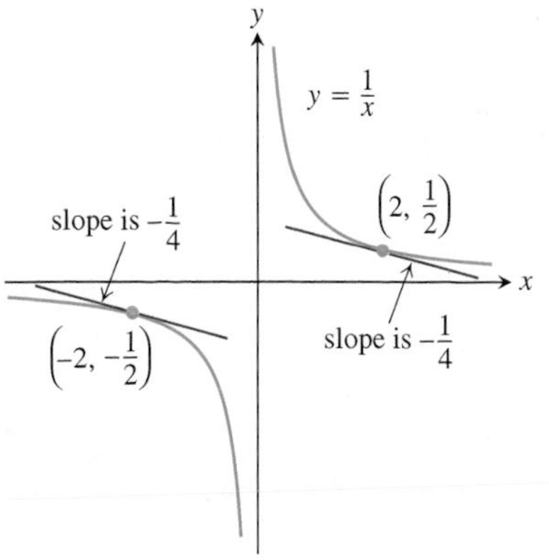

FIGURE 3.3 The two tangent lines to $y = 1/x$ having slope $-1/4$ (Example 1).

EXAMPLE 1

(a) Find the slope of the curve $y = 1/x$ at any point $x = a \neq 0$. What is the slope at the point $x = -1$?

(b) Where does the slope equal $-1/4$?

(c) What happens to the tangent to the curve at the point $(a, 1/a)$ as a changes?

Solution

(a) Here $f(x) = 1/x$. The slope at $(a, 1/a)$ is

$$\lim_{h\to 0} \frac{f(a+h) - f(a)}{h} = \lim_{h\to 0} \frac{\dfrac{1}{a+h} - \dfrac{1}{a}}{h} = \lim_{h\to 0} \frac{1}{h} \frac{a - (a+h)}{a(a+h)}$$

$$= \lim_{h\to 0} \frac{-h}{ha(a+h)} = \lim_{h\to 0} \frac{-1}{a(a+h)} = -\frac{1}{a^2}.$$

Notice how we had to keep writing "$\lim_{h\to 0}$" before each fraction until the stage where we could evaluate the limit by substituting $h = 0$. The number a may be positive or negative, but not 0. When $a = -1$, the slope is $-1/(-1)^2 = -1$ (Figure 3.2).

(b) The slope of $y = 1/x$ at the point where $x = a$ is $-1/a^2$. It will be $-1/4$ provided that

$$-\frac{1}{a^2} = -\frac{1}{4}.$$

This equation is equivalent to $a^2 = 4$, so $a = 2$ or $a = -2$. The curve has slope $-1/4$ at the two points $(2, 1/2)$ and $(-2, -1/2)$ (Figure 3.3).

(c) The slope $-1/a^2$ is always negative if $a \neq 0$. As $a \to 0^+$, the slope approaches $-\infty$ and the tangent becomes increasingly steep (Figure 3.2). We see this situation again as $a \to 0^-$. As a moves away from the origin in either direction, the slope approaches 0 and the tangent levels off to become horizontal. ■

Rates of Change: Derivative at a Point

The expression

$$\frac{f(x_0 + h) - f(x_0)}{h}, \quad h \neq 0$$

is called the **difference quotient of f at x_0 with increment h**. If the difference quotient has a limit as h approaches zero, that limit is given a special name and notation.

> **DEFINITION** The **derivative of a function f at a point x_0**, denoted $f'(x_0)$, is
>
> $$f'(x_0) = \lim_{h\to 0} \frac{f(x_0 + h) - f(x_0)}{h}$$
>
> provided this limit exists.

If we interpret the difference quotient as the slope of a secant line, then the derivative gives the slope of the curve $y = f(x)$ at the point $P(x_0, f(x_0))$. Exercise 31 shows that the derivative of the linear function $f(x) = mx + b$ at any point x_0 is simply the slope of the line, so

$$f'(x_0) = m,$$

which is consistent with our definition of slope.

If we interpret the difference quotient as an average rate of change (Section 2.1), the derivative gives the function's instantaneous rate of change with respect to x at the point $x = x_0$. We study this interpretation in Section 3.4.

EXAMPLE 2 In Examples 1 and 2 in Section 2.1, we studied the speed of a rock falling freely from rest near the surface of the earth. We knew that the rock fell $y = 16t^2$ feet during the first t sec, and we used a sequence of average rates over increasingly short intervals to estimate the rock's speed at the instant $t = 1$. What was the rock's *exact* speed at this time?

Solution We let $f(t) = 16t^2$. The average speed of the rock over the interval between $t = 1$ and $t = 1 + h$ seconds, for $h > 0$, was found to be

$$\frac{f(1 + h) - f(1)}{h} = \frac{16(1 + h)^2 - 16(1)^2}{h} = \frac{16(h^2 + 2h)}{h} = 16(h + 2).$$

The rock's speed at the instant $t = 1$ is then

$$\lim_{h \to 0} 16(h + 2) = 16(0 + 2) = 32 \text{ ft/sec}.$$

Our original estimate of 32 ft/ sec in Section 2.1 was right. ■

Summary

We have been discussing slopes of curves, lines tangent to a curve, the rate of change of a function, and the derivative of a function at a point. All of these ideas refer to the same limit.

The following are all interpretations for the limit of the difference quotient,

$$\lim_{h \to 0} \frac{f(x_0 + h) - f(x_0)}{h}.$$

1. The slope of the graph of $y = f(x)$ at $x = x_0$
2. The slope of the tangent to the curve $y = f(x)$ at $x = x_0$
3. The rate of change of $f(x)$ with respect to x at $x = x_0$
4. The derivative $f'(x_0)$ at a point

In the next sections, we allow the point x_0 to vary across the domain of the function f.

Exercises 3.1

Slopes and Tangent Lines

In Exercises 1–4, use the grid and a straight edge to make a rough estimate of the slope of the curve (in y-units per x-unit) at the points P_1 and P_2.

1.

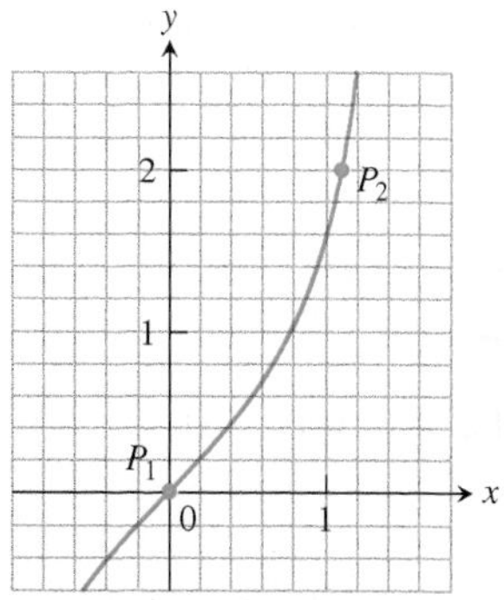

2.

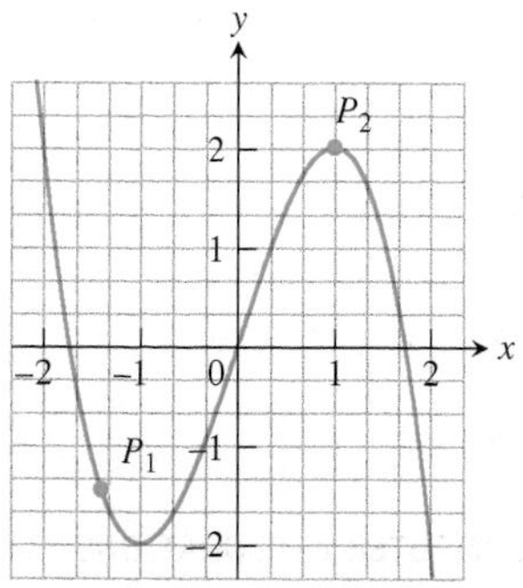

3.

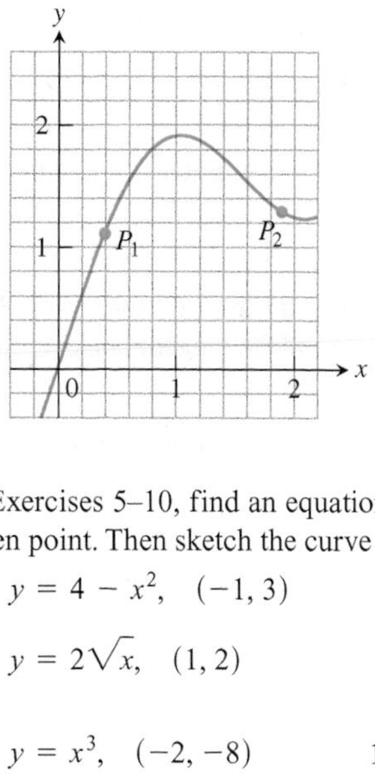

4.

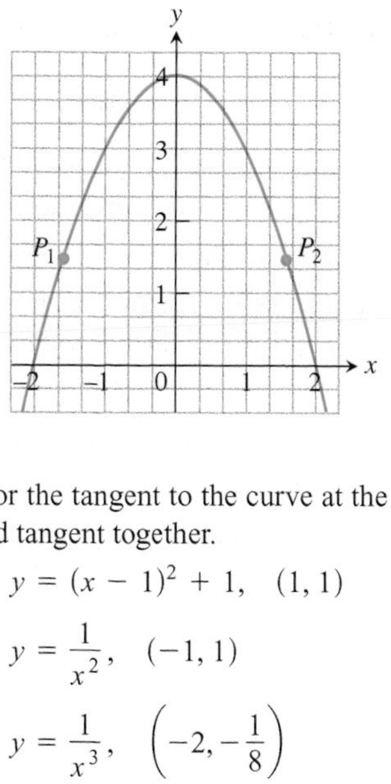

In Exercises 5–10, find an equation for the tangent to the curve at the given point. Then sketch the curve and tangent together.

5. $y = 4 - x^2, \quad (-1, 3)$

6. $y = (x - 1)^2 + 1, \quad (1, 1)$

7. $y = 2\sqrt{x}, \quad (1, 2)$

8. $y = \dfrac{1}{x^2}, \quad (-1, 1)$

9. $y = x^3, \quad (-2, -8)$

10. $y = \dfrac{1}{x^3}, \quad \left(-2, -\dfrac{1}{8}\right)$

In Exercises 11–18, find the slope of the function's graph at the given point. Then find an equation for the line tangent to the graph there.

11. $f(x) = x^2 + 1, \quad (2, 5)$

12. $f(x) = x - 2x^2, \quad (1, -1)$

13. $g(x) = \dfrac{x}{x - 2}, \quad (3, 3)$

14. $g(x) = \dfrac{8}{x^2}, \quad (2, 2)$

15. $h(t) = t^3, \quad (2, 8)$

16. $h(t) = t^3 + 3t, \quad (1, 4)$

17. $f(x) = \sqrt{x}, \quad (4, 2)$

18. $f(x) = \sqrt{x + 1}, \quad (8, 3)$

In Exercises 19–22, find the slope of the curve at the point indicated.

19. $y = 5x^2, \quad x = -1$

20. $y = 1 - x^2, \quad x = 2$

21. $y = \dfrac{1}{x - 1}, \quad x = 3$

22. $y = \dfrac{x - 1}{x + 1}, \quad x = 0$

Tangent Lines with Specified Slopes

At what points do the graphs of the functions in Exercises 23 and 24 have horizontal tangents?

23. $f(x) = x^2 + 4x - 1$

24. $g(x) = x^3 - 3x$

25. Find equations of all lines having slope -1 that are tangent to the curve $y = 1/(x - 1)$.

26. Find an equation of the straight line having slope $1/4$ that is tangent to the curve $y = \sqrt{x}$.

Rates of Change

27. Object dropped from a tower An object is dropped from the top of a 100-m-high tower. Its height above ground after t sec is $100 - 4.9t^2$ m. How fast is it falling 2 sec after it is dropped?

28. Speed of a rocket At t sec after liftoff, the height of a rocket is $3t^2$ ft. How fast is the rocket climbing 10 sec after liftoff?

29. Circle's changing area What is the rate of change of the area of a circle ($A = \pi r^2$) with respect to the radius when the radius is $r = 3$?

30. Ball's changing volume What is the rate of change of the volume of a ball ($V = (4/3)\pi r^3$) with respect to the radius when the radius is $r = 2$?

31. Show that the line $y = mx + b$ is its own tangent line at any point $(x_0, mx_0 + b)$.

32. Find the slope of the tangent to the curve $y = 1/\sqrt{x}$ at the point where $x = 4$.

Testing for Tangents

33. Does the graph of

$$f(x) = \begin{cases} x^2 \sin(1/x), & x \neq 0 \\ 0, & x = 0 \end{cases}$$

have a tangent at the origin? Give reasons for your answer.

34. Does the graph of

$$g(x) = \begin{cases} x \sin(1/x), & x \neq 0 \\ 0, & x = 0 \end{cases}$$

have a tangent at the origin? Give reasons for your answer.

Vertical Tangents

We say that a continuous curve $y = f(x)$ has a **vertical tangent** at the point where $x = x_0$ if $\lim_{h\to 0} (f(x_0 + h) - f(x_0))/h = \infty$ or $-\infty$. For example, $y = x^{1/3}$ has a vertical tangent at $x = 0$ (see accompanying figure):

$$\lim_{h\to 0} \frac{f(0 + h) - f(0)}{h} = \lim_{h\to 0} \frac{h^{1/3} - 0}{h} = \lim_{h\to 0} \frac{1}{h^{2/3}} = \infty.$$

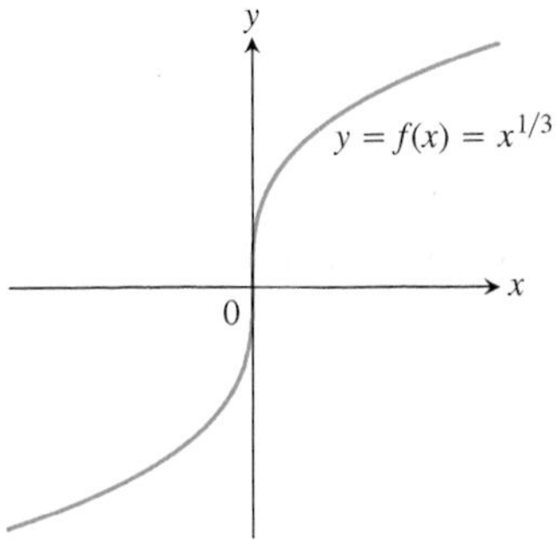

VERTICAL TANGENT AT ORIGIN

However, $y = x^{2/3}$ has *no* vertical tangent at $x = 0$ (see next figure):

$$\lim_{h\to 0} \frac{g(0+h) - g(0)}{h} = \lim_{h\to 0} \frac{h^{2/3} - 0}{h} = \lim_{h\to 0} \frac{1}{h^{1/3}}$$

does not exist, because the limit is ∞ from the right and $-\infty$ from the left.

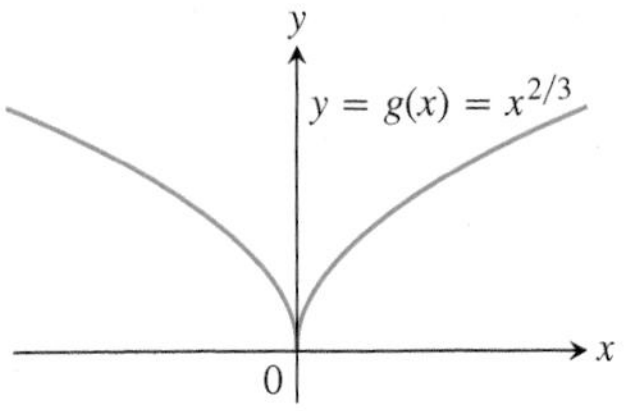

NO VERTICAL TANGENT AT ORIGIN

35. Does the graph of

$$f(x) = \begin{cases} -1, & x < 0 \\ 0, & x = 0 \\ 1, & x > 0 \end{cases}$$

have a vertical tangent at the origin? Give reasons for your answer.

36. Does the graph of

$$U(x) = \begin{cases} 0, & x < 0 \\ 1, & x \ge 0 \end{cases}$$

have a vertical tangent at the point (0, 1)? Give reasons for your answer.

T Graph the curves in Exercises 37–46.

a. Where do the graphs appear to have vertical tangents?

b. Confirm your findings in part (a) with limit calculations. But before you do, read the introduction to Exercises 35 and 36.

37. $y = x^{2/5}$ **38.** $y = x^{4/5}$

39. $y = x^{1/5}$ **40.** $y = x^{3/5}$

41. $y = 4x^{2/5} - 2x$ **42.** $y = x^{5/3} - 5x^{2/3}$

43. $y = x^{2/3} - (x - 1)^{1/3}$ **44.** $y = x^{1/3} + (x - 1)^{1/3}$

45. $y = \begin{cases} -\sqrt{|x|}, & x \le 0 \\ \sqrt{x}, & x > 0 \end{cases}$ **46.** $y = \sqrt{|4 - x|}$

COMPUTER EXPLORATIONS

Use a CAS to perform the following steps for the functions in Exercises 47–50:

a. Plot $y = f(x)$ over the interval $(x_0 - 1/2) \le x \le (x_0 + 3)$.

b. Holding x_0 fixed, the difference quotient

$$q(h) = \frac{f(x_0 + h) - f(x_0)}{h}$$

at x_0 becomes a function of the step size h. Enter this function into your CAS workspace.

c. Find the limit of q as $h \to 0$.

d. Define the secant lines $y = f(x_0) + q \cdot (x - x_0)$ for $h = 3, 2$, and 1. Graph them together with f and the tangent line over the interval in part (a).

47. $f(x) = x^3 + 2x, \quad x_0 = 0$ **48.** $f(x) = x + \frac{5}{x}, \quad x_0 = 1$

49. $f(x) = x + \sin(2x), \quad x_0 = \pi/2$

50. $f(x) = \cos x + 4\sin(2x), \quad x_0 = \pi$

3.2 The Derivative as a Function

HISTORICAL ESSAY

The Derivative

In the last section we defined the derivative of $y = f(x)$ at the point $x = x_0$ to be the limit

$$f'(x_0) = \lim_{h\to 0} \frac{f(x_0 + h) - f(x_0)}{h}.$$

We now investigate the derivative as a *function* derived from f by considering the limit at each point x in the domain of f.

DEFINITION The **derivative** of the function $f(x)$ with respect to the variable x is the function f' whose value at x is

$$f'(x) = \lim_{h\to 0} \frac{f(x + h) - f(x)}{h},$$

provided the limit exists.

We use the notation $f(x)$ in the definition to emphasize the independent variable x with respect to which the derivative function $f'(x)$ is being defined. The domain of f' is the set of points in the domain of f for which the limit exists, which means that the domain may be the same as or smaller than the domain of f. If f' exists at a particular x, we say that f is **differentiable (has a derivative) at x**. If f' exists at every point in the domain of f, we call f **differentiable.**

If we write $z = x + h$, then $h = z - x$ and h approaches 0 if and only if z approaches x. Therefore, an equivalent definition of the derivative is as follows (see Figure 3.4). This formula is sometimes more convenient to use when finding a derivative function.

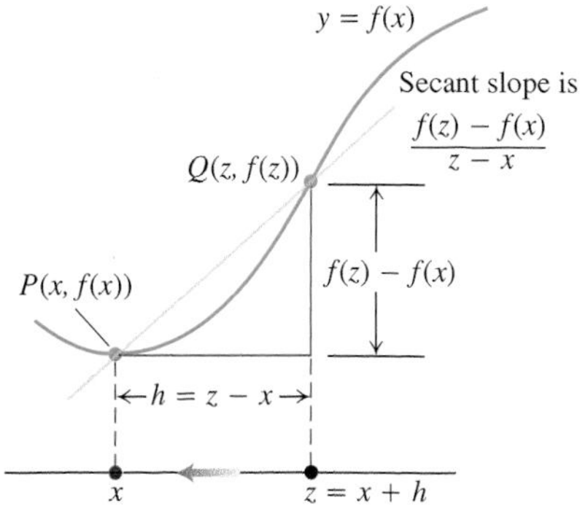

Derivative of f at x is

$$f'(x) = \lim_{h\to 0} \frac{f(x+h) - f(x)}{h}$$

$$= \lim_{z\to x} \frac{f(z) - f(x)}{z - x}$$

FIGURE 3.4 Two forms for the difference quotient.

Alternative Formula for the Derivative

$$f'(x) = \lim_{z\to x} \frac{f(z) - f(x)}{z - x}$$

Calculating Derivatives from the Definition

The process of calculating a derivative is called **differentiation**. To emphasize the idea that differentiation is an operation performed on a function $y = f(x)$, we use the notation

$$\frac{d}{dx} f(x)$$

as another way to denote the derivative $f'(x)$. Example 1 of Section 3.1 illustrated the differentiation process for the function $y = 1/x$ when $x = a$. For x representing any point in the domain, we get the formula

$$\frac{d}{dx}\left(\frac{1}{x}\right) = -\frac{1}{x^2}.$$

Derivative of the Reciprocal Function

$$\frac{d}{dx}\left(\frac{1}{x}\right) = -\frac{1}{x^2}, \quad x \neq 0$$

Here are two more examples in which we allow x to be any point in the domain of f.

EXAMPLE 1 Differentiate $f(x) = \dfrac{x}{x-1}$.

Solution We use the definition of derivative, which requires us to calculate $f(x + h)$ and then subtract $f(x)$ to obtain the numerator in the difference quotient. We have

$$f(x) = \frac{x}{x-1} \quad \text{and} \quad f(x+h) = \frac{(x+h)}{(x+h)-1}, \text{ so}$$

$$f'(x) = \lim_{h\to 0} \frac{f(x+h) - f(x)}{h} \qquad \text{Definition}$$

$$= \lim_{h\to 0} \frac{\dfrac{x+h}{x+h-1} - \dfrac{x}{x-1}}{h}$$

$$= \lim_{h\to 0} \frac{1}{h} \cdot \frac{(x+h)(x-1) - x(x+h-1)}{(x+h-1)(x-1)} \qquad \frac{a}{b} - \frac{c}{d} = \frac{ad - cb}{bd}$$

$$= \lim_{h\to 0} \frac{1}{h} \cdot \frac{-h}{(x+h-1)(x-1)} \qquad \text{Simplify.}$$

$$= \lim_{h\to 0} \frac{-1}{(x+h-1)(x-1)} = \frac{-1}{(x-1)^2}. \qquad \text{Cancel } h \neq 0.$$

■

EXAMPLE 2

(a) Find the derivative of $f(x) = \sqrt{x}$ for $x > 0$.

(b) Find the tangent line to the curve $y = \sqrt{x}$ at $x = 4$.

Derivative of the Square Root Function

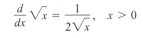

$$\frac{d}{dx}\sqrt{x} = \frac{1}{2\sqrt{x}}, \quad x > 0$$

Solution

(a) We use the alternative formula to calculate f':

$$\begin{aligned} f'(x) &= \lim_{z \to x} \frac{f(z) - f(x)}{z - x} \\ &= \lim_{z \to x} \frac{\sqrt{z} - \sqrt{x}}{z - x} \\ &= \lim_{z \to x} \frac{\sqrt{z} - \sqrt{x}}{\left(\sqrt{z} - \sqrt{x}\right)\left(\sqrt{z} + \sqrt{x}\right)} \\ &= \lim_{z \to x} \frac{1}{\sqrt{z} + \sqrt{x}} = \frac{1}{2\sqrt{x}}. \end{aligned}$$

(b) The slope of the curve at $x = 4$ is

$$f'(4) = \frac{1}{2\sqrt{4}} = \frac{1}{4}.$$

The tangent is the line through the point (4, 2) with slope 1/4 (Figure 3.5):

$$y = 2 + \frac{1}{4}(x - 4)$$

$$y = \frac{1}{4}x + 1.$$ ■

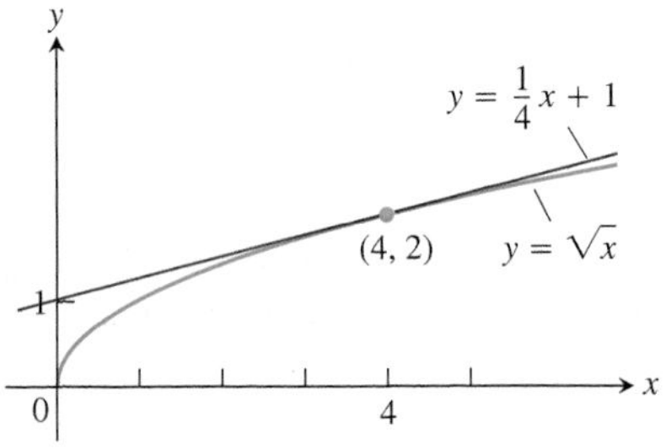

FIGURE 3.5 The curve $y = \sqrt{x}$ and its tangent at (4, 2). The tangent's slope is found by evaluating the derivative at $x = 4$ (Example 2).

Notations

There are many ways to denote the derivative of a function $y = f(x)$, where the independent variable is x and the dependent variable is y. Some common alternative notations for the derivative are

$$f'(x) = y' = \frac{dy}{dx} = \frac{df}{dx} = \frac{d}{dx}f(x) = D(f)(x) = D_x f(x).$$

The symbols d/dx and D indicate the operation of differentiation. We read dy/dx as "the derivative of y with respect to x," and df/dx and $(d/dx)f(x)$ as "the derivative of f with respect to x." The "prime" notations y' and f' come from notations that Newton used for derivatives. The d/dx notations are similar to those used by Leibniz. The symbol dy/dx should not be regarded as a ratio (until we introduce the idea of "differentials" in Section 3.11).

To indicate the value of a derivative at a specified number $x = a$, we use the notation

$$f'(a) = \left.\frac{dy}{dx}\right|_{x=a} = \left.\frac{df}{dx}\right|_{x=a} = \left.\frac{d}{dx}f(x)\right|_{x=a}.$$

For instance, in Example 2

$$f'(4) = \left.\frac{d}{dx}\sqrt{x}\right|_{x=4} = \left.\frac{1}{2\sqrt{x}}\right|_{x=4} = \frac{1}{2\sqrt{4}} = \frac{1}{4}.$$

Graphing the Derivative

We can often make a reasonable plot of the derivative of $y = f(x)$ by estimating the slopes on the graph of f. That is, we plot the points $(x, f'(x))$ in the xy-plane and connect them with a smooth curve, which represents $y = f'(x)$.

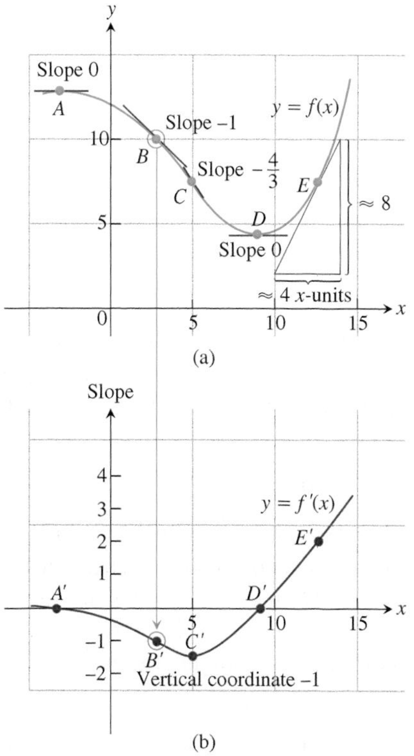

FIGURE 3.6 We made the graph of $y = f'(x)$ in (b) by plotting slopes from the graph of $y = f(x)$ in (a). The vertical coordinate of B' is the slope at B and so on. The slope at E is approximately $8/4 = 2$. In (b) we see that the rate of change of f is negative for x between A' and D'; the rate of change is positive for x to the right of D'.

EXAMPLE 3 Graph the derivative of the function $y = f(x)$ in Figure 3.6a.

Solution We sketch the tangents to the graph of f at frequent intervals and use their slopes to estimate the values of $f'(x)$ at these points. We plot the corresponding $(x, f'(x))$ pairs and connect them with a smooth curve as sketched in Figure 3.6b. ■

What can we learn from the graph of $y = f'(x)$? At a glance we can see

1. where the rate of change of f is positive, negative, or zero;
2. the rough size of the growth rate at any x and its size in relation to the size of $f(x)$;
3. where the rate of change itself is increasing or decreasing.

Differentiable on an Interval; One-Sided Derivatives

A function $y = f(x)$ is **differentiable on an open interval** (finite or infinite) if it has a derivative at each point of the interval. It is **differentiable on a closed interval** $[a, b]$ if it is differentiable on the interior (a, b) and if the limits

$$\lim_{h\to 0^+} \frac{f(a+h) - f(a)}{h} \qquad \textbf{Right-hand derivative at } a$$

$$\lim_{h\to 0^-} \frac{f(b+h) - f(b)}{h} \qquad \textbf{Left-hand derivative at } b$$

exist at the endpoints (Figure 3.7).

Right-hand and left-hand derivatives may be defined at any point of a function's domain. Because of Theorem 6, Section 2.4, a function has a derivative at a point if and only if it has left-hand and right-hand derivatives there, and these one-sided derivatives are equal.

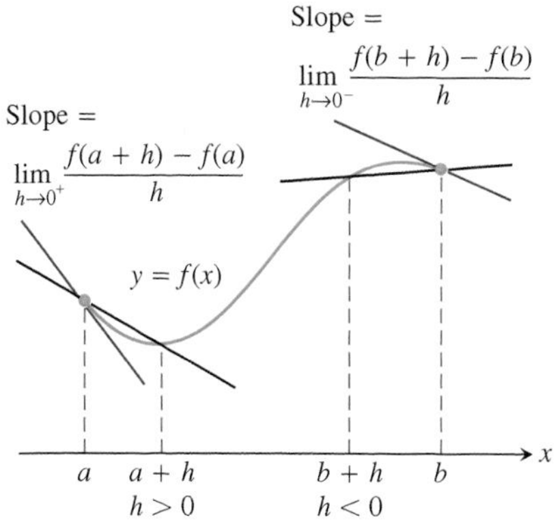

FIGURE 3.7 Derivatives at endpoints are one-sided limits.

EXAMPLE 4 Show that the function $y = |x|$ is differentiable on $(-\infty, 0)$ and $(0, \infty)$ but has no derivative at $x = 0$.

Solution From Section 3.1, the derivative of $y = mx + b$ is the slope m. Thus, to the right of the origin,

$$\frac{d}{dx}(|x|) = \frac{d}{dx}(x) = \frac{d}{dx}(1 \cdot x) = 1. \qquad \frac{d}{dx}(mx+b) = m,\ |x| = x$$

To the left,

$$\frac{d}{dx}(|x|) = \frac{d}{dx}(-x) = \frac{d}{dx}(-1 \cdot x) = -1 \qquad |x| = -x$$

(Figure 3.8). There is no derivative at the origin because the one-sided derivatives differ there:

$$\begin{aligned}
\text{Right-hand derivative of } |x| \text{ at zero} &= \lim_{h\to 0^+} \frac{|0+h| - |0|}{h} = \lim_{h\to 0^+} \frac{|h|}{h} \\
&= \lim_{h\to 0^+} \frac{h}{h} \qquad |h| = h \text{ when } h > 0 \\
&= \lim_{h\to 0^+} 1 = 1 \\
\text{Left-hand derivative of } |x| \text{ at zero} &= \lim_{h\to 0^-} \frac{|0+h| - |0|}{h} = \lim_{h\to 0^-} \frac{|h|}{h} \\
&= \lim_{h\to 0^-} \frac{-h}{h} \qquad |h| = -h \text{ when } h < 0 \\
&= \lim_{h\to 0^-} -1 = -1.
\end{aligned}$$

■

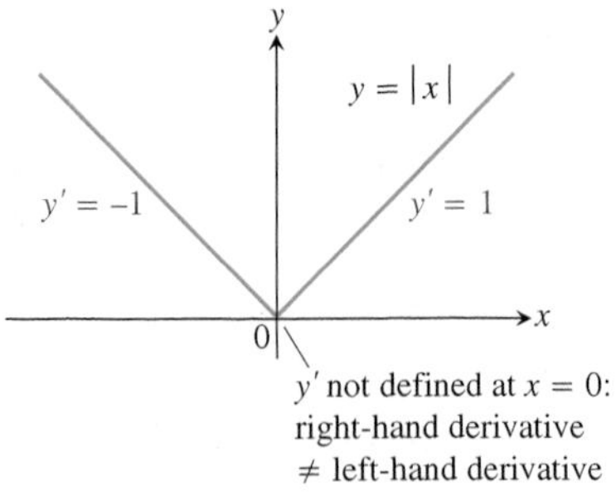

FIGURE 3.8 The function $y = |x|$ is not differentiable at the origin where the graph has a "corner" (Example 4).

EXAMPLE 5 In Example 2 we found that for $x > 0$,

$$\frac{d}{dx}\sqrt{x} = \frac{1}{2\sqrt{x}}.$$

We apply the definition to examine if the derivative exists at $x = 0$:

$$\lim_{h\to 0^+}\frac{\sqrt{0+h}-\sqrt{0}}{h} = \lim_{h\to 0^+}\frac{1}{\sqrt{h}} = \infty.$$

Since the (right-hand) limit is not finite, there is no derivative at $x = 0$. Since the slopes of the secant lines joining the origin to the points $(h, \sqrt{h})$ on a graph of $y = \sqrt{x}$ approach ∞, the graph has a *vertical tangent* at the origin. (See Figure 1.17 on page 9). ■

When Does a Function *Not* Have a Derivative at a Point?

A function has a derivative at a point x_0 if the slopes of the secant lines through $P(x_0, f(x_0))$ and a nearby point Q on the graph approach a finite limit as Q approaches P. Whenever the secants fail to take up a limiting position or become vertical as Q approaches P, the derivative does not exist. Thus differentiability is a "smoothness" condition on the graph of f. A function can fail to have a derivative at a point for many reasons, including the existence of points where the graph has

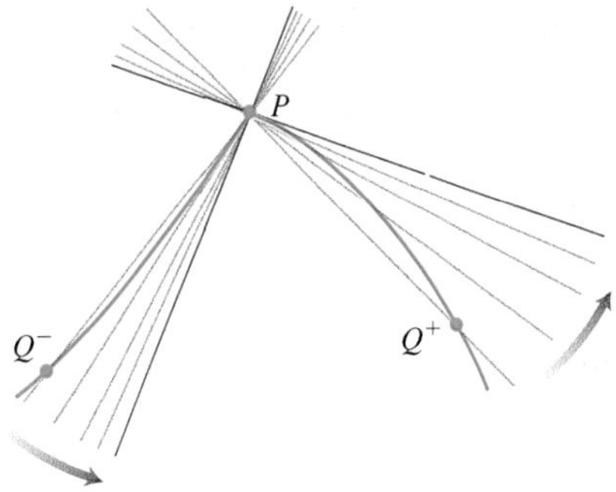

1. a *corner*, where the one-sided derivatives differ.

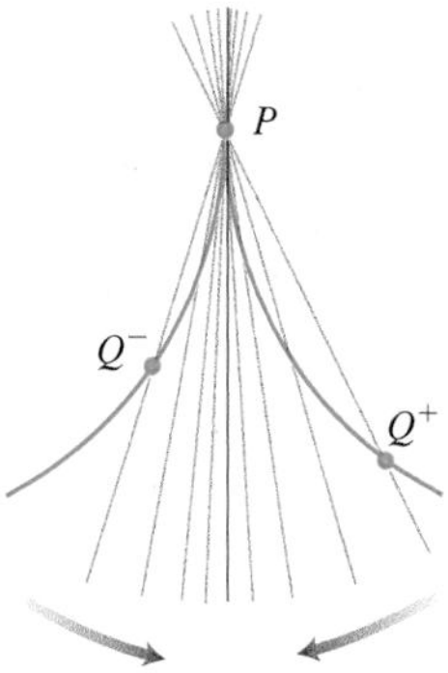

2. a *cusp*, where the slope of PQ approaches ∞ from one side and $-\infty$ from the other.

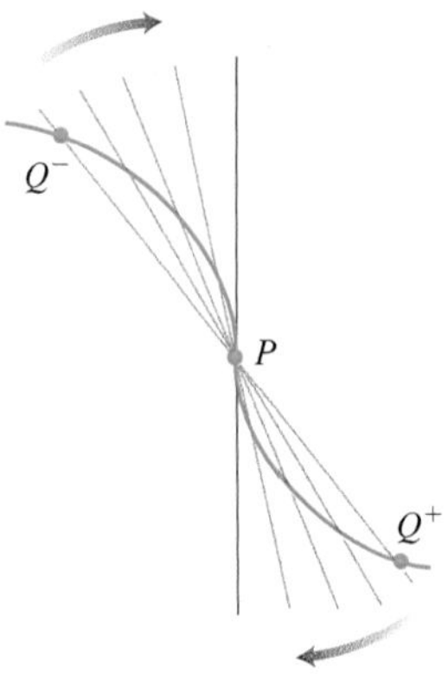

3. a *vertical tangent*, where the slope of PQ approaches ∞ from both sides or approaches $-\infty$ from both sides (here, $-\infty$).

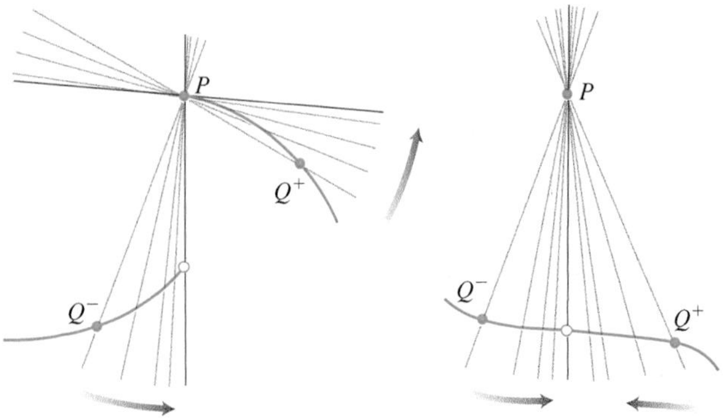

4. a *discontinuity* (two examples shown).

Another case in which the derivative may fail to exist occurs when the function's slope is oscillating rapidly near P, as with $f(x) = \sin(1/x)$ near the origin, where it is discontinuous (see Figure 2.31).

Differentiable Functions Are Continuous

A function is continuous at every point where it has a derivative.

> **THEOREM 1—Differentiability Implies Continuity** If f has a derivative at $x = c$, then f is continuous at $x = c$.

Proof Given that $f'(c)$ exists, we must show that $\lim_{x \to c} f(x) = f(c)$, or equivalently, that $\lim_{h \to 0} f(c + h) = f(c)$. If $h \neq 0$, then

$$\begin{aligned} f(c+h) &= f(c) + (f(c+h) - f(c)) \\ &= f(c) + \frac{f(c+h) - f(c)}{h} \cdot h. \end{aligned}$$

Now take limits as $h \to 0$. By Theorem 1 of Section 2.2,

$$\begin{aligned} \lim_{h \to 0} f(c+h) &= \lim_{h \to 0} f(c) + \lim_{h \to 0} \frac{f(c+h) - f(c)}{h} \cdot \lim_{h \to 0} h \\ &= f(c) + f'(c) \cdot 0 \\ &= f(c) + 0 \\ &= f(c). \end{aligned}$$

■

Similar arguments with one-sided limits show that if f has a derivative from one side (right or left) at $x = c$, then f is continuous from that side at $x = c$.

Theorem 1 says that if a function has a discontinuity at a point (for instance, a jump discontinuity), then it cannot be differentiable there. The greatest integer function $y = \lfloor x \rfloor$ fails to be differentiable at every integer $x = n$ (Example 4, Section 2.5).

Caution The converse of Theorem 1 is false. A function need not have a derivative at a point where it is continuous, as we saw in Example 4.

Exercises 3.2

Finding Derivative Functions and Values

Using the definition, calculate the derivatives of the functions in Exercises 1–6. Then find the values of the derivatives as specified.

1. $f(x) = 4 - x^2$; $f'(-3), f'(0), f'(1)$
2. $F(x) = (x - 1)^2 + 1$; $F'(-1), F'(0), F'(2)$
3. $g(t) = \dfrac{1}{t^2}$; $g'(-1), g'(2), g'(\sqrt{3})$
4. $k(z) = \dfrac{1 - z}{2z}$; $k'(-1), k'(1), k'(\sqrt{2})$
5. $p(\theta) = \sqrt{3\theta}$; $p'(1), p'(3), p'(2/3)$
6. $r(s) = \sqrt{2s + 1}$; $r'(0), r'(1), r'(1/2)$

In Exercises 7–12, find the indicated derivatives.

7. $\dfrac{dy}{dx}$ if $y = 2x^3$
8. $\dfrac{dr}{ds}$ if $r = s^3 - 2s^2 + 3$
9. $\dfrac{ds}{dt}$ if $s = \dfrac{t}{2t + 1}$
10. $\dfrac{dv}{dt}$ if $v = t - \dfrac{1}{t}$
11. $\dfrac{dp}{dq}$ if $p = \dfrac{1}{\sqrt{q + 1}}$
12. $\dfrac{dz}{dw}$ if $z = \dfrac{1}{\sqrt{3w - 2}}$

Slopes and Tangent Lines

In Exercises 13–16, differentiate the functions and find the slope of the tangent line at the given value of the independent variable.

13. $f(x) = x + \frac{9}{x}, \quad x = -3$ **14.** $k(x) = \frac{1}{2 + x}, \quad x = 2$

15. $s = t^3 - t^2, \quad t = -1$ **16.** $y = \frac{x + 3}{1 - x}, \quad x = -2$

In Exercises 17–18, differentiate the functions. Then find an equation of the tangent line at the indicated point on the graph of the function.

17. $y = f(x) = \frac{8}{\sqrt{x - 2}}, \quad (x, y) = (6, 4)$

18. $w = g(z) = 1 + \sqrt{4 - z}, \quad (z, w) = (3, 2)$

In Exercises 19–22, find the values of the derivatives.

19. $\left.\frac{ds}{dt}\right|_{t=-1}$ if $s = 1 - 3t^2$

20. $\left.\frac{dy}{dx}\right|_{x=\sqrt{3}}$ if $y = 1 - \frac{1}{x}$

21. $\left.\frac{dr}{d\theta}\right|_{\theta=0}$ if $r = \frac{2}{\sqrt{4 - \theta}}$

22. $\left.\frac{dw}{dz}\right|_{z=4}$ if $w = z + \sqrt{z}$

Using the Alternative Formula for Derivatives

Use the formula

$$f'(x) = \lim_{z \to x} \frac{f(z) - f(x)}{z - x}$$

to find the derivative of the functions in Exercises 23–26.

23. $f(x) = \frac{1}{x + 2}$ **24.** $f(x) = x^2 - 3x + 4$

25. $g(x) = \frac{x}{x - 1}$ **26.** $g(x) = 1 + \sqrt{x}$

Graphs

Match the functions graphed in Exercises 27–30 with the derivatives graphed in the accompanying figures (a)–(d).

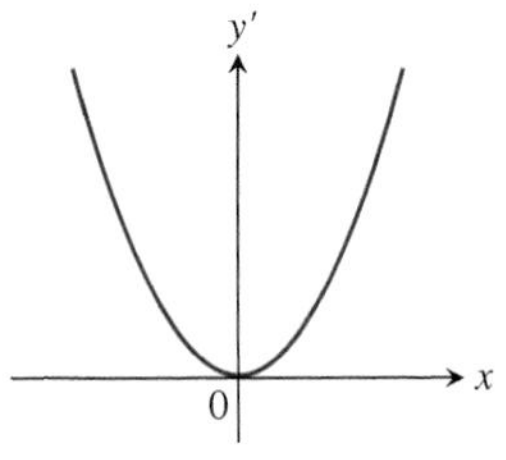

(a)

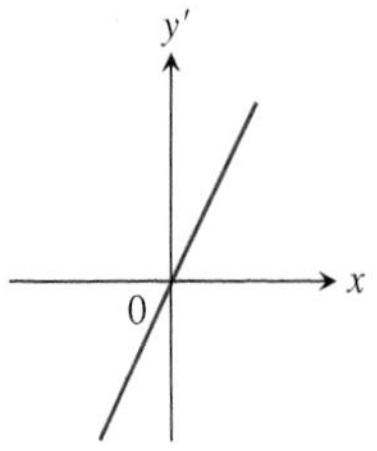

(b)

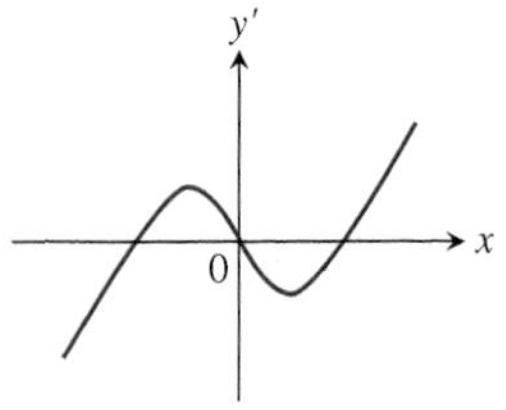

(c)

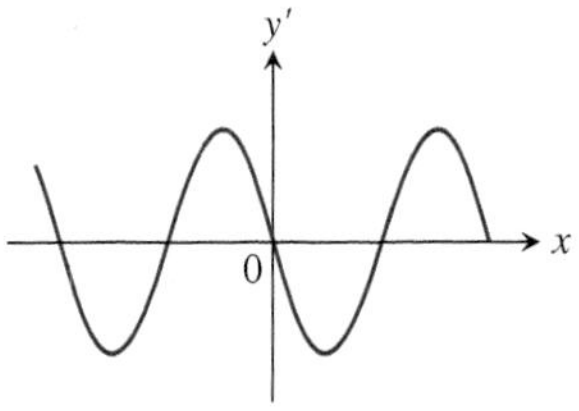

(d)

27.

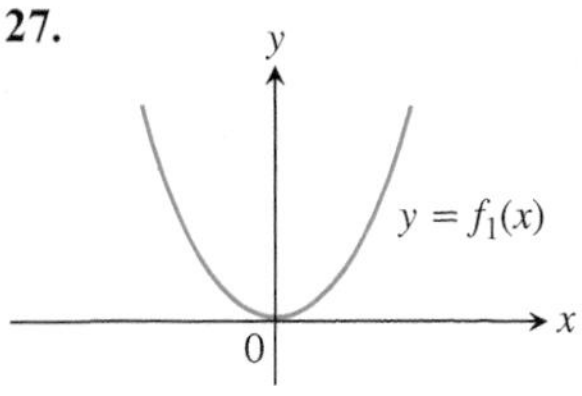

28.

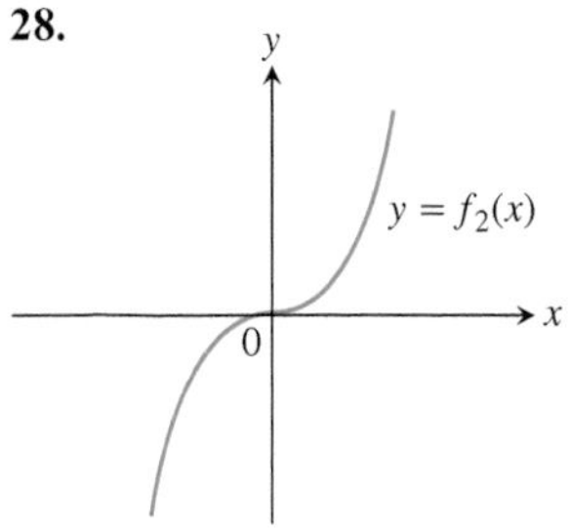

29.

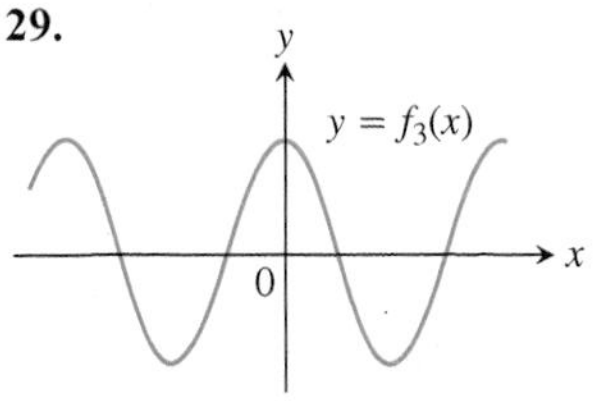

30.

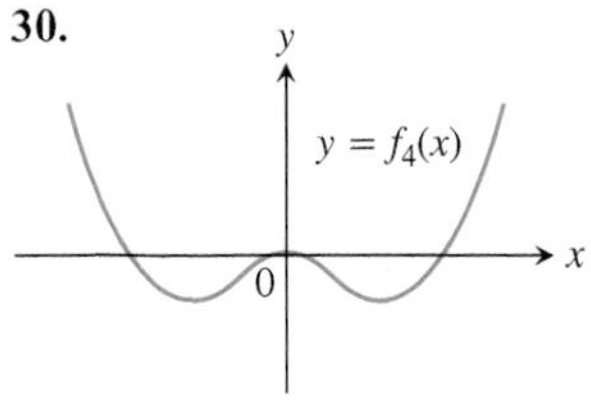

31. a. The graph in the accompanying figure is made of line segments joined end to end. At which points of the interval $[-4, 6]$ is f' not defined? Give reasons for your answer.

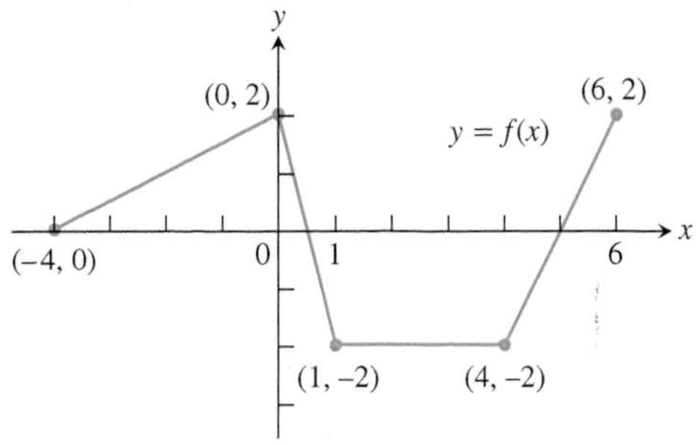

b. Graph the derivative of f.
The graph should show a step function.

32. Recovering a function from its derivative

a. Use the following information to graph the function f over the closed interval $[-2, 5]$.

i) The graph of f is made of closed line segments joined end to end.

ii) The graph starts at the point $(-2, 3)$.

iii) The derivative of f is the step function in the figure shown here.

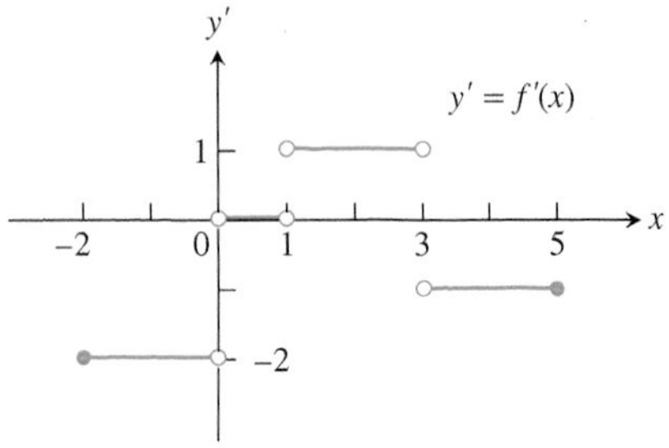

b. Repeat part (a), assuming that the graph starts at $(-2, 0)$ instead of $(-2, 3)$.

33. Growth in the economy The graph in the accompanying figure shows the average annual percentage change $y = f(t)$ in the U.S. gross national product (GNP) for the years 1983–1988. Graph dy/dt (where defined).

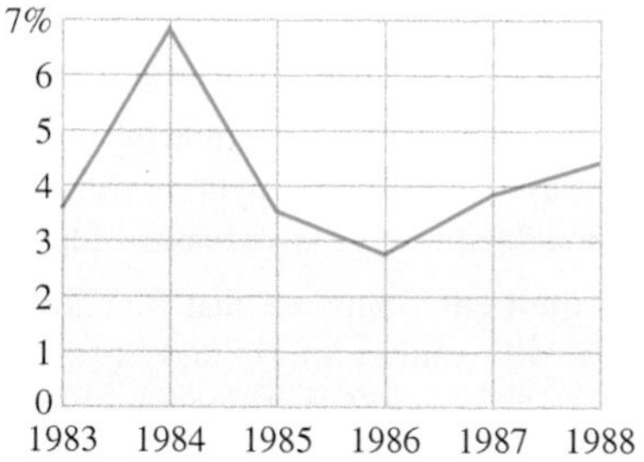

34. Fruit flies (*Continuation of Example 4, Section 2.1.*) Populations starting out in closed environments grow slowly at first, when there are relatively few members, then more rapidly as the number of reproducing individuals increases and resources are still abundant, then slowly again as the population reaches the carrying capacity of the environment.

a. Use the graphical technique of Example 3 to graph the derivative of the fruit fly population. The graph of the population is reproduced here.

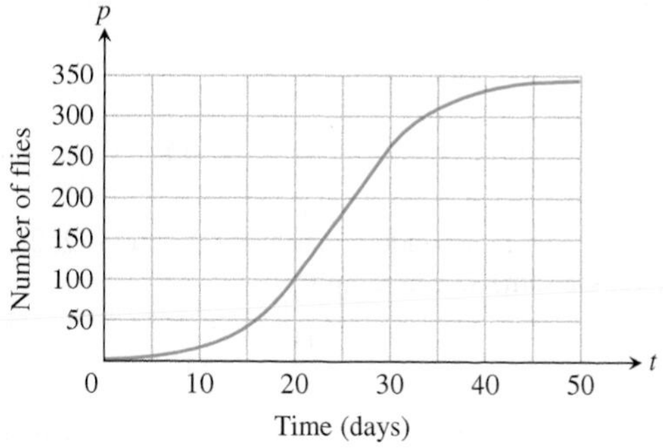

b. During what days does the population seem to be increasing fastest? Slowest?

35. Temperature The given graph shows the temperature T in °F at Davis, CA, on April 18, 2008, between 6 A.M. and 6 P.M.

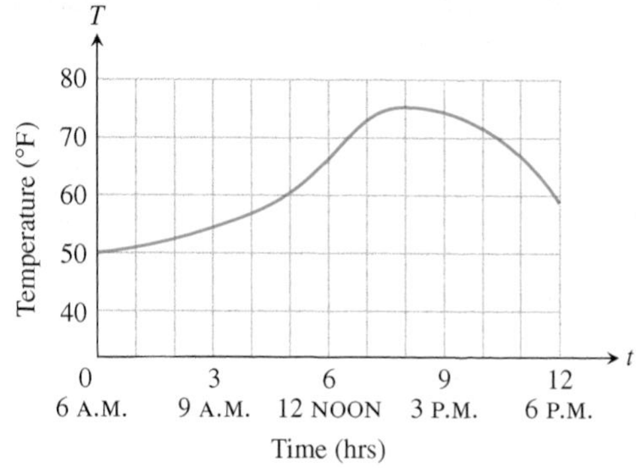

a. Estimate the rate of temperature change at the times

i) 7 A.M. **ii)** 9 A.M. **iii)** 2 P.M. **iv)** 4 P.M.

b. At what time does the temperature increase most rapidly? Decrease most rapidly? What is the rate for each of those times?

c. Use the graphical technique of Example 3 to graph the derivative of temperature T versus time t.

36. Weight loss Jared Fogle, also known as the "Subway Sandwich Guy," weighed 425 lb in 1997 before losing more than 240 lb in 12 months (http://en.wikipedia.org/wiki/Jared_Fogle). A chart showing his possible dramatic weight loss is given in the accompanying figure.

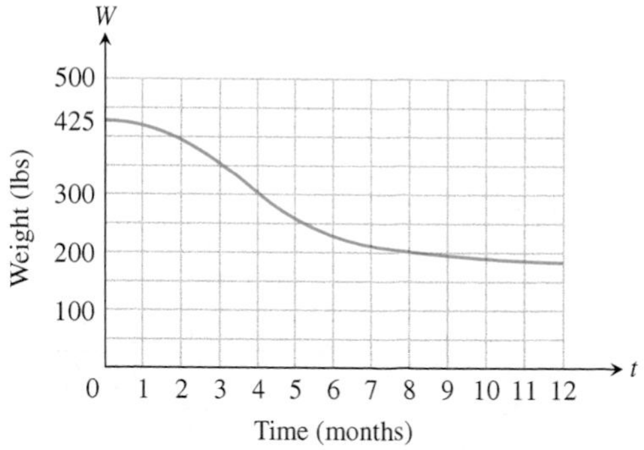

a. Estimate Jared's rate of weight loss when

i) $t = 1$ **ii)** $t = 4$ **iii)** $t = 11$

b. When does Jared lose weight most rapidly and what is this rate of weight loss?

c. Use the graphical technique of Example 3 to graph the derivative of weight W.

One-Sided Derivatives

Compute the right-hand and left-hand derivatives as limits to show that the functions in Exercises 37–40 are not differentiable at the point P.

37.

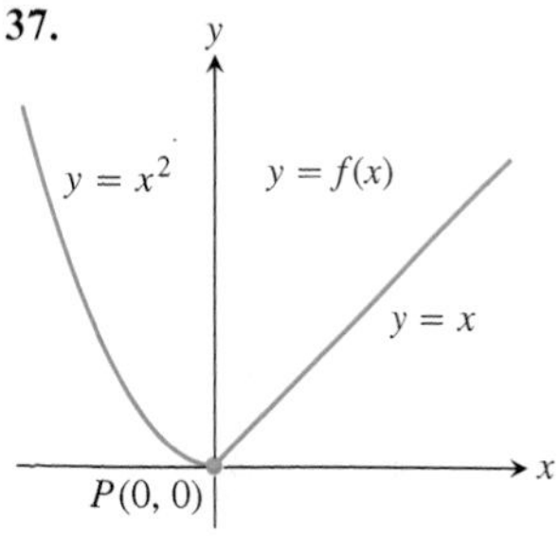

38.

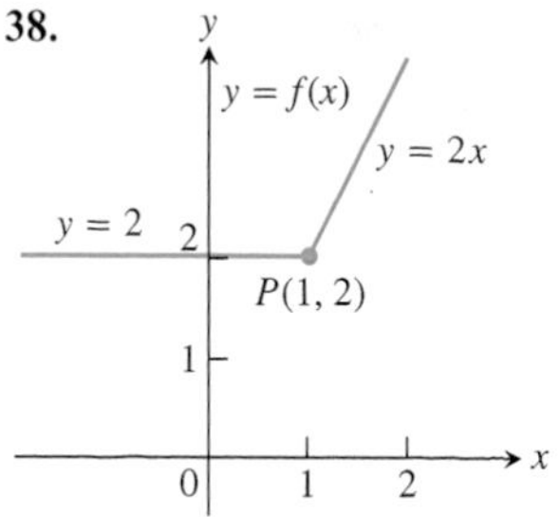

39.

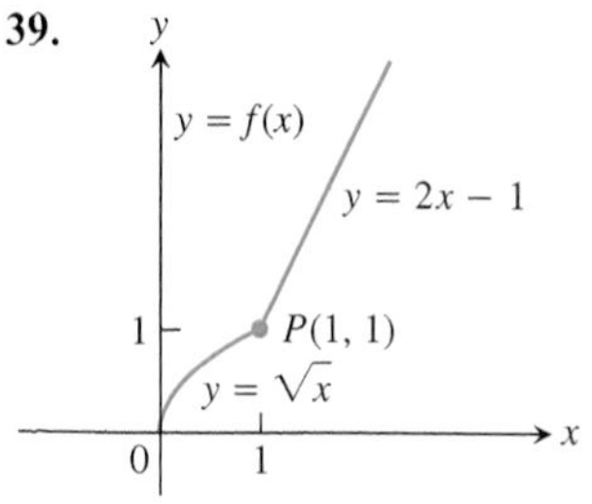

40.

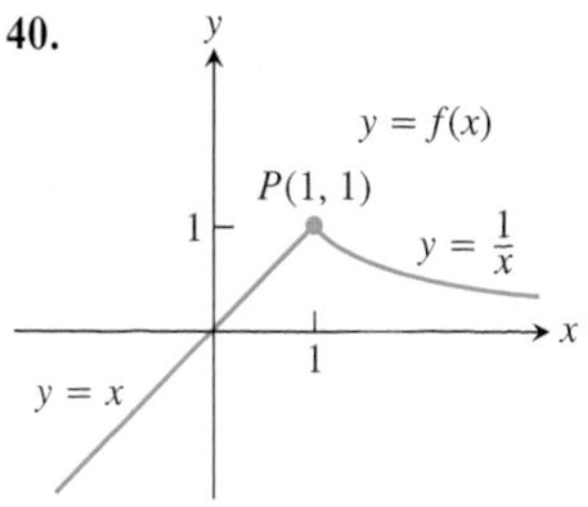

In Exercises 41 and 42, determine if the piecewise-defined function is differentiable at the origin.

41. $f(x) = \begin{cases} 2x - 1, & x \geq 0 \\ x^2 + 2x + 7, & x < 0 \end{cases}$

42. $g(x) = \begin{cases} x^{2/3}, & x \geq 0 \\ x^{1/3}, & x < 0 \end{cases}$

Differentiability and Continuity on an Interval

Each figure in Exercises 43–48 shows the graph of a function over a closed interval D. At what domain points does the function appear to be

a. differentiable?

b. continuous but not differentiable?

c. neither continuous nor differentiable?

Give reasons for your answers.

43.

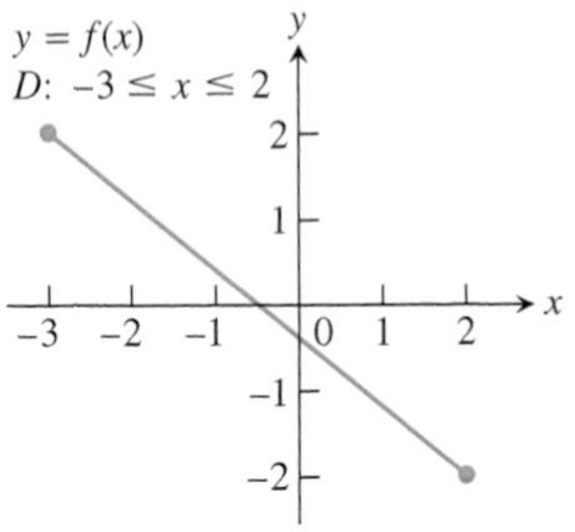

44.

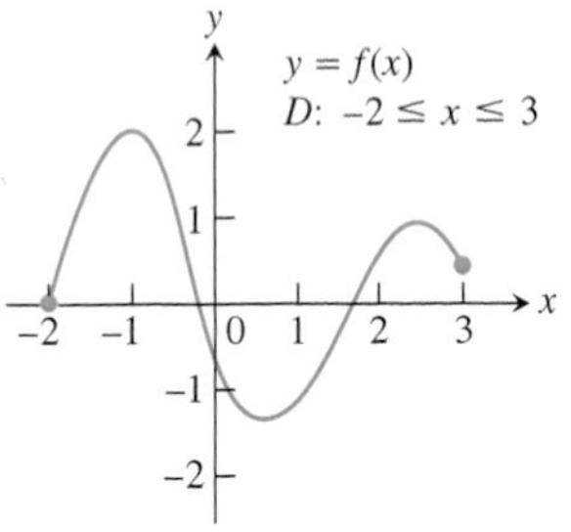

45.

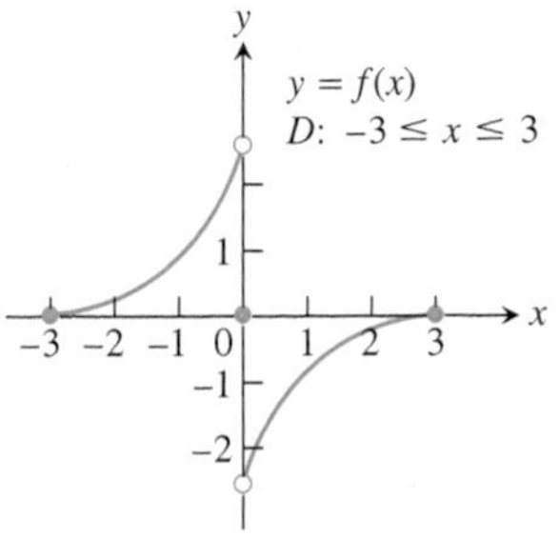

46.

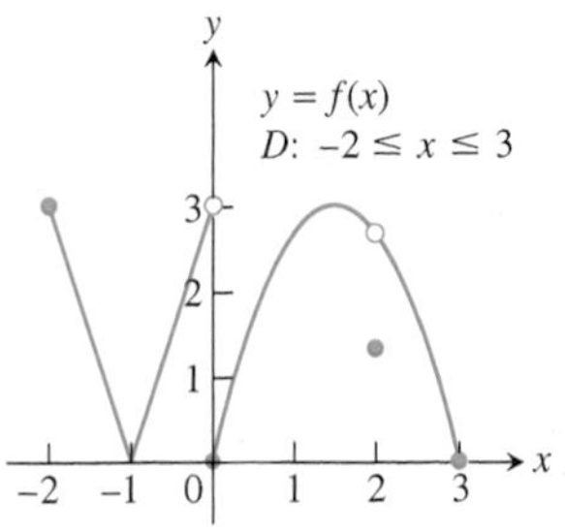

47.

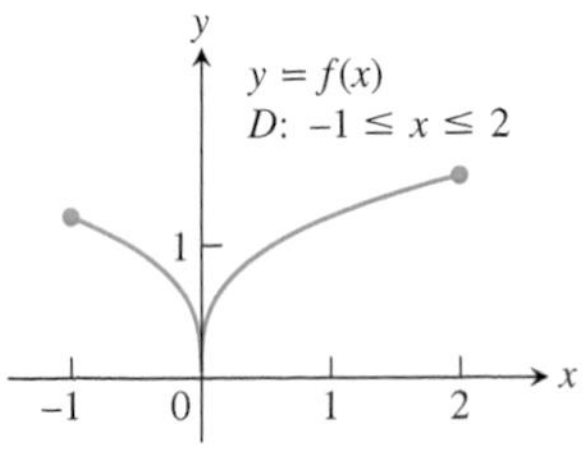

48.

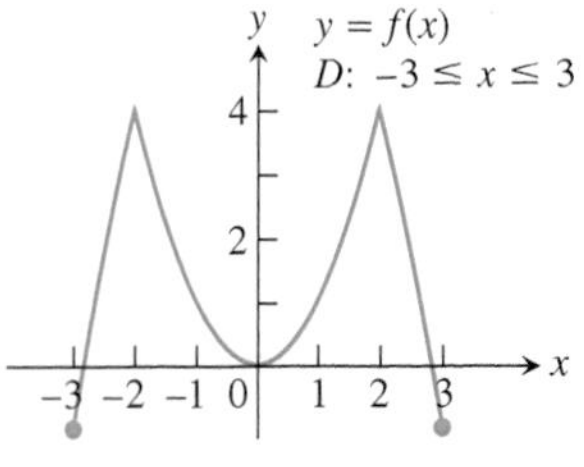

Theory and Examples

In Exercises 49–52,

a. Find the derivative $f'(x)$ of the given function $y = f(x)$.

b. Graph $y = f(x)$ and $y = f'(x)$ side by side using separate sets of coordinate axes, and answer the following questions.

c. For what values of x, if any, is f' positive? Zero? Negative?

d. Over what intervals of x-values, if any, does the function $y = f(x)$ increase as x increases? Decrease as x increases? How is this related to what you found in part (c)? (We will say more about this relationship in Section 4.3.)

49. $y = -x^2$ **50.** $y = -1/x$

51. $y = x^3/3$ **52.** $y = x^4/4$

53. Tangent to a parabola Does the parabola $y = 2x^2 - 13x + 5$ have a tangent whose slope is -1? If so, find an equation for the line and the point of tangency. If not, why not?

54. Tangent to $y = \sqrt{x}$ Does any tangent to the curve $y = \sqrt{x}$ cross the x-axis at $x = -1$? If so, find an equation for the line and the point of tangency. If not, why not?

55. Derivative of $-f$ Does knowing that a function $f(x)$ is differentiable at $x = x_0$ tell you anything about the differentiability of the function $-f$ at $x = x_0$? Give reasons for your answer.

56. Derivative of multiples Does knowing that a function $g(t)$ is differentiable at $t = 7$ tell you anything about the differentiability of the function $3g$ at $t = 7$? Give reasons for your answer.

57. Limit of a quotient Suppose that functions $g(t)$ and $h(t)$ are defined for all values of t and $g(0) = h(0) = 0$. Can $\lim_{t\to 0} (g(t))/(h(t))$ exist? If it does exist, must it equal zero? Give reasons for your answers.

58. a. Let $f(x)$ be a function satisfying $|f(x)| \le x^2$ for $-1 \le x \le 1$. Show that f is differentiable at $x = 0$ and find $f'(0)$.

b. Show that

$$f(x) = \begin{cases} x^2 \sin \dfrac{1}{x}, & x \neq 0 \\ 0, & x = 0 \end{cases}$$

is differentiable at $x = 0$ and find $f'(0)$.

T **59.** Graph $y = 1/(2\sqrt{x})$ in a window that has $0 \le x \le 2$. Then, on the same screen, graph

$$y = \frac{\sqrt{x + h} - \sqrt{x}}{h}$$

for $h = 1, 0.5, 0.1$. Then try $h = -1, -0.5, -0.1$. Explain what is going on.

T **60.** Graph $y = 3x^2$ in a window that has $-2 \le x \le 2, 0 \le y \le 3$. Then, on the same screen, graph

$$y = \frac{(x + h)^3 - x^3}{h}$$

for $h = 2, 1, 0.2$. Then try $h = -2, -1, -0.2$. Explain what is going on.

61. Derivative of $y = |x|$ Graph the derivative of $f(x) = |x|$. Then graph $y = (|x| - 0)/(x - 0) = |x|/x$. What can you conclude?

T **62. Weierstrass's nowhere differentiable continuous function** The sum of the first eight terms of the Weierstrass function $f(x) = \sum_{n=0}^{\infty} (2/3)^n \cos(9^n \pi x)$ is

$$g(x) = \cos(\pi x) + (2/3)^1 \cos(9\pi x) + (2/3)^2 \cos(9^2 \pi x) + (2/3)^3 \cos(9^3 \pi x) + \cdots + (2/3)^7 \cos(9^7 \pi x).$$

Graph this sum. Zoom in several times. How wiggly and bumpy is this graph? Specify a viewing window in which the displayed portion of the graph is smooth.

COMPUTER EXPLORATIONS

Use a CAS to perform the following steps for the functions in Exercises 63–68.

a. Plot $y = f(x)$ to see that function's global behavior.

b. Define the difference quotient q at a general point x, with general step size h.

c. Take the limit as $h \to 0$. What formula does this give?

d. Substitute the value $x = x_0$ and plot the function $y = f(x)$ together with its tangent line at that point.

e. Substitute various values for x larger and smaller than x_0 into the formula obtained in part (c). Do the numbers make sense with your picture?

f. Graph the formula obtained in part (c). What does it mean when its values are negative? Zero? Positive? Does this make sense with your plot from part (a)? Give reasons for your answer.

63. $f(x) = x^3 + x^2 - x, \quad x_0 = 1$

64. $f(x) = x^{1/3} + x^{2/3}, \quad x_0 = 1$

65. $f(x) = \dfrac{4x}{x^2 + 1}, \quad x_0 = 2$

66. $f(x) = \dfrac{x - 1}{3x^2 + 1}, \quad x_0 = -1$

67. $f(x) = \sin 2x, \quad x_0 = \pi/2$

68. $f(x) = x^2 \cos x, \quad x_0 = \pi/4$

3.3 Differentiation Rules

This section introduces several rules that allow us to differentiate constant functions, power functions, polynomials, exponential functions, rational functions, and certain combinations of them, simply and directly, without having to take limits each time.

Powers, Multiples, Sums, and Differences

A simple rule of differentiation is that the derivative of every constant function is zero.

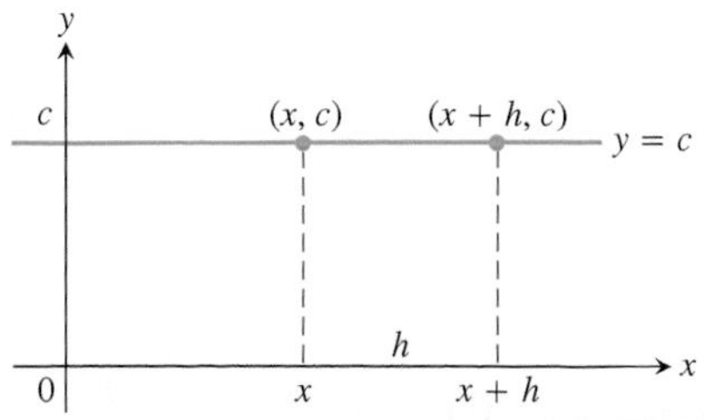

FIGURE 3.9 The rule $(d/dx)(c) = 0$ is another way to say that the values of constant functions never change and that the slope of a horizontal line is zero at every point.

Derivative of a Constant Function

If f has the constant value $f(x) = c$, then

$$\frac{df}{dx} = \frac{d}{dx}(c) = 0.$$

Proof We apply the definition of the derivative to $f(x) = c$, the function whose outputs have the constant value c (Figure 3.9). At every value of x, we find that

$$f'(x) = \lim_{h \to 0} \frac{f(x + h) - f(x)}{h} = \lim_{h \to 0} \frac{c - c}{h} = \lim_{h \to 0} 0 = 0. \qquad \blacksquare$$

From Section 3.1, we know that

$$\frac{d}{dx}\left(\frac{1}{x}\right) = -\frac{1}{x^2}, \quad \text{or} \quad \frac{d}{dx}\left(x^{-1}\right) = -x^{-2}.$$

From Example 2 of the last section we also know that

$$\frac{d}{dx}\left(\sqrt{x}\right) = \frac{1}{2\sqrt{x}}, \quad \text{or} \quad \frac{d}{dx}\left(x^{1/2}\right) = \frac{1}{2}x^{-1/2}.$$

These two examples illustrate a general rule for differentiating a power x^n. We first prove the rule when n is a positive integer.

Power Rule for Positive Integers:

If n is a positive integer, then

$$\frac{d}{dx}x^n = nx^{n-1}.$$

HISTORICAL BIOGRAPHY

Richard Courant
(1888–1972)

Proof of the Positive Integer Power Rule The formula

$$z^n - x^n = (z - x)(z^{n-1} + z^{n-2}x + \cdots + zx^{n-2} + x^{n-1})$$

can be verified by multiplying out the right-hand side. Then from the alternative formula for the definition of the derivative,

$$\begin{aligned} f'(x) &= \lim_{z\to x} \frac{f(z) - f(x)}{z - x} = \lim_{z\to x} \frac{z^n - x^n}{z - x} \\ &= \lim_{z\to x}(z^{n-1} + z^{n-2}x + \cdots + zx^{n-2} + x^{n-1}) \qquad n \text{ terms} \\ &= nx^{n-1}. \end{aligned}$$

■

The Power Rule is actually valid for all real numbers n. The number n could be a negative integer or a fractional power or an irrational number. To apply the Power Rule, we subtract 1 from the original exponent n and multiply the result by n. Here we state the general version of the rule, but postpone its proof until Section 3.8.

> **Power Rule (General Version)**
> If n is any real number, then
> $$\frac{d}{dx}x^n = nx^{n-1}$$
> for all x where the powers x^n and x^{n-1} are defined.

EXAMPLE 1 Differentiate the following powers of x.

(a) x^3 **(b)** $x^{2/3}$ **(c)** $x^{\sqrt{2}}$ **(d)** $\dfrac{1}{x^4}$ **(e)** $x^{-4/3}$ **(f)** $\sqrt{x^{2+\pi}}$

Solution

(a) $\dfrac{d}{dx}(x^3) = 3x^{3-1} = 3x^2$ **(b)** $\dfrac{d}{dx}(x^{2/3}) = \dfrac{2}{3}x^{(2/3)-1} = \dfrac{2}{3}x^{-1/3}$

(c) $\dfrac{d}{dx}\left(x^{\sqrt{2}}\right) = \sqrt{2}x^{\sqrt{2}-1}$ **(d)** $\dfrac{d}{dx}\left(\dfrac{1}{x^4}\right) = \dfrac{d}{dx}(x^{-4}) = -4x^{-4-1} = -4x^{-5} = -\dfrac{4}{x^5}$

(e) $\dfrac{d}{dx}(x^{-4/3}) = -\dfrac{4}{3}x^{-(4/3)-1} = -\dfrac{4}{3}x^{-7/3}$

(f) $\dfrac{d}{dx}\left(\sqrt{x^{2+\pi}}\right) = \dfrac{d}{dx}\left(x^{1+(\pi/2)}\right) = \left(1 + \dfrac{\pi}{2}\right)x^{1+(\pi/2)-1} = \dfrac{1}{2}(2 + \pi)\sqrt{x^{\pi}}$ ■

The next rule says that when a differentiable function is multiplied by a constant, its derivative is multiplied by the same constant.

> **Derivative Constant Multiple Rule**
> If u is a differentiable function of x, and c is a constant, then
> $$\frac{d}{dx}(cu) = c\frac{du}{dx}.$$

In particular, if n is any real number, then

$$\frac{d}{dx}(cx^n) = cnx^{n-1}.$$

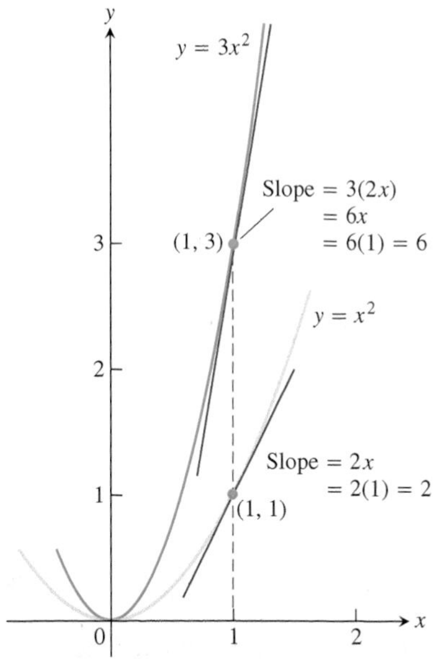

FIGURE 3.10 The graphs of $y = x^2$ and $y = 3x^2$. Tripling the y-coordinate triples the slope (Example 2).

Denoting Functions by u and v
The functions we are working with when we need a differentiation formula are likely to be denoted by letters like f and g. We do not want to use these same letters when stating general differentiation rules, so instead we use letters like u and v that are not likely to be already in use.

Proof

$$\frac{d}{dx}cu = \lim_{h\to 0}\frac{cu(x+h) - cu(x)}{h} \quad \text{Derivative definition with } f(x) = cu(x)$$

$$= c\lim_{h\to 0}\frac{u(x+h) - u(x)}{h} \quad \text{Constant Multiple Limit Property}$$

$$= c\frac{du}{dx} \quad u \text{ is differentiable.}$$ ■

EXAMPLE 2

(a) The derivative formula

$$\frac{d}{dx}(3x^2) = 3 \cdot 2x = 6x$$

says that if we rescale the graph of $y = x^2$ by multiplying each y-coordinate by 3, then we multiply the slope at each point by 3 (Figure 3.10).

(b) Negative of a function

The derivative of the negative of a differentiable function u is the negative of the function's derivative. The Constant Multiple Rule with $c = -1$ gives

$$\frac{d}{dx}(-u) = \frac{d}{dx}(-1 \cdot u) = -1 \cdot \frac{d}{dx}(u) = -\frac{du}{dx}.$$ ■

The next rule says that the derivative of the sum of two differentiable functions is the sum of their derivatives.

Derivative Sum Rule

If u and v are differentiable functions of x, then their sum $u + v$ is differentiable at every point where u and v are both differentiable. At such points,

$$\frac{d}{dx}(u + v) = \frac{du}{dx} + \frac{dv}{dx}.$$

For example, if $y = x^4 + 12x$, then y is the sum of $u(x) = x^4$ and $v(x) = 12x$. We then have

$$\frac{dy}{dx} = \frac{d}{dx}(x^4) + \frac{d}{dx}(12x) = 4x^3 + 12.$$

Proof We apply the definition of the derivative to $f(x) = u(x) + v(x)$:

$$\frac{d}{dx}[u(x) + v(x)] = \lim_{h\to 0}\frac{[u(x+h) + v(x+h)] - [u(x) + v(x)]}{h}$$

$$= \lim_{h\to 0}\left[\frac{u(x+h) - u(x)}{h} + \frac{v(x+h) - v(x)}{h}\right]$$

$$= \lim_{h\to 0}\frac{u(x+h) - u(x)}{h} + \lim_{h\to 0}\frac{v(x+h) - v(x)}{h} = \frac{du}{dx} + \frac{dv}{dx}.$$ ■

Combining the Sum Rule with the Constant Multiple Rule gives the **Difference Rule**, which says that the derivative of a *difference* of differentiable functions is the difference of their derivatives:

$$\frac{d}{dx}(u - v) = \frac{d}{dx}[u + (-1)v] = \frac{du}{dx} + (-1)\frac{dv}{dx} = \frac{du}{dx} - \frac{dv}{dx}.$$

The Sum Rule also extends to finite sums of more than two functions. If $u_1, u_2, \ldots, u_n$ are differentiable at x, then so is $u_1 + u_2 + \cdots + u_n$, and

$$\frac{d}{dx}(u_1 + u_2 + \cdots + u_n) = \frac{du_1}{dx} + \frac{du_2}{dx} + \cdots + \frac{du_n}{dx}.$$

For instance, to see that the rule holds for three functions we compute

$$\frac{d}{dx}(u_1 + u_2 + u_3) = \frac{d}{dx}((u_1 + u_2) + u_3) = \frac{d}{dx}(u_1 + u_2) + \frac{du_3}{dx} = \frac{du_1}{dx} + \frac{du_2}{dx} + \frac{du_3}{dx}.$$

A proof by mathematical induction for any finite number of terms is given in Appendix 2.

EXAMPLE 3 Find the derivative of the polynomial $y = x^3 + \frac{4}{3}x^2 - 5x + 1$.

Solution
$$\frac{dy}{dx} = \frac{d}{dx}x^3 + \frac{d}{dx}\left(\frac{4}{3}x^2\right) - \frac{d}{dx}(5x) + \frac{d}{dx}(1) \qquad \text{Sum and Difference Rules}$$
$$= 3x^2 + \frac{4}{3}\cdot 2x - 5 + 0 = 3x^2 + \frac{8}{3}x - 5$$
■

We can differentiate any polynomial term by term, the way we differentiated the polynomial in Example 3. All polynomials are differentiable at all values of x.

EXAMPLE 4 Does the curve $y = x^4 - 2x^2 + 2$ have any horizontal tangents? If so, where?

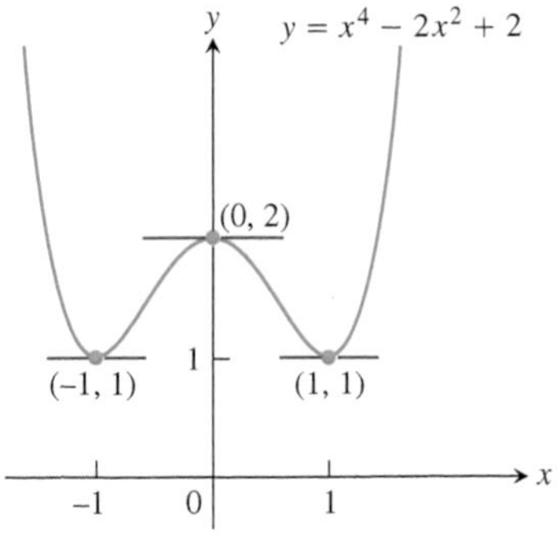

FIGURE 3.11 The curve in Example 4 and its horizontal tangents.

Solution The horizontal tangents, if any, occur where the slope dy/dx is zero. We have

$$\frac{dy}{dx} = \frac{d}{dx}(x^4 - 2x^2 + 2) = 4x^3 - 4x.$$

Now solve the equation $\frac{dy}{dx} = 0$ for x:

$$4x^3 - 4x = 0$$
$$4x(x^2 - 1) = 0$$
$$x = 0, 1, -1.$$

The curve $y = x^4 - 2x^2 + 2$ has horizontal tangents at $x = 0, 1$, and -1. The corresponding points on the curve are $(0, 2)$, $(1, 1)$, and $(-1, 1)$. See Figure 3.11. We will see in Chapter 4 that finding the values of x where the derivative of a function is equal to zero is an important and useful procedure. ■

Derivatives of Exponential Functions

We briefly reviewed exponential functions in Section 1.5. When we apply the definition of the derivative to $f(x) = a^x$, we get

$$\frac{d}{dx}(a^x) = \lim_{h\to 0}\frac{a^{x+h} - a^x}{h} \qquad \text{Derivative definition}$$
$$= \lim_{h\to 0}\frac{a^x\cdot a^h - a^x}{h} \qquad a^{x+h} = a^x\cdot a^h$$
$$= \lim_{h\to 0} a^x\cdot\frac{a^h - 1}{h} \qquad \text{Factoring out } a^x$$
$$= a^x\cdot\lim_{h\to 0}\frac{a^h - 1}{h} \qquad a^x \text{ is constant as } h \to 0.$$
$$= \underbrace{\left(\lim_{h\to 0}\frac{a^h - 1}{h}\right)}_{\text{a fixed number } L}\cdot a^x. \qquad (1)$$

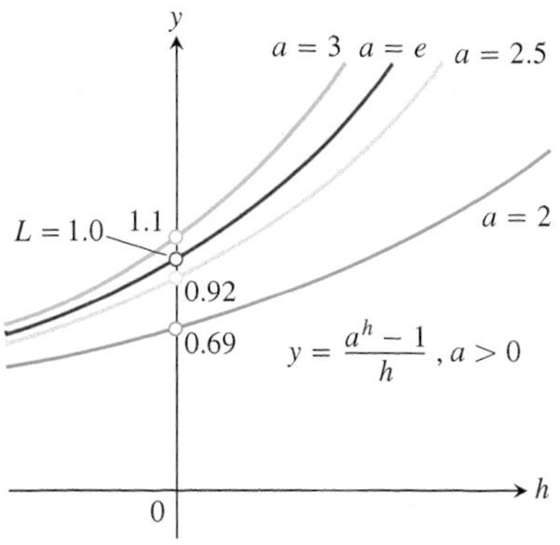

FIGURE 3.12 The position of the curve $y = (a^h - 1)/h$, $a > 0$, varies continuously with a. The limit L of y as $h \to 0$ changes with different values of a. The number e between $a = 2$ and $a = 3$ is the number for which the limit equals 1 as $h \to 0$.

Thus we see that the derivative of a^x is a constant multiple L of a^x. The constant L is a limit unlike any we have encountered before. Note, however, that it equals the derivative of $f(x) = a^x$ at $x = 0$:

$$f'(0) = \lim_{h \to 0} \frac{a^h - a^0}{h} = \lim_{h \to 0} \frac{a^h - 1}{h} = L.$$

The limit L is therefore the slope of the graph of $f(x) = a^x$ where it crosses the y-axis. In Chapter 7, where we carefully develop the logarithmic and exponential functions, we prove that the limit L exists and has the value $\ln a$. For now we investigate values of L by graphing the function $y = (a^h - 1)/h$ and studying its behavior as h approaches 0.

Figure 3.12 shows the graphs of $y = (a^h - 1)/h$ for four different values of a. The limit L is approximately 0.69 if $a = 2$, about 0.92 if $a = 2.5$, and about 1.1 if $a = 3$. It appears that the value of L is 1 at some number a chosen between 2.5 and 3. That number is given by $a = e \approx 2.718281828$. With this choice of base we obtain the natural exponential function $f(x) = e^x$ as in Section 1.5, and see that it satisfies the property

$$f'(0) = \lim_{h \to 0} \frac{e^h - 1}{h} = 1. \tag{2}$$

That the limit is 1 implies an important relationship between the natural exponential function e^x and its derivative:

$$\frac{d}{dx}(e^x) = \lim_{h \to 0} \left(\frac{e^h - 1}{h} \right) \cdot e^x \qquad \text{Eq. (1) with } a = e$$

$$= 1 \cdot e^x = e^x. \qquad \text{Eq. (2)}$$

Therefore the natural exponential function is its own derivative.

Derivative of the Natural Exponential Function

$$\frac{d}{dx}(e^x) = e^x$$

EXAMPLE 5 Find an equation for a line that is tangent to the graph of $y = e^x$ and goes through the origin.

Solution Since the line passes through the origin, its equation is of the form $y = mx$, where m is the slope. If it is tangent to the graph at the point (a, e^a), the slope is $m = (e^a - 0)/(a - 0)$. The slope of the natural exponential at $x = a$ is e^a. Because these slopes are the same, we then have that $e^a = e^a/a$. It follows that $a = 1$ and $m = e$, so the equation of the tangent line is $y = ex$. See Figure 3.13. ■

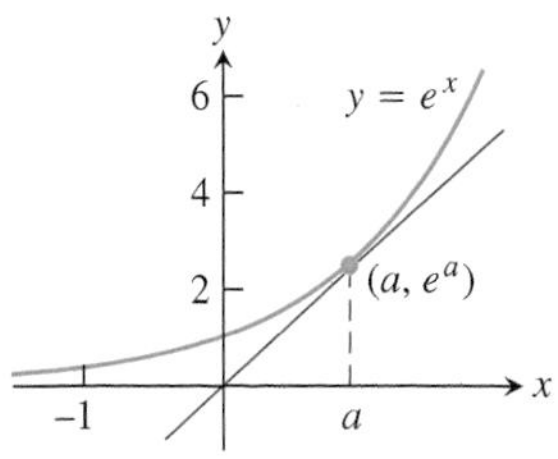

FIGURE 3.13 The line through the origin is tangent to the graph of $y = e^x$ when $a = 1$ (Example 5).

We might ask if there are functions *other* than the natural exponential function that are their own derivatives. The answer is that the only functions that satisfy the property that $f'(x) = f(x)$ are functions that are constant multiples of the natural exponential function, $f(x) = c \cdot e^x$, c any constant. We prove this fact in Section 7.2. Note from the Constant Multiple Rule that indeed

$$\frac{d}{dx}(c \cdot e^x) = c \cdot \frac{d}{dx}(e^x) = c \cdot e^x.$$

Products and Quotients

While the derivative of the sum of two functions is the sum of their derivatives, the derivative of the product of two functions is *not* the product of their derivatives. For instance,

$$\frac{d}{dx}(x \cdot x) = \frac{d}{dx}(x^2) = 2x, \qquad \text{while} \qquad \frac{d}{dx}(x) \cdot \frac{d}{dx}(x) = 1 \cdot 1 = 1.$$

The derivative of a product of two functions is the sum of *two* products, as we now explain.

Derivative Product Rule

If u and v are differentiable at x, then so is their product uv, and

$$\frac{d}{dx}(uv) = u\frac{dv}{dx} + v\frac{du}{dx}.$$

The derivative of the product uv is u times the derivative of v plus v times the derivative of u. In *prime notation*, $(uv)' = uv' + vu'$. In function notation,

$$\frac{d}{dx}[f(x)g(x)] = f(x)g'(x) + g(x)f'(x).$$

EXAMPLE 6 Find the derivative of **(a)** $y = \frac{1}{x}\left(x^2 + e^x\right)$, **(b)** $y = e^{2x}$.

Solution

(a) We apply the Product Rule with $u = 1/x$ and $v = x^2 + e^x$:

$$\frac{d}{dx}\left[\frac{1}{x}\left(x^2 + e^x\right)\right] = \frac{1}{x}\left(2x + e^x\right) + \left(x^2 + e^x\right)\left(-\frac{1}{x^2}\right)$$

$$= 2 + \frac{e^x}{x} - 1 - \frac{e^x}{x^2}$$

$$= 1 + (x - 1)\frac{e^x}{x^2}.$$

$\frac{d}{dx}(uv) = u\frac{dv}{dx} + v\frac{du}{dx}$, and

$\frac{d}{dx}\left(\frac{1}{x}\right) = -\frac{1}{x^2}$

(b) $\frac{d}{dx}(e^{2x}) = \frac{d}{dx}(e^x \cdot e^x) = e^x \cdot \frac{d}{dx}(e^x) + e^x \cdot \frac{d}{dx}(e^x) = 2e^x \cdot e^x = 2e^{2x}$ ■

Picturing the Product Rule

Suppose $u(x)$ and $v(x)$ are positive and increase when x increases, and $h > 0$.

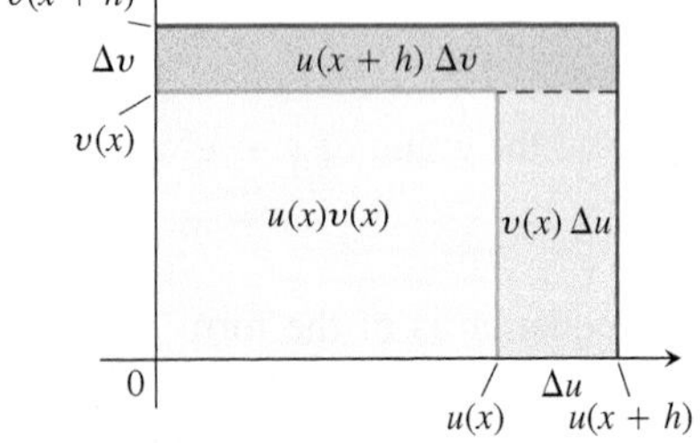

Then the change in the product uv is the difference in areas of the larger and smaller "squares," which is the sum of the upper and right-hand reddish-shaded rectangles. That is,

$$\Delta(uv) = u(x + h)v(x + h) - u(x)v(x)$$
$$= u(x + h)\Delta v + v(x)\Delta u.$$

Division by h gives

$$\frac{\Delta(uv)}{h} = u(x + h)\frac{\Delta v}{h} + v(x)\frac{\Delta u}{h}.$$

The limit as $h \to 0^+$ gives the Product Rule.

Proof of the Derivative Product Rule

$$\frac{d}{dx}(uv) = \lim_{h\to 0}\frac{u(x + h)v(x + h) - u(x)v(x)}{h}$$

To change this fraction into an equivalent one that contains difference quotients for the derivatives of u and v, we subtract and add $u(x + h)v(x)$ in the numerator:

$$\frac{d}{dx}(uv) = \lim_{h\to 0}\frac{u(x + h)v(x + h) - u(x + h)v(x) + u(x + h)v(x) - u(x)v(x)}{h}$$

$$= \lim_{h\to 0}\left[u(x + h)\frac{v(x + h) - v(x)}{h} + v(x)\frac{u(x + h) - u(x)}{h}\right]$$

$$= \lim_{h\to 0}u(x + h) \cdot \lim_{h\to 0}\frac{v(x + h) - v(x)}{h} + v(x) \cdot \lim_{h\to 0}\frac{u(x + h) - u(x)}{h}.$$

As h approaches zero, $u(x + h)$ approaches $u(x)$ because u, being differentiable at x, is continuous at x. The two fractions approach the values of dv/dx at x and du/dx at x. In short,

$$\frac{d}{dx}(uv) = u\frac{dv}{dx} + v\frac{du}{dx}.$$ ■

EXAMPLE 7 Find the derivative of $y = (x^2 + 1)(x^3 + 3)$.

Solution

(a) From the Product Rule with $u = x^2 + 1$ and $v = x^3 + 3$, we find

$$\begin{aligned}\frac{d}{dx}\left[(x^2 + 1)(x^3 + 3)\right] &= (x^2 + 1)(3x^2) + (x^3 + 3)(2x) \qquad \frac{d}{dx}(uv) = u\frac{dv}{dx} + v\frac{du}{dx}\\ &= 3x^4 + 3x^2 + 2x^4 + 6x\\ &= 5x^4 + 3x^2 + 6x.\end{aligned}$$

(b) This particular product can be differentiated as well (perhaps better) by multiplying out the original expression for y and differentiating the resulting polynomial:

$$\begin{aligned}y &= (x^2 + 1)(x^3 + 3) = x^5 + x^3 + 3x^2 + 3\\ \frac{dy}{dx} &= 5x^4 + 3x^2 + 6x.\end{aligned}$$

This is in agreement with our first calculation. ■

The derivative of the quotient of two functions is given by the Quotient Rule.

Derivative Quotient Rule

If u and v are differentiable at x and if $v(x) \neq 0$, then the quotient u/v is differentiable at x, and

$$\frac{d}{dx}\left(\frac{u}{v}\right) = \frac{v\dfrac{du}{dx} - u\dfrac{dv}{dx}}{v^2}.$$

In function notation,

$$\frac{d}{dx}\left[\frac{f(x)}{g(x)}\right] = \frac{g(x)f'(x) - f(x)g'(x)}{g^2(x)}.$$

EXAMPLE 8 Find the derivative of **(a)** $y = \dfrac{t^2 - 1}{t^3 + 1}$, **(b)** $y = e^{-x}$.

Solution

(a) We apply the Quotient Rule with $u = t^2 - 1$ and $v = t^3 + 1$:

$$\begin{aligned}\frac{dy}{dt} &= \frac{(t^3 + 1)\cdot 2t - (t^2 - 1)\cdot 3t^2}{(t^3 + 1)^2} \qquad \frac{d}{dt}\left(\frac{u}{v}\right) = \frac{v(du/dt) - u(dv/dt)}{v^2}\\ &= \frac{2t^4 + 2t - 3t^4 + 3t^2}{(t^3 + 1)^2}\\ &= \frac{-t^4 + 3t^2 + 2t}{(t^3 + 1)^2}.\end{aligned}$$

(b) $$\frac{d}{dx}(e^{-x}) = \frac{d}{dx}\left(\frac{1}{e^x}\right) = \frac{e^x\cdot 0 - 1\cdot e^x}{(e^x)^2} = \frac{-1}{e^x} = -e^{-x}$$ ■

Proof of the Derivative Quotient Rule

$$\frac{d}{dx}\left(\frac{u}{v}\right) = \lim_{h\to 0} \frac{\dfrac{u(x+h)}{v(x+h)} - \dfrac{u(x)}{v(x)}}{h}$$

$$= \lim_{h\to 0} \frac{v(x)u(x+h) - u(x)v(x+h)}{hv(x+h)v(x)}$$

To change the last fraction into an equivalent one that contains the difference quotients for the derivatives of u and v, we subtract and add $v(x)u(x)$ in the numerator. We then get

$$\frac{d}{dx}\left(\frac{u}{v}\right) = \lim_{h\to 0} \frac{v(x)u(x+h) - v(x)u(x) + v(x)u(x) - u(x)v(x+h)}{hv(x+h)v(x)}$$

$$= \lim_{h\to 0} \frac{v(x)\dfrac{u(x+h) - u(x)}{h} - u(x)\dfrac{v(x+h) - v(x)}{h}}{v(x+h)v(x)}.$$

Taking the limits in the numerator and denominator now gives the Quotient Rule. Exercise 74 outlines another proof. ■

The choice of which rules to use in solving a differentiation problem can make a difference in how much work you have to do. Here is an example.

EXAMPLE 9 Find the derivative of

$$y = \frac{(x-1)(x^2-2x)}{x^4}.$$

Solution Using the Quotient Rule here will result in a complicated expression with many terms. Instead, use some algebra to simplify the expression. First expand the numerator and divide by x^4:

$$y = \frac{(x-1)(x^2-2x)}{x^4} = \frac{x^3 - 3x^2 + 2x}{x^4} = x^{-1} - 3x^{-2} + 2x^{-3}.$$

Then use the Sum and Power Rules:

$$\frac{dy}{dx} = -x^{-2} - 3(-2)x^{-3} + 2(-3)x^{-4}$$

$$= -\frac{1}{x^2} + \frac{6}{x^3} - \frac{6}{x^4}.$$ ■

Second- and Higher-Order Derivatives

If $y = f(x)$ is a differentiable function, then its derivative $f'(x)$ is also a function. If f' is also differentiable, then we can differentiate f' to get a new function of x denoted by f''. So $f'' = (f')'$. The function f'' is called the **second derivative** of f because it is the derivative of the first derivative. It is written in several ways:

$$f''(x) = \frac{d^2y}{dx^2} = \frac{d}{dx}\left(\frac{dy}{dx}\right) = \frac{dy'}{dx} = y'' = D^2(f)(x) = D_x^2 f(x).$$

The symbol D^2 means the operation of differentiation is performed twice.

If $y = x^6$, then $y' = 6x^5$ and we have

$$y'' = \frac{dy'}{dx} = \frac{d}{dx}(6x^5) = 30x^4.$$

Thus $D^2(x^6) = 30x^4$.

How to Read the Symbols for Derivatives

y'	"y prime"
y''	"y double prime"
$\frac{d^2y}{dx^2}$	"d squared y dx squared"
y'''	"y triple prime"
$y^{(n)}$	"y super n"
$\frac{d^ny}{dx^n}$	"d to the n of y by dx to the n"
D^n	"D to the n"

If y'' is differentiable, its derivative, $y''' = dy''/dx = d^3y/dx^3$, is the **third derivative** of y with respect to x. The names continue as you imagine, with

$$y^{(n)} = \frac{d}{dx}y^{(n-1)} = \frac{d^ny}{dx^n} = D^ny$$

denoting the ***n*th derivative** of y with respect to x for any positive integer n.

We can interpret the second derivative as the rate of change of the slope of the tangent to the graph of $y = f(x)$ at each point. You will see in the next chapter that the second derivative reveals whether the graph bends upward or downward from the tangent line as we move off the point of tangency. In the next section, we interpret both the second and third derivatives in terms of motion along a straight line.

EXAMPLE 10 The first four derivatives of $y = x^3 - 3x^2 + 2$ are

First derivative: $y' = 3x^2 - 6x$

Second derivative: $y'' = 6x - 6$

Third derivative: $y''' = 6$

Fourth derivative: $y^{(4)} = 0.$

The function has derivatives of all orders, the fifth and later derivatives all being zero. ■

Exercises 3.3

Derivative Calculations

In Exercises 1–12, find the first and second derivatives.

1. $y = -x^2 + 3$ **2.** $y = x^2 + x + 8$

3. $s = 5t^3 - 3t^5$ **4.** $w = 3z^7 - 7z^3 + 21z^2$

5. $y = \frac{4x^3}{3} - x + 2e^x$ **6.** $y = \frac{x^3}{3} + \frac{x^2}{2} + \frac{x}{4}$

7. $w = 3z^{-2} - \frac{1}{z}$ **8.** $s = -2t^{-1} + \frac{4}{t^2}$

9. $y = 6x^2 - 10x - 5x^{-2}$ **10.** $y = 4 - 2x - x^{-3}$

11. $r = \frac{1}{3s^2} - \frac{5}{2s}$ **12.** $r = \frac{12}{\theta} - \frac{4}{\theta^3} + \frac{1}{\theta^4}$

In Exercises 13–16, find y' **(a)** by applying the Product Rule and **(b)** by multiplying the factors to produce a sum of simpler terms to differentiate.

13. $y = (3 - x^2)(x^3 - x + 1)$ **14.** $y = (2x + 3)(5x^2 - 4x)$

15. $y = (x^2 + 1)\left(x + 5 + \frac{1}{x}\right)$ **16.** $y = (1 + x^2)(x^{3/4} - x^{-3})$

Find the derivatives of the functions in Exercises 17–40.

17. $y = \frac{2x + 5}{3x - 2}$ **18.** $z = \frac{4 - 3x}{3x^2 + x}$

19. $g(x) = \frac{x^2 - 4}{x + 0.5}$ **20.** $f(t) = \frac{t^2 - 1}{t^2 + t - 2}$

21. $v = (1 - t)(1 + t^2)^{-1}$ **22.** $w = (2x - 7)^{-1}(x + 5)$

23. $f(s) = \frac{\sqrt{s} - 1}{\sqrt{s} + 1}$ **24.** $u = \frac{5x + 1}{2\sqrt{x}}$

25. $v = \frac{1 + x - 4\sqrt{x}}{x}$ **26.** $r = 2\left(\frac{1}{\sqrt{\theta}} + \sqrt{\theta}\right)$

27. $y = \frac{1}{(x^2 - 1)(x^2 + x + 1)}$ **28.** $y = \frac{(x + 1)(x + 2)}{(x - 1)(x - 2)}$

29. $y = 2e^{-x} + e^{3x}$ **30.** $y = \frac{x^2 + 3e^x}{2e^x - x}$

31. $y = x^3e^x$ **32.** $w = re^{-r}$

33. $y = x^{9/4} + e^{-2x}$ **34.** $y = x^{-3/5} + \pi^{3/2}$

35. $s = 2t^{3/2} + 3e^2$ **36.** $w = \frac{1}{z^{1.4}} + \frac{\pi}{\sqrt{z}}$

37. $y = \sqrt[7]{x^2} - x^e$ **38.** $y = \sqrt[3]{x^{9.6}} + 2e^{1.3}$

39. $r = \frac{e^s}{s}$ **40.** $r = e^\theta\left(\frac{1}{\theta^2} + \theta^{-\pi/2}\right)$

Find the derivatives of all orders of the functions in Exercises 41–44.

41. $y = \frac{x^4}{2} - \frac{3}{2}x^2 - x$ **42.** $y = \frac{x^5}{120}$

43. $y = (x - 1)(x^2 + 3x - 5)$ **44.** $y = (4x^3 + 3x)(2 - x)$

Find the first and second derivatives of the functions in Exercises 45–52.

45. $y = \frac{x^3 + 7}{x}$ **46.** $s = \frac{t^2 + 5t - 1}{t^2}$

47. $r = \frac{(\theta - 1)(\theta^2 + \theta + 1)}{\theta^3}$ **48.** $u = \frac{(x^2 + x)(x^2 - x + 1)}{x^4}$

49. $w = \left(\frac{1 + 3z}{3z}\right)(3 - z)$ **50.** $p = \frac{q^2 + 3}{(q - 1)^3 + (q + 1)^3}$

51. $w = 3z^2e^{2z}$ **52.** $w = e^z(z - 1)(z^2 + 1)$

53. Suppose u and v are functions of x that are differentiable at $x = 0$ and that

$$u(0) = 5, \quad u'(0) = -3, \quad v(0) = -1, \quad v'(0) = 2.$$

Find the values of the following derivatives at $x = 0$.

a. $\frac{d}{dx}(uv)$ **b.** $\frac{d}{dx}\left(\frac{u}{v}\right)$ **c.** $\frac{d}{dx}\left(\frac{v}{u}\right)$ **d.** $\frac{d}{dx}(7v - 2u)$

54. Suppose u and v are differentiable functions of x and that

$$u(1) = 2, \quad u'(1) = 0, \quad v(1) = 5, \quad v'(1) = -1.$$

Find the values of the following derivatives at $x = 1$.

a. $\frac{d}{dx}(uv)$ **b.** $\frac{d}{dx}\left(\frac{u}{v}\right)$ **c.** $\frac{d}{dx}\left(\frac{v}{u}\right)$ **d.** $\frac{d}{dx}(7v - 2u)$

Slopes and Tangents

55. **a. Normal to a curve** Find an equation for the line perpendicular to the tangent to the curve $y = x^3 - 4x + 1$ at the point (2, 1).

b. Smallest slope What is the smallest slope on the curve? At what point on the curve does the curve have this slope?

c. Tangents having specified slope Find equations for the tangents to the curve at the points where the slope of the curve is 8.

56. **a. Horizontal tangents** Find equations for the horizontal tangents to the curve $y = x^3 - 3x - 2$. Also find equations for the lines that are perpendicular to these tangents at the points of tangency.

b. Smallest slope What is the smallest slope on the curve? At what point on the curve does the curve have this slope? Find an equation for the line that is perpendicular to the curve's tangent at this point.

57. Find the tangents to *Newton's serpentine* (graphed here) at the origin and the point (1, 2).

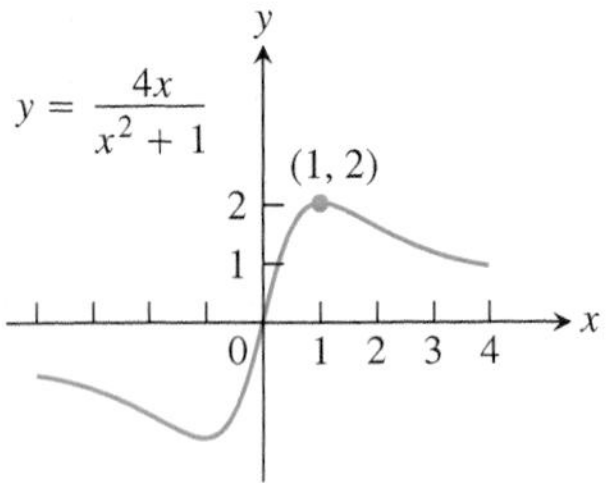

58. Find the tangent to the *Witch of Agnesi* (graphed here) at the point (2, 1).

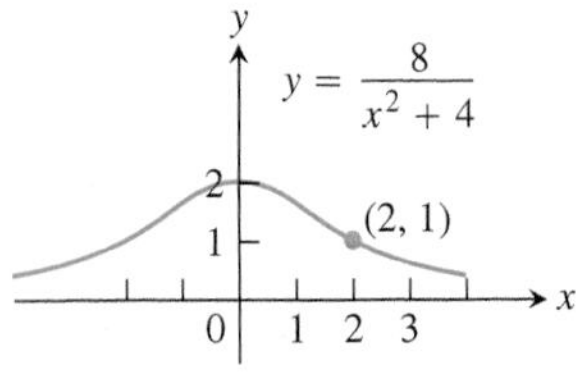

59. **Quadratic tangent to identity function** The curve $y = ax^2 + bx + c$ passes through the point (1, 2) and is tangent to the line $y = x$ at the origin. Find a, b, and c.

60. **Quadratics having a common tangent** The curves $y = x^2 + ax + b$ and $y = cx - x^2$ have a common tangent line at the point (1, 0). Find a, b, and c.

61. Find all points (x, y) on the graph of $f(x) = 3x^2 - 4x$ with tangent lines parallel to the line $y = 8x + 5$.

62. Find all points (x, y) on the graph of $g(x) = \frac{1}{3}x^3 - \frac{3}{2}x^2 + 1$ with tangent lines parallel to the line $8x - 2y = 1$.

63. Find all points (x, y) on the graph of $y = x/(x - 2)$ with tangent lines perpendicular to the line $y = 2x + 3$.

64. Find all points (x, y) on the graph of $f(x) = x^2$ with tangent lines passing through the point (3, 8).

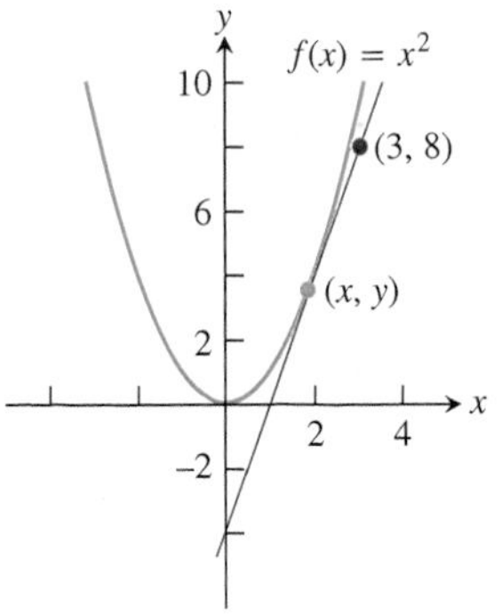

65. **a.** Find an equation for the line that is tangent to the curve $y = x^3 - x$ at the point $(-1, 0)$.

T **b.** Graph the curve and tangent line together. The tangent intersects the curve at another point. Use Zoom and Trace to estimate the point's coordinates.

T **c.** Confirm your estimates of the coordinates of the second intersection point by solving the equations for the curve and tangent simultaneously (Solver key).

66. **a.** Find an equation for the line that is tangent to the curve $y = x^3 - 6x^2 + 5x$ at the origin.

T **b.** Graph the curve and tangent together. The tangent intersects the curve at another point. Use Zoom and Trace to estimate the point's coordinates.

T **c.** Confirm your estimates of the coordinates of the second intersection point by solving the equations for the curve and tangent simultaneously (Solver key).

Theory and Examples

For Exercises 67 and 68 evaluate each limit by first converting each to a derivative at a particular x-value.

67. $\lim_{x \to 1} \frac{x^{50} - 1}{x - 1}$

68. $\lim_{x \to -1} \frac{x^{2/9} - 1}{x + 1}$

69. Find the value of a that makes the following function differentiable for all x-values.

$$g(x) = \begin{cases} ax, & \text{if } x < 0 \\ x^2 - 3x, & \text{if } x \geq 0 \end{cases}$$

70. Find the values of a and b that make the following function differentiable for all x-values.

$$f(x) = \begin{cases} ax + b, & x > -1 \\ bx^2 - 3, & x \leq -1 \end{cases}$$

71. The general polynomial of degree n has the form

$$P(x) = a_n x^n + a_{n-1} x^{n-1} + \cdots + a_2 x^2 + a_1 x + a_0$$

where $a_n \neq 0$. Find $P'(x)$.

72. The body's reaction to medicine The reaction of the body to a dose of medicine can sometimes be represented by an equation of the form

$$R = M^2\left(\frac{C}{2} - \frac{M}{3}\right),$$

where C is a positive constant and M is the amount of medicine absorbed in the blood. If the reaction is a change in blood pressure, R is measured in millimeters of mercury. If the reaction is a change in temperature, R is measured in degrees, and so on.

Find dR/dM. This derivative, as a function of M, is called the sensitivity of the body to the medicine. In Section 4.5, we will see how to find the amount of medicine to which the body is most sensitive.

73. Suppose that the function v in the Derivative Product Rule has a constant value c. What does the Derivative Product Rule then say? What does this say about the Derivative Constant Multiple Rule?

74. The Reciprocal Rule

a. The *Reciprocal Rule* says that at any point where the function $v(x)$ is differentiable and different from zero,

$$\frac{d}{dx}\left(\frac{1}{v}\right) = -\frac{1}{v^2}\frac{dv}{dx}.$$

Show that the Reciprocal Rule is a special case of the Derivative Quotient Rule.

b. Show that the Reciprocal Rule and the Derivative Product Rule together imply the Derivative Quotient Rule.

75. Generalizing the Product Rule The Derivative Product Rule gives the formula

$$\frac{d}{dx}(uv) = u\frac{dv}{dx} + v\frac{du}{dx}$$

for the derivative of the product uv of two differentiable functions of x.

a. What is the analogous formula for the derivative of the product uvw of *three* differentiable functions of x?

b. What is the formula for the derivative of the product $u_1u_2u_3u_4$ of *four* differentiable functions of x?

c. What is the formula for the derivative of a product $u_1u_2u_3 \cdots u_n$ of a finite number n of differentiable functions of x?

76. Power Rule for negative integers Use the Derivative Quotient Rule to prove the Power Rule for negative integers, that is,

$$\frac{d}{dx}(x^{-m}) = -mx^{-m-1}$$

where m is a positive integer.

77. Cylinder pressure If gas in a cylinder is maintained at a constant temperature T, the pressure P is related to the volume V by a formula of the form

$$P = \frac{nRT}{V - nb} - \frac{an^2}{V^2},$$

in which a, b, n, and R are constants. Find dP/dV. (See accompanying figure.)

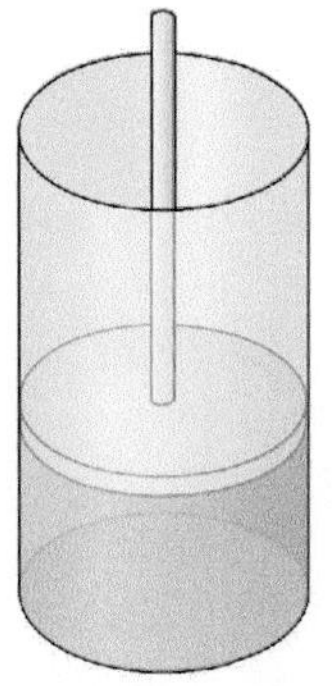

78. The best quantity to order One of the formulas for inventory management says that the average weekly cost of ordering, paying for, and holding merchandise is

$$A(q) = \frac{km}{q} + cm + \frac{hq}{2},$$

where q is the quantity you order when things run low (shoes, radios, brooms, or whatever the item might be); k is the cost of placing an order (the same, no matter how often you order); c is the cost of one item (a constant); m is the number of items sold each week (a constant); and h is the weekly holding cost per item (a constant that takes into account things such as space, utilities, insurance, and security). Find dA/dq and d^2A/dq^2.

3.4 The Derivative as a Rate of Change

In Section 2.1 we introduced average and instantaneous rates of change. In this section we study further applications in which derivatives model the rates at which things change. It is natural to think of a quantity changing with respect to time, but other variables can be treated in the same way. For example, an economist may want to study how the cost of producing steel varies with the number of tons produced, or an engineer may want to know how the power output of a generator varies with its temperature.

Instantaneous Rates of Change

If we interpret the difference quotient $(f(x + h) - f(x))/h$ as the average rate of change in f over the interval from x to $x + h$, we can interpret its limit as $h \to 0$ as the rate at which f is changing at the point x.

DEFINITION The **instantaneous rate of change** of f with respect to x at x_0 is the derivative

$$f'(x_0) = \lim_{h \to 0} \frac{f(x_0 + h) - f(x_0)}{h},$$

provided the limit exists.

Thus, instantaneous rates are limits of average rates.

It is conventional to use the word *instantaneous* even when x does not represent time. The word is, however, frequently omitted. When we say *rate of change*, we mean *instantaneous rate of change*.

EXAMPLE 1 The area A of a circle is related to its diameter by the equation

$$A = \frac{\pi}{4} D^2.$$

How fast does the area change with respect to the diameter when the diameter is 10 m?

Solution The rate of change of the area with respect to the diameter is

$$\frac{dA}{dD} = \frac{\pi}{4} \cdot 2D = \frac{\pi D}{2}.$$

When $D = 10$ m, the area is changing with respect to the diameter at the rate of $(\pi/2)10 = 5\pi\ \text{m}^2/\text{m} \approx 15.71\ \text{m}^2/\text{m}$. ■

Motion Along a Line: Displacement, Velocity, Speed, Acceleration, and Jerk

Suppose that an object is moving along a coordinate line (an s-axis), usually horizontal or vertical, so that we know its position s on that line as a function of time t:

$$s = f(t).$$

The **displacement** of the object over the time interval from t to $t + \Delta t$ (Figure 3.14) is

$$\Delta s = f(t + \Delta t) - f(t),$$

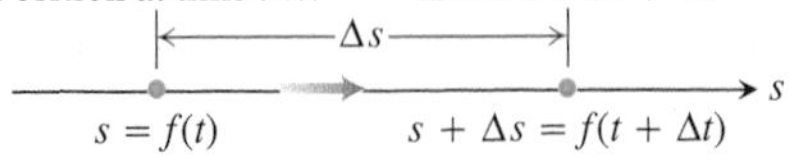

FIGURE 3.14 The positions of a body moving along a coordinate line at time t and shortly later at time $t + \Delta t$. Here the coordinate line is horizontal.

and the **average velocity** of the object over that time interval is

$$v_{av} = \frac{\text{displacement}}{\text{travel time}} = \frac{\Delta s}{\Delta t} = \frac{f(t + \Delta t) - f(t)}{\Delta t}.$$

To find the body's velocity at the exact instant t, we take the limit of the average velocity over the interval from t to $t + \Delta t$ as Δt shrinks to zero. This limit is the derivative of f with respect to t.

DEFINITION **Velocity (instantaneous velocity)** is the derivative of position with respect to time. If a body's position at time t is $s = f(t)$, then the body's velocity at time t is

$$v(t) = \frac{ds}{dt} = \lim_{\Delta t \to 0} \frac{f(t + \Delta t) - f(t)}{\Delta t}.$$

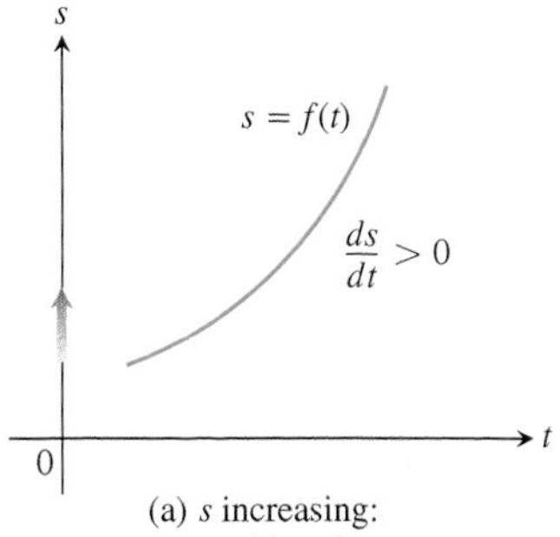

(a) s increasing: positive slope so moving upward

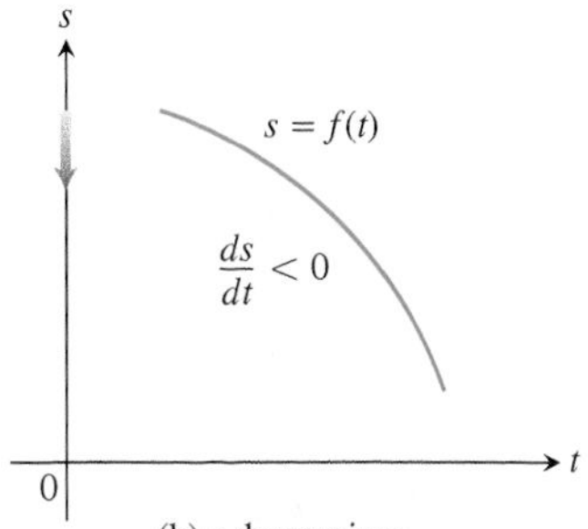

(b) s decreasing: negative slope so moving downward

FIGURE 3.15 For motion $s = f(t)$ along a straight line (the vertical axis), $v = ds/dt$ is (a) positive when s increases and (b) negative when s decreases.

Besides telling how fast an object is moving along the horizontal line in Figure 3.14, its velocity tells the direction of motion. When the object is moving forward (s increasing), the velocity is positive; when the object is moving backward (s decreasing), the velocity is negative. If the coordinate line is vertical, the object moves upward for positive velocity and downward for negative velocity. The blue curves in Figure 3.15 represent position along the line over time; they do not portray the path of motion, which lies along the s-axis.

If we drive to a friend's house and back at 30 mph, say, the speedometer will show 30 on the way over but it will not show -30 on the way back, even though our distance from home is decreasing. The speedometer always shows *speed*, which is the absolute value of velocity. Speed measures the rate of progress regardless of direction.

DEFINITION **Speed** is the absolute value of velocity.

$$\text{Speed} = |v(t)| = \left|\frac{ds}{dt}\right|$$

EXAMPLE 2 Figure 3.16 shows the graph of the velocity $v = f'(t)$ of a particle moving along a horizontal line (as opposed to showing a position function $s = f(t)$ such as in Figure 3.15). In the graph of the velocity function, it's not the slope of the curve that tells us if the particle is moving forward or backward along the line (which is not shown in the figure), but rather the sign of the velocity. Looking at Figure 3.16, we see that the particle moves forward for the first 3 sec (when the velocity is positive), moves backward for the next 2 sec (the velocity is negative), stands motionless for a full second, and then moves forward again. The particle is speeding up when its positive velocity increases during the first second, moves at a steady speed during the next second, and then slows down as the velocity decreases to zero during the third second. It stops for an instant at $t = 3$ sec (when the velocity is zero) and reverses direction as the velocity starts to become negative. The particle is now moving backward and gaining in speed until $t = 4$ sec, at which time it achieves its greatest speed during its backward motion. Continuing its backward motion at time $t = 4$, the particle starts to slow down again until it finally stops at time $t = 5$ (when the velocity is once again zero). The particle now remains motionless for one full second, and then moves forward again at $t = 6$ sec, speeding up during the final second of the forward motion indicated in the velocity graph. ■

HISTORICAL BIOGRAPHY

Bernard Bolzano (1781–1848)

The rate at which a body's velocity changes is the body's *acceleration*. The acceleration measures how quickly the body picks up or loses speed. In Chapter 12 we will study motion in the plane and in space, where acceleration of an object may also lead to a change in direction.

A sudden change in acceleration is called a *jerk*. When a ride in a car or a bus is jerky, it is not that the accelerations involved are necessarily large but that the changes in acceleration are abrupt.

DEFINITIONS **Acceleration** is the derivative of velocity with respect to time. If a body's position at time t is $s = f(t)$, then the body's acceleration at time t is

$$a(t) = \frac{dv}{dt} = \frac{d^2s}{dt^2}.$$

Jerk is the derivative of acceleration with respect to time:

$$j(t) = \frac{da}{dt} = \frac{d^3s}{dt^3}.$$

Near the surface of the Earth all bodies fall with the same constant acceleration. Galileo's experiments with free fall (see Section 2.1) lead to the equation

$$s = \frac{1}{2}gt^2,$$

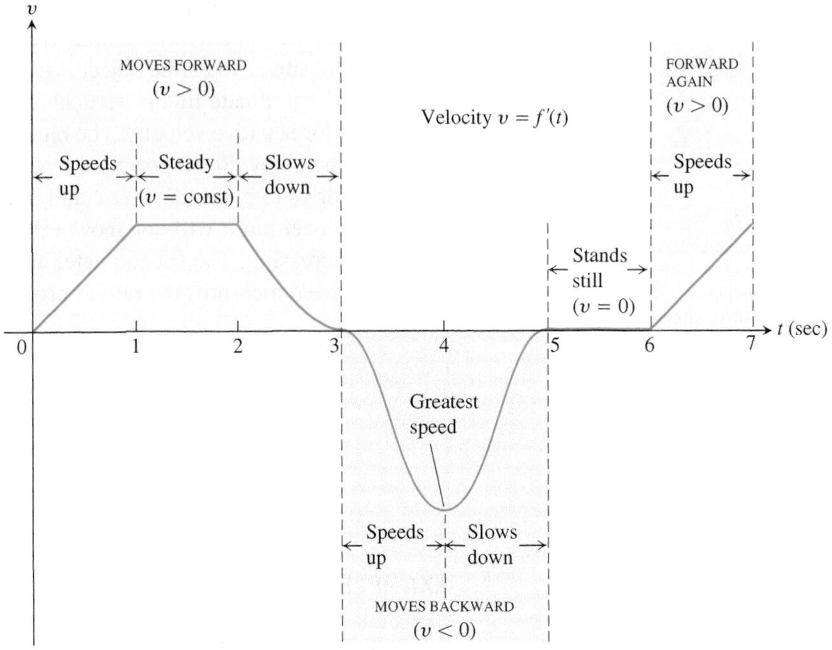

FIGURE 3.16 The velocity graph of a particle moving along a horizontal line, discussed in Example 2.

where s is the distance fallen and g is the acceleration due to Earth's gravity. This equation holds in a vacuum, where there is no air resistance, and closely models the fall of dense, heavy objects, such as rocks or steel tools, for the first few seconds of their fall, before the effects of air resistance are significant.

The value of g in the equation $s = (1/2)gt^2$ depends on the units used to measure t and s. With t in seconds (the usual unit), the value of g determined by measurement at sea level is approximately 32 ft/sec^2 (feet per second squared) in English units, and $g = 9.8$ m/sec^2 (meters per second squared) in metric units. (These gravitational constants depend on the distance from Earth's center of mass, and are slightly lower on top of Mt. Everest, for example.)

The jerk associated with the constant acceleration of gravity ($g = 32$ ft/sec^2) is zero:

$$j = \frac{d}{dt}(g) = 0.$$

An object does not exhibit jerkiness during free fall.

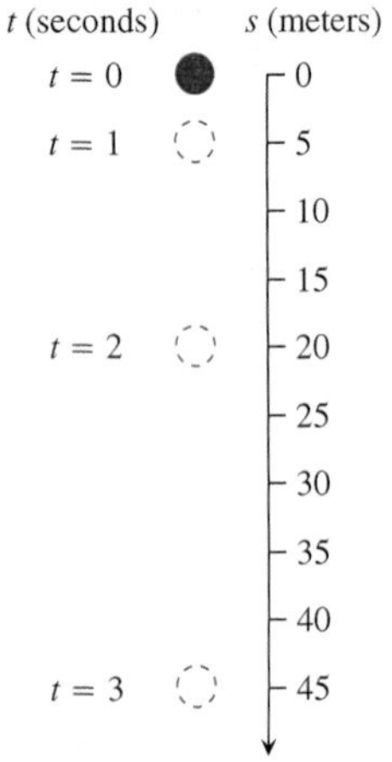

FIGURE 3.17 A ball bearing falling from rest (Example 3).

EXAMPLE 3 Figure 3.17 shows the free fall of a heavy ball bearing released from rest at time $t = 0$ sec.

(a) How many meters does the ball fall in the first 3 sec?

(b) What is its velocity, speed, and acceleration when $t = 3$?

Solution

(a) The metric free-fall equation is $s = 4.9t^2$. During the first 3 sec, the ball falls

$$s(3) = 4.9(3)^2 = 44.1 \text{ m}.$$

(b) At any time t, *velocity* is the derivative of position:

$$v(t) = s'(t) = \frac{d}{dt}(4.9t^2) = 9.8t.$$

At $t = 3$, the velocity is

$$v(3) = 29.4 \text{ m/sec}$$

in the downward (increasing s) direction. The *speed* at $t = 3$ is

$$\text{speed} = |v(3)| = 29.4 \text{ m/sec}.$$

The *acceleration* at any time t is

$$a(t) = v'(t) = s''(t) = 9.8 \text{ m/sec}^2.$$

At $t = 3$, the acceleration is 9.8 m/sec^2. ∎

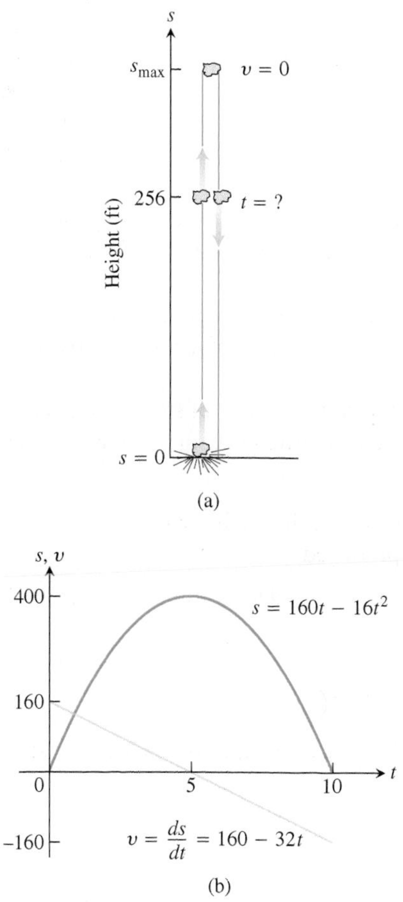

FIGURE 3.18 (a) The rock in Example 4. (b) The graphs of s and v as functions of time; s is largest when $v = ds/dt = 0$. The graph of s is *not* the path of the rock: It is a plot of height versus time. The slope of the plot is the rock's velocity, graphed here as a straight line.

EXAMPLE 4 A dynamite blast blows a heavy rock straight up with a launch velocity of 160 ft/sec (about 109 mph) (Figure 3.18a). It reaches a height of $s = 160t - 16t^2$ ft after t sec.

(a) How high does the rock go?

(b) What are the velocity and speed of the rock when it is 256 ft above the ground on the way up? On the way down?

(c) What is the acceleration of the rock at any time t during its flight (after the blast)?

(d) When does the rock hit the ground again?

Solution

(a) In the coordinate system we have chosen, s measures height from the ground up, so the velocity is positive on the way up and negative on the way down. The instant the rock is at its highest point is the one instant during the flight when the velocity is 0. To find the maximum height, all we need to do is to find when $v = 0$ and evaluate s at this time.

At any time t during the rock's motion, its velocity is

$$v = \frac{ds}{dt} = \frac{d}{dt}(160t - 16t^2) = 160 - 32t \text{ ft/sec}.$$

The velocity is zero when

$$160 - 32t = 0 \quad \text{or} \quad t = 5 \text{ sec}.$$

The rock's height at $t = 5$ sec is

$$s_{max} = s(5) = 160(5) - 16(5)^2 = 800 - 400 = 400 \text{ ft}.$$

See Figure 3.18b.

(b) To find the rock's velocity at 256 ft on the way up and again on the way down, we first find the two values of t for which

$$s(t) = 160t - 16t^2 = 256.$$

To solve this equation, we write

$$\begin{aligned} 16t^2 - 160t + 256 &= 0 \\ 16(t^2 - 10t + 16) &= 0 \\ (t - 2)(t - 8) &= 0 \\ t = 2 \text{ sec}, t &= 8 \text{ sec}. \end{aligned}$$

The rock is 256 ft above the ground 2 sec after the explosion and again 8 sec after the explosion. The rock's velocities at these times are

$$v(2) = 160 - 32(2) = 160 - 64 = 96 \text{ ft/sec}.$$
$$v(8) = 160 - 32(8) = 160 - 256 = -96 \text{ ft/sec}.$$

At both instants, the rock's speed is 96 ft/sec. Since $v(2) > 0$, the rock is moving upward (s is increasing) at $t = 2$ sec; it is moving downward (s is decreasing) at $t = 8$ because $v(8) < 0$.

(c) At any time during its flight following the explosion, the rock's acceleration is a constant

$$a = \frac{dv}{dt} = \frac{d}{dt}(160 - 32t) = -32 \text{ ft/sec}^2.$$

The acceleration is always downward. As the rock rises, it slows down; as it falls, it speeds up.

(d) The rock hits the ground at the positive time t for which $s = 0$. The equation $160t - 16t^2 = 0$ factors to give $16t(10 - t) = 0$, so it has solutions $t = 0$ and $t = 10$. At $t = 0$, the blast occurred and the rock was thrown upward. It returned to the ground 10 sec later. ■

Derivatives in Economics

Engineers use the terms *velocity* and *acceleration* to refer to the derivatives of functions describing motion. Economists, too, have a specialized vocabulary for rates of change and derivatives. They call them *marginals*.

In a manufacturing operation, the *cost of production* $c(x)$ is a function of x, the number of units produced. The **marginal cost of production** is the rate of change of cost with respect to level of production, so it is dc/dx.

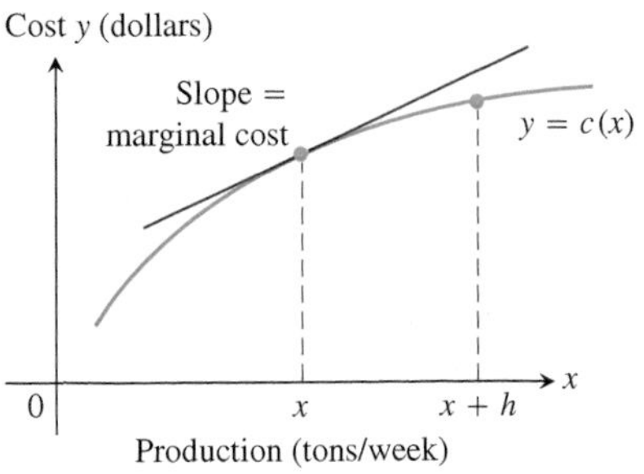

FIGURE 3.19 Weekly steel production: $c(x)$ is the cost of producing x tons per week. The cost of producing an additional h tons is $c(x + h) - c(x)$.

Suppose that $c(x)$ represents the dollars needed to produce x tons of steel in one week. It costs more to produce $x + h$ tons per week, and the cost difference, divided by h, is the average cost of producing each additional ton:

$$\frac{c(x + h) - c(x)}{h} = \begin{array}{l}\text{average cost of each of the additional}\\ h \text{ tons of steel produced.}\end{array}$$

The limit of this ratio as $h \to 0$ is the *marginal cost* of producing more steel per week when the current weekly production is x tons (Figure 3.19):

$$\frac{dc}{dx} = \lim_{h \to 0} \frac{c(x + h) - c(x)}{h} = \text{marginal cost of production}.$$

Sometimes the marginal cost of production is loosely defined to be the extra cost of producing one additional unit:

$$\frac{\Delta c}{\Delta x} = \frac{c(x + 1) - c(x)}{1},$$

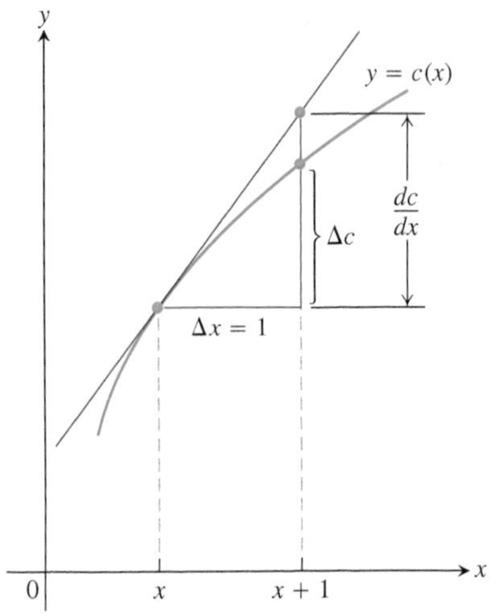

FIGURE 3.20 The marginal cost dc/dx is approximately the extra cost Δc of producing $\Delta x = 1$ more unit.

which is approximated by the value of dc/dx at x. This approximation is acceptable if the slope of the graph of c does not change quickly near x. Then the difference quotient will be close to its limit dc/dx, which is the rise in the tangent line if $\Delta x = 1$ (Figure 3.20). The approximation works best for large values of x.

Economists often represent a total cost function by a cubic polynomial

$$c(x) = \alpha x^3 + \beta x^2 + \gamma x + \delta$$

where δ represents *fixed costs*, such as rent, heat, equipment capitalization, and management costs. The other terms represent *variable costs*, such as the costs of raw materials, taxes, and labor. Fixed costs are independent of the number of units produced, whereas variable costs depend on the quantity produced. A cubic polynomial is usually adequate to capture the cost behavior on a realistic quantity interval.

EXAMPLE 5 Suppose that it costs

$$c(x) = x^3 - 6x^2 + 15x$$

dollars to produce x radiators when 8 to 30 radiators are produced and that

$$r(x) = x^3 - 3x^2 + 12x$$

gives the dollar revenue from selling x radiators. Your shop currently produces 10 radiators a day. About how much extra will it cost to produce one more radiator a day, and what is your estimated increase in revenue for selling 11 radiators a day?

Solution The cost of producing one more radiator a day when 10 are produced is about $c'(10)$:

$$c'(x) = \frac{d}{dx}\left(x^3 - 6x^2 + 15x\right) = 3x^2 - 12x + 15$$

$$c'(10) = 3(100) - 12(10) + 15 = 195.$$

The additional cost will be about \$195. The marginal revenue is

$$r'(x) = \frac{d}{dx}(x^3 - 3x^2 + 12x) = 3x^2 - 6x + 12.$$

The marginal revenue function estimates the increase in revenue that will result from selling one additional unit. If you currently sell 10 radiators a day, you can expect your revenue to increase by about

$$r'(10) = 3(100) - 6(10) + 12 = \$252$$

if you increase sales to 11 radiators a day. ■

EXAMPLE 6 To get some feel for the language of marginal rates, consider marginal tax rates. If your marginal income tax rate is 28% and your income increases by \$1000, you can expect to pay an extra \$280 in taxes. This does not mean that you pay 28% of your entire income in taxes. It just means that at your current income level I, the rate of increase of taxes T with respect to income is $dT/dI = 0.28$. You will pay \$0.28 in taxes out of every extra dollar you earn. Of course, if you earn a lot more, you may land in a higher tax bracket and your marginal rate will increase. ■

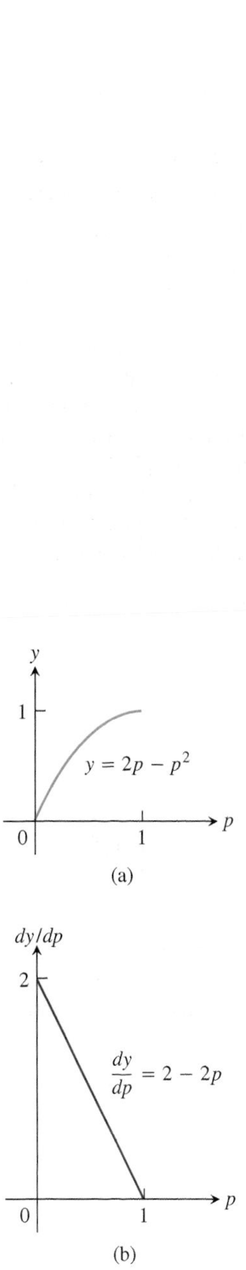

FIGURE 3.21 (a) The graph of $y = 2p - p^2$, describing the proportion of smooth-skinned peas in the next generation. (b) The graph of dy/dp (Example 7).

Sensitivity to Change

When a small change in x produces a large change in the value of a function $f(x)$, we say that the function is relatively **sensitive** to changes in x. The derivative $f'(x)$ is a measure of this sensitivity.

EXAMPLE 7 Genetic Data and Sensitivity to Change

The Austrian monk Gregor Johann Mendel (1822–1884), working with garden peas and other plants, provided the first scientific explanation of hybridization.

His careful records showed that if p (a number between 0 and 1) is the frequency of the gene for smooth skin in peas (dominant) and $(1 - p)$ is the frequency of the gene for wrinkled skin in peas, then the proportion of smooth-skinned peas in the next generation will be

$$y = 2p(1 - p) + p^2 = 2p - p^2.$$

The graph of y versus p in Figure 3.21a suggests that the value of y is more sensitive to a change in p when p is small than when p is large. Indeed, this fact is borne out by the derivative graph in Figure 3.21b, which shows that dy/dp is close to 2 when p is near 0 and close to 0 when p is near 1.

The implication for genetics is that introducing a few more smooth skin genes into a population where the frequency of wrinkled skin peas is large will have a more dramatic effect on later generations than will a similar increase when the population has a large proportion of smooth skin peas. ■

Exercises 3.4

Motion Along a Coordinate Line

Exercises 1–6 give the positions $s = f(t)$ of a body moving on a coordinate line, with s in meters and t in seconds.

a. Find the body's displacement and average velocity for the given time interval.

b. Find the body's speed and acceleration at the endpoints of the interval.

c. When, if ever, during the interval does the body change direction?

1. $s = t^2 - 3t + 2, \quad 0 \le t \le 2$

2. $s = 6t - t^2, \quad 0 \le t \le 6$

3. $s = -t^3 + 3t^2 - 3t, \quad 0 \le t \le 3$

4. $s = (t^4/4) - t^3 + t^2, \quad 0 \le t \le 3$

5. $s = \dfrac{25}{t^2} - \dfrac{5}{t}, \quad 1 \le t \le 5$

6. $s = \dfrac{25}{t + 5}, \quad -4 \le t \le 0$

7. Particle motion At time t, the position of a body moving along the s-axis is $s = t^3 - 6t^2 + 9t$ m.

a. Find the body's acceleration each time the velocity is zero.

b. Find the body's speed each time the acceleration is zero.

c. Find the total distance traveled by the body from $t = 0$ to $t = 2$.

8. Particle motion At time $t \ge 0$, the velocity of a body moving along the horizontal s-axis is $v = t^2 - 4t + 3$.

a. Find the body's acceleration each time the velocity is zero.

b. When is the body moving forward? Backward?

c. When is the body's velocity increasing? Decreasing?

Free-Fall Applications

9. Free fall on Mars and Jupiter The equations for free fall at the surfaces of Mars and Jupiter (s in meters, t in seconds) are $s = 1.86t^2$ on Mars and $s = 11.44t^2$ on Jupiter. How long does it take a rock falling from rest to reach a velocity of 27.8 m/sec (about 100 km/h) on each planet?

10. Lunar projectile motion A rock thrown vertically upward from the surface of the moon at a velocity of 24 m/sec (about 86 km/h) reaches a height of $s = 24t - 0.8t^2$ m in t sec.

a. Find the rock's velocity and acceleration at time t. (The acceleration in this case is the acceleration of gravity on the moon.)

b. How long does it take the rock to reach its highest point?

c. How high does the rock go?

d. How long does it take the rock to reach half its maximum height?

e. How long is the rock aloft?

11. Finding g on a small airless planet Explorers on a small airless planet used a spring gun to launch a ball bearing vertically upward from the surface at a launch velocity of 15 m/sec. Because the acceleration of gravity at the planet's surface was g_s m/sec^2, the explorers expected the ball bearing to reach a height of $s = 15t - (1/2)g_s t^2$ m t sec later. The ball bearing reached its maximum height 20 sec after being launched. What was the value of g_s?

12. Speeding bullet A 45-caliber bullet shot straight up from the surface of the moon would reach a height of $s = 832t - 2.6t^2$ ft after t sec. On Earth, in the absence of air, its height would be $s = 832t - 16t^2$ ft after t sec. How long will the bullet be aloft in each case? How high will the bullet go?

13. Free fall from the Tower of Pisa Had Galileo dropped a cannonball from the Tower of Pisa, 179 ft above the ground, the ball's height above the ground t sec into the fall would have been $s = 179 - 16t^2$.

a. What would have been the ball's velocity, speed, and acceleration at time t?

b. About how long would it have taken the ball to hit the ground?

c. What would have been the ball's velocity at the moment of impact?

14. Galileo's free-fall formula Galileo developed a formula for a body's velocity during free fall by rolling balls from rest down increasingly steep inclined planks and looking for a limiting formula that would predict a ball's behavior when the plank was vertical and the ball fell freely; see part (a) of the accompanying figure. He found that, for any given angle of the plank, the ball's velocity t sec into motion was a constant multiple of t. That is, the velocity was given by a formula of the form $v = kt$. The value of the constant k depended on the inclination of the plank.

In modern notation—part (b) of the figure—with distance in meters and time in seconds, what Galileo determined by experiment was that, for any given angle θ, the ball's velocity t sec into the roll was

$$v = 9.8(\sin \theta)t \text{ m/sec}.$$

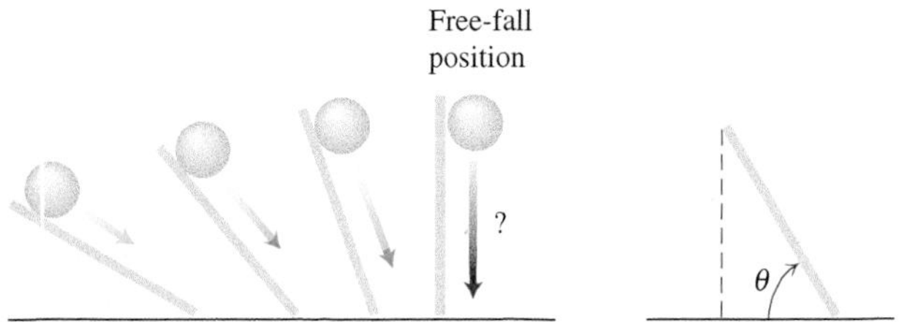

(a) (b)

a. What is the equation for the ball's velocity during free fall?

b. Building on your work in part (a), what constant acceleration does a freely falling body experience near the surface of Earth?

Understanding Motion from Graphs

15. The accompanying figure shows the velocity $v = ds/dt = f(t)$ (m/sec) of a body moving along a coordinate line.

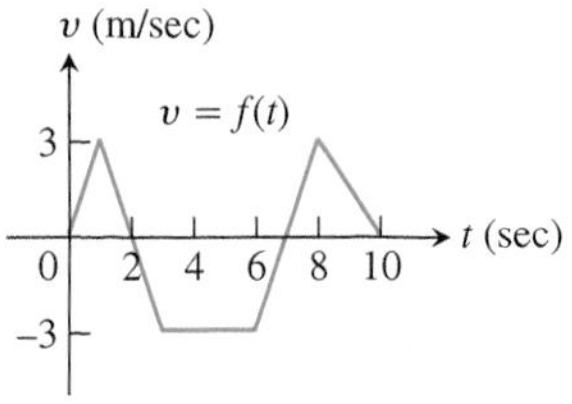

a. When does the body reverse direction?

b. When (approximately) is the body moving at a constant speed?

c. Graph the body's speed for $0 \le t \le 10$.

d. Graph the acceleration, where defined.

16. A particle P moves on the number line shown in part (a) of the accompanying figure. Part (b) shows the position of P as a function of time t.

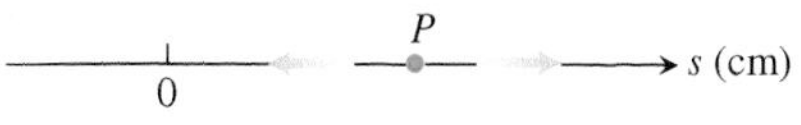

(a)

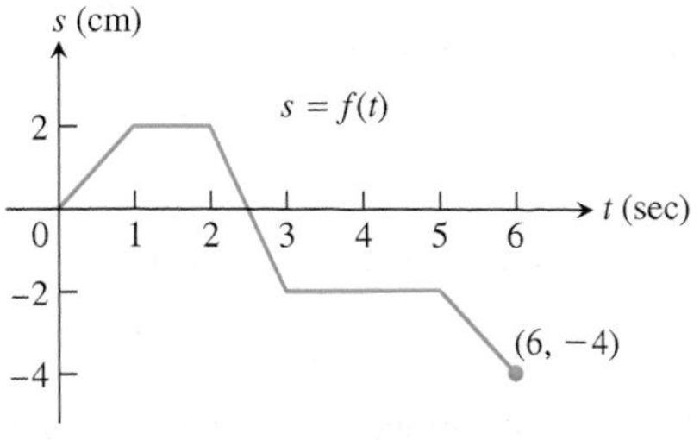

(b)

a. When is P moving to the left? Moving to the right? Standing still?

b. Graph the particle's velocity and speed (where defined).

17. Launching a rocket When a model rocket is launched, the propellant burns for a few seconds, accelerating the rocket upward. After burnout, the rocket coasts upward for a while and then begins to fall. A small explosive charge pops out a parachute shortly after the rocket starts down. The parachute slows the rocket to keep it from breaking when it lands.

The figure here shows velocity data from the flight of the model rocket. Use the data to answer the following.

a. How fast was the rocket climbing when the engine stopped?

b. For how many seconds did the engine burn?

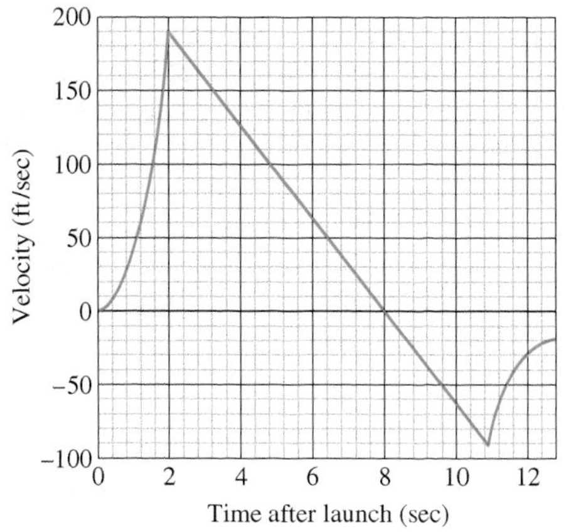

c. When did the rocket reach its highest point? What was its velocity then?

d. When did the parachute pop out? How fast was the rocket falling then?

e. How long did the rocket fall before the parachute opened?

f. When was the rocket's acceleration greatest?

g. When was the acceleration constant? What was its value then (to the nearest integer)?

18. The accompanying figure shows the velocity $v = f(t)$ of a particle moving on a horizontal coordinate line.

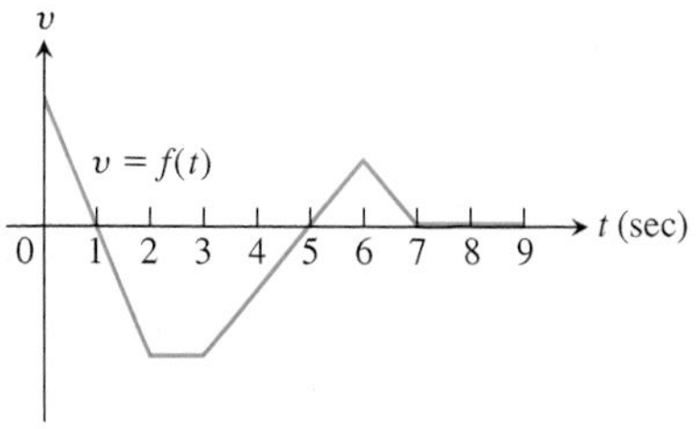

a. When does the particle move forward? Move backward? Speed up? Slow down?

b. When is the particle's acceleration positive? Negative? Zero?

c. When does the particle move at its greatest speed?

d. When does the particle stand still for more than an instant?

19. Two falling balls The multiflash photograph in the accompanying figure shows two balls falling from rest. The vertical rulers are marked in centimeters. Use the equation $s = 490t^2$ (the free-fall equation for s in centimeters and t in seconds) to answer the following questions.

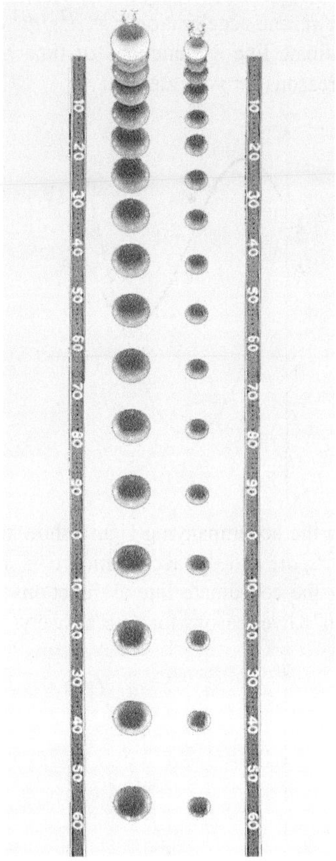

a. How long did it take the balls to fall the first 160 cm? What was their average velocity for the period?

b. How fast were the balls falling when they reached the 160-cm mark? What was their acceleration then?

c. About how fast was the light flashing (flashes per second)?

20. A traveling truck The accompanying graph shows the position s of a truck traveling on a highway. The truck starts at $t = 0$ and returns 15 h later at $t = 15$.

a. Use the technique described in Section 3.2, Example 3, to graph the truck's velocity $v = ds/dt$ for $0 \leq t \leq 15$. Then repeat the process, with the velocity curve, to graph the truck's acceleration dv/dt.

b. Suppose that $s = 15t^2 - t^3$. Graph ds/dt and d^2s/dt^2 and compare your graphs with those in part (a).

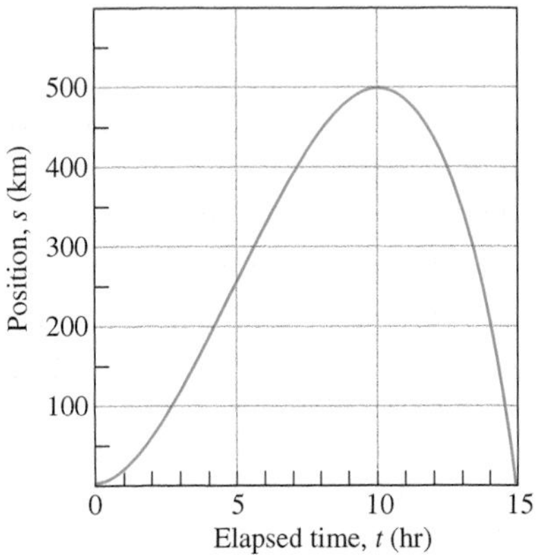

21. The graphs in the accompanying figure show the position s, velocity $v = ds/dt$, and acceleration $a = d^2s/dt^2$ of a body moving along a coordinate line as functions of time t. Which graph is which? Give reasons for your answers.

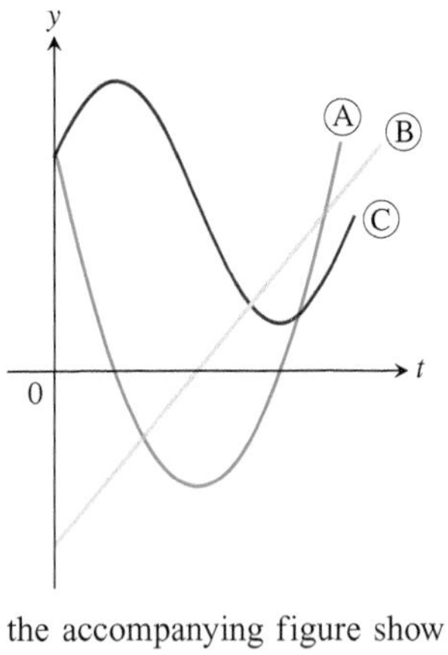

22. The graphs in the accompanying figure show the position s, the velocity $v = ds/dt$, and the acceleration $a = d^2s/dt^2$ of a body moving along the coordinate line as functions of time t. Which graph is which? Give reasons for your answers.

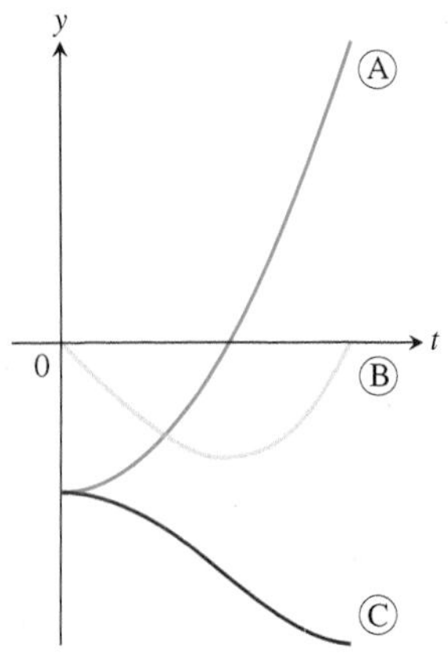

Economics

23. Marginal cost Suppose that the dollar cost of producing x washing machines is $c(x) = 2000 + 100x - 0.1x^2$.

a. Find the average cost per machine of producing the first 100 washing machines.

b. Find the marginal cost when 100 washing machines are produced.

c. Show that the marginal cost when 100 washing machines are produced is approximately the cost of producing one more washing machine after the first 100 have been made, by calculating the latter cost directly.

24. Marginal revenue Suppose that the revenue from selling x washing machines is

$$r(x) = 20{,}000\left(1 - \frac{1}{x}\right)$$

dollars.

a. Find the marginal revenue when 100 machines are produced.

b. Use the function $r'(x)$ to estimate the increase in revenue that will result from increasing production from 100 machines a week to 101 machines a week.

c. Find the limit of $r'(x)$ as $x \to \infty$. How would you interpret this number?

Additional Applications

25. Bacterium population When a bactericide was added to a nutrient broth in which bacteria were growing, the bacterium population continued to grow for a while, but then stopped growing and began to decline. The size of the population at time t (hours) was $b = 10^6 + 10^4t - 10^3t^2$. Find the growth rates at

a. $t = 0$ hours.

b. $t = 5$ hours.

c. $t = 10$ hours.

26. Draining a tank The number of gallons of water in a tank t minutes after the tank has started to drain is $Q(t) = 200(30 - t)^2$. How fast is the water running out at the end of 10 min? What is the average rate at which the water flows out during the first 10 min?

T **27. Draining a tank** It takes 12 hours to drain a storage tank by opening the valve at the bottom. The depth y of fluid in the tank t hours after the valve is opened is given by the formula

$$y = 6\left(1 - \frac{t}{12}\right)^2 \text{ m}.$$

a. Find the rate dy/dt (m/h) at which the tank is draining at time t.

b. When is the fluid level in the tank falling fastest? Slowest? What are the values of dy/dt at these times?

c. Graph y and dy/dt together and discuss the behavior of y in relation to the signs and values of dy/dt.

28. Inflating a balloon The volume $V = (4/3)\pi r^3$ of a spherical balloon changes with the radius.

a. At what rate (ft^3/ft) does the volume change with respect to the radius when $r = 2$ ft?

b. By approximately how much does the volume increase when the radius changes from 2 to 2.2 ft?

29. **Airplane takeoff** Suppose that the distance an aircraft travels along a runway before takeoff is given by $D = (10/9)t^2$, where D is measured in meters from the starting point and t is measured in seconds from the time the brakes are released. The aircraft will become airborne when its speed reaches 200 km/h. How long will it take to become airborne, and what distance will it travel in that time?

30. **Volcanic lava fountains** Although the November 1959 Kilauea Iki eruption on the island of Hawaii began with a line of fountains along the wall of the crater, activity was later confined to a single vent in the crater's floor, which at one point shot lava 1900 ft straight into the air (a Hawaiian record). What was the lava's exit velocity in feet per second? In miles per hour? (*Hint:* If v_0 is the exit velocity of a particle of lava, its height t sec later will be $s = v_0 t - 16t^2$ ft. Begin by finding the time at which $ds/dt = 0$. Neglect air resistance.)

Analyzing Motion Using Graphs

T Exercises 31–34 give the position function $s = f(t)$ of an object moving along the s-axis as a function of time t. Graph f together with the velocity function $v(t) = ds/dt = f'(t)$ and the acceleration function $a(t) = d^2s/dt^2 = f''(t)$. Comment on the object's behavior in relation to the signs and values of v and a. Include in your commentary such topics as the following:

a. When is the object momentarily at rest?

b. When does it move to the left (down) or to the right (up)?

c. When does it change direction?

d. When does it speed up and slow down?

e. When is it moving fastest (highest speed)? Slowest?

f. When is it farthest from the axis origin?

31. $s = 200t - 16t^2, \quad 0 \le t \le 12.5$ (a heavy object fired straight up from Earth's surface at 200 ft/sec)

32. $s = t^2 - 3t + 2, \quad 0 \le t \le 5$

33. $s = t^3 - 6t^2 + 7t, \quad 0 \le t \le 4$

34. $s = 4 - 7t + 6t^2 - t^3, \quad 0 \le t \le 4$

3.5 Derivatives of Trigonometric Functions

Many phenomena of nature are approximately periodic (electromagnetic fields, heart rhythms, tides, weather). The derivatives of sines and cosines play a key role in describing periodic changes. This section shows how to differentiate the six basic trigonometric functions.

Derivative of the Sine Function

To calculate the derivative of $f(x) = \sin x$, for x measured in radians, we combine the limits in Example 5a and Theorem 7 in Section 2.4 with the angle sum identity for the sine function:

$$\sin(x + h) = \sin x \cos h + \cos x \sin h.$$

If $f(x) = \sin x$, then

$$f'(x) = \lim_{h\to 0} \frac{f(x+h) - f(x)}{h} = \lim_{h\to 0} \frac{\sin(x+h) - \sin x}{h} \qquad \text{Derivative definition}$$

$$= \lim_{h\to 0} \frac{(\sin x \cos h + \cos x \sin h) - \sin x}{h} = \lim_{h\to 0} \frac{\sin x(\cos h - 1) + \cos x \sin h}{h}$$

$$= \lim_{h\to 0} \left(\sin x \cdot \frac{\cos h - 1}{h}\right) + \lim_{h\to 0} \left(\cos x \cdot \frac{\sin h}{h}\right)$$

$$= \sin x \cdot \underbrace{\lim_{h\to 0} \frac{\cos h - 1}{h}}_{\text{limit } 0} + \cos x \cdot \underbrace{\lim_{h\to 0} \frac{\sin h}{h}}_{\text{limit } 1} = \sin x \cdot 0 + \cos x \cdot 1 = \cos x. \qquad \text{Example 5a and Theorem 7, Section 2.4}$$

The derivative of the sine function is the cosine function:

$$\frac{d}{dx}(\sin x) = \cos x.$$

EXAMPLE 1 We find derivatives of the sine function involving differences, products, and quotients.

(a) $y = x^2 - \sin x$:

$$\frac{dy}{dx} = 2x - \frac{d}{dx}(\sin x) \qquad \text{Difference Rule}$$
$$= 2x - \cos x$$

(b) $y = e^x \sin x$:

$$\frac{dy}{dx} = e^x \frac{d}{dx}(\sin x) + \frac{d}{dx}(e^x)\sin x \qquad \text{Product Rule}$$
$$= e^x \cos x + e^x \sin x$$
$$= e^x(\cos x + \sin x)$$

(c) $y = \dfrac{\sin x}{x}$:

$$\frac{dy}{dx} = \frac{x \cdot \frac{d}{dx}(\sin x) - \sin x \cdot 1}{x^2} \qquad \text{Quotient Rule}$$
$$= \frac{x \cos x - \sin x}{x^2}$$

■

Derivative of the Cosine Function

With the help of the angle sum formula for the cosine function,

$$\cos(x + h) = \cos x \cos h - \sin x \sin h,$$

we can compute the limit of the difference quotient:

$$\frac{d}{dx}(\cos x) = \lim_{h\to 0} \frac{\cos(x + h) - \cos x}{h} \qquad \text{Derivative definition}$$
$$= \lim_{h\to 0} \frac{(\cos x \cos h - \sin x \sin h) - \cos x}{h} \qquad \text{Cosine angle sum identity}$$
$$= \lim_{h\to 0} \frac{\cos x(\cos h - 1) - \sin x \sin h}{h}$$
$$= \lim_{h\to 0} \cos x \cdot \frac{\cos h - 1}{h} - \lim_{h\to 0} \sin x \cdot \frac{\sin h}{h}$$
$$= \cos x \cdot \lim_{h\to 0} \frac{\cos h - 1}{h} - \sin x \cdot \lim_{h\to 0} \frac{\sin h}{h}$$
$$= \cos x \cdot 0 - \sin x \cdot 1 \qquad \text{Example 5a and Theorem 7, Section 2.4}$$
$$= -\sin x.$$

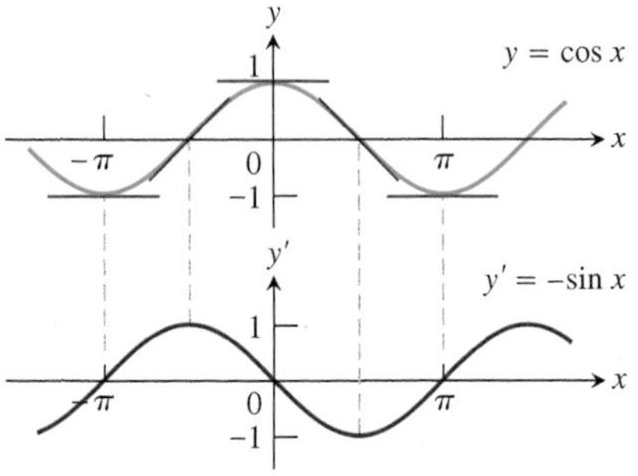

FIGURE 3.22 The curve $y' = -\sin x$ as the graph of the slopes of the tangents to the curve $y = \cos x$.

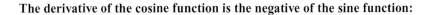

The derivative of the cosine function is the negative of the sine function:

$$\frac{d}{dx}(\cos x) = -\sin x.$$

Figure 3.22 shows a way to visualize this result in the same way we did for graphing derivatives in Section 3.2, Figure 3.6.

EXAMPLE 2 We find derivatives of the cosine function in combinations with other functions.

(a) $y = 5e^x + \cos x$:

$$\begin{aligned}\frac{dy}{dx} &= \frac{d}{dx}(5e^x) + \frac{d}{dx}(\cos x) && \text{Sum Rule}\\ &= 5e^x - \sin x\end{aligned}$$

(b) $y = \sin x \cos x$:

$$\begin{aligned}\frac{dy}{dx} &= \sin x \frac{d}{dx}(\cos x) + \cos x \frac{d}{dx}(\sin x) && \text{Product Rule}\\ &= \sin x(-\sin x) + \cos x(\cos x)\\ &= \cos^2 x - \sin^2 x\end{aligned}$$

(c) $y = \dfrac{\cos x}{1 - \sin x}$:

$$\begin{aligned}\frac{dy}{dx} &= \frac{(1 - \sin x)\frac{d}{dx}(\cos x) - \cos x \frac{d}{dx}(1 - \sin x)}{(1 - \sin x)^2} && \text{Quotient Rule}\\ &= \frac{(1 - \sin x)(-\sin x) - \cos x(0 - \cos x)}{(1 - \sin x)^2}\\ &= \frac{1 - \sin x}{(1 - \sin x)^2} && \sin^2 x + \cos^2 x = 1\\ &= \frac{1}{1 - \sin x}\end{aligned}$$

■

Simple Harmonic Motion

The motion of an object or weight bobbing freely up and down with no resistance on the end of a spring is an example of *simple harmonic motion*. The motion is periodic and repeats indefinitely, so we represent it using trigonometric functions. The next example describes a case in which there are no opposing forces such as friction to slow the motion.

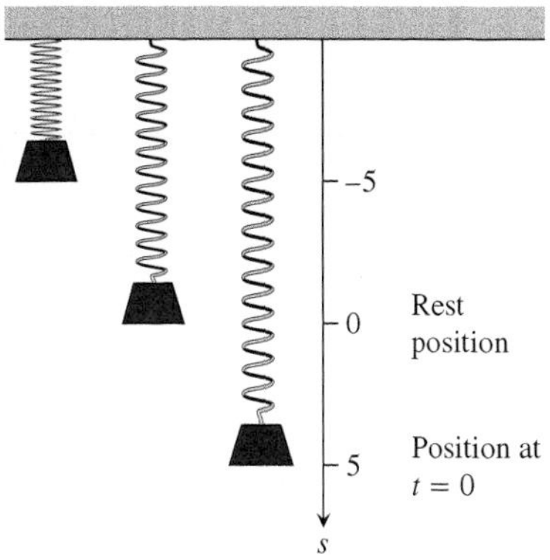

FIGURE 3.23 A weight hanging from a vertical spring and then displaced oscillates above and below its rest position (Example 3).

EXAMPLE 3 A weight hanging from a spring (Figure 3.23) is stretched down 5 units beyond its rest position and released at time $t = 0$ to bob up and down. Its position at any later time t is

$$s = 5 \cos t.$$

What are its velocity and acceleration at time t?

Solution We have

$$\begin{aligned}&\text{Position:} && s = 5\cos t\\ &\text{Velocity:} && v = \frac{ds}{dt} = \frac{d}{dt}(5\cos t) = -5\sin t\\ &\text{Acceleration:} && a = \frac{dv}{dt} = \frac{d}{dt}(-5\sin t) = -5\cos t.\end{aligned}$$

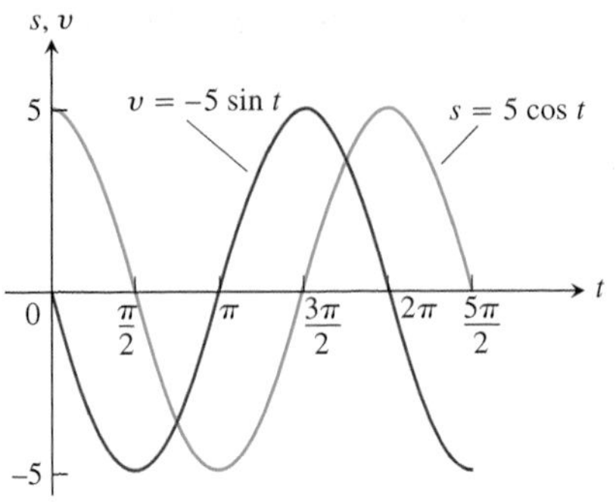

FIGURE 3.24 The graphs of the position and velocity of the weight in Example 3.

Notice how much we can learn from these equations:

1. As time passes, the weight moves down and up between $s = -5$ and $s = 5$ on the s-axis. The amplitude of the motion is 5. The period of the motion is 2π, the period of the cosine function.
2. The velocity $v = -5 \sin t$ attains its greatest magnitude, 5, when $\cos t = 0$, as the graphs show in Figure 3.24. Hence, the speed of the weight, $|v| = 5|\sin t|$, is greatest when $\cos t = 0$, that is, when $s = 0$ (the rest position). The speed of the weight is zero when $\sin t = 0$. This occurs when $s = 5 \cos t = \pm 5$, at the endpoints of the interval of motion.
3. The weight is acted on by the spring and by gravity. When the weight is below the rest position, the combined forces pull it up, and when it is above the rest position, they pull it down. The weight's acceleration is always proportional to the negative of its displacement. This property of springs is called *Hooke's Law*, and is studied further in Section 6.5.
4. The acceleration, $a = -5 \cos t$, is zero only at the rest position, where $\cos t = 0$ and the force of gravity and the force from the spring balance each other. When the weight is anywhere else, the two forces are unequal and acceleration is nonzero. The acceleration is greatest in magnitude at the points farthest from the rest position, where $\cos t = \pm 1$. ■

EXAMPLE 4 The jerk associated with the simple harmonic motion in Example 3 is

$$j = \frac{da}{dt} = \frac{d}{dt}(-5 \cos t) = 5 \sin t.$$

It has its greatest magnitude when $\sin t = \pm 1$, not at the extremes of the displacement but at the rest position, where the acceleration changes direction and sign. ■

Derivatives of the Other Basic Trigonometric Functions

Because $\sin x$ and $\cos x$ are differentiable functions of x, the related functions

$$\tan x = \frac{\sin x}{\cos x}, \qquad \cot x = \frac{\cos x}{\sin x}, \qquad \sec x = \frac{1}{\cos x}, \qquad \text{and} \qquad \csc x = \frac{1}{\sin x}$$

are differentiable at every value of x at which they are defined. Their derivatives, calculated from the Quotient Rule, are given by the following formulas. Notice the negative signs in the derivative formulas for the cofunctions.

The derivatives of the other trigonometric functions:

$$\frac{d}{dx}(\tan x) = \sec^2 x \qquad \frac{d}{dx}(\cot x) = -\csc^2 x$$

$$\frac{d}{dx}(\sec x) = \sec x \tan x \qquad \frac{d}{dx}(\csc x) = -\csc x \cot x$$

To show a typical calculation, we find the derivative of the tangent function. The other derivations are left to Exercise 60.

EXAMPLE 5 Find $d(\tan x)/dx$.

Solution We use the Derivative Quotient Rule to calculate the derivative:

$$\frac{d}{dx}(\tan x) = \frac{d}{dx}\left(\frac{\sin x}{\cos x}\right) = \frac{\cos x \frac{d}{dx}(\sin x) - \sin x \frac{d}{dx}(\cos x)}{\cos^2 x} \quad \text{Quotient Rule}$$

$$= \frac{\cos x \cos x - \sin x(-\sin x)}{\cos^2 x}$$

$$= \frac{\cos^2 x + \sin^2 x}{\cos^2 x}$$

$$= \frac{1}{\cos^2 x} = \sec^2 x.$$

■

EXAMPLE 6 Find y'' if $y = \sec x$.

Solution Finding the second derivative involves a combination of trigonometric derivatives.

$$y = \sec x$$

$$y' = \sec x \tan x \quad \text{Derivative rule for secant function}$$

$$y'' = \frac{d}{dx}(\sec x \tan x)$$

$$= \sec x \frac{d}{dx}(\tan x) + \tan x \frac{d}{dx}(\sec x) \quad \text{Derivative Product Rule}$$

$$= \sec x(\sec^2 x) + \tan x(\sec x \tan x) \quad \text{Derivative rules}$$

$$= \sec^3 x + \sec x \tan^2 x$$

■

The differentiability of the trigonometric functions throughout their domains gives another proof of their continuity at every point in their domains (Theorem 1, Section 3.2). So we can calculate limits of algebraic combinations and composites of trigonometric functions by direct substitution.

EXAMPLE 7 We can use direct substitution in computing limits provided there is no division by zero, which is algebraically undefined.

$$\lim_{x \to 0} \frac{\sqrt{2 + \sec x}}{\cos(\pi - \tan x)} = \frac{\sqrt{2 + \sec 0}}{\cos(\pi - \tan 0)} = \frac{\sqrt{2 + 1}}{\cos(\pi - 0)} = \frac{\sqrt{3}}{-1} = -\sqrt{3}$$

■

Exercises 3.5

Derivatives

In Exercises 1–18, find dy/dx.

1. $y = -10x + 3\cos x$
2. $y = \frac{3}{x} + 5\sin x$
3. $y = x^2 \cos x$
4. $y = \sqrt{x}\sec x + 3$
5. $y = \csc x - 4\sqrt{x} + 7$
6. $y = x^2 \cot x - \frac{1}{x^2}$
7. $f(x) = \sin x \tan x$
8. $g(x) = \csc x \cot x$
9. $y = (\sec x + \tan x)(\sec x - \tan x)$
10. $y = (\sin x + \cos x)\sec x$

11. $y = \dfrac{\cot x}{1 + \cot x}$ **12.** $y = \dfrac{\cos x}{1 + \sin x}$

13. $y = \dfrac{4}{\cos x} + \dfrac{1}{\tan x}$ **14.** $y = \dfrac{\cos x}{x} + \dfrac{x}{\cos x}$

15. $y = x^2 \sin x + 2x \cos x - 2 \sin x$

16. $y = x^2 \cos x - 2x \sin x - 2 \cos x$

17. $f(x) = x^3 \sin x \cos x$ **18.** $g(x) = (2 - x) \tan^2 x$

In Exercises 19–22, find ds/dt.

19. $s = \tan t - e^{-t}$ **20.** $s = t^2 - \sec t + 5e^t$

21. $s = \dfrac{1 + \csc t}{1 - \csc t}$ **22.** $s = \dfrac{\sin t}{1 - \cos t}$

In Exercises 23–26, find $dr/d\theta$.

23. $r = 4 - \theta^2 \sin \theta$ **24.** $r = \theta \sin \theta + \cos \theta$

25. $r = \sec \theta \csc \theta$ **26.** $r = (1 + \sec \theta) \sin \theta$

In Exercises 27–32, find dp/dq.

27. $p = 5 + \dfrac{1}{\cot q}$ **28.** $p = (1 + \csc q) \cos q$

29. $p = \dfrac{\sin q + \cos q}{\cos q}$ **30.** $p = \dfrac{\tan q}{1 + \tan q}$

31. $p = \dfrac{q \sin q}{q^2 - 1}$ **32.** $p = \dfrac{3q + \tan q}{q \sec q}$

33. Find y'' if

a. $y = \csc x$. **b.** $y = \sec x$.

34. Find $y^{(4)} = d^4 y/dx^4$ if

a. $y = -2 \sin x$. **b.** $y = 9 \cos x$.

Tangent Lines

In Exercises 35–38, graph the curves over the given intervals, together with their tangents at the given values of x. Label each curve and tangent with its equation.

35. $y = \sin x, \quad -3\pi/2 \le x \le 2\pi$

$x = -\pi, 0, 3\pi/2$

36. $y = \tan x, \quad -\pi/2 < x < \pi/2$

$x = -\pi/3, 0, \pi/3$

37. $y = \sec x, \quad -\pi/2 < x < \pi/2$

$x = -\pi/3, \pi/4$

38. $y = 1 + \cos x, \quad -3\pi/2 \le x \le 2\pi$

$x = -\pi/3, 3\pi/2$

T Do the graphs of the functions in Exercises 39–42 have any horizontal tangents in the interval $0 \le x \le 2\pi$? If so, where? If not, why not? Visualize your findings by graphing the functions with a grapher.

39. $y = x + \sin x$

40. $y = 2x + \sin x$

41. $y = x - \cot x$

42. $y = x + 2 \cos x$

43. Find all points on the curve $y = \tan x$, $-\pi/2 < x < \pi/2$, where the tangent line is parallel to the line $y = 2x$. Sketch the curve and tangent(s) together, labeling each with its equation.

44. Find all points on the curve $y = \cot x$, $0 < x < \pi$, where the tangent line is parallel to the line $y = -x$. Sketch the curve and tangent(s) together, labeling each with its equation.

In Exercises 45 and 46, find an equation for **(a)** the tangent to the curve at P and **(b)** the horizontal tangent to the curve at Q.

45.

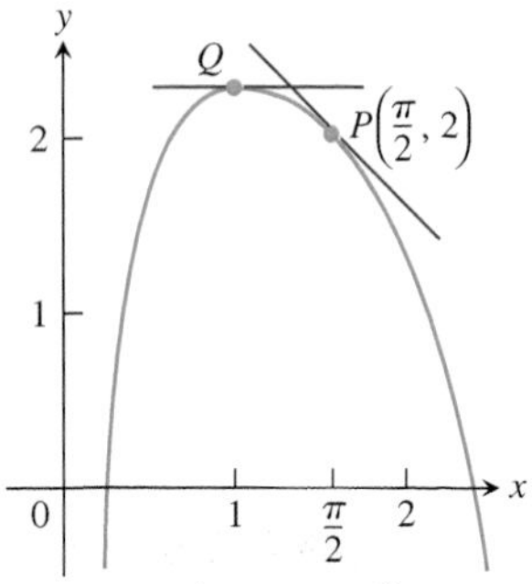

$y = 4 + \cot x - 2\csc x$

46.

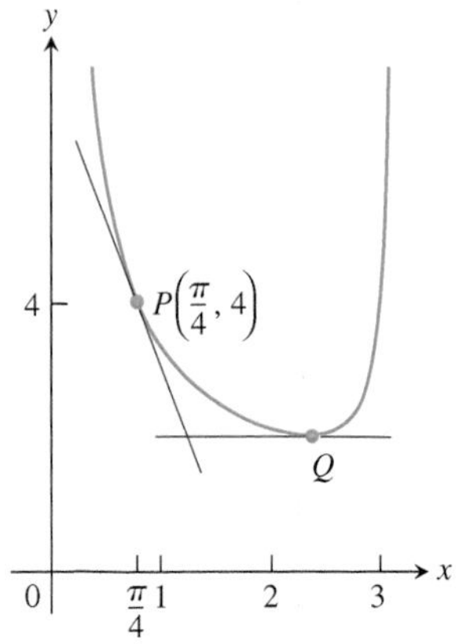

$y = 1 + \sqrt{2} \csc x + \cot x$

Trigonometric Limits

Find the limits in Exercises 47–54.

47. $\displaystyle\lim_{x \to 2} \sin\left(\frac{1}{x} - \frac{1}{2}\right)$

48. $\displaystyle\lim_{x \to -\pi/6} \sqrt{1 + \cos(\pi \csc x)}$

49. $\displaystyle\lim_{\theta \to \pi/6} \frac{\sin \theta - \frac{1}{2}}{\theta - \frac{\pi}{6}}$ **50.** $\displaystyle\lim_{\theta \to \pi/4} \frac{\tan \theta - 1}{\theta - \frac{\pi}{4}}$

51. $\displaystyle\lim_{x \to 0} \sec\left[e^x + \pi \tan\left(\frac{\pi}{4 \sec x}\right) - 1\right]$

52. $\displaystyle\lim_{x \to 0} \sin\left(\frac{\pi + \tan x}{\tan x - 2 \sec x}\right)$

53. $\displaystyle\lim_{t \to 0} \tan\left(1 - \frac{\sin t}{t}\right)$ **54.** $\displaystyle\lim_{\theta \to 0} \cos\left(\frac{\pi \theta}{\sin \theta}\right)$

Theory and Examples

The equations in Exercises 55 and 56 give the position $s = f(t)$ of a body moving on a coordinate line (s in meters, t in seconds). Find the body's velocity, speed, acceleration, and jerk at time $t = \pi/4$ sec.

55. $s = 2 - 2 \sin t$ **56.** $s = \sin t + \cos t$

57. Is there a value of c that will make

$$f(x) = \begin{cases} \dfrac{\sin^2 3x}{x^2}, & x \ne 0 \\ c, & x = 0 \end{cases}$$

continuous at $x = 0$? Give reasons for your answer.

58. Is there a value of b that will make

$$g(x) = \begin{cases} x + b, & x < 0 \\ \cos x, & x \ge 0 \end{cases}$$

continuous at $x = 0$? Differentiable at $x = 0$? Give reasons for your answers.

59. By computing the first few derivatives and looking for a pattern, find $d^{999}/dx^{999}(\cos x)$.

60. Derive the formula for the derivative with respect to x of

a. $\sec x$. **b.** $\csc x$. **c.** $\cot x$.

61. A weight is attached to a spring and reaches its equilibrium position ($x = 0$). It is then set in motion resulting in a displacement of

$$x = 10 \cos t,$$

where x is measured in centimeters and t is measured in seconds. See the accompanying figure.

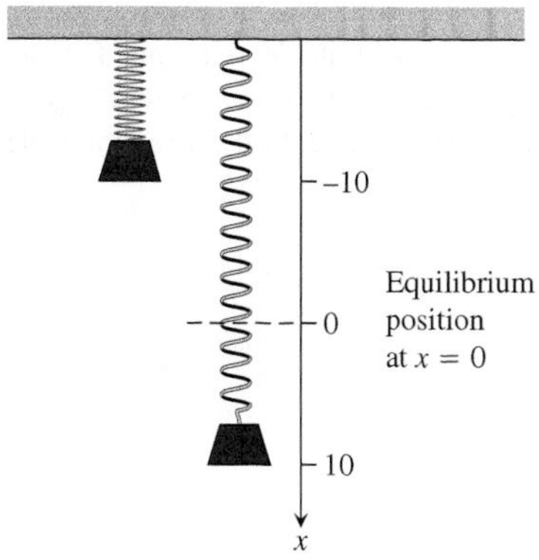

a. Find the spring's displacement when $t = 0, t = \pi/3$, and $t = 3\pi/4$.

b. Find the spring's velocity when $t = 0, t = \pi/3$, and $t = 3\pi/4$.

62. Assume that a particle's position on the x-axis is given by

$$x = 3 \cos t + 4 \sin t,$$

where x is measured in feet and t is measured in seconds.

a. Find the particle's position when $t = 0, t = \pi/2$, and $t = \pi$.

b. Find the particle's velocity when $t = 0, t = \pi/2$, and $t = \pi$.

63. Graph $y = \cos x$ for $-\pi \le x \le 2\pi$. On the same screen, graph

$$y = \frac{\sin(x + h) - \sin x}{h}$$

for $h = 1, 0.5, 0.3$, and 0.1. Then, in a new window, try $h = -1, -0.5$, and -0.3. What happens as $h \to 0^+$? As $h \to 0^-$? What phenomenon is being illustrated here?

64. Graph $y = -\sin x$ for $-\pi \le x \le 2\pi$. On the same screen, graph

$$y = \frac{\cos(x + h) - \cos x}{h}$$

for $h = 1, 0.5, 0.3$, and 0.1. Then, in a new window, try $h = -1, -0.5$, and -0.3. What happens as $h \to 0^+$? As $h \to 0^-$? What phenomenon is being illustrated here?

65. Centered difference quotients The *centered difference quotient*

$$\frac{f(x + h) - f(x - h)}{2h}$$

is used to approximate $f'(x)$ in numerical work because (1) its limit as $h \to 0$ equals $f'(x)$ when $f'(x)$ exists, and (2) it usually gives a better approximation of $f'(x)$ for a given value of h than the difference quotient

$$\frac{f(x + h) - f(x)}{h}.$$

See the accompanying figure.

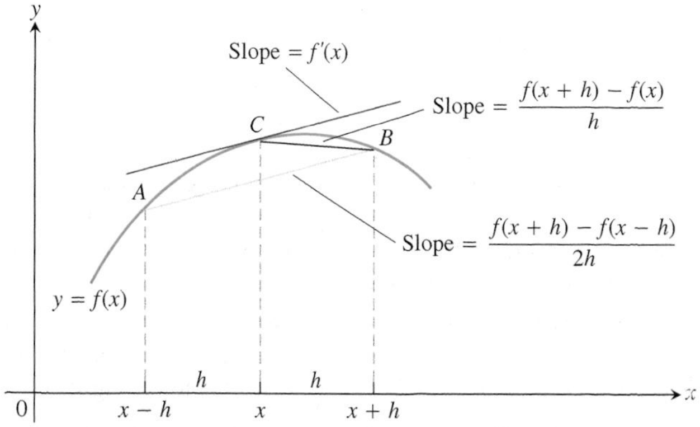

a. To see how rapidly the centered difference quotient for $f(x) = \sin x$ converges to $f'(x) = \cos x$, graph $y = \cos x$ together with

$$y = \frac{\sin(x + h) - \sin(x - h)}{2h}$$

over the interval $[-\pi, 2\pi]$ for $h = 1, 0.5$, and 0.3. Compare the results with those obtained in Exercise 63 for the same values of h.

b. To see how rapidly the centered difference quotient for $f(x) = \cos x$ converges to $f'(x) = -\sin x$, graph $y = -\sin x$ together with

$$y = \frac{\cos(x + h) - \cos(x - h)}{2h}$$

over the interval $[-\pi, 2\pi]$ for $h = 1, 0.5$, and 0.3. Compare the results with those obtained in Exercise 64 for the same values of h.

66. A caution about centered difference quotients (*Continuation of Exercise 65.*) The quotient

$$\frac{f(x + h) - f(x - h)}{2h}$$

may have a limit as $h \to 0$ when f has no derivative at x. As a case in point, take $f(x) = |x|$ and calculate

$$\lim_{h \to 0} \frac{|0 + h| - |0 - h|}{2h}.$$

As you will see, the limit exists even though $f(x) = |x|$ has no derivative at $x = 0$. *Moral:* Before using a centered difference quotient, be sure the derivative exists.

67. Slopes on the graph of the tangent function Graph $y = \tan x$ and its derivative together on $(-\pi/2, \pi/2)$. Does the graph of the tangent function appear to have a smallest slope? A largest slope? Is the slope ever negative? Give reasons for your answers.

T **68. Slopes on the graph of the cotangent function** Graph $y = \cot x$ and its derivative together for $0 < x < \pi$. Does the graph of the cotangent function appear to have a smallest slope? A largest slope? Is the slope ever positive? Give reasons for your answers.

T **69. Exploring $(\sin kx)/x$** Graph $y = (\sin x)/x$, $y = (\sin 2x)/x$, and $y = (\sin 4x)/x$ together over the interval $-2 \le x \le 2$. Where does each graph appear to cross the y-axis? Do the graphs really intersect the axis? What would you expect the graphs of $y = (\sin 5x)/x$ and $y = (\sin(-3x))/x$ to do as $x \to 0$? Why? What about the graph of $y = (\sin kx)/x$ for other values of k? Give reasons for your answers.

T **70. Radians versus degrees: degree mode derivatives** What happens to the derivatives of $\sin x$ and $\cos x$ if x is measured in degrees instead of radians? To find out, take the following steps.

a. With your graphing calculator or computer grapher in *degree mode*, graph

$$f(h) = \frac{\sin h}{h}$$

and estimate $\lim_{h \to 0} f(h)$. Compare your estimate with $\pi/180$. Is there any reason to believe the limit *should* be $\pi/180$?

b. With your grapher still in degree mode, estimate

$$\lim_{h \to 0} \frac{\cos h - 1}{h}.$$

c. Now go back to the derivation of the formula for the derivative of $\sin x$ in the text and carry out the steps of the derivation using degree-mode limits. What formula do you obtain for the derivative?

d. Work through the derivation of the formula for the derivative of $\cos x$ using degree-mode limits. What formula do you obtain for the derivative?

e. The disadvantages of the degree-mode formulas become apparent as you start taking derivatives of higher order. Try it. What are the second and third degree-mode derivatives of $\sin x$ and $\cos x$?

3.6 The Chain Rule

How do we differentiate $F(x) = \sin(x^2 - 4)$? This function is the composite $f \circ g$ of two functions $y = f(u) = \sin u$ and $u = g(x) = x^2 - 4$ that we know how to differentiate. The answer, given by the *Chain Rule*, says that the derivative is the product of the derivatives of f and g. We develop the rule in this section.

Derivative of a Composite Function

The function $y = \frac{3}{2}x = \frac{1}{2}(3x)$ is the composite of the functions $y = \frac{1}{2}u$ and $u = 3x$. We have

$$\frac{dy}{dx} = \frac{3}{2}, \quad \frac{dy}{du} = \frac{1}{2}, \quad \text{and} \quad \frac{du}{dx} = 3.$$

Since $\frac{3}{2} = \frac{1}{2} \cdot 3$, we see in this case that

$$\frac{dy}{dx} = \frac{dy}{du} \cdot \frac{du}{dx}.$$

FIGURE 3.25 When gear A makes x turns, gear B makes u turns and gear C makes y turns. By comparing circumferences or counting teeth, we see that $y = u/2$ (C turns one-half turn for each B turn) and $u = 3x$ (B turns three times for A's one), so $y = 3x/2$. Thus, $dy/dx = 3/2 = (1/2)(3) = (dy/du)(du/dx)$.

If we think of the derivative as a rate of change, our intuition allows us to see that this relationship is reasonable. If $y = f(u)$ changes half as fast as u and $u = g(x)$ changes three times as fast as x, then we expect y to change $3/2$ times as fast as x. This effect is much like that of a multiple gear train (Figure 3.25). Let's look at another example.

EXAMPLE 1 The function

$$y = (3x^2 + 1)^2$$

is the composite of $y = f(u) = u^2$ and $u = g(x) = 3x^2 + 1$. Calculating derivatives, we see that

$$\begin{aligned}\frac{dy}{du}\cdot\frac{du}{dx} &= 2u\cdot 6x\\ &= 2(3x^2+1)\cdot 6x\\ &= 36x^3 + 12x.\end{aligned}$$

Calculating the derivative from the expanded formula $(3x^2 + 1)^2 = 9x^4 + 6x^2 + 1$ gives the same result:

$$\begin{aligned}\frac{dy}{dx} &= \frac{d}{dx}(9x^4 + 6x^2 + 1)\\ &= 36x^3 + 12x.\end{aligned}$$

■

The derivative of the composite function $f(g(x))$ at x is the derivative of f at $g(x)$ times the derivative of g at x. This is known as the Chain Rule (Figure 3.26).

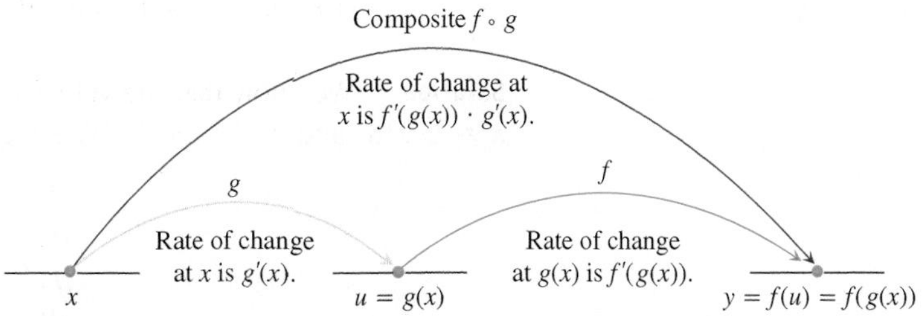

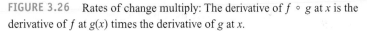

FIGURE 3.26 Rates of change multiply: The derivative of $f \circ g$ at x is the derivative of f at $g(x)$ times the derivative of g at x.

> **THEOREM 2—The Chain Rule** If $f(u)$ is differentiable at the point $u = g(x)$ and $g(x)$ is differentiable at x, then the composite function $(f \circ g)(x) = f(g(x))$ is differentiable at x, and
>
> $$(f \circ g)'(x) = f'(g(x))\cdot g'(x).$$
>
> In Leibniz's notation, if $y = f(u)$ and $u = g(x)$, then
>
> $$\frac{dy}{dx} = \frac{dy}{du}\cdot\frac{du}{dx},$$
>
> where dy/du is evaluated at $u = g(x)$.

A Proof of One Case of the Chain Rule:

Let Δu be the change in u when x changes by Δx, so that

$$\Delta u = g(x + \Delta x) - g(x).$$

Then the corresponding change in y is

$$\Delta y = f(u + \Delta u) - f(u).$$

If $\Delta u \neq 0$, we can write the fraction $\Delta y/\Delta x$ as the product

$$\frac{\Delta y}{\Delta x} = \frac{\Delta y}{\Delta u}\cdot\frac{\Delta u}{\Delta x} \qquad (1)$$

and take the limit as $\Delta x \to 0$:

$$\begin{aligned}
\frac{dy}{dx} &= \lim_{\Delta x \to 0} \frac{\Delta y}{\Delta x} \\
&= \lim_{\Delta x \to 0} \frac{\Delta y}{\Delta u} \cdot \frac{\Delta u}{\Delta x} \\
&= \lim_{\Delta x \to 0} \frac{\Delta y}{\Delta u} \cdot \lim_{\Delta x \to 0} \frac{\Delta u}{\Delta x} \\
&= \lim_{\Delta u \to 0} \frac{\Delta y}{\Delta u} \cdot \lim_{\Delta x \to 0} \frac{\Delta u}{\Delta x} \qquad \text{(Note that } \Delta u \to 0 \text{ as } \Delta x \to 0 \text{ since } g \text{ is continuous.)} \\
&= \frac{dy}{du} \cdot \frac{du}{dx}.
\end{aligned}$$

The problem with this argument is that if the function $g(x)$ oscillates rapidly near x, then Δu can be zero even when $\Delta x \neq 0$, so the cancellation of Δu in Equation (1) would be invalid. A complete proof requires a different approach that avoids this problem, and we give one such proof in Section 3.11. ■

EXAMPLE 2 An object moves along the x-axis so that its position at any time $t \geq 0$ is given by $x(t) = \cos(t^2 + 1)$. Find the velocity of the object as a function of t.

Solution We know that the velocity is dx/dt. In this instance, x is a composite function: $x = \cos(u)$ and $u = t^2 + 1$. We have

$$\begin{aligned}
\frac{dx}{du} &= -\sin(u) && x = \cos(u) \\
\frac{du}{dt} &= 2t. && u = t^2 + 1
\end{aligned}$$

By the Chain Rule,

$$\begin{aligned}
\frac{dx}{dt} &= \frac{dx}{du} \cdot \frac{du}{dt} \\
&= -\sin(u) \cdot 2t && \frac{dx}{du} \text{ evaluated at } u \\
&= -\sin(t^2 + 1) \cdot 2t \\
&= -2t \sin(t^2 + 1).
\end{aligned}$$

■

"Outside-Inside" Rule

A difficulty with the Leibniz notation is that it doesn't state specifically where the derivatives in the Chain Rule are supposed to be evaluated. So it sometimes helps to think about the Chain Rule using functional notation. If $y = f(g(x))$, then

$$\frac{dy}{dx} = f'(g(x)) \cdot g'(x).$$

In words, differentiate the "outside" function f and evaluate it at the "inside" function $g(x)$ left alone; then multiply by the derivative of the "inside function."

EXAMPLE 3 Differentiate $\sin(x^2 + e^x)$ with respect to x.

Solution We apply the Chain Rule directly and find

$$\frac{d}{dx} \sin \underbrace{(x^2 + e^x)}_{\text{inside}} = \cos \underbrace{(x^2 + e^x)}_{\substack{\text{inside} \\ \text{left alone}}} \cdot \underbrace{(2x + e^x)}_{\substack{\text{derivative of} \\ \text{the inside}}}.$$

■

EXAMPLE 4 Differentiate $y = e^{\cos x}$.

Solution Here the inside function is $u = g(x) = \cos x$ and the outside function is the exponential function $f(x) = e^x$. Applying the Chain Rule, we get

$$\frac{dy}{dx} = \frac{d}{dx}(e^{\cos x}) = e^{\cos x}\frac{d}{dx}(\cos x) = e^{\cos x}(-\sin x) = -e^{\cos x}\sin x. \qquad \blacksquare$$

Generalizing Example 4, we see that the Chain Rule gives the formula

$$\frac{d}{dx}e^u = e^u\frac{du}{dx}.$$

For example,

$$\frac{d}{dx}(e^{kx}) = e^{kx}\cdot\frac{d}{dx}(kx) = ke^{kx}, \qquad \text{for any constant } k$$

and

$$\frac{d}{dx}\left(e^{x^2}\right) = e^{x^2}\cdot\frac{d}{dx}(x^2) = 2xe^{x^2}.$$

Repeated Use of the Chain Rule

We sometimes have to use the Chain Rule two or more times to find a derivative.

HISTORICAL BIOGRAPHY

Johann Bernoulli
(1667–1748)

EXAMPLE 5 Find the derivative of $g(t) = \tan(5 - \sin 2t)$.

Solution Notice here that the tangent is a function of $5 - \sin 2t$, whereas the sine is a function of $2t$, which is itself a function of t. Therefore, by the Chain Rule,

$$\begin{aligned} g'(t) &= \frac{d}{dt}(\tan(5 - \sin 2t)) \\ &= \sec^2(5 - \sin 2t)\cdot\frac{d}{dt}(5 - \sin 2t) && \text{Derivative of } \tan u \text{ with } u = 5 - \sin 2t \\ &= \sec^2(5 - \sin 2t)\cdot\left(0 - \cos 2t\cdot\frac{d}{dt}(2t)\right) && \text{Derivative of } 5 - \sin u \text{ with } u = 2t \\ &= \sec^2(5 - \sin 2t)\cdot(-\cos 2t)\cdot 2 \\ &= -2(\cos 2t)\sec^2(5 - \sin 2t). \end{aligned} \qquad \blacksquare$$

The Chain Rule with Powers of a Function

If f is a differentiable function of u and if u is a differentiable function of x, then substituting $y = f(u)$ into the Chain Rule formula

$$\frac{dy}{dx} = \frac{dy}{du}\cdot\frac{du}{dx}$$

leads to the formula

$$\frac{d}{dx}f(u) = f'(u)\frac{du}{dx}.$$

If n is any real number and f is a power function, $f(u) = u^n$, the Power Rule tells us that $f'(u) = nu^{n-1}$. If u is a differentiable function of x, then we can use the Chain Rule to extend this to the **Power Chain Rule**:

$$\frac{d}{dx}(u^n) = nu^{n-1}\frac{du}{dx}. \qquad \frac{d}{du}(u^n) = nu^{n-1}$$

EXAMPLE 6 The Power Chain Rule simplifies computing the derivative of a power of an expression.

(a) $\frac{d}{dx}(5x^3 - x^4)^7 = 7(5x^3 - x^4)^6 \frac{d}{dx}(5x^3 - x^4)$ Power Chain Rule with $u = 5x^3 - x^4, n = 7$

$= 7(5x^3 - x^4)^6(5 \cdot 3x^2 - 4x^3)$

$= 7(5x^3 - x^4)^6(15x^2 - 4x^3)$

(b) $\frac{d}{dx}\left(\frac{1}{3x - 2}\right) = \frac{d}{dx}(3x - 2)^{-1}$

$= -1(3x - 2)^{-2}\frac{d}{dx}(3x - 2)$ Power Chain Rule with $u = 3x - 2, n = -1$

$= -1(3x - 2)^{-2}(3)$

$= -\frac{3}{(3x - 2)^2}$

In part (b) we could also find the derivative with the Derivative Quotient Rule.

(c) $\frac{d}{dx}(\sin^5 x) = 5\sin^4 x \cdot \frac{d}{dx}\sin x$ Power Chain Rule with $u = \sin x, n = 5$, because $\sin^n x$ means $(\sin x)^n$, $n \neq -1$.

$= 5\sin^4 x \cos x$

(d) $\frac{d}{dx}\left(e^{\sqrt{3x+1}}\right) = e^{\sqrt{3x+1}} \cdot \frac{d}{dx}\left(\sqrt{3x + 1}\right)$

$= e^{\sqrt{3x+1}} \cdot \frac{1}{2}(3x + 1)^{-1/2} \cdot 3$ Power Chain Rule with $u = 3x + 1, n = 1/2$

$= \frac{3}{2\sqrt{3x + 1}} e^{\sqrt{3x+1}}$ ■

EXAMPLE 7 In Section 3.2, we saw that the absolute value function $y = |x|$ is not differentiable at $x = 0$. However, the function *is* differentiable at all other real numbers, as we now show. Since $|x| = \sqrt{x^2}$, we can derive the following formula:

Derivative of the Absolute Value Function

$$\frac{d}{dx}(|x|) = \frac{x}{|x|}, \quad x \neq 0$$

$\frac{d}{dx}(|x|) = \frac{d}{dx}\sqrt{x^2}$

$= \frac{1}{2\sqrt{x^2}} \cdot \frac{d}{dx}(x^2)$ Power Chain Rule with $u = x^2, n = 1/2, x \neq 0$

$= \frac{1}{2|x|} \cdot 2x$ $\sqrt{x^2} = |x|$

$= \frac{x}{|x|}, \quad x \neq 0.$ ■

EXAMPLE 8 Show that the slope of every line tangent to the curve $y = 1/(1 - 2x)^3$ is positive.

Solution We find the derivative:

$\frac{dy}{dx} = \frac{d}{dx}(1 - 2x)^{-3}$

$= -3(1 - 2x)^{-4} \cdot \frac{d}{dx}(1 - 2x)$ Power Chain Rule with $u = (1 - 2x), n = -3$

$= -3(1 - 2x)^{-4} \cdot (-2)$

$= \frac{6}{(1 - 2x)^4}.$

At any point (x, y) on the curve, $x \neq 1/2$ and the slope of the tangent line is

$$\frac{dy}{dx} = \frac{6}{(1 - 2x)^4},$$

the quotient of two positive numbers. ∎

EXAMPLE 9 The formulas for the derivatives of both $\sin x$ and $\cos x$ were obtained under the assumption that x is measured in radians, *not* degrees. The Chain Rule gives us new insight into the difference between the two. Since $180° = \pi$ radians, $x° = \pi x/180$ radians where $x°$ is the size of the angle measured in degrees.

By the Chain Rule,

$$\frac{d}{dx}\sin(x°) = \frac{d}{dx}\sin\left(\frac{\pi x}{180}\right) = \frac{\pi}{180}\cos\left(\frac{\pi x}{180}\right) = \frac{\pi}{180}\cos(x°).$$

See Figure 3.27. Similarly, the derivative of $\cos(x°)$ is $-(\pi/180)\sin(x°)$.

The factor $\pi/180$ would compound with repeated differentiation. We see here the advantage for the use of radian measure in computations. ∎

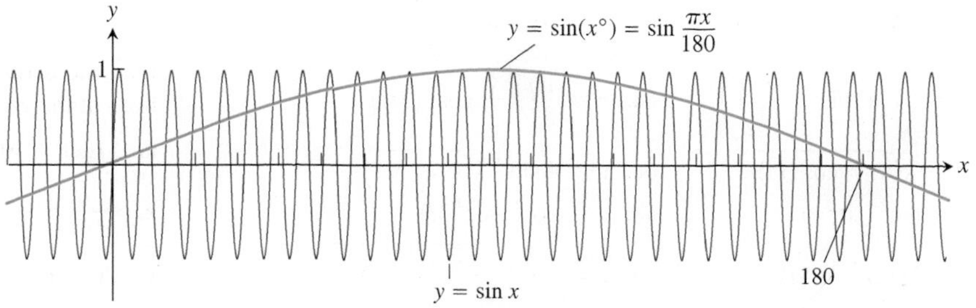

FIGURE 3.27 The function $\sin(x°)$ oscillates only $\pi/180$ times as often as $\sin x$ oscillates. Its maximum slope is $\pi/180$ at $x = 0$ (Example 9).

Exercises 3.6

Derivative Calculations

In Exercises 1–8, given $y = f(u)$ and $u = g(x)$, find $dy/dx = f'(g(x))g'(x)$.

1. $y = 6u - 9, \quad u = (1/2)x^4$
2. $y = 2u^3, \quad u = 8x - 1$
3. $y = \sin u, \quad u = 3x + 1$
4. $y = \cos u, \quad u = -x/3$
5. $y = \cos u, \quad u = \sin x$
6. $y = \sin u, \quad u = x - \cos x$
7. $y = \tan u, \quad u = 10x - 5$
8. $y = -\sec u, \quad u = x^2 + 7x$

In Exercises 9–22, write the function in the form $y = f(u)$ and $u = g(x)$. Then find dy/dx as a function of x.

9. $y = (2x + 1)^5$
10. $y = (4 - 3x)^9$
11. $y = \left(1 - \frac{x}{7}\right)^{-7}$
12. $y = \left(\frac{x}{2} - 1\right)^{-10}$
13. $y = \left(\frac{x^2}{8} + x - \frac{1}{x}\right)^4$
14. $y = \sqrt{3x^2 - 4x + 6}$
15. $y = \sec(\tan x)$
16. $y = \cot\left(\pi - \frac{1}{x}\right)$
17. $y = \sin^3 x$
18. $y = 5\cos^{-4} x$
19. $y = e^{-5x}$
20. $y = e^{2x/3}$
21. $y = e^{5-7x}$
22. $y = e^{\left(4\sqrt{x}+x^2\right)}$

Find the derivatives of the functions in Exercises 23–50.

23. $p = \sqrt{3 - t}$
24. $q = \sqrt[3]{2r - r^2}$
25. $s = \frac{4}{3\pi}\sin 3t + \frac{4}{5\pi}\cos 5t$
26. $s = \sin\left(\frac{3\pi t}{2}\right) + \cos\left(\frac{3\pi t}{2}\right)$
27. $r = (\csc\theta + \cot\theta)^{-1}$
28. $r = 6(\sec\theta - \tan\theta)^{3/2}$
29. $y = x^2\sin^4 x + x\cos^{-2} x$
30. $y = \frac{1}{x}\sin^{-5} x - \frac{x}{3}\cos^3 x$
31. $y = \frac{1}{21}(3x - 2)^7 + \left(4 - \frac{1}{2x^2}\right)^{-1}$
32. $y = (5 - 2x)^{-3} + \frac{1}{8}\left(\frac{2}{x} + 1\right)^4$
33. $y = (4x + 3)^4(x + 1)^{-3}$
34. $y = (2x - 5)^{-1}(x^2 - 5x)^6$
35. $y = xe^{-x} + e^{3x}$
36. $y = (1 + 2x)e^{-2x}$
37. $y = (x^2 - 2x + 2)e^{5x/2}$
38. $y = (9x^2 - 6x + 2)e^{x^3}$
39. $h(x) = x\tan\left(2\sqrt{x}\right) + 7$
40. $k(x) = x^2\sec\left(\frac{1}{x}\right)$

41. $f(x) = \sqrt{7 + x \sec x}$

42. $g(x) = \dfrac{\tan 3x}{(x + 7)^4}$

43. $f(\theta) = \left(\dfrac{\sin \theta}{1 + \cos \theta}\right)^2$

44. $g(t) = \left(\dfrac{1 + \sin 3t}{3 - 2t}\right)^{-1}$

45. $r = \sin(\theta^2)\cos(2\theta)$

46. $r = \sec\sqrt{\theta}\tan\left(\dfrac{1}{\theta}\right)$

47. $q = \sin\left(\dfrac{t}{\sqrt{t + 1}}\right)$

48. $q = \cot\left(\dfrac{\sin t}{t}\right)$

49. $y = \cos\left(e^{-\theta^2}\right)$

50. $y = \theta^3 e^{-2\theta}\cos 5\theta$

In Exercises 51–70, find dy/dt.

51. $y = \sin^2(\pi t - 2)$

52. $y = \sec^2 \pi t$

53. $y = (1 + \cos 2t)^{-4}$

54. $y = (1 + \cot(t/2))^{-2}$

55. $y = (t \tan t)^{10}$

56. $y = (t^{-3/4}\sin t)^{4/3}$

57. $y = e^{\cos^2(\pi t - 1)}$

58. $y = \left(e^{\sin(t/2)}\right)^3$

59. $y = \left(\dfrac{t^2}{t^3 - 4t}\right)^3$

60. $y = \left(\dfrac{3t - 4}{5t + 2}\right)^{-5}$

61. $y = \sin(\cos(2t - 5))$

62. $y = \cos\left(5\sin\left(\dfrac{t}{3}\right)\right)$

63. $y = \left(1 + \tan^4\left(\dfrac{t}{12}\right)\right)^3$

64. $y = \dfrac{1}{6}\left(1 + \cos^2(7t)\right)^3$

65. $y = \sqrt{1 + \cos(t^2)}$

66. $y = 4\sin\left(\sqrt{1 + \sqrt{t}}\right)$

67. $y = \tan^2(\sin^3 t)$

68. $y = \cos^4(\sec^2 3t)$

69. $y = 3t(2t^2 - 5)^4$

70. $y = \sqrt{3t + \sqrt{2 + \sqrt{1 - t}}}$

Second Derivatives

Find y'' in Exercises 71–78.

71. $y = \left(1 + \dfrac{1}{x}\right)^3$

72. $y = \left(1 - \sqrt{x}\right)^{-1}$

73. $y = \dfrac{1}{9}\cot(3x - 1)$

74. $y = 9\tan\left(\dfrac{x}{3}\right)$

75. $y = x(2x + 1)^4$

76. $y = x^2(x^3 - 1)^5$

77. $y = e^{x^2} + 5x$

78. $y = \sin(x^2 e^x)$

Finding Derivative Values

In Exercises 79–84, find the value of $(f \circ g)'$ at the given value of x.

79. $f(u) = u^5 + 1, \quad u = g(x) = \sqrt{x}, \quad x = 1$

80. $f(u) = 1 - \dfrac{1}{u}, \quad u = g(x) = \dfrac{1}{1 - x}, \quad x = -1$

81. $f(u) = \cot\dfrac{\pi u}{10}, \quad u = g(x) = 5\sqrt{x}, \quad x = 1$

82. $f(u) = u + \dfrac{1}{\cos^2 u}, \quad u = g(x) = \pi x, \quad x = 1/4$

83. $f(u) = \dfrac{2u}{u^2 + 1}, \quad u = g(x) = 10x^2 + x + 1, \quad x = 0$

84. $f(u) = \left(\dfrac{u - 1}{u + 1}\right)^2, \quad u = g(x) = \dfrac{1}{x^2} - 1, \quad x = -1$

85. Assume that $f'(3) = -1$, $g'(2) = 5$, $g(2) = 3$, and $y = f(g(x))$. What is y' at $x = 2$?

86. If $r = \sin(f(t))$, $f(0) = \pi/3$, and $f'(0) = 4$, then what is dr/dt at $t = 0$?

87. Suppose that functions f and g and their derivatives with respect to x have the following values at $x = 2$ and $x = 3$.

x	$f(x)$	$g(x)$	$f'(x)$	$g'(x)$
2	8	2	1/3	−3
3	3	−4	2π	5

Find the derivatives with respect to x of the following combinations at the given value of x.

a. $2f(x), \quad x = 2$

b. $f(x) + g(x), \quad x = 3$

c. $f(x)\cdot g(x), \quad x = 3$

d. $f(x)/g(x), \quad x = 2$

e. $f(g(x)), \quad x = 2$

f. $\sqrt{f(x)}, \quad x = 2$

g. $1/g^2(x), \quad x = 3$

h. $\sqrt{f^2(x) + g^2(x)}, \quad x = 2$

88. Suppose that the functions f and g and their derivatives with respect to x have the following values at $x = 0$ and $x = 1$.

x	$f(x)$	$g(x)$	$f'(x)$	$g'(x)$
0	1	1	5	1/3
1	3	−4	−1/3	−8/3

Find the derivatives with respect to x of the following combinations at the given value of x.

a. $5f(x) - g(x), \quad x = 1$

b. $f(x)g^3(x), \quad x = 0$

c. $\dfrac{f(x)}{g(x) + 1}, \quad x = 1$

d. $f(g(x)), \quad x = 0$

e. $g(f(x)), \quad x = 0$

f. $(x^{11} + f(x))^{-2}, \quad x = 1$

g. $f(x + g(x)), \quad x = 0$

89. Find ds/dt when $\theta = 3\pi/2$ if $s = \cos\theta$ and $d\theta/dt = 5$.

90. Find dy/dt when $x = 1$ if $y = x^2 + 7x - 5$ and $dx/dt = 1/3$.

Theory and Examples

What happens if you can write a function as a composite in different ways? Do you get the same derivative each time? The Chain Rule says you should. Try it with the functions in Exercises 91 and 92.

91. Find dy/dx if $y = x$ by using the Chain Rule with y as a composite of

a. $y = (u/5) + 7 \quad$ and $\quad u = 5x - 35$

b. $y = 1 + (1/u) \quad$ and $\quad u = 1/(x - 1)$.

92. Find dy/dx if $y = x^{3/2}$ by using the Chain Rule with y as a composite of

a. $y = u^3 \quad$ and $\quad u = \sqrt{x}$

b. $y = \sqrt{u} \quad$ and $\quad u = x^3$.

93. Find the tangent to $y = ((x - 1)/(x + 1))^2$ at $x = 0$.

94. Find the tangent to $y = \sqrt{x^2 - x + 7}$ at $x = 2$.

95. a. Find the tangent to the curve $y = 2\tan(\pi x/4)$ at $x = 1$.

b. Slopes on a tangent curve What is the smallest value the slope of the curve can ever have on the interval $-2 < x < 2$? Give reasons for your answer.

96. Slopes on sine curves

a. Find equations for the tangents to the curves $y = \sin 2x$ and $y = -\sin(x/2)$ at the origin. Is there anything special about how the tangents are related? Give reasons for your answer.

b. Can anything be said about the tangents to the curves $y = \sin mx$ and $y = -\sin(x/m)$ at the origin (m a constant $\neq 0$)? Give reasons for your answer.

c. For a given m, what are the largest values the slopes of the curves $y = \sin mx$ and $y = -\sin(x/m)$ can ever have? Give reasons for your answer.

d. The function $y = \sin x$ completes one period on the interval $[0, 2\pi]$, the function $y = \sin 2x$ completes two periods, the function $y = \sin(x/2)$ completes half a period, and so on. Is there any relation between the number of periods $y = \sin mx$ completes on $[0, 2\pi]$ and the slope of the curve $y = \sin mx$ at the origin? Give reasons for your answer.

97. Running machinery too fast Suppose that a piston is moving straight up and down and that its position at time t sec is

$$s = A\cos(2\pi bt),$$

with A and b positive. The value of A is the amplitude of the motion, and b is the frequency (number of times the piston moves up and down each second). What effect does doubling the frequency have on the piston's velocity, acceleration, and jerk? (Once you find out, you will know why some machinery breaks when you run it too fast.)

98. Temperatures in Fairbanks, Alaska The graph in the accompanying figure shows the average Fahrenheit temperature in Fairbanks, Alaska, during a typical 365-day year. The equation that approximates the temperature on day x is

$$y = 37\sin\left[\frac{2\pi}{365}(x - 101)\right] + 25$$

and is graphed in the accompanying figure.

a. On what day is the temperature increasing the fastest?

b. About how many degrees per day is the temperature increasing when it is increasing at its fastest?

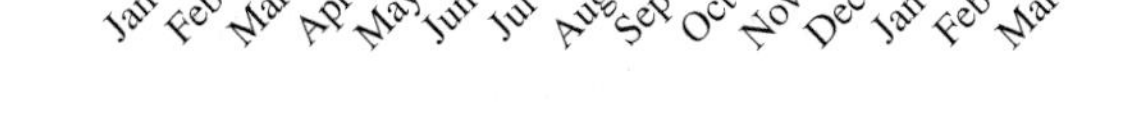

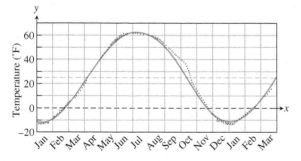

99. Particle motion The position of a particle moving along a coordinate line is $s = \sqrt{1 + 4t}$, with s in meters and t in seconds. Find the particle's velocity and acceleration at $t = 6$ sec.

100. Constant acceleration Suppose that the velocity of a falling body is $v = k\sqrt{s}$ m/sec (k a constant) at the instant the body has fallen s m from its starting point. Show that the body's acceleration is constant.

101. Falling meteorite The velocity of a heavy meteorite entering Earth's atmosphere is inversely proportional to $\sqrt{s}$ when it is s km from Earth's center. Show that the meteorite's acceleration is inversely proportional to s^2.

102. Particle acceleration A particle moves along the x-axis with velocity $dx/dt = f(x)$. Show that the particle's acceleration is $f(x)f'(x)$.

103. Temperature and the period of a pendulum For oscillations of small amplitude (short swings), we may safely model the relationship between the period T and the length L of a simple pendulum with the equation

$$T = 2\pi\sqrt{\frac{L}{g}},$$

where g is the constant acceleration of gravity at the pendulum's location. If we measure g in centimeters per second squared, we measure L in centimeters and T in seconds. If the pendulum is made of metal, its length will vary with temperature, either increasing or decreasing at a rate that is roughly proportional to L. In symbols, with u being temperature and k the proportionality constant,

$$\frac{dL}{du} = kL.$$

Assuming this to be the case, show that the rate at which the period changes with respect to temperature is $kT/2$.

104. Chain Rule Suppose that $f(x) = x^2$ and $g(x) = |x|$. Then the composites

$$(f \circ g)(x) = |x|^2 = x^2 \quad \text{and} \quad (g \circ f)(x) = |x^2| = x^2$$

are both differentiable at $x = 0$ even though g itself is not differentiable at $x = 0$. Does this contradict the Chain Rule? Explain.

T **105. The derivative of sin 2x** Graph the function $y = 2\cos 2x$ for $-2 \leq x \leq 3.5$. Then, on the same screen, graph

$$y = \frac{\sin 2(x + h) - \sin 2x}{h}$$

for $h = 1.0, 0.5$, and 0.2. Experiment with other values of h, including negative values. What do you see happening as $h \to 0$? Explain this behavior.

106. The derivative of $\cos(x^2)$ Graph $y = -2x\sin(x^2)$ for $-2 \leq x \leq 3$. Then, on the same screen, graph

$$y = \frac{\cos((x + h)^2) - \cos(x^2)}{h}$$

for $h = 1.0, 0.7$, and 0.3. Experiment with other values of h. What do you see happening as $h \to 0$? Explain this behavior.

Using the Chain Rule, show that the Power Rule $(d/dx)x^n = nx^{n-1}$ holds for the functions x^n in Exercises 107 and 108.

107. $x^{1/4} = \sqrt{\sqrt{x}}$

108. $x^{3/4} = \sqrt{x\sqrt{x}}$

COMPUTER EXPLORATIONS

Trigonometric Polynomials

109. As the accompanying figure shows, the trigonometric "polynomial"

$$s = f(t) = 0.78540 - 0.63662\cos 2t - 0.07074\cos 6t$$
$$- 0.02546\cos 10t - 0.01299\cos 14t$$

gives a good approximation of the sawtooth function $s = g(t)$ on the interval $[-\pi, \pi]$. How well does the derivative of f approximate the derivative of g at the points where dg/dt is defined? To find out, carry out the following steps.

a. Graph dg/dt (where defined) over $[-\pi, \pi]$.

b. Find df/dt.

c. Graph df/dt. Where does the approximation of dg/dt by df/dt seem to be best? Least good? Approximations by trigonometric polynomials are important in the theories of heat and oscillation, but we must not expect too much of them, as we see in the next exercise.

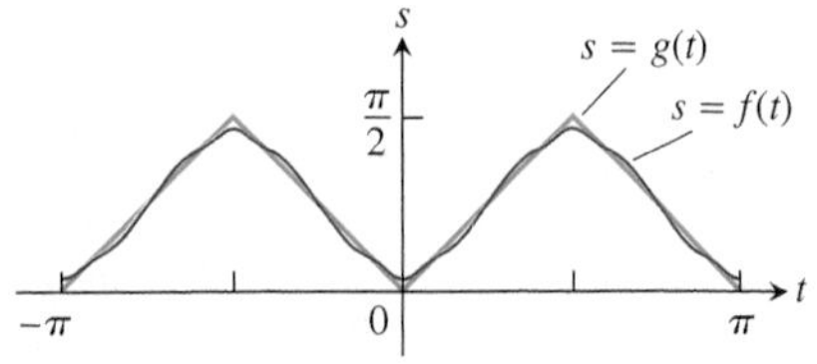

110. (*Continuation of Exercise 109.*) In Exercise 109, the trigonometric polynomial $f(t)$ that approximated the sawtooth function $g(t)$ on $[-\pi, \pi]$ had a derivative that approximated the derivative of the sawtooth function. It is possible, however, for a trigonometric polynomial to approximate a function in a reasonable way without its derivative approximating the function's derivative at all well. As a case in point, the "polynomial"

$$s = h(t) = 1.2732 \sin 2t + 0.4244 \sin 6t + 0.25465 \sin 10t + 0.18189 \sin 14t + 0.14147 \sin 18t$$

graphed in the accompanying figure approximates the step function $s = k(t)$ shown there. Yet the derivative of h is nothing like the derivative of k.

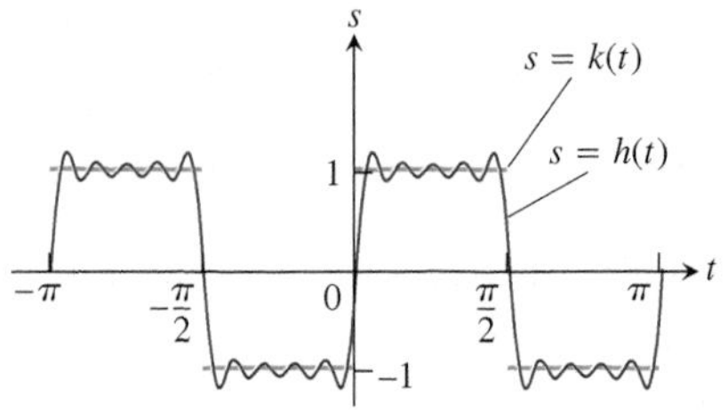

a. Graph dk/dt (where defined) over $[-\pi, \pi]$.

b. Find dh/dt.

c. Graph dh/dt to see how badly the graph fits the graph of dk/dt. Comment on what you see.

3.7 Implicit Differentiation

Most of the functions we have dealt with so far have been described by an equation of the form $y = f(x)$ that expresses y explicitly in terms of the variable x. We have learned rules for differentiating functions defined in this way. Another situation occurs when we encounter equations like

$$x^3 + y^3 - 9xy = 0, \qquad y^2 - x = 0, \qquad \text{or} \qquad x^2 + y^2 - 25 = 0.$$

(See Figures 3.28, 3.29, and 3.30.) These equations define an *implicit* relation between the variables x and y. In some cases we may be able to solve such an equation for y as an explicit function (or even several functions) of x. When we cannot put an equation $F(x, y) = 0$ in the form $y = f(x)$ to differentiate it in the usual way, we may still be able to find dy/dx by *implicit differentiation*. This section describes the technique.

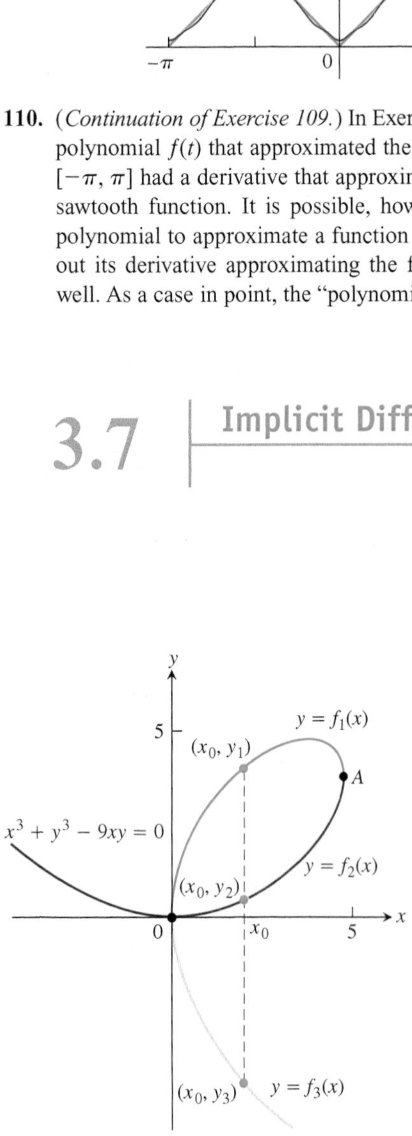

FIGURE 3.28 The curve $x^3 + y^3 - 9xy = 0$ is not the graph of any one function of x. The curve can, however, be divided into separate arcs that *are* the graphs of functions of x. This particular curve, called a *folium*, dates to Descartes in 1638.

Implicitly Defined Functions

We begin with examples involving familiar equations that we can solve for y as a function of x to calculate dy/dx in the usual way. Then we differentiate the equations implicitly, and find the derivative to compare the two methods. Following the examples, we summarize the steps involved in the new method. In the examples and exercises, it is always assumed that the given equation determines y implicitly as a differentiable function of x so that dy/dx exists.

EXAMPLE 1 Find dy/dx if $y^2 = x$.

Solution The equation $y^2 = x$ defines two differentiable functions of x that we can actually find, namely $y_1 = \sqrt{x}$ and $y_2 = -\sqrt{x}$ (Figure 3.29). We know how to calculate the derivative of each of these for $x > 0$:

$$\frac{dy_1}{dx} = \frac{1}{2\sqrt{x}} \quad \text{and} \quad \frac{dy_2}{dx} = -\frac{1}{2\sqrt{x}}.$$

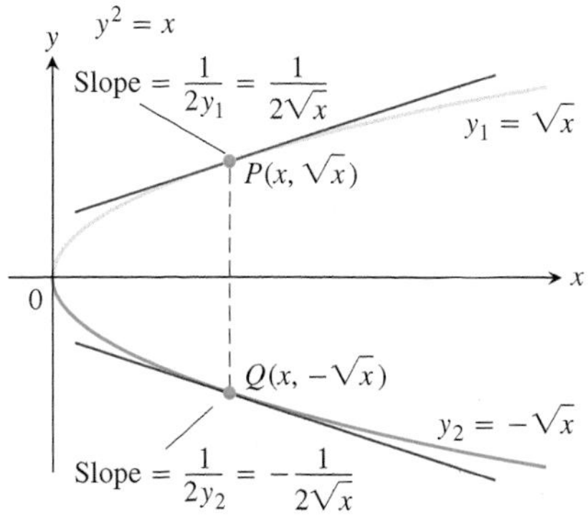

FIGURE 3.29 The equation $y^2 - x = 0$, or $y^2 = x$ as it is usually written, defines two differentiable functions of x on the interval $x > 0$. Example 1 shows how to find the derivatives of these functions without solving the equation $y^2 = x$ for y.

But suppose that we knew only that the equation $y^2 = x$ defined y as one or more differentiable functions of x for $x > 0$ without knowing exactly what these functions were. Could we still find dy/dx?

The answer is yes. To find dy/dx, we simply differentiate both sides of the equation $y^2 = x$ with respect to x, treating $y = f(x)$ as a differentiable function of x:

$$y^2 = x$$
$$2y\frac{dy}{dx} = 1$$
$$\frac{dy}{dx} = \frac{1}{2y}.$$

The Chain Rule gives $\frac{d}{dx}(y^2) = \frac{d}{dx}[f(x)]^2 = 2f(x)f'(x) = 2y\frac{dy}{dx}$.

This one formula gives the derivatives we calculated for *both* explicit solutions $y_1 = \sqrt{x}$ and $y_2 = -\sqrt{x}$:

$$\frac{dy_1}{dx} = \frac{1}{2y_1} = \frac{1}{2\sqrt{x}} \quad \text{and} \quad \frac{dy_2}{dx} = \frac{1}{2y_2} = \frac{1}{2(-\sqrt{x})} = -\frac{1}{2\sqrt{x}}.$$

■

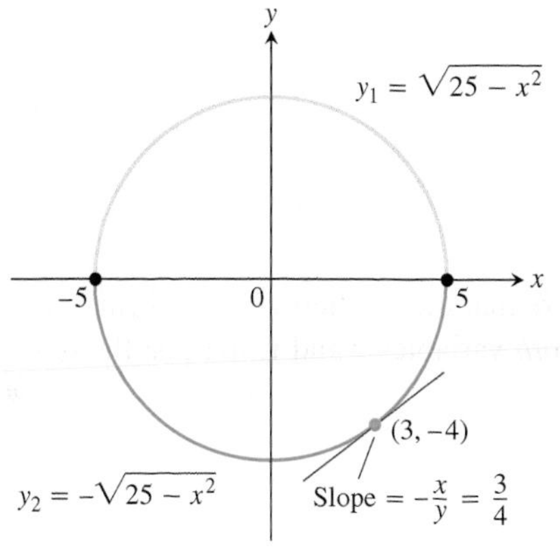

FIGURE 3.30 The circle combines the graphs of two functions. The graph of y_2 is the lower semicircle and passes through $(3, -4)$.

EXAMPLE 2 Find the slope of the circle $x^2 + y^2 = 25$ at the point $(3, -4)$.

Solution The circle is not the graph of a single function of x. Rather, it is the combined graphs of two differentiable functions, $y_1 = \sqrt{25 - x^2}$ and $y_2 = -\sqrt{25 - x^2}$ (Figure 3.30). The point $(3, -4)$ lies on the graph of y_2, so we can find the slope by calculating the derivative directly, using the Power Chain Rule:

$$\left.\frac{dy_2}{dx}\right|_{x=3} = -\left.\frac{-2x}{2\sqrt{25 - x^2}}\right|_{x=3} = -\frac{-6}{2\sqrt{25 - 9}} = \frac{3}{4}.$$

$\frac{d}{dx}\left(-(25 - x^2)^{1/2}\right) = -\frac{1}{2}(25 - x^2)^{-1/2}(-2x)$

We can solve this problem more easily by differentiating the given equation of the circle implicitly with respect to x:

$$\frac{d}{dx}(x^2) + \frac{d}{dx}(y^2) = \frac{d}{dx}(25)$$
$$2x + 2y\frac{dy}{dx} = 0$$
$$\frac{dy}{dx} = -\frac{x}{y}.$$

The slope at $(3, -4)$ is $\left.-\frac{x}{y}\right|_{(3,-4)} = -\frac{3}{-4} = \frac{3}{4}.$

Notice that unlike the slope formula for dy_2/dx, which applies only to points below the x-axis, the formula $dy/dx = -x/y$ applies everywhere the circle has a slope. Notice also that the derivative involves *both* variables x and y, not just the independent variable x. ■

To calculate the derivatives of other implicitly defined functions, we proceed as in Examples 1 and 2: We treat y as a differentiable implicit function of x and apply the usual rules to differentiate both sides of the defining equation.

> **Implicit Differentiation**
> 1. Differentiate both sides of the equation with respect to x, treating y as a differentiable function of x.
> 2. Collect the terms with dy/dx on one side of the equation and solve for dy/dx.

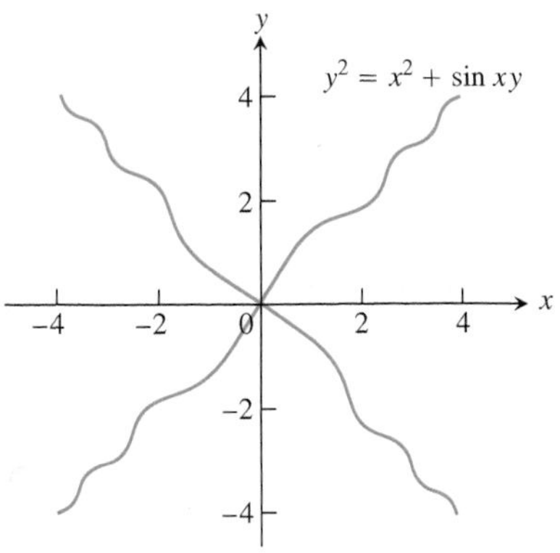

FIGURE 3.31 The graph of $y^2 = x^2 + \sin xy$ in Example 3.

EXAMPLE 3 Find dy/dx if $y^2 = x^2 + \sin xy$ (Figure 3.31).

Solution We differentiate the equation implicitly.

$$y^2 = x^2 + \sin xy$$

$$\frac{d}{dx}\left(y^2\right) = \frac{d}{dx}\left(x^2\right) + \frac{d}{dx}\left(\sin xy\right) \qquad \text{Differentiate both sides with respect to } x \ldots$$

$$2y\frac{dy}{dx} = 2x + (\cos xy)\frac{d}{dx}(xy) \qquad \ldots \text{treating } y \text{ as a function of } x \text{ and using the Chain Rule.}$$

$$2y\frac{dy}{dx} = 2x + (\cos xy)\left(y + x\frac{dy}{dx}\right) \qquad \text{Treat } xy \text{ as a product.}$$

$$2y\frac{dy}{dx} - (\cos xy)\left(x\frac{dy}{dx}\right) = 2x + (\cos xy)y \qquad \text{Collect terms with } dy/dx.$$

$$(2y - x\cos xy)\frac{dy}{dx} = 2x + y\cos xy$$

$$\frac{dy}{dx} = \frac{2x + y\cos xy}{2y - x\cos xy} \qquad \text{Solve for } dy/dx.$$

Notice that the formula for dy/dx applies everywhere that the implicitly defined curve has a slope. Notice again that the derivative involves *both* variables x and y, not just the independent variable x. ■

Derivatives of Higher Order

Implicit differentiation can also be used to find higher derivatives.

EXAMPLE 4 Find d^2y/dx^2 if $2x^3 - 3y^2 = 8$.

Solution To start, we differentiate both sides of the equation with respect to x in order to find $y' = dy/dx$.

$$\frac{d}{dx}(2x^3 - 3y^2) = \frac{d}{dx}(8)$$

$$6x^2 - 6yy' = 0 \qquad \text{Treat } y \text{ as a function of } x.$$

$$y' = \frac{x^2}{y}, \quad \text{when } y \neq 0 \qquad \text{Solve for } y'.$$

We now apply the Quotient Rule to find y''.

$$y'' = \frac{d}{dx}\left(\frac{x^2}{y}\right) = \frac{2xy - x^2y'}{y^2} = \frac{2x}{y} - \frac{x^2}{y^2}\cdot y'$$

Finally, we substitute $y' = x^2/y$ to express y'' in terms of x and y.

$$y'' = \frac{2x}{y} - \frac{x^2}{y^2}\left(\frac{x^2}{y}\right) = \frac{2x}{y} - \frac{x^4}{y^3}, \quad \text{when } y \neq 0$$

■

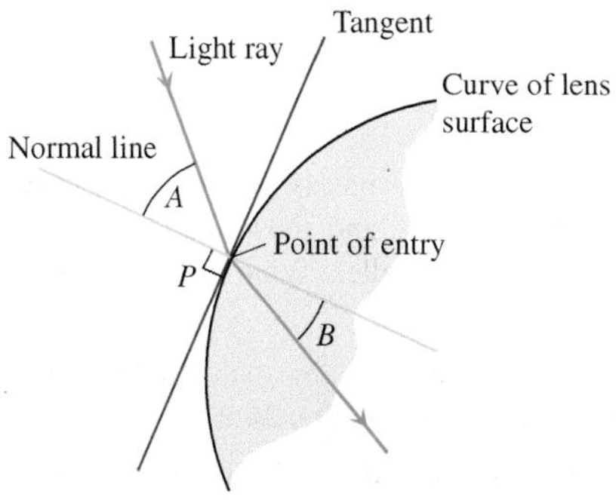

FIGURE 3.32 The profile of a lens, showing the bending (refraction) of a ray of light as it passes through the lens surface.

Lenses, Tangents, and Normal Lines

In the law that describes how light changes direction as it enters a lens, the important angles are the angles the light makes with the line perpendicular to the surface of the lens at the point of entry (angles A and B in Figure 3.32). This line is called the *normal* to the surface at the point of entry. In a profile view of a lens like the one in Figure 3.32, the **normal** is the line perpendicular to the tangent of the profile curve at the point of entry.

EXAMPLE 5 Show that the point (2, 4) lies on the curve $x^3 + y^3 - 9xy = 0$. Then find the tangent and normal to the curve there (Figure 3.33).

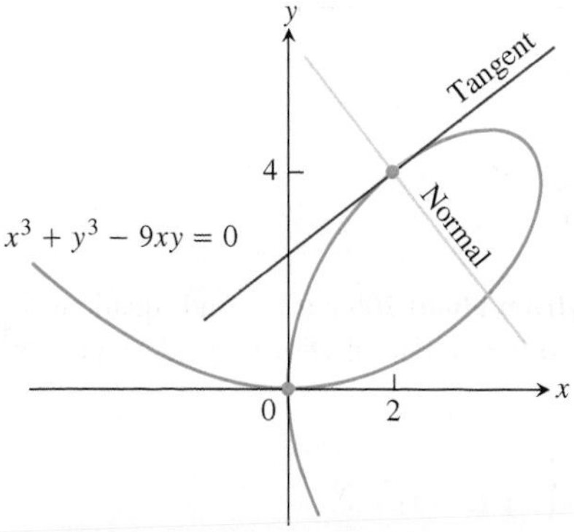

FIGURE 3.33 Example 5 shows how to find equations for the tangent and normal to the folium of Descartes at (2, 4).

Solution The point (2, 4) lies on the curve because its coordinates satisfy the equation given for the curve: $2^3 + 4^3 - 9(2)(4) = 8 + 64 - 72 = 0$.

To find the slope of the curve at (2, 4), we first use implicit differentiation to find a formula for dy/dx:

$$x^3 + y^3 - 9xy = 0$$

$$\frac{d}{dx}(x^3) + \frac{d}{dx}(y^3) - \frac{d}{dx}(9xy) = \frac{d}{dx}(0)$$

$$3x^2 + 3y^2\frac{dy}{dx} - 9\left(x\frac{dy}{dx} + y\frac{dx}{dx}\right) = 0 \qquad \text{Differentiate both sides with respect to } x.$$

$$(3y^2 - 9x)\frac{dy}{dx} + 3x^2 - 9y = 0 \qquad \text{Treat } xy \text{ as a product and } y \text{ as a function of } x.$$

$$3(y^2 - 3x)\frac{dy}{dx} = 9y - 3x^2$$

$$\frac{dy}{dx} = \frac{3y - x^2}{y^2 - 3x}. \qquad \text{Solve for } dy/dx.$$

We then evaluate the derivative at $(x, y) = (2, 4)$:

$$\left.\frac{dy}{dx}\right|_{(2,4)} = \left.\frac{3y - x^2}{y^2 - 3x}\right|_{(2,4)} = \frac{3(4) - 2^2}{4^2 - 3(2)} = \frac{8}{10} = \frac{4}{5}.$$

The tangent at (2, 4) is the line through (2, 4) with slope $4/5$:

$$y = 4 + \frac{4}{5}(x - 2)$$

$$y = \frac{4}{5}x + \frac{12}{5}.$$

The normal to the curve at (2, 4) is the line perpendicular to the tangent there, the line through (2, 4) with slope $-5/4$:

$$y = 4 - \frac{5}{4}(x - 2)$$

$$y = -\frac{5}{4}x + \frac{13}{2}.$$

■

Exercise 3.7

Differentiating Implicitly

Use implicit differentiation to find dy/dx in Exercises 1–16.

1. $x^2y + xy^2 = 6$

2. $x^3 + y^3 = 18xy$

3. $2xy + y^2 = x + y$

4. $x^3 - xy + y^3 = 1$

5. $x^2(x - y)^2 = x^2 - y^2$

6. $(3xy + 7)^2 = 6y$

7. $y^2 = \dfrac{x - 1}{x + 1}$

8. $x^3 = \dfrac{2x - y}{x + 3y}$

9. $x = \tan y$

10. $xy = \cot(xy)$

11. $x + \tan(xy) = 0$

12. $x^4 + \sin y = x^3y^2$

13. $y \sin\left(\dfrac{1}{y}\right) = 1 - xy$

14. $x \cos(2x + 3y) = y \sin x$

15. $e^{2x} = \sin(x + 3y)$

16. $e^{x^2y} = 2x + 2y$

Find $dr/d\theta$ in Exercises 17–20.

17. $\theta^{1/2} + r^{1/2} = 1$

18. $r - 2\sqrt{\theta} = \dfrac{3}{2}\theta^{2/3} + \dfrac{4}{3}\theta^{3/4}$

19. $\sin(r\theta) = \dfrac{1}{2}$

20. $\cos r + \cot\theta = e^{r\theta}$

Second Derivatives

In Exercises 21–26, use implicit differentiation to find dy/dx and then d^2y/dx^2.

21. $x^2 + y^2 = 1$

22. $x^{2/3} + y^{2/3} = 1$

23. $y^2 = e^{x^2} + 2x$

24. $y^2 - 2x = 1 - 2y$

25. $2\sqrt{y} = x - y$

26. $xy + y^2 = 1$

27. If $x^3 + y^3 = 16$, find the value of d^2y/dx^2 at the point $(2, 2)$.

28. If $xy + y^2 = 1$, find the value of d^2y/dx^2 at the point $(0, -1)$.

In Exercises 29 and 30, find the slope of the curve at the given points.

29. $y^2 + x^2 = y^4 - 2x$ at $(-2, 1)$ and $(-2, -1)$

30. $(x^2 + y^2)^2 = (x - y)^2$ at $(1, 0)$ and $(1, -1)$

Slopes, Tangents, and Normals

In Exercises 31–40, verify that the given point is on the curve and find the lines that are **(a)** tangent and **(b)** normal to the curve at the given point.

31. $x^2 + xy - y^2 = 1, \quad (2, 3)$

32. $x^2 + y^2 = 25, \quad (3, -4)$

33. $x^2y^2 = 9, \quad (-1, 3)$

34. $y^2 - 2x - 4y - 1 = 0, \quad (-2, 1)$

35. $6x^2 + 3xy + 2y^2 + 17y - 6 = 0, \quad (-1, 0)$

36. $x^2 - \sqrt{3}xy + 2y^2 = 5, \quad (\sqrt{3}, 2)$

37. $2xy + \pi \sin y = 2\pi, \quad (1, \pi/2)$

38. $x \sin 2y = y \cos 2x, \quad (\pi/4, \pi/2)$

39. $y = 2\sin(\pi x - y), \quad (1, 0)$

40. $x^2\cos^2 y - \sin y = 0, \quad (0, \pi)$

41. Parallel tangents Find the two points where the curve $x^2 + xy + y^2 = 7$ crosses the x-axis, and show that the tangents to the curve at these points are parallel. What is the common slope of these tangents?

42. Normals parallel to a line Find the normals to the curve $xy + 2x - y = 0$ that are parallel to the line $2x + y = 0$.

43. The eight curve Find the slopes of the curve $y^4 = y^2 - x^2$ at the two points shown here.

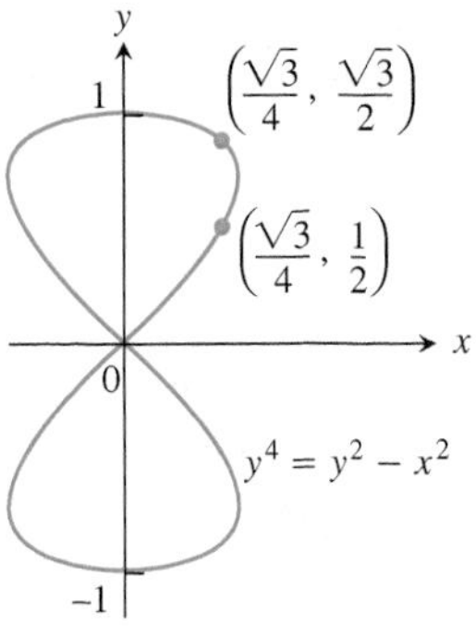

44. The cissoid of Diocles (from about 200 B.C.) Find equations for the tangent and normal to the cissoid of Diocles $y^2(2 - x) = x^3$ at $(1, 1)$.

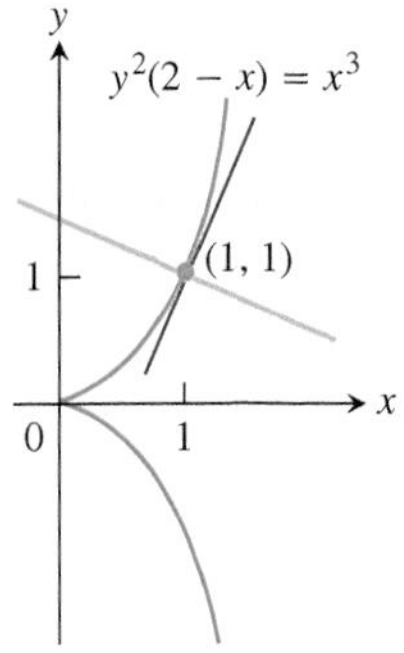

45. The devil's curve (Gabriel Cramer, 1750) Find the slopes of the devil's curve $y^4 - 4y^2 = x^4 - 9x^2$ at the four indicated points.

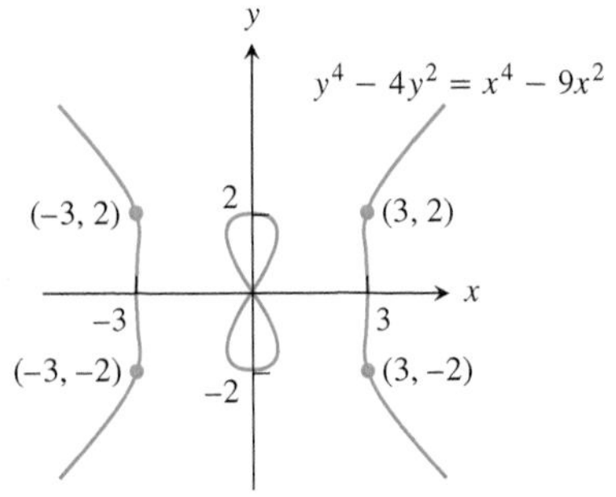

46. **The folium of Descartes** (See Figure 3.28.)

  a. Find the slope of the folium of Descartes $x^3 + y^3 - 9xy = 0$ at the points (4, 2) and (2, 4).

  b. At what point other than the origin does the folium have a horizontal tangent?

  c. Find the coordinates of the point A in Figure 3.28, where the folium has a vertical tangent.

Theory and Examples

47. **Intersecting normal** The line that is normal to the curve $x^2 + 2xy - 3y^2 = 0$ at (1, 1) intersects the curve at what other point?

48. **Power rule for rational exponents** Let p and q be integers with $q > 0$. If $y = x^{p/q}$, differentiate the equivalent equation $y^q = x^p$ implicitly and show that, for $y \neq 0$,

$$\frac{d}{dx}x^{p/q} = \frac{p}{q}x^{(p/q)-1}.$$

49. **Normals to a parabola** Show that if it is possible to draw three normals from the point $(a, 0)$ to the parabola $x = y^2$ shown in the accompanying diagram, then a must be greater than 1/2. One of the normals is the x-axis. For what value of a are the other two normals perpendicular?

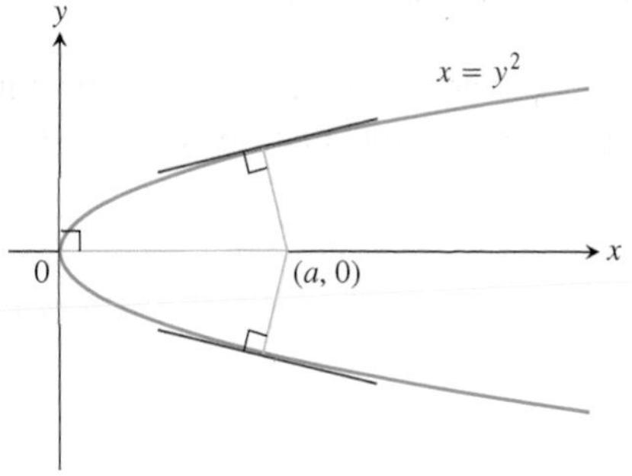

50. Is there anything special about the tangents to the curves $y^2 = x^3$ and $2x^2 + 3y^2 = 5$ at the points $(1, \pm 1)$? Give reasons for your answer.

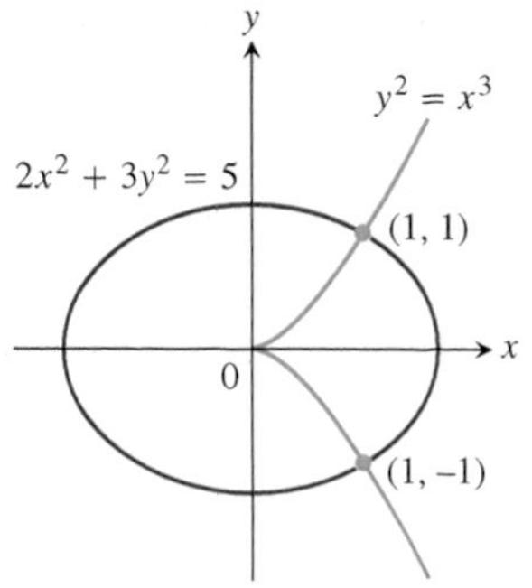

51. Verify that the following pairs of curves meet orthogonally.

  a. $x^2 + y^2 = 4, \quad x^2 = 3y^2$

  b. $x = 1 - y^2, \quad x = \frac{1}{3}y^2$

52. The graph of $y^2 = x^3$ is called a **semicubical parabola** and is shown in the accompanying figure. Determine the constant b so that the line $y = -\frac{1}{3}x + b$ meets this graph orthogonally.

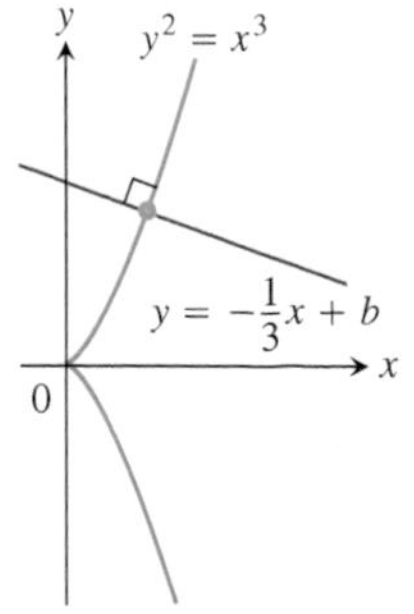

T In Exercises 53 and 54, find both dy/dx (treating y as a differentiable function of x) and dx/dy (treating x as a differentiable function of y). How do dy/dx and dx/dy seem to be related? Explain the relationship geometrically in terms of the graphs.

53. $xy^3 + x^2y = 6$

54. $x^3 + y^2 = \sin^2 y$

COMPUTER EXPLORATIONS

Use a CAS to perform the following steps in Exercises 55–62.

  a. Plot the equation with the implicit plotter of a CAS. Check to see that the given point P satisfies the equation.

  b. Using implicit differentiation, find a formula for the derivative dy/dx and evaluate it at the given point P.

  c. Use the slope found in part (b) to find an equation for the tangent line to the curve at P. Then plot the implicit curve and tangent line together on a single graph.

55. $x^3 - xy + y^3 = 7, \quad P(2, 1)$

56. $x^5 + y^3x + yx^2 + y^4 = 4, \quad P(1, 1)$

57. $y^2 + y = \frac{2 + x}{1 - x}, \quad P(0, 1)$

58. $y^3 + \cos xy = x^2, \quad P(1, 0)$

59. $x + \tan\left(\frac{y}{x}\right) = 2, \quad P\left(1, \frac{\pi}{4}\right)$

60. $xy^3 + \tan(x + y) = 1, \quad P\left(\frac{\pi}{4}, 0\right)$

61. $2y^2 + (xy)^{1/3} = x^2 + 2, \quad P(1, 1)$

62. $x\sqrt{1 + 2y} + y = x^2, \quad P(1, 0)$

3.8 Derivatives of Inverse Functions and Logarithms

In Section 1.6 we saw how the inverse of a function undoes, or inverts, the effect of that function. We defined there the natural logarithm function $f^{-1}(x) = \ln x$ as the inverse of the natural exponential function $f(x) = e^x$. This is one of the most important function-inverse pairs in mathematics and science. We learned how to differentiate the exponential function in Section 3.3. Here we learn a rule for differentiating the inverse of a differentiable function and we apply the rule to find the derivative of the natural logarithm function.

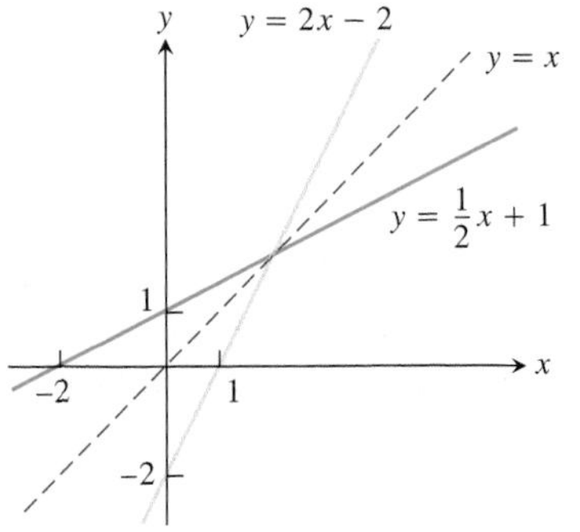

FIGURE 3.34 Graphing a line and its inverse together shows the graphs' symmetry with respect to the line $y = x$. The slopes are reciprocals of each other.

Derivatives of Inverses of Differentiable Functions

We calculated the inverse of the function $f(x) = (1/2)x + 1$ as $f^{-1}(x) = 2x - 2$ in Example 3 of Section 1.6. Figure 3.34 shows again the graphs of both functions. If we calculate their derivatives, we see that

$$\frac{d}{dx} f(x) = \frac{d}{dx}\left(\frac{1}{2}x + 1\right) = \frac{1}{2}$$

$$\frac{d}{dx} f^{-1}(x) = \frac{d}{dx}(2x - 2) = 2.$$

The derivatives are reciprocals of one another, so the slope of one line is the reciprocal of the slope of its inverse line. (See Figure 3.34.)

This is not a special case. Reflecting any nonhorizontal or nonvertical line across the line $y = x$ always inverts the line's slope. If the original line has slope $m \neq 0$, the reflected line has slope $1/m$.

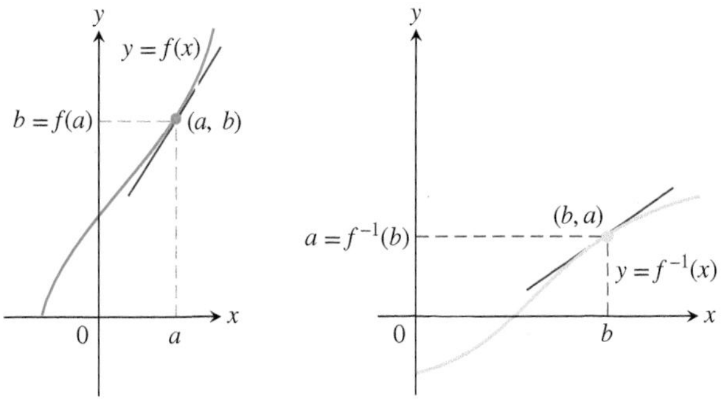

The slopes are reciprocal: $(f^{-1})'(b) = \dfrac{1}{f'(a)}$ or $(f^{-1})'(b) = \dfrac{1}{f'(f^{-1}(b))}$

FIGURE 3.35 The graphs of inverse functions have reciprocal slopes at corresponding points.

The reciprocal relationship between the slopes of f and f^{-1} holds for other functions as well, but we must be careful to compare slopes at corresponding points. If the slope of $y = f(x)$ at the point $(a, f(a))$ is $f'(a)$ and $f'(a) \neq 0$, then the slope of $y = f^{-1}(x)$ at the point $(f(a), a)$ is the reciprocal $1/f'(a)$ (Figure 3.35). If we set $b = f(a)$, then

$$(f^{-1})'(b) = \frac{1}{f'(a)} = \frac{1}{f'(f^{-1}(b))}.$$

If $y = f(x)$ has a horizontal tangent line at $(a, f(a))$, then the inverse function f^{-1} has a vertical tangent line at $(f(a), a)$, and this infinite slope implies that f^{-1} is not differentiable at $f(a)$. Theorem 3 gives the conditions under which f^{-1} is differentiable in its domain (which is the same as the range of f).

THEOREM 3—The Derivative Rule for Inverses If f has an interval I as domain and $f'(x)$ exists and is never zero on I, then f^{-1} is differentiable at every point in its domain (the range of f). The value of $(f^{-1})'$ at a point b in the domain of f^{-1} is the reciprocal of the value of f' at the point $a = f^{-1}(b)$:

$$(f^{-1})'(b) = \frac{1}{f'(f^{-1}(b))} \tag{1}$$

or

$$\left.\frac{df^{-1}}{dx}\right|_{x=b} = \frac{1}{\left.\dfrac{df}{dx}\right|_{x=f^{-1}(b)}}.$$

Theorem 3 makes two assertions. The first of these has to do with the conditions under which f^{-1} is differentiable; the second assertion is a formula for the derivative of f^{-1} when it exists. While we omit the proof of the first assertion, the second one is proved in the following way:

$$f(f^{-1}(x)) = x \qquad \text{Inverse function relationship}$$

$$\frac{d}{dx} f(f^{-1}(x)) = 1 \qquad \text{Differentiating both sides}$$

$$f'(f^{-1}(x)) \cdot \frac{d}{dx} f^{-1}(x) = 1 \qquad \text{Chain Rule}$$

$$\frac{d}{dx} f^{-1}(x) = \frac{1}{f'(f^{-1}(x))}. \qquad \text{Solving for the derivative}$$

EXAMPLE 1 The function $f(x) = x^2, x \geq 0$ and its inverse $f^{-1}(x) = \sqrt{x}$ have derivatives $f'(x) = 2x$ and $(f^{-1})'(x) = 1/(2\sqrt{x})$.

Let's verify that Theorem 3 gives the same formula for the derivative of $f^{-1}(x)$:

$$\begin{aligned}(f^{-1})'(x) &= \frac{1}{f'(f^{-1}(x))} \\ &= \frac{1}{2(f^{-1}(x))} \qquad f'(x) = 2x \text{ with } x \text{ replaced by } f^{-1}(x) \\ &= \frac{1}{2(\sqrt{x})}.\end{aligned}$$

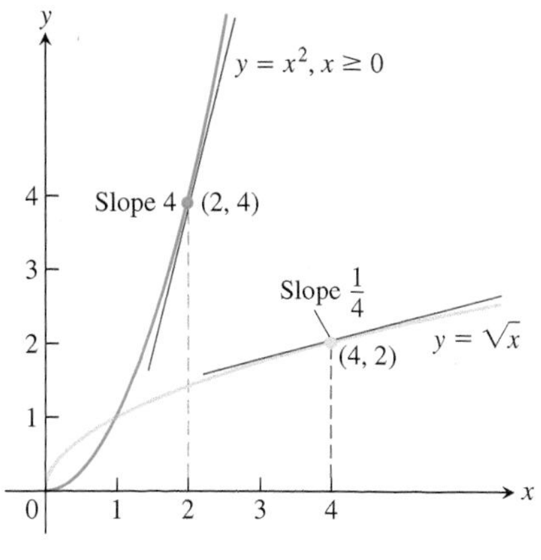

FIGURE 3.36 The derivative of $f^{-1}(x) = \sqrt{x}$ at the point (4, 2) is the reciprocal of the derivative of $f(x) = x^2$ at (2, 4) (Example 1).

Theorem 3 gives a derivative that agrees with the known derivative of the square root function.

Let's examine Theorem 3 at a specific point. We pick $x = 2$ (the number a) and $f(2) = 4$ (the value b). Theorem 3 says that the derivative of f at 2, $f'(2) = 4$, and the derivative of f^{-1} at $f(2)$, $(f^{-1})'(4)$, are reciprocals. It states that

$$(f^{-1})'(4) = \frac{1}{f'(f^{-1}(4))} = \frac{1}{f'(2)} = \left.\frac{1}{2x}\right|_{x=2} = \frac{1}{4}.$$

See Figure 3.36. ■

We will use the procedure illustrated in Example 1 to calculate formulas for the derivatives of many inverse functions throughout this chapter. Equation (1) sometimes enables us to find specific values of df^{-1}/dx without knowing a formula for f^{-1}.

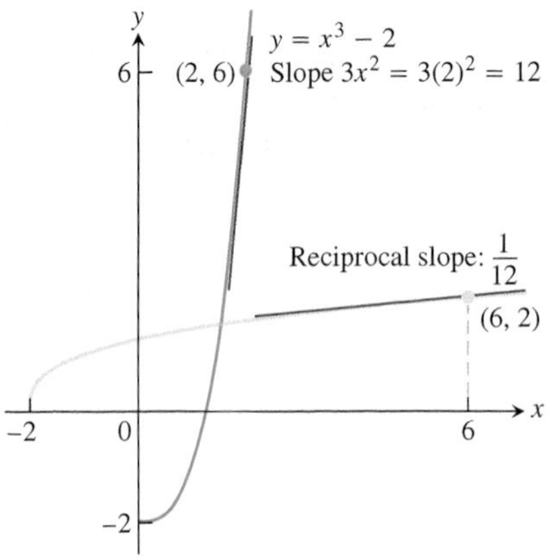

FIGURE 3.37 The derivative of $f(x) = x^3 - 2$ at $x = 2$ tells us the derivative of f^{-1} at $x = 6$ (Example 2).

EXAMPLE 2 Let $f(x) = x^3 - 2$. Find the value of df^{-1}/dx at $x = 6 = f(2)$ without finding a formula for $f^{-1}(x)$.

Solution We apply Theorem 3 to obtain the value of the derivative of f^{-1} at $x = 6$:

$$\left.\frac{df}{dx}\right|_{x=2} = 3x^2\Big|_{x=2} = 12$$

$$\left.\frac{df^{-1}}{dx}\right|_{x=f(2)} = \frac{1}{\left.\frac{df}{dx}\right|_{x=2}} = \frac{1}{12}. \qquad \text{Eq. (1)}$$

See Figure 3.37. ■

Derivative of the Natural Logarithm Function

Since we know the exponential function $f(x) = e^x$ is differentiable everywhere, we can apply Theorem 3 to find the derivative of its inverse $f^{-1}(x) = \ln x$:

$$\begin{aligned}(f^{-1})'(x) &= \frac{1}{f'(f^{-1}(x))} && \text{Theorem 3}\\ &= \frac{1}{e^{f^{-1}(x)}} && f'(u) = e^u\\ &= \frac{1}{e^{\ln x}}\\ &= \frac{1}{x}. && \text{Inverse function relationship}\end{aligned}$$

Alternate Derivation Instead of applying Theorem 3 directly, we can find the derivative of $y = \ln x$ using implicit differentiation, as follows:

$$\begin{aligned} y &= \ln x\\ e^y &= x && \text{Inverse function relationship}\\ \frac{d}{dx}(e^y) &= \frac{d}{dx}(x) && \text{Differentiate implicitly.}\\ e^y\frac{dy}{dx} &= 1 && \text{Chain Rule}\\ \frac{dy}{dx} &= \frac{1}{e^y} = \frac{1}{x}. && e^y = x\end{aligned}$$

No matter which derivation we use, the derivative of $y = \ln x$ with respect to x is

$$\frac{d}{dx}(\ln x) = \frac{1}{x}, \quad x > 0.$$

The Chain Rule extends this formula for positive functions $u(x)$:

$$\frac{d}{dx}\ln u = \frac{1}{u}\frac{du}{dx}, \qquad u > 0. \tag{2}$$

EXAMPLE 3 We use Equation (2) to find derivatives.

(a) $\frac{d}{dx}\ln 2x = \frac{1}{2x}\frac{d}{dx}(2x) = \frac{1}{2x}(2) = \frac{1}{x}, \quad x > 0$

(b) Equation (2) with $u = x^2 + 3$ gives

$$\frac{d}{dx}\ln(x^2+3) = \frac{1}{x^2+3}\cdot\frac{d}{dx}(x^2+3) = \frac{1}{x^2+3}\cdot 2x = \frac{2x}{x^2+3}.$$

(c) Equation (2) with $u = |x|$ gives an important derivative:

$$\begin{aligned}\frac{d}{dx}\ln|x| &= \frac{d}{du}\ln u\cdot\frac{du}{dx} && u = |x|, x \neq 0\\ &= \frac{1}{u}\cdot\frac{x}{|x|} && \frac{d}{dx}(|x|) = \frac{x}{|x|}\\ &= \frac{1}{|x|}\cdot\frac{x}{|x|} && \text{Substitute for } u.\\ &= \frac{x}{x^2}\\ &= \frac{1}{x}.\end{aligned}$$

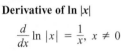

Derivative of ln |x|

$$\frac{d}{dx}\ln|x| = \frac{1}{x}, \quad x \neq 0$$

So $1/x$ is the derivative of $\ln x$ on the domain $x > 0$, and the derivative of $\ln(-x)$ on the domain $x < 0$. ■

Notice from Example 3a that the function $y = \ln 2x$ has the same derivative as the function $y = \ln x$. This is true of $y = \ln bx$ for any constant b, provided that $bx > 0$:

$$\frac{d}{dx}\ln bx = \frac{1}{bx}\cdot\frac{d}{dx}(bx) = \frac{1}{bx}(b) = \frac{1}{x}. \tag{3}$$

EXAMPLE 4 A line with slope m passes through the origin and is tangent to the graph of $y = \ln x$. What is the value of m?

Solution Suppose the point of tangency occurs at the unknown point $x = a > 0$. Then we know that the point $(a, \ln a)$ lies on the graph and that the tangent line at that point has slope $m = 1/a$ (Figure 3.38). Since the tangent line passes through the origin, its slope is

$$m = \frac{\ln a - 0}{a - 0} = \frac{\ln a}{a}.$$

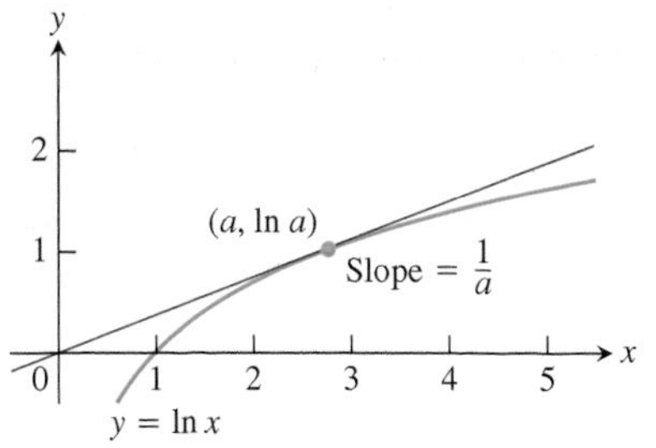

FIGURE 3.38 The tangent line intersects the curve at some point $(a, \ln a)$, where the slope of the curve is $1/a$ (Example 4).

Setting these two formulas for m equal to each other, we have

$$\begin{aligned}\frac{\ln a}{a} &= \frac{1}{a}\\ \ln a &= 1\\ e^{\ln a} &= e^1\\ a &= e\\ m &= \frac{1}{e}.\end{aligned}$$

■

The Derivatives of a^u and $\log_a u$

We start with the equation $a^x = e^{\ln(a^x)} = e^{x\ln a}$, which was seen in Section 1.6:

$$\begin{aligned}\frac{d}{dx}a^x &= \frac{d}{dx}e^{x\ln a} = e^{x\ln a}\cdot\frac{d}{dx}(x\ln a) && \frac{d}{dx}e^u = e^u\frac{du}{dx}\\ &= a^x\ln a.\end{aligned}$$

If $a > 0$, then

$$\frac{d}{dx} a^x = a^x \ln a. \tag{4}$$

This equation shows why e^x is the exponential function preferred in calculus. If $a = e$, then $\ln a = 1$ and the derivative of a^x simplifies to

$$\frac{d}{dx} e^x = e^x \ln e = e^x.$$

With the Chain Rule, we get a more general form for the derivative of a general exponential function.

If $a > 0$ and u is a differentiable function of x, then a^u is a differentiable function of x and

$$\frac{d}{dx} a^u = a^u \ln a \frac{du}{dx}. \tag{5}$$

EXAMPLE 5 Here are some derivatives of general exponential functions.

(a) $\frac{d}{dx} 3^x = 3^x \ln 3$ Eq. (5) with $a = 3, u = x$

(b) $\frac{d}{dx} 3^{-x} = 3^{-x}(\ln 3)\frac{d}{dx}(-x) = -3^{-x} \ln 3$ Eq. (5) with $a = 3, u = -x$

(c) $\frac{d}{dx} 3^{\sin x} = 3^{\sin x}(\ln 3)\frac{d}{dx}(\sin x) = 3^{\sin x}(\ln 3) \cos x$ $\ldots, u = \sin x$ ■

In Section 3.3 we looked at the derivative $f'(0)$ for the exponential functions $f(x) = a^x$ at various values of the base a. The number $f'(0)$ is the limit, $\lim_{h\to 0} (a^h - 1)/h$, and gives the slope of the graph of a^x when it crosses the y-axis at the point (0, 1). We now see from Equation (4) that the value of this slope is

$$\lim_{h\to 0} \frac{a^h - 1}{h} = \ln a. \tag{6}$$

In particular, when $a = e$ we obtain

$$\lim_{h\to 0} \frac{e^h - 1}{h} = \ln e = 1.$$

However, we have not fully justified that these limits actually exist. While all of the arguments given in deriving the derivatives of the exponential and logarithmic functions are correct, they do assume the existence of these limits. In Chapter 7 we will give another development of the theory of logarithmic and exponential functions which fully justifies that both limits do in fact exist and have the values derived above.

To find the derivative of $\log_a u$ for an arbitrary base ($a > 0, a \neq 1$), we start with the change-of-base formula for logarithms (reviewed in Section 1.6) and express $\log_a u$ in terms of natural logarithms,

$$\log_a x = \frac{\ln x}{\ln a}.$$

Taking derivatives, we have

$$\begin{aligned}
\frac{d}{dx}\log_a x &= \frac{d}{dx}\left(\frac{\ln x}{\ln a}\right) \\
&= \frac{1}{\ln a}\cdot\frac{d}{dx}\ln x \qquad \text{ln } a \text{ is a constant.} \\
&= \frac{1}{\ln a}\cdot\frac{1}{x} \\
&= \frac{1}{x\ln a}.
\end{aligned}$$

If u is a differentiable function of x and $u > 0$, the Chain Rule gives the following formula.

> For $a > 0$ and $a \neq 1$,
>
> $$\frac{d}{dx}\log_a u = \frac{1}{u\ln a}\frac{du}{dx}. \qquad (7)$$

Logarithmic Differentiation

The derivatives of positive functions given by formulas that involve products, quotients, and powers can often be found more quickly if we take the natural logarithm of both sides before differentiating. This enables us to use the laws of logarithms to simplify the formulas before differentiating. The process, called **logarithmic differentiation**, is illustrated in the next example.

EXAMPLE 6 Find dy/dx if

$$y = \frac{(x^2+1)(x+3)^{1/2}}{x-1}, \qquad x > 1.$$

Solution We take the natural logarithm of both sides and simplify the result with the algebraic properties of logarithms from Theorem 1 in Section 1.6:

$$\begin{aligned}
\ln y &= \ln\frac{(x^2+1)(x+3)^{1/2}}{x-1} \\
&= \ln\left((x^2+1)(x+3)^{1/2}\right) - \ln(x-1) \qquad \text{Rule 2} \\
&= \ln(x^2+1) + \ln(x+3)^{1/2} - \ln(x-1) \qquad \text{Rule 1} \\
&= \ln(x^2+1) + \frac{1}{2}\ln(x+3) - \ln(x-1). \qquad \text{Rule 4}
\end{aligned}$$

We then take derivatives of both sides with respect to x, using Equation (2) on the left:

$$\frac{1}{y}\frac{dy}{dx} = \frac{1}{x^2+1}\cdot 2x + \frac{1}{2}\cdot\frac{1}{x+3} - \frac{1}{x-1}.$$

Next we solve for dy/dx:

$$\frac{dy}{dx} = y\left(\frac{2x}{x^2+1} + \frac{1}{2x+6} - \frac{1}{x-1}\right).$$

Finally, we substitute for y:

$$\frac{dy}{dx} = \frac{(x^2 + 1)(x + 3)^{1/2}}{x - 1}\left(\frac{2x}{x^2 + 1} + \frac{1}{2x + 6} - \frac{1}{x - 1}\right).$$ ■

Irrational Exponents and the Power Rule (General Version)

The definition of the general exponential function enables us to raise any positive number to any real power n, rational or irrational. That is, we can define the power function $y = x^n$ for any exponent n.

DEFINITION For any $x > 0$ and for any real number n,

$$x^n = e^{n \ln x}.$$

Because the logarithm and exponential functions are inverses of each other, the definition gives

$$\ln x^n = n \ln x, \quad \text{for all real numbers } n.$$

That is, the rule for taking the natural logarithm of any power holds for *all* real exponents n, not just for rational exponents.

The definition of the power function also enables us to establish the derivative Power Rule for any real power n, as stated in Section 3.3.

General Power Rule for Derivatives

For $x > 0$ and any real number n,

$$\frac{d}{dx}x^n = nx^{n-1}.$$

If $x \leq 0$, then the formula holds whenever the derivative, x^n, and x^{n-1} all exist.

Proof Differentiating x^n with respect to x gives

$$\begin{aligned}
\frac{d}{dx}x^n &= \frac{d}{dx}e^{n \ln x} && \text{Definition of } x^n,\ x > 0\\
&= e^{n \ln x} \cdot \frac{d}{dx}(n \ln x) && \text{Chain Rule for } e^u\\
&= x^n \cdot \frac{n}{x} && \text{Definition and derivative of } \ln x\\
&= nx^{n-1}. && x^n \cdot x^{-1} = x^{n-1}
\end{aligned}$$

In short, whenever $x > 0$,

$$\frac{d}{dx}x^n = nx^{n-1}.$$

For $x < 0$, if $y = x^n$, y', and x^{n-1} all exist, then

$$\ln|y| = \ln|x|^n = n \ln|x|.$$

Using implicit differentiation (which *assumes* the existence of the derivative y') and Example 3(c), we have

$$\frac{y'}{y} = \frac{n}{x}.$$

Solving for the derivative,

$$y' = n\frac{y}{x} = n\frac{x^n}{x} = nx^{n-1}. \qquad y = x^n$$

It can be shown directly from the definition of the derivative that the derivative equals 0 when $x = 0$ and $n \geq 1$. This completes the proof of the general version of the Power Rule for all values of x. ■

EXAMPLE 7 Differentiate $f(x) = x^x$, $x > 0$.

Solution We note that $f(x) = x^x = e^{x \ln x}$, so differentiation gives

$$\begin{aligned} f'(x) &= \frac{d}{dx}(e^{x \ln x}) \\ &= e^{x \ln x}\frac{d}{dx}(x \ln x) && \tfrac{d}{dx}e^u,\ u = x \ln x \\ &= e^{x \ln x}\left(\ln x + x \cdot \frac{1}{x}\right) \\ &= x^x(\ln x + 1). && x > 0 \end{aligned}$$

■

The Number e Expressed as a Limit

In Section 1.5 we defined the number e as the base value for which the exponential function $y = a^x$ has slope 1 when it crosses the y-axis at (0, 1). Thus e is the constant that satisfies the equation

$$\lim_{h \to 0} \frac{e^h - 1}{h} = \ln e = 1. \qquad \text{Slope equals } \ln e \text{ from Eq. (6).}$$

We now prove that e can be calculated as a certain limit.

THEOREM 4—The Number e as a Limit The number e can be calculated as the limit

$$e = \lim_{x \to 0}(1 + x)^{1/x}.$$

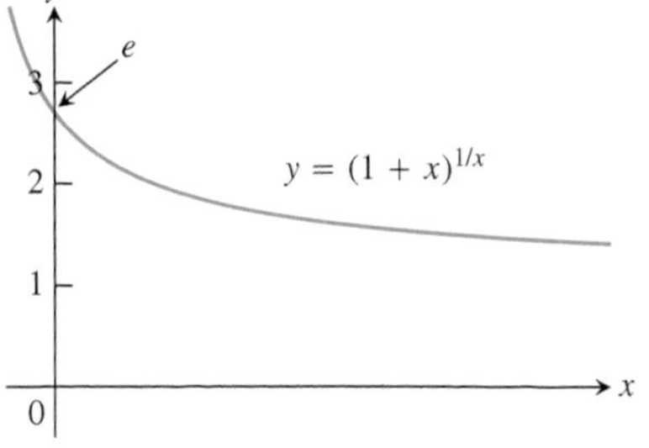

FIGURE 3.39 The number e is the limit of the function graphed here as $x \to 0$.

Proof If $f(x) = \ln x$, then $f'(x) = 1/x$, so $f'(1) = 1$. But, by the definition of derivative,

$$\begin{aligned} f'(1) &= \lim_{h \to 0}\frac{f(1+h) - f(1)}{h} = \lim_{x \to 0}\frac{f(1+x) - f(1)}{x} \\ &= \lim_{x \to 0}\frac{\ln(1+x) - \ln 1}{x} = \lim_{x \to 0}\frac{1}{x}\ln(1+x) && \ln 1 = 0 \\ &= \lim_{x \to 0}\ln(1+x)^{1/x} = \ln\left[\lim_{x \to 0}(1+x)^{1/x}\right]. && \text{ln is continuous, Theorem 10 in Chapter 2.} \end{aligned}$$

Because $f'(1) = 1$, we have

$$\ln\left[\lim_{x\to 0}(1+x)^{1/x}\right] = 1.$$

Therefore, exponentiating both sides we get

$$\lim_{x\to 0}(1+x)^{1/x} = e.$$

See Figure 3.39 on the previous page. ■

Approximating the limit in Theorem 4 by taking x very small gives approximations to e. Its value is $e \approx 2.718281828459045$ to 15 decimal places.

Exercises 3.8

Derivatives of Inverse Functions

In Exercises 1–4:

a. Find $f^{-1}(x)$.

b. Graph f and f^{-1} together.

c. Evaluate df/dx at $x = a$ and df^{-1}/dx at $x = f(a)$ to show that at these points $df^{-1}/dx = 1/(df/dx)$.

1. $f(x) = 2x + 3, \quad a = -1$

2. $f(x) = (1/5)x + 7, \quad a = -1$

3. $f(x) = 5 - 4x, \quad a = 1/2$

4. $f(x) = 2x^2, \quad x \geq 0, \quad a = 5$

5. a. Show that $f(x) = x^3$ and $g(x) = \sqrt[3]{x}$ are inverses of one another.

b. Graph f and g over an x-interval large enough to show the graphs intersecting at $(1, 1)$ and $(-1, -1)$. Be sure the picture shows the required symmetry about the line $y = x$.

c. Find the slopes of the tangents to the graphs of f and g at $(1, 1)$ and $(-1, -1)$ (four tangents in all).

d. What lines are tangent to the curves at the origin?

6. a. Show that $h(x) = x^3/4$ and $k(x) = (4x)^{1/3}$ are inverses of one another.

b. Graph h and k over an x-interval large enough to show the graphs intersecting at $(2, 2)$ and $(-2, -2)$. Be sure the picture shows the required symmetry about the line $y = x$.

c. Find the slopes of the tangents to the graphs at h and k at $(2, 2)$ and $(-2, -2)$.

d. What lines are tangent to the curves at the origin?

7. Let $f(x) = x^3 - 3x^2 - 1, x \geq 2$. Find the value of df^{-1}/dx at the point $x = -1 = f(3)$.

8. Let $f(x) = x^2 - 4x - 5, x > 2$. Find the value of df^{-1}/dx at the point $x = 0 = f(5)$.

9. Suppose that the differentiable function $y = f(x)$ has an inverse and that the graph of f passes through the point $(2, 4)$ and has a slope of $1/3$ there. Find the value of df^{-1}/dx at $x = 4$.

10. Suppose that the differentiable function $y = g(x)$ has an inverse and that the graph of g passes through the origin with slope 2. Find the slope of the graph of g^{-1} at the origin.

Derivatives of Logarithms

In Exercises 11–40, find the derivative of y with respect to x, t, or θ, as appropriate.

11. $y = \ln 3x$

12. $y = \ln kx$, k constant

13. $y = \ln(t^2)$

14. $y = \ln(t^{3/2})$

15. $y = \ln\frac{3}{x}$

16. $y = \ln\frac{10}{x}$

17. $y = \ln(\theta + 1)$

18. $y = \ln(2\theta + 2)$

19. $y = \ln x^3$

20. $y = (\ln x)^3$

21. $y = t(\ln t)^2$

22. $y = t\sqrt{\ln t}$

23. $y = \frac{x^4}{4}\ln x - \frac{x^4}{16}$

24. $y = (x^2 \ln x)^4$

25. $y = \frac{\ln t}{t}$

26. $y = \frac{1 + \ln t}{t}$

27. $y = \frac{\ln x}{1 + \ln x}$

28. $y = \frac{x \ln x}{1 + \ln x}$

29. $y = \ln(\ln x)$

30. $y = \ln(\ln(\ln x))$

31. $y = \theta(\sin(\ln\theta) + \cos(\ln\theta))$

32. $y = \ln(\sec\theta + \tan\theta)$

33. $y = \ln\frac{1}{x\sqrt{x+1}}$

34. $y = \frac{1}{2}\ln\frac{1+x}{1-x}$

35. $y = \frac{1 + \ln t}{1 - \ln t}$

36. $y = \sqrt{\ln\sqrt{t}}$

37. $y = \ln(\sec(\ln\theta))$

38. $y = \ln\left(\frac{\sqrt{\sin\theta\cos\theta}}{1 + 2\ln\theta}\right)$

39. $y = \ln\left(\frac{(x^2+1)^5}{\sqrt{1-x}}\right)$

40. $y = \ln\sqrt{\frac{(x+1)^5}{(x+2)^{20}}}$

Logarithmic Differentiation

In Exercises 41–54, use logarithmic differentiation to find the derivative of y with respect to the given independent variable.

41. $y = \sqrt{x(x+1)}$

42. $y = \sqrt{(x^2+1)(x-1)^2}$

43. $y = \sqrt{\frac{t}{t+1}}$

44. $y = \sqrt{\frac{1}{t(t+1)}}$

45. $y = (\sin\theta)\sqrt{\theta + 3}$

46. $y = (\tan\theta)\sqrt{2\theta + 1}$

47. $y = t(t+1)(t+2)$

48. $y = \frac{1}{t(t+1)(t+2)}$

49. $y = \frac{\theta + 5}{\theta\cos\theta}$

50. $y = \frac{\theta\sin\theta}{\sqrt{\sec\theta}}$

51. $y = \frac{x\sqrt{x^2+1}}{(x+1)^{2/3}}$

52. $y = \sqrt{\frac{(x+1)^{10}}{(2x+1)^5}}$

53. $y = \sqrt[3]{\dfrac{x(x-2)}{x^2+1}}$

54. $y = \sqrt[3]{\dfrac{x(x+1)(x-2)}{(x^2+1)(2x+3)}}$

Finding Derivatives

In Exercises 55–62, find the derivative of y with respect to x, t, or θ, as appropriate.

55. $y = \ln(\cos^2\theta)$

56. $y = \ln(3\theta e^{-\theta})$

57. $y = \ln(3te^{-t})$

58. $y = \ln(2e^{-t}\sin t)$

59. $y = \ln\left(\dfrac{e^\theta}{1+e^\theta}\right)$

60. $y = \ln\left(\dfrac{\sqrt{\theta}}{1+\sqrt{\theta}}\right)$

61. $y = e^{(\cos t + \ln t)}$

62. $y = e^{\sin t}(\ln t^2 + 1)$

In Exercises 63–66, find dy/dx.

63. $\ln y = e^y \sin x$

64. $\ln xy = e^{x+y}$

65. $x^y = y^x$

66. $\tan y = e^x + \ln x$

In Exercises 67–88, find the derivative of y with respect to the given independent variable.

67. $y = 2^x$

68. $y = 3^{-x}$

69. $y = 5^{\sqrt{s}}$

70. $y = 2^{(s^2)}$

71. $y = x^\pi$

72. $y = t^{1-e}$

73. $y = \log_2 5\theta$

74. $y = \log_3(1 + \theta\ln 3)$

75. $y = \log_4 x + \log_4 x^2$

76. $y = \log_{25} e^x - \log_5\sqrt{x}$

77. $y = \log_2 r \cdot \log_4 r$

78. $y = \log_3 r \cdot \log_9 r$

79. $y = \log_3\left(\left(\dfrac{x+1}{x-1}\right)^{\ln 3}\right)$

80. $y = \log_5\sqrt{\left(\dfrac{7x}{3x+2}\right)^{\ln 5}}$

81. $y = \theta\sin(\log_7\theta)$

82. $y = \log_7\left(\dfrac{\sin\theta\cos\theta}{e^\theta 2^\theta}\right)$

83. $y = \log_5 e^x$

84. $y = \log_2\left(\dfrac{x^2e^2}{2\sqrt{x+1}}\right)$

85. $y = 3^{\log_2 t}$

86. $y = 3\log_8(\log_2 t)$

87. $y = \log_2(8t^{\ln 2})$

88. $y = t\log_3\left(e^{(\sin t)(\ln 3)}\right)$

Logarithmic Differentiation with Exponentials

In Exercises 89–96, use logarithmic differentiation to find the derivative of y with respect to the given independent variable.

89. $y = (x+1)^x$

90. $y = x^{(x+1)}$

91. $y = (\sqrt{t})^t$

92. $y = t^{\sqrt{t}}$

93. $y = (\sin x)^x$

94. $y = x^{\sin x}$

95. $y = x^{\ln x}$

96. $y = (\ln x)^{\ln x}$

Theory and Applications

97. If we write $g(x)$ for $f^{-1}(x)$, Equation (1) can be written as

$$g'(f(a)) = \frac{1}{f'(a)}, \quad \text{or} \quad g'(f(a))\cdot f'(a) = 1.$$

If we then write x for a, we get

$$g'(f(x))\cdot f'(x) = 1.$$

The latter equation may remind you of the Chain Rule, and indeed there is a connection.

Assume that f and g are differentiable functions that are inverses of one another, so that $(g \circ f)(x) = x$. Differentiate both sides of this equation with respect to x, using the Chain Rule to express $(g \circ f)'(x)$ as a product of derivatives of g and f. What do you find? (This is not a proof of Theorem 3 because we assume here the theorem's conclusion that $g = f^{-1}$ is differentiable.)

98. Show that $\lim_{n\to\infty}\left(1+\dfrac{x}{n}\right)^n = e^x$ for any $x > 0$.

99. If $y = A\sin(\ln x) + B\cos(\ln x)$, where A and B are constants, show that

$$x^2y'' + xy' + y = 0.$$

100. Using mathematical induction, show that

$$\frac{d^n}{dx^n}\ln x = (-1)^{n-1}\frac{(n-1)!}{x^n}.$$

COMPUTER EXPLORATIONS

In Exercises 101–108, you will explore some functions and their inverses together with their derivatives and tangent line approximations at specified points. Perform the following steps using your CAS:

a. Plot the function $y = f(x)$ together with its derivative over the given interval. Explain why you know that f is one-to-one over the interval.

b. Solve the equation $y = f(x)$ for x as a function of y, and name the resulting inverse function g.

c. Find the equation for the tangent line to f at the specified point $(x_0, f(x_0))$.

d. Find the equation for the tangent line to g at the point $(f(x_0), x_0)$ located symmetrically across the 45° line $y = x$ (which is the graph of the identity function). Use Theorem 3 to find the slope of this tangent line.

e. Plot the functions f and g, the identity, the two tangent lines, and the line segment joining the points $(x_0, f(x_0))$ and $(f(x_0), x_0)$. Discuss the symmetries you see across the main diagonal.

101. $y = \sqrt{3x-2}, \quad \dfrac{2}{3} \le x \le 4, \quad x_0 = 3$

102. $y = \dfrac{3x+2}{2x-11}, \quad -2 \le x \le 2, \quad x_0 = 1/2$

103. $y = \dfrac{4x}{x^2+1}, \quad -1 \le x \le 1, \quad x_0 = 1/2$

104. $y = \dfrac{x^3}{x^2+1}, \quad -1 \le x \le 1, \quad x_0 = 1/2$

105. $y = x^3 - 3x^2 - 1, \quad 2 \le x \le 5, \quad x_0 = \dfrac{27}{10}$

106. $y = 2 - x - x^3, \quad -2 \le x \le 2, \quad x_0 = \dfrac{3}{2}$

107. $y = e^x, \quad -3 \le x \le 5, \quad x_0 = 1$

108. $y = \sin x, \quad -\dfrac{\pi}{2} \le x \le \dfrac{\pi}{2}, \quad x_0 = 1$

In Exercises 109 and 110, repeat the steps above to solve for the functions $y = f(x)$ and $x = f^{-1}(y)$ defined implicitly by the given equations over the interval.

109. $y^{1/3} - 1 = (x+2)^3, \quad -5 \le x \le 5, \quad x_0 = -3/2$

110. $\cos y = x^{1/5}, \quad 0 \le x \le 1, \quad x_0 = 1/2$

3.9 Inverse Trigonometric Functions

We introduced the six basic inverse trigonometric functions in Section 1.6, but focused there on the arcsine and arccosine functions. Here we complete the study of how all six inverse trigonometric functions are defined, graphed, and evaluated, and how their derivatives are computed.

Inverses of tan *x*, cot *x*, sec *x*, and csc *x*

The graphs of these four basic inverse trigonometric functions are shown again in Figure 3.40. We obtain these graphs by reflecting the graphs of the restricted trigonometric functions (as discussed in Section 1.6) through the line $y = x$. Let's take a closer look at the arctangent, arccotangent, arcsecant, and arccosecant functions.

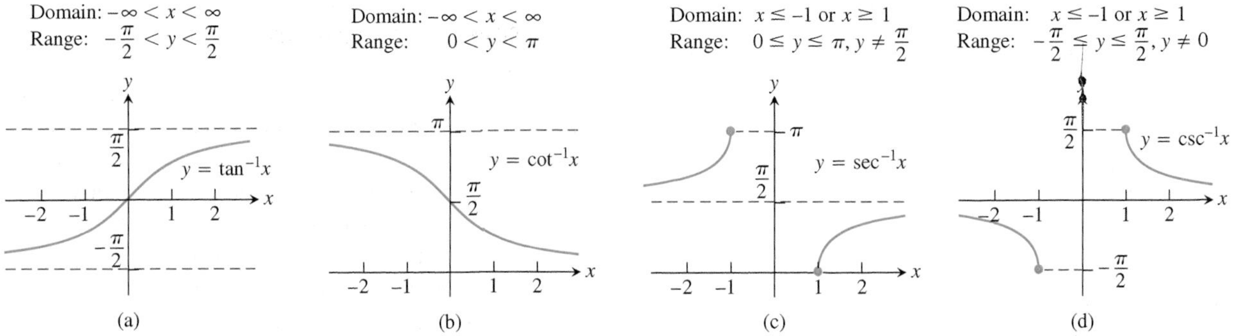

FIGURE 3.40 Graphs of the arctangent, arccotangent, arcsecant, and arccosecant functions.

The arctangent of x is a radian angle whose tangent is x. The arccotangent of x is an angle whose cotangent is x, and so forth. The angles belong to the restricted domains of the tangent, cotangent, secant, and cosecant functions.

DEFINITION

$y = \mathbf{tan^{-1}}\, \boldsymbol{x}$ is the number in $(-\pi/2, \pi/2)$ for which $\tan y = x$.

$y = \mathbf{cot^{-1}}\, \boldsymbol{x}$ is the number in $(0, \pi)$ for which $\cot y = x$.

$y = \mathbf{sec^{-1}}\, \boldsymbol{x}$ is the number in $[0, \pi/2) \cup (\pi/2, \pi]$ for which $\sec y = x$.

$y = \mathbf{csc^{-1}}\, \boldsymbol{x}$ is the number in $[-\pi/2, 0) \cup (0, \pi/2]$ for which $\csc y = x$.

We use open or half-open intervals when describing the ranges to avoid values where the tangent, cotangent, secant, and cosecant functions are undefined. (See Figure 3.40.)

The graph of $y = \tan^{-1} x$ is symmetric about the origin because it is a branch of the graph $x = \tan y$ that is symmetric about the origin (Figure 3.40a). Algebraically this means that

$$\tan^{-1}(-x) = -\tan^{-1} x;$$

the arctangent is an odd function. The graph of $y = \cot^{-1} x$ has no such symmetry (Figure 3.40b). Notice from Figure 3.40a that the graph of the arctangent function has two horizontal asymptotes; one at $y = \pi/2$ and the other at $y = -\pi/2$.

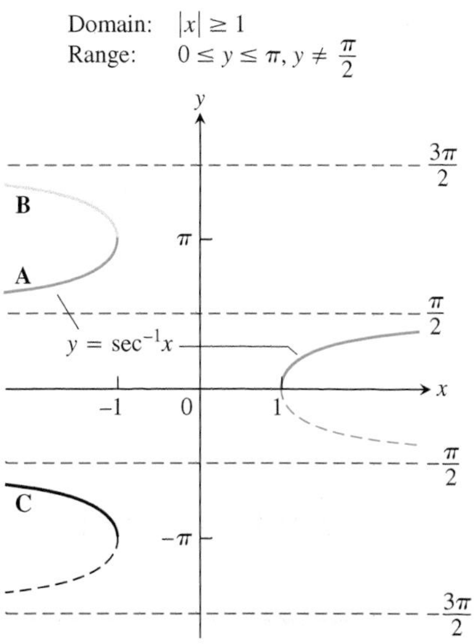

FIGURE 3.41 There are several logical choices for the left-hand branch of $y = \sec^{-1} x$. With choice **A**, $\sec^{-1} x = \cos^{-1}(1/x)$, a useful identity employed by many calculators.

The inverses of the restricted forms of sec x and csc x are chosen to be the functions graphed in Figures 3.40c and 3.40d.

Caution There is no general agreement about how to define $\sec^{-1} x$ for negative values of x. We chose angles in the second quadrant between $\pi/2$ and π. This choice makes $\sec^{-1} x = \cos^{-1}(1/x)$. It also makes $\sec^{-1} x$ an increasing function on each interval of its domain. Some tables choose $\sec^{-1} x$ to lie in $[-\pi, -\pi/2)$ for $x < 0$ and some texts choose it to lie in $[\pi, 3\pi/2)$ (Figure 3.41). These choices simplify the formula for the derivative (our formula needs absolute value signs) but fail to satisfy the computational equation $\sec^{-1} x = \cos^{-1}(1/x)$. From this, we can derive the identity

$$\sec^{-1} x = \cos^{-1}\left(\frac{1}{x}\right) = \frac{\pi}{2} - \sin^{-1}\left(\frac{1}{x}\right) \tag{1}$$

by applying Equation (5) in Section 1.6.

EXAMPLE 1 The accompanying figures show two values of $\tan^{-1} x$.

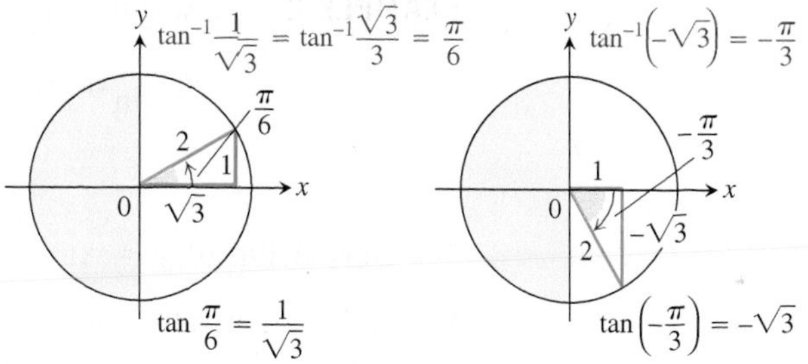

x	$\tan^{-1} x$
$\sqrt{3}$	$\pi/3$
1	$\pi/4$
$\sqrt{3}/3$	$\pi/6$
$-\sqrt{3}/3$	$-\pi/6$
-1	$-\pi/4$
$-\sqrt{3}$	$-\pi/3$

The angles come from the first and fourth quadrants because the range of $\tan^{-1} x$ is $(-\pi/2, \pi/2)$. ■

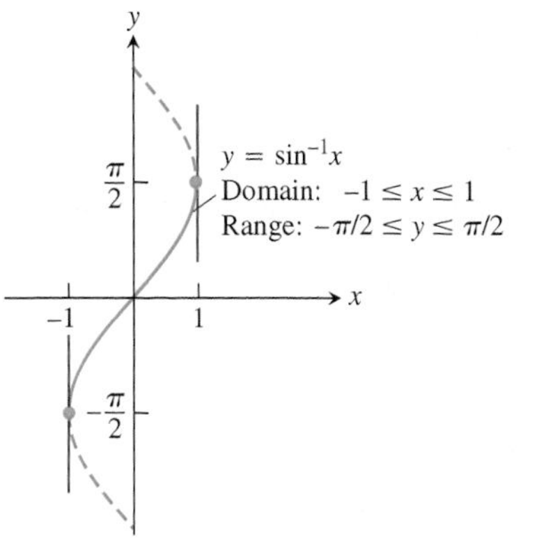

FIGURE 3.42 The graph of $y = \sin^{-1} x$ has vertical tangents at $x = -1$ and $x = 1$.

The Derivative of $y = \sin^{-1} u$

We know that the function $x = \sin y$ is differentiable in the interval $-\pi/2 < y < \pi/2$ and that its derivative, the cosine, is positive there. Theorem 3 in Section 3.8 therefore assures us that the inverse function $y = \sin^{-1} x$ is differentiable throughout the interval $-1 < x < 1$. We cannot expect it to be differentiable at $x = 1$ or $x = -1$ because the tangents to the graph are vertical at these points (see Figure 3.42).

We find the derivative of $y = \sin^{-1} x$ by applying Theorem 3 with $f(x) = \sin x$ and $f^{-1}(x) = \sin^{-1} x$:

$$\begin{aligned}
(f^{-1})'(x) &= \frac{1}{f'(f^{-1}(x))} && \text{Theorem 3} \\
&= \frac{1}{\cos(\sin^{-1} x)} && f'(u) = \cos u \\
&= \frac{1}{\sqrt{1 - \sin^2(\sin^{-1} x)}} && \cos u = \sqrt{1 - \sin^2 u} \\
&= \frac{1}{\sqrt{1 - x^2}}. && \sin(\sin^{-1} x) = x
\end{aligned}$$

If u is a differentiable function of x with $|u| < 1$, we apply the Chain Rule to get

$$\frac{d}{dx}(\sin^{-1} u) = \frac{1}{\sqrt{1 - u^2}} \frac{du}{dx}, \qquad |u| < 1.$$

EXAMPLE 2 Using the Chain Rule, we calculate the derivative

$$\frac{d}{dx}(\sin^{-1} x^2) = \frac{1}{\sqrt{1 - (x^2)^2}} \cdot \frac{d}{dx}(x^2) = \frac{2x}{\sqrt{1 - x^4}}.$$ ■

The Derivative of $y = \tan^{-1} u$

We find the derivative of $y = \tan^{-1} x$ by applying Theorem 3 with $f(x) = \tan x$ and $f^{-1}(x) = \tan^{-1} x$. Theorem 3 can be applied because the derivative of $\tan x$ is positive for $-\pi/2 < x < \pi/2$:

$$\begin{aligned}
(f^{-1})'(x) &= \frac{1}{f'(f^{-1}(x))} && \text{Theorem 3} \\
&= \frac{1}{\sec^2(\tan^{-1} x)} && f'(u) = \sec^2 u \\
&= \frac{1}{1 + \tan^2(\tan^{-1} x)} && \sec^2 u = 1 + \tan^2 u \\
&= \frac{1}{1 + x^2}. && \tan(\tan^{-1} x) = x
\end{aligned}$$

The derivative is defined for all real numbers. If u is a differentiable function of x, we get the Chain Rule form:

$$\frac{d}{dx}(\tan^{-1} u) = \frac{1}{1 + u^2} \frac{du}{dx}.$$

The Derivative of $y = \sec^{-1} u$

Since the derivative of $\sec x$ is positive for $0 < x < \pi/2$ and $\pi/2 < x < \pi$, Theorem 3 says that the inverse function $y = \sec^{-1} x$ is differentiable. Instead of applying the formula in Theorem 3 directly, we find the derivative of $y = \sec^{-1} x$, $|x| > 1$, using implicit differentiation and the Chain Rule as follows:

$$y = \sec^{-1} x$$

$$\sec y = x \qquad \text{Inverse function relationship}$$

$$\frac{d}{dx}(\sec y) = \frac{d}{dx}x \qquad \text{Differentiate both sides.}$$

$$\sec y \tan y \frac{dy}{dx} = 1 \qquad \text{Chain Rule}$$

$$\frac{dy}{dx} = \frac{1}{\sec y \tan y}. \qquad \text{Since } |x| > 1,\ y \text{ lies in } (0, \pi/2) \cup (\pi/2, \pi) \text{ and } \sec y \tan y \neq 0.$$

To express the result in terms of x, we use the relationships

$$\sec y = x \quad \text{and} \quad \tan y = \pm\sqrt{\sec^2 y - 1} = \pm\sqrt{x^2 - 1}$$

to get

$$\frac{dy}{dx} = \pm\frac{1}{x\sqrt{x^2 - 1}}.$$

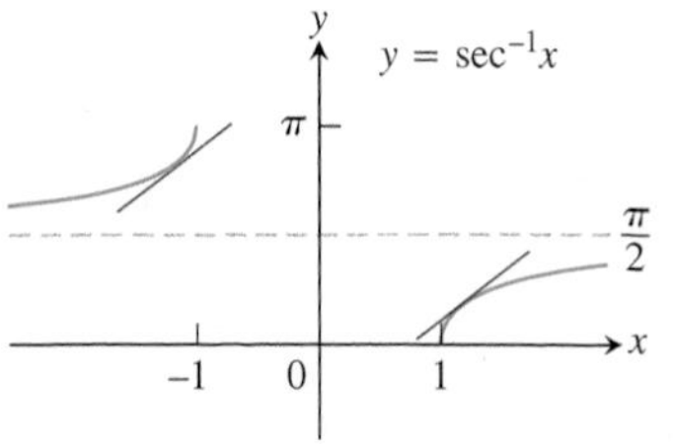

FIGURE 3.43 The slope of the curve $y = \sec^{-1} x$ is positive for both $x < -1$ and $x > 1$.

Can we do anything about the $\pm$ sign? A glance at Figure 3.43 shows that the slope of the graph $y = \sec^{-1} x$ is always positive. Thus,

$$\frac{d}{dx}\sec^{-1} x = \begin{cases} +\dfrac{1}{x\sqrt{x^2 - 1}} & \text{if } x > 1 \\ -\dfrac{1}{x\sqrt{x^2 - 1}} & \text{if } x < -1. \end{cases}$$

With the absolute value symbol, we can write a single expression that eliminates the "$\pm$" ambiguity:

$$\frac{d}{dx}\sec^{-1} x = \frac{1}{|x|\sqrt{x^2 - 1}}.$$

If u is a differentiable function of x with $|u| > 1$, we have the formula

$$\frac{d}{dx}(\sec^{-1} u) = \frac{1}{|u|\sqrt{u^2 - 1}}\frac{du}{dx}, \qquad |u| > 1.$$

EXAMPLE 3 Using the Chain Rule and derivative of the arcsecant function, we find

$$\begin{aligned} \frac{d}{dx}\sec^{-1}(5x^4) &= \frac{1}{|5x^4|\sqrt{(5x^4)^2 - 1}}\frac{d}{dx}(5x^4) \\ &= \frac{1}{5x^4\sqrt{25x^8 - 1}}(20x^3) \qquad 5x^4 > 1 > 0 \\ &= \frac{4}{x\sqrt{25x^8 - 1}}. \end{aligned}$$

■

Derivatives of the Other Three Inverse Trigonometric Functions

We could use the same techniques to find the derivatives of the other three inverse trigonometric functions—arccosine, arccotangent, and arccosecant—but there is an easier way, thanks to the following identities.

Inverse Function–Inverse Cofunction Identities

$$\cos^{-1} x = \pi/2 - \sin^{-1} x$$
$$\cot^{-1} x = \pi/2 - \tan^{-1} x$$
$$\csc^{-1} x = \pi/2 - \sec^{-1} x$$

We saw the first of these identities in Equation (5) of Section 1.6. The others are derived in a similar way. It follows easily that the derivatives of the inverse cofunctions are the negatives of the derivatives of the corresponding inverse functions. For example, the derivative of $\cos^{-1} x$ is calculated as follows:

$$\begin{aligned} \frac{d}{dx}(\cos^{-1} x) &= \frac{d}{dx}\left(\frac{\pi}{2} - \sin^{-1} x\right) && \text{Identity} \\ &= -\frac{d}{dx}(\sin^{-1} x) \\ &= -\frac{1}{\sqrt{1 - x^2}}. && \text{Derivative of arcsine} \end{aligned}$$

The derivatives of the inverse trigonometric functions are summarized in Table 3.1.

TABLE 3.1 Derivatives of the inverse trigonometric functions

1. $\dfrac{d(\sin^{-1} u)}{dx} = \dfrac{1}{\sqrt{1 - u^2}}\dfrac{du}{dx}, \quad |u| < 1$

2. $\dfrac{d(\cos^{-1} u)}{dx} = -\dfrac{1}{\sqrt{1 - u^2}}\dfrac{du}{dx}, \quad |u| < 1$

3. $\dfrac{d(\tan^{-1} u)}{dx} = \dfrac{1}{1 + u^2}\dfrac{du}{dx}$

4. $\dfrac{d(\cot^{-1} u)}{dx} = -\dfrac{1}{1 + u^2}\dfrac{du}{dx}$

5. $\dfrac{d(\sec^{-1} u)}{dx} = \dfrac{1}{|u|\sqrt{u^2 - 1}}\dfrac{du}{dx}, \quad |u| > 1$

6. $\dfrac{d(\csc^{-1} u)}{dx} = -\dfrac{1}{|u|\sqrt{u^2 - 1}}\dfrac{du}{dx}, \quad |u| > 1$

Exercises 3.9

Common Values

Use reference triangles in an appropriate quadrant, as in Example 1, to find the angles in Exercises 1–8.

1. **a.** $\tan^{-1} 1$ **b.** $\tan^{-1}(-\sqrt{3})$ **c.** $\tan^{-1}\left(\frac{1}{\sqrt{3}}\right)$

2. **a.** $\tan^{-1}(-1)$ **b.** $\tan^{-1}\sqrt{3}$ **c.** $\tan^{-1}\left(\frac{-1}{\sqrt{3}}\right)$

3. **a.** $\sin^{-1}\left(\frac{-1}{2}\right)$ **b.** $\sin^{-1}\left(\frac{1}{\sqrt{2}}\right)$ **c.** $\sin^{-1}\left(\frac{-\sqrt{3}}{2}\right)$

4. **a.** $\sin^{-1}\left(\frac{1}{2}\right)$ **b.** $\sin^{-1}\left(\frac{-1}{\sqrt{2}}\right)$ **c.** $\sin^{-1}\left(\frac{\sqrt{3}}{2}\right)$

5. **a.** $\cos^{-1}\left(\frac{1}{2}\right)$ **b.** $\cos^{-1}\left(\frac{-1}{\sqrt{2}}\right)$ **c.** $\cos^{-1}\left(\frac{\sqrt{3}}{2}\right)$

6. **a.** $\csc^{-1}\sqrt{2}$ **b.** $\csc^{-1}\left(\frac{-2}{\sqrt{3}}\right)$ **c.** $\csc^{-1} 2$

7. **a.** $\sec^{-1}(-\sqrt{2})$ **b.** $\sec^{-1}\left(\frac{2}{\sqrt{3}}\right)$ **c.** $\sec^{-1}(-2)$

8. **a.** $\cot^{-1}(-1)$ **b.** $\cot^{-1}(\sqrt{3})$ **c.** $\cot^{-1}\left(\frac{-1}{\sqrt{3}}\right)$

Evaluations

Find the values in Exercises 9–12.

9. $\sin\left(\cos^{-1}\left(\frac{\sqrt{2}}{2}\right)\right)$

10. $\sec\left(\cos^{-1}\frac{1}{2}\right)$

11. $\tan\left(\sin^{-1}\left(-\frac{1}{2}\right)\right)$

12. $\cot\left(\sin^{-1}\left(-\frac{\sqrt{3}}{2}\right)\right)$

Limits

Find the limits in Exercises 13–20. (If in doubt, look at the function's graph.)

13. $\lim_{x\to 1^-} \sin^{-1} x$

14. $\lim_{x\to -1^+} \cos^{-1} x$

15. $\lim_{x\to\infty} \tan^{-1} x$

16. $\lim_{x\to -\infty} \tan^{-1} x$

17. $\lim_{x\to\infty} \sec^{-1} x$

18. $\lim_{x\to -\infty} \sec^{-1} x$

19. $\lim_{x\to\infty} \csc^{-1} x$

20. $\lim_{x\to -\infty} \csc^{-1} x$

Finding Derivatives

In Exercises 21–42, find the derivative of y with respect to the appropriate variable.

21. $y = \cos^{-1}(x^2)$

22. $y = \cos^{-1}(1/x)$

23. $y = \sin^{-1}\sqrt{2}\, t$

24. $y = \sin^{-1}(1 - t)$

25. $y = \sec^{-1}(2s + 1)$

26. $y = \sec^{-1} 5s$

27. $y = \csc^{-1}(x^2 + 1), \quad x > 0$

28. $y = \csc^{-1}\frac{x}{2}$

29. $y = \sec^{-1}\frac{1}{t}, \quad 0 < t < 1$

30. $y = \sin^{-1}\frac{3}{t^2}$

31. $y = \cot^{-1}\sqrt{t}$

32. $y = \cot^{-1}\sqrt{t - 1}$

33. $y = \ln(\tan^{-1} x)$

34. $y = \tan^{-1}(\ln x)$

35. $y = \csc^{-1}(e^t)$

36. $y = \cos^{-1}(e^{-t})$

37. $y = s\sqrt{1 - s^2} + \cos^{-1} s$

38. $y = \sqrt{s^2 - 1} - \sec^{-1} s$

39. $y = \tan^{-1}\sqrt{x^2 - 1} + \csc^{-1} x, \quad x > 1$

40. $y = \cot^{-1}\frac{1}{x} - \tan^{-1} x$

41. $y = x\sin^{-1} x + \sqrt{1 - x^2}$

42. $y = \ln(x^2 + 4) - x\tan^{-1}\left(\frac{x}{2}\right)$

Theory and Examples

43. You are sitting in a classroom next to the wall looking at the blackboard at the front of the room. The blackboard is 12 ft long and starts 3 ft from the wall you are sitting next to. Show that your viewing angle is

$$\alpha = \cot^{-1}\frac{x}{15} - \cot^{-1}\frac{x}{3}$$

if you are x ft from the front wall.

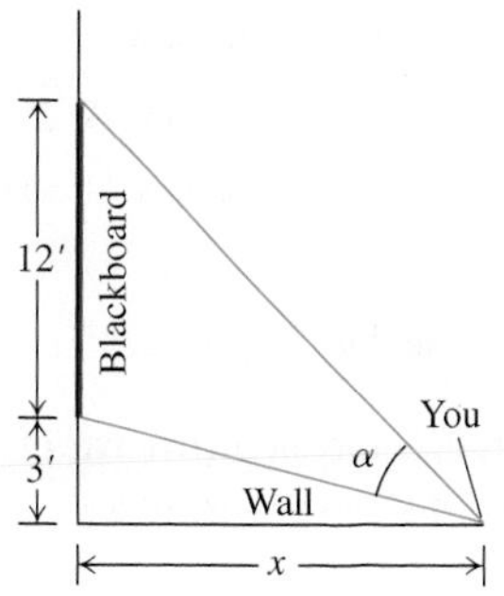

44. Find the angle α.

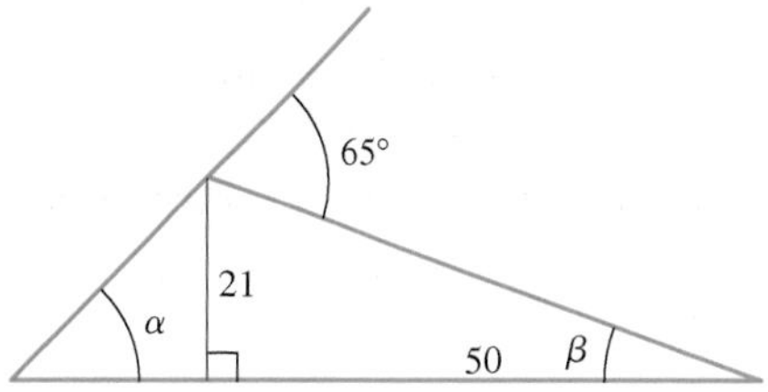

45. Here is an informal proof that $\tan^{-1} 1 + \tan^{-1} 2 + \tan^{-1} 3 = \pi$. Explain what is going on.

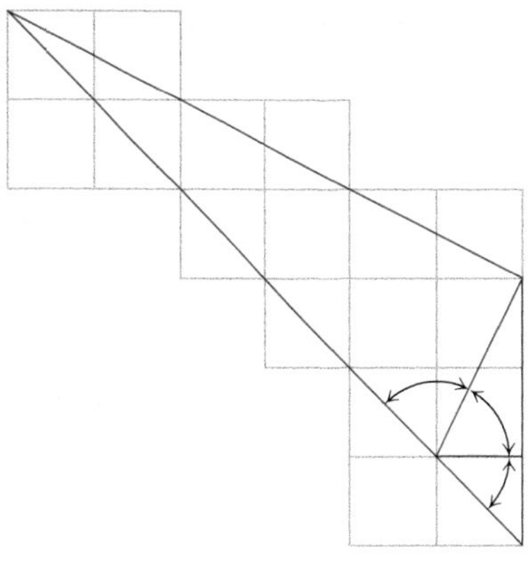

46. Two derivations of the identity $\sec^{-1}(-x) = \pi - \sec^{-1}x$

a. (*Geometric*) Here is a pictorial proof that $\sec^{-1}(-x) = \pi - \sec^{-1}x$. See if you can tell what is going on.

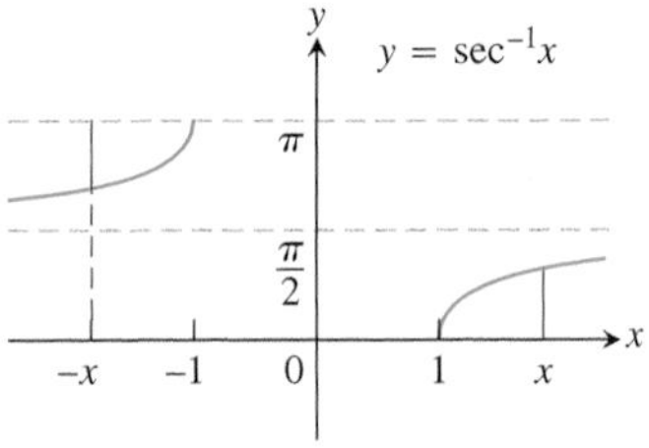

b. (*Algebraic*) Derive the identity $\sec^{-1}(-x) = \pi - \sec^{-1}x$ by combining the following two equations from the text:

$$\cos^{-1}(-x) = \pi - \cos^{-1}x \qquad \text{Eq. (4), Section 1.6}$$

$$\sec^{-1}x = \cos^{-1}(1/x) \qquad \text{Eq. (1)}$$

Which of the expressions in Exercises 47–50 are defined, and which are not? Give reasons for your answers.

47. a. $\tan^{-1} 2$ **b.** $\cos^{-1} 2$

48. a. $\csc^{-1}(1/2)$ **b.** $\csc^{-1} 2$

49. a. $\sec^{-1} 0$ **b.** $\sin^{-1}\sqrt{2}$

50. a. $\cot^{-1}(-1/2)$ **b.** $\cos^{-1}(-5)$

51. Use the identity

$$\csc^{-1}u = \frac{\pi}{2} - \sec^{-1}u$$

to derive the formula for the derivative of $\csc^{-1}u$ in Table 3.1 from the formula for the derivative of $\sec^{-1}u$.

52. Derive the formula

$$\frac{dy}{dx} = \frac{1}{1 + x^2}$$

for the derivative of $y = \tan^{-1}x$ by differentiating both sides of the equivalent equation $\tan y = x$.

53. Use the Derivative Rule in Section 3.8, Theorem 3, to derive

$$\frac{d}{dx}\sec^{-1}x = \frac{1}{|x|\sqrt{x^2 - 1}}, \quad |x| > 1.$$

54. Use the identity

$$\cot^{-1}u = \frac{\pi}{2} - \tan^{-1}u$$

to derive the formula for the derivative of $\cot^{-1}u$ in Table 3.1 from the formula for the derivative of $\tan^{-1}u$.

55. What is special about the functions

$$f(x) = \sin^{-1}\frac{x - 1}{x + 1}, \quad x \geq 0, \quad \text{and} \quad g(x) = 2\tan^{-1}\sqrt{x}?$$

Explain.

56. What is special about the functions

$$f(x) = \sin^{-1}\frac{1}{\sqrt{x^2 + 1}} \quad \text{and} \quad g(x) = \tan^{-1}\frac{1}{x}?$$

Explain.

T **57.** Find the values of

a. $\sec^{-1} 1.5$ **b.** $\csc^{-1}(-1.5)$ **c.** $\cot^{-1} 2$

T **58.** Find the values of

a. $\sec^{-1}(-3)$ **b.** $\csc^{-1} 1.7$ **c.** $\cot^{-1}(-2)$

T In Exercises 59–61, find the domain and range of each composite function. Then graph the composites on separate screens. Do the graphs make sense in each case? Give reasons for your answers. Comment on any differences you see.

59. a. $y = \tan^{-1}(\tan x)$ **b.** $y = \tan(\tan^{-1}x)$

60. a. $y = \sin^{-1}(\sin x)$ **b.** $y = \sin(\sin^{-1}x)$

61. a. $y = \cos^{-1}(\cos x)$ **b.** $y = \cos(\cos^{-1}x)$

T Use your graphing utility for Exercises 62–66.

62. Graph $y = \sec(\sec^{-1}x) = \sec(\cos^{-1}(1/x))$. Explain what you see.

63. Newton's serpentine Graph Newton's serpentine, $y = 4x/(x^2 + 1)$. Then graph $y = 2\sin(2\tan^{-1}x)$ in the same graphing window. What do you see? Explain.

64. Graph the rational function $y = (2 - x^2)/x^2$. Then graph $y = \cos(2\sec^{-1}x)$ in the same graphing window. What do you see? Explain.

65. Graph $f(x) = \sin^{-1}x$ together with its first two derivatives. Comment on the behavior of f and the shape of its graph in relation to the signs and values of f' and f''.

66. Graph $f(x) = \tan^{-1}x$ together with its first two derivatives. Comment on the behavior of f and the shape of its graph in relation to the signs and values of f' and f''.

3.10 Related Rates

In this section we look at problems that ask for the rate at which some variable changes when it is known how the rate of some other related variable (or perhaps several variables) changes. The problem of finding a rate of change from other known rates of change is called a *related rates problem*.

Related Rates Equations

Suppose we are pumping air into a spherical balloon. Both the volume and radius of the balloon are increasing over time. If V is the volume and r is the radius of the balloon at an instant of time, then

$$V = \frac{4}{3}\pi r^3.$$

Using the Chain Rule, we differentiate both sides with respect to t to find an equation relating the rates of change of V and r,

$$\frac{dV}{dt} = \frac{dV}{dr}\frac{dr}{dt} = 4\pi r^2 \frac{dr}{dt}.$$

So if we know the radius r of the balloon and the rate dV/dt at which the volume is increasing at a given instant of time, then we can solve this last equation for dr/dt to find how fast the radius is increasing at that instant. Note that it is easier to directly measure the rate of increase of the volume (the rate at which air is being pumped into the balloon) than it is to measure the increase in the radius. The related rates equation allows us to calculate dr/dt from dV/dt.

Very often the key to relating the variables in a related rates problem is drawing a picture that shows the geometric relations between them, as illustrated in the following example.

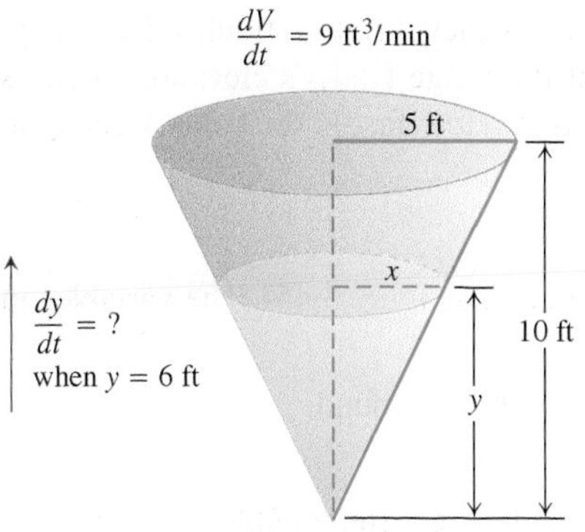

FIGURE 3.44 The geometry of the conical tank and the rate at which water fills the tank determine how fast the water level rises (Example 1).

EXAMPLE 1 Water runs into a conical tank at the rate of 9 ft^3/min. The tank stands point down and has a height of 10 ft and a base radius of 5 ft. How fast is the water level rising when the water is 6 ft deep?

Solution Figure 3.44 shows a partially filled conical tank. The variables in the problem are

V = volume (ft^3) of the water in the tank at time t (min)

x = radius (ft) of the surface of the water at time t

y = depth (ft) of the water in the tank at time t.

We assume that V, x, and y are differentiable functions of t. The constants are the dimensions of the tank. We are asked for dy/dt when

$$y = 6 \text{ ft} \quad \text{and} \quad \frac{dV}{dt} = 9 \text{ ft}^3/\text{min}.$$

The water forms a cone with volume

$$V = \frac{1}{3}\pi x^2 y.$$

This equation involves x as well as V and y. Because no information is given about x and dx/dt at the time in question, we need to eliminate x. The similar triangles in Figure 3.44 give us a way to express x in terms of y:

$$\frac{x}{y} = \frac{5}{10} \quad \text{or} \quad x = \frac{y}{2}.$$

Therefore, find

$$V = \frac{1}{3}\pi\left(\frac{y}{2}\right)^2 y = \frac{\pi}{12}y^3$$

to give the derivative

$$\frac{dV}{dt} = \frac{\pi}{12}\cdot 3y^2\frac{dy}{dt} = \frac{\pi}{4}y^2\frac{dy}{dt}.$$

Finally, use $y = 6$ and $dV/dt = 9$ to solve for dy/dt.

$$9 = \frac{\pi}{4}(6)^2 \frac{dy}{dt}$$

$$\frac{dy}{dt} = \frac{1}{\pi} \approx 0.32$$

At the moment in question, the water level is rising at about 0.32 ft/min. ■

Related Rates Problem Strategy

1. *Draw a picture and name the variables and constants.* Use t for time. Assume that all variables are differentiable functions of t.
2. *Write down the numerical information* (in terms of the symbols you have chosen).
3. *Write down what you are asked to find* (usually a rate, expressed as a derivative).
4. *Write an equation that relates the variables.* You may have to combine two or more equations to get a single equation that relates the variable whose rate you want to the variables whose rates you know.
5. *Differentiate with respect to t.* Then express the rate you want in terms of the rates and variables whose values you know.
6. *Evaluate.* Use known values to find the unknown rate.

EXAMPLE 2 A hot air balloon rising straight up from a level field is tracked by a range finder 150 m from the liftoff point. At the moment the range finder's elevation angle is $\pi/4$, the angle is increasing at the rate of 0.14 rad/min. How fast is the balloon rising at that moment?

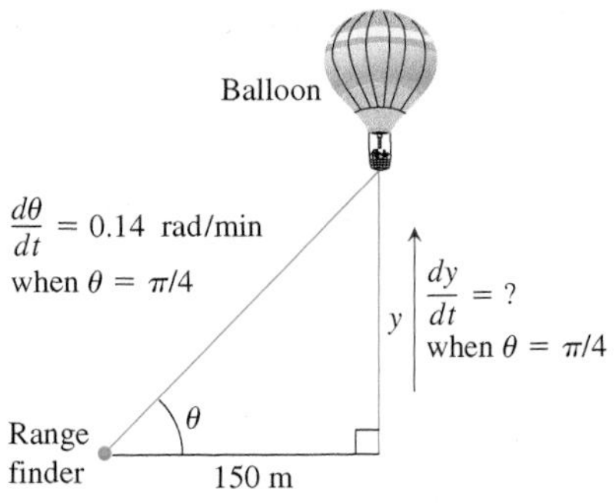

FIGURE 3.45 The rate of change of the balloon's height is related to the rate of change of the angle the range finder makes with the ground (Example 2).

Solution We answer the question in six steps.

1. *Draw a picture and name the variables and constants* (Figure 3.45). The variables in the picture are

   $\theta =$ the angle in radians the range finder makes with the ground.

   $y =$ the height in feet of the balloon.

We let t represent time in minutes and assume that θ and y are differentiable functions of t.

The one constant in the picture is the distance from the range finder to the liftoff point (150 m). There is no need to give it a special symbol.

2. *Write down the additional numerical information.*

$$\frac{d\theta}{dt} = 0.14 \text{ rad/min} \qquad \text{when} \qquad \theta = \frac{\pi}{4}$$

3. *Write down what we are to find.* We want dy/dt when $\theta = \pi/4$.
4. *Write an equation that relates the variables y and θ.*

$$\frac{y}{150} = \tan\theta \qquad \text{or} \qquad y = 150 \tan\theta$$

5. *Differentiate with respect to t using the Chain Rule.* The result tells how dy/dt (which we want) is related to $d\theta/dt$ (which we know).

$$\frac{dy}{dt} = 150\,(\sec^2\theta)\frac{d\theta}{dt}$$

6. *Evaluate with $\theta = \pi/4$ and $d\theta/dt = 0.14$ to find dy/dt.*

$$\frac{dy}{dt} = 150\left(\sqrt{2}\right)^2(0.14) = 42 \qquad \sec\frac{\pi}{4} = \sqrt{2}$$

At the moment in question, the balloon is rising at the rate of 42 m/min. ■

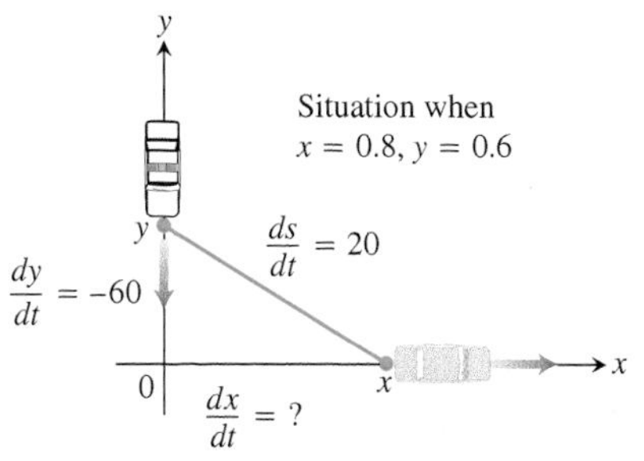

FIGURE 3.46 The speed of the car is related to the speed of the police cruiser and the rate of change of the distance between them (Example 3).

EXAMPLE 3 A police cruiser, approaching a right-angled intersection from the north, is chasing a speeding car that has turned the corner and is now moving straight east. When the cruiser is 0.6 mi north of the intersection and the car is 0.8 mi to the east, the police determine with radar that the distance between them and the car is increasing at 20 mph. If the cruiser is moving at 60 mph at the instant of measurement, what is the speed of the car?

Solution We picture the car and cruiser in the coordinate plane, using the positive x-axis as the eastbound highway and the positive y-axis as the southbound highway (Figure 3.46). We let t represent time and set

$$\begin{aligned} x &= \text{position of car at time } t \\ y &= \text{position of cruiser at time } t \\ s &= \text{distance between car and cruiser at time } t. \end{aligned}$$

We assume that x, y, and s are differentiable functions of t.

We want to find dx/dt when

$$x = 0.8 \text{ mi}, \qquad y = 0.6 \text{ mi}, \qquad \frac{dy}{dt} = -60 \text{ mph}, \qquad \frac{ds}{dt} = 20 \text{ mph}.$$

Note that dy/dt is negative because y is decreasing.

We differentiate the distance equation

$$s^2 = x^2 + y^2$$

(we could also use $s = \sqrt{x^2 + y^2}$), and obtain

$$\begin{aligned} 2s\frac{ds}{dt} &= 2x\frac{dx}{dt} + 2y\frac{dy}{dt} \\ \frac{ds}{dt} &= \frac{1}{s}\left(x\frac{dx}{dt} + y\frac{dy}{dt}\right) \\ &= \frac{1}{\sqrt{x^2 + y^2}}\left(x\frac{dx}{dt} + y\frac{dy}{dt}\right). \end{aligned}$$

Finally, we use $x = 0.8$, $y = 0.6$, $dy/dt = -60$, $ds/dt = 20$, and solve for dx/dt.

$$20 = \frac{1}{\sqrt{(0.8)^2 + (0.6)^2}}\left(0.8\frac{dx}{dt} + (0.6)(-60)\right)$$

$$\frac{dx}{dt} = \frac{20\sqrt{(0.8)^2 + (0.6)^2} + (0.6)(60)}{0.8} = 70$$

At the moment in question, the car's speed is 70 mph. ■

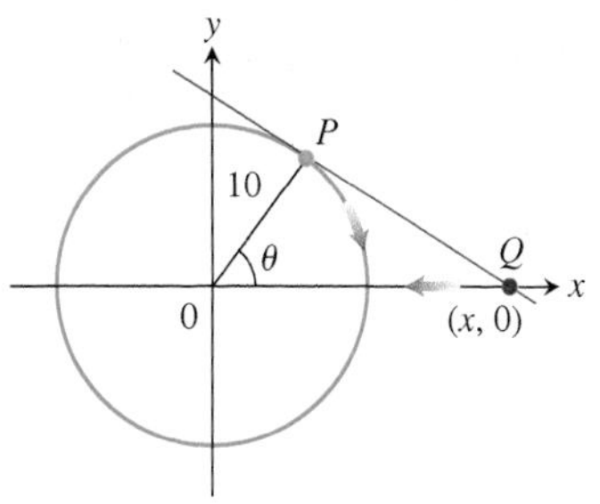

FIGURE 3.47 The particle P travels clockwise along the circle (Example 4).

EXAMPLE 4 A particle P moves clockwise at a constant rate along a circle of radius 10 m centered at the origin. The particle's initial position is (0, 10) on the y-axis, and its final destination is the point (10, 0) on the x-axis. Once the particle is in motion, the tangent line at P intersects the x-axis at a point Q (which moves over time). If it takes the particle 30 sec to travel from start to finish, how fast is the point Q moving along the x-axis when it is 20 m from the center of the circle?

Solution We picture the situation in the coordinate plane with the circle centered at the origin (see Figure 3.47). We let t represent time and let θ denote the angle from the x-axis to the radial line joining the origin to P. Since the particle travels from start to finish in 30 sec, it is traveling along the circle at a constant rate of $\pi/2$ radians in 1/2 min, or π rad/min. In other words, $d\theta/dt = -\pi$, with t being measured in minutes. The negative sign appears because θ is decreasing over time.

Setting $x(t)$ to be the distance at time t from the point Q to the origin, we want to find dx/dt when

$$x = 20 \text{ m} \qquad \text{and} \qquad \frac{d\theta}{dt} = -\pi \text{ rad/min}.$$

To relate the variables x and θ, we see from Figure 3.47 that $x \cos\theta = 10$, or $x = 10 \sec\theta$. Differentiation of this last equation gives

$$\frac{dx}{dt} = 10 \sec\theta \tan\theta \frac{d\theta}{dt} = -10\pi \sec\theta \tan\theta.$$

Note that dx/dt is negative because x is decreasing (Q is moving toward the origin).

When $x = 20$, $\cos\theta = 1/2$ and $\sec\theta = 2$. Also, $\tan\theta = \sqrt{\sec^2\theta - 1} = \sqrt{3}$. It follows that

$$\frac{dx}{dt} = (-10\pi)(2)(\sqrt{3}) = -20\sqrt{3}\pi.$$

At the moment in question, the point Q is moving toward the origin at the speed of $20\sqrt{3}\pi \approx 108.8$ m/min. ■

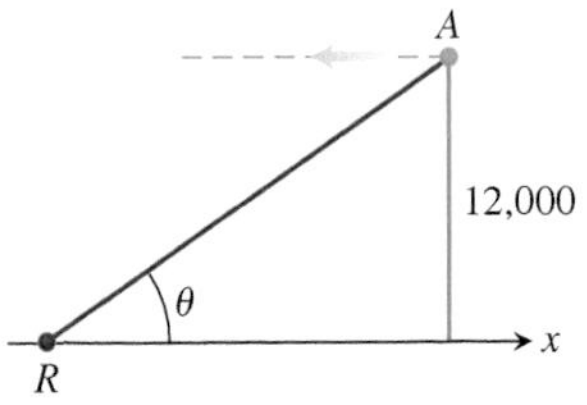

FIGURE 3.48 Jet airliner A traveling at constant altitude toward radar station R (Example 5).

EXAMPLE 5 A jet airliner is flying at a constant altitude of 12,000 ft above sea level as it approaches a Pacific island. The aircraft comes within the direct line of sight of a radar station located on the island, and the radar indicates the initial angle between sea level and its line of sight to the aircraft is 30°. How fast (in miles per hour) is the aircraft approaching the island when first detected by the radar instrument if it is turning upward (counterclockwise) at the rate of 2/3 deg/sec in order to keep the aircraft within its direct line of sight?

Solution The aircraft A and radar station R are pictured in the coordinate plane, using the positive x-axis as the horizontal distance at sea level from R to A, and the positive y-axis as the vertical altitude above sea level. We let t represent time and observe that $y = 12{,}000$ is a constant. The general situation and line-of-sight angle θ are depicted in Figure 3.48. We want to find dx/dt when $\theta = \pi/6$ rad and $d\theta/dt = 2/3$ deg/sec.

From Figure 3.48, we see that

$$\frac{12{,}000}{x} = \tan\theta \qquad \text{or} \qquad x = 12{,}000 \cot\theta.$$

Using miles instead of feet for our distance units, the last equation translates to

$$x = \frac{12{,}000}{5280} \cot\theta.$$

Differentiation with respect to t gives

$$\frac{dx}{dt} = -\frac{1200}{528} \csc^2\theta \frac{d\theta}{dt}.$$

When $\theta = \pi/6$, $\sin^2\theta = 1/4$, so $\csc^2\theta = 4$. Converting $d\theta/dt = 2/3$ deg/sec to radians per hour, we find

$$\frac{d\theta}{dt} = \frac{2}{3}\left(\frac{\pi}{180}\right)(3600) \text{ rad/hr.} \qquad \text{1 hr = 3600 sec, 1 deg = } \pi/180 \text{ rad}$$

Substitution into the equation for dx/dt then gives

$$\frac{dx}{dt} = \left(-\frac{1200}{528}\right)(4)\left(\frac{2}{3}\right)\left(\frac{\pi}{180}\right)(3600) \approx -380.$$

The negative sign appears because the distance x is decreasing, so the aircraft is approaching the island at a speed of approximately 380 mi/hr when first detected by the radar. ■

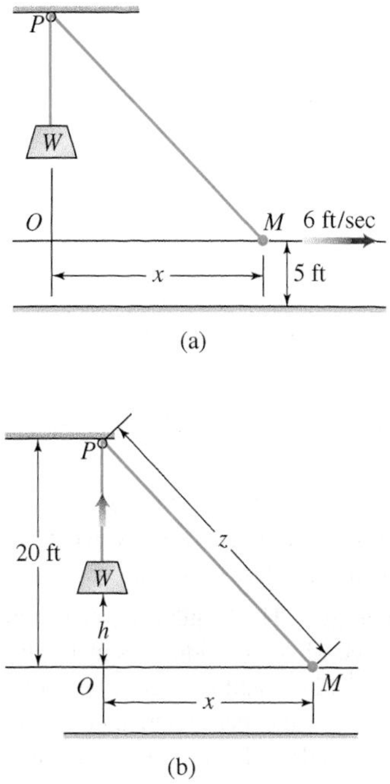

FIGURE 3.49 A worker at M walks to the right, pulling the weight W upward as the rope moves through the pulley P (Example 6).

EXAMPLE 6 Figure 3.49a shows a rope running through a pulley at P and bearing a weight W at one end. The other end is held 5 ft above the ground in the hand M of a worker. Suppose the pulley is 25 ft above ground, the rope is 45 ft long, and the worker is walking rapidly away from the vertical line PW at the rate of 6 ft/sec. How fast is the weight being raised when the worker's hand is 21 ft away from PW?

Solution We let OM be the horizontal line of length x ft from a point O directly below the pulley to the worker's hand M at any instant of time (Figure 3.49). Let h be the height of the weight W above O, and let z denote the length of rope from the pulley P to the worker's hand. We want to know dh/dt when $x = 21$ given that $dx/dt = 6$. Note that the height of P above O is 20 ft because O is 5 ft above the ground. We assume the angle at O is a right angle.

At any instant of time t we have the following relationships (see Figure 3.49b):

$$20 - h + z = 45 \qquad \text{Total length of rope is 45 ft.}$$

$$20^2 + x^2 = z^2. \qquad \text{Angle at } O \text{ is a right angle.}$$

If we solve for $z = 25 + h$ in the first equation, and substitute into the second equation, we have

$$20^2 + x^2 = (25 + h)^2. \tag{1}$$

Differentiating both sides with respect to t gives

$$2x\frac{dx}{dt} = 2(25 + h)\frac{dh}{dt},$$

and solving this last equation for dh/dt we find

$$\frac{dh}{dt} = \frac{x}{25 + h}\frac{dx}{dt}. \tag{2}$$

Since we know dx/dt, it remains only to find $25 + h$ at the instant when $x = 21$. From Equation (1),

$$20^2 + 21^2 = (25 + h)^2$$

so that

$$(25 + h)^2 = 841, \qquad \text{or} \qquad 25 + h = 29.$$

Equation (2) now gives

$$\frac{dh}{dt} = \frac{21}{29}\cdot 6 = \frac{126}{29} \approx 4.3 \text{ ft/sec}$$

as the rate at which the weight is being raised when $x = 21$ ft. ■

Exercises 3.10

1. **Area** Suppose that the radius r and area $A = \pi r^2$ of a circle are differentiable functions of t. Write an equation that relates dA/dt to dr/dt.
2. **Surface area** Suppose that the radius r and surface area $S = 4\pi r^2$ of a sphere are differentiable functions of t. Write an equation that relates dS/dt to dr/dt.
3. Assume that $y = 5x$ and $dx/dt = 2$. Find dy/dt.
4. Assume that $2x + 3y = 12$ and $dy/dt = -2$. Find dx/dt.
5. If $y = x^2$ and $dx/dt = 3$, then what is dy/dt when $x = -1$?
6. If $x = y^3 - y$ and $dy/dt = 5$, then what is dx/dt when $y = 2$?
7. If $x^2 + y^2 = 25$ and $dx/dt = -2$, then what is dy/dt when $x = 3$ and $y = -4$?
8. If $x^2y^3 = 4/27$ and $dy/dt = 1/2$, then what is dx/dt when $x = 2$?
9. If $L = \sqrt{x^2 + y^2}$, $dx/dt = -1$, and $dy/dt = 3$, find dL/dt when $x = 5$ and $y = 12$.
10. If $r + s^2 + v^3 = 12$, $dr/dt = 4$, and $ds/dt = -3$, find dv/dt when $r = 3$ and $s = 1$.

11. If the original 24 m edge length x of a cube decreases at the rate of 5 m/min, when $x = 3$ m at what rate does the cube's
    a. surface area change?
    b. volume change?

12. A cube's surface area increases at the rate of 72 in^2/sec. At what rate is the cube's volume changing when the edge length is $x = 3$ in?

13. **Volume** The radius r and height h of a right circular cylinder are related to the cylinder's volume V by the formula $V = \pi r^2 h$.
    a. How is dV/dt related to dh/dt if r is constant?
    b. How is dV/dt related to dr/dt if h is constant?
    c. How is dV/dt related to dr/dt and dh/dt if neither r nor h is constant?

14. **Volume** The radius r and height h of a right circular cone are related to the cone's volume V by the equation $V = (1/3)\pi r^2 h$.
    a. How is dV/dt related to dh/dt if r is constant?
    b. How is dV/dt related to dr/dt if h is constant?
    c. How is dV/dt related to dr/dt and dh/dt if neither r nor h is constant?

15. **Changing voltage** The voltage V (volts), current I (amperes), and resistance R (ohms) of an electric circuit like the one shown here are related by the equation $V = IR$. Suppose that V is increasing at the rate of 1 volt/sec while I is decreasing at the rate of 1/3 amp/sec. Let t denote time in seconds.

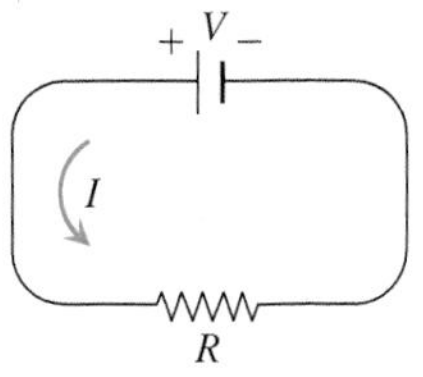

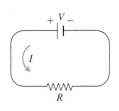

    a. What is the value of dV/dt?
    b. What is the value of dI/dt?
    c. What equation relates dR/dt to dV/dt and dI/dt?
    d. Find the rate at which R is changing when $V = 12$ volts and $I = 2$ amp. Is R increasing, or decreasing?

16. **Electrical power** The power P (watts) of an electric circuit is related to the circuit's resistance R (ohms) and current I (amperes) by the equation $P = RI^2$.
    a. How are dP/dt, dR/dt, and dI/dt related if none of P, R, and I are constant?
    b. How is dR/dt related to dI/dt if P is constant?

17. **Distance** Let x and y be differentiable functions of t and let $s = \sqrt{x^2 + y^2}$ be the distance between the points $(x, 0)$ and $(0, y)$ in the xy-plane.
    a. How is ds/dt related to dx/dt if y is constant?
    b. How is ds/dt related to dx/dt and dy/dt if neither x nor y is constant?
    c. How is dx/dt related to dy/dt if s is constant?

18. **Diagonals** If x, y, and z are lengths of the edges of a rectangular box, the common length of the box's diagonals is $s = \sqrt{x^2 + y^2 + z^2}$.
    a. Assuming that x, y, and z are differentiable functions of t, how is ds/dt related to dx/dt, dy/dt, and dz/dt?
    b. How is ds/dt related to dy/dt and dz/dt if x is constant?
    c. How are dx/dt, dy/dt, and dz/dt related if s is constant?

19. **Area** The area A of a triangle with sides of lengths a and b enclosing an angle of measure θ is

$$A = \frac{1}{2} ab \sin \theta .$$

    a. How is dA/dt related to $d\theta/dt$ if a and b are constant?
    b. How is dA/dt related to $d\theta/dt$ and da/dt if only b is constant?
    c. How is dA/dt related to $d\theta/dt$, da/dt, and db/dt if none of a, b, and θ are constant?

20. **Heating a plate** When a circular plate of metal is heated in an oven, its radius increases at the rate of 0.01 cm/min. At what rate is the plate's area increasing when the radius is 50 cm?

21. **Changing dimensions in a rectangle** The length l of a rectangle is decreasing at the rate of 2 cm/sec while the width w is increasing at the rate of 2 cm/sec. When $l = 12$ cm and $w = 5$ cm, find the rates of change of **(a)** the area, **(b)** the perimeter, and **(c)** the lengths of the diagonals of the rectangle. Which of these quantities are decreasing, and which are increasing?

22. **Changing dimensions in a rectangular box** Suppose that the edge lengths x, y, and z of a closed rectangular box are changing at the following rates:

$$\frac{dx}{dt} = 1 \text{ m/sec}, \quad \frac{dy}{dt} = -2 \text{ m/sec}, \quad \frac{dz}{dt} = 1 \text{ m/sec}.$$

Find the rates at which the box's **(a)** volume, **(b)** surface area, and **(c)** diagonal length $s = \sqrt{x^2 + y^2 + z^2}$ are changing at the instant when $x = 4$, $y = 3$, and $z = 2$.

23. **A sliding ladder** A 13-ft ladder is leaning against a house when its base starts to slide away (see accompanying figure). By the time the base is 12 ft from the house, the base is moving at the rate of 5 ft/sec.
    a. How fast is the top of the ladder sliding down the wall then?
    b. At what rate is the area of the triangle formed by the ladder, wall, and ground changing then?
    c. At what rate is the angle θ between the ladder and the ground changing then?

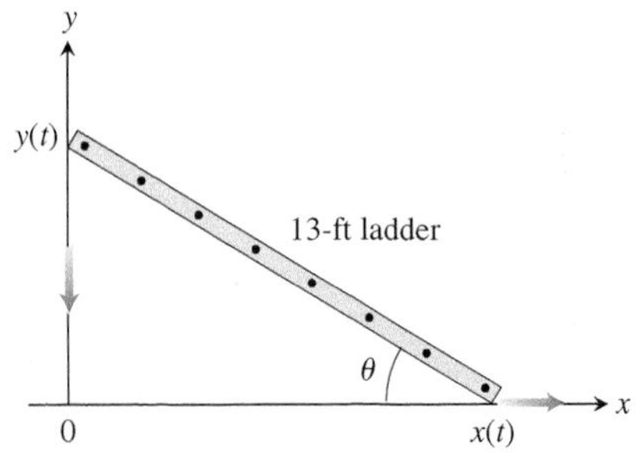

24. **Commercial air traffic** Two commercial airplanes are flying at an altitude of 40,000 ft along straight-line courses that intersect at right angles. Plane A is approaching the intersection point at a speed of 442 knots (nautical miles per hour; a nautical mile is 2000 yd). Plane B is approaching the intersection at 481 knots. At what rate is the distance between the planes changing when A is 5

nautical miles from the intersection point and B is 12 nautical miles from the intersection point?

25. **Flying a kite** A girl flies a kite at a height of 300 ft, the wind carrying the kite horizontally away from her at a rate of 25 ft/sec. How fast must she let out the string when the kite is 500 ft away from her?

26. **Boring a cylinder** The mechanics at Lincoln Automotive are reboring a 6-in.-deep cylinder to fit a new piston. The machine they are using increases the cylinder's radius one thousandth of an inch every 3 min. How rapidly is the cylinder volume increasing when the bore (diameter) is 3.800 in.?

27. **A growing sand pile** Sand falls from a conveyor belt at the rate of 10 m^3/min onto the top of a conical pile. The height of the pile is always three-eighths of the base diameter. How fast are the **(a)** height and **(b)** radius changing when the pile is 4 m high? Answer in centimeters per minute.

28. **A draining conical reservoir** Water is flowing at the rate of 50 m^3/min from a shallow concrete conical reservoir (vertex down) of base radius 45 m and height 6 m.

   a. How fast (centimeters per minute) is the water level falling when the water is 5 m deep?

   b. How fast is the radius of the water's surface changing then? Answer in centimeters per minute.

29. **A draining hemispherical reservoir** Water is flowing at the rate of 6 m^3/min from a reservoir shaped like a hemispherical bowl of radius 13 m, shown here in profile. Answer the following questions, given that the volume of water in a hemispherical bowl of radius R is $V = (\pi/3)y^2(3R - y)$ when the water is y meters deep.

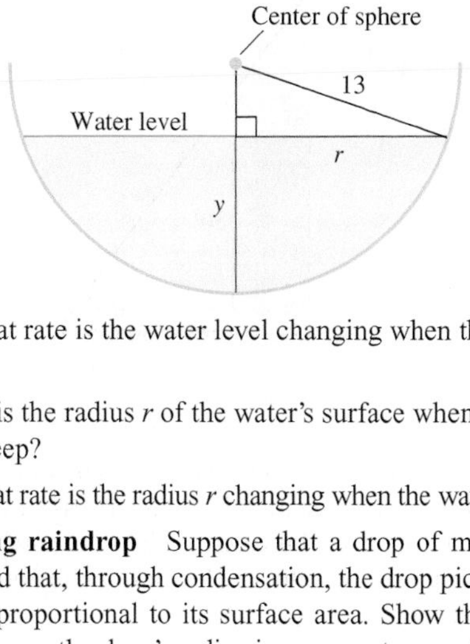

   a. At what rate is the water level changing when the water is 8 m deep?

   b. What is the radius r of the water's surface when the water is y m deep?

   c. At what rate is the radius r changing when the water is 8 m deep?

30. **A growing raindrop** Suppose that a drop of mist is a perfect sphere and that, through condensation, the drop picks up moisture at a rate proportional to its surface area. Show that under these circumstances the drop's radius increases at a constant rate.

31. **The radius of an inflating balloon** A spherical balloon is inflated with helium at the rate of 100π ft^3/min. How fast is the balloon's radius increasing at the instant the radius is 5 ft? How fast is the surface area increasing?

32. **Hauling in a dinghy** A dinghy is pulled toward a dock by a rope from the bow through a ring on the dock 6 ft above the bow. The rope is hauled in at the rate of 2 ft/sec.

   a. How fast is the boat approaching the dock when 10 ft of rope are out?

   b. At what rate is the angle θ changing at this instant (see the figure)?

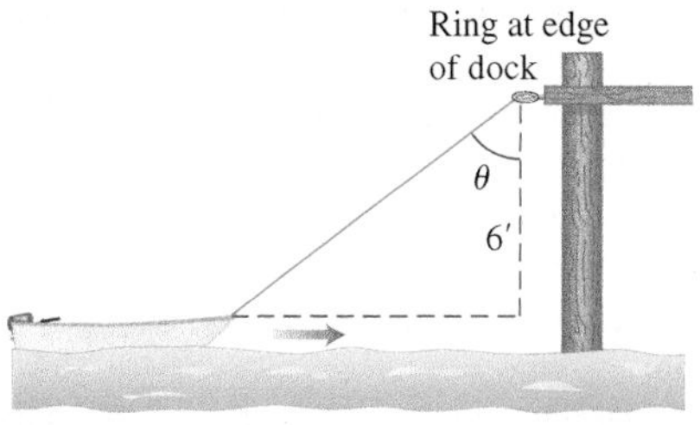

33. **A balloon and a bicycle** A balloon is rising vertically above a level, straight road at a constant rate of 1 ft/sec. Just when the balloon is 65 ft above the ground, a bicycle moving at a constant rate of 17 ft/sec passes under it. How fast is the distance $s(t)$ between the bicycle and balloon increasing 3 sec later?

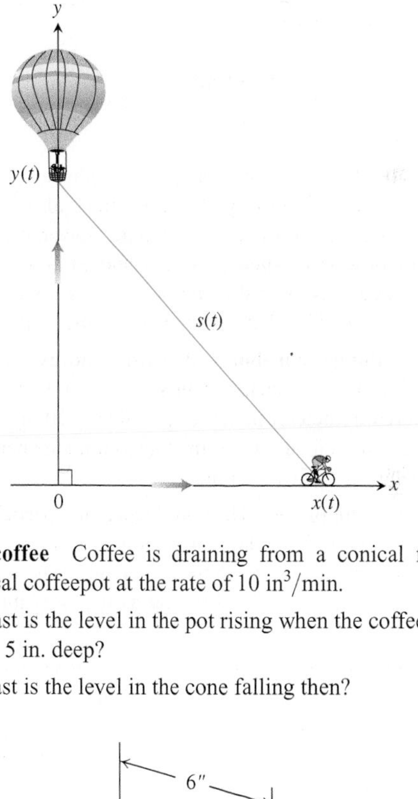

34. **Making coffee** Coffee is draining from a conical filter into a cylindrical coffeepot at the rate of 10 in^3/min.

   a. How fast is the level in the pot rising when the coffee in the cone is 5 in. deep?

   b. How fast is the level in the cone falling then?

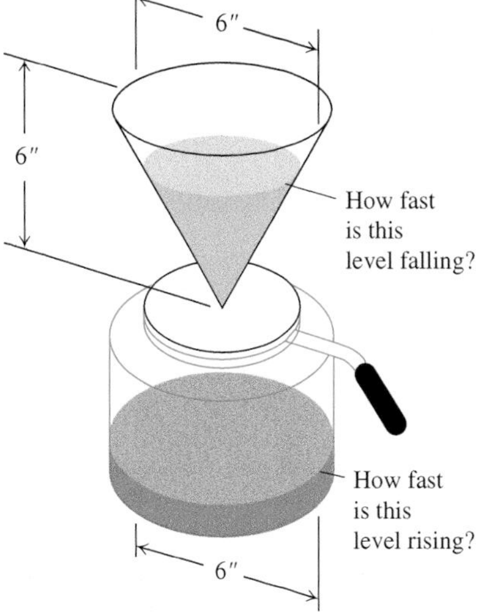

35. Cardiac output In the late 1860s, Adolf Fick, a professor of physiology in the Faculty of Medicine in Würzberg, Germany, developed one of the methods we use today for measuring how much blood your heart pumps in a minute. Your cardiac output as you read this sentence is probably about 7 L/min. At rest it is likely to be a bit under 6 L/min. If you are a trained marathon runner running a marathon, your cardiac output can be as high as 30 L/min.

Your cardiac output can be calculated with the formula

$$y = \frac{Q}{D},$$

where Q is the number of milliliters of CO_2 you exhale in a minute and D is the difference between the CO_2 concentration (ml/L) in the blood pumped to the lungs and the CO_2 concentration in the blood returning from the lungs. With $Q = 233$ ml/min and $D = 97 - 56 = 41$ ml/L,

$$y = \frac{233 \text{ ml/min}}{41 \text{ ml/L}} \approx 5.68 \text{ L/min},$$

fairly close to the 6 L/min that most people have at basal (resting) conditions. (Data courtesy of J. Kenneth Herd, M.D., Quillan College of Medicine, East Tennessee State University.)

Suppose that when $Q = 233$ and $D = 41$, we also know that D is decreasing at the rate of 2 units a minute but that Q remains unchanged. What is happening to the cardiac output?

36. Moving along a parabola A particle moves along the parabola $y = x^2$ in the first quadrant in such a way that its x-coordinate (measured in meters) increases at a steady 10 m/sec. How fast is the angle of inclination θ of the line joining the particle to the origin changing when $x = 3$ m?

37. Motion in the plane The coordinates of a particle in the metric xy-plane are differentiable functions of time t with $dx/dt = -1$ m/sec and $dy/dt = -5$ m/sec. How fast is the particle's distance from the origin changing as it passes through the point (5, 12)?

38. Videotaping a moving car You are videotaping a race from a stand 132 ft from the track, following a car that is moving at 180 mi/h (264 ft/sec), as shown in the accompanying figure. How fast will your camera angle θ be changing when the car is right in front of you? A half second later?

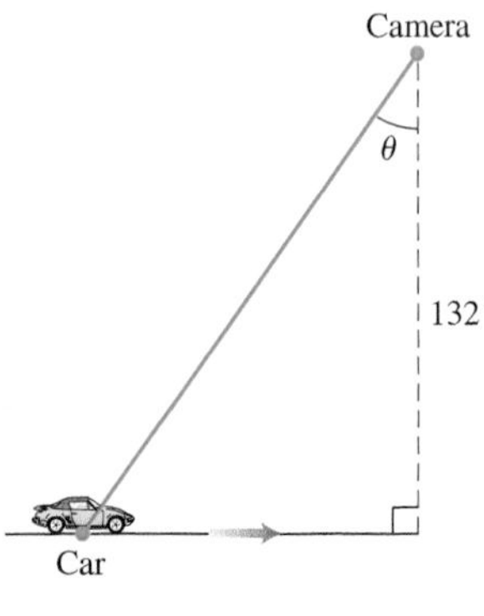

39. A moving shadow A light shines from the top of a pole 50 ft high. A ball is dropped from the same height from a point 30 ft away from the light. (See accompanying figure.) How fast is the shadow of the ball moving along the ground 1/2 sec later? (Assume the ball falls a distance $s = 16t^2$ ft in t sec.)

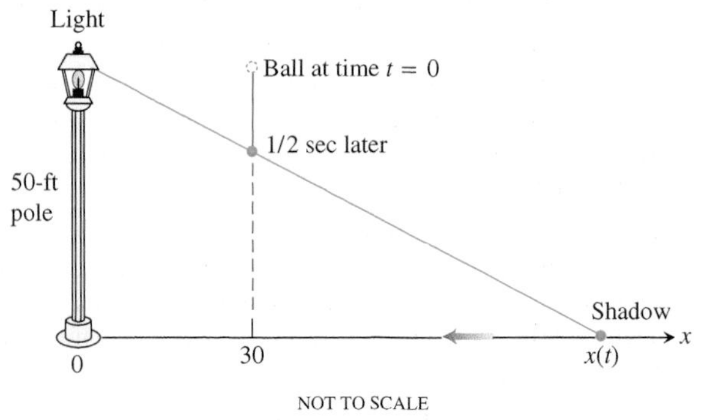

40. A building's shadow On a morning of a day when the sun will pass directly overhead, the shadow of an 80-ft building on level ground is 60 ft long. At the moment in question, the angle θ the sun makes with the ground is increasing at the rate of 0.27°/min. At what rate is the shadow decreasing? (Remember to use radians. Express your answer in inches per minute, to the nearest tenth.)

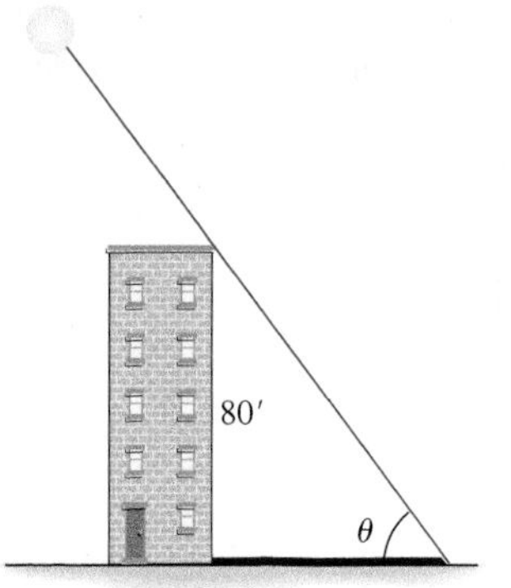

41. A melting ice layer A spherical iron ball 8 in. in diameter is coated with a layer of ice of uniform thickness. If the ice melts at the rate of 10 in^3/min, how fast is the thickness of the ice decreasing when it is 2 in. thick? How fast is the outer surface area of ice decreasing?

42. Highway patrol A highway patrol plane flies 3 mi above a level, straight road at a steady 120 mi/h. The pilot sees an oncoming car and with radar determines that at the instant the line-of-sight distance from plane to car is 5 mi, the line-of-sight distance is decreasing at the rate of 160 mi/h. Find the car's speed along the highway.

43. Baseball players A baseball diamond is a square 90 ft on a side. A player runs from first base to second at a rate of 16 ft/sec.

a. At what rate is the player's distance from third base changing when the player is 30 ft from first base?

b. At what rates are angles θ_1 and θ_2 (see the figure) changing at that time?

c. The player slides into second base at the rate of 15 ft/sec. At what rates are angles θ_1 and θ_2 changing as the player touches base?

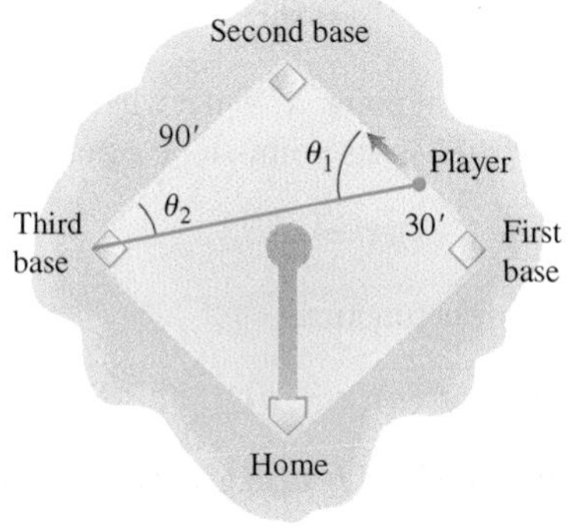

44. Ships Two ships are steaming straight away from a point O along routes that make a 120° angle. Ship A moves at 14 knots (nautical miles per hour; a nautical mile is 2000 yd). Ship B moves at 21 knots. How fast are the ships moving apart when $OA = 5$ and $OB = 3$ nautical miles?

3.11 Linearization and Differentials

Sometimes we can approximate complicated functions with simpler ones that give the accuracy we want for specific applications and are easier to work with. The approximating functions discussed in this section are called *linearizations*, and they are based on tangent lines. Other approximating functions, such as polynomials, are discussed in Chapter 9.

We introduce new variables dx and dy, called *differentials*, and define them in a way that makes Leibniz's notation for the derivative dy/dx a true ratio. We use dy to estimate error in measurement, which then provides for a precise proof of the Chain Rule (Section 3.6).

Linearization

As you can see in Figure 3.50, the tangent to the curve $y = x^2$ lies close to the curve near the point of tangency. For a brief interval to either side, the y-values along the tangent line

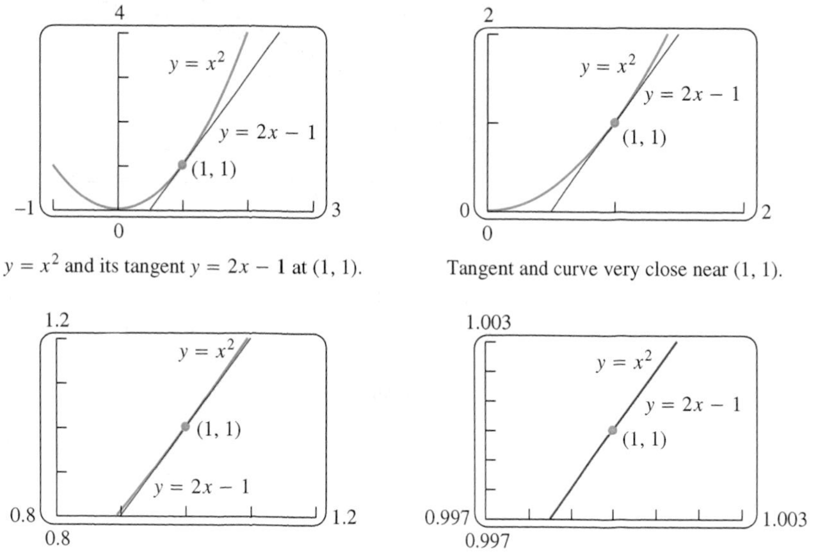

$y = x^2$ and its tangent $y = 2x - 1$ at (1, 1).

Tangent and curve very close near (1, 1).

Tangent and curve very close throughout entire x-interval shown.

Tangent and curve closer still. Computer screen cannot distinguish tangent from curve on this x-interval.

FIGURE 3.50 The more we magnify the graph of a function near a point where the function is differentiable, the flatter the graph becomes and the more it resembles its tangent.

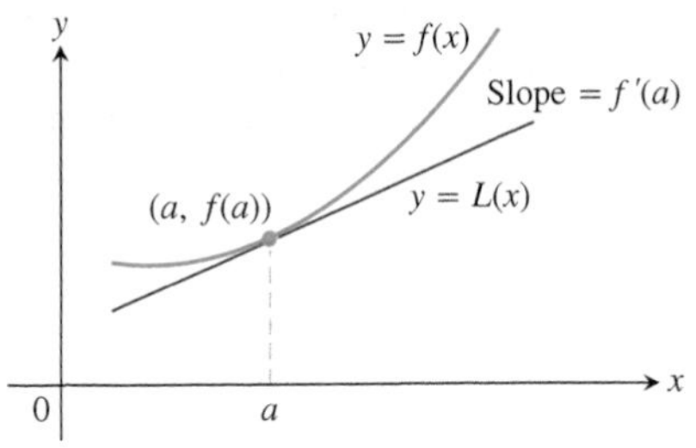

FIGURE 3.51 The tangent to the curve $y = f(x)$ at $x = a$ is the line $L(x) = f(a) + f'(a)(x - a)$.

give good approximations to the y-values on the curve. We observe this phenomenon by zooming in on the two graphs at the point of tangency or by looking at tables of values for the difference between $f(x)$ and its tangent line near the x-coordinate of the point of tangency. The phenomenon is true not just for parabolas; every differentiable curve behaves locally like its tangent line.

In general, the tangent to $y = f(x)$ at a point $x = a$, where f is differentiable (Figure 3.51), passes through the point $(a, f(a))$, so its point-slope equation is

$$y = f(a) + f'(a)(x - a).$$

Thus, this tangent line is the graph of the linear function

$$L(x) = f(a) + f'(a)(x - a).$$

For as long as this line remains close to the graph of f, $L(x)$ gives a good approximation to $f(x)$.

> **DEFINITIONS** If f is differentiable at $x = a$, then the approximating function
>
> $$L(x) = f(a) + f'(a)(x - a)$$
>
> is the **linearization** of f at a. The approximation
>
> $$f(x) \approx L(x)$$
>
> of f by L is the **standard linear approximation** of f at a. The point $x = a$ is the **center** of the approximation.

EXAMPLE 1 Find the linearization of $f(x) = \sqrt{1 + x}$ at $x = 0$ (Figure 3.52).

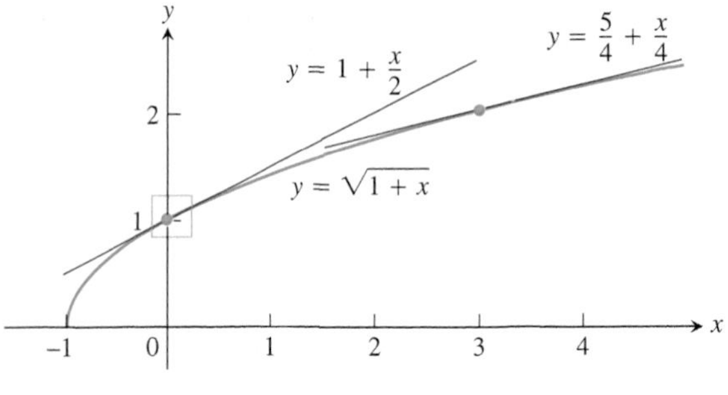

FIGURE 3.52 The graph of $y = \sqrt{1 + x}$ and its linearizations at $x = 0$ and $x = 3$. Figure 3.53 shows a magnified view of the small window about 1 on the y-axis.

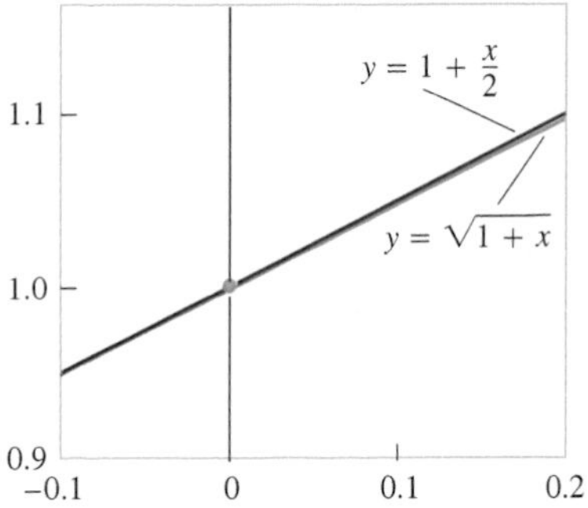

FIGURE 3.53 Magnified view of the window in Figure 3.52.

Solution Since

$$f'(x) = \frac{1}{2}(1 + x)^{-1/2},$$

we have $f(0) = 1$ and $f'(0) = 1/2$, giving the linearization

$$L(x) = f(a) + f'(a)(x - a) = 1 + \frac{1}{2}(x - 0) = 1 + \frac{x}{2}.$$

See Figure 3.53. ■

The following table shows how accurate the approximation $\sqrt{1 + x} \approx 1 + (x/2)$ from Example 1 is for some values of x near 0. As we move away from zero, we lose accuracy. For example, for $x = 2$, the linearization gives 2 as the approximation for $\sqrt{3}$, which is not even accurate to one decimal place.

Approximation	True value	|True value − approximation|
$\sqrt{1.2} \approx 1 + \frac{0.2}{2} = 1.10$	1.095445	$0.004555 < 10^{-2}$
$\sqrt{1.05} \approx 1 + \frac{0.05}{2} = 1.025$	1.024695	$0.000305 < 10^{-3}$
$\sqrt{1.005} \approx 1 + \frac{0.005}{2} = 1.00250$	1.002497	$0.000003 < 10^{-5}$

Do not be misled by the preceding calculations into thinking that whatever we do with a linearization is better done with a calculator. In practice, we would never use a linearization to find a particular square root. The utility of a linearization is its ability to replace a complicated formula by a simpler one over an entire interval of values. If we have to work with $\sqrt{1 + x}$ for x close to 0 and can tolerate the small amount of error involved, we can work with $1 + (x/2)$ instead. Of course, we then need to know how much error there is. We further examine the estimation of error in Chapter 9.

A linear approximation normally loses accuracy away from its center. As Figure 3.52 suggests, the approximation $\sqrt{1 + x} \approx 1 + (x/2)$ will probably be too crude to be useful near $x = 3$. There, we need the linearization at $x = 3$.

EXAMPLE 2 Find the linearization of $f(x) = \sqrt{1 + x}$ at $x = 3$.

Solution We evaluate the equation defining $L(x)$ at $a = 3$. With

$$f(3) = 2, \qquad f'(3) = \frac{1}{2}(1 + x)^{-1/2}\Big|_{x=3} = \frac{1}{4},$$

we have

$$L(x) = 2 + \frac{1}{4}(x - 3) = \frac{5}{4} + \frac{x}{4}. \qquad \blacksquare$$

At $x = 3.2$, the linearization in Example 2 gives

$$\sqrt{1 + x} = \sqrt{1 + 3.2} \approx \frac{5}{4} + \frac{3.2}{4} = 1.250 + 0.800 = 2.050,$$

which differs from the true value $\sqrt{4.2} \approx 2.04939$ by less than one one-thousandth. The linearization in Example 1 gives

$$\sqrt{1 + x} = \sqrt{1 + 3.2} \approx 1 + \frac{3.2}{2} = 1 + 1.6 = 2.6,$$

a result that is off by more than 25%.

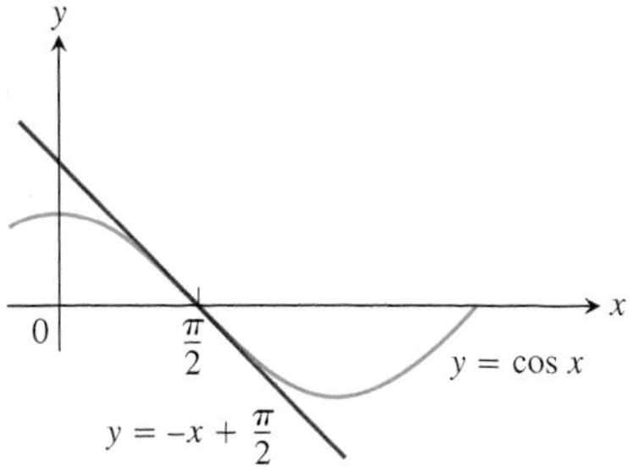

FIGURE 3.54 The graph of $f(x) = \cos x$ and its linearization at $x = \pi/2$. Near $x = \pi/2$, $\cos x \approx -x + (\pi/2)$ (Example 3).

EXAMPLE 3 Find the linearization of $f(x) = \cos x$ at $x = \pi/2$ (Figure 3.54).

Solution Since $f(\pi/2) = \cos(\pi/2) = 0$, $f'(x) = -\sin x$, and $f'(\pi/2) = -\sin(\pi/2) = -1$, we find the linearization at $a = \pi/2$ to be

$$\begin{aligned} L(x) &= f(a) + f'(a)(x - a) \\ &= 0 + (-1)\left(x - \frac{\pi}{2}\right) \\ &= -x + \frac{\pi}{2}. \end{aligned} \qquad \blacksquare$$

An important linear approximation for roots and powers is

$$(1+x)^k \approx 1 + kx \qquad (x \text{ near } 0; \text{ any number } k)$$

(Exercise 15). This approximation, good for values of x sufficiently close to zero, has broad application. For example, when x is small,

$$\sqrt{1+x} \approx 1 + \frac{1}{2}x \qquad k = 1/2$$

$$\frac{1}{1-x} = (1-x)^{-1} \approx 1 + (-1)(-x) = 1 + x \qquad k = -1;\ \text{replace } x \text{ by } -x.$$

$$\sqrt[3]{1+5x^4} = (1+5x^4)^{1/3} \approx 1 + \frac{1}{3}(5x^4) = 1 + \frac{5}{3}x^4 \qquad k = 1/3;\ \text{replace } x \text{ by } 5x^4.$$

$$\frac{1}{\sqrt{1-x^2}} = (1-x^2)^{-1/2} \approx 1 + \left(-\frac{1}{2}\right)(-x^2) = 1 + \frac{1}{2}x^2 \qquad k = -1/2;\ \text{replace } x \text{ by } -x^2.$$

Differentials

We sometimes use the Leibniz notation dy/dx to represent the derivative of y with respect to x. Contrary to its appearance, it is not a ratio. We now introduce two new variables dx and dy with the property that when their ratio exists, it is equal to the derivative.

DEFINITION Let $y = f(x)$ be a differentiable function. The **differential dx** is an independent variable. The **differential dy** is

$$dy = f'(x)\,dx.$$

Unlike the independent variable dx, the variable dy is always a dependent variable. It depends on both x and dx. If dx is given a specific value and x is a particular number in the domain of the function f, then these values determine the numerical value of dy.

EXAMPLE 4

(a) Find dy if $y = x^5 + 37x$.

(b) Find the value of dy when $x = 1$ and $dx = 0.2$.

Solution

(a) $dy = (5x^4 + 37)\,dx$

(b) Substituting $x = 1$ and $dx = 0.2$ in the expression for dy, we have

$$dy = (5 \cdot 1^4 + 37)0.2 = 8.4.$$

■

The geometric meaning of differentials is shown in Figure 3.55. Let $x = a$ and set $dx = \Delta x$. The corresponding change in $y = f(x)$ is

$$\Delta y = f(a + dx) - f(a).$$

The corresponding change in the tangent line L is

$$\begin{aligned}\Delta L &= L(a + dx) - L(a)\\ &= \underbrace{f(a) + f'(a)[(a + dx) - a]}_{L(a+dx)} - \underbrace{f(a)}_{L(a)}\\ &= f'(a)\,dx.\end{aligned}$$

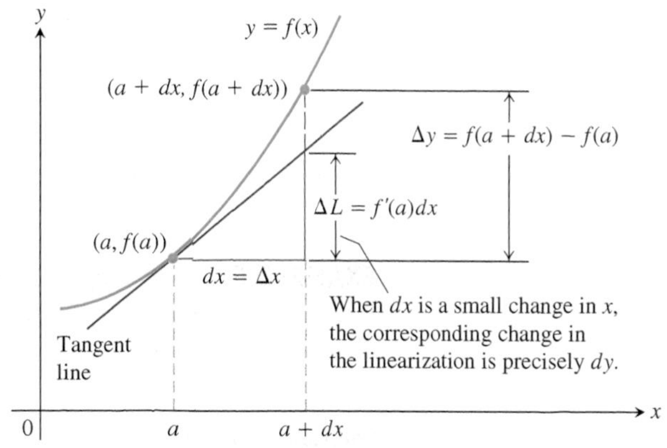

FIGURE 3.55 Geometrically, the differential dy is the change ΔL in the linearization of f when $x = a$ changes by an amount $dx = \Delta x$.

That is, the change in the linearization of f is precisely the value of the differential dy when $x = a$ and $dx = \Delta x$. Therefore, dy represents the amount the tangent line rises or falls when x changes by an amount $dx = \Delta x$.

If $dx \neq 0$, then the quotient of the differential dy by the differential dx is equal to the derivative $f'(x)$ because

$$dy \div dx = \frac{f'(x)\,dx}{dx} = f'(x) = \frac{dy}{dx}.$$

We sometimes write

$$df = f'(x)\,dx$$

in place of $dy = f'(x)\,dx$, calling df the **differential of f**. For instance, if $f(x) = 3x^2 - 6$, then

$$df = d(3x^2 - 6) = 6x\,dx.$$

Every differentiation formula like

$$\frac{d(u + v)}{dx} = \frac{du}{dx} + \frac{dv}{dx} \quad \text{or} \quad \frac{d(\sin u)}{dx} = \cos u \frac{du}{dx}$$

has a corresponding differential form like

$$d(u + v) = du + dv \quad \text{or} \quad d(\sin u) = \cos u\,du.$$

EXAMPLE 5 We can use the Chain Rule and other differentiation rules to find differentials of functions.

(a) $d(\tan 2x) = \sec^2(2x)\,d(2x) = 2\sec^2 2x\,dx$

(b) $d\left(\dfrac{x}{x + 1}\right) = \dfrac{(x + 1)\,dx - x\,d(x + 1)}{(x + 1)^2} = \dfrac{x\,dx + dx - x\,dx}{(x + 1)^2} = \dfrac{dx}{(x + 1)^2}$ ∎

Estimating with Differentials

Suppose we know the value of a differentiable function $f(x)$ at a point a and want to estimate how much this value will change if we move to a nearby point $a + dx$. If $dx = \Delta x$ is small, then we can see from Figure 3.55 that Δy is approximately equal to the differential dy. Since

$$f(a + dx) = f(a) + \Delta y, \qquad \Delta x = dx$$

the differential approximation gives

$$f(a + dx) \approx f(a) + dy$$

when $dx = \Delta x$. Thus the approximation $\Delta y \approx dy$ can be used to estimate $f(a + dx)$ when $f(a)$ is known and dx is small.

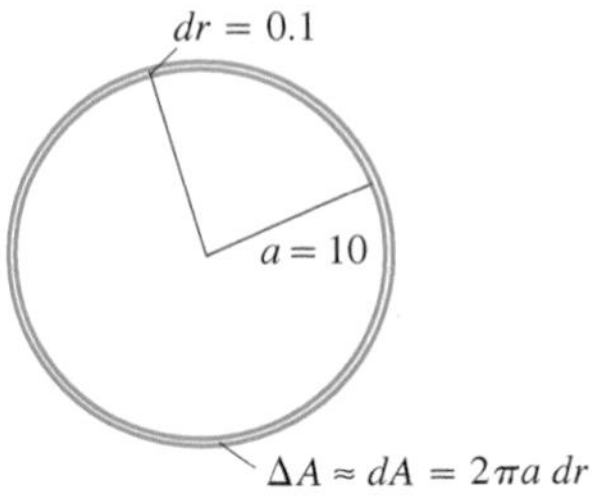

FIGURE 3.56 When dr is small compared with a, the differential dA gives the estimate $A(a + dr) = \pi a^2 + dA$ (Example 6).

EXAMPLE 6 The radius r of a circle increases from $a = 10$ m to 10.1 m (Figure 3.56). Use dA to estimate the increase in the circle's area A. Estimate the area of the enlarged circle and compare your estimate to the true area found by direct calculation.

Solution Since $A = \pi r^2$, the estimated increase is

$$dA = A'(a)\,dr = 2\pi a\,dr = 2\pi(10)(0.1) = 2\pi \text{ m}^2.$$

Thus, since $A(r + \Delta r) \approx A(r) + dA$, we have

$$\begin{aligned} A(10 + 0.1) &\approx A(10) + 2\pi \\ &= \pi(10)^2 + 2\pi = 102\pi. \end{aligned}$$

The area of a circle of radius 10.1 m is approximately 102π m^2.

The true area is

$$\begin{aligned} A(10.1) &= \pi(10.1)^2 \\ &= 102.01\pi \text{ m}^2. \end{aligned}$$

The error in our estimate is 0.01π m^2, which is the difference $\Delta A - dA$. ■

EXAMPLE 7 Use differentials to estimate

(a) $7.97^{1/3}$

(b) $\sin(\pi/6 + 0.01)$.

Solution

(a) The differential associated with the cube root function $y = x^{1/3}$ is

$$dy = \frac{1}{3x^{2/3}}\,dx.$$

We set $a = 8$, the closest number near 7.97 where we can easily compute $f(a)$ and $f'(a)$. To arrange that $a + dx = 7.97$, we choose $dx = -0.03$. Approximating with the differential gives

$$\begin{aligned} f(7.97) = f(a + dx) &\approx f(a) + dy \\ &= 8^{1/3} + \frac{1}{3(8)^{2/3}}(-0.03) \\ &= 2 + \frac{1}{12}(-0.03) = 1.9975 \end{aligned}$$

This gives an approximation to the true value of $7.97^{1/3}$, which is 1.997497 to 6 decimals.

(b) The differential associated with $y = \sin x$ is

$$dy = \cos x\,dx.$$

To estimate $\sin(\pi/6 + 0.01)$, we set $a = \pi/6$ and $dx = 0.01$. Then

$$\begin{aligned} f(\pi/6 + 0.01) = f(a + dx) &\approx f(a) + dy \\ &= \sin\frac{\pi}{6} + \left(\cos\frac{\pi}{6}\right)(0.01) \\ &= \frac{1}{2} + \frac{\sqrt{3}}{2}(0.01) \approx 0.5087 \end{aligned}$$

For comparison, the true value of $\sin(\pi/6 + 0.01)$ to 6 decimals is 0.508635. ■

The method in part (b) of Example 7 is used by some calculator and computer algorithms to give values of trigonometric functions. The algorithms store a large table of sine and cosine values between 0 and $\pi/4$. Values between these stored values are computed using differentials as in Example 7b. Values outside of $[0, \pi/4]$ are computed from values in this interval using trigonometric identities.

Error in Differential Approximation

Let $f(x)$ be differentiable at $x = a$ and suppose that $dx = \Delta x$ is an increment of x. We have two ways to describe the change in f as x changes from a to $a + \Delta x$:

The true change: $\Delta f = f(a + \Delta x) - f(a)$

The differential estimate: $df = f'(a)\,\Delta x.$

How well does df approximate Δf?

We measure the approximation error by subtracting df from Δf:

$$\begin{aligned} \text{Approximation error} &= \Delta f - df \\ &= \Delta f - f'(a)\Delta x \\ &= \underbrace{f(a + \Delta x) - f(a)}_{\Delta f} - f'(a)\Delta x \\ &= \underbrace{\left(\frac{f(a + \Delta x) - f(a)}{\Delta x} - f'(a)\right)}_{\text{Call this part } \epsilon.} \cdot \Delta x \\ &= \epsilon \cdot \Delta x. \end{aligned}$$

As $\Delta x \to 0$, the difference quotient

$$\frac{f(a + \Delta x) - f(a)}{\Delta x}$$

approaches $f'(a)$ (remember the definition of $f'(a)$), so the quantity in parentheses becomes a very small number (which is why we called it ϵ). In fact, $\epsilon \to 0$ as $\Delta x \to 0$. When Δx is small, the approximation error $\epsilon\,\Delta x$ is smaller still.

$$\underbrace{\Delta f}_{\substack{\text{true} \\ \text{change}}} = \underbrace{f'(a)\Delta x}_{\substack{\text{estimated} \\ \text{change}}} + \underbrace{\epsilon\,\Delta x}_{\text{error}}$$

Although we do not know the exact size of the error, it is the product $\epsilon \cdot \Delta x$ of two small quantities that both approach zero as $\Delta x \to 0$. For many common functions, whenever Δx is small, the error is still smaller.

Change in $y = f(x)$ near $x = a$

If $y = f(x)$ is differentiable at $x = a$ and x changes from a to $a + \Delta x$, the change Δy in f is given by

$$\Delta y = f'(a)\,\Delta x + \epsilon\,\Delta x \tag{1}$$

in which $\epsilon \to 0$ as $\Delta x \to 0$.

In Example 6 we found that

$$\Delta A = \pi(10.1)^2 - \pi(10)^2 = (102.01 - 100)\pi = (\underbrace{2\pi}_{dA} + \underbrace{0.01\pi}_{\text{error}})\,\mathrm{m}^2$$

so the approximation error is $\Delta A - dA = \epsilon\Delta r = 0.01\pi$ and $\epsilon = 0.01\pi/\Delta r = 0.01\pi/0.1 = 0.1\pi$ m.

Proof of the Chain Rule

Equation (1) enables us to prove the Chain Rule correctly. Our goal is to show that if $f(u)$ is a differentiable function of u and $u = g(x)$ is a differentiable function of x, then the composite $y = f(g(x))$ is a differentiable function of x. Since a function is differentiable if and only if it has a derivative at each point in its domain, we must show that whenever g is differentiable at x_0 and f is differentiable at $g(x_0)$, then the composite is differentiable at x_0 and the derivative of the composite satisfies the equation

$$\left.\frac{dy}{dx}\right|_{x=x_0} = f'(g(x_0)) \cdot g'(x_0).$$

Let Δx be an increment in x and let Δu and Δy be the corresponding increments in u and y. Applying Equation (1) we have

$$\Delta u = g'(x_0)\Delta x + \epsilon_1\,\Delta x = (g'(x_0) + \epsilon_1)\Delta x,$$

where $\epsilon_1 \to 0$ as $\Delta x \to 0$. Similarly,

$$\Delta y = f'(u_0)\Delta u + \epsilon_2\,\Delta u = (f'(u_0) + \epsilon_2)\Delta u,$$

where $\epsilon_2 \to 0$ as $\Delta u \to 0$. Notice also that $\Delta u \to 0$ as $\Delta x \to 0$. Combining the equations for Δu and Δy gives

$$\Delta y = (f'(u_0) + \epsilon_2)(g'(x_0) + \epsilon_1)\Delta x,$$

so

$$\frac{\Delta y}{\Delta x} = f'(u_0)g'(x_0) + \epsilon_2\, g'(x_0) + f'(u_0)\epsilon_1 + \epsilon_2\epsilon_1.$$

Since ϵ_1 and ϵ_2 go to zero as Δx goes to zero, three of the four terms on the right vanish in the limit, leaving

$$\left.\frac{dy}{dx}\right|_{x=x_0} = \lim_{\Delta x \to 0} \frac{\Delta y}{\Delta x} = f'(u_0)g'(x_0) = f'(g(x_0)) \cdot g'(x_0). \qquad \blacksquare$$

Sensitivity to Change

The equation $df = f'(x)\,dx$ tells how *sensitive* the output of f is to a change in input at different values of x. The larger the value of f' at x, the greater the effect of a given change dx. As we move from a to a nearby point $a + dx$, we can describe the change in f in three ways:

	True	Estimated
Absolute change	$\Delta f = f(a + dx) - f(a)$	$df = f'(a)\,dx$
Relative change	$\dfrac{\Delta f}{f(a)}$	$\dfrac{df}{f(a)}$
Percentage change	$\dfrac{\Delta f}{f(a)} \times 100$	$\dfrac{df}{f(a)} \times 100$

EXAMPLE 8 You want to calculate the depth of a well from the equation $s = 16t^2$ by timing how long it takes a heavy stone you drop to splash into the water below. How sensitive will your calculations be to a 0.1-sec error in measuring the time?

Solution The size of ds in the equation

$$ds = 32t\,dt$$

depends on how big t is. If $t = 2$ sec, the change caused by $dt = 0.1$ is about

$$ds = 32(2)(0.1) = 6.4 \text{ ft}.$$

Three seconds later at $t = 5$ sec, the change caused by the same dt is

$$ds = 32(5)(0.1) = 16 \text{ ft}.$$

For a fixed error in the time measurement, the error in using ds to estimate the depth is larger when it takes a longer time before the stone splashes into the water. ■

Exercises 3.11

Finding Linearizations

In Exercises 1–5, find the linearization $L(x)$ of $f(x)$ at $x = a$.

1. $f(x) = x^3 - 2x + 3, \quad a = 2$
2. $f(x) = \sqrt{x^2 + 9}, \quad a = -4$
3. $f(x) = x + \dfrac{1}{x}, \quad a = 1$
4. $f(x) = \sqrt[3]{x}, \quad a = -8$
5. $f(x) = \tan x, \quad a = \pi$
6. **Common linear approximations at $x = 0$** Find the linearizations of the following functions at $x = 0$.
   (a) $\sin x$ **(b)** $\cos x$ **(c)** $\tan x$ **(d)** e^x **(e)** $\ln(1 + x)$

Linearization for Approximation

In Exercises 7–14, find a linearization at a suitably chosen integer near a at which the given function and its derivative are easy to evaluate.

7. $f(x) = x^2 + 2x, \quad a = 0.1$
8. $f(x) = x^{-1}, \quad a = 0.9$
9. $f(x) = 2x^2 + 3x - 3, \quad a = -0.9$
10. $f(x) = 1 + x, \quad a = 8.1$
11. $f(x) = \sqrt[3]{x}, \quad a = 8.5$
12. $f(x) = \dfrac{x}{x + 1}, \quad a = 1.3$
13. $f(x) = e^{-x}, \quad a = -0.1$
14. $f(x) = \sin^{-1} x, \quad a = \pi/12$
15. Show that the linearization of $f(x) = (1 + x)^k$ at $x = 0$ is $L(x) = 1 + kx$.
16. Use the linear approximation $(1 + x)^k \approx 1 + kx$ to find an approximation for the function $f(x)$ for values of x near zero.
    a. $f(x) = (1 - x)^6$ **b.** $f(x) = \dfrac{2}{1 - x}$
    c. $f(x) = \dfrac{1}{\sqrt{1 + x}}$ **d.** $f(x) = \sqrt{2 + x^2}$
    e. $f(x) = (4 + 3x)^{1/3}$ **f.** $f(x) = \sqrt[3]{\left(1 - \dfrac{1}{2 + x}\right)^2}$
17. **Faster than a calculator** Use the approximation $(1 + x)^k \approx 1 + kx$ to estimate the following.
    a. $(1.0002)^{50}$ **b.** $\sqrt[3]{1.009}$
18. Find the linearization of $f(x) = \sqrt{x + 1} + \sin x$ at $x = 0$. How is it related to the individual linearizations of $\sqrt{x + 1}$ and $\sin x$ at $x = 0$?

Derivatives in Differential Form

In Exercises 19–38, find dy.

19. $y = x^3 - 3\sqrt{x}$
20. $y = x\sqrt{1 - x^2}$
21. $y = \dfrac{2x}{1 + x^2}$
22. $y = \dfrac{2\sqrt{x}}{3(1 + \sqrt{x})}$
23. $2y^{3/2} + xy - x = 0$
24. $xy^2 - 4x^{3/2} - y = 0$
25. $y = \sin(5\sqrt{x})$
26. $y = \cos(x^2)$
27. $y = 4\tan(x^3/3)$
28. $y = \sec(x^2 - 1)$
29. $y = 3\csc(1 - 2\sqrt{x})$
30. $y = 2\cot\left(\dfrac{1}{\sqrt{x}}\right)$
31. $y = e^{\sqrt{x}}$
32. $y = xe^{-x}$
33. $y = \ln(1 + x^2)$
34. $y = \ln\left(\dfrac{x + 1}{\sqrt{x - 1}}\right)$
35. $y = \tan^{-1}(e^{x^2})$
36. $y = \cot^{-1}\left(\dfrac{1}{x^2}\right) + \cos^{-1} 2x$
37. $y = \sec^{-1}(e^{-x})$
38. $y = e^{\tan^{-1}\sqrt{x^2+1}}$

Approximation Error

In Exercises 39–44, each function $f(x)$ changes value when x changes from x_0 to $x_0 + dx$. Find

a. the change $\Delta f = f(x_0 + dx) - f(x_0)$;

b. the value of the estimate $df = f'(x_0)\,dx$; and

c. the approximation error $|\Delta f - df|$.

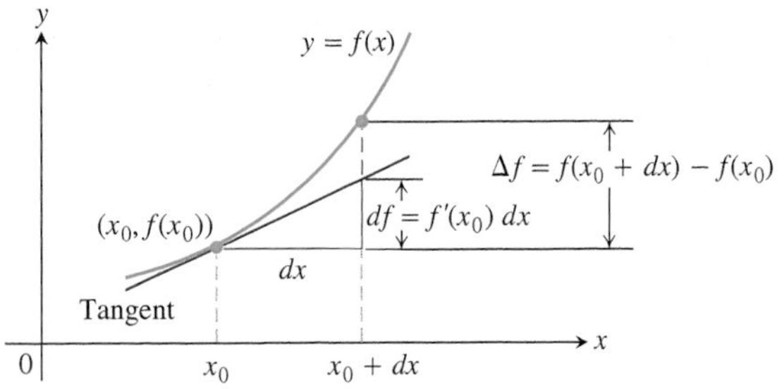

39. $f(x) = x^2 + 2x, \quad x_0 = 1, \quad dx = 0.1$
40. $f(x) = 2x^2 + 4x - 3, \quad x_0 = -1, \quad dx = 0.1$
41. $f(x) = x^3 - x, \quad x_0 = 1, \quad dx = 0.1$
42. $f(x) = x^4, \quad x_0 = 1, \quad dx = 0.1$
43. $f(x) = x^{-1}, \quad x_0 = 0.5, \quad dx = 0.1$
44. $f(x) = x^3 - 2x + 3, \quad x_0 = 2, \quad dx = 0.1$

Differential Estimates of Change

In Exercises 45–50, write a differential formula that estimates the given change in volume or surface area.

45. The change in the volume $V = (4/3)\pi r^3$ of a sphere when the radius changes from r_0 to $r_0 + dr$
46. The change in the volume $V = x^3$ of a cube when the edge lengths change from x_0 to $x_0 + dx$
47. The change in the surface area $S = 6x^2$ of a cube when the edge lengths change from x_0 to $x_0 + dx$
48. The change in the lateral surface area $S = \pi r\sqrt{r^2 + h^2}$ of a right circular cone when the radius changes from r_0 to $r_0 + dr$ and the height does not change
49. The change in the volume $V = \pi r^2 h$ of a right circular cylinder when the radius changes from r_0 to $r_0 + dr$ and the height does not change
50. The change in the lateral surface area $S = 2\pi rh$ of a right circular cylinder when the height changes from h_0 to $h_0 + dh$ and the radius does not change

Applications

51. The radius of a circle is increased from 2.00 to 2.02 m.
    a. Estimate the resulting change in area.
    b. Express the estimate as a percentage of the circle's original area.
52. The diameter of a tree was 10 in. During the following year, the circumference increased 2 in. About how much did the tree's diameter increase? The tree's cross-section area?
53. **Estimating volume** Estimate the volume of material in a cylindrical shell with length 30 in., radius 6 in., and shell thickness 0.5 in.

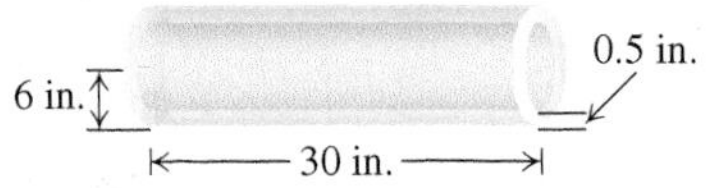

54. **Estimating height of a building** A surveyor, standing 30 ft from the base of a building, measures the angle of elevation to the top of the building to be 75°. How accurately must the angle be measured for the percentage error in estimating the height of the building to be less than 4%?
55. **Tolerance** The radius r of a circle is measured with an error of at most 2%. What is the maximum corresponding percentage error in computing the circle's
    a. circumference?
    b. area?
56. **Tolerance** The edge x of a cube is measured with an error of at most 0.5%. What is the maximum corresponding percentage error in computing the cube's
    a. surface area?
    b. volume?
57. **Tolerance** The height and radius of a right circular cylinder are equal, so the cylinder's volume is $V = \pi h^3$. The volume is to be calculated with an error of no more than 1% of the true value. Find approximately the greatest error that can be tolerated in the measurement of h, expressed as a percentage of h.
58. **Tolerance**
    a. About how accurately must the interior diameter of a 10-m-high cylindrical storage tank be measured to calculate the tank's volume to within 1% of its true value?
    b. About how accurately must the tank's exterior diameter be measured to calculate the amount of paint it will take to paint the side of the tank to within 5% of the true amount?
59. The diameter of a sphere is measured as 100 ± 1 cm and the volume is calculated from this measurement. Estimate the percentage error in the volume calculation.
60. Estimate the allowable percentage error in measuring the diameter D of a sphere if the volume is to be calculated correctly to within 3%.
61. **The effect of flight maneuvers on the heart** The amount of work done by the heart's main pumping chamber, the left ventricle, is given by the equation

$$W = PV + \frac{V\delta v^2}{2g},$$

where W is the work per unit time, P is the average blood pressure, V is the volume of blood pumped out during the unit of time, δ ("delta") is the weight density of the blood, v is the average velocity of the exiting blood, and g is the acceleration of gravity.

When P, V, δ, and v remain constant, W becomes a function of g, and the equation takes the simplified form

$$W = a + \frac{b}{g} \quad (a, b \text{ constant}).$$

As a member of NASA's medical team, you want to know how sensitive W is to apparent changes in g caused by flight maneuvers, and this depends on the initial value of g. As part of your investigation, you decide to compare the effect on W of a given change dg on the moon, where $g = 5.2$ ft/sec^2, with the effect the same change dg would have on Earth, where $g = 32$ ft/sec^2. Use the simplified equation above to find the ratio of dW_{moon} to dW_{Earth}.

62. **Measuring acceleration of gravity** When the length L of a clock pendulum is held constant by controlling its temperature, the pendulum's period T depends on the acceleration of gravity g. The period will therefore vary slightly as the clock is moved from place to place on the earth's surface, depending on the change in g. By keeping track of ΔT, we can estimate the variation in g from the equation $T = 2\pi(L/g)^{1/2}$ that relates T, g, and L.
   a. With L held constant and g as the independent variable, calculate dT and use it to answer parts (b) and (c).
   b. If g increases, will T increase or decrease? Will a pendulum clock speed up or slow down? Explain.
   c. A clock with a 100-cm pendulum is moved from a location where $g = 980$ cm/sec^2 to a new location. This increases the period by $dT = 0.001$ sec. Find dg and estimate the value of g at the new location.

63. **The linearization is the best linear approximation** Suppose that $y = f(x)$ is differentiable at $x = a$ and that $g(x) = m(x - a) + c$ is a linear function in which m and c are constants. If the error $E(x) = f(x) - g(x)$ were small enough near $x = a$, we might think of using g as a linear approximation of f instead of the linearization $L(x) = f(a) + f'(a)(x - a)$. Show that if we impose on g the conditions
   1. $E(a) = 0$ — The approximation error is zero at $x = a$.
   2. $\lim_{x \to a} \frac{E(x)}{x - a} = 0$ — The error is negligible when compared with $x - a$.

   then $g(x) = f(a) + f'(a)(x - a)$. Thus, the linearization $L(x)$ gives the only linear approximation whose error is both zero at $x = a$ and negligible in comparison with $x - a$.

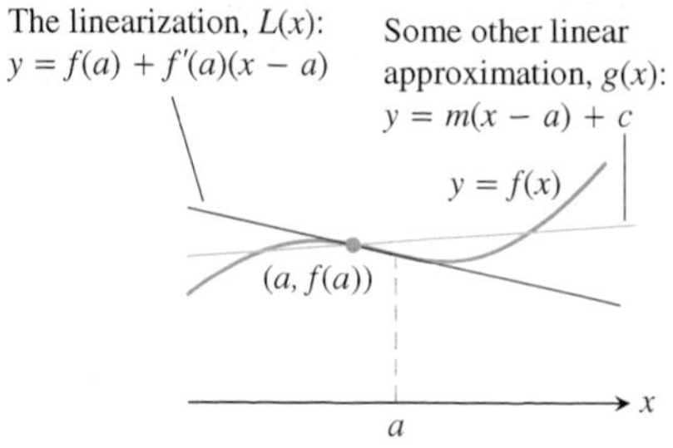

64. **Quadratic approximations**
   a. Let $Q(x) = b_0 + b_1(x - a) + b_2(x - a)^2$ be a quadratic approximation to $f(x)$ at $x = a$ with the properties:
      i) $Q(a) = f(a)$
      ii) $Q'(a) = f'(a)$
      iii) $Q''(a) = f''(a)$.

      Determine the coefficients b_0, b_1, and b_2.
   b. Find the quadratic approximation to $f(x) = 1/(1 - x)$ at $x = 0$.
   T c. Graph $f(x) = 1/(1 - x)$ and its quadratic approximation at $x = 0$. Then zoom in on the two graphs at the point (0, 1). Comment on what you see.
   T d. Find the quadratic approximation to $g(x) = 1/x$ at $x = 1$. Graph g and its quadratic approximation together. Comment on what you see.
   T e. Find the quadratic approximation to $h(x) = \sqrt{1 + x}$ at $x = 0$. Graph h and its quadratic approximation together. Comment on what you see.
   f. What are the linearizations of f, g, and h at the respective points in parts (b), (d), and (e)?

65. **The linearization of 2^x**
   a. Find the linearization of $f(x) = 2^x$ at $x = 0$. Then round its coefficients to two decimal places.
   T b. Graph the linearization and function together for $-3 \le x \le 3$ and $-1 \le x \le 1$.

66. **The linearization of $\log_3 x$**
   a. Find the linearization of $f(x) = \log_3 x$ at $x = 3$. Then round its coefficients to two decimal places.
   T b. Graph the linearization and function together in the window $0 \le x \le 8$ and $2 \le x \le 4$.

COMPUTER EXPLORATIONS

In Exercises 67–72, use a CAS to estimate the magnitude of the error in using the linearization in place of the function over a specified interval I. Perform the following steps:

a. Plot the function f over I.
b. Find the linearization L of the function at the point a.
c. Plot f and L together on a single graph.
d. Plot the absolute error $|f(x) - L(x)|$ over I and find its maximum value.
e. From your graph in part (d), estimate as large a $\delta > 0$ as you can, satisfying

$$|x - a| < \delta \quad \Rightarrow \quad |f(x) - L(x)| < \epsilon$$

for $\epsilon = 0.5$, 0.1, and 0.01. Then check graphically to see if your δ-estimate holds true.

67. $f(x) = x^3 + x^2 - 2x, \quad [-1, 2], \quad a = 1$

68. $f(x) = \frac{x - 1}{4x^2 + 1}, \quad \left[-\frac{3}{4}, 1\right], \quad a = \frac{1}{2}$

69. $f(x) = x^{2/3}(x - 2), \quad [-2, 3], \quad a = 2$

70. $f(x) = \sqrt{x} - \sin x, \quad [0, 2\pi], \quad a = 2$

71. $f(x) = x2^x, \quad [0, 2], \quad a = 1$

72. $f(x) = \sqrt{x}\sin^{-1} x, \quad [0, 1], \quad a = \frac{1}{2}$

Chapter Questions to Guide Your Review

1. What is the derivative of a function f? How is its domain related to the domain of f? Give examples.
2. What role does the derivative play in defining slopes, tangents, and rates of change?
3. How can you sometimes graph the derivative of a function when all you have is a table of the function's values?
4. What does it mean for a function to be differentiable on an open interval? On a closed interval?
5. How are derivatives and one-sided derivatives related?
6. Describe geometrically when a function typically does *not* have a derivative at a point.
7. How is a function's differentiability at a point related to its continuity there, if at all?
8. What rules do you know for calculating derivatives? Give some examples.
9. Explain how the three formulas
   a. $\dfrac{d}{dx}(x^n) = nx^{n-1}$
   b. $\dfrac{d}{dx}(cu) = c\dfrac{du}{dx}$
   c. $\dfrac{d}{dx}(u_1 + u_2 + \cdots + u_n) = \dfrac{du_1}{dx} + \dfrac{du_2}{dx} + \cdots + \dfrac{du_n}{dx}$

   enable us to differentiate any polynomial.
10. What formula do we need, in addition to the three listed in Question 9, to differentiate rational functions?
11. What is a second derivative? A third derivative? How many derivatives do the functions you know have? Give examples.
12. What is the derivative of the exponential function e^x? How does the domain of the derivative compare with the domain of the function?
13. What is the relationship between a function's average and instantaneous rates of change? Give an example.
14. How do derivatives arise in the study of motion? What can you learn about a body's motion along a line by examining the derivatives of the body's position function? Give examples.
15. How can derivatives arise in economics?
16. Give examples of still other applications of derivatives.
17. What do the limits $\lim_{h\to 0}((\sin h)/h)$ and $\lim_{h\to 0}((\cos h - 1)/h)$ have to do with the derivatives of the sine and cosine functions? What *are* the derivatives of these functions?
18. Once you know the derivatives of $\sin x$ and $\cos x$, how can you find the derivatives of $\tan x$, $\cot x$, $\sec x$, and $\csc x$? What *are* the derivatives of these functions?
19. At what points are the six basic trigonometric functions continuous? How do you know?
20. What is the rule for calculating the derivative of a composite of two differentiable functions? How is such a derivative evaluated? Give examples.
21. If u is a differentiable function of x, how do you find $(d/dx)(u^n)$ if n is an integer? If n is a real number? Give examples.
22. What is implicit differentiation? When do you need it? Give examples.
23. What is the derivative of the natural logarithm function $\ln x$? How does the domain of the derivative compare with the domain of the function?
24. What is the derivative of the exponential function a^x, $a > 0$ and $a \neq 1$? What is the geometric significance of the limit of $(a^h - 1)/h$ as $h \to 0$? What is the limit when a is the number e?
25. What is the derivative of $\log_a x$? Are there any restrictions on a?
26. What is logarithmic differentiation? Give an example.
27. How can you write any real power of x as a power of e? Are there any restrictions on x? How does this lead to the Power Rule for differentiating arbitrary real powers?
28. What is one way of expressing the special number e as a limit? What is an approximate numerical value of e correct to 7 decimal places?
29. What are the derivatives of the inverse trigonometric functions? How do the domains of the derivatives compare with the domains of the functions?
30. How do related rates problems arise? Give examples.
31. Outline a strategy for solving related rates problems. Illustrate with an example.
32. What is the linearization $L(x)$ of a function $f(x)$ at a point $x = a$? What is required of f at a for the linearization to exist? How are linearizations used? Give examples.
33. If x moves from a to a nearby value $a + dx$, how do you estimate the corresponding change in the value of a differentiable function $f(x)$? How do you estimate the relative change? The percentage change? Give an example.

Chapter Practice Exercises

Derivatives of Functions

Find the derivatives of the functions in Exercises 1–64.

1. $y = x^5 - 0.125x^2 + 0.25x$
2. $y = 3 - 0.7x^3 + 0.3x^7$
3. $y = x^3 - 3(x^2 + \pi^2)$
4. $y = x^7 + \sqrt{7x} - \dfrac{1}{\pi + 1}$
5. $y = (x + 1)^2(x^2 + 2x)$
6. $y = (2x - 5)(4 - x)^{-1}$
7. $y = (\theta^2 + \sec\theta + 1)^3$
8. $y = \left(-1 - \dfrac{\csc\theta}{2} - \dfrac{\theta^2}{4}\right)^2$
9. $s = \dfrac{\sqrt{t}}{1 + \sqrt{t}}$
10. $s = \dfrac{1}{\sqrt{t} - 1}$
11. $y = 2\tan^2 x - \sec^2 x$
12. $y = \dfrac{1}{\sin^2 x} - \dfrac{2}{\sin x}$

13. $s = \cos^4(1 - 2t)$

14. $s = \cot^3\left(\frac{2}{t}\right)$

15. $s = (\sec t + \tan t)^5$

16. $s = \csc^5(1 - t + 3t^2)$

17. $r = \sqrt{2\theta \sin \theta}$

18. $r = 2\theta\sqrt{\cos \theta}$

19. $r = \sin \sqrt{2\theta}$

20. $r = \sin\left(\theta + \sqrt{\theta + 1}\right)$

21. $y = \frac{1}{2}x^2 \csc \frac{2}{x}$

22. $y = 2\sqrt{x} \sin \sqrt{x}$

23. $y = x^{-1/2} \sec (2x)^2$

24. $y = \sqrt{x} \csc (x + 1)^3$

25. $y = 5 \cot x^2$

26. $y = x^2 \cot 5x$

27. $y = x^2 \sin^2(2x^2)$

28. $y = x^{-2} \sin^2(x^3)$

29. $s = \left(\frac{4t}{t + 1}\right)^{-2}$

30. $s = \frac{-1}{15(15t - 1)^3}$

31. $y = \left(\frac{\sqrt{x}}{1 + x}\right)^2$

32. $y = \left(\frac{2\sqrt{x}}{2\sqrt{x} + 1}\right)^2$

33. $y = \sqrt{\frac{x^2 + x}{x^2}}$

34. $y = 4x\sqrt{x + \sqrt{x}}$

35. $r = \left(\frac{\sin \theta}{\cos \theta - 1}\right)^2$

36. $r = \left(\frac{1 + \sin \theta}{1 - \cos \theta}\right)^2$

37. $y = (2x + 1)\sqrt{2x + 1}$

38. $y = 20(3x - 4)^{1/4}(3x - 4)^{-1/5}$

39. $y = \frac{3}{(5x^2 + \sin 2x)^{3/2}}$

40. $y = (3 + \cos^3 3x)^{-1/3}$

41. $y = 10e^{-x/5}$

42. $y = \sqrt{2}e^{\sqrt{2}x}$

43. $y = \frac{1}{4}xe^{4x} - \frac{1}{16}e^{4x}$

44. $y = x^2e^{-2/x}$

45. $y = \ln(\sin^2 \theta)$

46. $y = \ln(\sec^2 \theta)$

47. $y = \log_2(x^2/2)$

48. $y = \log_5(3x - 7)$

49. $y = 8^{-t}$

50. $y = 9^{2t}$

51. $y = 5x^{3.6}$

52. $y = \sqrt{2}x^{-\sqrt{2}}$

53. $y = (x + 2)^{x+2}$

54. $y = 2(\ln x)^{x/2}$

55. $y = \sin^{-1}\sqrt{1 - u^2}, \quad 0 < u < 1$

56. $y = \sin^{-1}\left(\frac{1}{\sqrt{v}}\right), \quad v > 1$

57. $y = \ln \cos^{-1} x$

58. $y = z \cos^{-1} z - \sqrt{1 - z^2}$

59. $y = t \tan^{-1} t - \frac{1}{2}\ln t$

60. $y = (1 + t^2) \cot^{-1} 2t$

61. $y = z \sec^{-1} z - \sqrt{z^2 - 1}, \quad z > 1$

62. $y = 2\sqrt{x - 1}\, \sec^{-1}\sqrt{x}$

63. $y = \csc^{-1}(\sec \theta), \quad 0 < \theta < \pi/2$

64. $y = (1 + x^2)e^{\tan^{-1} x}$

Implicit Differentiation

In Exercises 65–78, find dy/dx by implicit differentiation.

65. $xy + 2x + 3y = 1$

66. $x^2 + xy + y^2 - 5x = 2$

67. $x^3 + 4xy - 3y^{4/3} = 2x$

68. $5x^{4/5} + 10y^{6/5} = 15$

69. $\sqrt{xy} = 1$

70. $x^2y^2 = 1$

71. $y^2 = \frac{x}{x + 1}$

72. $y^2 = \sqrt{\frac{1 + x}{1 - x}}$

73. $e^{x+2y} = 1$

74. $y^2 = 2e^{-1/x}$

75. $\ln(x/y) = 1$

76. $x \sin^{-1} y = 1 + x^2$

77. $ye^{\tan^{-1} x} = 2$

78. $x^y = \sqrt{2}$

In Exercises 79 and 80, find dp/dq.

79. $p^3 + 4pq - 3q^2 = 2$

80. $q = (5p^2 + 2p)^{-3/2}$

In Exercises 81 and 82, find dr/ds.

81. $r \cos 2s + \sin^2 s = \pi$

82. $2rs - r - s + s^2 = -3$

83. Find d^2y/dx^2 by implicit differentiation:

a. $x^3 + y^3 = 1$ **b.** $y^2 = 1 - \frac{2}{x}$

84. a. By differentiating $x^2 - y^2 = 1$ implicitly, show that $dy/dx = x/y$.

b. Then show that $d^2y/dx^2 = -1/y^3$.

Numerical Values of Derivatives

85. Suppose that functions $f(x)$ and $g(x)$ and their first derivatives have the following values at $x = 0$ and $x = 1$.

x	$f(x)$	$g(x)$	$f'(x)$	$g'(x)$
0	1	1	-3	$1/2$
1	3	5	$1/2$	-4

Find the first derivatives of the following combinations at the given value of x.

a. $6f(x) - g(x), \quad x = 1$ **b.** $f(x)g^2(x), \quad x = 0$

c. $\frac{f(x)}{g(x) + 1}, \quad x = 1$ **d.** $f(g(x)), \quad x = 0$

e. $g(f(x)), \quad x = 0$ **f.** $(x + f(x))^{3/2}, \quad x = 1$

g. $f(x + g(x)), \quad x = 0$

86. Suppose that the function $f(x)$ and its first derivative have the following values at $x = 0$ and $x = 1$.

x	$f(x)$	$f'(x)$
0	9	-2
1	-3	$1/5$

Find the first derivatives of the following combinations at the given value of x.

a. $\sqrt{x}\, f(x), \quad x = 1$ **b.** $\sqrt{f(x)}, \quad x = 0$

c. $f(\sqrt{x}), \quad x = 1$ **d.** $f(1 - 5 \tan x), \quad x = 0$

e. $\frac{f(x)}{2 + \cos x}, \quad x = 0$ **f.** $10 \sin\left(\frac{\pi x}{2}\right) f^2(x), \quad x = 1$

87. Find the value of dy/dt at $t = 0$ if $y = 3 \sin 2x$ and $x = t^2 + \pi$.

88. Find the value of ds/du at $u = 2$ if $s = t^2 + 5t$ and $t = (u^2 + 2u)^{1/3}$.

89. Find the value of dw/ds at $s = 0$ if $w = \sin\left(e^{\sqrt{r}}\right)$ and $r = 3 \sin(s + \pi/6)$.

90. Find the value of dr/dt at $t = 0$ if $r = (\theta^2 + 7)^{1/3}$ and $\theta^2 t + \theta = 1$.

91. If $y^3 + y = 2\cos x$, find the value of d^2y/dx^2 at the point (0, 1).

92. If $x^{1/3} + y^{1/3} = 4$, find d^2y/dx^2 at the point (8, 8).

Applying the Derivative Definition

In Exercises 93 and 94, find the derivative using the definition.

93. $f(t) = \dfrac{1}{2t + 1}$

94. $g(x) = 2x^2 + 1$

95. a. Graph the function

$$f(x) = \begin{cases} x^2, & -1 \le x < 0 \\ -x^2, & 0 \le x \le 1. \end{cases}$$

b. Is f continuous at $x = 0$?

c. Is f differentiable at $x = 0$?

Give reasons for your answers.

96. a. Graph the function

$$f(x) = \begin{cases} x, & -1 \le x < 0 \\ \tan x, & 0 \le x \le \pi/4. \end{cases}$$

b. Is f continuous at $x = 0$?

c. Is f differentiable at $x = 0$?

Give reasons for your answers.

97. a. Graph the function

$$f(x) = \begin{cases} x, & 0 \le x \le 1 \\ 2 - x, & 1 < x \le 2. \end{cases}$$

b. Is f continuous at $x = 1$?

c. Is f differentiable at $x = 1$?

Give reasons for your answers.

98. For what value or values of the constant m, if any, is

$$f(x) = \begin{cases} \sin 2x, & x \le 0 \\ mx, & x > 0 \end{cases}$$

a. continuous at $x = 0$?

b. differentiable at $x = 0$?

Give reasons for your answers.

Slopes, Tangents, and Normals

99. Tangents with specified slope Are there any points on the curve $y = (x/2) + 1/(2x - 4)$ where the slope is $-3/2$? If so, find them.

100. Tangents with specified slope Are there any points on the curve $y = x - e^{-x}$ where the slope is 2? If so, find them.

101. Horizontal tangents Find the points on the curve $y = 2x^3 - 3x^2 - 12x + 20$ where the tangent is parallel to the x-axis.

102. Tangent intercepts Find the x- and y-intercepts of the line that is tangent to the curve $y = x^3$ at the point $(-2, -8)$.

103. Tangents perpendicular or parallel to lines Find the points on the curve $y = 2x^3 - 3x^2 - 12x + 20$ where the tangent is

a. perpendicular to the line $y = 1 - (x/24)$.

b. parallel to the line $y = \sqrt{2} - 12x$.

104. Intersecting tangents Show that the tangents to the curve $y = (\pi \sin x)/x$ at $x = \pi$ and $x = -\pi$ intersect at right angles.

105. Normals parallel to a line Find the points on the curve $y = \tan x$, $-\pi/2 < x < \pi/2$, where the normal is parallel to the line $y = -x/2$. Sketch the curve and normals together, labeling each with its equation.

106. Tangent and normal lines Find equations for the tangent and normal to the curve $y = 1 + \cos x$ at the point $(\pi/2, 1)$. Sketch the curve, tangent, and normal together, labeling each with its equation.

107. Tangent parabola The parabola $y = x^2 + C$ is to be tangent to the line $y = x$. Find C.

108. Slope of tangent Show that the tangent to the curve $y = x^3$ at any point (a, a^3) meets the curve again at a point where the slope is four times the slope at (a, a^3).

109. Tangent curve For what value of c is the curve $y = c/(x + 1)$ tangent to the line through the points $(0, 3)$ and $(5, -2)$?

110. Normal to a circle Show that the normal line at any point of the circle $x^2 + y^2 = a^2$ passes through the origin.

In Exercises 111–116, find equations for the lines that are tangent and normal to the curve at the given point.

111. $x^2 + 2y^2 = 9, \quad (1, 2)$

112. $e^x + y^2 = 2, \quad (0, 1)$

113. $xy + 2x - 5y = 2, \quad (3, 2)$

114. $(y - x)^2 = 2x + 4, \quad (6, 2)$

115. $x + \sqrt{xy} = 6, \quad (4, 1)$

116. $x^{3/2} + 2y^{3/2} = 17, \quad (1, 4)$

117. Find the slope of the curve $x^3y^3 + y^2 = x + y$ at the points $(1, 1)$ and $(1, -1)$.

118. The graph shown suggests that the curve $y = \sin(x - \sin x)$ might have horizontal tangents at the x-axis. Does it? Give reasons for your answer.

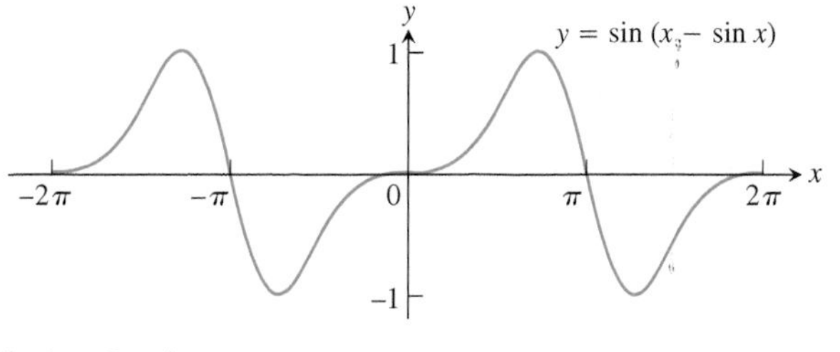

Analyzing Graphs

Each of the figures in Exercises 119 and 120 shows two graphs, the graph of a function $y = f(x)$ together with the graph of its derivative $f'(x)$. Which graph is which? How do you know?

119.

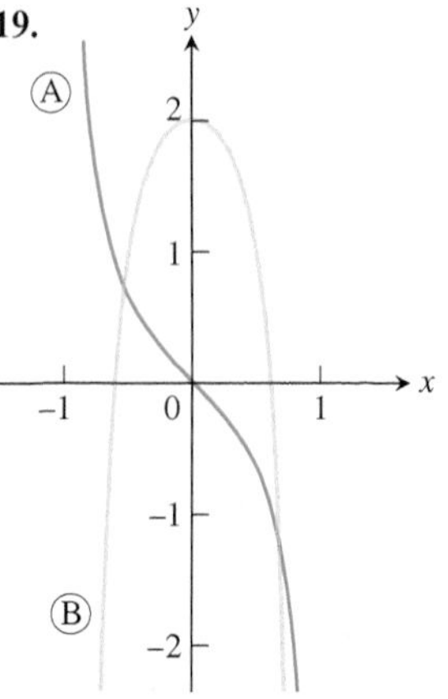

120.

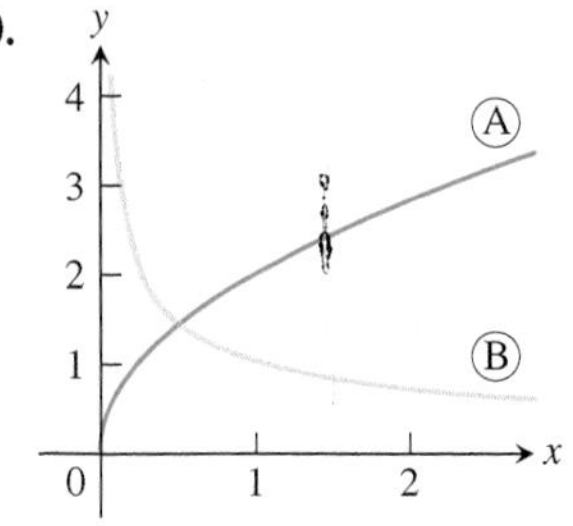

121. Use the following information to graph the function $y = f(x)$ for $-1 \le x \le 6$.

i) The graph of f is made of line segments joined end to end.

ii) The graph starts at the point $(-1, 2)$.

iii) The derivative of f, where defined, agrees with the step function shown here.

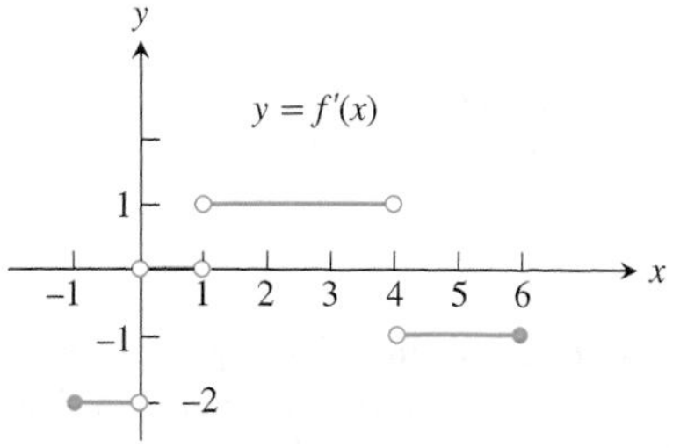

122. Repeat Exercise 121, supposing that the graph starts at $(-1, 0)$ instead of $(-1, 2)$.

Exercises 123 and 124 are about the accompanying graphs. The graphs in part (a) show the numbers of rabbits and foxes in a small arctic population. They are plotted as functions of time for 200 days. The number of rabbits increases at first, as the rabbits reproduce. But the foxes prey on rabbits and, as the number of foxes increases, the rabbit population levels off and then drops. Part (b) shows the graph of the derivative of the rabbit population, made by plotting slopes.

123. a. What is the value of the derivative of the rabbit population when the number of rabbits is largest? Smallest?

b. What is the size of the rabbit population when its derivative is largest? Smallest (negative value)?

124. In what units should the slopes of the rabbit and fox population curves be measured?

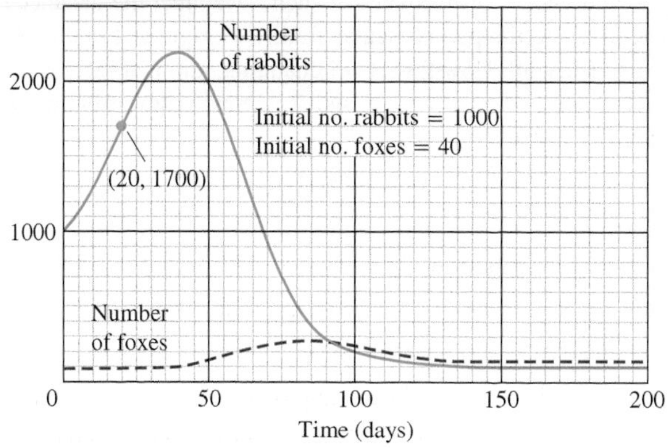

(a)

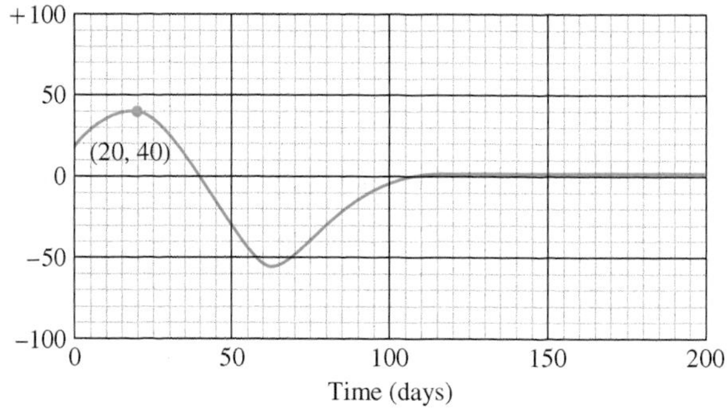

Derivative of the rabbit population

(b)

Trigonometric Limits

Find the limits in Exercises 125–132.

125. $\lim_{x \to 0} \dfrac{\sin x}{2x^2 - x}$

126. $\lim_{x \to 0} \dfrac{3x - \tan 7x}{2x}$

127. $\lim_{r \to 0} \dfrac{\sin r}{\tan 2r}$

128. $\lim_{\theta \to 0} \dfrac{\sin(\sin \theta)}{\theta}$

129. $\lim_{\theta \to (\pi/2)^-} \dfrac{4\tan^2\theta + \tan\theta + 1}{\tan^2\theta + 5}$

130. $\lim_{\theta \to 0^+} \dfrac{1 - 2\cot^2\theta}{5\cot^2\theta - 7\cot\theta - 8}$

131. $\lim_{x \to 0} \dfrac{x \sin x}{2 - 2\cos x}$

132. $\lim_{\theta \to 0} \dfrac{1 - \cos\theta}{\theta^2}$

Show how to extend the functions in Exercises 133 and 134 to be continuous at the origin.

133. $g(x) = \dfrac{\tan(\tan x)}{\tan x}$

134. $f(x) = \dfrac{\tan(\tan x)}{\sin(\sin x)}$

Logarithmic Differentiation

In Exercises 135–140, use logarithmic differentiation to find the derivative of y with respect to the appropriate variable.

135. $y = \dfrac{2(x^2 + 1)}{\sqrt{\cos 2x}}$

136. $y = \sqrt[10]{\dfrac{3x + 4}{2x - 4}}$

137. $y = \left(\dfrac{(t + 1)(t - 1)}{(t - 2)(t + 3)}\right)^5, \quad t > 2$

138. $y = \dfrac{2u2^u}{\sqrt{u^2 + 1}}$

139. $y = (\sin\theta)^{\sqrt{\theta}}$

140. $y = (\ln x)^{1/(\ln x)}$

Related Rates

141. Right circular cylinder The total surface area S of a right circular cylinder is related to the base radius r and height h by the equation $S = 2\pi r^2 + 2\pi rh$.

a. How is dS/dt related to dr/dt if h is constant?

b. How is dS/dt related to dh/dt if r is constant?

c. How is dS/dt related to dr/dt and dh/dt if neither r nor h is constant?

d. How is dr/dt related to dh/dt if S is constant?

142. Right circular cone The lateral surface area S of a right circular cone is related to the base radius r and height h by the equation $S = \pi r\sqrt{r^2 + h^2}$.

a. How is dS/dt related to dr/dt if h is constant?

b. How is dS/dt related to dh/dt if r is constant?

c. How is dS/dt related to dr/dt and dh/dt if neither r nor h is constant?

143. Circle's changing area The radius of a circle is changing at the rate of $-2/\pi$ m/sec. At what rate is the circle's area changing when $r = 10$ m?

144. Cube's changing edges The volume of a cube is increasing at the rate of $1200 \text{ cm}^3/\text{min}$ at the instant its edges are 20 cm long. At what rate are the lengths of the edges changing at that instant?

145. Resistors connected in parallel If two resistors of R_1 and R_2 ohms are connected in parallel in an electric circuit to make an R-ohm resistor, the value of R can be found from the equation

$$\frac{1}{R} = \frac{1}{R_1} + \frac{1}{R_2}.$$

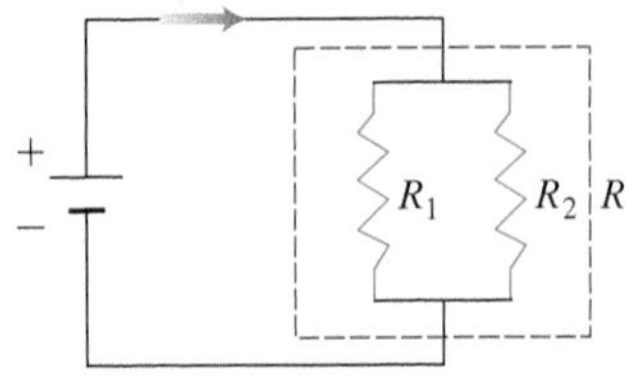

If R_1 is decreasing at the rate of 1 ohm/sec and R_2 is increasing at the rate of 0.5 ohm/sec, at what rate is R changing when $R_1 = 75$ ohms and $R_2 = 50$ ohms?

146. Impedance in a series circuit The impedance Z (ohms) in a series circuit is related to the resistance R (ohms) and reactance X (ohms) by the equation $Z = \sqrt{R^2 + X^2}$. If R is increasing at 3 ohms/sec and X is decreasing at 2 ohms/sec, at what rate is Z changing when $R = 10$ ohms and $X = 20$ ohms?

147. Speed of moving particle The coordinates of a particle moving in the metric xy-plane are differentiable functions of time t with $dx/dt = 10$ m/sec and $dy/dt = 5$ m/sec. How fast is the particle moving away from the origin as it passes through the point $(3, -4)$?

148. Motion of a particle A particle moves along the curve $y = x^{3/2}$ in the first quadrant in such a way that its distance from the origin increases at the rate of 11 units per second. Find dx/dt when $x = 3$.

149. Draining a tank Water drains from the conical tank shown in the accompanying figure at the rate of 5 ft^3/min.

a. What is the relation between the variables h and r in the figure?

b. How fast is the water level dropping when $h = 6$ ft?

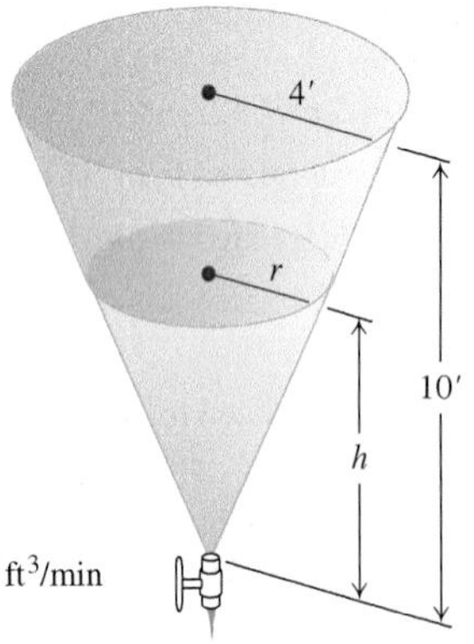

150. Rotating spool As television cable is pulled from a large spool to be strung from the telephone poles along a street, it unwinds from the spool in layers of constant radius (see accompanying figure). If the truck pulling the cable moves at a steady 6 ft/sec (a touch over 4 mph), use the equation $s = r\theta$ to find how fast (radians per second) the spool is turning when the layer of radius 1.2 ft is being unwound.

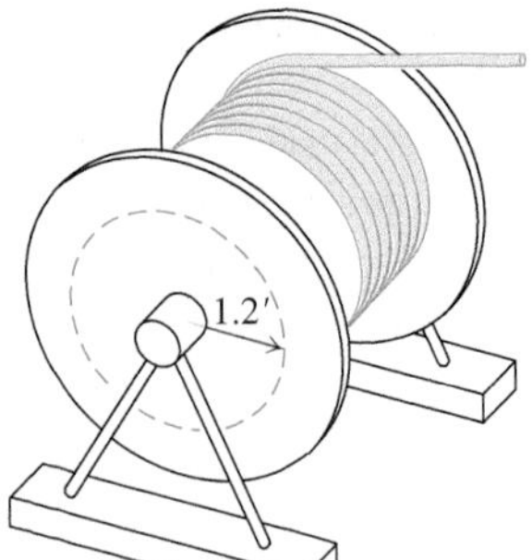

151. Moving searchlight beam The figure shows a boat 1 km offshore, sweeping the shore with a searchlight. The light turns at a constant rate, $d\theta/dt = -0.6$ rad/sec.

a. How fast is the light moving along the shore when it reaches point A?

b. How many revolutions per minute is 0.6 rad/sec?

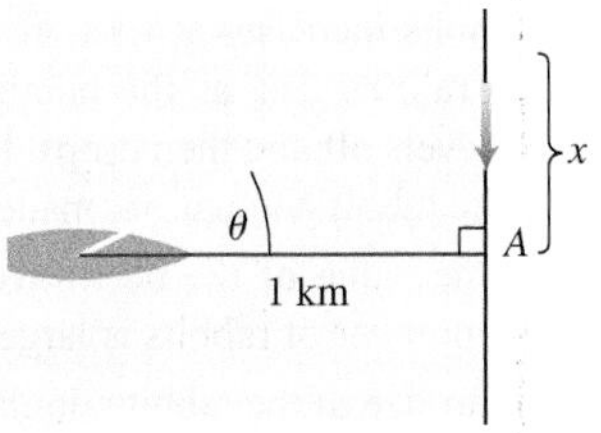

152. Points moving on coordinate axes Points A and B move along the x- and y-axes, respectively, in such a way that the distance r (meters) along the perpendicular from the origin to the line AB remains constant. How fast is OA changing, and is it increasing, or decreasing, when $OB = 2r$ and B is moving toward O at the rate of $0.3r$ m/sec?

Linearization

153. Find the linearizations of

a. $\tan x$ at $x = -\pi/4$ b. $\sec x$ at $x = -\pi/4$.

Graph the curves and linearizations together.

154. We can obtain a useful linear approximation of the function $f(x) = 1/(1 + \tan x)$ at $x = 0$ by combining the approximations

$$\frac{1}{1+x} \approx 1 - x \quad \text{and} \quad \tan x \approx x$$

to get

$$\frac{1}{1 + \tan x} \approx 1 - x.$$

Show that this result is the standard linear approximation of $1/(1 + \tan x)$ at $x = 0$.

155. Find the linearization of $f(x) = \sqrt{1 + x} + \sin x - 0.5$ at $x = 0$.

156. Find the linearization of $f(x) = 2/(1 - x) + \sqrt{1 + x} - 3.1$ at $x = 0$.

Differential Estimates of Change

157. Surface area of a cone Write a formula that estimates the change that occurs in the lateral surface area of a right circular cone when the height changes from h_0 to $h_0 + dh$ and the radius does not change.

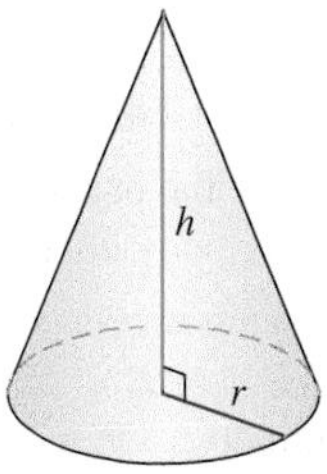

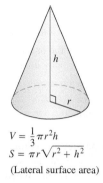

$$V = \frac{1}{3}\pi r^2 h$$
$$S = \pi r \sqrt{r^2 + h^2}$$
(Lateral surface area)

158. Controlling error

a. How accurately should you measure the edge of a cube to be reasonably sure of calculating the cube's surface area with an error of no more than 2%?

b. Suppose that the edge is measured with the accuracy required in part (a). About how accurately can the cube's volume be calculated from the edge measurement? To find out, estimate the percentage error in the volume calculation that might result from using the edge measurement.

159. Compounding error The circumference of the equator of a sphere is measured as 10 cm with a possible error of 0.4 cm. This measurement is used to calculate the radius. The radius is then used to calculate the surface area and volume of the sphere. Estimate the percentage errors in the calculated values of

a. the radius.

b. the surface area.

c. the volume.

160. Finding height To find the height of a lamppost (see accompanying figure), you stand a 6 ft pole 20 ft from the lamp and measure the length a of its shadow, finding it to be 15 ft, give or take an inch. Calculate the height of the lamppost using the value $a = 15$ and estimate the possible error in the result.

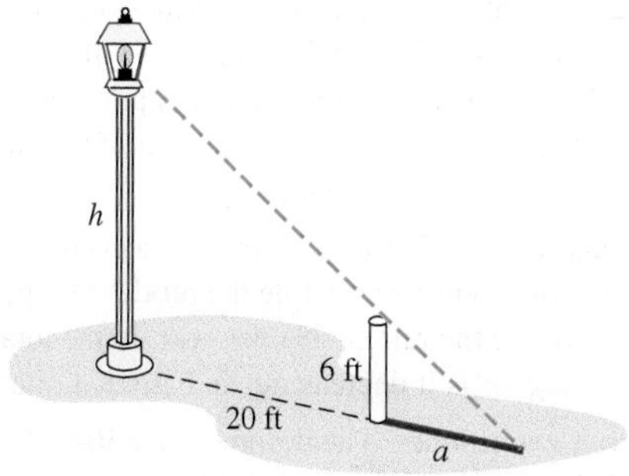

Chapter 3 Additional and Advanced Exercises

1. An equation like $\sin^2\theta + \cos^2\theta = 1$ is called an **identity** because it holds for all values of θ. An equation like $\sin\theta = 0.5$ is not an identity because it holds only for selected values of θ, not all. If you differentiate both sides of a trigonometric identity in θ with respect to θ, the resulting new equation will also be an identity.

Differentiate the following to show that the resulting equations hold for all θ.

a. $\sin 2\theta = 2\sin\theta\cos\theta$

b. $\cos 2\theta = \cos^2\theta - \sin^2\theta$

2. If the identity $\sin(x + a) = \sin x \cos a + \cos x \sin a$ is differentiated with respect to x, is the resulting equation also an identity? Does this principle apply to the equation $x^2 - 2x - 8 = 0$? Explain.

3. a. Find values for the constants a, b, and c that will make

$$f(x) = \cos x \quad \text{and} \quad g(x) = a + bx + cx^2$$

satisfy the conditions

$$f(0) = g(0), \quad f'(0) = g'(0), \quad \text{and} \quad f''(0) = g''(0).$$

b. Find values for b and c that will make

$$f(x) = \sin(x + a) \quad \text{and} \quad g(x) = b\sin x + c\cos x$$

satisfy the conditions

$$f(0) = g(0) \quad \text{and} \quad f'(0) = g'(0).$$

c. For the determined values of a, b, and c, what happens for the third and fourth derivatives of f and g in each of parts (a) and (b)?

4. Solutions to differential equations

a. Show that $y = \sin x$, $y = \cos x$, and $y = a\cos x + b\sin x$ (a and b constants) all satisfy the equation

$$y'' + y = 0.$$

b. How would you modify the functions in part (a) to satisfy the equation

$$y'' + 4y = 0?$$

Generalize this result.

5. An osculating circle Find the values of h, k, and a that make the circle $(x - h)^2 + (y - k)^2 = a^2$ tangent to the parabola $y = x^2 + 1$ at the point $(1, 2)$ and that also make the second derivatives d^2y/dx^2 have the same value on both curves there. Circles like this one that are tangent to a curve and have the same second derivative as the curve at the point of tangency are called *osculating circles* (from the Latin *osculari*, meaning "to kiss"). We encounter them again in Chapter 12.

6. **Marginal revenue** A bus will hold 60 people. The number x of people per trip who use the bus is related to the fare charged (p dollars) by the law $p = [3 - (x/40)]^2$. Write an expression for the total revenue $r(x)$ per trip received by the bus company. What number of people per trip will make the marginal revenue dr/dx equal to zero? What is the corresponding fare? (This fare is the one that maximizes the revenue, so the bus company should probably rethink its fare policy.)

7. **Industrial production**

   a. Economists often use the expression "rate of growth" in relative rather than absolute terms. For example, let $u = f(t)$ be the number of people in the labor force at time t in a given industry. (We treat this function as though it were differentiable even though it is an integer-valued step function.)

   Let $v = g(t)$ be the average production per person in the labor force at time t. The total production is then $y = uv$. If the labor force is growing at the rate of 4% per year ($du/dt = 0.04u$) and the production per worker is growing at the rate of 5% per year ($dv/dt = 0.05v$), find the rate of growth of the total production, y.

   b. Suppose that the labor force in part (a) is decreasing at the rate of 2% per year while the production per person is increasing at the rate of 3% per year. Is the total production increasing, or is it decreasing, and at what rate?

8. **Designing a gondola** The designer of a 30-ft-diameter spherical hot air balloon wants to suspend the gondola 8 ft below the bottom of the balloon with cables tangent to the surface of the balloon, as shown. Two of the cables are shown running from the top edges of the gondola to their points of tangency, $(-12, -9)$ and $(12, -9)$. How wide should the gondola be?

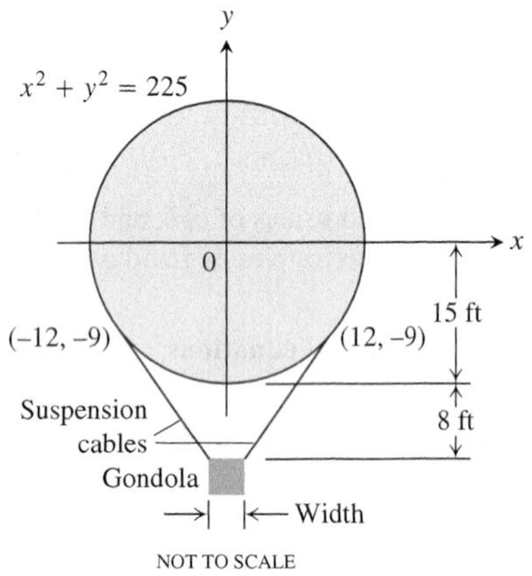

9. **Pisa by parachute** On August 5, 1988, Mike McCarthy of London jumped from the top of the Tower of Pisa. He then opened his parachute in what he said was a world record low-level parachute jump of 179 ft. Make a rough sketch to show the shape of the graph of his speed during the jump. (*Source: Boston Globe*, Aug. 6, 1988.)

10. **Motion of a particle** The position at time $t \geq 0$ of a particle moving along a coordinate line is

$$s = 10\cos(t + \pi/4).$$

   a. What is the particle's starting position ($t = 0$)?

   b. What are the points farthest to the left and right of the origin reached by the particle?

   c. Find the particle's velocity and acceleration at the points in part (b).

   d. When does the particle first reach the origin? What are its velocity, speed, and acceleration then?

11. **Shooting a paper clip** On Earth, you can easily shoot a paper clip 64 ft straight up into the air with a rubber band. In t sec after firing, the paper clip is $s = 64t - 16t^2$ ft above your hand.

   a. How long does it take the paper clip to reach its maximum height? With what velocity does it leave your hand?

   b. On the moon, the same acceleration will send the paper clip to a height of $s = 64t - 2.6t^2$ ft in t sec. About how long will it take the paper clip to reach its maximum height, and how high will it go?

12. **Velocities of two particles** At time t sec, the positions of two particles on a coordinate line are $s_1 = 3t^3 - 12t^2 + 18t + 5$ m and $s_2 = -t^3 + 9t^2 - 12t$ m. When do the particles have the same velocities?

13. **Velocity of a particle** A particle of constant mass m moves along the x-axis. Its velocity v and position x satisfy the equation

$$\frac{1}{2}m(v^2 - v_0{}^2) = \frac{1}{2}k(x_0{}^2 - x^2),$$

where k, v_0, and x_0 are constants. Show that whenever $v \neq 0$,

$$m\frac{dv}{dt} = -kx.$$

14. **Average and instantaneous velocity**

   a. Show that if the position x of a moving point is given by a quadratic function of t, $x = At^2 + Bt + C$, then the average velocity over any time interval $[t_1, t_2]$ is equal to the instantaneous velocity at the midpoint of the time interval.

   b. What is the geometric significance of the result in part (a)?

15. Find all values of the constants m and b for which the function

$$y = \begin{cases} \sin x, & x < \pi \\ mx + b, & x \geq \pi \end{cases}$$

is

   a. continuous at $x = \pi$.

   b. differentiable at $x = \pi$.

16. Does the function

$$f(x) = \begin{cases} \dfrac{1 - \cos x}{x}, & x \neq 0 \\ 0, & x = 0 \end{cases}$$

have a derivative at $x = 0$? Explain.

17. a. For what values of a and b will

$$f(x) = \begin{cases} ax, & x < 2 \\ ax^2 - bx + 3, & x \geq 2 \end{cases}$$

be differentiable for all values of x?

   b. Discuss the geometry of the resulting graph of f.

18. a. For what values of a and b will

$$g(x) = \begin{cases} ax + b, & x \le -1 \\ ax^3 + x + 2b, & x > -1 \end{cases}$$

be differentiable for all values of x?

b. Discuss the geometry of the resulting graph of g.

19. **Odd differentiable functions** Is there anything special about the derivative of an odd differentiable function of x? Give reasons for your answer.

20. **Even differentiable functions** Is there anything special about the derivative of an even differentiable function of x? Give reasons for your answer.

21. Suppose that the functions f and g are defined throughout an open interval containing the point x_0, that f is differentiable at x_0, that $f(x_0) = 0$, and that g is continuous at x_0. Show that the product fg is differentiable at x_0. This process shows, for example, that although $|x|$ is not differentiable at $x = 0$, the product $x|x|$ *is* differentiable at $x = 0$.

22. (*Continuation of Exercise 21.*) Use the result of Exercise 21 to show that the following functions are differentiable at $x = 0$.

a. $|x|\sin x$ b. $x^{2/3}\sin x$ c. $\sqrt[3]{x}(1 - \cos x)$

d. $h(x) = \begin{cases} x^2 \sin(1/x), & x \ne 0 \\ 0, & x = 0 \end{cases}$

23. Is the derivative of

$$h(x) = \begin{cases} x^2 \sin(1/x), & x \ne 0 \\ 0, & x = 0 \end{cases}$$

continuous at $x = 0$? How about the derivative of $k(x) = xh(x)$? Give reasons for your answers.

24. Suppose that a function f satisfies the following conditions for all real values of x and y:

i) $f(x + y) = f(x) \cdot f(y)$.

ii) $f(x) = 1 + xg(x)$, where $\lim_{x\to 0} g(x) = 1$.

Show that the derivative $f'(x)$ exists at every value of x and that $f'(x) = f(x)$.

25. **The generalized product rule** Use mathematical induction to prove that if $y = u_1 u_2 \cdots u_n$ is a finite product of differentiable functions, then y is differentiable on their common domain and

$$\frac{dy}{dx} = \frac{du_1}{dx} u_2 \cdots u_n + u_1 \frac{du_2}{dx} \cdots u_n + \cdots + u_1 u_2 \cdots u_{n-1} \frac{du_n}{dx}.$$

26. **Leibniz's rule for higher-order derivatives of products** Leibniz's rule for higher-order derivatives of products of differentiable functions says that

a. $\dfrac{d^2(uv)}{dx^2} = \dfrac{d^2u}{dx^2} v + 2\dfrac{du}{dx}\dfrac{dv}{dx} + u\dfrac{d^2v}{dx^2}.$

b. $\dfrac{d^3(uv)}{dx^3} = \dfrac{d^3u}{dx^3} v + 3\dfrac{d^2u}{dx^2}\dfrac{dv}{dx} + 3\dfrac{du}{dx}\dfrac{d^2v}{dx^2} + u\dfrac{d^3v}{dx^3}.$

c. $\dfrac{d^n(uv)}{dx^n} = \dfrac{d^nu}{dx^n} v + n\dfrac{d^{n-1}u}{dx^{n-1}}\dfrac{dv}{dx} + \cdots$

$$+ \frac{n(n-1)\cdots(n-k+1)}{k!} \frac{d^{n-k}u}{dx^{n-k}} \frac{d^kv}{dx^k}$$

$$+ \cdots + u\frac{d^nv}{dx^n}.$$

The equations in parts (a) and (b) are special cases of the equation in part (c). Derive the equation in part (c) by mathematical induction, using

$$\binom{m}{k} + \binom{m}{k+1} = \frac{m!}{k!(m-k)!} + \frac{m!}{(k+1)!(m-k-1)!}.$$

27. **The period of a clock pendulum** The period T of a clock pendulum (time for one full swing and back) is given by the formula $T^2 = 4\pi^2 L/g$, where T is measured in seconds, $g = 32.2$ ft/sec^2, and L, the length of the pendulum, is measured in feet. Find approximately

a. the length of a clock pendulum whose period is $T = 1$ sec.

b. the change dT in T if the pendulum in part (a) is lengthened 0.01 ft.

c. the amount the clock gains or loses in a day as a result of the period's changing by the amount dT found in part (b).

28. **The melting ice cube** Assume that an ice cube retains its cubical shape as it melts. If we call its edge length s, its volume is $V = s^3$ and its surface area is $6s^2$. We assume that V and s are differentiable functions of time t. We assume also that the cube's volume decreases at a rate that is proportional to its surface area. (This latter assumption seems reasonable enough when we think that the melting takes place at the surface: Changing the amount of surface changes the amount of ice exposed to melt.) In mathematical terms,

$$\frac{dV}{dt} = -k(6s^2), \qquad k > 0.$$

The minus sign indicates that the volume is decreasing. We assume that the proportionality factor k is constant. (It probably depends on many things, such as the relative humidity of the surrounding air, the air temperature, and the incidence or absence of sunlight, to name only a few.) Assume a particular set of conditions in which the cube lost 1/4 of its volume during the first hour, and that the volume is V_0 when $t = 0$. How long will it take the ice cube to melt?

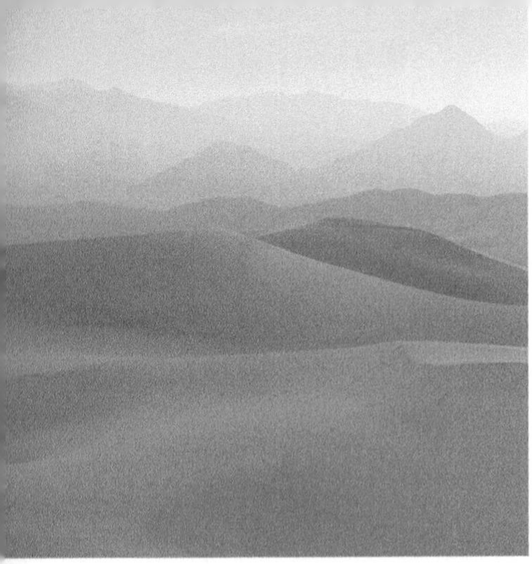

4

Applications of Derivatives

OVERVIEW In this chapter we use derivatives to find extreme values of functions, to determine and analyze the shapes of graphs, and to solve equations numerically. We also introduce the idea of recovering a function from its derivative. The key to many of these applications is the Mean Value Theorem, which paves the way to integral calculus in Chapter 5.

4.1 Extreme Values of Functions

This section shows how to locate and identify extreme (maximum or minimum) values of a function from its derivative. Once we can do this, we can solve a variety of problems in which we find the optimal (best) way to do something in a given situation (see Section 4.6). Finding maximum and minimum values is one of the most important applications of the derivative.

DEFINITIONS Let f be a function with domain D. Then f has an **absolute maximum** value on D at a point c if

$$f(x) \le f(c) \qquad \text{for all } x \text{ in } D$$

and an **absolute minimum** value on D at c if

$$f(x) \ge f(c) \qquad \text{for all } x \text{ in } D.$$

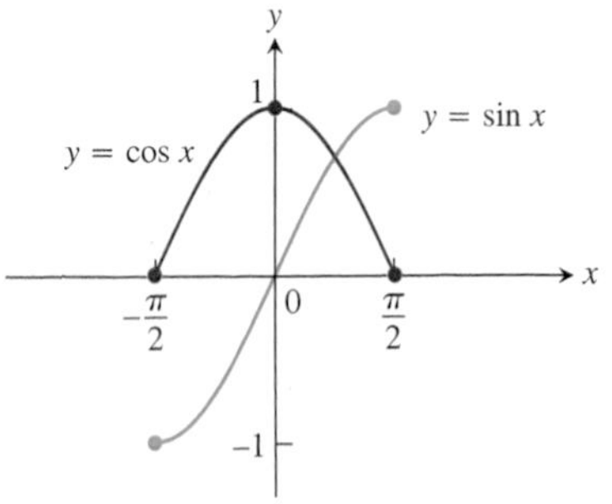

FIGURE 4.1 Absolute extrema for the sine and cosine functions on $[-\pi/2, \pi/2]$. These values can depend on the domain of a function.

Maximum and minimum values are called **extreme values** of the function f. Absolute maxima or minima are also referred to as **global** maxima or minima.

For example, on the closed interval $[-\pi/2, \pi/2]$ the function $f(x) = \cos x$ takes on an absolute maximum value of 1 (once) and an absolute minimum value of 0 (twice). On the same interval, the function $g(x) = \sin x$ takes on a maximum value of 1 and a minimum value of -1 (Figure 4.1).

Functions with the same defining rule or formula can have different extrema (maximum or minimum values), depending on the domain. We see this in the following example.

EXAMPLE 1 The absolute extrema of the following functions on their domains can be seen in Figure 4.2. Each function has the same defining equation, $y = x^2$, but the domains vary. Notice that a function might not have a maximum or minimum if the domain is unbounded or fails to contain an endpoint.

Function rule	Domain D	Absolute extrema on D
(a) $y = x^2$	$(-\infty, \infty)$	No absolute maximum Absolute minimum of 0 at $x = 0$
(b) $y = x^2$	$[0, 2]$	Absolute maximum of 4 at $x = 2$ Absolute minimum of 0 at $x = 0$
(c) $y = x^2$	$(0, 2]$	Absolute maximum of 4 at $x = 2$ No absolute minimum
(d) $y = x^2$	$(0, 2)$	No absolute extrema

■

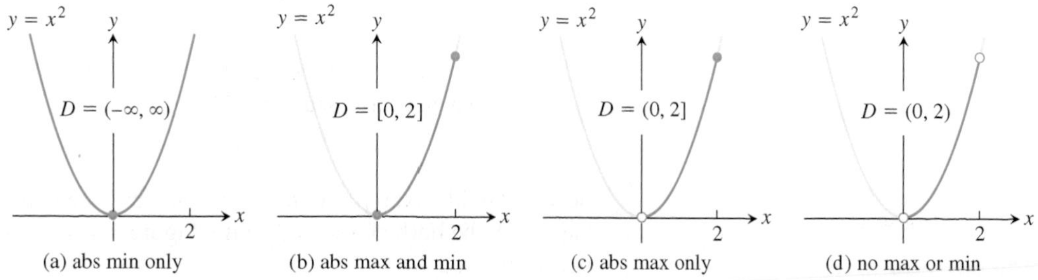

FIGURE 4.2 Graphs for Example 1.

HISTORICAL BIOGRAPHY

Daniel Bernoulli
(1700–1789)

Some of the functions in Example 1 did not have a maximum or a minimum value. The following theorem asserts that a function which is *continuous* at every point of a finite *closed* interval $[a, b]$ has an absolute maximum and an absolute minimum value on the interval. We look for these extreme values when we graph a function.

THEOREM 1—The Extreme Value Theorem If f is continuous on a closed interval $[a, b]$, then f attains both an absolute maximum value M and an absolute minimum value m in $[a, b]$. That is, there are numbers x_1 and x_2 in $[a, b]$ with $f(x_1) = m$, $f(x_2) = M$, and $m \le f(x) \le M$ for every other x in $[a, b]$.

The proof of the Extreme Value Theorem requires a detailed knowledge of the real number system (see Appendix 7) and we will not give it here. Figure 4.3 illustrates possible locations for the absolute extrema of a continuous function on a closed interval $[a, b]$. As we observed for the function $y = \cos x$, it is possible that an absolute minimum (or absolute maximum) may occur at two or more different points of the interval.

The requirements in Theorem 1 that the interval be closed and finite, and that the function be continuous, are key ingredients. Without them, the conclusion of the theorem

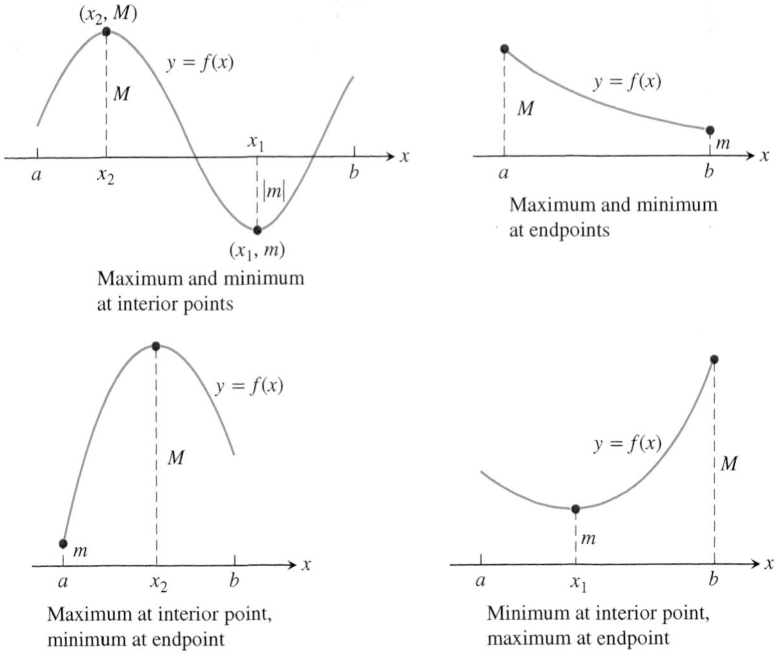

FIGURE 4.3 Some possibilities for a continuous function's maximum and minimum on a closed interval $[a, b]$.

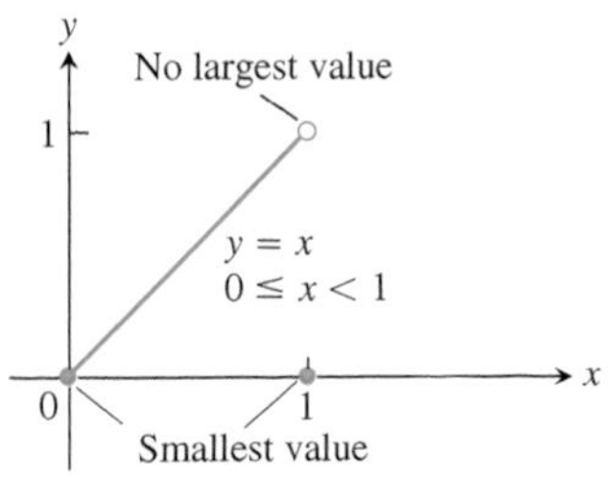

FIGURE 4.4 Even a single point of discontinuity can keep a function from having either a maximum or minimum value on a closed interval. The function

$$y = \begin{cases} x, & 0 \le x < 1 \\ 0, & x = 1 \end{cases}$$

is continuous at every point of $[0, 1]$ except $x = 1$, yet its graph over $[0, 1]$ does not have a highest point.

need not hold. Example 1 shows that an absolute extreme value may not exist if the interval fails to be both closed and finite. Figure 4.4 shows that the continuity requirement cannot be omitted.

Local (Relative) Extreme Values

Figure 4.5 shows a graph with five points where a function has extreme values on its domain $[a, b]$. The function's absolute minimum occurs at a even though at e the function's value is smaller than at any other point *nearby*. The curve rises to the left and falls to the right around c, making $f(c)$ a maximum locally. The function attains its absolute maximum at d. We now define what we mean by local extrema.

> **DEFINITIONS** A function f has a **local maximum** value at a point c within its domain D if $f(x) \le f(c)$ for all $x \in D$ lying in some open interval containing c.
>
> A function f has a **local minimum** value at a point c within its domain D if $f(x) \ge f(c)$ for all $x \in D$ lying in some open interval containing c.

If the domain of f is the closed interval $[a, b]$, then f has a local maximum at the endpoint $x = a$, if $f(x) \le f(a)$ for all x in some half-open interval $[a, a + \delta)$, $\delta > 0$. Likewise, f has a local maximum at an interior point $x = c$ if $f(x) \le f(c)$ for all x in some open interval $(c - \delta, c + \delta)$, $\delta > 0$, and a local maximum at the endpoint $x = b$ if $f(x) \le f(b)$ for all x in some half-open interval $(b - \delta, b]$, $\delta > 0$. The inequalities are reversed for local minimum values. In Figure 4.5, the function f has local maxima at c and d and local minima at a, e, and b. Local extrema are also called **relative extrema**. Some functions can have infinitely many local extrema, even over a finite interval. One example is the function $f(x) = \sin(1/x)$ on the interval $(0, 1]$. (We graphed this function in Figure 2.40.)

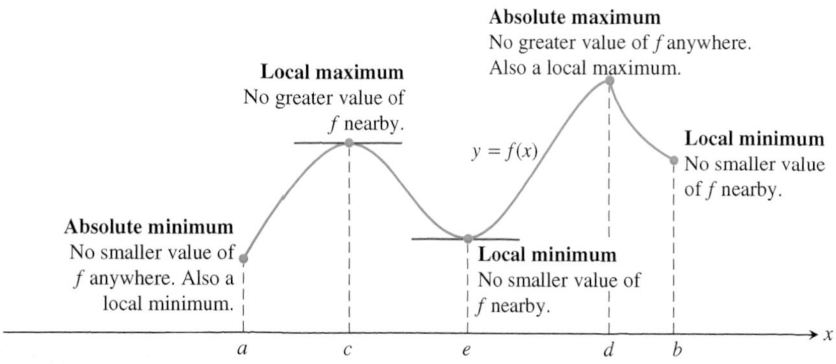

FIGURE 4.5 How to identify types of maxima and minima for a function with domain $a \leq x \leq b$.

An absolute maximum is also a local maximum. Being the largest value overall, it is also the largest value in its immediate neighborhood. Hence, *a list of all local maxima will automatically include the absolute maximum if there is one*. Similarly, *a list of all local minima will include the absolute minimum if there is one*.

Finding Extrema

The next theorem explains why we usually need to investigate only a few values to find a function's extrema.

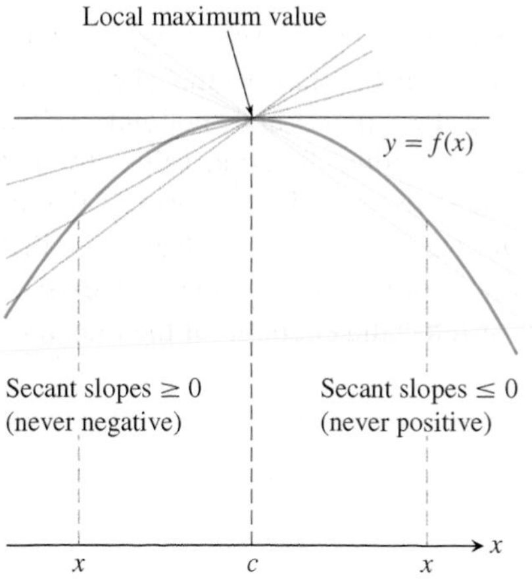

FIGURE 4.6 A curve with a local maximum value. The slope at c, simultaneously the limit of nonpositive numbers and nonnegative numbers, is zero.

> **THEOREM 2—The First Derivative Theorem for Local Extreme Values** If f has a local maximum or minimum value at an interior point c of its domain, and if f' is defined at c, then
>
> $$f'(c) = 0.$$

Proof To prove that $f'(c)$ is zero at a local extremum, we show first that $f'(c)$ cannot be positive and second that $f'(c)$ cannot be negative. The only number that is neither positive nor negative is zero, so that is what $f'(c)$ must be.

To begin, suppose that f has a local maximum value at $x = c$ (Figure 4.6) so that $f(x) - f(c) \leq 0$ for all values of x near enough to c. Since c is an interior point of f's domain, $f'(c)$ is defined by the two-sided limit

$$\lim_{x \to c} \frac{f(x) - f(c)}{x - c}.$$

This means that the right-hand and left-hand limits both exist at $x = c$ and equal $f'(c)$. When we examine these limits separately, we find that

$$f'(c) = \lim_{x \to c^+} \frac{f(x) - f(c)}{x - c} \leq 0. \qquad \text{Because } (x - c) > 0 \text{ and } f(x) \leq f(c) \qquad (1)$$

Similarly,

$$f'(c) = \lim_{x \to c^-} \frac{f(x) - f(c)}{x - c} \geq 0. \qquad \text{Because } (x - c) < 0 \text{ and } f(x) \leq f(c) \qquad (2)$$

Together, Equations (1) and (2) imply $f'(c) = 0$.

This proves the theorem for local maximum values. To prove it for local minimum values, we simply use $f(x) \geq f(c)$, which reverses the inequalities in Equations (1) and (2). ∎

Theorem 2 says that a function's first derivative is always zero at an interior point where the function has a local extreme value and the derivative is defined. Hence the only places where a function f can possibly have an extreme value (local or global) are

1. interior points where $f' = 0$, — At $x = c$ and $x = e$ in Fig. 4.5
2. interior points where f' is undefined, — At $x = d$ in Fig. 4.5
3. endpoints of the domain of f. — At $x = a$ and $x = b$ in Fig. 4.5

The following definition helps us to summarize.

DEFINITION An interior point of the domain of a function f where f' is zero or undefined is a **critical point** of f.

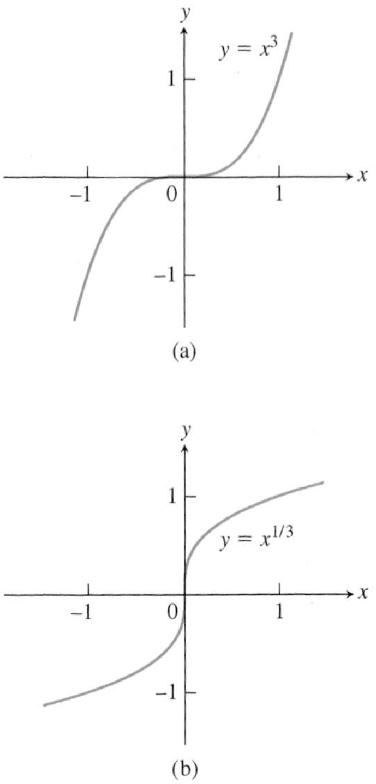

FIGURE 4.7 Critical points without extreme values. (a) $y' = 3x^2$ is 0 at $x = 0$, but $y = x^3$ has no extremum there. (b) $y' = (1/3)x^{-2/3}$ is undefined at $x = 0$, but $y = x^{1/3}$ has no extremum there.

Thus the only domain points where a function can assume extreme values are critical points and endpoints. However, be careful not to misinterpret what is being said here. A function may have a critical point at $x = c$ without having a local extreme value there. For instance, both of the functions $y = x^3$ and $y = x^{1/3}$ have critical points at the origin, but neither function has a local extreme value at the origin. Instead, each function has a *point of inflection* there (see Figure 4.7). We define and explore inflection points in Section 4.4.

Most problems that ask for extreme values call for finding the absolute extrema of a continuous function on a closed and finite interval. Theorem 1 assures us that such values exist; Theorem 2 tells us that they are taken on only at critical points and endpoints. Often we can simply list these points and calculate the corresponding function values to find what the largest and smallest values are, and where they are located. Of course, if the interval is not closed or not finite (such as $a < x < b$ or $a < x < \infty$), we have seen that absolute extrema need not exist. If an absolute maximum or minimum value does exist, it must occur at a critical point or at an included right- or left-hand endpoint of the interval.

How to Find the Absolute Extrema of a Continuous Function f on a Finite Closed Interval

1. Evaluate f at all critical points and endpoints.
2. Take the largest and smallest of these values.

EXAMPLE 2 Find the absolute maximum and minimum values of $f(x) = x^2$ on $[-2, 1]$.

Solution The function is differentiable over its entire domain, so the only critical point is where $f'(x) = 2x = 0$, namely $x = 0$. We need to check the function's values at $x = 0$ and at the endpoints $x = -2$ and $x = 1$:

Critical point value:	$f(0) = 0$
Endpoint values:	$f(-2) = 4$
	$f(1) = 1$.

The function has an absolute maximum value of 4 at $x = -2$ and an absolute minimum value of 0 at $x = 0$. ■

EXAMPLE 3 Find the absolute maximum and minimum values of $f(x) = 10x(2 - \ln x)$ on the interval $[1, e^2]$.

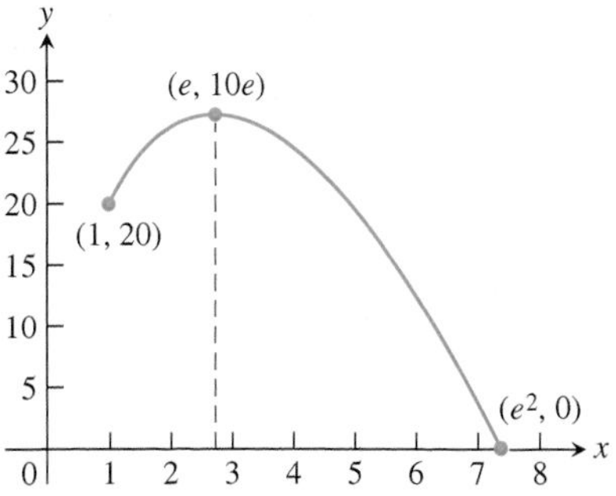

FIGURE 4.8 The extreme values of $f(x) = 10x(2 - \ln x)$ on $[1, e^2]$ occur at $x = e$ and $x = e^2$ (Example 3).

Solution Figure 4.8 suggests that f has its absolute maximum value near $x = 3$ and its absolute minimum value of 0 at $x = e^2$. Let's verify this observation.

We evaluate the function at the critical points and endpoints and take the largest and smallest of the resulting values.

The first derivative is

$$f'(x) = 10(2 - \ln x) - 10x\left(\frac{1}{x}\right) = 10(1 - \ln x).$$

The only critical point in the domain $[1, e^2]$ is the point $x = e$, where $\ln x = 1$. The values of f at this one critical point and at the endpoints are

Critical point value: $f(e) = 10e$

Endpoint values: $f(1) = 10(2 - \ln 1) = 20$

$f(e^2) = 10e^2(2 - 2\ln e) = 0.$

We can see from this list that the function's absolute maximum value is $10e \approx 27.2$; it occurs at the critical interior point $x = e$. The absolute minimum value is 0 and occurs at the right endpoint $x = e^2$. ■

EXAMPLE 4 Find the absolute maximum and minimum values of $f(x) = x^{2/3}$ on the interval $[-2, 3]$.

Solution We evaluate the function at the critical points and endpoints and take the largest and smallest of the resulting values.

The first derivative

$$f'(x) = \frac{2}{3}x^{-1/3} = \frac{2}{3\sqrt[3]{x}}$$

has no zeros but is undefined at the interior point $x = 0$. The values of f at this one critical point and at the endpoints are

Critical point value: $f(0) = 0$

Endpoint values: $f(-2) = (-2)^{2/3} = \sqrt[3]{4}$

$f(3) = (3)^{2/3} = \sqrt[3]{9}.$

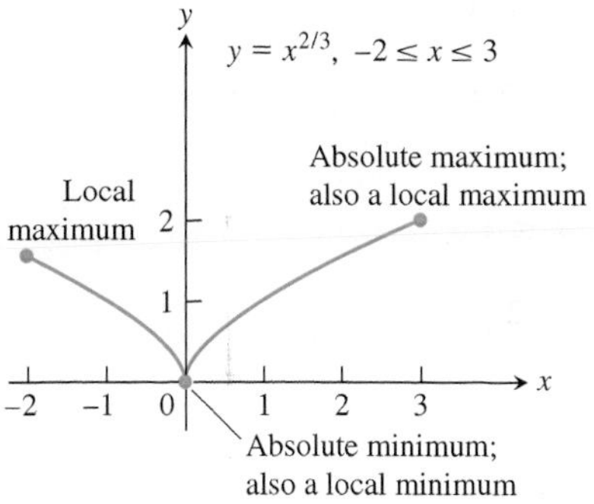

FIGURE 4.9 The extreme values of $f(x) = x^{2/3}$ on $[-2, 3]$ occur at $x = 0$ and $x = 3$ (Example 4).

We can see from this list that the function's absolute maximum value is $\sqrt[3]{9} \approx 2.08$, and it occurs at the right endpoint $x = 3$. The absolute minimum value is 0, and it occurs at the interior point $x = 0$ where the graph has a cusp (Figure 4.9). ■

Exercises 4.1

Finding Extrema from Graphs

In Exercises 1–6, determine from the graph whether the function has any absolute extreme values on $[a, b]$. Then explain how your answer is consistent with Theorem 1.

1.

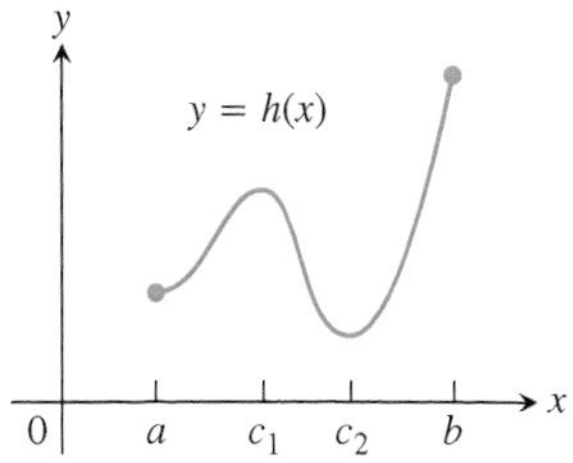

2.

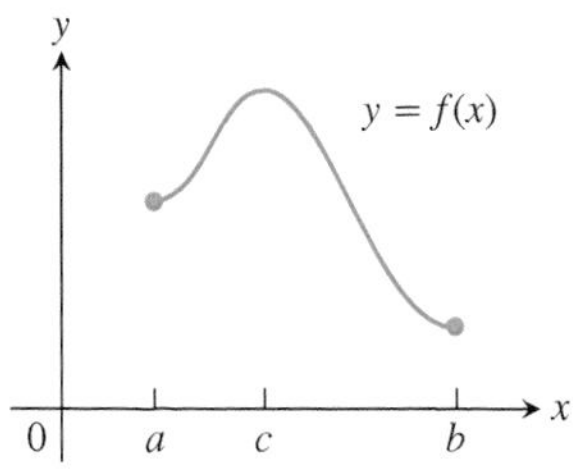

3.

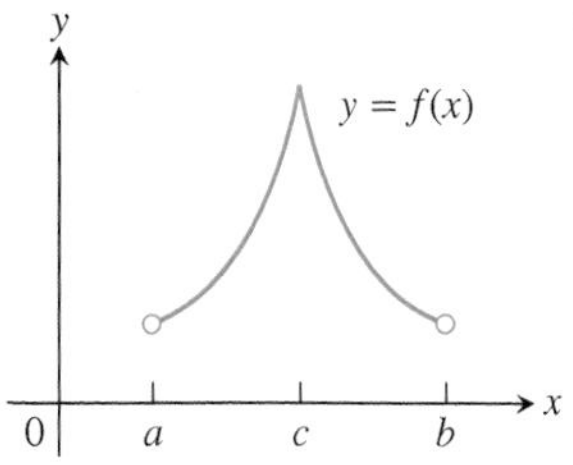

4.

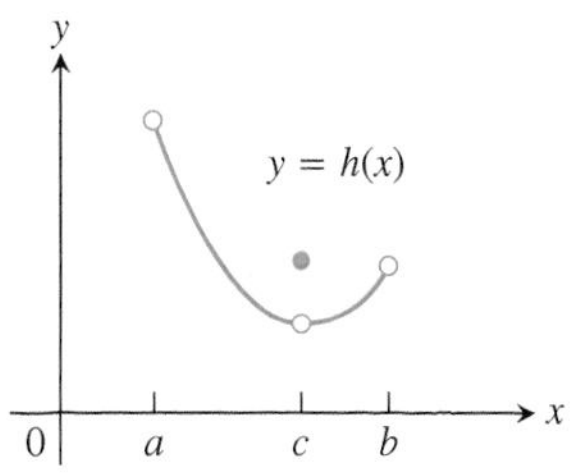

5.
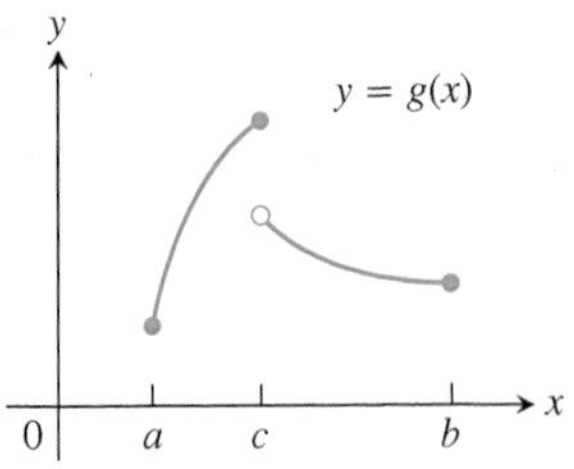

6.
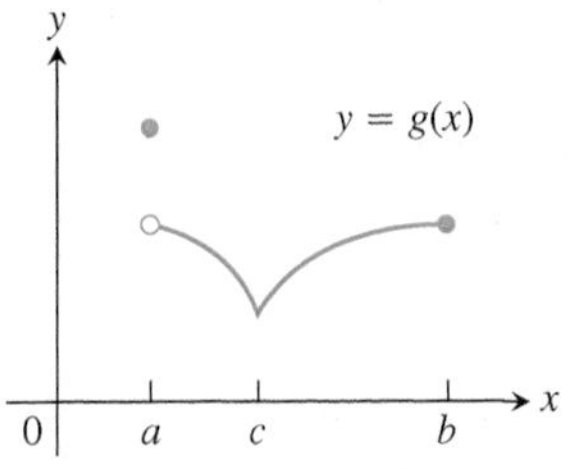

In Exercises 7–10, find the absolute extreme values and where they occur.

7.
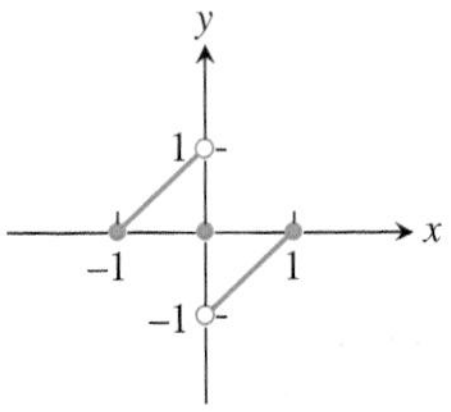

8.
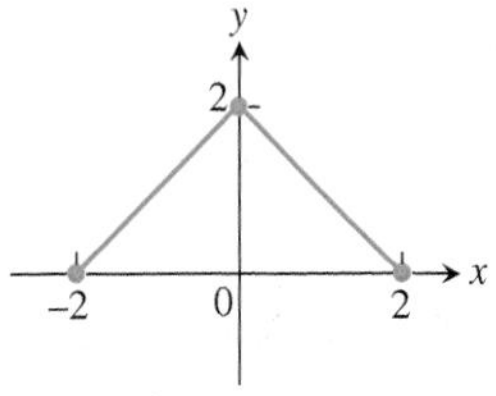

9.
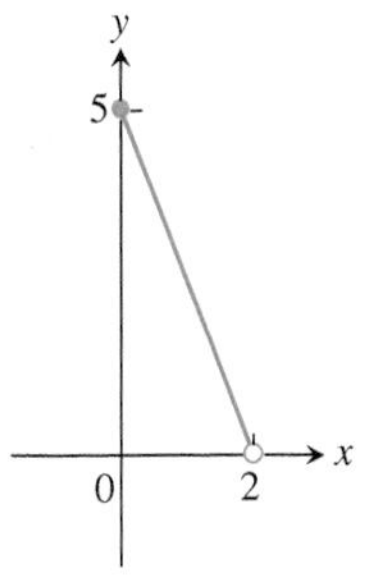

10.
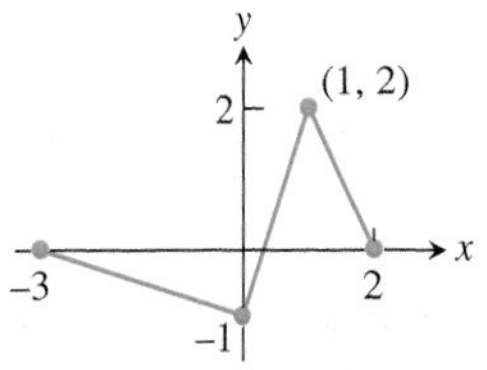

In Exercises 11–14, match the table with a graph.

11.

x	$f'(x)$
a	0
b	0
c	5

12.

x	$f'(x)$
a	0
b	0
c	-5

13.

x	$f'(x)$
a	does not exist
b	0
c	-2

14.

x	$f'(x)$
a	does not exist
b	does not exist
c	-1.7

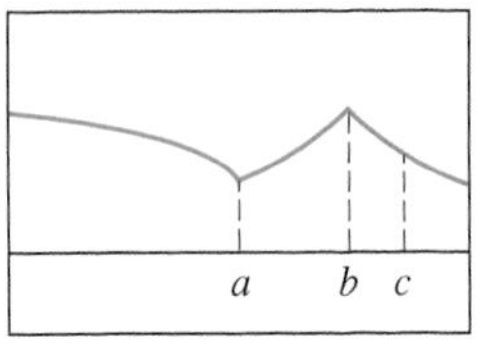

(a)

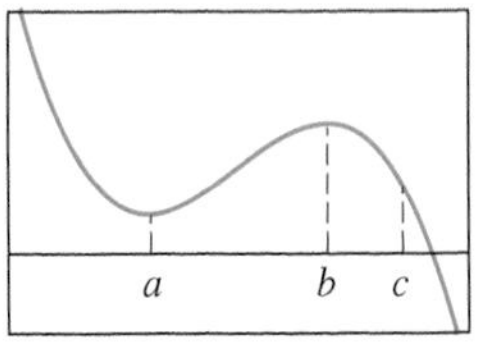

(b)

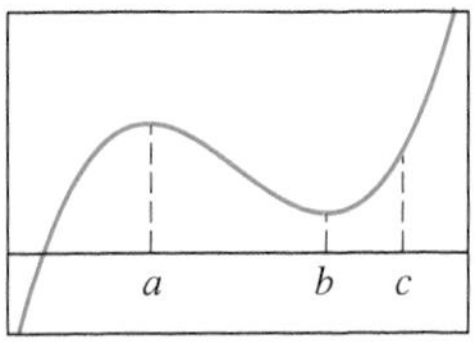

(c)

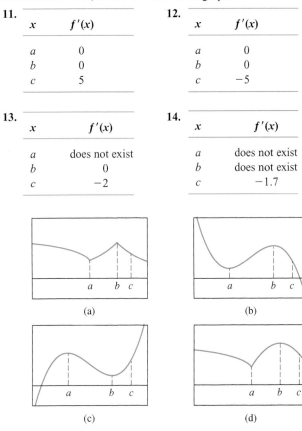

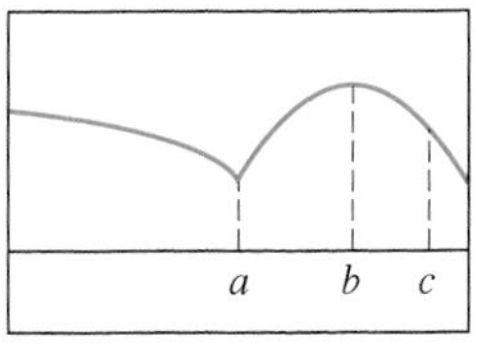

(d)

In Exercises 15–20, sketch the graph of each function and determine whether the function has any absolute extreme values on its domain. Explain how your answer is consistent with Theorem 1.

15. $f(x) = |x|, \quad -1 < x < 2$

16. $y = \dfrac{6}{x^2 + 2}, \quad -1 < x < 1$

17. $g(x) = \begin{cases} -x, & 0 \le x < 1 \\ x - 1, & 1 \le x \le 2 \end{cases}$

18. $h(x) = \begin{cases} \dfrac{1}{x}, & -1 \le x < 0 \\ \sqrt{x}, & 0 \le x \le 4 \end{cases}$

19. $y = 3 \sin x, \quad 0 < x < 2\pi$

20. $f(x) = \begin{cases} x + 1, & -1 \le x < 0 \\ \cos x, & 0 \le x \le \dfrac{\pi}{2} \end{cases}$

Absolute Extrema on Finite Closed Intervals

In Exercises 21–40, find the absolute maximum and minimum values of each function on the given interval. Then graph the function. Identify the points on the graph where the absolute extrema occur, and include their coordinates.

21. $f(x) = \dfrac{2}{3}x - 5, \quad -2 \le x \le 3$

22. $f(x) = -x - 4, \quad -4 \le x \le 1$

23. $f(x) = x^2 - 1, \quad -1 \le x \le 2$

24. $f(x) = 4 - x^2, \quad -3 \le x \le 1$

25. $F(x) = -\dfrac{1}{x^2}, \quad 0.5 \le x \le 2$

26. $F(x) = -\dfrac{1}{x}, \quad -2 \le x \le -1$

27. $h(x) = \sqrt[3]{x}, \quad -1 \le x \le 8$

28. $h(x) = -3x^{2/3}, \quad -1 \le x \le 1$

29. $g(x) = \sqrt{4 - x^2}, \quad -2 \le x \le 1$

30. $g(x) = -\sqrt{5 - x^2}, \quad -\sqrt{5} \le x \le 0$

31. $f(\theta) = \sin \theta, \quad -\dfrac{\pi}{2} \le \theta \le \dfrac{5\pi}{6}$

32. $f(\theta) = \tan \theta, \quad -\dfrac{\pi}{3} \le \theta \le \dfrac{\pi}{4}$

33. $g(x) = \csc x, \quad \dfrac{\pi}{3} \le x \le \dfrac{2\pi}{3}$

34. $g(x) = \sec x, \quad -\dfrac{\pi}{3} \le x \le \dfrac{\pi}{6}$

35. $f(t) = 2 - |t|, \quad -1 \le t \le 3$

36. $f(t) = |t - 5|, \quad 4 \le t \le 7$

37. $g(x) = xe^{-x}, \quad -1 \le x \le 1$

38. $h(x) = \ln(x + 1), \quad 0 \le x \le 3$

39. $f(x) = \dfrac{1}{x} + \ln x, \quad 0.5 \le x \le 4$

40. $g(x) = e^{-x^2}, \quad -2 \le x \le 1$

In Exercises 41–44, find the function's absolute maximum and minimum values and say where they are assumed.

41. $f(x) = x^{4/3}, \quad -1 \le x \le 8$

42. $f(x) = x^{5/3}, \quad -1 \le x \le 8$

43. $g(\theta) = \theta^{3/5}, \quad -32 \le \theta \le 1$

44. $h(\theta) = 3\theta^{2/3}, \quad -27 \le \theta \le 8$

Finding Critical Points

In Exercises 45–52, determine all critical points for each function.

45. $y = x^2 - 6x + 7$

46. $f(x) = 6x^2 - x^3$

47. $f(x) = x(4 - x)^3$

48. $g(x) = (x - 1)^2(x - 3)^2$

49. $y = x^2 + \dfrac{2}{x}$

50. $f(x) = \dfrac{x^2}{x - 2}$

51. $y = x^2 - 32\sqrt{x}$

52. $g(x) = \sqrt{2x - x^2}$

Finding Extreme Values

In Exercises 53–68, find the extreme values (absolute and local) of the function and where they occur.

53. $y = 2x^2 - 8x + 9$

54. $y = x^3 - 2x + 4$

55. $y = x^3 + x^2 - 8x + 5$

56. $y = x^3(x - 5)^2$

57. $y = \sqrt{x^2 - 1}$

58. $y = x - 4\sqrt{x}$

59. $y = \dfrac{1}{\sqrt[3]{1 - x^2}}$

60. $y = \sqrt{3 + 2x - x^2}$

61. $y = \dfrac{x}{x^2 + 1}$

62. $y = \dfrac{x + 1}{x^2 + 2x + 2}$

63. $y = e^x + e^{-x}$

64. $y = e^x - e^{-x}$

65. $y = x \ln x$

66. $y = x^2 \ln x$

67. $y = \cos^{-1}(x^2)$

68. $y = \sin^{-1}(e^x)$

Local Extrema and Critical Points

In Exercises 69–76, find the critical points, domain endpoints, and extreme values (absolute and local) for each function.

69. $y = x^{2/3}(x + 2)$

70. $y = x^{2/3}(x^2 - 4)$

71. $y = x\sqrt{4 - x^2}$

72. $y = x^2\sqrt{3 - x}$

73. $y = \begin{cases} 4 - 2x, & x \le 1 \\ x + 1, & x > 1 \end{cases}$

74. $y = \begin{cases} 3 - x, & x < 0 \\ 3 + 2x - x^2, & x \ge 0 \end{cases}$

75. $y = \begin{cases} -x^2 - 2x + 4, & x \le 1 \\ -x^2 + 6x - 4, & x > 1 \end{cases}$

76. $y = \begin{cases} -\frac{1}{4}x^2 - \frac{1}{2}x + \frac{15}{4}, & x \le 1 \\ x^3 - 6x^2 + 8x, & x > 1 \end{cases}$

In Exercises 77 and 78, give reasons for your answers.

77. Let $f(x) = (x - 2)^{2/3}$.

a. Does $f'(2)$ exist?

b. Show that the only local extreme value of f occurs at $x = 2$.

c. Does the result in part (b) contradict the Extreme Value Theorem?

d. Repeat parts (a) and (b) for $f(x) = (x - a)^{2/3}$, replacing 2 by a.

78. Let $f(x) = |x^3 - 9x|$.

a. Does $f'(0)$ exist?

b. Does $f'(3)$ exist?

c. Does $f'(-3)$ exist?

d. Determine all extrema of f.

Theory and Examples

79. A minimum with no derivative The function $f(x) = |x|$ has an absolute minimum value at $x = 0$ even though f is not differentiable at $x = 0$. Is this consistent with Theorem 2? Give reasons for your answer.

80. Even functions If an even function $f(x)$ has a local maximum value at $x = c$, can anything be said about the value of f at $x = -c$? Give reasons for your answer.

81. Odd functions If an odd function $g(x)$ has a local minimum value at $x = c$, can anything be said about the value of g at $x = -c$? Give reasons for your answer.

82. We know how to find the extreme values of a continuous function $f(x)$ by investigating its values at critical points and endpoints. But what if there *are* no critical points or endpoints? What happens then? Do such functions really exist? Give reasons for your answers.

83. The function

$$V(x) = x(10 - 2x)(16 - 2x), \qquad 0 < x < 5,$$

models the volume of a box.

a. Find the extreme values of V.

b. Interpret any values found in part (a) in terms of the volume of the box.

84. Cubic functions Consider the cubic function

$$f(x) = ax^3 + bx^2 + cx + d.$$

a. Show that f can have 0, 1, or 2 critical points. Give examples and graphs to support your argument.

b. How many local extreme values can f have?

85. Maximum height of a vertically moving body The height of a body moving vertically is given by

$$s = -\frac{1}{2}gt^2 + v_0 t + s_0, \qquad g > 0,$$

with s in meters and t in seconds. Find the body's maximum height.

86. Peak alternating current Suppose that at any given time t (in seconds) the current i (in amperes) in an alternating current circuit is $i = 2\cos t + 2\sin t$. What is the peak current for this circuit (largest magnitude)?

T Graph the functions in Exercises 87–90. Then find the extreme values of the function on the interval and say where they occur.

87. $f(x) = |x - 2| + |x + 3|, \quad -5 \le x \le 5$

88. $g(x) = |x - 1| - |x - 5|, \quad -2 \le x \le 7$

89. $h(x) = |x + 2| - |x - 3|, \quad -\infty < x < \infty$

90. $k(x) = |x + 1| + |x - 3|, \quad -\infty < x < \infty$

COMPUTER EXPLORATIONS

In Exercises 91–98, you will use a CAS to help find the absolute extrema of the given function over the specified closed interval. Perform the following steps.

a. Plot the function over the interval to see its general behavior there.

b. Find the interior points where $f' = 0$. (In some exercises, you may have to use the numerical equation solver to approximate a solution.) You may want to plot f' as well.

c. Find the interior points where f' does not exist.

d. Evaluate the function at all points found in parts (b) and (c) and at the endpoints of the interval.

e. Find the function's absolute extreme values on the interval and identify where they occur.

91. $f(x) = x^4 - 8x^2 + 4x + 2, \quad [-20/25, 64/25]$

92. $f(x) = -x^4 + 4x^3 - 4x + 1, \quad [-3/4, 3]$

93. $f(x) = x^{2/3}(3 - x), \quad [-2, 2]$

94. $f(x) = 2 + 2x - 3x^{2/3}, \quad [-1, 10/3]$

95. $f(x) = \sqrt{x} + \cos x, \quad [0, 2\pi]$

96. $f(x) = x^{3/4} - \sin x + \frac{1}{2}, \quad [0, 2\pi]$

97. $f(x) = \pi x^2 e^{-3x/2}, \quad [0, 5]$

98. $f(x) = \ln(2x + x \sin x), \quad [1, 15]$

4.2 The Mean Value Theorem

We know that constant functions have zero derivatives, but could there be a more complicated function whose derivative is always zero? If two functions have identical derivatives over an interval, how are the functions related? We answer these and other questions in this chapter by applying the Mean Value Theorem. First we introduce a special case, known as Rolle's Theorem, which is used to prove the Mean Value Theorem.

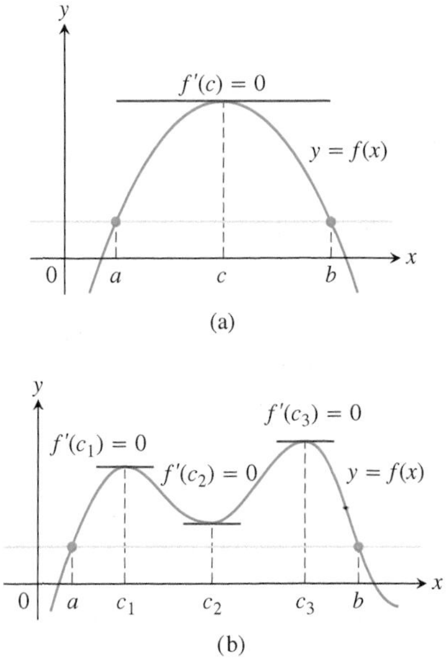

FIGURE 4.10 Rolle's Theorem says that a differentiable curve has at least one horizontal tangent between any two points where it crosses a horizontal line. It may have just one (a), or it may have more (b).

Rolle's Theorem

As suggested by its graph, if a differentiable function crosses a horizontal line at two different points, there is at least one point between them where the tangent to the graph is horizontal and the derivative is zero (Figure 4.10). We now state and prove this result.

> **THEOREM 3—Rolle's Theorem** Suppose that $y = f(x)$ is continuous at every point of the closed interval $[a, b]$ and differentiable at every point of its interior (a, b). If $f(a) = f(b)$, then there is at least one number c in (a, b) at which $f'(c) = 0$.

Proof Being continuous, f assumes absolute maximum and minimum values on $[a, b]$ by Theorem 1. These can occur only

1. at interior points where f' is zero,
2. at interior points where f' does not exist,
3. at the endpoints of the function's domain, in this case a and b.

By hypothesis, f has a derivative at every interior point. That rules out possibility (2), leaving us with interior points where $f' = 0$ and with the two endpoints a and b.

If either the maximum or the minimum occurs at a point c between a and b, then $f'(c) = 0$ by Theorem 2 in Section 4.1, and we have found a point for Rolle's Theorem.

If both the absolute maximum and the absolute minimum occur at the endpoints, then because $f(a) = f(b)$ it must be the case that f is a constant function with $f(x) = f(a) = f(b)$ for every $x \in [a, b]$. Therefore $f'(x) = 0$ and the point c can be taken anywhere in the interior (a, b). ■

HISTORICAL BIOGRAPHY

Michel Rolle
(1652–1719)

The hypotheses of Theorem 3 are essential. If they fail at even one point, the graph may not have a horizontal tangent (Figure 4.11).

Rolle's Theorem may be combined with the Intermediate Value Theorem to show when there is only one real solution of an equation $f(x) = 0$, as we illustrate in the next example.

EXAMPLE 1 Show that the equation

$$x^3 + 3x + 1 = 0$$

has exactly one real solution.

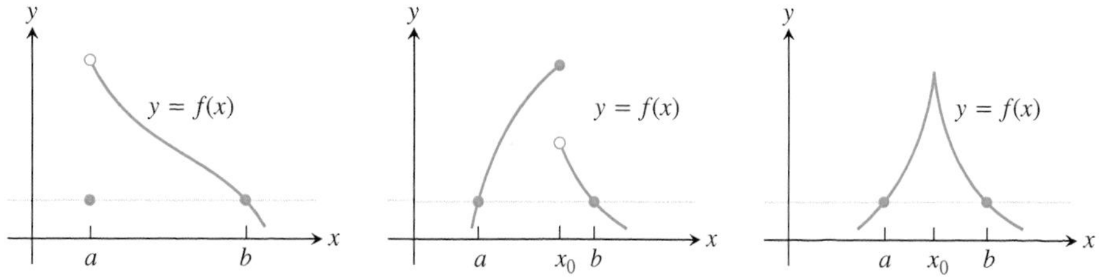

(a) Discontinuous at an endpoint of $[a, b]$

(b) Discontinuous at an interior point of $[a, b]$

(c) Continuous on $[a, b]$ but not differentiable at an interior point

FIGURE 4.11 There may be no horizontal tangent if the hypotheses of Rolle's Theorem do not hold.

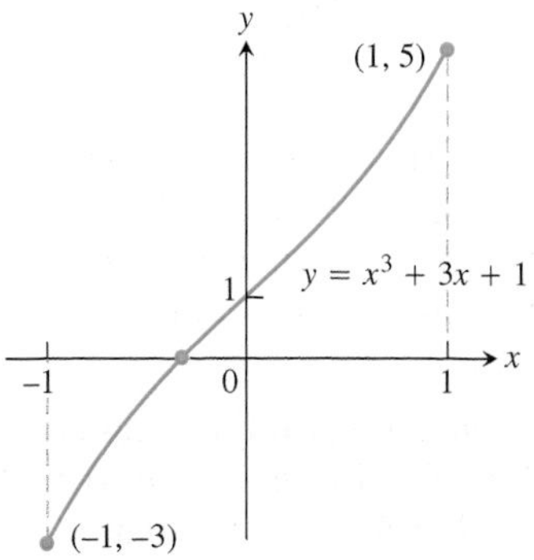

FIGURE 4.12 The only real zero of the polynomial $y = x^3 + 3x + 1$ is the one shown here where the curve crosses the x-axis between -1 and 0 (Example 1).

Solution We define the continuous function

$$f(x) = x^3 + 3x + 1.$$

Since $f(-1) = -3$ and $f(0) = 1$, the Intermediate Value Theorem tells us that the graph of f crosses the x-axis somewhere in the open interval $(-1, 0)$. (See Figure 4.12.) The derivative

$$f'(x) = 3x^2 + 3$$

is never zero (because it is always positive). Now, if there were even two points $x = a$ and $x = b$ where $f(x)$ was zero, Rolle's Theorem would guarantee the existence of a point $x = c$ in between them where f' was zero. Therefore, f has no more than one zero. ■

Our main use of Rolle's Theorem is in proving the Mean Value Theorem.

The Mean Value Theorem

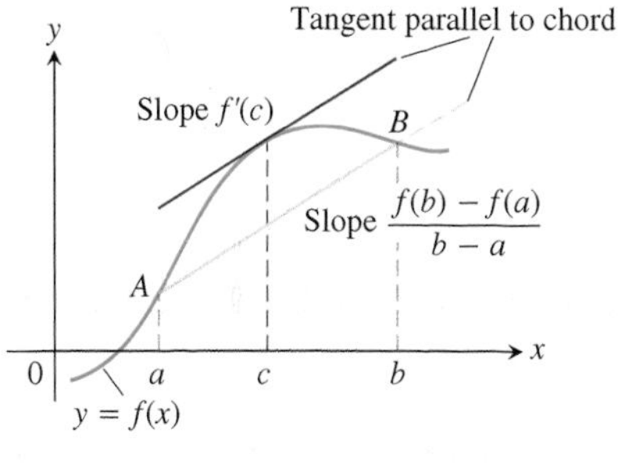

FIGURE 4.13 Geometrically, the Mean Value Theorem says that somewhere between a and b the curve has at least one tangent parallel to chord AB.

The Mean Value Theorem, which was first stated by Joseph-Louis Lagrange, is a slanted version of Rolle's Theorem (Figure 4.13). The Mean Value Theorem guarantees that there is a point where the tangent line is parallel to the chord AB.

THEOREM 4—The Mean Value Theorem Suppose $y = f(x)$ is continuous on a closed interval $[a, b]$ and differentiable on the interval's interior (a, b). Then there is at least one point c in (a, b) at which

$$\frac{f(b) - f(a)}{b - a} = f'(c). \tag{1}$$

Proof We picture the graph of f and draw a line through the points $A(a, f(a))$ and $B(b, f(b))$. (See Figure 4.14.) The line is the graph of the function

$$g(x) = f(a) + \frac{f(b) - f(a)}{b - a}(x - a) \tag{2}$$

(point-slope equation). The vertical difference between the graphs of f and g at x is

$$\begin{aligned} h(x) &= f(x) - g(x) \\ &= f(x) - f(a) - \frac{f(b) - f(a)}{b - a}(x - a). \end{aligned} \tag{3}$$

Figure 4.15 shows the graphs of f, g, and h together.

HISTORICAL BIOGRAPHY

Joseph-Louis Lagrange (1736–1813)

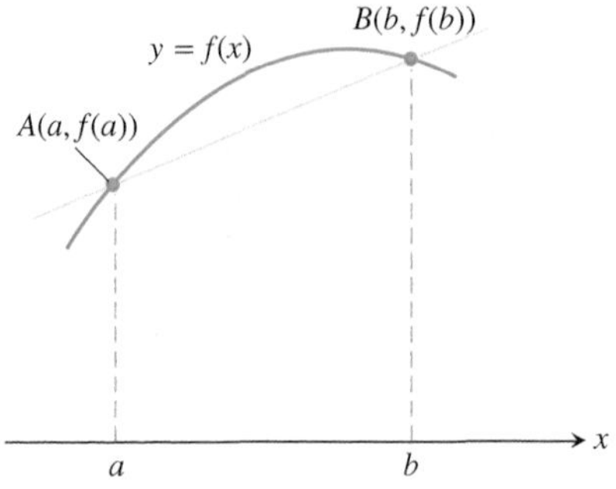

FIGURE 4.14 The graph of f and the chord AB over the interval $[a, b]$.

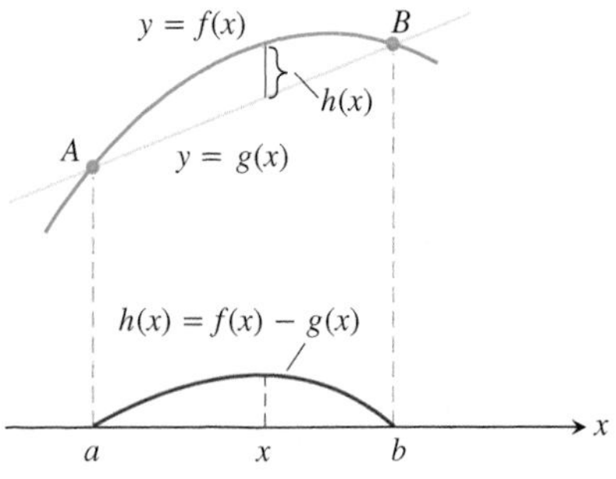

FIGURE 4.15 The chord AB is the graph of the function $g(x)$. The function $h(x) = f(x) - g(x)$ gives the vertical distance between the graphs of f and g at x.

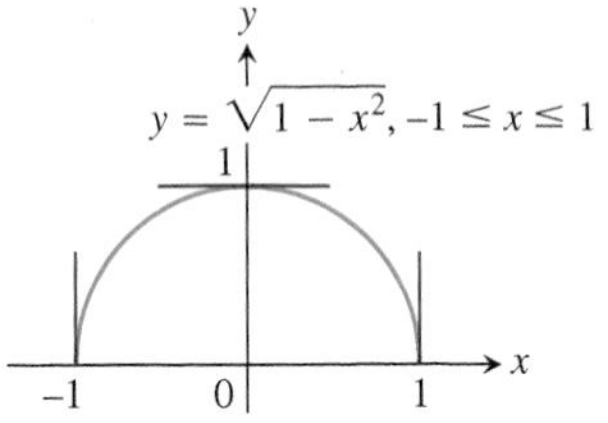

FIGURE 4.16 The function $f(x) = \sqrt{1 - x^2}$ satisfies the hypotheses (and conclusion) of the Mean Value Theorem on $[-1, 1]$ even though f is not differentiable at -1 and 1.

The function h satisfies the hypotheses of Rolle's Theorem on $[a, b]$. It is continuous on $[a, b]$ and differentiable on (a, b) because both f and g are. Also, $h(a) = h(b) = 0$ because the graphs of f and g both pass through A and B. Therefore $h'(c) = 0$ at some point $c \in (a, b)$. This is the point we want for Equation (1).

To verify Equation (1), we differentiate both sides of Equation (3) with respect to x and then set $x = c$:

$$h'(x) = f'(x) - \frac{f(b) - f(a)}{b - a} \qquad \text{Derivative of Eq. (3) . . .}$$

$$h'(c) = f'(c) - \frac{f(b) - f(a)}{b - a} \qquad \text{. . . with } x = c$$

$$0 = f'(c) - \frac{f(b) - f(a)}{b - a} \qquad h'(c) = 0$$

$$f'(c) = \frac{f(b) - f(a)}{b - a}, \qquad \text{Rearranged}$$

which is what we set out to prove. ■

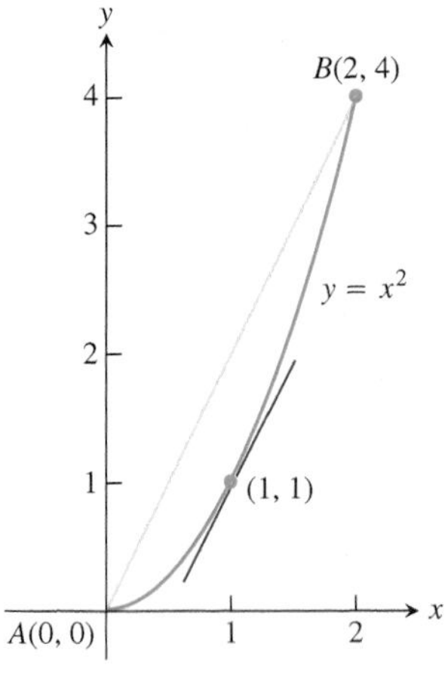

FIGURE 4.17 As we find in Example 2, $c = 1$ is where the tangent is parallel to the chord.

The hypotheses of the Mean Value Theorem do not require f to be differentiable at either a or b. Continuity at a and b is enough (Figure 4.16).

EXAMPLE 2 The function $f(x) = x^2$ (Figure 4.17) is continuous for $0 \le x \le 2$ and differentiable for $0 < x < 2$. Since $f(0) = 0$ and $f(2) = 4$, the Mean Value Theorem says that at some point c in the interval, the derivative $f'(x) = 2x$ must have the value $(4 - 0)/(2 - 0) = 2$. In this case we can identify c by solving the equation $2c = 2$ to get $c = 1$. However, it is not always easy to find c algebraically, even though we know it always exists. ■

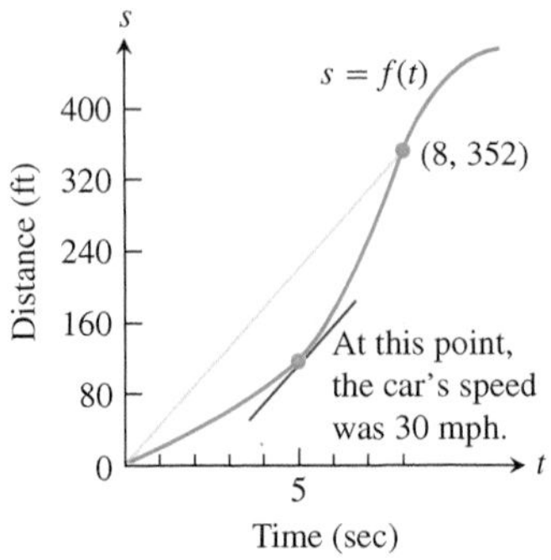

FIGURE 4.18 Distance versus elapsed time for the car in Example 3.

A Physical Interpretation

We can think of the number $(f(b) - f(a))/(b - a)$ as the average change in f over $[a, b]$ and $f'(c)$ as an instantaneous change. Then the Mean Value Theorem says that at some interior point the instantaneous change must equal the average change over the entire interval.

EXAMPLE 3 If a car accelerating from zero takes 8 sec to go 352 ft, its average velocity for the 8-sec interval is $352/8 = 44$ ft/sec. The Mean Value Theorem says that at some point during the acceleration the speedometer must read exactly 30 mph (44 ft/sec) (Figure 4.18). ■

Mathematical Consequences

At the beginning of the section, we asked what kind of function has a zero derivative over an interval. The first corollary of the Mean Value Theorem provides the answer that only constant functions have zero derivatives.

COROLLARY 1 If $f'(x) = 0$ at each point x of an open interval (a, b), then $f(x) = C$ for all $x \in (a, b)$, where C is a constant.

Proof We want to show that f has a constant value on the interval (a, b). We do so by showing that if x_1 and x_2 are any two points in (a, b) with $x_1 < x_2$, then $f(x_1) = f(x_2)$. Now f satisfies the hypotheses of the Mean Value Theorem on $[x_1, x_2]$: It is differentiable at every point of $[x_1, x_2]$ and hence continuous at every point as well. Therefore,

$$\frac{f(x_2) - f(x_1)}{x_2 - x_1} = f'(c)$$

at some point c between x_1 and x_2. Since $f' = 0$ throughout (a, b), this equation implies successively that

$$\frac{f(x_2) - f(x_1)}{x_2 - x_1} = 0, \qquad f(x_2) - f(x_1) = 0, \qquad \text{and} \qquad f(x_1) = f(x_2). \qquad \blacksquare$$

At the beginning of this section, we also asked about the relationship between two functions that have identical derivatives over an interval. The next corollary tells us that their values on the interval have a constant difference.

COROLLARY 2 If $f'(x) = g'(x)$ at each point x in an open interval (a, b), then there exists a constant C such that $f(x) = g(x) + C$ for all $x \in (a, b)$. That is, $f - g$ is a constant function on (a, b).

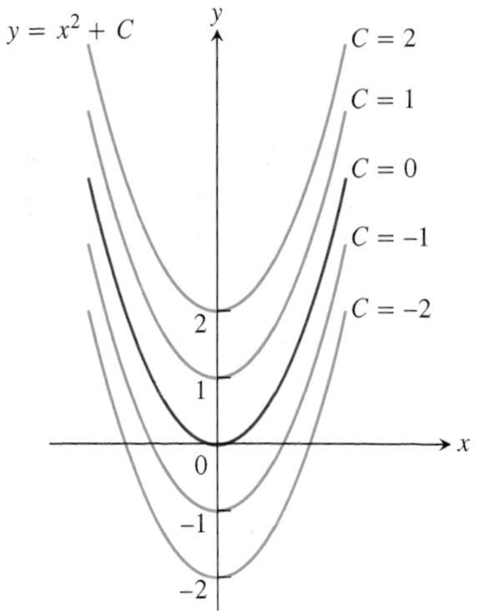

FIGURE 4.19 From a geometric point of view, Corollary 2 of the Mean Value Theorem says that the graphs of functions with identical derivatives on an interval can differ only by a vertical shift there. The graphs of the functions with derivative $2x$ are the parabolas $y = x^2 + C$, shown here for selected values of C.

Proof At each point $x \in (a, b)$ the derivative of the difference function $h = f - g$ is

$$h'(x) = f'(x) - g'(x) = 0.$$

Thus, $h(x) = C$ on (a, b) by Corollary 1. That is, $f(x) - g(x) = C$ on (a, b), so $f(x) = g(x) + C$. $\blacksquare$

Corollaries 1 and 2 are also true if the open interval (a, b) fails to be finite. That is, they remain true if the interval is (a, ∞), $(-\infty, b)$, or $(-\infty, \infty)$.

Corollary 2 plays an important role when we discuss antiderivatives in Section 4.8. It tells us, for instance, that since the derivative of $f(x) = x^2$ on $(-\infty, \infty)$ is $2x$, any other function with derivative $2x$ on $(-\infty, \infty)$ must have the formula $x^2 + C$ for some value of C (Figure 4.19).

EXAMPLE 4 Find the function $f(x)$ whose derivative is $\sin x$ and whose graph passes through the point $(0, 2)$.

Solution Since the derivative of $g(x) = -\cos x$ is $g'(x) = \sin x$, we see that f and g have the same derivative. Corollary 2 then says that $f(x) = -\cos x + C$ for some constant C. Since the graph of f passes through the point $(0, 2)$, the value of C is determined from the condition that $f(0) = 2$:

$$f(0) = -\cos(0) + C = 2, \qquad \text{so} \qquad C = 3.$$

The function is $f(x) = -\cos x + 3$. ■

Finding Velocity and Position from Acceleration

We can use Corollary 2 to find the velocity and position functions of an object moving along a vertical line. Assume the object or body is falling freely from rest with acceleration 9.8 m/sec^2. We assume the position $s(t)$ of the body is measured positive downward from the rest position (so the vertical coordinate line points *downward*, in the direction of the motion, with the rest position at 0).

We know that the velocity $v(t)$ is some function whose derivative is 9.8. We also know that the derivative of $g(t) = 9.8t$ is 9.8. By Corollary 2,

$$v(t) = 9.8t + C$$

for some constant C. Since the body falls from rest, $v(0) = 0$. Thus

$$9.8(0) + C = 0, \qquad \text{and} \qquad C = 0.$$

The velocity function must be $v(t) = 9.8t$. What about the position function $s(t)$?

We know that $s(t)$ is some function whose derivative is $9.8t$. We also know that the derivative of $f(t) = 4.9t^2$ is $9.8t$. By Corollary 2,

$$s(t) = 4.9t^2 + C$$

for some constant C. Since $s(0) = 0$,

$$4.9(0)^2 + C = 0, \qquad \text{and} \qquad C = 0.$$

The position function is $s(t) = 4.9t^2$ until the body hits the ground.

The ability to find functions from their rates of change is one of the very powerful tools of calculus. As we will see, it lies at the heart of the mathematical developments in Chapter 5.

Proofs of the Laws of Logarithms

The algebraic properties of logarithms were stated in Section 1.6. We can prove those properties by applying Corollary 2 of the Mean Value Theorem to each of them. The steps in the proofs are similar to those used in solving problems involving logarithms.

Proof that $\ln bx = \ln b + \ln x$ The argument starts by observing that $\ln bx$ and $\ln x$ have the same derivative:

$$\frac{d}{dx}\ln(bx) = \frac{b}{bx} = \frac{1}{x} = \frac{d}{dx}\ln x.$$

According to Corollary 2 of the Mean Value Theorem, then, the functions must differ by a constant, which means that

$$\ln bx = \ln x + C$$

for some C.

Since this last equation holds for all positive values of x, it must hold for $x = 1$. Hence,

$$\begin{aligned} \ln(b \cdot 1) &= \ln 1 + C \\ \ln b &= 0 + C \qquad \ln 1 = 0 \\ C &= \ln b. \end{aligned}$$

By substituting, we conclude

$$\ln bx = \ln b + \ln x. \qquad \blacksquare$$

Proof that $\ln x^r = r \ln x$ We use the same-derivative argument again. For all positive values of x,

$$\begin{aligned}\frac{d}{dx}\ln x^r &= \frac{1}{x^r}\frac{d}{dx}(x^r) && \text{Chain Rule}\\ &= \frac{1}{x^r} r x^{r-1} && \text{Derivative Power Rule}\\ &= r \cdot \frac{1}{x} = \frac{d}{dx}(r \ln x).\end{aligned}$$

Since $\ln x^r$ and $r \ln x$ have the same derivative,

$$\ln x^r = r \ln x + C$$

for some constant C. Taking x to be 1 identifies C as zero, and we're done. ■

You are asked to prove the Quotient Rule for logarithms,

$$\ln\left(\frac{b}{x}\right) = \ln b - \ln x,$$

in Exercise 75. The Reciprocal Rule, $\ln(1/x) = -\ln x$, is a special case of the Quotient Rule, obtained by taking $b = 1$ and noting that $\ln 1 = 0$.

Laws of Exponents

The laws of exponents for the natural exponential e^x are consequences of the algebraic properties of $\ln x$. They follow from the inverse relationship between these functions.

Laws of Exponents for e^x

For all numbers x, x_1, and x_2, the natural exponential e^x obeys the following laws:

1. $e^{x_1} \cdot e^{x_2} = e^{x_1 + x_2}$
2. $e^{-x} = \dfrac{1}{e^x}$
3. $\dfrac{e^{x_1}}{e^{x_2}} = e^{x_1 - x_2}$
4. $(e^{x_1})^{x_2} = e^{x_1 x_2} = (e^{x_2})^{x_1}$

Proof of Law 1 Let

$$y_1 = e^{x_1} \quad \text{and} \quad y_2 = e^{x_2}. \tag{4}$$

Then

$$\begin{aligned} x_1 &= \ln y_1 \quad \text{and} \quad x_2 = \ln y_2 && \text{Take logs of both sides of Eqs. (4).}\\ x_1 + x_2 &= \ln y_1 + \ln y_2 \\ &= \ln y_1 y_2 && \text{Product Rule for logarithms}\\ e^{x_1 + x_2} &= e^{\ln y_1 y_2} && \text{Exponentiate.}\\ &= y_1 y_2 && e^{\ln u} = u\\ &= e^{x_1} e^{x_2}. \end{aligned}$$

■

The proof of Law 4 is similar. Laws 2 and 3 follow from Law 1 (Exercises 77 and 78).

Exercises 4.2

Checking the Mean Value Theorem

Find the value or values of c that satisfy the equation

$$\frac{f(b) - f(a)}{b - a} = f'(c)$$

in the conclusion of the Mean Value Theorem for the functions and intervals in Exercises 1–8.

1. $f(x) = x^2 + 2x - 1, \quad [0, 1]$
2. $f(x) = x^{2/3}, \quad [0, 1]$
3. $f(x) = x + \frac{1}{x}, \quad \left[\frac{1}{2}, 2\right]$
4. $f(x) = \sqrt{x - 1}, \quad [1, 3]$
5. $f(x) = \sin^{-1} x, \quad [-1, 1]$
6. $f(x) = \ln (x - 1), \quad [2, 4]$
7. $f(x) = x^3 - x^2, \quad [-1, 2]$
8. $g(x) = \begin{cases} x^3, & -2 \le x \le 0 \\ x^2, & 0 < x \le 2 \end{cases}$

Which of the functions in Exercises 9–14 satisfy the hypotheses of the Mean Value Theorem on the given interval, and which do not? Give reasons for your answers.

9. $f(x) = x^{2/3}, \quad [-1, 8]$
10. $f(x) = x^{4/5}, \quad [0, 1]$
11. $f(x) = \sqrt{x(1 - x)}, \quad [0, 1]$
12. $f(x) = \begin{cases} \frac{\sin x}{x}, & -\pi \le x < 0 \\ 0, & x = 0 \end{cases}$
13. $f(x) = \begin{cases} x^2 - x, & -2 \le x \le -1 \\ 2x^2 - 3x - 3, & -1 < x \le 0 \end{cases}$
14. $f(x) = \begin{cases} 2x - 3, & 0 \le x \le 2 \\ 6x - x^2 - 7, & 2 < x \le 3 \end{cases}$
15. The function

$$f(x) = \begin{cases} x, & 0 \le x < 1 \\ 0, & x = 1 \end{cases}$$

is zero at $x = 0$ and $x = 1$ and differentiable on $(0, 1)$, but its derivative on $(0, 1)$ is never zero. How can this be? Doesn't Rolle's Theorem say the derivative has to be zero somewhere in $(0, 1)$? Give reasons for your answer.

16. For what values of a, m, and b does the function

$$f(x) = \begin{cases} 3, & x = 0 \\ -x^2 + 3x + a, & 0 < x < 1 \\ mx + b, & 1 \le x \le 2 \end{cases}$$

satisfy the hypotheses of the Mean Value Theorem on the interval $[0, 2]$?

Roots (Zeros)

17. **a.** Plot the zeros of each polynomial on a line together with the zeros of its first derivative.
    i) $y = x^2 - 4$
    ii) $y = x^2 + 8x + 15$
    iii) $y = x^3 - 3x^2 + 4 = (x + 1)(x - 2)^2$
    iv) $y = x^3 - 33x^2 + 216x = x(x - 9)(x - 24)$
    b. Use Rolle's Theorem to prove that between every two zeros of $x^n + a_{n-1}x^{n-1} + \cdots + a_1x + a_0$ there lies a zero of
    $$nx^{n-1} + (n - 1)a_{n-1}x^{n-2} + \cdots + a_1.$$
18. Suppose that f'' is continuous on $[a, b]$ and that f has three zeros in the interval. Show that f'' has at least one zero in (a, b). Generalize this result.
19. Show that if $f'' > 0$ throughout an interval $[a, b]$, then f' has at most one zero in $[a, b]$. What if $f'' < 0$ throughout $[a, b]$ instead?
20. Show that a cubic polynomial can have at most three real zeros.

Show that the functions in Exercises 21–28 have exactly one zero in the given interval.

21. $f(x) = x^4 + 3x + 1, \quad [-2, -1]$
22. $f(x) = x^3 + \frac{4}{x^2} + 7, \quad (-\infty, 0)$
23. $g(t) = \sqrt{t} + \sqrt{1 + t} - 4, \quad (0, \infty)$
24. $g(t) = \frac{1}{1 - t} + \sqrt{1 + t} - 3.1, \quad (-1, 1)$
25. $r(\theta) = \theta + \sin^2\left(\frac{\theta}{3}\right) - 8, \quad (-\infty, \infty)$
26. $r(\theta) = 2\theta - \cos^2 \theta + \sqrt{2}, \quad (-\infty, \infty)$
27. $r(\theta) = \sec \theta - \frac{1}{\theta^3} + 5, \quad (0, \pi/2)$
28. $r(\theta) = \tan \theta - \cot \theta - \theta, \quad (0, \pi/2)$

Finding Functions from Derivatives

29. Suppose that $f(-1) = 3$ and that $f'(x) = 0$ for all x. Must $f(x) = 3$ for all x? Give reasons for your answer.
30. Suppose that $f(0) = 5$ and that $f'(x) = 2$ for all x. Must $f(x) = 2x + 5$ for all x? Give reasons for your answer.
31. Suppose that $f'(x) = 2x$ for all x. Find $f(2)$ if
    a. $f(0) = 0$ **b.** $f(1) = 0$ **c.** $f(-2) = 3$.
32. What can be said about functions whose derivatives are constant? Give reasons for your answer.

In Exercises 33–38, find all possible functions with the given derivative.

33. **a.** $y' = x$ **b.** $y' = x^2$ **c.** $y' = x^3$
34. **a.** $y' = 2x$ **b.** $y' = 2x - 1$ **c.** $y' = 3x^2 + 2x - 1$
35. **a.** $y' = -\frac{1}{x^2}$ **b.** $y' = 1 - \frac{1}{x^2}$ **c.** $y' = 5 + \frac{1}{x^2}$

36. **a.** $y' = \dfrac{1}{2\sqrt{x}}$ **b.** $y' = \dfrac{1}{\sqrt{x}}$ **c.** $y' = 4x - \dfrac{1}{\sqrt{x}}$

37. **a.** $y' = \sin 2t$ **b.** $y' = \cos \dfrac{t}{2}$ **c.** $y' = \sin 2t + \cos \dfrac{t}{2}$

38. **a.** $y' = \sec^2 \theta$ **b.** $y' = \sqrt{\theta}$ **c.** $y' = \sqrt{\theta} - \sec^2 \theta$

In Exercises 39–42, find the function with the given derivative whose graph passes through the point P.

39. $f'(x) = 2x - 1, \quad P(0, 0)$

40. $g'(x) = \dfrac{1}{x^2} + 2x, \quad P(-1, 1)$

41. $f'(x) = e^{2x}, \quad P\left(0, \dfrac{3}{2}\right)$

42. $r'(t) = \sec t \tan t - 1, \quad P(0, 0)$

Finding Position from Velocity or Acceleration

Exercises 43–46 give the velocity $v = ds/dt$ and initial position of a body moving along a coordinate line. Find the body's position at time t.

43. $v = 9.8t + 5, \quad s(0) = 10$

44. $v = 32t - 2, \quad s(0.5) = 4$

45. $v = \sin \pi t, \quad s(0) = 0$

46. $v = \dfrac{2}{\pi} \cos \dfrac{2t}{\pi}, \quad s(\pi^2) = 1$

Exercises 47–50 give the acceleration $a = d^2s/dt^2$, initial velocity, and initial position of a body moving on a coordinate line. Find the body's position at time t.

47. $a = e^t, \quad v(0) = 20, \quad s(0) = 5$

48. $a = 9.8, \quad v(0) = -3, \quad s(0) = 0$

49. $a = -4 \sin 2t, \quad v(0) = 2, \quad s(0) = -3$

50. $a = \dfrac{9}{\pi^2} \cos \dfrac{3t}{\pi}, \quad v(0) = 0, \quad s(0) = -1$

Applications

51. Temperature change It took 14 sec for a mercury thermometer to rise from −19°C to 100°C when it was taken from a freezer and placed in boiling water. Show that somewhere along the way the mercury was rising at the rate of 8.5°C/sec.

52. A trucker handed in a ticket at a toll booth showing that in 2 hours she had covered 159 mi on a toll road with speed limit 65 mph. The trucker was cited for speeding. Why?

53. Classical accounts tell us that a 170-oar trireme (ancient Greek or Roman warship) once covered 184 sea miles in 24 hours. Explain why at some point during this feat the trireme's speed exceeded 7.5 knots (sea miles per hour).

54. A marathoner ran the 26.2-mi New York City Marathon in 2.2 hours. Show that at least twice the marathoner was running at exactly 11 mph, assuming the initial and final speeds are zero.

55. Show that at some instant during a 2-hour automobile trip the car's speedometer reading will equal the average speed for the trip.

56. Free fall on the moon On our moon, the acceleration of gravity is 1.6 m/sec^2. If a rock is dropped into a crevasse, how fast will it be going just before it hits bottom 30 sec later?

Theory and Examples

57. The geometric mean of *a* and *b* The *geometric mean* of two positive numbers a and b is the number $\sqrt{ab}$. Show that the value of c in the conclusion of the Mean Value Theorem for $f(x) = 1/x$ on an interval of positive numbers $[a, b]$ is $c = \sqrt{ab}$.

58. The arithmetic mean of *a* and *b* The *arithmetic mean* of two numbers a and b is the number $(a + b)/2$. Show that the value of c in the conclusion of the Mean Value Theorem for $f(x) = x^2$ on any interval $[a, b]$ is $c = (a + b)/2$.

T **59.** Graph the function

$$f(x) = \sin x \sin (x + 2) - \sin^2 (x + 1).$$

What does the graph do? Why does the function behave this way? Give reasons for your answers.

60. Rolle's Theorem

a. Construct a polynomial $f(x)$ that has zeros at $x = -2, -1, 0, 1$, and 2.

b. Graph f and its derivative f' together. How is what you see related to Rolle's Theorem?

c. Do $g(x) = \sin x$ and its derivative g' illustrate the same phenomenon as f and f'?

61. Unique solution Assume that f is continuous on $[a, b]$ and differentiable on (a, b). Also assume that $f(a)$ and $f(b)$ have opposite signs and that $f' \neq 0$ between a and b. Show that $f(x) = 0$ exactly once between a and b.

62. Parallel tangents Assume that f and g are differentiable on $[a, b]$ and that $f(a) = g(a)$ and $f(b) = g(b)$. Show that there is at least one point between a and b where the tangents to the graphs of f and g are parallel or the same line. Illustrate with a sketch.

63. Suppose that $f'(x) \le 1$ for $1 \le x \le 4$. Show that $f(4) - f(1) \le 3$.

64. Suppose that $0 < f'(x) < 1/2$ for all x-values. Show that $f(-1) < f(1) < 2 + f(-1)$.

65. Show that $|\cos x - 1| \le |x|$ for all x-values. (*Hint:* Consider $f(t) = \cos t$ on $[0, x]$.)

66. Show that for any numbers a and b, the sine inequality $|\sin b - \sin a| \le |b - a|$ is true.

67. If the graphs of two differentiable functions $f(x)$ and $g(x)$ start at the same point in the plane and the functions have the same rate of change at every point, do the graphs have to be identical? Give reasons for your answer.

68. If $|f(w) - f(x)| \le |w - x|$ for all values w and x and f is a differentiable function, show that $-1 \le f'(x) \le 1$ for all x-values.

69. Assume that f is differentiable on $a \le x \le b$ and that $f(b) < f(a)$. Show that f' is negative at some point between a and b.

70. Let f be a function defined on an interval $[a, b]$. What conditions could you place on f to guarantee that

$$\min f' \le \frac{f(b) - f(a)}{b - a} \le \max f',$$

where $\min f'$ and $\max f'$ refer to the minimum and maximum values of f' on $[a, b]$? Give reasons for your answers.

T **71.** Use the inequalities in Exercise 70 to estimate $f(0.1)$ if $f'(x) = 1/(1 + x^4 \cos x)$ for $0 \le x \le 0.1$ and $f(0) = 1$.

T **72.** Use the inequalities in Exercise 70 to estimate $f(0.1)$ if $f'(x) = 1/(1 - x^4)$ for $0 \le x \le 0.1$ and $f(0) = 2$.

73. Let f be differentiable at every value of x and suppose that $f(1) = 1$, that $f' < 0$ on $(-\infty, 1)$, and that $f' > 0$ on $(1, \infty)$.

a. Show that $f(x) \ge 1$ for all x.

b. Must $f'(1) = 0$? Explain.

74. Let $f(x) = px^2 + qx + r$ be a quadratic function defined on a closed interval $[a, b]$. Show that there is exactly one point c in (a, b) at which f satisfies the conclusion of the Mean Value Theorem.

75. Use the same-derivative argument, as was done to prove the Product and Power Rules for logarithms, to prove the Quotient Rule property.

76. Use the same-derivative argument to prove the identities

a. $\tan^{-1} x + \cot^{-1} x = \dfrac{\pi}{2}$ **b.** $\sec^{-1} x + \csc^{-1} x = \dfrac{\pi}{2}$

77. Starting with the equation $e^{x_1}e^{x_2} = e^{x_1+x_2}$, derived in the text, show that $e^{-x} = 1/e^x$ for any real number x. Then show that $e^{x_1}/e^{x_2} = e^{x_1-x_2}$ for any numbers x_1 and x_2.

78. Show that $(e^{x_1})^{x_2} = e^{x_1x_2} = (e^{x_2})^{x_1}$ for any numbers x_1 and x_2.

4.3 Monotonic Functions and the First Derivative Test

In sketching the graph of a differentiable function, it is useful to know where it increases (rises from left to right) and where it decreases (falls from left to right) over an interval. This section gives a test to determine where it increases and where it decreases. We also show how to test the critical points of a function to identify whether local extreme values are present.

Increasing Functions and Decreasing Functions

As another corollary to the Mean Value Theorem, we show that functions with positive derivatives are increasing functions and functions with negative derivatives are decreasing functions. A function that is increasing or decreasing on an interval is said to be **monotonic** on the interval.

> COROLLARY 3 Suppose that f is continuous on $[a, b]$ and differentiable on (a, b).
>
> If $f'(x) > 0$ at each point $x \in (a, b)$, then f is increasing on $[a, b]$.
> If $f'(x) < 0$ at each point $x \in (a, b)$, then f is decreasing on $[a, b]$.

Proof Let x_1 and x_2 be any two points in $[a, b]$ with $x_1 < x_2$. The Mean Value Theorem applied to f on $[x_1, x_2]$ says that

$$f(x_2) - f(x_1) = f'(c)(x_2 - x_1)$$

for some c between x_1 and x_2. The sign of the right-hand side of this equation is the same as the sign of $f'(c)$ because $x_2 - x_1$ is positive. Therefore, $f(x_2) > f(x_1)$ if f' is positive on (a, b) and $f(x_2) < f(x_1)$ if f' is negative on (a, b). ■

Corollary 3 tells us that $f(x) = \sqrt{x}$ is increasing on the interval $[0, b]$ for any $b > 0$ because $f'(x) = 1/\sqrt{x}$ is positive on $(0, b)$. The derivative does not exist at $x = 0$, but Corollary 3 still applies. The corollary is valid for infinite as well as finite intervals, so $f(x) = \sqrt{x}$ is increasing on $[0, \infty)$.

To find the intervals where a function f is increasing or decreasing, we first find all of the critical points of f. If $a < b$ are two critical points for f, and if the derivative f' is continuous but never zero on the interval (a, b), then by the Intermediate Value Theorem applied to f', the derivative must be everywhere positive on (a, b), or everywhere negative there. One way we can determine the sign of f' on (a, b) is simply by evaluating the derivative at a single point c in (a, b). If $f'(c) > 0$, then $f'(x) > 0$ for all x in (a, b) so f is increasing on $[a, b]$ by Corollary 3; if $f'(c) < 0$, then f is decreasing on $[a, b]$. The next example illustrates how we use this procedure.

EXAMPLE 1 Find the critical points of $f(x) = x^3 - 12x - 5$ and identify the intervals on which f is increasing and on which f is decreasing.

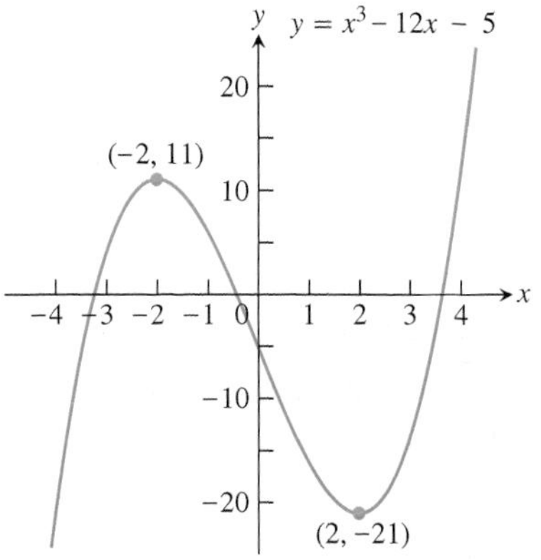

FIGURE 4.20 The function $f(x) = x^3 - 12x - 5$ is monotonic on three separate intervals (Example 1).

Solution The function f is everywhere continuous and differentiable. The first derivative

$$\begin{aligned} f'(x) &= 3x^2 - 12 = 3(x^2 - 4) \\ &= 3(x + 2)(x - 2) \end{aligned}$$

is zero at $x = -2$ and $x = 2$. These critical points subdivide the domain of f to create nonoverlapping open intervals $(-\infty, -2)$, $(-2, 2)$, and $(2, \infty)$ on which f' is either positive or negative. We determine the sign of f' by evaluating f' at a convenient point in each subinterval. The behavior of f is determined by then applying Corollary 3 to each subinterval. The results are summarized in the following table, and the graph of f is given in Figure 4.20.

Interval	$-\infty < x < -2$	$-2 < x < 2$	$2 < x < \infty$
f' evaluated	$f'(-3) = 15$	$f'(0) = -12$	$f'(3) = 15$
Sign of f'	$+$	$-$	$+$
Behavior of f	increasing	decreasing	increasing

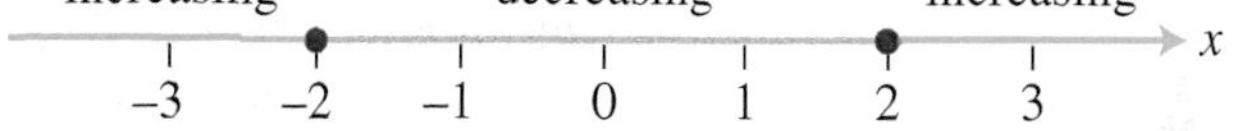

■

We used "strict" less-than inequalities to specify the intervals in the summary table for Example 1. Corollary 3 says that we could use $\le$ inequalities as well. That is, the function f in the example is increasing on $-\infty < x \le -2$, decreasing on $-2 \le x \le 2$, and increasing on $2 \le x < \infty$. We do not talk about whether a function is increasing or decreasing at a single point.

HISTORICAL BIOGRAPHY

Edmund Halley
(1656–1742)

First Derivative Test for Local Extrema

In Figure 4.21, at the points where f has a minimum value, $f' < 0$ immediately to the left and $f' > 0$ immediately to the right. (If the point is an endpoint, there is only one side to consider.) Thus, the function is decreasing on the left of the minimum value and it is increasing on its right. Similarly, at the points where f has a maximum value, $f' > 0$ immediately to the left and $f' < 0$ immediately to the right. Thus, the function is increasing on the left of the maximum value and decreasing on its right. In summary, at a local extreme point, the sign of $f'(x)$ changes.

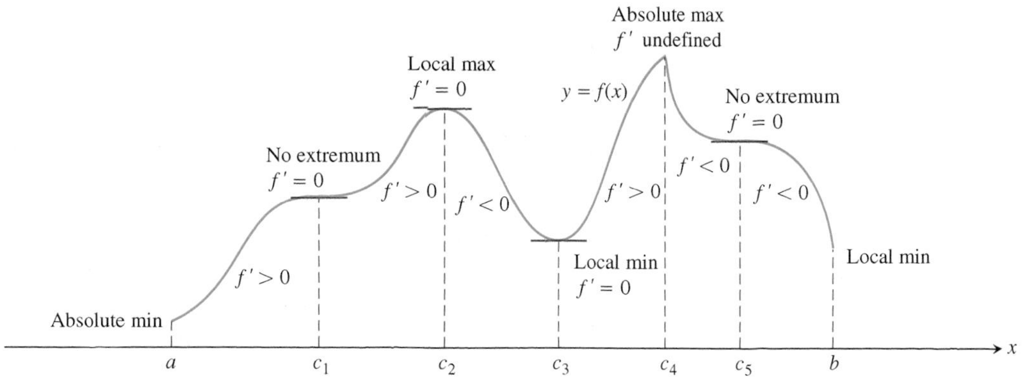

FIGURE 4.21 The critical points of a function locate where it is increasing and where it is decreasing. The first derivative changes sign at a critical point where a local extremum occurs.

These observations lead to a test for the presence and nature of local extreme values of differentiable functions.

First Derivative Test for Local Extrema

Suppose that c is a critical point of a continuous function f, and that f is differentiable at every point in some interval containing c except possibly at c itself. Moving across this interval from left to right,

1. if f' changes from negative to positive at c, then f has a local minimum at c;
2. if f' changes from positive to negative at c, then f has a local maximum at c;
3. if f' does not change sign at c (that is, f' is positive on both sides of c or negative on both sides), then f has no local extremum at c.

The test for local extrema at endpoints is similar, but there is only one side to consider.

Proof of the First Derivative Test Part (1). Since the sign of f' changes from negative to positive at c, there are numbers a and b such that $a < c < b$, $f' < 0$ on (a, c), and $f' > 0$ on (c, b). If $x \in (a, c)$, then $f(c) < f(x)$ because $f' < 0$ implies that f is decreasing on $[a, c]$. If $x \in (c, b)$, then $f(c) < f(x)$ because $f' > 0$ implies that f is increasing on $[c, b]$. Therefore, $f(x) \geq f(c)$ for every $x \in (a, b)$. By definition, f has a local minimum at c.

Parts (2) and (3) are proved similarly. ■

EXAMPLE 2 Find the critical points of

$$f(x) = x^{1/3}(x - 4) = x^{4/3} - 4x^{1/3}.$$

Identify the intervals on which f is increasing and decreasing. Find the function's local and absolute extreme values.

Solution The function f is continuous at all x since it is the product of two continuous functions, $x^{1/3}$ and $(x - 4)$. The first derivative

$$f'(x) = \frac{d}{dx}\left(x^{4/3} - 4x^{1/3}\right) = \frac{4}{3}x^{1/3} - \frac{4}{3}x^{-2/3}$$
$$= \frac{4}{3}x^{-2/3}\left(x - 1\right) = \frac{4(x - 1)}{3x^{2/3}}$$

is zero at $x = 1$ and undefined at $x = 0$. There are no endpoints in the domain, so the critical points $x = 0$ and $x = 1$ are the only places where f might have an extreme value.

The critical points partition the x-axis into intervals on which f' is either positive or negative. The sign pattern of f' reveals the behavior of f between and at the critical points, as summarized in the following table.

Interval	$x < 0$	$0 < x < 1$	$x > 1$
Sign of f'	$-$	$-$	$+$
Behavior of f	decreasing	decreasing	increasing

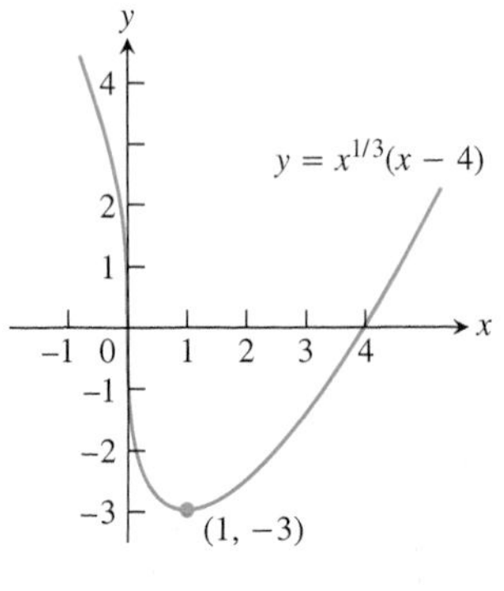

FIGURE 4.22 The function $f(x) = x^{1/3}(x - 4)$ decreases when $x < 1$ and increases when $x > 1$ (Example 2).

Corollary 3 to the Mean Value Theorem tells us that f decreases on $(-\infty, 0]$, decreases on $[0, 1]$, and increases on $[1, \infty)$. The First Derivative Test for Local Extrema tells us that f does not have an extreme value at $x = 0$ (f' does not change sign) and that f has a local minimum at $x = 1$ (f' changes from negative to positive).

The value of the local minimum is $f(1) = 1^{1/3}(1 - 4) = -3$. This is also an absolute minimum since f is decreasing on $(-\infty, 1]$ and increasing on $[1, \infty)$. Figure 4.22 shows this value in relation to the function's graph.

Note that $\lim_{x \to 0} f'(x) = -\infty$, so the graph of f has a vertical tangent at the origin. ■

EXAMPLE 3 Find the critical points of

$$f(x) = (x^2 - 3)e^x.$$

Identify the intervals on which f is increasing and decreasing. Find the function's local and absolute extreme values.

Solution The function f is continuous and differentiable for all real numbers, so the critical points occur only at the zeros of f'.

Using the Derivative Product Rule, we find the derivative

$$\begin{aligned} f'(x) &= (x^2 - 3)\cdot\frac{d}{dx}e^x + \frac{d}{dx}(x^2 - 3)\cdot e^x \\ &= (x^2 - 3)\cdot e^x + (2x)\cdot e^x \\ &= (x^2 + 2x - 3)e^x. \end{aligned}$$

Since e^x is never zero, the first derivative is zero if and only if

$$x^2 + 2x - 3 = 0$$
$$(x + 3)(x - 1) = 0.$$

The zeros $x = -3$ and $x = 1$ partition the x-axis into intervals as follows.

Interval	$x < -3$	$-3 < x < 1$	$1 < x$
Sign of f'	$+$	$-$	$+$
Behavior of f	increasing	decreasing	increasing

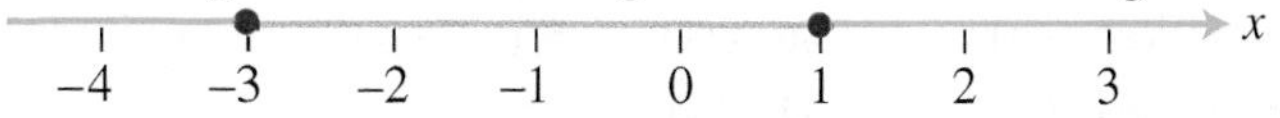

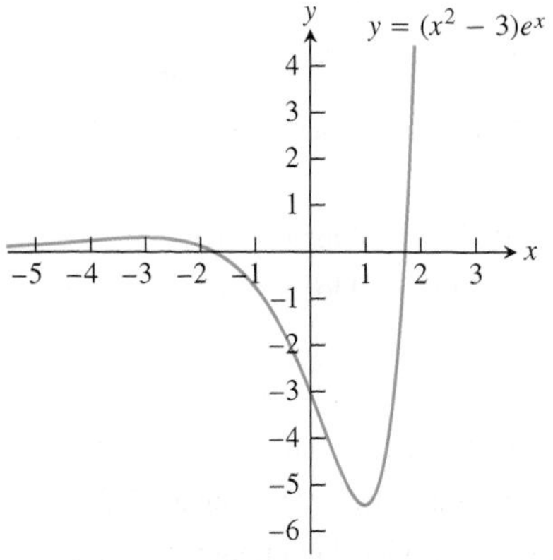

FIGURE 4.23 The graph of $f(x) = (x^2 - 3)e^x$ (Example 3).

We can see from the table that there is a local maximum (about 0.299) at $x = -3$ and a local minimum (about -5.437) at $x = 1$. The local minimum value is also an absolute minimum because $f(x) > 0$ for $|x| > \sqrt{3}$. There is no absolute maximum. The function increases on $(-\infty, -3)$ and $(1, \infty)$ and decreases on $(-3, 1)$. Figure 4.23 shows the graph. ■

Exercises 4.3

Analyzing Functions from Derivatives

Answer the following questions about the functions whose derivatives are given in Exercises 1–14:

a. What are the critical points of f?

b. On what intervals is f increasing or decreasing?

c. At what points, if any, does f assume local maximum and minimum values?

1. $f'(x) = x(x - 1)$ **2.** $f'(x) = (x - 1)(x + 2)$

3. $f'(x) = (x - 1)^2(x + 2)$ **4.** $f'(x) = (x - 1)^2(x + 2)^2$

5. $f'(x) = (x - 1)e^{-x}$

6. $f'(x) = (x - 7)(x + 1)(x + 5)$

7. $f'(x) = \dfrac{x^2(x - 1)}{x + 2}, \quad x \neq -2$

8. $f'(x) = \dfrac{(x - 2)(x + 4)}{(x + 1)(x - 3)}, \quad x \neq -1, 3$

9. $f'(x) = 1 - \dfrac{4}{x^2}, \quad x \neq 0$ **10.** $f'(x) = 3 - \dfrac{6}{\sqrt{x}}, \quad x \neq 0$

11. $f'(x) = x^{-1/3}(x + 2)$ **12.** $f'(x) = x^{-1/2}(x - 3)$

13. $f'(x) = (\sin x - 1)(2\cos x + 1), 0 \le x \le 2\pi$

14. $f'(x) = (\sin x + \cos x)(\sin x - \cos x), 0 \le x \le 2\pi$

Identifying Extrema

In Exercises 15–44:

a. Find the open intervals on which the function is increasing and decreasing.

b. Identify the function's local and absolute extreme values, if any, saying where they occur.

15.

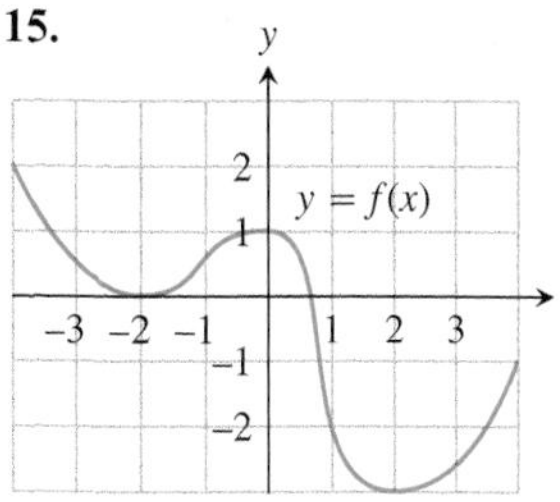

16.

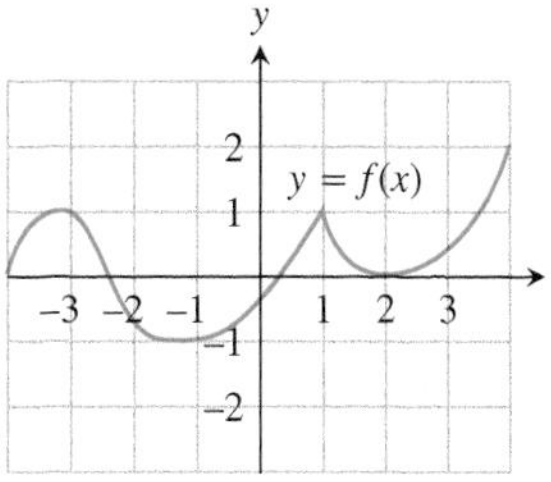

17.

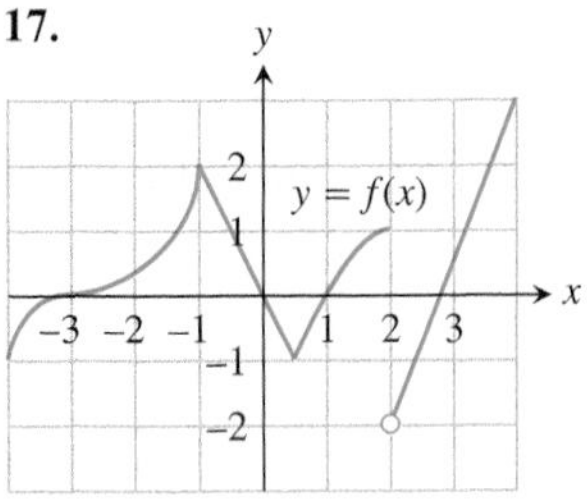

18.

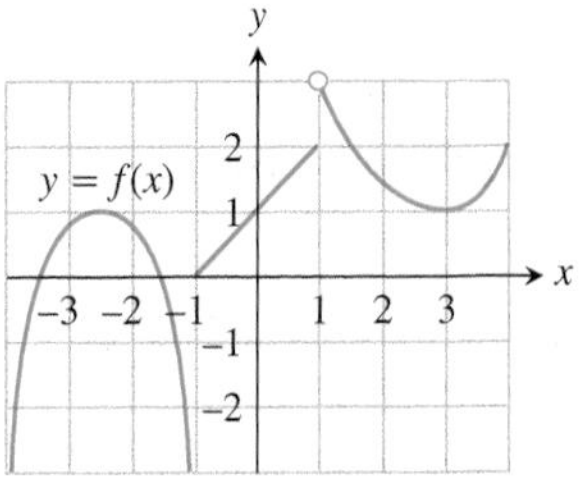

19. $g(t) = -t^2 - 3t + 3$

20. $g(t) = -3t^2 + 9t + 5$

21. $h(x) = -x^3 + 2x^2$

22. $h(x) = 2x^3 - 18x$

23. $f(\theta) = 3\theta^2 - 4\theta^3$

24. $f(\theta) = 6\theta - \theta^3$

25. $f(r) = 3r^3 + 16r$

26. $h(r) = (r + 7)^3$

27. $f(x) = x^4 - 8x^2 + 16$

28. $g(x) = x^4 - 4x^3 + 4x^2$

29. $H(t) = \frac{3}{2}t^4 - t^6$

30. $K(t) = 15t^3 - t^5$

31. $f(x) = x - 6\sqrt{x - 1}$

32. $g(x) = 4\sqrt{x} - x^2 + 3$

33. $g(x) = x\sqrt{8 - x^2}$

34. $g(x) = x^2\sqrt{5 - x}$

35. $f(x) = \frac{x^2 - 3}{x - 2}, \quad x \neq 2$

36. $f(x) = \frac{x^3}{3x^2 + 1}$

37. $f(x) = x^{1/3}(x + 8)$

38. $g(x) = x^{2/3}(x + 5)$

39. $h(x) = x^{1/3}(x^2 - 4)$

40. $k(x) = x^{2/3}(x^2 - 4)$

41. $f(x) = e^{2x} + e^{-x}$

42. $f(x) = e^{\sqrt{x}}$

43. $f(x) = x \ln x$

44. $f(x) = x^2 \ln x$

In Exercises 45–56:

a. Identify the function's local extreme values in the given domain, and say where they occur.

b. Which of the extreme values, if any, are absolute?

T **c.** Support your findings with a graphing calculator or computer grapher.

45. $f(x) = 2x - x^2, \quad -\infty < x \leq 2$

46. $f(x) = (x + 1)^2, \quad -\infty < x \leq 0$

47. $g(x) = x^2 - 4x + 4, \quad 1 \leq x < \infty$

48. $g(x) = -x^2 - 6x - 9, \quad -4 \leq x < \infty$

49. $f(t) = 12t - t^3, \quad -3 \leq t < \infty$

50. $f(t) = t^3 - 3t^2, \quad -\infty < t \leq 3$

51. $h(x) = \frac{x^3}{3} - 2x^2 + 4x, \quad 0 \leq x < \infty$

52. $k(x) = x^3 + 3x^2 + 3x + 1, \quad -\infty < x \leq 0$

53. $f(x) = \sqrt{25 - x^2}, \quad -5 \leq x \leq 5$

54. $f(x) = \sqrt{x^2 - 2x - 3}, \quad 3 \leq x < \infty$

55. $g(x) = \frac{x - 2}{x^2 - 1}, \quad 0 \leq x < 1$

56. $g(x) = \frac{x^2}{4 - x^2}, \quad -2 < x \leq 1$

In Exercises 57–64:

a. Find the local extrema of each function on the given interval, and say where they occur.

T **b.** Graph the function and its derivative together. Comment on the behavior of f in relation to the signs and values of f'.

57. $f(x) = \sin 2x, \quad 0 \leq x \leq \pi$

58. $f(x) = \sin x - \cos x, \quad 0 \leq x \leq 2\pi$

59. $f(x) = \sqrt{3}\cos x + \sin x, \quad 0 \leq x \leq 2\pi$

60. $f(x) = -2x + \tan x, \quad \frac{-\pi}{2} < x < \frac{\pi}{2}$

61. $f(x) = \frac{x}{2} - 2\sin\frac{x}{2}, \quad 0 \leq x \leq 2\pi$

62. $f(x) = -2\cos x - \cos^2 x, \quad -\pi \leq x \leq \pi$

63. $f(x) = \csc^2 x - 2\cot x, \quad 0 < x < \pi$

64. $f(x) = \sec^2 x - 2\tan x, \quad \frac{-\pi}{2} < x < \frac{\pi}{2}$

Theory and Examples

Show that the functions in Exercises 65 and 66 have local extreme values at the given values of θ, and say which kind of local extreme the function has.

65. $h(\theta) = 3\cos\frac{\theta}{2}, \quad 0 \leq \theta \leq 2\pi, \quad$ at $\theta = 0$ and $\theta = 2\pi$

66. $h(\theta) = 5\sin\frac{\theta}{2}, \quad 0 \leq \theta \leq \pi, \quad$ at $\theta = 0$ and $\theta = \pi$

67. Sketch the graph of a differentiable function $y = f(x)$ through the point $(1, 1)$ if $f'(1) = 0$ and

a. $f'(x) > 0$ for $x < 1$ and $f'(x) < 0$ for $x > 1$;

b. $f'(x) < 0$ for $x < 1$ and $f'(x) > 0$ for $x > 1$;

c. $f'(x) > 0$ for $x \neq 1$;

d. $f'(x) < 0$ for $x \neq 1$.

68. Sketch the graph of a differentiable function $y = f(x)$ that has

a. a local minimum at $(1, 1)$ and a local maximum at $(3, 3)$;

b. a local maximum at $(1, 1)$ and a local minimum at $(3, 3)$;

c. local maxima at $(1, 1)$ and $(3, 3)$;

d. local minima at $(1, 1)$ and $(3, 3)$.

69. Sketch the graph of a continuous function $y = g(x)$ such that

a. $g(2) = 2$, $0 < g' < 1$ for $x < 2$, $g'(x) \to 1^-$ as $x \to 2^-$, $-1 < g' < 0$ for $x > 2$, and $g'(x) \to -1^+$ as $x \to 2^+$;

b. $g(2) = 2$, $g' < 0$ for $x < 2$, $g'(x) \to -\infty$ as $x \to 2^-$, $g' > 0$ for $x > 2$, and $g'(x) \to \infty$ as $x \to 2^+$.

70. Sketch the graph of a continuous function $y = h(x)$ such that

a. $h(0) = 0$, $-2 \leq h(x) \leq 2$ for all x, $h'(x) \to \infty$ as $x \to 0^-$, and $h'(x) \to \infty$ as $x \to 0^+$;

b. $h(0) = 0$, $-2 \leq h(x) \leq 0$ for all x, $h'(x) \to \infty$ as $x \to 0^-$, and $h'(x) \to -\infty$ as $x \to 0^+$.

71. Discuss the extreme-value behavior of the function $f(x) = x\sin(1/x)$, $x \neq 0$. How many critical points does this function have? Where are they located on the x-axis? Does f have an absolute minimum? An absolute maximum? (See Exercise 49 in Section 2.3.)

72. Find the intervals on which the function $f(x) = ax^2 + bx + c$, $a \neq 0$, is increasing and decreasing. Describe the reasoning behind your answer.

73. Determine the values of constants a and b so that $f(x) = ax^2 + bx$ has an absolute maximum at the point $(1, 2)$.

74. Determine the values of constants a, b, c, and d so that $f(x) = ax^3 + bx^2 + cx + d$ has a local maximum at the point $(0, 0)$ and a local minimum at the point $(1, -1)$.

75. Locate and identify the absolute extreme values of

a. $\ln(\cos x)$ on $[-\pi/4, \pi/3]$,

b. $\cos(\ln x)$ on $[1/2, 2]$.

76. a. Prove that $f(x) = x - \ln x$ is increasing for $x > 1$.

b. Using part (a), show that $\ln x < x$ if $x > 1$.

77. Find the absolute maximum and minimum values of $f(x) = e^x - 2x$ on $[0, 1]$.

78. Where does the periodic function $f(x) = 2e^{\sin(x/2)}$ take on its extreme values and what are these values?

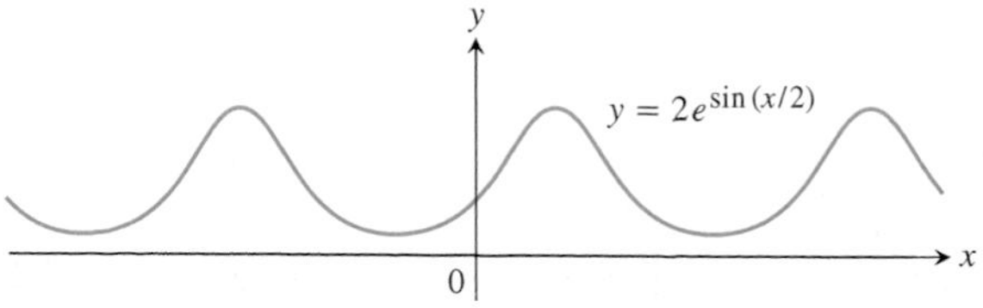

79. Find the absolute maximum value of $f(x) = x^2 \ln(1/x)$ and say where it is assumed.

80. a. Prove that $e^x \geq 1 + x$ if $x \geq 0$.

b. Use the result in part (a) to show that

$$e^x \geq 1 + x + \frac{1}{2}x^2.$$

81. Show that increasing functions and decreasing functions are one-to-one. That is, show that for any x_1 and x_2 in I, $x_2 \neq x_1$ implies $f(x_2) \neq f(x_1)$.

Use the results of Exercise 81 to show that the functions in Exercises 82–86 have inverses over their domains. Find a formula for df^{-1}/dx using Theorem 3, Section 3.8.

82. $f(x) = (1/3)x + (5/6)$

83. $f(x) = 27x^3$

84. $f(x) = 1 - 8x^3$

85. $f(x) = (1 - x)^3$

86. $f(x) = x^{5/3}$

4.4 Concavity and Curve Sketching

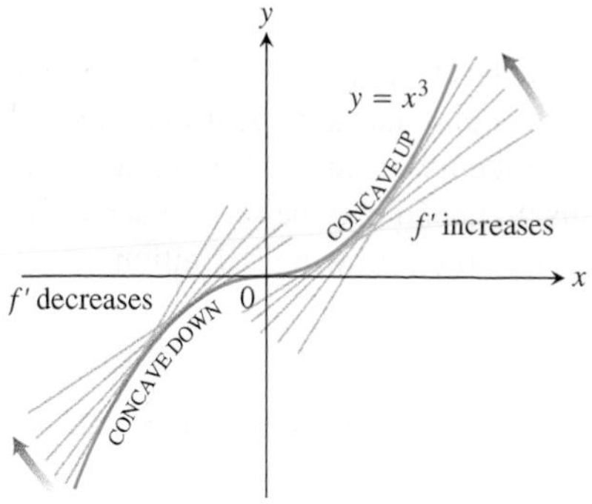

FIGURE 4.24 The graph of $f(x) = x^3$ is concave down on $(-\infty, 0)$ and concave up on $(0, \infty)$ (Example 1a).

We have seen how the first derivative tells us where a function is increasing, where it is decreasing, and whether a local maximum or local minimum occurs at a critical point. In this section we see that the second derivative gives us information about how the graph of a differentiable function bends or turns. With this knowledge about the first and second derivatives, coupled with our previous understanding of symmetry and asymptotic behavior studied in Sections 1.1 and 2.6, we can now draw an accurate graph of a function. By organizing all of these ideas into a coherent procedure, we give a method for sketching graphs and revealing visually the key features of functions. Identifying and knowing the locations of these features is of major importance in mathematics and its applications to science and engineering, especially in the graphical analysis and interpretation of data.

Concavity

As you can see in Figure 4.24, the curve $y = x^3$ rises as x increases, but the portions defined on the intervals $(-\infty, 0)$ and $(0, \infty)$ turn in different ways. As we approach the origin from the left along the curve, the curve turns to our right and falls below its tangents. The slopes of the tangents are decreasing on the interval $(-\infty, 0)$. As we move away from the origin along the curve to the right, the curve turns to our left and rises above its tangents. The slopes of the tangents are increasing on the interval $(0, \infty)$. This turning or bending behavior defines the *concavity* of the curve.

DEFINITION The graph of a differentiable function $y = f(x)$ is

(a) concave up on an open interval I if f' is increasing on I;

(b) concave down on an open interval I if f' is decreasing on I.

If $y = f(x)$ has a second derivative, we can apply Corollary 3 of the Mean Value Theorem to the first derivative function. We conclude that f' increases if $f'' > 0$ on I, and decreases if $f'' < 0$.

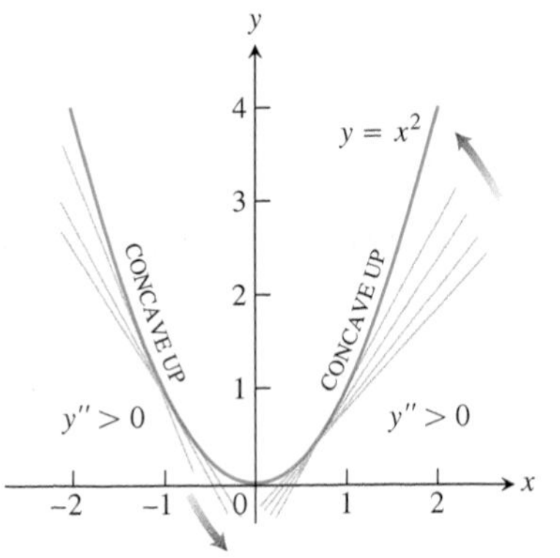

FIGURE 4.25 The graph of $f(x) = x^2$ is concave up on every interval (Example 1b).

The Second Derivative Test for Concavity

Let $y = f(x)$ be twice-differentiable on an interval I.

1. If $f'' > 0$ on I, the graph of f over I is concave up.
2. If $f'' < 0$ on I, the graph of f over I is concave down.

If $y = f(x)$ is twice-differentiable, we will use the notations f'' and y'' interchangeably when denoting the second derivative.

EXAMPLE 1

(a) The curve $y = x^3$ (Figure 4.24) is concave down on $(-\infty, 0)$ where $y'' = 6x < 0$ and concave up on $(0, \infty)$ where $y'' = 6x > 0$.

(b) The curve $y = x^2$ (Figure 4.25) is concave up on $(-\infty, \infty)$ because its second derivative $y'' = 2$ is always positive. ■

EXAMPLE 2 Determine the concavity of $y = 3 + \sin x$ on $[0, 2\pi]$.

Solution The first derivative of $y = 3 + \sin x$ is $y' = \cos x$, and the second derivative is $y'' = -\sin x$. The graph of $y = 3 + \sin x$ is concave down on $(0, \pi)$, where $y'' = -\sin x$ is negative. It is concave up on $(\pi, 2\pi)$, where $y'' = -\sin x$ is positive (Figure 4.26). ■

Points of Inflection

The curve $y = 3 + \sin x$ in Example 2 changes concavity at the point $(\pi, 3)$. Since the first derivative $y' = \cos x$ exists for all x, we see that the curve has a tangent line of slope -1 at the point $(\pi, 3)$. This point is called a *point of inflection* of the curve. Notice from Figure 4.26 that the graph crosses its tangent line at this point and that the second derivative $y'' = -\sin x$ has value 0 when $x = \pi$. In general, we have the following definition.

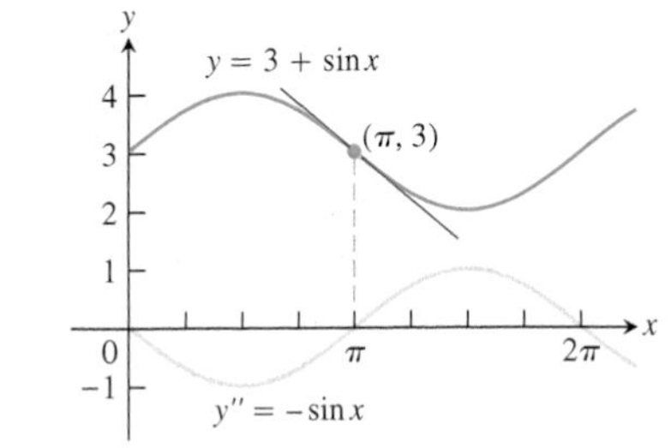

FIGURE 4.26 Using the sign of y'' to determine the concavity of y (Example 2).

DEFINITION A point where the graph of a function has a tangent line and where the concavity changes is a **point of inflection**.

We observed that the second derivative of $f(x) = 3 + \sin x$ is equal to zero at the inflection point $(\pi, 3)$. Generally, if the second derivative exists at a point of inflection $(c, f(c))$, then $f''(c) = 0$. This follows immediately from the Intermediate Value Theorem whenever f'' is continuous over an interval containing $x = c$ because the second derivative changes sign moving across this interval. Even if the continuity assumption is dropped, it is still true that $f''(c) = 0$, provided the second derivative exists (although a more advanced agrument is required in this noncontinuous case). Since a tangent line must exist at the point of inflection, either the first derivative $f'(c)$ exists (is finite) or a vertical tangent exists at the point. At a vertical tangent neither the first nor second derivative exists. In summary, we conclude the following result.

At a point of inflection $(c, f(c))$, either $f''(c) = 0$ or $f''(c)$ fails to exist.

The next example illustrates a function having a point of inflection where the first derivative exists, but the second derivative fails to exist.

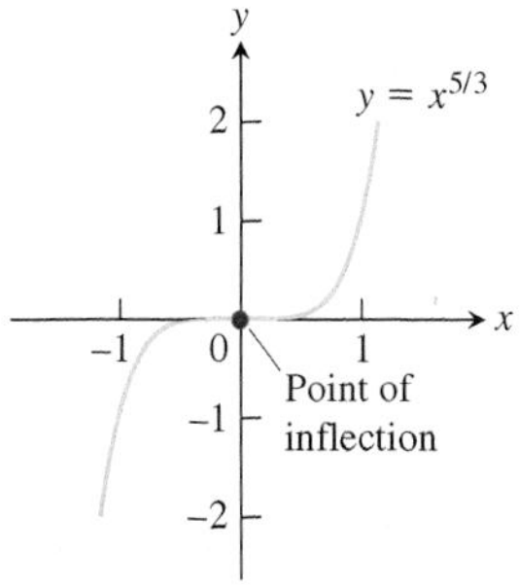

FIGURE 4.27 The graph of $f(x) = x^{5/3}$ has a horizontal tangent at the origin where the concavity changes, although f'' does not exist at $x = 0$ (Example 3).

EXAMPLE 3 The graph of $f(x) = x^{5/3}$ has a horizontal tangent at the origin because $f'(x) = (5/3)x^{2/3} = 0$ when $x = 0$. However, the second derivative

$$f''(x) = \frac{d}{dx}\left(\frac{5}{3}x^{2/3}\right) = \frac{10}{9}x^{-1/3}$$

fails to exist at $x = 0$. Nevertheless, $f''(x) < 0$ for $x < 0$ and $f''(x) > 0$ for $x > 0$, so the second derivative changes sign at $x = 0$ and there is a point of inflection at the origin. The graph is shown in Figure 4.27. ■

Here is an example showing that an inflection point need not occur even though both derivatives exist and $f'' = 0$.

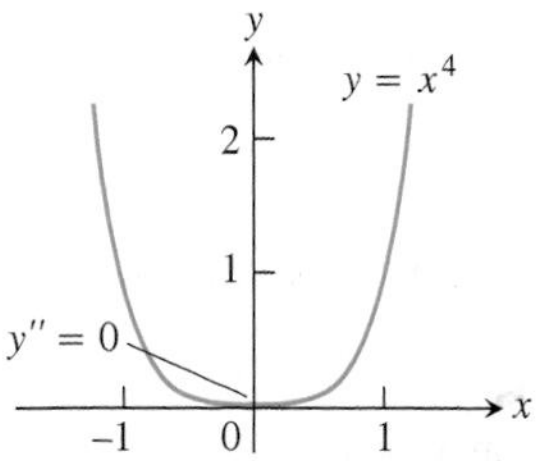

FIGURE 4.28 The graph of $y = x^4$ has no inflection point at the origin, even though $y'' = 0$ there (Example 4).

EXAMPLE 4 The curve $y = x^4$ has no inflection point at $x = 0$ (Figure 4.28). Even though the second derivative $y'' = 12x^2$ is zero there, it does not change sign. ■

As our final illustration, we show a situation in which a point of inflection occurs at a vertical tangent to the curve where neither the first nor the second derivative exists.

EXAMPLE 5 The graph of $y = x^{1/3}$ has a point of inflection at the origin because the second derivative is positive for $x < 0$ and negative for $x > 0$:

$$y'' = \frac{d^2}{dx^2}\left(x^{1/3}\right) = \frac{d}{dx}\left(\frac{1}{3}x^{-2/3}\right) = -\frac{2}{9}x^{-5/3}.$$

However, both $y' = x^{-2/3}/3$ and y'' fail to exist at $x = 0$, and there is a vertical tangent there. See Figure 4.29. ■

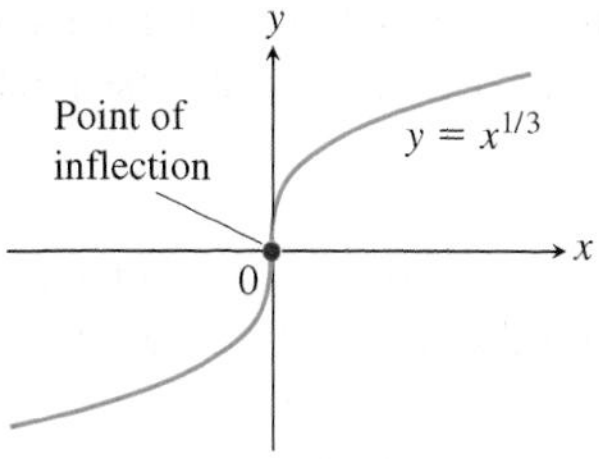

FIGURE 4.29 A point of inflection where y' and y'' fail to exist (Example 5).

To study the motion of an object moving along a line as a function of time, we often are interested in knowing when the object's acceleration, given by the second derivative, is positive or negative. The points of inflection on the graph of the object's position function reveal where the acceleration changes sign.

EXAMPLE 6 A particle is moving along a horizontal coordinate line (positive to the right) with position function

$$s(t) = 2t^3 - 14t^2 + 22t - 5, \qquad t \geq 0.$$

Find the velocity and acceleration, and describe the motion of the particle.

Solution The velocity is

$$v(t) = s'(t) = 6t^2 - 28t + 22 = 2(t - 1)(3t - 11),$$

and the acceleration is

$$a(t) = v'(t) = s''(t) = 12t - 28 = 4(3t - 7).$$

When the function $s(t)$ is increasing, the particle is moving to the right; when $s(t)$ is decreasing, the particle is moving to the left.

Notice that the first derivative ($v = s'$) is zero at the critical points $t = 1$ and $t = 11/3$.

Interval	$0 < t < 1$	$1 < t < 11/3$	$11/3 < t$
Sign of $v = s'$	+	−	+
Behavior of s	increasing	decreasing	increasing
Particle motion	right	left	right

The particle is moving to the right in the time intervals $[0, 1)$ and $(11/3, \infty)$, and moving to the left in $(1, 11/3)$. It is momentarily stationary (at rest) at $t = 1$ and $t = 11/3$.

The acceleration $a(t) = s''(t) = 4(3t - 7)$ is zero when $t = 7/3$.

Interval	$0 < t < 7/3$	$7/3 < t$
Sign of $a = s''$	$-$	$+$
Graph of s	concave down	concave up

The particle starts out moving to the right while slowing down, and then reverses and begins moving to the left at $t = 1$ under the influence of the leftward acceleration over the time interval $[0, 7/3)$. The acceleration then changes direction at $t = 7/3$ but the particle continues moving leftward, while slowing down under the rightward acceleration. At $t = 11/3$ the particle reverses direction again: moving to the right in the same direction as the acceleration. ■

Second Derivative Test for Local Extrema

Instead of looking for sign changes in f' at critical points, we can sometimes use the following test to determine the presence and nature of local extrema.

THEOREM 5—Second Derivative Test for Local Extrema Suppose f'' is continuous on an open interval that contains $x = c$.

1. If $f'(c) = 0$ and $f''(c) < 0$, then f has a local maximum at $x = c$.
2. If $f'(c) = 0$ and $f''(c) > 0$, then f has a local minimum at $x = c$.
3. If $f'(c) = 0$ and $f''(c) = 0$, then the test fails. The function f may have a local maximum, a local minimum, or neither.

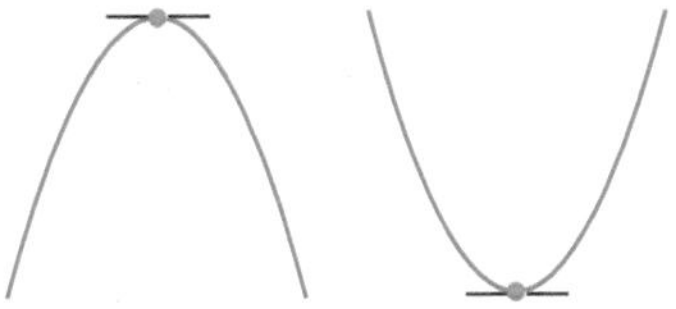

$f' = 0, f'' < 0$ $\Rightarrow$ local max

$f' = 0, f'' > 0$ $\Rightarrow$ local min

Proof Part (1). If $f''(c) < 0$, then $f''(x) < 0$ on some open interval I containing the point c, since f'' is continuous. Therefore, f' is decreasing on I. Since $f'(c) = 0$, the sign of f' changes from positive to negative at c so f has a local maximum at c by the First Derivative Test.

The proof of Part (2) is similar.

For Part (3), consider the three functions $y = x^4$, $y = -x^4$, and $y = x^3$. For each function, the first and second derivatives are zero at $x = 0$. Yet the function $y = x^4$ has a local minimum there, $y = -x^4$ has a local maximum, and $y = x^3$ is increasing in any open interval containing $x = 0$ (having neither a maximum nor a minimum there). Thus the test fails. ■

This test requires us to know f'' *only at c itself* and not in an interval about c. This makes the test easy to apply. That's the good news. The bad news is that the test is inconclusive if $f'' = 0$ or if f'' does not exist at $x = c$. When this happens, use the First Derivative Test for local extreme values.

Together f' and f'' tell us the shape of the function's graph—that is, where the critical points are located and what happens at a critical point, where the function is increasing and where it is decreasing, and how the curve is turning or bending as defined by its concavity. We use this information to sketch a graph of the function that captures its key features.

EXAMPLE 7 Sketch a graph of the function

$$f(x) = x^4 - 4x^3 + 10$$

using the following steps.

(a) Identify where the extrema of f occur.

(b) Find the intervals on which f is increasing and the intervals on which f is decreasing.

(c) Find where the graph of f is concave up and where it is concave down.

(d) Sketch the general shape of the graph for f.

(e) Plot some specific points, such as local maximum and minimum points, points of inflection, and intercepts. Then sketch the curve.

Solution The function f is continuous since $f'(x) = 4x^3 - 12x^2$ exists. The domain of f is $(-\infty, \infty)$, and the domain of f' is also $(-\infty, \infty)$. Thus, the critical points of f occur only at the zeros of f'. Since

$$f'(x) = 4x^3 - 12x^2 = 4x^2(x - 3),$$

the first derivative is zero at $x = 0$ and $x = 3$. We use these critical points to define intervals where f is increasing or decreasing.

Interval	$x < 0$	$0 < x < 3$	$3 < x$
Sign of f'	$-$	$-$	$+$
Behavior of f	decreasing	decreasing	increasing

(a) Using the First Derivative Test for local extrema and the table above, we see that there is no extremum at $x = 0$ and a local minimum at $x = 3$.

(b) Using the table above, we see that f is decreasing on $(-\infty, 0]$ and $[0, 3]$, and increasing on $[3, \infty)$.

(c) $f''(x) = 12x^2 - 24x = 12x(x - 2)$ is zero at $x = 0$ and $x = 2$. We use these points to define intervals where f is concave up or concave down.

Interval	$x < 0$	$0 < x < 2$	$2 < x$
Sign of f''	$+$	$-$	$+$
Behavior of f	concave up	concave down	concave up

We see that f is concave up on the intervals $(-\infty, 0)$ and $(2, \infty)$, and concave down on $(0, 2)$.

(d) Summarizing the information in the last two tables, we obtain the following.

$x < 0$	$0 < x < 2$	$2 < x < 3$	$3 < x$
decreasing concave up	decreasing concave down	decreasing concave up	increasing concave up

The general shape of the curve is shown in the accompanying figure.

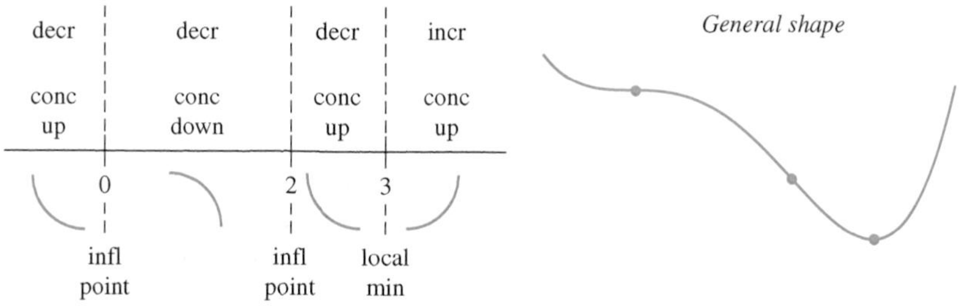

(e) Plot the curve's intercepts (if possible) and the points where y' and y'' are zero. Indicate any local extreme values and inflection points. Use the general shape as a guide to sketch the curve. (Plot additional points as needed.) Figure 4.30 shows the graph of f. ■

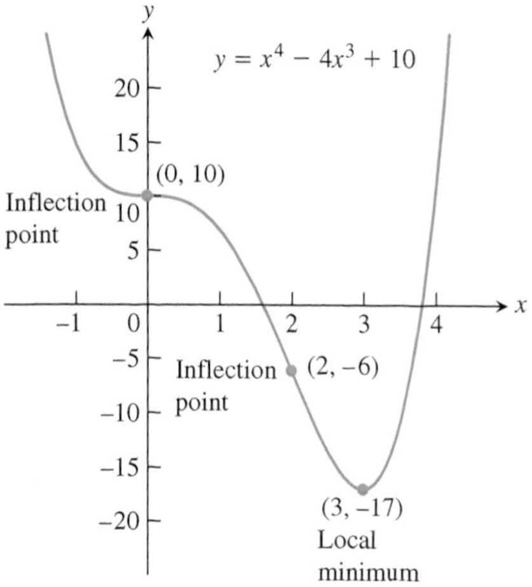

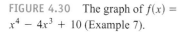

FIGURE 4.30 The graph of $f(x) = x^4 - 4x^3 + 10$ (Example 7).

The steps in Example 7 give a procedure for graphing the key features of a function.

Procedure for Graphing $y = f(x)$

1. Identify the domain of f and any symmetries the curve may have.
2. Find the derivatives y' and y''.
3. Find the critical points of f, if any, and identify the function's behavior at each one.
4. Find where the curve is increasing and where it is decreasing.
5. Find the points of inflection, if any occur, and determine the concavity of the curve.
6. Identify any asymptotes that may exist (see Section 2.6).
7. Plot key points, such as the intercepts and the points found in Steps 3–5, and sketch the curve together with any asymptotes that exist.

EXAMPLE 8 Sketch the graph of $f(x) = \dfrac{(x+1)^2}{1+x^2}$.

Solution

1. The domain of f is $(-\infty, \infty)$ and there are no symmetries about either axis or the origin (Section 1.1).
2. *Find f' and f''.*

$$f(x) = \frac{(x+1)^2}{1+x^2}$$

x-intercept at $x = -1$, y-intercept $(y = 1)$ at $x = 0$

$$f'(x) = \frac{(1+x^2)\cdot 2(x+1) - (x+1)^2\cdot 2x}{(1+x^2)^2}$$

$$= \frac{2(1-x^2)}{(1+x^2)^2}$$

Critical points: $x = -1, x = 1$

$$f''(x) = \frac{(1+x^2)^2\cdot 2(-2x) - 2(1-x^2)[2(1+x^2)\cdot 2x]}{(1+x^2)^4}$$

$$= \frac{4x(x^2-3)}{(1+x^2)^3}$$

After some algebra

3. *Behavior at critical points.* The critical points occur only at $x = \pm 1$ where $f'(x) = 0$ (Step 2) since f' exists everywhere over the domain of f. At $x = -1$, $f''(-1) = 1 > 0$, yielding a relative minimum by the Second Derivative Test. At $x = 1$, $f''(1) = -1 < 0$, yielding a relative maximum by the Second Derivative test.
4. *Increasing and decreasing.* We see that on the interval $(-\infty, -1)$ the derivative $f'(x) < 0$, and the curve is decreasing. On the interval $(-1, 1)$, $f'(x) > 0$ and the curve is increasing; it is decreasing on $(1, \infty)$ where $f'(x) < 0$ again.

5. *Inflection points*. Notice that the denominator of the second derivative (Step 2) is always positive. The second derivative f'' is zero when $x = -\sqrt{3}, 0$, and $\sqrt{3}$. The second derivative changes sign at each of these points: negative on $\left(-\infty, -\sqrt{3}\right)$, positive on $\left(-\sqrt{3}, 0\right)$, negative on $\left(0, \sqrt{3}\right)$, and positive again on $\left(\sqrt{3}, \infty\right)$. Thus each point is a point of inflection. The curve is concave down on the interval $\left(-\infty, -\sqrt{3}\right)$, concave up on $\left(-\sqrt{3}, 0\right)$, concave down on $\left(0, \sqrt{3}\right)$, and concave up again on $\left(\sqrt{3}, \infty\right)$.
6. *Asymptotes*. Expanding the numerator of $f(x)$ and then dividing both numerator and denominator by x^2 gives

$$f(x) = \frac{(x+1)^2}{1+x^2} = \frac{x^2+2x+1}{1+x^2} \qquad \text{Expanding numerator}$$

$$= \frac{1 + (2/x) + (1/x^2)}{(1/x^2) + 1}. \qquad \text{Dividing by } x^2$$

We see that $f(x) \to 1^+$ as $x \to \infty$ and that $f(x) \to 1^-$ as $x \to -\infty$. Thus, the line $y = 1$ is a horizontal asymptote.

Since f decreases on $(-\infty, -1)$ and then increases on $(-1, 1)$, we know that $f(-1) = 0$ is a local minimum. Although f decreases on $(1, \infty)$, it never crosses the horizontal asymptote $y = 1$ on that interval (it approaches the asymptote from above). So the graph never becomes negative, and $f(-1) = 0$ is an absolute minimum as well. Likewise, $f(1) = 2$ is an absolute maximum because the graph never crosses the asymptote $y = 1$ on the interval $(-\infty, -1)$, approaching it from below. Therefore, there are no vertical asymptotes (the range of f is $0 \le y \le 2$).

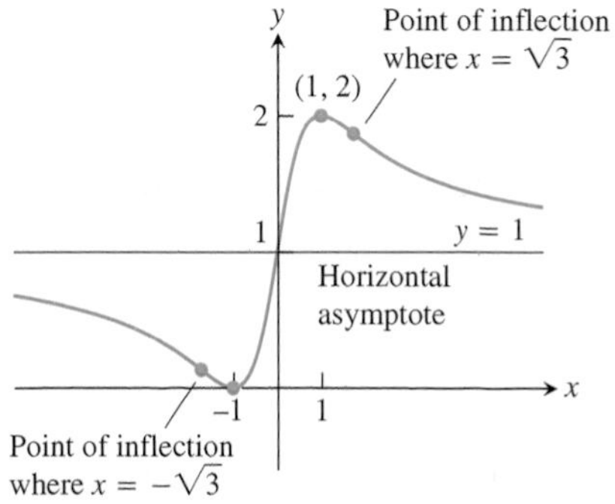

FIGURE 4.31 The graph of $y = \frac{(x+1)^2}{1+x^2}$ (Example 8).

7. The graph of f is sketched in Figure 4.31. Notice how the graph is concave down as it approaches the horizontal asymptote $y = 1$ as $x \to -\infty$, and concave up in its approach to $y = 1$ as $x \to \infty$. ■

EXAMPLE 9 Sketch the graph of $f(x) = \frac{x^2+4}{2x}$.

Solution

1. The domain of f is all nonzero real numbers. There are no intercepts because neither x nor $f(x)$ can be zero. Since $f(-x) = -f(x)$, we note that f is an odd function, so the graph of f is symmetric about the origin.
2. We calculate the derivatives of the function, but first rewrite it in order to simplify our computations:

$$f(x) = \frac{x^2+4}{2x} = \frac{x}{2} + \frac{2}{x} \qquad \text{Function simplified for differentiation}$$

$$f'(x) = \frac{1}{2} - \frac{2}{x^2} = \frac{x^2-4}{2x^2} \qquad \text{Combine fractions to solve easily } f'(x) = 0.$$

$$f''(x) = \frac{4}{x^3} \qquad \text{Exists throughout the entire domain of } f$$

3. The critical points occur at $x = \pm 2$ where $f'(x) = 0$. Since $f''(-2) < 0$ and $f''(2) > 0$, we see from the Second Derivative Test that a relative maximum occurs at $x = -2$ with $f(-2) = -2$, and a relative minimum occurs at $x = 2$ with $f(2) = 2$.

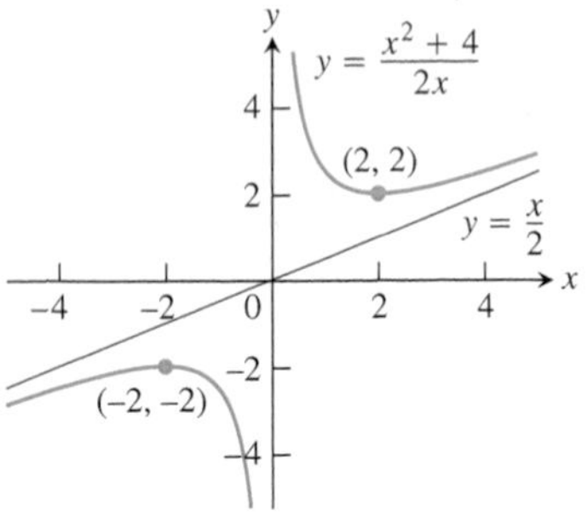

FIGURE 4.32 The graph of $y = \frac{x^2 + 4}{2x}$ (Example 9).

4. On the interval $(-\infty, -2)$ the derivative f' is positive because $x^2 - 4 > 0$ so the graph is increasing; on the interval $(-2, 0)$ the derivative is negative and the graph is decreasing. Similarly, the graph is decreasing on the interval $(0, 2)$ and increasing on $(2, \infty)$.
5. There are no points of inflection because $f''(x) < 0$ whenever $x < 0$, $f''(x) > 0$ whenever $x > 0$, and f'' exists everywhere and is never zero throughout the domain of f. The graph is concave down on the interval $(-\infty, 0)$ and concave up on the interval $(0, \infty)$.
6. From the rewritten formula for $f(x)$, we see that

$$\lim_{x \to 0^+} \left(\frac{x}{2} + \frac{2}{x}\right) = +\infty \quad \text{and} \quad \lim_{x \to 0^-} \left(\frac{x}{2} + \frac{2}{x}\right) = -\infty,$$

so the y-axis is a vertical asymptote. Also, as $x \to \infty$ or as $x \to -\infty$, the graph of $f(x)$ approaches the line $y = x/2$. Thus $y = x/2$ is an oblique asymptote.
7. The graph of f is sketched in Figure 4.32. ■

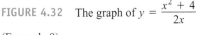

EXAMPLE 10 Sketch the graph of $f(x) = e^{2/x}$.

Solution The domain of f is $(-\infty, 0) \cup (0, \infty)$ and there are no symmetries about either axis or the origin. The derivatives of f are

$$f'(x) = e^{2/x}\left(-\frac{2}{x^2}\right) = -\frac{2e^{2/x}}{x^2}$$

and

$$f''(x) = \frac{x^2(2e^{2/x})(-2/x^2) - 2e^{2/x}(2x)}{x^4} = \frac{4e^{2/x}(1 + x)}{x^4}.$$

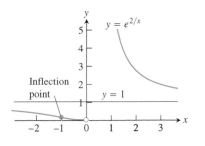

FIGURE 4.33 The graph of $y = e^{2/x}$ has a point of inflection at $(-1, e^{-2})$. The line $y = 1$ is a horizontal asymptote and $x = 0$ is a vertical asymptote (Example 10).

Both derivatives exist everywhere over the domain of f. Moreover, since $e^{2/x}$ and x^2 are both positive for all $x \neq 0$, we see that $f' < 0$ everywhere over the domain and the graph is everywhere decreasing. Examining the second derivative, we see that $f''(x) = 0$ at $x = -1$. Since $e^{2/x} > 0$ and $x^4 > 0$, we have $f'' < 0$ for $x < -1$ and $f'' > 0$ for $x > -1, x \neq 0$. Therefore, the point $(-1, e^{-2})$ is a point of inflection. The curve is concave down on the interval $(-\infty, -1)$ and concave up over $(-1, 0) \cup (0, \infty)$.

From Example 7, Section 2.6, we see that $\lim_{x \to 0^-} f(x) = 0$. As $x \to 0^+$, we see that $2/x \to \infty$, so $\lim_{x \to 0^+} f(x) = \infty$ and the y-axis is a vertical asymptote. Also, as $x \to -\infty$, $2/x \to 0^-$ and so $\lim_{x \to -\infty} f(x) = e^0 = 1$. Therefore, $y = 1$ is a horizontal asymptote. There are no absolute extrema since f never takes on the value 0. The graph of f is sketched in Figure 4.33. ■

Graphical Behavior of Functions from Derivatives

As we saw in Examples 7–10, we can learn much about a twice-differentiable function $y = f(x)$ by examining its first derivative. We can find where the function's graph rises and falls and where any local extrema are located. We can differentiate y' to learn how the graph bends as it passes over the intervals of rise and fall. We can determine the shape of the function's graph. Information we cannot get from the derivative is how to place the graph in the xy-plane. But, as we discovered in Section 4.2, the only additional information we need to position the graph is the value of f at one point. Information about the asymptotes is found using limits (Section 2.6). The following figure summarizes how the derivative and second derivative affect the shape of a graph.

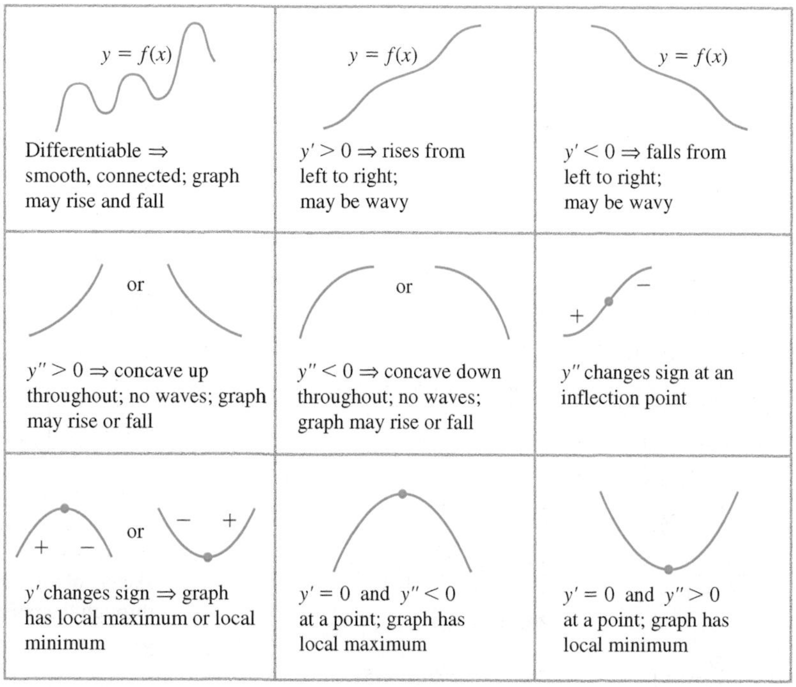
$y = f(x)$
Differentiable ⇒ smooth, connected; graph may rise and fall
$y = f(x)$
$y' > 0$ ⇒ rises from left to right; may be wavy
$y = f(x)$
$y' < 0$ ⇒ falls from left to right; may be wavy
or
$y'' > 0$ ⇒ concave up throughout; no waves; graph may rise or fall
or
$y'' < 0$ ⇒ concave down throughout; no waves; graph may rise or fall
+
−
y'' changes sign at an inflection point
+ −
or
− +
y' changes sign ⇒ graph has local maximum or local minimum
$y' = 0$ and $y'' < 0$ at a point; graph has local maximum
$y' = 0$ and $y'' > 0$ at a point; graph has local minimum

Exercises 4.4

Analyzing Functions from Graphs

Identify the inflection points and local maxima and minima of the functions graphed in Exercises 1–8. Identify the intervals on which the functions are concave up and concave down.

1. $y = \frac{x^3}{3} - \frac{x^2}{2} - 2x + \frac{1}{3}$

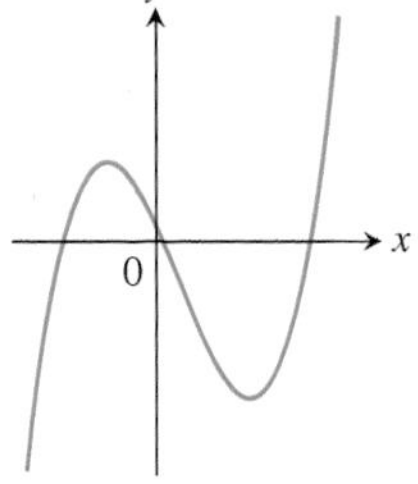

2. $y = \frac{x^4}{4} - 2x^2 + 4$

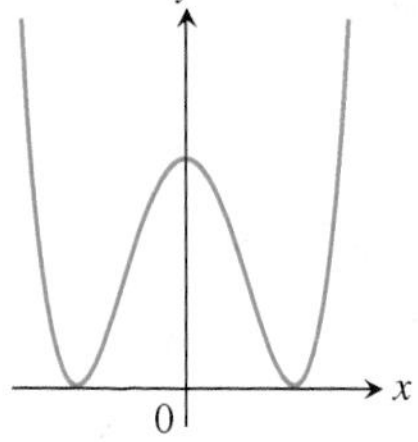

3. $y = \frac{3}{4}(x^2 - 1)^{2/3}$

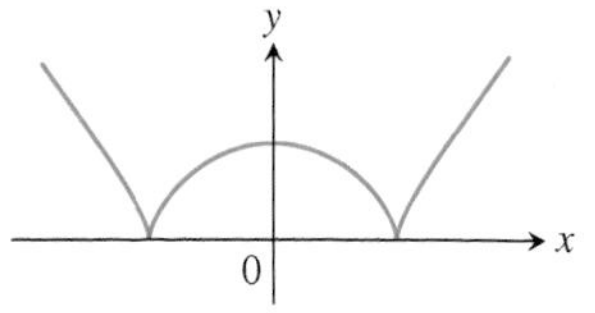

4. $y = \frac{9}{14}x^{1/3}(x^2 - 7)$

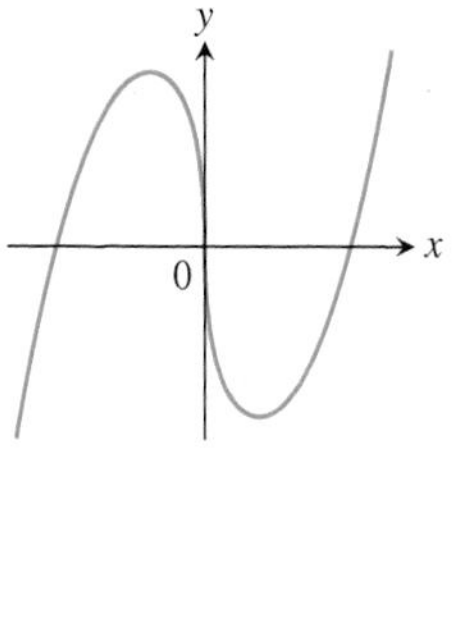

5. $y = x + \sin 2x, -\frac{2\pi}{3} \le x \le \frac{2\pi}{3}$

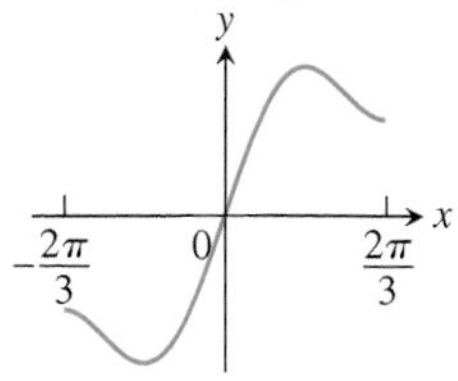

6. $y = \tan x - 4x, -\frac{\pi}{2} < x < \frac{\pi}{2}$

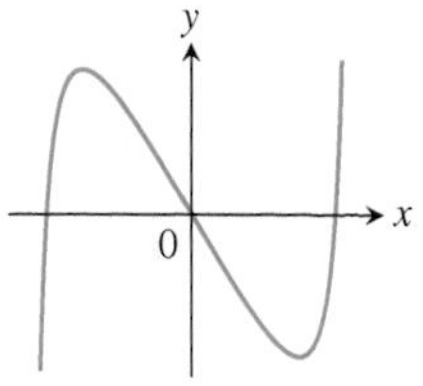

7. $y = \sin |x|, -2\pi \le x \le 2\pi$

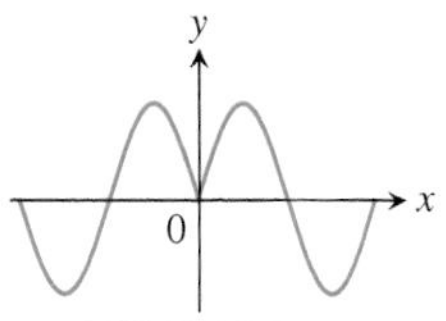

NOT TO SCALE

8. $y = 2\cos x - \sqrt{2}\,x, -\pi \le x \le \frac{3\pi}{2}$

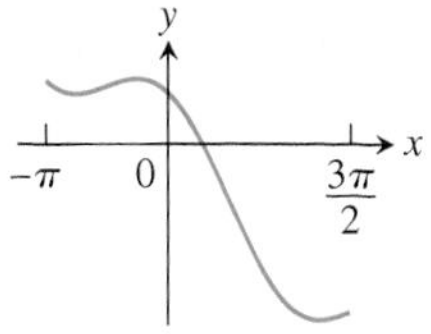

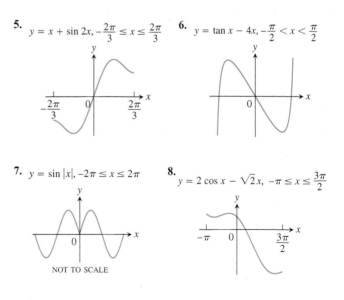

Graphing Equations

Use the steps of the graphing procedure on page 240 to graph the equations in Exercises 9–58. Include the coordinates of any local and absolute extreme points and inflection points.

9. $y = x^2 - 4x + 3$

10. $y = 6 - 2x - x^2$

11. $y = x^3 - 3x + 3$

12. $y = x(6 - 2x)^2$

13. $y = -2x^3 + 6x^2 - 3$

14. $y = 1 - 9x - 6x^2 - x^3$

15. $y = (x - 2)^3 + 1$

16. $y = 1 - (x + 1)^3$

17. $y = x^4 - 2x^2 = x^2(x^2 - 2)$

18. $y = -x^4 + 6x^2 - 4 = x^2(6 - x^2) - 4$

19. $y = 4x^3 - x^4 = x^3(4 - x)$

20. $y = x^4 + 2x^3 = x^3(x + 2)$

21. $y = x^5 - 5x^4 = x^4(x - 5)$

22. $y = x\left(\frac{x}{2} - 5\right)^4$

23. $y = x + \sin x, \quad 0 \le x \le 2\pi$

24. $y = x - \sin x, \quad 0 \le x \le 2\pi$

25. $y = \sqrt{3}x - 2\cos x, \quad 0 \le x \le 2\pi$

26. $y = \frac{4}{3}x - \tan x, \quad \frac{-\pi}{2} < x < \frac{\pi}{2}$

27. $y = \sin x \cos x, \quad 0 \le x \le \pi$

28. $y = \cos x + \sqrt{3}\sin x, \quad 0 \le x \le 2\pi$

29. $y = x^{1/5}$

30. $y = x^{2/5}$

31. $y = \frac{x}{\sqrt{x^2 + 1}}$

32. $y = \frac{\sqrt{1 - x^2}}{2x + 1}$

33. $y = 2x - 3x^{2/3}$

34. $y = 5x^{2/5} - 2x$

35. $y = x^{2/3}\left(\frac{5}{2} - x\right)$

36. $y = x^{2/3}(x - 5)$

37. $y = x\sqrt{8 - x^2}$

38. $y = (2 - x^2)^{3/2}$

39. $y = \sqrt{16 - x^2}$

40. $y = x^2 + \frac{2}{x}$

41. $y = \frac{x^2 - 3}{x - 2}$

42. $y = \sqrt[3]{x^3 + 1}$

43. $y = \frac{8x}{x^2 + 4}$

44. $y = \frac{5}{x^4 + 5}$

45. $y = |x^2 - 1|$

46. $y = |x^2 - 2x|$

47. $y = \sqrt{|x|} = \begin{cases} \sqrt{-x}, & x < 0 \\ \sqrt{x}, & x \ge 0 \end{cases}$

48. $y = \sqrt{|x - 4|}$

49. $y = xe^{1/x}$

50. $y = \frac{e^x}{x}$

51. $y = \ln(3 - x^2)$

52. $y = x(\ln x)^2$

53. $y = e^x - 2e^{-x} - 3x$

54. $y = xe^{-x}$

55. $y = \ln(\cos x)$

56. $y = \frac{\ln x}{\sqrt{x}}$

57. $y = \frac{1}{1 + e^{-x}}$

58. $y = \frac{e^x}{1 + e^x}$

Sketching the General Shape, Knowing y'

Each of Exercises 59–80 gives the first derivative of a continuous function $y = f(x)$. Find y'' and then use steps 2–4 of the graphing procedure on page 240 to sketch the general shape of the graph of f.

59. $y' = 2 + x - x^2$

60. $y' = x^2 - x - 6$

61. $y' = x(x - 3)^2$

62. $y' = x^2(2 - x)$

63. $y' = x(x^2 - 12)$

64. $y' = (x - 1)^2(2x + 3)$

65. $y' = (8x - 5x^2)(4 - x)^2$

66. $y' = (x^2 - 2x)(x - 5)^2$

67. $y' = \sec^2 x, \quad -\frac{\pi}{2} < x < \frac{\pi}{2}$

68. $y' = \tan x, \quad -\frac{\pi}{2} < x < \frac{\pi}{2}$

69. $y' = \cot \frac{\theta}{2}, \quad 0 < \theta < 2\pi$

70. $y' = \csc^2 \frac{\theta}{2}, \quad 0 < \theta < 2\pi$

71. $y' = \tan^2 \theta - 1, \quad -\frac{\pi}{2} < \theta < \frac{\pi}{2}$

72. $y' = 1 - \cot^2 \theta, \quad 0 < \theta < \pi$

73. $y' = \cos t, \quad 0 \le t \le 2\pi$

74. $y' = \sin t, \quad 0 \le t \le 2\pi$

75. $y' = (x + 1)^{-2/3}$

76. $y' = (x - 2)^{-1/3}$

77. $y' = x^{-2/3}(x - 1)$

78. $y' = x^{-4/5}(x + 1)$

79. $y' = 2|x| = \begin{cases} -2x, & x \le 0 \\ 2x, & x > 0 \end{cases}$

80. $y' = \begin{cases} -x^2, & x \le 0 \\ x^2, & x > 0 \end{cases}$

Sketching y from Graphs of y' and y''

Each of Exercises 81–84 shows the graphs of the first and second derivatives of a function $y = f(x)$. Copy the picture and add to it a sketch of the approximate graph of f, given that the graph passes through the point P.

81.

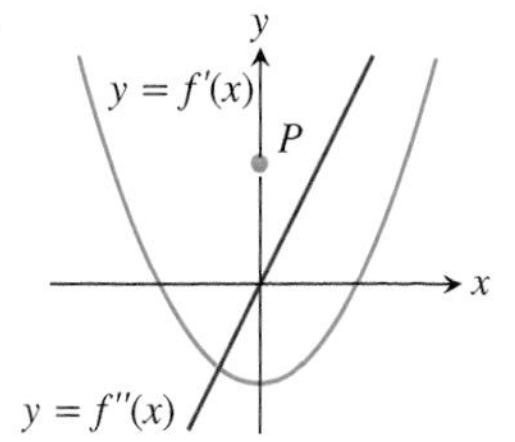

82.

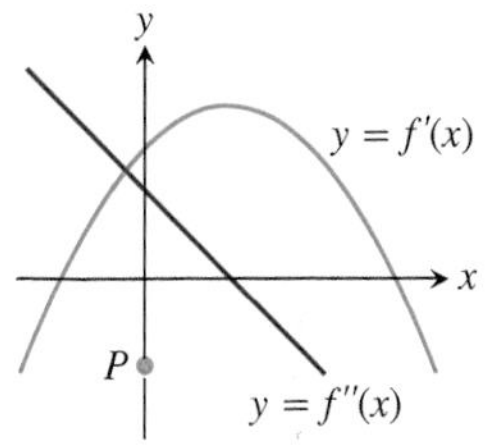

83.

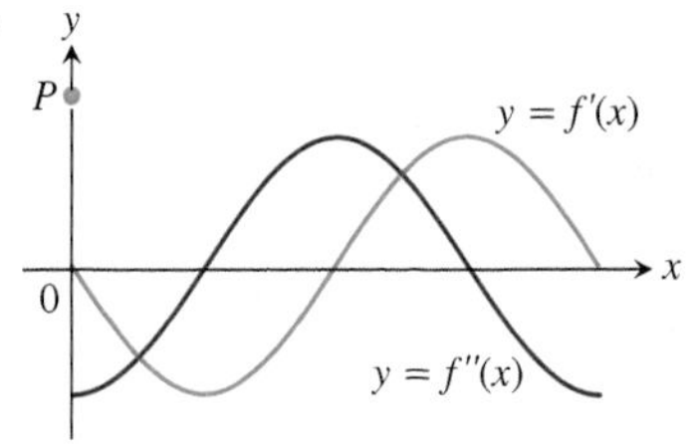

84.

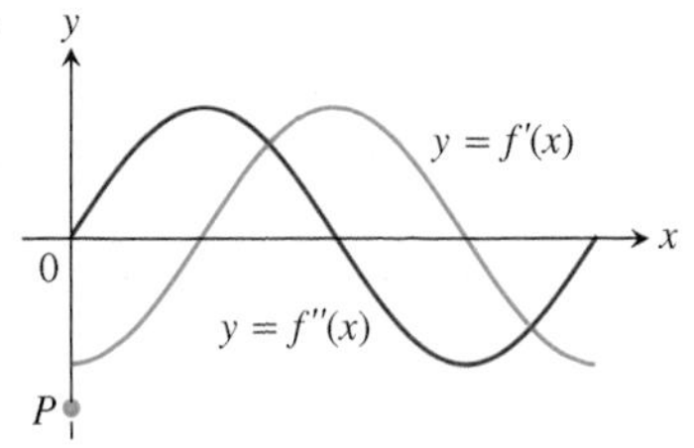

Graphing Rational Functions

Graph the rational functions in Exercises 85–102.

85. $y = \frac{2x^2 + x - 1}{x^2 - 1}$

86. $y = \frac{x^2 - 49}{x^2 + 5x - 14}$

87. $y = \frac{x^4 + 1}{x^2}$

88. $y = \frac{x^2 - 4}{2x}$

89. $y = \frac{1}{x^2 - 1}$

90. $y = \frac{x^2}{x^2 - 1}$

91. $y = -\dfrac{x^2 - 2}{x^2 - 1}$ **92.** $y = \dfrac{x^2 - 4}{x^2 - 2}$

93. $y = \dfrac{x^2}{x + 1}$ **94.** $y = -\dfrac{x^2 - 4}{x + 1}$

95. $y = \dfrac{x^2 - x + 1}{x - 1}$ **96.** $y = -\dfrac{x^2 - x + 1}{x - 1}$

97. $y = \dfrac{x^3 - 3x^2 + 3x - 1}{x^2 + x - 2}$ **98.** $y = \dfrac{x^3 + x - 2}{x - x^2}$

99. $y = \dfrac{x}{x^2 - 1}$ **100.** $y = \dfrac{x - 1}{x^2(x - 2)}$

101. $y = \dfrac{8}{x^2 + 4}$ (Agnesi's witch)

102. $y = \dfrac{4x}{x^2 + 4}$ (Newton's serpentine)

Theory and Examples

103. The accompanying figure shows a portion of the graph of a twice-differentiable function $y = f(x)$. At each of the five labeled points, classify y' and y'' as positive, negative, or zero.

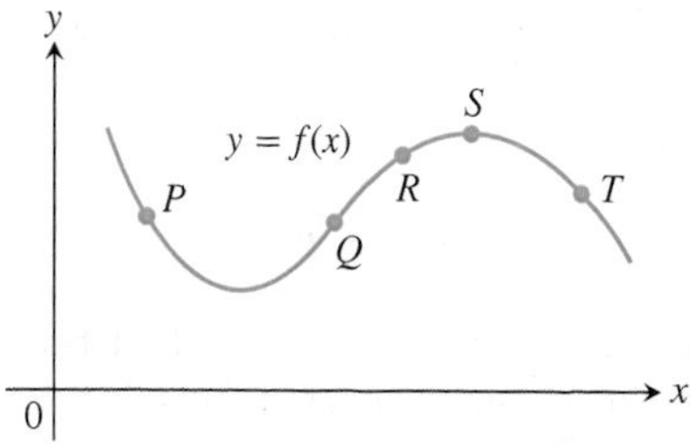

104. Sketch a smooth connected curve $y = f(x)$ with

$f(-2) = 8,$ $f'(2) = f'(-2) = 0,$

$f(0) = 4,$ $f'(x) < 0$ for $|x| < 2,$

$f(2) = 0,$ $f''(x) < 0$ for $x < 0,$

$f'(x) > 0$ for $|x| > 2,$ $f''(x) > 0$ for $x > 0.$

105. Sketch the graph of a twice-differentiable function $y = f(x)$ with the following properties. Label coordinates where possible.

x	y	Derivatives
$x < 2$		$y' < 0,\ y'' > 0$
2	1	$y' = 0,\ y'' > 0$
$2 < x < 4$		$y' > 0,\ y'' > 0$
4	4	$y' > 0,\ y'' = 0$
$4 < x < 6$		$y' > 0,\ y'' < 0$
6	7	$y' = 0,\ y'' < 0$
$x > 6$		$y' < 0,\ y'' < 0$

106. Sketch the graph of a twice-differentiable function $y = f(x)$ that passes through the points $(-2, 2)$, $(-1, 1)$, $(0, 0)$, $(1, 1)$, and $(2, 2)$ and whose first two derivatives have the following sign patterns.

y': + | −2 | − | 0 | + | 2 | −

y'': − | −1 | + | 1 | −

Motion Along a Line The graphs in Exercises 107 and 108 show the position $s = f(t)$ of an object moving up and down on a coordinate line. **(a)** When is the object moving away from the origin? Toward the origin? At approximately what times is the **(b)** velocity equal to zero? **(c)** Acceleration equal to zero? **(d)** When is the acceleration positive? Negative?

107.

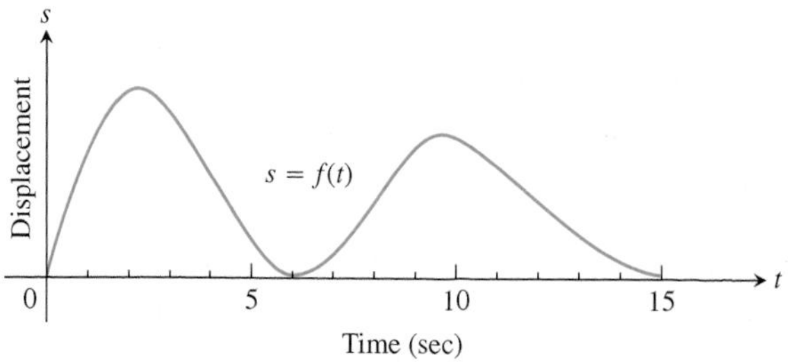

108.

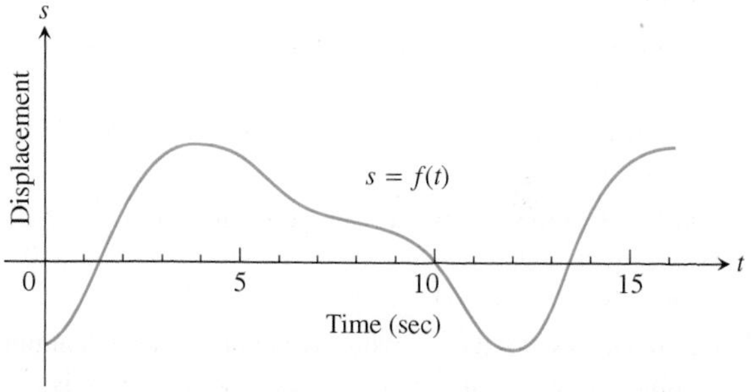

109. **Marginal cost** The accompanying graph shows the hypothetical cost $c = f(x)$ of manufacturing x items. At approximately what production level does the marginal cost change from decreasing to increasing?

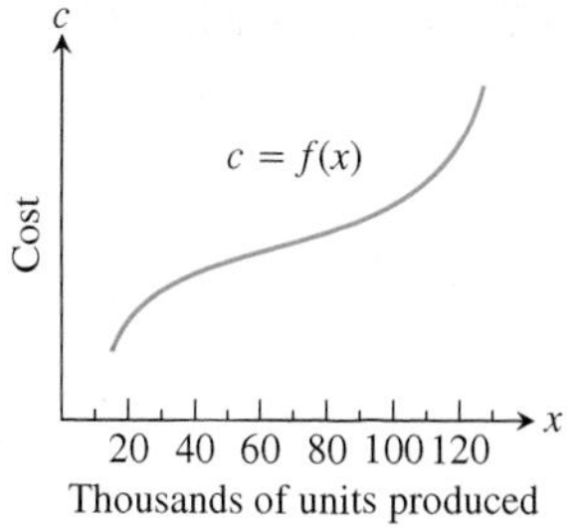

110. The accompanying graph shows the monthly revenue of the Widget Corporation for the last 12 years. During approximately what time intervals was the marginal revenue increasing? Decreasing?

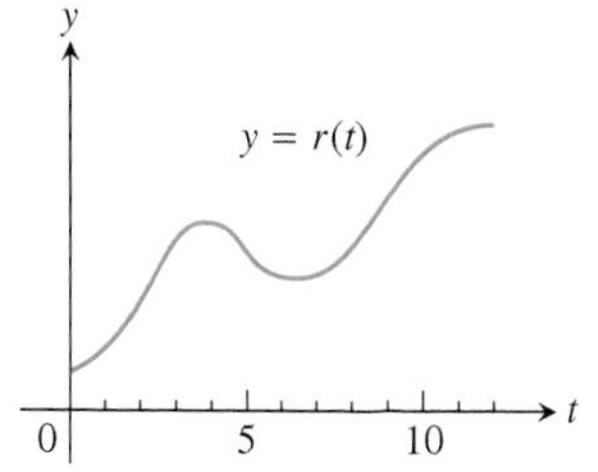

111. Suppose the derivative of the function $y = f(x)$ is

$$y' = (x - 1)^2(x - 2).$$

At what points, if any, does the graph of f have a local minimum, local maximum, or point of inflection? (*Hint:* Draw the sign pattern for y'.)

112. Suppose the derivative of the function $y = f(x)$ is

$$y' = (x - 1)^2(x - 2)(x - 4).$$

At what points, if any, does the graph of f have a local minimum, local maximum, or point of inflection?

113. For $x > 0$, sketch a curve $y = f(x)$ that has $f(1) = 0$ and $f'(x) = 1/x$. Can anything be said about the concavity of such a curve? Give reasons for your answer.

114. Can anything be said about the graph of a function $y = f(x)$ that has a continuous second derivative that is never zero? Give reasons for your answer.

115. If b, c, and d are constants, for what value of b will the curve $y = x^3 + bx^2 + cx + d$ have a point of inflection at $x = 1$? Give reasons for your answer.

116. Parabolas

a. Find the coordinates of the vertex of the parabola $y = ax^2 + bx + c, a \neq 0$.

b. When is the parabola concave up? Concave down? Give reasons for your answers.

117. Quadratic curves What can you say about the inflection points of a quadratic curve $y = ax^2 + bx + c, a \neq 0$? Give reasons for your answer.

118. Cubic curves What can you say about the inflection points of a cubic curve $y = ax^3 + bx^2 + cx + d, a \neq 0$? Give reasons for your answer.

119. Suppose that the second derivative of the function $y = f(x)$ is

$$y'' = (x + 1)(x - 2).$$

For what x-values does the graph of f have an inflection point?

120. Suppose that the second derivative of the function $y = f(x)$ is

$$y'' = x^2(x - 2)^3(x + 3).$$

For what x-values does the graph of f have an inflection point?

121. Find the values of constants a, b, and c so that the graph of $y = ax^3 + bx^2 + cx$ has a local maximum at $x = 3$, local minimum at $x = -1$, and inflection point at $(1, 11)$.

122. Find the values of constants a, b, and c so that the graph of $y = (x^2 + a)/(bx + c)$ has a local minimum at $x = 3$ and a local maximum at $(-1, -2)$.

COMPUTER EXPLORATIONS

In Exercises 123–126, find the inflection points (if any) on the graph of the function and the coordinates of the points on the graph where the function has a local maximum or local minimum value. Then graph the function in a region large enough to show all these points simultaneously. Add to your picture the graphs of the function's first and second derivatives. How are the values at which these graphs intersect the x-axis related to the graph of the function? In what other ways are the graphs of the derivatives related to the graph of the function?

123. $y = x^5 - 5x^4 - 240$ **124.** $y = x^3 - 12x^2$

125. $y = \frac{4}{5}x^5 + 16x^2 - 25$

126. $y = \frac{x^4}{4} - \frac{x^3}{3} - 4x^2 + 12x + 20$

127. Graph $f(x) = 2x^4 - 4x^2 + 1$ and its first two derivatives together. Comment on the behavior of f in relation to the signs and values of f' and f''.

128. Graph $f(x) = x \cos x$ and its second derivative together for $0 \leq x \leq 2\pi$. Comment on the behavior of the graph of f in relation to the signs and values of f''.

4.5 Indeterminate Forms and L'Hôpital's Rule

John (Johann) Bernoulli discovered a rule using derivatives to calculate limits of fractions whose numerators and denominators both approach zero or $+\infty$. The rule is known today as **l'Hôpital's Rule**, after Guillaume de l'Hôpital. He was a French nobleman who wrote the first introductory differential calculus text, where the rule first appeared in print. Limits involving transcendental functions often require some use of the rule for their calculation.

HISTORICAL BIOGRAPHY

Guillaume François Antoine de l'Hôpital (1661–1704)

Johann Bernoulli (1667–1748)

Indeterminate Form 0/0

If we want to know how the function

$$F(x) = \frac{x - \sin x}{x^3}$$

behaves *near* $x = 0$ (where it is undefined), we can examine the limit of $F(x)$ as $x \to 0$. We cannot apply the Quotient Rule for limits (Theorem 1 of Chapter 2) because the limit of the denominator is 0. Moreover, in this case, *both* the numerator and denominator approach 0, and $0/0$ is undefined. Such limits may or may not exist in general, but the limit does exist for the function $F(x)$ under discussion by applying l'Hôpital's Rule, as we will see in Example 1d.

If the continuous functions $f(x)$ and $g(x)$ are both zero at $x = a$, then

$$\lim_{x \to a} \frac{f(x)}{g(x)}$$

cannot be found by substituting $x = a$. The substitution produces $0/0$, a meaningless expression, which we cannot evaluate. We use $0/0$ as a notation for an expression known as an **indeterminate form**. Other meaningless expressions often occur, such as ∞/∞, $\infty \cdot 0$, $\infty - \infty$, 0^0, and 1^∞, which cannot be evaluated in a consistent way; these are called indeterminate forms as well. Sometimes, but not always, limits that lead to indeterminate forms may be found by cancellation, rearrangement of terms, or other algebraic manipulations. This was our experience in Chapter 2. It took considerable analysis in Section 2.4 to find $\lim_{x \to 0} (\sin x)/x$. But we have had success with the limit

$$f'(a) = \lim_{x \to a} \frac{f(x) - f(a)}{x - a},$$

from which we calculate derivatives and which produces the indeterminant form $0/0$ when we substitute $x = a$. L'Hôpital's Rule enables us to draw on our success with derivatives to evaluate limits that otherwise lead to indeterminate forms.

THEOREM 6— L'Hôpital's Rule Suppose that $f(a) = g(a) = 0$, that f and g are differentiable on an open interval I containing a, and that $g'(x) \neq 0$ on I if $x \neq a$. Then

$$\lim_{x \to a} \frac{f(x)}{g(x)} = \lim_{x \to a} \frac{f'(x)}{g'(x)},$$

assuming that the limit on the right side of this equation exists.

We give a proof of Theorem 6 at the end of this section.

Caution
To apply l'Hôpital's Rule to f/g, divide the derivative of f by the derivative of g. Do not fall into the trap of taking the derivative of f/g. The quotient to use is f'/g', not $(f/g)'$.

EXAMPLE 1 The following limits involve $0/0$ indeterminate forms, so we apply l'Hôpital's Rule. In some cases, it must be applied repeatedly.

(a) $$\lim_{x \to 0} \frac{3x - \sin x}{x} = \lim_{x \to 0} \frac{3 - \cos x}{1} = \left.\frac{3 - \cos x}{1}\right|_{x=0} = 2$$

(b) $$\lim_{x \to 0} \frac{\sqrt{1 + x} - 1}{x} = \lim_{x \to 0} \frac{\frac{1}{2\sqrt{1 + x}}}{1} = \frac{1}{2}$$

(c) $$\lim_{x \to 0} \frac{\sqrt{1 + x} - 1 - x/2}{x^2}$$ $\frac{0}{0}$; apply l'Hôpital's Rule.

$$= \lim_{x \to 0} \frac{(1/2)(1 + x)^{-1/2} - 1/2}{2x}$$ Still $\frac{0}{0}$; apply l'Hôpital's Rule again.

$$= \lim_{x \to 0} \frac{-(1/4)(1 + x)^{-3/2}}{2} = -\frac{1}{8}$$ Not $\frac{0}{0}$; limit is found.

(d) $\lim_{x \to 0} \dfrac{x - \sin x}{x^3}$ $\quad \frac{0}{0}$; apply l'Hôpital's Rule.

$= \lim_{x \to 0} \dfrac{1 - \cos x}{3x^2}$ $\quad$ Still $\frac{0}{0}$; apply l'Hôpital's Rule again.

$= \lim_{x \to 0} \dfrac{\sin x}{6x}$ $\quad$ Still $\frac{0}{0}$; apply l'Hôpital's Rule again.

$= \lim_{x \to 0} \dfrac{\cos x}{6} = \dfrac{1}{6}$ $\quad$ Not $\frac{0}{0}$; limit is found. ■

Here is a summary of the procedure we followed in Example 1.

Using L'Hôpital's Rule

To find

$$\lim_{x \to a} \frac{f(x)}{g(x)}$$

by l'Hôpital's Rule, continue to differentiate f and g, so long as we still get the form $0/0$ at $x = a$. But as soon as one or the other of these derivatives is different from zero at $x = a$ we stop differentiating. L'Hôpital's Rule does not apply when either the numerator or denominator has a finite nonzero limit.

EXAMPLE 2 Be careful to apply l'Hôpital's Rule correctly:

$$\lim_{x \to 0} \frac{1 - \cos x}{x + x^2} \qquad \frac{0}{0}$$

$$= \lim_{x \to 0} \frac{\sin x}{1 + 2x} \qquad \text{Not } \frac{0}{0}$$

It is tempting to try to apply l'Hôpital's Rule again, which would result in

$$\lim_{x \to 0} \frac{\cos x}{2} = \frac{1}{2},$$

but this is not the correct limit. l'Hôpital's Rule can be applied only to limits that give indeterminate forms, and $\lim_{x \to 0} (\sin x)/(1 + 2x)$ does not give an indeterminate form. Instead, this limit is $0/1 = 0$, and the correct answer for the original limit is 0. ■

L'Hôpital's Rule applies to one-sided limits as well.

EXAMPLE 3 In this example the one-sided limits are different.

(a) $\lim_{x \to 0^+} \dfrac{\sin x}{x^2}$ $\quad \frac{0}{0}$

$= \lim_{x \to 0^+} \dfrac{\cos x}{2x} = \infty$ $\quad$ Positive for $x > 0$

Recall that ∞ and $+\infty$ mean the same thing.

(b) $\lim_{x \to 0^-} \dfrac{\sin x}{x^2}$ $\quad \frac{0}{0}$

$= \lim_{x \to 0^-} \dfrac{\cos x}{2x} = -\infty$ $\quad$ Negative for $x < 0$ ■

Indeterminate Forms ∞/∞, $\infty \cdot 0$, $\infty - \infty$

Sometimes when we try to evaluate a limit as $x \to a$ by substituting $x = a$ we get an indeterminant form like ∞/∞, $\infty \cdot 0$, or $\infty - \infty$, instead of $0/0$. We first consider the form ∞/∞.

In more advanced treatments of calculus, it is proved that l'Hôpital's Rule applies to the indeterminate form ∞/∞ as well as to $0/0$. If $f(x) \to \pm\infty$ and $g(x) \to \pm\infty$ as $x \to a$, then

$$\lim_{x\to a} \frac{f(x)}{g(x)} = \lim_{x\to a} \frac{f'(x)}{g'(x)}$$

provided the limit on the right exists. In the notation $x \to a$, a may be either finite or infinite. Moreover, $x \to a$ may be replaced by the one-sided limits $x \to a^+$ or $x \to a^-$.

EXAMPLE 4 Find the limits of these ∞/∞ forms:

(a) $\displaystyle\lim_{x\to\pi/2} \frac{\sec x}{1 + \tan x}$ **(b)** $\displaystyle\lim_{x\to\infty} \frac{\ln x}{2\sqrt{x}}$ **(c)** $\displaystyle\lim_{x\to\infty} \frac{e^x}{x^2}$.

Solution

(a) The numerator and denominator are discontinuous at $x = \pi/2$, so we investigate the one-sided limits there. To apply l'Hôpital's Rule, we can choose I to be any open interval with $x = \pi/2$ as an endpoint.

$$\lim_{x\to(\pi/2)^-} \frac{\sec x}{1 + \tan x} \qquad \frac{\infty}{\infty} \text{ from the left so we apply l'Hôpital's Rule.}$$

$$= \lim_{x\to(\pi/2)^-} \frac{\sec x \tan x}{\sec^2 x} = \lim_{x\to(\pi/2)^-} \sin x = 1$$

The right-hand limit is 1 also, with $(-\infty)/(-\infty)$ as the indeterminate form. Therefore, the two-sided limit is equal to 1.

(b) $$\lim_{x\to\infty} \frac{\ln x}{2\sqrt{x}} = \lim_{x\to\infty} \frac{1/x}{1/\sqrt{x}} = \lim_{x\to\infty} \frac{1}{\sqrt{x}} = 0 \qquad \frac{1/x}{1/\sqrt{x}} = \frac{\sqrt{x}}{x} = \frac{1}{\sqrt{x}}$$

(c) $$\lim_{x\to\infty} \frac{e^x}{x^2} = \lim_{x\to\infty} \frac{e^x}{2x} = \lim_{x\to\infty} \frac{e^x}{2} = \infty$$ ■

Next we turn our attention to the indeterminate forms $\infty \cdot 0$ and $\infty - \infty$. Sometimes these forms can be handled by using algebra to convert them to a $0/0$ or ∞/∞ form. Here again we do not mean to suggest that $\infty \cdot 0$ or $\infty - \infty$ is a number. They are only notations for functional behaviors when considering limits. Here are examples of how we might work with these indeterminate forms.

EXAMPLE 5 Find the limits of these $\infty \cdot 0$ forms:

(a) $\displaystyle\lim_{x\to\infty} \left(x \sin\frac{1}{x}\right)$ **(b)** $\displaystyle\lim_{x\to 0^+} \sqrt{x} \ln x$

Solution

(a) $$\lim_{x\to\infty} \left(x \sin\frac{1}{x}\right) = \lim_{h\to 0^+} \left(\frac{1}{h} \sin h\right) = \lim_{h\to 0^+} \frac{\sin h}{h} = 1 \qquad \infty \cdot 0;\ \text{let } h = 1/x.$$

(b) $$\lim_{x\to 0^+} \sqrt{x} \ln x = \lim_{x\to 0^+} \frac{\ln x}{1/\sqrt{x}} \qquad \infty \cdot 0 \text{ converted to } \infty/\infty$$

$$= \lim_{x\to 0^+} \frac{1/x}{-1/2x^{3/2}} \qquad \text{l'Hôpital's Rule applied}$$

$$= \lim_{x\to 0^+} \left(-2\sqrt{x}\right) = 0$$ ■

EXAMPLE 6 Find the limit of this $\infty - \infty$ form:

$$\lim_{x\to 0}\left(\frac{1}{\sin x} - \frac{1}{x}\right).$$

Solution If $x \to 0^+$, then $\sin x \to 0^+$ and

$$\frac{1}{\sin x} - \frac{1}{x} \to \infty - \infty.$$

Similarly, if $x \to 0^-$, then $\sin x \to 0^-$ and

$$\frac{1}{\sin x} - \frac{1}{x} \to -\infty - (-\infty) = -\infty + \infty.$$

Neither form reveals what happens in the limit. To find out, we first combine the fractions:

$$\frac{1}{\sin x} - \frac{1}{x} = \frac{x - \sin x}{x \sin x} \qquad \text{Common denominator is } x \sin x.$$

Then we apply l'Hôpital's Rule to the result:

$$\begin{aligned}\lim_{x\to 0}\left(\frac{1}{\sin x} - \frac{1}{x}\right) &= \lim_{x\to 0} \frac{x - \sin x}{x \sin x} && \frac{0}{0} \\ &= \lim_{x\to 0} \frac{1 - \cos x}{\sin x + x \cos x} && \text{Still } \frac{0}{0} \\ &= \lim_{x\to 0} \frac{\sin x}{2\cos x - x \sin x} = \frac{0}{2} = 0.\end{aligned}$$

■

Indeterminate Powers

Limits that lead to the indeterminate forms 1^∞, 0^0, and ∞^0 can sometimes be handled by first taking the logarithm of the function. We use l'Hôpital's Rule to find the limit of the logarithm expression and then exponentiate the result to find the original function limit. This procedure is justified by the continuity of the exponential function and Theorem 10 in Section 2.5, and it is formulated as follows. (The formula is also valid for one-sided limits.)

If $\lim_{x\to a} \ln f(x) = L$, then

$$\lim_{x\to a} f(x) = \lim_{x\to a} e^{\ln f(x)} = e^L.$$

Here a may be either finite or infinite.

EXAMPLE 7 Apply l'Hôpital's Rule to show that $\lim_{x\to 0^+} (1 + x)^{1/x} = e$.

Solution The limit leads to the indeterminate form 1^∞. We let $f(x) = (1 + x)^{1/x}$ and find $\lim_{x\to 0^+} \ln f(x)$. Since

$$\ln f(x) = \ln (1 + x)^{1/x} = \frac{1}{x} \ln (1 + x),$$

l'Hôpital's Rule now applies to give

$$\lim_{x\to0^+}\ln f(x) = \lim_{x\to0^+}\frac{\ln(1+x)}{x} \qquad \frac{0}{0}$$

$$= \lim_{x\to0^+}\frac{\dfrac{1}{1+x}}{1} \qquad \text{l'Hôpital's Rule applied}$$

$$= \frac{1}{1} = 1.$$

Therefore, $\lim_{x\to0^+}(1+x)^{1/x} = \lim_{x\to0^+} f(x) = \lim_{x\to0^+} e^{\ln f(x)} = e^1 = e.$ ■

EXAMPLE 8 Find $\lim_{x\to\infty} x^{1/x}$.

Solution The limit leads to the indeterminate form ∞^0. We let $f(x) = x^{1/x}$ and find $\lim_{x\to\infty}\ln f(x)$. Since

$$\ln f(x) = \ln x^{1/x} = \frac{\ln x}{x},$$

l'Hôpital's Rule gives

$$\lim_{x\to\infty}\ln f(x) = \lim_{x\to\infty}\frac{\ln x}{x} \qquad \frac{\infty}{\infty}$$

$$= \lim_{x\to\infty}\frac{1/x}{1} \qquad \text{l'Hôpital's Rule applied}$$

$$= \frac{0}{1} = 0.$$

Therefore $\lim_{x\to\infty} x^{1/x} = \lim_{x\to\infty} f(x) = \lim_{x\to\infty} e^{\ln f(x)} = e^0 = 1.$ ■

Proof of L'Hôpital's Rule

HISTORICAL BIOGRAPHY

Augustin-Louis Cauchy (1789–1857)

The proof of l'Hôpital's Rule is based on Cauchy's Mean Value Theorem, an extension of the Mean Value Theorem that involves two functions instead of one. We prove Cauchy's Theorem first and then show how it leads to l'Hôpital's Rule.

When $g(x) = x$, Theorem 7 is the Mean Value Theorem.

THEOREM 7—Cauchy's Mean Value Theorem Suppose functions f and g are continuous on $[a, b]$ and differentiable throughout (a, b) and also suppose $g'(x) \neq 0$ throughout (a, b). Then there exists a number c in (a, b) at which

$$\frac{f'(c)}{g'(c)} = \frac{f(b) - f(a)}{g(b) - g(a)}.$$

Proof We apply the Mean Value Theorem of Section 4.2 twice. First we use it to show that $g(a) \neq g(b)$. For if $g(b)$ did equal $g(a)$, then the Mean Value Theorem would give

$$g'(c) = \frac{g(b) - g(a)}{b - a} = 0$$

for some c between a and b, which cannot happen because $g'(x) \neq 0$ in (a, b).

We next apply the Mean Value Theorem to the function

$$F(x) = f(x) - f(a) - \frac{f(b) - f(a)}{g(b) - g(a)}[g(x) - g(a)].$$

This function is continuous and differentiable where f and g are, and $F(b) = F(a) = 0$. Therefore, there is a number c between a and b for which $F'(c) = 0$. When expressed in terms of f and g, this equation becomes

$$F'(c) = f'(c) - \frac{f(b) - f(a)}{g(b) - g(a)}[g'(c)] = 0$$

so that

$$\frac{f'(c)}{g'(c)} = \frac{f(b) - f(a)}{g(b) - g(a)}.$$

■

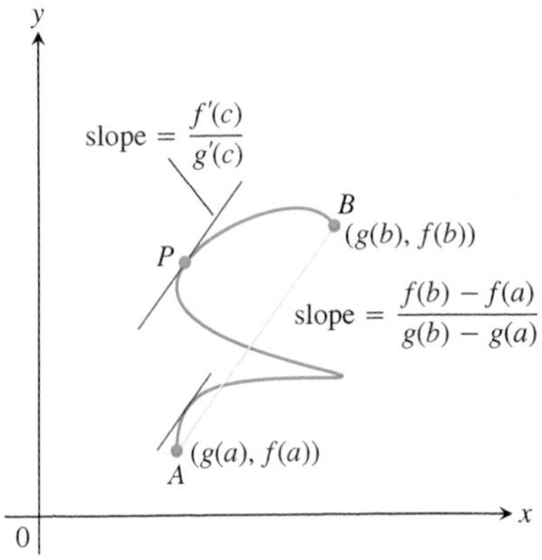

FIGURE 4.34 There is at least one point P on the curve C for which the slope of the tangent to the curve at P is the same as the slope of the secant line joining the points $A(g(a), f(a))$ and $B(g(b), f(b))$.

Cauchy's Mean Value Theorem has a geometric interpretation for a general winding curve C in the plane joining the two points $A = (g(a), f(a))$ and $B = (g(b), f(b))$. In Chapter 11 you will learn how the curve C can be formulated so that there is at least one point P on the curve for which the tangent to the curve at P is parallel to the secant line joining the points A and B. The slope of that tangent line turns out to be the quotient f'/g' evaluated at the number c in the interval (a, b), which is the left-hand side of the equation in Theorem 7. Because the slope of the secant line joining A and B is

$$\frac{f(b) - f(a)}{g(b) - g(a)},$$

the equation in Cauchy's Mean Value Theorem says that the slope of the tangent line equals the slope of the secant line. This geometric interpretation is shown in Figure 4.34. Notice from the figure that it is possible for more than one point on the curve C to have a tangent line that is parallel to the secant line joining A and B.

Proof of l'Hôpital's Rule We first establish the limit equation for the case $x \to a^+$. The method needs almost no change to apply to $x \to a^-$, and the combination of these two cases establishes the result.

Suppose that x lies to the right of a. Then $g'(x) \neq 0$, and we can apply Cauchy's Mean Value Theorem to the closed interval from a to x. This step produces a number c between a and x such that

$$\frac{f'(c)}{g'(c)} = \frac{f(x) - f(a)}{g(x) - g(a)}.$$

But $f(a) = g(a) = 0$, so

$$\frac{f'(c)}{g'(c)} = \frac{f(x)}{g(x)}.$$

As x approaches a, c approaches a because it always lies between a and x. Therefore,

$$\lim_{x \to a^+} \frac{f(x)}{g(x)} = \lim_{c \to a^+} \frac{f'(c)}{g'(c)} = \lim_{x \to a^+} \frac{f'(x)}{g'(x)},$$

which establishes l'Hôpital's Rule for the case where x approaches a from above. The case where x approaches a from below is proved by applying Cauchy's Mean Value Theorem to the closed interval $[x, a]$, $x < a$.

■

Exercises 4.5

Finding Limits in Two Ways

In Exercises 1–6, use l'Hôpital's Rule to evaluate the limit. Then evaluate the limit using a method studied in Chapter 2.

1. $\lim_{x\to-2} \frac{x+2}{x^2-4}$

2. $\lim_{x\to0} \frac{\sin 5x}{x}$

3. $\lim_{x\to\infty} \frac{5x^2-3x}{7x^2+1}$

4. $\lim_{x\to1} \frac{x^3-1}{4x^3-x-3}$

5. $\lim_{x\to0} \frac{1-\cos x}{x^2}$

6. $\lim_{x\to\infty} \frac{2x^2+3x}{x^3+x+1}$

Applying l'Hôpital's Rule

Use l'Hôpital's rule to find the limits in Exercises 7–50.

7. $\lim_{x\to2} \frac{x-2}{x^2-4}$

8. $\lim_{x\to-5} \frac{x^2-25}{x+5}$

9. $\lim_{t\to-3} \frac{t^3-4t+15}{t^2-t-12}$

10. $\lim_{t\to-1} \frac{3t^3+3}{4t^3-t+3}$

11. $\lim_{x\to\infty} \frac{5x^3-2x}{7x^3+3}$

12. $\lim_{x\to\infty} \frac{x-8x^2}{12x^2+5x}$

13. $\lim_{t\to0} \frac{\sin t^2}{t}$

14. $\lim_{t\to0} \frac{\sin 5t}{2t}$

15. $\lim_{x\to0} \frac{8x^2}{\cos x-1}$

16. $\lim_{x\to0} \frac{\sin x-x}{x^3}$

17. $\lim_{\theta\to\pi/2} \frac{2\theta-\pi}{\cos(2\pi-\theta)}$

18. $\lim_{\theta\to-\pi/3} \frac{3\theta+\pi}{\sin(\theta+(\pi/3))}$

19. $\lim_{\theta\to\pi/2} \frac{1-\sin\theta}{1+\cos 2\theta}$

20. $\lim_{x\to1} \frac{x-1}{\ln x-\sin \pi x}$

21. $\lim_{x\to0} \frac{x^2}{\ln(\sec x)}$

22. $\lim_{x\to\pi/2} \frac{\ln(\csc x)}{(x-(\pi/2))^2}$

23. $\lim_{t\to0} \frac{t(1-\cos t)}{t-\sin t}$

24. $\lim_{t\to0} \frac{t\sin t}{1-\cos t}$

25. $\lim_{x\to(\pi/2)^-} \left(x-\frac{\pi}{2}\right)\sec x$

26. $\lim_{x\to(\pi/2)^-} \left(\frac{\pi}{2}-x\right)\tan x$

27. $\lim_{\theta\to0} \frac{3^{\sin\theta}-1}{\theta}$

28. $\lim_{\theta\to0} \frac{(1/2)^\theta-1}{\theta}$

29. $\lim_{x\to0} \frac{x2^x}{2^x-1}$

30. $\lim_{x\to0} \frac{3^x-1}{2^x-1}$

31. $\lim_{x\to\infty} \frac{\ln(x+1)}{\log_2 x}$

32. $\lim_{x\to\infty} \frac{\log_2 x}{\log_3(x+3)}$

33. $\lim_{x\to0^+} \frac{\ln(x^2+2x)}{\ln x}$

34. $\lim_{x\to0^+} \frac{\ln(e^x-1)}{\ln x}$

35. $\lim_{y\to0} \frac{\sqrt{5y+25}-5}{y}$

36. $\lim_{y\to0} \frac{\sqrt{ay+a^2}-a}{y}, \quad a>0$

37. $\lim_{x\to\infty} (\ln 2x-\ln(x+1))$

38. $\lim_{x\to0^+} (\ln x-\ln\sin x)$

39. $\lim_{x\to0^+} \frac{(\ln x)^2}{\ln(\sin x)}$

40. $\lim_{x\to0^+} \left(\frac{3x+1}{x}-\frac{1}{\sin x}\right)$

41. $\lim_{x\to1^+} \left(\frac{1}{x-1}-\frac{1}{\ln x}\right)$

42. $\lim_{x\to0^+} (\csc x-\cot x+\cos x)$

43. $\lim_{\theta\to0} \frac{\cos\theta-1}{e^\theta-\theta-1}$

44. $\lim_{h\to0} \frac{e^h-(1+h)}{h^2}$

45. $\lim_{t\to\infty} \frac{e^t+t^2}{e^t-t}$

46. $\lim_{x\to\infty} x^2e^{-x}$

47. $\lim_{x\to0} \frac{x-\sin x}{x\tan x}$

48. $\lim_{x\to0} \frac{(e^x-1)^2}{x\sin x}$

49. $\lim_{\theta\to0} \frac{\theta-\sin\theta\cos\theta}{\tan\theta-\theta}$

50. $\lim_{x\to0} \frac{\sin 3x-3x+x^2}{\sin x\sin 2x}$

Indeterminate Powers and Products

Find the limits in Exercise 51–66.

51. $\lim_{x\to1^+} x^{1/(1-x)}$

52. $\lim_{x\to1^+} x^{1/(x-1)}$

53. $\lim_{x\to\infty} (\ln x)^{1/x}$

54. $\lim_{x\to e^+} (\ln x)^{1/(x-e)}$

55. $\lim_{x\to0^+} x^{-1/\ln x}$

56. $\lim_{x\to\infty} x^{1/\ln x}$

57. $\lim_{x\to\infty} (1+2x)^{1/(2\ln x)}$

58. $\lim_{x\to0} (e^x+x)^{1/x}$

59. $\lim_{x\to0^+} x^x$

60. $\lim_{x\to0^+} \left(1+\frac{1}{x}\right)^x$

61. $\lim_{x\to\infty} \left(\frac{x+2}{x-1}\right)^x$

62. $\lim_{x\to\infty} \left(\frac{x^2+1}{x+2}\right)^{1/x}$

63. $\lim_{x\to0^+} x^2\ln x$

64. $\lim_{x\to0^+} x(\ln x)^2$

65. $\lim_{x\to0^+} x\tan\left(\frac{\pi}{2}-x\right)$

66. $\lim_{x\to0^+} \sin x\cdot\ln x$

Theory and Applications

L'Hôpital's Rule does not help with the limits in Exercises 67–74. Try it—you just keep on cycling. Find the limits some other way.

67. $\lim_{x\to\infty} \frac{\sqrt{9x+1}}{\sqrt{x+1}}$

68. $\lim_{x\to0^+} \frac{\sqrt{x}}{\sqrt{\sin x}}$

69. $\lim_{x\to(\pi/2)^-} \frac{\sec x}{\tan x}$

70. $\lim_{x\to0^+} \frac{\cot x}{\csc x}$

71. $\lim_{x\to\infty} \frac{2^x-3^x}{3^x+4^x}$

72. $\lim_{x\to-\infty} \frac{2^x+4^x}{5^x-2^x}$

73. $\lim_{x\to\infty} \frac{e^{x^2}}{xe^x}$

74. $\lim_{x\to0^+} \frac{x}{e^{-1/x}}$

75. Which one is correct, and which one is wrong? Give reasons for your answers.

a. $\lim_{x\to3} \frac{x-3}{x^2-3} = \lim_{x\to3} \frac{1}{2x} = \frac{1}{6}$ **b.** $\lim_{x\to3} \frac{x-3}{x^2-3} = \frac{0}{6} = 0$

76. Which one is correct, and which one is wrong? Give reasons for your answers.

a. $\lim_{x\to0} \frac{x^2-2x}{x^2-\sin x} = \lim_{x\to0} \frac{2x-2}{2x-\cos x}$

$= \lim_{x\to0} \frac{2}{2+\sin x} = \frac{2}{2+0} = 1$

b. $\lim_{x\to0} \frac{x^2-2x}{x^2-\sin x} = \lim_{x\to0} \frac{2x-2}{2x-\cos x} = \frac{-2}{0-1} = 2$

77. Only one of these calculations is correct. Which one? Why are the others wrong? Give reasons for your answers.

a. $\lim_{x\to 0^+} x \ln x = 0 \cdot (-\infty) = 0$

b. $\lim_{x\to 0^+} x \ln x = 0 \cdot (-\infty) = -\infty$

c. $\lim_{x\to 0^+} x \ln x = \lim_{x\to 0^+} \dfrac{\ln x}{(1/x)} = \dfrac{-\infty}{\infty} = -1$

d. $\lim_{x\to 0^+} x \ln x = \lim_{x\to 0^+} \dfrac{\ln x}{(1/x)}$

$= \lim_{x\to 0^+} \dfrac{(1/x)}{(-1/x^2)} = \lim_{x\to 0^+} (-x) = 0$

78. Find all values of c that satisfy the conclusion of Cauchy's Mean Value Theorem for the given functions and interval.

a. $f(x) = x, \quad g(x) = x^2, \quad (a, b) = (-2, 0)$

b. $f(x) = x, \quad g(x) = x^2, \quad (a, b)$ arbitrary

c. $f(x) = x^3/3 - 4x, \quad g(x) = x^2, \quad (a, b) = (0, 3)$

79. Continuous extension Find a value of c that makes the function

$$f(x) = \begin{cases} \dfrac{9x - 3\sin 3x}{5x^3}, & x \neq 0 \\ c, & x = 0 \end{cases}$$

continuous at $x = 0$. Explain why your value of c works.

80. For what values of a and b is

$$\lim_{x\to 0} \left(\frac{\tan 2x}{x^3} + \frac{a}{x^2} + \frac{\sin bx}{x} \right) = 0?$$

T **81. $\infty - \infty$ Form**

a. Estimate the value of

$$\lim_{x\to\infty} \left(x - \sqrt{x^2 + x} \right)$$

by graphing $f(x) = x - \sqrt{x^2 + x}$ over a suitably large interval of x-values.

b. Now confirm your estimate by finding the limit with l'Hôpital's Rule. As the first step, multiply $f(x)$ by the fraction $(x + \sqrt{x^2 + x})/(x + \sqrt{x^2 + x})$ and simplify the new numerator.

82. Find $\lim_{x\to\infty} \left(\sqrt{x^2 + 1} - \sqrt{x} \right)$.

T **83. 0/0 Form** Estimate the value of

$$\lim_{x\to 1} \frac{2x^2 - (3x + 1)\sqrt{x} + 2}{x - 1}$$

by graphing. Then confirm your estimate with l'Hôpital's Rule.

84. This exercise explores the difference between the limit

$$\lim_{x\to\infty} \left(1 + \frac{1}{x^2} \right)^x$$

and the limit

$$\lim_{x\to\infty} \left(1 + \frac{1}{x} \right)^x = e.$$

a. Use l'Hôpital's Rule to show that

$$\lim_{x\to\infty} \left(1 + \frac{1}{x} \right)^x = e.$$

T **b.** Graph

$$f(x) = \left(1 + \frac{1}{x^2} \right)^x \quad \text{and} \quad g(x) = \left(1 + \frac{1}{x} \right)^x$$

together for $x \geq 0$. How does the behavior of f compare with that of g? Estimate the value of $\lim_{x\to\infty} f(x)$.

c. Confirm your estimate of $\lim_{x\to\infty} f(x)$ by calculating it with l'Hôpital's Rule.

85. Show that

$$\lim_{k\to\infty} \left(1 + \frac{r}{k} \right)^k = e^r.$$

86. Given that $x > 0$, find the maximum value, if any, of

a. $x^{1/x}$

b. x^{1/x^2}

c. x^{1/x^n} (n a positive integer)

d. Show that $\lim_{x\to\infty} x^{1/x^n} = 1$ for every positive integer n.

87. Use limits to find horizontal asymptotes for each function.

a. $y = x \tan\left(\dfrac{1}{x}\right)$ **b.** $y = \dfrac{3x + e^{2x}}{2x + e^{3x}}$

88. Find $f'(0)$ for $f(x) = \begin{cases} e^{-1/x^2}, & x \neq 0 \\ 0, & x = 0. \end{cases}$

T **89. The continuous extension of $(\sin x)^x$ to $[0, \pi]$**

a. Graph $f(x) = (\sin x)^x$ on the interval $0 \leq x \leq \pi$. What value would you assign to f to make it continuous at $x = 0$?

b. Verify your conclusion in part (a) by finding $\lim_{x\to 0^+} f(x)$ with l'Hôpital's Rule.

c. Returning to the graph, estimate the maximum value of f on $[0, \pi]$. About where is max f taken on?

d. Sharpen your estimate in part (c) by graphing f' in the same window to see where its graph crosses the x-axis. To simplify your work, you might want to delete the exponential factor from the expression for f' and graph just the factor that has a zero.

T **90. The function $(\sin x)^{\tan x}$** *(Continuation of Exercise 89.)*

a. Graph $f(x) = (\sin x)^{\tan x}$ on the interval $-7 \leq x \leq 7$. How do you account for the gaps in the graph? How wide are the gaps?

b. Now graph f on the interval $0 \leq x \leq \pi$. The function is not defined at $x = \pi/2$, but the graph has no break at this point. What is going on? What value does the graph appear to give for f at $x = \pi/2$? (*Hint:* Use l'Hôpital's Rule to find lim f as $x \to (\pi/2)^-$ and $x \to (\pi/2)^+$.)

c. Continuing with the graphs in part (b), find max f and min f as accurately as you can and estimate the values of x at which they are taken on.

4.6 Applied Optimization

What are the dimensions of a rectangle with fixed perimeter having *maximum area*? What are the dimensions for the *least expensive* cylindrical can of a given volume? How many items should be produced for the *most profitable* production run? Each of these questions asks for the best, or optimal, value of a given function. In this section we use derivatives to solve a variety of optimization problems in business, mathematics, physics, and economics.

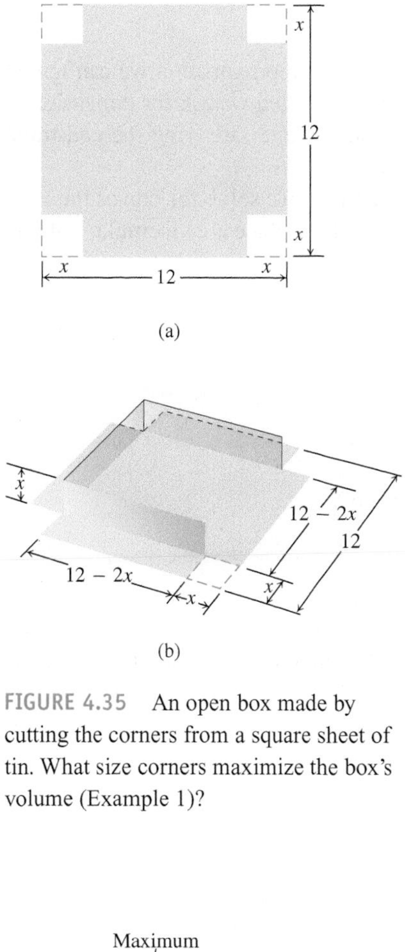

FIGURE 4.35 An open box made by cutting the corners from a square sheet of tin. What size corners maximize the box's volume (Example 1)?

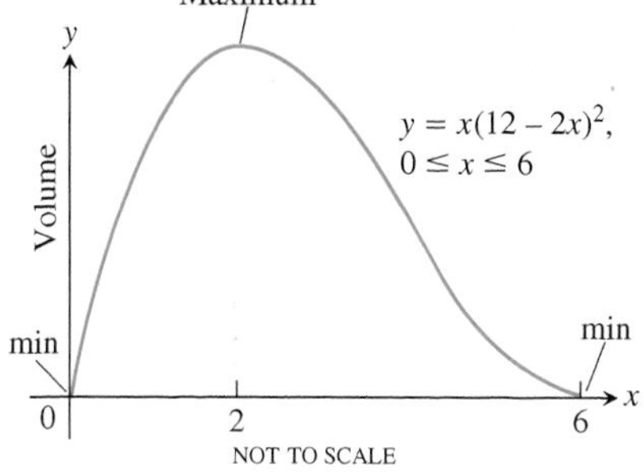

FIGURE 4.36 The volume of the box in Figure 4.35 graphed as a function of x.

Solving Applied Optimization Problems

1. *Read the problem.* Read the problem until you understand it. What is given? What is the unknown quantity to be optimized?
2. *Draw a picture.* Label any part that may be important to the problem.
3. *Introduce variables.* List every relation in the picture and in the problem as an equation or algebraic expression, and identify the unknown variable.
4. *Write an equation for the unknown quantity.* If you can, express the unknown as a function of a single variable or in two equations in two unknowns. This may require considerable manipulation.
5. *Test the critical points and endpoints in the domain of the unknown.* Use what you know about the shape of the function's graph. Use the first and second derivatives to identify and classify the function's critical points.

EXAMPLE 1 An open-top box is to be made by cutting small congruent squares from the corners of a 12-in.-by-12-in. sheet of tin and bending up the sides. How large should the squares cut from the corners be to make the box hold as much as possible?

Solution We start with a picture (Figure 4.35). In the figure, the corner squares are x in. on a side. The volume of the box is a function of this variable:

$$V(x) = x(12 - 2x)^2 = 144x - 48x^2 + 4x^3. \qquad V = hlw$$

Since the sides of the sheet of tin are only 12 in. long, $x \le 6$ and the domain of V is the interval $0 \le x \le 6$.

A graph of V (Figure 4.36) suggests a minimum value of 0 at $x = 0$ and $x = 6$ and a maximum near $x = 2$. To learn more, we examine the first derivative of V with respect to x:

$$\frac{dV}{dx} = 144 - 96x + 12x^2 = 12(12 - 8x + x^2) = 12(2 - x)(6 - x).$$

Of the two zeros, $x = 2$ and $x = 6$, only $x = 2$ lies in the interior of the function's domain and makes the critical-point list. The values of V at this one critical point and two endpoints are

$$\text{Critical-point value:} \quad V(2) = 128$$
$$\text{Endpoint values:} \quad V(0) = 0, \qquad V(6) = 0.$$

The maximum volume is 128 in^3. The cutout squares should be 2 in. on a side. ■

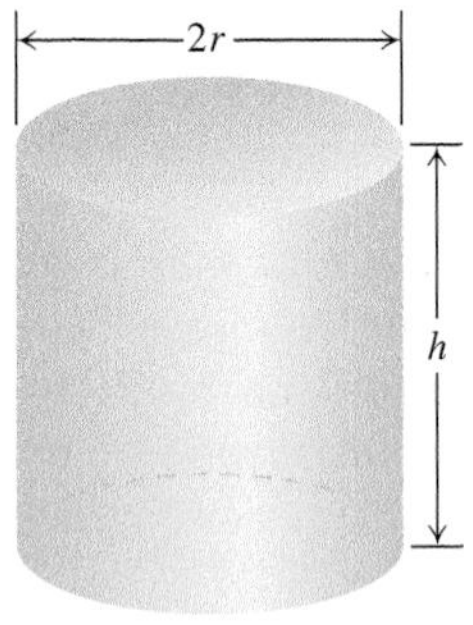

FIGURE 4.37 This one-liter can uses the least material when $h = 2r$ (Example 2).

EXAMPLE 2 You have been asked to design a one-liter can shaped like a right circular cylinder (Figure 4.37). What dimensions will use the least material?

Solution *Volume of can:* If r and h are measured in centimeters, then the volume of the can in cubic centimeters is

$$\pi r^2 h = 1000. \qquad \text{1 liter} = 1000 \text{ cm}^3$$

Surface area of can: $$A = \underbrace{2\pi r^2}_{\text{circular ends}} + \underbrace{2\pi r h}_{\text{cylindrical wall}}$$

How can we interpret the phrase "least material"? For a first approximation we can ignore the thickness of the material and the waste in manufacturing. Then we ask for dimensions r and h that make the total surface area as small as possible while satisfying the constraint $\pi r^2 h = 1000$.

To express the surface area as a function of one variable, we solve for one of the variables in $\pi r^2 h = 1000$ and substitute that expression into the surface area formula. Solving for h is easier:

$$h = \frac{1000}{\pi r^2}.$$

Thus,

$$\begin{aligned} A &= 2\pi r^2 + 2\pi r h \\ &= 2\pi r^2 + 2\pi r\left(\frac{1000}{\pi r^2}\right) \\ &= 2\pi r^2 + \frac{2000}{r}. \end{aligned}$$

Our goal is to find a value of $r > 0$ that minimizes the value of A. Figure 4.38 suggests that such a value exists.

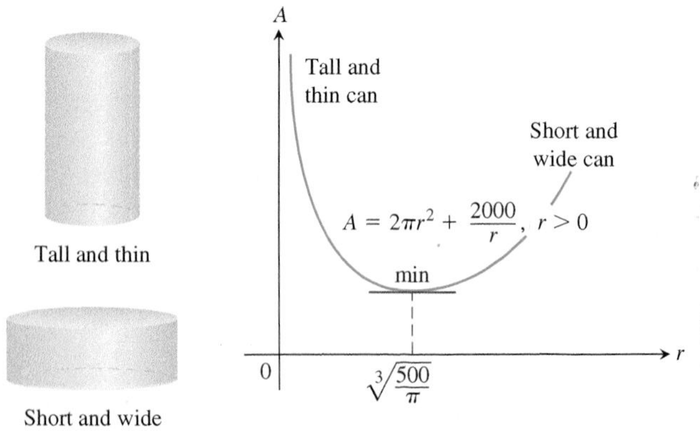

FIGURE 4.38 The graph of $A = 2\pi r^2 + 2000/r$ is concave up.

Notice from the graph that for small r (a tall, thin cylindrical container), the term $2000/r$ dominates (see Section 2.6) and A is large. For large r (a short, wide cylindrical container), the term $2\pi r^2$ dominates and A again is large.

Since A is differentiable on $r > 0$, an interval with no endpoints, it can have a minimum value only where its first derivative is zero.

$$\begin{aligned}\frac{dA}{dr} &= 4\pi r - \frac{2000}{r^2} \\ 0 &= 4\pi r - \frac{2000}{r^2} && \text{Set } dA/dr = 0. \\ 4\pi r^3 &= 2000 && \text{Multiply by } r^2. \\ r &= \sqrt[3]{\frac{500}{\pi}} \approx 5.42 && \text{Solve for } r.\end{aligned}$$

What happens at $r = \sqrt[3]{500/\pi}$?

The second derivative

$$\frac{d^2A}{dr^2} = 4\pi + \frac{4000}{r^3}$$

is positive throughout the domain of A. The graph is therefore everywhere concave up and the value of A at $r = \sqrt[3]{500/\pi}$ is an absolute minimum.

The corresponding value of h (after a little algebra) is

$$h = \frac{1000}{\pi r^2} = 2\sqrt[3]{\frac{500}{\pi}} = 2r.$$

The one-liter can that uses the least material has height equal to twice the radius, here with $r \approx 5.42$ cm and $h \approx 10.84$ cm. ■

Examples from Mathematics and Physics

EXAMPLE 3 A rectangle is to be inscribed in a semicircle of radius 2. What is the largest area the rectangle can have, and what are its dimensions?

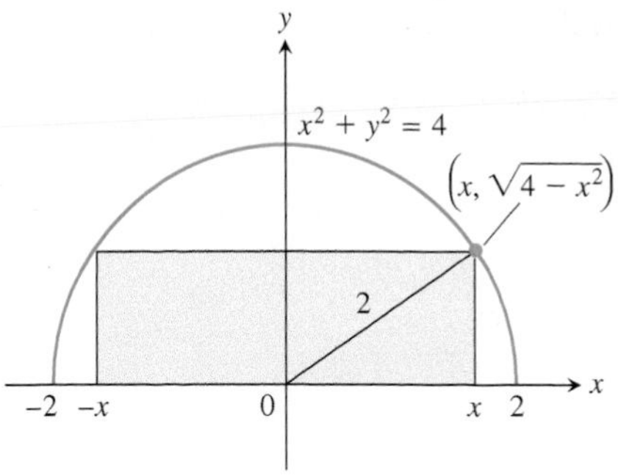

FIGURE 4.39 The rectangle inscribed in the semicircle in Example 3.

Solution Let $(x, \sqrt{4 - x^2})$ be the coordinates of the corner of the rectangle obtained by placing the circle and rectangle in the coordinate plane (Figure 4.39). The length, height, and area of the rectangle can then be expressed in terms of the position x of the lower right-hand corner:

$$\text{Length: } 2x, \qquad \text{Height: } \sqrt{4 - x^2}, \qquad \text{Area: } 2x\sqrt{4 - x^2}.$$

Notice that the values of x are to be found in the interval $0 \le x \le 2$, where the selected corner of the rectangle lies.

Our goal is to find the absolute maximum value of the function

$$A(x) = 2x\sqrt{4 - x^2}$$

on the domain $[0, 2]$.

The derivative

$$\frac{dA}{dx} = \frac{-2x^2}{\sqrt{4 - x^2}} + 2\sqrt{4 - x^2}$$

is not defined when $x = 2$ and is equal to zero when

$$\begin{aligned}\frac{-2x^2}{\sqrt{4 - x^2}} + 2\sqrt{4 - x^2} &= 0 \\ -2x^2 + 2(4 - x^2) &= 0 \\ 8 - 4x^2 &= 0 \\ x^2 = 2 \text{ or } x &= \pm\sqrt{2}.\end{aligned}$$

Of the two zeros, $x = \sqrt{2}$ and $x = -\sqrt{2}$, only $x = \sqrt{2}$ lies in the interior of A's domain and makes the critical-point list. The values of A at the endpoints and at this one critical point are

$$\text{Critical-point value:} \quad A(\sqrt{2}) = 2\sqrt{2}\sqrt{4-2} = 4$$
$$\text{Endpoint values:} \quad A(0) = 0, \quad A(2) = 0.$$

The area has a maximum value of 4 when the rectangle is $\sqrt{4-x^2} = \sqrt{2}$ units high and $2x = 2\sqrt{2}$ units long. ■

HISTORICAL BIOGRAPHY

Willebrord Snell van Royen (1580–1626)

EXAMPLE 4 The speed of light depends on the medium through which it travels, and is generally slower in denser media.

Fermat's principle in optics states that light travels from one point to another along a path for which the time of travel is a minimum. Describe the path that a ray of light will follow in going from a point A in a medium where the speed of light is c_1 to a point B in a second medium where its speed is c_2.

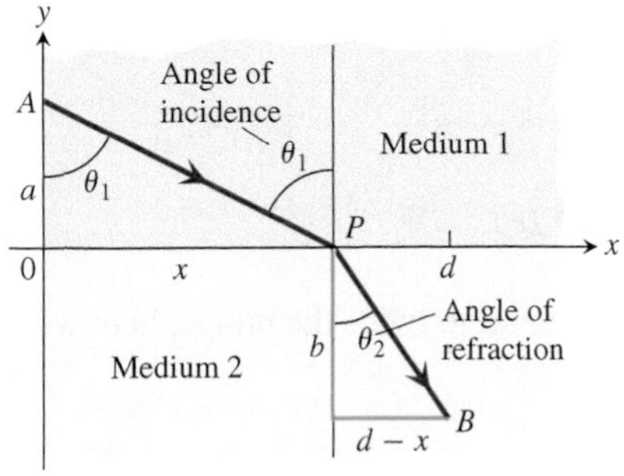

FIGURE 4.40 A light ray refracted (deflected from its path) as it passes from one medium to a denser medium (Example 4).

Solution Since light traveling from A to B follows the quickest route, we look for a path that will minimize the travel time. We assume that A and B lie in the xy-plane and that the line separating the two media is the x-axis (Figure 4.40).

In a uniform medium, where the speed of light remains constant, "shortest time" means "shortest path," and the ray of light will follow a straight line. Thus the path from A to B will consist of a line segment from A to a boundary point P, followed by another line segment from P to B. Distance traveled equals rate times time, so

$$\text{Time} = \frac{\text{distance}}{\text{rate}}.$$

From Figure 4.40, the time required for light to travel from A to P is

$$t_1 = \frac{AP}{c_1} = \frac{\sqrt{a^2+x^2}}{c_1}.$$

From P to B, the time is

$$t_2 = \frac{PB}{c_2} = \frac{\sqrt{b^2+(d-x)^2}}{c_2}.$$

The time from A to B is the sum of these:

$$t = t_1 + t_2 = \frac{\sqrt{a^2+x^2}}{c_1} + \frac{\sqrt{b^2+(d-x)^2}}{c_2}.$$

This equation expresses t as a differentiable function of x whose domain is $[0, d]$. We want to find the absolute minimum value of t on this closed interval. We find the derivative

$$\frac{dt}{dx} = \frac{x}{c_1\sqrt{a^2+x^2}} - \frac{d-x}{c_2\sqrt{b^2+(d-x)^2}}$$

and observe that it is continuous. In terms of the angles θ_1 and θ_2 in Figure 4.40,

$$\frac{dt}{dx} = \frac{\sin\theta_1}{c_1} - \frac{\sin\theta_2}{c_2}.$$

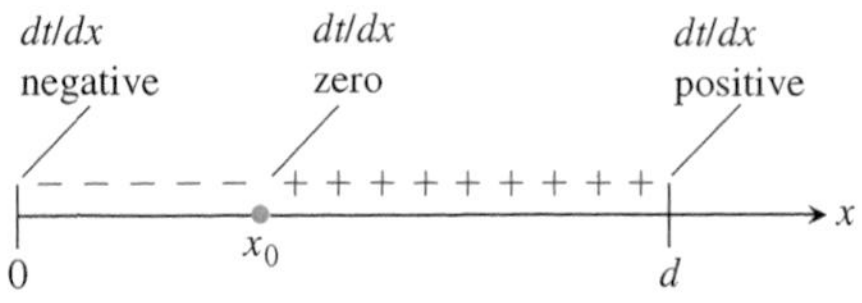

FIGURE 4.41 The sign pattern of dt/dx in Example 4.

The function t has a negative derivative at $x = 0$ and a positive derivative at $x = d$. Since dt/dx is continuous over the interval $[0, d]$, by the Intermediate Value Theorem for continuous functions (Section 2.5), there is a point $x_0 \in [0, d]$ where $dt/dx = 0$ (Figure 4.41).

There is only one such point because dt/dx is an increasing function of x (Exercise 62). At this unique point we then have

$$\frac{\sin\theta_1}{c_1} = \frac{\sin\theta_2}{c_2}.$$

This equation is **Snell's Law** or the **Law of Refraction**, and is an important principle in the theory of optics. It describes the path the ray of light follows. ■

Examples from Economics

Suppose that

$$r(x) = \text{the revenue from selling } x \text{ items}$$
$$c(x) = \text{the cost of producing the } x \text{ items}$$
$$p(x) = r(x) - c(x) = \text{the profit from producing and selling } x \text{ items}.$$

Although x is usually an integer in many applications, we can learn about the behavior of these functions by defining them for all nonzero real numbers and by assuming they are differentiable functions. Economists use the terms **marginal revenue**, **marginal cost**, and **marginal profit** to name the derivatives $r'(x)$, $c'(x)$, and $p'(x)$ of the revenue, cost, and profit functions. Let's consider the relationship of the profit p to these derivatives.

If $r(x)$ and $c(x)$ are differentiable for x in some interval of production possibilities, and if $p(x) = r(x) - c(x)$ has a maximum value there, it occurs at a critical point of $p(x)$ or at an endpoint of the interval. If it occurs at a critical point, then $p'(x) = r'(x) - c'(x) = 0$ and we see that $r'(x) = c'(x)$. In economic terms, this last equation means that

> At a production level yielding maximum profit, marginal revenue equals marginal cost (Figure 4.42).

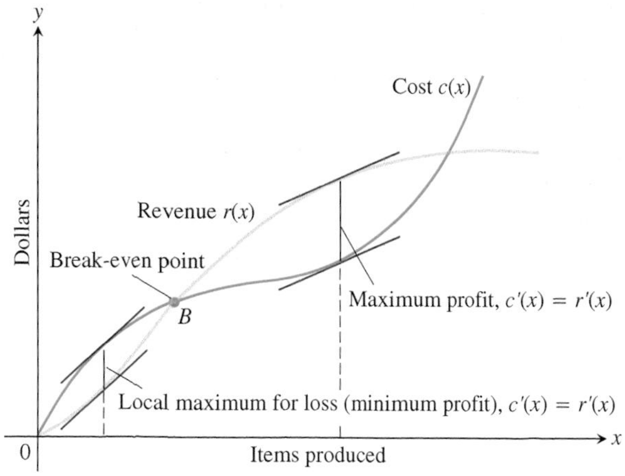

FIGURE 4.42 The graph of a typical cost function starts concave down and later turns concave up. It crosses the revenue curve at the break-even point B. To the left of B, the company operates at a loss. To the right, the company operates at a profit, with the maximum profit occurring where $c'(x) = r'(x)$. Farther to the right, cost exceeds revenue (perhaps because of a combination of rising labor and material costs and market saturation) and production levels become unprofitable again.

EXAMPLE 5 Suppose that $r(x) = 9x$ and $c(x) = x^3 - 6x^2 + 15x$, where x represents millions of MP3 players produced. Is there a production level that maximizes profit? If so, what is it?

Solution Notice that $r'(x) = 9$ and $c'(x) = 3x^2 - 12x + 15$.

$$3x^2 - 12x + 15 = 9 \qquad \text{Set } c'(x) = r'(x).$$
$$3x^2 - 12x + 6 = 0$$

The two solutions of the quadratic equation are

$$x_1 = \frac{12 - \sqrt{72}}{6} = 2 - \sqrt{2} \approx 0.586 \qquad \text{and}$$

$$x_2 = \frac{12 + \sqrt{72}}{6} = 2 + \sqrt{2} \approx 3.414.$$

The possible production levels for maximum profit are $x \approx 0.586$ million MP3 players or $x \approx 3.414$ million. The second derivative of $p(x) = r(x) - c(x)$ is $p''(x) = -c''(x)$ since $r''(x)$ is everywhere zero. Thus, $p''(x) = 6(2 - x)$, which is negative at $x = 2 + \sqrt{2}$ and positive at $x = 2 - \sqrt{2}$. By the Second Derivative Test, a maximum profit occurs at about $x = 3.414$ (where revenue exceeds costs) and maximum loss occurs at about $x = 0.586$. The graphs of $r(x)$ and $c(x)$ are shown in Figure 4.43. ■

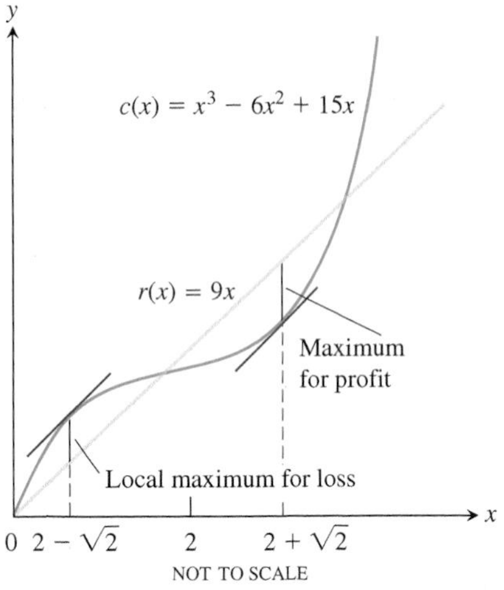

FIGURE 4.43 The cost and revenue curves for Example 5.

Exercises 4.6

Mathematical Applications

Whenever you are maximizing or minimizing a function of a single variable, we urge you to graph it over the domain that is appropriate to the problem you are solving. The graph will provide insight before you calculate and will furnish a visual context for understanding your answer.

1. **Minimizing perimeter** What is the smallest perimeter possible for a rectangle whose area is 16 in^2, and what are its dimensions?
2. Show that among all rectangles with an 8-m perimeter, the one with largest area is a square.
3. The figure shows a rectangle inscribed in an isosceles right triangle whose hypotenuse is 2 units long.
   a. Express the y-coordinate of P in terms of x. (*Hint:* Write an equation for the line AB.)
   b. Express the area of the rectangle in terms of x.
   c. What is the largest area the rectangle can have, and what are its dimensions?

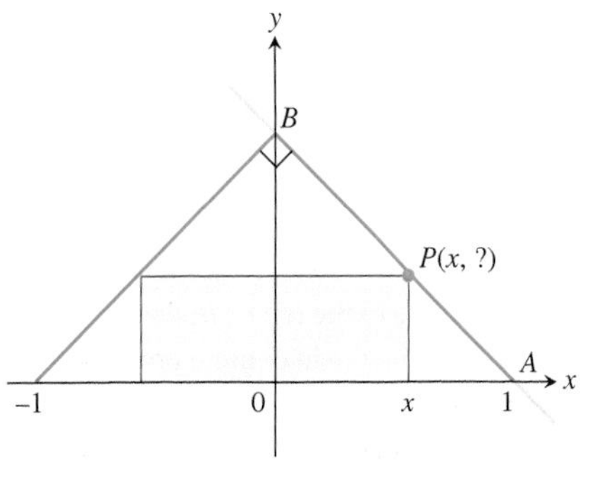

4. A rectangle has its base on the x-axis and its upper two vertices on the parabola $y = 12 - x^2$. What is the largest area the rectangle can have, and what are its dimensions?
5. You are planning to make an open rectangular box from an 8-in.-by-15-in. piece of cardboard by cutting congruent squares from the corners and folding up the sides. What are the dimensions of the box of largest volume you can make this way, and what is its volume?
6. You are planning to close off a corner of the first quadrant with a line segment 20 units long running from $(a, 0)$ to $(0, b)$. Show that the area of the triangle enclosed by the segment is largest when $a = b$.
7. **The best fencing plan** A rectangular plot of farmland will be bounded on one side by a river and on the other three sides by a single-strand electric fence. With 800 m of wire at your disposal, what is the largest area you can enclose, and what are its dimensions?
8. **The shortest fence** A 216 m^2 rectangular pea patch is to be enclosed by a fence and divided into two equal parts by another fence parallel to one of the sides. What dimensions for the outer rectangle will require the smallest total length of fence? How much fence will be needed?
9. **Designing a tank** Your iron works has contracted to design and build a 500 ft^3, square-based, open-top, rectangular steel holding tank for a paper company. The tank is to be made by welding thin stainless steel plates together along their edges. As the production engineer, your job is to find dimensions for the base and height that will make the tank weigh as little as possible.

a. What dimensions do you tell the shop to use?

b. Briefly describe how you took weight into account.

10. Catching rainwater A 1125 ft^3 open-top rectangular tank with a square base x ft on a side and y ft deep is to be built with its top flush with the ground to catch runoff water. The costs associated with the tank involve not only the material from which the tank is made but also an excavation charge proportional to the product xy.

a. If the total cost is

$$c = 5(x^2 + 4xy) + 10xy,$$

what values of x and y will minimize it?

b. Give a possible scenario for the cost function in part (a).

11. Designing a poster You are designing a rectangular poster to contain 50 in^2 of printing with a 4-in. margin at the top and bottom and a 2-in. margin at each side. What overall dimensions will minimize the amount of paper used?

12. Find the volume of the largest right circular cone that can be inscribed in a sphere of radius 3.

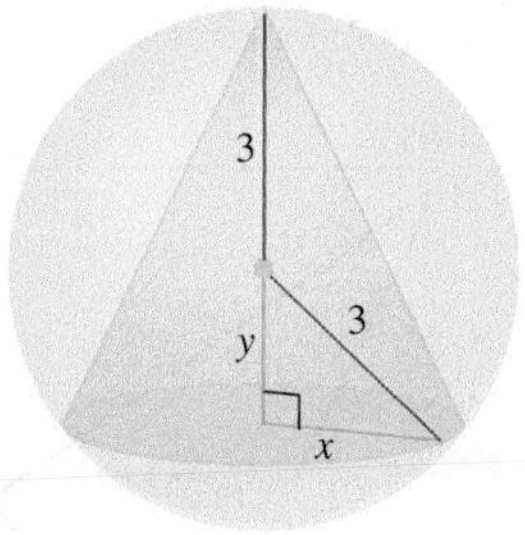

13. Two sides of a triangle have lengths a and b, and the angle between them is θ. What value of θ will maximize the triangle's area? (*Hint:* $A = (1/2)ab \sin \theta$.)

14. Designing a can What are the dimensions of the lightest open-top right circular cylindrical can that will hold a volume of 1000 cm^3? Compare the result here with the result in Example 2.

15. Designing a can You are designing a 1000 cm^3 right circular cylindrical can whose manufacture will take waste into account. There is no waste in cutting the aluminum for the side, but the top and bottom of radius r will be cut from squares that measure $2r$ units on a side. The total amount of aluminum used up by the can will therefore be

$$A = 8r^2 + 2\pi rh$$

rather than the $A = 2\pi r^2 + 2\pi rh$ in Example 2. In Example 2, the ratio of h to r for the most economical can was 2 to 1. What is the ratio now?

T **16. Designing a box with a lid** A piece of cardboard measures 10 in. by 15 in. Two equal squares are removed from the corners of a 10-in. side as shown in the figure. Two equal rectangles are removed from the other corners so that the tabs can be folded to form a rectangular box with lid.

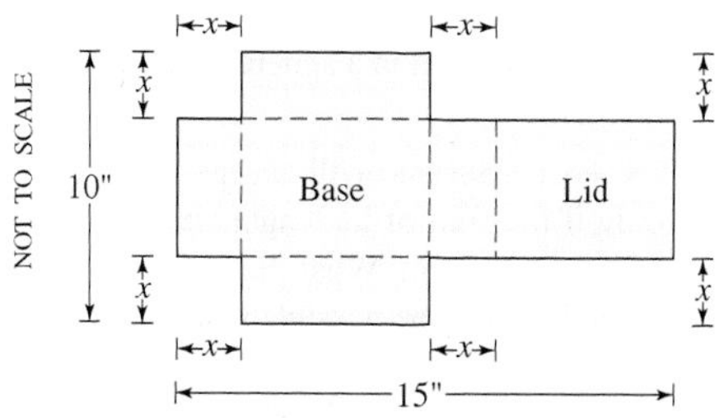

a. Write a formula $V(x)$ for the volume of the box.

b. Find the domain of V for the problem situation and graph V over this domain.

c. Use a graphical method to find the maximum volume and the value of x that gives it.

d. Confirm your result in part (c) analytically.

T **17. Designing a suitcase** A 24-in.-by-36-in. sheet of cardboard is folded in half to form a 24-in.-by-18-in. rectangle as shown in the accompanying figure. Then four congruent squares of side length x are cut from the corners of the folded rectangle. The sheet is unfolded, and the six tabs are folded up to form a box with sides and a lid.

a. Write a formula $V(x)$ for the volume of the box.

b. Find the domain of V for the problem situation and graph V over this domain.

c. Use a graphical method to find the maximum volume and the value of x that gives it.

d. Confirm your result in part (c) analytically.

e. Find a value of x that yields a volume of 1120 in^3.

f. Write a paragraph describing the issues that arise in part (b).

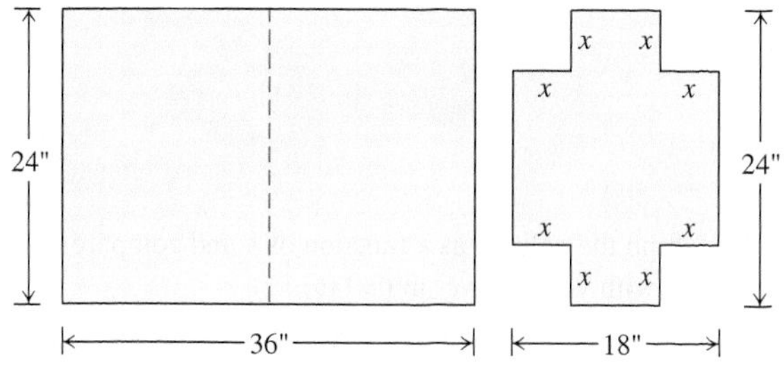

The sheet is then unfolded.

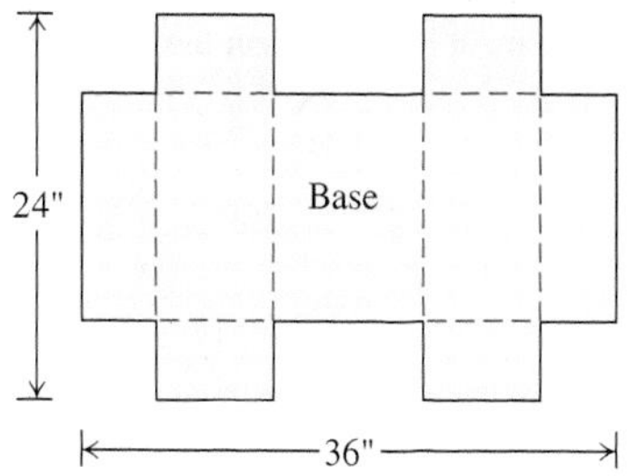

18. A rectangle is to be inscribed under the arch of the curve $y = 4 \cos (0.5x)$ from $x = -\pi$ to $x = \pi$. What are the dimensions of the rectangle with largest area, and what is the largest area?

19. Find the dimensions of a right circular cylinder of maximum volume that can be inscribed in a sphere of radius 10 cm. What is the maximum volume?

20. a. The U.S. Postal Service will accept a box for domestic shipment only if the sum of its length and girth (distance around) does not exceed 108 in. What dimensions will give a box with a square end the largest possible volume?

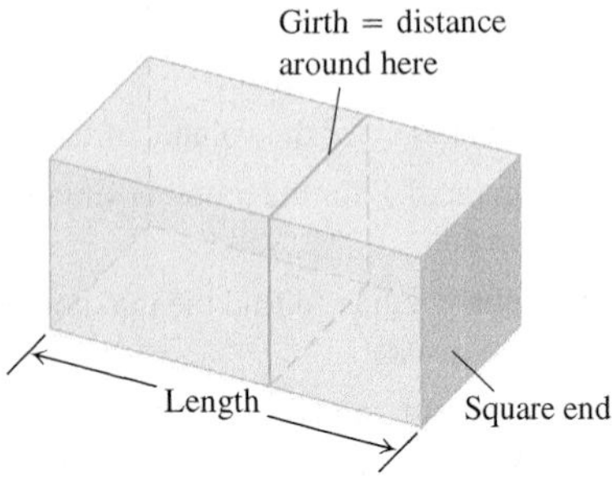

T b. Graph the volume of a 108-in. box (length plus girth equals 108 in.) as a function of its length and compare what you see with your answer in part (a).

21. (*Continuation of Exercise 20.*)

a. Suppose that instead of having a box with square ends you have a box with square sides so that its dimensions are h by h by w and the girth is $2h + 2w$. What dimensions will give the box its largest volume now?

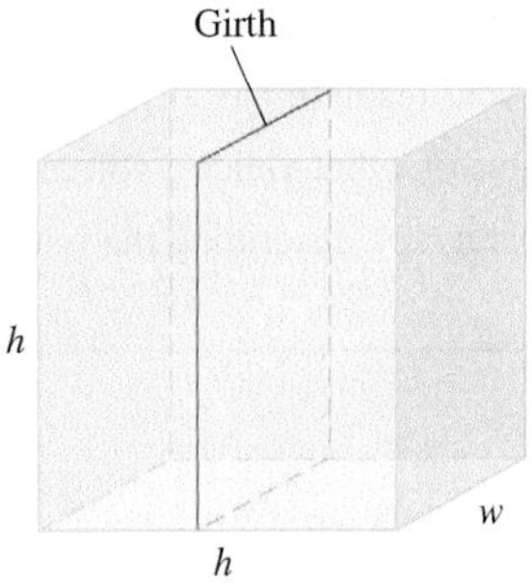

T b. Graph the volume as a function of h and compare what you see with your answer in part (a).

22. A window is in the form of a rectangle surmounted by a semicircle. The rectangle is of clear glass, whereas the semicircle is of tinted glass that transmits only half as much light per unit area as clear glass does. The total perimeter is fixed. Find the proportions of the window that will admit the most light. Neglect the thickness of the frame.

23. A silo (base not included) is to be constructed in the form of a cylinder surmounted by a hemisphere. The cost of construction per square unit of surface area is twice as great for the hemisphere as it is for the cylindrical sidewall. Determine the dimensions to be used if the volume is fixed and the cost of construction is to be kept to a minimum. Neglect the thickness of the silo and waste in construction.

24. The trough in the figure is to be made to the dimensions shown. Only the angle θ can be varied. What value of θ will maximize the trough's volume?

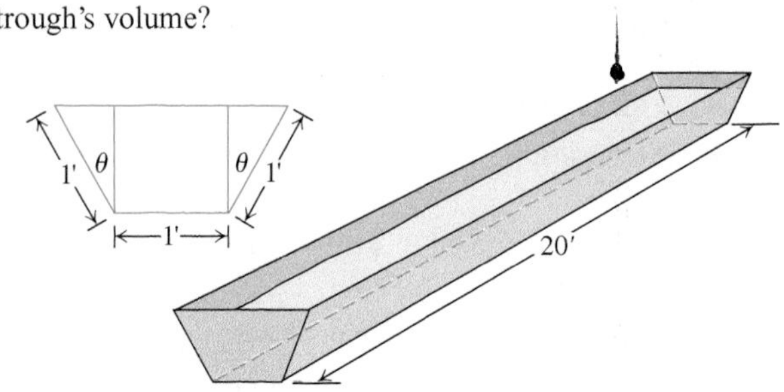

25. Paper folding A rectangular sheet of 8.5-in.-by-11-in. paper is placed on a flat surface. One of the corners is placed on the opposite longer edge, as shown in the figure, and held there as the paper is smoothed flat. The problem is to make the length of the crease as small as possible. Call the length L. Try it with paper.

a. Show that $L^2 = 2x^3/(2x - 8.5)$.

b. What value of x minimizes L^2?

c. What is the minimum value of L?

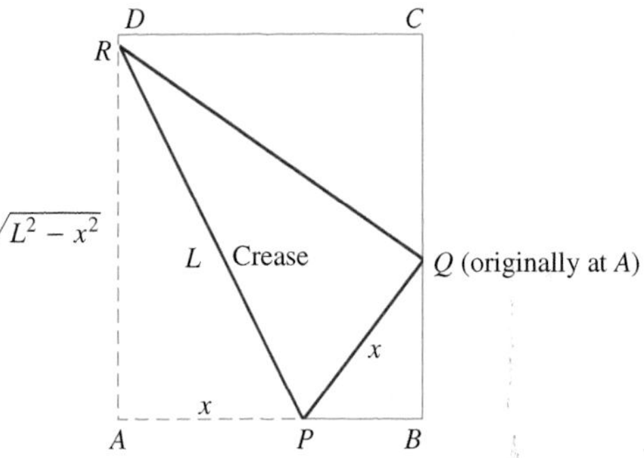

26. Constructing cylinders Compare the answers to the following two construction problems.

a. A rectangular sheet of perimeter 36 cm and dimensions x cm by y cm is to be rolled into a cylinder as shown in part (a) of the figure. What values of x and y give the largest volume?

b. The same sheet is to be revolved about one of the sides of length y to sweep out the cylinder as shown in part (b) of the figure. What values of x and y give the largest volume?

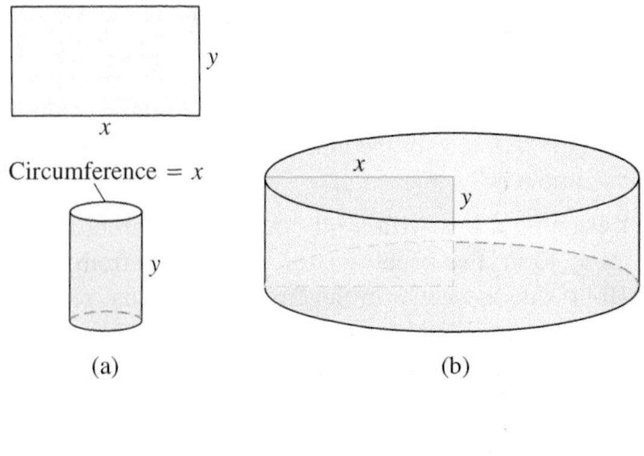

27. **Constructing cones** A right triangle whose hypotenuse is $\sqrt{3}$ m long is revolved about one of its legs to generate a right circular cone. Find the radius, height, and volume of the cone of greatest volume that can be made this way.

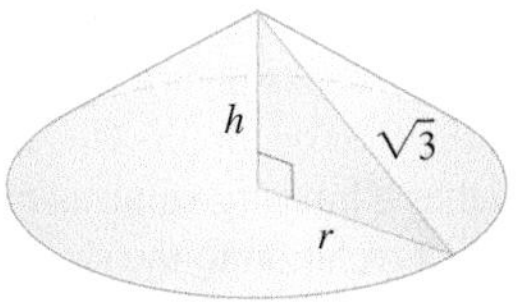

28. Find the point on the line $\frac{x}{a} + \frac{y}{b} = 1$ that is closest to the origin.

29. Find a positive number for which the sum of it and its reciprocal is the smallest (least) possible.

30. Find a postitive number for which the sum of its reciprocal and four times its square is the smallest possible.

31. A wire b m long is cut into two pieces. One piece is bent into an equilateral triangle and the other is bent into a circle. If the sum of the areas enclosed by each part is a minimum, what is the length of each part?

32. Answer Exercise 31 if one piece is bent into a square and the other into a circle.

33. Determine the dimensions of the rectangle of largest area that can be inscribed in the right triangle shown in the accompanying figure.

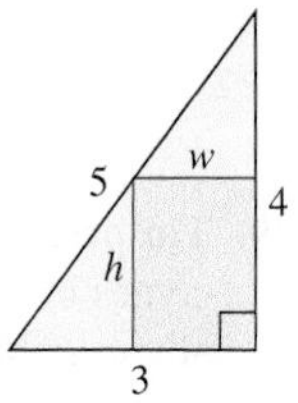

34. Determine the dimensions of the rectangle of largest area that can be inscribed in a semicircle of radius 3. (See accompanying figure.)

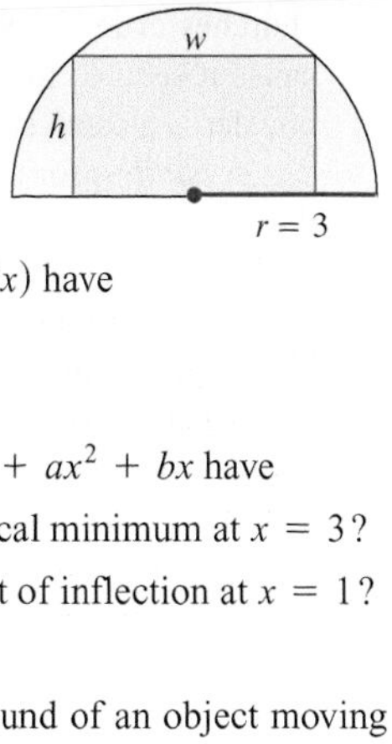

35. What value of a makes $f(x) = x^2 + (a/x)$ have

a. a local minimum at $x = 2$?

b. a point of inflection at $x = 1$?

36. What values of a and b make $f(x) = x^3 + ax^2 + bx$ have

a. a local maximum at $x = -1$ and a local minimum at $x = 3$?

b. a local minimum at $x = 4$ and a point of inflection at $x = 1$?

Physical Applications

37. **Vertical motion** The height above ground of an object moving vertically is given by

$$s = -16t^2 + 96t + 112,$$

with s in feet and t in seconds. Find

a. the object's velocity when $t = 0$;

b. its maximum height and when it occurs;

c. its velocity when $s = 0$.

38. **Quickest route** Jane is 2 mi offshore in a boat and wishes to reach a coastal village 6 mi down a straight shoreline from the point nearest the boat. She can row 2 mph and can walk 5 mph. Where should she land her boat to reach the village in the least amount of time?

39. **Shortest beam** The 8-ft wall shown here stands 27 ft from the building. Find the length of the shortest straight beam that will reach to the side of the building from the ground outside the wall.

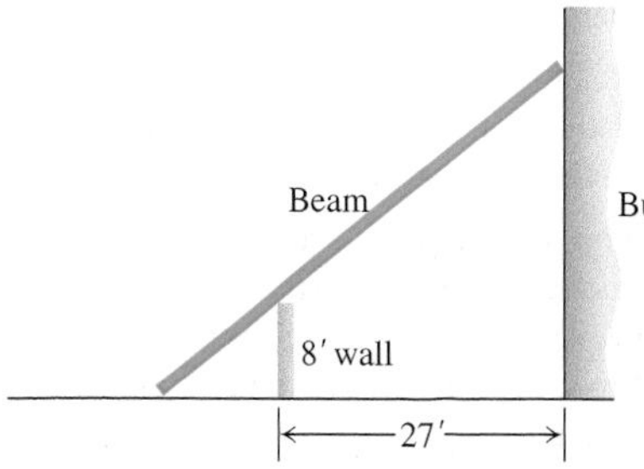

40. **Motion on a line** The positions of two particles on the s-axis are $s_1 = \sin t$ and $s_2 = \sin(t + \pi/3)$, with s_1 and s_2 in meters and t in seconds.

a. At what time(s) in the interval $0 \le t \le 2\pi$ do the particles meet?

b. What is the farthest apart that the particles ever get?

c. When in the interval $0 \le t \le 2\pi$ is the distance between the particles changing the fastest?

41. The intensity of illumination at any point from a light source is proportional to the square of the reciprocal of the distance between the point and the light source. Two lights, one having an intensity eight times that of the other, are 6 m apart. How far from the stronger light is the total illumination least?

42. **Projectile motion** The *range* R of a projectile fired from the origin over horizontal ground is the distance from the origin to the point of impact. If the projectile is fired with an initial velocity v_0 at an angle α with the horizontal, then in Chapter 12 we find that

$$R = \frac{v_0^2}{g} \sin 2\alpha,$$

where g is the downward acceleration due to gravity. Find the angle α for which the range R is the largest possible.

T 43. **Strength of a beam** The strength S of a rectangular wooden beam is proportional to its width times the square of its depth. (See the accompanying figure.)

a. Find the dimensions of the strongest beam that can be cut from a 12-in.-diameter cylindrical log.

b. Graph S as a function of the beam's width w, assuming the proportionality constant to be $k = 1$. Reconcile what you see with your answer in part (a).

c. On the same screen, graph S as a function of the beam's depth d, again taking $k = 1$. Compare the graphs with one another and with your answer in part (a). What would be the effect of changing to some other value of k? Try it.

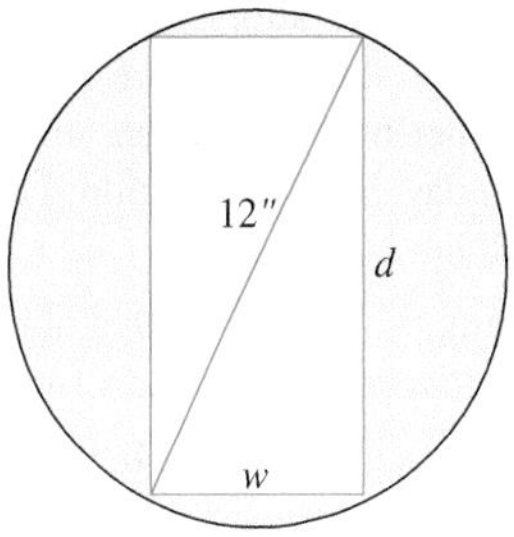

T **44. Stiffness of a beam** The stiffness S of a rectangular beam is proportional to its width times the cube of its depth.

a. Find the dimensions of the stiffest beam that can be cut from a 12-in.-diameter cylindrical log.

b. Graph S as a function of the beam's width w, assuming the proportionality constant to be $k = 1$. Reconcile what you see with your answer in part (a).

c. On the same screen, graph S as a function of the beam's depth d, again taking $k = 1$. Compare the graphs with one another and with your answer in part (a). What would be the effect of changing to some other value of k? Try it.

45. Frictionless cart A small frictionless cart, attached to the wall by a spring, is pulled 10 cm from its rest position and released at time $t = 0$ to roll back and forth for 4 sec. Its position at time t is $s = 10 \cos \pi t$.

a. What is the cart's maximum speed? When is the cart moving that fast? Where is it then? What is the magnitude of the acceleration then?

b. Where is the cart when the magnitude of the acceleration is greatest? What is the cart's speed then?

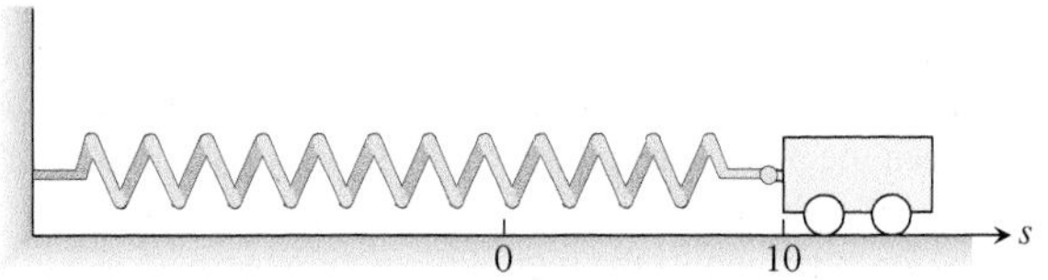

46. Two masses hanging side by side from springs have positions $s_1 = 2 \sin t$ and $s_2 = \sin 2t$, respectively.

a. At what times in the interval $0 < t$ do the masses pass each other? (*Hint:* $\sin 2t = 2 \sin t \cos t$.)

b. When in the interval $0 \le t \le 2\pi$ is the vertical distance between the masses the greatest? What is this distance? (*Hint:* $\cos 2t = 2 \cos^2 t - 1$.)

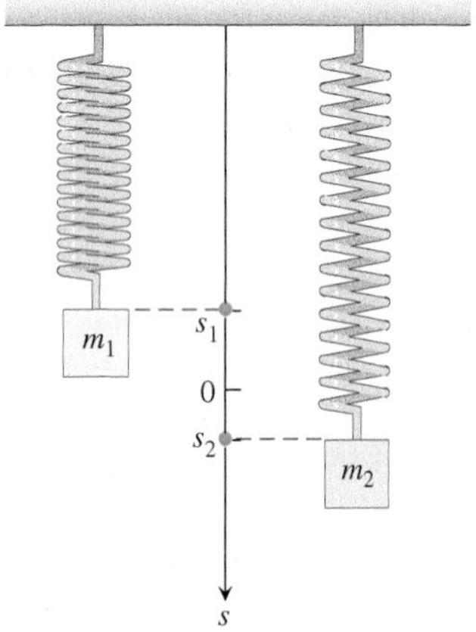

47. Distance between two ships At noon, ship A was 12 nautical miles due north of ship B. Ship A was sailing south at 12 knots (nautical miles per hour; a nautical mile is 2000 yd) and continued to do so all day. Ship B was sailing east at 8 knots and continued to do so all day.

a. Start counting time with $t = 0$ at noon and express the distance s between the ships as a function of t.

b. How rapidly was the distance between the ships changing at noon? One hour later?

c. The visibility that day was 5 nautical miles. Did the ships ever sight each other?

T **d.** Graph s and ds/dt together as functions of t for $-1 \le t \le 3$, using different colors if possible. Compare the graphs and reconcile what you see with your answers in parts (b) and (c).

e. The graph of ds/dt looks as if it might have a horizontal asymptote in the first quadrant. This in turn suggests that ds/dt approaches a limiting value as $t \to \infty$. What is this value? What is its relation to the ships' individual speeds?

48. Fermat's principle in optics Light from a source A is reflected by a plane mirror to a receiver at point B, as shown in the accompanying figure. Show that for the light to obey Fermat's principle, the angle of incidence must equal the angle of reflection, both measured from the line normal to the reflecting surface. (This result can also be derived without calculus. There is a purely geometric argument, which you may prefer.)

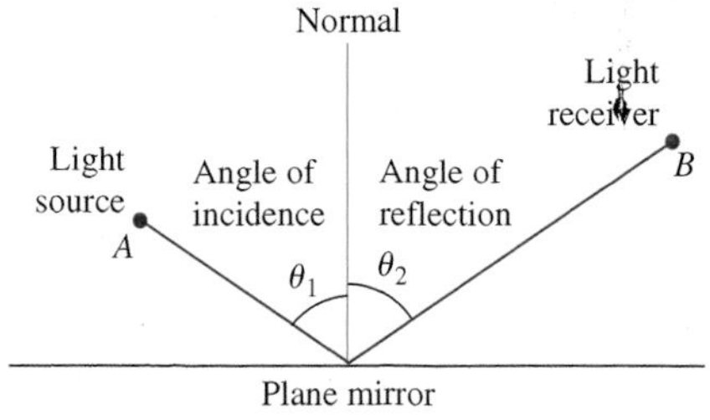

49. Tin pest When metallic tin is kept below 13.2°C, it slowly becomes brittle and crumbles to a gray powder. Tin objects eventually crumble to this gray powder spontaneously if kept in a cold climate for years. The Europeans who saw tin organ pipes in their churches crumble away years ago called the change *tin pest* because it seemed to be contagious, and indeed it was, for the gray powder is a catalyst for its own formation.

A *catalyst* for a chemical reaction is a substance that controls the rate of reaction without undergoing any permanent change in itself. An *autocatalytic reaction* is one whose product is a catalyst for its own formation. Such a reaction may proceed slowly at first if the amount of catalyst present is small and slowly again at the end, when most of the original substance is used up. But in between, when both the substance and its catalyst product are abundant, the reaction proceeds at a faster pace.

In some cases, it is reasonable to assume that the rate $v = dx/dt$ of the reaction is proportional both to the amount of the original substance present and to the amount of product. That is, v may be considered to be a function of x alone, and

$$v = kx(a - x) = kax - kx^2,$$

where

$x =$ the amount of product

$a =$ the amount of substance at the beginning

$k =$ a positive constant.

At what value of x does the rate v have a maximum? What is the maximum value of v?

50. Airplane landing path An airplane is flying at altitude H when it begins its descent to an airport runway that is at horizontal ground distance L from the airplane, as shown in the figure. Assume that the landing path of the airplane is the graph of a cubic polynomial function $y = ax^3 + bx^2 + cx + d$, where $y(-L) = H$ and $y(0) = 0$.

a. What is dy/dx at $x = 0$?

b. What is dy/dx at $x = -L$?

c. Use the values for dy/dx at $x = 0$ and $x = -L$ together with $y(0) = 0$ and $y(-L) = H$ to show that

$$y(x) = H\left[2\left(\frac{x}{L}\right)^3 + 3\left(\frac{x}{L}\right)^2\right].$$

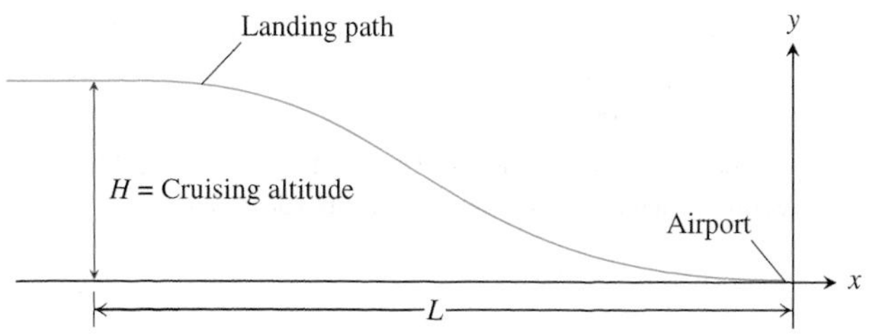

Business and Economics

51. It costs you c dollars each to manufacture and distribute backpacks. If the backpacks sell at x dollars each, the number sold is given by

$$n = \frac{a}{x - c} + b(100 - x),$$

where a and b are positive constants. What selling price will bring a maximum profit?

52. You operate a tour service that offers the following rates:

$200 per person if 50 people (the minimum number to book the tour) go on the tour.

For each additional person, up to a maximum of 80 people total, the rate per person is reduced by $2.

It costs $6000 (a fixed cost) plus $32 per person to conduct the tour. How many people does it take to maximize your profit?

53. Wilson lot size formula One of the formulas for inventory management says that the average weekly cost of ordering, paying for, and holding merchandise is

$$A(q) = \frac{km}{q} + cm + \frac{hq}{2},$$

where q is the quantity you order when things run low (shoes, radios, brooms, or whatever the item might be), k is the cost of placing an order (the same, no matter how often you order), c is the cost of one item (a constant), m is the number of items sold each week (a constant), and h is the weekly holding cost per item (a constant that takes into account things such as space, utilities, insurance, and security).

a. Your job, as the inventory manager for your store, is to find the quantity that will minimize $A(q)$. What is it? (The formula you get for the answer is called the *Wilson lot size formula*.)

b. Shipping costs sometimes depend on order size. When they do, it is more realistic to replace k by $k + bq$, the sum of k and a constant multiple of q. What is the most economical quantity to order now?

54. Production level Prove that the production level (if any) at which average cost is smallest is a level at which the average cost equals marginal cost.

55. Show that if $r(x) = 6x$ and $c(x) = x^3 - 6x^2 + 15x$ are your revenue and cost functions, then the best you can do is break even (have revenue equal cost).

56. Production level Suppose that $c(x) = x^3 - 20x^2 + 20{,}000x$ is the cost of manufacturing x items. Find a production level that will minimize the average cost of making x items.

57. You are to construct an open rectangular box with a square base and a volume of 48 ft^3. If material for the bottom costs \$6/ft^2 and material for the sides costs \$4/ft^2, what dimensions will result in the least expensive box? What is the minimum cost?

58. The 800-room Mega Motel chain is filled to capacity when the room charge is $50 per night. For each $10 increase in room charge, 40 fewer rooms are filled each night. What charge per room will result in the maximum revenue per night?

Biology

59. Sensitivity to medicine (*Continuation of Exercise 72, Section 3.3.*) Find the amount of medicine to which the body is most sensitive by finding the value of M that maximizes the derivative dR/dM, where

$$R = M^2\left(\frac{C}{2} - \frac{M}{3}\right)$$

and C is a constant.

60. How we cough

a. When we cough, the trachea (windpipe) contracts to increase the velocity of the air going out. This raises the questions of how much it should contract to maximize the velocity and whether it really contracts that much when we cough.

Under reasonable assumptions about the elasticity of the tracheal wall and about how the air near the wall is slowed by friction, the average flow velocity v can be modeled by the equation

$$v = c(r_0 - r)r^2 \text{ cm/sec}, \qquad \frac{r_0}{2} \le r \le r_0,$$

where r_0 is the rest radius of the trachea in centimeters and c is a positive constant whose value depends in part on the length of the trachea.

Show that v is greatest when $r = (2/3)r_0$; that is, when the trachea is about 33% contracted. The remarkable fact is that X-ray photographs confirm that the trachea contracts about this much during a cough.

T **b.** Take r_0 to be 0.5 and c to be 1 and graph v over the interval $0 \le r \le 0.5$. Compare what you see with the claim that v is at a maximum when $r = (2/3)r_0$.

Theory and Examples

61. An inequality for positive integers Show that if a, b, c, and d are positive integers, then

$$\frac{(a^2 + 1)(b^2 + 1)(c^2 + 1)(d^2 + 1)}{abcd} \ge 16.$$

62. The derivative dt/dx in Example 4

a. Show that

$$f(x) = \frac{x}{\sqrt{a^2 + x^2}}$$

is an increasing function of x.

b. Show that

$$g(x) = \frac{d - x}{\sqrt{b^2 + (d - x)^2}}$$

is a decreasing function of x.

c. Show that

$$\frac{dt}{dx} = \frac{x}{c_1\sqrt{a^2 + x^2}} - \frac{d - x}{c_2\sqrt{b^2 + (d - x)^2}}$$

is an increasing function of x.

63. Let $f(x)$ and $g(x)$ be the differentiable functions graphed here. Point c is the point where the vertical distance between the curves is the greatest. Is there anything special about the tangents to the two curves at c? Give reasons for your answer.

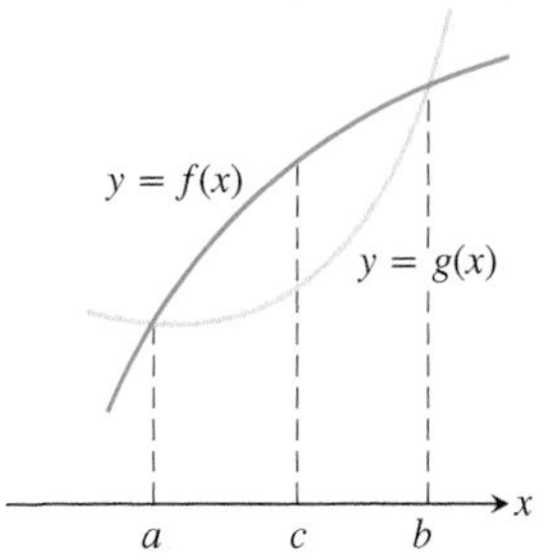

64. You have been asked to determine whether the function $f(x) = 3 + 4\cos x + \cos 2x$ is ever negative.

a. Explain why you need to consider values of x only in the interval $[0, 2\pi]$.

b. Is f ever negative? Explain.

65. a. The function $y = \cot x - \sqrt{2}\csc x$ has an absolute maximum value on the interval $0 < x < \pi$. Find it.

T **b.** Graph the function and compare what you see with your answer in part (a).

66. a. The function $y = \tan x + 3\cot x$ has an absolute minimum value on the interval $0 < x < \pi/2$. Find it.

T **b.** Graph the function and compare what you see with your answer in part (a).

67. a. How close does the curve $y = \sqrt{x}$ come to the point $(3/2, 0)$? (*Hint:* If you minimize the *square* of the distance, you can avoid square roots.)

T **b.** Graph the distance function $D(x)$ and $y = \sqrt{x}$ together and reconcile what you see with your answer in part (a).

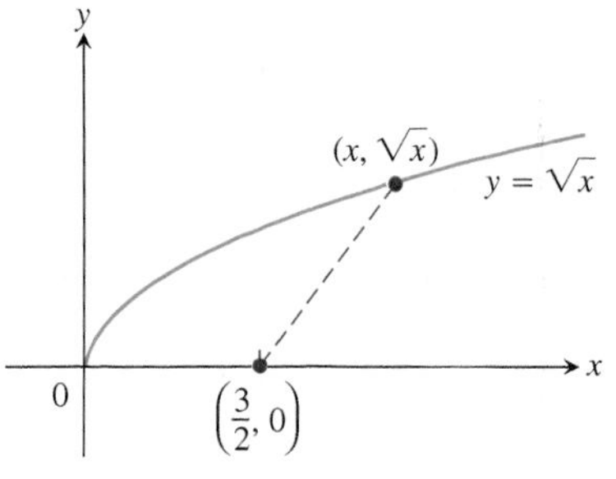

68. a. How close does the semicircle $y = \sqrt{16 - x^2}$ come to the point $(1, \sqrt{3})$?

T **b.** Graph the distance function and $y = \sqrt{16 - x^2}$ together and reconcile what you see with your answer in part (a).

4.7 Newton's Method

In this section we study a numerical method, called *Newton's method* or the *Newton–Raphson method*, which is a technique to approximate the solution to an equation $f(x) = 0$. Essentially it uses tangent lines in place of the graph of $y = f(x)$ near the points where f is zero. (A value of x where f is zero is a *root* of the function f and a *solution* of the equation $f(x) = 0$.)

Procedure for Newton's Method

The goal of Newton's method for estimating a solution of an equation $f(x) = 0$ is to produce a sequence of approximations that approach the solution. We pick the first number x_0 of the sequence. Then, under favorable circumstances, the method does the rest by moving step by step toward a point where the graph of f crosses the x-axis (Figure 4.44). At each step the method approximates a zero of f with a zero of one of its linearizations. Here is how it works.

The initial estimate, x_0, may be found by graphing or just plain guessing. The method then uses the tangent to the curve $y = f(x)$ at $(x_0, f(x_0))$ to approximate the curve, calling

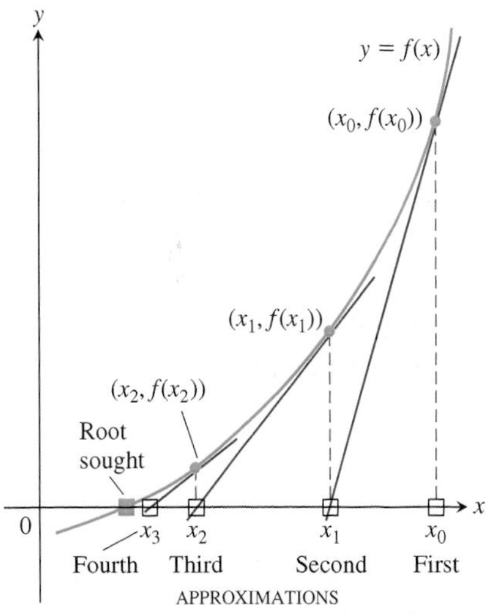

FIGURE 4.44 Newton's method starts with an initial guess x_0 and (under favorable circumstances) improves the guess one step at a time.

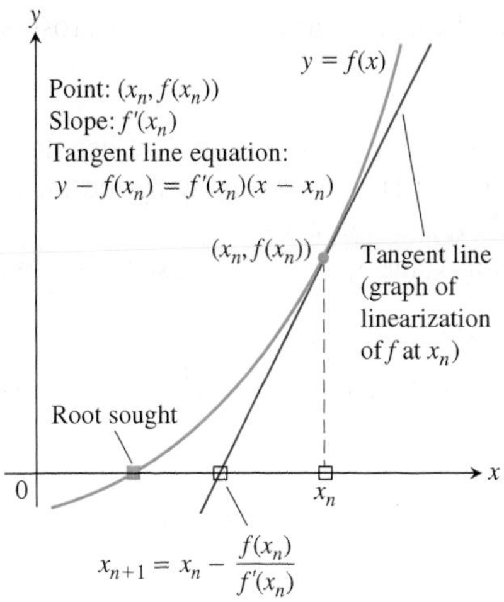

FIGURE 4.45 The geometry of the successive steps of Newton's method. From x_n we go up to the curve and follow the tangent line down to find x_{n+1}.

the point x_1 where the tangent meets the x-axis (Figure 4.44). The number x_1 is usually a better approximation to the solution than is x_0. The point x_2 where the tangent to the curve at $(x_1, f(x_1))$ crosses the x-axis is the next approximation in the sequence. We continue on, using each approximation to generate the next, until we are close enough to the root to stop.

We can derive a formula for generating the successive approximations in the following way. Given the approximation x_n, the point-slope equation for the tangent to the curve at $(x_n, f(x_n))$ is

$$y = f(x_n) + f'(x_n)(x - x_n).$$

We can find where it crosses the x-axis by setting $y = 0$ (Figure 4.45):

$$0 = f(x_n) + f'(x_n)(x - x_n)$$

$$-\frac{f(x_n)}{f'(x_n)} = x - x_n$$

$$x = x_n - \frac{f(x_n)}{f'(x_n)} \qquad \text{If } f'(x_n) \neq 0$$

This value of x is the next approximation x_{n+1}. Here is a summary of Newton's method.

Newton's Method

1. Guess a first approximation to a solution of the equation $f(x) = 0$. A graph of $y = f(x)$ may help.
2. Use the first approximation to get a second, the second to get a third, and so on, using the formula

$$x_{n+1} = x_n - \frac{f(x_n)}{f'(x_n)}, \qquad \text{if } f'(x_n) \neq 0. \tag{1}$$

Applying Newton's Method

Applications of Newton's method generally involve many numerical computations, making them well suited for computers or calculators. Nevertheless, even when the calculations are done by hand (which may be very tedious), they give a powerful way to find solutions of equations.

In our first example, we find decimal approximations to $\sqrt{2}$ by estimating the positive root of the equation $f(x) = x^2 - 2 = 0$.

EXAMPLE 1 Find the positive root of the equation

$$f(x) = x^2 - 2 = 0.$$

Solution With $f(x) = x^2 - 2$ and $f'(x) = 2x$, Equation (1) becomes

$$\begin{aligned} x_{n+1} &= x_n - \frac{x_n{}^2 - 2}{2x_n} \\ &= x_n - \frac{x_n}{2} + \frac{1}{x_n} \\ &= \frac{x_n}{2} + \frac{1}{x_n}. \end{aligned}$$

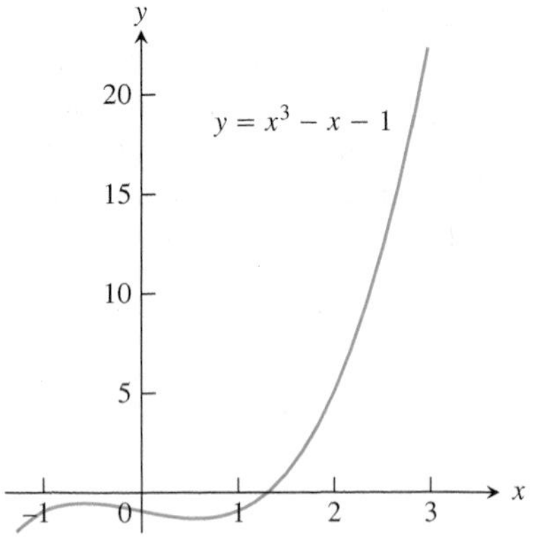

FIGURE 4.46 The graph of $f(x) = x^3 - x - 1$ crosses the x-axis once; this is the root we want to find (Example 2).

The equation

$$x_{n+1} = \frac{x_n}{2} + \frac{1}{x_n}$$

enables us to go from each approximation to the next with just a few keystrokes. With the starting value $x_0 = 1$, we get the results in the first column of the following table. (To five decimal places, $\sqrt{2} = 1.41421$.)

	Error	Number of correct digits
$x_0 = 1$	-0.41421	1
$x_1 = 1.5$	0.08579	1
$x_2 = 1.41667$	0.00246	3
$x_3 = 1.41422$	0.00001	5

■

Newton's method is the method used by most calculators to calculate roots because it converges so fast (more about this later). If the arithmetic in the table in Example 1 had been carried to 13 decimal places instead of 5, then going one step further would have given $\sqrt{2}$ correctly to more than 10 decimal places.

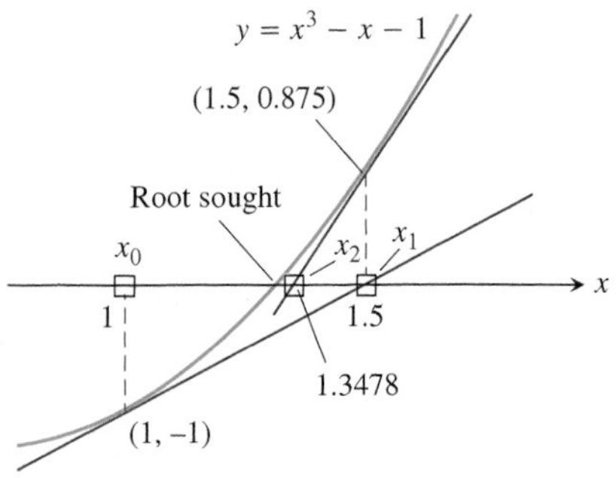

FIGURE 4.47 The first three x-values in Table 4.1 (four decimal places).

EXAMPLE 2 Find the x-coordinate of the point where the curve $y = x^3 - x$ crosses the horizontal line $y = 1$.

Solution The curve crosses the line when $x^3 - x = 1$ or $x^3 - x - 1 = 0$. When does $f(x) = x^3 - x - 1$ equal zero? Since $f(1) = -1$ and $f(2) = 5$, we know by the Intermediate Value Theorem there is a root in the interval $(1, 2)$ (Figure 4.46).

We apply Newton's method to f with the starting value $x_0 = 1$. The results are displayed in Table 4.1 and Figure 4.47.

At $n = 5$, we come to the result $x_6 = x_5 = 1.3247\ 17957$. When $x_{n+1} = x_n$, Equation (1) shows that $f(x_n) = 0$. We have found a solution of $f(x) = 0$ to nine decimals. ■

TABLE 4.1 The result of applying Newton's method to $f(x) = x^3 - x - 1$ with $x_0 = 1$

n	x_n	$f(x_n)$	$f'(x_n)$	$x_{n+1} = x_n - \dfrac{f(x_n)}{f'(x_n)}$
0	1	-1	2	1.5
1	1.5	0.875	5.75	1.3478 26087
2	1.3478 26087	0.1006 82173	4.4499 05482	1.3252 00399
3	1.3252 00399	0.0020 58362	4.2684 68292	1.3247 18174
4	1.3247 18174	0.0000 00924	4.2646 34722	1.3247 17957
5	1.3247 17957	$-1.8672\text{E}{-13}$	4.2646 32999	1.3247 17957

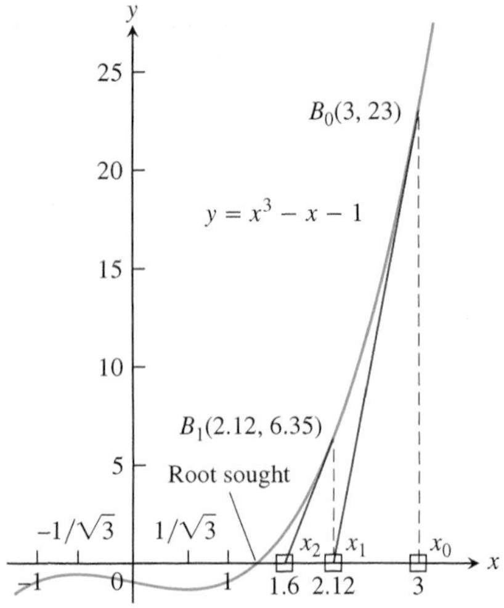

FIGURE 4.48 Any starting value x_0 to the right of $x = 1/\sqrt{3}$ will lead to the root.

In Figure 4.48 we have indicated that the process in Example 2 might have started at the point $B_0(3, 23)$ on the curve, with $x_0 = 3$. Point B_0 is quite far from the x-axis, but the tangent at B_0 crosses the x-axis at about $(2.12, 0)$, so x_1 is still an improvement over x_0. If we use Equation (1) repeatedly as before, with $f(x) = x^3 - x - 1$ and $f'(x) = 3x^2 - 1$, we obtain the nine-place solution $x_7 = x_6 = 1.3247\ 17957$ in seven steps.

Convergence of the Approximations

In Chapter 9 we define precisely the idea of *convergence* for the approximations x_n in Newton's method. Intuitively, we mean that as the number n of approximations increases without bound, the values x_n get arbitrarily close to the desired root r. (This notion is similar to the idea of the limit of a function $g(t)$ as t approaches infinity, as defined in Section 2.6.)

In practice, Newton's method usually gives convergence with impressive speed, but this is not guaranteed. One way to test convergence is to begin by graphing the function to estimate a good starting value for x_0. You can test that you are getting closer to a zero of the function by evaluating $|f(x_n)|$, and check that the approximations are converging by evaluating $|x_n - x_{n+1}|$.

Newton's method does not always converge. For instance, if

$$f(x) = \begin{cases} -\sqrt{r - x}, & x < r \\ \sqrt{x - r}, & x \geq r, \end{cases}$$

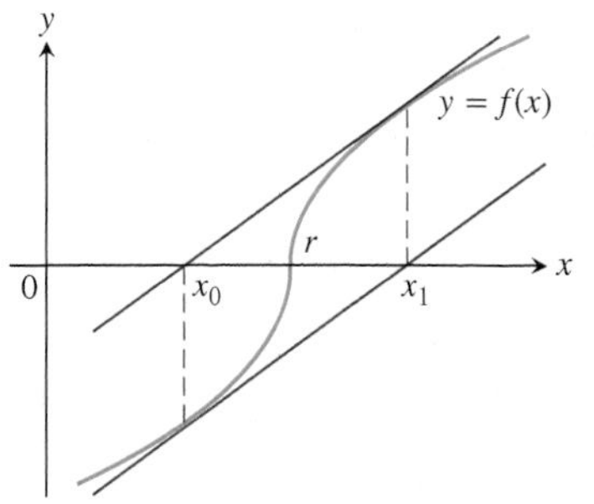

FIGURE 4.49 Newton's method fails to converge. You go from x_0 to x_1 and back to x_0, never getting any closer to r.

the graph will be like the one in Figure 4.49. If we begin with $x_0 = r - h$, we get $x_1 = r + h$, and successive approximations go back and forth between these two values. No amount of iteration brings us closer to the root than our first guess.

If Newton's method does converge, it converges to a root. Be careful, however. There are situations in which the method appears to converge but there is no root there. Fortunately, such situations are rare.

When Newton's method converges to a root, it may not be the root you have in mind. Figure 4.50 shows two ways this can happen.

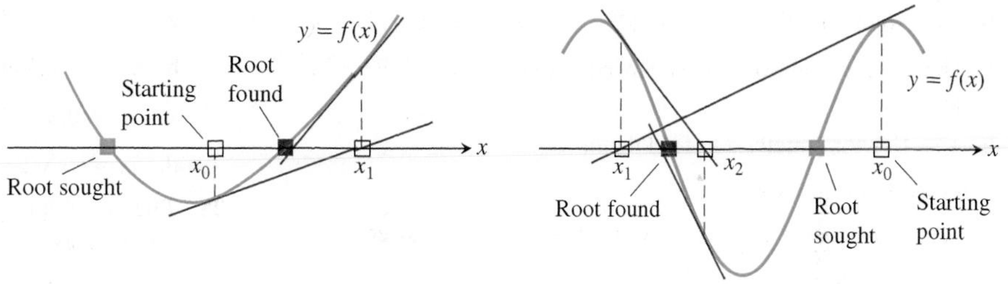

FIGURE 4.50 If you start too far away, Newton's method may miss the root you want.

Exercises 4.7

Root Finding

1. Use Newton's method to estimate the solutions of the equation $x^2 + x - 1 = 0$. Start with $x_0 = -1$ for the left-hand solution and with $x_0 = 1$ for the solution on the right. Then, in each case, find x_2.

2. Use Newton's method to estimate the one real solution of $x^3 + 3x + 1 = 0$. Start with $x_0 = 0$ and then find x_2.

3. Use Newton's method to estimate the two zeros of the function $f(x) = x^4 + x - 3$. Start with $x_0 = -1$ for the left-hand zero and with $x_0 = 1$ for the zero on the right. Then, in each case, find x_2.

4. Use Newton's method to estimate the two zeros of the function $f(x) = 2x - x^2 + 1$. Start with $x_0 = 0$ for the left-hand zero and with $x_0 = 2$ for the zero on the right. Then, in each case, find x_2.

5. Use Newton's method to find the positive fourth root of 2 by solving the equation $x^4 - 2 = 0$. Start with $x_0 = 1$ and find x_2.

6. Use Newton's method to find the negative fourth root of 2 by solving the equation $x^4 - 2 = 0$. Start with $x_0 = -1$ and find x_2.

7. **Guessing a root** Suppose that your first guess is lucky, in the sense that x_0 is a root of $f(x) = 0$. Assuming that $f'(x_0)$ is defined and not 0, what happens to x_1 and later approximations?

8. **Estimating pi** You plan to estimate $\pi/2$ to five decimal places by using Newton's method to solve the equation $\cos x = 0$. Does it matter what your starting value is? Give reasons for your answer.

Theory and Examples

9. **Oscillation** Show that if $h > 0$, applying Newton's method to

$$f(x) = \begin{cases} \sqrt{x}, & x \geq 0 \\ \sqrt{-x}, & x < 0 \end{cases}$$

leads to $x_1 = -h$ if $x_0 = h$ and to $x_1 = h$ if $x_0 = -h$. Draw a picture that shows what is going on.

10. **Approximations that get worse and worse** Apply Newton's method to $f(x) = x^{1/3}$ with $x_0 = 1$ and calculate x_1, x_2, x_3, and x_4. Find a formula for $|x_n|$. What happens to $|x_n|$ as $n \to \infty$? Draw a picture that shows what is going on.

11. Explain why the following four statements ask for the same information:
   i) Find the roots of $f(x) = x^3 - 3x - 1$.
   ii) Find the x-coordinates of the intersections of the curve $y = x^3$ with the line $y = 3x + 1$.
   iii) Find the x-coordinates of the points where the curve $y = x^3 - 3x$ crosses the horizontal line $y = 1$.
   iv) Find the values of x where the derivative of $g(x) = (1/4)x^4 - (3/2)x^2 - x + 5$ equals zero.

12. **Locating a planet** To calculate a planet's space coordinates, we have to solve equations like $x = 1 + 0.5 \sin x$. Graphing the function $f(x) = x - 1 - 0.5 \sin x$ suggests that the function has a root near $x = 1.5$. Use one application of Newton's method to improve this estimate. That is, start with $x_0 = 1.5$ and find x_1. (The value of the root is 1.49870 to five decimal places.) Remember to use radians.

T 13. **Intersecting curves** The curve $y = \tan x$ crosses the line $y = 2x$ between $x = 0$ and $x = \pi/2$. Use Newton's method to find where.

T 14. **Real solutions of a quartic** Use Newton's method to find the two real solutions of the equation $x^4 - 2x^3 - x^2 - 2x + 2 = 0$.

T 15. **a.** How many solutions does the equation $\sin 3x = 0.99 - x^2$ have?
   b. Use Newton's method to find them.

16. **Intersection of curves**
   a. Does $\cos 3x$ ever equal x? Give reasons for your answer.
   b. Use Newton's method to find where.

17. Find the four real zeros of the function $f(x) = 2x^4 - 4x^2 + 1$.

T 18. **Estimating pi** Estimate π to as many decimal places as your calculator will display by using Newton's method to solve the equation $\tan x = 0$ with $x_0 = 3$.

19. **Intersection of curves** At what value(s) of x does $\cos x = 2x$?

20. **Intersection of curves** At what value(s) of x does $\cos x = -x$?

21. The graphs of $y = x^2(x + 1)$ and $y = 1/x$ $(x > 0)$ intersect at one point $x = r$. Use Newton's method to estimate the value of r to four decimal places.

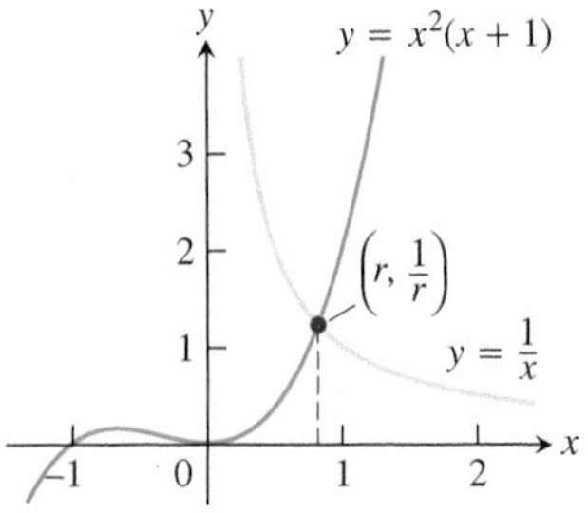

22. The graphs of $y = \sqrt{x}$ and $y = 3 - x^2$ intersect at one point $x = r$. Use Newton's method to estimate the value of r to four decimal places.

23. **Intersection of curves** At what value(s) of x does $e^{-x^2} = x^2 - x + 1$?

24. **Intersection of curves** At what value(s) of x does $\ln(1 - x^2) = x - 1$?

25. Use the Intermediate Value Theorem from Section 2.5 to show that $f(x) = x^3 + 2x - 4$ has a root between $x = 1$ and $x = 2$. Then find the root to five decimal places.

26. **Factoring a quartic** Find the approximate values of r_1 through r_4 in the factorization

$$8x^4 - 14x^3 - 9x^2 + 11x - 1 = 8(x - r_1)(x - r_2)(x - r_3)(x - r_4).$$

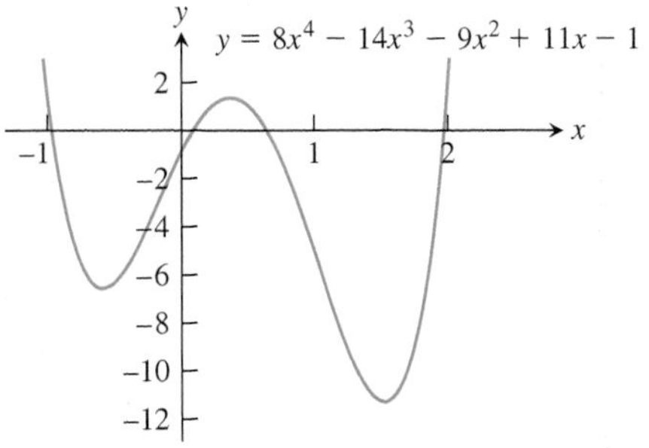

T 27. **Converging to different zeros** Use Newton's method to find the zeros of $f(x) = 4x^4 - 4x^2$ using the given starting values.
   a. $x_0 = -2$ and $x_0 = -0.8$, lying in $\left(-\infty, -\sqrt{2}/2\right)$
   b. $x_0 = -0.5$ and $x_0 = 0.25$, lying in $\left(-\sqrt{21}/7, \sqrt{21}/7\right)$
   c. $x_0 = 0.8$ and $x_0 = 2$, lying in $\left(\sqrt{2}/2, \infty\right)$
   d. $x_0 = -\sqrt{21}/7$ and $x_0 = \sqrt{21}/7$

28. **The sonobuoy problem** In submarine location problems, it is often necessary to find a submarine's closest point of approach (CPA) to a sonobuoy (sound detector) in the water. Suppose that the submarine travels on the parabolic path $y = x^2$ and that the buoy is located at the point $(2, -1/2)$.
   a. Show that the value of x that minimizes the distance between the submarine and the buoy is a solution of the equation $x = 1/(x^2 + 1)$.
   b. Solve the equation $x = 1/(x^2 + 1)$ with Newton's method.

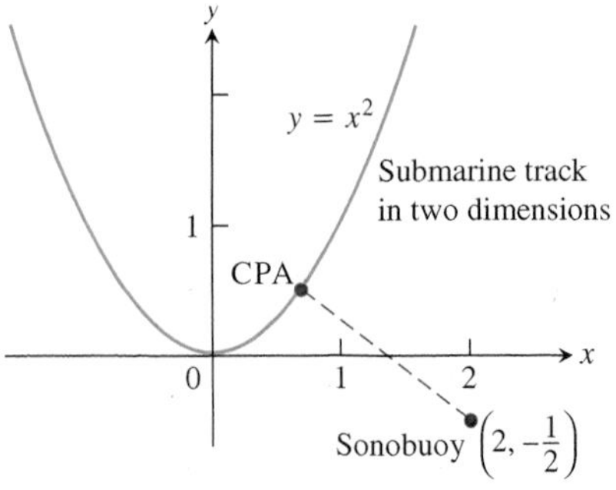

T 29. **Curves that are nearly flat at the root** Some curves are so flat that, in practice, Newton's method stops too far from the root to give a useful estimate. Try Newton's method on $f(x) = (x - 1)^{40}$ with a starting value of $x_0 = 2$ to see how close your machine comes to the root $x = 1$. See the accompanying graph.

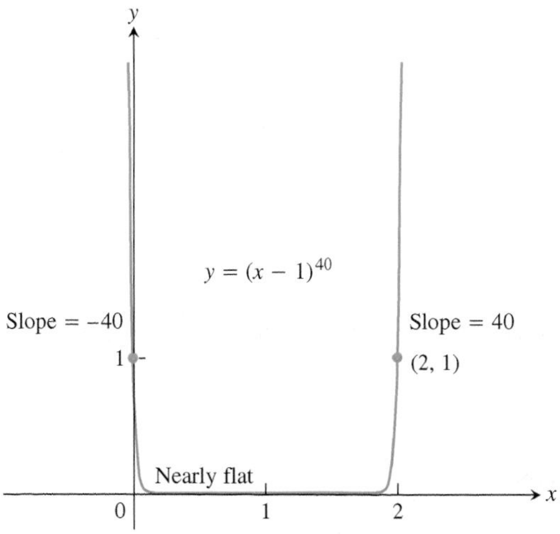

30. The accompanying figure shows a circle of radius r with a chord of length 2 and an arc s of length 3. Use Newton's method to solve for r and θ (radians) to four decimal places. Assume $0 < \theta < \pi$.

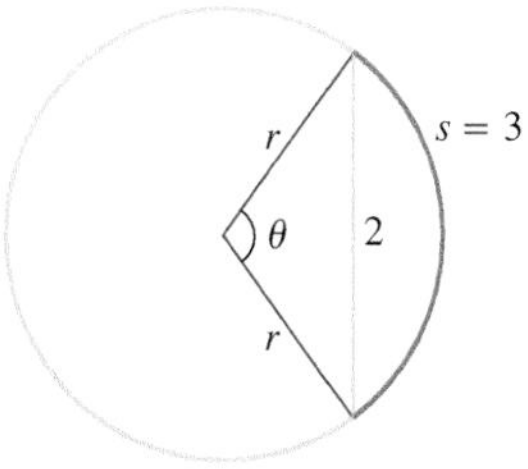

4.8 Antiderivatives

We have studied how to find the derivative of a function. However, many problems require that we recover a function from its known derivative (from its known rate of change). For instance, the laws of physics tell us the acceleration of an object falling from an initial height and we can use this to compute its velocity and its height at any time. More generally, starting with a function f, we want to find a function F whose derivative is f. If such a function F exists, it is called an *antiderivative* of f. We will see in the next chapter that antiderivatives are the link connecting the two major elements of calculus: derivatives and definite integrals.

Finding Antiderivatives

DEFINITION A function F is an **antiderivative** of f on an interval I if $F'(x) = f(x)$ for all x in I.

The process of recovering a function $F(x)$ from its derivative $f(x)$ is called *antidifferentiation*. We use capital letters such as F to represent an antiderivative of a function f, G to represent an antiderivative of g, and so forth.

EXAMPLE 1 Find an antiderivative for each of the following functions.

(a) $f(x) = 2x$ **(b)** $g(x) = \cos x$ **(c)** $h(x) = \frac{1}{x} + 2e^{2x}$

Solution We need to think backward here: What function do we know has a derivative equal to the given function?

(a) $F(x) = x^2$ **(b)** $G(x) = \sin x$ **(c)** $H(x) = \ln|x| + e^{2x}$

Each answer can be checked by differentiating. The derivative of $F(x) = x^2$ is $2x$. The derivative of $G(x) = \sin x$ is $\cos x$, and the derivative of $H(x) = \ln|x| + e^{2x}$ is $(1/x) + 2e^{2x}$. ∎

The function $F(x) = x^2$ is not the only function whose derivative is $2x$. The function $x^2 + 1$ has the same derivative. So does $x^2 + C$ for any constant C. Are there others?

Corollary 2 of the Mean Value Theorem in Section 4.2 gives the answer: Any two antiderivatives of a function differ by a constant. So the functions $x^2 + C$, where C is an **arbitrary constant**, form *all* the antiderivatives of $f(x) = 2x$. More generally, we have the following result.

THEOREM 8 If F is an antiderivative of f on an interval I, then the most general antiderivative of f on I is

$$F(x) + C$$

where C is an arbitrary constant.

Thus the most general antiderivative of f on I is a *family* of functions $F(x) + C$ whose graphs are vertical translations of one another. We can select a particular antiderivative from this family by assigning a specific value to C. Here is an example showing how such an assignment might be made.

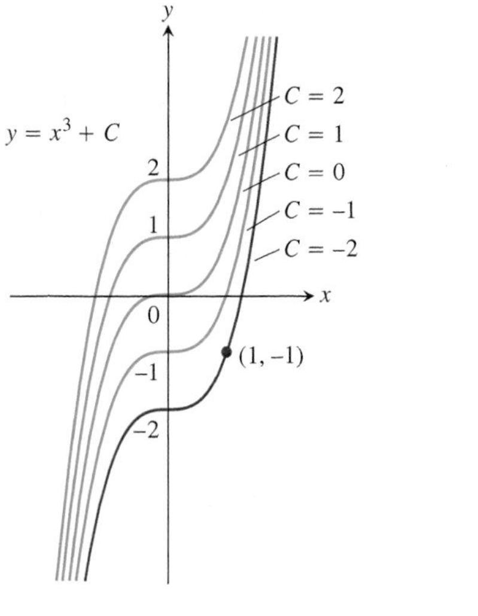

FIGURE 4.51 The curves $y = x^3 + C$ fill the coordinate plane without overlapping. In Example 2, we identify the curve $y = x^3 - 2$ as the one that passes through the given point $(1, -1)$.

EXAMPLE 2 Find an antiderivative of $f(x) = 3x^2$ that satisfies $F(1) = -1$.

Solution Since the derivative of x^3 is $3x^2$, the general antiderivative

$$F(x) = x^3 + C$$

gives all the antiderivatives of $f(x)$. The condition $F(1) = -1$ determines a specific value for C. Substituting $x = 1$ into $F(x) = x^3 + C$ gives

$$F(1) = (1)^3 + C = 1 + C.$$

Since $F(1) = -1$, solving $1 + C = -1$ for C gives $C = -2$. So

$$F(x) = x^3 - 2$$

is the antiderivative satisfying $F(1) = -1$. Notice that this assignment for C selects the particular curve from the family of curves $y = x^3 + C$ that passes through the point $(1, -1)$ in the plane (Figure 4.51). ∎

By working backward from assorted differentiation rules, we can derive formulas and rules for antiderivatives. In each case there is an arbitrary constant C in the general expression representing all antiderivatives of a given function. Table 4.2 gives antiderivative formulas for a number of important functions.

The rules in Table 4.2 are easily verified by differentiating the general antiderivative formula to obtain the function to its left. For example, the derivative of $(\tan kx)/k + C$ is $\sec^2 kx$, whatever the value of the constants C or $k \neq 0$, and this establishes Formula 4 for the most general antiderivative of $\sec^2 kx$.

EXAMPLE 3 Find the general antiderivative of each of the following functions.

(a) $f(x) = x^5$ **(b)** $g(x) = \dfrac{1}{\sqrt{x}}$ **(c)** $h(x) = \sin 2x$

(d) $i(x) = \cos \dfrac{x}{2}$ **(e)** $j(x) = e^{-3x}$ **(f)** $k(x) = 2^x$

TABLE 4.2 Antiderivative formulas, k a nonzero constant

	Function	General antiderivative		Function	General antiderivative
1.	x^n	$\frac{1}{n+1}x^{n+1} + C, \quad n \neq -1$	8.	e^{kx}	$\frac{1}{k}e^{kx} + C$
2.	$\sin kx$	$-\frac{1}{k}\cos kx + C$	9.	$\frac{1}{x}$	$\ln\lvert x\rvert + C, \quad x \neq 0$
3.	$\cos kx$	$\frac{1}{k}\sin kx + C$	10.	$\frac{1}{\sqrt{1-k^2x^2}}$	$\frac{1}{k}\sin^{-1} kx + C$
4.	$\sec^2 kx$	$\frac{1}{k}\tan kx + C$	11.	$\frac{1}{1+k^2x^2}$	$\frac{1}{k}\tan^{-1} kx + C$
5.	$\csc^2 kx$	$-\frac{1}{k}\cot kx + C$	12.	$\frac{1}{x\sqrt{k^2x^2-1}}$	$\sec^{-1} kx + C, \quad kx > 1$
6.	$\sec kx \tan kx$	$\frac{1}{k}\sec kx + C$	13.	a^{kx}	$\left(\frac{1}{k\ln a}\right)a^{kx} + C, \quad a > 0,\ a \neq 1$
7.	$\csc kx \cot kx$	$-\frac{1}{k}\csc kx + C$			

Solution In each case, we can use one of the formulas listed in Table 4.2.

(a) $F(x) = \frac{x^6}{6} + C$ — Formula 1 with $n = 5$

(b) $g(x) = x^{-1/2}$, so

$$G(x) = \frac{x^{1/2}}{1/2} + C = 2\sqrt{x} + C$$

Formula 1 with $n = -1/2$

(c) $H(x) = \frac{-\cos 2x}{2} + C$ — Formula 2 with $k = 2$

(d) $I(x) = \frac{\sin(x/2)}{1/2} + C = 2\sin\frac{x}{2} + C$ — Formula 3 with $k = 1/2$

(e) $J(x) = -\frac{1}{3}e^{-3x} + C$ — Formula 8 with $k = -3$

(f) $K(x) = \left(\frac{1}{\ln 2}\right)2^x + C$ — Formula 13 with $a = 2$, $k = 1$ ■

Other derivative rules also lead to corresponding antiderivative rules. We can add and subtract antiderivatives and multiply them by constants.

TABLE 4.3 Antiderivative linearity rules

		Function	General antiderivative
1.	*Constant Multiple Rule:*	$kf(x)$	$kF(x) + C$, k a constant
2.	*Negative Rule:*	$-f(x)$	$-F(x) + C$
3.	*Sum or Difference Rule:*	$f(x) \pm g(x)$	$F(x) \pm G(x) + C$

The formulas in Table 4.3 are easily proved by differentiating the antiderivatives and verifying that the result agrees with the original function. Formula 2 is the special case $k = -1$ in Formula 1.

EXAMPLE 4 Find the general antiderivative of

$$f(x) = \frac{3}{\sqrt{x}} + \sin 2x.$$

Solution We have that $f(x) = 3g(x) + h(x)$ for the functions g and h in Example 3. Since $G(x) = 2\sqrt{x}$ is an antiderivative of $g(x)$ from Example 3b, it follows from the Constant Multiple Rule for antiderivatives that $3G(x) = 3 \cdot 2\sqrt{x} = 6\sqrt{x}$ is an antiderivative of $3g(x) = 3/\sqrt{x}$. Likewise, from Example 3c we know that $H(x) = (-1/2)\cos 2x$ is an antiderivative of $h(x) = \sin 2x$. From the Sum Rule for antiderivatives, we then get that

$$\begin{aligned} F(x) &= 3G(x) + H(x) + C \\ &= 6\sqrt{x} - \frac{1}{2}\cos 2x + C \end{aligned}$$

is the general antiderivative formula for $f(x)$, where C is an arbitrary constant. ■

Initial Value Problems and Differential Equations

Antiderivatives play several important roles in mathematics and its applications. Methods and techniques for finding them are a major part of calculus, and we take up that study in Chapter 8. Finding an antiderivative for a function $f(x)$ is the same problem as finding a function $y(x)$ that satisfies the equation

$$\frac{dy}{dx} = f(x).$$

This is called a **differential equation**, since it is an equation involving an unknown function y that is being differentiated. To solve it, we need a function $y(x)$ that satisfies the equation. This function is found by taking the antiderivative of $f(x)$. We fix the arbitrary constant arising in the antidifferentiation process by specifying an initial condition

$$y(x_0) = y_0.$$

This condition means the function $y(x)$ has the value y_0 when $x = x_0$. The combination of a differential equation and an initial condition is called an **initial value problem**. Such problems play important roles in all branches of science.

The most general antiderivative $F(x) + C$ (such as $x^3 + C$ in Example 2) of the function $f(x)$ gives the **general solution** $y = F(x) + C$ of the differential equation $dy/dx = f(x)$. The general solution gives *all* the solutions of the equation (there are infinitely many, one for each value of C). We **solve** the differential equation by finding its general solution. We then solve the initial value problem by finding the **particular solution** that satisfies the initial condition $y(x_0) = y_0$. In Example 2, the function $y = x^3 - 2$ is the particular solution of the differential equation $dy/dx = 3x^2$ satisfying the initial condition $y(1) = -1$.

Antiderivatives and Motion

We have seen that the derivative of the position function of an object gives its velocity, and the derivative of its velocity function gives its acceleration. If we know an object's acceleration, then by finding an antiderivative we can recover the velocity, and from an antiderivative of the velocity we can recover its position function. This procedure was used as an application of Corollary 2 in Section 4.2. Now that we have a terminology and conceptual framework in terms of antiderivatives, we revisit the problem from the point of view of differential equations.

EXAMPLE 5 A hot-air balloon ascending at the rate of 12 ft/sec is at a height 80 ft above the ground when a package is dropped. How long does it take the package to reach the ground?

Solution Let $v(t)$ denote the velocity of the package at time t, and let $s(t)$ denote its height above the ground. The acceleration of gravity near the surface of the earth is 32 ft/sec^2. Assuming no other forces act on the dropped package, we have

$$\frac{dv}{dt} = -32. \qquad \text{Negative because gravity acts in the direction of decreasing } s$$

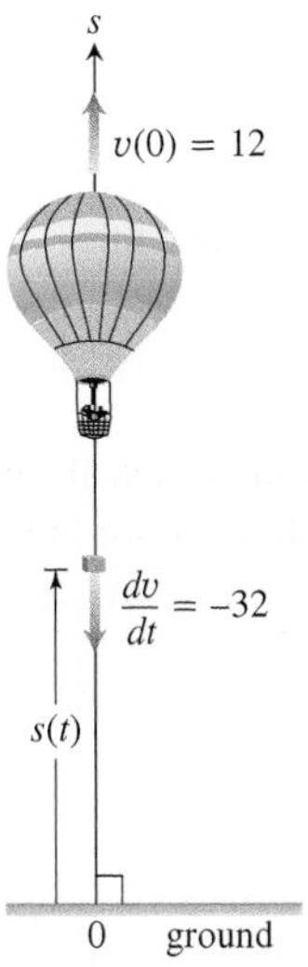

FIGURE 4.52 A package dropped from a rising hot-air balloon (Example 5).

This leads to the following initial value problem (Figure 4.52):

Differential equation: $\dfrac{dv}{dt} = -32$

Initial condition: $v(0) = 12.$ Balloon initially rising

This is our mathematical model for the package's motion. We solve the initial value problem to obtain the velocity of the package.

1. *Solve the differential equation*: The general formula for an antiderivative of -32 is

$$v = -32t + C.$$

Having found the general solution of the differential equation, we use the initial condition to find the particular solution that solves our problem.

2. *Evaluate C*:

$$12 = -32(0) + C \qquad \text{Initial condition } v(0) = 12$$

$$C = 12.$$

The solution of the initial value problem is

$$v = -32t + 12.$$

Since velocity is the derivative of height, and the height of the package is 80 ft at time $t = 0$ when it is dropped, we now have a second initial value problem.

Differential equation: $\dfrac{ds}{dt} = -32t + 12$ Set $v = ds/dt$ in the previous equation.

Initial condition: $s(0) = 80$

We solve this initial value problem to find the height as a function of t.

1. *Solve the differential equation*: Finding the general antiderivative of $-32t + 12$ gives

$$s = -16t^2 + 12t + C.$$

2. *Evaluate C*:

$$80 = -16(0)^2 + 12(0) + C \qquad \text{Initial condition } s(0) = 80$$

$$C = 80.$$

The package's height above ground at time t is

$$s = -16t^2 + 12t + 80.$$

Use the solution: To find how long it takes the package to reach the ground, we set s equal to 0 and solve for t:

$$-16t^2 + 12t + 80 = 0$$

$$-4t^2 + 3t + 20 = 0$$

$$t = \frac{-3 \pm \sqrt{329}}{-8} \qquad \text{Quadratic formula}$$

$$t \approx -1.89, \qquad t \approx 2.64.$$

The package hits the ground about 2.64 sec after it is dropped from the balloon. (The negative root has no physical meaning.) ■

Indefinite Integrals

A special symbol is used to denote the collection of all antiderivatives of a function f.

DEFINITION The collection of all antiderivatives of f is called the **indefinite integral** of f with respect to x, and is denoted by

$$\int f(x)\,dx.$$

The symbol $\int$ is an **integral sign**. The function f is the **integrand** of the integral, and x is the **variable of integration**.

After the integral sign in the notation we just defined, the integrand function is always followed by a differential to indicate the variable of integration. We will have more to say about why this is important in Chapter 5. Using this notation, we restate the solutions of Example 1, as follows:

$$\int 2x\,dx = x^2 + C,$$

$$\int \cos x\,dx = \sin x + C,$$

$$\int \left(\frac{1}{x} + 2e^{2x}\right) dx = \ln|x| + e^{2x} + C.$$

This notation is related to the main application of antiderivatives, which will be explored in Chapter 5. Antiderivatives play a key role in computing limits of certain infinite sums, an unexpected and wonderfully useful role that is described in a central result of Chapter 5, called the Fundamental Theorem of Calculus.

EXAMPLE 6 Evaluate

$$\int (x^2 - 2x + 5)\,dx.$$

Solution If we recognize that $(x^3/3) - x^2 + 5x$ is an antiderivative of $x^2 - 2x + 5$, we can evaluate the integral as

$$\int (x^2 - 2x + 5)\,dx = \overbrace{\frac{x^3}{3} - x^2 + 5x}^{\text{antiderivative}} + \underset{\text{arbitrary constant}}{\underbrace{C}}.$$

If we do not recognize the antiderivative right away, we can generate it term-by-term with the Sum, Difference, and Constant Multiple Rules:

$$\begin{aligned}\int (x^2 - 2x + 5)\,dx &= \int x^2\,dx - \int 2x\,dx + \int 5\,dx \\ &= \int x^2\,dx - 2\int x\,dx + 5\int 1\,dx \\ &= \left(\frac{x^3}{3} + C_1\right) - 2\left(\frac{x^2}{2} + C_2\right) + 5(x + C_3) \\ &= \frac{x^3}{3} + C_1 - x^2 - 2C_2 + 5x + 5C_3.\end{aligned}$$

This formula is more complicated than it needs to be. If we combine C_1, $-2C_2$, and $5C_3$ into a single arbitrary constant $C = C_1 - 2C_2 + 5C_3$, the formula simplifies to

$$\frac{x^3}{3} - x^2 + 5x + C$$

and *still* gives all the possible antiderivatives there are. For this reason, we recommend that you go right to the final form even if you elect to integrate term-by-term. Write

$$\int (x^2 - 2x + 5)\,dx = \int x^2\,dx - \int 2x\,dx + \int 5\,dx$$
$$= \frac{x^3}{3} - x^2 + 5x + C.$$

Find the simplest antiderivative you can for each part and add the arbitrary constant of integration at the end. ■

Exercises 4.8

Finding Antiderivatives

In Exercises 1–24, find an antiderivative for each function. Do as many as you can mentally. Check your answers by differentiation.

1. a. $2x$ b. x^2 c. $x^2 - 2x + 1$
2. a. $6x$ b. x^7 c. $x^7 - 6x + 8$
3. a. $-3x^{-4}$ b. x^{-4} c. $x^{-4} + 2x + 3$
4. a. $2x^{-3}$ b. $\frac{x^{-3}}{2} + x^2$ c. $-x^{-3} + x - 1$
5. a. $\frac{1}{x^2}$ b. $\frac{5}{x^2}$ c. $2 - \frac{5}{x^2}$
6. a. $-\frac{2}{x^3}$ b. $\frac{1}{2x^3}$ c. $x^3 - \frac{1}{x^3}$
7. a. $\frac{3}{2}\sqrt{x}$ b. $\frac{1}{2\sqrt{x}}$ c. $\sqrt{x} + \frac{1}{\sqrt{x}}$
8. a. $\frac{4}{3}\sqrt[3]{x}$ b. $\frac{1}{3\sqrt[3]{x}}$ c. $\sqrt[3]{x} + \frac{1}{\sqrt[3]{x}}$
9. a. $\frac{2}{3}x^{-1/3}$ b. $\frac{1}{3}x^{-2/3}$ c. $-\frac{1}{3}x^{-4/3}$
10. a. $\frac{1}{2}x^{-1/2}$ b. $-\frac{1}{2}x^{-3/2}$ c. $-\frac{3}{2}x^{-5/2}$
11. a. $\frac{1}{x}$ b. $\frac{7}{x}$ c. $1 - \frac{5}{x}$
12. a. $\frac{1}{3x}$ b. $\frac{2}{5x}$ c. $1 + \frac{4}{3x} - \frac{1}{x^2}$
13. a. $-\pi \sin \pi x$ b. $3 \sin x$ c. $\sin \pi x - 3 \sin 3x$
14. a. $\pi \cos \pi x$ b. $\frac{\pi}{2} \cos \frac{\pi x}{2}$ c. $\cos \frac{\pi x}{2} + \pi \cos x$
15. a. $\sec^2 x$ b. $\frac{2}{3} \sec^2 \frac{x}{3}$ c. $-\sec^2 \frac{3x}{2}$
16. a. $\csc^2 x$ b. $-\frac{3}{2} \csc^2 \frac{3x}{2}$ c. $1 - 8 \csc^2 2x$
17. a. $\csc x \cot x$ b. $-\csc 5x \cot 5x$ c. $-\pi \csc \frac{\pi x}{2} \cot \frac{\pi x}{2}$
18. a. $\sec x \tan x$ b. $4 \sec 3x \tan 3x$ c. $\sec \frac{\pi x}{2} \tan \frac{\pi x}{2}$
19. a. e^{3x} b. e^{-x} c. $e^{x/2}$
20. a. e^{-2x} b. $e^{4x/3}$ c. $e^{-x/5}$
21. a. 3^x b. 2^{-x} c. $\left(\frac{5}{3}\right)^x$
22. a. $x^{\sqrt{3}}$ b. x^{π} c. $x^{\sqrt{2}-1}$
23. a. $\frac{2}{\sqrt{1 - x^2}}$ b. $\frac{1}{2(x^2 + 1)}$ c. $\frac{1}{1 + 4x^2}$
24. a. $x - \left(\frac{1}{2}\right)^x$ b. $x^2 + 2^x$ c. $\pi^x - x^{-1}$

Finding Indefinite Integrals

In Exercises 25–70, find the most general antiderivative or indefinite integral. You may need to try a solution and then adjust your guess. Check your answers by differentiation.

25. $\int (x + 1)\,dx$
26. $\int (5 - 6x)\,dx$
27. $\int \left(3t^2 + \frac{t}{2}\right) dt$
28. $\int \left(\frac{t^2}{2} + 4t^3\right) dt$
29. $\int (2x^3 - 5x + 7)\,dx$
30. $\int (1 - x^2 - 3x^5)\,dx$
31. $\int \left(\frac{1}{x^2} - x^2 - \frac{1}{3}\right) dx$
32. $\int \left(\frac{1}{5} - \frac{2}{x^3} + 2x\right) dx$
33. $\int x^{-1/3}\,dx$
34. $\int x^{-5/4}\,dx$
35. $\int \left(\sqrt{x} + \sqrt[3]{x}\right) dx$
36. $\int \left(\frac{\sqrt{x}}{2} + \frac{2}{\sqrt{x}}\right) dx$
37. $\int \left(8y - \frac{2}{y^{1/4}}\right) dy$
38. $\int \left(\frac{1}{7} - \frac{1}{y^{5/4}}\right) dy$
39. $\int 2x(1 - x^{-3})\,dx$
40. $\int x^{-3}(x + 1)\,dx$
41. $\int \frac{t\sqrt{t} + \sqrt{t}}{t^2}\,dt$
42. $\int \frac{4 + \sqrt{t}}{t^3}\,dt$

43. $\int(-2\cos t)\,dt$

44. $\int(-5\sin t)\,dt$

45. $\int 7\sin\frac{\theta}{3}\,d\theta$

46. $\int 3\cos 5\theta\,d\theta$

47. $\int(-3\csc^2 x)\,dx$

48. $\int\left(-\frac{\sec^2 x}{3}\right)dx$

49. $\int\frac{\csc\theta\cot\theta}{2}\,d\theta$

50. $\int\frac{2}{5}\sec\theta\tan\theta\,d\theta$

51. $\int(e^{3x}+5e^{-x})\,dx$

52. $\int(2e^x-3e^{-2x})\,dx$

53. $\int(e^{-x}+4^x)\,dx$

54. $\int(1.3)^x\,dx$

55. $\int(4\sec x\tan x-2\sec^2 x)\,dx$

56. $\int\frac{1}{2}(\csc^2 x-\csc x\cot x)\,dx$

57. $\int(\sin 2x-\csc^2 x)\,dx$

58. $\int(2\cos 2x-3\sin 3x)\,dx$

59. $\int\frac{1+\cos 4t}{2}\,dt$

60. $\int\frac{1-\cos 6t}{2}\,dt$

61. $\int\left(\frac{1}{x}-\frac{5}{x^2+1}\right)dx$

62. $\int\left(\frac{2}{\sqrt{1-y^2}}-\frac{1}{y^{1/4}}\right)dy$

63. $\int 3x^{\sqrt{3}}\,dx$

64. $\int x^{\sqrt{2}-1}\,dx$

65. $\int(1+\tan^2\theta)\,d\theta$
(*Hint:* $1+\tan^2\theta=\sec^2\theta$)

66. $\int(2+\tan^2\theta)\,d\theta$

67. $\int\cot^2 x\,dx$
(*Hint:* $1+\cot^2 x=\csc^2 x$)

68. $\int(1-\cot^2 x)\,dx$

69. $\int\cos\theta\,(\tan\theta+\sec\theta)\,d\theta$

70. $\int\frac{\csc\theta}{\csc\theta-\sin\theta}\,d\theta$

Checking Antiderivative Formulas

Verify the formulas in Exercises 71–82 by differentiation.

71. $\int(7x-2)^3\,dx=\frac{(7x-2)^4}{28}+C$

72. $\int(3x+5)^{-2}\,dx=-\frac{(3x+5)^{-1}}{3}+C$

73. $\int\sec^2(5x-1)\,dx=\frac{1}{5}\tan(5x-1)+C$

74. $\int\csc^2\left(\frac{x-1}{3}\right)dx=-3\cot\left(\frac{x-1}{3}\right)+C$

75. $\int\frac{1}{(x+1)^2}\,dx=-\frac{1}{x+1}+C$

76. $\int\frac{1}{(x+1)^2}\,dx=\frac{x}{x+1}+C$

77. $\int\frac{1}{x+1}\,dx=\ln(x+1)+C,\quad x>-1$

78. $\int xe^x\,dx=xe^x-e^x+C$

79. $\int\frac{dx}{a^2+x^2}=\frac{1}{a}\tan^{-1}\left(\frac{x}{a}\right)+C$

80. $\int\frac{dx}{\sqrt{a^2-x^2}}=\sin^{-1}\left(\frac{x}{a}\right)+C$

81. $\int\frac{\tan^{-1}x}{x^2}\,dx=\ln x-\frac{1}{2}\ln(1+x^2)-\frac{\tan^{-1}x}{x}+C$

82. $\int(\sin^{-1}x)^2\,dx=x(\sin^{-1}x)^2-2x+2\sqrt{1-x^2}\sin^{-1}x+C$

83. Right, or wrong? Say which for each formula and give a brief reason for each answer.

a. $\int x\sin x\,dx=\frac{x^2}{2}\sin x+C$

b. $\int x\sin x\,dx=-x\cos x+C$

c. $\int x\sin x\,dx=-x\cos x+\sin x+C$

84. Right, or wrong? Say which for each formula and give a brief reason for each answer.

a. $\int\tan\theta\sec^2\theta\,d\theta=\frac{\sec^3\theta}{3}+C$

b. $\int\tan\theta\sec^2\theta\,d\theta=\frac{1}{2}\tan^2\theta+C$

c. $\int\tan\theta\sec^2\theta\,d\theta=\frac{1}{2}\sec^2\theta+C$

85. Right, or wrong? Say which for each formula and give a brief reason for each answer.

a. $\int(2x+1)^2\,dx=\frac{(2x+1)^3}{3}+C$

b. $\int 3(2x+1)^2\,dx=(2x+1)^3+C$

c. $\int 6(2x+1)^2\,dx=(2x+1)^3+C$

86. Right, or wrong? Say which for each formula and give a brief reason for each answer.

a. $\int\sqrt{2x+1}\,dx=\sqrt{x^2+x+C}$

b. $\int\sqrt{2x+1}\,dx=\sqrt{x^2+x}+C$

c. $\int\sqrt{2x+1}\,dx=\frac{1}{3}\left(\sqrt{2x+1}\right)^3+C$

87. Right, or wrong? Give a brief reason why.

$$\int\frac{-15(x+3)^2}{(x-2)^4}\,dx=\left(\frac{x+3}{x-2}\right)^3+C$$

88. Right, or wrong? Give a brief reason why.

$$\int\frac{x\cos(x^2)-\sin(x^2)}{x^2}\,dx=\frac{\sin(x^2)}{x}+C$$

Initial Value Problems

89. Which of the following graphs shows the solution of the initial value problem

$$\frac{dy}{dx} = 2x, \quad y = 4 \text{ when } x = 1?$$

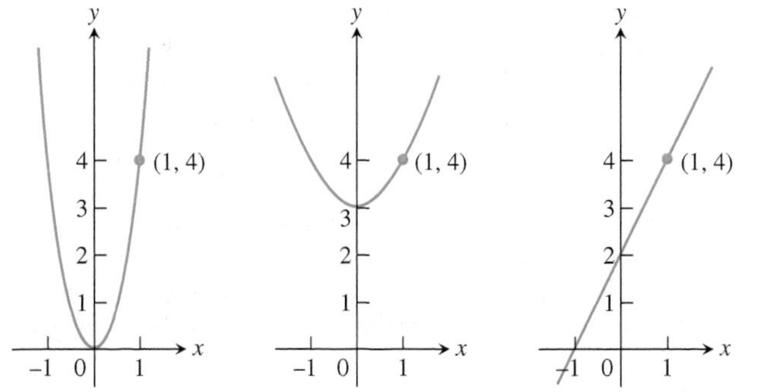

(a) (b) (c)

Give reasons for your answer.

90. Which of the following graphs shows the solution of the initial value problem

$$\frac{dy}{dx} = -x, \quad y = 1 \text{ when } x = -1?$$

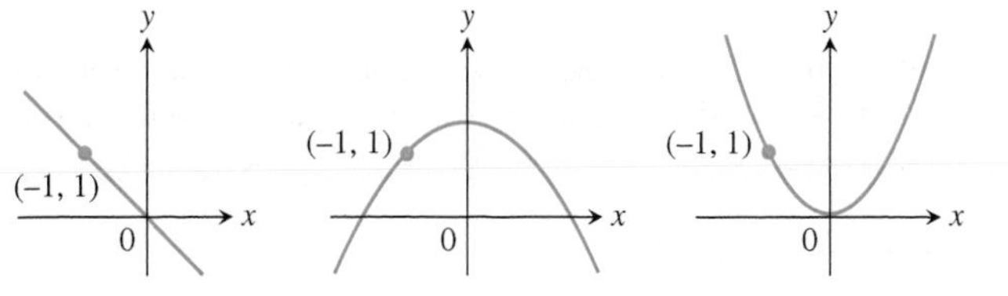

(a) (b) (c)

Give reasons for your answer.

Solve the initial value problems in Exercises 91–112.

91. $\frac{dy}{dx} = 2x - 7, \quad y(2) = 0$

92. $\frac{dy}{dx} = 10 - x, \quad y(0) = -1$

93. $\frac{dy}{dx} = \frac{1}{x^2} + x, \quad x > 0; \quad y(2) = 1$

94. $\frac{dy}{dx} = 9x^2 - 4x + 5, \quad y(-1) = 0$

95. $\frac{dy}{dx} = 3x^{-2/3}, \quad y(-1) = -5$

96. $\frac{dy}{dx} = \frac{1}{2\sqrt{x}}, \quad y(4) = 0$

97. $\frac{ds}{dt} = 1 + \cos t, \quad s(0) = 4$

98. $\frac{ds}{dt} = \cos t + \sin t, \quad s(\pi) = 1$

99. $\frac{dr}{d\theta} = -\pi \sin \pi\theta, \quad r(0) = 0$

100. $\frac{dr}{d\theta} = \cos \pi\theta, \quad r(0) = 1$

101. $\frac{dv}{dt} = \frac{1}{2} \sec t \tan t, \quad v(0) = 1$

102. $\frac{dv}{dt} = 8t + \csc^2 t, \quad v\left(\frac{\pi}{2}\right) = -7$

103. $\frac{dv}{dt} = \frac{3}{t\sqrt{t^2 - 1}}, \quad t > 1, v(2) = 0$

104. $\frac{dv}{dt} = \frac{8}{1 + t^2} + \sec^2 t, \quad v(0) = 1$

105. $\frac{d^2y}{dx^2} = 2 - 6x; \quad y'(0) = 4, \quad y(0) = 1$

106. $\frac{d^2y}{dx^2} = 0; \quad y'(0) = 2, \quad y(0) = 0$

107. $\frac{d^2r}{dt^2} = \frac{2}{t^3}; \quad \left.\frac{dr}{dt}\right|_{t=1} = 1, \quad r(1) = 1$

108. $\frac{d^2s}{dt^2} = \frac{3t}{8}; \quad \left.\frac{ds}{dt}\right|_{t=4} = 3, \quad s(4) = 4$

109. $\frac{d^3y}{dx^3} = 6; \quad y''(0) = -8, \quad y'(0) = 0, \quad y(0) = 5$

110. $\frac{d^3\theta}{dt^3} = 0; \quad \theta''(0) = -2, \quad \theta'(0) = -\frac{1}{2}, \quad \theta(0) = \sqrt{2}$

111. $y^{(4)} = -\sin t + \cos t;$

$y'''(0) = 7, \quad y''(0) = y'(0) = -1, \quad y(0) = 0$

112. $y^{(4)} = -\cos x + 8 \sin 2x;$

$y'''(0) = 0, \quad y''(0) = y'(0) = 1, \quad y(0) = 3$

113. Find the curve $y = f(x)$ in the xy-plane that passes through the point (9, 4) and whose slope at each point is $3\sqrt{x}$.

114. a. Find a curve $y = f(x)$ with the following properties:

i) $\frac{d^2y}{dx^2} = 6x$

ii) Its graph passes through the point (0, 1), and has a horizontal tangent there.

b. How many curves like this are there? How do you know?

Solution (Integral) Curves

Exercises 115–118 show solution curves of differential equations. In each exercise, find an equation for the curve through the labeled point.

115.

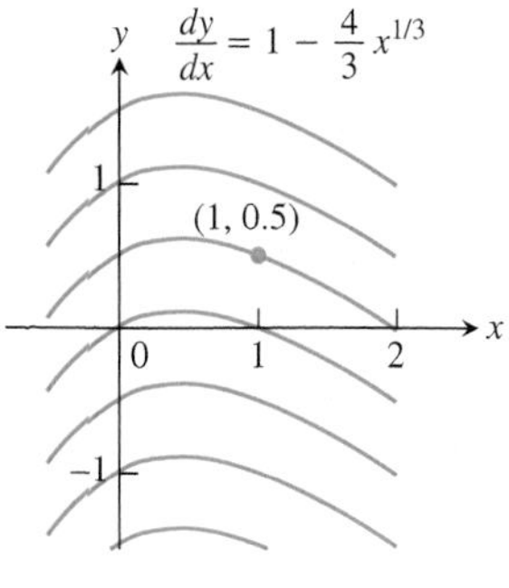

116.

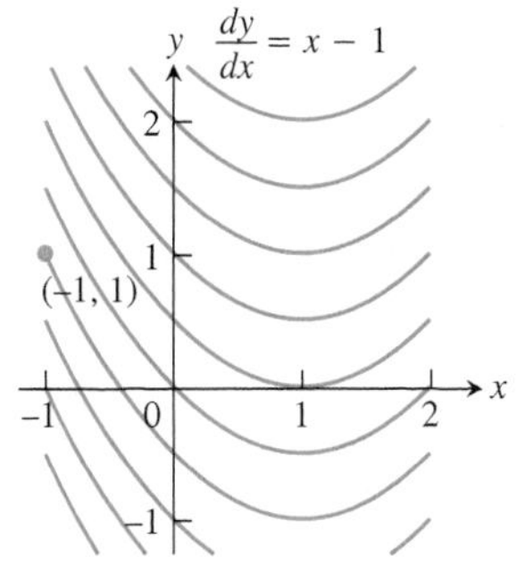

117. $\dfrac{dy}{dx} = \sin x - \cos x$

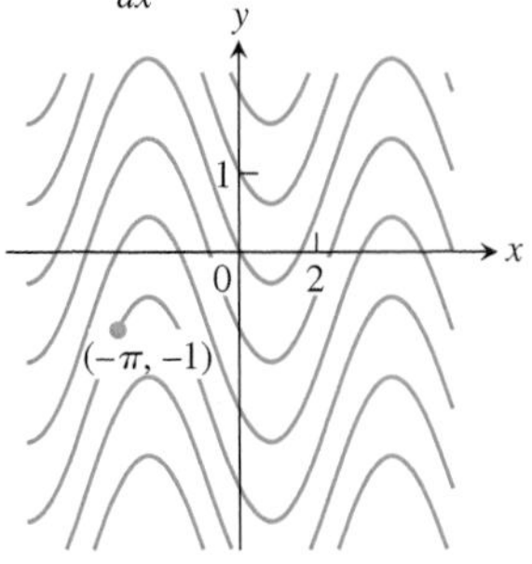

118. $\dfrac{dy}{dx} = \dfrac{1}{2\sqrt{x}} + \pi \sin \pi x$

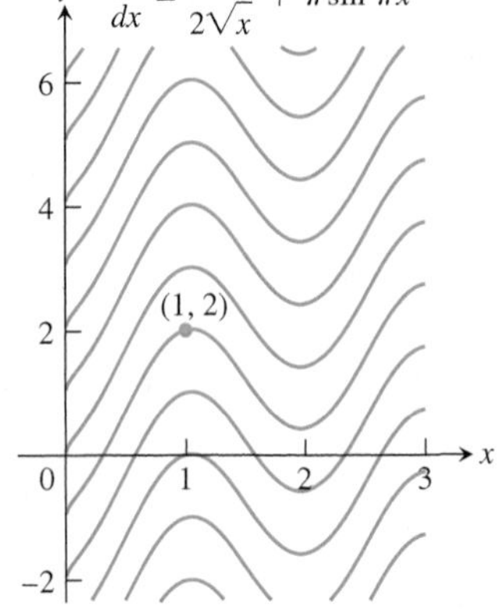

Applications

119. Finding displacement from an antiderivative of velocity

a. Suppose that the velocity of a body moving along the s-axis is

$$\frac{ds}{dt} = v = 9.8t - 3.$$

i) Find the body's displacement over the time interval from $t = 1$ to $t = 3$ given that $s = 5$ when $t = 0$.

ii) Find the body's displacement from $t = 1$ to $t = 3$ given that $s = -2$ when $t = 0$.

iii) Now find the body's displacement from $t = 1$ to $t = 3$ given that $s = s_0$ when $t = 0$.

b. Suppose that the position s of a body moving along a coordinate line is a differentiable function of time t. Is it true that once you know an antiderivative of the velocity function ds/dt you can find the body's displacement from $t = a$ to $t = b$ even if you do not know the body's exact position at either of those times? Give reasons for your answer.

120. Liftoff from Earth A rocket lifts off the surface of Earth with a constant acceleration of 20 m/sec^2. How fast will the rocket be going 1 min later?

121. Stopping a car in time You are driving along a highway at a steady 60 mph (88 ft/sec) when you see an accident ahead and slam on the brakes. What constant deceleration is required to stop your car in 242 ft? To find out, carry out the following steps.

1. Solve the initial value problem

Differential equation: $\dfrac{d^2s}{dt^2} = -k \quad (k \text{ constant})$

Initial conditions: $\dfrac{ds}{dt} = 88 \text{ and } s = 0 \text{ when } t = 0.$

Measuring time and distance from when the brakes are applied

2. Find the value of t that makes $ds/dt = 0$. (The answer will involve k.)

3. Find the value of k that makes $s = 242$ for the value of t you found in Step 2.

122. Stopping a motorcycle The State of Illinois Cycle Rider Safety Program requires motorcycle riders to be able to brake from 30 mph (44 ft/sec) to 0 in 45 ft. What constant deceleration does it take to do that?

123. Motion along a coordinate line A particle moves on a coordinate line with acceleration $a = d^2s/dt^2 = 15\sqrt{t} - \left(3/\sqrt{t}\right)$, subject to the conditions that $ds/dt = 4$ and $s = 0$ when $t = 1$. Find

a. the velocity $v = ds/dt$ in terms of t

b. the position s in terms of t.

T **124. The hammer and the feather** When *Apollo 15* astronaut David Scott dropped a hammer and a feather on the moon to demonstrate that in a vacuum all bodies fall with the same (constant) acceleration, he dropped them from about 4 ft above the ground. The television footage of the event shows the hammer and the feather falling more slowly than on Earth, where, in a vacuum, they would have taken only half a second to fall the 4 ft. How long did it take the hammer and feather to fall 4 ft on the moon? To find out, solve the following initial value problem for s as a function of t. Then find the value of t that makes s equal to 0.

Differential equation: $\dfrac{d^2s}{dt^2} = -5.2 \text{ ft/sec}^2$

Initial conditions: $\dfrac{ds}{dt} = 0 \text{ and } s = 4 \text{ when } t = 0$

125. Motion with constant acceleration The standard equation for the position s of a body moving with a constant acceleration a along a coordinate line is

$$s = \frac{a}{2}t^2 + v_0 t + s_0, \tag{1}$$

where v_0 and s_0 are the body's velocity and position at time $t = 0$. Derive this equation by solving the initial value problem

Differential equation: $\dfrac{d^2s}{dt^2} = a$

Initial conditions: $\dfrac{ds}{dt} = v_0 \text{ and } s = s_0 \text{ when } t = 0.$

126. Free fall near the surface of a planet For free fall near the surface of a planet where the acceleration due to gravity has a constant magnitude of g length-units/sec^2, Equation (1) in Exercise 125 takes the form

$$s = -\frac{1}{2}gt^2 + v_0 t + s_0, \tag{2}$$

where s is the body's height above the surface. The equation has a minus sign because the acceleration acts downward, in the direction of decreasing s. The velocity v_0 is positive if the object is rising at time $t = 0$ and negative if the object is falling.

Instead of using the result of Exercise 125, you can derive Equation (2) directly by solving an appropriate initial value problem. What initial value problem? Solve it to be sure you have the right one, explaining the solution steps as you go along.

127. Suppose that

$$f(x) = \frac{d}{dx}\left(1 - \sqrt{x}\right) \quad \text{and} \quad g(x) = \frac{d}{dx}(x + 2).$$

Find:

a. $\displaystyle\int f(x)\,dx$ **b.** $\displaystyle\int g(x)\,dx$

c. $\int [-f(x)]\, dx$

d. $\int [-g(x)]\, dx$

e. $\int [f(x) + g(x)]\, dx$

f. $\int [f(x) - g(x)]\, dx$

128. Uniqueness of solutions If differentiable functions $y = F(x)$ and $y = G(x)$ both solve the initial value problem

$$\frac{dy}{dx} = f(x), \qquad y(x_0) = y_0,$$

on an interval I, must $F(x) = G(x)$ for every x in I? Give reasons for your answer.

COMPUTER EXPLORATIONS

Use a CAS to solve the initial value problems in Exercises 129–132. Plot the solution curves.

129. $y' = \cos^2 x + \sin x, \quad y(\pi) = 1$

130. $y' = \frac{1}{x} + x, \quad y(1) = -1$

131. $y' = \frac{1}{\sqrt{4 - x^2}}, \quad y(0) = 2$

132. $y'' = \frac{2}{x} + \sqrt{x}, \quad y(1) = 0, \quad y'(1) = 0$

Chapter 4 Questions to Guide Your Review

1. What can be said about the extreme values of a function that is continuous on a closed interval?
2. What does it mean for a function to have a local extreme value on its domain? An absolute extreme value? How are local and absolute extreme values related, if at all? Give examples.
3. How do you find the absolute extrema of a continuous function on a closed interval? Give examples.
4. What are the hypotheses and conclusion of Rolle's Theorem? Are the hypotheses really necessary? Explain.
5. What are the hypotheses and conclusion of the Mean Value Theorem? What physical interpretations might the theorem have?
6. State the Mean Value Theorem's three corollaries.
7. How can you sometimes identify a function $f(x)$ by knowing f' and knowing the value of f at a point $x = x_0$? Give an example.
8. What is the First Derivative Test for Local Extreme Values? Give examples of how it is applied.
9. How do you test a twice-differentiable function to determine where its graph is concave up or concave down? Give examples.
10. What is an inflection point? Give an example. What physical significance do inflection points sometimes have?
11. What is the Second Derivative Test for Local Extreme Values? Give examples of how it is applied.
12. What do the derivatives of a function tell you about the shape of its graph?
13. List the steps you would take to graph a polynomial function. Illustrate with an example.
14. What is a cusp? Give examples.
15. List the steps you would take to graph a rational function. Illustrate with an example.
16. Outline a general strategy for solving max-min problems. Give examples.
17. Describe l'Hôpital's Rule. How do you know when to use the rule and when to stop? Give an example.
18. How can you sometimes handle limits that lead to indeterminate forms ∞/∞, $\infty \cdot 0$, and $\infty - \infty$? Give examples.
19. How can you sometimes handle limits that lead to indeterminate forms 1^∞, 0^0, and ∞^∞? Give examples.
20. Describe Newton's method for solving equations. Give an example. What is the theory behind the method? What are some of the things to watch out for when you use the method?
21. Can a function have more than one antiderivative? If so, how are the antiderivatives related? Explain.
22. What is an indefinite integral? How do you evaluate one? What general formulas do you know for finding indefinite integrals?
23. How can you sometimes solve a differential equation of the form $dy/dx = f(x)$?
24. What is an initial value problem? How do you solve one? Give an example.
25. If you know the acceleration of a body moving along a coordinate line as a function of time, what more do you need to know to find the body's position function? Give an example.

Chapter 4 Practice Exercises

Extreme Values

1. Does $f(x) = x^3 + 2x + \tan x$ have any local maximum or minimum values? Give reasons for your answer.
2. Does $g(x) = \csc x + 2 \cot x$ have any local maximum values? Give reasons for your answer.
3. Does $f(x) = (7 + x)(11 - 3x)^{1/3}$ have an absolute minimum value? An absolute maximum? If so, find them or give reasons why they fail to exist. List all critical points of f.

4. Find values of a and b such that the function

$$f(x) = \frac{ax + b}{x^2 - 1}$$

has a local extreme value of 1 at $x = 3$. Is this extreme value a local maximum, or a local minimum? Give reasons for your answer.

5. Does $g(x) = e^x - x$ have an absolute minimum value? An absolute maximum? If so, find them or give reasons why they fail to exist. List all critical points of g.

6. Does $f(x) = 2e^x/(1 + x^2)$ have an absolute minimum value? An absolute maximum? If so, find them or give reasons why they fail to exist. List all critical points of f.

In Exercises 7 and 8, find the absolute maximum and absolute minimum values of f over the interval.

7. $f(x) = x - 2 \ln x, \quad 1 \le x \le 3$

8. $f(x) = (4/x) + \ln x^2, \quad 1 \le x \le 4$

9. The greatest integer function $f(x) = \lfloor x \rfloor$, defined for all values of x, assumes a local maximum value of 0 at each point of $[0, 1)$. Could any of these local maximum values also be local minimum values of f? Give reasons for your answer.

10. **a.** Give an example of a differentiable function f whose first derivative is zero at some point c even though f has neither a local maximum nor a local minimum at c.

b. How is this consistent with Theorem 2 in Section 4.1? Give reasons for your answer.

11. The function $y = 1/x$ does not take on either a maximum or a minimum on the interval $0 < x < 1$ even though the function is continuous on this interval. Does this contradict the Extreme Value Theorem for continuous functions? Why?

12. What are the maximum and minimum values of the function $y = |x|$ on the interval $-1 \le x < 1$? Notice that the interval is not closed. Is this consistent with the Extreme Value Theorem for continuous functions? Why?

T 13. A graph that is large enough to show a function's global behavior may fail to reveal important local features. The graph of $f(x) = (x^8/8) - (x^6/2) - x^5 + 5x^3$ is a case in point.

a. Graph f over the interval $-2.5 \le x \le 2.5$. Where does the graph appear to have local extreme values or points of inflection?

b. Now factor $f'(x)$ and show that f has a local maximum at $x = \sqrt[3]{5} \approx 1.70998$ and local minima at $x = \pm\sqrt{3} \approx \pm 1.73205$.

c. Zoom in on the graph to find a viewing window that shows the presence of the extreme values at $x = \sqrt[3]{5}$ and $x = \sqrt{3}$.

The moral here is that without calculus the existence of two of the three extreme values would probably have gone unnoticed. On any normal graph of the function, the values would lie close enough together to fall within the dimensions of a single pixel on the screen.

(*Source*: *Uses of Technology in the Mathematics Curriculum*, by Benny Evans and Jerry Johnson, Oklahoma State University, published in 1990 under National Science Foundation Grant USE-8950044.)

T 14. (*Continuation of Exercise 13.*)

a. Graph $f(x) = (x^8/8) - (2/5)x^5 - 5x - (5/x^2) + 11$ over the interval $-2 \le x \le 2$. Where does the graph appear to have local extreme values or points of inflection?

b. Show that f has a local maximum value at $x = \sqrt[7]{5} \approx 1.2585$ and a local minimum value at $x = \sqrt[3]{2} \approx 1.2599$.

c. Zoom in to find a viewing window that shows the presence of the extreme values at $x = \sqrt[7]{5}$ and $x = \sqrt[3]{2}$.

The Mean Value Theorem

15. **a.** Show that $g(t) = \sin^2 t - 3t$ decreases on every interval in its domain.

b. How many solutions does the equation $\sin^2 t - 3t = 5$ have? Give reasons for your answer.

16. **a.** Show that $y = \tan \theta$ increases on every interval in its domain.

b. If the conclusion in part (a) is really correct, how do you explain the fact that $\tan \pi = 0$ is less than $\tan(\pi/4) = 1$?

17. **a.** Show that the equation $x^4 + 2x^2 - 2 = 0$ has exactly one solution on $[0, 1]$.

T **b.** Find the solution to as many decimal places as you can.

18. **a.** Show that $f(x) = x/(x + 1)$ increases on every interval in its domain.

b. Show that $f(x) = x^3 + 2x$ has no local maximum or minimum values.

19. **Water in a reservoir** As a result of a heavy rain, the volume of water in a reservoir increased by 1400 acre-ft in 24 hours. Show that at some instant during that period the reservoir's volume was increasing at a rate in excess of 225,000 gal/min. (An acre-foot is 43,560 ft^3, the volume that would cover 1 acre to the depth of 1 ft. A cubic foot holds 7.48 gal.)

20. The formula $F(x) = 3x + C$ gives a different function for each value of C. All of these functions, however, have the same derivative with respect to x, namely $F'(x) = 3$. Are these the only differentiable functions whose derivative is 3? Could there be any others? Give reasons for your answers.

21. Show that

$$\frac{d}{dx}\left(\frac{x}{x+1}\right) = \frac{d}{dx}\left(-\frac{1}{x+1}\right)$$

even though

$$\frac{x}{x+1} \neq -\frac{1}{x+1}.$$

Doesn't this contradict Corollary 2 of the Mean Value Theorem? Give reasons for your answer.

22. Calculate the first derivatives of $f(x) = x^2/(x^2 + 1)$ and $g(x) = -1/(x^2 + 1)$. What can you conclude about the graphs of these functions?

Analyzing Graphs

In Exercises 23 and 24, use the graph to answer the questions.

23. Identify any global extreme values of f and the values of x at which they occur.

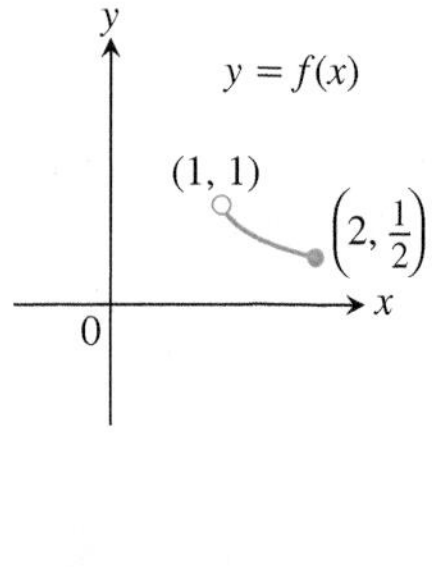

24. Estimate the intervals on which the function $y = f(x)$ is

a. increasing.

b. decreasing.

c. Use the given graph of f' to indicate where any local extreme values of the function occur, and whether each extreme is a relative maximum or minimum.

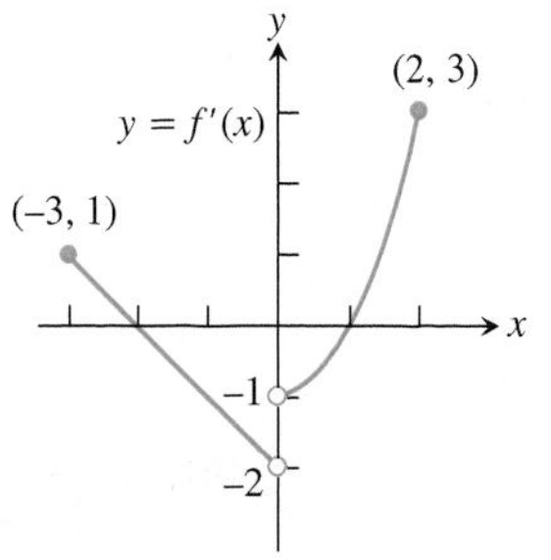

Each of the graphs in Exercises 25 and 26 is the graph of the position function $s = f(t)$ of an object moving on a coordinate line (t represents time). At approximately what times (if any) is each object's **(a)** velocity equal to zero? **(b)** Acceleration equal to zero? During approximately what time intervals does the object move **(c)** forward? **(d)** Backward?

25.

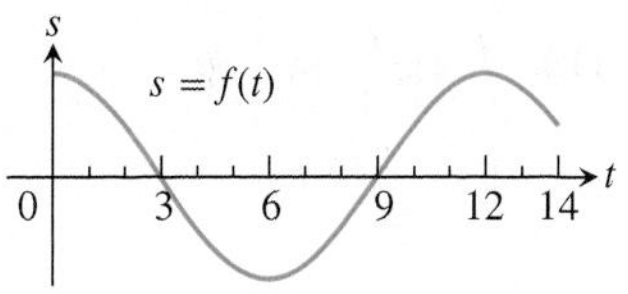

26.

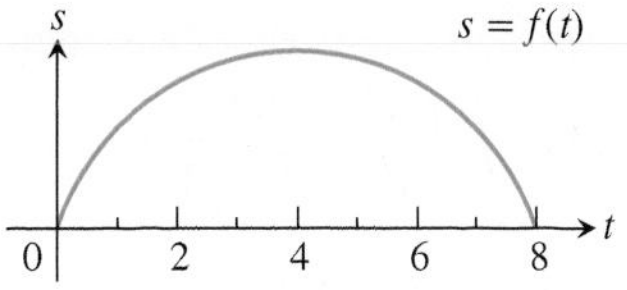

Graphs and Graphing

Graph the curves in Exercises 27–42.

27. $y = x^2 - (x^3/6)$

28. $y = x^3 - 3x^2 + 3$

29. $y = -x^3 + 6x^2 - 9x + 3$

30. $y = (1/8)(x^3 + 3x^2 - 9x - 27)$

31. $y = x^3(8 - x)$

32. $y = x^2(2x^2 - 9)$

33. $y = x - 3x^{2/3}$

34. $y = x^{1/3}(x - 4)$

35. $y = x\sqrt{3 - x}$

36. $y = x\sqrt{4 - x^2}$

37. $y = (x - 3)^2 e^x$

38. $y = xe^{-x^2}$

39. $y = \ln(x^2 - 4x + 3)$

40. $y = \ln(\sin x)$

41. $y = \sin^{-1}\left(\dfrac{1}{x}\right)$

42. $y = \tan^{-1}\left(\dfrac{1}{x}\right)$

Each of Exercises 43–48 gives the first derivative of a function $y = f(x)$. **(a)** At what points, if any, does the graph of f have a local maximum, local minimum, or inflection point? **(b)** Sketch the general shape of the graph.

43. $y' = 16 - x^2$

44. $y' = x^2 - x - 6$

45. $y' = 6x(x + 1)(x - 2)$

46. $y' = x^2(6 - 4x)$

47. $y' = x^4 - 2x^2$

48. $y' = 4x^2 - x^4$

In Exercises 49–52, graph each function. Then use the function's first derivative to explain what you see.

49. $y = x^{2/3} + (x - 1)^{1/3}$

50. $y = x^{2/3} + (x - 1)^{2/3}$

51. $y = x^{1/3} + (x - 1)^{1/3}$

52. $y = x^{2/3} - (x - 1)^{1/3}$

Sketch the graphs of the rational functions in Exercises 53–60.

53. $y = \dfrac{x + 1}{x - 3}$

54. $y = \dfrac{2x}{x + 5}$

55. $y = \dfrac{x^2 + 1}{x}$

56. $y = \dfrac{x^2 - x + 1}{x}$

57. $y = \dfrac{x^3 + 2}{2x}$

58. $y = \dfrac{x^4 - 1}{x^2}$

59. $y = \dfrac{x^2 - 4}{x^2 - 3}$

60. $y = \dfrac{x^2}{x^2 - 4}$

Using L'Hôpital's Rule

Use l'Hôpital's Rule to find the limits in Exercises 61–72.

61. $\displaystyle\lim_{x\to 1} \frac{x^2 + 3x - 4}{x - 1}$

62. $\displaystyle\lim_{x\to 1} \frac{x^a - 1}{x^b - 1}$

63. $\displaystyle\lim_{x\to \pi} \frac{\tan x}{x}$

64. $\displaystyle\lim_{x\to 0} \frac{\tan x}{x + \sin x}$

65. $\displaystyle\lim_{x\to 0} \frac{\sin^2 x}{\tan(x^2)}$

66. $\displaystyle\lim_{x\to 0} \frac{\sin mx}{\sin nx}$

67. $\displaystyle\lim_{x\to \pi/2^-} \sec 7x \cos 3x$

68. $\displaystyle\lim_{x\to 0^+} \sqrt{x} \sec x$

69. $\displaystyle\lim_{x\to 0} (\csc x - \cot x)$

70. $\displaystyle\lim_{x\to 0} \left(\frac{1}{x^4} - \frac{1}{x^2}\right)$

71. $\displaystyle\lim_{x\to \infty} \left(\sqrt{x^2 + x + 1} - \sqrt{x^2 - x}\right)$

72. $\displaystyle\lim_{x\to \infty} \left(\frac{x^3}{x^2 - 1} - \frac{x^3}{x^2 + 1}\right)$

Find the limits in Exercises 73–84.

73. $\displaystyle\lim_{x\to 0} \frac{10^x - 1}{x}$

74. $\displaystyle\lim_{\theta\to 0} \frac{3^\theta - 1}{\theta}$

75. $\displaystyle\lim_{x\to 0} \frac{2^{\sin x} - 1}{e^x - 1}$

76. $\displaystyle\lim_{x\to 0} \frac{2^{-\sin x} - 1}{e^x - 1}$

77. $\displaystyle\lim_{x\to 0} \frac{5 - 5\cos x}{e^x - x - 1}$

78. $\displaystyle\lim_{x\to 0} \frac{4 - 4e^x}{xe^x}$

79. $\displaystyle\lim_{t\to 0^+} \frac{t - \ln(1 + 2t)}{t^2}$

80. $\displaystyle\lim_{x\to 4} \frac{\sin^2(\pi x)}{e^{x-4} + 3 - x}$

81. $\displaystyle\lim_{t\to 0^+} \left(\frac{e^t}{t} - \frac{1}{t}\right)$

82. $\displaystyle\lim_{y\to 0^+} e^{-1/y} \ln y$

83. $\displaystyle\lim_{x\to \infty} \left(1 + \frac{b}{x}\right)^{kx}$

84. $\displaystyle\lim_{x\to \infty} \left(1 + \frac{2}{x} + \frac{7}{x^2}\right)$

Optimization

85. The sum of two nonnegative numbers is 36. Find the numbers if

a. the difference of their square roots is to be as large as possible.

b. the sum of their square roots is to be as large as possible.

86. The sum of two nonnegative numbers is 20. Find the numbers

a. if the product of one number and the square root of the other is to be as large as possible.

b. if one number plus the square root of the other is to be as large as possible.

87. An isosceles triangle has its vertex at the origin and its base parallel to the x-axis with the vertices above the axis on the curve $y = 27 - x^2$. Find the largest area the triangle can have.

88. A customer has asked you to design an open-top rectangular stainless steel vat. It is to have a square base and a volume of 32 ft^3, to be welded from quarter-inch plate, and to weigh no more than necessary. What dimensions do you recommend?

89. Find the height and radius of the largest right circular cylinder that can be put in a sphere of radius $\sqrt{3}$.

90. The figure here shows two right circular cones, one upside down inside the other. The two bases are parallel, and the vertex of the smaller cone lies at the center of the larger cone's base. What values of r and h will give the smaller cone the largest possible volume?

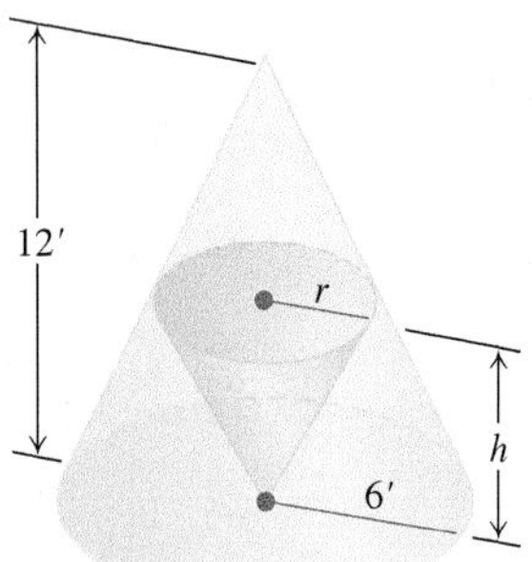

91. Manufacturing tires Your company can manufacture x hundred grade A tires and y hundred grade B tires a day, where $0 \le x \le 4$ and

$$y = \frac{40 - 10x}{5 - x}.$$

Your profit on a grade A tire is twice your profit on a grade B tire. What is the most profitable number of each kind to make?

92. Particle motion The positions of two particles on the s-axis are $s_1 = \cos t$ and $s_2 = \cos(t + \pi/4)$.

a. What is the farthest apart the particles ever get?

b. When do the particles collide?

T **93. Open-top box** An open-top rectangular box is constructed from a 10-in.-by-16-in. piece of cardboard by cutting squares of equal side length from the corners and folding up the sides. Find analytically the dimensions of the box of largest volume and the maximum volume. Support your answers graphically.

94. The ladder problem What is the approximate length (in feet) of the longest ladder you can carry horizontally around the corner of the corridor shown here? Round your answer down to the nearest foot.

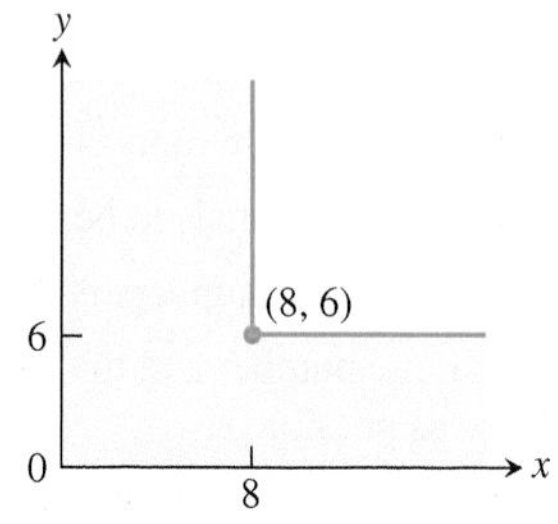

Newton's Method

95. Let $f(x) = 3x - x^3$. Show that the equation $f(x) = -4$ has a solution in the interval [2, 3] and use Newton's method to find it.

96. Let $f(x) = x^4 - x^3$. Show that the equation $f(x) = 75$ has a solution in the interval [3, 4] and use Newton's method to find it.

Finding Indefinite Integrals

Find the indefinite integrals (most general antiderivatives) in Exercises 97–120. You may need to try a solution and then adjust your guess. Check your answers by differentiation.

97. $\int (x^3 + 5x - 7)\, dx$

98. $\int \left(8t^3 - \frac{t^2}{2} + t\right) dt$

99. $\int \left(3\sqrt{t} + \frac{4}{t^2}\right) dt$

100. $\int \left(\frac{1}{2\sqrt{t}} - \frac{3}{t^4}\right) dt$

101. $\int \frac{dr}{(r + 5)^2}$

102. $\int \frac{6\, dr}{\left(r - \sqrt{2}\right)^3}$

103. $\int 3\theta\sqrt{\theta^2 + 1}\, d\theta$

104. $\int \frac{\theta}{\sqrt{7 + \theta^2}}\, d\theta$

105. $\int x^3(1 + x^4)^{-1/4}\, dx$

106. $\int (2 - x)^{3/5}\, dx$

107. $\int \sec^2 \frac{s}{10}\, ds$

108. $\int \csc^2 \pi s\, ds$

109. $\int \csc \sqrt{2}\theta \cot \sqrt{2}\theta\, d\theta$

110. $\int \sec \frac{\theta}{3} \tan \frac{\theta}{3}\, d\theta$

111. $\int \sin^2 \frac{x}{4}\, dx \quad \left(\textit{Hint: } \sin^2\theta = \frac{1 - \cos 2\theta}{2}\right)$

112. $\int \cos^2 \frac{x}{2}\, dx$

113. $\int \left(\frac{3}{x} - x\right) dx$

114. $\int \left(\frac{5}{x^2} + \frac{2}{x^2 + 1}\right) dx$

115. $\int \left(\frac{1}{2}e^t - e^{-t}\right) dt$

116. $\int (5^s + s^5)\, ds$

117. $\int \theta^{1-\pi}\, d\theta$

118. $\int 2^{\pi + r}\, dr$

119. $\int \frac{3}{2x\sqrt{x^2 - 1}}\, dx$

120. $\int \frac{d\theta}{\sqrt{16 - \theta^2}}$

Initial Value Problems

Solve the initial value problems in Exercises 121–124.

121. $\frac{dy}{dx} = \frac{x^2 + 1}{x^2}, \quad y(1) = -1$

122. $\frac{dy}{dx} = \left(x + \frac{1}{x}\right)^2, \quad y(1) = 1$

123. $\frac{d^2r}{dt^2} = 15\sqrt{t} + \frac{3}{\sqrt{t}}; \quad r'(1) = 8, \quad r(1) = 0$

124. $\frac{d^3r}{dt^3} = -\cos t; \quad r''(0) = r'(0) = 0, \quad r(0) = -1$

Applications and Examples

125. Can the integrations in (a) and (b) both be correct? Explain.

a. $\int \frac{dx}{\sqrt{1 - x^2}} = \sin^{-1} x + C$

b. $\int \frac{dx}{\sqrt{1 - x^2}} = -\int -\frac{dx}{\sqrt{1 - x^2}} = -\cos^{-1} x + C$

126. Can the integrations in (a) and (b) both be correct? Explain.

a. $\displaystyle\int \frac{dx}{\sqrt{1-x^2}} = -\int -\frac{dx}{\sqrt{1-x^2}} = -\cos^{-1} x + C$

b. $\displaystyle\int \frac{dx}{\sqrt{1-x^2}} = \int \frac{-du}{\sqrt{1-(-u)^2}}$ $\quad x = -u,\ dx = -du$

$\displaystyle = \int \frac{-du}{\sqrt{1-u^2}}$

$= \cos^{-1} u + C$

$= \cos^{-1}(-x) + C \quad u = -x$

127. The rectangle shown here has one side on the positive y-axis, one side on the positive x-axis, and its upper right-hand vertex on the curve $y = e^{-x^2}$. What dimensions give the rectangle its largest area, and what is that area?

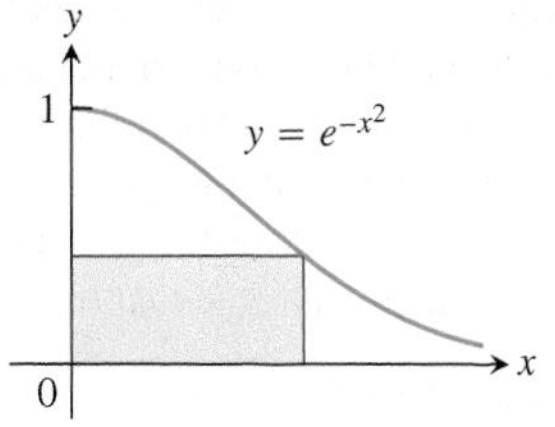

128. The rectangle shown here has one side on the positive y-axis, one side on the positive x-axis, and its upper right-hand vertex on the curve $y = (\ln x)/x^2$. What dimensions give the rectangle its largest area, and what is that area?

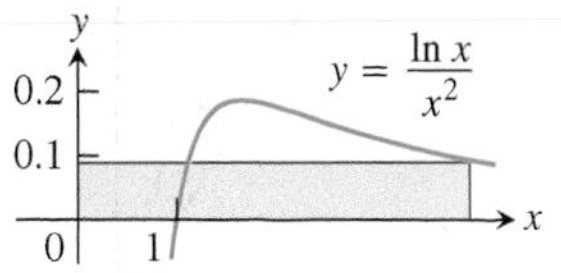

In Exercises 129 and 130, find the absolute maximum and minimum values of each function on the given interval.

129. $y = x \ln 2x - x, \quad \left[\frac{1}{2e}, \frac{e}{2}\right]$

130. $y = 10x(2 - \ln x), \quad (0, e^2]$

In Exercises 131 and 132, find the absolute maxima and minima of the functions and say where they are assumed.

131. $f(x) = e^{x/\sqrt{x^4+1}}$

132. $g(x) = e^{\sqrt{3-2x-x^2}}$

T **133.** Graph the following functions and use what you see to locate and estimate the extreme values, identify the coordinates of the inflection points, and identify the intervals on which the graphs are concave up and concave down. Then confirm your estimates by working with the functions' derivatives.

a. $y = (\ln x)/\sqrt{x}$ **b.** $y = e^{-x^2}$ **c.** $y = (1 + x)e^{-x}$

T **134.** Graph $f(x) = x \ln x$. Does the function appear to have an absolute minimum value? Confirm your answer with calculus.

T **135.** Graph $f(x) = (\sin x)^{\sin x}$ over $[0, 3\pi]$. Explain what you see.

136. A round underwater transmission cable consists of a core of copper wires surrounded by nonconducting insulation. If x denotes the ratio of the radius of the core to the thickness of the insulation, it is known that the speed of the transmission signal is given by the equation $v = x^2 \ln(1/x)$. If the radius of the core is 1 cm, what insulation thickness h will allow the greatest transmission speed?

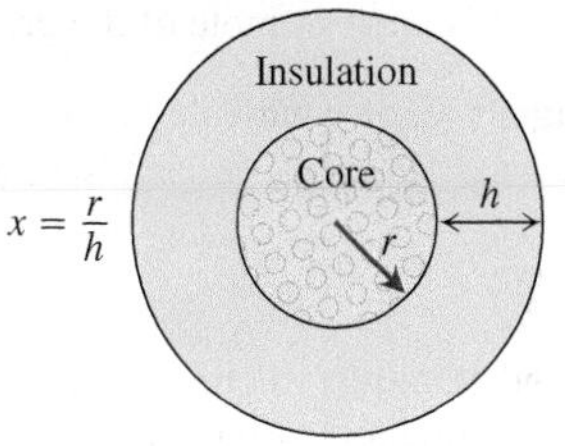

Chapter Additional and Advanced Exercises

Functions and Derivatives

1. What can you say about a function whose maximum and minimum values on an interval are equal? Give reasons for your answer.

2. Is it true that a discontinuous function cannot have both an absolute maximum and an absolute minimum value on a closed interval? Give reasons for your answer.

3. Can you conclude anything about the extreme values of a continuous function on an open interval? On a half-open interval? Give reasons for your answer.

4. Local extrema Use the sign pattern for the derivative

$$\frac{df}{dx} = 6(x-1)(x-2)^2(x-3)^3(x-4)^4$$

to identify the points where f has local maximum and minimum values.

5. Local extrema

a. Suppose that the first derivative of $y = f(x)$ is

$$y' = 6(x+1)(x-2)^2.$$

At what points, if any, does the graph of f have a local maximum, local minimum, or point of inflection?

b. Suppose that the first derivative of $y = f(x)$ is

$$y' = 6x(x+1)(x-2).$$

At what points, if any, does the graph of f have a local maximum, local minimum, or point of inflection?

6. If $f'(x) \le 2$ for all x, what is the most the values of f can increase on $[0, 6]$? Give reasons for your answer.

7. Bounding a function Suppose that f is continuous on $[a, b]$ and that c is an interior point of the interval. Show that if $f'(x) \le 0$ on $[a, c)$ and $f'(x) \ge 0$ on $(c, b]$, then $f(x)$ is never less than $f(c)$ on $[a, b]$.

8. An inequality

a. Show that $-1/2 \le x/(1 + x^2) \le 1/2$ for every value of x.

b. Suppose that f is a function whose derivative is $f'(x) = x/(1 + x^2)$. Use the result in part (a) to show that

$$|f(b) - f(a)| \le \frac{1}{2}|b - a|$$

for any a and b.

9. The derivative of $f(x) = x^2$ is zero at $x = 0$, but f is not a constant function. Doesn't this contradict the corollary of the Mean Value Theorem that says that functions with zero derivatives are constant? Give reasons for your answer.

10. Extrema and inflection points Let $h = fg$ be the product of two differentiable functions of x.

a. If f and g are positive, with local maxima at $x = a$, and if f' and g' change sign at a, does h have a local maximum at a?

b. If the graphs of f and g have inflection points at $x = a$, does the graph of h have an inflection point at a?

In either case, if the answer is yes, give a proof. If the answer is no, give a counterexample.

11. Finding a function Use the following information to find the values of a, b, and c in the formula $f(x) = (x + a)/(bx^2 + cx + 2)$.

i) The values of a, b, and c are either 0 or 1.

ii) The graph of f passes through the point $(-1, 0)$.

iii) The line $y = 1$ is an asymptote of the graph of f.

12. Horizontal tangent For what value or values of the constant k will the curve $y = x^3 + kx^2 + 3x - 4$ have exactly one horizontal tangent?

Optimization

13. Largest inscribed triangle Points A and B lie at the ends of a diameter of a unit circle and point C lies on the circumference. Is it true that the area of triangle ABC is largest when the triangle is isosceles? How do you know?

14. Proving the second derivative test The Second Derivative Test for Local Maxima and Minima (Section 4.4) says:

a. f has a local maximum value at $x = c$ if $f'(c) = 0$ and $f''(c) < 0$

b. f has a local minimum value at $x = c$ if $f'(c) = 0$ and $f''(c) > 0$.

To prove statement (a), let $\epsilon = (1/2)|f''(c)|$. Then use the fact that

$$f''(c) = \lim_{h \to 0} \frac{f'(c + h) - f'(c)}{h} = \lim_{h \to 0} \frac{f'(c + h)}{h}$$

to conclude that for some $\delta > 0$,

$$0 < |h| < \delta \quad \Rightarrow \quad \frac{f'(c + h)}{h} < f''(c) + \epsilon < 0.$$

Thus, $f'(c + h)$ is positive for $-\delta < h < 0$ and negative for $0 < h < \delta$. Prove statement (b) in a similar way.

15. Hole in a water tank You want to bore a hole in the side of the tank shown here at a height that will make the stream of water coming out hit the ground as far from the tank as possible. If you drill the hole near the top, where the pressure is low, the water will exit slowly but spend a relatively long time in the air. If you drill the hole near the bottom, the water will exit at a higher velocity but have only a short time to fall. Where is the best place, if any, for the hole? (*Hint:* How long will it take an exiting particle of water to fall from height y to the ground?)

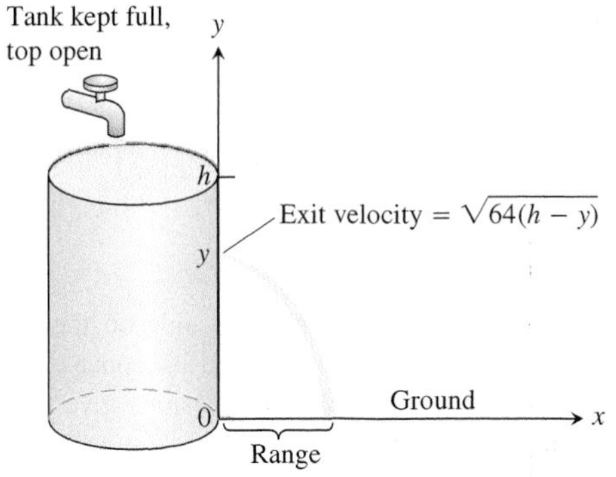

16. Kicking a field goal An American football player wants to kick a field goal with the ball being on a right hash mark. Assume that the goal posts are b feet apart and that the hash mark line is a distance $a > 0$ feet from the right goal post. (See the accompanying figure.) Find the distance h from the goal post line that gives the kicker his largest angle β. Assume that the football field is flat.

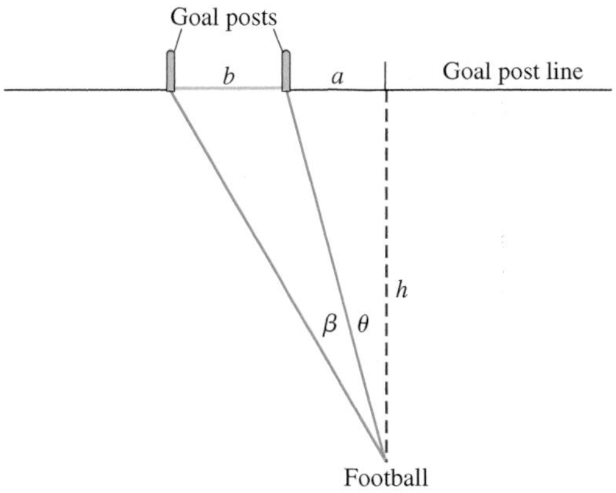

17. A max-min problem with a variable answer Sometimes the solution of a max-min problem depends on the proportions of the shapes involved. As a case in point, suppose that a right circular cylinder of radius r and height h is inscribed in a right circular cone of radius R and height H, as shown here. Find the value of r (in terms of R and H) that maximizes the total surface area of the cylinder (including top and bottom). As you will see, the solution depends on whether $H \le 2R$ or $H > 2R$.

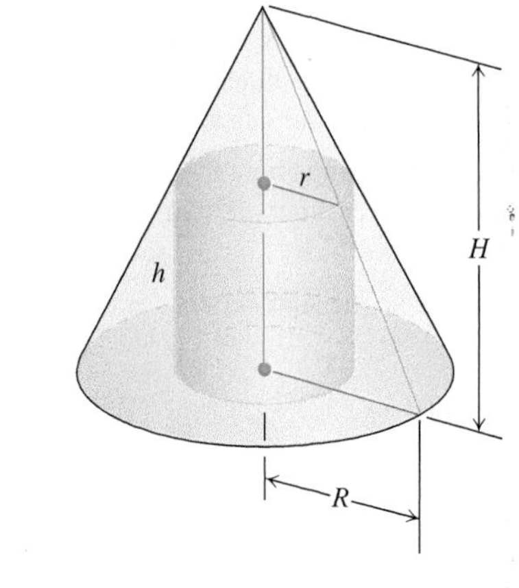

18. Minimizing a parameter Find the smallest value of the positive constant m that will make $mx - 1 + (1/x)$ greater than or equal to zero for all positive values of x.

Limits

19. Evaluate the following limits.

a. $\lim_{x\to 0} \frac{2 \sin 5x}{3x}$ b. $\lim_{x\to 0} \sin 5x \cot 3x$

c. $\lim_{x\to 0} x \csc^2 \sqrt{2x}$ d. $\lim_{x\to \pi/2} (\sec x - \tan x)$

e. $\lim_{x\to 0} \frac{x - \sin x}{x - \tan x}$ f. $\lim_{x\to 0} \frac{\sin x^2}{x \sin x}$

g. $\lim_{x\to 0} \frac{\sec x - 1}{x^2}$ h. $\lim_{x\to 2} \frac{x^3 - 8}{x^2 - 4}$

20. L'Hôpital's Rule does not help with the following limits. Find them some other way.

a. $\lim_{x\to\infty} \frac{\sqrt{x + 5}}{\sqrt{x} + 5}$ b. $\lim_{x\to\infty} \frac{2x}{x + 7\sqrt{x}}$

Theory and Examples

21. Suppose that it costs a company $y = a + bx$ dollars to produce x units per week. It can sell x units per week at a price of $P = c - ex$ dollars per unit. Each of a, b, c, and e represents a positive constant. **(a)** What production level maximizes the profit? **(b)** What is the corresponding price? **(c)** What is the weekly profit at this level of production? **(d)** At what price should each item be sold to maximize profits if the government imposes a tax of t dollars per item sold? Comment on the difference between this price and the price before the tax.

22. Estimating reciprocals without division You can estimate the value of the reciprocal of a number a without ever dividing by a if you apply Newton's method to the function $f(x) = (1/x) - a$. For example, if $a = 3$, the function involved is $f(x) = (1/x) - 3$.

a. Graph $y = (1/x) - 3$. Where does the graph cross the x-axis?

b. Show that the recursion formula in this case is

$$x_{n+1} = x_n(2 - 3x_n),$$

so there is no need for division.

23. To find $x = \sqrt[q]{a}$, we apply Newton's method to $f(x) = x^q - a$. Here we assume that a is a positive real number and q is a positive integer. Show that x_1 is a "weighted average" of x_0 and a/x_0^{q-1}, and find the coefficients m_0, m_1 such that

$$x_1 = m_0 x_0 + m_1\left(\frac{a}{x_0^{q-1}}\right), \qquad \begin{array}{l} m_0 > 0,\ m_1 > 0, \\ m_0 + m_1 = 1. \end{array}$$

What conclusion would you reach if x_0 and a/x_0^{q-1} were equal? What would be the value of x_1 in that case?

24. The family of straight lines $y = ax + b$ (a, b arbitrary constants) can be characterized by the relation $y'' = 0$. Find a similar relation satisfied by the family of all circles

$$(x - h)^2 + (y - h)^2 = r^2,$$

where h and r are arbitrary constants. (*Hint:* Eliminate h and r from the set of three equations including the given one and two obtained by successive differentiation.)

25. Free fall in the fourteenth century In the middle of the fourteenth century, Albert of Saxony (1316–1390) proposed a model of free fall that assumed that the velocity of a falling body was proportional to the distance fallen. It seemed reasonable to think that a body that had fallen 20 ft might be moving twice as fast as a body that had fallen 10 ft. And besides, none of the instruments in use at the time were accurate enough to prove otherwise. Today we can see just how far off Albert of Saxony's model was by solving the initial value problem implicit in his model. Solve the problem and compare your solution graphically with the equation $s = 16t^2$. You will see that it describes a motion that starts too slowly at first and then becomes too fast too soon to be realistic.

T **26. Group blood testing** During World War II it was necessary to administer blood tests to large numbers of recruits. There are two standard ways to administer a blood test to N people. In method 1, each person is tested separately. In method 2, the blood samples of x people are pooled and tested as one large sample. If the test is negative, this one test is enough for all x people. If the test is positive, then each of the x people is tested separately, requiring a total of $x + 1$ tests. Using the second method and some probability theory it can be shown that, on the average, the total number of tests y will be

$$y = N\left(1 - q^x + \frac{1}{x}\right).$$

With $q = 0.99$ and $N = 1000$, find the integer value of x that minimizes y. Also find the integer value of x that maximizes y. (This second result is not important to the real-life situation.) The group testing method was used in World War II with a savings of 80% over the individual testing method, but not with the given value of q.

27. Assume that the brakes of an automobile produce a constant deceleration of k ft/sec^2. **(a)** Determine what k must be to bring an automobile traveling 60 mi/hr (88 ft/sec) to rest in a distance of 100 ft from the point where the brakes are applied. **(b)** With the same k, how far would a car traveling 30 mi/hr travel before being brought to a stop?

28. Let $f(x)$, $g(x)$ be two continuously differentiable functions satisfying the relationships $f'(x) = g(x)$ and $f''(x) = -f(x)$. Let $h(x) = f^2(x) + g^2(x)$. If $h(0) = 5$, find $h(10)$.

29. Can there be a curve satisfying the following conditions? d^2y/dx^2 is everywhere equal to zero and, when $x = 0$, $y = 0$ and $dy/dx = 1$. Give a reason for your answer.

30. Find the equation for the curve in the xy-plane that passes through the point $(1, -1)$ if its slope at x is always $3x^2 + 2$.

31. A particle moves along the x-axis. Its acceleration is $a = -t^2$. At $t = 0$, the particle is at the origin. In the course of its motion, it reaches the point $x = b$, where $b > 0$, but no point beyond b. Determine its velocity at $t = 0$.

32. A particle moves with acceleration $a = \sqrt{t} - (1/\sqrt{t})$. Assuming that the velocity $v = 4/3$ and the position $s = -4/15$ when $t = 0$, find

a. the velocity v in terms of t.

b. the position s in terms of t.

33. Given $f(x) = ax^2 + 2bx + c$ with $a > 0$. By considering the minimum, prove that $f(x) \geq 0$ for all real x if and only if $b^2 - ac \leq 0$.

34. Schwarz's inequality

a. In Exercise 33, let

$$f(x) = (a_1 x + b_1)^2 + (a_2 x + b_2)^2 + \cdots + (a_n x + b_n)^2,$$

and deduce Schwarz's inequality:

$$(a_1 b_1 + a_2 b_2 + \cdots + a_n b_n)^2 \le \left(a_1^2 + a_2^2 + \cdots + a_n^2\right)\left(b_1^2 + b_2^2 + \cdots + b_n^2\right).$$

b. Show that equality holds in Schwarz's inequality only if there exists a real number x that makes $a_i x$ equal $-b_i$ for every value of i from 1 to n.

35. The best branching angles for blood vessels and pipes When a smaller pipe branches off from a larger one in a flow system, we may want it to run off at an angle that is best from some energy-saving point of view. We might require, for instance, that energy loss due to friction be minimized along the section AOB shown in the accompanying figure. In this diagram, B is a given point to be reached by the smaller pipe, A is a point in the larger pipe upstream from B, and O is the point where the branching occurs. A law due to Poiseuille states that the loss of energy due to friction in nonturbulent flow is proportional to the length of the path and inversely proportional to the fourth power of the radius. Thus, the loss along AO is $(kd_1)/R^4$ and along OB is $(kd_2)/r^4$, where k is a constant, d_1 is the length of AO, d_2 is the length of OB, R is the radius of the larger pipe, and r is the radius of the smaller pipe. The angle θ is to be chosen to minimize the sum of these two losses:

$$L = k\frac{d_1}{R^4} + k\frac{d_2}{r^4}.$$

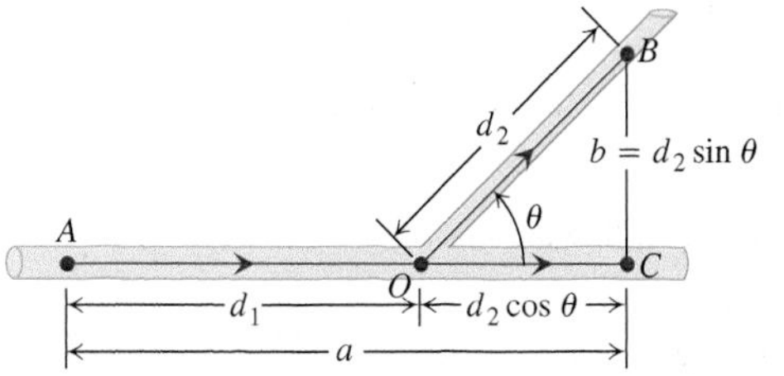

In our model, we assume that $AC = a$ and $BC = b$ are fixed. Thus we have the relations

$$d_1 + d_2 \cos\theta = a \qquad d_2 \sin\theta = b,$$

so that

$$d_2 = b \csc\theta,$$
$$d_1 = a - d_2\cos\theta = a - b\cot\theta.$$

We can express the total loss L as a function of θ:

$$L = k\left(\frac{a - b\cot\theta}{R^4} + \frac{b\csc\theta}{r^4}\right).$$

a. Show that the critical value of θ for which $dL/d\theta$ equals zero is

$$\theta_c = \cos^{-1}\frac{r^4}{R^4}.$$

b. If the ratio of the pipe radii is $r/R = 5/6$, estimate to the nearest degree the optimal branching angle given in part (a).

5

INTEGRATION

OVERVIEW A great achievement of classical geometry was obtaining formulas for the areas and volumes of triangles, spheres, and cones. In this chapter we develop a method to calculate the areas and volumes of very general shapes. This method, called *integration*, is a tool for calculating much more than areas and volumes. The *integral* is of fundamental importance in statistics, the sciences, and engineering. As with the derivative, the integral also arises as a limit, this time of increasingly fine approximations. We use it to calculate quantities ranging from probabilities and averages to energy consumption and the forces against a dam's floodgates. We study a variety of these applications in the next chapter, but in this chapter we focus on the integral concept and its use in computing areas of various regions with curved boundaries.

5.1 Area and Estimating with Finite Sums

The *definite integral* is the key tool in calculus for defining and calculating quantities important to mathematics and science, such as areas, volumes, lengths of curved paths, probabilities, and the weights of various objects, just to mention a few. The idea behind the integral is that we can effectively compute such quantities by breaking them into small pieces and then summing the contributions from each piece. We then consider what happens when more and more, smaller and smaller pieces are taken in the summation process. Finally, if the number of terms contributing to the sum approaches infinity and we take the limit of these sums in the way described in Section 5.3, the result is a definite integral. We prove in Section 5.4 that integrals are connected to antiderivatives, a connection that is one of the most important relationships in calculus.

The basis for formulating definite integrals is the construction of appropriate finite sums. Although we need to define precisely what we mean by the area of a general region in the plane, or the average value of a function over a closed interval, we do have intuitive ideas of what these notions mean. So in this section we begin our approach to integration by *approximating* these quantities with finite sums. We also consider what happens when we take more and more terms in the summation process. In subsequent sections we look at taking the limit of these sums as the number of terms goes to infinity, which then leads to precise definitions of the quantities being approximated here.

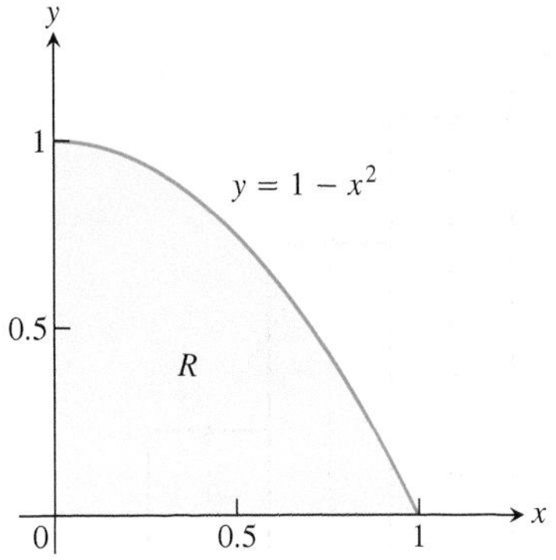

FIGURE 5.1 The area of the region R cannot be found by a simple formula.

Area

Suppose we want to find the area of the shaded region R that lies above the x-axis, below the graph of $y = 1 - x^2$, and between the vertical lines $x = 0$ and $x = 1$ (Figure 5.1). Unfortunately, there is no simple geometric formula for calculating the areas of general shapes having curved boundaries like the region R. How, then, can we find the area of R?

While we do not yet have a method for determining the exact area of R, we can approximate it in a simple way. Figure 5.2a shows two rectangles that together contain the region R. Each rectangle has width $1/2$ and they have heights 1 and $3/4$, moving from left to right. The height of each rectangle is the maximum value of the function f,

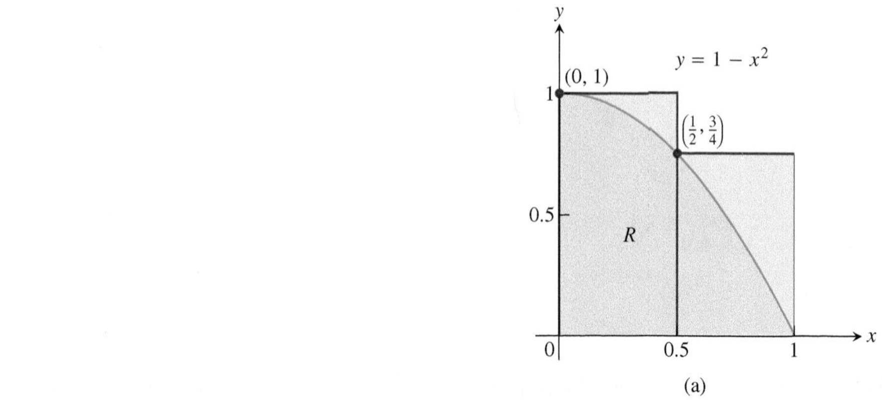

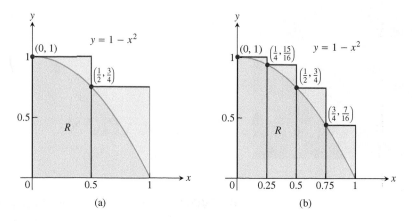

FIGURE 5.2 (a) We get an upper estimate of the area of R by using two rectangles containing R. (b) Four rectangles give a better upper estimate. Both estimates overshoot the true value for the area by the amount shaded in light red.

obtained by evaluating f at the left endpoint of the subinterval of [0, 1] forming the base of the rectangle. The total area of the two rectangles approximates the area A of the region R,

$$A \approx 1 \cdot \frac{1}{2} + \frac{3}{4} \cdot \frac{1}{2} = \frac{7}{8} = 0.875.$$

This estimate is larger than the true area A since the two rectangles contain R. We say that 0.875 is an **upper sum** because it is obtained by taking the height of each rectangle as the maximum (uppermost) value of $f(x)$ for a point x in the base interval of the rectangle. In Figure 5.2b, we improve our estimate by using four thinner rectangles, each of width 1/4, which taken together contain the region R. These four rectangles give the approximation

$$A \approx 1 \cdot \frac{1}{4} + \frac{15}{16} \cdot \frac{1}{4} + \frac{3}{4} \cdot \frac{1}{4} + \frac{7}{16} \cdot \frac{1}{4} = \frac{25}{32} = 0.78125,$$

which is still greater than A since the four rectangles contain R.

Suppose instead we use four rectangles contained *inside* the region R to estimate the area, as in Figure 5.3a. Each rectangle has width 1/4 as before, but the rectangles are

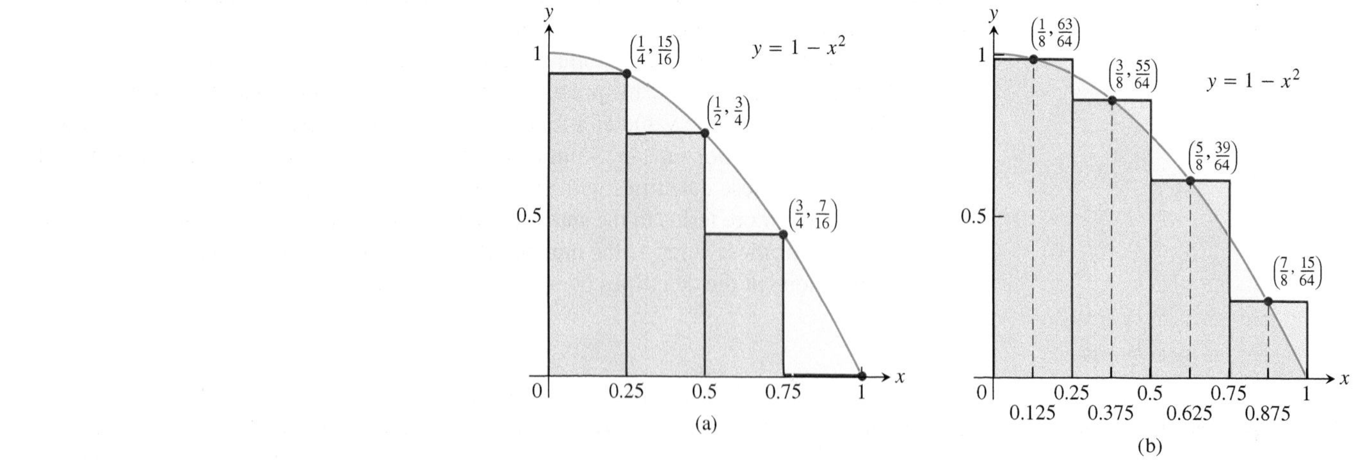

FIGURE 5.3 (a) Rectangles contained in R give an estimate for the area that undershoots the true value by the amount shaded in light blue. (b) The midpoint rule uses rectangles whose height is the value of $y = f(x)$ at the midpoints of their bases. The estimate appears closer to the true value of the area because the light red overshoot areas roughly balance the light blue undershoot areas.

shorter and lie entirely beneath the graph of f. The function $f(x) = 1 - x^2$ is decreasing on $[0, 1]$, so the height of each of these rectangles is given by the value of f at the right endpoint of the subinterval forming its base. The fourth rectangle has zero height and therefore contributes no area. Summing these rectangles with heights equal to the minimum value of $f(x)$ for a point x in each base subinterval gives a **lower sum** approximation to the area,

$$A \approx \frac{15}{16}\cdot\frac{1}{4} + \frac{3}{4}\cdot\frac{1}{4} + \frac{7}{16}\cdot\frac{1}{4} + 0\cdot\frac{1}{4} = \frac{17}{32} = 0.53125.$$

This estimate is smaller than the area A since the rectangles all lie inside of the region R. The true value of A lies somewhere between these lower and upper sums:

$$0.53125 < A < 0.78125.$$

By considering both lower and upper sum approximations, we get not only estimates for the area, but also a bound on the size of the possible error in these estimates since the true value of the area lies somewhere between them. Here the error cannot be greater than the difference $0.78125 - 0.53125 = 0.25$.

Yet another estimate can be obtained by using rectangles whose heights are the values of f at the midpoints of their bases (Figure 5.3b). This method of estimation is called the **midpoint rule** for approximating the area. The midpoint rule gives an estimate that is between a lower sum and an upper sum, but it is not quite so clear whether it overestimates or underestimates the true area. With four rectangles of width $1/4$ as before, the midpoint rule estimates the area of R to be

$$A \approx \frac{63}{64}\cdot\frac{1}{4} + \frac{55}{64}\cdot\frac{1}{4} + \frac{39}{64}\cdot\frac{1}{4} + \frac{15}{64}\cdot\frac{1}{4} = \frac{172}{64}\cdot\frac{1}{4} = 0.671875.$$

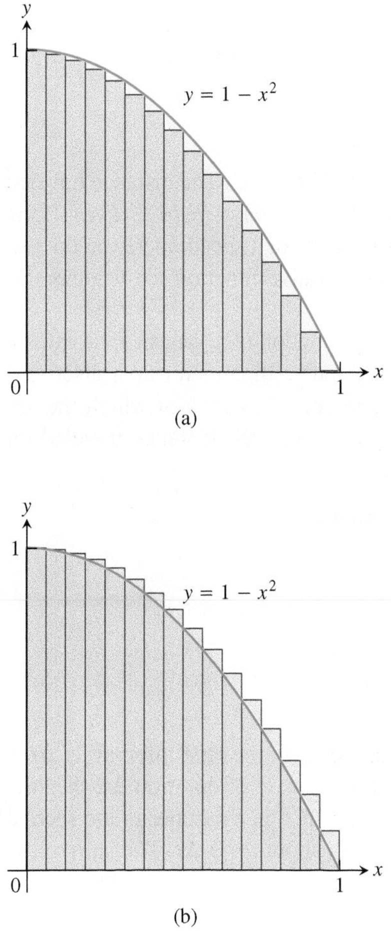

FIGURE 5.4 (a) A lower sum using 16 rectangles of equal width $\Delta x = 1/16$. (b) An upper sum using 16 rectangles.

In each of our computed sums, the interval $[a, b]$ over which the function f is defined was subdivided into n subintervals of equal width (also called length) $\Delta x = (b - a)/n$, and f was evaluated at a point in each subinterval: c_1 in the first subinterval, c_2 in the second subinterval, and so on. The finite sums then all take the form

$$f(c_1)\,\Delta x + f(c_2)\,\Delta x + f(c_3)\,\Delta x + \cdots + f(c_n)\,\Delta x.$$

By taking more and more rectangles, with each rectangle thinner than before, it appears that these finite sums give better and better approximations to the true area of the region R.

Figure 5.4a shows a lower sum approximation for the area of R using 16 rectangles of equal width. The sum of their areas is 0.634765625, which appears close to the true area, but is still smaller since the rectangles lie inside R.

Figure 5.4b shows an upper sum approximation using 16 rectangles of equal width. The sum of their areas is 0.697265625, which is somewhat larger than the true area because the rectangles taken together contain R. The midpoint rule for 16 rectangles gives a total area approximation of 0.6669921875, but it is not immediately clear whether this estimate is larger or smaller than the true area.

EXAMPLE 1 Table 5.1 shows the values of upper and lower sum approximations to the area of R, using up to 1000 rectangles. In Section 5.2 we will see how to get an exact value of the areas of regions such as R by taking a limit as the base width of each rectangle goes to zero and the number of rectangles goes to infinity. With the techniques developed there, we will be able to show that the area of R is exactly $2/3$. ■

Distance Traveled

Suppose we know the velocity function $v(t)$ of a car moving down a highway, without changing direction, and want to know how far it traveled between times $t = a$ and $t = b$. The position function $s(t)$ of the car has derivative $v(t)$. If we can find an antiderivative $F(t)$ of $v(t)$ then

TABLE 5.1 Finite approximations for the area of R

Number of subintervals	Lower sum	Midpoint rule	Upper sum
2	0.375	0.6875	0.875
4	0.53125	0.671875	0.78125
16	0.634765625	0.6669921875	0.697265625
50	0.6566	0.6667	0.6766
100	0.66165	0.666675	0.67165
1000	0.6661665	0.66666675	0.6671665

we can find the car's position function $s(t)$ by setting $s(t) = F(t) + C$. The distance traveled can then be found by calculating the change in position, $s(b) - s(a) = F(b) - F(a)$. If the velocity function is known only by the readings at various times of a speedometer on the car, then we have no formula from which to obtain an antiderivative function for velocity. So what do we do in this situation?

When we don't know an antiderivative for the velocity function $v(t)$, we can approximate the distance traveled with finite sums in a way similar to our estimates for area discussed before. We subdivide the interval $[a, b]$ into short time intervals on each of which the velocity is considered to be fairly constant. Then we approximate the distance traveled on each time subinterval with the usual distance formula

$$\text{distance} = \text{velocity} \times \text{time}$$

and add the results across $[a, b]$.

Suppose the subdivided interval looks like

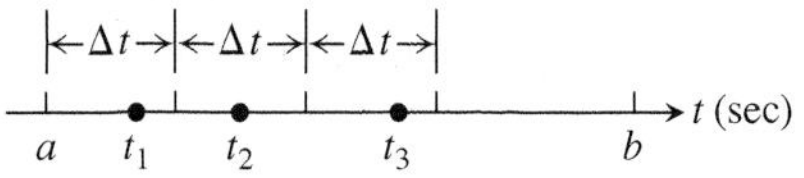

with the subintervals all of equal length Δt. Pick a number t_1 in the first interval. If Δt is so small that the velocity barely changes over a short time interval of duration Δt, then the distance traveled in the first time interval is about $v(t_1)\,\Delta t$. If t_2 is a number in the second interval, the distance traveled in the second time interval is about $v(t_2)\,\Delta t$. The sum of the distances traveled over all the time intervals is

$$D \approx v(t_1)\,\Delta t + v(t_2)\,\Delta t + \cdots + v(t_n)\,\Delta t,$$

where n is the total number of subintervals.

EXAMPLE 2 The velocity function of a projectile fired straight into the air is $f(t) = 160 - 9.8t$ m/sec. Use the summation technique just described to estimate how far the projectile rises during the first 3 sec. How close do the sums come to the exact value of 435.9 m?

Solution We explore the results for different numbers of intervals and different choices of evaluation points. Notice that $f(t)$ is decreasing, so choosing left endpoints gives an upper sum estimate; choosing right endpoints gives a lower sum estimate.

(a) *Three subintervals of length* 1, *with* f *evaluated at left endpoints giving an upper sum*:

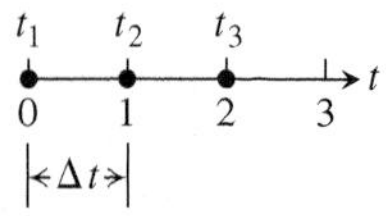

With f evaluated at $t = 0, 1$, and 2, we have

$$\begin{aligned} D &\approx f(t_1)\,\Delta t + f(t_2)\,\Delta t + f(t_3)\,\Delta t \\ &= [160 - 9.8(0)](1) + [160 - 9.8(1)](1) + [160 - 9.8(2)](1) \\ &= 450.6. \end{aligned}$$

(b) *Three subintervals of length* 1, *with f evaluated at right endpoints giving a lower sum*:

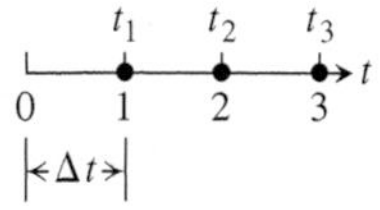

With f evaluated at $t = 1, 2$, and 3, we have

$$\begin{aligned} D &\approx f(t_1)\,\Delta t + f(t_2)\,\Delta t + f(t_3)\,\Delta t \\ &= [160 - 9.8(1)](1) + [160 - 9.8(2)](1) + [160 - 9.8(3)](1) \\ &= 421.2. \end{aligned}$$

(c) *With six subintervals of length* $1/2$, *we get*

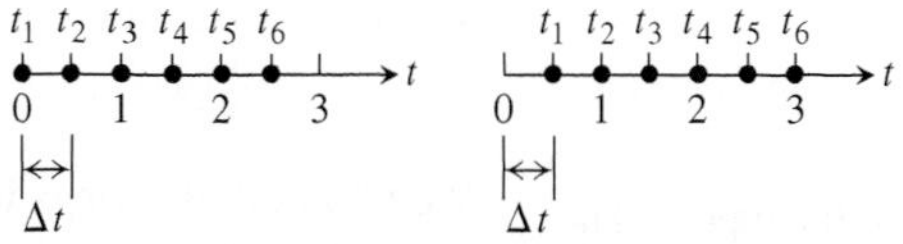

These estimates give an upper sum using left endpoints: $D \approx 443.25$; and a lower sum using right endpoints: $D \approx 428.55$. These six-interval estimates are somewhat closer than the three-interval estimates. The results improve as the subintervals get shorter.

As we can see in Table 5.2, the left-endpoint upper sums approach the true value 435.9 from above, whereas the right-endpoint lower sums approach it from below. The true value lies between these upper and lower sums. The magnitude of the error in the closest entries is 0.23, a small percentage of the true value.

$$\begin{aligned} \text{Error magnitude} &= |\text{true value} - \text{calculated value}| \\ &= |435.9 - 435.67| = 0.23. \end{aligned}$$

$$\text{Error percentage} = \frac{0.23}{435.9} \approx 0.05\%.$$

It would be reasonable to conclude from the table's last entries that the projectile rose about 436 m during its first 3 sec of flight. ■

TABLE 5.2 Travel-distance estimates

Number of subintervals	Length of each subinterval	Upper sum	Lower sum
3	1	450.6	421.2
6	1/2	443.25	428.55
12	1/4	439.58	432.23
24	1/8	437.74	434.06
48	1/16	436.82	434.98
96	1/32	436.36	435.44
192	1/64	436.13	435.67

Displacement Versus Distance Traveled

If an object with position function $s(t)$ moves along a coordinate line without changing direction, we can calculate the total distance it travels from $t = a$ to $t = b$ by summing the distance traveled over small intervals, as in Example 2. If the object reverses direction one or more times during the trip, then we need to use the object's *speed* $|v(t)|$, which is the absolute value of its velocity function, $v(t)$, to find the total distance traveled. Using the velocity itself, as in Example 2, gives instead an estimate to the object's **displacement**, $s(b) - s(a)$, the difference between its initial and final positions.

To see why using the velocity function in the summation process gives an estimate to the displacement, partition the time interval $[a, b]$ into small enough equal subintervals Δt so that the object's velocity does not change very much from time t_{k-1} to t_k. Then $v(t_k)$ gives a good approximation of the velocity throughout the interval. Accordingly, the change in the object's position coordinate during the time interval is about

$$v(t_k)\ \Delta t.$$

The change is positive if $v(t_k)$ is positive and negative if $v(t_k)$ is negative.

In either case, the distance traveled by the object during the subinterval is about

$$|v(t_k)|\ \Delta t.$$

The **total distance traveled** is approximately the sum

$$|v(t_1)|\ \Delta t + |v(t_2)|\Delta t + \cdots + |v(t_n)|\ \Delta t.$$

We revisit these ideas in Section 5.4.

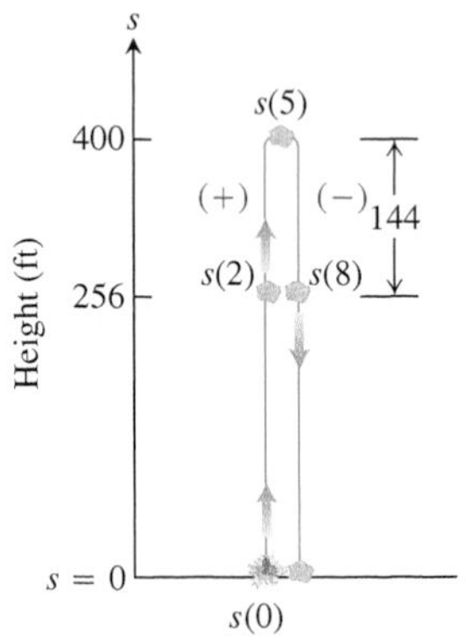

FIGURE 5.5 The rock in Example 3. The height $s = 256$ ft is reached at $t = 2$ and $t = 8$ sec. The rock falls 144 ft from its maximum height when $t = 8$.

EXAMPLE 3 In Example 4 in Section 3.4, we analyzed the motion of a heavy rock blown straight up by a dynamite blast. In that example, we found the velocity of the rock at any time during its motion to be $v(t) = 160 - 32t$ ft/sec. The rock was 256 ft above the ground 2 sec after the explosion, continued upward to reach a maximum height of 400 ft at 5 sec after the explosion, and then fell back down to reach the height of 256 ft again at $t = 8$ sec after the explosion. (See Figure 5.5.)

If we follow a procedure like that presented in Example 2, and use the velocity function $v(t)$ in the summation process over the time interval [0, 8], we will obtain an estimate to 256 ft, the rock's *height* above the ground at $t = 8$. The positive upward motion (which yields a positive distance change of 144 ft from the height of 256 ft to the maximum height) is canceled by the negative downward motion (giving a negative change of 144 ft from the maximum height down to 256 ft again), so the displacement or height above the ground is being estimated from the velocity function.

On the other hand, if the absolute value $|v(t)|$ is used in the summation process, we will obtain an estimate to the *total distance* the rock has traveled: the maximum height reached of 400 ft plus the additional distance of 144 ft it has fallen back down from that maximum when it again reaches the height of 256 ft at $t = 8$ sec. That is, using the absolute value of the velocity function in the summation process over the time interval [0, 8], we obtain an estimate to 544 ft, the total distance up and down that the rock has traveled in 8 sec. There is no cancelation of distance changes due to sign changes in the velocity function, so we estimate distance traveled rather than displacement when we use the absolute value of the velocity function (that is, the speed of the rock).

As an illustration of our discussion, we subdivide the interval [0, 8] into sixteen subintervals of length $\Delta t = 1/2$ and take the right endpoint of each subinterval in our calculations. Table 5.3 shows the values of the velocity function at these endpoints.

TABLE 5.3 Velocity Function

t	$v(t)$	t	$v(t)$
0	160	4.5	16
0.5	144	5.0	0
1.0	128	5.5	−16
1.5	112	6.0	−32
2.0	96	6.5	−48
2.5	80	7.0	−64
3.0	64	7.5	−80
3.5	48	8.0	−96
4.0	32		

Using $v(t)$ in the summation process, we estimate the displacement at $t = 8$:

$$(144 + 128 + 112 + 96 + 80 + 64 + 48 + 32 + 16$$
$$+ 0 - 16 - 32 - 48 - 64 - 80 - 96) \cdot \frac{1}{2} = 192$$
$$\text{Error magnitude} = 256 - 192 = 64$$

Using $|v(t)|$ in the summation process, we estimate the total distance traveled over the time interval [0, 8]:

$$(144 + 128 + 112 + 96 + 80 + 64 + 48 + 32 + 16$$
$$+ 0 + 16 + 32 + 48 + 64 + 80 + 96) \cdot \frac{1}{2} = 528$$
$$\text{Error magnitude} = 544 - 528 = 16$$

If we take more and more subintervals of [0, 8] in our calculations, the estimates to 256 ft and 544 ft improve, approaching their true values. ■

Average Value of a Nonnegative Continuous Function

The average value of a collection of n numbers $x_1, x_2, \ldots, x_n$ is obtained by adding them together and dividing by n. But what is the average value of a continuous function f on an interval $[a, b]$? Such a function can assume infinitely many values. For example, the temperature at a certain location in a town is a continuous function that goes up and down each day. What does it mean to say that the average temperature in the town over the course of a day is 73 degrees?

When a function is constant, this question is easy to answer. A function with constant value c on an interval $[a, b]$ has average value c. When c is positive, its graph over $[a, b]$ gives a rectangle of height c. The average value of the function can then be interpreted geometrically as the area of this rectangle divided by its width $b - a$ (Figure 5.6a).

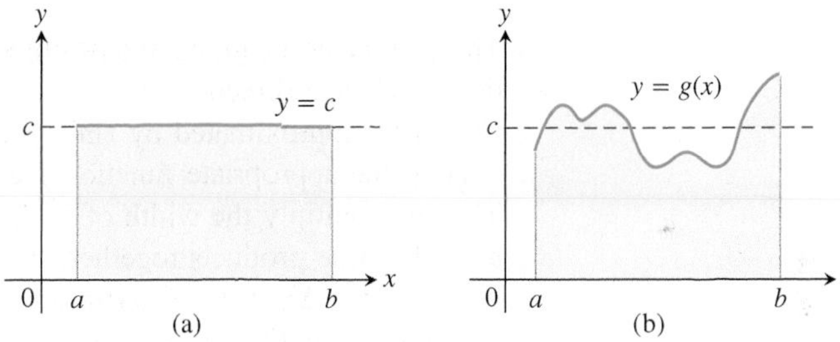

FIGURE 5.6 (a) The average value of $f(x) = c$ on $[a, b]$ is the area of the rectangle divided by $b - a$. (b) The average value of $g(x)$ on $[a, b]$ is the area beneath its graph divided by $b - a$.

What if we want to find the average value of a nonconstant function, such as the function g in Figure 5.6b? We can think of this graph as a snapshot of the height of some water that is sloshing around in a tank between enclosing walls at $x = a$ and $x = b$. As the water moves, its height over each point changes, but its average height remains the same. To get the average height of the water, we let it settle down until it is level and its height is constant. The resulting height c equals the area under the graph of g divided by $b - a$. We are led to *define* the average value of a nonnegative function on an interval $[a, b]$ to be the area under its graph divided by $b - a$. For this definition to be valid, we need a precise understanding of what is meant by the area under a graph. This will be obtained in Section 5.3, but for now we look at an example.

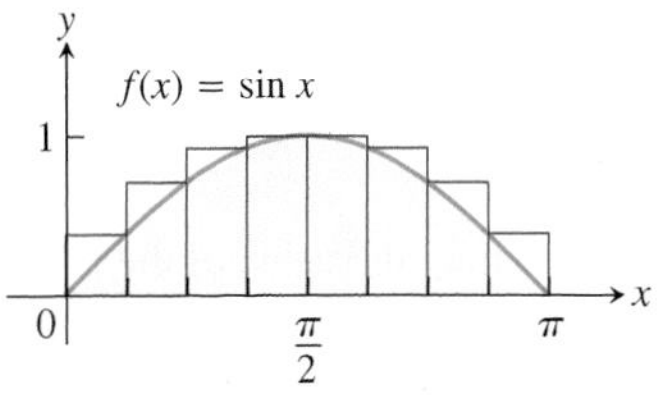

FIGURE 5.7 Approximating the area under $f(x) = \sin x$ between 0 and π to compute the average value of $\sin x$ over $[0, \pi]$, using eight rectangles (Example 4).

EXAMPLE 4 Estimate the average value of the function $f(x) = \sin x$ on the interval $[0, \pi]$.

Solution Looking at the graph of $\sin x$ between 0 and π in Figure 5.7, we can see that its average height is somewhere between 0 and 1. To find the average we need to calculate the area A under the graph and then divide this area by the length of the interval, $\pi - 0 = \pi$.

We do not have a simple way to determine the area, so we approximate it with finite sums. To get an upper sum approximation, we add the areas of eight rectangles of equal width $\pi/8$ that together contain the region beneath the graph of $y = \sin x$ and above the x-axis on $[0, \pi]$. We choose the heights of the rectangles to be the largest value of $\sin x$ on each subinterval. Over a particular subinterval, this largest value may occur at the left endpoint, the right endpoint, or somewhere between them. We evaluate $\sin x$ at this point to get the height of the rectangle for an upper sum. The sum of the rectangle areas then estimates the total area (Figure 5.7):

$$A \approx \left(\sin\frac{\pi}{8} + \sin\frac{\pi}{4} + \sin\frac{3\pi}{8} + \sin\frac{\pi}{2} + \sin\frac{\pi}{2} + \sin\frac{5\pi}{8} + \sin\frac{3\pi}{4} + \sin\frac{7\pi}{8}\right)\cdot\frac{\pi}{8}$$

$$\approx (.38 + .71 + .92 + 1 + 1 + .92 + .71 + .38)\cdot\frac{\pi}{8} = (6.02)\cdot\frac{\pi}{8} \approx 2.365.$$

To estimate the average value of $\sin x$ we divide the estimated area by π and obtain the approximation $2.365/\pi \approx 0.753$.

Since we used an upper sum to approximate the area, this estimate is greater than the actual average value of $\sin x$ over $[0, \pi]$. If we use more and more rectangles, with each rectangle getting thinner and thinner, we get closer and closer to the true average value. Using the techniques covered in Section 5.3, we will show that the true average value is $2/\pi \approx 0.64$.

As before, we could just as well have used rectangles lying under the graph of $y = \sin x$ and calculated a lower sum approximation, or we could have used the midpoint rule. In Section 5.3 we will see that in each case, the approximations are close to the true area if all the rectangles are sufficiently thin. ■

Summary

The area under the graph of a positive function, the distance traveled by a moving object that doesn't change direction, and the average value of a nonnegative function over an interval can all be approximated by finite sums. First we subdivide the interval into subintervals, treating the appropriate function f as if it were constant over each particular subinterval. Then we multiply the width of each subinterval by the value of f at some point within it, and add these products together. If the interval $[a, b]$ is subdivided into n subintervals of equal widths $\Delta x = (b - a)/n$, and if $f(c_k)$ is the value of f at the chosen point c_k in the kth subinterval, this process gives a finite sum of the form

$$f(c_1)\,\Delta x + f(c_2)\,\Delta x + f(c_3)\,\Delta x + \cdots + f(c_n)\,\Delta x.$$

The choices for the c_k could maximize or minimize the value of f in the kth subinterval, or give some value in between. The true value lies somewhere between the approximations given by upper sums and lower sums. The finite sum approximations we looked at improved as we took more subintervals of thinner width.

Exercises 5.1

Area

In Exercises 1–4, use finite approximations to estimate the area under the graph of the function using

a. a lower sum with two rectangles of equal width.

b. a lower sum with four rectangles of equal width.

c. an upper sum with two rectangles of equal width.

d. an upper sum with four rectangles of equal width.

1. $f(x) = x^2$ between $x = 0$ and $x = 1$.

2. $f(x) = x^3$ between $x = 0$ and $x = 1$.

3. $f(x) = 1/x$ between $x = 1$ and $x = 5$.

4. $f(x) = 4 - x^2$ between $x = -2$ and $x = 2$.

Using rectangles whose height is given by the value of the function at the midpoint of the rectangle's base (*the midpoint rule*), estimate the area under the graphs of the following functions, using first two and then four rectangles.

5. $f(x) = x^2$ between $x = 0$ and $x = 1$.

6. $f(x) = x^3$ between $x = 0$ and $x = 1$.

7. $f(x) = 1/x$ between $x = 1$ and $x = 5$.

8. $f(x) = 4 - x^2$ between $x = -2$ and $x = 2$.

Distance

9. **Distance traveled** The accompanying table shows the velocity of a model train engine moving along a track for 10 sec. Estimate the distance traveled by the engine using 10 subintervals of length 1 with

a. left-endpoint values.

b. right-endpoint values.

Time (sec)	Velocity (in./sec)	Time (sec)	Velocity (in./sec)
0	0	6	11
1	12	7	6
2	22	8	2
3	10	9	6
4	5	10	0
5	13		

10. **Distance traveled upstream** You are sitting on the bank of a tidal river watching the incoming tide carry a bottle upstream. You record the velocity of the flow every 5 minutes for an hour, with the results shown in the accompanying table. About how far upstream did the bottle travel during that hour? Find an estimate using 12 subintervals of length 5 with

a. left-endpoint values.

b. right-endpoint values.

Time (min)	Velocity (m/sec)	Time (min)	Velocity (m/sec)
0	1	35	1.2
5	1.2	40	1.0
10	1.7	45	1.8
15	2.0	50	1.5
20	1.8	55	1.2
25	1.6	60	0
30	1.4		

11. **Length of a road** You and a companion are about to drive a twisty stretch of dirt road in a car whose speedometer works but whose odometer (mileage counter) is broken. To find out how long this particular stretch of road is, you record the car's velocity at 10-sec intervals, with the results shown in the accompanying table. Estimate the length of the road using

a. left-endpoint values.

b. right-endpoint values.

Time (sec)	Velocity (converted to ft/sec) (30 mi/h = 44 ft/sec)	Time (sec)	Velocity (converted to ft/sec) (30 mi/h = 44 ft/sec)
0	0	70	15
10	44	80	22
20	15	90	35
30	35	100	44
40	30	110	30
50	44	120	35
60	35		

12. **Distance from velocity data** The accompanying table gives data for the velocity of a vintage sports car accelerating from 0 to 142 mi/h in 36 sec (10 thousandths of an hour).

Time (h)	Velocity (mi/h)	Time (h)	Velocity (mi/h)
0.0	0	0.006	116
0.001	40	0.007	125
0.002	62	0.008	132
0.003	82	0.009	137
0.004	96	0.010	142
0.005	108		

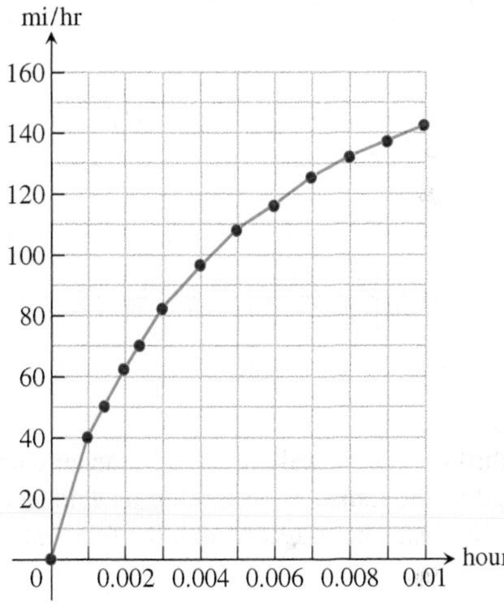

a. Use rectangles to estimate how far the car traveled during the 36 sec it took to reach 142 mi/h.

b. Roughly how many seconds did it take the car to reach the halfway point? About how fast was the car going then?

13. **Free fall with air resistance** An object is dropped straight down from a helicopter. The object falls faster and faster but its acceleration (rate of change of its velocity) decreases over time because of air resistance. The acceleration is measured in ft/sec^2 and recorded every second after the drop for 5 sec, as shown:

t	0	1	2	3	4	5
a	32.00	19.41	11.77	7.14	4.33	2.63

a. Find an upper estimate for the speed when $t = 5$.

b. Find a lower estimate for the speed when $t = 5$.

c. Find an upper estimate for the distance fallen when $t = 3$.

14. **Distance traveled by a projectile** An object is shot straight upward from sea level with an initial velocity of 400 ft/sec.

a. Assuming that gravity is the only force acting on the object, give an upper estimate for its velocity after 5 sec have elapsed. Use $g = 32$ ft/sec^2 for the gravitational acceleration.

b. Find a lower estimate for the height attained after 5 sec.

Average Value of a Function

In Exercises 15–18, use a finite sum to estimate the average value of f on the given interval by partitioning the interval into four subintervals of equal length and evaluating f at the subinterval midpoints.

15. $f(x) = x^3$ on $[0, 2]$ **16.** $f(x) = 1/x$ on $[1, 9]$

17. $f(t) = (1/2) + \sin^2 \pi t$ on $[0, 2]$

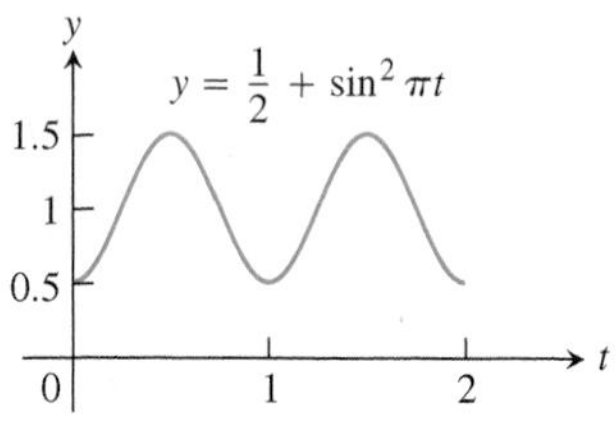

18. $f(t) = 1 - \left(\cos \frac{\pi t}{4}\right)^4$ on $[0, 4]$

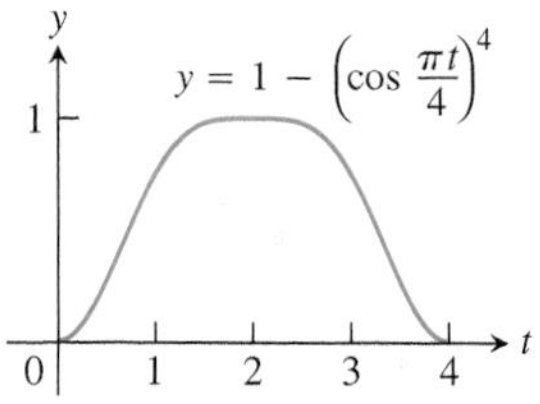

Examples of Estimations

19. Water pollution Oil is leaking out of a tanker damaged at sea. The damage to the tanker is worsening as evidenced by the increased leakage each hour, recorded in the following table.

Time (h)	0	1	2	3	4
Leakage (gal/h)	50	70	97	136	190

Time (h)	5	6	7	8
Leakage (gal/h)	265	369	516	720

a. Give an upper and a lower estimate of the total quantity of oil that has escaped after 5 hours.

b. Repeat part (a) for the quantity of oil that has escaped after 8 hours.

c. The tanker continues to leak 720 gal/h after the first 8 hours. If the tanker originally contained 25,000 gal of oil, approximately how many more hours will elapse in the worst case before all the oil has spilled? In the best case?

20. Air pollution A power plant generates electricity by burning oil. Pollutants produced as a result of the burning process are removed by scrubbers in the smokestacks. Over time, the scrubbers become less efficient and eventually they must be replaced when the amount of pollution released exceeds government standards. Measurements are taken at the end of each month determining the rate at which pollutants are released into the atmosphere, recorded as follows.

Month	Jan	Feb	Mar	Apr	May	Jun
Pollutant release rate (tons/day)	0.20	0.25	0.27	0.34	0.45	0.52

Month	Jul	Aug	Sep	Oct	Nov	Dec
Pollutant release rate (tons/day)	0.63	0.70	0.81	0.85	0.89	0.95

a. Assuming a 30-day month and that new scrubbers allow only 0.05 ton/day to be released, give an upper estimate of the total tonnage of pollutants released by the end of June. What is a lower estimate?

b. In the best case, approximately when will a total of 125 tons of pollutants have been released into the atmosphere?

21. Inscribe a regular n-sided polygon inside a circle of radius 1 and compute the area of the polygon for the following values of n:

a. 4 (square) **b.** 8 (octagon) **c.** 16

d. Compare the areas in parts (a), (b), and (c) with the area of the circle.

22. (*Continuation of Exercise 21.*)

a. Inscribe a regular n-sided polygon inside a circle of radius 1 and compute the area of one of the n congruent triangles formed by drawing radii to the vertices of the polygon.

b. Compute the limit of the area of the inscribed polygon as $n \to \infty$.

c. Repeat the computations in parts (a) and (b) for a circle of radius r.

COMPUTER EXPLORATIONS

In Exercises 23–26, use a CAS to perform the following steps.

a. Plot the functions over the given interval.

b. Subdivide the interval into $n = 100, 200$, and 1000 subintervals of equal length and evaluate the function at the midpoint of each subinterval.

c. Compute the average value of the function values generated in part (b).

d. Solve the equation $f(x) =$ (average value) for x using the average value calculated in part (c) for the $n = 1000$ partitioning.

23. $f(x) = \sin x$ on $[0, \pi]$ **24.** $f(x) = \sin^2 x$ on $[0, \pi]$

25. $f(x) = x \sin \frac{1}{x}$ on $\left[\frac{\pi}{4}, \pi\right]$ **26.** $f(x) = x \sin^2 \frac{1}{x}$ on $\left[\frac{\pi}{4}, \pi\right]$

5.2 Sigma Notation and Limits of Finite Sums

In estimating with finite sums in Section 5.1, we encountered sums with many terms (up to 1000 in Table 5.1, for instance). In this section we introduce a more convenient notation for sums with a large number of terms. After describing the notation and stating several of its properties, we look at what happens to a finite sum approximation as the number of terms approaches infinity.

Finite Sums and Sigma Notation

Sigma notation enables us to write a sum with many terms in the compact form

$$\sum_{k=1}^{n} a_k = a_1 + a_2 + a_3 + \cdots + a_{n-1} + a_n.$$

The Greek letter Σ (capital sigma, corresponding to our letter S), stands for "sum." The **index of summation** k tells us where the sum begins (at the number below the Σ symbol) and where it ends (at the number above Σ). Any letter can be used to denote the index, but the letters i, j, and k are customary.

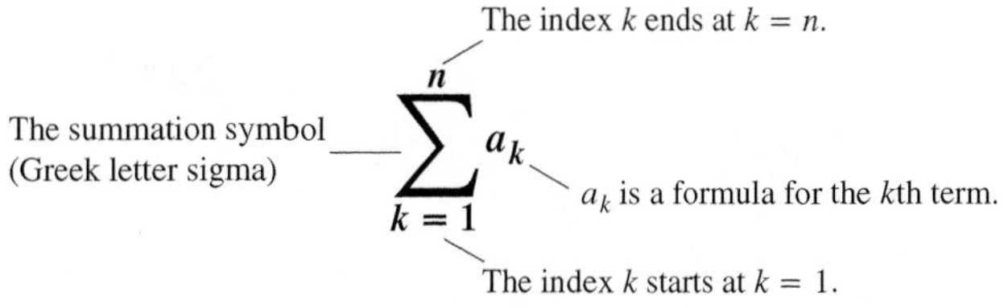
The index k ends at k = n.
The summation symbol (Greek letter sigma)
a_k is a formula for the kth term.
The index k starts at k = 1.

Thus we can write

$$1^2 + 2^2 + 3^2 + 4^2 + 5^2 + 6^2 + 7^2 + 8^2 + 9^2 + 10^2 + 11^2 = \sum_{k=1}^{11} k^2,$$

and

$$f(1) + f(2) + f(3) + \cdots + f(100) = \sum_{i=1}^{100} f(i).$$

The lower limit of summation does not have to be 1; it can be any integer.

EXAMPLE 1

A sum in sigma notation	The sum written out, one term for each value of k	The value of the sum
$\sum_{k=1}^{5} k$	$1 + 2 + 3 + 4 + 5$	15
$\sum_{k=1}^{3} (-1)^k k$	$(-1)^1(1) + (-1)^2(2) + (-1)^3(3)$	$-1 + 2 - 3 = -2$
$\sum_{k=1}^{2} \frac{k}{k+1}$	$\frac{1}{1+1} + \frac{2}{2+1}$	$\frac{1}{2} + \frac{2}{3} = \frac{7}{6}$
$\sum_{k=4}^{5} \frac{k^2}{k-1}$	$\frac{4^2}{4-1} + \frac{5^2}{5-1}$	$\frac{16}{3} + \frac{25}{4} = \frac{139}{12}$

■

EXAMPLE 2 Express the sum $1 + 3 + 5 + 7 + 9$ in sigma notation.

Solution The formula generating the terms changes with the lower limit of summation, but the terms generated remain the same. It is often simplest to start with $k = 0$ or $k = 1$, but we can start with any integer.

Starting with $k = 0$: $$1 + 3 + 5 + 7 + 9 = \sum_{k=0}^{4}(2k + 1)$$

Starting with $k = 1$: $$1 + 3 + 5 + 7 + 9 = \sum_{k=1}^{5}(2k - 1)$$

Starting with $k = 2$: $$1 + 3 + 5 + 7 + 9 = \sum_{k=2}^{6}(2k - 3)$$

Starting with $k = -3$: $$1 + 3 + 5 + 7 + 9 = \sum_{k=-3}^{1}(2k + 7)$$ ■

When we have a sum such as

$$\sum_{k=1}^{3}(k + k^2)$$

we can rearrange its terms,

$$\begin{aligned}\sum_{k=1}^{3}(k + k^2) &= (1 + 1^2) + (2 + 2^2) + (3 + 3^2)\\ &= (1 + 2 + 3) + (1^2 + 2^2 + 3^2) \qquad \text{Regroup terms.}\\ &= \sum_{k=1}^{3} k + \sum_{k=1}^{3} k^2.\end{aligned}$$

This illustrates a general rule for finite sums:

$$\sum_{k=1}^{n}(a_k + b_k) = \sum_{k=1}^{n} a_k + \sum_{k=1}^{n} b_k.$$

Four such rules are given below. A proof that they are valid can be obtained using mathematical induction (see Appendix 2).

Algebra Rules for Finite Sums

1. *Sum Rule:* $$\sum_{k=1}^{n}(a_k + b_k) = \sum_{k=1}^{n} a_k + \sum_{k=1}^{n} b_k$$
2. *Difference Rule:* $$\sum_{k=1}^{n}(a_k - b_k) = \sum_{k=1}^{n} a_k - \sum_{k=1}^{n} b_k$$
3. *Constant Multiple Rule:* $$\sum_{k=1}^{n} ca_k = c \cdot \sum_{k=1}^{n} a_k$$ (Any number c)
4. *Constant Value Rule:* $$\sum_{k=1}^{n} c = n \cdot c$$ (c is any constant value.)

EXAMPLE 3 We demonstrate the use of the algebra rules.

(a) $$\sum_{k=1}^{n}(3k - k^2) = 3\sum_{k=1}^{n} k - \sum_{k=1}^{n} k^2$$ Difference Rule and Constant Multiple Rule

(b) $$\sum_{k=1}^{n}(-a_k) = \sum_{k=1}^{n}(-1) \cdot a_k = -1 \cdot \sum_{k=1}^{n} a_k = -\sum_{k=1}^{n} a_k$$ Constant Multiple Rule

(c) $\sum_{k=1}^{3}(k+4) = \sum_{k=1}^{3}k + \sum_{k=1}^{3}4$ — Sum Rule

$= (1+2+3) + (3 \cdot 4)$ — Constant Value Rule

$= 6 + 12 = 18$

(d) $\sum_{k=1}^{n}\frac{1}{n} = n \cdot \frac{1}{n} = 1$ — Constant Value Rule ($1/n$ is constant) ■

HISTORICAL BIOGRAPHY

Carl Friedrich Gauss (1777–1855)

Over the years people have discovered a variety of formulas for the values of finite sums. The most famous of these are the formula for the sum of the first n integers (Gauss is said to have discovered it at age 8) and the formulas for the sums of the squares and cubes of the first n integers.

EXAMPLE 4 Show that the sum of the first n integers is

$$\sum_{k=1}^{n} k = \frac{n(n+1)}{2}.$$

Solution The formula tells us that the sum of the first 4 integers is

$$\frac{(4)(5)}{2} = 10.$$

Addition verifies this prediction:

$$1 + 2 + 3 + 4 = 10.$$

To prove the formula in general, we write out the terms in the sum twice, once forward and once backward.

$$\begin{array}{ccccccccc} 1 & + & 2 & + & 3 & + & \cdots & + & n \\ n & + & (n-1) & + & (n-2) & + & \cdots & + & 1 \end{array}$$

If we add the two terms in the first column we get $1 + n = n + 1$. Similarly, if we add the two terms in the second column we get $2 + (n-1) = n + 1$. The two terms in any column sum to $n + 1$. When we add the n columns together we get n terms, each equal to $n + 1$, for a total of $n(n+1)$. Since this is twice the desired quantity, the sum of the first n integers is $(n)(n+1)/2$. ■

Formulas for the sums of the squares and cubes of the first n integers are proved using mathematical induction (see Appendix 2). We state them here.

The first n squares: $\sum_{k=1}^{n} k^2 = \frac{n(n+1)(2n+1)}{6}$

The first n cubes: $\sum_{k=1}^{n} k^3 = \left(\frac{n(n+1)}{2}\right)^2$

Limits of Finite Sums

The finite sum approximations we considered in Section 5.1 became more accurate as the number of terms increased and the subinterval widths (lengths) narrowed. The next example shows how to calculate a limiting value as the widths of the subintervals go to zero and their number grows to infinity.

EXAMPLE 5 Find the limiting value of lower sum approximations to the area of the region R below the graph of $y = 1 - x^2$ and above the interval $[0, 1]$ on the x-axis using equal-width rectangles whose widths approach zero and whose number approaches infinity. (See Figure 5.4a.)

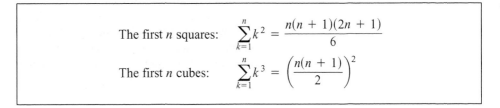

Solution We compute a lower sum approximation using n rectangles of equal width $\Delta x = (1 - 0)/n$, and then we see what happens as $n \to \infty$. We start by subdividing $[0, 1]$ into n equal width subintervals

$$\left[0, \frac{1}{n}\right], \left[\frac{1}{n}, \frac{2}{n}\right], \ldots, \left[\frac{n-1}{n}, \frac{n}{n}\right].$$

Each subinterval has width $1/n$. The function $1 - x^2$ is decreasing on $[0, 1]$, and its smallest value in a subinterval occurs at the subinterval's right endpoint. So a lower sum is constructed with rectangles whose height over the subinterval $[(k-1)/n, k/n]$ is $f(k/n) = 1 - (k/n)^2$, giving the sum

$$\left[f\left(\frac{1}{n}\right)\right]\left(\frac{1}{n}\right) + \left[f\left(\frac{2}{n}\right)\right]\left(\frac{1}{n}\right) + \cdots + \left[f\left(\frac{k}{n}\right)\right]\left(\frac{1}{n}\right) + \cdots + \left[f\left(\frac{n}{n}\right)\right]\left(\frac{1}{n}\right).$$

We write this in sigma notation and simplify,

$$\begin{aligned}
\sum_{k=1}^{n} f\left(\frac{k}{n}\right)\left(\frac{1}{n}\right) &= \sum_{k=1}^{n}\left(1 - \left(\frac{k}{n}\right)^2\right)\left(\frac{1}{n}\right) \\
&= \sum_{k=1}^{n}\left(\frac{1}{n} - \frac{k^2}{n^3}\right) \\
&= \sum_{k=1}^{n}\frac{1}{n} - \sum_{k=1}^{n}\frac{k^2}{n^3} && \text{Difference Rule} \\
&= n \cdot \frac{1}{n} - \frac{1}{n^3}\sum_{k=1}^{n} k^2 && \text{Constant Value and Constant Multiple Rules} \\
&= 1 - \left(\frac{1}{n^3}\right)\frac{(n)(n+1)(2n+1)}{6} && \text{Sum of the First } n \text{ Squares} \\
&= 1 - \frac{2n^3 + 3n^2 + n}{6n^3}. && \text{Numerator expanded}
\end{aligned}$$

We have obtained an expression for the lower sum that holds for any n. Taking the limit of this expression as $n \to \infty$, we see that the lower sums converge as the number of subintervals increases and the subinterval widths approach zero:

$$\lim_{n\to\infty}\left(1 - \frac{2n^3 + 3n^2 + n}{6n^3}\right) = 1 - \frac{2}{6} = \frac{2}{3}.$$

The lower sum approximations converge to $2/3$. A similar calculation shows that the upper sum approximations also converge to $2/3$. Any finite sum approximation $\sum_{k=1}^{n} f(c_k)(1/n)$ also converges to the same value, $2/3$. This is because it is possible to show that any finite sum approximation is trapped between the lower and upper sum approximations. For this reason we are led to *define* the area of the region R as this limiting value. In Section 5.3 we study the limits of such finite approximations in a general setting. ■

Riemann Sums

HISTORICAL BIOGRAPHY

Georg Friedrich Bernhard Riemann (1826–1866)

The theory of limits of finite approximations was made precise by the German mathematician Bernhard Riemann. We now introduce the notion of a *Riemann sum*, which underlies the theory of the definite integral studied in the next section.

We begin with an arbitrary bounded function f defined on a closed interval $[a, b]$. Like the function pictured in Figure 5.8, f may have negative as well as positive values. We subdivide the interval $[a, b]$ into subintervals, not necessarily of equal widths (or lengths), and form sums in the same way as for the finite approximations in Section 5.1. To do so, we choose $n - 1$ points $\{x_1, x_2, x_3, \ldots, x_{n-1}\}$ between a and b and satisfying

$$a < x_1 < x_2 < \cdots < x_{n-1} < b.$$

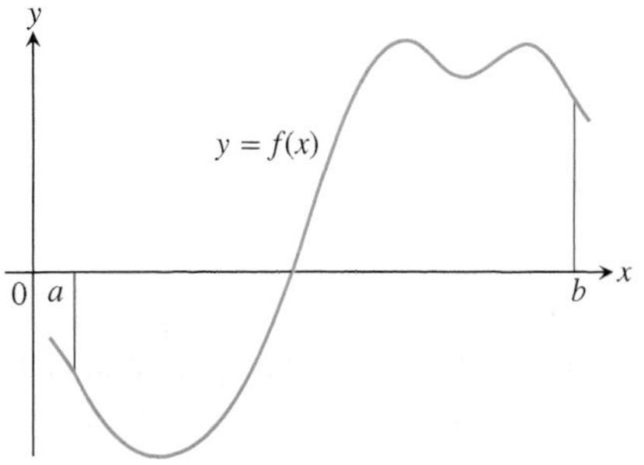

FIGURE 5.8 A typical continuous function $y = f(x)$ over a closed interval $[a, b]$.

To make the notation consistent, we denote a by x_0 and b by x_n, so that

$$a = x_0 < x_1 < x_2 < \cdots < x_{n-1} < x_n = b.$$

The set

$$P = \{x_0, x_1, x_2, \ldots, x_{n-1}, x_n\}$$

is called a **partition** of $[a, b]$.

The partition P divides $[a, b]$ into n closed subintervals

$$[x_0, x_1], [x_1, x_2], \ldots, [x_{n-1}, x_n].$$

The first of these subintervals is $[x_0, x_1]$, the second is $[x_1, x_2]$, and the ***k*th subinterval of** P is $[x_{k-1}, x_k]$, for k an integer between 1 and n.

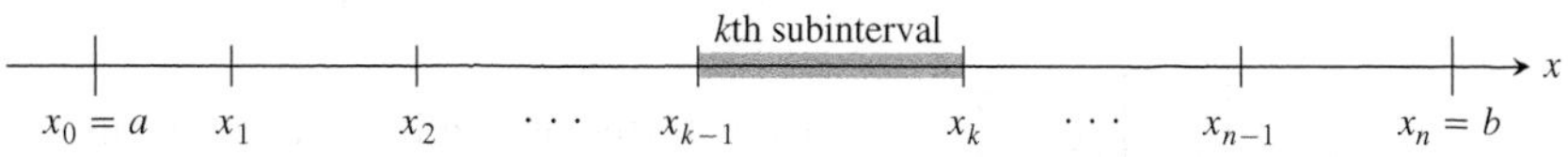

The width of the first subinterval $[x_0, x_1]$ is denoted Δx_1, the width of the second $[x_1, x_2]$ is denoted Δx_2, and the width of the kth subinterval is $\Delta x_k = x_k - x_{k-1}$. If all n subintervals have equal width, then the common width Δx is equal to $(b - a)/n$.

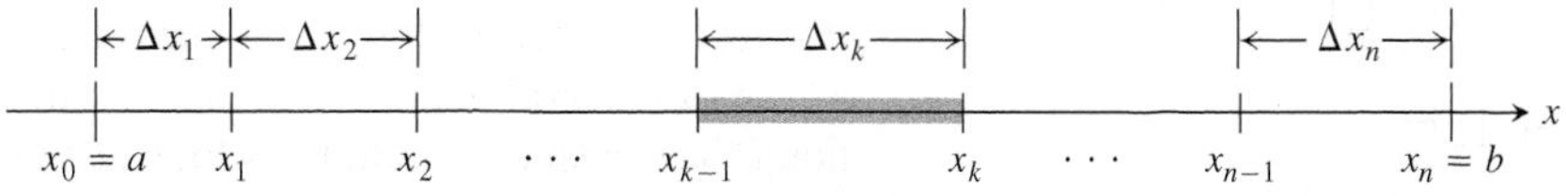

In each subinterval we select some point. The point chosen in the kth subinterval $[x_{k-1}, x_k]$ is called c_k. Then on each subinterval we stand a vertical rectangle that stretches from the x-axis to touch the curve at $(c_k, f(c_k))$. These rectangles can be above or below the x-axis, depending on whether $f(c_k)$ is positive or negative, or on the x-axis if $f(c_k) = 0$ (Figure 5.9).

On each subinterval we form the product $f(c_k) \cdot \Delta x_k$. This product is positive, negative, or zero, depending on the sign of $f(c_k)$. When $f(c_k) > 0$, the product $f(c_k) \cdot \Delta x_k$ is the area of a rectangle with height $f(c_k)$ and width Δx_k. When $f(c_k) < 0$, the product $f(c_k) \cdot \Delta x_k$ is a negative number, the negative of the area of a rectangle of width Δx_k that drops from the x-axis to the negative number $f(c_k)$.

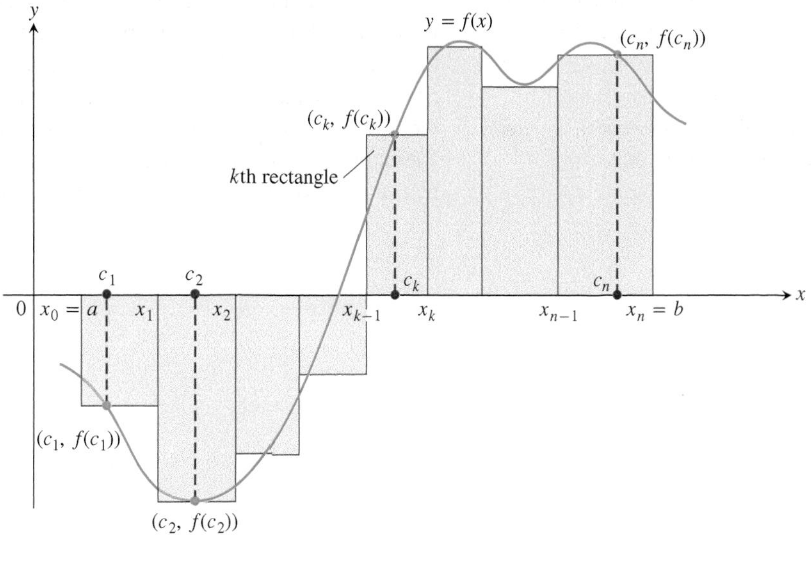

FIGURE 5.9 The rectangles approximate the region between the graph of the function $y = f(x)$ and the x-axis. Figure 5.8 has been enlarged to enhance the partition of $[a, b]$ and selection of points c_k that produce the rectangles.

Finally we sum all these products to get

$$S_P = \sum_{k=1}^{n} f(c_k)\,\Delta x_k .$$

The sum S_P is called a **Riemann sum for f on the interval $[a, b]$**. There are many such sums, depending on the partition P we choose, and the choices of the points c_k in the subintervals. For instance, we could choose n subintervals all having equal width $\Delta x = (b - a)/n$ to partition $[a, b]$, and then choose the point c_k to be the right-hand endpoint of each subinterval when forming the Riemann sum (as we did in Example 5). This choice leads to the Riemann sum formula

$$S_n = \sum_{k=1}^{n} f\left(a + k\frac{b-a}{n}\right)\cdot\left(\frac{b-a}{n}\right).$$

Similar formulas can be obtained if instead we choose c_k to be the left-hand endpoint, or the midpoint, of each subinterval.

In the cases in which the subintervals all have equal width $\Delta x = (b - a)/n$, we can make them thinner by simply increasing their number n. When a partition has subintervals of varying widths, we can ensure they are all thin by controlling the width of a widest (longest) subinterval. We define the **norm** of a partition P, written $\|P\|$, to be the largest of all the subinterval widths. If $\|P\|$ is a small number, then all of the subintervals in the partition P have a small width. Let's look at an example of these ideas.

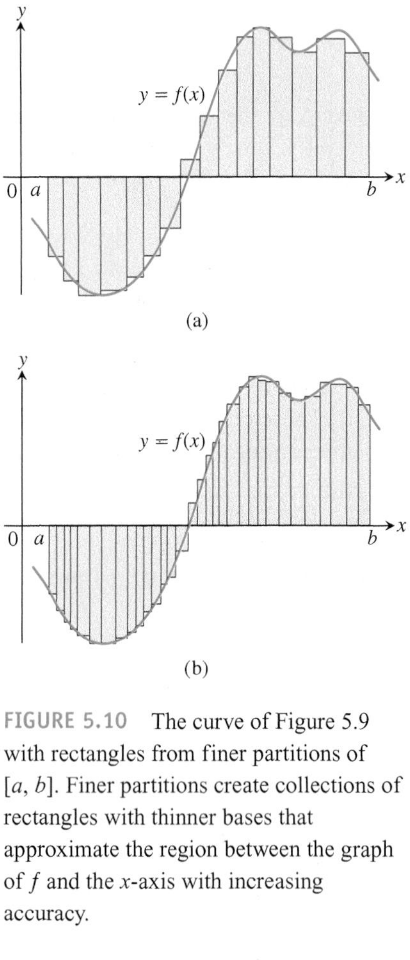

FIGURE 5.10 The curve of Figure 5.9 with rectangles from finer partitions of $[a, b]$. Finer partitions create collections of rectangles with thinner bases that approximate the region between the graph of f and the x-axis with increasing accuracy.

EXAMPLE 6 The set $P = \{0, 0.2, 0.6, 1, 1.5, 2\}$ is a partition of $[0, 2]$. There are five subintervals of P: $[0, 0.2]$, $[0.2, 0.6]$, $[0.6, 1]$, $[1, 1.5]$, and $[1.5, 2]$:

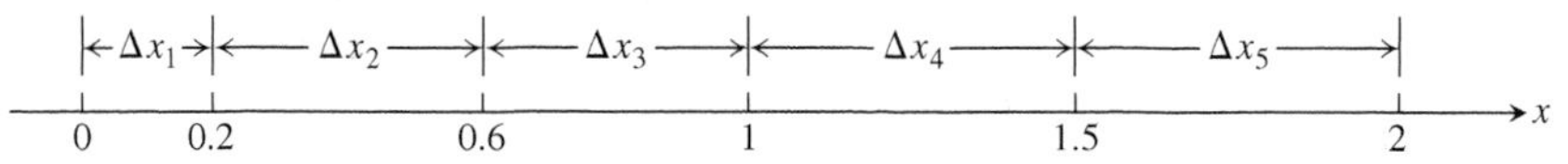

The lengths of the subintervals are $\Delta x_1 = 0.2$, $\Delta x_2 = 0.4$, $\Delta x_3 = 0.4$, $\Delta x_4 = 0.5$, and $\Delta x_5 = 0.5$. The longest subinterval length is 0.5, so the norm of the partition is $\|P\| = 0.5$. In this example, there are two subintervals of this length. ■

Any Riemann sum associated with a partition of a closed interval $[a, b]$ defines rectangles that approximate the region between the graph of a continuous function f and the x-axis. Partitions with norm approaching zero lead to collections of rectangles that approximate this region with increasing accuracy, as suggested by Figure 5.10. We will see in the next section that if the function f is continuous over the closed interval $[a, b]$, then no matter how we choose the partition P and the points c_k in its subintervals to construct a Riemann sum, a single limiting value is approached as the subinterval widths, controlled by the norm of the partition, approach zero.

Exercises 5.2

Sigma Notation

Write the sums in Exercises 1–6 without sigma notation. Then evaluate them.

1. $\displaystyle\sum_{k=1}^{2} \frac{6k}{k+1}$

2. $\displaystyle\sum_{k=1}^{3} \frac{k-1}{k}$

3. $\displaystyle\sum_{k=1}^{4} \cos k\pi$

4. $\displaystyle\sum_{k=1}^{5} \sin k\pi$

5. $\displaystyle\sum_{k=1}^{3} (-1)^{k+1} \sin\frac{\pi}{k}$

6. $\displaystyle\sum_{k=1}^{4} (-1)^{k} \cos k\pi$

7. Which of the following express $1 + 2 + 4 + 8 + 16 + 32$ in sigma notation?

   a. $\displaystyle\sum_{k=1}^{6} 2^{k-1}$ b. $\displaystyle\sum_{k=0}^{5} 2^{k}$ c. $\displaystyle\sum_{k=-1}^{4} 2^{k+1}$

8. Which of the following express $1 - 2 + 4 - 8 + 16 - 32$ in sigma notation?

   a. $\displaystyle\sum_{k=1}^{6} (-2)^{k-1}$ b. $\displaystyle\sum_{k=0}^{5} (-1)^{k} 2^{k}$ c. $\displaystyle\sum_{k=-2}^{3} (-1)^{k+1} 2^{k+2}$

9. Which formula is not equivalent to the other two?

a. $\sum_{k=2}^{4} \frac{(-1)^{k-1}}{k-1}$ **b.** $\sum_{k=0}^{2} \frac{(-1)^k}{k+1}$ **c.** $\sum_{k=-1}^{1} \frac{(-1)^k}{k+2}$

10. Which formula is not equivalent to the other two?

a. $\sum_{k=1}^{4} (k-1)^2$ **b.** $\sum_{k=-1}^{3} (k+1)^2$ **c.** $\sum_{k=-3}^{-1} k^2$

Express the sums in Exercises 11–16 in sigma notation. The form of your answer will depend on your choice of the lower limit of summation.

11. $1 + 2 + 3 + 4 + 5 + 6$ **12.** $1 + 4 + 9 + 16$

13. $\frac{1}{2} + \frac{1}{4} + \frac{1}{8} + \frac{1}{16}$ **14.** $2 + 4 + 6 + 8 + 10$

15. $1 - \frac{1}{2} + \frac{1}{3} - \frac{1}{4} + \frac{1}{5}$ **16.** $-\frac{1}{5} + \frac{2}{5} - \frac{3}{5} + \frac{4}{5} - \frac{5}{5}$

Values of Finite Sums

17. Suppose that $\sum_{k=1}^{n} a_k = -5$ and $\sum_{k=1}^{n} b_k = 6$. Find the values of

a. $\sum_{k=1}^{n} 3a_k$ **b.** $\sum_{k=1}^{n} \frac{b_k}{6}$ **c.** $\sum_{k=1}^{n} (a_k + b_k)$

d. $\sum_{k=1}^{n} (a_k - b_k)$ **e.** $\sum_{k=1}^{n} (b_k - 2a_k)$

18. Suppose that $\sum_{k=1}^{n} a_k = 0$ and $\sum_{k=1}^{n} b_k = 1$. Find the values of

a. $\sum_{k=1}^{n} 8a_k$ **b.** $\sum_{k=1}^{n} 250b_k$

c. $\sum_{k=1}^{n} (a_k + 1)$ **d.** $\sum_{k=1}^{n} (b_k - 1)$

Evaluate the sums in Exercises 19–32.

19. a. $\sum_{k=1}^{10} k$ **b.** $\sum_{k=1}^{10} k^2$ **c.** $\sum_{k=1}^{10} k^3$

20. a. $\sum_{k=1}^{13} k$ **b.** $\sum_{k=1}^{13} k^2$ **c.** $\sum_{k=1}^{13} k^3$

21. $\sum_{k=1}^{7} (-2k)$ **22.** $\sum_{k=1}^{5} \frac{\pi k}{15}$

23. $\sum_{k=1}^{6} (3 - k^2)$ **24.** $\sum_{k=1}^{6} (k^2 - 5)$

25. $\sum_{k=1}^{5} k(3k + 5)$ **26.** $\sum_{k=1}^{7} k(2k + 1)$

27. $\sum_{k=1}^{5} \frac{k^3}{225} + \left(\sum_{k=1}^{5} k\right)^3$ **28.** $\left(\sum_{k=1}^{7} k\right)^2 - \sum_{k=1}^{7} \frac{k^3}{4}$

29. a. $\sum_{k=1}^{7} 3$ **b.** $\sum_{k=1}^{500} 7$ **c.** $\sum_{k=3}^{264} 10$

30. a. $\sum_{k=9}^{36} k$ **b.** $\sum_{k=3}^{17} k^2$ **c.** $\sum_{k=18}^{71} k(k-1)$

31. a. $\sum_{k=1}^{n} 4$ **b.** $\sum_{k=1}^{n} c$ **c.** $\sum_{k=1}^{n} (k-1)$

32. a. $\sum_{k=1}^{n} \left(\frac{1}{n} + 2n\right)$ **b.** $\sum_{k=1}^{n} \frac{c}{n}$ **c.** $\sum_{k=1}^{n} \frac{k}{n^2}$

Riemann Sums

In Exercises 33–36, graph each function $f(x)$ over the given interval. Partition the interval into four subintervals of equal length. Then add to your sketch the rectangles associated with the Riemann sum $\Sigma_{k=1}^{4} f(c_k)\,\Delta x_k$, given that c_k is the **(a)** left-hand endpoint, **(b)** right-hand endpoint, **(c)** midpoint of the kth subinterval. (Make a separate sketch for each set of rectangles.)

33. $f(x) = x^2 - 1, \quad [0, 2]$ **34.** $f(x) = -x^2, \quad [0, 1]$

35. $f(x) = \sin x, \quad [-\pi, \pi]$ **36.** $f(x) = \sin x + 1, \quad [-\pi, \pi]$

37. Find the norm of the partition $P = \{0, 1.2, 1.5, 2.3, 2.6, 3\}$.

38. Find the norm of the partition $P = \{-2, -1.6, -0.5, 0, 0.8, 1\}$.

Limits of Riemann Sums

For the functions in Exercises 39–46, find a formula for the Riemann sum obtained by dividing the interval $[a, b]$ into n equal subintervals and using the right-hand endpoint for each c_k. Then take a limit of these sums as $n \to \infty$ to calculate the area under the curve over $[a, b]$.

39. $f(x) = 1 - x^2$ over the interval $[0, 1]$.

40. $f(x) = 2x$ over the interval $[0, 3]$.

41. $f(x) = x^2 + 1$ over the interval $[0, 3]$.

42. $f(x) = 3x^2$ over the interval $[0, 1]$.

43. $f(x) = x + x^2$ over the interval $[0, 1]$.

44. $f(x) = 3x + 2x^2$ over the interval $[0, 1]$.

45. $f(x) = 2x^3$ over the interval $[0, 1]$.

46. $f(x) = x^2 - x^3$ over the interval $[-1, 0]$.

5.3 The Definite Integral

In Section 5.2 we investigated the limit of a finite sum for a function defined over a closed interval $[a, b]$ using n subintervals of equal width (or length), $(b - a)/n$. In this section we consider the limit of more general Riemann sums as the norm of the partitions of $[a, b]$ approaches zero. For general Riemann sums the subintervals of the partitions need not have equal widths. The limiting process then leads to the definition of the *definite integral* of a function over a closed interval $[a, b]$.

Definition of the Definite Integral

The definition of the definite integral is based on the idea that for certain functions, as the norm of the partitions of $[a, b]$ approaches zero, the values of the corresponding Riemann sums approach a limiting value J. What we mean by this limit is that a Riemann sum will be close to the number J provided that the norm of its partition is sufficiently small (so that all of its subintervals have thin enough widths). We introduce the symbol ϵ as a small positive number that specifies how close to J the Riemann sum must be, and the symbol δ as a second small positive number that specifies how small the norm of a partition must be in order for convergence to happen. We now define this limit precisely.

DEFINITION Let $f(x)$ be a function defined on a closed interval $[a, b]$. We say that a number J is the **definite integral of f over $[a, b]$** and that J is the limit of the Riemann sums $\sum_{k=1}^{n} f(c_k)\,\Delta x_k$ if the following condition is satisfied:

Given any number $\epsilon > 0$ there is a corresponding number $\delta > 0$ such that for every partition $P = \{x_0, x_1, \ldots, x_n\}$ of $[a, b]$ with $\|P\| < \delta$ and any choice of c_k in $[x_{k-1}, x_k]$, we have

$$\left| \sum_{k=1}^{n} f(c_k)\,\Delta x_k - J \right| < \epsilon .$$

The definition involves a limiting process in which the norm of the partition goes to zero. In the cases where the subintervals all have equal width $\Delta x = (b - a)/n$, we can form each Riemann sum as

$$S_n = \sum_{k=1}^{n} f(c_k)\,\Delta x_k = \sum_{k=1}^{n} f(c_k)\left(\frac{b-a}{n}\right), \qquad \Delta x_k = \Delta x = (b-a)/n \text{ for all } k$$

where c_k is chosen in the subinterval Δx_k. If the limit of these Riemann sums as $n \to \infty$ exists and is equal to J, then J is the definite integral of f over $[a, b]$, so

$$J = \lim_{n\to\infty} \sum_{k=1}^{n} f(c_k)\left(\frac{b-a}{n}\right) = \lim_{n\to\infty} \sum_{k=1}^{n} f(c_k)\,\Delta x. \qquad \Delta x = (b-a)/n$$

Leibniz introduced a notation for the definite integral that captures its construction as a limit of Riemann sums. He envisioned the finite sums $\sum_{k=1}^{n} f(c_k)\,\Delta x_k$ becoming an infinite sum of function values $f(x)$ multiplied by "infinitesimal" subinterval widths dx. The sum symbol $\sum$ is replaced in the limit by the integral symbol $\int$, whose origin is in the letter "S." The function values $f(c_k)$ are replaced by a continuous selection of function values $f(x)$. The subinterval widths Δx_k become the differential dx. It is as if we are summing all products of the form $f(x) \cdot dx$ as x goes from a to b. While this notation captures the process of constructing an integral, it is Riemann's definition that gives a precise meaning to the definite integral.

The symbol for the number J in the definition of the definite integral is

$$\int_a^b f(x)\,dx,$$

which is read as "the integral from a to b of f of x dee x" or sometimes as "the integral from a to b of f of x with respect to x." The component parts in the integral symbol also have names:

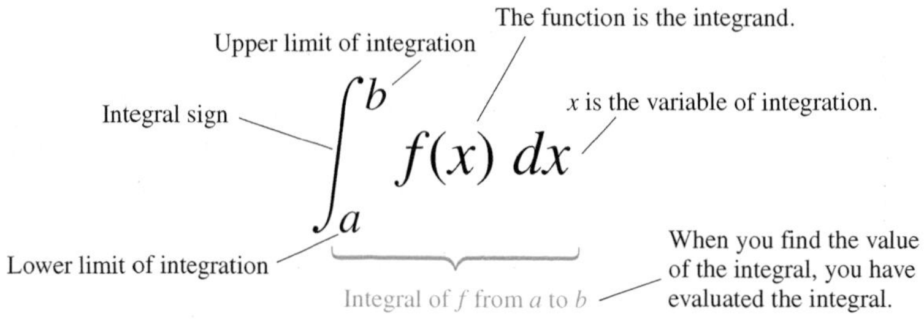

When the condition in the definition is satisfied, we say that the Riemann sums of f on $[a, b]$ **converge** to the definite integral $J = \int_a^b f(x)\,dx$ and that f is **integrable** over $[a, b]$.

We have many choices for a partition P with norm going to zero, and many choices of points c_k for each partition. The definite integral exists when we always get the same limit J, no matter what choices are made. When the limit exists we write it as the definite integral

$$\lim_{\|P\|\to 0} \sum_{k=1}^{n} f(c_k)\,\Delta x_k = J = \int_a^b f(x)\,dx.$$

The limit of any Riemann sum is always taken as the norm of the partitions approaches zero and the number of subintervals goes to infinity.

If we choose the partitions with n equal subintervals of width $\Delta x = (b - a)/n$, and we pick the point c_k at the right endpoint of the kth subinterval, so $c_k = a + k\,\Delta x = a + k(b - a)/n$, then the formula for the definite integral becomes

$$\int_a^b f(x)\,dx = \lim_{n\to\infty} \sum_{k=1}^{n} f\left(a + k\frac{(b-a)}{n}\right)\left(\frac{b-a}{n}\right) \tag{1}$$

Equation (1) gives an explicit formula that can be used to compute definite integrals. Other choices of partitions and locations of points c_k result in the same value for the definite integral when we take the limit as $n \to \infty$ provided that the norm of the partition approaches zero.

The value of the definite integral of a function over any particular interval depends on the function, not on the letter we choose to represent its independent variable. If we decide to use t or u instead of x, we simply write the integral as

$$\int_a^b f(t)\,dt \qquad \text{or} \qquad \int_a^b f(u)\,du \qquad \text{instead of} \qquad \int_a^b f(x)\,dx.$$

No matter how we write the integral, it is still the same number that is defined as a limit of Riemann sums. Since it does not matter what letter we use, the variable of integration is called a dummy variable.

Integrable and Nonintegrable Functions

Not every function defined over the closed interval $[a, b]$ is integrable there, even if the function is bounded. That is, the Riemann sums for some functions may not converge to the same limiting value, or to any value at all. A full development of exactly which functions defined over $[a, b]$ are integrable requires advanced mathematical analysis, but fortunately most functions that commonly occur in applications are integrable. In particular, every *continuous* function over $[a, b]$ is integrable over this interval, and so is every function having no more than a finite number of jump discontinuities on $[a, b]$. (See Figures 1.9 and 1.10. The latter functions are called *piecewise-continuous functions,* and they are defined in Additional Exercises 11–18 at the end of this chapter.) The following theorem, which is proved in more advanced courses, establishes these results.

THEOREM 1—Integrability of Continuous Functions If a function f is continuous over the interval $[a, b]$, or if f has at most finitely many jump discontinuities there, then the definite integral $\int_a^b f(x)\,dx$ exists and f is integrable over $[a, b]$.

The idea behind Theorem 1 for continuous functions is given in Exercises 86 and 87. Briefly, when f is continuous we can choose each c_k so that $f(c_k)$ gives the maximum value of f on the subinterval $[x_{k-1}, x_k]$, resulting in an upper sum. Likewise, we can choose c_k to give the minimum value of f on $[x_{k-1}, x_k]$ to obtain a lower sum. The upper and lower sums can be shown to converge to the same limiting value as the norm of the partition P tends to zero. Moreover, every Riemann sum is trapped between the values of the upper and lower sums, so every Riemann sum converges to the same limit as well. Therefore, the number J in the definition of the definite integral exists, and the continuous function f is integrable over $[a, b]$.

For integrability to fail, a function needs to be sufficiently discontinuous that the region between its graph and the x-axis cannot be approximated well by increasingly thin rectangles. The next example shows a function that is not integrable over a closed interval.

EXAMPLE 1 The function

$$f(x) = \begin{cases} 1, & \text{if } x \text{ is rational} \\ 0, & \text{if } x \text{ is irrational} \end{cases}$$

has no Riemann integral over $[0, 1]$. Underlying this is the fact that between any two numbers there is both a rational number and an irrational number. Thus the function jumps up and down too erratically over $[0, 1]$ to allow the region beneath its graph and above the x-axis to be approximated by rectangles, no matter how thin they are. We show, in fact, that upper sum approximations and lower sum approximations converge to different limiting values.

If we pick a partition P of $[0, 1]$ and choose c_k to be the point giving the maximum value for f on $[x_{k-1}, x_k]$ then the corresponding Riemann sum is

$$U = \sum_{k=1}^{n} f(c_k)\,\Delta x_k = \sum_{k=1}^{n} (1)\,\Delta x_k = 1,$$

since each subinterval $[x_{k-1}, x_k]$ contains a rational number where $f(c_k) = 1$. Note that the lengths of the intervals in the partition sum to 1, $\sum_{k=1}^{n} \Delta x_k = 1$. So each such Riemann sum equals 1, and a limit of Riemann sums using these choices equals 1.

On the other hand, if we pick c_k to be the point giving the minimum value for f on $[x_{k-1}, x_k]$, then the Riemann sum is

$$L = \sum_{k=1}^{n} f(c_k)\,\Delta x_k = \sum_{k=1}^{n} (0)\,\Delta x_k = 0,$$

since each subinterval $[x_{k-1}, x_k]$ contains an irrational number c_k where $f(c_k) = 0$. The limit of Riemann sums using these choices equals zero. Since the limit depends on the choices of c_k, the function f is not integrable. ■

Theorem 1 says nothing about how to *calculate* definite integrals. A method of calculation will be developed in Section 5.4, through a connection to the process of taking antiderivatives.

Properties of Definite Integrals

In defining $\int_a^b f(x)\,dx$ as a limit of sums $\sum_{k=1}^{n} f(c_k)\,\Delta x_k$, we moved from left to right across the interval $[a, b]$. What would happen if we instead move right to left, starting with $x_0 = b$ and ending at $x_n = a$? Each Δx_k in the Riemann sum would change its sign, with $x_k - x_{k-1}$ now negative instead of positive. With the same choices of c_k in each subinterval, the sign of any Riemann sum would change, as would the sign of the limit, the integral $\int_b^a f(x)\,dx$. Since we have not previously given a meaning to integrating backward, we are led to define

$$\int_b^a f(x)\,dx = -\int_a^b f(x)\,dx.$$

Although we have only defined the integral over an interval $[a, b]$ when $a < b$, it is convenient to have a definition for the integral over $[a, b]$ when $a = b$, that is, for the integral over an interval of zero width. Since $a = b$ gives $\Delta x = 0$, whenever $f(a)$ exists we define

$$\int_a^a f(x)\,dx = 0.$$

Theorem 2 states basic properties of integrals, given as rules that they satisfy, including the two just discussed. These rules, listed in Table 5.4, become very useful in the process of computing integrals. We will refer to them repeatedly to simplify our calculations. Rules 2 through 7 have geometric interpretations, shown in Figure 5.11. The graphs in these figures are of positive functions, but the rules apply to general integrable functions.

THEOREM 2 When f and g are integrable over the interval $[a, b]$, the definite integral satisfies the rules in Table 5.4.

TABLE 5.4 Rules satisfied by definite integrals

1.	*Order of Integration:*	$\int_b^a f(x)\,dx = -\int_a^b f(x)\,dx$	A definition
2.	*Zero Width Interval:*	$\int_a^a f(x)\,dx = 0$	A definition when $f(a)$ exists
3.	*Constant Multiple:*	$\int_a^b kf(x)\,dx = k\int_a^b f(x)\,dx$	Any constant k
4.	*Sum and Difference:*	$\int_a^b (f(x) \pm g(x))\,dx = \int_a^b f(x)\,dx \pm \int_a^b g(x)\,dx$	
5.	*Additivity:*	$\int_a^b f(x)\,dx + \int_b^c f(x)\,dx = \int_a^c f(x)\,dx$	
6.	*Max-Min Inequality:*	If f has maximum value max f and minimum value min f on $[a, b]$, then $\min f \cdot (b-a) \le \int_a^b f(x)\,dx \le \max f \cdot (b-a).$	
7.	*Domination:*	$f(x) \ge g(x)$ on $[a, b] \Rightarrow \int_a^b f(x)\,dx \ge \int_a^b g(x)\,dx$	
		$f(x) \ge 0$ on $[a, b] \Rightarrow \int_a^b f(x)\,dx \ge 0$	(Special case)

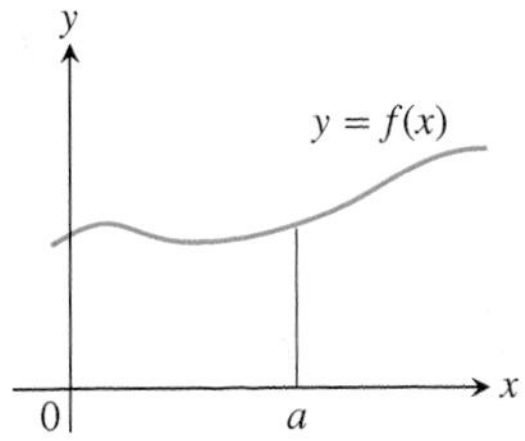

(a) *Zero Width Interval:*

$$\int_a^a f(x)\,dx = 0$$

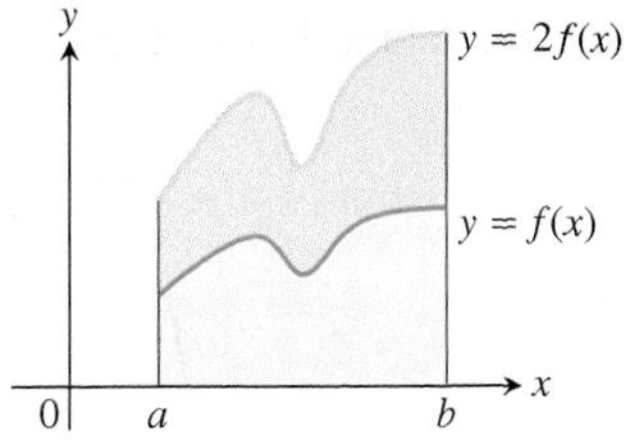

(b) *Constant Multiple:* ($k = 2$)

$$\int_a^b kf(x)\,dx = k\int_a^b f(x)\,dx$$

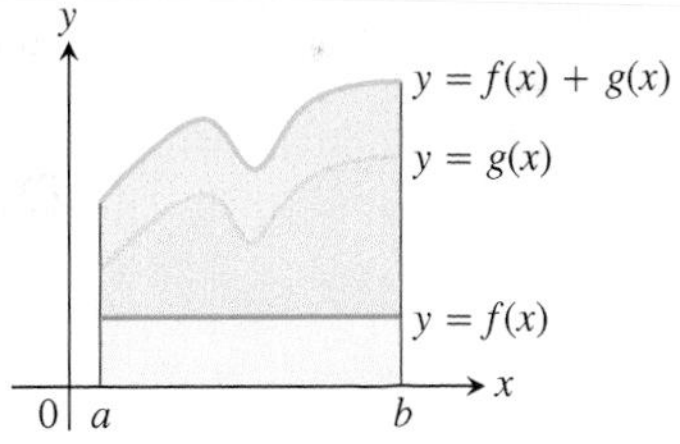

(c) *Sum:* (*areas add*)

$$\int_a^b (f(x) + g(x))\,dx = \int_a^b f(x)\,dx + \int_a^b g(x)\,dx$$

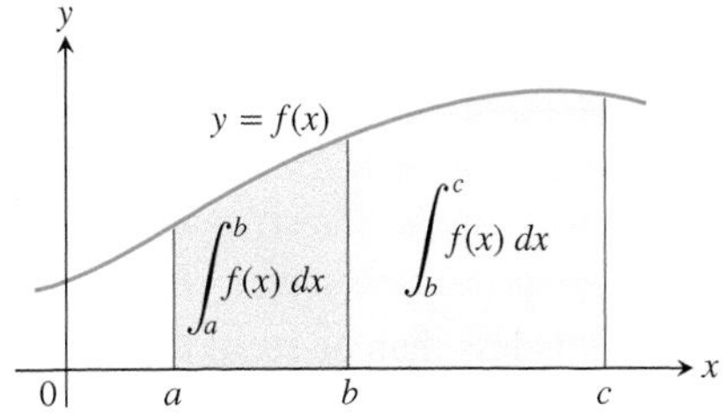

(d) *Additivity for definite integrals:*

$$\int_a^b f(x)\,dx + \int_b^c f(x)\,dx = \int_a^c f(x)\,dx$$

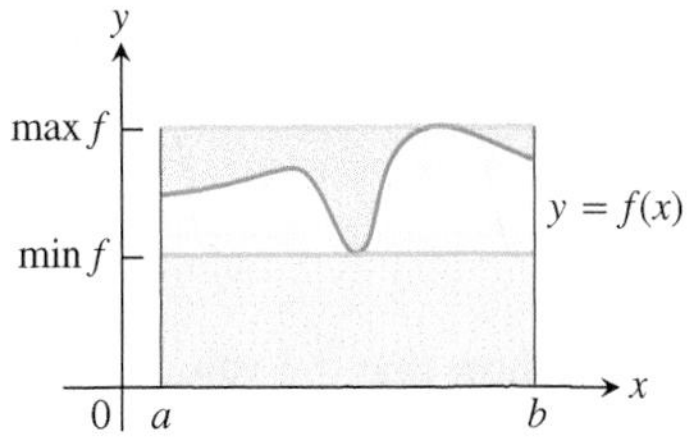

(e) *Max-Min Inequality:*

$$\min f \cdot (b-a) \le \int_a^b f(x)\,dx \le \max f \cdot (b-a)$$

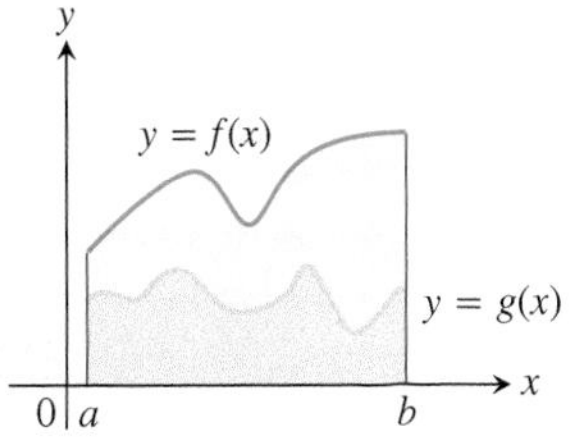

(f) *Domination:*

$$f(x) \ge g(x) \text{ on } [a, b] \Rightarrow \int_a^b f(x)\,dx \ge \int_a^b g(x)\,dx$$

FIGURE 5.11 Geometric interpretations of Rules 2–7 in Table 5.4.

While Rules 1 and 2 are definitions, Rules 3 to 7 of Table 5.4 must be proved. The following is a proof of Rule 6. Similar proofs can be given to verify the other properties in Table 5.4.

Proof of Rule 6 Rule 6 says that the integral of f over $[a, b]$ is never smaller than the minimum value of f times the length of the interval and never larger than the maximum value of f times the length of the interval. The reason is that for every partition of $[a, b]$ and for every choice of the points c_k,

$$
\begin{aligned}
\min f \cdot (b - a) &= \min f \cdot \sum_{k=1}^{n} \Delta x_k && \sum_{k=1}^{n} \Delta x_k = b - a \\
&= \sum_{k=1}^{n} \min f \cdot \Delta x_k && \text{Constant Multiple Rule} \\
&\le \sum_{k=1}^{n} f(c_k)\, \Delta x_k && \min f \le f(c_k) \\
&\le \sum_{k=1}^{n} \max f \cdot \Delta x_k && f(c_k) \le \max f \\
&= \max f \cdot \sum_{k=1}^{n} \Delta x_k && \text{Constant Multiple Rule} \\
&= \max f \cdot (b - a).
\end{aligned}
$$

In short, all Riemann sums for f on $[a, b]$ satisfy the inequality

$$\min f \cdot (b - a) \le \sum_{k=1}^{n} f(c_k)\, \Delta x_k \le \max f \cdot (b - a).$$

Hence their limit, the integral, does too. ■

EXAMPLE 2 To illustrate some of the rules, we suppose that

$$\int_{-1}^{1} f(x)\, dx = 5, \qquad \int_{1}^{4} f(x)\, dx = -2, \quad \text{and} \quad \int_{-1}^{1} h(x)\, dx = 7.$$

Then

1. $\displaystyle \int_{4}^{1} f(x)\, dx = -\int_{1}^{4} f(x)\, dx = -(-2) = 2$ — Rule 1

2. $\displaystyle \int_{-1}^{1} [2f(x) + 3h(x)]\, dx = 2\int_{-1}^{1} f(x)\, dx + 3\int_{-1}^{1} h(x)\, dx = 2(5) + 3(7) = 31$ — Rules 3 and 4

3. $\displaystyle \int_{-1}^{4} f(x)\, dx = \int_{-1}^{1} f(x)\, dx + \int_{1}^{4} f(x)\, dx = 5 + (-2) = 3$ — Rule 5 ■

EXAMPLE 3 Show that the value of $\int_0^1 \sqrt{1 + \cos x}\, dx$ is less than or equal to $\sqrt{2}$.

Solution The Max-Min Inequality for definite integrals (Rule 6) says that $\min f \cdot (b - a)$ is a *lower bound* for the value of $\int_a^b f(x)\, dx$ and that $\max f \cdot (b - a)$ is an *upper bound*. The maximum value of $\sqrt{1 + \cos x}$ on $[0, 1]$ is $\sqrt{1 + 1} = \sqrt{2}$, so

$$\int_0^1 \sqrt{1 + \cos x}\, dx \le \sqrt{2} \cdot (1 - 0) = \sqrt{2}.$$ ■

Area Under the Graph of a Nonnegative Function

We now return to the problem that started this chapter, that of defining what we mean by the *area* of a region having a curved boundary. In Section 5.1 we approximated the area under the graph of a nonnegative continuous function using several types of finite sums of areas of rectangles capturing the region—upper sums, lower sums, and sums using the midpoints of each subinterval—all being cases of Riemann sums constructed in special ways. Theorem 1 guarantees that all of these Riemann sums converge to a single definite integral as the norm of the partitions approaches zero and the number of subintervals goes to infinity. As a result, we can now *define* the area under the graph of a nonnegative integrable function to be the value of that definite integral.

DEFINITION If $y = f(x)$ is nonnegative and integrable over a closed interval $[a, b]$, then the **area under the curve $y = f(x)$ over $[a, b]$** is the integral of f from a to b,

$$A = \int_a^b f(x)\, dx.$$

For the first time we have a rigorous definition for the area of a region whose boundary is the graph of any continuous function. We now apply this to a simple example, the area under a straight line, where we can verify that our new definition agrees with our previous notion of area.

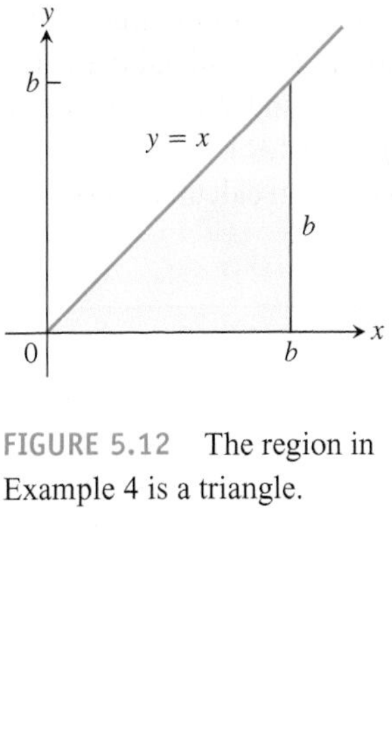

FIGURE 5.12 The region in Example 4 is a triangle.

EXAMPLE 4 Compute $\int_0^b x\, dx$ and find the area A under $y = x$ over the interval $[0, b]$, $b > 0$.

Solution The region of interest is a triangle (Figure 5.12). We compute the area in two ways.

(a) To compute the definite integral as the limit of Riemann sums, we calculate $\lim_{\|P\|\to 0} \sum_{k=1}^{n} f(c_k)\, \Delta x_k$ for partitions whose norms go to zero. Theorem 1 tells us that it does not matter how we choose the partitions or the points c_k as long as the norms approach zero. All choices give the exact same limit. So we consider the partition P that subdivides the interval $[0, b]$ into n subintervals of equal width $\Delta x = (b - 0)/n = b/n$, and we choose c_k to be the right endpoint in each subinterval. The partition is $P = \left\{0, \frac{b}{n}, \frac{2b}{n}, \frac{3b}{n}, \ldots, \frac{nb}{n}\right\}$ and $c_k = \frac{kb}{n}$. So

$$\sum_{k=1}^{n} f(c_k)\, \Delta x = \sum_{k=1}^{n} \frac{kb}{n} \cdot \frac{b}{n} \qquad f(c_k) = c_k$$

$$= \sum_{k=1}^{n} \frac{kb^2}{n^2}$$

$$= \frac{b^2}{n^2} \sum_{k=1}^{n} k \qquad \text{Constant Multiple Rule}$$

$$= \frac{b^2}{n^2} \cdot \frac{n(n+1)}{2} \qquad \text{Sum of First } n \text{ Integers}$$

$$= \frac{b^2}{2}\left(1 + \frac{1}{n}\right).$$

As $n \to \infty$ and $\|P\| \to 0$, this last expression on the right has the limit $b^2/2$. Therefore,

$$\int_0^b x\,dx = \frac{b^2}{2}.$$

(b) Since the area equals the definite integral for a nonnegative function, we can quickly derive the definite integral by using the formula for the area of a triangle having base length b and height $y = b$. The area is $A = (1/2)\,b \cdot b = b^2/2$. Again we conclude that $\int_0^b x\,dx = b^2/2$. ■

Example 4 can be generalized to integrate $f(x) = x$ over any closed interval $[a, b]$, $0 < a < b$.

$$\begin{aligned}\int_a^b x\,dx &= \int_a^0 x\,dx + \int_0^b x\,dx && \text{Rule 5}\\ &= -\int_0^a x\,dx + \int_0^b x\,dx && \text{Rule 1}\\ &= -\frac{a^2}{2} + \frac{b^2}{2}. && \text{Example 4}\end{aligned}$$

In conclusion, we have the following rule for integrating $f(x) = x$:

$$\int_a^b x\,dx = \frac{b^2}{2} - \frac{a^2}{2}, \qquad a < b \tag{2}$$

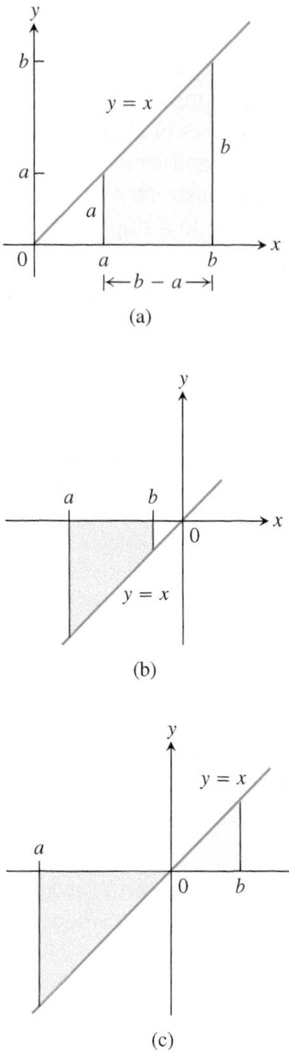

FIGURE 5.13 (a) The area of this trapezoidal region is $A = (b^2 - a^2)/2$. (b) The definite integral in Equation (2) gives the negative of the area of this trapezoidal region. (c) The definite integral in Equation (2) gives the area of the blue triangular region added to the negative of the area of the gold triangular region.

This computation gives the area of a trapezoid (Figure 5.13a). Equation (2) remains valid when a and b are negative. When $a < b < 0$, the definite integral value $(b^2 - a^2)/2$ is a negative number, the negative of the area of a trapezoid dropping down to the line $y = x$ below the x-axis (Figure 5.13b). When $a < 0$ and $b > 0$, Equation (2) is still valid and the definite integral gives the difference between two areas, the area under the graph and above $[0, b]$ minus the area below $[a, 0]$ and over the graph (Figure 5.13c).

The following results can also be established using a Riemann sum calculation similar to that in Example 4 (Exercises 63 and 65).

$$\int_a^b c\,dx = c(b - a), \qquad c \text{ any constant} \tag{3}$$

$$\int_a^b x^2\,dx = \frac{b^3}{3} - \frac{a^3}{3}, \qquad a < b \tag{4}$$

Average Value of a Continuous Function Revisited

In Section 5.1 we introduced informally the average value of a nonnegative continuous function f over an interval $[a, b]$, leading us to define this average as the area under the graph of $y = f(x)$ divided by $b - a$. In integral notation we write this as

$$\text{Average} = \frac{1}{b - a}\int_a^b f(x)\,dx.$$

We can use this formula to give a precise definition of the average value of any continuous (or integrable) function, whether positive, negative, or both.

Alternatively, we can use the following reasoning. We start with the idea from arithmetic that the average of n numbers is their sum divided by n. A continuous function f on $[a, b]$ may have infinitely many values, but we can still sample them in an orderly way.

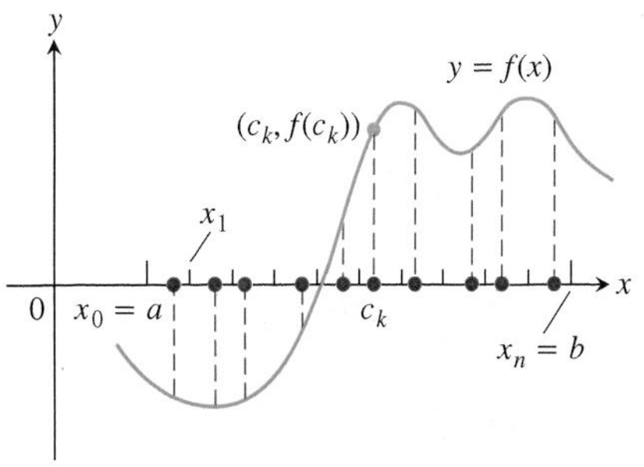

FIGURE 5.14 A sample of values of a function on an interval $[a, b]$.

We divide $[a, b]$ into n subintervals of equal width $\Delta x = (b - a)/n$ and evaluate f at a point c_k in each (Figure 5.14). The average of the n sampled values is

$$\begin{aligned}\frac{f(c_1) + f(c_2) + \cdots + f(c_n)}{n} &= \frac{1}{n}\sum_{k=1}^{n} f(c_k) \\ &= \frac{\Delta x}{b - a}\sum_{k=1}^{n} f(c_k) \qquad \Delta x = \frac{b-a}{n}, \text{ so } \frac{1}{n} = \frac{\Delta x}{b-a} \\ &= \frac{1}{b - a}\sum_{k=1}^{n} f(c_k)\,\Delta x. \qquad \text{Constant Multiple Rule}\end{aligned}$$

The average is obtained by dividing a Riemann sum for f on $[a, b]$ by $(b - a)$. As we increase the size of the sample and let the norm of the partition approach zero, the average approaches $(1/(b - a))\int_a^b f(x)\,dx$. Both points of view lead us to the following definition.

DEFINITION If f is integrable on $[a, b]$, then its **average value on $[a, b]$**, also called its **mean**, is

$$\text{av}(f) = \frac{1}{b - a}\int_a^b f(x)\,dx.$$

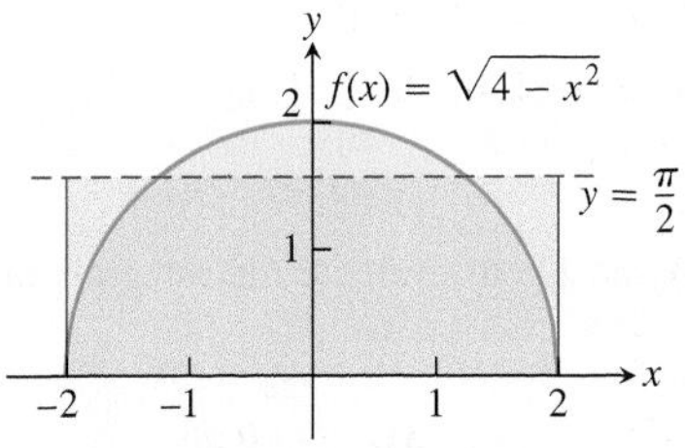

FIGURE 5.15 The average value of $f(x) = \sqrt{4 - x^2}$ on $[-2, 2]$ is $\pi/2$ (Example 5). The area of the rectangle shown here is $4 \cdot (\pi/2) = 2\pi$, which is also the area of the semicircle.

EXAMPLE 5 Find the average value of $f(x) = \sqrt{4 - x^2}$ on $[-2, 2]$.

Solution We recognize $f(x) = \sqrt{4 - x^2}$ as a function whose graph is the upper semicircle of radius 2 centered at the origin (Figure 5.15).

Since we know the area inside a circle, we do not need to take the limit of Riemann sums. The area between the semicircle and the x-axis from -2 to 2 can be computed using the geometry formula

$$\text{Area} = \frac{1}{2}\cdot \pi r^2 = \frac{1}{2}\cdot \pi(2)^2 = 2\pi.$$

Because f is nonnegative, the area is also the value of the integral of f from -2 to 2,

$$\int_{-2}^{2}\sqrt{4 - x^2}\,dx = 2\pi.$$

Therefore, the average value of f is

$$\text{av}(f) = \frac{1}{2 - (-2)}\int_{-2}^{2}\sqrt{4 - x^2}\,dx = \frac{1}{4}(2\pi) = \frac{\pi}{2}.$$

Notice that the average value of f over $[-2, 2]$ is the same as the height of a rectangle over $[-2, 2]$ whose area equals the area of the upper semicircle (see Figure 5.15). ■

Exercises 5.3

Interpreting Limits as Integrals

Express the limits in Exercises 1–8 as definite integrals.

1. $\lim_{\|P\|\to 0}\sum_{k=1}^{n} c_k^2\,\Delta x_k$, where P is a partition of $[0, 2]$

2. $\lim_{\|P\|\to 0}\sum_{k=1}^{n} 2c_k^3\,\Delta x_k$, where P is a partition of $[-1, 0]$

3. $\lim_{\|P\|\to 0}\sum_{k=1}^{n} (c_k^2 - 3c_k)\,\Delta x_k$, where P is a partition of $[-7, 5]$

4. $\lim_{\|P\|\to 0}\sum_{k=1}^{n}\left(\frac{1}{c_k}\right)\Delta x_k$, where P is a partition of $[1, 4]$

5. $\lim_{\|P\|\to 0}\sum_{k=1}^{n}\frac{1}{1 - c_k}\,\Delta x_k$, where P is a partition of $[2, 3]$

6. $\lim_{\|P\|\to 0} \sum_{k=1}^{n} \sqrt{4 - c_k^2}\,\Delta x_k$, where P is a partition of $[0, 1]$

7. $\lim_{\|P\|\to 0} \sum_{k=1}^{n} (\sec c_k)\,\Delta x_k$, where P is a partition of $[-\pi/4, 0]$

8. $\lim_{\|P\|\to 0} \sum_{k=1}^{n} (\tan c_k)\,\Delta x_k$, where P is a partition of $[0, \pi/4]$

Using the Definite Integral Rules

9. Suppose that f and g are integrable and that

$$\int_1^2 f(x)\,dx = -4, \quad \int_1^5 f(x)\,dx = 6, \quad \int_1^5 g(x)\,dx = 8.$$

Use the rules in Table 5.4 to find

a. $\int_2^2 g(x)\,dx$ b. $\int_5^1 g(x)\,dx$

c. $\int_1^2 3f(x)\,dx$ d. $\int_2^5 f(x)\,dx$

e. $\int_1^5 [f(x) - g(x)]\,dx$ f. $\int_1^5 [4f(x) - g(x)]\,dx$

10. Suppose that f and h are integrable and that

$$\int_1^9 f(x)\,dx = -1, \quad \int_7^9 f(x)\,dx = 5, \quad \int_7^9 h(x)\,dx = 4.$$

Use the rules in Table 5.4 to find

a. $\int_1^9 -2f(x)\,dx$ b. $\int_7^9 [f(x) + h(x)]\,dx$

c. $\int_7^9 [2f(x) - 3h(x)]\,dx$ d. $\int_9^1 f(x)\,dx$

e. $\int_1^7 f(x)\,dx$ f. $\int_9^7 [h(x) - f(x)]\,dx$

11. Suppose that $\int_1^2 f(x)\,dx = 5$. Find

a. $\int_1^2 f(u)\,du$ b. $\int_1^2 \sqrt{3}f(z)\,dz$

c. $\int_2^1 f(t)\,dt$ d. $\int_1^2 [-f(x)]\,dx$

12. Suppose that $\int_{-3}^0 g(t)\,dt = \sqrt{2}$. Find

a. $\int_0^{-3} g(t)\,dt$ b. $\int_{-3}^0 g(u)\,du$

c. $\int_{-3}^0 [-g(x)]\,dx$ d. $\int_{-3}^0 \frac{g(r)}{\sqrt{2}}\,dr$

13. Suppose that f is integrable and that $\int_0^3 f(z)\,dz = 3$ and $\int_0^4 f(z)\,dz = 7$. Find

a. $\int_3^4 f(z)\,dz$ b. $\int_4^3 f(t)\,dt$

14. Suppose that h is integrable and that $\int_{-1}^1 h(r)\,dr = 0$ and $\int_{-1}^3 h(r)\,dr = 6$. Find

a. $\int_1^3 h(r)\,dr$ b. $-\int_3^1 h(u)\,du$

Using Known Areas to Find Integrals

In Exercises 15–22, graph the integrands and use areas to evaluate the integrals.

15. $\int_{-2}^4 \left(\frac{x}{2} + 3\right) dx$ 16. $\int_{1/2}^{3/2} (-2x + 4)\,dx$

17. $\int_{-3}^3 \sqrt{9 - x^2}\,dx$ 18. $\int_{-4}^0 \sqrt{16 - x^2}\,dx$

19. $\int_{-2}^1 |x|\,dx$ 20. $\int_{-1}^1 (1 - |x|)\,dx$

21. $\int_{-1}^1 (2 - |x|)\,dx$ 22. $\int_{-1}^1 \left(1 + \sqrt{1 - x^2}\right) dx$

Use areas to evaluate the integrals in Exercises 23–28.

23. $\int_0^b \frac{x}{2}\,dx, \quad b > 0$ 24. $\int_0^b 4x\,dx, \quad b > 0$

25. $\int_a^b 2s\,ds, \quad 0 < a < b$ 26. $\int_a^b 3t\,dt, \quad 0 < a < b$

27. $f(x) = \sqrt{4 - x^2}$ on **a.** $[-2, 2]$, **b.** $[0, 2]$

28. $f(x) = 3x + \sqrt{1 - x^2}$ on **a.** $[-1, 0]$, **b.** $[-1, 1]$

Evaluating Definite Integrals

Use the results of Equations (2) and (4) to evaluate the integrals in Exercises 29–40.

29. $\int_1^{\sqrt{2}} x\,dx$ 30. $\int_{0.5}^{2.5} x\,dx$ 31. $\int_\pi^{2\pi} \theta\,d\theta$

32. $\int_{\sqrt{2}}^{5\sqrt{2}} r\,dr$ 33. $\int_0^{\sqrt[3]{7}} x^2\,dx$ 34. $\int_0^{0.3} s^2\,ds$

35. $\int_0^{1/2} t^2\,dt$ 36. $\int_0^{\pi/2} \theta^2\,d\theta$ 37. $\int_a^{2a} x\,dx$

38. $\int_a^{\sqrt{3}a} x\,dx$ 39. $\int_0^{\sqrt[3]{b}} x^2\,dx$ 40. $\int_0^{3b} x^2\,dx$

Use the rules in Table 5.4 and Equations (2)–(4) to evaluate the integrals in Exercises 41–50.

41. $\int_3^1 7\,dx$ 42. $\int_0^2 5x\,dx$

43. $\int_0^2 (2t - 3)\,dt$ 44. $\int_0^{\sqrt{2}} \left(t - \sqrt{2}\right) dt$

45. $\int_2^1 \left(1 + \frac{z}{2}\right) dz$ 46. $\int_3^0 (2z - 3)\,dz$

47. $\int_1^2 3u^2\,du$ 48. $\int_{1/2}^1 24u^2\,du$

49. $\int_0^2 (3x^2 + x - 5)\,dx$ 50. $\int_1^0 (3x^2 + x - 5)\,dx$

Finding Area by Definite Integrals

In Exercises 51–54, use a definite integral to find the area of the region between the given curve and the x-axis on the interval $[0, b]$.

51. $y = 3x^2$ 52. $y = \pi x^2$

53. $y = 2x$ 54. $y = \frac{x}{2} + 1$

Finding Average Value

In Exercises 55–62, graph the function and find its average value over the given interval.

55. $f(x) = x^2 - 1$ on $\left[0, \sqrt{3}\right]$

56. $f(x) = -\dfrac{x^2}{2}$ on $[0, 3]$ **57.** $f(x) = -3x^2 - 1$ on $[0, 1]$

58. $f(x) = 3x^2 - 3$ on $[0, 1]$

59. $f(t) = (t - 1)^2$ on $[0, 3]$

60. $f(t) = t^2 - t$ on $[-2, 1]$

61. $g(x) = |x| - 1$ on **a.** $[-1, 1]$, **b.** $[1, 3]$, and **c.** $[-1, 3]$

62. $h(x) = -|x|$ on **a.** $[-1, 0]$, **b.** $[0, 1]$, and **c.** $[-1, 1]$

Definite Integrals as Limits

Use the method of Example 4a or Equation (1) to evaluate the definite integrals in Exercises 63–70.

63. $\displaystyle\int_a^b c\,dx$ **64.** $\displaystyle\int_0^2 (2x + 1)\,dx$

65. $\displaystyle\int_a^b x^2\,dx, \quad a < b$ **66.** $\displaystyle\int_{-1}^0 (x - x^2)\,dx$

67. $\displaystyle\int_{-1}^2 (3x^2 - 2x + 1)\,dx$ **68.** $\displaystyle\int_{-1}^1 x^3\,dx$

69. $\displaystyle\int_a^b x^3\,dx, \quad a < b$ **70.** $\displaystyle\int_0^1 (3x - x^3)\,dx$

Theory and Examples

71. What values of a and b maximize the value of

$$\int_a^b (x - x^2)\,dx?$$

(*Hint:* Where is the integrand positive?)

72. What values of a and b minimize the value of

$$\int_a^b (x^4 - 2x^2)\,dx?$$

73. Use the Max-Min Inequality to find upper and lower bounds for the value of

$$\int_0^1 \frac{1}{1 + x^2}\,dx.$$

74. (*Continuation of Exercise 73.*) Use the Max-Min Inequality to find upper and lower bounds for

$$\int_0^{0.5} \frac{1}{1 + x^2}\,dx \quad \text{and} \quad \int_{0.5}^1 \frac{1}{1 + x^2}\,dx.$$

Add these to arrive at an improved estimate of

$$\int_0^1 \frac{1}{1 + x^2}\,dx.$$

75. Show that the value of $\int_0^1 \sin(x^2)\,dx$ cannot possibly be 2.

76. Show that the value of $\int_0^1 \sqrt{x + 8}\,dx$ lies between $2\sqrt{2} \approx 2.8$ and 3.

77. Integrals of nonnegative functions Use the Max-Min Inequality to show that if f is integrable then

$$f(x) \geq 0 \quad \text{on} \quad [a, b] \quad \Rightarrow \quad \int_a^b f(x)\,dx \geq 0.$$

78. Integrals of nonpositive functions Show that if f is integrable then

$$f(x) \leq 0 \quad \text{on} \quad [a, b] \quad \Rightarrow \quad \int_a^b f(x)\,dx \leq 0.$$

79. Use the inequality $\sin x \leq x$, which holds for $x \geq 0$, to find an upper bound for the value of $\int_0^1 \sin x\,dx$.

80. The inequality $\sec x \geq 1 + (x^2/2)$ holds on $(-\pi/2, \pi/2)$. Use it to find a lower bound for the value of $\int_0^1 \sec x\,dx$.

81. If av(f) really is a typical value of the integrable function $f(x)$ on $[a, b]$, then the constant function av(f) should have the same integral over $[a, b]$ as f. Does it? That is, does

$$\int_a^b \text{av}(f)\,dx = \int_a^b f(x)\,dx?$$

Give reasons for your answer.

82. It would be nice if average values of integrable functions obeyed the following rules on an interval $[a, b]$.

a. $\text{av}(f + g) = \text{av}(f) + \text{av}(g)$

b. $\text{av}(kf) = k\,\text{av}(f)$ (any number k)

c. $\text{av}(f) \leq \text{av}(g)$ if $f(x) \leq g(x)$ on $[a, b]$.

Do these rules ever hold? Give reasons for your answers.

83. Upper and lower sums for increasing functions

a. Suppose the graph of a continuous function $f(x)$ rises steadily as x moves from left to right across an interval $[a, b]$. Let P be a partition of $[a, b]$ into n subintervals of length $\Delta x = (b - a)/n$. Show by referring to the accompanying figure that the difference between the upper and lower sums for f on this partition can be represented graphically as the area of a rectangle R whose dimensions are $[f(b) - f(a)]$ by Δx. (*Hint:* The difference $U - L$ is the sum of areas of rectangles whose diagonals $Q_0Q_1, Q_1Q_2, \ldots, Q_{n-1}Q_n$ lie along the curve. There is no overlapping when these rectangles are shifted horizontally onto R.)

b. Suppose that instead of being equal, the lengths Δx_k of the subintervals of the partition of $[a, b]$ vary in size. Show that

$$U - L \leq |f(b) - f(a)|\,\Delta x_{\max},$$

where $\Delta x_{\max}$ is the norm of P, and hence that $\lim_{\|P\|\to 0} (U - L) = 0$.

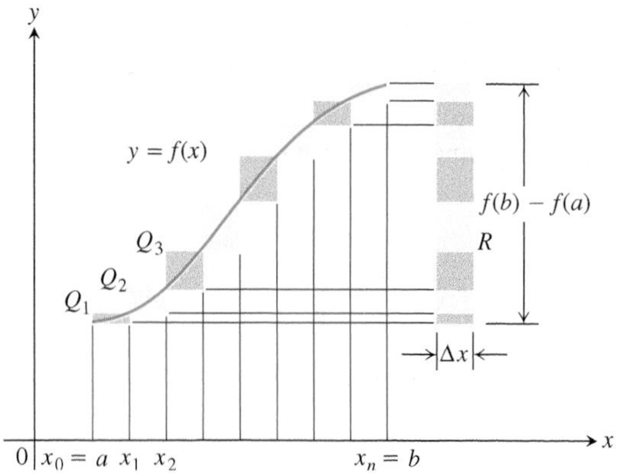

84. Upper and lower sums for decreasing functions *(Continuation of Exercise 83.)*

a. Draw a figure like the one in Exercise 83 for a continuous function $f(x)$ whose values decrease steadily as x moves from left to right across the interval $[a, b]$. Let P be a partition of $[a, b]$ into subintervals of equal length. Find an expression for $U - L$ that is analogous to the one you found for $U - L$ in Exercise 83a.

b. Suppose that instead of being equal, the lengths Δx_k of the subintervals of P vary in size. Show that the inequality

$$U - L \le |f(b) - f(a)|\, \Delta x_{\max}$$

of Exercise 83b still holds and hence that $\lim_{\|P\|\to 0} (U - L) = 0$.

85. Use the formula

$$\sin h + \sin 2h + \sin 3h + \cdots + \sin mh = \frac{\cos(h/2) - \cos((m + (1/2))h)}{2\sin(h/2)}$$

to find the area under the curve $y = \sin x$ from $x = 0$ to $x = \pi/2$ in two steps:

a. Partition the interval $[0, \pi/2]$ into n subintervals of equal length and calculate the corresponding upper sum U; then

b. Find the limit of U as $n \to \infty$ and $\Delta x = (b - a)/n \to 0$.

86. Suppose that f is continuous and nonnegative over $[a, b]$, as in the accompanying figure. By inserting points

$$x_1, x_2, \ldots, x_{k-1}, x_k, \ldots, x_{n-1}$$

as shown, divide $[a, b]$ into n subintervals of lengths $\Delta x_1 = x_1 - a$, $\Delta x_2 = x_2 - x_1, \ldots, \Delta x_n = b - x_{n-1}$, which need not be equal.

a. If $m_k = \min\{f(x) \text{ for } x \text{ in the } k\text{th subinterval}\}$, explain the connection between the **lower sum**

$$L = m_1\,\Delta x_1 + m_2\,\Delta x_2 + \cdots + m_n\,\Delta x_n$$

and the shaded regions in the first part of the figure.

b. If $M_k = \max\{f(x) \text{ for } x \text{ in the } k\text{th subinterval}\}$, explain the connection between the **upper sum**

$$U = M_1\,\Delta x_1 + M_2\,\Delta x_2 + \cdots + M_n\,\Delta x_n$$

and the shaded regions in the second part of the figure.

c. Explain the connection between $U - L$ and the shaded regions along the curve in the third part of the figure.

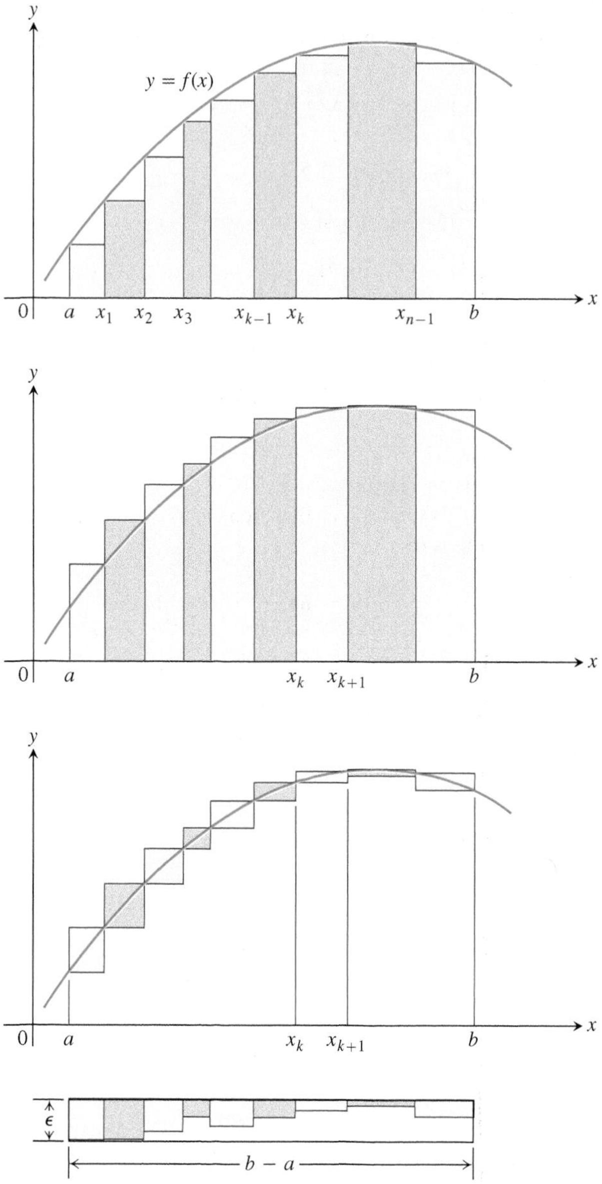

87. We say f is **uniformly continuous** on $[a, b]$ if given any $\epsilon > 0$, there is a $\delta > 0$ such that if x_1, x_2 are in $[a, b]$ and $|x_1 - x_2| < \delta$, then $|f(x_1) - f(x_2)| < \epsilon$. It can be shown that a continuous function on $[a, b]$ is uniformly continuous. Use this and the figure for Exercise 86 to show that if f is continuous and $\epsilon > 0$ is given, it is possible to make $U - L \le \epsilon \cdot (b - a)$ by making the largest of the Δx_k's sufficiently small.

88. If you average 30 mi/h on a 150-mi trip and then return over the same 150 mi at the rate of 50 mi/h, what is your average speed for the trip? Give reasons for your answer.

COMPUTER EXPLORATIONS

If your CAS can draw rectangles associated with Riemann sums, use it to draw rectangles associated with Riemann sums that converge to the integrals in Exercises 89–94. Use $n = 4$, 10, 20, and 50 subintervals of equal length in each case.

89. $\displaystyle\int_0^1 (1 - x)\,dx = \frac{1}{2}$

90. $\int_0^1 (x^2 + 1)\, dx = \frac{4}{3}$

91. $\int_{-\pi}^{\pi} \cos x\, dx = 0$

92. $\int_0^{\pi/4} \sec^2 x\, dx = 1$

93. $\int_{-1}^{1} |x|\, dx = 1$

94. $\int_1^2 \frac{1}{x}\, dx$ (The integral's value is about 0.693.)

In Exercises 95–102, use a CAS to perform the following steps:

a. Plot the functions over the given interval.

b. Partition the interval into $n = 100, 200$, and 1000 subintervals of equal length, and evaluate the function at the midpoint of each subinterval.

c. Compute the average value of the function values generated in part (b).

d. Solve the equation $f(x) =$ (average value) for x using the average value calculated in part (c) for the $n = 1000$ partitioning.

95. $f(x) = \sin x$ on $[0, \pi]$

96. $f(x) = \sin^2 x$ on $[0, \pi]$

97. $f(x) = x \sin \frac{1}{x}$ on $\left[\frac{\pi}{4}, \pi\right]$

98. $f(x) = x \sin^2 \frac{1}{x}$ on $\left[\frac{\pi}{4}, \pi\right]$

99. $f(x) = xe^{-x}$ on $[0, 1]$

100. $f(x) = e^{-x^2}$ on $[0, 1]$

101. $f(x) = \frac{\ln x}{x}$ on $[2, 5]$

102. $f(x) = \frac{1}{\sqrt{1 - x^2}}$ on $\left[0, \frac{1}{2}\right]$

5.4 The Fundamental Theorem of Calculus

HISTORICAL BIOGRAPHY

Sir Isaac Newton
(1642–1727)

In this section we present the Fundamental Theorem of Calculus, which is the central theorem of integral calculus. It connects integration and differentiation, enabling us to compute integrals using an antiderivative of the integrand function rather than by taking limits of Riemann sums as we did in Section 5.3. Leibniz and Newton exploited this relationship and started mathematical developments that fueled the scientific revolution for the next 200 years.

Along the way, we present an integral version of the Mean Value Theorem, which is another important theorem of integral calculus and is used to prove the Fundamental Theorem.

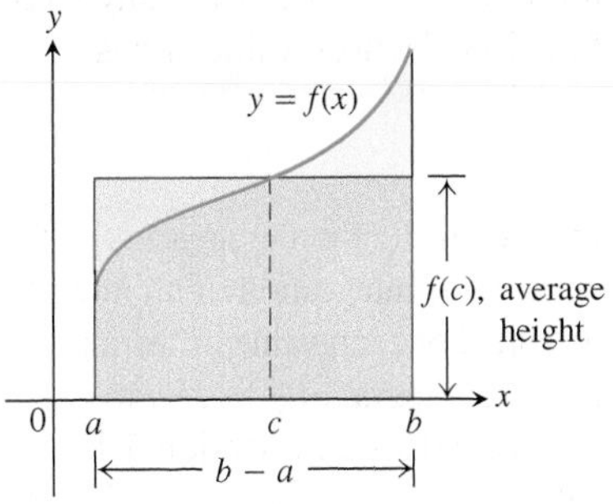

FIGURE 5.16 The value $f(c)$ in the Mean Value Theorem is, in a sense, the average (or *mean*) height of f on $[a, b]$. When $f \geq 0$, the area of the rectangle is the area under the graph of f from a to b,

$$f(c)(b - a) = \int_a^b f(x)\, dx.$$

Mean Value Theorem for Definite Integrals

In the previous section we defined the average value of a continuous function over a closed interval $[a, b]$ as the definite integral $\int_a^b f(x)\, dx$ divided by the length or width $b - a$ of the interval. The Mean Value Theorem for Definite Integrals asserts that this average value is *always* taken on at least once by the function f in the interval.

The graph in Figure 5.16 shows a *positive* continuous function $y = f(x)$ defined over the interval $[a, b]$. Geometrically, the Mean Value Theorem says that there is a number c in $[a, b]$ such that the rectangle with height equal to the average value $f(c)$ of the function and base width $b - a$ has exactly the same area as the region beneath the graph of f from a to b.

THEOREM 3—The Mean Value Theorem for Definite Integrals If f is continuous on $[a, b]$, then at some point c in $[a, b]$,

$$f(c) = \frac{1}{b - a} \int_a^b f(x)\, dx.$$

Proof If we divide both sides of the Max-Min Inequality (Table 5.4, Rule 6) by $(b - a)$, we obtain

$$\min f \leq \frac{1}{b - a} \int_a^b f(x)\, dx \leq \max f.$$

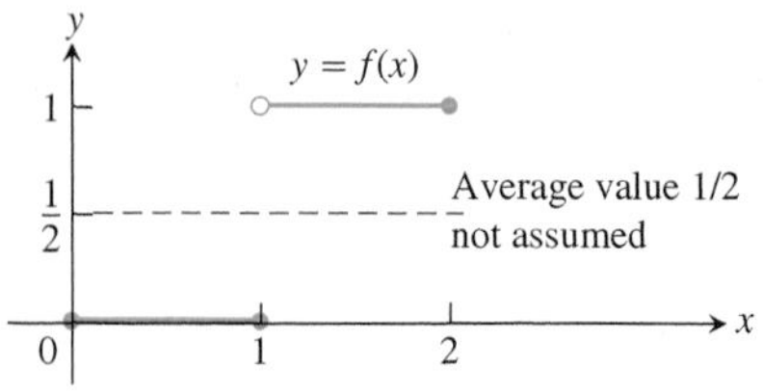

FIGURE 5.17 A discontinuous function need not assume its average value.

Since f is continuous, the Intermediate Value Theorem for Continuous Functions (Section 2.5) says that f must assume every value between min f and max f. It must therefore assume the value $(1/(b-a))\int_a^b f(x)\,dx$ at some point c in $[a, b]$. ■

The continuity of f is important here. It is possible that a discontinuous function never equals its average value (Figure 5.17).

EXAMPLE 1 Show that if f is continuous on $[a, b]$, $a \neq b$, and if

$$\int_a^b f(x)\,dx = 0,$$

then $f(x) = 0$ at least once in $[a, b]$.

Solution The average value of f on $[a, b]$ is

$$\text{av}(f) = \frac{1}{b-a}\int_a^b f(x)\,dx = \frac{1}{b-a}\cdot 0 = 0.$$

By the Mean Value Theorem, f assumes this value at some point $c \in [a, b]$. ■

Fundamental Theorem, Part 1

It can be very difficult to compute definite integrals by taking the limit of Riemann sums. We now develop a powerful new method for evaluating definite integrals, based on using antiderivatives. This method combines the two strands of calculus. One strand involves the idea of taking the limits of finite sums to obtain a definite integral, and the other strand contains derivatives and antiderivatives. They come together in the Fundamental Theorem of Calculus. We begin by considering how to differentiate a certain type of function that is described as an integral.

If $f(t)$ is an integrable function over a finite interval I, then the integral from any fixed number $a \in I$ to another number $x \in I$ defines a new function F whose value at x is

$$F(x) = \int_a^x f(t)\,dt. \tag{1}$$

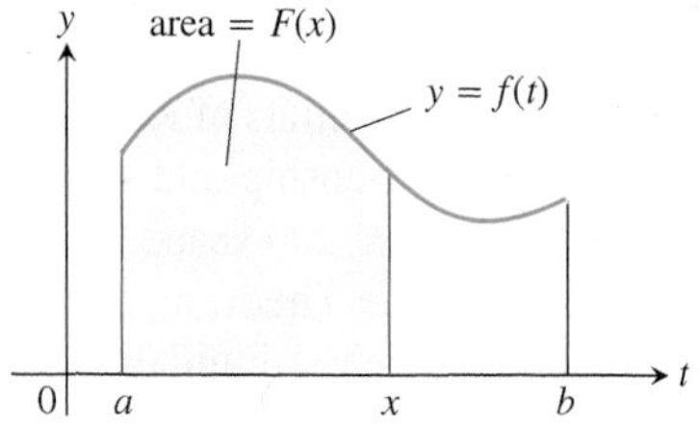

FIGURE 5.18 The function $F(x)$ defined by Equation (1) gives the area under the graph of f from a to x when f is nonnegative and $x > a$.

For example, if f is nonnegative and x lies to the right of a, then $F(x)$ is the area under the graph from a to x (Figure 5.18). The variable x is the upper limit of integration of an integral, but F is just like any other real-valued function of a real variable. For each value of the input x, there is a well-defined numerical output, in this case the definite integral of f from a to x.

Equation (1) gives a way to define new functions (as we will see in Section 7.1), but its importance now is the connection it makes between integrals and derivatives. If f is any continuous function, then the Fundamental Theorem asserts that F is a differentiable function of x whose derivative is f itself. At every value of x, it asserts that

$$\frac{d}{dx}F(x) = f(x).$$

To gain some insight into why this result holds, we look at the geometry behind it.

If $f \geq 0$ on $[a, b]$, then the computation of $F'(x)$ from the definition of the derivative means taking the limit as $h \to 0$ of the difference quotient

$$\frac{F(x+h) - F(x)}{h}.$$

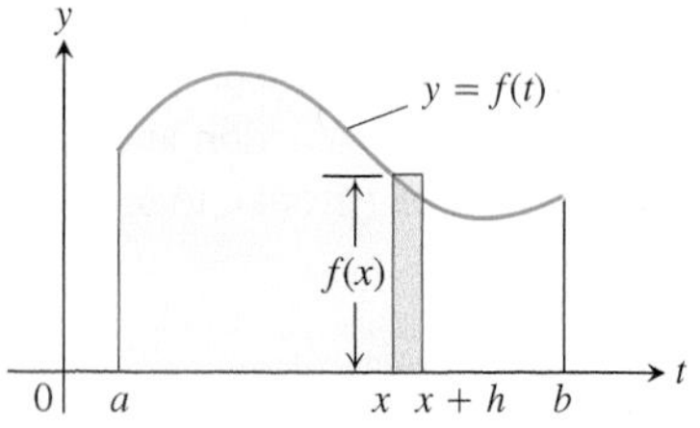

FIGURE 5.19 In Equation (1), $F(x)$ is the area to the left of x. Also, $F(x+h)$ is the area to the left of $x+h$. The difference quotient $[F(x+h) - F(x)]/h$ is then approximately equal to $f(x)$, the height of the rectangle shown here.

For $h > 0$, the numerator is obtained by subtracting two areas, so it is the area under the graph of f from x to $x+h$ (Figure 5.19). If h is small, this area is approximately equal to the area of the rectangle of height $f(x)$ and width h, which can be seen from Figure 5.19. That is,

$$F(x+h) - F(x) \approx hf(x).$$

Dividing both sides of this approximation by h and letting $h \to 0$, it is reasonable to expect that

$$F'(x) = \lim_{h\to 0}\frac{F(x+h) - F(x)}{h} = f(x).$$

This result is true even if the function f is not positive, and it forms the first part of the Fundamental Theorem of Calculus.

THEOREM 4—The Fundamental Theorem of Calculus, Part 1 If f is continuous on $[a, b]$, then $F(x) = \int_a^x f(t)\,dt$ is continuous on $[a, b]$ and differentiable on (a, b) and its derivative is $f(x)$:

$$F'(x) = \frac{d}{dx}\int_a^x f(t)\,dt = f(x). \qquad (2)$$

Before proving Theorem 4, we look at several examples to gain a better understanding of what it says. In each example, notice that the independent variable appears in a limit of integration, possibly in a formula.

EXAMPLE 2 Use the Fundamental Theorem to find dy/dx if

(a) $y = \int_a^x (t^3 + 1)\,dt$ **(b)** $y = \int_x^5 3t \sin t\,dt$

(c) $y = \int_1^{x^2} \cos t\,dt$ **(d)** $y = \int_{1+3x^2}^4 \frac{1}{2 + e^t}\,dt$

Solution We calculate the derivatives with respect to the independent variable x.

(a) $\frac{dy}{dx} = \frac{d}{dx}\int_a^x (t^3 + 1)\,dt = x^3 + 1$ Eq. (2) with $f(t) = t^3 + 1$

(b) $\frac{dy}{dx} = \frac{d}{dx}\int_x^5 3t \sin t\,dt = \frac{d}{dx}\left(-\int_5^x 3t \sin t\,dt\right)$ Table 5.4, Rule 1

$= -\frac{d}{dx}\int_5^x 3t \sin t\,dt$

$= -3x \sin x$ Eq. (2) with $f(t) = 3t \sin t$

(c) The upper limit of integration is not x but x^2. This makes y a composite of the two functions,

$$y = \int_1^u \cos t\,dt \quad \text{and} \quad u = x^2.$$

We must therefore apply the Chain Rule when finding dy/dx.

$$\begin{aligned}\frac{dy}{dx} &= \frac{dy}{du}\cdot\frac{du}{dx}\\ &= \left(\frac{d}{du}\int_1^u \cos t\,dt\right)\cdot\frac{du}{dx}\\ &= \cos u \cdot \frac{du}{dx}\\ &= \cos(x^2)\cdot 2x\\ &= 2x \cos x^2\end{aligned}$$

(d) $\frac{d}{dx}\int_{1+3x^2}^4 \frac{1}{2 + e^t}\,dt = \frac{d}{dx}\left(-\int_4^{1+3x^2} \frac{1}{2 + e^t}\,dt\right)$ Rule 1

$= -\frac{d}{dx}\int_4^{1+3x^2} \frac{1}{2 + e^t}\,dt$

$= -\frac{1}{2 + e^{(1+3x^2)}}\frac{d}{dx}(1 + 3x^2)$ Eq. (2) and the Chain Rule

$= -\frac{6x}{2 + e^{(1+3x^2)}}$ ■

Proof of Theorem 4 We prove the Fundamental Theorem, Part 1, by applying the definition of the derivative directly to the function $F(x)$, when x and $x + h$ are in (a, b). This means writing out the difference quotient

$$\frac{F(x+h) - F(x)}{h} \tag{3}$$

and showing that its limit as $h \to 0$ is the number $f(x)$ for each x in (a, b). Thus,

$$\begin{aligned} F'(x) &= \lim_{h\to 0} \frac{F(x+h) - F(x)}{h} \\ &= \lim_{h\to 0} \frac{1}{h}\left[\int_a^{x+h} f(t)\,dt - \int_a^x f(t)\,dt\right] \\ &= \lim_{h\to 0} \frac{1}{h}\int_x^{x+h} f(t)\,dt \qquad \text{Table 5.4, Rule 5} \end{aligned}$$

According to the Mean Value Theorem for Definite Integrals, the value before taking the limit in the last expression is one of the values taken on by f in the interval between x and $x + h$. That is, for some number c in this interval,

$$\frac{1}{h}\int_x^{x+h} f(t)\,dt = f(c). \tag{4}$$

As $h \to 0$, $x + h$ approaches x, forcing c to approach x also (because c is trapped between x and $x + h$). Since f is continuous at x, $f(c)$ approaches $f(x)$:

$$\lim_{h\to 0} f(c) = f(x). \tag{5}$$

In conclusion, we have

$$\begin{aligned} F'(x) &= \lim_{h\to 0} \frac{1}{h}\int_x^{x+h} f(t)\,dt \\ &= \lim_{h\to 0} f(c) \qquad \text{Eq. (4)} \\ &= f(x). \qquad \text{Eq. (5)} \end{aligned}$$

If $x = a$ or b, then the limit of Equation (3) is interpreted as a one-sided limit with $h \to 0^+$ or $h \to 0^-$, respectively. Then Theorem 1 in Section 3.2 shows that F is continuous for every point in $[a, b]$. This concludes the proof. ■

Fundamental Theorem, Part 2 (The Evaluation Theorem)

We now come to the second part of the Fundamental Theorem of Calculus. This part describes how to evaluate definite integrals without having to calculate limits of Riemann sums. Instead we find and evaluate an antiderivative at the upper and lower limits of integration.

THEOREM 4 (Continued)—The Fundamental Theorem of Calculus, Part 2 If f is continuous at every point in $[a, b]$ and F is any antiderivative of f on $[a, b]$, then

$$\int_a^b f(x)\,dx = F(b) - F(a).$$

Proof Part 1 of the Fundamental Theorem tells us that an antiderivative of f exists, namely

$$G(x) = \int_a^x f(t)\,dt.$$

Thus, if F is *any* antiderivative of f, then $F(x) = G(x) + C$ for some constant C for $a < x < b$ (by Corollary 2 of the Mean Value Theorem for Derivatives, Section 4.2).

Since both F and G are continuous on $[a, b]$, we see that $F(x) = G(x) + C$ also holds when $x = a$ and $x = b$ by taking one-sided limits (as $x \to a^+$ and $x \to b^-$).

Evaluating $F(b) - F(a)$, we have

$$\begin{aligned} F(b) - F(a) &= [G(b) + C] - [G(a) + C] \\ &= G(b) - G(a) \\ &= \int_a^b f(t)\,dt - \int_a^a f(t)\,dt \\ &= \int_a^b f(t)\,dt - 0 \\ &= \int_a^b f(t)\,dt. \end{aligned}$$

■

The Evaluation Theorem is important because it says that to calculate the definite integral of f over an interval $[a, b]$ we need do only two things:

1. Find an antiderivative F of f, and
2. Calculate the number $F(b) - F(a)$, which is equal to $\int_a^b f(x)\,dx$.

This process is much easier than using a Riemann sum computation. The power of the theorem follows from the realization that the definite integral, which is defined by a complicated process involving all of the values of the function f over $[a, b]$, can be found by knowing the values of *any* antiderivative F at only the two endpoints a and b. The usual notation for the difference $F(b) - F(a)$ is

$$F(x)\Big]_a^b \qquad \text{or} \qquad \Big[F(x)\Big]_a^b,$$

depending on whether F has one or more terms.

EXAMPLE 3 We calculate several definite integrals using the Evaluation Theorem, rather than by taking limits of Riemann sums.

(a) $$\begin{aligned} \int_0^{\pi} \cos x\,dx &= \sin x\Big]_0^{\pi} \\ &= \sin \pi - \sin 0 = 0 - 0 = 0 \end{aligned}$$

$\frac{d}{dx}\sin x = \cos x$

(b) $$\begin{aligned} \int_{-\pi/4}^{0} \sec x \tan x\,dx &= \sec x\Big]_{-\pi/4}^{0} \\ &= \sec 0 - \sec\left(-\frac{\pi}{4}\right) = 1 - \sqrt{2} \end{aligned}$$

$\frac{d}{dx}\sec x = \sec x \tan x$

(c) $$\begin{aligned} \int_1^4 \left(\frac{3}{2}\sqrt{x} - \frac{4}{x^2}\right) dx &= \left[x^{3/2} + \frac{4}{x}\right]_1^4 \\ &= \left[(4)^{3/2} + \frac{4}{4}\right] - \left[(1)^{3/2} + \frac{4}{1}\right] \\ &= [8 + 1] - [5] = 4 \end{aligned}$$

$\frac{d}{dx}\left(x^{3/2} + \frac{4}{x}\right) = \frac{3}{2}x^{1/2} - \frac{4}{x^2}$

(d) $$\begin{aligned} \int_0^1 \frac{dx}{x + 1} &= \ln|x + 1|\Big]_0^1 \\ &= \ln 2 - \ln 1 = \ln 2 \end{aligned}$$

$\frac{d}{dx}\ln|x + 1| = \frac{1}{x + 1}$

(e) $$\begin{aligned} \int_0^1 \frac{dx}{x^2 + 1} &= \tan^{-1} x\Big]_0^1 \\ &= \tan^{-1} 1 - \tan^{-1} 0 = \frac{\pi}{4} - 0 = \frac{\pi}{4}. \end{aligned}$$

$\frac{d}{dx}\tan^{-1} x = \frac{1}{x^2 + 1}$

■

Exercise 82 offers another proof of the Evaluation Theorem, bringing together the ideas of Riemann sums, the Mean Value Theorem, and the definition of the definite integral.

The Integral of a Rate

We can interpret Part 2 of the Fundamental Theorem in another way. If F is any antiderivative of f, then $F' = f$. The equation in the theorem can then be rewritten as

$$\int_a^b F'(x)\,dx = F(b) - F(a).$$

Now $F'(x)$ represents the rate of change of the function $F(x)$ with respect to x, so the last equation asserts that the integral of F' is just the *net change* in F as x changes from a to b. Formally, we have the following result.

THEOREM 5—The Net Change Theorem The net change in a differentiable function $F(x)$ over an interval $a \le x \le b$ is the integral of its rate of change:

$$F(b) - F(a) = \int_a^b F'(x)\,dx. \tag{6}$$

EXAMPLE 4 Here are several interpretations of the Net Change Theorem.

(a) If $c(x)$ is the cost of producing x units of a certain commodity, then $c'(x)$ is the marginal cost (Section 3.4). From Theorem 5,

$$\int_{x_1}^{x_2} c'(x)\,dx = c(x_2) - c(x_1),$$

which is the cost of increasing production from x_1 units to x_2 units.

(b) If an object with position function $s(t)$ moves along a coordinate line, its velocity is $v(t) = s'(t)$. Theorem 5 says that

$$\int_{t_1}^{t_2} v(t)\,dt = s(t_2) - s(t_1),$$

so the integral of velocity is the **displacement** over the time interval $t_1 \le t \le t_2$. On the other hand, the integral of the speed $|v(t)|$ is the **total distance traveled** over the time interval. This is consistent with our discussion in Section 5.1. ■

If we rearrange Equation (6) as

$$F(b) = F(a) + \int_a^b F'(x)\,dx,$$

we see that the Net Change Theorem also says that the final value of a function $F(x)$ over an interval $[a, b]$ equals its initial value $F(a)$ plus its net change over the interval. So if $v(t)$ represents the velocity function of an object moving along a coordinate line, this means that the object's final position $s(t_2)$ over a time interval $t_1 \le t \le t_2$ is its initial position $s(t_1)$ plus its net change in position along the line (see Example 4b).

EXAMPLE 5 Consider again our analysis of a heavy rock blown straight up from the ground by a dynamite blast (Example 3, Section 5.1). The velocity of the rock at any time t during its motion was given as $v(t) = 160 - 32t$ ft/sec.

(a) Find the displacement of the rock during the time period $0 \le t \le 8$.

(b) Find the total distance traveled during this time period.

Solution

(a) From Example 4b, the displacement is the integral

$$\int_0^8 v(t)\,dt = \int_0^8 (160 - 32t)\,dt = \Big[160t - 16t^2\Big]_0^8$$
$$= (160)(8) - (16)(64) = 256.$$

This means that the height of the rock is 256 ft above the ground 8 sec after the explosion, which agrees with our conclusion in Example 3, Section 5.1.

(b) As we noted in Table 5.3, the velocity function $v(t)$ is positive over the time interval $[0, 5]$ and negative over the interval $[5, 8]$. Therefore, from Example 4b, the total distance traveled is the integral

$$\int_0^8 |v(t)|\,dt = \int_0^5 |v(t)|\,dt + \int_5^8 |v(t)|\,dt$$
$$= \int_0^5 (160 - 32t)\,dt - \int_5^8 (160 - 32t)\,dt$$
$$= \Big[160t - 16t^2\Big]_0^5 - \Big[160t - 16t^2\Big]_5^8$$
$$= [(160)(5) - (16)(25)] - [(160)(8) - (16)(64) - ((160)(5) - (16)(25))]$$
$$= 400 - (-144) = 544.$$

Again, this calculation agrees with our conclusion in Example 3, Section 5.1. That is, the total distance of 544 ft traveled by the rock during the time period $0 \le t \le 8$ is (i) the maximum height of 400 ft it reached over the time interval $[0, 5]$ plus (ii) the additional distance of 144 ft the rock fell over the time interval $[5, 8]$. ■

The Relationship Between Integration and Differentiation

The conclusions of the Fundamental Theorem tell us several things. Equation (2) can be rewritten as

$$\frac{d}{dx}\int_a^x f(t)\,dt = f(x),$$

which says that if you first integrate the function f and then differentiate the result, you get the function f back again. Likewise, replacing b by x and x by t in Equation (6) gives

$$\int_a^x F'(t)\,dt = F(x) - F(a),$$

so that if you first differentiate the function F and then integrate the result, you get the function F back (adjusted by an integration constant). In a sense, the processes of integration and differentiation are "inverses" of each other. The Fundamental Theorem also says that every continuous function f has an antiderivative F. It shows the importance of finding antiderivatives in order to evaluate definite integrals easily. Furthermore, it says that the differential equation $dy/dx = f(x)$ has a solution (namely, any of the functions $y = F(x) + C$) for every continuous function f.

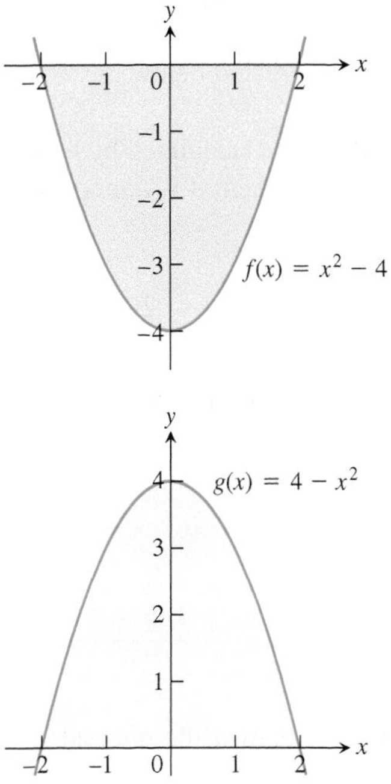

FIGURE 5.20 These graphs enclose the same amount of area with the x-axis, but the definite integrals of the two functions over $[-2, 2]$ differ in sign (Example 6).

Total Area

The Riemann sum contains terms such as $f(c_k)\,\Delta x_k$ that give the area of a rectangle when $f(c_k)$ is positive. When $f(c_k)$ is negative, then the product $f(c_k)\,\Delta x_k$ is the negative of the rectangle's area. When we add up such terms for a negative function, we get the negative of the area between the curve and the x-axis. If we then take the absolute value, we obtain the correct positive area.

EXAMPLE 6 Figure 5.20 shows the graph of $f(x) = x^2 - 4$ and its mirror image $g(x) = 4 - x^2$ reflected across the x-axis. For each function, compute

(a) the definite integral over the interval $[-2, 2]$, and

(b) the area between the graph and the x-axis over $[-2, 2]$.

Solution

(a) $$\int_{-2}^{2} f(x)\,dx = \left[\frac{x^3}{3} - 4x\right]_{-2}^{2} = \left(\frac{8}{3} - 8\right) - \left(-\frac{8}{3} + 8\right) = -\frac{32}{3},$$

and

$$\int_{-2}^{2} g(x)\,dx = \left[4x - \frac{x^3}{3}\right]_{-2}^{2} = \frac{32}{3}.$$

(b) In both cases, the area between the curve and the x-axis over $[-2, 2]$ is $32/3$ units. Although the definite integral of $f(x)$ is negative, the area is still positive. ■

To compute the area of the region bounded by the graph of a function $y = f(x)$ and the x-axis when the function takes on both positive and negative values, we must be careful to break up the interval $[a, b]$ into subintervals on which the function doesn't change sign. Otherwise we might get cancellation between positive and negative signed areas, leading to an incorrect total. The correct total area is obtained by adding the absolute value of the definite integral over each subinterval where $f(x)$ does not change sign. The term "area" will be taken to mean this *total area*.

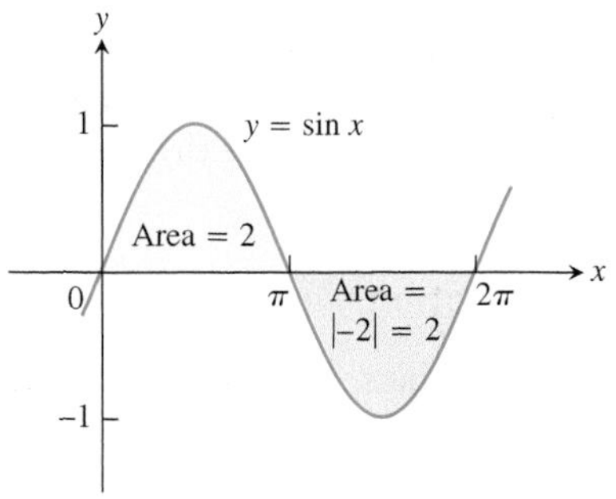

FIGURE 5.21 The total area between $y = \sin x$ and the x-axis for $0 \le x \le 2\pi$ is the sum of the absolute values of two integrals (Example 7).

EXAMPLE 7 Figure 5.21 shows the graph of the function $f(x) = \sin x$ between $x = 0$ and $x = 2\pi$. Compute

(a) the definite integral of $f(x)$ over $[0, 2\pi]$.

(b) the area between the graph of $f(x)$ and the x-axis over $[0, 2\pi]$.

Solution The definite integral for $f(x) = \sin x$ is given by

$$\int_{0}^{2\pi} \sin x\,dx = -\cos x\Big]_{0}^{2\pi} = -[\cos 2\pi - \cos 0] = -[1 - 1] = 0.$$

The definite integral is zero because the portions of the graph above and below the x-axis make canceling contributions.

The area between the graph of $f(x)$ and the x-axis over $[0, 2\pi]$ is calculated by breaking up the domain of $\sin x$ into two pieces: the interval $[0, \pi]$ over which it is nonnegative and the interval $[\pi, 2\pi]$ over which it is nonpositive.

$$\int_{0}^{\pi} \sin x\,dx = -\cos x\Big]_{0}^{\pi} = -[\cos \pi - \cos 0] = -[-1 - 1] = 2$$

$$\int_{\pi}^{2\pi} \sin x\,dx = -\cos x\Big]_{\pi}^{2\pi} = -[\cos 2\pi - \cos \pi] = -[1 - (-1)] = -2$$

The second integral gives a negative value. The area between the graph and the axis is obtained by adding the absolute values

$$\text{Area} = |2| + |-2| = 4.$$ ■

Summary:

To find the area between the graph of $y = f(x)$ and the x-axis over the interval $[a, b]$:

1. Subdivide $[a, b]$ at the zeros of f.
2. Integrate f over each subinterval.
3. Add the absolute values of the integrals.

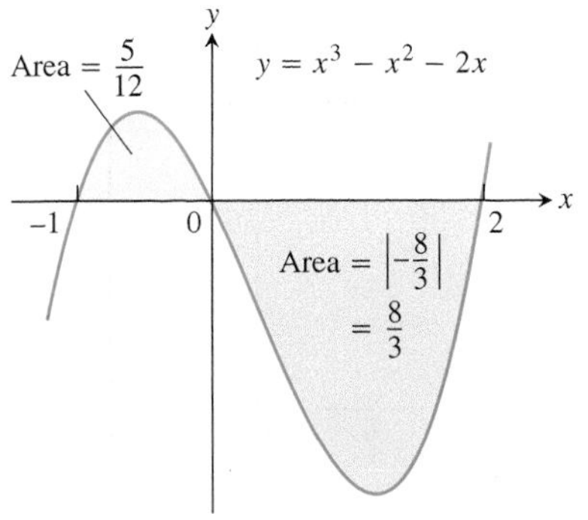

FIGURE 5.22 The region between the curve $y = x^3 - x^2 - 2x$ and the x-axis (Example 8).

EXAMPLE 8 Find the area of the region between the x-axis and the graph of $f(x) = x^3 - x^2 - 2x, -1 \le x \le 2$.

Solution First find the zeros of f. Since

$$f(x) = x^3 - x^2 - 2x = x(x^2 - x - 2) = x(x + 1)(x - 2),$$

the zeros are $x = 0, -1$, and 2 (Figure 5.22). The zeros subdivide $[-1, 2]$ into two subintervals: $[-1, 0]$, on which $f \ge 0$, and $[0, 2]$, on which $f \le 0$. We integrate f over each subinterval and add the absolute values of the calculated integrals.

$$\int_{-1}^{0}(x^3 - x^2 - 2x)\,dx = \left[\frac{x^4}{4} - \frac{x^3}{3} - x^2\right]_{-1}^{0} = 0 - \left[\frac{1}{4} + \frac{1}{3} - 1\right] = \frac{5}{12}$$

$$\int_{0}^{2}(x^3 - x^2 - 2x)\,dx = \left[\frac{x^4}{4} - \frac{x^3}{3} - x^2\right]_{0}^{2} = \left[4 - \frac{8}{3} - 4\right] - 0 = -\frac{8}{3}$$

The total enclosed area is obtained by adding the absolute values of the calculated integrals.

$$\text{Total enclosed area} = \frac{5}{12} + \left|-\frac{8}{3}\right| = \frac{37}{12}$$ ■

Exercises 5.4

Evaluating Integrals

Evaluate the integrals in Exercises 1–34.

1. $\int_{-2}^{0}(2x + 5)\,dx$
2. $\int_{-3}^{4}\left(5 - \frac{x}{2}\right)dx$
3. $\int_{0}^{2}x(x - 3)\,dx$
4. $\int_{-1}^{1}(x^2 - 2x + 3)\,dx$
5. $\int_{0}^{4}\left(3x - \frac{x^3}{4}\right)dx$
6. $\int_{-2}^{2}(x^3 - 2x + 3)\,dx$
7. $\int_{0}^{1}\left(x^2 + \sqrt{x}\right)dx$
8. $\int_{1}^{32}x^{-6/5}\,dx$
9. $\int_{0}^{\pi/3}2\sec^2 x\,dx$
10. $\int_{0}^{\pi}(1 + \cos x)\,dx$
11. $\int_{\pi/4}^{3\pi/4}\csc\theta\cot\theta\,d\theta$
12. $\int_{0}^{\pi/3}4\sec u\tan u\,du$
13. $\int_{\pi/2}^{0}\frac{1 + \cos 2t}{2}\,dt$
14. $\int_{-\pi/3}^{\pi/3}\frac{1 - \cos 2t}{2}\,dt$
15. $\int_{0}^{\pi/4}\tan^2 x\,dx$
16. $\int_{0}^{\pi/6}(\sec x + \tan x)^2\,dx$
17. $\int_{0}^{\pi/8}\sin 2x\,dx$
18. $\int_{-\pi/3}^{-\pi/4}\left(4\sec^2 t + \frac{\pi}{t^2}\right)dt$
19. $\int_{1}^{-1}(r + 1)^2\,dr$
20. $\int_{-\sqrt{3}}^{\sqrt{3}}(t + 1)(t^2 + 4)\,dt$
21. $\int_{\sqrt{2}}^{1}\left(\frac{u^7}{2} - \frac{1}{u^5}\right)du$
22. $\int_{-3}^{-1}\frac{y^5 - 2y}{y^3}\,dy$
23. $\int_{1}^{\sqrt{2}}\frac{s^2 + \sqrt{s}}{s^2}\,ds$
24. $\int_{1}^{8}\frac{(x^{1/3} + 1)(2 - x^{2/3})}{x^{1/3}}\,dx$
25. $\int_{\pi/2}^{\pi}\frac{\sin 2x}{2\sin x}\,dx$
26. $\int_{0}^{\pi/3}(\cos x + \sec x)^2\,dx$
27. $\int_{-4}^{4}|x|\,dx$
28. $\int_{0}^{\pi}\frac{1}{2}(\cos x + |\cos x|)\,dx$
29. $\int_{0}^{\ln 2}e^{3x}\,dx$
30. $\int_{1}^{2}\left(\frac{1}{x} - e^{-x}\right)dx$
31. $\int_{0}^{1/2}\frac{4}{\sqrt{1 - x^2}}\,dx$
32. $\int_{0}^{1/\sqrt{3}}\frac{dx}{1 + 4x^2}$
33. $\int_{2}^{4}x^{\pi-1}\,dx$
34. $\int_{-1}^{0}\pi^{x-1}\,dx$

In Exercises 35–38, guess an antiderivative for the integrand function. Validate your guess by differentiation and then evaluate the given definite integral. (*Hint:* Keep in mind the Chain Rule in guessing an antiderivative. You will learn how to find such antiderivatives in the next section.)

35. $\int_{0}^{1}xe^{x^2}\,dx$
36. $\int_{1}^{2}\frac{\ln x}{x}\,dx$
37. $\int_{2}^{5}\frac{x\,dx}{\sqrt{1 + x^2}}$
38. $\int_{0}^{\pi/3}\sin^2 x\cos x\,dx$

Derivatives of Integrals

Find the derivatives in Exercises 39–44.

a. by evaluating the integral and differentiating the result.
b. by differentiating the integral directly.

39. $\dfrac{d}{dx}\displaystyle\int_0^{\sqrt{x}} \cos t\, dt$

40. $\dfrac{d}{dx}\displaystyle\int_1^{\sin x} 3t^2\, dt$

41. $\dfrac{d}{dt}\displaystyle\int_0^{t^4} \sqrt{u}\, du$

42. $\dfrac{d}{d\theta}\displaystyle\int_0^{\tan\theta} \sec^2 y\, dy$

43. $\dfrac{d}{dx}\displaystyle\int_0^{x^3} e^{-t}\, dt$

44. $\dfrac{d}{dt}\displaystyle\int_0^{\sqrt{t}} \left(x^4 + \frac{3}{\sqrt{1-x^2}}\right) dx$

Find dy/dx in Exercises 45–56.

45. $y = \displaystyle\int_0^x \sqrt{1+t^2}\, dt$

46. $y = \displaystyle\int_1^x \frac{1}{t}\, dt, \quad x > 0$

47. $y = \displaystyle\int_{\sqrt{x}}^0 \sin(t^2)\, dt$

48. $y = x\displaystyle\int_2^{x^2} \sin(t^3)\, dt$

49. $y = \displaystyle\int_{-1}^x \frac{t^2}{t^2+4}\, dt - \int_3^x \frac{t^2}{t^2+4}\, dt$

50. $y = \left(\displaystyle\int_0^x (t^3+1)^{10}\, dt\right)^3$

51. $y = \displaystyle\int_0^{\sin x} \frac{dt}{\sqrt{1-t^2}}, \quad |x| < \frac{\pi}{2}$

52. $y = \displaystyle\int_{\tan x}^0 \frac{dt}{1+t^2}$

53. $y = \displaystyle\int_0^{e^{x^2}} \frac{1}{\sqrt{t}}\, dt$

54. $y = \displaystyle\int_{2^x}^1 \sqrt[3]{t}\, dt$

55. $y = \displaystyle\int_0^{\sin^{-1} x} \cos t\, dt$

56. $y = \displaystyle\int_{-1}^{x^{1/\pi}} \sin^{-1} t\, dt$

Area

In Exercises 57–60, find the total area between the region and the x-axis.

57. $y = -x^2 - 2x, \quad -3 \le x \le 2$

58. $y = 3x^2 - 3, \quad -2 \le x \le 2$

59. $y = x^3 - 3x^2 + 2x, \quad 0 \le x \le 2$

60. $y = x^{1/3} - x, \quad -1 \le x \le 8$

Find the areas of the shaded regions in Exercises 61–64.

61.

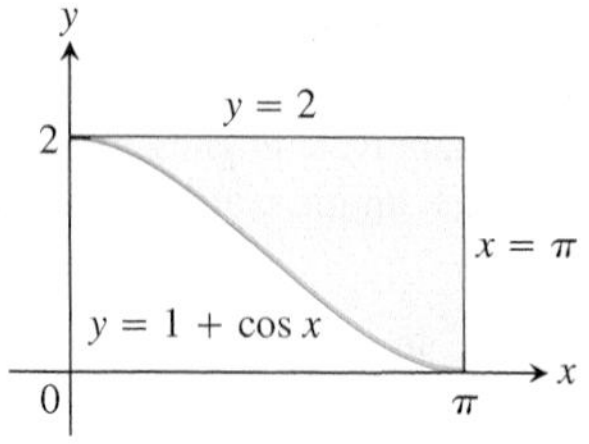

62.

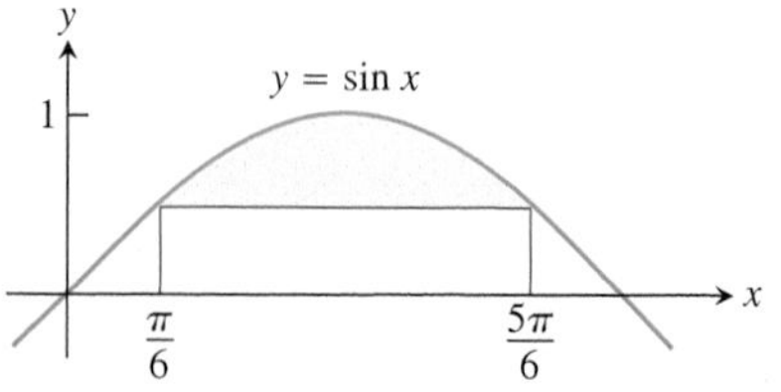

63.

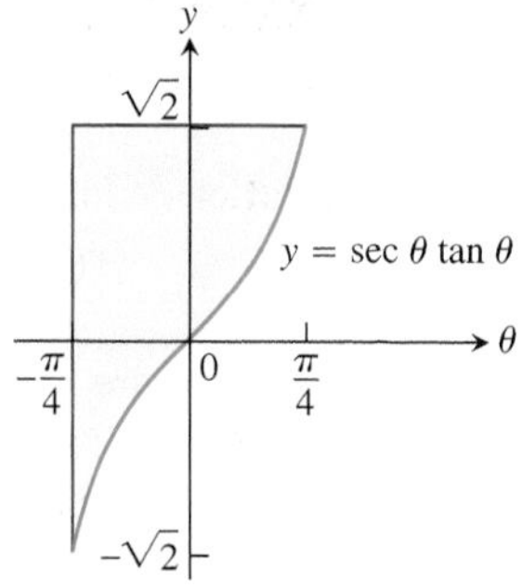

64.

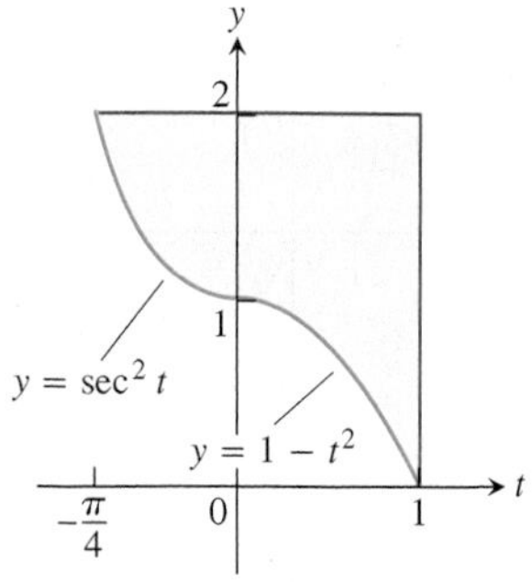

Initial Value Problems

Each of the following functions solves one of the initial value problems in Exercises 65–68. Which function solves which problem? Give brief reasons for your answers.

a. $y = \displaystyle\int_1^x \frac{1}{t}\, dt - 3$

b. $y = \displaystyle\int_0^x \sec t\, dt + 4$

c. $y = \displaystyle\int_{-1}^x \sec t\, dt + 4$

d. $y = \displaystyle\int_\pi^x \frac{1}{t}\, dt - 3$

65. $\dfrac{dy}{dx} = \dfrac{1}{x}, \quad y(\pi) = -3$

66. $y' = \sec x, \quad y(-1) = 4$

67. $y' = \sec x, \quad y(0) = 4$

68. $y' = \dfrac{1}{x}, \quad y(1) = -3$

Express the solutions of the initial value problems in Exercises 69 and 70 in terms of integrals.

69. $\dfrac{dy}{dx} = \sec x, \quad y(2) = 3$

70. $\dfrac{dy}{dx} = \sqrt{1+x^2}, \quad y(1) = -2$

Theory and Examples

71. **Archimedes' area formula for parabolic arches** Archimedes (287–212 B.C.), inventor, military engineer, physicist, and the greatest mathematician of classical times in the Western world, discovered that the area under a parabolic arch is two-thirds the base times the height. Sketch the parabolic arch $y = h - (4h/b^2)x^2$, $-b/2 \le x \le b/2$, assuming that h and b are positive. Then use calculus to find the area of the region enclosed between the arch and the x-axis.

72. Show that if k is a positive constant, then the area between the x-axis and one arch of the curve $y = \sin kx$ is $2/k$.

73. **Cost from marginal cost** The marginal cost of printing a poster when x posters have been printed is

$$\frac{dc}{dx} = \frac{1}{2\sqrt{x}}$$

dollars. Find $c(100) - c(1)$, the cost of printing posters 2–100.

74. **Revenue from marginal revenue** Suppose that a company's marginal revenue from the manufacture and sale of eggbeaters is

$$\frac{dr}{dx} = 2 - 2/(x+1)^2,$$

where r is measured in thousands of dollars and x in thousands of units. How much money should the company expect from a production run of $x = 3$ thousand eggbeaters? To find out, integrate the marginal revenue from $x = 0$ to $x = 3$.

75. The temperature T (°F) of a room at time t minutes is given by

$$T = 85 - 3\sqrt{25 - t} \quad \text{for} \quad 0 \le t \le 25.$$

a. Find the room's temperature when $t = 0$, $t = 16$, and $t = 25$.

b. Find the room's average temperature for $0 \le t \le 25$.

76. The height H (ft) of a palm tree after growing for t years is given by

$$H = \sqrt{t + 1} + 5t^{1/3} \quad \text{for} \quad 0 \le t \le 8.$$

a. Find the tree's height when $t = 0$, $t = 4$, and $t = 8$.

b. Find the tree's average height for $0 \le t \le 8$.

77. Suppose that $\int_1^x f(t)\,dt = x^2 - 2x + 1$. Find $f(x)$.

78. Find $f(4)$ if $\int_0^x f(t)\,dt = x \cos \pi x$.

79. Find the linearization of

$$f(x) = 2 - \int_2^{x+1} \frac{9}{1 + t}\,dt$$

at $x = 1$.

80. Find the linearization of

$$g(x) = 3 + \int_1^{x^2} \sec(t - 1)\,dt$$

at $x = -1$.

81. Suppose that f has a positive derivative for all values of x and that $f(1) = 0$. Which of the following statements must be true of the function

$$g(x) = \int_0^x f(t)\,dt?$$

Give reasons for your answers.

a. g is a differentiable function of x.

b. g is a continuous function of x.

c. The graph of g has a horizontal tangent at $x = 1$.

d. g has a local maximum at $x = 1$.

e. g has a local minimum at $x = 1$.

f. The graph of g has an inflection point at $x = 1$.

g. The graph of dg/dx crosses the x-axis at $x = 1$.

82. Another proof of the Evaluation Theorem

a. Let $a = x_0 < x_1 < x_2 \cdots < x_n = b$ be any partition of $[a, b]$, and let F be any antiderivative of f. Show that

$$F(b) - F(a) = \sum_{i=1}^{n} [F(x_i) - F(x_{i-1})].$$

b. Apply the Mean Value Theorem to each term to show that $F(x_i) - F(x_{i-1}) = f(c_i)(x_i - x_{i-1})$ for some c_i in the interval (x_{i-1}, x_i). Then show that $F(b) - F(a)$ is a Riemann sum for f on $[a, b]$.

c. From part (b) and the definition of the definite integral, show that

$$F(b) - F(a) = \int_a^b f(x)\,dx.$$

83. Suppose that f is the differentiable function shown in the accompanying graph and that the position at time t (sec) of a particle moving along a coordinate axis is

$$s = \int_0^t f(x)\,dx$$

meters. Use the graph to answer the following questions. Give reasons for your answers.

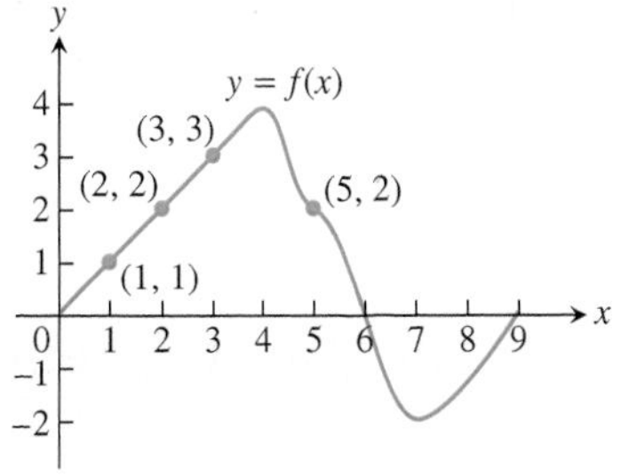

a. What is the particle's velocity at time $t = 5$?

b. Is the acceleration of the particle at time $t = 5$ positive, or negative?

c. What is the particle's position at time $t = 3$?

d. At what time during the first 9 sec does s have its largest value?

e. Approximately when is the acceleration zero?

f. When is the particle moving toward the origin? Away from the origin?

g. On which side of the origin does the particle lie at time $t = 9$?

84. Find $\displaystyle\lim_{x\to\infty} \frac{1}{\sqrt{x}} \int_1^x \frac{dt}{\sqrt{t}}$.

COMPUTER EXPLORATIONS

In Exercises 85–88, let $F(x) = \int_a^x f(t)\,dt$ for the specified function f and interval $[a, b]$. Use a CAS to perform the following steps and answer the questions posed.

a. Plot the functions f and F together over $[a, b]$.

b. Solve the equation $F'(x) = 0$. What can you see to be true about the graphs of f and F at points where $F'(x) = 0$? Is your observation borne out by Part 1 of the Fundamental Theorem coupled with information provided by the first derivative? Explain your answer.

c. Over what intervals (approximately) is the function F increasing and decreasing? What is true about f over those intervals?

d. Calculate the derivative f' and plot it together with F. What can you see to be true about the graph of F at points where $f'(x) = 0$? Is your observation borne out by Part 1 of the Fundamental Theorem? Explain your answer.

85. $f(x) = x^3 - 4x^2 + 3x, \quad [0, 4]$

86. $f(x) = 2x^4 - 17x^3 + 46x^2 - 43x + 12, \quad \left[0, \frac{9}{2}\right]$

87. $f(x) = \sin 2x \cos \frac{x}{3}, \quad [0, 2\pi]$

88. $f(x) = x \cos \pi x, \quad [0, 2\pi]$

In Exercises 89–92, let $F(x) = \int_a^{u(x)} f(t)\,dt$ for the specified a, u, and f. Use a CAS to perform the following steps and answer the questions posed.

a. Find the domain of F.

b. Calculate $F'(x)$ and determine its zeros. For what points in its domain is F increasing? Decreasing?

c. Calculate $F''(x)$ and determine its zero. Identify the local extrema and the points of inflection of F.

d. Using the information from parts (a)–(c), draw a rough hand-sketch of $y = F(x)$ over its domain. Then graph $F(x)$ on your CAS to support your sketch.

89. $a = 1, \quad u(x) = x^2, \quad f(x) = \sqrt{1 - x^2}$

90. $a = 0, \quad u(x) = x^2, \quad f(x) = \sqrt{1 - x^2}$

91. $a = 0, \quad u(x) = 1 - x, \quad f(x) = x^2 - 2x - 3$

92. $a = 0, \quad u(x) = 1 - x^2, \quad f(x) = x^2 - 2x - 3$

In Exercises 93 and 94, assume that f is continuous and $u(x)$ is twice-differentiable.

93. Calculate $\dfrac{d}{dx}\displaystyle\int_a^{u(x)} f(t)\,dt$ and check your answer using a CAS.

94. Calculate $\dfrac{d^2}{dx^2}\displaystyle\int_a^{u(x)} f(t)\,dt$ and check your answer using a CAS.

5.5 Indefinite Integrals and the Substitution Method

The Fundamental Theorem of Calculus says that a definite integral of a continuous function can be computed directly if we can find an antiderivative of the function. In Section 4.8 we defined the **indefinite integral** of the function f with respect to x as the set of *all* antiderivatives of f, symbolized by

$$\int f(x)\,dx.$$

Since any two antiderivatives of f differ by a constant, the indefinite integral $\int$ notation means that for any antiderivative F of f,

$$\int f(x)\,dx = F(x) + C,$$

where C is any arbitrary constant.

The connection between antiderivatives and the definite integral stated in the Fundamental Theorem now explains this notation. When finding the indefinite integral of a function f, remember that it always includes an arbitrary constant C.

We must distinguish carefully between definite and indefinite integrals. A definite integral $\int_a^b f(x)\,dx$ is a *number*. An indefinite integral $\int f(x)\,dx$ is a *function* plus an arbitrary constant C.

So far, we have only been able to find antiderivatives of functions that are clearly recognizable as derivatives. In this section we begin to develop more general techniques for finding antiderivatives.

Substitution: Running the Chain Rule Backwards

If u is a differentiable function of x and n is any number different from -1, the Chain Rule tells us that

$$\frac{d}{dx}\left(\frac{u^{n+1}}{n+1}\right) = u^n \frac{du}{dx}.$$

From another point of view, this same equation says that $u^{n+1}/(n+1)$ is one of the antiderivatives of the function $u^n(du/dx)$. Therefore,

$$\int u^n \frac{du}{dx}\,dx = \frac{u^{n+1}}{n+1} + C. \qquad (1)$$

The integral in Equation (1) is equal to the simpler integral

$$\int u^n \, du = \frac{u^{n+1}}{n+1} + C,$$

which suggests that the simpler expression du can be substituted for $(du/dx)\,dx$ when computing an integral. Leibniz, one of the founders of calculus, had the insight that indeed this substitution could be done, leading to the *substitution method* for computing integrals. As with differentials, when computing integrals we have

$$du = \frac{du}{dx}\,dx.$$

EXAMPLE 1 Find the integral $\int (x^3 + x)^5(3x^2 + 1)\,dx$.

Solution We set $u = x^3 + x$. Then

$$du = \frac{du}{dx}\,dx = (3x^2 + 1)\,dx,$$

so that by substitution we have

$$\int (x^3 + x)^5(3x^2 + 1)\,dx = \int u^5\,du \qquad \text{Let } u = x^3 + x,\ du = (3x^2 + 1)\,dx.$$

$$= \frac{u^6}{6} + C \qquad \text{Integrate with respect to } u.$$

$$= \frac{(x^3 + x)^6}{6} + C \qquad \text{Substitute } x^3 + x \text{ for } u. \quad \blacksquare$$

EXAMPLE 2 Find $\int \sqrt{2x + 1}\,dx$.

Solution The integral does not fit the formula

$$\int u^n\,du,$$

with $u = 2x + 1$ and $n = 1/2$, because

$$du = \frac{du}{dx}\,dx = 2\,dx$$

is not precisely dx. The constant factor 2 is missing from the integral. However, we can introduce this factor after the integral sign if we compensate for it by a factor of $1/2$ in front of the integral sign. So we write

$$\int \sqrt{2x + 1}\,dx = \frac{1}{2}\int \underbrace{\sqrt{2x + 1}}_{u} \cdot \underbrace{2\,dx}_{du}$$

$$= \frac{1}{2}\int u^{1/2}\,du \qquad \text{Let } u = 2x + 1,\ du = 2\,dx.$$

$$= \frac{1}{2}\frac{u^{3/2}}{3/2} + C \qquad \text{Integrate with respect to } u.$$

$$= \frac{1}{3}(2x + 1)^{3/2} + C \qquad \text{Substitute } 2x + 1 \text{ for } u. \quad \blacksquare$$

The substitutions in Examples 1 and 2 are instances of the following general rule.

THEOREM 6—The Substitution Rule If $u = g(x)$ is a differentiable function whose range is an interval I, and f is continuous on I, then

$$\int f(g(x))g'(x)\,dx = \int f(u)\,du.$$

Proof By the Chain Rule, $F(g(x))$ is an antiderivative of $f(g(x)) \cdot g'(x)$ whenever F is an antiderivative of f:

$$\begin{aligned}\frac{d}{dx}F(g(x)) &= F'(g(x)) \cdot g'(x) && \text{Chain Rule}\\ &= f(g(x)) \cdot g'(x). && F' = f\end{aligned}$$

If we make the substitution $u = g(x)$, then

$$\begin{aligned}\int f(g(x))g'(x)\,dx &= \int \frac{d}{dx}F(g(x))\,dx\\ &= F(g(x)) + C && \text{Fundamental Theorem}\\ &= F(u) + C && u = g(x)\\ &= \int F'(u)\,du && \text{Fundamental Theorem}\\ &= \int f(u)\,du && F' = f\end{aligned}$$

■

The Substitution Rule provides the following **substitution method** to evaluate the integral

$$\int f(g(x))g'(x)\,dx,$$

when f and g' are continuous functions:

1. Substitute $u = g(x)$ and $du = (du/dx)\,dx = g'(x)\,dx$ to obtain the integral

$$\int f(u)\,du.$$

2. Integrate with respect to u.
3. Replace u by $g(x)$ in the result.

EXAMPLE 3 Find $\displaystyle\int \sec^2(5t + 1) \cdot 5\,dt$.

Solution We substitute $u = 5t + 1$ and $du = 5\,dt$. Then,

$$\begin{aligned}\int \sec^2(5t + 1) \cdot 5\,dt &= \int \sec^2 u\,du && \text{Let } u = 5t + 1,\ du = 5\,dt.\\ &= \tan u + C && \frac{d}{du}\tan u = \sec^2 u\\ &= \tan(5t + 1) + C && \text{Substitute } 5t + 1 \text{ for } u.\end{aligned}$$

■

EXAMPLE 4 Find $\displaystyle\int \cos(7\theta + 3)\,d\theta$.

Solution We let $u = 7\theta + 3$ so that $du = 7\,d\theta$. The constant factor 7 is missing from the $d\theta$ term in the integral. We can compensate for it by multiplying and dividing by 7, using the same procedure as in Example 2. Then,

$$\begin{aligned}
\int \cos(7\theta + 3)\,d\theta &= \frac{1}{7}\int \cos(7\theta + 3)\cdot 7\,d\theta && \text{Place factor } 1/7 \text{ in front of integral.}\\
&= \frac{1}{7}\int \cos u\,du && \text{Let } u = 7\theta + 3,\ du = 7\,d\theta.\\
&= \frac{1}{7}\sin u + C && \text{Integrate.}\\
&= \frac{1}{7}\sin(7\theta + 3) + C && \text{Substitute } 7\theta + 3 \text{ for } u.
\end{aligned}$$

There is another approach to this problem. With $u = 7\theta + 3$ and $du = 7\,d\theta$ as before, we solve for $d\theta$ to obtain $d\theta = (1/7)\,du$. Then the integral becomes

$$\begin{aligned}
\int \cos(7\theta + 3)\,d\theta &= \int \cos u\cdot\frac{1}{7}\,du && \text{Let } u = 7\theta + 3,\ du = 7\,d\theta, \text{ and } d\theta = (1/7)\,du.\\
&= \frac{1}{7}\sin u + C && \text{Integrate.}\\
&= \frac{1}{7}\sin(7\theta + 3) + C && \text{Substitute } 7\theta + 3 \text{ for } u.
\end{aligned}$$

We can verify this solution by differentiating and checking that we obtain the original function $\cos(7\theta + 3)$. ■

EXAMPLE 5 Sometimes we observe that a power of x appears in the integrand that is one less than the power of x appearing in the argument of a function we want to integrate. This observation immediately suggests we try a substitution for the higher power of x. This situation occurs in the following integration.

$$\begin{aligned}
\int x^2 e^{x^3}\,dx &= \int e^{x^3}\cdot x^2\,dx\\
&= \int e^u\cdot\frac{1}{3}\,du && \text{Let } u = x^3,\ du = 3x^2\,dx,\ (1/3)\,du = x^2\,dx.\\
&= \frac{1}{3}\int e^u\,du\\
&= \frac{1}{3}e^u + C && \text{Integrate with respect to } u.\\
&= \frac{1}{3}e^{x^3} + C && \text{Replace } u \text{ by } x^3.
\end{aligned}$$

■

HISTORICAL BIOGRAPHY

George David Birkhoff (1884–1944)

EXAMPLE 6 An integrand may require some algebraic manipulation before the substitution method can be applied. This example gives two integrals obtained by multiplying the integrand by an algebraic form equal to 1, leading to an appropriate substitution.

(a)
$$\begin{aligned}
\int \frac{dx}{e^x + e^{-x}} &= \int \frac{e^x\,dx}{e^{2x} + 1} && \text{Multiply by } (e^x/e^x) = 1.\\
&= \int \frac{du}{u^2 + 1} && \text{Let } u = e^x,\ u^2 = e^{2x},\ du = e^x\,dx.\\
&= \tan^{-1}u + C && \text{Integrate with respect to } u.\\
&= \tan^{-1}(e^x) + C && \text{Replace } u \text{ by } e^x.
\end{aligned}$$

(b) $$\int \sec x\,dx = \int (\sec x)(1)\,dx = \int \sec x \cdot \frac{\sec x + \tan x}{\sec x + \tan x}\,dx$$ $\frac{\sec x + \tan x}{\sec x + \tan x}$ is a form of 1

$$= \int \frac{\sec^2 x + \sec x \tan x}{\sec x + \tan x}\,dx$$

$$= \int \frac{du}{u}$$ $u = \tan x + \sec x$, $du = (\sec^2 x + \sec x \tan x)\,dx$

$$= \ln|u| + C = \ln|\sec x + \tan x| + C.$$ ■

EXAMPLE 7 Sometimes we can use trigonometric identities to transform integrals we do not know how to evaluate into ones we can evaluate using the Substitution Rule.

(a) $$\int \sin^2 x\,dx = \int \frac{1 - \cos 2x}{2}\,dx$$ $\sin^2 x = \frac{1 - \cos 2x}{2}$

$$= \frac{1}{2}\int (1 - \cos 2x)\,dx$$

$$= \frac{1}{2}x - \frac{1}{2}\frac{\sin 2x}{2} + C = \frac{x}{2} - \frac{\sin 2x}{4} + C$$

(b) $$\int \cos^2 x\,dx = \int \frac{1 + \cos 2x}{2}\,dx = \frac{x}{2} + \frac{\sin 2x}{4} + C$$ $\cos^2 x = \frac{1 + \cos 2x}{2}$ ■

It may happen that an extra factor of x appears in the integrand when we try a substitution $u = g(x)$. In that case, it may be possible to solve the equation $u = g(x)$ for x in terms of u. Replacing the extra factor of x with that expression may then allow for an integral we can evaluate. Here's an example of this situation.

EXAMPLE 8 Evaluate $\int x\sqrt{2x + 1}\,dx$.

Solution Our previous integration in Example 2 suggests the substitution $u = 2x + 1$ with $du = 2\,dx$. Then,

$$\sqrt{2x + 1}\,dx = \frac{1}{2}\sqrt{u}\,du.$$

However, in this case the integrand contains an extra factor of x multiplying the term $\sqrt{2x + 1}$. To adjust for this, we solve the substitution equation $u = 2x + 1$ to obtain $x = (u - 1)/2$, and find that

$$x\sqrt{2x + 1}\,dx = \frac{1}{2}(u - 1)\cdot\frac{1}{2}\sqrt{u}\,du.$$

The integration now becomes

$$\int x\sqrt{2x + 1}\,dx = \frac{1}{4}\int (u - 1)\sqrt{u}\,du = \frac{1}{4}\int (u - 1)u^{1/2}\,du$$ Substitute.

$$= \frac{1}{4}\int (u^{3/2} - u^{1/2})\,du$$ Multiply terms.

$$= \frac{1}{4}\left(\frac{2}{5}u^{5/2} - \frac{2}{3}u^{3/2}\right) + C$$ Integrate.

$$= \frac{1}{10}(2x + 1)^{5/2} - \frac{1}{6}(2x + 1)^{3/2} + C.$$ Replace u by $2x + 1$. ■

The success of the substitution method depends on finding a substitution that changes an integral we cannot evaluate directly into one that we can. If the first substitution fails, try to simplify the integrand further with additional substitutions (see Exercises 67 and 68).

EXAMPLE 9 Evaluate $\int \frac{2z\,dz}{\sqrt[3]{z^2+1}}$.

Solution We can use the substitution method of integration as an exploratory tool: Substitute for the most troublesome part of the integrand and see how things work out. For the integral here, we might try $u = z^2 + 1$ or we might even press our luck and take u to be the entire cube root. Here is what happens in each case.

Solution 1: Substitute $u = z^2 + 1$.

$$\int \frac{2z\,dz}{\sqrt[3]{z^2+1}} = \int \frac{du}{u^{1/3}} \qquad \text{Let } u = z^2+1,\ du = 2z\,dz.$$

$$= \int u^{-1/3}\,du \qquad \text{In the form } \int u^n\,du$$

$$= \frac{u^{2/3}}{2/3} + C \qquad \text{Integrate.}$$

$$= \frac{3}{2}u^{2/3} + C$$

$$= \frac{3}{2}(z^2+1)^{2/3} + C \qquad \text{Replace } u \text{ by } z^2+1.$$

Solution 2: Substitute $u = \sqrt[3]{z^2+1}$ instead.

$$\int \frac{2z\,dz}{\sqrt[3]{z^2+1}} = \int \frac{3u^2\,du}{u} \qquad \text{Let } u = \sqrt[3]{z^2+1},\ u^3 = z^2+1,\ 3u^2\,du = 2z\,dz.$$

$$= 3\int u\,du$$

$$= 3\cdot\frac{u^2}{2} + C \qquad \text{Integrate.}$$

$$= \frac{3}{2}(z^2+1)^{2/3} + C \qquad \text{Replace } u \text{ by } (z^2+1)^{1/3}. \blacksquare$$

Exercises 5.5

Evaluating Indefinite Integrals

Evaluate the indefinite integrals in Exercises 1–16 by using the given substitutions to reduce the integrals to standard form.

1. $\int 2(2x+4)^5\,dx, \quad u = 2x+4$

2. $\int 7\sqrt{7x-1}\,dx, \quad u = 7x-1$

3. $\int 2x(x^2+5)^{-4}\,dx, \quad u = x^2+5$

4. $\int \frac{4x^3}{(x^4+1)^2}\,dx, \quad u = x^4+1$

5. $\int (3x+2)(3x^2+4x)^4\,dx, \quad u = 3x^2+4x$

6. $\int \frac{\left(1+\sqrt{x}\right)^{1/3}}{\sqrt{x}}\,dx, \quad u = 1+\sqrt{x}$

7. $\int \sin 3x\,dx, \quad u = 3x$

8. $\int x \sin(2x^2)\, dx, \quad u = 2x^2$

9. $\int \sec 2t \tan 2t\, dt, \quad u = 2t$

10. $\int \left(1 - \cos\frac{t}{2}\right)^2 \sin\frac{t}{2}\, dt, \quad u = 1 - \cos\frac{t}{2}$

11. $\int \frac{9r^2\, dr}{\sqrt{1 - r^3}}, \quad u = 1 - r^3$

12. $\int 12(y^4 + 4y^2 + 1)^2(y^3 + 2y)\, dy, \quad u = y^4 + 4y^2 + 1$

13. $\int \sqrt{x} \sin^2(x^{3/2} - 1)\, dx, \quad u = x^{3/2} - 1$

14. $\int \frac{1}{x^2} \cos^2\left(\frac{1}{x}\right) dx, \quad u = -\frac{1}{x}$

15. $\int \csc^2 2\theta \cot 2\theta\, d\theta$

a. Using $u = \cot 2\theta$ b. Using $u = \csc 2\theta$

16. $\int \frac{dx}{\sqrt{5x + 8}}$

a. Using $u = 5x + 8$ b. Using $u = \sqrt{5x + 8}$

Evaluate the integrals in Exercises 17–66.

17. $\int \sqrt{3 - 2s}\, ds$

18. $\int \frac{1}{\sqrt{5s + 4}}\, ds$

19. $\int \theta \sqrt[4]{1 - \theta^2}\, d\theta$

20. $\int 3y\sqrt{7 - 3y^2}\, dy$

21. $\int \frac{1}{\sqrt{x}(1 + \sqrt{x})^2}\, dx$

22. $\int \cos(3z + 4)\, dz$

23. $\int \sec^2(3x + 2)\, dx$

24. $\int \tan^2 x \sec^2 x\, dx$

25. $\int \sin^5\frac{x}{3} \cos\frac{x}{3}\, dx$

26. $\int \tan^7\frac{x}{2} \sec^2\frac{x}{2}\, dx$

27. $\int r^2\left(\frac{r^3}{18} - 1\right)^5 dr$

28. $\int r^4\left(7 - \frac{r^5}{10}\right)^3 dr$

29. $\int x^{1/2} \sin(x^{3/2} + 1)\, dx$

30. $\int \csc\left(\frac{v - \pi}{2}\right) \cot\left(\frac{v - \pi}{2}\right) dv$

31. $\int \frac{\sin(2t + 1)}{\cos^2(2t + 1)}\, dt$

32. $\int \frac{\sec z \tan z}{\sqrt{\sec z}}\, dz$

33. $\int \frac{1}{t^2} \cos\left(\frac{1}{t} - 1\right) dt$

34. $\int \frac{1}{\sqrt{t}} \cos(\sqrt{t} + 3)\, dt$

35. $\int \frac{1}{\theta^2} \sin\frac{1}{\theta} \cos\frac{1}{\theta}\, d\theta$

36. $\int \frac{\cos\sqrt{\theta}}{\sqrt{\theta}\sin^2\sqrt{\theta}}\, d\theta$

37. $\int t^3(1 + t^4)^3\, dt$

38. $\int \sqrt{\frac{x - 1}{x^5}}\, dx$

39. $\int \frac{1}{x^2}\sqrt{2 - \frac{1}{x}}\, dx$

40. $\int \frac{1}{x^3}\sqrt{\frac{x^2 - 1}{x^2}}\, dx$

41. $\int \sqrt{\frac{x^3 - 3}{x^{11}}}\, dx$

42. $\int \sqrt{\frac{x^4}{x^3 - 1}}\, dx$

43. $\int x(x - 1)^{10}\, dx$

44. $\int x\sqrt{4 - x}\, dx$

45. $\int (x + 1)^2(1 - x)^5\, dx$

46. $\int (x + 5)(x - 5)^{1/3}\, dx$

47. $\int x^3\sqrt{x^2 + 1}\, dx$

48. $\int 3x^5\sqrt{x^3 + 1}\, dx$

49. $\int \frac{x}{(x^2 - 4)^3}\, dx$

50. $\int \frac{x}{(x - 4)^3}\, dx$

51. $\int (\cos x)\, e^{\sin x}\, dx$

52. $\int (\sin 2\theta)\, e^{\sin^2\theta}\, d\theta$

53. $\int \frac{1}{\sqrt{x e^{-\sqrt{x}}}} \sec^2(e^{\sqrt{x}} + 1)\, dx$

54. $\int \frac{1}{x^2} e^{1/x} \sec(1 + e^{1/x}) \tan(1 + e^{1/x})\, dx$

55. $\int \frac{dx}{x \ln x}$

56. $\int \frac{\ln\sqrt{t}}{t}\, dt$

57. $\int \frac{dz}{1 + e^z}$

58. $\int \frac{dx}{x\sqrt{x^4 - 1}}$

59. $\int \frac{5}{9 + 4r^2}\, dr$

60. $\int \frac{1}{\sqrt{e^{2\theta} - 1}}\, d\theta$

61. $\int \frac{e^{\sin^{-1}x}\, dx}{\sqrt{1 - x^2}}$

62. $\int \frac{e^{\cos^{-1}x}\, dx}{\sqrt{1 - x^2}}$

63. $\int \frac{(\sin^{-1}x)^2\, dx}{\sqrt{1 - x^2}}$

64. $\int \frac{\sqrt{\tan^{-1}x}\, dx}{1 + x^2}$

65. $\int \frac{dy}{(\tan^{-1}y)(1 + y^2)}$

66. $\int \frac{dy}{(\sin^{-1}y)\sqrt{1 - y^2}}$

If you do not know what substitution to make, try reducing the integral step by step, using a trial substitution to simplify the integral a bit and then another to simplify it some more. You will see what we mean if you try the sequences of substitutions in Exercises 67 and 68.

67. $\int \frac{18\tan^2 x \sec^2 x}{(2 + \tan^3 x)^2}\, dx$

a. $u = \tan x$, followed by $v = u^3$, then by $w = 2 + v$

b. $u = \tan^3 x$, followed by $v = 2 + u$

c. $u = 2 + \tan^3 x$

68. $\int \sqrt{1 + \sin^2(x - 1)} \sin(x - 1)\cos(x - 1)\, dx$

a. $u = x - 1$, followed by $v = \sin u$, then by $w = 1 + v^2$

b. $u = \sin(x - 1)$, followed by $v = 1 + u^2$

c. $u = 1 + \sin^2(x - 1)$

Evaluate the integrals in Exercises 69 and 70.

69. $\int \frac{(2r - 1)\cos\sqrt{3(2r - 1)^2 + 6}}{\sqrt{3(2r - 1)^2 + 6}}\, dr$

70. $\int \frac{\sin\sqrt{\theta}}{\sqrt{\theta\cos^3\sqrt{\theta}}}\, d\theta$

Initial Value Problems

Solve the initial value problems in Exercises 71–76.

71. $\frac{ds}{dt} = 12t\,(3t^2 - 1)^3, \quad s(1) = 3$

72. $\frac{dy}{dx} = 4x\,(x^2 + 8)^{-1/3}, \quad y(0) = 0$

73. $\frac{ds}{dt} = 8\sin^2\left(t + \frac{\pi}{12}\right), \quad s(0) = 8$

74. $\frac{dr}{d\theta} = 3\cos^2\left(\frac{\pi}{4} - \theta\right), \quad r(0) = \frac{\pi}{8}$

75. $\frac{d^2s}{dt^2} = -4\sin\left(2t - \frac{\pi}{2}\right), \quad s'(0) = 100, \quad s(0) = 0$

76. $\frac{d^2y}{dx^2} = 4\sec^2 2x \tan 2x, \quad y'(0) = 4, \quad y(0) = -1$

77. The velocity of a particle moving back and forth on a line is $v = ds/dt = 6\sin 2t$ m/sec for all t. If $s = 0$ when $t = 0$, find the value of s when $t = \pi/2$ sec.

78. The acceleration of a particle moving back and forth on a line is $a = d^2s/dt^2 = \pi^2 \cos \pi t$ m/sec^2 for all t. If $s = 0$ and $v = 8$ m/sec when $t = 0$, find s when $t = 1$ sec.

5.6 Substitution and Area Between Curves

There are two methods for evaluating a definite integral by substitution. One method is to find an antiderivative using substitution and then to evaluate the definite integral by applying the Evaluation Theorem. The other method extends the process of substitution directly to *definite* integrals by changing the limits of integration. We apply the new formula introduced here to the problem of computing the area between two curves.

The Substitution Formula

The following formula shows how the limits of integration change when the variable of integration is changed by substitution.

THEOREM 7—Substitution in Definite Integrals If g' is continuous on the interval $[a, b]$ and f is continuous on the range of $g(x) = u$, then

$$\int_a^b f(g(x)) \cdot g'(x)\,dx = \int_{g(a)}^{g(b)} f(u)\,du.$$

Proof Let F denote any antiderivative of f. Then,

$$\begin{aligned}\int_a^b f(g(x)) \cdot g'(x)\,dx &= F(g(x))\Big]_{x=a}^{x=b} \\ &= F(g(b)) - F(g(a)) \\ &= F(u)\Big]_{u=g(a)}^{u=g(b)} \\ &= \int_{g(a)}^{g(b)} f(u)\,du.\end{aligned}$$

$\frac{d}{dx}F(g(x)) = F'(g(x))g'(x) = f(g(x))g'(x)$

Fundamental Theorem, Part 2 ■

To use the formula, make the same u-substitution $u = g(x)$ and $du = g'(x)\,dx$ you would use to evaluate the corresponding indefinite integral. Then integrate the transformed integral with respect to u from the value $g(a)$ (the value of u at $x = a$) to the value $g(b)$ (the value of u at $x = b$).

EXAMPLE 1 Evaluate $\int_{-1}^{1} 3x^2\sqrt{x^3+1}\,dx$.

Solution We have two choices.

Method 1: Transform the integral and evaluate the transformed integral with the transformed limits given in Theorem 7.

$$\int_{-1}^{1} 3x^2\sqrt{x^3+1}\,dx \qquad \text{Let } u = x^3+1,\ du = 3x^2\,dx. \text{ When } x=-1,\ u=(-1)^3+1=0. \text{ When } x=1,\ u=(1)^3+1=2.$$

$$= \int_0^2 \sqrt{u}\,du$$

$$= \frac{2}{3}u^{3/2}\Big]_0^2 \qquad \text{Evaluate the new definite integral.}$$

$$= \frac{2}{3}\left[2^{3/2}-0^{3/2}\right] = \frac{2}{3}\left[2\sqrt{2}\right] = \frac{4\sqrt{2}}{3}$$

Method 2: Transform the integral as an indefinite integral, integrate, change back to x, and use the original x-limits.

$$\int 3x^2\sqrt{x^3+1}\,dx = \int \sqrt{u}\,du \qquad \text{Let } u = x^3+1,\ du = 3x^2\,dx.$$

$$= \frac{2}{3}u^{3/2}+C \qquad \text{Integrate with respect to } u.$$

$$= \frac{2}{3}(x^3+1)^{3/2}+C \qquad \text{Replace } u \text{ by } x^3+1.$$

$$\int_{-1}^{1} 3x^2\sqrt{x^3+1}\,dx = \frac{2}{3}(x^3+1)^{3/2}\Big]_{-1}^{1} \qquad \text{Use the integral just found, with limits of integration for } x.$$

$$= \frac{2}{3}\left[((1)^3+1)^{3/2}-((-1)^3+1)^{3/2}\right]$$

$$= \frac{2}{3}\left[2^{3/2}-0^{3/2}\right] = \frac{2}{3}\left[2\sqrt{2}\right] = \frac{4\sqrt{2}}{3}$$

■

Which method is better—evaluating the transformed definite integral with transformed limits using Theorem 7, or transforming the integral, integrating, and transforming back to use the original limits of integration? In Example 1, the first method seems easier, but that is not always the case. Generally, it is best to know both methods and to use whichever one seems better at the time.

EXAMPLE 2 We use the method of transforming the limits of integration.

(a) $$\int_{\pi/4}^{\pi/2} \cot\theta\csc^2\theta\,d\theta = \int_1^0 u\cdot(-du) \qquad \text{Let } u=\cot\theta,\ du=-\csc^2\theta\,d\theta,\ -du=\csc^2\theta\,d\theta. \text{ When } \theta=\pi/4,\ u=\cot(\pi/4)=1. \text{ When } \theta=\pi/2,\ u=\cot(\pi/2)=0.$$

$$= -\int_1^0 u\,du$$

$$= -\left[\frac{u^2}{2}\right]_1^0$$

$$= -\left[\frac{(0)^2}{2}-\frac{(1)^2}{2}\right] = \frac{1}{2}$$

$$\textbf{(b)} \int_{-\pi/4}^{\pi/4} \tan x\, dx = \int_{-\pi/4}^{\pi/4} \frac{\sin x}{\cos x}\, dx$$

$$= -\int_{\sqrt{2}/2}^{\sqrt{2}/2} \frac{du}{u}$$

Let $u = \cos x$, $du = -\sin x\, dx$. When $x = -\pi/4$, $u = \sqrt{2}/2$. When $x = \pi/4$, $u = \sqrt{2}/2$.

$$= -\ln|u| \Big]_{\sqrt{2}/2}^{\sqrt{2}/2} = 0$$

Integrate, zero-width interval ■

Definite Integrals of Symmetric Functions

The Substitution Formula in Theorem 7 simplifies the calculation of definite integrals of even and odd functions (Section 1.1) over a symmetric interval $[-a, a]$ (Figure 5.23).

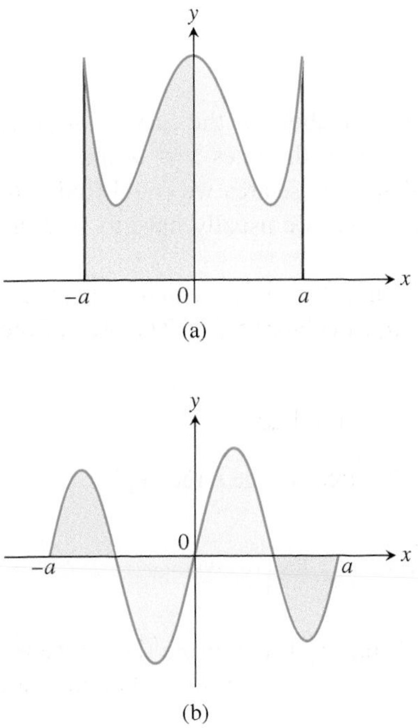

FIGURE 5.23 (a) For f an even function, the integral from $-a$ to a is twice the integral from 0 to a.
(b) For f an odd function, the integral from $-a$ to a equals 0.

THEOREM 8 Let f be continuous on the symmetric interval $[-a, a]$.

(a) If f is even, then $\int_{-a}^{a} f(x)\, dx = 2\int_{0}^{a} f(x)\, dx$.

(b) If f is odd, then $\int_{-a}^{a} f(x)\, dx = 0$.

Proof of Part (a)

$$\int_{-a}^{a} f(x)\, dx = \int_{-a}^{0} f(x)\, dx + \int_{0}^{a} f(x)\, dx$$

Additivity Rule for Definite Integrals

$$= -\int_{0}^{-a} f(x)\, dx + \int_{0}^{a} f(x)\, dx$$

Order of Integration Rule

$$= -\int_{0}^{a} f(-u)(-du) + \int_{0}^{a} f(x)\, dx$$

Let $u = -x$, $du = -dx$. When $x = 0$, $u = 0$. When $x = -a$, $u = a$.

$$= \int_{0}^{a} f(-u)\, du + \int_{0}^{a} f(x)\, dx$$

$$= \int_{0}^{a} f(u)\, du + \int_{0}^{a} f(x)\, dx$$

f is even, so $f(-u) = f(u)$.

$$= 2\int_{0}^{a} f(x)\, dx$$

The proof of part (b) is entirely similar and you are asked to give it in Exercise 114. ■

The assertions of Theorem 8 remain true when f is an integrable function (rather than having the stronger property of being continuous).

EXAMPLE 3 Evaluate $\int_{-2}^{2} (x^4 - 4x^2 + 6)\, dx$.

Solution Since $f(x) = x^4 - 4x^2 + 6$ satisfies $f(-x) = f(x)$, it is even on the symmetric interval $[-2, 2]$, so

$$\begin{aligned}\int_{-2}^{2}(x^4 - 4x^2 + 6)\,dx &= 2\int_{0}^{2}(x^4 - 4x^2 + 6)\,dx \\ &= 2\left[\frac{x^5}{5} - \frac{4}{3}x^3 + 6x\right]_0^2 \\ &= 2\left(\frac{32}{5} - \frac{32}{3} + 12\right) = \frac{232}{15}.\end{aligned}$$

Areas Between Curves

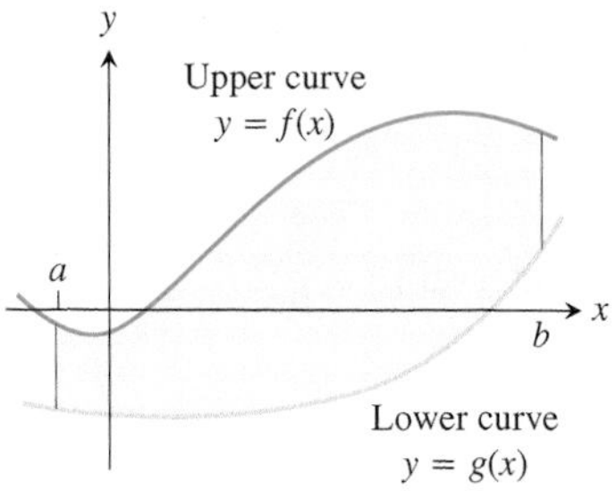

FIGURE 5.24 The region between the curves $y = f(x)$ and $y = g(x)$ and the lines $x = a$ and $x = b$.

Suppose we want to find the area of a region that is bounded above by the curve $y = f(x)$, below by the curve $y = g(x)$, and on the left and right by the lines $x = a$ and $x = b$ (Figure 5.24). The region might accidentally have a shape whose area we could find with geometry, but if f and g are arbitrary continuous functions, we usually have to find the area with an integral.

To see what the integral should be, we first approximate the region with n vertical rectangles based on a partition $P = \{x_0, x_1, \ldots, x_n\}$ of $[a, b]$ (Figure 5.25). The area of the kth rectangle (Figure 5.26) is

$$\Delta A_k = \text{height} \times \text{width} = [f(c_k) - g(c_k)]\,\Delta x_k.$$

We then approximate the area of the region by adding the areas of the n rectangles:

$$A \approx \sum_{k=1}^{n} \Delta A_k = \sum_{k=1}^{n} [f(c_k) - g(c_k)]\,\Delta x_k. \qquad \text{Riemann sum}$$

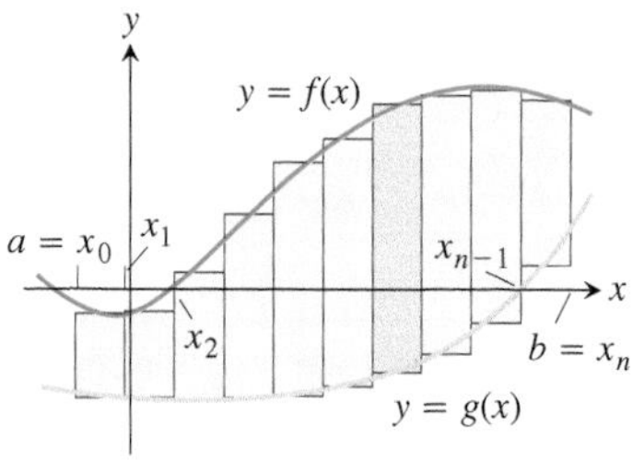

FIGURE 5.25 We approximate the region with rectangles perpendicular to the x-axis.

As $\|P\| \to 0$, the sums on the right approach the limit $\int_a^b [f(x) - g(x)]\,dx$ because f and g are continuous. We take the area of the region to be the value of this integral. That is,

$$A = \lim_{\|P\|\to 0} \sum_{k=1}^{n} [f(c_k) - g(c_k)]\,\Delta x_k = \int_a^b [f(x) - g(x)]\,dx.$$

DEFINITION If f and g are continuous with $f(x) \geq g(x)$ throughout $[a, b]$, then the **area of the region between the curves $y = f(x)$ and $y = g(x)$ from a to b** is the integral of $(f - g)$ from a to b:

$$A = \int_a^b [f(x) - g(x)]\,dx.$$

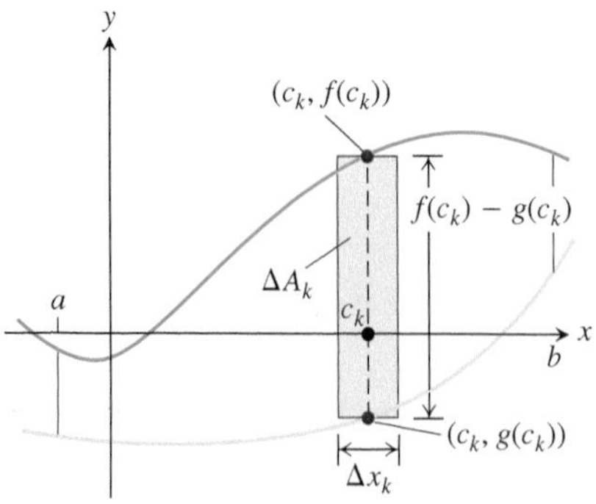

FIGURE 5.26 The area ΔA_k of the kth rectangle is the product of its height, $f(c_k) - g(c_k)$, and its width, Δx_k.

When applying this definition it is helpful to graph the curves. The graph reveals which curve is the upper curve f and which is the lower curve g. It also helps you find the limits of integration if they are not given. You may need to find where the curves intersect to determine the limits of integration, and this may involve solving the equation $f(x) = g(x)$ for values of x. Then you can integrate the function $f - g$ for the area between the intersections.

EXAMPLE 4 Find the area of the region bounded above by the curve $y = 2e^{-x} + x$, below by the curve $y = e^x/2$, on the left by $x = 0$, and on the right by $x = 1$.

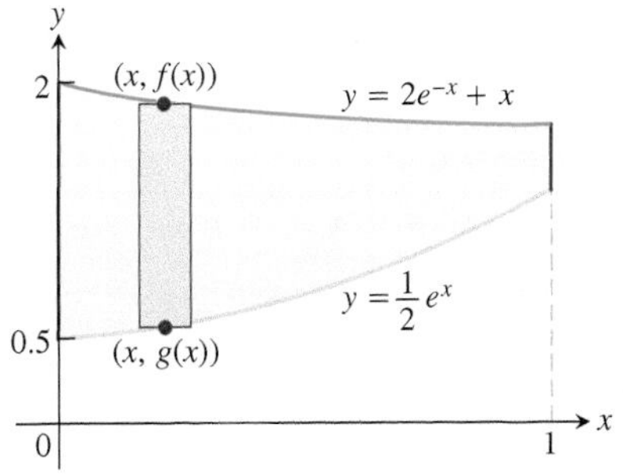

FIGURE 5.27 The region in Example 4 with a typical approximating rectangle.

Solution Figure 5.27 displays the graphs of the curves and the region whose area we want to find. The area between the curves over the interval $0 \leq x \leq 1$ is given by

$$A = \int_0^1 \left[(2e^{-x} + x) - \frac{1}{2}e^x\right] dx = \left[-2e^{-x} + \frac{1}{2}x^2 - \frac{1}{2}e^x\right]_0^1$$

$$= \left(-2e^{-1} + \frac{1}{2} - \frac{1}{2}e\right) - \left(-2 + 0 - \frac{1}{2}\right)$$

$$= 3 - \frac{2}{e} - \frac{e}{2} \approx 0.9051.$$ ■

EXAMPLE 5 Find the area of the region enclosed by the parabola $y = 2 - x^2$ and the line $y = -x$.

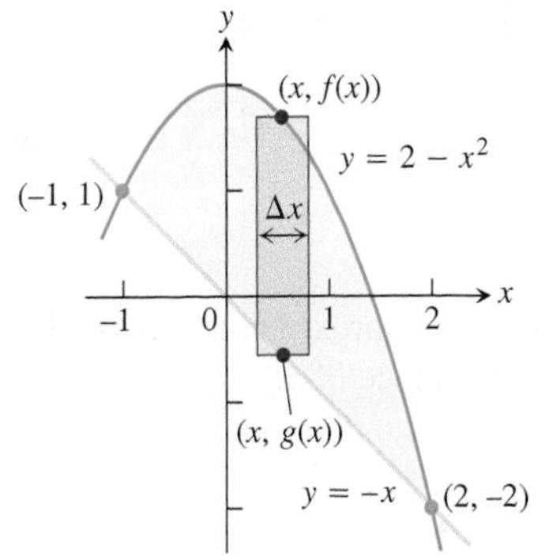

FIGURE 5.28 The region in Example 5 with a typical approximating rectangle.

Solution First we sketch the two curves (Figure 5.28). The limits of integration are found by solving $y = 2 - x^2$ and $y = -x$ simultaneously for x.

$2 - x^2 = -x$	Equate $f(x)$ and $g(x)$.
$x^2 - x - 2 = 0$	Rewrite.
$(x + 1)(x - 2) = 0$	Factor.
$x = -1, \quad x = 2.$	Solve.

The region runs from $x = -1$ to $x = 2$. The limits of integration are $a = -1$, $b = 2$.

The area between the curves is

$$A = \int_a^b [f(x) - g(x)]\,dx = \int_{-1}^2 [(2 - x^2) - (-x)]\,dx$$

$$= \int_{-1}^2 (2 + x - x^2)\,dx = \left[2x + \frac{x^2}{2} - \frac{x^3}{3}\right]_{-1}^2$$

$$= \left(4 + \frac{4}{2} - \frac{8}{3}\right) - \left(-2 + \frac{1}{2} + \frac{1}{3}\right) = \frac{9}{2}.$$ ■

HISTORICAL BIOGRAPHY

Richard Dedekind
(1831–1916)

If the formula for a bounding curve changes at one or more points, we subdivide the region into subregions that correspond to the formula changes and apply the formula for the area between curves to each subregion.

EXAMPLE 6 Find the area of the region in the first quadrant that is bounded above by $y = \sqrt{x}$ and below by the x-axis and the line $y = x - 2$.

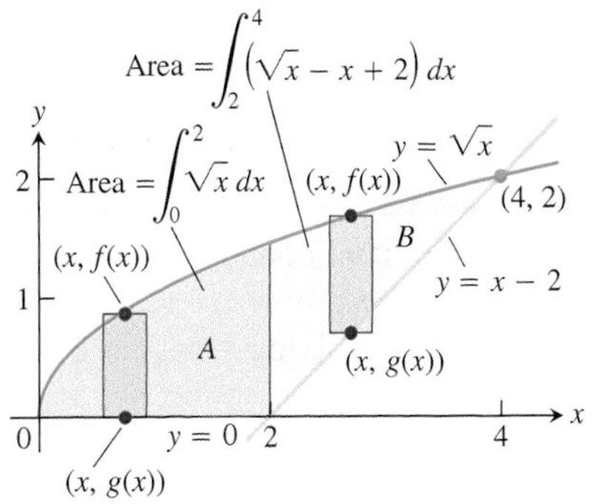

FIGURE 5.29 When the formula for a bounding curve changes, the area integral changes to become the sum of integrals to match, one integral for each of the shaded regions shown here for Example 6.

Solution The sketch (Figure 5.29) shows that the region's upper boundary is the graph of $f(x) = \sqrt{x}$. The lower boundary changes from $g(x) = 0$ for $0 \leq x \leq 2$ to $g(x) = x - 2$ for $2 \leq x \leq 4$ (both formulas agree at $x = 2$). We subdivide the region at $x = 2$ into subregions A and B, shown in Figure 5.29.

The limits of integration for region A are $a = 0$ and $b = 2$. The left-hand limit for region B is $a = 2$. To find the right-hand limit, we solve the equations $y = \sqrt{x}$ and $y = x - 2$ simultaneously for x:

$\sqrt{x} = x - 2$	Equate $f(x)$ and $g(x)$.
$x = (x - 2)^2 = x^2 - 4x + 4$	Square both sides.
$x^2 - 5x + 4 = 0$	Rewrite.
$(x - 1)(x - 4) = 0$	Factor.
$x = 1, \quad x = 4.$	Solve.

Only the value $x = 4$ satisfies the equation $\sqrt{x} = x - 2$. The value $x = 1$ is an extraneous root introduced by squaring. The right-hand limit is $b = 4$.

$$\text{For } 0 \le x \le 2: \quad f(x) - g(x) = \sqrt{x} - 0 = \sqrt{x}$$
$$\text{For } 2 \le x \le 4: \quad f(x) - g(x) = \sqrt{x} - (x - 2) = \sqrt{x} - x + 2$$

We add the areas of subregions A and B to find the total area:

$$\text{Total area} = \underbrace{\int_0^2 \sqrt{x}\,dx}_{\text{area of } A} + \underbrace{\int_2^4 (\sqrt{x} - x + 2)\,dx}_{\text{area of } B}$$
$$= \left[\frac{2}{3}x^{3/2}\right]_0^2 + \left[\frac{2}{3}x^{3/2} - \frac{x^2}{2} + 2x\right]_2^4$$
$$= \frac{2}{3}(2)^{3/2} - 0 + \left(\frac{2}{3}(4)^{3/2} - 8 + 8\right) - \left(\frac{2}{3}(2)^{3/2} - 2 + 4\right)$$
$$= \frac{2}{3}(8) - 2 = \frac{10}{3}.$$

■

Integration with Respect to y

If a region's bounding curves are described by functions of y, the approximating rectangles are horizontal instead of vertical and the basic formula has y in place of x.

For regions like these:

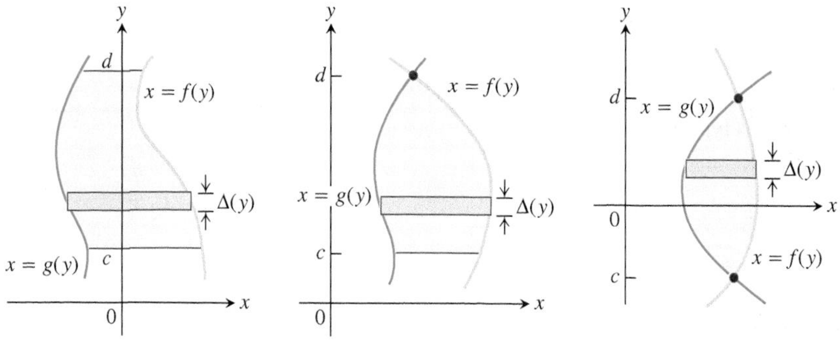

use the formula

$$A = \int_c^d [f(y) - g(y)]\,dy.$$

In this equation f always denotes the right-hand curve and g the left-hand curve, so $f(y) - g(y)$ is nonnegative.

EXAMPLE 7 Find the area of the region in Example 6 by integrating with respect to y.

Solution We first sketch the region and a typical *horizontal* rectangle based on a partition of an interval of y-values (Figure 5.30). The region's right-hand boundary is the line $x = y + 2$, so $f(y) = y + 2$. The left-hand boundary is the curve $x = y^2$, so $g(y) = y^2$. The lower limit of integration is $y = 0$. We find the upper limit by solving $x = y + 2$ and $x = y^2$ simultaneously for y:

$$y + 2 = y^2 \qquad \text{Equate } f(y) = y + 2 \text{ and } g(y) = y^2.$$
$$y^2 - y - 2 = 0 \qquad \text{Rewrite.}$$
$$(y + 1)(y - 2) = 0 \qquad \text{Factor.}$$
$$y = -1, \quad y = 2 \qquad \text{Solve.}$$

The upper limit of integration is $b = 2$. (The value $y = -1$ gives a point of intersection *below* the x-axis.)

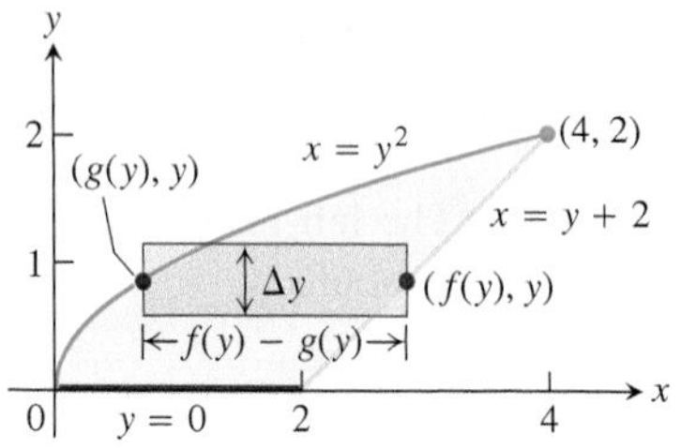

FIGURE 5.30 It takes two integrations to find the area of this region if we integrate with respect to x. It takes only one if we integrate with respect to y (Example 7).

The area of the region is

$$\begin{aligned} A = \int_c^d [f(y) - g(y)]\,dy &= \int_0^2 [y + 2 - y^2]\,dy \\ &= \int_0^2 [2 + y - y^2]\,dy \\ &= \left[2y + \frac{y^2}{2} - \frac{y^3}{3}\right]_0^2 \\ &= 4 + \frac{4}{2} - \frac{8}{3} = \frac{10}{3}. \end{aligned}$$

This is the result of Example 6, found with less work. ■

Exercises 5.6

Evaluating Definite Integrals

Use the Substitution Formula in Theorem 7 to evaluate the integrals in Exercises 1–46.

1. a. $\int_0^3 \sqrt{y+1}\,dy$ b. $\int_{-1}^0 \sqrt{y+1}\,dy$

2. a. $\int_0^1 r\sqrt{1-r^2}\,dr$ b. $\int_{-1}^1 r\sqrt{1-r^2}\,dr$

3. a. $\int_0^{\pi/4} \tan x \sec^2 x\,dx$ b. $\int_{-\pi/4}^0 \tan x \sec^2 x\,dx$

4. a. $\int_0^{\pi} 3\cos^2 x \sin x\,dx$ b. $\int_{2\pi}^{3\pi} 3\cos^2 x \sin x\,dx$

5. a. $\int_0^1 t^3(1+t^4)^3\,dt$ b. $\int_{-1}^1 t^3(1+t^4)^3\,dt$

6. a. $\int_0^{\sqrt{7}} t(t^2+1)^{1/3}\,dt$ b. $\int_{-\sqrt{7}}^0 t(t^2+1)^{1/3}\,dt$

7. a. $\int_{-1}^1 \frac{5r}{(4+r^2)^2}\,dr$ b. $\int_0^1 \frac{5r}{(4+r^2)^2}\,dr$

8. a. $\int_0^1 \frac{10\sqrt{v}}{(1+v^{3/2})^2}\,dv$ b. $\int_1^4 \frac{10\sqrt{v}}{(1+v^{3/2})^2}\,dv$

9. a. $\int_0^{\sqrt{3}} \frac{4x}{\sqrt{x^2+1}}\,dx$ b. $\int_{-\sqrt{3}}^{\sqrt{3}} \frac{4x}{\sqrt{x^2+1}}\,dx$

10. a. $\int_0^1 \frac{x^3}{\sqrt{x^4+9}}\,dx$ b. $\int_{-1}^0 \frac{x^3}{\sqrt{x^4+9}}\,dx$

11. a. $\int_0^{\pi/6} (1-\cos 3t)\sin 3t\,dt$ b. $\int_{\pi/6}^{\pi/3} (1-\cos 3t)\sin 3t\,dt$

12. a. $\int_{-\pi/2}^0 \left(2+\tan\frac{t}{2}\right)\sec^2\frac{t}{2}\,dt$ b. $\int_{-\pi/2}^{\pi/2} \left(2+\tan\frac{t}{2}\right)\sec^2\frac{t}{2}\,dt$

13. a. $\int_0^{2\pi} \frac{\cos z}{\sqrt{4+3\sin z}}\,dz$ b. $\int_{-\pi}^{\pi} \frac{\cos z}{\sqrt{4+3\sin z}}\,dz$

14. a. $\int_{-\pi/2}^0 \frac{\sin w}{(3+2\cos w)^2}\,dw$ b. $\int_0^{\pi/2} \frac{\sin w}{(3+2\cos w)^2}\,dw$

15. $\int_0^1 \sqrt{t^5+2t}\,(5t^4+2)\,dt$

16. $\int_1^4 \frac{dy}{2\sqrt{y}\,(1+\sqrt{y})^2}$

17. $\int_0^{\pi/6} \cos^{-3} 2\theta \sin 2\theta\,d\theta$

18. $\int_{\pi}^{3\pi/2} \cot^5\left(\frac{\theta}{6}\right)\sec^2\left(\frac{\theta}{6}\right)d\theta$

19. $\int_0^{\pi} 5(5-4\cos t)^{1/4}\sin t\,dt$

20. $\int_0^{\pi/4} (1-\sin 2t)^{3/2}\cos 2t\,dt$

21. $\int_0^1 (4y-y^2+4y^3+1)^{-2/3}(12y^2-2y+4)\,dy$

22. $\int_0^1 (y^3+6y^2-12y+9)^{-1/2}(y^2+4y-4)\,dy$

23. $\int_0^{\sqrt[3]{\pi^2}} \sqrt{\theta}\cos^2(\theta^{3/2})\,d\theta$

24. $\int_{-1}^{-1/2} t^{-2}\sin^2\left(1+\frac{1}{t}\right)dt$

25. $\int_0^{\pi/4} (1+e^{\tan\theta})\sec^2\theta\,d\theta$

26. $\int_{\pi/4}^{\pi/2} (1+e^{\cot\theta})\csc^2\theta\,d\theta$

27. $\int_0^{\pi} \frac{\sin t}{2-\cos t}\,dt$

28. $\int_0^{\pi/3} \frac{4\sin\theta}{1-4\cos\theta}\,d\theta$

29. $\int_1^2 \frac{2\ln x}{x}\,dx$

30. $\int_2^4 \frac{dx}{x\ln x}$

31. $\int_2^4 \frac{dx}{x(\ln x)^2}$

32. $\int_2^{16} \frac{dx}{2x\sqrt{\ln x}}$

33. $\int_0^{\pi/2} \tan\frac{x}{2}\,dx$

34. $\int_{\pi/4}^{\pi/2} \cot t\,dt$

35. $\int_{\pi/2}^{\pi} 2\cot\frac{\theta}{3}\,d\theta$

36. $\int_0^{\pi/12} 6\tan 3x\,dx$

37. $\int_{-\pi/2}^{\pi/2} \frac{2\cos\theta\,d\theta}{1+(\sin\theta)^2}$

38. $\int_{\pi/6}^{\pi/4} \frac{\csc^2 x\,dx}{1+(\cot x)^2}$

39. $\int_0^{\ln\sqrt{3}} \frac{e^x\,dx}{1+e^{2x}}$

40. $\int_1^{e^{\pi/4}} \frac{4\,dt}{t(1+\ln^2 t)}$

41. $\int_0^1 \frac{4\,ds}{\sqrt{4-s^2}}$

42. $\int_0^{3\sqrt{2}/4} \frac{ds}{\sqrt{9-4s^2}}$

43. $\int_{\sqrt{2}}^2 \frac{\sec^2(\sec^{-1}x)\,dx}{x\sqrt{x^2-1}}$

44. $\int_{2/\sqrt{3}}^2 \frac{\cos(\sec^{-1}x)\,dx}{x\sqrt{x^2-1}}$

45. $\int_{-1}^{-\sqrt{2}/2} \frac{dy}{y\sqrt{4y^2-1}}$

46. $\int_{-2/3}^{-\sqrt{2}/3} \frac{dy}{y\sqrt{9y^2-1}}$

Area

Find the total areas of the shaded regions in Exercises 47–62.

47.

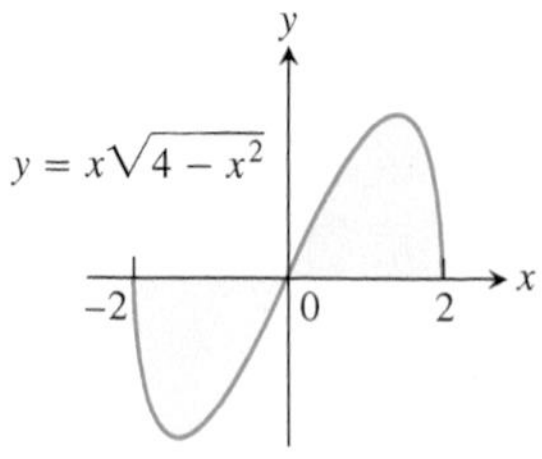

48.

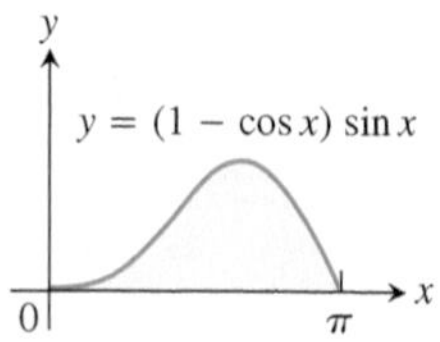

49.

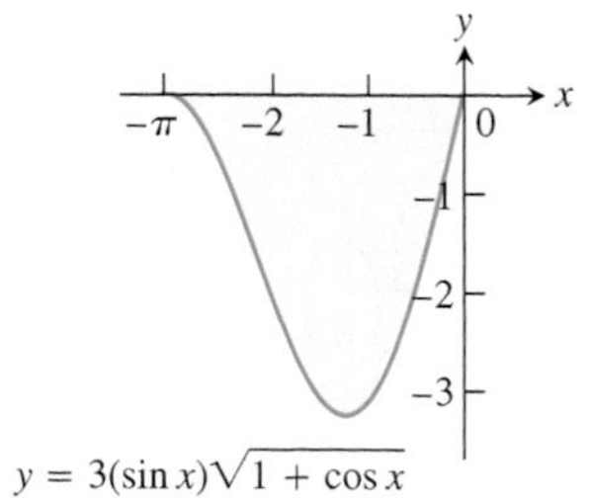

50.

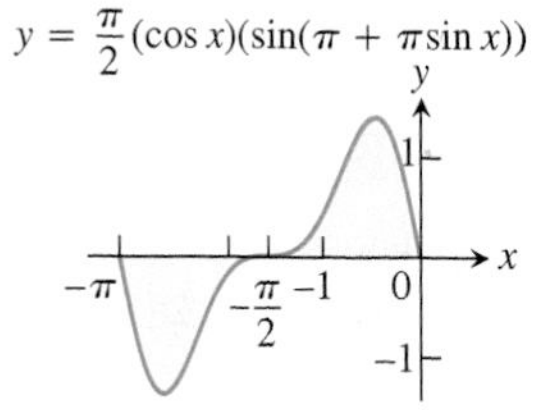

51.

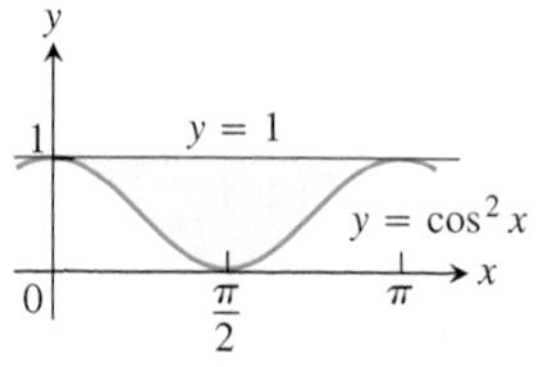

52.

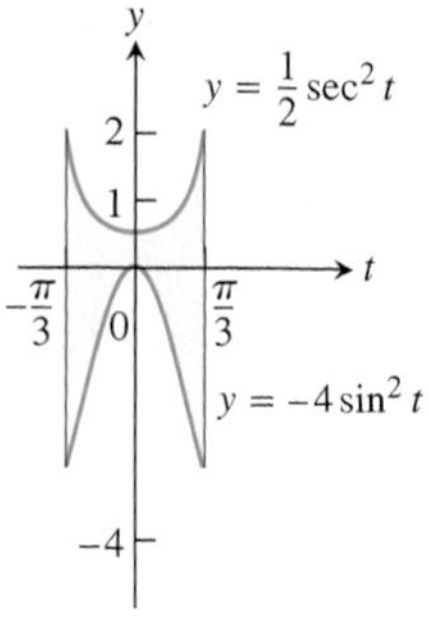

53.

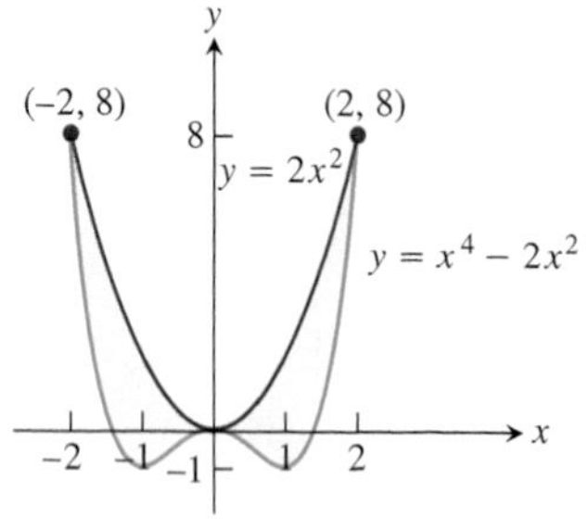

NOT TO SCALE

54.

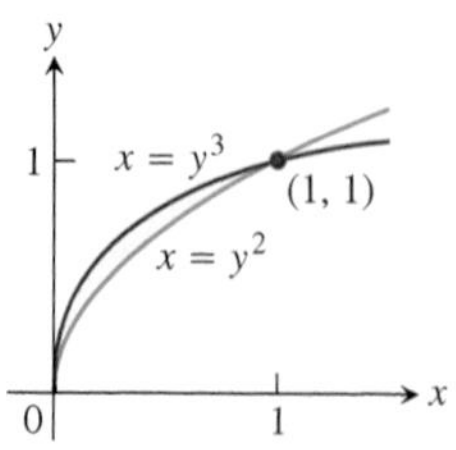

55.

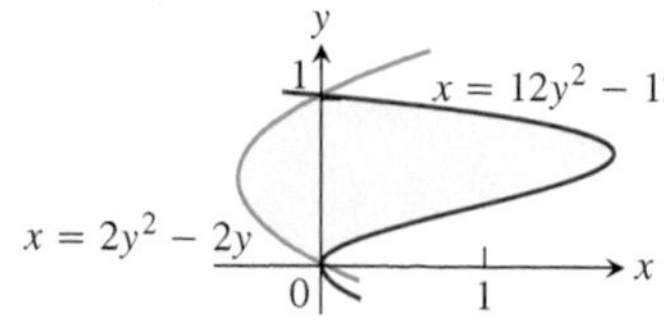

56.

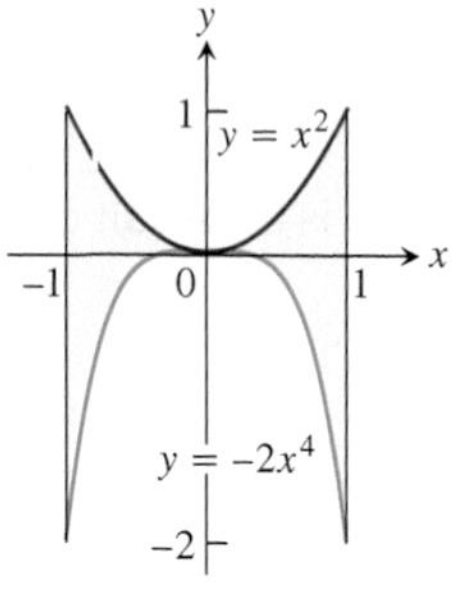

57.

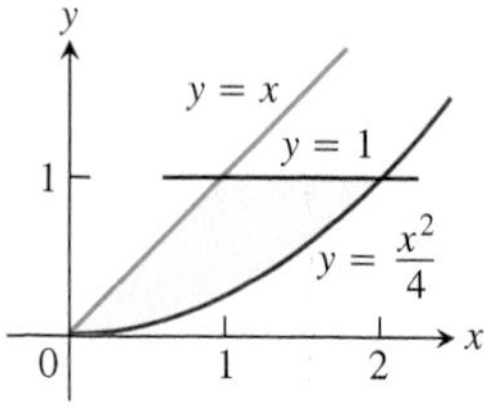

58.

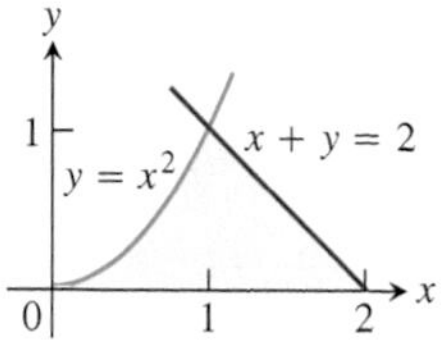

59.

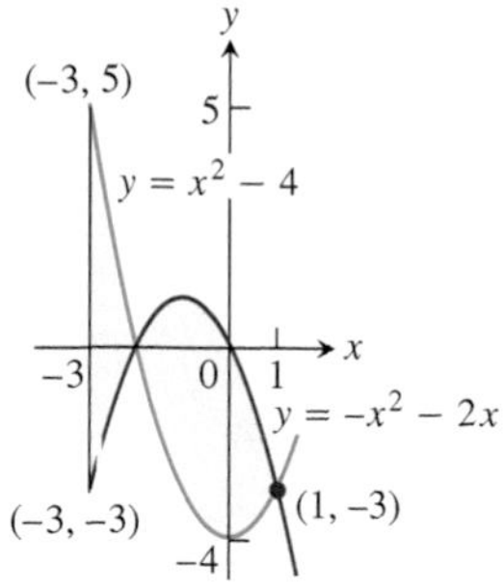

60.

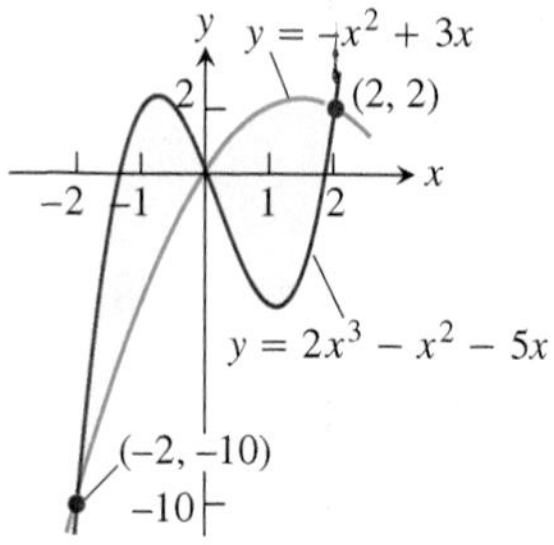

61.

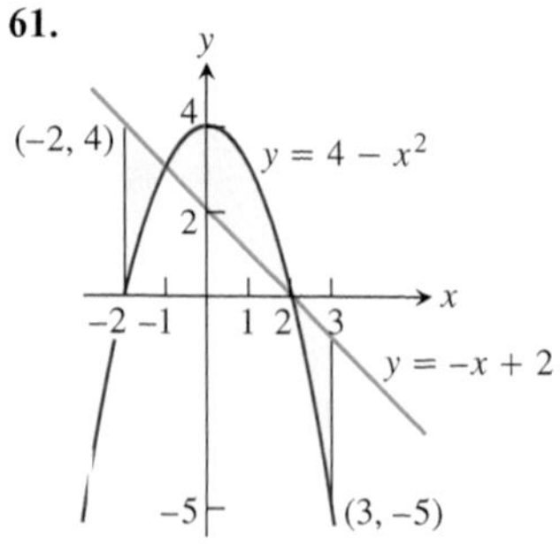

62.

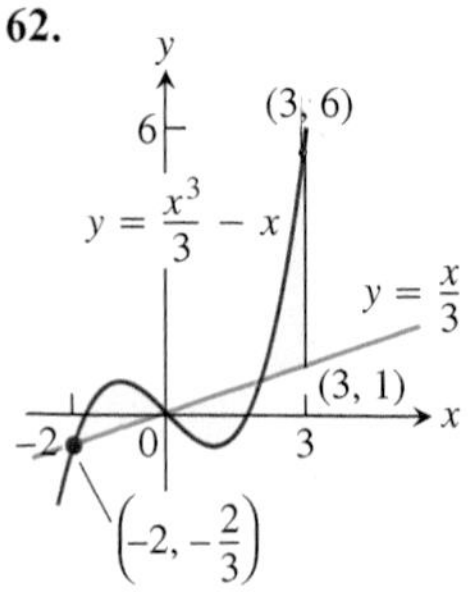

Find the areas of the regions enclosed by the lines and curves in Exercises 63–72.

63. $y = x^2 - 2$ and $y = 2$

64. $y = 2x - x^2$ and $y = -3$

65. $y = x^4$ and $y = 8x$

66. $y = x^2 - 2x$ and $y = x$

67. $y = x^2$ and $y = -x^2 + 4x$

68. $y = 7 - 2x^2$ and $y = x^2 + 4$

69. $y = x^4 - 4x^2 + 4$ and $y = x^2$

70. $y = x\sqrt{a^2 - x^2}$, $a > 0$, and $y = 0$

71. $y = \sqrt{|x|}$ and $5y = x + 6$ (How many intersection points are there?)

72. $y = |x^2 - 4|$ and $y = (x^2/2) + 4$

Find the areas of the regions enclosed by the lines and curves in Exercises 73–80.

73. $x = 2y^2$, $x = 0$, and $y = 3$

74. $x = y^2$ and $x = y + 2$

75. $y^2 - 4x = 4$ and $4x - y = 16$

76. $x - y^2 = 0$ and $x + 2y^2 = 3$

77. $x + y^2 = 0$ and $x + 3y^2 = 2$

78. $x - y^{2/3} = 0$ and $x + y^4 = 2$

79. $x = y^2 - 1$ and $x = |y|\sqrt{1 - y^2}$

80. $x = y^3 - y^2$ and $x = 2y$

Find the areas of the regions enclosed by the curves in Exercises 81–84.

81. $4x^2 + y = 4$ and $x^4 - y = 1$

82. $x^3 - y = 0$ and $3x^2 - y = 4$

83. $x + 4y^2 = 4$ and $x + y^4 = 1$, for $x \geq 0$

84. $x + y^2 = 3$ and $4x + y^2 = 0$

Find the areas of the regions enclosed by the lines and curves in Exercises 85–92.

85. $y = 2\sin x$ and $y = \sin 2x$, $0 \leq x \leq \pi$

86. $y = 8\cos x$ and $y = \sec^2 x$, $-\pi/3 \leq x \leq \pi/3$

87. $y = \cos(\pi x/2)$ and $y = 1 - x^2$

88. $y = \sin(\pi x/2)$ and $y = x$

89. $y = \sec^2 x$, $y = \tan^2 x$, $x = -\pi/4$, and $x = \pi/4$

90. $x = \tan^2 y$ and $x = -\tan^2 y$, $-\pi/4 \leq y \leq \pi/4$

91. $x = 3\sin y\sqrt{\cos y}$ and $x = 0$, $0 \leq y \leq \pi/2$

92. $y = \sec^2(\pi x/3)$ and $y = x^{1/3}$, $-1 \leq x \leq 1$

Area Between Curves

93. Find the area of the propeller-shaped region enclosed by the curve $x - y^3 = 0$ and the line $x - y = 0$.

94. Find the area of the propeller-shaped region enclosed by the curves $x - y^{1/3} = 0$ and $x - y^{1/5} = 0$.

95. Find the area of the region in the first quadrant bounded by the line $y = x$, the line $x = 2$, the curve $y = 1/x^2$, and the x-axis.

96. Find the area of the "triangular" region in the first quadrant bounded on the left by the y-axis and on the right by the curves $y = \sin x$ and $y = \cos x$.

97. Find the area between the curves $y = \ln x$ and $y = \ln 2x$ from $x = 1$ to $x = 5$.

98. Find the area between the curve $y = \tan x$ and the x-axis from $x = -\pi/4$ to $x = \pi/3$.

99. Find the area of the "triangular" region in the first quadrant that is bounded above by the curve $y = e^{2x}$, below by the curve $y = e^x$, and on the right by the line $x = \ln 3$.

100. Find the area of the "triangular" region in the first quadrant that is bounded above by the curve $y = e^{x/2}$, below by the curve $y = e^{-x/2}$, and on the right by the line $x = 2\ln 2$.

101. Find the area of the region between the curve $y = 2x/(1 + x^2)$ and the interval $-2 \leq x \leq 2$ of the x-axis.

102. Find the area of the region between the curve $y = 2^{1-x}$ and the interval $-1 \leq x \leq 1$ of the x-axis.

103. The region bounded below by the parabola $y = x^2$ and above by the line $y = 4$ is to be partitioned into two subsections of equal area by cutting across it with the horizontal line $y = c$.

a. Sketch the region and draw a line $y = c$ across it that looks about right. In terms of c, what are the coordinates of the points where the line and parabola intersect? Add them to your figure.

b. Find c by integrating with respect to y. (This puts c in the limits of integration.)

c. Find c by integrating with respect to x. (This puts c into the integrand as well.)

104. Find the area of the region between the curve $y = 3 - x^2$ and the line $y = -1$ by integrating with respect to **a.** x, **b.** y.

105. Find the area of the region in the first quadrant bounded on the left by the y-axis, below by the line $y = x/4$, above left by the curve $y = 1 + \sqrt{x}$, and above right by the curve $y = 2/\sqrt{x}$.

106. Find the area of the region in the first quadrant bounded on the left by the y-axis, below by the curve $x = 2\sqrt{y}$, above left by the curve $x = (y - 1)^2$, and above right by the line $x = 3 - y$.

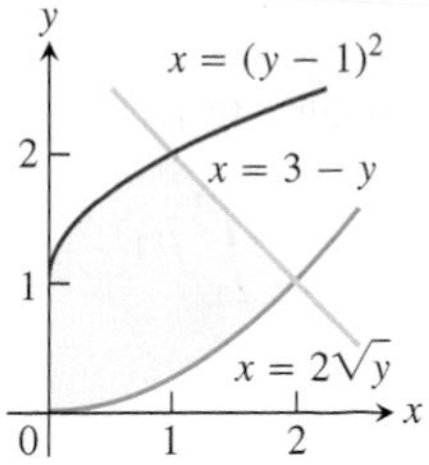

107. The figure here shows triangle AOC inscribed in the region cut from the parabola $y = x^2$ by the line $y = a^2$. Find the limit of the ratio of the area of the triangle to the area of the parabolic region as a approaches zero.

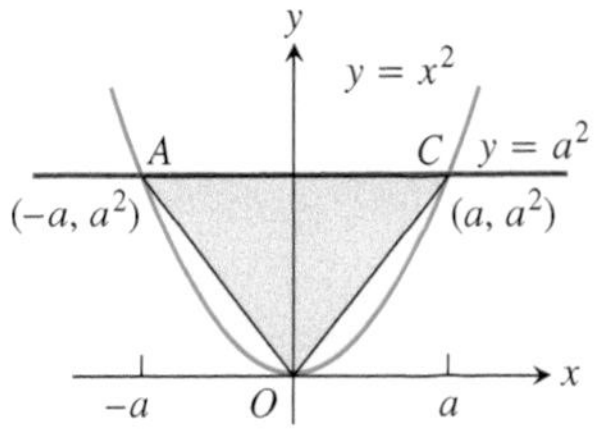

108. Suppose the area of the region between the graph of a positive continuous function f and the x-axis from $x = a$ to $x = b$ is 4 square units. Find the area between the curves $y = f(x)$ and $y = 2f(x)$ from $x = a$ to $x = b$.

109. Which of the following integrals, if either, calculates the area of the shaded region shown here? Give reasons for your answer.

a. $\int_{-1}^{1}(x-(-x))\,dx=\int_{-1}^{1}2x\,dx$

b. $\int_{-1}^{1}(-x-(x))\,dx=\int_{-1}^{1}-2x\,dx$

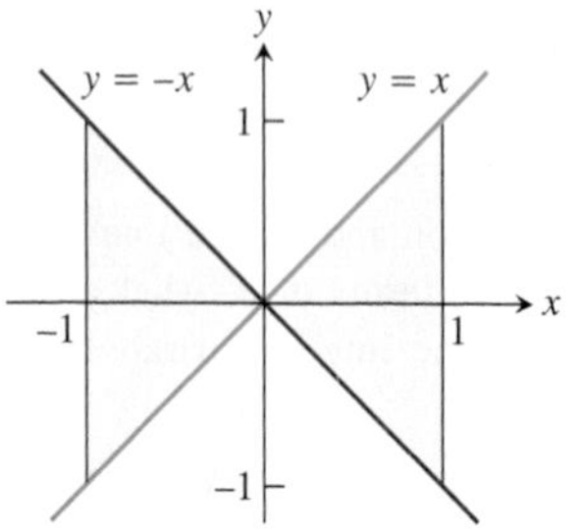

110. True, sometimes true, or never true? The area of the region between the graphs of the continuous functions $y=f(x)$ and $y=g(x)$ and the vertical lines $x=a$ and $x=b$ $(a<b)$ is

$$\int_a^b [f(x)-g(x)]\,dx.$$

Give reasons for your answer.

Theory and Examples

111. Suppose that $F(x)$ is an antiderivative of $f(x)=(\sin x)/x$, $x>0$. Express

$$\int_1^3 \frac{\sin 2x}{x}\,dx$$

in terms of F.

112. Show that if f is continuous, then

$$\int_0^1 f(x)\,dx=\int_0^1 f(1-x)\,dx.$$

113. Suppose that

$$\int_0^1 f(x)\,dx=3.$$

Find

$$\int_{-1}^0 f(x)\,dx$$

if **a.** f is odd, **b.** f is even.

114. a. Show that if f is odd on $[-a,a]$, then

$$\int_{-a}^{a} f(x)\,dx=0.$$

b. Test the result in part (a) with $f(x)=\sin x$ and $a=\pi/2$.

115. If f is a continuous function, find the value of the integral

$$I=\int_0^a \frac{f(x)\,dx}{f(x)+f(a-x)}$$

by making the substitution $u=a-x$ and adding the resulting integral to I.

116. By using a substitution, prove that for all positive numbers x and y,

$$\int_x^{xy}\frac{1}{t}\,dt=\int_1^y\frac{1}{t}\,dt.$$

The Shift Property for Definite Integrals A basic property of definite integrals is their invariance under translation, as expressed by the equation

$$\int_a^b f(x)\,dx=\int_{a-c}^{b-c} f(x+c)\,dx. \qquad (1)$$

The equation holds whenever f is integrable and defined for the necessary values of x. For example in the accompanying figure, show that

$$\int_{-2}^{-1}(x+2)^3\,dx=\int_0^1 x^3\,dx$$

because the areas of the shaded regions are congruent.

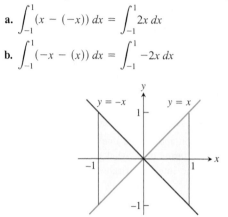

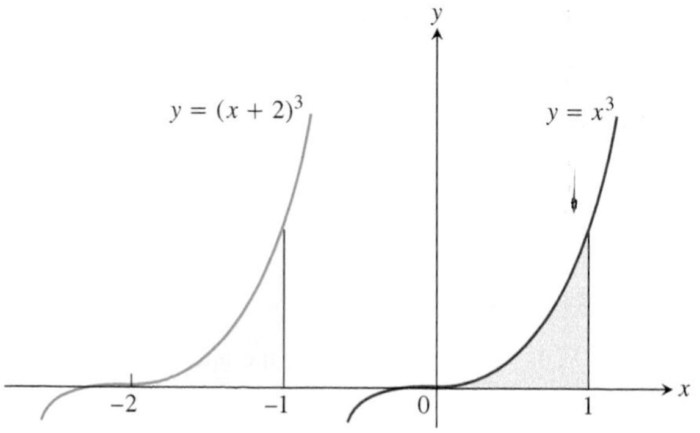

117. Use a substitution to verify Equation (1).

118. For each of the following functions, graph $f(x)$ over $[a,b]$ and $f(x+c)$ over $[a-c, b-c]$ to convince yourself that Equation (1) is reasonable.

a. $f(x)=x^2,\quad a=0,\quad b=1,\quad c=1$

b. $f(x)=\sin x,\quad a=0,\quad b=\pi,\quad c=\pi/2$

c. $f(x)=\sqrt{x-4},\quad a=4,\quad b=8,\quad c=5$

COMPUTER EXPLORATIONS

In Exercises 119–122, you will find the area between curves in the plane when you cannot find their points of intersection using simple algebra. Use a CAS to perform the following steps:

a. Plot the curves together to see what they look like and how many points of intersection they have.

b. Use the numerical equation solver in your CAS to find all the points of intersection.

c. Integrate $|f(x)-g(x)|$ over consecutive pairs of intersection values.

d. Sum together the integrals found in part (c).

119. $f(x)=\frac{x^3}{3}-\frac{x^2}{2}-2x+\frac{1}{3},\quad g(x)=x-1$

120. $f(x)=\frac{x^4}{2}-3x^3+10,\quad g(x)=8-12x$

121. $f(x)=x+\sin(2x),\quad g(x)=x^3$

122. $f(x)=x^2\cos x,\quad g(x)=x^3-x$

Chapter Questions to Guide Your Review

1. How can you sometimes estimate quantities like distance traveled, area, and average value with finite sums? Why might you want to do so?
2. What is sigma notation? What advantage does it offer? Give examples.
3. What is a Riemann sum? Why might you want to consider such a sum?
4. What is the norm of a partition of a closed interval?
5. What is the definite integral of a function f over a closed interval $[a, b]$? When can you be sure it exists?
6. What is the relation between definite integrals and area? Describe some other interpretations of definite integrals.
7. What is the average value of an integrable function over a closed interval? Must the function assume its average value? Explain.
8. Describe the rules for working with definite integrals (Table 5.4). Give examples.
9. What is the Fundamental Theorem of Calculus? Why is it so important? Illustrate each part of the theorem with an example.
10. What is the Net Change Theorem? What does it say about the integral of velocity? The integral of marginal cost?
11. Discuss how the processes of integration and differentiation can be considered as "inverses" of each other.
12. How does the Fundamental Theorem provide a solution to the initial value problem $dy/dx = f(x),\ y(x_0) = y_0$, when f is continuous?
13. How is integration by substitution related to the Chain Rule?
14. How can you sometimes evaluate indefinite integrals by substitution? Give examples.
15. How does the method of substitution work for definite integrals? Give examples.
16. How do you define and calculate the area of the region between the graphs of two continuous functions? Give an example.

Chapter 5 Practice Exercises

Finite Sums and Estimates

1. The accompanying figure shows the graph of the velocity (ft/sec) of a model rocket for the first 8 sec after launch. The rocket accelerated straight up for the first 2 sec and then coasted to reach its maximum height at $t = 8$ sec.

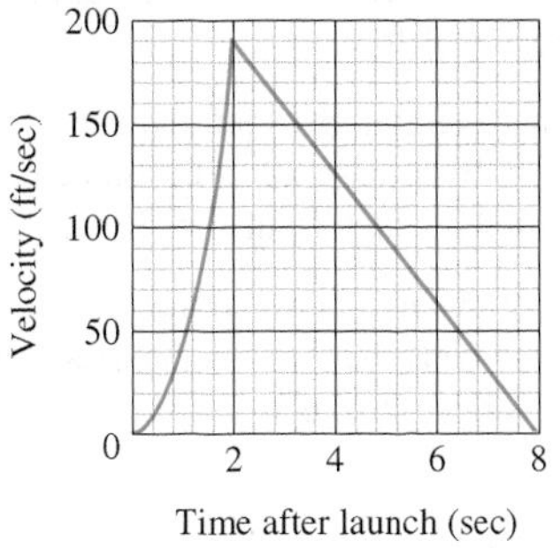

   a. Assuming that the rocket was launched from ground level, about how high did it go? (This is the rocket in Section 3.3, Exercise 17, but you do not need to do Exercise 17 to do the exercise here.)

   b. Sketch a graph of the rocket's height aboveground as a function of time for $0 \le t \le 8$.

2. a. The accompanying figure shows the velocity (m/sec) of a body moving along the s-axis during the time interval from $t = 0$ to $t = 10$ sec. About how far did the body travel during those 10 sec?

   b. Sketch a graph of s as a function of t for $0 \le t \le 10$ assuming $s(0) = 0$.

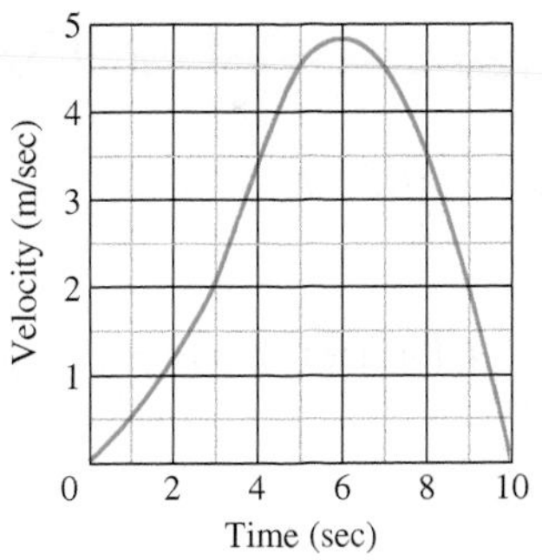

3. Suppose that $\sum_{k=1}^{10} a_k = -2$ and $\sum_{k=1}^{10} b_k = 25$. Find the value of

   a. $\sum_{k=1}^{10} \frac{a_k}{4}$

   b. $\sum_{k=1}^{10} (b_k - 3a_k)$

   c. $\sum_{k=1}^{10} (a_k + b_k - 1)$

   d. $\sum_{k=1}^{10} \left(\frac{5}{2} - b_k\right)$

4. Suppose that $\sum_{k=1}^{20} a_k = 0$ and $\sum_{k=1}^{20} b_k = 7$. Find the values of

   a. $\sum_{k=1}^{20} 3a_k$

   b. $\sum_{k=1}^{20} (a_k + b_k)$

   c. $\sum_{k=1}^{20} \left(\frac{1}{2} - \frac{2b_k}{7}\right)$

   d. $\sum_{k=1}^{20} (a_k - 2)$

Definite Integrals

In Exercises 5–8, express each limit as a definite integral. Then evaluate the integral to find the value of the limit. In each case, P is a partition of the given interval and the numbers c_k are chosen from the subintervals of P.

5. $\lim_{\|P\|\to 0} \sum_{k=1}^{n} (2c_k - 1)^{-1/2} \Delta x_k$, where P is a partition of $[1, 5]$

6. $\lim_{\|P\|\to 0} \sum_{k=1}^{n} c_k(c_k^2 - 1)^{1/3} \Delta x_k$, where P is a partition of $[1, 3]$

7. $\lim_{\|P\|\to 0} \sum_{k=1}^{n} \left(\cos\left(\frac{c_k}{2}\right)\right) \Delta x_k$, where P is a partition of $[-\pi, 0]$

8. $\lim_{\|P\|\to 0} \sum_{k=1}^{n} (\sin c_k)(\cos c_k) \Delta x_k$, where P is a partition of $[0, \pi/2]$

9. If $\int_{-2}^{2} 3f(x)\,dx = 12$, $\int_{-2}^{5} f(x)\,dx = 6$, and $\int_{-2}^{5} g(x)\,dx = 2$, find the values of the following.

a. $\int_{-2}^{2} f(x)\,dx$ **b.** $\int_{2}^{5} f(x)\,dx$

c. $\int_{5}^{-2} g(x)\,dx$ **d.** $\int_{-2}^{5} (-\pi g(x))\,dx$

e. $\int_{-2}^{5} \left(\frac{f(x) + g(x)}{5}\right) dx$

10. If $\int_{0}^{2} f(x)\,dx = \pi$, $\int_{0}^{2} 7g(x)\,dx = 7$, and $\int_{0}^{1} g(x)\,dx = 2$, find the values of the following.

a. $\int_{0}^{2} g(x)\,dx$ **b.** $\int_{1}^{2} g(x)\,dx$

c. $\int_{2}^{0} f(x)\,dx$ **d.** $\int_{0}^{2} \sqrt{2}\, f(x)\,dx$

e. $\int_{0}^{2} (g(x) - 3f(x))\,dx$

Area

In Exercises 11–14, find the total area of the region between the graph of f and the x-axis.

11. $f(x) = x^2 - 4x + 3, \quad 0 \le x \le 3$

12. $f(x) = 1 - (x^2/4), \quad -2 \le x \le 3$

13. $f(x) = 5 - 5x^{2/3}, \quad -1 \le x \le 8$

14. $f(x) = 1 - \sqrt{x}, \quad 0 \le x \le 4$

Find the areas of the regions enclosed by the curves and lines in Exercises 15–26.

15. $y = x, \quad y = 1/x^2, \quad x = 2$

16. $y = x, \quad y = 1/\sqrt{x}, \quad x = 2$

17. $\sqrt{x} + \sqrt{y} = 1, \quad x = 0, \quad y = 0$

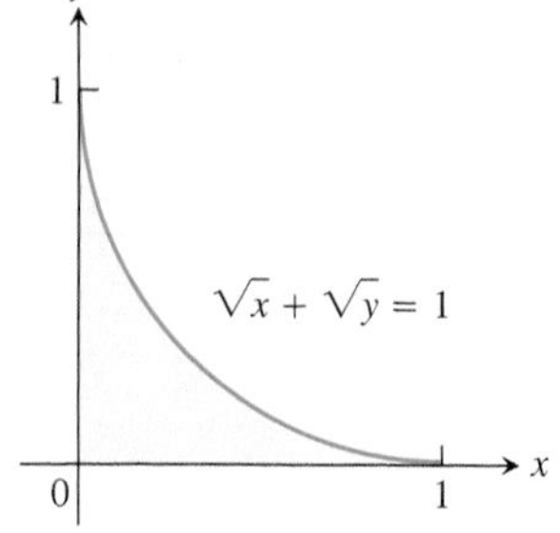

18. $x^3 + \sqrt{y} = 1, \quad x = 0, \quad y = 0, \quad$ for $\quad 0 \le x \le 1$

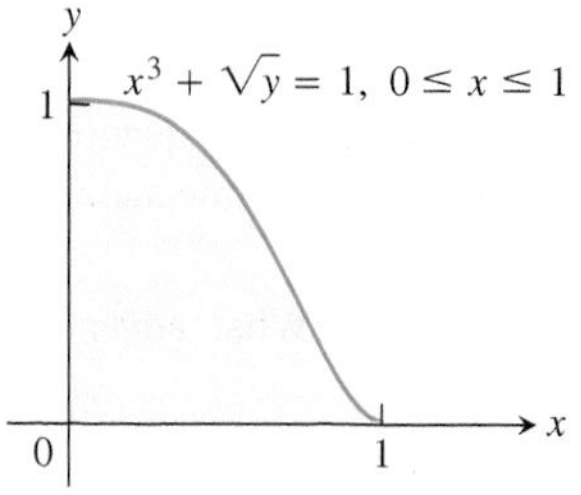

19. $x = 2y^2, \quad x = 0, \quad y = 3$ **20.** $x = 4 - y^2, \quad x = 0$

21. $y^2 = 4x, \quad y = 4x - 2$

22. $y^2 = 4x + 4, \quad y = 4x - 16$

23. $y = \sin x, \quad y = x, \quad 0 \le x \le \pi/4$

24. $y = |\sin x|, \quad y = 1, \quad -\pi/2 \le x \le \pi/2$

25. $y = 2\sin x, \quad y = \sin 2x, \quad 0 \le x \le \pi$

26. $y = 8\cos x, \quad y = \sec^2 x, \quad -\pi/3 \le x \le \pi/3$

27. Find the area of the "triangular" region bounded on the left by $x + y = 2$, on the right by $y = x^2$, and above by $y = 2$.

28. Find the area of the "triangular" region bounded on the left by $y = \sqrt{x}$, on the right by $y = 6 - x$, and below by $y = 1$.

29. Find the extreme values of $f(x) = x^3 - 3x^2$ and find the area of the region enclosed by the graph of f and the x-axis.

30. Find the area of the region cut from the first quadrant by the curve $x^{1/2} + y^{1/2} = a^{1/2}$.

31. Find the total area of the region enclosed by the curve $x = y^{2/3}$ and the lines $x = y$ and $y = -1$.

32. Find the total area of the region between the curves $y = \sin x$ and $y = \cos x$ for $0 \le x \le 3\pi/2$.

33. Area Find the area between the curve $y = 2(\ln x)/x$ and the x-axis from $x = 1$ to $x = e$.

34. a. Show that the area between the curve $y = 1/x$ and the x-axis from $x = 10$ to $x = 20$ is the same as the area between the curve and the x-axis from $x = 1$ to $x = 2$.

b. Show that the area between the curve $y = 1/x$ and the x-axis from ka to kb is the same as the area between the curve and the x-axis from $x = a$ to $x = b$ $(0 < a < b, k > 0)$.

Initial Value Problems

35. Show that $y = x^2 + \int_{1}^{x} \frac{1}{t}\,dt$ solves the initial value problem

$$\frac{d^2y}{dx^2} = 2 - \frac{1}{x^2}; \quad y'(1) = 3, \quad y(1) = 1.$$

36. Show that $y = \int_{0}^{x} \left(1 + 2\sqrt{\sec t}\right) dt$ solves the initial value problem

$$\frac{d^2y}{dx^2} = \sqrt{\sec x}\tan x; \quad y'(0) = 3, \quad y(0) = 0.$$

Express the solutions of the initial value problems in Exercises 37 and 38 in terms of integrals.

37. $\frac{dy}{dx} = \frac{\sin x}{x}, \quad y(5) = -3$

38. $\frac{dy}{dx} = \sqrt{2 - \sin^2 x}, \quad y(-1) = 2$

Solve the initial value problems in Exercises 39–42.

39. $\frac{dy}{dx} = \frac{1}{\sqrt{1 - x^2}}, \quad y(0) = 0$

40. $\frac{dy}{dx} = \frac{1}{x^2 + 1} - 1, \quad y(0) = 1$

41. $\frac{dy}{dx} = \frac{1}{x\sqrt{x^2 - 1}}, \quad x > 1; \quad y(2) = \pi$

42. $\frac{dy}{dx} = \frac{1}{1 + x^2} - \frac{2}{\sqrt{1 - x^2}}, \quad y(0) = 2$

Evaluating Indefinite Integrals

Evaluate the integrals in Exercises 43–72.

43. $\int 2(\cos x)^{-1/2} \sin x \, dx$

44. $\int (\tan x)^{-3/2} \sec^2 x \, dx$

45. $\int (2\theta + 1 + 2\cos(2\theta + 1)) \, d\theta$

46. $\int \left(\frac{1}{\sqrt{2\theta - \pi}} + 2\sec^2(2\theta - \pi) \right) d\theta$

47. $\int \left(t - \frac{2}{t} \right)\left(t + \frac{2}{t} \right) dt$

48. $\int \frac{(t + 1)^2 - 1}{t^4} \, dt$

49. $\int \sqrt{t} \sin(2t^{3/2}) \, dt$

50. $\int (\sec\theta \tan\theta) \sqrt{1 + \sec\theta} \, d\theta$

51. $\int e^x \sec^2(e^x - 7) \, dx$

52. $\int e^y \csc(e^y + 1) \cot(e^y + 1) \, dy$

53. $\int (\sec^2 x) \, e^{\tan x} \, dx$

54. $\int (\csc^2 x) \, e^{\cot x} \, dx$

55. $\int_{-1}^{1} \frac{dx}{3x - 4}$

56. $\int_{1}^{e} \frac{\sqrt{\ln x}}{x} \, dx$

57. $\int_{0}^{4} \frac{2t}{t^2 - 25} \, dt$

58. $\int \frac{\tan(\ln v)}{v} \, dv$

59. $\int \frac{(\ln x)^{-3}}{x} \, dx$

60. $\int \frac{1}{r} \csc^2(1 + \ln r) \, dr$

61. $\int x 3^{x^2} \, dx$

62. $\int 2^{\tan x} \sec^2 x \, dx$

63. $\int \frac{3 \, dr}{\sqrt{1 - 4(r - 1)^2}}$

64. $\int \frac{6 \, dr}{\sqrt{4 - (r + 1)^2}}$

65. $\int \frac{dx}{2 + (x - 1)^2}$

66. $\int \frac{dx}{1 + (3x + 1)^2}$

67. $\int \frac{dx}{(2x - 1)\sqrt{(2x - 1)^2 - 4}}$

68. $\int \frac{dx}{(x + 3)\sqrt{(x + 3)^2 - 25}}$

69. $\int \frac{e^{\sin^{-1}\sqrt{x}} \, dx}{2\sqrt{x - x^2}}$

70. $\int \frac{\sqrt{\sin^{-1} x} \, dx}{\sqrt{1 - x^2}}$

71. $\int \frac{dy}{\sqrt{\tan^{-1} y}\,(1 + y^2)}$

72. $\int \frac{(\tan^{-1} x)^2 \, dx}{1 + x^2}$

Evaluating Definite Integrals

Evaluate the integrals in Exercises 73–112.

73. $\int_{-1}^{1} (3x^2 - 4x + 7) \, dx$

74. $\int_{0}^{1} (8s^3 - 12s^2 + 5) \, ds$

75. $\int_{1}^{2} \frac{4}{v^2} \, dv$

76. $\int_{1}^{27} x^{-4/3} \, dx$

77. $\int_{1}^{4} \frac{dt}{t\sqrt{t}}$

78. $\int_{1}^{4} \frac{\left(1 + \sqrt{u}\right)^{1/2}}{\sqrt{u}} \, du$

79. $\int_{0}^{1} \frac{36 \, dx}{(2x + 1)^3}$

80. $\int_{0}^{1} \frac{dr}{\sqrt[3]{(7 - 5r)^2}}$

81. $\int_{1/8}^{1} x^{-1/3}(1 - x^{2/3})^{3/2} \, dx$

82. $\int_{0}^{1/2} x^3(1 + 9x^4)^{-3/2} \, dx$

83. $\int_{0}^{\pi} \sin^2 5r \, dr$

84. $\int_{0}^{\pi/4} \cos^2\left(4t - \frac{\pi}{4}\right) dt$

85. $\int_{0}^{\pi/3} \sec^2\theta \, d\theta$

86. $\int_{\pi/4}^{3\pi/4} \csc^2 x \, dx$

87. $\int_{\pi}^{3\pi} \cot^2 \frac{x}{6} \, dx$

88. $\int_{0}^{\pi} \tan^2 \frac{\theta}{3} \, d\theta$

89. $\int_{-\pi/3}^{0} \sec x \tan x \, dx$

90. $\int_{\pi/4}^{3\pi/4} \csc z \cot z \, dz$

91. $\int_{0}^{\pi/2} 5(\sin x)^{3/2} \cos x \, dx$

92. $\int_{-\pi/2}^{\pi/2} 15 \sin^4 3x \cos 3x \, dx$

93. $\int_{0}^{\pi/2} \frac{3 \sin x \cos x}{\sqrt{1 + 3\sin^2 x}} \, dx$

94. $\int_{0}^{\pi/4} \frac{\sec^2 x}{(1 + 7\tan x)^{2/3}} \, dx$

95. $\int_{1}^{4} \left(\frac{x}{8} + \frac{1}{2x} \right) dx$

96. $\int_{1}^{8} \left(\frac{2}{3x} - \frac{8}{x^2} \right) dx$

97. $\int_{-2}^{-1} e^{-(x+1)} \, dx$

98. $\int_{-\ln 2}^{0} e^{2w} \, dw$

99. $\int_{0}^{\ln 5} e^r(3e^r + 1)^{-3/2} \, dr$

100. $\int_{0}^{\ln 9} e^{\theta}(e^{\theta} - 1)^{1/2} \, d\theta$

101. $\int_{1}^{e} \frac{1}{x}(1 + 7\ln x)^{-1/3} \, dx$

102. $\int_{1}^{3} \frac{(\ln(v + 1))^2}{v + 1} \, dv$

103. $\int_{1}^{8} \frac{\log_4 \theta}{\theta} \, d\theta$

104. $\int_{1}^{e} \frac{8 \ln 3 \log_3 \theta}{\theta} \, d\theta$

105. $\int_{-3/4}^{3/4} \frac{6 \, dx}{\sqrt{9 - 4x^2}}$

106. $\int_{-1/5}^{1/5} \frac{6 \, dx}{\sqrt{4 - 25x^2}}$

107. $\int_{-2}^{2} \frac{3 \, dt}{4 + 3t^2}$

108. $\int_{\sqrt{3}}^{3} \frac{dt}{3 + t^2}$

109. $\int \frac{dy}{y\sqrt{4y^2 - 1}}$

110. $\int \frac{24 \, dy}{y\sqrt{y^2 - 16}}$

111. $\int_{\sqrt{2}/3}^{2/3} \frac{dy}{|y|\sqrt{9y^2 - 1}}$

112. $\int_{-2/\sqrt{5}}^{-\sqrt{6}/\sqrt{5}} \frac{dy}{|y|\sqrt{5y^2 - 3}}$

Average Values

113. Find the average value of $f(x) = mx + b$
   a. over $[-1, 1]$
   b. over $[-k, k]$

114. Find the average value of
   a. $y = \sqrt{3x}$ over $[0, 3]$
   b. $y = \sqrt{ax}$ over $[0, a]$

115. Let f be a function that is differentiable on $[a, b]$. In Chapter 2 we defined the average rate of change of f over $[a, b]$ to be

$$\frac{f(b) - f(a)}{b - a}$$

and the instantaneous rate of change of f at x to be $f'(x)$. In this chapter we defined the average value of a function. For the new definition of average to be consistent with the old one, we should have

$$\frac{f(b) - f(a)}{b - a} = \text{average value of } f' \text{ on } [a, b].$$

Is this the case? Give reasons for your answer.

116. Is it true that the average value of an integrable function over an interval of length 2 is half the function's integral over the interval? Give reasons for your answer.

117. a. Verify that $\int \ln x\, dx = x \ln x - x + C$.

b. Find the average value of $\ln x$ over $[1, e]$.

118. Find the average value of $f(x) = 1/x$ on $[1, 2]$.

T **119.** Compute the average value of the temperature function

$$f(x) = 37 \sin\left(\frac{2\pi}{365}(x - 101)\right) + 25$$

for a 365-day year. (See Exercise 98, Section 3.6.) This is one way to estimate the annual mean air temperature in Fairbanks, Alaska. The National Weather Service's official figure, a numerical average of the daily normal mean air temperatures for the year, is 25.7°F, which is slightly higher than the average value of $f(x)$.

T **120. Specific heat of a gas** Specific heat C_v is the amount of heat required to raise the temperature of one mole (gram molecule) of a gas with constant volume by 1°C. The specific heat of oxygen depends on its temperature T and satisfies the formula

$$C_v = 8.27 + 10^{-5}(26T - 1.87T^2).$$

Find the average value of C_v for $20° \le T \le 675°\text{C}$ and the temperature at which it is attained.

Differentiating Integrals

In Exercises 121–128, find dy/dx.

121. $y = \displaystyle\int_2^x \sqrt{2 + \cos^3 t}\, dt$

122. $y = \displaystyle\int_2^{7x^2} \sqrt{2 + \cos^3 t}\, dt$

123. $y = \displaystyle\int_x^1 \frac{6}{3 + t^4}\, dt$

124. $y = \displaystyle\int_{\sec x}^2 \frac{1}{t^2 + 1}\, dt$

125. $y = \displaystyle\int_{\ln x^2}^0 e^{\cos t}\, dt$

126. $y = \displaystyle\int_1^{e^{\sqrt{x}}} \ln(t^2 + 1)\, dt$

127. $y = \displaystyle\int_0^{\sin^{-1} x} \frac{dt}{\sqrt{1 - 2t^2}}$

128. $y = \displaystyle\int_{\tan^{-1} x}^{\pi/4} e^{\sqrt{t}}\, dt$

Theory and Examples

129. Is it true that every function $y = f(x)$ that is differentiable on $[a, b]$ is itself the derivative of some function on $[a, b]$? Give reasons for your answer.

130. Suppose that $F(x)$ is an antiderivative of $f(x) = \sqrt{1 + x^4}$. Express $\int_0^1 \sqrt{1 + x^4}\, dx$ in terms of F and give a reason for your answer.

131. Find dy/dx if $y = \int_x^1 \sqrt{1 + t^2}\, dt$. Explain the main steps in your calculation.

132. Find dy/dx if $y = \int_{\cos x}^0 (1/(1 - t^2))\, dt$. Explain the main steps in your calculation.

133. A new parking lot To meet the demand for parking, your town has allocated the area shown here. As the town engineer, you have been asked by the town council to find out if the lot can be built for \$10,000. The cost to clear the land will be \$0.10 a square foot, and the lot will cost \$2.00 a square foot to pave. Can the job be done for \$10,000? Use a lower sum estimate to see. (Answers may vary slightly, depending on the estimate used.)

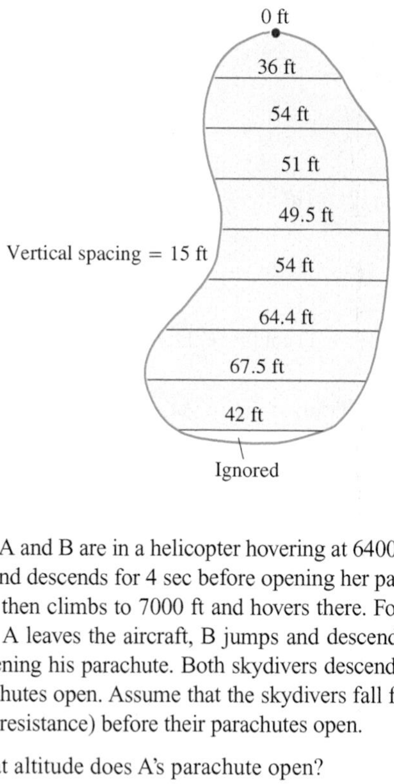

134. Skydivers A and B are in a helicopter hovering at 6400 ft. Skydiver A jumps and descends for 4 sec before opening her parachute. The helicopter then climbs to 7000 ft and hovers there. Forty-five seconds after A leaves the aircraft, B jumps and descends for 13 sec before opening his parachute. Both skydivers descend at 16 ft/sec with parachutes open. Assume that the skydivers fall freely (no effective air resistance) before their parachutes open.

a. At what altitude does A's parachute open?

b. At what altitude does B's parachute open?

c. Which skydiver lands first?

Chapter Additional and Advanced Exercises

Theory and Examples

1. a. If $\int_0^1 7f(x)\,dx = 7$, does $\int_0^1 f(x)\,dx = 1$?

 b. If $\int_0^1 f(x)\,dx = 4$ and $f(x) \geq 0$, does

$$\int_0^1 \sqrt{f(x)}\,dx = \sqrt{4} = 2?$$

 Give reasons for your answers.

2. Suppose $\int_{-2}^2 f(x)\,dx = 4, \int_2^5 f(x)\,dx = 3, \int_{-2}^5 g(x)\,dx = 2.$ Which, if any, of the following statements are true?

 a. $\int_5^2 f(x)\,dx = -3$ b. $\int_{-2}^5 (f(x) + g(x)) = 9$

 c. $f(x) \leq g(x)$ on the interval $-2 \leq x \leq 5$

3. **Initial value problem** Show that

$$y = \frac{1}{a}\int_0^x f(t)\sin a(x - t)\,dt$$

 solves the initial value problem

$$\frac{d^2y}{dx^2} + a^2y = f(x), \quad \frac{dy}{dx} = 0 \text{ and } y = 0 \text{ when } x = 0.$$

 (*Hint:* $\sin(ax - at) = \sin ax \cos at - \cos ax \sin at$.)

4. **Proportionality** Suppose that x and y are related by the equation

$$x = \int_0^y \frac{1}{\sqrt{1 + 4t^2}}\,dt.$$

 Show that d^2y/dx^2 is proportional to y and find the constant of proportionality.

5. Find $f(4)$ if

 a. $\int_0^{x^2} f(t)\,dt = x\cos\pi x$ b. $\int_0^{f(x)} t^2\,dt = x\cos\pi x.$

6. Find $f(\pi/2)$ from the following information.

 i) f is positive and continuous.

 ii) The area under the curve $y = f(x)$ from $x = 0$ to $x = a$ is

$$\frac{a^2}{2} + \frac{a}{2}\sin a + \frac{\pi}{2}\cos a.$$

7. The area of the region in the xy-plane enclosed by the x-axis, the curve $y = f(x)$, $f(x) \geq 0$, and the lines $x = 1$ and $x = b$ is equal to $\sqrt{b^2 + 1} - \sqrt{2}$ for all $b > 1$. Find $f(x)$.

8. Prove that

$$\int_0^x \left(\int_0^u f(t)\,dt\right) du = \int_0^x f(u)(x - u)\,du.$$

 (*Hint:* Express the integral on the right-hand side as the difference of two integrals. Then show that both sides of the equation have the same derivative with respect to x.)

9. **Finding a curve** Find the equation for the curve in the xy-plane that passes through the point $(1, -1)$ if its slope at x is always $3x^2 + 2$.

10. **Shoveling dirt** You sling a shovelful of dirt up from the bottom of a hole with an initial velocity of 32 ft/sec. The dirt must rise 17 ft above the release point to clear the edge of the hole. Is that enough speed to get the dirt out, or had you better duck?

Piecewise Continuous Functions

Although we are mainly interested in continuous functions, many functions in applications are piecewise continuous. A function $f(x)$ is **piecewise continuous on a closed interval I** if f has only finitely many discontinuities in I, the limits

$$\lim_{x \to c^-} f(x) \quad \text{and} \quad \lim_{x \to c^+} f(x)$$

exist and are finite at every interior point of I, and the appropriate one-sided limits exist and are finite at the endpoints of I. All piecewise continuous functions are integrable. The points of discontinuity subdivide I into open and half-open subintervals on which f is continuous, and the limit criteria above guarantee that f has a continuous extension to the closure of each subinterval. To integrate a piecewise continuous function, we integrate the individual extensions and add the results. The integral of

$$f(x) = \begin{cases} 1 - x, & -1 \leq x < 0 \\ x^2, & 0 \leq x < 2 \\ -1, & 2 \leq x \leq 3 \end{cases}$$

(Figure 5.32) over $[-1, 3]$ is

$$\begin{aligned} \int_{-1}^3 f(x)\,dx &= \int_{-1}^0 (1 - x)\,dx + \int_0^2 x^2\,dx + \int_2^3 (-1)\,dx \\ &= \left[x - \frac{x^2}{2}\right]_{-1}^0 + \left[\frac{x^3}{3}\right]_0^2 + \left[-x\right]_2^3 \\ &= \frac{3}{2} + \frac{8}{3} - 1 = \frac{19}{6}. \end{aligned}$$

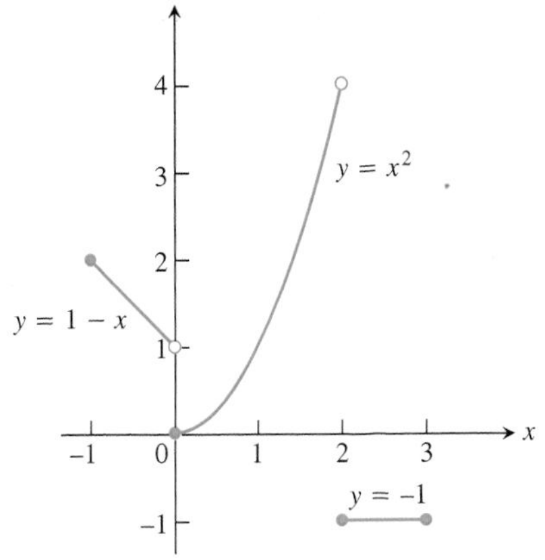

FIGURE 5.32 Piecewise continuous functions like this are integrated piece by piece.

The Fundamental Theorem applies to piecewise continuous functions with the restriction that $(d/dx)\int_a^x f(t)\,dt$ is expected to equal $f(x)$ only at values of x at which f is continuous. There is a similar restriction on Leibniz's Rule (see Exercises 31–38).

Graph the functions in Exercises 11–16 and integrate them over their domains.

11. $f(x) = \begin{cases} x^{2/3}, & -8 \le x < 0 \\ -4, & 0 \le x \le 3 \end{cases}$

12. $f(x) = \begin{cases} \sqrt{-x}, & -4 \le x < 0 \\ x^2 - 4, & 0 \le x \le 3 \end{cases}$

13. $g(t) = \begin{cases} t, & 0 \le t < 1 \\ \sin \pi t, & 1 \le t \le 2 \end{cases}$

14. $h(z) = \begin{cases} \sqrt{1 - z}, & 0 \le z < 1 \\ (7z - 6)^{-1/3}, & 1 \le z \le 2 \end{cases}$

15. $f(x) = \begin{cases} 1, & -2 \le x < -1 \\ 1 - x^2, & -1 \le x < 1 \\ 2, & 1 \le x \le 2 \end{cases}$

16. $h(r) = \begin{cases} r, & -1 \le r < 0 \\ 1 - r^2, & 0 \le r < 1 \\ 1, & 1 \le r \le 2 \end{cases}$

17. Find the average value of the function graphed in the accompanying figure.

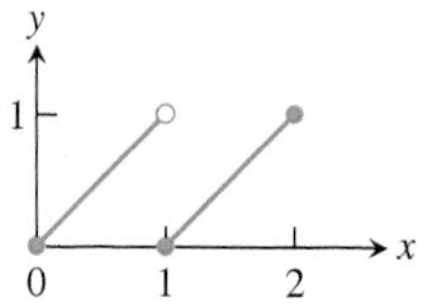

18. Find the average value of the function graphed in the accompanying figure.

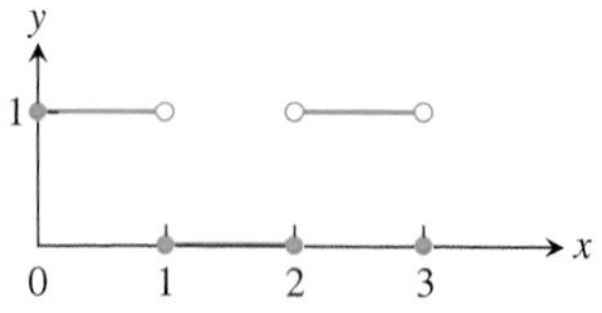

Limits

Find the limits in Exercises 19–22.

19. $\displaystyle\lim_{b \to 1^-} \int_0^b \frac{dx}{\sqrt{1 - x^2}}$

20. $\displaystyle\lim_{x \to \infty} \frac{1}{x} \int_0^x \tan^{-1} t\, dt$

21. $\displaystyle\lim_{n \to \infty} \left(\frac{1}{n + 1} + \frac{1}{n + 2} + \cdots + \frac{1}{2n} \right)$

22. $\displaystyle\lim_{n \to \infty} \frac{1}{n} \left(e^{1/n} + e^{2/n} + \cdots + e^{(n-1)/n} + e^{n/n} \right)$

Approximating Finite Sums with Integrals

In many applications of calculus, integrals are used to approximate finite sums—the reverse of the usual procedure of using finite sums to approximate integrals.

For example, let's estimate the sum of the square roots of the first n positive integers, $\sqrt{1} + \sqrt{2} + \cdots + \sqrt{n}$. The integral

$$\int_0^1 \sqrt{x}\, dx = \frac{2}{3} x^{3/2} \bigg]_0^1 = \frac{2}{3}$$

is the limit of the upper sums

$$S_n = \sqrt{\frac{1}{n}} \cdot \frac{1}{n} + \sqrt{\frac{2}{n}} \cdot \frac{1}{n} + \cdots + \sqrt{\frac{n}{n}} \cdot \frac{1}{n}$$

$$= \frac{\sqrt{1} + \sqrt{2} + \cdots + \sqrt{n}}{n^{3/2}}.$$

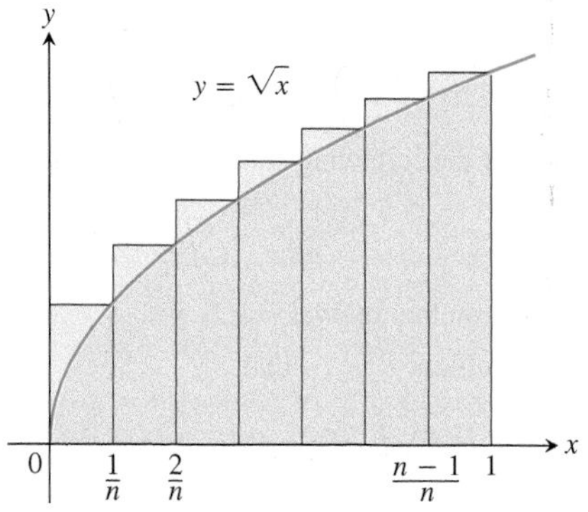

Therefore, when n is large, S_n will be close to $2/3$ and we will have

$$\text{Root sum} = \sqrt{1} + \sqrt{2} + \cdots + \sqrt{n} = S_n \cdot n^{3/2} \approx \frac{2}{3} n^{3/2}.$$

The following table shows how good the approximation can be.

n	**Root sum**	$(2/3)n^{3/2}$	**Relative error**
10	22.468	21.082	$1.386/22.468 \approx 6\%$
50	239.04	235.70	1.4%
100	671.46	666.67	0.7%
1000	21,097	21,082	0.07%

23. Evaluate

$$\lim_{n \to \infty} \frac{1^5 + 2^5 + 3^5 + \cdots + n^5}{n^6}$$

by showing that the limit is

$$\int_0^1 x^5\, dx$$

and evaluating the integral.

24. See Exercise 23. Evaluate

$$\lim_{n \to \infty} \frac{1}{n^4} (1^3 + 2^3 + 3^3 + \cdots + n^3).$$

25. Let $f(x)$ be a continuous function. Express

$$\lim_{n \to \infty} \frac{1}{n} \left[f\left(\frac{1}{n}\right) + f\left(\frac{2}{n}\right) + \cdots + f\left(\frac{n}{n}\right) \right]$$

as a definite integral.

26. Use the result of Exercise 25 to evaluate

a. $\lim_{n\to\infty} \frac{1}{n^2}(2 + 4 + 6 + \cdots + 2n)$,

b. $\lim_{n\to\infty} \frac{1}{n^{16}}(1^{15} + 2^{15} + 3^{15} + \cdots + n^{15})$,

c. $\lim_{n\to\infty} \frac{1}{n}\left(\sin\frac{\pi}{n} + \sin\frac{2\pi}{n} + \sin\frac{3\pi}{n} + \cdots + \sin\frac{n\pi}{n}\right)$.

What can be said about the following limits?

d. $\lim_{n\to\infty} \frac{1}{n^{17}}(1^{15} + 2^{15} + 3^{15} + \cdots + n^{15})$

e. $\lim_{n\to\infty} \frac{1}{n^{15}}(1^{15} + 2^{15} + 3^{15} + \cdots + n^{15})$

27. a. Show that the area A_n of an n-sided regular polygon in a circle of radius r is

$$A_n = \frac{nr^2}{2}\sin\frac{2\pi}{n}.$$

b. Find the limit of A_n as $n \to \infty$. Is this answer consistent with what you know about the area of a circle?

28. Let

$$S_n = \frac{1^2}{n^3} + \frac{2^2}{n^3} + \cdots + \frac{(n-1)^2}{n^3}.$$

To calculate $\lim_{n\to\infty} S_n$, show that

$$S_n = \frac{1}{n}\left[\left(\frac{1}{n}\right)^2 + \left(\frac{2}{n}\right)^2 + \cdots + \left(\frac{n-1}{n}\right)^2\right]$$

and interpret S_n as an approximating sum of the integral

$$\int_0^1 x^2\,dx.$$

(*Hint:* Partition [0, 1] into n intervals of equal length and write out the approximating sum for inscribed rectangles.)

Defining Functions Using the Fundamental Theorem

29. **A function defined by an integral** The graph of a function f consists of a semicircle and two line segments as shown. Let $g(x) = \int_1^x f(t)\,dt$.

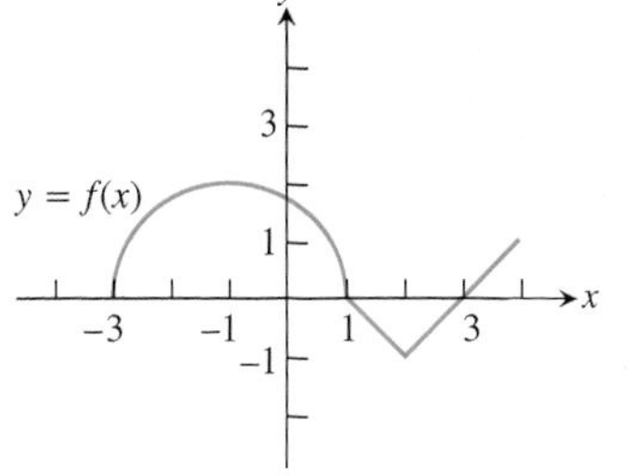

a. Find $g(1)$.

b. Find $g(3)$.

c. Find $g(-1)$.

d. Find all values of x on the open interval $(-3, 4)$ at which g has a relative maximum.

e. Write an equation for the line tangent to the graph of g at $x = -1$.

f. Find the x-coordinate of each point of inflection of the graph of g on the open interval $(-3, 4)$.

g. Find the range of g.

30. **A differential equation** Show that both of the following conditions are satisfied by $y = \sin x + \int_x^\pi \cos 2t\,dt + 1$:

i) $y'' = -\sin x + 2\sin 2x$

ii) $y = 1$ and $y' = -2$ when $x = \pi$.

Leibniz's Rule In applications, we sometimes encounter functions like

$$f(x) = \int_{\sin x}^{x^2} (1 + t)\,dt \quad \text{and} \quad g(x) = \int_{\sqrt{x}}^{2\sqrt{x}} \sin t^2\,dt,$$

defined by integrals that have variable upper limits of integration and variable lower limits of integration at the same time. The first integral can be evaluated directly, but the second cannot. We may find the derivative of either integral, however, by a formula called **Leibniz's Rule**.

Leibniz's Rule

If f is continuous on $[a, b]$ and if $u(x)$ and $v(x)$ are differentiable functions of x whose values lie in $[a, b]$, then

$$\frac{d}{dx}\int_{u(x)}^{v(x)} f(t)\,dt = f(v(x))\frac{dv}{dx} - f(u(x))\frac{du}{dx}.$$

Figure 5.33 gives a geometric interpretation of Leibniz's Rule. It shows a carpet of variable width $f(t)$ that is being rolled up at the left at the same time x as it is being unrolled at the right. (In this interpretation, time is x, not t.) At time x, the floor is covered from $u(x)$ to $v(x)$. The rate du/dx at which the carpet is being rolled up need not be the same as the rate dv/dx at which the carpet is being laid down. At any given time x, the area covered by carpet is

$$A(x) = \int_{u(x)}^{v(x)} f(t)\,dt.$$

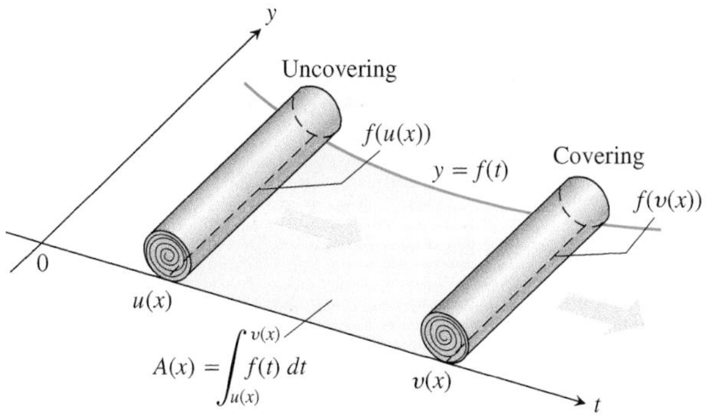

FIGURE 5.33 Rolling and unrolling a carpet gives a geometric interpretation of Leibniz's Rule:

$$\frac{dA}{dx} = f(v(x))\frac{dv}{dx} - f(u(x))\frac{du}{dx}.$$

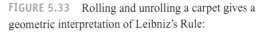

At what rate is the covered area changing? At the instant x, $A(x)$ is increasing by the width $f(v(x))$ of the unrolling carpet times the rate dv/dx at which the carpet is being unrolled. That is, $A(x)$ is being increased at the rate

$$f(v(x))\frac{dv}{dx}.$$

At the same time, A is being decreased at the rate

$$f(u(x))\frac{du}{dx},$$

the width at the end that is being rolled up times the rate du/dx. The net rate of change in A is

$$\frac{dA}{dx} = f(v(x))\frac{dv}{dx} - f(u(x))\frac{du}{dx},$$

which is precisely Leibniz's Rule.

To prove the rule, let F be an antiderivative of f on $[a, b]$. Then

$$\int_{u(x)}^{v(x)} f(t)\,dt = F(v(x)) - F(u(x)).$$

Differentiating both sides of this equation with respect to x gives the equation we want:

$$\begin{aligned}\frac{d}{dx}\int_{u(x)}^{v(x)} f(t)\,dt &= \frac{d}{dx}\Big[F(v(x)) - F(u(x))\Big] \\ &= F'(v(x))\frac{dv}{dx} - F'(u(x))\frac{du}{dx} \qquad \text{Chain Rule} \\ &= f(v(x))\frac{dv}{dx} - f(u(x))\frac{du}{dx}.\end{aligned}$$

Use Leibniz's Rule to find the derivatives of the functions in Exercises 31–38.

31. $f(x) = \displaystyle\int_{1/x}^{x} \frac{1}{t}\,dt$

32. $f(x) = \displaystyle\int_{\cos x}^{\sin x} \frac{1}{1 - t^2}\,dt$

33. $g(y) = \displaystyle\int_{\sqrt{y}}^{2\sqrt{y}} \sin t^2\,dt$

34. $g(y) = \displaystyle\int_{\sqrt{y}}^{y^2} \frac{e^t}{t}\,dt$

35. $y = \displaystyle\int_{x^2/2}^{x^2} \ln\sqrt{t}\,dt$

36. $y = \displaystyle\int_{\sqrt{x}}^{\sqrt[3]{x}} \ln t\,dt$

37. $y = \displaystyle\int_{0}^{\ln x} \sin e^t\,dt$

38. $y = \displaystyle\int_{e^{4\sqrt{x}}}^{e^{2x}} \ln t\,dt$

Theory and Examples

39. Use Leibniz's Rule to find the value of x that maximizes the value of the integral

$$\int_{x}^{x+3} t(5 - t)\,dt.$$

40. For what $x > 0$ does $x^{(x^x)} = (x^x)^x$? Give reasons for your answer.

41. Find the areas between the curves $y = 2(\log_2 x)/x$ and $y = 2(\log_4 x)/x$ and the x-axis from $x = 1$ to $x = e$. What is the ratio of the larger area to the smaller?

42. **a.** Find df/dx if

$$f(x) = \int_{1}^{e^x} \frac{2\ln t}{t}\,dt.$$

b. Find $f(0)$.

c. What can you conclude about the graph of f? Give reasons for your answer.

43. Find $f'(2)$ if $f(x) = e^{g(x)}$ and $g(x) = \displaystyle\int_{2}^{x} \frac{t}{1 + t^4}\,dt.$

44. Use the accompanying figure to show that

$$\int_{0}^{\pi/2} \sin x\,dx = \frac{\pi}{2} - \int_{0}^{1} \sin^{-1} x\,dx.$$

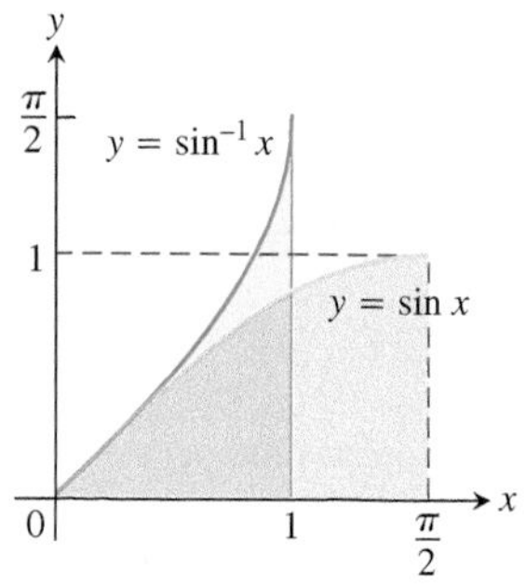

45. **Napier's inequality** Here are two pictorial proofs that

$$b > a > 0 \quad \Rightarrow \quad \frac{1}{b} < \frac{\ln b - \ln a}{b - a} < \frac{1}{a}.$$

Explain what is going on in each case.

a.

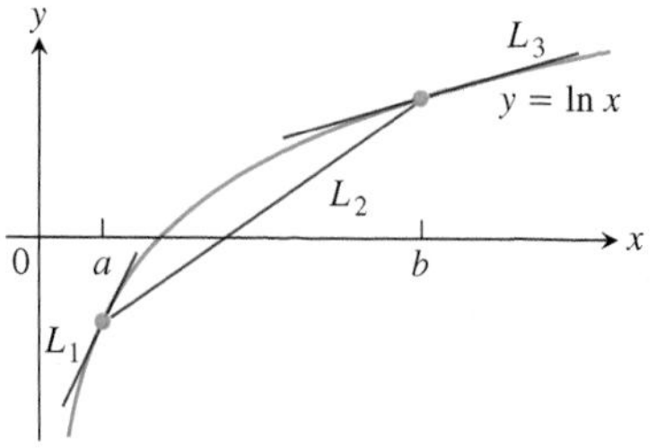

b.

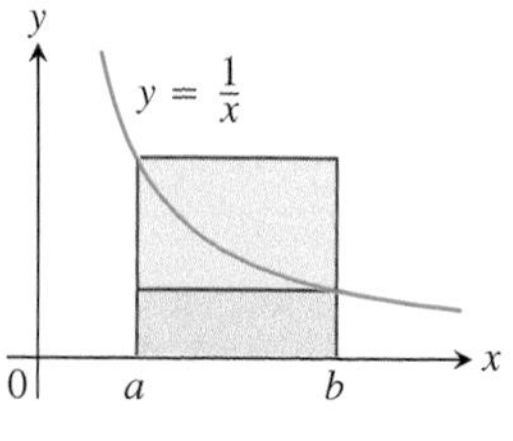

(*Source:* Roger B. Nelson, *College Mathematics Journal*, Vol. 24, No. 2, March 1993, p. 165.)

6

Applications of Definite Integrals

OVERVIEW In Chapter 5 we saw that a continuous function over a closed interval has a definite integral, which is the limit of any Riemann sum for the function. We proved that we could evaluate definite integrals using the Fundamental Theorem of Calculus. We also found that the area under a curve and the area between two curves could be computed as definite integrals.

In this chapter we extend the applications of definite integrals to finding volumes, lengths of plane curves, and areas of surfaces of revolution. We also use integrals to solve physical problems involving the work done by a force, and to find the location of an object's center of mass. Each application comes from a process leading to an approximation by a Riemann sum, and then taking a limit to obtain an appropriate definite integral.

6.1 Volumes Using Cross-Sections

In this section we define volumes of solids using the areas of their cross-sections. A **cross-section** of a solid S is the plane region formed by intersecting S with a plane (Figure 6.1). We present three different methods for obtaining the cross-sections appropriate to finding the volume of a particular solid: the method of slicing, the disk method, and the washer method.

Suppose we want to find the volume of a solid S like the one in Figure 6.1. We begin by extending the definition of a cylinder from classical geometry to cylindrical solids with arbitrary bases (Figure 6.2). If the cylindrical solid has a known base area A and height h, then the volume of the cylindrical solid is

$$\text{Volume} = \text{area} \times \text{height} = A \cdot h.$$

This equation forms the basis for defining the volumes of many solids that are not cylinders, like the one in Figure 6.1. If the cross-section of the solid S at each point x in the interval $[a, b]$ is a region $S(x)$ of area $A(x)$, and A is a continuous function of x, we can define and calculate the volume of the solid S as the definite integral of $A(x)$. We now show how this integral is obtained by the **method of slicing**.

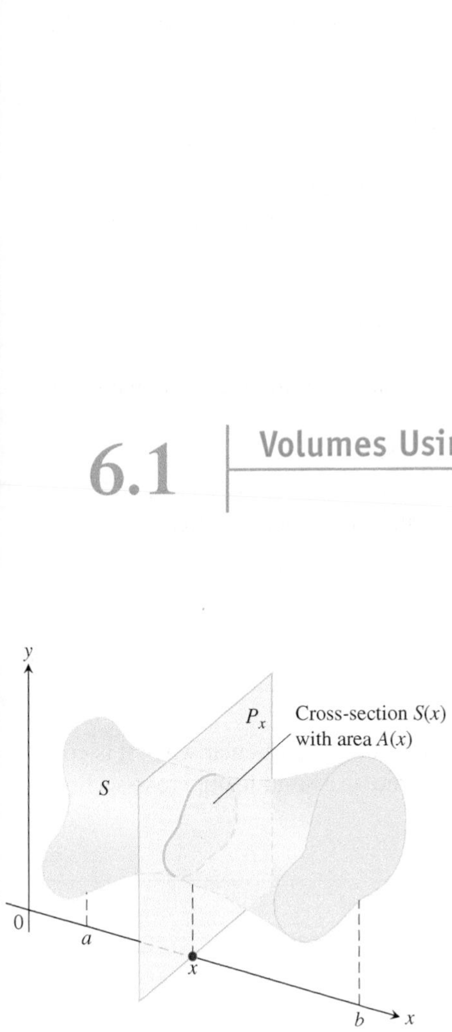

FIGURE 6.1 A cross-section $S(x)$ of the solid S formed by intersecting S with a plane P_x perpendicular to the x-axis through the point x in the interval $[a, b]$.

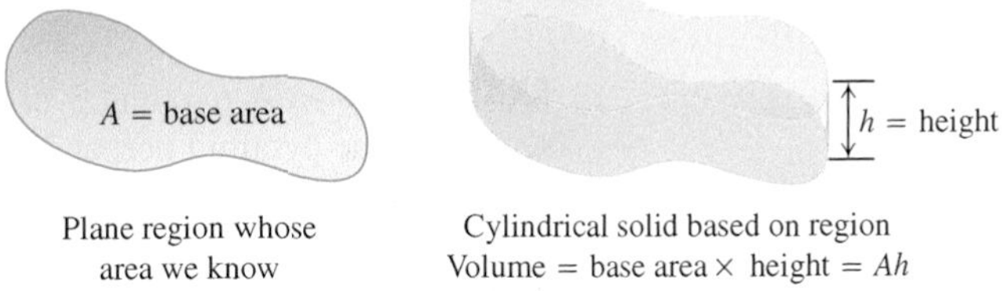

FIGURE 6.2 The volume of a cylindrical solid is always defined to be its base area times its height.

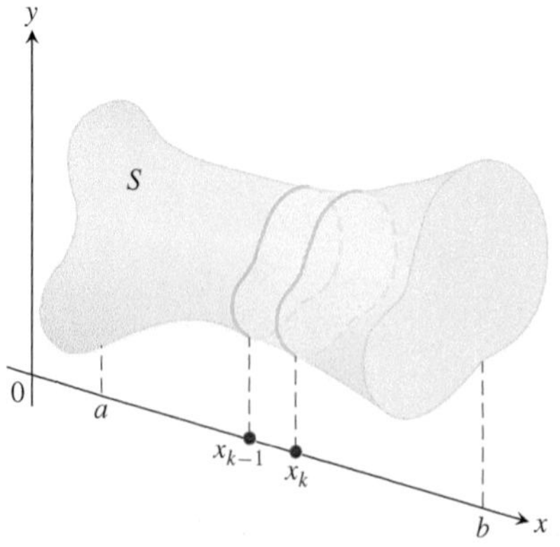

FIGURE 6.3 A typical thin slab in the solid S.

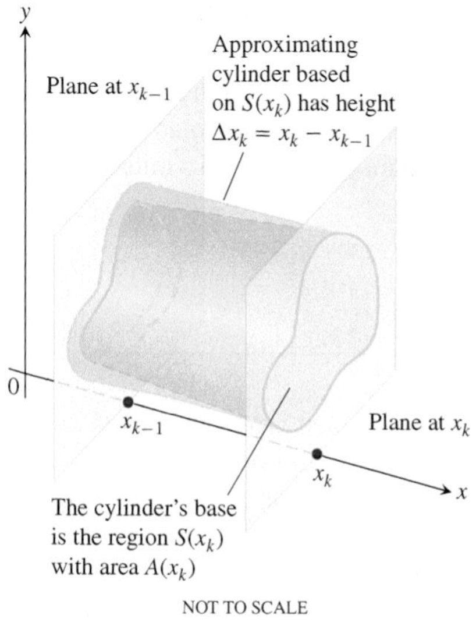

FIGURE 6.4 The solid thin slab in Figure 6.3 is shown enlarged here. It is approximated by the cylindrical solid with base $S(x_k)$ having area $A(x_k)$ and height $\Delta x_k = x_k - x_{k-1}$.

Slicing by Parallel Planes

We partition $[a, b]$ into subintervals of width (length) Δx_k and slice the solid, as we would a loaf of bread, by planes perpendicular to the x-axis at the partition points $a = x_0 < x_1 < \cdots < x_n = b$. The planes P_{x_k}, perpendicular to the x-axis at the partition points, slice S into thin "slabs" (like thin slices of a loaf of bread). A typical slab is shown in Figure 6.3. We approximate the slab between the plane at x_{k-1} and the plane at x_k by a cylindrical solid with base area $A(x_k)$ and height $\Delta x_k = x_k - x_{k-1}$ (Figure 6.4). The volume V_k of this cylindrical solid is $A(x_k) \cdot \Delta x_k$, which is approximately the same volume as that of the slab:

$$\text{Volume of the } k\text{th slab} \approx V_k = A(x_k)\,\Delta x_k.$$

The volume V of the entire solid S is therefore approximated by the sum of these cylindrical volumes,

$$V \approx \sum_{k=1}^{n} V_k = \sum_{k=1}^{n} A(x_k)\,\Delta x_k.$$

This is a Riemann sum for the function $A(x)$ on $[a, b]$. We expect the approximations from these sums to improve as the norm of the partition of $[a, b]$ goes to zero. Taking a partition of $[a, b]$ into n subintervals with $\|P\| \to 0$ gives

$$\lim_{n\to\infty} \sum_{k=1}^{n} A(x_k)\,\Delta x_k = \int_a^b A(x)\,dx.$$

So we define the limiting definite integral of the Riemann sum to be the volume of the solid S.

> **DEFINITION** The **volume** of a solid of integrable cross-sectional area $A(x)$ from $x = a$ to $x = b$ is the integral of A from a to b,
>
> $$V = \int_a^b A(x)\,dx.$$

This definition applies whenever $A(x)$ is integrable, and in particular when it is continuous. To apply the definition to calculate the volume of a solid using cross-sections perpendicular to the x-axis, take the following steps:

> **Calculating the Volume of a Solid**
>
> 1. *Sketch the solid and a typical cross-section.*
> 2. *Find a formula for* $A(x)$, the area of a typical cross-section.
> 3. *Find the limits of integration.*
> 4. *Integrate* $A(x)$ to find the volume.

EXAMPLE 1 A pyramid 3 m high has a square base that is 3 m on a side. The cross-section of the pyramid perpendicular to the altitude x m down from the vertex is a square x m on a side. Find the volume of the pyramid.

Solution

1. *A sketch.* We draw the pyramid with its altitude along the x-axis and its vertex at the origin and include a typical cross-section (Figure 6.5).

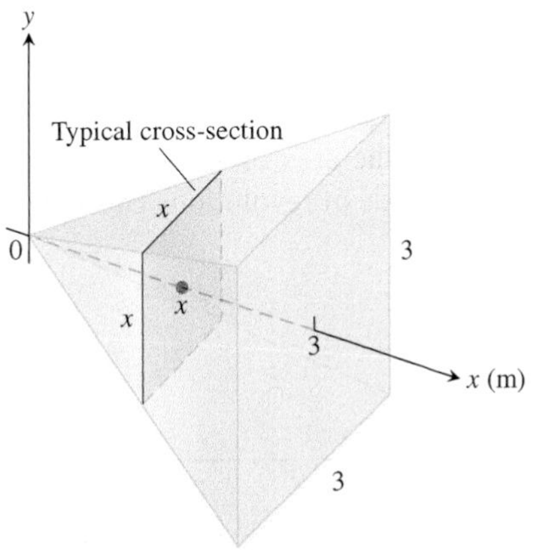

FIGURE 6.5 The cross-sections of the pyramid in Example 1 are squares.

2. *A formula for A(x).* The cross-section at x is a square x meters on a side, so its area is

$$A(x) = x^2.$$

3. *The limits of integration.* The squares lie on the planes from $x = 0$ to $x = 3$.

4. *Integrate to find the volume*:

$$V = \int_0^3 A(x)\,dx = \int_0^3 x^2\,dx = \frac{x^3}{3}\bigg]_0^3 = 9\text{ m}^3.$$ ■

EXAMPLE 2 A curved wedge is cut from a circular cylinder of radius 3 by two planes. One plane is perpendicular to the axis of the cylinder. The second plane crosses the first plane at a 45° angle at the center of the cylinder. Find the volume of the wedge.

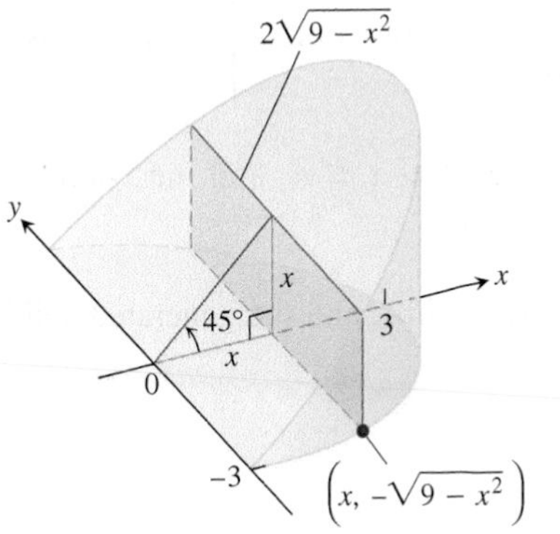

FIGURE 6.6 The wedge of Example 2, sliced perpendicular to the x-axis. The cross-sections are rectangles.

Solution We draw the wedge and sketch a typical cross-section perpendicular to the x-axis (Figure 6.6). The base of the wedge in the figure is the semicircle with $x \geq 0$ that is cut from the circle $x^2 + y^2 = 9$ by the 45° plane when it intersects the y-axis. For any x in the interval [0, 3], the y-values in this semicircular base vary from $y = -\sqrt{9 - x^2}$ to $y = \sqrt{9 - x^2}$. When we slice through the wedge by a plane perpendicular to the x-axis, we obtain a cross-section at x which is a rectangle of height x whose width extends across the semicircular base. The area of this cross-section is

$$\begin{aligned} A(x) &= (\text{height})(\text{width}) = (x)\left(2\sqrt{9 - x^2}\right) \\ &= 2x\sqrt{9 - x^2}. \end{aligned}$$

The rectangles run from $x = 0$ to $x = 3$, so we have

$$\begin{aligned} V &= \int_a^b A(x)\,dx = \int_0^3 2x\sqrt{9 - x^2}\,dx \\ &= -\frac{2}{3}(9 - x^2)^{3/2}\bigg]_0^3 \\ &= 0 + \frac{2}{3}(9)^{3/2} \\ &= 18. \end{aligned}$$

Let $u = 9 - x^2$, $du = -2x\,dx$, integrate, and substitute back.

■

EXAMPLE 3 Cavalieri's principle says that solids with equal altitudes and identical cross-sectional areas at each height have the same volume (Figure 6.7). This follows immediately from the definition of volume, because the cross-sectional area function $A(x)$ and the interval $[a, b]$ are the same for both solids.

HISTORICAL BIOGRAPHY

Bonaventura Cavalieri
(1598–1647)

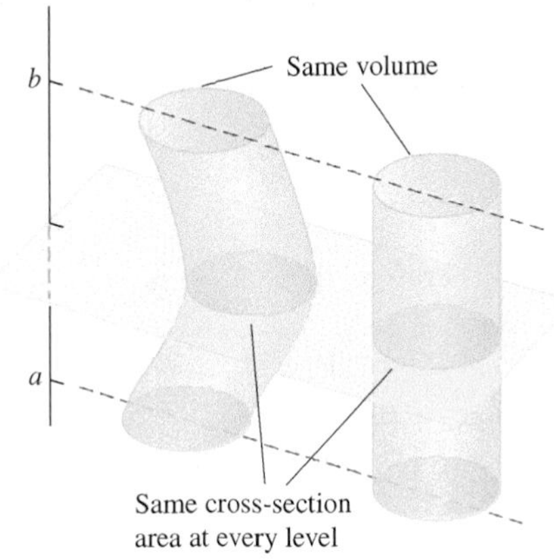

FIGURE 6.7 *Cavalieri's principle:* These solids have the same volume, which can be illustrated with stacks of coins. ■

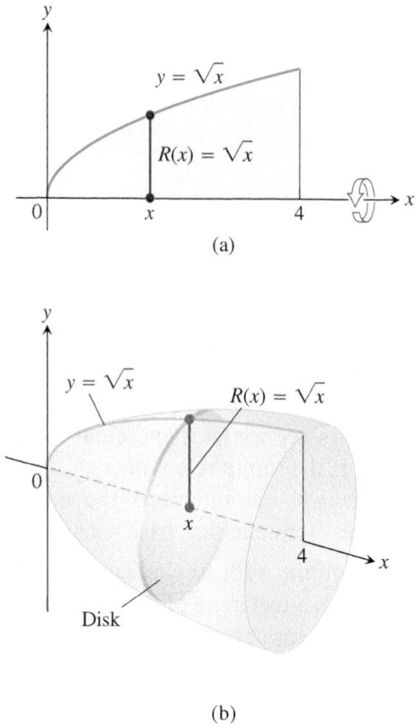

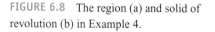

FIGURE 6.8 The region (a) and solid of revolution (b) in Example 4.

Solids of Revolution: The Disk Method

The solid generated by rotating (or revolving) a plane region about an axis in its plane is called a **solid of revolution**. To find the volume of a solid like the one shown in Figure 6.8, we need only observe that the cross-sectional area $A(x)$ is the area of a disk of radius $R(x)$, the distance of the planar region's boundary from the axis of revolution. The area is then

$$A(x) = \pi(\text{radius})^2 = \pi[R(x)]^2.$$

So the definition of volume in this case gives

Volume by Disks for Rotation About the x-axis

$$V = \int_a^b A(x)\,dx = \int_a^b \pi[R(x)]^2\,dx.$$

This method for calculating the volume of a solid of revolution is often called the **disk method** because a cross-section is a circular disk of radius $R(x)$.

EXAMPLE 4 The region between the curve $y = \sqrt{x}$, $0 \le x \le 4$, and the x-axis is revolved about the x-axis to generate a solid. Find its volume.

Solution We draw figures showing the region, a typical radius, and the generated solid (Figure 6.8). The volume is

$$\begin{aligned} V &= \int_a^b \pi[R(x)]^2\,dx \\ &= \int_0^4 \pi\left[\sqrt{x}\right]^2 dx \qquad \text{Radius } R(x) = \sqrt{x} \text{ for rotation around } x\text{-axis} \\ &= \pi\int_0^4 x\,dx = \pi\frac{x^2}{2}\bigg]_0^4 = \pi\frac{(4)^2}{2} = 8\pi. \end{aligned}$$

■

EXAMPLE 5 The circle

$$x^2 + y^2 = a^2$$

is rotated about the x-axis to generate a sphere. Find its volume.

Solution We imagine the sphere cut into thin slices by planes perpendicular to the x-axis (Figure 6.9). The cross-sectional area at a typical point x between $-a$ and a is

$$A(x) = \pi y^2 = \pi(a^2 - x^2). \qquad R(x) = \sqrt{a^2 - x^2} \text{ for rotation around } x\text{-axis}$$

Therefore, the volume is

$$V = \int_{-a}^{a} A(x)\,dx = \int_{-a}^{a} \pi(a^2 - x^2)\,dx = \pi\left[a^2x - \frac{x^3}{3}\right]_{-a}^{a} = \frac{4}{3}\pi a^3.$$

■

The axis of revolution in the next example is not the x-axis, but the rule for calculating the volume is the same: Integrate $\pi(\text{radius})^2$ between appropriate limits.

EXAMPLE 6 Find the volume of the solid generated by revolving the region bounded by $y = \sqrt{x}$ and the lines $y = 1$, $x = 4$ about the line $y = 1$.

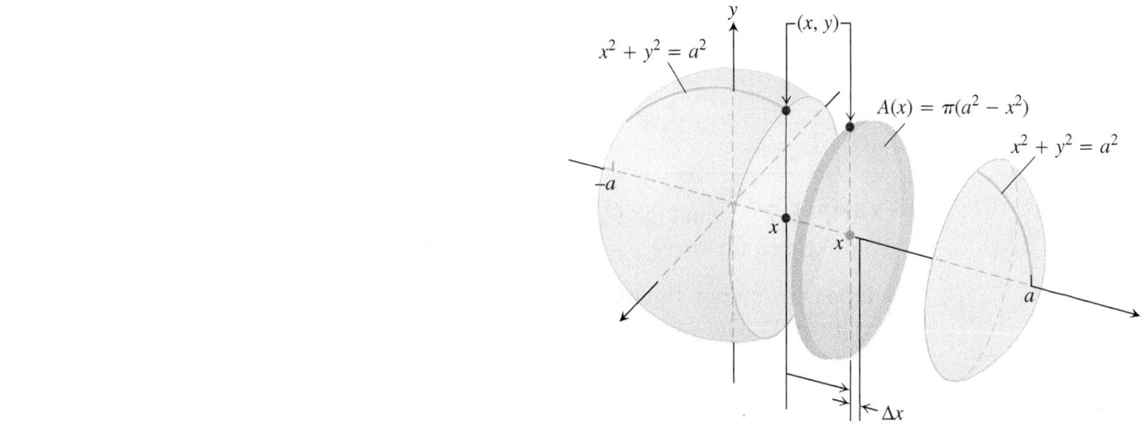

FIGURE 6.9 The sphere generated by rotating the circle $x^2 + y^2 = a^2$ about the x-axis. The radius is $R(x) = y = \sqrt{a^2 - x^2}$ (Example 5).

Solution We draw figures showing the region, a typical radius, and the generated solid (Figure 6.10). The volume is

$$\begin{aligned} V &= \int_1^4 \pi[R(x)]^2\,dx \\ &= \int_1^4 \pi\left[\sqrt{x} - 1\right]^2 dx && \text{Radius } R(x) = \sqrt{x} - 1 \text{ for rotation around } y = 1 \\ &= \pi \int_1^4 \left[x - 2\sqrt{x} + 1\right] dx && \text{Expand integrand.} \\ &= \pi\left[\frac{x^2}{2} - 2 \cdot \frac{2}{3}x^{3/2} + x\right]_1^4 = \frac{7\pi}{6}. && \text{Integrate.} \end{aligned}$$

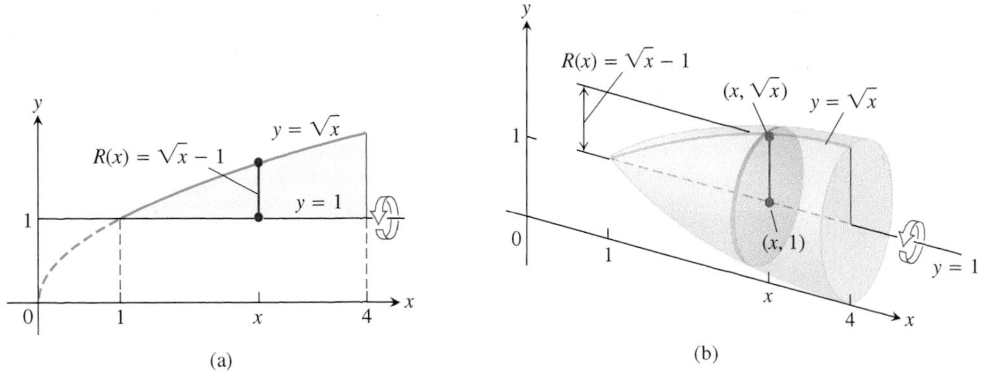

FIGURE 6.10 The region (a) and solid of revolution (b) in Example 6. ■

To find the volume of a solid generated by revolving a region between the y-axis and a curve $x = R(y)$, $c \le y \le d$, about the y-axis, we use the same method with x replaced by y. In this case, the circular cross-section is

$$A(y) = \pi[\text{radius}]^2 = \pi[R(y)]^2,$$

and the definition of volume gives

Volume by Disks for Rotation About the y-axis

$$V = \int_c^d A(y)\,dy = \int_c^d \pi[R(y)]^2\,dy.$$

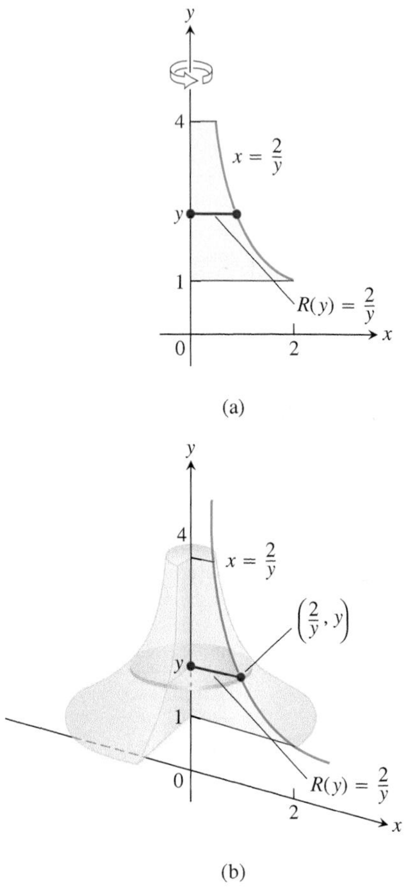

FIGURE 6.11 The region (a) and part of the solid of revolution (b) in Example 7.

EXAMPLE 7 Find the volume of the solid generated by revolving the region between the y-axis and the curve $x = 2/y$, $1 \le y \le 4$, about the y-axis.

Solution We draw figures showing the region, a typical radius, and the generated solid (Figure 6.11). The volume is

$$\begin{aligned} V &= \int_1^4 \pi[R(y)]^2\,dy \\ &= \int_1^4 \pi\left(\frac{2}{y}\right)^2 dy \qquad \text{Radius } R(y) = \frac{2}{y} \text{ for rotation around } y\text{-axis} \\ &= \pi\int_1^4 \frac{4}{y^2}\,dy = 4\pi\left[-\frac{1}{y}\right]_1^4 = 4\pi\left[\frac{3}{4}\right] = 3\pi. \end{aligned}$$

■

EXAMPLE 8 Find the volume of the solid generated by revolving the region between the parabola $x = y^2 + 1$ and the line $x = 3$ about the line $x = 3$.

Solution We draw figures showing the region, a typical radius, and the generated solid (Figure 6.12). Note that the cross-sections are perpendicular to the line $x = 3$ and have y-coordinates from $y = -\sqrt{2}$ to $y = \sqrt{2}$. The volume is

$$\begin{aligned} V &= \int_{-\sqrt{2}}^{\sqrt{2}} \pi[R(y)]^2\,dy \qquad y = \pm\sqrt{2} \text{ when } x = 3 \\ &= \int_{-\sqrt{2}}^{\sqrt{2}} \pi[2 - y^2]^2\,dy \qquad \text{Radius } R(y) = 3 - (y^2 + 1) \text{ for rotation around axis } x = 3 \\ &= \pi\int_{-\sqrt{2}}^{\sqrt{2}} [4 - 4y^2 + y^4]\,dy \qquad \text{Expand integrand.} \\ &= \pi\left[4y - \frac{4}{3}y^3 + \frac{y^5}{5}\right]_{-\sqrt{2}}^{\sqrt{2}} \qquad \text{Integrate.} \\ &= \frac{64\pi\sqrt{2}}{15}. \end{aligned}$$

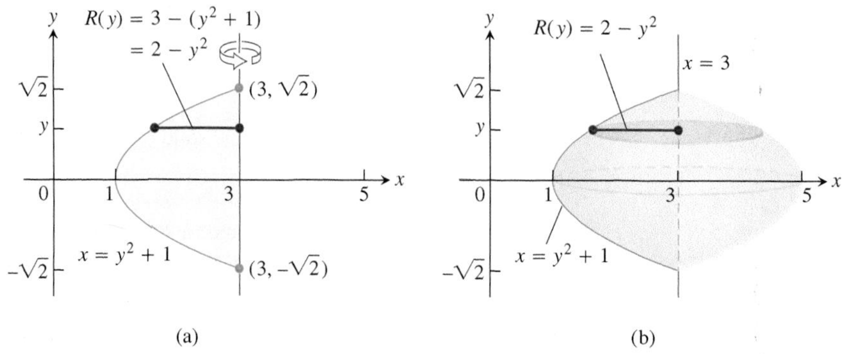

FIGURE 6.12 The region (a) and solid of revolution (b) in Example 8.

■

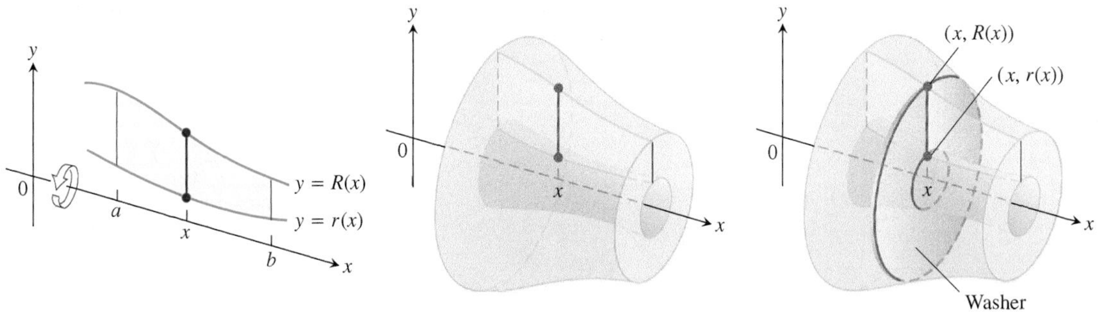

FIGURE 6.13 The cross-sections of the solid of revolution generated here are washers, not disks, so the integral $\int_a^b A(x)\,dx$ leads to a slightly different formula.

Solids of Revolution: The Washer Method

If the region we revolve to generate a solid does not border on or cross the axis of revolution, the solid has a hole in it (Figure 6.13). The cross-sections perpendicular to the axis of revolution are *washers* (the purplish circular surface in Figure 6.13) instead of disks. The dimensions of a typical washer are

Outer radius: $R(x)$

Inner radius: $r(x)$

The washer's area is

$$A(x) = \pi[R(x)]^2 - \pi[r(x)]^2 = \pi([R(x)]^2 - [r(x)]^2).$$

Consequently, the definition of volume in this case gives

Volume by Washers for Rotation About the x-axis

$$V = \int_a^b A(x)\,dx = \int_a^b \pi([R(x)]^2 - [r(x)]^2)\,dx.$$

This method for calculating the volume of a solid of revolution is called the **washer method** because a thin slab of the solid resembles a circular washer of outer radius $R(x)$ and inner radius $r(x)$.

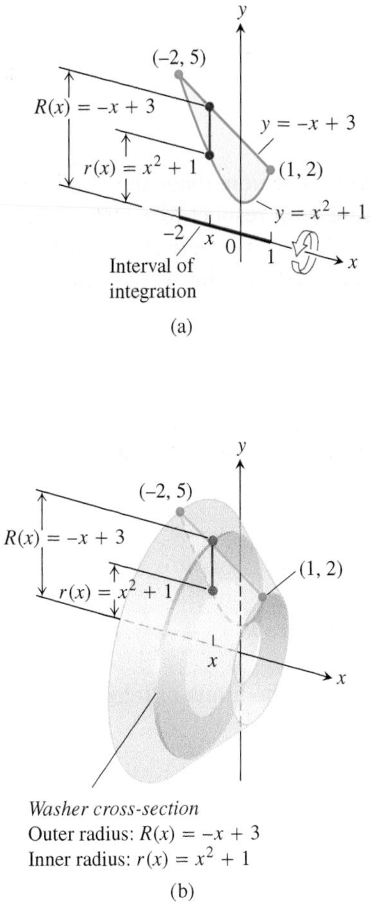

FIGURE 6.14 (a) The region in Example 9 spanned by a line segment perpendicular to the axis of revolution. (b) When the region is revolved about the x-axis, the line segment generates a washer.

EXAMPLE 9 The region bounded by the curve $y = x^2 + 1$ and the line $y = -x + 3$ is revolved about the x-axis to generate a solid. Find the volume of the solid.

Solution We use the four steps for calculating the volume of a solid as discussed early in this section.

1. Draw the region and sketch a line segment across it perpendicular to the axis of revolution (the red segment in Figure 6.14a).

2. Find the outer and inner radii of the washer that would be swept out by the line segment if it were revolved about the x-axis along with the region.

   These radii are the distances of the ends of the line segment from the axis of revolution (Figure 6.14).

   Outer radius: $R(x) = -x + 3$

   Inner radius: $r(x) = x^2 + 1$

3. Find the limits of integration by finding the x-coordinates of the intersection points of the curve and line in Figure 6.14a.

$$\begin{aligned} x^2 + 1 &= -x + 3 \\ x^2 + x - 2 &= 0 \\ (x + 2)(x - 1) &= 0 \\ x = -2, \quad x &= 1 \end{aligned}$$

Limits of integration

4. Evaluate the volume integral.

$$\begin{aligned} V &= \int_a^b \pi([R(x)]^2 - [r(x)]^2)\, dx && \text{Rotation around } x\text{-axis} \\ &= \int_{-2}^{1} \pi((-x + 3)^2 - (x^2 + 1)^2)\, dx && \text{Values from Steps 2 and 3} \\ &= \pi \int_{-2}^{1} (8 - 6x - x^2 - x^4)\, dx && \text{Simplify algebraically.} \\ &= \pi \left[8x - 3x^2 - \frac{x^3}{3} - \frac{x^5}{5} \right]_{-2}^{1} = \frac{117\pi}{5} \end{aligned}$$

■

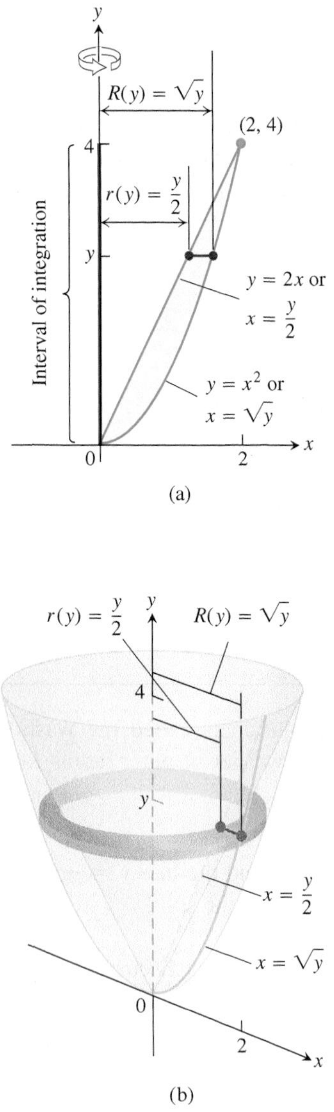

FIGURE 6.15 (a) The region being rotated about the y-axis, the washer radii, and limits of integration in Example 10. (b) The washer swept out by the line segment in part (a).

To find the volume of a solid formed by revolving a region about the y-axis, we use the same procedure as in Example 9, but integrate with respect to y instead of x. In this situation the line segment sweeping out a typical washer is perpendicular to the y-axis (the axis of revolution), and the outer and inner radii of the washer are functions of y.

EXAMPLE 10 The region bounded by the parabola $y = x^2$ and the line $y = 2x$ in the first quadrant is revolved about the y-axis to generate a solid. Find the volume of the solid.

Solution First we sketch the region and draw a line segment across it perpendicular to the axis of revolution (the y-axis). See Figure 6.15a.

The radii of the washer swept out by the line segment are $R(y) = \sqrt{y}$, $r(y) = y/2$ (Figure 6.15).

The line and parabola intersect at $y = 0$ and $y = 4$, so the limits of integration are $c = 0$ and $d = 4$. We integrate to find the volume:

$$\begin{aligned} V &= \int_c^d \pi([R(y)]^2 - [r(y)]^2)\, dy && \text{Rotation around } y\text{-axis} \\ &= \int_0^4 \pi\left(\left[\sqrt{y}\right]^2 - \left[\frac{y}{2}\right]^2\right) dy && \text{Substitute for radii and limits of integration.} \\ &= \pi \int_0^4 \left(y - \frac{y^2}{4}\right) dy = \pi \left[\frac{y^2}{2} - \frac{y^3}{12}\right]_0^4 = \frac{8}{3}\pi. \end{aligned}$$

■

Exercises 6.1

Volumes by Slicing

Find the volumes of the solids in Exercises 1–10.

1. The solid lies between planes perpendicular to the x-axis at $x = 0$ and $x = 4$. The cross-sections perpendicular to the axis on the interval $0 \le x \le 4$ are squares whose diagonals run from the parabola $y = -\sqrt{x}$ to the parabola $y = \sqrt{x}$.

2. The solid lies between planes perpendicular to the x-axis at $x = -1$ and $x = 1$. The cross-sections perpendicular to the x-axis are circular disks whose diameters run from the parabola $y = x^2$ to the parabola $y = 2 - x^2$.

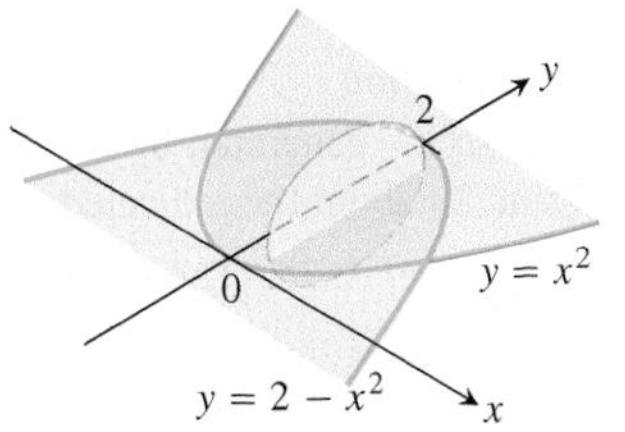

3. The solid lies between planes perpendicular to the x-axis at $x = -1$ and $x = 1$. The cross-sections perpendicular to the x-axis between these planes are squares whose bases run from the semicircle $y = -\sqrt{1 - x^2}$ to the semicircle $y = \sqrt{1 - x^2}$.

4. The solid lies between planes perpendicular to the x-axis at $x = -1$ and $x = 1$. The cross-sections perpendicular to the x-axis between these planes are squares whose diagonals run from the semicircle $y = -\sqrt{1 - x^2}$ to the semicircle $y = \sqrt{1 - x^2}$.

5. The base of a solid is the region between the curve $y = 2\sqrt{\sin x}$ and the interval $[0, \pi]$ on the x-axis. The cross-sections perpendicular to the x-axis are

   a. equilateral triangles with bases running from the x-axis to the curve as shown in the accompanying figure.

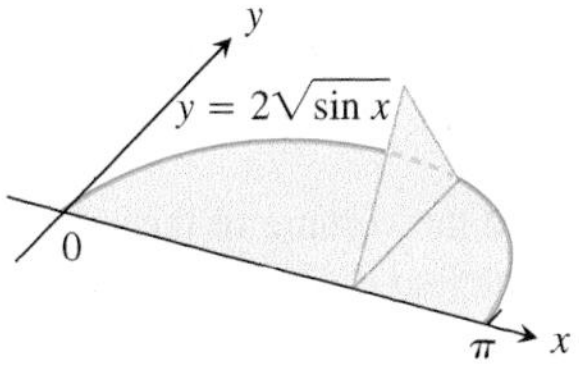

   b. squares with bases running from the x-axis to the curve.

6. The solid lies between planes perpendicular to the x-axis at $x = -\pi/3$ and $x = \pi/3$. The cross-sections perpendicular to the x-axis are

   a. circular disks with diameters running from the curve $y = \tan x$ to the curve $y = \sec x$.

   b. squares whose bases run from the curve $y = \tan x$ to the curve $y = \sec x$.

7. The base of a solid is the region bounded by the graphs of $y = 3x$, $y = 6$, and $x = 0$. The cross-sections perpendicular to the x-axis are

   a. rectangles of height 10.

   b. rectangles of perimeter 20.

8. The base of a solid is the region bounded by the graphs of $y = \sqrt{x}$ and $y = x/2$. The cross-sections perpendicular to the x-axis are

   a. isosceles triangles of height 6.

   b. semi-circles with diameters running across the base of the solid.

9. The solid lies between planes perpendicular to the y-axis at $y = 0$ and $y = 2$. The cross-sections perpendicular to the y-axis are circular disks with diameters running from the y-axis to the parabola $x = \sqrt{5}y^2$.

10. The base of the solid is the disk $x^2 + y^2 \le 1$. The cross-sections by planes perpendicular to the y-axis between $y = -1$ and $y = 1$ are isosceles right triangles with one leg in the disk.

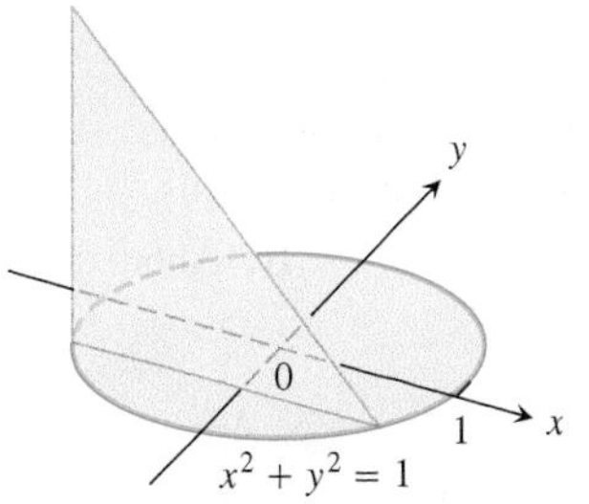

11. Find the volume of the given tetrahedron. (Hint: Consider slices perpendicular to one of the labeled edges.)

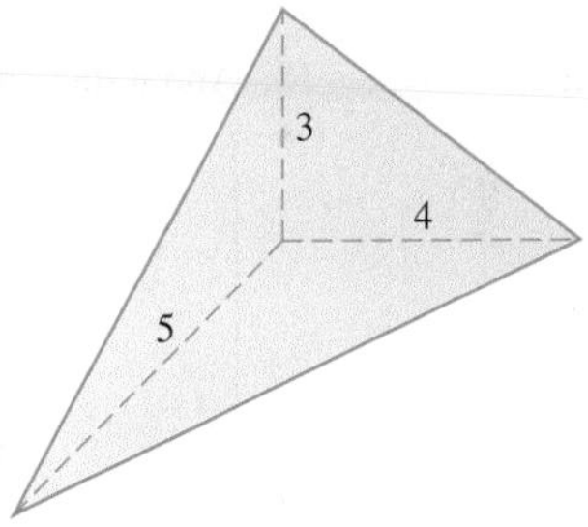

12. Find the volume of the given pyramid, which has a square base of area 9 and height 5.

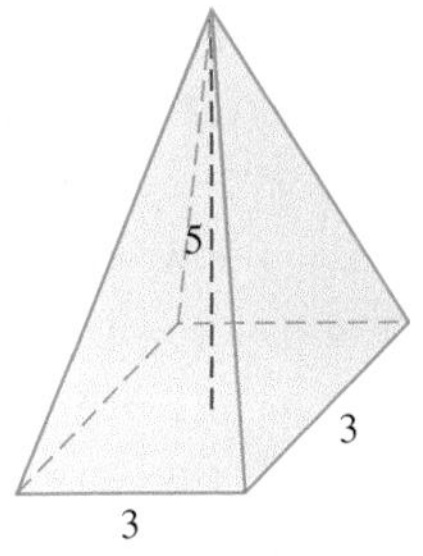

13. **A twisted solid** A square of side length s lies in a plane perpendicular to a line L. One vertex of the square lies on L. As this square moves a distance h along L, the square turns one revolution about L to generate a corkscrew-like column with square cross-sections.

   a. Find the volume of the column.

   b. What will the volume be if the square turns twice instead of once? Give reasons for your answer.

14. **Cavalieri's principle** A solid lies between planes perpendicular to the x-axis at $x = 0$ and $x = 12$. The cross-sections by planes perpendicular to the x-axis are circular disks whose diameters run from the line $y = x/2$ to the line $y = x$ as shown in the accompanying figure. Explain why the solid has the same volume as a right circular cone with base radius 3 and height 12.

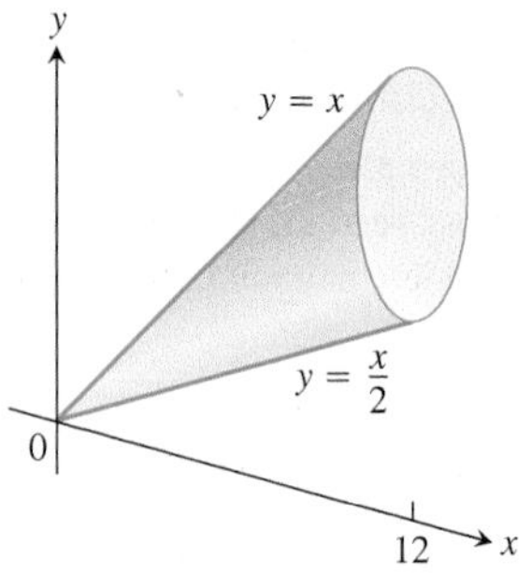

Volumes by the Disk Method

In Exercises 15–18, find the volume of the solid generated by revolving the shaded region about the given axis.

15. About the x-axis

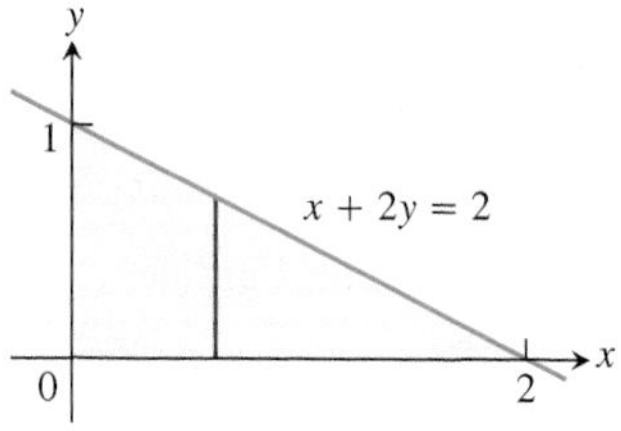

16. About the y-axis

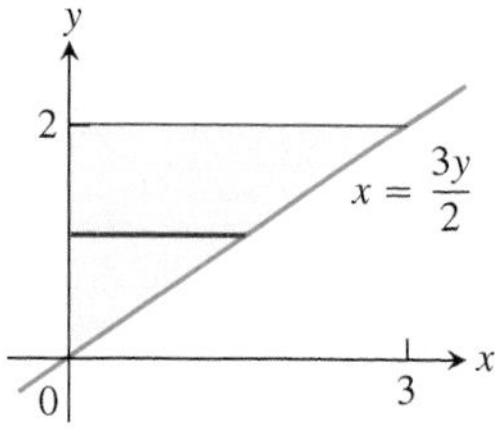

17. About the y-axis

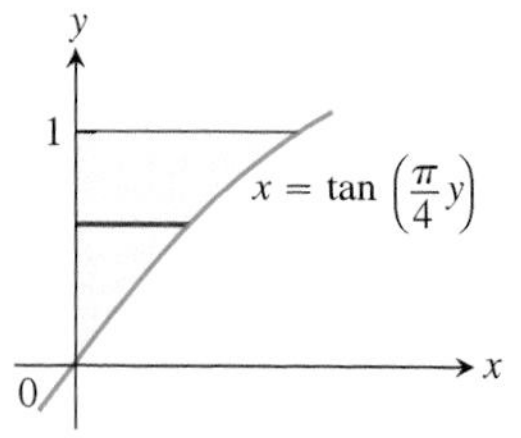

18. About the x-axis

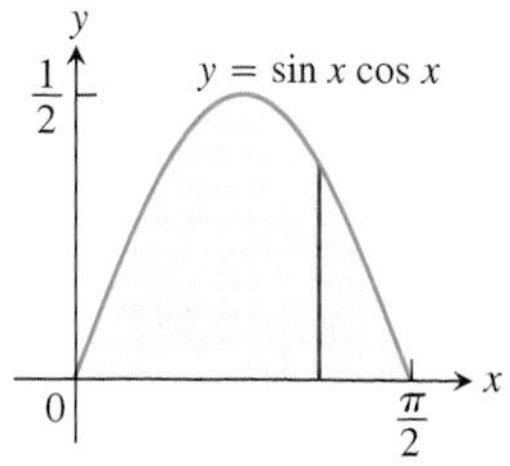

Find the volumes of the solids generated by revolving the regions bounded by the lines and curves in Exercises 19–28 about the x-axis.

19. $y = x^2, \quad y = 0, \quad x = 2$
20. $y = x^3, \quad y = 0, \quad x = 2$
21. $y = \sqrt{9 - x^2}, \quad y = 0$
22. $y = x - x^2, \quad y = 0$
23. $y = \sqrt{\cos x}, \quad 0 \le x \le \pi/2, \quad y = 0, \quad x = 0$
24. $y = \sec x, \quad y = 0, \quad x = -\pi/4, \quad x = \pi/4$
25. $y = e^{-x}, \quad y = 0, \quad x = 0, \quad x = 1$
26. The region between the curve $y = \sqrt{\cot x}$ and the x-axis from $x = \pi/6$ to $x = \pi/2$.
27. The region between the curve $y = 1/(2\sqrt{x})$ and the x-axis from $x = 1/4$ to $x = 4$.
28. $y = e^{x-1}, \quad y = 0, \quad x = 1, \quad x = 3$

In Exercises 29 and 30, find the volume of the solid generated by revolving the region about the given line.

29. The region in the first quadrant bounded above by the line $y = \sqrt{2}$, below by the curve $y = \sec x \tan x$, and on the left by the y-axis, about the line $y = \sqrt{2}$
30. The region in the first quadrant bounded above by the line $y = 2$, below by the curve $y = 2 \sin x$, $0 \le x \le \pi/2$, and on the left by the y-axis, about the line $y = 2$

Find the volumes of the solids generated by revolving the regions bounded by the lines and curves in Exercises 31–36 about the y-axis.

31. The region enclosed by $x = \sqrt{5}y^2, \quad x = 0, \quad y = -1, \quad y = 1$
32. The region enclosed by $x = y^{3/2}, \quad x = 0, \quad y = 2$
33. The region enclosed by $x = \sqrt{2 \sin 2y}, \quad 0 \le y \le \pi/2, \quad x = 0$
34. The region enclosed by $x = \sqrt{\cos(\pi y/4)}, \quad -2 \le y \le 0$, $x = 0$
35. $x = 2/\sqrt{y + 1}, \quad x = 0, \quad y = 0, \quad y = 3$
36. $x = \sqrt{2y}/(y^2 + 1), \quad x = 0, \quad y = 1$

Volumes by the Washer Method

Find the volumes of the solids generated by revolving the shaded regions in Exercises 37 and 38 about the indicated axes.

37. The x-axis

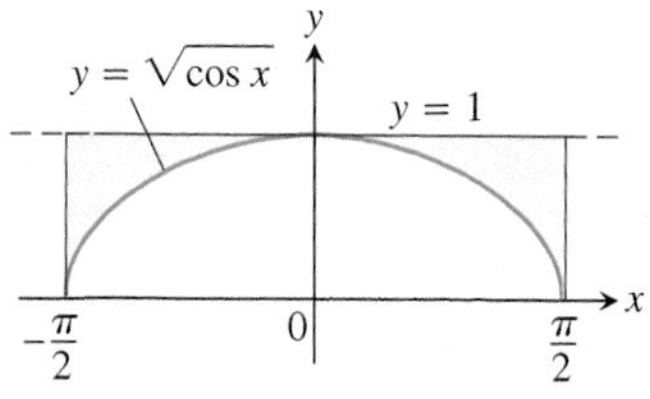

38. The y-axis

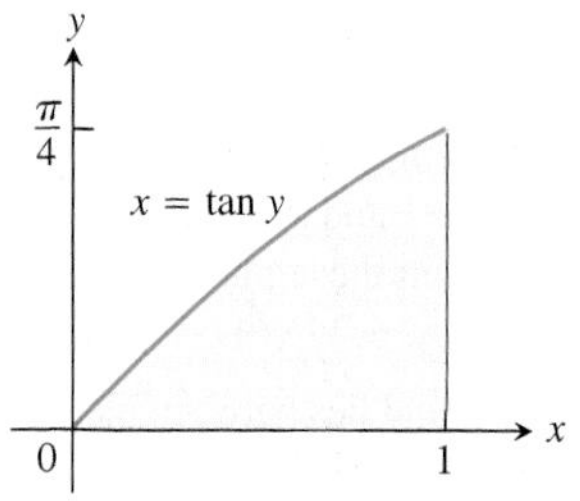

Find the volumes of the solids generated by revolving the regions bounded by the lines and curves in Exercises 39–44 about the x-axis.

39. $y = x, \quad y = 1, \quad x = 0$
40. $y = 2\sqrt{x}, \quad y = 2, \quad x = 0$
41. $y = x^2 + 1, \quad y = x + 3$
42. $y = 4 - x^2, \quad y = 2 - x$
43. $y = \sec x, \quad y = \sqrt{2}, \quad -\pi/4 \le x \le \pi/4$
44. $y = \sec x, \quad y = \tan x, \quad x = 0, \quad x = 1$

In Exercises 45–48, find the volume of the solid generated by revolving each region about the y-axis.

45. The region enclosed by the triangle with vertices (1, 0), (2, 1), and (1, 1)
46. The region enclosed by the triangle with vertices (0, 1), (1, 0), and (1, 1)
47. The region in the first quadrant bounded above by the parabola $y = x^2$, below by the x-axis, and on the right by the line $x = 2$
48. The region in the first quadrant bounded on the left by the circle $x^2 + y^2 = 3$, on the right by the line $x = \sqrt{3}$, and above by the line $y = \sqrt{3}$

In Exercises 49 and 50, find the volume of the solid generated by revolving each region about the given axis.

49. The region in the first quadrant bounded above by the curve $y = x^2$, below by the x-axis, and on the right by the line $x = 1$, about the line $x = -1$

50. The region in the second quadrant bounded above by the curve $y = -x^3$, below by the x-axis, and on the left by the line $x = -1$, about the line $x = -2$

Volumes of Solids of Revolution

51. Find the volume of the solid generated by revolving the region bounded by $y = \sqrt{x}$ and the lines $y = 2$ and $x = 0$ about
 a. the x-axis. **b.** the y-axis.
 c. the line $y = 2$. **d.** the line $x = 4$.

52. Find the volume of the solid generated by revolving the triangular region bounded by the lines $y = 2x$, $y = 0$, and $x = 1$ about
 a. the line $x = 1$. **b.** the line $x = 2$.

53. Find the volume of the solid generated by revolving the region bounded by the parabola $y = x^2$ and the line $y = 1$ about
 a. the line $y = 1$. **b.** the line $y = 2$.
 c. the line $y = -1$.

54. By integration, find the volume of the solid generated by revolving the triangular region with vertices $(0, 0)$, $(b, 0)$, $(0, h)$ about
 a. the x-axis. **b.** the y-axis.

Theory and Applications

55. **The volume of a torus** The disk $x^2 + y^2 \le a^2$ is revolved about the line $x = b$ $(b > a)$ to generate a solid shaped like a doughnut and called a *torus*. Find its volume. (*Hint:* $\int_{-a}^{a} \sqrt{a^2 - y^2}\,dy = \pi a^2/2$, since it is the area of a semicircle of radius a.)

56. **Volume of a bowl** A bowl has a shape that can be generated by revolving the graph of $y = x^2/2$ between $y = 0$ and $y = 5$ about the y-axis.
 a. Find the volume of the bowl.
 b. Related rates If we fill the bowl with water at a constant rate of 3 cubic units per second, how fast will the water level in the bowl be rising when the water is 4 units deep?

57. **Volume of a bowl**
 a. A hemispherical bowl of radius a contains water to a depth h. Find the volume of water in the bowl.
 b. Related rates Water runs into a sunken concrete hemispherical bowl of radius 5 m at the rate of 0.2 m^3/sec. How fast is the water level in the bowl rising when the water is 4 m deep?

58. Explain how you could estimate the volume of a solid of revolution by measuring the shadow cast on a table parallel to its axis of revolution by a light shining directly above it.

59. **Volume of a hemisphere** Derive the formula $V = (2/3)\pi R^3$ for the volume of a hemisphere of radius R by comparing its cross-sections with the cross-sections of a solid right circular cylinder of radius R and height R from which a solid right circular cone of base radius R and height R has been removed, as suggested by the accompanying figure.

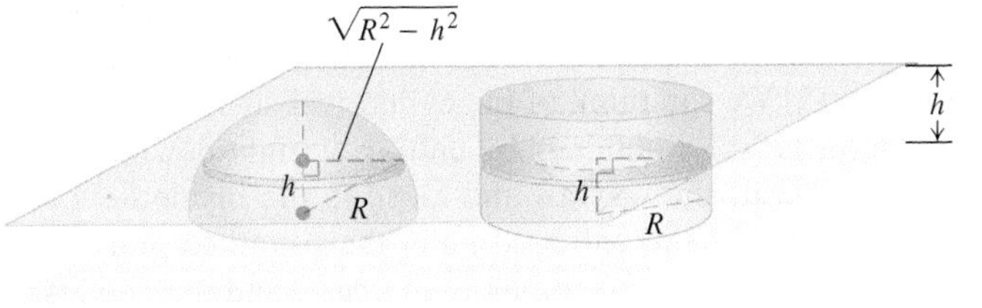

60. **Designing a plumb bob** Having been asked to design a brass plumb bob that will weigh in the neighborhood of 190 g, you decide to shape it like the solid of revolution shown here. Find the plumb bob's volume. If you specify a brass that weighs 8.5 g/cm^3, how much will the plumb bob weigh (to the nearest gram)?

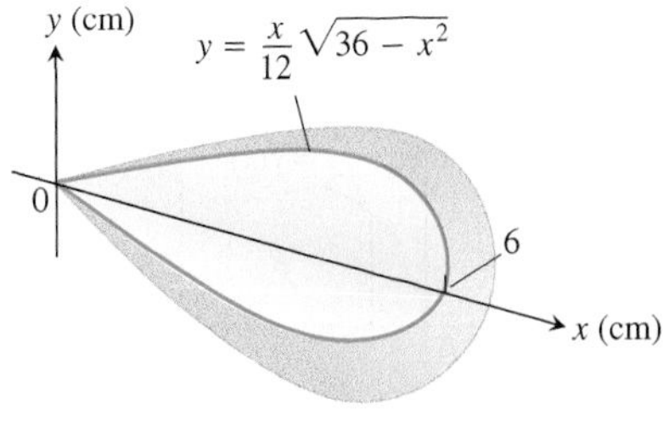

61. **Designing a wok** You are designing a wok frying pan that will be shaped like a spherical bowl with handles. A bit of experimentation at home persuades you that you can get one that holds about 3 L if you make it 9 cm deep and give the sphere a radius of 16 cm. To be sure, you picture the wok as a solid of revolution, as shown here, and calculate its volume with an integral. To the nearest cubic centimeter, what volume do you really get? (1 L = 1000 cm^3.)

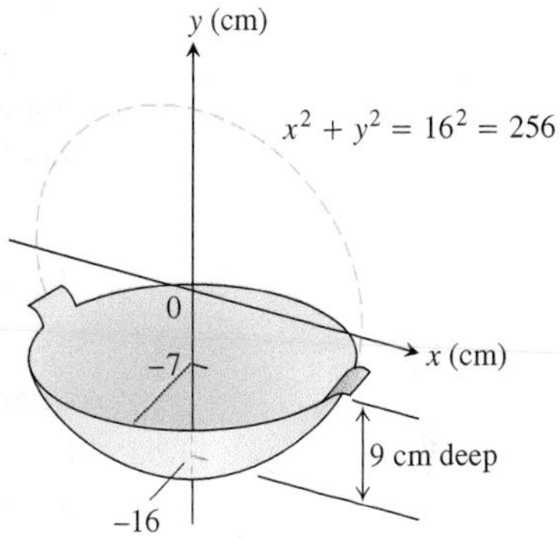

62. **Max-min** The arch $y = \sin x$, $0 \le x \le \pi$, is revolved about the line $y = c$, $0 \le c \le 1$, to generate the solid in the accompanying figure.
 a. Find the value of c that minimizes the volume of the solid. What is the minimum volume?
 b. What value of c in $[0, 1]$ maximizes the volume of the solid?
 T **c.** Graph the solid's volume as a function of c, first for $0 \le c \le 1$ and then on a larger domain. What happens to the volume of the solid as c moves away from $[0, 1]$? Does this make sense physically? Give reasons for your answers.

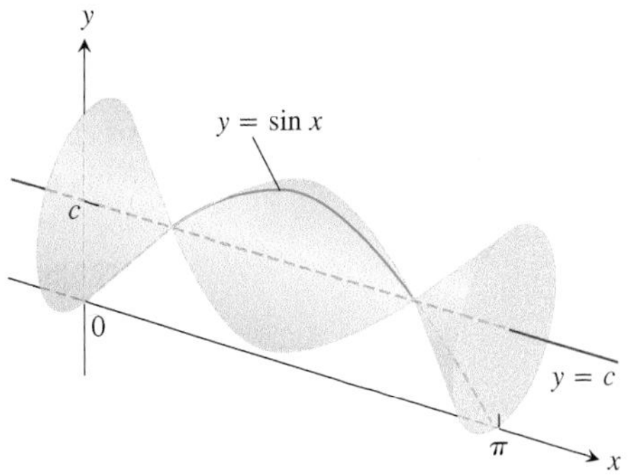

63. Consider the region R bounded by the graphs of $y = f(x) > 0$, $x = a > 0$, $x = b > a$, and $y = 0$ (see accompanying figure). If the volume of the solid formed by revolving R about the x-axis is 4π, and the volume of the solid formed by revolving R about the line $y = -1$ is 8π, find the area of R.

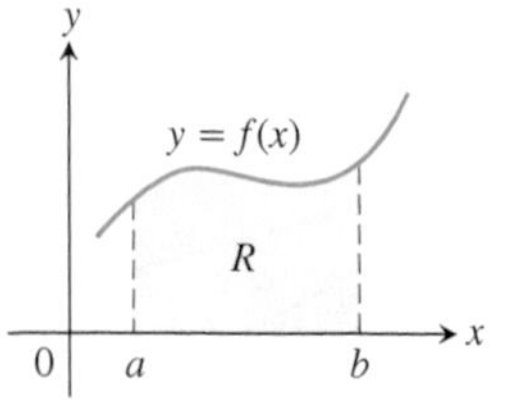

64. Consider the region R given in Exercise 63. If the volume of the solid formed by revolving R around the x-axis is 6π, and the volume of the solid formed by revolving R around the line $y = -2$ is 10π, find the area of R.

6.2 Volumes Using Cylindrical Shells

In Section 6.1 we defined the volume of a solid as the definite integral $V = \int_a^b A(x)\,dx$, where $A(x)$ is an integrable cross-sectional area of the solid from $x = a$ to $x = b$. The area $A(x)$ was obtained by slicing through the solid with a plane perpendicular to the x-axis. However, this method of slicing is sometimes awkward to apply, as we will illustrate in our first example. To overcome this difficulty, we use the same integral definition for volume, but obtain the area by slicing through the solid in a different way.

Slicing with Cylinders

Suppose we slice through the solid using circular cylinders of increasing radii, like cookie cutters. We slice straight down through the solid so that the axis of each cylinder is parallel to the y-axis. The vertical axis of each cylinder is the same line, but the radii of the cylinders increase with each slice. In this way the solid is sliced up into thin cylindrical shells of constant thickness that grow outward from their common axis, like circular tree rings. Unrolling a cylindrical shell shows that its volume is approximately that of a rectangular slab with area $A(x)$ and thickness Δx. This slab interpretation allows us to apply the same integral definition for volume as before. The following example provides some insight before we derive the general method.

EXAMPLE 1 The region enclosed by the x-axis and the parabola $y = f(x) = 3x - x^2$ is revolved about the vertical line $x = -1$ to generate a solid (Figure 6.16). Find the volume of the solid.

Solution Using the washer method from Section 6.1 would be awkward here because we would need to express the x-values of the left and right sides of the parabola in Figure 6.16a in terms of y. (These x-values are the inner and outer radii for a typical washer, requiring us to solve $y = 3x - x^2$ for x, which leads to complicated formulas.) Instead of rotating a horizontal strip of thickness Δy, we rotate a *vertical strip* of thickness Δx. This rotation produces a *cylindrical shell* of height y_k above a point x_k within the base of the vertical strip and of thickness Δx. An example of a cylindrical shell is shown as the orange-shaded region in Figure 6.17. We can think of the cylindrical shell shown in the figure as approximating a slice of the solid obtained by cutting straight down through it, parallel to the axis of revolution, all the way around close to the inside hole. We then cut another cylindrical slice around the enlarged hole, then another, and so on, obtaining n cylinders. The radii of the cylinders gradually increase, and the heights of

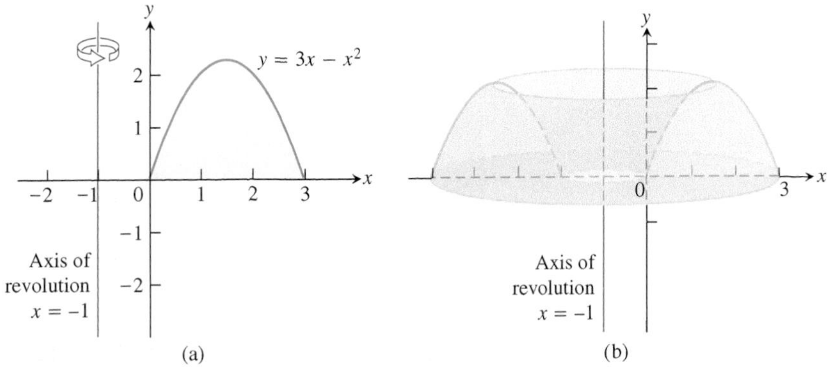

FIGURE 6.16 (a) The graph of the region in Example 1, before revolution. (b) The solid formed when the region in part (a) is revolved about the axis of revolution $x = -1$.

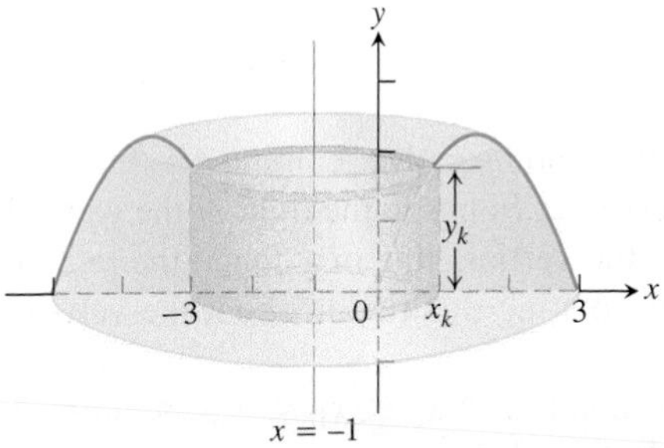

FIGURE 6.17 A cylindrical shell of height y_k obtained by rotating a vertical strip of thickness Δx_k about the line $x = -1$. The outer radius of the cylinder occurs at x_k, where the height of the parabola is $y_k = 3x_k - x_k^2$ (Example 1).

the cylinders follow the contour of the parabola: shorter to taller, then back to shorter (Figure 6.16a).

Each slice is sitting over a subinterval of the x-axis of length (width) Δx_k. Its radius is approximately $(1 + x_k)$, and its height is approximately $3x_k - x_k^2$. If we unroll the cylinder at x_k and flatten it out, it becomes (approximately) a rectangular slab with thickness Δx_k (Figure 6.18). The outer circumference of the kth cylinder is $2\pi \cdot \text{radius} = 2\pi(1 + x_k)$, and this is the length of the rolled-out rectangular slab. Its volume is approximated by that of a rectangular solid,

$$\begin{aligned}\Delta V_k &= \text{circumference} \times \text{height} \times \text{thickness}\\ &= 2\pi(1 + x_k) \cdot \left(3x_k - x_k^2\right) \cdot \Delta x_k.\end{aligned}$$

Summing together the volumes ΔV_k of the individual cylindrical shells over the interval $[0, 3]$ gives the Riemann sum

$$\sum_{k=1}^{n} \Delta V_k = \sum_{k=1}^{n} 2\pi(x_k + 1)\left(3x_k - x_k^2\right) \Delta x_k.$$

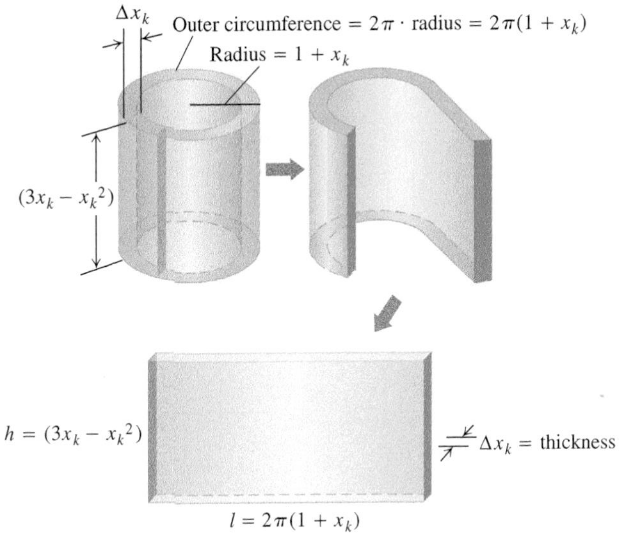

FIGURE 6.18 Cutting and unrolling a cylindrical shell gives a nearly rectangular solid (Example 1).

Taking the limit as the thickness $\Delta x_k \to 0$ and $n \to \infty$ gives the volume integral

$$\begin{aligned} V &= \lim_{n\to\infty} \sum_{k=1}^{n} 2\pi(x_k + 1)\left(3x_k - x_k^2\right) \Delta x_k \\ &= \int_0^3 2\pi(x + 1)(3x - x^2)\, dx \\ &= \int_0^3 2\pi(3x^2 + 3x - x^3 - x^2)\, dx \\ &= 2\pi \int_0^3 (2x^2 + 3x - x^3)\, dx \\ &= 2\pi\left[\frac{2}{3}x^3 + \frac{3}{2}x^2 - \frac{1}{4}x^4\right]_0^3 = \frac{45\pi}{2}. \end{aligned}$$

We now generalize the procedure used in Example 1.

The Shell Method

Suppose the region bounded by the graph of a nonnegative continuous function $y = f(x)$ and the x-axis over the finite closed interval $[a, b]$ lies to the right of the vertical line $x = L$ (Figure 6.19a). We assume $a \ge L$, so the vertical line may touch the region, but not pass through it. We generate a solid S by rotating this region about the vertical line L.

Let P be a partition of the interval $[a, b]$ by the points $a = x_0 < x_1 < \cdots < x_n = b$, and let c_k be the midpoint of the kth subinterval $[x_{k-1}, x_k]$. We approximate the region in Figure 6.19a with rectangles based on this partition of $[a, b]$. A typical approximating rectangle has height $f(c_k)$ and width $\Delta x_k = x_k - x_{k-1}$. If this rectangle is rotated about the vertical line $x = L$, then a shell is swept out, as in Figure 6.19b. A formula from geometry tells us that the volume of the shell swept out by the rectangle is

$$\begin{aligned} \Delta V_k &= 2\pi \times \text{average shell radius} \times \text{shell height} \times \text{thickness} \\ &= 2\pi \cdot (c_k - L) \cdot f(c_k) \cdot \Delta x_k. \end{aligned}$$

The volume of a cylindrical shell of height h with inner radius r and outer radius R is

$$\pi R^2 h - \pi r^2 h = 2\pi\left(\frac{R + r}{2}\right)(h)(R - r).$$

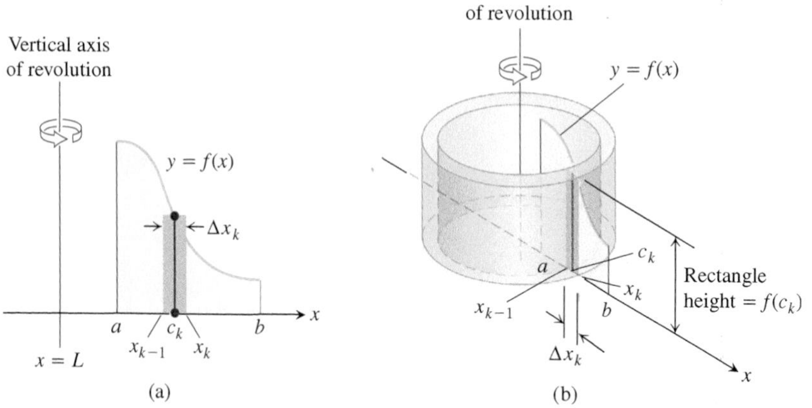

FIGURE 6.19 When the region shown in (a) is revolved about the vertical line $x = L$, a solid is produced which can be sliced into cylindrical shells. A typical shell is shown in (b).

We approximate the volume of the solid S by summing the volumes of the shells swept out by the n rectangles based on P:

$$V \approx \sum_{k=1}^{n} \Delta V_k.$$

The limit of this Riemann sum as each $\Delta x_k \to 0$ and $n \to \infty$ gives the volume of the solid as a definite integral:

$$V = \lim_{n\to\infty} \sum_{k=1}^{n} \Delta V_k = \int_a^b 2\pi(\text{shell radius})(\text{shell height})\, dx.$$

$$= \int_a^b 2\pi(x - L)f(x)\, dx.$$

We refer to the variable of integration, here x, as the **thickness variable**. We use the first integral, rather than the second containing a formula for the integrand, to emphasize the *process* of the shell method. This will allow for rotations about a horizontal line L as well.

Shell Formula for Revolution About a Vertical Line

The volume of the solid generated by revolving the region between the x-axis and the graph of a continuous function $y = f(x) \geq 0$, $L \leq a \leq x \leq b$, about a vertical line $x = L$ is

$$V = \int_a^b 2\pi \begin{pmatrix}\text{shell}\\ \text{radius}\end{pmatrix} \begin{pmatrix}\text{shell}\\ \text{height}\end{pmatrix} dx.$$

EXAMPLE 2 The region bounded by the curve $y = \sqrt{x}$, the x-axis, and the line $x = 4$ is revolved about the y-axis to generate a solid. Find the volume of the solid.

Solution Sketch the region and draw a line segment across it *parallel* to the axis of revolution (Figure 6.20a). Label the segment's height (shell height) and distance from the axis of revolution (shell radius). (We drew the shell in Figure 6.20b, but you need not do that.)

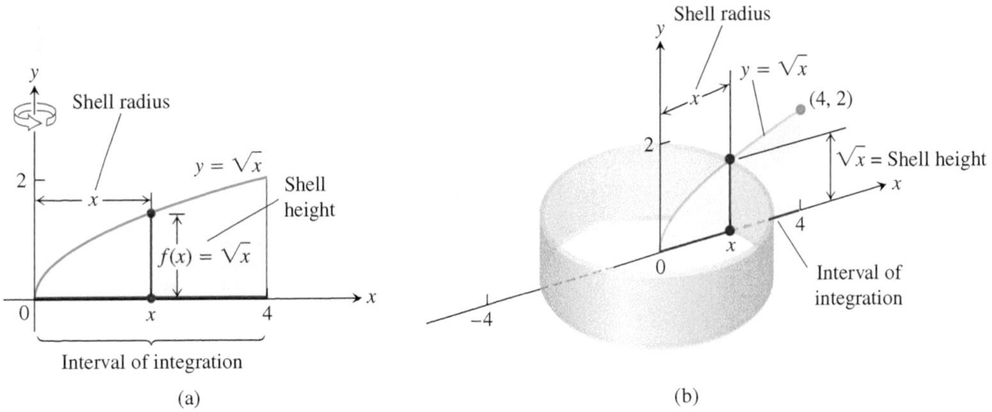

FIGURE 6.20 (a) The region, shell dimensions, and interval of integration in Example 2. (b) The shell swept out by the vertical segment in part (a) with a width Δx.

The shell thickness variable is x, so the limits of integration for the shell formula are $a = 0$ and $b = 4$ (Figure 6.20). The volume is then

$$\begin{aligned} V &= \int_a^b 2\pi \begin{pmatrix}\text{shell}\\ \text{radius}\end{pmatrix}\begin{pmatrix}\text{shell}\\ \text{height}\end{pmatrix} dx \\ &= \int_0^4 2\pi(x)\left(\sqrt{x}\right) dx \\ &= 2\pi \int_0^4 x^{3/2}\, dx = 2\pi\left[\frac{2}{5}x^{5/2}\right]_0^4 = \frac{128\pi}{5}. \end{aligned}$$

■

So far, we have used vertical axes of revolution. For horizontal axes, we replace the x's with y's.

EXAMPLE 3 The region bounded by the curve $y = \sqrt{x}$, the x-axis, and the line $x = 4$ is revolved about the x-axis to generate a solid. Find the volume of the solid by the shell method.

Solution This is the solid whose volume was found by the disk method in Example 4 of Section 6.1. Now we find its volume by the shell method. First, sketch the region and draw a line segment across it *parallel* to the axis of revolution (Figure 6.21a). Label the segment's length (shell height) and distance from the axis of revolution (shell radius). (We drew the shell in Figure 6.21b, but you need not do that.)

In this case, the shell thickness variable is y, so the limits of integration for the shell formula method are $a = 0$ and $b = 2$ (along the y-axis in Figure 6.21). The volume of the solid is

$$\begin{aligned} V &= \int_a^b 2\pi \begin{pmatrix}\text{shell}\\ \text{radius}\end{pmatrix}\begin{pmatrix}\text{shell}\\ \text{height}\end{pmatrix} dy \\ &= \int_0^2 2\pi(y)(4 - y^2)\, dy \\ &= 2\pi \int_0^2 (4y - y^3)\, dy \\ &= 2\pi\left[2y^2 - \frac{y^4}{4}\right]_0^2 = 8\pi. \end{aligned}$$

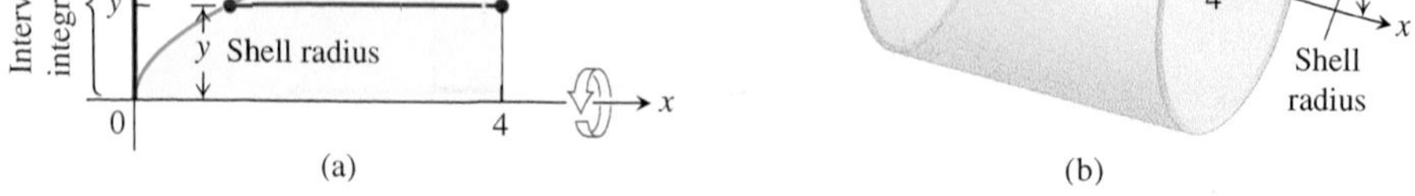

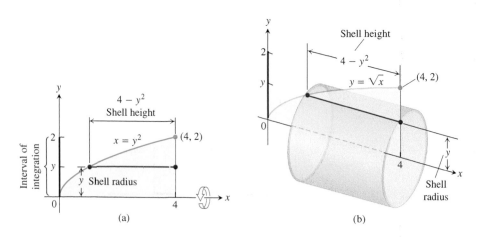

FIGURE 6.21 (a) The region, shell dimensions, and interval of integration in Example 3. (b) The shell swept out by the horizontal segment in part (a) with a width Δy.

■

> **Summary of the Shell Method**
>
> Regardless of the position of the axis of revolution (horizontal or vertical), the steps for implementing the shell method are these.
>
> 1. *Draw the region and sketch a line segment* across it *parallel* to the axis of revolution. *Label* the segment's height or length (shell height) and distance from the axis of revolution (shell radius).
> 2. *Find the limits of integration* for the thickness variable.
> 3. *Integrate* the product 2π (shell radius) (shell height) with respect to the thickness variable (x or y) to find the volume.

The shell method gives the same answer as the washer method when both are used to calculate the volume of a region. We do not prove that result here, but it is illustrated in Exercises 37 and 38. (Exercise 45 outlines a proof.) Both volume formulas are actually special cases of a general volume formula we will look at when studying double and triple integrals in Chapter 14. That general formula also allows for computing volumes of solids other than those swept out by regions of revolution.

Exercises 6.2

Revolution About the Axes

In Exercises 1–6, use the shell method to find the volumes of the solids generated by revolving the shaded region about the indicated axis.

1.

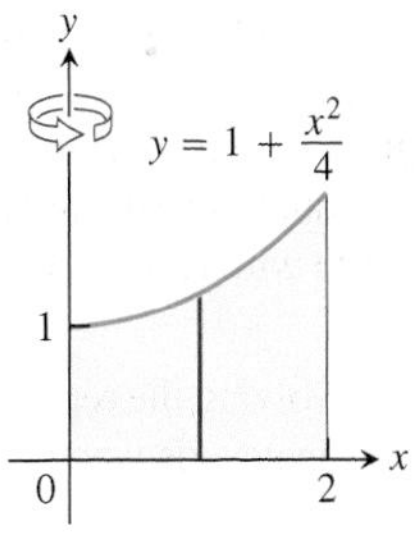

2.

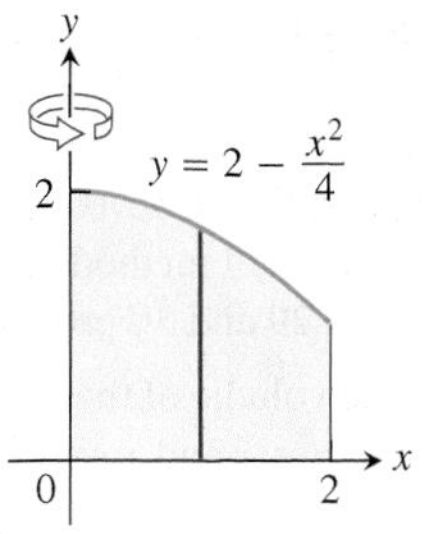

3.

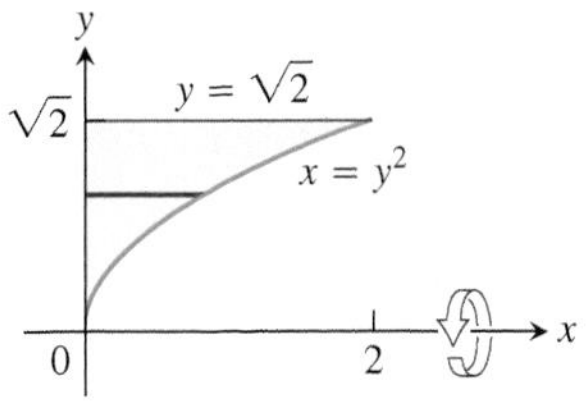

4.

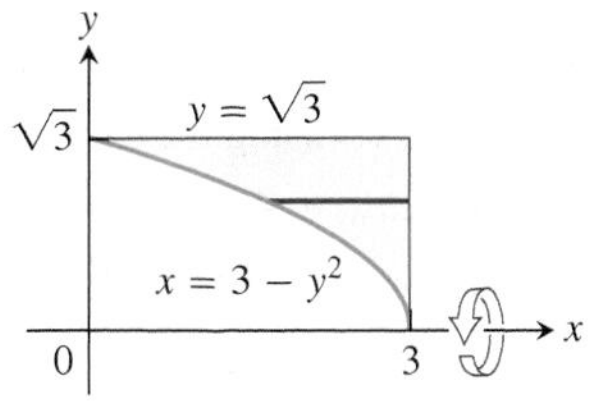

5. The y-axis

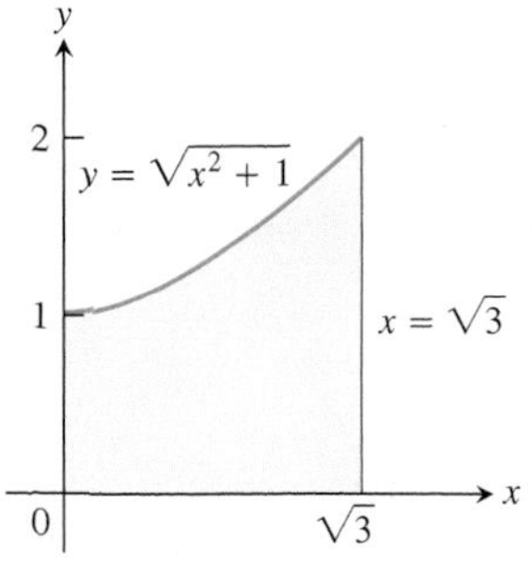

6. The y-axis

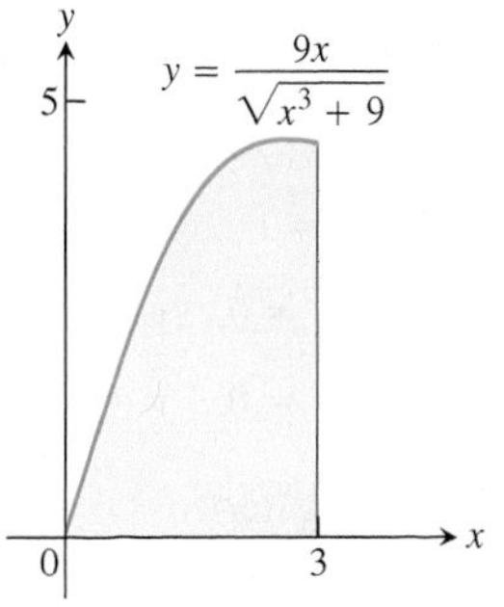

Revolution About the y-Axis

Use the shell method to find the volumes of the solids generated by revolving the regions bounded by the curves and lines in Exercises 7–12 about the y-axis.

7. $y = x, \quad y = -x/2, \quad x = 2$

8. $y = 2x, \quad y = x/2, \quad x = 1$

9. $y = x^2, \quad y = 2 - x, \quad x = 0, \quad$ for $x \geq 0$

10. $y = 2 - x^2, \quad y = x^2, \quad x = 0$

11. $y = 2x - 1, \quad y = \sqrt{x}, \quad x = 0$

12. $y = 3/(2\sqrt{x}), \quad y = 0, \quad x = 1, \quad x = 4$

13. Let $f(x) = \begin{cases} (\sin x)/x, & 0 < x \le \pi \\ 1, & x = 0 \end{cases}$

a. Show that $x f(x) = \sin x,\ 0 \le x \le \pi$.

b. Find the volume of the solid generated by revolving the shaded region about the y-axis in the accompanying figure.

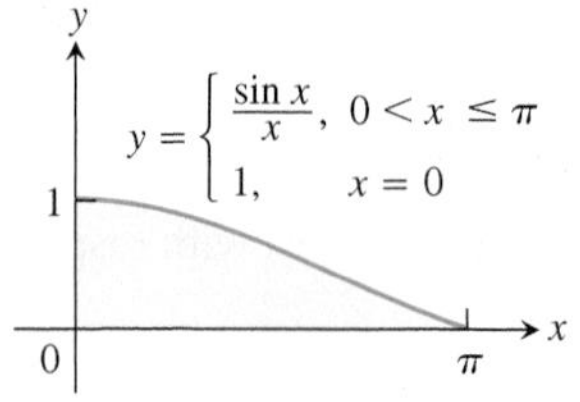

14. Let $g(x) = \begin{cases} (\tan x)^2/x, & 0 < x \le \pi/4 \\ 0, & x = 0 \end{cases}$

a. Show that $x g(x) = (\tan x)^2,\ 0 \le x \le \pi/4$.

b. Find the volume of the solid generated by revolving the shaded region about the y-axis in the accompanying figure.

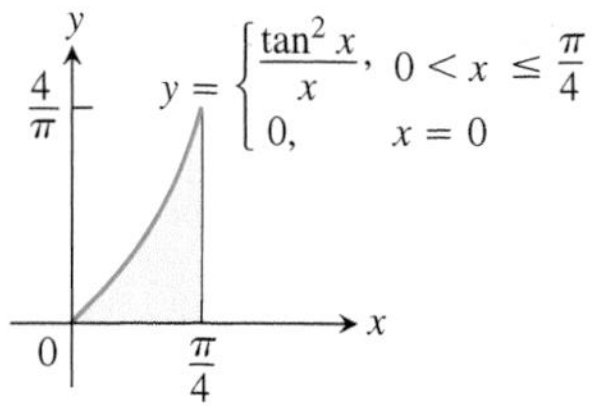

Revolution About the x-Axis

Use the shell method to find the volumes of the solids generated by revolving the regions bounded by the curves and lines in Exercises 15–22 about the x-axis.

15. $x = \sqrt{y},\quad x = -y,\quad y = 2$

16. $x = y^2,\quad x = -y,\quad y = 2,\quad y \ge 0$

17. $x = 2y - y^2,\quad x = 0$

18. $x = 2y - y^2,\quad x = y$

19. $y = |x|,\quad y = 1$

20. $y = x,\quad y = 2x,\quad y = 2$

21. $y = \sqrt{x},\quad y = 0,\quad y = x - 2$

22. $y = \sqrt{x},\quad y = 0,\quad y = 2 - x$

Revolution About Horizontal and Vertical Lines

In Exercises 23–26, use the shell method to find the volumes of the solids generated by revolving the regions bounded by the given curves about the given lines.

23. $y = 3x,\quad y = 0,\quad x = 2$

a. The y-axis
b. The line $x = 4$
c. The line $x = -1$
d. The x-axis
e. The line $y = 7$
f. The line $y = -2$

24. $y = x^3,\quad y = 8,\quad x = 0$

a. The y-axis
b. The line $x = 3$
c. The line $x = -2$
d. The x-axis
e. The line $y = 8$
f. The line $y = -1$

25. $y = x + 2,\quad y = x^2$

a. The line $x = 2$
b. The line $x = -1$
c. The x-axis
d. The line $y = 4$

26. $y = x^4,\quad y = 4 - 3x^2$

a. The line $x = 1$
c. The x-axis

In Exercises 27 and 28, use the shell method to find the volumes of the solids generated by revolving the shaded regions about the indicated axes.

27. **a.** The x-axis
b. The line $y = 1$
c. The line $y = 8/5$
d. The line $y = -2/5$

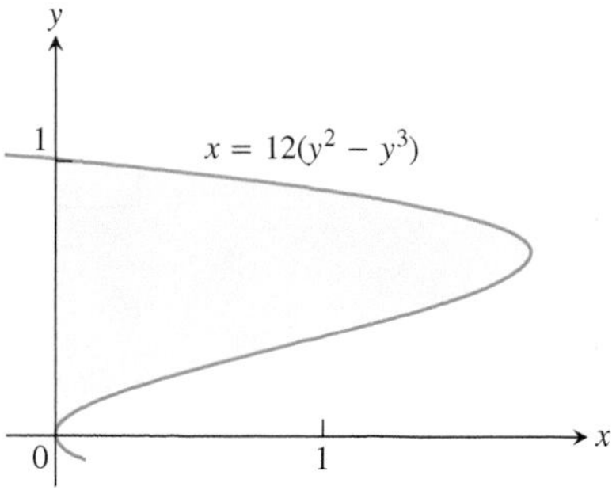

28. **a.** The x-axis
b. The line $y = 2$
c. The line $y = 5$
d. The line $y = -5/8$

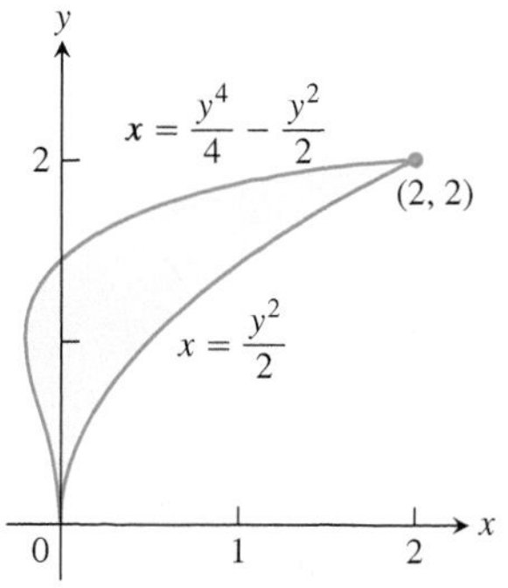

Choosing the Washer Method or Shell Method

For some regions, both the washer and shell methods work well for the solid generated by revolving the region about the coordinate axes, but this is not always the case. When a region is revolved about the y-axis, for example, and washers are used, we must integrate with respect to y. It may not be possible, however, to express the integrand in terms of y. In such a case, the shell method allows us to integrate with respect to x instead. Exercises 29 and 30 provide some insight.

29. Compute the volume of the solid generated by revolving the region bounded by $y = x$ and $y = x^2$ about each coordinate axis using

a. the shell method.
b. the washer method.

30. Compute the volume of the solid generated by revolving the triangular region bounded by the lines $2y = x + 4$, $y = x$, and $x = 0$ about

a. the x-axis using the washer method.
b. the y-axis using the shell method.
c. the line $x = 4$ using the shell method.
d. the line $y = 8$ using the washer method.

In Exercises 31–36, find the volumes of the solids generated by revolving the regions about the given axes. If you think it would be better to use washers in any given instance, feel free to do so.

31. The triangle with vertices (1, 1), (1, 2), and (2, 2) about

a. the x-axis **b.** the y-axis

c. the line $x = 10/3$ **d.** the line $y = 1$

32. The region bounded by $y = \sqrt{x}$, $y = 2$, $x = 0$ about

a. the x-axis **b.** the y-axis

c. the line $x = 4$ **d.** the line $y = 2$

33. The region in the first quadrant bounded by the curve $x = y - y^3$ and the y-axis about

a. the x-axis **b.** the line $y = 1$

34. The region in the first quadrant bounded by $x = y - y^3$, $x = 1$, and $y = 1$ about

a. the x-axis **b.** the y-axis

c. the line $x = 1$ **d.** the line $y = 1$

35. The region bounded by $y = \sqrt{x}$ and $y = x^2/8$ about

a. the x-axis **b.** the y-axis

36. The region bounded by $y = 2x - x^2$ and $y = x$ about

a. the y-axis **b.** the line $x = 1$

37. The region in the first quadrant that is bounded above by the curve $y = 1/x^{1/4}$, on the left by the line $x = 1/16$, and below by the line $y = 1$ is revolved about the x-axis to generate a solid. Find the volume of the solid by

a. the washer method. **b.** the shell method.

38. The region in the first quadrant that is bounded above by the curve $y = 1/\sqrt{x}$, on the left by the line $x = 1/4$, and below by the line $y = 1$ is revolved about the y-axis to generate a solid. Find the volume of the solid by

a. the washer method. **b.** the shell method.

Theory and Examples

39. The region shown here is to be revolved about the x-axis to generate a solid. Which of the methods (disk, washer, shell) could you use to find the volume of the solid? How many integrals would be required in each case? Explain.

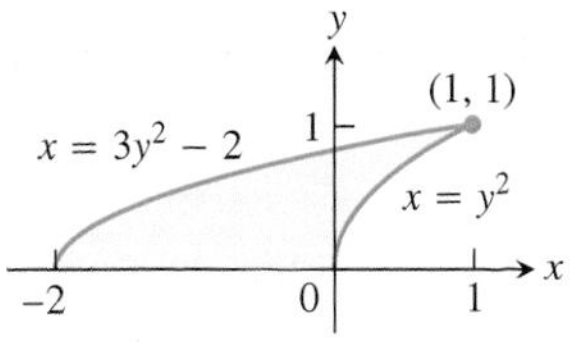

40. The region shown here is to be revolved about the y-axis to generate a solid. Which of the methods (disk, washer, shell) could you use to find the volume of the solid? How many integrals would be required in each case? Give reasons for your answers.

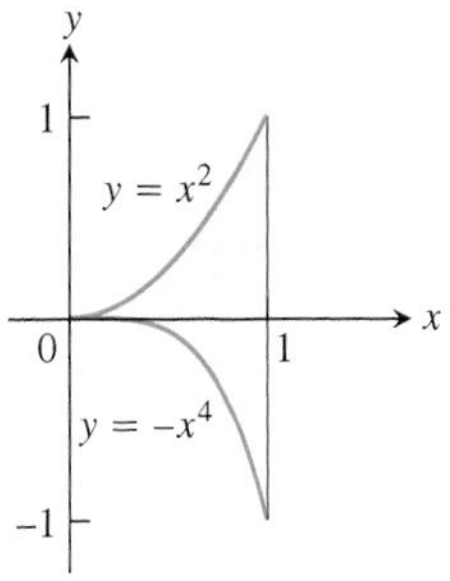

41. A bead is formed from a sphere of radius 5 by drilling through a diameter of the sphere with a drill bit of radius 3.

a. Find the volume of the bead.

b. Find the volume of the removed portion of the sphere.

42. A Bundt cake, well known for having a ringed shape, is formed by revolving around the y-axis the region bounded by the graph of $y = \sin(x^2 - 1)$ and the x-axis over the interval $1 \le x \le \sqrt{1 + \pi}$. Find the volume of the cake.

43. Derive the formula for the volume of a right circular cone of height h and radius r using an appropriate solid of revolution.

44. Derive the equation for the volume of a sphere of radius r using the shell method.

45. Equivalence of the washer and shell methods for finding volume Let f be differentiable and increasing on the interval $a \le x \le b$, with $a > 0$, and suppose that f has a differentiable inverse, f^{-1}. Revolve about the y-axis the region bounded by the graph of f and the lines $x = a$ and $y = f(b)$ to generate a solid. Then the values of the integrals given by the washer and shell methods for the volume have identical values:

$$\int_{f(a)}^{f(b)} \pi\left((f^{-1}(y))^2 - a^2\right) dy = \int_a^b 2\pi x(f(b) - f(x))\, dx.$$

To prove this equality, define

$$W(t) = \int_{f(a)}^{f(t)} \pi((f^{-1}(y))^2 - a^2)\, dy$$

$$S(t) = \int_a^t 2\pi x(f(t) - f(x))\, dx.$$

Then show that the functions W and S agree at a point of $[a, b]$ and have identical derivatives on $[a, b]$. As you saw in Section 4.8, Exercise 128, this will guarantee $W(t) = S(t)$ for all t in $[a, b]$. In particular, $W(b) = S(b)$. (*Source:* "Disks and Shells Revisited," by Walter Carlip, *American Mathematical Monthly*, Vol. 98, No. 2, Feb. 1991, pp. 154–156.)

46. The region between the curve $y = \sec^{-1} x$ and the x-axis from $x = 1$ to $x = 2$ (shown here) is revolved about the y-axis to generate a solid. Find the volume of the solid.

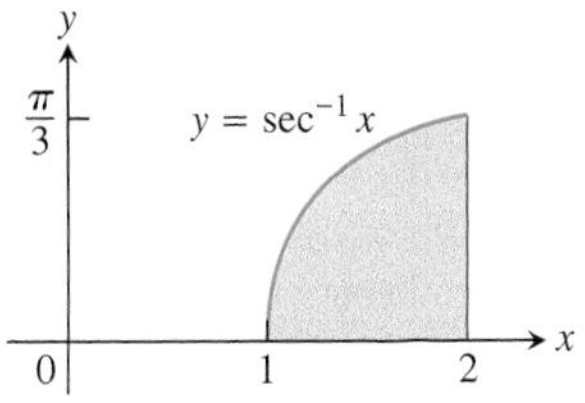

47. Find the volume of the solid generated by revolving the region enclosed by the graphs of $y = e^{-x^2}$, $y = 0$, $x = 0$, and $x = 1$ about the y-axis.

48. Find the volume of the solid generated by revolving the region enclosed by the graphs of $y = e^{x/2}$, $y = 1$, and $x = \ln 3$ about the x-axis.

6.3 Arc Length

We know what is meant by the length of a straight line segment, but without calculus, we have no precise definition of the length of a general winding curve. If the curve is the graph of a continuous function defined over an interval, then we can find the length of the curve using a procedure similar to that we used for defining the area between the curve and the x-axis. This procedure results in a division of the curve from point A to point B into many pieces and joining successive points of division by straight line segments. We then sum the lengths of all these line segments and define the length of the curve to be the limiting value of this sum as the number of segments goes to infinity.

Length of a Curve $y = f(x)$

Suppose the curve whose length we want to find is the graph of the function $y = f(x)$ from $x = a$ to $x = b$. In order to derive an integral formula for the length of the curve, we assume that f has a continuous derivative at every point of $[a, b]$. Such a function is called **smooth**, and its graph is a **smooth curve** because it does not have any breaks, corners, or cusps.

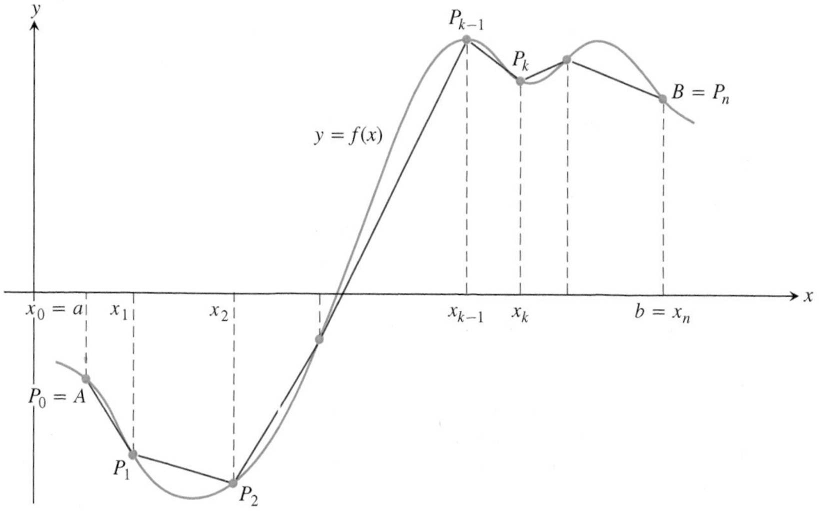

FIGURE 6.22 The length of the polygonal path $P_0P_1P_2 \cdots P_n$ approximates the length of the curve $y = f(x)$ from point A to point B.

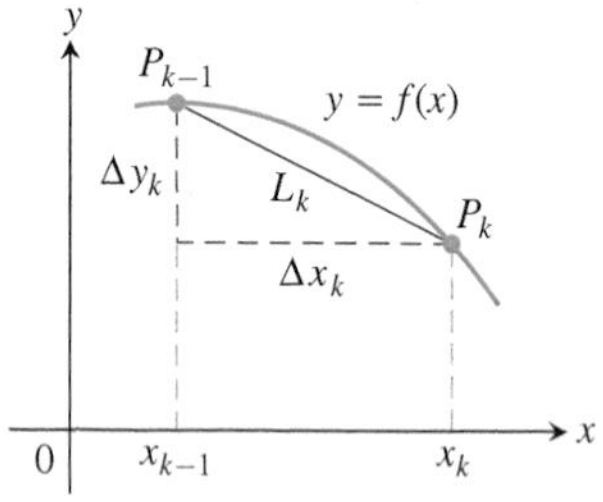

FIGURE 6.23 The arc $P_{k-1}P_k$ of the curve $y = f(x)$ is approximated by the straight line segment shown here, which has length $L_k = \sqrt{(\Delta x_k)^2 + (\Delta y_k)^2}$.

We partition the interval $[a, b]$ into n subintervals with $a = x_0 < x_1 < x_2 < \cdots < x_n = b$. If $y_k = f(x_k)$, then the corresponding point $P_k(x_k, y_k)$ lies on the curve. Next we connect successive points P_{k-1} and P_k with straight line segments that, taken together, form a polygonal path whose length approximates the length of the curve (Figure 6.22). If $\Delta x_k = x_k - x_{k-1}$ and $\Delta y_k = y_k - y_{k-1}$, then a representative line segment in the path has length (see Figure 6.23)

$$L_k = \sqrt{(\Delta x_k)^2 + (\Delta y_k)^2},$$

so the length of the curve is approximated by the sum

$$\sum_{k=1}^{n} L_k = \sum_{k=1}^{n} \sqrt{(\Delta x_k)^2 + (\Delta y_k)^2}. \tag{1}$$

We expect the approximation to improve as the partition of $[a, b]$ becomes finer. Now, by the Mean Value Theorem, there is a point c_k, with $x_{k-1} < c_k < x_k$, such that

$$\Delta y_k = f'(c_k)\,\Delta x_k.$$

With this substitution for Δy_k, the sums in Equation (1) take the form

$$\sum_{k=1}^{n} L_k = \sum_{k=1}^{n} \sqrt{(\Delta x_k)^2 + (f'(c_k)\Delta x_k)^2} = \sum_{k=1}^{n} \sqrt{1 + [f'(c_k)]^2}\, \Delta x_k. \quad (2)$$

Because $\sqrt{1 + [f'(x)]^2}$ is continuous on $[a, b]$, the limit of the Riemann sum on the right-hand side of Equation (2) exists as the norm of the partition goes to zero, giving

$$\lim_{n\to\infty} \sum_{k=1}^{n} L_k = \lim_{n\to\infty} \sum_{k=1}^{n} \sqrt{1 + [f'(c_k)]^2}\, \Delta x_k = \int_a^b \sqrt{1 + [f'(x)]^2}\, dx.$$

We define the value of this limiting integral to be the length of the curve.

DEFINITION If f' is continuous on $[a, b]$, then the **length (arc length)** of the curve $y = f(x)$ from the point $A = (a, f(a))$ to the point $B = (b, f(b))$ is the value of the integral

$$L = \int_a^b \sqrt{1 + [f'(x)]^2}\, dx = \int_a^b \sqrt{1 + \left(\frac{dy}{dx}\right)^2}\, dx. \quad (3)$$

EXAMPLE 1 Find the length of the curve (Figure 6.24)

$$y = \frac{4\sqrt{2}}{3}x^{3/2} - 1, \qquad 0 \le x \le 1.$$

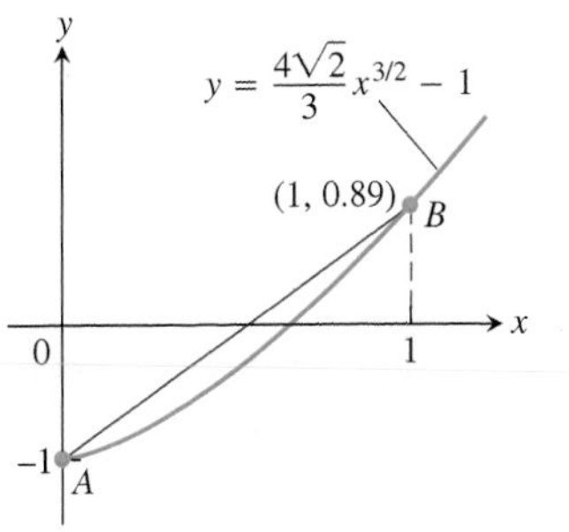

FIGURE 6.24 The length of the curve is slightly larger than the length of the line segment joining points A and B (Example 1).

Solution We use Equation (3) with $a = 0$, $b = 1$, and

$$y = \frac{4\sqrt{2}}{3}x^{3/2} - 1 \qquad x = 1, y \approx 0.89$$

$$\frac{dy}{dx} = \frac{4\sqrt{2}}{3} \cdot \frac{3}{2}x^{1/2} = 2\sqrt{2}x^{1/2}$$

$$\left(\frac{dy}{dx}\right)^2 = \left(2\sqrt{2}x^{1/2}\right)^2 = 8x.$$

The length of the curve over $x = 0$ to $x = 1$ is

$$L = \int_0^1 \sqrt{1 + \left(\frac{dy}{dx}\right)^2}\, dx = \int_0^1 \sqrt{1 + 8x}\, dx \qquad \text{Eq. (3) with } a = 0, b = 1$$

$$= \frac{2}{3} \cdot \frac{1}{8}(1 + 8x)^{3/2}\Big]_0^1 = \frac{13}{6} \approx 2.17. \qquad \text{Let } u = 1 + 8x \text{, integrate, and replace } u \text{ by } 1 + 8x.$$

Notice that the length of the curve is slightly larger than the length of the straight-line segment joining the points $A = (0, -1)$ and $B = \left(1, 4\sqrt{2}/3 - 1\right)$ on the curve (see Figure 6.24):

$$2.17 > \sqrt{1^2 + (1.89)^2} \approx 2.14 \qquad \text{Decimal approximations}$$ ■

EXAMPLE 2 Find the length of the graph of

$$f(x) = \frac{x^3}{12} + \frac{1}{x}, \qquad 1 \le x \le 4.$$

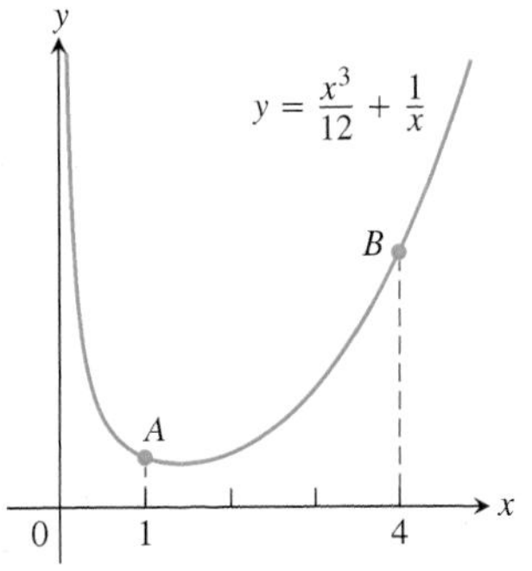

FIGURE 6.25 The curve in Example 2, where $A = (1, 13/12)$ and $B = (4, 67/12)$.

Solution A graph of the function is shown in Figure 6.25. To use Equation (3), we find

$$f'(x) = \frac{x^2}{4} - \frac{1}{x^2}$$

so

$$1 + [f'(x)]^2 = 1 + \left(\frac{x^2}{4} - \frac{1}{x^2}\right)^2 = 1 + \left(\frac{x^4}{16} - \frac{1}{2} + \frac{1}{x^4}\right)$$
$$= \frac{x^4}{16} + \frac{1}{2} + \frac{1}{x^4} = \left(\frac{x^2}{4} + \frac{1}{x^2}\right)^2.$$

The length of the graph over [1, 4] is

$$L = \int_1^4 \sqrt{1 + [f'(x)]^2}\, dx = \int_1^4 \left(\frac{x^2}{4} + \frac{1}{x^2}\right) dx$$
$$= \left[\frac{x^3}{12} - \frac{1}{x}\right]_1^4 = \left(\frac{64}{12} - \frac{1}{4}\right) - \left(\frac{1}{12} - 1\right) = \frac{72}{12} = 6.$$

■

EXAMPLE 3 Find the length of the curve

$$y = \frac{1}{2}(e^x + e^{-x}), \qquad 0 \le x \le 2.$$

Solution We use Equation (3) with $a = 0$, $b = 2$, and

$$y = \frac{1}{2}(e^x + e^{-x})$$
$$\frac{dy}{dx} = \frac{1}{2}(e^x - e^{-x})$$
$$\left(\frac{dy}{dx}\right)^2 = \frac{1}{4}(e^{2x} - 2 + e^{-2x})$$
$$1 + \left(\frac{dy}{dx}\right)^2 = \frac{1}{4}(e^{2x} + 2 + e^{-2x}) = \left[\frac{1}{2}(e^x + e^{-x})\right]^2.$$

The length of the curve from $x = 0$ to $x = 2$ is

$$L = \int_0^2 \sqrt{1 + \left(\frac{dy}{dx}\right)^2}\, dx = \int_0^2 \frac{1}{2}(e^x + e^{-x})\, dx \qquad \text{Eq. (3) with } a = 0, b = 2$$
$$= \frac{1}{2}\left[e^x - e^{-x}\right]_0^2 = \frac{1}{2}(e^2 - e^{-2}) \approx 3.63.$$

■

Dealing with Discontinuities in dy/dx

At a point on a curve where dy/dx fails to exist, dx/dy may exist. In this case, we may be able to find the curve's length by expressing x as a function of y and applying the following analogue of Equation (3):

Formula for the Length of $x = g(y)$, $c \le y \le d$

If g' is continuous on $[c, d]$, the length of the curve $x = g(y)$ from $A = (g(c), c)$ to $B = (g(d), d)$ is

$$L = \int_c^d \sqrt{1 + \left(\frac{dx}{dy}\right)^2}\, dy = \int_c^d \sqrt{1 + [g'(y)]^2}\, dy. \qquad (4)$$

EXAMPLE 4 Find the length of the curve $y = (x/2)^{2/3}$ from $x = 0$ to $x = 2$.

Solution The derivative

$$\frac{dy}{dx} = \frac{2}{3}\left(\frac{x}{2}\right)^{-1/3}\left(\frac{1}{2}\right) = \frac{1}{3}\left(\frac{2}{x}\right)^{1/3}$$

is not defined at $x = 0$, so we cannot find the curve's length with Equation (3).

We therefore rewrite the equation to express x in terms of y:

$$y = \left(\frac{x}{2}\right)^{2/3}$$

$$y^{3/2} = \frac{x}{2} \qquad \text{Raise both sides to the power 3/2.}$$

$$x = 2y^{3/2}. \qquad \text{Solve for } x.$$

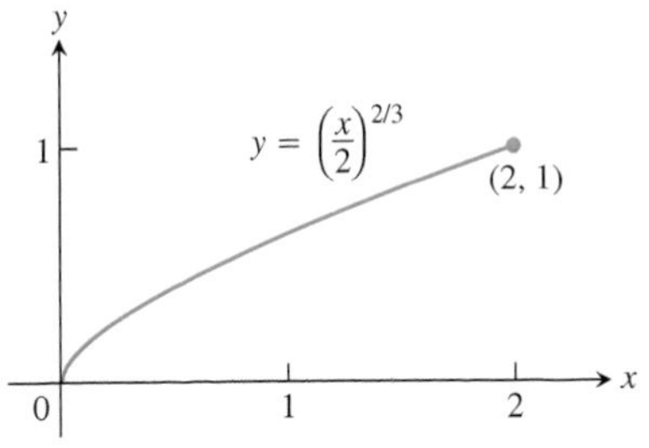

FIGURE 6.26 The graph of $y = (x/2)^{2/3}$ from $x = 0$ to $x = 2$ is also the graph of $x = 2y^{3/2}$ from $y = 0$ to $y = 1$ (Example 4).

From this we see that the curve whose length we want is also the graph of $x = 2y^{3/2}$ from $y = 0$ to $y = 1$ (Figure 6.26).

The derivative

$$\frac{dx}{dy} = 2\left(\frac{3}{2}\right)y^{1/2} = 3y^{1/2}$$

is continuous on $[0, 1]$. We may therefore use Equation (4) to find the curve's length:

$$\begin{aligned} L &= \int_c^d \sqrt{1 + \left(\frac{dx}{dy}\right)^2}\, dy = \int_0^1 \sqrt{1 + 9y}\, dy \\ &= \frac{1}{9}\cdot\frac{2}{3}(1 + 9y)^{3/2}\Big]_0^1 \\ &= \frac{2}{27}\left(10\sqrt{10} - 1\right) \approx 2.27. \end{aligned}$$

Eq. (4) with $c = 0, d = 1$. Let $u = 1 + 9y$, $du/9 = dy$, integrate, and substitute back. ■

The Differential Formula for Arc Length

If $y = f(x)$ and if f' is continuous on $[a, b]$, then by the Fundamental Theorem of Calculus we can define a new function

$$s(x) = \int_a^x \sqrt{1 + [f'(t)]^2}\, dt. \tag{5}$$

From Equation (3) and Figure 6.22, we see that this function $s(x)$ is continuous and measures the length along the curve $y = f(x)$ from the initial point $P_0(a, f(a))$ to the point $Q(x, f(x))$ for each $x \in [a, b]$. The function s is called the **arc length function** for $y = f(x)$. From the Fundamental Theorem, the function s is differentiable on (a, b) and

$$\frac{ds}{dx} = \sqrt{1 + [f'(x)]^2} = \sqrt{1 + \left(\frac{dy}{dx}\right)^2}.$$

Then the differential of arc length is

$$ds = \sqrt{1 + \left(\frac{dy}{dx}\right)^2}\, dx. \tag{6}$$

A useful way to remember Equation (6) is to write

$$ds = \sqrt{dx^2 + dy^2}, \tag{7}$$

which can be integrated between appropriate limits to give the total length of a curve. From this point of view, all the arc length formulas are simply different expressions for the equation

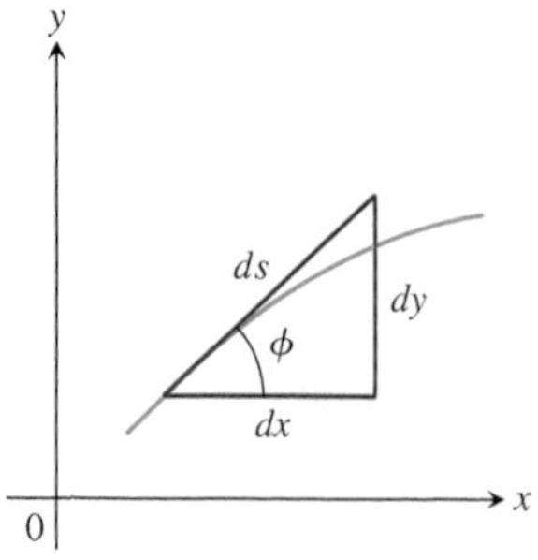

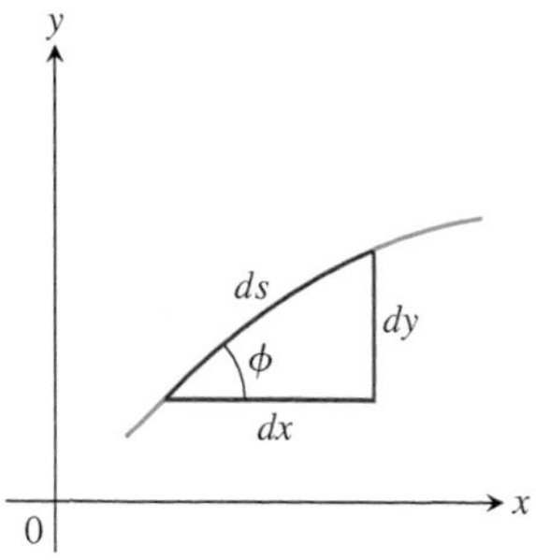

FIGURE 6.27 Diagrams for remembering the equation $ds = \sqrt{dx^2 + dy^2}$.

$L = \int ds$. Figure 6.27a gives the exact interpretation of ds corresponding to Equation (7). Figure 6.27b is not strictly accurate, but is to be thought of as a simplified approximation of Figure 6.27a. That is, $ds \approx \Delta s$.

EXAMPLE 5 Find the arc length function for the curve in Example 2 taking $A = (1, 13/12)$ as the starting point (see Figure 6.25).

Solution In the solution to Example 2, we found that

$$1 + [f'(x)]^2 = \left(\frac{x^2}{4} + \frac{1}{x^2}\right)^2.$$

Therefore the arc length function is given by

$$\begin{aligned} s(x) &= \int_1^x \sqrt{1 + [f'(t)]^2}\, dt = \int_1^x \left(\frac{t^2}{4} + \frac{1}{t^2}\right) dt \\ &= \left[\frac{t^3}{12} - \frac{1}{t}\right]_1^x = \frac{x^3}{12} - \frac{1}{x} + \frac{11}{12}. \end{aligned}$$

To compute the arc length along the curve from $A = (1, 13/12)$ to $B = (4, 67/12)$, for instance, we simply calculate

$$s(4) = \frac{4^3}{12} - \frac{1}{4} + \frac{11}{12} = 6.$$

This is the same result we obtained in Example 2. ■

Exercises 6.3

Finding Lengths of Curves

Find the lengths of the curves in Exercises 1–14. If you have a grapher, you may want to graph these curves to see what they look like.

1. $y = (1/3)(x^2 + 2)^{3/2}$ from $x = 0$ to $x = 3$
2. $y = x^{3/2}$ from $x = 0$ to $x = 4$
3. $x = (y^3/3) + 1/(4y)$ from $y = 1$ to $y = 3$
4. $x = (y^{3/2}/3) - y^{1/2}$ from $y = 1$ to $y = 9$
5. $x = (y^4/4) + 1/(8y^2)$ from $y = 1$ to $y = 2$
6. $x = (y^3/6) + 1/(2y)$ from $y = 2$ to $y = 3$
7. $y = (3/4)x^{4/3} - (3/8)x^{2/3} + 5, \quad 1 \le x \le 8$
8. $y = (x^3/3) + x^2 + x + 1/(4x + 4), \quad 0 \le x \le 2$
9. $y = \ln x - \dfrac{x^2}{8}$ from $x = 1$ to $x = 2$
10. $y = \dfrac{x^2}{2} - \dfrac{\ln x}{4}$ from $x = 1$ to $x = 3$
11. $y = \dfrac{x^3}{3} + \dfrac{1}{4x}, \quad 1 \le x \le 3$
12. $y = \dfrac{x^5}{5} + \dfrac{1}{12x^3}, \quad \dfrac{1}{2} \le x \le 1$
13. $x = \displaystyle\int_0^y \sqrt{\sec^4 t - 1}\, dt, \quad -\pi/4 \le y \le \pi/4$
14. $y = \displaystyle\int_{-2}^x \sqrt{3t^4 - 1}\, dt, \quad -2 \le x \le -1$

T Finding Integrals for Lengths of Curves

In Exercises 15–22, do the following.

a. Set up an integral for the length of the curve.

b. Graph the curve to see what it looks like.

c. Use your grapher's or computer's integral evaluator to find the curve's length numerically.

15. $y = x^2, \quad -1 \le x \le 2$
16. $y = \tan x, \quad -\pi/3 \le x \le 0$
17. $x = \sin y, \quad 0 \le y \le \pi$
18. $x = \sqrt{1 - y^2}, \quad -1/2 \le y \le 1/2$
19. $y^2 + 2y = 2x + 1$ from $(-1, -1)$ to $(7, 3)$
20. $y = \sin x - x\cos x, \quad 0 \le x \le \pi$
21. $y = \displaystyle\int_0^x \tan t\, dt, \quad 0 \le x \le \pi/6$
22. $x = \displaystyle\int_0^y \sqrt{\sec^2 t - 1}\, dt, \quad -\pi/3 \le y \le \pi/4$

Theory and Examples

23. **a.** Find a curve through the point (1, 1) whose length integral (Equation 3) is

$$L = \int_1^4 \sqrt{1 + \frac{1}{4x}}\, dx.$$

b. How many such curves are there? Give reasons for your answer.

24. a. Find a curve through the point (0, 1) whose length integral (Equation 4) is
$$L = \int_1^2 \sqrt{1 + \frac{1}{y^4}}\, dy.$$
b. How many such curves are there? Give reasons for your answer.

25. Find the length of the curve
$$y = \int_0^x \sqrt{\cos 2t}\, dt$$
from $x = 0$ to $x = \pi/4$.

26. **The length of an astroid** The graph of the equation $x^{2/3} + y^{2/3} = 1$ is one of a family of curves called *astroids* (not "asteroids") because of their starlike appearance (see the accompanying figure). Find the length of this particular astroid by finding the length of half the first-quadrant portion, $y = (1 - x^{2/3})^{3/2}$, $\sqrt{2}/4 \le x \le 1$, and multiplying by 8.

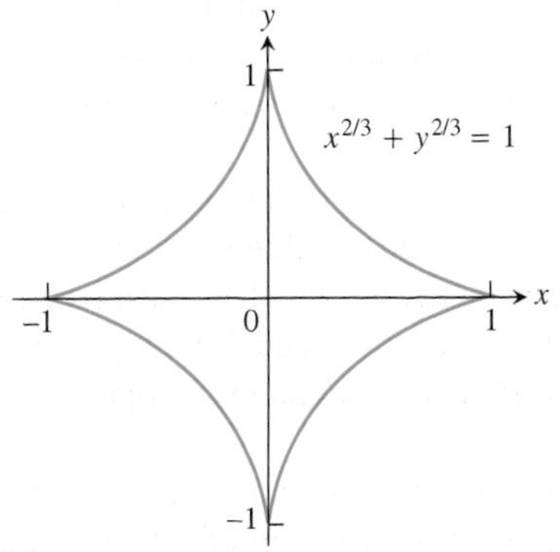

27. **Length of a line segment** Use the arc length formula (Equation 3) to find the length of the line segment $y = 3 - 2x$, $0 \le x \le 2$. Check your answer by finding the length of the segment as the hypotenuse of a right triangle.

28. **Circumference of a circle** Set up an integral to find the circumference of a circle of radius r centered at the origin. You will learn how to evaluate the integral in Section 8.3.

29. If $9x^2 = y(y - 3)^2$, show that
$$ds^2 = \frac{(y + 1)^2}{4y} dy^2.$$

30. If $4x^2 - y^2 = 64$, show that
$$ds^2 = \frac{4}{y^2}\left(5x^2 - 16\right) dx^2.$$

31. Is there a smooth (continuously differentiable) curve $y = f(x)$ whose length over the interval $0 \le x \le a$ is always $\sqrt{2}a$? Give reasons for your answer.

32. **Using tangent fins to derive the length formula for curves** Assume that f is smooth on $[a, b]$ and partition the interval $[a, b]$ in the usual way. In each subinterval $[x_{k-1}, x_k]$, construct the *tangent fin* at the point $(x_{k-1}, f(x_{k-1}))$, as shown in the accompanying figure.

a. Show that the length of the kth tangent fin over the interval $[x_{k-1}, x_k]$ equals $\sqrt{(\Delta x_k)^2 + (f'(x_{k-1})\,\Delta x_k)^2}$.

b. Show that
$$\lim_{n\to\infty} \sum_{k=1}^{n} (\text{length of } k\text{th tangent fin}) = \int_a^b \sqrt{1 + (f'(x))^2}\, dx,$$
which is the length L of the curve $y = f(x)$ from a to b.

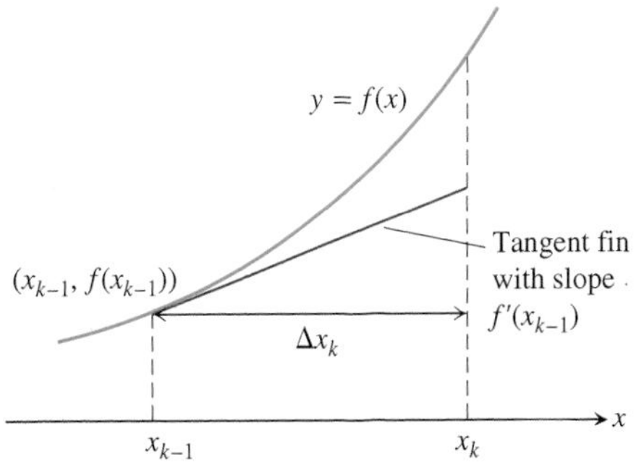

33. Approximate the arc length of one-quarter of the unit circle (which is $\pi/2$) by computing the length of the polygonal approximation with $n = 4$ segments (see accompanying figure).

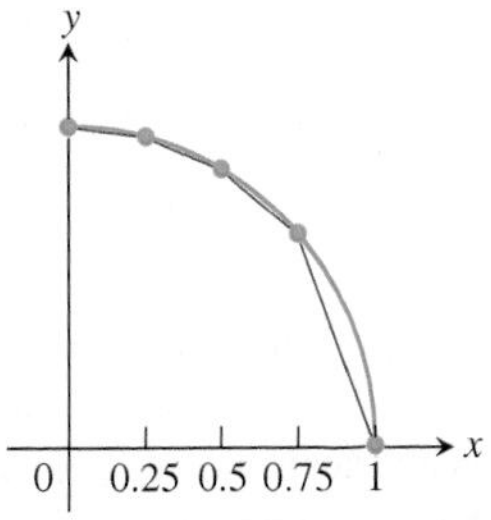

34. **Distance between two points** Assume that the two points (x_1, y_1) and (x_2, y_2) lie on the graph of the straight line $y = mx + b$. Use the arc length formula (Equation 3) to find the distance between the two points.

35. Find the arc length function for the graph of $f(x) = 2x^{3/2}$ using (0, 0) as the starting point. What is the length of the curve from (0, 0) to (1, 2)?

36. Find the arc length function for the curve in Exercise 8, using (0, 1/4) as the starting point. What is the length of the curve from (0, 1/4) to (1, 59/24)?

COMPUTER EXPLORATIONS

In Exercises 37–42, use a CAS to perform the following steps for the given graph of the function over the closed interval.

a. Plot the curve together with the polygonal path approximations for $n = 2, 4, 8$ partition points over the interval. (See Figure 6.22.)

b. Find the corresponding approximation to the length of the curve by summing the lengths of the line segments.

c. Evaluate the length of the curve using an integral. Compare your approximations for $n = 2, 4, 8$ with the actual length given by the integral. How does the actual length compare with the approximations as n increases? Explain your answer.

37. $f(x) = \sqrt{1 - x^2}$, $-1 \le x \le 1$

38. $f(x) = x^{1/3} + x^{2/3}$, $0 \le x \le 2$

39. $f(x) = \sin(\pi x^2)$, $0 \le x \le \sqrt{2}$

40. $f(x) = x^2 \cos x$, $0 \le x \le \pi$

41. $f(x) = \dfrac{x - 1}{4x^2 + 1}$, $-\dfrac{1}{2} \le x \le 1$

42. $f(x) = x^3 - x^2$, $-1 \le x \le 1$

6.4 Areas of Surfaces of Revolution

When you jump rope, the rope sweeps out a surface in the space around you similar to what is called a *surface of revolution*. The surface surrounds a volume of revolution, and many applications require that we know the area of the surface rather than the volume it encloses. In this section we define areas of surfaces of revolution. More general surfaces are treated in Chapter 15.

Defining Surface Area

If you revolve a region in the plane that is bounded by the graph of a function over an interval, it sweeps out a solid of revolution, as we saw earlier in the chapter. However, if you revolve only the bounding curve itself, it does not sweep out any interior volume but rather a surface that surrounds the solid and forms part of its boundary. Just as we were interested in defining and finding the length of a curve in the last section, we are now interested in defining and finding the area of a surface generated by revolving a curve about an axis.

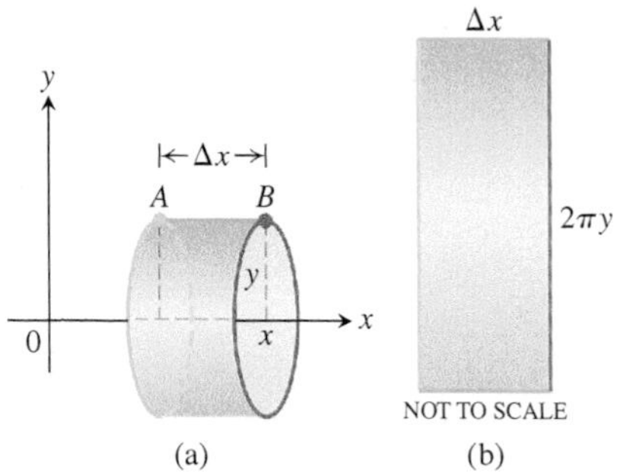

FIGURE 6.28 (a) A cylindrical surface generated by rotating the horizontal line segment AB of length Δx about the x-axis has area $2\pi y \Delta x$. (b) The cut and rolled-out cylindrical surface as a rectangle.

Before considering general curves, we begin by rotating horizontal and slanted line segments about the x-axis. If we rotate the horizontal line segment AB having length Δx about the x-axis (Figure 6.28a), we generate a cylinder with surface area $2\pi y \Delta x$. This area is the same as that of a rectangle with side lengths Δx and $2\pi y$ (Figure 6.28b). The length $2\pi y$ is the circumference of the circle of radius y generated by rotating the point (x, y) on the line AB about the x-axis.

Suppose the line segment AB has length L and is slanted rather than horizontal. Now when AB is rotated about the x-axis, it generates a frustum of a cone (Figure 6.29a). From classical geometry, the surface area of this frustum is $2\pi y^* L$, where $y^* = (y_1 + y_2)/2$ is the average height of the slanted segment AB above the x-axis. This surface area is the same as that of a rectangle with side lengths L and $2\pi y^*$ (Figure 6.29b).

Let's build on these geometric principles to define the area of a surface swept out by revolving more general curves about the x-axis. Suppose we want to find the area of the surface swept out by revolving the graph of a nonnegative continuous function $y = f(x)$, $a \le x \le b$, about the x-axis. We partition the closed interval $[a, b]$ in the usual way and use the points in the partition to subdivide the graph into short arcs. Figure 6.30 shows a typical arc PQ and the band it sweeps out as part of the graph of f.

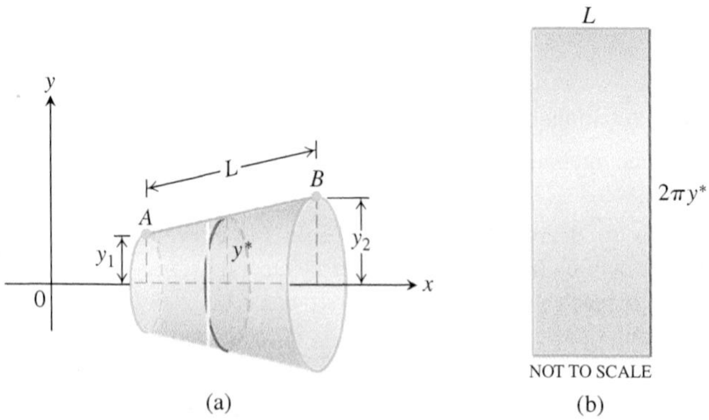

FIGURE 6.29 (a) The frustum of a cone generated by rotating the slanted line segment AB of length L about the x-axis has area $2\pi y^* L$. (b) The area of the rectangle for $y^* = \dfrac{y_1 + y_2}{2}$, the average height of AB above the x-axis.

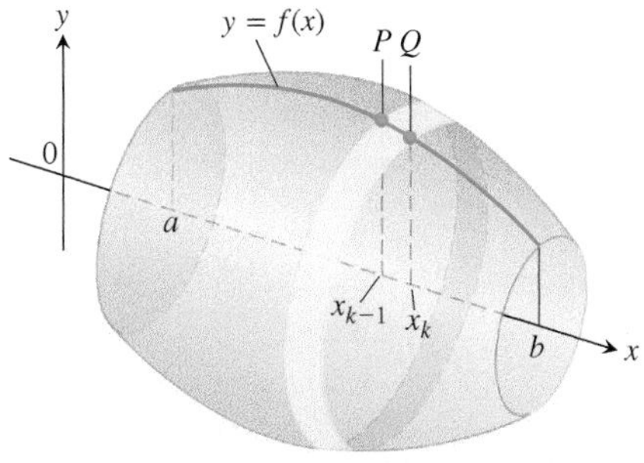

FIGURE 6.30 The surface generated by revolving the graph of a nonnegative function $y = f(x)$, $a \le x \le b$, about the x-axis. The surface is a union of bands like the one swept out by the arc PQ.

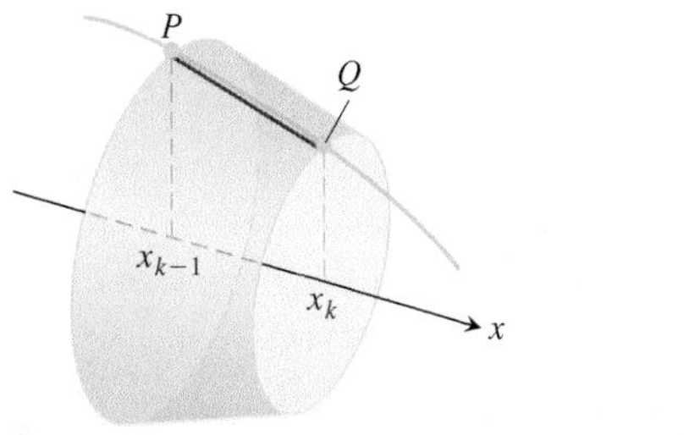

FIGURE 6.31 The line segment joining P and Q sweeps out a frustum of a cone.

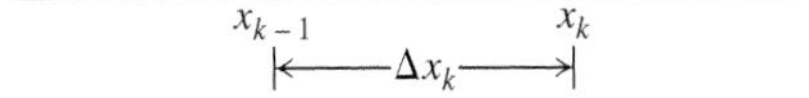

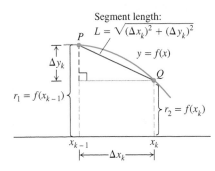

FIGURE 6.32 Dimensions associated with the arc and line segment PQ.

As the arc PQ revolves about the x-axis, the line segment joining P and Q sweeps out a frustum of a cone whose axis lies along the x-axis (Figure 6.31). The surface area of this frustum approximates the surface area of the band swept out by the arc PQ. The surface area of the frustum of the cone shown in Figure 6.31 is $2\pi y^* L$, where y^* is the average height of the line segment joining P and Q, and L is its length (just as before). Since $f \ge 0$, from Figure 6.32 we see that the average height of the line segment is $y^* = (f(x_{k-1}) + f(x_k))/2$, and the slant length is $L = \sqrt{(\Delta x_k)^2 + (\Delta y_k)^2}$. Therefore,

$$\begin{aligned}\text{Frustum surface area} &= 2\pi \cdot \frac{f(x_{k-1}) + f(x_k)}{2} \cdot \sqrt{(\Delta x_k)^2 + (\Delta y_k)^2} \\ &= \pi(f(x_{k-1}) + f(x_k))\sqrt{(\Delta x_k)^2 + (\Delta y_k)^2}.\end{aligned}$$

The area of the original surface, being the sum of the areas of the bands swept out by arcs like arc PQ, is approximated by the frustum area sum

$$\sum_{k=1}^{n} \pi(f(x_{k-1}) + f(x_k))\sqrt{(\Delta x_k)^2 + (\Delta y_k)^2}. \qquad (1)$$

We expect the approximation to improve as the partition of $[a, b]$ becomes finer. Moreover, if the function f is differentiable, then by the Mean Value Theorem, there is a point $(c_k, f(c_k))$ on the curve between P and Q where the tangent is parallel to the segment PQ (Figure 6.33). At this point,

$$f'(c_k) = \frac{\Delta y_k}{\Delta x_k},$$

$$\Delta y_k = f'(c_k)\, \Delta x_k.$$

With this substitution for Δy_k, the sums in Equation (1) take the form

$$\begin{aligned}&\sum_{k=1}^{n} \pi(f(x_{k-1}) + f(x_k))\sqrt{(\Delta x_k)^2 + (f'(c_k)\,\Delta x_k)^2} \\ &= \sum_{k=1}^{n} \pi(f(x_{k-1}) + f(x_k))\sqrt{1 + (f'(c_k))^2}\,\Delta x_k. \qquad (2)\end{aligned}$$

These sums are not the Riemann sums of any function because the points x_{k-1}, x_k, and c_k are not the same. However, it can be proved that as the norm of the partition of $[a, b]$ goes to zero, the sums in Equation (2) converge to the integral

$$\int_a^b 2\pi f(x)\sqrt{1 + (f'(x))^2}\, dx.$$

We therefore define this integral to be the area of the surface swept out by the graph of f from a to b.

DEFINITION If the function $f(x) \ge 0$ is continuously differentiable on $[a, b]$, the **area of the surface** generated by revolving the graph of $y = f(x)$ about the x-axis is

$$S = \int_a^b 2\pi y\sqrt{1 + \left(\frac{dy}{dx}\right)^2}\, dx = \int_a^b 2\pi f(x)\sqrt{1 + (f'(x))^2}\, dx. \qquad (3)$$

The square root in Equation (3) is the same one that appears in the formula for the arc length differential of the generating curve in Equation (6) of Section 6.3.

EXAMPLE 1 Find the area of the surface generated by revolving the curve $y = 2\sqrt{x}$, $1 \le x \le 2$, about the x-axis (Figure 6.34).

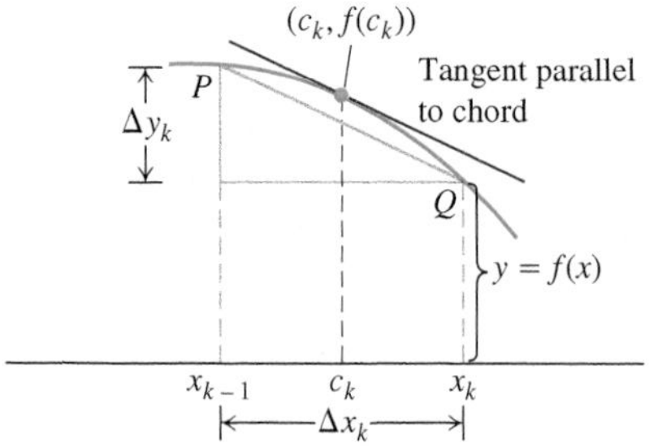

FIGURE 6.33 If f is smooth, the Mean Value Theorem guarantees the existence of a point c_k where the tangent is parallel to segment PQ.

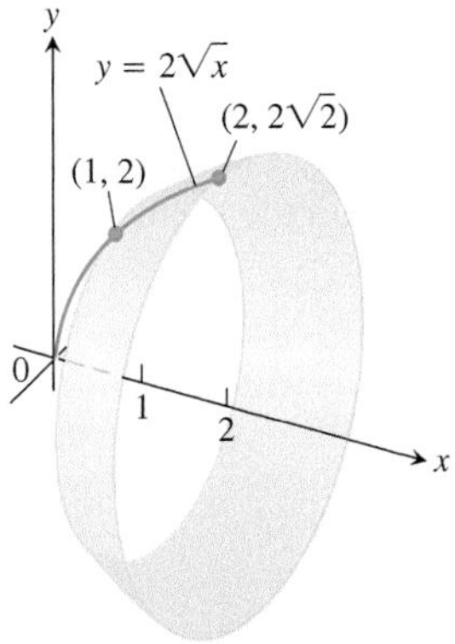

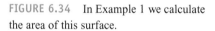

FIGURE 6.34 In Example 1 we calculate the area of this surface.

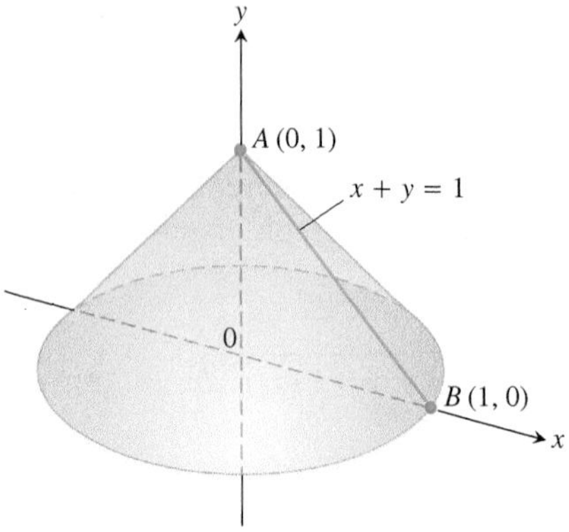

FIGURE 6.35 Revolving line segment AB about the y-axis generates a cone whose lateral surface area we can now calculate in two different ways (Example 2).

Solution We evaluate the formula

$$S = \int_a^b 2\pi y \sqrt{1 + \left(\frac{dy}{dx}\right)^2}\, dx \qquad \text{Eq. (3)}$$

with

$$a = 1, \qquad b = 2, \qquad y = 2\sqrt{x}, \qquad \frac{dy}{dx} = \frac{1}{\sqrt{x}}.$$

First, we perform some algebraic manipulation on the radical in the integrand to transform it into an expression that is easier to integrate.

$$\sqrt{1 + \left(\frac{dy}{dx}\right)^2} = \sqrt{1 + \left(\frac{1}{\sqrt{x}}\right)^2}$$

$$= \sqrt{1 + \frac{1}{x}} = \sqrt{\frac{x+1}{x}} = \frac{\sqrt{x+1}}{\sqrt{x}}.$$

With these substitutions, we have

$$S = \int_1^2 2\pi \cdot 2\sqrt{x}\frac{\sqrt{x+1}}{\sqrt{x}}\, dx = 4\pi \int_1^2 \sqrt{x+1}\, dx$$

$$= 4\pi \cdot \frac{2}{3}(x+1)^{3/2}\Big]_1^2 = \frac{8\pi}{3}\left(3\sqrt{3} - 2\sqrt{2}\right).$$

■

Revolution About the y-Axis

For revolution about the y-axis, we interchange x and y in Equation (3).

> **Surface Area for Revolution About the y-Axis**
> If $x = g(y) \geq 0$ is continuously differentiable on $[c, d]$, the area of the surface generated by revolving the graph of $x = g(y)$ about the y-axis is
>
> $$S = \int_c^d 2\pi x \sqrt{1 + \left(\frac{dx}{dy}\right)^2}\, dy = \int_c^d 2\pi g(y)\sqrt{1 + (g'(y))^2}\, dy. \qquad (4)$$

EXAMPLE 2 The line segment $x = 1 - y$, $0 \leq y \leq 1$, is revolved about the y-axis to generate the cone in Figure 6.35. Find its lateral surface area (which excludes the base area).

Solution Here we have a calculation we can check with a formula from geometry:

$$\text{Lateral surface area} = \frac{\text{base circumference}}{2} \times \text{slant height} = \pi\sqrt{2}.$$

To see how Equation (4) gives the same result, we take

$$c = 0, \qquad d = 1, \qquad x = 1 - y, \qquad \frac{dx}{dy} = -1,$$

$$\sqrt{1 + \left(\frac{dx}{dy}\right)^2} = \sqrt{1 + (-1)^2} = \sqrt{2}$$

and calculate

$$\begin{aligned} S &= \int_c^d 2\pi x \sqrt{1 + \left(\frac{dx}{dy}\right)^2}\, dy = \int_0^1 2\pi(1 - y)\sqrt{2}\, dy \\ &= 2\pi\sqrt{2}\left[y - \frac{y^2}{2}\right]_0^1 = 2\pi\sqrt{2}\left(1 - \frac{1}{2}\right) \\ &= \pi\sqrt{2}. \end{aligned}$$

The results agree, as they should. ■

Exercises 6.4

Finding Integrals for Surface Area

In Exercises 1–8:

a. Set up an integral for the area of the surface generated by revolving the given curve about the indicated axis.

T b. Graph the curve to see what it looks like. If you can, graph the surface too.

T c. Use your grapher's or computer's integral evaluator to find the surface's area numerically.

1. $y = \tan x, \quad 0 \le x \le \pi/4; \quad x\text{-axis}$
2. $y = x^2, \quad 0 \le x \le 2; \quad x\text{-axis}$
3. $xy = 1, \quad 1 \le y \le 2; \quad y\text{-axis}$
4. $x = \sin y, \quad 0 \le y \le \pi; \quad y\text{-axis}$
5. $x^{1/2} + y^{1/2} = 3$ from $(4, 1)$ to $(1, 4)$; x-axis
6. $y + 2\sqrt{y} = x, \quad 1 \le y \le 2; \quad y\text{-axis}$
7. $x = \displaystyle\int_0^y \tan t\, dt, \quad 0 \le y \le \pi/3; \quad y\text{-axis}$
8. $y = \displaystyle\int_1^x \sqrt{t^2 - 1}\, dt, \quad 1 \le x \le \sqrt{5}; \quad x\text{-axis}$

Finding Surface Area

9. Find the lateral (side) surface area of the cone generated by revolving the line segment $y = x/2$, $0 \le x \le 4$, about the x-axis. Check your answer with the geometry formula

$$\text{Lateral surface area} = \frac{1}{2} \times \text{base circumference} \times \text{slant height}.$$

10. Find the lateral surface area of the cone generated by revolving the line segment $y = x/2$, $0 \le x \le 4$, about the y-axis. Check your answer with the geometry formula

$$\text{Lateral surface area} = \frac{1}{2} \times \text{base circumference} \times \text{slant height}.$$

11. Find the surface area of the cone frustum generated by revolving the line segment $y = (x/2) + (1/2)$, $1 \le x \le 3$, about the x-axis. Check your result with the geometry formula

$$\text{Frustum surface area} = \pi(r_1 + r_2) \times \text{slant height}.$$

12. Find the surface area of the cone frustum generated by revolving the line segment $y = (x/2) + (1/2)$, $1 \le x \le 3$, about the y-axis. Check your result with the geometry formula

$$\text{Frustum surface area} = \pi(r_1 + r_2) \times \text{slant height}.$$

Find the areas of the surfaces generated by revolving the curves in Exercises 13–23 about the indicated axes. If you have a grapher, you may want to graph these curves to see what they look like.

13. $y = x^3/9, \quad 0 \le x \le 2; \quad x\text{-axis}$
14. $y = \sqrt{x}, \quad 3/4 \le x \le 15/4; \quad x\text{-axis}$
15. $y = \sqrt{2x - x^2}, \quad 0.5 \le x \le 1.5; \quad x\text{-axis}$
16. $y = \sqrt{x + 1}, \quad 1 \le x \le 5; \quad x\text{-axis}$
17. $x = y^3/3, \quad 0 \le y \le 1; \quad y\text{-axis}$
18. $x = (1/3)y^{3/2} - y^{1/2}, \quad 1 \le y \le 3; \quad y\text{-axis}$
19. $x = 2\sqrt{4 - y}, \quad 0 \le y \le 15/4; \quad y\text{-axis}$

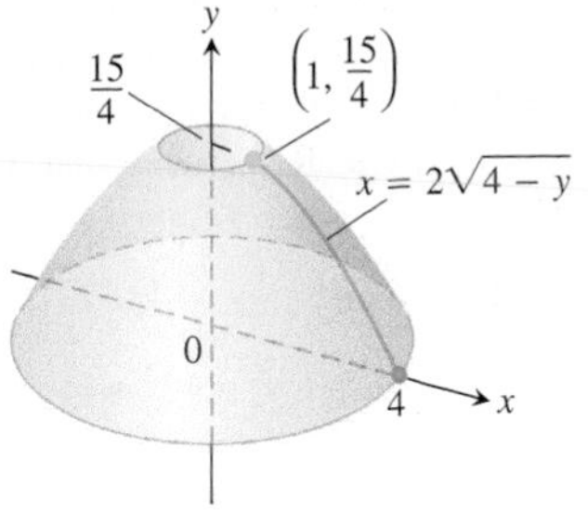

20. $x = \sqrt{2y - 1}, \quad 5/8 \le y \le 1; \quad y\text{-axis}$

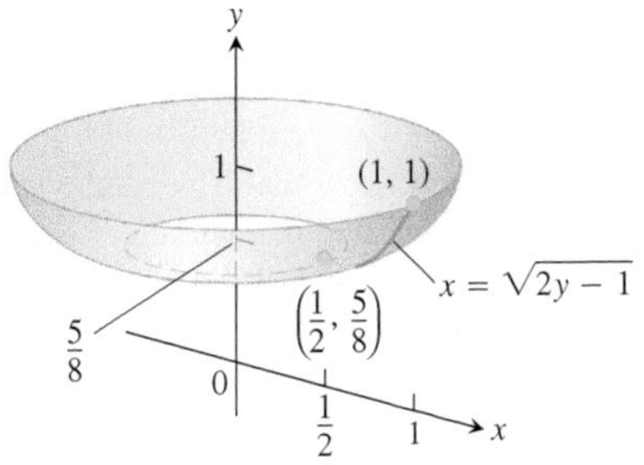

21. $x = (e^y + e^{-y})/2, \quad 0 \le y \le \ln 2; \quad y\text{-axis}$

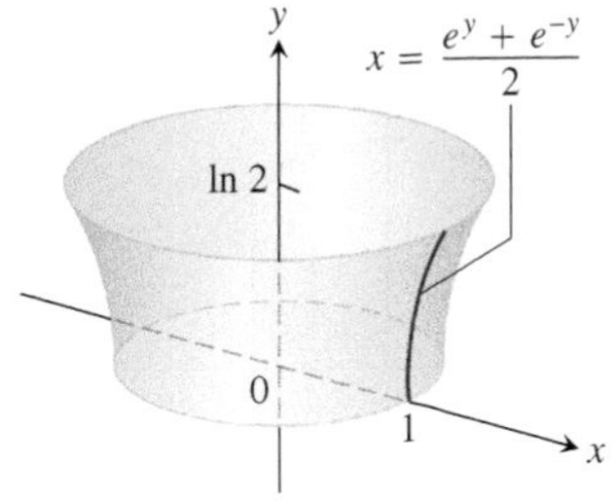

22. $y = (1/3)(x^2 + 2)^{3/2}$, $0 \le x \le \sqrt{2}$; y-axis (*Hint:* Express $ds = \sqrt{dx^2 + dy^2}$ in terms of dx, and evaluate the integral $S = \int 2\pi x\, ds$ with appropriate limits.)

23. $x = (y^4/4) + 1/(8y^2)$, $1 \le y \le 2$; x-axis (*Hint:* Express $ds = \sqrt{dx^2 + dy^2}$ in terms of dy, and evaluate the integral $S = \int 2\pi y\, ds$ with appropriate limits.)

24. Write an integral for the area of the surface generated by revolving the curve $y = \cos x$, $-\pi/2 \le x \le \pi/2$, about the x-axis. In Section 8.4 we will see how to evaluate such integrals.

25. **Testing the new definition** Show that the surface area of a sphere of radius a is still $4\pi a^2$ by using Equation (3) to find the area of the surface generated by revolving the curve $y = \sqrt{a^2 - x^2}$, $-a \le x \le a$, about the x-axis.

26. **Testing the new definition** The lateral (side) surface area of a cone of height h and base radius r should be $\pi r\sqrt{r^2 + h^2}$, the semiperimeter of the base times the slant height. Show that this is still the case by finding the area of the surface generated by revolving the line segment $y = (r/h)x$, $0 \le x \le h$, about the x-axis.

T 27. **Enameling woks** Your company decided to put out a deluxe version of a wok you designed. The plan is to coat it inside with white enamel and outside with blue enamel. Each enamel will be sprayed on 0.5 mm thick before baking. (See accompanying figure.) Your manufacturing department wants to know how much enamel to have on hand for a production run of 5000 woks. What do you tell them? (Neglect waste and unused material and give your answer in liters. Remember that $1\ \text{cm}^3 = 1\ \text{mL}$, so $1\ \text{L} = 1000\ \text{cm}^3$.)

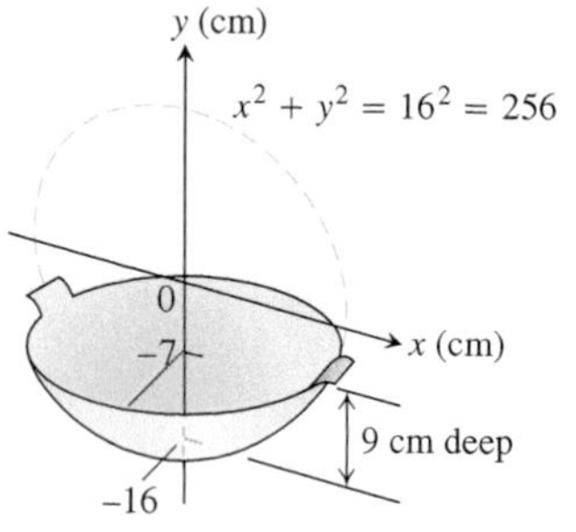

28. **Slicing bread** Did you know that if you cut a spherical loaf of bread into slices of equal width, each slice will have the same amount of crust? To see why, suppose the semicircle $y = \sqrt{r^2 - x^2}$ shown here is revolved about the x-axis to generate a sphere. Let AB be an arc of the semicircle that lies above an interval of length h on the x-axis. Show that the area swept out by AB does not depend on the location of the interval. (It does depend on the length of the interval.)

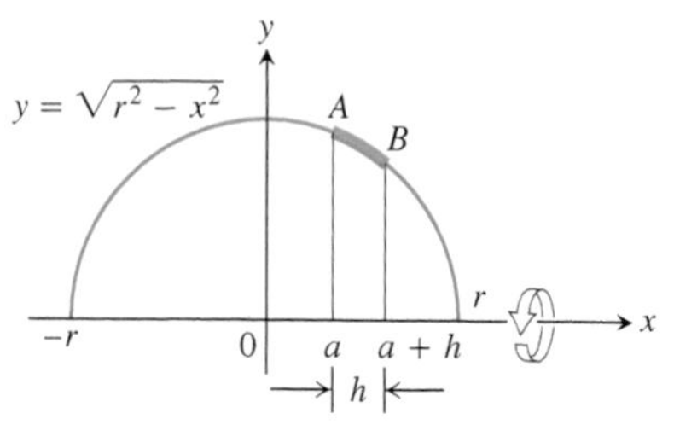

29. The shaded band shown here is cut from a sphere of radius R by parallel planes h units apart. Show that the surface area of the band is $2\pi Rh$.

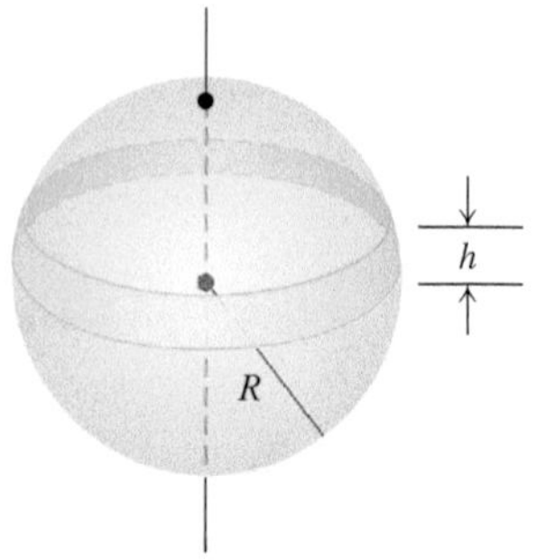

30. Here is a schematic drawing of the 90-ft dome used by the U.S. National Weather Service to house radar in Bozeman, Montana.

a. How much outside surface is there to paint (not counting the bottom)?

T b. Express the answer to the nearest square foot.

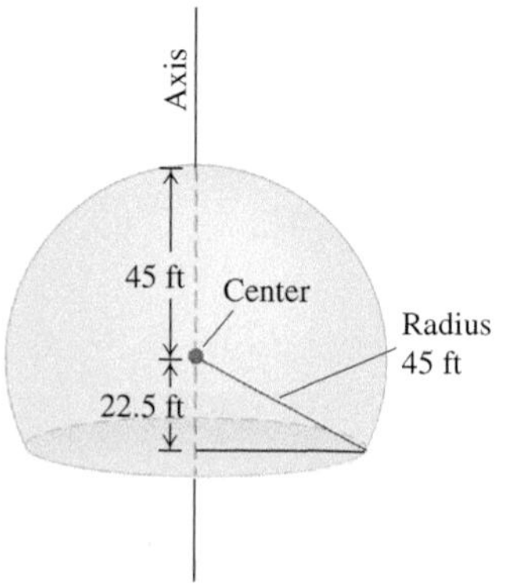

31. **An alternative derivation of the surface area formula** Assume f is smooth on $[a, b]$ and partition $[a, b]$ in the usual way. In the kth subinterval $[x_{k-1}, x_k]$, construct the tangent line to the curve at the midpoint $m_k = (x_{k-1} + x_k)/2$, as in the accompanying figure.

a. Show that

$$r_1 = f(m_k) - f'(m_k)\frac{\Delta x_k}{2} \quad \text{and} \quad r_2 = f(m_k) + f'(m_k)\frac{\Delta x_k}{2}.$$

b. Show that the length L_k of the tangent line segment in the kth subinterval is $L_k = \sqrt{(\Delta x_k)^2 + (f'(m_k)\,\Delta x_k)^2}$.

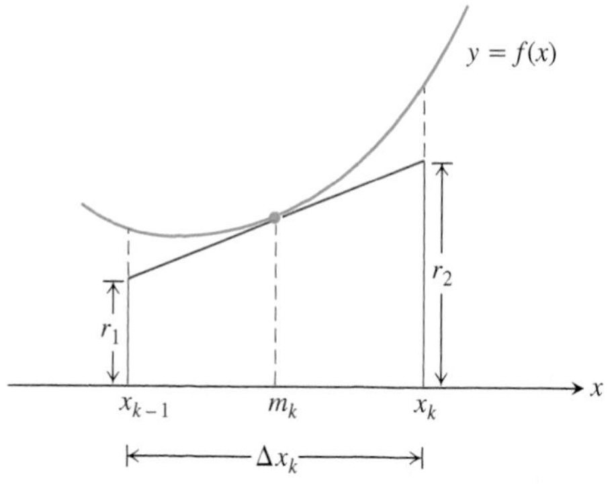

c. Show that the lateral surface area of the frustum of the cone swept out by the tangent line segment as it revolves about the x-axis is $2\pi f(m_k)\sqrt{1+(f'(m_k))^2}\,\Delta x_k$.

d. Show that the area of the surface generated by revolving $y = f(x)$ about the x-axis over $[a, b]$ is

$$\lim_{n\to\infty}\sum_{k=1}^{n}\begin{pmatrix}\text{lateral surface area}\\ \text{of } k\text{th frustum}\end{pmatrix} = \int_a^b 2\pi f(x)\sqrt{1+(f'(x))^2}\,dx.$$

32. The surface of an astroid Find the area of the surface generated by revolving about the x-axis the portion of the astroid $x^{2/3} + y^{2/3} = 1$ shown in the accompanying figure.

(*Hint:* Revolve the first-quadrant portion $y = (1 - x^{2/3})^{3/2}$, $0 \le x \le 1$, about the x-axis and double your result.)

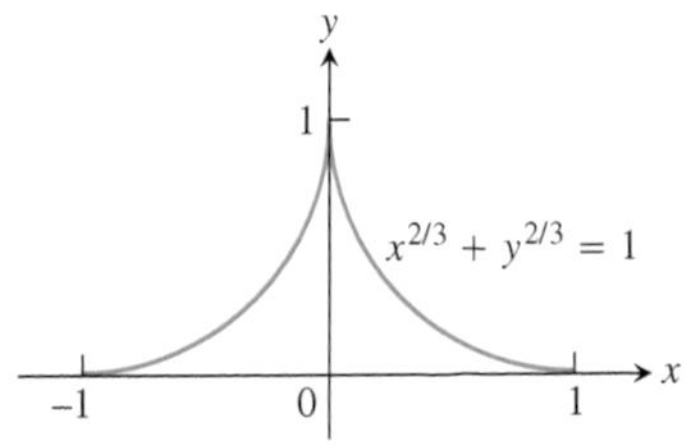

6.5 Work

In everyday life, *work* means an activity that requires muscular or mental effort. In science, the term refers specifically to a force acting on a body (or object) and the body's subsequent displacement. This section shows how to calculate work. The applications run from compressing railroad car springs and emptying subterranean tanks to forcing subatomic particles to collide and lifting satellites into orbit.

Work Done by a Constant Force

When a body moves a distance d along a straight line as a result of being acted on by a force of constant magnitude F in the direction of motion, we define the **work** W done by the force on the body with the formula

$$W = Fd \qquad \text{(Constant-force formula for work).} \tag{1}$$

From Equation (1) we see that the unit of work in any system is the unit of force multiplied by the unit of distance. In SI units (SI stands for *Système International*, or International System), the unit of force is a newton, the unit of distance is a meter, and the unit of work is a newton-meter $(\text{N}\cdot\text{m})$. This combination appears so often it has a special name, the **joule**. In the British system, the unit of work is the foot-pound, a unit frequently used by engineers.

Joules
The joule, abbreviated J, is named after the English physicist James Prescott Joule (1818–1889). The defining equation is

$$1 \text{ joule} = (1 \text{ newton})(1 \text{ meter}).$$

In symbols, $1\text{ J} = 1\text{ N}\cdot\text{m}$.

EXAMPLE 1 Suppose you jack up the side of a 2000-lb car 1.25 ft to change a tire. The jack applies a constant vertical force of about 1000 lb in lifting the side of the car (but because of the mechanical advantage of the jack, the force you apply to the jack itself is only about 30 lb). The total work performed by the jack on the car is $1000 \times 1.25 = 1250$ ft-lb. In SI units, the jack has applied a force of 4448 N through a distance of 0.381 m to do $4448 \times 0.381 \approx 1695$ J of work. ■

Work Done by a Variable Force Along a Line

If the force you apply varies along the way, as it will if you are stretching or compressing a spring, the formula $W = Fd$ has to be replaced by an integral formula that takes the variation in F into account.

Suppose that the force performing the work acts on an object moving along a straight line, which we take to be the x-axis. We assume that the magnitude of the force is a continuous function F of the object's position x. We want to find the work done over the interval from $x = a$ to $x = b$. We partition $[a, b]$ in the usual way and choose an arbitrary point c_k in each subinterval $[x_{k-1}, x_k]$. If the subinterval is short enough, the continuous function F

will not vary much from x_{k-1} to x_k. The amount of work done across the interval will be about $F(c_k)$ times the distance Δx_k, the same as it would be if F were constant and we could apply Equation (1). The total work done from a to b is therefore approximated by the Riemann sum

$$\text{Work} \approx \sum_{k=1}^{n} F(c_k)\,\Delta x_k.$$

We expect the approximation to improve as the norm of the partition goes to zero, so we define the work done by the force from a to b to be the integral of F from a to b:

$$\lim_{n\to\infty} \sum_{k=1}^{n} F(c_k)\,\Delta x_k = \int_a^b F(x)\,dx.$$

DEFINITION The **work** done by a variable force $F(x)$ in the direction of motion along the x-axis from $x = a$ to $x = b$ is

$$W = \int_a^b F(x)\,dx. \tag{2}$$

The units of the integral are joules if F is in newtons and x is in meters, and foot-pounds if F is in pounds and x is in feet. So the work done by a force of $F(x) = 1/x^2$ newtons in moving an object along the x-axis from $x = 1$ m to $x = 10$ m is

$$W = \int_1^{10} \frac{1}{x^2}\,dx = -\frac{1}{x}\bigg]_1^{10} = -\frac{1}{10} + 1 = 0.9 \text{ J}.$$

Hooke's Law for Springs: $F = kx$

Hooke's Law says that the force required to hold a stretched or compressed spring x units from its natural (unstressed) length is proportional to x. In symbols,

$$F = kx. \tag{3}$$

The constant k, measured in force units per unit length, is a characteristic of the spring, called the **force constant** (or **spring constant**) of the spring. Hooke's Law, Equation (3), gives good results as long as the force doesn't distort the metal in the spring. We assume that the forces in this section are too small to do that.

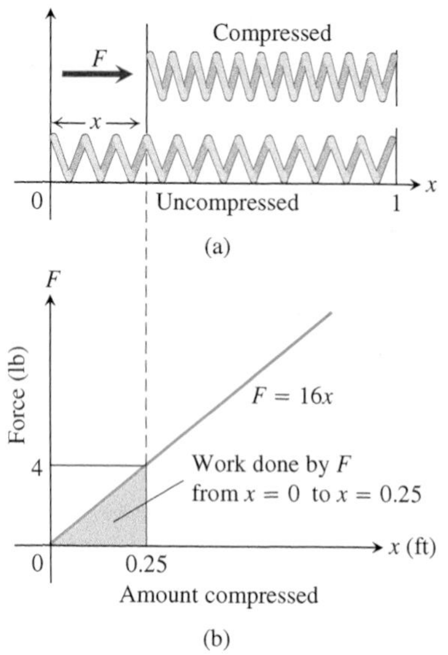

FIGURE 6.36 The force F needed to hold a spring under compression increases linearly as the spring is compressed (Example 2).

EXAMPLE 2 Find the work required to compress a spring from its natural length of 1 ft to a length of 0.75 ft if the force constant is $k = 16$ lb/ft.

Solution We picture the uncompressed spring laid out along the x-axis with its movable end at the origin and its fixed end at $x = 1$ ft (Figure 6.36). This enables us to describe the force required to compress the spring from 0 to x with the formula $F = 16x$. To compress the spring from 0 to 0.25 ft, the force must increase from

$$F(0) = 16 \cdot 0 = 0 \text{ lb} \quad \text{to} \quad F(0.25) = 16 \cdot 0.25 = 4 \text{ lb}.$$

The work done by F over this interval is

$$W = \int_0^{0.25} 16x\,dx = 8x^2\bigg]_0^{0.25} = 0.5 \text{ ft-lb}.$$

Eq. (2) with $a = 0, b = 0.25$, $F(x) = 16x$ ■

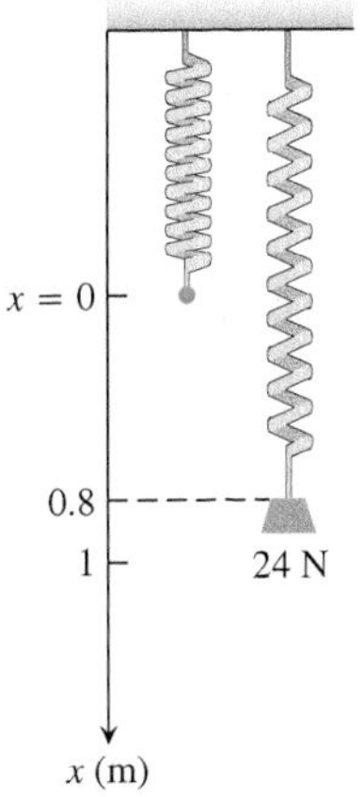

FIGURE 6.37 A 24-N weight stretches this spring 0.8 m beyond its unstressed length (Example 3).

EXAMPLE 3 A spring has a natural length of 1 m. A force of 24 N holds the spring stretched to a total length of 1.8 m.

(a) Find the force constant k.

(b) How much work will it take to stretch the spring 2 m beyond its natural length?

(c) How far will a 45-N force stretch the spring?

Solution

(a) *The force constant.* We find the force constant from Equation (3). A force of 24 N maintains the spring at a position where it is stretched 0.8 m from its natural length, so

$$24 = k(0.8) \qquad \text{Eq. (3) with } F = 24, x = 0.8$$
$$k = 24/0.8 = 30 \text{ N/m}.$$

(b) *The work to stretch the spring* 2 m. We imagine the unstressed spring hanging along the x-axis with its free end at $x = 0$ (Figure 6.37). The force required to stretch the spring x m beyond its natural length is the force required to hold the free end of the spring x units from the origin. Hooke's Law with $k = 30$ says that this force is

$$F(x) = 30x.$$

The work done by F on the spring from $x = 0$ m to $x = 2$ m is

$$W = \int_0^2 30x\,dx = 15x^2\Big]_0^2 = 60 \text{ J}.$$

(c) *How far will a* 45-N *force stretch the spring?* We substitute $F = 45$ in the equation $F = 30x$ to find

$$45 = 30x, \qquad \text{or} \qquad x = 1.5 \text{ m}.$$

A 45-N force will keep the spring stretched 1.5 m beyond its natural length. ■

The work integral is useful to calculate the work done in lifting objects whose weights vary with their elevation.

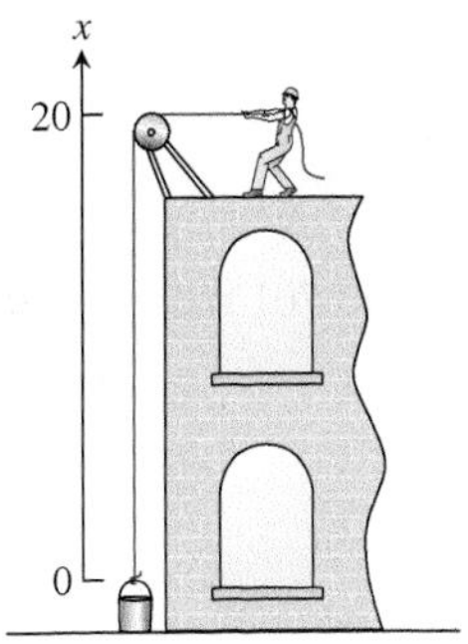

FIGURE 6.38 Lifting the bucket in Example 4.

EXAMPLE 4 A 5-lb bucket is lifted from the ground into the air by pulling in 20 ft of rope at a constant speed (Figure 6.38). The rope weighs 0.08 lb/ft. How much work was spent lifting the bucket and rope?

Solution The bucket has constant weight, so the work done lifting it alone is weight × distance = $5 \cdot 20 = 100$ ft-lb.

The weight of the rope varies with the bucket's elevation, because less of it is freely hanging. When the bucket is x ft off the ground, the remaining proportion of the rope still being lifted weighs $(0.08) \cdot (20 - x)$ lb. So the work in lifting the rope is

$$\text{Work on rope} = \int_0^{20} (0.08)(20 - x)\,dx = \int_0^{20} (1.6 - 0.08x)\,dx$$
$$= \left[1.6x - 0.04x^2\right]_0^{20} = 32 - 16 = 16 \text{ ft-lb}.$$

The total work for the bucket and rope combined is

$$100 + 16 = 116 \text{ ft-lb}.$$ ■

Pumping Liquids from Containers

How much work does it take to pump all or part of the liquid from a container? Engineers often need to know the answer in order to design or choose the right pump to transport water or some other liquid from one place to another. To find out how much work is required to pump the liquid, we imagine lifting the liquid out one thin horizontal slab at a time and applying the equation $W = Fd$ to each slab. We then evaluate the integral this leads to as the slabs become thinner and more numerous. The integral we get each time depends on the weight of the liquid and the dimensions of the container, but the way we find the integral is always the same. The next example shows what to do.

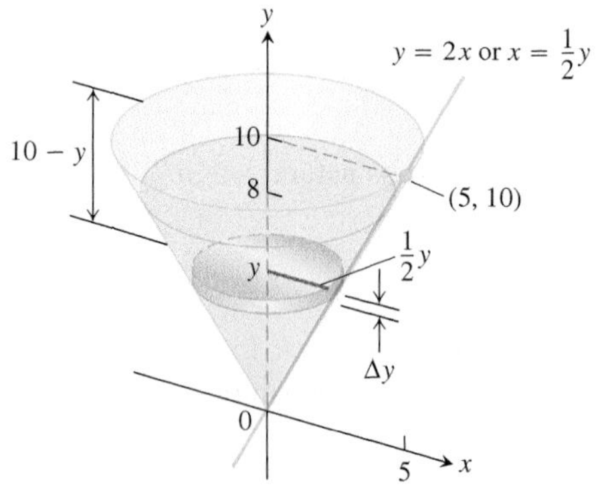

FIGURE 6.39 The olive oil and tank in Example 5.

EXAMPLE 5 The conical tank in Figure 6.39 is filled to within 2 ft of the top with olive oil weighing 57 lb/ft³. How much work does it take to pump the oil to the rim of the tank?

Solution We imagine the oil divided into thin slabs by planes perpendicular to the y-axis at the points of a partition of the interval [0, 8].

The typical slab between the planes at y and $y + \Delta y$ has a volume of about

$$\Delta V = \pi(\text{radius})^2(\text{thickness}) = \pi\left(\frac{1}{2}y\right)^2 \Delta y = \frac{\pi}{4}y^2\,\Delta y \text{ ft}^3.$$

The force $F(y)$ required to lift this slab is equal to its weight,

$$F(y) = 57\,\Delta V = \frac{57\pi}{4}y^2\,\Delta y \text{ lb.}$$

Weight = (weight per unit volume) × volume

The distance through which $F(y)$ must act to lift this slab to the level of the rim of the cone is about $(10 - y)$ ft, so the work done lifting the slab is about

$$\Delta W = \frac{57\pi}{4}(10 - y)y^2\,\Delta y \text{ ft-lb.}$$

Assuming there are n slabs associated with the partition of [0, 8], and that $y = y_k$ denotes the plane associated with the kth slab of thickness Δy_k, we can approximate the work done lifting all of the slabs with the Riemann sum

$$W \approx \sum_{k=1}^{n} \frac{57\pi}{4}(10 - y_k){y_k}^2\,\Delta y_k \text{ ft-lb.}$$

The work of pumping the oil to the rim is the limit of these sums as the norm of the partition goes to zero and the number of slabs tends to infinity:

$$\begin{aligned} W = \lim_{n\to\infty}\sum_{k=1}^{n}\frac{57\pi}{4}(10 - y_k){y_k}^2\,\Delta y_k &= \int_0^8 \frac{57\pi}{4}(10 - y)y^2\,dy \\ &= \frac{57\pi}{4}\int_0^8 (10y^2 - y^3)\,dy \\ &= \frac{57\pi}{4}\left[\frac{10y^3}{3} - \frac{y^4}{4}\right]_0^8 \approx 30{,}561 \text{ ft-lb.} \end{aligned}$$

■

Exercises 6.5

Springs

1. **Spring constant** It took 1800 J of work to stretch a spring from its natural length of 2 m to a length of 5 m. Find the spring's force constant.

2. **Stretching a spring** A spring has a natural length of 10 in. An 800-lb force stretches the spring to 14 in.
   a. Find the force constant.
   b. How much work is done in stretching the spring from 10 in. to 12 in.?
   c. How far beyond its natural length will a 1600-lb force stretch the spring?

3. **Stretching a rubber band** A force of 2 N will stretch a rubber band 2 cm (0.02 m). Assuming that Hooke's Law applies, how far will a 4-N force stretch the rubber band? How much work does it take to stretch the rubber band this far?

4. **Stretching a spring** If a force of 90 N stretches a spring 1 m beyond its natural length, how much work does it take to stretch the spring 5 m beyond its natural length?

5. **Subway car springs** It takes a force of 21,714 lb to compress a coil spring assembly on a New York City Transit Authority subway car from its free height of 8 in. to its fully compressed height of 5 in.
   a. What is the assembly's force constant?
   b. How much work does it take to compress the assembly the first half inch? the second half inch? Answer to the nearest in.-lb.

6. **Bathroom scale** A bathroom scale is compressed 1/16 in. when a 150-lb person stands on it. Assuming that the scale behaves like a spring that obeys Hooke's Law, how much does someone who compresses the scale 1/8 in. weigh? How much work is done compressing the scale 1/8 in.?

Work Done by a Variable Force

7. **Lifting a rope** A mountain climber is about to haul up a 50-m length of hanging rope. How much work will it take if the rope weighs 0.624 N/m?

8. **Leaky sandbag** A bag of sand originally weighing 144 lb was lifted at a constant rate. As it rose, sand also leaked out at a constant rate. The sand was half gone by the time the bag had been lifted to 18 ft. How much work was done lifting the sand this far? (Neglect the weight of the bag and lifting equipment.)

9. **Lifting an elevator cable** An electric elevator with a motor at the top has a multistrand cable weighing 4.5 lb/ft. When the car is at the first floor, 180 ft of cable are paid out, and effectively 0 ft are out when the car is at the top floor. How much work does the motor do just lifting the cable when it takes the car from the first floor to the top?

10. **Force of attraction** When a particle of mass m is at $(x, 0)$, it is attracted toward the origin with a force whose magnitude is k/x^2. If the particle starts from rest at $x = b$ and is acted on by no other forces, find the work done on it by the time it reaches $x = a$, $0 < a < b$.

11. **Leaky bucket** Assume the bucket in Example 4 is leaking. It starts with 2 gal of water (16 lb) and leaks at a constant rate. It finishes draining just as it reaches the top. How much work was spent lifting the water alone? (*Hint:* Do not include the rope and bucket, and find the proportion of water left at elevation x ft.)

12. (*Continuation of Exercise 11.*) The workers in Example 4 and Exercise 11 changed to a larger bucket that held 5 gal (40 lb) of water, but the new bucket had an even larger leak so that it, too, was empty by the time it reached the top. Assuming that the water leaked out at a steady rate, how much work was done lifting the water alone? (Do not include the rope and bucket.)

Pumping Liquids from Containers

13. **Pumping water** The rectangular tank shown here, with its top at ground level, is used to catch runoff water. Assume that the water weighs 62.4 lb/ft^3.

    a. How much work does it take to empty the tank by pumping the water back to ground level once the tank is full?

    b. If the water is pumped to ground level with a (5/11)-horsepower (hp) motor (work output 250 ft-lb/sec), how long will it take to empty the full tank (to the nearest minute)?

    c. Show that the pump in part (b) will lower the water level 10 ft (halfway) during the first 25 min of pumping.

    d. **The weight of water** What are the answers to parts (a) and (b) in a location where water weighs 62.26 lb/ft^3? 62.59 lb/ft^3?

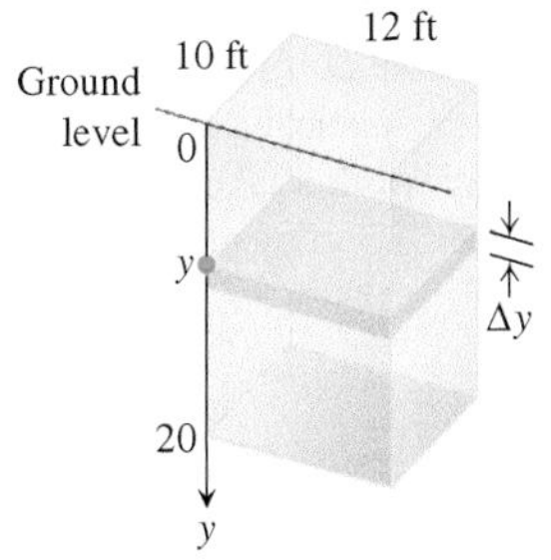

14. **Emptying a cistern** The rectangular cistern (storage tank for rainwater) shown has its top 10 ft below ground level. The cistern, currently full, is to be emptied for inspection by pumping its contents to ground level.

    a. How much work will it take to empty the cistern?

    b. How long will it take a 1/2-hp pump, rated at 275 ft-lb/sec, to pump the tank dry?

    c. How long will it take the pump in part (b) to empty the tank halfway? (It will be less than half the time required to empty the tank completely.)

    d. **The weight of water** What are the answers to parts (a) through (c) in a location where water weighs 62.26 lb/ft^3? 62.59 lb/ft^3?

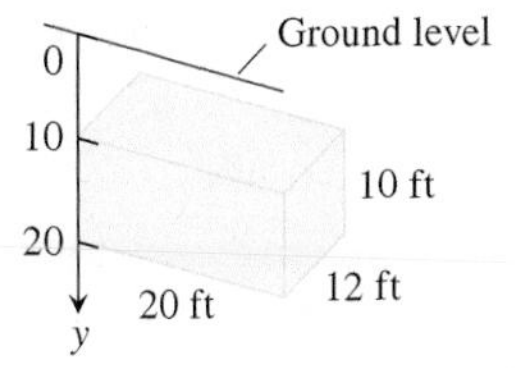

15. **Pumping oil** How much work would it take to pump oil from the tank in Example 5 to the level of the top of the tank if the tank were completely full?

16. **Pumping a half-full tank** Suppose that, instead of being full, the tank in Example 5 is only half full. How much work does it take to pump the remaining oil to a level 4 ft above the top of the tank?

17. **Emptying a tank** A vertical right-circular cylindrical tank measures 30 ft high and 20 ft in diameter. It is full of kerosene weighing 51.2 lb/ft^3. How much work does it take to pump the kerosene to the level of the top of the tank?

18. a. **Pumping milk** Suppose that the conical container in Example 5 contains milk (weighing 64.5 lb/ft^3) instead of olive oil. How much work will it take to pump the contents to the rim?

    b. **Pumping oil** How much work will it take to pump the oil in Example 5 to a level 3 ft above the cone's rim?

19. The graph of $y = x^2$ on $0 \leq x \leq 2$ is revolved about the y-axis to form a tank that is then filled with salt water from the Dead Sea (weighing approximately 73 lb/ft^3). How much work does it take to pump all of the water to the top of the tank?

20. A right-circular cylindrical tank of height 10 ft and radius 5 ft is lying horizontally and is full of diesel fuel weighing 53 lb/ft^3. How much work is required to pump all of the fuel to a point 15 ft above the top of the tank?

21. Emptying a water reservoir We model pumping from spherical containers the way we do from other containers, with the axis of integration along the vertical axis of the sphere. Use the figure here to find how much work it takes to empty a full hemispherical water reservoir of radius 5 m by pumping the water to a height of 4 m above the top of the reservoir. Water weighs 9800 N/m^3.

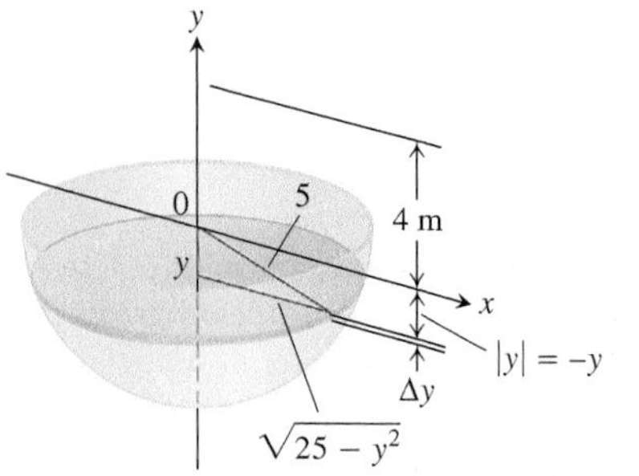

22. You are in charge of the evacuation and repair of the storage tank shown here. The tank is a hemisphere of radius 10 ft and is full of benzene weighing 56 lb/ft^3. A firm you contacted says it can empty the tank for 1/2¢ per foot-pound of work. Find the work required to empty the tank by pumping the benzene to an outlet 2 ft above the top of the tank. If you have \$5000 budgeted for the job, can you afford to hire the firm?

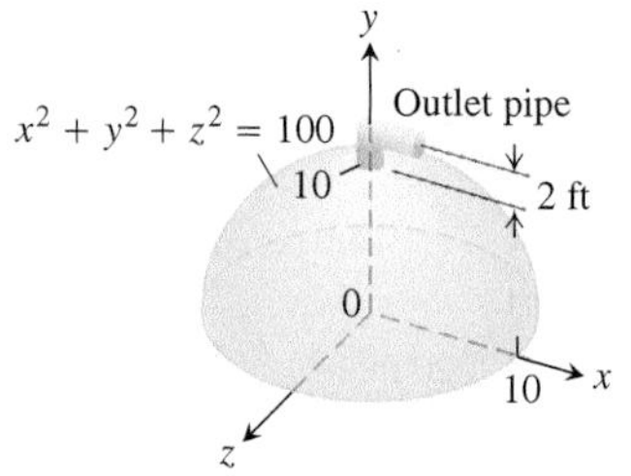

Work and Kinetic Energy

23. Kinetic energy If a variable force of magnitude $F(x)$ moves a body of mass m along the x-axis from x_1 to x_2, the body's velocity v can be written as dx/dt (where t represents time). Use Newton's second law of motion $F = m(dv/dt)$ and the Chain Rule

$$\frac{dv}{dt} = \frac{dv}{dx}\frac{dx}{dt} = v\frac{dv}{dx}$$

to show that the net work done by the force in moving the body from x_1 to x_2 is

$$W = \int_{x_1}^{x_2} F(x)\, dx = \frac{1}{2}m{v_2}^2 - \frac{1}{2}m{v_1}^2,$$

where v_1 and v_2 are the body's velocities at x_1 and x_2. In physics, the expression $(1/2)mv^2$ is called the *kinetic energy* of a body of mass m moving with velocity v. Therefore, *the work done by the force equals the change in the body's kinetic energy*, and we can find the work by calculating this change.

In Exercises 24–28, use the result of Exercise 23.

24. Tennis A 2-oz tennis ball was served at 160 ft/sec (about 109 mph). How much work was done on the ball to make it go this fast? (To find the ball's mass from its weight, express the weight in pounds and divide by 32 ft/sec^2, the acceleration of gravity.)

25. Baseball How many foot-pounds of work does it take to throw a baseball 90 mph? A baseball weighs 5 oz, or 0.3125 lb.

26. Golf A 1.6-oz golf ball is driven off the tee at a speed of 280 ft/sec (about 191 mph). How many foot-pounds of work are done on the ball getting it into the air?

27. On June 11, 2004, in a tennis match between Andy Roddick and Paradorn Srichaphan at the Stella Artois tournament in London, England, Roddick hit a serve measured at 153 mi/h. How much work was required by Andy to serve a 2-oz tennis ball at that speed?

28. Softball How much work has to be performed on a 6.5-oz softball to pitch it 132 ft/sec (90 mph)?

29. Drinking a milkshake The truncated conical container shown here is full of strawberry milkshake that weighs 4/9 oz/in^3. As you can see, the container is 7 in. deep, 2.5 in. across at the base, and 3.5 in. across at the top (a standard size at Brigham's in Boston). The straw sticks up an inch above the top. About how much work does it take to suck up the milkshake through the straw (neglecting friction)? Answer in inch-ounces.

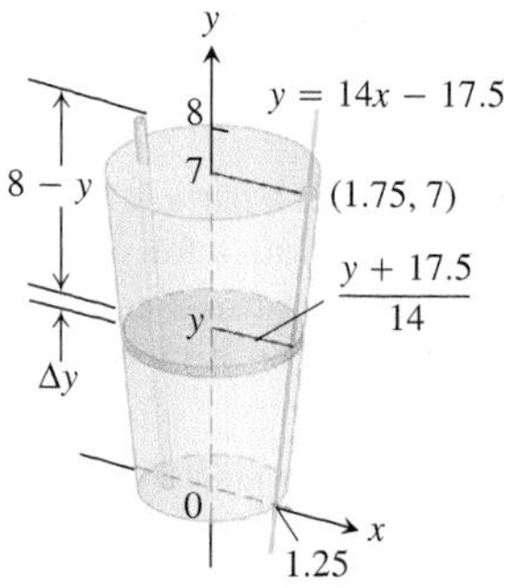

Dimensions in inches

30. Water tower Your town has decided to drill a well to increase its water supply. As the town engineer, you have determined that a water tower will be necessary to provide the pressure needed for distribution, and you have designed the system shown here. The water is to be pumped from a 300-ft well through a vertical 4-in. pipe into the base of a cylindrical tank 20 ft in diameter and 25 ft high. The base of the tank will be 60 ft above ground. The pump is a 3-hp pump, rated at 1650 ft · lb/sec. To the nearest hour, how long will it take to fill the tank the first time? (Include the time it takes to fill the pipe.) Assume that water weighs 62.4 lb/ft^3.

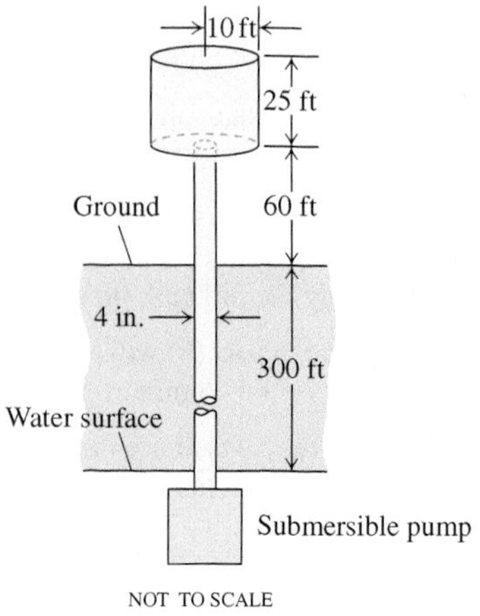

31. **Putting a satellite in orbit** The strength of Earth's gravitational field varies with the distance r from Earth's center, and the magnitude of the gravitational force experienced by a satellite of mass m during and after launch is

$$F(r) = \frac{mMG}{r^2}.$$

Here, $M = 5.975 \times 10^{24}$ kg is Earth's mass, $G = 6.6720 \times 10^{-11}\ \text{N} \cdot \text{m}^2\ \text{kg}^{-2}$ is the universal gravitational constant, and r is measured in meters. The work it takes to lift a 1000-kg satellite from Earth's surface to a circular orbit 35,780 km above Earth's center is therefore given by the integral

$$\text{Work} = \int_{6{,}370{,}000}^{35{,}780{,}000} \frac{1000MG}{r^2}\,dr \text{ joules}.$$

Evaluate the integral. The lower limit of integration is Earth's radius in meters at the launch site. (This calculation does not take into account energy spent lifting the launch vehicle or energy spent bringing the satellite to orbit velocity.)

32. **Forcing electrons together** Two electrons r meters apart repel each other with a force of

$$F = \frac{23 \times 10^{-29}}{r^2} \text{ newtons.}$$

a. Suppose one electron is held fixed at the point $(1, 0)$ on the x-axis (units in meters). How much work does it take to move a second electron along the x-axis from the point $(-1, 0)$ to the origin?

b. Suppose an electron is held fixed at each of the points $(-1, 0)$ and $(1, 0)$. How much work does it take to move a third electron along the x-axis from $(5, 0)$ to $(3, 0)$?

6.6 Moments and Centers of Mass

Many structures and mechanical systems behave as if their masses were concentrated at a single point, called the *center of mass* (Figure 6.40). It is important to know how to locate this point, and doing so is basically a mathematical enterprise. Here we consider masses distributed along a line or region in the plane. Masses distributed across a region or curve in three-dimensional space are treated in Chapters 14 and 15.

Masses Along a Line

We develop our mathematical model in stages. The first stage is to imagine masses m_1, m_2, and m_3 on a rigid x-axis supported by a fulcrum at the origin.

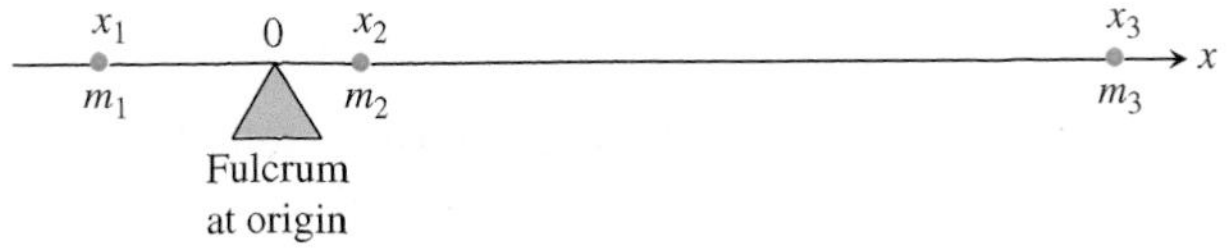

The resulting system might balance, or it might not, depending on how large the masses are and how they are arranged along the x-axis.

Each mass m_k exerts a downward force $m_k g$ (the weight of m_k) equal to the magnitude of the mass times the acceleration due to gravity. Note that gravitational acceleration is downward, hence negative. Each of these forces has a tendency to turn the x-axis about the origin, the way a child turns a seesaw. This turning effect, called a **torque**, is measured by multiplying the force $m_k g$ by the signed distance x_k from the point of application to the origin. By convention, a positive torque induces a counterclockwise turn. Masses to the left of the origin exert positive (counterclockwise) torque. Masses to the right of the origin exert negative (clockwise) torque.

The sum of the torques measures the tendency of a system to rotate about the origin. This sum is called the **system torque**.

$$\text{System torque} = m_1 g x_1 + m_2 g x_2 + m_3 g x_3 \tag{1}$$

The system will balance if and only if its torque is zero.

FIGURE 6.40 A wrench gliding on ice turning about its center of mass as the center glides in a vertical line.

If we factor out the g in Equation (1), we see that the system torque is

$$\underbrace{g}_{\text{a feature of the environment}} \cdot \underbrace{(m_1x_1 + m_2x_2 + m_3x_3)}_{\text{a feature of the system}}.$$

Thus, the torque is the product of the gravitational acceleration g, which is a feature of the environment in which the system happens to reside, and the number $(m_1x_1 + m_2x_2 + m_3x_3)$, which is a feature of the system itself, a constant that stays the same no matter where the system is placed.

The number $(m_1x_1 + m_2x_2 + m_3x_3)$ is called the **moment of the system about the origin**. It is the sum of the **moments** m_1x_1, m_2x_2, m_3x_3 of the individual masses.

$$M_0 = \text{Moment of system about origin} = \sum m_kx_k$$

(We shift to sigma notation here to allow for sums with more terms.)

We usually want to know where to place the fulcrum to make the system balance, that is, at what point $\bar{x}$ to place it to make the torques add to zero.

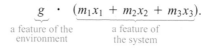

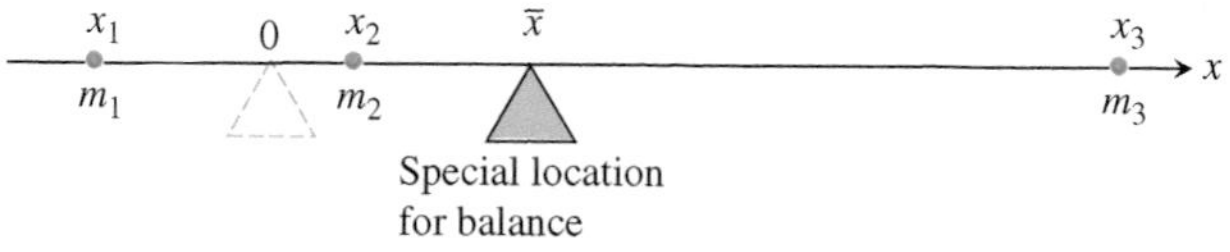

The torque of each mass about the fulcrum in this special location is

$$\begin{aligned}\text{Torque of } m_k \text{ about } \bar{x} &= \begin{pmatrix}\text{signed distance}\\ \text{of } m_k \text{ from } \bar{x}\end{pmatrix}\begin{pmatrix}\text{downward}\\ \text{force}\end{pmatrix}\\ &= (x_k - \bar{x})m_kg.\end{aligned}$$

When we write the equation that says that the sum of these torques is zero, we get an equation we can solve for $\bar{x}$:

$$\sum (x_k - \bar{x})m_kg = 0 \qquad \text{Sum of the torques equals zero.}$$

$$\bar{x} = \frac{\sum m_kx_k}{\sum m_k}. \qquad \text{Solved for } \bar{x}$$

This last equation tells us to find $\bar{x}$ by dividing the system's moment about the origin by the system's total mass:

$$\bar{x} = \frac{\sum m_kx_k}{\sum m_k} = \frac{\text{system moment about origin}}{\text{system mass}}. \tag{2}$$

The point $\bar{x}$ is called the system's **center of mass**.

Masses Distributed over a Plane Region

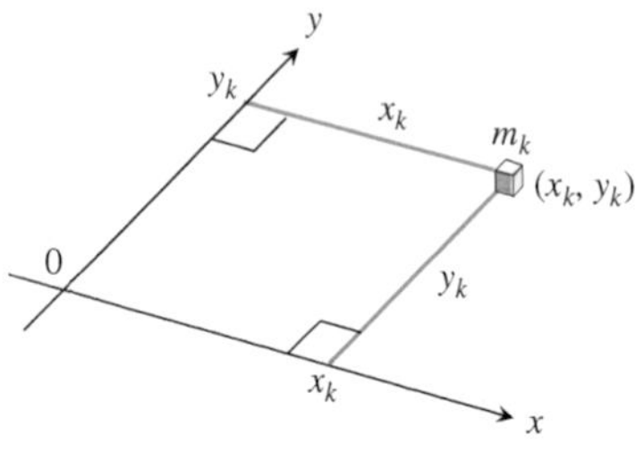

FIGURE 6.41 Each mass m_k has a moment about each axis.

Suppose that we have a finite collection of masses located in the plane, with mass m_k at the point (x_k, y_k) (see Figure 6.41). The mass of the system is

$$\text{System mass:} \quad M = \sum m_k.$$

Each mass m_k has a moment about each axis. Its moment about the x-axis is m_ky_k, and its moment about the y-axis is m_kx_k. The moments of the entire system about the two axes are

$$\text{Moment about } x\text{-axis:} \quad M_x = \sum m_ky_k,$$

$$\text{Moment about } y\text{-axis:} \quad M_y = \sum m_kx_k.$$

The x-coordinate of the system's center of mass is defined to be

$$\bar{x} = \frac{M_y}{M} = \frac{\sum m_k x_k}{\sum m_k}. \tag{3}$$

With this choice of $\bar{x}$, as in the one-dimensional case, the system balances about the line $x = \bar{x}$ (Figure 6.42).

The y-coordinate of the system's center of mass is defined to be

$$\bar{y} = \frac{M_x}{M} = \frac{\sum m_k y_k}{\sum m_k}. \tag{4}$$

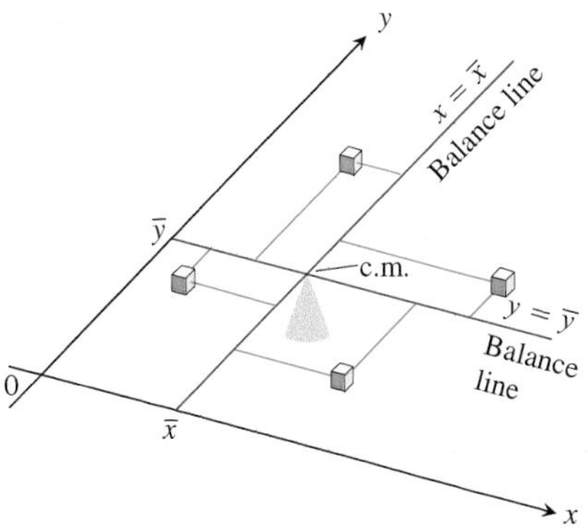

FIGURE 6.42 A two-dimensional array of masses balances on its center of mass.

With this choice of $\bar{y}$, the system balances about the line $y = \bar{y}$ as well. The torques exerted by the masses about the line $y = \bar{y}$ cancel out. Thus, as far as balance is concerned, the system behaves as if all its mass were at the single point $(\bar{x}, \bar{y})$. We call this point the system's **center of mass.**

Thin, Flat Plates

In many applications, we need to find the center of mass of a thin, flat plate: a disk of aluminum, say, or a triangular sheet of steel. In such cases, we assume the distribution of mass to be continuous, and the formulas we use to calculate $\bar{x}$ and $\bar{y}$ contain integrals instead of finite sums. The integrals arise in the following way.

Imagine that the plate occupying a region in the xy-plane is cut into thin strips parallel to one of the axes (in Figure 6.43, the y-axis). The center of mass of a typical strip is $(\tilde{x}, \tilde{y})$. We treat the strip's mass Δm as if it were concentrated at $(\tilde{x}, \tilde{y})$. The moment of the strip about the y-axis is then $\tilde{x}\,\Delta m$. The moment of the strip about the x-axis is $\tilde{y}\,\Delta m$. Equations (3) and (4) then become

$$\bar{x} = \frac{M_y}{M} = \frac{\sum \tilde{x}\,\Delta m}{\sum \Delta m}, \qquad \bar{y} = \frac{M_x}{M} = \frac{\sum \tilde{y}\,\Delta m}{\sum \Delta m}.$$

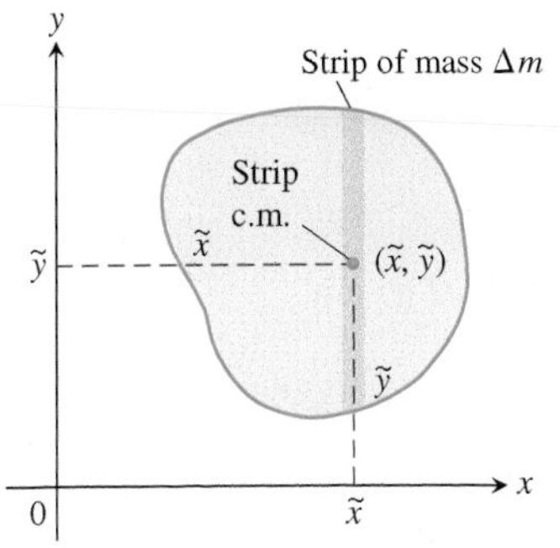

FIGURE 6.43 A plate cut into thin strips parallel to the y-axis. The moment exerted by a typical strip about each axis is the moment its mass Δm would exert if concentrated at the strip's center of mass $(\tilde{x}, \tilde{y})$.

The sums are Riemann sums for integrals and approach these integrals as limiting values as the strips into which the plate is cut become narrower and narrower. We write these integrals symbolically as

$$\bar{x} = \frac{\int \tilde{x}\,dm}{\int dm} \quad \text{and} \quad \bar{y} = \frac{\int \tilde{y}\,dm}{\int dm}.$$

Moments, Mass, and Center of Mass of a Thin Plate Covering a Region in the xy-Plane

$$\begin{aligned}
&\text{Moment about the } x\text{-axis:} && M_x = \int \tilde{y}\,dm \\
&\text{Moment about the } y\text{-axis:} && M_y = \int \tilde{x}\,dm \\
&\text{Mass:} && M = \int dm \\
&\text{Center of mass:} && \bar{x} = \frac{M_y}{M}, \quad \bar{y} = \frac{M_x}{M}
\end{aligned} \tag{5}$$

Density
A material's density is its mass per unit area. For wires, rods, and narrow strips, we use mass per unit length.

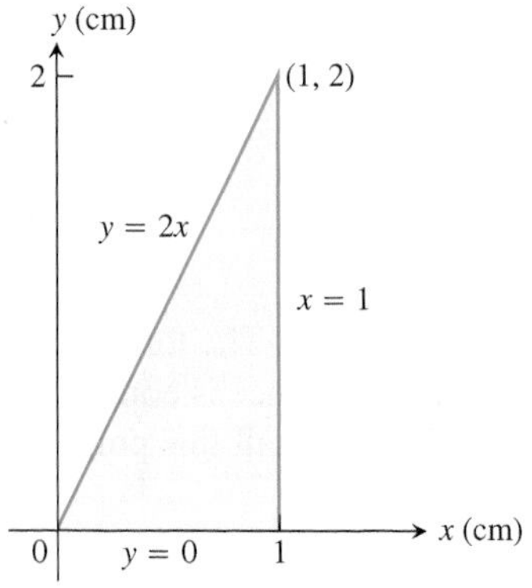

FIGURE 6.44 The plate in Example 1.

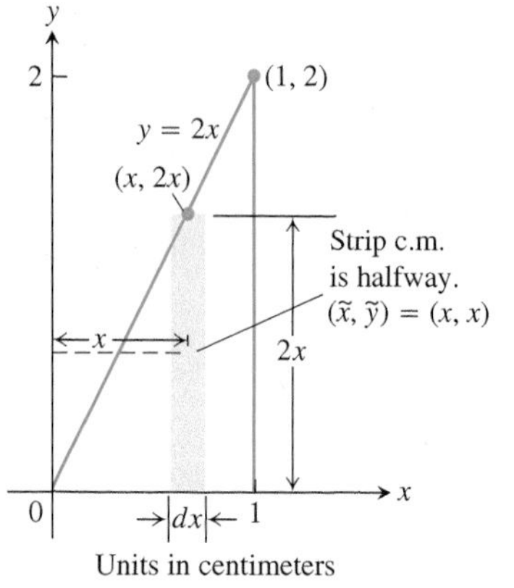

FIGURE 6.45 Modeling the plate in Example 1 with vertical strips.

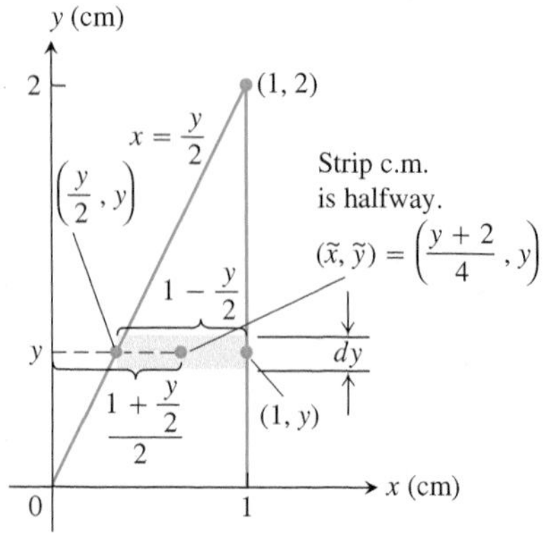

FIGURE 6.46 Modeling the plate in Example 1 with horizontal strips.

The differential dm is the mass of the strip. Assuming the density δ of the plate to be a continuous function, the mass differential dm equals the product $\delta\, dA$ (mass per unit area times area). Here dA represents the area of the strip.

To evaluate the integrals in Equations (5), we picture the plate in the coordinate plane and sketch a strip of mass parallel to one of the coordinate axes. We then express the strip's mass dm and the coordinates $(\tilde{x}, \tilde{y})$ of the strip's center of mass in terms of x or y. Finally, we integrate $\tilde{y}\, dm$, $\tilde{x}\, dm$, and dm between limits of integration determined by the plate's location in the plane.

EXAMPLE 1 The triangular plate shown in Figure 6.44 has a constant density of $\delta = 3\text{ g/cm}^2$. Find

(a) the plate's moment M_y about the y-axis. **(b)** the plate's mass M.

(c) the x-coordinate of the plate's center of mass (c.m.).

Solution **Method 1: Vertical Strips** (Figure 6.45)

(a) The moment M_y: The typical vertical strip has the following relevant data.

center of mass (c.m.):	$(\tilde{x}, \tilde{y}) = (x, x)$
length:	$2x$
width:	dx
area:	$dA = 2x\, dx$
mass:	$dm = \delta\, dA = 3 \cdot 2x\, dx = 6x\, dx$
distance of c.m. from y-axis:	$\tilde{x} = x$

The moment of the strip about the y-axis is

$$\tilde{x}\, dm = x \cdot 6x\, dx = 6x^2\, dx.$$

The moment of the plate about the y-axis is therefore

$$M_y = \int \tilde{x}\, dm = \int_0^1 6x^2\, dx = 2x^3\Big]_0^1 = 2\text{ g}\cdot\text{cm}.$$

(b) The plate's mass:

$$M = \int dm = \int_0^1 6x\, dx = 3x^2\Big]_0^1 = 3\text{ g}.$$

(c) The x-coordinate of the plate's center of mass:

$$\bar{x} = \frac{M_y}{M} = \frac{2\text{ g}\cdot\text{cm}}{3\text{ g}} = \frac{2}{3}\text{ cm}.$$

By a similar computation, we could find M_x and $\bar{y} = M_x/M$.

Method 2: Horizontal Strips (Figure 6.46)

(a) The moment M_y: The y-coordinate of the center of mass of a typical horizontal strip is y (see the figure), so

$$\tilde{y} = y.$$

The x-coordinate is the x-coordinate of the point halfway across the triangle. This makes it the average of $y/2$ (the strip's left-hand x-value) and 1 (the strip's right-hand x-value):

$$\tilde{x} = \frac{(y/2) + 1}{2} = \frac{y}{4} + \frac{1}{2} = \frac{y+2}{4}.$$

We also have

$$\text{length: } 1 - \frac{y}{2} = \frac{2-y}{2}$$
$$\text{width: } dy$$
$$\text{area: } dA = \frac{2-y}{2}\,dy$$
$$\text{mass: } dm = \delta\,dA = 3\cdot\frac{2-y}{2}\,dy$$
$$\text{distance of c.m. to } y\text{-axis: } \tilde{x} = \frac{y+2}{4}.$$

The moment of the strip about the y-axis is

$$\tilde{x}\,dm = \frac{y+2}{4}\cdot 3\cdot\frac{2-y}{2}\,dy = \frac{3}{8}(4-y^2)\,dy.$$

The moment of the plate about the y-axis is

$$M_y = \int \tilde{x}\,dm = \int_0^2 \frac{3}{8}(4-y^2)\,dy = \frac{3}{8}\left[4y - \frac{y^3}{3}\right]_0^2 = \frac{3}{8}\left(\frac{16}{3}\right) = 2\text{ g}\cdot\text{cm}.$$

(b) The plate's mass:

$$M = \int dm = \int_0^2 \frac{3}{2}(2-y)\,dy = \frac{3}{2}\left[2y - \frac{y^2}{2}\right]_0^2 = \frac{3}{2}(4-2) = 3\text{ g}.$$

(c) The x-coordinate of the plate's center of mass:

$$\bar{x} = \frac{M_y}{M} = \frac{2\text{ g}\cdot\text{cm}}{3\text{ g}} = \frac{2}{3}\text{ cm}.$$

By a similar computation, we could find M_x and $\bar{y}$. ■

If the distribution of mass in a thin, flat plate has an axis of symmetry, the center of mass will lie on this axis. If there are two axes of symmetry, the center of mass will lie at their intersection. These facts often help to simplify our work.

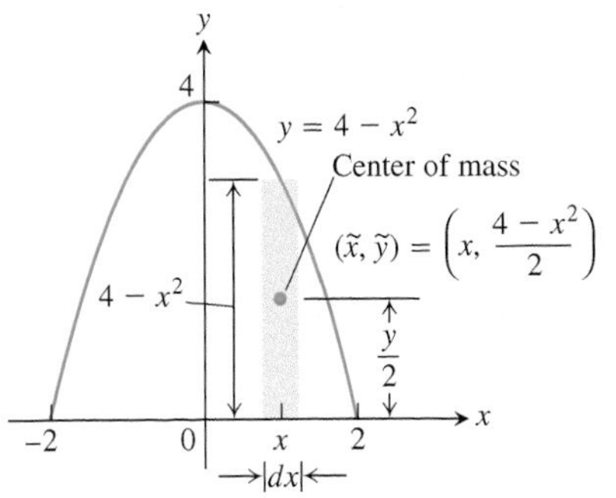

FIGURE 6.47 Modeling the plate in Example 2 with vertical strips.

EXAMPLE 2 Find the center of mass of a thin plate covering the region bounded above by the parabola $y = 4 - x^2$ and below by the x-axis (Figure 6.47). Assume the density of the plate at the point (x, y) is $\delta = 2x^2$, which is twice the square of the distance from the point to the y-axis.

Solution The mass distribution is symmetric about the y-axis, so $\bar{x} = 0$. We model the distribution of mass with vertical strips since the density is given as a function of the variable x. The typical vertical strip (see Figure 6.47) has the following relevant data.

$$\text{center of mass (c.m.): } (\tilde{x}, \tilde{y}) = \left(x, \frac{4-x^2}{2}\right)$$
$$\text{length: } 4 - x^2$$
$$\text{width: } dx$$
$$\text{area: } dA = (4-x^2)\,dx$$
$$\text{mass: } dm = \delta\,dA = \delta(4-x^2)\,dx$$
$$\text{distance from c.m. to } x\text{-axis: } \tilde{y} = \frac{4-x^2}{2}$$

The moment of the strip about the x-axis is

$$\tilde{y}\,dm = \frac{4-x^2}{2}\cdot\delta(4-x^2)\,dx = \frac{\delta}{2}(4-x^2)^2\,dx.$$

The moment of the plate about the x-axis is

$$M_x = \int \tilde{y}\, dm = \int_{-2}^{2} \frac{\delta}{2}(4 - x^2)^2\, dx = \int_{-2}^{2} x^2(4 - x^2)^2\, dx$$
$$= \int_{-2}^{2} (16x^2 - 8x^4 + x^6)\, dx = \frac{2048}{105}$$
$$M = \int dm = \int_{-2}^{2} \delta(4 - x^2)\, dx = \int_{-2}^{2} 2x^2(4 - x^2)\, dx$$
$$= \int_{-2}^{2} (8x^2 - 2x^4)\, dx = \frac{256}{15}.$$

Therefore,

$$\bar{y} = \frac{M_x}{M} = \frac{2048}{105} \cdot \frac{15}{256} = \frac{8}{7}.$$

The plate's center of mass is

$$(\bar{x}, \bar{y}) = \left(0, \frac{8}{7}\right).$$

■

Plates Bounded by Two Curves

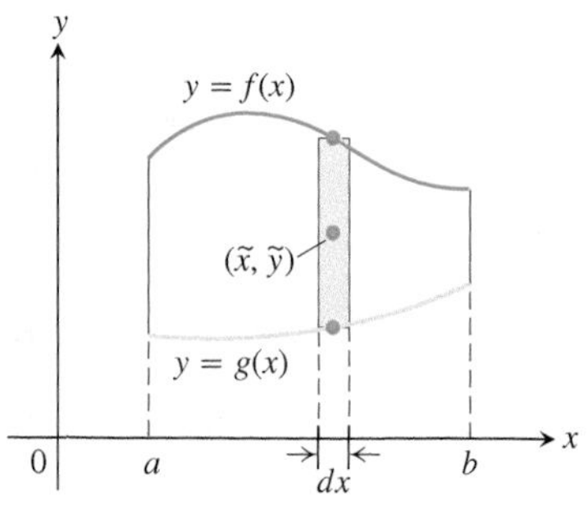

FIGURE 6.48 Modeling the plate bounded by two curves with vertical strips. The strip c.m. is halfway, so $\tilde{y} = \frac{1}{2}[f(x) + g(x)]$.

Suppose a plate covers a region that lies between two curves $y = g(x)$ and $y = f(x)$, where $f(x) \geq g(x)$ and $a \leq x \leq b$. The typical vertical strip (see Figure 6.48) has

center of mass (c.m.): $(\tilde{x}, \tilde{y}) = (x, \frac{1}{2}[f(x) + g(x)])$
length: $f(x) - g(x)$
width: dx
area: $dA = [f(x) - g(x)]\, dx$
mass: $dm = \delta\, dA = \delta[f(x) - g(x)]\, dx.$

The moment of the plate about the y-axis is

$$M_y = \int x\, dm = \int_a^b x\delta[f(x) - g(x)]\, dx,$$

and the moment about the x-axis is

$$M_x = \int y\, dm = \int_a^b \frac{1}{2}[f(x) + g(x)] \cdot \delta[f(x) - g(x)]\, dx$$
$$= \int_a^b \frac{\delta}{2}[f^2(x) - g^2(x)]\, dx.$$

These moments give the formulas

$$\bar{x} = \frac{1}{M}\int_a^b \delta x\,[f(x) - g(x)]\, dx \qquad (6)$$

$$\bar{y} = \frac{1}{M}\int_a^b \frac{\delta}{2}[f^2(x) - g^2(x)]\, dx \qquad (7)$$

EXAMPLE 3 Find the center of mass for the thin plate bounded by the curves $g(x) = x/2$ and $f(x) = \sqrt{x}$, $0 \le x \le 1$, (Figure 6.49) using Equations (6) and (7) with the density function $\delta(x) = x^2$.

Solution We first compute the mass of the plate, where $dm = \delta[f(x) - g(x)]\,dx$:

$$M = \int_0^1 x^2\left(\sqrt{x} - \frac{x}{2}\right)dx = \int_0^1 \left(x^{5/2} - \frac{x^3}{2}\right)dx = \left[\frac{2}{7}x^{7/2} - \frac{1}{8}x^4\right]_0^1 = \frac{9}{56}.$$

Then from Equations (6) and (7) we get

$$\bar{x} = \frac{56}{9}\int_0^1 x^2 \cdot x\left(\sqrt{x} - \frac{x}{2}\right)dx$$
$$= \frac{56}{9}\int_0^1 \left(x^{7/2} - \frac{x^4}{2}\right)dx$$
$$= \frac{56}{9}\left[\frac{2}{9}x^{9/2} - \frac{1}{10}x^5\right]_0^1 = \frac{308}{405},$$

and

$$\bar{y} = \frac{56}{9}\int_0^1 \frac{x^2}{2}\left(x - \frac{x^2}{4}\right)dx$$
$$= \frac{28}{9}\int_0^1 \left(x^3 - \frac{x^4}{4}\right)dx$$
$$= \frac{28}{9}\left[\frac{1}{4}x^4 - \frac{1}{20}x^5\right]_0^1 = \frac{252}{405}.$$

The center of mass is shown in Figure 6.49. ■

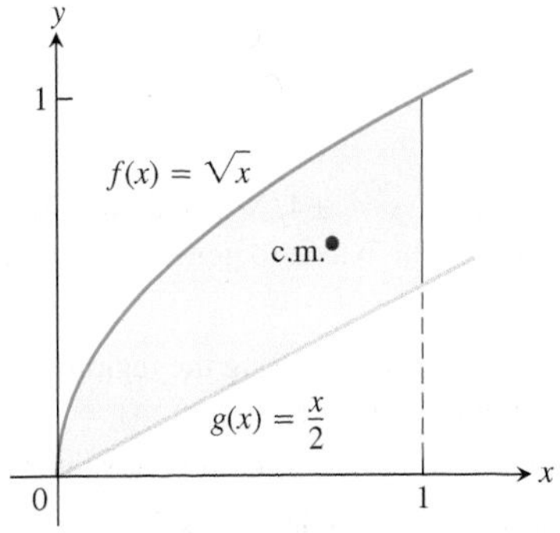

FIGURE 6.49 The region in Example 3.

Centroids

The center of mass in Example 3 is not located at the geometric center of the region. This is due to the region's non-uniform density. When the density function is constant, it cancels out of the numerator and denominator of the formulas for $\bar{x}$ and $\bar{y}$. Thus, when the density is constant, the location of the center of mass is a feature of the geometry of the object and not of the material from which it is made. In such cases, engineers may call the center of mass the **centroid** of the shape, as in "Find the centroid of a triangle or a solid cone." To do so, just set δ equal to 1 and proceed to find $\bar{x}$ and $\bar{y}$ as before, by dividing moments by masses.

EXAMPLE 4 Find the center of mass (centroid) of a thin wire of constant density δ shaped like a semicircle of radius a.

Solution We model the wire with the semicircle $y = \sqrt{a^2 - x^2}$ (Figure 6.50). The distribution of mass is symmetric about the y-axis, so $\bar{x} = 0$. To find $\bar{y}$, we imagine the wire divided into short subarc segments. If $(\tilde{x}, \tilde{y})$ is the center of mass of a subarc and θ is the angle between the x-axis and the radial line joining the origin to $(\tilde{x}, \tilde{y})$, then $\tilde{y} = a \sin\theta$ is a function of the angle θ measured in radians (see Figure 6.50a). The length ds of the subarc containing $(\tilde{x}, \tilde{y})$ subtends an angle of $d\theta$ radians, so $ds = a\,d\theta$. Thus a typical subarc segment has these relevant data for calculating $\bar{y}$:

length:	$ds = a\,d\theta$	
mass:	$dm = \delta\,ds = \delta a\,d\theta$	Mass per unit length times length
distance of c.m. to x-axis:	$\tilde{y} = a\sin\theta.$	

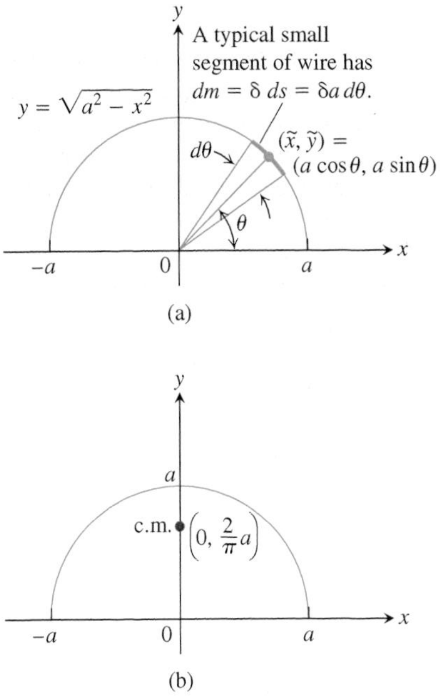

FIGURE 6.50 The semicircular wire in Example 4. (a) The dimensions and variables used in finding the center of mass. (b) The center of mass does not lie on the wire.

Hence,

$$\bar{y} = \frac{\int \tilde{y}\, dm}{\int dm} = \frac{\int_0^{\pi} a \sin\theta \cdot \delta a\, d\theta}{\int_0^{\pi} \delta a\, d\theta} = \frac{\delta a^2\big[-\cos\theta\big]_0^{\pi}}{\delta a \pi} = \frac{2}{\pi} a.$$

The center of mass lies on the axis of symmetry at the point $(0, 2a/\pi)$, about two-thirds of the way up from the origin (Figure 6.50b). Notice how δ cancels in the equation for $\bar{y}$, so we could have set $\delta = 1$ everywhere and obtained the same value for $\bar{y}$. ■

In Example 4 we found the center of mass of a thin wire lying along the graph of a differentiable function in the xy-plane. In Chapter 15 we will learn how to find the center of mass of wires lying along more general smooth curves in the plane (or in space).

Exercises 6.6

Thin Plates with Constant Density

In Exercises 1–14, find the center of mass of a thin plate of constant density δ covering the given region.

1. The region bounded by the parabola $y = x^2$ and the line $y = 4$
2. The region bounded by the parabola $y = 25 - x^2$ and the x-axis
3. The region bounded by the parabola $y = x - x^2$ and the line $y = -x$
4. The region enclosed by the parabolas $y = x^2 - 3$ and $y = -2x^2$
5. The region bounded by the y-axis and the curve $x = y - y^3$, $0 \le y \le 1$
6. The region bounded by the parabola $x = y^2 - y$ and the line $y = x$
7. The region bounded by the x-axis and the curve $y = \cos x$, $-\pi/2 \le x \le \pi/2$
8. The region between the curve $y = \sec^2 x$, $-\pi/4 \le x \le \pi/4$ and the x-axis
9. T The region between the curve $y = 1/x$ and the x-axis from $x = 1$ to $x = 2$. Give the coordinates to two decimal places.
10. **a.** The region cut from the first quadrant by the circle $x^2 + y^2 = 9$
    b. The region bounded by the x-axis and the semicircle $y = \sqrt{9 - x^2}$
    Compare your answer in part (b) with the answer in part (a).
11. The region in the first and fourth quadrants enclosed by the curves $y = 1/(1 + x^2)$ and $y = -1/(1 + x^2)$ and by the lines $x = 0$ and $x = 1$
12. The region bounded by the parabolas $y = 2x^2 - 4x$ and $y = 2x - x^2$
13. The region between the curve $y = 1/\sqrt{x}$ and the x-axis from $x = 1$ to $x = 16$
14. The region bounded above by the curve $y = 1/x^3$, below by the curve $y = -1/x^3$, and on the left and right by the lines $x = 1$ and $x = a > 1$. Also, find $\lim_{a\to\infty} \bar{x}$.

Thin Plates with Varying Density

15. Find the center of mass of a thin plate covering the region between the x-axis and the curve $y = 2/x^2$, $1 \le x \le 2$, if the plate's density at the point (x, y) is $\delta(x) = x^2$.
16. Find the center of mass of a thin plate covering the region bounded below by the parabola $y = x^2$ and above by the line $y = x$ if the plate's density at the point (x, y) is $\delta(x) = 12x$.
17. The region bounded by the curves $y = \pm 4/\sqrt{x}$ and the lines $x = 1$ and $x = 4$ is revolved about the y-axis to generate a solid.
    a. Find the volume of the solid.
    b. Find the center of mass of a thin plate covering the region if the plate's density at the point (x, y) is $\delta(x) = 1/x$.
    c. Sketch the plate and show the center of mass in your sketch.
18. The region between the curve $y = 2/x$ and the x-axis from $x = 1$ to $x = 4$ is revolved about the x-axis to generate a solid.
    a. Find the volume of the solid.
    b. Find the center of mass of a thin plate covering the region if the plate's density at the point (x, y) is $\delta(x) = \sqrt{x}$.
    c. Sketch the plate and show the center of mass in your sketch.

Centroids of Triangles

19. **The centroid of a triangle lies at the intersection of the triangle's medians** You may recall that the point inside a triangle that lies one-third of the way from each side toward the opposite vertex is the point where the triangle's three medians intersect. Show that the centroid lies at the intersection of the medians by showing that it too lies one-third of the way from each side toward the opposite vertex. To do so, take the following steps.
    i) Stand one side of the triangle on the x-axis as in part (b) of the accompanying figure. Express dm in terms of L and dy.
    ii) Use similar triangles to show that $L = (b/h)(h - y)$. Substitute this expression for L in your formula for dm.
    iii) Show that $\bar{y} = h/3$.
    iv) Extend the argument to the other sides.

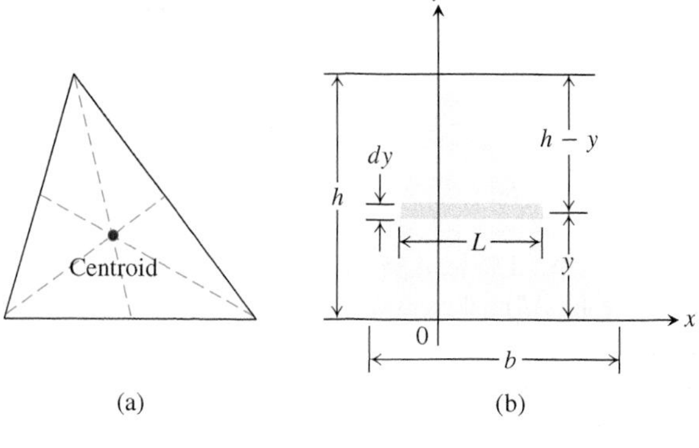

Use the result in Exercise 19 to find the centroids of the triangles whose vertices appear in Exercises 20–24. Assume $a, b > 0$.

20. $(-1, 0), (1, 0), (0, 3)$

21. $(0, 0), (1, 0), (0, 1)$

22. $(0, 0), (a, 0), (0, a)$

23. $(0, 0), (a, 0), (0, b)$

24. $(0, 0), (a, 0), (a/2, b)$

Thin Wires

25. Constant density Find the moment about the x-axis of a wire of constant density that lies along the curve $y = \sqrt{x}$ from $x = 0$ to $x = 2$.

26. Constant density Find the moment about the x-axis of a wire of constant density that lies along the curve $y = x^3$ from $x = 0$ to $x = 1$.

27. Variable density Suppose that the density of the wire in Example 4 is $\delta = k \sin \theta$ (k constant). Find the center of mass.

28. Variable density Suppose that the density of the wire in Example 4 is $\delta = 1 + k|\cos \theta|$ (k constant). Find the center of mass.

Plates Bounded by Two Curves

In Exercises 29–32, find the centroid of the thin plate bounded by the graphs of the given functions. Use Equations (6) and (7) with $\delta = 1$ and M = area of the region covered by the plate.

29. $g(x) = x^2$ and $f(x) = x + 6$

30. $g(x) = x^2(x + 1)$, $f(x) = 2$, and $x = 0$

31. $g(x) = x^2(x - 1)$ and $f(x) = x^2$

32. $g(x) = 0$, $f(x) = 2 + \sin x$, $x = 0$, and $x = 2\pi$

(*Hint:* $\int x \sin x \, dx = \sin x - x \cos x + C$.)

Theory and Examples

Verify the statements and formulas in Exercises 33 and 34.

33. The coordinates of the centroid of a differentiable plane curve are

$$\bar{x} = \frac{\int x \, ds}{\text{length}}, \qquad \bar{y} = \frac{\int y \, ds}{\text{length}}.$$

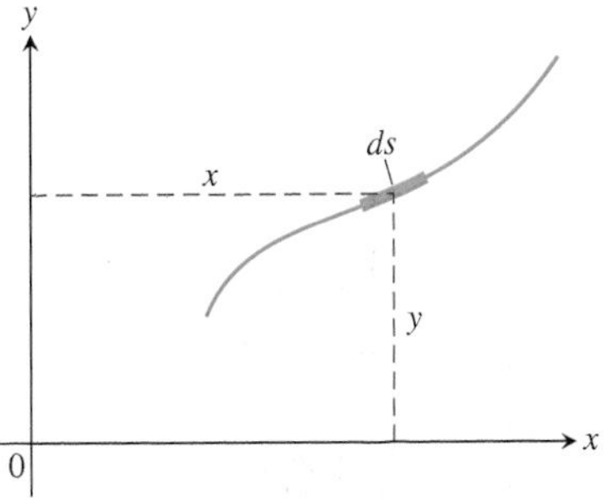

34. Whatever the value of $p > 0$ in the equation $y = x^2/(4p)$, the y-coordinate of the centroid of the parabolic segment shown here is $\bar{y} = (3/5)a$.

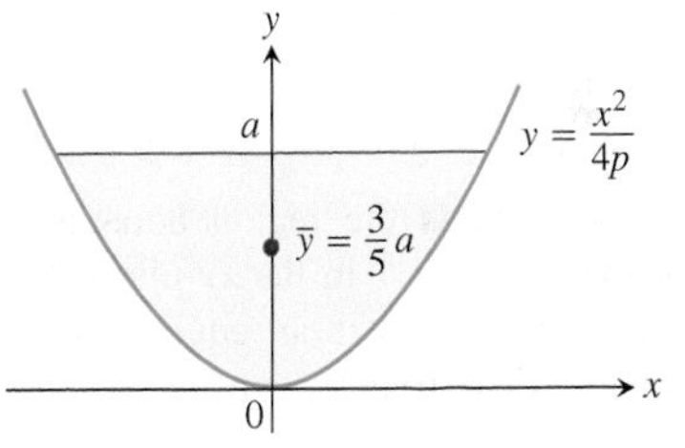

Chapter 6 Questions to Guide Your Review

1. How do you define and calculate the volumes of solids by the method of slicing? Give an example.
2. How are the disk and washer methods for calculating volumes derived from the method of slicing? Give examples of volume calculations by these methods.
3. Describe the method of cylindrical shells. Give an example.
4. How do you find the length of the graph of a smooth function over a closed interval?. Give an example. What about functions that do not have continuous first derivatives?
5. How do you define and calculate the area of the surface swept out by revolving the graph of a smooth function $y = f(x)$, $a \le x \le b$, about the x-axis? Give an example.
6. How do you define and calculate the work done by a variable force directed along a portion of the x-axis? How do you calculate the work it takes to pump a liquid from a tank? Give examples.
7. How do you calculate the force exerted by a liquid against a portion of a flat vertical wall? Give an example.
8. What is a center of mass? a centroid?
9. How do you locate the center of mass of a thin flat plate of material? Give an example.
10. How do you locate the center of mass of a thin plate bounded by two curves $y = f(x)$ and $y = g(x)$ over $a \le x \le b$?

Chapter 6 Practice Exercises

Volumes

Find the volumes of the solids in Exercises 1–16.

1. The solid lies between planes perpendicular to the x-axis at $x = 0$ and $x = 1$. The cross-sections perpendicular to the x-axis between these planes are circular disks whose diameters run from the parabola $y = x^2$ to the parabola $y = \sqrt{x}$.

2. The base of the solid is the region in the first quadrant between the line $y = x$ and the parabola $y = 2\sqrt{x}$. The cross-sections of the solid perpendicular to the x-axis are equilateral triangles whose bases stretch from the line to the curve.

3. The solid lies between planes perpendicular to the x-axis at $x = \pi/4$ and $x = 5\pi/4$. The cross-sections between these planes are circular disks whose diameters run from the curve $y = 2\cos x$ to the curve $y = 2\sin x$.

4. The solid lies between planes perpendicular to the x-axis at $x = 0$ and $x = 6$. The cross-sections between these planes are squares whose bases run from the x-axis up to the curve $x^{1/2} + y^{1/2} = \sqrt{6}$.

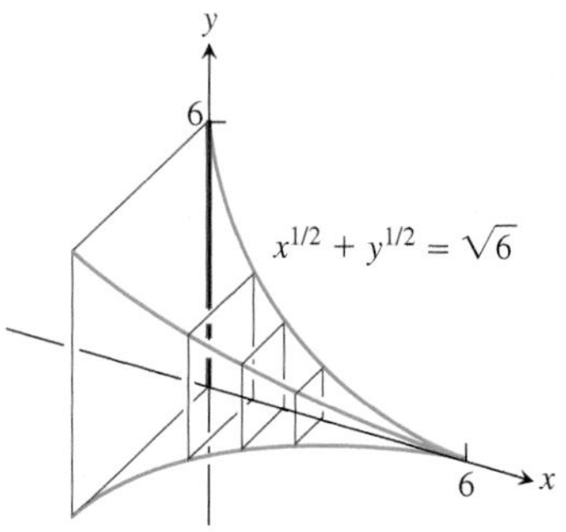

5. The solid lies between planes perpendicular to the x-axis at $x = 0$ and $x = 4$. The cross-sections of the solid perpendicular to the x-axis between these planes are circular disks whose diameters run from the curve $x^2 = 4y$ to the curve $y^2 = 4x$.

6. The base of the solid is the region bounded by the parabola $y^2 = 4x$ and the line $x = 1$ in the xy-plane. Each cross-section perpendicular to the x-axis is an equilateral triangle with one edge in the plane. (The triangles all lie on the same side of the plane.)

7. Find the volume of the solid generated by revolving the region bounded by the x-axis, the curve $y = 3x^4$, and the lines $x = 1$ and $x = -1$ about **(a)** the x-axis; **(b)** the y-axis; **(c)** the line $x = 1$; **(d)** the line $y = 3$.

8. Find the volume of the solid generated by revolving the "triangular" region bounded by the curve $y = 4/x^3$ and the lines $x = 1$ and $y = 1/2$ about **(a)** the x-axis; **(b)** the y-axis; **(c)** the line $x = 2$; **(d)** the line $y = 4$.

9. Find the volume of the solid generated by revolving the region bounded on the left by the parabola $x = y^2 + 1$ and on the right by the line $x = 5$ about **(a)** the x-axis; **(b)** the y-axis; **(c)** the line $x = 5$.

10. Find the volume of the solid generated by revolving the region bounded by the parabola $y^2 = 4x$ and the line $y = x$ about **(a)** the x-axis; **(b)** the y-axis; **(c)** the line $x = 4$; **(d)** the line $y = 4$.

11. Find the volume of the solid generated by revolving the "triangular" region bounded by the x-axis, the line $x = \pi/3$, and the curve $y = \tan x$ in the first quadrant about the x-axis.

12. Find the volume of the solid generated by revolving the region bounded by the curve $y = \sin x$ and the lines $x = 0$, $x = \pi$, and $y = 2$ about the line $y = 2$.

13. Find the volume of the solid generated by revolving the region bounded by the curve $x = e^{y^2}$ and the lines $y = 0$, $x = 0$, and $y = 1$ about the x-axis.

14. Find the volume of the solid generated by revolving about the x-axis the region bounded by $y = 2\tan x$, $y = 0$, $x = -\pi/4$, and $x = \pi/4$. (The region lies in the first and third quadrants and resembles a skewed bowtie.)

15. Volume of a solid sphere hole A round hole of radius $\sqrt{3}$ ft is bored through the center of a solid sphere of a radius 2 ft. Find the volume of material removed from the sphere.

16. Volume of a football The profile of a football resembles the ellipse shown here. Find the football's volume to the nearest cubic inch.

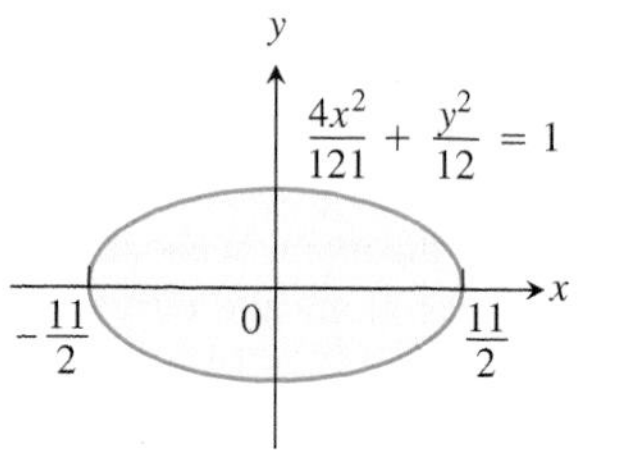

Lengths of Curves

Find the lengths of the curves in Exercises 17–20.

17. $y = x^{1/2} - (1/3)x^{3/2}, \quad 1 \le x \le 4$

18. $x = y^{2/3}, \quad 1 \le y \le 8$

19. $y = x^2 - (\ln x)/8, \quad 1 \le x \le 2$

20. $x = (y^3/12) + (1/y), \quad 1 \le y \le 2$

Areas of Surfaces of Revolution

In Exercises 21–24, find the areas of the surfaces generated by revolving the curves about the given axes.

21. $y = \sqrt{2x + 1}, \quad 0 \le x \le 3;$ x-axis

22. $y = x^3/3, \quad 0 \le x \le 1;$ x-axis

23. $x = \sqrt{4y - y^2}, \quad 1 \le y \le 2;$ y-axis

24. $x = \sqrt{y}, \quad 2 \le y \le 6;$ y-axis

Work

25. Lifting equipment A rock climber is about to haul up 100 N (about 22.5 lb) of equipment that has been hanging beneath her on 40 m of rope that weighs 0.8 newton per meter. How much work will it take? (*Hint:* Solve for the rope and equipment separately, then add.)

26. Leaky tank truck You drove an 800-gal tank truck of water from the base of Mt. Washington to the summit and discovered on arrival that the tank was only half full. You started with a full tank, climbed at a steady rate, and accomplished the 4750-ft elevation change in 50 min. Assuming that the water leaked out at a steady rate, how much work was spent in carrying water to the top? Do not count the work done in getting yourself and the truck there. Water weighs 8 lb/U.S. gal.

27. Stretching a spring If a force of 20 lb is required to hold a spring 1 ft beyond its unstressed length, how much work does it take to stretch the spring this far? An additional foot?

28. Garage door spring A force of 200 N will stretch a garage door spring 0.8 m beyond its unstressed length. How far will a 300-N force stretch the spring? How much work does it take to stretch the spring this far from its unstressed length?

29. Pumping a reservoir A reservoir shaped like a right-circular cone, point down, 20 ft across the top and 8 ft deep, is full of water. How much work does it take to pump the water to a level 6 ft above the top?

30. **Pumping a reservoir** (*Continuation of Exercise 29.*) The reservoir is filled to a depth of 5 ft, and the water is to be pumped to the same level as the top. How much work does it take?

31. **Pumping a conical tank** A right-circular conical tank, point down, with top radius 5 ft and height 10 ft is filled with a liquid whose weight-density is 60 lb/ft^3. How much work does it take to pump the liquid to a point 2 ft above the tank? If the pump is driven by a motor rated at 275 ft-lb/sec (1/2 hp), how long will it take to empty the tank?

32. **Pumping a cylindrical tank** A storage tank is a right-circular cylinder 20 ft long and 8 ft in diameter with its axis horizontal. If the tank is half full of olive oil weighing 57 lb/ft^3, find the work done in emptying it through a pipe that runs from the bottom of the tank to an outlet that is 6 ft above the top of the tank.

Centers of Mass and Centroids

33. Find the centroid of a thin, flat plate covering the region enclosed by the parabolas $y = 2x^2$ and $y = 3 - x^2$.

34. Find the centroid of a thin, flat plate covering the region enclosed by the x-axis, the lines $x = 2$ and $x = -2$, and the parabola $y = x^2$.

35. Find the centroid of a thin, flat plate covering the "triangular" region in the first quadrant bounded by the y-axis, the parabola $y = x^2/4$, and the line $y = 4$.

36. Find the centroid of a thin, flat plate covering the region enclosed by the parabola $y^2 = x$ and the line $x = 2y$.

37. Find the center of mass of a thin, flat plate covering the region enclosed by the parabola $y^2 = x$ and the line $x = 2y$ if the density function is $\delta(y) = 1 + y$. (Use horizontal strips.)

38. **a.** Find the center of mass of a thin plate of constant density covering the region between the curve $y = 3/x^{3/2}$ and the x-axis from $x = 1$ to $x = 9$.

b. Find the plate's center of mass if, instead of being constant, the density is $\delta(x) = x$. (Use vertical strips.)

Chapter 6 Additional and Advanced Exercises

Volume and Length

1. A solid is generated by revolving about the x-axis the region bounded by the graph of the positive continuous function $y = f(x)$, the x-axis, and the fixed line $x = a$ and the variable line $x = b, b > a$. Its volume, for all b, is $b^2 - ab$. Find $f(x)$.

2. A solid is generated by revolving about the x-axis the region bounded by the graph of the positive continuous function $y = f(x)$, the x-axis, and the lines $x = 0$ and $x = a$. Its volume, for all $a > 0$, is $a^2 + a$. Find $f(x)$.

3. Suppose that the increasing function $f(x)$ is smooth for $x \geq 0$ and that $f(0) = a$. Let $s(x)$ denote the length of the graph of f from $(0, a)$ to $(x, f(x)), x > 0$. Find $f(x)$ if $s(x) = Cx$ for some constant C. What are the allowable values for C?

4. **a.** Show that for $0 < \alpha \leq \pi/2$,

$$\int_0^\alpha \sqrt{1 + \cos^2\theta}\, d\theta > \sqrt{\alpha^2 + \sin^2\alpha}.$$

b. Generalize the result in part (a).

5. Find the volume of the solid formed by revolving the region bounded by the graphs of $y = x$ and $y = x^2$ about the line $y = x$.

6. Consider a right-circular cylinder of diameter 1. Form a wedge by making one slice parallel to the base of the cylinder completely through the cylinder, and another slice at an angle of 45° to the first slice and intersecting the first slice at the opposite edge of the cylinder (see accompanying diagram). Find the volume of the wedge.

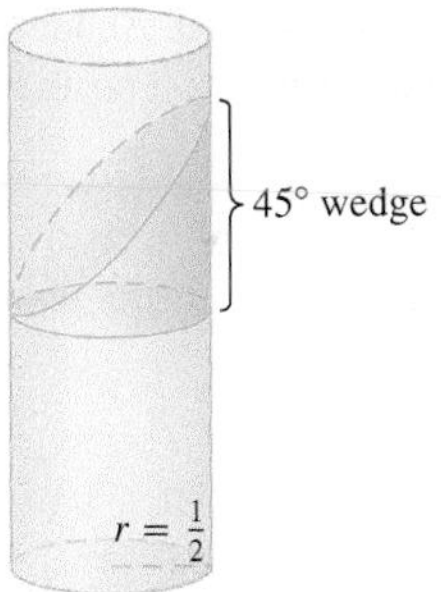

Surface Area

7. At points on the curve $y = 2\sqrt{x}$, line segments of length $h = y$ are drawn perpendicular to the xy-plane. (See accompanying figure.) Find the area of the surface formed by these perpendiculars from $(0, 0)$ to $(3, 2\sqrt{3})$.

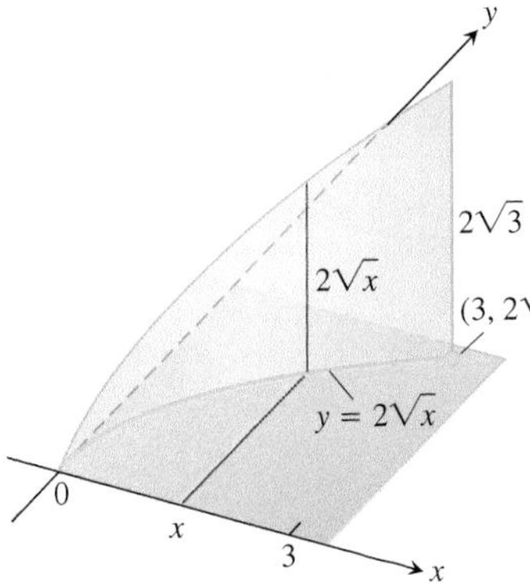

8. At points on a circle of radius a, line segments are drawn perpendicular to the plane of the circle, the perpendicular at each point P being of length ks, where s is the length of the arc of the circle measured counterclockwise from $(a, 0)$ to P and k is a positive constant, as shown here. Find the area of the surface formed by the perpendiculars along the arc beginning at $(a, 0)$ and extending once around the circle.

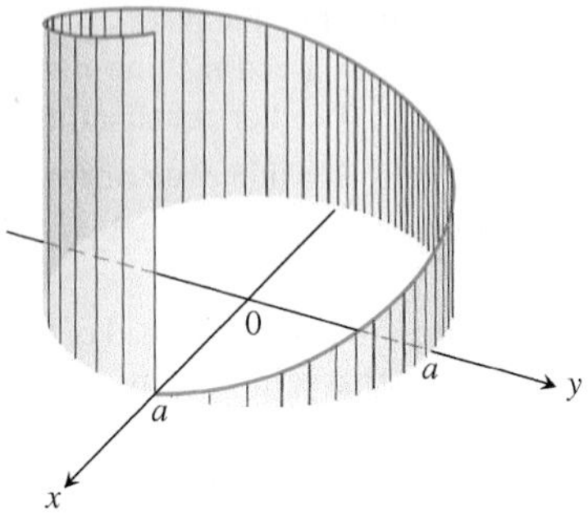

Work

9. A particle of mass m starts from rest at time $t = 0$ and is moved along the x-axis with constant acceleration a from $x = 0$ to $x = h$ against a variable force of magnitude $F(t) = t^2$. Find the work done.

10. **Work and kinetic energy** Suppose a 1.6-oz golf ball is placed on a vertical spring with force constant $k = 2$ lb/in. The spring is compressed 6 in. and released. About how high does the ball go (measured from the spring's rest position)?

Centers of Mass

11. Find the centroid of the region bounded below by the x-axis and above by the curve $y = 1 - x^n$, n an even positive integer. What is the limiting position of the centroid as $n \to \infty$?

12. If you haul a telephone pole on a two-wheeled carriage behind a truck, you want the wheels to be 3 ft or so behind the pole's center of mass to provide an adequate "tongue" weight. The 40-ft wooden telephone poles used by Verizon have a 27-in. circumference at the top and a 43.5-in. circumference at the base. About how far from the top is the center of mass?

13. Suppose that a thin metal plate of area A and constant density δ occupies a region R in the xy-plane, and let M_y be the plate's moment about the y-axis. Show that the plate's moment about the line $x = b$ is
   a. $M_y - b\delta A$ if the plate lies to the right of the line, and
   b. $b\delta A - M_y$ if the plate lies to the left of the line.

14. Find the center of mass of a thin plate covering the region bounded by the curve $y^2 = 4ax$ and the line $x = a$, $a =$ positive constant, if the density at (x, y) is directly proportional to **(a)** x, **(b)** $|y|$.

15. **a.** Find the centroid of the region in the first quadrant bounded by two concentric circles and the coordinate axes, if the circles have radii a and b, $0 < a < b$, and their centers are at the origin.
   b. Find the limits of the coordinates of the centroid as a approaches b and discuss the meaning of the result.

16. A triangular corner is cut from a square 1 ft on a side. The area of the triangle removed is 36 in^2. If the centroid of the remaining region is 7 in. from one side of the original square, how far is it from the remaining sides?

7

INTEGRALS AND TRANSCENDENTAL FUNCTIONS

OVERVIEW Our treatment of the logarithmic and exponential functions has been rather informal until now, appealing to intuition and graphs to describe what they mean and to explain some of their characteristics. In this chapter, we give a rigorous approach to the definitions and properties of these functions, and we study a wide range of applied problems in which they play a role. We also introduce the hyperbolic functions and their inverses, with their applications to integration and hanging cables.

7.1 The Logarithm Defined as an Integral

In Chapter 1, we introduced the natural logarithm function $\ln x$ as the inverse of the exponential function e^x. The function e^x was chosen as that function in the family of general exponential functions a^x, $a > 0$, whose graph has slope 1 as it crosses the y-axis. The function a^x was presented intuitively, however, based on its graph at rational values of x.

In this section we recreate the theory of logarithmic and exponential functions from an entirely different point of view. Here we define these functions analytically and recover their behaviors. To begin, we use the Fundamental Theorem of Calculus to define the natural logarithm function $\ln x$ as an integral. We quickly develop its properties, including the algebraic, geometric, and analytic properties as seen before. Next we introduce the function e^x as the inverse function of $\ln x$, and establish its previously seen properties. Defining $\ln x$ as an integral and e^x as its inverse is an indirect approach. While it may at first seem strange, it gives an elegant and powerful way to obtain the key properties of logarithmic and exponential functions.

Definition of the Natural Logarithm Function

The natural logarithm of a positive number x, written as $\ln x$, is the value of an integral.

DEFINITION The **natural logarithm** is the function given by

$$\ln x = \int_1^x \frac{1}{t}\,dt, \qquad x > 0.$$

From the Fundamental Theorem of Calculus, $\ln x$ is a continuous function. Geometrically, if $x > 1$, then $\ln x$ is the area under the curve $y = 1/t$ from $t = 1$ to $t = x$ (Figure 7.1). For $0 < x < 1$, $\ln x$ gives the negative of the area under the curve from x to 1.

The function is not defined for $x \leq 0$. From the Zero Width Interval Rule for definite integrals, we also have

$$\ln 1 = \int_1^1 \frac{1}{t}\,dt = 0.$$

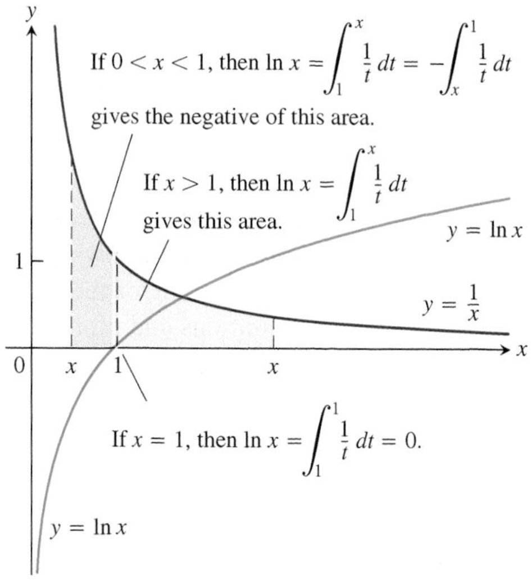
If $0 < x < 1$, then $\ln x = \int_1^x \frac{1}{t}\,dt = -\int_x^1 \frac{1}{t}\,dt$
gives the negative of this area.
If $x > 1$, then $\ln x = \int_1^x \frac{1}{t}\,dt$
gives this area.
$y = \ln x$
$y = \frac{1}{x}$
If $x = 1$, then $\ln x = \int_1^1 \frac{1}{t}\,dt = 0.$
$y = \ln x$
y
x
1
0
x
1
x

FIGURE 7.1 The graph of $y = \ln x$ and its relation to the function $y = 1/x, x > 0$. The graph of the logarithm rises above the x-axis as x moves from 1 to the right, and it falls below the axis as x moves from 1 to the left.

Notice that we show the graph of $y = 1/x$ in Figure 7.1 but use $y = 1/t$ in the integral. Using x for everything would have us writing

$$\ln x = \int_1^x \frac{1}{x}\,dx,$$

with x meaning two different things. So we change the variable of integration to t.

By using rectangles to obtain finite approximations of the area under the graph of $y = 1/t$ and over the interval between $t = 1$ and $t = x$, as in Section 5.1, we can approximate the values of the function $\ln x$. Several values are given in Table 7.1. There is an important number between $x = 2$ and $x = 3$ whose natural logarithm equals 1. This number, which we now define, exists because $\ln x$ is a continuous function and therefore satisfies the Intermediate Value Theorem on [2, 3].

TABLE 7.1 Typical 2-place values of $\ln x$

x	$\ln x$
0	undefined
0.05	-3.00
0.5	-0.69
1	0
2	0.69
3	1.10
4	1.39
10	2.30

DEFINITION The **number *e*** is that number in the domain of the natural logarithm satisfying

$$\ln(e) = \int_1^e \frac{1}{t}\,dt = 1.$$

Interpreted geometrically, the number e corresponds to the point on the x-axis for which the area under the graph of $y = 1/t$ and above the interval $[1, e]$ equals the area of the unit square. That is, the area of the region shaded blue in Figure 7.1 is 1 sq unit when $x = e$. We will see further on that this is the same number $e \approx 2.718281828$ we have encountered before.

The Derivative of $y = \ln x$

By the first part of the Fundamental Theorem of Calculus (Section 5.4),

$$\frac{d}{dx}\ln x = \frac{d}{dx}\int_1^x \frac{1}{t}\,dt = \frac{1}{x}.$$

For every positive value of x, we have

$$\frac{d}{dx}\ln x = \frac{1}{x}. \tag{1}$$

Therefore, the function $y = \ln x$ is a solution to the initial value problem $dy/dx = 1/x$, $x > 0$, with $y(1) = 0$. Notice that the derivative is always positive.

If u is a differentiable function of x whose values are positive, so that $\ln u$ is defined, then applying the Chain Rule we obtain

$$\frac{d}{dx}\ln u = \frac{1}{u}\frac{du}{dx}, \qquad u > 0. \tag{2}$$

As established in Example 3(c) of Section 3.8, we also have

$$\frac{d}{dx}\ln |x| = \frac{1}{x}, \qquad x \neq 0. \tag{3}$$

Moreover, if b is any constant with $bx > 0$

$$\frac{d}{dx}\ln bx = \frac{1}{bx}\cdot\frac{d}{dx}(bx) = \frac{1}{bx}(b) = \frac{1}{x}.$$

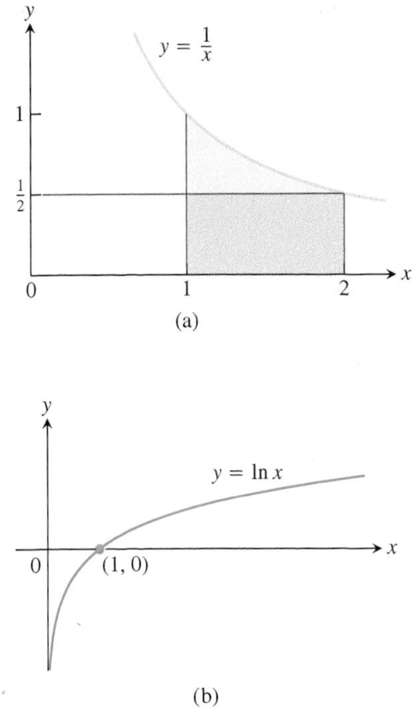

FIGURE 7.2 (a) The rectangle of height $y = 1/2$ fits beneath the graph of $y = 1/x$ for the interval $1 \le x \le 2$. (b) The graph of the natural logarithm.

The Graph and Range of $\ln x$

The derivative $d(\ln x)/dx = 1/x$ is positive for $x > 0$, so $\ln x$ is an increasing function of x. The second derivative, $-1/x^2$, is negative, so the graph of $\ln x$ is concave down. (See Figure 7.2.)

The function $\ln x$ has the following familiar algebraic properties, which we stated in Section 1.6. In Section 4.2 we showed these properties are a consequence of Corollary 2 of the Mean Value Theorem.

1. $\ln bx = \ln b + \ln x$	**2.** $\ln \frac{b}{x} = \ln b - \ln x$
3. $\ln \frac{1}{x} = -\ln x$	**4.** $\ln x^r = r \ln x$, r rational

We can estimate the value of ln 2 by considering the area under the graph of $y = 1/2$ and above the interval $[1, 2]$. In Figure 7.2(a) a rectangle of height $1/2$ over the interval $[1, 2]$

fits under the graph. Therefore, the area under the graph, which is ln 2, is greater than the area, $1/2$, of the rectangle. So $\ln 2 > 1/2$. Knowing this we have

$$\ln 2^n = n \ln 2 > n\left(\frac{1}{2}\right) = \frac{n}{2}.$$

This result shows that $\ln(2^n) \to \infty$ as $n \to \infty$. Since $\ln x$ is an increasing function, we get that

$$\lim_{x \to \infty} \ln x = \infty.$$

We also have

$$\lim_{x \to 0^+} \ln x = \lim_{t \to \infty} \ln t^{-1} = \lim_{t \to \infty} (-\ln t) = -\infty. \qquad x = 1/t = t^{-1}$$

We defined $\ln x$ for $x > 0$, so the domain of $\ln x$ is the set of positive real numbers. The above discussion and the Intermediate Value Theorem show that its range is the entire real line, giving the graph of $y = \ln x$ shown in Figure 7.2(b).

The Integral $\int (1/u)\, du$

Equation (3) leads to the following integral formula.

If u is a differentiable function that is never zero,

$$\int \frac{1}{u}\, du = \ln |u| + C. \tag{4}$$

Equation (4) applies anywhere on the domain of $1/u$, the points where $u \neq 0$. It says that integrals of a certain *form* lead to logarithms. If $u = f(x)$, then $du = f'(x)\, dx$ and

$$\int \frac{f'(x)}{f(x)}\, dx = \ln |f(x)| + C$$

whenever $f(x)$ is a differentiable function that is never zero.

EXAMPLE 1 Here we recognize an integral of the form $\displaystyle\int \frac{du}{u}$.

$$\begin{aligned}
\int_{-\pi/2}^{\pi/2} \frac{4 \cos \theta}{3 + 2 \sin \theta}\, d\theta &= \int_1^5 \frac{2}{u}\, du && u = 3 + 2 \sin \theta, \quad du = 2 \cos \theta\, d\theta, \\
& && u(-\pi/2) = 1, \quad u(\pi/2) = 5 \\
&= 2 \ln |u| \Big]_1^5 \\
&= 2 \ln |5| - 2 \ln |1| = 2 \ln 5
\end{aligned}$$

Note that $u = 3 + 2 \sin \theta$ is always positive on $[-\pi/2, \pi/2]$, so Equation (4) applies. ■

The Integrals of tan x, cot x, sec x, and csc x

Equation (4) tells us how to integrate these trigonometric functions.

$$\begin{aligned}
\int \tan x\, dx &= \int \frac{\sin x}{\cos x}\, dx = \int \frac{-du}{u} && u = \cos x > 0 \text{ on } (-\pi/2, \pi/2), \\
& && du = -\sin x\, dx \\
&= -\ln |u| + C = -\ln |\cos x| + C \\
&= \ln \frac{1}{|\cos x|} + C = \ln |\sec x| + C && \text{Reciprocal Rule}
\end{aligned}$$

For the cotangent,

$$\int \cot x\,dx = \int \frac{\cos x\,dx}{\sin x} = \int \frac{du}{u} \qquad \begin{aligned} &u = \sin x,\\ &du = \cos x\,dx\end{aligned}$$

$$= \ln|u| + C = \ln|\sin x| + C = -\ln|\csc x| + C.$$

To integrate $\sec x$, we multiply and divide by $(\sec x + \tan x)$.

$$\int \sec x\,dx = \int \sec x\,\frac{(\sec x + \tan x)}{(\sec x + \tan x)}\,dx = \int \frac{\sec^2 x + \sec x \tan x}{\sec x + \tan x}\,dx$$

$$= \int \frac{du}{u} = \ln|u| + C = \ln|\sec x + \tan x| + C \qquad \begin{aligned} &u = \sec x + \tan x,\\ &du = (\sec x \tan x + \sec^2 x)\,dx\end{aligned}$$

For $\csc x$, we multiply and divide by $(\csc x + \cot x)$.

$$\int \csc x\,dx = \int \csc x\,\frac{(\csc x + \cot x)}{(\csc x + \cot x)}\,dx = \int \frac{\csc^2 x + \csc x \cot x}{\csc x + \cot x}\,dx$$

$$= \int \frac{-du}{u} = -\ln|u| + C = -\ln|\csc x + \cot x| + C \qquad \begin{aligned} &u = \csc x + \cot x,\\ &du = (-\csc x \cot x - \csc^2 x)\,dx\end{aligned}$$

Integrals of the tangent, cotangent, secant, and cosecant functions

$$\int \tan u\,du = \ln|\sec u| + C \qquad \int \sec u\,du = \ln|\sec u + \tan u| + C$$

$$\int \cot u\,du = \ln|\sin u| + C \qquad \int \csc u\,du = -\ln|\csc u + \cot u| + C$$

The Inverse of ln *x* and the Number *e*

The function $\ln x$, being an increasing function of x with domain $(0, \infty)$ and range $(-\infty, \infty)$, has an inverse $\ln^{-1} x$ with domain $(-\infty, \infty)$ and range $(0, \infty)$. The graph of $\ln^{-1} x$ is the graph of $\ln x$ reflected across the line $y = x$. As you can see in Figure 7.3,

$$\lim_{x\to\infty} \ln^{-1} x = \infty \qquad \text{and} \qquad \lim_{x\to-\infty} \ln^{-1} x = 0.$$

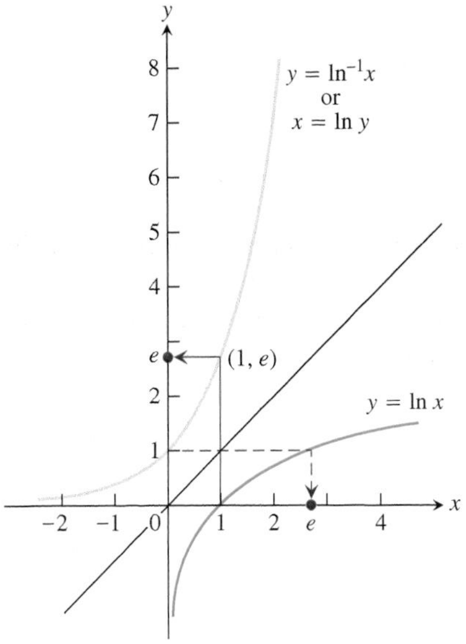

FIGURE 7.3 The graphs of $y = \ln x$ and $y = \ln^{-1} x = \exp x$. The number e is $\ln^{-1} 1 = \exp(1)$.

The function $\ln^{-1} x$ is also denoted by $\exp x$. We now show that $\ln^{-1} x = \exp x$ is an exponential function with base e.

The number e was defined to satisfy the equation $\ln(e) = 1$, so $e = \exp(1)$. We can raise the number e to a rational power r using algebra:

$$e^2 = e \cdot e, \qquad e^{-2} = \frac{1}{e^2}, \qquad e^{1/2} = \sqrt{e}, \qquad e^{2/3} = \sqrt[3]{e^2},$$

and so on. Since e is positive, e^r is positive too. Thus, e^r has a logarithm. When we take the logarithm, we find that for r rational

$$\ln e^r = r \ln e = r \cdot 1 = r.$$

Then applying the function $\ln^{-1}$ to both sides of the equation $\ln e^r = r$, we find that

$$e^r = \exp r \qquad \text{for } r \text{ rational.} \qquad \text{exp is } \ln^{-1}. \tag{5}$$

We have not yet found a way to give an exact meaning to e^x for x irrational. But $\ln^{-1} x$ has meaning for any x, rational or irrational. So Equation (5) provides a way to extend the definition of e^x to irrational values of x. The function $\exp x$ is defined for all x, so we use it to assign a value to e^x at every point.

Typical values of e^x

x	e^x (rounded)
-1	0.37
0	1
1	2.72
2	7.39
10	22026
100	2.6881×10^{43}

DEFINITION For every real number x, we define the **natural exponential function** to be $e^x = \exp x$.

For the first time we have a precise meaning for a number raised to an irrational power. Usually the exponential function is denoted by e^x rather than $\exp x$. Since $\ln x$ and e^x are inverses of one another, we have

Inverse Equations for e^x and $\ln x$

$$e^{\ln x} = x \qquad (\text{all } x > 0)$$
$$\ln(e^x) = x \qquad (\text{all } x)$$

Transcendental Numbers and Transcendental Functions

Numbers that are solutions of polynomial equations with rational coefficients are called **algebraic**: -2 is algebraic because it satisfies the equation $x + 2 = 0$, and $\sqrt{3}$ is algebraic because it satisfies the equation $x^2 - 3 = 0$. Numbers such as e and π that are not algebraic are called **transcendental**.

We call a function $y = f(x)$ algebraic if it satisfies an equation of the form

$$P_n y^n + \cdots + P_1 y + P_0 = 0$$

in which the P's are polynomials in x with rational coefficients. The function $y = 1/\sqrt{x+1}$ is algebraic because it satisfies the equation $(x+1)y^2 - 1 = 0$. Here the polynomials are $P_2 = x + 1$, $P_1 = 0$, and $P_0 = -1$. Functions that are not algebraic are called transcendental.

The Derivative and Integral of e^x

The exponential function is differentiable because it is the inverse of a differentiable function whose derivative is never zero. We calculate its derivative using Theorem 3 of Section 3.8 and our knowledge of the derivative of $\ln x$. Let

$$f(x) = \ln x \qquad \text{and} \qquad y = e^x = \ln^{-1} x = f^{-1}(x).$$

Then,

$$\begin{aligned}
\frac{dy}{dx} = \frac{d}{dx}(e^x) &= \frac{d}{dx}\ln^{-1} x \\
&= \frac{d}{dx} f^{-1}(x) \\
&= \frac{1}{f'(f^{-1}(x))} && \text{Theorem 3, Section 3.8} \\
&= \frac{1}{f'(e^x)} && f^{-1}(x) = e^x \\
&= \frac{1}{\left(\frac{1}{e^x}\right)} && f'(z) = \frac{1}{z} \text{ with } z = e^x \\
&= e^x.
\end{aligned}$$

That is, for $y = e^x$, we find that $dy/dx = e^x$ so the natural exponential function e^x is its own derivative, just as we claimed in Section 3.3. We will see in the next section that the only functions that behave this way are constant multiples of e^x. The Chain Rule extends the derivative result in the usual way to a more general form.

If u is any differentiable function of x, then

$$\frac{d}{dx} e^u = e^u \frac{du}{dx}. \qquad (6)$$

Since $e^x > 0$, its derivative is also everywhere positive, so it is an increasing and continuous function for all x, having limits

$$\lim_{x \to -\infty} e^x = 0 \qquad \text{and} \qquad \lim_{x \to \infty} e^x = \infty.$$

It follows that the x-axis ($y = 0$) is a horizontal asymptote of the graph $y = e^x$ (see Figure 7.3).

Equation (6) also tells us the antiderivative of e^u.

$$\int e^u\,du = e^u + C$$

If $f(x) = e^x$, then from Equation (6), $f'(0) = e^0 = 1$. That is, the exponential function e^x has slope 1 as it crosses the y-axis at $x = 0$. This agrees with our assertion for the natural exponential in Section 3.3.

Laws of Exponents

Even though e^x is defined in a seemingly roundabout way as $\ln^{-1} x$, it obeys the familiar laws of exponents from algebra. Theorem 1 shows us that these laws are consequences of the definitions of $\ln x$ and e^x. We proved the laws in Section 4.2, and they are still valid because of the inverse relationship between $\ln x$ and e^x.

THEOREM 1—Laws of Exponents for e^x

For all numbers x, x_1, and x_2, the natural exponential e^x obeys the following laws:

1. $e^{x_1} \cdot e^{x_2} = e^{x_1 + x_2}$

2. $e^{-x} = \dfrac{1}{e^x}$

3. $\dfrac{e^{x_1}}{e^{x_2}} = e^{x_1 - x_2}$

4. $(e^{x_1})^{x_2} = e^{x_1 x_2} = (e^{x_2})^{x_1}$

The General Exponential Function a^x

Since $a = e^{\ln a}$ for any positive number a, we can think of a^x as $(e^{\ln a})^x = e^{x \ln a}$. We therefore make the following definition, consistent with what we stated in Section 1.6.

DEFINITION For any numbers $a > 0$ and x, the exponential function with base a is given by

$$a^x = e^{x \ln a}.$$

The General Power Function

x^r is the function $e^{r \ln x}$

When $a = e$, the definition gives $a^x = e^{x \ln a} = e^{x \ln e} = e^{x \cdot 1} = e^x$. Similarly, the power function $f(x) = x^r$ is defined to be $x^r = e^{r \ln x}$ for any real number r, rational or irrational.

Theorem 1 is also valid for a^x, the exponential function with base a. For example,

$$\begin{aligned} a^{x_1} \cdot a^{x_2} &= e^{x_1 \ln a} \cdot e^{x_2 \ln a} && \text{Definition of } a^x \\ &= e^{x_1 \ln a + x_2 \ln a} && \text{Law 1} \\ &= e^{(x_1 + x_2)\ln a} && \text{Factor } \ln a \\ &= a^{x_1 + x_2}. && \text{Definition of } a^x \end{aligned}$$

Starting with the definition $a^x = e^{x \ln a}$, $a > 0$, we get the derivative

$$\frac{d}{dx} a^x = \frac{d}{dx} e^{x \ln a} = (\ln a) e^{x \ln a} = (\ln a) a^x,$$

so

$$\frac{d}{dx} a^x = a^x \ln a.$$

Alternatively, we get the same derivative rule by applying logarithmic differentiation:

$$\begin{aligned} y &= a^x \\ \ln y &= x \ln a && \text{Taking logarithms} \\ \frac{1}{y}\frac{dy}{dx} &= \ln a && \text{Differentiating with respect to } x \\ \frac{dy}{dx} &= y \ln a = a^x \ln a. \end{aligned}$$

With the Chain Rule, we get a more general form, as in Section 3.8.

If $a > 0$ and u is a differentiable function of x, then a^u is a differentiable function of x and

$$\frac{d}{dx} a^u = a^u \ln a \, \frac{du}{dx}.$$

The integral equivalent of this last result is

$$\int a^u \, du = \frac{a^u}{\ln a} + C.$$

Logarithms with Base a

If a is any positive number other than 1, the function a^x is one-to-one and has a nonzero derivative at every point. It therefore has a differentiable inverse.

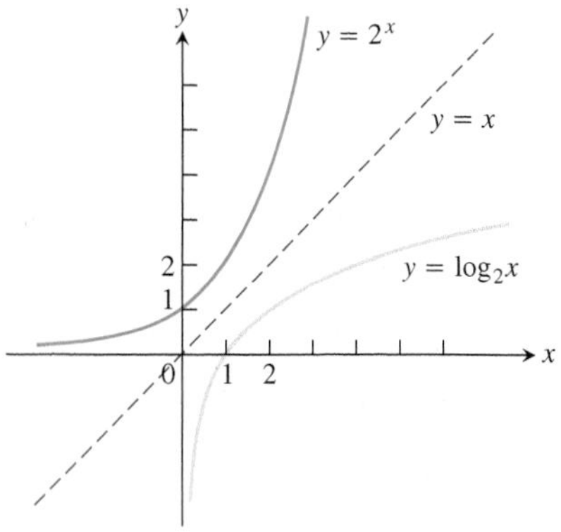

FIGURE 7.4 The graph of 2^x and its inverse, $\log_2 x$.

DEFINITION For any positive number $a \neq 1$, the **logarithm of x with base a**, denoted by $\log_a x$, is the inverse function of a^x.

The graph of $y = \log_a x$ can be obtained by reflecting the graph of $y = a^x$ across the 45° line $y = x$ (Figure 7.4). When $a = e$, we have $\log_e x = \text{inverse of } e^x = \ln x$. Since $\log_a x$ and a^x are inverses of one another, composing them in either order gives the identity function.

Inverse Equations for a^x and $\log_a x$

$$a^{\log_a x} = x \qquad (x > 0)$$
$$\log_a (a^x) = x \qquad (\text{all } x)$$

As stated in Section 1.6, the function $\log_a x$ is just a numerical multiple of $\ln x$. We see this from the following derivation:

$$\begin{aligned} y &= \log_a x && \text{Defining equation for } y \\ a^y &= x && \text{Equivalent equation} \\ \ln a^y &= \ln x && \text{Natural log of both sides} \\ y \ln a &= \ln x && \text{Algebra Rule 4 for natural log} \\ y &= \frac{\ln x}{\ln a} && \text{Solve for } y. \\ \log_a x &= \frac{\ln x}{\ln a} && \text{Substitute for } y. \end{aligned}$$

TABLE 7.2 Rules for base a logarithms

For any numbers $x > 0$ and $y > 0$,

1. *Product Rule:* $\log_a xy = \log_a x + \log_a y$
2. *Quotient Rule:* $\log_a \frac{x}{y} = \log_a x - \log_a y$
3. *Reciprocal Rule:* $\log_a \frac{1}{y} = -\log_a y$
4. *Power Rule:* $\log_a x^y = y \log_a x$

It then follows easily that the arithmetic rules satisfied by $\log_a x$ are the same as the ones for $\ln x$. These rules, given in Table 7.2, can be proved by dividing the corresponding rules for the natural logarithm function by $\ln a$. For example,

$$\ln xy = \ln x + \ln y \qquad \text{Rule 1 for natural logarithms} \ldots$$

$$\frac{\ln xy}{\ln a} = \frac{\ln x}{\ln a} + \frac{\ln y}{\ln a} \qquad \ldots \text{divided by } \ln a \ldots$$

$$\log_a xy = \log_a x + \log_a y. \qquad \ldots \text{gives Rule 1 for base } a \text{ logarithms.}$$

Derivatives and Integrals Involving $\log_a x$

To find derivatives or integrals involving base a logarithms, we convert them to natural logarithms. If u is a positive differentiable function of x, then

$$\frac{d}{dx}(\log_a u) = \frac{d}{dx}\left(\frac{\ln u}{\ln a}\right) = \frac{1}{\ln a}\frac{d}{dx}(\ln u) = \frac{1}{\ln a} \cdot \frac{1}{u}\frac{du}{dx}.$$

$$\boxed{\frac{d}{dx}(\log_a u) = \frac{1}{\ln a} \cdot \frac{1}{u}\frac{du}{dx}}$$

EXAMPLE 2 We illustrate the derivative and integral results.

(a) $$\frac{d}{dx}\log_{10}(3x + 1) = \frac{1}{\ln 10} \cdot \frac{1}{3x + 1}\frac{d}{dx}(3x + 1) = \frac{3}{(\ln 10)(3x + 1)}$$

(b) $$\int \frac{\log_2 x}{x}\,dx = \frac{1}{\ln 2}\int \frac{\ln x}{x}\,dx \qquad \log_2 x = \frac{\ln x}{\ln 2}$$

$$= \frac{1}{\ln 2}\int u\,du \qquad u = \ln x, \quad du = \frac{1}{x}dx$$

$$= \frac{1}{\ln 2}\frac{u^2}{2} + C = \frac{1}{\ln 2}\frac{(\ln x)^2}{2} + C = \frac{(\ln x)^2}{2 \ln 2} + C$$ ■

Summary

In this section we used calculus to give precise definitions of the logarithmic and exponential functions. This approach is somewhat different from our earlier treatments of the polynomial, rational, and trigonometric functions. There we first defined the function and then we studied its derivatives and integrals. Here we started with an integral from which the functions of interest were obtained. The motivation behind this approach was to avoid mathematical difficulties that arise when we attempt to define functions such as a^x for any real number x, rational or irrational. Defining $\ln x$ as the integral of the function $1/t$ from $t = 1$ to $t = x$ enabled us to define all of the exponential and logarithmic functions, and then derive their key algebraic and analytic properties.

Exercises 7.1

Integration

Evaluate the integrals in Exercises 1–46.

1. $\int_{-3}^{-2} \frac{dx}{x}$

2. $\int_{-1}^{0} \frac{3\,dx}{3x - 2}$

3. $\int \frac{2y\,dy}{y^2 - 25}$

4. $\int \frac{8r\,dr}{4r^2 - 5}$

5. $\int \frac{3\sec^2 t}{6 + 3\tan t}\,dt$

6. $\int \frac{\sec y \tan y}{2 + \sec y}\,dy$

7. $\int \frac{dx}{2\sqrt{x} + 2x}$

8. $\int \frac{\sec x\, dx}{\sqrt{\ln(\sec x + \tan x)}}$

9. $\int_{\ln 2}^{\ln 3} e^x\, dx$

10. $\int 8e^{(x+1)}\, dx$

11. $\int_1^4 \frac{(\ln x)^3}{2x}\, dx$

12. $\int \frac{\ln(\ln x)}{x \ln x}\, dx$

13. $\int_{\ln 4}^{\ln 9} e^{x/2}\, dx$

14. $\int \tan x \ln(\cos x)\, dx$

15. $\int \frac{e^{\sqrt{r}}}{\sqrt{r}}\, dr$

16. $\int \frac{e^{-\sqrt{r}}}{\sqrt{r}}\, dr$

17. $\int 2t\, e^{-t^2}\, dt$

18. $\int \frac{\ln x\, dx}{x\sqrt{\ln^2 x + 1}}$

19. $\int \frac{e^{1/x}}{x^2}\, dx$

20. $\int \frac{e^{-1/x^2}}{x^3}\, dx$

21. $\int e^{\sec \pi t} \sec \pi t \tan \pi t\, dt$

22. $\int e^{\csc(\pi + t)} \csc(\pi + t) \cot(\pi + t)\, dt$

23. $\int_{\ln(\pi/6)}^{\ln(\pi/2)} 2e^v \cos e^v\, dv$

24. $\int_0^{\sqrt{\ln \pi}} 2xe^{x^2} \cos(e^{x^2})\, dx$

25. $\int \frac{e^r}{1 + e^r}\, dr$

26. $\int \frac{dx}{1 + e^x}$

27. $\int_0^1 2^{-\theta}\, d\theta$

28. $\int_{-2}^0 5^{-\theta}\, d\theta$

29. $\int_1^{\sqrt{2}} x2^{(x^2)}\, dx$

30. $\int_1^4 \frac{2^{\sqrt{x}}}{\sqrt{x}}\, dx$

31. $\int_0^{\pi/2} 7^{\cos t} \sin t\, dt$

32. $\int_0^{\pi/4} \left(\frac{1}{3}\right)^{\tan t} \sec^2 t\, dt$

33. $\int_2^4 x^{2x}(1 + \ln x)\, dx$

34. $\int_1^2 \frac{2^{\ln x}}{x}\, dx$

35. $\int_0^3 (\sqrt{2} + 1)x^{\sqrt{2}}\, dx$

36. $\int_1^e x^{(\ln 2) - 1}\, dx$

37. $\int \frac{\log_{10} x}{x}\, dx$

38. $\int_1^4 \frac{\log_2 x}{x}\, dx$

39. $\int_1^4 \frac{\ln 2 \log_2 x}{x}\, dx$

40. $\int_1^e \frac{2 \ln 10 \log_{10} x}{x}\, dx$

41. $\int_0^2 \frac{\log_2(x + 2)}{x + 2}\, dx$

42. $\int_{1/10}^{10} \frac{\log_{10}(10x)}{x}\, dx$

43. $\int_0^9 \frac{2\log_{10}(x + 1)}{x + 1}\, dx$

44. $\int_2^3 \frac{2\log_2(x - 1)}{x - 1}\, dx$

45. $\int \frac{dx}{x \log_{10} x}$

46. $\int \frac{dx}{x(\log_8 x)^2}$

Initial Value Problems

Solve the initial value problems in Exercises 47–52.

47. $\frac{dy}{dt} = e^t \sin(e^t - 2), \quad y(\ln 2) = 0$

48. $\frac{dy}{dt} = e^{-t} \sec^2(\pi e^{-t}), \quad y(\ln 4) = 2/\pi$

49. $\frac{d^2y}{dx^2} = 2e^{-x}, \quad y(0) = 1 \quad \text{and} \quad y'(0) = 0$

50. $\frac{d^2y}{dt^2} = 1 - e^{2t}, \quad y(1) = -1 \quad \text{and} \quad y'(1) = 0$

51. $\frac{dy}{dx} = 1 + \frac{1}{x}, \quad y(1) = 3$

52. $\frac{d^2y}{dx^2} = \sec^2 x, \quad y(0) = 0 \quad \text{and} \quad y'(0) = 1$

Theory and Applications

53. The region between the curve $y = 1/x^2$ and the x-axis from $x = 1/2$ to $x = 2$ is revolved about the y-axis to generate a solid. Find the volume of the solid.

54. In Section 6.2, Exercise 6, we revolved about the y-axis the region between the curve $y = 9x/\sqrt{x^3 + 9}$ and the x-axis from $x = 0$ to $x = 3$ to generate a solid of volume 36π. What volume do you get if you revolve the region about the x-axis instead? (See Section 6.2, Exercise 6, for a graph.)

Find the lengths of the curves in Exercises 55 and 56.

55. $y = (x^2/8) - \ln x, \quad 4 \le x \le 8$

56. $x = (y/4)^2 - 2\ln(y/4), \quad 4 \le y \le 12$

T 57. **The linearization of $\ln(1 + x)$ at $x = 0$** Instead of approximating $\ln x$ near $x = 1$, we approximate $\ln(1 + x)$ near $x = 0$. We get a simpler formula this way.

a. Derive the linearization $\ln(1 + x) \approx x$ at $x = 0$.

b. Estimate to five decimal places the error involved in replacing $\ln(1 + x)$ by x on the interval $[0, 0.1]$.

c. Graph $\ln(1 + x)$ and x together for $0 \le x \le 0.5$. Use different colors, if available. At what points does the approximation of $\ln(1 + x)$ seem best? Least good? By reading coordinates from the graphs, find as good an upper bound for the error as your grapher will allow.

58. **The linearization of e^x at $x = 0$**

a. Derive the linear approximation $e^x \approx 1 + x$ at $x = 0$.

T b. Estimate to five decimal places the magnitude of the error involved in replacing e^x by $1 + x$ on the interval $[0, 0.2]$.

T c. Graph e^x and $1 + x$ together for $-2 \le x \le 2$. Use different colors, if available. On what intervals does the approximation appear to overestimate e^x? Underestimate e^x?

59. Show that for any number $a > 1$

$$\int_1^a \ln x\, dx + \int_0^{\ln a} e^y\, dy = a \ln a.$$

(See accompanying figure.)

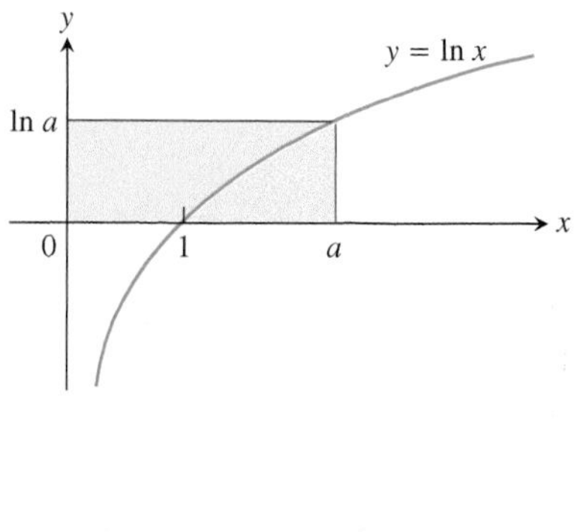

60. The geometric, logarithmic, and arithmetic mean inequality

a. Show that the graph of e^x is concave up over every interval of x-values.

b. Show, by reference to the accompanying figure, that if $0 < a < b$ then

$$e^{(\ln a+\ln b)/2}\cdot(\ln b-\ln a)<\int_{\ln a}^{\ln b} e^x\,dx<\frac{e^{\ln a}+e^{\ln b}}{2}\cdot(\ln b-\ln a).$$

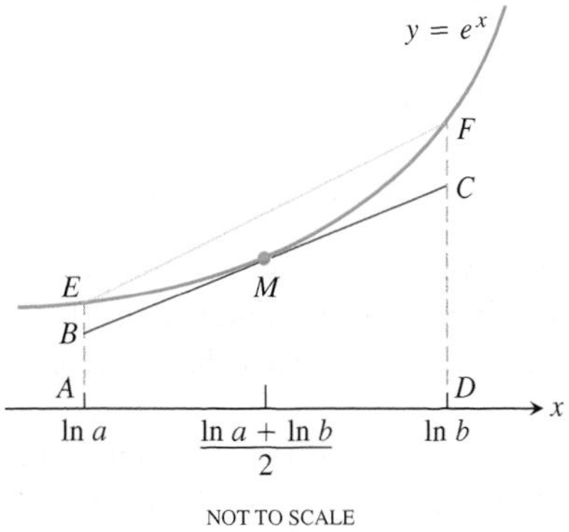

c. Use the inequality in part (b) to conclude that

$$\sqrt{ab}<\frac{b-a}{\ln b-\ln a}<\frac{a+b}{2}.$$

This inequality says that the geometric mean of two positive numbers is less than their logarithmic mean, which in turn is less than their arithmetic mean.

(For more about this inequality, see "The Geometric, Logarithmic, and Arithmetic Mean Inequality" by Frank Burk, *American Mathematical Monthly*, Vol. 94, No. 6, June–July 1987, pp. 527–528.)

Grapher Explorations

61. Graph $\ln x$, $\ln 2x$, $\ln 4x$, $\ln 8x$, and $\ln 16x$ (as many as you can) together for $0 < x \le 10$. What is going on? Explain.

62. Graph $y = \ln|\sin x|$ in the window $0 \le x \le 22$, $-2 \le y \le 0$. Explain what you see. How could you change the formula to turn the arches upside down?

63. a. Graph $y = \sin x$ and the curves $y = \ln(a + \sin x)$ for $a = 2$, 4, 8, 20, and 50 together for $0 \le x \le 23$.

b. Why do the curves flatten as a increases? (*Hint:* Find an a-dependent upper bound for $|y'|$.)

64. Does the graph of $y = \sqrt{x} - \ln x$, $x > 0$, have an inflection point? Try to answer the question **(a)** by graphing, **(b)** by using calculus.

T 65. The equation $x^2 = 2^x$ has three solutions: $x = 2$, $x = 4$, and one other. Estimate the third solution as accurately as you can by graphing.

T 66. Could $x^{\ln 2}$ possibly be the same as $2^{\ln x}$ for $x > 0$? Graph the two functions and explain what you see.

T 67. **Which is bigger, π^e or e^π?** Calculators have taken some of the mystery out of this once-challenging question. (Go ahead and check; you will see that it is a surprisingly close call.) You can answer the question without a calculator, though.

a. Find an equation for the line through the origin tangent to the graph of $y = \ln x$.

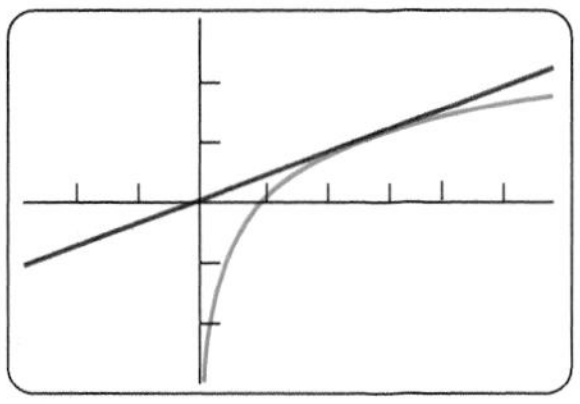

[−3, 6] by [−3, 3]

b. Give an argument based on the graphs of $y = \ln x$ and the tangent line to explain why $\ln x < x/e$ for all positive $x \ne e$.

c. Show that $\ln(x^e) < x$ for all positive $x \ne e$.

d. Conclude that $x^e < e^x$ for all positive $x \ne e$.

e. So which is bigger, π^e or e^π?

T 68. **A decimal representation of e** Find e to as many decimal places as your calculator allows by solving the equation $\ln x = 1$ using Newton's method in Section 4.7.

Calculations with Other Bases

T 69. Most scientific calculators have keys for $\log_{10} x$ and $\ln x$. To find logarithms to other bases, we use the equation $\log_a x = (\ln x)/(\ln a)$.

Find the following logarithms to five decimal places.

a. $\log_3 8$ b. $\log_7 0.5$ c. $\log_{20} 17$ d. $\log_{0.5} 7$

e. $\ln x$, given that $\log_{10} x = 2.3$

f. $\ln x$, given that $\log_2 x = 1.4$

g. $\ln x$, given that $\log_2 x = -1.5$

h. $\ln x$, given that $\log_{10} x = -0.7$

70. **Conversion factors**

a. Show that the equation for converting base 10 logarithms to base 2 logarithms is

$$\log_2 x = \frac{\ln 10}{\ln 2}\log_{10} x.$$

b. Show that the equation for converting base a logarithms to base b logarithms is

$$\log_b x = \frac{\ln a}{\ln b}\log_a x.$$

7.2 Exponential Change and Separable Differential Equations

Exponential functions increase or decrease very rapidly with changes in the independent variable. They describe growth or decay in many natural and industrial situations. The variety of models based on these functions partly accounts for their importance. We now investigate the basic proportionality assumption that leads to such *exponential change.*

Exponential Change

In modeling many real-world situations, a quantity y increases or decreases at a rate proportional to its size at a given time t. Examples of such quantities include the amount of a decaying radioactive material, the size of a population, and the temperature difference between a hot object and its surrounding medium. Such quantities are said to undergo **exponential change**.

If the amount present at time $t = 0$ is called y_0, then we can find y as a function of t by solving the following initial value problem:

$$\text{Differential equation:} \quad \frac{dy}{dt} = ky \tag{1a}$$

$$\text{Initial condition:} \quad y = y_0 \quad \text{when} \quad t = 0. \tag{1b}$$

If y is positive and increasing, then k is positive, and we use Equation (1a) to say that the rate of growth is proportional to what has already been accumulated. If y is positive and decreasing, then k is negative, and we use Equation (1a) to say that the rate of decay is proportional to the amount still left.

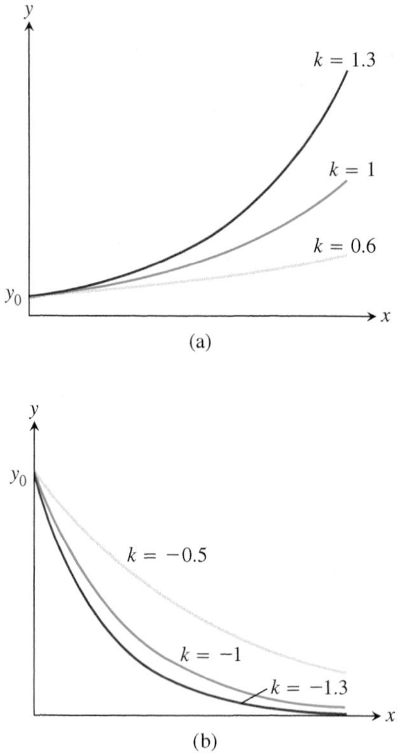

FIGURE 7.5 Graphs of (a) exponential growth and (b) exponential decay. As $|k|$ increases, the growth ($k > 0$) or decay ($k < 0$) intensifies.

We see right away that the constant function $y = 0$ is a solution of Equation (1a) if $y_0 = 0$. To find the nonzero solutions, we divide Equation (1a) by y:

$$\begin{aligned}
\frac{1}{y} \cdot \frac{dy}{dt} &= k && y \neq 0 \\
\int \frac{1}{y}\frac{dy}{dt}\,dt &= \int k\,dt && \text{Integrate with respect to } t; \\
\ln|y| &= kt + C && \int (1/u)\,du = \ln|u| + C. \\
|y| &= e^{kt+C} && \text{Exponentiate.} \\
|y| &= e^C \cdot e^{kt} && e^{a+b} = e^a \cdot e^b \\
y &= \pm e^C e^{kt} && \text{If } |y| = r, \text{ then } y = \pm r. \\
y &= Ae^{kt}. && A \text{ is a shorter name for } \pm e^C.
\end{aligned}$$

By allowing A to take on the value 0 in addition to all possible values $\pm e^C$, we can include the solution $y = 0$ in the formula.

We find the value of A for the initial value problem by solving for A when $y = y_0$ and $t = 0$:

$$y_0 = Ae^{k \cdot 0} = A.$$

The solution of the initial value problem in Equations (1a) and (1b) is therefore

$$y = y_0 e^{kt}. \tag{2}$$

Quantities changing in this way are said to undergo **exponential growth** if $k > 0$ and **exponential decay** if $k < 0$. The number k is called the **rate constant** of the change. (See Figure 7.5.)

The derivation of Equation (2) shows also that the only functions that are their own derivatives are constant multiples of the exponential function.

Before presenting several examples of exponential change, let's consider the process we used to derive it.

Separable Differential Equations

Exponential change is modeled by a differential equation of the form $dy/dx = ky$ for some nonzero constant k. More generally, suppose we have a differential equation of the form

$$\frac{dy}{dx} = f(x, y), \tag{3}$$

where f is a function of *both* the independent and dependent variables. A **solution** of the equation is a differentiable function $y = y(x)$ defined on an interval of x-values (perhaps infinite) such that

$$\frac{d}{dx}y(x) = f(x, y(x))$$

on that interval. That is, when $y(x)$ and its derivative $y'(x)$ are substituted into the differential equation, the resulting equation is true for all x in the solution interval. The **general solution** is a solution $y(x)$ that contains all possible solutions and it always contains an arbitrary constant.

Equation (3) is **separable** if f can be expressed as a product of a function of x and a function of y. The differential equation then has the form

$$\frac{dy}{dx} = g(x)H(y).$$

g is a function of x; H is a function of y.

When we rewrite this equation in the form

$$\frac{dy}{dx} = \frac{g(x)}{h(y)},$$

$H(y) = \dfrac{1}{h(y)}$

its differential form allows us to collect all y terms with dy and all x terms with dx:

$$h(y)\,dy = g(x)\,dx.$$

Now we simply integrate both sides of this equation:

$$\int h(y)\,dy = \int g(x)\,dx. \tag{4}$$

After completing the integrations we obtain the solution y defined implicitly as a function of x.

The justification that we can simply integrate both sides in Equation (4) is based on the Substitution Rule (Section 5.5):

$$\begin{aligned}\int h(y)\,dy &= \int h(y(x))\frac{dy}{dx}\,dx \\ &= \int h(y(x))\frac{g(x)}{h(y(x))}\,dx \qquad \frac{dy}{dx} = \frac{g(x)}{h(y)} \\ &= \int g(x)\,dx.\end{aligned}$$

EXAMPLE 1 Solve the differential equation

$$\frac{dy}{dx} = (1 + y)e^x, \quad y > -1.$$

Solution Since $1 + y$ is never zero for $y > -1$, we can solve the equation by separating the variables.

$$\begin{aligned}\frac{dy}{dx} &= (1 + y)e^x \\ dy &= (1 + y)e^x\,dx && \text{Treat } dy/dx \text{ as a quotient of differentials and multiply both sides by } dx. \\ \frac{dy}{1 + y} &= e^x\,dx && \text{Divide by } (1 + y). \\ \int \frac{dy}{1 + y} &= \int e^x\,dx && \text{Integrate both sides.} \\ \ln(1 + y) &= e^x + C && C \text{ represents the combined constants of integration.}\end{aligned}$$

The last equation gives y as an implicit function of x. ■

EXAMPLE 2 Solve the equation $y(x+1)\dfrac{dy}{dx} = x(y^2+1)$.

Solution We change to differential form, separate the variables, and integrate:

$$y(x+1)\,dy = x(y^2+1)\,dx$$

$$\frac{y\,dy}{y^2+1} = \frac{x\,dx}{x+1} \qquad x \neq -1$$

$$\int \frac{y\,dy}{1+y^2} = \int \left(1 - \frac{1}{x+1}\right) dx \qquad \text{Divide } x \text{ by } x+1.$$

$$\frac{1}{2}\ln(1+y^2) = x - \ln|x+1| + C.$$

The last equation gives the solution y as an implicit function of x. ∎

The initial value problem

$$\frac{dy}{dt} = ky, \qquad y(0) = y_0$$

involves a separable differential equation, and the solution $y = y_0e^{kt}$ expresses exponential change. We now present several examples of such change.

Unlimited Population Growth

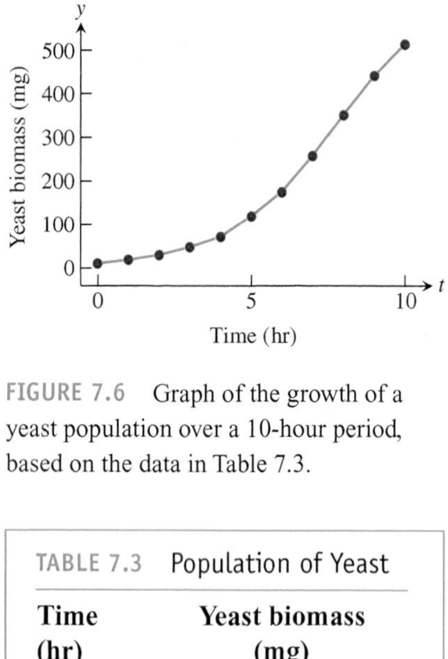

FIGURE 7.6 Graph of the growth of a yeast population over a 10-hour period, based on the data in Table 7.3.

TABLE 7.3 Population of Yeast

Time (hr)	Yeast biomass (mg)
0	9.6
1	18.3
2	29.0
3	47.2
4	71.1
5	119.1
6	174.6
7	257.3
8	350.7
9	441.0
10	513.3

Strictly speaking, the number of individuals in a population (of people, plants, animals, or bacteria, for example) is a discontinuous function of time because it takes on discrete values. However, when the number of individuals becomes large enough, the population can be approximated by a continuous function. Differentiability of the approximating function is another reasonable hypothesis in many settings, allowing for the use of calculus to model and predict population sizes.

If we assume that the proportion of reproducing individuals remains constant and assume a constant fertility, then at any instant t the birth rate is proportional to the number $y(t)$ of individuals present. Let's assume, too, that the death rate of the population is stable and proportional to $y(t)$. If, further, we neglect departures and arrivals, the growth rate dy/dt is the birth rate minus the death rate, which is the difference of the two proportionalities under our assumptions. In other words, $dy/dt = ky$ so that $y = y_0e^{kt}$, where y_0 is the size of the population at time $t = 0$. As with all kinds of growth, there may be limitations imposed by the surrounding environment, but we will not go into these here. When k is positive, the proportionality $dy/dt = ky$ models *unlimited population growth.* (See Figure 7.6.)

EXAMPLE 3 The biomass of a yeast culture in an experiment is initially 12 grams. After 10 minutes the mass is 15 grams. Assuming that the equation for unlimited population growth gives a good model for the growth of the yeast when the mass is below 100 grams, how long will it take for the mass to double from its initial value?

Solution Let $y(t)$ be the yeast biomass after t minutes. We use the exponential growth model $dy/dt = ky$ for unlimited population growth, with solution $y = y_0e^{kt}$.

We have $y_0 = y(0) = 12$. We are also told that,

$$y(10) = 12e^{k(10)} = 15.$$

Solving this equation for k, we find

$$e^{k(10)} = \frac{15}{12}$$

$$10k = \ln\left(\frac{5}{4}\right)$$

$$k = \frac{1}{10}\ln\left(\frac{5}{4}\right) \approx 0.022314.$$

Then the mass of the yeast in grams after t minutes is given by the equation

$$y = 12e^{(0.022314)t}.$$

To solve the problem we find the time t for which $y(t) = 24$, which is twice the initial amout:

$$\begin{aligned} 12e^{(0.022314)t} &= 24 \\ (0.022314)t &= \ln\left(\frac{24}{12}\right) \\ t &= \frac{\ln 2}{0.022314} \approx 31.06 \end{aligned}$$

It takes about 31 minutes for the yeast population to double. ■

In the next example we model the number of people within a given population who are infected by a disease which is being eradicated from the population. Here the constant of proportionality k is negative, and the model describes an exponentially decaying number of infected individuals.

EXAMPLE 4 One model for the way diseases die out when properly treated assumes that the rate dy/dt at which the number of infected people changes is proportional to the number y. The number of people cured is proportional to the number y that are infected with the disease. Suppose that in the course of any given year the number of cases of a disease is reduced by 20%. If there are 10,000 cases today, how many years will it take to reduce the number to 1000?

Solution We use the equation $y = y_0 e^{kt}$. There are three things to find: the value of y_0, the value of k, and the time t when $y = 1000$.

The value of y_0. We are free to count time beginning anywhere we want. If we count from today, then $y = 10{,}000$ when $t = 0$, so $y_0 = 10{,}000$. Our equation is now

$$y = 10{,}000e^{kt}. \tag{5}$$

The value of k. When $t = 1$ year, the number of cases will be 80% of its present value, or 8000. Hence,

$$\begin{aligned} 8000 &= 10{,}000e^{k(1)} && \text{Eq. (5) with } t = 1 \text{ and } y = 8000 \\ e^k &= 0.8 \\ \ln(e^k) &= \ln 0.8 && \text{Logs of both sides} \\ k &= \ln 0.8 < 0. && \ln 0.8 \approx -0.223 \end{aligned}$$

At any given time t,

$$y = 10{,}000e^{(\ln 0.8)t}. \tag{6}$$

The value of t that makes $y = 1000$. We set y equal to 1000 in Equation (6) and solve for t:

$$\begin{aligned} 1000 &= 10{,}000e^{(\ln 0.8)t} \\ e^{(\ln 0.8)t} &= 0.1 \\ (\ln 0.8)t &= \ln 0.1 && \text{Logs of both sides} \\ t &= \frac{\ln 0.1}{\ln 0.8} \approx 10.32 \text{ years}. \end{aligned}$$

It will take a little more than 10 years to reduce the number of cases to 1000. (See Figure 7.7) ■

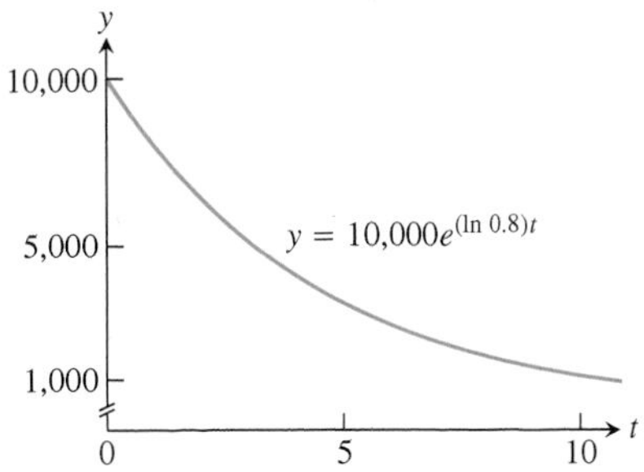

FIGURE 7.7 A graph of the number of people infected by a disease exhibits exponential decay (Example 4).

Radioactivity

Some atoms are unstable and can spontaneously emit mass or radiation. This process is called **radioactive decay**, and an element whose atoms go spontaneously through this process is called **radioactive**. Sometimes when an atom emits some of its mass through this process of radioactivity, the remainder of the atom re-forms to make an atom of some new element. For example, radioactive carbon-14 decays into nitrogen; radium, through a number of intermediate radioactive steps, decays into lead.

Experiments have shown that at any given time the rate at which a radioactive element decays (as measured by the number of nuclei that change per unit time) is approximately proportional to the number of radioactive nuclei present. Thus, the decay of a radioactive element is described by the equation $dy/dt = -ky$, $k > 0$. It is conventional to use $-k$, with $k > 0$, to emphasize that y is decreasing. If y_0 is the number of radioactive nuclei present at time zero, the number still present at any later time t will be

$$y = y_0 e^{-kt}, \qquad k > 0.$$

For radon-222 gas, t is measured in days and $k = 0.18$. For radium-226, which used to be painted on watch dials to make them glow at night (a dangerous practice), t is measured in years and $k = 4.3 \times 10^{-4}$.

In Section 1.6, we defined the **half-life** of a radioactive element to be the time required for half of the radioactive nuclei present in a sample to decay. It is an interesting fact that the half-life is a constant that does not depend on the number of radioactive nuclei initially present in the sample, but only on the radioactive substance. We found the half-life is given by

$$\text{Half-life} = \frac{\ln 2}{k} \tag{7}$$

For example, the half-life for radon-222 is

$$\text{half-life} = \frac{\ln 2}{0.18} \approx 3.9 \text{ days}.$$

EXAMPLE 5 The decay of radioactive elements can sometimes be used to date events from Earth's past. In a living organism, the ratio of radioactive carbon, carbon-14, to ordinary carbon stays fairly constant during the lifetime of the organism, being approximately equal to the ratio in the organism's atmosphere at the time. After the organism's death, however, no new carbon is ingested, and the proportion of carbon-14 in the organism's remains decreases as the carbon-14 decays.

Scientists who do carbon-14 dating use a figure of 5730 years for its half-life. Find the age of a sample in which 10% of the radioactive nuclei originally present have decayed.

Solution We use the decay equation $y = y_0 e^{-kt}$. There are two things to find: the value of k and the value of t when y is $0.9y_0$ (90% of the radioactive nuclei are still present). That is, find t when $y_0 e^{-kt} = 0.9y_0$, or $e^{-kt} = 0.9$.

The value of k. We use the half-life Equation (7):

$$k = \frac{\ln 2}{\text{half-life}} = \frac{\ln 2}{5730} \qquad (\text{about } 1.2 \times 10^{-4}).$$

The value of t that makes $e^{-kt} = 0.9$.

$$e^{-kt} = 0.9$$

$$e^{-(\ln 2/5730)t} = 0.9$$

$$-\frac{\ln 2}{5730}t = \ln 0.9 \qquad \text{Logs of both sides}$$

$$t = -\frac{5730 \ln 0.9}{\ln 2} \approx 871 \text{ years}$$

The sample is about 871 years old. ■

Heat Transfer: Newton's Law of Cooling

Hot soup left in a tin cup cools to the temperature of the surrounding air. A hot silver bar immersed in a large tub of water cools to the temperature of the surrounding water. In situations like these, the rate at which an object's temperature is changing at any given time is roughly proportional to the difference between its temperature and the temperature of the surrounding medium. This observation is called *Newton's Law of Cooling*, although it applies to warming as well.

If H is the temperature of the object at time t and H_S is the constant surrounding temperature, then the differential equation is

$$\frac{dH}{dt} = -k(H - H_S). \tag{8}$$

If we substitute y for $(H - H_S)$, then

$$\begin{aligned}
\frac{dy}{dt} &= \frac{d}{dt}(H - H_S) = \frac{dH}{dt} - \frac{d}{dt}(H_S) \\
&= \frac{dH}{dt} - 0 && H_S \text{ is a constant.} \\
&= \frac{dH}{dt} \\
&= -k(H - H_S) && \text{Eq. (8)} \\
&= -ky. && H - H_S = y
\end{aligned}$$

Now we know that the solution of $dy/dt = -ky$ is $y = y_0 e^{-kt}$, where $y(0) = y_0$. Substituting $(H - H_S)$ for y, this says that

$$H - H_S = (H_0 - H_S)e^{-kt}, \tag{9}$$

where H_0 is the temperature at $t = 0$. This equation is the solution to Newton's Law of Cooling.

EXAMPLE 6 A hard-boiled egg at 98°C is put in a sink of 18°C water. After 5 min, the egg's temperature is 38°C. Assuming that the water has not warmed appreciably, how much longer will it take the egg to reach 20°C?

Solution We find how long it would take the egg to cool from 98°C to 20°C and subtract the 5 min that have already elapsed. Using Equation (9) with $H_S = 18$ and $H_0 = 98$, the egg's temperature t min after it is put in the sink is

$$H = 18 + (98 - 18)e^{-kt} = 18 + 80e^{-kt}.$$

To find k, we use the information that $H = 38$ when $t = 5$:

$$\begin{aligned}
38 &= 18 + 80e^{-5k} \\
e^{-5k} &= \frac{1}{4} \\
-5k &= \ln\frac{1}{4} = -\ln 4 \\
k &= \frac{1}{5}\ln 4 = 0.2\ln 4 \qquad (\text{about } 0.28).
\end{aligned}$$

The egg's temperature at time t is $H = 18 + 80e^{-(0.2\ln 4)t}$. Now find the time t when $H = 20$:

$$\begin{aligned}
20 &= 18 + 80e^{-(0.2\ln 4)t} \\
80e^{-(0.2\ln 4)t} &= 2 \\
e^{-(0.2\ln 4)t} &= \frac{1}{40} \\
-(0.2\ln 4)t &= \ln\frac{1}{40} = -\ln 40 \\
t &= \frac{\ln 40}{0.2\ln 4} \approx 13 \text{ min}.
\end{aligned}$$

The egg's temperature will reach 20°C about 13 min after it is put in the water to cool. Since it took 5 min to reach 38°C, it will take about 8 min more to reach 20°C. ■

Exercises 7.2

Verifying Solutions

In Exercises 1–4, show that each function $y = f(x)$ is a solution of the accompanying differential equation.

1. $2y' + 3y = e^{-x}$

   a. $y = e^{-x}$ b. $y = e^{-x} + e^{-(3/2)x}$

   c. $y = e^{-x} + Ce^{-(3/2)x}$

2. $y' = y^2$

   a. $y = -\frac{1}{x}$ b. $y = -\frac{1}{x+3}$ c. $y = -\frac{1}{x+C}$

3. $y = \frac{1}{x}\int_1^x \frac{e^t}{t}\,dt, \quad x^2y' + xy = e^x$

4. $y = \frac{1}{\sqrt{1+x^4}}\int_1^x \sqrt{1+t^4}\,dt, \quad y' + \frac{2x^3}{1+x^4}y = 1$

Initial Value Problems

In Exercises 5–8, show that each function is a solution of the given initial value problem.

	Differential equation	Initial condition	Solution candidate
5.	$y' + y = \frac{2}{1+4e^{2x}}$	$y(-\ln 2) = \frac{\pi}{2}$	$y = e^{-x}\tan^{-1}(2e^x)$
6.	$y' = e^{-x^2} - 2xy$	$y(2) = 0$	$y = (x-2)e^{-x^2}$
7.	$xy' + y = -\sin x,$ $x > 0$	$y\left(\frac{\pi}{2}\right) = 0$	$y = \frac{\cos x}{x}$
8.	$x^2y' = xy - y^2,$ $x > 1$	$y(e) = e$	$y = \frac{x}{\ln x}$

Separable Differential Equations

Solve the differential equation in Exercises 9–22.

9. $2\sqrt{xy}\frac{dy}{dx} = 1, \quad x, y > 0$

10. $\frac{dy}{dx} = x^2\sqrt{y}, \quad y > 0$

11. $\frac{dy}{dx} = e^{x-y}$

12. $\frac{dy}{dx} = 3x^2e^{-y}$

13. $\frac{dy}{dx} = \sqrt{y}\cos^2\sqrt{y}$

14. $\sqrt{2xy}\frac{dy}{dx} = 1$

15. $\sqrt{x}\frac{dy}{dx} = e^{y+\sqrt{x}}, \quad x > 0$

16. $(\sec x)\frac{dy}{dx} = e^{y+\sin x}$

17. $\frac{dy}{dx} = 2x\sqrt{1-y^2}, \quad -1 < y < 1$

18. $\frac{dy}{dx} = \frac{e^{2x-y}}{e^{x+y}}$

19. $y^2\frac{dy}{dx} = 3x^2y^3 - 6x^2$

20. $\frac{dy}{dx} = xy + 3x - 2y - 6$

21. $\frac{1}{x}\frac{dy}{dx} = ye^{x^2} + 2\sqrt{y}e^{x^2}$

22. $\frac{dy}{dx} = e^{x-y} + e^x + e^{-y} + 1$

Applications and Examples

The answers to most of the following exercises are in terms of logarithms and exponentials. A calculator can be helpful, enabling you to express the answers in decimal form.

23. **Human evolution continues** The analysis of tooth shrinkage by C. Loring Brace and colleagues at the University of Michigan's Museum of Anthropology indicates that human tooth size is continuing to decrease and that the evolutionary process did not come to a halt some 30,000 years ago as many scientists contend. In northern Europeans, for example, tooth size reduction now has a rate of 1% per 1000 years.

    a. If t represents time in years and y represents tooth size, use the condition that $y = 0.99y_0$ when $t = 1000$ to find the value of k in the equation $y = y_0e^{kt}$. Then use this value of k to answer the following questions.

    b. In about how many years will human teeth be 90% of their present size?

    c. What will be our descendants' tooth size 20,000 years from now (as a percentage of our present tooth size)?

24. **Atmospheric pressure** The earth's atmospheric pressure p is often modeled by assuming that the rate dp/dh at which p changes with the altitude h above sea level is proportional to p. Suppose that the pressure at sea level is 1013 millibars (about 14.7 pounds per square inch) and that the pressure at an altitude of 20 km is 90 millibars.

    a. Solve the initial value problem

    Differential equation: $dp/dh = kp$ (k a constant)
    Initial condition: $p = p_0$ when $h = 0$

    to express p in terms of h. Determine the values of p_0 and k from the given altitude-pressure data.

    b. What is the atmospheric pressure at $h = 50$ km?

    c. At what altitude does the pressure equal 900 millibars?

25. **First-order chemical reactions** In some chemical reactions, the rate at which the amount of a substance changes with time is proportional to the amount present. For the change of δ-glucono lactone into gluconic acid, for example,

$$\frac{dy}{dt} = -0.6y$$

when t is measured in hours. If there are 100 grams of δ-glucono lactone present when $t = 0$, how many grams will be left after the first hour?

26. **The inversion of sugar** The processing of raw sugar has a step called "inversion" that changes the sugar's molecular structure. Once the process has begun, the rate of change of the amount of raw sugar is proportional to the amount of raw sugar remaining. If 1000 kg of raw sugar reduces to 800 kg of raw sugar during the first 10 hours, how much raw sugar will remain after another 14 hours?

27. **Working underwater** The intensity $L(x)$ of light x feet beneath the surface of the ocean satisfies the differential equation

$$\frac{dL}{dx} = -kL.$$

As a diver, you know from experience that diving to 18 ft in the Caribbean Sea cuts the intensity in half. You cannot work without artificial light when the intensity falls below one-tenth of the surface value. About how deep can you expect to work without artificial light?

28. **Voltage in a discharging capacitor** Suppose that electricity is draining from a capacitor at a rate that is proportional to the voltage V across its terminals and that, if t is measured in seconds,

$$\frac{dV}{dt} = -\frac{1}{40}V.$$

Solve this equation for V, using V_0 to denote the value of V when $t = 0$. How long will it take the voltage to drop to 10% of its original value?

29. **Cholera bacteria** Suppose that the bacteria in a colony can grow unchecked, by the law of exponential change. The colony starts with 1 bacterium and doubles every half-hour. How many bacteria will the colony contain at the end of 24 hours? (Under favorable laboratory conditions, the number of cholera bacteria can double every 30 min. In an infected person, many bacteria are destroyed, but this example helps explain why a person who feels well in the morning may be dangerously ill by evening.)

30. **Growth of bacteria** A colony of bacteria is grown under ideal conditions in a laboratory so that the population increases exponentially with time. At the end of 3 hours there are 10,000 bacteria. At the end of 5 hours there are 40,000. How many bacteria were present initially?

31. **The incidence of a disease** (*Continuation of Example 3.*) Suppose that in any given year the number of cases can be reduced by 25% instead of 20%.
   a. How long will it take to reduce the number of cases to 1000?
   b. How long will it take to eradicate the disease, that is, reduce the number of cases to less than 1?

32. **The U.S. population** The U.S. Census Bureau keeps a running clock totaling the U.S. population. On March 26, 2008, the total was increasing at the rate of 1 person every 13 sec. The population figure for 2:31 P.M. EST on that day was 303,714,725.
   a. Assuming exponential growth at a constant rate, find the rate constant for the population's growth (people per 365-day year).
   b. At this rate, what will the U.S. population be at 2:31 P.M. EST on March 26, 2015?

33. **Oil depletion** Suppose the amount of oil pumped from one of the canyon wells in Whittier, California, decreases at the continuous rate of 10% per year. When will the well's output fall to one-fifth of its present value?

34. **Continuous price discounting** To encourage buyers to place 100-unit orders, your firm's sales department applies a continuous discount that makes the unit price a function $p(x)$ of the number of units x ordered. The discount decreases the price at the rate of \$0.01 per unit ordered. The price per unit for a 100-unit order is $p(100) = \$20.09$.
   a. Find $p(x)$ by solving the following initial value problem:

   Differential equation: $\dfrac{dp}{dx} = -\dfrac{1}{100}p$

   Initial condition: $p(100) = 20.09.$

   b. Find the unit price $p(10)$ for a 10-unit order and the unit price $p(90)$ for a 90-unit order.
   c. The sales department has asked you to find out if it is discounting so much that the firm's revenue, $r(x) = x \cdot p(x)$, will actually be less for a 100-unit order than, say, for a 90-unit order. Reassure them by showing that r has its maximum value at $x = 100$.
   d. Graph the revenue function $r(x) = xp(x)$ for $0 \le x \le 200$.

35. **Plutonium-239** The half-life of the plutonium isotope is 24,360 years. If 10 g of plutonium is released into the atmosphere by a nuclear accident, how many years will it take for 80% of the isotope to decay?

36. **Polonium-210** The half-life of polonium is 139 days, but your sample will not be useful to you after 95% of the radioactive nuclei present on the day the sample arrives has disintegrated. For about how many days after the sample arrives will you be able to use the polonium?

37. **The mean life of a radioactive nucleus** Physicists using the radioactivity equation $y = y_0e^{-kt}$ call the number $1/k$ the *mean life* of a radioactive nucleus. The mean life of a radon nucleus is about $1/0.18 = 5.6$ days. The mean life of a carbon-14 nucleus is more than 8000 years. Show that 95% of the radioactive nuclei originally present in a sample will disintegrate within three mean lifetimes, i.e., by time $t = 3/k$. Thus, the mean life of a nucleus gives a quick way to estimate how long the radioactivity of a sample will last.

38. **Californium-252** What costs \$27 million per gram and can be used to treat brain cancer, analyze coal for its sulfur content, and detect explosives in luggage? The answer is californium-252, a radioactive isotope so rare that only 8 g of it have been made in the Western world since its discovery by Glenn Seaborg in 1950. The half-life of the isotope is 2.645 years—long enough for a useful service life and short enough to have a high radioactivity per unit mass. One microgram of the isotope releases 170 million neutrons per minute.
   a. What is the value of k in the decay equation for this isotope?
   b. What is the isotope's mean life? (See Exercise 37.)
   c. How long will it take 95% of a sample's radioactive nuclei to disintegrate?

39. **Cooling soup** Suppose that a cup of soup cooled from 90°C to 60°C after 10 min in a room whose temperature was 20°C. Use Newton's Law of Cooling to answer the following questions.
   a. How much longer would it take the soup to cool to 35°C?
   b. Instead of being left to stand in the room, the cup of 90°C soup is put in a freezer whose temperature is -15°C. How long will it take the soup to cool from 90°C to 35°C?

40. **A beam of unknown temperature** An aluminum beam was brought from the outside cold into a machine shop where the temperature was held at 65°F. After 10 min, the beam warmed to 35°F and after another 10 min it was 50°F. Use Newton's Law of Cooling to estimate the beam's initial temperature.

41. **Surrounding medium of unknown temperature** A pan of warm water (46°C) was put in a refrigerator. Ten minutes later, the water's temperature was 39°C; 10 min after that, it was 33°C. Use Newton's Law of Cooling to estimate how cold the refrigerator was.

42. **Silver cooling in air** The temperature of an ingot of silver is 60°C above room temperature right now. Twenty minutes ago, it was 70°C above room temperature. How far above room temperature will the silver be
   a. 15 min from now? b. 2 hours from now?
   c. When will the silver be 10°C above room temperature?

43. **The age of Crater Lake** The charcoal from a tree killed in the volcanic eruption that formed Crater Lake in Oregon contained 44.5% of the carbon-14 found in living matter. About how old is Crater Lake?

44. **The sensitivity of carbon-14 dating to measurement** To see the effect of a relatively small error in the estimate of the amount of carbon-14 in a sample being dated, consider this hypothetical situation:
   a. A bone fragment found in central Illinois in the year 2000 contains 17% of its original carbon-14 content. Estimate the year the animal died.
   b. Repeat part (a) assuming 18% instead of 17%.
   c. Repeat part (a) assuming 16% instead of 17%.

45. Carbon-14 The oldest known frozen human mummy, discovered in the Schnalstal glacier of the Italian Alps in 1991 and called *Otzi*, was found wearing straw shoes and a leather coat with goat fur, and holding a copper ax and stone dagger. It was estimated that Otzi died 5000 years before he was discovered in the melting glacier. How much of the original carbon-14 remained in Otzi at the time of his discovery?

46. Art forgery A painting attributed to Vermeer (1632–1675), which should contain no more than 96.2% of its original carbon-14, contains 99.5% instead. About how old is the forgery?

7.3 Hyperbolic Functions

The hyperbolic functions are formed by taking combinations of the two exponential functions e^x and e^{-x}. The hyperbolic functions simplify many mathematical expressions and occur frequently in mathematical and engineering applications. In this section we give a brief introduction to these functions, their graphs, their derivatives, their integrals, and their inverse functions.

Definitions and Identities

The hyperbolic sine and hyperbolic cosine functions are defined by the equations

$$\sinh x = \frac{e^x - e^{-x}}{2} \quad \text{and} \quad \cosh x = \frac{e^x + e^{-x}}{2}.$$

We pronounce $\sinh x$ as "cinch x," rhyming with "pinch x," and $\cosh x$ as "kosh x," rhyming with "gosh x." From this basic pair, we define the hyperbolic tangent, cotangent, secant, and cosecant functions. The defining equations and graphs of these functions are shown in Table 7.4. We will see that the hyperbolic functions bear many similarities to the trigonometric functions after which they are named.

TABLE 7.4 The six basic hyperbolic functions

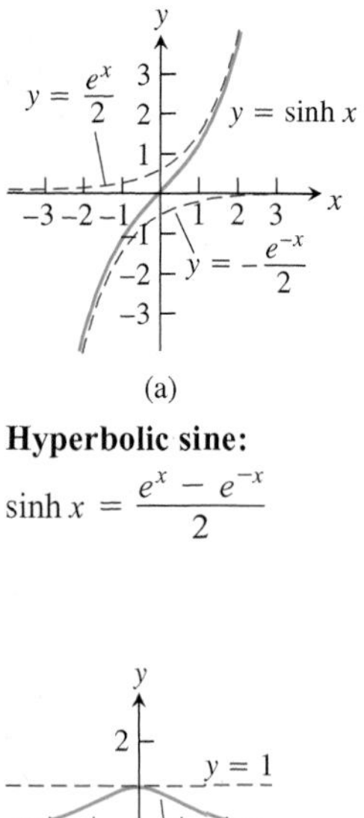

(a)

Hyperbolic sine:

$$\sinh x = \frac{e^x - e^{-x}}{2}$$

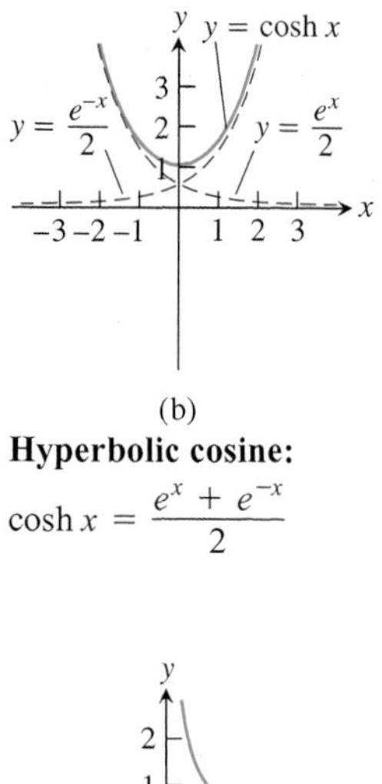

(b)

Hyperbolic cosine:

$$\cosh x = \frac{e^x + e^{-x}}{2}$$

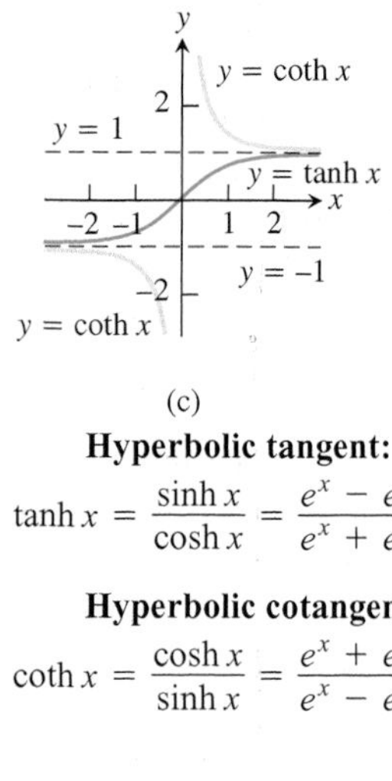

(c)

Hyperbolic tangent:

$$\tanh x = \frac{\sinh x}{\cosh x} = \frac{e^x - e^{-x}}{e^x + e^{-x}}$$

Hyperbolic cotangent:

$$\coth x = \frac{\cosh x}{\sinh x} = \frac{e^x + e^{-x}}{e^x - e^{-x}}$$

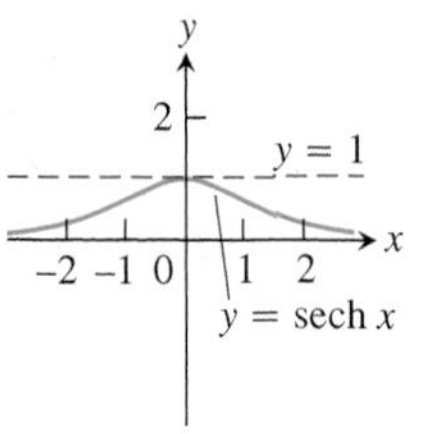

(d)

Hyperbolic secant:

$$\operatorname{sech} x = \frac{1}{\cosh x} = \frac{2}{e^x + e^{-x}}$$

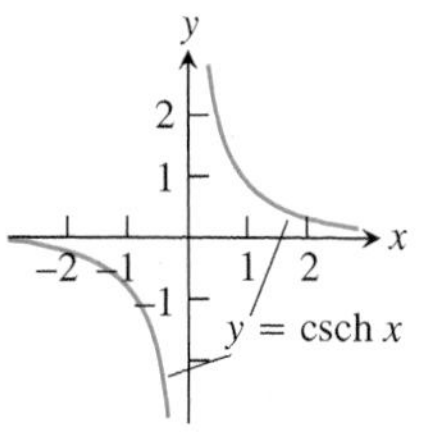

(e)

Hyperbolic cosecant:

$$\operatorname{csch} x = \frac{1}{\sinh x} = \frac{2}{e^x - e^{-x}}$$

TABLE 7.5 Identities for hyperbolic functions

$$\cosh^2 x - \sinh^2 x = 1$$
$$\sinh 2x = 2 \sinh x \cosh x$$
$$\cosh 2x = \cosh^2 x + \sinh^2 x$$
$$\cosh^2 x = \frac{\cosh 2x + 1}{2}$$
$$\sinh^2 x = \frac{\cosh 2x - 1}{2}$$
$$\tanh^2 x = 1 - \operatorname{sech}^2 x$$
$$\coth^2 x = 1 + \operatorname{csch}^2 x$$

TABLE 7.6 Derivatives of hyperbolic functions

$$\frac{d}{dx}(\sinh u) = \cosh u \frac{du}{dx}$$
$$\frac{d}{dx}(\cosh u) = \sinh u \frac{du}{dx}$$
$$\frac{d}{dx}(\tanh u) = \operatorname{sech}^2 u \frac{du}{dx}$$
$$\frac{d}{dx}(\coth u) = -\operatorname{csch}^2 u \frac{du}{dx}$$
$$\frac{d}{dx}(\operatorname{sech} u) = -\operatorname{sech} u \tanh u \frac{du}{dx}$$
$$\frac{d}{dx}(\operatorname{csch} u) = -\operatorname{csch} u \coth u \frac{du}{dx}$$

TABLE 7.7 Integral formulas for hyperbolic functions

$$\int \sinh u \, du = \cosh u + C$$
$$\int \cosh u \, du = \sinh u + C$$
$$\int \operatorname{sech}^2 u \, du = \tanh u + C$$
$$\int \operatorname{csch}^2 u \, du = -\coth u + C$$
$$\int \operatorname{sech} u \tanh u \, du = -\operatorname{sech} u + C$$
$$\int \operatorname{csch} u \coth u \, du = -\operatorname{csch} u + C$$

Hyperbolic functions satisfy the identities in Table 7.5. Except for differences in sign, these resemble identities we know for the trigonometric functions. The identities are proved directly from the definitions, as we show here for the second one:

$$\begin{aligned} 2 \sinh x \cosh x &= 2\left(\frac{e^x - e^{-x}}{2}\right)\left(\frac{e^x + e^{-x}}{2}\right) \\ &= \frac{e^{2x} - e^{-2x}}{2} \\ &= \sinh 2x. \end{aligned}$$

The other identities are obtained similarly, by substituting in the definitions of the hyperbolic functions and using algebra. Like many standard functions, hyperbolic functions and their inverses are easily evaluated with calculators, which often have special keys for that purpose.

For any real number u, we know the point with coordinates $(\cos u, \sin u)$ lies on the unit circle $x^2 + y^2 = 1$. So the trigonometric functions are sometimes called the *circular* functions. Because of the first identity

$$\cosh^2 u - \sinh^2 u = 1,$$

with u substituted for x in Table 7.5, the point having coordinates $(\cosh u, \sinh u)$ lies on the right-hand branch of the hyperbola $x^2 - y^2 = 1$. This is where the *hyperbolic* functions get their names (see Exercise 86).

Derivatives and Integrals of Hyperbolic Functions

The six hyperbolic functions, being rational combinations of the differentiable functions e^x and e^{-x}, have derivatives at every point at which they are defined (Table 7.6). Again, there are similarities with trigonometric functions.

The derivative formulas are derived from the derivative of e^u:

$$\begin{aligned} \frac{d}{dx}(\sinh u) &= \frac{d}{dx}\left(\frac{e^u - e^{-u}}{2}\right) && \text{Definition of } \sinh u \\ &= \frac{e^u\, du/dx + e^{-u}\, du/dx}{2} && \text{Derivative of } e^u \\ &= \cosh u \frac{du}{dx}. && \text{Definition of } \cosh u \end{aligned}$$

This gives the first derivative formula. From the definition, we can calculate the derivative of the hyperbolic cosecant function, as follows:

$$\begin{aligned} \frac{d}{dx}(\operatorname{csch} u) &= \frac{d}{dx}\left(\frac{1}{\sinh u}\right) && \text{Definition of } \operatorname{csch} u \\ &= -\frac{\cosh u}{\sinh^2 u}\frac{du}{dx} && \text{Quotient Rule} \\ &= -\frac{1}{\sinh u}\frac{\cosh u}{\sinh u}\frac{du}{dx} && \text{Rearrange terms.} \\ &= -\operatorname{csch} u \coth u \frac{du}{dx} && \text{Definitions of } \operatorname{csch} u \text{ and } \coth u \end{aligned}$$

The other formulas in Table 7.6 are obtained similarly.

The derivative formulas lead to the integral formulas in Table 7.7.

EXAMPLE 1

(a) $$\frac{d}{dt}\left(\tanh\sqrt{1+t^2}\right) = \operatorname{sech}^2\sqrt{1+t^2}\cdot\frac{d}{dt}\left(\sqrt{1+t^2}\right)$$
$$= \frac{t}{\sqrt{1+t^2}}\operatorname{sech}^2\sqrt{1+t^2}$$

(b) $$\int \coth 5x\,dx = \int \frac{\cosh 5x}{\sinh 5x}\,dx = \frac{1}{5}\int\frac{du}{u}$$
$u = \sinh 5x$, $du = 5\cosh 5x\,dx$
$$= \frac{1}{5}\ln|u| + C = \frac{1}{5}\ln|\sinh 5x| + C$$

(c) $$\int_0^1 \sinh^2 x\,dx = \int_0^1 \frac{\cosh 2x - 1}{2}\,dx$$
Table 7.5
$$= \frac{1}{2}\int_0^1 (\cosh 2x - 1)\,dx = \frac{1}{2}\left[\frac{\sinh 2x}{2} - x\right]_0^1$$
$$= \frac{\sinh 2}{4} - \frac{1}{2} \approx 0.40672$$
Evaluate with a calculator.

(d) $$\int_0^{\ln 2} 4e^x \sinh x\,dx = \int_0^{\ln 2} 4e^x\frac{e^x - e^{-x}}{2}\,dx = \int_0^{\ln 2}(2e^{2x} - 2)\,dx$$
$$= \left[e^{2x} - 2x\right]_0^{\ln 2} = (e^{2\ln 2} - 2\ln 2) - (1 - 0)$$
$$= 4 - 2\ln 2 - 1 \approx 1.6137$$ ■

Inverse Hyperbolic Functions

The inverses of the six basic hyperbolic functions are very useful in integration (see Chapter 8). Since $d(\sinh x)/dx = \cosh x > 0$, the hyperbolic sine is an increasing function of x. We denote its inverse by

$$y = \sinh^{-1} x.$$

For every value of x in the interval $-\infty < x < \infty$, the value of $y = \sinh^{-1} x$ is the number whose hyperbolic sine is x. The graphs of $y = \sinh x$ and $y = \sinh^{-1} x$ are shown in Figure 7.8a.

The function $y = \cosh x$ is not one-to-one because its graph in Table 7.4 does not pass the horizontal line test. The restricted function $y = \cosh x$, $x \ge 0$, however, is one-to-one and therefore has an inverse, denoted by

$$y = \cosh^{-1} x.$$

For every value of $x \ge 1$, $y = \cosh^{-1} x$ is the number in the interval $0 \le y < \infty$ whose hyperbolic cosine is x. The graphs of $y = \cosh x$, $x \ge 0$, and $y = \cosh^{-1} x$ are shown in Figure 7.8b.

Like $y = \cosh x$, the function $y = \operatorname{sech} x = 1/\cosh x$ fails to be one-to-one, but its restriction to nonnegative values of x does have an inverse, denoted by

$$y = \operatorname{sech}^{-1} x.$$

For every value of x in the interval $(0, 1]$, $y = \operatorname{sech}^{-1} x$ is the nonnegative number whose hyperbolic secant is x. The graphs of $y = \operatorname{sech} x$, $x \ge 0$, and $y = \operatorname{sech}^{-1} x$ are shown in Figure 7.8c.

The hyperbolic tangent, cotangent, and cosecant are one-to-one on their domains and therefore have inverses, denoted by

$$y = \tanh^{-1} x, \qquad y = \coth^{-1} x, \qquad y = \operatorname{csch}^{-1} x.$$

These functions are graphed in Figure 7.9.

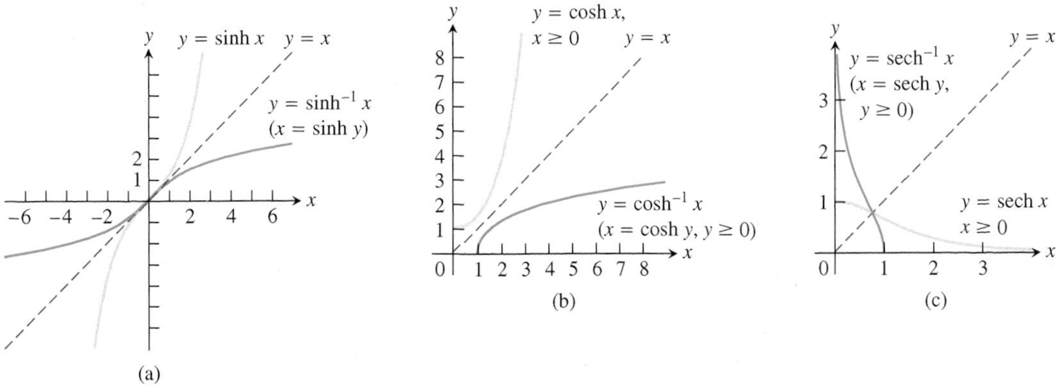

FIGURE 7.8 The graphs of the inverse hyperbolic sine, cosine, and secant of x. Notice the symmetries about the line $y = x$.

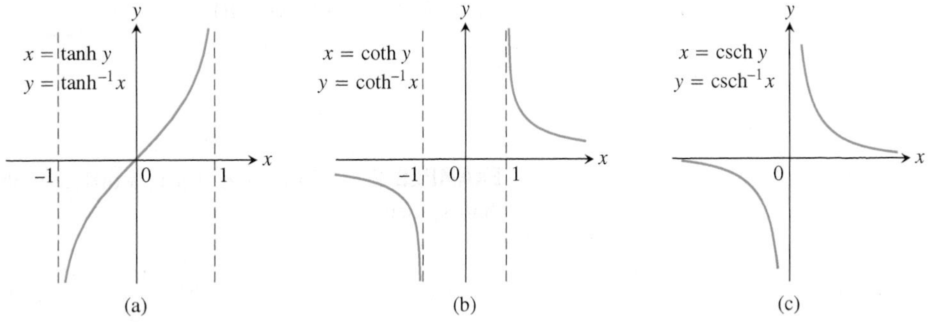

FIGURE 7.9 The graphs of the inverse hyperbolic tangent, cotangent, and cosecant of x.

Useful Identities

TABLE 7.8 Identities for inverse hyperbolic functions

$$\operatorname{sech}^{-1} x = \cosh^{-1} \frac{1}{x}$$

$$\operatorname{csch}^{-1} x = \sinh^{-1} \frac{1}{x}$$

$$\coth^{-1} x = \tanh^{-1} \frac{1}{x}$$

We use the identities in Table 7.8 to calculate the values of $\operatorname{sech}^{-1} x$, $\operatorname{csch}^{-1} x$, and $\coth^{-1} x$ on calculators that give only $\cosh^{-1} x$, $\sinh^{-1} x$, and $\tanh^{-1} x$. These identities are direct consequences of the definitions. For example, if $0 < x \le 1$, then

$$\operatorname{sech}\left(\cosh^{-1}\left(\frac{1}{x}\right)\right) = \frac{1}{\cosh\left(\cosh^{-1}\left(\frac{1}{x}\right)\right)} = \frac{1}{\left(\frac{1}{x}\right)} = x.$$

We also know that $\operatorname{sech}(\operatorname{sech}^{-1} x) = x$, so because the hyperbolic secant is one-to-one on $(0, 1]$, we have

$$\cosh^{-1}\left(\frac{1}{x}\right) = \operatorname{sech}^{-1} x.$$

Derivatives of Inverse Hyperbolic Functions

An important use of inverse hyperbolic functions lies in antiderivatives that reverse the derivative formulas in Table 7.9.

The restrictions $|u| < 1$ and $|u| > 1$ on the derivative formulas for $\tanh^{-1} u$ and $\coth^{-1} u$ come from the natural restrictions on the values of these functions. (See Figure 7.9a and b.) The distinction between $|u| < 1$ and $|u| > 1$ becomes important when we convert the derivative formulas into integral formulas.

We illustrate how the derivatives of the inverse hyperbolic functions are found in Example 2, where we calculate $d(\cosh^{-1} u)/dx$. The other derivatives are obtained by similar calculations.

TABLE 7.9 Derivatives of inverse hyperbolic functions

$$\frac{d(\sinh^{-1} u)}{dx} = \frac{1}{\sqrt{1 + u^2}} \frac{du}{dx}$$

$$\frac{d(\cosh^{-1} u)}{dx} = \frac{1}{\sqrt{u^2 - 1}} \frac{du}{dx}, \qquad u > 1$$

$$\frac{d(\tanh^{-1} u)}{dx} = \frac{1}{1 - u^2} \frac{du}{dx}, \qquad |u| < 1$$

$$\frac{d(\coth^{-1} u)}{dx} = \frac{1}{1 - u^2} \frac{du}{dx}, \qquad |u| > 1$$

$$\frac{d(\operatorname{sech}^{-1} u)}{dx} = -\frac{1}{u\sqrt{1 - u^2}} \frac{du}{dx}, \qquad 0 < u < 1$$

$$\frac{d(\operatorname{csch}^{-1} u)}{dx} = -\frac{1}{|u|\sqrt{1 + u^2}} \frac{du}{dx}, \qquad u \neq 0$$

EXAMPLE 2 Show that if u is a differentiable function of x whose values are greater than 1, then

$$\frac{d}{dx}(\cosh^{-1} u) = \frac{1}{\sqrt{u^2 - 1}} \frac{du}{dx}.$$

Solution First we find the derivative of $y = \cosh^{-1} x$ for $x > 1$ by applying Theorem 3 of Section 3.8 with $f(x) = \cosh x$ and $f^{-1}(x) = \cosh^{-1} x$. Theorem 3 can be applied because the derivative of $\cosh x$ is positive for $0 < x$.

$$
\begin{aligned}
(f^{-1})'(x) &= \frac{1}{f'(f^{-1}(x))} && \text{Theorem 3, Section 3.8} \\
&= \frac{1}{\sinh(\cosh^{-1} x)} && f'(u) = \sinh u \\
&= \frac{1}{\sqrt{\cosh^2(\cosh^{-1} x) - 1}} && \cosh^2 u - \sinh^2 u = 1, \ \sinh u = \sqrt{\cosh^2 u - 1} \\
&= \frac{1}{\sqrt{x^2 - 1}} && \cosh(\cosh^{-1} x) = x
\end{aligned}
$$

HISTORICAL BIOGRAPHY

Sonya Kovalevsky
(1850–1891)

The Chain Rule gives the final result:

$$\frac{d}{dx}(\cosh^{-1} u) = \frac{1}{\sqrt{u^2 - 1}} \frac{du}{dx}.$$ ■

With appropriate substitutions, the derivative formulas in Table 7.9 lead to the integration formulas in Table 7.10. Each of the formulas in Table 7.10 can be verified by differentiating the expression on the right-hand side.

EXAMPLE 3 Evaluate

$$\int_0^1 \frac{2\,dx}{\sqrt{3 + 4x^2}}.$$

TABLE 7.10 Integrals leading to inverse hyperbolic functions

1. $\displaystyle\int \frac{du}{\sqrt{a^2 + u^2}} = \sinh^{-1}\left(\frac{u}{a}\right) + C, \qquad a > 0$

2. $\displaystyle\int \frac{du}{\sqrt{u^2 - a^2}} = \cosh^{-1}\left(\frac{u}{a}\right) + C, \qquad u > a > 0$

3. $\displaystyle\int \frac{du}{a^2 - u^2} = \begin{cases} \dfrac{1}{a}\tanh^{-1}\left(\dfrac{u}{a}\right) + C, & u^2 < a^2 \\[2ex] \dfrac{1}{a}\coth^{-1}\left(\dfrac{u}{a}\right) + C, & u^2 > a^2 \end{cases}$

4. $\displaystyle\int \frac{du}{u\sqrt{a^2 - u^2}} = -\frac{1}{a}\operatorname{sech}^{-1}\left(\frac{u}{a}\right) + C, \qquad 0 < u < a$

5. $\displaystyle\int \frac{du}{u\sqrt{a^2 + u^2}} = -\frac{1}{a}\operatorname{csch}^{-1}\left|\frac{u}{a}\right| + C, \qquad u \neq 0 \text{ and } a > 0$

Solution The indefinite integral is

$$\int \frac{2\,dx}{\sqrt{3 + 4x^2}} = \int \frac{du}{\sqrt{a^2 + u^2}} \qquad u = 2x, \quad du = 2\,dx, \quad a = \sqrt{3}$$

$$= \sinh^{-1}\left(\frac{u}{a}\right) + C \qquad \text{Formula from Table 7.10}$$

$$= \sinh^{-1}\left(\frac{2x}{\sqrt{3}}\right) + C.$$

Therefore,

$$\int_0^1 \frac{2\,dx}{\sqrt{3 + 4x^2}} = \sinh^{-1}\left(\frac{2x}{\sqrt{3}}\right)\Big]_0^1 = \sinh^{-1}\left(\frac{2}{\sqrt{3}}\right) - \sinh^{-1}(0)$$

$$= \sinh^{-1}\left(\frac{2}{\sqrt{3}}\right) - 0 \approx 0.98665. \qquad \blacksquare$$

Exercises 7.3

Values and Identities

Each of Exercises 1–4 gives a value of $\sinh x$ or $\cosh x$. Use the definitions and the identity $\cosh^2 x - \sinh^2 x = 1$ to find the values of the remaining five hyperbolic functions.

1. $\sinh x = -\dfrac{3}{4}$

2. $\sinh x = \dfrac{4}{3}$

3. $\cosh x = \dfrac{17}{15}, \quad x > 0$

4. $\cosh x = \dfrac{13}{5}, \quad x > 0$

Rewrite the expressions in Exercises 5–10 in terms of exponentials and simplify the results as much as you can.

5. $2 \cosh(\ln x)$

6. $\sinh(2 \ln x)$

7. $\cosh 5x + \sinh 5x$

8. $\cosh 3x - \sinh 3x$

9. $(\sinh x + \cosh x)^4$

10. $\ln(\cosh x + \sinh x) + \ln(\cosh x - \sinh x)$

11. Prove the identities

$$\sinh(x + y) = \sinh x \cosh y + \cosh x \sinh y,$$
$$\cosh(x + y) = \cosh x \cosh y + \sinh x \sinh y.$$

Then use them to show that

a. $\sinh 2x = 2 \sinh x \cosh x.$

b. $\cosh 2x = \cosh^2 x + \sinh^2 x.$

12. Use the definitions of $\cosh x$ and $\sinh x$ to show that

$$\cosh^2 x - \sinh^2 x = 1.$$

Finding Derivatives

In Exercises 13–24, find the derivative of y with respect to the appropriate variable.

13. $y = 6 \sinh \dfrac{x}{3}$

14. $y = \dfrac{1}{2}\sinh(2x + 1)$

15. $y = 2\sqrt{t}\tanh\sqrt{t}$

16. $y = t^2\tanh\frac{1}{t}$

17. $y = \ln(\sinh z)$

18. $y = \ln(\cosh z)$

19. $y = \operatorname{sech}\theta(1 - \ln\operatorname{sech}\theta)$

20. $y = \operatorname{csch}\theta(1 - \ln\operatorname{csch}\theta)$

21. $y = \ln\cosh v - \frac{1}{2}\tanh^2 v$

22. $y = \ln\sinh v - \frac{1}{2}\coth^2 v$

23. $y = (x^2 + 1)\operatorname{sech}(\ln x)$

(*Hint:* Before differentiating, express in terms of exponentials and simplify.)

24. $y = (4x^2 - 1)\operatorname{csch}(\ln 2x)$

In Exercises 25–36, find the derivative of y with respect to the appropriate variable.

25. $y = \sinh^{-1}\sqrt{x}$

26. $y = \cosh^{-1}2\sqrt{x+1}$

27. $y = (1 - \theta)\tanh^{-1}\theta$

28. $y = (\theta^2 + 2\theta)\tanh^{-1}(\theta + 1)$

29. $y = (1 - t)\coth^{-1}\sqrt{t}$

30. $y = (1 - t^2)\coth^{-1}t$

31. $y = \cos^{-1}x - x\operatorname{sech}^{-1}x$

32. $y = \ln x + \sqrt{1 - x^2}\operatorname{sech}^{-1}x$

33. $y = \operatorname{csch}^{-1}\left(\frac{1}{2}\right)^\theta$

34. $y = \operatorname{csch}^{-1}2^\theta$

35. $y = \sinh^{-1}(\tan x)$

36. $y = \cosh^{-1}(\sec x),\quad 0 < x < \pi/2$

Integration Formulas

Verify the integration formulas in Exercises 37–40.

37. a. $\int \operatorname{sech} x\,dx = \tan^{-1}(\sinh x) + C$

b. $\int \operatorname{sech} x\,dx = \sin^{-1}(\tanh x) + C$

38. $\int x\operatorname{sech}^{-1}x\,dx = \frac{x^2}{2}\operatorname{sech}^{-1}x - \frac{1}{2}\sqrt{1 - x^2} + C$

39. $\int x\coth^{-1}x\,dx = \frac{x^2 - 1}{2}\coth^{-1}x + \frac{x}{2} + C$

40. $\int \tanh^{-1}x\,dx = x\tanh^{-1}x + \frac{1}{2}\ln(1 - x^2) + C$

Evaluating Integrals

Evaluate the integrals in Exercises 41–60.

41. $\int \sinh 2x\,dx$

42. $\int \sinh\frac{x}{5}\,dx$

43. $\int 6\cosh\left(\frac{x}{2} - \ln 3\right)dx$

44. $\int 4\cosh(3x - \ln 2)\,dx$

45. $\int \tanh\frac{x}{7}\,dx$

46. $\int \coth\frac{\theta}{\sqrt{3}}\,d\theta$

47. $\int \operatorname{sech}^2\left(x - \frac{1}{2}\right)dx$

48. $\int \operatorname{csch}^2(5 - x)\,dx$

49. $\int \frac{\operatorname{sech}\sqrt{t}\tanh\sqrt{t}\,dt}{\sqrt{t}}$

50. $\int \frac{\operatorname{csch}(\ln t)\coth(\ln t)\,dt}{t}$

51. $\int_{\ln 2}^{\ln 4}\coth x\,dx$

52. $\int_0^{\ln 2}\tanh 2x\,dx$

53. $\int_{-\ln 4}^{-\ln 2} 2e^\theta\cosh\theta\,d\theta$

54. $\int_0^{\ln 2} 4e^{-\theta}\sinh\theta\,d\theta$

55. $\int_{-\pi/4}^{\pi/4}\cosh(\tan\theta)\sec^2\theta\,d\theta$

56. $\int_0^{\pi/2} 2\sinh(\sin\theta)\cos\theta\,d\theta$

57. $\int_1^2 \frac{\cosh(\ln t)}{t}\,dt$

58. $\int_1^4 \frac{8\cosh\sqrt{x}}{\sqrt{x}}\,dx$

59. $\int_{-\ln 2}^0 \cosh^2\left(\frac{x}{2}\right)dx$

60. $\int_0^{\ln 10} 4\sinh^2\left(\frac{x}{2}\right)dx$

Inverse Hyperbolic Functions and Integrals

When hyperbolic function keys are not available on a calculator, it is still possible to evaluate the inverse hyperbolic functions by expressing them as logarithms, as shown here.

$\sinh^{-1}x = \ln\left(x + \sqrt{x^2 + 1}\right),$	$-\infty < x < \infty$
$\cosh^{-1}x = \ln\left(x + \sqrt{x^2 - 1}\right),$	$x \ge 1$
$\tanh^{-1}x = \frac{1}{2}\ln\frac{1 + x}{1 - x},$	$\lvert x\rvert < 1$
$\operatorname{sech}^{-1}x = \ln\left(\frac{1 + \sqrt{1 - x^2}}{x}\right),$	$0 < x \le 1$
$\operatorname{csch}^{-1}x = \ln\left(\frac{1}{x} + \frac{\sqrt{1 + x^2}}{\lvert x\rvert}\right),$	$x \ne 0$
$\coth^{-1}x = \frac{1}{2}\ln\frac{x + 1}{x - 1},$	$\lvert x\rvert > 1$

Use the formulas in the box here to express the numbers in Exercises 61–66 in terms of natural logarithms.

61. $\sinh^{-1}(-5/12)$

62. $\cosh^{-1}(5/3)$

63. $\tanh^{-1}(-1/2)$

64. $\coth^{-1}(5/4)$

65. $\operatorname{sech}^{-1}(3/5)$

66. $\operatorname{csch}^{-1}(-1/\sqrt{3})$

Evaluate the integrals in Exercises 67–74 in terms of

a. inverse hyperbolic functions.

b. natural logarithms.

67. $\int_0^{2\sqrt{3}}\frac{dx}{\sqrt{4 + x^2}}$

68. $\int_0^{1/3}\frac{6\,dx}{\sqrt{1 + 9x^2}}$

69. $\int_{5/4}^2\frac{dx}{1 - x^2}$

70. $\int_0^{1/2}\frac{dx}{1 - x^2}$

71. $\int_{1/5}^{3/13}\frac{dx}{x\sqrt{1 - 16x^2}}$

72. $\int_1^2\frac{dx}{x\sqrt{4 + x^2}}$

73. $\int_0^\pi\frac{\cos x\,dx}{\sqrt{1 + \sin^2 x}}$

74. $\int_1^e\frac{dx}{x\sqrt{1 + (\ln x)^2}}$

Applications and Examples

75. Show that if a function f is defined on an interval symmetric about the origin (so that f is defined at $-x$ whenever it is defined at x), then

$$f(x) = \frac{f(x) + f(-x)}{2} + \frac{f(x) - f(-x)}{2}. \tag{1}$$

Then show that $(f(x) + f(-x))/2$ is even and that $(f(x) - f(-x))/2$ is odd.

76. Derive the formula $\sinh^{-1} x = \ln\left(x + \sqrt{x^2 + 1}\right)$ for all real x. Explain in your derivation why the plus sign is used with the square root instead of the minus sign.

77. **Skydiving** If a body of mass m falling from rest under the action of gravity encounters an air resistance proportional to the square of the velocity, then the body's velocity t sec into the fall satisfies the differential equation

$$m\frac{dv}{dt} = mg - kv^2,$$

where k is a constant that depends on the body's aerodynamic properties and the density of the air. (We assume that the fall is short enough so that the variation in the air's density will not affect the outcome significantly.)

a. Show that

$$v = \sqrt{\frac{mg}{k}}\tanh\left(\sqrt{\frac{gk}{m}}\,t\right)$$

satisfies the differential equation and the initial condition that $v = 0$ when $t = 0$.

b. Find the body's *limiting velocity*, $\lim_{t\to\infty} v$.

c. For a 160-lb skydiver $(mg = 160)$, with time in seconds and distance in feet, a typical value for k is 0.005. What is the diver's limiting velocity?

78. **Accelerations whose magnitudes are proportional to displacement** Suppose that the position of a body moving along a coordinate line at time t is

a. $s = a\cos kt + b\sin kt$.

b. $s = a\cosh kt + b\sinh kt$.

Show in both cases that the acceleration d^2s/dt^2 is proportional to s but that in the first case it is directed toward the origin, whereas in the second case it is directed away from the origin.

79. **Volume** A region in the first quadrant is bounded above by the curve $y = \cosh x$, below by the curve $y = \sinh x$, and on the left and right by the y-axis and the line $x = 2$, respectively. Find the volume of the solid generated by revolving the region about the x-axis.

80. **Volume** The region enclosed by the curve $y = \operatorname{sech} x$, the x-axis, and the lines $x = \pm\ln\sqrt{3}$ is revolved about the x-axis to generate a solid. Find the volume of the solid.

81. **Arc length** Find the length of the graph of $y = (1/2)\cosh 2x$ from $x = 0$ to $x = \ln\sqrt{5}$.

82. Use the definitions of the hyperbolic functions to find each of the following limits.

(a) $\lim_{x\to\infty} \tanh x$ (b) $\lim_{x\to-\infty} \tanh x$

(c) $\lim_{x\to\infty} \sinh x$ (d) $\lim_{x\to-\infty} \sinh x$

(e) $\lim_{x\to\infty} \operatorname{sech} x$ (f) $\lim_{x\to\infty} \coth x$

(g) $\lim_{x\to 0^+} \coth x$ (h) $\lim_{x\to 0^-} \coth x$

(i) $\lim_{x\to-\infty} \operatorname{csch} x$

83. **Hanging cables** Imagine a cable, like a telephone line or TV cable, strung from one support to another and hanging freely. The cable's weight per unit length is a constant w and the horizontal tension at its lowest point is a *vector* of length H. If we choose a coordinate system for the plane of the cable in which the x-axis is horizontal, the force of gravity is straight down, the positive y-axis points straight up, and the lowest point of the cable lies at the point $y = H/w$ on the y-axis (see accompanying figure), then it can be shown that the cable lies along the graph of the hyperbolic cosine

$$y = \frac{H}{w}\cosh\frac{w}{H}x.$$

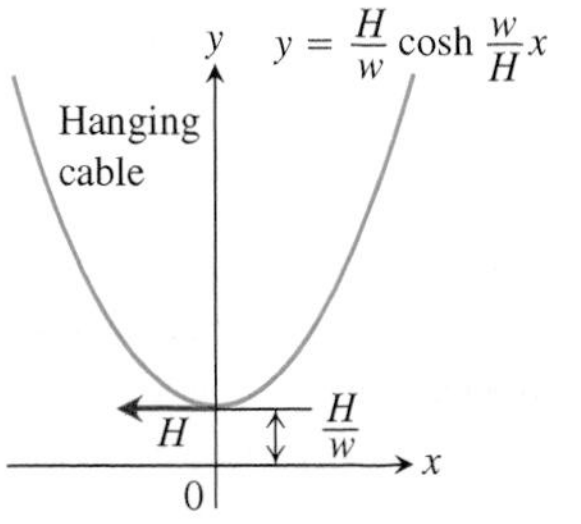

Such a curve is sometimes called a **chain curve** or a **catenary**, the latter deriving from the Latin *catena*, meaning "chain."

a. Let $P(x, y)$ denote an arbitrary point on the cable. The next accompanying figure displays the tension at P as a vector of length (magnitude) T, as well as the tension H at the lowest point A. Show that the cable's slope at P is

$$\tan\phi = \frac{dy}{dx} = \sinh\frac{w}{H}x.$$

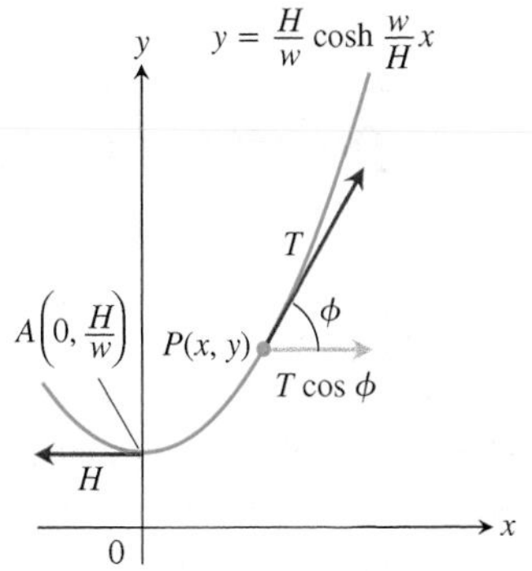

b. Using the result from part (a) and the fact that the horizontal tension at P must equal H (the cable is not moving), show that $T = wy$. Hence, the magnitude of the tension at $P(x, y)$ is exactly equal to the weight of y units of cable.

84. (*Continuation of Exercise 83.*) The length of arc AP in the Exercise 83 figure is $s = (1/a)\sinh ax$, where $a = w/H$. Show that the coordinates of P may be expressed in terms of s as

$$x = \frac{1}{a}\sinh^{-1} as, \qquad y = \sqrt{s^2 + \frac{1}{a^2}}.$$

85. **Area** Show that the area of the region in the first quadrant enclosed by the curve $y = (1/a)\cosh ax$, the coordinate axes, and the line $x = b$ is the same as the area of a rectangle of height $1/a$ and length s, where s is the length of the curve from $x = 0$ to $x = b$. Draw a figure illustrating this result.

86. **The hyperbolic in hyperbolic functions** Just as $x = \cos u$ and $y = \sin u$ are identified with points (x, y) on the unit circle, the functions $x = \cosh u$ and $y = \sinh u$ are identified with

points (x, y) on the right-hand branch of the unit hyperbola, $x^2 - y^2 = 1$.

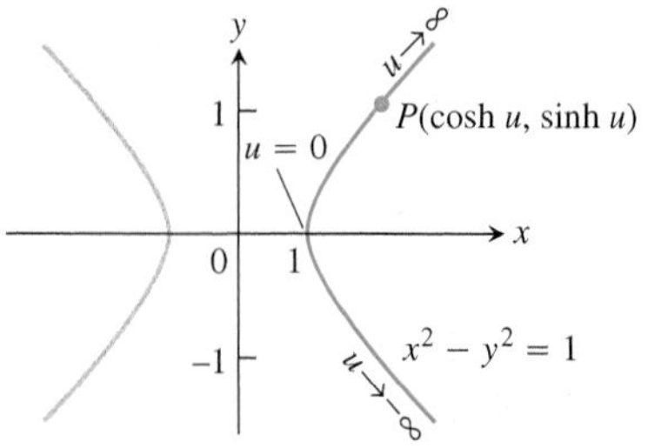

Since $\cosh^2 u - \sinh^2 u = 1$, the point $(\cosh u, \sinh u)$ lies on the right-hand branch of the hyperbola $x^2 - y^2 = 1$ for every value of u (Exercise 86).

Another analogy between hyperbolic and circular functions is that the variable u in the coordinates $(\cosh u, \sinh u)$ for the points of the right-hand branch of the hyperbola $x^2 - y^2 = 1$ is twice the area of the sector AOP pictured in the accompanying figure. To see why this is so, carry out the following steps.

a. Show that the area $A(u)$ of sector AOP is

$$A(u) = \frac{1}{2}\cosh u \sinh u - \int_1^{\cosh u} \sqrt{x^2 - 1}\, dx.$$

b. Differentiate both sides of the equation in part (a) with respect to u to show that

$$A'(u) = \frac{1}{2}.$$

c. Solve this last equation for $A(u)$. What is the value of $A(0)$? What is the value of the constant of integration C in your solution? With C determined, what does your solution say about the relationship of u to $A(u)$?

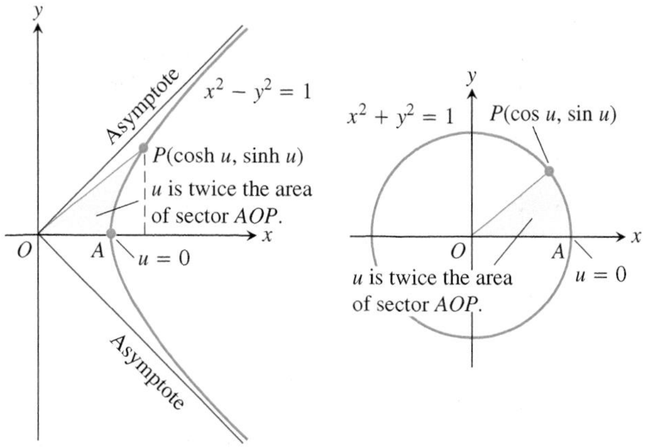

One of the analogies between hyperbolic and circular functions is revealed by these two diagrams (Exercise 86).

Chapter Questions to Guide Your Review

1. How is the natural logarithm function defined as an integral? What are its domain, range, and derivative? What arithmetic properties does it have? Comment on its graph.
2. What integrals lead to logarithms? Give examples.
3. What are the integrals of $\tan x$ and $\cot x$? $\sec x$ and $\csc x$?
4. How is the exponential function e^x defined? What are its domain, range, and derivative? What laws of exponents does it obey? Comment on its graph.
5. How are the functions a^x and $\log_a x$ defined? Are there any restrictions on a? How is the graph of $\log_a x$ related to the graph of $\ln x$? What truth is there in the statement that there is really only one exponential function and one logarithmic function?
6. How do you solve separable first-order differential equations?
7. What is the law of exponential change? How can it be derived from an initial value problem? What are some of the applications of the law?
8. What are the six basic hyperbolic functions? Comment on their domains, ranges, and graphs. What are some of the identities relating them?
9. What are the derivatives of the six basic hyperbolic functions? What are the corresponding integral formulas? What similarities do you see here with the six basic trigonometric functions?
10. How are the inverse hyperbolic functions defined? Comment on their domains, ranges, and graphs. How can you find values of $\text{sech}^{-1} x$, $\text{csch}^{-1} x$, and $\coth^{-1} x$ using a calculator's keys for $\cosh^{-1} x$, $\sinh^{-1} x$, and $\tanh^{-1} x$?
11. What integrals lead naturally to inverse hyperbolic functions?

Chapter Practice Exercises

Integration

Evaluate the integrals in Exercises 1–12.

1. $\int e^x \sin(e^x)\, dx$
2. $\int e^t \cos(3e^t - 2)\, dt$
3. $\int_0^{\pi} \tan\frac{x}{3}\, dx$
4. $\int_{1/6}^{1/4} 2\cot \pi x\, dx$
5. $\int_{-\pi/2}^{\pi/6} \frac{\cos t}{1 - \sin t}\, dt$
6. $\int e^x \sec e^x\, dx$

7. $\int \frac{\ln (x-5)}{x-5} dx$

8. $\int \frac{\cos (1 - \ln v)}{v} dv$

9. $\int_1^7 \frac{3}{x} dx$

10. $\int_1^{32} \frac{1}{5x} dx$

11. $\int_e^{e^2} \frac{1}{x\sqrt{\ln x}} dx$

12. $\int_2^4 (1 + \ln t)t \ln t \, dt$

Solving Equations with Logarithmic or Exponential Terms

In Exercises 13–18, solve for y.

13. $3^y = 2^{y+1}$

14. $4^{-y} = 3^{y+2}$

15. $9e^{2y} = x^2$

16. $3^y = 3 \ln x$

17. $\ln (y - 1) = x + \ln y$

18. $\ln (10 \ln y) = \ln 5x$

Theory and Applications

19. The function $f(x) = e^x + x$, being differentiable and one-to-one, has a differentiable inverse $f^{-1}(x)$. Find the value of df^{-1}/dx at the point $f(\ln 2)$.

20. Find the inverse of the function $f(x) = 1 + (1/x), x \neq 0$. Then show that $f^{-1}(f(x)) = f(f^{-1}(x)) = x$ and that

$$\left.\frac{df^{-1}}{dx}\right|_{f(x)} = \frac{1}{f'(x)}.$$

21. A particle is traveling upward and to the right along the curve $y = \ln x$. Its x-coordinate is increasing at the rate $(dx/dt) = \sqrt{x}$ m/sec. At what rate is the y-coordinate changing at the point $(e^2, 2)$?

22. A girl is sliding down a slide shaped like the curve $y = 9e^{-x/3}$. Her y-coordinate is changing at the rate $dy/dt = (-1/4)\sqrt{9 - y}$ ft/sec. At approximately what rate is her x-coordinate changing when she reaches the bottom of the slide at $x = 9$ ft? (Take e^3 to be 20 and round your answer to the nearest ft/sec.)

23. The functions $f(x) = \ln 5x$ and $g(x) = \ln 3x$ differ by a constant. What constant? Give reasons for your answer.

24. **a.** If $(\ln x)/x = (\ln 2)/2$, must $x = 2$?
b. If $(\ln x)/x = -2 \ln 2$, must $x = 1/2$?
Give reasons for your answers.

25. The quotient $(\log_4 x)/(\log_2 x)$ has a constant value. What value? Give reasons for your answer.

T 26. **$\log_x (2)$ vs. $\log_2 (x)$** How does $f(x) = \log_x (2)$ compare with $g(x) = \log_2 (x)$? Here is one way to find out.
a. Use the equation $\log_a b = (\ln b)/(\ln a)$ to express $f(x)$ and $g(x)$ in terms of natural logarithms.
b. Graph f and g together. Comment on the behavior of f in relation to the signs and values of g.

In Exercises 27–30, solve the differential equation.

27. $\frac{dy}{dx} = \sqrt{y} \cos^2 \sqrt{y}$

28. $y' = \frac{3y(x+1)^2}{y-1}$

29. $yy' = \sec y^2 \sec^2 x$

30. $y \cos^2 x \, dy + \sin x \, dx = 0$

In Exercises 31–34, solve the initial value problem.

31. $\frac{dy}{dx} = e^{-x-y-2}, \; y(0) = -2$

32. $\frac{dy}{dx} = \frac{y \ln y}{1 + x^2}, \; y(0) = e^2$

33. $x \, dy - \left(y + \sqrt{y}\right) dx = 0, \; y(1) = 1$

34. $y^{-2} \frac{dx}{dy} = \frac{e^x}{e^{2x} + 1}, \; y(0) = 1$

35. What is the age of a sample of charcoal in which 90% of the carbon-14 originally present has decayed?

36. **Cooling a pie** A deep-dish apple pie, whose internal temperature was 220°F when removed from the oven, was set out on a breezy 40°F porch to cool. Fifteen minutes later, the pie's internal temperature was 180°F. How long did it take the pie to cool from there to 70°F?

Chapter 7 Additional and Advanced Exercises

1. Let $A(t)$ be the area of the region in the first quadrant enclosed by the coordinate axes, the curve $y = e^{-x}$, and the vertical line $x = t, t > 0$. Let $V(t)$ be the volume of the solid generated by revolving the region about the x-axis. Find the following limits.
a. $\lim_{t\to\infty} A(t)$ **b.** $\lim_{t\to\infty} V(t)/A(t)$ **c.** $\lim_{t\to 0^+} V(t)/A(t)$

2. **Varying a logarithm's base**
a. Find $\lim \log_a 2$ as $a \to 0^+, 1^-, 1^+$, and ∞.
T **b.** Graph $y = \log_a 2$ as a function of a over the interval $0 < a \le 4$.

T 3. Graph $f(x) = \tan^{-1} x + \tan^{-1}(1/x)$ for $-5 \le x \le 5$. Then use calculus to explain what you see. How would you expect f to behave beyond the interval $[-5, 5]$? Give reasons for your answer.

T 4. Graph $f(x) = (\sin x)^{\sin x}$ over $[0, 3\pi]$. Explain what you see.

5. **Even-odd decompositions**
a. Suppose that g is an even function of x and h is an odd function of x. Show that if $g(x) + h(x) = 0$ for all x then $g(x) = 0$ for all x and $h(x) = 0$ for all x.
b. Use the result in part (a) to show that if $f(x) = f_E(x) + f_O(x)$ is the sum of an even function $f_E(x)$ and an odd function $f_O(x)$, then

$$f_E(x) = (f(x) + f(-x))/2 \quad \text{and} \quad f_O(x) = (f(x) - f(-x))/2.$$

c. What is the significance of the result in part (b)?

6. Let g be a function that is differentiable throughout an open interval containing the origin. Suppose g has the following properties:

   i. $g(x+y) = \dfrac{g(x)+g(y)}{1-g(x)g(y)}$ for all real numbers x, y, and $x+y$ in the domain of g.

   ii. $\lim_{h\to 0} g(h) = 0$

   iii. $\lim_{h\to 0} \dfrac{g(h)}{h} = 1$

   a. Show that $g(0) = 0$.

   b. Show that $g'(x) = 1 + [g(x)]^2$.

   c. Find $g(x)$ by solving the differential equation in part (b).

7. **Center of mass** Find the center of mass of a thin plate of constant density covering the region in the first and fourth quadrants enclosed by the curves $y = 1/(1+x^2)$ and $y = -1/(1+x^2)$ and by the lines $x = 0$ and $x = 1$.

8. **Solid of revolution** The region between the curve $y = 1/(2\sqrt{x})$ and the x-axis from $x = 1/4$ to $x = 4$ is revolved about the x-axis to generate a solid.

   a. Find the volume of the solid.

   b. Find the centroid of the region.

9. **The Rule of 70** If you use the approximation $\ln 2 \approx 0.70$ (in place of $0.69314\ldots$), you can derive a rule of thumb that says, "To estimate how many years it will take an amount of money to double when invested at r percent compounded continuously, divide r into 70." For instance, an amount of money invested at 5% will double in about $70/5 = 14$ years. If you want it to double in 10 years instead, you have to invest it at $70/10 = 7\%$. Show how the Rule of 70 is derived. (A similar "Rule of 72" uses 72 instead of 70, because 72 has more integer factors.)

T 10. **Urban gardening** A vegetable garden 50 ft wide is to be grown between two buildings, which are 500 ft apart along an east-west line. If the buildings are 200 ft and 350 ft tall, where should the garden be placed in order to receive the maximum number of hours of sunlight exposure? (*Hint:* Determine the value of x in the accompanying figure that maximizes sunlight exposure for the garden.)

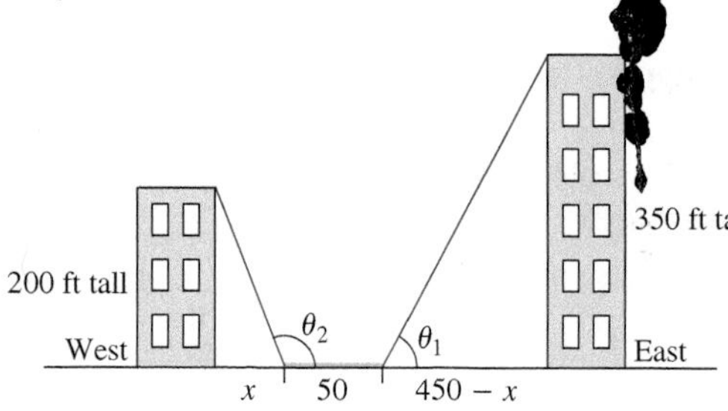

8 TECHNIQUES OF INTEGRATION

OVERVIEW The Fundamental Theorem tells us how to evaluate a definite integral once we have an antiderivative for the integrand function. Table 8.1 summarizes the forms of antiderivatives for many of the functions we have studied so far, and the substitution method helps us use the table to evaluate more complicated functions involving these basic ones. In this chapter we study a number of other important techniques for finding antiderivatives (or indefinite integrals) for many combinations of functions whose antiderivatives cannot be found using the methods presented before.

TABLE 8.1 Basic integration formulas

1. $\int k\,dx = kx + C \quad$ (any number k)
2. $\int x^n\,dx = \frac{x^{n+1}}{n+1} + C \quad (n \neq -1)$
3. $\int \frac{dx}{x} = \ln|x| + C$
4. $\int e^x\,dx = e^x + C$
5. $\int a^x\,dx = \frac{a^x}{\ln a} + C \quad (a > 0, a \neq 1)$
6. $\int \sin x\,dx = -\cos x + C$
7. $\int \cos x\,dx = \sin x + C$
8. $\int \sec^2 x\,dx = \tan x + C$
9. $\int \csc^2 x\,dx = -\cot x + C$
10. $\int \sec x \tan x\,dx = \sec x + C$
11. $\int \csc x \cot x\,dx = -\csc x + C$
12. $\int \tan x\,dx = \ln|\sec x| + C$
13. $\int \cot x\,dx = \ln|\sin x| + C$
14. $\int \sec x\,dx = \ln|\sec x + \tan x| + C$
15. $\int \csc x\,dx = -\ln|\csc x + \cot x| + C$
16. $\int \sinh x\,dx = \cosh x + C$
17. $\int \cosh x\,dx = \sinh x + C$
18. $\int \frac{dx}{\sqrt{a^2 - x^2}} = \sin^{-1}\left(\frac{x}{a}\right) + C$
19. $\int \frac{dx}{a^2 + x^2} = \frac{1}{a}\tan^{-1}\left(\frac{x}{a}\right) + C$
20. $\int \frac{dx}{x\sqrt{x^2 - a^2}} = \frac{1}{a}\sec^{-1}\left|\frac{x}{a}\right| + C$
21. $\int \frac{dx}{\sqrt{a^2 + x^2}} = \sinh^{-1}\left(\frac{x}{a}\right) + C \quad (a > 0)$
22. $\int \frac{dx}{\sqrt{x^2 - a^2}} = \cosh^{-1}\left(\frac{x}{a}\right) + C \quad (x > a > 0)$

8.1 Integration by Parts

Integration by parts is a technique for simplifying integrals of the form

$$\int f(x)g(x)\,dx.$$

It is useful when f can be differentiated repeatedly and g can be integrated repeatedly without difficulty. The integrals

$$\int x\cos x\,dx \qquad \text{and} \qquad \int x^2e^x\,dx$$

are such integrals because $f(x) = x$ or $f(x) = x^2$ can be differentiated repeatedly to become zero, and $g(x) = \cos x$ or $g(x) = e^x$ can be integrated repeatedly without difficulty. Integration by parts also applies to integrals like

$$\int \ln x\,dx \qquad \text{and} \qquad \int e^x\cos x\,dx.$$

In the first case, $f(x) = \ln x$ is easy to differentiate and $g(x) = 1$ easily integrates to x. In the second case, each part of the integrand appears again after repeated differentiation or integration.

Product Rule in Integral Form

If f and g are differentiable functions of x, the Product Rule says that

$$\frac{d}{dx}[f(x)g(x)] = f'(x)g(x) + f(x)g'(x).$$

In terms of indefinite integrals, this equation becomes

$$\int \frac{d}{dx}[f(x)g(x)]\,dx = \int [f'(x)g(x) + f(x)g'(x)]\,dx$$

or

$$\int \frac{d}{dx}[f(x)g(x)]\,dx = \int f'(x)g(x)\,dx + \int f(x)g'(x)\,dx.$$

Rearranging the terms of this last equation, we get

$$\int f(x)g'(x)\,dx = \int \frac{d}{dx}[f(x)g(x)]\,dx - \int f'(x)g(x)\,dx,$$

leading to the **integration by parts** formula

$$\int f(x)g'(x)\,dx = f(x)g(x) - \int f'(x)g(x)\,dx \qquad (1)$$

Sometimes it is easier to remember the formula if we write it in differential form. Let $u = f(x)$ and $v = g(x)$. Then $du = f'(x)\,dx$ and $dv = g'(x)\,dx$. Using the Substitution Rule, the integration by parts formula becomes

Integration by Parts Formula

$$\int u\,dv = uv - \int v\,du \tag{2}$$

This formula expresses one integral, $\int u\,dv$, in terms of a second integral, $\int v\,du$. With a proper choice of u and v, the second integral may be easier to evaluate than the first. In using the formula, various choices may be available for u and dv. The next examples illustrate the technique. To avoid mistakes, we always list our choices for u and dv, then we add to the list our calculated new terms du and v, and finally we apply the formula in Equation (2).

EXAMPLE 1 Find

$$\int x\cos x\,dx.$$

Solution We use the formula $\displaystyle\int u\,dv = uv - \int v\,du$ with

$$u = x, \qquad dv = \cos x\,dx,$$
$$du = dx, \qquad v = \sin x. \qquad \text{Simplest antiderivative of } \cos x$$

Then

$$\int x\cos x\,dx = x\sin x - \int \sin x\,dx = x\sin x + \cos x + C. \qquad \blacksquare$$

There are four choices available for u and dv in Example 1:

1. Let $u = 1$ and $dv = x\cos x\,dx$.
2. Let $u = x$ and $dv = \cos x\,dx$.
3. Let $u = x\cos x$ and $dv = dx$.
4. Let $u = \cos x$ and $dv = x\,dx$.

Choice 2 was used in Example 1. The other three choices lead to integrals we don't know how to integrate. For instance, Choice 3 leads to the integral

$$\int (x\cos x - x^2\sin x)\,dx.$$

The goal of integration by parts is to go from an integral $\int u\,dv$ that we don't see how to evaluate to an integral $\int v\,du$ that we can evaluate. Generally, you choose dv first to be as much of the integrand, including dx, as you can readily integrate; u is the leftover part. When finding v from dv, any antiderivative will work and we usually pick the simplest one; no arbitrary constant of integration is needed in v because it would simply cancel out of the right-hand side of Equation (2).

EXAMPLE 2 Find

$$\int \ln x\,dx.$$

Solution Since $\int \ln x\,dx$ can be written as $\int \ln x \cdot 1\,dx$, we use the formula $\int u\,dv = uv - \int v\,du$ with

$$u = \ln x \quad \text{Simplifies when differentiated} \qquad dv = dx \quad \text{Easy to integrate}$$

$$du = \frac{1}{x}\,dx, \qquad v = x. \quad \text{Simplest antiderivative}$$

Then from Equation (2),

$$\int \ln x\,dx = x\ln x - \int x\cdot\frac{1}{x}\,dx = x\ln x - \int dx = x\ln x - x + C. \qquad \blacksquare$$

Sometimes we have to use integration by parts more than once.

EXAMPLE 3 Evaluate

$$\int x^2 e^x\,dx.$$

Solution With $u = x^2$, $dv = e^x\,dx$, $du = 2x\,dx$, and $v = e^x$, we have

$$\int x^2 e^x\,dx = x^2 e^x - 2\int x e^x\,dx.$$

The new integral is less complicated than the original because the exponent on x is reduced by one. To evaluate the integral on the right, we integrate by parts again with $u = x$, $dv = e^x\,dx$. Then $du = dx$, $v = e^x$, and

$$\int xe^x\,dx = xe^x - \int e^x\,dx = xe^x - e^x + C.$$

Using this last evaluation, we then obtain

$$\begin{aligned}\int x^2 e^x\,dx &= x^2 e^x - 2\int xe^x\,dx \\ &= x^2 e^x - 2xe^x + 2e^x + C. \qquad \blacksquare\end{aligned}$$

The technique of Example 3 works for any integral $\int x^n e^x\,dx$ in which n is a positive integer, because differentiating x^n will eventually lead to zero and integrating e^x is easy.

Integrals like the one in the next example occur in electrical engineering. Their evaluation requires two integrations by parts, followed by solving for the unknown integral.

EXAMPLE 4 Evaluate

$$\int e^x \cos x\,dx.$$

Solution Let $u = e^x$ and $dv = \cos x\,dx$. Then $du = e^x\,dx$, $v = \sin x$, and

$$\int e^x \cos x\,dx = e^x \sin x - \int e^x \sin x\,dx.$$

The second integral is like the first except that it has $\sin x$ in place of $\cos x$. To evaluate it, we use integration by parts with

$$u = e^x, \qquad dv = \sin x\,dx, \qquad v = -\cos x, \qquad du = e^x\,dx.$$

Then

$$\begin{aligned}\int e^x \cos x\,dx &= e^x \sin x - \left(-e^x \cos x - \int (-\cos x)(e^x\,dx)\right) \\ &= e^x \sin x + e^x \cos x - \int e^x \cos x\,dx.\end{aligned}$$

The unknown integral now appears on both sides of the equation. Adding the integral to both sides and adding the constant of integration give

$$2\int e^x \cos x\, dx = e^x \sin x + e^x \cos x + C_1.$$

Dividing by 2 and renaming the constant of integration give

$$\int e^x \cos x\, dx = \frac{e^x \sin x + e^x \cos x}{2} + C. \qquad \blacksquare$$

EXAMPLE 5 Obtain a formula that expresses the integral

$$\int \cos^n x\, dx$$

in terms of an integral of a lower power of $\cos x$.

Solution We may think of $\cos^n x$ as $\cos^{n-1} x \cdot \cos x$. Then we let

$$u = \cos^{n-1} x \quad \text{and} \quad dv = \cos x\, dx,$$

so that

$$du = (n - 1)\cos^{n-2} x\,(-\sin x\, dx) \quad \text{and} \quad v = \sin x.$$

Integration by parts then gives

$$\begin{aligned}\int \cos^n x\, dx &= \cos^{n-1} x \sin x + (n - 1)\int \sin^2 x \cos^{n-2} x\, dx \\ &= \cos^{n-1} x \sin x + (n - 1)\int (1 - \cos^2 x)\cos^{n-2} x\, dx \\ &= \cos^{n-1} x \sin x + (n - 1)\int \cos^{n-2} x\, dx - (n - 1)\int \cos^n x\, dx.\end{aligned}$$

If we add

$$(n - 1)\int \cos^n x\, dx$$

to both sides of this equation, we obtain

$$n\int \cos^n x\, dx = \cos^{n-1} x \sin x + (n - 1)\int \cos^{n-2} x\, dx.$$

We then divide through by n, and the final result is

$$\int \cos^n x\, dx = \frac{\cos^{n-1} x \sin x}{n} + \frac{n - 1}{n}\int \cos^{n-2} x\, dx. \qquad \blacksquare$$

The formula found in Example 5 is called a **reduction formula** because it replaces an integral containing some power of a function with an integral of the same form having the power reduced. When n is a positive integer, we may apply the formula repeatedly until the remaining integral is easy to evaluate. For example, the result in Example 5 tells us that

$$\begin{aligned}\int \cos^3 x\, dx &= \frac{\cos^2 x \sin x}{3} + \frac{2}{3}\int \cos x\, dx \\ &= \frac{1}{3}\cos^2 x \sin x + \frac{2}{3}\sin x + C.\end{aligned}$$

Evaluating Definite Integrals by Parts

The integration by parts formula in Equation (1) can be combined with Part 2 of the Fundamental Theorem in order to evaluate definite integrals by parts. Assuming that both f' and g' are continuous over the interval $[a, b]$, Part 2 of the Fundamental Theorem gives

Integration by Parts Formula for Definite Integrals

$$\int_a^b f(x)g'(x)\,dx = f(x)g(x)\Big]_a^b - \int_a^b f'(x)g(x)\,dx \qquad (3)$$

In applying Equation (3), we normally use the u and v notation from Equation (2) because it is easier to remember. Here is an example.

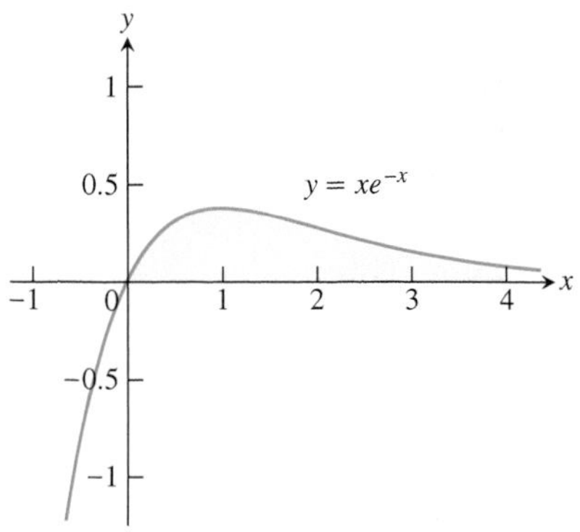

FIGURE 8.1 The region in Example 6.

EXAMPLE 6 Find the area of the region bounded by the curve $y = xe^{-x}$ and the x-axis from $x = 0$ to $x = 4$.

Solution The region is shaded in Figure 8.1. Its area is

$$\int_0^4 xe^{-x}\,dx.$$

Let $u = x$, $dv = e^{-x}\,dx$, $v = -e^{-x}$, and $du = dx$. Then,

$$\begin{aligned}\int_0^4 xe^{-x}\,dx &= -xe^{-x}\Big]_0^4 - \int_0^4 (-e^{-x})\,dx \\ &= [-4e^{-4} - (0)] + \int_0^4 e^{-x}\,dx \\ &= -4e^{-4} - e^{-x}\Big]_0^4 \\ &= -4e^{-4} - e^{-4} - (-e^0) = 1 - 5e^{-4} \approx 0.91.\end{aligned}$$

■

Exercises 8.1

Integration by Parts

Evaluate the integrals in Exercises 1–24 using integration by parts.

1. $\int x \sin \frac{x}{2}\,dx$
2. $\int \theta \cos \pi\theta\,d\theta$
3. $\int t^2 \cos t\,dt$
4. $\int x^2 \sin x\,dx$
5. $\int_1^2 x \ln x\,dx$
6. $\int_1^e x^3 \ln x\,dx$
7. $\int xe^x\,dx$
8. $\int xe^{3x}\,dx$
9. $\int x^2 e^{-x}\,dx$
10. $\int (x^2 - 2x + 1)\,e^{2x}\,dx$
11. $\int \tan^{-1} y\,dy$
12. $\int \sin^{-1} y\,dy$
13. $\int x \sec^2 x\,dx$
14. $\int 4x \sec^2 2x\,dx$
15. $\int x^3 e^x\,dx$
16. $\int p^4 e^{-p}\,dp$
17. $\int (x^2 - 5x)e^x\,dx$
18. $\int (r^2 + r + 1)e^r\,dr$
19. $\int x^5 e^x\,dx$
20. $\int t^2 e^{4t}\,dt$
21. $\int e^\theta \sin \theta\,d\theta$
22. $\int e^{-y} \cos y\,dy$
23. $\int e^{2x} \cos 3x\,dx$
24. $\int e^{-2x} \sin 2x\,dx$

Using Substitution

Evaluate the integrals in Exercises 25–30 by using a substitution prior to integration by parts.

25. $\int e^{\sqrt{3s+9}}\,ds$
26. $\int_0^1 x\sqrt{1 - x}\,dx$

27. $\int_0^{\pi/3} x \tan^2 x \, dx$

28. $\int \ln (x + x^2) \, dx$

29. $\int \sin (\ln x) \, dx$

30. $\int z(\ln z)^2 \, dz$

Evaluating Integrals

Evaluate the integrals in Exercises 31–50. Some integrals do not require integration by parts.

31. $\int x \sec x^2 \, dx$

32. $\int \frac{\cos \sqrt{x}}{\sqrt{x}} \, dx$

33. $\int x (\ln x)^2 \, dx$

34. $\int \frac{1}{x (\ln x)^2} \, dx$

35. $\int \frac{\ln x}{x^2} \, dx$

36. $\int \frac{(\ln x)^3}{x} \, dx$

37. $\int x^3 e^{x^4} \, dx$

38. $\int x^5 e^{x^3} \, dx$

39. $\int x^3 \sqrt{x^2 + 1} \, dx$

40. $\int x^2 \sin x^3 \, dx$

41. $\int \sin 3x \cos 2x \, dx$

42. $\int \sin 2x \cos 4x \, dx$

43. $\int e^x \sin e^x \, dx$

44. $\int \frac{e^{\sqrt{x}}}{\sqrt{x}} \, dx$

45. $\int \cos \sqrt{x} \, dx$

46. $\int \sqrt{x} \, e^{\sqrt{x}} \, dx$

47. $\int_0^{\pi/2} \theta^2 \sin 2\theta \, d\theta$

48. $\int_0^{\pi/2} x^3 \cos 2x \, dx$

49. $\int_{2/\sqrt{3}}^{2} t \sec^{-1} t \, dt$

50. $\int_0^{1/\sqrt{2}} 2x \sin^{-1} (x^2) \, dx$

Theory and Examples

51. **Finding area** Find the area of the region enclosed by the curve $y = x \sin x$ and the x-axis (see the accompanying figure) for

   a. $0 \le x \le \pi$.

   b. $\pi \le x \le 2\pi$.

   c. $2\pi \le x \le 3\pi$.

   d. What pattern do you see here? What is the area between the curve and the x-axis for $n\pi \le x \le (n + 1)\pi$, n an arbitrary nonnegative integer? Give reasons for your answer.

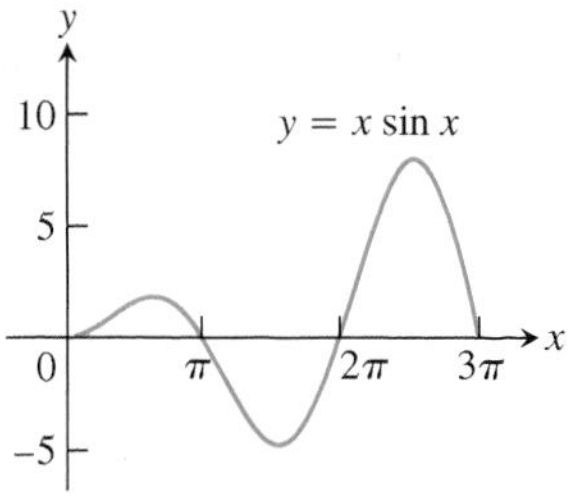

52. **Finding area** Find the area of the region enclosed by the curve $y = x \cos x$ and the x-axis (see the accompanying figure) for

   a. $\pi/2 \le x \le 3\pi/2$.

   b. $3\pi/2 \le x \le 5\pi/2$.

   c. $5\pi/2 \le x \le 7\pi/2$.

   d. What pattern do you see? What is the area between the curve and the x-axis for

$$\left(\frac{2n - 1}{2}\right)\pi \le x \le \left(\frac{2n + 1}{2}\right)\pi,$$

   n an arbitrary positive integer? Give reasons for your answer.

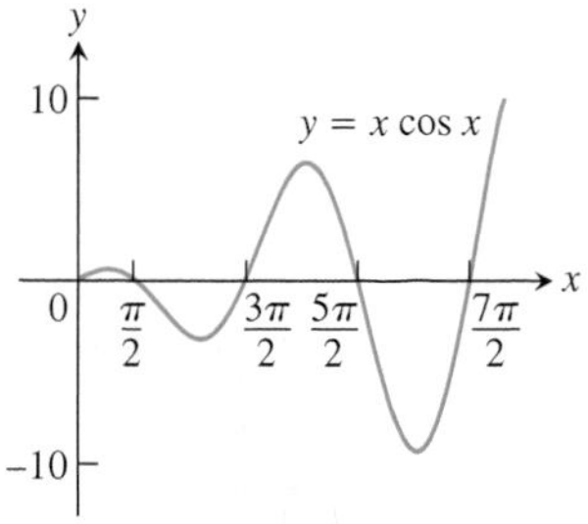

53. **Finding volume** Find the volume of the solid generated by revolving the region in the first quadrant bounded by the coordinate axes, the curve $y = e^x$, and the line $x = \ln 2$ about the line $x = \ln 2$.

54. **Finding volume** Find the volume of the solid generated by revolving the region in the first quadrant bounded by the coordinate axes, the curve $y = e^{-x}$, and the line $x = 1$

   a. about the y-axis.

   b. about the line $x = 1$.

55. **Finding volume** Find the volume of the solid generated by revolving the region in the first quadrant bounded by the coordinate axes and the curve $y = \cos x$, $0 \le x \le \pi/2$, about

   a. the y-axis.

   b. the line $x = \pi/2$.

56. **Finding volume** Find the volume of the solid generated by revolving the region bounded by the x-axis and the curve $y = x \sin x$, $0 \le x \le \pi$, about

   a. the y-axis.

   b. the line $x = \pi$.

   (See Exercise 51 for a graph.)

57. Consider the region bounded by the graphs of $y = \ln x$, $y = 0$, and $x = e$.

   a. Find the area of the region.

   b. Find the volume of the solid formed by revolving this region about the x-axis.

   c. Find the volume of the solid formed by revolving this region about the line $x = -2$.

   d. Find the centroid of the region.

58. Consider the region bounded by the graphs of $y = \tan^{-1} x$, $y = 0$, and $x = 1$.

   a. Find the area of the region.

   b. Find the volume of the solid formed by revolving this region about the y-axis.

59. **Average value** A retarding force, symbolized by the dashpot in the accompanying figure, slows the motion of the weighted spring so that the mass's position at time t is

$$y = 2e^{-t} \cos t, \qquad t \ge 0.$$

Find the average value of y over the interval $0 \le t \le 2\pi$.

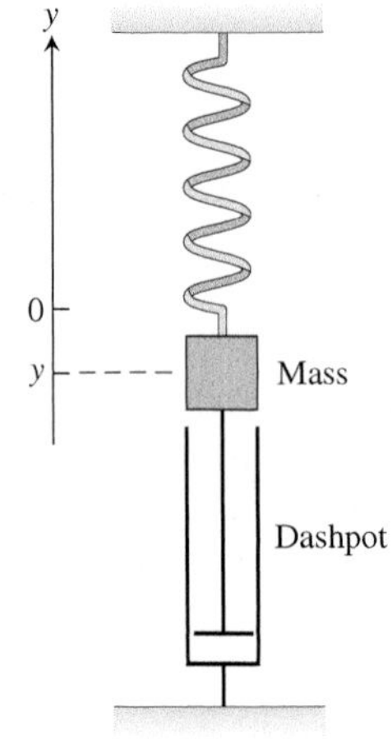

60. Average value In a mass-spring-dashpot system like the one in Exercise 59, the mass's position at time t is

$$y = 4e^{-t}(\sin t - \cos t), \qquad t \ge 0.$$

Find the average value of y over the interval $0 \le t \le 2\pi$.

Reduction Formulas

In Exercises 61–64, use integration by parts to establish the reduction formula.

61. $\displaystyle\int x^n \cos x\,dx = x^n \sin x - n\int x^{n-1}\sin x\,dx$

62. $\displaystyle\int x^n \sin x\,dx = -x^n \cos x + n\int x^{n-1}\cos x\,dx$

63. $\displaystyle\int x^n e^{ax}\,dx = \frac{x^n e^{ax}}{a} - \frac{n}{a}\int x^{n-1}e^{ax}\,dx, \quad a \ne 0$

64. $\displaystyle\int (\ln x)^n\,dx = x(\ln x)^n - n\int (\ln x)^{n-1}\,dx$

65. Show that

$$\int_a^b\left(\int_x^b f(t)\,dt\right)dx = \int_a^b (x-a)f(x)\,dx.$$

66. Use integration by parts to obtain the formula

$$\int \sqrt{1-x^2}\,dx = \frac{1}{2}x\sqrt{1-x^2} + \frac{1}{2}\int\frac{1}{\sqrt{1-x^2}}\,dx.$$

Integrating Inverses of Functions

Integration by parts leads to a rule for integrating inverses that usually gives good results:

$$\begin{aligned}\int f^{-1}(x)\,dx &= \int y f'(y)\,dy && y = f^{-1}(x),\quad x = f(y)\\ &&& dx = f'(y)\,dy\\ &= yf(y) - \int f(y)\,dy && \text{Integration by parts with}\\ &&& u = y,\ dv = f'(y)\,dy\\ &= xf^{-1}(x) - \int f(y)\,dy\end{aligned}$$

The idea is to take the most complicated part of the integral, in this case $f^{-1}(x)$, and simplify it first. For the integral of $\ln x$, we get

$$\begin{aligned}\int \ln x\,dx &= \int ye^y\,dy && y = \ln x,\quad x = e^y\\ &&& dx = e^y\,dy\\ &= ye^y - e^y + C\\ &= x\ln x - x + C.\end{aligned}$$

For the integral of $\cos^{-1}x$ we get

$$\begin{aligned}\int \cos^{-1}x\,dx &= x\cos^{-1}x - \int \cos y\,dy && y = \cos^{-1}x\\ &= x\cos^{-1}x - \sin y + C\\ &= x\cos^{-1}x - \sin(\cos^{-1}x) + C.\end{aligned}$$

Use the formula

$$\int f^{-1}(x)\,dx = xf^{-1}(x) - \int f(y)\,dy \qquad y = f^{-1}(x) \qquad (4)$$

to evaluate the integrals in Exercises 67–70. Express your answers in terms of x.

67. $\displaystyle\int \sin^{-1}x\,dx$

68. $\displaystyle\int \tan^{-1}x\,dx$

69. $\displaystyle\int \sec^{-1}x\,dx$

70. $\displaystyle\int \log_2 x\,dx$

Another way to integrate $f^{-1}(x)$ (when f^{-1} is integrable, of course) is to use integration by parts with $u = f^{-1}(x)$ and $dv = dx$ to rewrite the integral of f^{-1} as

$$\int f^{-1}(x)\,dx = xf^{-1}(x) - \int x\left(\frac{d}{dx}f^{-1}(x)\right)dx. \qquad (5)$$

Exercises 71 and 72 compare the results of using Equations (4) and (5).

71. Equations (4) and (5) give different formulas for the integral of $\cos^{-1}x$:

a. $\displaystyle\int \cos^{-1}x\,dx = x\cos^{-1}x - \sin(\cos^{-1}x) + C$ Eq. (4)

b. $\displaystyle\int \cos^{-1}x\,dx = x\cos^{-1}x - \sqrt{1-x^2} + C$ Eq. (5)

Can both integrations be correct? Explain.

72. Equations (4) and (5) lead to different formulas for the integral of $\tan^{-1}x$:

a. $\displaystyle\int \tan^{-1}x\,dx = x\tan^{-1}x - \ln\sec(\tan^{-1}x) + C$ Eq. (4)

b. $\displaystyle\int \tan^{-1}x\,dx = x\tan^{-1}x - \ln\sqrt{1+x^2} + C$ Eq. (5)

Can both integrations be correct? Explain.

Evaluate the integrals in Exercises 73 and 74 with **(a)** Eq. (4) and **(b)** Eq. (5). In each case, check your work by differentiating your answer with respect to x.

73. $\displaystyle\int \sinh^{-1}x\,dx$

74. $\displaystyle\int \tanh^{-1}x\,dx$

8.2 Trigonometric Integrals

Trigonometric integrals involve algebraic combinations of the six basic trigonometric functions. In principle, we can always express such integrals in terms of sines and cosines, but it is often simpler to work with other functions, as in the integral

$$\int \sec^2 x\, dx = \tan x + C.$$

The general idea is to use identities to transform the integrals we have to find into integrals that are easier to work with.

Products of Powers of Sines and Cosines

We begin with integrals of the form:

$$\int \sin^m x \cos^n x\, dx,$$

where m and n are nonnegative integers (positive or zero). We can divide the appropriate substitution into three cases according to m and n being odd or even.

Case 1 If ***m* is odd**, we write m as $2k + 1$ and use the identity $\sin^2 x = 1 - \cos^2 x$ to obtain

$$\sin^m x = \sin^{2k+1} x = (\sin^2 x)^k \sin x = (1 - \cos^2 x)^k \sin x. \tag{1}$$

Then we combine the single $\sin x$ with dx in the integral and set $\sin x\, dx$ equal to $-d(\cos x)$.

Case 2 If ***m* is even and *n* is odd** in $\int \sin^m x \cos^n x\, dx$, we write n as $2k + 1$ and use the identity $\cos^2 x = 1 - \sin^2 x$ to obtain

$$\cos^n x = \cos^{2k+1} x = (\cos^2 x)^k \cos x = (1 - \sin^2 x)^k \cos x.$$

We then combine the single $\cos x$ with dx and set $\cos x\, dx$ equal to $d(\sin x)$.

Case 3 If **both *m* and *n* are even** in $\int \sin^m x \cos^n x\, dx$, we substitute

$$\sin^2 x = \frac{1 - \cos 2x}{2}, \qquad \cos^2 x = \frac{1 + \cos 2x}{2} \tag{2}$$

to reduce the integrand to one in lower powers of $\cos 2x$.

Here are some examples illustrating each case.

EXAMPLE 1 Evaluate

$$\int \sin^3 x \cos^2 x\, dx.$$

Solution This is an example of Case 1.

$$\begin{aligned}
\int \sin^3 x \cos^2 x\, dx &= \int \sin^2 x \cos^2 x \sin x\, dx && m \text{ is odd.} \\
&= \int (1 - \cos^2 x) \cos^2 x\, (-d\,(\cos x)) && \sin x\, dx = -d(\cos x) \\
&= \int (1 - u^2)(u^2)(-du) && u = \cos x \\
&= \int (u^4 - u^2)\, du && \text{Multiply terms.} \\
&= \frac{u^5}{5} - \frac{u^3}{3} + C = \frac{\cos^5 x}{5} - \frac{\cos^3 x}{3} + C
\end{aligned}$$

■

EXAMPLE 2 Evaluate

$$\int \cos^5 x\, dx.$$

Solution This is an example of Case 2, where $m = 0$ is even and $n = 5$ is odd.

$$\begin{aligned}
\int \cos^5 x\, dx = \int \cos^4 x \cos x\, dx &= \int (1 - \sin^2 x)^2\, d(\sin x) && \cos x\, dx = d(\sin x) \\
&= \int (1 - u^2)^2\, du && u = \sin x \\
&= \int (1 - 2u^2 + u^4)\, du && \text{Square } 1 - u^2. \\
&= u - \frac{2}{3}u^3 + \frac{1}{5}u^5 + C = \sin x - \frac{2}{3}\sin^3 x + \frac{1}{5}\sin^5 x + C
\end{aligned}$$

■

EXAMPLE 3 Evaluate

$$\int \sin^2 x \cos^4 x\, dx.$$

Solution This is an example of Case 3.

$$\begin{aligned}
\int \sin^2 x \cos^4 x\, dx &= \int \left(\frac{1 - \cos 2x}{2}\right)\left(\frac{1 + \cos 2x}{2}\right)^2 dx && m \text{ and } n \text{ both even} \\
&= \frac{1}{8}\int (1 - \cos 2x)(1 + 2\cos 2x + \cos^2 2x)\, dx \\
&= \frac{1}{8}\int (1 + \cos 2x - \cos^2 2x - \cos^3 2x)\, dx \\
&= \frac{1}{8}\left[x + \frac{1}{2}\sin 2x - \int (\cos^2 2x + \cos^3 2x)\, dx\right]
\end{aligned}$$

For the term involving $\cos^2 2x$, we use

$$\begin{aligned}
\int \cos^2 2x\, dx &= \frac{1}{2}\int (1 + \cos 4x)\, dx \\
&= \frac{1}{2}\left(x + \frac{1}{4}\sin 4x\right). && \text{Omitting the constant of integration until the final result}
\end{aligned}$$

For the $\cos^3 2x$ term, we have

$$\int \cos^3 2x\,dx = \int (1 - \sin^2 2x)\cos 2x\,dx$$

$u = \sin 2x,$
$du = 2\cos 2x\,dx$

$$= \frac{1}{2}\int (1 - u^2)\,du = \frac{1}{2}\left(\sin 2x - \frac{1}{3}\sin^3 2x\right).$$

Again omitting C

Combining everything and simplifying, we get

$$\int \sin^2 x \cos^4 x\,dx = \frac{1}{16}\left(x - \frac{1}{4}\sin 4x + \frac{1}{3}\sin^3 2x\right) + C.$$ ■

Eliminating Square Roots

In the next example, we use the identity $\cos^2\theta = (1 + \cos 2\theta)/2$ to eliminate a square root.

EXAMPLE 4 Evaluate

$$\int_0^{\pi/4} \sqrt{1 + \cos 4x}\,dx.$$

Solution To eliminate the square root, we use the identity

$$\cos^2\theta = \frac{1 + \cos 2\theta}{2} \quad \text{or} \quad 1 + \cos 2\theta = 2\cos^2\theta.$$

With $\theta = 2x$, this becomes

$$1 + \cos 4x = 2\cos^2 2x.$$

Therefore,

$$\int_0^{\pi/4} \sqrt{1 + \cos 4x}\,dx = \int_0^{\pi/4} \sqrt{2\cos^2 2x}\,dx = \int_0^{\pi/4} \sqrt{2}\sqrt{\cos^2 2x}\,dx$$

$$= \sqrt{2}\int_0^{\pi/4} |\cos 2x|\,dx = \sqrt{2}\int_0^{\pi/4} \cos 2x\,dx$$

$\cos 2x \geq 0$ on $[0, \pi/4]$

$$= \sqrt{2}\left[\frac{\sin 2x}{2}\right]_0^{\pi/4} = \frac{\sqrt{2}}{2}[1 - 0] = \frac{\sqrt{2}}{2}.$$ ■

Integrals of Powers of tan *x* and sec *x*

We know how to integrate the tangent and secant and their squares. To integrate higher powers, we use the identities $\tan^2 x = \sec^2 x - 1$ and $\sec^2 x = \tan^2 x + 1$, and integrate by parts when necessary to reduce the higher powers to lower powers.

EXAMPLE 5 Evaluate

$$\int \tan^4 x\,dx.$$

Solution

$$\int \tan^4 x\,dx = \int \tan^2 x \cdot \tan^2 x\,dx = \int \tan^2 x \cdot (\sec^2 x - 1)\,dx$$

$$= \int \tan^2 x \sec^2 x\,dx - \int \tan^2 x\,dx$$

$$= \int \tan^2 x \sec^2 x\,dx - \int (\sec^2 x - 1)\,dx$$

$$= \int \tan^2 x \sec^2 x\,dx - \int \sec^2 x\,dx + \int dx$$

In the first integral, we let

$$u = \tan x, \qquad du = \sec^2 x\,dx$$

and have

$$\int u^2\,du = \frac{1}{3}u^3 + C_1.$$

The remaining integrals are standard forms, so

$$\int \tan^4 x\, dx = \frac{1}{3}\tan^3 x - \tan x + x + C. \quad \blacksquare$$

EXAMPLE 6 Evaluate

$$\int \sec^3 x\, dx.$$

Solution We integrate by parts using

$$u = \sec x, \qquad dv = \sec^2 x\, dx, \qquad v = \tan x, \qquad du = \sec x \tan x\, dx.$$

Then

$$\begin{aligned}\int \sec^3 x\, dx &= \sec x \tan x - \int (\tan x)(\sec x \tan x\, dx)\\ &= \sec x \tan x - \int (\sec^2 x - 1)\sec x\, dx && \tan^2 x = \sec^2 x - 1\\ &= \sec x \tan x + \int \sec x\, dx - \int \sec^3 x\, dx.\end{aligned}$$

Combining the two secant-cubed integrals gives

$$2\int \sec^3 x\, dx = \sec x \tan x + \int \sec x\, dx$$

and

$$\int \sec^3 x\, dx = \frac{1}{2}\sec x \tan x + \frac{1}{2}\ln|\sec x + \tan x| + C. \quad \blacksquare$$

EXAMPLE 7 Evaluate

$$\int \tan^4 x \sec^4 x\, dx.$$

Solution

$$\begin{aligned}\int (\tan^4 x)(\sec^4 x)\, dx &= \int (\tan^4 x)(1 + \tan^2 x)(\sec^2 x)\, dx && \sec^2 x = 1 + \tan^2 x\\ &= \int (\tan^4 x + \tan^6 x)(\sec^2 x)\, dx\\ &= \int (\tan^4 x)(\sec^2 x)\, dx + \int (\tan^6 x)(\sec^2 x)\, dx\\ &= \int u^4\, du + \int u^6\, du = \frac{u^5}{5} + \frac{u^7}{7} + C && \sec^2 x = 1 + \tan^2 x\\ &= \frac{\tan^5 x}{5} + \frac{\tan^7 x}{7} + C \quad \blacksquare\end{aligned}$$

Products of Sines and Cosines

The integrals

$$\int \sin mx \sin nx\, dx, \qquad \int \sin mx \cos nx\, dx, \qquad \text{and} \qquad \int \cos mx \cos nx\, dx$$

arise in many applications involving periodic functions. We can evaluate these integrals through integration by parts, but two such integrations are required in each case. It is simpler to use the identities

$$\sin mx \sin nx = \frac{1}{2}[\cos(m - n)x - \cos(m + n)x], \tag{3}$$

$$\sin mx \cos nx = \frac{1}{2}[\sin(m - n)x + \sin(m + n)x], \tag{4}$$

$$\cos mx \cos nx = \frac{1}{2}[\cos(m - n)x + \cos(m + n)x]. \tag{5}$$

These identities come from the angle sum formulas for the sine and cosine functions (Section 1.3). They give functions whose antiderivatives are easily found.

EXAMPLE 8 Evaluate

$$\int \sin 3x \cos 5x \, dx.$$

Solution From Equation (4) with $m = 3$ and $n = 5$, we get

$$\begin{aligned}\int \sin 3x \cos 5x \, dx &= \frac{1}{2}\int [\sin(-2x) + \sin 8x]\, dx \\ &= \frac{1}{2}\int (\sin 8x - \sin 2x)\, dx \\ &= -\frac{\cos 8x}{16} + \frac{\cos 2x}{4} + C.\end{aligned}$$

Exercises 8.2

Powers of Sines and Cosines

Evaluate the integrals in Exercises 1–22.

1. $\int \cos 2x \, dx$
2. $\int_0^{\pi} 3 \sin \frac{x}{3} \, dx$
3. $\int \cos^3 x \sin x \, dx$
4. $\int \sin^4 2x \cos 2x \, dx$
5. $\int \sin^3 x \, dx$
6. $\int \cos^3 4x \, dx$
7. $\int \sin^5 x \, dx$
8. $\int_0^{\pi} \sin^5 \frac{x}{2} \, dx$
9. $\int \cos^3 x \, dx$
10. $\int_0^{\pi/6} 3 \cos^5 3x \, dx$
11. $\int \sin^3 x \cos^3 x \, dx$
12. $\int \cos^3 2x \sin^5 2x \, dx$
13. $\int \cos^2 x \, dx$
14. $\int_0^{\pi/2} \sin^2 x \, dx$
15. $\int_0^{\pi/2} \sin^7 y \, dy$
16. $\int 7 \cos^7 t \, dt$
17. $\int_0^{\pi} 8 \sin^4 x \, dx$
18. $\int 8 \cos^4 2\pi x \, dx$
19. $\int 16 \sin^2 x \cos^2 x \, dx$
20. $\int_0^{\pi} 8 \sin^4 y \cos^2 y \, dy$
21. $\int 8 \cos^3 2\theta \sin 2\theta \, d\theta$
22. $\int_0^{\pi/2} \sin^2 2\theta \cos^3 2\theta \, d\theta$

Integrating Square Roots

Evaluate the integrals in Exercises 23–32.

23. $\int_0^{2\pi} \sqrt{\frac{1 - \cos x}{2}} \, dx$
24. $\int_0^{\pi} \sqrt{1 - \cos 2x} \, dx$
25. $\int_0^{\pi} \sqrt{1 - \sin^2 t} \, dt$
26. $\int_0^{\pi} \sqrt{1 - \cos^2 \theta} \, d\theta$
27. $\int_{\pi/3}^{\pi/2} \frac{\sin^2 x}{\sqrt{1 - \cos x}} \, dx$
28. $\int_0^{\pi/6} \sqrt{1 + \sin x} \, dx$

    $\left(\textit{Hint}: \text{Multiply by } \sqrt{\frac{1 - \sin x}{1 - \sin x}}.\right)$
29. $\int_{5\pi/6}^{\pi} \frac{\cos^4 x}{\sqrt{1 - \sin x}} \, dx$
30. $\int_{\pi/2}^{3\pi/4} \sqrt{1 - \sin 2x} \, dx$
31. $\int_0^{\pi/2} \theta\sqrt{1 - \cos 2\theta} \, d\theta$
32. $\int_{-\pi}^{\pi} (1 - \cos^2 t)^{3/2} \, dt$

Powers of Tangents and Secants

Evaluate the integrals in Exercises 33–50.

33. $\int \sec^2 x \tan x \, dx$
34. $\int \sec x \tan^2 x \, dx$
35. $\int \sec^3 x \tan x \, dx$
36. $\int \sec^3 x \tan^3 x \, dx$
37. $\int \sec^2 x \tan^2 x \, dx$
38. $\int \sec^4 x \tan^2 x \, dx$
39. $\int_{-\pi/3}^{0} 2 \sec^3 x \, dx$
40. $\int e^x \sec^3 e^x \, dx$
41. $\int \sec^4 \theta \, d\theta$
42. $\int 3 \sec^4 3x \, dx$
43. $\int_{\pi/4}^{\pi/2} \csc^4 \theta \, d\theta$
44. $\int \sec^6 x \, dx$
45. $\int 4 \tan^3 x \, dx$
46. $\int_{-\pi/4}^{\pi/4} 6 \tan^4 x \, dx$
47. $\int \tan^5 x \, dx$
48. $\int \cot^6 2x \, dx$
49. $\int_{\pi/6}^{\pi/3} \cot^3 x \, dx$
50. $\int 8 \cot^4 t \, dt$

Products of Sines and Cosines

Evaluate the integrals in Exercises 51–56.

51. $\int \sin 3x \cos 2x\, dx$

52. $\int \sin 2x \cos 3x\, dx$

53. $\int_{-\pi}^{\pi} \sin 3x \sin 3x\, dx$

54. $\int_{0}^{\pi/2} \sin x \cos x\, dx$

55. $\int \cos 3x \cos 4x\, dx$

56. $\int_{-\pi/2}^{\pi/2} \cos x \cos 7x\, dx$

Exercises 57–62 require the use of various trigonometric identities before you evaluate the integrals.

57. $\int \sin^2 \theta \cos 3\theta\, d\theta$

58. $\int \cos^2 2\theta \sin \theta\, d\theta$

59. $\int \cos^3 \theta \sin 2\theta\, d\theta$

60. $\int \sin^3 \theta \cos 2\theta\, d\theta$

61. $\int \sin \theta \cos \theta \cos 3\theta\, d\theta$

62. $\int \sin \theta \sin 2\theta \sin 3\theta\, d\theta$

Assorted Integrations

Use any method to evaluate the integrals in Exercises 63–68.

63. $\int \frac{\sec^3 x}{\tan x}\, dx$

64. $\int \frac{\sin^3 x}{\cos^4 x}\, dx$

65. $\int \frac{\tan^2 x}{\csc x}\, dx$

66. $\int \frac{\cot x}{\cos^2 x}\, dx$

67. $\int x \sin^2 x\, dx$

68. $\int x \cos^3 x\, dx$

Applications

69. Arc length Find the length of the curve

$$y = \ln(\sec x), \quad 0 \le x \le \pi/4.$$

70. Center of gravity Find the center of gravity of the region bounded by the x-axis, the curve $y = \sec x$, and the lines $x = -\pi/4$, $x = \pi/4$.

71. Volume Find the volume generated by revolving one arch of the curve $y = \sin x$ about the x-axis.

72. Area Find the area between the x-axis and the curve $y = \sqrt{1 + \cos 4x}$, $0 \le x \le \pi$.

73. Centroid Find the centroid of the region bounded by the graphs of $y = x + \cos x$ and $y = 0$ for $0 \le x \le 2\pi$.

74. Volume Find the volume of the solid formed by revolving the region bounded by the graphs of $y = \sin x + \sec x$, $y = 0$, $x = 0$, and $x = \pi/3$ about the x-axis.

8.3 Trigonometric Substitutions

Trigonometric substitutions occur when we replace the variable of integration by a trigonometric function. The most common substitutions are $x = a \tan \theta$, $x = a \sin \theta$, and $x = a \sec \theta$. These substitutions are effective in transforming integrals involving $\sqrt{a^2 + x^2}$, $\sqrt{a^2 - x^2}$, and $\sqrt{x^2 - a^2}$ into integrals we can evaluate directly since they come from the reference right triangles in Figure 8.2.

With $x = a \tan \theta$,

$$a^2 + x^2 = a^2 + a^2 \tan^2 \theta = a^2(1 + \tan^2 \theta) = a^2 \sec^2 \theta.$$

With $x = a \sin \theta$,

$$a^2 - x^2 = a^2 - a^2 \sin^2 \theta = a^2(1 - \sin^2 \theta) = a^2 \cos^2 \theta.$$

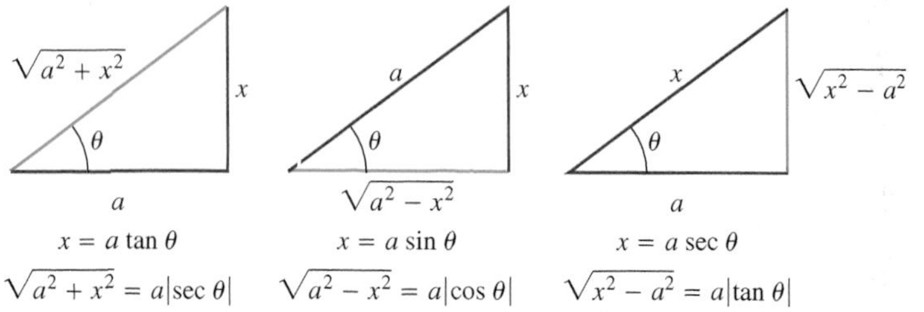

FIGURE 8.2 Reference triangles for the three basic substitutions identifying the sides labeled x and a for each substitution.

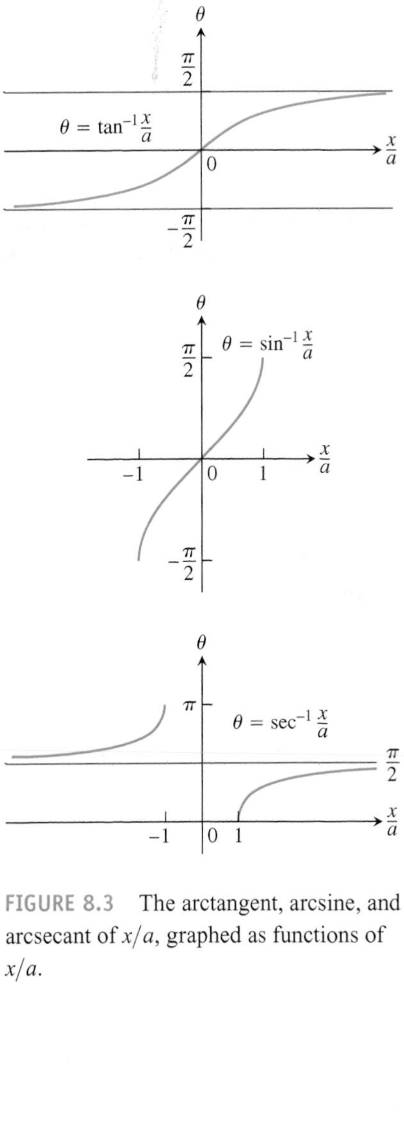

FIGURE 8.3 The arctangent, arcsine, and arcsecant of x/a, graphed as functions of x/a.

With $x = a \sec\theta$,

$$x^2 - a^2 = a^2\sec^2\theta - a^2 = a^2(\sec^2\theta - 1) = a^2\tan^2\theta.$$

We want any substitution we use in an integration to be reversible so that we can change back to the original variable afterward. For example, if $x = a\tan\theta$, we want to be able to set $\theta = \tan^{-1}(x/a)$ after the integration takes place. If $x = a\sin\theta$, we want to be able to set $\theta = \sin^{-1}(x/a)$ when we're done, and similarly for $x = a\sec\theta$.

As we know from Section 1.6, the functions in these substitutions have inverses only for selected values of θ (Figure 8.3). For reversibility,

$$x = a\tan\theta \quad \text{requires} \quad \theta = \tan^{-1}\left(\frac{x}{a}\right) \quad \text{with} \quad -\frac{\pi}{2} < \theta < \frac{\pi}{2},$$

$$x = a\sin\theta \quad \text{requires} \quad \theta = \sin^{-1}\left(\frac{x}{a}\right) \quad \text{with} \quad -\frac{\pi}{2} \le \theta \le \frac{\pi}{2},$$

$$x = a\sec\theta \quad \text{requires} \quad \theta = \sec^{-1}\left(\frac{x}{a}\right) \quad \text{with} \quad \begin{cases} 0 \le \theta < \dfrac{\pi}{2} & \text{if } \dfrac{x}{a} \ge 1, \\ \dfrac{\pi}{2} < \theta \le \pi & \text{if } \dfrac{x}{a} \le -1. \end{cases}$$

To simplify calculations with the substitution $x = a\sec\theta$, we will restrict its use to integrals in which $x/a \ge 1$. This will place θ in $[0, \pi/2)$ and make $\tan\theta \ge 0$. We will then have $\sqrt{x^2 - a^2} = \sqrt{a^2\tan^2\theta} = |a\tan\theta| = a\tan\theta$, free of absolute values, provided $a > 0$.

Procedure For a Trigonometric Substitution

1. Write down the substitution for x, calculate the differential dx, and specify the selected values of θ for the substitution.
2. Substitute the trigonometric expression and the calculated differential into the integrand, and then simplify the results algebraically.
3. Integrate the trigonometric integral, keeping in mind the restrictions on the angle θ for reversibility.
4. Draw an appropriate reference triangle to reverse the substitution in the integration result and convert it back to the original variable x.

EXAMPLE 1 Evaluate

$$\int \frac{dx}{\sqrt{4 + x^2}}.$$

Solution We set

$$x = 2\tan\theta, \qquad dx = 2\sec^2\theta\,d\theta, \qquad -\frac{\pi}{2} < \theta < \frac{\pi}{2},$$

$$4 + x^2 = 4 + 4\tan^2\theta = 4(1 + \tan^2\theta) = 4\sec^2\theta.$$

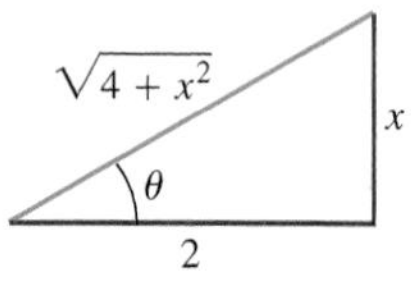

FIGURE 8.4 Reference triangle for $x = 2\tan\theta$ (Example 1):

$$\tan\theta = \frac{x}{2}$$

and

$$\sec\theta = \frac{\sqrt{4+x^2}}{2}.$$

Then

$$\int \frac{dx}{\sqrt{4+x^2}} = \int \frac{2\sec^2\theta\, d\theta}{\sqrt{4\sec^2\theta}} = \int \frac{\sec^2\theta\, d\theta}{|\sec\theta|} \qquad \sqrt{\sec^2\theta} = |\sec\theta|$$

$$= \int \sec\theta\, d\theta \qquad \sec\theta > 0 \text{ for } -\frac{\pi}{2} < \theta < \frac{\pi}{2}$$

$$= \ln|\sec\theta + \tan\theta| + C$$

$$= \ln\left|\frac{\sqrt{4+x^2}}{2} + \frac{x}{2}\right| + C. \qquad \text{From Fig. 8.4}$$

Notice how we expressed $\ln|\sec\theta + \tan\theta|$ in terms of x: We drew a reference triangle for the original substitution $x = 2\tan\theta$ (Figure 8.4) and read the ratios from the triangle. ■

EXAMPLE 2 Evaluate

$$\int \frac{x^2\, dx}{\sqrt{9-x^2}}.$$

Solution We set

$$x = 3\sin\theta, \qquad dx = 3\cos\theta\, d\theta, \qquad -\frac{\pi}{2} < \theta < \frac{\pi}{2}$$

$$9 - x^2 = 9 - 9\sin^2\theta = 9(1 - \sin^2\theta) = 9\cos^2\theta.$$

Then

$$\int \frac{x^2\, dx}{\sqrt{9-x^2}} = \int \frac{9\sin^2\theta \cdot 3\cos\theta\, d\theta}{|3\cos\theta|}$$

$$= 9\int \sin^2\theta\, d\theta \qquad \cos\theta > 0 \text{ for } -\frac{\pi}{2} < \theta < \frac{\pi}{2}$$

$$= 9\int \frac{1-\cos 2\theta}{2}\, d\theta$$

$$= \frac{9}{2}\left(\theta - \frac{\sin 2\theta}{2}\right) + C$$

$$= \frac{9}{2}(\theta - \sin\theta\cos\theta) + C \qquad \sin 2\theta = 2\sin\theta\cos\theta$$

$$= \frac{9}{2}\left(\sin^{-1}\frac{x}{3} - \frac{x}{3}\cdot\frac{\sqrt{9-x^2}}{3}\right) + C \qquad \text{From Fig. 8.5}$$

$$= \frac{9}{2}\sin^{-1}\frac{x}{3} - \frac{x}{2}\sqrt{9-x^2} + C.$$ ■

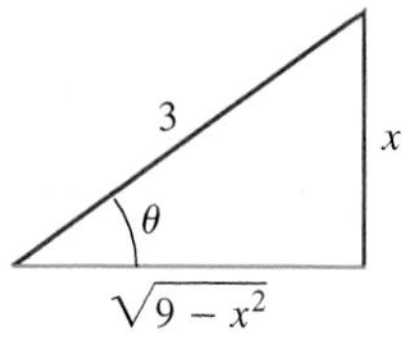

FIGURE 8.5 Reference triangle for $x = 3\sin\theta$ (Example 2):

$$\sin\theta = \frac{x}{3}$$

and

$$\cos\theta = \frac{\sqrt{9-x^2}}{3}.$$

EXAMPLE 3 Evaluate

$$\int \frac{dx}{\sqrt{25x^2-4}}, \qquad x > \frac{2}{5}.$$

Solution We first rewrite the radical as

$$\sqrt{25x^2-4} = \sqrt{25\left(x^2 - \frac{4}{25}\right)}$$

$$= 5\sqrt{x^2 - \left(\frac{2}{5}\right)^2}$$

to put the radicand in the form $x^2 - a^2$. We then substitute

$$x = \frac{2}{5}\sec\theta, \qquad dx = \frac{2}{5}\sec\theta\tan\theta\,d\theta, \qquad 0 < \theta < \frac{\pi}{2}$$

$$\begin{aligned} x^2 - \left(\frac{2}{5}\right)^2 &= \frac{4}{25}\sec^2\theta - \frac{4}{25} \\ &= \frac{4}{25}(\sec^2\theta - 1) = \frac{4}{25}\tan^2\theta \end{aligned}$$

$$\sqrt{x^2 - \left(\frac{2}{5}\right)^2} = \frac{2}{5}|\tan\theta| = \frac{2}{5}\tan\theta. \qquad \tan\theta > 0 \text{ for } 0 < \theta < \pi/2$$

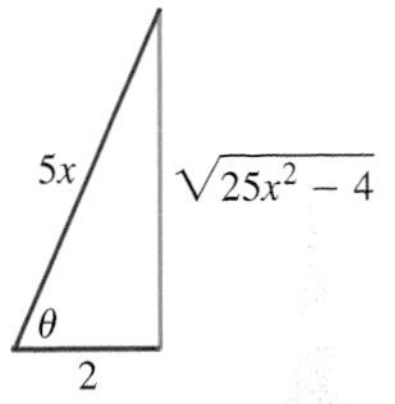

FIGURE 8.6 If $x = (2/5)\sec\theta$, $0 < \theta < \pi/2$, then $\theta = \sec^{-1}(5x/2)$, and we can read the values of the other trigonometric functions of θ from this right triangle (Example 3).

With these substitutions, we have

$$\begin{aligned} \int \frac{dx}{\sqrt{25x^2 - 4}} &= \int \frac{dx}{5\sqrt{x^2 - (4/25)}} = \int \frac{(2/5)\sec\theta\tan\theta\,d\theta}{5\cdot(2/5)\tan\theta} \\ &= \frac{1}{5}\int \sec\theta\,d\theta = \frac{1}{5}\ln|\sec\theta + \tan\theta| + C \\ &= \frac{1}{5}\ln\left|\frac{5x}{2} + \frac{\sqrt{25x^2 - 4}}{2}\right| + C. \qquad \text{From Fig. 8.6} \end{aligned}$$

■

EXERCISES 8.3

Using Trigonometric Substitutions

Evaluate the integrals in Exercises 1–14.

1. $\int \frac{dx}{\sqrt{9 + x^2}}$
2. $\int \frac{3\,dx}{\sqrt{1 + 9x^2}}$
3. $\int_{-2}^{2} \frac{dx}{4 + x^2}$
4. $\int_{0}^{2} \frac{dx}{8 + 2x^2}$
5. $\int_{0}^{3/2} \frac{dx}{\sqrt{9 - x^2}}$
6. $\int_{0}^{1/2\sqrt{2}} \frac{2\,dx}{\sqrt{1 - 4x^2}}$
7. $\int \sqrt{25 - t^2}\,dt$
8. $\int \sqrt{1 - 9t^2}\,dt$
9. $\int \frac{dx}{\sqrt{4x^2 - 49}}, \quad x > \frac{7}{2}$
10. $\int \frac{5\,dx}{\sqrt{25x^2 - 9}}, \quad x > \frac{3}{5}$
11. $\int \frac{\sqrt{y^2 - 49}}{y}\,dy, \quad y > 7$
12. $\int \frac{\sqrt{y^2 - 25}}{y^3}\,dy, \quad y > 5$
13. $\int \frac{dx}{x^2\sqrt{x^2 - 1}}, \quad x > 1$
14. $\int \frac{2\,dx}{x^3\sqrt{x^2 - 1}}, \quad x > 1$

Assorted Integrations

Use any method to evaluate the integrals in Exercises 15–34. Most will require trigonometric substitutions, but some can be evaluated by other methods.

15. $\int \frac{x}{\sqrt{9 - x^2}}\,dx$
16. $\int \frac{x^2}{4 + x^2}\,dx$
17. $\int \frac{x^3\,dx}{\sqrt{x^2 + 4}}$
18. $\int \frac{dx}{x^2\sqrt{x^2 + 1}}$
19. $\int \frac{8\,dw}{w^2\sqrt{4 - w^2}}$
20. $\int \frac{\sqrt{9 - w^2}}{w^2}\,dw$
21. $\int \frac{100}{36 + 25x^2}\,dx$
22. $\int x\sqrt{x^2 - 4}\,dx$
23. $\int_{0}^{\sqrt{3}/2} \frac{4x^2\,dx}{(1 - x^2)^{3/2}}$
24. $\int_{0}^{1} \frac{dx}{(4 - x^2)^{3/2}}$
25. $\int \frac{dx}{(x^2 - 1)^{3/2}}, \quad x > 1$
26. $\int \frac{x^2\,dx}{(x^2 - 1)^{5/2}}, \quad x > 1$
27. $\int \frac{(1 - x^2)^{3/2}}{x^6}\,dx$
28. $\int \frac{(1 - x^2)^{1/2}}{x^4}\,dx$
29. $\int \frac{8\,dx}{(4x^2 + 1)^2}$
30. $\int \frac{6\,dt}{(9t^2 + 1)^2}$
31. $\int \frac{x^3\,dx}{x^2 - 1}$
32. $\int \frac{x\,dx}{25 + 4x^2}$
33. $\int \frac{v^2\,dv}{(1 - v^2)^{5/2}}$
34. $\int \frac{(1 - r^2)^{5/2}}{r^8}\,dr$

In Exercises 35–48, use an appropriate substitution and then a trigonometric substitution to evaluate the integrals.

35. $\int_{0}^{\ln 4} \frac{e^t\,dt}{\sqrt{e^{2t} + 9}}$
36. $\int_{\ln(3/4)}^{\ln(4/3)} \frac{e^t\,dt}{(1 + e^{2t})^{3/2}}$
37. $\int_{1/12}^{1/4} \frac{2\,dt}{\sqrt{t} + 4t\sqrt{t}}$
38. $\int_{1}^{e} \frac{dy}{y\sqrt{1 + (\ln y)^2}}$

39. $\displaystyle\int \frac{dx}{x\sqrt{x^2-1}}$

40. $\displaystyle\int \frac{dx}{1+x^2}$

41. $\displaystyle\int \frac{x\,dx}{\sqrt{x^2-1}}$

42. $\displaystyle\int \frac{dx}{\sqrt{1-x^2}}$

43. $\displaystyle\int \frac{x\,dx}{\sqrt{1+x^4}}$

44. $\displaystyle\int \frac{\sqrt{1-(\ln x)^2}}{x\ln x}\,dx$

45. $\displaystyle\int \sqrt{\frac{4-x}{x}}\,dx$

(*Hint*: Let $x = u^2$.)

46. $\displaystyle\int \sqrt{\frac{x}{1-x^3}}\,dx$

(*Hint*: Let $u = x^{3/2}$.)

47. $\displaystyle\int \sqrt{x}\sqrt{1-x}\,dx$

48. $\displaystyle\int \frac{\sqrt{x-2}}{\sqrt{x-1}}\,dx$

Initial Value Problems

Solve the initial value problems in Exercises 49–52 for y as a function of x.

49. $x\dfrac{dy}{dx} = \sqrt{x^2-4}, \quad x \ge 2, \quad y(2) = 0$

50. $\sqrt{x^2-9}\dfrac{dy}{dx} = 1, \quad x > 3, \quad y(5) = \ln 3$

51. $(x^2+4)\dfrac{dy}{dx} = 3, \quad y(2) = 0$

52. $(x^2+1)^2\dfrac{dy}{dx} = \sqrt{x^2+1}, \quad y(0) = 1$

Applications and Examples

53. **Area** Find the area of the region in the first quadrant that is enclosed by the coordinate axes and the curve $y = \sqrt{9-x^2}/3$.

54. **Area** Find the area enclosed by the ellipse

$$\frac{x^2}{a^2} + \frac{y^2}{b^2} = 1.$$

55. Consider the region bounded by the graphs of $y = \sin^{-1} x$, $y = 0$, and $x = 1/2$.

a. Find the area of the region.

b. Find the centroid of the region.

56. Consider the region bounded by the graphs of $y = \sqrt{x}\tan^{-1} x$ and $y = 0$ for $0 \le x \le 1$. Find the volume of the solid formed by revolving this region about the x-axis (see accompanying figure).

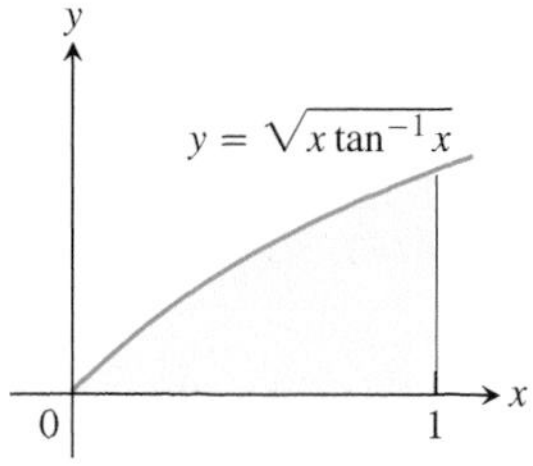

57. Evaluate $\int x^3\sqrt{1-x^2}\,dx$ using

a. integration by parts.

b. a u-substitution.

c. a trigonometric substitution.

58. **Path of a water skier** Suppose that a boat is positioned at the origin with a water skier tethered to the boat at the point (30, 0) on a rope 30 ft long. As the boat travels along the positive y-axis, the skier is pulled behind the boat along an unknown path $y = f(x)$, as shown in the accompanying figure.

a. Show that $f'(x) = \dfrac{-\sqrt{900-x^2}}{x}$.

(*Hint*: Assume that the skier is always pointed directly at the boat and the rope is on a line tangent to the path $y = f(x)$.)

b. Solve the equation in part (a) for $f(x)$, using $f(30) = 0$.

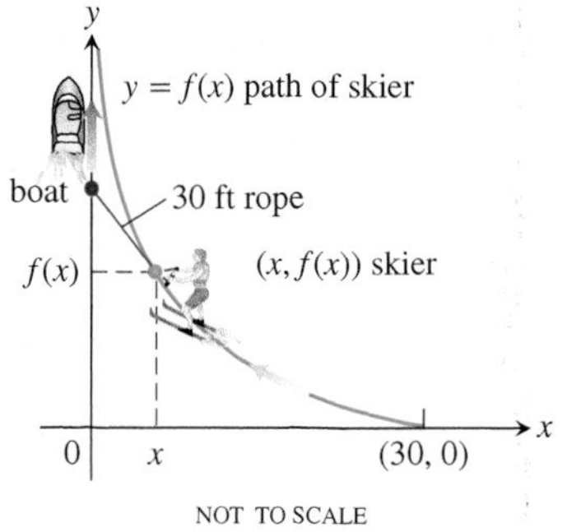

8.4 Integration of Rational Functions by Partial Fractions

This section shows how to express a rational function (a quotient of polynomials) as a sum of simpler fractions, called *partial fractions*, which are easily integrated. For instance, the rational function $(5x-3)/(x^2-2x-3)$ can be rewritten as

$$\frac{5x-3}{x^2-2x-3} = \frac{2}{x+1} + \frac{3}{x-3}.$$

You can verify this equation algebraically by placing the fractions on the right side over a common denominator $(x+1)(x-3)$. The skill acquired in writing rational functions as such a sum is useful in other settings as well (for instance, when using certain transform methods to solve differential equations). To integrate the rational function

$(5x - 3)/(x^2 - 2x - 3)$ on the left side of our previous expression, we simply sum the integrals of the fractions on the right side:

$$\int \frac{5x - 3}{(x + 1)(x - 3)}\, dx = \int \frac{2}{x + 1}\, dx + \int \frac{3}{x - 3}\, dx$$
$$= 2 \ln |x + 1| + 3 \ln |x - 3| + C.$$

The method for rewriting rational functions as a sum of simpler fractions is called **the method of partial fractions**. In the case of the preceding example, it consists of finding constants A and B such that

$$\frac{5x - 3}{x^2 - 2x - 3} = \frac{A}{x + 1} + \frac{B}{x - 3}. \tag{1}$$

(Pretend for a moment that we do not know that $A = 2$ and $B = 3$ will work.) We call the fractions $A/(x + 1)$ and $B/(x - 3)$ **partial fractions** because their denominators are only part of the original denominator $x^2 - 2x - 3$. We call A and B **undetermined coefficients** until proper values for them have been found.

To find A and B, we first clear Equation (1) of fractions and regroup in powers of x, obtaining

$$5x - 3 = A(x - 3) + B(x + 1) = (A + B)x - 3A + B.$$

This will be an identity in x if and only if the coefficients of like powers of x on the two sides are equal:

$$A + B = 5, \qquad -3A + B = -3.$$

Solving these equations simultaneously gives $A = 2$ and $B = 3$.

General Description of the Method

Success in writing a rational function $f(x)/g(x)$ as a sum of partial fractions depends on two things:

- *The degree of $f(x)$ must be less than the degree of $g(x)$.* That is, the fraction must be proper. If it isn't, divide $f(x)$ by $g(x)$ and work with the remainder term. See Example 3 of this section.
- *We must know the factors of $g(x)$.* In theory, any polynomial with real coefficients can be written as a product of real linear factors and real quadratic factors. In practice, the factors may be hard to find.

Here is how we find the partial fractions of a proper fraction $f(x)/g(x)$ when the factors of g are known. A quadratic polynomial (or factor) is **irreducible** if it cannot be written as the product of two linear factors with real coefficients. That is, the polynomial has no real roots.

Method of Partial Fractions ($f(x)/g(x)$ Proper)

1. Let $x - r$ be a linear factor of $g(x)$. Suppose that $(x - r)^m$ is the highest power of $x - r$ that divides $g(x)$. Then, to this factor, assign the sum of the m partial fractions:

$$\frac{A_1}{(x - r)} + \frac{A_2}{(x - r)^2} + \cdots + \frac{A_m}{(x - r)^m}.$$

Do this for each distinct linear factor of $g(x)$.

continued

2. Let $x^2 + px + q$ be an irreducible quadratic factor of $g(x)$ so that $x^2 + px + q$ has no real roots. Suppose that $(x^2 + px + q)^n$ is the highest power of this factor that divides $g(x)$. Then, to this factor, assign the sum of the n partial fractions:

$$\frac{B_1x + C_1}{(x^2 + px + q)} + \frac{B_2x + C_2}{(x^2 + px + q)^2} + \cdots + \frac{B_nx + C_n}{(x^2 + px + q)^n}.$$

Do this for each distinct quadratic factor of $g(x)$.

3. Set the original fraction $f(x)/g(x)$ equal to the sum of all these partial fractions. Clear the resulting equation of fractions and arrange the terms in decreasing powers of x.

4. Equate the coefficients of corresponding powers of x and solve the resulting equations for the undetermined coefficients.

EXAMPLE 1 Use partial fractions to evaluate

$$\int \frac{x^2 + 4x + 1}{(x - 1)(x + 1)(x + 3)}\,dx.$$

Solution The partial fraction decomposition has the form

$$\frac{x^2 + 4x + 1}{(x - 1)(x + 1)(x + 3)} = \frac{A}{x - 1} + \frac{B}{x + 1} + \frac{C}{x + 3}.$$

To find the values of the undetermined coefficients A, B, and C, we clear fractions and get

$$\begin{aligned} x^2 + 4x + 1 &= A(x + 1)(x + 3) + B(x - 1)(x + 3) + C(x - 1)(x + 1) \\ &= A(x^2 + 4x + 3) + B(x^2 + 2x - 3) + C(x^2 - 1) \\ &= (A + B + C)x^2 + (4A + 2B)x + (3A - 3B - C). \end{aligned}$$

The polynomials on both sides of the above equation are identical, so we equate coefficients of like powers of x, obtaining

Coefficient of x^2:	$A + B + C = 1$
Coefficient of x^1:	$4A + 2B = 4$
Coefficient of x^0:	$3A - 3B - C = 1$

There are several ways of solving such a system of linear equations for the unknowns A, B, and C, including elimination of variables or the use of a calculator or computer. Whatever method is used, the solution is $A = 3/4$, $B = 1/2$, and $C = -1/4$. Hence we have

$$\begin{aligned} \int \frac{x^2 + 4x + 1}{(x - 1)(x + 1)(x + 3)}\,dx &= \int \left[\frac{3}{4}\frac{1}{x - 1} + \frac{1}{2}\frac{1}{x + 1} - \frac{1}{4}\frac{1}{x + 3}\right] dx \\ &= \frac{3}{4}\ln|x - 1| + \frac{1}{2}\ln|x + 1| - \frac{1}{4}\ln|x + 3| + K, \end{aligned}$$

where K is the arbitrary constant of integration (to avoid confusion with the undetermined coefficient we labeled as C). ■

EXAMPLE 2 Use partial fractions to evaluate

$$\int \frac{6x + 7}{(x + 2)^2}\,dx.$$

Solution First we express the integrand as a sum of partial fractions with undetermined coefficients.

$$\frac{6x+7}{(x+2)^2} = \frac{A}{x+2} + \frac{B}{(x+2)^2}$$

$$6x+7 = A(x+2) + B \qquad \text{Multiply both sides by } (x+2)^2.$$

$$= Ax + (2A+B)$$

Equating coefficients of corresponding powers of x gives

$$A = 6 \quad \text{and} \quad 2A + B = 12 + B = 7, \quad \text{or} \quad A = 6 \quad \text{and} \quad B = -5.$$

Therefore,

$$\int \frac{6x+7}{(x+2)^2}\,dx = \int \left(\frac{6}{x+2} - \frac{5}{(x+2)^2}\right) dx$$

$$= 6\int \frac{dx}{x+2} - 5\int (x+2)^{-2}\,dx$$

$$= 6\ln|x+2| + 5(x+2)^{-1} + C. \qquad \blacksquare$$

EXAMPLE 3 Use partial fractions to evaluate

$$\int \frac{2x^3 - 4x^2 - x - 3}{x^2 - 2x - 3}\,dx.$$

Solution First we divide the denominator into the numerator to get a polynomial plus a proper fraction.

$$\begin{array}{r} 2x \\ x^2 - 2x - 3\,\overline{)\,2x^3 - 4x^2 - x - 3} \\ \underline{2x^3 - 4x^2 - 6x} \\ 5x - 3 \end{array}$$

Then we write the improper fraction as a polynomial plus a proper fraction.

$$\frac{2x^3 - 4x^2 - x - 3}{x^2 - 2x - 3} = 2x + \frac{5x - 3}{x^2 - 2x - 3}$$

We found the partial fraction decomposition of the fraction on the right in the opening example, so

$$\int \frac{2x^3 - 4x^2 - x - 3}{x^2 - 2x - 3}\,dx = \int 2x\,dx + \int \frac{5x-3}{x^2 - 2x - 3}\,dx$$

$$= \int 2x\,dx + \int \frac{2}{x+1}\,dx + \int \frac{3}{x-3}\,dx$$

$$= x^2 + 2\ln|x+1| + 3\ln|x-3| + C. \qquad \blacksquare$$

EXAMPLE 4 Use partial fractions to evaluate

$$\int \frac{-2x+4}{(x^2+1)(x-1)^2}\,dx.$$

Solution The denominator has an irreducible quadratic factor as well as a repeated linear factor, so we write

$$\frac{-2x+4}{(x^2+1)(x-1)^2} = \frac{Ax+B}{x^2+1} + \frac{C}{x-1} + \frac{D}{(x-1)^2}. \tag{2}$$

Clearing the equation of fractions gives

$$\begin{aligned}-2x + 4 &= (Ax + B)(x - 1)^2 + C(x - 1)(x^2 + 1) + D(x^2 + 1)\\ &= (A + C)x^3 + (-2A + B - C + D)x^2\\ &\quad + (A - 2B + C)x + (B - C + D).\end{aligned}$$

Equating coefficients of like terms gives

Coefficients of x^3:	$0 = A + C$
Coefficients of x^2:	$0 = -2A + B - C + D$
Coefficients of x^1:	$-2 = A - 2B + C$
Coefficients of x^0:	$4 = B - C + D$

We solve these equations simultaneously to find the values of A, B, C, and D:

$-4 = -2A, \quad A = 2$	Subtract fourth equation from second.
$C = -A = -2$	From the first equation
$B = (A + C + 2)/2 = 1$	From the third equation and $C = -A$
$D = 4 - B + C = 1.$	From the fourth equation

We substitute these values into Equation (2), obtaining

$$\frac{-2x + 4}{(x^2 + 1)(x - 1)^2} = \frac{2x + 1}{x^2 + 1} - \frac{2}{x - 1} + \frac{1}{(x - 1)^2}.$$

Finally, using the expansion above we can integrate:

$$\begin{aligned}\int \frac{-2x + 4}{(x^2 + 1)(x - 1)^2}\, dx &= \int \left(\frac{2x + 1}{x^2 + 1} - \frac{2}{x - 1} + \frac{1}{(x - 1)^2}\right) dx\\ &= \int \left(\frac{2x}{x^2 + 1} + \frac{1}{x^2 + 1} - \frac{2}{x - 1} + \frac{1}{(x - 1)^2}\right) dx\\ &= \ln(x^2 + 1) + \tan^{-1} x - 2\ln|x - 1| - \frac{1}{x - 1} + C. \quad \blacksquare\end{aligned}$$

EXAMPLE 5 Use partial fractions to evaluate

$$\int \frac{dx}{x(x^2 + 1)^2}.$$

Solution The form of the partial fraction decomposition is

$$\frac{1}{x(x^2 + 1)^2} = \frac{A}{x} + \frac{Bx + C}{x^2 + 1} + \frac{Dx + E}{(x^2 + 1)^2}.$$

Multiplying by $x(x^2 + 1)^2$, we have

$$\begin{aligned}1 &= A(x^2 + 1)^2 + (Bx + C)x(x^2 + 1) + (Dx + E)x\\ &= A(x^4 + 2x^2 + 1) + B(x^4 + x^2) + C(x^3 + x) + Dx^2 + Ex\\ &= (A + B)x^4 + Cx^3 + (2A + B + D)x^2 + (C + E)x + A.\end{aligned}$$

If we equate coefficients, we get the system

$$A + B = 0, \qquad C = 0, \qquad 2A + B + D = 0, \qquad C + E = 0, \qquad A = 1.$$

Solving this system gives $A = 1, B = -1, C = 0, D = -1$, and $E = 0$. Thus,

$$\int \frac{dx}{x(x^2+1)^2} = \int \left[\frac{1}{x} + \frac{-x}{x^2+1} + \frac{-x}{(x^2+1)^2}\right] dx$$

$$= \int \frac{dx}{x} - \int \frac{x\,dx}{x^2+1} - \int \frac{x\,dx}{(x^2+1)^2}$$

$$= \int \frac{dx}{x} - \frac{1}{2}\int \frac{du}{u} - \frac{1}{2}\int \frac{du}{u^2} \qquad u = x^2+1,\ du = 2x\,dx$$

$$= \ln|x| - \frac{1}{2}\ln|u| + \frac{1}{2u} + K$$

$$= \ln|x| - \frac{1}{2}\ln(x^2+1) + \frac{1}{2(x^2+1)} + K$$

$$= \ln\frac{|x|}{\sqrt{x^2+1}} + \frac{1}{2(x^2+1)} + K.$$ ■

Another Way to Determine the Coefficients

EXAMPLE 6 Find A, B, and C in the equation

$$\frac{x-1}{(x+1)^3} = \frac{A}{x+1} + \frac{B}{(x+1)^2} + \frac{C}{(x+1)^3}$$

by clearing fractions, differentiating the result, and substituting $x = -1$.

Solution We first clear fractions:

$$x - 1 = A(x+1)^2 + B(x+1) + C.$$

Substituting $x = -1$ shows $C = -2$. We then differentiate both sides with respect to x, obtaining

$$1 = 2A(x+1) + B.$$

Substituting $x = -1$ shows $B = 1$. We differentiate again to get $0 = 2A$, which shows $A = 0$. Hence,

$$\frac{x-1}{(x+1)^3} = \frac{1}{(x+1)^2} - \frac{2}{(x+1)^3}.$$ ■

In some problems, assigning appropriate small values to x, such as $x = 0, \pm 1, \pm 2$, to get equations in A, B, and C provides an alternative method to finding the constants that appear in partial fractions.

EXAMPLE 7 Find A, B, and C in the expression

$$\frac{x^2+1}{(x-1)(x-2)(x-3)} = \frac{A}{x-1} + \frac{B}{x-2} + \frac{C}{x-3}$$

by assigning numerical values to x.

Solution Clear fractions to get

$$x^2 + 1 = A(x - 2)(x - 3) + B(x - 1)(x - 3) + C(x - 1)(x - 2).$$

Then let $x = 1, 2, 3$ successively to find A, B, and C:

$$x = 1: \quad (1)^2 + 1 = A(-1)(-2) + B(0) + C(0)$$
$$2 = 2A$$
$$A = 1$$
$$x = 2: \quad (2)^2 + 1 = A(0) + B(1)(-1) + C(0)$$
$$5 = -B$$
$$B = -5$$
$$x = 3: \quad (3)^2 + 1 = A(0) + B(0) + C(2)(1)$$
$$10 = 2C$$
$$C = 5.$$

Conclusion:

$$\frac{x^2 + 1}{(x - 1)(x - 2)(x - 3)} = \frac{1}{x - 1} - \frac{5}{x - 2} + \frac{5}{x - 3}.$$ ■

Exercises 8.4

Expanding Quotients into Partial Fractions

Expand the quotients in Exercises 1–8 by partial fractions.

1. $\dfrac{5x - 13}{(x - 3)(x - 2)}$
2. $\dfrac{5x - 7}{x^2 - 3x + 2}$
3. $\dfrac{x + 4}{(x + 1)^2}$
4. $\dfrac{2x + 2}{x^2 - 2x + 1}$
5. $\dfrac{z + 1}{z^2(z - 1)}$
6. $\dfrac{z}{z^3 - z^2 - 6z}$
7. $\dfrac{t^2 + 8}{t^2 - 5t + 6}$
8. $\dfrac{t^4 + 9}{t^4 + 9t^2}$

Nonrepeated Linear Factors

In Exercises 9–16, express the integrand as a sum of partial fractions and evaluate the integrals.

9. $\displaystyle\int \frac{dx}{1 - x^2}$
10. $\displaystyle\int \frac{dx}{x^2 + 2x}$
11. $\displaystyle\int \frac{x + 4}{x^2 + 5x - 6}\,dx$
12. $\displaystyle\int \frac{2x + 1}{x^2 - 7x + 12}\,dx$
13. $\displaystyle\int_4^8 \frac{y\,dy}{y^2 - 2y - 3}$
14. $\displaystyle\int_{1/2}^1 \frac{y + 4}{y^2 + y}\,dy$
15. $\displaystyle\int \frac{dt}{t^3 + t^2 - 2t}$
16. $\displaystyle\int \frac{x + 3}{2x^3 - 8x}\,dx$

Repeated Linear Factors

In Exercises 17–20, express the integrand as a sum of partial fractions and evaluate the integrals.

17. $\displaystyle\int_0^1 \frac{x^3\,dx}{x^2 + 2x + 1}$
18. $\displaystyle\int_{-1}^0 \frac{x^3\,dx}{x^2 - 2x + 1}$
19. $\displaystyle\int \frac{dx}{(x^2 - 1)^2}$
20. $\displaystyle\int \frac{x^2\,dx}{(x - 1)(x^2 + 2x + 1)}$

Irreducible Quadratic Factors

In Exercises 21–32, express the integrand as a sum of partial fractions and evaluate the integrals.

21. $\displaystyle\int_0^1 \frac{dx}{(x + 1)(x^2 + 1)}$
22. $\displaystyle\int_1^{\sqrt{3}} \frac{3t^2 + t + 4}{t^3 + t}\,dt$
23. $\displaystyle\int \frac{y^2 + 2y + 1}{(y^2 + 1)^2}\,dy$
24. $\displaystyle\int \frac{8x^2 + 8x + 2}{(4x^2 + 1)^2}\,dx$
25. $\displaystyle\int \frac{2s + 2}{(s^2 + 1)(s - 1)^3}\,ds$
26. $\displaystyle\int \frac{s^4 + 81}{s(s^2 + 9)^2}\,ds$
27. $\displaystyle\int \frac{x^2 - x + 2}{x^3 - 1}\,dx$
28. $\displaystyle\int \frac{1}{x^4 + x}\,dx$
29. $\displaystyle\int \frac{x^2}{x^4 - 1}\,dx$
30. $\displaystyle\int \frac{x^2 + x}{x^4 - 3x^2 - 4}\,dx$
31. $\displaystyle\int \frac{2\theta^3 + 5\theta^2 + 8\theta + 4}{(\theta^2 + 2\theta + 2)^2}\,d\theta$
32. $\displaystyle\int \frac{\theta^4 - 4\theta^3 + 2\theta^2 - 3\theta + 1}{(\theta^2 + 1)^3}\,d\theta$

Improper Fractions

In Exercises 33–38, perform long division on the integrand, write the proper fraction as a sum of partial fractions, and then evaluate the integral.

33. $\displaystyle\int \frac{2x^3 - 2x^2 + 1}{x^2 - x}\,dx$
34. $\displaystyle\int \frac{x^4}{x^2 - 1}\,dx$

35. $\displaystyle\int \frac{9x^3 - 3x + 1}{x^3 - x^2}\,dx$

36. $\displaystyle\int \frac{16x^3}{4x^2 - 4x + 1}\,dx$

37. $\displaystyle\int \frac{y^4 + y^2 - 1}{y^3 + y}\,dy$

38. $\displaystyle\int \frac{2y^4}{y^3 - y^2 + y - 1}\,dy$

Evaluating Integrals

Evaluate the integrals in Exercises 39–50.

39. $\displaystyle\int \frac{e^t\,dt}{e^{2t} + 3e^t + 2}$

40. $\displaystyle\int \frac{e^{4t} + 2e^{2t} - e^t}{e^{2t} + 1}\,dt$

41. $\displaystyle\int \frac{\cos y\,dy}{\sin^2 y + \sin y - 6}$

42. $\displaystyle\int \frac{\sin\theta\,d\theta}{\cos^2\theta + \cos\theta - 2}$

43. $\displaystyle\int \frac{(x-2)^2\tan^{-1}(2x) - 12x^3 - 3x}{(4x^2+1)(x-2)^2}\,dx$

44. $\displaystyle\int \frac{(x+1)^2\tan^{-1}(3x) + 9x^3 + x}{(9x^2+1)(x+1)^2}\,dx$

45. $\displaystyle\int \frac{1}{x^{3/2} - \sqrt{x}}\,dx$

46. $\displaystyle\int \frac{1}{(x^{1/3} - 1)\sqrt{x}}\,dx$

(*Hint*: Let $x = u^6$.)

47. $\displaystyle\int \frac{\sqrt{x+1}}{x}\,dx$

(*Hint*: Let $x + 1 = u^2$.)

48. $\displaystyle\int \frac{1}{x\sqrt{x+9}}\,dx$

49. $\displaystyle\int \frac{1}{x(x^4+1)}\,dx$

$\left(\textit{Hint}\text{: Multiply by } \frac{x^3}{x^3}.\right)$

50. $\displaystyle\int \frac{1}{x^6(x^5+4)}\,dx$

Initial Value Problems

Solve the initial value problems in Exercises 51–54 for x as a function of t.

51. $(t^2 - 3t + 2)\dfrac{dx}{dt} = 1 \quad (t > 2), \quad x(3) = 0$

52. $(3t^4 + 4t^2 + 1)\dfrac{dx}{dt} = 2\sqrt{3}, \quad x(1) = -\pi\sqrt{3}/4$

53. $(t^2 + 2t)\dfrac{dx}{dt} = 2x + 2 \quad (t, x > 0), \quad x(1) = 1$

54. $(t + 1)\dfrac{dx}{dt} = x^2 + 1 \quad (t > -1), \quad x(0) = 0$

Applications and Examples

In Exercises 55 and 56, find the volume of the solid generated by revolving the shaded region about the indicated axis.

55. The x-axis

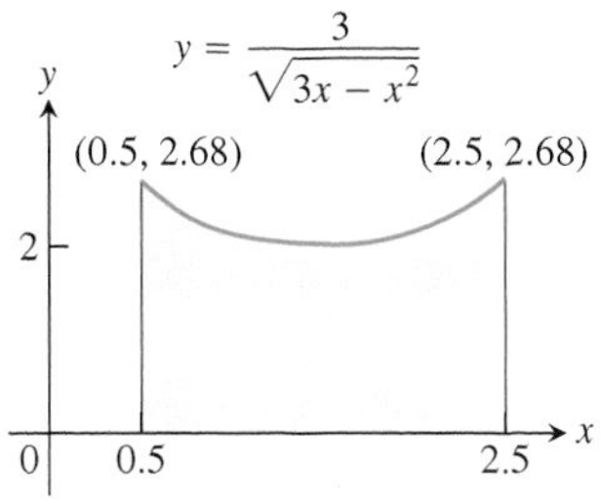

56. The y-axis

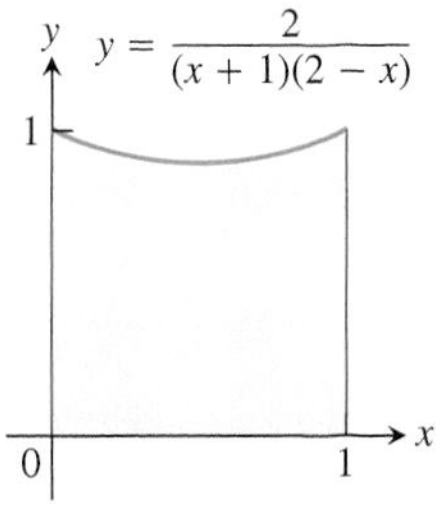

57. Find, to two decimal places, the x-coordinate of the centroid of the region in the first quadrant bounded by the x-axis, the curve $y = \tan^{-1} x$, and the line $x = \sqrt{3}$.

58. Find the x-coordinate of the centroid of this region to two decimal places.

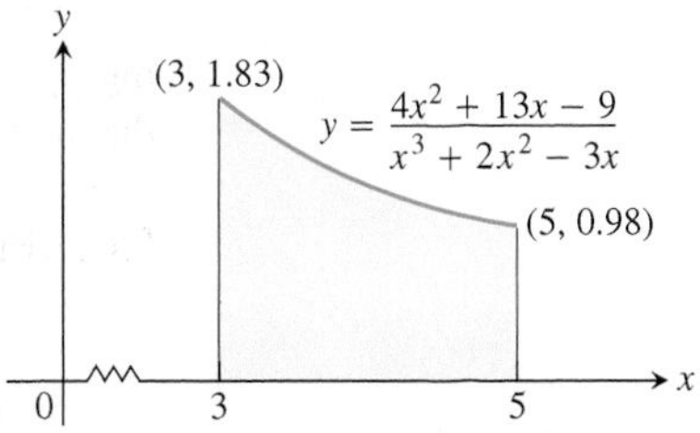

59. **Social diffusion** Sociologists sometimes use the phrase "social diffusion" to describe the way information spreads through a population. The information might be a rumor, a cultural fad, or news about a technical innovation. In a sufficiently large population, the number of people x who have the information is treated as a differentiable function of time t, and the rate of diffusion, dx/dt, is assumed to be proportional to the number of people who have the information times the number of people who do not. This leads to the equation

$$\frac{dx}{dt} = kx(N - x),$$

where N is the number of people in the population.

Suppose t is in days, $k = 1/250$, and two people start a rumor at time $t = 0$ in a population of $N = 1000$ people.

a. Find x as a function of t.

b. When will half the population have heard the rumor? (This is when the rumor will be spreading the fastest.)

60. **Second-order chemical reactions** Many chemical reactions are the result of the interaction of two molecules that undergo a change to produce a new product. The rate of the reaction typically depends on the concentrations of the two kinds of molecules. If a is the amount of substance A and b is the amount of substance B at time $t = 0$, and if x is the amount of product at time t, then the rate of formation of x may be given by the differential equation

$$\frac{dx}{dt} = k(a - x)(b - x),$$

or

$$\frac{1}{(a - x)(b - x)}\frac{dx}{dt} = k,$$

where k is a constant for the reaction. Integrate both sides of this equation to obtain a relation between x and t **(a)** if $a = b$, and **(b)** if $a \neq b$. Assume in each case that $x = 0$ when $t = 0$.

8.5 Integral Tables and Computer Algebra Systems

In this section we discuss how to use tables and computer algebra systems to evaluate integrals.

Integral Tables

A Brief Table of Integrals is provided at the back of the book, after the index. (More extensive tables appear in compilations such as *CRC Mathematical Tables*, which contain thousands of integrals.) The integration formulas are stated in terms of constants a, b, c, m, n, and so on. These constants can usually assume any real value and need not be integers. Occasional limitations on their values are stated with the formulas. Formula 21 requires $n \neq -1$, for example, and Formula 27 requires $n \neq -2$.

The formulas also assume that the constants do not take on values that require dividing by zero or taking even roots of negative numbers. For example, Formula 24 assumes that $a \neq 0$, and Formulas 29a and 29b cannot be used unless b is positive.

EXAMPLE 1 Find

$$\int x(2x + 5)^{-1}\, dx.$$

Solution We use Formula 24 at the back of the book (not 22, which requires $n \neq -1$):

$$\int x(ax + b)^{-1}\, dx = \frac{x}{a} - \frac{b}{a^2} \ln |ax + b| + C.$$

With $a = 2$ and $b = 5$, we have

$$\int x(2x + 5)^{-1}\, dx = \frac{x}{2} - \frac{5}{4} \ln |2x + 5| + C.$$ ■

EXAMPLE 2 Find

$$\int \frac{dx}{x\sqrt{2x - 4}}.$$

Solution We use Formula 29b:

$$\int \frac{dx}{x\sqrt{ax - b}} = \frac{2}{\sqrt{b}} \tan^{-1} \sqrt{\frac{ax - b}{b}} + C.$$

With $a = 2$ and $b = 4$, we have

$$\int \frac{dx}{x\sqrt{2x - 4}} = \frac{2}{\sqrt{4}} \tan^{-1} \sqrt{\frac{2x - 4}{4}} + C = \tan^{-1} \sqrt{\frac{x - 2}{2}} + C.$$ ■

EXAMPLE 3 Find

$$\int x \sin^{-1} x\, dx.$$

Solution We begin by using Formula 106:

$$\int x^n \sin^{-1} ax\, dx = \frac{x^{n+1}}{n + 1} \sin^{-1} ax - \frac{a}{n + 1} \int \frac{x^{n+1}\, dx}{\sqrt{1 - a^2x^2}}, \qquad n \neq -1.$$

With $n = 1$ and $a = 1$, we have

$$\int x \sin^{-1} x \, dx = \frac{x^2}{2} \sin^{-1} x - \frac{1}{2} \int \frac{x^2 \, dx}{\sqrt{1 - x^2}}.$$

Next we use Formula 49 to find the integral on the right:

$$\int \frac{x^2}{\sqrt{a^2 - x^2}} dx = \frac{a^2}{2} \sin^{-1}\left(\frac{x}{a}\right) - \frac{1}{2} x \sqrt{a^2 - x^2} + C.$$

With $a = 1$,

$$\int \frac{x^2 \, dx}{\sqrt{1 - x^2}} = \frac{1}{2} \sin^{-1} x - \frac{1}{2} x \sqrt{1 - x^2} + C.$$

The combined result is

$$\begin{aligned} \int x \sin^{-1} x \, dx &= \frac{x^2}{2} \sin^{-1} x - \frac{1}{2}\left(\frac{1}{2} \sin^{-1} x - \frac{1}{2} x \sqrt{1 - x^2} + C\right) \\ &= \left(\frac{x^2}{2} - \frac{1}{4}\right) \sin^{-1} x + \frac{1}{4} x \sqrt{1 - x^2} + C'. \end{aligned}$$

■

Reduction Formulas

The time required for repeated integrations by parts can sometimes be shortened by applying reduction formulas like

$$\int \tan^n x \, dx = \frac{1}{n - 1} \tan^{n-1} x - \int \tan^{n-2} x \, dx \tag{1}$$

$$\int (\ln x)^n \, dx = x(\ln x)^n - n \int (\ln x)^{n-1} \, dx \tag{2}$$

$$\int \sin^n x \cos^m x \, dx = -\frac{\sin^{n-1} x \cos^{m+1} x}{m + n} + \frac{n - 1}{m + n} \int \sin^{n-2} x \cos^m x \, dx \quad (n \neq -m). \tag{3}$$

By applying such a formula repeatedly, we can eventually express the original integral in terms of a power low enough to be evaluated directly. The next example illustrates this procedure.

EXAMPLE 4 Find

$$\int \tan^5 x \, dx.$$

Solution We apply Equation (1) with $n = 5$ to get

$$\int \tan^5 x \, dx = \frac{1}{4} \tan^4 x - \int \tan^3 x \, dx.$$

We then apply Equation (1) again, with $n = 3$, to evaluate the remaining integral:

$$\int \tan^3 x \, dx = \frac{1}{2} \tan^2 x - \int \tan x \, dx = \frac{1}{2} \tan^2 x + \ln |\cos x| + C.$$

The combined result is

$$\int \tan^5 x \, dx = \frac{1}{4} \tan^4 x - \frac{1}{2} \tan^2 x - \ln |\cos x| + C'.$$

■

As their form suggests, reduction formulas are derived using integration by parts. (See Example 5 in Section 8.1.)

Integration with a CAS

A powerful capability of computer algebra systems is their ability to integrate symbolically. This is performed with the **integrate command** specified by the particular system (for example, **int** in Maple, **Integrate** in Mathematica).

EXAMPLE 5 Suppose that you want to evaluate the indefinite integral of the function

$$f(x) = x^2\sqrt{a^2 + x^2}.$$

Using Maple, you first define or name the function:

$$> f := x\char`^2 * \text{sqrt}\,(a\char`^2 + x\char`^2);$$

Then you use the integrate command on f, identifying the variable of integration:

$$> \text{int}(f, x);$$

Maple returns the answer

$$\frac{1}{4}x(a^2 + x^2)^{3/2} - \frac{1}{8}a^2x\sqrt{a^2 + x^2} - \frac{1}{8}a^4\ln\left(x + \sqrt{a^2 + x^2}\right).$$

If you want to see if the answer can be simplified, enter

$$> \text{simplify}(\%);$$

Maple returns

$$\frac{1}{8}a^2x\sqrt{a^2 + x^2} + \frac{1}{4}x^3\sqrt{a^2 + x^2} - \frac{1}{8}a^4\ln\left(x + \sqrt{a^2 + x^2}\right).$$

If you want the definite integral for $0 \le x \le \pi/2$, you can use the format

$$> \text{int}(f, x = 0..\text{Pi}/2);$$

Maple will return the expression

$$\frac{1}{64}\pi(4a^2 + \pi^2)^{(3/2)} - \frac{1}{32}a^2\pi\sqrt{4a^2 + \pi^2} + \frac{1}{8}a^4\ln(2) - \frac{1}{8}a^4\ln\left(\pi + \sqrt{4a^2 + \pi^2}\right) + \frac{1}{16}a^4\ln(a^2).$$

You can also find the definite integral for a particular value of the constant a:

$$> a := 1;$$
$$> \text{int}(f, x = 0..1);$$

Maple returns the numerical answer

$$\frac{3}{8}\sqrt{2} + \frac{1}{8}\ln\left(\sqrt{2} - 1\right).$$

■

EXAMPLE 6 Use a CAS to find

$$\int \sin^2 x \cos^3 x\, dx.$$

Solution With Maple, we have the entry

$$> \text{int}\,((\sin\char`^2)(x) * (\cos\char`^3)(x), x);$$

with the immediate return

$$-\frac{1}{5}\sin(x)\cos(x)^4 + \frac{1}{15}\cos(x)^2\sin(x) + \frac{2}{15}\sin(x).$$

■

Computer algebra systems vary in how they process integrations. We used Maple in Examples 5 and 6. Mathematica would have returned somewhat different results:

1. In Example 5, given

$$\textit{In [1]:=}\ \text{Integrate}\ [x\text{^}2 * \text{Sqrt}\ [a\text{^}2 + x\text{^}2], x]$$

Mathematica returns

$$\textit{Out [1]=}\ \sqrt{a^2 + x^2}\left(\frac{a^2 x}{8} + \frac{x^3}{4}\right) - \frac{1}{8}a^4\,\text{Log}\left[x + \sqrt{a^2 + x^2}\right]$$

without having to simplify an intermediate result. The answer is close to Formula 22 in the integral tables.

2. The Mathematica answer to the integral

$$\textit{In [2]:=}\ \text{Integrate}\ [\text{Sin}\ [x]\text{^}2 * \text{Cos}\ [x]\text{^}3, x]$$

in Example 6 is

$$\textit{Out [2]=}\ \frac{\text{Sin}\ [x]}{8} - \frac{1}{48}\text{Sin}\ [3\,x] - \frac{1}{80}\text{Sin}\ [5\,x]$$

differing from the Maple answer. Both answers are correct.

Although a CAS is very powerful and can aid us in solving difficult problems, each CAS has its own limitations. There are even situations where a CAS may further complicate a problem (in the sense of producing an answer that is extremely difficult to use or interpret). Note, too, that neither Maple nor Mathematica returns an arbitrary constant $+C$. On the other hand, a little mathematical thinking on your part may reduce the problem to one that is quite easy to handle. We provide an example in Exercise 67.

Nonelementary Integrals

The development of computers and calculators that find antiderivatives by symbolic manipulation has led to a renewed interest in determining which antiderivatives can be expressed as finite combinations of elementary functions (the functions we have been studying) and which cannot. Integrals of functions that do not have elementary antiderivatives are called **nonelementary** integrals. These integrals can sometimes be expressed with infinite series (Chapter 9) or approximated using numerical methods for their evaluation (Section 8.6). Examples of nonelementary integrals include the error function (which measures the probability of random errors)

$$\operatorname{erf}(x) = \frac{2}{\sqrt{\pi}}\int_0^x e^{-t^2}\,dt$$

and integrals such as

$$\int \sin x^2\,dx \qquad \text{and} \qquad \int \sqrt{1 + x^4}\,dx$$

that arise in engineering and physics. These and a number of others, such as

$$\int \frac{e^x}{x}\,dx, \qquad \int e^{(e^x)}\,dx, \qquad \int \frac{1}{\ln x}\,dx, \qquad \int \ln(\ln x)\,dx, \qquad \int \frac{\sin x}{x}\,dx,$$

$$\int \sqrt{1 - k^2 \sin^2 x}\,dx, \qquad 0 < k < 1,$$

look so easy they tempt us to try them just to see how they turn out. It can be proved, however, that there is no way to express these integrals as finite combinations of elementary functions. The same applies to integrals that can be changed into these by substitution. The integrands all have antiderivatives, as a consequence of the Fundamental Theorem of Calculus, Part 1, because they are continuous. However, none of the antiderivatives are elementary.

None of the integrals you are asked to evaluate in the present chapter fall into this category, but you may encounter nonelementary integrals in your other work.

Exercises 8.5

Using Integral Tables

Use the table of integrals at the back of the book to evaluate the integrals in Exercises 1–26.

1. $\int \frac{dx}{x\sqrt{x-3}}$
2. $\int \frac{dx}{x\sqrt{x+4}}$
3. $\int \frac{x\,dx}{\sqrt{x-2}}$
4. $\int \frac{x\,dx}{(2x+3)^{3/2}}$
5. $\int x\sqrt{2x-3}\,dx$
6. $\int x(7x+5)^{3/2}\,dx$
7. $\int \frac{\sqrt{9-4x}}{x^2}\,dx$
8. $\int \frac{dx}{x^2\sqrt{4x-9}}$
9. $\int x\sqrt{4x-x^2}\,dx$
10. $\int \frac{\sqrt{x-x^2}}{x}\,dx$
11. $\int \frac{dx}{x\sqrt{7+x^2}}$
12. $\int \frac{dx}{x\sqrt{7-x^2}}$
13. $\int \frac{\sqrt{4-x^2}}{x}\,dx$
14. $\int \frac{\sqrt{x^2-4}}{x}\,dx$
15. $\int e^{2t}\cos 3t\,dt$
16. $\int e^{-3t}\sin 4t\,dt$
17. $\int x\cos^{-1}x\,dx$
18. $\int x\tan^{-1}x\,dx$
19. $\int x^2\tan^{-1}x\,dx$
20. $\int \frac{\tan^{-1}x}{x^2}\,dx$
21. $\int \sin 3x\cos 2x\,dx$
22. $\int \sin 2x\cos 3x\,dx$
23. $\int 8\sin 4t\sin\frac{t}{2}\,dt$
24. $\int \sin\frac{t}{3}\sin\frac{t}{6}\,dt$
25. $\int \cos\frac{\theta}{3}\cos\frac{\theta}{4}\,d\theta$
26. $\int \cos\frac{\theta}{2}\cos 7\theta\,d\theta$

Substitution and Integral Tables

In Exercises 27–40, use a substitution to change the integral into one you can find in the table. Then evaluate the integral.

27. $\int \frac{x^3+x+1}{(x^2+1)^2}\,dx$
28. $\int \frac{x^2+6x}{(x^2+3)^2}\,dx$
29. $\int \sin^{-1}\sqrt{x}\,dx$
30. $\int \frac{\cos^{-1}\sqrt{x}}{\sqrt{x}}\,dx$
31. $\int \frac{\sqrt{x}}{\sqrt{1-x}}\,dx$
32. $\int \frac{\sqrt{2-x}}{\sqrt{x}}\,dx$
33. $\int \cot t\sqrt{1-\sin^2 t}\,dt, \quad 0 < t < \pi/2$
34. $\int \frac{dt}{\tan t\sqrt{4-\sin^2 t}}$
35. $\int \frac{dy}{y\sqrt{3+(\ln y)^2}}$
36. $\int \tan^{-1}\sqrt{y}\,dy$
37. $\int \frac{1}{\sqrt{x^2+2x+5}}\,dx$ (*Hint*: Complete the square.)
38. $\int \frac{x^2}{\sqrt{x^2-4x+5}}\,dx$
39. $\int \sqrt{5-4x-x^2}\,dx$
40. $\int x^2\sqrt{2x-x^2}\,dx$

Using Reduction Formulas

Use reduction formulas to evaluate the integrals in Exercises 41–50.

41. $\int \sin^5 2x\,dx$
42. $\int 8\cos^4 2\pi t\,dt$
43. $\int \sin^2 2\theta\cos^3 2\theta\,d\theta$
44. $\int 2\sin^2 t\sec^4 t\,dt$
45. $\int 4\tan^3 2x\,dx$
46. $\int 8\cot^4 t\,dt$
47. $\int 2\sec^3 \pi x\,dx$
48. $\int 3\sec^4 3x\,dx$
49. $\int \csc^5 x\,dx$
50. $\int 16x^3(\ln x)^2\,dx$

Evaluate the integrals in Exercises 51–56 by making a substitution (possibly trigonometric) and then applying a reduction formula.

51. $\int e^t\sec^3(e^t-1)\,dt$
52. $\int \frac{\csc^3\sqrt{\theta}}{\sqrt{\theta}}\,d\theta$
53. $\int_0^1 2\sqrt{x^2+1}\,dx$
54. $\int_0^{\sqrt{3}/2} \frac{dy}{(1-y^2)^{5/2}}$
55. $\int_1^2 \frac{(r^2-1)^{3/2}}{r}\,dr$
56. $\int_0^{1/\sqrt{3}} \frac{dt}{(t^2+1)^{7/2}}$

Applications

57. **Surface area** Find the area of the surface generated by revolving the curve $y = \sqrt{x^2+2}$, $0 \le x \le \sqrt{2}$, about the x-axis.

58. **Arc length** Find the length of the curve $y = x^2$, $0 \le x \le \sqrt{3}/2$.

59. **Centroid** Find the centroid of the region cut from the first quadrant by the curve $y = 1/\sqrt{x+1}$ and the line $x = 3$.

60. **Moment about y-axis** A thin plate of constant density $\delta = 1$ occupies the region enclosed by the curve $y = 36/(2x+3)$ and the line $x = 3$ in the first quadrant. Find the moment of the plate about the y-axis.

T 61. Use the integral table and a calculator to find to two decimal places the area of the surface generated by revolving the curve $y = x^2$, $-1 \le x \le 1$, about the x-axis.

62. **Volume** The head of your firm's accounting department has asked you to find a formula she can use in a computer program to calculate the year-end inventory of gasoline in the company's tanks. A typical tank is shaped like a right circular cylinder of radius r and length L, mounted horizontally, as shown in the accompanying figure. The data come to the accounting office as depth measurements taken with a vertical measuring stick marked in centimeters.

a. Show, in the notation of the figure, that the volume of gasoline that fills the tank to a depth d is

$$V = 2L\int_{-r}^{-r+d}\sqrt{r^2 - y^2}\,dy.$$

b. Evaluate the integral.

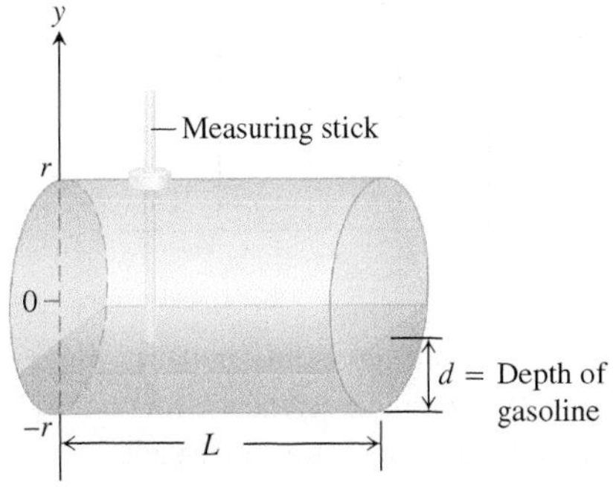

63. What is the largest value

$$\int_a^b \sqrt{x - x^2}\,dx$$

can have for any a and b? Give reasons for your answer.

64. What is the largest value

$$\int_a^b x\sqrt{2x - x^2}\,dx$$

can have for any a and b? Give reasons for your answer.

COMPUTER EXPLORATIONS

In Exercises 65 and 66, use a CAS to perform the integrations.

65. Evaluate the integrals

a. $\int x \ln x\,dx$ **b.** $\int x^2 \ln x\,dx$ **c.** $\int x^3 \ln x\,dx$.

d. What pattern do you see? Predict the formula for $\int x^4 \ln x\,dx$ and then see if you are correct by evaluating it with a CAS.

e. What is the formula for $\int x^n \ln x\,dx$, $n \ge 1$? Check your answer using a CAS.

66. Evaluate the integrals

a. $\int \frac{\ln x}{x^2}\,dx$ **b.** $\int \frac{\ln x}{x^3}\,dx$ **c.** $\int \frac{\ln x}{x^4}\,dx$.

d. What pattern do you see? Predict the formula for

$$\int \frac{\ln x}{x^5}\,dx$$

and then see if you are correct by evaluating it with a CAS.

e. What is the formula for

$$\int \frac{\ln x}{x^n}\,dx, \quad n \ge 2?$$

Check your answer using a CAS.

67. a. Use a CAS to evaluate

$$\int_0^{\pi/2} \frac{\sin^n x}{\sin^n x + \cos^n x}\,dx$$

where n is an arbitrary positive integer. Does your CAS find the result?

b. In succession, find the integral when $n = 1, 2, 3, 5$, and 7. Comment on the complexity of the results.

c. Now substitute $x = (\pi/2) - u$ and add the new and old integrals. What is the value of

$$\int_0^{\pi/2} \frac{\sin^n x}{\sin^n x + \cos^n x}\,dx?$$

This exercise illustrates how a little mathematical ingenuity solves a problem not immediately amenable to solution by a CAS.

8.6 Numerical Integration

The antiderivatives of some functions, like $\sin(x^2)$, $1/\ln x$, and $\sqrt{1 + x^4}$, have no elementary formulas. When we cannot find a workable antiderivative for a function f that we have to integrate, we can partition the interval of integration, replace f by a closely fitting polynomial on each subinterval, integrate the polynomials, and add the results to approximate the integral of f. This procedure is an example of numerical integration. In this section we study two such methods, the *Trapezoidal Rule* and *Simpson's Rule*. In our presentation we assume that f is positive, but the only requirement is for it to be continuous over the interval of integration $[a, b]$.

Trapezoidal Approximations

The Trapezoidal Rule for the value of a definite integral is based on approximating the region between a curve and the x-axis with trapezoids instead of rectangles, as in

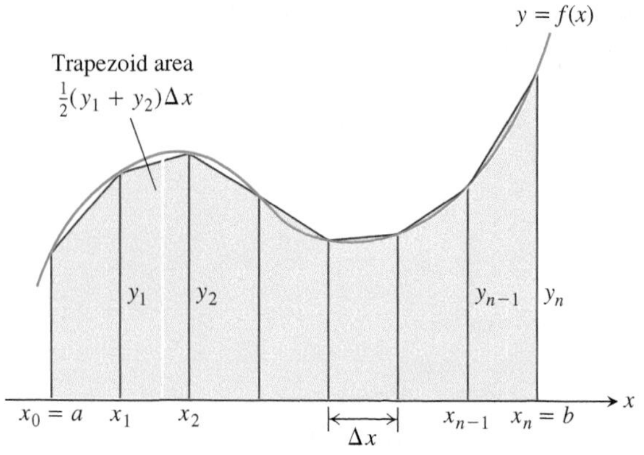

FIGURE 8.7 The Trapezoidal Rule approximates short stretches of the curve $y = f(x)$ with line segments. To approximate the integral of f from a to b, we add the areas of the trapezoids made by joining the ends of the segments to the x-axis.

Figure 8.7. It is not necessary for the subdivision points $x_0, x_1, x_2, \ldots, x_n$ in the figure to be evenly spaced, but the resulting formula is simpler if they are. We therefore assume that the length of each subinterval is

$$\Delta x = \frac{b - a}{n}.$$

The length $\Delta x = (b - a)/n$ is called the **step size** or **mesh size**. The area of the trapezoid that lies above the ith subinterval is

$$\Delta x\left(\frac{y_{i-1} + y_i}{2}\right) = \frac{\Delta x}{2}(y_{i-1} + y_i),$$

where $y_{i-1} = f(x_{i-1})$ and $y_i = f(x_i)$. This area is the length Δx of the trapezoid's horizontal "altitude" times the average of its two vertical "bases." (See Figure 8.7.) The area below the curve $y = f(x)$ and above the x-axis is then approximated by adding the areas of all the trapezoids:

$$\begin{aligned} T &= \frac{1}{2}(y_0 + y_1)\Delta x + \frac{1}{2}(y_1 + y_2)\Delta x + \cdots \\ &\quad + \frac{1}{2}(y_{n-2} + y_{n-1})\Delta x + \frac{1}{2}(y_{n-1} + y_n)\Delta x \\ &= \Delta x\left(\frac{1}{2}y_0 + y_1 + y_2 + \cdots + y_{n-1} + \frac{1}{2}y_n\right) \\ &= \frac{\Delta x}{2}(y_0 + 2y_1 + 2y_2 + \cdots + 2y_{n-1} + y_n), \end{aligned}$$

where

$$y_0 = f(a), \qquad y_1 = f(x_1), \qquad \ldots, \qquad y_{n-1} = f(x_{n-1}), \qquad y_n = f(b).$$

The Trapezoidal Rule says: Use T to estimate the integral of f from a to b. It is equivalent to the midpoint rule discussed in Section 5.1.

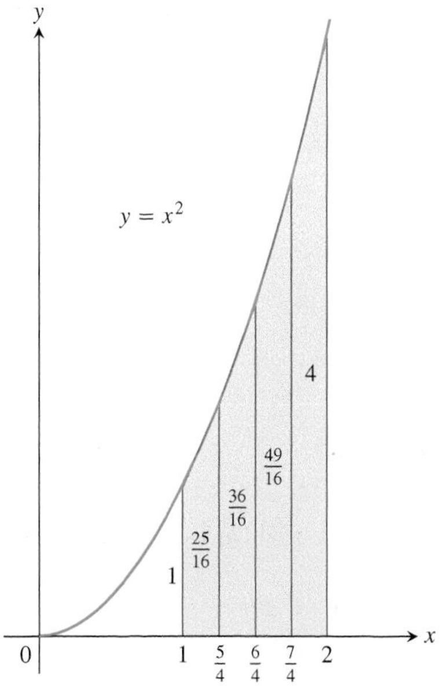

FIGURE 8.8 The trapezoidal approximation of the area under the graph of $y = x^2$ from $x = 1$ to $x = 2$ is a slight overestimate (Example 1).

The Trapezoidal Rule

To approximate $\int_a^b f(x)\,dx$, use

$$T = \frac{\Delta x}{2}\left(y_0 + 2y_1 + 2y_2 + \cdots + 2y_{n-1} + y_n\right).$$

The y's are the values of f at the partition points

$$x_0 = a, x_1 = a + \Delta x, x_2 = a + 2\Delta x, \ldots, x_{n-1} = a + (n-1)\Delta x, x_n = b,$$

where $\Delta x = (b - a)/n$.

EXAMPLE 1 Use the Trapezoidal Rule with $n = 4$ to estimate $\int_1^2 x^2\,dx$. Compare the estimate with the exact value.

Solution Partition [1, 2] into four subintervals of equal length (Figure 8.8). Then evaluate $y = x^2$ at each partition point (Table 8.2).

Using these y values, $n = 4$, and $\Delta x = (2 - 1)/4 = 1/4$ in the Trapezoidal Rule, we have

$$\begin{aligned} T &= \frac{\Delta x}{2}\left(y_0 + 2y_1 + 2y_2 + 2y_3 + y_4\right) \\ &= \frac{1}{8}\left(1 + 2\left(\frac{25}{16}\right) + 2\left(\frac{36}{16}\right) + 2\left(\frac{49}{16}\right) + 4\right) \\ &= \frac{75}{32} = 2.34375. \end{aligned}$$

TABLE 8.2

x	$y = x^2$
1	1
$\frac{5}{4}$	$\frac{25}{16}$
$\frac{6}{4}$	$\frac{36}{16}$
$\frac{7}{4}$	$\frac{49}{16}$
2	4

Since the parabola is concave *up*, the approximating segments lie above the curve, giving each trapezoid slightly more area than the corresponding strip under the curve. The exact value of the integral is

$$\int_1^2 x^2\,dx = \frac{x^3}{3}\Big]_1^2 = \frac{8}{3} - \frac{1}{3} = \frac{7}{3}.$$

The T approximation overestimates the integral by about half a percent of its true value of $7/3$. The percentage error is $(2.34375 - 7/3)/(7/3) \approx 0.00446$, or 0.446%. ■

Simpson's Rule: Approximations Using Parabolas

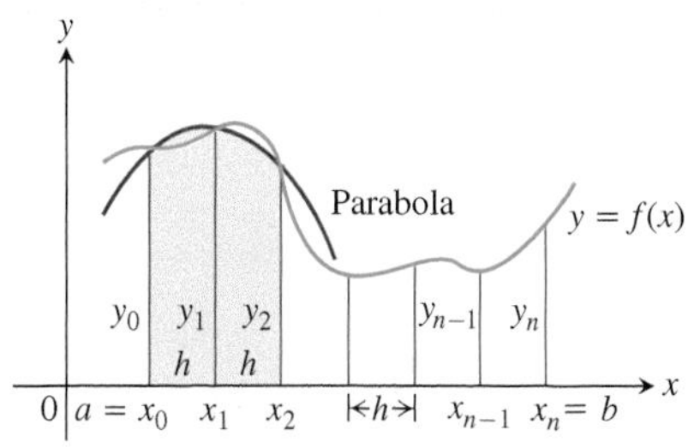

FIGURE 8.9 Simpson's Rule approximates short stretches of the curve with parabolas.

Another rule for approximating the definite integral of a continuous function results from using parabolas instead of the straight line segments that produced trapezoids. As before, we partition the interval $[a, b]$ into n subintervals of equal length $h = \Delta x = (b - a)/n$, but this time we require that n be an *even* number. On each consecutive pair of intervals we approximate the curve $y = f(x) \geq 0$ by a parabola, as shown in Figure 8.9. A typical parabola passes through three consecutive points (x_{i-1}, y_{i-1}), (x_i, y_i), and (x_{i+1}, y_{i+1}) on the curve.

Let's calculate the shaded area beneath a parabola passing through three consecutive points. To simplify our calculations, we first take the case where $x_0 = -h$, $x_1 = 0$, and

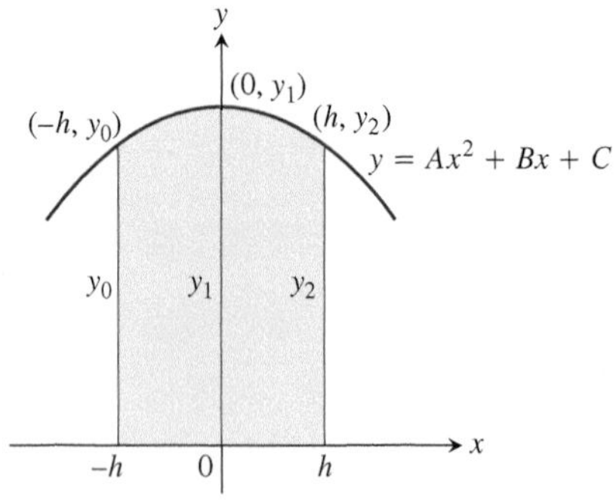

FIGURE 8.10 By integrating from $-h$ to h, we find the shaded area to be

$$\frac{h}{3}(y_0 + 4y_1 + y_2).$$

$x_2 = h$ (Figure 8.10), where $h = \Delta x = (b - a)/n$. The area under the parabola will be the same if we shift the y-axis to the left or right. The parabola has an equation of the form

$$y = Ax^2 + Bx + C,$$

so the area under it from $x = -h$ to $x = h$ is

$$\begin{aligned} A_p &= \int_{-h}^{h} (Ax^2 + Bx + C)\,dx \\ &= \frac{Ax^3}{3} + \frac{Bx^2}{2} + Cx \Big]_{-h}^{h} \\ &= \frac{2Ah^3}{3} + 2Ch = \frac{h}{3}(2Ah^2 + 6C). \end{aligned}$$

Since the curve passes through the three points $(-h, y_0)$, $(0, y_1)$, and (h, y_2), we also have

$$y_0 = Ah^2 - Bh + C, \qquad y_1 = C, \qquad y_2 = Ah^2 + Bh + C,$$

from which we obtain

$$\begin{aligned} C &= y_1, \\ Ah^2 - Bh &= y_0 - y_1, \\ Ah^2 + Bh &= y_2 - y_1, \\ 2Ah^2 &= y_0 + y_2 - 2y_1. \end{aligned}$$

Hence, expressing the area A_p in terms of the ordinates y_0, y_1, and y_2, we have

$$A_p = \frac{h}{3}(2Ah^2 + 6C) = \frac{h}{3}((y_0 + y_2 - 2y_1) + 6y_1) = \frac{h}{3}(y_0 + 4y_1 + y_2).$$

Now shifting the parabola horizontally to its shaded position in Figure 8.9 does not change the area under it. Thus the area under the parabola through (x_0, y_0), (x_1, y_1), and (x_2, y_2) in Figure 8.9 is still

$$\frac{h}{3}(y_0 + 4y_1 + y_2).$$

Similarly, the area under the parabola through the points (x_2, y_2), (x_3, y_3), and (x_4, y_4) is

$$\frac{h}{3}(y_2 + 4y_3 + y_4).$$

Computing the areas under all the parabolas and adding the results gives the approximation

$$\begin{aligned} \int_a^b f(x)\,dx &\approx \frac{h}{3}(y_0 + 4y_1 + y_2) + \frac{h}{3}(y_2 + 4y_3 + y_4) + \cdots \\ &\quad + \frac{h}{3}(y_{n-2} + 4y_{n-1} + y_n) \\ &= \frac{h}{3}(y_0 + 4y_1 + 2y_2 + 4y_3 + 2y_4 + \cdots + 2y_{n-2} + 4y_{n-1} + y_n). \end{aligned}$$

The result is known as Simpson's Rule. The function need not be positive, as in our derivation, but the number n of subintervals must be even to apply the rule because each parabolic arc uses two subintervals.

HISTORICAL BIOGRAPHY

Thomas Simpson
(1720–1761)

Simpson's Rule

To approximate $\int_a^b f(x)\,dx$, use

$$S = \frac{\Delta x}{3}(y_0 + 4y_1 + 2y_2 + 4y_3 + \cdots + 2y_{n-2} + 4y_{n-1} + y_n).$$

The y's are the values of f at the partition points

$$x_0 = a, x_1 = a + \Delta x, x_2 = a + 2\Delta x, \ldots, x_{n-1} = a + (n-1)\Delta x, x_n = b.$$

The number n is even, and $\Delta x = (b - a)/n$.

Note the pattern of the coefficients in the above rule: 1, 4, 2, 4, 2, 4, 2, . . . , 4, 1.

EXAMPLE 2 Use Simpson's Rule with $n = 4$ to approximate $\int_0^2 5x^4\,dx$.

TABLE 8.3

x	$y = 5x^4$
0	0
$\frac{1}{2}$	$\frac{5}{16}$
1	5
$\frac{3}{2}$	$\frac{405}{16}$
2	80

Solution Partition [0, 2] into four subintervals and evaluate $y = 5x^4$ at the partition points (Table 8.3). Then apply Simpson's Rule with $n = 4$ and $\Delta x = 1/2$:

$$\begin{aligned} S &= \frac{\Delta x}{3}\left(y_0 + 4y_1 + 2y_2 + 4y_3 + y_4\right) \\ &= \frac{1}{6}\left(0 + 4\left(\frac{5}{16}\right) + 2(5) + 4\left(\frac{405}{16}\right) + 80\right) \\ &= 32\frac{1}{12}. \end{aligned}$$

This estimate differs from the exact value (32) by only 1/12, a percentage error of less than three-tenths of one percent, and this was with just four subintervals. ■

Error Analysis

Whenever we use an approximation technique, the issue arises as to how accurate the approximation might be. The following theorem gives formulas for estimating the errors when using the Trapezoidal Rule and Simpson's Rule. The **error** is the difference between the approximation obtained by the rule and the actual value of the definite integral $\int_a^b f(x)\,dx$.

THEOREM 1—Error Estimates in the Trapezoidal and Simpson's Rules If f'' is continuous and M is any upper bound for the values of $|f''|$ on $[a, b]$, then the error E_T in the trapezoidal approximation of the integral of f from a to b for n steps satisfies the inequality

$$|E_T| \le \frac{M(b-a)^3}{12n^2}. \qquad \text{Trapezoidal Rule}$$

If $f^{(4)}$ is continuous and M is any upper bound for the values of $|f^{(4)}|$ on $[a, b]$, then the error E_S in the Simpson's Rule approximation of the integral of f from a to b for n steps satisfies the inequality

$$|E_S| \le \frac{M(b-a)^5}{180n^4}. \qquad \text{Simpson's Rule}$$

To see why Theorem 1 is true in the case of the Trapezoidal Rule, we begin with a result from advanced calculus, which says that if f'' is continuous on the interval $[a, b]$, then

$$\int_a^b f(x)\,dx = T - \frac{b-a}{12}\cdot f''(c)(\Delta x)^2$$

for some number c between a and b. Thus, as Δx approaches zero, the error defined by

$$E_T = -\frac{b-a}{12} \cdot f''(c)(\Delta x)^2$$

approaches zero as the *square* of Δx.

The inequality

$$|E_T| \leq \frac{b-a}{12} \max|f''(x)|(\Delta x)^2$$

where max refers to the interval $[a, b]$, gives an upper bound for the magnitude of the error. In practice, we usually cannot find the exact value of $\max|f''(x)|$ and have to estimate an upper bound or "worst case" value for it instead. If M is any upper bound for the values of $|f''(x)|$ on $[a, b]$, so that $|f''(x)| \leq M$ on $[a, b]$, then

$$|E_T| \leq \frac{b-a}{12} M(\Delta x)^2.$$

If we substitute $(b-a)/n$ for Δx, we get

$$|E_T| \leq \frac{M(b-a)^3}{12n^2}.$$

To estimate the error in Simpson's Rule, we start with a result from advanced calculus that says that if the fourth derivative $f^{(4)}$ is continuous, then

$$\int_a^b f(x)\,dx = S - \frac{b-a}{180} \cdot f^{(4)}(c)(\Delta x)^4$$

for some point c between a and b. Thus, as Δx approaches zero, the error,

$$E_S = -\frac{b-a}{180} \cdot f^{(4)}(c)(\Delta x)^4,$$

approaches zero as the *fourth power* of Δx. (This helps to explain why Simpson's Rule is likely to give better results than the Trapezoidal Rule.)

The inequality

$$|E_S| \leq \frac{b-a}{180} \max|f^{(4)}(x)|(\Delta x)^4,$$

where max refers to the interval $[a, b]$, gives an upper bound for the magnitude of the error. As with $\max|f''|$ in the error formula for the Trapezoidal Rule, we usually cannot find the exact value of $\max|f^{(4)}(x)|$ and have to replace it with an upper bound. If M is any upper bound for the values of $|f^{(4)}|$ on $[a, b]$, then

$$|E_S| \leq \frac{b-a}{180} M(\Delta x)^4.$$

Substituting $(b-a)/n$ for Δx in this last expression gives

$$|E_S| \leq \frac{M(b-a)^5}{180n^4}.$$

EXAMPLE 3 Find an upper bound for the error in estimating $\int_0^2 5x^4\,dx$ using Simpson's Rule with $n = 4$ (Example 2).

Solution To estimate the error, we first find an upper bound M for the magnitude of the fourth derivative of $f(x) = 5x^4$ on the interval $0 \leq x \leq 2$. Since the fourth derivative has the constant value $f^{(4)}(x) = 120$, we take $M = 120$. With $b - a = 2$ and $n = 4$, the error estimate for Simpson's Rule gives

$$|E_S| \leq \frac{M(b-a)^5}{180n^4} = \frac{120(2)^5}{180 \cdot 4^4} = \frac{1}{12}.$$

This estimate is consistent with the result of Example 2. ■

Theorem 1 can also be used to estimate the number of subintervals required when using the Trapezoidal or Simpson's Rule if we specify a certain tolerance for the error.

EXAMPLE 4 Estimate the minimum number of subintervals needed to approximate the integral in Example 3 using Simpson's Rule with an error of magnitude less than 10^{-4}.

Solution Using the inequality in Theorem 1, if we choose the number of subintervals n to satisfy

$$\frac{M(b-a)^5}{180n^4} < 10^{-4},$$

then the error E_S in Simpson's Rule satisfies $|E_S| < 10^{-4}$ as required.

From the solution in Example 3, we have $M = 120$ and $b - a = 2$, so we want n to satisfy

$$\frac{120(2)^5}{180n^4} < \frac{1}{10^4}$$

or, equivalently,

$$n^4 > \frac{64 \cdot 10^4}{3}.$$

It follows that

$$n > 10\left(\frac{64}{3}\right)^{1/4} \approx 21.5.$$

Since n must be even in Simpson's Rule, we estimate the minimum number of subintervals required for the error tolerance to be $n = 22$. ■

EXAMPLE 5 As we saw in Chapter 7, the value of ln 2 can be calculated from the integral

$$\ln 2 = \int_1^2 \frac{1}{x}\,dx.$$

Table 8.4 shows T and S values for approximations of $\int_1^2 (1/x)\,dx$ using various values of n. Notice how Simpson's Rule dramatically improves over the Trapezoidal Rule.

TABLE 8.4 Trapezoidal Rule approximations (T_n) and Simpson's Rule approximations (S_n) of $\ln 2 = \int_1^2 (1/x)\,dx$

n	T_n	|Error| less than . . .	S_n	|Error| less than . . .
10	0.6937714032	0.0006242227	0.6931502307	0.0000030502
20	0.6933033818	0.0001562013	0.6931473747	0.0000001942
30	0.6932166154	0.0000694349	0.6931472190	0.0000000385
40	0.6931862400	0.0000390595	0.6931471927	0.0000000122
50	0.6931721793	0.0000249988	0.6931471856	0.0000000050
100	0.6931534305	0.0000062500	0.6931471809	0.0000000004

In particular, notice that when we double the value of n (thereby halving the value of $h = \Delta x$), the T error is divided by 2 *squared*, whereas the S error is divided by 2 *to the fourth*.

This has a dramatic effect as $\Delta x = (2 - 1)/n$ gets very small. The Simpson approximation for $n = 50$ rounds accurately to seven places and for $n = 100$ agrees to nine decimal places (billionths)! ■

If $f(x)$ is a polynomial of degree less than four, then its fourth derivative is zero, and

$$E_S = -\frac{b-a}{180} f^{(4)}(c)(\Delta x)^4 = -\frac{b-a}{180}(0)(\Delta x)^4 = 0.$$

Thus, there will be no error in the Simpson approximation of any integral of f. In other words, if f is a constant, a linear function, or a quadratic or cubic polynomial, Simpson's Rule will give the value of any integral of f exactly, whatever the number of subdivisions. Similarly, if f is a constant or a linear function, then its second derivative is zero, and

$$E_T = -\frac{b-a}{12} f''(c)(\Delta x)^2 = -\frac{b-a}{12}(0)(\Delta x)^2 = 0.$$

The Trapezoidal Rule will therefore give the exact value of any integral of f. This is no surprise, for the trapezoids fit the graph perfectly.

Although decreasing the step size Δx reduces the error in the Simpson and Trapezoidal approximations in theory, it may fail to do so in practice. When Δx is very small, say $\Delta x = 10^{-5}$, computer or calculator round-off errors in the arithmetic required to evaluate S and T may accumulate to such an extent that the error formulas no longer describe what is going on. Shrinking Δx below a certain size can actually make things worse. You should consult a text on numerical analysis for more sophisticated methods if you are having problems with round-off error using the rules discussed in this section.

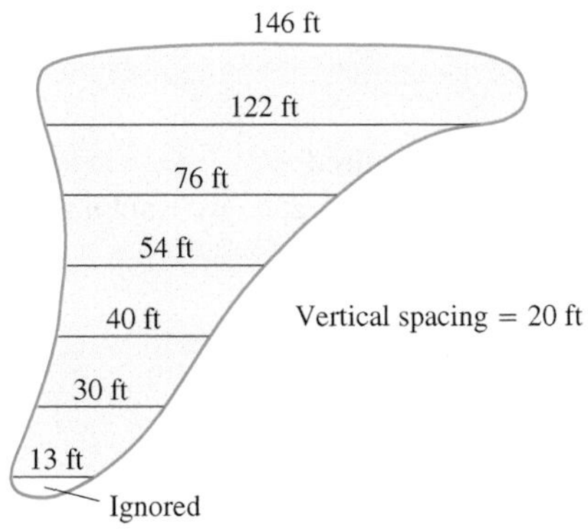

FIGURE 8.11 The dimensions of the swamp in Example 6.

EXAMPLE 6 A town wants to drain and fill a small polluted swamp (Figure 8.11). The swamp averages 5 ft deep. About how many cubic yards of dirt will it take to fill the area after the swamp is drained?

Solution To calculate the volume of the swamp, we estimate the surface area and multiply by 5. To estimate the area, we use Simpson's Rule with $\Delta x = 20$ ft and the y's equal to the distances measured across the swamp, as shown in Figure 8.11.

$$\begin{aligned} S &= \frac{\Delta x}{3}(y_0 + 4y_1 + 2y_2 + 4y_3 + 2y_4 + 4y_5 + y_6) \\ &= \frac{20}{3}(146 + 488 + 152 + 216 + 80 + 120 + 13) = 8100 \end{aligned}$$

The volume is about $(8100)(5) = 40{,}500$ ft^3 or 1500 yd^3. ■

Exercises 8.6

Estimating Integrals

The instructions for the integrals in Exercises 1–10 have two parts, one for the Trapezoidal Rule and one for Simpson's Rule.

I. Using the Trapezoidal Rule

a. Estimate the integral with $n = 4$ steps and find an upper bound for $|E_T|$.

b. Evaluate the integral directly and find $|E_T|$.

c. Use the formula $(|E_T|/(\text{true value})) \times 100$ to express $|E_T|$ as a percentage of the integral's true value.

II. Using Simpson's Rule

a. Estimate the integral with $n = 4$ steps and find an upper bound for $|E_S|$.

b. Evaluate the integral directly and find $|E_S|$.

c. Use the formula $(|E_S|/(\text{true value})) \times 100$ to express $|E_S|$ as a percentage of the integral's true value.

1. $\displaystyle\int_1^2 x\,dx$

2. $\displaystyle\int_1^3 (2x-1)\,dx$

3. $\int_{-1}^{1}(x^2+1)\,dx$

4. $\int_{-2}^{0}(x^2-1)\,dx$

5. $\int_{0}^{2}(t^3+t)\,dt$

6. $\int_{-1}^{1}(t^3+1)\,dt$

7. $\int_{1}^{2}\frac{1}{s^2}\,ds$

8. $\int_{2}^{4}\frac{1}{(s-1)^2}\,ds$

9. $\int_{0}^{\pi}\sin t\,dt$

10. $\int_{0}^{1}\sin \pi t\,dt$

Estimating the Number of Subintervals

In Exercises 11–22, estimate the minimum number of subintervals needed to approximate the integrals with an error of magnitude less than 10^{-4} by **(a)** the Trapezoidal Rule and **(b)** Simpson's Rule. (The integrals in Exercises 11–18 are the integrals from Exercises 1–8.)

11. $\int_{1}^{2}x\,dx$

12. $\int_{1}^{3}(2x-1)\,dx$

13. $\int_{-1}^{1}(x^2+1)\,dx$

14. $\int_{-2}^{0}(x^2-1)\,dx$

15. $\int_{0}^{2}(t^3+t)\,dt$

16. $\int_{-1}^{1}(t^3+1)\,dt$

17. $\int_{1}^{2}\frac{1}{s^2}\,ds$

18. $\int_{2}^{4}\frac{1}{(s-1)^2}\,ds$

19. $\int_{0}^{3}\sqrt{x+1}\,dx$

20. $\int_{0}^{3}\frac{1}{\sqrt{x+1}}\,dx$

21. $\int_{0}^{2}\sin(x+1)\,dx$

22. $\int_{-1}^{1}\cos(x+\pi)\,dx$

Estimates with Numerical Data

23. **Volume of water in a swimming pool** A rectangular swimming pool is 30 ft wide and 50 ft long. The accompanying table shows the depth $h(x)$ of the water at 5-ft intervals from one end of the pool to the other. Estimate the volume of water in the pool using the Trapezoidal Rule with $n = 10$ applied to the integral

$$V = \int_{0}^{50} 30 \cdot h(x)\,dx.$$

Position (ft) x	Depth (ft) $h(x)$	Position (ft) x	Depth (ft) $h(x)$
0	6.0	30	11.5
5	8.2	35	11.9
10	9.1	40	12.3
15	9.9	45	12.7
20	10.5	50	13.0
25	11.0		

24. **Distance traveled** The accompanying table shows time-to-speed data for a sports car accelerating from rest to 130 mph. How far had the car traveled by the time it reached this speed? (Use trapezoids to estimate the area under the velocity curve, but be careful: The time intervals vary in length.)

Speed change	Time (sec)
Zero to 30 mph	2.2
40 mph	3.2
50 mph	4.5
60 mph	5.9
70 mph	7.8
80 mph	10.2
90 mph	12.7
100 mph	16.0
110 mph	20.6
120 mph	26.2
130 mph	37.1

25. **Wing design** The design of a new airplane requires a gasoline tank of constant cross-sectional area in each wing. A scale drawing of a cross-section is shown here. The tank must hold 5000 lb of gasoline, which has a density of 42 lb/ft^3. Estimate the length of the tank by Simpson's Rule.

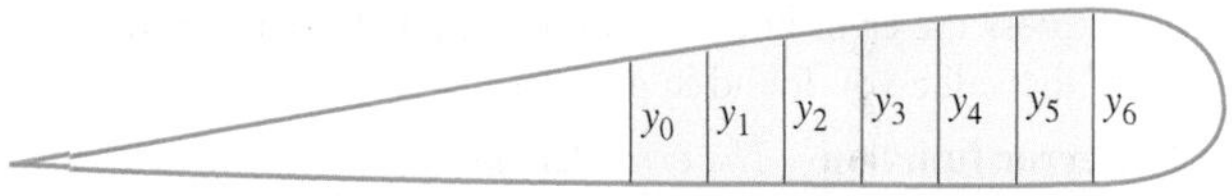

$y_0 = 1.5$ ft, $y_1 = 1.6$ ft, $y_2 = 1.8$ ft, $y_3 = 1.9$ ft,
$y_4 = 2.0$ ft, $y_5 = y_6 = 2.1$ ft Horizontal spacing $= 1$ ft

26. **Oil consumption on Pathfinder Island** A diesel generator runs continuously, consuming oil at a gradually increasing rate until it must be temporarily shut down to have the filters replaced. Use the Trapezoidal Rule to estimate the amount of oil consumed by the generator during that week.

Day	Oil consumption rate (liters/h)
Sun	0.019
Mon	0.020
Tue	0.021
Wed	0.023
Thu	0.025
Fri	0.028
Sat	0.031
Sun	0.035

Theory and Examples

27. **Usable values of the sine-integral function** *The sine-integral function,*

$$\mathrm{Si}(x) = \int_{0}^{x}\frac{\sin t}{t}\,dt, \qquad \text{"Sine integral of } x\text{"}$$

is one of the many functions in engineering whose formulas cannot be simplified. There is no elementary formula for the antiderivative of $(\sin t)/t$. The values of Si(x), however, are readily estimated by numerical integration.

Although the notation does not show it explicitly, the function being integrated is

$$f(t) = \begin{cases} \dfrac{\sin t}{t}, & t \neq 0 \\ 1, & t = 0, \end{cases}$$

the continuous extension of $(\sin t)/t$ to the interval $[0, x]$. The function has derivatives of all orders at every point of its domain. Its graph is smooth, and you can expect good results from Simpson's Rule.

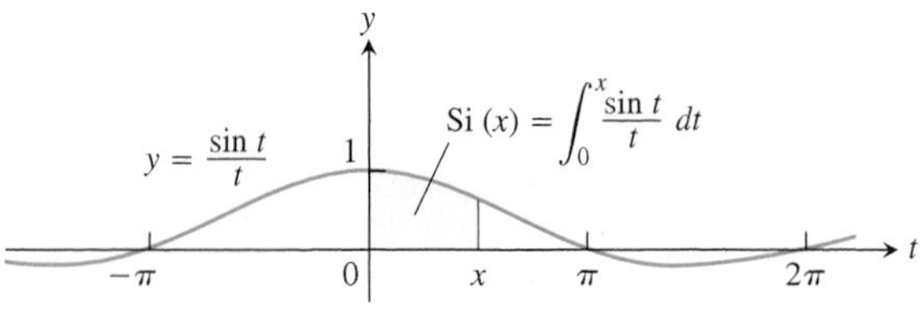

a. Use the fact that $|f^{(4)}| \le 1$ on $[0, \pi/2]$ to give an upper bound for the error that will occur if

$$\mathrm{Si}\left(\frac{\pi}{2}\right) = \int_0^{\pi/2} \frac{\sin t}{t}\,dt$$

is estimated by Simpson's Rule with $n = 4$.

b. Estimate $\mathrm{Si}(\pi/2)$ by Simpson's Rule with $n = 4$.

c. Express the error bound you found in part (a) as a percentage of the value you found in part (b).

28. The error function *The error function,*

$$\operatorname{erf}(x) = \frac{2}{\sqrt{\pi}} \int_0^x e^{-t^2}\,dt,$$

important in probability and in the theories of heat flow and signal transmission, must be evaluated numerically because there is no elementary expression for the antiderivative of e^{-t^2}.

a. Use Simpson's Rule with $n = 10$ to estimate erf (1).

b. In [0, 1],

$$\left|\frac{d^4}{dt^4}\left(e^{-t^2}\right)\right| \le 12.$$

Give an upper bound for the magnitude of the error of the estimate in part (a).

29. Prove that the sum T in the Trapezoidal Rule for $\int_a^b f(x)\,dx$ is a Riemann sum for f continuous on $[a, b]$. (*Hint:* Use the Intermediate Value Theorem to show the existence of c_k in the subinterval $[x_{k-1}, x_k]$ satisfying $f(c_k) = (f(x_{k-1}) + f(x_k))/2$.)

30. Prove that the sum S in Simpson's Rule for $\int_a^b f(x)\,dx$ is a Riemann sum for f continuous on $[a, b]$. (See Exercise 29.)

T **31. Elliptic integrals** The length of the ellipse

$$\frac{x^2}{a^2} + \frac{y^2}{b^2} = 1$$

turns out to be

$$\text{Length} = 4a \int_0^{\pi/2} \sqrt{1 - e^2 \cos^2 t}\,dt,$$

where $e = \sqrt{a^2 - b^2}/a$ is the ellipse's eccentricity. The integral in this formula, called an *elliptic integral*, is nonelementary except when $e = 0$ or 1.

a. Use the Trapezoidal Rule with $n = 10$ to estimate the length of the ellipse when $a = 1$ and $e = 1/2$.

b. Use the fact that the absolute value of the second derivative of $f(t) = \sqrt{1 - e^2 \cos^2 t}$ is less than 1 to find an upper bound for the error in the estimate you obtained in part (a).

Applications

T **32.** The length of one arch of the curve $y = \sin x$ is given by

$$L = \int_0^{\pi} \sqrt{1 + \cos^2 x}\,dx.$$

Estimate L by Simpson's Rule with $n = 8$.

T **33.** Your metal fabrication company is bidding for a contract to make sheets of corrugated iron roofing like the one shown here. The cross-sections of the corrugated sheets are to conform to the curve

$$y = \sin \frac{3\pi}{20} x, \quad 0 \le x \le 20 \text{ in}.$$

If the roofing is to be stamped from flat sheets by a process that does not stretch the material, how wide should the original material be? To find out, use numerical integration to approximate the length of the sine curve to two decimal places.

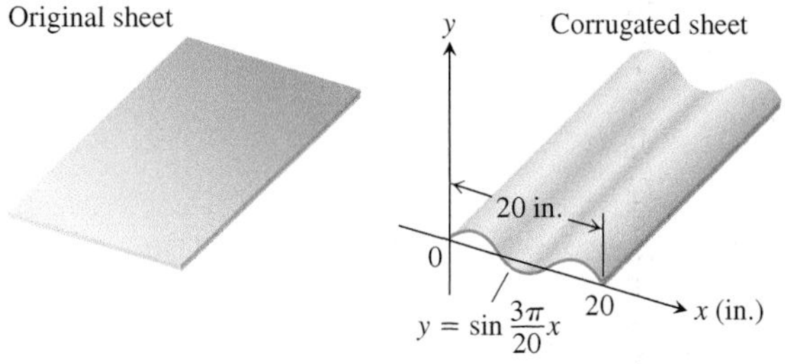

T **34.** Your engineering firm is bidding for the contract to construct the tunnel shown here. The tunnel is 300 ft long and 50 ft wide at the base. The cross-section is shaped like one arch of the curve $y = 25 \cos(\pi x/50)$. Upon completion, the tunnel's inside surface (excluding the roadway) will be treated with a waterproof sealer that costs \$1.75 per square foot to apply. How much will it cost to apply the sealer? (*Hint:* Use numerical integration to find the length of the cosine curve.)

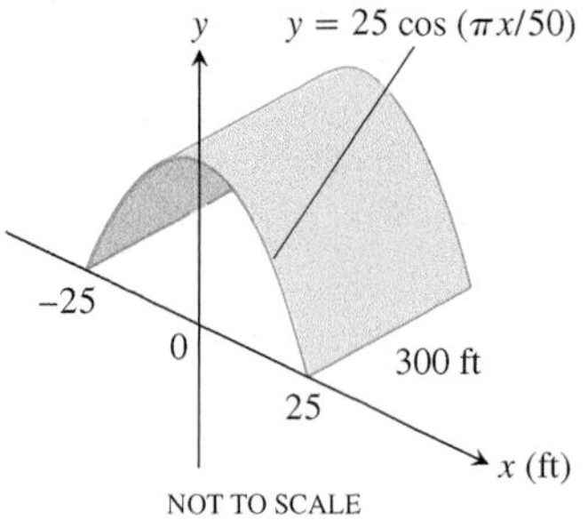

Find, to two decimal places, the areas of the surfaces generated by revolving the curves in Exercises 35 and 36 about the x-axis.

35. $y = \sin x, \quad 0 \le x \le \pi$

36. $y = x^2/4, \quad 0 \le x \le 2$

37. Use numerical integration to estimate the value of

$$\sin^{-1} 0.6 = \int_0^{0.6} \frac{dx}{\sqrt{1 - x^2}}.$$

For reference, $\sin^{-1} 0.6 = 0.64350$ to five decimal places.

38. Use numerical integration to estimate the value of

$$\pi = 4 \int_0^1 \frac{1}{1 + x^2}\,dx.$$

8.7 Improper Integrals

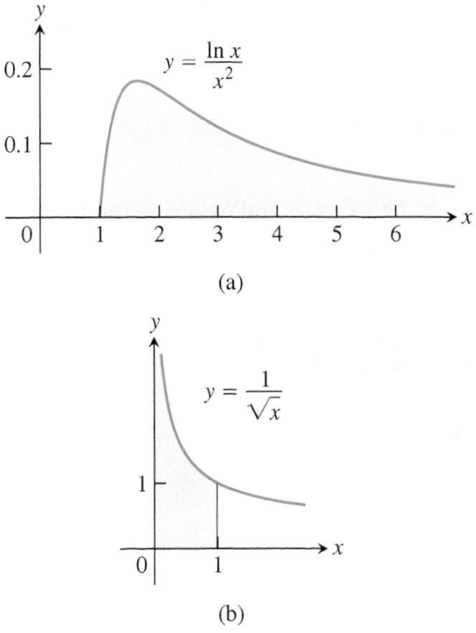

FIGURE 8.12 Are the areas under these infinite curves finite? We will see that the answer is yes for both curves.

Up to now, we have required definite integrals to have two properties. First, that the domain of integration $[a, b]$ be finite. Second, that the range of the integrand be finite on this domain. In practice, we may encounter problems that fail to meet one or both of these conditions. The integral for the area under the curve $y = (\ln x)/x^2$ from $x = 1$ to $x = \infty$ is an example for which the domain is infinite (Figure 8.12a). The integral for the area under the curve of $y = 1/\sqrt{x}$ between $x = 0$ and $x = 1$ is an example for which the range of the integrand is infinite (Figure 8.12b). In either case, the integrals are said to be *improper* and are calculated as limits. We will see in Chapter 9 that improper integrals play an important role when investigating the convergence of certain infinite series.

Infinite Limits of Integration

Consider the infinite region that lies under the curve $y = e^{-x/2}$ in the first quadrant (Figure 8.13a). You might think this region has infinite area, but we will see that the value is finite. We assign a value to the area in the following way. First find the area $A(b)$ of the portion of the region that is bounded on the right by $x = b$ (Figure 8.13b).

$$A(b) = \int_0^b e^{-x/2}\,dx = -2e^{-x/2}\Big]_0^b = -2e^{-b/2} + 2$$

Then find the limit of $A(b)$ as $b \to \infty$

$$\lim_{b\to\infty} A(b) = \lim_{b\to\infty} (-2e^{-b/2} + 2) = 2.$$

The value we assign to the area under the curve from 0 to ∞ is

$$\int_0^\infty e^{-x/2}\,dx = \lim_{b\to\infty} \int_0^b e^{-x/2}\,dx = 2.$$

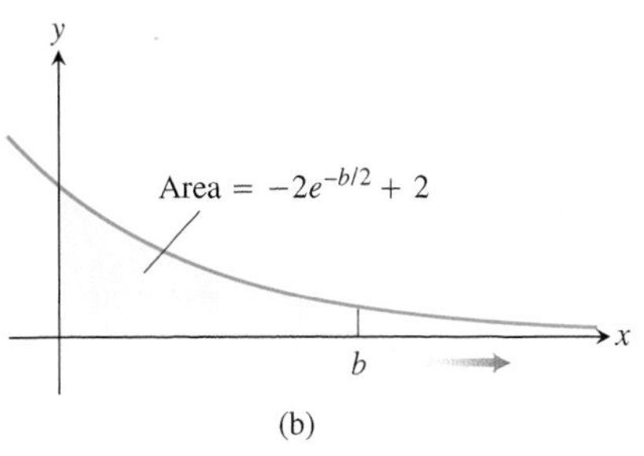

FIGURE 8.13 (a) The area in the first quadrant under the curve $y = e^{-x/2}$.
(b) The area is an improper integral of the first type.

DEFINITION Integrals with infinite limits of integration are **improper integrals of Type I**.

1. If $f(x)$ is continuous on $[a, \infty)$, then

$$\int_a^\infty f(x)\,dx = \lim_{b\to\infty} \int_a^b f(x)\,dx.$$

2. If $f(x)$ is continuous on $(-\infty, b]$, then

$$\int_{-\infty}^b f(x)\,dx = \lim_{a\to-\infty} \int_a^b f(x)\,dx.$$

3. If $f(x)$ is continuous on $(-\infty, \infty)$, then

$$\int_{-\infty}^\infty f(x)\,dx = \int_{-\infty}^c f(x)\,dx + \int_c^\infty f(x)\,dx,$$

where c is any real number.

In each case, if the limit is finite we say that the improper integral **converges** and that the limit is the **value** of the improper integral. If the limit fails to exist, the improper integral **diverges**.

It can be shown that the choice of c in Part 3 of the definition is unimportant. We can evaluate or determine the convergence or divergence of $\int_{-\infty}^{\infty} f(x)\,dx$ with any convenient choice.

Any of the integrals in the above definition can be interpreted as an area if $f \geq 0$ on the interval of integration. For instance, we interpreted the improper integral in Figure 8.13 as an area. In that case, the area has the finite value 2. If $f \geq 0$ and the improper integral diverges, we say the area under the curve is **infinite**.

EXAMPLE 1 Is the area under the curve $y = (\ln x)/x^2$ from $x = 1$ to $x = \infty$ finite? If so, what is its value?

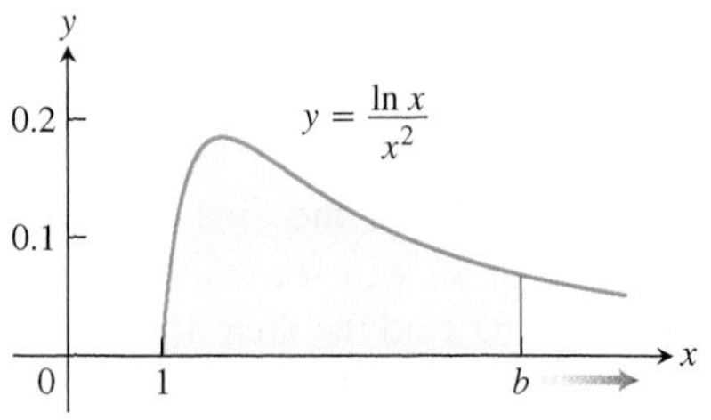

FIGURE 8.14 The area under this curve is an improper integral (Example 1).

Solution We find the area under the curve from $x = 1$ to $x = b$ and examine the limit as $b \to \infty$. If the limit is finite, we take it to be the area under the curve (Figure 8.14). The area from 1 to b is

$$\int_1^b \frac{\ln x}{x^2}\,dx = \left[(\ln x)\left(-\frac{1}{x}\right)\right]_1^b - \int_1^b \left(-\frac{1}{x}\right)\left(\frac{1}{x}\right)dx$$

Integration by parts with $u = \ln x$, $dv = dx/x^2$, $du = dx/x$, $v = -1/x$

$$= -\frac{\ln b}{b} - \left[\frac{1}{x}\right]_1^b$$

$$= -\frac{\ln b}{b} - \frac{1}{b} + 1.$$

The limit of the area as $b \to \infty$ is

$$\int_1^\infty \frac{\ln x}{x^2}\,dx = \lim_{b\to\infty} \int_1^b \frac{\ln x}{x^2}\,dx$$

$$= \lim_{b\to\infty}\left[-\frac{\ln b}{b} - \frac{1}{b} + 1\right]$$

$$= -\left[\lim_{b\to\infty} \frac{\ln b}{b}\right] - 0 + 1$$

$$= -\left[\lim_{b\to\infty} \frac{1/b}{1}\right] + 1 = 0 + 1 = 1.$$

l'Hôpital's Rule

Thus, the improper integral converges and the area has finite value 1. ■

EXAMPLE 2 Evaluate

$$\int_{-\infty}^{\infty} \frac{dx}{1+x^2}.$$

Solution According to the definition (Part 3), we can choose $c = 0$ and write

$$\int_{-\infty}^{\infty} \frac{dx}{1+x^2} = \int_{-\infty}^{0} \frac{dx}{1+x^2} + \int_{0}^{\infty} \frac{dx}{1+x^2}.$$

HISTORICAL BIOGRAPHY

Lejeune Dirichlet
(1805–1859)

Next we evaluate each improper integral on the right side of the equation above.

$$\int_{-\infty}^{0} \frac{dx}{1+x^2} = \lim_{a\to-\infty} \int_{a}^{0} \frac{dx}{1+x^2}$$

$$= \lim_{a\to-\infty} \tan^{-1} x \Big]_a^0$$

$$= \lim_{a\to-\infty} (\tan^{-1} 0 - \tan^{-1} a) = 0 - \left(-\frac{\pi}{2}\right) = \frac{\pi}{2}$$

$$\int_0^{\infty} \frac{dx}{1+x^2} = \lim_{b\to\infty} \int_0^b \frac{dx}{1+x^2}$$
$$= \lim_{b\to\infty} \tan^{-1} x \Big]_0^b$$
$$= \lim_{b\to\infty} (\tan^{-1} b - \tan^{-1} 0) = \frac{\pi}{2} - 0 = \frac{\pi}{2}$$

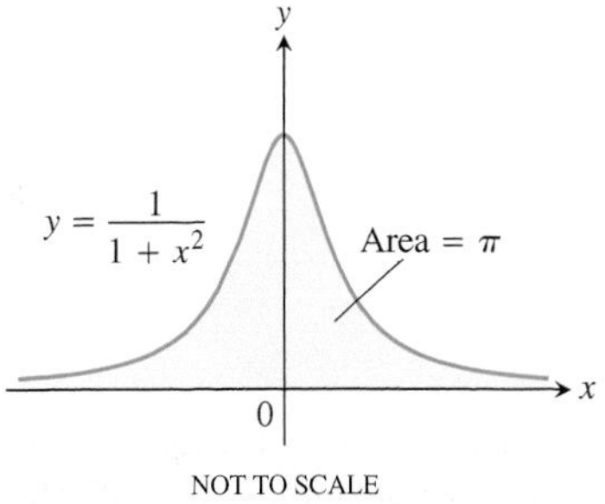

FIGURE 8.15 The area under this curve is finite (Example 2).

Thus,

$$\int_{-\infty}^{\infty} \frac{dx}{1+x^2} = \frac{\pi}{2} + \frac{\pi}{2} = \pi.$$

Since $1/(1+x^2) > 0$, the improper integral can be interpreted as the (finite) area beneath the curve and above the x-axis (Figure 8.15). ■

The Integral $\int_1^{\infty} \frac{dx}{x^p}$

The function $y = 1/x$ is the boundary between the convergent and divergent improper integrals with integrands of the form $y = 1/x^p$. As the next example shows, the improper integral converges if $p > 1$ and diverges if $p \le 1$.

EXAMPLE 3 For what values of p does the integral $\int_1^{\infty} dx/x^p$ converge? When the integral does converge, what is its value?

Solution If $p \neq 1$,

$$\int_1^b \frac{dx}{x^p} = \frac{x^{-p+1}}{-p+1}\Big]_1^b = \frac{1}{1-p}(b^{-p+1} - 1) = \frac{1}{1-p}\left(\frac{1}{b^{p-1}} - 1\right).$$

Thus,

$$\int_1^{\infty} \frac{dx}{x^p} = \lim_{b\to\infty} \int_1^b \frac{dx}{x^p}$$
$$= \lim_{b\to\infty}\left[\frac{1}{1-p}\left(\frac{1}{b^{p-1}} - 1\right)\right] = \begin{cases} \dfrac{1}{p-1}, & p > 1 \\ \infty, & p < 1 \end{cases}$$

because

$$\lim_{b\to\infty} \frac{1}{b^{p-1}} = \begin{cases} 0, & p > 1 \\ \infty, & p < 1. \end{cases}$$

Therefore, the integral converges to the value $1/(p-1)$ if $p > 1$ and it diverges if $p < 1$.

If $p = 1$, the integral also diverges:

$$\begin{aligned}\int_1^\infty \frac{dx}{x^p} &= \int_1^\infty \frac{dx}{x} \\ &= \lim_{b\to\infty} \int_1^b \frac{dx}{x} \\ &= \lim_{b\to\infty} \ln x\Big]_1^b \\ &= \lim_{b\to\infty} (\ln b - \ln 1) = \infty.\end{aligned}$$

■

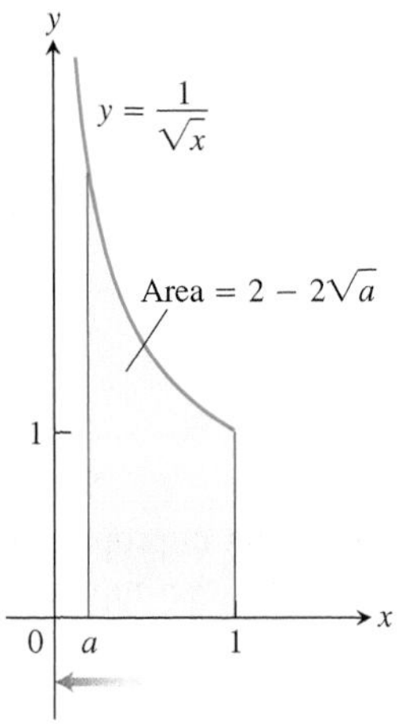

FIGURE 8.16 The area under this curve is an example of an improper integral of the second kind.

Integrands with Vertical Asymptotes

Another type of improper integral arises when the integrand has a vertical asymptote—an infinite discontinuity—at a limit of integration or at some point between the limits of integration. If the integrand f is positive over the interval of integration, we can again interpret the improper integral as the area under the graph of f and above the x-axis between the limits of integration.

Consider the region in the first quadrant that lies under the curve $y = 1/\sqrt{x}$ from $x = 0$ to $x = 1$ (Figure 8.12b). First we find the area of the portion from a to 1 (Figure 8.16).

$$\int_a^1 \frac{dx}{\sqrt{x}} = 2\sqrt{x}\Big]_a^1 = 2 - 2\sqrt{a}.$$

Then we find the limit of this area as $a \to 0^+$:

$$\lim_{a\to 0^+} \int_a^1 \frac{dx}{\sqrt{x}} = \lim_{a\to 0^+} \left(2 - 2\sqrt{a}\right) = 2.$$

Therefore the area under the curve from 0 to 1 is finite and is defined to be

$$\int_0^1 \frac{dx}{\sqrt{x}} = \lim_{a\to 0^+} \int_a^1 \frac{dx}{\sqrt{x}} = 2.$$

DEFINITION Integrals of functions that become infinite at a point within the interval of integration are **improper integrals of Type II**.

1. If $f(x)$ is continuous on $(a, b]$ and discontinuous at a, then

$$\int_a^b f(x)\,dx = \lim_{c\to a^+} \int_c^b f(x)\,dx.$$

2. If $f(x)$ is continuous on $[a, b)$ and discontinuous at b, then

$$\int_a^b f(x)\,dx = \lim_{c\to b^-} \int_a^c f(x)\,dx.$$

3. If $f(x)$ is discontinuous at c, where $a < c < b$, and continuous on $[a, c) \cup (c, b]$, then

$$\int_a^b f(x)\,dx = \int_a^c f(x)\,dx + \int_c^b f(x)\,dx.$$

In each case, if the limit is finite we say the improper integral **converges** and that the limit is the **value** of the improper integral. If the limit does not exist, the integral **diverges**.

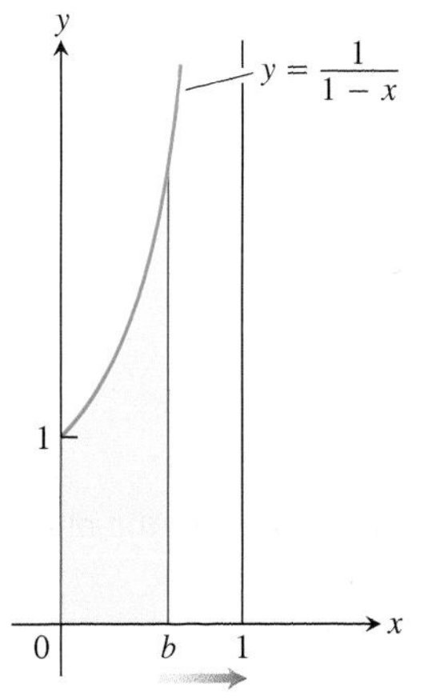

FIGURE 8.17 The area beneath the curve and above the x-axis for $[0, 1)$ is not a real number (Example 4).

In Part 3 of the definition, the integral on the left side of the equation converges if *both* integrals on the right side converge; otherwise it diverges.

EXAMPLE 4 Investigate the convergence of

$$\int_0^1 \frac{1}{1-x}\,dx.$$

Solution The integrand $f(x) = 1/(1-x)$ is continuous on $[0, 1)$ but is discontinuous at $x = 1$ and becomes infinite as $x \to 1^-$ (Figure 8.17). We evaluate the integral as

$$\begin{aligned}\lim_{b\to 1^-}\int_0^b \frac{1}{1-x}\,dx &= \lim_{b\to 1^-}\Big[-\ln|1-x|\Big]_0^b \\ &= \lim_{b\to 1^-}\left[-\ln(1-b) + 0\right] = \infty.\end{aligned}$$

The limit is infinite, so the integral diverges. ■

EXAMPLE 5 Evaluate

$$\int_0^3 \frac{dx}{(x-1)^{2/3}}.$$

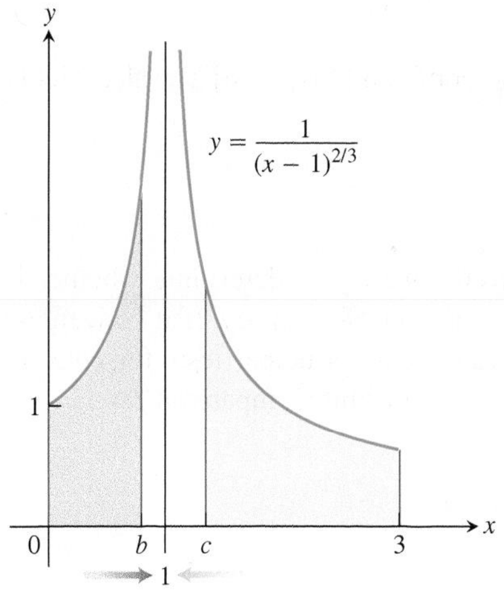

FIGURE 8.18 Example 5 shows that the area under the curve exists (so it is a real number).

Solution The integrand has a vertical asymptote at $x = 1$ and is continuous on $[0, 1)$ and $(1, 3]$ (Figure 8.18). Thus, by Part 3 of the definition above,

$$\int_0^3 \frac{dx}{(x-1)^{2/3}} = \int_0^1 \frac{dx}{(x-1)^{2/3}} + \int_1^3 \frac{dx}{(x-1)^{2/3}}.$$

Next, we evaluate each improper integral on the right-hand side of this equation.

$$\begin{aligned}\int_0^1 \frac{dx}{(x-1)^{2/3}} &= \lim_{b\to 1^-}\int_0^b \frac{dx}{(x-1)^{2/3}} \\ &= \lim_{b\to 1^-} 3(x-1)^{1/3}\Big]_0^b \\ &= \lim_{b\to 1^-}\left[3(b-1)^{1/3} + 3\right] = 3\end{aligned}$$

$$\begin{aligned}\int_1^3 \frac{dx}{(x-1)^{2/3}} &= \lim_{c\to 1^+}\int_c^3 \frac{dx}{(x-1)^{2/3}} \\ &= \lim_{c\to 1^+} 3(x-1)^{1/3}\Big]_c^3 \\ &= \lim_{c\to 1^+}\left[3(3-1)^{1/3} - 3(c-1)^{1/3}\right] = 3\sqrt[3]{2}\end{aligned}$$

We conclude that

$$\int_0^3 \frac{dx}{(x-1)^{2/3}} = 3 + 3\sqrt[3]{2}.$$ ■

Improper Integrals with a CAS

Computer algebra systems can evaluate many convergent improper integrals. To evaluate the integral

$$\int_2^\infty \frac{x+3}{(x-1)(x^2+1)}\,dx$$

(which converges) using Maple, enter

$$> f{:=}\ (x + 3)/((x - 1) * (x\hat{}2 + 1));$$

Then use the integration command

$$> \text{int}(f, x = 2..\text{infinity});$$

Maple returns the answer

$$-\frac{1}{2}\pi + \ln(5) + \arctan(2).$$

To obtain a numerical result, use the evaluation command **evalf** and specify the number of digits as follows:

$$> \text{evalf}(\%, 6);$$

The symbol % instructs the computer to evaluate the last expression on the screen, in this case $(-1/2)\pi + \ln(5) + \arctan(2)$. Maple returns 1.14579.

Using Mathematica, entering

$$\textit{In [1]:=}\ \text{Integrate}\ [(x + 3)/((x - 1)(x\hat{}2 + 1)),\ \{x, 2, \text{Infinity}\}]$$

returns

$$\textit{Out [1]=}\ \frac{-\pi}{2} + \text{ArcTan}\,[2] + \text{Log}\,[5].$$

To obtain a numerical result with six digits, use the command "N[%, 6]"; it also yields 1.14579.

Tests for Convergence and Divergence

When we cannot evaluate an improper integral directly, we try to determine whether it converges or diverges. If the integral diverges, that's the end of the story. If it converges, we can use numerical methods to approximate its value. The principal tests for convergence or divergence are the Direct Comparison Test and the Limit Comparison Test.

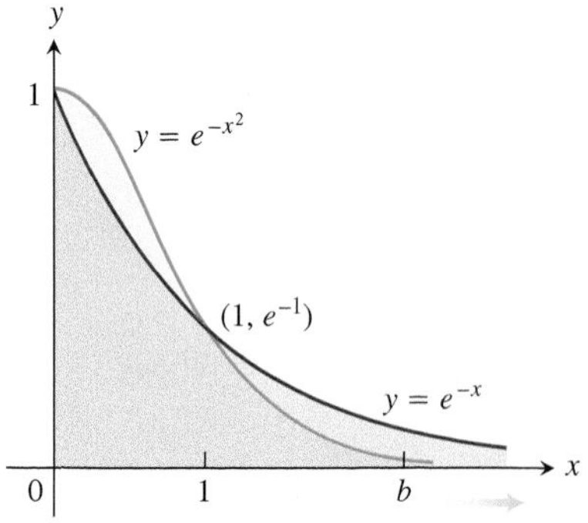

FIGURE 8.19 The graph of e^{-x^2} lies below the graph of e^{-x} for $x > 1$ (Example 6).

EXAMPLE 6 Does the integral $\int_1^{\infty} e^{-x^2}\,dx$ converge?

Solution By definition,

$$\int_1^{\infty} e^{-x^2}\,dx = \lim_{b\to\infty}\int_1^{b} e^{-x^2}\,dx.$$

We cannot evaluate this integral directly because it is nonelementary. But we *can* show that its limit as $b \to \infty$ is finite. We know that $\int_1^b e^{-x^2}\,dx$ is an increasing function of b. Therefore either it becomes infinite as $b \to \infty$ or it has a finite limit as $b \to \infty$. It does not become infinite: For every value of $x \ge 1$, we have $e^{-x^2} \le e^{-x}$ (Figure 8.19) so that

$$\int_1^b e^{-x^2}\,dx \le \int_1^b e^{-x}\,dx = -e^{-b} + e^{-1} < e^{-1} \approx 0.36788.$$

Hence,

$$\int_1^{\infty} e^{-x^2}\,dx = \lim_{b\to\infty}\int_1^{b} e^{-x^2}\,dx$$

converges to some definite finite value. We do not know exactly what the value is except that it is something positive and less than 0.37. Here we are relying on the completeness property of the real numbers, discussed in Appendix 7. ■

The comparison of e^{-x^2} and e^{-x} in Example 6 is a special case of the following test.

HISTORICAL BIOGRAPHY

Karl Weierstrass
(1815–1897)

THEOREM 2—Direct Comparison Test Let f and g be continuous on $[a, \infty)$ with $0 \leq f(x) \leq g(x)$ for all $x \geq a$. Then

1. $\displaystyle\int_a^{\infty} f(x)\,dx$ converges if $\displaystyle\int_a^{\infty} g(x)\,dx$ converges.

2. $\displaystyle\int_a^{\infty} g(x)\,dx$ diverges if $\displaystyle\int_a^{\infty} f(x)\,dx$ diverges.

Proof The reasoning behind the argument establishing Theorem 2 is similar to that in Example 6. If $0 \leq f(x) \leq g(x)$ for $x \geq a$, then from Rule 7 in Theorem 2 of Section 5.3 we have

$$\int_a^b f(x)\,dx \leq \int_a^b g(x)\,dx, \qquad b > a.$$

From this it can be argued, as in Example 6, that

$$\int_a^{\infty} f(x)\,dx \quad \text{converges if} \quad \int_a^{\infty} g(x)\,dx \quad \text{converges.}$$

Turning this around says that

$$\int_a^{\infty} g(x)\,dx \quad \text{diverges if} \quad \int_a^{\infty} f(x)\,dx \quad \text{diverges.}$$

■

EXAMPLE 7 These examples illustrate how we use Theorem 2.

(a) $\displaystyle\int_1^{\infty} \frac{\sin^2 x}{x^2}\,dx$ converges because

$$0 \leq \frac{\sin^2 x}{x^2} \leq \frac{1}{x^2} \quad \text{on} \quad [1, \infty) \quad \text{and} \quad \int_1^{\infty} \frac{1}{x^2}\,dx \quad \text{converges.}$$

Example 3

(b) $\displaystyle\int_1^{\infty} \frac{1}{\sqrt{x^2 - 0.1}}\,dx$ diverges because

$$\frac{1}{\sqrt{x^2 - 0.1}} \geq \frac{1}{x} \quad \text{on} \quad [1, \infty) \quad \text{and} \quad \int_1^{\infty} \frac{1}{x}\,dx \quad \text{diverges.}$$

Example 3 ■

THEOREM 3—Limit Comparison Test If the positive functions f and g are continuous on $[a, \infty)$, and if

$$\lim_{x \to \infty} \frac{f(x)}{g(x)} = L, \qquad 0 < L < \infty,$$

then

$$\int_a^{\infty} f(x)\,dx \quad \text{and} \quad \int_a^{\infty} g(x)\,dx$$

both converge or both diverge.

We omit the more advanced proof of Theorem 3.

Although the improper integrals of two functions from a to ∞ may both converge, this does not mean that their integrals necessarily have the same value, as the next example shows.

EXAMPLE 8 Show that

$$\int_1^\infty \frac{dx}{1+x^2}$$

converges by comparison with $\int_1^\infty (1/x^2)\,dx$. Find and compare the two integral values.

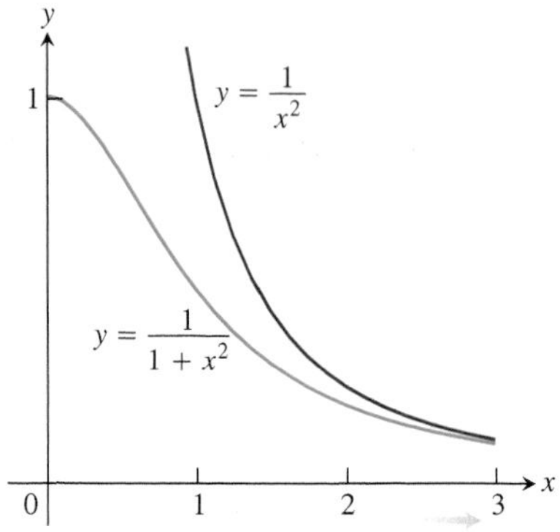

FIGURE 8.20 The functions in Example 8.

Solution The functions $f(x) = 1/x^2$ and $g(x) = 1/(1+x^2)$ are positive and continuous on $[1, \infty)$. Also,

$$\lim_{x\to\infty} \frac{f(x)}{g(x)} = \lim_{x\to\infty} \frac{1/x^2}{1/(1+x^2)} = \lim_{x\to\infty} \frac{1+x^2}{x^2}$$
$$= \lim_{x\to\infty} \left(\frac{1}{x^2} + 1\right) = 0 + 1 = 1,$$

a positive finite limit (Figure 8.20). Therefore, $\int_1^\infty \frac{dx}{1+x^2}$ converges because $\int_1^\infty \frac{dx}{x^2}$ converges.

The integrals converge to different values, however:

$$\int_1^\infty \frac{dx}{x^2} = \frac{1}{2-1} = 1 \qquad \text{Example 3}$$

and

$$\int_1^\infty \frac{dx}{1+x^2} = \lim_{b\to\infty} \int_1^b \frac{dx}{1+x^2}$$
$$= \lim_{b\to\infty} [\tan^{-1} b - \tan^{-1} 1] = \frac{\pi}{2} - \frac{\pi}{4} = \frac{\pi}{4}. \qquad \blacksquare$$

EXAMPLE 9 Investigate the convergence of $\int_1^\infty \frac{1-e^{-x}}{x}\,dx$.

Solution The integrand suggests a comparison of $f(x) = (1 - e^{-x})/x$ with $g(x) = 1/x$. However, we cannot use the Direct Comparison Test because $f(x) \le g(x)$ and the integral of $g(x)$ *diverges*. On the other hand, using the Limit Comparison Test we find that

$$\lim_{x\to\infty} \frac{f(x)}{g(x)} = \lim_{x\to\infty} \left(\frac{1-e^{-x}}{x}\right)\left(\frac{x}{1}\right) = \lim_{x\to\infty} (1 - e^{-x}) = 1,$$

which is a positive finite limit. Therefore, $\int_1^\infty \frac{1-e^{-x}}{x}\,dx$ diverges because $\int_1^\infty \frac{dx}{x}$ diverges. Approximations to the improper integral are given in Table 8.5. Note that the values do not appear to approach any fixed limiting value as $b \to \infty$. $\blacksquare$

TABLE 8.5

b	$\int_1^b \frac{1-e^{-x}}{x}\,dx$
2	0.5226637569
5	1.3912002736
10	2.0832053156
100	4.3857862516
1000	6.6883713446
10000	8.9909564376
100000	11.2935415306

Exercises 8.7

Evaluating Improper Integrals

The integrals in Exercises 1–34 converge. Evaluate the integrals without using tables.

1. $\int_0^\infty \frac{dx}{x^2+1}$
2. $\int_1^\infty \frac{dx}{x^{1.001}}$
3. $\int_0^1 \frac{dx}{\sqrt{x}}$
4. $\int_0^4 \frac{dx}{\sqrt{4-x}}$
5. $\int_{-1}^1 \frac{dx}{x^{2/3}}$
6. $\int_{-8}^1 \frac{dx}{x^{1/3}}$
7. $\int_0^1 \frac{dx}{\sqrt{1-x^2}}$
8. $\int_0^1 \frac{dr}{r^{0.999}}$
9. $\int_{-\infty}^{-2} \frac{2\,dx}{x^2-1}$
10. $\int_{-\infty}^{2} \frac{2\,dx}{x^2+4}$
11. $\int_2^\infty \frac{2}{v^2-v}\,dv$
12. $\int_2^\infty \frac{2\,dt}{t^2-1}$
13. $\int_{-\infty}^\infty \frac{2x\,dx}{(x^2+1)^2}$
14. $\int_{-\infty}^\infty \frac{x\,dx}{(x^2+4)^{3/2}}$
15. $\int_0^1 \frac{\theta+1}{\sqrt{\theta^2+2\theta}}\,d\theta$
16. $\int_0^2 \frac{s+1}{\sqrt{4-s^2}}\,ds$
17. $\int_0^\infty \frac{dx}{(1+x)\sqrt{x}}$
18. $\int_1^\infty \frac{1}{x\sqrt{x^2-1}}\,dx$
19. $\int_0^\infty \frac{dv}{(1+v^2)(1+\tan^{-1} v)}$
20. $\int_0^\infty \frac{16\tan^{-1} x}{1+x^2}\,dx$
21. $\int_{-\infty}^0 \theta e^\theta\,d\theta$
22. $\int_0^\infty 2e^{-\theta}\sin\theta\,d\theta$
23. $\int_{-\infty}^0 e^{-|x|}\,dx$
24. $\int_{-\infty}^\infty 2xe^{-x^2}\,dx$
25. $\int_0^1 x\ln x\,dx$
26. $\int_0^1 (-\ln x)\,dx$
27. $\int_0^2 \frac{ds}{\sqrt{4-s^2}}$
28. $\int_0^1 \frac{4r\,dr}{\sqrt{1-r^4}}$
29. $\int_1^2 \frac{ds}{s\sqrt{s^2-1}}$
30. $\int_2^4 \frac{dt}{t\sqrt{t^2-4}}$
31. $\int_{-1}^4 \frac{dx}{\sqrt{|x|}}$
32. $\int_0^2 \frac{dx}{\sqrt{|x-1|}}$
33. $\int_{-1}^\infty \frac{d\theta}{\theta^2+5\theta+6}$
34. $\int_0^\infty \frac{dx}{(x+1)(x^2+1)}$

Testing for Convergence

In Exercises 35–64, use integration, the Direct Comparison Test, or the Limit Comparison Test to test the integrals for convergence. If more than one method applies, use whatever method you prefer.

35. $\int_0^{\pi/2} \tan\theta\,d\theta$
36. $\int_0^{\pi/2} \cot\theta\,d\theta$
37. $\int_0^\pi \frac{\sin\theta\,d\theta}{\sqrt{\pi-\theta}}$
38. $\int_{-\pi/2}^{\pi/2} \frac{\cos\theta\,d\theta}{(\pi-2\theta)^{1/3}}$
39. $\int_0^{\ln 2} x^{-2}e^{-1/x}\,dx$
40. $\int_0^1 \frac{e^{-\sqrt{x}}}{\sqrt{x}}\,dx$
41. $\int_0^\pi \frac{dt}{\sqrt{t}+\sin t}$
42. $\int_0^1 \frac{dt}{t-\sin t}$ (*Hint:* $t \ge \sin t$ for $t \ge 0$)
43. $\int_0^2 \frac{dx}{1-x^2}$
44. $\int_0^2 \frac{dx}{1-x}$
45. $\int_{-1}^1 \ln|x|\,dx$
46. $\int_{-1}^1 -x\ln|x|\,dx$
47. $\int_1^\infty \frac{dx}{x^3+1}$
48. $\int_4^\infty \frac{dx}{\sqrt{x}-1}$
49. $\int_2^\infty \frac{dv}{\sqrt{v-1}}$
50. $\int_0^\infty \frac{d\theta}{1+e^\theta}$
51. $\int_0^\infty \frac{dx}{\sqrt{x^6+1}}$
52. $\int_2^\infty \frac{dx}{\sqrt{x^2-1}}$
53. $\int_1^\infty \frac{\sqrt{x+1}}{x^2}\,dx$
54. $\int_2^\infty \frac{x\,dx}{\sqrt{x^4-1}}$
55. $\int_\pi^\infty \frac{2+\cos x}{x}\,dx$
56. $\int_\pi^\infty \frac{1+\sin x}{x^2}\,dx$
57. $\int_4^\infty \frac{2\,dt}{t^{3/2}-1}$
58. $\int_2^\infty \frac{1}{\ln x}\,dx$
59. $\int_1^\infty \frac{e^x}{x}\,dx$
60. $\int_{e^e}^\infty \ln(\ln x)\,dx$
61. $\int_1^\infty \frac{1}{\sqrt{e^x-x}}\,dx$
62. $\int_1^\infty \frac{1}{e^x-2^x}\,dx$
63. $\int_{-\infty}^\infty \frac{dx}{\sqrt{x^4+1}}$
64. $\int_{-\infty}^\infty \frac{dx}{e^x+e^{-x}}$

Theory and Examples

65. Find the values of p for which each integral converges.

 a. $\int_1^2 \frac{dx}{x(\ln x)^p}$ b. $\int_2^\infty \frac{dx}{x(\ln x)^p}$

66. **$\int_{-\infty}^\infty f(x)\,dx$ may not equal $\lim_{b\to\infty}\int_{-b}^b f(x)\,dx$** Show that

$$\int_0^\infty \frac{2x\,dx}{x^2+1}$$

diverges and hence that

$$\int_{-\infty}^\infty \frac{2x\,dx}{x^2+1}$$

diverges. Then show that

$$\lim_{b\to\infty}\int_{-b}^b \frac{2x\,dx}{x^2+1} = 0.$$

Exercises 67–70 are about the infinite region in the first quadrant between the curve $y = e^{-x}$ and the x-axis.

67. Find the area of the region.
68. Find the centroid of the region.
69. Find the volume of the solid generated by revolving the region about the y-axis.

70. Find the volume of the solid generated by revolving the region about the x-axis.

71. Find the area of the region that lies between the curves $y = \sec x$ and $y = \tan x$ from $x = 0$ to $x = \pi/2$.

72. The region in Exercise 71 is revolved about the x-axis to generate a solid.

a. Find the volume of the solid.

b. Show that the inner and outer surfaces of the solid have infinite area.

73. Estimating the value of a convergent improper integral whose domain is infinite

a. Show that

$$\int_3^{\infty} e^{-3x}\,dx = \frac{1}{3}e^{-9} < 0.000042,$$

and hence that $\int_3^{\infty} e^{-x^2}\,dx < 0.000042$. Explain why this means that $\int_0^{\infty} e^{-x^2}\,dx$ can be replaced by $\int_0^{3} e^{-x^2}\,dx$ without introducing an error of magnitude greater than 0.000042.

T **b.** Evaluate $\int_0^{3} e^{-x^2}\,dx$ numerically.

74. The infinite paint can or Gabriel's horn As Example 3 shows, the integral $\int_1^{\infty} (dx/x)$ diverges. This means that the integral

$$\int_1^{\infty} 2\pi \frac{1}{x}\sqrt{1 + \frac{1}{x^4}}\,dx,$$

which measures the *surface area* of the solid of revolution traced out by revolving the curve $y = 1/x$, $1 \le x$, about the x-axis, diverges also. By comparing the two integrals, we see that, for every finite value $b > 1$,

$$\int_1^{b} 2\pi \frac{1}{x}\sqrt{1 + \frac{1}{x^4}}\,dx > 2\pi \int_1^{b} \frac{1}{x}\,dx.$$

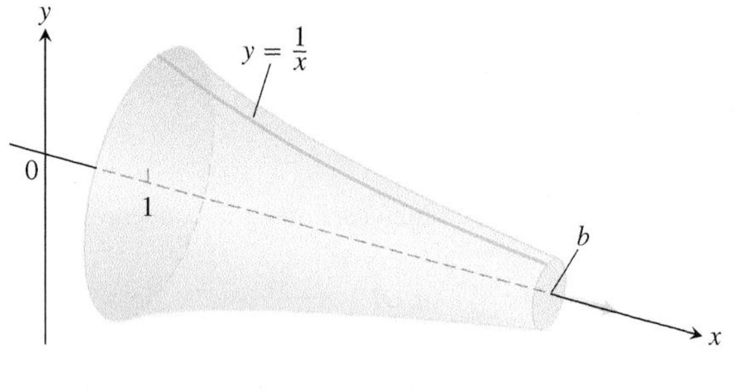

However, the integral

$$\int_1^{\infty} \pi\left(\frac{1}{x}\right)^2 dx$$

for the *volume* of the solid converges.

a. Calculate it.

b. This solid of revolution is sometimes described as a can that does not hold enough paint to cover its own interior. Think about that for a moment. It is common sense that a finite amount of paint cannot cover an infinite surface. But if we fill the horn with paint (a finite amount), then we *will* have covered an infinite surface. Explain the apparent contradiction.

75. Sine-integral function The integral

$$\mathrm{Si}(x) = \int_0^{x} \frac{\sin t}{t}\,dt,$$

called the *sine-integral function*, has important applications in optics.

T **a.** Plot the integrand $(\sin t)/t$ for $t > 0$. Is the sine-integral function everywhere increasing or decreasing? Do you think $\mathrm{Si}(x) = 0$ for $x > 0$? Check your answers by graphing the function $\mathrm{Si}(x)$ for $0 \le x \le 25$.

b. Explore the convergence of

$$\int_0^{\infty} \frac{\sin t}{t}\,dt.$$

If it converges, what is its value?

76. Error function The function

$$\mathrm{erf}(x) = \int_0^{x} \frac{2e^{-t^2}}{\sqrt{\pi}}\,dt,$$

called the *error function*, has important applications in probability and statistics.

T **a.** Plot the error function for $0 \le x \le 25$.

b. Explore the convergence of

$$\int_0^{\infty} \frac{2e^{-t^2}}{\sqrt{\pi}}\,dt.$$

If it converges, what appears to be its value? You will see how to confirm your estimate in Section 14.4, Exercise 41.

77. Normal probability distribution The function

$$f(x) = \frac{1}{\sigma\sqrt{2\pi}}e^{-\frac{1}{2}\left(\frac{x-\mu}{\sigma}\right)^2}$$

is called the *normal probability density function* with mean μ and standard deviation σ. The number μ tells where the distribution is centered, and σ measures the "scatter" around the mean.

From the theory of probability, it is known that

$$\int_{-\infty}^{\infty} f(x)\,dx = 1.$$

In what follows, let $\mu = 0$ and $\sigma = 1$.

T **a.** Draw the graph of f. Find the intervals on which f is increasing, the intervals on which f is decreasing, and any local extreme values and where they occur.

b. Evaluate

$$\int_{-n}^{n} f(x)\,dx$$

for $n = 1$, 2, and 3.

c. Give a convincing argument that

$$\int_{-\infty}^{\infty} f(x)\,dx = 1.$$

(*Hint:* Show that $0 < f(x) < e^{-x/2}$ for $x > 1$, and for $b > 1$,

$$\int_b^{\infty} e^{-x/2}\,dx \to 0 \quad \text{as} \quad b \to \infty.)$$

78. Show that if $f(x)$ is integrable on every interval of real numbers and a and b are real numbers with $a < b$, then

a. $\int_{-\infty}^{a} f(x)\,dx$ and $\int_a^{\infty} f(x)\,dx$ both converge if and only if $\int_{-\infty}^{b} f(x)\,dx$ and $\int_b^{\infty} f(x)\,dx$ both converge.

b. $\int_{-\infty}^{a} f(x)\,dx + \int_a^{\infty} f(x)\,dx = \int_{-\infty}^{b} f(x)\,dx + \int_b^{\infty} f(x)\,dx$ when the integrals involved converge.

COMPUTER EXPLORATIONS

In Exercises 79–82, use a CAS to explore the integrals for various values of p (include noninteger values). For what values of p does the integral converge? What is the value of the integral when it does converge? Plot the integrand for various values of p.

79. $\int_0^e x^p \ln x\, dx$

80. $\int_e^\infty x^p \ln x\, dx$

81. $\int_0^\infty x^p \ln x\, dx$

82. $\int_{-\infty}^\infty x^p \ln |x|\, dx$

Chapter 8 Questions to Guide Your Review

1. What is the formula for integration by parts? Where does it come from? Why might you want to use it?
2. When applying the formula for integration by parts, how do you choose the u and dv? How can you apply integration by parts to an integral of the form $\int f(x)\, dx$?
3. If an integrand is a product of the form $\sin^n x \cos^m x$, where m and n are nonnegative integers, how do you evaluate the integral? Give a specific example of each case.
4. What substitutions are made to evaluate integrals of $\sin mx \sin nx$, $\sin mx \cos nx$, and $\cos mx \cos nx$? Give an example of each case.
5. What substitutions are sometimes used to transform integrals involving $\sqrt{a^2 - x^2}$, $\sqrt{a^2 + x^2}$, and $\sqrt{x^2 - a^2}$ into integrals that can be evaluated directly? Give an example of each case.
6. What restrictions can you place on the variables involved in the three basic trigonometric substitutions to make sure the substitutions are reversible (have inverses)?
7. What is the goal of the method of partial fractions?
8. When the degree of a polynomial $f(x)$ is less than the degree of a polynomial $g(x)$, how do you write $f(x)/g(x)$ as a sum of partial fractions if $g(x)$
   a. is a product of distinct linear factors?
   b. consists of a repeated linear factor?
   c. contains an irreducible quadratic factor?
   What do you do if the degree of f is *not* less than the degree of g?
9. How are integral tables typically used? What do you do if a particular integral you want to evaluate is not listed in the table?
10. What is a reduction formula? How are reduction formulas used? Give an example.
11. How would you compare the relative merits of Simpson's Rule and the Trapezoidal Rule?
12. What is an improper integral of Type I? Type II? How are the values of various types of improper integrals defined? Give examples.
13. What tests are available for determining the convergence and divergence of improper integrals that cannot be evaluated directly? Give examples of their use.

Chapter 8 Practice Exercises

Integration by Parts

Evaluate the integrals in Exercises 1–8 using integration by parts.

1. $\int \ln(x+1)\, dx$

2. $\int x^2 \ln x\, dx$

3. $\int \tan^{-1} 3x\, dx$

4. $\int \cos^{-1}\left(\frac{x}{2}\right) dx$

5. $\int (x+1)^2 e^x\, dx$

6. $\int x^2 \sin(1-x)\, dx$

7. $\int e^x \cos 2x\, dx$

8. $\int e^{-2x} \sin 3x\, dx$

Partial Fractions

Evaluate the integrals in Exercises 9–28. It may be necessary to use a substitution first.

9. $\int \frac{x\, dx}{x^2 - 3x + 2}$

10. $\int \frac{x\, dx}{x^2 + 4x + 3}$

11. $\int \frac{dx}{x(x+1)^2}$

12. $\int \frac{x+1}{x^2(x-1)}\, dx$

13. $\int \frac{\sin\theta\, d\theta}{\cos^2\theta + \cos\theta - 2}$

14. $\int \frac{\cos\theta\, d\theta}{\sin^2\theta + \sin\theta - 6}$

15. $\int \frac{3x^2 + 4x + 4}{x^3 + x}\, dx$

16. $\int \frac{4x\, dx}{x^3 + 4x}$

17. $\int \frac{v+3}{2v^3 - 8v}\, dv$

18. $\int \frac{(3v - 7)\, dv}{(v-1)(v-2)(v-3)}$

19. $\int \frac{dt}{t^4 + 4t^2 + 3}$

20. $\int \frac{t\, dt}{t^4 - t^2 - 2}$

21. $\int \frac{x^3 + x^2}{x^2 + x - 2}\, dx$

22. $\int \frac{x^3 + 1}{x^3 - x}\, dx$

23. $\int \frac{x^3 + 4x^2}{x^2 + 4x + 3}\, dx$

24. $\int \frac{2x^3 + x^2 - 21x + 24}{x^2 + 2x - 8}\, dx$

25. $\int \frac{dx}{x(3\sqrt{x+1})}$

26. $\int \frac{dx}{x(1 + \sqrt[3]{x})}$

27. $\int \frac{ds}{e^s - 1}$

28. $\int \frac{ds}{\sqrt{e^s + 1}}$

Trigonometric Substitutions

Evaluate the integrals in Exercises 29–32 **(a)** without using a trigonometric substitution, **(b)** using a trigonometric substitution.

29. $\displaystyle\int \frac{y\,dy}{\sqrt{16-y^2}}$ **30.** $\displaystyle\int \frac{x\,dx}{\sqrt{4+x^2}}$

31. $\displaystyle\int \frac{x\,dx}{4-x^2}$ **32.** $\displaystyle\int \frac{t\,dt}{\sqrt{4t^2-1}}$

Evaluate the integrals in Exercises 33–36.

33. $\displaystyle\int \frac{x\,dx}{9-x^2}$ **34.** $\displaystyle\int \frac{dx}{x(9-x^2)}$

35. $\displaystyle\int \frac{dx}{9-x^2}$ **36.** $\displaystyle\int \frac{dx}{\sqrt{9-x^2}}$

Trigonometric Integrals

Evaluate the integrals in Exercises 37–44.

37. $\displaystyle\int \sin^3 x \cos^4 x\,dx$ **38.** $\displaystyle\int \cos^5 x \sin^5 x\,dx$

39. $\displaystyle\int \tan^4 x \sec^2 x\,dx$ **40.** $\displaystyle\int \tan^3 x \sec^3 x\,dx$

41. $\displaystyle\int \sin 5\theta \cos 6\theta\,d\theta$ **42.** $\displaystyle\int \cos 3\theta \cos 3\theta\,d\theta$

43. $\displaystyle\int \sqrt{1+\cos(t/2)}\,dt$ **44.** $\displaystyle\int e^t\sqrt{\tan^2 e^t + 1}\,dt$

Numerical Integration

45. According to the error-bound formula for Simpson's Rule, how many subintervals should you use to be sure of estimating the value of

$$\ln 3 = \int_1^3 \frac{1}{x}\,dx$$

by Simpson's Rule with an error of no more than 10^{-4} in absolute value? (Remember that for Simpson's Rule, the number of subintervals has to be even.)

46. A brief calculation shows that if $0 \le x \le 1$, then the second derivative of $f(x) = \sqrt{1+x^4}$ lies between 0 and 8. Based on this, about how many subdivisions would you need to estimate the integral of f from 0 to 1 with an error no greater than 10^{-3} in absolute value using the Trapezoidal Rule?

47. A direct calculation shows that

$$\int_0^{\pi} 2\sin^2 x\,dx = \pi.$$

How close do you come to this value by using the Trapezoidal Rule with $n = 6$? Simpson's Rule with $n = 6$? Try them and find out.

48. You are planning to use Simpson's Rule to estimate the value of the integral

$$\int_1^2 f(x)\,dx$$

with an error magnitude less than 10^{-5}. You have determined that $|f^{(4)}(x)| \le 3$ throughout the interval of integration. How many subintervals should you use to assure the required accuracy? (Remember that for Simpson's Rule the number has to be even.)

T **49. Mean temperature** Use Simpson's Rule to approximate the average value of the temperature function

$$f(x) = 37\sin\left(\frac{2\pi}{365}(x-101)\right) + 25$$

for a 365-day year. This is one way to estimate the annual mean air temperature in Fairbanks, Alaska. The National Weather Service's official figure, a numerical average of the daily normal mean air temperatures for the year, is 25.7°F, which is slightly higher than the average value of $f(x)$.

50. Heat capacity of a gas Heat capacity C_v is the amount of heat required to raise the temperature of a given mass of gas with constant volume by 1°C, measured in units of cal/deg-mol (calories per degree gram molecular weight). The heat capacity of oxygen depends on its temperature T and satisfies the formula

$$C_v = 8.27 + 10^{-5}(26T - 1.87T^2).$$

Use Simpson's Rule to find the average value of C_v and the temperature at which it is attained for $20° \le T \le 675°$C.

51. Fuel efficiency An automobile computer gives a digital readout of fuel consumption in gallons per hour. During a trip, a passenger recorded the fuel consumption every 5 min for a full hour of travel.

Time	Gal/h	Time	Gal/h
0	2.5	35	2.5
5	2.4	40	2.4
10	2.3	45	2.3
15	2.4	50	2.4
20	2.4	55	2.4
25	2.5	60	2.3
30	2.6		

a. Use the Trapezoidal Rule to approximate the total fuel consumption during the hour.

b. If the automobile covered 60 mi in the hour, what was its fuel efficiency (in miles per gallon) for that portion of the trip?

52. A new parking lot To meet the demand for parking, your town has allocated the area shown here. As the town engineer, you have been asked by the town council to find out if the lot can be built for \$11,000. The cost to clear the land will be \$0.10 a square foot, and the lot will cost \$2.00 a square foot to pave. Use Simpson's Rule to find out if the job can be done for \$11,000.

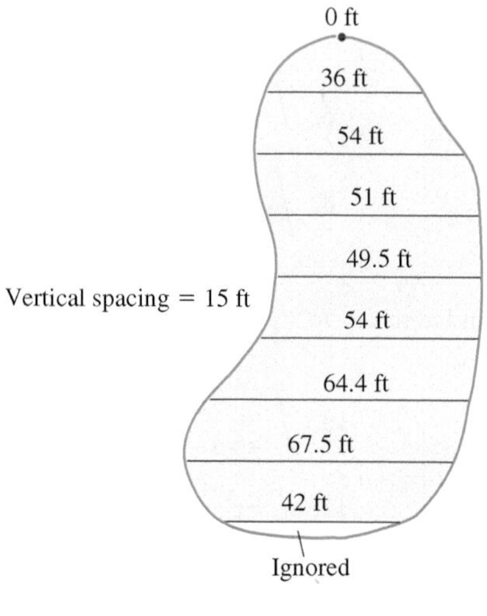

Improper Integrals

Evaluate the improper integrals in Exercises 53–62.

53. $\displaystyle\int_0^3 \frac{dx}{\sqrt{9-x^2}}$

54. $\displaystyle\int_0^1 \ln x\, dx$

55. $\displaystyle\int_0^2 \frac{dy}{(y-1)^{2/3}}$

56. $\displaystyle\int_{-2}^0 \frac{d\theta}{(\theta+1)^{3/5}}$

57. $\displaystyle\int_3^\infty \frac{2\, du}{u^2-2u}$

58. $\displaystyle\int_1^\infty \frac{3v-1}{4v^3-v^2}\, dv$

59. $\displaystyle\int_0^\infty x^2 e^{-x}\, dx$

60. $\displaystyle\int_{-\infty}^0 xe^{3x}\, dx$

61. $\displaystyle\int_{-\infty}^\infty \frac{dx}{4x^2+9}$

62. $\displaystyle\int_{-\infty}^\infty \frac{4\, dx}{x^2+16}$

Which of the improper integrals in Exercises 63–68 converge and which diverge?

63. $\displaystyle\int_6^\infty \frac{d\theta}{\sqrt{\theta^2+1}}$

64. $\displaystyle\int_0^\infty e^{-u}\cos u\, du$

65. $\displaystyle\int_1^\infty \frac{\ln z}{z}\, dz$

66. $\displaystyle\int_1^\infty \frac{e^{-t}}{\sqrt{t}}\, dt$

67. $\displaystyle\int_{-\infty}^\infty \frac{2\, dx}{e^x+e^{-x}}$

68. $\displaystyle\int_{-\infty}^\infty \frac{dx}{x^2(1+e^x)}$

Assorted Integrations

Evaluate the integrals in Exercises 69–116. The integrals are listed in random order so you need to decide which integration technique to use.

69. $\displaystyle\int \frac{x\, dx}{1+\sqrt{x}}$

70. $\displaystyle\int \frac{x^3+2}{4-x^2}\, dx$

71. $\displaystyle\int \frac{dx}{x(x^2+1)^2}$

72. $\displaystyle\int \frac{dx}{\sqrt{-2x-x^2}}$

73. $\displaystyle\int \frac{2-\cos x+\sin x}{\sin^2 x}\, dx$

74. $\displaystyle\int \frac{\sin^2\theta}{\cos^2\theta}\, d\theta$

75. $\displaystyle\int \frac{9\, dv}{81-v^4}$

76. $\displaystyle\int_2^\infty \frac{dx}{(x-1)^2}$

77. $\displaystyle\int \theta\cos(2\theta+1)\, d\theta$

78. $\displaystyle\int \frac{x^3\, dx}{x^2-2x+1}$

79. $\displaystyle\int \frac{\sin 2\theta\, d\theta}{(1+\cos 2\theta)^2}$

80. $\displaystyle\int_{\pi/4}^{\pi/2} \sqrt{1+\cos 4x}\, dx$

81. $\displaystyle\int \frac{x\, dx}{\sqrt{2-x}}$

82. $\displaystyle\int \frac{\sqrt{1-v^2}}{v^2}\, dv$

83. $\displaystyle\int \frac{dy}{y^2-2y+2}$

84. $\displaystyle\int \frac{x\, dx}{\sqrt{8-2x^2-x^4}}$

85. $\displaystyle\int \frac{z+1}{z^2(z^2+4)}\, dz$

86. $\displaystyle\int x^3 e^{(x^2)}\, dx$

87. $\displaystyle\int \frac{t\, dt}{\sqrt{9-4t^2}}$

88. $\displaystyle\int \frac{\tan^{-1} x}{x^2}\, dx$

89. $\displaystyle\int \frac{e^t\, dt}{e^{2t}+3e^t+2}$

90. $\displaystyle\int \tan^3 t\, dt$

91. $\displaystyle\int_1^\infty \frac{\ln y}{y^3}\, dy$

92. $\displaystyle\int \frac{\cot v\, dv}{\ln \sin v}$

93. $\displaystyle\int e^{\ln\sqrt{x}}\, dx$

94. $\displaystyle\int e^\theta\sqrt{3+4e^\theta}\, d\theta$

95. $\displaystyle\int \frac{\sin 5t\, dt}{1+(\cos 5t)^2}$

96. $\displaystyle\int \frac{dv}{\sqrt{e^{2v}-1}}$

97. $\displaystyle\int \frac{dr}{1+\sqrt{r}}$

98. $\displaystyle\int \frac{4x^3-20x}{x^4-10x^2+9}\, dx$

99. $\displaystyle\int \frac{x^3}{1+x^2}\, dx$

100. $\displaystyle\int \frac{x^2}{1+x^3}\, dx$

101. $\displaystyle\int \frac{1+x^2}{1+x^3}\, dx$

102. $\displaystyle\int \frac{1+x^2}{(1+x)^3}\, dx$

103. $\displaystyle\int \sqrt{x}\cdot\sqrt{1+\sqrt{x}}\, dx$

104. $\displaystyle\int \sqrt{1+\sqrt{1+x}}\, dx$

105. $\displaystyle\int \frac{1}{\sqrt{x}\sqrt{1+x}}\, dx$

106. $\displaystyle\int_0^{1/2} \sqrt{1+\sqrt{1-x^2}}\, dx$

107. $\displaystyle\int \frac{\ln x}{x+x\ln x}\, dx$

108. $\displaystyle\int \frac{1}{x\cdot\ln x\cdot\ln(\ln x)}\, dx$

109. $\displaystyle\int \frac{x^{\ln x}\ln x}{x}\, dx$

110. $\displaystyle\int (\ln x)^{\ln x}\left[\frac{1}{x}+\frac{\ln(\ln x)}{x}\right] dx$

111. $\displaystyle\int \frac{1}{x\sqrt{1-x^4}}\, dx$

112. $\displaystyle\int \frac{\sqrt{1-x}}{x}\, dx$

113. a. Show that $\int_0^a f(x)\, dx = \int_0^a f(a-x)\, dx$.

b. Use part (a) to evaluate

$$\int_0^{\pi/2} \frac{\sin x}{\sin x+\cos x}\, dx.$$

114. $\displaystyle\int \frac{\sin x}{\sin x+\cos x}\, dx$

115. $\displaystyle\int \frac{\sin^2 x}{1+\sin^2 x}\, dx$

116. $\displaystyle\int \frac{1-\cos x}{1+\cos x}\, dx$

Chapter Additional and Advanced Exercises

Evaluating Integrals

Evaluate the integrals in Exercises 1–6.

1. $\displaystyle\int (\sin^{-1} x)^2\, dx$

2. $\displaystyle\int \frac{dx}{x(x+1)(x+2)\cdots(x+m)}$

3. $\displaystyle\int x\sin^{-1} x\, dx$

4. $\displaystyle\int \sin^{-1}\sqrt{y}\, dy$

5. $\displaystyle\int \frac{dt}{t - \sqrt{1 - t^2}}$

6. $\displaystyle\int \frac{dx}{x^4 + 4}$

Evaluate the limits in Exercises 7 and 8.

7. $\displaystyle\lim_{x\to\infty} \int_{-x}^{x} \sin t\, dt$

8. $\displaystyle\lim_{x\to 0^+} x \int_{x}^{1} \frac{\cos t}{t^2}\, dt$

Evaluate the limits in Exercises 9 and 10 by identifying them with definite integrals and evaluating the integrals.

9. $\displaystyle\lim_{n\to\infty} \sum_{k=1}^{n} \ln \sqrt[n]{1 + \frac{k}{n}}$

10. $\displaystyle\lim_{n\to\infty} \sum_{k=0}^{n-1} \frac{1}{\sqrt{n^2 - k^2}}$

Applications

11. **Finding arc length** Find the length of the curve

$$y = \int_0^x \sqrt{\cos 2t}\, dt, \quad 0 \le x \le \pi/4.$$

12. **Finding arc length** Find the length of the graph of the function $y = \ln(1 - x^2)$, $0 \le x \le 1/2$.

13. **Finding volume** The region in the first quadrant that is enclosed by the x-axis and the curve $y = 3x\sqrt{1 - x}$ is revolved about the y-axis to generate a solid. Find the volume of the solid.

14. **Finding volume** The region in the first quadrant that is enclosed by the x-axis, the curve $y = 5/\left(x\sqrt{5 - x}\right)$, and the lines $x = 1$ and $x = 4$ is revolved about the x-axis to generate a solid. Find the volume of the solid.

15. **Finding volume** The region in the first quadrant enclosed by the coordinate axes, the curve $y = e^x$, and the line $x = 1$ is revolved about the y-axis to generate a solid. Find the volume of the solid.

16. **Finding volume** The region in the first quadrant that is bounded above by the curve $y = e^x - 1$, below by the x-axis, and on the right by the line $x = \ln 2$ is revolved about the line $x = \ln 2$ to generate a solid. Find the volume of the solid.

17. **Finding volume** Let R be the "triangular" region in the first quadrant that is bounded above by the line $y = 1$, below by the curve $y = \ln x$, and on the left by the line $x = 1$. Find the volume of the solid generated by revolving R about

 a. the x-axis. **b.** the line $y = 1$.

18. **Finding volume** (*Continuation of Exercise 17.*) Find the volume of the solid generated by revolving the region R about

 a. the y-axis. **b.** the line $x = 1$.

19. **Finding volume** The region between the x-axis and the curve

$$y = f(x) = \begin{cases} 0, & x = 0 \\ x \ln x, & 0 < x \le 2 \end{cases}$$

is revolved about the x-axis to generate the solid shown here.

 a. Show that f is continuous at $x = 0$.

 b. Find the volume of the solid.

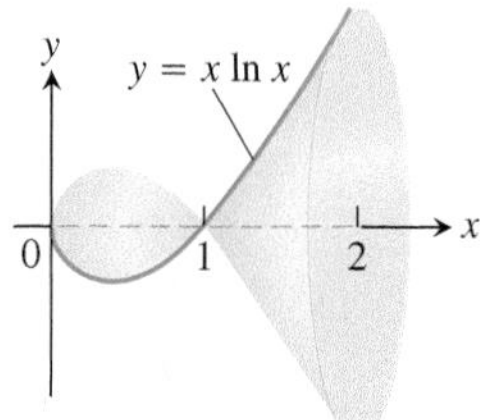

20. **Finding volume** The infinite region bounded by the coordinate axes and the curve $y = -\ln x$ in the first quadrant is revolved about the x-axis to generate a solid. Find the volume of the solid.

21. **Centroid of a region** Find the centroid of the region in the first quadrant that is bounded below by the x-axis, above by the curve $y = \ln x$, and on the right by the line $x = e$.

22. **Centroid of a region** Find the centroid of the region in the plane enclosed by the curves $y = \pm(1 - x^2)^{-1/2}$ and the lines $x = 0$ and $x = 1$.

23. **Length of a curve** Find the length of the curve $y = \ln x$ from $x = 1$ to $x = e$.

24. **Finding surface area** Find the area of the surface generated by revolving the curve in Exercise 23 about the y-axis.

25. **The surface generated by an astroid** The graph of the equation $x^{2/3} + y^{2/3} = 1$ is an *astroid* (see accompanying figure). Find the area of the surface generated by revolving the curve about the x-axis.

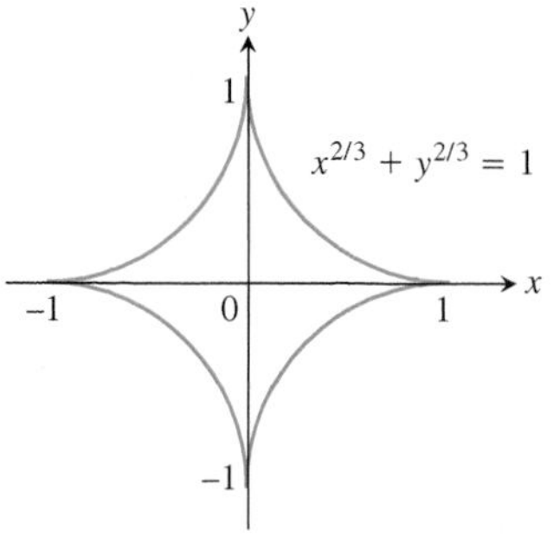

26. **Length of a curve** Find the length of the curve

$$y = \int_1^x \sqrt{\sqrt{t} - 1}\, dt, \qquad 1 \le x \le 16.$$

27. For what value or values of a does

$$\int_1^\infty \left(\frac{ax}{x^2 + 1} - \frac{1}{2x}\right) dx$$

converge? Evaluate the corresponding integral(s).

28. For each $x > 0$, let $G(x) = \int_0^\infty e^{-xt}\, dt$. Prove that $xG(x) = 1$ for each $x > 0$.

29. **Infinite area and finite volume** What values of p have the following property: The area of the region between the curve $y = x^{-p}$, $1 \le x < \infty$, and the x-axis is infinite but the volume of the solid generated by revolving the region about the x-axis is finite.

30. **Infinite area and finite volume** What values of p have the following property: The area of the region in the first quadrant enclosed by the curve $y = x^{-p}$, the y-axis, the line $x = 1$, and the interval $[0, 1]$ on the x-axis is infinite but the volume of the solid generated by revolving the region about one of the coordinate axes is finite.

The Gamma Function and Stirling's Formula

Euler's gamma function $\Gamma(x)$ ("gamma of x"; Γ is a Greek capital g) uses an integral to extend the factorial function from the nonnegative integers to other real values. The formula is

$$\Gamma(x) = \int_0^\infty t^{x-1} e^{-t}\, dt, \quad x > 0.$$

For each positive x, the number $\Gamma(x)$ is the integral of $t^{x-1}e^{-t}$ with respect to t from 0 to ∞. Figure 8.21 shows the graph of Γ near the origin. You will see how to calculate $\Gamma(1/2)$ if you do Additional Exercise 23 in Chapter 14.

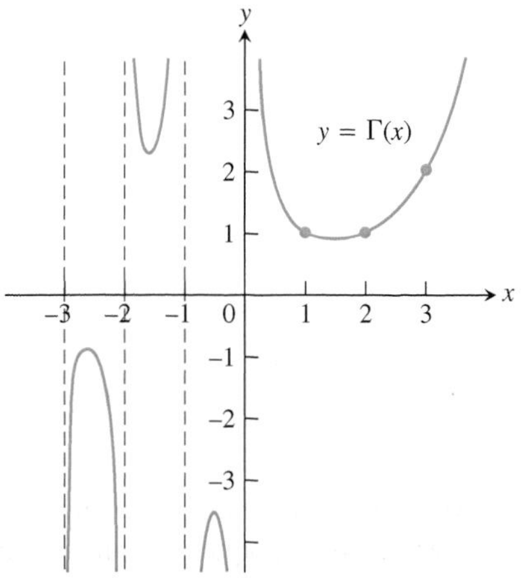

FIGURE 8.21 Euler's gamma function $\Gamma(x)$ is a continuous function of x whose value at each positive integer $n + 1$ is $n!$. The defining integral formula for Γ is valid only for $x > 0$, but we can extend Γ to negative noninteger values of x with the formula $\Gamma(x) = (\Gamma(x + 1))/x$, which is the subject of Exercise 31.

31. If n is a nonnegative integer, $\Gamma(n + 1) = n!$

a. Show that $\Gamma(1) = 1$.

b. Then apply integration by parts to the integral for $\Gamma(x + 1)$ to show that $\Gamma(x + 1) = x\Gamma(x)$. This gives

$$\begin{aligned}\Gamma(2) &= 1\Gamma(1) = 1\\ \Gamma(3) &= 2\Gamma(2) = 2\\ \Gamma(4) &= 3\Gamma(3) = 6\\ &\vdots\\ \Gamma(n+1) &= n\,\Gamma(n) = n! \qquad (1)\end{aligned}$$

c. Use mathematical induction to verify Equation (1) for every nonnegative integer n.

32. Stirling's formula Scottish mathematician James Stirling (1692–1770) showed that

$$\lim_{x\to\infty}\left(\frac{e}{x}\right)^x\sqrt{\frac{x}{2\pi}}\,\Gamma(x) = 1,$$

so, for large x,

$$\Gamma(x) = \left(\frac{x}{e}\right)^x\sqrt{\frac{2\pi}{x}}\,(1 + \epsilon(x)), \qquad \epsilon(x)\to 0 \text{ as } x\to\infty. \qquad (2)$$

Dropping $\epsilon(x)$ leads to the approximation

$$\Gamma(x) \approx \left(\frac{x}{e}\right)^x\sqrt{\frac{2\pi}{x}} \qquad \textbf{(Stirling's formula)}. \qquad (3)$$

a. Stirling's approximation for $n!$ Use Equation (3) and the fact that $n! = n\Gamma(n)$ to show that

$$n! \approx \left(\frac{n}{e}\right)^n\sqrt{2n\pi} \qquad \textbf{(Stirling's approximation)}. \qquad (4)$$

As you will see if you do Exercise 104 in Section 10.1, Equation (4) leads to the approximation

$$\sqrt[n]{n!} \approx \frac{n}{e}. \qquad (5)$$

T **b.** Compare your calculator's value for $n!$ with the value given by Stirling's approximation for $n = 10, 20, 30, \ldots$, as far as your calculator can go.

T **c.** A refinement of Equation (2) gives

$$\Gamma(x) = \left(\frac{x}{e}\right)^x\sqrt{\frac{2\pi}{x}}\,e^{1/(12x)}(1 + \epsilon(x))$$

or

$$\Gamma(x) \approx \left(\frac{x}{e}\right)^x\sqrt{\frac{2\pi}{x}}\,e^{1/(12x)},$$

which tells us that

$$n! \approx \left(\frac{n}{e}\right)^n\sqrt{2n\pi}\,e^{1/(12n)}. \qquad (6)$$

Compare the values given for 10! by your calculator, Stirling's approximation, and Equation (6).

9 Infinite Sequences and Series

OVERVIEW Everyone knows how to add two numbers together, or even several. But how do you add infinitely many numbers together? In this chapter we answer this question, which is part of the theory of infinite sequences and series.

An important application of this theory is a method for representing a known differentiable function $f(x)$ as an infinite sum of powers of x, so it looks like a "polynomial with infinitely many terms." Moreover, the method extends our knowledge of how to evaluate, differentiate, and integrate polynomials, so we can work with even more general functions than those encountered so far. These new functions are often solutions to important problems in science and engineering.

9.1 Sequences

HISTORICAL ESSAY

Sequences and Series

Sequences are fundamental to the study of infinite series and many applications of mathematics. We have already seen an example of a sequence when we studied Newton's Method in Section 4.7. There we produced a sequence of approximations x_n that became closer and closer to the root of a differentiable function. Now we will explore general sequences of numbers and the conditions under which they converge to a finite number.

Representing Sequences

A sequence is a list of numbers

$$a_1, a_2, a_3, \ldots, a_n, \ldots$$

in a given order. Each of a_1, a_2, a_3 and so on represents a number. These are the **terms** of the sequence. For example, the sequence

$$2, 4, 6, 8, 10, 12, \ldots, 2n, \ldots$$

has first term $a_1 = 2$, second term $a_2 = 4$, and nth term $a_n = 2n$. The integer n is called the **index** of a_n, and indicates where a_n occurs in the list. Order is important. The sequence 2, 4, 6, 8 . . . is not the same as the sequence 4, 2, 6, 8 . . . .

We can think of the sequence

$$a_1, a_2, a_3, \ldots, a_n, \ldots$$

as a function that sends 1 to a_1, 2 to a_2, 3 to a_3, and in general sends the positive integer n to the nth term a_n. More precisely, an **infinite sequence** of numbers is a function whose domain is the set of positive integers.

The function associated with the sequence

$$2, 4, 6, 8, 10, 12, \ldots, 2n, \ldots$$

sends 1 to $a_1 = 2$, 2 to $a_2 = 4$, and so on. The general behavior of this sequence is described by the formula $a_n = 2n$.

We can equally well make the domain the integers larger than a given number n_0, and we allow sequences of this type also. For example, the sequence

$$12, 14, 16, 18, 20, 22 \ldots$$

is described by the formula $a_n = 10 + 2n$. It can also be described by the simpler formula $b_n = 2n$, where the index n starts at 6 and increases. To allow such simpler formulas, we let the first index of the sequence be any integer. In the sequence above, $\{a_n\}$ starts with a_1 while $\{b_n\}$ starts with b_6.

Sequences can be described by writing rules that specify their terms, such as

$$a_n = \sqrt{n}, \qquad b_n = (-1)^{n+1}\frac{1}{n}, \qquad c_n = \frac{n-1}{n}, \qquad d_n = (-1)^{n+1},$$

or by listing terms:

$$\{a_n\} = \left\{\sqrt{1}, \sqrt{2}, \sqrt{3}, \ldots, \sqrt{n}, \ldots\right\}$$
$$\{b_n\} = \left\{1, -\frac{1}{2}, \frac{1}{3}, -\frac{1}{4}, \ldots, (-1)^{n+1}\frac{1}{n}, \ldots\right\}$$
$$\{c_n\} = \left\{0, \frac{1}{2}, \frac{2}{3}, \frac{3}{4}, \frac{4}{5}, \ldots, \frac{n-1}{n}, \ldots\right\}$$
$$\{d_n\} = \{1, -1, 1, -1, 1, -1, \ldots, (-1)^{n+1}, \ldots\}.$$

We also sometimes write

$$\{a_n\} = \left\{\sqrt{n}\right\}_{n=1}^{\infty}.$$

Figure 9.1 shows two ways to represent sequences graphically. The first marks the first few points from $a_1, a_2, a_3, \ldots, a_n, \ldots$ on the real axis. The second method shows the graph of the function defining the sequence. The function is defined only on integer inputs, and the graph consists of some points in the xy-plane located at $(1, a_1), (2, a_2), \ldots, (n, a_n), \ldots$.

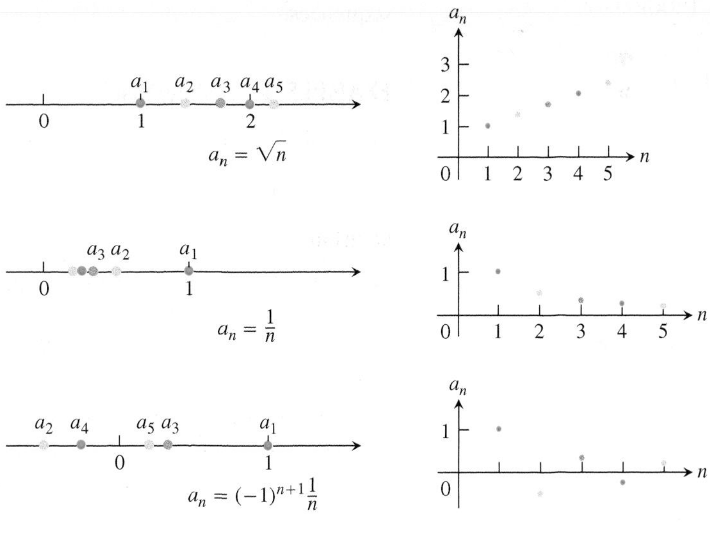

FIGURE 9.1 Sequences can be represented as points on the real line or as points in the plane where the horizontal axis n is the index number of the term and the vertical axis a_n is its value.

Convergence and Divergence

Sometimes the numbers in a sequence approach a single value as the index n increases. This happens in the sequence

$$\left\{1, \frac{1}{2}, \frac{1}{3}, \frac{1}{4}, \ldots, \frac{1}{n}, \ldots\right\}$$

whose terms approach 0 as n gets large, and in the sequence

$$\left\{0, \frac{1}{2}, \frac{2}{3}, \frac{3}{4}, \frac{4}{5}, \ldots, 1 - \frac{1}{n}, \ldots\right\}$$

whose terms approach 1. On the other hand, sequences like

$$\{\sqrt{1}, \sqrt{2}, \sqrt{3}, \ldots, \sqrt{n}, \ldots\}$$

have terms that get larger than any number as n increases, and sequences like

$$\{1, -1, 1, -1, 1, -1, \ldots, (-1)^{n+1}, \ldots\}$$

bounce back and forth between 1 and -1, never converging to a single value. The following definition captures the meaning of having a sequence converge to a limiting value. It says that if we go far enough out in the sequence, by taking the index n to be larger than some value N, the difference between a_n and the limit of the sequence becomes less than any preselected number $\epsilon > 0$.

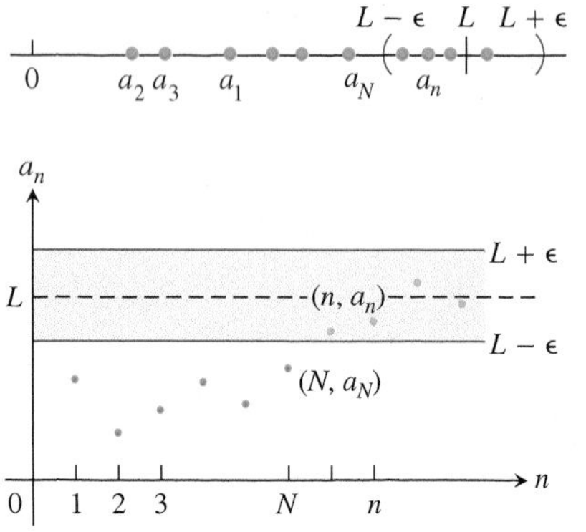

FIGURE 9.2 In the representation of a sequence as points in the plane, $a_n \to L$ if $y = L$ is a horizontal asymptote of the sequence of points $\{(n, a_n)\}$. In this figure, all the a_n's after a_N lie within ϵ of L.

DEFINITIONS The sequence $\{a_n\}$ **converges** to the number L if for every positive number ϵ there corresponds an integer N such that for all n,

$$n > N \qquad \Rightarrow \qquad |a_n - L| < \epsilon.$$

If no such number L exists, we say that $\{a_n\}$ **diverges**.

If $\{a_n\}$ converges to L, we write $\lim_{n\to\infty} a_n = L$, or simply $a_n \to L$, and call L the **limit** of the sequence (Figure 9.2).

The definition is very similar to the definition of the limit of a function $f(x)$ as x tends to ∞ ($\lim_{x\to\infty} f(x)$ in Section 2.6). We will exploit this connection to calculate limits of sequences.

HISTORICAL BIOGRAPHY

Nicole Oresme
(ca. 1320–1382)

EXAMPLE 1 Show that

(a) $\lim\limits_{n\to\infty} \frac{1}{n} = 0$ **(b)** $\lim\limits_{n\to\infty} k = k$ (any constant k)

Solution

(a) Let $\epsilon > 0$ be given. We must show that there exists an integer N such that for all n,

$$n > N \qquad \Rightarrow \qquad \left|\frac{1}{n} - 0\right| < \epsilon.$$

This implication will hold if $(1/n) < \epsilon$ or $n > 1/\epsilon$. If N is any integer greater than $1/\epsilon$, the implication will hold for all $n > N$. This proves that $\lim_{n\to\infty}(1/n) = 0$.

(b) Let $\epsilon > 0$ be given. We must show that there exists an integer N such that for all n,

$$n > N \qquad \Rightarrow \qquad |k - k| < \epsilon.$$

Since $k - k = 0$, we can use any positive integer for N and the implication will hold. This proves that $\lim_{n\to\infty} k = k$ for any constant k. ■

EXAMPLE 2 Show that the sequence $\{1, -1, 1, -1, 1, -1, \ldots, (-1)^{n+1}, \ldots\}$ diverges.

Solution Suppose the sequence converges to some number L. By choosing $\epsilon = 1/2$ in the definition of the limit, all terms a_n of the sequence with index n larger than some N must lie within $\epsilon = 1/2$ of L. Since the number 1 appears repeatedly as every other term of the sequence, we must have that the number 1 lies within the distance $\epsilon = 1/2$ of L.

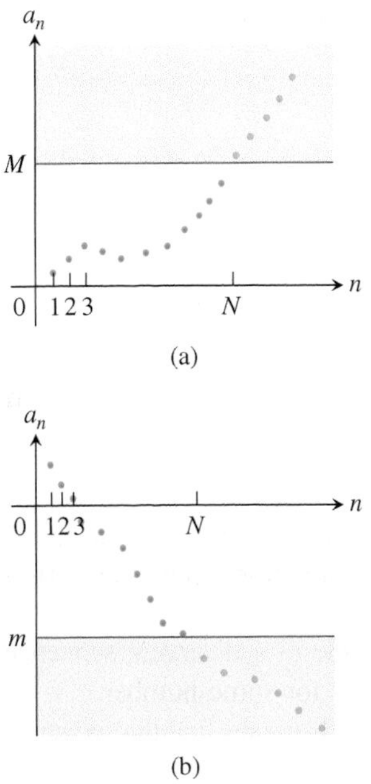

FIGURE 9.3 (a) The sequence diverges to ∞ because no matter what number M is chosen, the terms of the sequence after some index N all lie in the yellow band above M. (b) The sequence diverges to $-\infty$ because all terms after some index N lie below any chosen number m.

It follows that $|L - 1| < 1/2$, or equivalently, $1/2 < L < 3/2$. Likewise, the number -1 appears repeatedly in the sequence with arbitrarily high index. So we must also have that $|L - (-1)| < 1/2$, or equivalently, $-3/2 < L < -1/2$. But the number L cannot lie in both of the intervals $(1/2, 3/2)$ and $(-3/2, -1/2)$ because they have no overlap. Therefore, no such limit L exists and so the sequence diverges.

Note that the same argument works for any positive number ϵ smaller than 1, not just $1/2$. ∎

The sequence $\{\sqrt{n}\}$ also diverges, but for a different reason. As n increases, its terms become larger than any fixed number. We describe the behavior of this sequence by writing

$$\lim_{n\to\infty} \sqrt{n} = \infty.$$

In writing infinity as the limit of a sequence, we are not saying that the differences between the terms a_n and ∞ become small as n increases. Nor are we asserting that there is some number infinity that the sequence approaches. We are merely using a notation that captures the idea that a_n eventually gets and stays larger than any fixed number as n gets large (see Figure 9.3a). The terms of a sequence might also decrease to negative infinity, as in Figure 9.3b.

DEFINITION The sequence $\{a_n\}$ **diverges to infinity** if for every number M there is an integer N such that for all n larger than N, $a_n > M$. If this condition holds we write

$$\lim_{n\to\infty} a_n = \infty \qquad \text{or} \qquad a_n \to \infty.$$

Similarly, if for every number m there is an integer N such that for all $n > N$ we have $a_n < m$, then we say $\{a_n\}$ **diverges to negative infinity** and write

$$\lim_{n\to\infty} a_n = -\infty \qquad \text{or} \qquad a_n \to -\infty.$$

A sequence may diverge without diverging to infinity or negative infinity, as we saw in Example 2. The sequences $\{1, -2, 3, -4, 5, -6, 7, -8, \dots\}$ and $\{1, 0, 2, 0, 3, 0, \dots\}$ are also examples of such divergence.The convergence or divergence of a sequence is not affected by the values of any number of its initial terms (whether we omit or change the first 10, 1000, or even the first million terms does not matter). From Figure 9.2, we can see that only the part of the sequence that remains after discarding some initial number of terms determines whether the sequence has a limit and the value of that limit when it does exist.

Calculating Limits of Sequences

Since sequences are functions with domain restricted to the positive integers, it is not surprising that the theorems on limits of functions given in Chapter 2 have versions for sequences.

THEOREM 1 Let $\{a_n\}$ and $\{b_n\}$ be sequences of real numbers, and let A and B be real numbers. The following rules hold if $\lim_{n\to\infty} a_n = A$ and $\lim_{n\to\infty} b_n = B$.

1. *Sum Rule:* $\lim_{n\to\infty}(a_n + b_n) = A + B$
2. *Difference Rule:* $\lim_{n\to\infty}(a_n - b_n) = A - B$
3. *Constant Multiple Rule:* $\lim_{n\to\infty}(k \cdot b_n) = k \cdot B$ (any number k)
4. *Product Rule:* $\lim_{n\to\infty}(a_n \cdot b_n) = A \cdot B$
5. *Quotient Rule:* $\lim_{n\to\infty} \dfrac{a_n}{b_n} = \dfrac{A}{B}$ if $B \neq 0$

The proof is similar to that of Theorem 1 of Section 2.2 and is omitted.

EXAMPLE 3 By combining Theorem 1 with the limits of Example 1, we have:

(a) $\lim_{n\to\infty}\left(-\frac{1}{n}\right) = -1 \cdot \lim_{n\to\infty}\frac{1}{n} = -1 \cdot 0 = 0$ Constant Multiple Rule and Example 1a

(b) $\lim_{n\to\infty}\left(\frac{n-1}{n}\right) = \lim_{n\to\infty}\left(1-\frac{1}{n}\right) = \lim_{n\to\infty} 1 - \lim_{n\to\infty}\frac{1}{n} = 1 - 0 = 1$ Difference Rule and Example 1a

(c) $\lim_{n\to\infty}\frac{5}{n^2} = 5 \cdot \lim_{n\to\infty}\frac{1}{n} \cdot \lim_{n\to\infty}\frac{1}{n} = 5 \cdot 0 \cdot 0 = 0$ Product Rule

(d) $\lim_{n\to\infty}\frac{4-7n^6}{n^6+3} = \lim_{n\to\infty}\frac{(4/n^6)-7}{1+(3/n^6)} = \frac{0-7}{1+0} = -7.$ Sum and Quotient Rules ■

Be cautious in applying Theorem 1. It does not say, for example, that each of the sequences $\{a_n\}$ and $\{b_n\}$ have limits if their sum $\{a_n + b_n\}$ has a limit. For instance, $\{a_n\} = \{1, 2, 3, \ldots\}$ and $\{b_n\} = \{-1, -2, -3, \ldots\}$ both diverge, but their sum $\{a_n + b_n\} = \{0, 0, 0, \ldots\}$ clearly converges to 0.

One consequence of Theorem 1 is that every nonzero multiple of a divergent sequence $\{a_n\}$ diverges. For suppose, to the contrary, that $\{ca_n\}$ converges for some number $c \neq 0$. Then, by taking $k = 1/c$ in the Constant Multiple Rule in Theorem 1, we see that the sequence

$$\left\{\frac{1}{c} \cdot ca_n\right\} = \{a_n\}$$

converges. Thus, $\{ca_n\}$ cannot converge unless $\{a_n\}$ also converges. If $\{a_n\}$ does not converge, then $\{ca_n\}$ does not converge.

The next theorem is the sequence version of the Sandwich Theorem in Section 2.2. You are asked to prove the theorem in Exercise 109. (See Figure 9.4.)

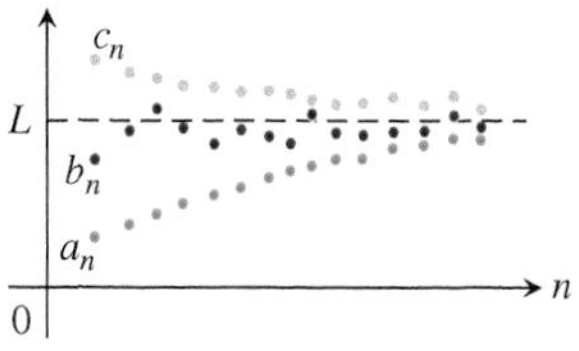

FIGURE 9.4 The terms of sequence $\{b_n\}$ are sandwiched between those of $\{a_n\}$ and $\{c_n\}$, forcing them to the same common limit L.

> **THEOREM 2—The Sandwich Theorem for Sequences** Let $\{a_n\}$, $\{b_n\}$, and $\{c_n\}$ be sequences of real numbers. If $a_n \leq b_n \leq c_n$ holds for all n beyond some index N, and if $\lim_{n\to\infty} a_n = \lim_{n\to\infty} c_n = L$, then $\lim_{n\to\infty} b_n = L$ also.

An immediate consequence of Theorem 2 is that, if $|b_n| \leq c_n$ and $c_n \to 0$, then $b_n \to 0$ because $-c_n \leq b_n \leq c_n$. We use this fact in the next example.

EXAMPLE 4 Since $1/n \to 0$, we know that

(a) $\frac{\cos n}{n} \to 0$ because $-\frac{1}{n} \leq \frac{\cos n}{n} \leq \frac{1}{n}$;

(b) $\frac{1}{2^n} \to 0$ because $0 \leq \frac{1}{2^n} \leq \frac{1}{n}$;

(c) $(-1)^n \frac{1}{n} \to 0$ because $-\frac{1}{n} \leq (-1)^n \frac{1}{n} \leq \frac{1}{n}$. ■

The application of Theorems 1 and 2 is broadened by a theorem stating that applying a continuous function to a convergent sequence produces a convergent sequence. We state the theorem, leaving the proof as an exercise (Exercise 110).

> **THEOREM 3—The Continuous Function Theorem for Sequences** Let $\{a_n\}$ be a sequence of real numbers. If $a_n \to L$ and if f is a function that is continuous at L and defined at all a_n, then $f(a_n) \to f(L)$.

EXAMPLE 5 Show that $\sqrt{(n + 1)/n} \rightarrow 1$.

Solution We know that $(n + 1)/n \rightarrow 1$. Taking $f(x) = \sqrt{x}$ and $L = 1$ in Theorem 3 gives $\sqrt{(n + 1)/n} \rightarrow \sqrt{1} = 1$. ■

EXAMPLE 6 The sequence $\{1/n\}$ converges to 0. By taking $a_n = 1/n$, $f(x) = 2^x$, and $L = 0$ in Theorem 3, we see that $2^{1/n} = f(1/n) \rightarrow f(L) = 2^0 = 1$. The sequence $\{2^{1/n}\}$ converges to 1 (Figure 9.5). ■

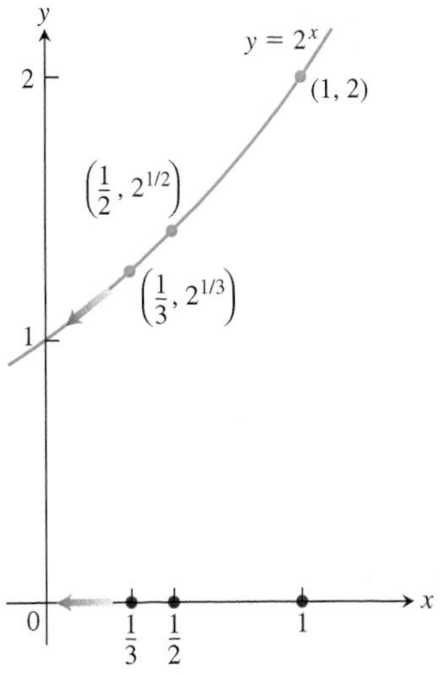

FIGURE 9.5 As $n \rightarrow \infty$, $1/n \rightarrow 0$ and $2^{1/n} \rightarrow 2^0$ (Example 6). The terms of $\{1/n\}$ are shown on the x-axis; the terms of $\{2^{1/n}\}$ are shown as the y-values on the graph of $f(x) = 2^x$.

Using L'Hôpital's Rule

The next theorem formalizes the connection between $\lim_{n\rightarrow\infty} a_n$ and $\lim_{x\rightarrow\infty} f(x)$. It enables us to use l'Hôpital's Rule to find the limits of some sequences.

THEOREM 4 Suppose that $f(x)$ is a function defined for all $x \geq n_0$ and that $\{a_n\}$ is a sequence of real numbers such that $a_n = f(n)$ for $n \geq n_0$. Then

$$\lim_{x\rightarrow\infty} f(x) = L \quad \Rightarrow \quad \lim_{n\rightarrow\infty} a_n = L.$$

Proof Suppose that $\lim_{x\rightarrow\infty} f(x) = L$. Then for each positive number ϵ there is a number M such that for all x,

$$x > M \quad \Rightarrow \quad |f(x) - L| < \epsilon.$$

Let N be an integer greater than M and greater than or equal to n_0. Then

$$n > N \quad \Rightarrow \quad a_n = f(n) \quad \text{and} \quad |a_n - L| = |f(n) - L| < \epsilon. \quad ■$$

EXAMPLE 7 Show that

$$\lim_{n\rightarrow\infty} \frac{\ln n}{n} = 0.$$

Solution The function $(\ln x)/x$ is defined for all $x \geq 1$ and agrees with the given sequence at positive integers. Therefore, by Theorem 4, $\lim_{n\rightarrow\infty}(\ln n)/n$ will equal $\lim_{x\rightarrow\infty}(\ln x)/x$ if the latter exists. A single application of l'Hôpital's Rule shows that

$$\lim_{x\rightarrow\infty} \frac{\ln x}{x} = \lim_{x\rightarrow\infty} \frac{1/x}{1} = \frac{0}{1} = 0.$$

We conclude that $\lim_{n\rightarrow\infty}(\ln n)/n = 0$. ■

When we use l'Hôpital's Rule to find the limit of a sequence, we often treat n as a continuous real variable and differentiate directly with respect to n. This saves us from having to rewrite the formula for a_n as we did in Example 7.

EXAMPLE 8 Does the sequence whose nth term is

$$a_n = \left(\frac{n + 1}{n - 1}\right)^n$$

converge? If so, find $\lim_{n\rightarrow\infty} a_n$.

Solution The limit leads to the indeterminate form 1^{∞}. We can apply l'Hôpital's Rule if we first change the form to $\infty \cdot 0$ by taking the natural logarithm of a_n:

$$\begin{aligned}\ln a_n &= \ln\left(\frac{n+1}{n-1}\right)^n \\ &= n\ln\left(\frac{n+1}{n-1}\right).\end{aligned}$$

Then,

$$\begin{aligned}\lim_{n\to\infty} \ln a_n &= \lim_{n\to\infty} n\ln\left(\frac{n+1}{n-1}\right) && \infty \cdot 0 \text{ form} \\ &= \lim_{n\to\infty} \frac{\ln\left(\frac{n+1}{n-1}\right)}{1/n} && \frac{0}{0} \text{ form} \\ &= \lim_{n\to\infty} \frac{-2/(n^2-1)}{-1/n^2} && \text{L'Hôpital's Rule: differentiate numerator and denominator.} \\ &= \lim_{n\to\infty} \frac{2n^2}{n^2-1} = 2.\end{aligned}$$

Since $\ln a_n \to 2$ and $f(x) = e^x$ is continuous, Theorem 4 tells us that

$$a_n = e^{\ln a_n} \to e^2.$$

The sequence $\{a_n\}$ converges to e^2. ■

Commonly Occurring Limits

The next theorem gives some limits that arise frequently.

THEOREM 5 The following six sequences converge to the limits listed below:

1. $\lim_{n\to\infty} \frac{\ln n}{n} = 0$
2. $\lim_{n\to\infty} \sqrt[n]{n} = 1$
3. $\lim_{n\to\infty} x^{1/n} = 1 \quad (x > 0)$
4. $\lim_{n\to\infty} x^n = 0 \quad (|x| < 1)$
5. $\lim_{n\to\infty} \left(1 + \frac{x}{n}\right)^n = e^x \quad (\text{any } x)$
6. $\lim_{n\to\infty} \frac{x^n}{n!} = 0 \quad (\text{any } x)$

In Formulas (3) through (6), x remains fixed as $n \to \infty$.

Proof The first limit was computed in Example 7. The next two can be proved by taking logarithms and applying Theorem 4 (Exercises 107 and 108). The remaining proofs are given in Appendix 6. ■

EXAMPLE 9 These are examples of the limits in Theorem 5.

(a) $\frac{\ln(n^2)}{n} = \frac{2\ln n}{n} \to 2 \cdot 0 = 0$ — Formula 1

(b) $\sqrt[n]{n^2} = n^{2/n} = (n^{1/n})^2 \to (1)^2 = 1$ — Formula 2

(c) $\sqrt[n]{3n} = 3^{1/n}(n^{1/n}) \to 1 \cdot 1 = 1$ — Formula 3 with $x = 3$ and Formula 2

(d) $\left(-\frac{1}{2}\right)^n \to 0$ — Formula 4 with $x = -\frac{1}{2}$

Factorial Notation
The notation $n!$ ("n factorial") means the product $1 \cdot 2 \cdot 3 \cdots n$ of the integers from 1 to n. Notice that $(n + 1)! = (n + 1) \cdot n!$. Thus, $4! = 1 \cdot 2 \cdot 3 \cdot 4 = 24$ and $5! = 1 \cdot 2 \cdot 3 \cdot 4 \cdot 5 = 5 \cdot 4! = 120$. We define 0! to be 1. Factorials grow even faster than exponentials, as the table suggests. The values in the table are rounded.

n	e^n	$n!$
1	3	1
5	148	120
10	22,026	3,628,800
20	4.9×10^8	2.4×10^{18}

(e) $\left(\dfrac{n-2}{n}\right)^n = \left(1 + \dfrac{-2}{n}\right)^n \rightarrow e^{-2}$ Formula 5 with $x = -2$

(f) $\dfrac{100^n}{n!} \rightarrow 0$ Formula 6 with $x = 100$ ■

Recursive Definitions

So far, we have calculated each a_n directly from the value of n. But sequences are often defined **recursively** by giving

1. The value(s) of the initial term or terms, and
2. A rule, called a **recursion formula**, for calculating any later term from terms that precede it.

EXAMPLE 10

(a) The statements $a_1 = 1$ and $a_n = a_{n-1} + 1$ for $n > 1$ define the sequence $1, 2, 3, \ldots, n, \ldots$ of positive integers. With $a_1 = 1$, we have $a_2 = a_1 + 1 = 2$, $a_3 = a_2 + 1 = 3$, and so on.

(b) The statements $a_1 = 1$ and $a_n = n \cdot a_{n-1}$ for $n > 1$ define the sequence $1, 2, 6, 24, \ldots, n!, \ldots$ of factorials. With $a_1 = 1$, we have $a_2 = 2 \cdot a_1 = 2$, $a_3 = 3 \cdot a_2 = 6$, $a_4 = 4 \cdot a_3 = 24$, and so on.

(c) The statements $a_1 = 1$, $a_2 = 1$, and $a_{n+1} = a_n + a_{n-1}$ for $n > 2$ define the sequence $1, 1, 2, 3, 5, \ldots$ of **Fibonacci numbers**. With $a_1 = 1$ and $a_2 = 1$, we have $a_3 = 1 + 1 = 2$, $a_4 = 2 + 1 = 3$, $a_5 = 3 + 2 = 5$, and so on.

(d) As we can see by applying Newton's method (see Exercise 133), the statements $x_0 = 1$ and $x_{n+1} = x_n - [(\sin x_n - x_n^2)/(\cos x_n - 2x_n)]$ for $n > 0$ define a sequence that, when it converges, gives a solution to the equation $\sin x - x^2 = 0$. ■

Bounded Monotonic Sequences

Two concepts that play a key role in determining the convergence of a sequence are those of a *bounded* sequence and a *monotonic* sequence.

DEFINITIONS A sequence $\{a_n\}$ is **bounded from above** if there exists a number M such that $a_n \leq M$ for all n. The number M is an **upper bound** for $\{a_n\}$. If M is an upper bound for $\{a_n\}$ but no number less than M is an upper bound for $\{a_n\}$, then M is the **least upper bound** for $\{a_n\}$.

A sequence $\{a_n\}$ is **bounded from below** if there exists a number m such that $a_n \geq m$ for all n. The number m is a **lower bound** for $\{a_n\}$. If m is a lower bound for $\{a_n\}$ but no number greater than m is a lower bound for $\{a_n\}$, then m is the **greatest lower bound** for $\{a_n\}$.

If $\{a_n\}$ is bounded from above and below, the $\{a_n\}$ is **bounded**. If $\{a_n\}$ is not bounded, then we say that $\{a_n\}$ is an **unbounded** sequence.

EXAMPLE 11

(a) The sequence $1, 2, 3, \ldots, n, \ldots$ has no upper bound since it eventually surpasses every number M. However, it is bounded below by every real number less than or equal to 1. The number $m = 1$ is the greatest lower bound of the sequence.

(b) The sequence $\dfrac{1}{2}, \dfrac{2}{3}, \dfrac{3}{4}, \ldots, \dfrac{n}{n+1}, \ldots$ is bounded above by every real number greater than or equal to 1. The upper bound $M = 1$ is the least upper bound (Exercise 125). The sequence is also bounded below by every number less than or equal to $\frac{1}{2}$, which is its greatest lower bound. ■

Convergent sequences are bounded

If a sequence $\{a_n\}$ converges to the number L, then by definition there is a number N such that $|a_n - L| < 1$ if $n > N$. That is,

$$L - 1 < a_n < L + 1 \quad \text{for } n > N.$$

If M is a number larger than $L + 1$ and all of the finitely many numbers $a_1, a_2, \ldots, a_N$, then for every index n we have $a_n \le M$ so that $\{a_n\}$ is bounded from above. Similarly, if m is a number smaller than $L - 1$ and all of the numbers $a_1, a_2, \ldots, a_N$, then m is a lower bound of the sequence. Therefore, all convergent sequences are bounded.

Although it is true that every convergent sequence is bounded, there are bounded sequences that fail to converge. One example is the bounded sequence $\{(-1)^{n+1}\}$ discussed in Example 2. The problem here is that some bounded sequences bounce around in the band determined by any lower bound m and any upper bound M (Figure 9.6). An important type of sequence that does not behave that way is one for which each term is at least as large, or at least as small, as its predecessor.

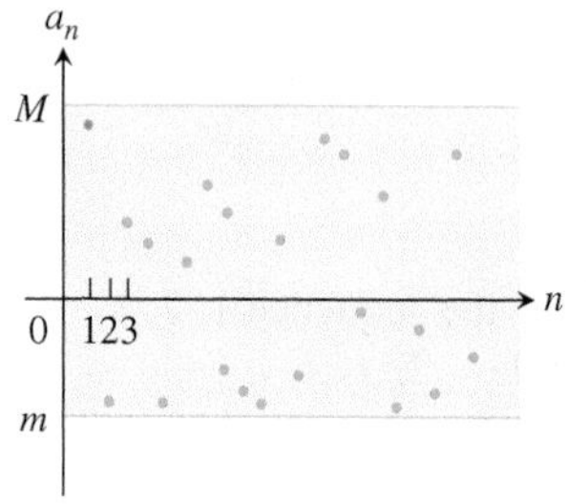

FIGURE 9.6 Some bounded sequences bounce around between their bounds and fail to converge to any limiting value.

DEFINITION A sequence $\{a_n\}$ is **nondecreasing** if $a_n \le a_{n+1}$ for all n. That is, $a_1 \le a_2 \le a_3 \le \ldots$. The sequence is **nonincreasing** if $a_n \ge a_{n+1}$ for all n. The sequence $\{a_n\}$ is **monotonic** if it is either nondecreasing or nonincreasing.

EXAMPLE 12

(a) The sequence $1, 2, 3, \ldots, n, \ldots$ is nondecreasing.

(b) The sequence $\frac{1}{2}, \frac{2}{3}, \frac{3}{4}, \ldots, \frac{n}{n+1}, \ldots$ is nondecreasing.

(c) The sequence $1, \frac{1}{2}, \frac{1}{4}, \frac{1}{8}, \ldots, \frac{1}{2^n}, \ldots$ is nonincreasing.

(d) The constant sequence $3, 3, 3, \ldots, 3, \ldots$ is both nondecreasing and nonincreasing.

(e) The sequence $1, -1, 1, -1, 1, -1, \ldots$ is not monotonic. ■

A nondecreasing sequence that is bounded from above always has a least upper bound. Likewise, a nonincreasing sequence bounded from below always has a greatest lower bound. These results are based on the *completeness property* of the real numbers, discussed in Appendix 7. We now prove that if L is the least upper bound of a nondecreasing sequence then the sequence converges to L, and that if L is the greatest lower bound of a nonincreasing sequence then the sequence converges to L.

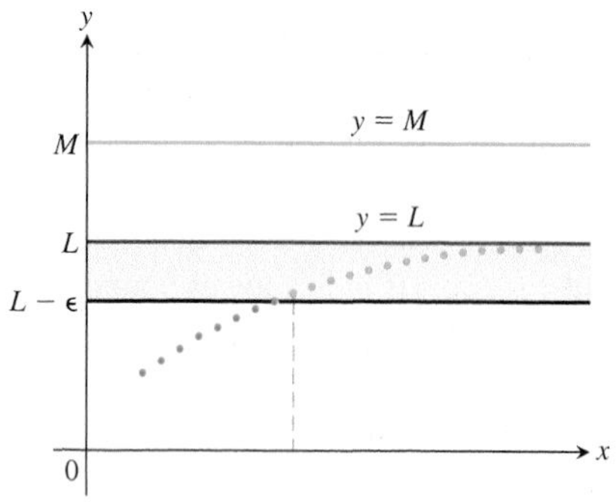

FIGURE 9.7 If the terms of a nondecreasing sequence have an upper bound M, they have a limit $L \le M$.

THEOREM 6—The Monotonic Sequence Theorem If a sequence $\{a_n\}$ is both bounded and monotonic, then the sequence converges.

Proof Suppose $\{a_n\}$ is nondecreasing, L is its least upper bound, and we plot the points $(1, a_1), (2, a_2), \ldots, (n, a_n), \ldots$ in the xy-plane. If M is an upper bound of the sequence, all these points will lie on or below the line $y = M$ (Figure 9.7). The line $y = L$ is the lowest such line. None of the points (n, a_n) lies above $y = L$, but some do lie above any lower line $y = L - \epsilon$, if ϵ is a positive number. The sequence converges to L because

(a) $a_n \le L$ for *all* values of n, and

(b) given any $\epsilon > 0$, there exists at least one integer N for which $a_N > L - \epsilon$.

The fact that $\{a_n\}$ is nondecreasing tells us further that

$$a_n \ge a_N > L - \epsilon \quad \text{for all } n \ge N.$$

Thus, *all* the numbers a_n beyond the Nth number lie within ϵ of L. This is precisely the condition for L to be the limit of the sequence $\{a_n\}$.

The proof for nonincreasing sequences bounded from below is similar. ■

It is important to realize that Theorem 6 does not say that convergent sequences are monotonic. The sequence $\{(-1)^{n+1}/n\}$ converges and is bounded, but it is not monotonic since it alternates between positive and negative values as it tends toward zero. What the theorem does say is that a nondecreasing sequence converges when it is bounded from above, but it diverges to infinity otherwise.

Exercises 9.1

Finding Terms of a Sequence

Each of Exercises 1–6 gives a formula for the nth term a_n of a sequence $\{a_n\}$. Find the values of a_1, a_2, a_3, and a_4.

1. $a_n = \dfrac{1-n}{n^2}$ **2.** $a_n = \dfrac{1}{n!}$

3. $a_n = \dfrac{(-1)^{n+1}}{2n-1}$ **4.** $a_n = 2 + (-1)^n$

5. $a_n = \dfrac{2^n}{2^{n+1}}$ **6.** $a_n = \dfrac{2^n - 1}{2^n}$

Each of Exercises 7–12 gives the first term or two of a sequence along with a recursion formula for the remaining terms. Write out the first ten terms of the sequence.

7. $a_1 = 1, \quad a_{n+1} = a_n + (1/2^n)$

8. $a_1 = 1, \quad a_{n+1} = a_n/(n+1)$

9. $a_1 = 2, \quad a_{n+1} = (-1)^{n+1}a_n/2$

10. $a_1 = -2, \quad a_{n+1} = na_n/(n+1)$

11. $a_1 = a_2 = 1, \quad a_{n+2} = a_{n+1} + a_n$

12. $a_1 = 2, \quad a_2 = -1, \quad a_{n+2} = a_{n+1}/a_n$

Finding a Sequence's Formula

In Exercises 13–26, find a formula for the nth term of the sequence.

13. The sequence $1, -1, 1, -1, 1, \ldots$ 1's with alternating signs

14. The sequence $-1, 1, -1, 1, -1, \ldots$ 1's with alternating signs

15. The sequence $1, -4, 9, -16, 25, \ldots$ Squares of the positive integers, with alternating signs

16. The sequence $1, -\frac{1}{4}, \frac{1}{9}, -\frac{1}{16}, \frac{1}{25}, \ldots$ Reciprocals of squares of the positive integers, with alternating signs

17. $\frac{1}{9}, \frac{2}{12}, \frac{2^2}{15}, \frac{2^3}{18}, \frac{2^4}{21}, \ldots$ Powers of 2 divided by multiples of 3

18. $-\frac{3}{2}, -\frac{1}{6}, \frac{1}{12}, \frac{3}{20}, \frac{5}{30}, \ldots$ Integers differing by 2 divided by products of consecutive integers

19. The sequence $0, 3, 8, 15, 24, \ldots$ Squares of the positive integers diminished by 1

20. The sequence $-3, -2, -1, 0, 1, \ldots$ Integers, beginning with -3

21. The sequence $1, 5, 9, 13, 17, \ldots$ Every other odd positive integer

22. The sequence $2, 6, 10, 14, 18, \ldots$ Every other even positive integer

23. $\frac{5}{1}, \frac{8}{2}, \frac{11}{6}, \frac{14}{24}, \frac{17}{120}, \ldots$ Integers differing by 3 divided by factorials

24. $\frac{1}{25}, \frac{8}{125}, \frac{27}{625}, \frac{64}{3125}, \frac{125}{15{,}625}, \ldots$ Cubes of positive integers divided by powers of 5

25. The sequence $1, 0, 1, 0, 1, \ldots$ Alternating 1's and 0's

26. The sequence $0, 1, 1, 2, 2, 3, 3, 4, \ldots$ Each positive integer repeated

Convergence and Divergence

Which of the sequences $\{a_n\}$ in Exercises 27–90 converge, and which diverge? Find the limit of each convergent sequence.

27. $a_n = 2 + (0.1)^n$ **28.** $a_n = \dfrac{n + (-1)^n}{n}$

29. $a_n = \dfrac{1-2n}{1+2n}$ **30.** $a_n = \dfrac{2n+1}{1-3\sqrt{n}}$

31. $a_n = \dfrac{1-5n^4}{n^4+8n^3}$ **32.** $a_n = \dfrac{n+3}{n^2+5n+6}$

33. $a_n = \dfrac{n^2-2n+1}{n-1}$ **34.** $a_n = \dfrac{1-n^3}{70-4n^2}$

35. $a_n = 1 + (-1)^n$ **36.** $a_n = (-1)^n\left(1 - \dfrac{1}{n}\right)$

37. $a_n = \left(\dfrac{n+1}{2n}\right)\left(1 - \dfrac{1}{n}\right)$ **38.** $a_n = \left(2 - \dfrac{1}{2^n}\right)\left(3 + \dfrac{1}{2^n}\right)$

39. $a_n = \dfrac{(-1)^{n+1}}{2n-1}$ **40.** $a_n = \left(-\dfrac{1}{2}\right)^n$

41. $a_n = \sqrt{\dfrac{2n}{n+1}}$ **42.** $a_n = \dfrac{1}{(0.9)^n}$

43. $a_n = \sin\left(\dfrac{\pi}{2} + \dfrac{1}{n}\right)$ **44.** $a_n = n\pi\cos(n\pi)$

45. $a_n = \dfrac{\sin n}{n}$ **46.** $a_n = \dfrac{\sin^2 n}{2^n}$

47. $a_n = \dfrac{n}{2^n}$ **48.** $a_n = \dfrac{3^n}{n^3}$

49. $a_n = \dfrac{\ln(n+1)}{\sqrt{n}}$ **50.** $a_n = \dfrac{\ln n}{\ln 2n}$

51. $a_n = 8^{1/n}$ **52.** $a_n = (0.03)^{1/n}$

53. $a_n = \left(1 + \dfrac{7}{n}\right)^n$ **54.** $a_n = \left(1 - \dfrac{1}{n}\right)^n$

55. $a_n = \sqrt[n]{10n}$ **56.** $a_n = \sqrt[n]{n^2}$

57. $a_n = \left(\dfrac{3}{n}\right)^{1/n}$ **58.** $a_n = (n+4)^{1/(n+4)}$

59. $a_n = \dfrac{\ln n}{n^{1/n}}$ **60.** $a_n = \ln n - \ln(n+1)$

61. $a_n = \sqrt[n]{4^n n}$

62. $a_n = \sqrt[n]{3^{2n+1}}$

63. $a_n = \dfrac{n!}{n^n}$ (*Hint:* Compare with $1/n$.)

64. $a_n = \dfrac{(-4)^n}{n!}$

65. $a_n = \dfrac{n!}{10^{6n}}$

66. $a_n = \dfrac{n!}{2^n \cdot 3^n}$

67. $a_n = \left(\dfrac{1}{n}\right)^{1/(\ln n)}$

68. $a_n = \ln\left(1 + \dfrac{1}{n}\right)^n$

69. $a_n = \left(\dfrac{3n + 1}{3n - 1}\right)^n$

70. $a_n = \left(\dfrac{n}{n + 1}\right)^n$

71. $a_n = \left(\dfrac{x^n}{2n + 1}\right)^{1/n}, \quad x > 0$

72. $a_n = \left(1 - \dfrac{1}{n^2}\right)^n$

73. $a_n = \dfrac{3^n \cdot 6^n}{2^{-n} \cdot n!}$

74. $a_n = \dfrac{(10/11)^n}{(9/10)^n + (11/12)^n}$

75. $a_n = \tanh n$

76. $a_n = \sinh(\ln n)$

77. $a_n = \dfrac{n^2}{2n - 1} \sin \dfrac{1}{n}$

78. $a_n = n\left(1 - \cos \dfrac{1}{n}\right)$

79. $a_n = \sqrt{n} \sin \dfrac{1}{\sqrt{n}}$

80. $a_n = (3^n + 5^n)^{1/n}$

81. $a_n = \tan^{-1} n$

82. $a_n = \dfrac{1}{\sqrt{n}} \tan^{-1} n$

83. $a_n = \left(\dfrac{1}{3}\right)^n + \dfrac{1}{\sqrt{2^n}}$

84. $a_n = \sqrt[n]{n^2 + n}$

85. $a_n = \dfrac{(\ln n)^{200}}{n}$

86. $a_n = \dfrac{(\ln n)^5}{\sqrt{n}}$

87. $a_n = n - \sqrt{n^2 - n}$

88. $a_n = \dfrac{1}{\sqrt{n^2 - 1} - \sqrt{n^2 + n}}$

89. $a_n = \dfrac{1}{n} \displaystyle\int_1^n \dfrac{1}{x}\, dx$

90. $a_n = \displaystyle\int_1^n \dfrac{1}{x^p}\, dx, \quad p > 1$

Recursively Defined Sequences

In Exercises 91–98, assume that each sequence converges and find its limit.

91. $a_1 = 2, \quad a_{n+1} = \dfrac{72}{1 + a_n}$

92. $a_1 = -1, \quad a_{n+1} = \dfrac{a_n + 6}{a_n + 2}$

93. $a_1 = -4, \quad a_{n+1} = \sqrt{8 + 2a_n}$

94. $a_1 = 0, \quad a_{n+1} = \sqrt{8 + 2a_n}$

95. $a_1 = 5, \quad a_{n+1} = \sqrt{5a_n}$

96. $a_1 = 3, \quad a_{n+1} = 12 - \sqrt{a_n}$

97. $2, 2 + \dfrac{1}{2}, 2 + \dfrac{1}{2 + \frac{1}{2}}, 2 + \dfrac{1}{2 + \frac{1}{2 + \frac{1}{2}}}, \ldots$

98. $\sqrt{1}, \sqrt{1 + \sqrt{1}}, \sqrt{1 + \sqrt{1 + \sqrt{1}}},$
$\sqrt{1 + \sqrt{1 + \sqrt{1 + \sqrt{1}}}}, \ldots$

Theory and Examples

99. The first term of a sequence is $x_1 = 1$. Each succeeding term is the sum of all those that come before it:

$$x_{n+1} = x_1 + x_2 + \cdots + x_n.$$

Write out enough early terms of the sequence to deduce a general formula for x_n that holds for $n \geq 2$.

100. A sequence of rational numbers is described as follows:

$$\frac{1}{1}, \frac{3}{2}, \frac{7}{5}, \frac{17}{12}, \ldots, \frac{a}{b}, \frac{a + 2b}{a + b}, \ldots.$$

Here the numerators form one sequence, the denominators form a second sequence, and their ratios form a third sequence. Let x_n and y_n be, respectively, the numerator and the denominator of the nth fraction $r_n = x_n/y_n$.

a. Verify that $x_1^2 - 2y_1^2 = -1, x_2^2 - 2y_2^2 = +1$ and, more generally, that if $a^2 - 2b^2 = -1$ or $+1$, then

$$(a + 2b)^2 - 2(a + b)^2 = +1 \quad \text{or} \quad -1,$$

respectively.

b. The fractions $r_n = x_n/y_n$ approach a limit as n increases. What is that limit? (*Hint:* Use part (a) to show that $r_n^2 - 2 = \pm(1/y_n)^2$ and that y_n is not less than n.)

101. Newton's method The following sequences come from the recursion formula for Newton's method,

$$x_{n+1} = x_n - \frac{f(x_n)}{f'(x_n)}.$$

Do the sequences converge? If so, to what value? In each case, begin by identifying the function f that generates the sequence.

a. $x_0 = 1, \quad x_{n+1} = x_n - \dfrac{x_n^2 - 2}{2x_n} = \dfrac{x_n}{2} + \dfrac{1}{x_n}$

b. $x_0 = 1, \quad x_{n+1} = x_n - \dfrac{\tan x_n - 1}{\sec^2 x_n}$

c. $x_0 = 1, \quad x_{n+1} = x_n - 1$

102. a. Suppose that $f(x)$ is differentiable for all x in $[0, 1]$ and that $f(0) = 0$. Define sequence $\{a_n\}$ by the rule $a_n = nf(1/n)$. Show that $\lim_{n\to\infty} a_n = f'(0)$. Use the result in part (a) to find the limits of the following sequences $\{a_n\}$.

b. $a_n = n \tan^{-1} \dfrac{1}{n}$

c. $a_n = n(e^{1/n} - 1)$

d. $a_n = n \ln\left(1 + \dfrac{2}{n}\right)$

103. Pythagorean triples A triple of positive integers a, b, and c is called a **Pythagorean triple** if $a^2 + b^2 = c^2$. Let a be an odd positive integer and let

$$b = \left\lfloor \frac{a^2}{2} \right\rfloor \quad \text{and} \quad c = \left\lceil \frac{a^2}{2} \right\rceil$$

be, respectively, the integer floor and ceiling for $a^2/2$.

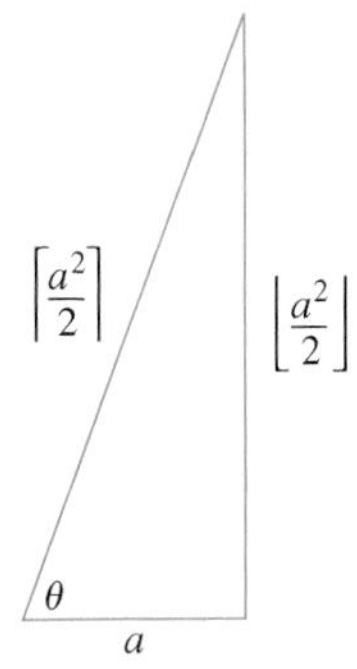

a. Show that $a^2 + b^2 = c^2$. (*Hint:* Let $a = 2n + 1$ and express b and c in terms of n.)

b. By direct calculation, or by appealing to the accompanying figure, find

$$\lim_{a \to \infty} \frac{\left\lfloor \frac{a^2}{2} \right\rfloor}{\left\lceil \frac{a^2}{2} \right\rceil}.$$

104. The nth root of n!

a. Show that $\lim_{n\to\infty} (2n\pi)^{1/(2n)} = 1$ and hence, using Stirling's approximation (Chapter 8, Additional Exercise 32a), that

$$\sqrt[n]{n!} \approx \frac{n}{e} \quad \text{for large values of } n.$$

T **b.** Test the approximation in part (a) for $n = 40, 50, 60, \ldots$, as far as your calculator will allow.

105. a. Assuming that $\lim_{n\to\infty} (1/n^c) = 0$ if c is any positive constant, show that

$$\lim_{n\to\infty} \frac{\ln n}{n^c} = 0$$

if c is any positive constant.

b. Prove that $\lim_{n\to\infty} (1/n^c) = 0$ if c is any positive constant. (*Hint:* If $\epsilon = 0.001$ and $c = 0.04$, how large should N be to ensure that $|1/n^c - 0| < \epsilon$ if $n > N$?)

106. The zipper theorem Prove the "zipper theorem" for sequences: If $\{a_n\}$ and $\{b_n\}$ both converge to L, then the sequence

$$a_1, b_1, a_2, b_2, \ldots, a_n, b_n, \ldots$$

converges to L.

107. Prove that $\lim_{n\to\infty} \sqrt[n]{n} = 1$.

108. Prove that $\lim_{n\to\infty} x^{1/n} = 1, (x > 0)$.

109. Prove Theorem 2. **110.** Prove Theorem 3.

In Exercises 111–114, determine if the sequence is monotonic and if it is bounded.

111. $a_n = \dfrac{3n + 1}{n + 1}$ **112.** $a_n = \dfrac{(2n + 3)!}{(n + 1)!}$

113. $a_n = \dfrac{2^n 3^n}{n!}$ **114.** $a_n = 2 - \dfrac{2}{n} - \dfrac{1}{2^n}$

Which of the sequences in Exercises 115–124 converge, and which diverge? Give reasons for your answers.

115. $a_n = 1 - \dfrac{1}{n}$ **116.** $a_n = n - \dfrac{1}{n}$

117. $a_n = \dfrac{2^n - 1}{2^n}$ **118.** $a_n = \dfrac{2^n - 1}{3^n}$

119. $a_n = ((-1)^n + 1)\left(\dfrac{n + 1}{n}\right)$

120. The first term of a sequence is $x_1 = \cos(1)$. The next terms are $x_2 = x_1$ or $\cos(2)$, whichever is larger; and $x_3 = x_2$ or $\cos(3)$, whichever is larger (farther to the right). In general,

$$x_{n+1} = \max\{x_n, \cos(n + 1)\}.$$

121. $a_n = \dfrac{1 + \sqrt{2n}}{\sqrt{n}}$ **122.** $a_n = \dfrac{n + 1}{n}$

123. $a_n = \dfrac{4^{n+1} + 3^n}{4^n}$

124. $a_1 = 1, \quad a_{n+1} = 2a_n - 3$

125. The sequence $\{n/(n + 1)\}$ has a least upper bound of 1 Show that if M is a number less than 1, then the terms of $\{n/(n + 1)\}$ eventually exceed M. That is, if $M < 1$ there is an integer N such that $n/(n + 1) > M$ whenever $n > N$. Since $n/(n + 1) < 1$ for every n, this proves that 1 is a least upper bound for $\{n/(n + 1)\}$.

126. Uniqueness of least upper bounds Show that if M_1 and M_2 are least upper bounds for the sequence $\{a_n\}$, then $M_1 = M_2$. That is, a sequence cannot have two different least upper bounds.

127. Is it true that a sequence $\{a_n\}$ of positive numbers must converge if it is bounded from above? Give reasons for your answer.

128. Prove that if $\{a_n\}$ is a convergent sequence, then to every positive number ϵ there corresponds an integer N such that for all m and n,

$$m > N \quad \text{and} \quad n > N \quad \Rightarrow \quad |a_m - a_n| < \epsilon.$$

129. Uniqueness of limits Prove that limits of sequences are unique. That is, show that if L_1 and L_2 are numbers such that $a_n \to L_1$ and $a_n \to L_2$, then $L_1 = L_2$.

130. Limits and subsequences If the terms of one sequence appear in another sequence in their given order, we call the first sequence a **subsequence** of the second. Prove that if two subsequences of a sequence $\{a_n\}$ have different limits $L_1 \neq L_2$, then $\{a_n\}$ diverges.

131. For a sequence $\{a_n\}$ the terms of even index are denoted by a_{2k} and the terms of odd index by a_{2k+1}. Prove that if $a_{2k} \to L$ and $a_{2k+1} \to L$, then $a_n \to L$.

132. Prove that a sequence $\{a_n\}$ converges to 0 if and only if the sequence of absolute values $\{|a_n|\}$ converges to 0.

133. Sequences generated by Newton's method Newton's method, applied to a differentiable function $f(x)$, begins with a starting value x_0 and constructs from it a sequence of numbers $\{x_n\}$ that under favorable circumstances converges to a zero of f. The recursion formula for the sequence is

$$x_{n+1} = x_n - \frac{f(x_n)}{f'(x_n)}.$$

a. Show that the recursion formula for $f(x) = x^2 - a, a > 0$, can be written as $x_{n+1} = (x_n + a/x_n)/2$.

T **b.** Starting with $x_0 = 1$ and $a = 3$, calculate successive terms of the sequence until the display begins to repeat. What number is being approximated? Explain.

T **134. A recursive definition of $\pi/2$** If you start with $x_1 = 1$ and define the subsequent terms of $\{x_n\}$ by the rule $x_n = x_{n-1} + \cos x_{n-1}$, you generate a sequence that converges rapidly to $\pi/2$. **(a)** Try it. **(b)** Use the accompanying figure to explain why the convergence is so rapid.

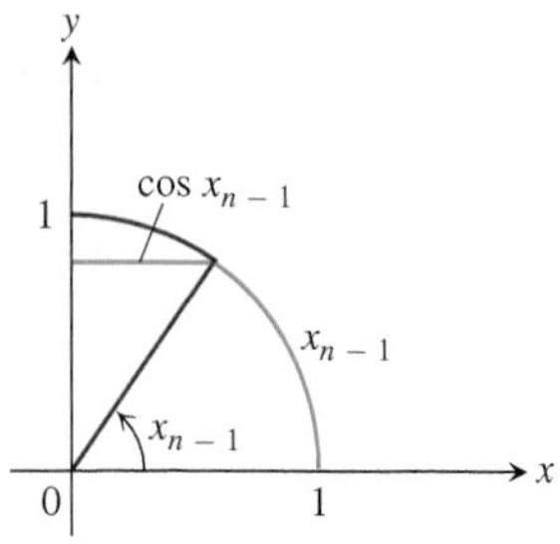

COMPUTER EXPLORATIONS

Use a CAS to perform the following steps for the sequences in Exercises 135–146.

a. Calculate and then plot the first 25 terms of the sequence. Does the sequence appear to be bounded from above or below? Does it appear to converge or diverge? If it does converge, what is the limit L?

b. If the sequence converges, find an integer N such that $|a_n - L| \le 0.01$ for $n \ge N$. How far in the sequence do you have to get for the terms to lie within 0.0001 of L?

135. $a_n = \sqrt[n]{n}$

136. $a_n = \left(1 + \frac{0.5}{n}\right)^n$

137. $a_1 = 1, \quad a_{n+1} = a_n + \frac{1}{5^n}$

138. $a_1 = 1, \quad a_{n+1} = a_n + (-2)^n$

139. $a_n = \sin n$

140. $a_n = n \sin \frac{1}{n}$

141. $a_n = \frac{\sin n}{n}$

142. $a_n = \frac{\ln n}{n}$

143. $a_n = (0.9999)^n$

144. $a_n = (123456)^{1/n}$

145. $a_n = \frac{8^n}{n!}$

146. $a_n = \frac{n^{41}}{19^n}$

9.2 Infinite Series

An *infinite series* is the sum of an infinite sequence of numbers

$$a_1 + a_2 + a_3 + \cdots + a_n + \cdots$$

The goal of this section is to understand the meaning of such an infinite sum and to develop methods to calculate it. Since there are infinitely many terms to add in an infinite series, we cannot just keep adding to see what comes out. Instead we look at the result of summing the first n terms of the sequence and stopping. The sum of the first n terms

$$s_n = a_1 + a_2 + a_3 + \cdots + a_n$$

is an ordinary finite sum and can be calculated by normal addition. It is called the *nth partial sum*. As n gets larger, we expect the partial sums to get closer and closer to a limiting value in the same sense that the terms of a sequence approach a limit, as discussed in Section 9.1.

For example, to assign meaning to an expression like

$$1 + \frac{1}{2} + \frac{1}{4} + \frac{1}{8} + \frac{1}{16} + \cdots$$

we add the terms one at a time from the beginning and look for a pattern in how these partial sums grow.

Partial sum		Value	Suggestive expression for partial sum
First:	$s_1 = 1$	1	$2 - 1$
Second:	$s_2 = 1 + \frac{1}{2}$	$\frac{3}{2}$	$2 - \frac{1}{2}$
Third:	$s_3 = 1 + \frac{1}{2} + \frac{1}{4}$	$\frac{7}{4}$	$2 - \frac{1}{4}$
⋮	⋮	⋮	⋮
nth:	$s_n = 1 + \frac{1}{2} + \frac{1}{4} + \cdots + \frac{1}{2^{n-1}}$	$\frac{2^n - 1}{2^{n-1}}$	$2 - \frac{1}{2^{n-1}}$

Indeed there is a pattern. The partial sums form a sequence whose nth term is

$$s_n = 2 - \frac{1}{2^{n-1}}.$$

This sequence of partial sums converges to 2 because $\lim_{n\to\infty}(1/2^{n-1}) = 0$. We say

$$\text{"the sum of the infinite series } 1 + \frac{1}{2} + \frac{1}{4} + \cdots + \frac{1}{2^{n-1}} + \cdots \text{ is 2."}$$

Is the sum of any finite number of terms in this series equal to 2? No. Can we actually add an infinite number of terms one by one? No. But we can still define their sum by defining it to be the limit of the sequence of partial sums as $n \to \infty$, in this case 2 (Figure 9.8). Our knowledge of sequences and limits enables us to break away from the confines of finite sums.

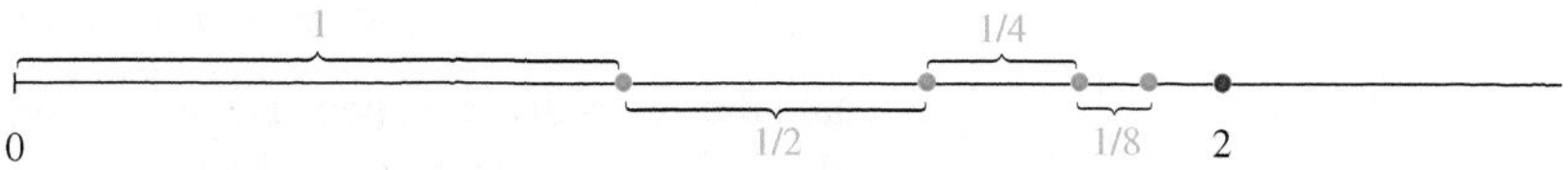

FIGURE 9.8 As the lengths $1, \frac{1}{2}, \frac{1}{4}, \frac{1}{8}, \ldots$ are added one by one, the sum approaches 2.

HISTORICAL BIOGRAPHY

Blaise Pascal (1623–1662)

DEFINITIONS Given a sequence of numbers $\{a_n\}$, an expression of the form

$$a_1 + a_2 + a_3 + \cdots + a_n + \cdots$$

is an **infinite series**. The number a_n is the ***n*th term** of the series. The sequence $\{s_n\}$ defined by

$$\begin{aligned} s_1 &= a_1 \\ s_2 &= a_1 + a_2 \\ &\vdots \\ s_n &= a_1 + a_2 + \cdots + a_n = \sum_{k=1}^{n} a_k \\ &\vdots \end{aligned}$$

is the **sequence of partial sums** of the series, the number s_n being the ***n*th partial sum**. If the sequence of partial sums converges to a limit L, we say that the series **converges** and that its **sum** is L. In this case, we also write

$$a_1 + a_2 + \cdots + a_n + \cdots = \sum_{n=1}^{\infty} a_n = L.$$

If the sequence of partial sums of the series does not converge, we say that the series **diverges**.

When we begin to study a given series $a_1 + a_2 + \cdots + a_n + \cdots$, we might not know whether it converges or diverges. In either case, it is convenient to use sigma notation to write the series as

$$\sum_{n=1}^{\infty} a_n, \qquad \sum_{k=1}^{\infty} a_k, \qquad \text{or} \qquad \sum a_n$$

A useful shorthand when summation from 1 to ∞ is understood

Geometric Series

Geometric series are series of the form

$$a + ar + ar^2 + \cdots + ar^{n-1} + \cdots = \sum_{n=1}^{\infty} ar^{n-1}$$

in which a and r are fixed real numbers and $a \neq 0$. The series can also be written as $\sum_{n=0}^{\infty} ar^n$. The **ratio** r can be positive, as in

$$1 + \frac{1}{2} + \frac{1}{4} + \cdots + \left(\frac{1}{2}\right)^{n-1} + \cdots, \qquad r = 1/2,\ a = 1$$

or negative, as in

$$1 - \frac{1}{3} + \frac{1}{9} - \cdots + \left(-\frac{1}{3}\right)^{n-1} + \cdots. \qquad r = -1/3,\ a = 1$$

If $r = 1$, the nth partial sum of the geometric series is

$$s_n = a + a(1) + a(1)^2 + \cdots + a(1)^{n-1} = na,$$

and the series diverges because $\lim_{n\to\infty} s_n = \pm\infty$, depending on the sign of a. If $r = -1$, the series diverges because the nth partial sums alternate between a and 0. If $|r| \neq 1$, we can determine the convergence or divergence of the series in the following way:

$$s_n = a + ar + ar^2 + \cdots + ar^{n-1}$$

$$rs_n = ar + ar^2 + \cdots + ar^{n-1} + ar^n \qquad \text{Multiply } s_n \text{ by } r.$$

$$s_n - rs_n = a - ar^n \qquad \text{Subtract } rs_n \text{ from } s_n. \text{ Most of the terms on the right cancel.}$$

$$s_n(1 - r) = a(1 - r^n) \qquad \text{Factor.}$$

$$s_n = \frac{a(1 - r^n)}{1 - r}, \quad (r \neq 1). \qquad \text{We can solve for } s_n \text{ if } r \neq 1.$$

If $|r| < 1$, then $r^n \to 0$ as $n \to \infty$ (as in Section 9.1) and $s_n \to a/(1 - r)$. If $|r| > 1$, then $|r^n| \to \infty$ and the series diverges.

If $|r| < 1$, the geometric series $a + ar + ar^2 + \cdots + ar^{n-1} + \cdots$ converges to $a/(1 - r)$:

$$\sum_{n=1}^{\infty} ar^{n-1} = \frac{a}{1 - r}, \qquad |r| < 1.$$

If $|r| \geq 1$, the series diverges.

We have determined when a geometric series converges or diverges, and to what value. Often we can determine that a series converges without knowing the value to which it converges, as we will see in the next several sections. The formula $a/(1 - r)$ for the sum of a geometric series applies *only* when the summation index begins with $n = 1$ in the expression $\sum_{n=1}^{\infty} ar^{n-1}$ (or with the index $n = 0$ if we write the series as $\sum_{n=0}^{\infty} ar^n$).

EXAMPLE 1 The geometric series with $a = 1/9$ and $r = 1/3$ is

$$\frac{1}{9} + \frac{1}{27} + \frac{1}{81} + \cdots = \sum_{n=1}^{\infty} \frac{1}{9}\left(\frac{1}{3}\right)^{n-1} = \frac{1/9}{1 - (1/3)} = \frac{1}{6}.$$ ■

EXAMPLE 2 The series

$$\sum_{n=0}^{\infty} \frac{(-1)^n 5}{4^n} = 5 - \frac{5}{4} + \frac{5}{16} - \frac{5}{64} + \cdots$$

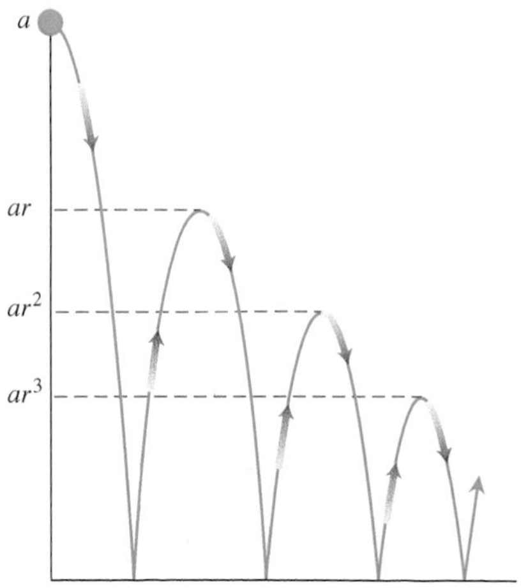

(a)

(b)

FIGURE 9.9 (a) Example 3 shows how to use a geometric series to calculate the total vertical distance traveled by a bouncing ball if the height of each rebound is reduced by the factor r. (b) A stroboscopic photo of a bouncing ball.

is a geometric series with $a = 5$ and $r = -1/4$. It converges to

$$\frac{a}{1-r} = \frac{5}{1+(1/4)} = 4.$$

EXAMPLE 3 You drop a ball from a meters above a flat surface. Each time the ball hits the surface after falling a distance h, it rebounds a distance rh, where r is positive but less than 1. Find the total distance the ball travels up and down (Figure 9.9).

Solution The total distance is

$$s = a + \underbrace{2ar + 2ar^2 + 2ar^3 + \cdots}_{\text{This sum is } 2ar/(1-r).} = a + \frac{2ar}{1-r} = a\frac{1+r}{1-r}.$$

If $a = 6$ m and $r = 2/3$, for instance, the distance is

$$s = 6\frac{1+(2/3)}{1-(2/3)} = 6\left(\frac{5/3}{1/3}\right) = 30 \text{ m}.$$

EXAMPLE 4 Express the repeating decimal 5.232323 . . . as the ratio of two integers.

Solution From the definition of a decimal number, we get a geometric series

$$5.232323\ldots = 5 + \frac{23}{100} + \frac{23}{(100)^2} + \frac{23}{(100)^3} + \cdots$$

$$= 5 + \frac{23}{100}\underbrace{\left(1 + \frac{1}{100} + \left(\frac{1}{100}\right)^2 + \cdots\right)}_{1/(1-0.01)} \qquad \begin{matrix} a = 1, \\ r = 1/100 \end{matrix}$$

$$= 5 + \frac{23}{100}\left(\frac{1}{0.99}\right) = 5 + \frac{23}{99} = \frac{518}{99}$$

Unfortunately, formulas like the one for the sum of a convergent geometric series are rare and we usually have to settle for an estimate of a series' sum (more about this later). The next example, however, is another case in which we can find the sum exactly.

EXAMPLE 5 Find the sum of the "telescoping" series $\displaystyle\sum_{n=1}^{\infty} \frac{1}{n(n+1)}$.

Solution We look for a pattern in the sequence of partial sums that might lead to a formula for s_k. The key observation is the partial fraction decomposition

$$\frac{1}{n(n+1)} = \frac{1}{n} - \frac{1}{n+1},$$

so

$$\sum_{n=1}^{k} \frac{1}{n(n+1)} = \sum_{n=1}^{k} \left(\frac{1}{n} - \frac{1}{n+1}\right)$$

and

$$s_k = \left(\frac{1}{1} - \frac{1}{2}\right) + \left(\frac{1}{2} - \frac{1}{3}\right) + \left(\frac{1}{3} - \frac{1}{4}\right) + \cdots + \left(\frac{1}{k} - \frac{1}{k+1}\right).$$

Removing parentheses and canceling adjacent terms of opposite sign collapses the sum to

$$s_k = 1 - \frac{1}{k+1}.$$

We now see that $s_k \to 1$ as $k \to \infty$. The series converges, and its sum is 1:

$$\sum_{n=1}^{\infty} \frac{1}{n(n+1)} = 1.$$

The *n*th-Term Test for a Divergent Series

One reason that a series may fail to converge is that its terms don't become small.

EXAMPLE 6 The series

$$\sum_{n=1}^{\infty} \frac{n+1}{n} = \frac{2}{1} + \frac{3}{2} + \frac{4}{3} + \cdots + \frac{n+1}{n} + \cdots$$

diverges because the partial sums eventually outgrow every preassigned number. Each term is greater than 1, so the sum of n terms is greater than n. ■

Notice that $\lim_{n\to\infty} a_n$ must equal zero if the series $\sum_{n=1}^{\infty} a_n$ converges. To see why, let S represent the series' sum and $s_n = a_1 + a_2 + \cdots + a_n$ the nth partial sum. When n is large, both s_n and s_{n-1} are close to S, so their difference, a_n, is close to zero. More formally,

$$a_n = s_n - s_{n-1} \quad\rightarrow\quad S - S = 0.$$ Difference Rule for sequences

This establishes the following theorem.

Caution
Theorem 7 *does not say* that $\sum_{n=1}^{\infty} a_n$ converges if $a_n \to 0$. It is possible for a series to diverge when $a_n \to 0$.

THEOREM 7 If $\sum_{n=1}^{\infty} a_n$ converges, then $a_n \to 0$.

Theorem 7 leads to a test for detecting the kind of divergence that occurred in Example 6.

The *n*th-Term Test for Divergence
$\sum_{n=1}^{\infty} a_n$ diverges if $\lim_{n\to\infty} a_n$ fails to exist or is different from zero.

EXAMPLE 7 The following are all examples of divergent series.

(a) $\sum_{n=1}^{\infty} n^2$ diverges because $n^2 \to \infty$.

(b) $\sum_{n=1}^{\infty} \frac{n+1}{n}$ diverges because $\frac{n+1}{n} \to 1$. $\lim_{n\to\infty} a_n \neq 0$

(c) $\sum_{n=1}^{\infty} (-1)^{n+1}$ diverges because $\lim_{n\to\infty}(-1)^{n+1}$ does not exist.

(d) $\sum_{n=1}^{\infty} \frac{-n}{2n+5}$ diverges because $\lim_{n\to\infty} \frac{-n}{2n+5} = -\frac{1}{2} \neq 0$. ■

EXAMPLE 8 The series

$$1 + \underbrace{\frac{1}{2} + \frac{1}{2}}_{2\text{ terms}} + \underbrace{\frac{1}{4} + \frac{1}{4} + \frac{1}{4} + \frac{1}{4}}_{4\text{ terms}} + \cdots + \underbrace{\frac{1}{2^n} + \frac{1}{2^n} + \cdots + \frac{1}{2^n}}_{2^n\text{ terms}} + \cdots$$

diverges because the terms can be grouped into infinitely many clusters each of which adds to 1, so the partial sums increase without bound. However, the terms of the series form a sequence that converges to 0. Example 1 of Section 9.3 shows that the harmonic series also behaves in this manner. ■

Combining Series

Whenever we have two convergent series, we can add them term by term, subtract them term by term, or multiply them by constants to make new convergent series.

THEOREM 8 If $\sum a_n = A$ and $\sum b_n = B$ are convergent series, then

1. *Sum Rule:* $\sum(a_n + b_n) = \sum a_n + \sum b_n = A + B$
2. *Difference Rule:* $\sum(a_n - b_n) = \sum a_n - \sum b_n = A - B$
3. *Constant Multiple Rule:* $\sum ka_n = k\sum a_n = kA$ (any number k).

Proof The three rules for series follow from the analogous rules for sequences in Theorem 1, Section 9.1. To prove the Sum Rule for series, let

$$A_n = a_1 + a_2 + \cdots + a_n, \quad B_n = b_1 + b_2 + \cdots + b_n.$$

Then the partial sums of $\sum(a_n + b_n)$ are

$$\begin{aligned} s_n &= (a_1 + b_1) + (a_2 + b_2) + \cdots + (a_n + b_n) \\ &= (a_1 + \cdots + a_n) + (b_1 + \cdots + b_n) \\ &= A_n + B_n. \end{aligned}$$

Since $A_n \to A$ and $B_n \to B$, we have $s_n \to A + B$ by the Sum Rule for sequences. The proof of the Difference Rule is similar.

To prove the Constant Multiple Rule for series, observe that the partial sums of $\sum ka_n$ form the sequence

$$s_n = ka_1 + ka_2 + \cdots + ka_n = k(a_1 + a_2 + \cdots + a_n) = kA_n,$$

which converges to kA by the Constant Multiple Rule for sequences. ■

As corollaries of Theorem 8, we have the following results. We omit the proofs.

1. Every nonzero constant multiple of a divergent series diverges.
2. If $\sum a_n$ converges and $\sum b_n$ diverges, then $\sum(a_n + b_n)$ and $\sum(a_n - b_n)$ both diverge.

Caution Remember that $\sum(a_n + b_n)$ can converge when $\sum a_n$ and $\sum b_n$ both diverge. For example, $\sum a_n = 1 + 1 + 1 + \cdots$ and $\sum b_n = (-1) + (-1) + (-1) + \cdots$ diverge, whereas $\sum(a_n + b_n) = 0 + 0 + 0 + \cdots$ converges to 0.

EXAMPLE 9 Find the sums of the following series.

(a)
$$\begin{aligned} \sum_{n=1}^{\infty} \frac{3^{n-1} - 1}{6^{n-1}} &= \sum_{n=1}^{\infty} \left(\frac{1}{2^{n-1}} - \frac{1}{6^{n-1}}\right) \\ &= \sum_{n=1}^{\infty} \frac{1}{2^{n-1}} - \sum_{n=1}^{\infty} \frac{1}{6^{n-1}} && \text{Difference Rule} \\ &= \frac{1}{1 - (1/2)} - \frac{1}{1 - (1/6)} && \text{Geometric series with } a = 1 \text{ and } r = 1/2,\ 1/6 \\ &= 2 - \frac{6}{5} = \frac{4}{5} \end{aligned}$$

(b) $$\sum_{n=0}^{\infty} \frac{4}{2^n} = 4\sum_{n=0}^{\infty} \frac{1}{2^n} \qquad \text{Constant Multiple Rule}$$

$$= 4\left(\frac{1}{1 - (1/2)}\right) \qquad \text{Geometric series with } a = 1, r = 1/2$$

$$= 8$$ ∎

Adding or Deleting Terms

We can add a finite number of terms to a series or delete a finite number of terms without altering the series' convergence or divergence, although in the case of convergence this will usually change the sum. If $\sum_{n=1}^{\infty} a_n$ converges, then $\sum_{n=k}^{\infty} a_n$ converges for any $k > 1$ and

$$\sum_{n=1}^{\infty} a_n = a_1 + a_2 + \cdots + a_{k-1} + \sum_{n=k}^{\infty} a_n.$$

Conversely, if $\sum_{n=k}^{\infty} a_n$ converges for any $k > 1$, then $\sum_{n=1}^{\infty} a_n$ converges. Thus,

$$\sum_{n=1}^{\infty} \frac{1}{5^n} = \frac{1}{5} + \frac{1}{25} + \frac{1}{125} + \sum_{n=4}^{\infty} \frac{1}{5^n}$$

and

$$\sum_{n=4}^{\infty} \frac{1}{5^n} = \left(\sum_{n=1}^{\infty} \frac{1}{5^n}\right) - \frac{1}{5} - \frac{1}{25} - \frac{1}{125}.$$

The convergence or divergence of a series is not affected by its first few terms. Only the "tail" of the series, the part that remains when we sum beyond some finite number of initial terms, influences whether it converges or diverges.

HISTORICAL BIOGRAPHY

Richard Dedekind
(1831–1916)

Reindexing

As long as we preserve the order of its terms, we can reindex any series without altering its convergence. To raise the starting value of the index h units, replace the n in the formula for a_n by $n - h$:

$$\sum_{n=1}^{\infty} a_n = \sum_{n=1+h}^{\infty} a_{n-h} = a_1 + a_2 + a_3 + \cdots.$$

To lower the starting value of the index h units, replace the n in the formula for a_n by $n + h$:

$$\sum_{n=1}^{\infty} a_n = \sum_{n=1-h}^{\infty} a_{n+h} = a_1 + a_2 + a_3 + \cdots.$$

We saw this reindexing in starting a geometric series with the index $n = 0$ instead of the index $n = 1$, but we can use any other starting index value as well. We usually give preference to indexings that lead to simple expressions.

EXAMPLE 10 We can write the geometric series

$$\sum_{n=1}^{\infty} \frac{1}{2^{n-1}} = 1 + \frac{1}{2} + \frac{1}{4} + \cdots$$

as

$$\sum_{n=0}^{\infty} \frac{1}{2^n}, \qquad \sum_{n=5}^{\infty} \frac{1}{2^{n-5}}, \qquad \text{or even} \qquad \sum_{n=-4}^{\infty} \frac{1}{2^{n+4}}.$$

The partial sums remain the same no matter what indexing we choose. ∎

Exercises 9.2

Finding *n*th Partial Sums

In Exercises 1–6, find a formula for the *n*th partial sum of each series and use it to find the series' sum if the series converges.

1. $2 + \frac{2}{3} + \frac{2}{9} + \frac{2}{27} + \cdots + \frac{2}{3^{n-1}} + \cdots$

2. $\frac{9}{100} + \frac{9}{100^2} + \frac{9}{100^3} + \cdots + \frac{9}{100^n} + \cdots$

3. $1 - \frac{1}{2} + \frac{1}{4} - \frac{1}{8} + \cdots + (-1)^{n-1}\frac{1}{2^{n-1}} + \cdots$

4. $1 - 2 + 4 - 8 + \cdots + (-1)^{n-1}2^{n-1} + \cdots$

5. $\frac{1}{2 \cdot 3} + \frac{1}{3 \cdot 4} + \frac{1}{4 \cdot 5} + \cdots + \frac{1}{(n+1)(n+2)} + \cdots$

6. $\frac{5}{1 \cdot 2} + \frac{5}{2 \cdot 3} + \frac{5}{3 \cdot 4} + \cdots + \frac{5}{n(n+1)} + \cdots$

Series with Geometric Terms

In Exercises 7–14, write out the first eight terms of each series to show how the series starts. Then find the sum of the series or show that it diverges.

7. $\sum_{n=0}^{\infty} \frac{(-1)^n}{4^n}$

8. $\sum_{n=2}^{\infty} \frac{1}{4^n}$

9. $\sum_{n=1}^{\infty} \left(1 - \frac{7}{4^n}\right)$

10. $\sum_{n=0}^{\infty} (-1)^n \frac{5}{4^n}$

11. $\sum_{n=0}^{\infty} \left(\frac{5}{2^n} + \frac{1}{3^n}\right)$

12. $\sum_{n=0}^{\infty} \left(\frac{5}{2^n} - \frac{1}{3^n}\right)$

13. $\sum_{n=0}^{\infty} \left(\frac{1}{2^n} + \frac{(-1)^n}{5^n}\right)$

14. $\sum_{n=0}^{\infty} \left(\frac{2^{n+1}}{5^n}\right)$

In Exercises 15–18, determine if the geometric series converges or diverges. If a series converges, find its sum.

15. $1 + \left(\frac{2}{5}\right) + \left(\frac{2}{5}\right)^2 + \left(\frac{2}{5}\right)^3 + \left(\frac{2}{5}\right)^4 + \cdots$

16. $1 + (-3) + (-3)^2 + (-3)^3 + (-3)^4 + \cdots$

17. $\left(\frac{1}{8}\right) + \left(\frac{1}{8}\right)^2 + \left(\frac{1}{8}\right)^3 + \left(\frac{1}{8}\right)^4 + \left(\frac{1}{8}\right)^5 + \cdots$

18. $\left(\frac{-2}{3}\right)^2 + \left(\frac{-2}{3}\right)^3 + \left(\frac{-2}{3}\right)^4 + \left(\frac{-2}{3}\right)^5 + \left(\frac{-2}{3}\right)^6 + \cdots$

Repeating Decimals

Express each of the numbers in Exercises 19–26 as the ratio of two integers.

19. $0.\overline{23} = 0.23\ 23\ 23 \ldots$

20. $0.\overline{234} = 0.234\ 234\ 234 \ldots$

21. $0.\overline{7} = 0.7777 \ldots$

22. $0.\overline{d} = 0.dddd \ldots$, where d is a digit

23. $0.0\overline{6} = 0.06666 \ldots$

24. $1.\overline{414} = 1.414\ 414\ 414 \ldots$

25. $1.24\overline{123} = 1.24\ 123\ 123\ 123 \ldots$

26. $3.\overline{142857} = 3.142857\ 142857 \ldots$

Using the *n*th-Term Test

In Exercises 27–34, use the *n*th-Term Test for divergence to show that the series is divergent, or state that the test is inconclusive.

27. $\sum_{n=1}^{\infty} \frac{n}{n+10}$

28. $\sum_{n=1}^{\infty} \frac{n(n+1)}{(n+2)(n+3)}$

29. $\sum_{n=0}^{\infty} \frac{1}{n+4}$

30. $\sum_{n=1}^{\infty} \frac{n}{n^2+3}$

31. $\sum_{n=1}^{\infty} \cos\frac{1}{n}$

32. $\sum_{n=0}^{\infty} \frac{e^n}{e^n+n}$

33. $\sum_{n=1}^{\infty} \ln\frac{1}{n}$

34. $\sum_{n=0}^{\infty} \cos n\pi$

Telescoping Series

In Exercises 35–40, find a formula for the *n*th partial sum of the series and use it to determine if the series converges or diverges. If a series converges, find its sum.

35. $\sum_{n=1}^{\infty} \left(\frac{1}{n} - \frac{1}{n+1}\right)$

36. $\sum_{n=1}^{\infty} \left(\frac{3}{n^2} - \frac{3}{(n+1)^2}\right)$

37. $\sum_{n=1}^{\infty} \left(\ln\sqrt{n+1} - \ln\sqrt{n}\right)$

38. $\sum_{n=1}^{\infty} (\tan(n) - \tan(n-1))$

39. $\sum_{n=1}^{\infty} \left(\cos^{-1}\left(\frac{1}{n+1}\right) - \cos^{-1}\left(\frac{1}{n+2}\right)\right)$

40. $\sum_{n=1}^{\infty} \left(\sqrt{n+4} - \sqrt{n+3}\right)$

Find the sum of each series in Exercises 41–48.

41. $\sum_{n=1}^{\infty} \frac{4}{(4n-3)(4n+1)}$

42. $\sum_{n=1}^{\infty} \frac{6}{(2n-1)(2n+1)}$

43. $\sum_{n=1}^{\infty} \frac{40n}{(2n-1)^2(2n+1)^2}$

44. $\sum_{n=1}^{\infty} \frac{2n+1}{n^2(n+1)^2}$

45. $\sum_{n=1}^{\infty} \left(\frac{1}{\sqrt{n}} - \frac{1}{\sqrt{n+1}}\right)$

46. $\sum_{n=1}^{\infty} \left(\frac{1}{2^{1/n}} - \frac{1}{2^{1/(n+1)}}\right)$

47. $\sum_{n=1}^{\infty} \left(\frac{1}{\ln(n+2)} - \frac{1}{\ln(n+1)}\right)$

48. $\sum_{n=1}^{\infty} (\tan^{-1}(n) - \tan^{-1}(n+1))$

Convergence or Divergence

Which series in Exercises 49–68 converge, and which diverge? Give reasons for your answers. If a series converges, find its sum.

49. $\sum_{n=0}^{\infty} \left(\frac{1}{\sqrt{2}}\right)^n$

50. $\sum_{n=0}^{\infty} (\sqrt{2})^n$

51. $\sum_{n=1}^{\infty} (-1)^{n+1}\frac{3}{2^n}$

52. $\sum_{n=1}^{\infty} (-1)^{n+1}n$

53. $\sum_{n=0}^{\infty} \cos n\pi$

54. $\sum_{n=0}^{\infty} \frac{\cos n\pi}{5^n}$

55. $\sum_{n=0}^{\infty} e^{-2n}$

56. $\sum_{n=1}^{\infty} \ln \frac{1}{3^n}$

57. $\sum_{n=1}^{\infty} \frac{2}{10^n}$

58. $\sum_{n=0}^{\infty} \frac{1}{x^n}, \quad |x| > 1$

59. $\sum_{n=0}^{\infty} \frac{2^n - 1}{3^n}$

60. $\sum_{n=1}^{\infty} \left(1 - \frac{1}{n}\right)^n$

61. $\sum_{n=0}^{\infty} \frac{n!}{1000^n}$

62. $\sum_{n=1}^{\infty} \frac{n^n}{n!}$

63. $\sum_{n=1}^{\infty} \frac{2^n + 3^n}{4^n}$

64. $\sum_{n=1}^{\infty} \frac{2^n + 4^n}{3^n + 4^n}$

65. $\sum_{n=1}^{\infty} \ln\left(\frac{n}{n+1}\right)$

66. $\sum_{n=1}^{\infty} \ln\left(\frac{n}{2n+1}\right)$

67. $\sum_{n=0}^{\infty} \left(\frac{e}{\pi}\right)^n$

68. $\sum_{n=0}^{\infty} \frac{e^{n\pi}}{\pi^{ne}}$

Geometric Series with a Variable x

In each of the geometric series in Exercises 69–72, write out the first few terms of the series to find a and r, and find the sum of the series. Then express the inequality $|r| < 1$ in terms of x and find the values of x for which the inequality holds and the series converges.

69. $\sum_{n=0}^{\infty} (-1)^n x^n$

70. $\sum_{n=0}^{\infty} (-1)^n x^{2n}$

71. $\sum_{n=0}^{\infty} 3\left(\frac{x-1}{2}\right)^n$

72. $\sum_{n=0}^{\infty} \frac{(-1)^n}{2}\left(\frac{1}{3 + \sin x}\right)^n$

In Exercises 73–78, find the values of x for which the given geometric series converges. Also, find the sum of the series (as a function of x) for those values of x.

73. $\sum_{n=0}^{\infty} 2^n x^n$

74. $\sum_{n=0}^{\infty} (-1)^n x^{-2n}$

75. $\sum_{n=0}^{\infty} (-1)^n (x+1)^n$

76. $\sum_{n=0}^{\infty} \left(-\frac{1}{2}\right)^n (x-3)^n$

77. $\sum_{n=0}^{\infty} \sin^n x$

78. $\sum_{n=0}^{\infty} (\ln x)^n$

Theory and Examples

79. The series in Exercise 5 can also be written as

$$\sum_{n=1}^{\infty} \frac{1}{(n+1)(n+2)} \quad \text{and} \quad \sum_{n=-1}^{\infty} \frac{1}{(n+3)(n+4)}.$$

Write it as a sum beginning with **(a)** $n = -2$, **(b)** $n = 0$, **(c)** $n = 5$.

80. The series in Exercise 6 can also be written as

$$\sum_{n=1}^{\infty} \frac{5}{n(n+1)} \quad \text{and} \quad \sum_{n=0}^{\infty} \frac{5}{(n+1)(n+2)}.$$

Write it as a sum beginning with **(a)** $n = -1$, **(b)** $n = 3$, **(c)** $n = 20$.

81. Make up an infinite series of nonzero terms whose sum is

a. 1 **b.** -3 **c.** 0.

82. (*Continuation of Exercise 81.*) Can you make an infinite series of nonzero terms that converges to any number you want? Explain.

83. Show by example that $\sum(a_n/b_n)$ may diverge even though $\sum a_n$ and $\sum b_n$ converge and no b_n equals 0.

84. Find convergent geometric series $A = \sum a_n$ and $B = \sum b_n$ that illustrate the fact that $\sum a_n b_n$ may converge without being equal to AB.

85. Show by example that $\sum(a_n/b_n)$ may converge to something other than A/B even when $A = \sum a_n$, $B = \sum b_n \neq 0$, and no b_n equals 0.

86. If $\sum a_n$ converges and $a_n > 0$ for all n, can anything be said about $\sum(1/a_n)$? Give reasons for your answer.

87. What happens if you add a finite number of terms to a divergent series or delete a finite number of terms from a divergent series? Give reasons for your answer.

88. If $\sum a_n$ converges and $\sum b_n$ diverges, can anything be said about their term-by-term sum $\sum(a_n + b_n)$? Give reasons for your answer.

89. Make up a geometric series $\sum ar^{n-1}$ that converges to the number 5 if

a. $a = 2$ **b.** $a = 13/2$.

90. Find the value of b for which

$$1 + e^b + e^{2b} + e^{3b} + \cdots = 9.$$

91. For what values of r does the infinite series

$$1 + 2r + r^2 + 2r^3 + r^4 + 2r^5 + r^6 + \cdots$$

converge? Find the sum of the series when it converges.

92. Show that the error $(L - s_n)$ obtained by replacing a convergent geometric series with one of its partial sums s_n is $ar^n/(1 - r)$.

93. The accompanying figure shows the first five of a sequence of squares. The outermost square has an area of 4 m^2. Each of the other squares is obtained by joining the midpoints of the sides of the squares before it. Find the sum of the areas of all the squares.

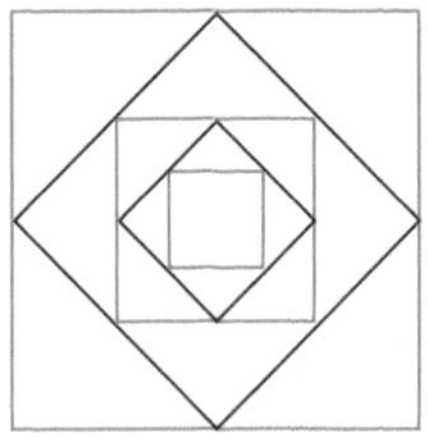

94. **Helga von Koch's snowflake curve** Helga von Koch's snowflake is a curve of infinite length that encloses a region of finite area. To see why this is so, suppose the curve is generated by starting with an equilateral triangle whose sides have length 1.

a. Find the length L_n of the nth curve C_n and show that $\lim_{n\to\infty} L_n = \infty$.

b. Find the area A_n of the region enclosed by C_n and show that $\lim_{n\to\infty} A_n = (8/5)A_1$.

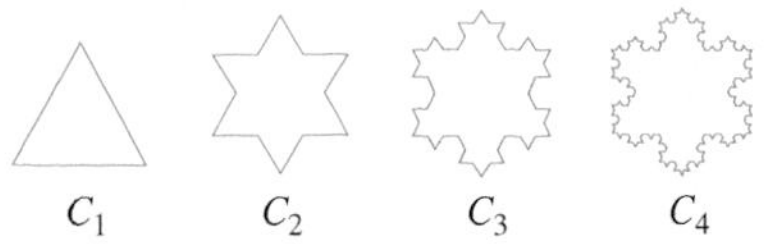

9.3 The Integral Test

Given a series, the most basic question we can ask is whether it converges or not. In this section and the next two, we study this question, starting with series that have nonnegative terms. Such a series converges if its sequence of partial sums is bounded. If we establish that a given series does converge, we generally do not have a formula available for its sum, so we investigate methods to approximate the sum instead.

Nondecreasing Partial Sums

Suppose that $\sum_{n=1}^{\infty} a_n$ is an infinite series with $a_n \geq 0$ for all n. Then each partial sum is greater than or equal to its predecessor because $s_{n+1} = s_n + a_n$:

$$s_1 \leq s_2 \leq s_3 \leq \cdots \leq s_n \leq s_{n+1} \leq \cdots.$$

Since the partial sums form a nondecreasing sequence, the Monotonic Sequence Theorem (Theorem 6, Section 9.1) gives the following result.

Corollary of Theorem 6 A series $\sum_{n=1}^{\infty} a_n$ of nonnegative terms converges if and only if its partial sums are bounded from above.

EXAMPLE 1 The series

$$\sum_{n=1}^{\infty} \frac{1}{n} = 1 + \frac{1}{2} + \frac{1}{3} + \cdots + \frac{1}{n} + \cdots$$

is called the **harmonic series**. The harmonic series is divergent, but this doesn't follow from the nth-Term Test. The nth term $1/n$ does go to zero, but the series still diverges. The reason it diverges is because there is no upper bound for its partial sums. To see why, group the terms of the series in the following way:

$$1 + \frac{1}{2} + \underbrace{\left(\frac{1}{3} + \frac{1}{4}\right)}_{> \frac{2}{4} = \frac{1}{2}} + \underbrace{\left(\frac{1}{5} + \frac{1}{6} + \frac{1}{7} + \frac{1}{8}\right)}_{> \frac{4}{8} = \frac{1}{2}} + \underbrace{\left(\frac{1}{9} + \frac{1}{10} + \cdots + \frac{1}{16}\right)}_{> \frac{8}{16} = \frac{1}{2}} + \cdots.$$

The sum of the first two terms is 1.5. The sum of the next two terms is $1/3 + 1/4$, which is greater than $1/4 + 1/4 = 1/2$. The sum of the next four terms is $1/5 + 1/6 + 1/7 + 1/8$, which is greater than $1/8 + 1/8 + 1/8 + 1/8 = 1/2$. The sum of the next eight terms is $1/9 + 1/10 + 1/11 + 1/12 + 1/13 + 1/14 + 1/15 + 1/16$, which is greater than $8/16 = 1/2$. The sum of the next 16 terms is greater than $16/32 = 1/2$, and so on. In general, the sum of 2^n terms ending with $1/2^{n+1}$ is greater than $2^n/2^{n+1} = 1/2$. The sequence of partial sums is not bounded from above: If $n = 2^k$, the partial sum s_n is greater than $k/2$. The harmonic series diverges. ■

The Integral Test

We now introduce the Integral Test with a series that is related to the harmonic series, but whose nth term is $1/n^2$ instead of $1/n$.

EXAMPLE 2 Does the following series converge?

$$\sum_{n=1}^{\infty} \frac{1}{n^2} = 1 + \frac{1}{4} + \frac{1}{9} + \frac{1}{16} + \cdots + \frac{1}{n^2} + \cdots$$

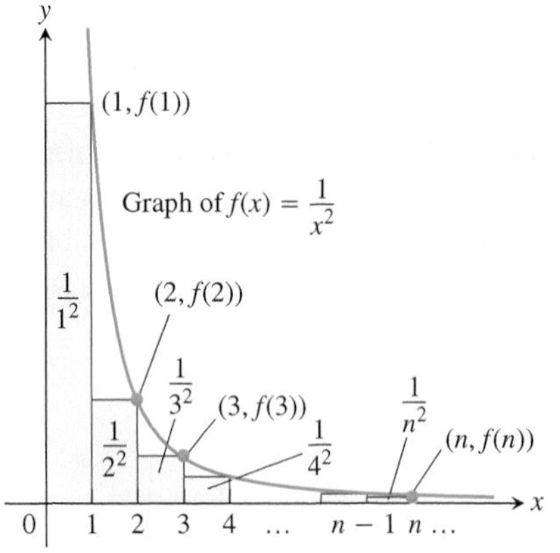

FIGURE 9.10 The sum of the areas of the rectangles under the graph of $f(x) = 1/x^2$ is less than the area under the graph (Example 2).

Solution We determine the convergence of $\sum_{n=1}^{\infty}(1/n^2)$ by comparing it with $\int_1^{\infty}(1/x^2)\,dx$. To carry out the comparison, we think of the terms of the series as values of the function $f(x) = 1/x^2$ and interpret these values as the areas of rectangles under the curve $y = 1/x^2$.

As Figure 9.10 shows,

$$
\begin{aligned}
s_n &= \frac{1}{1^2} + \frac{1}{2^2} + \frac{1}{3^2} + \cdots + \frac{1}{n^2} \\
&= f(1) + f(2) + f(3) + \cdots + f(n) \\
&< f(1) + \int_1^n \frac{1}{x^2}\,dx && \text{Rectangle areas sum to less than area under graph.} \\
&< 1 + \int_1^{\infty} \frac{1}{x^2}\,dx && \int_1^n (1/x^2)\,dx < \int_1^{\infty}(1/x^2)\,dx \\
&< 1 + 1 = 2. && \text{As in Section 8.7, Example 3, } \int_1^{\infty}(1/x^2)\,dx = 1.
\end{aligned}
$$

Thus the partial sums of $\sum_{n=1}^{\infty}(1/n^2)$ are bounded from above (by 2) and the series converges. The sum of the series is known to be $\pi^2/6 \approx 1.64493$. ■

Caution
The series and integral need not have the same value in the convergent case. As we noted in Example 2, $\sum_{n=1}^{\infty}(1/n^2) = \pi^2/6$ while $\int_1^{\infty}(1/x^2)\,dx = 1$.

THEOREM 9—The Integral Test Let $\{a_n\}$ be a sequence of positive terms. Suppose that $a_n = f(n)$, where f is a continuous, positive, decreasing function of x for all $x \geq N$ (N a positive integer). Then the series $\sum_{n=N}^{\infty} a_n$ and the integral $\int_N^{\infty} f(x)\,dx$ both converge or both diverge.

Proof We establish the test for the case $N = 1$. The proof for general N is similar.

We start with the assumption that f is a decreasing function with $f(n) = a_n$ for every n. This leads us to observe that the rectangles in Figure 9.11a, which have areas $a_1, a_2, \ldots, a_n$, collectively enclose more area than that under the curve $y = f(x)$ from $x = 1$ to $x = n + 1$. That is,

$$\int_1^{n+1} f(x)\,dx \leq a_1 + a_2 + \cdots + a_n.$$

In Figure 9.11b the rectangles have been faced to the left instead of to the right. If we momentarily disregard the first rectangle of area a_1, we see that

$$a_2 + a_3 + \cdots + a_n \leq \int_1^n f(x)\,dx.$$

If we include a_1, we have

$$a_1 + a_2 + \cdots + a_n \leq a_1 + \int_1^n f(x)\,dx.$$

Combining these results gives

$$\int_1^{n+1} f(x)\,dx \leq a_1 + a_2 + \cdots + a_n \leq a_1 + \int_1^n f(x)\,dx.$$

These inequalities hold for each n, and continue to hold as $n \to \infty$.

If $\int_1^{\infty} f(x)\,dx$ is finite, the right-hand inequality shows that $\sum a_n$ is finite. If $\int_1^{\infty} f(x)\,dx$ is infinite, the left-hand inequality shows that $\sum a_n$ is infinite. Hence the series and the integral are both finite or both infinite. ■

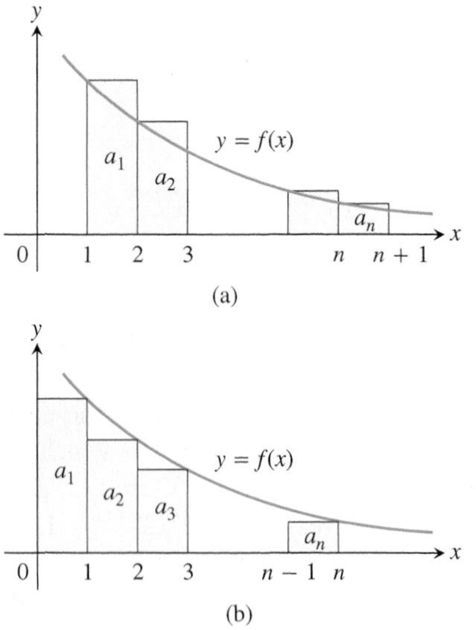

FIGURE 9.11 Subject to the conditions of the Integral Test, the series $\sum_{n=1}^{\infty} a_n$ and the integral $\int_1^{\infty} f(x)\,dx$ both converge or both diverge.

EXAMPLE 3 Show that the ***p*-series**

$$\sum_{n=1}^{\infty} \frac{1}{n^p} = \frac{1}{1^p} + \frac{1}{2^p} + \frac{1}{3^p} + \cdots + \frac{1}{n^p} + \cdots$$

(p a real constant) converges if $p > 1$, and diverges if $p \le 1$.

Solution If $p > 1$, then $f(x) = 1/x^p$ is a positive decreasing function of x. Since

$$\begin{aligned}\int_1^{\infty} \frac{1}{x^p}\,dx &= \int_1^{\infty} x^{-p}\,dx = \lim_{b\to\infty}\left[\frac{x^{-p+1}}{-p+1}\right]_1^b \\ &= \frac{1}{1-p}\lim_{b\to\infty}\left(\frac{1}{b^{p-1}} - 1\right) \\ &= \frac{1}{1-p}(0-1) = \frac{1}{p-1},\end{aligned}$$

$b^{p-1} \to \infty$ as $b \to \infty$ because $p - 1 > 0$.

the series converges by the Integral Test. We emphasize that the sum of the p-series is *not* $1/(p-1)$. The series converges, but we don't know the value it converges to.

The *p*-series $\sum_{n=1}^{\infty} \frac{1}{n^p}$ converges if $p > 1$, diverges if $p \le 1$.

If $p < 1$, then $1 - p > 0$ and

$$\int_1^{\infty} \frac{1}{x^p}\,dx = \frac{1}{1-p}\lim_{b\to\infty}(b^{1-p} - 1) = \infty.$$

The series diverges by the Integral Test.

If $p = 1$, we have the (divergent) harmonic series

$$1 + \frac{1}{2} + \frac{1}{3} + \cdots + \frac{1}{n} + \cdots.$$

We have convergence for $p > 1$ but divergence for all other values of p. ■

The p-series with $p = 1$ is the **harmonic series** (Example 1). The p-Series Test shows that the harmonic series is just *barely* divergent; if we increase p to 1.000000001, for instance, the series converges!

The slowness with which the partial sums of the harmonic series approach infinity is impressive. For instance, it takes more than 178 million terms of the harmonic series to move the partial sums beyond 20. (See also Exercise 43b.)

EXAMPLE 4 The series $\sum_{n=1}^{\infty}(1/(n^2+1))$ is not a p-series, but it converges by the Integral Test. The function $f(x) = 1/(x^2+1)$ is positive, continuous, and decreasing for $x \ge 1$, and

$$\begin{aligned}\int_1^{\infty} \frac{1}{x^2+1}\,dx &= \lim_{b\to\infty}\left[\arctan x\right]_1^b \\ &= \lim_{b\to\infty}[\arctan b - \arctan 1] \\ &= \frac{\pi}{2} - \frac{\pi}{4} = \frac{\pi}{4}.\end{aligned}$$

The series converges, but $\pi/4$ is *not* the sum of the series. ■

Error Estimation

For some convergent series, such as the geometric series or the telescoping series in Example 5 of Section 9.2, we can actually find the total sum of the series. That is, we can find the limiting value S of the sequence of partial sums. For most convergent series, however, we cannot easily find the total sum. Nevertheless, we can *estimate* the sum by adding the first n terms to get s_n, but then we need to know how far off s_n is from the total sum S.

Suppose that a series Σa_n is shown to be convergent by the Integral Test, and we want to estimate the size of the **remainder** R_n between the total sum S of the series and its nth partial sum s_n. That is, we wish to estimate

$$R_n = S - s_n = a_{n+1} + a_{n+2} + a_{n+3} + \cdots.$$

To get a lower bound for the remainder, we compare the sum of the areas of the rectangles with the area under the curve $y = f(x)$ for $x \geq n$ (see Figure 9.11a). We see that

$$R_n = a_{n+1} + a_{n+2} + a_{n+3} + \cdots \geq \int_{n+1}^{\infty} f(x)\, dx.$$

Similarly, from Figure 9.11b, we find an upper bound with

$$R_n = a_{n+1} + a_{n+2} + a_{n+3} + \cdots \leq \int_{n}^{\infty} f(x)\, dx.$$

These comparisons prove the following result, giving bounds on the size of the remainder.

Bounds for the Remainder in the Integral Test

Suppose $\{a_k\}$ is a sequence of positive terms with $a_k = f(k)$, where f is a continuous positive decreasing function of x for all $x \geq n$, and that Σa_n converges to S. Then the remainder $R_n = S - s_n$ satisfies the inequalities

$$\int_{n+1}^{\infty} f(x)\, dx \leq R_n \leq \int_{n}^{\infty} f(x)\, dx. \tag{1}$$

If we add the partial sum s_n to each side of the inequalities in (1), we get

$$s_n + \int_{n+1}^{\infty} f(x)\, dx \leq S \leq s_n + \int_{n}^{\infty} f(x)\, dx \tag{2}$$

since $s_n + R_n = S$. The inequalities in (2) are useful for estimating the error in approximating the sum of a series known to converge by the Integral Test. The error can be no larger than the length of the interval containing S, as given by (2).

EXAMPLE 5 Estimate the sum of the series $\Sigma(1/n^2)$ using the inequalities in (2) and $n = 10$.

Solution We have that

$$\int_{n}^{\infty} \frac{1}{x^2}\, dx = \lim_{b\to\infty} \left[-\frac{1}{x}\right]_n^b = \lim_{b\to\infty} \left(-\frac{1}{b} + \frac{1}{n}\right) = \frac{1}{n}.$$

Using this result with the inequalities in (2), we get

$$s_{10} + \frac{1}{11} \leq S \leq s_{10} + \frac{1}{10}.$$

Taking $s_{10} = 1 + (1/4) + (1/9) + (1/16) + \cdots + (1/100) \approx 1.54977$, these last inequalities give

$$1.64068 \leq S \leq 1.64997.$$

If we approximate the sum S by the midpoint of this interval, we find that

$$\sum_{n=1}^{\infty} \frac{1}{n^2} \approx 1.6453.$$

The error in this approximation is less than half the length of the interval, so the error is less than 0.005. ■

Exercises 9.3

Applying the Integral Test

Use the Integral Test to determine if the series in Exercises 1–10 converge or diverge. Be sure to check that the conditions of the Integral Test are satisfied.

1. $\sum_{n=1}^{\infty} \frac{1}{n^2}$

2. $\sum_{n=1}^{\infty} \frac{1}{n^{0.2}}$

3. $\sum_{n=1}^{\infty} \frac{1}{n^2 + 4}$

4. $\sum_{n=1}^{\infty} \frac{1}{n + 4}$

5. $\sum_{n=1}^{\infty} e^{-2n}$

6. $\sum_{n=2}^{\infty} \frac{1}{n(\ln n)^2}$

7. $\sum_{n=1}^{\infty} \frac{n}{n^2 + 4}$

8. $\sum_{n=2}^{\infty} \frac{\ln (n^2)}{n}$

9. $\sum_{n=1}^{\infty} \frac{n^2}{e^{n/3}}$

10. $\sum_{n=2}^{\infty} \frac{n - 4}{n^2 - 2n + 1}$

Determining Convergence or Divergence

Which of the series in Exercises 11–40 converge, and which diverge? Give reasons for your answers. (When you check an answer, remember that there may be more than one way to determine the series' convergence or divergence.)

11. $\sum_{n=1}^{\infty} \frac{1}{10^n}$

12. $\sum_{n=1}^{\infty} e^{-n}$

13. $\sum_{n=1}^{\infty} \frac{n}{n + 1}$

14. $\sum_{n=1}^{\infty} \frac{5}{n + 1}$

15. $\sum_{n=1}^{\infty} \frac{3}{\sqrt{n}}$

16. $\sum_{n=1}^{\infty} \frac{-2}{n\sqrt{n}}$

17. $\sum_{n=1}^{\infty} -\frac{1}{8^n}$

18. $\sum_{n=1}^{\infty} \frac{-8}{n}$

19. $\sum_{n=2}^{\infty} \frac{\ln n}{n}$

20. $\sum_{n=2}^{\infty} \frac{\ln n}{\sqrt{n}}$

21. $\sum_{n=1}^{\infty} \frac{2^n}{3^n}$

22. $\sum_{n=1}^{\infty} \frac{5^n}{4^n + 3}$

23. $\sum_{n=0}^{\infty} \frac{-2}{n + 1}$

24. $\sum_{n=1}^{\infty} \frac{1}{2n - 1}$

25. $\sum_{n=1}^{\infty} \frac{2^n}{n + 1}$

26. $\sum_{n=1}^{\infty} \frac{1}{\sqrt{n}\left(\sqrt{n} + 1\right)}$

27. $\sum_{n=2}^{\infty} \frac{\sqrt{n}}{\ln n}$

28. $\sum_{n=1}^{\infty} \left(1 + \frac{1}{n}\right)^n$

29. $\sum_{n=1}^{\infty} \frac{1}{(\ln 2)^n}$

30. $\sum_{n=1}^{\infty} \frac{1}{(\ln 3)^n}$

31. $\sum_{n=3}^{\infty} \frac{(1/n)}{(\ln n)\sqrt{\ln^2 n - 1}}$

32. $\sum_{n=1}^{\infty} \frac{1}{n(1 + \ln^2 n)}$

33. $\sum_{n=1}^{\infty} n \sin \frac{1}{n}$

34. $\sum_{n=1}^{\infty} n \tan \frac{1}{n}$

35. $\sum_{n=1}^{\infty} \frac{e^n}{1 + e^{2n}}$

36. $\sum_{n=1}^{\infty} \frac{2}{1 + e^n}$

37. $\sum_{n=1}^{\infty} \frac{8 \tan^{-1} n}{1 + n^2}$

38. $\sum_{n=1}^{\infty} \frac{n}{n^2 + 1}$

39. $\sum_{n=1}^{\infty} \operatorname{sech} n$

40. $\sum_{n=1}^{\infty} \operatorname{sech}^2 n$

Theory and Examples

For what values of a, if any, do the series in Exercises 41 and 42 converge?

41. $\sum_{n=1}^{\infty} \left(\frac{a}{n + 2} - \frac{1}{n + 4}\right)$

42. $\sum_{n=3}^{\infty} \left(\frac{1}{n - 1} - \frac{2a}{n + 1}\right)$

43. **a.** Draw illustrations like those in Figures 9.7 and 9.8 to show that the partial sums of the harmonic series satisfy the inequalities

$$\ln (n + 1) = \int_1^{n+1} \frac{1}{x}\, dx \le 1 + \frac{1}{2} + \cdots + \frac{1}{n}$$
$$\le 1 + \int_1^n \frac{1}{x}\, dx = 1 + \ln n.$$

T **b.** There is absolutely no empirical evidence for the divergence of the harmonic series even though we know it diverges. The partial sums just grow too slowly. To see what we mean, suppose you had started with $s_1 = 1$ the day the universe was formed, 13 billion years ago, and added a new term every *second*. About how large would the partial sum s_n be today, assuming a 365-day year?

44. Are there any values of x for which $\sum_{n=1}^{\infty} (1/nx)$ converges? Give reasons for your answer.

45. Is it true that if $\sum_{n=1}^{\infty} a_n$ is a divergent series of positive numbers, then there is also a divergent series $\sum_{n=1}^{\infty} b_n$ of positive numbers with $b_n < a_n$ for every n? Is there a "smallest" divergent series of positive numbers? Give reasons for your answers.

46. (*Continuation of Exercise 45.*) Is there a "largest" convergent series of positive numbers? Explain.

47. **$\sum_{n=1}^{\infty} \left(1/\sqrt{n+1}\right)$ diverges**

a. Use the accompanying graph to show that the partial sum

$s_{50} = \sum_{n=1}^{50} \left(1/\sqrt{n + 1}\right)$ satisfies

$$\int_1^{51} \frac{1}{\sqrt{x + 1}}\, dx < s_{50} < \int_0^{50} \frac{1}{\sqrt{x + 1}}\, dx.$$

Conclude that $11.5 < s_{50} < 12.3$.

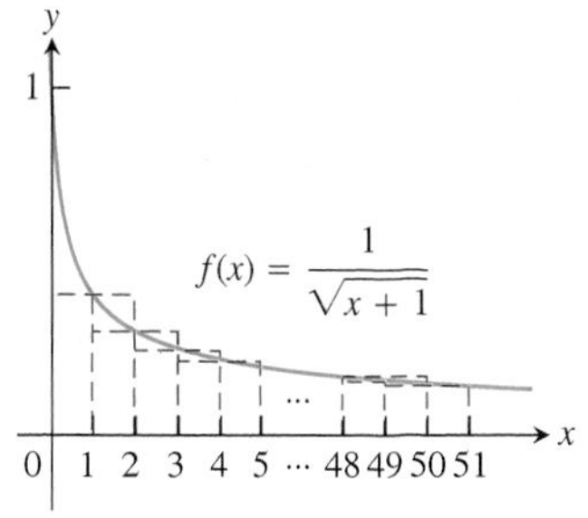

b. What should n be in order that the partial sum

$s_n = \sum_{i=1}^{n} \left(1/\sqrt{i + 1}\right)$ satisfy $s_n > 1000$?

48. $\sum_{n=1}^{\infty}(1/n^4)$ **converges**

a. Use the accompanying graph to determine the error if $s_{30} = \sum_{n=1}^{30}(1/n^4)$ is used to estimate the value of $\sum_{n=1}^{\infty}(1/n^4)$.

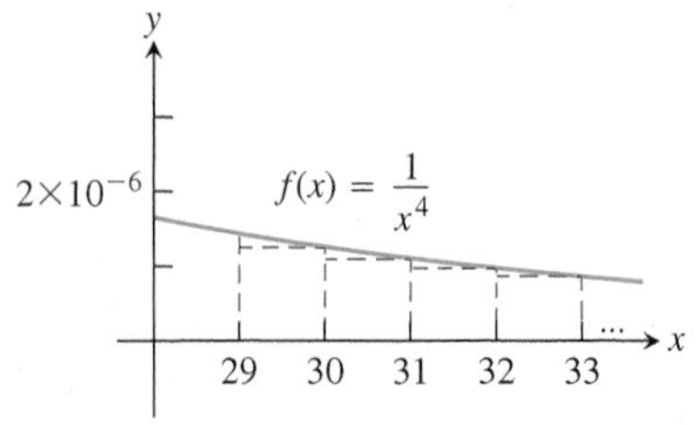

b. Find n so that the partial sum $s_n = \sum_{i=1}^{n}(1/i^4)$ estimates the value of $\sum_{n=1}^{\infty}(1/n^4)$ with an error of at most 0.000001.

49. Estimate the value of $\sum_{n=1}^{\infty}(1/n^3)$ to within 0.01 of its exact value.

50. Estimate the value of $\sum_{n=2}^{\infty}(1/(n^2+4))$ to within 0.1 of its exact value.

51. How many terms of the convergent series $\sum_{n=1}^{\infty}(1/n^{1.1})$ should be used to estimate its value with error at most 0.00001?

52. How many terms of the convergent series $\sum_{n=4}^{\infty}(1/n(\ln n)^3)$ should be used to estimate its value with error at most 0.01?

53. The Cauchy condensation test The Cauchy condensation test says: Let $\{a_n\}$ be a nonincreasing sequence ($a_n \ge a_{n+1}$ for all n) of positive terms that converges to 0. Then $\sum a_n$ converges if and only if $\sum 2^n a_{2^n}$ converges. For example, $\sum(1/n)$ diverges because $\sum 2^n \cdot (1/2^n) = \sum 1$ diverges. Show why the test works.

54. Use the Cauchy condensation test from Exercise 53 to show that

a. $\displaystyle\sum_{n=2}^{\infty}\frac{1}{n\ln n}$ diverges;

b. $\displaystyle\sum_{n=1}^{\infty}\frac{1}{n^p}$ converges if $p > 1$ and diverges if $p \le 1$.

55. Logarithmic *p*-series

a. Show that the improper integral

$$\int_2^{\infty}\frac{dx}{x(\ln x)^p}\quad (p \text{ a positive constant})$$

converges if and only if $p > 1$.

b. What implications does the fact in part (a) have for the convergence of the series

$$\sum_{n=2}^{\infty}\frac{1}{n(\ln n)^p}?$$

Give reasons for your answer.

56. (*Continuation of Exercise 55.*) Use the result in Exercise 55 to determine which of the following series converge and which diverge. Support your answer in each case.

a. $\displaystyle\sum_{n=2}^{\infty}\frac{1}{n(\ln n)}$ b. $\displaystyle\sum_{n=2}^{\infty}\frac{1}{n(\ln n)^{1.01}}$

c. $\displaystyle\sum_{n=2}^{\infty}\frac{1}{n\ln(n^3)}$ d. $\displaystyle\sum_{n=2}^{\infty}\frac{1}{n(\ln n)^3}$

57. Euler's constant Graphs like those in Figure 9.11 suggest that as n increases there is little change in the difference between the sum

$$1 + \frac{1}{2} + \cdots + \frac{1}{n}$$

and the integral

$$\ln n = \int_1^n \frac{1}{x}\,dx.$$

To explore this idea, carry out the following steps.

a. By taking $f(x) = 1/x$ in the proof of Theorem 9, show that

$$\ln(n+1) \le 1 + \frac{1}{2} + \cdots + \frac{1}{n} \le 1 + \ln n$$

or

$$0 < \ln(n+1) - \ln n \le 1 + \frac{1}{2} + \cdots + \frac{1}{n} - \ln n \le 1.$$

Thus, the sequence

$$a_n = 1 + \frac{1}{2} + \cdots + \frac{1}{n} - \ln n$$

is bounded from below and from above.

b. Show that

$$\frac{1}{n+1} < \int_n^{n+1}\frac{1}{x}\,dx = \ln(n+1) - \ln n,$$

and use this result to show that the sequence $\{a_n\}$ in part (a) is decreasing.

Since a decreasing sequence that is bounded from below converges, the numbers a_n defined in part (a) converge:

$$1 + \frac{1}{2} + \cdots + \frac{1}{n} - \ln n \to \gamma.$$

The number γ, whose value is 0.5772 . . . , is called *Euler's constant.*

58. Use the Integral Test to show that the series

$$\sum_{n=0}^{\infty} e^{-n^2}$$

converges.

59. a. For the series $\sum(1/n^3)$, use the inequalities in Equation (2) with $n = 10$ to find an interval containing the sum S.

b. As in Example 5, use the midpoint of the interval found in part (a) to approximate the sum of the series. What is the maximum error for your approximation?

60. Repeat Exercise 59 using the series $\sum(1/n^4)$.

9.4 Comparison Tests

We have seen how to determine the convergence of geometric series, *p*-series, and a few others. We can test the convergence of many more series by comparing their terms to those of a series whose convergence is known.

THEOREM 10—The Comparison Test Let $\sum a_n$, $\sum c_n$, and $\sum d_n$ be series with nonnegative terms. Suppose that for some integer N

$$d_n \le a_n \le c_n \qquad \text{for all} \qquad n > N.$$

(a) If $\sum c_n$ converges, then $\sum a_n$ also converges.
(b) If $\sum d_n$ diverges, then $\sum a_n$ also diverges.

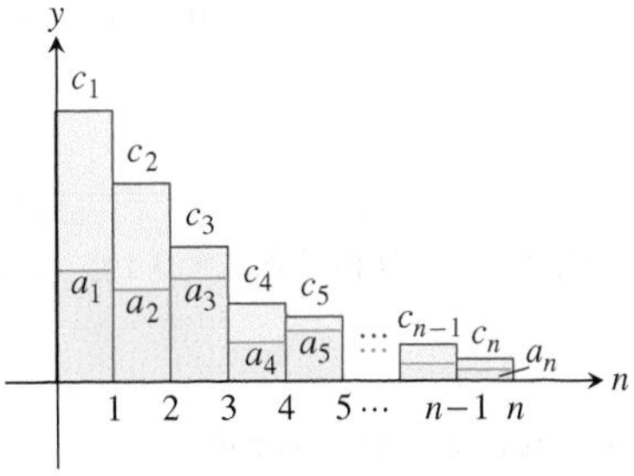

FIGURE 9.12 If the total area $\sum c_n$ of the taller c_n rectangles is finite, then so is the total area $\sum a_n$ of the shorter a_n rectangles.

Proof In Part (a), the partial sums of $\sum a_n$ are bounded above by

$$M = a_1 + a_2 + \cdots + a_N + \sum_{n=N+1}^{\infty} c_n.$$

They therefore form a nondecreasing sequence with a limit $L \le M$. That is, if $\sum c_n$ converges, then so does $\sum a_n$. Figure 9.12 depicts this result, where each term of each series is interpreted as the area of a rectangle (just like we did for the integral test in Figure 9.11).

In Part (b), the partial sums of $\sum a_n$ are not bounded from above. If they were, the partial sums for $\sum d_n$ would be bounded by

$$M^* = d_1 + d_2 + \cdots + d_N + \sum_{n=N+1}^{\infty} a_n$$

and $\sum d_n$ would have to converge instead of diverge. ■

EXAMPLE 1 We apply Theorem 10 to several series.

(a) The series

$$\sum_{n=1}^{\infty} \frac{5}{5n-1}$$

diverges because its nth term

$$\frac{5}{5n-1} = \frac{1}{n - \frac{1}{5}} > \frac{1}{n}$$

is greater than the nth term of the divergent harmonic series.

HISTORICAL BIOGRAPHY

Albert of Saxony
(ca. 1316–1390)

(b) The series

$$\sum_{n=0}^{\infty} \frac{1}{n!} = 1 + \frac{1}{1!} + \frac{1}{2!} + \frac{1}{3!} + \cdots$$

converges because its terms are all positive and less than or equal to the corresponding terms of

$$1 + \sum_{n=0}^{\infty} \frac{1}{2^n} = 1 + 1 + \frac{1}{2} + \frac{1}{2^2} + \cdots.$$

The geometric series on the left converges and we have

$$1 + \sum_{n=0}^{\infty} \frac{1}{2^n} = 1 + \frac{1}{1-(1/2)} = 3.$$

The fact that 3 is an upper bound for the partial sums of $\sum_{n=0}^{\infty}(1/n!)$ does not mean that the series converges to 3. As we will see in Section 9.9, the series converges to e.

(c) The series

$$5 + \frac{2}{3} + \frac{1}{7} + 1 + \frac{1}{2+\sqrt{1}} + \frac{1}{4+\sqrt{2}} + \frac{1}{8+\sqrt{3}} + \cdots + \frac{1}{2^n+\sqrt{n}} + \cdots$$

converges. To see this, we ignore the first three terms and compare the remaining terms with those of the convergent geometric series $\sum_{n=0}^{\infty}(1/2^n)$. The term $1/(2^n + \sqrt{n})$ of the truncated sequence is less than the corresponding term $1/2^n$ of the geometric series. We see that term by term we have the comparison

$$1 + \frac{1}{2 + \sqrt{1}} + \frac{1}{4 + \sqrt{2}} + \frac{1}{8 + \sqrt{3}} + \cdots \leq 1 + \frac{1}{2} + \frac{1}{4} + \frac{1}{8} + \cdots.$$

So the truncated series and the original series converge by an application of the Comparison Test. ■

The Limit Comparison Test

We now introduce a comparison test that is particularly useful for series in which a_n is a rational function of n.

THEOREM 11—Limit Comparison Test Suppose that $a_n > 0$ and $b_n > 0$ for all $n \geq N$ (N an integer).

1. If $\lim_{n\to\infty} \frac{a_n}{b_n} = c > 0$, then $\sum a_n$ and $\sum b_n$ both converge or both diverge.

2. If $\lim_{n\to\infty} \frac{a_n}{b_n} = 0$ and $\sum b_n$ converges, then $\sum a_n$ converges.

3. If $\lim_{n\to\infty} \frac{a_n}{b_n} = \infty$ and $\sum b_n$ diverges, then $\sum a_n$ diverges.

Proof We will prove Part 1. Parts 2 and 3 are left as Exercises 55a and b.
Since $c/2 > 0$, there exists an integer N such that for all n

$$n > N \Rightarrow \left|\frac{a_n}{b_n} - c\right| < \frac{c}{2}.$$

Limit definition with $\epsilon = c/2$, $L = c$, and a_n replaced by a_n/b_n

Thus, for $n > N$,

$$-\frac{c}{2} < \frac{a_n}{b_n} - c < \frac{c}{2},$$

$$\frac{c}{2} < \frac{a_n}{b_n} < \frac{3c}{2},$$

$$\left(\frac{c}{2}\right)b_n < a_n < \left(\frac{3c}{2}\right)b_n.$$

If $\sum b_n$ converges, then $\sum(3c/2)b_n$ converges and $\sum a_n$ converges by the Direct Comparison Test. If $\sum b_n$ diverges, then $\sum(c/2)b_n$ diverges and $\sum a_n$ diverges by the Direct Comparison Test. ■

EXAMPLE 2 Which of the following series converge, and which diverge?

(a) $\frac{3}{4} + \frac{5}{9} + \frac{7}{16} + \frac{9}{25} + \cdots = \sum_{n=1}^{\infty} \frac{2n+1}{(n+1)^2} = \sum_{n=1}^{\infty} \frac{2n+1}{n^2+2n+1}$

(b) $\frac{1}{1} + \frac{1}{3} + \frac{1}{7} + \frac{1}{15} + \cdots = \sum_{n=1}^{\infty} \frac{1}{2^n - 1}$

(c) $\frac{1 + 2\ln 2}{9} + \frac{1 + 3\ln 3}{14} + \frac{1 + 4\ln 4}{21} + \cdots = \sum_{n=2}^{\infty} \frac{1 + n\ln n}{n^2 + 5}$

Solution We apply the Limit Comparison Test to each series.

(a) Let $a_n = (2n + 1)/(n^2 + 2n + 1)$. For large n, we expect a_n to behave like $2n/n^2 = 2/n$ since the leading terms dominate for large n, so we let $b_n = 1/n$. Since

$$\sum_{n=1}^{\infty} b_n = \sum_{n=1}^{\infty} \frac{1}{n} \text{ diverges}$$

and

$$\lim_{n\to\infty} \frac{a_n}{b_n} = \lim_{n\to\infty} \frac{2n^2 + n}{n^2 + 2n + 1} = 2,$$

$\sum a_n$ diverges by Part 1 of the Limit Comparison Test. We could just as well have taken $b_n = 2/n$, but $1/n$ is simpler.

(b) Let $a_n = 1/(2^n - 1)$. For large n, we expect a_n to behave like $1/2^n$, so we let $b_n = 1/2^n$. Since

$$\sum_{n=1}^{\infty} b_n = \sum_{n=1}^{\infty} \frac{1}{2^n} \text{ converges}$$

and

$$\begin{aligned} \lim_{n\to\infty} \frac{a_n}{b_n} &= \lim_{n\to\infty} \frac{2^n}{2^n - 1} \\ &= \lim_{n\to\infty} \frac{1}{1 - (1/2^n)} \\ &= 1, \end{aligned}$$

$\sum a_n$ converges by Part 1 of the Limit Comparison Test.

(c) Let $a_n = (1 + n \ln n)/(n^2 + 5)$. For large n, we expect a_n to behave like $(n \ln n)/n^2 = (\ln n)/n$, which is greater than $1/n$ for $n \ge 3$, so we let $b_n = 1/n$. Since

$$\sum_{n=2}^{\infty} b_n = \sum_{n=2}^{\infty} \frac{1}{n} \text{ diverges}$$

and

$$\begin{aligned} \lim_{n\to\infty} \frac{a_n}{b_n} &= \lim_{n\to\infty} \frac{n + n^2 \ln n}{n^2 + 5} \\ &= \infty, \end{aligned}$$

$\sum a_n$ diverges by Part 3 of the Limit Comparison Test. ■

EXAMPLE 3 Does $\displaystyle\sum_{n=1}^{\infty} \frac{\ln n}{n^{3/2}}$ converge?

Solution Because $\ln n$ grows more slowly than n^c for any positive constant c (Section 9.1, Exercise 105), we can compare the series to a convergent p-series. To get the p-series, we see that

$$\frac{\ln n}{n^{3/2}} < \frac{n^{1/4}}{n^{3/2}} = \frac{1}{n^{5/4}}$$

for n sufficiently large. Then taking $a_n = (\ln n)/n^{3/2}$ and $b_n = 1/n^{5/4}$, we have

$$\begin{aligned} \lim_{n\to\infty} \frac{a_n}{b_n} &= \lim_{n\to\infty} \frac{\ln n}{n^{1/4}} \\ &= \lim_{n\to\infty} \frac{1/n}{(1/4)n^{-3/4}} \qquad \text{l'Hôpital's Rule} \\ &= \lim_{n\to\infty} \frac{4}{n^{1/4}} = 0. \end{aligned}$$

Since $\sum b_n = \sum(1/n^{5/4})$ is a p-series with $p > 1$, it converges, so $\sum a_n$ converges by Part 2 of the Limit Comparison Test. ■

Exercises 9.4

Comparison Test

In Exercises 1–8, use the Comparison Test to determine if each series converges or diverges.

1. $\sum_{n=1}^{\infty} \frac{1}{n^2 + 30}$

2. $\sum_{n=1}^{\infty} \frac{n - 1}{n^4 + 2}$

3. $\sum_{n=2}^{\infty} \frac{1}{\sqrt{n} - 1}$

4. $\sum_{n=2}^{\infty} \frac{n + 2}{n^2 - n}$

5. $\sum_{n=1}^{\infty} \frac{\cos^2 n}{n^{3/2}}$

6. $\sum_{n=1}^{\infty} \frac{1}{n3^n}$

7. $\sum_{n=1}^{\infty} \sqrt{\frac{n + 4}{n^4 + 4}}$

8. $\sum_{n=1}^{\infty} \frac{\sqrt{n} + 1}{\sqrt{n^2 + 3}}$

Limit Comparison Test

In Exercises 9–16, use the Limit Comparison Test to determine if each series converges or diverges.

9. $\sum_{n=1}^{\infty} \frac{n - 2}{n^3 - n^2 + 3}$

(*Hint:* Limit Comparison with $\sum_{n=1}^{\infty} (1/n^2)$)

10. $\sum_{n=1}^{\infty} \sqrt{\frac{n + 1}{n^2 + 2}}$

(*Hint:* Limit Comparison with $\sum_{n=1}^{\infty} (1/\sqrt{n})$)

11. $\sum_{n=2}^{\infty} \frac{n(n + 1)}{(n^2 + 1)(n - 1)}$

12. $\sum_{n=1}^{\infty} \frac{2^n}{3 + 4^n}$

13. $\sum_{n=1}^{\infty} \frac{5^n}{\sqrt{n}\, 4^n}$

14. $\sum_{n=1}^{\infty} \left(\frac{2n + 3}{5n + 4}\right)^n$

15. $\sum_{n=2}^{\infty} \frac{1}{\ln n}$

(*Hint:* Limit Comparison with $\sum_{n=2}^{\infty} (1/n)$)

16. $\sum_{n=1}^{\infty} \ln\left(1 + \frac{1}{n^2}\right)$

(*Hint:* Limit Comparison with $\sum_{n=1}^{\infty} (1/n^2)$)

Determining Convergence or Divergence

Which of the series in Exercises 17–54 converge, and which diverge? Use any method, and give reasons for your answers.

17. $\sum_{n=1}^{\infty} \frac{1}{2\sqrt{n} + \sqrt[3]{n}}$

18. $\sum_{n=1}^{\infty} \frac{3}{n + \sqrt{n}}$

19. $\sum_{n=1}^{\infty} \frac{\sin^2 n}{2^n}$

20. $\sum_{n=1}^{\infty} \frac{1 + \cos n}{n^2}$

21. $\sum_{n=1}^{\infty} \frac{2n}{3n - 1}$

22. $\sum_{n=1}^{\infty} \frac{n + 1}{n^2\sqrt{n}}$

23. $\sum_{n=1}^{\infty} \frac{10n + 1}{n(n + 1)(n + 2)}$

24. $\sum_{n=3}^{\infty} \frac{5n^3 - 3n}{n^2(n - 2)(n^2 + 5)}$

25. $\sum_{n=1}^{\infty} \left(\frac{n}{3n + 1}\right)^n$

26. $\sum_{n=1}^{\infty} \frac{1}{\sqrt{n^3 + 2}}$

27. $\sum_{n=3}^{\infty} \frac{1}{\ln(\ln n)}$

28. $\sum_{n=1}^{\infty} \frac{(\ln n)^2}{n^3}$

29. $\sum_{n=2}^{\infty} \frac{1}{\sqrt{n}\ln n}$

30. $\sum_{n=1}^{\infty} \frac{(\ln n)^2}{n^{3/2}}$

31. $\sum_{n=1}^{\infty} \frac{1}{1 + \ln n}$

32. $\sum_{n=2}^{\infty} \frac{\ln(n + 1)}{n + 1}$

33. $\sum_{n=2}^{\infty} \frac{1}{n\sqrt{n^2 - 1}}$

34. $\sum_{n=1}^{\infty} \frac{\sqrt{n}}{n^2 + 1}$

35. $\sum_{n=1}^{\infty} \frac{1 - n}{n2^n}$

36. $\sum_{n=1}^{\infty} \frac{n + 2^n}{n^2 2^n}$

37. $\sum_{n=1}^{\infty} \frac{1}{3^{n-1} + 1}$

38. $\sum_{n=1}^{\infty} \frac{3^{n-1} + 1}{3^n}$

39. $\sum_{n=1}^{\infty} \frac{n + 1}{n^2 + 3n} \cdot \frac{1}{5n}$

40. $\sum_{n=1}^{\infty} \frac{2^n + 3^n}{3^n + 4^n}$

41. $\sum_{n=1}^{\infty} \frac{2^n - n}{n2^n}$

42. $\sum_{n=1}^{\infty} \ln\left(\frac{n}{n + 1}\right)$

43. $\sum_{n=2}^{\infty} \frac{1}{n!}$

(*Hint:* First show that $(1/n!) \le (1/n(n - 1))$ for $n \ge 2$.)

44. $\sum_{n=1}^{\infty} \frac{(n - 1)!}{(n + 2)!}$

45. $\sum_{n=1}^{\infty} \sin \frac{1}{n}$

46. $\sum_{n=1}^{\infty} \tan \frac{1}{n}$

47. $\sum_{n=1}^{\infty} \frac{\tan^{-1} n}{n^{1.1}}$

48. $\sum_{n=1}^{\infty} \frac{\sec^{-1} n}{n^{1.3}}$

49. $\sum_{n=1}^{\infty} \frac{\coth n}{n^2}$

50. $\sum_{n=1}^{\infty} \frac{\tanh n}{n^2}$

51. $\sum_{n=1}^{\infty} \frac{1}{n\sqrt[n]{n}}$

52. $\sum_{n=1}^{\infty} \frac{\sqrt[n]{n}}{n^2}$

53. $\sum_{n=1}^{\infty} \frac{1}{1 + 2 + 3 + \cdots + n}$

54. $\sum_{n=1}^{\infty} \frac{1}{1 + 2^2 + 3^2 + \cdots + n^2}$

Theory and Examples

55. Prove **(a)** Part 2 and **(b)** Part 3 of the Limit Comparison Test.

56. If $\sum_{n=1}^{\infty} a_n$ is a convergent series of nonnegative numbers, can anything be said about $\sum_{n=1}^{\infty} (a_n/n)$? Explain.

57. Suppose that $a_n > 0$ and $b_n > 0$ for $n \ge N$ (N an integer). If $\lim_{n\to\infty} (a_n/b_n) = \infty$ and $\sum a_n$ converges, can anything be said about $\sum b_n$? Give reasons for your answer.

58. Prove that if $\sum a_n$ is a convergent series of nonnegative terms, then $\sum a_n^2$ converges.

59. Suppose that $a_n > 0$ and $\lim_{n\to\infty} a_n = \infty$. Prove that $\sum a_n$ diverges.

60. Suppose that $a_n > 0$ and $\lim_{n\to\infty} n^2 a_n = 0$. Prove that $\sum a_n$ converges.

61. Show that $\sum_{n=2}^{\infty} ((\ln n)^q/n^p)$ converges for $-\infty < q < \infty$ and $p > 1$.

(*Hint:* Limit Comparison with $\sum_{n=2}^{\infty} 1/n^r$ for $1 < r < p$.)

62. (*Continuation of Exercise 61.*) Show that $\sum_{n=2}^{\infty} ((\ln n)^q/n^p)$ diverges for $-\infty < q < \infty$ and $0 < p \le 1$.

(*Hint:* Limit Comparison with an appropriate p-series.)

In Exercises 63–68, use the results of Exercises 61 and 62 to determine if each series converges or diverges.

63. $\sum_{n=2}^{\infty} \frac{(\ln n)^3}{n^4}$

64. $\sum_{n=2}^{\infty} \sqrt{\frac{\ln n}{n}}$

65. $\sum_{n=2}^{\infty} \frac{(\ln n)^{1000}}{n^{1.001}}$

66. $\sum_{n=2}^{\infty} \frac{(\ln n)^{1/5}}{n^{0.99}}$

67. $\sum_{n=2}^{\infty} \frac{1}{n^{1.1}(\ln n)^3}$

68. $\sum_{n=2}^{\infty} \frac{1}{\sqrt{n} \cdot \ln n}$

COMPUTER EXPLORATIONS

69. It is not yet known whether the series

$$\sum_{n=1}^{\infty} \frac{1}{n^3 \sin^2 n}$$

converges or diverges. Use a CAS to explore the behavior of the series by performing the following steps.

a. Define the sequence of partial sums

$$s_k = \sum_{n=1}^{k} \frac{1}{n^3 \sin^2 n}.$$

What happens when you try to find the limit of s_k as $k \rightarrow \infty$? Does your CAS find a closed form answer for this limit?

b. Plot the first 100 points (k, s_k) for the sequence of partial sums. Do they appear to converge? What would you estimate the limit to be?

c. Next plot the first 200 points (k, s_k). Discuss the behavior in your own words.

d. Plot the first 400 points (k, s_k). What happens when $k = 355$? Calculate the number $355/113$. Explain from your calculation what happened at $k = 355$. For what values of k would you guess this behavior might occur again?

70. a. Use Theorem 8 to show that

$$S = \sum_{n=1}^{\infty} \frac{1}{n(n+1)} + \sum_{n=1}^{\infty} \left(\frac{1}{n^2} - \frac{1}{n(n+1)}\right)$$

where $S = \sum_{n=1}^{\infty} (1/n^2)$, the sum of a convergent p-series.

b. From Example 5, Section 9.2, show that

$$S = 1 + \sum_{n=1}^{\infty} \frac{1}{n^2(n+1)}.$$

c. Explain why taking the first M terms in the series in part (b) gives a better approximation to S than taking the first M terms in the original series $\sum_{n=1}^{\infty} (1/n^2)$.

d. The exact value of S is known to be $\pi^2/6$. Which of the sums

$$\sum_{n=1}^{1000000} \frac{1}{n^2} \quad \text{or} \quad 1 + \sum_{n=1}^{1000} \frac{1}{n^2(n+1)}$$

gives a better approximation to S?

9.5 The Ratio and Root Tests

The Ratio Test measures the rate of growth (or decline) of a series by examining the ratio a_{n+1}/a_n. For a geometric series $\sum ar^n$, this rate is a constant $((ar^{n+1})/(ar^n) = r)$, and the series converges if and only if its ratio is less than 1 in absolute value. The Ratio Test is a powerful rule extending that result.

THEOREM 12—The Ratio Test Let $\sum a_n$ be a series with positive terms and suppose that

$$\lim_{n \to \infty} \frac{a_{n+1}}{a_n} = \rho.$$

Then **(a)** the series *converges* if $\rho < 1$, **(b)** the series *diverges* if $\rho > 1$ or ρ is infinite, **(c)** the test is *inconclusive* if $\rho = 1$.

Proof

(a) $\boldsymbol{\rho < 1}$**.** Let r be a number between ρ and 1. Then the number $\epsilon = r - \rho$ is positive. Since

$$\frac{a_{n+1}}{a_n} \rightarrow \rho,$$

a_{n+1}/a_n must lie within ϵ of ρ when n is large enough, say for all $n \geq N$. In particular,

$$\frac{a_{n+1}}{a_n} < \rho + \epsilon = r, \qquad \text{when } n \geq N.$$

That is,

$$\begin{aligned}
a_{N+1} &< ra_N, \\
a_{N+2} &< ra_{N+1} < r^2 a_N, \\
a_{N+3} &< ra_{N+2} < r^3 a_N, \\
&\vdots \\
a_{N+m} &< ra_{N+m-1} < r^m a_N.
\end{aligned}$$

These inequalities show that the terms of our series, after the Nth term, approach zero more rapidly than the terms in a geometric series with ratio $r < 1$. More precisely, consider the series $\sum c_n$, where $c_n = a_n$ for $n = 1, 2, \ldots, N$ and $c_{N+1} = ra_N$, $c_{N+2} = r^2 a_N, \ldots, c_{N+m} = r^m a_N, \ldots$. Now $a_n \le c_n$ for all n, and

$$\begin{aligned}
\sum_{n=1}^{\infty} c_n &= a_1 + a_2 + \cdots + a_{N-1} + a_N + ra_N + r^2 a_N + \cdots \\
&= a_1 + a_2 + \cdots + a_{N-1} + a_N(1 + r + r^2 + \cdots).
\end{aligned}$$

The geometric series $1 + r + r^2 + \cdots$ converges because $|r| < 1$, so $\sum c_n$ converges. Since $a_n \le c_n$, $\sum a_n$ also converges.

(b) $\boldsymbol{1 < \rho \le \infty}$**.** From some index M on,

$$\frac{a_{n+1}}{a_n} > 1 \quad \text{and} \quad a_M < a_{M+1} < a_{M+2} < \cdots.$$

The terms of the series do not approach zero as n becomes infinite, and the series diverges by the nth-Term Test.

(c) $\boldsymbol{\rho = 1}$**.** The two series

$$\sum_{n=1}^{\infty} \frac{1}{n} \quad \text{and} \quad \sum_{n=1}^{\infty} \frac{1}{n^2}$$

show that some other test for convergence must be used when $\rho = 1$.

$$\text{For } \sum_{n=1}^{\infty} \frac{1}{n}: \quad \frac{a_{n+1}}{a_n} = \frac{1/(n+1)}{1/n} = \frac{n}{n+1} \to 1.$$

$$\text{For } \sum_{n=1}^{\infty} \frac{1}{n^2}: \quad \frac{a_{n+1}}{a_n} = \frac{1/(n+1)^2}{1/n^2} = \left(\frac{n}{n+1}\right)^2 \to 1^2 = 1.$$

In both cases, $\rho = 1$, yet the first series diverges, whereas the second converges. ■

The Ratio Test is often effective when the terms of a series contain factorials of expressions involving n or expressions raised to a power involving n.

EXAMPLE 1 Investigate the convergence of the following series.

(a) $\displaystyle\sum_{n=0}^{\infty} \frac{2^n + 5}{3^n}$ **(b)** $\displaystyle\sum_{n=1}^{\infty} \frac{(2n)!}{n!n!}$ **(c)** $\displaystyle\sum_{n=1}^{\infty} \frac{4^n n! n!}{(2n)!}$

Solution We apply the Ratio Test to each series.

(a) For the series $\sum_{n=0}^{\infty} (2^n + 5)/3^n$,

$$\frac{a_{n+1}}{a_n} = \frac{(2^{n+1} + 5)/3^{n+1}}{(2^n + 5)/3^n} = \frac{1}{3} \cdot \frac{2^{n+1} + 5}{2^n + 5} = \frac{1}{3} \cdot \left(\frac{2 + 5 \cdot 2^{-n}}{1 + 5 \cdot 2^{-n}}\right) \to \frac{1}{3} \cdot \frac{2}{1} = \frac{2}{3}.$$

The series converges because $\rho = 2/3$ is less than 1. This does *not* mean that $2/3$ is the sum of the series. In fact,

$$\sum_{n=0}^{\infty} \frac{2^n + 5}{3^n} = \sum_{n=0}^{\infty} \left(\frac{2}{3}\right)^n + \sum_{n=0}^{\infty} \frac{5}{3^n} = \frac{1}{1 - (2/3)} + \frac{5}{1 - (1/3)} = \frac{21}{2}.$$

(b) If $a_n = \dfrac{(2n)!}{n!n!}$, then $a_{n+1} = \dfrac{(2n+2)!}{(n+1)!(n+1)!}$ and

$$\frac{a_{n+1}}{a_n} = \frac{n!n!(2n+2)(2n+1)(2n)!}{(n+1)!(n+1)!(2n)!}$$
$$= \frac{(2n+2)(2n+1)}{(n+1)(n+1)} = \frac{4n+2}{n+1} \to 4.$$

The series diverges because $\rho = 4$ is greater than 1.

(c) If $a_n = 4^n n!n!/(2n)!$, then

$$\frac{a_{n+1}}{a_n} = \frac{4^{n+1}(n+1)!(n+1)!}{(2n+2)(2n+1)(2n)!} \cdot \frac{(2n)!}{4^n n!n!}$$
$$= \frac{4(n+1)(n+1)}{(2n+2)(2n+1)} = \frac{2(n+1)}{2n+1} \to 1.$$

Because the limit is $\rho = 1$, we cannot decide from the Ratio Test whether the series converges. When we notice that $a_{n+1}/a_n = (2n+2)/(2n+1)$, we conclude that a_{n+1} is always greater than a_n because $(2n+2)/(2n+1)$ is always greater than 1. Therefore, all terms are greater than or equal to $a_1 = 2$, and the nth term does not approach zero as $n \to \infty$. The series diverges. ■

The Root Test

The convergence tests we have so far for $\sum a_n$ work best when the formula for a_n is relatively simple. However, consider the series with the terms

$$a_n = \begin{cases} n/2^n, & n \text{ odd} \\ 1/2^n, & n \text{ even.} \end{cases}$$

To investigate convergence we write out several terms of the series:

$$\sum_{n=1}^{\infty} a_n = \frac{1}{2^1} + \frac{1}{2^2} + \frac{3}{2^3} + \frac{1}{2^4} + \frac{5}{2^5} + \frac{1}{2^6} + \frac{7}{2^7} + \cdots$$
$$= \frac{1}{2} + \frac{1}{4} + \frac{3}{8} + \frac{1}{16} + \frac{5}{32} + \frac{1}{64} + \frac{7}{128} + \cdots.$$

Clearly, this is not a geometric series. The nth term approaches zero as $n \to \infty$, so the nth-Term Test does not tell us if the series diverges. The Integral Test does not look promising. The Ratio Test produces

$$\frac{a_{n+1}}{a_n} = \begin{cases} \dfrac{1}{2n}, & n \text{ odd} \\[2ex] \dfrac{n+1}{2}, & n \text{ even.} \end{cases}$$

As $n \to \infty$, the ratio is alternately small and large and has no limit. However, we will see that the following test establishes that the series converges.

> **THEOREM 13—The Root Test** Let $\sum a_n$ be a series with $a_n \geq 0$ for $n \geq N$, and suppose that
>
> $$\lim_{n\to\infty} \sqrt[n]{a_n} = \rho.$$
>
> Then **(a)** the series *converges* if $\rho < 1$, **(b)** the series *diverges* if $\rho > 1$ or ρ is infinite, **(c)** the test is *inconclusive* if $\rho = 1$.

Proof

(a) $\rho < 1$**.** Choose an $\epsilon > 0$ so small that $\rho + \epsilon < 1$. Since $\sqrt[n]{a_n} \to \rho$, the terms $\sqrt[n]{a_n}$ eventually get closer than ϵ to ρ. In other words, there exists an index $M \geq N$ such that

$$\sqrt[n]{a_n} < \rho + \epsilon \qquad \text{when } n \geq M.$$

Then it is also true that

$$a_n < (\rho + \epsilon)^n \qquad \text{for } n \geq M.$$

Now, $\sum_{n=M}^{\infty} (\rho + \epsilon)^n$, a geometric series with ratio $(\rho + \epsilon) < 1$, converges. By comparison, $\sum_{n=M}^{\infty} a_n$ converges, from which it follows that

$$\sum_{n=1}^{\infty} a_n = a_1 + \cdots + a_{M-1} + \sum_{n=M}^{\infty} a_n$$

converges.

(b) $1 < \rho \leq \infty$**.** For all indices beyond some integer M, we have $\sqrt[n]{a_n} > 1$, so that $a_n > 1$ for $n > M$. The terms of the series do not converge to zero. The series diverges by the nth-Term Test.

(c) $\rho = 1$**.** The series $\sum_{n=1}^{\infty} (1/n)$ and $\sum_{n=1}^{\infty} (1/n^2)$ show that the test is not conclusive when $\rho = 1$. The first series diverges and the second converges, but in both cases $\sqrt[n]{a_n} \to 1$. ■

EXAMPLE 2 Consider again the series with terms $a_n = \begin{cases} n/2^n, & n \text{ odd} \\ 1/2^n, & n \text{ even.} \end{cases}$

Does $\sum a_n$ converge?

Solution We apply the Root Test, finding that

$$\sqrt[n]{a_n} = \begin{cases} \sqrt[n]{n}/2, & n \text{ odd} \\ 1/2, & n \text{ even.} \end{cases}$$

Therefore,

$$\frac{1}{2} \leq \sqrt[n]{a_n} \leq \frac{\sqrt[n]{n}}{2}.$$

Since $\sqrt[n]{n} \to 1$ (Section 9.1, Theorem 5), we have $\lim_{n\to\infty} \sqrt[n]{a_n} = 1/2$ by the Sandwich Theorem. The limit is less than 1, so the series converges by the Root Test. ■

EXAMPLE 3 Which of the following series converge, and which diverge?

(a) $\sum_{n=1}^{\infty} \frac{n^2}{2^n}$ **(b)** $\sum_{n=1}^{\infty} \frac{2^n}{n^3}$ **(c)** $\sum_{n=1}^{\infty} \left(\frac{1}{1+n}\right)^n$

Solution We apply the Root Test to each series.

(a) $\sum_{n=1}^{\infty} \frac{n^2}{2^n}$ converges because $\sqrt[n]{\frac{n^2}{2^n}} = \frac{\sqrt[n]{n^2}}{\sqrt[n]{2^n}} = \frac{\left(\sqrt[n]{n}\right)^2}{2} \to \frac{1^2}{2} < 1.$

(b) $\sum_{n=1}^{\infty} \frac{2^n}{n^3}$ diverges because $\sqrt[n]{\frac{2^n}{n^3}} = \frac{2}{\left(\sqrt[n]{n}\right)^3} \to \frac{2}{1^3} > 1.$

(c) $\sum_{n=1}^{\infty} \left(\frac{1}{1+n}\right)^n$ converges because $\sqrt[n]{\left(\frac{1}{1+n}\right)^n} = \frac{1}{1+n} \to 0 < 1.$ ■

Exercises 9.5

Using the Ratio Test

In Exercises 1–8, use the Ratio Test to determine if each series converges or diverges.

1. $\sum_{n=1}^{\infty} \frac{2^n}{n!}$

2. $\sum_{n=1}^{\infty} \frac{n+2}{3^n}$

3. $\sum_{n=1}^{\infty} \frac{(n-1)!}{(n+1)^2}$

4. $\sum_{n=1}^{\infty} \frac{2^{n+1}}{n3^{n-1}}$

5. $\sum_{n=1}^{\infty} \frac{n^4}{4^n}$

6. $\sum_{n=2}^{\infty} \frac{3^{n+2}}{\ln n}$

7. $\sum_{n=1}^{\infty} \frac{n^2(n+2)!}{n!\,3^{2n}}$

8. $\sum_{n=1}^{\infty} \frac{n5^n}{(2n+3)\ln(n+1)}$

Using the Root Test

In Exercises 9–16, use the Root Test to determine if each series converges or diverges.

9. $\sum_{n=1}^{\infty} \frac{7}{(2n+5)^n}$

10. $\sum_{n=1}^{\infty} \frac{4^n}{(3n)^n}$

11. $\sum_{n=1}^{\infty} \left(\frac{4n+3}{3n-5}\right)^n$

12. $\sum_{n=1}^{\infty} \left(\ln\left(e^2+\frac{1}{n}\right)\right)^{n+1}$

13. $\sum_{n=1}^{\infty} \frac{8}{(3+(1/n))^{2n}}$

14. $\sum_{n=1}^{\infty} \sin^n\left(\frac{1}{\sqrt{n}}\right)$

15. $\sum_{n=1}^{\infty} \left(1-\frac{1}{n}\right)^{n^2}$

(*Hint:* $\lim_{n\to\infty}(1+x/n)^n = e^x$)

16. $\sum_{n=2}^{\infty} \frac{1}{n^{1+n}}$

Determining Convergence or Divergence

In Exercises 17–44, use any method to determine if the series converges or diverges. Give reasons for your answer.

17. $\sum_{n=1}^{\infty} \frac{n^{\sqrt{2}}}{2^n}$

18. $\sum_{n=1}^{\infty} n^2 e^{-n}$

19. $\sum_{n=1}^{\infty} n!\,e^{-n}$

20. $\sum_{n=1}^{\infty} \frac{n!}{10^n}$

21. $\sum_{n=1}^{\infty} \frac{n^{10}}{10^n}$

22. $\sum_{n=1}^{\infty} \left(\frac{n-2}{n}\right)^n$

23. $\sum_{n=1}^{\infty} \frac{2+(-1)^n}{1.25^n}$

24. $\sum_{n=1}^{\infty} \frac{(-2)^n}{3^n}$

25. $\sum_{n=1}^{\infty} \left(1-\frac{3}{n}\right)^n$

26. $\sum_{n=1}^{\infty} \left(1-\frac{1}{3n}\right)^n$

27. $\sum_{n=1}^{\infty} \frac{\ln n}{n^3}$

28. $\sum_{n=1}^{\infty} \frac{(\ln n)^n}{n^n}$

29. $\sum_{n=1}^{\infty} \left(\frac{1}{n}-\frac{1}{n^2}\right)$

30. $\sum_{n=1}^{\infty} \left(\frac{1}{n}-\frac{1}{n^2}\right)^n$

31. $\sum_{n=1}^{\infty} \frac{\ln n}{n}$

32. $\sum_{n=1}^{\infty} \frac{n\ln n}{2^n}$

33. $\sum_{n=1}^{\infty} \frac{(n+1)(n+2)}{n!}$

34. $\sum_{n=1}^{\infty} e^{-n}(n^3)$

35. $\sum_{n=1}^{\infty} \frac{(n+3)!}{3!\,n!\,3^n}$

36. $\sum_{n=1}^{\infty} \frac{n2^n(n+1)!}{3^n n!}$

37. $\sum_{n=1}^{\infty} \frac{n!}{(2n+1)!}$

38. $\sum_{n=1}^{\infty} \frac{n!}{n^n}$

39. $\sum_{n=2}^{\infty} \frac{n}{(\ln n)^n}$

40. $\sum_{n=2}^{\infty} \frac{n}{(\ln n)^{(n/2)}}$

41. $\sum_{n=1}^{\infty} \frac{n!\ln n}{n(n+2)!}$

42. $\sum_{n=1}^{\infty} \frac{3^n}{n^3 2^n}$

43. $\sum_{n=1}^{\infty} \frac{(n!)^2}{(2n)!}$

44. $\sum_{n=1}^{\infty} \frac{(2n+3)(2^n+3)}{3^n+2}$

Recursively Defined Terms Which of the series $\sum_{n=1}^{\infty} a_n$ defined by the formulas in Exercises 45–54 converge, and which diverge? Give reasons for your answers.

45. $a_1 = 2, \quad a_{n+1} = \frac{1+\sin n}{n} a_n$

46. $a_1 = 1, \quad a_{n+1} = \frac{1+\tan^{-1} n}{n} a_n$

47. $a_1 = \frac{1}{3}, \quad a_{n+1} = \frac{3n-1}{2n+5} a_n$

48. $a_1 = 3, \quad a_{n+1} = \frac{n}{n+1} a_n$

49. $a_1 = 2, \quad a_{n+1} = \frac{2}{n} a_n$

50. $a_1 = 5, \quad a_{n+1} = \frac{\sqrt[n]{n}}{2} a_n$

51. $a_1 = 1, \quad a_{n+1} = \frac{1+\ln n}{n} a_n$

52. $a_1 = \frac{1}{2}, \quad a_{n+1} = \frac{n+\ln n}{n+10} a_n$

53. $a_1 = \frac{1}{3}, \quad a_{n+1} = \sqrt[n]{a_n}$

54. $a_1 = \frac{1}{2}, \quad a_{n+1} = (a_n)^{n+1}$

Convergence or Divergence

Which of the series in Exercises 55–62 converge, and which diverge? Give reasons for your answers.

55. $\sum_{n=1}^{\infty} \frac{2^n n!\,n!}{(2n)!}$

56. $\sum_{n=1}^{\infty} \frac{(3n)!}{n!(n+1)!(n+2)!}$

57. $\sum_{n=1}^{\infty} \frac{(n!)^n}{(n^n)^2}$

58. $\sum_{n=1}^{\infty} \frac{(n!)^n}{n^{(n^2)}}$

59. $\sum_{n=1}^{\infty} \frac{n^n}{2^{(n^2)}}$

60. $\sum_{n=1}^{\infty} \frac{n^n}{(2^n)^2}$

61. $\sum_{n=1}^{\infty} \frac{1\cdot 3\cdot \cdots \cdot(2n-1)}{4^n 2^n n!}$

62. $\sum_{n=1}^{\infty} \frac{1\cdot 3\cdot \cdots \cdot(2n-1)}{[2\cdot 4\cdot \cdots \cdot(2n)](3^n+1)}$

Theory and Examples

63. Neither the Ratio Test nor the Root Test helps with p-series. Try them on

$$\sum_{n=1}^{\infty} \frac{1}{n^p}$$

and show that both tests fail to provide information about convergence.

64. Show that neither the Ratio Test nor the Root Test provides information about the convergence of

$$\sum_{n=2}^{\infty} \frac{1}{(\ln n)^p} \qquad (p \text{ constant}).$$

65. Let $a_n = \begin{cases} n/2^n, & \text{if } n \text{ is a prime number} \\ 1/2^n, & \text{otherwise.} \end{cases}$

Does $\sum a_n$ converge? Give reasons for your answer.

66. Show that $\sum_{n=1}^{\infty} 2^{(n^2)}/n!$ diverges. Recall from the Laws of Exponents that $2^{(n^2)} = (2^n)^n$.

9.6 Alternating Series, Absolute and Conditional Convergence

A series in which the terms are alternately positive and negative is an **alternating series**. Here are three examples:

$$1 - \frac{1}{2} + \frac{1}{3} - \frac{1}{4} + \frac{1}{5} - \cdots + \frac{(-1)^{n+1}}{n} + \cdots \tag{1}$$

$$-2 + 1 - \frac{1}{2} + \frac{1}{4} - \frac{1}{8} + \cdots + \frac{(-1)^n 4}{2^n} + \cdots \tag{2}$$

$$1 - 2 + 3 - 4 + 5 - 6 + \cdots + (-1)^{n+1} n + \cdots \tag{3}$$

We see from these examples that the nth term of an alternating series is of the form

$$a_n = (-1)^{n+1} u_n \qquad \text{or} \qquad a_n = (-1)^n u_n$$

where $u_n = |a_n|$ is a positive number.

Series (1), called the **alternating harmonic series**, converges, as we will see in a moment. Series (2), a geometric series with ratio $r = -1/2$, converges to $-2/[1 + (1/2)] = -4/3$. Series (3) diverges because the nth term does not approach zero.

We prove the convergence of the alternating harmonic series by applying the Alternating Series Test. This test is for convergence of an alternating series and cannot be used to conclude that such a series diverges. The test is also valid for the alternating series $-u_1 + u_2 - u_3 + \cdots$, like the one in Series (2) given above.

THEOREM 14—The Alternating Series Test The series

$$\sum_{n=1}^{\infty} (-1)^{n+1} u_n = u_1 - u_2 + u_3 - u_4 + \cdots$$

converges if all three of the following conditions are satisfied:

1. The u_n's are all positive.
2. The positive u_n's are (eventually) nonincreasing: $u_n \geq u_{n+1}$ for all $n \geq N$, for some integer N.
3. $u_n \to 0$.

Proof Assume $N = 1$. If n is an even integer, say $n = 2m$, then the sum of the first n terms is

$$\begin{aligned} s_{2m} &= (u_1 - u_2) + (u_3 - u_4) + \cdots + (u_{2m-1} - u_{2m}) \\ &= u_1 - (u_2 - u_3) - (u_4 - u_5) - \cdots - (u_{2m-2} - u_{2m-1}) - u_{2m}. \end{aligned}$$

The first equality shows that s_{2m} is the sum of m nonnegative terms since each term in parentheses is positive or zero. Hence $s_{2m+2} \geq s_{2m}$, and the sequence $\{s_{2m}\}$ is nondecreasing. The second equality shows that $s_{2m} \leq u_1$. Since $\{s_{2m}\}$ is nondecreasing and bounded from above, it has a limit, say

$$\lim_{m\to\infty} s_{2m} = L. \tag{4}$$

If n is an odd integer, say $n = 2m + 1$, then the sum of the first n terms is $s_{2m+1} = s_{2m} + u_{2m+1}$. Since $u_n \to 0$,

$$\lim_{m\to\infty} u_{2m+1} = 0$$

and, as $m \to \infty$,

$$s_{2m+1} = s_{2m} + u_{2m+1} \to L + 0 = L. \tag{5}$$

Combining the results of Equations (4) and (5) gives $\lim_{n\to\infty} s_n = L$ (Section 9.1, Exercise 131). ■

EXAMPLE 1 The alternating harmonic series

$$\sum_{n=1}^{\infty} (-1)^{n+1} \frac{1}{n} = 1 - \frac{1}{2} + \frac{1}{3} - \frac{1}{4} + \cdots$$

clearly satisfies the three requirements of Theorem 14 with $N = 1$; it therefore converges. ■

Rather than directly verifying the definition $u_n \geq u_{n+1}$, a second way to show that the sequence $\{u_n\}$ is nonincreasing is to define a differentiable function $f(x)$ satisfying $f(n) = u_n$. That is, the values of f match the values of the sequence at every positive integer n. If $f'(x) \leq 0$ for all x greater than or equal to some positive integer N, then $f(x)$ is nonincreasing for $x \geq N$. It follows that $f(n) \geq f(n + 1)$, or $u_n \geq u_{n+1}$, for $n \geq N$.

EXAMPLE 2 Consider the sequence where $u_n = 10n/(n^2 + 16)$. Define $f(x) = 10x/(x^2 + 16)$. Then from the Derivative Quotient Rule,

$$f'(x) = \frac{10(16 - x^2)}{(x^2 + 16)^2} \leq 0 \qquad \text{whenever } x \geq 4.$$

It follows that $u_n \geq u_{n+1}$ for $n \geq 4$. That is, the sequence $\{u_n\}$ is nonincreasing for $n \geq 4$. ■

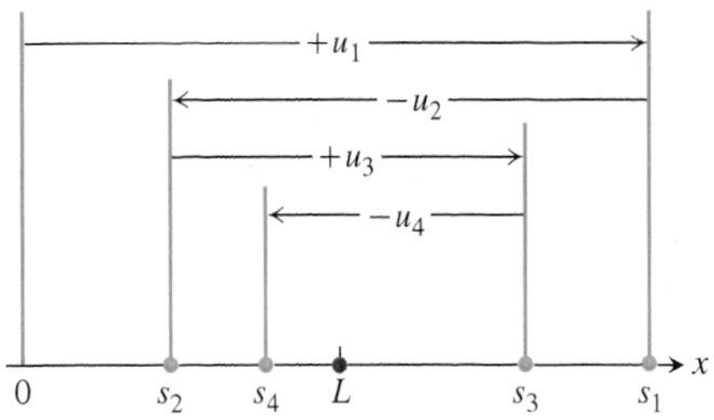

FIGURE 9.13 The partial sums of an alternating series that satisfies the hypotheses of Theorem 14 for $N = 1$ straddle the limit from the beginning.

A graphical interpretation of the partial sums (Figure 9.13) shows how an alternating series converges to its limit L when the three conditions of Theorem 14 are satisfied with $N = 1$. Starting from the origin of the x-axis, we lay off the positive distance $s_1 = u_1$. To find the point corresponding to $s_2 = u_1 - u_2$, we back up a distance equal to u_2. Since $u_2 \leq u_1$, we do not back up any farther than the origin. We continue in this seesaw fashion, backing up or going forward as the signs in the series demand. But for $n \geq N$, each forward or backward step is shorter than (or at most the same size as) the preceding step because $u_{n+1} \leq u_n$. And since the nth term approaches zero as n increases, the size of step we take forward or backward gets smaller and smaller. We oscillate across the limit L, and the amplitude of oscillation approaches zero. The limit L lies between any two successive sums s_n and s_{n+1} and hence differs from s_n by an amount less than u_{n+1}.

Because

$$|L - s_n| < u_{n+1} \qquad \text{for } n \geq N,$$

we can make useful estimates of the sums of convergent alternating series.

THEOREM 15—The Alternating Series Estimation Theorem If the alternating series $\sum_{n=1}^{\infty}(-1)^{n+1}u_n$ satisfies the three conditions of Theorem 14, then for $n \geq N$,

$$s_n = u_1 - u_2 + \cdots + (-1)^{n+1}u_n$$

approximates the sum L of the series with an error whose absolute value is less than u_{n+1}, the absolute value of the first unused term. Furthermore, the sum L lies between any two successive partial sums s_n and s_{n+1}, and the remainder, $L - s_n$, has the same sign as the first unused term.

We leave the verification of the sign of the remainder for Exercise 61.

EXAMPLE 3 We try Theorem 15 on a series whose sum we know:

$$\sum_{n=0}^{\infty}(-1)^n\frac{1}{2^n} = 1 - \frac{1}{2} + \frac{1}{4} - \frac{1}{8} + \frac{1}{16} - \frac{1}{32} + \frac{1}{64} - \frac{1}{128} \,\vdots\, + \frac{1}{256} - \cdots.$$

The theorem says that if we truncate the series after the eighth term, we throw away a total that is positive and less than $1/256$. The sum of the first eight terms is $s_8 = 0.6640625$ and the sum of the first nine terms is $s_9 = 0.66796875$. The sum of the geometric series is

$$\frac{1}{1-(-1/2)} = \frac{1}{3/2} = \frac{2}{3},$$

and we note that $0.6640625 < (2/3) < 0.66796875$. The difference, $(2/3) - 0.6640625 = 0.0026041666\ldots$, is positive and is less than $(1/256) = 0.00390625$. ■

Absolute and Conditional Convergence

We can apply the tests for convergence studied before to the series of absolute values of a series with both positive and negative terms.

DEFINITION A series $\sum a_n$ **converges absolutely** (is **absolutely convergent**) if the corresponding series of absolute values, $\sum|a_n|$, converges.

The geometric series in Example 3 converges absolutely because the corresponding series of absolute values

$$\sum_{n=0}^{\infty}\frac{1}{2^n} = 1 + \frac{1}{2} + \frac{1}{4} + \frac{1}{8} + \cdots$$

converges. The alternating harmonic series does not converge absolutely because the corresponding series of absolute values is the (divergent) harmonic series.

DEFINITION A series that converges but does not converge absolutely **converges conditionally**.

The alternating harmonic series converges conditionally.

Absolute convergence is important for two reasons. First, we have good tests for convergence of series of positive terms. Second, if a series converges absolutely, then it converges, as we now prove.

THEOREM 16—The Absolute Convergence Test If $\sum_{n=1}^{\infty} |a_n|$ converges, then $\sum_{n=1}^{\infty} a_n$ converges.

Proof For each n,

$$-|a_n| \le a_n \le |a_n|, \qquad \text{so} \qquad 0 \le a_n + |a_n| \le 2|a_n|.$$

If $\sum_{n=1}^{\infty} |a_n|$ converges, then $\sum_{n=1}^{\infty} 2|a_n|$ converges and, by the Direct Comparison Test, the nonnegative series $\sum_{n=1}^{\infty} (a_n + |a_n|)$ converges. The equality $a_n = (a_n + |a_n|) - |a_n|$ now lets us express $\sum_{n=1}^{\infty} a_n$ as the difference of two convergent series:

$$\sum_{n=1}^{\infty} a_n = \sum_{n=1}^{\infty} (a_n + |a_n| - |a_n|) = \sum_{n=1}^{\infty} (a_n + |a_n|) - \sum_{n=1}^{\infty} |a_n|.$$

Therefore, $\sum_{n=1}^{\infty} a_n$ converges. ■

Caution We can rephrase Theorem 16 to say that every absolutely convergent series converges. However, the converse statement is false: Many convergent series do not converge absolutely (such as the alternating harmonic series in Example 1).

EXAMPLE 4 This example gives two series that converge absolutely.

(a) For $\sum_{n=1}^{\infty} (-1)^{n+1} \frac{1}{n^2} = 1 - \frac{1}{4} + \frac{1}{9} - \frac{1}{16} + \cdots$, the corresponding series of absolute values is the convergent series

$$\sum_{n=1}^{\infty} \frac{1}{n^2} = 1 + \frac{1}{4} + \frac{1}{9} + \frac{1}{16} + \cdots.$$

The original series converges because it converges absolutely.

(b) For $\sum_{n=1}^{\infty} \frac{\sin n}{n^2} = \frac{\sin 1}{1} + \frac{\sin 2}{4} + \frac{\sin 3}{9} + \cdots$, which contains both positive and negative terms, the corresponding series of absolute values is

$$\sum_{n=1}^{\infty} \left| \frac{\sin n}{n^2} \right| = \frac{|\sin 1|}{1} + \frac{|\sin 2|}{4} + \cdots,$$

which converges by comparison with $\sum_{n=1}^{\infty} (1/n^2)$ because $|\sin n| \le 1$ for every n. The original series converges absolutely; therefore it converges. ■

EXAMPLE 5 If p is a positive constant, the sequence $\{1/n^p\}$ is a decreasing sequence with limit zero. Therefore the alternating p-series

$$\sum_{n=1}^{\infty} \frac{(-1)^{n-1}}{n^p} = 1 - \frac{1}{2^p} + \frac{1}{3^p} - \frac{1}{4^p} + \cdots, \qquad p > 0$$

converges.

If $p > 1$, the series converges absolutely. If $0 < p \le 1$, the series converges conditionally.

$$\text{Conditional convergence:} \qquad 1 - \frac{1}{\sqrt{2}} + \frac{1}{\sqrt{3}} - \frac{1}{\sqrt{4}} + \cdots$$

$$\text{Absolute convergence:} \qquad 1 - \frac{1}{2^{3/2}} + \frac{1}{3^{3/2}} - \frac{1}{4^{3/2}} + \cdots$$

■

Rearranging Series

We can always rearrange the terms of a *finite* sum. The same result is true for an infinite series that is absolutely convergent (see Exercise 68 for an outline of the proof).

THEOREM 17—The Rearrangement Theorem for Absolutely Convergent Series If $\sum_{n=1}^{\infty} a_n$ converges absolutely, and $b_1, b_2, \ldots, b_n, \ldots$ is any arrangement of the sequence $\{a_n\}$, then $\sum b_n$ converges absolutely and

$$\sum_{n=1}^{\infty} b_n = \sum_{n=1}^{\infty} a_n.$$

If we rearrange the terms of a conditionally convergent series, we get different results. In fact, it can be proved that for any real number r, a given conditionally convergent series can be rearranged so its sum is equal to r. (We omit the proof of this fact.) Here's an example of summing the terms of a conditionally convergent series with different orderings, with each ordering giving a different value for the sum.

EXAMPLE 6 We know that the alternating harmonic series $\sum_{n=1}^{\infty} (-1)^{n+1}/n$ converges to some number L. Moreover, by Theorem 15, L lies between the successive partial sums $s_2 = 1/2$ and $s_3 = 5/6$, so $L \neq 0$. If we multiply the series by 2 we obtain

$$\begin{aligned} 2L = 2\sum_{n=1}^{\infty} \frac{(-1)^{n+1}}{n} &= 2\left(1 - \frac{1}{2} + \frac{1}{3} - \frac{1}{4} + \frac{1}{5} - \frac{1}{6} + \frac{1}{7} - \frac{1}{8} + \frac{1}{9} - \frac{1}{10} + \frac{1}{11} - \cdots\right) \\ &= 2 - 1 + \frac{2}{3} - \frac{1}{2} + \frac{2}{5} - \frac{1}{3} + \frac{2}{7} - \frac{1}{4} + \frac{2}{9} - \frac{1}{5} + \frac{2}{11} - \cdots. \end{aligned}$$

Now we change the order of this last sum by grouping each pair of terms with the same odd denominator, but leaving the negative terms with the even denominators as they are placed (so the denominators are the positive integers in their natural order). This rearrangement gives

$$\begin{aligned} (2 - 1) - \frac{1}{2} + \left(\frac{2}{3} - \frac{1}{3}\right) - \frac{1}{4} + \left(\frac{2}{5} - \frac{1}{5}\right) - \frac{1}{6} + \left(\frac{2}{7} - \frac{1}{7}\right) - \frac{1}{8} + \cdots \\ = \left(1 - \frac{1}{2} + \frac{1}{3} - \frac{1}{4} + \frac{1}{5} - \frac{1}{6} + \frac{1}{7} - \frac{1}{8} + \frac{1}{9} - \frac{1}{10} + \frac{1}{11} - \cdots\right) \\ = \sum_{n=1}^{\infty} \frac{(-1)^{n+1}}{n} = L. \end{aligned}$$

So by rearranging the terms of the conditionally convergent series $\sum_{n=1}^{\infty} 2(-1)^{n+1}/n$, the series becomes $\sum_{n=1}^{\infty} (-1)^{n+1}/n$, which is the alternating harmonic series itself. If the two series are the same, it would imply that $2L = L$, which is clearly false since $L \neq 0$. ■

Example 6 shows that we cannot rearrange the terms of a conditionally convergent series and expect the new series to be the same as the original one. When we are using a conditionally convergent series, the terms must be added together in the order they are given to obtain a correct result. On the other hand, Theorem 17 guarantees that the terms of an absolutely convergent series can be summed in any order without affecting the result.

Summary of Tests

We have developed a variety of tests to determine convergence or divergence for an infinite series of constants. There are other tests we have not presented which are sometimes given in more advanced courses. Here is a summary of the tests we have considered.

1. **The nth-Term Test:** Unless $a_n \to 0$, the series diverges.
2. **Geometric series:** $\sum ar^n$ converges if $|r| < 1$; otherwise it diverges.
3. **p-series:** $\sum 1/n^p$ converges if $p > 1$; otherwise it diverges.
4. **Series with nonnegative terms:** Try the Integral Test, Ratio Test, or Root Test. Try comparing to a known series with the Comparison Test or the Limit Comparison Test.
5. **Series with some negative terms:** Does $\sum |a_n|$ converge? If yes, so does $\sum a_n$ since absolute convergence implies convergence.
6. **Alternating series:** $\sum a_n$ converges if the series satisfies the conditions of the Alternating Series Test.

Exercises 9.6

Determining Convergence or Divergence

In Exercises 1–14, determine if the alternating series converges or diverges. Some of the series do not satisfy the conditions of the Alternating Series Test.

1. $\sum_{n=1}^{\infty} (-1)^{n+1} \frac{1}{\sqrt{n}}$
2. $\sum_{n=1}^{\infty} (-1)^{n+1} \frac{1}{n^{3/2}}$
3. $\sum_{n=1}^{\infty} (-1)^{n+1} \frac{1}{n3^n}$
4. $\sum_{n=2}^{\infty} (-1)^{n} \frac{4}{(\ln n)^2}$
5. $\sum_{n=1}^{\infty} (-1)^{n} \frac{n}{n^2+1}$
6. $\sum_{n=1}^{\infty} (-1)^{n+1} \frac{n^2+5}{n^2+4}$
7. $\sum_{n=1}^{\infty} (-1)^{n+1} \frac{2^n}{n^2}$
8. $\sum_{n=1}^{\infty} (-1)^{n} \frac{10^n}{(n+1)!}$
9. $\sum_{n=1}^{\infty} (-1)^{n+1} \left(\frac{n}{10}\right)^n$
10. $\sum_{n=2}^{\infty} (-1)^{n+1} \frac{1}{\ln n}$
11. $\sum_{n=1}^{\infty} (-1)^{n+1} \frac{\ln n}{n}$
12. $\sum_{n=1}^{\infty} (-1)^{n} \ln\left(1+\frac{1}{n}\right)$
13. $\sum_{n=1}^{\infty} (-1)^{n+1} \frac{\sqrt{n}+1}{n+1}$
14. $\sum_{n=1}^{\infty} (-1)^{n+1} \frac{3\sqrt{n+1}}{\sqrt{n}+1}$

Absolute and Conditional Convergence

Which of the series in Exercises 15–48 converge absolutely, which converge, and which diverge? Give reasons for your answers.

15. $\sum_{n=1}^{\infty} (-1)^{n+1}(0.1)^n$
16. $\sum_{n=1}^{\infty} (-1)^{n+1} \frac{(0.1)^n}{n}$
17. $\sum_{n=1}^{\infty} (-1)^{n} \frac{1}{\sqrt{n}}$
18. $\sum_{n=1}^{\infty} \frac{(-1)^n}{1+\sqrt{n}}$
19. $\sum_{n=1}^{\infty} (-1)^{n+1} \frac{n}{n^3+1}$
20. $\sum_{n=1}^{\infty} (-1)^{n+1} \frac{n!}{2^n}$
21. $\sum_{n=1}^{\infty} (-1)^{n} \frac{1}{n+3}$
22. $\sum_{n=1}^{\infty} (-1)^{n} \frac{\sin n}{n^2}$
23. $\sum_{n=1}^{\infty} (-1)^{n+1} \frac{3+n}{5+n}$
24. $\sum_{n=1}^{\infty} \frac{(-2)^{n+1}}{n+5^n}$
25. $\sum_{n=1}^{\infty} (-1)^{n+1} \frac{1+n}{n^2}$
26. $\sum_{n=1}^{\infty} (-1)^{n+1}\left(\sqrt[n]{10}\right)$
27. $\sum_{n=1}^{\infty} (-1)^{n} n^2 (2/3)^n$
28. $\sum_{n=2}^{\infty} (-1)^{n+1} \frac{1}{n \ln n}$
29. $\sum_{n=1}^{\infty} (-1)^{n} \frac{\tan^{-1} n}{n^2+1}$
30. $\sum_{n=1}^{\infty} (-1)^{n} \frac{\ln n}{n - \ln n}$
31. $\sum_{n=1}^{\infty} (-1)^{n} \frac{n}{n+1}$
32. $\sum_{n=1}^{\infty} (-5)^{-n}$
33. $\sum_{n=1}^{\infty} \frac{(-100)^n}{n!}$
34. $\sum_{n=1}^{\infty} \frac{(-1)^{n-1}}{n^2+2n+1}$
35. $\sum_{n=1}^{\infty} \frac{\cos n\pi}{n\sqrt{n}}$
36. $\sum_{n=1}^{\infty} \frac{\cos n\pi}{n}$
37. $\sum_{n=1}^{\infty} \frac{(-1)^n (n+1)^n}{(2n)^n}$
38. $\sum_{n=1}^{\infty} \frac{(-1)^{n+1} (n!)^2}{(2n)!}$
39. $\sum_{n=1}^{\infty} (-1)^{n} \frac{(2n)!}{2^n n! n}$
40. $\sum_{n=1}^{\infty} (-1)^{n} \frac{(n!)^2 3^n}{(2n+1)!}$
41. $\sum_{n=1}^{\infty} (-1)^{n}\left(\sqrt{n+1} - \sqrt{n}\right)$
42. $\sum_{n=1}^{\infty} (-1)^{n}\left(\sqrt{n^2+n} - n\right)$
43. $\sum_{n=1}^{\infty} (-1)^{n}\left(\sqrt{n+\sqrt{n}} - \sqrt{n}\right)$
44. $\sum_{n=1}^{\infty} \frac{(-1)^n}{\sqrt{n}+\sqrt{n+1}}$
45. $\sum_{n=1}^{\infty} (-1)^{n} \operatorname{sech} n$
46. $\sum_{n=1}^{\infty} (-1)^{n} \operatorname{csch} n$
47. $\frac{1}{4} - \frac{1}{6} + \frac{1}{8} - \frac{1}{10} + \frac{1}{12} - \frac{1}{14} + \cdots$
48. $1 + \frac{1}{4} - \frac{1}{9} - \frac{1}{16} + \frac{1}{25} + \frac{1}{36} - \frac{1}{49} - \frac{1}{64} + \cdots$

Error Estimation

In Exercises 49–52, estimate the magnitude of the error involved in using the sum of the first four terms to approximate the sum of the entire series.

49. $\sum_{n=1}^{\infty} (-1)^{n+1} \frac{1}{n}$
50. $\sum_{n=1}^{\infty} (-1)^{n+1} \frac{1}{10^n}$

51. $\sum_{n=1}^{\infty}(-1)^{n+1}\frac{(0.01)^n}{n}$ As you will see in Section 9.7, the sum is $\ln(1.01)$.

52. $\frac{1}{1+t} = \sum_{n=0}^{\infty}(-1)^n t^n, \quad 0 < t < 1$

In Exercises 53–56, determine how many terms should be used to estimate the sum of the entire series with an error of less than 0.001.

53. $\sum_{n=1}^{\infty}(-1)^n\frac{1}{n^2+3}$

54. $\sum_{n=1}^{\infty}(-1)^{n+1}\frac{n}{n^2+1}$

55. $\sum_{n=1}^{\infty}(-1)^{n+1}\frac{1}{\left(n+3\sqrt{n}\right)^3}$

56. $\sum_{n=1}^{\infty}(-1)^n\frac{1}{\ln(\ln(n+2))}$

T Approximate the sums in Exercises 57 and 58 with an error of magnitude less than 5×10^{-6}.

57. $\sum_{n=0}^{\infty}(-1)^n\frac{1}{(2n)!}$ As you will see in Section 9.9, the sum is cos 1, the cosine of 1 radian.

58. $\sum_{n=0}^{\infty}(-1)^n\frac{1}{n!}$ As you will see in Section 9.9, the sum is e^{-1}.

Theory and Examples

59. a. The series

$$\frac{1}{3}-\frac{1}{2}+\frac{1}{9}-\frac{1}{4}+\frac{1}{27}-\frac{1}{8}+\cdots+\frac{1}{3^n}-\frac{1}{2^n}+\cdots$$

does not meet one of the conditions of Theorem 14. Which one?

b. Use Theorem 17 to find the sum of the series in part (a).

T 60. The limit L of an alternating series that satisfies the conditions of Theorem 14 lies between the values of any two consecutive partial sums. This suggests using the average

$$\frac{s_n + s_{n+1}}{2} = s_n + \frac{1}{2}(-1)^{n+2}a_{n+1}$$

to estimate L. Compute

$$s_{20} + \frac{1}{2}\cdot\frac{1}{21}$$

as an approximation to the sum of the alternating harmonic series. The exact sum is $\ln 2 = 0.69314718\ldots$.

61. The sign of the remainder of an alternating series that satisfies the conditions of Theorem 14 Prove the assertion in Theorem 15 that whenever an alternating series satisfying the conditions of Theorem 14 is approximated with one of its partial sums, then the remainder (sum of the unused terms) has the same sign as the first unused term. (*Hint:* Group the remainder's terms in consecutive pairs.)

62. Show that the sum of the first $2n$ terms of the series

$$1-\frac{1}{2}+\frac{1}{2}-\frac{1}{3}+\frac{1}{3}-\frac{1}{4}+\frac{1}{4}-\frac{1}{5}+\frac{1}{5}-\frac{1}{6}+\cdots$$

is the same as the sum of the first n terms of the series

$$\frac{1}{1\cdot 2}+\frac{1}{2\cdot 3}+\frac{1}{3\cdot 4}+\frac{1}{4\cdot 5}+\frac{1}{5\cdot 6}+\cdots.$$

Do these series converge? What is the sum of the first $2n+1$ terms of the first series? If the series converge, what is their sum?

63. Show that if $\sum_{n=1}^{\infty} a_n$ diverges, then $\sum_{n=1}^{\infty}|a_n|$ diverges.

64. Show that if $\sum_{n=1}^{\infty} a_n$ converges absolutely, then

$$\left|\sum_{n=1}^{\infty} a_n\right| \le \sum_{n=1}^{\infty}|a_n|.$$

65. Show that if $\sum_{n=1}^{\infty} a_n$ and $\sum_{n=1}^{\infty} b_n$ both converge absolutely, then so do the following.

a. $\sum_{n=1}^{\infty}(a_n+b_n)$

b. $\sum_{n=1}^{\infty}(a_n-b_n)$

c. $\sum_{n=1}^{\infty} ka_n$ (k any number)

66. Show by example that $\sum_{n=1}^{\infty} a_n b_n$ may diverge even if $\sum_{n=1}^{\infty} a_n$ and $\sum_{n=1}^{\infty} b_n$ both converge.

T 67. In the alternating harmonic series, suppose the goal is to arrange the terms to get a new series that converges to $-1/2$. Start the new arrangement with the first negative term, which is $-1/2$. Whenever you have a sum that is less than or equal to $-1/2$, start introducing positive terms, taken in order, until the new total is greater than $-1/2$. Then add negative terms until the total is less than or equal to $-1/2$ again. Continue this process until your partial sums have been above the target at least three times and finish at or below it. If s_n is the sum of the first n terms of your new series, plot the points (n, s_n) to illustrate how the sums are behaving.

68. Outline of the proof of the Rearrangement Theorem (Theorem 17)

a. Let ϵ be a positive real number, let $L = \sum_{n=1}^{\infty} a_n$, and let $s_k = \sum_{n=1}^{k} a_n$. Show that for some index N_1 and for some index $N_2 \ge N_1$,

$$\sum_{n=N_1}^{\infty}|a_n| < \frac{\epsilon}{2} \quad\text{and}\quad |s_{N_2} - L| < \frac{\epsilon}{2}.$$

Since all the terms $a_1, a_2, \ldots, a_{N_2}$ appear somewhere in the sequence $\{b_n\}$, there is an index $N_3 \ge N_2$ such that if $n \ge N_3$, then $\left(\sum_{k=1}^{n} b_k\right) - s_{N_2}$ is at most a sum of terms a_m with $m \ge N_1$. Therefore, if $n \ge N_3$,

$$\left|\sum_{k=1}^{n} b_k - L\right| \le \left|\sum_{k=1}^{n} b_k - s_{N_2}\right| + |s_{N_2} - L|$$
$$\le \sum_{k=N_1}^{\infty}|a_k| + |s_{N_2} - L| < \epsilon.$$

b. The argument in part (a) shows that if $\sum_{n=1}^{\infty} a_n$ converges absolutely then $\sum_{n=1}^{\infty} b_n$ converges and $\sum_{n=1}^{\infty} b_n = \sum_{n=1}^{\infty} a_n$. Now show that because $\sum_{n=1}^{\infty}|a_n|$ converges, $\sum_{n=1}^{\infty}|b_n|$ converges to $\sum_{n=1}^{\infty}|a_n|$.

9.7 Power Series

Now that we can test many infinite series of numbers for convergence, we can study sums that look like "infinite polynomials." We call these sums *power series* because they are defined as infinite series of powers of some variable, in our case x. Like polynomials, power series can be added, subtracted, multiplied, differentiated, and integrated to give new power series. With power series we can extend the methods of calculus we have developed to a vast array of functions making the techniques of calculus applicable in a much wider setting.

Power Series and Convergence

We begin with the formal definition, which specifies the notation and terminology used for power series.

DEFINITIONS A **power series about $x = 0$** is a series of the form

$$\sum_{n=0}^{\infty} c_n x^n = c_0 + c_1 x + c_2 x^2 + \cdots + c_n x^n + \cdots. \tag{1}$$

A **power series about $x = a$** is a series of the form

$$\sum_{n=0}^{\infty} c_n (x-a)^n = c_0 + c_1(x-a) + c_2(x-a)^2 + \cdots + c_n(x-a)^n + \cdots \tag{2}$$

in which the **center** a and the **coefficients** $c_0, c_1, c_2, \ldots, c_n, \ldots$ are constants.

Equation (1) is the special case obtained by taking $a = 0$ in Equation (2). We will see that a power series defines a function $f(x)$ on a certain interval where it converges. Moreover, this function will be shown to be continuous and differentiable over the interior of that interval.

EXAMPLE 1 Taking all the coefficients to be 1 in Equation (1) gives the geometric power series

$$\sum_{n=0}^{\infty} x^n = 1 + x + x^2 + \cdots + x^n + \cdots.$$

This is the geometric series with first term 1 and ratio x. It converges to $1/(1-x)$ for $|x| < 1$. We express this fact by writing

$$\frac{1}{1-x} = 1 + x + x^2 + \cdots + x^n + \cdots, \qquad -1 < x < 1. \tag{3}$$

■

Reciprocal Power Series

$$\frac{1}{1-x} = \sum_{n=0}^{\infty} x^n, \quad |x| < 1$$

Up to now, we have used Equation (3) as a formula for the sum of the series on the right. We now change the focus: We think of the partial sums of the series on the right as polynomials $P_n(x)$ that approximate the function on the left. For values of x near zero, we need take only a few terms of the series to get a good approximation. As we move toward $x = 1$, or -1, we must take more terms. Figure 9.14 shows the graphs of $f(x) = 1/(1-x)$ and the approximating polynomials $y_n = P_n(x)$ for $n = 0, 1, 2$, and 8. The function $f(x) = 1/(1-x)$ is not continuous on intervals containing $x = 1$, where it has a vertical asymptote. The approximations do not apply when $x \geq 1$.

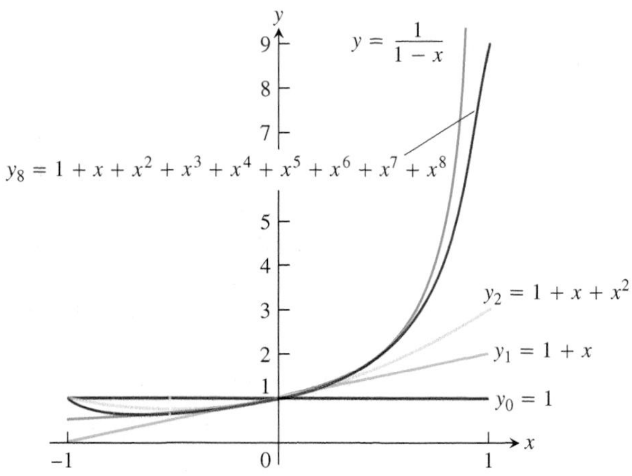

FIGURE 9.14 The graphs of $f(x) = 1/(1 - x)$ in Example 1 and four of its polynomial approximations.

EXAMPLE 2 The power series

$$1 - \frac{1}{2}(x - 2) + \frac{1}{4}(x - 2)^2 + \cdots + \left(-\frac{1}{2}\right)^n (x - 2)^n + \cdots \tag{4}$$

matches Equation (2) with $a = 2$, $c_0 = 1$, $c_1 = -1/2$, $c_2 = 1/4, \ldots, c_n = (-1/2)^n$. This is a geometric series with first term 1 and ratio $r = -\frac{x-2}{2}$. The series converges for $\left|\frac{x-2}{2}\right| < 1$ or $0 < x < 4$. The sum is

$$\frac{1}{1 - r} = \frac{1}{1 + \frac{x-2}{2}} = \frac{2}{x},$$

so

$$\frac{2}{x} = 1 - \frac{(x-2)}{2} + \frac{(x-2)^2}{4} - \cdots + \left(-\frac{1}{2}\right)^n (x - 2)^n + \cdots, \qquad 0 < x < 4.$$

Series (4) generates useful polynomial approximations of $f(x) = 2/x$ for values of x near 2:

$$P_0(x) = 1$$

$$P_1(x) = 1 - \frac{1}{2}(x - 2) = 2 - \frac{x}{2}$$

$$P_2(x) = 1 - \frac{1}{2}(x - 2) + \frac{1}{4}(x - 2)^2 = 3 - \frac{3x}{2} + \frac{x^2}{4},$$

and so on (Figure 9.15). ■

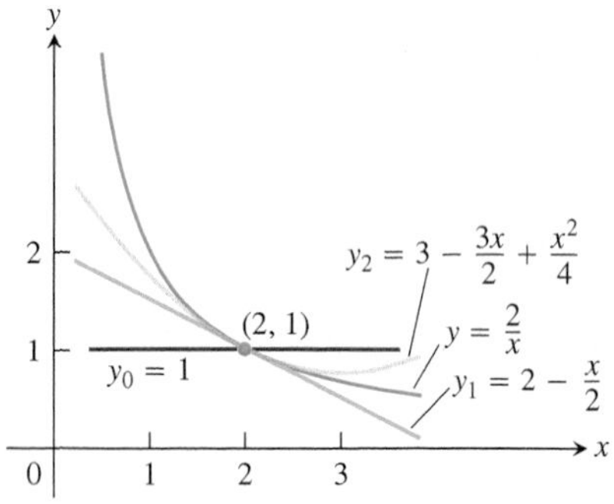

FIGURE 9.15 The graphs of $f(x) = 2/x$ and its first three polynomial approximations (Example 2).

The following example illustrates how we test a power series for convergence by using the Ratio Test to see where it converges and diverges.

EXAMPLE 3 For what values of x do the following power series converge?

(a) $\sum_{n=1}^{\infty} (-1)^{n-1} \frac{x^n}{n} = x - \frac{x^2}{2} + \frac{x^3}{3} - \cdots$

(b) $\sum_{n=1}^{\infty}(-1)^{n-1}\frac{x^{2n-1}}{2n-1} = x - \frac{x^3}{3} + \frac{x^5}{5} - \cdots$

(c) $\sum_{n=0}^{\infty}\frac{x^n}{n!} = 1 + x + \frac{x^2}{2!} + \frac{x^3}{3!} + \cdots$

(d) $\sum_{n=0}^{\infty} n!x^n = 1 + x + 2!x^2 + 3!x^3 + \cdots$

Solution Apply the Ratio Test to the series $\sum|u_n|$, where u_n is the nth term of the power series in question. (Recall that the Ratio Test applies to series with nonnegative terms.)

(a) $$\left|\frac{u_{n+1}}{u_n}\right| = \left|\frac{x^{n+1}}{n+1}\cdot\frac{n}{x}\right| = \frac{n}{n+1}|x| \to |x|.$$

The series converges absolutely for $|x| < 1$. It diverges if $|x| > 1$ because the nth term does not converge to zero. At $x = 1$, we get the alternating harmonic series $1 - 1/2 + 1/3 - 1/4 + \cdots$, which converges. At $x = -1$, we get $-1 - 1/2 - 1/3 - 1/4 - \cdots$, the negative of the harmonic series; it diverges. Series (a) converges for $-1 < x \le 1$ and diverges elsewhere.

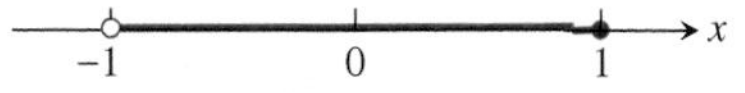

(b) $$\left|\frac{u_{n+1}}{u_n}\right| = \left|\frac{x^{2n+1}}{2n+1}\cdot\frac{2n-1}{x^{2n-1}}\right| = \frac{2n-1}{2n+1}x^2 \to x^2.$$

$2(n+1) - 1 = 2n + 1$

The series converges absolutely for $x^2 < 1$. It diverges for $x^2 > 1$ because the nth term does not converge to zero. At $x = 1$ the series becomes $1 - 1/3 + 1/5 - 1/7 + \cdots$, which converges by the Alternating Series Theorem. It also converges at $x = -1$ because it is again an alternating series that satisfies the conditions for convergence. The value at $x = -1$ is the negative of the value at $x = 1$. Series (b) converges for $-1 \le x \le 1$ and diverges elsewhere.

(c) $$\left|\frac{u_{n+1}}{u_n}\right| = \left|\frac{x^{n+1}}{(n+1)!}\cdot\frac{n!}{x^n}\right| = \frac{|x|}{n+1} \to 0 \text{ for every } x.$$

$\frac{n!}{(n+1)!} = \frac{1\cdot 2\cdot 3\cdots n}{1\cdot 2\cdot 3\cdots n\cdot(n+1)}$

The series converges absolutely for all x.

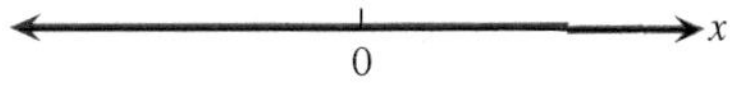

(d) $$\left|\frac{u_{n+1}}{u_n}\right| = \left|\frac{(n+1)!x^{n+1}}{n!x^n}\right| = (n+1)|x| \to \infty \text{ unless } x = 0.$$

The series diverges for all values of x except $x = 0$.

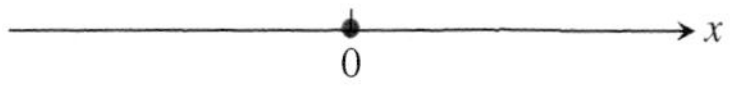

■

The previous example illustrated how a power series might converge. The next result shows that if a power series converges at more than one value, then it converges over an entire interval of values. The interval might be finite or infinite and contain one, both, or none of its endpoints. We will see that each endpoint of a finite interval must be tested independently for convergence or divergence.

THEOREM 18—The Convergence Theorem for Power Series If the power series

$$\sum_{n=0}^{\infty} a_n x^n = a_0 + a_1 x + a_2 x^2 + \cdots$$

converges at $x = c \neq 0$, then it converges absolutely for all x with $|x| < |c|$. If the series diverges at $x = d$, then it diverges for all x with $|x| > |d|$.

Proof The proof uses the Comparison Test, with the given series compared to a converging geometric series.

Suppose the series $\sum_{n=0}^{\infty} a_n c^n$ converges. Then $\lim_{n\to\infty} a_n c^n = 0$ by the nth-Term Test. Hence, there is an integer N such that $|a_n c^n| < 1$ for all $n > N$, so that

$$|a_n| < \frac{1}{|c|^n} \qquad \text{for } n > N. \tag{5}$$

Now take any x such that $|x| < |c|$, so that $|x|/|c| < 1$. Multiplying both sides of Equation (5) by $|x|^n$ gives

$$|a_n||x|^n < \frac{|x|^n}{|c|^n} \qquad \text{for } n > N.$$

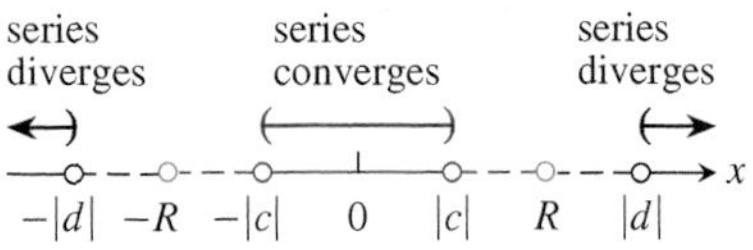

FIGURE 9.16 Convergence of $\sum a_n x^n$ at $x = c$ implies absolute convergence on the interval $-|c| < x < |c|$; divergence at $x = d$ implies divergence for $|x| > |d|$. The corollary to Theorem 18 asserts the existence of a radius of convergence $R \geq 0$. For $|x| < R$ the series converges absolutely and for $|x| > R$ it diverges.

Since $|x/c| < 1$, it follows that the geometric series $\sum_{n=0}^{\infty} |x/c|^n$ converges. By the Comparison Test (Theorem 10), the series $\sum_{n=0}^{\infty} |a_n||x^n|$ converges, so the original power series $\sum_{n=0}^{\infty} a_n x^n$ converges absolutely for $-|c| < x < |c|$ as claimed by the theorem. (See Figure 9.16.)

Now suppose that the series $\sum_{n=0}^{\infty} a_n x^n$ diverges at $x = d$. If x is a number with $|x| > |d|$ and the series converges at x, then the first half of the theorem shows that the series also converges at d, contrary to our assumption. So the series diverges for all x with $|x| > |d|$. ■

To simplify the notation, Theorem 18 deals with the convergence of series of the form $\sum a_n x^n$. For series of the form $\sum a_n (x - a)^n$ we can replace $x - a$ by x' and apply the results to the series $\sum a_n (x')^n$.

The Radius of Convergence of a Power Series

The theorem we have just proved and the examples we have studied lead to the conclusion that a power series $\sum c_n (x - a)^n$ behaves in one of three possible ways. It might converge only at $x = a$, or converge everywhere, or converge on some interval of radius R centered at $x = a$. We prove this as a Corollary to Theorem 18.

COROLLARY TO THEOREM 18 The convergence of the series $\sum c_n (x - a)^n$ is described by one of the following three cases:

1. There is a positive number R such that the series diverges for x with $|x - a| > R$ but converges absolutely for x with $|x - a| < R$. The series may or may not converge at either of the endpoints $x = a - R$ and $x = a + R$.
2. The series converges absolutely for every x $(R = \infty)$.
3. The series converges at $x = a$ and diverges elsewhere $(R = 0)$.

Proof We first consider the case where $a = 0$, so that we have a power series $\sum_{n=0}^{\infty} c_n x^n$ centered at 0. If the series converges everywhere we are in Case 2. If it converges only at $x = 0$ then we are in Case 3. Otherwise there is a nonzero number d such that $\sum_{n=0}^{\infty} c_n d^n$ diverges. Let S be the set of values of x for which $\sum_{n=0}^{\infty} c_n x^n$ converges. The set S does not include any x with $|x| > |d|$, since Theorem 18 implies the series diverges at all such values. So the set S is bounded. By the Completeness Property of the Real Numbers (Appendix 7) S has a least upper bound R. (This is the smallest number with the property that all elements of S are less than or equal to R.) Since we are not in Case 3, the series converges at some number $b \neq 0$ and, by Theorem 18, also on the open interval $(-|b|, |b|)$. Therefore $R > 0$.

If $|x| < R$ then there is a number c in S with $|x| < c < R$, since otherwise R would not be the least upper bound for S. The series converges at c since $c \in S$, so by Theorem 18 the series converges absolutely at x.

Now suppose $|x| > R$. If the series converges at x, then Theorem 18 implies it converges absolutely on the open interval $(-|x|, |x|)$, so that S contains this interval. Since R is an upper bound for S, it follows that $|x| \leq R$, which is a contradiction. So if $|x| > R$ then the series diverges. This proves the theorem for power series centered at $a = 0$.

For a power series centered at an arbitrary point $x = a$, set $x' = x - a$ and repeat the argument above, replacing x with x'. Since $x' = 0$ when $x = a$, convergence of the series $\sum_{n=0}^{\infty} |c_n (x')^n|$ on a radius R open interval centered at $x' = 0$ corresponds to convergence of the series $\sum_{n=0}^{\infty} |c_n (x - a)^n|$ on a radius R open interval centered at $x = a$. ∎

R is called the **radius of convergence** of the power series, and the interval of radius R centered at $x = a$ is called the **interval of convergence**. The interval of convergence may be open, closed, or half-open, depending on the particular series. At points x with $|x - a| < R$, the series converges absolutely. If the series converges for all values of x, we say its radius of convergence is infinite. If it converges only at $x = a$, we say its radius of convergence is zero.

How to Test a Power Series for Convergence

1. *Use the Ratio Test (or Root Test) to find the interval where the series converges absolutely.* Ordinarily, this is an open interval

$$|x - a| < R \qquad \text{or} \qquad a - R < x < a + R.$$

2. *If the interval of absolute convergence is finite, test for convergence or divergence at each endpoint*, as in Examples 3a and b. Use a Comparison Test, the Integral Test, or the Alternating Series Test.
3. *If the interval of absolute convergence is $a - R < x < a + R$, the series diverges for $|x - a| > R$* (it does not even converge conditionally) because the nth term does not approach zero for those values of x.

Operations on Power Series

On the intersection of their intervals of convergence, two power series can be added and subtracted term by term just like series of constants (Theorem 8). They can be multiplied just as we multiply polynomials, but we often limit the computation of the product to the first few terms, which are the most important. The following result gives a formula for the coefficients in the product, but we omit the proof. (Power series can also be divided in a way similar to division of polynomials, but we do not give a formula for the general coefficient here.)

THEOREM 19—The Series Multiplication Theorem for Power Series If $A(x) = \sum_{n=0}^{\infty} a_n x^n$ and $B(x) = \sum_{n=0}^{\infty} b_n x^n$ converge absolutely for $|x| < R$, and

$$c_n = a_0 b_n + a_1 b_{n-1} + a_2 b_{n-2} + \cdots + a_{n-1} b_1 + a_n b_0 = \sum_{k=0}^{n} a_k b_{n-k},$$

then $\sum_{n=0}^{\infty} c_n x^n$ converges absolutely to $A(x)B(x)$ for $|x| < R$:

$$\left(\sum_{n=0}^{\infty} a_n x^n\right) \cdot \left(\sum_{n=0}^{\infty} b_n x^n\right) = \sum_{n=0}^{\infty} c_n x^n.$$

Finding the general coefficient c_n in the product of two power series can be very tedious and the term may be unwieldy. The following computation provides an illustration of a product where we find the first few terms by multiplying the terms of the second series by each term of the first series:

$$\left(\sum_{n=0}^{\infty} x^n\right) \cdot \left(\sum_{n=0}^{\infty} (-1)^n \frac{x^{n+1}}{n+1}\right)$$

$$= (1 + x + x^2 + \cdots)\left(x - \frac{x^2}{2} + \frac{x^3}{3} - \cdots\right) \qquad \text{Multiply second series . . .}$$

$$= \underbrace{\left(x - \frac{x^2}{2} + \frac{x^3}{3} - \cdots\right)}_{\text{by } 1} + \underbrace{\left(x^2 - \frac{x^3}{2} + \frac{x^4}{3} - \cdots\right)}_{\text{by } x} + \underbrace{\left(x^3 - \frac{x^4}{2} + \frac{x^5}{3} - \cdots\right)}_{\text{by } x^2} + \cdots$$

$$= x + \frac{x^2}{2} + \frac{5x^3}{6} - \frac{x^4}{6} \cdots. \qquad \text{and gather the first four powers.}$$

We can also substitute a function $f(x)$ for x in a convergent power series.

THEOREM 20 If $\sum_{n=0}^{\infty} a_n x^n$ converges absolutely for $|x| < R$, then $\sum_{n=0}^{\infty} a_n (f(x))^n$ converges absolutely for any continuous function f on $|f(x)| < R$.

Since $1/(1 - x) = \sum_{n=0}^{\infty} x^n$ converges absolutely for $|x| < 1$, it follows from Theorem 20 that $1/(1 - 4x^2) = \sum_{n=0}^{\infty} (4x^2)^n$ converges absolutely for $|4x^2| < 1$ or $|x| < 1/2$.

A theorem from advanced calculus says that a power series can be differentiated term by term at each interior point of its interval of convergence.

THEOREM 21—The Term-by-Term Differentiation Theorem If $\sum c_n (x - a)^n$ has radius of convergence $R > 0$, it defines a function

$$f(x) = \sum_{n=0}^{\infty} c_n (x - a)^n \qquad \text{on the interval} \qquad a - R < x < a + R.$$

This function f has derivatives of all orders inside the interval, and we obtain the derivatives by differentiating the original series term by term:

$$f'(x) = \sum_{n=1}^{\infty} n c_n (x - a)^{n-1},$$

$$f''(x) = \sum_{n=2}^{\infty} n(n - 1) c_n (x - a)^{n-2},$$

and so on. Each of these derived series converges at every point of the interval $a - R < x < a + R$.

EXAMPLE 4 Find series for $f'(x)$ and $f''(x)$ if

$$f(x) = \frac{1}{1-x} = 1 + x + x^2 + x^3 + x^4 + \cdots + x^n + \cdots$$
$$= \sum_{n=0}^{\infty} x^n, \qquad -1 < x < 1.$$

Solution We differentiate the power series on the right term by term:

$$f'(x) = \frac{1}{(1-x)^2} = 1 + 2x + 3x^2 + 4x^3 + \cdots + nx^{n-1} + \cdots$$
$$= \sum_{n=1}^{\infty} nx^{n-1}, \qquad -1 < x < 1;$$
$$f''(x) = \frac{2}{(1-x)^3} = 2 + 6x + 12x^2 + \cdots + n(n-1)x^{n-2} + \cdots$$
$$= \sum_{n=2}^{\infty} n(n-1)x^{n-2}, \qquad -1 < x < 1.$$

■

Caution Term-by-term differentiation might not work for other kinds of series. For example, the trigonometric series

$$\sum_{n=1}^{\infty} \frac{\sin(n!x)}{n^2}$$

converges for all x. But if we differentiate term by term we get the series

$$\sum_{n=1}^{\infty} \frac{n!\cos(n!x)}{n^2},$$

which diverges for all x. This is not a power series since it is not a sum of positive integer powers of x.

It is also true that a power series can be integrated term by term throughout its interval of convergence. This result is proved in a more advanced course.

THEOREM 22—The Term-by-Term Integration Theorem Suppose that

$$f(x) = \sum_{n=0}^{\infty} c_n(x-a)^n$$

converges for $a - R < x < a + R$ $(R > 0)$. Then

$$\sum_{n=0}^{\infty} c_n \frac{(x-a)^{n+1}}{n+1}$$

converges for $a - R < x < a + R$ and

$$\int f(x)\,dx = \sum_{n=0}^{\infty} c_n \frac{(x-a)^{n+1}}{n+1} + C$$

for $a - R < x < a + R$.

EXAMPLE 5 Identify the function

$$f(x) = \sum_{n=0}^{\infty} \frac{(-1)^n x^{2n+1}}{2n+1} = x - \frac{x^3}{3} + \frac{x^5}{5} - \cdots, \qquad -1 \le x \le 1.$$

Solution We differentiate the original series term by term and get

$$f'(x) = 1 - x^2 + x^4 - x^6 + \cdots, \qquad -1 < x < 1. \qquad \text{Theorem 21}$$

This is a geometric series with first term 1 and ratio $-x^2$, so

$$f'(x) = \frac{1}{1 - (-x^2)} = \frac{1}{1 + x^2}.$$

We can now integrate $f'(x) = 1/(1 + x^2)$ to get

$$\int f'(x)\,dx = \int \frac{dx}{1 + x^2} = \tan^{-1} x + C.$$

The series for $f(x)$ is zero when $x = 0$, so $C = 0$. Hence

$$f(x) = x - \frac{x^3}{3} + \frac{x^5}{5} - \frac{x^7}{7} + \cdots = \tan^{-1} x, \qquad -1 < x < 1. \tag{6}$$

The Number π as a Series

$$\frac{\pi}{4} = \tan^{-1} 1 = \sum_{n=0}^{\infty} \frac{(-1)^n}{2n + 1}$$

It can be shown that the series also converges to $\tan^{-1} x$ at the endpoints $x = \pm 1$, but we omit the proof. ■

Notice that the original series in Example 5 converges at both endpoints of the original interval of convergence, but Theorem 22 can guarantee the convergence of the differentiated series only inside the interval.

EXAMPLE 6 The series

$$\frac{1}{1 + t} = 1 - t + t^2 - t^3 + \cdots$$

converges on the open interval $-1 < t < 1$. Therefore,

$$\ln(1 + x) = \int_0^x \frac{1}{1 + t}\,dt = t - \frac{t^2}{2} + \frac{t^3}{3} - \frac{t^4}{4} + \cdots \Big]_0^x \qquad \text{Theorem 22}$$

$$= x - \frac{x^2}{2} + \frac{x^3}{3} - \frac{x^4}{4} + \cdots$$

or

$$\ln(1 + x) = \sum_{n=1}^{\infty} \frac{(-1)^{n-1} x^n}{n}, \qquad -1 < x < 1.$$

Alternating Harmonic Series Sum

$$\ln 2 = \sum_{n=1}^{\infty} \frac{(-1)^{n-1}}{n}$$

It can also be shown that the series converges at $x = 1$ to the number ln 2, but that was not guaranteed by the theorem. ■

Exercises 9.7

Intervals of Convergence

In Exercises 1–36, **(a)** find the series' radius and interval of convergence. For what values of x does the series converge **(b)** absolutely, **(c)** conditionally?

1. $\sum_{n=0}^{\infty} x^n$

2. $\sum_{n=0}^{\infty} (x + 5)^n$

3. $\sum_{n=0}^{\infty} (-1)^n (4x + 1)^n$

4. $\sum_{n=1}^{\infty} \frac{(3x - 2)^n}{n}$

5. $\sum_{n=0}^{\infty} \frac{(x - 2)^n}{10^n}$

6. $\sum_{n=0}^{\infty} (2x)^n$

7. $\sum_{n=0}^{\infty} \frac{nx^n}{n + 2}$

8. $\sum_{n=1}^{\infty} \frac{(-1)^n (x + 2)^n}{n}$

9. $\sum_{n=1}^{\infty} \frac{x^n}{n\sqrt{n}\,3^n}$

10. $\sum_{n=1}^{\infty} \frac{(x - 1)^n}{\sqrt{n}}$

11. $\sum_{n=0}^{\infty} \frac{(-1)^n x^n}{n!}$

12. $\sum_{n=0}^{\infty} \frac{3^n x^n}{n!}$

13. $\sum_{n=1}^{\infty} \frac{4^n x^{2n}}{n}$

14. $\sum_{n=1}^{\infty} \frac{(x - 1)^n}{n^3 3^n}$

15. $\sum_{n=0}^{\infty} \frac{x^n}{\sqrt{n^2 + 3}}$

16. $\sum_{n=0}^{\infty} \frac{(-1)^n x^{n+1}}{\sqrt{n + 3}}$

17. $\sum_{n=0}^{\infty} \frac{n(x+3)^n}{5^n}$

18. $\sum_{n=0}^{\infty} \frac{nx^n}{4^n(n^2+1)}$

19. $\sum_{n=0}^{\infty} \frac{\sqrt{n}x^n}{3^n}$

20. $\sum_{n=1}^{\infty} \sqrt[n]{n}(2x+5)^n$

21. $\sum_{n=1}^{\infty} (2+(-1)^n)\cdot(x+1)^{n-1}$

22. $\sum_{n=1}^{\infty} \frac{(-1)^n 3^{2n}(x-2)^n}{3n}$

23. $\sum_{n=1}^{\infty} \left(1+\frac{1}{n}\right)^n x^n$

24. $\sum_{n=1}^{\infty} (\ln n)x^n$

25. $\sum_{n=1}^{\infty} n^n x^n$

26. $\sum_{n=0}^{\infty} n!(x-4)^n$

27. $\sum_{n=1}^{\infty} \frac{(-1)^{n+1}(x+2)^n}{n2^n}$

28. $\sum_{n=0}^{\infty} (-2)^n(n+1)(x-1)^n$

29. $\sum_{n=2}^{\infty} \frac{x^n}{n(\ln n)^2}$ Get the information you need about $\sum 1/(n(\ln n)^2)$ from Section 9.3, Exercise 55.

30. $\sum_{n=2}^{\infty} \frac{x^n}{n \ln n}$ Get the information you need about $\sum 1/(n \ln n)$ from Section 9.3, Exercise 54.

31. $\sum_{n=1}^{\infty} \frac{(4x-5)^{2n+1}}{n^{3/2}}$

32. $\sum_{n=1}^{\infty} \frac{(3x+1)^{n+1}}{2n+2}$

33. $\sum_{n=1}^{\infty} \frac{1}{2\cdot 4\cdot 8\cdots(2n)}x^n$

34. $\sum_{n=1}^{\infty} \frac{3\cdot 5\cdot 7\cdots(2n+1)}{n^2\cdot 2^n}x^{n+1}$

35. $\sum_{n=1}^{\infty} \frac{1+2+3+\cdots+n}{1^2+2^2+3^2+\cdots+n^2}x^n$

36. $\sum_{n=1}^{\infty} \left(\sqrt{n+1}-\sqrt{n}\right)(x-3)^n$

In Exercises 37–40, find the series' radius of convergence.

37. $\sum_{n=1}^{\infty} \frac{n!}{3\cdot 6\cdot 9\cdots 3n}x^n$

38. $\sum_{n=1}^{\infty} \left(\frac{2\cdot 4\cdot 6\cdots(2n)}{2\cdot 5\cdot 8\cdots(3n-1)}\right)^2 x^n$

39. $\sum_{n=1}^{\infty} \frac{(n!)^2}{2^n(2n)!}x^n$

40. $\sum_{n=1}^{\infty} \left(\frac{n}{n+1}\right)^{n^2} x^n$

(*Hint:* Apply the Root Test.)

In Exercises 41–48, use Theorem 20 to find the series' interval of convergence and, within this interval, the sum of the series as a function of x.

41. $\sum_{n=0}^{\infty} 3^n x^n$

42. $\sum_{n=0}^{\infty} (e^x-4)^n$

43. $\sum_{n=0}^{\infty} \frac{(x-1)^{2n}}{4^n}$

44. $\sum_{n=0}^{\infty} \frac{(x+1)^{2n}}{9^n}$

45. $\sum_{n=0}^{\infty} \left(\frac{\sqrt{x}}{2}-1\right)^n$

46. $\sum_{n=0}^{\infty} (\ln x)^n$

47. $\sum_{n=0}^{\infty} \left(\frac{x^2+1}{3}\right)^n$

48. $\sum_{n=0}^{\infty} \left(\frac{x^2-1}{2}\right)^n$

Theory and Examples

49. For what values of x does the series

$$1-\frac{1}{2}(x-3)+\frac{1}{4}(x-3)^2+\cdots+\left(-\frac{1}{2}\right)^n(x-3)^n+\cdots$$

converge? What is its sum? What series do you get if you differentiate the given series term by term? For what values of x does the new series converge? What is its sum?

50. If you integrate the series in Exercise 49 term by term, what new series do you get? For what values of x does the new series converge, and what is another name for its sum?

51. The series

$$\sin x = x-\frac{x^3}{3!}+\frac{x^5}{5!}-\frac{x^7}{7!}+\frac{x^9}{9!}-\frac{x^{11}}{11!}+\cdots$$

converges to $\sin x$ for all x.

a. Find the first six terms of a series for $\cos x$. For what values of x should the series converge?

b. By replacing x by $2x$ in the series for $\sin x$, find a series that converges to $\sin 2x$ for all x.

c. Using the result in part (a) and series multiplication, calculate the first six terms of a series for $2 \sin x \cos x$. Compare your answer with the answer in part (b).

52. The series

$$e^x = 1+x+\frac{x^2}{2!}+\frac{x^3}{3!}+\frac{x^4}{4!}+\frac{x^5}{5!}+\cdots$$

converges to e^x for all x.

a. Find a series for $(d/dx)e^x$. Do you get the series for e^x? Explain your answer.

b. Find a series for $\int e^x\,dx$. Do you get the series for e^x? Explain your answer.

c. Replace x by $-x$ in the series for e^x to find a series that converges to e^{-x} for all x. Then multiply the series for e^x and e^{-x} to find the first six terms of a series for $e^{-x}\cdot e^x$.

53. The series

$$\tan x = x+\frac{x^3}{3}+\frac{2x^5}{15}+\frac{17x^7}{315}+\frac{62x^9}{2835}+\cdots$$

converges to $\tan x$ for $-\pi/2 < x < \pi/2$.

a. Find the first five terms of the series for $\ln|\sec x|$. For what values of x should the series converge?

b. Find the first five terms of the series for $\sec^2 x$. For what values of x should this series converge?

c. Check your result in part (b) by squaring the series given for $\sec x$ in Exercise 54.

54. The series

$$\sec x = 1+\frac{x^2}{2}+\frac{5}{24}x^4+\frac{61}{720}x^6+\frac{277}{8064}x^8+\cdots$$

converges to $\sec x$ for $-\pi/2 < x < \pi/2$.

a. Find the first five terms of a power series for the function $\ln|\sec x+\tan x|$. For what values of x should the series converge?

b. Find the first four terms of a series for $\sec x \tan x$. For what values of x should the series converge?

c. Check your result in part (b) by multiplying the series for $\sec x$ by the series given for $\tan x$ in Exercise 53.

55. Uniqueness of convergent power series

a. Show that if two power series $\sum_{n=0}^{\infty} a_n x^n$ and $\sum_{n=0}^{\infty} b_n x^n$ are convergent and equal for all values of x in an open interval $(-c, c)$, then $a_n = b_n$ for every n. (*Hint:* Let $f(x) = \sum_{n=0}^{\infty} a_n x^n = \sum_{n=0}^{\infty} b_n x^n$. Differentiate term by term to show that a_n and b_n both equal $f^{(n)}(0)/(n!)$.)

b. Show that if $\sum_{n=0}^{\infty} a_n x^n = 0$ for all x in an open interval $(-c, c)$, then $a_n = 0$ for every n.

56. The sum of the series $\sum_{n=0}^{\infty} (n^2/2^n)$ To find the sum of this series, express $1/(1 - x)$ as a geometric series, differentiate both sides of the resulting equation with respect to x, multiply both sides of the result by x, differentiate again, multiply by x again, and set x equal to $1/2$. What do you get?

9.8 Taylor and Maclaurin Series

This section shows how functions that are infinitely differentiable generate power series called Taylor series. In many cases, these series can provide useful polynomial approximations of the generating functions. Because they are used routinely by mathematicians and scientists, Taylor series are considered one of the most important topics of this chapter.

Series Representations

We know from Theorem 21 that within its interval of convergence the sum of a power series is a continuous function with derivatives of all orders. But what about the other way around? If a function $f(x)$ has derivatives of all orders on an interval I, can it be expressed as a power series on I? And if it can, what will its coefficients be?

We can answer the last question readily if we assume that $f(x)$ is the sum of a power series

$$\begin{aligned} f(x) &= \sum_{n=0}^{\infty} a_n (x - a)^n \\ &= a_0 + a_1(x - a) + a_2(x - a)^2 + \cdots + a_n(x - a)^n + \cdots \end{aligned}$$

with a positive radius of convergence. By repeated term-by-term differentiation within the interval of convergence I, we obtain

$$\begin{aligned} f'(x) &= a_1 + 2a_2(x - a) + 3a_3(x - a)^2 + \cdots + na_n(x - a)^{n-1} + \cdots, \\ f''(x) &= 1 \cdot 2a_2 + 2 \cdot 3a_3(x - a) + 3 \cdot 4a_4(x - a)^2 + \cdots, \\ f'''(x) &= 1 \cdot 2 \cdot 3a_3 + 2 \cdot 3 \cdot 4a_4(x - a) + 3 \cdot 4 \cdot 5a_5(x - a)^2 + \cdots, \end{aligned}$$

with the nth derivative, for all n, being

$$f^{(n)}(x) = n!a_n + \text{a sum of terms with } (x - a) \text{ as a factor}.$$

Since these equations all hold at $x = a$, we have

$$f'(a) = a_1, \qquad f''(a) = 1 \cdot 2a_2, \qquad f'''(a) = 1 \cdot 2 \cdot 3a_3,$$

and, in general,

$$f^{(n)}(a) = n!a_n.$$

These formulas reveal a pattern in the coefficients of any power series $\sum_{n=0}^{\infty} a_n(x - a)^n$ that converges to the values of f on I ("represents f on I"). If there *is* such a series (still an open question), then there is only one such series, and its nth coefficient is

$$a_n = \frac{f^{(n)}(a)}{n!}.$$

If f has a series representation, then the series must be

$$f(x) = f(a) + f'(a)(x - a) + \frac{f''(a)}{2!}(x - a)^2 + \cdots + \frac{f^{(n)}(a)}{n!}(x - a)^n + \cdots. \tag{1}$$

But if we start with an arbitrary function f that is infinitely differentiable on an interval I centered at $x = a$ and use it to generate the series in Equation (1), will the series then converge to $f(x)$ at each x in the interior of I? The answer is maybe—for some functions it will but for other functions it will not, as we will see.

Taylor and Maclaurin Series

The series on the right-hand side of Equation (1) is the most important and useful series we will study in this chapter.

HISTORICAL BIOGRAPHIES

Brook Taylor (1685–1731)

Colin Maclaurin (1698–1746)

DEFINITIONS Let f be a function with derivatives of all orders throughout some interval containing a as an interior point. Then the **Taylor series generated by f at $x = a$** is

$$\sum_{k=0}^{\infty} \frac{f^{(k)}(a)}{k!}(x - a)^k = f(a) + f'(a)(x - a) + \frac{f''(a)}{2!}(x - a)^2 + \cdots + \frac{f^{(n)}(a)}{n!}(x - a)^n + \cdots.$$

The **Maclaurin series generated by f** is

$$\sum_{k=0}^{\infty} \frac{f^{(k)}(0)}{k!}x^k = f(0) + f'(0)x + \frac{f''(0)}{2!}x^2 + \cdots + \frac{f^{(n)}(0)}{n!}x^n + \cdots,$$

the Taylor series generated by f at $x = 0$.

The Maclaurin series generated by f is often just called the Taylor series of f.

EXAMPLE 1 Find the Taylor series generated by $f(x) = 1/x$ at $a = 2$. Where, if anywhere, does the series converge to $1/x$?

Solution We need to find $f(2), f'(2), f''(2), \ldots$. Taking derivatives we get

$$f(x) = x^{-1}, \quad f'(x) = -x^{-2}, \quad f''(x) = 2!x^{-3}, \quad \cdots, \quad f^{(n)}(x) = (-1)^n n! x^{-(n+1)},$$

so that

$$f(2) = 2^{-1} = \frac{1}{2}, \quad f'(2) = -\frac{1}{2^2}, \quad \frac{f''(2)}{2!} = 2^{-3} = \frac{1}{2^3}, \quad \cdots, \quad \frac{f^{(n)}(2)}{n!} = \frac{(-1)^n}{2^{n+1}}.$$

The Taylor series is

$$f(2) + f'(2)(x - 2) + \frac{f''(2)}{2!}(x - 2)^2 + \cdots + \frac{f^{(n)}(2)}{n!}(x - 2)^n + \cdots$$

$$= \frac{1}{2} - \frac{(x - 2)}{2^2} + \frac{(x - 2)^2}{2^3} - \cdots + (-1)^n \frac{(x - 2)^n}{2^{n+1}} + \cdots.$$

This is a geometric series with first term $1/2$ and ratio $r = -(x - 2)/2$. It converges absolutely for $|x - 2| < 2$ and its sum is

$$\frac{1/2}{1 + (x - 2)/2} = \frac{1}{2 + (x - 2)} = \frac{1}{x}.$$

In this example the Taylor series generated by $f(x) = 1/x$ at $a = 2$ converges to $1/x$ for $|x - 2| < 2$ or $0 < x < 4$. ■

Taylor Polynomials

The linearization of a differentiable function f at a point a is the polynomial of degree one given by

$$P_1(x) = f(a) + f'(a)(x - a).$$

In Section 3.11 we used this linearization to approximate $f(x)$ at values of x near a. If f has derivatives of higher order at a, then it has higher-order polynomial approximations as well, one for each available derivative. These polynomials are called the Taylor polynomials of f.

DEFINITION Let f be a function with derivatives of order k for $k = 1, 2, \ldots, N$ in some interval containing a as an interior point. Then for any integer n from 0 through N, the **Taylor polynomial of order n** generated by f at $x = a$ is the polynomial

$$P_n(x) = f(a) + f'(a)(x - a) + \frac{f''(a)}{2!}(x - a)^2 + \cdots + \frac{f^{(k)}(a)}{k!}(x - a)^k + \cdots + \frac{f^{(n)}(a)}{n!}(x - a)^n.$$

We speak of a Taylor polynomial of *order n* rather than *degree n* because $f^{(n)}(a)$ may be zero. The first two Taylor polynomials of $f(x) = \cos x$ at $x = 0$, for example, are $P_0(x) = 1$ and $P_1(x) = 1$. The first-order Taylor polynomial has degree zero, not one.

Just as the linearization of f at $x = a$ provides the best linear approximation of f in the neighborhood of a, the higher-order Taylor polynomials provide the "best" polynomial approximations of their respective degrees. (See Exercise 40.)

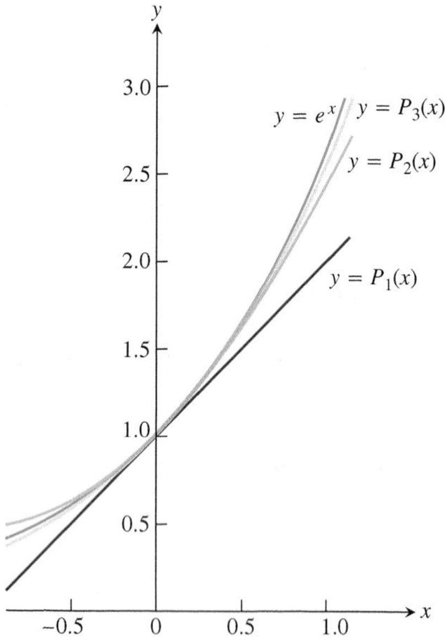

FIGURE 9.17 The graph of $f(x) = e^x$ and its Taylor polynomials

$P_1(x) = 1 + x$

$P_2(x) = 1 + x + (x^2/2!)$

$P_3(x) = 1 + x + (x^2/2!) + (x^3/3!)$.

Notice the very close agreement near the center $x = 0$ (Example 2).

EXAMPLE 2 Find the Taylor series and the Taylor polynomials generated by $f(x) = e^x$ at $x = 0$.

Solution Since $f^{(n)}(x) = e^x$ and $f^{(n)}(0) = 1$ for every $n = 0, 1, 2, \ldots$, the Taylor series generated by f at $x = 0$ (see Figure 9.17) is

$$f(0) + f'(0)x + \frac{f''(0)}{2!}x^2 + \cdots + \frac{f^{(n)}(0)}{n!}x^n + \cdots$$

$$= 1 + x + \frac{x^2}{2} + \cdots + \frac{x^n}{n!} + \cdots$$

$$= \sum_{k=0}^{\infty} \frac{x^k}{k!}.$$

This is also the Maclaurin series for e^x. In the next section we will see that the series converges to e^x at every x.

The Taylor polynomial of order n at $x = 0$ is

$$P_n(x) = 1 + x + \frac{x^2}{2} + \cdots + \frac{x^n}{n!}. \qquad \blacksquare$$

EXAMPLE 3 Find the Taylor series and Taylor polynomials generated by $f(x) = \cos x$ at $x = 0$.

Solution The cosine and its derivatives are

$$\begin{aligned} f(x) &= \cos x, & f'(x) &= -\sin x, \\ f''(x) &= -\cos x, & f^{(3)}(x) &= \sin x, \\ &\vdots & &\vdots \\ f^{(2n)}(x) &= (-1)^n \cos x, & f^{(2n+1)}(x) &= (-1)^{n+1} \sin x. \end{aligned}$$

At $x = 0$, the cosines are 1 and the sines are 0, so

$$f^{(2n)}(0) = (-1)^n, \qquad f^{(2n+1)}(0) = 0.$$

The Taylor series generated by f at 0 is

$$\begin{aligned} f(0) + f'(0)x + \frac{f''(0)}{2!}x^2 + \frac{f'''(0)}{3!}x^3 + \cdots + \frac{f^{(n)}(0)}{n!}x^n + \cdots \\ = 1 + 0 \cdot x - \frac{x^2}{2!} + 0 \cdot x^3 + \frac{x^4}{4!} + \cdots + (-1)^n \frac{x^{2n}}{(2n)!} + \cdots \\ = \sum_{k=0}^{\infty} \frac{(-1)^k x^{2k}}{(2k)!}. \end{aligned}$$

This is also the Maclaurin series for $\cos x$. Notice that only even powers of x occur in the Taylor series generated by the cosine function, which is consistent with the fact that it is an even function. In Section 9.9, we will see that the series converges to $\cos x$ at every x.

Because $f^{(2n+1)}(0) = 0$, the Taylor polynomials of orders $2n$ and $2n + 1$ are identical:

$$P_{2n}(x) = P_{2n+1}(x) = 1 - \frac{x^2}{2!} + \frac{x^4}{4!} - \cdots + (-1)^n \frac{x^{2n}}{(2n)!}.$$

Figure 9.18 shows how well these polynomials approximate $f(x) = \cos x$ near $x = 0$. Only the right-hand portions of the graphs are given because the graphs are symmetric about the y-axis. $\blacksquare$

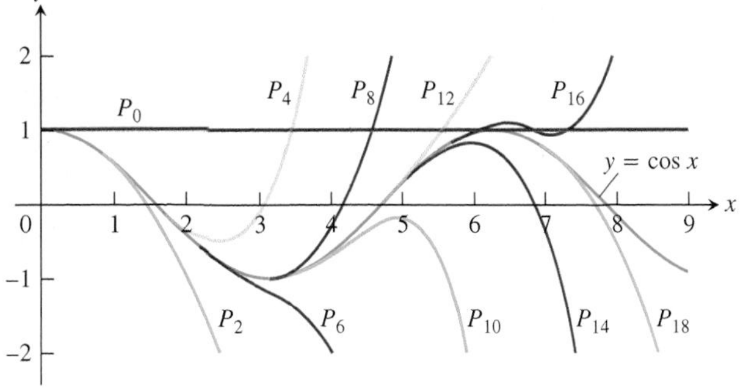

FIGURE 9.18 The polynomials

$$P_{2n}(x) = \sum_{k=0}^{n} \frac{(-1)^k x^{2k}}{(2k)!}$$

converge to $\cos x$ as $n \to \infty$. We can deduce the behavior of $\cos x$ arbitrarily far away solely from knowing the values of the cosine and its derivatives at $x = 0$ (Example 3).

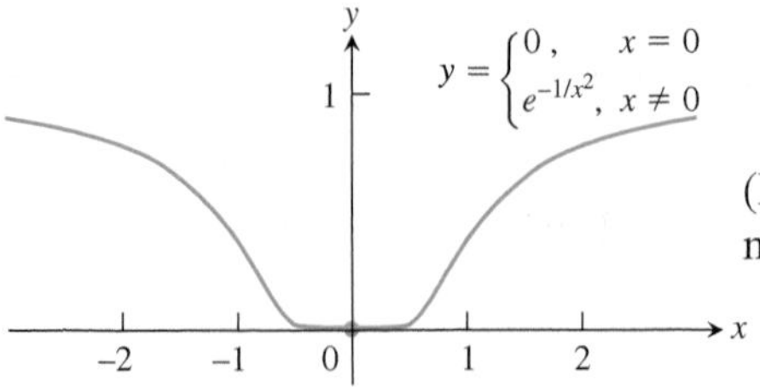

FIGURE 9.19 The graph of the continuous extension of $y = e^{-1/x^2}$ is so flat at the origin that all of its derivatives there are zero (Example 4). Therefore its Taylor series is not the function itself.

EXAMPLE 4 It can be shown (though not easily) that

$$f(x) = \begin{cases} 0, & x = 0 \\ e^{-1/x^2}, & x \neq 0 \end{cases}$$

(Figure 9.19) has derivatives of all orders at $x = 0$ and that $f^{(n)}(0) = 0$ for all n. This means that the Taylor series generated by f at $x = 0$ is

$$\begin{aligned} f(0) + f'(0)x + \frac{f''(0)}{2!}x^2 + \cdots + \frac{f^{(n)}(0)}{n!}x^n + \cdots \\ = 0 + 0 \cdot x + 0 \cdot x^2 + \cdots + 0 \cdot x^n + \cdots \\ = 0 + 0 + \cdots + 0 + \cdots. \end{aligned}$$

The series converges for every x (its sum is 0) but converges to $f(x)$ only at $x = 0$. That is, the Taylor series generated by $f(x)$ in this example is *not* equal to the function $f(x)$ itself. ■

Two questions still remain.

1. For what values of x can we normally expect a Taylor series to converge to its generating function?
2. How accurately do a function's Taylor polynomials approximate the function on a given interval?

The answers are provided by a theorem of Taylor in the next section.

Exercises 9.8

Finding Taylor Polynomials

In Exercises 1–10, find the Taylor polynomials of orders 0, 1, 2, and 3 generated by f at a.

1. $f(x) = e^{2x}, \quad a = 0$
2. $f(x) = \sin x, \quad a = 0$
3. $f(x) = \ln x, \quad a = 1$
4. $f(x) = \ln(1 + x), \quad a = 0$
5. $f(x) = 1/x, \quad a = 2$
6. $f(x) = 1/(x + 2), \quad a = 0$
7. $f(x) = \sin x, \quad a = \pi/4$
8. $f(x) = \tan x, \quad a = \pi/4$
9. $f(x) = \sqrt{x}, \quad a = 4$
10. $f(x) = \sqrt{1 - x}, \quad a = 0$

Finding Taylor Series at $x = 0$ (Maclaurin Series)

Find the Maclaurin series for the functions in Exercises 11–22.

11. e^{-x}
12. xe^x
13. $\dfrac{1}{1 + x}$
14. $\dfrac{2 + x}{1 - x}$
15. $\sin 3x$
16. $\sin \dfrac{x}{2}$
17. $7 \cos(-x)$
18. $5 \cos \pi x$
19. $\cosh x = \dfrac{e^x + e^{-x}}{2}$
20. $\sinh x = \dfrac{e^x - e^{-x}}{2}$
21. $x^4 - 2x^3 - 5x + 4$
22. $\dfrac{x^2}{x + 1}$

Finding Taylor and Maclaurin Series

In Exercises 23–32, find the Taylor series generated by f at $x = a$.

23. $f(x) = x^3 - 2x + 4, \quad a = 2$
24. $f(x) = 2x^3 + x^2 + 3x - 8, \quad a = 1$
25. $f(x) = x^4 + x^2 + 1, \quad a = -2$
26. $f(x) = 3x^5 - x^4 + 2x^3 + x^2 - 2, \quad a = -1$
27. $f(x) = 1/x^2, \quad a = 1$
28. $f(x) = 1/(1 - x)^3, \quad a = 0$
29. $f(x) = e^x, \quad a = 2$
30. $f(x) = 2^x, \quad a = 1$
31. $f(x) = \cos(2x + (\pi/2)), \quad a = \pi/4$
32. $f(x) = \sqrt{x + 1}, \quad a = 0$

In Exercises 33–36, find the first three nonzero terms of the Maclaurin series for each function and the values of x for which the series converges absolutely.

33. $f(x) = \cos x - (2/(1 - x))$
34. $f(x) = (1 - x + x^2)\, e^x$
35. $f(x) = (\sin x) \ln(1 + x)$
36. $f(x) = x \sin^2 x$

Theory and Examples

37. Use the Taylor series generated by e^x at $x = a$ to show that
$$e^x = e^a\left[1 + (x - a) + \frac{(x - a)^2}{2!} + \cdots\right].$$
38. (*Continuation of Exercise 37.*) Find the Taylor series generated by e^x at $x = 1$. Compare your answer with the formula in Exercise 37.
39. Let $f(x)$ have derivatives through order n at $x = a$. Show that the Taylor polynomial of order n and its first n derivatives have the same values that f and its first n derivatives have at $x = a$.

40. Approximation properties of Taylor polynomials Suppose that $f(x)$ is differentiable on an interval centered at $x = a$ and that $g(x) = b_0 + b_1(x - a) + \cdots + b_n(x - a)^n$ is a polynomial of degree n with constant coefficients $b_0, \ldots, b_n$. Let $E(x) = f(x) - g(x)$. Show that if we impose on g the conditions

i) $E(a) = 0$ — The approximation error is zero at $x = a$.

ii) $\lim_{x \to a} \dfrac{E(x)}{(x - a)^n} = 0,$ — The error is negligible when compared to $(x - a)^n$.

then

$$g(x) = f(a) + f'(a)(x - a) + \frac{f''(a)}{2!}(x - a)^2 + \cdots + \frac{f^{(n)}(a)}{n!}(x - a)^n.$$

Thus, the Taylor polynomial $P_n(x)$ is the only polynomial of degree less than or equal to n whose error is both zero at $x = a$ and negligible when compared with $(x - a)^n$.

Quadratic Approximations The Taylor polynomial of order 2 generated by a twice-differentiable function $f(x)$ at $x = a$ is called the *quadratic approximation* of f at $x = a$. In Exercises 41–46, find the **(a)** linearization (Taylor polynomial of order 1) and **(b)** quadratic approximation of f at $x = 0$.

41. $f(x) = \ln(\cos x)$

42. $f(x) = e^{\sin x}$

43. $f(x) = 1/\sqrt{1 - x^2}$

44. $f(x) = \cosh x$

45. $f(x) = \sin x$

46. $f(x) = \tan x$

9.9 Convergence of Taylor Series

In the last section we asked when a Taylor series for a function can be expected to converge to that (generating) function. We answer the question in this section with the following theorem.

THEOREM 23—Taylor's Theorem If f and its first n derivatives $f', f'', \ldots, f^{(n)}$ are continuous on the closed interval between a and b, and $f^{(n)}$ is differentiable on the open interval between a and b, then there exists a number c between a and b such that

$$f(b) = f(a) + f'(a)(b - a) + \frac{f''(a)}{2!}(b - a)^2 + \cdots + \frac{f^{(n)}(a)}{n!}(b - a)^n + \frac{f^{(n+1)}(c)}{(n + 1)!}(b - a)^{n+1}.$$

Taylor's Theorem is a generalization of the Mean Value Theorem (Exercise 45). There is a proof of Taylor's Theorem at the end of this section.

When we apply Taylor's Theorem, we usually want to hold a fixed and treat b as an independent variable. Taylor's formula is easier to use in circumstances like these if we change b to x. Here is a version of the theorem with this change.

Taylor's Formula

If f has derivatives of all orders in an open interval I containing a, then for each positive integer n and for each x in I,

$$f(x) = f(a) + f'(a)(x - a) + \frac{f''(a)}{2!}(x - a)^2 + \cdots + \frac{f^{(n)}(a)}{n!}(x - a)^n + R_n(x), \quad (1)$$

where

$$R_n(x) = \frac{f^{(n+1)}(c)}{(n + 1)!}(x - a)^{n+1} \quad \text{for some } c \text{ between } a \text{ and } x. \quad (2)$$

When we state Taylor's theorem this way, it says that for each $x \in I$,

$$f(x) = P_n(x) + R_n(x).$$

The function $R_n(x)$ is determined by the value of the $(n + 1)$st derivative $f^{(n+1)}$ at a point c that depends on both a and x, and that lies somewhere between them. For any value of n we want, the equation gives both a polynomial approximation of f of that order and a formula for the error involved in using that approximation over the interval I.

Equation (1) is called **Taylor's formula**. The function $R_n(x)$ is called the **remainder of order n** or the **error term** for the approximation of f by $P_n(x)$ over I.

> If $R_n(x) \to 0$ as $n \to \infty$ for all $x \in I$, we say that the Taylor series generated by f at $x = a$ **converges** to f on I, and we write
>
> $$f(x) = \sum_{k=0}^{\infty} \frac{f^{(k)}(a)}{k!}(x - a)^k.$$

Often we can estimate R_n without knowing the value of c, as the following example illustrates.

EXAMPLE 1 Show that the Taylor series generated by $f(x) = e^x$ at $x = 0$ converges to $f(x)$ for every real value of x.

Solution The function has derivatives of all orders throughout the interval $I = (-\infty, \infty)$. Equations (1) and (2) with $f(x) = e^x$ and $a = 0$ give

$$e^x = 1 + x + \frac{x^2}{2!} + \cdots + \frac{x^n}{n!} + R_n(x) \qquad \text{Polynomial from Section 9.8, Example 2}$$

and

$$R_n(x) = \frac{e^c}{(n + 1)!}x^{n+1} \quad \text{for some } c \text{ between 0 and } x.$$

Since e^x is an increasing function of x, e^c lies between $e^0 = 1$ and e^x. When x is negative, so is c, and $e^c < 1$. When x is zero, $e^x = 1$ and $R_n(x) = 0$. When x is positive, so is c, and $e^c < e^x$. Thus, for $R_n(x)$ given as above,

$$|R_n(x)| \le \frac{|x|^{n+1}}{(n + 1)!} \quad \text{when } x \le 0, \qquad e^c < 1$$

and

$$|R_n(x)| < e^x \frac{x^{n+1}}{(n + 1)!} \quad \text{when } x > 0. \qquad e^c < e^x$$

Finally, because

$$\lim_{n\to\infty} \frac{x^{n+1}}{(n + 1)!} = 0 \quad \text{for every } x, \qquad \text{Section 9.1, Theorem 5}$$

$\lim_{n\to\infty} R_n(x) = 0$, and the series converges to e^x for every x. Thus,

$$e^x = \sum_{k=0}^{\infty} \frac{x^k}{k!} = 1 + x + \frac{x^2}{2!} + \cdots + \frac{x^k}{k!} + \cdots. \tag{3}$$

■

The Number e as a Series

$$e = \sum_{n=0}^{\infty} \frac{1}{n!}$$

We can use the result of Example 1 with $x = 1$ to write

$$e = 1 + 1 + \frac{1}{2!} + \cdots + \frac{1}{n!} + R_n(1),$$

where for some c between 0 and 1,

$$R_n(1) = e^c \frac{1}{(n+1)!} < \frac{3}{(n+1)!}. \qquad e^c < e^1 < 3$$

Estimating the Remainder

It is often possible to estimate $R_n(x)$ as we did in Example 1. This method of estimation is so convenient that we state it as a theorem for future reference.

THEOREM 24—The Remainder Estimation Theorem If there is a positive constant M such that $|f^{(n+1)}(t)| \le M$ for all t between x and a, inclusive, then the remainder term $R_n(x)$ in Taylor's Theorem satisfies the inequality

$$|R_n(x)| \le M \frac{|x-a|^{n+1}}{(n+1)!}.$$

If this inequality holds for every n and the other conditions of Taylor's Theorem are satisfied by f, then the series converges to $f(x)$.

The next two examples use Theorem 24 to show that the Taylor series generated by the sine and cosine functions do in fact converge to the functions themselves.

EXAMPLE 2 Show that the Taylor series for $\sin x$ at $x = 0$ converges for all x.

Solution The function and its derivatives are

$$\begin{aligned} f(x) &= \sin x, & f'(x) &= \cos x, \\ f''(x) &= -\sin x, & f'''(x) &= -\cos x, \\ &\vdots & &\vdots \\ f^{(2k)}(x) &= (-1)^k \sin x, & f^{(2k+1)}(x) &= (-1)^k \cos x, \end{aligned}$$

so

$$f^{(2k)}(0) = 0 \quad \text{and} \quad f^{(2k+1)}(0) = (-1)^k.$$

The series has only odd-powered terms and, for $n = 2k + 1$, Taylor's Theorem gives

$$\sin x = x - \frac{x^3}{3!} + \frac{x^5}{5!} - \cdots + \frac{(-1)^k x^{2k+1}}{(2k+1)!} + R_{2k+1}(x).$$

All the derivatives of $\sin x$ have absolute values less than or equal to 1, so we can apply the Remainder Estimation Theorem with $M = 1$ to obtain

$$|R_{2k+1}(x)| \le 1 \cdot \frac{|x|^{2k+2}}{(2k+2)!}.$$

From Theorem 5, Rule 6, we have $(|x|^{2k+2}/(2k+2)!) \to 0$ as $k \to \infty$, whatever the value of x, so $R_{2k+1}(x) \to 0$ and the Maclaurin series for $\sin x$ converges to $\sin x$ for every x. Thus,

$$\sin x = \sum_{k=0}^{\infty} \frac{(-1)^k x^{2k+1}}{(2k+1)!} = x - \frac{x^3}{3!} + \frac{x^5}{5!} - \frac{x^7}{7!} + \cdots. \tag{4}$$

■

EXAMPLE 3 Show that the Taylor series for $\cos x$ at $x = 0$ converges to $\cos x$ for every value of x.

Solution We add the remainder term to the Taylor polynomial for $\cos x$ (Section 9.8, Example 3) to obtain Taylor's formula for $\cos x$ with $n = 2k$:

$$\cos x = 1 - \frac{x^2}{2!} + \frac{x^4}{4!} - \cdots + (-1)^k \frac{x^{2k}}{(2k)!} + R_{2k}(x).$$

Because the derivatives of the cosine have absolute value less than or equal to 1, the Remainder Estimation Theorem with $M = 1$ gives

$$|R_{2k}(x)| \leq 1 \cdot \frac{|x|^{2k+1}}{(2k+1)!}.$$

For every value of x, $R_{2k}(x) \to 0$ as $k \to \infty$. Therefore, the series converges to $\cos x$ for every value of x. Thus,

$$\cos x = \sum_{k=0}^{\infty} \frac{(-1)^k x^{2k}}{(2k)!} = 1 - \frac{x^2}{2!} + \frac{x^4}{4!} - \frac{x^6}{6!} + \cdots. \tag{5}$$

■

Using Taylor Series

Since every Taylor series is a power series, the operations of adding, subtracting, and multiplying Taylor series are all valid on the intersection of their intervals of convergence.

EXAMPLE 4 Using known series, find the first few terms of the Taylor series for the given function using power series operations.

(a) $\frac{1}{3}(2x + x\cos x)$ **(b)** $e^x \cos x$

Solution

(a) $$\frac{1}{3}(2x + x\cos x) = \frac{2}{3}x + \frac{1}{3}x\left(1 - \frac{x^2}{2!} + \frac{x^4}{4!} - \cdots + (-1)^k \frac{x^{2k}}{(2k)!} + \cdots\right)$$

$$= \frac{2}{3}x + \frac{1}{3}x - \frac{x^3}{3!} + \frac{x^5}{3 \cdot 4!} - \cdots = x - \frac{x^3}{6} + \frac{x^5}{72} - \cdots$$

(b) $$e^x \cos x = \left(1 + x + \frac{x^2}{2!} + \frac{x^3}{3!} + \frac{x^4}{4!} + \cdots\right) \cdot \left(1 - \frac{x^2}{2!} + \frac{x^4}{4!} - \cdots\right)$$

Multiply the first series by each term of the second series.

$$= \left(1 + x + \frac{x^2}{2!} + \frac{x^3}{3!} + \frac{x^4}{4!} + \cdots\right) - \left(\frac{x^2}{2!} + \frac{x^3}{2!} + \frac{x^4}{2!2!} + \frac{x^5}{2!3!} + \cdots\right)$$

$$+ \left(\frac{x^4}{4!} + \frac{x^5}{4!} + \frac{x^6}{2!4!} + \cdots\right) + \cdots$$

$$= 1 + x - \frac{x^3}{3} - \frac{x^4}{6} + \cdots$$

■

By Theorem 20, we can use the Taylor series of the function f to find the Taylor series of $f(u(x))$ where $u(x)$ is any continuous function. The Taylor series resulting from this substitution will converge for all x such that $u(x)$ lies within the interval of convergence of the Taylor series of f. For instance, we can find the Taylor series for cos $2x$ by substituting $2x$ for x in the Taylor series for cos x:

$$\cos 2x = \sum_{k=0}^{\infty} \frac{(-1)^k (2x)^{2k}}{(2k)!} = 1 - \frac{(2x)^2}{2!} + \frac{(2x)^4}{4!} - \frac{(2x)^6}{6!} + \cdots$$

Eq. (5) with $2x$ for x

$$= 1 - \frac{2^2 x^2}{2!} + \frac{2^4 x^4}{4!} - \frac{2^6 x^6}{6!} + \cdots$$

$$= \sum_{k=0}^{\infty} (-1)^k \frac{2^{2k} x^{2k}}{(2k)!}.$$

EXAMPLE 5 For what values of x can we replace $\sin x$ by $x - (x^3/3!)$ with an error of magnitude no greater than 3×10^{-4}?

Solution Here we can take advantage of the fact that the Taylor series for $\sin x$ is an alternating series for every nonzero value of x. According to the Alternating Series Estimation Theorem (Section 9.6), the error in truncating

$$\sin x = x - \frac{x^3}{3!} \;\vdots\; + \frac{x^5}{5!} - \cdots$$

after $(x^3/3!)$ is no greater than

$$\left|\frac{x^5}{5!}\right| = \frac{|x|^5}{120}.$$

Therefore the error will be less than or equal to 3×10^{-4} if

$$\frac{|x|^5}{120} < 3 \times 10^{-4} \qquad \text{or} \qquad |x| < \sqrt[5]{360 \times 10^{-4}} \approx 0.514.$$

Rounded down, to be safe

The Alternating Series Estimation Theorem tells us something that the Remainder Estimation Theorem does not: namely, that the estimate $x - (x^3/3!)$ for $\sin x$ is an underestimate when x is positive, because then $x^5/120$ is positive.

Figure 9.20 shows the graph of $\sin x$, along with the graphs of a number of its approximating Taylor polynomials. The graph of $P_3(x) = x - (x^3/3!)$ is almost indistinguishable from the sine curve when $0 \le x \le 1$. ■

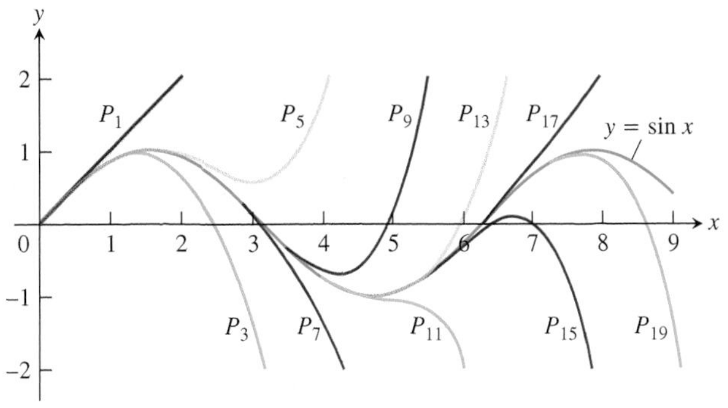

FIGURE 9.20 The polynomials

$$P_{2n+1}(x) = \sum_{k=0}^{n} \frac{(-1)^k x^{2k+1}}{(2k+1)!}$$

converge to $\sin x$ as $n \to \infty$. Notice how closely $P_3(x)$ approximates the sine curve for $x \le 1$ (Example 5).

A Proof of Taylor's Theorem

We prove Taylor's theorem assuming $a < b$. The proof for $a > b$ is nearly the same.

The Taylor polynomial

$$P_n(x) = f(a) + f'(a)(x - a) + \frac{f''(a)}{2!}(x - a)^2 + \cdots + \frac{f^{(n)}(a)}{n!}(x - a)^n$$

and its first n derivatives match the function f and its first n derivatives at $x = a$. We do not disturb that matching if we add another term of the form $K(x - a)^{n+1}$, where K is any constant, because such a term and its first n derivatives are all equal to zero at $x = a$. The new function

$$\phi_n(x) = P_n(x) + K(x - a)^{n+1}$$

and its first n derivatives still agree with f and its first n derivatives at $x = a$.

We now choose the particular value of K that makes the curve $y = \phi_n(x)$ agree with the original curve $y = f(x)$ at $x = b$. In symbols,

$$f(b) = P_n(b) + K(b - a)^{n+1}, \qquad \text{or} \qquad K = \frac{f(b) - P_n(b)}{(b - a)^{n+1}}. \tag{6}$$

With K defined by Equation (6), the function

$$F(x) = f(x) - \phi_n(x)$$

measures the difference between the original function f and the approximating function ϕ_n for each x in $[a, b]$.

We now use Rolle's Theorem (Section 4.2). First, because $F(a) = F(b) = 0$ and both F and F' are continuous on $[a, b]$, we know that

$$F'(c_1) = 0 \qquad \text{for some } c_1 \text{ in } (a, b).$$

Next, because $F'(a) = F'(c_1) = 0$ and both F' and F'' are continuous on $[a, c_1]$, we know that

$$F''(c_2) = 0 \qquad \text{for some } c_2 \text{ in } (a, c_1).$$

Rolle's Theorem, applied successively to $F'', F''', \ldots, F^{(n-1)}$ implies the existence of

$$\begin{aligned} &c_3 \quad \text{in } (a, c_2) && \text{such that } F'''(c_3) = 0, \\ &c_4 \quad \text{in } (a, c_3) && \text{such that } F^{(4)}(c_4) = 0, \\ &\ \vdots \\ &c_n \quad \text{in } (a, c_{n-1}) && \text{such that } F^{(n)}(c_n) = 0. \end{aligned}$$

Finally, because $F^{(n)}$ is continuous on $[a, c_n]$ and differentiable on (a, c_n), and $F^{(n)}(a) = F^{(n)}(c_n) = 0$, Rolle's Theorem implies that there is a number c_{n+1} in (a, c_n) such that

$$F^{(n+1)}(c_{n+1}) = 0. \tag{7}$$

If we differentiate $F(x) = f(x) - P_n(x) - K(x - a)^{n+1}$ a total of $n + 1$ times, we get

$$F^{(n+1)}(x) = f^{(n+1)}(x) - 0 - (n + 1)!K. \tag{8}$$

Equations (7) and (8) together give

$$K = \frac{f^{(n+1)}(c)}{(n + 1)!} \qquad \text{for some number } c = c_{n+1} \text{ in } (a, b). \tag{9}$$

Equations (6) and (9) give

$$f(b) = P_n(b) + \frac{f^{(n+1)}(c)}{(n+1)!}(b-a)^{n+1}.$$

This concludes the proof. ■

Exercises 9.9

Finding Taylor Series

Use substitution (as in Example 4) to find the Taylor series at $x = 0$ of the functions in Exercises 1–10.

1. e^{-5x} **2.** $e^{-x/2}$ **3.** $5 \sin(-x)$

4. $\sin\left(\frac{\pi x}{2}\right)$ **5.** $\cos 5x^2$ **6.** $\cos\left(x^{2/3}/\sqrt{2}\right)$

7. $\ln(1 + x^2)$ **8.** $\tan^{-1}(3x^4)$ **9.** $\frac{1}{1 + \frac{3}{4}x^3}$

10. $\frac{1}{2 - x}$

Use power series operations to find the Taylor series at $x = 0$ for the functions in Exercises 11–28.

11. xe^x **12.** $x^2 \sin x$ **13.** $\frac{x^2}{2} - 1 + \cos x$

14. $\sin x - x + \frac{x^3}{3!}$ **15.** $x \cos \pi x$ **16.** $x^2 \cos(x^2)$

17. $\cos^2 x$ (*Hint:* $\cos^2 x = (1 + \cos 2x)/2$.)

18. $\sin^2 x$ **19.** $\frac{x^2}{1 - 2x}$ **20.** $x \ln(1 + 2x)$

21. $\frac{1}{(1 - x)^2}$ **22.** $\frac{2}{(1 - x)^3}$ **23.** $x \tan^{-1} x^2$

24. $\sin x \cdot \cos x$ **25.** $e^x + \frac{1}{1 + x}$ **26.** $\cos x - \sin x$

27. $\frac{x}{3} \ln(1 + x^2)$ **28.** $\ln(1 + x) - \ln(1 - x)$

Find the first four nonzero terms in the Maclaurin series for the functions in Exercises 29–34.

29. $e^x \sin x$ **30.** $\frac{\ln(1 + x)}{1 - x}$ **31.** $(\tan^{-1} x)^2$

32. $\cos^2 x \cdot \sin x$ **33.** $e^{\sin x}$ **34.** $\sin(\tan^{-1} x)$

Error Estimates

35. Estimate the error if $P_3(x) = x - (x^3/6)$ is used to estimate the value of $\sin x$ at $x = 0.1$.

36. Estimate the error if $P_4(x) = 1 + x + (x^2/2) + (x^3/6) + (x^4/24)$ is used to estimate the value of e^x at $x = 1/2$.

37. For approximately what values of x can you replace $\sin x$ by $x - (x^3/6)$ with an error of magnitude no greater than 5×10^{-4}? Give reasons for your answer.

38. If $\cos x$ is replaced by $1 - (x^2/2)$ and $|x| < 0.5$, what estimate can be made of the error? Does $1 - (x^2/2)$ tend to be too large, or too small? Give reasons for your answer.

39. How close is the approximation $\sin x = x$ when $|x| < 10^{-3}$? For which of these values of x is $x < \sin x$?

40. The estimate $\sqrt{1 + x} = 1 + (x/2)$ is used when x is small. Estimate the error when $|x| < 0.01$.

41. The approximation $e^x = 1 + x + (x^2/2)$ is used when x is small. Use the Remainder Estimation Theorem to estimate the error when $|x| < 0.1$.

42. (*Continuation of Exercise 41.*) When $x < 0$, the series for e^x is an alternating series. Use the Alternating Series Estimation Theorem to estimate the error that results from replacing e^x by $1 + x + (x^2/2)$ when $-0.1 < x < 0$. Compare your estimate with the one you obtained in Exercise 41.

Theory and Examples

43. Use the identity $\sin^2 x = (1 - \cos 2x)/2$ to obtain the Maclaurin series for $\sin^2 x$. Then differentiate this series to obtain the Maclaurin series for $2 \sin x \cos x$. Check that this is the series for $\sin 2x$.

44. (*Continuation of Exercise 43.*) Use the identity $\cos^2 x = \cos 2x + \sin^2 x$ to obtain a power series for $\cos^2 x$.

45. Taylor's Theorem and the Mean Value Theorem Explain how the Mean Value Theorem (Section 4.2, Theorem 4) is a special case of Taylor's Theorem.

46. Linearizations at inflection points Show that if the graph of a twice-differentiable function $f(x)$ has an inflection point at $x = a$, then the linearization of f at $x = a$ is also the quadratic approximation of f at $x = a$. This explains why tangent lines fit so well at inflection points.

47. The (second) second derivative test Use the equation

$$f(x) = f(a) + f'(a)(x - a) + \frac{f''(c_2)}{2}(x - a)^2$$

to establish the following test.

Let f have continuous first and second derivatives and suppose that $f'(a) = 0$. Then

a. f has a local maximum at a if $f'' \le 0$ throughout an interval whose interior contains a;

b. f has a local minimum at a if $f'' \ge 0$ throughout an interval whose interior contains a.

48. A cubic approximation Use Taylor's formula with $a = 0$ and $n = 3$ to find the standard cubic approximation of $f(x) = 1/(1 - x)$ at $x = 0$. Give an upper bound for the magnitude of the error in the approximation when $|x| \leq 0.1$.

49. **a.** Use Taylor's formula with $n = 2$ to find the quadratic approximation of $f(x) = (1 + x)^k$ at $x = 0$ (k a constant).

b. If $k = 3$, for approximately what values of x in the interval $[0, 1]$ will the error in the quadratic approximation be less than $1/100$?

50. Improving approximations of π

a. Let P be an approximation of π accurate to n decimals. Show that $P + \sin P$ gives an approximation correct to $3n$ decimals. (*Hint:* Let $P = \pi + x$.)

T **b.** Try it with a calculator.

51. The Taylor series generated by $f(x) = \sum_{n=0}^{\infty} a_n x^n$ is $\sum_{n=0}^{\infty} a_n x^n$ A function defined by a power series $\sum_{n=0}^{\infty} a_n x^n$ with a radius of convergence $R > 0$ has a Taylor series that converges to the function at every point of $(-R, R)$. Show this by showing that the Taylor series generated by $f(x) = \sum_{n=0}^{\infty} a_n x^n$ is the series $\sum_{n=0}^{\infty} a_n x^n$ itself.

An immediate consequence of this is that series like

$$x \sin x = x^2 - \frac{x^4}{3!} + \frac{x^6}{5!} - \frac{x^8}{7!} + \cdots$$

and

$$x^2 e^x = x^2 + x^3 + \frac{x^4}{2!} + \frac{x^5}{3!} + \cdots,$$

obtained by multiplying Taylor series by powers of x, as well as series obtained by integration and differentiation of convergent power series, are themselves the Taylor series generated by the functions they represent.

52. Taylor series for even functions and odd functions (*Continuation of Section 9.7, Exercise 55.*) Suppose that $f(x) = \sum_{n=0}^{\infty} a_n x^n$ converges for all x in an open interval $(-R, R)$. Show that

a. If f is even, then $a_1 = a_3 = a_5 = \cdots = 0$, i.e., the Taylor series for f at $x = 0$ contains only even powers of x.

b. If f is odd, then $a_0 = a_2 = a_4 = \cdots = 0$, i.e., the Taylor series for f at $x = 0$ contains only odd powers of x.

COMPUTER EXPLORATIONS

Taylor's formula with $n = 1$ and $a = 0$ gives the linearization of a function at $x = 0$. With $n = 2$ and $n = 3$ we obtain the standard quadratic and cubic approximations. In these exercises we explore the errors associated with these approximations. We seek answers to two questions:

a. For what values of x can the function be replaced by each approximation with an error less than 10^{-2}?

b. What is the maximum error we could expect if we replace the function by each approximation over the specified interval?

Using a CAS, perform the following steps to aid in answering questions (a) and (b) for the functions and intervals in Exercises 53–58.

Step 1: Plot the function over the specified interval.

Step 2: Find the Taylor polynomials $P_1(x)$, $P_2(x)$, and $P_3(x)$ at $x = 0$.

Step 3: Calculate the $(n + 1)$st derivative $f^{(n+1)}(c)$ associated with the remainder term for each Taylor polynomial. Plot the derivative as a function of c over the specified interval and estimate its maximum absolute value, M.

Step 4: Calculate the remainder $R_n(x)$ for each polynomial. Using the estimate M from Step 3 in place of $f^{(n+1)}(c)$, plot $R_n(x)$ over the specified interval. Then estimate the values of x that answer question (a).

Step 5: Compare your estimated error with the actual error $E_n(x) = |f(x) - P_n(x)|$ by plotting $E_n(x)$ over the specified interval. This will help answer question (b).

Step 6: Graph the function and its three Taylor approximations together. Discuss the graphs in relation to the information discovered in Steps 4 and 5.

53. $f(x) = \dfrac{1}{\sqrt{1 + x}}, \quad |x| \leq \dfrac{3}{4}$

54. $f(x) = (1 + x)^{3/2}, \quad -\dfrac{1}{2} \leq x \leq 2$

55. $f(x) = \dfrac{x}{x^2 + 1}, \quad |x| \leq 2$

56. $f(x) = (\cos x)(\sin 2x), \quad |x| \leq 2$

57. $f(x) = e^{-x} \cos 2x, \quad |x| \leq 1$

58. $f(x) = e^{x/3} \sin 2x, \quad |x| \leq 2$

9.10 The Binomial Series and Applications of Taylor Series

We can use Taylor series to solve problems that would otherwise be intractable. For example, many functions have antiderivatives that cannot be expressed using familiar functions. In this section we show how to evaluate integrals of such functions by giving them as Taylor series. We also show how to use Taylor series to evaluate limits that lead to indeterminate forms and how Taylor series can be used to extend the exponential function from real to complex numbers. We begin with a discussion of the binomial series, which comes from the Taylor series of the function $f(x) = (1 + x)^m$, and conclude the section with a table of commonly used series.

The Binomial Series for Powers and Roots

The Taylor series generated by $f(x) = (1 + x)^m$, when m is constant, is

$$1 + mx + \frac{m(m-1)}{2!}x^2 + \frac{m(m-1)(m-2)}{3!}x^3 + \cdots$$
$$+ \frac{m(m-1)(m-2)\cdots(m-k+1)}{k!}x^k + \cdots. \tag{1}$$

This series, called the **binomial series**, converges absolutely for $|x| < 1$. To derive the series, we first list the function and its derivatives:

$$\begin{aligned}
f(x) &= (1+x)^m \\
f'(x) &= m(1+x)^{m-1} \\
f''(x) &= m(m-1)(1+x)^{m-2} \\
f'''(x) &= m(m-1)(m-2)(1+x)^{m-3} \\
&\vdots \\
f^{(k)}(x) &= m(m-1)(m-2)\cdots(m-k+1)(1+x)^{m-k}.
\end{aligned}$$

We then evaluate these at $x = 0$ and substitute into the Taylor series formula to obtain Series (1).

If m is an integer greater than or equal to zero, the series stops after $(m + 1)$ terms because the coefficients from $k = m + 1$ on are zero.

If m is not a positive integer or zero, the series is infinite and converges for $|x| < 1$. To see why, let u_k be the term involving x^k. Then apply the Ratio Test for absolute convergence to see that

$$\left|\frac{u_{k+1}}{u_k}\right| = \left|\frac{m-k}{k+1}x\right| \to |x| \quad \text{as } k \to \infty.$$

Our derivation of the binomial series shows only that it is generated by $(1 + x)^m$ and converges for $|x| < 1$. The derivation does not show that the series converges to $(1 + x)^m$. It does, but we leave the proof to Exercise 64.

The Binomial Series

For $-1 < x < 1$,

$$(1+x)^m = 1 + \sum_{k=1}^{\infty} \binom{m}{k} x^k,$$

where we define

$$\binom{m}{1} = m, \qquad \binom{m}{2} = \frac{m(m-1)}{2!},$$

and

$$\binom{m}{k} = \frac{m(m-1)(m-2)\cdots(m-k+1)}{k!} \qquad \text{for } k \geq 3.$$

EXAMPLE 1 If $m = -1$,

$$\binom{-1}{1} = -1, \qquad \binom{-1}{2} = \frac{-1(-2)}{2!} = 1,$$

and

$$\binom{-1}{k} = \frac{-1(-2)(-3)\cdots(-1-k+1)}{k!} = (-1)^k\left(\frac{k!}{k!}\right) = (-1)^k.$$

With these coefficient values and with x replaced by $-x$, the binomial series formula gives the familiar geometric series

$$(1+x)^{-1} = 1 + \sum_{k=1}^{\infty}(-1)^k x^k = 1 - x + x^2 - x^3 + \cdots + (-1)^k x^k + \cdots. \quad \blacksquare$$

EXAMPLE 2 We know from Section 3.11, Example 1, that $\sqrt{1+x} \approx 1 + (x/2)$ for $|x|$ small. With $m = 1/2$, the binomial series gives quadratic and higher-order approximations as well, along with error estimates that come from the Alternating Series Estimation Theorem:

$$(1+x)^{1/2} = 1 + \frac{x}{2} + \frac{\left(\frac{1}{2}\right)\left(-\frac{1}{2}\right)}{2!}x^2 + \frac{\left(\frac{1}{2}\right)\left(-\frac{1}{2}\right)\left(-\frac{3}{2}\right)}{3!}x^3 + \frac{\left(\frac{1}{2}\right)\left(-\frac{1}{2}\right)\left(-\frac{3}{2}\right)\left(-\frac{5}{2}\right)}{4!}x^4 + \cdots$$

$$= 1 + \frac{x}{2} - \frac{x^2}{8} + \frac{x^3}{16} - \frac{5x^4}{128} + \cdots.$$

Substitution for x gives still other approximations. For example,

$$\sqrt{1-x^2} \approx 1 - \frac{x^2}{2} - \frac{x^4}{8} \qquad \text{for } |x^2| \text{ small}$$

$$\sqrt{1-\frac{1}{x}} \approx 1 - \frac{1}{2x} - \frac{1}{8x^2} \qquad \text{for } \left|\frac{1}{x}\right| \text{ small, that is, } |x| \text{ large.} \quad \blacksquare$$

Evaluating Nonelementary Integrals

Sometimes we can use a familiar Taylor series to find the sum of a given power series in terms of a known function. For example,

$$x^2 - \frac{x^6}{3!} + \frac{x^{10}}{5!} - \frac{x^{14}}{7!} + \cdots = (x^2) - \frac{(x^2)^3}{3!} + \frac{(x^2)^5}{5!} - \frac{(x^2)^7}{7!} + \cdots = \sin x^2.$$

Additional examples are provided in Exercises 59–62.

Taylor series can be used to express nonelementary integrals in terms of series. Integrals like $\int \sin x^2\,dx$ arise in the study of the diffraction of light.

EXAMPLE 3 Express $\int \sin x^2\,dx$ as a power series.

Solution From the series for $\sin x$ we substitute x^2 for x to obtain

$$\sin x^2 = x^2 - \frac{x^6}{3!} + \frac{x^{10}}{5!} - \frac{x^{14}}{7!} + \frac{x^{18}}{9!} - \cdots.$$

Therefore,

$$\int \sin x^2\,dx = C + \frac{x^3}{3} - \frac{x^7}{7\cdot 3!} + \frac{x^{11}}{11\cdot 5!} - \frac{x^{15}}{15\cdot 7!} + \frac{x^{10}}{19\cdot 9!} - \cdots. \quad \blacksquare$$

EXAMPLE 4 Estimate $\int_0^1 \sin x^2\, dx$ with an error of less than 0.001.

Solution From the indefinite integral in Example 3, we easily find that

$$\int_0^1 \sin x^2\, dx = \frac{1}{3} - \frac{1}{7\cdot 3!} + \frac{1}{11\cdot 5!} - \frac{1}{15\cdot 7!} + \frac{1}{19\cdot 9!} - \cdots.$$

The series on the right-hand side alternates, and we find by numerical evaluations that

$$\frac{1}{11\cdot 5!} \approx 0.00076$$

is the first term to be numerically less than 0.001. The sum of the preceding two terms gives

$$\int_0^1 \sin x^2\, dx \approx \frac{1}{3} - \frac{1}{42} \approx 0.310.$$

With two more terms we could estimate

$$\int_0^1 \sin x^2\, dx \approx 0.310268$$

with an error of less than 10^{-6}. With only one term beyond that we have

$$\int_0^1 \sin x^2\, dx \approx \frac{1}{3} - \frac{1}{42} + \frac{1}{1320} - \frac{1}{75600} + \frac{1}{6894720} \approx 0.310268303,$$

with an error of about 1.08×10^{-9}. To guarantee this accuracy with the error formula for the Trapezoidal Rule would require using about 8000 subintervals. ■

Arctangents

In Section 9.7, Example 5, we found a series for $\tan^{-1} x$ by differentiating to get

$$\frac{d}{dx}\tan^{-1} x = \frac{1}{1+x^2} = 1 - x^2 + x^4 - x^6 + \cdots$$

and then integrating to get

$$\tan^{-1} x = x - \frac{x^3}{3} + \frac{x^5}{5} - \frac{x^7}{7} + \cdots.$$

However, we did not prove the term-by-term integration theorem on which this conclusion depended. We now derive the series again by integrating both sides of the finite formula

$$\frac{1}{1+t^2} = 1 - t^2 + t^4 - t^6 + \cdots + (-1)^n t^{2n} + \frac{(-1)^{n+1}t^{2n+2}}{1+t^2}, \tag{2}$$

in which the last term comes from adding the remaining terms as a geometric series with first term $a = (-1)^{n+1}t^{2n+2}$ and ratio $r = -t^2$. Integrating both sides of Equation (2) from $t = 0$ to $t = x$ gives

$$\tan^{-1} x = x - \frac{x^3}{3} + \frac{x^5}{5} - \frac{x^7}{7} + \cdots + (-1)^n \frac{x^{2n+1}}{2n+1} + R_n(x),$$

where

$$R_n(x) = \int_0^x \frac{(-1)^{n+1}t^{2n+2}}{1+t^2}\, dt.$$

The denominator of the integrand is greater than or equal to 1; hence

$$|R_n(x)| \le \int_0^{|x|} t^{2n+2}\, dt = \frac{|x|^{2n+3}}{2n+3}.$$

If $|x| \le 1$, the right side of this inequality approaches zero as $n \to \infty$. Therefore $\lim_{n\to\infty} R_n(x) = 0$ if $|x| \le 1$ and

$$\tan^{-1} x = \sum_{n=0}^{\infty} \frac{(-1)^n x^{2n+1}}{2n+1}, \qquad |x| \le 1.$$
$$\tan^{-1} x = x - \frac{x^3}{3} + \frac{x^5}{5} - \frac{x^7}{7} + \cdots, \qquad |x| \le 1. \tag{3}$$

We take this route instead of finding the Taylor series directly because the formulas for the higher-order derivatives of $\tan^{-1} x$ are unmanageable. When we put $x = 1$ in Equation (3), we get **Leibniz's formula**:

$$\frac{\pi}{4} = 1 - \frac{1}{3} + \frac{1}{5} - \frac{1}{7} + \frac{1}{9} - \cdots + \frac{(-1)^n}{2n+1} + \cdots.$$

Because this series converges very slowly, it is not used in approximating π to many decimal places. The series for $\tan^{-1} x$ converges most rapidly when x is near zero. For that reason, people who use the series for $\tan^{-1} x$ to compute π use various trigonometric identities.

For example, if

$$\alpha = \tan^{-1}\frac{1}{2} \quad \text{and} \quad \beta = \tan^{-1}\frac{1}{3},$$

then

$$\tan(\alpha + \beta) = \frac{\tan\alpha + \tan\beta}{1 - \tan\alpha\tan\beta} = \frac{\frac{1}{2} + \frac{1}{3}}{1 - \frac{1}{6}} = 1 = \tan\frac{\pi}{4}$$

and

$$\frac{\pi}{4} = \alpha + \beta = \tan^{-1}\frac{1}{2} + \tan^{-1}\frac{1}{3}.$$

Now Equation (3) may be used with $x = 1/2$ to evaluate $\tan^{-1}(1/2)$ and with $x = 1/3$ to give $\tan^{-1}(1/3)$. The sum of these results, multiplied by 4, gives π.

Evaluating Indeterminate Forms

We can sometimes evaluate indeterminate forms by expressing the functions involved as Taylor series.

EXAMPLE 5 Evaluate

$$\lim_{x\to 1} \frac{\ln x}{x - 1}.$$

Solution We represent $\ln x$ as a Taylor series in powers of $x - 1$. This can be accomplished by calculating the Taylor series generated by $\ln x$ at $x = 1$ directly or by replacing x by $x - 1$ in the series for $\ln(1 + x)$ in Section 9.7, Example 6. Either way, we obtain

$$\ln x = (x - 1) - \frac{1}{2}(x - 1)^2 + \cdots,$$

from which we find that

$$\lim_{x\to 1} \frac{\ln x}{x - 1} = \lim_{x\to 1} \left(1 - \frac{1}{2}(x - 1) + \cdots\right) = 1. \quad \blacksquare$$

EXAMPLE 6 Evaluate

$$\lim_{x\to 0} \frac{\sin x - \tan x}{x^3}.$$

Solution The Taylor series for $\sin x$ and $\tan x$, to terms in x^5, are

$$\sin x = x - \frac{x^3}{3!} + \frac{x^5}{5!} - \cdots, \qquad \tan x = x + \frac{x^3}{3} + \frac{2x^5}{15} + \cdots.$$

Subtracting the series term by term, it follows that

$$\sin x - \tan x = -\frac{x^3}{2} - \frac{x^5}{8} - \cdots = x^3\left(-\frac{1}{2} - \frac{x^2}{8} - \cdots\right).$$

Division of both sides by x^3 and taking limits then gives

$$\begin{aligned}\lim_{x\to 0}\frac{\sin x - \tan x}{x^3} &= \lim_{x\to 0}\left(-\frac{1}{2} - \frac{x^2}{8} - \cdots\right)\\ &= -\frac{1}{2}.\end{aligned}$$

■

If we apply series to calculate $\lim_{x\to 0}((1/\sin x) - (1/x))$, we not only find the limit successfully but also discover an approximation formula for $\csc x$.

EXAMPLE 7 Find $\lim_{x\to 0}\left(\frac{1}{\sin x} - \frac{1}{x}\right)$.

Solution Using algebra and the Taylor series for $\sin x$, we have

$$\begin{aligned}\frac{1}{\sin x} - \frac{1}{x} = \frac{x - \sin x}{x \sin x} &= \frac{x - \left(x - \dfrac{x^3}{3!} + \dfrac{x^5}{5!} - \cdots\right)}{x\cdot\left(x - \dfrac{x^3}{3!} + \dfrac{x^5}{5!} - \cdots\right)}\\ &= \frac{x^3\left(\dfrac{1}{3!} - \dfrac{x^2}{5!} + \cdots\right)}{x^2\left(1 - \dfrac{x^2}{3!} + \cdots\right)} = x\,\frac{\dfrac{1}{3!} - \dfrac{x^2}{5!} + \cdots}{1 - \dfrac{x^2}{3!} + \cdots}.\end{aligned}$$

Therefore,

$$\lim_{x\to 0}\left(\frac{1}{\sin x} - \frac{1}{x}\right) = \lim_{x\to 0}\left(x\,\frac{\dfrac{1}{3!} - \dfrac{x^2}{5!} + \cdots}{1 - \dfrac{x^2}{3!} + \cdots}\right) = 0.$$

From the quotient on the right, we can see that if $|x|$ is small, then

$$\frac{1}{\sin x} - \frac{1}{x} \approx x\cdot\frac{1}{3!} = \frac{x}{6} \quad\text{or}\quad \csc x \approx \frac{1}{x} + \frac{x}{6}.$$

■

Euler's Identity

A complex number is a number of the form $a + bi$, where a and b are real numbers and $i = \sqrt{-1}$ (see Appendix 8). If we substitute $x = i\theta$ (θ real) in the Taylor series for e^x and use the relations

$$i^2 = -1, \qquad i^3 = i^2 i = -i, \qquad i^4 = i^2 i^2 = 1, \qquad i^5 = i^4 i = i,$$

and so on, to simplify the result, we obtain

$$e^{i\theta} = 1 + \frac{i\theta}{1!} + \frac{i^2\theta^2}{2!} + \frac{i^3\theta^3}{3!} + \frac{i^4\theta^4}{4!} + \frac{i^5\theta^5}{5!} + \frac{i^6\theta^6}{6!} + \cdots$$

$$= \left(1 - \frac{\theta^2}{2!} + \frac{\theta^4}{4!} - \frac{\theta^6}{6!} + \cdots\right) + i\left(\theta - \frac{\theta^3}{3!} + \frac{\theta^5}{5!} - \cdots\right) = \cos\theta + i\sin\theta.$$

This does not *prove* that $e^{i\theta} = \cos\theta + i\sin\theta$ because we have not yet defined what it means to raise e to an imaginary power. Rather, it says how to define $e^{i\theta}$ to be consistent with other things we know about the exponential function for real numbers.

DEFINITION

For any real number θ, $e^{i\theta} = \cos\theta + i\sin\theta$. (4)

Equation (4), called **Euler's identity**, enables us to define e^{a+bi} to be $e^a \cdot e^{bi}$ for any complex number $a + bi$. One consequence of the identity is the equation

$$e^{i\pi} = -1.$$

When written in the form $e^{i\pi} + 1 = 0$, this equation combines five of the most important constants in mathematics.

TABLE 9.1 Frequently used Taylor series

$$\frac{1}{1-x} = 1 + x + x^2 + \cdots + x^n + \cdots = \sum_{n=0}^{\infty} x^n, \quad |x| < 1$$

$$\frac{1}{1+x} = 1 - x + x^2 - \cdots + (-x)^n + \cdots = \sum_{n=0}^{\infty} (-1)^n x^n, \quad |x| < 1$$

$$e^x = 1 + x + \frac{x^2}{2!} + \cdots + \frac{x^n}{n!} + \cdots = \sum_{n=0}^{\infty} \frac{x^n}{n!}, \quad |x| < \infty$$

$$\sin x = x - \frac{x^3}{3!} + \frac{x^5}{5!} - \cdots + (-1)^n \frac{x^{2n+1}}{(2n+1)!} + \cdots = \sum_{n=0}^{\infty} \frac{(-1)^n x^{2n+1}}{(2n+1)!}, \quad |x| < \infty$$

$$\cos x = 1 - \frac{x^2}{2!} + \frac{x^4}{4!} - \cdots + (-1)^n \frac{x^{2n}}{(2n)!} + \cdots = \sum_{n=0}^{\infty} \frac{(-1)^n x^{2n}}{(2n)!}, \quad |x| < \infty$$

$$\ln(1+x) = x - \frac{x^2}{2} + \frac{x^3}{3} - \cdots + (-1)^{n-1} \frac{x^n}{n} + \cdots = \sum_{n=1}^{\infty} \frac{(-1)^{n-1} x^n}{n}, \quad -1 < x \le 1$$

$$\tan^{-1} x = x - \frac{x^3}{3} + \frac{x^5}{5} - \cdots + (-1)^n \frac{x^{2n+1}}{2n+1} + \cdots = \sum_{n=0}^{\infty} \frac{(-1)^n x^{2n+1}}{2n+1}, \quad |x| \le 1$$

Exercises 9.10

Binomial Series

Find the first four terms of the binomial series for the functions in Exercises 1–10.

1. $(1 + x)^{1/2}$

2. $(1 + x)^{1/3}$

3. $(1 - x)^{-1/2}$

4. $(1 - 2x)^{1/2}$

5. $\left(1 + \frac{x}{2}\right)^{-2}$

6. $\left(1 - \frac{x}{3}\right)^{4}$

7. $(1 + x^3)^{-1/2}$

8. $(1 + x^2)^{-1/3}$

9. $\left(1+\frac{1}{x}\right)^{1/2}$ **10.** $\frac{x}{\sqrt[3]{1+x}}$

Find the binomial series for the functions in Exercises 11–14.

11. $(1+x)^4$ **12.** $(1+x^2)^3$

13. $(1-2x)^3$ **14.** $\left(1-\frac{x}{2}\right)^4$

Approximations and Nonelementary Integrals

T In Exercises 15–18, use series to estimate the integrals' values with an error of magnitude less than 10^{-3}. (The answer section gives the integrals' values rounded to five decimal places.)

15. $\int_0^{0.2} \sin x^2\, dx$ **16.** $\int_0^{0.2} \frac{e^{-x}-1}{x}\, dx$

17. $\int_0^{0.1} \frac{1}{\sqrt{1+x^4}}\, dx$ **18.** $\int_0^{0.25} \sqrt[3]{1+x^2}\, dx$

T Use series to approximate the values of the integrals in Exercises 19–22 with an error of magnitude less than 10^{-8}.

19. $\int_0^{0.1} \frac{\sin x}{x}\, dx$ **20.** $\int_0^{0.1} e^{-x^2}\, dx$

21. $\int_0^{0.1} \sqrt{1+x^4}\, dx$ **22.** $\int_0^{1} \frac{1-\cos x}{x^2}\, dx$

23. Estimate the error if $\cos t^2$ is approximated by $1 - \frac{t^4}{2} + \frac{t^8}{4!}$ in the integral $\int_0^1 \cos t^2\, dt$.

24. Estimate the error if $\cos\sqrt{t}$ is approximated by $1 - \frac{t}{2} + \frac{t^2}{4!} - \frac{t^3}{6!}$ in the integral $\int_0^1 \cos\sqrt{t}\, dt$.

In Exercises 25–28, find a polynomial that will approximate $F(x)$ throughout the given interval with an error of magnitude less than 10^{-3}.

25. $F(x) = \int_0^x \sin t^2\, dt$, $[0, 1]$

26. $F(x) = \int_0^x t^2 e^{-t^2}\, dt$, $[0, 1]$

27. $F(x) = \int_0^x \tan^{-1} t\, dt$, **(a)** $[0, 0.5]$ **(b)** $[0, 1]$

28. $F(x) = \int_0^x \frac{\ln(1+t)}{t}\, dt$, **(a)** $[0, 0.5]$ **(b)** $[0, 1]$

Indeterminate Forms

Use series to evaluate the limits in Exercises 29–40.

29. $\lim_{x\to 0} \frac{e^x - (1+x)}{x^2}$ **30.** $\lim_{x\to 0} \frac{e^x - e^{-x}}{x}$

31. $\lim_{t\to 0} \frac{1-\cos t - (t^2/2)}{t^4}$ **32.** $\lim_{\theta\to 0} \frac{\sin\theta - \theta + (\theta^3/6)}{\theta^5}$

33. $\lim_{y\to 0} \frac{y - \tan^{-1} y}{y^3}$ **34.** $\lim_{y\to 0} \frac{\tan^{-1} y - \sin y}{y^3 \cos y}$

35. $\lim_{x\to\infty} x^2(e^{-1/x^2} - 1)$ **36.** $\lim_{x\to\infty} (x+1)\sin\frac{1}{x+1}$

37. $\lim_{x\to 0} \frac{\ln(1+x^2)}{1-\cos x}$ **38.** $\lim_{x\to 2} \frac{x^2-4}{\ln(x-1)}$

39. $\lim_{x\to 0} \frac{\sin 3x^2}{1-\cos 2x}$ **40.** $\lim_{x\to 0} \frac{\ln(1+x^3)}{x\cdot\sin x^2}$

Using Table 9.1

In Exercises 41–52, use Table 9.1 to find the sum of each series.

41. $1 + 1 + \frac{1}{2!} + \frac{1}{3!} + \frac{1}{4!} + \cdots$

42. $\left(\frac{1}{4}\right)^3 + \left(\frac{1}{4}\right)^4 + \left(\frac{1}{4}\right)^5 + \left(\frac{1}{4}\right)^6 + \cdots$

43. $1 - \frac{3^2}{4^2\cdot 2!} + \frac{3^4}{4^4\cdot 4!} - \frac{3^6}{4^6\cdot 6!} + \cdots$

44. $\frac{1}{2} - \frac{1}{2\cdot 2^2} + \frac{1}{3\cdot 2^3} - \frac{1}{4\cdot 2^4} + \cdots$

45. $\frac{\pi}{3} - \frac{\pi^3}{3^3\cdot 3!} + \frac{\pi^5}{3^5\cdot 5!} - \frac{\pi^7}{3^7\cdot 7!} + \cdots$

46. $\frac{2}{3} - \frac{2^3}{3^3\cdot 3} + \frac{2^5}{3^5\cdot 5} - \frac{2^7}{3^7\cdot 7} + \cdots$

47. $x^3 + x^4 + x^5 + x^6 + \cdots$

48. $1 - \frac{3^2x^2}{2!} + \frac{3^4x^4}{4!} - \frac{3^6x^6}{6!} + \cdots$

49. $x^3 - x^5 + x^7 - x^9 + x^{11} - \cdots$

50. $x^2 - 2x^3 + \frac{2^2x^4}{2!} - \frac{2^3x^5}{3!} + \frac{2^4x^6}{4!} - \cdots$

51. $-1 + 2x - 3x^2 + 4x^3 - 5x^4 + \cdots$

52. $1 + \frac{x}{2} + \frac{x^2}{3} + \frac{x^3}{4} + \frac{x^4}{5} + \cdots$

Theory and Examples

53. Replace x by $-x$ in the Taylor series for $\ln(1+x)$ to obtain a series for $\ln(1-x)$. Then subtract this from the Taylor series for $\ln(1+x)$ to show that for $|x| < 1$,

$$\ln\frac{1+x}{1-x} = 2\left(x + \frac{x^3}{3} + \frac{x^5}{5} + \cdots\right).$$

54. How many terms of the Taylor series for $\ln(1+x)$ should you add to be sure of calculating $\ln(1.1)$ with an error of magnitude less than 10^{-8}? Give reasons for your answer.

55. According to the Alternating Series Estimation Theorem, how many terms of the Taylor series for $\tan^{-1} 1$ would you have to add to be sure of finding $\pi/4$ with an error of magnitude less than 10^{-3}? Give reasons for your answer.

56. Show that the Taylor series for $f(x) = \tan^{-1} x$ diverges for $|x| > 1$.

T **57. Estimating Pi** About how many terms of the Taylor series for $\tan^{-1} x$ would you have to use to evaluate each term on the right-hand side of the equation

$$\pi = 48\tan^{-1}\frac{1}{18} + 32\tan^{-1}\frac{1}{57} - 20\tan^{-1}\frac{1}{239}$$

with an error of magnitude less than 10^{-6}? In contrast, the convergence of $\sum_{n=1}^{\infty}(1/n^2)$ to $\pi^2/6$ is so slow that even 50 terms will not yield two-place accuracy.

58. Integrate the first three nonzero terms of the Taylor series for $\tan t$ from 0 to x to obtain the first three nonzero terms of the Taylor series for $\ln \sec x$.

59. a. Use the binomial series and the fact that

$$\frac{d}{dx}\sin^{-1}x = (1 - x^2)^{-1/2}$$

to generate the first four nonzero terms of the Taylor series for $\sin^{-1}x$. What is the radius of convergence?

b. Series for $\cos^{-1}x$ Use your result in part (a) to find the first five nonzero terms of the Taylor series for $\cos^{-1}x$.

60. a. Series for $\sinh^{-1}x$ Find the first four nonzero terms of the Taylor series for

$$\sinh^{-1}x = \int_0^x \frac{dt}{\sqrt{1 + t^2}}.$$

T **b.** Use the first *three* terms of the series in part (a) to estimate $\sinh^{-1} 0.25$. Give an upper bound for the magnitude of the estimation error.

61. Obtain the Taylor series for $1/(1 + x)^2$ from the series for $-1/(1 + x)$.

62. Use the Taylor series for $1/(1 - x^2)$ to obtain a series for $2x/(1 - x^2)^2$.

T **63. Estimating Pi** The English mathematician Wallis discovered the formula

$$\frac{\pi}{4} = \frac{2\cdot4\cdot4\cdot6\cdot6\cdot8\cdot\cdots}{3\cdot3\cdot5\cdot5\cdot7\cdot7\cdot\cdots}.$$

Find π to two decimal places with this formula.

64. Use the following steps to prove that the binomial series in Equation (1) converges to $(1 + x)^m$.

a. Differentiate the series

$$f(x) = 1 + \sum_{k=1}^{\infty}\binom{m}{k}x^k$$

to show that

$$f'(x) = \frac{mf(x)}{1 + x}, \quad -1 < x < 1.$$

b. Define $g(x) = (1 + x)^{-m} f(x)$ and show that $g'(x) = 0$.

c. From part (b), show that

$$f(x) = (1 + x)^m.$$

65. Series for $\sin^{-1}x$ Integrate the binomial series for $(1 - x^2)^{-1/2}$ to show that for $|x| < 1$,

$$\sin^{-1}x = x + \sum_{n=1}^{\infty}\frac{1\cdot3\cdot5\cdot\cdots\cdot(2n-1)}{2\cdot4\cdot6\cdot\cdots\cdot(2n)}\frac{x^{2n+1}}{2n+1}.$$

66. Series for $\tan^{-1}x$ for $|x| > 1$ Derive the series

$$\tan^{-1}x = \frac{\pi}{2} - \frac{1}{x} + \frac{1}{3x^3} - \frac{1}{5x^5} + \cdots, \quad x > 1$$

$$\tan^{-1}x = -\frac{\pi}{2} - \frac{1}{x} + \frac{1}{3x^3} - \frac{1}{5x^5} + \cdots, \quad x < -1,$$

by integrating the series

$$\frac{1}{1 + t^2} = \frac{1}{t^2}\cdot\frac{1}{1 + (1/t^2)} = \frac{1}{t^2} - \frac{1}{t^4} + \frac{1}{t^6} - \frac{1}{t^8} + \cdots$$

in the first case from x to ∞ and in the second case from $-\infty$ to x.

Euler's Identity

67. Use Equation (4) to write the following powers of e in the form $a + bi$.

a. $e^{-i\pi}$ **b.** $e^{i\pi/4}$ **c.** $e^{-i\pi/2}$

68. Use Equation (4) to show that

$$\cos\theta = \frac{e^{i\theta} + e^{-i\theta}}{2} \quad \text{and} \quad \sin\theta = \frac{e^{i\theta} - e^{-i\theta}}{2i}.$$

69. Establish the equations in Exercise 68 by combining the formal Taylor series for $e^{i\theta}$ and $e^{-i\theta}$.

70. Show that

a. $\cosh i\theta = \cos\theta$, **b.** $\sinh i\theta = i\sin\theta$.

71. By multiplying the Taylor series for e^x and $\sin x$, find the terms through x^5 of the Taylor series for $e^x \sin x$. This series is the imaginary part of the series for

$$e^x\cdot e^{ix} = e^{(1+i)x}.$$

Use this fact to check your answer. For what values of x should the series for $e^x \sin x$ converge?

72. When a and b are real, we define $e^{(a+ib)x}$ with the equation

$$e^{(a+ib)x} = e^{ax}\cdot e^{ibx} = e^{ax}(\cos bx + i\sin bx).$$

Differentiate the right-hand side of this equation to show that

$$\frac{d}{dx}e^{(a+ib)x} = (a + ib)e^{(a+ib)x}.$$

Thus the familiar rule $(d/dx)e^{kx} = ke^{kx}$ holds for k complex as well as real.

73. Use the definition of $e^{i\theta}$ to show that for any real numbers θ, θ_1, and θ_2,

a. $e^{i\theta_1}e^{i\theta_2} = e^{i(\theta_1+\theta_2)}$, **b.** $e^{-i\theta} = 1/e^{i\theta}$.

74. Two complex numbers $a + ib$ and $c + id$ are equal if and only if $a = c$ and $b = d$. Use this fact to evaluate

$$\int e^{ax}\cos bx\,dx \quad \text{and} \quad \int e^{ax}\sin bx\,dx$$

from

$$\int e^{(a+ib)x}\,dx = \frac{a - ib}{a^2 + b^2}e^{(a+ib)x} + C,$$

where $C = C_1 + iC_2$ is a complex constant of integration.

Chapter Questions to Guide Your Review

1. What is an infinite sequence? What does it mean for such a sequence to converge? To diverge? Give examples.
2. What is a monotonic sequence? Under what circumstances does such a sequence have a limit? Give examples.
3. What theorems are available for calculating limits of sequences? Give examples.
4. What theorem sometimes enables us to use l'Hôpital's Rule to calculate the limit of a sequence? Give an example.
5. What are the six commonly occurring limits in Theorem 5 that arise frequently when you work with sequences and series?
6. What is an infinite series? What does it mean for such a series to converge? To diverge? Give examples.
7. What is a geometric series? When does such a series converge? Diverge? When it does converge, what is its sum? Give examples.
8. Besides geometric series, what other convergent and divergent series do you know?
9. What is the nth-Term Test for Divergence? What is the idea behind the test?
10. What can be said about term-by-term sums and differences of convergent series? About constant multiples of convergent and divergent series?
11. What happens if you add a finite number of terms to a convergent series? A divergent series? What happens if you delete a finite number of terms from a convergent series? A divergent series?
12. How do you reindex a series? Why might you want to do this?
13. Under what circumstances will an infinite series of nonnegative terms converge? Diverge? Why study series of nonnegative terms?
14. What is the Integral Test? What is the reasoning behind it? Give an example of its use.
15. When do p-series converge? Diverge? How do you know? Give examples of convergent and divergent p-series.
16. What are the Direct Comparison Test and the Limit Comparison Test? What is the reasoning behind these tests? Give examples of their use.
17. What are the Ratio and Root Tests? Do they always give you the information you need to determine convergence or divergence? Give examples.
18. What is an alternating series? What theorem is available for determining the convergence of such a series?
19. How can you estimate the error involved in approximating the sum of an alternating series with one of the series' partial sums? What is the reasoning behind the estimate?
20. What is absolute convergence? Conditional convergence? How are the two related?
21. What do you know about rearranging the terms of an absolutely convergent series? Of a conditionally convergent series?
22. What is a power series? How do you test a power series for convergence? What are the possible outcomes?
23. What are the basic facts about
    a. sums, differences, and products of power series?
    b. substitution of a function for x in a power series?
    c. term-by-term differentiation of power series?
    d. term-by-term integration of power series?

    Give examples.
24. What is the Taylor series generated by a function $f(x)$ at a point $x = a$? What information do you need about f to construct the series? Give an example.
25. What is a Maclaurin series?
26. Does a Taylor series always converge to its generating function? Explain.
27. What are Taylor polynomials? Of what use are they?
28. What is Taylor's formula? What does it say about the errors involved in using Taylor polynomials to approximate functions? In particular, what does Taylor's formula say about the error in a linearization? A quadratic approximation?
29. What is the binomial series? On what interval does it converge? How is it used?
30. How can you sometimes use power series to estimate the values of nonelementary definite integrals? To find limits?
31. What are the Taylor series for $1/(1 - x)$, $1/(1 + x)$, e^x, $\sin x$, $\cos x$, $\ln(1 + x)$, and $\tan^{-1} x$? How do you estimate the errors involved in replacing these series with their partial sums?

Chapter Practice Exercises

Determining Convergence of Sequences

Which of the sequences whose nth terms appear in Exercises 1–18 converge, and which diverge? Find the limit of each convergent sequence.

1. $a_n = 1 + \dfrac{(-1)^n}{n}$
2. $a_n = \dfrac{1 - (-1)^n}{\sqrt{n}}$
3. $a_n = \dfrac{1 - 2^n}{2^n}$
4. $a_n = 1 + (0.9)^n$
5. $a_n = \sin \dfrac{n\pi}{2}$
6. $a_n = \sin n\pi$
7. $a_n = \dfrac{\ln(n^2)}{n}$
8. $a_n = \dfrac{\ln(2n + 1)}{n}$
9. $a_n = \dfrac{n + \ln n}{n}$
10. $a_n = \dfrac{\ln(2n^3 + 1)}{n}$
11. $a_n = \left(\dfrac{n - 5}{n}\right)^n$
12. $a_n = \left(1 + \dfrac{1}{n}\right)^{-n}$

13. $a_n = \sqrt[n]{\frac{3^n}{n}}$

14. $a_n = \left(\frac{3}{n}\right)^{1/n}$

15. $a_n = n(2^{1/n} - 1)$

16. $a_n = \sqrt[n]{2n + 1}$

17. $a_n = \frac{(n + 1)!}{n!}$

18. $a_n = \frac{(-4)^n}{n!}$

Convergent Series

Find the sums of the series in Exercises 19–24.

19. $\sum_{n=3}^{\infty} \frac{1}{(2n - 3)(2n - 1)}$

20. $\sum_{n=2}^{\infty} \frac{-2}{n(n + 1)}$

21. $\sum_{n=1}^{\infty} \frac{9}{(3n - 1)(3n + 2)}$

22. $\sum_{n=3}^{\infty} \frac{-8}{(4n - 3)(4n + 1)}$

23. $\sum_{n=0}^{\infty} e^{-n}$

24. $\sum_{n=1}^{\infty} (-1)^n \frac{3}{4^n}$

Determining Convergence of Series

Which of the series in Exercises 25–40 converge absolutely, which converge conditionally, and which diverge? Give reasons for your answers.

25. $\sum_{n=1}^{\infty} \frac{1}{\sqrt{n}}$

26. $\sum_{n=1}^{\infty} \frac{-5}{n}$

27. $\sum_{n=1}^{\infty} \frac{(-1)^n}{\sqrt{n}}$

28. $\sum_{n=1}^{\infty} \frac{1}{2n^3}$

29. $\sum_{n=1}^{\infty} \frac{(-1)^n}{\ln (n + 1)}$

30. $\sum_{n=2}^{\infty} \frac{1}{n (\ln n)^2}$

31. $\sum_{n=1}^{\infty} \frac{\ln n}{n^3}$

32. $\sum_{n=3}^{\infty} \frac{\ln n}{\ln (\ln n)}$

33. $\sum_{n=1}^{\infty} \frac{(-1)^n}{n\sqrt{n^2 + 1}}$

34. $\sum_{n=1}^{\infty} \frac{(-1)^n 3n^2}{n^3 + 1}$

35. $\sum_{n=1}^{\infty} \frac{n + 1}{n!}$

36. $\sum_{n=1}^{\infty} \frac{(-1)^n(n^2 + 1)}{2n^2 + n - 1}$

37. $\sum_{n=1}^{\infty} \frac{(-3)^n}{n!}$

38. $\sum_{n=1}^{\infty} \frac{2^n 3^n}{n^n}$

39. $\sum_{n=1}^{\infty} \frac{1}{\sqrt{n(n + 1)(n + 2)}}$

40. $\sum_{n=2}^{\infty} \frac{1}{n\sqrt{n^2 - 1}}$

Power Series

In Exercises 41–50, **(a)** find the series' radius and interval of convergence. Then identify the values of x for which the series converges **(b)** absolutely and **(c)** conditionally.

41. $\sum_{n=1}^{\infty} \frac{(x + 4)^n}{n3^n}$

42. $\sum_{n=1}^{\infty} \frac{(x - 1)^{2n-2}}{(2n - 1)!}$

43. $\sum_{n=1}^{\infty} \frac{(-1)^{n-1}(3x - 1)^n}{n^2}$

44. $\sum_{n=0}^{\infty} \frac{(n + 1)(2x + 1)^n}{(2n + 1)2^n}$

45. $\sum_{n=1}^{\infty} \frac{x^n}{n^n}$

46. $\sum_{n=1}^{\infty} \frac{x^n}{\sqrt{n}}$

47. $\sum_{n=0}^{\infty} \frac{(n + 1)x^{2n-1}}{3^n}$

48. $\sum_{n=0}^{\infty} \frac{(-1)^n(x - 1)^{2n+1}}{2n + 1}$

49. $\sum_{n=1}^{\infty} (\operatorname{csch} n)x^n$

50. $\sum_{n=1}^{\infty} (\coth n)x^n$

Maclaurin Series

Each of the series in Exercises 51–56 is the value of the Taylor series at $x = 0$ of a function $f(x)$ at a particular point. What function and what point? What is the sum of the series?

51. $1 - \frac{1}{4} + \frac{1}{16} - \cdots + (-1)^n \frac{1}{4^n} + \cdots$

52. $\frac{2}{3} - \frac{4}{18} + \frac{8}{81} - \cdots + (-1)^{n-1} \frac{2^n}{n3^n} + \cdots$

53. $\pi - \frac{\pi^3}{3!} + \frac{\pi^5}{5!} - \cdots + (-1)^n \frac{\pi^{2n+1}}{(2n + 1)!} + \cdots$

54. $1 - \frac{\pi^2}{9 \cdot 2!} + \frac{\pi^4}{81 \cdot 4!} - \cdots + (-1)^n \frac{\pi^{2n}}{3^{2n}(2n)!} + \cdots$

55. $1 + \ln 2 + \frac{(\ln 2)^2}{2!} + \cdots + \frac{(\ln 2)^n}{n!} + \cdots$

56. $\frac{1}{\sqrt{3}} - \frac{1}{9\sqrt{3}} + \frac{1}{45\sqrt{3}} - \cdots + (-1)^{n-1} \frac{1}{(2n - 1)\left(\sqrt{3}\right)^{2n-1}} + \cdots$

Find Taylor series at $x = 0$ for the functions in Exercises 57–64.

57. $\frac{1}{1 - 2x}$

58. $\frac{1}{1 + x^3}$

59. $\sin \pi x$

60. $\sin \frac{2x}{3}$

61. $\cos (x^{5/3})$

62. $\cos \frac{x^3}{\sqrt{5}}$

63. $e^{(\pi x/2)}$

64. e^{-x^2}

Taylor Series

In Exercises 65–68, find the first four nonzero terms of the Taylor series generated by f at $x = a$.

65. $f(x) = \sqrt{3 + x^2}$ at $x = -1$

66. $f(x) = 1/(1 - x)$ at $x = 2$

67. $f(x) = 1/(x + 1)$ at $x = 3$

68. $f(x) = 1/x$ at $x = a > 0$

Nonelementary Integrals

Use series to approximate the values of the integrals in Exercises 69–72 with an error of magnitude less than 10^{-8}. (The answer section gives the integrals' values rounded to 10 decimal places.)

69. $\int_0^{1/2} e^{-x^3}\, dx$

70. $\int_0^1 x \sin (x^3)\, dx$

71. $\int_0^{1/2} \frac{\tan^{-1} x}{x}\, dx$

72. $\int_0^{1/64} \frac{\tan^{-1} x}{\sqrt{x}}\, dx$

Using Series to Find Limits

In Exercises 73–78:

a. Use power series to evaluate the limit.

T **b.** Then use a grapher to support your calculation.

73. $\lim_{x \to 0} \frac{7 \sin x}{e^{2x} - 1}$

74. $\lim_{\theta \to 0} \frac{e^{\theta} - e^{-\theta} - 2\theta}{\theta - \sin \theta}$

75. $\lim_{t \to 0} \left(\frac{1}{2 - 2 \cos t} - \frac{1}{t^2}\right)$

76. $\lim_{h \to 0} \frac{(\sin h)/h - \cos h}{h^2}$

77. $\lim_{z \to 0} \frac{1 - \cos^2 z}{\ln(1 - z) + \sin z}$

78. $\lim_{y \to 0} \frac{y^2}{\cos y - \cosh y}$

Theory and Examples

79. Use a series representation of sin 3x to find values of r and s for which

$$\lim_{x \to 0} \left(\frac{\sin 3x}{x^3} + \frac{r}{x^2} + s \right) = 0.$$

T 80. Compare the accuracies of the approximations $\sin x \approx x$ and $\sin x \approx 6x/(6 + x^2)$ by comparing the graphs of $f(x) = \sin x - x$ and $g(x) = \sin x - (6x/(6 + x^2))$. Describe what you find.

81. Find the radius of convergence of the series

$$\sum_{n=1}^{\infty} \frac{2 \cdot 5 \cdot 8 \cdot \cdots \cdot (3n - 1)}{2 \cdot 4 \cdot 6 \cdot \cdots \cdot (2n)} x^n.$$

82. Find the radius of convergence of the series

$$\sum_{n=1}^{\infty} \frac{3 \cdot 5 \cdot 7 \cdot \cdots \cdot (2n + 1)}{4 \cdot 9 \cdot 14 \cdot \cdots \cdot (5n - 1)} (x - 1)^n.$$

83. Find a closed-form formula for the nth partial sum of the series $\sum_{n=2}^{\infty} \ln(1 - (1/n^2))$ and use it to determine the convergence or divergence of the series.

84. Evaluate $\sum_{k=2}^{\infty} (1/(k^2 - 1))$ by finding the limits as $n \to \infty$ of the series' nth partial sum.

85. **a.** Find the interval of convergence of the series

$$y = 1 + \frac{1}{6}x^3 + \frac{1}{180}x^6 + \cdots + \frac{1 \cdot 4 \cdot 7 \cdot \cdots \cdot (3n - 2)}{(3n)!} x^{3n} + \cdots.$$

b. Show that the function defined by the series satisfies a differential equation of the form

$$\frac{d^2 y}{dx^2} = x^a y + b$$

and find the values of the constants a and b.

86. **a.** Find the Maclaurin series for the function $x^2/(1 + x)$.

b. Does the series converge at $x = 1$? Explain.

87. If $\sum_{n=1}^{\infty} a_n$ and $\sum_{n=1}^{\infty} b_n$ are convergent series of nonnegative numbers, can anything be said about $\sum_{n=1}^{\infty} a_n b_n$? Give reasons for your answer.

88. If $\sum_{n=1}^{\infty} a_n$ and $\sum_{n=1}^{\infty} b_n$ are divergent series of nonnegative numbers, can anything be said about $\sum_{n=1}^{\infty} a_n b_n$? Give reasons for your answer.

89. Prove that the sequence $\{x_n\}$ and the series $\sum_{k=1}^{\infty} (x_{k+1} - x_k)$ both converge or both diverge.

90. Prove that $\sum_{n=1}^{\infty} (a_n/(1 + a_n))$ converges if $a_n > 0$ for all n and $\sum_{n=1}^{\infty} a_n$ converges.

91. Suppose that $a_1, a_2, a_3, \ldots, a_n$ are positive numbers satisfying the following conditions:

i) $a_1 \geq a_2 \geq a_3 \geq \cdots$;

ii) the series $a_2 + a_4 + a_8 + a_{16} + \cdots$ diverges.

Show that the series

$$\frac{a_1}{1} + \frac{a_2}{2} + \frac{a_3}{3} + \cdots$$

diverges.

92. Use the result in Exercise 91 to show that

$$1 + \sum_{n=2}^{\infty} \frac{1}{n \ln n}$$

diverges.

Chapter 9 Additional and Advanced Exercises

Determining Convergence of Series

Which of the series $\sum_{n=1}^{\infty} a_n$ defined by the formulas in Exercises 1–4 converge, and which diverge? Give reasons for your answers.

1. $\sum_{n=1}^{\infty} \frac{1}{(3n - 2)^{n+(1/2)}}$

2. $\sum_{n=1}^{\infty} \frac{(\tan^{-1} n)^2}{n^2 + 1}$

3. $\sum_{n=1}^{\infty} (-1)^n \tanh n$

4. $\sum_{n=2}^{\infty} \frac{\log_n (n!)}{n^3}$

Which of the series $\sum_{n=1}^{\infty} a_n$ defined by the formulas in Exercises 5–8 converge, and which diverge? Give reasons for your answers.

5. $a_1 = 1, \quad a_{n+1} = \frac{n(n + 1)}{(n + 2)(n + 3)} a_n$

(*Hint:* Write out several terms, see which factors cancel, and then generalize.)

6. $a_1 = a_2 = 7, \quad a_{n+1} = \frac{n}{(n - 1)(n + 1)} a_n \quad$ if $n \geq 2$

7. $a_1 = a_2 = 1, \quad a_{n+1} = \frac{1}{1 + a_n} \quad$ if $n \geq 2$

8. $a_n = 1/3^n$ if n is odd, $\quad a_n = n/3^n$ if n is even

Choosing Centers for Taylor Series

Taylor's formula

$$f(x) = f(a) + f'(a)(x - a) + \frac{f''(a)}{2!}(x - a)^2 + \cdots + \frac{f^{(n)}(a)}{n!}(x - a)^n + \frac{f^{(n+1)}(c)}{(n + 1)!}(x - a)^{n+1}$$

expresses the value of f at x in terms of the values of f and its derivatives at $x = a$. In numerical computations, we therefore need a to be a point where we know the values of f and its derivatives. We also need a to be close enough to the values of f we are interested in to make $(x - a)^{n+1}$ so small we can neglect the remainder.

In Exercises 9–14, what Taylor series would you choose to represent the function near the given value of x? (There may be more than one good answer.) Write out the first four nonzero terms of the series you choose.

9. $\cos x$ near $x = 1$

10. $\sin x$ near $x = 6.3$

11. e^x near $x = 0.4$

12. $\ln x$ near $x = 1.3$

13. $\cos x$ near $x = 69$

14. $\tan^{-1} x$ near $x = 2$

Theory and Examples

15. Let a and b be constants with $0 < a < b$. Does the sequence $\{(a^n + b^n)^{1/n}\}$ converge? If it does converge, what is the limit?

16. Find the sum of the infinite series

$$1 + \frac{2}{10} + \frac{3}{10^2} + \frac{7}{10^3} + \frac{2}{10^4} + \frac{3}{10^5} + \frac{7}{10^6} + \frac{2}{10^7} + \frac{3}{10^8} + \frac{7}{10^9} + \cdots.$$

17. Evaluate

$$\sum_{n=0}^{\infty} \int_{n}^{n+1} \frac{1}{1+x^2}\, dx.$$

18. Find all values of x for which

$$\sum_{n=1}^{\infty} \frac{nx^n}{(n+1)(2x+1)^n}$$

converges absolutely.

T **19. a.** Does the value of

$$\lim_{n\to\infty} \left(1 - \frac{\cos(a/n)}{n}\right)^n, \quad a \text{ constant},$$

appear to depend on the value of a? If so, how?

b. Does the value of

$$\lim_{n\to\infty} \left(1 - \frac{\cos(a/n)}{bn}\right)^n, \quad a \text{ and } b \text{ constant}, b \neq 0,$$

appear to depend on the value of b? If so, how?

c. Use calculus to confirm your findings in parts (a) and (b).

20. Show that if $\sum_{n=1}^{\infty} a_n$ converges, then

$$\sum_{n=1}^{\infty} \left(\frac{1 + \sin(a_n)}{2}\right)^n$$

converges.

21. Find a value for the constant b that will make the radius of convergence of the power series

$$\sum_{n=2}^{\infty} \frac{b^n x^n}{\ln n}$$

equal to 5.

22. How do you know that the functions $\sin x$, $\ln x$, and e^x are not polynomials? Give reasons for your answer.

23. Find the value of a for which the limit

$$\lim_{x\to 0} \frac{\sin(ax) - \sin x - x}{x^3}$$

is finite and evaluate the limit.

24. Find values of a and b for which

$$\lim_{x\to 0} \frac{\cos(ax) - b}{2x^2} = -1.$$

25. Raabe's (or Gauss's) Test The following test, which we state without proof, is an extension of the Ratio Test.

Raabe's Test: If $\sum_{n=1}^{\infty} u_n$ is a series of positive constants and there exist constants C, K, and N such that

$$\frac{u_n}{u_{n+1}} = 1 + \frac{C}{n} + \frac{f(n)}{n^2},$$

where $|f(n)| < K$ for $n \geq N$, then $\sum_{n=1}^{\infty} u_n$ converges if $C > 1$ and diverges if $C \leq 1$.

Show that the results of Raabe's Test agree with what you know about the series $\sum_{n=1}^{\infty} (1/n^2)$ and $\sum_{n=1}^{\infty} (1/n)$.

26. (*Continuation of Exercise 25.*) Suppose that the terms of $\sum_{n=1}^{\infty} u_n$ are defined recursively by the formulas

$$u_1 = 1, \quad u_{n+1} = \frac{(2n-1)^2}{(2n)(2n+1)} u_n.$$

Apply Raabe's Test to determine whether the series converges.

27. If $\sum_{n=1}^{\infty} a_n$ converges, and if $a_n \neq 1$ and $a_n > 0$ for all n,

a. Show that $\sum_{n=1}^{\infty} a_n{}^2$ converges.

b. Does $\sum_{n=1}^{\infty} a_n/(1 - a_n)$ converge? Explain.

28. (*Continuation of Exercise 27.*) If $\sum_{n=1}^{\infty} a_n$ converges, and if $1 > a_n > 0$ for all n, show that $\sum_{n=1}^{\infty} \ln(1 - a_n)$ converges.

(*Hint:* First show that $|\ln(1 - a_n)| \leq a_n/(1 - a_n)$.)

29. Nicole Oresme's Theorem Prove Nicole Oresme's Theorem that

$$1 + \frac{1}{2}\cdot 2 + \frac{1}{4}\cdot 3 + \cdots + \frac{n}{2^{n-1}} + \cdots = 4.$$

(*Hint:* Differentiate both sides of the equation $1/(1-x) = 1 + \sum_{n=1}^{\infty} x^n$.)

30. a. Show that

$$\sum_{n=1}^{\infty} \frac{n(n+1)}{x^n} = \frac{2x^2}{(x-1)^3}$$

for $|x| > 1$ by differentiating the identity

$$\sum_{n=1}^{\infty} x^{n+1} = \frac{x^2}{1-x}$$

twice, multiplying the result by x, and then replacing x by $1/x$.

b. Use part (a) to find the real solution greater than 1 of the equation

$$x = \sum_{n=1}^{\infty} \frac{n(n+1)}{x^n}.$$

10
Parametric Equations and Polar Coordinates

OVERVIEW In this chapter we study new ways to define curves in the plane. Instead of thinking of a curve as the graph of a function or equation, we consider a more general way of thinking of a curve as the path of a moving particle whose position is changing over time. Then each of the x- and y-coordinates of the particle's position becomes a function of a third variable t. We can also change the way in which points in the plane themselves are described by using *polar coordinates* rather than the rectangular or Cartesian system. Both of these new tools are useful for describing motion, like that of planets and satellites, or projectiles moving in the plane or space. Parabolas, ellipses, and hyperbolas (called *conic sections,* or *conics,* and reviewed in Appendix 4) model the paths traveled by projectiles, planets, or any other object moving under the sole influence of a gravitational or electromagnetic force.

10.1 Parametrizations of Plane Curves

In previous chapters, we have studied curves as the graphs of functions or equations involving the two variables x and y. We are now going to introduce another way to describe a curve by expressing both coordinates as functions of a third variable t.

Parametric Equations

Figure 10.1 shows the path of a moving particle in the xy-plane. Notice that the path fails the vertical line test, so it cannot be described as the graph of a function of the variable x. However, we can sometimes describe the path by a pair of equations, $x = f(t)$ and $y = g(t)$, where f and g are continuous functions. When studying motion, t usually denotes time. Equations like these describe more general curves than those like $y = f(x)$ and provide not only the graph of the path traced out but also the location of the particle $(x, y) = (f(t), g(t))$ at any time t.

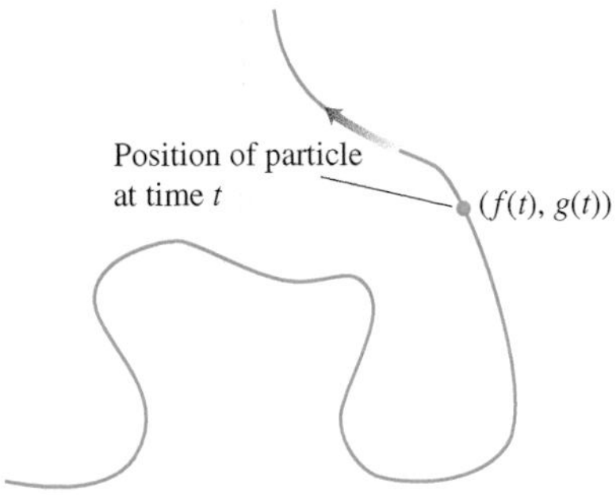

FIGURE 10.1 The curve or path traced by a particle moving in the xy-plane is not always the graph of a function or single equation.

DEFINITION If x and y are given as functions

$$x = f(t), \qquad y = g(t)$$

over an interval I of t-values, then the set of points $(x, y) = (f(t), g(t))$ defined by these equations is a **parametric curve**. The equations are **parametric equations** for the curve.

The variable t is a **parameter** for the curve, and its domain I is the **parameter interval**. If I is a closed interval, $a \le t \le b$, the point $(f(a), g(a))$ is the **initial point** of the curve and $(f(b), g(b))$ is the **terminal point**. When we give parametric equations and a parameter interval for a curve, we say that we have **parametrized** the curve. The equations and interval together constitute a **parametrization** of the curve. A given curve can be represented by different sets of parametric equations. (See Exercises 19 and 20.)

EXAMPLE 1 Sketch the curve defined by the parametric equations

$$x = t^2, \qquad y = t + 1, \qquad -\infty < t < \infty.$$

Solution We make a brief table of values (Table 10.1), plot the points (x, y), and draw a smooth curve through them (Figure 10.2). Each value of t gives a point (x, y) on the curve, such as $t = 1$ giving the point $(1, 2)$ recorded in Table 10.1. If we think of the curve as the path of a moving particle, then the particle moves along the curve in the direction of the arrows shown in Figure 10.2. Although the time intervals in the table are equal, the consecutive points plotted along the curve are not at equal arc length distances. The reason for this is that the particle slows down at it gets nearer to the y-axis along the lower branch of the curve as t increases, and then speeds up after reaching the y-axis at $(0, 1)$ and moving along the upper branch. Since the interval of values for t is all real numbers, there is no initial point and no terminal point for the curve. ■

TABLE 10.1 Values of $x = t^2$ and $y = t + 1$ for selected values of t.

t	x	y
−3	9	−2
−2	4	−1
−1	1	0
0	0	1
1	1	2
2	4	3
3	9	4

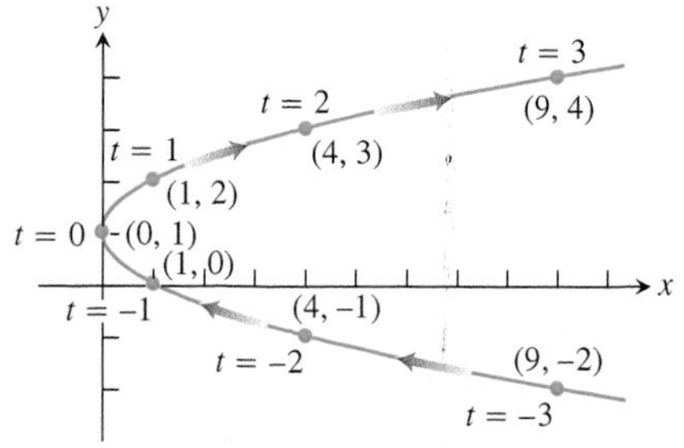

FIGURE 10.2 The curve given by the parametric equations $x = t^2$ and $y = t + 1$ (Example 1).

EXAMPLE 2 Identify geometrically the curve in Example 1 (Figure 10.2) by eliminating the parameter t and obtaining an algebraic equation in x and y.

Solution We solve the equation $y = t + 1$ for the parameter t and substitute the result into the parametric equation for x. This procedure gives $t = y - 1$ and

$$x = t^2 = (y - 1)^2 = y^2 - 2y + 1.$$

The equation $x = y^2 - 2y + 1$ represents a parabola, as displayed in Figure 10.2. It is sometimes quite difficult, or even impossible, to eliminate the parameter from a pair of parametric equations, as we did here. ■

EXAMPLE 3 Graph the parametric curves

(a) $x = \cos t, \qquad y = \sin t, \qquad 0 \le t \le 2\pi.$

(b) $x = a\cos t, \qquad y = a\sin t, \qquad 0 \le t \le 2\pi.$

Solution

(a) Since $x^2 + y^2 = \cos^2 t + \sin^2 t = 1$, the parametric curve lies along the unit circle $x^2 + y^2 = 1$. As t increases from 0 to 2π, the point $(x, y) = (\cos t, \sin t)$ starts at $(1, 0)$ and traces the entire circle once counterclockwise (Figure 10.3).

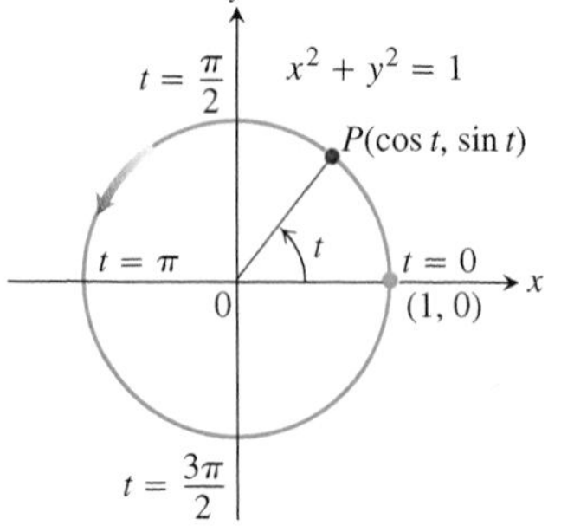

FIGURE 10.3 The equations $x = \cos t$ and $y = \sin t$ describe motion on the circle $x^2 + y^2 = 1$. The arrow shows the direction of increasing t (Example 3).

(b) For $x = a\cos t$, $y = a\sin t$, $0 \le t \le 2\pi$, we have $x^2 + y^2 = a^2\cos^2 t + a^2\sin^2 t = a^2$. The parametrization describes a motion that begins at the point $(a, 0)$ and traverses the circle $x^2 + y^2 = a^2$ once counterclockwise, returning to $(a, 0)$ at $t = 2\pi$. The graph is a circle centered at the origin with radius $r = a$ and coordinate points $(a\cos t, a\sin t)$. ■

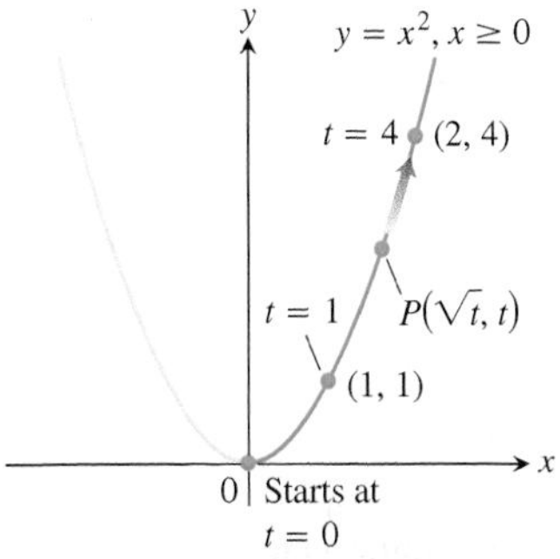

FIGURE 10.4 The equations $x = \sqrt{t}$ and $y = t$ and the interval $t \ge 0$ describe the path of a particle that traces the right-hand half of the parabola $y = x^2$ (Example 4).

EXAMPLE 4 The position $P(x, y)$ of a particle moving in the xy-plane is given by the equations and parameter interval

$$x = \sqrt{t}, \qquad y = t, \qquad t \ge 0.$$

Identify the path traced by the particle and describe the motion.

Solution We try to identify the path by eliminating t between the equations $x = \sqrt{t}$ and $y = t$. With any luck, this will produce a recognizable algebraic relation between x and y. We find that

$$y = t = \left(\sqrt{t}\right)^2 = x^2.$$

Thus, the particle's position coordinates satisfy the equation $y = x^2$, so the particle moves along the parabola $y = x^2$.

It would be a mistake, however, to conclude that the particle's path is the entire parabola $y = x^2$; it is only half the parabola. The particle's x-coordinate is never negative. The particle starts at (0, 0) when $t = 0$ and rises into the first quadrant as t increases (Figure 10.4). The parameter interval is $[0, \infty)$ and there is no terminal point. ■

The graph of any function $y = f(x)$ can always be given a natural parametrization $x = t$ and $y = f(t)$. The domain of the parameter in this case is the same as the domain of the function f.

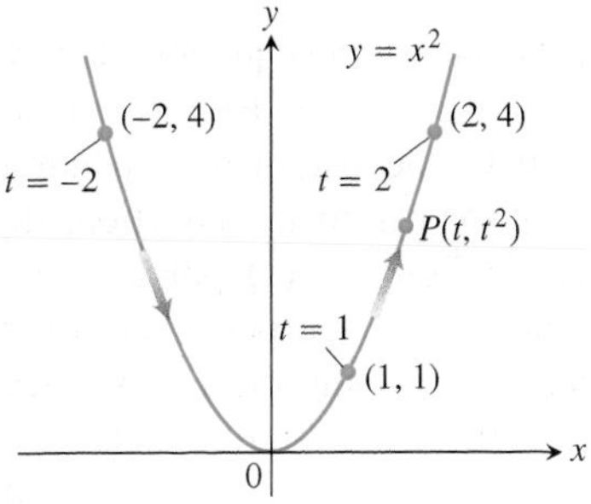

FIGURE 10.5 The path defined by $x = t, y = t^2, -\infty < t < \infty$ is the entire parabola $y = x^2$ (Example 5).

EXAMPLE 5 A parametrization of the graph of the function $f(x) = x^2$ is given by

$$x = t, \qquad y = f(t) = t^2, \qquad -\infty < t < \infty.$$

When $t \ge 0$, this parametrization gives the same path in the xy-plane as we had in Example 4. However, since the parameter t here can now also be negative, we obtain the left-hand part of the parabola as well; that is, we have the entire parabolic curve. For this parametrization, there is no starting point and no terminal point (Figure 10.5). ■

Notice that a parametrization also specifies *when* (the value of the parameter) a particle moving along the curve is *located* at a specific point along the curve. In Example 4, the point (2, 4) is reached when $t = 4$; in Example 5, it is reached "earlier" when $t = 2$. You can see the implications of this aspect of parametrizations when considering the possibility of two objects coming into collision: They have to be at the exact same location point $P(x, y)$ for some (possibly different) values of their respective parameters. We will say more about this aspect of parametrizations when we study motion in Chapter 12.

EXAMPLE 6 Find a parametrization for the line through the point (a, b) having slope m.

Solution A Cartesian equation of the line is $y - b = m(x - a)$. If we set the parameter $t = x - a$, we find that $x = a + t$ and $y - b = mt$. That is,

$$x = a + t, \qquad y = b + mt, \qquad -\infty < t < \infty$$

parametrizes the line. This parametrization differs from the one we would obtain by the technique used in Example 5 when $t = x$. However, both parametrizations give the same line. ■

TABLE 10.2 Values of $x = t + (1/t)$ and $y = t - (1/t)$ for selected values of t.

t	$1/t$	x	y
0.1	10.0	10.1	−9.9
0.2	5.0	5.2	−4.8
0.4	2.5	2.9	−2.1
1.0	1.0	2.0	0.0
2.0	0.5	2.5	1.5
5.0	0.2	5.2	4.8
10.0	0.1	10.1	9.9

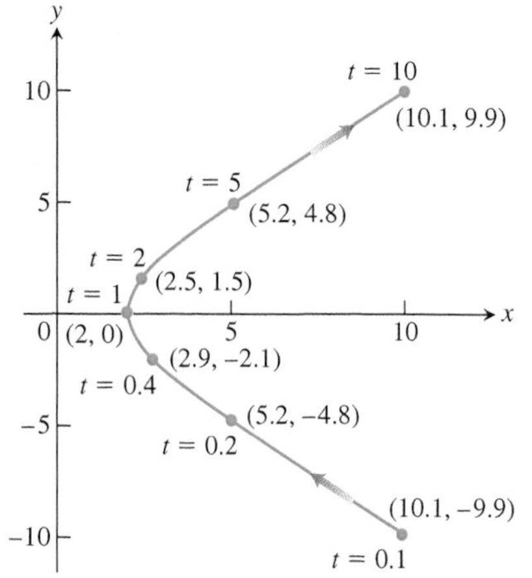

FIGURE 10.6 The curve for $x = t + (1/t)$, $y = t - (1/t)$, $t > 0$ in Example 7. (The part shown is for $0.1 \le t \le 10$.)

EXAMPLE 7 Sketch and identify the path traced by the point $P(x, y)$ if

$$x = t + \frac{1}{t}, \qquad y = t - \frac{1}{t}, \qquad t > 0.$$

Solution We make a brief table of values in Table 10.2, plot the points, and draw a smooth curve through them, as we did in Example 1. Next we eliminate the parameter t from the equations. The procedure is more complicated than in Example 2. Taking the difference between x and y as given by the parametric equations, we find that

$$x - y = \left(t + \frac{1}{t}\right) - \left(t - \frac{1}{t}\right) = \frac{2}{t}.$$

If we add the two parametric equations, we get

$$x + y = \left(t + \frac{1}{t}\right) + \left(t - \frac{1}{t}\right) = 2t.$$

We can then eliminate the parameter t by multiplying these last equations together:

$$(x - y)(x + y) = \left(\frac{2}{t}\right)(2t) = 4,$$

or, multiplying together the terms on the left-hand side, we obtain a standard equation for a hyperbola (reviewed in Appendix 4):

$$x^2 - y^2 = 4. \tag{1}$$

Thus the coordinates of all the points $P(x, y)$ described by the parametric equations satisfy Equation (1). However, Equation (1) does not require that the x-coordinate be positive. So there are points (x, y) on the hyperbola that do not satisfy the parametric equation $x = t + (1/t)$, $t > 0$, for which x is always positive. That is, the parametric equations do not yield any points on the left branch of the hyperbola given by Equation (1), points where the x-coordinate would be negative. For small positive values of t, the path lies in the fourth quadrant and rises into the first quadrant as t increases, crossing the x-axis when $t = 1$ (see Figure 10.6). The parameter domain is $(0, \infty)$, and there is no starting point and no terminal point for the path. ■

Examples 4, 5, and 6 illustrate that a given curve, or portion of it, can be represented by different parametrizations. In the case of Example 7, we can also represent the right-hand branch of the hyperbola by the parametrization

$$x = \sqrt{4 + t^2}, \qquad y = t, \qquad -\infty < t < \infty,$$

which is obtained by solving Equation (1) for $x \ge 0$ and letting y be the parameter. Still another parametrization for the right-hand branch of the hyperbola given by Equation (1) is

$$x = 2 \sec t, \qquad y = 2 \tan t, \qquad -\frac{\pi}{2} < t < \frac{\pi}{2}.$$

This parametrization follows from the trigonometric identity $\sec^2 t - \tan^2 t = 1$, so

$$x^2 - y^2 = 4 \sec^2 t - 4 \tan^2 t = 4(\sec^2 t - \tan^2 t) = 4.$$

As t runs between $-\pi/2$ and $\pi/2$, $x = \sec t$ remains positive and $y = \tan t$ runs between $-\infty$ and ∞, so P traverses the hyperbola's right-hand branch. It comes in along the branch's lower half as $t \to 0^-$, reaches $(2, 0)$ at $t = 0$, and moves out into the first quadrant as t increases steadily toward $\pi/2$. This is the same hyperbola branch for which a portion is shown in Figure 10.6.

HISTORICAL BIOGRAPHY

Christian Huygens
(1629–1695)

Cycloids

The problem with a pendulum clock whose bob swings in a circular arc is that the frequency of the swing depends on the amplitude of the swing. The wider the swing, the longer it takes the bob to return to center (its lowest position).

This does not happen if the bob can be made to swing in a *cycloid*. In 1673, Christian Huygens designed a pendulum clock whose bob would swing in a cycloid, a curve we define in Example 8. He hung the bob from a fine wire constrained by guards that caused it to draw up as it swung away from center (Figure 10.7).

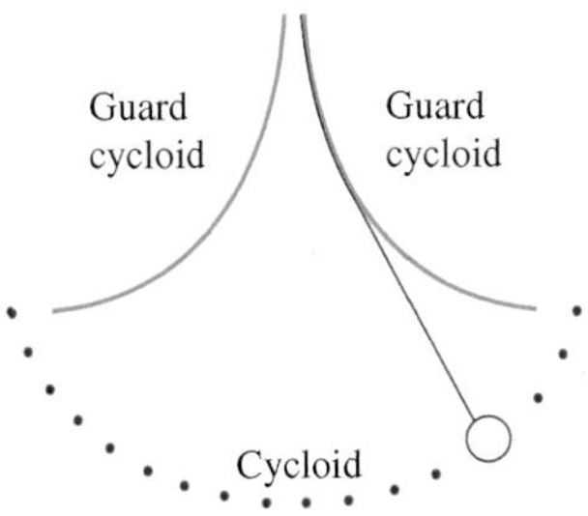

FIGURE 10.7 In Huygens' pendulum clock, the bob swings in a cycloid, so the frequency is independent of the amplitude.

EXAMPLE 8 A wheel of radius a rolls along a horizontal straight line. Find parametric equations for the path traced by a point P on the wheel's circumference. The path is called a **cycloid**.

Solution We take the line to be the x-axis, mark a point P on the wheel, start the wheel with P at the origin, and roll the wheel to the right. As parameter, we use the angle t through which the wheel turns, measured in radians. Figure 10.8 shows the wheel a short while later when its base lies at units from the origin. The wheel's center C lies at (at, a) and the coordinates of P are

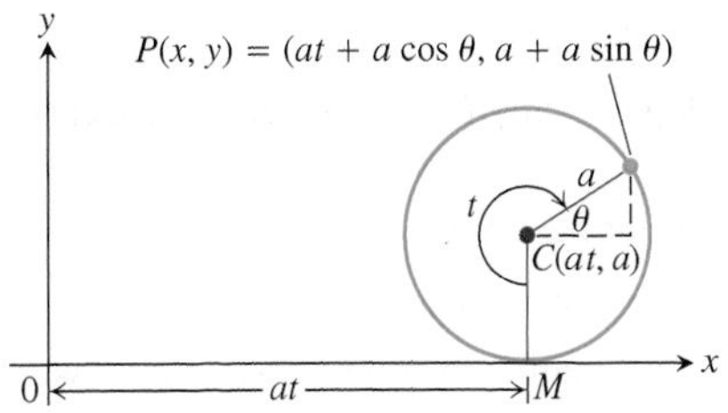

FIGURE 10.8 The position of $P(x, y)$ on the rolling wheel at angle t (Example 8).

$$x = at + a\cos\theta, \qquad y = a + a\sin\theta.$$

To express θ in terms of t, we observe that $t + \theta = 3\pi/2$ in the figure, so that

$$\theta = \frac{3\pi}{2} - t.$$

This makes

$$\cos\theta = \cos\left(\frac{3\pi}{2} - t\right) = -\sin t, \qquad \sin\theta = \sin\left(\frac{3\pi}{2} - t\right) = -\cos t.$$

The equations we seek are

$$x = at - a\sin t, \qquad y = a - a\cos t.$$

These are usually written with the a factored out:

$$x = a(t - \sin t), \qquad y = a(1 - \cos t). \tag{2}$$

Figure 10.9 shows the first arch of the cycloid and part of the next. ■

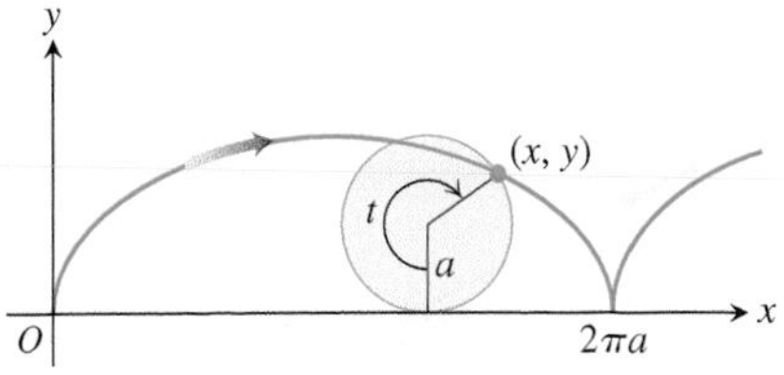

FIGURE 10.9 The cycloid curve for $t \geq 0$ given by Eqs. (2) derived in Example 8.

Brachistochrones and Tautochrones

If we turn Figure 10.9 upside down, Equations (2) still apply and the resulting curve (Figure 10.10) has two interesting physical properties. The first relates to the origin O and the point B at the bottom of the first arch. Among all smooth curves joining these points, the cycloid is the curve along which a frictionless bead, subject only to the force of gravity, will slide from O to B the fastest. This makes the cycloid a **brachistochrone** ("brah-*kiss*-toe-krone"), or shortest-time curve for these points. The second property is that even if you start the bead partway down the curve toward B, it will still take the bead the same amount of time to reach B. This makes the cycloid a **tautochrone** ("*taw*-toe-krone"), or same-time curve for O and B. It can be shown that the cycloid from O to B is the one and only brachistochrone for O and B. We omit the argument here.

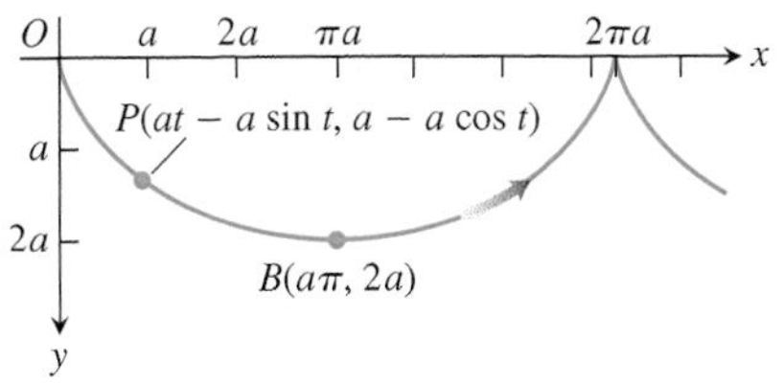

FIGURE 10.10 To study motion along an upside-down cycloid under the influence of gravity, we turn Figure 10.9 upside down. This points the y-axis in the direction of the gravitational force and makes the downward y-coordinates positive. The equations and parameter interval for the cycloid are still

$$x = a(t - \sin t),$$
$$y = a(1 - \cos t), \quad t \geq 0.$$

The arrow shows the direction of increasing t.

Exercises 10.1

Finding Cartesian from Parametric Equations

Exercises 1–18 give parametric equations and parameter intervals for the motion of a particle in the xy-plane. Identify the particle's path by finding a Cartesian equation for it. Graph the Cartesian equation. (The graphs will vary with the equation used.) Indicate the portion of the graph traced by the particle and the direction of motion.

1. $x = 3t, \quad y = 9t^2, \quad -\infty < t < \infty$

2. $x = -\sqrt{t}, \quad y = t, \quad t \geq 0$

3. $x = 2t - 5, \quad y = 4t - 7, \quad -\infty < t < \infty$

4. $x = 3 - 3t, \quad y = 2t, \quad 0 \leq t \leq 1$

5. $x = \cos 2t, \quad y = \sin 2t, \quad 0 \leq t \leq \pi$

6. $x = \cos(\pi - t), \quad y = \sin(\pi - t), \quad 0 \leq t \leq \pi$

7. $x = 4\cos t, \quad y = 2\sin t, \quad 0 \leq t \leq 2\pi$

8. $x = 4\sin t, \quad y = 5\cos t, \quad 0 \leq t \leq 2\pi$

9. $x = \sin t, \quad y = \cos 2t, \quad -\frac{\pi}{2} \leq t \leq \frac{\pi}{2}$

10. $x = 1 + \sin t, \quad y = \cos t - 2, \quad 0 \leq t \leq \pi$

11. $x = t^2, \quad y = t^6 - 2t^4, \quad -\infty < t < \infty$

12. $x = \frac{t}{t - 1}, \quad y = \frac{t - 2}{t + 1}, \quad -1 < t < 1$

13. $x = t, \quad y = \sqrt{1 - t^2}, \quad -1 \leq t \leq 0$

14. $x = \sqrt{t + 1}, \quad y = \sqrt{t}, \quad t \geq 0$

15. $x = \sec^2 t - 1, \quad y = \tan t, \quad -\pi/2 < t < \pi/2$

16. $x = -\sec t, \quad y = \tan t, \quad -\pi/2 < t < \pi/2$

17. $x = -\cosh t, \quad y = \sinh t, \quad -\infty < t < \infty$

18. $x = 2\sinh t, \quad y = 2\cosh t, \quad -\infty < t < \infty$

Finding Parametric Equations

19. Find parametric equations and a parameter interval for the motion of a particle that starts at $(a, 0)$ and traces the circle $x^2 + y^2 = a^2$

a. once clockwise.
b. once counterclockwise.
c. twice clockwise.
d. twice counterclockwise.

(There are many ways to do these, so your answers may not be the same as the ones in the back of the book.)

20. Find parametric equations and a parameter interval for the motion of a particle that starts at $(a, 0)$ and traces the ellipse $(x^2/a^2) + (y^2/b^2) = 1$

a. once clockwise.
b. once counterclockwise.
c. twice clockwise.
d. twice counterclockwise.

(As in Exercise 19, there are many correct answers.)

In Exercises 21–26, find a parametrization for the curve.

21. the line segment with endpoints $(-1, -3)$ and $(4, 1)$

22. the line segment with endpoints $(-1, 3)$ and $(3, -2)$

23. the lower half of the parabola $x - 1 = y^2$

24. the left half of the parabola $y = x^2 + 2x$

25. the ray (half line) with initial point $(2, 3)$ that passes through the point $(-1, -1)$

26. the ray (half line) with initial point $(-1, 2)$ that passes through the point $(0, 0)$

27. Find parametric equations and a parameter interval for the motion of a particle starting at the point $(2, 0)$ and tracing the top half of the circle $x^2 + y^2 = 4$ four times.

28. Find parametric equations and a parameter interval for the motion of a particle that moves along the graph of $y = x^2$ in the following way: beginning at $(0, 0)$ it moves to $(3, 9)$, and then travels back and forth from $(3, 9)$ to $(-3, 9)$ infinitely many times.

29. Find parametric equations for the semicircle

$$x^2 + y^2 = a^2, \quad y > 0,$$

using as parameter the slope $t = dy/dx$ of the tangent to the curve at (x, y).

30. Find parametric equations for the circle

$$x^2 + y^2 = a^2,$$

using as parameter the arc length s measured counterclockwise from the point $(a, 0)$ to the point (x, y).

31. Find a parametrization for the line segment joining points $(0, 2)$ and $(4, 0)$ using the angle θ in the accompanying figure as the parameter.

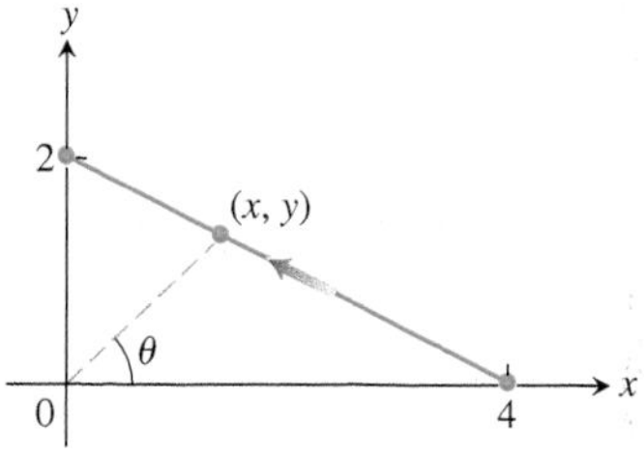

32. Find a parametrization for the curve $y = \sqrt{x}$ with terminal point $(0, 0)$ using the angle θ in the accompanying figure as the parameter.

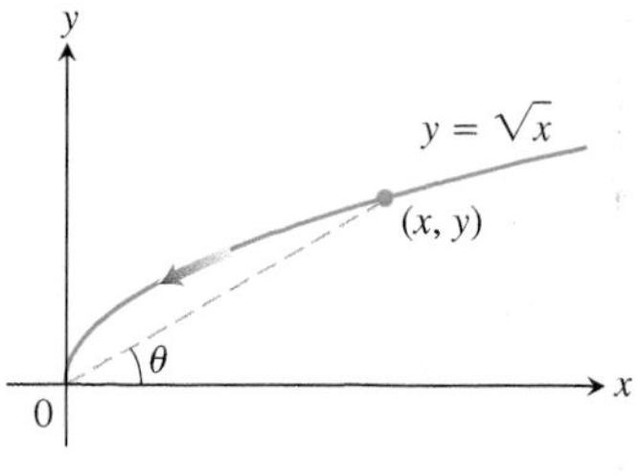

33. Find a parametrization for the circle $(x - 2)^2 + y^2 = 1$ starting at $(1, 0)$ and moving clockwise once around the circle, using the central angle θ in the accompanying figure as the parameter.

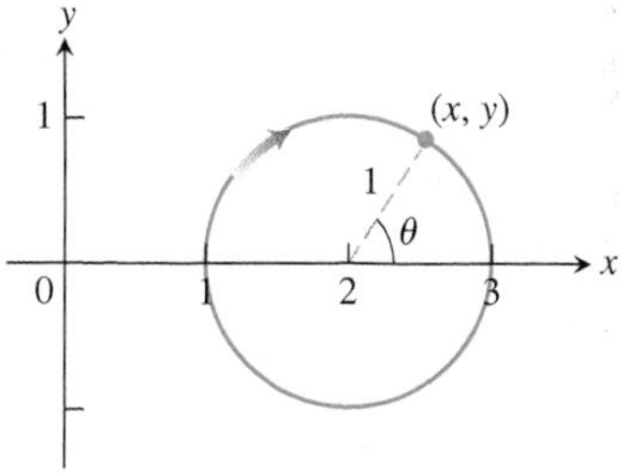

34. Find a parametrization for the circle $x^2 + y^2 = 1$ starting at $(1, 0)$ and moving counterclockwise to the terminal point $(0, 1)$, using the angle θ in the accompanying figure as the parameter.

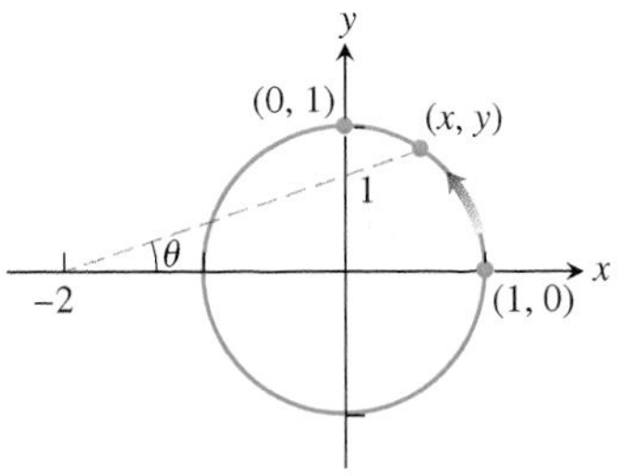

35. **The witch of Maria Agnesi** The bell-shaped witch of Maria Agnesi can be constructed in the following way. Start with a circle of radius 1, centered at the point $(0, 1)$, as shown in the accompanying figure. Choose a point A on the line $y = 2$ and connect it to the origin with a line segment. Call the point where the segment crosses the circle B. Let P be the point where the vertical line through A crosses the horizontal line through B. The witch is the curve traced by P as A moves along the line $y = 2$. Find parametric equations and a parameter interval for the witch by expressing the coordinates of P in terms of t, the radian measure of the angle that segment OA makes with the positive x-axis. The following equalities (which you may assume) will help.

a. $x = AQ$ **b.** $y = 2 - AB \sin t$

c. $AB \cdot OA = (AQ)^2$

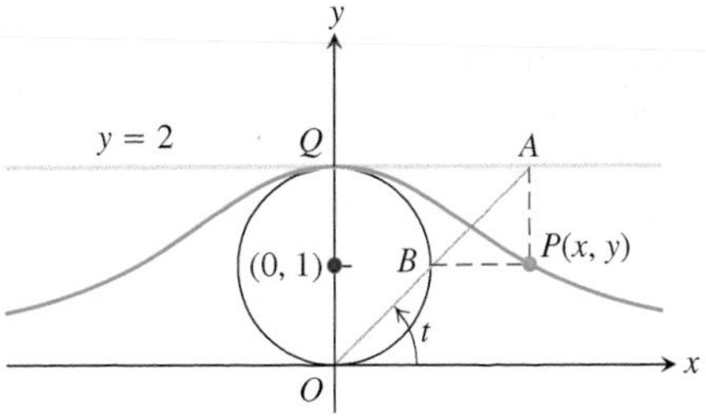

36. **Hypocycloid** When a circle rolls on the inside of a fixed circle, any point P on the circumference of the rolling circle describes a *hypocycloid*. Let the fixed circle be $x^2 + y^2 = a^2$, let the radius of the rolling circle be b, and let the initial position of the tracing point P be $A\ (a, 0)$. Find parametric equations for the hypocycloid, using as the parameter the angle θ from the positive x-axis to the line joining the circles' centers. In particular, if $b = a/4$, as in the accompanying figure, show that the hypocycloid is the astroid

$$x = a \cos^3 \theta, \quad y = a \sin^3 \theta.$$

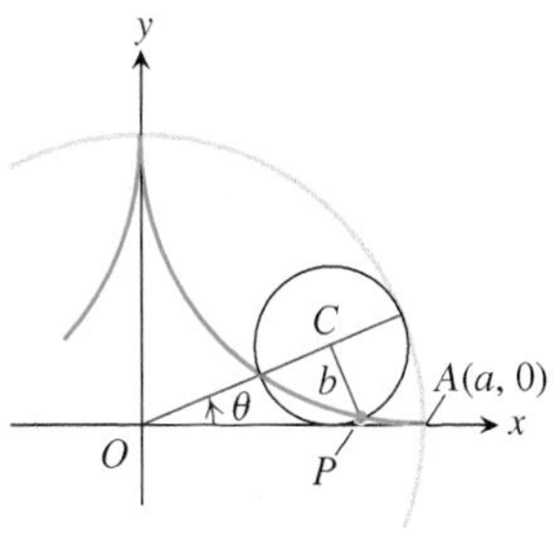

37. As the point N moves along the line $y = a$ in the accompanying figure, P moves in such a way that $OP = MN$. Find parametric equations for the coordinates of P as functions of the angle t that the line ON makes with the positive y-axis.

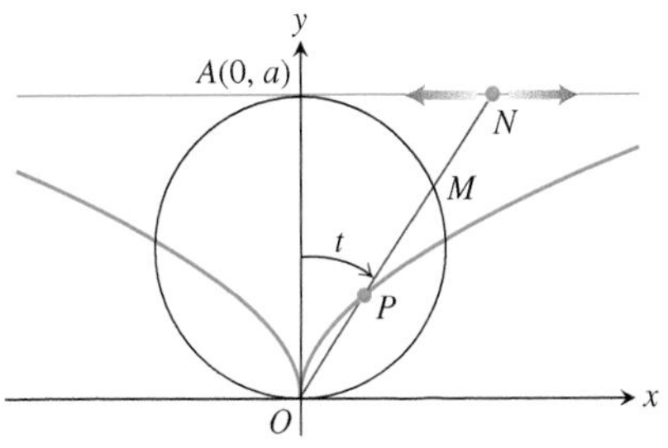

38. **Trochoids** A wheel of radius a rolls along a horizontal straight line without slipping. Find parametric equations for the curve traced out by a point P on a spoke of the wheel b units from its center. As parameter, use the angle θ through which the wheel turns. The curve is called a *trochoid*, which is a cycloid when $b = a$.

Distance Using Parametric Equations

39. Find the point on the parabola $x = t, y = t^2, -\infty < t < \infty$, closest to the point $(2, 1/2)$. (*Hint:* Minimize the square of the distance as a function of t.)

40. Find the point on the ellipse $x = 2 \cos t, y = \sin t, 0 \le t \le 2\pi$ closest to the point $(3/4, 0)$. (*Hint:* Minimize the square of the distance as a function of t.)

T GRAPHER EXPLORATIONS

If you have a parametric equation grapher, graph the equations over the given intervals in Exercises 41–48.

41. **Ellipse** $x = 4 \cos t, \quad y = 2 \sin t,$ over

a. $0 \le t \le 2\pi$ **b.** $0 \le t \le \pi$

c. $-\pi/2 \le t \le \pi/2$.

42. **Hyperbola branch** $x = \sec t$ (enter as $1/\cos(t)$), $y = \tan t$ (enter as $\sin(t)/\cos(t)$), over

a. $-1.5 \le t \le 1.5$ **b.** $-0.5 \le t \le 0.5$

c. $-0.1 \le t \le 0.1$.

43. **Parabola** $x = 2t + 3, \quad y = t^2 - 1, \quad -2 \le t \le 2$

44. **Cycloid** $x = t - \sin t, \quad y = 1 - \cos t,$ over

a. $0 \le t \le 2\pi$ **b.** $0 \le t \le 4\pi$

c. $\pi \le t \le 3\pi$.

45. **Deltoid**

$$x = 2 \cos t + \cos 2t, \quad y = 2 \sin t - \sin 2t; \quad 0 \le t \le 2\pi$$

What happens if you replace 2 with −2 in the equations for x and y? Graph the new equations and find out.

46. **A nice curve**

$$x = 3 \cos t + \cos 3t, \quad y = 3 \sin t - \sin 3t; \quad 0 \le t \le 2\pi$$

What happens if you replace 3 with −3 in the equations for x and y? Graph the new equations and find out.

47. a. Epicycloid

$x = 9\cos t - \cos 9t, \quad y = 9\sin t - \sin 9t; \quad 0 \le t \le 2\pi$

b. Hypocycloid

$x = 8\cos t + 2\cos 4t, \quad y = 8\sin t - 2\sin 4t; \quad 0 \le t \le 2\pi$

c. Hypotrochoid

$x = \cos t + 5\cos 3t, \quad y = 6\cos t - 5\sin 3t; \quad 0 \le t \le 2\pi$

48. a. $x = 6\cos t + 5\cos 3t, \quad y = 6\sin t - 5\sin 3t;$
$0 \le t \le 2\pi$

b. $x = 6\cos 2t + 5\cos 6t, \quad y = 6\sin 2t - 5\sin 6t;$
$0 \le t \le \pi$

c. $x = 6\cos t + 5\cos 3t, \quad y = 6\sin 2t - 5\sin 3t;$
$0 \le t \le 2\pi$

d. $x = 6\cos 2t + 5\cos 6t, \quad y = 6\sin 4t - 5\sin 6t;$
$0 \le t \le \pi$

10.2 Calculus with Parametric Curves

In this section we apply calculus to parametric curves. Specifically, we find slopes, lengths, and areas associated with parametrized curves.

Tangents and Areas

A parametrized curve $x = f(t)$ and $y = g(t)$ is **differentiable** at t if f and g are differentiable at t. At a point on a differentiable parametrized curve where y is also a differentiable function of x, the derivatives dy/dt, dx/dt, and dy/dx are related by the Chain Rule:

$$\frac{dy}{dt} = \frac{dy}{dx} \cdot \frac{dx}{dt}.$$

If $dx/dt \neq 0$, we may divide both sides of this equation by dx/dt to solve for dy/dx.

Parametric Formula for dy/dx

If all three derivatives exist and $dx/dt \neq 0$,

$$\frac{dy}{dx} = \frac{dy/dt}{dx/dt}. \tag{1}$$

If parametric equations define y as a twice-differentiable function of x, we can apply Equation (1) to the function $dy/dx = y'$ to calculate d^2y/dx^2 as a function of t:

$$\frac{d^2y}{dx^2} = \frac{d}{dx}(y') = \frac{dy'/dt}{dx/dt}. \qquad \text{Eq. (1) with } y' \text{ in place of } y$$

Parametric Formula for d^2y/dx^2

If the equations $x = f(t)$, $y = g(t)$ define y as a twice-differentiable function of x, then at any point where $dx/dt \neq 0$ and $y' = dy/dx$,

$$\frac{d^2y}{dx^2} = \frac{dy'/dt}{dx/dt}. \tag{2}$$

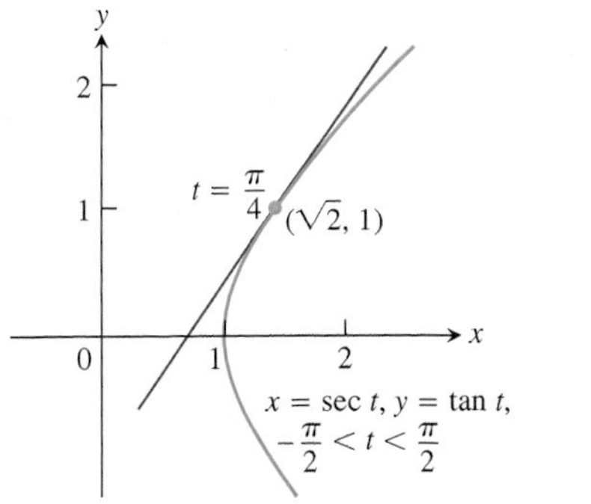

FIGURE 10.11 The curve in Example 1 is the right-hand branch of the hyperbola $x^2 - y^2 = 1$.

EXAMPLE 1 Find the tangent to the curve

$$x = \sec t, \qquad y = \tan t, \qquad -\frac{\pi}{2} < t < \frac{\pi}{2},$$

at the point $(\sqrt{2}, 1)$, where $t = \pi/4$ (Figure 10.11).

Solution The slope of the curve at t is

$$\frac{dy}{dx} = \frac{dy/dt}{dx/dt} = \frac{\sec^2 t}{\sec t \tan t} = \frac{\sec t}{\tan t}. \qquad \text{Eq. (1)}$$

Setting t equal to $\pi/4$ gives

$$\left.\frac{dy}{dx}\right|_{t=\pi/4} = \frac{\sec(\pi/4)}{\tan(\pi/4)}$$

$$= \frac{\sqrt{2}}{1} = \sqrt{2}.$$

The tangent line is

$$y - 1 = \sqrt{2}(x - \sqrt{2})$$

$$y = \sqrt{2}x - 2 + 1$$

$$y = \sqrt{2}x - 1.$$

■

EXAMPLE 2 Find d^2y/dx^2 as a function of t if $x = t - t^2$, $y = t - t^3$.

Finding d^2y/dx^2 in Terms of t
1. Express $y' = dy/dx$ in terms of t.
2. Find dy'/dt.
3. Divide dy'/dt by dx/dt.

Solution

1. Express $y' = dy/dx$ in terms of t.

$$y' = \frac{dy}{dx} = \frac{dy/dt}{dx/dt} = \frac{1 - 3t^2}{1 - 2t}$$

2. Differentiate y' with respect to t.

$$\frac{dy'}{dt} = \frac{d}{dt}\left(\frac{1 - 3t^2}{1 - 2t}\right) = \frac{2 - 6t + 6t^2}{(1 - 2t)^2} \qquad \text{Derivative Quotient Rule}$$

3. Divide dy'/dt by dx/dt.

$$\frac{d^2y}{dx^2} = \frac{dy'/dt}{dx/dt} = \frac{(2 - 6t + 6t^2)/(1 - 2t)^2}{1 - 2t} = \frac{2 - 6t + 6t^2}{(1 - 2t)^3} \qquad \text{Eq. (2)}$$

■

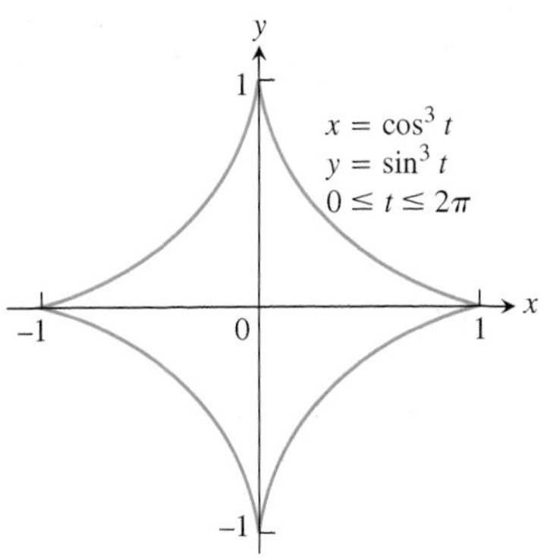

FIGURE 10.12 The astroid in Example 3.

EXAMPLE 3 Find the area enclosed by the astroid (Figure 10.12)

$$x = \cos^3 t, \qquad y = \sin^3 t, \qquad 0 \le t \le 2\pi.$$

Solution By symmetry, the enclosed area is 4 times the area beneath the curve in the first quadrant where $0 \le t \le \pi/2$. We can apply the definite integral formula for area studied in Chapter 5, using substitution to express the curve and differential dx in terms of the parameter t. So,

$$
\begin{aligned}
A &= 4\int_0^1 y\,dx \\
&= 4\int_0^{\pi/2} \sin^3 t \cdot 3\cos^2 t \sin t\,dt && \text{Substitution for } y \text{ and } dx \\
&= 12\int_0^{\pi/2} \left(\frac{1-\cos 2t}{2}\right)^2 \left(\frac{1+\cos 2t}{2}\right) dt && \sin^4 t = \left(\frac{1-\cos 2t}{2}\right)^2 \\
&= \frac{3}{2}\int_0^{\pi/2} (1 - 2\cos 2t + \cos^2 2t)(1+\cos 2t)\,dt && \text{Expand square term.} \\
&= \frac{3}{2}\int_0^{\pi/2} (1 - \cos 2t - \cos^2 2t + \cos^3 2t)\,dt && \text{Multiply terms.} \\
&= \frac{3}{2}\left[\int_0^{\pi/2} (1-\cos 2t)\,dt - \int_0^{\pi/2} \cos^2 2t\,dt + \int_0^{\pi/2} \cos^3 2t\,dt\right] \\
&= \frac{3}{2}\left[\left(t - \frac{1}{2}\sin 2t\right) - \frac{1}{2}\left(t + \frac{1}{4}\sin 2t\right) + \frac{1}{2}\left(\sin 2t - \frac{1}{3}\sin^3 2t\right)\right]_0^{\pi/2} && \text{Section 8.2, Example 3} \\
&= \frac{3}{2}\left[\left(\frac{\pi}{2} - 0 - 0 - 0\right) - \frac{1}{2}\left(\frac{\pi}{2} + 0 - 0 - 0\right) + \frac{1}{2}(0 - 0 - 0 + 0)\right] && \text{Evaluate.} \\
&= \frac{3\pi}{8}.
\end{aligned}
$$

■

Length of a Parametrically Defined Curve

Let C be a curve given parametrically by the equations

$$x = f(t) \quad \text{and} \quad y = g(t), \quad a \le t \le b.$$

We assume the functions f and g are **continuously differentiable** (meaning they have continuous first derivatives) on the interval $[a, b]$. We also assume that the derivatives $f'(t)$ and $g'(t)$ are not simultaneously zero, which prevents the curve C from having any corners or cusps. Such a curve is called a **smooth curve**. We subdivide the path (or arc) AB into n pieces at points $A = P_0, P_1, P_2, \dots, P_n = B$ (Figure 10.13). These points correspond to a partition of the interval $[a, b]$ by $a = t_0 < t_1 < t_2 < \cdots < t_n = b$, where $P_k = (f(t_k), g(t_k))$. Join successive points of this subdivision by straight line segments (Figure 10.13). A representative line segment has length

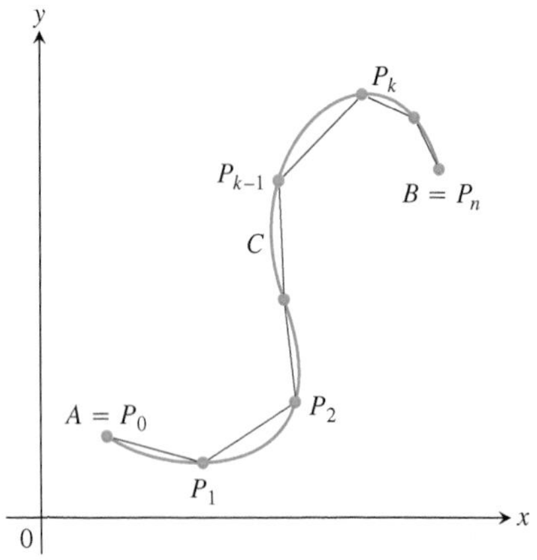

FIGURE 10.13 The smooth curve C defined parametrically by the equations $x = f(t)$ and $y = g(t)$, $a \le t \le b$. The length of the curve from A to B is approximated by the sum of the lengths of the polygonal path (straight line segments) starting at $A = P_0$, then to P_1, and so on, ending at $B = P_n$.

$$
\begin{aligned}
L_k &= \sqrt{(\Delta x_k)^2 + (\Delta y_k)^2} \\
&= \sqrt{[f(t_k) - f(t_{k-1})]^2 + [g(t_k) - g(t_{k-1})]^2}
\end{aligned}
$$

(see Figure 10.14). If Δt_k is small, the length L_k is approximately the length of arc $P_{k-1}P_k$. By the Mean Value Theorem there are numbers t_k^* and t_k^{**} in $[t_{k-1}, t_k]$ such that

$$
\begin{aligned}
\Delta x_k &= f(t_k) - f(t_{k-1}) = f'(t_k^*)\,\Delta t_k, \\
\Delta y_k &= g(t_k) - g(t_{k-1}) = g'(t_k^{**})\,\Delta t_k.
\end{aligned}
$$

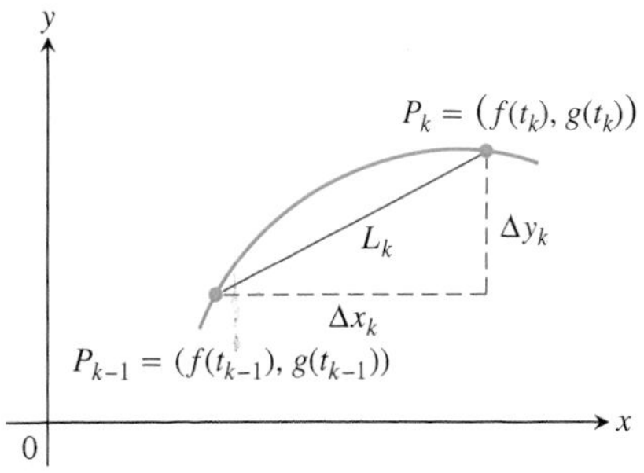

FIGURE 10.14 The arc $P_{k-1}P_k$ is approximated by the straight line segment shown here, which has length $L_k = \sqrt{(\Delta x_k)^2 + (\Delta y_k)^2}$.

Assuming the path from A to B is traversed exactly once as t increases from $t = a$ to $t = b$, with no doubling back or retracing, an approximation to the (yet to be defined) "length" of the curve AB is the sum of all the lengths L_k:

$$\sum_{k=1}^{n} L_k = \sum_{k=1}^{n} \sqrt{(\Delta x_k)^2 + (\Delta y_k)^2}$$

$$= \sum_{k=1}^{n} \sqrt{[f'(t_k^*)]^2 + [g'(t_k^{**})]^2}\, \Delta t_k.$$

Although this last sum on the right is not exactly a Riemann sum (because f' and g' are evaluated at different points), it can be shown that its limit, as the norm of the partition tends to zero and the number of segments $n \to \infty$, is the definite integral

$$\lim_{\|P\| \to 0} \sum_{k=1}^{n} \sqrt{[f'(t_k^*)]^2 + [g'(t_k^{**})]^2}\, \Delta t_k = \int_a^b \sqrt{[f'(t)]^2 + [g'(t)]^2}\, dt.$$

Therefore, it is reasonable to define the length of the curve from A to B as this integral.

DEFINITION If a curve C is defined parametrically by $x = f(t)$ and $y = g(t)$, $a \le t \le b$, where f' and g' are continuous and not simultaneously zero on $[a, b]$, and C is traversed exactly once as t increases from $t = a$ to $t = b$, then **the length of C** is the definite integral

$$L = \int_a^b \sqrt{[f'(t)]^2 + [g'(t)]^2}\, dt.$$

A smooth curve C does not double back or reverse the direction of motion over the time interval $[a, b]$ since $(f')^2 + (g')^2 > 0$ throughout the interval. At a point where a curve does start to double back on itself, either the curve fails to be differentiable or both derivatives must simultaneously equal zero. We will examine this phenomenon in Chapter 12, where we study tangent vectors to curves.

If $x = f(t)$ and $y = g(t)$, then using the Leibniz notation we have the following result for arc length:

$$L = \int_a^b \sqrt{\left(\frac{dx}{dt}\right)^2 + \left(\frac{dy}{dt}\right)^2}\, dt. \qquad (3)$$

What if there are two different parametrizations for a curve C whose length we want to find; does it matter which one we use? The answer is no, as long as the parametrization we choose meets the conditions stated in the definition of the length of C (see Exercise 41 for an example).

EXAMPLE 4 Using the definition, find the length of the circle of radius r defined parametrically by

$$x = r\cos t \quad \text{and} \quad y = r\sin t, \qquad 0 \le t \le 2\pi.$$

Solution As t varies from 0 to 2π, the circle is traversed exactly once, so the circumference is

$$L = \int_0^{2\pi} \sqrt{\left(\frac{dx}{dt}\right)^2 + \left(\frac{dy}{dt}\right)^2}\, dt.$$

We find

$$\frac{dx}{dt} = -r\sin t, \qquad \frac{dy}{dt} = r\cos t$$

and

$$\left(\frac{dx}{dt}\right)^2 + \left(\frac{dy}{dt}\right)^2 = r^2(\sin^2 t + \cos^2 t) = r^2.$$

So

$$L = \int_0^{2\pi} \sqrt{r^2}\, dt = r\left[t\right]_0^{2\pi} = 2\pi r. \qquad \blacksquare$$

EXAMPLE 5 Find the length of the astroid (Figure 10.12)

$$x = \cos^3 t, \qquad y = \sin^3 t, \qquad 0 \le t \le 2\pi.$$

Solution Because of the curve's symmetry with respect to the coordinate axes, its length is four times the length of the first-quadrant portion. We have

$$x = \cos^3 t, \qquad y = \sin^3 t$$

$$\left(\frac{dx}{dt}\right)^2 = [3\cos^2 t(-\sin t)]^2 = 9\cos^4 t\sin^2 t$$

$$\left(\frac{dy}{dt}\right)^2 = [3\sin^2 t(\cos t)]^2 = 9\sin^4 t\cos^2 t$$

$$\begin{aligned}\sqrt{\left(\frac{dx}{dt}\right)^2 + \left(\frac{dy}{dt}\right)^2} &= \sqrt{9\cos^2 t\sin^2 t\underbrace{(\cos^2 t + \sin^2 t)}_{1}} \\ &= \sqrt{9\cos^2 t\sin^2 t} \\ &= 3|\cos t\sin t| \\ &= 3\cos t\sin t.\end{aligned}$$

$\cos t \sin t \ge 0$ for $0 \le t \le \pi/2$

Therefore,

$$\begin{aligned}\text{Length of first-quadrant portion} &= \int_0^{\pi/2} 3\cos t\sin t\, dt \\ &= \frac{3}{2}\int_0^{\pi/2} \sin 2t\, dt \\ &= -\frac{3}{4}\cos 2t\Big]_0^{\pi/2} = \frac{3}{2}.\end{aligned}$$

$\cos t \sin t = (1/2)\sin 2t$

The length of the astroid is four times this: $4(3/2) = 6$. ■

HISTORICAL BIOGRAPHY

Gregory St. Vincent
(1584–1667)

Length of a Curve $y = f(x)$

The length formula in Section 6.3 is a special case of Equation (3). Given a continuously differentiable function $y = f(x)$, $a \le x \le b$, we can assign $x = t$ as a parameter. The graph of the function f is then the curve C defined parametrically by

$$x = t \quad \text{and} \quad y = f(t), \qquad a \le t \le b,$$

a special case of what we considered before. Then,

$$\frac{dx}{dt} = 1 \quad \text{and} \quad \frac{dy}{dt} = f'(t).$$

From Equation (1), we have

$$\frac{dy}{dx} = \frac{dy/dt}{dx/dt} = f'(t),$$

giving

$$\begin{aligned}\left(\frac{dx}{dt}\right)^2 + \left(\frac{dy}{dt}\right)^2 &= 1 + [f'(t)]^2 \\ &= 1 + [f'(x)]^2. \qquad t = x\end{aligned}$$

Substitution into Equation (3) gives the arc length formula for the graph of $y = f(x)$, consistent with Equation (3) in Section 6.3.

The Arc Length Differential

Consistent with our discussion in Section 6.3, we can define the arc length function for a parametrically defined curve $x = f(t)$ and $y = g(t)$, $a \le t \le b$, by

$$s(t) = \int_a^t \sqrt{[f'(z)]^2 + [g'(z)]^2}\, dz.$$

Then, by the Fundamental Theorem of Calculus,

$$\frac{ds}{dt} = \sqrt{[f'(t)]^2 + [g'(t)]^2} = \sqrt{\left(\frac{dx}{dt}\right)^2 + \left(\frac{dy}{dt}\right)^2}.$$

The differential of arc length is

$$ds = \sqrt{\left(\frac{dx}{dt}\right)^2 + \left(\frac{dy}{dt}\right)^2}\, dt. \qquad (4)$$

Equation (4) is often abbreviated to

$$ds = \sqrt{dx^2 + dy^2}.$$

Just as in Section 6.3, we can integrate the differential ds between appropriate limits to find the total length of a curve.

Here's an example where we use the arc length formula to find the centroid of an arc.

EXAMPLE 6 Find the centroid of the first-quadrant arc of the astroid in Example 5.

Solution We take the curve's density to be $\delta = 1$ and calculate the curve's mass and moments about the coordinate axes as we did in Section 6.6.

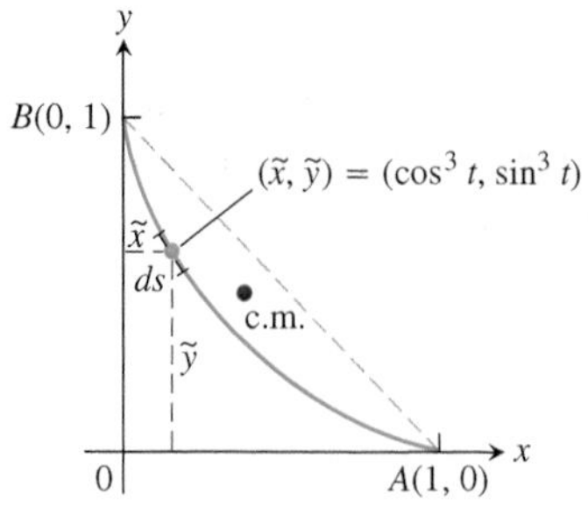

FIGURE 10.15 The centroid (c.m.) of the astroid arc in Example 6.

The distribution of mass is symmetric about the line $y = x$, so $\bar{x} = \bar{y}$. A typical segment of the curve (Figure 10.15) has mass

$$dm = 1 \cdot ds = \sqrt{\left(\frac{dx}{dt}\right)^2 + \left(\frac{dy}{dt}\right)^2}\, dt = 3 \cos t \sin t \, dt. \qquad \text{From Example 5}$$

The curve's mass is

$$M = \int_0^{\pi/2} dm = \int_0^{\pi/2} 3 \cos t \sin t \, dt = \frac{3}{2}. \qquad \text{Again from Example 5}$$

The curve's moment about the x-axis is

$$M_x = \int \tilde{y}\, dm = \int_0^{\pi/2} \sin^3 t \cdot 3 \cos t \sin t \, dt$$

$$= 3 \int_0^{\pi/2} \sin^4 t \cos t \, dt = 3 \cdot \frac{\sin^5 t}{5}\bigg]_0^{\pi/2} = \frac{3}{5}.$$

It follows that

$$\bar{y} = \frac{M_x}{M} = \frac{3/5}{3/2} = \frac{2}{5}.$$

The centroid is the point $(2/5, 2/5)$. ■

Areas of Surfaces of Revolution

In Section 6.4 we found integral formulas for the area of a surface when a curve is revolved about a coordinate axis. Specifically, we found that the surface area is $S = \int 2\pi y \, ds$ for revolution about the x-axis, and $S = \int 2\pi x \, ds$ for revolution about the y-axis. If the curve is parametrized by the equations $x = f(t)$ and $y = g(t)$, $a \le t \le b$, where f and g are continuously differentiable and $(f')^2 + (g')^2 > 0$ on $[a, b]$, then the arc length differential ds is given by Equation (4). This observation leads to the following formulas for area of surfaces of revolution for smooth parametrized curves.

Area of Surface of Revolution for Parametrized Curves

If a smooth curve $x = f(t)$, $y = g(t)$, $a \le t \le b$, is traversed exactly once as t increases from a to b, then the areas of the surfaces generated by revolving the curve about the coordinate axes are as follows.

1. Revolution about the x-axis ($y \ge 0$):

$$S = \int_a^b 2\pi y \sqrt{\left(\frac{dx}{dt}\right)^2 + \left(\frac{dy}{dt}\right)^2}\, dt \qquad (5)$$

2. Revolution about the y-axis ($x \ge 0$):

$$S = \int_a^b 2\pi x \sqrt{\left(\frac{dx}{dt}\right)^2 + \left(\frac{dy}{dt}\right)^2}\, dt \qquad (6)$$

As with length, we can calculate surface area from any convenient parametrization that meets the stated criteria.

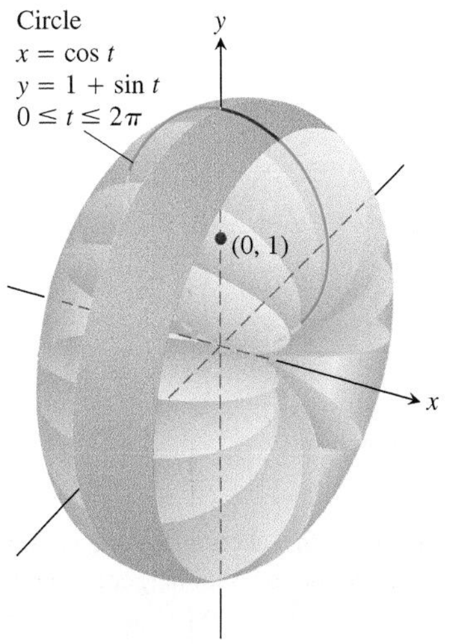

FIGURE 10.16 In Example 7 we calculate the area of the surface of revolution swept out by this parametrized curve.

EXAMPLE 7 The standard parametrization of the circle of radius 1 centered at the point (0, 1) in the xy-plane is

$$x = \cos t, \qquad y = 1 + \sin t, \qquad 0 \le t \le 2\pi.$$

Use this parametrization to find the area of the surface swept out by revolving the circle about the x-axis (Figure 10.16).

Solution We evaluate the formula

$$S = \int_a^b 2\pi y \sqrt{\left(\frac{dx}{dt}\right)^2 + \left(\frac{dy}{dt}\right)^2}\, dt \qquad \text{Eq. (5) for revolution about the } x\text{-axis; } y = 1 + \sin t \ge 0$$

$$= \int_0^{2\pi} 2\pi(1 + \sin t)\underbrace{\sqrt{(-\sin t)^2 + (\cos t)^2}}_{1}\, dt$$

$$= 2\pi \int_0^{2\pi} (1 + \sin t)\, dt$$

$$= 2\pi\Big[t - \cos t\Big]_0^{2\pi} = 4\pi^2.$$ ■

Exercises 10.2

Tangents to Parametrized Curves

In Exercises 1–14, find an equation for the line tangent to the curve at the point defined by the given value of t. Also, find the value of d^2y/dx^2 at this point.

1. $x = 2\cos t, \quad y = 2\sin t, \quad t = \pi/4$
2. $x = \sin 2\pi t, \quad y = \cos 2\pi t, \quad t = -1/6$
3. $x = 4\sin t, \quad y = 2\cos t, \quad t = \pi/4$
4. $x = \cos t, \quad y = \sqrt{3}\cos t, \quad t = 2\pi/3$
5. $x = t, \quad y = \sqrt{t}, \quad t = 1/4$
6. $x = \sec^2 t - 1, \quad y = \tan t, \quad t = -\pi/4$
7. $x = \sec t, \quad y = \tan t, \quad t = \pi/6$
8. $x = -\sqrt{t+1}, \quad y = \sqrt{3t}, \quad t = 3$
9. $x = 2t^2 + 3, \quad y = t^4, \quad t = -1$
10. $x = 1/t, \quad y = -2 + \ln t, \quad t = 1$
11. $x = t - \sin t, \quad y = 1 - \cos t, \quad t = \pi/3$
12. $x = \cos t, \quad y = 1 + \sin t, \quad t = \pi/2$
13. $x = \dfrac{1}{t+1}, \quad y = \dfrac{t}{t-1}, \quad t = 2$
14. $x = t + e^t, \quad y = 1 - e^t, \quad t = 0$

Implicitly Defined Parametrizations

Assuming that the equations in Exercises 15–20 define x and y implicitly as differentiable functions $x = f(t), y = g(t)$, find the slope of the curve $x = f(t), y = g(t)$ at the given value of t.

15. $x^3 + 2t^2 = 9, \quad 2y^3 - 3t^2 = 4, \quad t = 2$
16. $x = \sqrt{5 - \sqrt{t}}, \quad y(t-1) = \sqrt{t}, \quad t = 4$
17. $x + 2x^{3/2} = t^2 + t, \quad y\sqrt{t+1} + 2t\sqrt{y} = 4, \quad t = 0$
18. $x\sin t + 2x = t, \quad t\sin t - 2t = y, \quad t = \pi$
19. $x = t^3 + t, \quad y + 2t^3 = 2x + t^2, \quad t = 1$
20. $t = \ln(x - t), \quad y = te^t, \quad t = 0$

Area

21. Find the area under one arch of the cycloid
$$x = a(t - \sin t), \quad y = a(1 - \cos t).$$
22. Find the area enclosed by the y-axis and the curve
$$x = t - t^2, \quad y = 1 + e^{-t}.$$
23. Find the area enclosed by the ellipse
$$x = a\cos t, \quad y = b\sin t, \quad 0 \le t \le 2\pi.$$
24. Find the area under $y = x^3$ over [0, 1] using the following parametrizations.
   a. $x = t^2, \quad y = t^6$ **b.** $x = t^3, \quad y = t^9$

Lengths of Curves

Find the lengths of the curves in Exercises 25–30.

25. $x = \cos t, \quad y = t + \sin t, \quad 0 \le t \le \pi$
26. $x = t^3, \quad y = 3t^2/2, \quad 0 \le t \le \sqrt{3}$
27. $x = t^2/2, \quad y = (2t+1)^{3/2}/3, \quad 0 \le t \le 4$
28. $x = (2t+3)^{3/2}/3, \quad y = t + t^2/2, \quad 0 \le t \le 3$
29. $x = 8\cos t + 8t\sin t$
   $y = 8\sin t - 8t\cos t,$
   $0 \le t \le \pi/2$
30. $x = \ln(\sec t + \tan t) - \sin t$
   $y = \cos t, \quad 0 \le t \le \pi/3$

Surface Area

Find the areas of the surfaces generated by revolving the curves in Exercises 31–34 about the indicated axes.

31. $x = \cos t, \quad y = 2 + \sin t, \quad 0 \le t \le 2\pi; \quad x$-axis

32. $x = (2/3)t^{3/2}, \quad y = 2\sqrt{t}, \quad 0 \le t \le \sqrt{3}$; y-axis

33. $x = t + \sqrt{2}, \quad y = (t^2/2) + \sqrt{2}t, \quad -\sqrt{2} \le t \le \sqrt{2}$; y-axis

34. $x = \ln(\sec t + \tan t) - \sin t, \ y = \cos t, \ 0 \le t \le \pi/3$; x-axis

35. A cone frustum The line segment joining the points (0, 1) and (2, 2) is revolved about the x-axis to generate a frustum of a cone. Find the surface area of the frustum using the parametrization $x = 2t, y = t + 1, 0 \le t \le 1$. Check your result with the geometry formula: Area $= \pi(r_1 + r_2)$(slant height).

36. A cone The line segment joining the origin to the point (h, r) is revolved about the x-axis to generate a cone of height h and base radius r. Find the cone's surface area with the parametric equations $x = ht, \ y = rt, \ 0 \le t \le 1$. Check your result with the geometry formula: Area $= \pi r$(slant height).

Centroids

37. Find the coordinates of the centroid of the curve

$$x = \cos t + t \sin t, \quad y = \sin t - t \cos t, \quad 0 \le t \le \pi/2.$$

38. Find the coordinates of the centroid of the curve

$$x = e^t \cos t, \quad y = e^t \sin t, \quad 0 \le t \le \pi.$$

39. Find the coordinates of the centroid of the curve

$$x = \cos t, \quad y = t + \sin t, \quad 0 \le t \le \pi.$$

T **40.** Most centroid calculations for curves are done with a calculator or computer that has an integral evaluation program. As a case in point, find, to the nearest hundredth, the coordinates of the centroid of the curve

$$x = t^3, \quad y = 3t^2/2, \quad 0 \le t \le \sqrt{3}.$$

Theory and Examples

41. Length is independent of parametrization To illustrate the fact that the numbers we get for length do not depend on the way we parametrize our curves (except for the mild restrictions preventing doubling back mentioned earlier), calculate the length of the semicircle $y = \sqrt{1 - x^2}$ with these two different parametrizations:

a. $x = \cos 2t, \quad y = \sin 2t, \quad 0 \le t \le \pi/2.$

b. $x = \sin \pi t, \quad y = \cos \pi t, \quad -1/2 \le t \le 1/2.$

42. a. Show that the Cartesian formula

$$L = \int_c^d \sqrt{1 + \left(\frac{dx}{dy}\right)^2}\, dy$$

for the length of the curve $x = g(y), c \le y \le d$ (Section 6.3, Equation 4), is a special case of the parametric length formula

$$L = \int_a^b \sqrt{\left(\frac{dx}{dt}\right)^2 + \left(\frac{dy}{dt}\right)^2}\, dt.$$

Use this result to find the length of each curve.

b. $x = y^{3/2}, \quad 0 \le y \le 4/3$

c. $x = \frac{3}{2}y^{2/3}, \quad 0 \le y \le 1$

43. The curve with parametric equations

$$x = (1 + 2\sin\theta)\cos\theta, \quad y = (1 + 2\sin\theta)\sin\theta$$

is called a *limaçon* and is shown in the accompanying figure. Find the points (x, y) and the slopes of the tangent lines at these points for

a. $\theta = 0$. **b.** $\theta = \pi/2$. **c.** $\theta = 4\pi/3$.

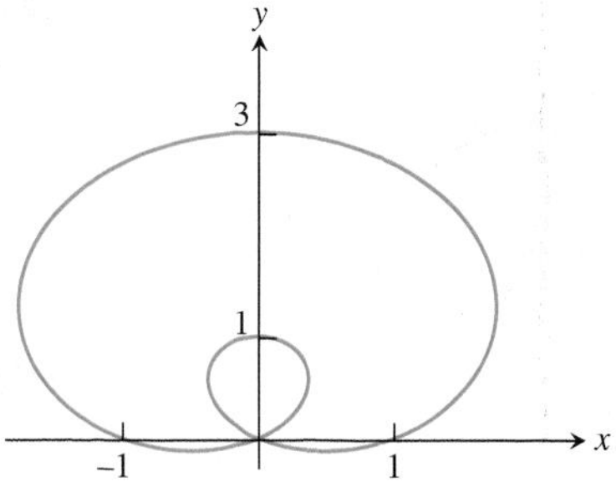

44. The curve with parametric equations

$$x = t, \quad y = 1 - \cos t, \quad 0 \le t \le 2\pi$$

is called a *sinusoid* and is shown in the accompanying figure. Find the point (x, y) where the slope of the tangent line is

a. largest **b.** smallest.

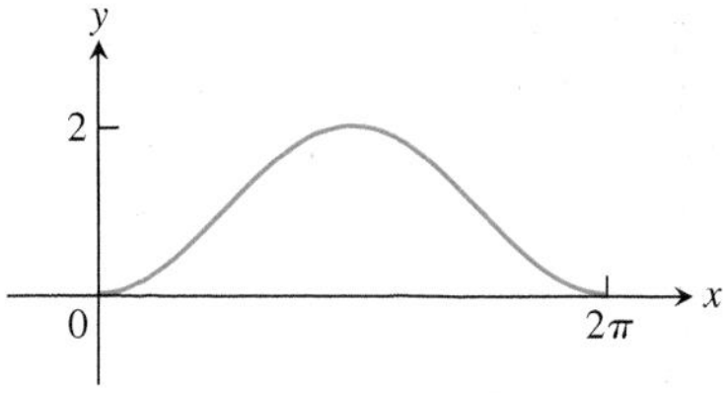

T The curves in Exercises 45 and 46 are called *Bowditch curves* or *Lissajous figures*. In each case, find the point in the interior of the first quadrant where the tangent to the curve is horizontal, and find the equations of the two tangents at the origin.

45.

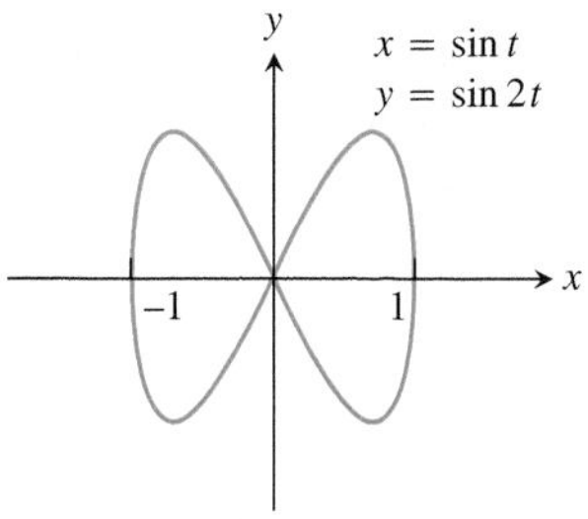

46.

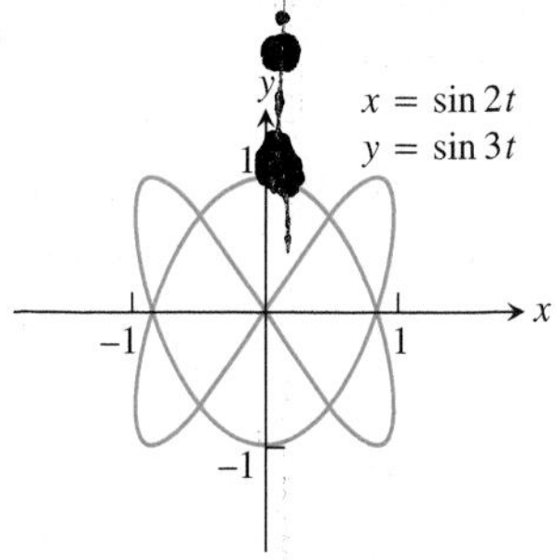

47. Cycloid

a. Find the length of one arch of the cycloid

$$x = a(t - \sin t), \quad y = a(1 - \cos t).$$

b. Find the area of the surface generated by revolving one arch of the cycloid in part (a) about the x-axis for $a = 1$.

48. Volume Find the volume swept out by revolving the region bounded by the x-axis and one arch of the cycloid

$$x = t - \sin t, \quad y = 1 - \cos t$$

about the x-axis.

COMPUTER EXPLORATIONS

In Exercises 49–52, use a CAS to perform the following steps for the given curve over the closed interval.

a. Plot the curve together with the polygonal path approximations for $n = 2, 4, 8$ partition points over the interval. (See Figure 10.13.)

b. Find the corresponding approximation to the length of the curve by summing the lengths of the line segments.

c. Evaluate the length of the curve using an integral. Compare your approximations for $n = 2, 4, 8$ with the actual length given by the integral. How does the actual length compare with the approximations as n increases? Explain your answer.

49. $x = \frac{1}{3}t^3, \quad y = \frac{1}{2}t^2, \quad 0 \le t \le 1$

50. $x = 2t^3 - 16t^2 + 25t + 5, \quad y = t^2 + t - 3, \quad 0 \le t \le 6$

51. $x = t - \cos t, \quad y = 1 + \sin t, \quad -\pi \le t \le \pi$

52. $x = e^t \cos t, \quad y = e^t \sin t, \quad 0 \le t \le \pi$

10.3 Polar Coordinates

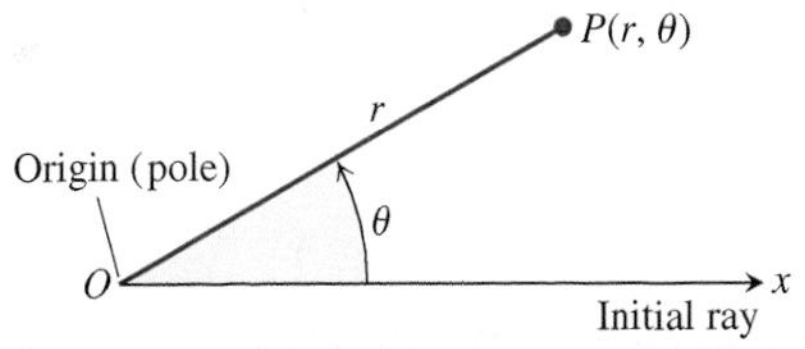

FIGURE 10.17 To define polar coordinates for the plane, we start with an origin, called the pole, and an initial ray.

In this section we study polar coordinates and their relation to Cartesian coordinates. You will see that polar coordinates are very useful for calculating many multiple integrals studied in Chapter 14.

Definition of Polar Coordinates

To define polar coordinates, we first fix an **origin** O (called the **pole**) and an **initial ray** from O (Figure 10.17). Usually the positive x-axis is chosen as the initial ray. Then each point P can be located by assigning to it a **polar coordinate pair** (r, θ) in which r gives the directed distance from O to P and θ gives the directed angle from the initial ray to ray OP. So we label the point P as

$$P(r, \theta)$$

Directed distance from O to P — Directed angle from initial ray to OP

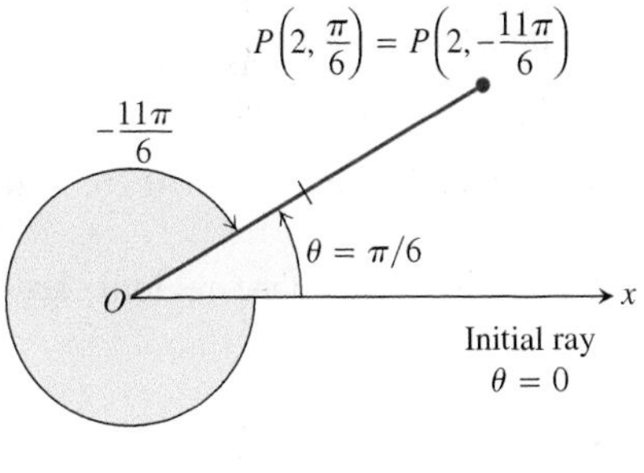

FIGURE 10.18 Polar coordinates are not unique.

As in trigonometry, θ is positive when measured counterclockwise and negative when measured clockwise. The angle associated with a given point is not unique. While a point in the plane has just one pair of Cartesian coordinates, it has infinitely many pairs of polar coordinates. For instance, the point 2 units from the origin along the ray $\theta = \pi/6$ has polar coordinates $r = 2, \theta = \pi/6$. It also has coordinates $r = 2, \theta = -11\pi/6$ (Figure 10.18). In some situations we allow r to be negative. That is why we use directed distance in defining $P(r, \theta)$. The point $P(2, 7\pi/6)$ can be reached by turning $7\pi/6$ radians counterclockwise from the initial ray and going forward 2 units (Figure 10.19). It can also be reached by turning $\pi/6$ radians counterclockwise from the initial ray and going *backward* 2 units. So the point also has polar coordinates $r = -2, \theta = \pi/6$.

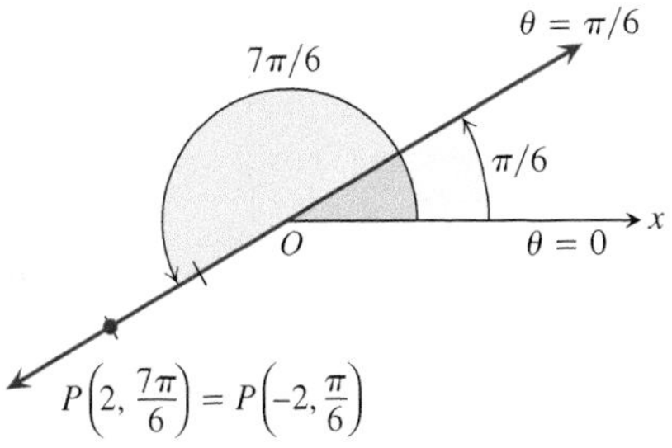

FIGURE 10.19 Polar coordinates can have negative r-values.

EXAMPLE 1 Find all the polar coordinates of the point $P(2, \pi/6)$.

Solution We sketch the initial ray of the coordinate system, draw the ray from the origin that makes an angle of $\pi/6$ radians with the initial ray, and mark the point $(2, \pi/6)$ (Figure 10.20). We then find the angles for the other coordinate pairs of P in which $r = 2$ and $r = -2$.

For $r = 2$, the complete list of angles is

$$\frac{\pi}{6}, \quad \frac{\pi}{6} \pm 2\pi, \quad \frac{\pi}{6} \pm 4\pi, \quad \frac{\pi}{6} \pm 6\pi, \ldots .$$

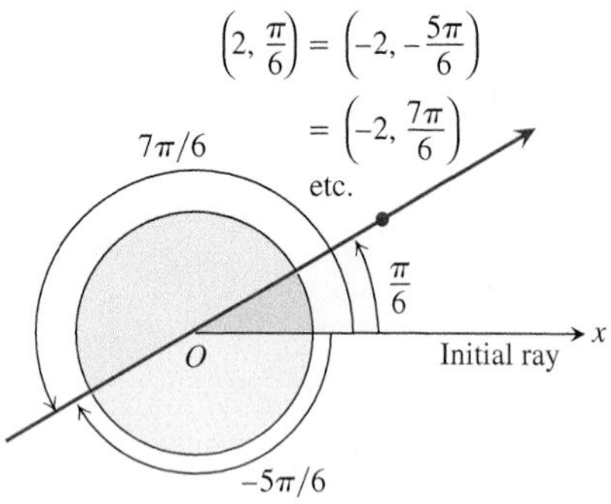

FIGURE 10.20 The point $P(2, \pi/6)$ has infinitely many polar coordinate pairs (Example 1).

For $r = -2$, the angles are

$$-\frac{5\pi}{6}, \quad -\frac{5\pi}{6} \pm 2\pi, \quad -\frac{5\pi}{6} \pm 4\pi, \quad -\frac{5\pi}{6} \pm 6\pi, \ldots.$$

The corresponding coordinate pairs of P are

$$\left(2, \frac{\pi}{6} + 2n\pi\right), \qquad n = 0, \pm 1, \pm 2, \ldots$$

and

$$\left(-2, -\frac{5\pi}{6} + 2n\pi\right), \qquad n = 0, \pm 1, \pm 2, \ldots.$$

When $n = 0$, the formulas give $(2, \pi/6)$ and $(-2, -5\pi/6)$. When $n = 1$, they give $(2, 13\pi/6)$ and $(-2, 7\pi/6)$, and so on. ■

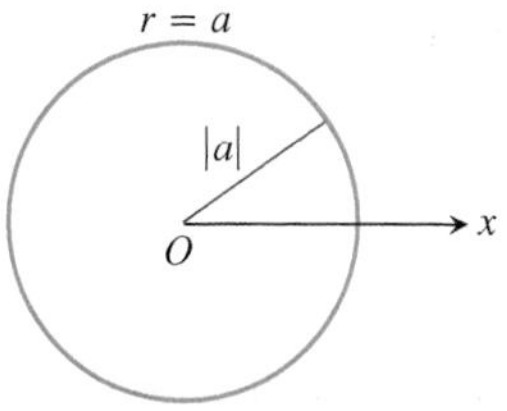

FIGURE 10.21 The polar equation for a circle is $r = a$.

Polar Equations and Graphs

If we hold r fixed at a constant value $r = a \neq 0$, the point $P(r, \theta)$ will lie $|a|$ units from the origin O. As θ varies over any interval of length 2π, P then traces a circle of radius $|a|$ centered at O (Figure 10.21).

If we hold θ fixed at a constant value $\theta = \theta_0$ and let r vary between $-\infty$ and ∞, the point $P(r, \theta)$ traces the line through O that makes an angle of measure θ_0 with the initial ray. (See Figure 10.19 for an example.)

EXAMPLE 2 A circle or line can have more than one polar equation.

(a) $r = 1$ and $r = -1$ are equations for the circle of radius 1 centered at O.

(b) $\theta = \pi/6$, $\theta = 7\pi/6$, and $\theta = -5\pi/6$ are equations for the line in Figure 10.20. ■

Equations of the form $r = a$ and $\theta = \theta_0$ can be combined to define regions, segments, and rays.

EXAMPLE 3 Graph the sets of points whose polar coordinates satisfy the following conditions.

(a) $1 \leq r \leq 2$ and $0 \leq \theta \leq \frac{\pi}{2}$

(b) $-3 \leq r \leq 2$ and $\theta = \frac{\pi}{4}$

(c) $\frac{2\pi}{3} \leq \theta \leq \frac{5\pi}{6}$ (no restriction on r)

Solution The graphs are shown in Figure 10.22. ■

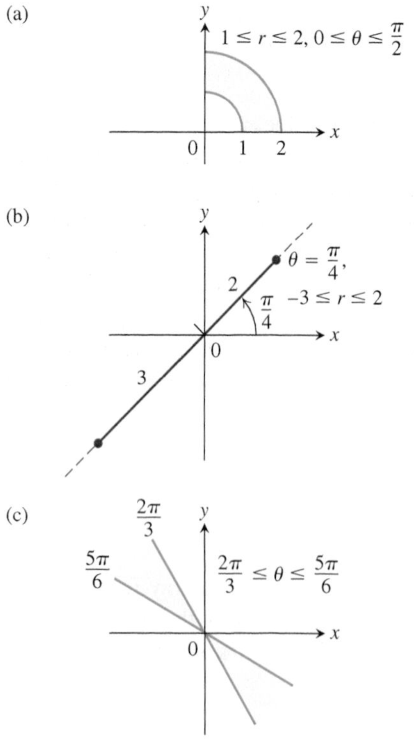

FIGURE 10.22 The graphs of typical inequalities in r and θ (Example 3).

Relating Polar and Cartesian Coordinates

When we use both polar and Cartesian coordinates in a plane, we place the two origins together and take the initial polar ray as the positive x-axis. The ray $\theta = \pi/2, r > 0$,

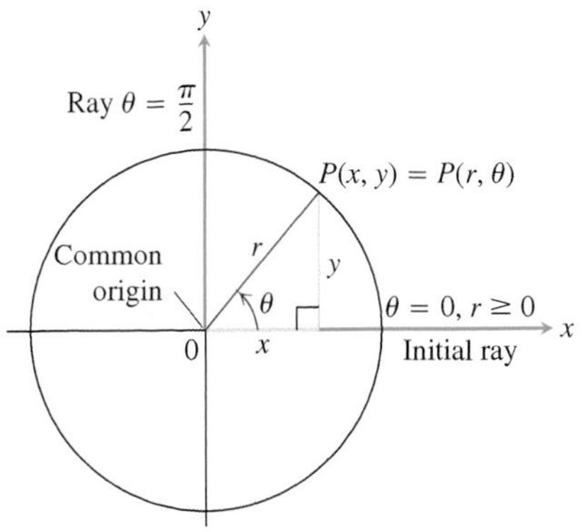

FIGURE 10.23 The usual way to relate polar and Cartesian coordinates.

becomes the positive y-axis (Figure 10.23). The two coordinate systems are then related by the following equations.

Equations Relating Polar and Cartesian Coordinates

$$x = r\cos\theta, \qquad y = r\sin\theta, \qquad r^2 = x^2 + y^2, \qquad \tan\theta = \frac{y}{x}$$

The first two of these equations uniquely determine the Cartesian coordinates x and y given the polar coordinates r and θ. On the other hand, if x and y are given, the third equation gives two possible choices for r (a positive and a negative value). For each $(x, y) \neq (0, 0)$, there is a unique $\theta \in [0, 2\pi)$ satisfying the first two equations, each then giving a polar coordinate representation of the Cartesian point (x, y). The other polar coordinate representations for the point can be determined from these two, as in Example 1.

EXAMPLE 4 Here are some plane curves expressed in terms of both polar coordinate and Cartesian coordinate equations.

Polar equation	Cartesian equivalent
$r\cos\theta = 2$	$x = 2$
$r^2\cos\theta\sin\theta = 4$	$xy = 4$
$r^2\cos^2\theta - r^2\sin^2\theta = 1$	$x^2 - y^2 = 1$
$r = 1 + 2r\cos\theta$	$y^2 - 3x^2 - 4x - 1 = 0$
$r = 1 - \cos\theta$	$x^4 + y^4 + 2x^2y^2 + 2x^3 + 2xy^2 - y^2 = 0$

Some curves are more simply expressed with polar coordinates; others are not. ■

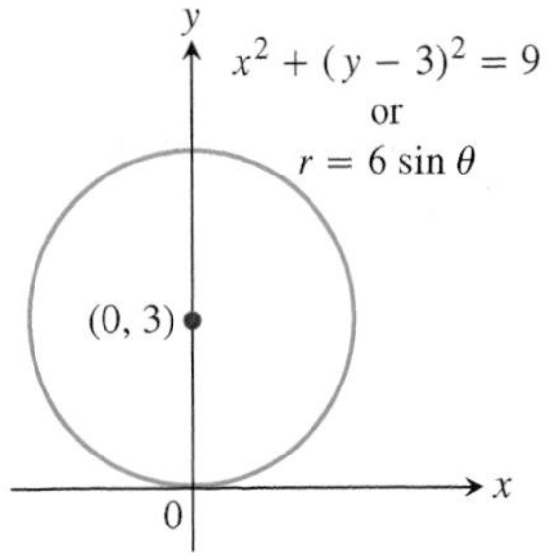

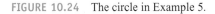

FIGURE 10.24 The circle in Example 5.

EXAMPLE 5 Find a polar equation for the circle $x^2 + (y - 3)^2 = 9$ (Figure 10.24).

Solution We apply the equations relating polar and Cartesian coordinates:

$$
\begin{aligned}
x^2 + (y - 3)^2 &= 9 \\
x^2 + y^2 - 6y + 9 &= 9 && \text{Expand } (y-3)^2. \\
x^2 + y^2 - 6y &= 0 && \text{Cancellation} \\
r^2 - 6r\sin\theta &= 0 && x^2 + y^2 = r^2,\ y = r\sin\theta \\
r = 0 \quad \text{or} \quad r - 6\sin\theta &= 0 \\
r &= 6\sin\theta && \text{Includes both possibilities}
\end{aligned}
$$

■

EXAMPLE 6 Replace the following polar equations by equivalent Cartesian equations and identify their graphs.

(a) $r\cos\theta = -4$

(b) $r^2 = 4r\cos\theta$

(c) $r = \dfrac{4}{2\cos\theta - \sin\theta}$

Solution We use the substitutions $r\cos\theta = x$, $r\sin\theta = y$, and $r^2 = x^2 + y^2$.

(a) $r\cos\theta = -4$

The Cartesian equation:

$$
\begin{aligned}
r\cos\theta &= -4 \\
x &= -4 && \text{Substitution}
\end{aligned}
$$

The graph: Vertical line through $x = -4$ on the x-axis

(b) $r^2 = 4r\cos\theta$

The Cartesian equation:

$$r^2 = 4r\cos\theta$$

$$x^2 + y^2 = 4x \quad \text{Substitution}$$

$$x^2 - 4x + y^2 = 0$$

$$x^2 - 4x + 4 + y^2 = 4 \quad \text{Completing the square}$$

$$(x - 2)^2 + y^2 = 4 \quad \text{Factoring}$$

The graph: Circle, radius 2, center $(h, k) = (2, 0)$

(c) $r = \dfrac{4}{2\cos\theta - \sin\theta}$

The Cartesian equation:

$$r(2\cos\theta - \sin\theta) = 4$$

$$2r\cos\theta - r\sin\theta = 4 \quad \text{Multiplying by } r$$

$$2x - y = 4 \quad \text{Substitution}$$

$$y = 2x - 4 \quad \text{Solve for } y.$$

The graph: Line, slope $m = 2$, y-intercept $b = -4$ ■

Exercises 10.3

Polar Coordinates

1. Which polar coordinate pairs label the same point?

a. $(3, 0)$ **b.** $(-3, 0)$ **c.** $(2, 2\pi/3)$
d. $(2, 7\pi/3)$ **e.** $(-3, \pi)$ **f.** $(2, \pi/3)$
g. $(-3, 2\pi)$ **h.** $(-2, -\pi/3)$

2. Which polar coordinate pairs label the same point?

a. $(-2, \pi/3)$ **b.** $(2, -\pi/3)$ **c.** (r, θ)
d. $(r, \theta + \pi)$ **e.** $(-r, \theta)$ **f.** $(2, -2\pi/3)$
g. $(-r, \theta + \pi)$ **h.** $(-2, 2\pi/3)$

3. Plot the following points (given in polar coordinates). Then find all the polar coordinates of each point.

a. $(2, \pi/2)$ **b.** $(2, 0)$
c. $(-2, \pi/2)$ **d.** $(-2, 0)$

4. Plot the following points (given in polar coordinates). Then find all the polar coordinates of each point.

a. $(3, \pi/4)$ **b.** $(-3, \pi/4)$
c. $(3, -\pi/4)$ **d.** $(-3, -\pi/4)$

Polar to Cartesian Coordinates

5. Find the Cartesian coordinates of the points in Exercise 1.

6. Find the Cartesian coordinates of the following points (given in polar coordinates).

a. $(\sqrt{2}, \pi/4)$ **b.** $(1, 0)$
c. $(0, \pi/2)$ **d.** $(-\sqrt{2}, \pi/4)$
e. $(-3, 5\pi/6)$ **f.** $(5, \tan^{-1}(4/3))$
g. $(-1, 7\pi)$ **h.** $(2\sqrt{3}, 2\pi/3)$

Cartesian to Polar Coordinates

7. Find the polar coordinates, $0 \le \theta < 2\pi$ and $r \ge 0$, of the following points given in Cartesian coordinates.

a. $(1, 1)$ **b.** $(-3, 0)$
c. $(\sqrt{3}, -1)$ **d.** $(-3, 4)$

8. Find the polar coordinates, $-\pi \le \theta < \pi$ and $r \ge 0$, of the following points given in Cartesian coordinates.

a. $(-2, -2)$ **b.** $(0, 3)$
c. $(-\sqrt{3}, 1)$ **d.** $(5, -12)$

9. Find the polar coordinates, $0 \le \theta < 2\pi$ and $r \le 0$, of the following points given in Cartesian coordinates.

a. $(3, 3)$ **b.** $(-1, 0)$
c. $(-1, \sqrt{3})$ **d.** $(4, -3)$

10. Find the polar coordinates, $-\pi \le \theta < 2\pi$ and $r \le 0$, of the following points given in Cartesian coordinates.

a. $(-2, 0)$ **b.** $(1, 0)$
c. $(0, -3)$ **d.** $\left(\frac{\sqrt{3}}{2}, \frac{1}{2}\right)$

Graphing in Polar Coordinates

Graph the sets of points whose polar coordinates satisfy the equations and inequalities in Exercises 11–26.

11. $r = 2$ **12.** $0 \le r \le 2$
13. $r \ge 1$ **14.** $1 \le r \le 2$

15. $0 \le \theta \le \pi/6, \quad r \ge 0$

16. $\theta = 2\pi/3, \quad r \le -2$

17. $\theta = \pi/3, \quad -1 \le r \le 3$

18. $\theta = 11\pi/4, \quad r \ge -1$

19. $\theta = \pi/2, \quad r \ge 0$

20. $\theta = \pi/2, \quad r \le 0$

21. $0 \le \theta \le \pi, \quad r = 1$

22. $0 \le \theta \le \pi, \quad r = -1$

23. $\pi/4 \le \theta \le 3\pi/4, \quad 0 \le r \le 1$

24. $-\pi/4 \le \theta \le \pi/4, \quad -1 \le r \le 1$

25. $-\pi/2 \le \theta \le \pi/2, \quad 1 \le r \le 2$

26. $0 \le \theta \le \pi/2, \quad 1 \le |r| \le 2$

Polar to Cartesian Equations

Replace the polar equations in Exercises 27–52 with equivalent Cartesian equations. Then describe or identify the graph.

27. $r\cos\theta = 2$

28. $r\sin\theta = -1$

29. $r\sin\theta = 0$

30. $r\cos\theta = 0$

31. $r = 4\csc\theta$

32. $r = -3\sec\theta$

33. $r\cos\theta + r\sin\theta = 1$

34. $r\sin\theta = r\cos\theta$

35. $r^2 = 1$

36. $r^2 = 4r\sin\theta$

37. $r = \dfrac{5}{\sin\theta - 2\cos\theta}$

38. $r^2\sin 2\theta = 2$

39. $r = \cot\theta\csc\theta$

40. $r = 4\tan\theta\sec\theta$

41. $r = \csc\theta\, e^{r\cos\theta}$

42. $r\sin\theta = \ln r + \ln\cos\theta$

43. $r^2 + 2r^2\cos\theta\sin\theta = 1$

44. $\cos^2\theta = \sin^2\theta$

45. $r^2 = -4r\cos\theta$

46. $r^2 = -6r\sin\theta$

47. $r = 8\sin\theta$

48. $r = 3\cos\theta$

49. $r = 2\cos\theta + 2\sin\theta$

50. $r = 2\cos\theta - \sin\theta$

51. $r\sin\left(\theta + \dfrac{\pi}{6}\right) = 2$

52. $r\sin\left(\dfrac{2\pi}{3} - \theta\right) = 5$

Cartesian to Polar Equations

Replace the Cartesian equations in Exercises 53–66 with equivalent polar equations.

53. $x = 7$

54. $y = 1$

55. $x = y$

56. $x - y = 3$

57. $x^2 + y^2 = 4$

58. $x^2 - y^2 = 1$

59. $\dfrac{x^2}{9} + \dfrac{y^2}{4} = 1$

60. $xy = 2$

61. $y^2 = 4x$

62. $x^2 + xy + y^2 = 1$

63. $x^2 + (y - 2)^2 = 4$

64. $(x - 5)^2 + y^2 = 25$

65. $(x - 3)^2 + (y + 1)^2 = 4$

66. $(x + 2)^2 + (y - 5)^2 = 16$

67. Find all polar coordinates of the origin.

68. Vertical and horizontal lines

a. Show that every vertical line in the xy-plane has a polar equation of the form $r = a\sec\theta$.

b. Find the analogous polar equation for horizontal lines in the xy-plane.

10.4 Graphing in Polar Coordinates

It is often helpful to have the graph of an equation in polar coordinates. This section describes some techniques for graphing these equations using symmetries and tangents to the graph.

Symmetry

Figure 10.25 illustrates the standard polar coordinate tests for symmetry. The following summary says how the symmetric points are related.

> **Symmetry Tests for Polar Graphs**
>
> 1. *Symmetry about the x-axis:* If the point (r, θ) lies on the graph, then the point $(r, -\theta)$ or $(-r, \pi - \theta)$ lies on the graph (Figure 10.25a).
> 2. *Symmetry about the y-axis:* If the point (r, θ) lies on the graph, then the point $(r, \pi - \theta)$ or $(-r, -\theta)$ lies on the graph (Figure 10.25b).
> 3. *Symmetry about the origin:* If the point (r, θ) lies on the graph, then the point $(-r, \theta)$ or $(r, \theta + \pi)$ lies on the graph (Figure 10.25c).

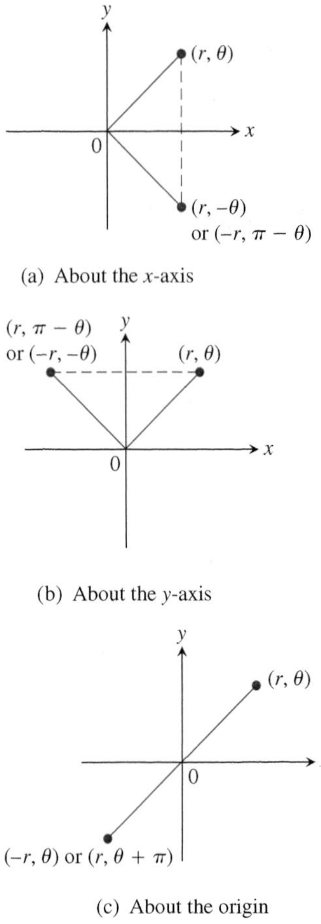

FIGURE 10.25 Three tests for symmetry in polar coordinates.

Slope

The slope of a polar curve $r = f(\theta)$ in the xy-plane is still given by dy/dx, which is not $r' = df/d\theta$. To see why, think of the graph of f as the graph of the parametric equations

$$x = r\cos\theta = f(\theta)\cos\theta, \qquad y = r\sin\theta = f(\theta)\sin\theta.$$

If f is a differentiable function of θ, then so are x and y and, when $dx/d\theta \neq 0$, we can calculate dy/dx from the parametric formula

$$\begin{aligned}\frac{dy}{dx} &= \frac{dy/d\theta}{dx/d\theta} && \text{Section 10.2, Eq. (1) with } t = \theta\\ &= \frac{\dfrac{d}{d\theta}(f(\theta)\cdot\sin\theta)}{\dfrac{d}{d\theta}(f(\theta)\cdot\cos\theta)}\\ &= \frac{\dfrac{df}{d\theta}\sin\theta + f(\theta)\cos\theta}{\dfrac{df}{d\theta}\cos\theta - f(\theta)\sin\theta} && \text{Product Rule for derivatives}\end{aligned}$$

Therefore we see that dy/dx is not the same as $df/d\theta$.

> **Slope of the Curve $r = f(\theta)$**
>
> $$\left.\frac{dy}{dx}\right|_{(r,\theta)} = \frac{f'(\theta)\sin\theta + f(\theta)\cos\theta}{f'(\theta)\cos\theta - f(\theta)\sin\theta}$$
>
> provided $dx/d\theta \neq 0$ at (r, θ).

If the curve $r = f(\theta)$ passes through the origin at $\theta = \theta_0$, then $f(\theta_0) = 0$, and the slope equation gives

$$\left.\frac{dy}{dx}\right|_{(0,\theta_0)} = \frac{f'(\theta_0)\sin\theta_0}{f'(\theta_0)\cos\theta_0} = \tan\theta_0.$$

If the graph of $r = f(\theta)$ passes through the origin at the value $\theta = \theta_0$, the slope of the curve there is $\tan\theta_0$. The reason we say "slope at $(0, \theta_0)$" and not just "slope at the origin" is that a polar curve may pass through the origin (or any point) more than once, with different slopes at different θ-values. This is not the case in our first example, however.

EXAMPLE 1 Graph the curve $r = 1 - \cos\theta$.

Solution The curve is symmetric about the x-axis because

$$\begin{aligned}(r, \theta) \text{ on the graph} &\Rightarrow r = 1 - \cos\theta\\ &\Rightarrow r = 1 - \cos(-\theta) && \cos\theta = \cos(-\theta)\\ &\Rightarrow (r, -\theta) \text{ on the graph.}\end{aligned}$$

θ	$r = 1 - \cos\theta$
0	0
$\frac{\pi}{3}$	$\frac{1}{2}$
$\frac{\pi}{2}$	1
$\frac{2\pi}{3}$	$\frac{3}{2}$
π	2

(a)

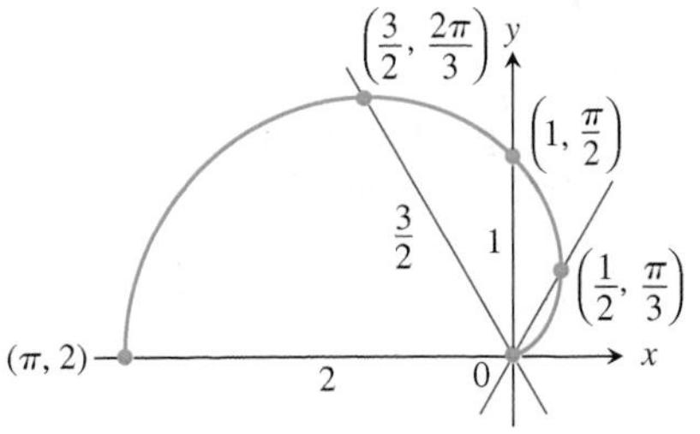

(b)

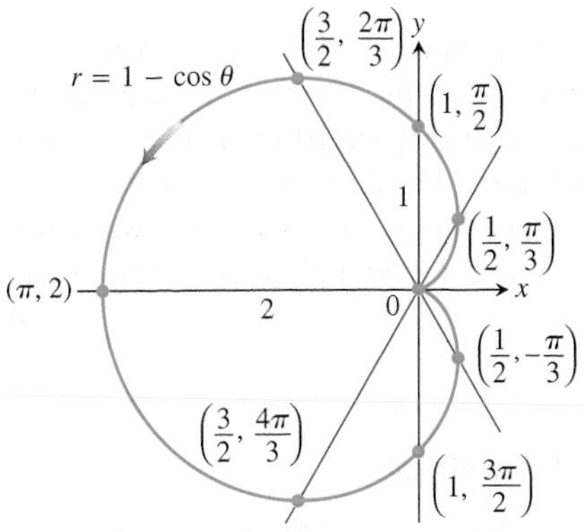

(c)

FIGURE 10.26 The steps in graphing the cardioid $r = 1 - \cos\theta$ (Example 1). The arrow shows the direction of increasing θ.

As θ increases from 0 to π, $\cos\theta$ decreases from 1 to -1, and $r = 1 - \cos\theta$ increases from a minimum value of 0 to a maximum value of 2. As θ continues on from π to 2π, $\cos\theta$ increases from -1 back to 1 and r decreases from 2 back to 0. The curve starts to repeat when $\theta = 2\pi$ because the cosine has period 2π.

The curve leaves the origin with slope $\tan(0) = 0$ and returns to the origin with slope $\tan(2\pi) = 0$.

We make a table of values from $\theta = 0$ to $\theta = \pi$, plot the points, draw a smooth curve through them with a horizontal tangent at the origin, and reflect the curve across the x-axis to complete the graph (Figure 10.26). The curve is called a *cardioid* because of its heart shape. ■

EXAMPLE 2 Graph the curve $r^2 = 4\cos\theta$.

Solution The equation $r^2 = 4\cos\theta$ requires $\cos\theta \geq 0$, so we get the entire graph by running θ from $-\pi/2$ to $\pi/2$. The curve is symmetric about the x-axis because

$$(r, \theta) \text{ on the graph} \Rightarrow r^2 = 4\cos\theta$$
$$\Rightarrow r^2 = 4\cos(-\theta) \qquad \cos\theta = \cos(-\theta)$$
$$\Rightarrow (r, -\theta) \text{ on the graph.}$$

The curve is also symmetric about the origin because

$$(r, \theta) \text{ on the graph} \Rightarrow r^2 = 4\cos\theta$$
$$\Rightarrow (-r)^2 = 4\cos\theta$$
$$\Rightarrow (-r, \theta) \text{ on the graph.}$$

Together, these two symmetries imply symmetry about the y-axis.

The curve passes through the origin when $\theta = -\pi/2$ and $\theta = \pi/2$. It has a vertical tangent both times because $\tan\theta$ is infinite.

For each value of θ in the interval between $-\pi/2$ and $\pi/2$, the formula $r^2 = 4\cos\theta$ gives two values of r:

$$r = \pm 2\sqrt{\cos\theta}.$$

We make a short table of values, plot the corresponding points, and use information about symmetry and tangents to guide us in connecting the points with a smooth curve (Figure 10.27).

θ	$\cos\theta$	$r = \pm 2\sqrt{\cos\theta}$
0	1	± 2
$\pm\frac{\pi}{6}$	$\frac{\sqrt{3}}{2}$	$\approx \pm 1.9$
$\pm\frac{\pi}{4}$	$\frac{1}{\sqrt{2}}$	$\approx \pm 1.7$
$\pm\frac{\pi}{3}$	$\frac{1}{2}$	$\approx \pm 1.4$
$\pm\frac{\pi}{2}$	0	0

(a)

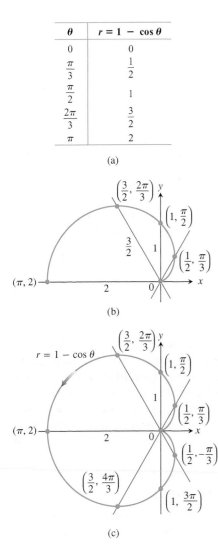

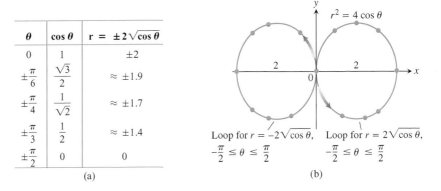

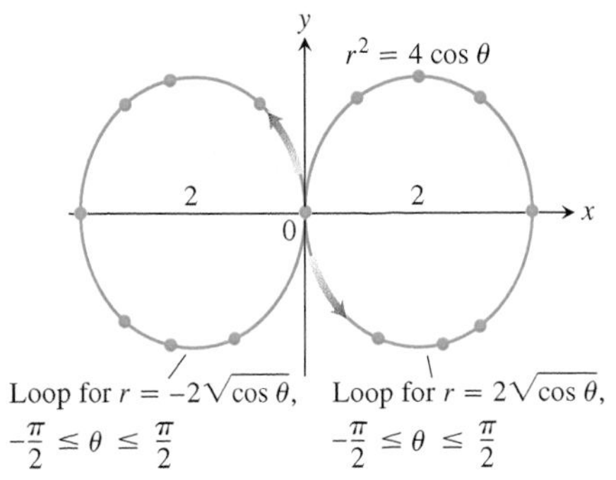

(b)

FIGURE 10.27 The graph of $r^2 = 4\cos\theta$. The arrows show the direction of increasing θ. The values of r in the table are rounded (Example 2). ■

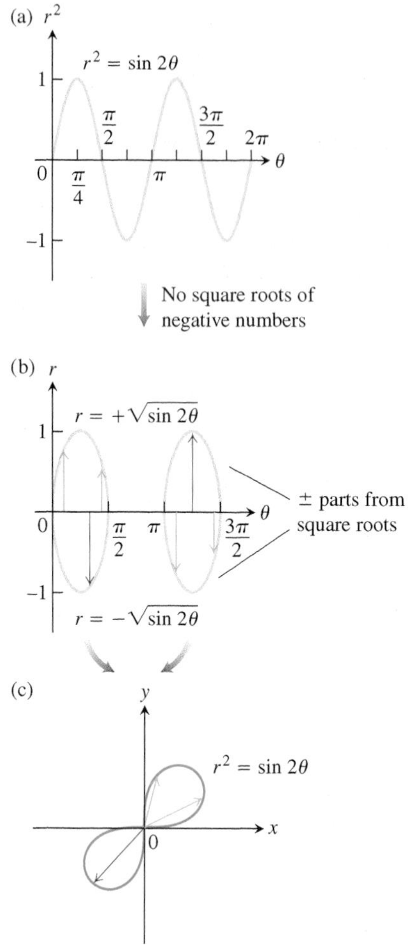

FIGURE 10.28 To plot $r = f(\theta)$ in the Cartesian $r\theta$-plane in (b), we first plot $r^2 = \sin 2\theta$ in the $r^2\theta$-plane in (a) and then ignore the values of θ for which $\sin 2\theta$ is negative. The radii from the sketch in (b) cover the polar graph of the lemniscate in (c) twice (Example 3).

Converting a Graph from the $r\theta$- to xy-Plane

One way to graph a polar equation $r = f(\theta)$ in the xy-plane is to make a table of (r, θ)-values, plot the corresponding points there and connect them in order of increasing θ. This can work well if enough points have been plotted to reveal all the loops and dimples in the graph. Another method of graphing is to

1. first graph the function $r = f(\theta)$ in the *Cartesian* $r\theta$-plane,
2. then use that Cartesian graph as a "table" and guide to sketch the *polar* coordinate graph in the xy-plane

This method is sometimes better than simple point plotting because the first Cartesian graph, even when hastily drawn, shows at a glance where r is positive, negative, and nonexistent, as well as where r is increasing and decreasing. Here's an example.

EXAMPLE 3 Graph the *lemniscate* curve

$$r^2 = \sin 2\theta.$$

Solution Here we begin by plotting r^2 (not r) as a function of θ in the Cartesian $r^2\theta$-plane. See Figure 10.28a. We pass from there to the graph of $r = \pm\sqrt{\sin 2\theta}$ in the $r\theta$-plane (Figure 10.28b), and then draw the polar graph (Figure 10.28c). The graph in Figure 10.28b "covers" the final polar graph in Figure 10.28c twice. We could have managed with either loop alone, with the two upper halves, or with the two lower halves. The double covering does no harm, however, and we actually learn a little more about the behavior of the function this way. ■

USING TECHNOLOGY **Graphing Polar Curves Parametrically**

For complicated polar curves we may need to use a graphing calculator or computer to graph the curve. If the device does not plot polar graphs directly, we can convert $r = f(\theta)$ into parametric form using the equations

$$x = r\cos\theta = f(\theta)\cos\theta, \qquad y = r\sin\theta = f(\theta)\sin\theta.$$

Then we use the device to draw a parametrized curve in the Cartesian xy-plane. It may be necessary to use the parameter t rather than θ for the graphing device.

Exercises 10.4

Symmetries and Polar Graphs

Identify the symmetries of the curves in Exercises 1–12. Then sketch the curves.

1. $r = 1 + \cos\theta$

2. $r = 2 - 2\cos\theta$

3. $r = 1 - \sin\theta$

4. $r = 1 + \sin\theta$

5. $r = 2 + \sin\theta$

6. $r = 1 + 2\sin\theta$

7. $r = \sin(\theta/2)$

8. $r = \cos(\theta/2)$

9. $r^2 = \cos\theta$

10. $r^2 = \sin\theta$

11. $r^2 = -\sin\theta$

12. $r^2 = -\cos\theta$

Graph the lemniscates in Exercises 13–16. What symmetries do these curves have?

13. $r^2 = 4\cos 2\theta$

14. $r^2 = 4\sin 2\theta$

15. $r^2 = -\sin 2\theta$

16. $r^2 = -\cos 2\theta$

Slopes of Polar Curves

Find the slopes of the curves in Exercises 17–20 at the given points. Sketch the curves along with their tangents at these points.

17. Cardioid $r = -1 + \cos\theta;\ \theta = \pm\pi/2$

18. Cardioid $r = -1 + \sin\theta;\ \theta = 0, \pi$

19. Four-leaved rose $r = \sin 2\theta;\ \theta = \pm\pi/4, \pm 3\pi/4$

20. Four-leaved rose $r = \cos 2\theta;\ \theta = 0, \pm\pi/2, \pi$

Graphing Limaçons

Graph the limaçons in Exercises 21–24. Limaçon ("*lee*-ma-sahn") is Old French for "snail." You will understand the name when you graph the limaçons in Exercise 21. Equations for limaçons have the form $r = a \pm b\cos\theta$ or $r = a \pm b\sin\theta$. There are four basic shapes.

21. Limaçons with an inner loop

a. $r = \frac{1}{2} + \cos\theta$ **b.** $r = \frac{1}{2} + \sin\theta$

22. Cardioids

a. $r = 1 - \cos\theta$ **b.** $r = -1 + \sin\theta$

23. Dimpled limaçons

a. $r = \frac{3}{2} + \cos\theta$ **b.** $r = \frac{3}{2} - \sin\theta$

24. Oval limaçons

a. $r = 2 + \cos\theta$ **b.** $r = -2 + \sin\theta$

Graphing Polar Regions and Curves

25. Sketch the region defined by the inequalities $-1 \le r \le 2$ and $-\pi/2 \le \theta \le \pi/2$.

26. Sketch the region defined by the inequalities $0 \le r \le 2\sec\theta$ and $-\pi/4 \le \theta \le \pi/4$.

In Exercises 27 and 28, sketch the region defined by the inequality.

27. $0 \le r \le 2 - 2\cos\theta$ **28.** $0 \le r^2 \le \cos\theta$

T **29.** Which of the following has the same graph as $r = 1 - \cos\theta$?

a. $r = -1 - \cos\theta$

b. $r = 1 + \cos\theta$

Confirm your answer with algebra.

T **30.** Which of the following has the same graph as $r = \cos 2\theta$?

a. $r = -\sin(2\theta + \pi/2)$

b. $r = -\cos(\theta/2)$

Confirm your answer with algebra.

T **31. A rose within a rose** Graph the equation $r = 1 - 2\sin 3\theta$.

T **32. The nephroid of Freeth** Graph the nephroid of Freeth:

$$r = 1 + 2\sin\frac{\theta}{2}.$$

T **33. Roses** Graph the roses $r = \cos m\theta$ for $m = 1/3, 2, 3$, and 7.

T **34. Spirals** Polar coordinates are just the thing for defining spirals. Graph the following spirals.

a. $r = \theta$

b. $r = -\theta$

c. *A logarithmic spiral:* $r = e^{\theta/10}$

d. *A hyperbolic spiral:* $r = 8/\theta$

e. *An equilateral hyperbola:* $r = \pm 10/\sqrt{\theta}$

(Use different colors for the two branches.)

10.5 Areas and Lengths in Polar Coordinates

This section shows how to calculate areas of plane regions and lengths of curves in polar coordinates. The defining ideas are the same as before, but the formulas are different in polar versus Cartesian coordinates.

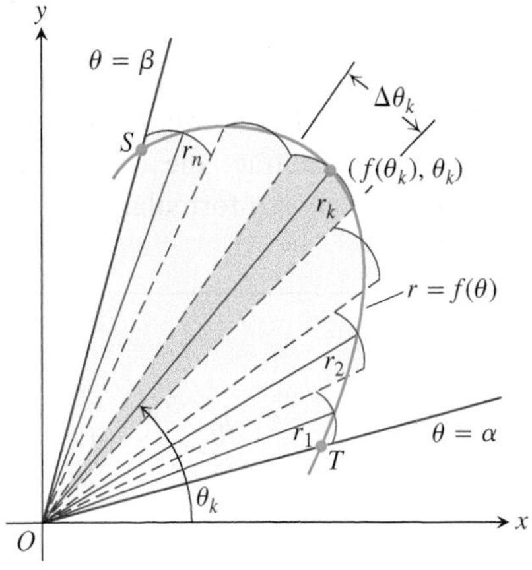

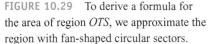

FIGURE 10.29 To derive a formula for the area of region *OTS*, we approximate the region with fan-shaped circular sectors.

Area in the Plane

The region *OTS* in Figure 10.29 is bounded by the rays $\theta = \alpha$ and $\theta = \beta$ and the curve $r = f(\theta)$. We approximate the region with n nonoverlapping fan-shaped circular sectors based on a partition P of angle *TOS*. The typical sector has radius $r_k = f(\theta_k)$ and central angle of radian measure $\Delta\theta_k$. Its area is $\Delta\theta_k/2\pi$ times the area of a circle of radius r_k, or

$$A_k = \frac{1}{2}r_k^2\,\Delta\theta_k = \frac{1}{2}\left(f(\theta_k)\right)^2\Delta\theta_k.$$

The area of region *OTS* is approximately

$$\sum_{k=1}^{n} A_k = \sum_{k=1}^{n}\frac{1}{2}\left(f(\theta_k)\right)^2\Delta\theta_k.$$

If f is continuous, we expect the approximations to improve as the norm of the partition P goes to zero, where the norm of P is the largest value of $\Delta\theta_k$. We are then led to the following formula defining the region's area:

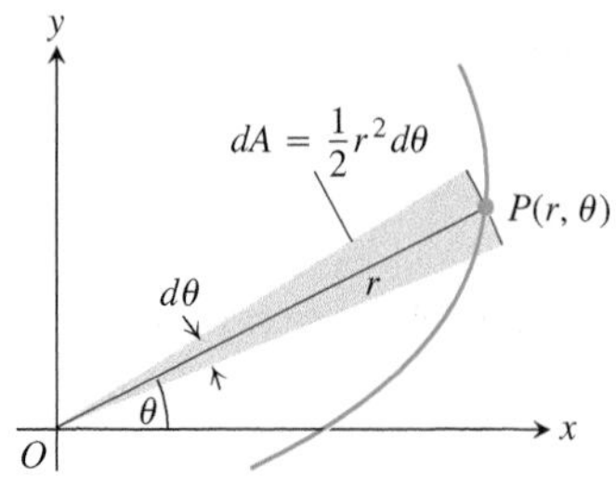

FIGURE 10.30 The area differential dA for the curve $r = f(\theta)$.

$$A = \lim_{\|P\|\to 0} \sum_{k=1}^{n} \frac{1}{2}\left(f(\theta_k)\right)^2 \Delta\theta_k$$

$$= \int_{\alpha}^{\beta} \frac{1}{2}\left(f(\theta)\right)^2 d\theta.$$

Area of the Fan-Shaped Region Between the Origin and the Curve $r = f(\theta),\ \alpha \le \theta \le \beta$

$$A = \int_{\alpha}^{\beta} \frac{1}{2} r^2 \, d\theta.$$

This is the integral of the **area differential** (Figure 10.30)

$$dA = \frac{1}{2} r^2 \, d\theta = \frac{1}{2}\left(f(\theta)\right)^2 d\theta.$$

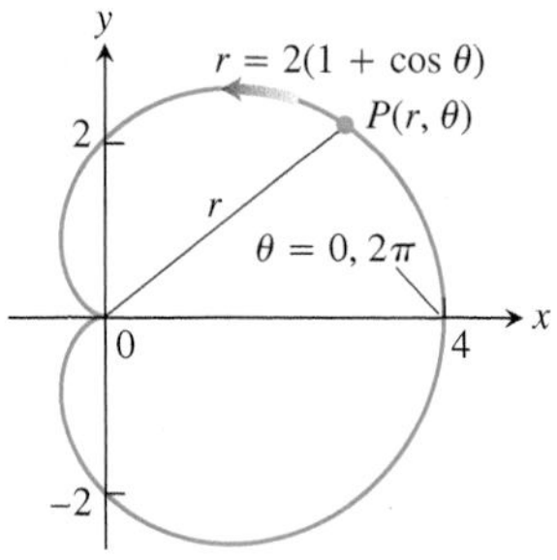

FIGURE 10.31 The cardioid in Example 1.

EXAMPLE 1 Find the area of the region in the plane enclosed by the cardioid $r = 2(1 + \cos\theta)$.

Solution We graph the cardioid (Figure 10.31) and determine that the radius OP sweeps out the region exactly once as θ runs from 0 to 2π. The area is therefore

$$\int_{\theta=0}^{\theta=2\pi} \frac{1}{2} r^2 \, d\theta = \int_0^{2\pi} \frac{1}{2} \cdot 4(1 + \cos\theta)^2 \, d\theta$$

$$= \int_0^{2\pi} 2(1 + 2\cos\theta + \cos^2\theta)\, d\theta$$

$$= \int_0^{2\pi} \left(2 + 4\cos\theta + 2\,\frac{1 + \cos 2\theta}{2}\right) d\theta$$

$$= \int_0^{2\pi} (3 + 4\cos\theta + \cos 2\theta)\, d\theta$$

$$= \left[3\theta + 4\sin\theta + \frac{\sin 2\theta}{2}\right]_0^{2\pi} = 6\pi - 0 = 6\pi.$$ ■

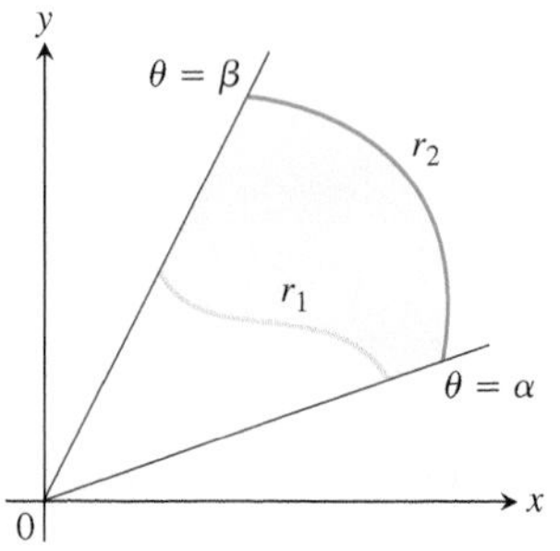

FIGURE 10.32 The area of the shaded region is calculated by subtracting the area of the region between r_1 and the origin from the area of the region between r_2 and the origin.

To find the area of a region like the one in Figure 10.32, which lies between two polar curves $r_1 = r_1(\theta)$ and $r_2 = r_2(\theta)$ from $\theta = \alpha$ to $\theta = \beta$, we subtract the integral of $(1/2)r_1^2\, d\theta$ from the integral of $(1/2)r_2^2\, d\theta$. This leads to the following formula.

Area of the Region $0 \le r_1(\theta) \le r \le r_2(\theta),\ \alpha \le \theta \le \beta$

$$A = \int_{\alpha}^{\beta} \frac{1}{2} r_2^2 \, d\theta - \int_{\alpha}^{\beta} \frac{1}{2} r_1^2 \, d\theta = \int_{\alpha}^{\beta} \frac{1}{2}\left(r_2^2 - r_1^2\right) d\theta \qquad (1)$$

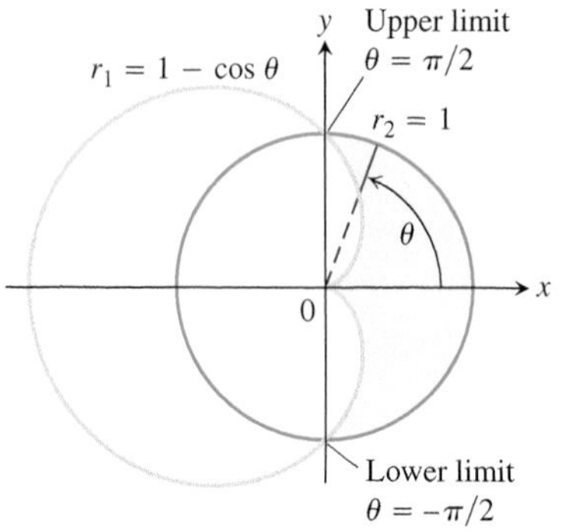

FIGURE 10.33 The region and limits of integration in Example 2.

EXAMPLE 2 Find the area of the region that lies inside the circle $r = 1$ and outside the cardioid $r = 1 - \cos\theta$.

Solution We sketch the region to determine its boundaries and find the limits of integration (Figure 10.33). The outer curve is $r_2 = 1$, the inner curve is $r_1 = 1 - \cos\theta$, and θ runs from $-\pi/2$ to $\pi/2$. The area, from Equation (1), is

$$\begin{aligned}
A &= \int_{-\pi/2}^{\pi/2} \frac{1}{2}\left(r_2^2 - r_1^2\right) d\theta \\
&= 2\int_{0}^{\pi/2} \frac{1}{2}\left(r_2^2 - r_1^2\right) d\theta && \text{Symmetry} \\
&= \int_{0}^{\pi/2} (1 - (1 - 2\cos\theta + \cos^2\theta))\, d\theta && \text{Square } r_1. \\
&= \int_{0}^{\pi/2} (2\cos\theta - \cos^2\theta)\, d\theta = \int_{0}^{\pi/2} \left(2\cos\theta - \frac{1 + \cos 2\theta}{2}\right) d\theta \\
&= \left[2\sin\theta - \frac{\theta}{2} - \frac{\sin 2\theta}{4}\right]_0^{\pi/2} = 2 - \frac{\pi}{4}.
\end{aligned}$$

■

The fact that we can represent a point in different ways in polar coordinates requires extra care in deciding when a point lies on the graph of a polar equation and in determining the points in which polar graphs intersect. (We needed intersection points in Example 2.) In Cartesian coordinates, we can always find the points where two curves cross by solving their equations simultaneously. In polar coordinates, the story is different. Simultaneous solution may reveal some intersection points without revealing others, so it is sometimes difficult to find all points of intersection of two polar curves. One way to identify all the points of intersection is to graph the equations.

Length of a Polar Curve

We can obtain a polar coordinate formula for the length of a curve $r = f(\theta)$, $\alpha \le \theta \le \beta$, by parametrizing the curve as

$$x = r\cos\theta = f(\theta)\cos\theta, \qquad y = r\sin\theta = f(\theta)\sin\theta, \qquad \alpha \le \theta \le \beta. \tag{2}$$

The parametric length formula, Equation (3) from Section 10.2, then gives the length as

$$L = \int_{\alpha}^{\beta} \sqrt{\left(\frac{dx}{d\theta}\right)^2 + \left(\frac{dy}{d\theta}\right)^2}\, d\theta.$$

This equation becomes

$$L = \int_{\alpha}^{\beta} \sqrt{r^2 + \left(\frac{dr}{d\theta}\right)^2}\, d\theta$$

when Equations (2) are substituted for x and y (Exercise 29).

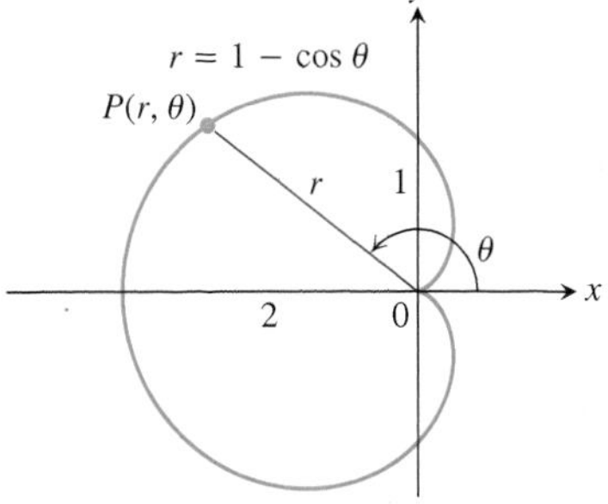

FIGURE 10.34 Calculating the length of a cardioid (Example 3).

> **Length of a Polar Curve**
> If $r = f(\theta)$ has a continuous first derivative for $\alpha \le \theta \le \beta$ and if the point $P(r, \theta)$ traces the curve $r = f(\theta)$ exactly once as θ runs from α to β, then the length of the curve is
>
> $$L = \int_{\alpha}^{\beta} \sqrt{r^2 + \left(\frac{dr}{d\theta}\right)^2}\, d\theta. \tag{3}$$

EXAMPLE 3 Find the length of the cardioid $r = 1 - \cos\theta$.

Solution We sketch the cardioid to determine the limits of integration (Figure 10.34). The point $P(r, \theta)$ traces the curve once, counterclockwise as θ runs from 0 to 2π, so these are the values we take for α and β.

With

$$r = 1 - \cos\theta, \qquad \frac{dr}{d\theta} = \sin\theta,$$

we have

$$\begin{aligned} r^2 + \left(\frac{dr}{d\theta}\right)^2 &= (1 - \cos\theta)^2 + (\sin\theta)^2 \\ &= 1 - 2\cos\theta + \underbrace{\cos^2\theta + \sin^2\theta}_{1} = 2 - 2\cos\theta \end{aligned}$$

and

$$\begin{aligned} L &= \int_\alpha^\beta \sqrt{r^2 + \left(\frac{dr}{d\theta}\right)^2}\, d\theta = \int_0^{2\pi} \sqrt{2 - 2\cos\theta}\, d\theta \\ &= \int_0^{2\pi} \sqrt{4\sin^2\frac{\theta}{2}}\, d\theta \qquad 1 - \cos\theta = 2\sin^2(\theta/2) \\ &= \int_0^{2\pi} 2\left|\sin\frac{\theta}{2}\right| d\theta \\ &= \int_0^{2\pi} 2\sin\frac{\theta}{2}\, d\theta \qquad \sin(\theta/2) \geq 0 \quad \text{for} \quad 0 \leq \theta \leq 2\pi \\ &= \left[-4\cos\frac{\theta}{2}\right]_0^{2\pi} = 4 + 4 = 8. \end{aligned}$$

■

EXERCISES 10.5

Finding Polar Areas

Find the areas of the regions in Exercises 1–8.

1. Bounded by the spiral $r = \theta$ for $0 \leq \theta \leq \pi$

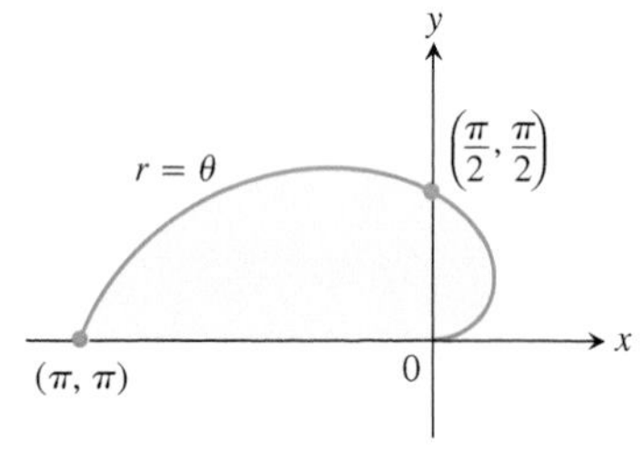

2. Bounded by the circle $r = 2\sin\theta$ for $\pi/4 \leq \theta \leq \pi/2$

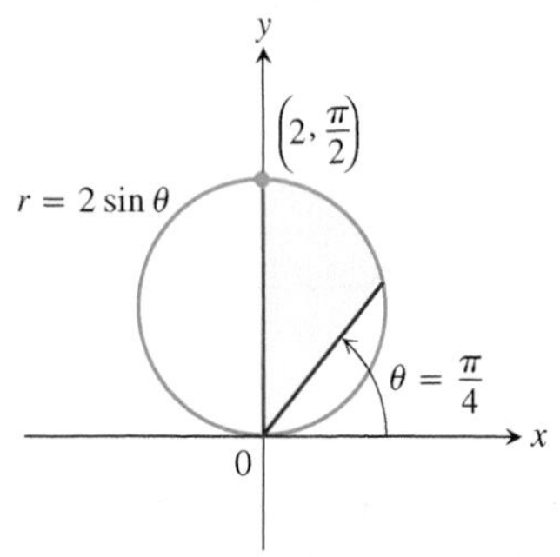

3. Inside the oval limaçon $r = 4 + 2\cos\theta$

4. Inside the cardioid $r = a(1 + \cos\theta), \quad a > 0$

5. Inside one leaf of the four-leaved rose $r = \cos 2\theta$

6. Inside one leaf of the three-leaved rose $r = \cos 3\theta$

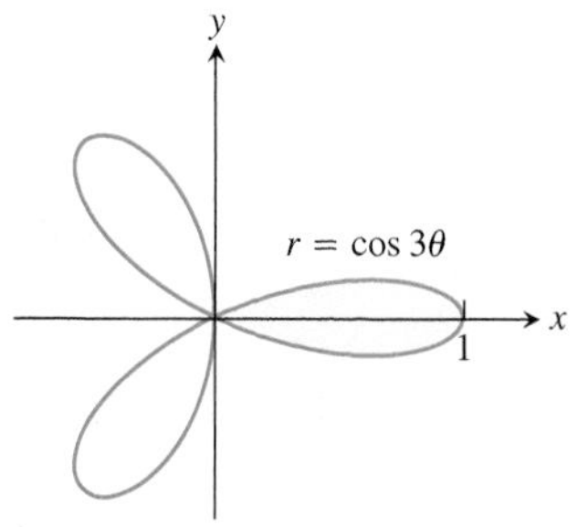

7. Inside one loop of the lemniscate $r^2 = 4\sin 2\theta$

8. Inside the six-leaved rose $r^2 = 2\sin 3\theta$

Find the areas of the regions in Exercises 9–16.

9. Shared by the circles $r = 2\cos\theta$ and $r = 2\sin\theta$

10. Shared by the circles $r = 1$ and $r = 2\sin\theta$

11. Shared by the circle $r = 2$ and the cardioid $r = 2(1 - \cos\theta)$

12. Shared by the cardioids $r = 2(1 + \cos\theta)$ and $r = 2(1 - \cos\theta)$

13. Inside the lemniscate $r^2 = 6\cos 2\theta$ and outside the circle $r = \sqrt{3}$

14. Inside the circle $r = 3a \cos \theta$ and outside the cardioid $r = a(1 + \cos \theta), a > 0$

15. Inside the circle $r = -2 \cos \theta$ and outside the circle $r = 1$

16. Inside the circle $r = 6$ above the line $r = 3 \csc \theta$

17. Inside the circle $r = 4 \cos \theta$ and to the right of the vertical line $r = \sec \theta$

18. Inside the circle $r = 4 \sin \theta$ and below the horizontal line $r = 3 \csc \theta$

19. **a.** Find the area of the shaded region in the accompanying figure.

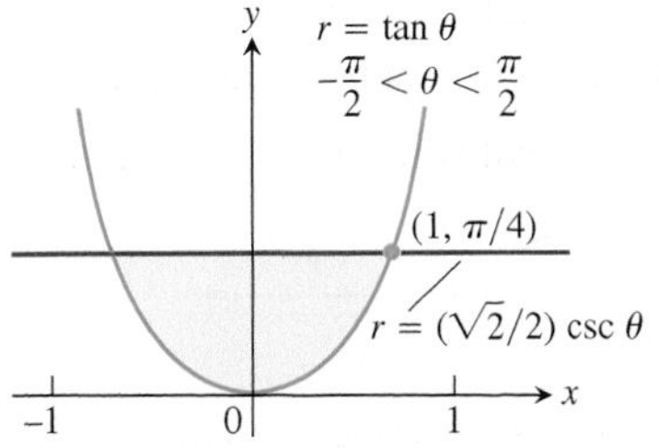

b. It looks as if the graph of $r = \tan \theta, -\pi/2 < \theta < \pi/2$, could be asymptotic to the lines $x = 1$ and $x = -1$. Is it? Give reasons for your answer.

20. The area of the region that lies inside the cardioid curve $r = \cos \theta + 1$ and outside the circle $r = \cos \theta$ is not

$$\frac{1}{2}\int_0^{2\pi} [(\cos \theta + 1)^2 - \cos^2 \theta]\, d\theta = \pi.$$

Why not? What *is* the area? Give reasons for your answers.

Finding Lengths of Polar Curves

Find the lengths of the curves in Exercises 21–28.

21. The spiral $r = \theta^2, \quad 0 \le \theta \le \sqrt{5}$

22. The spiral $r = e^\theta/\sqrt{2}, \quad 0 \le \theta \le \pi$

23. The cardioid $r = 1 + \cos \theta$

24. The curve $r = a \sin^2 (\theta/2), \quad 0 \le \theta \le \pi, \quad a > 0$

25. The parabolic segment $r = 6/(1 + \cos \theta), \quad 0 \le \theta \le \pi/2$

26. The parabolic segment $r = 2/(1 - \cos \theta), \quad \pi/2 \le \theta \le \pi$

27. The curve $r = \cos^3 (\theta/3), \quad 0 \le \theta \le \pi/4$

28. The curve $r = \sqrt{1 + \sin 2\theta}, \quad 0 \le \theta \le \pi\sqrt{2}$

29. **The length of the curve $r = f(\theta), \alpha \le \theta \le \beta$** Assuming that the necessary derivatives are continuous, show how the substitutions

$$x = f(\theta) \cos \theta, \quad y = f(\theta) \sin \theta$$

(Equations 2 in the text) transform

$$L = \int_\alpha^\beta \sqrt{\left(\frac{dx}{d\theta}\right)^2 + \left(\frac{dy}{d\theta}\right)^2}\, d\theta$$

into

$$L = \int_\alpha^\beta \sqrt{r^2 + \left(\frac{dr}{d\theta}\right)^2}\, d\theta.$$

30. **Circumferences of circles** As usual, when faced with a new formula, it is a good idea to try it on familiar objects to be sure it gives results consistent with past experience. Use the length formula in Equation (3) to calculate the circumferences of the following circles ($a > 0$).

a. $r = a$ **b.** $r = a \cos \theta$ **c.** $r = a \sin \theta$

Theory and Examples

31. **Average value** If f is continuous, the average value of the polar coordinate r over the curve $r = f(\theta), \alpha \le \theta \le \beta$, with respect to θ is given by the formula

$$r_{\text{av}} = \frac{1}{\beta - \alpha}\int_\alpha^\beta f(\theta)\, d\theta.$$

Use this formula to find the average value of r with respect to θ over the following curves ($a > 0$).

a. The cardioid $r = a(1 - \cos \theta)$

b. The circle $r = a$

c. The circle $r = a \cos \theta, \quad -\pi/2 \le \theta \le \pi/2$

32. **$r = f(\theta)$ *vs.* $r = 2f(\theta)$** Can anything be said about the relative lengths of the curves $r = f(\theta), \alpha \le \theta \le \beta$, and $r = 2f(\theta), \alpha \le \theta \le \beta$? Give reasons for your answer.

10.6 Conics in Polar Coordinates

Polar coordinates are especially important in astronomy and astronautical engineering because satellites, moons, planets, and comets all move approximately along ellipses, parabolas, and hyperbolas that can be described with a single relatively simple polar coordinate equation. (The standard Cartesian equations for the conics are reviewed in Appendix 4.) We develop the polar coordinate equation here after first introducing the idea of a conic section's *eccentricity*. The eccentricity reveals the conic section's type (circle, ellipse, parabola, or hyperbola) and the degree to which it is "squashed" or flattened.

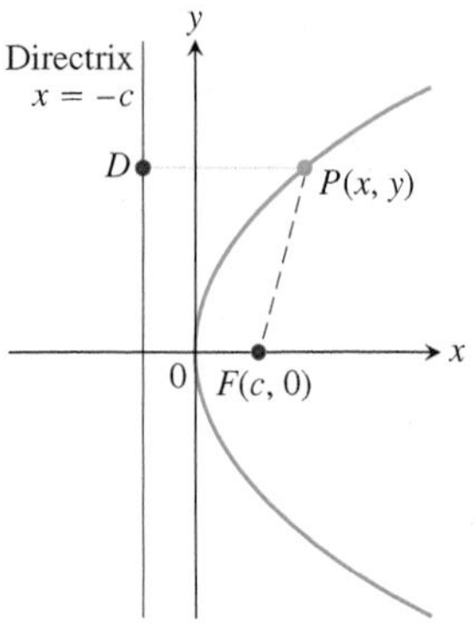

FIGURE 10.35 The distance from the focus F to any point P on a parabola equals the distance from P to the nearest point D on the directrix, so $PF = PD$.

Eccentricity

Although the center-to-focus distance c (see Appendix 4) does not appear in the standard Cartesian equation

$$\frac{x^2}{a^2} + \frac{y^2}{b^2} = 1, \qquad (a > b)$$

for an ellipse, we can still determine c from the equation $c = \sqrt{a^2 - b^2}$. If we fix a and vary c over the interval $0 \le c \le a$, the resulting ellipses will vary in shape. They are circles if $c = 0$ (so that $a = b$) and flatten as c increases. If $c = a$, the foci and vertices overlap and the ellipse degenerates into a line segment. Thus we are led to consider the ratio $e = c/a$. We use this ratio for hyperbolas as well—only in this case c equals $\sqrt{a^2 + b^2}$ instead of $\sqrt{a^2 - b^2}$—and define these ratios with the term *eccentricity*.

DEFINITION

The **eccentricity** of the ellipse $(x^2/a^2) + (y^2/b^2) = 1$ $(a > b)$ is

$$e = \frac{c}{a} = \frac{\sqrt{a^2 - b^2}}{a}.$$

The **eccentricity** of the hyperbola $(x^2/a^2) - (y^2/b^2) = 1$ is

$$e = \frac{c}{a} = \frac{\sqrt{a^2 + b^2}}{a}.$$

The **eccentricity** of a parabola is $e = 1$.

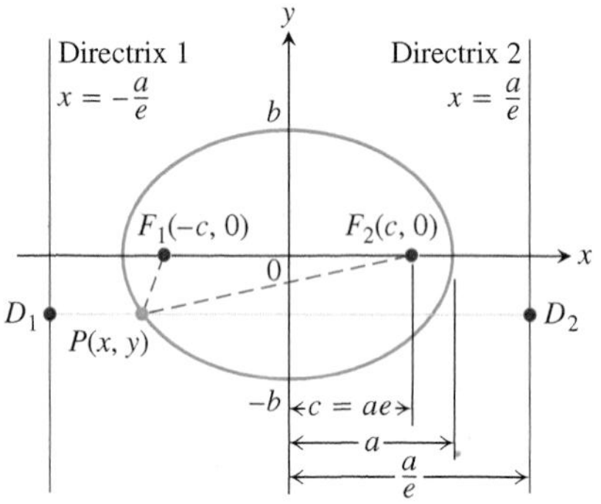

FIGURE 10.36 The foci and directrices of the ellipse $(x^2/a^2) + (y^2/b^2) = 1$. Directrix 1 corresponds to focus F_1 and directrix 2 to focus F_2.

Whereas a parabola has one focus and one directrix, each **ellipse** has two foci and two **directrices**. These are the lines perpendicular to the major axis at distances $\pm a/e$ from the center. From Figure 10.35 we see that a parabola has the property

$$PF = 1 \cdot PD \tag{1}$$

for any point P on it, where F is the focus and D is the point nearest P on the directrix. For an ellipse, it can be shown that the equations that replace Equation (1) are

$$PF_1 = e \cdot PD_1, \qquad PF_2 = e \cdot PD_2. \tag{2}$$

Here, e is the eccentricity, P is any point on the ellipse, F_1 and F_2 are the foci, and D_1 and D_2 are the points on the directrices nearest P (Figure 10.36).

In both Equations (2) the directrix and focus must correspond; that is, if we use the distance from P to F_1, we must also use the distance from P to the directrix at the same end of the ellipse. The directrix $x = -a/e$ corresponds to $F_1(-c, 0)$, and the directrix $x = a/e$ corresponds to $F_2(c, 0)$.

As with the ellipse, it can be shown that the lines $x = \pm a/e$ act as **directrices** for the **hyperbola** and that

$$PF_1 = e \cdot PD_1 \qquad \text{and} \qquad PF_2 = e \cdot PD_2. \tag{3}$$

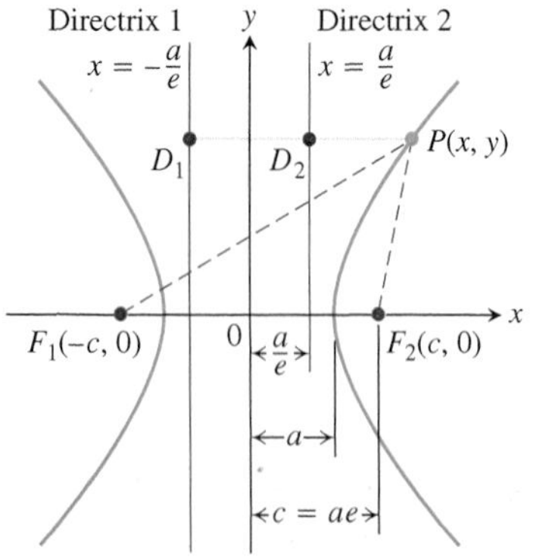

FIGURE 10.37 The foci and directrices of the hyperbola $(x^2/a^2) - (y^2/b^2) = 1$. No matter where P lies on the hyperbola, $PF_1 = e \cdot PD_1$ and $PF_2 = e \cdot PD_2$.

Here P is any point on the hyperbola, F_1 and F_2 are the foci, and D_1 and D_2 are the points nearest P on the directrices (Figure 10.37).

In both the ellipse and the hyperbola, the eccentricity is the ratio of the distance between the foci to the distance between the vertices (because $c/a = 2c/2a$).

$$\text{Eccentricity} = \frac{\text{distance between foci}}{\text{distance between vertices}}$$

In an ellipse, the foci are closer together than the vertices and the ratio is less than 1. In a hyperbola, the foci are farther apart than the vertices and the ratio is greater than 1.

The "focus–directrix" equation $PF = e \cdot PD$ unites the parabola, ellipse, and hyperbola in the following way. Suppose that the distance PF of a point P from a fixed point F (the focus) is a constant multiple of its distance from a fixed line (the directrix). That is, suppose

$$PF = e \cdot PD, \tag{4}$$

where e is the constant of proportionality. Then the path traced by P is

(a) a *parabola* if $e = 1$,

(b) an *ellipse* of eccentricity e if $e < 1$, and

(c) a *hyperbola* of eccentricity e if $e > 1$.

There are no coordinates in Equation (4), and when we try to translate it into coordinate form, it translates in different ways depending on the size of e. At least, that is what happens in Cartesian coordinates. However, as we are about to see, in polar coordinates the equation $PF = e \cdot PD$ translates into a single equation regardless of the value of e.

Given the focus and corresponding directrix of a hyperbola centered at the origin and with foci on the x-axis, we can use the dimensions shown in Figure 10.37 to find e. Knowing e, we can derive a Cartesian equation for the hyperbola from the equation $PF = e \cdot PD$, as in the next example. We can find equations for ellipses centered at the origin and with foci on the x-axis in a similar way, using the dimensions shown in Figure 10.36.

EXAMPLE 1 Find a Cartesian equation for the hyperbola centered at the origin that has a focus at $(3, 0)$ and the line $x = 1$ as the corresponding directrix.

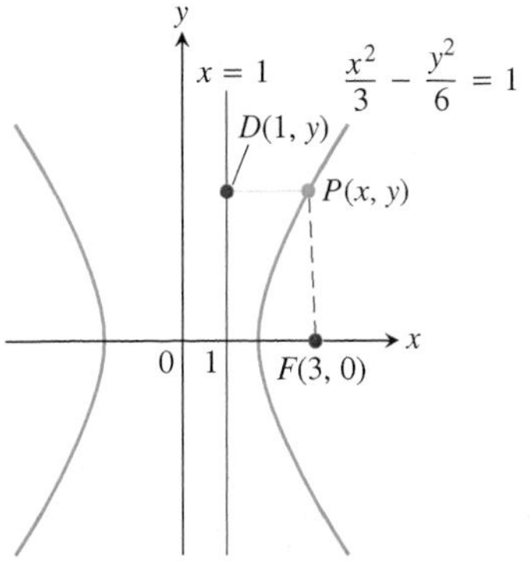

FIGURE 10.38 The hyperbola and directrix in Example 1.

Solution We first use the dimensions shown in Figure 10.37 to find the hyperbola's eccentricity. The focus is (see Figure 10.38)

$$(c, 0) = (3, 0), \qquad \text{so} \qquad c = 3.$$

Again from Figure 10.37, the directrix is the line

$$x = \frac{a}{e} = 1, \qquad \text{so} \qquad a = e.$$

When combined with the equation $e = c/a$ that defines eccentricity, these results give

$$e = \frac{c}{a} = \frac{3}{e}, \qquad \text{so} \qquad e^2 = 3 \quad \text{and} \quad e = \sqrt{3}.$$

Knowing e, we can now derive the equation we want from the equation $PF = e \cdot PD$. In the coordinates of Figure 10.38, we have

$$\begin{aligned} PF &= e \cdot PD && \text{Eq. (4)} \\ \sqrt{(x-3)^2 + (y-0)^2} &= \sqrt{3}\,|x-1| && e = \sqrt{3} \\ x^2 - 6x + 9 + y^2 &= 3(x^2 - 2x + 1) \\ 2x^2 - y^2 &= 6 \\ \frac{x^2}{3} - \frac{y^2}{6} &= 1. \end{aligned}$$

■

Polar Equations

To find a polar equation for an ellipse, parabola, or hyperbola, we place one focus at the origin and the corresponding directrix to the right of the origin along the vertical line $x = k$ (Figure 10.39). In polar coordinates, this makes

$$PF = r$$

and

$$PD = k - FB = k - r\cos\theta.$$

The conic's focus–directrix equation $PF = e \cdot PD$ then becomes

$$r = e(k - r\cos\theta),$$

which can be solved for r to obtain the following expression.

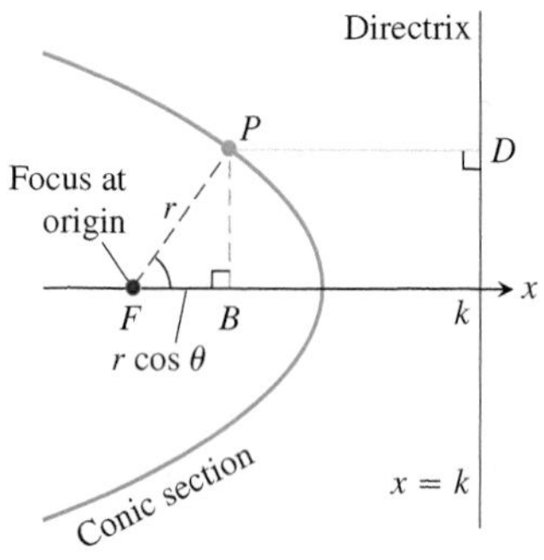

FIGURE 10.39 If a conic section is put in the position with its focus placed at the origin and a directrix perpendicular to the initial ray and right of the origin, we can find its polar equation from the conic's focus–directrix equation.

Polar Equation for a Conic with Eccentricity e

$$r = \frac{ke}{1 + e\cos\theta}, \tag{5}$$

where $x = k > 0$ is the vertical directrix.

EXAMPLE 2 Here are polar equations for three conics. The eccentricity values identifying the conic are the same for both polar and Cartesian coordinates.

$$\begin{aligned} e = \frac{1}{2}: &\quad \text{ellipse} \quad && r = \frac{k}{2 + \cos\theta} \\ e = 1: &\quad \text{parabola} \quad && r = \frac{k}{1 + \cos\theta} \\ e = 2: &\quad \text{hyperbola} \quad && r = \frac{2k}{1 + 2\cos\theta} \end{aligned}$$

■

You may see variations of Equation (5), depending on the location of the directrix. If the directrix is the line $x = -k$ to the left of the origin (the origin is still a focus), we replace Equation (5) with

$$r = \frac{ke}{1 - e\cos\theta}.$$

The denominator now has a $(-)$ instead of a $(+)$. If the directrix is either of the lines $y = k$ or $y = -k$, the equations have sines in them instead of cosines, as shown in Figure 10.40.

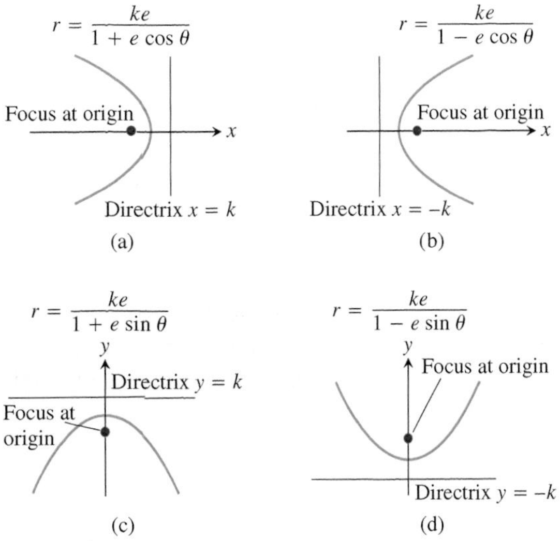

FIGURE 10.40 Equations for conic sections with eccentricity $e > 0$ but different locations of the directrix. The graphs here show a parabola, so $e = 1$.

EXAMPLE 3 Find an equation for the hyperbola with eccentricity $3/2$ and directrix $x = 2$.

Solution We use Equation (5) with $k = 2$ and $e = 3/2$:

$$r = \frac{2(3/2)}{1 + (3/2)\cos\theta} \quad \text{or} \quad r = \frac{6}{2 + 3\cos\theta}.$$ ■

EXAMPLE 4 Find the directrix of the parabola

$$r = \frac{25}{10 + 10\cos\theta}.$$

Solution We divide the numerator and denominator by 10 to put the equation in standard polar form:

$$r = \frac{5/2}{1 + \cos\theta}.$$

This is the equation

$$r = \frac{ke}{1 + e\cos\theta}$$

with $k = 5/2$ and $e = 1$. The equation of the directrix is $x = 5/2$. ■

From the ellipse diagram in Figure 10.41, we see that k is related to the eccentricity e and the semimajor axis a by the equation

$$k = \frac{a}{e} - ea.$$

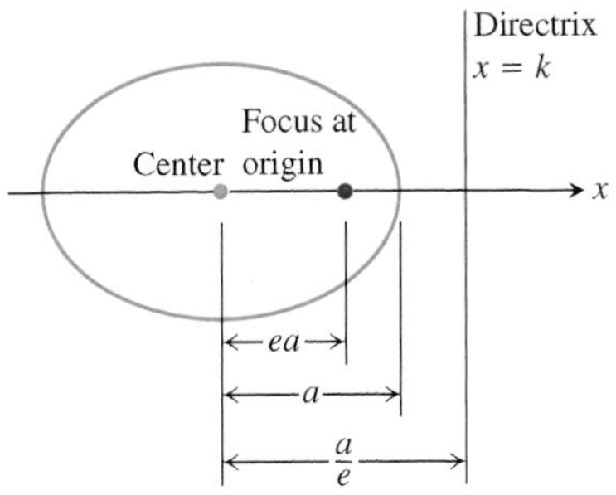

FIGURE 10.41 In an ellipse with semimajor axis a, the focus–directrix distance is $k = (a/e) - ea$, so $ke = a(1 - e^2)$.

From this, we find that $ke = a(1 - e^2)$. Replacing ke in Equation (5) by $a(1 - e^2)$ gives the standard polar equation for an ellipse.

Polar Equation for the Ellipse with Eccentricity e and Semimajor Axis a

$$r = \frac{a(1 - e^2)}{1 + e \cos \theta} \tag{6}$$

Notice that when $e = 0$, Equation (6) becomes $r = a$, which represents a circle.

Lines

Suppose the perpendicular from the origin to line L meets L at the point $P_0(r_0, \theta_0)$, with $r_0 \geq 0$ (Figure 10.42). Then, if $P(r, \theta)$ is any other point on L, the points P, P_0, and O are the vertices of a right triangle, from which we can read the relation

$$r_0 = r \cos(\theta - \theta_0).$$

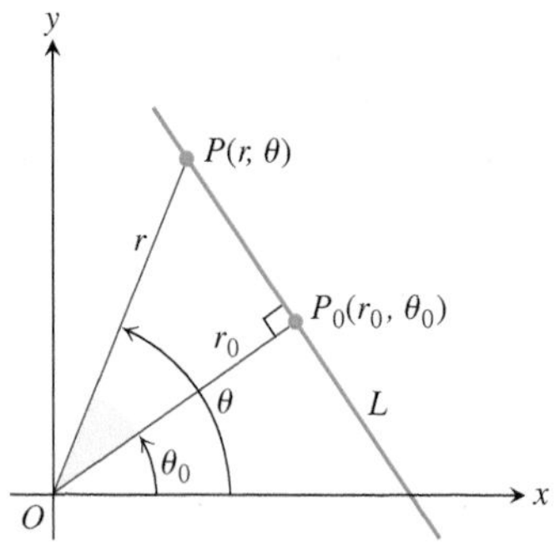

FIGURE 10.42 We can obtain a polar equation for line L by reading the relation $r_0 = r \cos(\theta - \theta_0)$ from the right triangle OP_0P.

The Standard Polar Equation for Lines

If the point $P_0(r_0, \theta_0)$ is the foot of the perpendicular from the origin to the line L, and $r_0 \geq 0$, then an equation for L is

$$r \cos(\theta - \theta_0) = r_0. \tag{7}$$

For example, if $\theta_0 = \pi/3$ and $r_0 = 2$, we find that

$$r \cos\left(\theta - \frac{\pi}{3}\right) = 2$$

$$r\left(\cos\theta \cos\frac{\pi}{3} + \sin\theta \sin\frac{\pi}{3}\right) = 2$$

$$\frac{1}{2} r \cos\theta + \frac{\sqrt{3}}{2} r \sin\theta = 2, \quad \text{or} \quad x + \sqrt{3}\, y = 4.$$

Circles

To find a polar equation for the circle of radius a centered at $P_0(r_0, \theta_0)$, we let $P(r, \theta)$ be a point on the circle and apply the Law of Cosines to triangle OP_0P (Figure 10.43). This gives

$$a^2 = r_0^2 + r^2 - 2r_0 r \cos(\theta - \theta_0).$$

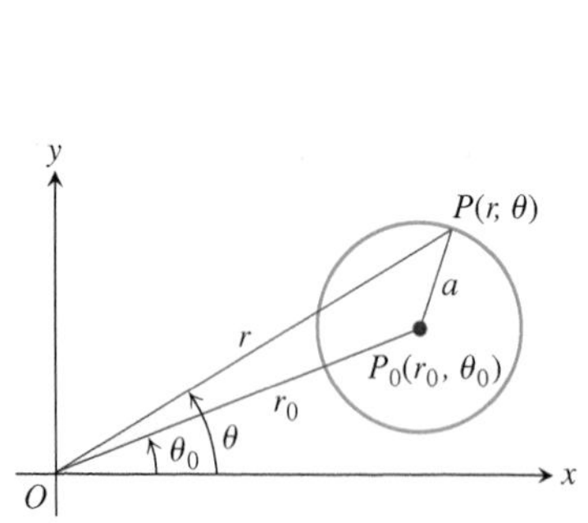

FIGURE 10.43 We can get a polar equation for this circle by applying the Law of Cosines to triangle OP_0P.

If the circle passes through the origin, then $r_0 = a$ and this equation simplifies to

$$a^2 = a^2 + r^2 - 2ar \cos(\theta - \theta_0)$$

$$r^2 = 2ar \cos(\theta - \theta_0)$$

$$r = 2a \cos(\theta - \theta_0).$$

If the circle's center lies on the positive x-axis, $\theta_0 = 0$ and we get the further simplification

$$r = 2a \cos\theta. \tag{8}$$

If the center lies on the positive y-axis, $\theta = \pi/2$, $\cos(\theta - \pi/2) = \sin\theta$, and the equation $r = 2a\cos(\theta - \theta_0)$ becomes

$$r = 2a \sin\theta. \qquad (9)$$

Equations for circles through the origin centered on the negative x- and y-axes can be obtained by replacing r with $-r$ in the above equations.

EXAMPLE 5 Here are several polar equations given by Equations (8) and (9) for circles through the origin and having centers that lie on the x- or y-axis.

Radius	Center (polar coordinates)	Polar equation
3	$(3, 0)$	$r = 6\cos\theta$
2	$(2, \pi/2)$	$r = 4\sin\theta$
1/2	$(-1/2, 0)$	$r = -\cos\theta$
1	$(-1, \pi/2)$	$r = -2\sin\theta$

■

Exercises 10.6

Ellipses and Eccentricity

In Exercises 1–8, find the eccentricity of the ellipse. Then find and graph the ellipse's foci and directrices.

1. $16x^2 + 25y^2 = 400$
2. $7x^2 + 16y^2 = 112$
3. $2x^2 + y^2 = 2$
4. $2x^2 + y^2 = 4$
5. $3x^2 + 2y^2 = 6$
6. $9x^2 + 10y^2 = 90$
7. $6x^2 + 9y^2 = 54$
8. $169x^2 + 25y^2 = 4225$

Exercises 9–12 give the foci or vertices and the eccentricities of ellipses centered at the origin of the xy-plane. In each case, find the ellipse's standard-form equation in Cartesian coordinates.

9. Foci: $(0, \pm 3)$
   Eccentricity: 0.5
10. Foci: $(\pm 8, 0)$
    Eccentricity: 0.2
11. Vertices: $(0, \pm 70)$
    Eccentricity: 0.1
12. Vertices: $(\pm 10, 0)$
    Eccentricity: 0.24

Exercises 13–16 give foci and corresponding directrices of ellipses centered at the origin of the xy-plane. In each case, use the dimensions in Figure 10.36 to find the eccentricity of the ellipse. Then find the ellipse's standard-form equation in Cartesian coordinates.

13. Focus: $(\sqrt{5}, 0)$
    Directrix: $x = \dfrac{9}{\sqrt{5}}$
14. Focus: $(4, 0)$
    Directrix: $x = \dfrac{16}{3}$
15. Focus: $(-4, 0)$
    Directrix: $x = -16$
16. Focus: $(-\sqrt{2}, 0)$
    Directrix: $x = -2\sqrt{2}$

Hyperbolas and Eccentricity

In Exercises 17–24, find the eccentricity of the hyperbola. Then find and graph the hyperbola's foci and directrices.

17. $x^2 - y^2 = 1$
18. $9x^2 - 16y^2 = 144$
19. $y^2 - x^2 = 8$
20. $y^2 - x^2 = 4$
21. $8x^2 - 2y^2 = 16$
22. $y^2 - 3x^2 = 3$
23. $8y^2 - 2x^2 = 16$
24. $64x^2 - 36y^2 = 2304$

Exercises 25–28 give the eccentricities and the vertices or foci of hyperbolas centered at the origin of the xy-plane. In each case, find the hyperbola's standard-form equation in Cartesian coordinates.

25. Eccentricity: 3
    Vertices: $(0, \pm 1)$
26. Eccentricity: 2
    Vertices: $(\pm 2, 0)$
27. Eccentricity: 3
    Foci: $(\pm 3, 0)$
28. Eccentricity: 1.25
    Foci: $(0, \pm 5)$

Eccentricities and Directrices

Exercises 29–36 give the eccentricities of conic sections with one focus at the origin along with the directrix corresponding to that focus. Find a polar equation for each conic section.

29. $e = 1, \quad x = 2$
30. $e = 1, \quad y = 2$
31. $e = 5, \quad y = -6$
32. $e = 2, \quad x = 4$
33. $e = 1/2, \quad x = 1$
34. $e = 1/4, \quad x = -2$
35. $e = 1/5, \quad y = -10$
36. $e = 1/3, \quad y = 6$

Parabolas and Ellipses

Sketch the parabolas and ellipses in Exercises 37–44. Include the directrix that corresponds to the focus at the origin. Label the vertices with appropriate polar coordinates. Label the centers of the ellipses as well.

37. $r = \dfrac{1}{1 + \cos\theta}$
38. $r = \dfrac{6}{2 + \cos\theta}$
39. $r = \dfrac{25}{10 - 5\cos\theta}$
40. $r = \dfrac{4}{2 - 2\cos\theta}$
41. $r = \dfrac{400}{16 + 8\sin\theta}$
42. $r = \dfrac{12}{3 + 3\sin\theta}$
43. $r = \dfrac{8}{2 - 2\sin\theta}$
44. $r = \dfrac{4}{2 - \sin\theta}$

Lines

Sketch the lines in Exercises 45–48 and find Cartesian equations for them.

45. $r\cos\left(\theta - \frac{\pi}{4}\right) = \sqrt{2}$ **46.** $r\cos\left(\theta + \frac{3\pi}{4}\right) = 1$

47. $r\cos\left(\theta - \frac{2\pi}{3}\right) = 3$ **48.** $r\cos\left(\theta + \frac{\pi}{3}\right) = 2$

Find a polar equation in the form $r\cos(\theta - \theta_0) = r_0$ for each of the lines in Exercises 49–52.

49. $\sqrt{2}x + \sqrt{2}y = 6$ **50.** $\sqrt{3}x - y = 1$

51. $y = -5$ **52.** $x = -4$

Circles

Sketch the circles in Exercises 53–56. Give polar coordinates for their centers and identify their radii.

53. $r = 4\cos\theta$ **54.** $r = 6\sin\theta$

55. $r = -2\cos\theta$ **56.** $r = -8\sin\theta$

Find polar equations for the circles in Exercises 57–64. Sketch each circle in the coordinate plane and label it with both its Cartesian and polar equations.

57. $(x - 6)^2 + y^2 = 36$ **58.** $(x + 2)^2 + y^2 = 4$

59. $x^2 + (y - 5)^2 = 25$ **60.** $x^2 + (y + 7)^2 = 49$

61. $x^2 + 2x + y^2 = 0$ **62.** $x^2 - 16x + y^2 = 0$

63. $x^2 + y^2 + y = 0$ **64.** $x^2 + y^2 - \frac{4}{3}y = 0$

Graphs of Polar Equations, and Examples

T Graph the lines and conic sections in Exercises 65–74.

65. $r = 3\sec(\theta - \pi/3)$ **66.** $r = 4\sec(\theta + \pi/6)$

67. $r = 4\sin\theta$ **68.** $r = -2\cos\theta$

69. $r = 8/(4 + \cos\theta)$ **70.** $r = 8/(4 + \sin\theta)$

71. $r = 1/(1 - \sin\theta)$ **72.** $r = 1/(1 + \cos\theta)$

73. $r = 1/(1 + 2\sin\theta)$ **74.** $r = 1/(1 + 2\cos\theta)$

75. Perihelion and aphelion A planet travels about its sun in an ellipse whose semimajor axis has length a. (See accompanying figure.)

a. Show that $r = a(1 - e)$ when the planet is closest to the sun and that $r = a(1 + e)$ when the planet is farthest from the sun.

b. Use the data in the table in Exercise 76 to find how close each planet in our solar system comes to the sun and how far away each planet gets from the sun.

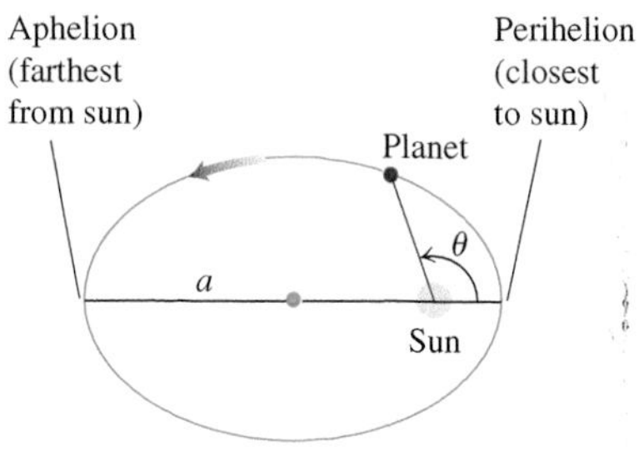

76. Planetary orbits Use the data in the table below and Equation (6) to find polar equations for the orbits of the planets.

Planet	Semimajor axis (astronomical units)	Eccentricity
Mercury	0.3871	0.2056
Venus	0.7233	0.0068
Earth	1.000	0.0167
Mars	1.524	0.0934
Jupiter	5.203	0.0484
Saturn	9.539	0.0543
Uranus	19.18	0.0460
Neptune	30.06	0.0082

Chapter 10 Questions to Guide Your Review

1. What is a parametrization of a curve in the xy-plane? Does a function $y = f(x)$ always have a parametrization? Are parametrizations of a curve unique? Give examples.
2. Give some typical parametrizations for lines, circles, parabolas, ellipses, and hyperbolas. How might the parametrized curve differ from the graph of its Cartesian equation?
3. What is a cycloid? What are typical parametric equations for cycloids? What physical properties account for the importance of cycloids?
4. What is the formula for the slope dy/dx of a parametrized curve $x = f(t), y = g(t)$? When does the formula apply? When can you expect to be able to find d^2y/dx^2 as well? Give examples.
5. How can you sometimes find the area bounded by a parametrized curve and one of the coordinate axes?
6. How do you find the length of a smooth parametrized curve $x = f(t), y = g(t), a \le t \le b$? What does smoothness have to do with length? What else do you need to know about the parametrization in order to find the curve's length? Give examples.
7. What is the arc length function for a smooth parametrized curve? What is its arc length differential?
8. Under what conditions can you find the area of the surface generated by revolving a curve $x = f(t), y = g(t), a \le t \le b$, about the x-axis? the y-axis? Give examples.
9. How do you find the centroid of a smooth parametrized curve $x = f(t), y = g(t), a \le t \le b$? Give an example.
10. What are polar coordinates? What equations relate polar coordinates to Cartesian coordinates? Why might you want to change from one coordinate system to the other?
11. What consequence does the lack of uniqueness of polar coordinates have for graphing? Give an example.
12. How do you graph equations in polar coordinates? Include in your discussion symmetry, slope, behavior at the origin, and the use of Cartesian graphs. Give examples.
13. How do you find the area of a region $0 \le r_1(\theta) \le r \le r_2(\theta)$, $\alpha \le \theta \le \beta$, in the polar coordinate plane? Give examples.

14. Under what conditions can you find the length of a curve $r = f(\theta)$, $\alpha \le \theta \le \beta$, in the polar coordinate plane? Give an example of a typical calculation.

15. What is the eccentricity of a conic section? How can you classify conic sections by eccentricity? How are an ellipse's shape and eccentricity related?

16. Explain the equation $PF = e \cdot PD$.

17. What are the standard equations for lines and conic sections in polar coordinates? Give examples.

Chapter 10 Practice Exercises

Identifying Parametric Equations in the Plane

Exercises 1–6 give parametric equations and parameter intervals for the motion of a particle in the xy-plane. Identify the particle's path by finding a Cartesian equation for it. Graph the Cartesian equation and indicate the direction of motion and the portion traced by the particle.

1. $x = t/2, \quad y = t + 1; \quad -\infty < t < \infty$

2. $x = \sqrt{t}, \quad y = 1 - \sqrt{t}; \quad t \ge 0$

3. $x = (1/2)\tan t, \quad y = (1/2)\sec t; \quad -\pi/2 < t < \pi/2$

4. $x = -2\cos t, \quad y = 2\sin t; \quad 0 \le t \le \pi$

5. $x = -\cos t, \quad y = \cos^2 t; \quad 0 \le t \le \pi$

6. $x = 4\cos t, \quad y = 9\sin t; \quad 0 \le t \le 2\pi$

Finding Parametric Equations and Tangent Lines

7. Find parametric equations and a parameter interval for the motion of a particle in the xy-plane that traces the ellipse $16x^2 + 9y^2 = 144$ once counterclockwise. (There are many ways to do this.)

8. Find parametric equations and a parameter interval for the motion of a particle that starts at the point $(-2, 0)$ in the xy-plane and traces the circle $x^2 + y^2 = 4$ three times clockwise. (There are many ways to do this.)

In Exercises 9 and 10, find an equation for the line in the xy-plane that is tangent to the curve at the point corresponding to the given value of t. Also, find the value of d^2y/dx^2 at this point.

9. $x = (1/2)\tan t, \quad y = (1/2)\sec t; \quad t = \pi/3$

10. $x = 1 + 1/t^2, \quad y = 1 - 3/t; \quad t = 2$

11. Eliminate the parameter to express the curve in the form $y = f(x)$.

a. $x = 4t^2, \quad y = t^3 - 1$ **b.** $x = \cos t, \quad y = \tan t$

12. Find parametric equations for the given curve.

a. Line through $(1, -2)$ with slope 3

b. $(x - 1)^2 + (y + 2)^2 = 9$

c. $y = 4x^2 - x$

d. $9x^2 + 4y^2 = 36$

Lengths of Curves

Find the lengths of the curves in Exercises 13–19.

13. $y = x^{1/2} - (1/3)x^{3/2}, \quad 1 \le x \le 4$

14. $x = y^{2/3}, \quad 1 \le y \le 8$

15. $y = (5/12)x^{6/5} - (5/8)x^{4/5}, \quad 1 \le x \le 32$

16. $x = (y^3/12) + (1/y), \quad 1 \le y \le 2$

17. $x = 5\cos t - \cos 5t, \quad y = 5\sin t - \sin 5t, \quad 0 \le t \le \pi/2$

18. $x = t^3 - 6t^2, \quad y = t^3 + 6t^2, \quad 0 \le t \le 1$

19. $x = 3\cos\theta, \quad y = 3\sin\theta, \quad 0 \le \theta \le \dfrac{3\pi}{2}$

20. Find the length of the enclosed loop $x = t^2, y = (t^3/3) - t$ shown here. The loop starts at $t = -\sqrt{3}$ and ends at $t = \sqrt{3}$.

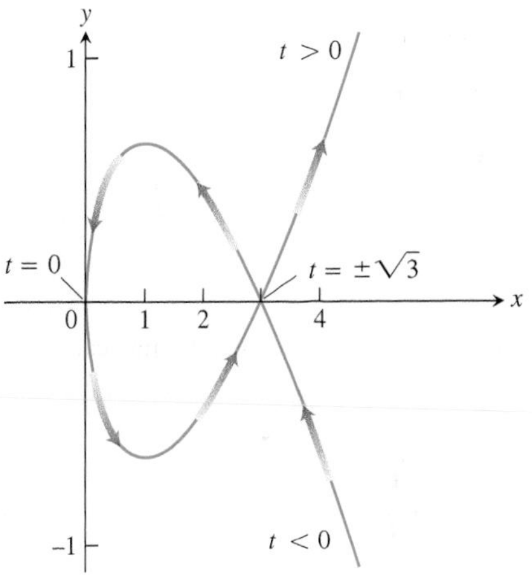

Surface Areas

Find the areas of the surfaces generated by revolving the curves in Exercises 21 and 22 about the indicated axes.

21. $x = t^2/2, \quad y = 2t, \quad 0 \le t \le \sqrt{5}$; x-axis

22. $x = t^2 + 1/(2t), \quad y = 4\sqrt{t}, \quad 1/\sqrt{2} \le t \le 1$; y-axis

Polar to Cartesian Equations

Sketch the lines in Exercises 23–28. Also, find a Cartesian equation for each line.

23. $r\cos\left(\theta + \dfrac{\pi}{3}\right) = 2\sqrt{3}$ **24.** $r\cos\left(\theta - \dfrac{3\pi}{4}\right) = \dfrac{\sqrt{2}}{2}$

25. $r = 2\sec\theta$ **26.** $r = -\sqrt{2}\sec\theta$

27. $r = -(3/2)\csc\theta$ **28.** $r = \left(3\sqrt{3}\right)\csc\theta$

Find Cartesian equations for the circles in Exercises 29–32. Sketch each circle in the coordinate plane and label it with both its Cartesian and polar equations.

29. $r = -4\sin\theta$ **30.** $r = 3\sqrt{3}\sin\theta$

31. $r = 2\sqrt{2}\cos\theta$ **32.** $r = -6\cos\theta$

Cartesian to Polar Equations

Find polar equations for the circles in Exercises 33–36. Sketch each circle in the coordinate plane and label it with both its Cartesian and polar equations.

33. $x^2 + y^2 + 5y = 0$ **34.** $x^2 + y^2 - 2y = 0$

35. $x^2 + y^2 - 3x = 0$ **36.** $x^2 + y^2 + 4x = 0$

Graphs in Polar Coordinates

Sketch the regions defined by the polar coordinate inequalities in Exercises 37 and 38.

37. $0 \le r \le 6 \cos \theta$ **38.** $-4 \sin \theta \le r \le 0$

Match each graph in Exercises 39–46 with the appropriate equation (a)–(l). There are more equations than graphs, so some equations will not be matched.

a. $r = \cos 2\theta$ **b.** $r \cos \theta = 1$ **c.** $r = \dfrac{6}{1 - 2\cos\theta}$

d. $r = \sin 2\theta$ **e.** $r = \theta$ **f.** $r^2 = \cos 2\theta$

g. $r = 1 + \cos\theta$ **h.** $r = 1 - \sin\theta$ **i.** $r = \dfrac{2}{1 - \cos\theta}$

j. $r^2 = \sin 2\theta$ **k.** $r = -\sin\theta$ **l.** $r = 2\cos\theta + 1$

39. Four-leaved rose

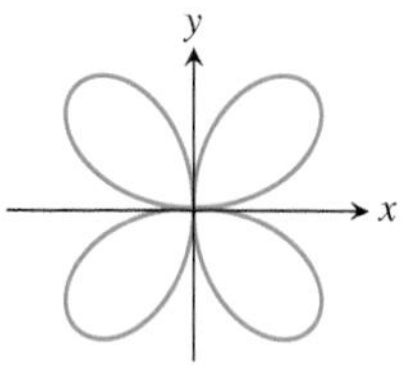

40. Spiral

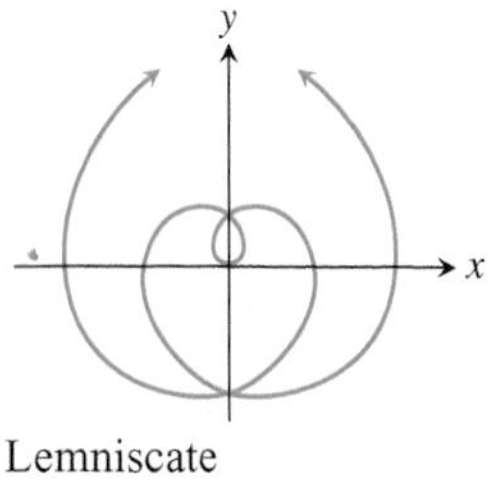

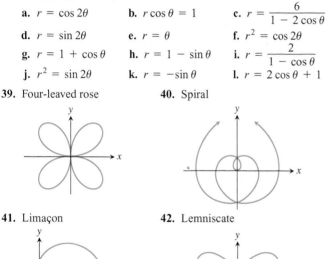

41. Limaçon

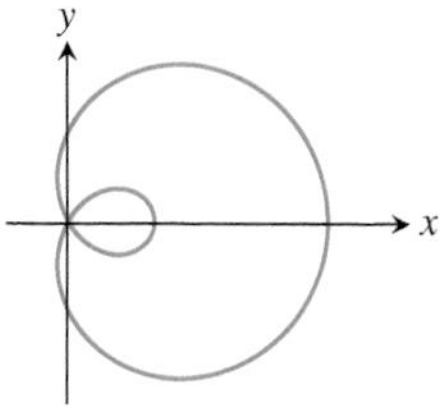

42. Lemniscate

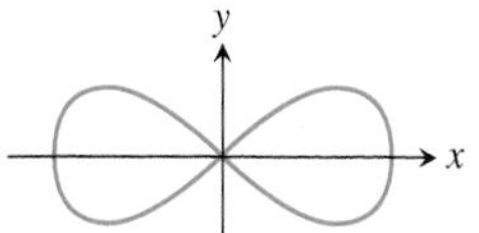

43. Circle

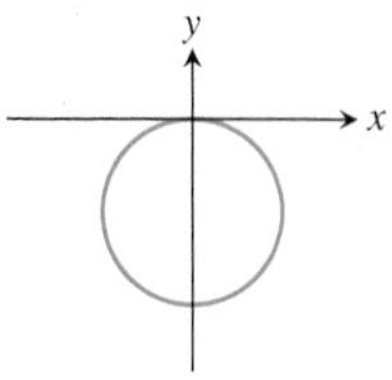

44. Cardioid

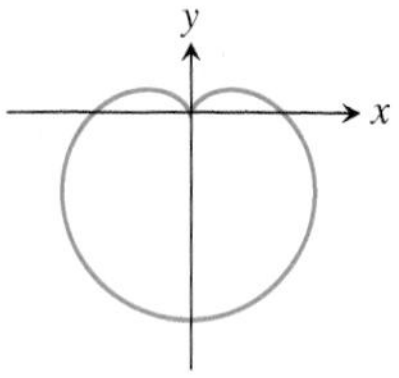

45. Parabola

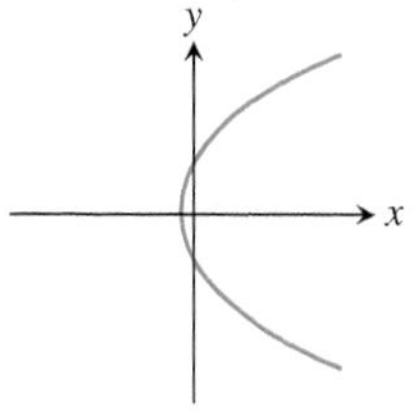

46. Lemniscate

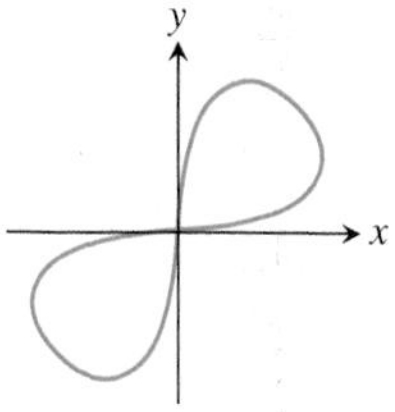

Area in Polar Coordinates

Find the areas of the regions in the polar coordinate plane described in Exercises 47–50.

47. Enclosed by the limaçon $r = 2 - \cos\theta$

48. Enclosed by one leaf of the three-leaved rose $r = \sin 3\theta$

49. Inside the "figure eight" $r = 1 + \cos 2\theta$ and outside the circle $r = 1$

50. Inside the cardioid $r = 2(1 + \sin\theta)$ and outside the circle $r = 2\sin\theta$

Length in Polar Coordinates

Find the lengths of the curves given by the polar coordinate equations in Exercises 51–54.

51. $r = -1 + \cos\theta$

52. $r = 2\sin\theta + 2\cos\theta, \quad 0 \le \theta \le \pi/2$

53. $r = 8\sin^3(\theta/3), \quad 0 \le \theta \le \pi/4$

54. $r = \sqrt{1 + \cos 2\theta}, \quad -\pi/2 \le \theta \le \pi/2$

Conics in Polar Coordinates

Sketch the conic sections whose polar coordinate equations are given in Exercises 55–58. Give polar coordinates for the vertices and, in the case of ellipses, for the centers as well.

55. $r = \dfrac{2}{1 + \cos\theta}$ **56.** $r = \dfrac{8}{2 + \cos\theta}$

57. $r = \dfrac{6}{1 - 2\cos\theta}$ **58.** $r = \dfrac{12}{3 + \sin\theta}$

Exercises 59–62 give the eccentricities of conic sections with one focus at the origin of the polar coordinate plane, along with the directrix for that focus. Find a polar equation for each conic section.

59. $e = 2, \quad r\cos\theta = 2$ **60.** $e = 1, \quad r\cos\theta = -4$

61. $e = 1/2, \quad r\sin\theta = 2$ **62.** $e = 1/3, \quad r\sin\theta = -6$

Chapter Additional and Advanced Exercises

Polar Coordinates

1. a. Find an equation in polar coordinates for the curve

$$x = e^{2t}\cos t, \quad y = e^{2t}\sin t; \quad -\infty < t < \infty.$$

b. Find the length of the curve from $t = 0$ to $t = 2\pi$.

2. Find the length of the curve $r = 2\sin^3(\theta/3), 0 \le \theta \le 3\pi$, in the polar coordinate plane.

Exercises 3–6 give the eccentricities of conic sections with one focus at the origin of the polar coordinate plane, along with the directrix for that focus. Find a polar equation for each conic section.

3. $e = 2, \quad r\cos\theta = 2$ **4.** $e = 1, \quad r\cos\theta = -4$

5. $e = 1/2, \quad r\sin\theta = 2$ **6.** $e = 1/3, \quad r\sin\theta = -6$

Theory and Examples

7. **Epicycloids** When a circle rolls externally along the circumference of a second, fixed circle, any point P on the circumference of the rolling circle describes an *epicycloid*, as shown here. Let the fixed circle have its center at the origin O and have radius a.

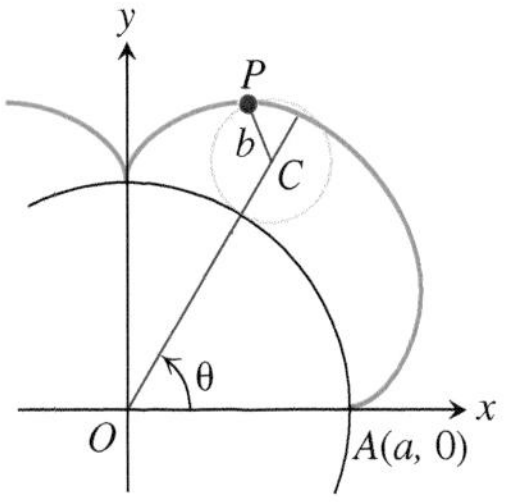

Let the radius of the rolling circle be b and let the initial position of the tracing point P be $A(a, 0)$. Find parametric equations for the epicycloid, using as the parameter the angle θ from the positive x-axis to the line through the circles' centers.

8. Find the centroid of the region enclosed by the x-axis and the cycloid arch

$$x = a(t - \sin t), \quad y = a(1 - \cos t); \quad 0 \le t \le 2\pi.$$

The Angle Between the Radius Vector and the Tangent Line to a Polar Coordinate Curve In Cartesian coordinates, when we want to discuss the direction of a curve at a point, we use the angle ϕ measured counterclockwise from the positive x-axis to the tangent line. In polar coordinates, it is more convenient to calculate the angle ψ from the *radius vector* to the tangent line (see the accompanying figure). The angle ϕ can then be calculated from the relation

$$\phi = \theta + \psi, \tag{1}$$

which comes from applying the Exterior Angle Theorem to the triangle in the accompanying figure.

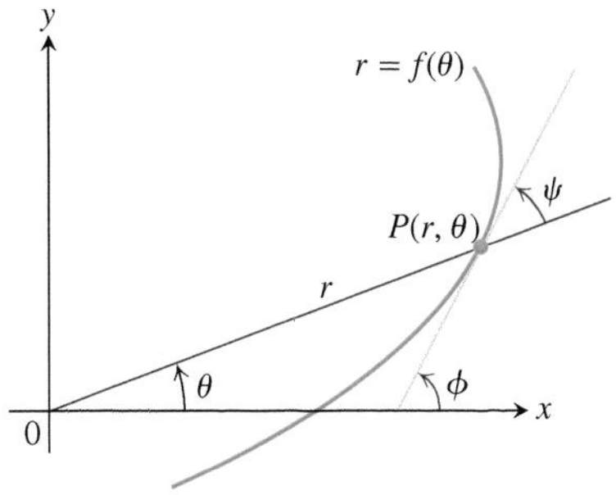

Suppose the equation of the curve is given in the form $r = f(\theta)$, where $f(\theta)$ is a differentiable function of θ. Then

$$x = r\cos\theta \quad \text{and} \quad y = r\sin\theta \tag{2}$$

are differentiable functions of θ with

$$\frac{dx}{d\theta} = -r\sin\theta + \cos\theta\frac{dr}{d\theta},$$

$$\frac{dy}{d\theta} = r\cos\theta + \sin\theta\frac{dr}{d\theta}. \tag{3}$$

Since $\psi = \phi - \theta$ from (1),

$$\tan\psi = \tan(\phi - \theta) = \frac{\tan\phi - \tan\theta}{1 + \tan\phi\tan\theta}.$$

Furthermore,

$$\tan\phi = \frac{dy}{dx} = \frac{dy/d\theta}{dx/d\theta}$$

because $\tan\phi$ is the slope of the curve at P. Also,

$$\tan\theta = \frac{y}{x}.$$

Hence

$$\tan\psi = \frac{\dfrac{dy/d\theta}{dx/d\theta} - \dfrac{y}{x}}{1 + \dfrac{y}{x}\dfrac{dy/d\theta}{dx/d\theta}} = \frac{x\dfrac{dy}{d\theta} - y\dfrac{dx}{d\theta}}{x\dfrac{dx}{d\theta} + y\dfrac{dy}{d\theta}}. \tag{4}$$

9. From Equations (2), (3), and (4), show that

$$\tan\psi = \frac{r}{dr/d\theta}. \tag{5}$$

This is the equation we use for finding ψ as a function of θ.

10. Find the value of $\tan\psi$ for the curve $r = \sin^4(\theta/4)$.

11. Find the angle between the radius vector to the curve $r = 2a\sin 3\theta$ and its tangent when $\theta = \pi/6$.

T 12. **a.** Graph the hyperbolic spiral $r\theta = 1$. What appears to happen to ψ as the spiral winds in around the origin?

b. Confirm your finding in part (a) analytically.

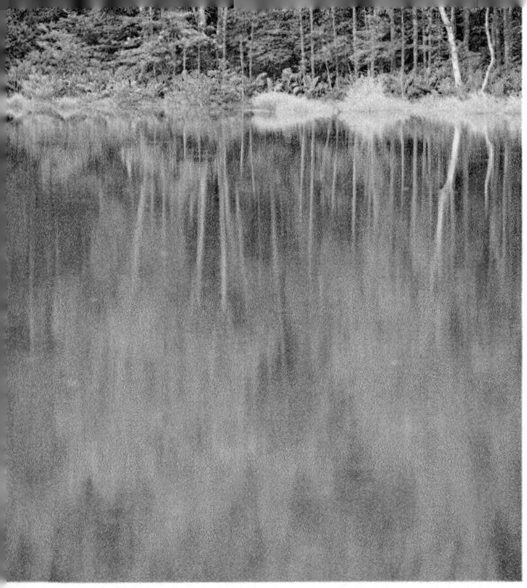

APPENDICES

A.1 Real Numbers and the Real Line

This section reviews real numbers, inequalities, intervals, and absolute values.

Real Numbers

Much of calculus is based on properties of the real number system. **Real numbers** are numbers that can be expressed as decimals, such as

$$-\frac{3}{4} = -0.75000\ldots$$
$$\frac{1}{3} = 0.33333\ldots$$
$$\sqrt{2} = 1.4142\ldots$$

The dots ... in each case indicate that the sequence of decimal digits goes on forever. Every conceivable decimal expansion represents a real number, although some numbers have two representations. For instance, the infinite decimals .999... and 1.000... represent the same real number 1. A similar statement holds for any number with an infinite tail of 9's.

The real numbers can be represented geometrically as points on a number line called the **real line**.

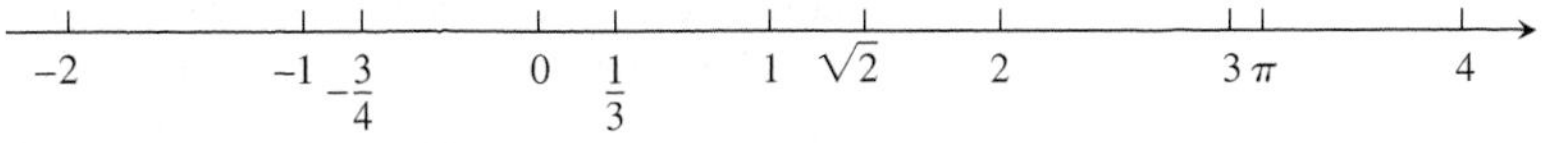

The symbol $\mathbb{R}$ denotes either the real number system or, equivalently, the real line.

The properties of the real number system fall into three categories: algebraic properties, order properties, and completeness. The **algebraic properties** say that the real numbers can be added, subtracted, multiplied, and divided (except by 0) to produce more real numbers under the usual rules of arithmetic. *You can never divide by* 0.

The **order properties** of real numbers are given in Appendix 7. The useful rules at the left can be derived from them, where the symbol $\Rightarrow$ means "implies."

Rules for inequalities

If a, b, and c are real numbers, then:

1. $a < b \Rightarrow a + c < b + c$

2. $a < b \Rightarrow a - c < b - c$

3. $a < b$ and $c > 0 \Rightarrow ac < bc$

4. $a < b$ and $c < 0 \Rightarrow bc < ac$
Special case: $a < b \Rightarrow -b < -a$

5. $a > 0 \Rightarrow \frac{1}{a} > 0$

6. If a and b are both positive or both negative, then $a < b \Rightarrow \frac{1}{b} < \frac{1}{a}$

Notice the rules for multiplying an inequality by a number. Multiplying by a positive number preserves the inequality; multiplying by a negative number reverses the inequality. Also, reciprocation reverses the inequality for numbers of the same sign. For example, $2 < 5$ but $-2 > -5$ and $1/2 > 1/5$.

The **completeness property** of the real number system is deeper and harder to define precisely. However, the property is essential to the idea of a limit (Chapter 2). Roughly speaking, it says that there are enough real numbers to "complete" the real number line, in the sense that there are no "holes" or "gaps" in it. Many theorems of calculus would fail if the real number system were not complete. The topic is best saved for a more advanced course, but Appendix 7 hints about what is involved and how the real numbers are constructed.

We distinguish three special subsets of real numbers.

1. The **natural numbers**, namely 1, 2, 3, 4, ...
2. The **integers**, namely $0, \pm 1, \pm 2, \pm 3, \ldots$
3. The **rational numbers**, namely the numbers that can be expressed in the form of a fraction m/n, where m and n are integers and $n \neq 0$. Examples are

$$\frac{1}{3}, \quad -\frac{4}{9} = \frac{-4}{9} = \frac{4}{-9}, \quad \frac{200}{13}, \qquad \text{and} \qquad 57 = \frac{57}{1}.$$

The rational numbers are precisely the real numbers with decimal expansions that are either

(a) terminating (ending in an infinite string of zeros), for example,

$$\frac{3}{4} = 0.75000\ldots = 0.75 \qquad \text{or}$$

(b) eventually repeating (ending with a block of digits that repeats over and over), for example,

$$\frac{23}{11} = 2.090909\ldots = 2.\overline{09}$$

The bar indicates the block of repeating digits.

A terminating decimal expansion is a special type of repeating decimal, since the ending zeros repeat.

The set of rational numbers has all the algebraic and order properties of the real numbers but lacks the completeness property. For example, there is no rational number whose square is 2; there is a "hole" in the rational line where $\sqrt{2}$ should be.

Real numbers that are not rational are called **irrational numbers**. They are characterized by having nonterminating and nonrepeating decimal expansions. Examples are π, $\sqrt{2}$, $\sqrt[3]{5}$, and $\log_{10} 3$. Since every decimal expansion represents a real number, it should be clear that there are infinitely many irrational numbers. Both rational and irrational numbers are found arbitrarily close to any point on the real line.

Set notation is very useful for specifying a particular subset of real numbers. A **set** is a collection of objects, and these objects are the **elements** of the set. If S is a set, the notation $a \in S$ means that a is an element of S, and $a \notin S$ means that a is not an element of S. If S and T are sets, then $S \cup T$ is their **union** and consists of all elements belonging either to S or T (or to both S and T). The **intersection** $S \cap T$ consists of all elements belonging to both S and T. The **empty set** $\emptyset$ is the set that contains no elements. For example, the intersection of the rational numbers and the irrational numbers is the empty set.

Some sets can be described by *listing* their elements in braces. For instance, the set A consisting of the natural numbers (or positive integers) less than 6 can be expressed as

$$A = \{1, 2, 3, 4, 5\}.$$

The entire set of integers is written as

$$\{0, \pm 1, \pm 2, \pm 3, \ldots\}.$$

Another way to describe a set is to enclose in braces a rule that generates all the elements of the set. For instance, the set

$$A = \{x \mid x \text{ is an integer and } 0 < x < 6\}$$

is the set of positive integers less than 6.

Intervals

A subset of the real line is called an **interval** if it contains at least two numbers and contains all the real numbers lying between any two of its elements. For example, the set of all real numbers x such that $x > 6$ is an interval, as is the set of all x such that $-2 \leq x \leq 5$. The set of all nonzero real numbers is not an interval; since 0 is absent, the set fails to contain every real number between -1 and 1 (for example).

Geometrically, intervals correspond to rays and line segments on the real line, along with the real line itself. Intervals of numbers corresponding to line segments are **finite intervals**; intervals corresponding to rays and the real line are **infinite intervals**.

A finite interval is said to be **closed** if it contains both of its endpoints, **half-open** if it contains one endpoint but not the other, and **open** if it contains neither endpoint. The endpoints are also called **boundary points**; they make up the interval's **boundary**. The remaining points of the interval are **interior points** and together comprise the interval's **interior**. Infinite intervals are closed if they contain a finite endpoint, and open otherwise. The entire real line $\mathbb{R}$ is an infinite interval that is both open and closed. Table A.1 summarizes the various types of intervals.

TABLE A.1 Types of intervals

Notation	Set description	Type	Picture
(a, b)	$\{x \mid a < x < b\}$	Open	
$[a, b]$	$\{x \mid a \leq x \leq b\}$	Closed	
$[a, b)$	$\{x \mid a \leq x < b\}$	Half-open	
$(a, b]$	$\{x \mid a < x \leq b\}$	Half-open	
(a, ∞)	$\{x \mid x > a\}$	Open	
$[a, \infty)$	$\{x \mid x \geq a\}$	Closed	
$(-\infty, b)$	$\{x \mid x < b\}$	Open	
$(-\infty, b]$	$\{x \mid x \leq b\}$	Closed	
$(-\infty, \infty)$	$\mathbb{R}$ (set of all real numbers)	Both open and closed	

Solving Inequalities

The process of finding the interval or intervals of numbers that satisfy an inequality in x is called **solving** the inequality.

EXAMPLE 1 Solve the following inequalities and show their solution sets on the real line.

(a) $2x - 1 < x + 3$ **(b)** $-\frac{x}{3} < 2x + 1$ **(c)** $\frac{6}{x - 1} \geq 5$

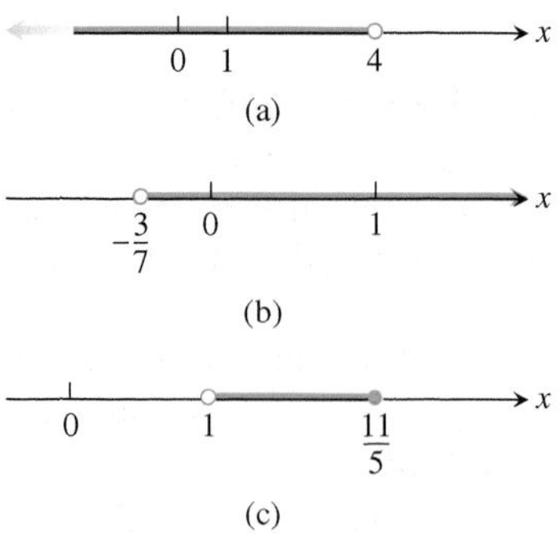

FIGURE A.1 Solution sets for the inequalities in Example 1.

Solution

(a)

$$2x - 1 < x + 3$$
$$2x < x + 4 \quad \text{Add 1 to both sides.}$$
$$x < 4 \quad \text{Subtract } x \text{ from both sides.}$$

The solution set is the open interval $(-\infty, 4)$ (Figure A.1a).

(b)

$$-\frac{x}{3} < 2x + 1$$
$$-x < 6x + 3 \quad \text{Multiply both sides by 3.}$$
$$0 < 7x + 3 \quad \text{Add } x \text{ to both sides.}$$
$$-3 < 7x \quad \text{Subtract 3 from both sides.}$$
$$-\frac{3}{7} < x \quad \text{Divide by 7.}$$

The solution set is the open interval $(-3/7, \infty)$ (Figure A.1b).

(c) The inequality $6/(x - 1) \geq 5$ can hold only if $x > 1$, because otherwise $6/(x - 1)$ is undefined or negative. Therefore, $(x - 1)$ is positive and the inequality will be preserved if we multiply both sides by $(x - 1)$, and we have

$$\frac{6}{x - 1} \geq 5$$
$$6 \geq 5x - 5 \quad \text{Multiply both sides by } (x - 1).$$
$$11 \geq 5x \quad \text{Add 5 to both sides.}$$
$$\frac{11}{5} \geq x. \quad \text{Or } x \leq \frac{11}{5}.$$

The solution set is the half-open interval $(1, 11/5]$ (Figure A.1c). ■

Absolute Value

The **absolute value** of a number x, denoted by $|x|$, is defined by the formula

$$|x| = \begin{cases} x, & x \geq 0 \\ -x, & x < 0. \end{cases}$$

EXAMPLE 2 $|3| = 3, \quad |0| = 0, \quad |-5| = -(-5) = 5, \quad |-|a|| = |a|$ ■

Geometrically, the absolute value of x is the distance from x to 0 on the real number line. Since distances are always positive or 0, we see that $|x| \geq 0$ for every real number x, and $|x| = 0$ if and only if $x = 0$. Also,

$$|x - y| = \text{the distance between } x \text{ and } y$$

on the real line (Figure A.2).

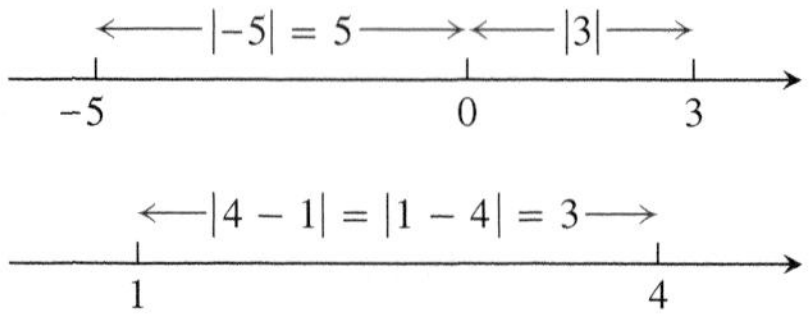

FIGURE A.2 Absolute values give distances between points on the number line.

Since the symbol $\sqrt{a}$ always denotes the *nonnegative* square root of a, an alternate definition of $|x|$ is

$$|x| = \sqrt{x^2}.$$

It is important to remember that $\sqrt{a^2} = |a|$. Do not write $\sqrt{a^2} = a$ unless you already know that $a \geq 0$.

The absolute value has the following properties. (You are asked to prove these properties in the exercises.)

Absolute Value Properties

1. $\lvert -a \rvert = \lvert a \rvert$	A number and its additive inverse or negative have the same absolute value.
2. $\lvert ab \rvert = \lvert a \rvert \lvert b \rvert$	The absolute value of a product is the product of the absolute values.
3. $\left\lvert \frac{a}{b} \right\rvert = \frac{\lvert a \rvert}{\lvert b \rvert}$	The absolute value of a quotient is the quotient of the absolute values.
4. $\lvert a + b \rvert \le \lvert a \rvert + \lvert b \rvert$	The **triangle inequality**. The absolute value of the sum of two numbers is less than or equal to the sum of their absolute values.

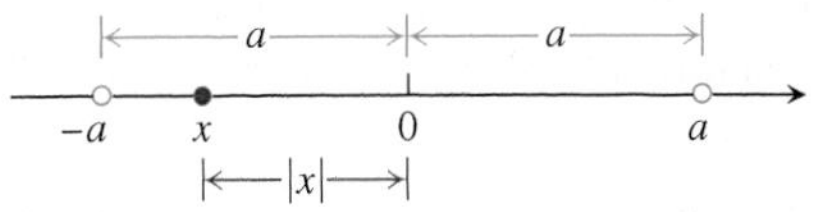

FIGURE A.3 $\lvert x \rvert < a$ means x lies between $-a$ and a.

Absolute values and intervals

If a is any positive number, then

5. $\lvert x \rvert = a$	$\Leftrightarrow$	$x = \pm a$
6. $\lvert x \rvert < a$	$\Leftrightarrow$	$-a < x < a$
7. $\lvert x \rvert > a$	$\Leftrightarrow$	$x > a$ or $x < -a$
8. $\lvert x \rvert \le a$	$\Leftrightarrow$	$-a \le x \le a$
9. $\lvert x \rvert \ge a$	$\Leftrightarrow$	$x \ge a$ or $x \le -a$

Note that $\lvert -a \rvert \ne -\lvert a \rvert$. For example, $\lvert -3 \rvert = 3$, whereas $-\lvert 3 \rvert = -3$. If a and b differ in sign, then $\lvert a + b \rvert$ is less than $\lvert a \rvert + \lvert b \rvert$. In all other cases, $\lvert a + b \rvert$ equals $\lvert a \rvert + \lvert b \rvert$. Absolute value bars in expressions like $\lvert -3 + 5 \rvert$ work like parentheses: We do the arithmetic inside *before* taking the absolute value.

EXAMPLE 3

$$\lvert -3 + 5 \rvert = \lvert 2 \rvert = 2 < \lvert -3 \rvert + \lvert 5 \rvert = 8$$
$$\lvert 3 + 5 \rvert = \lvert 8 \rvert = \lvert 3 \rvert + \lvert 5 \rvert$$
$$\lvert -3 - 5 \rvert = \lvert -8 \rvert = 8 = \lvert -3 \rvert + \lvert -5 \rvert \qquad \blacksquare$$

The inequality $\lvert x \rvert < a$ says that the distance from x to 0 is less than the positive number a. This means that x must lie between $-a$ and a, as we can see from Figure A.3.

The statements in the table are all consequences of the definition of absolute value and are often helpful when solving equations or inequalities involving absolute values.

The symbol $\Leftrightarrow$ is often used by mathematicians to denote the "if and only if" logical relationship. It also means "implies and is implied by."

EXAMPLE 4 Solve the equation $\lvert 2x - 3 \rvert = 7$.

Solution By Property 5, $2x - 3 = \pm 7$, so there are two possibilities:

$$2x - 3 = 7 \qquad 2x - 3 = -7 \qquad \text{Equivalent equations without absolute values}$$
$$2x = 10 \qquad 2x = -4 \qquad \text{Solve as usual.}$$
$$x = 5 \qquad x = -2$$

The solutions of $\lvert 2x - 3 \rvert = 7$ are $x = 5$ and $x = -2$. ■

EXAMPLE 5 Solve the inequality $\left\lvert 5 - \frac{2}{x} \right\rvert < 1$.

Solution We have

$$\left\lvert 5 - \frac{2}{x} \right\rvert < 1 \Leftrightarrow -1 < 5 - \frac{2}{x} < 1 \qquad \text{Property 6}$$
$$\Leftrightarrow -6 < -\frac{2}{x} < -4 \qquad \text{Subtract 5.}$$
$$\Leftrightarrow 3 > \frac{1}{x} > 2 \qquad \text{Multiply by } -\frac{1}{2}.$$
$$\Leftrightarrow \frac{1}{3} < x < \frac{1}{2}. \qquad \text{Take reciprocals.}$$

Notice how the various rules for inequalities were used here. Multiplying by a negative number reverses the inequality. So does taking reciprocals in an inequality in which both sides are positive. The original inequality holds if and only if $(1/3) < x < (1/2)$. The solution set is the open interval $(1/3, 1/2)$. ■

Exercises A.1

1. Express $1/9$ as a repeating decimal, using a bar to indicate the repeating digits. What are the decimal representations of $2/9$? $3/9$? $8/9$? $9/9$?

2. If $2 < x < 6$, which of the following statements about x are necessarily true, and which are not necessarily true?

   a. $0 < x < 4$ **b.** $0 < x - 2 < 4$

   c. $1 < \frac{x}{2} < 3$ **d.** $\frac{1}{6} < \frac{1}{x} < \frac{1}{2}$

   e. $1 < \frac{6}{x} < 3$ **f.** $|x - 4| < 2$

   g. $-6 < -x < 2$ **h.** $-6 < -x < -2$

In Exercises 3–6, solve the inequalities and show the solution sets on the real line.

3. $-2x > 4$
4. $5x - 3 \leq 7 - 3x$
5. $2x - \frac{1}{2} \geq 7x + \frac{7}{6}$
6. $\frac{4}{5}(x - 2) < \frac{1}{3}(x - 6)$

Solve the equations in Exercises 7–9.

7. $|y| = 3$
8. $|2t + 5| = 4$
9. $|8 - 3s| = \frac{9}{2}$

Solve the inequalities in Exercises 10–17, expressing the solution sets as intervals or unions of intervals. Also, show each solution set on the real line.

10. $|x| < 2$
11. $|t - 1| \leq 3$
12. $|3y - 7| < 4$
13. $\left|\frac{z}{5} - 1\right| \leq 1$
14. $\left|3 - \frac{1}{x}\right| < \frac{1}{2}$
15. $|2s| \geq 4$
16. $|1 - x| > 1$
17. $\left|\frac{r + 1}{2}\right| \geq 1$

Solve the inequalities in Exercises 18–21. Express the solution sets as intervals or unions of intervals and show them on the real line. Use the result $\sqrt{a^2} = |a|$ as appropriate.

18. $x^2 < 2$
19. $4 < x^2 < 9$
20. $(x - 1)^2 < 4$
21. $x^2 - x < 0$
22. Do not fall into the trap of thinking $|-a| = a$. For what real numbers a is this equation true? For what real numbers is it false?
23. Solve the equation $|x - 1| = 1 - x$.
24. **A proof of the triangle inequality** Give the reason justifying each of the numbered steps in the following proof of the triangle inequality.

$$
\begin{aligned}
|a + b|^2 &= (a + b)^2 && (1)\\
&= a^2 + 2ab + b^2 &&\\
&\leq a^2 + 2|a||b| + b^2 && (2)\\
&= |a|^2 + 2|a||b| + |b|^2 && (3)\\
&= (|a| + |b|)^2 &&\\
|a + b| &\leq |a| + |b| && (4)
\end{aligned}
$$

25. Prove that $|ab| = |a||b|$ for any numbers a and b.
26. If $|x| \leq 3$ and $x > -1/2$, what can you say about x?
27. Graph the inequality $|x| + |y| \leq 1$.
28. For any number a, prove that $|-a| = |a|$.
29. Let a be any positive number. Prove that $|x| > a$ if and only if $x > a$ or $x < -a$.
30. **a.** If b is any nonzero real number, prove that $|1/b| = 1/|b|$.

    b. Prove that $\left|\frac{a}{b}\right| = \frac{|a|}{|b|}$ for any numbers a and $b \neq 0$.

A.2 Mathematical Induction

Many formulas, like

$$1 + 2 + \cdots + n = \frac{n(n + 1)}{2},$$

can be shown to hold for every positive integer n by applying an axiom called the *mathematical induction principle.* A proof that uses this axiom is called a *proof by mathematical induction* or a *proof by induction.*

The steps in proving a formula by induction are the following:

1. Check that the formula holds for $n = 1$.
2. Prove that if the formula holds for any positive integer $n = k$, then it also holds for the next integer, $n = k + 1$.

The induction axiom says that once these steps are completed, the formula holds for all positive integers n. By Step 1 it holds for $n = 1$. By Step 2 it holds for $n = 2$, and therefore by Step 2 also for $n = 3$, and by Step 2 again for $n = 4$, and so on. If the first domino falls, and the kth domino always knocks over the $(k + 1)$st when it falls, all the dominoes fall.

From another point of view, suppose we have a sequence of statements S_1, $S_2, \ldots, S_n, \ldots$, one for each positive integer. Suppose we can show that assuming any one of the statements to be true implies that the next statement in line is true. Suppose that we can also show that S_1 is true. Then we may conclude that the statements are true from S_1 on.

EXAMPLE 1 Use mathematical induction to prove that for every positive integer n,

$$1 + 2 + \cdots + n = \frac{n(n + 1)}{2}.$$

Solution We accomplish the proof by carrying out the two steps above.

1. The formula holds for $n = 1$ because

$$1 = \frac{1(1 + 1)}{2}.$$

2. If the formula holds for $n = k$, does it also hold for $n = k + 1$? The answer is yes, as we now show. If

$$1 + 2 + \cdots + k = \frac{k(k + 1)}{2},$$

then

$$\begin{aligned} 1 + 2 + \cdots + k + (k + 1) &= \frac{k(k + 1)}{2} + (k + 1) = \frac{k^2 + k + 2k + 2}{2} \\ &= \frac{(k + 1)(k + 2)}{2} = \frac{(k + 1)((k + 1) + 1)}{2}. \end{aligned}$$

The last expression in this string of equalities is the expression $n(n + 1)/2$ for $n = (k + 1)$.

The mathematical induction principle now guarantees the original formula for all positive integers n. ■

In Example 4 of Section 5.2 we gave another proof for the formula giving the sum of the first n integers. However, proof by mathematical induction is more general. It can be used to find the sums of the squares and cubes of the first n integers (Exercises 9 and 10). Here is another example.

EXAMPLE 2 Show by mathematical induction that for all positive integers n,

$$\frac{1}{2^1} + \frac{1}{2^2} + \cdots + \frac{1}{2^n} = 1 - \frac{1}{2^n}.$$

Solution We accomplish the proof by carrying out the two steps of mathematical induction.

1. The formula holds for $n = 1$ because

$$\frac{1}{2^1} = 1 - \frac{1}{2^1}.$$

2. If

$$\frac{1}{2^1} + \frac{1}{2^2} + \cdots + \frac{1}{2^k} = 1 - \frac{1}{2^k},$$

then

$$\frac{1}{2^1} + \frac{1}{2^2} + \cdots + \frac{1}{2^k} + \frac{1}{2^{k+1}} = 1 - \frac{1}{2^k} + \frac{1}{2^{k+1}} = 1 - \frac{1 \cdot 2}{2^k \cdot 2} + \frac{1}{2^{k+1}}$$

$$= 1 - \frac{2}{2^{k+1}} + \frac{1}{2^{k+1}} = 1 - \frac{1}{2^{k+1}}.$$

Thus, the original formula holds for $n = (k + 1)$ whenever it holds for $n = k$.

With these steps verified, the mathematical induction principle now guarantees the formula for every positive integer n. ■

Other Starting Integers

Instead of starting at $n = 1$ some induction arguments start at another integer. The steps for such an argument are as follows.

1. Check that the formula holds for $n = n_1$ (the first appropriate integer).
2. Prove that if the formula holds for any integer $n = k \geq n_1$, then it also holds for $n = (k + 1)$.

Once these steps are completed, the mathematical induction principle guarantees the formula for all $n \geq n_1$.

EXAMPLE 3 Show that $n! > 3^n$ if n is large enough.

Solution How large is large enough? We experiment:

n	1	2	3	4	5	6	7
$n!$	1	2	6	24	120	720	5040
3^n	3	9	27	81	243	729	2187

It looks as if $n! > 3^n$ for $n \geq 7$. To be sure, we apply mathematical induction. We take $n_1 = 7$ in Step 1 and complete Step 2.

Suppose $k! > 3^k$ for some $k \geq 7$. Then

$$(k + 1)! = (k + 1)(k!) > (k + 1)3^k > 7 \cdot 3^k > 3^{k+1}.$$

Thus, for $k \geq 7$,

$$k! > 3^k \quad \text{implies} \quad (k + 1)! > 3^{k+1}.$$

The mathematical induction principle now guarantees $n! \geq 3^n$ for all $n \geq 7$. ■

Proof of the Derivative Sum Rule for Sums of Finitely Many Functions

We prove the statement

$$\frac{d}{dx}(u_1 + u_2 + \cdots + u_n) = \frac{du_1}{dx} + \frac{du_2}{dx} + \cdots + \frac{du_n}{dx}$$

by mathematical induction. The statement is true for $n = 2$, as was proved in Section 3.3. This is Step 1 of the induction proof.

Step 2 is to show that if the statement is true for any positive integer $n = k$, where $k \geq n_0 = 2$, then it is also true for $n = k + 1$. So suppose that

$$\frac{d}{dx}(u_1 + u_2 + \cdots + u_k) = \frac{du_1}{dx} + \frac{du_2}{dx} + \cdots + \frac{du_k}{dx}. \quad (1)$$

Then

$$\frac{d}{dx}(\underbrace{u_1 + u_2 + \cdots + u_k}_{\text{Call the function defined by this sum } u.} + \underbrace{u_{k+1}}_{\text{Call this function } v.})$$

$$= \frac{d}{dx}(u_1 + u_2 + \cdots + u_k) + \frac{du_{k+1}}{dx} \qquad \text{Sum Rule for } \frac{d}{dx}(u + v)$$

$$= \frac{du_1}{dx} + \frac{du_2}{dx} + \cdots + \frac{du_k}{dx} + \frac{du_{k+1}}{dx}. \qquad \text{Eq. (1)}$$

With these steps verified, the mathematical induction principle now guarantees the Sum Rule for every integer $n \geq 2$.

Exercises A.2

1. Assuming that the triangle inequality $|a + b| \leq |a| + |b|$ holds for any two numbers a and b, show that

$$|x_1 + x_2 + \cdots + x_n| \leq |x_1| + |x_2| + \cdots + |x_n|$$

for any n numbers.

2. Show that if $r \neq 1$, then

$$1 + r + r^2 + \cdots + r^n = \frac{1 - r^{n+1}}{1 - r}$$

for every positive integer n.

3. Use the Product Rule, $\frac{d}{dx}(uv) = u\frac{dv}{dx} + v\frac{du}{dx}$, and the fact that $\frac{d}{dx}(x) = 1$ to show that $\frac{d}{dx}(x^n) = nx^{n-1}$ for every positive integer n.

4. Suppose that a function $f(x)$ has the property that $f(x_1x_2) = f(x_1) + f(x_2)$ for any two positive numbers x_1 and x_2. Show that

$$f(x_1x_2\cdots x_n) = f(x_1) + f(x_2) + \cdots + f(x_n)$$

for the product of any n positive numbers $x_1, x_2, \ldots, x_n$.

5. Show that

$$\frac{2}{3^1} + \frac{2}{3^2} + \cdots + \frac{2}{3^n} = 1 - \frac{1}{3^n}$$

for all positive integers n.

6. Show that $n! > n^3$ if n is large enough.

7. Show that $2^n > n^2$ if n is large enough.

8. Show that $2^n \geq 1/8$ for $n \geq -3$.

9. **Sums of squares** Show that the sum of the squares of the first n positive integers is

$$\frac{n\left(n + \frac{1}{2}\right)(n + 1)}{3}.$$

10. **Sums of cubes** Show that the sum of the cubes of the first n positive integers is $(n(n + 1)/2)^2$.

11. **Rules for finite sums** Show that the following finite sum rules hold for every positive integer n. (See Section 5.2.)

    a. $\sum_{k=1}^{n}(a_k + b_k) = \sum_{k=1}^{n} a_k + \sum_{k=1}^{n} b_k$

    b. $\sum_{k=1}^{n}(a_k - b_k) = \sum_{k=1}^{n} a_k - \sum_{k=1}^{n} b_k$

    c. $\sum_{k=1}^{n} ca_k = c \cdot \sum_{k=1}^{n} a_k$ (any number c)

    d. $\sum_{k=1}^{n} a_k = n \cdot c$ (if a_k has the constant value c)

12. Show that $|x^n| = |x|^n$ for every positive integer n and every real number x.

A.3 Lines, Circles, and Parabolas

This section reviews coordinates, lines, distance, circles, and parabolas in the plane. The notion of increment is also discussed.

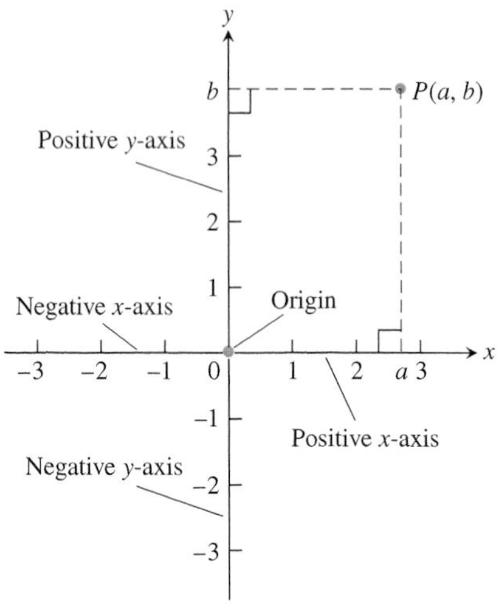

FIGURE A.4 Cartesian coordinates in the plane are based on two perpendicular axes intersecting at the origin.

HISTORICAL BIOGRAPHY

René Descartes
(1596–1650)

Cartesian Coordinates in the Plane

In Appendix 1 we identified the points on the line with real numbers by assigning them coordinates. Points in the plane can be identified with ordered pairs of real numbers. To begin, we draw two perpendicular coordinate lines that intersect at the 0-point of each line. These lines are called **coordinate axes** in the plane. On the horizontal x-axis, numbers are denoted by x and increase to the right. On the vertical y-axis, numbers are denoted by y and increase upward (Figure A.4). Thus "upward" and "to the right" are positive directions, whereas "downward" and "to the left" are considered as negative. The **origin** O, also labeled 0, of the coordinate system is the point in the plane where x and y are both zero.

If P is any point in the plane, it can be located by exactly one ordered pair of real numbers in the following way. Draw lines through P perpendicular to the two coordinate axes. These lines intersect the axes at points with coordinates a and b (Figure A.4). The ordered pair (a, b) is assigned to the point P and is called its **coordinate pair**. The first number a is the ***x*-coordinate** (or **abscissa**) of P; the second number b is the ***y*-coordinate** (or **ordinate**) of P. The x-coordinate of every point on the y-axis is 0. The y-coordinate of every point on the x-axis is 0. The origin is the point $(0, 0)$.

Starting with an ordered pair (a, b), we can reverse the process and arrive at a corresponding point P in the plane. Often we identify P with the ordered pair and write $P(a, b)$. We sometimes also refer to "the point (a, b)" and it will be clear from the context when (a, b) refers to a point in the plane and not to an open interval on the real line. Several points labeled by their coordinates are shown in Figure A.5.

This coordinate system is called the **rectangular coordinate system** or **Cartesian coordinate system** (after the sixteenth-century French mathematician René Descartes). The coordinate axes of this coordinate or Cartesian plane divide the plane into four regions called **quadrants**, numbered counterclockwise as shown in Figure A.5.

The **graph** of an equation or inequality in the variables x and y is the set of all points $P(x, y)$ in the plane whose coordinates satisfy the equation or inequality. When we plot data in the coordinate plane or graph formulas whose variables have different units of measure, we do not need to use the same scale on the two axes. If we plot time vs. thrust for a rocket motor, for example, there is no reason to place the mark that shows 1 sec on the time axis the same distance from the origin as the mark that shows 1 lb on the thrust axis.

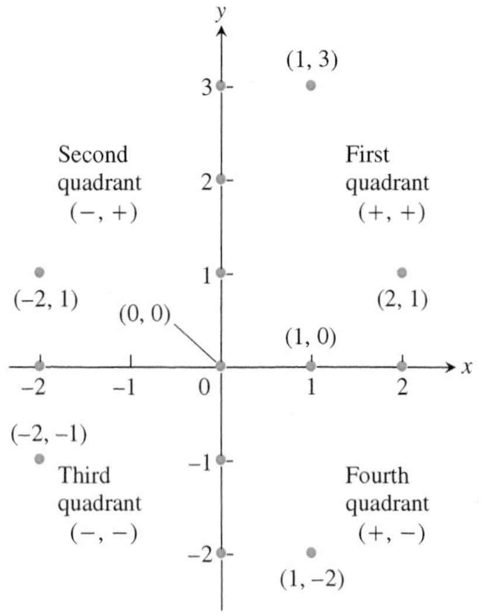

FIGURE A.5 Points labeled in the xy-coordinate or Cartesian plane. The points on the axes all have coordinate pairs but are usually labeled with single real numbers, (so $(1, 0)$ on the x-axis is labeled as 1). Notice the coordinate sign patterns of the quadrants.

Usually when we graph functions whose variables do not represent physical measurements and when we draw figures in the coordinate plane to study their geometry and trigonometry, we try to make the scales on the axes identical. A vertical unit of distance then looks the same as a horizontal unit. As on a surveyor's map or a scale drawing, line segments that are supposed to have the same length will look as if they do and angles that are supposed to be congruent will look congruent.

Computer displays and calculator displays are another matter. The vertical and horizontal scales on machine-generated graphs usually differ, and there are corresponding distortions in distances, slopes, and angles. Circles may look like ellipses, rectangles may look like squares, right angles may appear to be acute or obtuse, and so on. We discuss these displays and distortions in greater detail in Section 1.4.

Increments and Straight Lines

When a particle moves from one point in the plane to another, the net changes in its coordinates are called *increments*. They are calculated by subtracting the coordinates of the

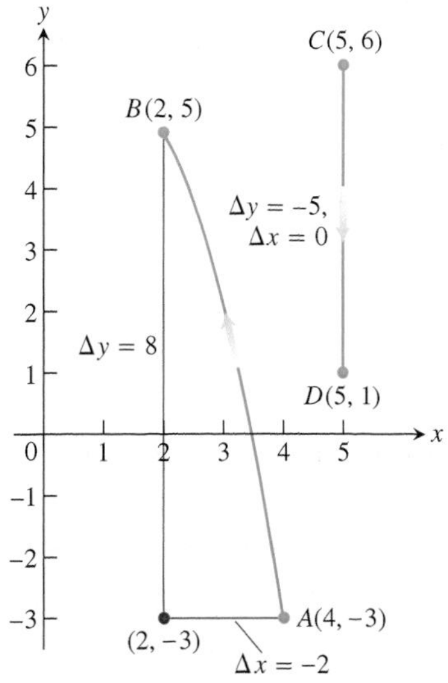

FIGURE A.6 Coordinate increments may be positive, negative, or zero (Example 1).

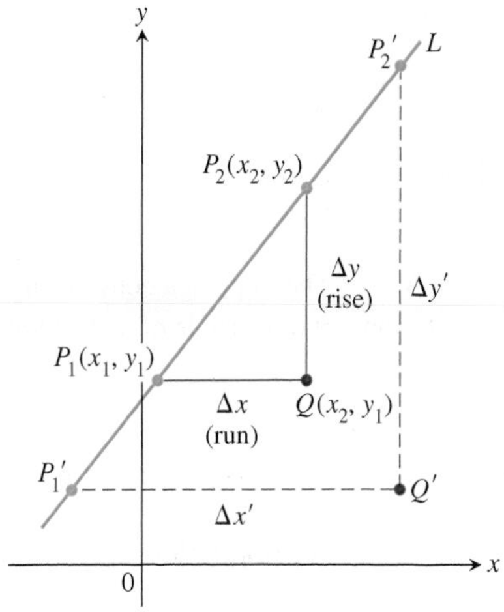

FIGURE A.7 Triangles P_1QP_2 and $P_1'Q'P_2'$ are similar, so the ratio of their sides has the same value for any two points on the line. This common value is the line's slope.

starting point from the coordinates of the ending point. If x changes from x_1 to x_2, the **increment** in x is

$$\Delta x = x_2 - x_1.$$

EXAMPLE 1 In going from the point $A(4, -3)$ to the point $B(2, 5)$ the increments in the x- and y-coordinates are

$$\Delta x = 2 - 4 = -2, \qquad \Delta y = 5 - (-3) = 8.$$

From $C(5, 6)$ to $D(5, 1)$ the coordinate increments are

$$\Delta x = 5 - 5 = 0, \qquad \Delta y = 1 - 6 = -5.$$

See Figure A.6. ■

Given two points $P_1(x_1, y_1)$ and $P_2(x_2, y_2)$ in the plane, we call the increments $\Delta x = x_2 - x_1$ and $\Delta y = y_2 - y_1$ the **run** and the **rise**, respectively, between P_1 and P_2. Two such points always determine a unique straight line (usually called simply a line) passing through them both. We call the line P_1P_2.

Any nonvertical line in the plane has the property that the ratio

$$m = \frac{\text{rise}}{\text{run}} = \frac{\Delta y}{\Delta x} = \frac{y_2 - y_1}{x_2 - x_1}$$

has the same value for every choice of the two points $P_1(x_1, y_1)$ and $P_2(x_2, y_2)$ on the line (Figure A.7). This is because the ratios of corresponding sides for similar triangles are equal.

DEFINITION The constant ratio

$$m = \frac{\text{rise}}{\text{run}} = \frac{\Delta y}{\Delta x} = \frac{y_2 - y_1}{x_2 - x_1}$$

is the **slope** of the nonvertical line P_1P_2.

The slope tells us the direction (uphill, downhill) and steepness of a line. A line with positive slope rises uphill to the right; one with negative slope falls downhill to the right (Figure A.8). The greater the absolute value of the slope, the more rapid the rise or fall. The slope of a vertical line is *undefined*. Since the run Δx is zero for a vertical line, we cannot form the slope ratio m.

The direction and steepness of a line can also be measured with an angle. The **angle of inclination** of a line that crosses the x-axis is the smallest counterclockwise angle from the x-axis to the line (Figure A.9). The inclination of a horizontal line is 0°. The inclination of a vertical line is 90°. If ϕ (the Greek letter phi) is the inclination of a line, then $0 \le \phi < 180°$.

The relationship between the slope m of a nonvertical line and the line's angle of inclination ϕ is shown in Figure A.10:

$$m = \tan \phi.$$

Straight lines have relatively simple equations. All points on the *vertical line* through the point a on the x-axis have x-coordinates equal to a. Thus, $x = a$ is an equation for the vertical line. Similarly, $y = b$ is an equation for the *horizontal line* meeting the y-axis at b. (See Figure A.11.)

We can write an equation for a nonvertical straight line L if we know its slope m and the coordinates of one point $P_1(x_1, y_1)$ on it. If $P(x, y)$ is *any* other point on L, then we can

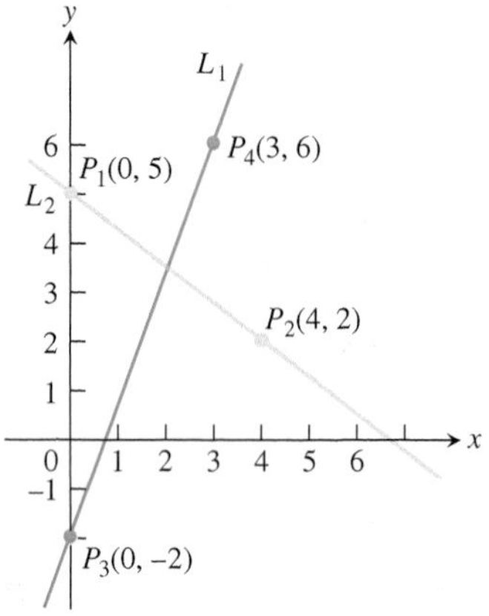

FIGURE A.8 The slope of L_1 is

$$m = \frac{\Delta y}{\Delta x} = \frac{6 - (-2)}{3 - 0} = \frac{8}{3}.$$

That is, y increases 8 units every time x increases 3 units. The slope of L_2 is

$$m = \frac{\Delta y}{\Delta x} = \frac{2 - 5}{4 - 0} = \frac{-3}{4}.$$

That is, y decreases 3 units every time x increases 4 units.

use the two points P_1 and P to compute the slope,

$$m = \frac{y - y_1}{x - x_1}$$

so that

$$y - y_1 = m(x - x_1), \qquad \text{or} \qquad y = y_1 + m(x - x_1).$$

> The equation
>
> $$y = y_1 + m(x - x_1)$$
>
> is the **point-slope equation** of the line that passes through the point (x_1, y_1) and has slope m.

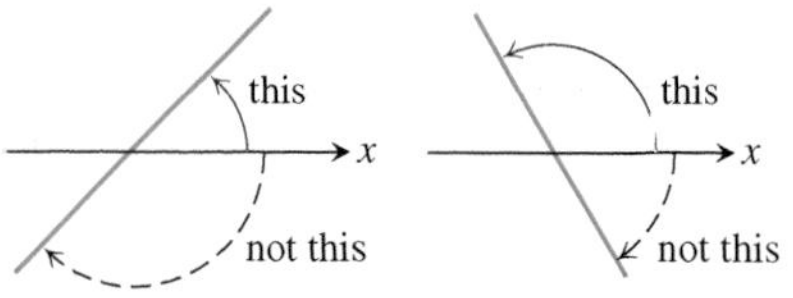

FIGURE A.9 Angles of inclination are measured counterclockwise from the x-axis.

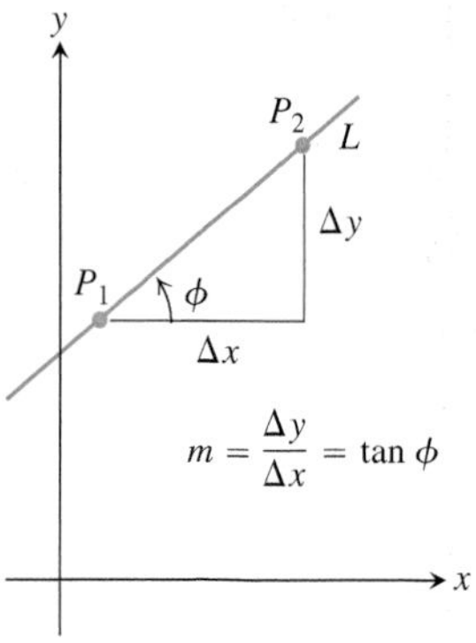

FIGURE A.10 The slope of a nonvertical line is the tangent of its angle of inclination.

EXAMPLE 2 Write an equation for the line through the point (2, 3) with slope $-3/2$.

Solution We substitute $x_1 = 2, y_1 = 3$, and $m = -3/2$ into the point-slope equation and obtain

$$y = 3 - \frac{3}{2}(x - 2), \qquad \text{or} \qquad y = -\frac{3}{2}x + 6.$$

When $x = 0$, $y = 6$ so the line intersects the y-axis at $y = 6$. ■

EXAMPLE 3 Write an equation for the line through $(-2, -1)$ and $(3, 4)$.

Solution The line's slope is

$$m = \frac{-1 - 4}{-2 - 3} = \frac{-5}{-5} = 1.$$

We can use this slope with either of the two given points in the point-slope equation:

With $(x_1, y_1) = (-2, -1)$	With $(x_1, y_1) = (3, 4)$
$y = -1 + 1 \cdot (x - (-2))$	$y = 4 + 1 \cdot (x - 3)$
$y = -1 + x + 2$	$y = 4 + x - 3$
$y = x + 1$	$y = x + 1$

Same result

Either way, $y = x + 1$ is an equation for the line (Figure A.12). ■

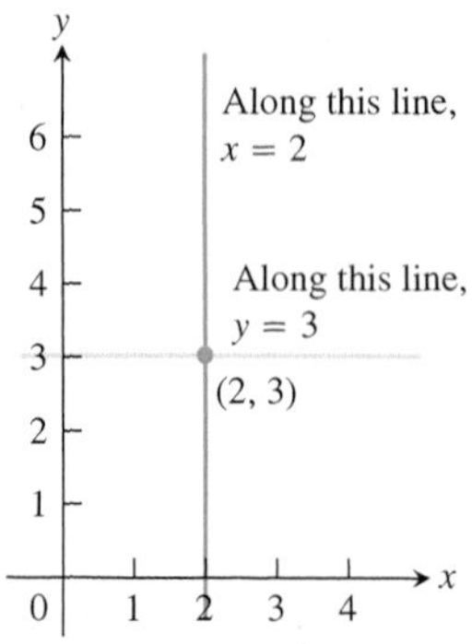

FIGURE A.11 The standard equations for the vertical and horizontal lines through (2, 3) are $x = 2$ and $y = 3$.

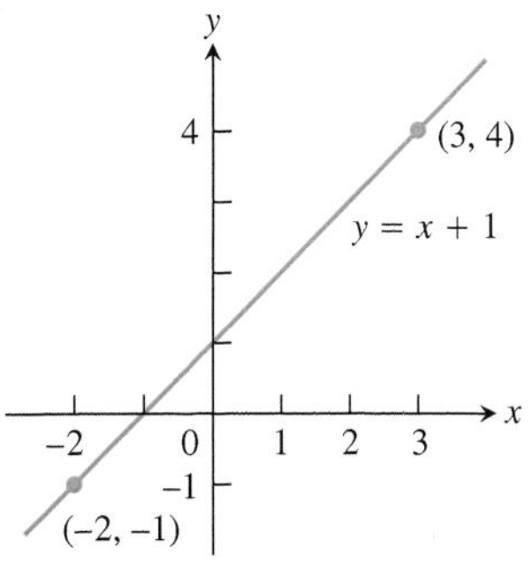

FIGURE A.12 The line in Example 3.

The y-coordinate of the point where a nonvertical line intersects the y-axis is called the ***y*-intercept** of the line. Similarly, the ***x*-intercept** of a nonhorizontal line is the x-coordinate of the point where it crosses the x-axis (Figure A.13). A line with slope m and y-intercept b passes through the point $(0, b)$, so it has equation

$$y = b + m(x - 0), \qquad \text{or, more simply,} \qquad y = mx + b.$$

> The equation
>
> $$y = mx + b$$
>
> is called the **slope-intercept equation** of the line with slope m and y-intercept b.

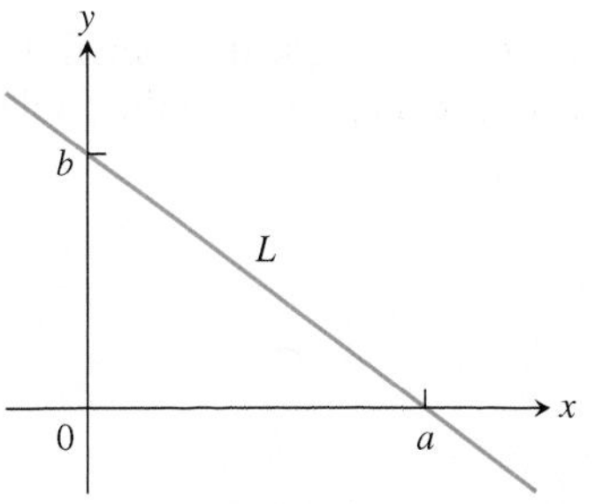

FIGURE A.13 Line L has x-intercept a and y-intercept b.

Lines with equations of the form $y = mx$ have y-intercept 0 and so pass through the origin. Equations of lines are called **linear** equations.

The equation

$$Ax + By = C \qquad (A \text{ and } B \text{ not both } 0)$$

is called the **general linear equation** in x and y because its graph always represents a line and every line has an equation in this form (including lines with undefined slope).

Parallel and Perpendicular Lines

Lines that are parallel have equal angles of inclination, so they have the same slope (if they are not vertical). Conversely, lines with equal slopes have equal angles of inclination and so are parallel.

If two nonvertical lines L_1 and L_2 are perpendicular, their slopes m_1 and m_2 satisfy $m_1 m_2 = -1$, so each slope is the *negative reciprocal* of the other:

$$m_1 = -\frac{1}{m_2}, \qquad m_2 = -\frac{1}{m_1}.$$

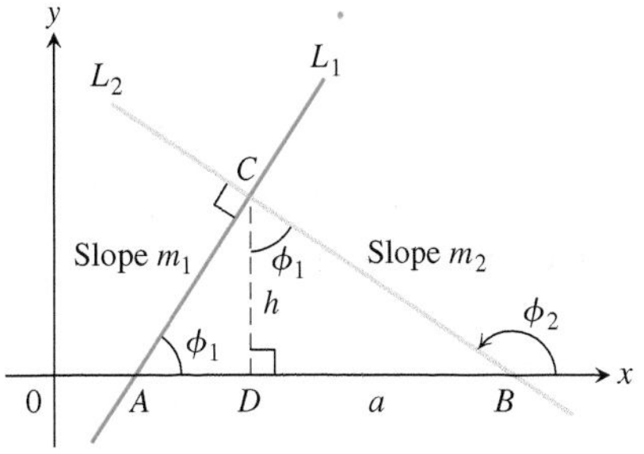

FIGURE A.14 ΔADC is similar to ΔCDB. Hence ϕ_1 is also the upper angle in ΔCDB. From the sides of ΔCDB, we read $\tan \phi_1 = a/h$.

To see this, notice by inspecting similar triangles in Figure A.14 that $m_1 = a/h$, and $m_2 = -h/a$. Hence, $m_1 m_2 = (a/h)(-h/a) = -1$.

Distance and Circles in the Plane

The distance between points in the plane is calculated with a formula that comes from the Pythagorean theorem (Figure A.15).

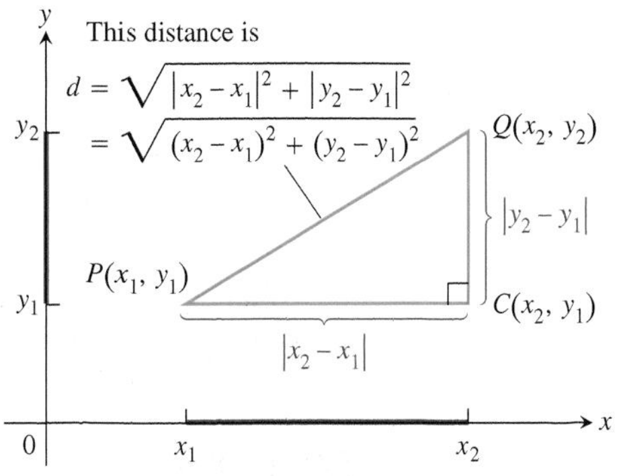

FIGURE A.15 To calculate the distance between $P(x_1, y_1)$ and $Q(x_2, y_2)$, apply the Pythagorean theorem to triangle PCQ.

> **Distance Formula for Points in the Plane**
> The distance between $P(x_1, y_1)$ and $Q(x_2, y_2)$ is
> $$d = \sqrt{(\Delta x)^2 + (\Delta y)^2} = \sqrt{(x_2 - x_1)^2 + (y_2 - y_1)^2}.$$

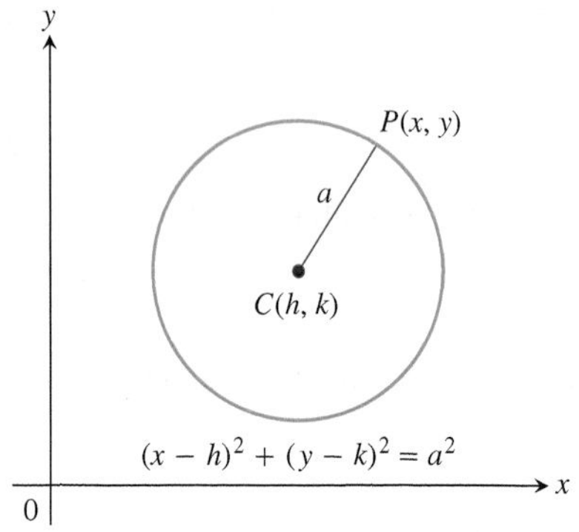

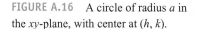

FIGURE A.16 A circle of radius a in the xy-plane, with center at (h, k).

EXAMPLE 4

(a) The distance between $P(-1, 2)$ and $Q(3, 4)$ is

$$\sqrt{(3 - (-1))^2 + (4 - 2)^2} = \sqrt{(4)^2 + (2)^2} = \sqrt{20} = \sqrt{4 \cdot 5} = 2\sqrt{5}.$$

(b) The distance from the origin to $P(x, y)$ is

$$\sqrt{(x - 0)^2 + (y - 0)^2} = \sqrt{x^2 + y^2}.$$ ■

By definition, a **circle** of radius a is the set of all points $P(x, y)$ whose distance from some center $C(h, k)$ equals a (Figure A.16). From the distance formula, P lies on the circle if and only if

$$\sqrt{(x - h)^2 + (y - k)^2} = a,$$

so

$$(x - h)^2 + (y - k)^2 = a^2. \qquad (1)$$

Equation (1) is the **standard equation** of a circle with center (h, k) and radius a. The circle of radius $a = 1$ and centered at the origin is the **unit circle** with equation

$$x^2 + y^2 = 1.$$

EXAMPLE 5

(a) The standard equation for the circle of radius 2 centered at (3, 4) is

$$(x - 3)^2 + (y - 4)^2 = 2^2 = 4.$$

(b) The circle

$$(x - 1)^2 + (y + 5)^2 = 3$$

has $h = 1$, $k = -5$, and $a = \sqrt{3}$. The center is the point $(h, k) = (1, -5)$ and the radius is $a = \sqrt{3}$. ■

If an equation for a circle is not in standard form, we can find the circle's center and radius by first converting the equation to standard form. The algebraic technique for doing so is *completing the square*.

EXAMPLE 6 Find the center and radius of the circle

$$x^2 + y^2 + 4x - 6y - 3 = 0.$$

Solution We convert the equation to standard form by completing the squares in x and y:

$$x^2 + y^2 + 4x - 6y - 3 = 0$$ Start with the given equation.

$$(x^2 + 4x) + (y^2 - 6y) = 3$$ Gather terms. Move the constant to the right-hand side.

$$\left(x^2 + 4x + \left(\frac{4}{2}\right)^2\right) + \left(y^2 - 6y + \left(\frac{-6}{2}\right)^2\right) = 3 + \left(\frac{4}{2}\right)^2 + \left(\frac{-6}{2}\right)^2$$ Add the square of half the coefficient of x to each side of the equation. Do the same for y. The parenthetical expressions on the left-hand side are now perfect squares.

$$(x^2 + 4x + 4) + (y^2 - 6y + 9) = 3 + 4 + 9$$

$$(x + 2)^2 + (y - 3)^2 = 16$$ Write each quadratic as a squared linear expression.

The center is $(-2, 3)$ and the radius is $a = 4$. ■

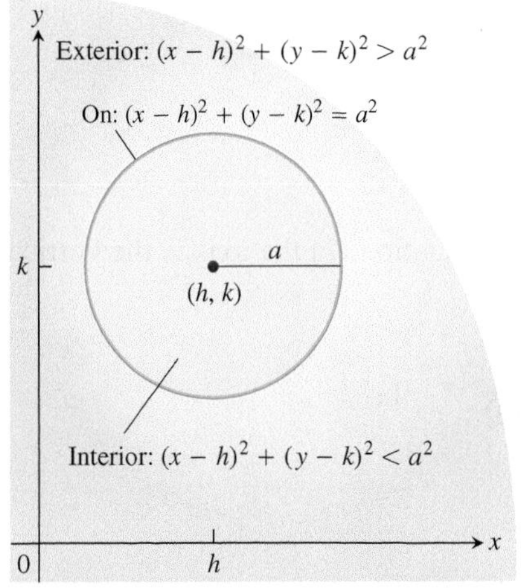

FIGURE A.17 The interior and exterior of the circle $(x - h)^2 + (y - k)^2 = a^2$.

The points (x, y) satisfying the inequality

$$(x - h)^2 + (y - k)^2 < a^2$$

make up the **interior** region of the circle with center (h, k) and radius a (Figure A.17). The circle's **exterior** consists of the points (x, y) satisfying

$$(x - h)^2 + (y - k)^2 > a^2.$$

Parabolas

The geometric definition and properties of general parabolas are reviewed in Appendix 4. Here we look at parabolas arising as the graphs of equations of the form $y = ax^2 + bx + c$.

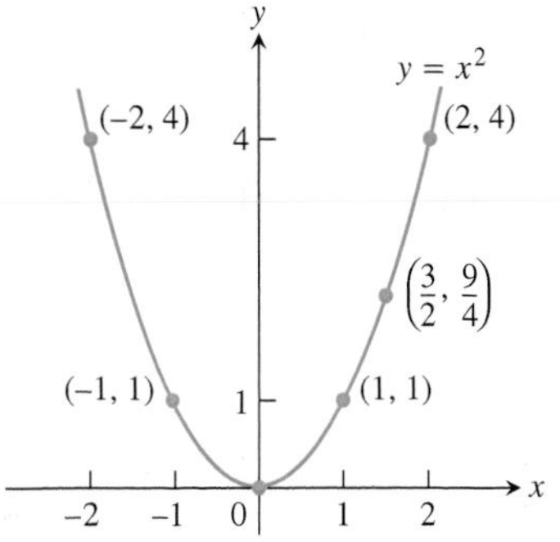

FIGURE A.18 The parabola $y = x^2$ (Example 7).

EXAMPLE 7 Consider the equation $y = x^2$. Some points whose coordinates satisfy this equation are $(0, 0)$, $(1, 1)$, $\left(\frac{3}{2}, \frac{9}{4}\right)$, $(-1, 1)$, $(2, 4)$, and $(-2, 4)$. These points (and all others satisfying the equation) make up a smooth curve called a parabola (Figure A.18). ■

The graph of an equation of the form

$$y = ax^2$$

is a **parabola** whose **axis** (axis of symmetry) is the y-axis. The parabola's **vertex** (point where the parabola and axis cross) lies at the origin. The parabola opens upward if $a > 0$ and downward if $a < 0$. The larger the value of $|a|$, the narrower the parabola (Figure A.19).

Generally, the graph of $y = ax^2 + bx + c$ is a shifted and scaled version of the parabola $y = x^2$. We discuss shifting and scaling of graphs in more detail in Section 1.2.

The Graph of $y = ax^2 + bx + c, \quad a \neq 0$

The graph of the equation $y = ax^2 + bx + c$, $a \neq 0$, is a parabola. The parabola opens upward if $a > 0$ and downward if $a < 0$. The **axis** is the line

$$x = -\frac{b}{2a}. \qquad (2)$$

The **vertex** of the parabola is the point where the axis and parabola intersect. Its x-coordinate is $x = -b/2a$; its y-coordinate is found by substituting $x = -b/2a$ in the parabola's equation.

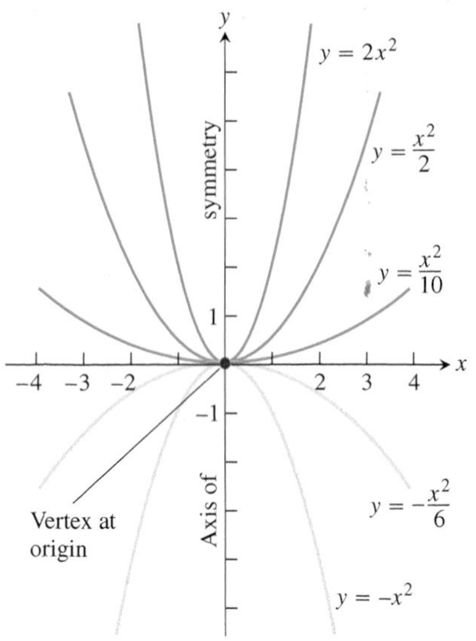

FIGURE A.19 Besides determining the direction in which the parabola $y = ax^2$ opens, the number a is a scaling factor. The parabola widens as a approaches zero and narrows as $|a|$ becomes large.

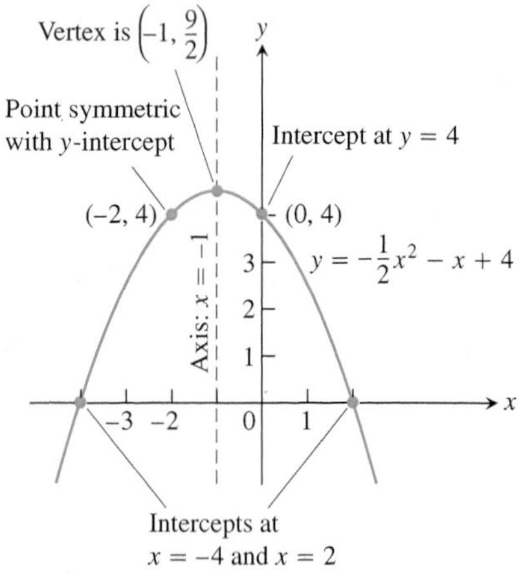

FIGURE A.20 The parabola in Example 8.

Notice that if $a = 0$, then we have $y = bx + c$, which is an equation for a line. The axis, given by Equation (2), can be found by completing the square.

EXAMPLE 8 Graph the equation $y = -\frac{1}{2}x^2 - x + 4$.

Solution Comparing the equation with $y = ax^2 + bx + c$ we see that

$$a = -\frac{1}{2}, \qquad b = -1, \qquad c = 4.$$

Since $a < 0$, the parabola opens downward. From Equation (2) the axis is the vertical line

$$x = -\frac{b}{2a} = -\frac{(-1)}{2(-1/2)} = -1.$$

When $x = -1$, we have

$$y = -\frac{1}{2}(-1)^2 - (-1) + 4 = \frac{9}{2}.$$

The vertex is $(-1, 9/2)$.

The x-intercepts are where $y = 0$:

$$\begin{aligned} -\frac{1}{2}x^2 - x + 4 &= 0 \\ x^2 + 2x - 8 &= 0 \\ (x - 2)(x + 4) &= 0 \\ x = 2, \qquad x &= -4 \end{aligned}$$

We plot some points, sketch the axis, and use the direction of opening to complete the graph in Figure A.20. ■

Exercises A.3

Distance, Slopes, and Lines

In Exercises 1 and 2, a particle moves from A to B in the coordinate plane. Find the increments Δx and Δy in the particle's coordinates. Also find the distance from A to B.

1. $A(-3, 2)$, $B(-1, -2)$ **2.** $A(-3.2, -2)$, $B(-8.1, -2)$

Describe the graphs of the equations in Exercises 3 and 4.

3. $x^2 + y^2 = 1$ **4.** $x^2 + y^2 \leq 3$

Plot the points in Exercises 5 and 6 and find the slope (if any) of the line they determine. Also find the common slope (if any) of the lines perpendicular to line AB.

5. $A(-1, 2)$, $B(-2, -1)$ **6.** $A(2, 3)$, $B(-1, 3)$

In Exercises 7 and 8, find an equation for **(a)** the vertical line and **(b)** the horizontal line through the given point.

7. $(-1, 4/3)$ **8.** $\left(0, -\sqrt{2}\right)$

In Exercises 9–15, write an equation for each line described.

9. Passes through $(-1, 1)$ with slope -1

10. Passes through $(3, 4)$ and $(-2, 5)$

11. Has slope $-5/4$ and y-intercept 6

12. Passes through $(-12, -9)$ and has slope 0

13. Has y-intercept 4 and x-intercept -1

14. Passes through $(5, -1)$ and is parallel to the line $2x + 5y = 15$

15. Passes through $(4, 10)$ and is perpendicular to the line $6x - 3y = 5$

In Exercises 16 and 17, find the line's x- and y-intercepts and use this information to graph the line.

16. $3x + 4y = 12$ **17.** $\sqrt{2}x - \sqrt{3}y = \sqrt{6}$

18. Is there anything special about the relationship between the lines $Ax + By = C_1$ and $Bx - Ay = C_2$ $(A \neq 0, B \neq 0)$? Give reasons for your answer.

19. A particle starts at $A(-2, 3)$ and its coordinates change by increments $\Delta x = 5$, $\Delta y = -6$. Find its new position.

20. The coordinates of a particle change by $\Delta x = 5$ and $\Delta y = 6$ as it moves from $A(x, y)$ to $B(3, -3)$. Find x and y.

Circles

In Exercises 21–23, find an equation for the circle with the given center $C(h, k)$ and radius a. Then sketch the circle in the xy-plane. Include the circle's center in your sketch. Also, label the circle's x- and y-intercepts, if any, with their coordinate pairs.

21. $C(0, 2)$, $a = 2$ **22.** $C(-1, 5)$, $a = \sqrt{10}$

23. $C(-\sqrt{3}, -2)$, $a = 2$

Graph the circles whose equations are given in Exercises 24–26. Label each circle's center and intercepts (if any) with their coordinate pairs.

24. $x^2 + y^2 + 4x - 4y + 4 = 0$

25. $x^2 + y^2 - 3y - 4 = 0$ **26.** $x^2 + y^2 - 4x + 4y = 0$

Parabolas

Graph the parabolas in Exercises 27–30. Label the vertex, axis, and intercepts in each case.

27. $y = x^2 - 2x - 3$ **28.** $y = -x^2 + 4x$

29. $y = -x^2 - 6x - 5$ **30.** $y = \frac{1}{2}x^2 + x + 4$

Inequalities

Describe the regions defined by the inequalities and pairs of inequalities in Exercises 31–34.

31. $x^2 + y^2 > 7$ **32.** $(x - 1)^2 + y^2 \leq 4$

33. $x^2 + y^2 > 1$, $x^2 + y^2 < 4$

34. $x^2 + y^2 + 6y < 0$, $y > -3$

35. Write an inequality that describes the points that lie inside the circle with center $(-2, 1)$ and radius $\sqrt{6}$.

36. Write a pair of inequalities that describe the points that lie inside or on the circle with center $(0, 0)$ and radius $\sqrt{2}$, and on or to the right of the vertical line through $(1, 0)$.

Theory and Examples

In Exercises 37–40, graph the two equations and find the points at which the graphs intersect.

37. $y = 2x$, $x^2 + y^2 = 1$ **38.** $y - x = 1$, $y = x^2$

39. $y = -x^2$, $y = 2x^2 - 1$

40. $x^2 + y^2 = 1$, $(x - 1)^2 + y^2 = 1$

41. Insulation By measuring slopes in the figure, estimate the temperature change in degrees per inch for **(a)** the gypsum wallboard; **(b)** the fiberglass insulation; **(c)** the wood sheathing.

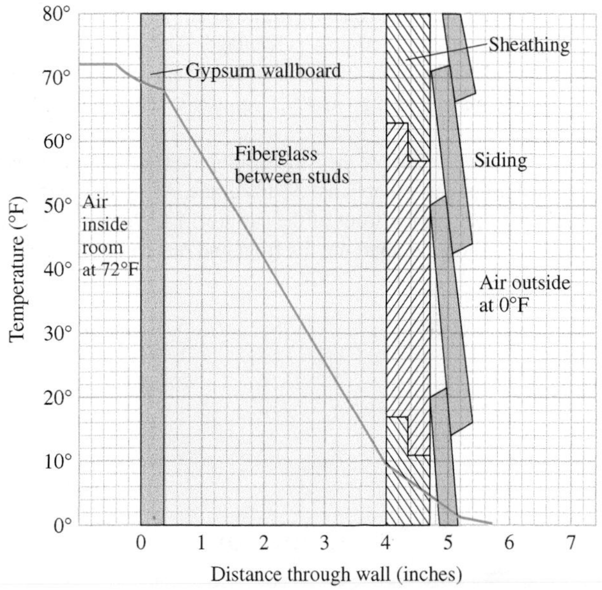

The temperature changes in the wall in Exercises 41 and 42.

42. Insulation According to the figure in Exercise 41, which of the materials is the best insulator? The poorest? Explain.

43. Pressure under water The pressure p experienced by a diver under water is related to the diver's depth d by an equation of the form $p = kd + 1$ (k a constant). At the surface, the pressure is 1 atmosphere. The pressure at 100 meters is about 10.94 atmospheres. Find the pressure at 50 meters.

44. Reflected light A ray of light comes in along the line $x + y = 1$ from the second quadrant and reflects off the x-axis (see the accompanying figure). The angle of incidence is equal to the angle of reflection. Write an equation for the line along which the departing light travels.

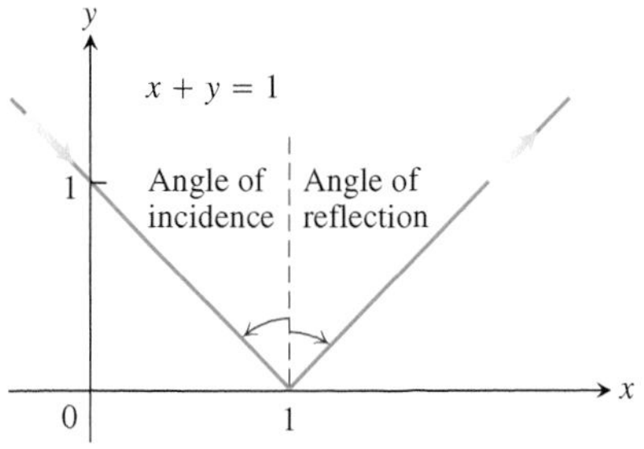

The path of the light ray in Exercise 44. Angles of incidence and reflection are measured from the perpendicular.

45. **Fahrenheit vs. Celsius** In the FC-plane, sketch the graph of the equation

$$C = \frac{5}{9}(F - 32)$$

linking Fahrenheit and Celsius temperatures. On the same graph sketch the line $C = F$. Is there a temperature at which a Celsius thermometer gives the same numerical reading as a Fahrenheit thermometer? If so, find it.

46. **The Mt. Washington Cog Railway** Civil engineers calculate the slope of roadbed as the ratio of the distance it rises or falls to the distance it runs horizontally. They call this ratio the **grade** of the roadbed, usually written as a percentage. Along the coast, commercial railroad grades are usually less than 2%. In the mountains, they may go as high as 4%. Highway grades are usually less than 5%.

    The steepest part of the Mt. Washington Cog Railway in New Hampshire has an exceptional 37.1% grade. Along this part of the track, the seats in the front of the car are 14 ft above those in the rear. About how far apart are the front and rear rows of seats?

47. By calculating the lengths of its sides, show that the triangle with vertices at the points $A(1, 2)$, $B(5, 5)$, and $C(4, -2)$ is isosceles but not equilateral.

48. Show that the triangle with vertices $A(0, 0)$, $B(1, \sqrt{3})$, and $C(2, 0)$ is equilateral.

49. Show that the points $A(2, -1)$, $B(1, 3)$, and $C(-3, 2)$ are vertices of a square, and find the fourth vertex.

50. Three different parallelograms have vertices at $(-1, 1)$, $(2, 0)$, and $(2, 3)$. Sketch them and find the coordinates of the fourth vertex of each.

51. For what value of k is the line $2x + ky = 3$ perpendicular to the line $4x + y = 1$? For what value of k are the lines parallel?

52. **Midpoint of a line segment** Show that the point with coordinates

$$\left(\frac{x_1 + x_2}{2}, \frac{y_1 + y_2}{2}\right)$$

is the midpoint of the line segment joining $P(x_1, y_1)$ to $Q(x_2, y_2)$.

A.4 Conic Sections

In this appendix we define and review parabolas, ellipses, and hyperbolas geometrically and derive their standard Cartesian equations. These curves are called *conic sections* or *conics* because they are formed by cutting a double cone with a plane (Figure A.21). This geometry method was the only way they could be described by Greek mathematicians who did not have our tools of Cartesian or polar coordinates.

Parabolas

DEFINITIONS A set that consists of all the points in a plane equidistant from a given fixed point and a given fixed line in the plane is a **parabola**. The fixed point is the **focus** of the parabola. The fixed line is the **directrix**.

If the focus F lies on the directrix L, the parabola is the line through F perpendicular to L. We consider this to be a degenerate case and assume henceforth that F does not lie on L.

A parabola has its simplest equation when its focus and directrix straddle one of the coordinate axes. For example, suppose that the focus lies at the point $F(0, p)$ on the positive y-axis and that the directrix is the line $y = -p$ (Figure A.22). In the notation of the figure, a point $P(x, y)$ lies on the parabola if and only if $PF = PQ$. From the distance formula,

$$PF = \sqrt{(x - 0)^2 + (y - p)^2} = \sqrt{x^2 + (y - p)^2}$$

$$PQ = \sqrt{(x - x)^2 + (y - (-p))^2} = \sqrt{(y + p)^2}.$$

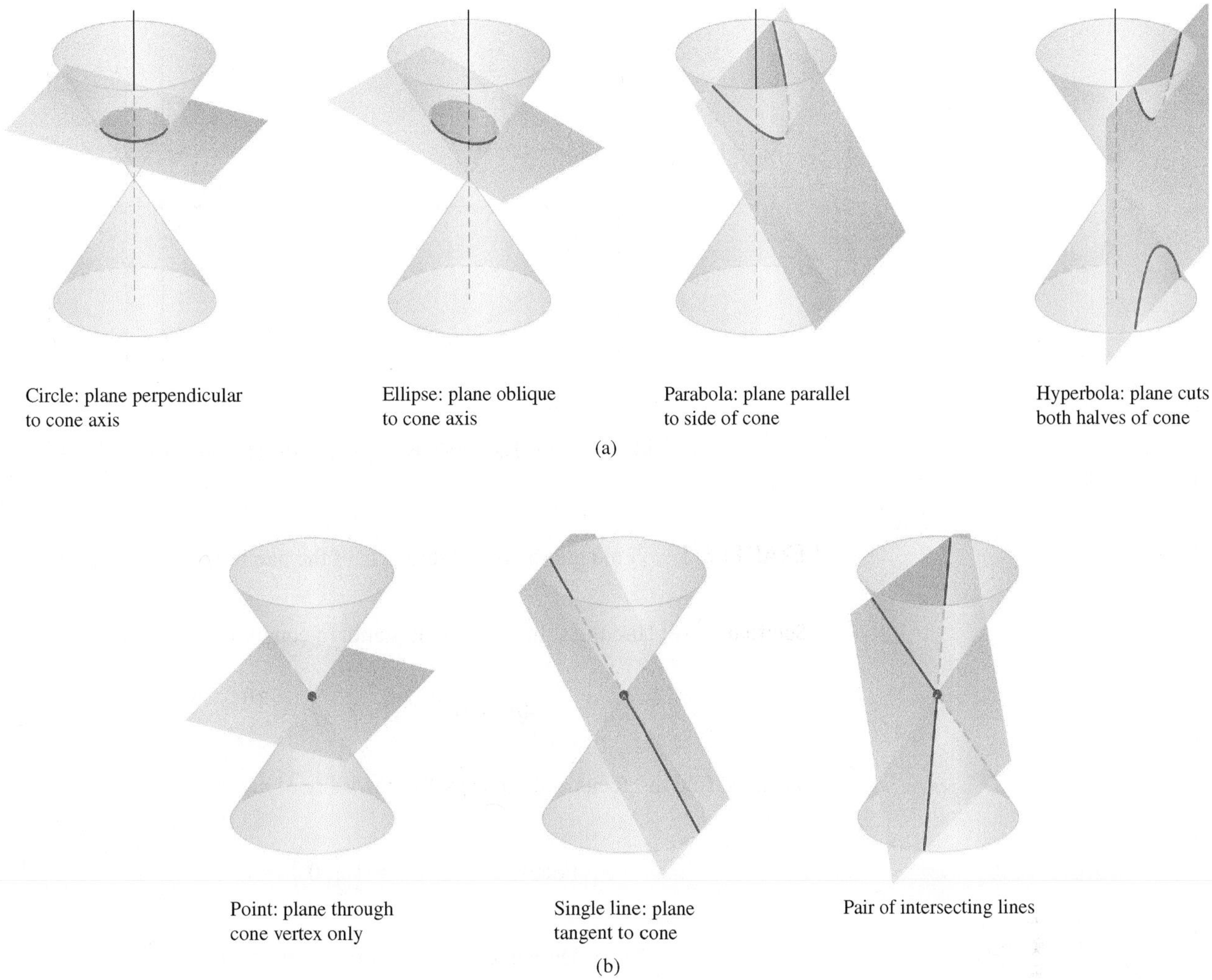

FIGURE A.21 The standard conic sections (a) are the curves in which a plane cuts a *double* cone. Hyperbolas come in two parts, called *branches*. The point and lines obtained by passing the plane through the cone's vertex (b) are *degenerate* conic sections.

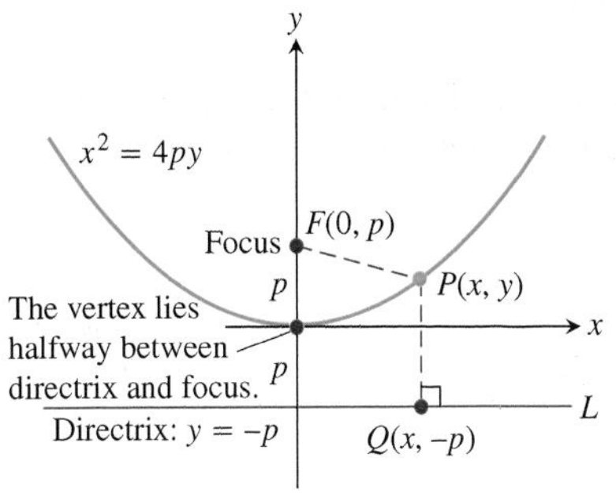

FIGURE A.22 The standard form of the parabola $x^2 = 4py, p > 0$.

When we equate these expressions, square, and simplify, we get

$$y = \frac{x^2}{4p} \quad \text{or} \quad x^2 = 4py. \qquad \text{Standard form} \tag{1}$$

These equations reveal the parabola's symmetry about the y-axis. We call the y-axis the **axis** of the parabola (short for "axis of symmetry").

The point where a parabola crosses its axis is the **vertex**. The vertex of the parabola $x^2 = 4py$ lies at the origin (Figure A.22). The positive number p is the parabola's **focal length**.

If the parabola opens downward, with its focus at $(0, -p)$ and its directrix the line $y = p$, then Equations (1) become

$$y = -\frac{x^2}{4p} \quad \text{and} \quad x^2 = -4py.$$

By interchanging the variables x and y, we obtain similar equations for parabolas opening to the right or to the left (Figure A.23).

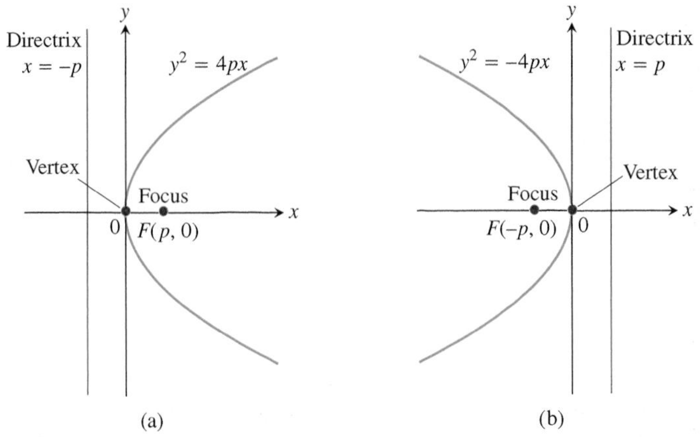

FIGURE A.23 (a) The parabola $y^2 = 4px$. (b) The parabola $y^2 = -4px$.

EXAMPLE 1 Find the focus and directrix of the parabola $y^2 = 10x$.

Solution We find the value of p in the standard equation $y^2 = 4px$:

$$4p = 10, \qquad \text{so} \qquad p = \frac{10}{4} = \frac{5}{2}.$$

Then we find the focus and directrix for this value of p:

$$\text{Focus:} \qquad (p, 0) = \left(\frac{5}{2}, 0\right)$$

$$\text{Directrix:} \qquad x = -p \qquad \text{or} \qquad x = -\frac{5}{2}.$$

■

Ellipses

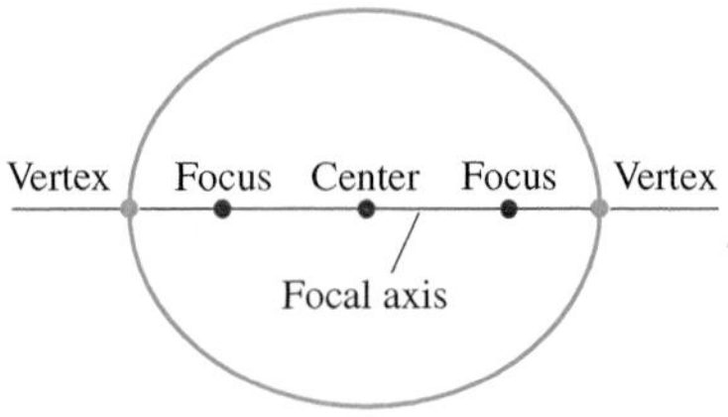

FIGURE A.24 Points on the focal axis of an ellipse.

> **DEFINITIONS** An **ellipse** is the set of points in a plane whose distances from two fixed points in the plane have a constant sum. The two fixed points are the **foci** of the ellipse.
>
> The line through the foci of an ellipse is the ellipse's **focal axis**. The point on the axis halfway between the foci is the **center**. The points where the focal axis and ellipse cross are the ellipse's **vertices** (Figure A.24).

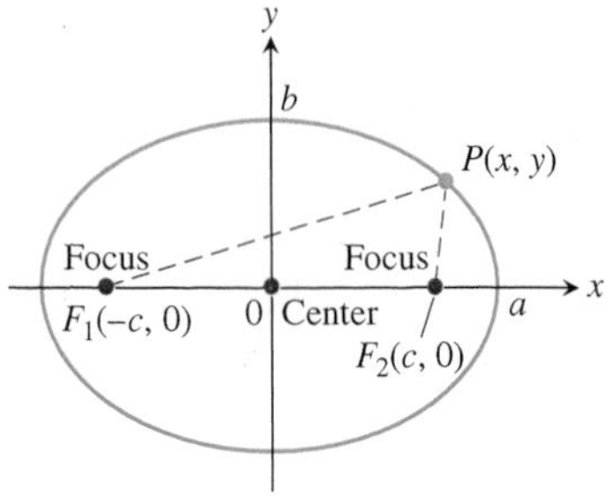

FIGURE A.25 The ellipse defined by the equation $PF_1 + PF_2 = 2a$ is the graph of the equation $(x^2/a^2) + (y^2/b^2) = 1$, where $b^2 = a^2 - c^2$.

If the foci are $F_1(-c, 0)$ and $F_2(c, 0)$ (Figure A.25), and $PF_1 + PF_2$ is denoted by $2a$, then the coordinates of a point P on the ellipse satisfy the equation

$$\sqrt{(x + c)^2 + y^2} + \sqrt{(x - c)^2 + y^2} = 2a.$$

To simplify this equation, we move the second radical to the right-hand side, square, isolate the remaining radical, and square again, obtaining

$$\frac{x^2}{a^2} + \frac{y^2}{a^2 - c^2} = 1. \tag{2}$$

Since $PF_1 + PF_2$ is greater than the length F_1F_2 (by the triangle inequality for triangle PF_1F_2), the number $2a$ is greater than $2c$. Accordingly, $a > c$ and the number $a^2 - c^2$ in Equation (2) is positive.

The algebraic steps leading to Equation (2) can be reversed to show that every point P whose coordinates satisfy an equation of this form with $0 < c < a$ also satisfies the equation $PF_1 + PF_2 = 2a$. A point therefore lies on the ellipse if and only if its coordinates satisfy Equation (2).

If

$$b = \sqrt{a^2 - c^2}, \tag{3}$$

then $a^2 - c^2 = b^2$ and Equation (2) takes the form

$$\frac{x^2}{a^2} + \frac{y^2}{b^2} = 1. \tag{4}$$

Equation (4) reveals that this ellipse is symmetric with respect to the origin and both coordinate axes. It lies inside the rectangle bounded by the lines $x = \pm a$ and $y = \pm b$. It crosses the axes at the points $(\pm a, 0)$ and $(0, \pm b)$. The tangents at these points are perpendicular to the axes because

$$\frac{dy}{dx} = -\frac{b^2x}{a^2y} \qquad \text{Obtained from Eq. (4) by implicit differentiation}$$

is zero if $x = 0$ and infinite if $y = 0$.

The **major axis** of the ellipse in Equation (4) is the line segment of length $2a$ joining the points $(\pm a, 0)$. The **minor axis** is the line segment of length $2b$ joining the points $(0, \pm b)$. The number a itself is the **semimajor axis**, the number b the **semiminor axis**. The number c, found from Equation (3) as

$$c = \sqrt{a^2 - b^2},$$

is the **center-to-focus distance** of the ellipse. If $a = b$, the ellipse is a circle.

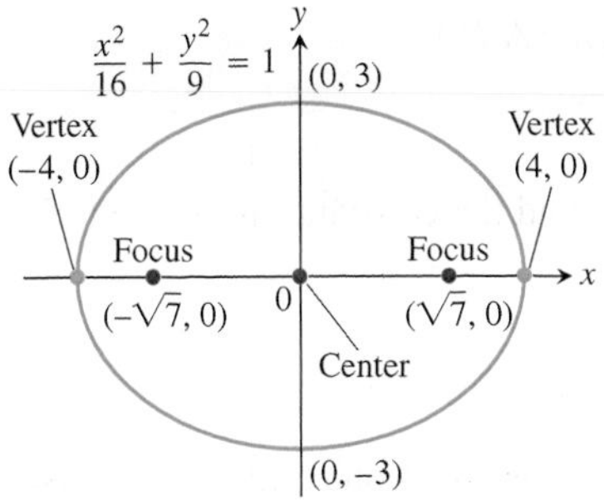

FIGURE A.26 An ellipse with its major axis horizontal (Example 2).

EXAMPLE 2 The ellipse

$$\frac{x^2}{16} + \frac{y^2}{9} = 1 \tag{5}$$

(Figure A.26) has

Semimajor axis: $a = \sqrt{16} = 4$, Semiminor axis: $b = \sqrt{9} = 3$

Center-to-focus distance: $c = \sqrt{16 - 9} = \sqrt{7}$

Foci: $(\pm c, 0) = \left(\pm\sqrt{7}, 0\right)$

Vertices: $(\pm a, 0) = (\pm 4, 0)$

Center: $(0, 0)$. ■

If we interchange x and y in Equation (5), we have the equation

$$\frac{x^2}{9} + \frac{y^2}{16} = 1. \tag{6}$$

The major axis of this ellipse is now vertical instead of horizontal, with the foci and vertices on the y-axis. There is no confusion in analyzing Equations (5) and (6). If we find the intercepts on the coordinate axes, we will know which way the major axis runs because it is the longer of the two axes.

Standard-Form Equations for Ellipses Centered at the Origin

Foci on the x-axis: $\dfrac{x^2}{a^2} + \dfrac{y^2}{b^2} = 1 \quad (a > b)$

Center-to-focus distance: $c = \sqrt{a^2 - b^2}$

Foci: $(\pm c, 0)$

Vertices: $(\pm a, 0)$

Foci on the y-axis: $\dfrac{x^2}{b^2} + \dfrac{y^2}{a^2} = 1 \quad (a > b)$

Center-to-focus distance: $c = \sqrt{a^2 - b^2}$

Foci: $(0, \pm c)$

Vertices: $(0, \pm a)$

In each case, a is the semimajor axis and b is the semiminor axis.

Hyperbolas

DEFINITIONS A **hyperbola** is the set of points in a plane whose distances from two fixed points in the plane have a constant difference. The two fixed points are the **foci** of the hyperbola.

The line through the foci of a hyperbola is the **focal axis**. The point on the axis halfway between the foci is the hyperbola's **center**. The points where the focal axis and hyperbola cross are the **vertices** (Figure A.27).

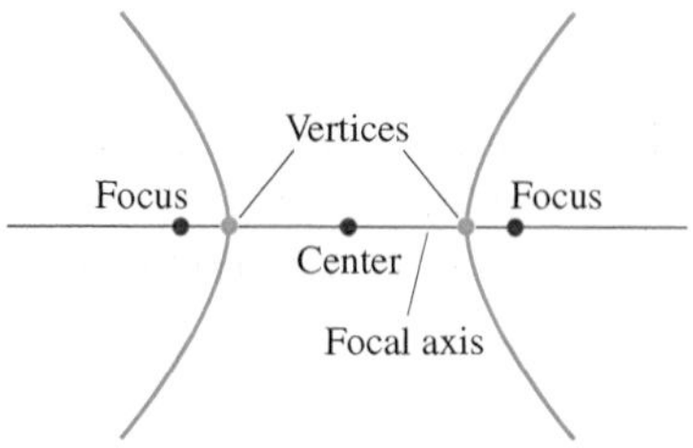

FIGURE A.27 Points on the focal axis of a hyperbola.

If the foci are $F_1(-c, 0)$ and $F_2(c, 0)$ (Figure A.28) and the constant difference is $2a$, then a point (x, y) lies on the hyperbola if and only if

$$\sqrt{(x + c)^2 + y^2} - \sqrt{(x - c)^2 + y^2} = \pm 2a. \tag{7}$$

To simplify this equation, we move the second radical to the right-hand side, square, isolate the remaining radical, and square again, obtaining

$$\frac{x^2}{a^2} + \frac{y^2}{a^2 - c^2} = 1. \tag{8}$$

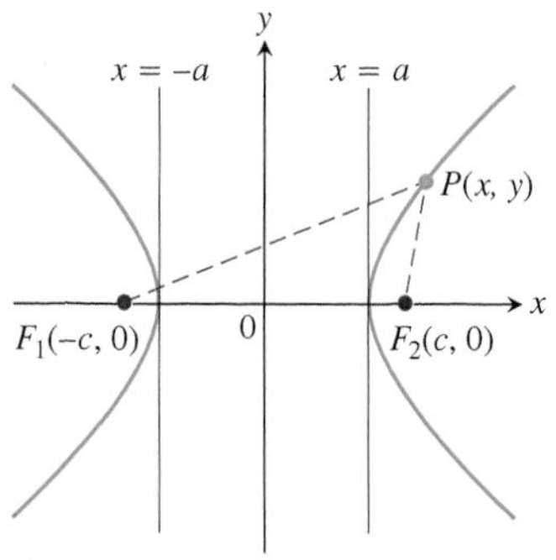

FIGURE A.28 Hyperbolas have two branches. For points on the right-hand branch of the hyperbola shown here, $PF_1 - PF_2 = 2a$. For points on the left-hand branch, $PF_2 - PF_1 = 2a$. We then let $b = \sqrt{c^2 - a^2}$.

So far, this looks just like the equation for an ellipse. But now $a^2 - c^2$ is negative because $2a$, being the difference of two sides of triangle PF_1F_2, is less than $2c$, the third side.

The algebraic steps leading to Equation (8) can be reversed to show that every point P whose coordinates satisfy an equation of this form with $0 < a < c$ also satisfies Equation (7). A point therefore lies on the hyperbola if and only if its coordinates satisfy Equation (8).

If we let b denote the positive square root of $c^2 - a^2$,

$$b = \sqrt{c^2 - a^2}, \tag{9}$$

then $a^2 - c^2 = -b^2$ and Equation (8) takes the more compact form

$$\frac{x^2}{a^2} - \frac{y^2}{b^2} = 1. \tag{10}$$

The differences between Equation (10) and the equation for an ellipse (Equation 4) are the minus sign and the new relation

$$c^2 = a^2 + b^2. \qquad \text{From Eq. (9)}$$

Like the ellipse, the hyperbola is symmetric with respect to the origin and coordinate axes. It crosses the x-axis at the points $(\pm a, 0)$. The tangents at these points are vertical because

$$\frac{dy}{dx} = \frac{b^2x}{a^2y} \qquad \text{Obtained from Eq. (10) by implicit differentiation}$$

is infinite when $y = 0$. The hyperbola has no y-intercepts; in fact, no part of the curve lies between the lines $x = -a$ and $x = a$.

The lines

$$y = \pm\frac{b}{a}x$$

are the two **asymptotes** of the hyperbola defined by Equation (10). The fastest way to find the equations of the asymptotes is to replace the 1 in Equation (10) by 0 and solve the new equation for y:

$$\underbrace{\frac{x^2}{a^2} - \frac{y^2}{b^2} = 1}_{\text{hyperbola}} \rightarrow \underbrace{\frac{x^2}{a^2} - \frac{y^2}{b^2} = 0}_{\text{0 for 1}} \rightarrow \underbrace{y = \pm\frac{b}{a}x.}_{\text{asymptotes}}$$

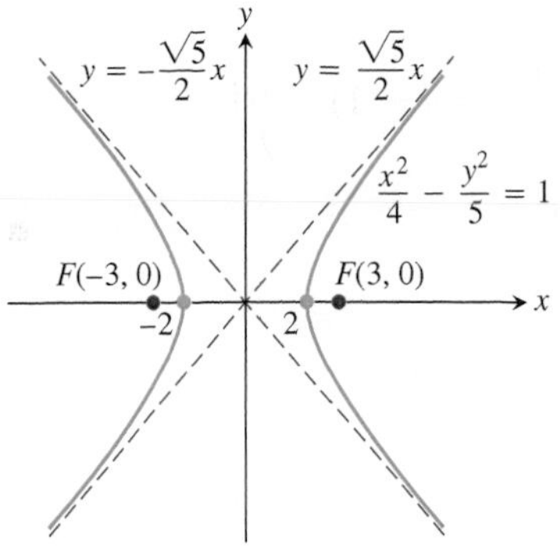

FIGURE A.29 The hyperbola and its asymptotes in Example 3.

EXAMPLE 3 The equation

$$\frac{x^2}{4} - \frac{y^2}{5} = 1 \tag{11}$$

is Equation (10) with $a^2 = 4$ and $b^2 = 5$ (Figure A.29). We have

Center-to-focus distance: $c = \sqrt{a^2 + b^2} = \sqrt{4 + 5} = 3$

Foci: $(\pm c, 0) = (\pm 3, 0)$, Vertices: $(\pm a, 0) = (\pm 2, 0)$

Center: $(0, 0)$

Asymptotes: $\frac{x^2}{4} - \frac{y^2}{5} = 0$ or $y = \pm\frac{\sqrt{5}}{2}x.$ ■

If we interchange x and y in Equation (11), the foci and vertices of the resulting hyperbola will lie along the y-axis. We still find the asymptotes in the same way as before, but now their equations will be $y = \pm 2x/\sqrt{5}$.

Standard-Form Equations for Hyperbolas Centered at the Origin

Foci on the x-axis: $\frac{x^2}{a^2} - \frac{y^2}{b^2} = 1$

Center-to-focus distance: $c = \sqrt{a^2 + b^2}$

Foci: $(\pm c, 0)$

Vertices: $(\pm a, 0)$

Asymptotes: $\frac{x^2}{a^2} - \frac{y^2}{b^2} = 0$ or $y = \pm\frac{b}{a}x$

Foci on the y-axis: $\frac{y^2}{a^2} - \frac{x^2}{b^2} = 1$

Center-to-focus distance: $c = \sqrt{a^2 + b^2}$

Foci: $(0, \pm c)$

Vertices: $(0, \pm a)$

Asymptotes: $\frac{y^2}{a^2} - \frac{x^2}{b^2} = 0$ or $y = \pm\frac{a}{b}x$

Notice the difference in the asymptote equations (b/a in the first, a/b in the second).

We shift conics using the principles reviewed in Section 1.2, replacing x by $x + h$ and y by $y + k$.

EXAMPLE 4 Show that the equation $x^2 - 4y^2 + 2x + 8y - 7 = 0$ represents a hyperbola. Find its center, asymptotes, and foci.

Solution We reduce the equation to standard form by completing the square in x and y as follows:

$$(x^2 + 2x) - 4(y^2 - 2y) = 7$$

$$(x^2 + 2x + 1) - 4(y^2 - 2y + 1) = 7 + 1 - 4$$

$$\frac{(x + 1)^2}{4} - (y - 1)^2 = 1.$$

This is the standard form Equation (10) of a hyperbola with x replaced by $x + 1$ and y replaced by $y - 1$. The hyperbola is shifted one unit to the left and one unit upward, and it has center $x + 1 = 0$ and $y - 1 = 0$, or $x = -1$ and $y = 1$. Moreover,

$$a^2 = 4, \qquad b^2 = 1, \qquad c^2 = a^2 + b^2 = 5,$$

so the asymptotes are the two lines

$$\frac{x + 1}{2} - (y - 1) = 0 \qquad \text{and} \qquad \frac{x + 1}{2} + (y - 1) = 0.$$

The shifted foci have coordinates $\left(-1 \pm \sqrt{5}, 1\right)$. ■

Exercises A.4

Identifying Graphs

Match the parabolas in Exercises 1–4 with the following equations:

$$x^2 = 2y, \quad x^2 = -6y, \quad y^2 = 8x, \quad y^2 = -4x.$$

Then find each parabola's focus and directrix.

1.

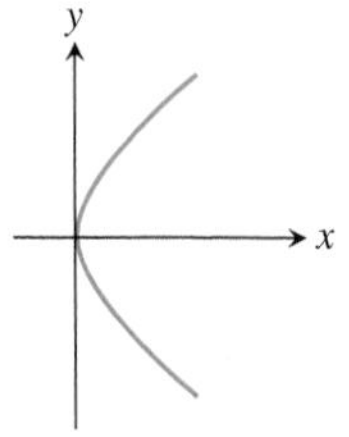

2.

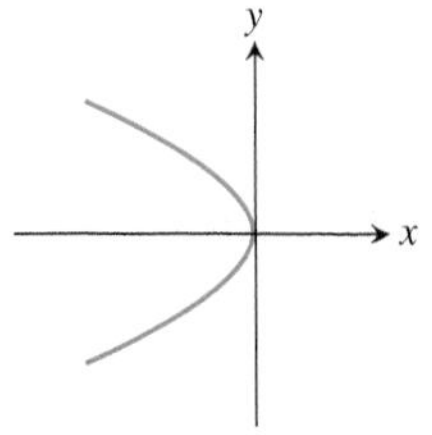

3.

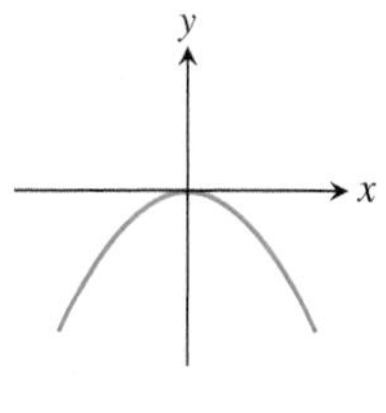

4.

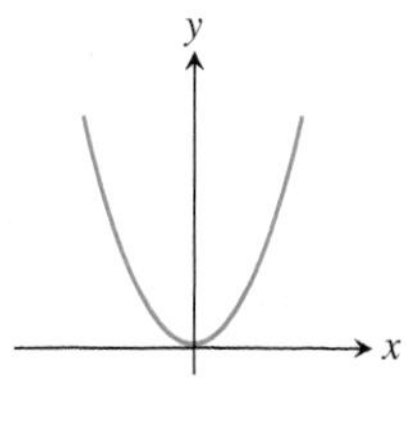

Match each conic section in Exercises 5–8 with one of these equations:

$$\frac{x^2}{4} + \frac{y^2}{9} = 1, \qquad \frac{x^2}{2} + y^2 = 1,$$

$$\frac{y^2}{4} - x^2 = 1, \qquad \frac{x^2}{4} - \frac{y^2}{9} = 1.$$

Then find the conic section's foci and vertices. If the conic section is a hyperbola, find its asymptotes as well.

5.

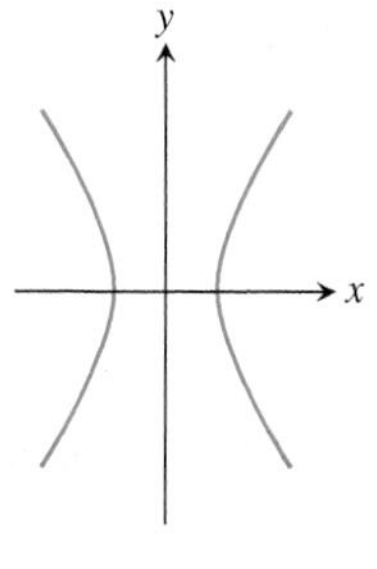

6.

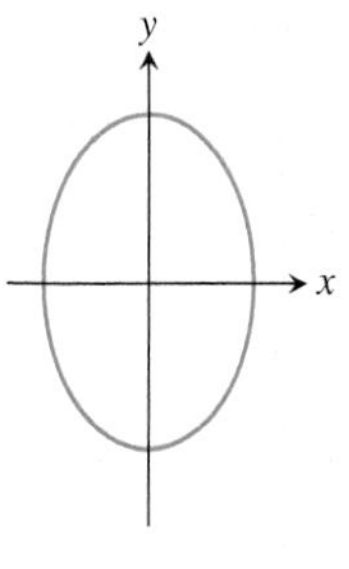

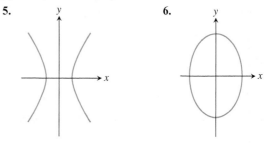

7.

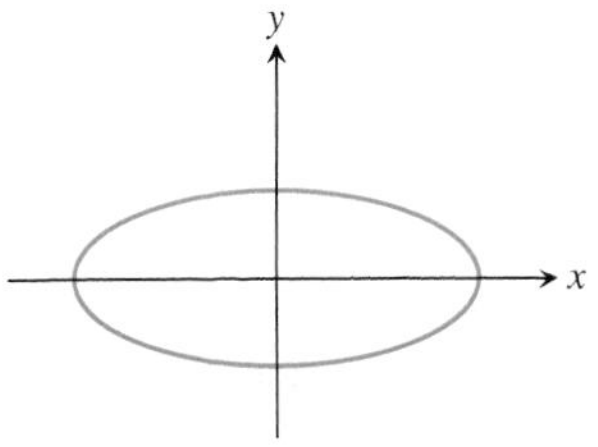

8.

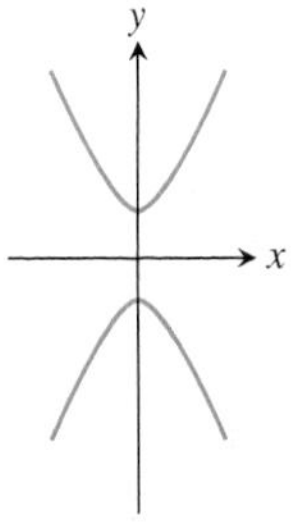

Parabolas

Exercises 9–16 give equations of parabolas. Find each parabola's focus and directrix. Then sketch the parabola. Include the focus and directrix in your sketch.

9. $y^2 = 12x$ **10.** $x^2 = 6y$ **11.** $x^2 = -8y$

12. $y^2 = -2x$ **13.** $y = 4x^2$ **14.** $y = -8x^2$

15. $x = -3y^2$ **16.** $x = 2y^2$

Ellipses

Exercises 17–24 give equations for ellipses. Put each equation in standard form. Then sketch the ellipse. Include the foci in your sketch.

17. $16x^2 + 25y^2 = 400$ **18.** $7x^2 + 16y^2 = 112$

19. $2x^2 + y^2 = 2$ **20.** $2x^2 + y^2 = 4$

21. $3x^2 + 2y^2 = 6$ **22.** $9x^2 + 10y^2 = 90$

23. $6x^2 + 9y^2 = 54$ **24.** $169x^2 + 25y^2 = 4225$

Exercises 25 and 26 give information about the foci and vertices of ellipses centered at the origin of the xy-plane. In each case, find the ellipse's standard-form equation from the given information.

25. Foci: $\left(\pm\sqrt{2}, 0\right)$ Vertices: $(\pm 2, 0)$

26. Foci: $(0, \pm 4)$ Vertices: $(0, \pm 5)$

Hyperbolas

Exercises 27–34 give equations for hyperbolas. Put each equation in standard form and find the hyperbola's asymptotes. Then sketch the hyperbola. Include the asymptotes and foci in your sketch.

27. $x^2 - y^2 = 1$ **28.** $9x^2 - 16y^2 = 144$

29. $y^2 - x^2 = 8$ **30.** $y^2 - x^2 = 4$

31. $8x^2 - 2y^2 = 16$ **32.** $y^2 - 3x^2 = 3$

33. $8y^2 - 2x^2 = 16$ **34.** $64x^2 - 36y^2 = 2304$

Exercises 35–38 give information about the foci, vertices, and asymptotes of hyperbolas centered at the origin of the xy-plane. In each case, find the hyperbola's standard-form equation from the information given.

35. Foci: $\left(0, \pm\sqrt{2}\right)$

Asymptotes: $y = \pm x$

36. Foci: $(\pm 2, 0)$

Asymptotes: $y = \pm\frac{1}{\sqrt{3}}x$

37. Vertices: $(\pm 3, 0)$

Asymptotes: $y = \pm\frac{4}{3}x$

38. Vertices: $(0, \pm 2)$

Asymptotes: $y = \pm\frac{1}{2}x$

Shifting Conic Sections

You may wish to review Section 1.2 before solving Exercises 39–56.

39. The parabola $y^2 = 8x$ is shifted down 2 units and right 1 unit to generate the parabola $(y + 2)^2 = 8(x - 1)$.

a. Find the new parabola's vertex, focus, and directrix.

b. Plot the new vertex, focus, and directrix, and sketch in the parabola.

40. The parabola $x^2 = -4y$ is shifted left 1 unit and up 3 units to generate the parabola $(x + 1)^2 = -4(y - 3)$.

a. Find the new parabola's vertex, focus, and directrix.

b. Plot the new vertex, focus, and directrix, and sketch in the parabola.

41. The ellipse $(x^2/16) + (y^2/9) = 1$ is shifted 4 units to the right and 3 units up to generate the ellipse

$$\frac{(x-4)^2}{16} + \frac{(y-3)^2}{9} = 1.$$

a. Find the foci, vertices, and center of the new ellipse.

b. Plot the new foci, vertices, and center, and sketch in the new ellipse.

42. The ellipse $(x^2/9) + (y^2/25) = 1$ is shifted 3 units to the left and 2 units down to generate the ellipse

$$\frac{(x+3)^2}{9} + \frac{(y+2)^2}{25} = 1.$$

a. Find the foci, vertices, and center of the new ellipse.

b. Plot the new foci, vertices, and center, and sketch in the new ellipse.

43. The hyperbola $(x^2/16) - (y^2/9) = 1$ is shifted 2 units to the right to generate the hyperbola

$$\frac{(x-2)^2}{16} - \frac{y^2}{9} = 1.$$

a. Find the center, foci, vertices, and asymptotes of the new hyperbola.

b. Plot the new center, foci, vertices, and asymptotes, and sketch in the hyperbola.

44. The hyperbola $(y^2/4) - (x^2/5) = 1$ is shifted 2 units down to generate the hyperbola

$$\frac{(y+2)^2}{4} - \frac{x^2}{5} = 1.$$

a. Find the center, foci, vertices, and asymptotes of the new hyperbola.

b. Plot the new center, foci, vertices, and asymptotes, and sketch in the hyperbola.

Exercises 45–48 give equations for parabolas and tell how many units up or down and to the right or left each parabola is to be shifted. Find an equation for the new parabola, and find the new vertex, focus, and directrix.

45. $y^2 = 4x$, left 2, down 3 **46.** $y^2 = -12x$, right 4, up 3

47. $x^2 = 8y$, right 1, down 7 **48.** $x^2 = 6y$, left 3, down 2

Exercises 49–52 give equations for ellipses and tell how many units up or down and to the right or left each ellipse is to be shifted. Find an equation for the new ellipse, and find the new foci, vertices, and center.

49. $\frac{x^2}{6} + \frac{y^2}{9} = 1,\quad$ left 2, down 1

50. $\frac{x^2}{2} + y^2 = 1,\quad$ right 3, up 4

51. $\frac{x^2}{3} + \frac{y^2}{2} = 1,\quad$ right 2, up 3

52. $\frac{x^2}{16} + \frac{y^2}{25} = 1,\quad$ left 4, down 5

Exercises 53–56 give equations for hyperbolas and tell how many units up or down and to the right or left each hyperbola is to be shifted. Find an equation for the new hyperbola, and find the new center, foci, vertices, and asymptotes.

53. $\frac{x^2}{4} - \frac{y^2}{5} = 1,\quad$ right 2, up 2

54. $\frac{x^2}{16} - \frac{y^2}{9} = 1,\quad$ left 2, down 1

55. $y^2 - x^2 = 1,\quad$ left 1, down 1

56. $\frac{y^2}{3} - x^2 = 1,\quad$ right 1, up 3

Find the center, foci, vertices, asymptotes, and radius, as appropriate, of the conic sections in Exercises 57–68.

57. $x^2 + 4x + y^2 = 12$

58. $2x^2 + 2y^2 - 28x + 12y + 114 = 0$

59. $x^2 + 2x + 4y - 3 = 0$

60. $y^2 - 4y - 8x - 12 = 0$

61. $x^2 + 5y^2 + 4x = 1$

62. $9x^2 + 6y^2 + 36y = 0$

63. $x^2 + 2y^2 - 2x - 4y = -1$

64. $4x^2 + y^2 + 8x - 2y = -1$

65. $x^2 - y^2 - 2x + 4y = 4$

66. $x^2 - y^2 + 4x - 6y = 6$

67. $2x^2 - y^2 + 6y = 3$

68. $y^2 - 4x^2 + 16x = 24$

A.5 Proofs of Limit Theorems

This appendix proves Theorem 1, Parts 2–5, and Theorem 4 from Section 2.2.

THEOREM 1—Limit Laws If L, M, c, and k are real numbers and

$$\lim_{x\to c} f(x) = L \quad \text{and} \quad \lim_{x\to c} g(x) = M, \quad \text{then}$$

1. *Sum Rule*: $\lim_{x\to c}(f(x) + g(x)) = L + M$
2. *Difference Rule*: $\lim_{x\to c}(f(x) - g(x)) = L - M$
3. *Constant Multiple Rule*: $\lim_{x\to c}(k \cdot f(x)) = k \cdot L$
4. *Product Rule*: $\lim_{x\to c}(f(x) \cdot g(x)) = L \cdot M$
5. *Quotient Rule*: $\lim_{x\to c}\frac{f(x)}{g(x)} = \frac{L}{M},\quad M \neq 0$
6. *Power Rule*: $\lim_{x\to c}[f(x)]^n = L^n$, n a positive integer
7. *Root Rule*: $\lim_{x\to c}\sqrt[n]{f(x)} = \sqrt[n]{L} = L^{1/n}$, n a positive integer

(If n is even, we assume that $\lim_{x\to c} f(x) = L > 0$.)

We proved the Sum Rule in Section 2.3 and the Power and Root Rules are proved in more advanced texts. We obtain the Difference Rule by replacing $g(x)$ by $-g(x)$ and M by $-M$ in the Sum Rule. The Constant Multiple Rule is the special case $g(x) = k$ of the Product Rule. This leaves only the Product and Quotient Rules.

Proof of the Limit Product Rule We show that for any $\epsilon > 0$ there exists a $\delta > 0$ such that for all x in the intersection D of the domains of f and g,

$$0 < |x - c| < \delta \quad \Rightarrow \quad |f(x)g(x) - LM| < \epsilon.$$

Suppose then that ϵ is a positive number, and write $f(x)$ and $g(x)$ as

$$f(x) = L + (f(x) - L), \qquad g(x) = M + (g(x) - M).$$

Multiply these expressions together and subtract LM:

$$\begin{aligned} f(x)\cdot g(x) - LM &= (L + (f(x) - L))(M + (g(x) - M)) - LM \\ &= LM + L(g(x) - M) + M(f(x) - L) \\ &\quad + (f(x) - L)(g(x) - M) - LM \\ &= L(g(x) - M) + M(f(x) - L) + (f(x) - L)(g(x) - M). \end{aligned} \tag{1}$$

Since f and g have limits L and M as $x \to c$, there exist positive numbers δ_1, δ_2, δ_3, and δ_4 such that for all x in D

$$\begin{aligned} 0 < |x - c| < \delta_1 &\quad\Rightarrow\quad |f(x) - L| < \sqrt{\epsilon/3} \\ 0 < |x - c| < \delta_2 &\quad\Rightarrow\quad |g(x) - M| < \sqrt{\epsilon/3} \\ 0 < |x - c| < \delta_3 &\quad\Rightarrow\quad |f(x) - L| < \epsilon/(3(1 + |M|)) \\ 0 < |x - c| < \delta_4 &\quad\Rightarrow\quad |g(x) - M| < \epsilon/(3(1 + |L|)). \end{aligned} \tag{2}$$

If we take δ to be the smallest numbers δ_1 through δ_4, the inequalities on the right-hand side of the Implications (2) will hold simultaneously for $0 < |x - c| < \delta$. Therefore, for all x in D, $0 < |x - c| < \delta$ implies

$$\begin{aligned} &|f(x)\cdot g(x) - LM| && \text{Triangle inequality applied to Eq. (1)} \\ &\quad \le |L||g(x) - M| + |M||f(x) - L| + |f(x) - L||g(x) - M| \\ &\quad \le (1 + |L|)|g(x) - M| + (1 + |M|)|f(x) - L| + |f(x) - L||g(x) - M| \\ &\quad < \frac{\epsilon}{3} + \frac{\epsilon}{3} + \sqrt{\frac{\epsilon}{3}}\sqrt{\frac{\epsilon}{3}} = \epsilon. && \text{Values from (2)} \end{aligned}$$

This completes the proof of the Limit Product Rule. ■

Proof of the Limit Quotient Rule We show that $\lim_{x\to c}(1/g(x)) = 1/M$. We can then conclude that

$$\lim_{x\to c}\frac{f(x)}{g(x)} = \lim_{x\to c}\left(f(x)\cdot\frac{1}{g(x)}\right) = \lim_{x\to c} f(x)\cdot\lim_{x\to c}\frac{1}{g(x)} = L\cdot\frac{1}{M} = \frac{L}{M}$$

by the Limit Product Rule.

Let $\epsilon > 0$ be given. To show that $\lim_{x\to c}(1/g(x)) = 1/M$, we need to show that there exists a $\delta > 0$ such that for all x

$$0 < |x - c| < \delta \quad\Rightarrow\quad \left|\frac{1}{g(x)} - \frac{1}{M}\right| < \epsilon.$$

Since $|M| > 0$, there exists a positive number δ_1 such that for all x

$$0 < |x - c| < \delta_1 \quad\Rightarrow\quad |g(x) - M| < \frac{M}{2}. \tag{3}$$

For any numbers A and B it can be shown that $|A| - |B| \le |A - B|$ and $|B| - |A| \le |A - B|$, from which it follows that $||A| - |B|| \le |A - B|$. With $A = g(x)$ and $B = M$, this becomes

$$||g(x)| - |M|| \le |g(x) - M|,$$

which can be combined with the inequality on the right in Implication (3) to get, in turn,

$$\begin{aligned}
\big|\,|g(x)| - |M|\,\big| &< \frac{|M|}{2} \\
-\frac{|M|}{2} < |g(x)| - |M| &< \frac{|M|}{2} \\
\frac{|M|}{2} < |g(x)| &< \frac{3|M|}{2} \\
|M| < 2|g(x)| &< 3|M| \\
\frac{1}{|g(x)|} < \frac{2}{|M|} &< \frac{3}{|g(x)|}.
\end{aligned} \tag{4}$$

Therefore, $0 < |x - c| < \delta_1$ implies that

$$\begin{aligned}
\left|\frac{1}{g(x)} - \frac{1}{M}\right| = \left|\frac{M - g(x)}{Mg(x)}\right| &\le \frac{1}{|M|}\cdot\frac{1}{|g(x)|}\cdot|M - g(x)| \\
&< \frac{1}{|M|}\cdot\frac{2}{|M|}\cdot|M - g(x)|. \qquad \text{Inequality (4)}
\end{aligned} \tag{5}$$

Since $(1/2)|M|^2\epsilon > 0$, there exists a number $\delta_2 > 0$ such that for all x

$$0 < |x - c| < \delta_2 \quad \Rightarrow \quad |M - g(x)| < \frac{\epsilon}{2}|M|^2. \tag{6}$$

If we take δ to be the smaller of δ_1 and δ_2, the conclusions in (5) and (6) both hold for all x such that $0 < |x - c| < \delta$. Combining these conclusions gives

$$0 < |x - c| < \delta \quad \Rightarrow \quad \left|\frac{1}{g(x)} - \frac{1}{M}\right| < \epsilon.$$

This concludes the proof of the Limit Quotient Rule. ■

THEOREM 4—The Sandwich Theorem Suppose that $g(x) \le f(x) \le h(x)$ for all x in some open interval I containing c, except possibly at $x = c$ itself. Suppose also that $\lim_{x\to c} g(x) = \lim_{x\to c} h(x) = L$. Then $\lim_{x\to c} f(x) = L$.

Proof for Right-Hand Limits Suppose $\lim_{x\to c^+} g(x) = \lim_{x\to c^+} h(x) = L$. Then for any $\epsilon > 0$ there exists a $\delta > 0$ such that for all x the interval $c < x < c + \delta$ is contained in I and the inequality implies

$$L - \epsilon < g(x) < L + \epsilon \qquad \text{and} \qquad L - \epsilon < h(x) < L + \epsilon.$$

These inequalities combine with the inequality $g(x) \le f(x) \le h(x)$ to give

$$\begin{aligned}
L - \epsilon < g(x) \le f(x) \le h(x) &< L + \epsilon, \\
L - \epsilon < f(x) &< L + \epsilon, \\
-\epsilon < f(x) - L &< \epsilon.
\end{aligned}$$

Therefore, for all x, the inequality $c < x < c + \delta$ implies $|f(x) - L| < \epsilon$.

Proof for Left-Hand Limits Suppose $\lim_{x\to c^-} g(x) = \lim_{x\to c^-} h(x) = L$. Then for any $\epsilon > 0$ there exists a $\delta > 0$ such that for all x the interval $c - \delta < x < c$ is contained in I and the inequality implies

$$L - \epsilon < g(x) < L + \epsilon \quad \text{and} \quad L - \epsilon < h(x) < L + \epsilon.$$

We conclude as before that for all x, $c - \delta < x < c$ implies $|f(x) - L| < \epsilon$.

Proof for Two-Sided Limits If $\lim_{x\to c} g(x) = \lim_{x\to c} h(x) = L$, then $g(x)$ and $h(x)$ both approach L as $x \to c^+$ and as $x \to c^-$; so $\lim_{x\to c^+} f(x) = L$ and $\lim_{x\to c^-} f(x) = L$. Hence $\lim_{x\to c} f(x)$ exists and equals L. ■

Exercises A.5

1. Suppose that functions $f_1(x)$, $f_2(x)$, and $f_3(x)$ have limits L_1, L_2, and L_3, respectively, as $x \to c$. Show that their sum has limit $L_1 + L_2 + L_3$. Use mathematical induction (Appendix 2) to generalize this result to the sum of any finite number of functions.

2. Use mathematical induction and the Limit Product Rule in Theorem 1 to show that if functions $f_1(x), f_2(x), \dots, f_n(x)$ have limits $L_1, L_2, \dots, L_n$ as $x \to c$, then
$$\lim_{x\to c} f_1(x)\cdot f_2(x)\cdot\cdots\cdot f_n(x) = L_1\cdot L_2\cdot\cdots\cdot L_n.$$

3. Use the fact that $\lim_{x\to c} x = c$ and the result of Exercise 2 to show that $\lim_{x\to c} x^n = c^n$ for any integer $n > 1$.

4. **Limits of polynomials** Use the fact that $\lim_{x\to c}(k) = k$ for any number k together with the results of Exercises 1 and 3 to show that $\lim_{x\to c} f(x) = f(c)$ for any polynomial function
$$f(x) = a_n x^n + a_{n-1}x^{n-1} + \cdots + a_1 x + a_0.$$

5. **Limits of rational functions** Use Theorem 1 and the result of Exercise 4 to show that if $f(x)$ and $g(x)$ are polynomial functions and $g(c) \neq 0$, then
$$\lim_{x\to c} \frac{f(x)}{g(x)} = \frac{f(c)}{g(c)}.$$

6. **Composites of continuous functions** Figure A.30 gives the diagram for a proof that the composite of two continuous functions is continuous. Reconstruct the proof from the diagram. The statement to be proved is this: If f is continuous at $x = c$ and g is continuous at $f(c)$, then $g \circ f$ is continuous at c.
   Assume that c is an interior point of the domain of f and that $f(c)$ is an interior point of the domain of g. This will make the limits involved two-sided. (The arguments for the cases that involve one-sided limits are similar.)

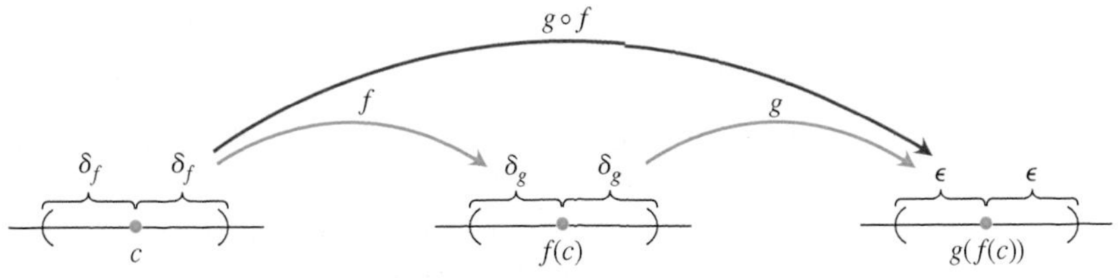

FIGURE A.30 The diagram for a proof that the composite of two continuous functions is continuous.

A.6 Commonly Occurring Limits

This appendix verifies limits (4)–(6) in Theorem 5 of Section 9.1.

Limit 4: If $|x| < 1$, $\lim_{n\to\infty} x^n = 0$ We need to show that to each $\epsilon > 0$ there corresponds an integer N so large that $|x^n| < \epsilon$ for all n greater than N. Since $\epsilon^{1/n} \to 1$, while $|x| < 1$, there exists an integer N for which $\epsilon^{1/N} > |x|$. In other words,

$$|x^N| = |x|^N < \epsilon. \tag{1}$$

This is the integer we seek because, if $|x| < 1$, then

$$|x^n| < |x^N| \quad \text{for all } n > N. \tag{2}$$

Combining (1) and (2) produces $|x^n| < \epsilon$ for all $n > N$, concluding the proof. ■

Limit 5: For any number x, $\lim_{n\to\infty}\left(1 + \frac{x}{n}\right)^n = e^x$ Let

$$a_n = \left(1 + \frac{x}{n}\right)^n.$$

Then

$$\ln a_n = \ln\left(1 + \frac{x}{n}\right)^n = n \ln\left(1 + \frac{x}{n}\right) \to x,$$

as we can see by the following application of l'Hôpital's Rule, in which we differentiate with respect to n:

$$\begin{aligned}\lim_{n\to\infty} n \ln\left(1 + \frac{x}{n}\right) &= \lim_{n\to\infty} \frac{\ln(1 + x/n)}{1/n} \\ &= \lim_{n\to\infty} \frac{\left(\dfrac{1}{1 + x/n}\right)\cdot\left(-\dfrac{x}{n^2}\right)}{-1/n^2} = \lim_{n\to\infty} \frac{x}{1 + x/n} = x.\end{aligned}$$

Apply Theorem 3, Section 9.1, with $f(x) = e^x$ to conclude that

$$\left(1 + \frac{x}{n}\right)^n = a_n = e^{\ln a_n} \to e^x.$$

■

Limit 6: For any number x, $\lim_{n\to\infty} \frac{x^n}{n!} = 0$ Since

$$-\frac{|x|^n}{n!} \le \frac{x^n}{n!} \le \frac{|x|^n}{n!},$$

all we need to show is that $|x|^n/n! \to 0$. We can then apply the Sandwich Theorem for Sequences (Section 9.1, Theorem 2) to conclude that $x^n/n! \to 0$.

The first step in showing that $|x|^n/n! \to 0$ is to choose an integer $M > |x|$, so that $(|x|/M) < 1$. By Limit 4, just proved, we then have $(|x|/M)^n \to 0$. We then restrict our attention to values of $n > M$. For these values of n, we can write

$$\begin{aligned}\frac{|x|^n}{n!} &= \frac{|x|^n}{1\cdot 2\cdot \cdots \cdot M\cdot \underbrace{(M + 1)\cdot (M + 2)\cdot \cdots \cdot n}_{(n - M)\text{ factors}}} \\ &\le \frac{|x|^n}{M!M^{n-M}} = \frac{|x|^n M^M}{M!M^n} = \frac{M^M}{M!}\left(\frac{|x|}{M}\right)^n.\end{aligned}$$

Thus,

$$0 \le \frac{|x|^n}{n!} \le \frac{M^M}{M!}\left(\frac{|x|}{M}\right)^n.$$

Now, the constant $M^M/M!$ does not change as n increases. Thus the Sandwich Theorem tells us that $|x|^n/n! \to 0$ because $(|x|/M)^n \to 0$. ■

Answers to Odd-Numbered Exercises

CHAPTER 1

Section 1.1, pp. 11–13

1. $D: (-\infty, \infty)$, $R: [1, \infty)$ **3.** $D: [-2, \infty)$, $R: [0, \infty)$

5. $D: (-\infty, 3) \cup (3, \infty)$, $R: (-\infty, 0) \cup (0, \infty)$

7. **(a)** Not a function of x because some values of x have two values of y
(b) A function of x because for every x there is only one possible y

9. $A = \frac{\sqrt{3}}{4}x^2$, $p = 3x$ **11.** $x = \frac{d}{\sqrt{3}}$, $A = 2d^2$, $V = \frac{d^3}{3\sqrt{3}}$

13. $L = \frac{\sqrt{20x^2 - 20x + 25}}{4}$

15. $(-\infty, \infty)$

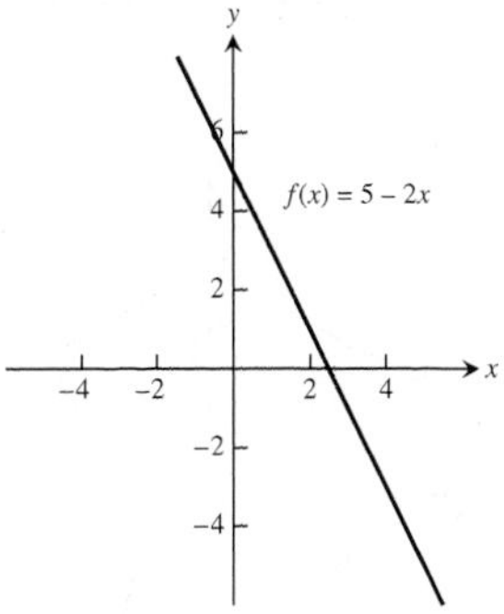

17. $(-\infty, \infty)$

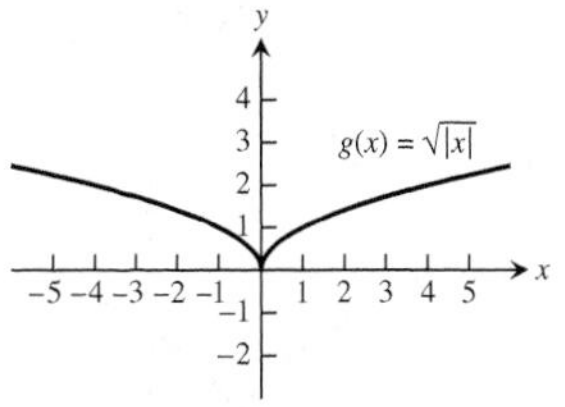

19. $(-\infty, 0) \cup (0, \infty)$

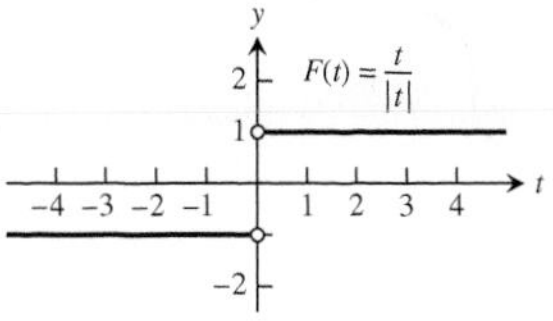

21. $(-\infty, -5) \cup (-5, -3] \cup [3, 5) \cup (5, \infty)$

23. **(a)** For each positive value of x, there are two values of y. **(b)** For each value of $x \neq 0$, there are two values of y.

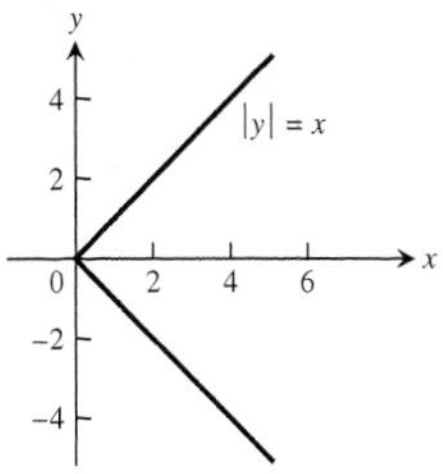

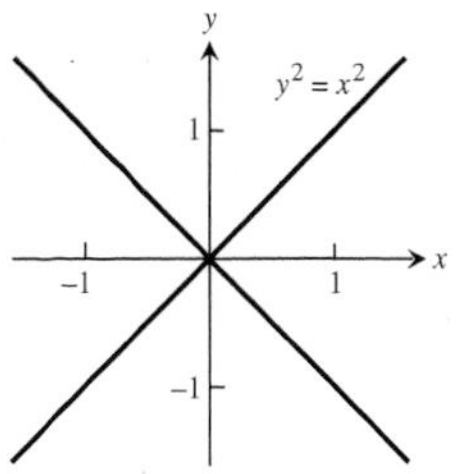

25.

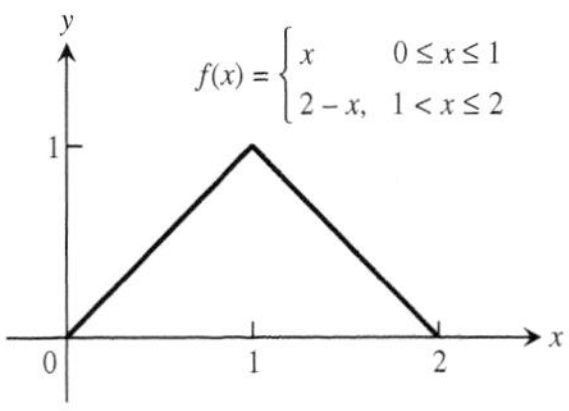

27.

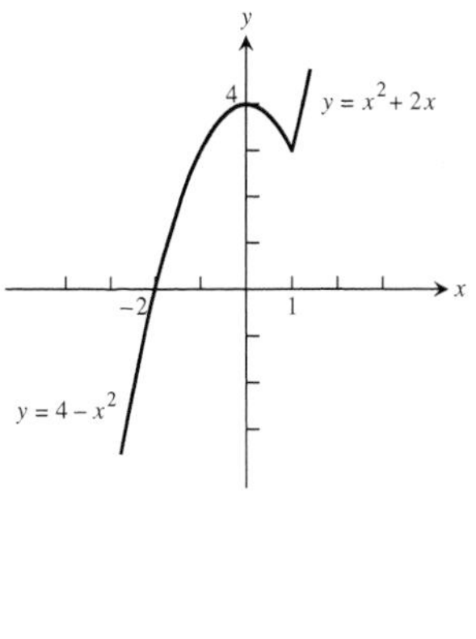

29. **(a)** $f(x) = \begin{cases} x, & 0 \le x \le 1 \\ -x + 2, & 1 < x \le 2 \end{cases}$

(b) $f(x) = \begin{cases} 2, & 0 \le x < 1 \\ 0, & 1 \le x < 2 \\ 2, & 2 \le x < 3 \\ 0, & 3 \le x \le 4 \end{cases}$

31. **(a)** $f(x) = \begin{cases} -x, & -1 \le x < 0 \\ 1, & 0 < x \le 1 \\ -\frac{1}{2}x + \frac{3}{2}, & 1 < x < 3 \end{cases}$

(b) $f(x) = \begin{cases} \frac{1}{2}x, & -2 \le x \le 0 \\ -2x + 2, & 0 < x \le 1 \\ -1, & 1 < x \le 3 \end{cases}$

33. **(a)** $0 \le x < 1$ **(b)** $-1 < x \le 0$ **35.** Yes

37. Symmetric about the origin

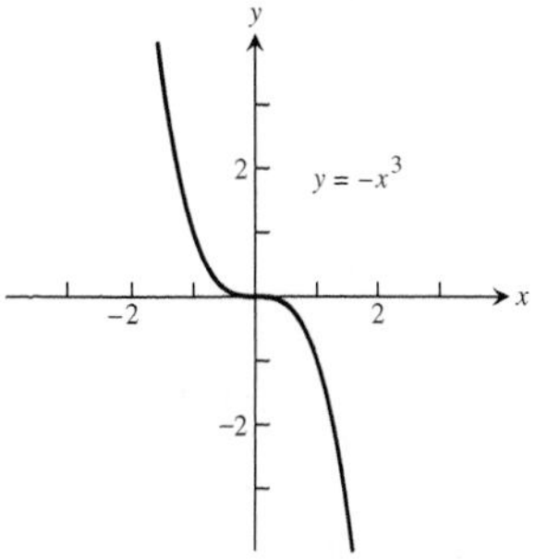

Dec. $-\infty < x < \infty$

39. Symmetric about the origin

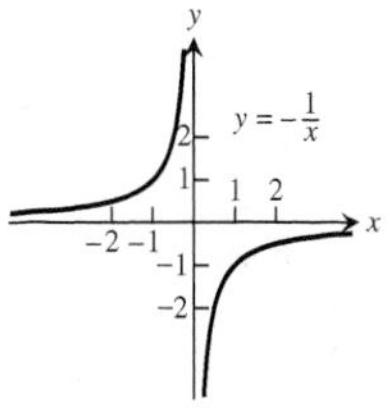

Inc. $-\infty < x < 0$ and $0 < x < \infty$

41. Symmetric about the y-axis

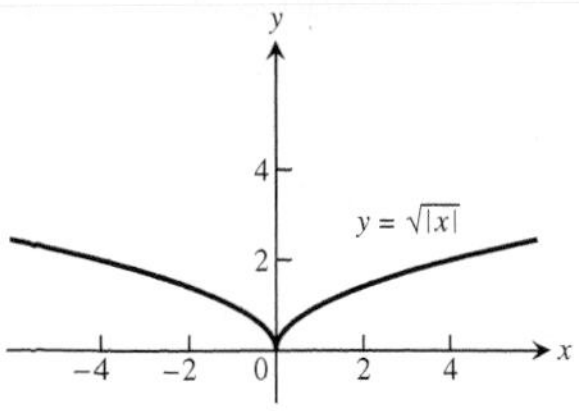

Dec. $-\infty < x \le 0$;
Inc. $0 \le x < \infty$

43. Symmetric about the origin

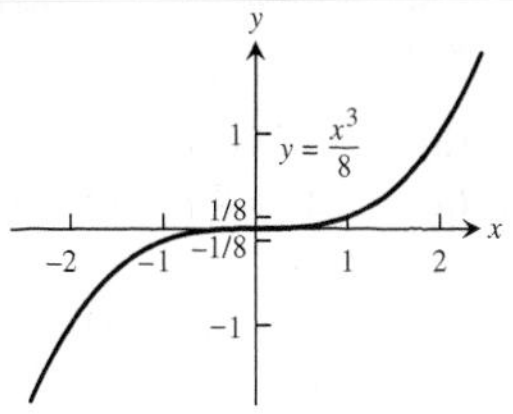

Inc. $-\infty < x < \infty$

45. No symmetry

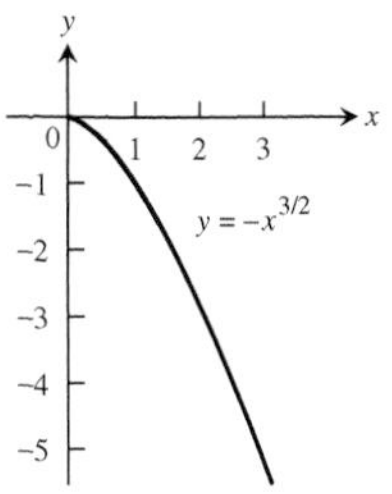

Dec. $0 \le x < \infty$

47. Even **49.** Even **51.** Odd **53.** Even

55. Neither **57.** Neither **59.** $t = 180$ **61.** $s = 2.4$

63. $V = x(14 - 2x)(22 - 2x)$

65. **(a)** h **(b)** f **(c)** g **67.** **(a)** $(-2, 0) \cup (4, \infty)$

71. $C = 5(2 + \sqrt{2})h$

Section 1.2, pp. 18–21

1. $D_f: -\infty < x < \infty,\quad D_g: x \ge 1,\quad R_f: -\infty < y < \infty,$ $R_g: y \ge 0,\quad D_{f+g} = D_{f\cdot g} = D_g,\quad R_{f+g}: y \ge 1,\quad R_{f\cdot g}: y \ge 0$

3. $D_f: -\infty < x < \infty,\quad D_g: -\infty < x < \infty,\quad R_f: y = 2,$ $R_g: y \ge 1,\quad D_{f/g}: -\infty < x < \infty,\quad R_{f/g}: 0 < y \le 2,$ $D_{g/f}: -\infty < x < \infty,\quad R_{g/f}: y \ge 1/2$

5. **(a)** 2 **(b)** 22 **(c)** $x^2 + 2$ **(d)** $x^2 + 10x + 22$ **(e)** 5 **(f)** -2 **(g)** $x + 10$ **(h)** $x^4 - 6x^2 + 6$

7. $13 - 3x$ **9.** $\sqrt{\dfrac{5x+1}{4x+1}}$

11. **(a)** $f(g(x))$ **(b)** $j(g(x))$ **(c)** $g(g(x))$ **(d)** $j(j(x))$ **(e)** $g(h(f(x)))$ **(f)** $h(j(f(x)))$

13.

	$g(x)$	$f(x)$	$(f \circ g)(x)$
(a)	$x - 7$	$\sqrt{x}$	$\sqrt{x - 7}$
(b)	$x + 2$	$3x$	$3x + 6$
(c)	x^2	$\sqrt{x - 5}$	$\sqrt{x^2 - 5}$
(d)	$\dfrac{x}{x-1}$	$\dfrac{x}{x-1}$	x
(e)	$\dfrac{1}{x-1}$	$1 + \dfrac{1}{x}$	x
(f)	$\dfrac{1}{x}$	$\dfrac{1}{x}$	x

15. **(a)** 1 **(b)** 2 **(c)** -2 **(d)** 0 **(e)** -1 **(f)** 0

17. **(a)** $f(g(x)) = \sqrt{\dfrac{1}{x} + 1},\ g(f(x)) = \dfrac{1}{\sqrt{x+1}}$
(b) $D_{f\circ g} = (-\infty, -1] \cup (0, \infty),\ D_{g\circ f} = (-1, \infty)$
(c) $R_{f\circ g} = [0, 1) \cup (1, \infty),\ R_{g\circ f} = (0, \infty)$

19. $g(x) = \dfrac{2x}{x - 1}$

21. **(a)** $y = -(x + 7)^2$ **(b)** $y = -(x - 4)^2$

23. **(a)** Position 4 **(b)** Position 1 **(c)** Position 2 **(d)** Position 3

25. $(x + 2)^2 + (y + 3)^2 = 49$

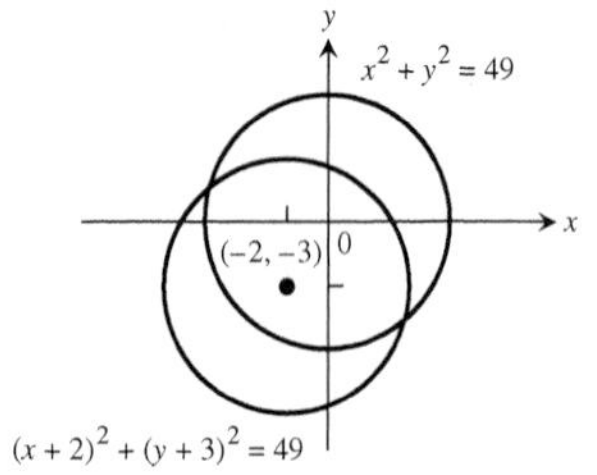

27. $y + 1 = (x + 1)^3$

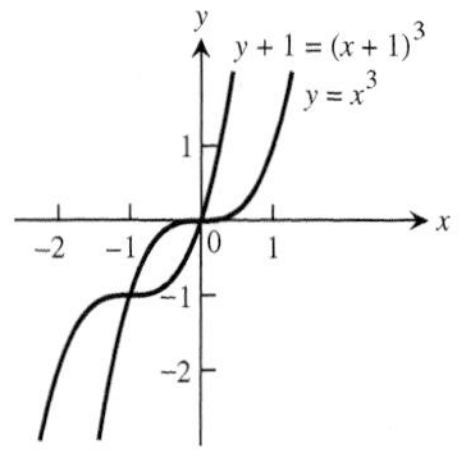

29. $y = \sqrt{x + 0.81}$

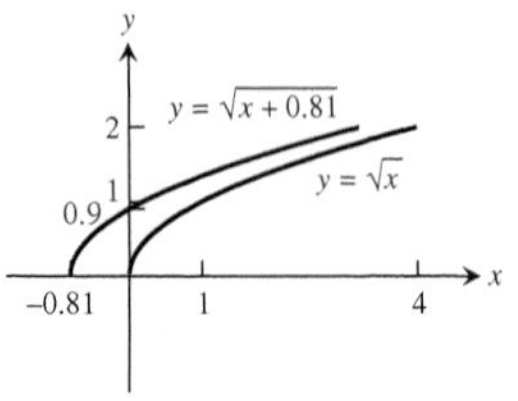

31. $y = 2x$

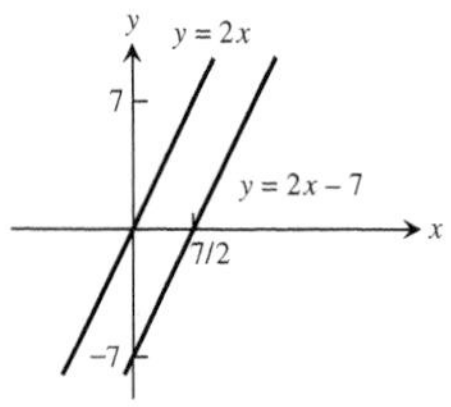

33. $y - 1 = \dfrac{1}{x - 1}$

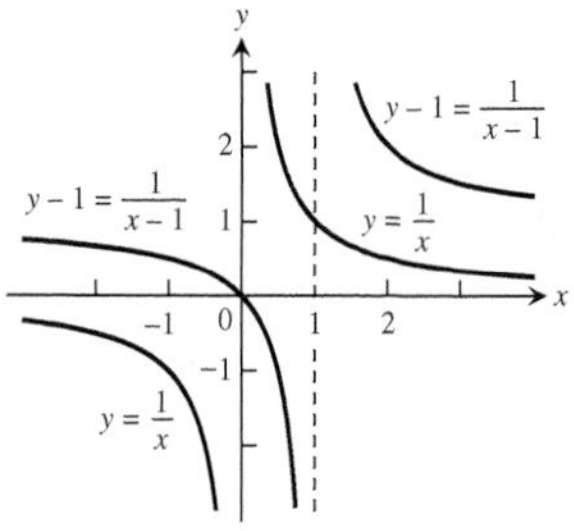

35.

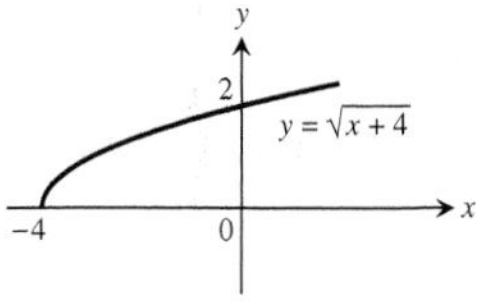

37.

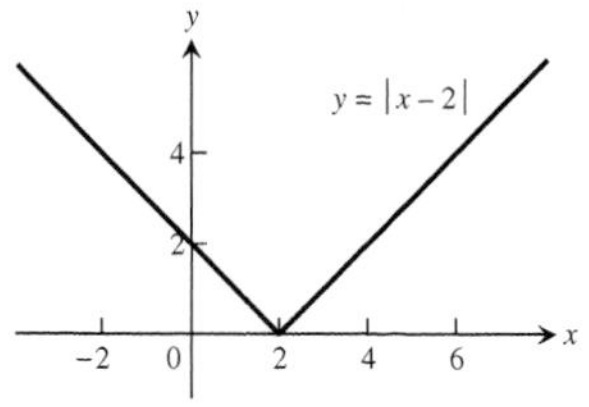

39.

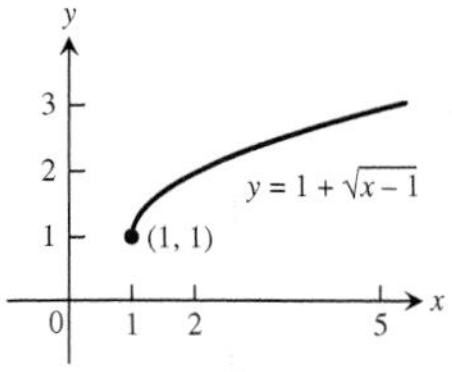

41.

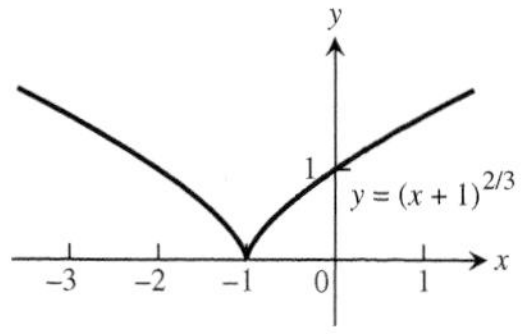

43.

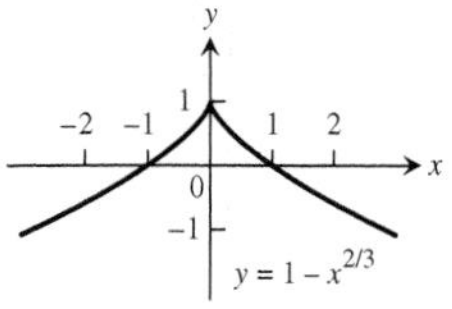

45.

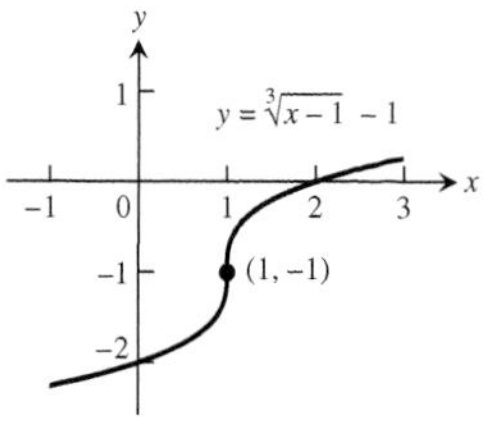

47.

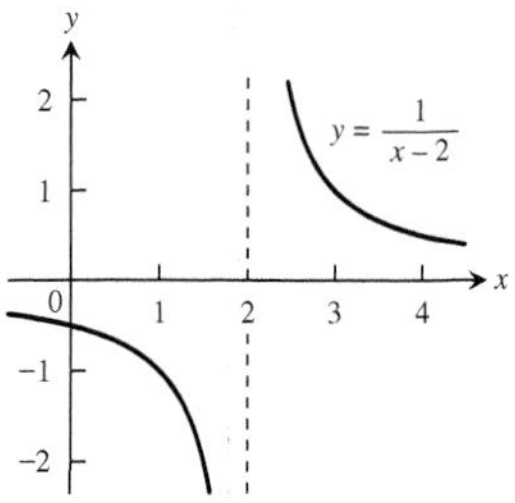

49.

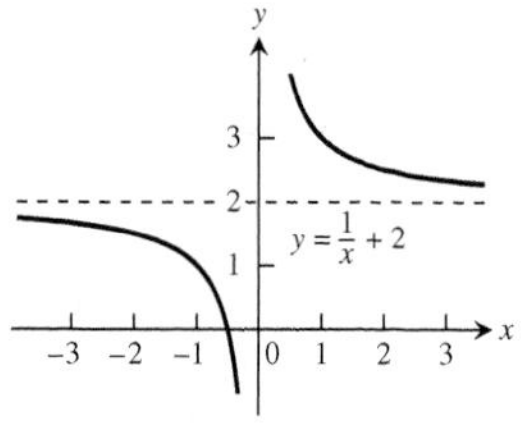

51.

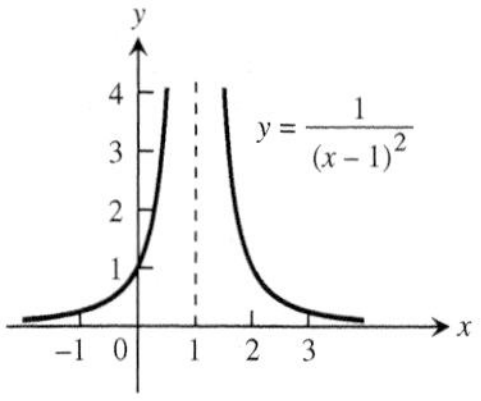

53.

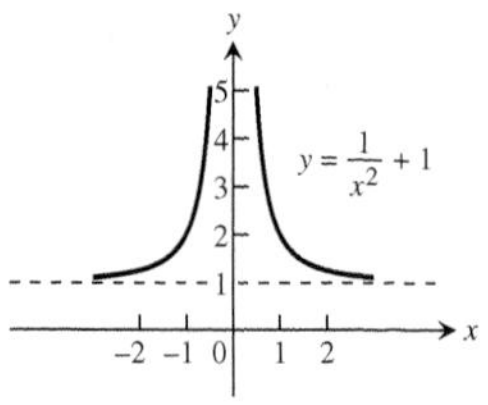

55. **(a)** $D: [0, 2],\quad R: [2, 3]$

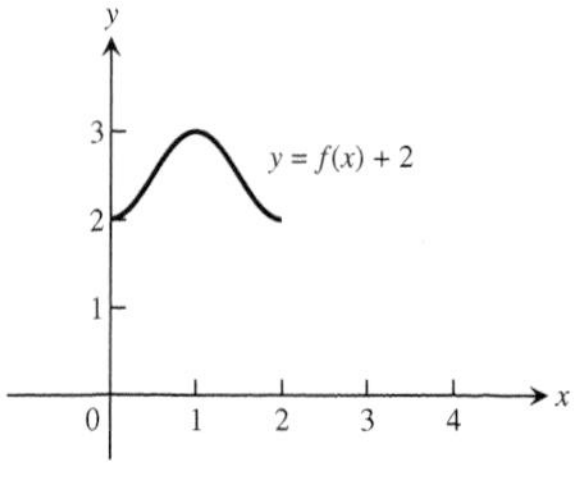

(b) $D: [0, 2],\quad R: [-1, 0]$

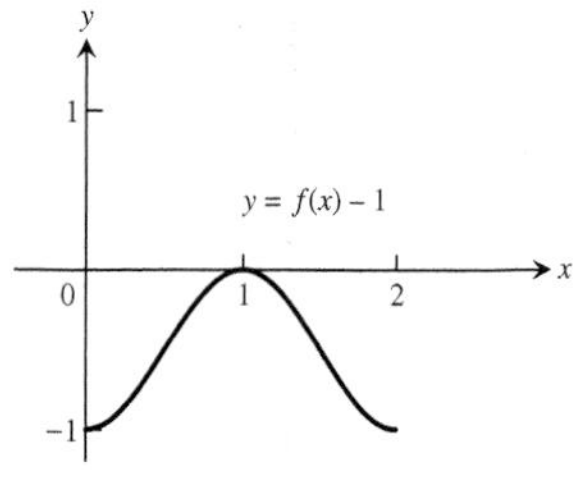

(c) $D: [0, 2], \quad R: [0, 2]$

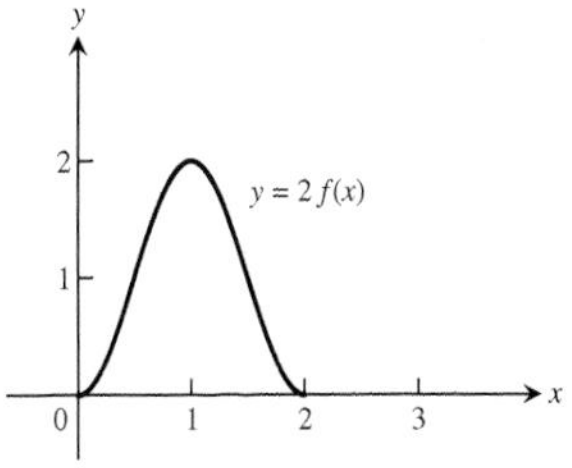

(d) $D: [0, 2], \quad R: [-1, 0]$

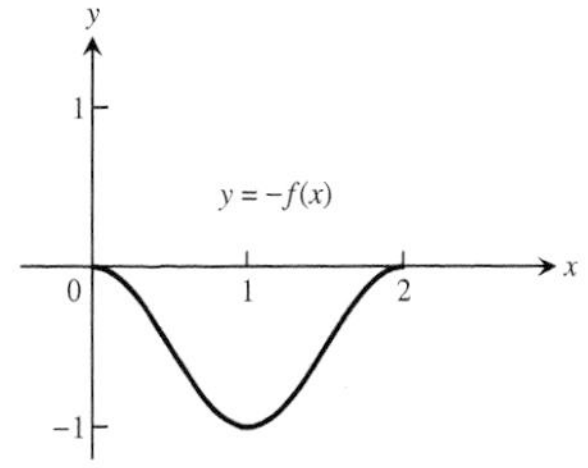

(e) $D: [-2, 0], \quad R: [0, 1]$

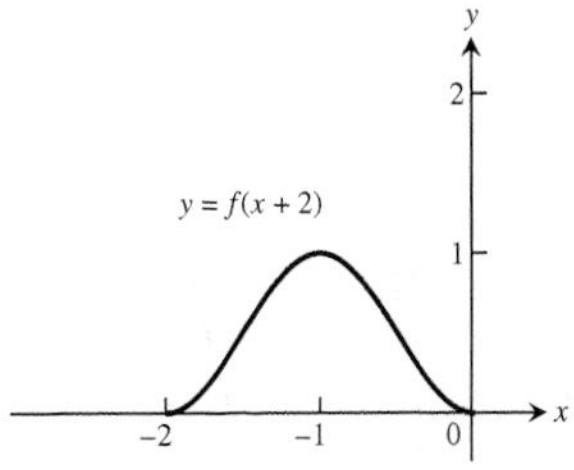

(f) $D: [1, 3], \quad R: [0, 1]$

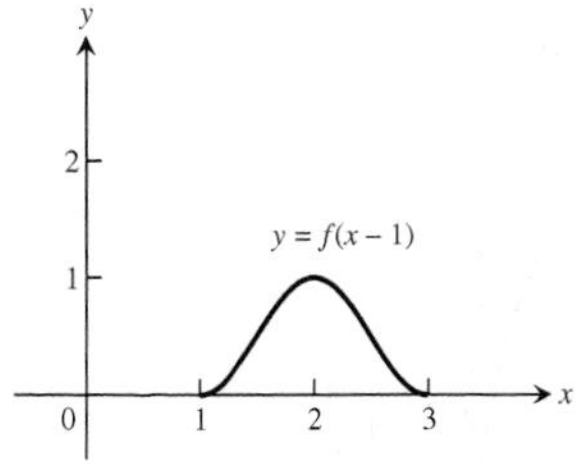

(g) $D: [-2, 0], \quad R: [0, 1]$

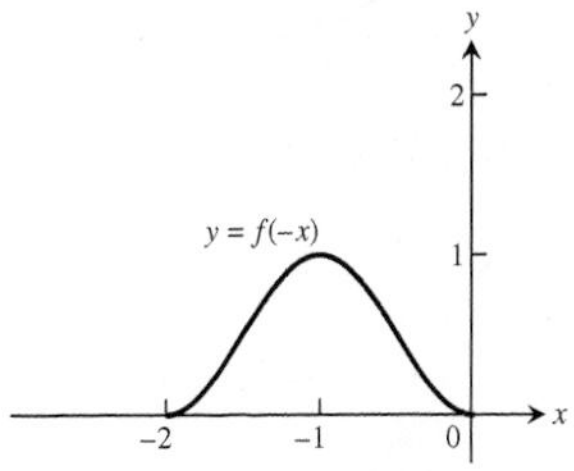

(h) $D: [-1, 1], \quad R: [0, 1]$

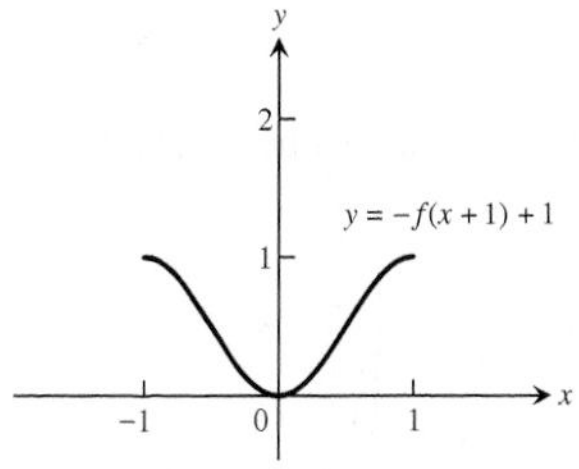

57. $y = 3x^2 - 3$ **59.** $y = \frac{1}{2} + \frac{1}{2x^2}$ **61.** $y = \sqrt{4x + 1}$

63. $y = \sqrt{4 - \frac{x^2}{4}}$ **65.** $y = 1 - 27x^3$

67.

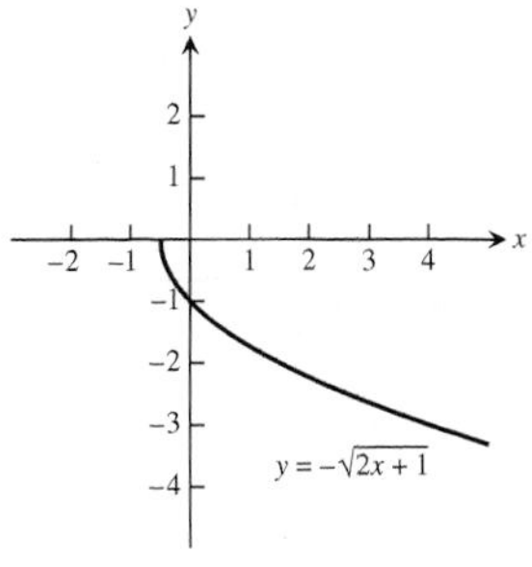

69.

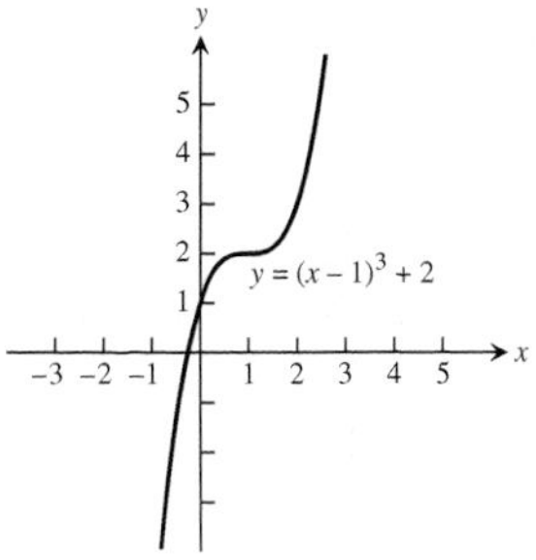

71.

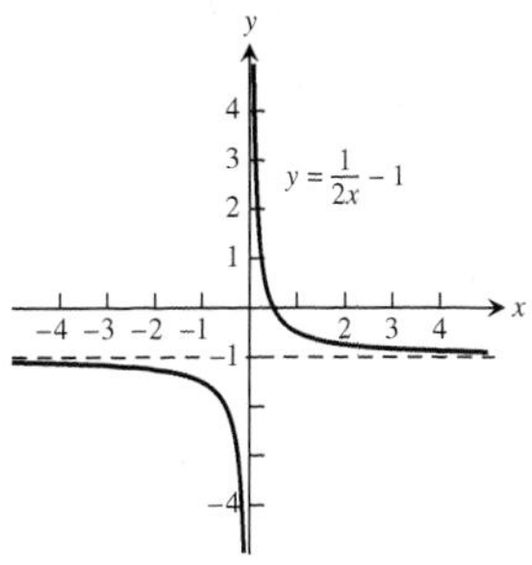

73.

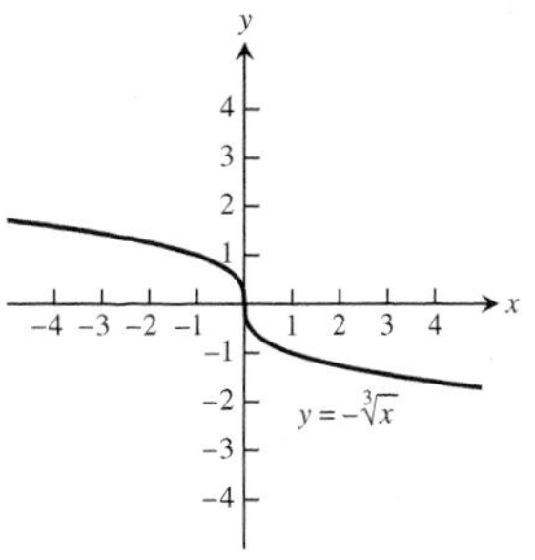

75.

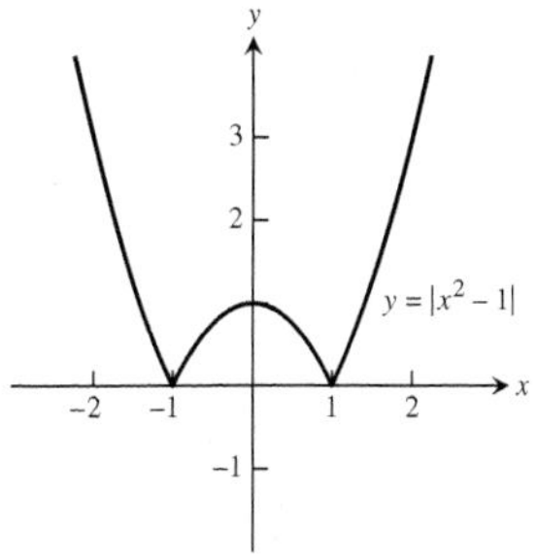

77. **(a)** Odd **(b)** Odd **(c)** Odd **(d)** Even **(e)** Even **(f)** Even **(g)** Even **(h)** Even **(i)** Odd

Section 1.3, pp. 27–29

1. **(a)** 8π m **(b)** $\frac{55\pi}{9}$ m **3.** 8.4 in.

5.

θ	$-\pi$	$-2\pi/3$	0	$\pi/2$	$3\pi/4$
$\sin\theta$	0	$-\frac{\sqrt{3}}{2}$	0	1	$\frac{1}{\sqrt{2}}$
$\cos\theta$	-1	$-\frac{1}{2}$	1	0	$-\frac{1}{\sqrt{2}}$
$\tan\theta$	0	$\sqrt{3}$	0	UND	-1
$\cot\theta$	UND	$\frac{1}{\sqrt{3}}$	UND	0	-1
$\sec\theta$	-1	-2	1	UND	$-\sqrt{2}$
$\csc\theta$	UND	$-\frac{2}{\sqrt{3}}$	UND	1	$\sqrt{2}$

7. $\cos x = -4/5, \tan x = -3/4$

9. $\sin x = -\frac{\sqrt{8}}{3}, \tan x = -\sqrt{8}$

11. $\sin x = -\frac{1}{\sqrt{5}}, \cos x = -\frac{2}{\sqrt{5}}$

13. Period π

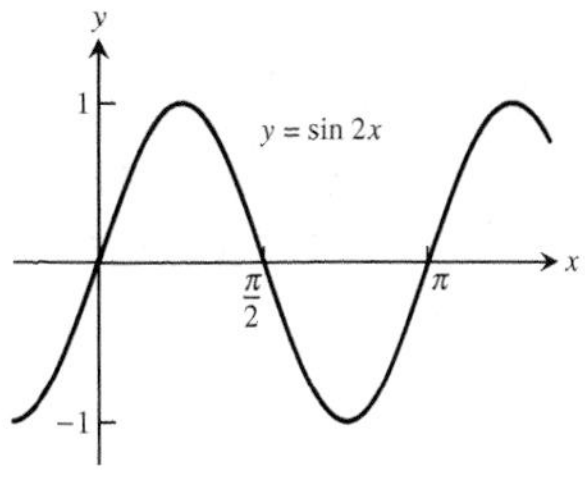

15. Period 2

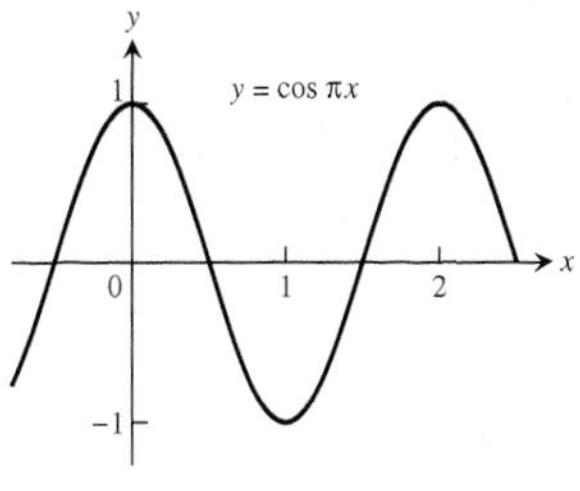

17. Period 6

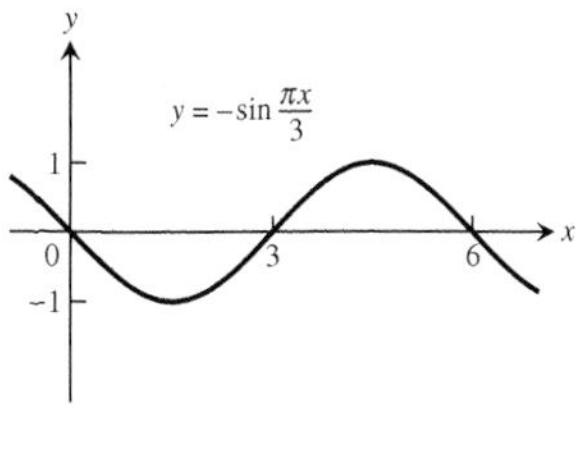

19. Period 2π

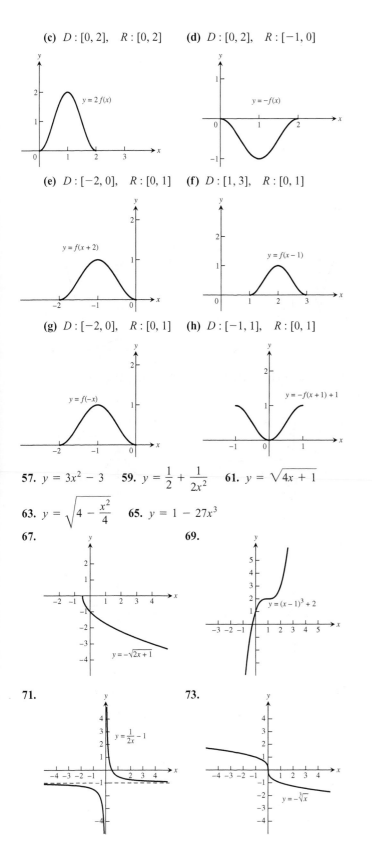

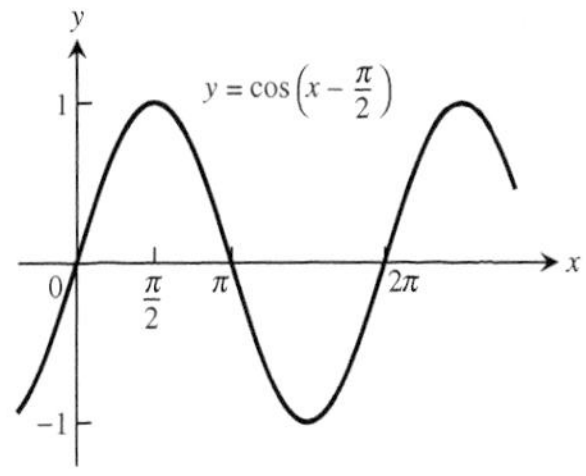

21. Period 2π

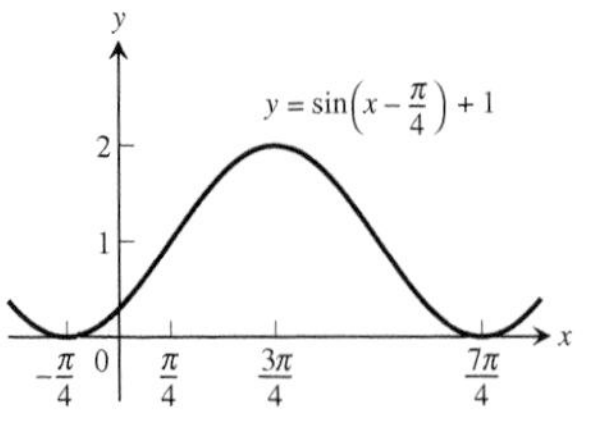

23. Period $\pi/2$, symmetric about the origin

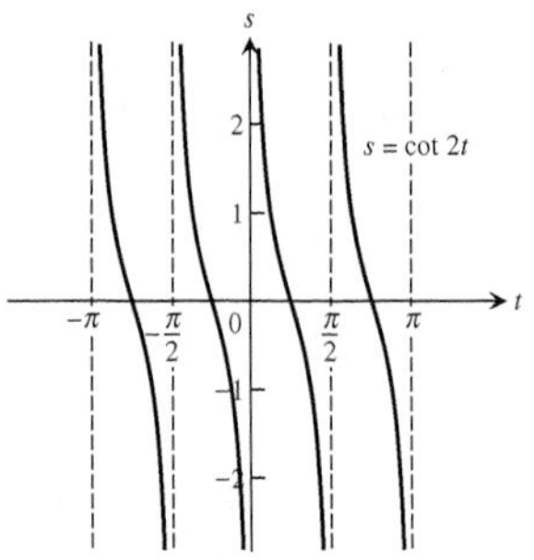

25. Period 4, symmetric about the y-axis

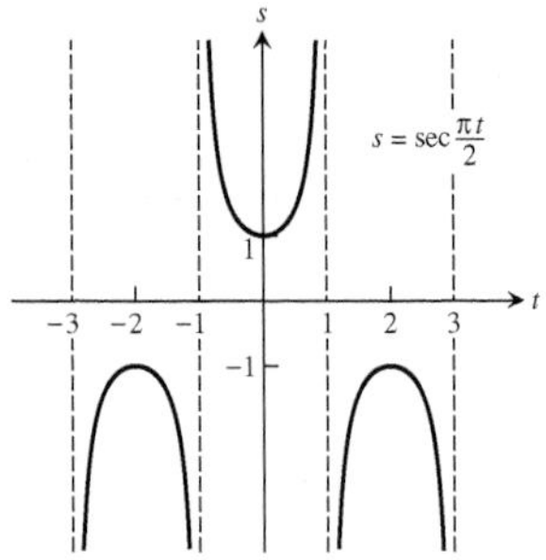

29. $D: (-\infty, \infty)$, $R: y = -1, 0, 1$

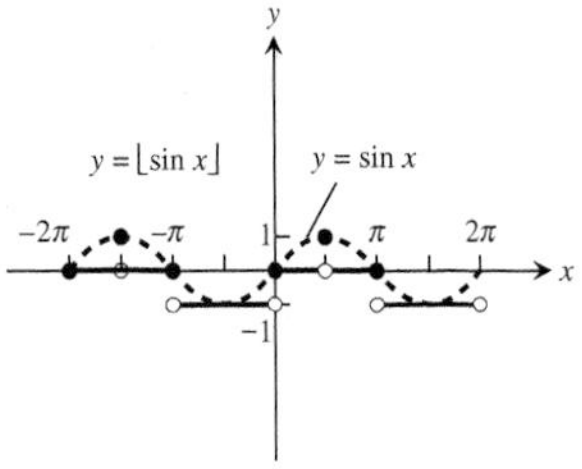

39. $-\cos x$ **41.** $-\cos x$ **43.** $\frac{\sqrt{6} + \sqrt{2}}{4}$ **45.** $\frac{\sqrt{2} + \sqrt{6}}{4}$

47. $\frac{2 + \sqrt{2}}{4}$ **49.** $\frac{2 - \sqrt{3}}{4}$ **51.** $\frac{\pi}{3}, \frac{2\pi}{3}, \frac{4\pi}{3}, \frac{5\pi}{3}$

53. $\frac{\pi}{6}, \frac{\pi}{2}, \frac{5\pi}{6}, \frac{3\pi}{2}$ **59.** $\sqrt{7} \approx 2.65$ **63.** $a = 1.464$

65. $A = 2, B = 2\pi,$ $C = -\pi, D = -1$

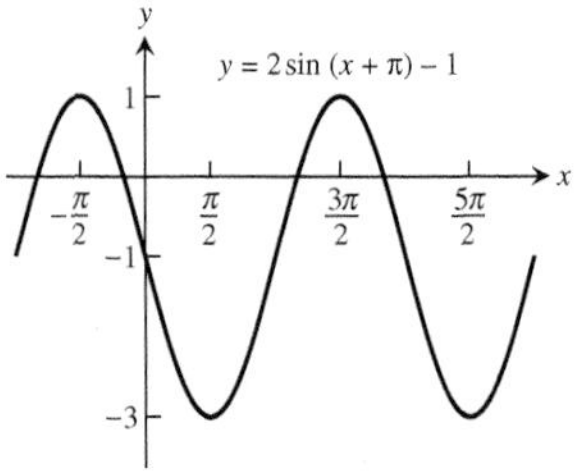

67. $A = -\frac{2}{\pi}, B = 4,$ $C = 0, D = \frac{1}{\pi}$

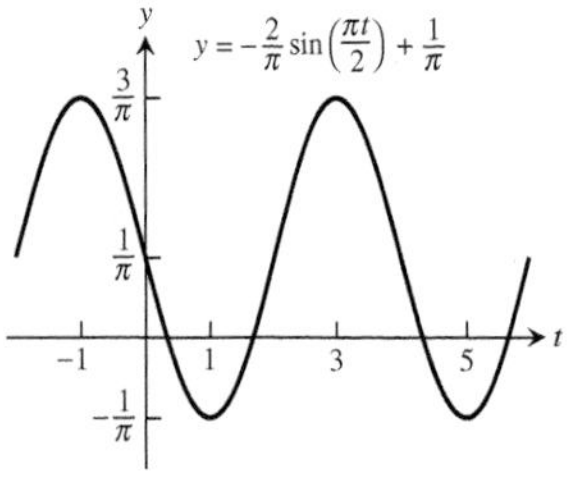

Section 1.4, p. 33

1. d **3.** d

5. $[-3, 5]$ by $[-15, 40]$

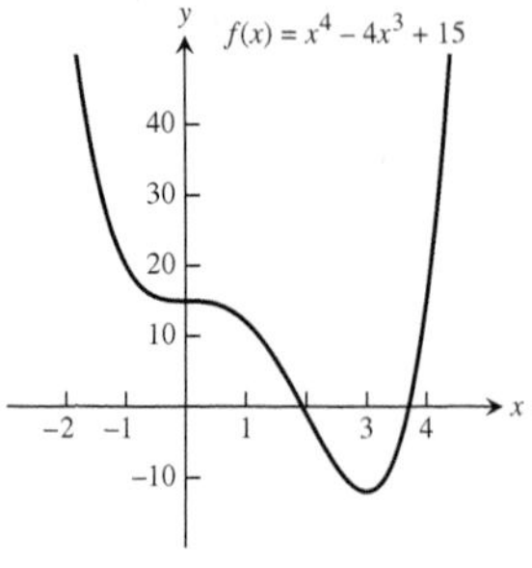

7. $[-3, 6]$ by $[-250, 50]$

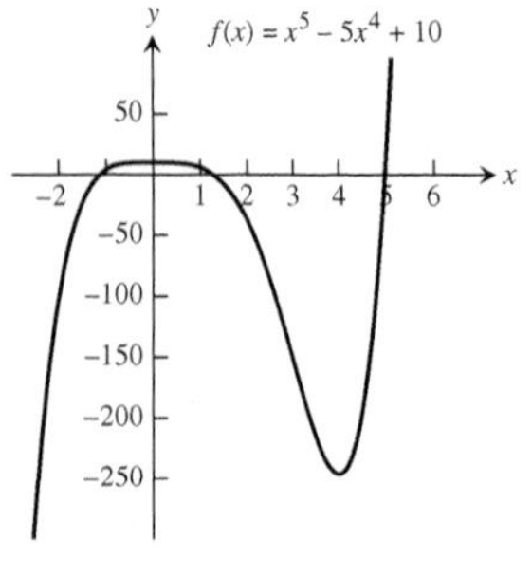

9. $[-5, 5]$ by $[-6, 6]$

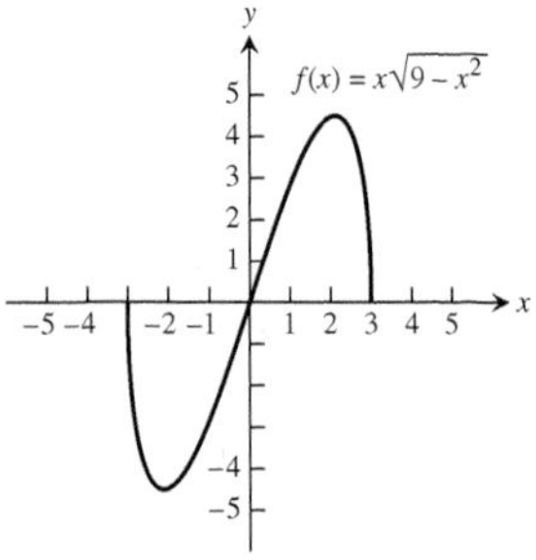

11. $[-2, 6]$ by $[-5, 4]$

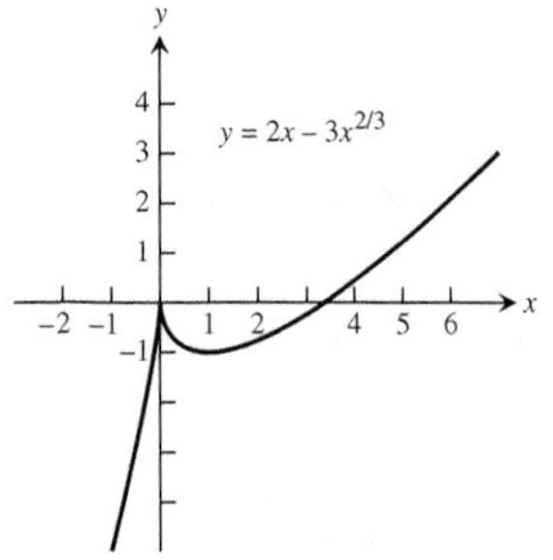

13. $[-2, 8]$ by $[-5, 10]$

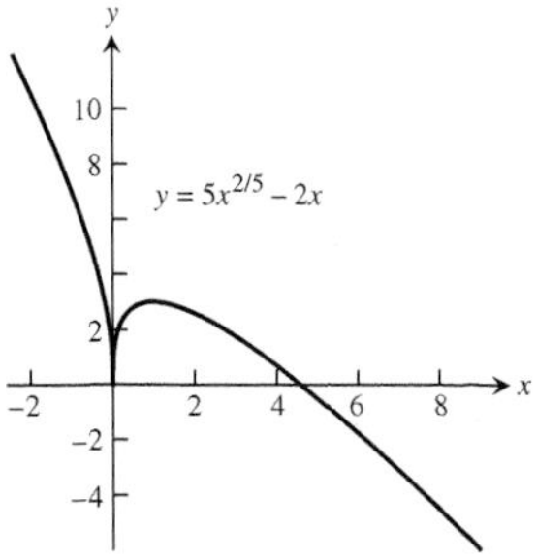

15. $[-3, 3]$ by $[0, 10]$

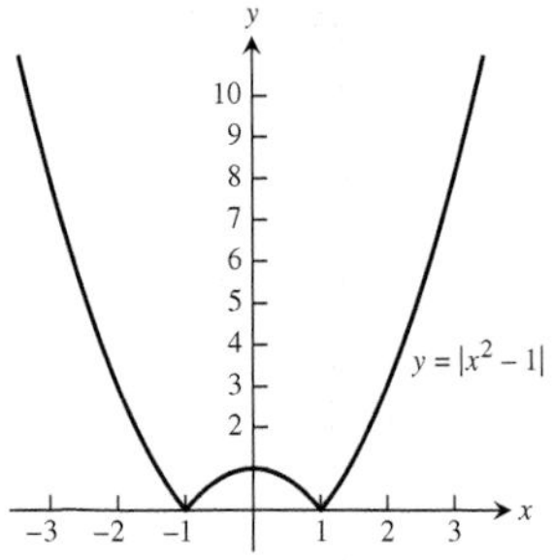

17. $[-10, 10]$ by $[-10, 10]$

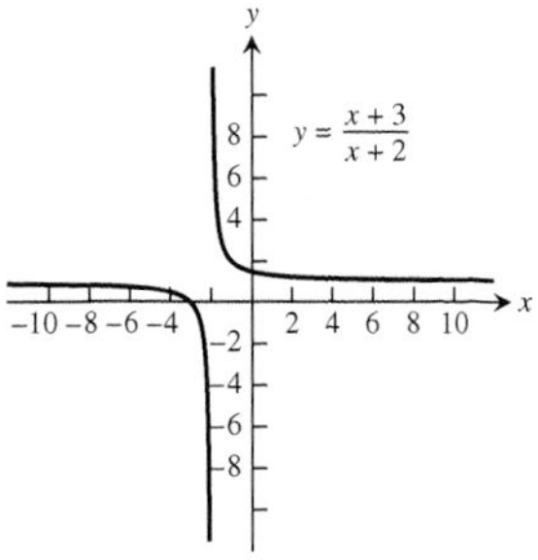

19. $[-4, 4]$ by $[0, 3]$

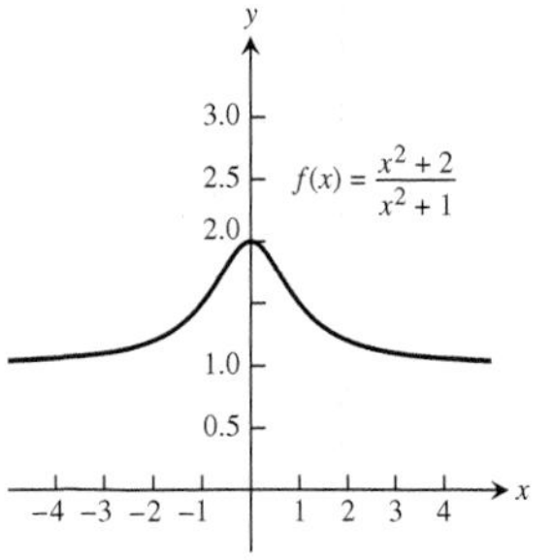

21. $[-10, 10]$ by $[-6, 6]$

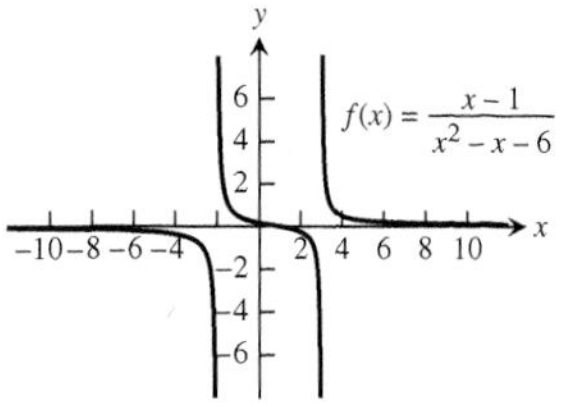

23. $[-6, 10]$ by $[-6, 6]$

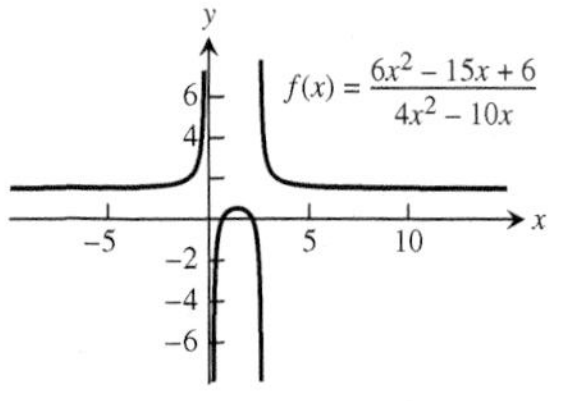

25. $\left[-\frac{\pi}{125}, \frac{\pi}{125}\right]$ by $[-1.25, 1.25]$

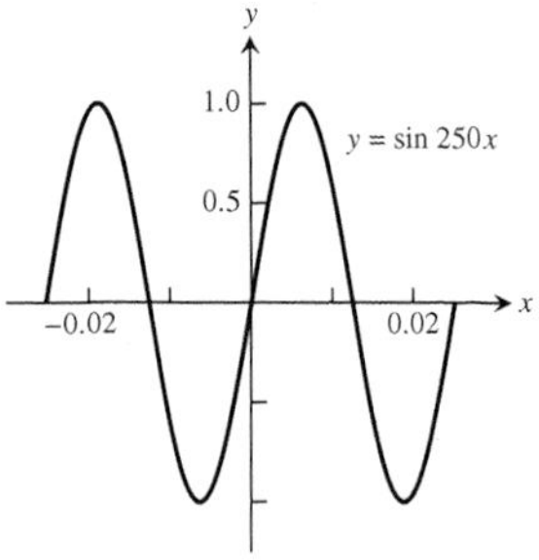

27. $[-100\pi, 100\pi]$ by $[-1.25, 1.25]$

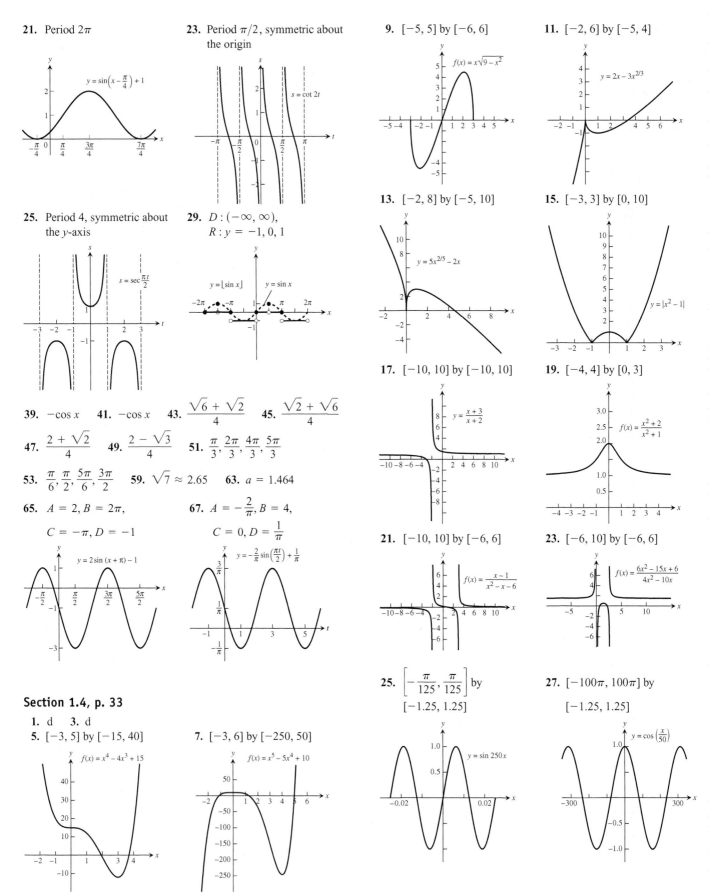

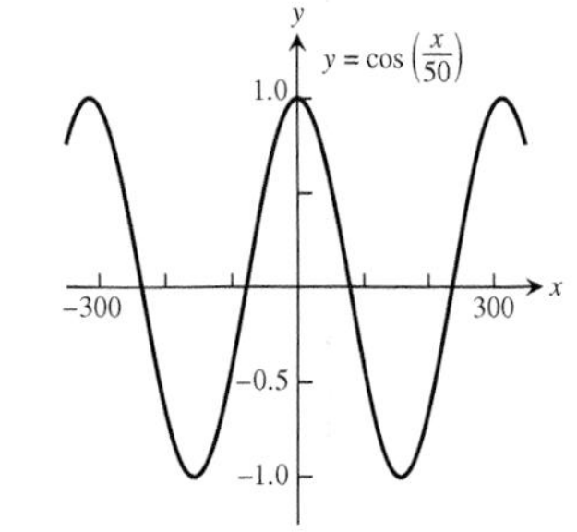

29. $\left[-\frac{\pi}{15}, \frac{\pi}{15}\right]$ by $[-0.25, 0.25]$

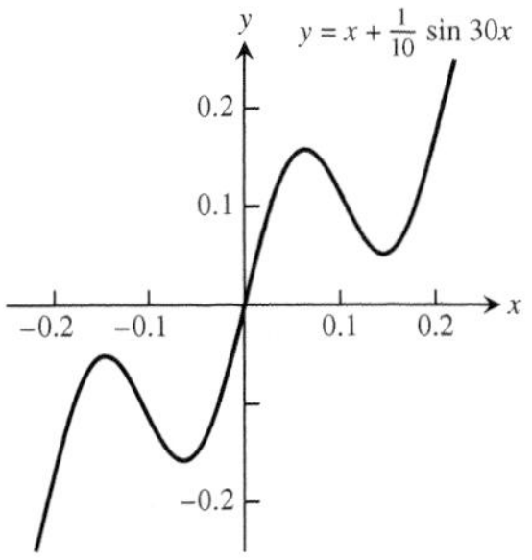

31.

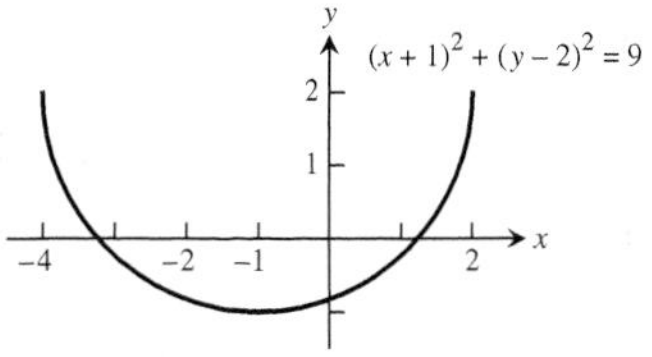

33.

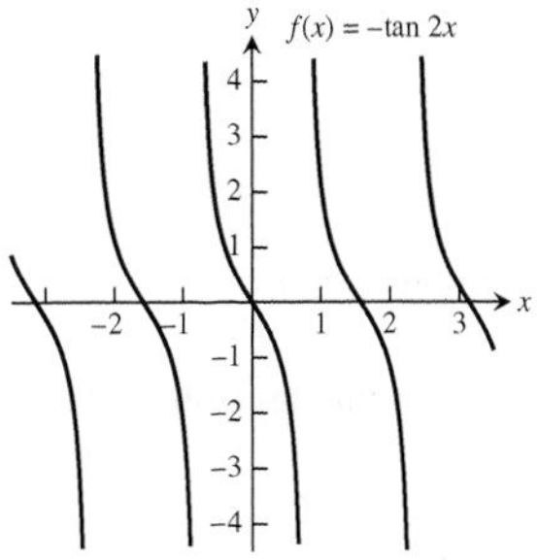

35.

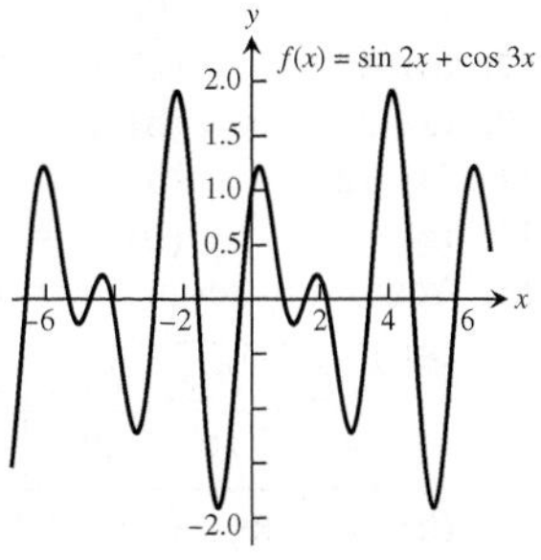

37.

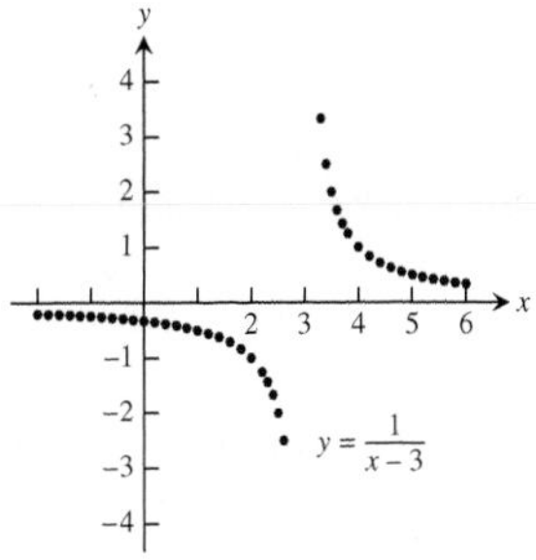

39.

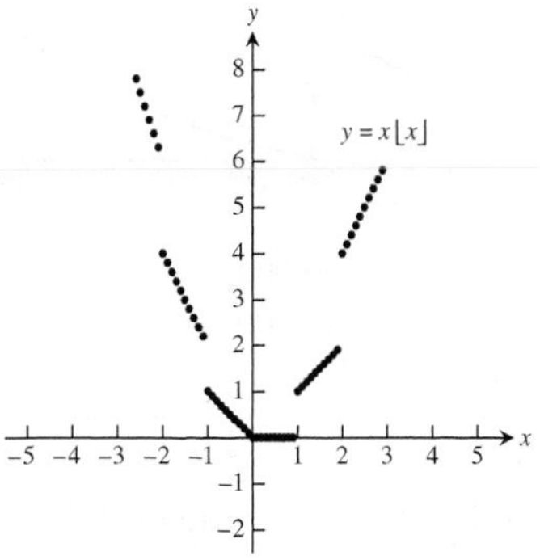

Section 1.5, pp. 38–39

1.

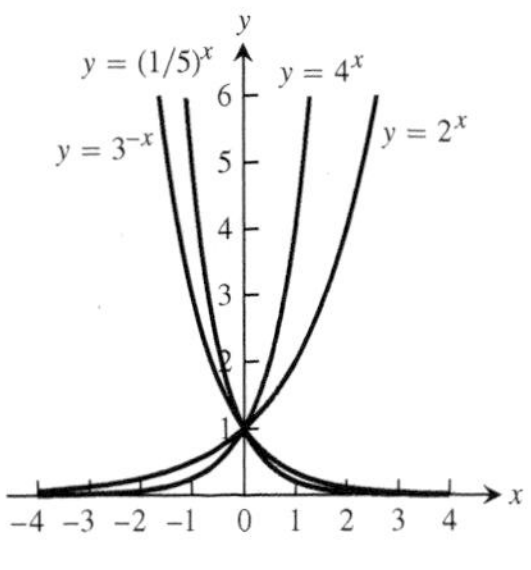

3.

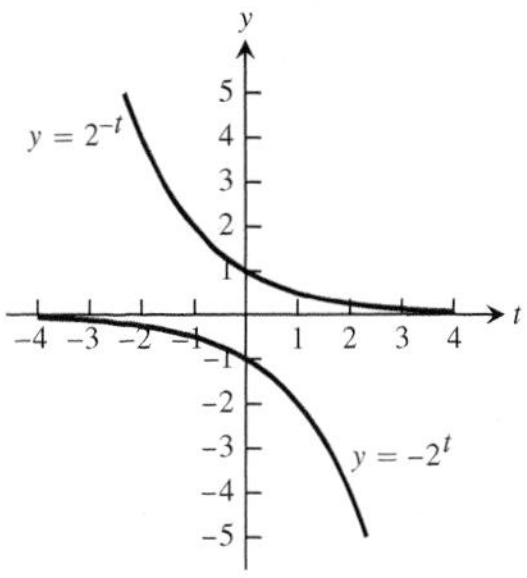

5.

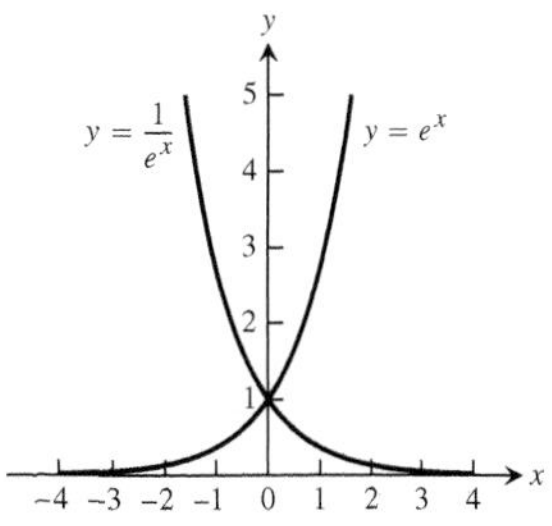

7.

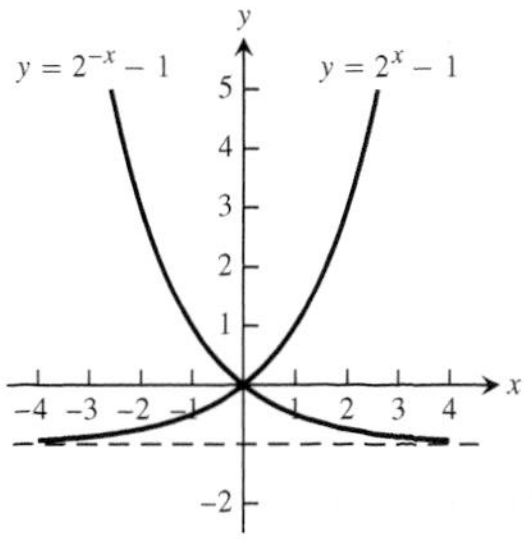

9.

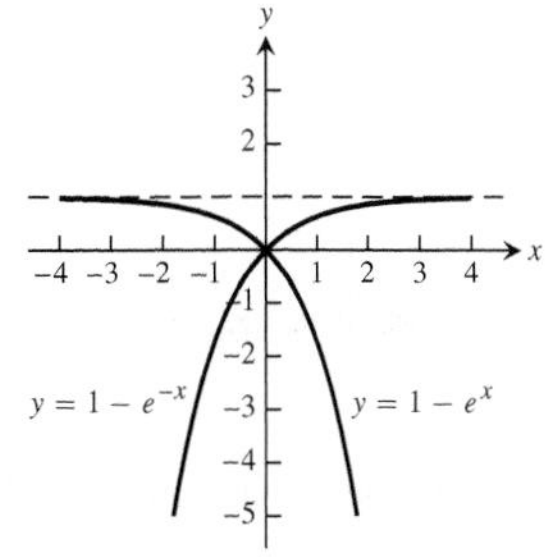

11. $16^{1/4} = 2$ **13.** $4^{1/2} = 2$ **15.** 5 **17.** $14^{\sqrt{3}}$ **19.** 4

21. D: $-\infty < x < \infty$; R: $0 < y < 1/2$

23. D: $-\infty < t < \infty$; R: $1 < y < \infty$

25. $x \approx 2.3219$ **27.** $x \approx -0.6309$ **29.** After 19 years

31. (a) $A(t) = 6.6\left(\frac{1}{2}\right)^{t/14}$ **(b)** About 38 days later

33. ≈ 11.433 years, or when interest is paid

35. $2^{48} \approx 2.815 \times 10^{14}$

Section 1.6, pp. 49–51

1. One-to-one **3.** Not one-to-one **5.** One-to-one

7. Not one-to-one **9.** One-to-one

11. D: $(0, 1]$ R: $[0, \infty)$

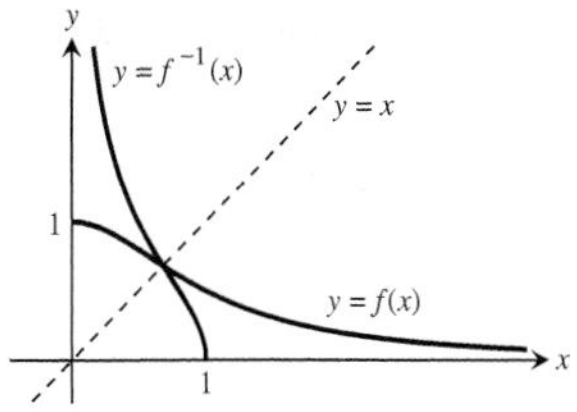

13. D: $[-1, 1]$ R: $[-\pi/2, \pi/2]$

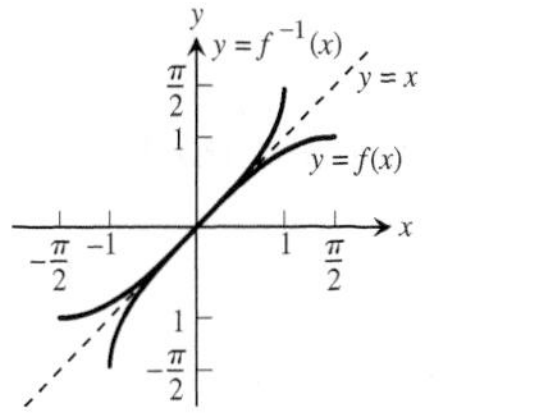

15. D: $[0, 6]$ R: $[0, 3]$

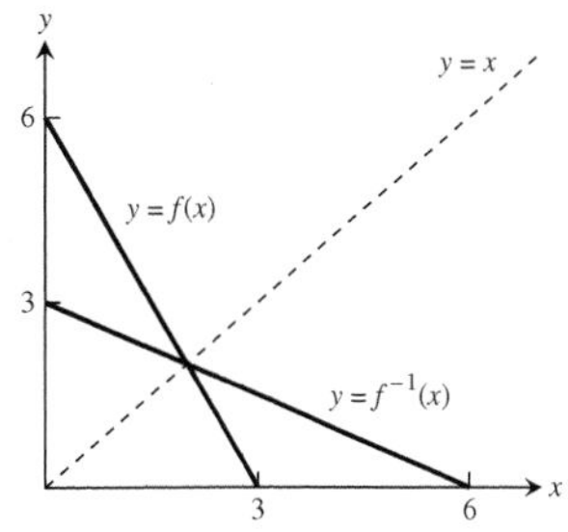

17. (a) Symmetric about the line $y = x$

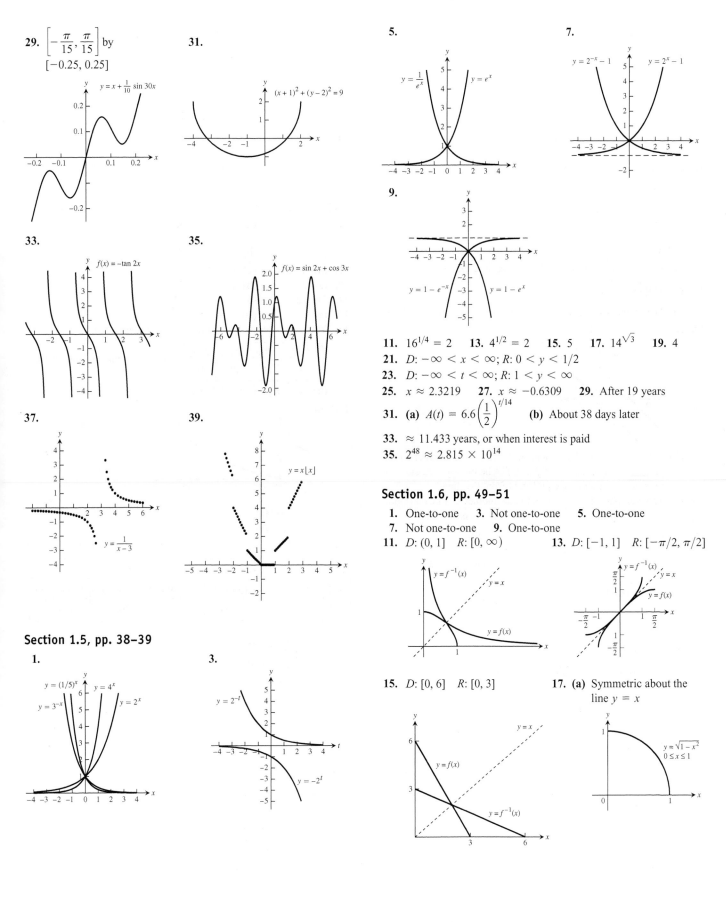

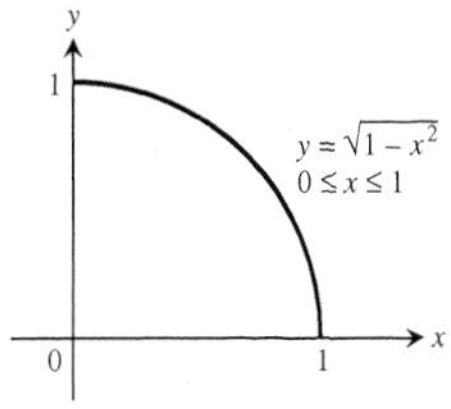

19. $f^{-1}(x) = \sqrt{x} - 1$ **21.** $f^{-1}(x) = \sqrt[3]{x+1}$

23. $f^{-1}(x) = \sqrt{x} - 1$

25. $f^{-1}(x) = \sqrt[5]{x}$; $D: -\infty < x < \infty$; $R: -\infty < y < \infty$

27. $f^{-1}(x) = \sqrt[3]{x-1}$; $D: -\infty < x < \infty$; $R: -\infty < y < \infty$

29. $f^{-1}(x) = \dfrac{1}{\sqrt{x}}$; $D: x > 0$; $R: y > 0$

31. $f^{-1}(x) = \dfrac{2x+3}{x-1}$; $D: -\infty < x < \infty, x \neq 1$; $R: -\infty < y < \infty, y \neq 2$

33. $f^{-1}(x) = 1 - \sqrt{x+1}$; $D: -1 \le x < \infty$; $R: -\infty < y \le 1$

35. $f^{-1}(x) = \dfrac{2x+b}{x-1}$; $D: -\infty < x < \infty, x \neq 1,\quad R: -\infty < y < \infty, y \neq 2$

37. **(a)** $f^{-1}(x) = \dfrac{1}{m}x$
(b) The graph of f^{-1} is the line through the origin with slope $1/m$.

39. **(a)** $f^{-1}(x) = x - 1$

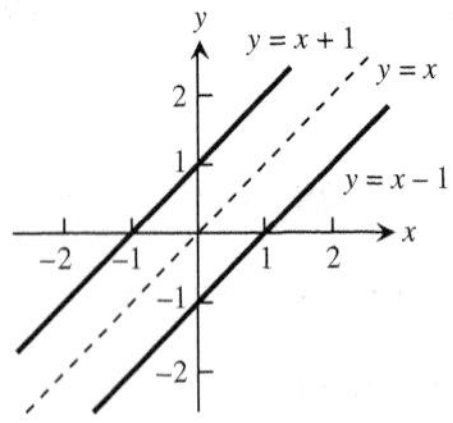

(b) $f^{-1}(x) = x - b$. The graph of f^{-1} is a line parallel to the graph of f. The graphs of f and f^{-1} lie on opposite sides of the line $y = x$ and are equidistant from that line.
(c) Their graphs will be parallel to one another and lie on opposite sides of the line $y = x$ equidistant from that line.

41. **(a)** $\ln 3 - 2\ln 2$ **(b)** $2(\ln 2 - \ln 3)$ **(c)** $-\ln 2$ **(d)** $\frac{2}{3}\ln 3$ **(e)** $\ln 3 + \frac{1}{2}\ln 2$ **(f)** $\frac{1}{2}(3\ln 3 - \ln 2)$

43. **(a)** $\ln 5$ **(b)** $\ln(x-3)$ **(c)** $\ln\left(\dfrac{2t^2}{b}\right)$

45. **(a)** 7.2 **(b)** $\dfrac{1}{x^2}$ **(c)** $\dfrac{x}{y}$

47. **(a)** 1 **(b)** 1 **(c)** $-x^2 - y^2$

49. e^{2t+4} **51.** $e^{5t} + b$ **53.** $y = 2xe^x + 1$

55. **(a)** $k = \ln 2$ **(b)** $k = (1/10)\ln 2$ **(c)** $k = 1000\ln a$

57. **(a)** $t = -10\ln 3$ **(b)** $t = -\dfrac{\ln 2}{k}$ **(c)** $t = \dfrac{\ln .4}{\ln .2}$

59. $4(\ln x)^2$

61. **(a)** 7 **(b)** $\sqrt{2}$ **(c)** 75 **(d)** 2 **(e)** 0.5 **(f)** -1

63. **(a)** $\sqrt{x}$ **(b)** x^2 **(c)** $\sin x$ **65.** **(a)** $\dfrac{\ln 3}{\ln 2}$ **(b)** 3 **(c)** 2

67. **(a)** $-\pi/6$ **(b)** $\pi/4$ **(c)** $-\pi/3$

69. **(a)** π **(b)** $\pi/2$

71. Yes, $g(x)$ is also one-to-one.

73. Yes, $f \circ g$ is also one-to-one.

75. **(a)** $f^{-1}(x) = \log_2\left(\dfrac{x}{100-x}\right)$ **(b)** $f^{-1}(x) = \log_{1.1}\left(\dfrac{x}{50-x}\right)$

77. **(a)** $y = \ln x - 3$ **(b)** $y = \ln(x-1)$ **(c)** $y = 3 + \ln(x+1)$ **(d)** $y = \ln(x-2) - 4$ **(e)** $y = \ln(-x)$ **(f)** $y = e^x$

79. -0.7667

81. **(a)** Amount $= 8\left(\dfrac{1}{2}\right)^{t/12}$ **(b)** 36 hours

83. ≈ 43.592 years

CHAPTER 2

Section 2.1, pp. 57–59

1. **(a)** 19 **(b)** 1

3. **(a)** $-\dfrac{4}{\pi}$ **(b)** $-\dfrac{3\sqrt{3}}{\pi}$ **5.** 1

7. **(a)** 4 **(b)** $y = 4x - 7$

9. **(a)** 2 **(b)** $y = 2x - 7$

11. **(a)** 12 **(b)** $y = 12x - 16$

13. **(a)** -9 **(b)** $y = -9x - 2$

15. Your estimates may not completely agree with these.

(a)

PQ_1	PQ_2	PQ_3	PQ_4
43	46	49	50

The appropriate units are m/sec.

(b) $\approx$ 50 m/sec or 180 km/h

17. **(a)**

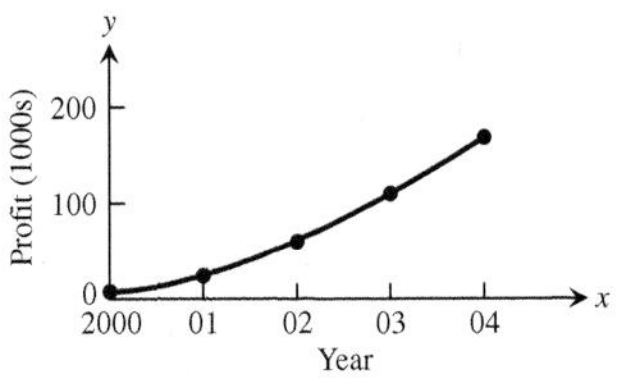

(b) $\approx$ \$56,000/year
(c) $\approx$ \$42,000/year

19. **(a)** 0.414213, 0.449489, $(\sqrt{1+h} - 1)/h$ **(b)** $g(x) = \sqrt{x}$

$1 + h$	1.1	1.01	1.001	1.0001
$\sqrt{1+h}$	1.04880	1.004987	1.0004998	1.0000499
$(\sqrt{1+h} - 1)/h$	0.4880	0.4987	0.4998	0.499

1.00001	1.000001
1.000005	1.0000005
0.5	0.5

(c) 0.5 **(d)** 0.5

21. **(a)** 15 mph, 3.3 mph, 10 mph **(b)** 10 mph, 0 mph, 4 mph
(c) 20 mph when $t = 3.5$ hr

Section 2.2, pp. 67–70

1. **(a)** Does not exist. As x approaches 1 from the right, $g(x)$ approaches 0. As x approaches 1 from the left, $g(x)$ approaches 1. There is no single number L that all the values $g(x)$ get arbitrarily close to as $x \to 1$.
(b) 1 **(c)** 0 **(d)** 1/2

3. **(a)** True **(b)** True **(c)** False **(d)** False **(e)** False **(f)** True **(g)** True

5. As x approaches 0 from the left, $x/|x|$ approaches -1. As x approaches 0 from the right, $x/|x|$ approaches 1. There is no single number L that the function values all get arbitrarily close to as $x \to 0$.
7. Nothing can be said. **9.** No; no; no **11.** -9 **13.** -8
15. $5/8$ **17.** 27 **19.** 16 **21.** $3/2$ **23.** $1/10$ **25.** -7
27. $3/2$ **29.** $-1/2$ **31.** -1 **33.** $4/3$ **35.** $1/6$ **37.** 4
39. $1/2$ **41.** $3/2$ **43.** -1 **45.** 1 **47.** $1/3$ **49.** $\sqrt{4-\pi}$
51. **(a)** Quotient Rule **(b)** Difference and Power Rules
(c) Sum and Constant Multiple Rules
53. **(a)** -10 **(b)** -20 **(c)** -1 **(d)** $5/7$
55. **(a)** 4 **(b)** -21 **(c)** -12 **(d)** $-7/3$
57. 2 **59.** 3 **61.** $1/(2\sqrt{7})$ **63.** $\sqrt{5}$
65. **(a)** The limit is 1.
67. **(a)** $f(x) = (x^2 - 9)/(x + 3)$

x	-3.1	-3.01	-3.001	-3.0001	-3.00001	-3.000001
$f(x)$	-6.1	-6.01	-6.001	-6.0001	-6.00001	-6.000001

x	-2.9	-2.99	-2.999	-2.9999	-2.99999	-2.999999
$f(x)$	-5.9	-5.99	-5.999	-5.9999	-5.99999	-5.999999

(c) $\lim_{x\to-3} f(x) = -6$

69. **(a)** $G(x) = (x + 6)/(x^2 + 4x - 12)$

x	-5.9	-5.99	-5.999	-5.9999
$G(x)$	$-.126582$	$-.1251564$	$-.1250156$	$-.1250015$

-5.99999	-5.999999
$-.1250001$	$-.1250000$

x	-6.1	-6.01	-6.001	-6.0001
$G(x)$	$-.123456$	$-.124843$	$-.124984$	$-.124998$

-6.00001	-6.000001
$-.124999$	$-.124999$

(c) $\lim_{x\to-6} G(x) = -1/8 = -0.125$

71. **(a)** $f(x) = (x^2 - 1)/(|x| - 1)$

x	-1.1	-1.01	-1.001	-1.0001	-1.00001	-1.000001
$f(x)$	2.1	2.01	2.001	2.0001	2.00001	2.000001

x	$-.9$	$-.99$	$-.999$	$-.9999$	$-.99999$	$-.999999$
$f(x)$	1.9	1.99	1.999	1.9999	1.99999	1.999999

(c) $\lim_{x\to-1} f(x) = 2$

73. **(a)** $g(\theta) = (\sin\theta)/\theta$

θ	.1	.01	.001	.0001	.00001	.000001
$g(\theta)$	.998334	.999983	.999999	.999999	.999999	.999999

θ	$-.1$	$-.01$	$-.001$	$-.0001$	$-.00001$	$-.000001$
$g(\theta)$	.998334	.999983	.999999	.999999	.999999	.999999

$\lim_{\theta\to0} g(\theta) = 1$

75. **(a)** $f(x) = x^{1/(1-x)}$

x	.9	.99	.999	.9999	.99999	.999999
$f(x)$	.348678	.366032	.367695	.367861	.367877	.367879

x	1.1	1.01	1.001	1.0001	1.00001	1.000001
$f(x)$	.385543	.369711	.368063	.367897	.367881	.367878

$\lim_{x\to1} f(x) \approx 0.36788$

77. $c = 0, 1, -1$; the limit is 0 at $c = 0$, and 1 at $c = 1, -1$.
79. 7 **81.** **(a)** 5 **(b)** 5 **83.** **(a)** 0 **(b)** 0

Section 2.3, pp. 76–79

1. $\delta = 2$

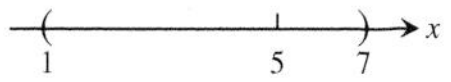

3. $\delta = 1/2$

5. $\delta = 1/18$

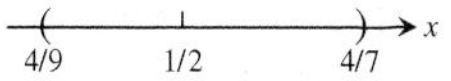

7. $\delta = 0.1$ **9.** $\delta = 7/16$ **11.** $\delta = \sqrt{5} - 2$ **13.** $\delta = 0.36$
15. $(3.99, 4.01)$, $\delta = 0.01$ **17.** $(-0.19, 0.21)$, $\delta = 0.19$
19. $(3, 15)$, $\delta = 5$ **21.** $(10/3, 5)$, $\delta = 2/3$
23. $(-\sqrt{4.5}, -\sqrt{3.5})$, $\delta = \sqrt{4.5} - 2 \approx 0.12$
25. $(\sqrt{15}, \sqrt{17})$, $\delta = \sqrt{17} - 4 \approx 0.12$
27. $\left(2 - \frac{0.03}{m}, 2 + \frac{0.03}{m}\right)$, $\delta = \frac{0.03}{m}$
29. $\left(\frac{1}{2} - \frac{c}{m}, \frac{c}{m} + \frac{1}{2}\right)$, $\delta = \frac{c}{m}$ **31.** $L = -3$, $\delta = 0.01$
33. $L = 4$, $\delta = 0.05$ **35.** $L = 4$, $\delta = 0.75$
55. [3.384, 3.387]. To be safe, the left endpoint was rounded up and the right endpoint rounded down.
59. The limit does not exist as x approaches 3.

Section 2.4, pp. 84–86

1. **(a)** True **(b)** True **(c)** False **(d)** True **(e)** True
(f) True **(g)** False **(h)** False **(i)** False **(j)** False
(k) True **(l)** False
3. **(a)** 2, 1 **(b)** No, $\lim_{x\to2^+} f(x) \neq \lim_{x\to2^-} f(x)$
(c) 3, 3 **(d)** Yes, 3
5. **(a)** No **(b)** Yes, 0 **(c)** No
7. **(a)**

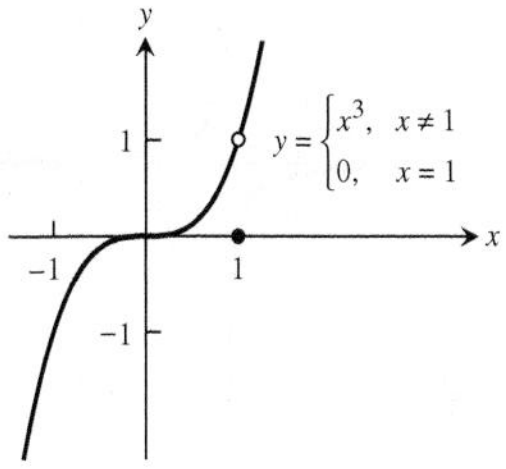

(b) 1, 1 **(c)** Yes, 1

9. **(a)** $D: 0 \le x \le 2$, $R: 0 < y \le 1$ and $y = 2$
(b) $(0, 1) \cup (1, 2)$ **(c)** $x = 2$ **(d)** $x = 0$

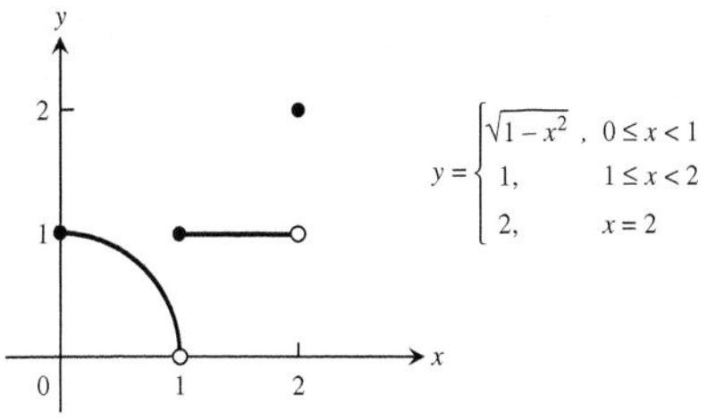

11. $\sqrt{3}$ **13.** 1 **15.** $2/\sqrt{5}$ **17.** **(a)** 1 **(b)** -1
19. **(a)** 1 **(b)** $2/3$ **21.** 1 **23.** $3/4$ **25.** 2 **27.** $1/2$
29. 2 **31.** 0 **33.** 1 **35.** $1/2$ **37.** 0 **39.** $3/8$
41. 3 **47.** $\delta = \epsilon^2$, $\lim_{x\to5^+} \sqrt{x-5} = 0$
51. **(a)** 400 **(b)** 399 **(c)** The limit does not exist.

Section 2.5, pp. 95–97

1. No; discontinuous at $x = 2$; not defined at $x = 2$
3. Continuous **5. (a)** Yes **(b)** Yes **(c)** Yes **(d)** Yes
7. (a) No **(b)** No **9.** 0 **11.** 1, nonremovable; 0, removable
13. All x except $x = 2$ **15.** All x except $x = 3, x = 1$
17. All x **19.** All x except $x = 0$
21. All x except $n\pi/2$, n any integer
23. All x except $n\pi/2$, n an odd integer
25. All $x \geq -3/2$ **27.** All x **29.** All x
31. 0; continuous at $x = \pi$ **33.** 1; continuous at $y = 1$
35. $\sqrt{2}/2$; continuous at $t = 0$ **37.** 1; continuous at $x = 0$
39. $g(3) = 6$ **41.** $f(1) = 3/2$ **43.** $a = 4/3$ **45.** $a = -2, 3$
47. $a = 5/2, b = -1/2$ **71.** $x \approx 1.8794, -1.5321, -0.3473$
73. $x \approx 1.7549$ **75.** $x \approx 3.5156$ **77.** $x \approx 0.7391$

Section 2.6, pp. 108–110

1. (a) 0 **(b)** -2 **(c)** 2 **(d)** Does not exist **(e)** -1
(f) ∞ **(g)** Does not exist **(h)** 1 **(i)** 0
3. (a) -3 **(b)** -3 **5. (a)** $1/2$ **(b)** $1/2$ **7. (a)** $-5/3$
(b) $-5/3$ **9.** 0 **11.** -1 **13. (a)** $2/5$ **(b)** $2/5$
15. (a) 0 **(b)** 0 **17. (a)** 7 **(b)** 7 **19. (a)** 0 **(b)** 0
21. (a) $-2/3$ **(b)** $-2/3$ **23.** 2 **25.** ∞ **27.** 0 **29.** 1
31. ∞ **33.** 1 **35.** $1/2$ **37.** ∞ **39.** $-\infty$ **41.** $-\infty$
43. ∞ **45. (a)** ∞ **(b)** $-\infty$ **47.** ∞ **49.** ∞ **51.** $-\infty$
53. (a) ∞ **(b)** $-\infty$ **(c)** $-\infty$ **(d)** ∞
55. (a) $-\infty$ **(b)** ∞ **(c)** 0 **(d)** $3/2$
57. (a) $-\infty$ **(b)** $1/4$ **(c)** $1/4$ **(d)** $1/4$ **(e)** It will be $-\infty$.
59. (a) $-\infty$ **(b)** ∞
61. (a) ∞ **(b)** ∞ **(c)** ∞ **(d)** ∞

63.

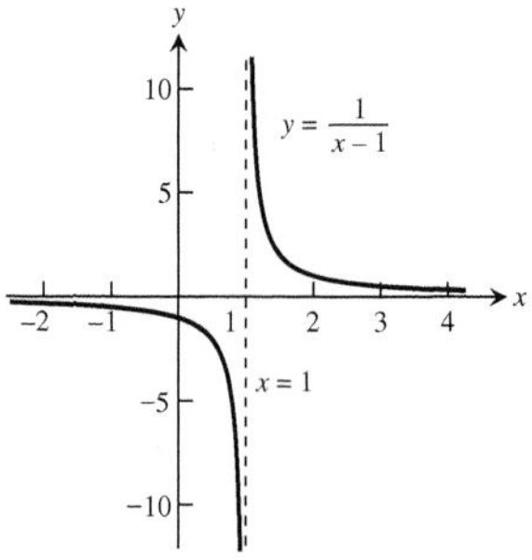

65.

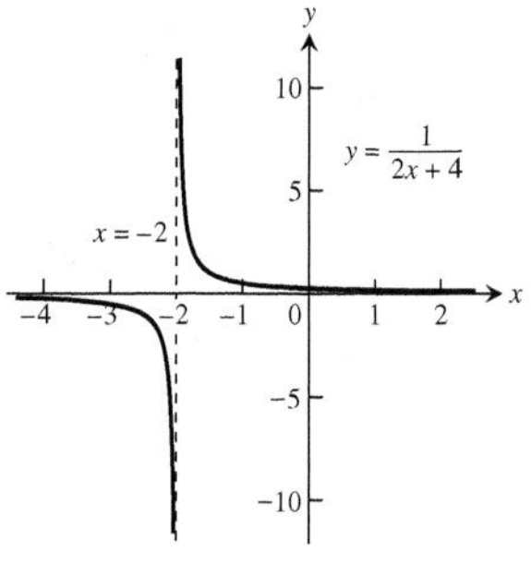

67.

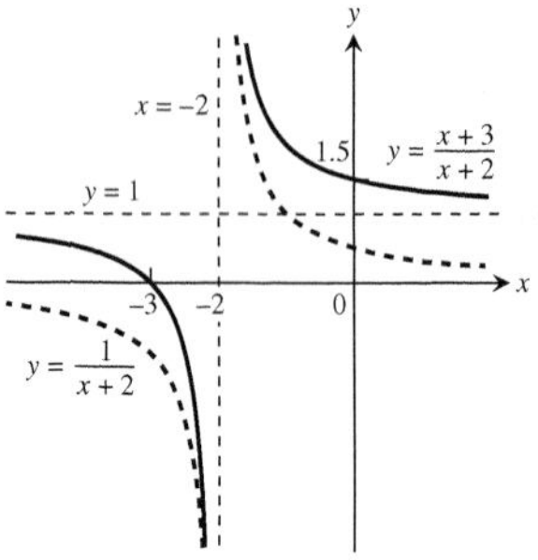

69. Here is one possibility.

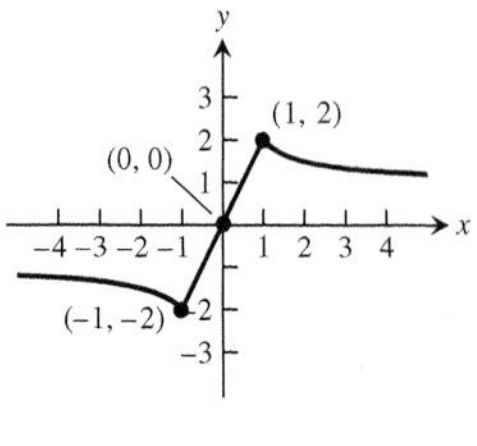

71. Here is one possibility.

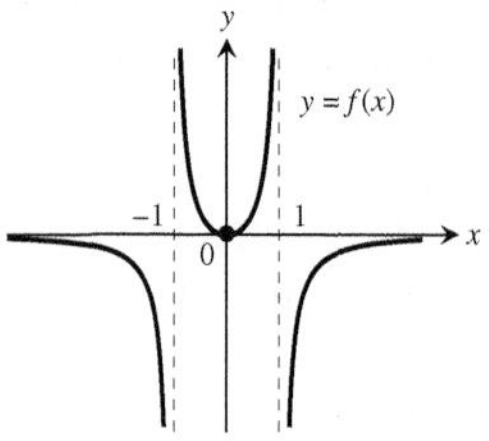

73. Here is one possibility.

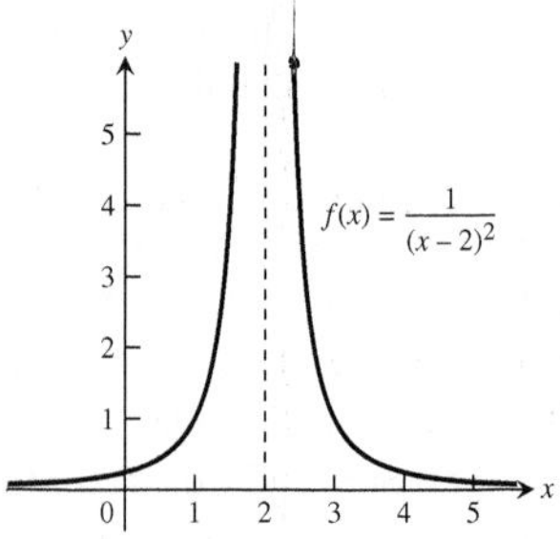

75. Here is one possibility.

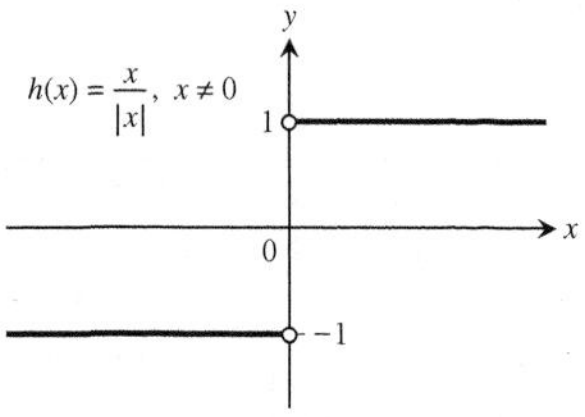

79. At most one

81. 0 **83.** $-3/4$ **85.** $5/2$

93. (a) For every positive real number B there exists a corresponding number $\delta > 0$ such that for all x

$$c - \delta < x < c \Rightarrow f(x) > B.$$

(b) For every negative real number $-B$ there exists a corresponding number $\delta > 0$ such that for all x

$$c < x < c + \delta \Rightarrow f(x) < -B.$$

(c) For every negative real number $-B$ there exists a corresponding number $\delta > 0$ such that for all x

$$c - \delta < x < c \Rightarrow f(x) < -B.$$

99.

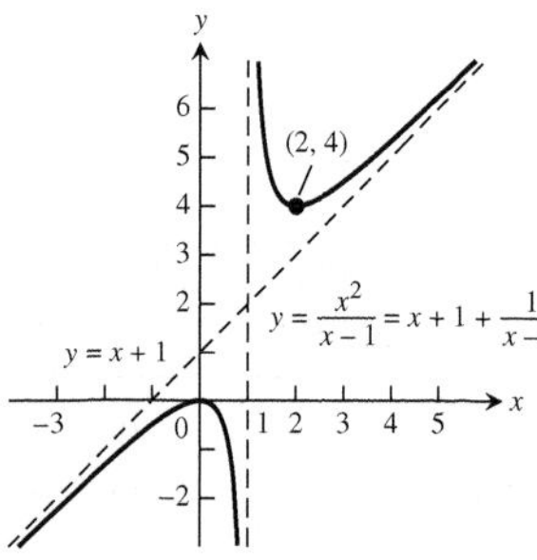

101.

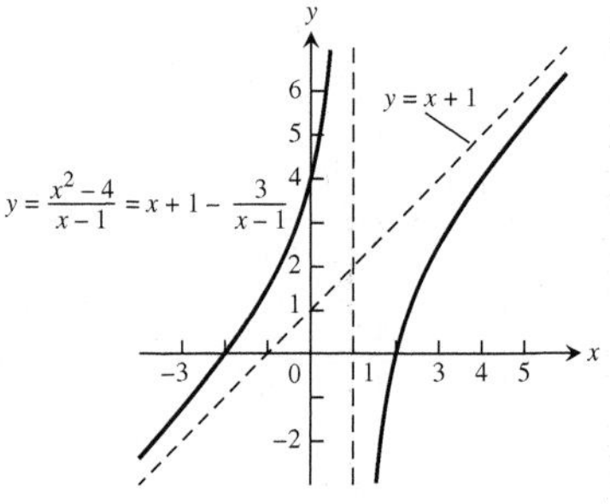

103.

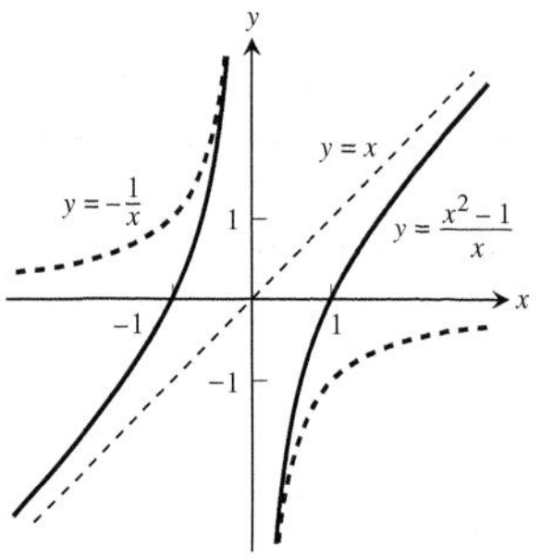

105.

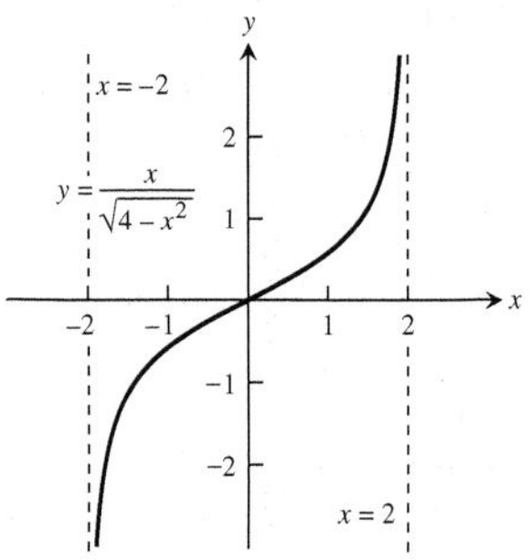

107.

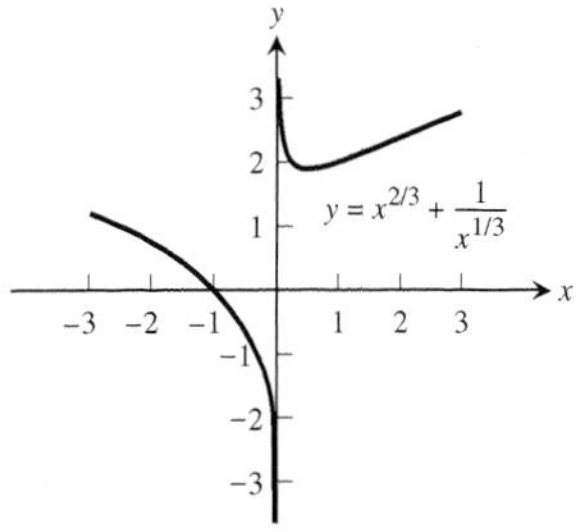

109. At ∞: ∞, at $-\infty$: 0

Practice Exercises, pp. 111–113

1. At $x = -1$: $\lim_{x\to -1^-} f(x) = \lim_{x\to -1^+} f(x) = 1$, so $\lim_{x\to -1} f(x) = 1 = f(-1)$; continuous at $x = -1$

At $x = 0$: $\lim_{x\to 0^-} f(x) = \lim_{x\to 0^+} f(x) = 0$, so $\lim_{x\to 0} f(x) = 0$. However, $f(0) \neq 0$, so f is discontinuous at $x = 0$. The discontinuity can be removed by redefining $f(0)$ to be 0.

At $x = 1$: $\lim_{x\to 1^-} f(x) = -1$ and $\lim_{x\to 1^+} f(x) = 1$, so $\lim_{x\to 1} f(x)$ does not exist. The function is discontinuous at $x = 1$, and the discontinuity is not removable.

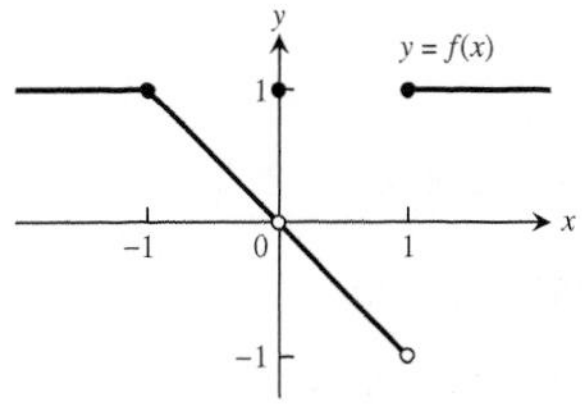

3. (a) -21 **(b)** 49 **(c)** 0 **(d)** 1 **(e)** 1 **(f)** 7 **(g)** -7 **(h)** $-\frac{1}{7}$ **5.** 4

7. (a) $(-\infty, +\infty)$ **(b)** $[0, \infty)$ **(c)** $(-\infty, 0)$ and $(0, \infty)$ **(d)** $(0, \infty)$

9. (a) Does not exist **(b)** 0

11. $\frac{1}{2}$ **13.** $2x$ **15.** $-\frac{1}{4}$ **17.** $2/3$ **19.** $2/\pi$ **21.** 1

23. 4 **25.** $-\infty$ **27.** 0 **29.** 2 **31.** 0

35. No in both cases, because $\lim_{x\to 1} f(x)$ does not exist, and $\lim_{x\to -1} f(x)$ does not exist.

37. Yes, f does have a continuous extension, to $a = 1$ with $f(1) = 4/3$.

39. No **41.** $2/5$ **43.** 0 **45.** $-\infty$ **47.** 0 **49.** 1 **51.** 1

53. $-\pi/2$ **55. (a)** $x = 3$ **(b)** $x = 1$ **(c)** $x = -4$

Additional and Advanced Exercises, pp. 113–115

3. 0; the left-hand limit was needed because the function is undefined for $v > c$. **5.** $65 < t < 75$; within 5°F

13. (a) B **(b)** A **(c)** A **(d)** A

21. (a) $\lim_{a\to 0} r_+(a) = 0.5$, $\lim_{a\to -1^+} r_+(a) = 1$

(b) $\lim_{a\to 0} r_-(a)$ does not exist, $\lim_{a\to -1^+} r_-(a) = 1$

25. 0 **27.** 1 **29.** 4 **31.** $y = 2x$ **33.** $y = x$, $y = -x$

CHAPTER 3

Section 3.1, pp. 119–120

1. P_1: $m_1 = 1$, P_2: $m_2 = 5$ **3.** P_1: $m_1 = 5/2$, P_2: $m_2 = -1/2$

5. $y = 2x + 5$ **7.** $y = x + 1$

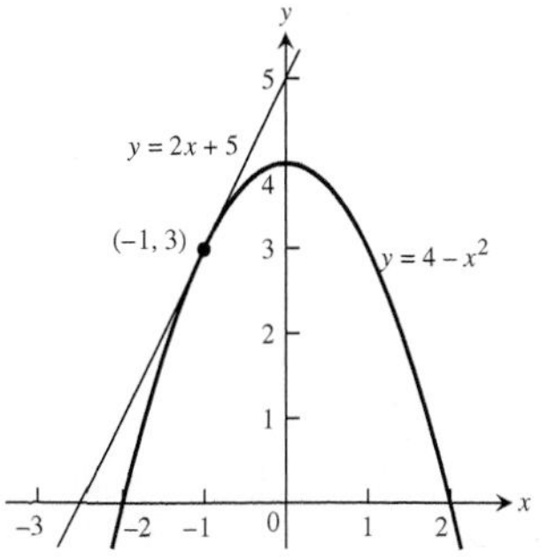

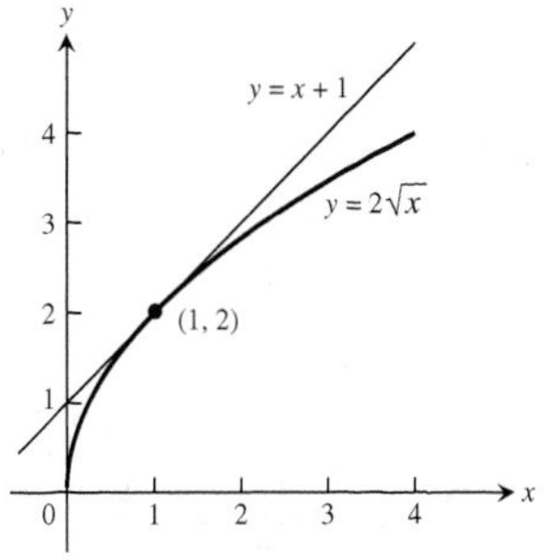

9. $y = 12x + 16$

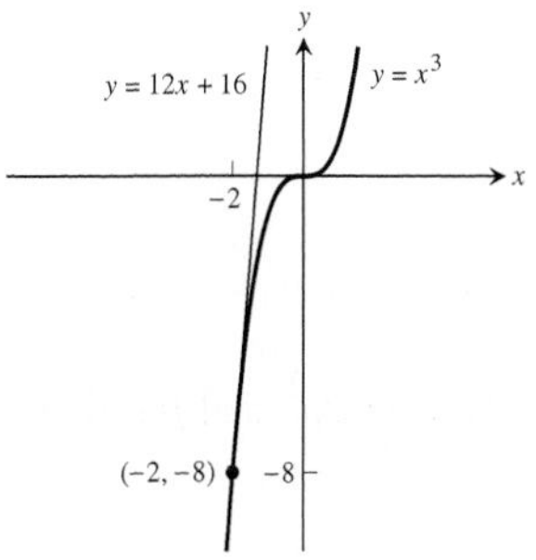

11. $m = 4, y - 5 = 4(x - 2)$

13. $m = -2, y - 3 = -2(x - 3)$

15. $m = 12, y - 8 = 12(t - 2)$

17. $m = \frac{1}{4}, y - 2 = \frac{1}{4}(x - 4)$

19. $m = -10$ **21.** $m = -1/4$ **23.** $(-2, -5)$

25. $y = -(x + 1), y = -(x - 3)$ **27.** 19.6 m/sec

29. 6π **33.** Yes **35.** Yes **37. (a)** Nowhere

39. (a) At $x = 0$ **41. (a)** Nowhere **43. (a)** At $x = 1$

45. (a) At $x = 0$

Section 3.2, pp. 125–129

1. $-2x, 6, 0, -2$ **3.** $-\frac{2}{t^3}, 2, -\frac{1}{4}, -\frac{2}{3\sqrt{3}}$

5. $\frac{3}{2\sqrt{3\theta}}, \frac{3}{2\sqrt{3}}, \frac{1}{2}, \frac{3}{2\sqrt{2}}$ **7.** $6x^2$ **9.** $\frac{1}{(2t + 1)^2}$

11. $\frac{-1}{2(q + 1)\sqrt{q + 1}}$ **13.** $1 - \frac{9}{x^2}, 0$ **15.** $3t^2 - 2t, 5$

17. $\frac{-4}{(x - 2)\sqrt{x - 2}}$, $y - 4 = -\frac{1}{2}(x - 6)$ **19.** 6

21. $1/8$ **23.** $\frac{-1}{(x + 2)^2}$ **25.** $\frac{-1}{(x - 1)^2}$ **27.** (b) **29.** (d)

31. **(a)** $x = 0, 1, 4$
(b)

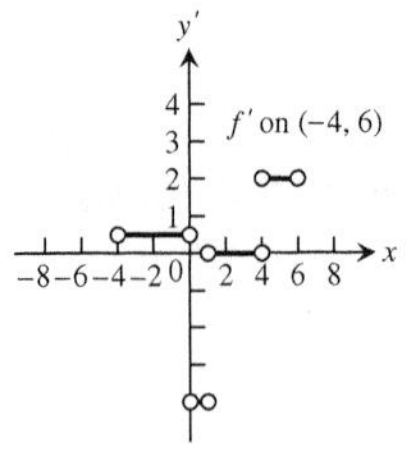

33.

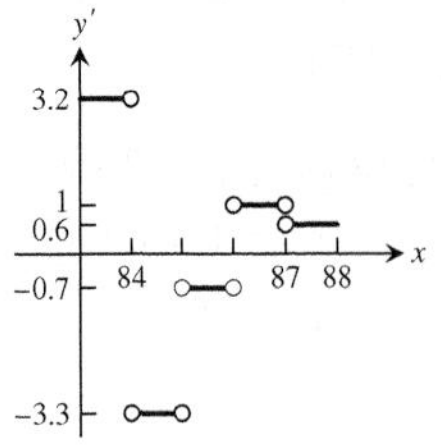

35. **(a)** **i)** 1.5 °F/hr **ii)** 2.9 °F/hr **iii)** 0 °F/hr **iv)** −3.7 °F/hr
(b) 7.3 °F/hr at 12 P.M., −11 °F/hr at 6 P.M.
(c)

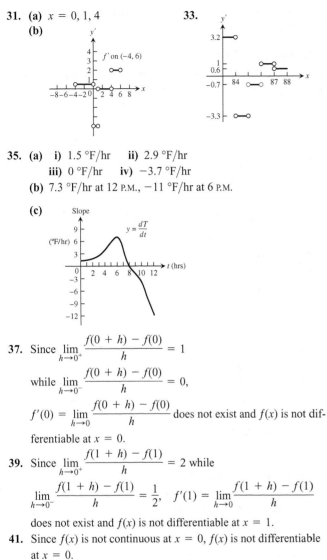

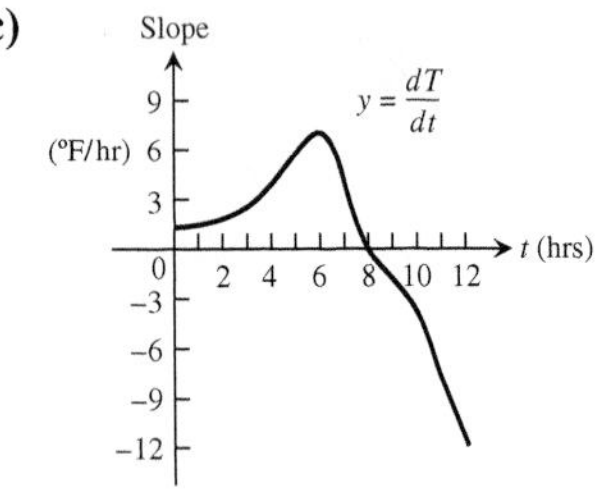

37. Since $\lim_{h\to 0^+} \frac{f(0+h) - f(0)}{h} = 1$ while $\lim_{h\to 0^-} \frac{f(0+h) - f(0)}{h} = 0$, $f'(0) = \lim_{h\to 0} \frac{f(0+h) - f(0)}{h}$ does not exist and $f(x)$ is not differentiable at $x = 0$.

39. Since $\lim_{h\to 0^+} \frac{f(1+h) - f(1)}{h} = 2$ while $\lim_{h\to 0^-} \frac{f(1+h) - f(1)}{h} = \frac{1}{2}$, $f'(1) = \lim_{h\to 0} \frac{f(1+h) - f(1)}{h}$ does not exist and $f(x)$ is not differentiable at $x = 1$.

41. Since $f(x)$ is not continuous at $x = 0$, $f(x)$ is not differentiable at $x = 0$.

43. **(a)** $-3 \le x \le 2$ **(b)** None **(c)** None
45. **(a)** $-3 \le x < 0, 0 < x \le 3$ **(b)** None **(c)** $x = 0$
47. **(a)** $-1 \le x < 0, 0 < x \le 2$ **(b)** $x = 0$ **(c)** None

Section 3.3, pp. 137–139

1. $\frac{dy}{dx} = -2x, \frac{d^2y}{dx^2} = -2$

3. $\frac{ds}{dt} = 15t^2 - 15t^4, \frac{d^2s}{dt^2} = 30t - 60t^3$

5. $\frac{dy}{dx} = 4x^2 - 1 + 2e^x, \frac{d^2y}{dx^2} = 8x + 2e^x$

7. $\frac{dw}{dz} = -\frac{6}{z^3} + \frac{1}{z^2}, \frac{d^2w}{dz^2} = \frac{18}{z^4} - \frac{2}{z^3}$

9. $\frac{dy}{dx} = 12x - 10 + 10x^{-3}, \frac{d^2y}{dx^2} = 12 - 30x^{-4}$

11. $\frac{dr}{ds} = \frac{-2}{3s^3} + \frac{5}{2s^2}, \frac{d^2r}{ds^2} = \frac{2}{s^4} - \frac{5}{s^3}$

13. $y' = -5x^4 + 12x^2 - 2x - 3$

15. $y' = 3x^2 + 10x + 2 - \frac{1}{x^2}$ **17.** $y' = \frac{-19}{(3x - 2)^2}$

19. $g'(x) = \frac{x^2 + x + 4}{(x + 0.5)^2}$ **21.** $\frac{dv}{dt} = \frac{t^2 - 2t - 1}{(1 + t^2)^2}$

23. $f'(s) = \frac{1}{\sqrt{s}(\sqrt{s} + 1)^2}$ **25.** $v' = -\frac{1}{x^2} + 2x^{-3/2}$

27. $y' = \frac{-4x^3 - 3x^2 + 1}{(x^2 - 1)^2(x^2 + x + 1)^2}$ **29.** $y' = -2e^{-x} + 3e^{3x}$

31. $y' = 3x^2e^x + x^3e^x$ **33.** $y' = \frac{9}{4}x^{5/4} - 2e^{-2x}$

35. $\frac{ds}{dt} = 3t^{1/2}$ **37.** $y' = \frac{2}{7x^{5/7}} - ex^{e-1}$ **39.** $\frac{dr}{ds} = \frac{se^s - e^s}{s^2}$

41. $y' = 2x^3 - 3x - 1, y'' = 6x^2 - 3, y''' = 12x, y^{(4)} = 12$, $y^{(n)} = 0$ for $n \ge 5$

43. $y' = 3x^2 + 4x - 8, y'' = 6x + 4, y''' = 6$, $y^{(n)} = 0$ for $n \ge 4$

45. $y' = 2x - 7x^{-2}, y'' = 2 + 14x^{-3}$

47. $\frac{dr}{d\theta} = 3\theta^{-4}, \frac{d^2r}{d\theta^2} = -12\theta^{-5}$

49. $\frac{dw}{dz} = -z^{-2} - 1, \frac{d^2w}{dz^2} = 2z^{-3}$

51. $\frac{dw}{dz} = 6ze^{2z}(1 + z), \frac{d^2w}{dz^2} = 6e^{2z}(1 + 4z + 2z^2)$

53. **(a)** 13 **(b)** −7 **(c)** 7/25 **(d)** 20

55. **(a)** $y = -\frac{x}{8} + \frac{5}{4}$ **(b)** $m = -4$ at $(0, 1)$
(c) $y = 8x - 15, y = 8x + 17$

57. $y = 4x, y = 2$ **59.** $a = 1, b = 1, c = 0$

61. (2, 4) **63.** (0, 0), (4, 2) **65.** **(a)** $y = 2x + 2$ **(c)** (2, 6)

67. 50 **69.** $a = -3$

71. $P'(x) = na_nx^{n-1} + (n - 1)a_{n-1}x^{n-2} + \cdots + 2a_2x + a_1$

73. The Product Rule is then the Constant Multiple Rule, so the latter is a special case of the Product Rule.

75. **(a)** $\frac{d}{dx}(uvw) = uvw' + uv'w + u'vw$

(b) $\frac{d}{dx}(u_1u_2u_3u_4) = u_1u_2u_3u_4' + u_1u_2u_3'u_4 + u_1u_2'u_3u_4 + u_1'u_2u_3u_4$

(c) $\frac{d}{dx}(u_1 \cdots u_n) = u_1u_2 \cdots u_{n-1}u_n' + u_1u_2 \cdots u_{n-2}u_{n-1}'u_n + \cdots + u_1'u_2 \cdots u_n$

77. $\frac{dP}{dV} = -\frac{nRT}{(V - nb)^2} + \frac{2an^2}{V^3}$

Section 3.4, pp. 146–149

1. **(a)** −2 m, −1 m/sec
(b) 3 m/sec, 1 m/sec; 2 m/sec^2, 2 m/sec^2
(c) Changes direction at $t = 3/2$ sec

3. **(a)** −9 m, −3 m/sec
(b) 3 m/sec, 12 m/sec; 6 m/sec^2, −12 m/sec^2
(c) No change in direction

5. **(a)** -20 m, -5 m/sec
(b) 45 m/sec, (1/5) m/sec; 140 m/sec^2, (4/25) m/sec^2
(c) No change in direction

7. **(a)** $a(1) = -6$ m/sec^2, $a(3) = 6$ m/sec^2
(b) $v(2) = 3$ m/sec **(c)** 6 m

9. Mars: ≈ 7.5 sec, Jupiter: ≈ 1.2 sec **11.** $g_s = 0.75$ m/sec^2

13. **(a)** $v = -32t, |v| = 32t$ ft/sec, $a = -32$ ft/sec^2
(b) $t \approx 3.3$ sec **(c)** $v \approx -107.0$ ft/sec

15. **(a)** $t = 2, t = 7$ **(b)** $3 \le t \le 6$
(c)

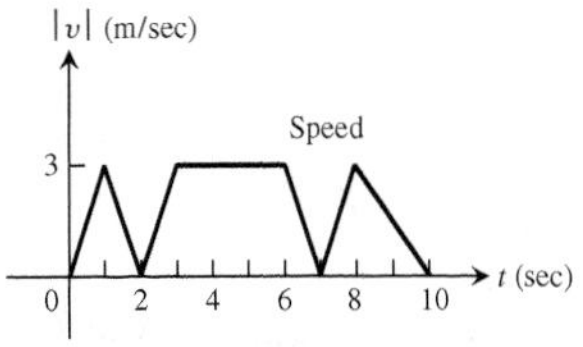

(d)

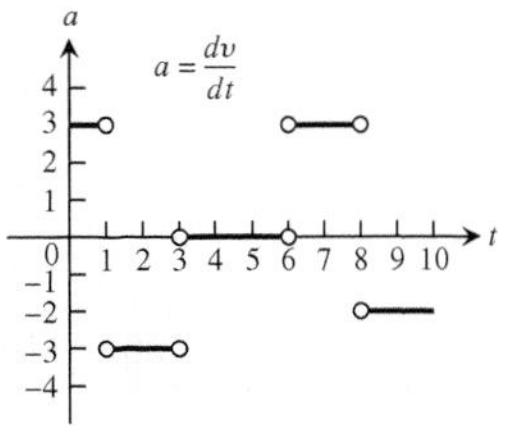

17. **(a)** 190 ft/sec **(b)** 2 sec **(c)** 8 sec, 0 ft/sec
(d) 10.8 sec, 90 ft/sec **(e)** 2.8 sec
(f) Greatest acceleration happens 2 sec after launch
(g) Constant acceleration between 2 and 10.8 sec, -32 ft/sec^2

19. **(a)** $\frac{4}{7}$ sec, 280 cm/sec **(b)** 560 cm/sec, 980 cm/sec^2
(c) 29.75 flashes/sec

21. C = position, A = velocity, B = acceleration

23. **(a)** \$110/machine **(b)** \$80 **(c)** \$79.90

25. **(a)** $b'(0) = 10^4$ bacteria/h **(b)** $b'(5) = 0$ bacteria/h
(c) $b'(10) = -10^4$ bacteria/h

27. **(a)** $\frac{dy}{dt} = \frac{t}{12} - 1$
(b) The largest value of $\frac{dy}{dt}$ is 0 m/h when $t = 12$ and the smallest value of $\frac{dy}{dt}$ is -1 m/h when $t = 0$.
(c)

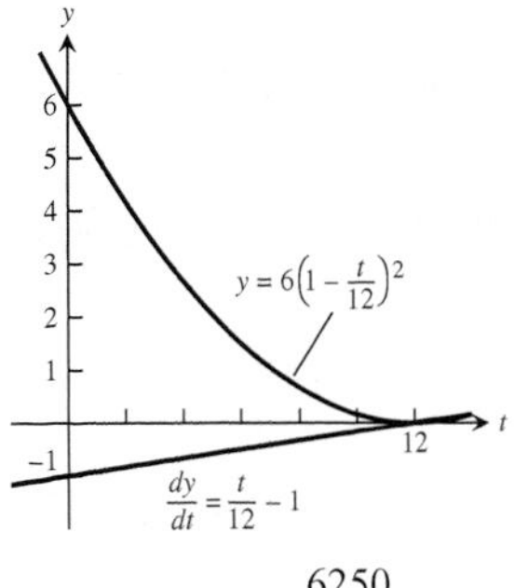

29. $t = 25$ sec $D = \frac{6250}{9}$ m

31.

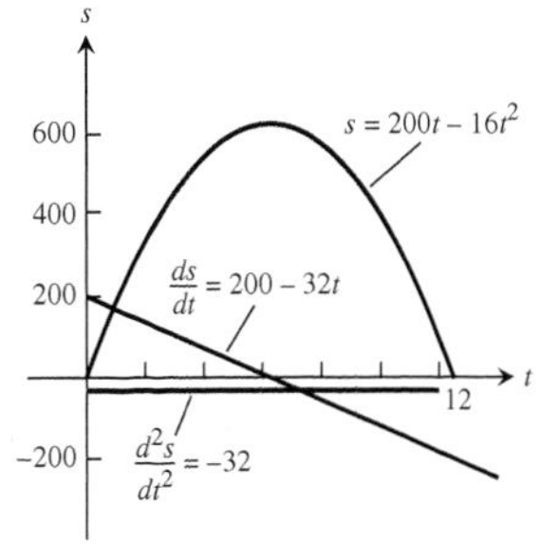

(a) $v = 0$ when $t = 6.25$ sec
(b) $v > 0$ when $0 \le t < 6.25 \Rightarrow$ the object moves up; $v < 0$ when $6.25 < t \le 12.5 \Rightarrow$ the object moves down.
(c) The object changes direction at $t = 6.25$ sec.
(d) The object speeds up on (6.25, 12.5] and slows down on [0, 6.25).
(e) The object is moving fastest at the endpoints $t = 0$ and $t = 12.5$ when it is traveling 200 ft/sec. It's moving slowest at $t = 6.25$ when the speed is 0.
(f) When $t = 6.25$ the object is $s = 625$ m from the origin and farthest away.

33.

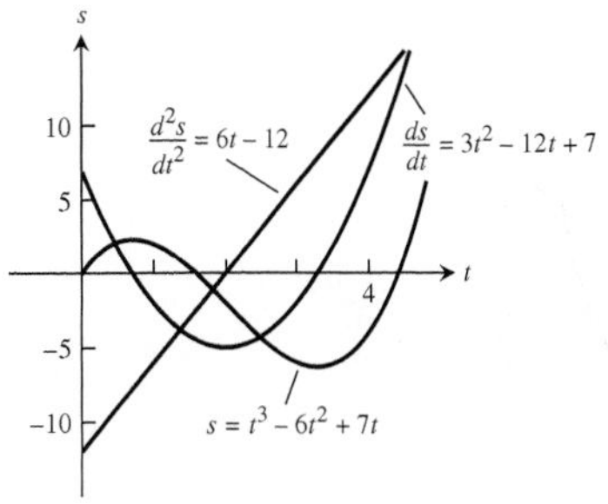

(a) $v = 0$ when $t = \frac{6 \pm \sqrt{15}}{3}$ sec
(b) $v < 0$ when $\frac{6 - \sqrt{15}}{3} < t < \frac{6 + \sqrt{15}}{3} \Rightarrow$ the object moves left; $v > 0$ when $0 \le t < \frac{6 - \sqrt{15}}{3}$ or $\frac{6 + \sqrt{15}}{3} < t \le 4 \Rightarrow$ the object moves right.
(c) The object changes direction at $t = \frac{6 \pm \sqrt{15}}{3}$ sec.
(d) The object speeds up on $\left(\frac{6 - \sqrt{15}}{3}, 2\right) \cup \left(\frac{6 + \sqrt{15}}{3}, 4\right]$ and slows down on $\left[0, \frac{6 - \sqrt{15}}{3}\right) \cup \left(2, \frac{6 + \sqrt{15}}{3}\right)$.
(e) The object is moving fastest at $t = 0$ and $t = 4$ when it is moving 7 units/sec and slowest at $t = \frac{6 \pm \sqrt{15}}{3}$ sec.
(f) When $t = \frac{6 + \sqrt{15}}{3}$ the object is at position $s \approx -6.303$ units and farthest from the origin.

Section 3.5, pp. 153–156

1. $-10 - 3 \sin x$ **3.** $2x \cos x - x^2 \sin x$

5. $-\csc x \cot x - \frac{2}{\sqrt{x}}$ **7.** $\sin x \sec^2 x + \sin x$ **9.** 0

11. $\frac{-\csc^2 x}{(1 + \cot x)^2}$ **13.** $4 \tan x \sec x - \csc^2 x$ **15.** $x^2 \cos x$

17. $3x^2 \sin x \cos x + x^3 \cos^2 x - x^3 \sin^2 x$

19. $\sec^2 t + e^{-t}$ **21.** $\frac{-2 \csc t \cot t}{(1 - \csc t)^2}$ **23.** $-\theta(\theta \cos \theta + 2 \sin \theta)$

25. $\sec \theta \csc \theta (\tan \theta - \cot \theta) = \sec^2 \theta - \csc^2 \theta$

27. $\sec^2 q$ **29.** $\sec^2 q$

31. $\dfrac{q^3 \cos q - q^2 \sin q - q \cos q - \sin q}{(q^2 - 1)^2}$

33. **(a)** $2 \csc^3 x - \csc x$ **(b)** $2 \sec^3 x - \sec x$

35.

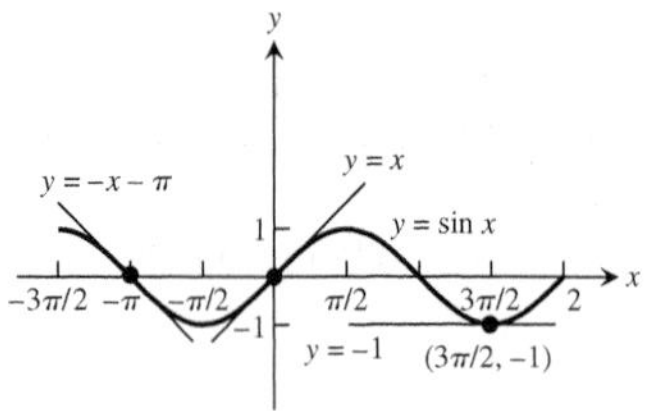

37.

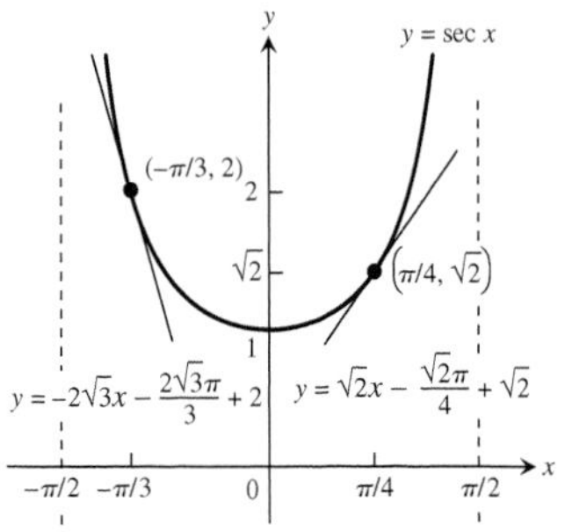

39. Yes, at $x = \pi$ **41.** No

43. $\left(-\dfrac{\pi}{4}, -1\right); \left(\dfrac{\pi}{4}, 1\right)$

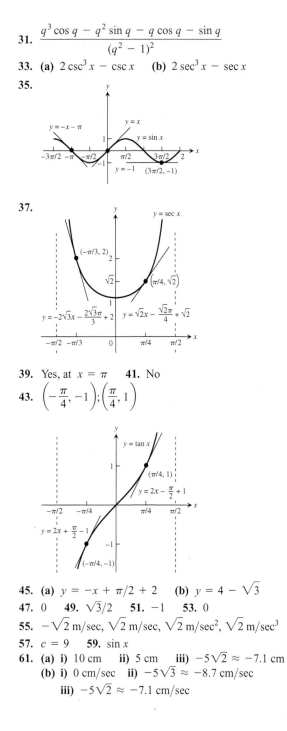

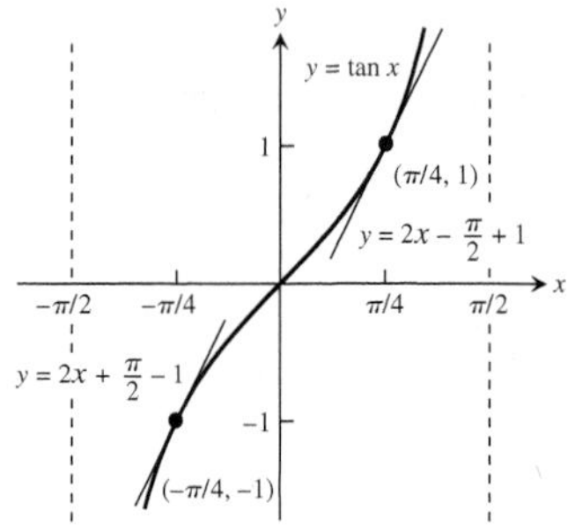

45. **(a)** $y = -x + \pi/2 + 2$ **(b)** $y = 4 - \sqrt{3}$

47. 0 **49.** $\sqrt{3}/2$ **51.** -1 **53.** 0

55. $-\sqrt{2}$ m/sec, $\sqrt{2}$ m/sec, $\sqrt{2}$ m/sec^2, $\sqrt{2}$ m/sec^3

57. $c = 9$ **59.** $\sin x$

61. **(a)** **i)** 10 cm **ii)** 5 cm **iii)** $-5\sqrt{2} \approx -7.1$ cm
(b) **i)** 0 cm/sec **ii)** $-5\sqrt{3} \approx -8.7$ cm/sec
iii) $-5\sqrt{2} \approx -7.1$ cm/sec

Section 3.6, pp. 161–164

1. $12x^3$ **3.** $3 \cos(3x + 1)$ **5.** $-\sin(\sin x) \cos x$

7. $10 \sec^2(10x - 5)$

9. With $u = (2x + 1), y = u^5 : \dfrac{dy}{dx} = \dfrac{dy}{du}\dfrac{du}{dx} = 5u^4 \cdot 2 = 10(2x + 1)^4$

11. With $u = (1 - (x/7)), y = u^{-7} : \dfrac{dy}{dx} = \dfrac{dy}{du}\dfrac{du}{dx} = -7u^{-8} \cdot \left(-\dfrac{1}{7}\right) = \left(1 - \dfrac{x}{7}\right)^{-8}$

13. With $u = ((x^2/8) + x - (1/x)), y = u^4 : \dfrac{dy}{dx} = \dfrac{dy}{du}\dfrac{du}{dx} = 4u^3 \cdot \left(\dfrac{x}{4} + 1 + \dfrac{1}{x^2}\right) = 4\left(\dfrac{x^2}{8} + x - \dfrac{1}{x}\right)^3 \left(\dfrac{x}{4} + 1 + \dfrac{1}{x^2}\right)$

15. With $u = \tan x, y = \sec u : \dfrac{dy}{dx} = \dfrac{dy}{du}\dfrac{du}{dx} = (\sec u \tan u)(\sec^2 x) = \sec(\tan x) \tan(\tan x) \sec^2 x$

17. With $u = \sin x, y = u^3 : \dfrac{dy}{dx} = \dfrac{dy}{du}\dfrac{du}{dx} = 3u^2 \cos x = 3 \sin^2 x (\cos x)$

19. $y = e^u, u = -5x, \dfrac{dy}{dx} = -5e^{-5x}$

21. $y = e^u, u = 5 - 7x, \dfrac{dy}{dx} = -7e^{(5-7x)}$

23. $-\dfrac{1}{2\sqrt{3 - t}}$ **25.** $\dfrac{4}{\pi}(\cos 3t - \sin 5t)$ **27.** $\dfrac{\csc \theta}{\cot \theta + \csc \theta}$

29. $2x \sin^4 x + 4x^2 \sin^3 x \cos x + \cos^{-2} x + 2x \cos^{-3} x \sin x$

31. $(3x - 2)^6 - \dfrac{1}{x^3\left(4 - \dfrac{1}{2x^2}\right)^2}$ **33.** $\dfrac{(4x + 3)^3(4x + 7)}{(x + 1)^4}$

35. $(1 - x)e^{-x} + 3e^{3x}$ **37.** $\left(\dfrac{5}{2}x^2 - 3x + 3\right)e^{5x/2}$

39. $\sqrt{x} \sec^2(2\sqrt{x}) + \tan(2\sqrt{x})$ **41.** $\dfrac{x \sec x \tan x + \sec x}{2\sqrt{7 + x \sec x}}$

43. $\dfrac{2 \sin \theta}{(1 + \cos \theta)^2}$ **45.** $-2 \sin(\theta^2) \sin 2\theta + 2\theta \cos(2\theta) \cos(\theta^2)$

47. $\left(\dfrac{t + 2}{2(t + 1)^{3/2}}\right) \cos\left(\dfrac{t}{\sqrt{t + 1}}\right)$ **49.** $2\theta e^{-\theta^2} \sin\left(e^{-\theta^2}\right)$

51. $2\pi \sin(\pi t - 2) \cos(\pi t - 2)$ **53.** $\dfrac{8 \sin(2t)}{(1 + \cos 2t)^5}$

55. $10t^{10} \tan^9 t \sec^2 t + 10t^9 \tan^{10} t$

57. $\dfrac{dy}{dt} = -2\pi \sin(\pi t - 1) \cdot \cos(\pi t - 1) \cdot e^{\cos^2(\pi t - 1)}$

59. $\dfrac{-3t^6(t^2 + 4)}{(t^3 - 4t)^4}$ **61.** $-2 \cos(\cos(2t - 5))(\sin(2t - 5))$

63. $\left(1 + \tan^4\left(\dfrac{t}{12}\right)\right)^2 \left(\tan^3\left(\dfrac{t}{12}\right) \sec^2\left(\dfrac{t}{12}\right)\right)$

65. $-\dfrac{t \sin(t^2)}{\sqrt{1 + \cos(t^2)}}$ **67.** $6 \tan(\sin^3 t) \sec^2(\sin^3 t) \sin^2 t \cos t$

69. $3(2t^2 - 5)^3(18t^2 - 5)$ **71.** $\dfrac{6}{x^3}\left(1 + \dfrac{1}{x}\right)\left(1 + \dfrac{2}{x}\right)$

73. $2 \csc^2(3x - 1) \cot(3x - 1)$ **75.** $16(2x + 1)^2(5x + 1)$

77. $2(2x^2 + 1)e^{x^2}$ **79.** $5/2$ **81.** $-\pi/4$ **83.** 0 **85.** -5

87. **(a)** $2/3$ **(b)** $2\pi + 5$ **(c)** $15 - 8\pi$ **(d)** $37/6$ **(e)** -1 **(f)** $\sqrt{2}/24$ **(g)** $5/32$ **(h)** $-5/(3\sqrt{17})$ **89.** 5

91. **(a)** 1 **(b)** 1 **93.** $y = 1 - 4x$

95. **(a)** $y = \pi x + 2 - \pi$ **(b)** $\pi/2$

97. It multiplies the velocity, acceleration, and jerk by 2, 4, and 8, respectively.

99. $v(6) = \dfrac{2}{5}$ m/sec, $a(6) = -\dfrac{4}{125}$ m/sec^2

Section 3.7, pp. 168–169

1. $\dfrac{-2xy - y^2}{x^2 + 2xy}$ **3.** $\dfrac{1 - 2y}{2x + 2y - 1}$

5. $\dfrac{-2x^3 + 3x^2y - xy^2 + x}{x^2y - x^3 + y}$ **7.** $\dfrac{1}{y(x+1)^2}$ **9.** $\cos^2 y$

11. $\dfrac{-\cos^2(xy) - y}{x}$ **13.** $\dfrac{-y^2}{y \sin\left(\frac{1}{y}\right) - \cos\left(\frac{1}{y}\right) + xy}$

15. $\dfrac{2e^{2x} - \cos(x + 3y)}{3\cos(x + 3y)}$ **17.** $-\dfrac{\sqrt{r}}{\sqrt{\theta}}$ **19.** $\dfrac{-r}{\theta}$

21. $y' = -\dfrac{x}{y}, y'' = \dfrac{-y^2 - x^2}{y^3}$

23. $\dfrac{dy}{dx} = \dfrac{xe^{x^2} + 1}{y}, \dfrac{d^2y}{dx^2} = \dfrac{(2x^2y^2 + y^2 - 2x)e^{x^2} - x^2e^{2x^2} - 1}{y^3}$

25. $y' = \dfrac{\sqrt{y}}{\sqrt{y} + 1}, y'' = \dfrac{1}{2(\sqrt{y} + 1)^3}$

27. -2 **29.** $(-2, 1): m = -1, (-2, -1): m = 1$

31. **(a)** $y = \frac{7}{4}x - \frac{1}{2}$ **(b)** $y = -\frac{4}{7}x + \frac{29}{7}$

33. **(a)** $y = 3x + 6$ **(b)** $y = -\frac{1}{3}x + \frac{8}{3}$

35. **(a)** $y = \frac{6}{7}x + \frac{6}{7}$ **(b)** $y = -\frac{7}{6}x - \frac{7}{6}$

37. **(a)** $y = -\frac{\pi}{2}x + \pi$ **(b)** $y = \frac{2}{\pi}x - \frac{2}{\pi} + \frac{\pi}{2}$

39. **(a)** $y = 2\pi x - 2\pi$ **(b)** $y = -\frac{x}{2\pi} + \frac{1}{2\pi}$

41. Points: $(-\sqrt{7}, 0)$ and $(\sqrt{7}, 0)$, Slope: -2

43. $m = -1$ at $\left(\frac{\sqrt{3}}{4}, \frac{\sqrt{3}}{2}\right)$, $m = \sqrt{3}$ at $\left(\frac{\sqrt{3}}{4}, \frac{1}{2}\right)$

45. $(-3, 2): m = -\frac{27}{8}$; $(-3, -2): m = \frac{27}{8}$; $(3, 2): m = \frac{27}{8}$; $(3, -2): m = -\frac{27}{8}$

47. $(3, -1)$

53. $\dfrac{dy}{dx} = -\dfrac{y^3 + 2xy}{x^2 + 3xy^2}, \dfrac{dx}{dy} = -\dfrac{x^2 + 3xy^2}{y^3 + 2xy}, \dfrac{dx}{dy} = \dfrac{1}{dy/dx}$

Section 3.8, pp. 178–179

1. **(a)** $f^{-1}(x) = \frac{x}{2} - \frac{3}{2}$

(b)

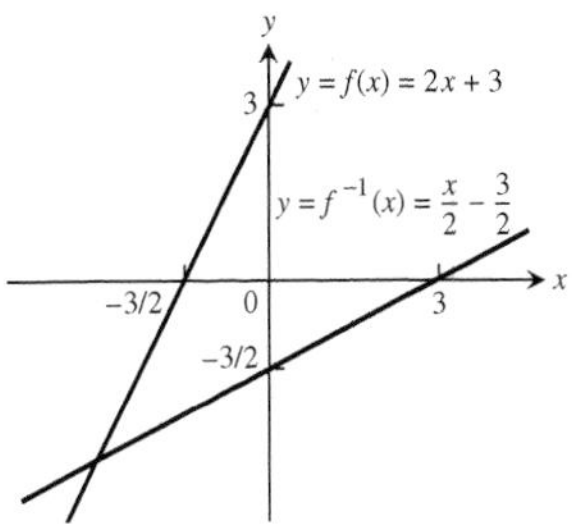

(c) 2, 1/2

3. **(a)** $f^{-1}(x) = -\frac{x}{4} + \frac{5}{4}$

(b)

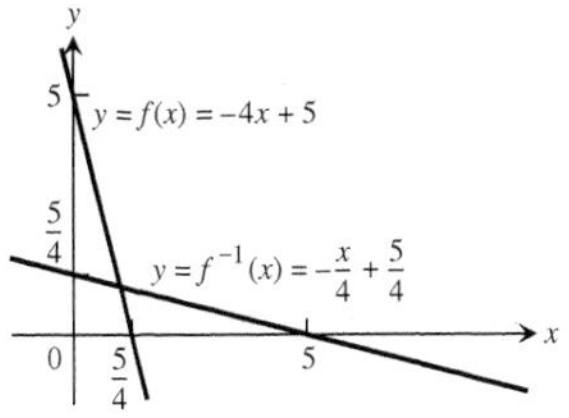

(c) $-4, -1/4$

5. **(b)**

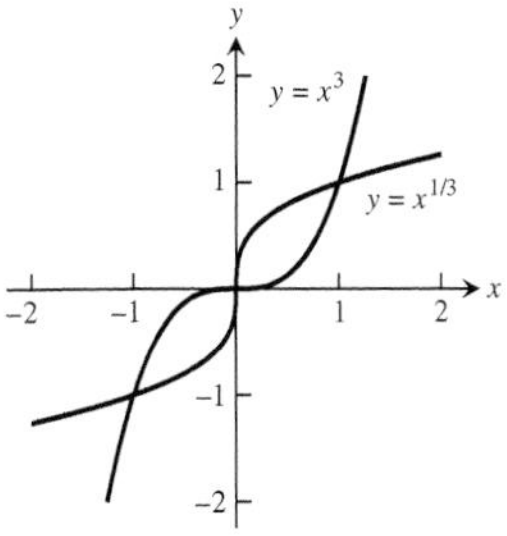

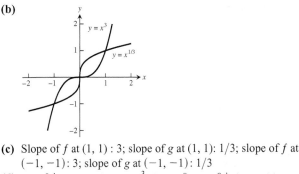

(c) Slope of f at $(1, 1)$: 3; slope of g at $(1, 1)$: 1/3; slope of f at $(-1, -1)$: 3; slope of g at $(-1, -1)$: 1/3
(d) $y = 0$ is tangent to $y = x^3$ at $x = 0$; $x = 0$ is tangent to $y = \sqrt[3]{x}$ at $x = 0$.

7. 1/9 **9.** 3 **11.** $1/x$ **13.** $2/t$ **15.** $-1/x$ **17.** $\dfrac{1}{\theta + 1}$

19. $3/x$ **21.** $2(\ln t) + (\ln t)^2$ **23.** $x^3 \ln x$ **25.** $\dfrac{1 - \ln t}{t^2}$

27. $\dfrac{1}{x(1 + \ln x)^2}$ **29.** $\dfrac{1}{x \ln x}$ **31.** $2\cos(\ln \theta)$

33. $-\dfrac{3x + 2}{2x(x + 1)}$ **35.** $\dfrac{2}{t(1 - \ln t)^2}$ **37.** $\dfrac{\tan(\ln \theta)}{\theta}$

39. $\dfrac{10x}{x^2 + 1} + \dfrac{1}{2(1 - x)}$

41. $\left(\frac{1}{2}\right)\sqrt{x(x + 1)}\left(\frac{1}{x} + \frac{1}{x + 1}\right) = \dfrac{2x + 1}{2\sqrt{x(x + 1)}}$

43. $\left(\frac{1}{2}\right)\sqrt{\frac{t}{t + 1}}\left(\frac{1}{t} - \frac{1}{t + 1}\right) = \dfrac{1}{2\sqrt{t}(t + 1)^{3/2}}$

45. $\sqrt{\theta + 3}(\sin\theta)\left(\frac{1}{2(\theta + 3)} + \cot\theta\right)$

47. $t(t + 1)(t + 2)\left[\frac{1}{t} + \frac{1}{t + 1} + \frac{1}{t + 2}\right] = 3t^2 + 6t + 2$

49. $\dfrac{\theta + 5}{\theta\cos\theta}\left[\frac{1}{\theta + 5} - \frac{1}{\theta} + \tan\theta\right]$

51. $\dfrac{x\sqrt{x^2 + 1}}{(x + 1)^{2/3}}\left[\frac{1}{x} + \frac{x}{x^2 + 1} - \frac{2}{3(x + 1)}\right]$

53. $\dfrac{1}{3}\sqrt[3]{\dfrac{x(x - 2)}{x^2 + 1}}\left(\frac{1}{x} + \frac{1}{x - 2} - \frac{2x}{x^2 + 1}\right)$ **55.** $-2\tan\theta$

57. $\dfrac{1 - t}{t}$ **59.** $1/(1 + e^{\theta})$ **61.** $e^{\cos t}(1 - t\sin t)$

63. $\dfrac{ye^y \cos x}{1 - ye^y \sin x}$ **65.** $\dfrac{dy}{dx} = \dfrac{y^2 - xy\ln y}{x^2 - xy\ln x}$ **67.** $2^x \ln x$

69. $\left(\dfrac{\ln 5}{2\sqrt{s}}\right)5^{\sqrt{s}}$ **71.** $\pi x^{(\pi - 1)}$ **73.** $\dfrac{1}{\theta \ln 2}$ **75.** $\dfrac{3}{x \ln 4}$

77. $\dfrac{2(\ln r)}{r(\ln 2)(\ln 4)}$ **79.** $\dfrac{-2}{(x + 1)(x - 1)}$

81. $\sin(\log_7 \theta) + \dfrac{1}{\ln 7}\cos(\log_7 \theta)$ **83.** $\dfrac{1}{\ln 5}$

85. $\dfrac{1}{t}(\log_2 3)3^{\log_2 t}$ **87.** $\dfrac{1}{t}$ **89.** $(x + 1)^x\left(\dfrac{x}{x + 1} + \ln(x + 1)\right)$

91. $(\sqrt{t})^t\left(\dfrac{\ln t}{2} + \dfrac{1}{2}\right)$ **93.** $(\sin x)^x(\ln \sin x + x\cot x)$

95. $(x^{\ln x})\left(\dfrac{\ln x^2}{x}\right)$

Section 3.9, pp. 185–186

1. **(a)** $\pi/4$ **(b)** $-\pi/3$ **(c)** $\pi/6$
3. **(a)** $-\pi/6$ **(b)** $\pi/4$ **(c)** $-\pi/3$
5. **(a)** $\pi/3$ **(b)** $3\pi/4$ **(c)** $\pi/6$
7. **(a)** $3\pi/4$ **(b)** $\pi/6$ **(c)** $2\pi/3$
9. $1/\sqrt{2}$ **11.** $-1/\sqrt{3}$ **13.** $\pi/2$ **15.** $\pi/2$ **17.** $\pi/2$

19. 0 **21.** $\dfrac{-2x}{\sqrt{1-x^4}}$ **23.** $\dfrac{\sqrt{2}}{\sqrt{1-2t^2}}$

25. $\dfrac{1}{|2s+1|\sqrt{s^2+s}}$ **27.** $\dfrac{-2x}{(x^2+1)\sqrt{x^4+2x^2}}$

29. $\dfrac{-1}{\sqrt{1-t^2}}$ **31.** $\dfrac{-1}{2\sqrt{t}\,(1+t)}$ **33.** $\dfrac{1}{(\tan^{-1}x)(1+x^2)}$

35. $\dfrac{-e^t}{|e^t|\sqrt{(e^t)^2-1}} = \dfrac{-1}{\sqrt{e^{2t}-1}}$ **37.** $\dfrac{-2s^2}{\sqrt{1-s^2}}$ **39.** 0

41. $\sin^{-1}x$
47. **(a)** Defined; there is an angle whose tangent is 2.
(b) Not defined; there is no angle whose cosine is 2.
49. **(a)** Not defined; no angle has secant 0.
(b) Not defined; no angle has sine $\sqrt{2}$.
59. **(a)** Domain: all real numbers except those having the form $\dfrac{\pi}{2} + k\pi$ where k is an integer; range: $-\pi/2 < y < \pi/2$
(b) Domain: $-\infty < x < \infty$; range: $-\infty < y < \infty$
61. **(a)** Domain: $-\infty < x < \infty$; range: $0 \le y \le \pi$
(b) Domain: $-1 \le x \le 1$; range: $-1 \le y \le 1$
63. The graphs are identical.

Section 3.10, pp. 191–195

1. $\dfrac{dA}{dt} = 2\pi r\dfrac{dr}{dt}$ **3.** 10 **5.** -6 **7.** $-3/2$
9. 31/13 **11.** **(a)** $-180\text{ m}^2/\text{min}$ **(b)** $-135\text{ m}^3/\text{min}$

13. **(a)** $\dfrac{dV}{dt} = \pi r^2\dfrac{dh}{dt}$ **(b)** $\dfrac{dV}{dt} = 2\pi hr\dfrac{dr}{dt}$

(c) $\dfrac{dV}{dt} = \pi r^2\dfrac{dh}{dt} + 2\pi hr\dfrac{dr}{dt}$

15. **(a)** 1 volt/sec **(b)** $-\dfrac{1}{3}$ amp/sec

(c) $\dfrac{dR}{dt} = \dfrac{1}{I}\left(\dfrac{dV}{dt} - \dfrac{V}{I}\dfrac{dI}{dt}\right)$

(d) 3/2 ohms/sec, R is increasing.

17. **(a)** $\dfrac{ds}{dt} = \dfrac{x}{\sqrt{x^2+y^2}}\dfrac{dx}{dt}$

(b) $\dfrac{ds}{dt} = \dfrac{x}{\sqrt{x^2+y^2}}\dfrac{dx}{dt} + \dfrac{y}{\sqrt{x^2+y^2}}\dfrac{dy}{dt}$ **(c)** $\dfrac{dx}{dt} = -\dfrac{y}{x}\dfrac{dy}{dt}$

19. **(a)** $\dfrac{dA}{dt} = \dfrac{1}{2}ab\cos\theta\,\dfrac{d\theta}{dt}$

(b) $\dfrac{dA}{dt} = \dfrac{1}{2}ab\cos\theta\,\dfrac{d\theta}{dt} + \dfrac{1}{2}b\sin\theta\,\dfrac{da}{dt}$

(c) $\dfrac{dA}{dt} = \dfrac{1}{2}ab\cos\theta\,\dfrac{d\theta}{dt} + \dfrac{1}{2}b\sin\theta\,\dfrac{da}{dt} + \dfrac{1}{2}a\sin\theta\,\dfrac{db}{dt}$

21. **(a)** $14\text{ cm}^2/\text{sec}$, increasing **(b)** 0 cm/sec, constant
(c) $-14/13$ cm/sec, decreasing
23. **(a)** -12 ft/sec **(b)** $-59.5\text{ ft}^2/\text{sec}$ **(c)** -1 rad/sec
25. 20 ft/sec

27. **(a)** $\dfrac{dh}{dt} = 11.19$ cm/min **(b)** $\dfrac{dr}{dt} = 14.92$ cm/min

29. **(a)** $\dfrac{-1}{24\pi}$ m/min **(b)** $r = \sqrt{26y - y^2}$ m

(c) $\dfrac{dr}{dt} = -\dfrac{5}{288\pi}$ m/min

31. 1 ft/min, $40\pi\text{ ft}^2/\text{min}$ **33.** 11 ft/sec
35. Increasing at $466/1681\text{ L/min}^2$
37. -5 m/sec **39.** -1500 ft/sec

41. $\dfrac{5}{72\pi}$ in./min, $\dfrac{10}{3}\text{ in}^2/\text{min}$

43. **(a)** $-32/\sqrt{13} \approx -8.875$ ft/sec
(b) $d\theta_1/dt = 8/65$ rad/sec, $d\theta_2/dt = -8/65$ rad/sec
(c) $d\theta_1/dt = 1/6$ rad/sec, $d\theta_2/dt = -1/6$ rad/sec

Section 3.11, pp. 203–205

1. $L(x) = 10x - 13$ **3.** $L(x) = 2$ **5.** $L(x) = x - \pi$

7. $2x$ **9.** $-x - 5$ **11.** $\dfrac{1}{12}x + \dfrac{4}{3}$ **13.** $1 - x$

15. $f(0) = 1$. Also, $f'(x) = k(1+x)^{k-1}$, so $f'(0) = k$. This means the linearization at $x = 0$ is $L(x) = 1 + kx$.
17. **(a)** 1.01 **(b)** 1.003

19. $\left(3x^2 - \dfrac{3}{2\sqrt{x}}\right)dx$ **21.** $\dfrac{2-2x^2}{(1+x^2)^2}\,dx$

23. $\dfrac{1-y}{3\sqrt{y}+x}\,dx$ **25.** $\dfrac{5}{2\sqrt{x}}\cos(5\sqrt{x})\,dx$

27. $(4x^2)\sec^2\left(\dfrac{x^3}{3}\right)dx$

29. $\dfrac{3}{\sqrt{x}}(\csc(1-2\sqrt{x})\cot(1-2\sqrt{x}))\,dx$

31. $\dfrac{1}{2\sqrt{x}}\cdot e^{\sqrt{x}}\,dx$ **33.** $\dfrac{2x}{1+x^2}\,dx$ **35.** $\dfrac{2xe^{x^2}}{1+e^{2x^2}}\,dx$

37. $\dfrac{-1}{\sqrt{e^{-2x}-1}}\,dx$ **39.** **(a)** .41 **(b)** .4 **(c)** .01

41. **(a)** .231 **(b)** .2 **(c)** .031
43. **(a)** $-1/3$ **(b)** $-2/5$ **(c)** $1/15$ **45.** $dV = 4\pi r_0^2\,dr$
47. $dS = 12x_0\,dx$ **49.** $dV = 2\pi r_0 h\,dr$
51. **(a)** $0.08\pi\text{ m}^2$ **(b)** 2% **53.** $dV \approx 565.5\text{ in}^3$
55. **(a)** 2% **(b)** 4% **57.** $\dfrac{1}{3}$% **59.** 3%
61. The ratio equals 37.87, so a change in the acceleration of gravity on the moon has about 38 times the effect that a change of the same magnitude has on Earth.
65. **(a)** $L(x) = x\ln 2 + 1 \approx 0.69x + 1$
(b)

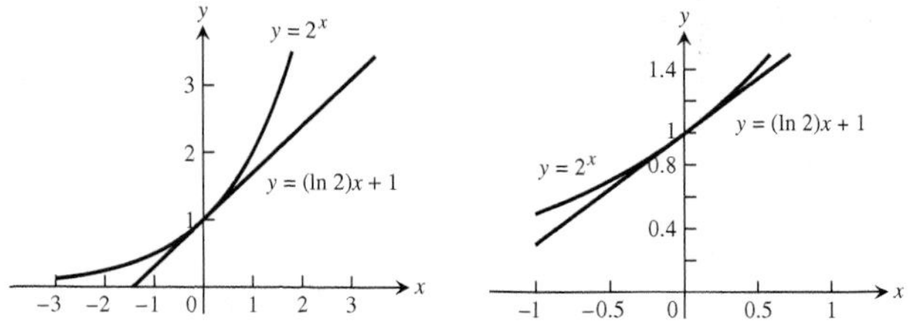

Practice Exercises, pp. 206–211

1. $5x^4 - 0.25x + 0.25$ **3.** $3x(x-2)$
5. $2(x+1)(2x^2+4x+1)$
7. $3(\theta^2 + \sec\theta + 1)^2(2\theta + \sec\theta\tan\theta)$

9. $\frac{1}{2\sqrt{t}(1+\sqrt{t})^2}$ **11.** $2\sec^2 x \tan x$

13. $8\cos^3(1-2t)\sin(1-2t)$

15. $5(\sec t)(\sec t + \tan t)^5$

17. $\frac{\theta\cos\theta + \sin\theta}{\sqrt{2\theta\sin\theta}}$ **19.** $\frac{\cos\sqrt{2\theta}}{\sqrt{2\theta}}$

21. $x\csc\left(\frac{2}{x}\right) + \csc\left(\frac{2}{x}\right)\cot\left(\frac{2}{x}\right)$

23. $\frac{1}{2}x^{1/2}\sec(2x)^2\left[16\tan(2x)^2 - x^{-2}\right]$

25. $-10x\csc^2(x^2)$ **27.** $8x^3\sin(2x^2)\cos(2x^2) + 2x\sin^2(2x^2)$

29. $\frac{-(t+1)}{8t^3}$ **31.** $\frac{1-x}{(x+1)^3}$ **33.** $\frac{-1}{2x^2\left(1+\frac{1}{x}\right)^{1/2}}$

35. $\frac{-2\sin\theta}{(\cos\theta-1)^2}$ **37.** $3\sqrt{2x+1}$ **39.** $-9\left[\frac{5x+\cos 2x}{(5x^2+\sin 2x)^{5/2}}\right]$

41. $-2e^{-x/5}$ **43.** xe^{4x} **45.** $\frac{2\sin\theta\cos\theta}{\sin^2\theta} = 2\cot\theta$

47. $\frac{2}{(\ln 2)x}$ **49.** $-8^{-t}(\ln 8)$ **51.** $18x^{2.6}$

53. $(x+2)^{x+2}(\ln(x+2)+1)$ **55.** $-\frac{1}{\sqrt{1-u^2}}$

57. $\frac{-1}{\sqrt{1-x^2}\cos^{-1}x}$ **59.** $\tan^{-1}(t) + \frac{t}{1+t^2} - \frac{1}{2t}$

61. $\frac{1-z}{\sqrt{z^2-1}} + \sec^{-1}z$ **63.** -1 **65.** $-\frac{y+2}{x+3}$

67. $\frac{-3x^2-4y+2}{4x-4y^{1/3}}$ **69.** $-\frac{y}{x}$ **71.** $\frac{1}{2y(x+1)^2}$

73. $-1/2$ **75.** y/x **77.** $-\frac{2e^{-\tan^{-1}x}}{1+x^2}$ **79.** $\frac{dp}{dq} = \frac{6q-4p}{3p^2+4q}$

81. $\frac{dr}{ds} = (2r-1)(\tan 2s)$

83. **(a)** $\frac{d^2y}{dx^2} = \frac{-2xy^3-2x^4}{y^5}$ **(b)** $\frac{d^2y}{dx^2} = \frac{-2xy^2-1}{x^4y^3}$

85. **(a)** 7 **(b)** -2 **(c)** $5/12$ **(d)** $1/4$ **(e)** 12 **(f)** $9/2$ **(g)** $3/4$

87. 0 **89.** $\frac{3\sqrt{2}e^{\sqrt{3/2}}}{4}\cos\left(e^{\sqrt{3/2}}\right)$ **91.** $-\frac{1}{2}$ **93.** $\frac{-2}{(2t+1)^2}$

95. **(a)**

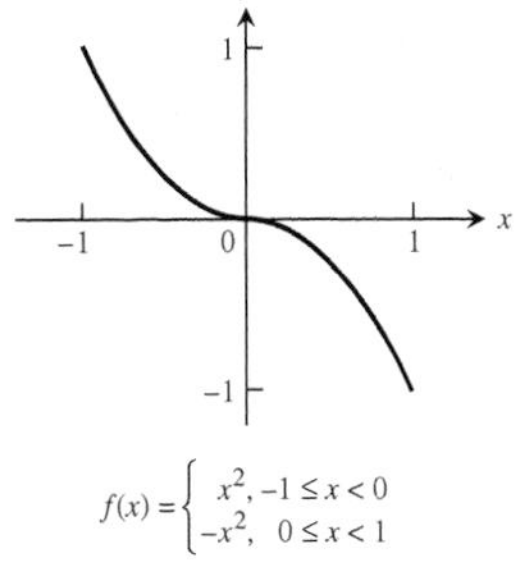

(b) Yes **(c)** Yes

97. **(a)**

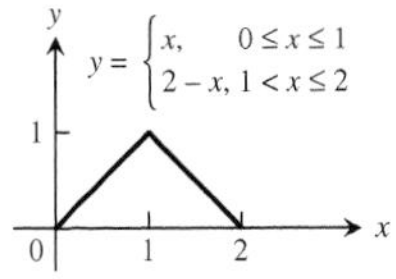

(b) Yes **(c)** No

99. $\left(\frac{5}{2}, \frac{9}{4}\right)$ and $\left(\frac{3}{2}, -\frac{1}{4}\right)$ **101.** $(-1, 27)$ and $(2, 0)$

103. **(a)** $(-2, 16), (3, 11)$ **(b)** $(0, 20), (1, 7)$

105.

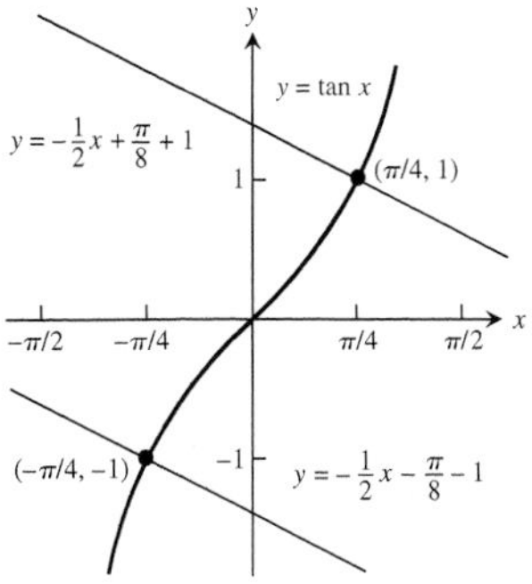

107. $\frac{1}{4}$ **109.** 4

111. Tangent: $y = -\frac{1}{4}x + \frac{9}{4}$, normal: $y = 4x - 2$

113. Tangent: $y = 2x - 4$, normal: $y = -\frac{1}{2}x + \frac{7}{2}$

115. Tangent: $y = -\frac{5}{4}x + 6$, normal: $y = \frac{4}{5}x - \frac{11}{5}$

117. $(1, 1)$: $m = -\frac{1}{2}$; $(1, -1)$: m not defined

119. B = graph of f, A = graph of f'

121.

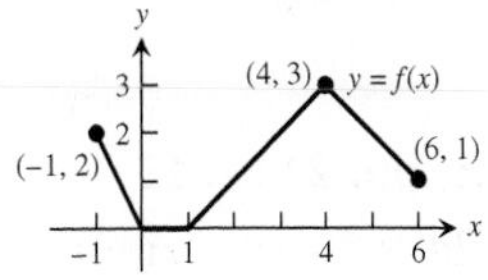

123. **(a)** 0, 0 **(b)** 1700 rabbits, ≈1400 rabbits

125. -1 **127.** $1/2$ **129.** 4 **131.** 1

133. To make g continuous at the origin, define $g(0) = 1$.

135. $\frac{2(x^2+1)}{\sqrt{\cos 2x}}\left[\frac{2x}{x^2+1} + \tan 2x\right]$

137. $5\left[\frac{(t+1)(t-1)}{(t-2)(t+3)}\right]^5\left[\frac{1}{t+1} + \frac{1}{t-1} - \frac{1}{t-2} - \frac{1}{t+3}\right]$

139. $\frac{1}{\sqrt{\theta}}(\sin\theta)^{\sqrt{\theta}}\left(\frac{\ln\sin\theta}{2} + \theta\cot\theta\right)$

141. **(a)** $\frac{dS}{dt} = (4\pi r + 2\pi h)\frac{dr}{dt}$ **(b)** $\frac{dS}{dt} = 2\pi r\frac{dh}{dt}$

(c) $\frac{dS}{dt} = (4\pi r + 2\pi h)\frac{dr}{dt} + 2\pi r\frac{dh}{dt}$

(d) $\frac{dr}{dt} = -\frac{r}{2r+h}\frac{dh}{dt}$

143. $-40\ \text{m}^2/\text{sec}$ **145.** 0.02 ohm/sec **147.** 2 m/sec

149. **(a)** $r = \frac{2}{5}h$ **(b)** $-\frac{125}{144\pi}$ ft/min

151. **(a)** $\frac{3}{5}$ km/sec or 600 m/sec **(b)** $\frac{18}{\pi}$ rpm

153. (a) $L(x) = 2x + \dfrac{\pi - 2}{2}$

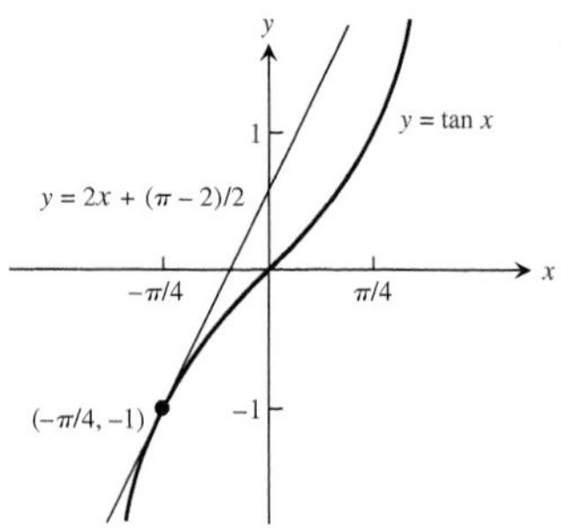

(b) $L(x) = -\sqrt{2}x + \dfrac{\sqrt{2}(4 - \pi)}{4}$

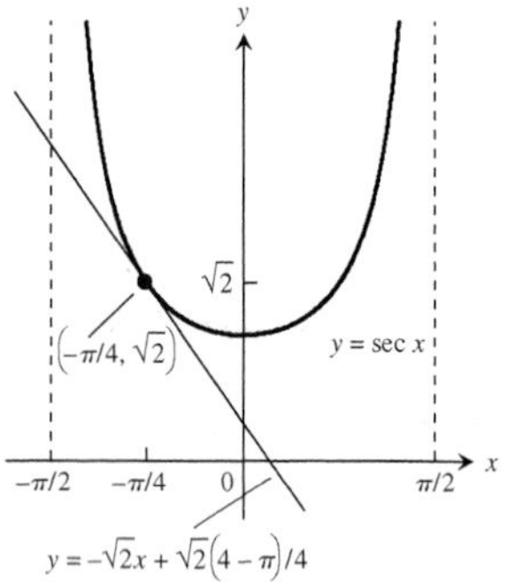

155. $L(x) = 1.5x + 0.5$ **157.** $dS = \dfrac{\pi r h_0}{\sqrt{r^2 + h_0^2}}\,dh$

159. (a) 4% **(b)** 8% **(c)** 12%

Additional and Advanced Exercises, pp. 211–213

1. (a) $\sin 2\theta = 2\sin\theta\cos\theta$; $2\cos 2\theta = 2\sin\theta(-\sin\theta) + \cos\theta(2\cos\theta)$; $2\cos 2\theta = -2\sin^2\theta + 2\cos^2\theta$; $\cos 2\theta = \cos^2\theta - \sin^2\theta$

(b) $\cos 2\theta = \cos^2\theta - \sin^2\theta$; $-2\sin 2\theta = 2\cos\theta(-\sin\theta) - 2\sin\theta(\cos\theta)$; $\sin 2\theta = \cos\theta\sin\theta + \sin\theta\cos\theta$; $\sin 2\theta = 2\sin\theta\cos\theta$

3. (a) $a = 1, b = 0, c = -\dfrac{1}{2}$ **(b)** $b = \cos a$, $c = \sin a$

5. $h = -4, k = \dfrac{9}{2}, a = \dfrac{5\sqrt{5}}{2}$

7. (a) $0.09y$ **(b)** Increasing at 1% per year

9. Answers will vary. Here is one possibility.

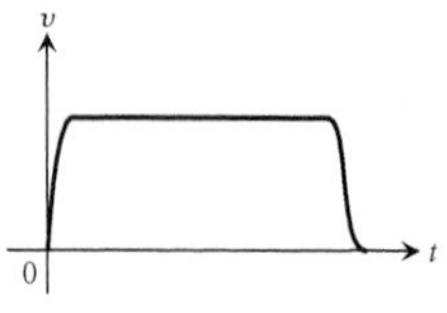

11. (a) 2 sec, 64 ft/sec **(b)** 12.31 sec, 393.85 ft

15. (a) $m = -\dfrac{b}{\pi}$ **(b)** $m = -1, b = \pi$

17. (a) $a = \dfrac{3}{4}, b = \dfrac{9}{4}$ **19.** f odd $\Rightarrow f'$ is even

23. h' is defined but not continuous at $x = 0$; k' is defined *and* continuous at $x = 0$.

27. (a) 0.8156 ft **(b)** 0.00613 sec **(c)** It will lose about 8.83 min/day.

CHAPTER 4

Section 4.1, pp. 219–222

1. Absolute minimum at $x = c_2$; absolute maximum at $x = b$

3. Absolute maximum at $x = c$; no absolute minimum

5. Absolute minimum at $x = a$; absolute maximum at $x = c$

7. No absolute minimum; no absolute maximum

9. Absolute maximum at (0, 5) **11.** (c) **13.** (d)

15. Absolute minimum at $x = 0$; no absolute maximum

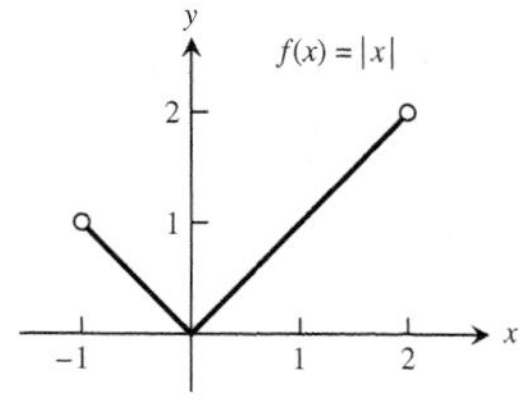

17. Absolute maximum at $x = 2$; no absolute minimum

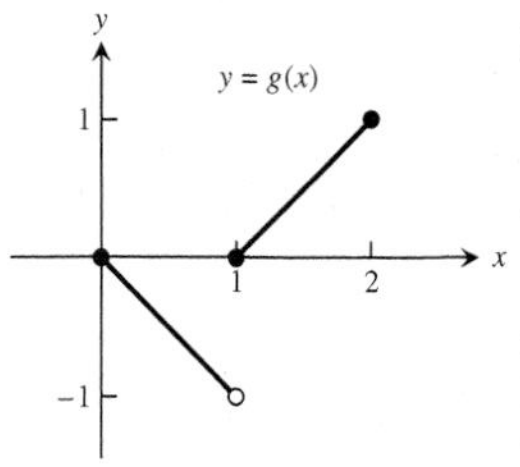

19. Absolute maximum at $x = \pi/2$; absolute minimum at $x = 3\pi/2$

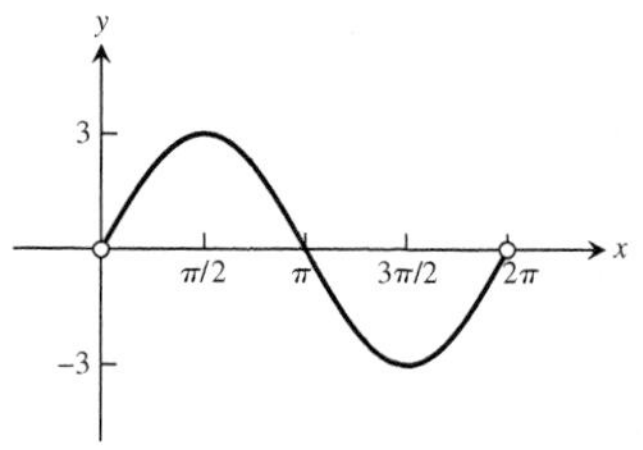

21. Absolute maximum: -3; absolute minimum: $-19/3$

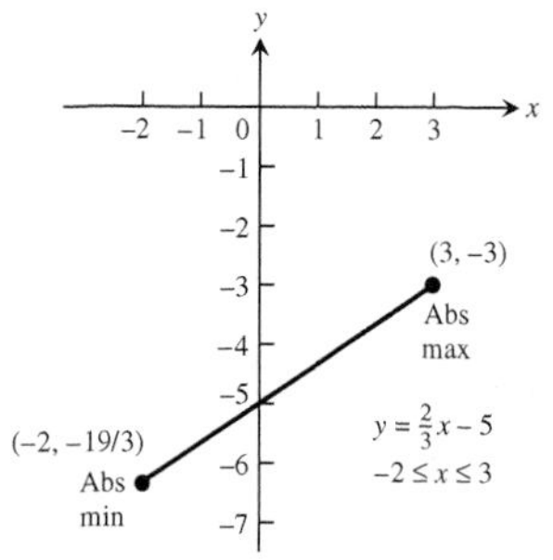

23. Absolute maximum: 3; absolute minimum: -1

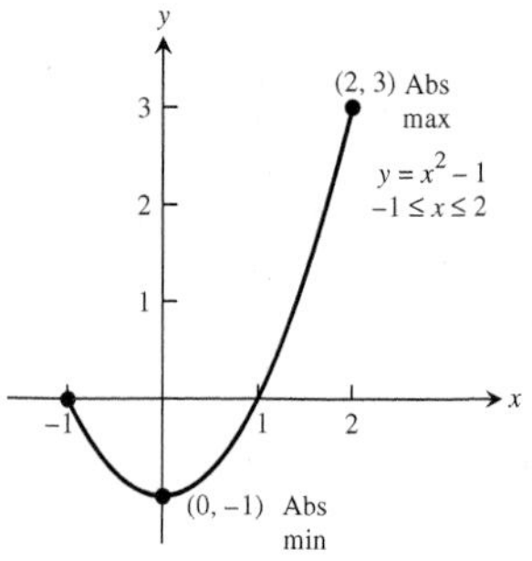

25. Absolute maximum: -0.25; absolute minimum: -4

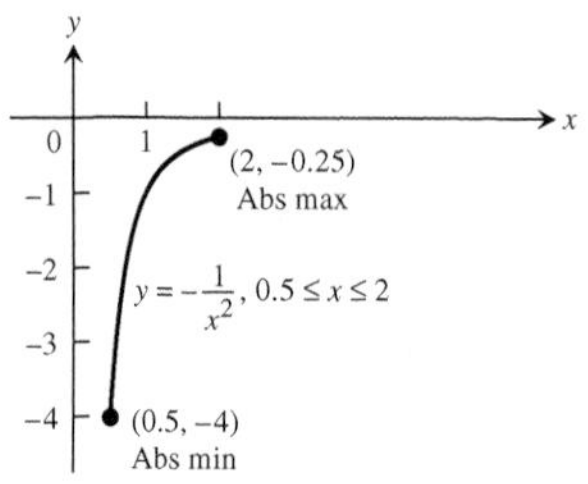

27. Absolute maximum: 2; absolute minimum: -1

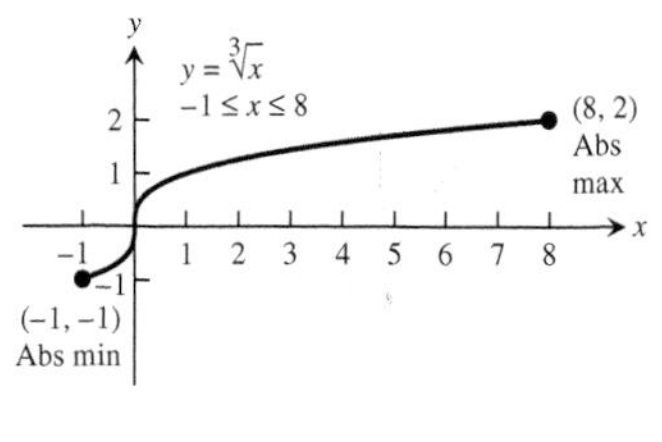

29. Absolute maximum: 2; absolute minimum: 0

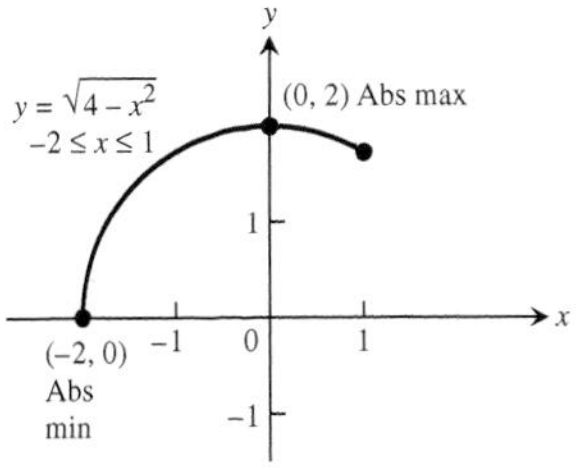

31. Absolute maximum: 1; absolute minimum: −1

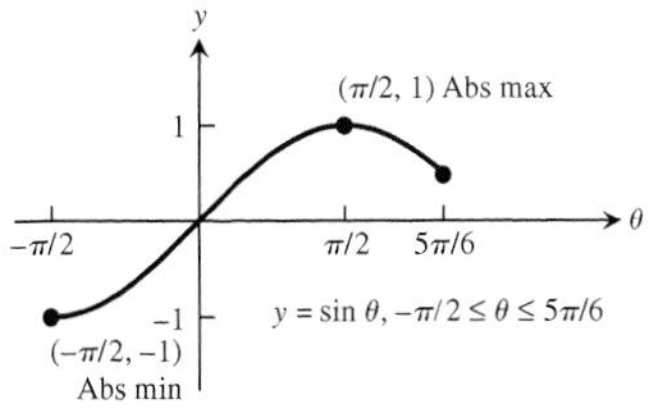

33. Absolute maximum: $2/\sqrt{3}$; absolute minimum: 1

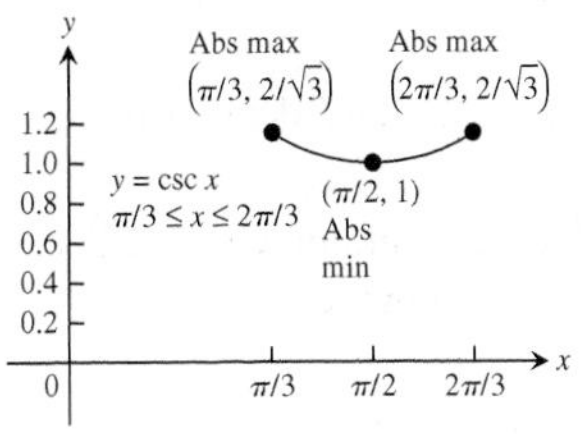

35. Absolute maximum: 2; absolute minimum: −1

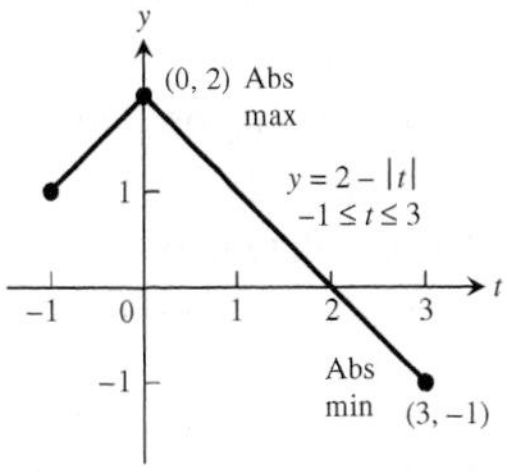

37. Absolute maximum is $1/e$ at $x = 1$; absolute minimum is $-e$ at $x = -1$.

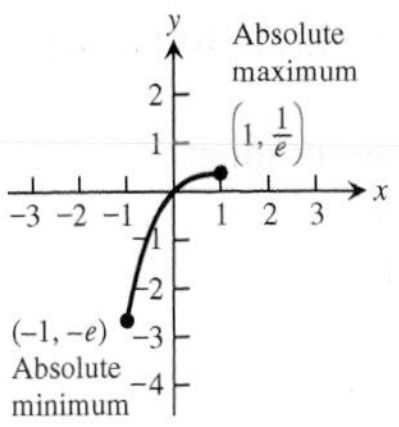

39. Absolute maximum value is $(1/4) + \ln 4$ at $x = 4$; absolute minimum value is 1 at $x = 1$; local maximum at $(1/2, 2 - \ln 2)$.

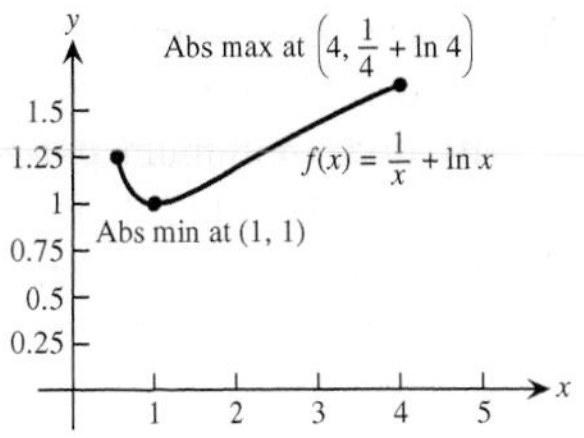

41. Increasing on (0, 8), decreasing on $(-1, 0)$; absolute maximum: 16 at $x = 8$; absolute minimum: 0 at $x = 0$

43. Increasing on $(-32, 1)$; absolute maximum: 1 at $\theta = 1$; absolute minimum: -8 at $\theta = -32$

45. $x = 3$

47. $x = 1, x = 4$

49. $x = 1$

51. $x = 0$ and $x = 4$

53. Minimum value is 1 at $x = 2$.

55. Local maximum at $(-2, 17)$; local minimum at $\left(\frac{4}{3}, -\frac{41}{27}\right)$

57. Minimum value is 0 at $x = -1$ and $x = 1$.

59. There is a local minimum at (0, 1).

61. Maximum value is $\frac{1}{2}$ at $x = 1$; minimum value is $-\frac{1}{2}$ at $x = -1$.

63. The minimum value is 2 at $x = 0$.

65. The minimum value is $-\frac{1}{e}$ at $x = \frac{1}{e}$.

67. The maximum value is $\frac{\pi}{2}$ at $x = 0$; an absolute minimum value is 0 at $x = 1$ and $x = -1$.

69.

Critical point or endpoint	Derivative	Extremum	Value
$x = -\frac{4}{5}$	0	Local max	$\frac{12}{25}10^{1/3} \approx 1.034$
$x = 0$	Undefined	Local min	0

71.

Critical point or endpoint	Derivative	Extremum	Value
$x = -2$	Undefined	Local max	0
$x = -\sqrt{2}$	0	Minimum	−2
$x = \sqrt{2}$	0	Maximum	2
$x = 2$	Undefined	Local min	0

73.

Critical point or endpoint	Derivative	Extremum	Value
$x = 1$	Undefined	Minimum	2

75.

Critical point or endpoint	Derivative	Extremum	Value
$x = -1$	0	Maximum	5
$x = 1$	Undefined	Local min	1
$x = 3$	0	Maximum	5

77. **(a)** No
(b) The derivative is defined and nonzero for $x \ne 2$. Also, $f(2) = 0$ and $f(x) > 0$ for all $x \ne 2$.
(c) No, because $(-\infty, \infty)$ is not a closed interval.
(d) The answers are the same as parts (a) and (b) with 2 replaced by a.

79. Yes **81.** g assumes a local maximum at $-c$.

83. **(a)** Maximum value is 144 at $x = 2$.
(b) The largest volume of the box is 144 cubic units, and it occurs when $x = 2$.

85. $\dfrac{{v_0}^2}{2g} + s_0$

87. Maximum value is 11 at $x = 5$; minimum value is 5 on the interval $[-3, 2]$; local maximum at $(-5, 9)$.

89. Maximum value is 5 on the interval $[3, \infty)$; minimum value is -5 on the interval $(-\infty, -2]$.

Section 4.2, pp. 228–230

1. $1/2$ **3.** 1 **5.** $\pm\sqrt{1 - \frac{4}{\pi^2}} \approx \pm 0.771$

7. $\frac{1}{3}\left(1 + \sqrt{7}\right) \approx 1.22, \frac{1}{3}\left(1 - \sqrt{7}\right) \approx -0.549$

9. Does not; f is not differentiable at the interior domain point $x = 0$.

11. Does **13.** Does not; f is not differentiable at $x = -1$.

17. **(a)**

i) 

ii) 

iii) 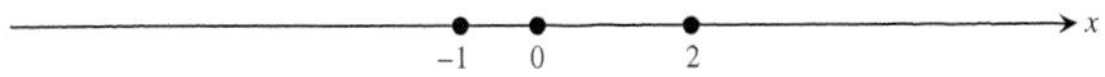

iv) 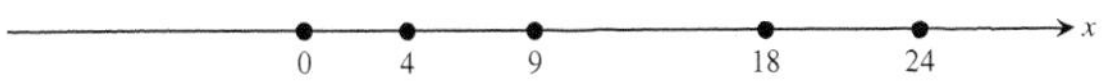

29. Yes **31. (a)** 4 **(b)** 3 **(c)** 3

33. (a) $\frac{x^2}{2} + C$ **(b)** $\frac{x^3}{3} + C$ **(c)** $\frac{x^4}{4} + C$

35. (a) $\frac{1}{x} + C$ **(b)** $x + \frac{1}{x} + C$ **(c)** $5x - \frac{1}{x} + C$

37. (a) $-\frac{1}{2}\cos 2t + C$ **(b)** $2\sin\frac{t}{2} + C$

(c) $-\frac{1}{2}\cos 2t + 2\sin\frac{t}{2} + C$

39. $f(x) = x^2 - x$ **41.** $f(x) = 1 + \frac{e^{2x}}{2}$

43. $s = 4.9t^2 + 5t + 10$ **45.** $s = \frac{1 - \cos(\pi t)}{\pi}$

47. $s = e^t + 19t + 4$ **49.** $s = \sin(2t) - 3$

51. If $T(t)$ is the temperature of the thermometer at time t, then $T(0) = -19$ °C and $T(14) = 100$ °C. From the Mean Value Theorem, there exists a $0 < t_0 < 14$ such that $\frac{T(14) - T(0)}{14 - 0} = 8.5$ °C/sec $= T'(t_0)$, the rate at which the temperature was changing at $t = t_0$ as measured by the rising mercury on the thermometer.

53. Because its average speed was approximately 7.667 knots, and by the Mean Value Theorem, it must have been going that speed at least once during the trip.

57. The conclusion of the Mean Value Theorem yields

$$\frac{\frac{1}{b} - \frac{1}{a}}{b - a} = -\frac{1}{c^2} \Rightarrow c^2\left(\frac{a - b}{ab}\right) = a - b \Rightarrow c = \sqrt{ab}.$$

61. $f(x)$ must be zero at least once between a and b by the Intermediate Value Theorem. Now suppose that $f(x)$ is zero twice between a and b. Then, by the Mean Value Theorem, $f'(x)$ would have to be zero at least once between the two zeros of $f(x)$, but this can't be true since we are given that $f'(x) \neq 0$ on this interval. Therefore, $f(x)$ is zero once and only once between a and b.

71. $1.09999 \leq f(0.1) \leq 1.1$

Section 4.3, pp. 233–235

1. (a) 0, 1
(b) Increasing on $(-\infty, 0)$ and $(1, \infty)$; decreasing on $(0, 1)$
(c) Local maximum at $x = 0$; local minimum at $x = 1$

3. (a) $-2, 1$
(b) Increasing on $(-2, 1)$ and $(1, \infty)$; decreasing on $(-\infty, -2)$
(c) No local maximum; local minimum at $x = -2$

5. (a) Critical point at $x = 1$
(b) Decreasing on $(-\infty, 1)$, increasing on $(1, \infty)$
(c) Local (and absolute) minimum at $x = 1$

7. (a) 0, 1
(b) Increasing on $(-\infty, -2)$ and $(1, \infty)$; decreasing on $(-2, 0)$ and $(0, 1)$
(c) Local minimum at $x = 1$

9. (a) $-2, 2$
(b) Increasing on $(-\infty, -2)$ and $(2, \infty)$; decreasing on $(-2, 0)$ and $(0, 2)$
(c) Local maximum at $x = -2$; local minimum at $x = 2$

11. (a) $-2, 0$
(b) Increasing on $(-\infty, -2)$ and $(0, \infty)$; decreasing on $(-2, 0)$
(c) Local maximum at $x = -2$; local minimum at $x = 0$

13. (a) $\frac{\pi}{2}, \frac{2\pi}{3}, \frac{4\pi}{3}$
(b) Increasing on $\left(\frac{2\pi}{3}, \frac{4\pi}{3}\right)$; decreasing on $\left(0, \frac{\pi}{2}\right)$, $\left(\frac{\pi}{2}, \frac{2\pi}{3}\right)$, and $\left(\frac{4\pi}{3}, 2\pi\right)$
(c) Local maximum at $x = 0$ and $x = \frac{4\pi}{3}$; local minimum at $x = \frac{2\pi}{3}$ and $x = 2\pi$

15. (a) Increasing on $(-2, 0)$ and $(2, 4)$; decreasing on $(-4, -2)$ and $(0, 2)$
(b) Absolute maximum at $(-4, 2)$; local maximum at $(0, 1)$ and $(4, -1)$; absolute minimum at $(2, -3)$; local minimum at $(-2, 0)$

17. (a) Increasing on $(-4, -1)$, $(1/2, 2)$, and $(2, 4)$; decreasing on $(-1, 1/2)$
(b) Absolute maximum at $(4, 3)$; local maximum at $(-1, 2)$ and $(2, 1)$; no absolute minimum; local minimum at $(-4, -1)$ and $(1/2, -1)$

19. (a) Increasing on $(-\infty, -1.5)$; decreasing on $(-1.5, \infty)$
(b) Local maximum: 5.25 at $t = -1.5$; absolute maximum: 5.25 at $t = -1.5$

21. (a) Decreasing on $(-\infty, 0)$; increasing on $(0, 4/3)$; decreasing on $(4/3, \infty)$
(b) Local minimum at $x = 0$ $(0, 0)$; local maximum at $x = 4/3$ $(4/3, 32/27)$; no absolute extrema

23. (a) Decreasing on $(-\infty, 0)$; increasing on $(0, 1/2)$; decreasing on $(1/2, \infty)$
(b) Local minimum at $\theta = 0$ $(0, 0)$; local maximum at $\theta = 1/2$ $(1/2, 1/4)$; no absolute extrema

25. (a) Increasing on $(-\infty, \infty)$; never decreasing
(b) No local extrema; no absolute extrema

27. (a) Increasing on $(-2, 0)$ and $(2, \infty)$; decreasing on $(-\infty, -2)$ and $(0, 2)$
(b) Local maximum: 16 at $x = 0$; local minimum: 0 at $x = \pm 2$; no absolute maximum; absolute minimum: 0 at $x = \pm 2$

29. (a) Increasing on $(-\infty, -1)$; decreasing on $(-1, 0)$; increasing on $(0, 1)$; decreasing on $(1, \infty)$
(b) Local maximum: 0.5 at $x = \pm 1$; local minimum: 0 at $x = 0$; absolute maximum: 1/2 at $x = \pm 1$; no absolute minimum

31. (a) Increasing on $(10, \infty)$; decreasing on $(1, 10)$
(b) Local maximum: 1 at $x = 1$; local minimum: -8 at $x = 10$; absolute minimum: -8 at $x = 10$

33. (a) Decreasing on $(-2\sqrt{2}, -2)$; increasing on $(-2, 2)$; decreasing on $(2, 2\sqrt{2})$
(b) Local minima: $g(-2) = -4$, $g(2\sqrt{2}) = 0$; local maxima: $g(-2\sqrt{2}) = 0$, $g(2) = 4$; absolute maximum: 4 at $x = 2$; absolute minimum: -4 at $x = -2$

35. (a) Increasing on $(-\infty, 1)$; decreasing when $1 < x < 2$, decreasing when $2 < x < 3$; discontinuous at $x = 2$; increasing on $(3, \infty)$
(b) Local minimum at $x = 3$ $(3, 6)$; local maximum at $x = 1$ $(1, 2)$; no absolute extrema

37. (a) Increasing on $(-2, 0)$ and $(0, \infty)$; decreasing on $(-\infty, -2)$
(b) Local minimum: $-6\sqrt[3]{2}$ at $x = -2$; no absolute maximum; absolute minimum: $-6\sqrt[3]{2}$ at $x = -2$

39. **(a)** Increasing on $(-\infty, -2/\sqrt{7})$ and $(2/\sqrt{7}, \infty)$; decreasing on $(-2/\sqrt{7}, 0)$ and $(0, 2/\sqrt{7})$
(b) Local maximum: $24\sqrt[3]{2}/7^{7/6} \approx 3.12$ at $x = -2/\sqrt{7}$; local minimum: $-24\sqrt[3]{2}/7^{7/6} \approx -3.12$ at $x = 2/\sqrt{7}$; no absolute extrema

41. **(a)** Increasing on $((1/3)\ln(1/2), \infty)$, decreasing on $(-\infty, (1/3)\ln(1/2))$
(b) Local minimum is $\frac{3}{2^{2/3}}$ at $x = (1/3)\ln(1/2)$; no local maximum; absolute minimum is $\frac{3}{2^{2/3}}$ at $x = (1/3)\ln(1/2)$; no absolute maximum

43. **(a)** Increasing on (e^{-1}, ∞), decreasing on $(0, e^{-1})$
(b) A local minimum is $-e^{-1}$ at $x = e^{-1}$, no local maximum; absolute minimum is $-e^{-1}$ at $x = e^{-1}$, no absolute maximum

45. **(a)** Local maximum: 1 at $x = 1$; local minimum: 0 at $x = 2$
(b) Absolute maximum: 1 at $x = 1$; no absolute minimum

47. **(a)** Local maximum: 1 at $x = 1$; local minimum: 0 at $x = 2$
(b) No absolute maximum; absolute minimum: 0 at $x = 2$

49. **(a)** Local maxima: -9 at $t = -3$ and 16 at $t = 2$; local minimum: -16 at $t = -2$
(b) Absolute maximum: 16 at $t = 2$; no absolute minimum

51. **(a)** Local minimum: 0 at $x = 0$
(b) No absolute maximum; absolute minimum: 0 at $x = 0$

53. **(a)** Local maximum: 5 at $x = 0$; local minimum: 0 at $x = -5$ and $x = 5$
(b) Absolute maximum: 5 at $x = 0$; absolute minimum: 0 at $x = -5$ and $x = 5$

55. **(a)** Local maximum: 2 at $x = 0$; local minimum: $\frac{\sqrt{3}}{4\sqrt{3} - 6}$ at $x = 2 - \sqrt{3}$
(b) No absolute maximum; an absolute minimum at $x = 2 - \sqrt{3}$

57. **(a)** Local maximum: 1 at $x = \pi/4$; local maximum: 0 at $x = \pi$; local minimum: 0 at $x = 0$; local minimum: -1 at $x = 3\pi/4$

59. Local maximum: 2 at $x = \pi/6$; local maximum: $\sqrt{3}$ at $x = 2\pi$; local minimum: -2 at $x = 7\pi/6$; local minimum: $\sqrt{3}$ at $x = 0$

61. **(a)** Local minimum: $(\pi/3) - \sqrt{3}$ at $x = 2\pi/3$; local maximum: 0 at $x = 0$; local maximum: π at $x = 2\pi$

63. **(a)** Local minimum: 0 at $x = \pi/4$

65. Local maximum: 3 at $\theta = 0$; local minimum: -3 at $\theta = 2\pi$

67.

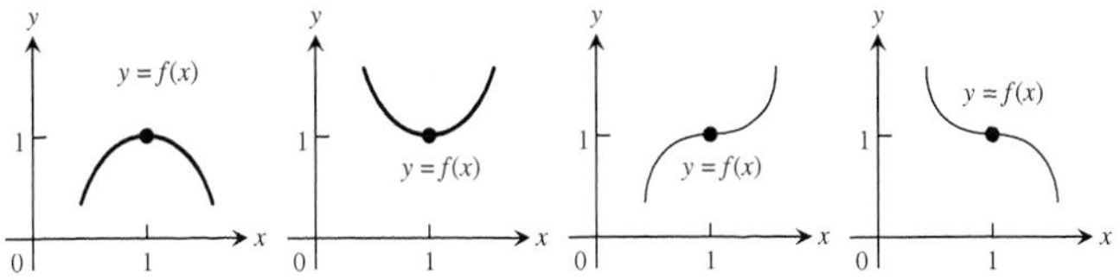

(a) (b) (c) (d)

69. **(a)** **(b)**

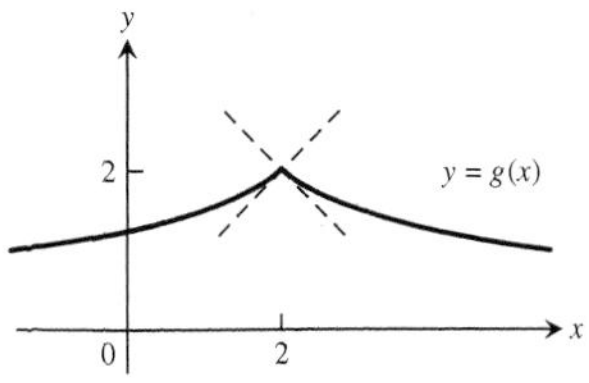

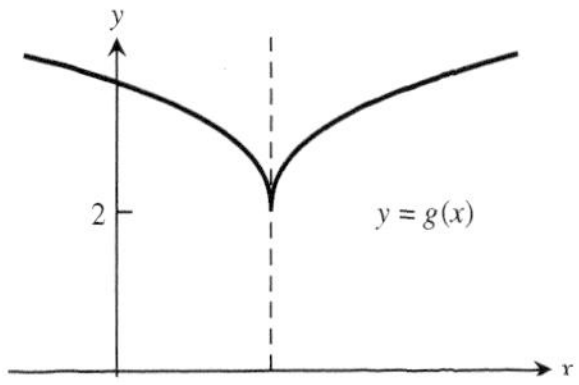

73. $a = -2, b = 4$

75. **(a)** Absolute minimum occurs at $x = \pi/3$ with $f(\pi/3) = -\ln 2$, and the absolute maximum occurs at $x = 0$ with $f(0) = 0$.
(b) Absolute minimum occurs at $x = 1/2$ and $x = 2$ with $f(1/2) = f(2) = \cos(\ln 2)$, and the absolute maximum occurs at $x = 1$ with $f(1) = 1$.

77. Minimum of $2 - 2\ln 2 \approx 0.613706$ at $x = \ln 2$; maximum of 1 at $x = 0$

79. Absolute maximum value of $1/2e$ assumed at $x = 1/\sqrt{e}$

83. Increasing; $\frac{df^{-1}}{dx} = \frac{1}{9}x^{-2/3}$

85. Decreasing; $\frac{df^{-1}}{dx} = -\frac{1}{3}x^{-2/3}$

Section 4.4, pp. 243–246

1. Local maximum: $3/2$ at $x = -1$; local minimum: -3 at $x = 2$; point of inflection at $(1/2, -3/4)$; rising on $(-\infty, -1)$ and $(2, \infty)$; falling on $(-1, 2)$; concave up on $(1/2, \infty)$; concave down on $(-\infty, 1/2)$

3. Local maximum: $3/4$ at $x = 0$; local minimum: 0 at $x = \pm 1$; points of inflection at $\left(-\sqrt{3}, \frac{3\sqrt[3]{4}}{4}\right)$ and $\left(\sqrt{3}, \frac{3\sqrt[3]{4}}{4}\right)$; rising on $(-1, 0)$ and $(1, \infty)$; falling on $(-\infty, -1)$ and $(0, 1)$; concave up on $(-\infty, -\sqrt{3})$ and $(\sqrt{3}, \infty)$; concave down on $(-\sqrt{3}, \sqrt{3})$

5. Local maxima: $\frac{-2\pi}{3} + \frac{\sqrt{3}}{2}$ at $x = -2\pi/3$, $\frac{\pi}{3} + \frac{\sqrt{3}}{2}$ at $x = \pi/3$; local minima: $-\frac{\pi}{3} - \frac{\sqrt{3}}{2}$ at $x = -\pi/3$, $\frac{2\pi}{3} - \frac{\sqrt{3}}{2}$ at $x = 2\pi/3$; points of inflection at $(-\pi/2, -\pi/2)$, $(0, 0)$, and $(\pi/2, \pi/2)$, rising on $(-\pi/3, \pi/3)$; falling on $(-2\pi/3, -\pi/3)$ and $(\pi/3, 2\pi/3)$, concave up on $(-\pi/2, 0)$ and $(\pi/2, 2\pi/3)$; concave down on $(-2\pi/3, -\pi/2)$ and $(0, \pi/2)$

7. Local maxima: 1 at $x = -\pi/2$ and $x = \pi/2$, 0 at $x = -2\pi$ and $x = 2\pi$; local minima: -1 at $x = -3\pi/2$ and $x = 3\pi/2$, 0 at $x = 0$; points of inflection at $(-\pi, 0)$ and $(\pi, 0)$; rising on $(-3\pi/2, -\pi/2)$, $(0, \pi/2)$, and $(3\pi/2, 2\pi)$; falling on $(-2\pi, -3\pi/2)$, $(-\pi/2, 0)$, and $(\pi/2, 3\pi/2)$; concave up on $(-2\pi, -\pi)$ and $(\pi, 2\pi)$; concave down on $(-\pi, 0)$ and $(0, \pi)$

9.

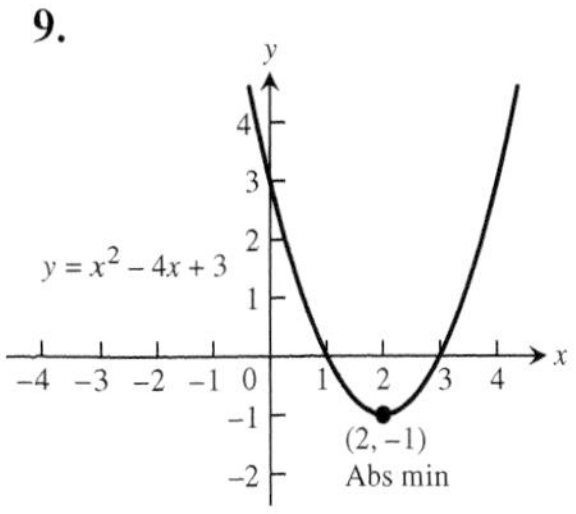

11.

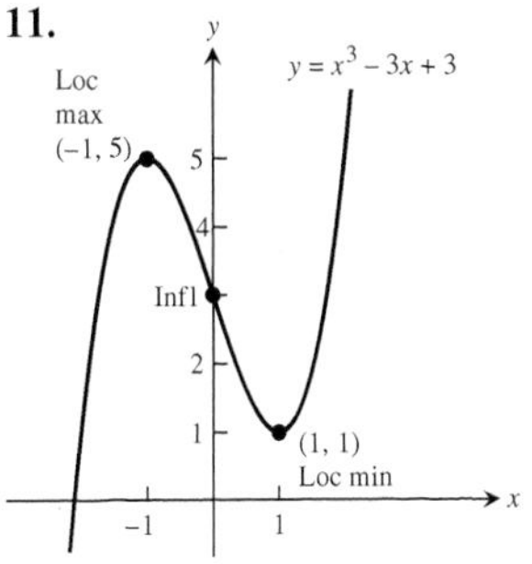

13.

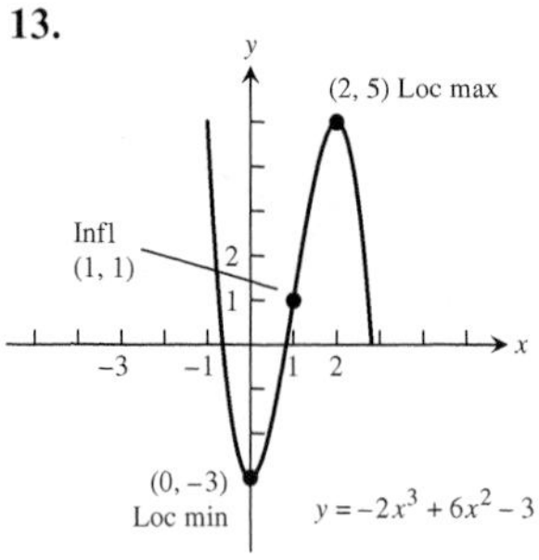

15.

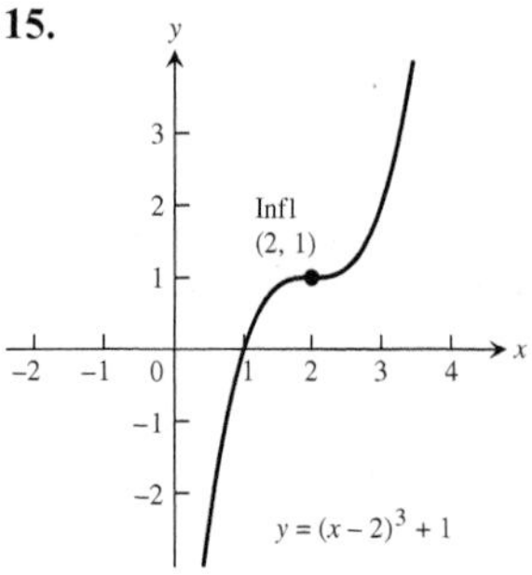

17.

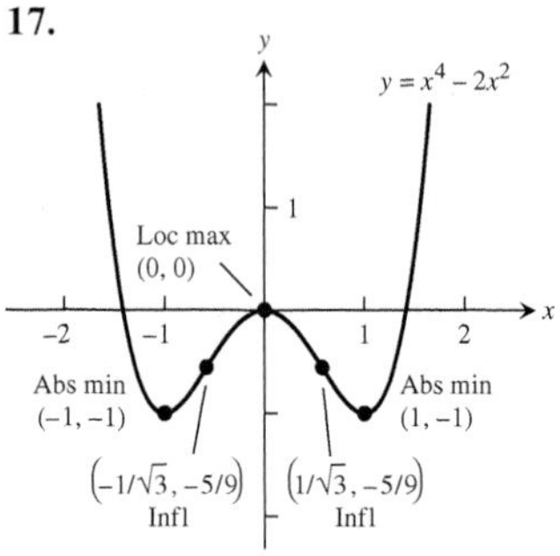

19.

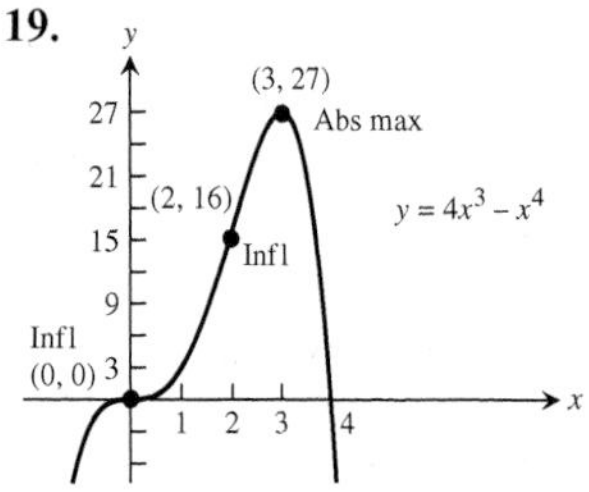

21.

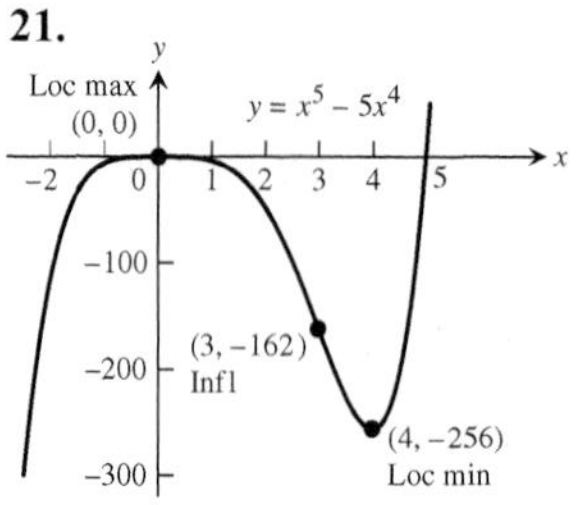

23.

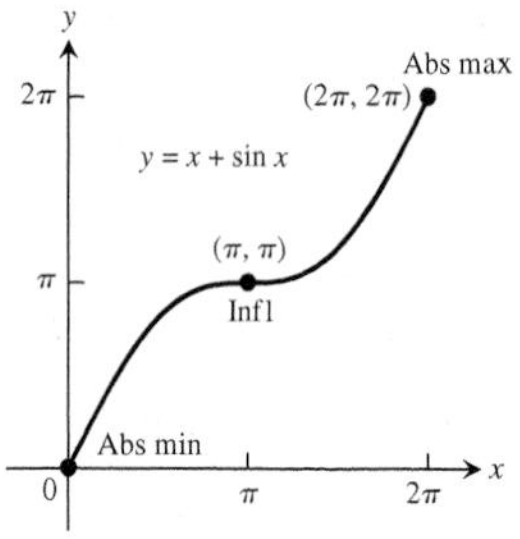

25.

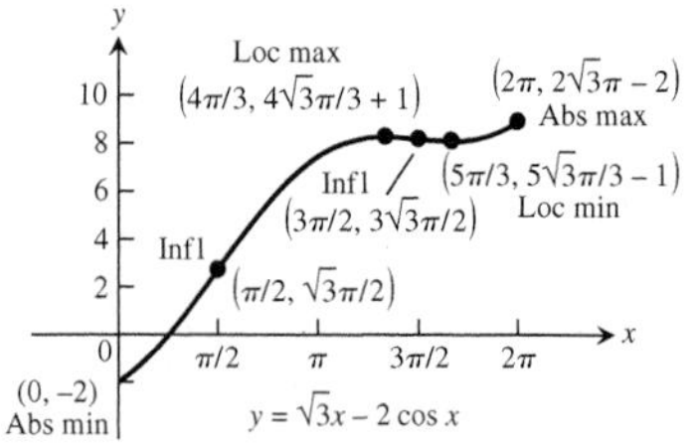

27.

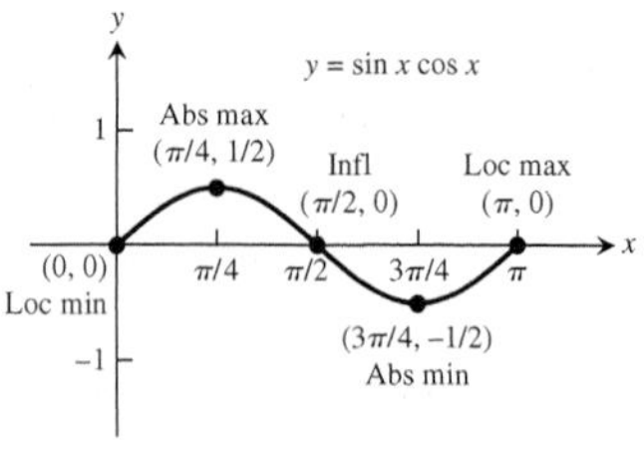

29.

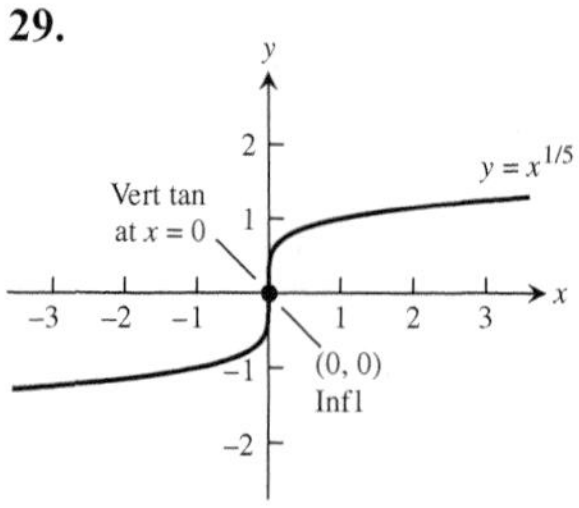

31.

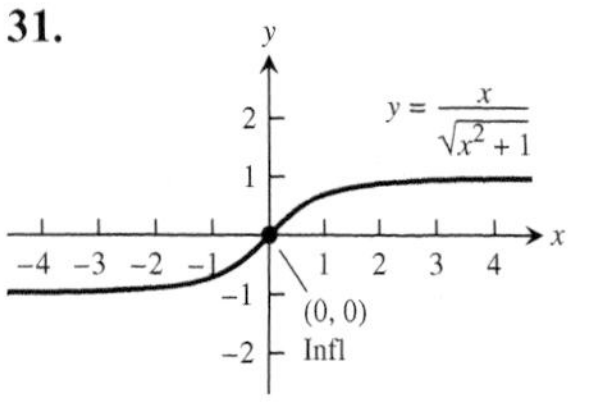

33.

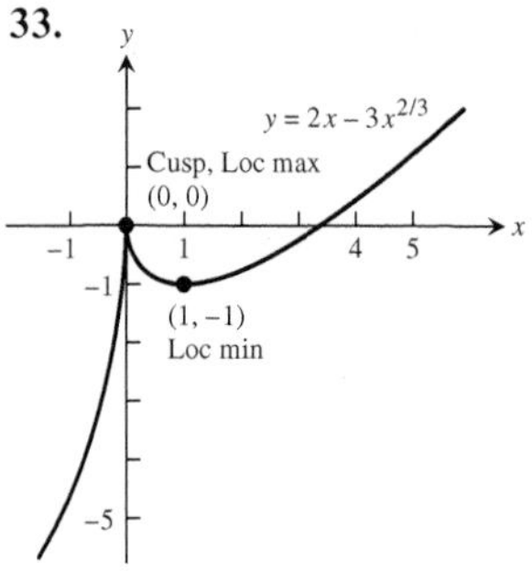

35.

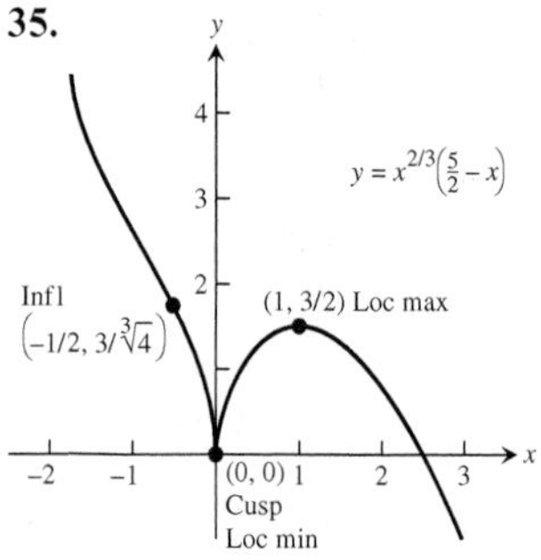

37.

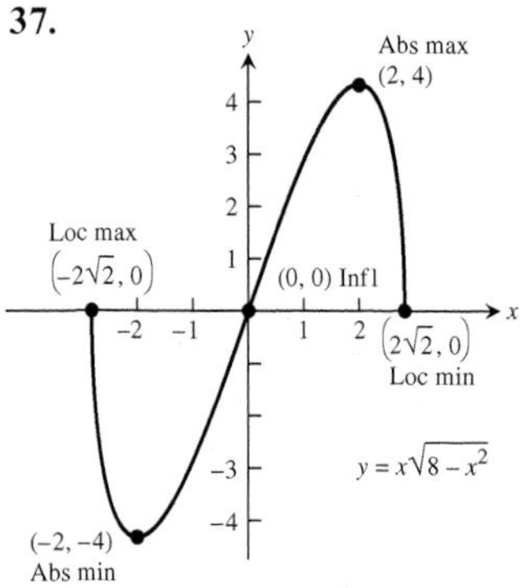

39.

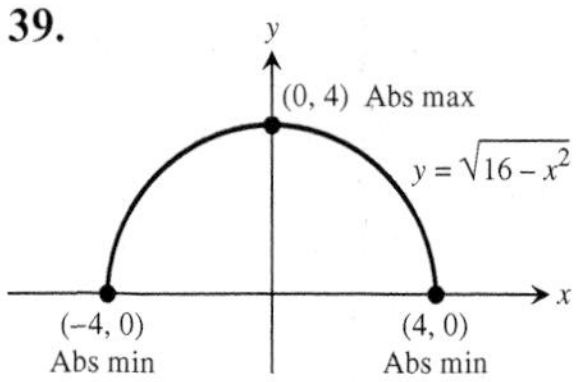

41.

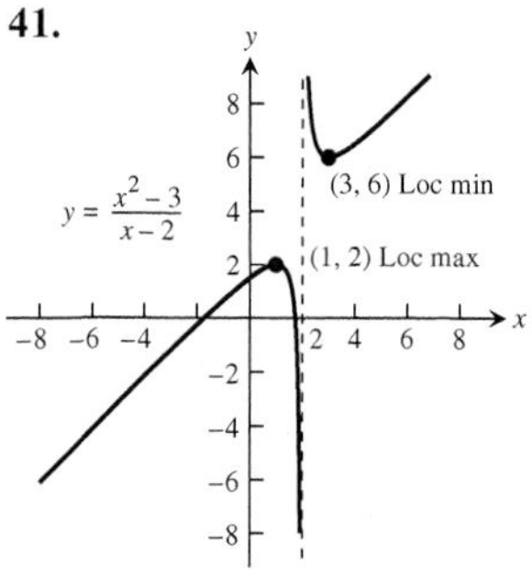

43.

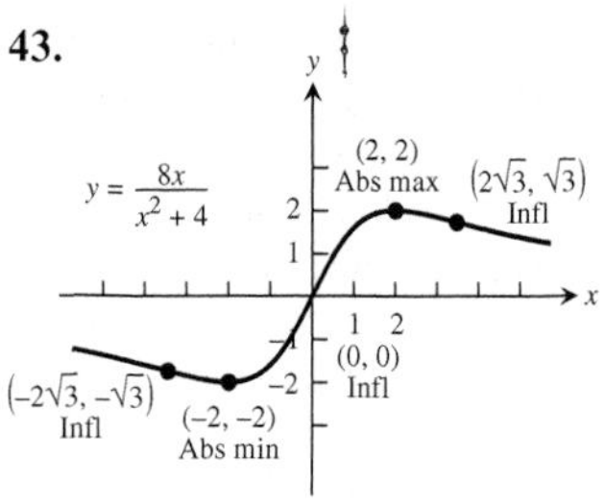

45.

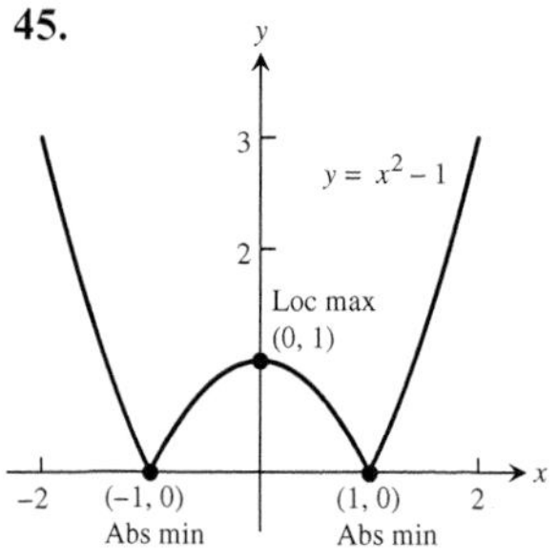

47.

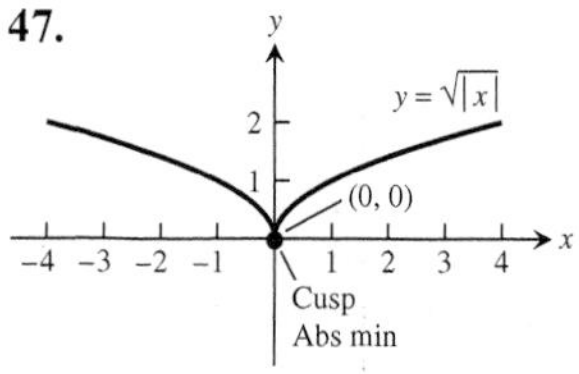

49.

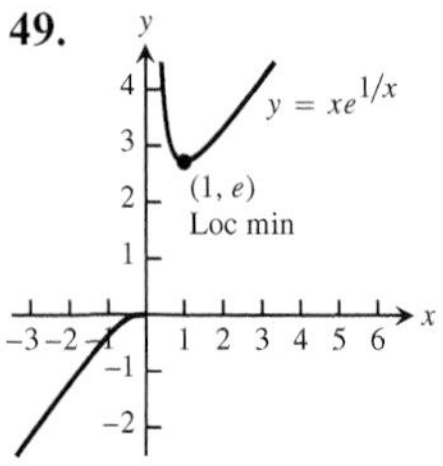

51.

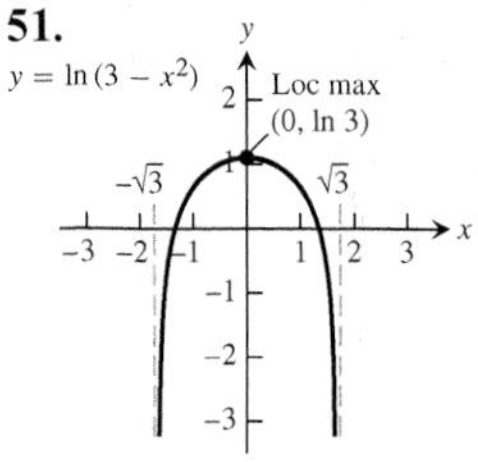

53.

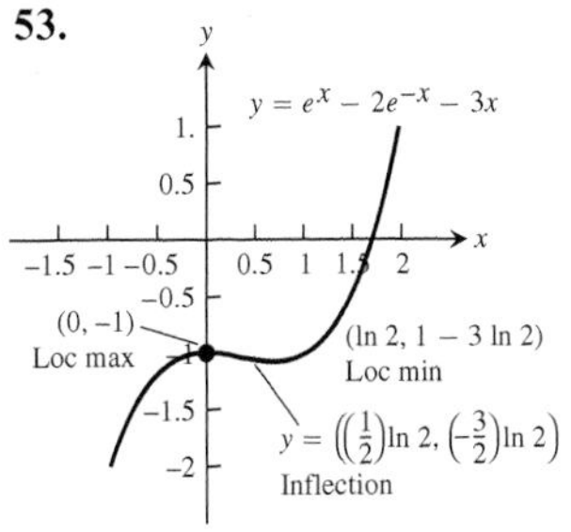

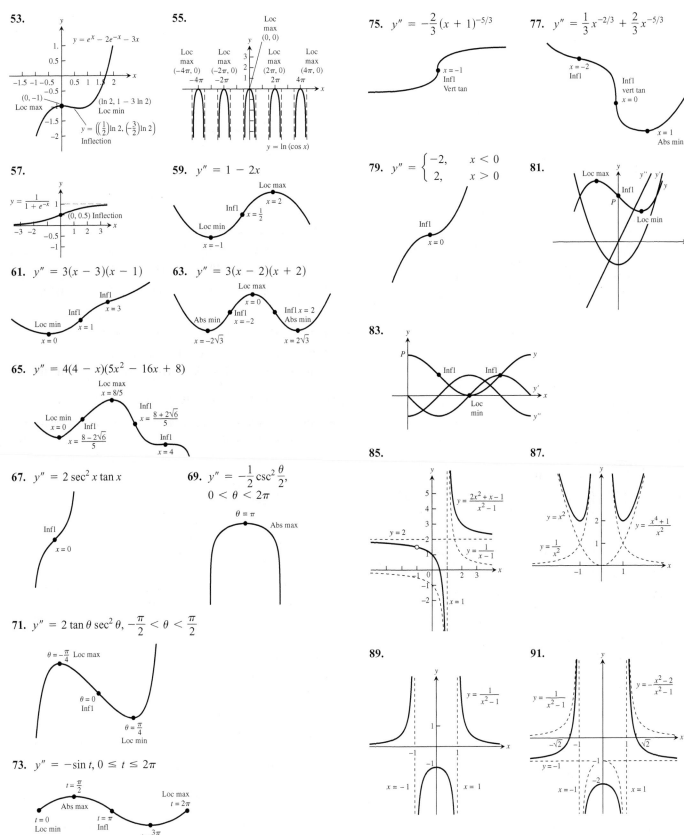

55.

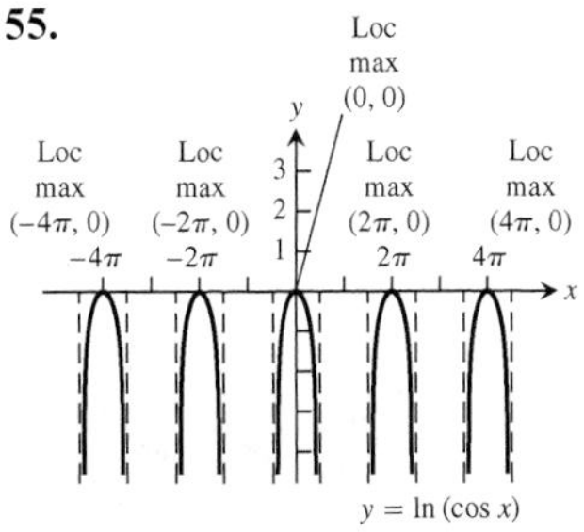

57.

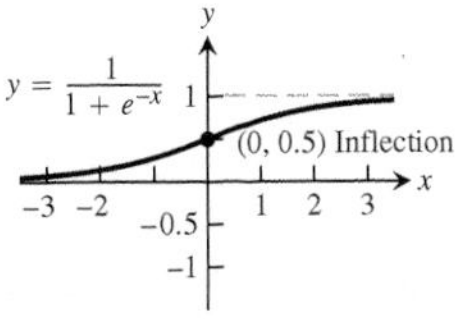

59. $y'' = 1 - 2x$

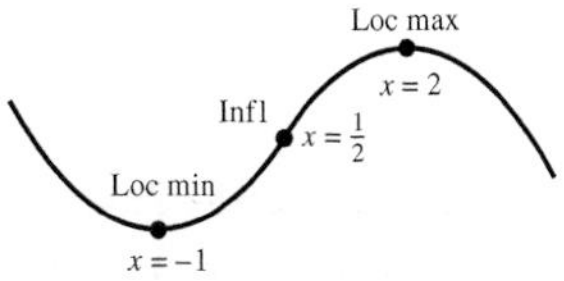

61. $y'' = 3(x - 3)(x - 1)$

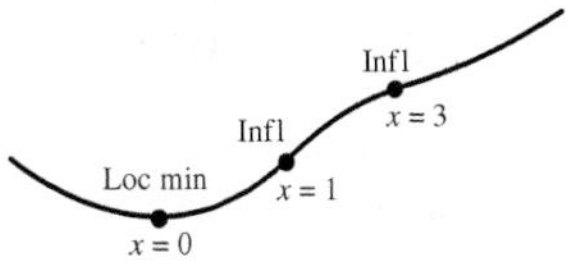

63. $y'' = 3(x - 2)(x + 2)$

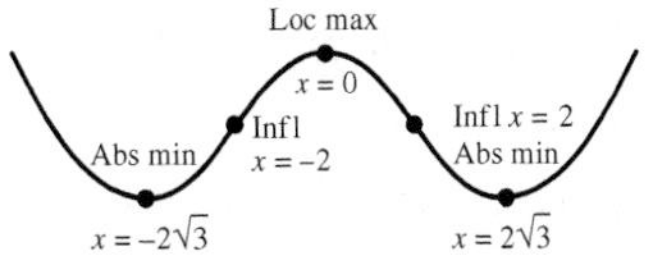

65. $y'' = 4(4 - x)(5x^2 - 16x + 8)$

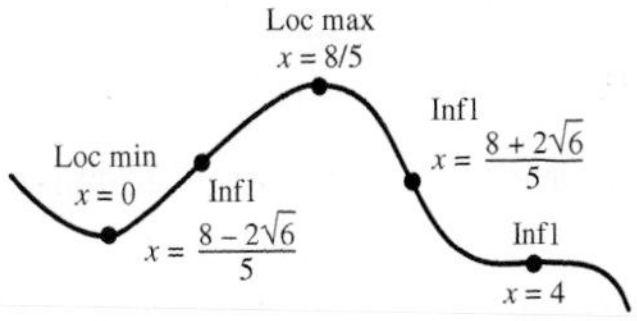

67. $y'' = 2\sec^2 x \tan x$

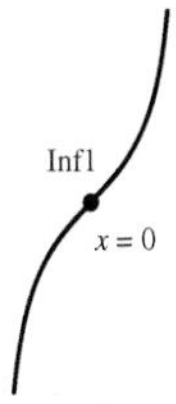

69. $y'' = -\frac{1}{2}\csc^2\frac{\theta}{2}$, $0 < \theta < 2\pi$

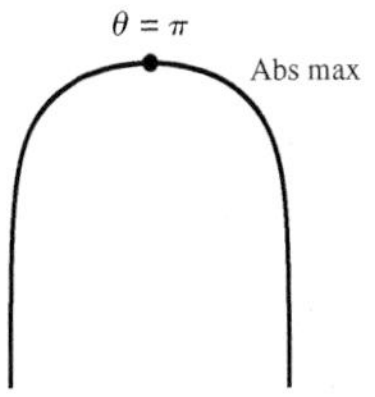

71. $y'' = 2\tan\theta\sec^2\theta$, $-\frac{\pi}{2} < \theta < \frac{\pi}{2}$

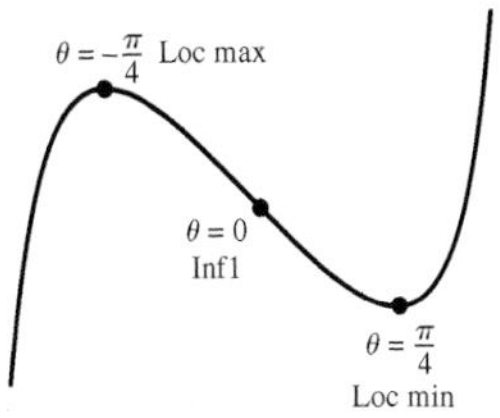

73. $y'' = -\sin t$, $0 \le t \le 2\pi$

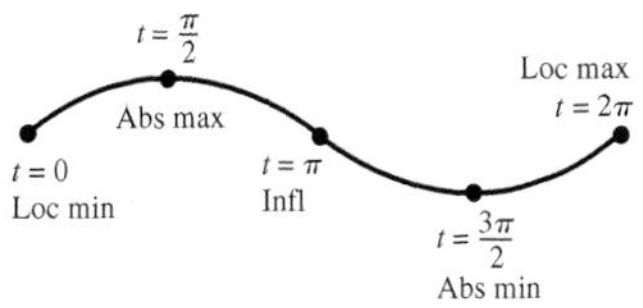

75. $y'' = -\frac{2}{3}(x + 1)^{-5/3}$

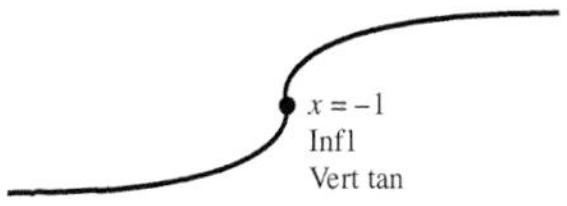

77. $y'' = \frac{1}{3}x^{-2/3} + \frac{2}{3}x^{-5/3}$

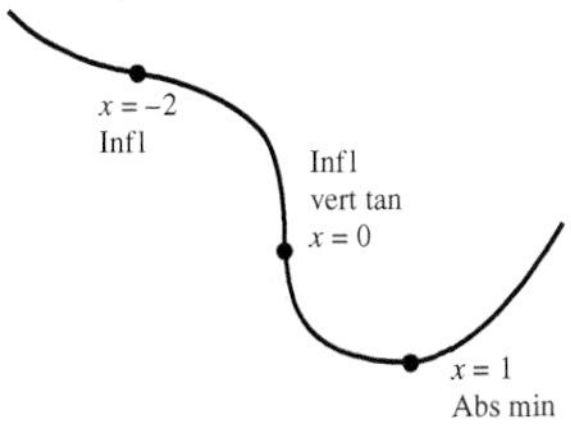

79. $y'' = \begin{cases} -2, & x < 0 \\ 2, & x > 0 \end{cases}$

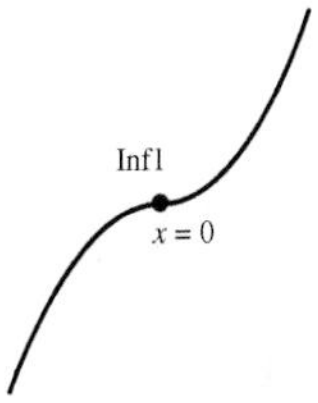

81.

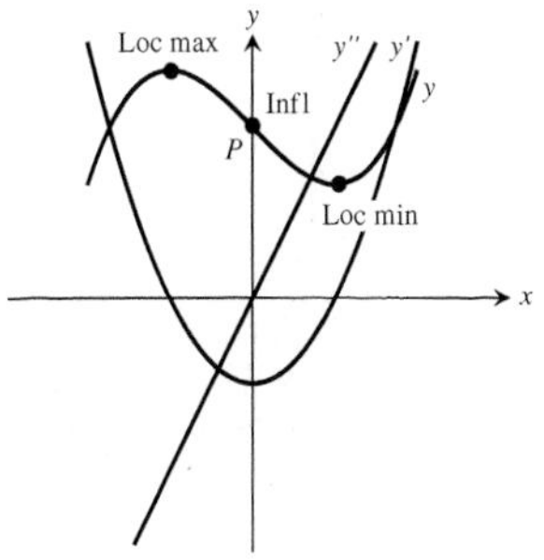

83.

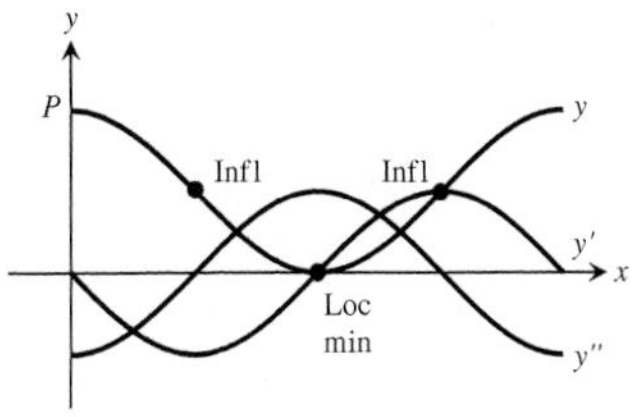

85.

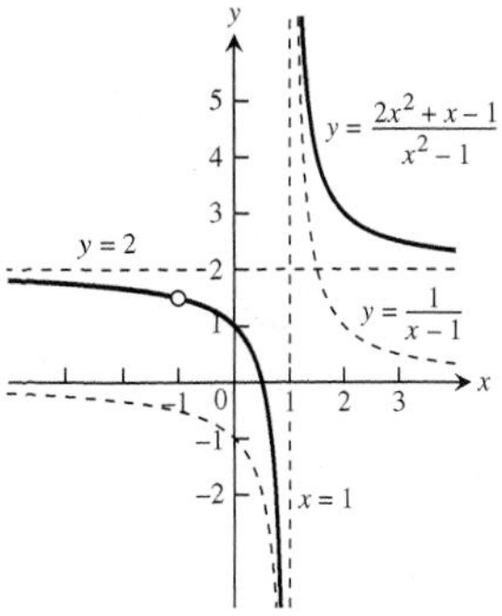

87.

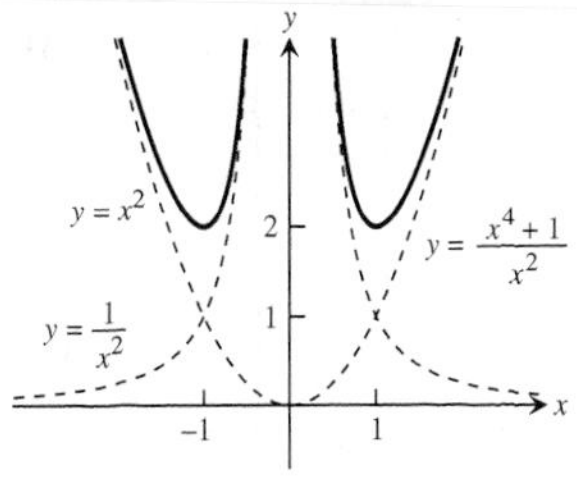

89.

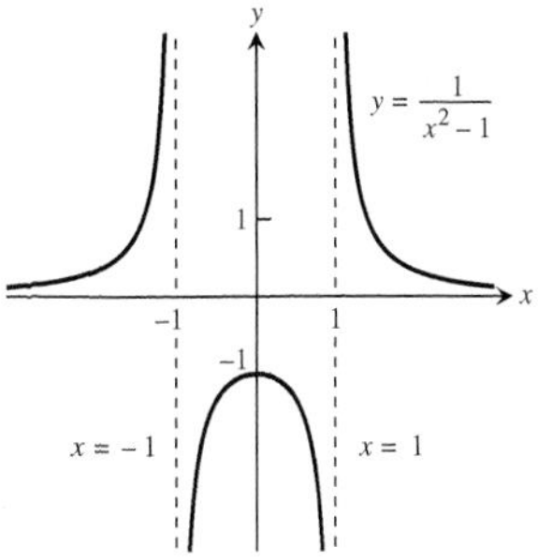

91.

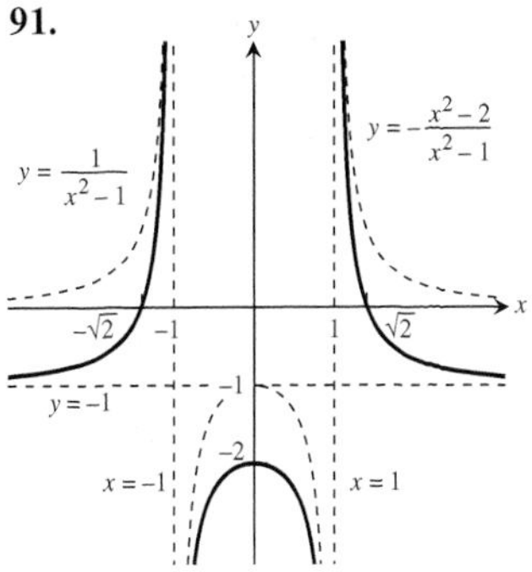

93.

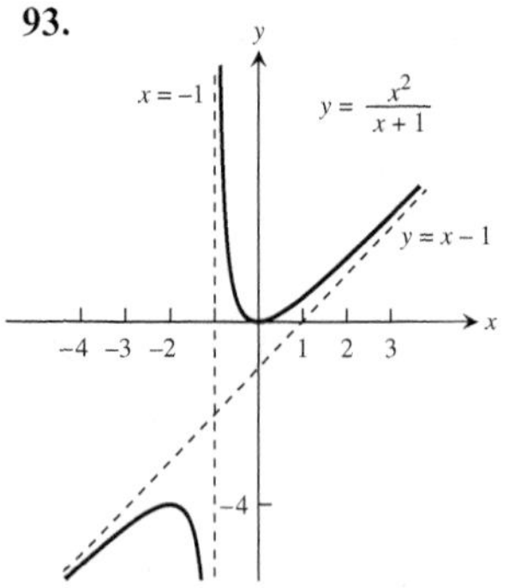

95.

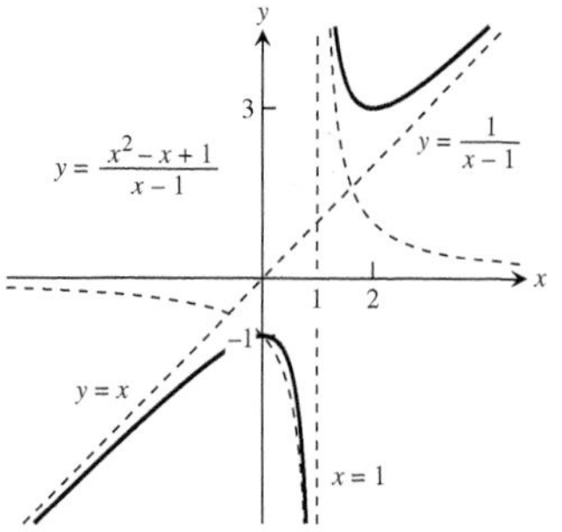

97.

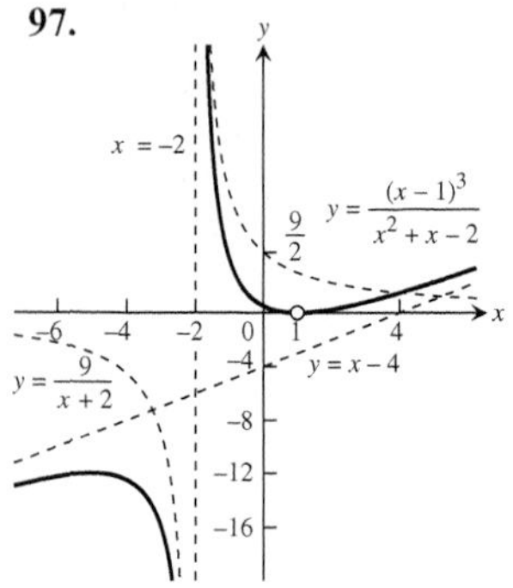

99.

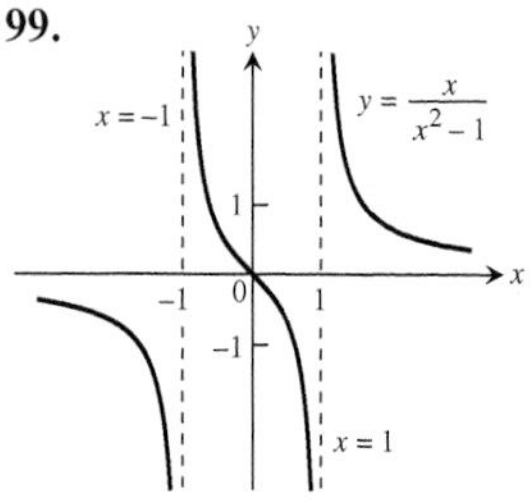

101.

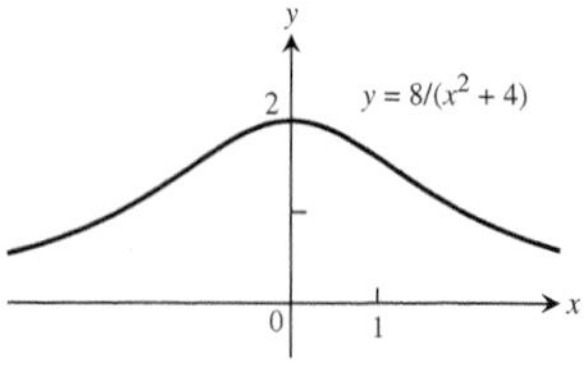

103.

Point	y'	y''
P	−	+
Q	+	0
R	+	−
S	0	−
T	−	−

105.

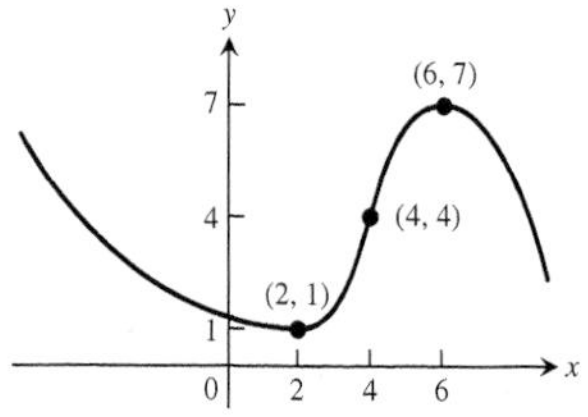

107. **(a)** Toward origin: $0 \le t < 2$ and $6 \le t \le 10$; away from origin: $2 \le t \le 6$ and $10 \le t \le 15$

(b) $t = 2, t = 6, t = 10$ **(c)** $t = 5, t = 7, t = 13$

(d) Positive: $5 \le t \le 7$, $13 \le t \le 15$; negative: $0 \le t \le 5$, $7 \le t \le 13$

109. ≈ 60 thousand units

111. Local minimum at $x = 2$; inflection points at $x = 1$ and $x = 5/3$

115. $b = -3$

119. $-1, 2$

121. $a = -1, b = 3, c = 9$

123. The zeros of $y' = 0$ and $y'' = 0$ are extrema and points of inflection, respectively. Inflection at $x = 3$, local maximum at $x = 0$, local minimum at $x = 4$.

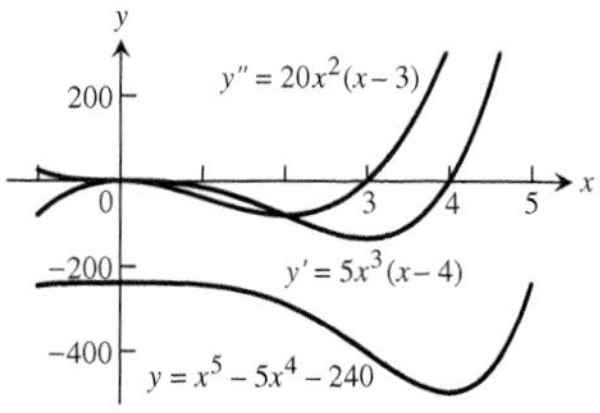

125. The zeros of $y' = 0$ and $y'' = 0$ are extrema and points of inflection, respectively. Inflection at $x = -\sqrt[3]{2}$; local maximum at $x = -2$; local minimum at $x = 0$.

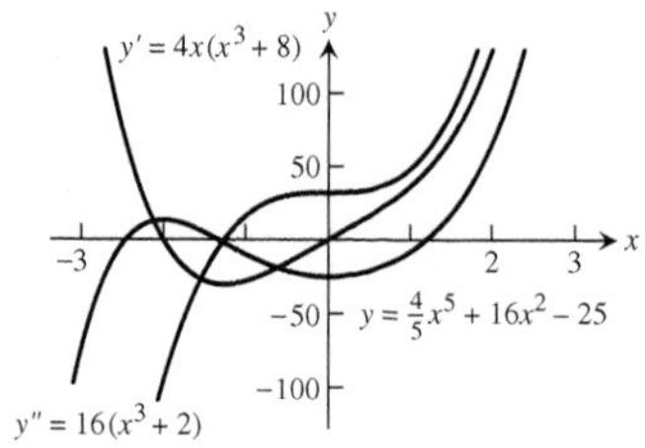

Section 4.5, pp. 253–254

1. $-1/4$ **3.** $5/7$ **5.** $1/2$ **7.** $1/4$ **9.** $-23/7$ **11.** $5/7$ **13.** 0 **15.** -16 **17.** -2 **19.** $1/4$ **21.** 2 **23.** 3 **25.** -1 **27.** $\ln 3$ **29.** $\frac{1}{\ln 2}$ **31.** $\ln 2$ **33.** 1 **35.** $1/2$ **37.** $\ln 2$ **39.** $-\infty$ **41.** $-1/2$ **43.** -1 **45.** 1 **47.** 0 **49.** 2 **51.** $1/e$ **53.** 1 **55.** $1/e$ **57.** $e^{1/2}$ **59.** 1 **61.** e^3 **63.** 0 **65.** 1 **67.** 3 **69.** 1 **71.** 0 **73.** ∞ **75.** (b) is correct. **77.** (d) is correct. **79.** $c = \frac{27}{10}$ **81.** **(b)** $\frac{-1}{2}$ **83.** -1 **87.** **(a)** $y = 1$ **(b)** $y = 0, y = \frac{3}{2}$

89. **(a)** We should assign the value 1 to $f(x) = (\sin x)^x$ to make it continuous at $x = 0$.

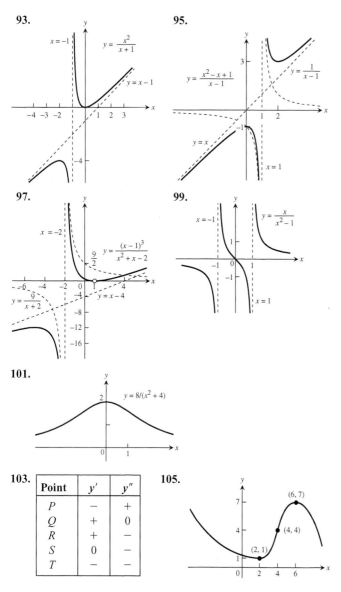

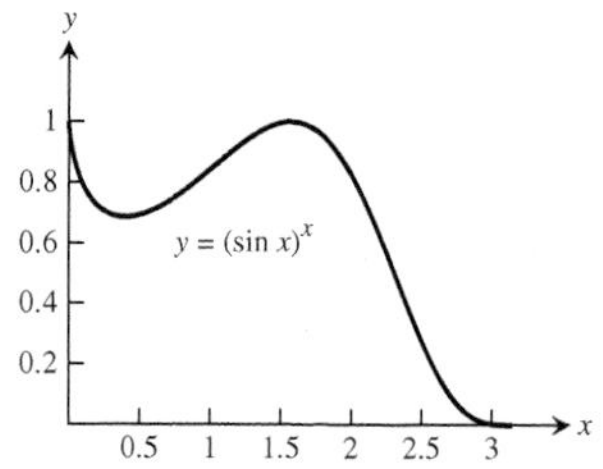

(c) The maximum value of $f(x)$ is close to 1 near the point $x \approx 1.55$ (see the graph in part (a)).

Section 4.6, pp. 260–266

1. 16 in., 4 in. by 4 in.

3. **(a)** $(x, 1 - x)$ **(b)** $A(x) = 2x(1 - x)$

(c) $\frac{1}{2}$ square units, 1 by $\frac{1}{2}$

5. $\frac{14}{3} \times \frac{35}{3} \times \frac{5}{3}$ in., $\frac{2450}{27}$ in^3 **7.** 80,000 m^2; 400 m by 200 m

9. **(a)** The optimum dimensions of the tank are 10 ft on the base edges and 5 ft deep.

(b) Minimizing the surface area of the tank minimizes its weight for a given wall thickness. The thickness of the steel walls would likely be determined by other considerations such as structural requirements.

11. 9×18 in. **13.** $\frac{\pi}{2}$ **15.** $h : r = 8 : \pi$

17. **(a)** $V(x) = 2x(24 - 2x)(18 - 2x)$ **(b)** Domain: $(0, 9)$

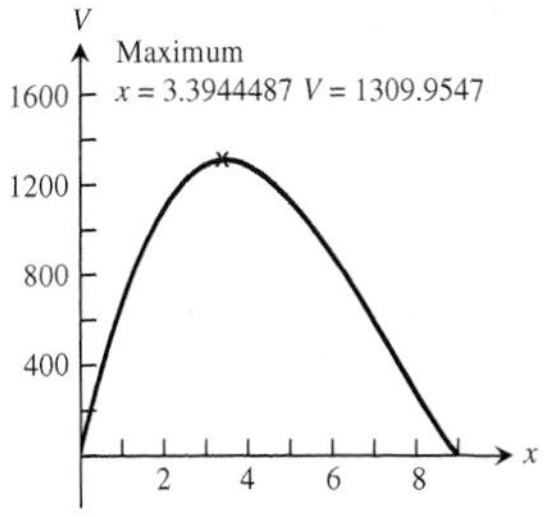

(c) Maximum volume $\approx 1309.95\ \text{in}^3$ when $x \approx 3.39$ in.
(d) $V'(x) = 24x^2 - 336x + 864$, so the critical point is at $x = 7 - \sqrt{13}$, which confirms the result in part (c).
(e) $x = 2$ in. or $x = 5$ in.

19. $\approx 2418.40\ \text{cm}^3$

21. **(a)** $h = 24$, $w = 18$
(b)

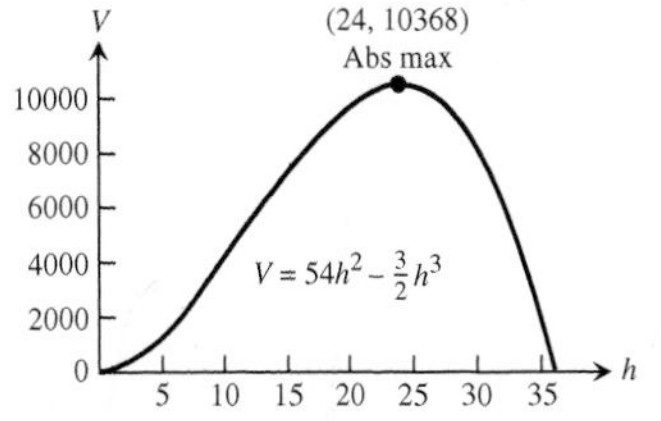

23. If r is the radius of the hemisphere, h the height of the cylinder, and V the volume, then $r = \left(\dfrac{3V}{8\pi}\right)^{1/3}$ and $h = \left(\dfrac{3V}{\pi}\right)^{1/3}$.

25. **(b)** $x = \dfrac{51}{8}$ **(c)** $L \approx 11$ in.

27. Radius $= \sqrt{2}$ m, height $= 1$ m, volume $= \dfrac{2\pi}{3}\ \text{m}^3$

29. 1 **31.** $\dfrac{9b}{9 + \sqrt{3}\pi}$ m, triangle; $\dfrac{b\sqrt{3}\pi}{9 + \sqrt{3}\pi}$ m, circle

33. $\dfrac{3}{2} \times 2$ **35.** **(a)** 16 **(b)** -1

37. **(a)** $v(0) = 96$ ft/sec
(b) 256 ft at $t = 3$ sec
(c) Velocity when $s = 0$ is $v(7) = -128$ ft/sec.

39. ≈ 46.87 ft **41.** **(a)** $6 \times 6\sqrt{3}$ in.

43. **(a)** $4\sqrt{3} \times 4\sqrt{6}$ in.

45. **(a)** $10\pi \approx 31.42$ cm/sec; when $t = 0.5$ sec, 1.5 sec, 2.5 sec, 3.5 sec; $s = 0$, acceleration is 0.
(b) 10 cm from rest position; speed is 0.

47. **(a)** $s = ((12 - 12t)^2 + 64t^2)^{1/2}$
(b) -12 knots, 8 knots
(c) No
(e) $4\sqrt{13}$. This limit is the square root of the sums of the squares of the individual speeds.

49. $x = \dfrac{a}{2}, v = \dfrac{ka^2}{4}$ **51.** $\dfrac{c}{2} + 50$

53. **(a)** $\sqrt{\dfrac{2km}{h}}$ **(b)** $\sqrt{\dfrac{2km}{h}}$

57. $4 \times 4 \times 3$ ft, \$288 **59.** $M = \dfrac{C}{2}$ **65.** **(a)** $y = -1$

67. **(a)** The minimum distance is $\dfrac{\sqrt{5}}{2}$.
(b) The minimum distance is from the point $(3/2, 0)$ to the point $(1, 1)$ on the graph of $y = \sqrt{x}$, and this occurs at the value $x = 1$, where $D(x)$, the distance squared, has its minimum value.

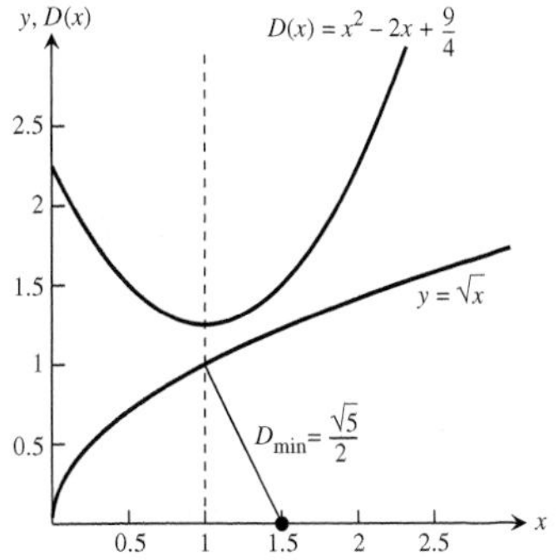

Section 4.7, pp. 269–271

1. $x_2 = -\dfrac{5}{3}, \dfrac{13}{21}$ **3.** $x_2 = -\dfrac{51}{31}, \dfrac{5763}{4945}$ **5.** $x_2 = \dfrac{2387}{2000}$

7. x_1, and all later approximations will equal x_0.

9.

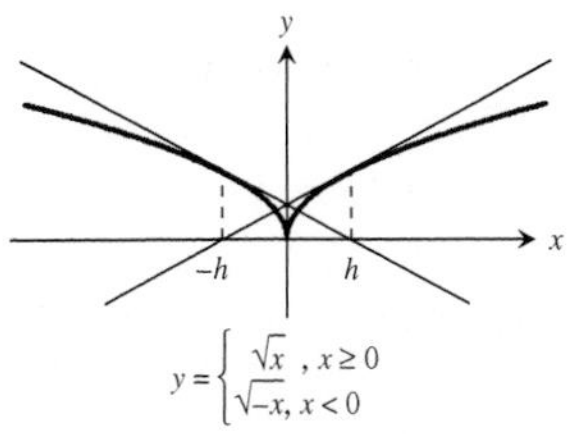

11. The points of intersection of $y = x^3$ and $y = 3x + 1$ or $y = x^3 - 3x$ and $y = 1$ have the same x-values as the roots of part (i) or the solutions of part (iv). **13.** 1.165561185

15. **(a)** Two **(b)** 0.35003501505249 and -1.0261731615301

17. ± 1.3065629648764, ± 0.5411961001462 **19.** $x \approx 0.45$

21. 0.8192 **23.** 0, 0.53485 **25.** The root is 1.17951.

27. **(a)** For $x_0 = -2$ or $x_0 = -0.8$, $x_i \to -1$ as i gets large.
(b) For $x_0 = -0.5$ or $x_0 = 0.25$, $x_i \to 0$ as i gets large.
(c) For $x_0 = 0.8$ or $x_0 = 2$, $x_i \to 1$ as i gets large.
(d) For $x_0 = -\sqrt{21}/7$ or $x_0 = \sqrt{21}/7$, Newton's method does not converge. The values of x_i alternate between $-\sqrt{21}/7$ and $\sqrt{21}/7$ as i increases.

29. Answers will vary with machine speed.

Section 4.8, pp. 277–281

1. **(a)** x^2 **(b)** $\dfrac{x^3}{3}$ **(c)** $\dfrac{x^3}{3} - x^2 + x$

3. **(a)** x^{-3} **(b)** $-\dfrac{1}{3}x^{-3}$ **(c)** $-\dfrac{1}{3}x^{-3} + x^2 + 3x$

5. **(a)** $-\dfrac{1}{x}$ **(b)** $-\dfrac{5}{x}$ **(c)** $2x + \dfrac{5}{x}$

7. **(a)** $\sqrt{x^3}$ **(b)** $\sqrt{x}$ **(c)** $\dfrac{2\sqrt{x^3}}{3} + 2\sqrt{x}$

9. **(a)** $x^{2/3}$ **(b)** $x^{1/3}$ **(c)** $x^{-1/3}$

11. **(a)** $\ln x$ **(b)** $7 \ln x$ **(c)** $x - 5 \ln x$

13. **(a)** $\cos(\pi x)$ **(b)** $-3 \cos x$ **(c)** $-\dfrac{1}{\pi}\cos(\pi x) + \cos(3x)$

15. **(a)** $\tan x$ **(b)** $2\tan\left(\frac{x}{3}\right)$ **(c)** $-\frac{2}{3}\tan\left(\frac{3x}{2}\right)$

17. **(a)** $-\csc x$ **(b)** $\frac{1}{5}\csc(5x)$ **(c)** $2\csc\left(\frac{\pi x}{2}\right)$

19. **(a)** $\frac{1}{3}e^{3x}$ **(b)** $-e^{-x}$ **(c)** $2e^{x/2}$

21. **(a)** $\frac{1}{\ln 3}3^x$ **(b)** $\frac{-1}{\ln 2}2^{-x}$ **(c)** $\frac{1}{\ln(5/3)}\left(\frac{5}{3}\right)^x$

23. **(a)** $2\sin^{-1}x$ **(b)** $\frac{1}{2}\tan^{-1}x$ **(c)** $\frac{1}{2}\tan^{-1}2x$

25. $\frac{x^2}{2}+x+C$ **27.** $t^3+\frac{t^2}{4}+C$ **29.** $\frac{x^4}{2}-\frac{5x^2}{2}+7x+C$

31. $-\frac{1}{x}-\frac{x^3}{3}-\frac{x}{3}+C$ **33.** $\frac{3}{2}x^{2/3}+C$

35. $\frac{2}{3}x^{3/2}+\frac{3}{4}x^{4/3}+C$ **37.** $4y^2-\frac{8}{3}y^{3/4}+C$

39. $x^2+\frac{2}{x}+C$ **41.** $2\sqrt{t}-\frac{2}{\sqrt{t}}+C$ **43.** $-2\sin t+C$

45. $-21\cos\frac{\theta}{3}+C$ **47.** $3\cot x+C$ **49.** $-\frac{1}{2}\csc\theta+C$

51. $\frac{1}{3}e^{3x}-5e^{-x}+C$ **53.** $-e^{-x}+\frac{4^x}{\ln 4}+C$

55. $4\sec x-2\tan x+C$ **57.** $-\frac{1}{2}\cos 2x+\cot x+C$

59. $\frac{t}{2}+\frac{\sin 4t}{8}+C$ **61.** $\ln|x|-5\tan^{-1}x+C$

63. $\frac{3x^{(\sqrt{3}+1)}}{\sqrt{3}+1}+C$ **65.** $\tan\theta+C$ **67.** $-\cot x-x+C$

69. $-\cos\theta+\theta+C$

83. **(a)** Wrong: $\frac{d}{dx}\left(\frac{x^2}{2}\sin x+C\right)=\frac{2x}{2}\sin x+\frac{x^2}{2}\cos x=x\sin x+\frac{x^2}{2}\cos x$

(b) Wrong: $\frac{d}{dx}(-x\cos x+C)=-\cos x+x\sin x$

(c) Right: $\frac{d}{dx}(-x\cos x+\sin x+C)=-\cos x+x\sin x+\cos x=x\sin x$

85. **(a)** Wrong: $\frac{d}{dx}\left(\frac{(2x+1)^3}{3}+C\right)=\frac{3(2x+1)^2(2)}{3}=2(2x+1)^2$

(b) Wrong: $\frac{d}{dx}((2x+1)^3+C)=3(2x+1)^2(2)=6(2x+1)^2$

(c) Right: $\frac{d}{dx}((2x+1)^3+C)=6(2x+1)^2$

87. Right **89.** (b) **91.** $y=x^2-7x+10$

93. $y=-\frac{1}{x}+\frac{x^2}{2}-\frac{1}{2}$ **95.** $y=9x^{1/3}+4$

97. $s=t+\sin t+4$ **99.** $r=\cos(\pi\theta)-1$

101. $v=\frac{1}{2}\sec t+\frac{1}{2}$ **103.** $v=3\sec^{-1}t-\pi$

105. $y=x^2-x^3+4x+1$ **107.** $r=\frac{1}{t}+2t-2$

109. $y=x^3-4x^2+5$ **111.** $y=-\sin t+\cos t+t^3-1$

113. $y=2x^{3/2}-50$ **115.** $y=x-x^{4/3}+\frac{1}{2}$

117. $y=-\sin x-\cos x-2$

119. **(a)** **(i)** 33.2 units, **(ii)** 33.2 units, **(iii)** 33.2 units **(b)** True

121. $t=88/k,\ k=16$

123. **(a)** $v=10t^{3/2}-6t^{1/2}$ **(b)** $s=4t^{5/2}-4t^{3/2}$

127. **(a)** $-\sqrt{x}+C$ **(b)** $x+C$ **(c)** $\sqrt{x}+C$ **(d)** $-x+C$ **(e)** $x-\sqrt{x}+C$ **(f)** $-x-\sqrt{x}+C$

Practice Exercises, pp. 281–285

1. No **3.** No minimum; absolute maximum: $f(1)=16$; critical points: $x=1$ and $11/3$

5. Absolute minimum: $g(0)=1$; no absolute maximum; critical point: $x=0$

7. Absolute minimum: $2-2\ln 2$ at $x=2$; absolute maximum 1 at $x=1$

9. Yes, except at $x=0$ **11.** No **15.** **(b)** one

17. **(b)** 0.8555 99677 2 **23.** Global minimum value of $\frac{1}{2}$ at $x=2$

25. **(a)** $t=0,6,12$ **(b)** $t=3,9$ **(c)** $6<t<12$ **(d)** $0<t<6,\ 12<t<14$

27.

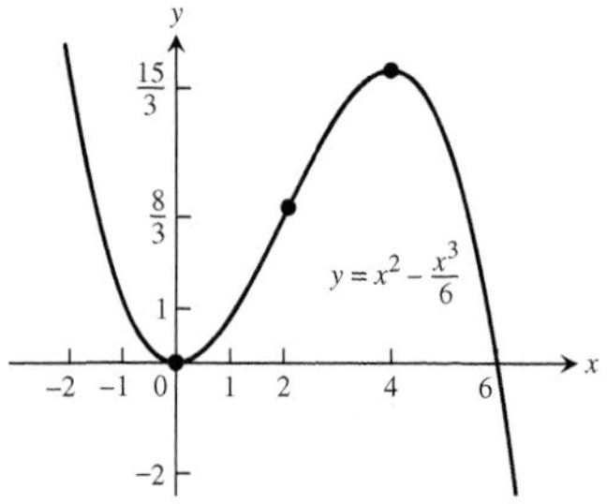

29.

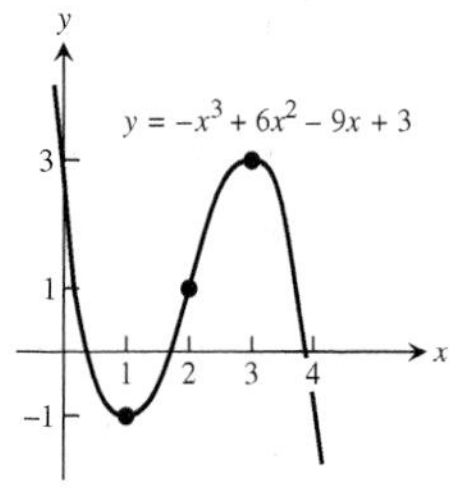

31.

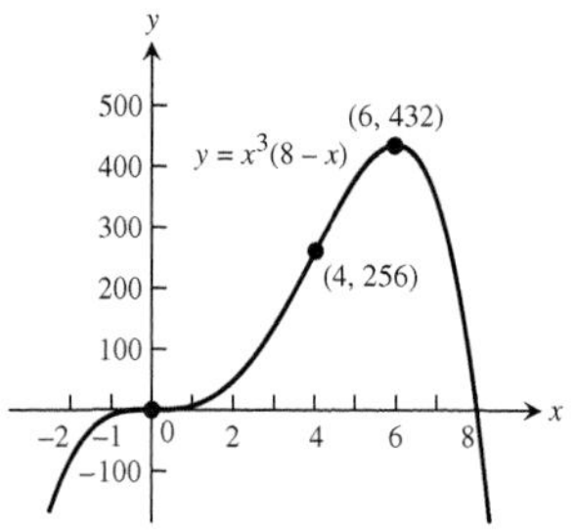

33.

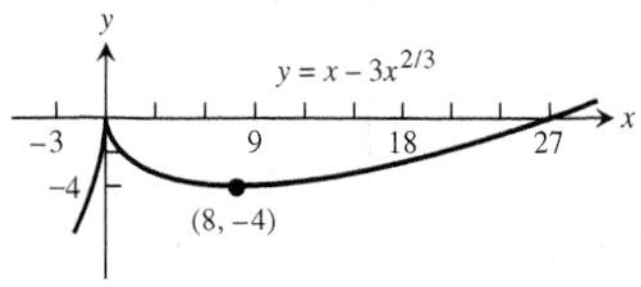

35.

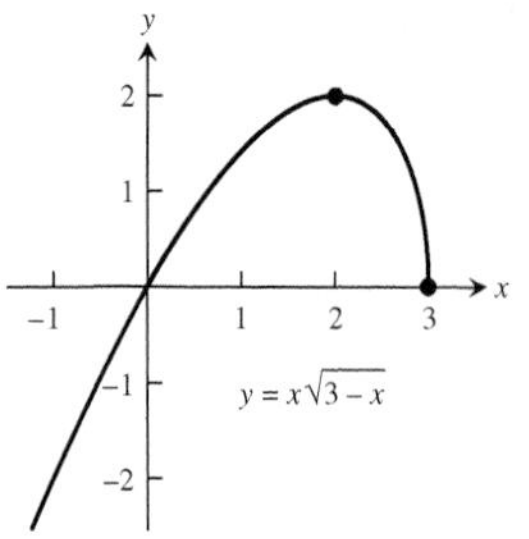

37.

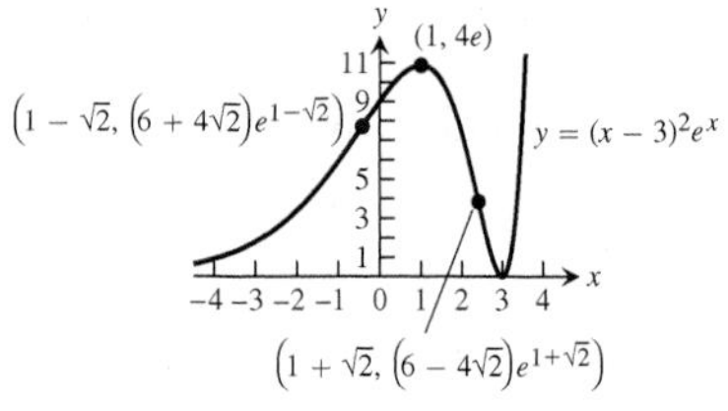

39.

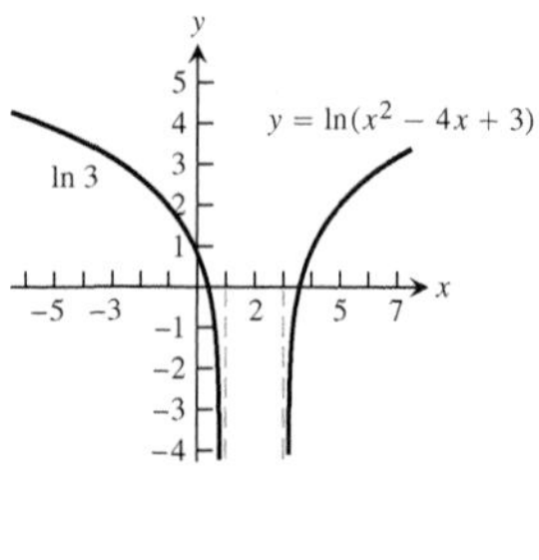

41.

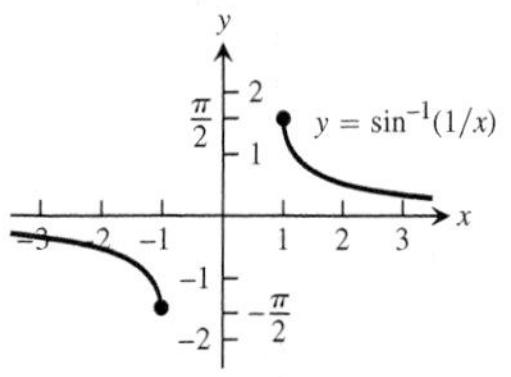

43. **(a)** Local maximum at $x = 4$, local minimum at $x = -4$, inflection point at $x = 0$

(b)

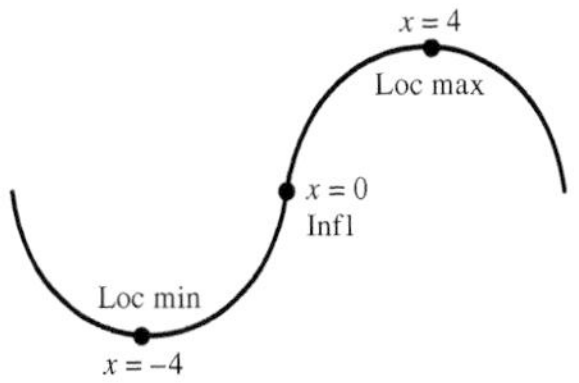

45. **(a)** Local maximum at $x = 0$, local minima at $x = -1$ and $x = 2$, inflection points at $x = (1 \pm \sqrt{7})/3$

(b)

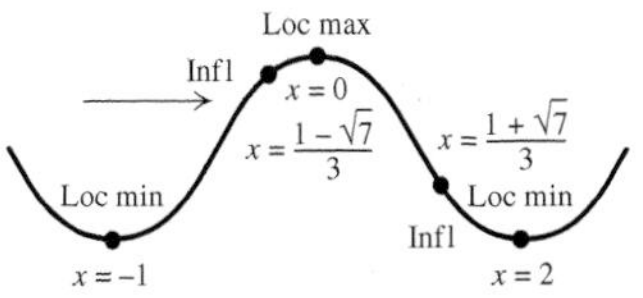

47. **(a)** Local maximum at $x = -\sqrt{2}$, local minimum at $x = \sqrt{2}$, inflection points at $x = \pm 1$ and 0

(b)

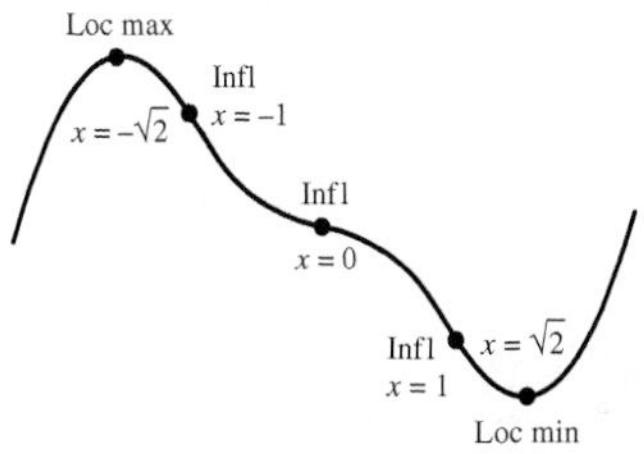

53.

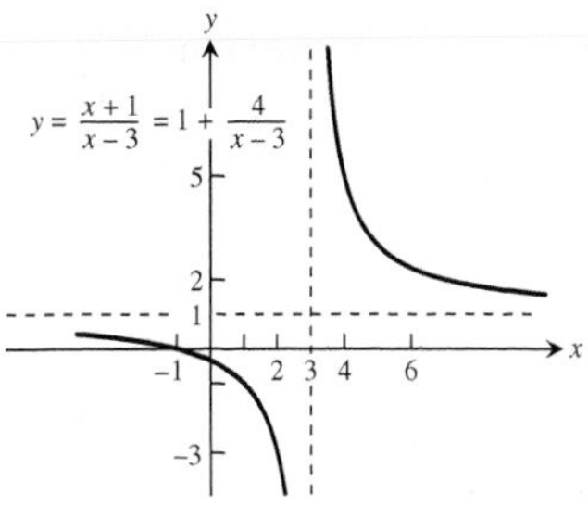

55.

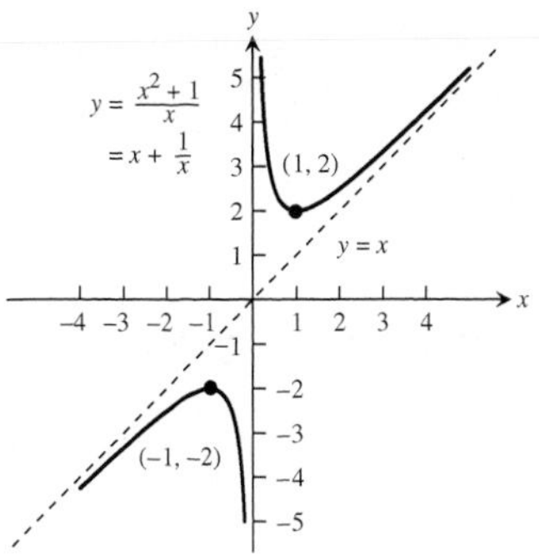

57.

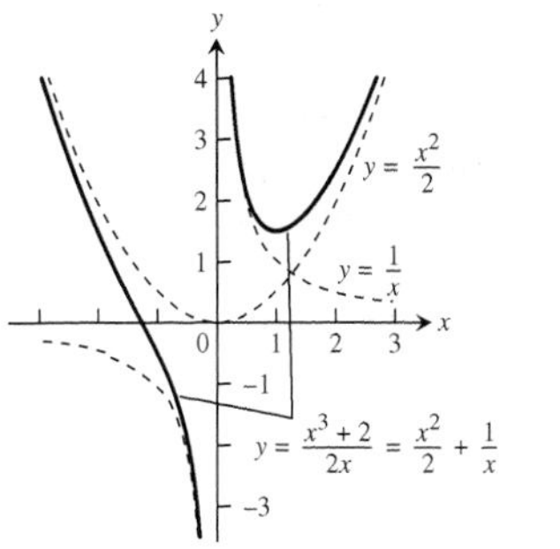

59.

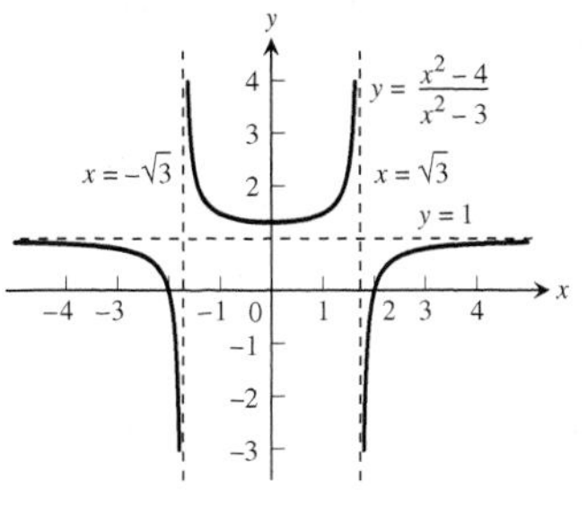

61. 5 **63.** 0 **65.** 1 **67.** 3/7 **69.** 0 **71.** 1
73. ln 10 **75.** ln 2 **77.** 5 **79.** $-\infty$ **81.** 1 **83.** e^{bk}
85. **(a)** 0, 36 **(b)** 18, 18 **87.** 54 square units
89. height = 2, radius = $\sqrt{2}$

91. $x = 5 - \sqrt{5}$ hundred ≈ 276 tires, $y = 2(5 - \sqrt{5})$ hundred ≈ 553 tires
93. Dimensions: base is 6 in. by 12 in., height = 2 in.; maximum volume = 144 in.^{3}
95. $x_5 = 2.1958\ 23345$ **97.** $\frac{x^4}{4} + \frac{5}{2}x^2 - 7x + C$
99. $2t^{3/2} - \frac{4}{t} + C$ **101.** $-\frac{1}{r+5} + C$ **103.** $(\theta^2 + 1)^{3/2} + C$
105. $\frac{1}{3}(1 + x^4)^{3/4} + C$ **107.** $10 \tan \frac{s}{10} + C$
109. $-\frac{1}{\sqrt{2}} \csc \sqrt{2}\,\theta + C$ **111.** $\frac{1}{2}x - \sin \frac{x}{2} + C$
113. $3 \ln x - \frac{x^2}{2} + C$ **115.** $\frac{1}{2}e^t + e^{-t} + C$
117. $\frac{\theta^{2-\pi}}{2 - \pi} + C$ **119.** $\frac{3}{2} \sec^{-1}|x| + C$
121. $y = x - \frac{1}{x} - 1$ **123.** $r = 4t^{5/2} + 4t^{3/2} - 8t$
125. Yes, $\sin^{-1}(x)$ and $-\cos^{-1}(x)$ differ by the constant $\pi/2$.
127. $1/\sqrt{2}$ units long by $1/\sqrt{e}$ units high, $A = 1/\sqrt{2e} \approx 0.43$ units^2
129. Absolute maximum = 0 at $x = e/2$, absolute minimum = -0.5 at $x = 0.5$
131. $x = \pm 1$ are the critical points; $y = 1$ is a horizontal asymptote in both directions; absolute minimum value of the function is $e^{-\sqrt{2}/2}$ at $x = -1$, and absolute maximum value is $e^{\sqrt{2}/2}$ at $x = 1$.
133. **(a)** Absolute maximum of $2/e$ at $x = e^2$, inflection point $(e^{8/3}, (8/3)e^{-4/3})$, concave up on $(e^{8/3}, \infty)$, concave down on $(0, e^{8/3})$
(b) Absolute maximum of 1 at $x = 0$, inflection points $(\pm 1/\sqrt{2}, 1/\sqrt{e})$, concave up on $(-\infty, -1/\sqrt{2}) \cup (1/\sqrt{2}, \infty)$, concave down on $(-1/\sqrt{2}, 1/\sqrt{2})$
(c) Absolute maximum of 1 at $x = 0$, inflection point $(1, 2/e)$, concave up on $(1, \infty)$, concave down on $(-\infty, 1)$

Additional and Advanced Exercises, pp. 285–288

1. The function is constant on the interval.
3. The extreme points will not be at the end of an open interval.
5. **(a)** A local minimum at $x = -1$, points of inflection at $x = 0$ and $x = 2$ **(b)** A local maximum at $x = 0$ and local minima at $x = -1$ and $x = 2$, points of inflection at $x = \frac{1 \pm \sqrt{7}}{3}$
9. No **11.** $a = 1, b = 0, c = 1$ **13.** Yes
15. Drill the hole at $y = h/2$.
17. $r = \frac{RH}{2(H - R)}$ for $H > 2R$, $r = R$ if $H \le 2R$
19. **(a)** $\frac{10}{3}$ **(b)** $\frac{5}{3}$ **(c)** $\frac{1}{2}$ **(d)** 0 **(e)** $-\frac{1}{2}$ **(f)** 1 **(g)** $\frac{1}{2}$ **(h)** 3
21. **(a)** $\frac{c - b}{2e}$ **(b)** $\frac{c + b}{2}$ **(c)** $\frac{b^2 - 2bc + c^2 + 4ae}{4e}$ **(d)** $\frac{c + b + t}{2}$
23. $m_0 = 1 - \frac{1}{q}, m_1 = \frac{1}{q}$

25. $s = ce^{kt}$

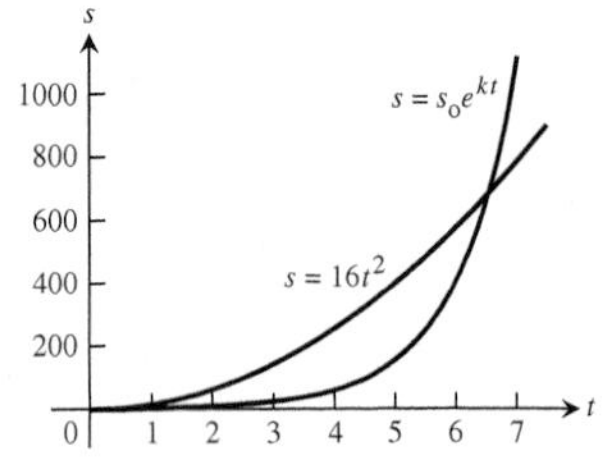

27. **(a)** $k = -38.72$ **(b)** 25 ft

29. Yes, $y = x + C$ **31.** $v_0 = \dfrac{2\sqrt{2}}{3}b^{3/4}$

CHAPTER 5

Section 5.1, pp. 296–298

1. **(a)** 0.125 **(b)** 0.21875 **(c)** 0.625 **(d)** 0.46875
3. **(a)** 1.066667 **(b)** 1.283333 **(c)** 2.666667 **(d)** 2.083333
5. 0.3125, 0.328125 **7.** 1.5, 1.574603
9. **(a)** 87 in. **(b)** 87 in. **11.** **(a)** 3490 ft **(b)** 3840 ft
13. **(a)** 74.65 ft/sec **(b)** 45.28 ft/sec **(c)** 146.59 ft
15. $\dfrac{31}{16}$ **17.** 1
19. **(a)** Upper = 758 gal, lower = 543 gal
(b) Upper = 2363 gal, lower = 1693 gal
(c) ≈ 31.4 h, ≈ 32.4 h
21. **(a)** 2 **(b)** $2\sqrt{2} \approx 2.828$
(c) $8\sin\left(\dfrac{\pi}{8}\right) \approx 3.061$
(d) Each area is less than the area of the circle, π. As n increases, the polygon area approaches π.

Section 5.2, pp. 304–305

1. $\dfrac{6(1)}{1+1} + \dfrac{6(2)}{2+1} = 7$
3. $\cos(1)\pi + \cos(2)\pi + \cos(3)\pi + \cos(4)\pi = 0$
5. $\sin\pi - \sin\dfrac{\pi}{2} + \sin\dfrac{\pi}{3} = \dfrac{\sqrt{3}-2}{2}$ **7.** All of them **9.** b
11. $\sum_{k=1}^{6} k$ **13.** $\sum_{k=1}^{4} \dfrac{1}{2^k}$ **15.** $\sum_{k=1}^{5} (-1)^{k+1}\dfrac{1}{k}$
17. **(a)** -15 **(b)** 1 **(c)** 1 **(d)** -11 **(e)** 16
19. **(a)** 55 **(b)** 385 **(c)** 3025
21. -56 **23.** -73 **25.** 240 **27.** 3376
29. **(a)** 21 **(b)** 3500 **(c)** 2620
31. **(a)** $4n$ **(b)** cn **(c)** $(n^2 - n)/2$
33. **(a)**

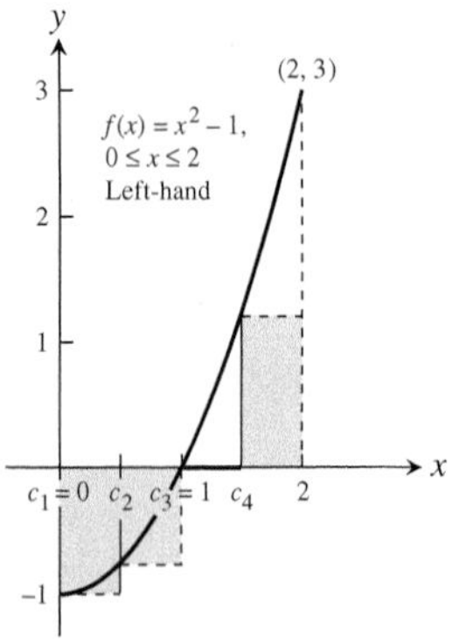

(b)

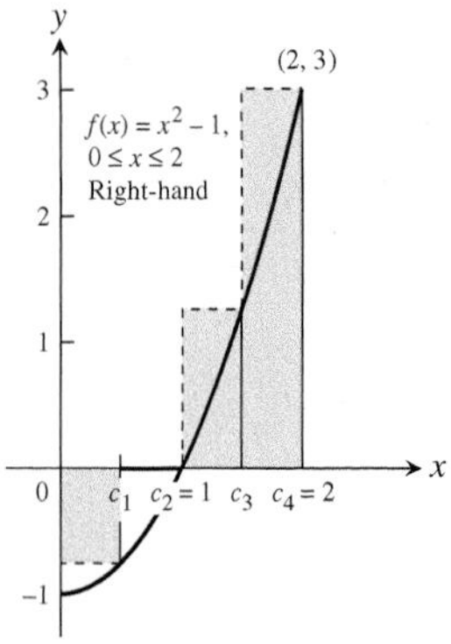

(c)

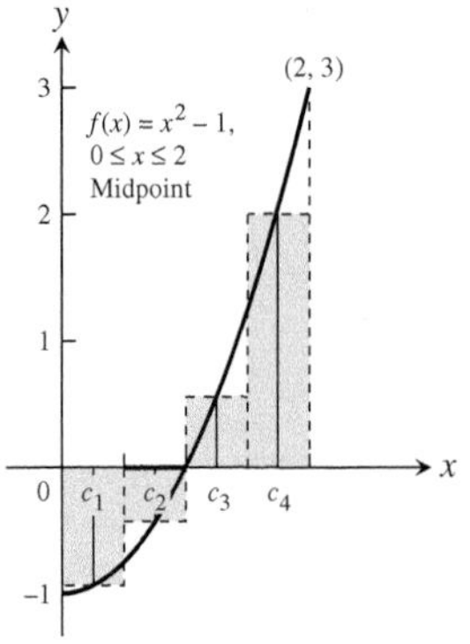

35. **(a)**

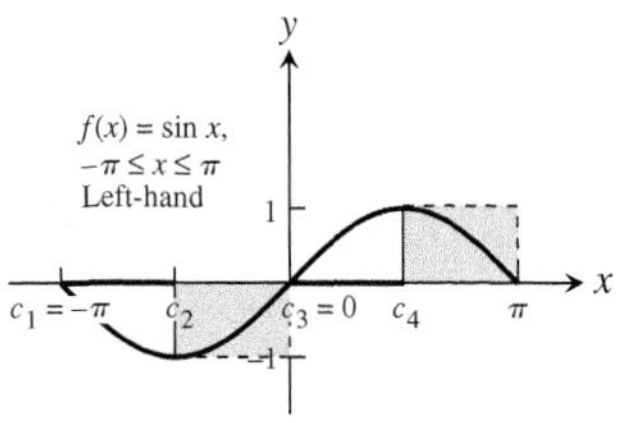

(b)

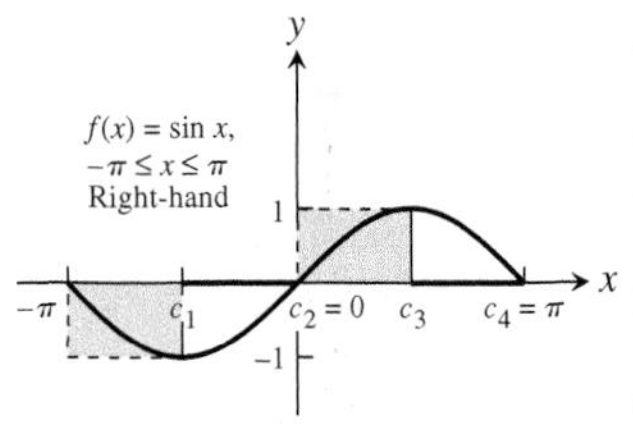

(c)

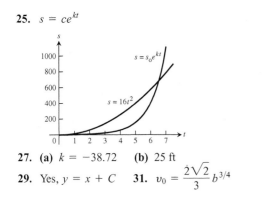

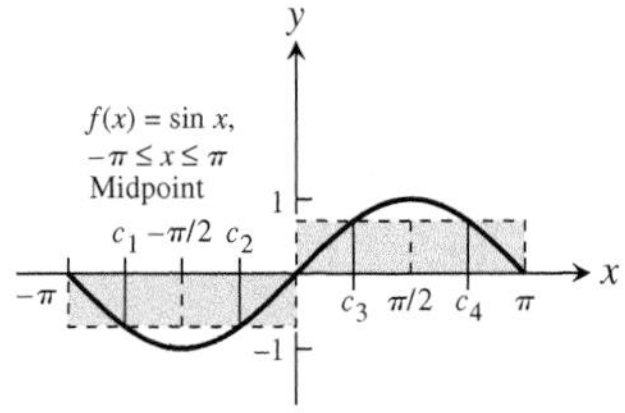

37. 1.2 **39.** $\dfrac{2}{3} - \dfrac{1}{2n} - \dfrac{1}{6n^2}, \dfrac{2}{3}$ **41.** $12 + \dfrac{27n+9}{2n^2}$, 12
43. $\dfrac{5}{6} + \dfrac{6n+1}{6n^2}, \dfrac{5}{6}$ **45.** $\dfrac{1}{2} + \dfrac{1}{n} + \dfrac{1}{2n^2}, \dfrac{1}{2}$

Section 5.3, pp. 313–317

1. $\int_0^2 x^2\,dx$ **3.** $\int_{-7}^5 (x^2 - 3x)\,dx$ **5.** $\int_2^3 \dfrac{1}{1-x}\,dx$
7. $\int_{-\pi/4}^0 \sec x\,dx$
9. **(a)** 0 **(b)** -8 **(c)** -12 **(d)** 10 **(e)** -2 **(f)** 16
11. **(a)** 5 **(b)** $5\sqrt{3}$ **(c)** -5 **(d)** -5
13. **(a)** 4 **(b)** -4 **15.** Area = 21 square units
17. Area = $9\pi/2$ square units **19.** Area = 2.5 square units
21. Area = 3 square units **23.** $b^2/4$ **25.** $b^2 - a^2$
27. **(a)** 2π **(b)** π **29.** 1/2 **31.** $3\pi^2/2$ **33.** 7/3
35. 1/24 **37.** $3a^2/2$ **39.** $b/3$ **41.** -14 **43.** -2
45. $-7/4$ **47.** 7 **49.** 0
51. Using n subintervals of length $\Delta x = b/n$ and right-endpoint values:

$$\text{Area} = \int_0^b 3x^2\,dx = b^3$$

53. Using n subintervals of length $\Delta x = b/n$ and right-endpoint values:

$$\text{Area} = \int_0^b 2x\,dx = b^2$$

55. $\text{av}(f) = 0$ **57.** $\text{av}(f) = -2$ **59.** $\text{av}(f) = 1$
61. (a) $\text{av}(g) = -1/2$ **(b)** $\text{av}(g) = 1$ **(c)** $\text{av}(g) = 1/4$
63. $c(b - a)$ **65.** $b^3/3 - a^3/3$ **67.** 9 **69.** $b^4/4 - a^4/4$
71. $a = 0$ and $b = 1$ maximize the integral.
73. Upper bound = 1, lower bound = 1/2
75. For example, $\int_0^1 \sin(x^2)\,dx \le \int_0^1 dx = 1$
77. $\int_a^b f(x)\,dx \ge \int_a^b 0\,dx = 0$ **79.** Upper bound = 1/2

Section 5.4, pp. 325–328

1. 6 **3.** $-10/3$ **5.** 8 **7.** 1 **9.** $2\sqrt{3}$ **11.** 0
13. $-\pi/4$ **15.** $1 - \frac{\pi}{4}$ **17.** $\frac{2 - \sqrt{2}}{4}$ **19.** $-8/3$
21. $-3/4$ **23.** $\sqrt{2} - \sqrt[4]{8} + 1$ **25.** -1 **27.** 16
29. $7/3$ **31.** $2\pi/3$ **33.** $\frac{1}{\pi}(4^\pi - 2^\pi)$ **35.** $\frac{1}{2}(e - 1)$
37. $\sqrt{26} - \sqrt{5}$ **39.** $(\cos\sqrt{x})\left(\frac{1}{2\sqrt{x}}\right)$ **41.** $4t^5$
43. $3x^2e^{-x^3}$ **45.** $\sqrt{1 + x^2}$ **47.** $-\frac{1}{2}x^{-1/2}\sin x$ **49.** 0
51. 1 **53.** $2xe^{(1/2)x^2}$ **55.** 1 **57.** $28/3$ **59.** $1/2$ **61.** π
63. $\frac{\sqrt{2\pi}}{2}$ **65.** d, since $y' = \frac{1}{x}$ and $y(\pi) = \int_\pi^\pi \frac{1}{t}\,dt - 3 = -3$
67. b, since $y' = \sec x$ and $y(0) = \int_0^0 \sec t\,dt + 4 = 4$
69. $y = \int_2^x \sec t\,dt + 3$ **71.** $\frac{2}{3}bh$ **73.** \$9.00
75. a. $T(0) = 70°\text{F}$, $T(16) = 76°\text{F}$
$T(25) = 85°\text{F}$
b. $\text{av}(T) = 75°\text{F}$
77. $2x - 2$ **79.** $-3x + 5$
81. (a) True. Since f is continuous, g is differentiable by Part 1 of the Fundamental Theorem of Calculus.
(b) True: g is continuous because it is differentiable.
(c) True, since $g'(1) = f(1) = 0$.
(d) False, since $g''(1) = f'(1) > 0$.
(e) True, since $g'(1) = 0$ and $g''(1) = f'(1) > 0$.
(f) False: $g''(x) = f'(x) > 0$, so g'' never changes sign.
(g) True, since $g'(1) = f(1) = 0$ and $g'(x) = f(x)$ is an increasing function of x (because $f'(x) > 0$).
83. (a) $v = \frac{ds}{dt} = \frac{d}{dt}\int_0^t f(x)\,dx = f(t) \Rightarrow v(5) = f(5) = 2$ m/sec
(b) $a = df/dt$ is negative since the slope of the tangent line at $t = 5$ is negative.
(c) $s = \int_0^3 f(x)\,dx = \frac{1}{2}(3)(3) = \frac{9}{2}$ m since the integral is the area of the triangle formed by $y = f(x)$, the x-axis, and $x = 3$.
(d) $t = 6$ since after $t = 6$ to $t = 9$, the region lies below the x-axis.
(e) At $t = 4$ and $t = 7$, since there are horizontal tangents there.
(f) Toward the origin between $t = 6$ and $t = 9$ since the velocity is negative on this interval. Away from the origin between $t = 0$ and $t = 6$ since the velocity is positive there.
(g) Right or positive side, because the integral of f from 0 to 9 is positive, there being more area above the x-axis than below.

Section 5.5, pp. 333–335

1. $\frac{1}{6}(2x + 4)^6 + C$ **3.** $-\frac{1}{3}(x^2 + 5)^{-3} + C$
5. $\frac{1}{10}(3x^2 + 4x)^5 + C$ **7.** $-\frac{1}{3}\cos 3x + C$
9. $\frac{1}{2}\sec 2t + C$ **11.** $-6(1 - r^3)^{1/2} + C$
13. $\frac{1}{3}(x^{3/2} - 1) - \frac{1}{6}\sin(2x^{3/2} - 2) + C$
15. (a) $-\frac{1}{4}(\cot^2 2\theta) + C$ **(b)** $-\frac{1}{4}(\csc^2 2\theta) + C$
17. $-\frac{1}{3}(3 - 2s)^{3/2} + C$ **19.** $-\frac{2}{5}(1 - \theta^2)^{5/4} + C$
21. $(-2/(1 + \sqrt{x})) + C$ **23.** $\frac{1}{3}\tan(3x + 2) + C$
25. $\frac{1}{2}\sin^6\left(\frac{x}{3}\right) + C$ **27.** $\left(\frac{r^3}{18} - 1\right)^6 + C$
29. $-\frac{2}{3}\cos(x^{3/2} + 1) + C$ **31.** $\frac{1}{2\cos(2t + 1)} + C$
33. $-\sin\left(\frac{1}{t} - 1\right) + C$ **35.** $-\frac{\sin^2(1/\theta)}{2} + C$
37. $\frac{1}{16}(1 + t^4)^4 + C$ **39.** $\frac{2}{3}\left(2 - \frac{1}{x}\right)^{3/2} + C$
41. $\frac{2}{27}\left(1 - \frac{3}{x^3}\right)^{3/2} + C$
43. $\frac{1}{12}(x - 1)^{12} + \frac{1}{11}(x - 1)^{11} + C$
45. $-\frac{1}{8}(1 - x)^8 + \frac{4}{7}(1 - x)^7 - \frac{2}{3}(1 - x)^6 + C$
47. $\frac{1}{5}(x^2 + 1)^{5/2} - \frac{1}{3}(x^2 + 1)^{3/2} + C$ **49.** $\frac{-1}{4(x^2 - 4)^2} + C$
51. $e^{\sin x} + C$ **53.** $2\tan\left(e^{\sqrt{x}} + 1\right) + C$ **55.** $\ln|\ln x| + C$
57. $z - \ln(1 + e^z) + C$ **59.** $\frac{5}{6}\tan^{-1}\left(\frac{2r}{3}\right) + C$
61. $e^{\sin^{-1} x} + C$ **63.** $\frac{1}{3}(\sin^{-1} x)^3 + C$ **65.** $\ln|\tan^{-1} y| + C$
67. (a) $-\frac{6}{2 + \tan^3 x} + C$ **(b)** $-\frac{6}{2 + \tan^3 x} + C$
(c) $-\frac{6}{2 + \tan^3 x} + C$
69. $\frac{1}{6}\sin\sqrt{3(2r - 1)^2 + 6} + C$ **71.** $s = \frac{1}{2}(3t^2 - 1)^4 - 5$
73. $s = 4t - 2\sin\left(2t + \frac{\pi}{6}\right) + 9$
75. $s = \sin\left(2t - \frac{\pi}{2}\right) + 100t + 1$ **77.** 6 m

Section 5.6, pp. 341–344

1. **(a)** 14/3 **(b)** 2/3 **3.** **(a)** 1/2 **(b)** −1/2
5. **(a)** 15/16 **(b)** 0 **7.** **(a)** 0 **(b)** 1/8 **9.** **(a)** 4 **(b)** 0
11. **(a)** 1/6 **(b)** 1/2 **13.** **(a)** 0 **(b)** 0 **15.** $2\sqrt{3}$
17. 3/4 **19.** $3^{5/2} - 1$ **21.** 3 **23.** $\pi/3$ **25.** e
27. ln 3 **29.** $(\ln 2)^2$ **31.** $\frac{1}{\ln 4}$ **33.** ln 2 **35.** ln 27 **37.** π
39. $\pi/12$ **41.** $2\pi/3$ **43.** $\sqrt{3} - 1$ **45.** $-\pi/12$
47. 16/3 **49.** $2^{5/2}$ **51.** $\pi/2$ **53.** 128/15 **55.** 4/3
57. 5/6 **59.** 38/3 **61.** 49/6 **63.** 32/3 **65.** 48/5
67. 8/3 **69.** 8 **71.** 5/3 (There are three intersection points.)
73. 18 **75.** 243/8 **77.** 8/3 **79.** 2 **81.** 104/15
83. 56/15 **85.** 4 **87.** $\frac{4}{3} - \frac{4}{\pi}$ **89.** $\pi/2$ **91.** 2 **93.** 1/2
95. 1 **97.** ln 16 **99.** 2 **101.** 2 ln 5
103. **(a)** $(\pm\sqrt{c}, c)$ **(b)** $c = 4^{2/3}$ **(c)** $c = 4^{2/3}$
105. 11/3 **107.** 3/4 **109.** Neither **111.** $F(6) - F(2)$
113. **(a)** −3 **(b)** 3 **115.** $I = a/2$

Practice Exercises, pp. 345–348

1. **(a)** About 680 ft **(b)**

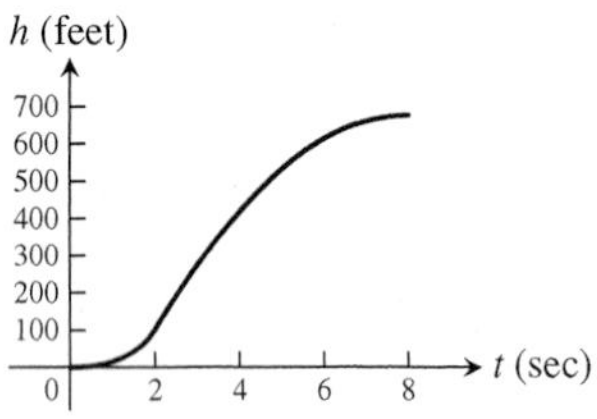

3. **(a)** −1/2 **(b)** 31 **(c)** 13 **(d)** 0
5. $\int_1^5 (2x - 1)^{-1/2}\, dx = 2$ **7.** $\int_{-\pi}^{0} \cos\frac{x}{2}\, dx = 2$
9. **(a)** 4 **(b)** 2 **(c)** −2 **(d)** -2π **(e)** 8/5
11. 8/3 **13.** 62 **15.** 1 **17.** 1/6 **19.** 18 **21.** 9/8
23. $\frac{\pi^2}{32} + \frac{\sqrt{2}}{2} - 1$ **25.** 4 **27.** $\frac{8\sqrt{2} - 7}{6}$
29. Min: −4, max: 0, area: 27/4 **31.** 6/5 **33.** 1
37. $y = \int_5^x \left(\frac{\sin t}{t}\right) dt - 3$ **39.** $y = \sin^{-1} x$
41. $y = \sec^{-1} x + \frac{2\pi}{3}, x > 1$ **43.** $-4(\cos x)^{1/2} + C$
45. $\theta^2 + \theta + \sin(2\theta + 1) + C$ **47.** $\frac{t^3}{3} + \frac{4}{t} + C$
49. $-\frac{1}{3}\cos(2t^{3/2}) + C$ **51.** $\tan(e^x - 7) + C$ **53.** $e^{\tan x} + C$
55. $\frac{-\ln 7}{3}$ **57.** ln (9/25) **59.** $-\frac{1}{2}(\ln x)^{-2} + C$
61. $\frac{1}{2\ln 3}\left(3^{x^2}\right) + C$ **63.** $\frac{3}{2}\sin^{-1} 2(r - 1) + C$
65. $\frac{\sqrt{2}}{2}\tan^{-1}\left(\frac{x - 1}{\sqrt{2}}\right) + C$ **67.** $\frac{1}{4}\sec^{-1}\left|\frac{2x - 1}{2}\right| + C$
69. $e^{\sin^{-1}\sqrt{x}} + C$ **71.** $2\sqrt{\tan^{-1} y} + C$ **73.** 16
75. 2 **77.** 1 **79.** 8 **81.** $27\sqrt{3}/160$ **83.** $\pi/2$
85 $\sqrt{3}$ **87.** $6\sqrt{3} - 2\pi$ **89.** −1 **91.** 2 **93.** 1
95. 15/16 + ln 2 **97.** $e - 1$ **99.** 1/6 **101.** 9/14
103. $\frac{9\ln 2}{4}$ **105.** π **107.** $\pi/\sqrt{3}$ **109.** $\sec^{-1}|2y| + C$
111. $\pi/12$ **113.** **(a)** b **(b)** b
117. **(a)** $\frac{d}{dx}(x\ln x - x + C) = x \cdot \frac{1}{x} + \ln x - 1 + 0 = \ln x$
(b) $\frac{1}{e - 1}$
119. 25°F **121.** $\sqrt{2 + \cos^3 x}$ **123.** $\frac{-6}{3 + x^4}$
125. $\frac{dy}{dx} = \frac{-2}{x}e^{\cos(2\ln x)}$ **127.** $\frac{dy}{dx} = \frac{1}{\sqrt{1 - x^2}\sqrt{1 - 2(\sin^{-1} x)^2}}$
129. Yes **131.** $-\sqrt{1 + x^2}$
133. Cost ≈ \$10,899 using a lower sum estimate

Additional and Advanced Exercises, pp. 349–352

1. **(a)** Yes **(b)** No **5.** **(a)** 1/4 **(b)** $\sqrt[3]{12}$
7. $f(x) = \frac{x}{\sqrt{x^2 + 1}}$ **9.** $y = x^3 + 2x - 4$
11. 36/5

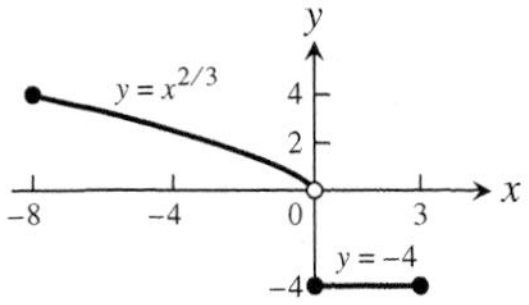

13. $\frac{1}{2} - \frac{2}{\pi}$

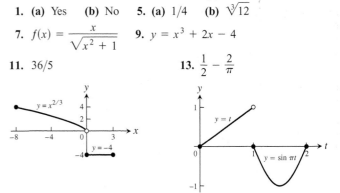

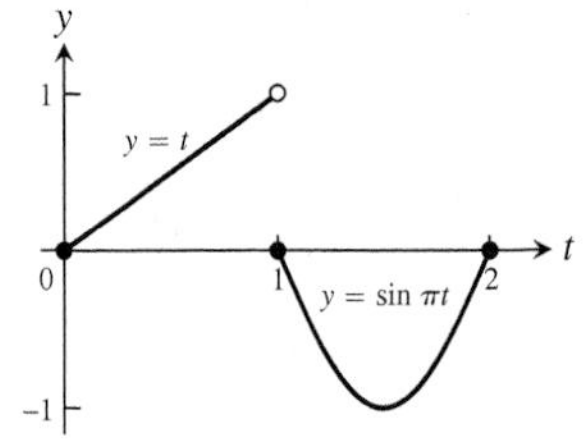

15. 13/3

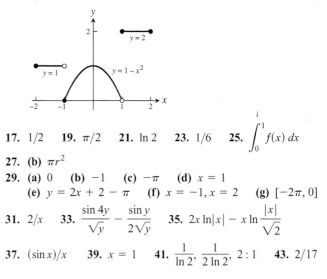

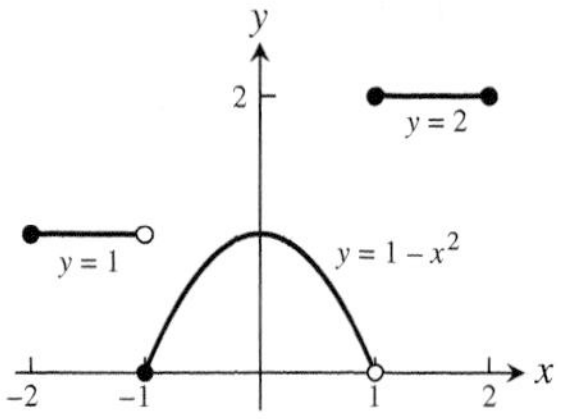

17. 1/2 **19.** $\pi/2$ **21.** ln 2 **23.** 1/6 **25.** $\int_0^1 f(x)\, dx$
27. **(b)** πr^2
29. **(a)** 0 **(b)** −1 **(c)** $-\pi$ **(d)** $x = 1$
(e) $y = 2x + 2 - \pi$ **(f)** $x = -1, x = 2$ **(g)** $[-2\pi, 0]$
31. $2/x$ **33.** $\frac{\sin 4y}{\sqrt{y}} - \frac{\sin y}{2\sqrt{y}}$ **35.** $2x\ln|x| - x\ln\frac{|x|}{\sqrt{2}}$
37. $(\sin x)/x$ **39.** $x = 1$ **41.** $\frac{1}{\ln 2}, \frac{1}{2\ln 2}$, 2 : 1 **43.** 2/17

CHAPTER 6

Section 6.1, pp. 361–364

1. 16 **3.** 16/3 **5.** **(a)** $2\sqrt{3}$ **(b)** 8 **7.** **(a)** 60 **(b)** 36
9. 8π **11.** 10 **13.** **(a)** s^2h **(b)** s^2h **15.** $\frac{2\pi}{3}$
17. $4 - \pi$ **19.** $\frac{32\pi}{5}$ **21.** 36π **23.** π **25.** $\frac{\pi}{2}\left(1 - \frac{1}{e^2}\right)$
27. $\frac{\pi}{2}\ln 4$ **29.** $\pi\left(\frac{\pi}{2} + 2\sqrt{2} - \frac{11}{3}\right)$ **31.** 2π **33.** 2π
35. $4\pi\ln 4$ **37.** $\pi^2 - 2\pi$ **39.** $\frac{2\pi}{3}$ **41.** $\frac{117\pi}{5}$
43. $\pi(\pi - 2)$ **45.** $\frac{4\pi}{3}$ **47.** 8π **49.** $\frac{7\pi}{6}$

51. **(a)** 8π **(b)** $\frac{32\pi}{5}$ **(c)** $\frac{8\pi}{3}$ **(d)** $\frac{224\pi}{15}$

53. **(a)** $\frac{16\pi}{15}$ **(b)** $\frac{56\pi}{15}$ **(c)** $\frac{64\pi}{15}$ **55.** $V = 2a^2b\pi^2$

57. **(a)** $V = \frac{\pi h^2(3a - h)}{3}$ **(b)** $\frac{1}{120\pi}$ m/sec

61. $V = 3308 \text{ cm}^3$ **63.** $\frac{4 - b + a}{2}$

Section 6.2, pp. 369–371

1. 6π **3.** 2π **5.** $14\pi/3$ **7.** 8π **9.** $5\pi/6$

11. $\frac{7\pi}{15}$ **13.** **(b)** 4π **15.** $\frac{16\pi}{15}(3\sqrt{2} + 5)$

17. $\frac{8\pi}{3}$ **19.** $\frac{4\pi}{3}$ **21.** $\frac{16\pi}{3}$

23. **(a)** 16π **(b)** 32π **(c)** 28π
(d) 24π **(e)** 60π **(f)** 48π

25. **(a)** $\frac{27\pi}{2}$ **(b)** $\frac{27\pi}{2}$ **(c)** $\frac{72\pi}{5}$ **(d)** $\frac{108\pi}{5}$

27. **(a)** $\frac{6\pi}{5}$ **(b)** $\frac{4\pi}{5}$ **(c)** 2π **(d)** 2π

29. **(a)** About the x-axis: $V = \frac{2\pi}{15}$; about the y-axis: $V = \frac{\pi}{6}$
(b) About the x-axis: $V = \frac{2\pi}{15}$; about the y-axis: $V = \frac{\pi}{6}$

31. **(a)** $\frac{5\pi}{3}$ **(b)** $\frac{4\pi}{3}$ **(c)** 2π **(d)** $\frac{2\pi}{3}$

33. **(a)** $\frac{4\pi}{15}$ **(b)** $\frac{7\pi}{30}$

35. **(a)** $\frac{24\pi}{5}$ **(b)** $\frac{48\pi}{5}$

37. **(a)** $\frac{9\pi}{16}$ **(b)** $\frac{9\pi}{16}$

39. Disk: 2 integrals; washer: 2 integrals; shell: 1 integral

41. **(a)** $\frac{256\pi}{3}$ **(b)** $\frac{244\pi}{3}$ **47.** $\pi\left(1 - \frac{1}{e}\right)$

Section 6.3, pp. 376–377

1. 12 **3.** $\frac{53}{6}$ **5.** $\frac{123}{32}$ **7.** $\frac{99}{8}$ **9.** $\ln 2 + \frac{3}{8}$ **11.** $\frac{53}{6}$ **13.** 2

15. **(a)** $\int_{-1}^{2} \sqrt{1 + 4x^2}\, dx$ **(c)** ≈ 6.13

17. **(a)** $\int_{0}^{\pi} \sqrt{1 + \cos^2 y}\, dy$ **(c)** ≈ 3.82

19. **(a)** $\int_{-1}^{3} \sqrt{1 + (y + 1)^2}\, dy$ **(c)** ≈ 9.29

21. **(a)** $\int_{0}^{\pi/6} \sec x\, dx$ **(c)** ≈ 0.55

23. **(a)** $y = \sqrt{x}$ from (1, 1) to (4, 2)
(b) Only one. We know the derivative of the function and the value of the function at one value of x.

25. 1 **27.** Yes, $f(x) = \pm x + C$ where C is any real number.

35. $\frac{2}{27}(10^{3/2} - 1)$

Section 6.4, pp. 381–383

1. **(a)** $2\pi \int_{0}^{\pi/4} (\tan x) \sqrt{1 + \sec^4 x}\, dx$ **(c)** $S \approx 3.84$

(b)

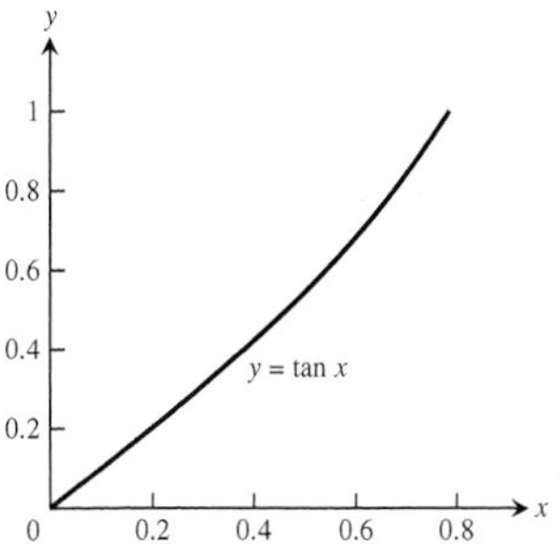

3. **(a)** $2\pi \int_{1}^{2} \frac{1}{y}\sqrt{1 + y^{-4}}\, dy$ **(c)** $S \approx 5.02$

(b)

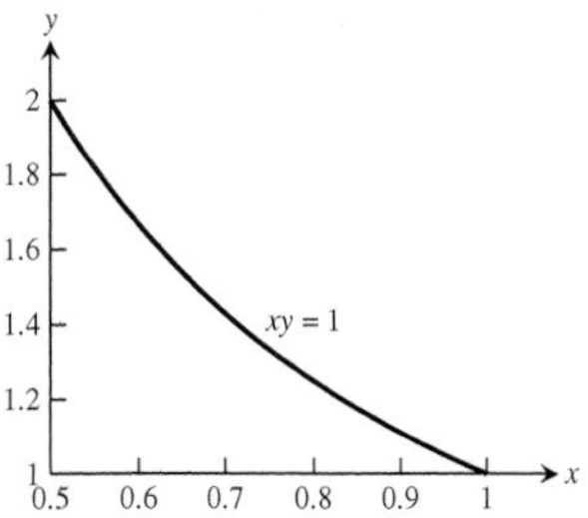

5. **(a)** $2\pi \int_{1}^{4} (3 - x^{1/2})^2 \sqrt{1 + (1 - 3x^{-1/2})^2}\, dx$ **(c)** $S \approx 63.37$

(b)

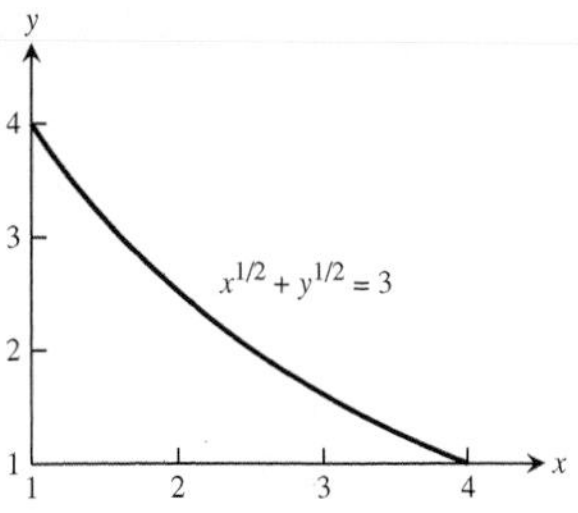

7. **(a)** $2\pi \int_{0}^{\pi/3} \left(\int_{0}^{y} \tan t\, dt\right) \sec y\, dy$ **(c)** $S \approx 2.08$

(b)

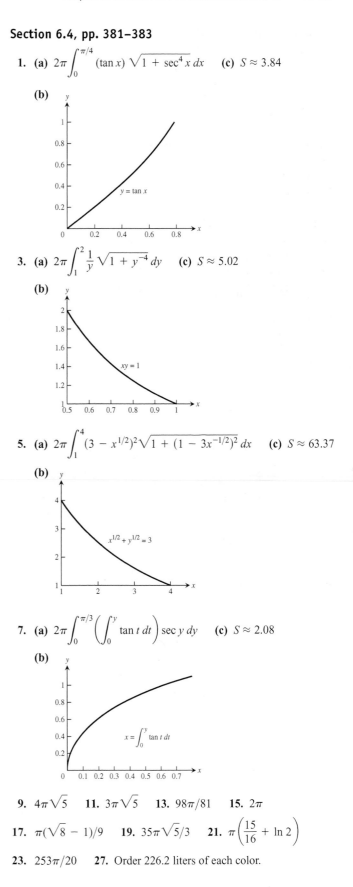

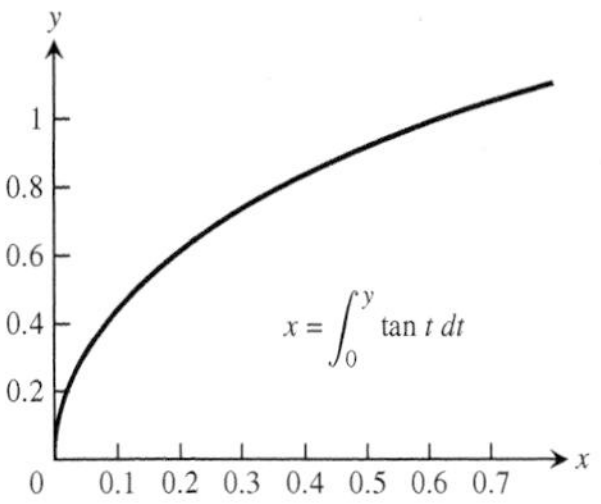

9. $4\pi\sqrt{5}$ **11.** $3\pi\sqrt{5}$ **13.** $98\pi/81$ **15.** 2π

17. $\pi(\sqrt{8} - 1)/9$ **19.** $35\pi\sqrt{5}/3$ **21.** $\pi\left(\frac{15}{16} + \ln 2\right)$

23. $253\pi/20$ **27.** Order 226.2 liters of each color.

Section 6.5, pp. 386–389

1. 400 N/m **3.** 4 cm, 0.08 J
5. **(a)** 7238 lb/in. **(b)** 905 in.-lb, 2714 in.-lb
7. 780 J **9.** 72,900 ft-lb **11.** 160 ft-lb
13. **(a)** 1,497,600 ft-lb **(b)** 1 hr, 40 min
(d) At 62.26 lb/ft^3: a) 1,494,240 ft-lb b) 1 hr, 40 min
At 62.59 lb/ft^3: a) 1,502,160 ft-lb b) 1 hr, 40.1 min
15. 37,306 ft-lb **17.** 7,238,299.47 ft-lb
19. 2446.25 ft-lb **21.** 15,073,099.75 J
25. 85.1 ft-lb **27.** 98.35 ft-lb **29.** 91.32 in.-oz
31. 5.144×10^{10} J

Section 6.6, pp. 396–397

1. $\bar{x} = 0, \bar{y} = 12/5$ **3.** $\bar{x} = 1, \bar{y} = -3/5$
5. $\bar{x} = 16/105, \bar{y} = 8/15$ **7.** $\bar{x} = 0, \bar{y} = \pi/8$
9. $\bar{x} \approx 1.44, \bar{y} \approx 0.36$
11. $\bar{x} = \dfrac{\ln 4}{\pi}, \bar{y} = 0$ **13.** $\bar{x} = 7, \bar{y} = \dfrac{\ln 16}{12}$
15. $\bar{x} = 3/2, \bar{y} = 1/2$
17. **(a)** $\dfrac{224\pi}{3}$ **(b)** $\bar{x} = 2, \bar{y} = 0$
(c)

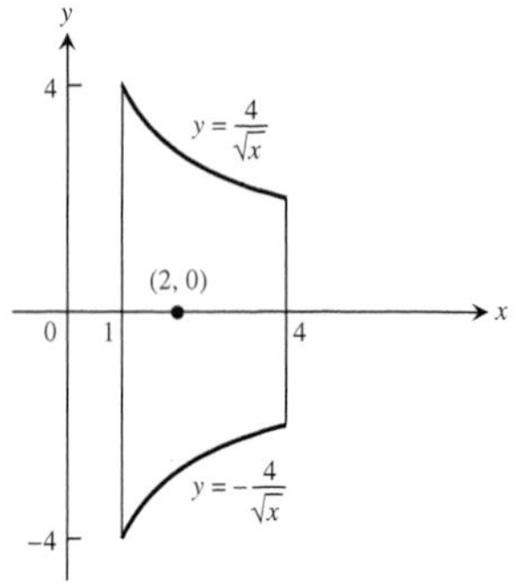

21. $\bar{x} = \bar{y} = 1/3$ **23.** $\bar{x} = a/3, \bar{y} = b/3$ **25.** $13\delta/6$
27. $\bar{x} = 0, \bar{y} = \dfrac{a\pi}{4}$
29. $\bar{x} = 1/2, \bar{y} = 4$ **31.** $\bar{x} = 6/5, \bar{y} = 8/7$

Practice Exercises, pp. 397–399

1. $\dfrac{9\pi}{280}$ **3.** π^2 **5.** $\dfrac{72\pi}{35}$
7. **(a)** 2π **(b)** π **(c)** $12\pi/5$ **(d)** $26\pi/5$
9. **(a)** 8π **(b)** $1088\pi/15$ **(c)** $512\pi/15$
11. $\pi(3\sqrt{3} - \pi)/3$ **13.** $\pi(e - 1)$
15. $\dfrac{28\pi}{3}$ ft^3 **17.** $\dfrac{10}{3}$ **19.** $3 + \dfrac{1}{8}\ln 2$
21. $28\pi\sqrt{2}/3$ **23.** 4π **25.** 4640 J
27. 10 ft-lb, 30 ft-lb **29.** 418,208.81 ft-lb
31. $22{,}500\pi$ ft-lb, 257 sec **33.** $\bar{x} = 0, \bar{y} = 8/5$
35. $\bar{x} = 3/2, \bar{y} = 12/5$ **37.** $\bar{x} = 9/5, \bar{y} = 11/10$

Additional and Advanced Exercises, pp. 399–400

1. $f(x) = \sqrt{\dfrac{2x - a}{\pi}}$ **3.** $f(x) = \sqrt{C^2 - 1}\,x + a$, where $C \geq 1$
5. $\dfrac{\pi}{30\sqrt{2}}$ **7.** 28/3 **9.** $\dfrac{4h\sqrt{3mh}}{3}$
11. $\bar{x} = 0, \bar{y} = \dfrac{n}{2n + 1}$, (0, 1/2)
15. **(a)** $\bar{x} = \bar{y} = 4(a^2 + ab + b^2)/(3\pi(a + b))$
(b) $(2a/\pi, 2a/\pi)$

CHAPTER 7

Section 7.1, pp. 409–411

1. $\ln\left(\dfrac{2}{3}\right)$ **3.** $\ln|y^2 - 25| + C$ **5.** $\ln|6 + 3\tan t| + C$
7. $\ln(1 + \sqrt{x}) + C$ **9.** 1 **11.** $2(\ln 2)^4$ **13.** 2
15. $2e^{\sqrt{r}} + C$ **17.** $-e^{-t^2} + C$ **19.** $-e^{1/x} + C$
21. $\dfrac{1}{\pi}e^{\sec \pi t} + C$ **23.** 1 **25.** $\ln(1 + e^r) + C$ **27.** $\dfrac{1}{2\ln 2}$
29. $\dfrac{1}{\ln 2}$ **31.** $\dfrac{6}{\ln 7}$ **33.** 32760 **35.** $3^{\sqrt{2}+1}$
37. $\dfrac{1}{\ln 10}\left(\dfrac{(\ln x)^2}{2}\right) + C$ **39.** $2(\ln 2)^2$ **41.** $\dfrac{3\ln 2}{2}$ **43.** $\ln 10$
45. $(\ln 10)\ln|\ln x| + C$ **47.** $y = 1 - \cos(e^t - 2)$
49. $y = 2(e^{-x} + x) - 1$ **51.** $y = x + \ln|x| + 2$ **53.** $\pi \ln 16$
55. $6 + \ln 2$ **57.** **(b)** 0.00469
69. **(a)** 1.89279 **(b)** −0.35621 **(c)** 0.94575 **(d)** −2.80735
(e) 5.29595 **(f)** 0.97041 **(g)** −1.03972 **(h)** −1.61181

Section 7.2, pp. 418–420

9. $\dfrac{2}{3}y^{3/2} - x^{1/2} = C$ **11.** $e^y - e^x = C$
13. $-x + 2\tan\sqrt{y} = C$ **15.** $e^{-y} + 2e^{\sqrt{x}} = C$
17. $y = \sin(x^2 + C)$ **19.** $\dfrac{1}{3}\ln|y^3 - 2| = x^3 + C$
21. $4\ln(\sqrt{y} + 2) = e^{x^2} + C$
23. **(a)** −0.00001 **(b)** 10,536 years **(c)** 82%
25. 54.88 g **27.** 59.8 ft **29.** 2.8147498×10^{14}
31. **(a)** 8 years **(b)** 32.02 years
33. 15.28 years **35.** 56,562 years
39. **(a)** 17.5 min **(b)** 13.26 min
41. −3°C **43.** About 6693 years **45.** 54.62%

Section 7.3, pp. 425–428

1. $\cosh x = 5/4, \tanh x = -3/5, \coth x = -5/3,$
$\operatorname{sech} x = 4/5, \operatorname{csch} x = -4/3$
3. $\sinh x = 8/15, \tanh x = 8/17, \coth x = 17/8, \operatorname{sech} x = 15/17,$
$\operatorname{csch} x = 15/8$
5. $x + \dfrac{1}{x}$ **7.** e^{5x} **9.** e^{4x} **13.** $2\cosh\dfrac{x}{3}$
15. $\operatorname{sech}^2\sqrt{t} + \dfrac{\tanh\sqrt{t}}{\sqrt{t}}$ **17.** $\coth z$
19. $(\ln \operatorname{sech}\theta)(\operatorname{sech}\theta \tanh\theta)$ **21.** $\tanh^3 v$ **23.** 2
25. $\dfrac{1}{2\sqrt{x(1 + x)}}$ **27.** $\dfrac{1}{1 + \theta} - \tanh^{-1}\theta$
29. $\dfrac{1}{2\sqrt{t}} - \coth^{-1}\sqrt{t}$ **31.** $-\operatorname{sech}^{-1} x$ **33.** $\dfrac{\ln 2}{\sqrt{1 + \left(\frac{1}{2}\right)^{2\theta}}}$

35. $|\sec x|$ **41.** $\dfrac{\cosh 2x}{2} + C$

43. $12 \sinh\left(\dfrac{x}{2} - \ln 3\right) + C$ **45.** $7 \ln|e^{x/7} + e^{-x/7}| + C$

47. $\tanh\left(x - \dfrac{1}{2}\right) + C$ **49.** $-2\,\mathrm{sech}\sqrt{t} + C$ **51.** $\ln\dfrac{5}{2}$

53. $\dfrac{3}{32} + \ln 2$ **55.** $e - e^{-1}$ **57.** $3/4$ **59.** $\dfrac{3}{8} + \ln\sqrt{2}$

61. $\ln(2/3)$ **63.** $\dfrac{-\ln 3}{2}$ **65.** $\ln 3$

67. **(a)** $\sinh^{-1}(\sqrt{3})$ **(b)** $\ln(\sqrt{3} + 2)$

69. **(a)** $\coth^{-1}(2) - \coth^{-1}(5/4)$ **(b)** $\left(\dfrac{1}{2}\right)\ln\left(\dfrac{1}{3}\right)$

71. **(a)** $-\mathrm{sech}^{-1}\left(\dfrac{12}{13}\right) + \mathrm{sech}^{-1}\left(\dfrac{4}{5}\right)$

(b) $-\ln\left(\dfrac{1 + \sqrt{1 - (12/13)^2}}{(12/13)}\right) + \ln\left(\dfrac{1 + \sqrt{1 - (4/5)^2}}{(4/5)}\right)$

$= -\ln\left(\dfrac{3}{2}\right) + \ln(2) = \ln(4/3)$

73. **(a)** 0 **(b)** 0

77. **(b)** $\sqrt{\dfrac{mg}{k}}$ **(c)** $80\sqrt{5} \approx 178.89$ ft/sec **79.** 2π **81.** $\dfrac{6}{5}$

Practice Exercises, pp. 428–429

1. $-\cos e^x + C$ **3.** $\ln 8$ **5.** $2 \ln 2$ **7.** $\dfrac{1}{2}(\ln(x - 5))^2 + C$

9. $3 \ln 7$ **11.** $2(\sqrt{2} - 1)$ **13.** $y = \dfrac{\ln 2}{\ln(3/2)}$

15. $y = \ln x - \ln 3$ **17.** $y = \dfrac{1}{1 - e^x}$

19. $1/3$ **21.** $1/e$ m/sec **23.** $\ln 5x - \ln 3x = \ln(5/3)$

25. $1/2$ **27.** $y = \left(\tan^{-1}\left(\dfrac{x + C}{2}\right)\right)^2$

29. $y^2 = \sin^{-1}(2 \tan x + C)$

31. $y = -2 + \ln(2 - e^{-x})$ **33.** $y = 4x - 4\sqrt{x} + 1$

35. 19,035 years

Additional and Advanced Exercises, pp. 429–430

1. **(a)** 1 **(b)** $\pi/2$ **(c)** π

3. $\tan^{-1}x + \tan^{-1}\left(\dfrac{1}{x}\right)$ is a constant and the constant is $\dfrac{\pi}{2}$ for $x > 0$; it is $-\dfrac{\pi}{2}$ for $x < 0$.

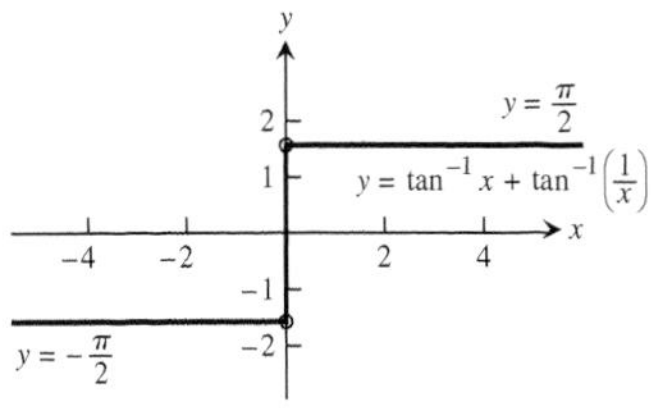

7. $\bar{x} = \dfrac{\ln 4}{\pi}$, $\bar{y} = 0$

CHAPTER 8

Section 8.1, pp. 436–438

1. $-2x \cos(x/2) + 4 \sin(x/2) + C$

3. $t^2 \sin t + 2t \cos t - 2 \sin t + C$ **5.** $\ln 4 - \dfrac{3}{4}$

7. $xe^x - e^x + C$ **9.** $-(x^2 + 2x + 2)e^{-x} + C$

11. $y \tan^{-1}(y) - \ln\sqrt{1 + y^2} + C$

13. $x \tan x + \ln|\cos x| + C$

15. $(x^3 - 3x^2 + 6x - 6)e^x + C$

17. $(x^2 - 7x + 7)e^x + C$

19. $(x^5 - 5x^4 + 20x^3 - 60x^2 + 120x - 120)e^x + C$

21. $\dfrac{1}{2}(-e^\theta \cos\theta + e^\theta \sin\theta) + C$

23. $\dfrac{e^{2x}}{13}(3 \sin 3x + 2 \cos 3x) + C$

25. $\dfrac{2}{3}\left(\sqrt{3s + 9}\, e^{\sqrt{3s+9}} - e^{\sqrt{3s+9}}\right) + C$

27. $\dfrac{\pi\sqrt{3}}{3} - \ln(2) - \dfrac{\pi^2}{18}$

29. $\dfrac{1}{2}[-x \cos(\ln x) + x \sin(\ln x)] + C$

31. $\dfrac{1}{2}\ln|\sec x^2 + \tan x^2| + C$

33. $\dfrac{1}{2}x^2(\ln x)^2 - \dfrac{1}{2}x^2 \ln x + \dfrac{1}{4}x^2 + C$

35. $-\dfrac{1}{x}\ln x - \dfrac{1}{x} + C$ **37.** $\dfrac{1}{4}e^{x^4} + C$

39. $\dfrac{1}{3}x^2(x^2 + 1)^{3/2} - \dfrac{2}{15}(x^2 + 1)^{5/2} + C$

41. $-\dfrac{2}{5}\sin 3x \sin 2x - \dfrac{3}{5}\cos 3x \cos 2x + C$

43. $-\cos e^x + C$ **45.** $2\sqrt{x}\sin\sqrt{x} + 2\cos\sqrt{x} + C$

47. $\dfrac{\pi^2 - 4}{8}$ **49.** $\dfrac{5\pi - 3\sqrt{3}}{9}$

51. **(a)** π **(b)** 3π **(c)** 5π **(d)** $(2n + 1)\pi$

53. $2\pi(1 - \ln 2)$ **55.** **(a)** $\pi(\pi - 2)$ **(b)** 2π

57. **(a)** 1 **(b)** $(e - 2)\pi$ **(c)** $\dfrac{\pi}{2}(e^2 + 9)$

(d) $\bar{x} = \dfrac{1}{4}(e^2 + 1), \bar{y} = \dfrac{1}{2}(e - 2)$

59. $\dfrac{1}{2\pi}(1 - e^{-2\pi})$ **61.** $u = x^n, dv = \cos x\, dx$

63. $u = x^n, dv = e^{ax}\, dx$ **67.** $x \sin^{-1} x + \cos(\sin^{-1} x) + C$

69. $x \sec^{-1} x - \ln\left|x + \sqrt{x^2 - 1}\right| + C$ **71.** Yes

73. **(a)** $x \sinh^{-1} x - \cosh(\sinh^{-1} x) + C$

(b) $x \sinh^{-1} x - (1 + x^2)^{1/2} + C$

Section 8.2, pp. 443–444

1. $\dfrac{1}{2}\sin 2x + C$ **3.** $-\dfrac{1}{4}\cos^4 x + C$ **5.** $\dfrac{1}{3}\cos^3 x - \cos x + C$

7. $-\cos x + \dfrac{2}{3}\cos^3 x - \dfrac{1}{5}\cos^5 x + C$ **9.** $\sin x - \dfrac{1}{3}\sin^3 x + C$

11. $\dfrac{1}{4}\sin^4 x - \dfrac{1}{6}\sin^6 x + C$ **13.** $\dfrac{1}{2}x + \dfrac{1}{4}\sin 2x + C$

15. 16/35 **17.** 3π

19. $-4\sin x\cos^3 x + 2\cos x\sin x + 2x + C$

21. $-\cos^4 2\theta + C$ **23.** 4 **25.** 2

27. $\sqrt{\frac{3}{2}} - \frac{2}{3}$ **29.** $\frac{4}{5}\left(\frac{3}{2}\right)^{5/2} - \frac{18}{35} - \frac{2}{7}\left(\frac{3}{2}\right)^{7/2}$ **31.** $\sqrt{2}$

33. $\frac{1}{2}\tan^2 x + C$ **35.** $\frac{1}{3}\sec^3 x + C$ **37.** $\frac{1}{3}\tan^3 x + C$

39. $2\sqrt{3} + \ln(2 + \sqrt{3})$ **41.** $\frac{2}{3}\tan\theta + \frac{1}{3}\sec^2\theta\tan\theta + C$

43. 4/3 **45.** $2\tan^2 x - 2\ln(1 + \tan^2 x) + C$

47. $\frac{1}{4}\tan^4 x - \frac{1}{2}\tan^2 x + \ln|\sec x| + C$

49. $\frac{4}{3} - \ln\sqrt{3}$ **51.** $-\frac{1}{10}\cos 5x - \frac{1}{2}\cos x + C$ **53.** π

55. $\frac{1}{2}\sin x + \frac{1}{14}\sin 7x + C$

57. $\frac{1}{6}\sin 3\theta - \frac{1}{4}\sin\theta - \frac{1}{20}\sin 5\theta + C$

59. $-\frac{2}{5}\cos^5\theta + C$ **61.** $\frac{1}{4}\cos\theta - \frac{1}{20}\cos 5\theta + C$

63. $\sec x - \ln|\csc x + \cot x| + C$ **65.** $\cos x + \sec x + C$

67. $\frac{1}{4}x^2 - \frac{1}{4}x\sin 2x - \frac{1}{8}\cos 2x + C$ **69.** $\ln(1 + \sqrt{2})$

71. $\pi^2/2$ **73.** $\bar{x} = \frac{4\pi}{3}, \bar{y} = \frac{8\pi^2 + 3}{12\pi}$

Section 8.3, pp. 447–448

1. $\ln|\sqrt{9 + x^2} + x| + C$ **3.** $\pi/4$ **5.** $\pi/6$

7. $\frac{25}{2}\sin^{-1}\left(\frac{t}{5}\right) + \frac{t\sqrt{25 - t^2}}{2} + C$

9. $\frac{1}{2}\ln\left|\frac{2x}{7} + \frac{\sqrt{4x^2 - 49}}{7}\right| + C$

11. $7\left[\frac{\sqrt{y^2 - 49}}{7} - \sec^{-1}\left(\frac{y}{7}\right)\right] + C$ **13.** $\frac{\sqrt{x^2 - 1}}{x} + C$

15. $-\sqrt{9 - x^2} + C$ **17.** $\frac{1}{3}(x^2 + 4)^{3/2} - 4\sqrt{x^2 + 4} + C$

19. $\frac{-2\sqrt{4 - w^2}}{w} + C$ **21.** $\frac{10}{3}\tan^{-1}\frac{5x}{6} + C$

23. $4\sqrt{3} - \frac{4\pi}{3}$ **25.** $-\frac{x}{\sqrt{x^2 - 1}} + C$

27. $-\frac{1}{5}\left(\frac{\sqrt{1 - x^2}}{x}\right)^5 + C$ **29.** $2\tan^{-1} 2x + \frac{4x}{(4x^2 + 1)} + C$

31. $\frac{1}{2}x^2 + \frac{1}{2}\ln|x^2 - 1| + C$ **33.** $\frac{1}{3}\left(\frac{v}{\sqrt{1 - v^2}}\right)^3 + C$

35. $\ln 9 - \ln(1 + \sqrt{10})$ **37.** $\pi/6$ **39.** $\sec^{-1}|x| + C$

41. $\sqrt{x^2 - 1} + C$ **43.** $\frac{1}{2}\ln|\sqrt{1 + x^4} + x^2| + C$

45. $4\sin^{-1}\frac{\sqrt{x}}{2} + \sqrt{x}\sqrt{4 - x} + C$

47. $\frac{1}{4}\sin^{-1}\sqrt{x} - \frac{1}{4}\sqrt{x}\sqrt{1 - x}(1 - 2x) + C$

49. $y = 2\left[\frac{\sqrt{x^2 - 4}}{2} - \sec^{-1}\left(\frac{x}{2}\right)\right]$

51. $y = \frac{3}{2}\tan^{-1}\left(\frac{x}{2}\right) - \frac{3\pi}{8}$ **53.** $3\pi/4$

55. **(a)** $\frac{1}{12}(\pi + 6\sqrt{3} - 12)$

(b) $\bar{x} = \frac{3\sqrt{3} - \pi}{4(\pi + 6\sqrt{3} - 12)}, \bar{y} = \frac{\pi^2 + 12\sqrt{3}\pi - 72}{12(\pi + 6\sqrt{3} - 12)}$

57. **(a)** $-\frac{1}{3}x^2(1 - x^2)^{3/2} - \frac{2}{15}(1 - x^2)^{5/2} + C$

(b) $-\frac{1}{3}(1 - x^2)^{3/2} + \frac{1}{5}(1 - x^2)^{5/2} + C$

(c) $\frac{1}{5}(1 - x^2)^{5/2} - \frac{1}{3}(1 - x^2)^{3/2} + C$

Section 8.4, pp. 454–455

1. $\frac{2}{x - 3} + \frac{3}{x - 2}$ **3.** $\frac{1}{x + 1} + \frac{3}{(x + 1)^2}$

5. $\frac{-2}{z} + \frac{-1}{z^2} + \frac{2}{z - 1}$ **7.** $1 + \frac{17}{t - 3} + \frac{-12}{t - 2}$

9. $\frac{1}{2}[\ln|1 + x| - \ln|1 - x|] + C$

11. $\frac{1}{7}\ln|(x + 6)^2(x - 1)^5| + C$ **13.** $(\ln 15)/2$

15. $-\frac{1}{2}\ln|t| + \frac{1}{6}\ln|t + 2| + \frac{1}{3}\ln|t - 1| + C$ **17.** $3\ln 2 - 2$

19. $\frac{1}{4}\ln\left|\frac{x + 1}{x - 1}\right| - \frac{x}{2(x^2 - 1)} + C$ **21.** $(\pi + 2\ln 2)/8$

23. $\tan^{-1} y - \frac{1}{y^2 + 1} + C$

25. $-(s - 1)^{-2} + (s - 1)^{-1} + \tan^{-1} s + C$

27. $\frac{2}{3}\ln|x - 1| + \frac{1}{6}\ln|x^2 + x + 1| - \sqrt{3}\tan^{-1}\left(\frac{2x + 1}{\sqrt{3}}\right) + C$

29. $\frac{1}{4}\ln\left|\frac{x - 1}{x + 1}\right| + \frac{1}{2}\tan^{-1} x + C$

31. $\frac{-1}{\theta^2 + 2\theta + 2} + \ln(\theta^2 + 2\theta + 2) - \tan^{-1}(\theta + 1) + C$

33. $x^2 + \ln\left|\frac{x - 1}{x}\right| + C$

35. $9x + 2\ln|x| + \frac{1}{x} + 7\ln|x - 1| + C$

37. $\frac{y^2}{2} - \ln|y| + \frac{1}{2}\ln(1 + y^2) + C$ **39.** $\ln\left(\frac{e^t + 1}{e^t + 2}\right) + C$

41. $\frac{1}{5}\ln\left|\frac{\sin y - 2}{\sin y + 3}\right| + C$

43. $\frac{(\tan^{-1} 2x)^2}{4} - 3\ln|x - 2| + \frac{6}{x - 2} + C$

45. $\ln\left|\frac{\sqrt{x} - 1}{\sqrt{x} + 1}\right| + C$ **47.** $2\sqrt{1 + x} + \ln\left|\frac{\sqrt{x + 1} - 1}{\sqrt{x + 1} + 1}\right| + C$

49. $\frac{1}{4}\ln\left|\frac{x^4}{x^4+1}\right| + C$

51. $x = \ln|t-2| - \ln|t-1| + \ln 2$ **53.** $x = \frac{6t}{t+2} - 1$

55. $3\pi \ln 25$ **57.** 1.10 **59. (a)** $x = \frac{1000e^{4t}}{499 + e^{4t}}$ **(b)** 1.55 days

Section 8.5, pp. 460–461

1. $\frac{2}{\sqrt{3}}\left(\tan^{-1}\sqrt{\frac{x-3}{3}}\right) + C$

3. $\sqrt{x-2}\left(\frac{2(x-2)}{3} + 4\right) + C$

5. $\frac{(2x-3)^{3/2}(x+1)}{5} + C$

7. $\frac{-\sqrt{9-4x}}{x} - \frac{2}{3}\ln\left|\frac{\sqrt{9-4x}-3}{\sqrt{9-4x}+3}\right| + C$

9. $\frac{(x+2)(2x-6)\sqrt{4x-x^2}}{6} + 4\sin^{-1}\left(\frac{x-2}{2}\right) + C$

11. $-\frac{1}{\sqrt{7}}\ln\left|\frac{\sqrt{7}+\sqrt{7+x^2}}{x}\right| + C$

13. $\sqrt{4-x^2} - 2\ln\left|\frac{2+\sqrt{4-x^2}}{x}\right| + C$

15. $\frac{e^{2t}}{13}(2\cos 3t + 3\sin 3t) + C$

17. $\frac{x^2}{2}\cos^{-1}x + \frac{1}{4}\sin^{-1}x - \frac{1}{4}x\sqrt{1-x^2} + C$

19. $\frac{x^3}{3}\tan^{-1}x - \frac{x^2}{6} + \frac{1}{6}\ln(1+x^2) + C$

21. $-\frac{\cos 5x}{10} - \frac{\cos x}{2} + C$ **23.** $8\left[\frac{\sin(7t/2)}{7} - \frac{\sin(9t/2)}{9}\right] + C$

25. $6\sin(\theta/12) + \frac{6}{7}\sin(7\theta/12) + C$

27. $\frac{1}{2}\ln(x^2+1) + \frac{x}{2(1+x^2)} + \frac{1}{2}\tan^{-1}x + C$

29. $\left(x - \frac{1}{2}\right)\sin^{-1}\sqrt{x} + \frac{1}{2}\sqrt{x-x^2} + C$

31. $\sin^{-1}\sqrt{x} - \sqrt{x-x^2} + C$

33. $\sqrt{1-\sin^2 t} - \ln\left|\frac{1+\sqrt{1-\sin^2 t}}{\sin t}\right| + C$

35. $\ln\left|\ln y + \sqrt{3+(\ln y)^2}\right| + C$

37. $\ln\left|x + 1 + \sqrt{x^2+2x+5}\right| + C$

39. $\frac{x+2}{2}\sqrt{5-4x-x^2} + \frac{9}{2}\sin^{-1}\left(\frac{x+2}{3}\right) + C$

41. $-\frac{\sin^4 2x\cos 2x}{10} - \frac{2\sin^2 2x\cos 2x}{15} - \frac{4\cos 2x}{15} + C$

43. $\frac{\sin^3 2\theta\cos^2 2\theta}{10} + \frac{\sin^3 2\theta}{15} + C$

45. $\tan^2 2x - 2\ln|\sec 2x| + C$

47. $\frac{(\sec \pi x)(\tan \pi x)}{\pi} + \frac{1}{\pi}\ln|\sec \pi x + \tan \pi x| + C$

49. $\frac{-\csc^3 x\cot x}{4} - \frac{3\csc x\cot x}{8} - \frac{3}{8}\ln|\csc x + \cot x| + C$

51. $\frac{1}{2}[\sec(e^t-1)\tan(e^t-1) + \ln|\sec(e^t-1) + \tan(e^t-1)|] + C$

53. $\sqrt{2} + \ln\left(\sqrt{2}+1\right)$ **55.** $\pi/3$

57. $2\pi\sqrt{3} + \pi\sqrt{2}\ln(\sqrt{2}+\sqrt{3})$

59. $\bar{x} = 4/3,\ \bar{y} = \ln\sqrt{2}$ **61.** 7.62 **63.** $\pi/8$ **67.** $\pi/4$

Section 8.6, pp. 468–470

1. I: (a) 1.5, 0 **(b)** 1.5, 0 **(c)** 0%
II: (a) 1.5, 0 **(b)** 1.5, 0 **(c)** 0%

3. I: (a) 2.75, 0.08 **(b)** 2.67, 0.08 **(c)** $0.0312 \approx 3\%$
II: (a) 2.67, 0 **(b)** 2.67, 0 **(c)** 0%

5. I: (a) 6.25, 0.5 **(b)** 6, 0.25 **(c)** $0.0417 \approx 4\%$
II: (a) 6, 0 **(b)** 6, 0 **(c)** 0%

7. I: (a) 0.509, 0.03125 **(b)** 0.5, 0.009 **(c)** $0.018 \approx 2\%$
II: (a) 0.5, 0.002604 **(b)** 0.5, 0.4794 **(c)** 0%

9. I: (a) 1.8961, 0.161 **(b)** 2, 0.1039 **(c)** $0.052 \approx 5\%$
II: (a) 2.0045, 0.0066 **(b)** 2, 0.00454 **(c)** 0.2%

11. (a) 1 **(b)** 2 **13. (a)** 116 **(b)** 2

15. (a) 283 **(b)** 2 **17. (a)** 71 **(b)** 10

19. (a) 76 **(b)** 12 **21. (a)** 82 **(b)** 8

23. 15,990 ft^3 **25.** ≈ 10.63 ft

27. (a) ≈ 0.00021 **(b)** ≈ 1.37079 **(c)** $\approx 0.015\%$

31. (a) ≈ 5.870 **(b)** $|E_T| \le 0.0032$

33. 21.07 in. **35.** 14.4

Section 8.7, pp. 479–481

1. $\pi/2$ **3.** 2 **5.** 6 **7.** $\pi/2$ **9.** $\ln 3$ **11.** $\ln 4$ **13.** 0

15. $\sqrt{3}$ **17.** π **19.** $\ln\left(1 + \frac{\pi}{2}\right)$ **21.** -1 **23.** 1

25. $-1/4$ **27.** $\pi/2$ **29.** $\pi/3$ **31.** 6 **33.** $\ln 2$

35. Diverges **37.** Converges **39.** Converges **41.** Converges

43. Diverges **45.** Converges **47.** Converges **49.** Diverges

51. Converges **53.** Converges **55.** Diverges **57.** Converges

59. Diverges **61.** Converges **63.** Converges

65. (a) Converges when $p < 1$ **(b)** Converges when $p > 1$

67. 1 **69.** 2π **71.** $\ln 2$ **73. (b)** ≈ 0.88621

75. (a)

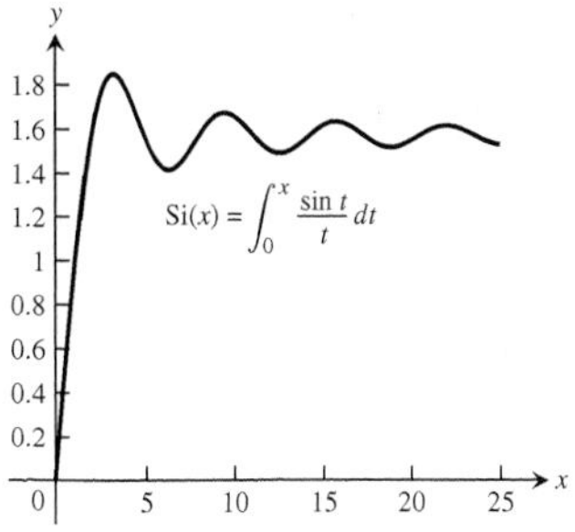

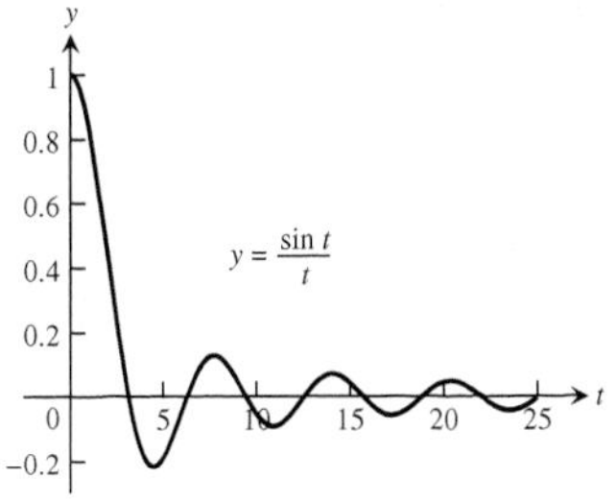

(b) $\pi/2$

77. (a)

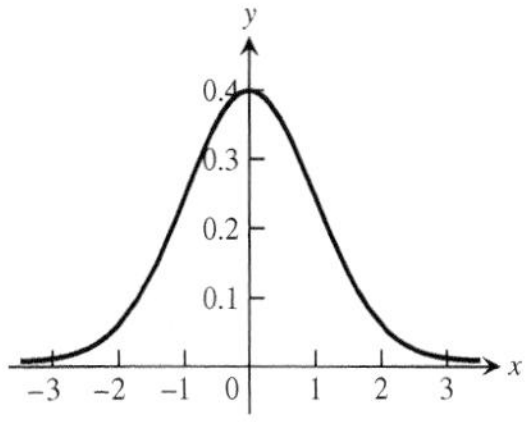

(b) ≈ 0.683, ≈ 0.954, ≈ 0.997

Practice Exercises, pp. 481–483

1. $(x+1)(\ln(x+1)) - (x+1) + C$

3. $x\tan^{-1}(3x) - \frac{1}{6}\ln(1+9x^2) + C$

5. $(x+1)^2e^x - 2(x+1)e^x + 2e^x + C$

7. $\frac{2e^x\sin 2x}{5} + \frac{e^x\cos 2x}{5} + C$

9. $2\ln|x-2| - \ln|x-1| + C$

11. $\ln|x| - \ln|x+1| + \frac{1}{x+1} + C$

13. $-\frac{1}{3}\ln\left|\frac{\cos\theta - 1}{\cos\theta + 2}\right| + C$

15. $4\ln|x| - \frac{1}{2}\ln(x^2+1) + 4\tan^{-1}x + C$

17. $\frac{1}{16}\ln\left|\frac{(v-2)^5(v+2)}{v^6}\right| + C$

19. $\frac{1}{2}\tan^{-1}t - \frac{\sqrt{3}}{6}\tan^{-1}\frac{t}{\sqrt{3}} + C$

21. $\frac{x^2}{2} + \frac{4}{3}\ln|x+2| + \frac{2}{3}\ln|x-1| + C$

23. $\frac{x^2}{2} - \frac{9}{2}\ln|x+3| + \frac{3}{2}\ln|x+1| + C$

25. $\frac{1}{3}\ln\left|\frac{\sqrt{x+1}-1}{\sqrt{x+1}+1}\right| + C$ 27. $\ln|1-e^{-s}| + C$

29. $-\sqrt{16-y^2} + C$ 31. $-\frac{1}{2}\ln|4-x^2| + C$

33. $\ln\frac{1}{\sqrt{9-x^2}} + C$ 35. $\frac{1}{6}\ln\left|\frac{x+3}{x-3}\right| + C$

37. $-\frac{\cos^5 x}{5} + \frac{\cos^7 x}{7} + C$ 39. $\frac{\tan^5 x}{5} + C$

41. $\frac{\cos\theta}{2} - \frac{\cos 11\theta}{22} + C$ 43. $4\sqrt{1-\cos(t/2)} + C$

45. At least 16 47. $T = \pi, S = \pi$ 49. 25°F

51. (a) ≈ 2.42 gal (b) ≈ 24.83 mi/gal

53. $\pi/2$ 55. 6 57. $\ln 3$ 59. 2 61. $\pi/6$

63. Diverges 65. Diverges 67. Converges

69. $\frac{2x^{3/2}}{3} - x + 2\sqrt{x} - 2\ln(\sqrt{x}+1) + C$

71. $\ln\left|\frac{\sqrt{x}}{\sqrt{x^2+1}}\right| - \frac{1}{2}\left(\frac{x}{\sqrt{x^2+1}}\right)^2 + C$

73. $-2\cot x - \ln|\csc x + \cot x| + \csc x + C$

75. $\frac{1}{12}\ln\left|\frac{3+v}{3-v}\right| + \frac{1}{6}\tan^{-1}\frac{v}{3} + C$

77. $\frac{\theta\sin(2\theta+1)}{2} + \frac{\cos(2\theta+1)}{4} + C$ 79. $\frac{1}{4}\sec^2\theta + C$

81. $2\left(\frac{(\sqrt{2-x})^3}{3} - 2\sqrt{2-x}\right) + C$ 83. $\tan^{-1}(y-1) + C$

85. $\frac{1}{4}\ln|z| - \frac{1}{4z} - \frac{1}{4}\left[\frac{1}{2}\ln(z^2+4) + \frac{1}{2}\tan^{-1}\left(\frac{z}{2}\right)\right] + C$

87. $-\frac{1}{4}\sqrt{9-4t^2} + C$ 89. $\ln\left(\frac{e^t+1}{e^t+2}\right) + C$ 91. 1/4

93. $\frac{2}{3}x^{3/2} + C$ 95. $-\frac{1}{5}\tan^{-1}(\cos 5t) + C$

97. $2\sqrt{r} - 2\ln(1+\sqrt{r}) + C$

99. $\frac{1}{2}x^2 - \frac{1}{2}\ln(x^2+1) + C$

101. $\frac{2}{3}\ln|x+1| + \frac{1}{6}\ln|x^2-x+1| + \frac{1}{\sqrt{3}}\tan^{-1}\left(\frac{2x-1}{\sqrt{3}}\right) + C$

103. $\frac{4}{7}(1+\sqrt{x})^{7/2} - \frac{8}{5}(1+\sqrt{x})^{5/2} + \frac{4}{3}(1+\sqrt{x})^{3/2} + C$

105. $2\ln|\sqrt{x} + \sqrt{1+x}| + C$

107. $\ln x - \ln|1 + \ln x| + C$

109. $\frac{1}{2}x^{\ln x} + C$ 111. $\frac{1}{2}\ln\left|\frac{1-\sqrt{1-x^4}}{x^2}\right| + C$

113. (b) $\frac{\pi}{4}$ 115. $x - \frac{1}{\sqrt{2}}\tan^{-1}(\sqrt{2}\tan x) + C$

Additional and Advanced Exercises, pp. 483–485

1. $x(\sin^{-1}x)^2 + 2(\sin^{-1}x)\sqrt{1-x^2} - 2x + C$

3. $\frac{x^2\sin^{-1}x}{2} + \frac{x\sqrt{1-x^2} - \sin^{-1}x}{4} + C$

5. $\frac{1}{2}\left(\ln\left(t - \sqrt{1-t^2}\right) - \sin^{-1}t\right) + C$

7. 0 9. $\ln(4) - 1$ 11. 1 13. $32\pi/35$ 15. 2π

17. (a) π (b) $\pi(2e-5)$

19. (b) $\pi\left(\frac{8(\ln 2)^2}{3} - \frac{16(\ln 2)}{9} + \frac{16}{27}\right)$ 21. $\left(\frac{e^2+1}{4}, \frac{e-2}{2}\right)$

23. $\sqrt{1+e^2} - \ln\left(\frac{\sqrt{1+e^2}}{e} + \frac{1}{e}\right) - \sqrt{2} + \ln(1+\sqrt{2})$

25. $\frac{12\pi}{5}$ 27. $a = \frac{1}{2}, -\frac{\ln 2}{4}$ 29. $\frac{1}{2} < p \le 1$

CHAPTER 9

Section 9.1, pp. 495–498

1. $a_1 = 0, a_2 = -1/4, a_3 = -2/9, a_4 = -3/16$

3. $a_1 = 1, a_2 = -1/3, a_3 = 1/5, a_4 = -1/7$

5. $a_1 = 1/2, a_2 = 1/2, a_3 = 1/2, a_4 = 1/2$

7. $1, \frac{3}{2}, \frac{7}{4}, \frac{15}{8}, \frac{31}{16}, \frac{63}{32}, \frac{127}{64}, \frac{255}{128}, \frac{511}{256}, \frac{1023}{512}$

9. $2, 1, -\frac{1}{2}, -\frac{1}{4}, \frac{1}{8}, \frac{1}{16}, -\frac{1}{32}, -\frac{1}{64}, \frac{1}{128}, \frac{1}{256}$

11. 1, 1, 2, 3, 5, 8, 13, 21, 34, 55 13. $a_n = (-1)^{n+1}, n \ge 1$

15. $a_n = (-1)^{n+1}(n)^2, n \ge 1$ 17. $a_n = \frac{2^{n-1}}{3(n+2)}, n \ge 1$

19. $a_n = n^2 - 1, n \ge 1$ 21. $a_n = 4n - 3, n \ge 1$

23. $a_n = \frac{3n+2}{n!}, n \ge 1$ 25. $a_n = \frac{1+(-1)^{n+1}}{2}, n \ge 1$

27. Converges, 2 29. Converges, −1 31. Converges, −5

33. Diverges **35.** Diverges **37.** Converges, $1/2$
39. Converges, 0 **41.** Converges, $\sqrt{2}$ **43.** Converges, 1
45. Converges, 0 **47.** Converges, 0 **49.** Converges, 0
51. Converges, 1 **53.** Converges, e^7 **55.** Converges, 1
57. Converges, 1 **59.** Diverges **61.** Converges, 4
63. Converges, 0 **65.** Diverges **67.** Converges, e^{-1}
69. Converges, $e^{2/3}$ **71.** Converges, $x\ (x > 0)$
73. Converges, 0 **75.** Converges, 1 **77.** Converges, $1/2$
79. Converges, 1 **81.** Converges, $\pi/2$ **83.** Converges, 0
85. Converges, 0 **87.** Converges, $1/2$ **89.** Converges, 0
91. 8 **93.** 4 **95.** 5 **97.** $1 + \sqrt{2}$ **99.** $x_n = 2^{n-2}$
101. **(a)** $f(x) = x^2 - 2,\ 1.414213562 \approx \sqrt{2}$
(b) $f(x) = \tan(x) - 1,\ 0.7853981635 \approx \pi/4$
(c) $f(x) = e^x$, diverges
103. **(b)** 1 **111.** Nondecreasing, bounded
113. Not nondecreasing, bounded
115. Converges, nondecreasing sequence theorem
117. Converges, nondecreasing sequence theorem
119. Diverges, definition of divergence **121.** Converges
123. Converges **133.** **(b)** $\sqrt{3}$

Section 9.2, pp. 505–506

1. $s_n = \dfrac{2(1 - (1/3)^n)}{1 - (1/3)}, 3$ **3.** $s_n = \dfrac{1 - (-1/2)^n}{1 - (-1/2)}, 2/3$

5. $s_n = \dfrac{1}{2} - \dfrac{1}{n + 2}, \dfrac{1}{2}$ **7.** $1 - \dfrac{1}{4} + \dfrac{1}{16} - \dfrac{1}{64} + \cdots, \dfrac{4}{5}$

9. $-\dfrac{3}{4} + \dfrac{9}{16} + \dfrac{57}{64} + \dfrac{249}{256} + \cdots$, diverges.

11. $(5 + 1) + \left(\dfrac{5}{2} + \dfrac{1}{3}\right) + \left(\dfrac{5}{4} + \dfrac{1}{9}\right) + \left(\dfrac{5}{8} + \dfrac{1}{27}\right) + \cdots, \dfrac{23}{2}$

13. $(1 + 1) + \left(\dfrac{1}{2} - \dfrac{1}{5}\right) + \left(\dfrac{1}{4} + \dfrac{1}{25}\right) + \left(\dfrac{1}{8} - \dfrac{1}{125}\right) + \cdots, \dfrac{17}{6}$

15. Converges, $5/3$ **17.** Converges, $1/7$ **19.** $23/99$ **21.** $7/9$
23. $1/15$ **25.** $41333/33300$ **27.** Diverges
29. Inconclusive **31.** Diverges **33.** Diverges

35. $s_n = 1 - \dfrac{1}{n + 1}$; converges, 1 **37.** $s_n = \ln\sqrt{n + 1}$; diverges

39. $s_n = \dfrac{\pi}{3} - \cos^{-1}\left(\dfrac{1}{n + 2}\right)$; converges, $-\dfrac{\pi}{6}$

41. 1 **43.** 5 **45.** 1 **47.** $-\dfrac{1}{\ln 2}$ **49.** Converges, $2 + \sqrt{2}$

51. Converges, 1 **53.** Diverges **55.** Converges, $\dfrac{e^2}{e^2 - 1}$

57. Converges, $2/9$ **59.** Converges, $3/2$ **61.** Diverges
63. Converges, 4 **65.** Diverges **67.** Converges, $\dfrac{\pi}{\pi - e}$
69. $a = 1, r = -x$; converges to $1/(1 + x)$ for $|x| < 1$
71. $a = 3, r = (x - 1)/2$; converges to $6/(3 - x)$ for x in $(-1, 3)$

73. $|x| < \dfrac{1}{2}, \dfrac{1}{1 - 2x}$ **75.** $-2 < x < 0, \dfrac{1}{2 + x}$

77. $x \neq (2k + 1)\dfrac{\pi}{2}$, k an integer; $\dfrac{1}{1 - \sin x}$

79. **(a)** $\displaystyle\sum_{n=-2}^{\infty} \frac{1}{(n + 4)(n + 5)}$ **(b)** $\displaystyle\sum_{n=0}^{\infty} \frac{1}{(n + 2)(n + 3)}$

(c) $\displaystyle\sum_{n=5}^{\infty} \frac{1}{(n - 3)(n - 2)}$

89. **(a)** $r = 3/5$ **(b)** $r = -3/10$

91. $|r| < 1, \dfrac{1 + 2r}{1 - r^2}$ **93.** $8\ \text{m}^2$

Section 9.3, pp. 511–512

1. Converges **3.** Converges **5.** Converges **7.** Diverges
9. Converges **11.** Converges; geometric series, $r = \dfrac{1}{10} < 1$
13. Diverges; $\lim\limits_{n\to\infty} \dfrac{n}{n + 1} = 1 \neq 0$ **15.** Diverges; p-series, $p < 1$

17. Converges; geometric series, $r = \dfrac{1}{8} < 1$
19. Diverges; Integral Test
21. Converges; geometric series, $r = 2/3 < 1$

23. Diverges; Integral Test **25.** Diverges; $\lim\limits_{n\to\infty} \dfrac{2^n}{n + 1} \neq 0$

27. Diverges; $\lim_{n\to\infty}\left(\sqrt{n}/\ln n\right) \neq 0$

29. Diverges; geometric series, $r = \dfrac{1}{\ln 2} > 1$

31. Converges; Integral Test **33.** Diverges; nth-Term Test
35. Converges; Integral Test **37.** Converges; Integral Test
39. Converges; Integral Test **41.** $a = 1$
43. **(a)**

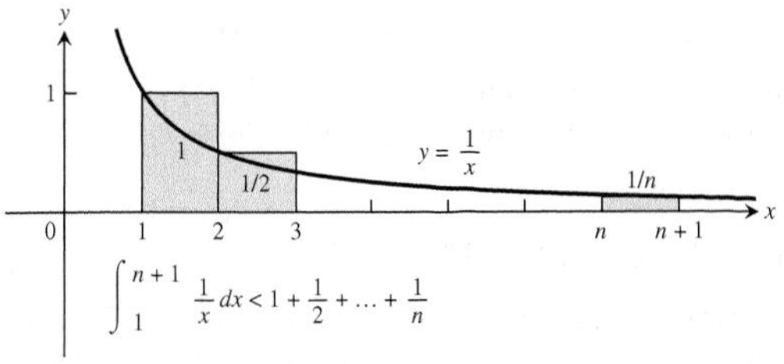

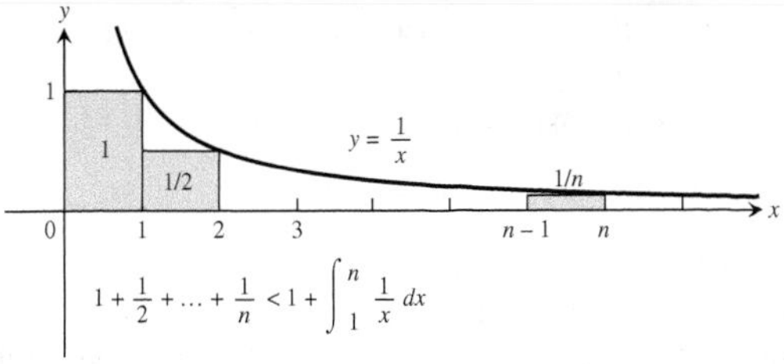

(b) ≈ 41.55
45. True **47.** **(b)** $n \geq 251{,}415$

49. $s_8 = \displaystyle\sum_{n=1}^{8} \frac{1}{n^3} \approx 1.195$ **51.** 10^{60}

59. **(a)** $1.20166 \leq S \leq 1.20253$ **(b)** $S \approx 1.2021$, error < 0.0005

Section 9.4, pp. 516–517

1. Converges; compare with $\Sigma\,(1/n^2)$
3. Diverges; compare with $\Sigma\left(1/\sqrt{n}\right)$
5. Converges; compare with $\Sigma\,(1/n^{3/2})$
7. Converges; compare with $\Sigma\sqrt{\dfrac{n + 4n}{n^4 + 0}} = \sqrt{5}\,\Sigma\,\dfrac{1}{n^{3/2}}$
9. Converges **11.** Diverges; limit comparison with $\Sigma\,(1/n)$
13. Diverges; limit comparison with $\Sigma\left(1/\sqrt{n}\right)$ **15.** Diverges
17. Diverges; limit comparison with $\Sigma\left(1/\sqrt{n}\right)$

19. Converges; compare with $\sum(1/2^n)$
21. Diverges; nth-Term Test
23. Converges; compare with $\sum(1/n^2)$
25. Converges; $\left(\frac{n}{3n+1}\right)^n < \left(\frac{n}{3n}\right)^n = \left(\frac{1}{3}\right)^n$
27. Diverges; direct comparison with $\sum(1/n)$
29. Diverges; limit comparison with $\sum(1/n)$
31. Diverges; limit comparison with $\sum(1/n)$
33. Converges; compare with $\sum(1/n^{3/2})$
35. Converges; $\frac{1}{n2^n} \le \frac{1}{2^n}$ **37.** Converges; $\frac{1}{3^{n-1}+1} < \frac{1}{3^{n-1}}$
39. Converges; comparison with $\sum(1/5n^2)$
41. Diverges; comparison with $\sum(1/n)$
43. Converges; comparison with $\sum \frac{1}{n(n-1)}$ or limit comparison with $\sum(1/n^2)$
45. Diverges; limit comparison with $\sum(1/n)$
47. Converges; $\frac{\tan^{-1} n}{n^{1.1}} < \frac{\pi/2}{n^{1.1}}$
49. Converges; compare with $\sum(1/n^2)$
51. Diverges; limit comparison with $\sum(1/n)$
53. Converges; limit comparison with $\sum(1/n^2)$
63. Converges **65.** Converges **67.** Converges

Section 9.5, pp. 521–522

1. Converges **3.** Diverges **5.** Converges **7.** Converges
9. Converges **11.** Diverges **13.** Converges **15.** Converges
17. Converges; Ratio Test **19.** Diverges; Ratio Test
21. Converges; Ratio Test
23. Converges; compare with $\sum(3/(1.25)^n)$
25. Diverges; $\lim_{n\to\infty}\left(1 - \frac{3}{n}\right)^n = e^{-3} \ne 0$
27. Converges; compare with $\sum(1/n^2)$
29. Diverges; compare with $\sum(1/(2n))$
31. Diverges; compare with $\sum(1/n)$ **33.** Converges; Ratio Test
35. Converges; Ratio Test **37.** Converges; Ratio Test
39. Converges; Root Test **41.** Converges; compare with $\sum(1/n^2)$
43. Converges; Ratio Test **45.** Converges; Ratio Test
47. Diverges; Ratio Test **49.** Converges; Ratio Test
51. Converges; Ratio Test **53.** Diverges; $a_n = \left(\frac{1}{3}\right)^{(1/n!)} \to 1$
55. Converges; Ratio Test **57.** Diverges; Root Test
59. Converges; Root Test **61.** Converges; Ratio Test **65.** Yes

Section 9.6, pp. 527–528

1. Converges by Theorem 16
3. Converges; Alternating Series Test
5. Converges; Alternating Series Test
7. Diverges; $a_n \nrightarrow 0$
9. Diverges; $a_n \nrightarrow 0$
11. Converges; Alternating Series Test
13. Converges by Theorem 16
15. Converges absolutely. Series of absolute values is a convergent geometric series.
17. Converges conditionally; $1/\sqrt{n} \to 0$ but $\sum_{n=1}^{\infty} \frac{1}{\sqrt{n}}$ diverges.
19. Converges absolutely; compare with $\sum_{n=1}^{\infty}(1/n^2)$.
21. Converges conditionally; $1/(n+3) \to 0$ but $\sum_{n=1}^{\infty} \frac{1}{n+3}$ diverges (compare with $\sum_{n=1}^{\infty}(1/n)$).
23. Diverges; $\frac{3+n}{5+n} \to 1$
25. Converges conditionally; $\left(\frac{1}{n^2} + \frac{1}{n}\right) \to 0$ but $(1+n)/n^2 > 1/n$
27. Converges absolutely; Ratio Test
29. Converges absolutely by Integral Test **31.** Diverges; $a_n \nrightarrow 0$
33. Converges absolutely by Ratio Test
35. Converges absolutely since $\left|\frac{\cos n\pi}{n\sqrt{n}}\right| = \left|\frac{(-1)^{n+1}}{n^{3/2}}\right| = \frac{1}{n^{3/2}}$ (convergent p-series)
37. Converges absolutely by Root Test **39.** Diverges; $a_n \to \infty$
41. Converges conditionally; $\sqrt{n+1} - \sqrt{n} = 1/(\sqrt{n} + \sqrt{n+1}) \to 0$, but series of absolute values diverges (compare with $\sum(1/\sqrt{n})$).
43. Diverges, $a_n \to 1/2 \ne 0$
45. Converges absolutely; $\operatorname{sech} n = \frac{2}{e^n + e^{-n}} = \frac{2e^n}{e^{2n}+1} < \frac{2e^n}{e^{2n}} = \frac{2}{e^n}$, a term from a convergent geometric series.
47. Converges conditionally; $\sum(-1)\frac{1}{2(n+1)}$ converges by Alternating Series Test; $\sum \frac{1}{2(n+1)}$ diverges by limit comparison with $\sum(1/n)$.
49. $|\text{Error}| < 0.2$ **51.** $|\text{Error}| < 2 \times 10^{-11}$
53. $n \ge 31$ **55.** $n \ge 4$ **57.** 0.54030
59. (a) $a_n \ge a_{n+1}$ (b) $-1/2$

Section 9.7, pp. 536–538

1. (a) $1, -1 < x < 1$ (b) $-1 < x < 1$ (c) none
3. (a) $1/4, -1/2 < x < 0$ (b) $-1/2 < x < 0$ (c) none
5. (a) $10, -8 < x < 12$ (b) $-8 < x < 12$ (c) none
7. (a) $1, -1 < x < 1$ (b) $-1 < x < 1$ (c) none
9. (a) $3, -3 \le x \le 3$ (b) $-3 \le x \le 3$ (c) none
11. (a) ∞, for all x (b) for all x (c) none
13. (a) $1/2, -1/2 \le x < 1/2$ (b) $-1/2 < x < 1/2$ (c) $-1/2$
15. (a) $1, -1 \le x < 1$ (b) $-1 < x < 1$ (c) $x = -1$
17. (a) $5, -8 < x < 2$ (b) $-8 < x < 2$ (c) none
19. (a) $3, -3 < x < 3$ (b) $-3 < x < 3$ (c) none
21. (a) $1, -2 < x < 0$ (b) $-2 < x < 0$ (c) none
23. (a) $1, -1 < x < 1$ (b) $-1 < x < 1$ (c) none
25. (a) $0, x = 0$ (b) $x = 0$ (c) none
27. (a) $2, -4 < x \le 0$ (b) $-4 < x < 0$ (c) $x = 0$
29. (a) $1, -1 \le x \le 1$ (b) $-1 \le x \le 1$ (c) none
31. (a) $1/4, 1 \le x \le 3/2$ (b) $1 \le x \le 3/2$ (c) none
33. (a) ∞, for all x (b) for all x (c) none
35. (a) $1, -1 \le x < 1$ (b) $-1 < x < 1$ (c) -1
37. 3 **39.** 8 **41.** $-1/3 < x < 1/3$, $1/(1-3x)$
43. $-1 < x < 3$, $4/(3 + 2x - x^2)$
45. $0 < x < 16$, $2/(4 - \sqrt{x})$

47. $-\sqrt{2} < x < \sqrt{2},\ 3/(2 - x^2)$

49. $1 < x < 5,\ 2/(x - 1),\ 1 < x < 5,\ -2/(x - 1)^2$

51. **(a)** $\cos x = 1 - \frac{x^2}{2!} + \frac{x^4}{4!} - \frac{x^6}{6!} + \frac{x^8}{8!} - \frac{x^{10}}{10!} + \cdots;$ converges for all x

(b) Same answer as part (c)

(c) $2x - \frac{2^3x^3}{3!} + \frac{2^5x^5}{5!} - \frac{2^7x^7}{7!} + \frac{2^9x^9}{9!} - \frac{2^{11}x^{11}}{11!} + \cdots$

53. **(a)** $\frac{x^2}{2} + \frac{x^4}{12} + \frac{x^6}{45} + \frac{17x^8}{2520} + \frac{31x^{10}}{14175},\ -\frac{\pi}{2} < x < \frac{\pi}{2}$

(b) $1 + x^2 + \frac{2x^4}{3} + \frac{17x^6}{45} + \frac{62x^8}{315} + \cdots,\ -\frac{\pi}{2} < x < \frac{\pi}{2}$

Section 9.8, pp. 542–543

1. $P_0(x) = 1, P_1(x) = 1 + 2x, P_2(x) = 1 + 2x + 2x^2,$

$P_3(x) = 1 + 2x + 2x^2 + \frac{4}{3}x^3$

3. $P_0(x) = 0, P_1(x) = x - 1, P_2(x) = (x - 1) - \frac{1}{2}(x - 1)^2,$

$P_3(x) = (x - 1) - \frac{1}{2}(x - 1)^2 + \frac{1}{3}(x - 1)^3$

5. $P_0(x) = \frac{1}{2}, P_1(x) = \frac{1}{2} - \frac{1}{4}(x - 2),$

$P_2(x) = \frac{1}{2} - \frac{1}{4}(x - 2) + \frac{1}{8}(x - 2)^2,$

$P_3(x) = \frac{1}{2} - \frac{1}{4}(x - 2) + \frac{1}{8}(x - 2)^2 - \frac{1}{16}(x - 2)^3$

7. $P_0(x) = \frac{\sqrt{2}}{2}, P_1(x) = \frac{\sqrt{2}}{2} + \frac{\sqrt{2}}{2}\left(x - \frac{\pi}{4}\right),$

$P_2(x) = \frac{\sqrt{2}}{2} + \frac{\sqrt{2}}{2}\left(x - \frac{\pi}{4}\right) - \frac{\sqrt{2}}{4}\left(x - \frac{\pi}{4}\right)^2,$

$P_3(x) = \frac{\sqrt{2}}{2} + \frac{\sqrt{2}}{2}\left(x - \frac{\pi}{4}\right) - \frac{\sqrt{2}}{4}\left(x - \frac{\pi}{4}\right)^2 - \frac{\sqrt{2}}{12}\left(x - \frac{\pi}{4}\right)^3$

9. $P_0(x) = 2, P_1(x) = 2 + \frac{1}{4}(x - 4),$

$P_2(x) = 2 + \frac{1}{4}(x - 4) - \frac{1}{64}(x - 4)^2,$

$P_3(x) = 2 + \frac{1}{4}(x - 4) - \frac{1}{64}(x - 4)^2 + \frac{1}{512}(x - 4)^3$

11. $\sum_{n=0}^{\infty} \frac{(-x)^n}{n!} = 1 - x + \frac{x^2}{2!} - \frac{x^3}{3!} + \frac{x^4}{4!} - \cdots$

13. $\sum_{n=0}^{\infty} (-1)^n x^n = 1 - x + x^2 - x^3 + \cdots$

15. $\sum_{n=0}^{\infty} \frac{(-1)^n 3^{2n+1} x^{2n+1}}{(2n + 1)!}$ **17.** $7\sum_{n=0}^{\infty} \frac{(-1)^n x^{2n}}{(2n)!}$ **19.** $\sum_{n=0}^{\infty} \frac{x^{2n}}{(2n)!}$

21. $x^4 - 2x^3 - 5x + 4$

23. $8 + 10(x - 2) + 6(x - 2)^2 + (x - 2)^3$

25. $21 - 36(x + 2) + 25(x + 2)^2 - 8(x + 2)^3 + (x + 2)^4$

27. $\sum_{n=0}^{\infty} (-1)^n (n + 1)(x - 1)^n$ **29.** $\sum_{n=0}^{\infty} \frac{e^2}{n!}(x - 2)^n$

31. $\sum_{n=0}^{\infty} (-1)^{n+1} \frac{2^{2n}}{(2n)!}\left(x - \frac{\pi}{4}\right)^{2n}$

33. $-1 - 2x - \frac{5}{2}x^2 - \cdots, -1 < x < 1$

35. $x^2 - \frac{1}{2}x^3 + \frac{1}{6}x^4 + \cdots, -1 < x < 1$

41. $L(x) = 0, Q(x) = -x^2/2$ **43.** $L(x) = 1, Q(x) = 1 + x^2/2$

45. $L(x) = x, Q(x) = x$

Section 9.9, pp. 549–550

1. $\sum_{n=0}^{\infty} \frac{(-5x)^n}{n!} = 1 - 5x + \frac{5^2x^2}{2!} - \frac{5^3x^3}{3!} + \cdots$

3. $\sum_{n=0}^{\infty} \frac{5(-1)^n(-x)^{2n+1}}{(2n + 1)!} = \sum_{n=0}^{\infty} \frac{5(-1)^{n+1}x^{2n+1}}{(2n + 1)!}$

$= -5x + \frac{5x^3}{3!} - \frac{5x^5}{5!} + \frac{5x^7}{7!} + \cdots$

5. $\sum_{n=0}^{\infty} \frac{(-1)^n(5x^2)^{2n}}{(2n)!} = 1 - \frac{25x^4}{2!} + \frac{625x^8}{4!} - \cdots$

7. $\sum_{n=1}^{\infty} (-1)^{n+1} \frac{x^{2n}}{n} = x^2 - \frac{x^4}{2} + \frac{x^6}{3} - \frac{x^8}{4} + \cdots$

9. $\sum_{n=0}^{\infty} (-1)^n \left(\frac{3}{4}\right)^n x^{3n} = 1 - \frac{3}{4}x^3 + \frac{3^2}{4^2}x^6 - \frac{3^3}{4^3}x^9 + \cdots$

11. $\sum_{n=0}^{\infty} \frac{x^{n+1}}{n!} = x + x^2 + \frac{x^3}{2!} + \frac{x^4}{3!} + \frac{x^5}{4!} + \cdots$

13. $\sum_{n=2}^{\infty} \frac{(-1)^n x^{2n}}{(2n)!} = \frac{x^4}{4!} - \frac{x^6}{6!} + \frac{x^8}{8!} - \frac{x^{10}}{10!} + \cdots$

15. $x - \frac{\pi^2x^3}{2!} + \frac{\pi^4x^5}{4!} - \frac{\pi^6x^7}{6!} + \cdots = \sum_{n=0}^{\infty} \frac{(-1)^n\pi^{2n}x^{2n+1}}{(2n)!}$

17. $1 + \sum_{n=1}^{\infty} \frac{(-1)^n(2x)^{2n}}{2\cdot(2n)!} =$

$1 - \frac{(2x)^2}{2\cdot 2!} + \frac{(2x)^4}{2\cdot 4!} - \frac{(2x)^6}{2\cdot 6!} + \frac{(2x)^8}{2\cdot 8!} - \cdots$

19. $x^2\sum_{n=0}^{\infty} (2x)^n = x^2 + 2x^3 + 4x^4 + \cdots$

21. $\sum_{n=1}^{\infty} nx^{n-1} = 1 + 2x + 3x^2 + 4x^3 + \cdots$

23. $\sum_{n=1}^{\infty} (-1)^{n+1} \frac{x^{4n-1}}{2n - 1} = x^3 - \frac{x^7}{3} + \frac{x^{11}}{5} - \frac{x^{15}}{7} + \cdots$

25. $\sum_{n=0}^{\infty} \left(\frac{1}{n!} + (-1)^n\right)x^n = 2 + \frac{3}{2}x^2 - \frac{5}{6}x^3 + \frac{25}{24}x^4 - \cdots$

27. $\sum_{n=1}^{\infty} \frac{(-1)^{n-1}x^{2n+1}}{3n} = \frac{x^3}{3} - \frac{x^5}{6} + \frac{x^7}{9} - \cdots$

29. $x + x^2 + \frac{x^3}{3} - \frac{x^5}{30} + \cdots$

31. $x^2 - \frac{2}{3}x^4 + \frac{23}{45}x^6 - \frac{44}{105}x^8 + \cdots$

33. $1 + x + \frac{1}{2}x^2 - \frac{1}{8}x^4 + \cdots$

35. $|\text{Error}| \le \frac{1}{10^4\cdot 4!} < 4.2 \times 10^{-6}$

37. $|x| < (0.06)^{1/5} < 0.56968$

39. $|\text{Error}| < (10^{-3})^3/6 < 1.67 \times 10^{-10}, \quad -10^{-3} < x < 0$

41. $|\text{Error}| < (3^{0.1})(0.1)^3/6 < 1.87 \times 10^{-4}$

49. **(a)** $Q(x) = 1 + kx + \frac{k(k - 1)}{2}x^2$ **(b)** $0 \le x < 100^{-1/3}$

Section 9.10, pp. 556–558

1. $1 + \frac{x}{2} - \frac{x^2}{8} + \frac{x^3}{16}$ **3.** $1 + \frac{1}{2}x + \frac{3}{8}x^2 + \frac{5}{16}x^3 + \cdots$

5. $1 - x + \frac{3x^2}{4} - \frac{x^3}{2}$ **7.** $1 - \frac{x^3}{2} + \frac{3x^6}{8} - \frac{5x^9}{16}$

9. $1 + \frac{1}{2x} - \frac{1}{8x^2} + \frac{1}{16x^3}$

11. $(1 + x)^4 = 1 + 4x + 6x^2 + 4x^3 + x^4$

13. $(1 - 2x)^3 = 1 - 6x + 12x^2 - 8x^3$

15. 0.00267 **17.** 0.10000 **19.** 0.09994 **21.** 0.10000

23. $\frac{1}{13 \cdot 6!} \approx 0.00011$ **25.** $\frac{x^3}{3} - \frac{x^7}{7 \cdot 3!} + \frac{x^{11}}{11 \cdot 5!}$

27. **(a)** $\frac{x^2}{2} - \frac{x^4}{12}$

(b) $\frac{x^2}{2} - \frac{x^4}{3 \cdot 4} + \frac{x^6}{5 \cdot 6} - \frac{x^8}{7 \cdot 8} + \cdots + (-1)^{15}\frac{x^{32}}{31 \cdot 32}$

29. $1/2$ **31.** $-1/24$ **33.** $1/3$ **35.** -1 **37.** 2

39. $3/2$ **41.** e **43.** $\cos\frac{3}{4}$ **45.** $\sqrt{3}/2$ **47.** $\frac{x^3}{1 - x}$

49. $\frac{x^3}{1 + x^2}$ **51.** $\frac{-1}{(1 + x)^2}$ **55.** 500 terms **57.** 4 terms

59. **(a)** $x + \frac{x^3}{6} + \frac{3x^5}{40} + \frac{5x^7}{112}$, radius of convergence = 1

(b) $\frac{\pi}{2} - x - \frac{x^3}{6} - \frac{3x^5}{40} - \frac{5x^7}{112}$

61. $1 - 2x + 3x^2 - 4x^3 + \cdots$

67. **(a)** -1 **(b)** $(1/\sqrt{2})(1 + i)$ **(c)** $-i$

71. $x + x^2 + \frac{1}{3}x^3 - \frac{1}{30}x^5 + \cdots$, for all x

Practice Exercises, pp. 559–561

1. Converges to 1 **3.** Converges to -1 **5.** Diverges
7. Converges to 0 **9.** Converges to 1 **11.** Converges to e^{-5}
13. Converges to 3 **15.** Converges to ln 2 **17.** Diverges
19. $1/6$ **21.** $3/2$ **23.** $e/(e - 1)$ **25.** Diverges
27. Converges conditionally **29.** Converges conditionally
31. Converges absolutely **33.** Converges absolutely
35. Converges absolutely **37.** Converges absolutely
39. Converges absolutely
41. **(a)** $3, -7 \le x < -1$ **(b)** $-7 < x < -1$ **(c)** $x = -7$
43. **(a)** $1/3, 0 \le x \le 2/3$ **(b)** $0 \le x \le 2/3$ **(c)** None
45. **(a)** ∞, for all x **(b)** For all x **(c)** None
47. **(a)** $\sqrt{3}, -\sqrt{3} < x < \sqrt{3}$ **(b)** $-\sqrt{3} < x < \sqrt{3}$
(c) None
49. **(a)** $e, -e < x < e$ **(b)** $-e < x < e$ **(c)** Empty set

51. $\frac{1}{1 + x}, \frac{1}{4}, \frac{4}{5}$ **53.** $\sin x, \pi, 0$ **55.** e^x, ln 2, 2 **57.** $\sum_{n=0}^{\infty} 2^n x^n$

59. $\sum_{n=0}^{\infty} \frac{(-1)^n \pi^{2n+1} x^{2n+1}}{(2n + 1)!}$ **61.** $\sum_{n=0}^{\infty} \frac{(-1)^n x^{10n/3}}{(2n)!}$ **63.** $\sum_{n=0}^{\infty} \frac{((\pi x)/2)^n}{n!}$

65. $2 - \frac{(x + 1)}{2 \cdot 1!} + \frac{3(x + 1)^2}{2^3 \cdot 2!} + \frac{9(x + 1)^3}{2^5 \cdot 3!} + \cdots$

67. $\frac{1}{4} - \frac{1}{4^2}(x - 3) + \frac{1}{4^3}(x - 3)^2 - \frac{1}{4^4}(x - 3)^3$

69. 0.4849171431 **71.** 0.4872223583 **73.** $7/2$ **75.** $1/12$

77. -2 **79.** $r = -3, s = 9/2$ **81.** $2/3$

83. $\ln\left(\frac{n + 1}{2n}\right)$; the series converges to $\ln\left(\frac{1}{2}\right)$.

85. **(a)** ∞ **(b)** $a = 1, b = 0$ **87.** It converges.

Additional and Advanced Exercises, pp. 561–562

1. Converges; Comparison Test **3.** Diverges; nth-Term Test
5. Converges; Comparison Test **7.** Diverges; nth-Term Test

9. With $a = \pi/3$, $\cos x = \frac{1}{2} - \frac{\sqrt{3}}{2}(x - \pi/3) - \frac{1}{4}(x - \pi/3)^2 + \frac{\sqrt{3}}{12}(x - \pi/3)^3 + \cdots$

11. With $a = 0$, $e^x = 1 + x + \frac{x^2}{2!} + \frac{x^3}{3!} + \cdots$

13. With $a = 22\pi$, $\cos x = 1 - \frac{1}{2}(x - 22\pi)^2 + \frac{1}{4!}(x - 22\pi)^4 - \frac{1}{6!}(x - 22\pi)^6 + \cdots$

15. Converges, limit $= b$ **17.** $\pi/2$ **21.** $b = \pm\frac{1}{5}$

23. $a = 2, L = -7/6$ **27.** **(b)** Yes

CHAPTER 10

Section 10.1, pp. 568–570

1.

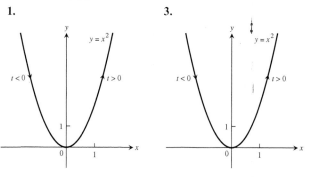

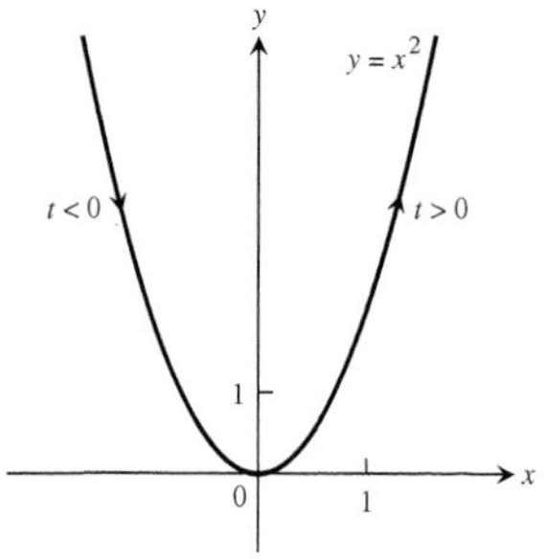

3.

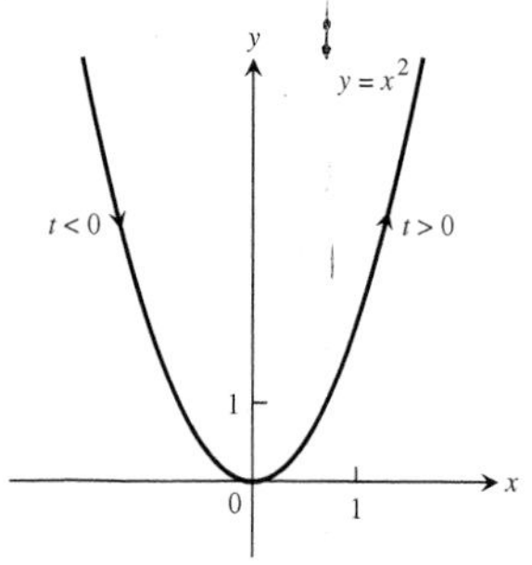

5.

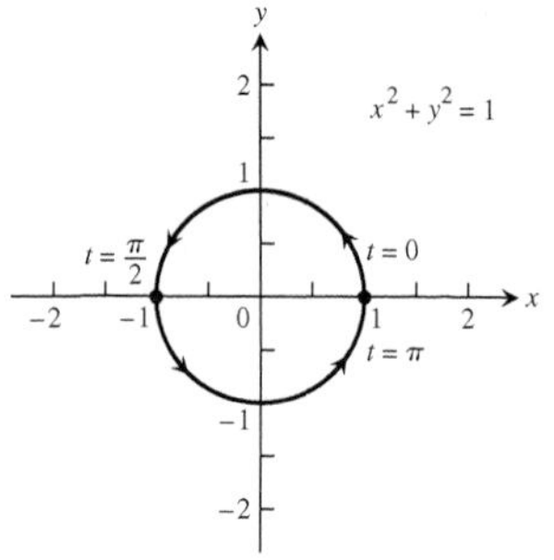

7.

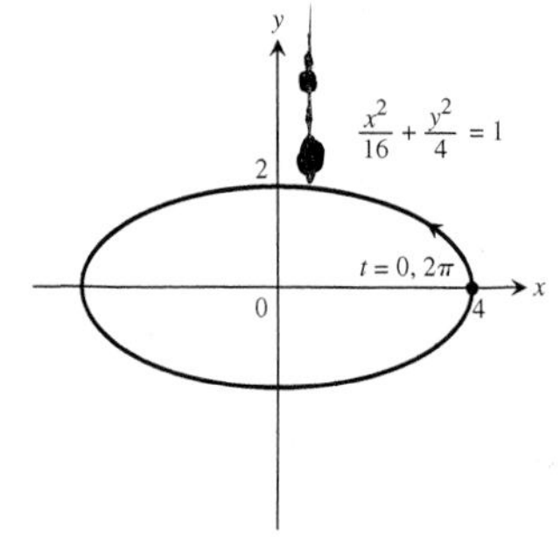

9.

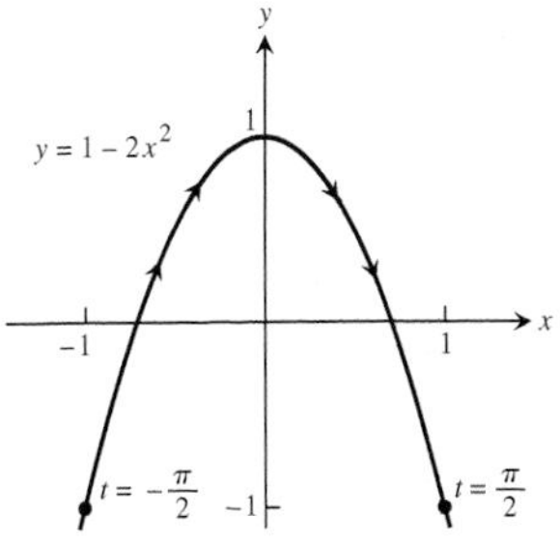

11.

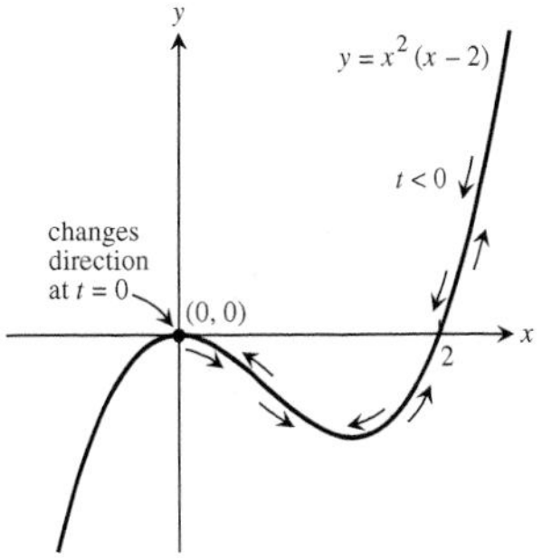

13.

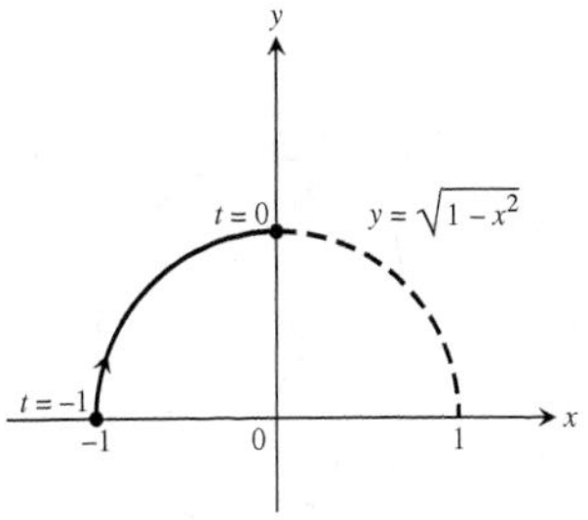

15.

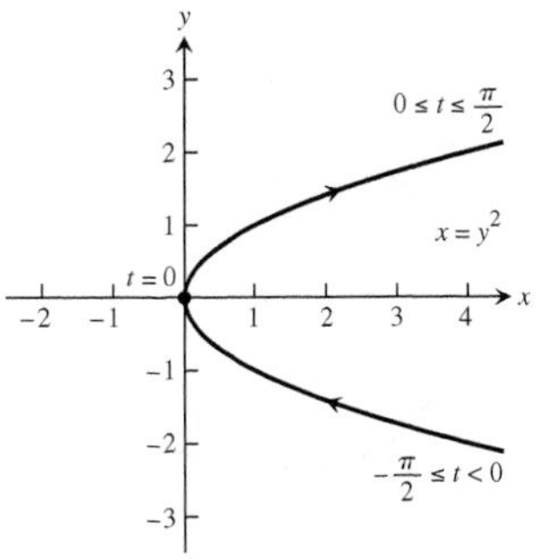

17.

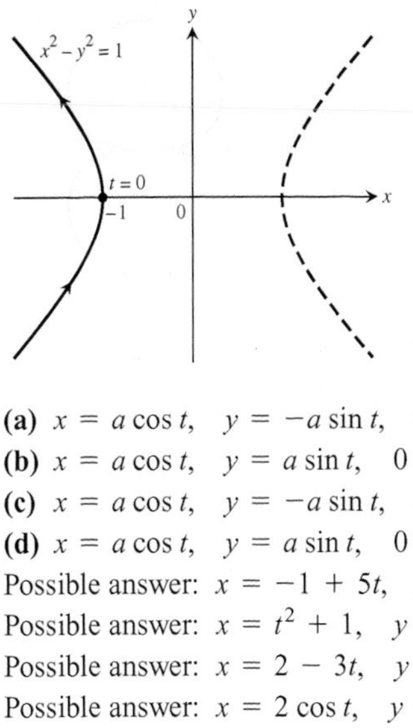

19. **(a)** $x = a\cos t,\quad y = -a\sin t,\quad 0 \le t \le 2\pi$
(b) $x = a\cos t,\quad y = a\sin t,\quad 0 \le t \le 2\pi$
(c) $x = a\cos t,\quad y = -a\sin t,\quad 0 \le t \le 4\pi$
(d) $x = a\cos t,\quad y = a\sin t,\quad 0 \le t \le 4\pi$

21. Possible answer: $x = -1 + 5t,\quad y = -3 + 4t,\quad 0 \le t \le 1$

23. Possible answer: $x = t^2 + 1,\quad y = t,\quad t \le 0$

25. Possible answer: $x = 2 - 3t,\quad y = 3 - 4t,\quad t \ge 0$

27. Possible answer: $x = 2\cos t,\quad y = 2\,|\sin t|,\quad 0 \le t \le 4\pi$

29. Possible answer: $x = \dfrac{-at}{\sqrt{1 + t^2}},\quad y = \dfrac{a}{\sqrt{1 + t^2}},$
$-\infty < t < \infty$

31. Possible answer: $x = \dfrac{4}{1 + 2\tan\theta},\quad y = \dfrac{4\tan\theta}{1 + 2\tan\theta},$
$0 \le \theta < \pi/2$ and $x = 0, y = 2$ if $\theta = \pi/2$

33. Possible answer: $x = 2 - \cos t,\quad y = \sin t,\quad 0 \le t \le 2\pi$

35. $x = 2\cot t,\quad y = 2\sin^2 t,\quad 0 < t < \pi$

37. $x = a\sin^2 t\tan t,\quad y = a\,\sin^2 t,\quad 0 \le t < \pi/2$ **39.** $(1, 1)$

Section 10.2, pp. 577–579

1. $y = -x + 2\sqrt{2},\quad \dfrac{d^2y}{dx^2} = -\sqrt{2}$

3. $y = -\dfrac{1}{2}x + 2\sqrt{2},\quad \dfrac{d^2y}{dx^2} = -\dfrac{\sqrt{2}}{4}$

5. $y = x + \dfrac{1}{4},\quad \dfrac{d^2y}{dx^2} = -2$ **7.** $y = 2x - \sqrt{3},\quad \dfrac{d^2y}{dx^2} = -3\sqrt{3}$

9. $y = x - 4,\quad \dfrac{d^2y}{dx^2} = \dfrac{1}{2}$

11. $y = \sqrt{3}x - \dfrac{\pi\sqrt{3}}{3} + 2,\quad \dfrac{d^2y}{dx^2} = -4$

13. $y = 9x - 1,\quad \dfrac{d^2y}{dx^2} = 108$ **15.** $-\dfrac{3}{16}$ **17.** -6

19. 1 **21.** $3a^2\pi$ **23.** $ab\pi$ **25.** 4 **27.** 12

29. π^2 **31.** $8\pi^2$ **33.** $\dfrac{52\pi}{3}$ **35.** $3\pi\sqrt{5}$

37. $(\bar{x}, \bar{y}) = \left(\dfrac{12}{\pi} - \dfrac{24}{\pi^2}, \dfrac{24}{\pi^2} - 2\right)$

39. $(\bar{x}, \bar{y}) = \left(\dfrac{1}{3}, \pi - \dfrac{4}{3}\right)$ **41.** **(a)** π **(b)** π

43. **(a)** $x = 1,\quad y = 0,\quad \dfrac{dy}{dx} = \dfrac{1}{2}$ **(b)** $x = 0,\quad y = 3,\quad \dfrac{dy}{dx} = 0$
(c) $x = \dfrac{\sqrt{3} - 1}{2},\quad y = \dfrac{3 - \sqrt{3}}{2},\quad \dfrac{dy}{dx} = \dfrac{2\sqrt{3} - 1}{\sqrt{3} - 2}$

45. $\left(\dfrac{\sqrt{2}}{2}, 1\right),\quad y = 2x$ at $t = 0,\quad y = -2x$ at $t = \pi$

47. **(a)** $8a$ **(b)** $\dfrac{64\pi}{3}$

Section 10.3, pp. 582–583

1. a, e; b, g; c, h; d, f **3.**

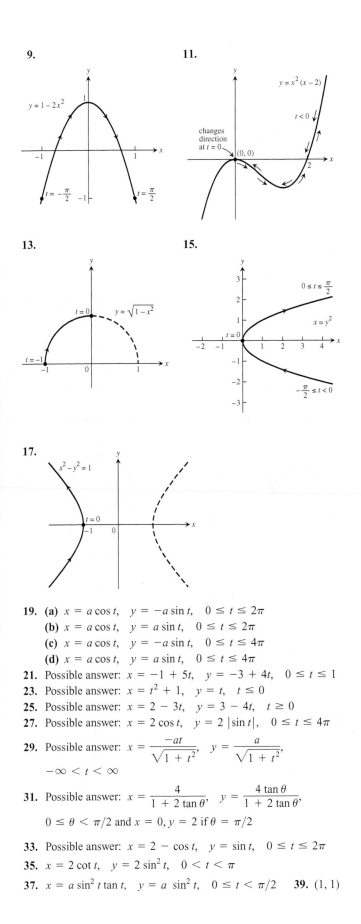

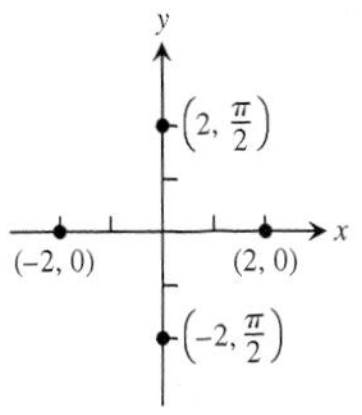

(a) $\left(2, \dfrac{\pi}{2} + 2n\pi\right)$ and $\left(-2, \dfrac{\pi}{2} + (2n + 1)\pi\right)$, n an integer
(b) $(2, 2n\pi)$ and $(-2, (2n + 1)\pi)$, n an integer
(c) $\left(2, \dfrac{3\pi}{2} + 2n\pi\right)$ and $\left(-2, \dfrac{3\pi}{2} + (2n + 1)\pi\right)$, n an integer
(d) $(2, (2n + 1)\pi)$ and $(-2, 2n\pi)$, n an integer

5. **(a)** $(3, 0)$ **(b)** $(-3, 0)$ **(c)** $\left(-1, \sqrt{3}\right)$ **(d)** $\left(1, \sqrt{3}\right)$
(e) $(3, 0)$ **(f)** $\left(1, \sqrt{3}\right)$ **(g)** $(-3, 0)$ **(h)** $\left(-1, \sqrt{3}\right)$

7. **(a)** $\left(\sqrt{2}, \dfrac{\pi}{4}\right)$ **(b)** $(3, \pi)$
(c) $\left(2, \dfrac{11\pi}{6}\right)$ **(d)** $\left(5, \pi - \tan^{-1}\dfrac{4}{3}\right)$

9. **(a)** $\left(-3\sqrt{2}, \frac{5\pi}{4}\right)$ **(b)** $(-1, 0)$

(c) $\left(-2, \frac{5\pi}{3}\right)$ **(d)** $\left(-5, \pi - \tan^{-1}\frac{3}{4}\right)$

11.

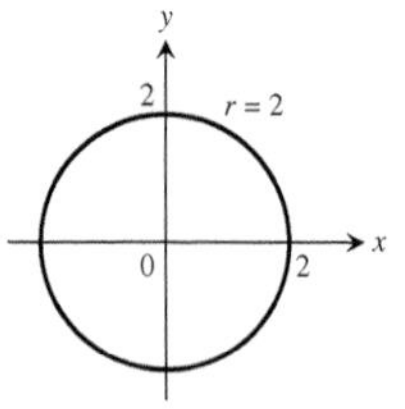

13.

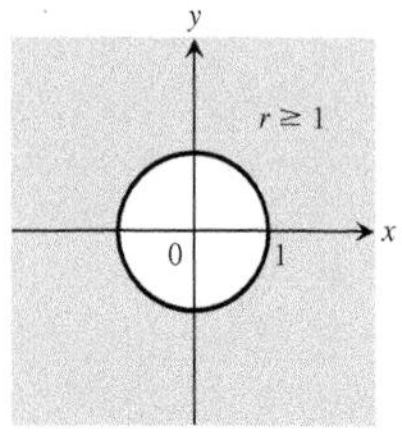

15.

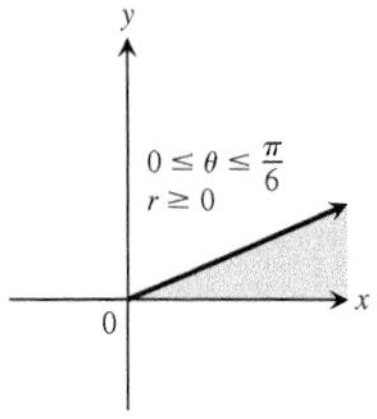

17.

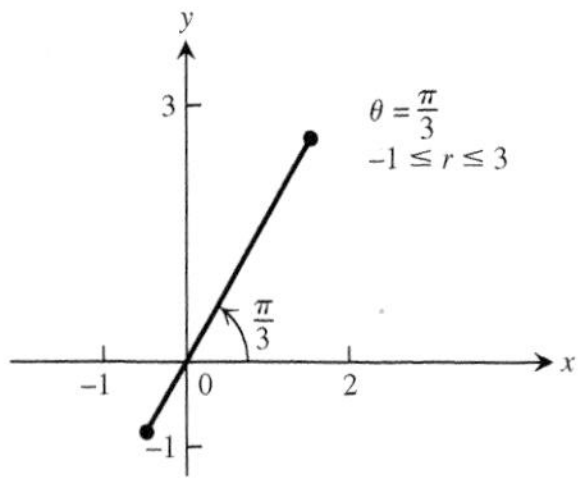

19.

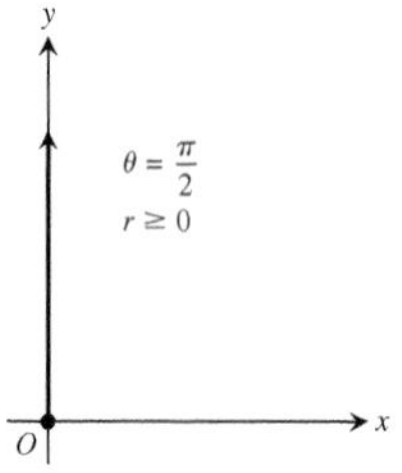

21.

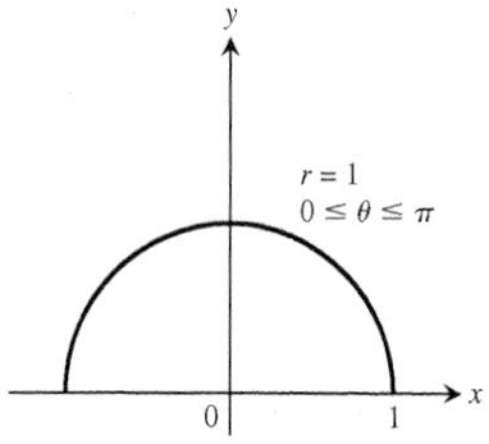

23.

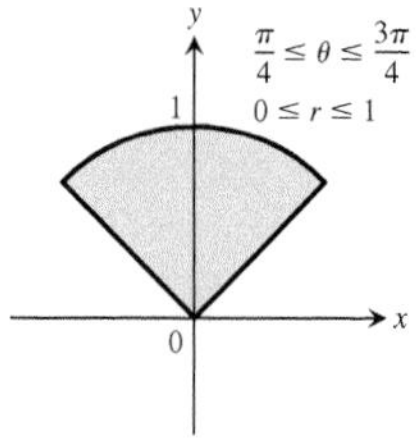

25.

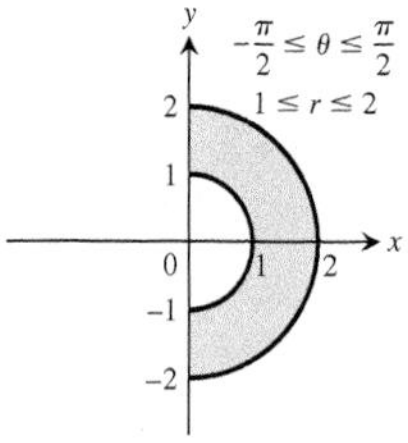

27. $x = 2$, vertical line through $(2, 0)$ **29.** $y = 0$, the x-axis
31. $y = 4$, horizontal line through $(0, 4)$
33. $x + y = 1$, line, $m = -1, b = 1$
35. $x^2 + y^2 = 1$, circle, $C(0, 0)$, radius 1
37. $y - 2x = 5$, line, $m = 2, b = 5$
39. $y^2 = x$, parabola, vertex $(0, 0)$, opens right
41. $y = e^x$, graph of natural exponential function
43. $x + y = \pm 1$, two straight lines of slope -1, y-intercepts $b = \pm 1$
45. $(x + 2)^2 + y^2 = 4$, circle, $C(-2, 0)$, radius 2
47. $x^2 + (y - 4)^2 = 16$, circle, $C(0, 4)$, radius 4
49. $(x - 1)^2 + (y - 1)^2 = 2$, circle, $C(1, 1)$, radius $\sqrt{2}$
51. $\sqrt{3}y + x = 4$ **53.** $r\cos\theta = 7$ **55.** $\theta = \pi/4$
57. $r = 2$ or $r = -2$ **59.** $4r^2\cos^2\theta + 9r^2\sin^2\theta = 36$
61. $r\sin^2\theta = 4\cos\theta$ **63.** $r = 4\sin\theta$
65. $r^2 = 6r\cos\theta - 2r\sin\theta - 6$ **67.** $(0, \theta)$, where θ is any angle

Section 10.4, pp. 586–587

1. x-axis

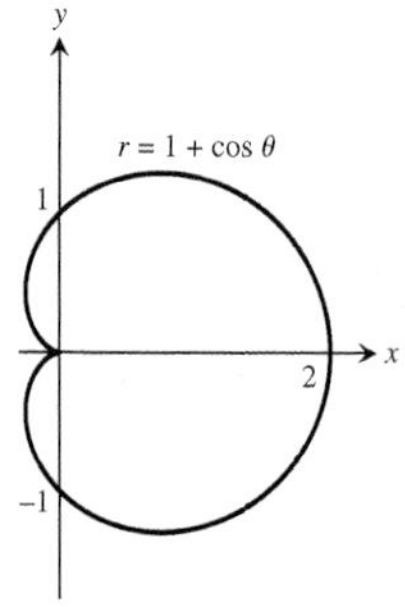

3. y-axis

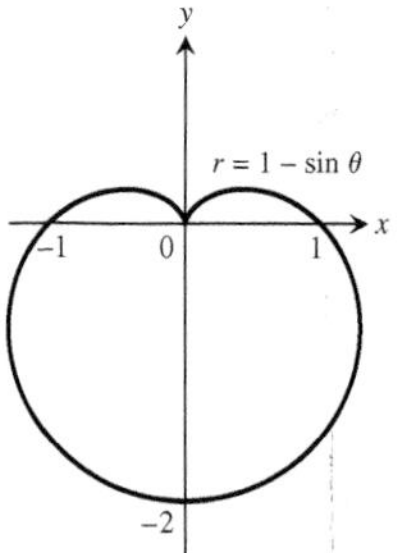

5. y-axis

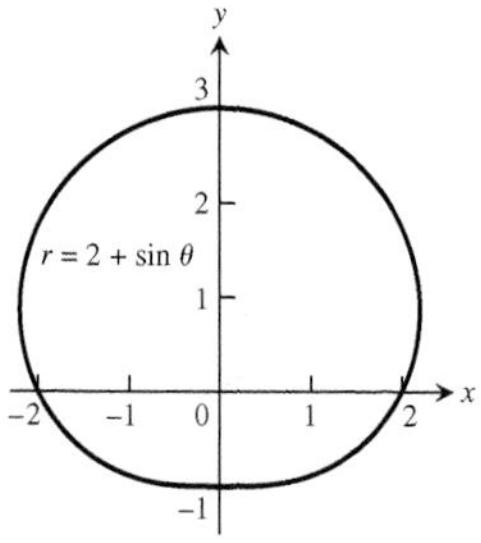

7. x-axis, y-axis, origin

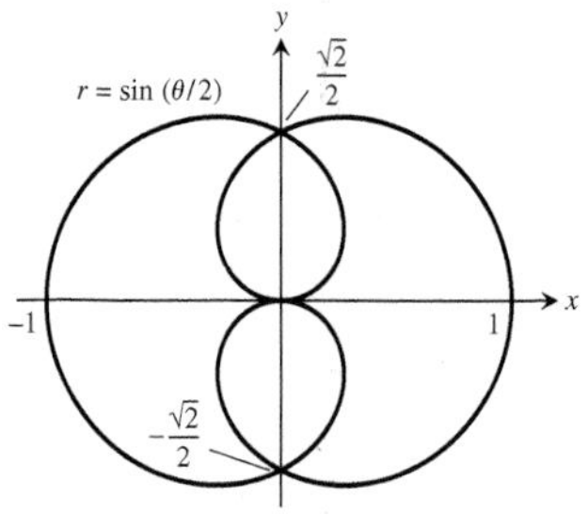

9. x-axis, y-axis, origin

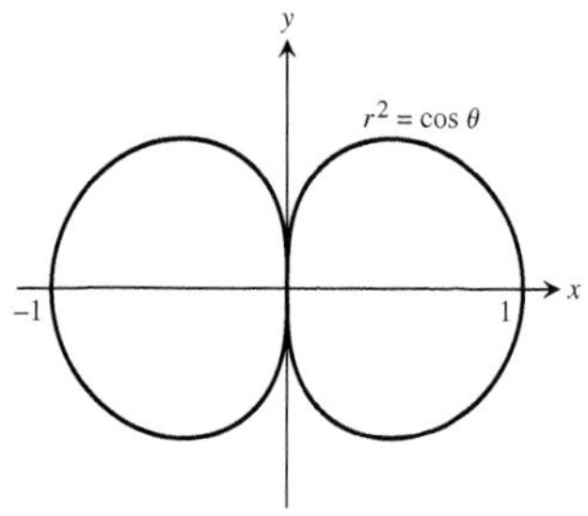

11. y-axis, x-axis, origin

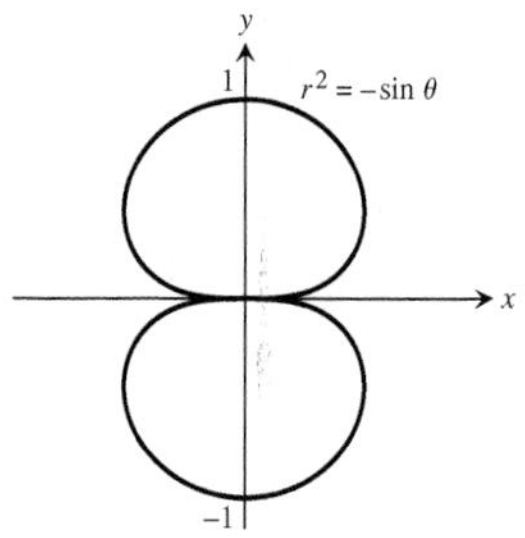

13. x-axis, y-axis, origin **15.** Origin
17. The slope at $(-1, \pi/2)$ is -1, at $(-1, -\pi/2)$ is 1.

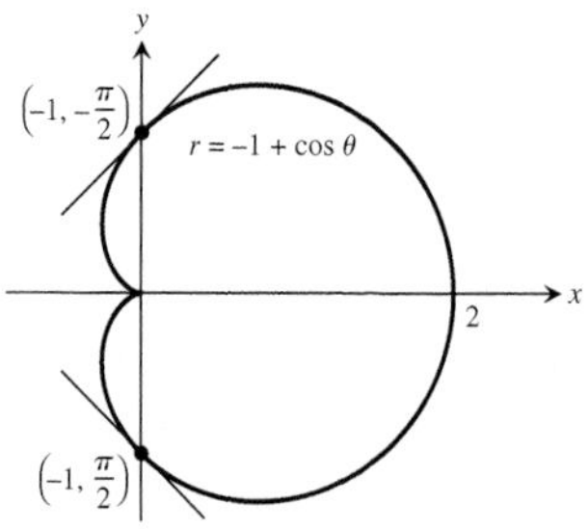

19. The slope at $(1, \pi/4)$ is -1, at $(-1, -\pi/4)$ is 1, at $(-1, 3\pi/4)$ is 1, at $(1, -3\pi/4)$ is -1.

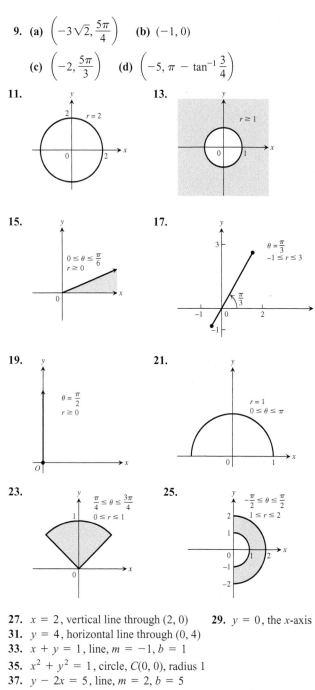

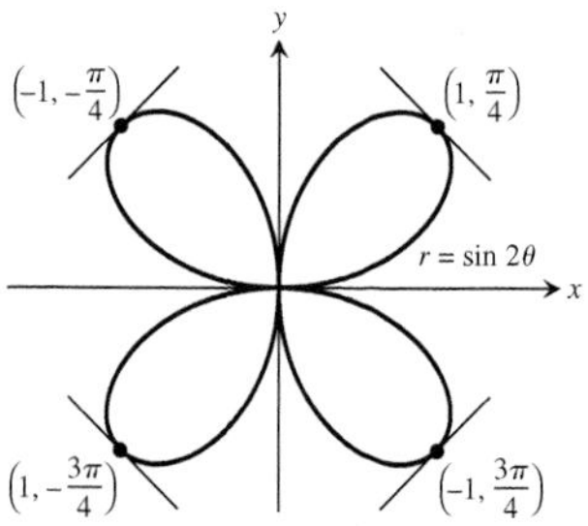

21. **(a)**

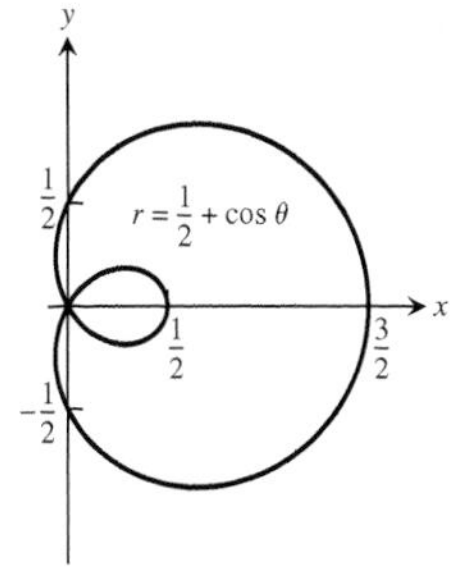

(b)

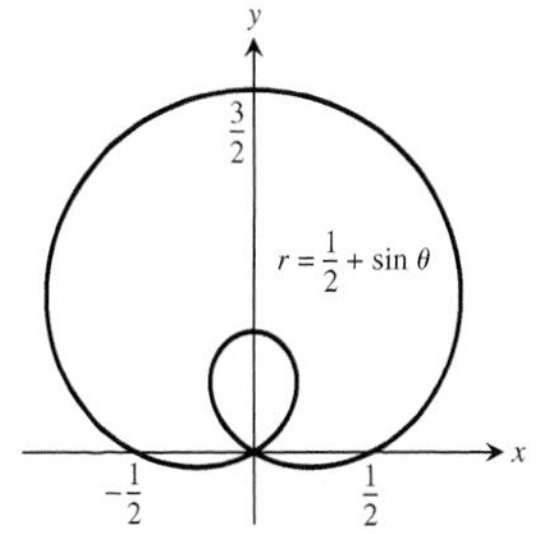

23. **(a)**

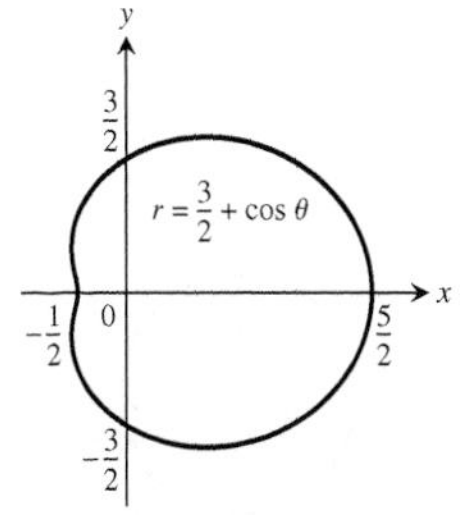

(b)

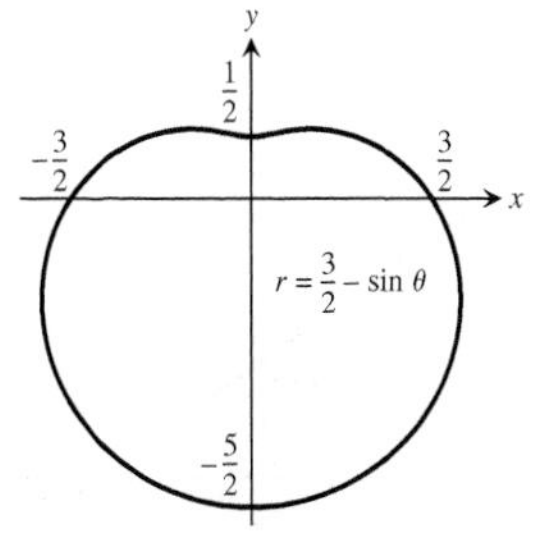

25.

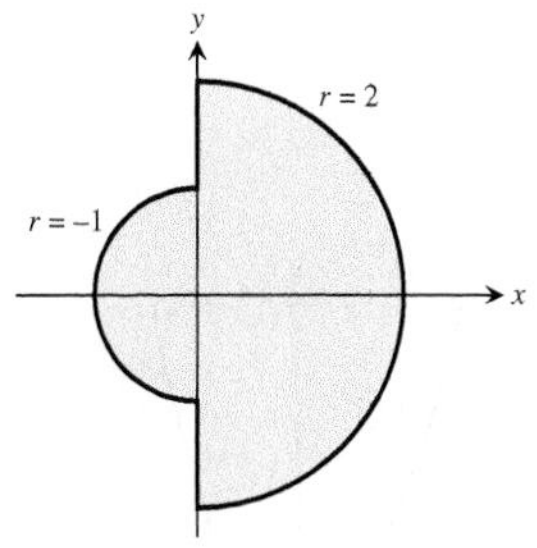

27.

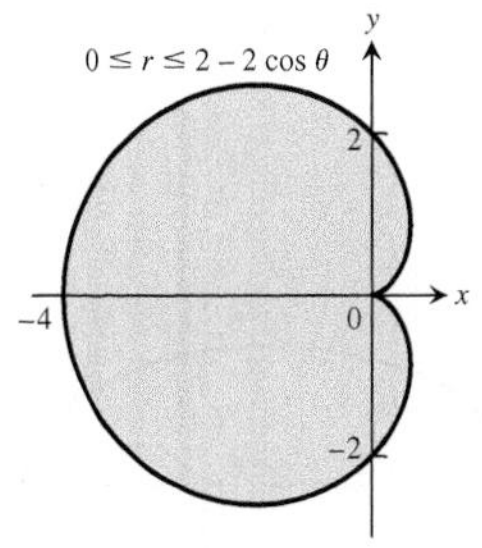

29. (a)

Section 10.5, pp. 590–591

1. $\frac{1}{6}\pi^3$ **3.** 18π **5.** $\frac{\pi}{8}$ **7.** 2 **9.** $\frac{\pi}{2} - 1$ **11.** $5\pi - 8$

13. $3\sqrt{3} - \pi$ **15.** $\frac{\pi}{3} + \frac{\sqrt{3}}{2}$ **17.** $\frac{8\pi}{3} + \sqrt{3}$

19. **(a)** $\frac{3}{2} - \frac{\pi}{4}$ **21.** $19/3$ **23.** 8

25. $3\left(\sqrt{2} + \ln\left(1 + \sqrt{2}\right)\right)$ **27.** $\frac{\pi}{8} + \frac{3}{8}$

Section 10.6, pp. 597–598

1. $e = \frac{3}{5}$, $F(\pm 3, 0)$; directrices are $x = \pm\frac{25}{3}$.

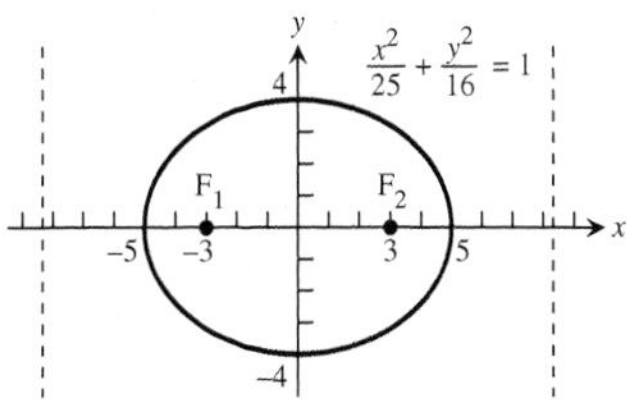

3. $e = \frac{1}{\sqrt{2}}$; $F(0, \pm 1)$; directrices are $y = \pm 2$.

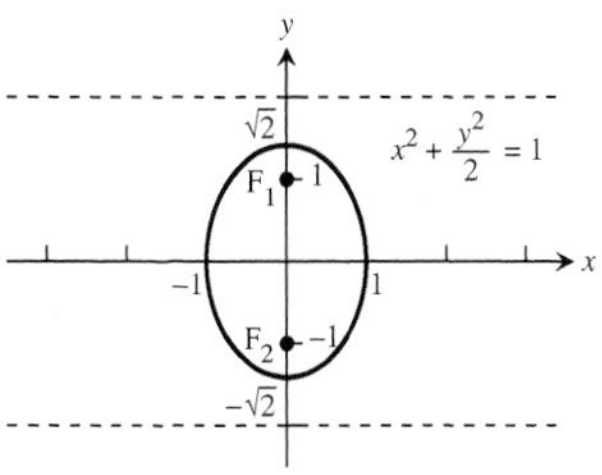

5. $e = \frac{1}{\sqrt{3}}$; $F(0, \pm 1)$; directrices are $y = \pm 3$.

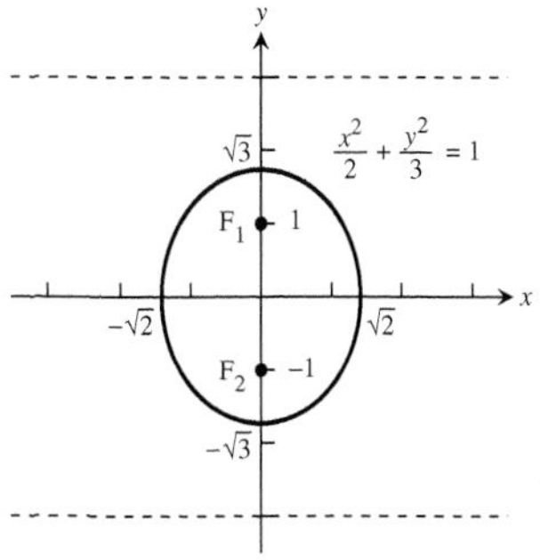

7. $e = \frac{\sqrt{3}}{3}$; $F\left(\pm\sqrt{3}, 0\right)$; directrices are $x = \pm 3\sqrt{3}$.

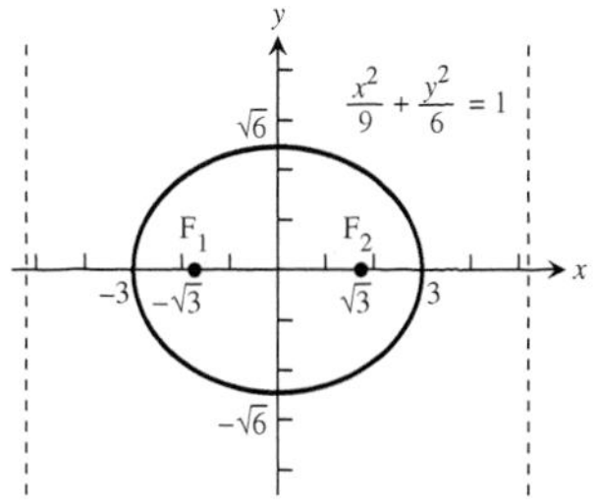

9. $\frac{x^2}{27} + \frac{y^2}{36} = 1$ **11.** $\frac{x^2}{4851} + \frac{y^2}{4900} = 1$

13. $\frac{x^2}{9} + \frac{y^2}{4} = 1$ **15.** $\frac{x^2}{64} + \frac{y^2}{48} = 1$

17. $e = \sqrt{2}$; $F\left(\pm\sqrt{2}, 0\right)$; directrices are $x = \pm\frac{1}{\sqrt{2}}$.

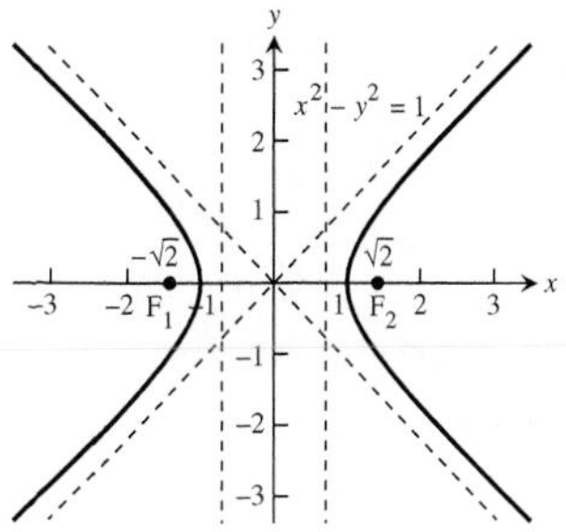

19. $e = \sqrt{2}$; $F(0, \pm 4)$; directrices are $y = \pm 2$.

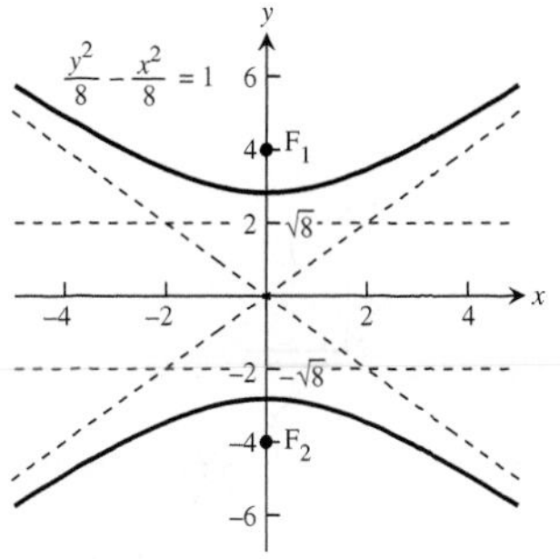

21. $e = \sqrt{5}$; $F\left(\pm\sqrt{10}, 0\right)$; directrices are $x = \pm\frac{2}{\sqrt{10}}$.

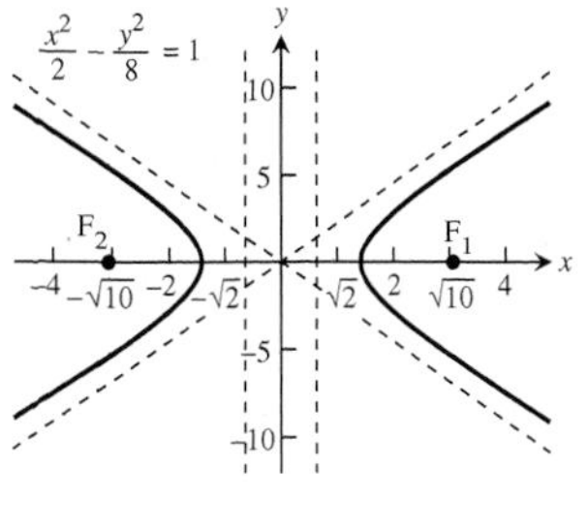

23. $e = \sqrt{5}$; $F\left(0, \pm\sqrt{10}\right)$; directrices are $y = \pm\frac{2}{\sqrt{10}}$.

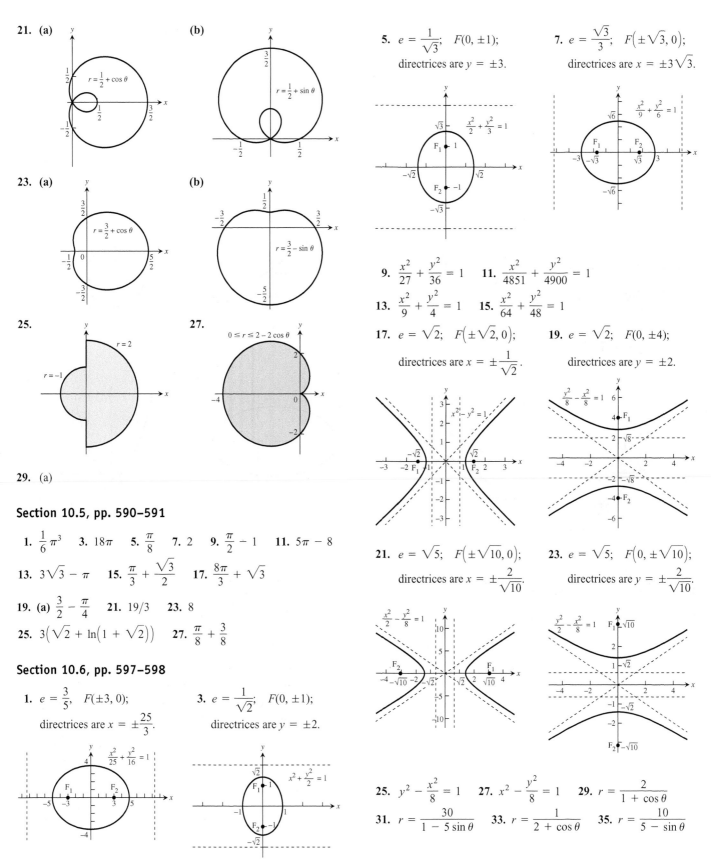

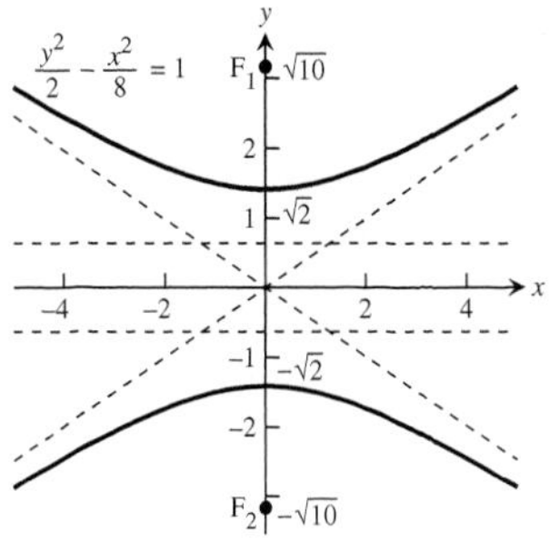

25. $y^2 - \frac{x^2}{8} = 1$ **27.** $x^2 - \frac{y^2}{8} = 1$ **29.** $r = \frac{2}{1 + \cos\theta}$

31. $r = \frac{30}{1 - 5\sin\theta}$ **33.** $r = \frac{1}{2 + \cos\theta}$ **35.** $r = \frac{10}{5 - \sin\theta}$

37.

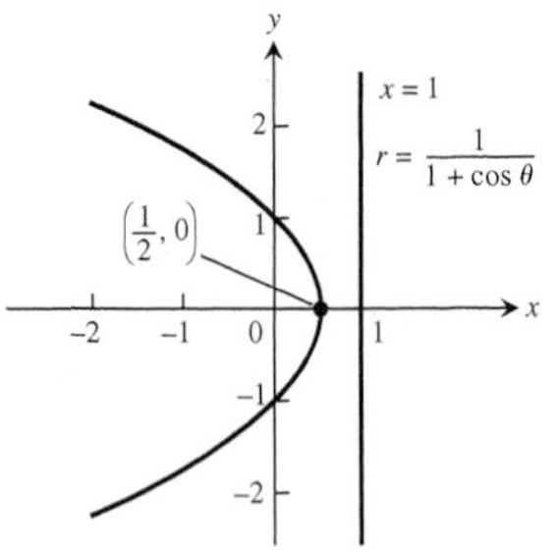

39.

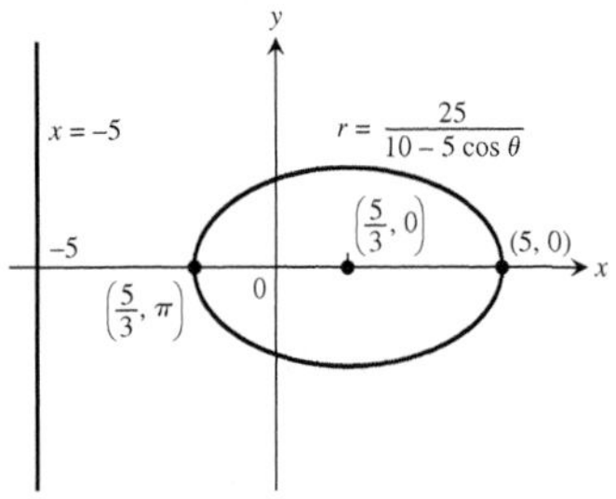

61. $r = -2\cos\theta$

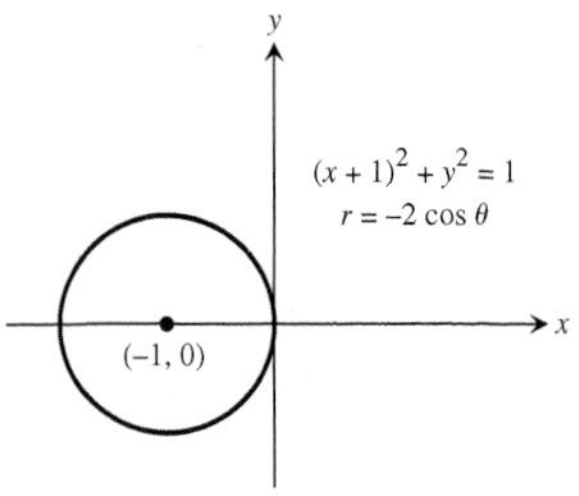

63. $r = -\sin\theta$

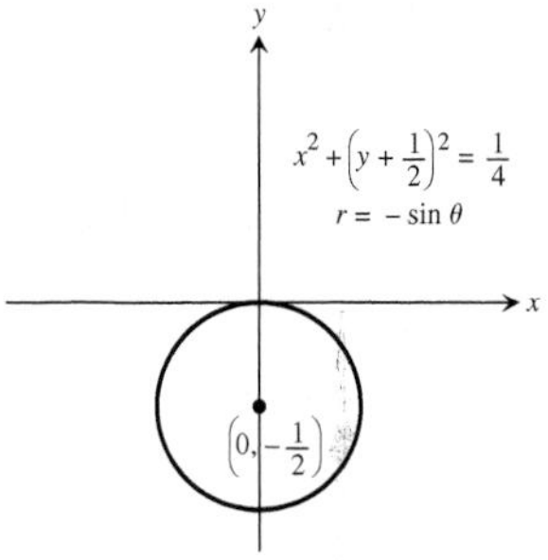

41.

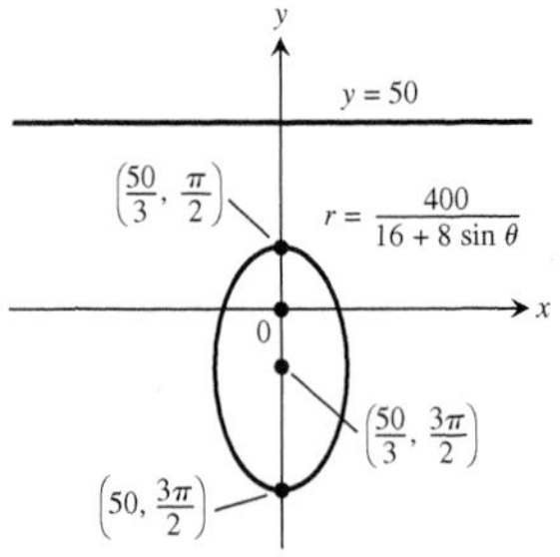

43.

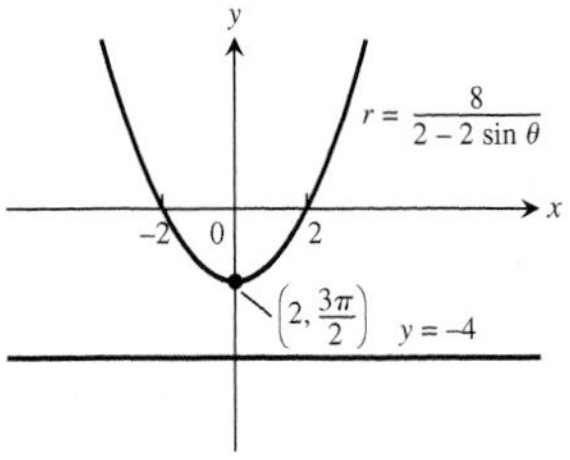

65.

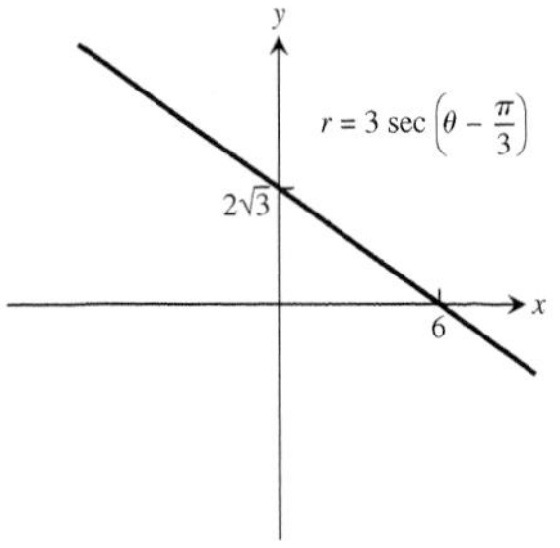

67.

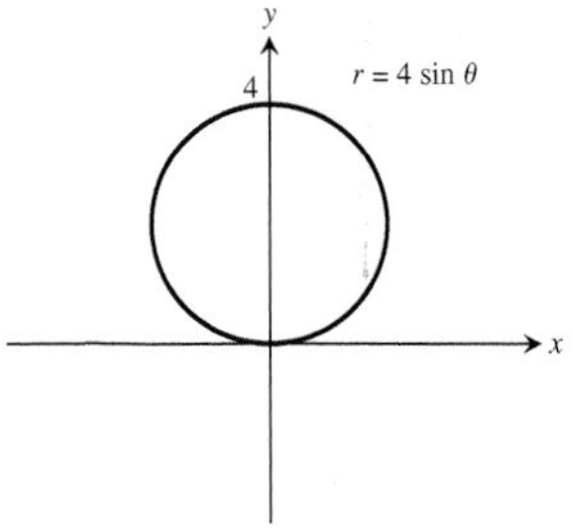

45. $y = 2 - x$

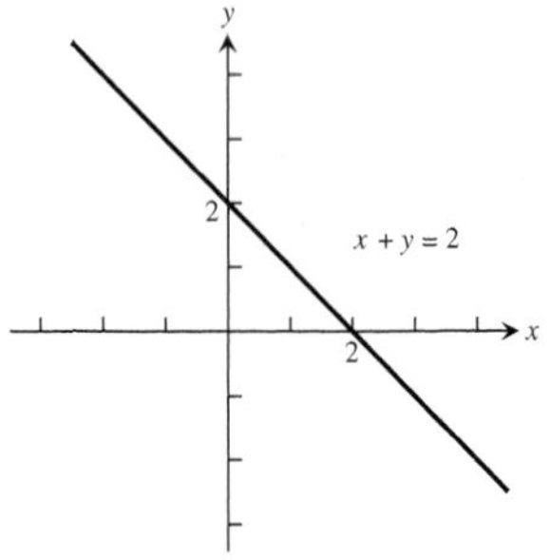

47. $y = \frac{\sqrt{3}}{3}x + 2\sqrt{3}$

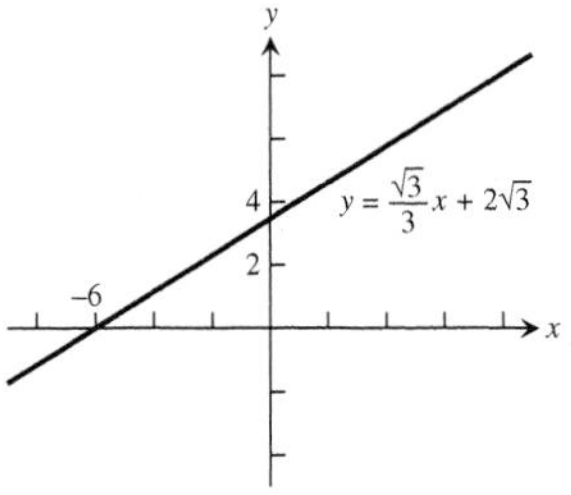

69.

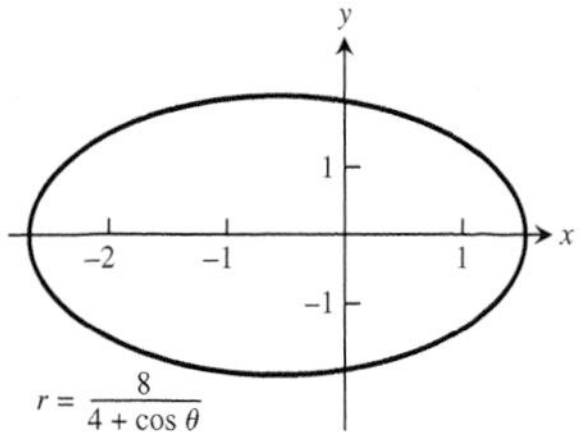

71.

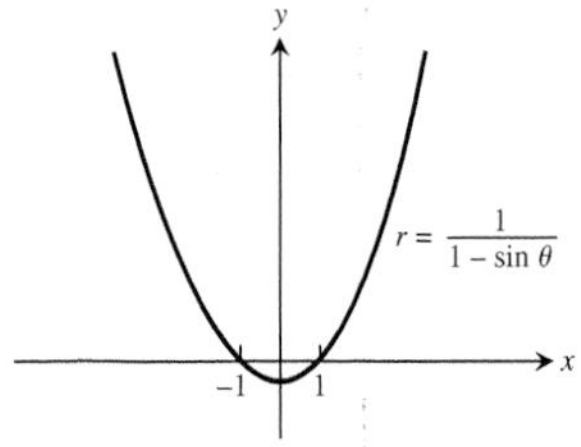

73.

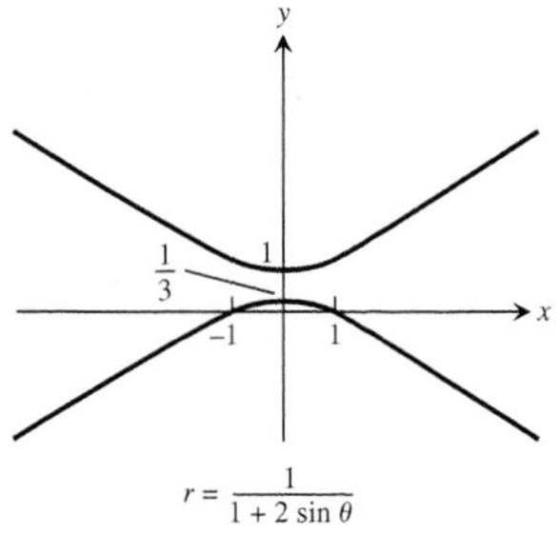

49. $r\cos\left(\theta - \frac{\pi}{4}\right) = 3$ **51.** $r\cos\left(\theta + \frac{\pi}{2}\right) = 5$

53.

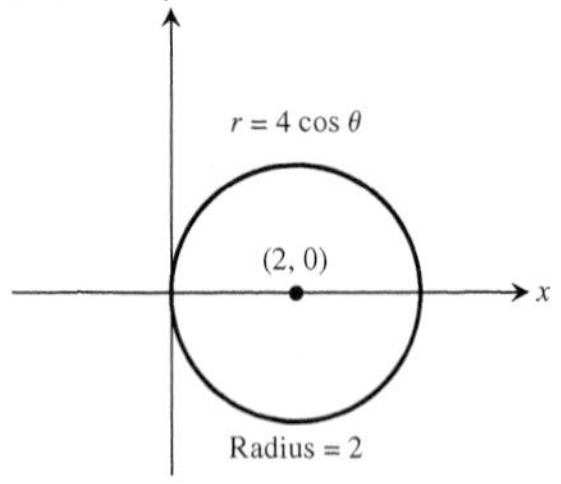

55.

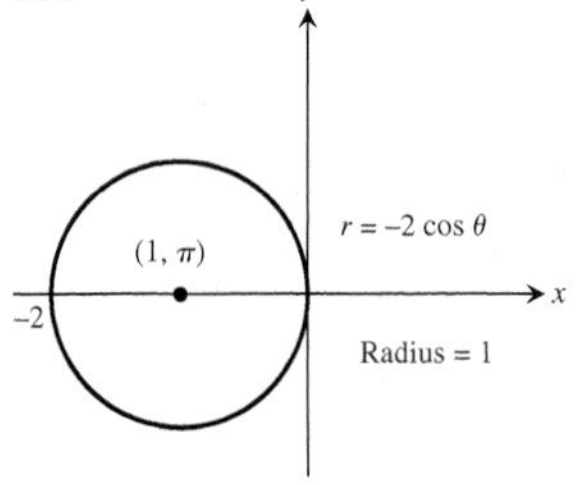

57. $r = 12\cos\theta$

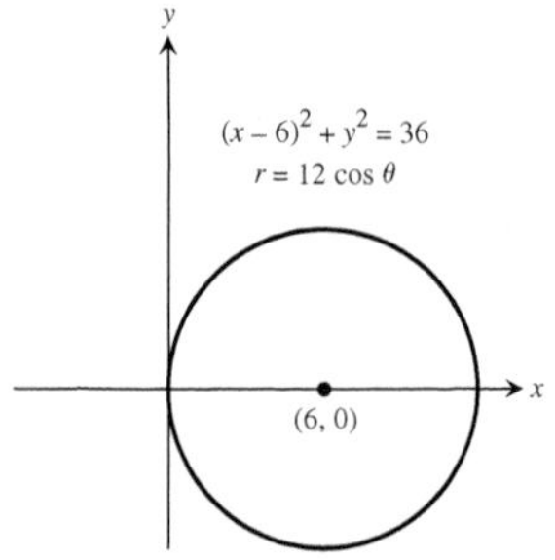

59. $r = 10\sin\theta$

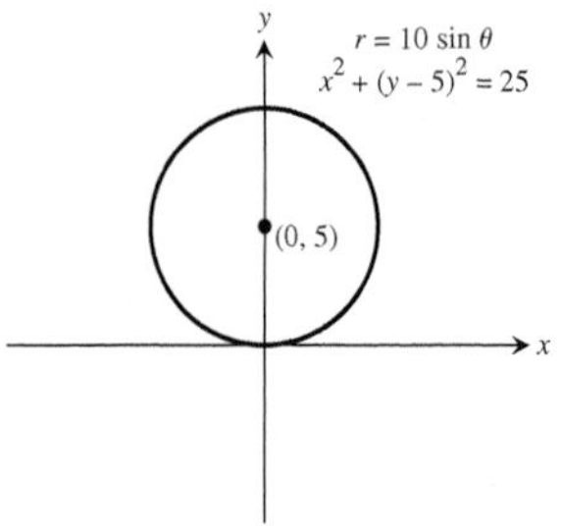

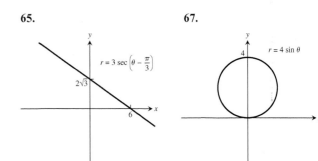

75. (b)

Planet	Perihelion	Aphelion
Mercury	0.3075 AU	0.4667 AU
Venus	0.7184 AU	0.7282 AU
Earth	0.9833 AU	1.0167 AU
Mars	1.3817 AU	1.6663 AU
Jupiter	4.9512 AU	5.4548 AU
Saturn	9.0210 AU	10.0570 AU
Uranus	18.2977 AU	20.0623 AU
Neptune	29.8135 AU	30.3065 AU

Practice Exercises, pp. 599–600

1.

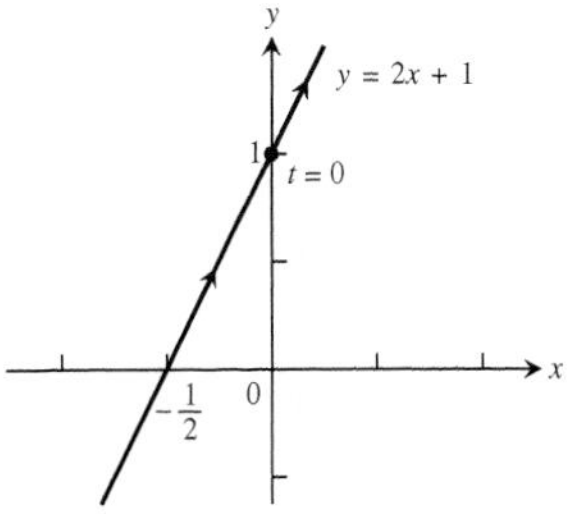

3.

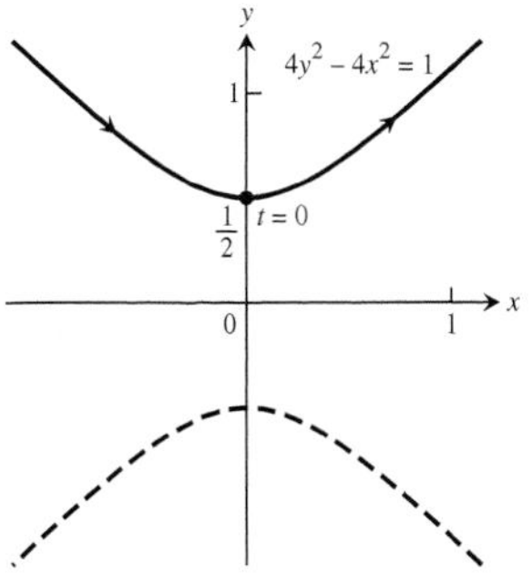

5.

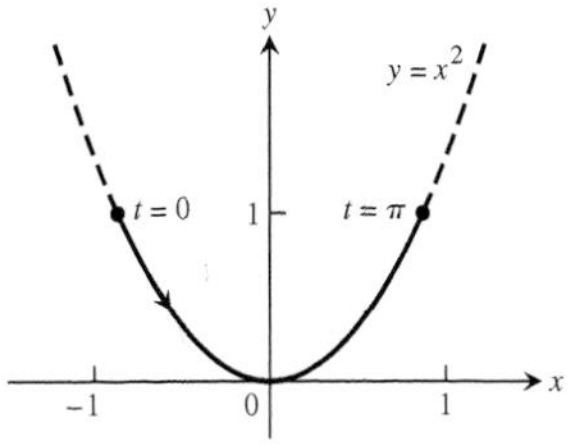

7. $x = 3\cos t,\quad y = 4\sin t,\quad 0 \le t \le 2\pi$

9. $y = \dfrac{\sqrt{3}}{2}x + \dfrac{1}{4}, \dfrac{1}{4}$

11. **(a)** $y = \dfrac{\pm|x|^{3/2}}{8} - 1$ **(b)** $y = \dfrac{\pm\sqrt{1 - x^2}}{x}$

13. $\dfrac{10}{3}$ **15.** $\dfrac{285}{8}$ **17.** 10 **19.** $\dfrac{9\pi}{2}$ **21.** $\dfrac{76\pi}{3}$

23. $y = \dfrac{\sqrt{3}}{3}x - 4$

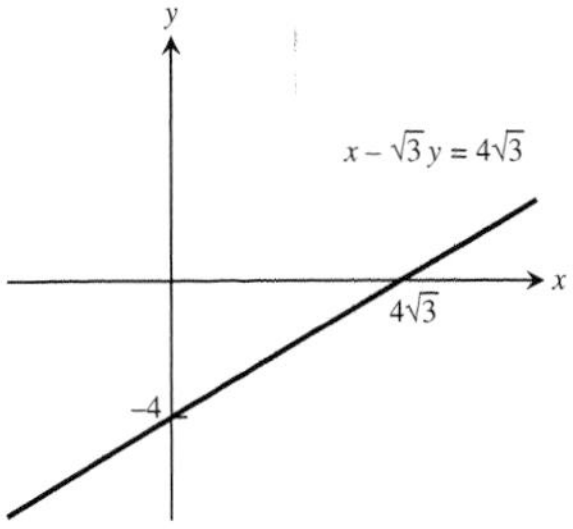

25. $x = 2$

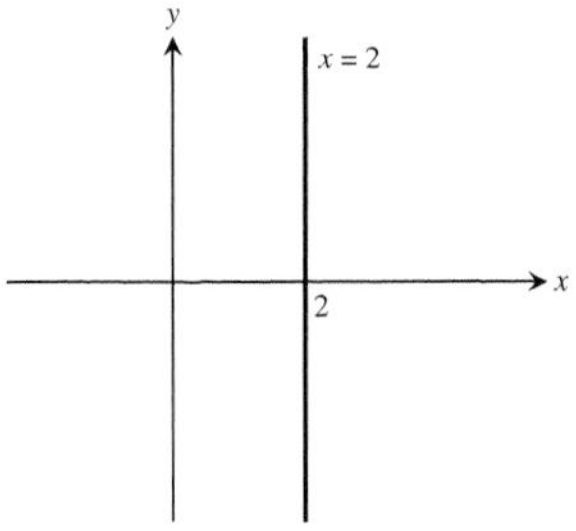

27. $y = -\dfrac{3}{2}$

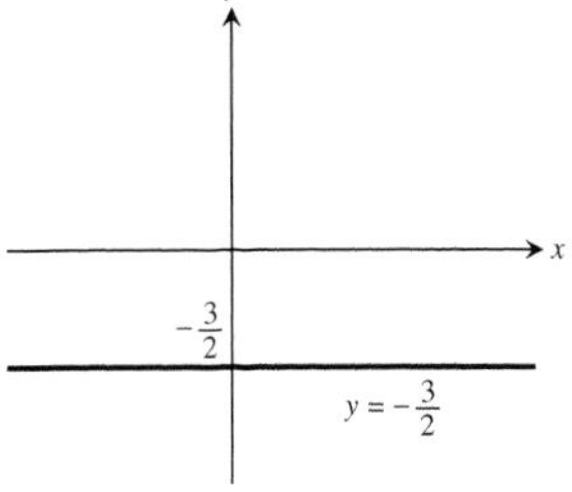

29. $x^2 + (y + 2)^2 = 4$

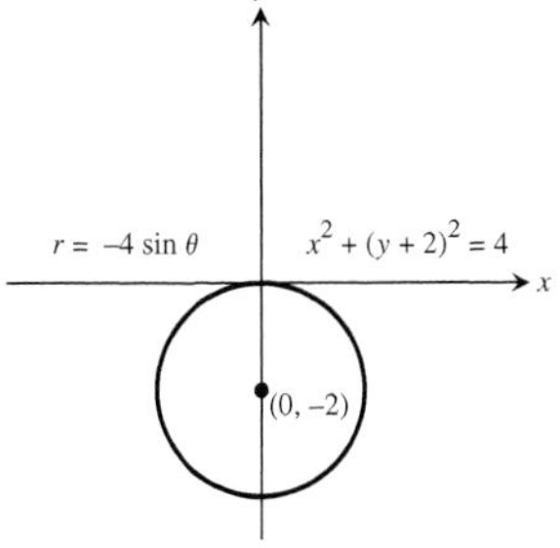

31. $\left(x - \sqrt{2}\right)^2 + y^2 = 2$

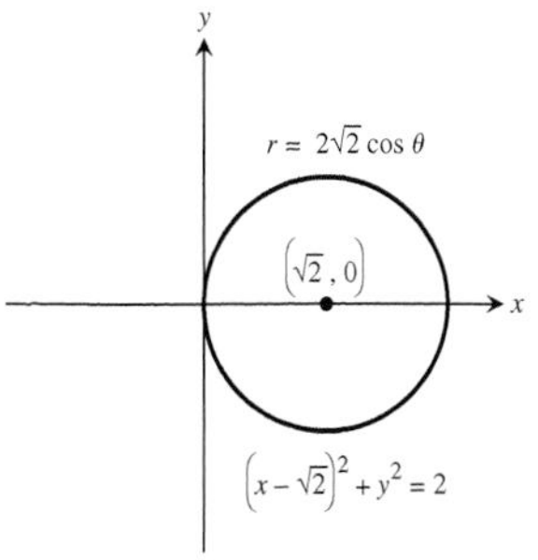

33. $r = -5\sin\theta$

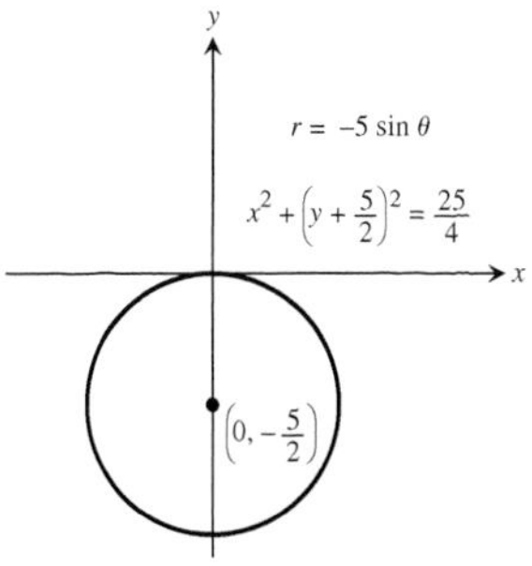

35. $r = 3\cos\theta$

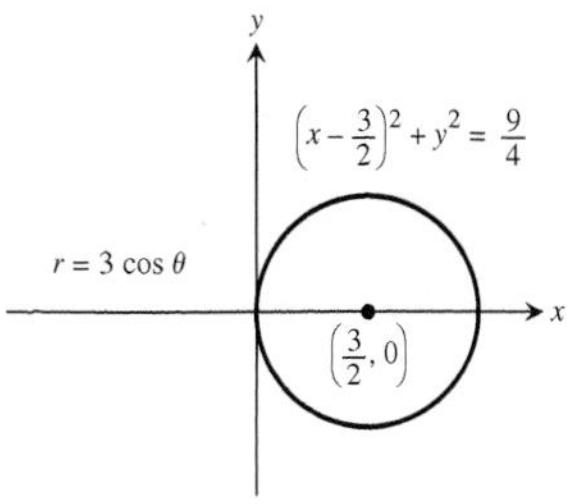

37.

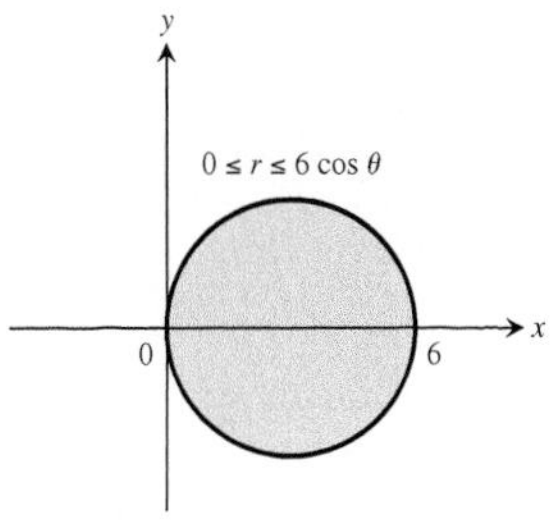

39. d **41.** l **43.** k **45.** i **47.** $\dfrac{9}{2}\pi$ **49.** $2 + \dfrac{\pi}{4}$

51. 8 **53.** $\pi - 3$

55. $V(1, 0)$

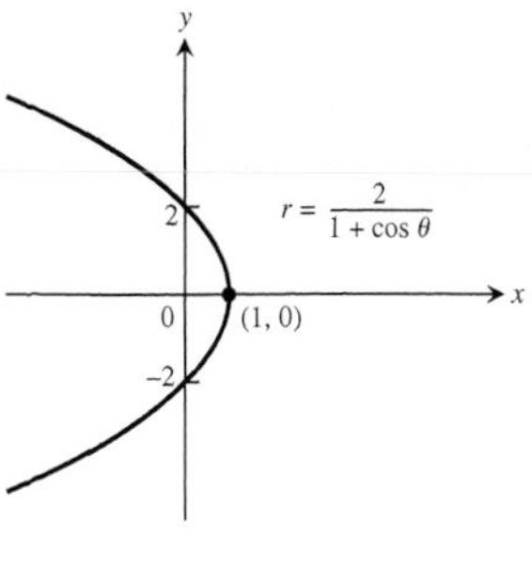

57. $V(2, \pi)$ and $V(6, \pi)$

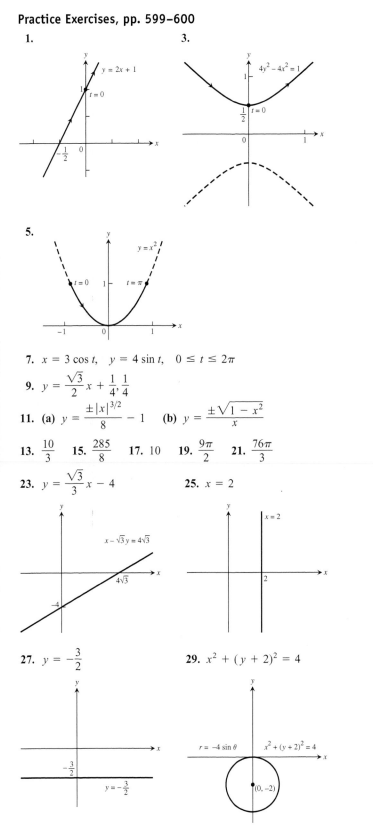

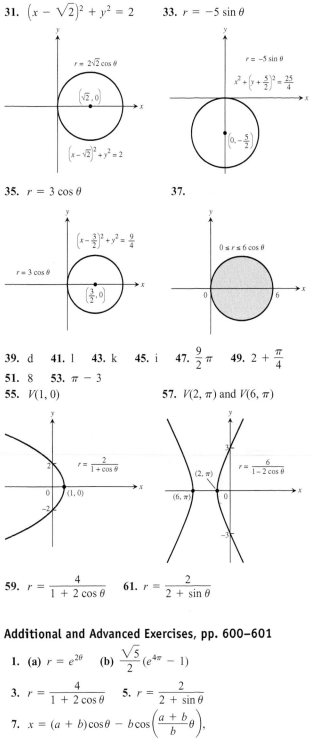

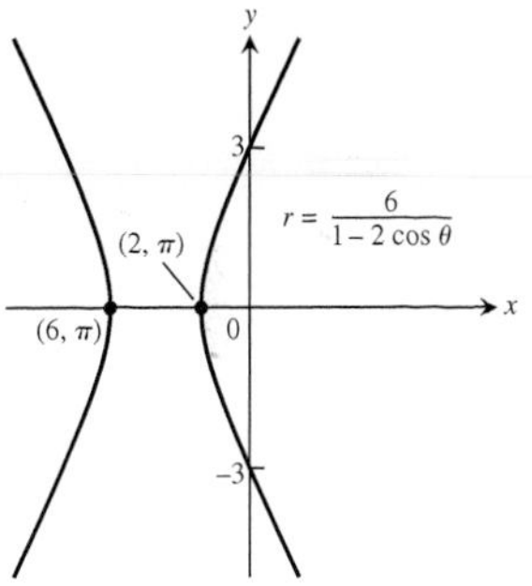

59. $r = \dfrac{4}{1 + 2\cos\theta}$ **61.** $r = \dfrac{2}{2 + \sin\theta}$

Additional and Advanced Exercises, pp. 600–601

1. **(a)** $r = e^{2\theta}$ **(b)** $\dfrac{\sqrt{5}}{2}(e^{4\pi} - 1)$

3. $r = \dfrac{4}{1 + 2\cos\theta}$ **5.** $r = \dfrac{2}{2 + \sin\theta}$

7. $x = (a + b)\cos\theta - b\cos\left(\dfrac{a + b}{b}\theta\right)$,

$y = (a + b)\sin\theta - b\sin\left(\dfrac{a + b}{b}\theta\right)$

11. $\dfrac{\pi}{2}$

Index

CONTENTS

The following content was taken from *Fundamentals of Precalculus,* Second Edition by Mark Dugopolski.

1 Graphs and Functions

2 Polynomial and Rational Functions

3 Trigonometric Functions

CHAPTER

1 Graphs and Functions

The Brooklyn Bridge

Location Manhattan and Brooklyn, New York

Completion Date 1883

Cost $18 million

Length 3460 feet

Longest Single Span 1595 feet

Engineers John Roebling, Washington Roebling

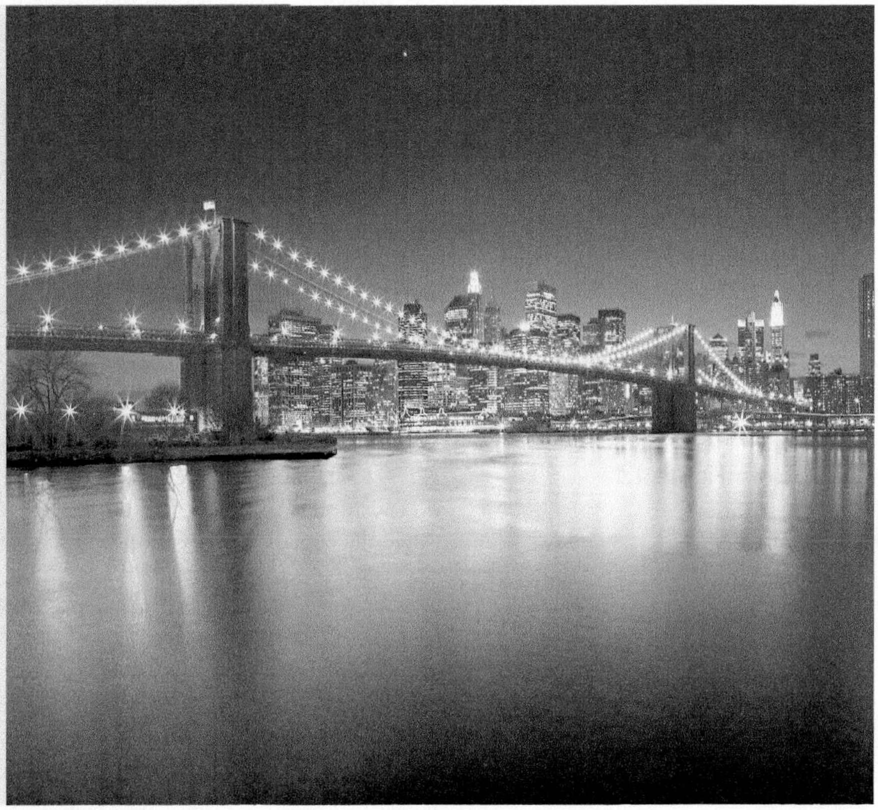

CONSIDERED a brilliant feat of 19th-century engineering, the Brooklyn Bridge was the first suspension bridge to use steel for its cable wire. In 1883 it was the longest suspension bridge in the world. But the bridge was not built without problems. Before construction began, the bridge's chief engineer, John Roebling, died from tetanus. The project was taken over and seen to completion by his son, Washington Roebling. Three years later, Roebling was crippled by an illness that is known today as "the bends." The bedridden engineer watched the bridge's progress for the next 11 years from his apartment with a telescope and passed on orders to workers through his wife, Emily. Today, the Brooklyn Bridge is the second busiest bridge in New York City. One hundred forty-four thousand vehicles cross the bridge every day.

1.1 Real Numbers and Their Properties

The numbers that we use the most in calculus are the real numbers. So we begin our preparation for calculus by reviewing the set of real numbers and their properties.

The Real Numbers

A **set** is a collection of objects or **elements.** The set containing the numbers 1, 2, and 3 is written as $\{1, 2, 3\}$. To indicate a continuing pattern, we use three dots as in $\{1, 2, 3, \ldots\}$. The set of real numbers is a collection of many types of numbers. To better understand the real numbers we recall some of the basic subsets of the real numbers:

Subset	Name (symbol)
$\{1, 2, 3, \ldots\}$	**Counting** or **natural numbers** (N)
$\{0, 1, 2, 3, \ldots\}$	**Whole numbers** (W)
$\{\ldots, -3, -2, -1, 0, 1, 2, 3, \ldots\}$	**Integers** (Z)

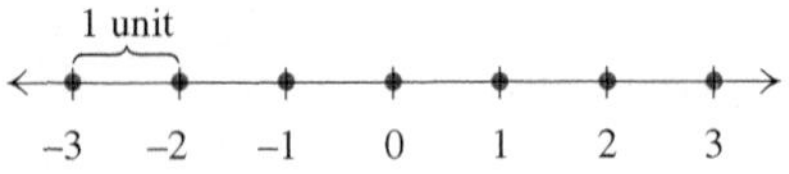

Figure 1.1

Numbers can be pictured as points on a line, the **number line.** To draw a number line, draw a line and label any convenient point with the number 0. Now choose a convenient length, one **unit,** and use it to locate evenly spaced points as shown in Fig. 1.1. The positive integers are located to the right of zero and the negative integers to the left of zero. The numbers corresponding to the points on the line are called the **coordinates** of the points.

The integers and their ratios form the set of **rational numbers,** Q. The rational numbers also correspond to points on the number line. For example, the rational number $1/2$ is found halfway between 0 and 1 on the number line. In set notation, the set of rational numbers is written as

$$\left\{\frac{a}{b} \,\middle|\, a \text{ and } b \text{ are integers with } b \neq 0\right\}.$$

This notation is read "The set of all numbers of the form a/b such that a and b are integers with b not equal to zero." In our set notation we used letters to represent integers. A letter that is used to represent a number is called a **variable.**

There are infinitely many rational numbers located between each pair of consecutive integers, yet there are infinitely many points on the number line that do not correspond to rational numbers. The numbers that correspond to those points are called **irrational** numbers. In decimal notation, the rational numbers are the numbers that are repeating or terminating decimals, and the irrational numbers are the nonrepeating nonterminating decimals. For example, the number 0.595959 . . . is a rational number because the pair 59 repeats indefinitely. By contrast, notice that in the number 5.010010001 . . . , each group of zeros contains one more zero than the previous group. Because no group of digits repeats, 5.010010001 . . . is an irrational number.

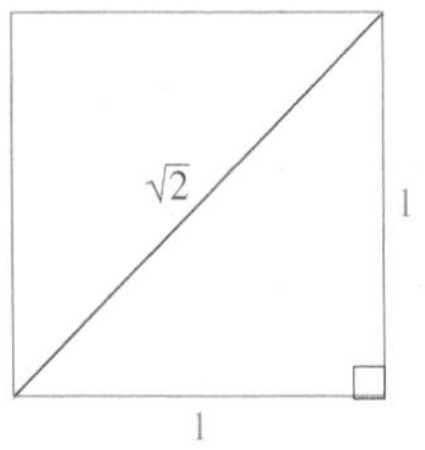

Figure 1.2

Numbers such as $\sqrt{2}$ or π are also irrational. We can visualize $\sqrt{2}$ as the length of the diagonal of a square whose sides are one unit in length. See Fig. 1.2. In any circle, the ratio of the circumference c to the diameter d is π ($\pi = c/d$).

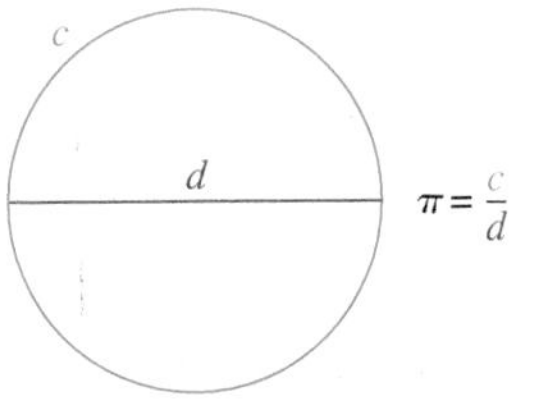

Figure 1.3

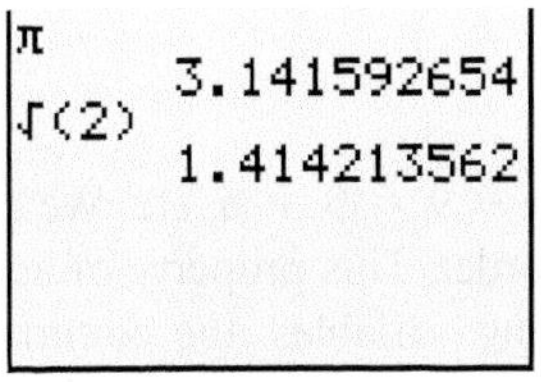

Figure 1.4

See Fig. 1.3. It is difficult to see that numbers like $\sqrt{2}$ and π are irrational because their decimal representations are not apparent. However, the irrationality of π was proven in 1767 by Johann Heinrich Lambert, and it can be shown that the square root of any positive integer that is not a perfect square is irrational.

Since a calculator operates with a fixed number of decimal places, it gives us a *rational approximation* for an irrational number such as $\sqrt{2}$ or π. See Fig. 1.4. □

The set of rational numbers, Q, together with the set of irrational numbers, I, is called the set of **real numbers,** R. The following are examples of real numbers:

$$-3, \quad -0.025, \quad 0, \quad \frac{1}{3}, \quad 0.595959\ldots, \quad \sqrt{2}, \quad \pi, \quad 5.010010001\ldots$$

These numbers are **graphed** on a number line in Fig. 1.5.

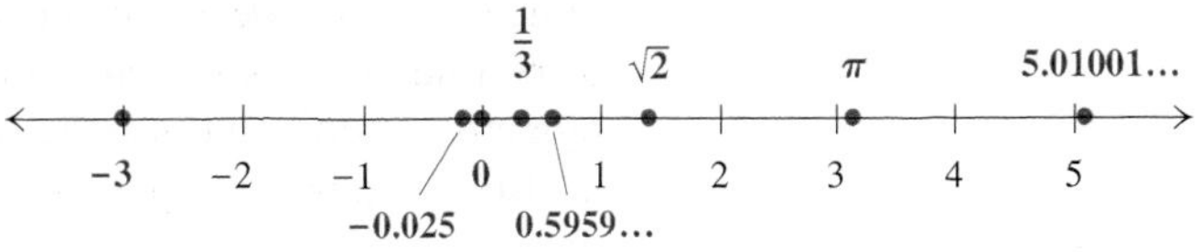

Figure 1.5

Since there is a one-to-one correspondence between the points of the number line and the real numbers, we often refer to a real number as a point. Figure 1.6 shows how the various subsets of the real numbers are related to one another.

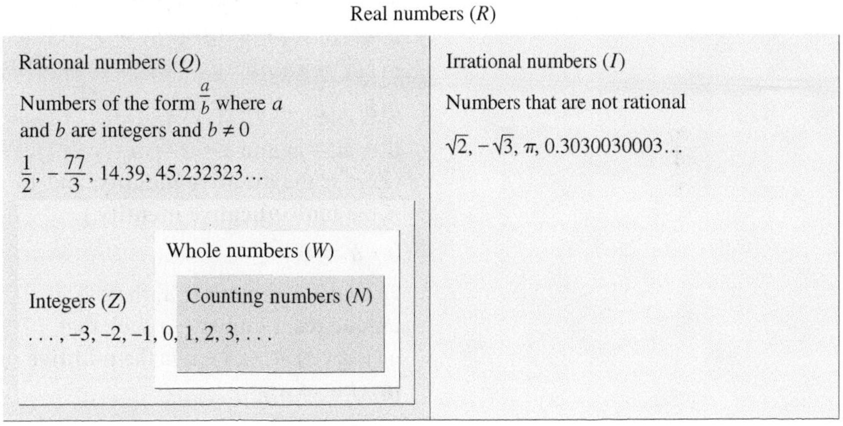

Figure 1.6

To indicate that a number is a member of a set, we write $a \in A$, which is read "a is a member of set A." We write $a \notin A$ for "a is not a member of set A." Set A is a subset of set B ($A \subseteq B$) means that every member of set A is also a member of set B, and A is not a subset of B ($A \not\subseteq B$) means that there is at least one member of A that is not a member of B.

Example 1 Classifying numbers and sets of numbers

Determine whether each statement is true or false and explain. See Fig. 1.6.

a. $0 \in R$ **b.** $\pi \in Q$ **c.** $R \subseteq Q$ **d.** $I \not\subseteq Q$ **e.** $\sqrt{5} \in Q$

Historical Note

Johann Heinrich Lambert (1728–1777) was a German mathematician, physicist, and astronomer. His father was a poor tailor, so Johann had to struggle to gain an education. Lambert studied light intensity and was the first to introduce hyberbolic functions into trigonometry. He proved that π is an irrational number. Lambert also devised theorems regarding conic sections that made the calculation of the orbits of comets simpler.

Solution

a. True, because 0 is a member of the set of whole numbers, a subset of the set of real numbers.

b. False, because π is irrational.

c. False, because every irrational number is a member of R but not Q.

d. True, because the irrational numbers and the rational numbers have no numbers in common.

e. False, because the square root of any integer that is not a perfect square is irrational. ■

Properties of the Real Numbers

In arithmetic we can observe that $3 + 4 = 4 + 3$, $6 + 9 = 9 + 6$, etc. We get the same sum when we add two real numbers in either order. This property of addition of real numbers is the **commutative property.** Using variables, the commutative property of addition is stated as $a + b = b + a$ for any real numbers a and b. There is also a commutative property of multiplication, which is written as $a \cdot b = b \cdot a$ or $ab = ba$. There are many properties concerning the operations of addition and multiplication on the real numbers that are useful in algebra.

Properties of the Real Numbers

For any real numbers a, b, and c:

$a + b$ and ab are real numbers	**Closure property**
$a + b = b + a$ and $ab = ba$	**Commutative properties**
$a + (b + c) = (a + b) + c$ and $a(bc) = (ab)c$	**Associative properties**
$a(b + c) = ab + ac$	**Distributive property**
$0 + a = a$ and $1 \cdot a = a$ (Zero is the **additive identity,** and 1 is the **multiplicative identity.**)	**Identity properties**
$0 \cdot a = 0$	**Multiplication property of zero**
For each real number a, there is a unique real number $-a$ such that $a + (-a) = 0$. ($-a$ is the **additive inverse** of a.)	**Additive inverse property**
For each nonzero real number a, there is a unique real number $1/a$ such that $a \cdot 1/a = 1$. ($1/a$ is the **multiplicative inverse** or **reciprocal** of a.)	**Multiplicative inverse property**

The closure property indicates that the sum and product of any pair of real numbers is a real number. The commutative properties indicate that we can add or multiply in either order and get the same result. Since we can add or multiply only a pair of numbers, the associative properties indicate two different ways to obtain the result when adding or multiplying three numbers. The operations within parentheses are performed first. Because of the commutative property, the distributive property can be used also in the form $(b + c)a = ab + ac$.

Note that the properties stated here involve only addition and multiplication, considered the basic operations of the real numbers. Subtraction and division are defined in terms of addition and multiplication. By definition $a - b = a + (-b)$ and $a \div b = a \cdot 1/b$ for $b \neq 0$. Note that $a - b$ is called the **difference** of a and b and $a \div b$ is called the **quotient** of a and b.

Example 2 Using the properties

Complete each statement using the property named.

a. $a7 =$ ______, commutative
b. $2x + 4 =$ ______, distributive
c. $8($______$) = 1$, multiplicative inverse
d. $\frac{1}{3}(3x) =$ ______, associative

Solution

a. $a7 = 7a$ **b.** $2x + 4 = 2(x + 2)$

c. $8\left(\frac{1}{8}\right) = 1$ **d.** $\frac{1}{3}(3x) = \left(\frac{1}{3} \cdot 3\right)x$ ■

Additive Inverses

The negative sign is used to indicate negative numbers as in -7 (negative seven). If the negative sign precedes a variable as in $-b$ it is read as "additive inverse" or "opposite" because $-b$ could be positive or negative. If b is positive then $-b$ is negative and if b is negative then $-b$ is positive.

Using two "opposite" signs has a cancellation effect. For example, $-(-5) = 5$ and $-(-(-3)) = -3$. Note that the additive inverse of a number can be obtained by multiplying the number by -1. For example, $-1 \cdot 3 = -3$.

Calculators usually use the negative sign (-) to indicate opposite or negative and the subtraction sign $(-)$ for subtraction as shown in Fig. 1.7. □

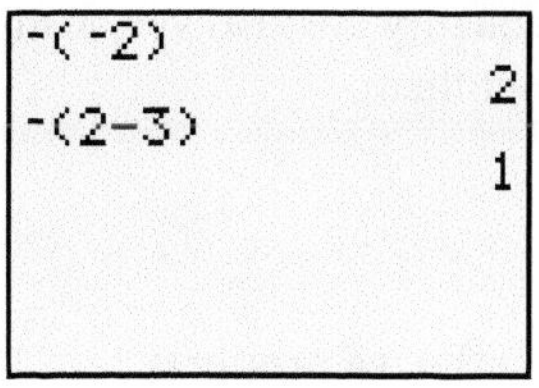

Figure 1.7

We know that $a + b = b + a$ for any real numbers a and b, but is $a - b = b - a$ for any real numbers a and b? In general, $a - b$ is not equal to $b - a$. For example, $7 - 3 = 4$ and $3 - 7 = -4$. So subtraction is not commutative. Since $a - b + b - a = 0$, we can conclude that $a - b$ and $b - a$ are opposites or additive inverses of each other. We summarize these properties of opposites as follows.

Properties of Opposites

For any real numbers a and b:

1. $-1 \cdot a = -a$ (The product of -1 and a is the opposite of a.)
2. $-(-a) = a$ (The opposite of the opposite of a is a.)
3. $-(a - b) = b - a$ (The opposite of $a - b$ is $b - a$.)

Example 3 Using properties of opposites

Use the properties of opposites to complete each equation.

a. $-(-\pi) =$ ______ **b.** $-1(-2) =$ ______ **c.** $-1(x - h) =$ ______

Solution

a. $-(-\pi) = \pi$
b. $-1(-2) = -(-2) = 2$
c. $-1(x - h) = -(x - h) = h - x$ ■

Relations

Symbols such as $<$, $>$, $=$, $\leq$, and $\geq$ are called **relations** because they indicate how numbers are related. We can visualize these relations by using a number line. For example, $\sqrt{2}$ is located to the right of 0 in Fig. 1.5, so $\sqrt{2} > 0$. Since $\sqrt{2}$ is to the left of π in Fig. 1.5, $\sqrt{2} < \pi$. In fact, if a and b are any two real numbers, we say that a is less than b (written $a < b$) provided that a is to the left of b on the number line. We say that a is greater than b (written $a > b$) if a is to the right of b on the number line. We say $a = b$ if a and b correspond to the same point on the number line. The fact that there are only three possibilities for ordering a pair of real numbers is called the **trichotomy property.**

Trichotomy Property

For any two real numbers a and b, exactly one of the following is true: $a < b$, $a = b$, or $a > b$.

The trichotomy property is very natural to use. For example, if we know that $r = t$ is false, then we can conclude (using the trichotomy property) that either $r > t$ or $r < t$ is true. If we know that $w + 6 > z$ is false, then we can conclude that $w + 6 \leq z$ is true. The following four properties of equality are also very natural to use, and we often use them without even thinking about them.

Properties of Equality

For any real numbers a, b, and c:

1. $a = a$	**Reflexive property**
2. If $a = b$, then $b = a$.	**Symmetric property**
3. If $a = b$ and $b = c$, then $a = c$.	**Transitive property**
4. If $a = b$, then a and b may be substituted for one another in any expression involving a or b.	**Substitution property**

Absolute Value

The **absolute value** of a (in symbols, $|a|$) can be thought of as the distance from a to 0 on a number line. Since both 3 and -3 are three units from 0 on a number line as shown in Fig. 1.8, $|3| = 3$ and $|-3| = 3$:

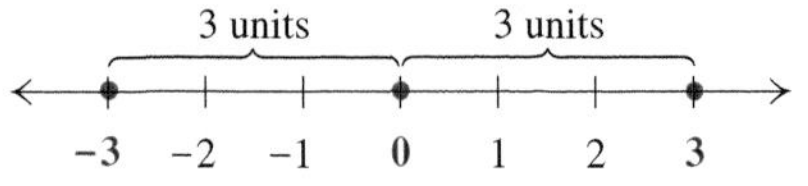

Figure 1.8

A symbolic definition of absolute value is written as follows.

Definition: Absolute Value

For any real number a,

$$|a| = \begin{cases} a & \text{if } a \geq 0 \\ -a & \text{if } a < 0. \end{cases}$$

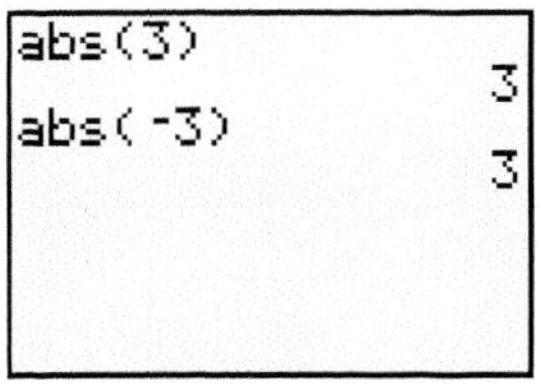

Figure 1.9

A calculator typically uses **abs** for absolute value as shown in Fig. 1.9. □

The symbolic definition of absolute value indicates that for $a \geq 0$ we use the equation $|a| = a$ (the absolute value of a is just a). For $a < 0$ we use the equation $|a| = -a$ (the absolute value of a is the opposite of a, a positive number).

Example 4 Using the definition of absolute value

Use the symbolic definition of absolute value to simplify each expression.

a. $|5.6|$ **b.** $|0|$ **c.** $|-3|$

Solution

a. Since $5.6 \geq 0$, we use the equation $|a| = a$ to get $|5.6| = 5.6$.
b. Since $0 \geq 0$, we use the equation $|a| = a$ to get $|0| = 0$.
c. Since $-3 < 0$, we use the equation $|a| = -a$ to get $|-3| = -(-3) = 3$. ■

The definition of absolute value guarantees that the absolute value of any number is nonnegative. The definition also implies that additive inverses (or opposites) have the same absolute value. These properties of absolute value and two others are stated as follows.

Properties of Absolute Value

For any real numbers a and b:

1. $|a| \geq 0$ (The absolute value of any number is nonnegative.)
2. $|-a| = |a|$ (Additive inverses have the same absolute value.)
3. $|a \cdot b| = |a| \cdot |b|$ (The absolute value of a product is the product of the absolute values.)
4. $\left|\frac{a}{b}\right| = \frac{|a|}{|b|}, b \neq 0$ (The absolute value of a quotient is the quotient of the absolute values.)

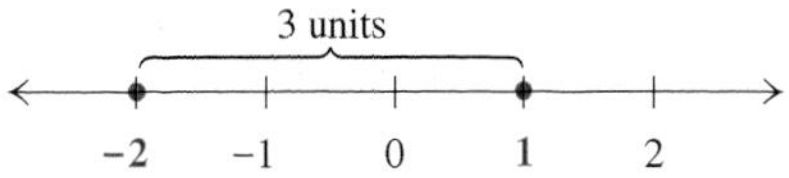

Figure 1.10

Absolute value is used in finding the distance between points on a number line. Since 9 lies four units to the right of 5, the distance between 5 and 9 is 4. In symbols, $d(5, 9) = 4$. We can obtain 4 by $9 - 5 = 4$ or $|5 - 9| = 4$. In general, $|a - b|$ gives the distance between a and b for any values of a and b. For example, the distance between -2 and 1 in Fig. 1.10 is three units and

$$d(-2, 1) = |-2 - 1| = |-3| = 3.$$

Distance Between Two Points on the Number Line

If a and b are any two points on the number line, then the distance between a and b is $|a - b|$. In symbols, $d(a, b) = |a - b|$.

Note that $d(a, 0) = |a - 0| = |a|$, which is consistent with the definition of absolute value of a as the distance between a and 0 on the number line.

Example 5 Distance between two points on a number line

Find the distance between -3 and 5 on the number line.

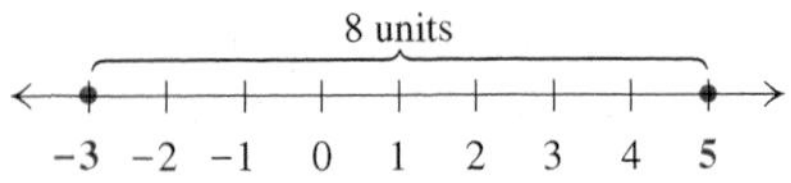

Figure 1.11

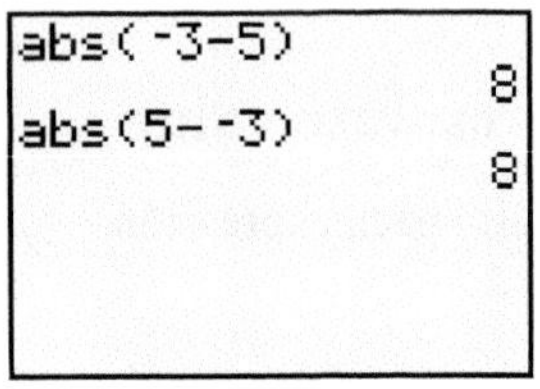

Figure 1.12

Solution

The points corresponding to -3 and 5 are shown on the number line in Fig. 1.11. The distances between these points is found as follows:

$$d(-3, 5) = |-3 - 5| = |-8| = 8$$

Notice that $d(-3, 5) = d(5, -3)$:

$$d(5, -3) = |5 - (-3)| = |8| = 8$$

When you use a calculator to find the absolute value of a difference or a sum, you must use parentheses as shown in Fig. 1.12. ■

Example 6 Absolute value equations for distance

Translate each sentence into an absolute value equation and solve it.

a. The distance between x and 3 is 6 units.
b. The distance between -2 and x is 5 units.

Solution

a. If x is 6 units away from 3, then $|x - 3| = 6$. Since both -3 and 9 are 6 units away from 3, the solution set is $\{-3, 9\}$.
b. If x is 5 units away from -2, then $|x - (-2)| = 5$ or $|x + 2| = 5$. Since both -7 and 3 are 5 units away from -2, the solution set is $\{-7, 3\}$. ■

Equations Involving Absolute Value

Not all absolute value equations are solved as easily as those in Example 6. To solve equations involving absolute value, remember that $|x| = x$ if $x \geq 0$, and $|x| = -x$ if $x < 0$. The absolute value of x is greater than or equal to 0 for any real number x. So an equation such as $|x| = -6$ has no solution. Since a number and its opposite have the same absolute value, $|x| = 4$ is equivalent to $x = 4$ or $x = -4$. The only number that has 0 absolute value is 0. These ideas are summarized as follows.

SUMMARY **Basic Absolute Value Equations**

Absolute value equation	Equivalent statement	Solution set
$\|x\| = k\ (k > 0)$	$x = -k$ or $x = k$	$\{-k, k\}$
$\|x\| = 0$	$x = 0$	$\{0\}$
$\|x\| = k\ (k < 0)$		$\varnothing$

Example 7 Equations involving absolute value

Solve each equation.

a. $|3x| = 12$
b. $2|x + 8| + 6 = 0$

Solution

a. First write an equivalent statement without absolute value symbols.

$$|3x| = 12$$

$$3x = -12 \quad \text{or} \quad 3x = 12$$

$$x = -4 \quad \text{or} \quad x = 4$$

Check that $|3(4)| = 12$ and $|3(-4)| = 12$. The solution set is $\{-4, 4\}$.

b. First isolate $|x + 8|$.

$$2|x + 8| + 6 = 0$$

$$2|x + 8| = -6$$

$$|x + 8| = -3$$

Since the left side of the equation is nonnegative, the solution set is $\varnothing$. ■

For Thought

True or False? Explain.

1. Zero is the only number that is both rational and irrational.
2. Every real number has a multiplicative inverse.
3. If a is not less than and not equal to 3, then a is greater than 3.
4. If $a \le w$ and $w \le z$, then $a < z$.
5. For any real numbers a, b, and c, $a - (b - c) = (a - b) - c$.
6. If a and b are any two real numbers, then the distance between a and b on the number line is $a - b$.
7. Calculators give only rational answers.
8. For any real numbers a and b, the opposite of $a + b$ is $a - b$.
9. The solution set to $|x - 9| = 2$ is $\{7, 11\}$.
10. The solution set to $|x - 5| = -3$ is $\varnothing$.

1.1 Exercises

Match each given statement with its symbolic form and determine whether the statement is true or false. If the statement is false, correct it.

1. The number $\sqrt{2}$ is a real number.
2. The number $\sqrt{3}$ is rational.
3. The number 0 is not an irrational number.
4. The number -6 is not an integer.
5. The set of integers is a subset of the real numbers.
6. The set of irrational numbers is a subset of the rationals.

7. The set of real numbers is not a subset of the rational numbers.

8. The set of natural numbers is not a subset of the whole numbers.

a. $\sqrt{3} \in Q$ **b.** $-6 \notin Z$ **c.** $R \not\subseteq Q$

d. $I \subseteq Q$ **e.** $\sqrt{2} \in R$ **f.** $N \not\subseteq W$

g. $Z \subseteq R$ **h.** $0 \notin I$

Determine which elements of the set $\{-3.5, -\sqrt{2}, -1, 0, 1, \sqrt{3}, 3.14, \pi, 4.3535\ldots, 5.090090009\ldots\}$ *are members of the following sets.*

9. Real numbers **10.** Rational numbers

11. Irrational numbers **12.** Integers

13. Whole numbers **14.** Natural numbers

Complete each statement using the property named.

15. $7 + x =$ ______, commutative

16. $5(4y) =$ ______, associative

17. $5(x + 3) =$ ______, distributive

18. $-3(x - 4) =$ ______, distributive

19. $5x + 5 =$ ______, distributive

20. $-5x + 10 =$ ______, distributive

21. $-13 + (4 + x) =$ ______, associative

22. $yx =$ ______, commutative

23. $0.125($______$) = 1$, multiplicative inverse

24. $-3 + ($______$) = 0$, additive inverse

Use the properties of opposites to complete each equation.

25. $-(-\sqrt{3}) =$ ______ **26.** $-1(-6.4) =$ ______

27. $-1(x^2 - y^2) =$ ______ **28.** $-(1 - a^2) =$ ______

Use the symbolic definition of absolute value to simplify each expression.

29. $|7.2|$ **30.** $|0/3|$ **31.** $|-\sqrt{5}|$ **32.** $|-3/4|$

Find the distance on the number line between each pair of numbers.

33. 8, 13 **34.** 1, 99 **35.** -5, 17 **36.** 22, -9

37. -6, -18 **38.** -3, -14 **39.** $-\frac{1}{2}, \frac{1}{4}$ **40.** $-\frac{1}{2}, -\frac{3}{4}$

Translate each sentence into an absolute value equation and solve it.

41. The distance between x and 7 is 3 units.

42. The distance between x and 2 is 7 units.

43. The distance between -1 and x is 3 units.

44. The distance between -4 and x is 8 units.

45. The distance between x and -9 is 4 units.

46. The distance between x and -6 is 5 units.

Solve each absolute value equation.

47. $|x| = 9$ **48.** $|x| = 13.6$

49. $|5x - 4| = 0$ **50.** $|4 - 3x| = 0$

51. $|2x - 3| = 7$ **52.** $|3x + 4| = 12$

53. $2|x + 5| - 10 = 0$ **54.** $6 - 4|x + 3| = -2$

55. $8|3x - 2| = 0$ **56.** $5|6 - 3x| = 0$

57. $2|x| + 7 = 6$ **58.** $5 + 3|x - 4| = 0$

Solve each problem.

59. Graph the numbers $\frac{1}{2}, -\frac{1}{2}, \frac{1}{3}, -\frac{1}{3}, 0, \frac{5}{12}$, and $-\frac{5}{12}$ on a number line. Explain how you decided where to put the numbers. Arrange these same numbers in order from smallest to largest. Explain your method. Did you use a calculator? If so, explain how it could be done without one.

60. Use a calculator to arrange the numbers $\frac{10}{3}, \sqrt{10}, \frac{22}{7}, \pi$, and $\frac{157}{50}$ in order from smallest to largest. Explain what you did to make your decisions on the order of these numbers. Could these numbers be arranged without using a calculator? How do these numbers differ from those in the previous exercise?

Thinking Outside the Box I

Paying Up A king agreed to pay his gardener one dollar's worth of titanium per day for seven days of work on the castle grounds. The king has a seven-dollar bar of titanium that is segmented so that it can be broken into seven one-dollar pieces, but it is bad luck to break a seven-dollar bar of titanium more than twice. How can the king make two breaks in the bar and pay the gardener exactly one dollar's worth of titanium per day for seven days?

Figure for Thinking Outside the Box I

1.1 Pop Quiz

1. Is 0 an irrational number?
2. Simplify $|-2|$.
3. Simplify $-(1 - y)$.
4. Find the distance between -3 and 9.
5. Write an absolute value equation that indicates that the distance between x and -3 is 6.
6. Solve $|2x - 3| = 1$.
7. Solve $|x + 2| = 0$.
8. Solve $|3x - 7| + 6 = 2$.

1.2 Linear and Absolute Value Inequalities

An equation states that two algebraic expressions are equal, while an **inequality** or **simple inequality** is a statement that two algebraic expressions are not equal in a particular way. Inequalities are stated using less than ($<$), less than or equal to ($\leq$), greater than ($>$), or greater than or equal to ($\geq$). In this section we study some basic inequalities.

Interval Notation

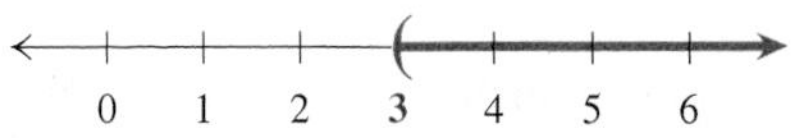

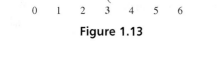

Figure 1.13

Figure 1.14

The solution set to an inequality is the set of all real numbers for which the inequality is true. The solution set to the inequality $x > 3$ is written $\{x | x > 3\}$ and consists of all real numbers to the right of 3 on the number line. This set is also called the **interval** of numbers greater than 3, and it is written in **interval notation** as $(3, \infty)$. The graph of the interval $(3, \infty)$ is shown in Fig. 1.13. A parenthesis is used next to the 3 to indicate that 3 is not in the interval or the solution set. The infinity symbol (∞) is not used as a number, but only to indicate that there is no bound on the numbers greater than 3.

The solution set to $x \leq 4$ is written in set notation as $\{x | x \leq 4\}$ and in interval notation as $(-\infty, 4]$. The symbol $-\infty$ means that all numbers to the left of 4 on the number line are in the set and the bracket means that 4 is in the set. The graph of the interval $(-\infty, 4]$ is shown in Fig. 1.14. Intervals that use the infinity symbol are **unbounded** intervals. The following summary lists the different types of unbounded intervals used in interval notation and the graphs of those intervals on a number line. An unbounded interval with an endpoint is **open** if the endpoint is not included in the interval and **closed** if the endpoint is included. Graphs of inequalities are also drawn using an open circle instead of a parenthesis when an endpoint is not included and a solid circle instead of a bracket when an endpoint is included. The advantage of the parenthesis and bracket notation is that it corresponds to the interval notation.

SUMMARY Interval Notation for Unbounded Intervals

Set	Interval notation	Type	Graph
$\{x \mid x > a\}$	(a, ∞)	Open	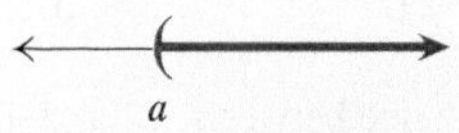
$\{x \mid x < a\}$	$(-\infty, a)$	Open	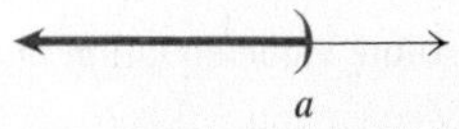
$\{x \mid x \geq a\}$	$[a, \infty)$	Closed	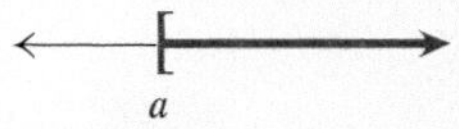
$\{x \mid x \leq a\}$	$(-\infty, a]$	Closed	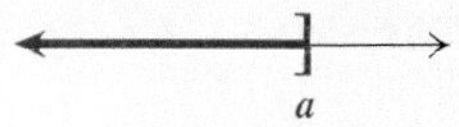
Real numbers	$(-\infty, \infty)$	Open	

We use a parenthesis when an endpoint of an interval is not included in the solution set and a bracket when an endpoint is included. A bracket is never used next to ∞ because infinity is not a number. On the graphs above, the number lines are shaded, showing that the solutions include all real numbers in the given interval.

Example 1 Interval notation

Write an inequality whose solution set is the given interval.

a. $(-\infty, -9)$ **b.** $[0, \infty)$

Solution

a. The interval $(-\infty, -9)$ represents all real numbers less than -9. It is the solution set to $x < -9$.

b. The interval $[0, \infty)$ represents all real numbers greater than or equal to 0. It is the solution set to $x \geq 0$. ■

Linear Inequalities

Replacing the equal sign in the general linear equation $ax + b = 0$ by any of the symbols $<, \leq, >$, or $\geq$ gives a **linear inequality.** Two inequalities are **equivalent** if they have the same solution set. We solve linear inequalities like we solve linear equations by performing operations on each side to get equivalent inequalities. However, the rules for inequalities are slightly different from the rules for equations.

Adding any real number to both sides of an inequality results in an equivalent inequality. For example, adding 3 to both sides of $-4 < 5$ yields $-1 < 8$, which is true. Adding or subtracting the same number simply moves the original numbers to the right or left along the number line and does not change their order.

The order of two numbers will also be unchanged when they are multiplied or divided by the same positive real number. For example, $10 < 20$, and after dividing both numbers by 10 we have $1 < 2$. Multiplying or dividing two numbers by a negative number will change the order. For example, $4 > 2$, but after multiplying both numbers by -1 we have $-4 < -2$. Likewise, $-10 < 20$, but after dividing both numbers by -10 we have $1 > -2$. *When an inequality is multiplied or divided by a negative number, the direction of the inequality symbol is reversed.* These ideas are stated symbolically in the following box for $<$, but they also hold for $>$, $\leq$, and $\geq$.

Properties of Inequality

If A and B are algebraic expressions and C is a nonzero real number, then the inequality $A < B$ is equivalent to

1. $A \pm C < B \pm C$,
2. $CA < CB$ (for C positive), $CA > CB$ (for C negative),
3. $\frac{A}{C} < \frac{B}{C}$ (for C positive), $\frac{A}{C} > \frac{B}{C}$ (for C negative).

Example 2 Solving a linear inequality

Solve $-3x - 9 < 0$. Write the solution set in interval notation and graph it.

Solution

Isolate the variable as is done in solving equations.

$$-3x - 9 < 0$$

$$-3x - 9 + 9 < 0 + 9 \quad \text{Add 9 to each side.}$$

$$-3x < 9$$

$$x > -3 \quad \text{Divide each side by } -3\text{, reversing the inequality.}$$

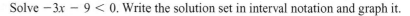

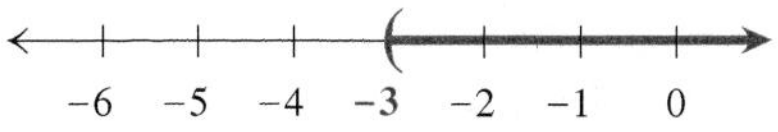

Figure 1.15

The solution set is the interval $(-3, \infty)$ and its graph is shown in Fig. 1.15. Checking the solution to an inequality is generally not as simple as checking an equation, because usually there are infinitely many solutions. We can do a "partial check" by checking one number in $(-3, \infty)$ and one number not in $(-3, \infty)$. For example, $0 > -3$ and $-3(0) - 9 < 0$ is correct, while $-6 < -3$ and $-3(-6) - 9 < 0$ is incorrect. ■

We can also perform operations on each side of an inequality using a variable expression. Addition or subtraction with variable expressions will give equivalent inequalities. However, we must always watch for undefined expressions. *Multiplication and division with a variable expression are usually avoided because we do not know whether the expression is positive or negative.*

Example 3 Solving a linear inequality

Solve $\frac{1}{2}x - 3 \geq \frac{1}{4}x + 2$ and graph the solution set.

Solution

Multiply each side by the LCD to eliminate the fractions.

$$\frac{1}{2}x - 3 \ge \frac{1}{4}x + 2$$

$$4\left(\frac{1}{2}x - 3\right) \ge 4\left(\frac{1}{4}x + 2\right) \quad \text{Multiply each side by 4.}$$

$$2x - 12 \ge x + 8$$

$$x - 12 \ge 8$$

$$x \ge 20$$

Figure 1.16

The solution set is the interval $[20, \infty)$. See Fig. 1.16 for its graph. ■

Compound Inequalities

A **compound inequality** is a sentence containing two simple inequalities connected with "and" or "or." The solution to a compound inequality can be an interval of real numbers that does not involve infinity, a **bounded** interval of real numbers. For example, the solution set to the compound inequality $x \ge 2$ and $x \le 5$ is the set of real numbers between 2 and 5, inclusive. This inequality is also written as $2 \le x \le 5$. Its solution set is $\{x \mid 2 \le x \le 5\}$, which is written in interval notation as $[2, 5]$. Because $[2, 5]$ contains both of its endpoints, the interval is **closed.** The following summary lists the different types of bounded intervals used in interval notation and the graphs of those intervals on a number line.

SUMMARY Interval Notation for Bounded Intervals

Set	Interval notation	Type	Graph
$\{x \mid a < x < b\}$	(a, b)	Open	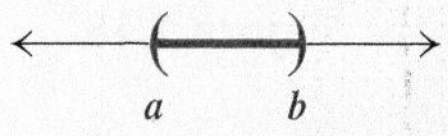
$\{x \mid a \le x \le b\}$	$[a, b]$	Closed	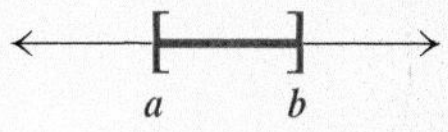
$\{x \mid a \le x < b\}$	$[a, b)$	Half open or half closed	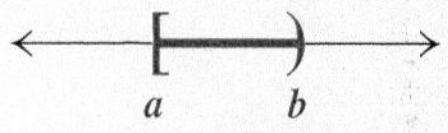
$\{x \mid a < x \le b\}$	$(a, b]$	Half open or half closed	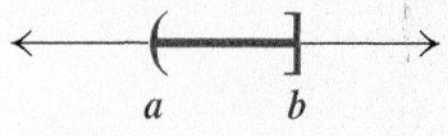

The notation $a < x < b$ is used only when x is between a and b, and a is less than b. We do *not* write inequalities such as $5 < x < 3$, $4 > x < 9$, or $2 < x > 8$.

The **intersection** of sets A and B is the set $A \cap B$ (read "A intersect B"), where $x \in A \cap B$ if and only if $x \in A$ and $x \in B$. (The symbol $\in$ means "belongs to.") The **union** of sets A and B is the set $A \cup B$ (read "A union B"), where $x \in A \cup B$ if and only if $x \in A$ or $x \in B$. In solving compounded inequalities it is often necessary to find intersections and unions of intervals.

Example 4 Intersections and unions of intervals

Let $A = (1, 5)$, $B = [3, 7)$, and $C = (6, \infty)$. Write each of the following sets in interval notation.

a. $A \cup B$ **b.** $A \cap B$ **c.** $A \cup C$ **d.** $A \cap C$

Solution

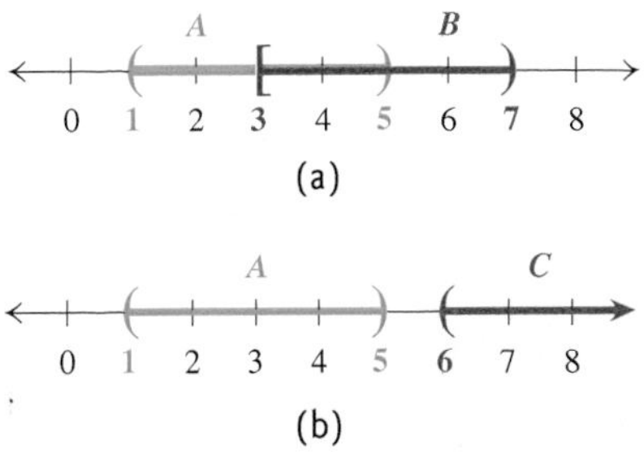

Figure 1.17

a. Graph both intervals on the number line as shown in Fig. 1.17(a). The union of two intervals is the set of points that are in one, the other, or both intervals. For a union, nothing is omitted. The union consists of all points shaded in the figure. So $A \cup B = (1, 7)$.

b. The intersection of A and B is the set of points that belong to both intervals. The intersection consist of the points that are shaded twice in Fig. 1.17(a). So $A \cap B = [3, 5)$.

c. Graph both intervals on the number line as shown in Fig. 1.17(b). For a union, nothing is omitted. So $A \cup C = (1, 5) \cup (6, \infty)$. Note that $A \cup C$ cannot be written as a single interval.

d. Since there are no points shaded twice in Fig. 1.17(b), $A \cap C = \varnothing$. ■

The solution set to a compound inequality using the connector "or" is the union of the two solution sets, and the solution set to a compound inequality using "and" is the intersection of the two solution sets.

Example 5 Solving compound inequalities

Solve each compound inequality. Write the solution set using interval notation and graph it.

a. $2x - 3 > 5$ and $4 - x \le 3$ **b.** $4 - 3x < -2$ or $3(x - 2) \le -6$
c. $-4 \le 3x - 1 < 5$

Solution

a.
$$2x - 3 > 5 \quad \text{and} \quad 4 - x \le 3$$
$$2x > 8 \quad \text{and} \quad -x \le -1$$
$$x > 4 \quad \text{and} \quad x \ge 1$$

Graph $(4, \infty)$ and $[1, \infty)$ on the number line as shown in Fig. 1.18(a). The intersection of the intervals is the set of points that are shaded twice in Fig. 1.18(a). So the intersection is the interval $(4, \infty)$ and $(4, \infty)$ is the solution set to the compound inequality. Its graph is shown in Fig. 1.18(b).

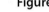

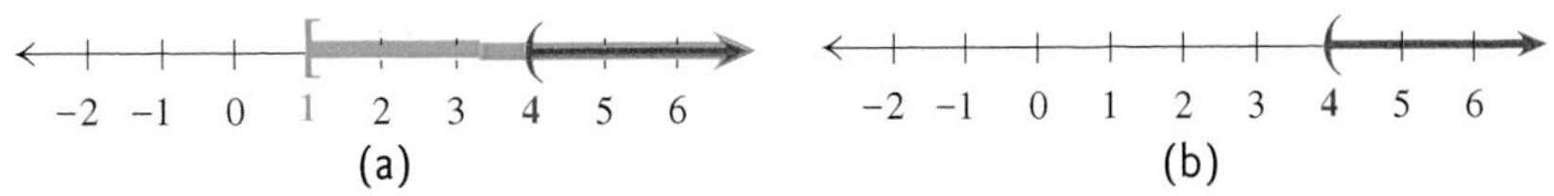

Figure 1.18

b.
$$4 - 3x < -2 \quad \text{or} \quad 3(x - 2) \le -6$$
$$-3x < -6 \quad \text{or} \quad x - 2 \le -2$$
$$x > 2 \quad \text{or} \quad x \le 0$$

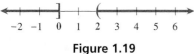

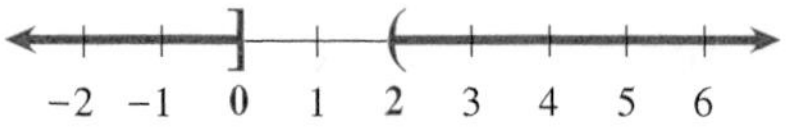
Figure 1.19

The union of the intervals $(2, \infty)$ and $(-\infty, 0]$ consists of all points that are shaded in Fig. 1.19. This set cannot be written as a single interval. So the solution set is $(-\infty, 0] \cup (2, \infty)$ and its graph is shown in Fig. 1.19.

c. We could write $-4 \leq 3x - 1 < 5$ as the compound inequality $-4 \leq 3x - 1$ and $3x - 1 < 5$, and then solve each simple inequality. Since each is solved using the same sequence of steps, we can solve the original inequality without separating it:

$$-4 \leq 3x - 1 < 5$$

$$-4 + 1 \leq 3x - 1 + 1 < 5 + 1 \quad \text{Add 1 to each part of the inequality.}$$

$$-3 \leq 3x < 6$$

$$\frac{-3}{3} \leq \frac{3x}{3} < \frac{6}{3} \quad \text{Divide each part by 3.}$$

$$-1 \leq x < 2$$

Figure 1.20

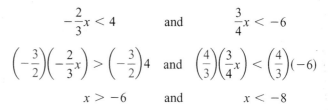

The solution set is the half-open interval $[-1, 2)$, graphed in Fig. 1.20. ■

It is possible that all real numbers satisfy a compound inequality or no real numbers satisfy a compound inequality.

Example 6 All or nothing

Solve each compound inequality.

a. $3x - 9 \leq 9$ or $4 - x \leq 3$ **b.** $-\frac{2}{3}x < 4$ and $\frac{3}{4}x < -6$

Solution

a. Solve each simple inequality and find the union of their solution sets:

$$3x - 9 \leq 9 \quad \text{or} \quad 4 - x \leq 3$$

$$3x \leq 18 \quad \text{or} \quad -x \leq -1$$

$$x \leq 6 \quad \text{or} \quad x \geq 1$$

The union of $(-\infty, 6]$ and $[1, \infty)$ is the set of all real numbers, $(-\infty, \infty)$.

b. Solve each simple inequality and find the intersection of their solution sets:

$$-\frac{2}{3}x < 4 \quad \text{and} \quad \frac{3}{4}x < -6$$

$$\left(-\frac{3}{2}\right)\left(-\frac{2}{3}x\right) > \left(-\frac{3}{2}\right)4 \quad \text{and} \quad \left(\frac{4}{3}\right)\left(\frac{3}{4}x\right) < \left(\frac{4}{3}\right)(-6)$$

$$x > -6 \quad \text{and} \quad x < -8$$

Since $(-6, \infty) \cap (-\infty, -8) = \varnothing$, there is no solution to the compound inequality. ■

Absolute Value Inequalities

Recall that the absolute value of a number is the number's distance from 0 on the number line. The inequality $|x| < 3$ means that x is less than three units from 0. See Fig. 1.21. The real numbers that are less than three units from 0 are precisely the numbers that satisfy $-3 < x < 3$. So the solution set to $|x| < 3$ is the open interval $(-3, 3)$.

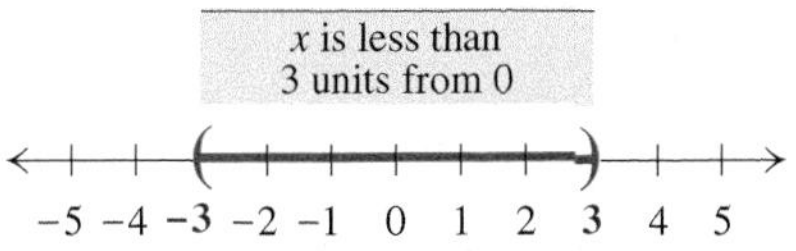

Figure 1.21

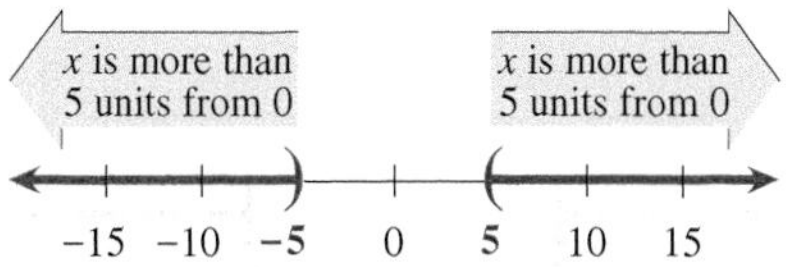

Figure 1.22

The inequality $|x| > 5$ means that x is more than five units from 0 on the number line, which is equivalent to the compound inequality $x > 5$ or $x < -5$. See Fig. 1.22. So the solution to $|x| > 5$ is the union of two intervals, $(-\infty, -5) \cup (5, \infty)$. These ideas about absolute value inequalities are summarized as follows.

SUMMARY

Basic Absolute Value Inequalities (for $k > 0$)

Absolute value inequality	Equivalent statement	Solution set in interval notation	Graph of solution set
$\|x\| > k$	$x < -k$ or $x > k$	$(-\infty, -k) \cup (k, \infty)$	
$\|x\| \geq k$	$x \leq -k$ or $x \geq k$	$(-\infty, -k] \cup [k, \infty)$	
$\|x\| < k$	$-k < x < k$	$(-k, k)$	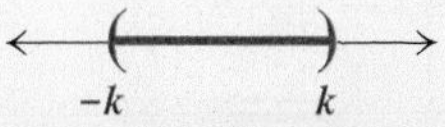
$\|x\| \leq k$	$-k \leq x \leq k$	$[-k, k]$	

In the next example we use the rules for basic absolute value inequalities to solve more complicated absolute value inequalities.

Example 7 Absolute value inequalities

Solve each absolute value inequality and graph the solution set.

a. $|3x + 2| < 7$ **b.** $-2|4 - x| \leq -4$ **c.** $|7x - 9| \geq -3$

Solution

a.

$$|3x + 2| < 7$$

$$-7 < 3x + 2 < 7 \quad \text{Write the equivalent compound inequality.}$$

$$-7 - 2 < 3x + 2 - 2 < 7 - 2 \quad \text{Subtract 2 from each part.}$$

$$-9 < 3x < 5$$

$$-3 < x < \frac{5}{3} \quad \text{Divide each part by 3.}$$

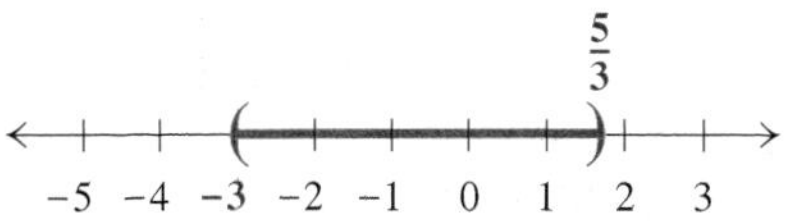

Figure 1.23

The solution set is the open interval $\left(-3, \frac{5}{3}\right)$. The graph is shown in Fig. 1.23.

b. $-2|4 - x| \le -4$ Divide each side by -2, reversing the inequality.

$$|4 - x| \ge 2$$

$$4 - x \le -2 \quad \text{or} \quad 4 - x \ge 2$$ Write the equivalent compound inequality.

$$-x \le -6 \quad \text{or} \quad -x \ge -2$$

$$x \ge 6 \quad \text{or} \quad x \le 2$$ Multiply each side by

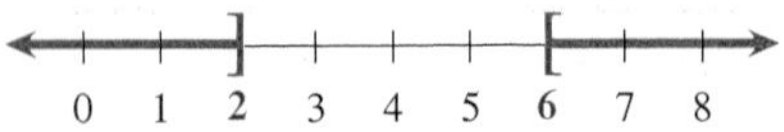

Figure 1.24

The solution set is $(-\infty, 2] \cup [6, \infty)$. Its graph is shown in Fig. 1.24. Check 8, 4, and 0 in the original inequality. If $x = 8$, we get $-2|4 - 8| \le -4$, which is true. If $x = 4$, we get $-2|4 - 4| \le -4$, which is false. If $x = 0$, we get $-2|4 - 0| \le -4$, which is true.

Figure 1.25

c. The expression $|7x - 9|$ has a nonnegative value for every real number x. So the inequality $|7x - 9| \ge -3$ is satisfied by every real number. The solution set is $(-\infty, \infty)$, and its graph is shown in Fig. 1.25. ■

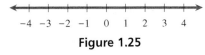

Modeling with Inequalities

Inequalities occur in applications just as equations do. In fact, in real life, equality in anything is usually the exception. The solution to a problem involving an inequality is generally an interval of real numbers. In this case we often ask for the range of values that solve the problem.

Example 8 An application involving inequality

Remington scored 74 on his midterm exam in history. If he is to get a B, the average of his midterm and final exam must be between 80 and 89 inclusive. In what range must his final exam score lie for him to get a B in the course?

Solution

Let x represent Remington's final exam score. The average of his midterm and final must satisfy the following inequality:

$$80 \le \frac{74 + x}{2} \le 89$$

$$160 \le 74 + x \le 178$$

$$86 \le x \le 104$$

His final exam score must lie in the interval $[86, 104]$ if he is to get a B. ■

When discussing the error made in a measurement, we may refer to the *absolute error* or the *relative error*. For example, if L is the actual length of an object and x is the length determined by a measurement, then the absolute error is $|x - L|$ and the relative error is $|x - L|/L$.

■ **Foreshadowing Calculus**

In Example 9 we find values for x that determine the size of the relative error. This same idea is used in calculus in the study of limits.

Example 9 Application of absolute value inequality

A technician is testing a scale with a 50 lb block of steel. The scale passes this test if the relative error when weighing this block is less than 0.1%. If x is the reading on the scale, then for what values of x does the scale pass this test?

Solution

If the relative error must be less than 0.1%, then x must satisfy the following inequality:

$$\frac{|x - 50|}{50} < 0.001$$

Solve the inequality for x:

$$|x - 50| < 0.05$$
$$-0.05 < x - 50 < 0.05$$
$$49.95 < x < 50.05$$

So the scale passes the test if it shows a weight in the interval (49.95, 50.05). ■

Absolute value inequalities like the one in Example 9 are used to measure "closeness" in the study of limits in calculus. For example, $|x - 2| < 0.01$ indicates that x differs from 2 by less than 0.01. So x is really close to 2. Note that $x - 2 < 0.01$ does not mean that x is close to 2 because this inequality is satisfied even if x is -1000.

For Thought

True or False? Explain.

1. The inequality $-3 < x + 6$ is equivalent to $x + 6 > -3$.
2. The inequality $-2x < -6$ is equivalent to $\frac{-2x}{-2} < \frac{-6}{-2}$.
3. The smallest real number that satisfies $x > 12$ is 13.
4. The number -6 satisfies $|x - 6| > -1$.
5. $(-\infty, -3) \cap (-\infty, -2) = (-\infty, -2)$
6. $(5, \infty) \cap (-\infty, -3) = (-3, 5)$
7. All negative numbers satisfy $|x - 2| < 0$.
8. The compound inequality $x < -3$ or $x > 3$ is equivalent to $|x| < -3$.
9. The inequality $|x| + 2 < 5$ is equivalent to $-5 < x + 2 < 5$.
10. The fact that the difference between your age, y, and my age, m, is at most 5 years is written $|y - m| \leq 5$.

1.2 Exercises

For each interval write an inequality whose solution set is the interval, and for each inequality write the solution set in interval notation. See the summary of interval notation for unbounded intervals on page 12.

1. $(-\infty, 12)$ **2.** $(-\infty, -3]$ **3.** $[-7, \infty)$

4. $(1.2, \infty)$ **5.** $x \geq -8$ **6.** $x < 54$

7. $x < \pi/2$ **8.** $x \geq \sqrt{3}$

Solve each inequality. Write the solution set using interval notation and graph it.

9. $3x - 6 > 9$ **10.** $2x + 1 < 6$

11. $7 - 5x \leq -3$ **12.** $-1 - 4x \geq 7$

13. $\frac{1}{2}x - 4 < \frac{1}{3}x + 5$ **14.** $\frac{1}{2} - x > \frac{x}{3} + \frac{1}{4}$

15. $\dfrac{7 - 3x}{2} \geq -3$

16. $\dfrac{5 - x}{3} \leq -2$

17. $\dfrac{2x - 3}{-5} \geq 0$

18. $\dfrac{5 - 3x}{-7} \leq 0$

19. $-2(3x - 2) \geq 4 - x$

20. $-5x \leq 3(x - 9)$

Write as a single interval. See the summary of interval notation for bounded intervals on page 14.

21. $(-3, \infty) \cup (5, \infty)$

22. $(-\infty, 0) \cup (-\infty, 6)$

23. $(3, 5) \cup (-3, \infty)$

24. $(4, 7) \cap (3, \infty)$

25. $(-\infty, -2) \cap (-5, \infty)$

26. $(-3, \infty) \cap (2, \infty)$

27. $(-\infty, -5) \cap (-2, \infty)$

28. $(-\infty, -3) \cup (-7, \infty)$

29. $(-\infty, 4) \cup [4, 5]$

30. $[3, 5] \cup [5, 7]$

Solve each compound inequality. Write the solution set using interval notation and graph it.

31. $5 > 8 - x$ and $1 + 0.5x < 4$

32. $5 - x < 4$ and $0.2x - 5 < 1$

33. $\dfrac{2x - 5}{-2} < 2$ and $\dfrac{2x + 1}{3} > 0$

34. $\dfrac{4 - x}{2} > 1$ and $\dfrac{2x - 7}{-3} < 1$

35. $1 - x < 7 + x$ or $4x + 3 > x$

36. $5 + x > 3 - x$ or $2x - 3 > x$

37. $\dfrac{1}{2}(x + 1) > 3$ or $0 < 7 - x$

38. $\dfrac{1}{2}(x + 6) > 3$ or $4(x - 1) < 3x - 4$

39. $1 - \dfrac{3}{2}x < 4$ and $\dfrac{1}{4}x - 2 \leq -3$

40. $\dfrac{3}{5}x - 1 > 2$ and $5 - \dfrac{2}{5}x \geq 3$

41. $1 < 3x - 5 < 7$

42. $-3 \leq 4x + 9 \leq 17$

43. $-2 \leq 4 - 6x < 22$

44. $-13 < 5 - 9x \leq 41$

Solve each absolute value inequality. Write the solution set using interval notation and graph it. See the summary of basic absolute value inequalities on page 17.

45. $|3x - 1| < 2$

46. $|4x - 3| \leq 5$

47. $|5 - 4x| \leq 1$

48. $|6 - x| < 6$

49. $5 \geq |4 - x|$

50. $3 < |2x - 1|$

51. $|5 - 4x| < 0$

52. $|3x - 7| \geq -5$

53. $|4 - 5x| < -1$

54. $|2 - 9x| \geq 0$

55. $3|x - 2| + 6 > 9$

56. $3|x - 1| + 2 < 8$

57. $\left|\dfrac{x - 3}{2}\right| > 1$

58. $\left|\dfrac{9 - 4x}{2}\right| < 3$

Write an inequality of the form $|x - a| < k$ or of the form $|x - a| > k$ so that the inequality has the given solution set. (Hint: $|x - a| < k$ means that x is less than k units from a and $|x - a| > k$ means that x is more than k units from a on the number line.)

59. $(-5, 5)$

60. $(-2, 2)$

61. $(-\infty, -3) \cup (3, \infty)$

62. $(-\infty, -1) \cup (1, \infty)$

63. $(4, 8)$

64. $(-3, 9)$

65. $(-\infty, 3) \cup (5, \infty)$

66. $(-\infty, -1) \cup (5, \infty)$

For each graph write an absolute value inequality that has the given solution set.

67.

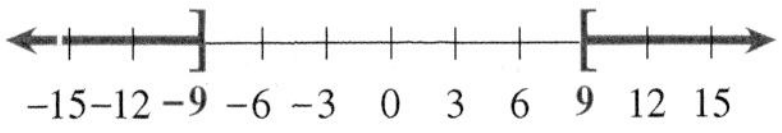

68.

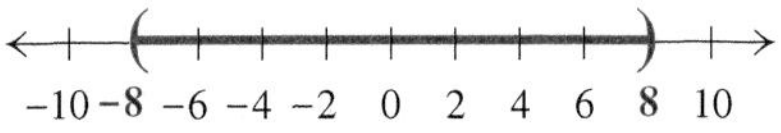

69.

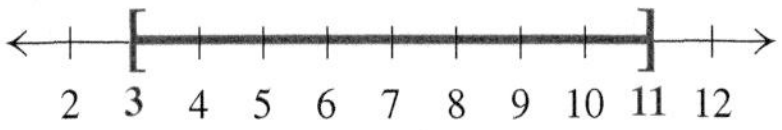

70.

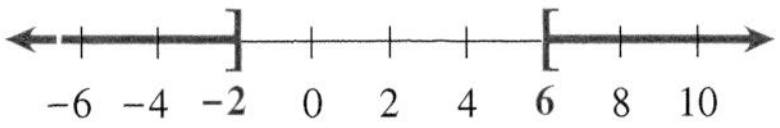

71.

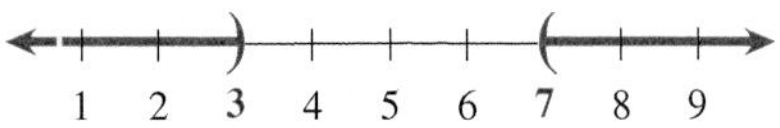

72.

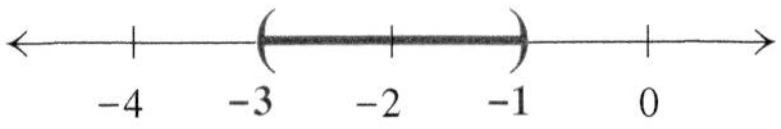

Solve each problem.

73. *Final Exam Score* Lucky scored 65 on his Psychology 101 midterm. If the average of his midterm and final must be between 79 and 90 for a B, then for what range of scores on the final exam would Lucky get a B?

74. *Bringing Up Your Average* Felix scored 52 and 64 on his first two tests in Sociology 212. What must he get on the third test to get an average for the three tests above 70?

75. *Weighted Average with Whole Numbers* Ingrid scored 65 on her calculus midterm. If her final exam counts twice as much as her midterm exam, then for what range of scores on her final would she get an average between 79 and 90?

76. *Weighted Average with Fractions* Elizabeth scored 62, 76, and 80 on three equally weighted tests in French. If the final exam score counts for two-thirds of the grade and the tests count for one-third, then what range of scores on the final exam would give her a final average over 70?

77. *Price Range for a Car* Yolanda is shopping for a used car in a city where the sales tax is 10% and the title and license fee is $300. If the maximum that she can spend is $8000, then she should look at cars in what price range?

78. *Price of a Burger* The price of Elaine's favorite Big Salad at the corner restaurant is 10 cents more than the price of Jerry's hamburger. After treating a group of friends to lunch, Jerry is certain that for 10 hamburgers and 5 salads he spent more than $9.14, but not more than $13.19, including tax at 8% and a 50 cent tip. In what price range is a hamburger?

79. *Bicycle Gear Ratio* The gear ratio r for a bicycle is defined by the formula

$$r = \frac{Nw}{n},$$

where N is the number of teeth on the chainring (by the pedal), n is the number of teeth on the cog (by the wheel), and w is the wheel diameter in inches. The following chart gives uses for the various gear ratios.

Ratio	Use	
$r > 90$	down hill	
$70 < r \leq 90$	level	
$50 < r \leq 70$	mild hill	
$35 < r \leq 50$	long hill	

A bicycle with a 27-in. diameter wheel has 50 teeth on the chainring and 5 cogs with 14, 17, 20, 24, and 29 teeth. Find the gear ratio with each of the five cogs. Does this bicycle have a gear ratio for each of the four types of pedaling described in the table?

80. *Selecting the Cogs* Use the formula from the previous exercise to answer the following.

a. If a single-speed 27-in. bicycle has 17 teeth on the cog, then for what numbers of teeth on the chainring will the gear ratio be between 60 and 80?

b. If a 26-in. bicycle has 40 teeth on the chainring, then for what numbers of teeth on the cog will the gear ratio be between 60 and 75?

81. *Expensive Models* The prices of the 2006 BMW 745 Li and 760 Li differ by more than $25,000. The list price of the 745 Li is $74,595. Assuming that you do not know which model is more expensive, write an absolute value inequality that describes the price of the 760 Li. What are the possibilities for the price of the 760 Li?

82. *Difference in Prices* There is less than $800 difference between the price of a $14,200 Ford and a comparable Chevrolet. Express this as an absolute value inequality. What are the possibilities for the price of the Chevrolet?

83. *Controlling Temperature* Michelle is trying to keep the water temperature in her chemistry experiment at 35°C. For the experiment to work, the relative error for the actual temperature must be less than 1%. Write an absolute value inequality for the actual temperature. Find the interval in which the actual temperature must lie.

84. *Laying Out a Track* Melvin is attempting to lay out a track for a 100 m race. According to the rules of competition, the relative error of the actual length must be less than 0.5%. Write an absolute value inequality for the actual length. Find the interval in which the actual length must fall.

85. *Acceptable Bearings* A spherical bearing is to have a circumference of 7.2 cm with an error of no more than 0.1 cm. Use an absolute value inequality to find the acceptable range of values for the diameter of the bearing.

86. *Acceptable Targets* A manufacturer makes circular targets that have an area of 15 ft^2. According to competition rules, the area can be in error by no more than 0.5 ft^2. Use an absolute value inequality to find the acceptable range of values for the radius.

Figure for Exercise 86

Thinking Outside the Box II

One in a Million If you write the integers from 1 through 1,000,000 inclusive, then how many ones will you write?

1.2 Pop Quiz

Solve each inequality. Write the solution set using interval notation.

1. $x - \sqrt{2} \geq 0$

2. $6 - 2x < 0$

3. $x > 4$ or $x \geq -1$

4. $x - 1 > 5$ and $2x < 18$

5. $|x| > 6$

6. $|x - 1| \leq 2$

1.3 Equations and Graphs in Two Variables

In algebra and calculus we study relationships between two variables. For example, p might represent the price of gasoline and n the number of gallons consumed in a month; r might be the radius of a circle and A its area; x might be the number of toppings on a medium pizza and y the cost of the pizza. We can visualize the relationship between two variables in a two-dimensional coordinate system.

Table 1.1

Toppings x	Cost y
0	\$ 5
1	7
2	9
3	11
4	13

The Cartesian Coordinate System

If x and y are real numbers, then (x, y) is called an **ordered pair** of real numbers. The numbers x and y are the **coordinates** of the ordered pair, with x being the **first coordinate** or **abscissa,** and y being the **second coordinate** or **ordinate.** For example, Table 1.1 shows the number of toppings on a medium pizza and the corresponding cost. The ordered pair (3, 11) indicates that a three-topping pizza costs \$11. The order of the numbers matters. In this context, (11, 3) would indicate that an 11-topping pizza costs \$3.

To picture ordered pairs of real numbers we use the **rectangular coordinate system** or **Cartesian coordinate system,** named after the French mathematician René Descartes (1596–1650). The Cartesian coordinate system consists of two number lines drawn perpendicular to one another, intersecting at zero on each number line as shown in Fig. 1.26. The point of intersection of the number lines is called the

Historical Note

René Descartes (1596–1650) was a noted French philosopher, mathematician, and scientist. He has been called the "founder of modern philosophy" and the "father of modern mathematics." He ranks as one of the most important and influential thinkers of modern times.

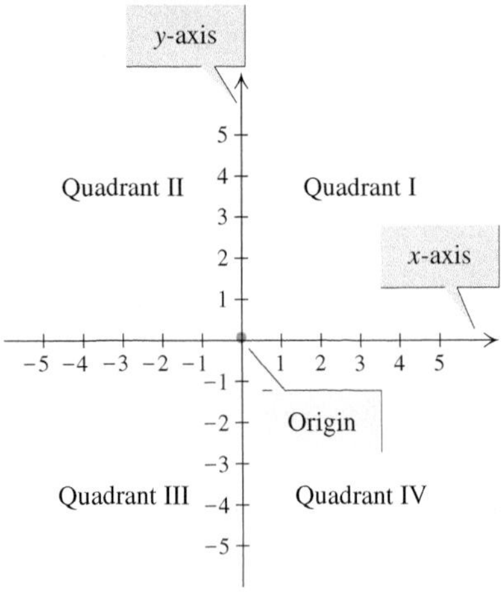

Figure 1.26

origin. The horizontal number line is the **x-axis** and its positive numbers are to the right of the origin. The vertical number line is the **y-axis** and its positive numbers are above the origin. The two number lines divide the plane into four regions called **quadrants,** numbered as shown in Fig. 1.26. The quadrants do not include any points on the axes. We call a plane with a rectangular coordinate system the **coordinate plane** or the **xy-plane.**

Just as every real number corresponds to a point on the number line, every ordered pair of real numbers (a, b) corresponds to a point P in the xy-plane. For this reason, ordered pairs of numbers are often called **points.** So a and b are the coordinates of (a, b) or the coordinates of the point P. Locating the point P that corresponds to (a, b) in the xy-plane is referred to as **plotting** or **graphing** the point, and P is called the *graph* of (a, b). In general, a **graph** is a set of points in the rectangular coordinate system.

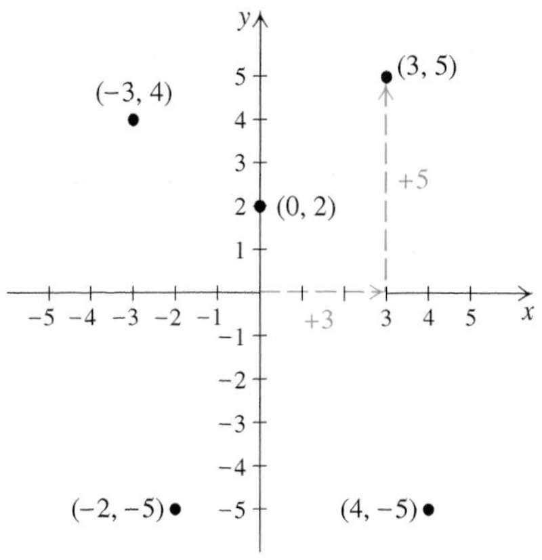

Figure 1.27

Example 1 Plotting points

Plot the points $(3, 5)$, $(4, -5)$, $(-3, 4)$, $(-2, -5)$, and $(0, 2)$ in the xy-plane.

Solution

The point $(3, 5)$ is located three units to the right of the origin and five units above the x-axis as shown in Fig. 1.27. The point $(4, -5)$ is located four units to the right of the origin and five units below the x-axis. The point $(-3, 4)$ is located three units to the left of the origin and four units above the x-axis. The point $(-2, -5)$ is located two units to the left of the origin and five units below the x-axis. The point $(0, 2)$ is on the y-axis because its first coordinate is zero. ■

Historical Note

Pythagoras of Samos (582 B.C.–507 B.C.) was a Greek mathematician and philosopher. He founded the mystic, religious, and scientific society called Pythagoreans. He is best known for the Pythagorean theorem. Pythagoras made influential contributions to philosophy and religious teaching in the late 6th century B.C. Pythagoras and his students believed that everything was related to mathematics and, through mathematics, everything could be predicted and measured in rhythmic patterns or cycles.

Note that for points in quadrant I, both coordinates are positive. In quadrant II the first coordinate is negative and the second is positive, while in quadrant III, both coordinates are negative. In quadrant IV the first coordinate is positive and the second is negative.

The Distance Formula

If a and b are real numbers, then the distance between them on the number line is $|a - b|$. Now consider the points $A(x_1, y_1)$ and $B(x_2, y_2)$ shown in Fig. 1.28. Let AB represent the length of line segment $\overline{AB}$. Now $\overline{AB}$ is the hypotenuse of the right triangle in Fig. 1.28. Since A and C lie on a horizontal line, the distance between them

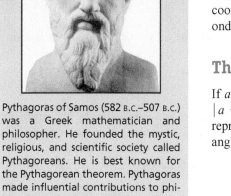

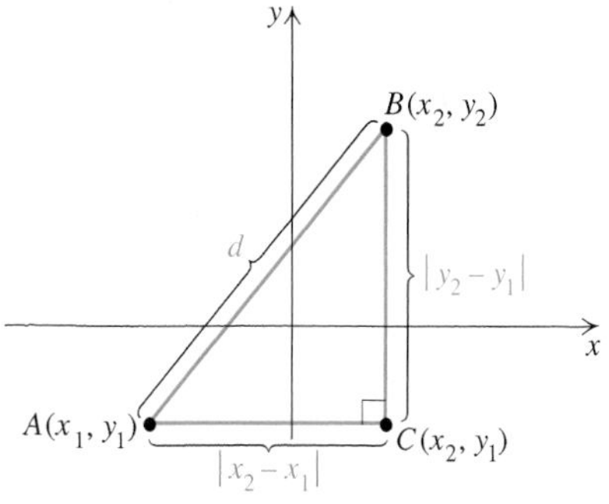

Figure 1.28

is $|x_2 - x_1|$. Likewise $CB = |y_2 - y_1|$. Since the sum of the squares of the legs of a right triangle is equal to the square of the hypotenuse (the Pythagorean theorem) we have

$$d^2 = |x_2 - x_1|^2 + |y_2 - y_1|^2.$$

Since the distance between two points is a nonnegative real number, we have $d = \sqrt{(x_2 - x_1)^2 + (y_2 - y_1)^2}$. The absolute value symbols are replaced with parentheses, because $|a - b|^2 = (a - b)^2$ for any real numbers a and b.

Theorem: The Distance Formula

The distance d between the points (x_1, y_1) and (x_2, y_2) is given by the formula

$$d = \sqrt{(x_2 - x_1)^2 + (y_2 - y_1)^2}.$$

Example 2 Finding the distance between two points

Find the distance between $(5, -3)$ and $(-1, -6)$.

Solution

Let $(x_1, y_1) = (5, -3)$ and $(x_2, y_2) = (-1, -6)$. These points are shown on the graph in Fig. 1.29. Substitute these values into the distance formula:

$$\begin{aligned} d &= \sqrt{(-1 - 5)^2 + (-6 - (-3))^2} \\ &= \sqrt{(-6)^2 + (-3)^2} \\ &= \sqrt{36 + 9} = \sqrt{45} = 3\sqrt{5} \end{aligned}$$

The exact distance between the points is $3\sqrt{5}$. ■

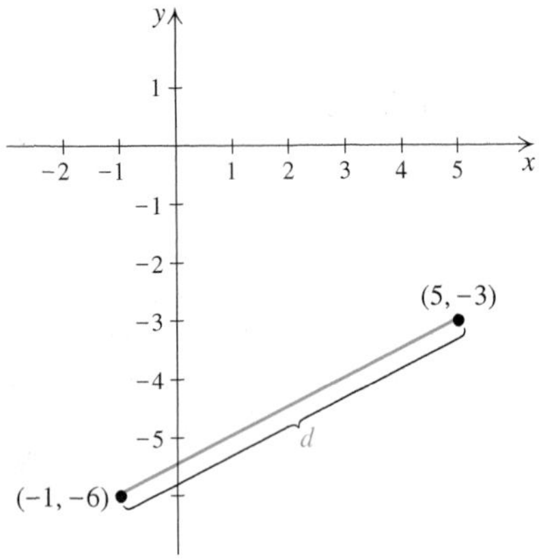

Figure 1.29

Note that the distance between two points is the same regardless of which point is chosen as (x_1, y_1) or (x_2, y_2).

The Midpoint Formula

When you average two test scores (by finding their sum and dividing by 2), you are finding a number midway between the two scores. Likewise, the midpoint of the line segment with endpoints -1 and 7 in Fig. 1.30 is $(-1 + 7)/2$ or 3. In general, $(a + b)/2$ is the midpoint of the line segment with endpoints a and b shown in Fig. 1.31.

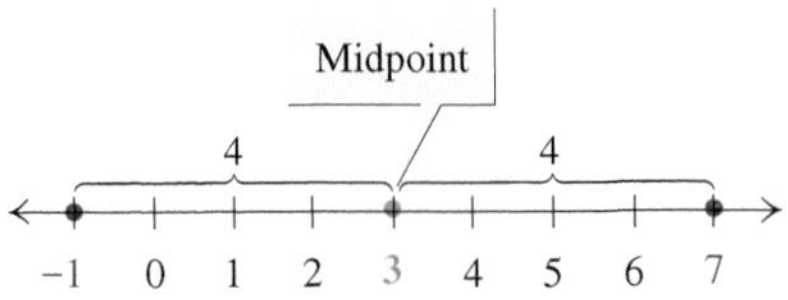

Figure 1.30

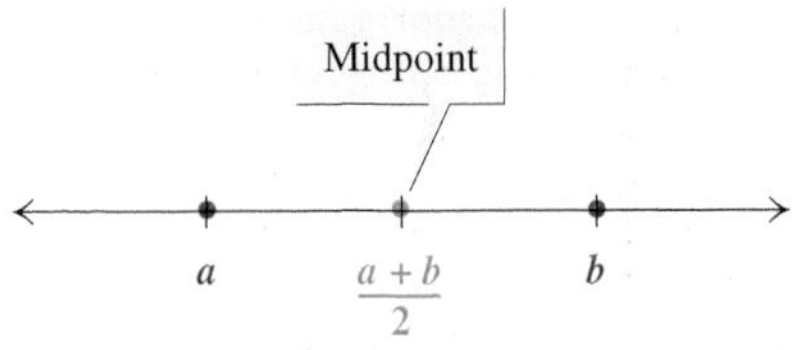

Figure 1.31

Theorem: Midpoint on a Number Line

If a and b are real numbers, then $\dfrac{a + b}{2}$ is midway between them on the number line.

PROOF The distance between two numbers on the number line is the absolute value of their difference. So

$$\left|a - \frac{a+b}{2}\right| = \left|\frac{2a}{2} - \frac{a+b}{2}\right| = \left|\frac{a-b}{2}\right| = \frac{|a-b|}{2}$$

and

$$\left|b - \frac{a+b}{2}\right| = \left|\frac{2b}{2} - \frac{a+b}{2}\right| = \left|\frac{b-a}{2}\right| = \frac{|b-a|}{2}.$$

Since $|a - b| = |b - a|$, the distances from $\frac{a+b}{2}$ to a and from $\frac{a+b}{2}$ to b are equal. Since $\frac{a+b}{2}$ is equidistant from a and b it must be between a and b. ■

We can find the midpoint of a line segment in the xy-plane in the same manner.

Theorem: The Midpoint Formula

The midpoint of the line segment with endpoints (x_1, y_1) and (x_2, y_2) is

$$\left(\frac{x_1 + x_2}{2}, \frac{y_1 + y_2}{2}\right).$$

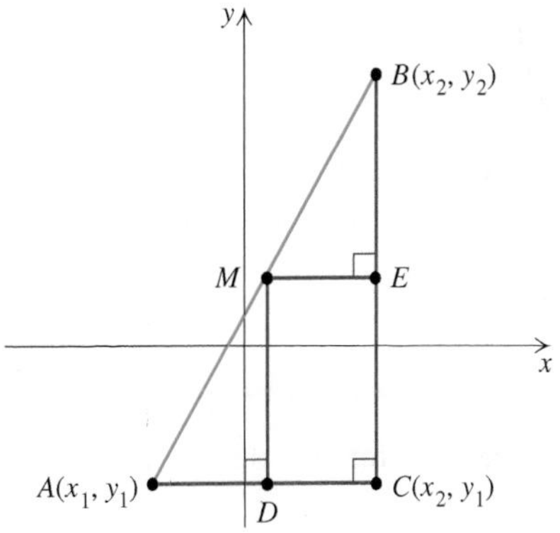

Figure 1.32

PROOF Start with a line segment with endpoints $A(x_1, y_1)$ and $B(x_2, y_2)$ as shown in Fig. 1.32. Let M be the midpoint of $\overline{AB}$. Draw horizontal and vertical line segments as shown in Fig. 1.32 forming three right triangles. Since M is the midpoint of $\overline{AB}$ the two small right triangles are congruent. So D is the midpoint of $\overline{AC}$ and E is the midpoint of $\overline{BC}$. Since the midpoint on a number line is found by adding and dividing by two, the x-coordinate of D is $\frac{x_1 + x_2}{2}$ and the y-coordinate of E is $\frac{y_1 + y_2}{2}$. So the midpoint M is $\left(\frac{x_1 + x_2}{2}, \frac{y_1 + y_2}{2}\right)$. ■

Example 3 Finding a midpoint

Find the midpoint of the line segment that has endpoints $(5, -3)$ and $(-1, 6)$.

Solution

Let $(x_1, y_1) = (5, -3)$ and $(x_2, y_2) = (-1, 6)$ in the midpoint formula:

$$\left(\frac{x_1 + x_2}{2}, \frac{y_1 + y_2}{2}\right) = \left(\frac{5 + (-1)}{2}, \frac{-3 + (-6)}{2}\right) = \left(2, -\frac{9}{2}\right)$$

So the midpoint of the line segment is $(2, -9/2)$. ■

The Circle

An ordered pair is a **solution to** or **satisfies** an equation in two variables if the equation is correct when the variables are replaced by the coordinates of the ordered pair. For example, $(3, 11)$ satisfies $y = 2x + 5$ because $11 = 2(3) + 5$ is correct. The **solution set** to an equation in two variables is the set of all ordered pairs that satisfy the equation. The graph of (the solution set to) an equation is a geometric object that gives us a visual image of an algebraic object. Circles provide a nice example of this relationship between algebra and geometry.

A **circle** is the set of all points in a plane that lie a fixed distance from a given point in the plane. The fixed distance is called the **radius,** and the given point is the **center.** The distance formula can be used to write an equation for the circle shown in Fig. 1.33 with center (h, k) and radius r for $r > 0$. A point (x, y) is on the circle if and only if it satisfies the equation

$$\sqrt{(x - h)^2 + (y - k)^2} = r.$$

Since both sides of $\sqrt{(x - h)^2 + (y - k)^2} = r$ are positive, we can square each side to get the following **standard form** for the equation of a circle.

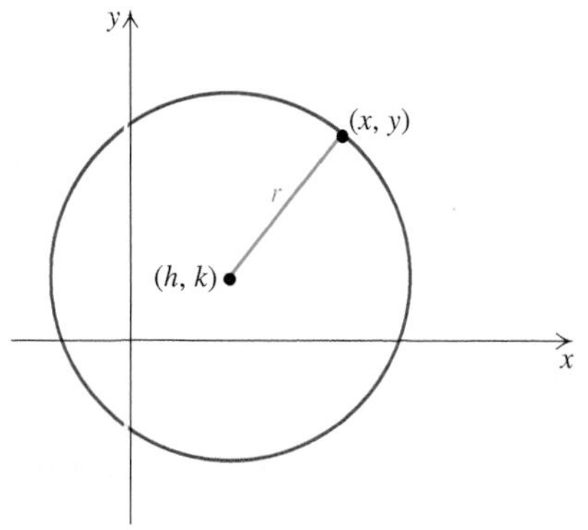

Figure 1.33

Theorem: Equation for a Circle in Standard Form

The equation for a circle with center (h, k) and radius r for $r > 0$ is

$$(x - h)^2 + (y - k)^2 = r^2.$$

A circle centered at the origin has equation $x^2 + y^2 = r^2$.

Note that squaring both sides of an equation produces an equivalent equation only when both sides are positive. If we square both sides of $\sqrt{x} = -3$, we get $x = 9$. But $\sqrt{9} \neq -3$ since the square root symbol always represents the nonnegative square root. Raising both sides of an equation to a power is discussed further in Section 2.5.

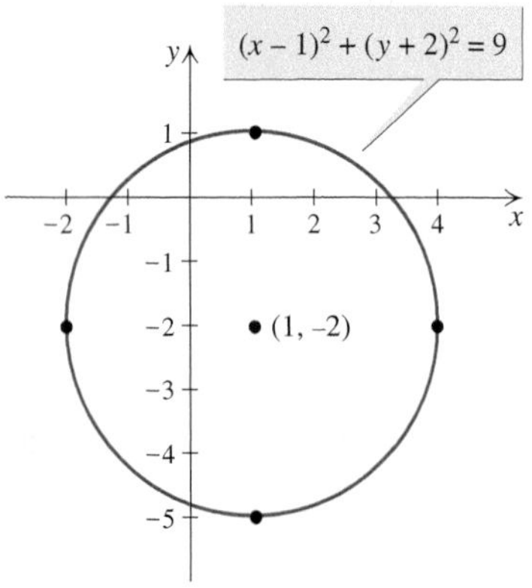

Figure 1.34

Example 4 Graphing a circle

Sketch the graph of the equation $(x - 1)^2 + (y + 2)^2 = 9$.

Solution

Since $(x - h)^2 + (y - k)^2 = r^2$ is a circle with center (h, k) and radius r (for $r > 0$), the graph of $(x - 1)^2 + (y + 2)^2 = 9$ is a circle with center $(1, -2)$ and radius 3. You can draw the circle as in Fig. 1.34 with a compass. To draw a circle by hand, locate the points that lie 3 units above, below, right, and left of the center, as shown in Fig. 1.34. Then sketch a circle through these points.

To support these results with a graphing calculator you must first solve the equation for y:

$$\begin{aligned} (x-1)^2 + (y+2)^2 &= 9 \\ (y+2)^2 &= 9 - (x-1)^2 \\ y + 2 &= \pm\sqrt{9-(x-1)^2} \\ y &= -2 \pm \sqrt{9-(x-1)^2} \end{aligned}$$

Now enter y_1 and y_2 as in Fig. 1.35(a). Set the viewing window as in Fig. 1.35(b). The graph in Fig. 1.35(c) supports our previous conclusion. A circle looks round only if the same unit distance is used on both axes. Some calculators automatically draw the graph with the same unit distance on both axes given the correct command (Zsquare on a TI-83).

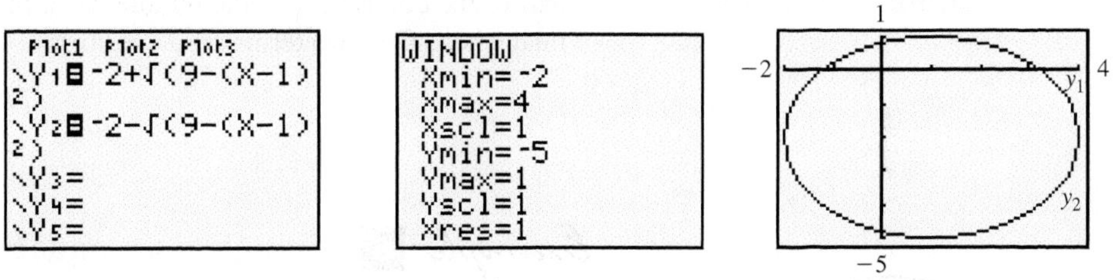

(a) (b) (c)

Figure 1.35 ■

Note that an equation such as $(x-1)^2 + (y+2)^2 = -9$ is not satisfied by any pair of real numbers, because the left-hand side is a nonnegative real number, while the right-hand side is negative. The equation $(x-1)^2 + (y+2)^2 = 0$ is satisfied only by $(1, -2)$. Since only one point satisfies $(x-1)^2 + (y+2)^2 = 0$, its graph is sometimes called a degenerate circle with radius zero. We study circles again later in this text when we study the conic sections.

In the next example we start with a description of a circle and write its equation.

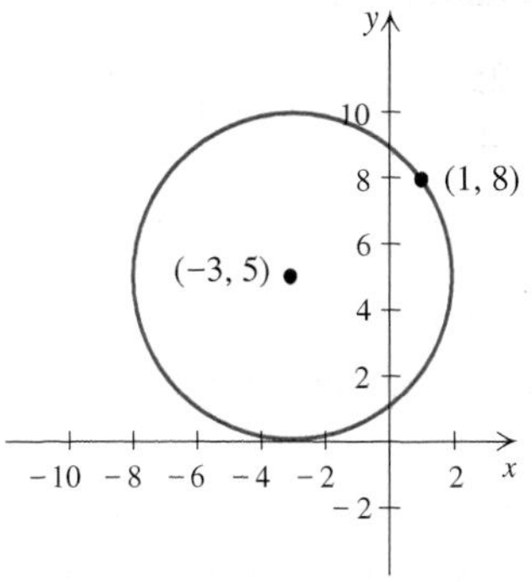

Figure 1.36

Example 5 Writing an equation of a circle

Write the standard equation for the circle with the center $(-3, 5)$ and passing through $(1, 8)$ as shown in Fig. 1.36.

Solution

The radius of this circle is the distance between $(-3, 5)$ and $(1, 8)$:

$$r = \sqrt{(8-5)^2 + (1-(-3))^2} = \sqrt{9+16} = 5$$

Now use $h = -3$, $k = 5$, and $r = 5$ in the standard equation of the circle $(x-h)^2 + (y-k)^2 = r^2$.

$$(x-(-3))^2 + (y-5)^2 = 5^2$$

So the equation of the circle is $(x+3)^2 + (y-5)^2 = 25$. ■

If the equation of a circle is not given in standard form, we can convert it to standard form using a process called **completing the square.** Completing the square means finding the third term of a perfect square trinomial when given the first two. That is, if we start with $x^2 + bx$, then what third term will make a perfect square trinomial? Since

$$\left(x + \frac{b}{2}\right)^2 = x^2 + 2 \cdot \frac{b}{2} \cdot x + \left(\frac{b}{2}\right)^2 = x^2 + bx + \left(\frac{b}{2}\right)^2$$

adding $\left(\frac{b}{2}\right)^2$ to $x^2 + bx$ completes the square. For example, the perfect square trinomial that starts with $x^2 + 6x$ is $x^2 + 6x + 9$. Note that 9 can be found by taking one-half of 6 and squaring.

Rule for Completing the Square of $x^2 + bx + ?$

The last term of a perfect square trinomial (with $a = 1$) is the square of one-half of the coefficient of the middle term. In symbols, the perfect square trinomial whose first two terms are $x^2 + bx$ is

$$x^2 + bx + \left(\frac{b}{2}\right)^2.$$

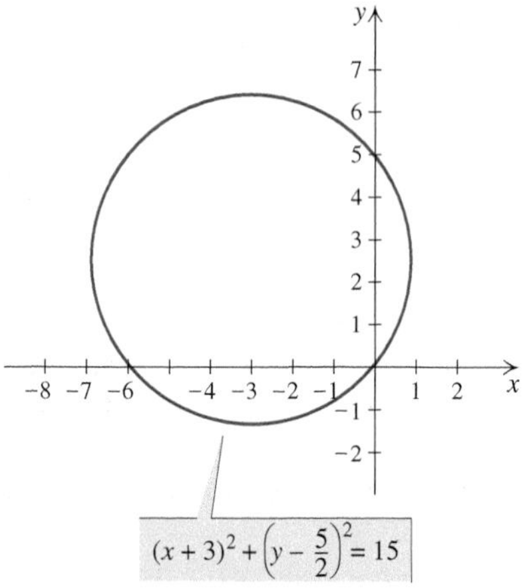

Figure 1.37

Example 6 Changing an equation of a circle to standard form

Graph the equation $x^2 + 6x + y^2 - 5y = -\frac{1}{4}$.

Solution

Complete the square for both x and y to get the standard form.

$$x^2 + 6x + 9 + y^2 - 5y + \frac{25}{4} = -\frac{1}{4} + 9 + \frac{25}{4} \qquad \left(\frac{1}{2} \cdot 6\right)^2 = 9, \left(\frac{1}{2} \cdot 5\right)^2 = \frac{25}{4}$$

$$(x + 3)^2 + \left(y - \frac{5}{2}\right)^2 = 15 \qquad \text{Factor the trinomials on the left side.}$$

The graph is a circle with center $\left(-3, \frac{5}{2}\right)$ and radius $\sqrt{15}$. See Fig. 1.37. ■

Whether an equation of the form $x^2 + y^2 + Ax + By = C$ is a circle depends on the value of C. We can always complete the squares for $x^2 + Ax$ and $y^2 + By$ by adding $(A/2)^2$ and $(B/2)^2$ to each side of the equation. Since a circle must have a positive radius we will have a circle only if $C + (A/2)^2 + (B/2)^2 > 0$.

The Line

For the circle, we started with the geometric definition and developed the algebraic equation. We would like to do the same thing for lines, but geometric definitions of lines are rather vague. Euclid's definition was "length without breadth." A modern geometry textbook states that a line is "a straight set of points extending infinitely in both directions." Another modern textbook defines lines algebraically as the graph of an equation of the form $Ax + By = C$. So we will accept the following theorem without proof.

Theorem: Equation of a Line in Standard Form

If A, B, and C are real numbers, then the graph of the equation

$$Ax + By = C$$

is a straight line, provided A and B are not both zero. Every straight line in the coordinate plane has an equation in the form $Ax + By = C$, the **standard form** for the equation of a line.

An equation of the form $Ax + By = C$ is called a **linear equation in two variables.** The equations,

$$2x + 3y = 5, \quad x = 4, \quad \text{and} \quad y = 5$$

are linear equations in standard form. An equation such as $y = 3x - 1$ that can be rewritten in standard form is also called a linear equation.

There is only one line containing any two distinct points. So to graph a linear equation we simply find two points that satisfy the equation and draw a line through them. We often use the point where the line crosses the x-axis, the ***x*-intercept,** and the point where the line crosses the y-axis, the ***y*-intercept.** Since every point on the x-axis has y-coordinate 0, we find the x-intercept by replacing y with 0 and then solving the equation for x. Since every point on the y-axis has x-coordinate 0, we find the y-intercept by replacing x with 0 and then solving for y. If the x- and y-intercepts are both at the origin, then you must find another point that satisfies the equation.

Example 7 Graphing lines and showing the intercepts

Graph each equation. Be sure to find and show the intercepts.

a. $2x - 3y = 9$ **b.** $y = 40 - x$

Solution

a. Since the y-coordinate of the x-intercept is 0, we replace y by 0 in the equation:

$$2x - 3(0) = 9$$
$$2x = 9$$
$$x = 4.5$$

To find the y-intercept, we replace x by 0 in the equation:

$$2(0) - 3y = 9$$
$$-3y = 9$$
$$y = -3$$

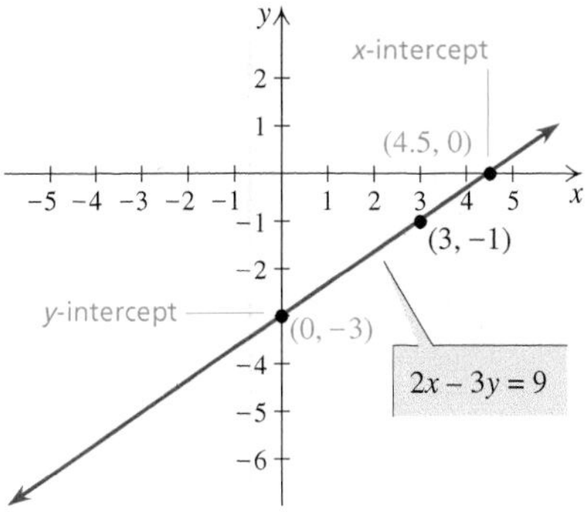

Figure 1.38

The x-intercept is (4.5, 0) and the y-intercept is $(0, -3)$. Locate the intercepts and draw the line as shown in Fig. 1.38. To check, locate a point such as $(3, -1)$, which also satisfies the equation, and see if the line goes through it.

b. If $x = 0$, then $y = 40 - 0 = 40$ and the y-intercept is (0, 40). If $y = 0$, then $0 = 40 - x$ or $x = 40$. The x-intercept is (40, 0). Draw a line through these points as shown in Fig. 1.39 on the next page. Check that (10, 30) and (20, 20) also satisfy $y = 40 - x$ and the line goes through these points.

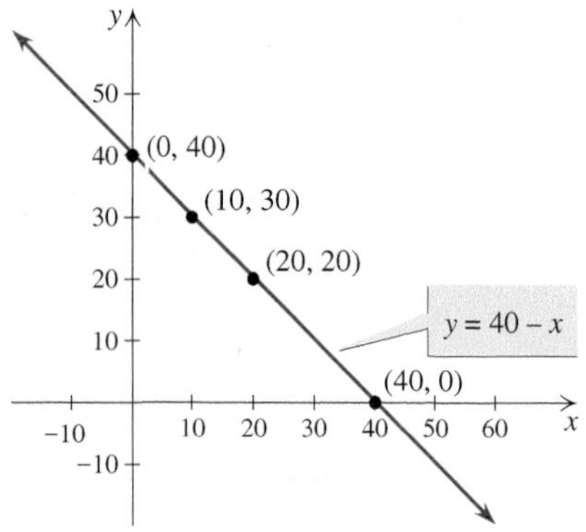

Figure 1.39

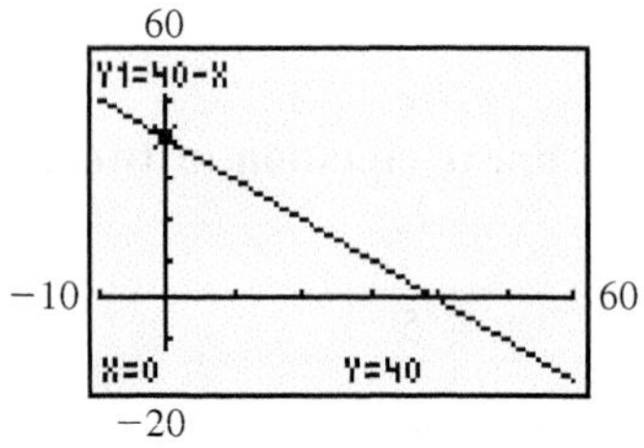

Figure 1.40

The calculator graph shown in Fig. 1.40 is consistent with the graph in Fig. 1.39. Note that the viewing window is set to show the intercepts. ■

Example 8 Graphing horizontal and vertical lines

Sketch the graph of each equation in the rectangular coordinate system.

a. $y = 3$ **b.** $x = 4$

Solution

a. The equation $y = 3$ is equivalent to $0 \cdot x + y = 3$. Because x is multiplied by 0, we can choose any value for x as long as we choose 3 for y. So ordered pairs such as $(-3, 3)$, $(-2, 3)$, and $(4, 3)$ satisfy the equation $y = 3$. The graph of $y = 3$ is the horizontal line shown in Fig. 1.41.

b. The equation $x = 4$ is equivalent to $x + 0 \cdot y = 4$. Because y is multiplied by 0, we can choose any value for y as long as we choose 4 for x. So ordered pairs such as $(4, -3)$, $(4, 2)$, and $(4, 5)$ satisfy the equation $x = 4$. The graph of $x = 4$ is the vertical line shown in Fig. 1.42.

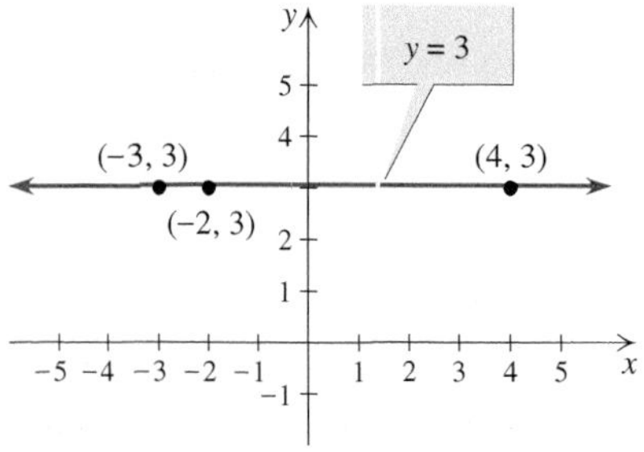

Figure 1.41

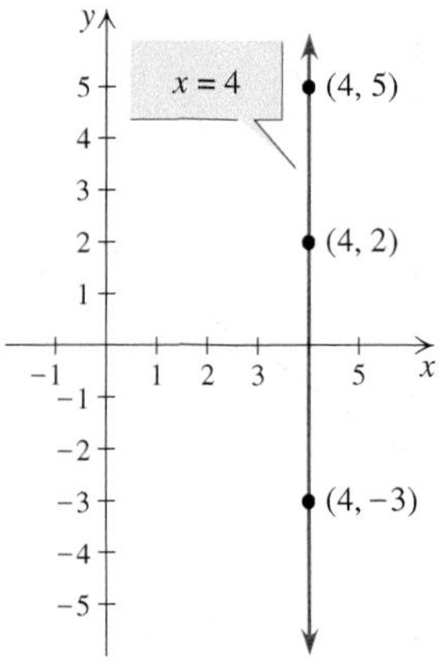

Figure 1.42

Note that you cannot graph $x = 4$ using the Y= key on your calculator. You can graph it on a calculator using polar coordinates or parametric equations (discussed later in this text). ■

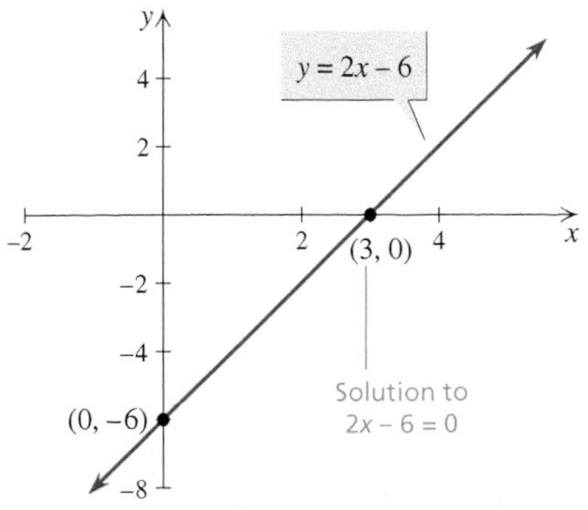

Figure 1.43

In the context of two variables the equation $x = 4$ has infinitely many solutions. Every ordered pair on the vertical line in Fig. 1.42 satisfies $x = 4$. In the context of one variable $x = 4$ has only one solution, 4.

Using a Graph to Solve an Equation

Graphing and solving equations go hand in hand. For example, the graph of $y = 2x - 6$ in Fig. 1.43 has x-intercept (3, 0), because if $x = 3$ then $y = 0$. Of course 3 is also the solution to the corresponding equation $2x - 6 = 0$ (where y is replaced by 0). For this reason, the solution to an equation is also called a **zero** or **root** of the equation. Every x-intercept on a graph provides us a solution to the corresponding equation. However, an x-intercept on a graph may not be easy to identify. In the next example we see how a graphing calculator identifies an x-intercept and thus gives us the approximate solution to an equation.

Example 9 Using a graph to solve an equation

Use a graphing calculator to solve $0.55(x - 3.45) + 13.98 = 0$.

Solution

First graph $y = 0.55(x - 3.45) + 13.98$ using a viewing window that shows the x-intercept as in Fig. 1.44(a). Next press ZERO or ROOT on the CALC menu. The calculator can find a zero between a *left bound* and a *right bound*, which you must enter. The calculator also asks you to make a guess. See Fig. 1.44(b). The more accurate the guess, the faster the calculator will find the zero. The solution to the equation rounded to two decimal places is −21.97. See Fig. 1.44(c). As always, consult your calulator manual if you are having difficulty.

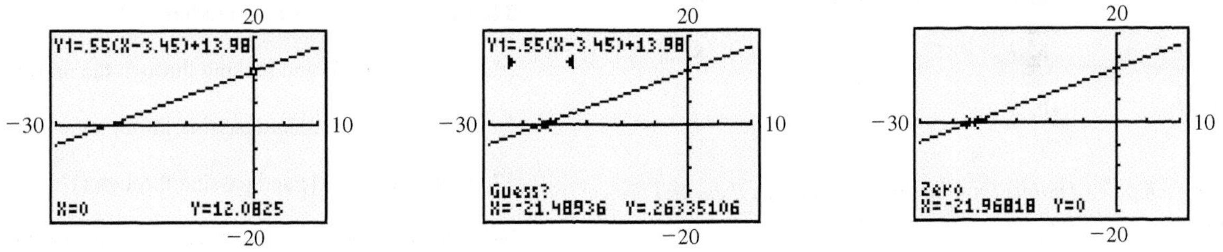

(a) (b) (c)

Figure 1.44

■

For Thought

True or False? Explain.

1. The point $(2, -3)$ is in quadrant II.
2. The point (4, 0) is in quadrant I.
3. The distance between (a, b) and (c, d) is $\sqrt{(a - b)^2 + (c - d)^2}$.
4. The equation $3x^2 + y = 5$ is a linear equation.
5. The solution to $7x - 9 = 0$ is the x-coordinate of the x-intercept of $y = 7x - 9$.

6. $\sqrt{7^2 + 9^2} = 7 + 9$

7. The origin lies midway between $(1, 3)$ and $(-1, -3)$.

8. The distance between $(3, -7)$ and $(3, 3)$ is 10.

9. The x-intercept for the graph of $3x - 2y = 7$ is $(7/3, 0)$.

10. The graph of $(x + 2)^2 + (y - 1)^2 = 5$ is a circle centered at $(-2, 1)$ with radius 5.

1.3 Exercises

For each point shown in the xy-plane, write the corresponding ordered pair and name the quadrant in which it lies or the axis on which it lies.

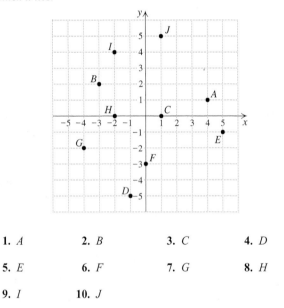

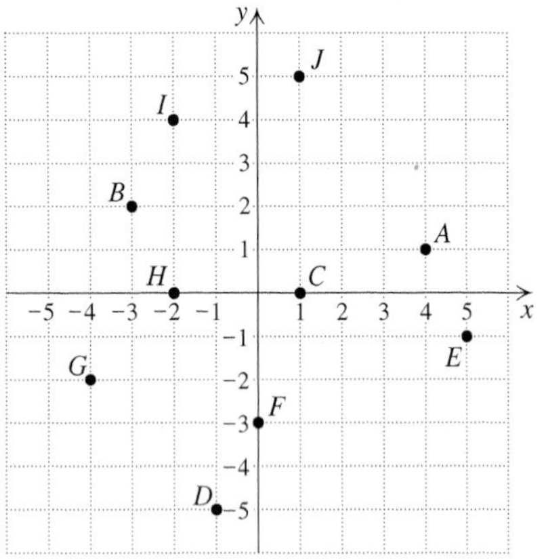

1. *A* 2. *B* 3. *C* 4. *D*

5. *E* 6. *F* 7. *G* 8. *H*

9. *I* 10. *J*

For each pair of points find the distance between them and the midpoint of the line segment joining them.

11. $(1, 3), (4, 7)$

12. $(-3, -2), (9, 3)$

13. $(-1, -2), (1, 0)$

14. $(-1, 0), (1, 2)$

15. $(-1, 1), \left(-1 + 3\sqrt{3}, 4\right)$

16. $\left(1 + \sqrt{2}, -2\right), \left(1 - \sqrt{2}, 2\right)$

17. $(1.2, 4.8), (-3.8, -2.2)$

18. $(-2.3, 1.5), (4.7, -7.5)$

19. $(a, 0), (b, 0)$

20. $(a, 0), \left(\dfrac{a + b}{2}, 0\right)$

21. $(\pi, 0), (\pi/2, 1)$

22. $(0, 0), (\pi/2, 1)$

Determine the center and radius of each circle and sketch the graph.

23. $x^2 + y^2 = 16$

24. $x^2 + y^2 = 1$

25. $(x + 6)^2 + y^2 = 36$

26. $x^2 + (y - 2)^2 = 16$

27. $y^2 = 25 - (x + 1)^2$

28. $x^2 = 9 - (y - 3)^2$

29. $(x - 2)^2 = 8 - (y + 2)^2$

30. $(y + 2)^2 = 20 - (x - 4)^2$

Write the standard equation for each circle.

31. Center at $(0, 0)$ with radius 7

32. Center at $(0, 0)$ with radius 5

33. Center at $(-2, 5)$ with radius $1/2$

34. Center at $(-1, -6)$ with radius $1/3$

35. Center at $(3, 5)$ and passing through the origin

36. Center at $(-3, 9)$ and passing through the origin

37. Center at $(5, -1)$ and passing through $(1, 3)$

38. Center at $(-2, -3)$ and passing through $(2, 5)$

Determine the center and radius of each circle and sketch the graph. See the rule for completing the square on page 28.

39. $x^2 + y^2 = 9$

40. $x^2 + y^2 = 100$

41. $x^2 + y^2 + 6y = 0$

42. $x^2 + y^2 = 4x$

43. $x^2 - 6x + y^2 - 8y = 0$

44. $x^2 + 10x + y^2 - 8y = -40$

45. $x^2 + y^2 = 4x + 3y$

46. $x^2 + y^2 = 5x - 6y$

47. $x^2 + y^2 = \dfrac{x}{2} - \dfrac{y}{3} - \dfrac{1}{16}$

48. $x^2 + y^2 = x - y + \dfrac{1}{2}$

Write the standard equation for each of the following circles.

49. a.

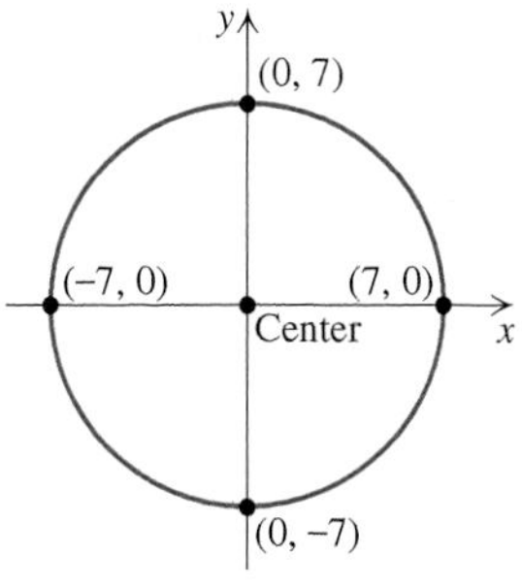

b.

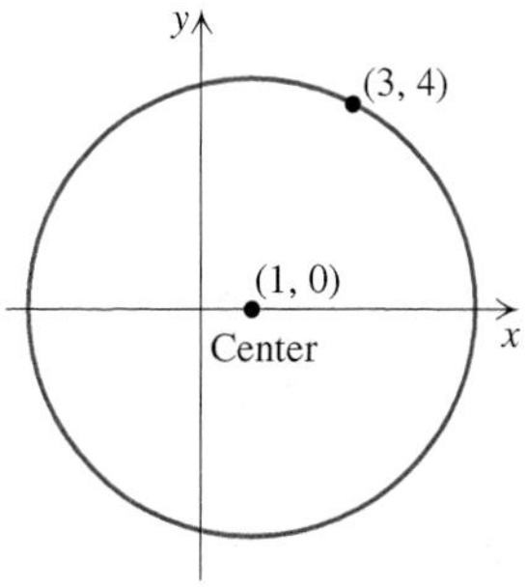

c.

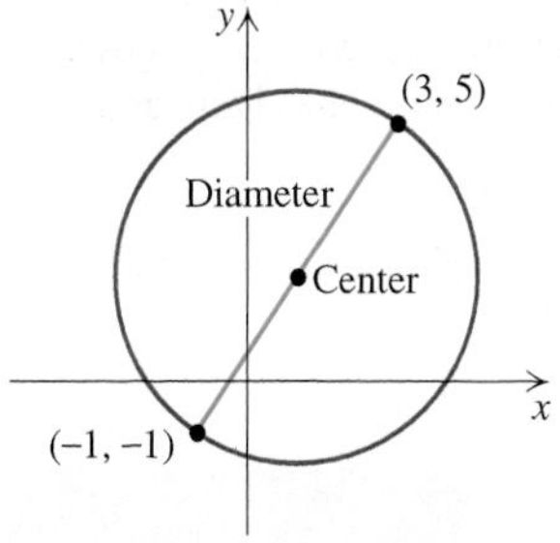

50. a.

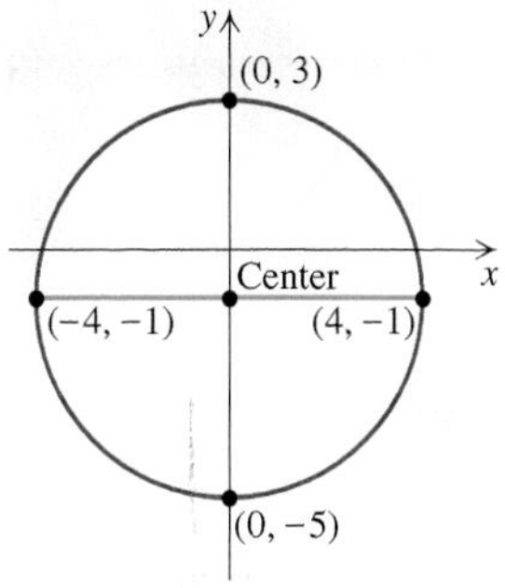

b.

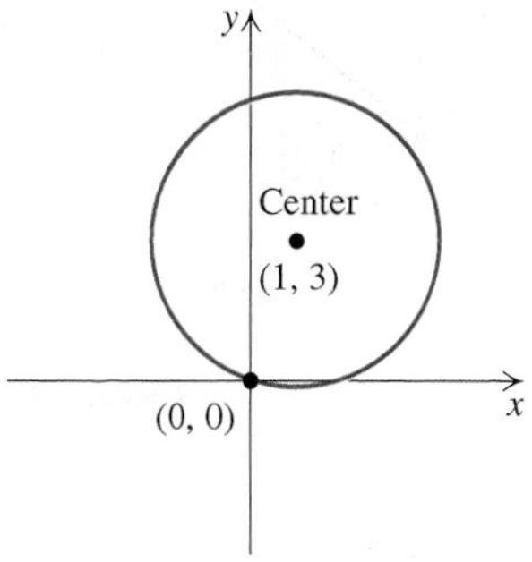

c.

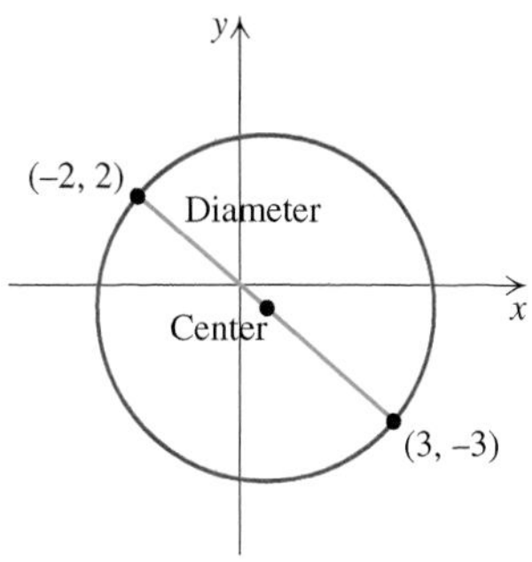

Write the equation of each circle in standard form. The coordinates of the center and the radius for each circle are integers.

51. a.

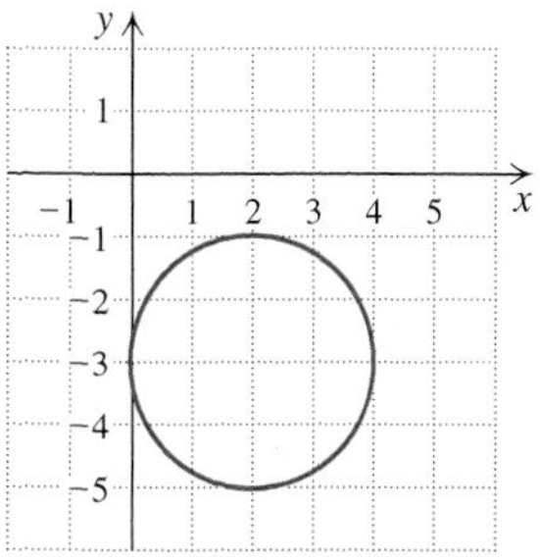

b.

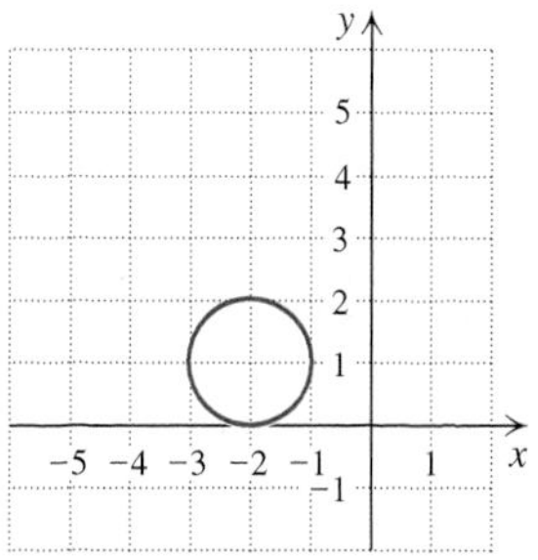

c.

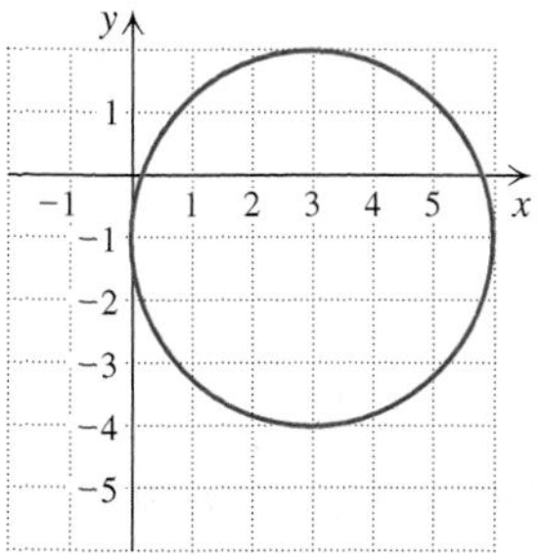

d.

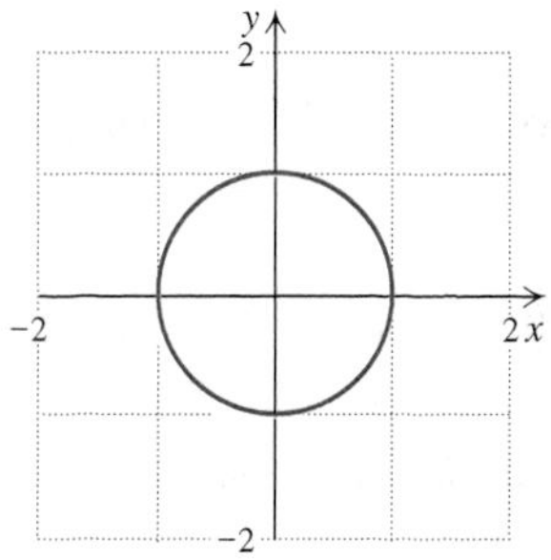

52. a.

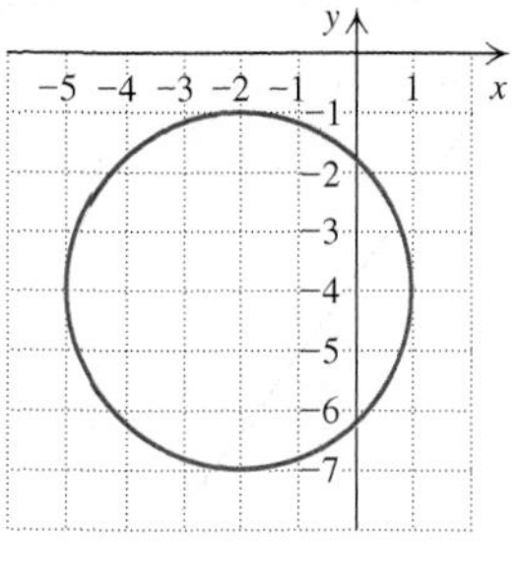

b.

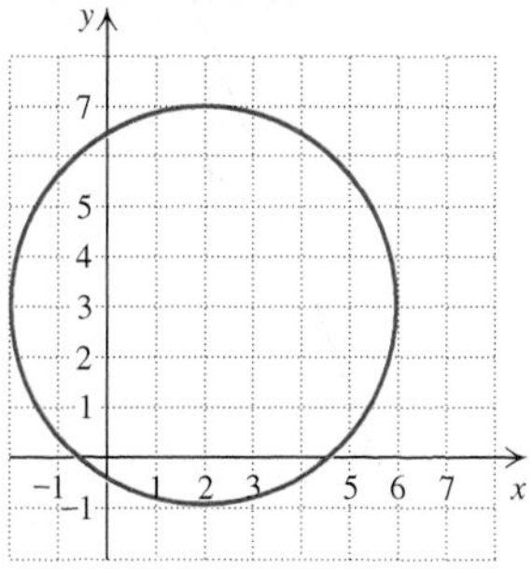

c.

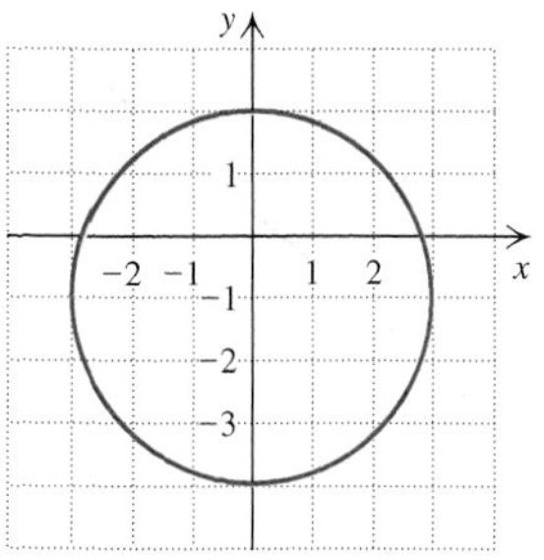

d.

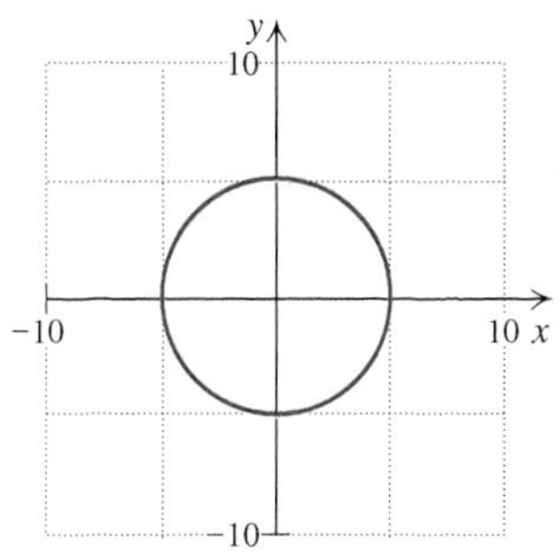

Sketch the graph of each linear equation. Be sure to find and show the x- and y-intercepts.

53. $y = 3x - 4$

54. $y = 5x - 5$

55. $3x - y = 6$

56. $5x - 2y = 10$

57. $x = 3y - 90$

58. $x = 80 - 2y$

59. $\frac{2}{3}y - \frac{1}{2}x = 400$

60. $\frac{1}{2}x - \frac{1}{3}y = 600$

61. $2x + 4y = 0.01$

62. $3x - 5y = 1.5$

63. $0.03x + 0.06y = 150$

64. $0.09x - 0.06y = 54$

Graph each equation in the rectangular coordinate system.

65. $x = 5$

66. $y = -2$

67. $y = 4$

68. $x = -3$

69. $x = -4$

70. $y = 5$

71. $y - 1 = 0$

72. $5 - x = 4$

Find the solution to each equation by reading the accompanying graph.

73. $2.4x - 8.64 = 0$

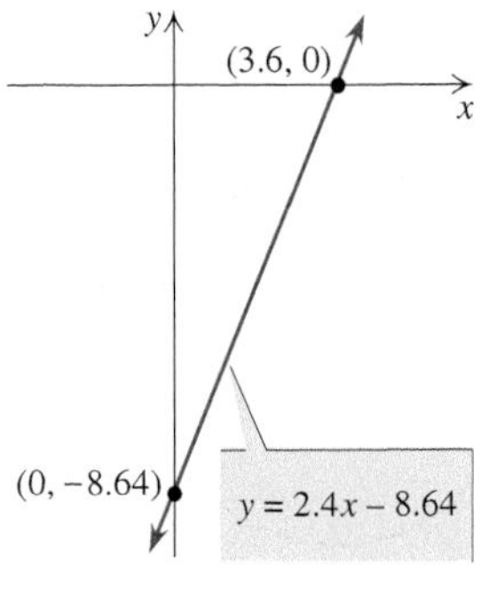

74. $8.84 - 1.3x = 0$

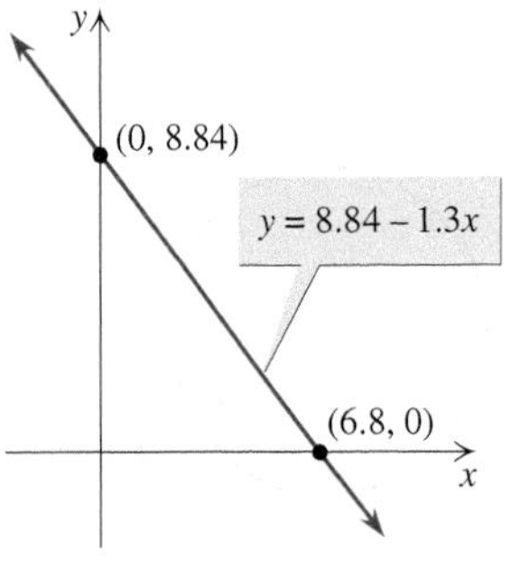

75. $-\frac{3}{7}x + 6 = 0$

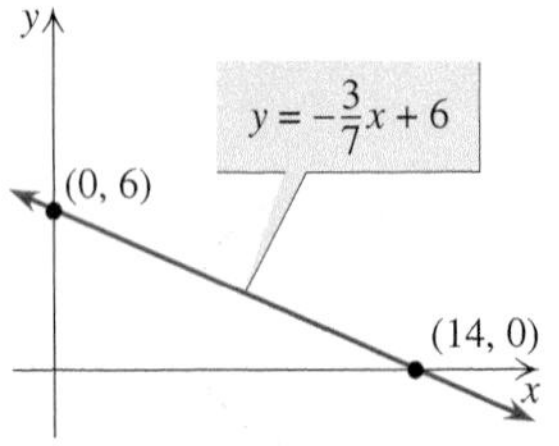

76. $\frac{5}{6}x + 30 = 0$

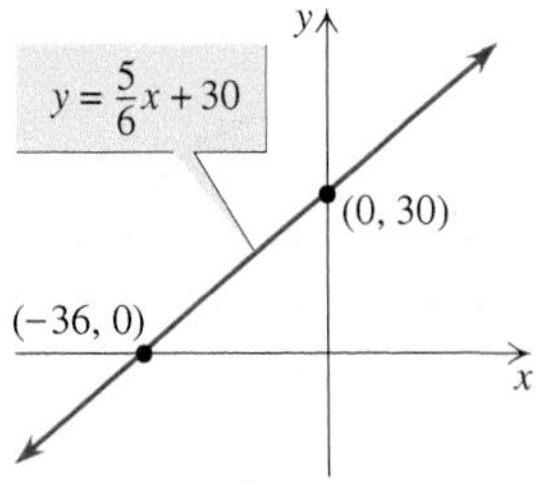

Use a graphing calculator to estimate the solution to each equation to two decimal places. Then find the solution algebraically and compare it with your estimate.

77. $1.2x + 3.4 = 0$

78. $3.2x - 4.5 = 0$

79. $0.03x - 3497 = 0$

80. $0.09x + 2000 = 0$

81. $4.3 - 3.1(2.3x - 9.9) = 0$

82. $9.4x - 4.37(3.5x - 9.76) = 0$

Solve each problem.

83. *First Marriage* The median age at first marriage for women went from 20.8 in 1970 to 25.1 in 2000 as shown in the accompanying figure (U.S. Census Bureau, www.census.gov).

a. Find the midpoint of the line segment in the figure and interpret your result.

b. Find the distance between the two points shown in the figure and interpret your result.

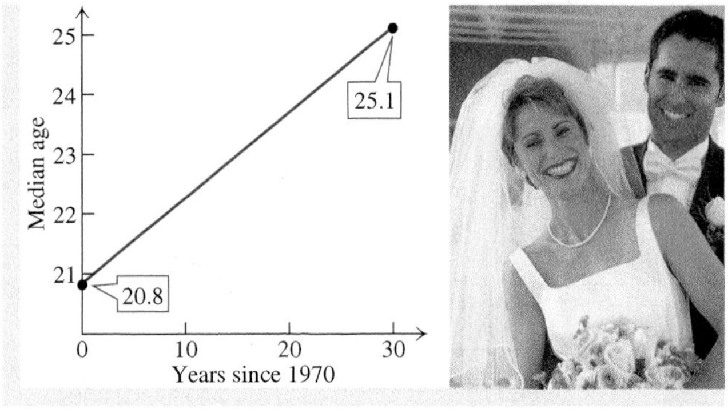

Figure for Exercise 83

84. *Unmarried Couples* The number of unmarried-couple households h (in millions), can be modeled using the equation $h = 0.171n + 2.913$, where n is the number of years since 1990 (U.S. Census Bureau, www.census.gov).

a. Find and interpret the n-intercept for the line. Does it make sense?

b. Find and interpret the h-intercept for the line.

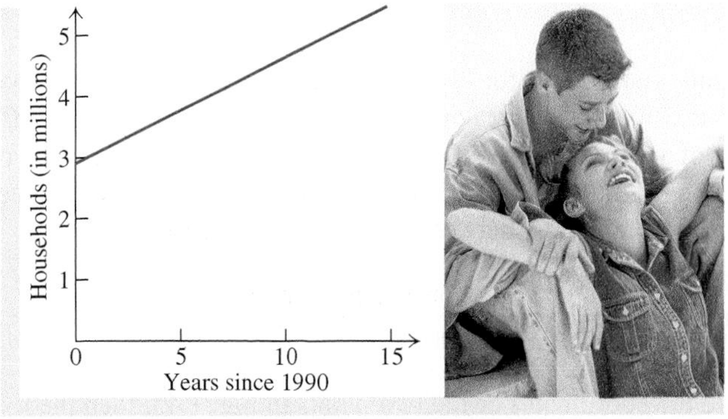

Figure for Exercise 84

85. *Capsize Control* The capsize screening value C is an indicator of a sailboat's suitability for extended offshore sailing. C is determined by the formula

$$C = 4D^{-1/3}B,$$

where D is the displacement of the boat in pounds and B is its beam (or width) in feet. Sketch the graph of this equation for B ranging from 0 to 20 ft assuming that D is fixed at 22,800 lbs. Find C for the Island Packet 40, which has a displacement of 22,800 pounds and a beam of 12 ft 11 in. (Island Packet Yachts, www.ipy.com).

86. *Limiting the Beam* The International Offshore Rules require that the capsize screening value C (from the previous exercise) be less than or equal to 2 for safety. What is the maximum allowable beam (to the nearest inch) for a boat with a displacement of 22,800 lbs? For a fixed displacement, is a boat more or less likely to capsize as its beam gets larger?

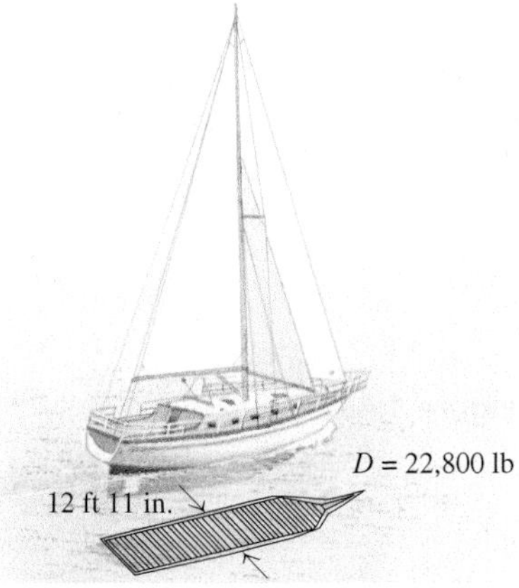

Figure for Exercises 85 and 86

Thinking Outside the Box III

Methodical Mower Eugene is mowing a rectangular lawn that is 300 ft by 400 ft. He starts at one corner and mows a swath of uniform width around the outside edge in a clockwise direction. He continues going clockwise, widening the swath that is mowed and shrinking the rectangular section that is yet to be mowed. When he is half done with the lawn, how wide is the swath?

1.3 Pop Quiz

1. Find the distance between $(-1, 3)$ and $(3, 5)$.
2. Find the center and radius for the circle
$$(x - 3)^2 + (y + 5)^2 = 81.$$
3. Find the center and radius for the circle
$$x^2 + 4x + y^2 - 10y = -28.$$
4. Find the equation of the circle that passes through the origin and has center at $(3, 4)$.
5. Find all intercepts for $2x - 3y = 12$.
6. Which point is on both of the lines $x = 5$ and $y = -1$?

1.4 Linear Equations in Two Variables

In Section 1.3 we graphed lines, including horizontal and vertical lines. We learned that every line has an equation in standard form $Ax + By = C$. In this section we will continue to study lines.

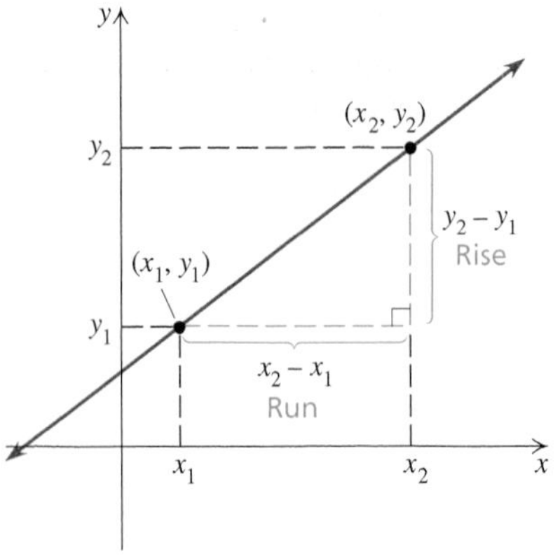

Figure 1.45

Slope of a Line

A road that has a 5% grade rises 5 feet for every horizontal run of 100 feet. A roof that has a 5–12 pitch rises 5 feet for every horizontal run of 12 feet. The grade of a road and the pitch of a roof are measurements of *steepness*. The steepness or *slope* of a line in the xy-coordinate system is the ratio of the **rise** (the change in y-coordinates) to the **run** (the change in x-coordinates) between two points on the line:

$$\text{slope} = \frac{\text{change in } y\text{-coordinates}}{\text{change in } x\text{-coordinates}} = \frac{\text{rise}}{\text{run}}$$

If (x_1, y_1) and (x_2, y_2) are the coordinates of the two points in Fig. 1.45, then the rise is $y_2 - y_1$ and the run is $x_2 - x_1$:

Definition: Slope

The **slope** of the line through (x_1, y_1) and (x_2, y_2) with $x_1 \neq x_2$ is

$$\frac{y_2 - y_1}{x_2 - x_1}.$$

Note that if (x_1, y_1) and (x_2, y_2) are two points for which $x_1 = x_2$ then the line through them is a vertical line. Since this case is not included in the definition of slope, a vertical line does not have a slope. We also say that the slope of a vertical line is undefined. If we choose two points on a horizontal line then $y_1 = y_2$ and $y_2 - y_1 = 0$. For any horizontal line the rise between two points is 0 and the slope is 0.

Example 1 Finding the slope

In each case find the slope of the line that contains the two given points.

a. $(-3, 4), (-1, -2)$ **b.** $(-3, 7), (5, 7)$ **c.** $(-3, 5), (-3, 8)$

Solution

a. Use $(x_1, y_1) = (-3, 4)$ and $(x_2, y_2) = (-1, -2)$ in the formula:

$$\text{slope} = \frac{y_2 - y_1}{x_2 - x_1} = \frac{-2 - 4}{-1 - (-3)} = \frac{-6}{2} = -3$$

The slope of the line is -3.

b. Use $(x_1, y_1) = (-3, 7)$ and $(x_2, y_2) = (5, 7)$ in the formula:

$$\text{slope} = \frac{y_2 - y_1}{x_2 - x_1} = \frac{7 - 7}{5 - (-3)} = \frac{0}{8} = 0$$

The slope of this horizontal line is 0.

c. The line through $(-3, 5)$ and $(-3, 8)$ is a vertical line and so it does not have a slope. ■

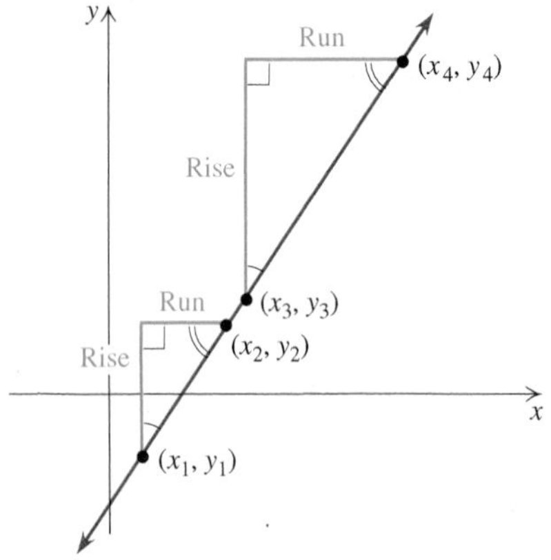

Figure 1.46

The slope of a line is the same number regardless of which two points on the line are used in the calculation of the slope. To understand why, consider the two triangles shown in Fig. 1.46. These triangles have the same shape and are called similar triangles. Because the ratios of corresponding sides of similar triangles are equal, the ratio of rise to run is the same for either triangle.

Point-Slope Form

Suppose that a line through (x_1, y_1) has slope m. Every other point (x, y) on the line must satisfy the equation

$$\frac{y - y_1}{x - x_1} = m$$

because any two points can be used to find the slope. Multiply both sides by $x - x_1$ to get $y - y_1 = m(x - x_1)$, which is the **point-slope form** of the equation of a line.

Theorem: Point-Slope Form

> The equation of the line (in point-slope form) through (x_1, y_1) with slope m is
> $$y - y_1 = m(x - x_1).$$

In Section 1.3 we started with the equation of a line and graphed the line. Using the point-slope form, we can start with a graph of a line or a description of the line and write the equation for the line.

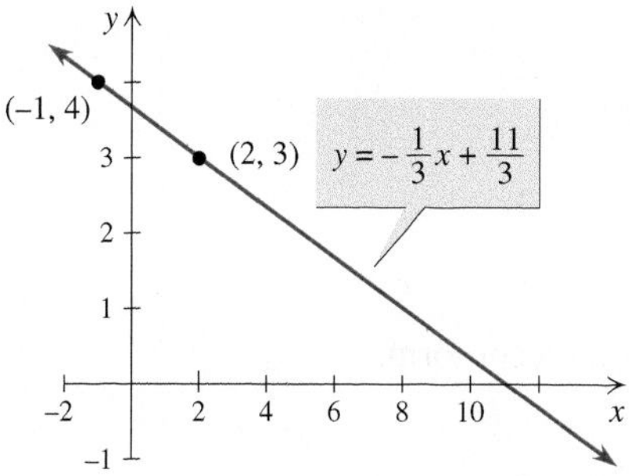

Figure 1.47

Example 2 The equation of a line given two points

In each case graph the line through the given pair of points. Then find the equation of the line and solve it for y if possible.

a. $(-1, 4), (2, 3)$ **b.** $(2, 5), (-6, 5)$ **c.** $(3, -1), (3, 9)$

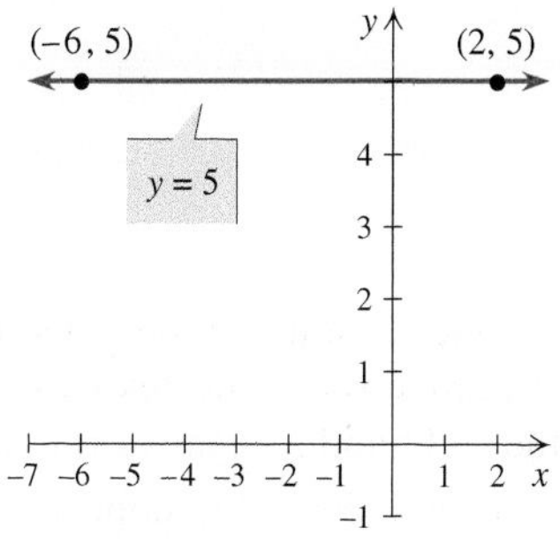

Figure 1.48

Solution

a. Find the slope of the line shown in Fig. 1.47 as follows:

$$m = \frac{y_2 - y_1}{x_2 - x_1} = \frac{3 - 4}{2 - (-1)} = \frac{-1}{3} = -\frac{1}{3}$$

Now use a point, say (2, 3), and $m = -\frac{1}{3}$ in the point-slope form:

$$y - y_1 = m(x - x_1)$$

$$y - 3 = -\frac{1}{3}(x - 2) \quad \text{The equation in point-slope form}$$

$$y - 3 = -\frac{1}{3}x + \frac{2}{3}$$

$$y = -\frac{1}{3}x + \frac{11}{3} \quad \text{The equation solved for } y$$

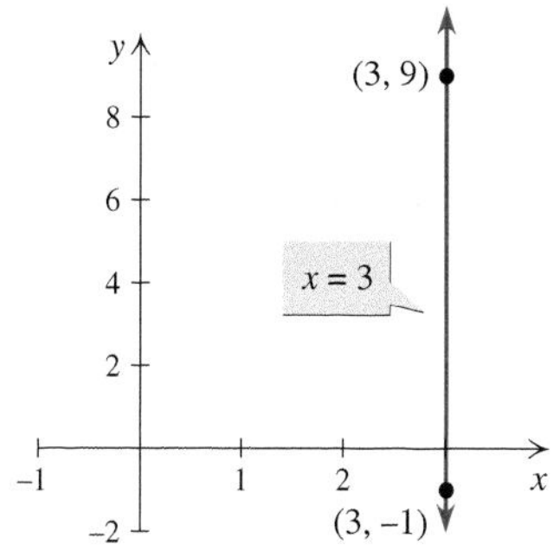

Figure 1.49

b. The slope of the line through (2, 5) and $(-6, 5)$ shown in Fig. 1.48 is 0. The equation of this horizontal line is $y = 5$.

c. The line through $(3, -1)$ and $(3, 9)$ shown in Fig. 1.49 is vertical and it does not have slope. Its equation is $x = 3$. ■

Slope-Intercept Form

The line $y = mx + b$ goes through $(0, b)$ and $(1, m + b)$. Between these two points the rise is m and the run is 1. So the slope is m. Since $(0, b)$ is the y-intercept and m is the slope, $y = mx + b$ is called **slope-intercept form.** Any equation in standard form $Ax + By = C$ can be rewritten in slope-intercept form by solving the equation for y provided $B \neq 0$. If $B = 0$ the line is vertical and has no slope.

Theorem: Slope-Intercept Form

> The equation of a line (in slope-intercept form) with slope m and y-intercept $(0, b)$ is
>
> $$y = mx + b.$$
>
> Every nonvertical line has an equation in slope-intercept form.

If you know the slope and y-intercept for a line then you can use slope-intercept form to write its equation. For example, the equation of the line through $(0, 9)$ with slope 4 is $y = 4x + 9$. In the next example we use the slope-intercept form to determine the slope and y-intercept for a line.

Example 3 Find the slope and y-intercept

Identify the slope and y-intercept for the line $2x - 3y = 6$.

Solution

First solve the equation for y to get it in slope-intercept form:

$$\begin{aligned} 2x - 3y &= 6 \\ -3y &= -2x + 6 \\ y &= \frac{2}{3}x - 2 \end{aligned}$$

So the slope is $\frac{2}{3}$ and the y-intercept is $(0, -2)$. ■

Using Slope to Graph a Line

Slope is the ratio $\frac{\text{rise}}{\text{run}}$ that results from moving from one point to another on a line. A positive rise indicates a motion upward and a negative rise indicates a motion downward. A positive run indicates a motion to the right and a negative run indicates a motion to the left. If you start at any point on a line with slope $\frac{1}{2}$, then moving up 1 unit and 2 units to the right will bring you back to the line. On a line with slope -3 or $\frac{-3}{1}$, moving down 3 units and 1 unit to the right will bring you back to the line.

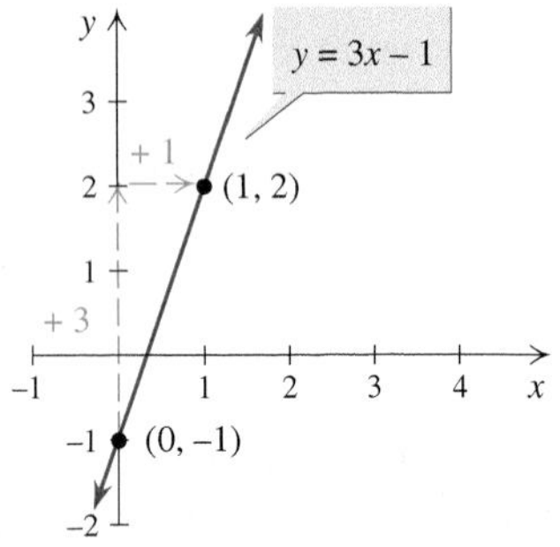

Figure 1.50

Example 4 Graphing a line using its slope and y-intercept

Graph each line.

a. $y = 3x - 1$ **b.** $y = -\frac{2}{3}x + 4$

Solution

a. The line $y = 3x - 1$ has y-intercept $(0, -1)$ and slope 3 or $\frac{3}{1}$. Starting at $(0, -1)$ we obtain a second point on the line by moving up 3 units and 1 unit to the right. So the line goes through $(0, -1)$ and $(1, 2)$ as shown in Fig. 1.50.

b. The line $y = -\frac{2}{3}x + 4$ has y-intercept $(0, 4)$ and slope $-\frac{2}{3}$ or $\frac{-2}{3}$. Starting at $(0, 4)$ we obtain a second point on the line by moving down 2 units and then 3 units to the right. So the line goes through $(0, 4)$ and $(3, 2)$ as shown in Fig. 1.51. ■

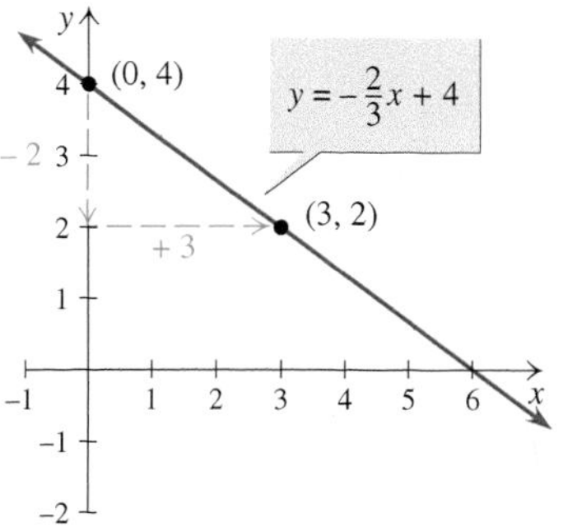

Figure 1.51

As the x-coordinate increases on a line with positive slope, the y-coordinate increases also. As the x-coordinate increases on a line with negative slope, the y-coordinate decreases. Figure 1.52 shows some lines of the form $y = mx$ with positive slopes and negative slopes. Observe the effect that the slope has on the position of the line.

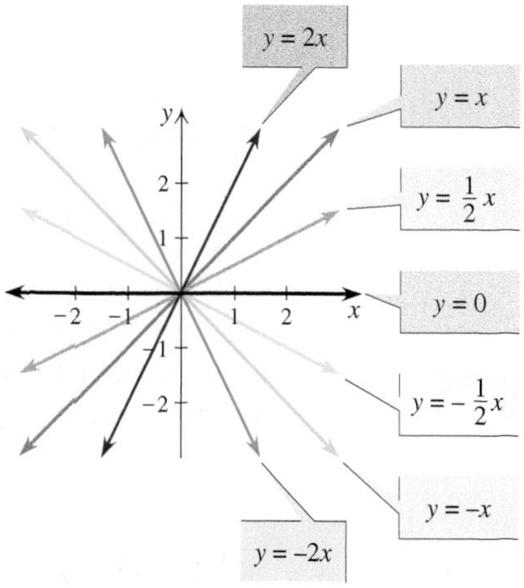

Graphs of $y = mx$

Figure 1.52

The Three Forms for the Equation of a Line

There are three forms for the equation of a line. The following strategy will help you decide when and how to use these forms.

STRATEGY

Finding the Equation of a Line

1. Since vertical lines have no slope they cannot be written in slope-intercept form $y = mx + b$ or point-slope form $y - y_1 = m(x - x_1)$. All lines can be described by an equation in standard form $Ax + By = C$.
2. For any constant k, $y = k$ is a horizontal line and $x = k$ is a vertical line.
3. If you know two points on a line, then find the slope.
4. If you know the slope and point on the line, use point-slope form. If the point is the y-intercept, then use slope-intercept form.
5. Final answers are usually written in slope-intercept or standard form. Standard form is often simplified by using only integers for the coefficients.

Example 5 Standard form using integers

Find the equation of the line through $\left(0, \frac{1}{3}\right)$ with slope $\frac{1}{2}$. Write the equation in standard form using only integers.

Solution

Since we know the slope and y-intercept, start with slope-intercept form:

$$y = \frac{1}{2}x + \frac{1}{3} \quad \text{Slope-intercept form}$$

$$-\frac{1}{2}x + y = \frac{1}{3}$$

$$-6\left(-\frac{1}{2}x + y\right) = -6 \cdot \frac{1}{3} \quad \text{Multiply by } -6 \text{ to get integers.}$$

$$3x - 6y = -2 \quad \text{Standard form with integers}$$

Any integral multiple of $3x - 6y = -2$ would also be standard form, but we usually use the smallest possible positive coefficient for x. ■

Parallel Lines

Two lines in a plane are said to be **parallel** if they have no points in common. Any two vertical lines are parallel, and slope can be used to determine whether nonvertical lines are parallel. For example, the lines $y = 3x - 4$ and $y = 3x + 1$ are parallel because their slopes are equal.

Theorem: Parallel Lines

Two nonvertical lines in the coordinate plane are parallel if and only if their slopes are equal.

PROOF Suppose that $y = m_1x + b_1$ and $y = m_2x + b_2$ are two lines with different y-intercepts ($b_1 \neq b_2$). These lines are parallel if and only if $m_1x + b_1 = m_2x + b_2$ has no solution. This equation has no solution if and only if $m_1 = m_2$. ■

Example 6 Writing equations of parallel lines

Find the equation in slope-intercept form of the line through $(1, -4)$ that is parallel to $y = 3x + 2$.

Solution

Since $y = 3x + 2$ has slope 3, any line parallel to it also has slope 3. Write the equation of the line through $(1, -4)$ with slope 3 in point-slope form:

$$y - (-4) = 3(x - 1) \quad \text{Point-slope form}$$

$$y + 4 = 3x - 3$$

$$y = 3x - 7 \quad \text{Slope-intercept form}$$

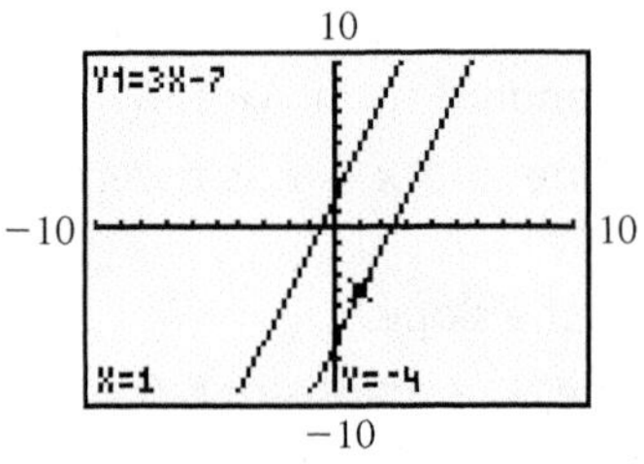

Figure 1.53

The line $y = 3x - 7$ goes through $(1, -4)$ and is parallel to $y = 3x + 2$.

The graphs of $y_1 = 3x - 7$ and $y_2 = 3x + 2$ in Fig. 1.53 support the answer. ■

Perpendicular Lines

Two lines are **perpendicular** if they intersect at a right angle. Slope can be used to determine whether lines are perpendicular. For example, lines with slopes such as $2/3$ and $-3/2$ are perpendicular. The slope $-3/2$ is the opposite of the reciprocal of $2/3$. In the following theorem we use the equivalent condition that the product of the slopes of two perpendicular lines is -1, provided they both have slopes.

Theorem: Perpendicular Lines

Two lines with slopes m_1 and m_2 are perpendicular if and only if $m_1 m_2 = -1$.

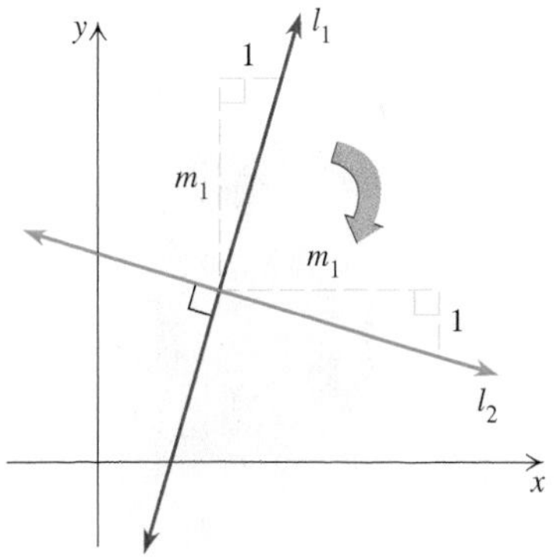

Figure 1.54

PROOF The phrase "if and only if" means that there are two statements to prove. First we prove that if l_1 with slope m_1 and l_2 with slope m_2 are perpendicular, then $m_1 m_2 = -1$. Assume that $m_1 > 0$. At the intersection of the lines draw a right triangle using a rise of m_1 and a run of 1, as shown in the Fig. 1.54. Rotate l_1 (along with the right triangle) 90 degrees so that it coincides with l_2. Now use the triangle in its new position to determine that $m_2 = \frac{1}{-m_1}$ or $m_1 m_2 = -1$.

The second statement to prove is that $m_1 m_2 = -1$ or $m_2 = \frac{1}{-m_1}$ implies that the lines are perpendicular. Start with the two intersecting lines and the two congruent right triangles as shown in Fig. 1.54. It takes a rotation of 90 degrees to get the vertical side marked m_1 to coincide with the horizontal side marked m_1. Since the triangles are congruent, rotating 90 degrees makes the triangles coincide and the lines coincide. So the lines are perpendicular. ■

Example 7 Writing equations of perpendicular lines

Find the equation of the line perpendicular to the line $3x - 4y = 8$ and containing the point $(-2, 1)$. Write the answer in slope-intercept form.

Solution

Rewrite $3x - 4y = 8$ in slope-intercept form:

$$-4y = -3x + 8$$

$$y = \frac{3}{4}x - 2 \qquad \text{Slope of this line is } 3/4.$$

Since the product of the slopes of perpendicular lines is -1, the slope of the line that we seek is $-4/3$. Use the slope $-4/3$ and the point $(-2, 1)$ in the point-slope form:

$$y - 1 = -\frac{4}{3}(x - (-2))$$

$$y - 1 = -\frac{4}{3}x - \frac{8}{3}$$

$$y = -\frac{4}{3}x - \frac{5}{3}$$

The last equation is the required equation in slope-intercept form. The graphs of these two equations should look perpendicular.

If you graph $y_1 = \frac{3}{4}x - 2$ and $y_2 = -\frac{4}{3}x - \frac{5}{3}$ with a graphing calculator, the graphs will not appear perpendicular in the standard viewing window because each axis has a different unit length. The graphs appear perpendicular in Fig. 1.55 because the unit lengths were made equal with the ZSquare feature of the TI-83. ■

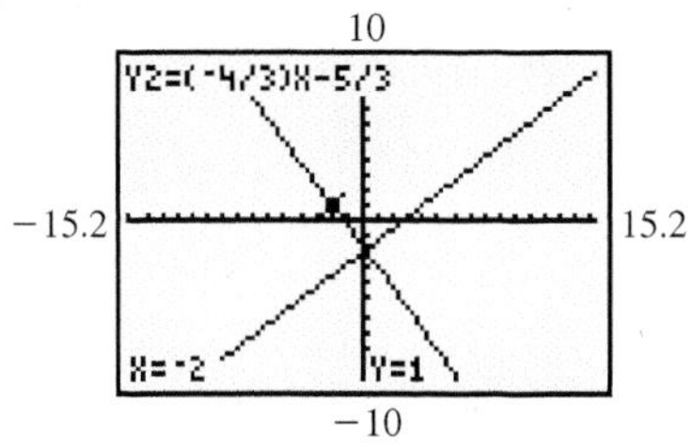

Figure 1.55

Applications

Example 8 Finding a linear equation

The monthly cost for a cell phone is \$35 for 100 minutes and \$45 for 200 minutes. See Fig. 1.56. The cost C is determined from the time t by a linear equation.

a. Find the linear equation.
b. What is the cost for 400 minutes per month?

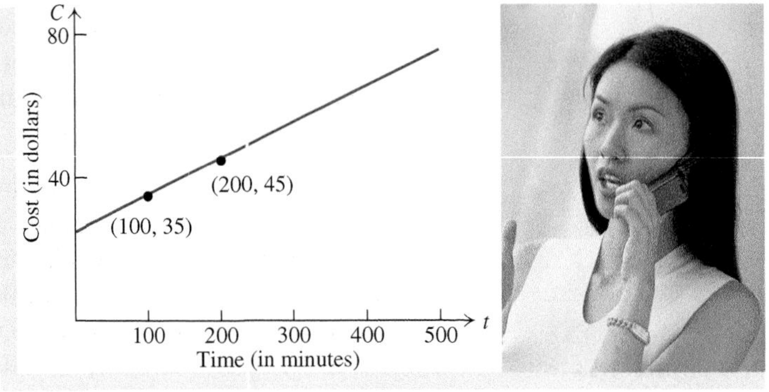

Figure 1.56

Solution

a. First find the slope:

$$m = \frac{C_2 - C_1}{t_2 - t_1} = \frac{45 - 35}{200 - 100} = \frac{10}{100} = 0.10$$

The slope is \$0.10 per minute. Now find b by using $C = 35, t = 100$, and $m = 0.10$ in the slope-intercept form $C = mt + b$:

$$35 = 0.10(100) + b$$
$$35 = 10 + b$$
$$25 = b$$

So the formula is $C = 0.10t + 25$.

b. Use $t = 400$ in the formula $C = 0.10t + 25$:

$$C = 0.10(400) + 25 = 65$$

The cost for 400 minutes per month is \$65. ■

Note that in Example 8 we could have used the point-slope form $C - C_1 = m(t - t_1)$ to get the formula $C = 0.10t + 25$. Try it.

For Thought

True or False? Explain.

1. The slope of the line through (2, 2) and (3, 3) is 3/2.
2. The slope of the line through (−3, 1) and (−3, 5) is 0.
3. Any two distinct parallel lines have equal slopes.
4. The graph of $x = 3$ in the coordinate plane is the single point (3, 0).

5. Two lines with slopes m_1 and m_2 are perpendicular if $m_1 = -1/m_2$.

6. Every line in the coordinate plane has an equation in slope-intercept form.

7. The slope of the line $y = 3 - 2x$ is 3.

8. Every line in the coordinate plane has an equation in standard form.

9. The line $y = 3x$ is parallel to the line $y = -3x$.

10. The line $x - 3y = 4$ contains the point $(1, -1)$ and has slope $1/3$.

1.4 Exercises

Find the slope of the line containing each pair of points.

1. $(-2, 3), (4, 5)$
2. $(-1, 2), (3, 6)$
3. $(1, 3), (3, -5)$
4. $(2, -1), (5, -3)$
5. $(5, 2), (-3, 2)$
6. $(0, 0), (5, 0)$
7. $\left(\frac{1}{8}, \frac{1}{4}\right), \left(\frac{1}{4}, \frac{1}{2}\right)$
8. $\left(-\frac{1}{3}, \frac{1}{2}\right), \left(\frac{1}{6}, \frac{1}{3}\right)$
9. $(5, -1), (5, 3)$
10. $(-7, 2), (-7, -6)$

Find the equation of the line through the given pair of points. Solve it for y if possible.

11. $(-1, -1), (3, 4)$
12. $(-2, 1), (3, 5)$
13. $(-2, 6), (4, -1)$
14. $(-3, 5), (2, 1)$
15. $(3, 5), (-3, 5)$
16. $(-6, 4), (2, 4)$
17. $(4, -3), (4, 12)$
18. $(-5, 6), (-5, 4)$

Write an equation in slope-intercept form for each of the lines shown.

19.

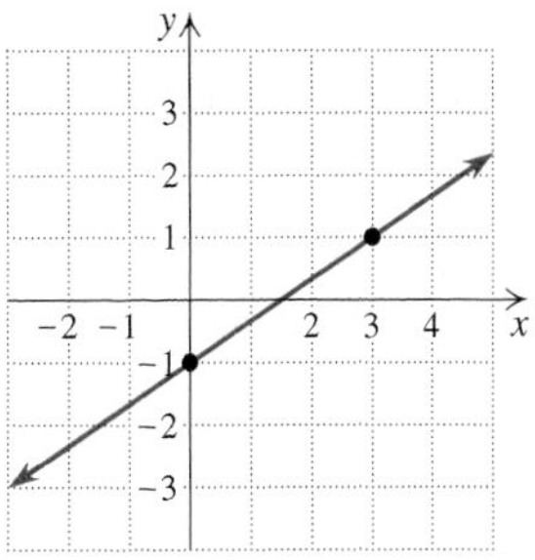

20.

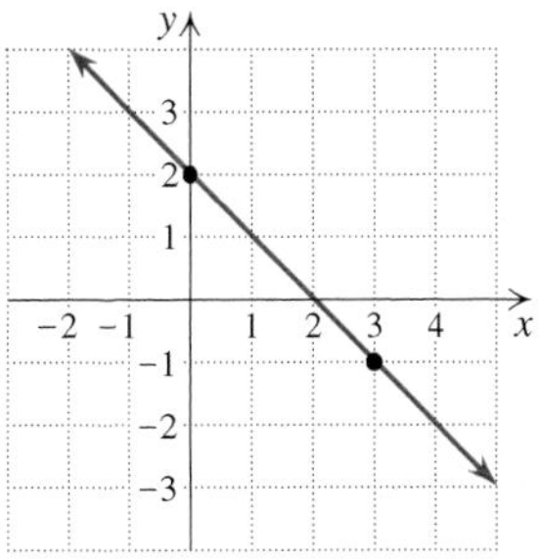

21.

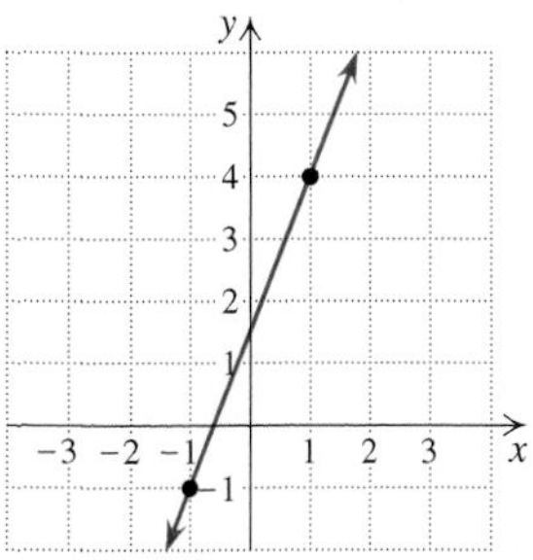

22.

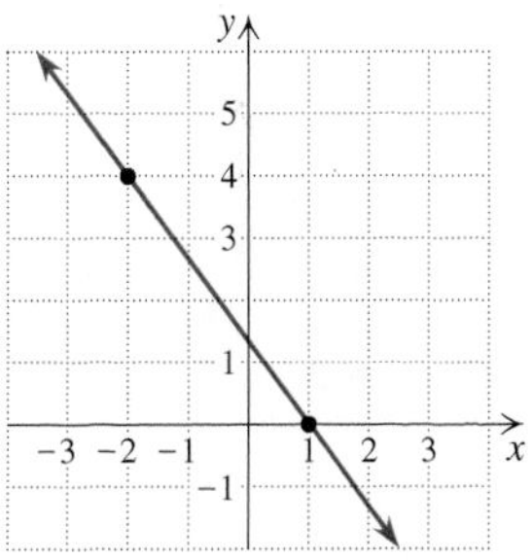

23.

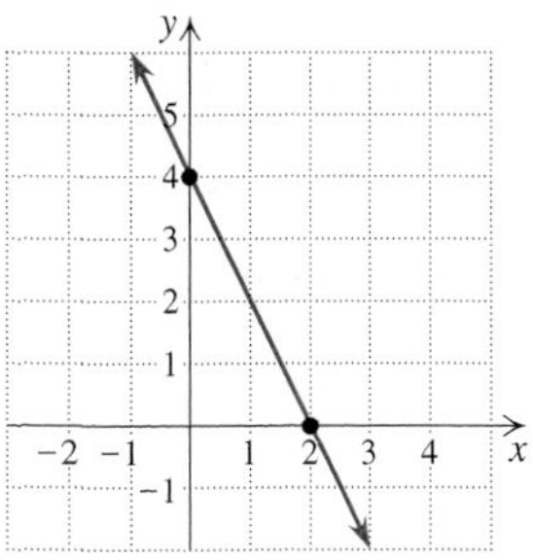

24.

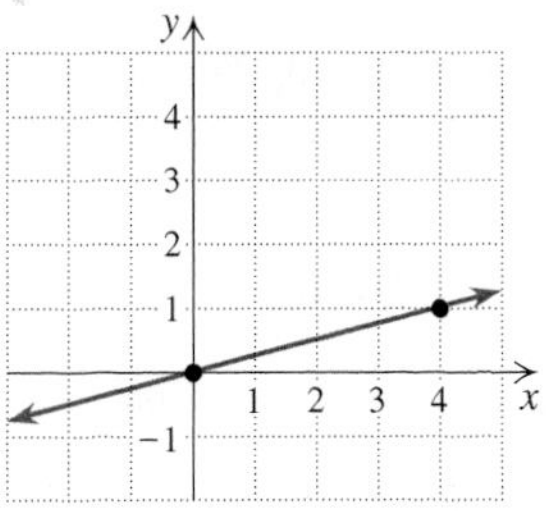

25.

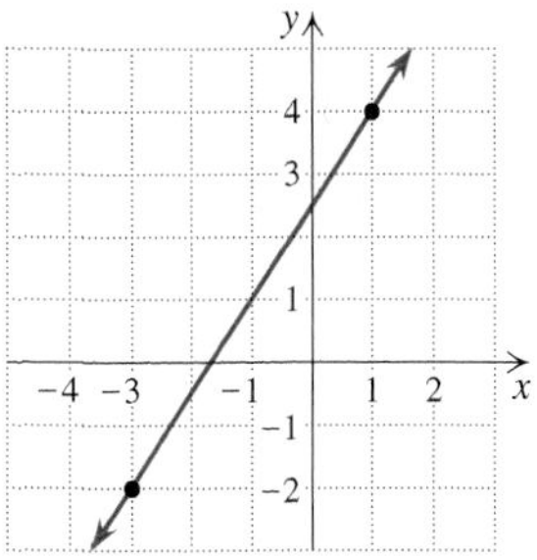

26.

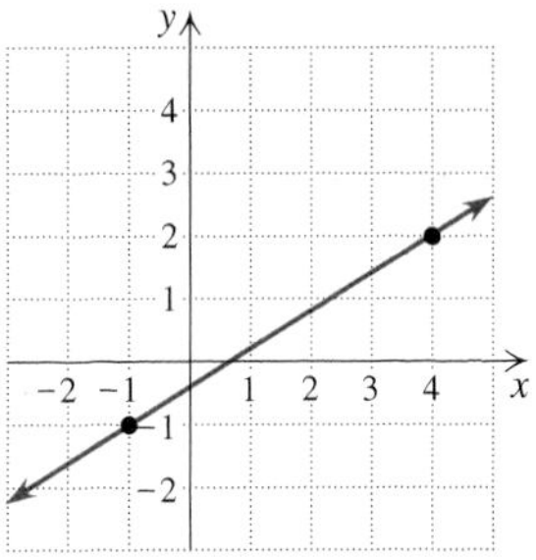

Write each equation in slope-intercept form and identify the slope and y-intercept of the line.

27. $3x - 5y = 10$

28. $2x - 2y = 1$

29. $y - 3 = 2(x - 4)$

30. $y + 5 = -3(x - (-1))$

31. $y + 1 = \frac{1}{2}(x - (-3))$

32. $y - 2 = -\frac{3}{2}(x + 5)$

33. $y - 4 = 0$

34. $-y + 5 = 0$

35. $y - 0.4 = 0.03(x - 100)$

36. $y + 0.2 = 0.02(x - 3)$

Use the y-intercept and slope to sketch the graph of each equation.

37. $y = \frac{1}{2}x - 2$

38. $y = \frac{2}{3}x + 1$

39. $y = -3x + 1$

40. $y = -x + 3$

41. $y = -\frac{3}{4}x - 1$

42. $y = -\frac{3}{2}x$

43. $x - y = 3$

44. $2x - 3y = 6$

45. $y - 5 = 0$

46. $6 - y = 0$

Find the equation of the line through the given pair of points in standard form using only integers. See the strategy for finding the equation of a line on page 39.

47. $(3, 0)$ and $(0, -4)$

48. $(-2, 0)$ and $(0, 3)$

49. $(2, 3)$ and $(-3, -1)$

50. $(4, -1)$ and $(-2, -6)$

51. $(-4, 2)$ and $(-4, 5)$

52. $(-3, 6)$ and $(9, 6)$

Find the slope of each line described.

53. A line parallel to $y = 0.5x - 9$

54. A line parallel to $3x - 9y = 4$

55. A line perpendicular to $3y - 3x = 7$

56. A line perpendicular to $2x - 3y = 8$

57. A line perpendicular to the line $x = 4$

58. A line parallel to $y = 5$

Write an equation in standard form using only integers for each of the lines described. In each case make a sketch.

59. The line with slope 2, going through $(1, -2)$

60. The line with slope -3, going through $(-3, 4)$

61. The line through $(1, 4)$, parallel to $y = -3x$

62. The line through $(-2, 3)$ parallel to $y = \frac{1}{2}x + 6$

63. The line perpendicular to $x - 2y = 3$ and containing $(-3, 1)$

64. The line perpendicular to $3x - y = 9$ and containing $(0, 0)$

65. The line perpendicular to $x = 4$ and containing $(2, 5)$

66. The line perpendicular to $y = 9$ and containing $(-1, 3)$

Solve each problem.

67. *Celsius to Fahrenheit Formula* Fahrenheit temperature F is determined from Celsius temperature C by a linear equation. Water freezes at 0°C or 32°F and boils at 100°C or 212°F. Use the point-slope formula to write F in terms of C. Find the Fahrenheit temperature of an oven that is 150°C.

68. *Cost of Business Cards* Speedy Printing charges \$23 for 200 deluxe business cards and \$35 for 500 deluxe business cards. Speedy uses a linear equation to determine the cost from the number of cards. Find the equation and find the cost of 700 deluxe business cards.

69. *Volume Discount* Mona Kalini gives a bus tour of Honolulu to one person for \$49, two people for \$48 each, three people for \$47 each, etc. Write a linear equation that gives the cost per person c in terms of the number of people n. What is her revenue for a bus load of 40 people?

70. *Ticket Pricing* At \$10 per ticket, the Rhythm Kings will fill all 8000 seats in the Saint Cloud Arena. For every \$1 increase in ticket price, 500 tickets will go unsold. Find a linear equation that gives the number of tickets sold n in terms of the ticket price p. Find the revenue if the tickets are \$20 each.

71. *Computers and Printers* An office manager will spend a total of \$60,000 on computers at \$2000 each and printers at \$1500 each. Find a linear equation that gives the number of computers purchased c in terms of the number of printers purchased p. Interpret the slope.

72. *Carpenters and Helpers* A contractor plans to distribute a total of \$2400 in bonus money to nine carpenters and three helpers. The carpenters all get the same amount and the helpers all get the same amount. Find a linear equation that gives the helpers' bonus h in terms of the carpenters' bonus c. Interpret the slope.

Thinking Outside the Box IV

Army of Ants An army of ants is marching across the kitchen floor. If they form columns with 10 ants in each column, then there are 6 ants left over. If they form columns with 7, 11, or 13 ants in each column, then there are 2 ants left over. What is the smallest number of ants that could be in this army?

1.4 Pop Quiz

1. Find the slope of the line through $(-4, 9)$ and $(5, 6)$.
2. Find the equation of the line through $(3, 4)$ and $(6, 8)$.
3. What is the slope of the line $2x - 7y = 1$?
4. Find the equation of the line with y-intercept $(0, 7)$ that is parallel to $y = 3x - 1$.
5. Find the equation of the line with y-intercept $(0, 8)$ that is perpendicular to $y = \frac{1}{2}x + 4$.

1.5 Functions

From this section to the end of this text we will be studying functions. This important concept is discussed extensively in calculus and also in most other areas of mathematics.

The Function Concept

If you spend \$10 on gasoline, then the price per gallon determines the number of gallons that you get. There is a rule: the number of gallons is \$10 divided by the price per gallon. The number of hours that you sleep before a test might be related to your grade on the test, but does not determine your grade. There is no rule that will determine your grade from the number of hours of sleep. If the value of a variable y is determined by the value of another variable x, then y **is a function of** x. The phrase "is a function of" means "is determined by." If there is more than one value for y corresponding to a particular x-value, then y is not determined by x and y is not a function of x.

Example 1 Using the phrase "is a function of"

Decide whether a is a function of b, b is a function of a, or neither.

a. Let a represent a positive integer smaller than 100 and b represent the number of divisors of a.
b. Let a represent the age of a United States citizen and b represent the number of days since his/her birth.
c. Let a represent the age of a United States citizen and b represent his/her annual income.

Solution

a. We can determine the number of divisors of any positive integer smaller than 100. So b is a function of a. We cannot determine the integer knowing the number of its divisors, because different integers have the same number of divisors. So a is not a function of b.
b. The number of days since a person's birth certainly determines the age of the person in the usual way. So a is a function of b. However, you cannot determine the number of days since a person's birth from their age. You need more information. For example, the number of days since birth for two 1-year-olds could be 370 and 380 days. So b is not a function of a.

c. We cannot determine the income from the age or the age from the income. We would need more information. Even though age and income are related, the relationship is not strong enough to say that either one is a function of the other. ■

To make the function concept clearer, we now define the noun "function." A *function* is often defined as a rule that assigns each element in one set to a unique element in a second set. Of course understanding this definition depends on knowing the meanings of the words *rule, assigns,* and *unique*. Using the language of ordered pairs we can make the following precise definition in which there are no undefined words.

Definition: Function

A **function** is a set of ordered pairs in which no two ordered pairs have the same first coordinate and different second coordinates.

If we start with two related variables, we can identify one as the first variable and the other as the second variable and consider the set of ordered pairs containing their corresponding values. If the set of ordered pairs satisfies the function definition, then we say that the second variable is a function of the first. The variable corresponding to the first coordinate is the **independent variable** and the variable corresponding to the second coordinate is the **dependent variable.**

Identifying Functions

A **relation** is a set of ordered pairs. A relation can also be indicated by a verbal description, a graph, a formula or equation, or a table. Not every relation is a function. A function is a special relation. No matter how a relation or function is given there is always an underlying set of ordered pairs.

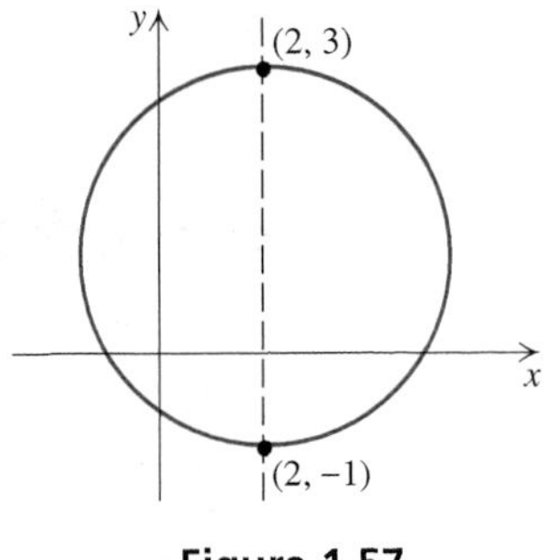

Figure 1.57

When a relation is given by a graph, we can visually check whether there are two ordered pairs with the same first coordinate and different second coordinates. For example, the circle shown in Fig. 1.57 is not the graph of a function, because there are two points on the circle with the same first coordinate. These points lie on a vertical line. In general, if there is a vertical line that crosses a graph more than once, the graph is not the graph of a function. This criterion is known as the **vertical line test.**

Theorem: The Vertical Line Test

A graph is the graph of a function if and only if there is no vertical line that crosses the graph more than once.

Every nonvertical line is the graph of a function, because every vertical line crosses a nonvertical line exactly once. Note that the vertical line test makes sense only because we always put the independent variable on the horizontal axis.

Example 2 Identifying a function from a graph

Determine which of the graphs shown in Fig. 1.58 are graphs of functions.

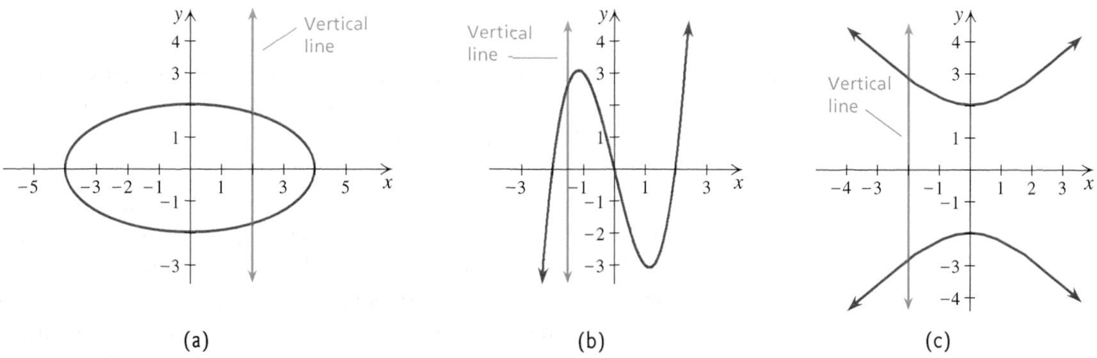

Figure 1.58

Solution

For each graph we want to decide whether y is a function of x. That is, can y be uniquely determined from x? In parts (a) and (c) we can draw a vertical line that crosses the graph more than once. So in each case there is an x-coordinate that corresponds to two different y-coordinates. So in parts (a) and (c) we cannot always determine a unique value of y from a given x-coordinate. So y is not a function of x in parts (a) and (c). The graph in Fig. 1.58(b) is the graph of a function because every vertical line appears to cross the graph at most once. So in this case we can determine y for a given x-coordinate and y is a function of x. ■

A calculator is a virtual function machine. Built-in functions on a calculator are marked with symbols such as $\sqrt{x}$, x^2, $x!$, 10^x, e^x, $\ln(x)$, $\sin(x)$, $\cos(x)$, etc. When you provide an x-coordinate and use one of these symbols, the calculator finds the appropriate y-coordinate. The ordered pairs certainly satisfy the definition of function because the calculator will not produce two different second coordinates corresponding to one first coordinate.

In the next example we determine whether a relation is a function when the relation is given as a list of ordered pairs or as a table.

Example 3 Identifying a function from a list or table

Determine whether each relation is a function.

a. $\{(1, 3), (2, 3), (4, 9)\}$ **b.** $\{(9, -3), (9, 3), (4, 2), (0, 0)\}$

c.

Quantity	Price each
1–5	\$9.40
5–10	\$8.75

Solution

a. This set of ordered pairs is a function because no two ordered pairs have the same first coordinate and different second coordinates. The second coordinate is a function of the first coordinate.

b. This set of ordered pairs is not a function because both (9, 3) and (9, −3) are in the set and they have the same first coordinate and different second coordinates. The second coordinate is not a function of the first coordinate.

c. The quantity 5 corresponds to a price of \$9.40 and also to a price of \$8.75. Assuming that quantity is the first coordinate, the ordered pairs (5, \$9.40) and (5, \$8.75) both belong to this relation. If you are purchasing items whose price was determined from this table, you would certainly say that something is wrong, the table has a mistake in it, or the price you should pay is not clear. The price is not a function of the quantity purchased. ■

We have seen and used many functions as formulas. For example, the formula $c = \pi d$ defines a set of ordered pairs in which the first coordinate is the diameter of a circle and the second coordinate is the circumference. Since each diameter corresponds to a unique circumference, the circumference is a function of the diameter. If the set of ordered pairs satisfying an equation is a function, then we say that the equation is a function or the equation defines a function. Other well-known formulas such as $C = \frac{5}{9}(F - 32)$, $A = \pi r^2$, and $V = \frac{4}{3}\pi r^3$ are also functions, but, as we will see in the next example, not every equation defines a function. The variables in the next example and all others in this text represent real numbers unless indicated otherwise.

Example 4 Identifying a function from an equation

Determine whether each equation defines y as a function of x.

a. $|y| = x$ **b.** $y = x^2 - 3x + 2$ **c.** $x^2 + y^2 = 1$ **d.** $3x - 4y = 8$

Solution

a. We must determine whether there are any values of x for which there is more than one y-value satisfying the equation. We arbitrarily select a number for x and see. If we select $x = 2$, then the equation is $|y| = 2$, which is satisfied if $y = \pm 2$. So both (2, 2) and (2, −2) satisfy $|y| = x$. So this equation does *not* define y as a function of x.

b. If we select any number for x, then y is calculated by the equation $y = x^2 - 3x + 2$. Since there is only one result when $x^2 - 3x + 2$ is calculated, there is only one y for any given x. So this equation *does* define y as a function of x.

c. Is it possible to pick a number for x for which there is more than one y-value? If we select $x = 0$, then the equation is $0^2 + y^2 = 1$ or $y = \pm 1$. So (0, 1) and (0, −1) both satisfy $x^2 + y^2 = 1$ and this equation does *not* define y as a function of x. Note that $x^2 + y^2 = 1$ is equivalent to $y = \pm\sqrt{1 - x^2}$, which indicates that there are many values for x that would produce two different y-coordinates.

d. The equation $3x - 4y = 8$ is equivalent to $y = \frac{3}{4}x - 2$. Since there is only one result when $\frac{3}{4}x - 2$ is calculated, there is only one y corresponding to any given x. So $3x - 4y = 8$ *does* define y as a function of x. ■

Domain and Range

A relation is a set of ordered pairs. The **domain** of a relation is the set of all first coordinates of the ordered pairs. The **range** of a relation is the set of all second coordinates of the ordered pairs. The relation

$$\{(19, 2.4), (27, 3.0), (19, 3.6), (22, 2.4), (36, 3.8)\}$$

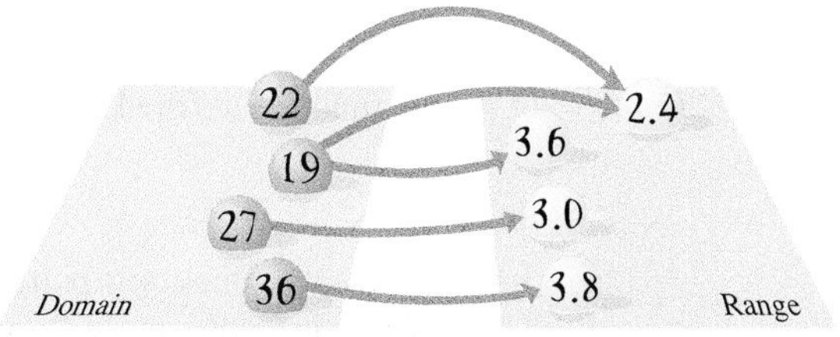

Figure 1.59

shows the ages and grade point averages of five randomly selected students. The domain of this relation is the set of ages, $\{19, 22, 27, 36\}$. The range is the set of grade point averages, $\{2.4, 3.0, 3.6, 3.8\}$. This relation matches elements of the domain (ages) with elements of the range (grade point averages), as shown in Fig. 1.59. Is this relation a function?

For some relations, all of the ordered pairs are listed, but for others, only an equation is given for determining the ordered pairs. When the domain of the relation is not stated, it is understood that the domain consists of only values of the independent variable that can be used in the expression defining the relation. When we use x and y for the variables, we always assume that x is the independent variable and y is the dependent variable.

Example 5 Determining domain and range

State the domain and range of each relation and whether the relation is a function.

a. $\{(-1, 1), (3, 9), (3, -9)\}$ **b.** $y = \sqrt{2x - 1}$ **c.** $x = |y|$

Solution

a. The domain is the set of first coordinates $\{-1, 3\}$, and the range is the set of second coordinates $\{1, 9, -9\}$. Note that an element of a set is not listed more than once. Since (3, 9) and (3, −9) are in the relation, the relation is not a function.

b. Since y is determined uniquely from x by the formula $y = \sqrt{2x - 1}$, y is a function of x. We are discussing only real numbers. So $\sqrt{2x - 1}$ is a real number provided that $2x - 1 \geq 0$, or $x \geq 1/2$. So the domain of the function is the interval $[1/2, \infty)$. If $2x - 1 \geq 0$ and $y = \sqrt{2x - 1}$, we have $y \geq 0$. So the range of the function is the interval $[0, \infty)$.

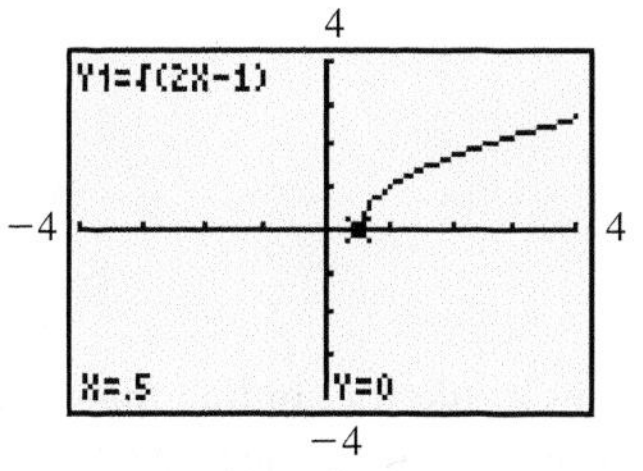

Figure 1.60

The graph of $y = \sqrt{2x - 1}$ shown in Fig. 1.60 supports these answers because the points that are plotted appear to have $x \geq 1/2$ and $y \geq 0$. □

c. The expression $|y|$ is defined for any real number y. So the range is the interval of all real numbers, $(-\infty, \infty)$. Since $|y|$ is nonnegative, the values of x must be nonnegative. So the domain is $[0, \infty)$. Since ordered pairs such as (2, 2) and (2, −2) satisfy $x = |y|$, this equation does not give y as a function of x. ■

In Example 5(b) and (c) we found the domain and range by examining an equation defining a relation. If the relation is a function as in Example 5(b), you can easily draw the graph with a graphing calculator and use it to support your answer. However, to choose an appropriate viewing window you must know the domain and range to begin with. So it is best to use a calculator graph to support your conclusions about domain and range rather than to make conclusions about domain and range. □

Function Notation

A function defined by a set of ordered pairs can be named with a letter. For example,

$$f = \{(2, 5), (3, 8)\}.$$

Since the function f pairs 2 with 5 we write $f(2) = 5$, which is read as "the value of f at 2 is 5" or simply "f of 2 is 5." We also have $f(3) = 8$.

A function defined by an equation can also be named with a letter. For example, the function $y = x^2$ could be named by a new letter, say g. We can then use $g(x)$, read "g of x" as a symbol for the second coordinate when the first coordinate is x. Since y and $g(x)$ are both symbols for the second coordinate we can write $y = g(x)$ and $g(x) = x^2$. Since $3^2 = 9$, the function g pairs 3 with 9 and we write $g(3) = 9$. This notation is called **function notation.**

Example 6 Using function notation

Let $h = \{(1, 4), (6, 0), (7, 9)\}$ and $f(x) = \sqrt{x - 3}$. Find each of the following.

a. $h(7)$ **b.** w, if $h(w) = 0$ **c.** $f(7)$ **d.** x, if $f(x) = 5$

Solution

a. The expression $h(7)$ is the second coordinate when the first coordinate is 7 in the function named h. So $h(7) = 9$.

b. We are looking for a number w for which $h(w) = 0$. That is, the second coordinate is 0 for some unknown first coordinate w. By examining the function h we see that $w = 6$.

c. To find $f(7)$ replace x by 7 in $f(x) = \sqrt{x - 3}$:

$$f(7) = \sqrt{7 - 3} = \sqrt{4} = 2$$

d. To find x for which $f(x) = 5$ we replace $f(x)$ by 5 in $f(x) = \sqrt{x - 3}$:

$$5 = \sqrt{x - 3}$$
$$25 = x - 3$$
$$28 = x$$

■

Function notation such as $f(x) = 3x + 1$ provides a rule for finding the second coordinate: Multiply the first coordinate (whatever it is) by 3 and then add 1. The x in this notation is called a **dummy variable** because the letter used is unimportant. We could write $f(t) = 3t + 1$,

$$f(\text{first coordinate}) = 3(\text{first coordinate}) + 1,$$

or even $f(\ ) = 3(\ ) + 1$ to convey the same idea. Whatever appears in the parentheses following f must be used in place of x on the other side of the equation.

Example 7 Using function notation with variables

Given that $f(x) = x^2 - 2$ and $g(x) = 2x - 3$, find and simplify each of the following expressions.

a. $f(a)$ **b.** $f(a + 1)$ **c.** $f(x + h) - f(x)$ **d.** $g(x - 2)$ **e.** $g(x + h) - g(x)$

Solution

a. Replace x by a in $f(x) = x^2 - 2$ to get $f(a) = a^2 - 2$.

b. $f(a + 1) = (a + 1)^2 - 2$ Replace x by $a + 1$ in $f(x) = x^2 - 2$.

$= a^2 + 2a - 1$

c. $f(x + h) - f(x) = (x + h)^2 - x^2$ Replace x with $x + h$ to get $f(x + h)$.

$= x^2 + 2hx + h^2 - x^2$

$= 2hx + h^2$

d. $g(x - 2) = 2(x - 2) - 3$

$= 2x - 7$

e. $g(x + h) - g(x) = 2(x + h) - 3 - (2x - 3)$

$= 2x + 2h - 3 - 2x + 3$

$= 2h$ ■

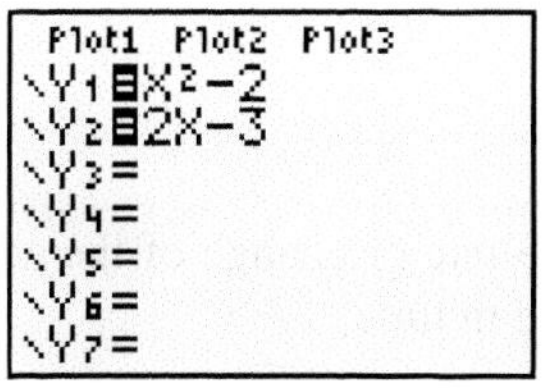

(a)

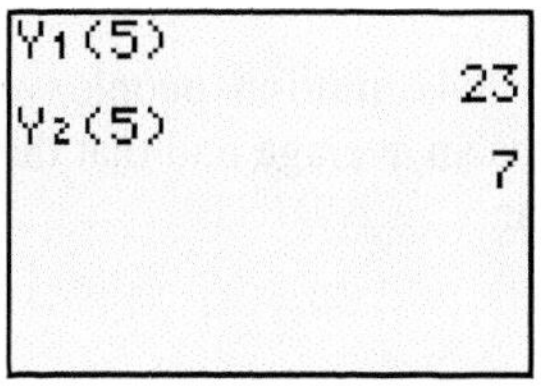

(b)

Figure 1.61

A graphing calculator uses subscripts to indicate different functions. For example, if $y_1 = x^2 - 2$ and $y_2 = 2x - 3$, then $y_1(5) = 23$ and $y_2(5) = 7$ as shown in Fig. 1.61(a) and (b). □

If a function describes some real application, then a letter that fits the situation is usually used. For example, if watermelons are \$3 each, then the cost of x watermelons is given by the function $C(x) = 3x$. The cost of five watermelons is $C(5) = 3 \cdot 5 = \$15$. In trigonometry the abbreviations sin, cos, and tan are used rather than a single letter to name the trigonometric functions. The dependent variables are written as $\sin(x)$, $\cos(x)$, and $\tan(x)$.

The Average Rate of Change of a Function

In Section 1.4 we defined the slope of the line through (x_1, y_1) and (x_2, y_2) as $\frac{y_2 - y_1}{x_2 - x_1}$. We now extend that idea to any function (linear or not).

Definition: Average Rate of Change from x_1 to x_2

If (x_1, y_1) and (x_2, y_2) are two ordered pairs of a function, we define the **average rate of change** of the function as x varies from x_1 to x_2 as

$$\frac{y_2 - y_1}{x_2 - x_1}.$$

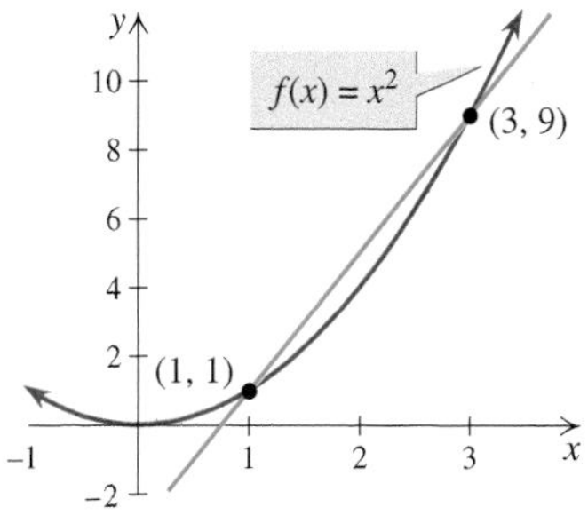

Figure 1.62

Note that the x-values can be specified with interval notation. For example, the average rate of change $f(x) = x^2$ on $[1, 3]$ is found as follows:

$$\frac{f(3) - f(1)}{3 - 1} = \frac{9 - 1}{3 - 1} = 4$$

The average rate of change is simply the slope of the line that passes through two points on the graph of the function as shown in Fig. 1.62.

It is not necessary to have a formula for a function to find an average rate of change, as is shown in the next example.

Example 8 Finding the average rate of change

The population of California was 29.8 million in 1990 and 33.9 million in 2000 (U.S. Census Bureau, www.census.gov). What was the average rate of change of the population over that time interval?

Solution

The population is a function of the year. The average rate of change of the population is the change in population divided by the change in time:

$$\frac{33.9 - 29.8}{2000 - 1990} = \frac{4.1}{10} = 0.41$$

The average rate of change of the population was 0.41 million people/year or 410,000 people/year. Note that 410,000 people/year is an average and that the population did not actually increase by 410,000 every year. ■

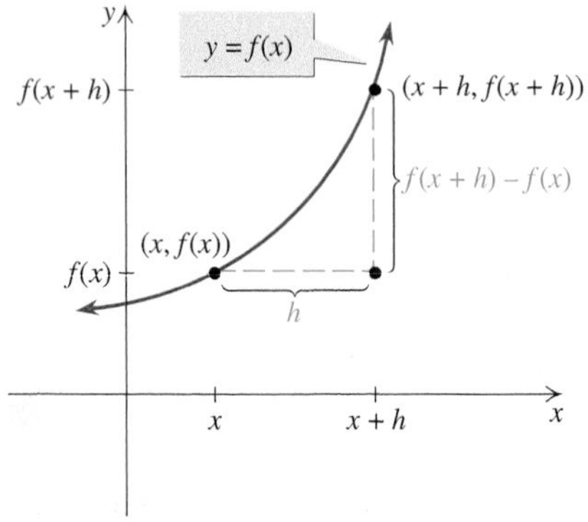

Figure 1.63

The expression $\frac{f(x + h) - f(x)}{h}$ is called the **difference quotient.** The difference quotient is the average rate of change between two points that are labeled as shown in Fig. 1.63. In calculus it is often necessary to find and simplify the difference quotient for a function.

Example 9 Finding a difference quotient

Find and simplify the difference quotient for each of the following functions.

a. $j(x) = 3x + 2$ **b.** $f(x) = x^2 - 2x$ **c.** $g(x) = \sqrt{x}$ **d.** $y = \frac{5}{x}$

Solution

a. $$\frac{j(x + h) - j(x)}{h} = \frac{3(x + h) + 2 - (3x + 2)}{h}$$

$$= \frac{3x + 3h + 2 - 3x - 2}{h}$$

$$= \frac{3h}{h} = 3$$

b. $$\frac{f(x + h) - f(x)}{h} = \frac{[(x + h)^2 - 2(x + h)] - (x^2 - 2x)}{h}$$

$$= \frac{x^2 + 2xh + h^2 - 2x - 2h - x^2 + 2x}{h}$$

$$= \frac{2xh + h^2 - 2h}{h}$$

$$= 2x + h - 2$$

■ Foreshadowing Calculus

The difference quotient or average rate of change of a function is the rate of change of y over some interval of x-values. In calculus this idea is extended to the instantaneous rate of change, which is the rate of change of y at a single value of x.

c. $$\frac{g(x+h)-g(x)}{h} = \frac{\sqrt{x+h}-\sqrt{x}}{h}$$

$$= \frac{\left(\sqrt{x+h}-\sqrt{x}\right)\left(\sqrt{x+h}+\sqrt{x}\right)}{h\left(\sqrt{x+h}+\sqrt{x}\right)}$$ Rationalize the numerator.

$$= \frac{x+h-x}{h(\sqrt{x+h}+\sqrt{x})}$$

$$= \frac{1}{\sqrt{x+h}+\sqrt{x}}$$

d. Use the function notation $f(x) = \frac{5}{x}$ for the function $y = \frac{5}{x}$:

$$\frac{f(x+h)-f(x)}{h} = \frac{\frac{5}{x+h}-\frac{5}{x}}{h} = \frac{\left(\frac{5}{x+h}-\frac{5}{x}\right)x(x+h)}{h \cdot x(x+h)}$$

$$= \frac{5x-5(x+h)}{hx(x+h)} = \frac{-5h}{hx(x+h)} = \frac{-5}{x(x+h)}$$ ■

Note that in Examples 9(b), 9(c), and 9(d) the average rate of change of the function depends on the values of x and h, while in Example 9(a) the average rate of change of the function is constant. In Example 9(c) the expression does not look much different after rationalizing the numerator than it did before. However, we did remove h as a factor of the denominator, and in calculus it is often necessary to perform this step.

Constructing Functions

In the next example we find a formula for, or **construct,** a function relating two variables in a geometric figure.

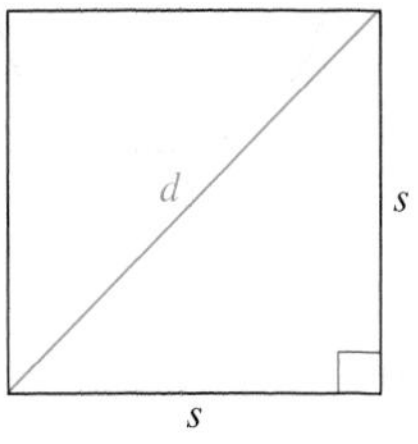

Figure 1.64

Example 10 Constructing a function

Given that a square has diagonal of length d and side of length s, write the area A as a function of the length of the diagonal.

Solution

The area of any square is given by $A = s^2$. The diagonal is the hypotenuse of a right triangle as shown in Fig. 1.64. By the Pythagorean theorem, $d^2 = s^2 + s^2$, $d^2 = 2s^2$, or $s^2 = d^2/2$. Since $A = s^2$ and $s^2 = d^2/2$, we get the formula

$$A = \frac{d^2}{2}$$

expressing the area of the square as a function of the length of the diagonal. ■

For Thought

True or False? Explain.

1. Any set of ordered pairs is a function.
2. If $f = \{(1, 1), (2, 4), (3, 9)\}$, then $f(5) = 25$.
3. The domain of $f(x) = 1/x$ is $(-\infty, 0) \cup (0, \infty)$.
4. Each student's exam grade is a function of the student's IQ.
5. If $f(x) = x^2$, then $f(x + h) = x^2 + h$.
6. The domain of $g(x) = |x - 3|$ is $[3, \infty)$.
7. The range of $y = 8 - x^2$ is $(-\infty, 8]$.
8. The equation $x = y^2$ does not define y as a function of x.
9. If $f(t) = \dfrac{t - 2}{t + 2}$, then $f(0) = -1$.
10. The set $\left\{\left(\frac{3}{8}, 8\right), \left(\frac{4}{7}, 7\right), \left(0.16, 6\right), \left(\frac{3}{8}, 5\right)\right\}$ is a function.

1.5 Exercises

For each pair of variables determine whether a is a function of b, b is a function of a, or neither.

1. a is the radius of any U.S. coin and b is its circumference.
2. a is the length of any rectangle with a width of 5 in. and b is its perimeter.
3. a is the length of any piece of U.S. paper currency and b is its denomination.
4. a is the diameter of any U.S. coin and b is its value.
5. a is the universal product code for an item at Wal-Mart and b is its price.
6. a is the final exam score for a student in your class and b is his/her semester grade.
7. a is the time spent studying for the final exam for a student in your class and b is the student's final exam score.
8. a is the age of an adult male and b is his shoe size.
9. a is the height of a car in inches and b is its height in centimeters.
10. a is the cost for mailing a first-class letter and b is its weight.

Use the vertical line test on each graph in Exercises 11–16 to determine whether y is a function of x.

11.

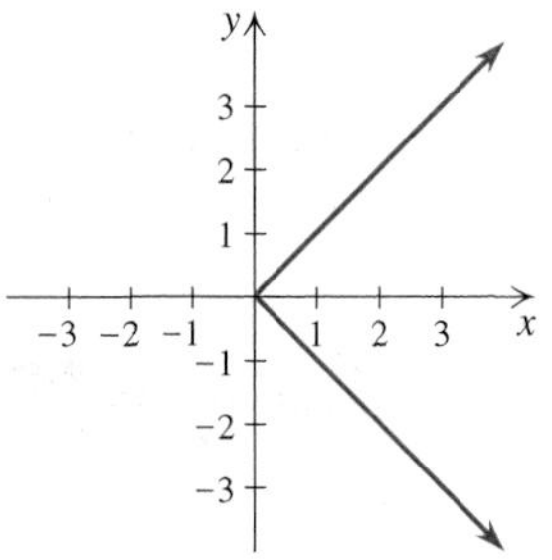

12.

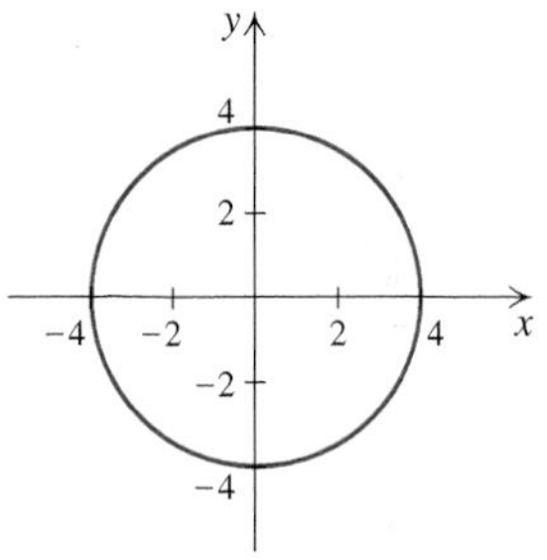

13.

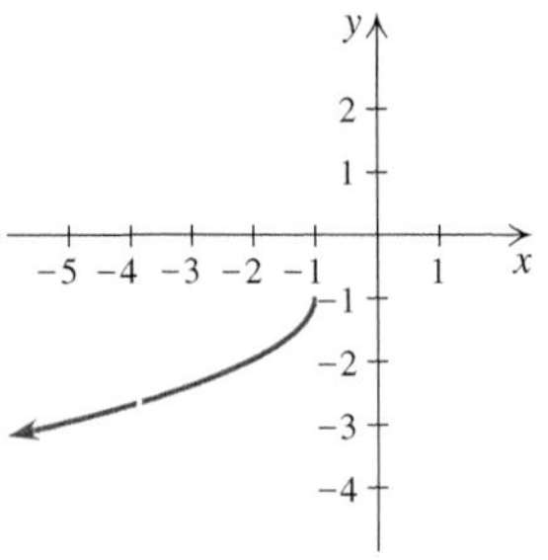

14.

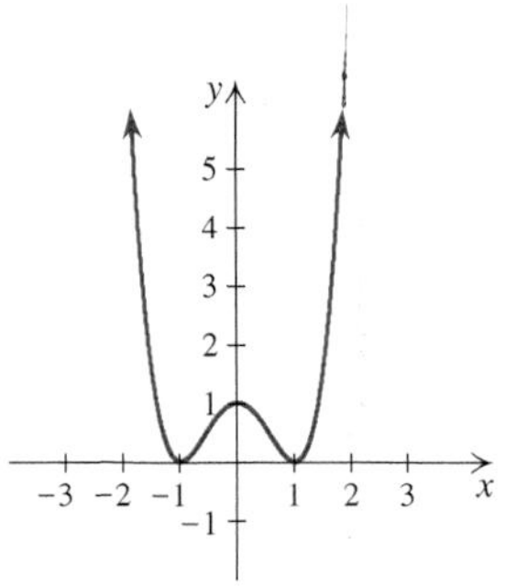

15.

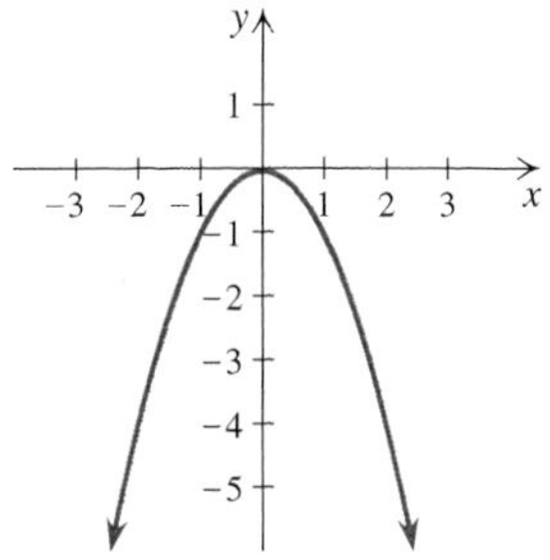

16.

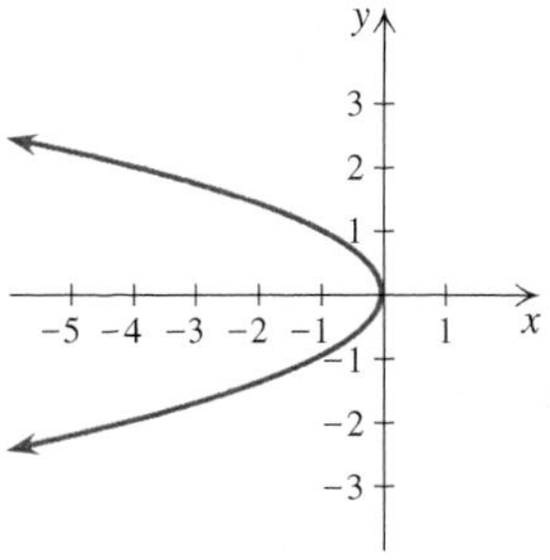

Determine whether each relation is a function.

17. $\{(-1, -1), (2, 2), (3, 3)\}$

18. $\{(0.5, 7), (0, 7), (1, 7), (9, 7)\}$

19. $\{(25, 5), (25, -5), (0, 0)\}$

20. $\{(1, \pi), (30, \pi/2), (60, \pi/4)\}$

21.

x	y
3	6
4	9
3	12

22.

x	y
1	6.98
5	5.98
9	6.98

23.

x	y
−1	1
1	1
−5	1
5	1

24.

x	y
1	1
2	4
3	9
4	16

Determine whether each equation defines y as a function of x.

25. $y = 3x - 8$

26. $y = x^2 - 3x + 7$

27. $x = 3y - 9$

28. $x = y^3$

29. $x^2 = y^2$

30. $y^2 - x^2 = 9$

31. $x = \sqrt{y}$

32. $x = \sqrt[3]{y}$

33. $y + 2 = |x|$

34. $y - 1 = x^2$

35. $x = |2y|$

36. $x = y^2 + 1$

Determine the domain and range of each relation.

37. $\{(-3, 1), (4, 2), (-3, 6), (5, 6)\}$

38. $\{(1, 2), (2, 4), (3, 8), (4, 16)\}$

39. $\{(x, y) | y = 4\}$

40. $\{(x, y) | x = 5\}$

41. $y = |x| + 5$

42. $y = x^2 + 8$

43. $x + 3 = |y|$

44. $x + 2 = \sqrt{y}$

45. $y = \sqrt{x - 4}$

46. $y = \sqrt{5 - x}$

47. $x = -y^2$

48. $x = -|y|$

Let $f = \{(2, 6), (3, 8), (4, 5)\}$ and $g(x) = 3x + 5$. Find the following.

49. $f(2)$

50. $f(4)$

51. $g(2)$

52. $g(4)$

53. x, if $f(x) = 8$

54. x, if $f(x) = 6$

55. x, if $g(x) = 26$

56. x, if $g(x) = -4$

57. $f(4) + g(4)$

58. $f(3) - g(3)$

Let $f(x) = 3x^2 - x$ and $g(x) = 4x - 2$. Find the following.

59. $f(a)$

60. $f(w)$

61. $g(a + 2)$

62. $g(a - 5)$

63. $f(x + 1)$

64. $f(x - 3)$

65. $g(x + h)$

66. $f(x + h)$

67. $f(x + h) - f(x)$

68. $g(x + h) - g(x)$

The following problems involve average rate of change.

69. *Depreciation of a Mustang* If a new Mustang is valued at \$16,000 and five years later it is valued at \$4000, then what is the average rate of change of its value during those five years?

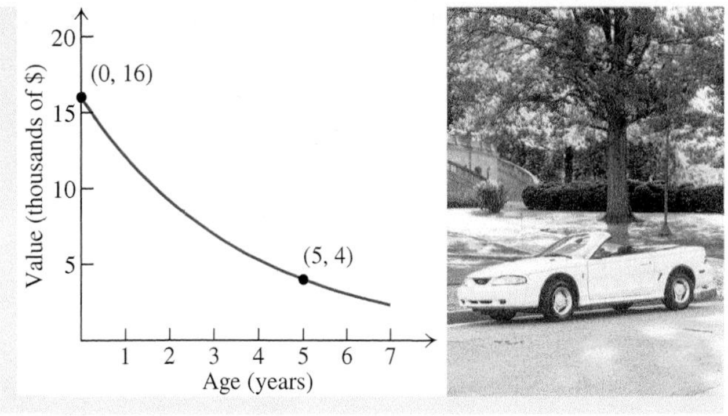

Figure for Exercise 69

70. *Cost of Gravel* Wilson's Sand and Gravel will deliver 12 yd^3 of gravel for \$240, 30 yd^3 for \$528, and 60 yd^3 for \$948. What is the average rate of change of the cost as the number of cubic yards varies from 12 to 30? What is the average rate of change as the number of cubic yards varies from 30 to 60?

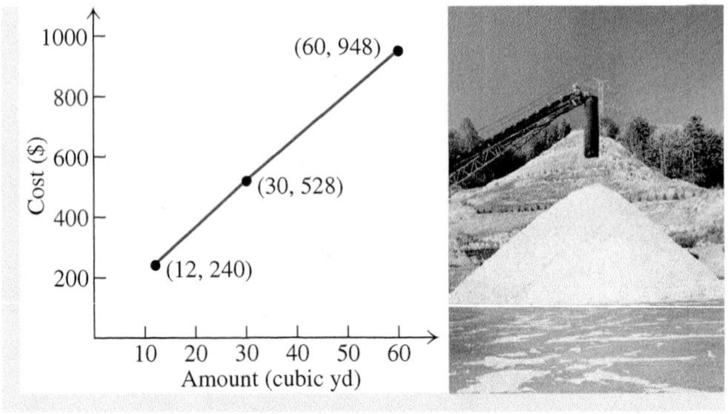

Figure for Exercise 70

Foreshadowing Calculus

In calculus we determine what happens to the average rate of change as the length of the interval for the independent variable approaches zero. You can get a hint of that process in the next exercise.

71. *Dropping a Watermelon* If a comedian drops a watermelon from a height of 64 ft, then its height (in feet) above the ground is given by the function $h(t) = -16t^2 + 64$ where t is time (in seconds). To get an idea of how fast the watermelon is traveling when it hits the ground find the average rate of change of the height on each of the time intervals [0, 2], [1, 2], [1.9, 2], [1.99, 2], and [1.999, 2].

72. *Bungee Jumping* Billy Joe McCallister jumped off the Tallahatchie Bridge, 70 ft above the water, with a bungee cord tied to his legs. If he was 6 ft above the water 2 sec after jumping, then what was the average rate of change of his altitude as the time varied from 0 to 2 sec?

Find the difference quotient $\frac{f(x+h)-f(x)}{h}$ *for each function and simplify it.*

73. $f(x) = 4x$

74. $f(x) = \frac{1}{2}x$

75. $f(x) = 3x + 5$

76. $f(x) = -2x + 3$

77. $y = x^2 + x$

78. $y = x^2 - 2x$

79. $y = -x^2 + x - 2$

80. $y = x^2 - x + 3$

81. $g(x) = 3\sqrt{x}$

82. $g(x) = -2\sqrt{x}$

83. $f(x) = \sqrt{x+2}$

84. $f(x) = \sqrt{\frac{x}{2}}$

85. $g(x) = \frac{1}{x}$

86. $g(x) = \frac{3}{x}$

87. $g(x) = \frac{3}{x+2}$

88. $g(x) = 3 + \frac{2}{x-1}$

Solve each problem.

89. *Constructing Functions* Consider a square with side of length s, diagonal of length d, perimeter P, and area A.

a. Write A as a function of s. **b.** Write s as a function of A.

c. Write s as a function of d. **d.** Write d as a function of s.

e. Write P as a function of s. **f.** Write s as a function of P.

g. Write A as a function of P. **h.** Write d as a function of A.

90. *Constructing Functions* Consider a circle with area A, circumference C, radius r, and diameter d.

a. Write A as a function of r. **b.** Write r as a function of A.

c. Write C as a function of r. **d.** Write d as a function of r.

e. Write d as a function of C. **f.** Write A as a function of d.

g. Write d as a function of A.

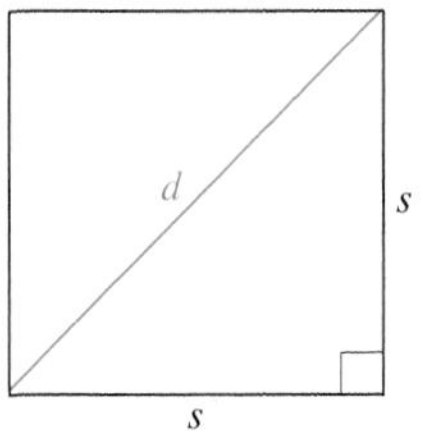

Figure for Exercise 89

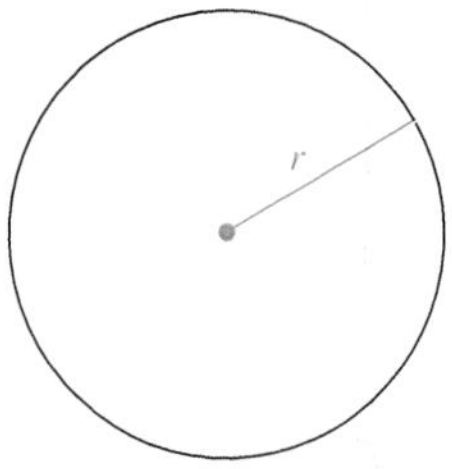

Figure for Exercise 90

91. *Below Sea Level* The accompanying table shows the depth below sea level d and the atmospheric pressure A (www.sportsfigures.espn.com). The equation $A(d) = 0.03d + 1$ expresses A as a function of d.

a. Find the atmospheric pressure for a depth of 100 ft, where nitrogen narcosis begins.

b. Find the depth at which the pressure is 4.9 atm, the maximum depth for intermediate divers.

Table for Exercise 91

Depth (ft)	Atmospheric Pressure (atm)
21	1.63
60	2.8
100	
	4.9
200	7.0
250	8.5

92. *Computer Spending* The amount spent online for computers in the year $2000 + n$ can be modeled by the function $C(n) = 0.95n + 5.8$ where n is a whole number and $C(n)$ is billions of dollars.

a. What does $C(4)$ represent and what is it?

b. Find the year in which online spending for computers will reach \$15 billion?

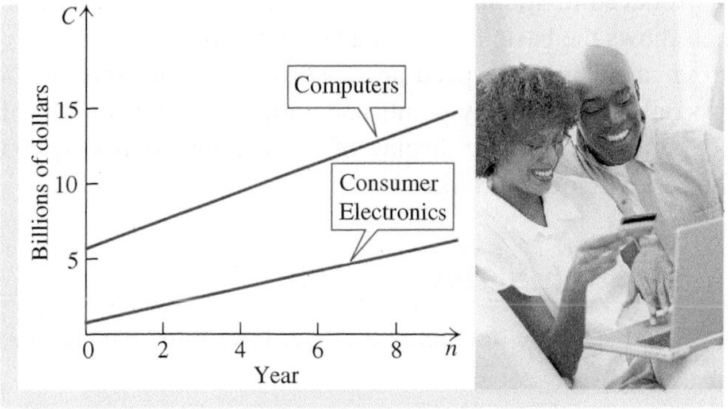

Figure for Exercise 92

93. *Pile of Pipes* Six pipes, each with radius a, are stacked as shown in the accompanying figure. Construct a function that gives the height h of the pile in terms of a.

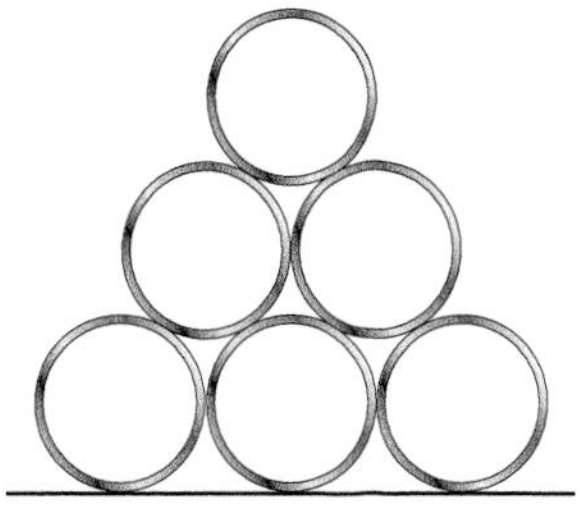

Figure for Exercise 93

94. *Angle Bisectors* The angle bisectors of any triangle meet at a single point. Let a be the length of the hypotenuse of a 30-60-90 triangle and d be the distance from the vertex of the right angle to the point where the angle bisectors meet. Write d as function of a.

Thinking Outside the Box V

Lucky Lucy Lucy's teacher asked her to evaluate $(20 + 25)^2$. As she was trying to figure out what to do she mumbled, "twenty twenty-five." Her teacher said, "Good, 2025 is correct." Find another pair of two digit whole numbers for which the square of their sum can be found by Lucy's method.

1.5 Pop Quiz

1. Is the radius of a circle a function of its area?
2. Is $\{(2, 4), (1, 8), (2, -4)\}$ a function?
3. Does $x^2 + y^2 = 1$ define y as a function of x?
4. What is the domain of $y = \sqrt{x - 1}$?
5. What is the range of $y = x^2 + 2$?
6. What is $f(2)$ if $f = \{(1, 8), (2, 9)\}$?
7. What is a if $f(a) = 1$ and $f(x) = 2x$?
8. If the cost was \$20 in 1998 and \$40 in 2008, then what is the average rate of change of the cost for that time period?
9. Find and simplify the difference quotient for $f(x) = x^2 + 3$.

1.6 Graphs of Relations and Functions

When we graph the set of ordered pairs that satisfy an equation, we are combining algebra with geometry. We saw in Section 1.3 that the graph of any equation of the form $(x - h)^2 + (y - k)^2 = r^2$ is a circle and that the graph of any equation of the form $Ax + By = C$ is a straight line. In this section we will see that graphs of equations have many different geometric shapes.

Graphing Equations

The circle and the line provide nice examples of how algebra and geometry are interrelated. When you see an equation that you recognize as the equation of a circle or a line, sketching a graph is easy to do. Other equations have graphs that are not such familiar shapes. Until we learn to recognize the kinds of graphs that other equations have, we graph other equations by calculating enough ordered pairs to determine the shape of the graph. When you graph equations, try to anticipate what the graph will look like, and after the graph is drawn, pause to reflect on the shape of the graph and the type of equation that produced it. You might wish to look ahead to the Function Gallery on page 79, which shows the basic functions that we will be studying.

Of course a graphing calculator can speed up this process. Remember that a graphing calculator shows only finitely many points and a graph usually consists of infinitely many points. After looking at the display of a graphing calculator, you must still decide what the entire graph looks like. □

Example 1 The square function

Graph the equation $y = x^2$ and state the domain and range. Determine whether the relation is a function.

Solution

Make a table of ordered pairs that satisfy $y = x^2$:

x is any real number

x	0	1	-1	2	-2
$y = x^2$	0	1	1	4	4

$y \geq 0$

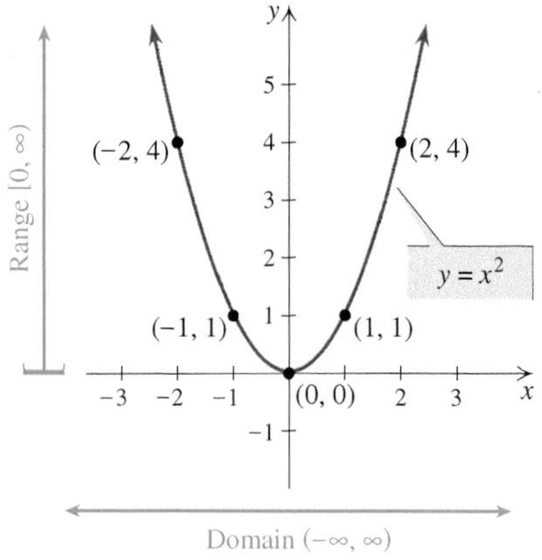

Figure 1.65

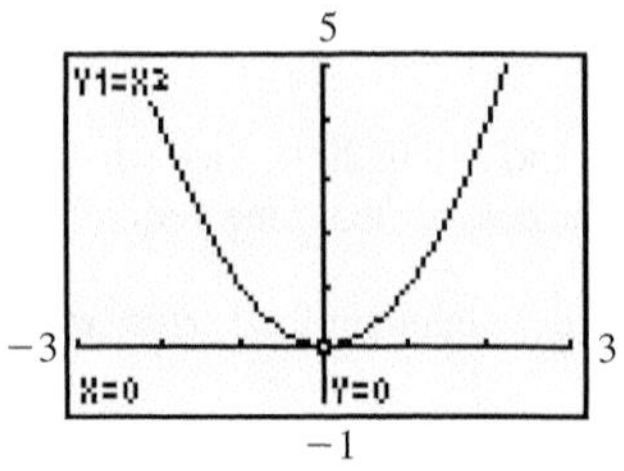

Figure 1.66

These ordered pairs indicate a graph in the shape shown in Fig. 1.65. The domain is $(-\infty, \infty)$ because any real number can be used for x in $y = x^2$. Since all y-coordinates are nonnegative, the range is $[0, \infty)$. Because no vertical line crosses this curve more than once, $y = x^2$ is a function.

The calculator graph shown in Fig. 1.66 supports these conclusions. ■

The graph of $y = x^2$ is called a **parabola.** We study parabolas in detail in Chapter 2. The graph of the **square-root function** $y = \sqrt{x}$ is half of a parabola.

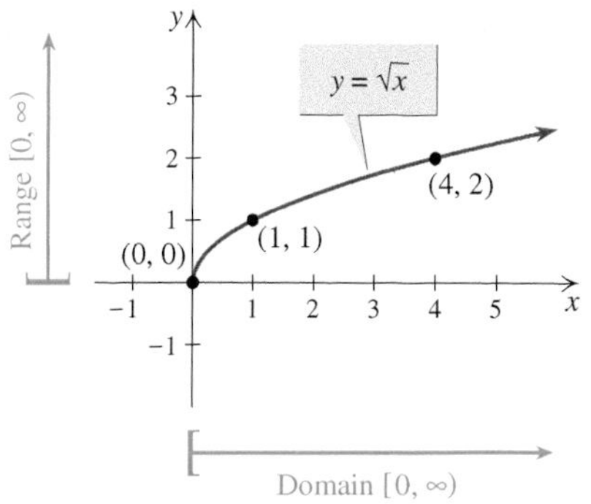

Figure 1.67

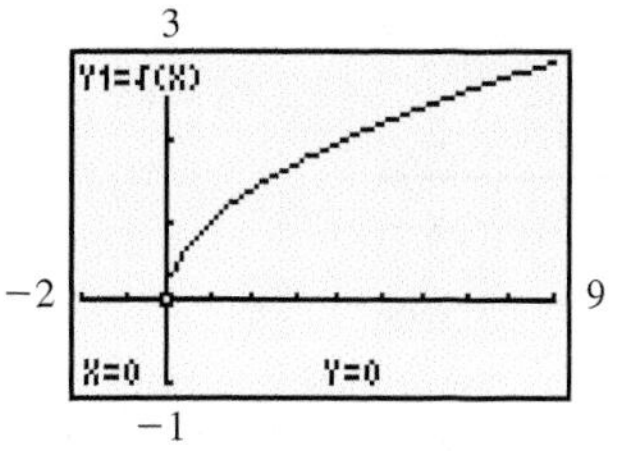

Figure 1.68

Example 2 The square-root function

Graph $y = \sqrt{x}$ and state the domain and range of the relation. Determine whether the relation is a function.

Solution

Make a table listing ordered pairs that satisfy $y = \sqrt{x}$:

$x \geq 0$

x	0	1	4	9
$y = \sqrt{x}$	0	1	2	3

$y \geq 0$

Plotting these ordered pairs suggests the graph shown in Fig. 1.67. The domain of the relation is $[0, \infty)$ and the range is $[0, \infty)$. Because no vertical line can cross this graph more than once, $y = \sqrt{x}$ is a function.

The calculator graph in Fig. 1.68 supports these conclusions. ■

In the next example we graph $x = y^2$ and see that its graph is also a parabola.

Example 3 A parabola opening to the right

Graph $x = y^2$ and state the domain and range of the relation. Determine whether the relation is a function.

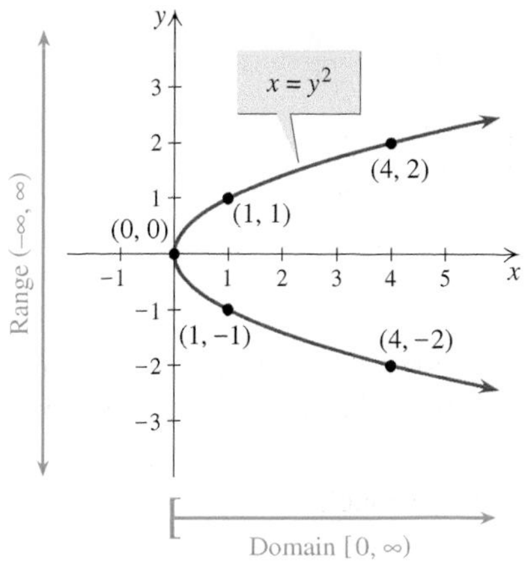

Figure 1.69

Solution

Make a table listing ordered pairs that satisfy $x = y^2$. In this case choose y and calculate x:

$x \geq 0$

$x = y^2$	0	1	1	4	4
y	0	1	−1	2	−2

y is any real number

Note that these ordered pairs are the same ones that satisfy $y = x^2$ except that the coordinates are reversed. For this reason the graph of $x = y^2$ in Fig. 1.69 has the same shape as the parabola in Fig. 1.65 and it is also a parabola. The domain of $x = y^2$ is $[0, \infty)$ and the range is $(-\infty, \infty)$. Because we can draw a vertical line that crosses this parabola twice, $x = y^2$ does not define y as a function of x. (Of course, $x = y^2$ does express x as a function of y.) ■

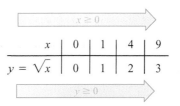

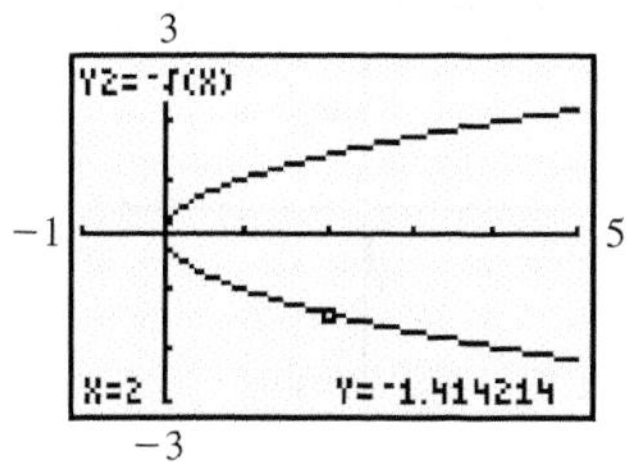

Figure 1.70

Because $x = y^2$ is equivalent to $y = \pm\sqrt{x}$, the top half of the graph of $x = y^2$ is $y = \sqrt{x}$ and the bottom half is $y = -\sqrt{x}$.

To support these conclusions with a graphing calculator, graph $y_1 = \sqrt{x}$ and $y_2 = -\sqrt{x}$ as shown in Fig. 1.70. □

In the next example we graph the **cube function** $y = x^3$ and the **cube-root function** $y = \sqrt[3]{x}$.

Example 4 Cube and cube-root functions

Graph each equation. State the domain and range.

a. $y = x^3$ **b.** $y = \sqrt[3]{x}$

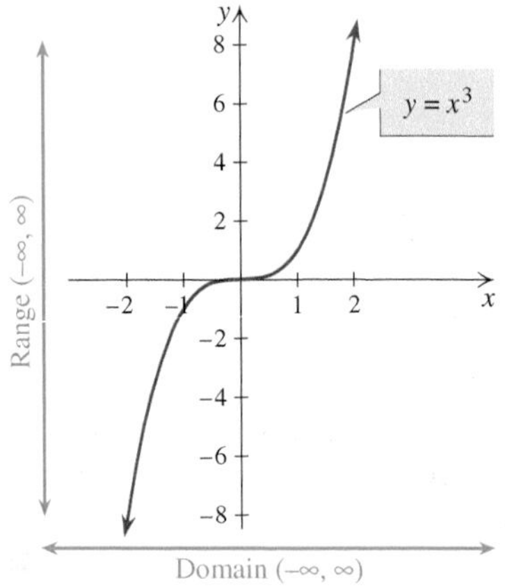

Figure 1.71

Solution

a. Make a table of ordered pairs that satisfy $y = x^3$:

x is any real number

x	-2	-1	0	1	2
$y = x^3$	-8	-1	0	1	8

y is any real number

These ordered pairs indicate a graph in the shape shown in Fig. 1.71. The domain is $(-\infty, \infty)$ and the range is $(-\infty, \infty)$. By the vertical line test, this graph is the graph of a function because no vertical line crosses the curve more than once.

b. Make a table of ordered pairs that satisfy $y = \sqrt[3]{x}$. Note that this table is simply the table for $y = x^3$ with the coordinates reversed.

x is any real number

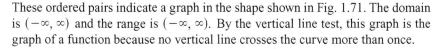

x	-8	-1	0	1	8
$y = \sqrt[3]{x}$	-2	-1	0	1	2

y is any real number

These ordered pairs indicate a graph in the shape shown in Fig. 1.72. The domain is $(-\infty, \infty)$ and the range is $(-\infty, \infty)$. Because no vertical line crosses this graph more than once, $y = \sqrt[3]{x}$ is a function.

The calculator graph in Fig. 1.73 supports these conclusions.

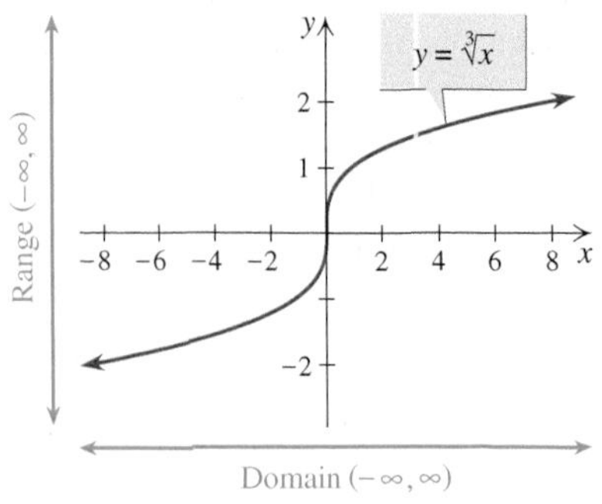

Figure 1.72

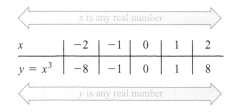

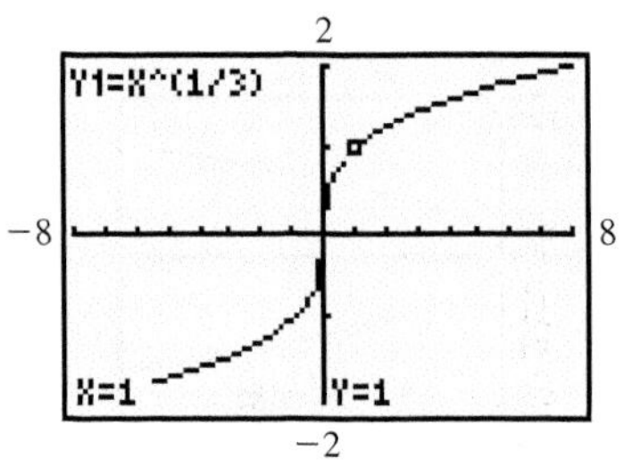

Figure 1.73

Semicircles

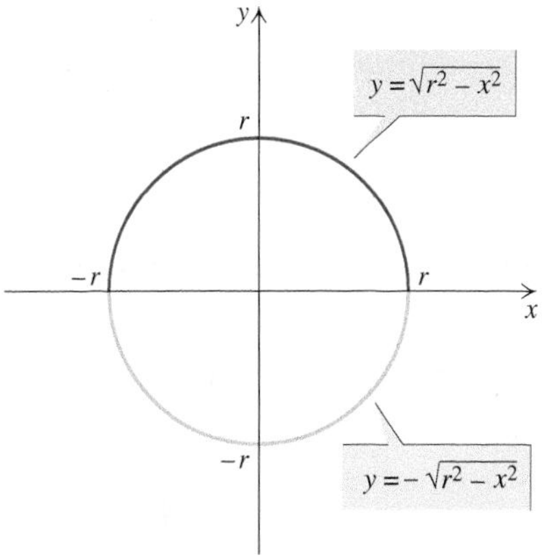

Figure 1.74

The graph of $x^2 + y^2 = r^2$ $(r > 0)$ is a circle centered at the origin of radius r. The circle does not pass the vertical line test, and a circle is not the graph of a function. We can find an equivalent equation by solving for y:

$$x^2 + y^2 = r^2$$
$$y^2 = r^2 - x^2$$
$$y = \pm\sqrt{r^2 - x^2}$$

The equation $y = \sqrt{r^2 - x^2}$ does define y as a function of x. Because y is nonnegative in this equation, the graph is the top semicircle in Fig. 1.74. The top semicircle passes the vertical line test. Likewise, the equation $y = -\sqrt{r^2 - x^2}$ defines y as a function of x, and its graph is the bottom semicircle in Fig. 1.74.

Example 5 Graphing a semicircle

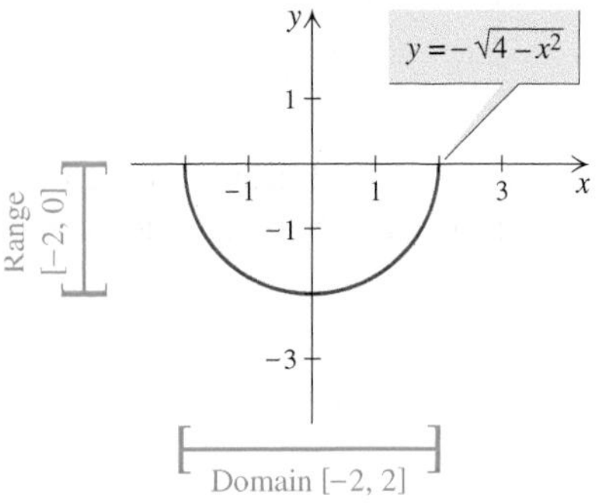

Figure 1.75

Sketch the graph of each function and state the domain and range of the function.

a. $y = -\sqrt{4 - x^2}$ **b.** $y = \sqrt{9 - x^2}$

Solution

a. Rewrite the equation in the standard form for a circle:

$$y = -\sqrt{4 - x^2}$$
$$y^2 = 4 - x^2 \quad \text{Square each side.}$$
$$x^2 + y^2 = 4 \quad \text{Standard form for the equation of a circle.}$$

The graph of $x^2 + y^2 = 4$ is a circle of radius 2 centered at (0, 0). Since y must be negative in $y = -\sqrt{4 - x^2}$, the graph of $y = -\sqrt{4 - x^2}$ is the semicircle shown in Fig. 1.75. We can see from the graph that the domain is $[-2, 2]$ and the range is $[-2, 0]$.

b. Rewrite the equation in the standard form for a circle:

$$y = \sqrt{9 - x^2}$$
$$y^2 = 9 - x^2 \quad \text{Square each side.}$$
$$x^2 + y^2 = 9$$

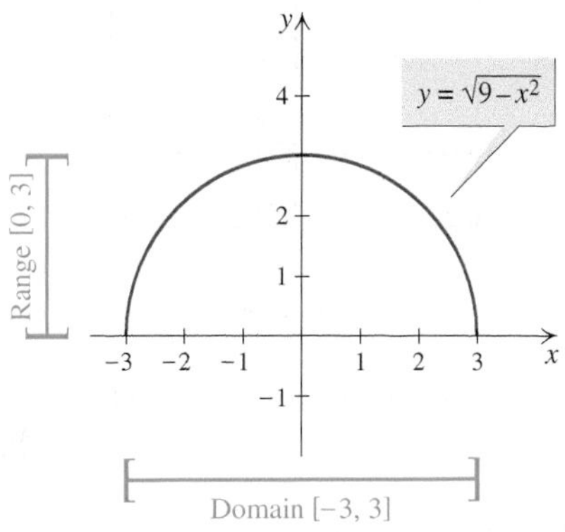

Figure 1.76

The graph of $x^2 + y^2 = 9$ is a circle with center (0, 0) and radius 3. But this equation is not equivalent to the original. The value of y in $y = \sqrt{9 - x^2}$ is nonnegative. So the graph of the original equation is the semicircle shown in Fig. 1.76. We can read the domain $[-3, 3]$ and the range $[0, 3]$ from the graph. ■

Piecewise Functions

For some functions, different formulas are used in different regions of the domain. Such functions are called **piecewise functions.** The simplest example of such a function is the **absolute value function** $f(x) = |x|$, which can be written as

$$f(x) = \begin{cases} x & \text{for } x \geq 0 \\ -x & \text{for } x < 0. \end{cases}$$

For $x \geq 0$ the equation $f(x) = x$ is used to obtain the second coordinate, and for $x < 0$ the equation $f(x) = -x$ is used. The graph of the absolute value function is shown in the next example.

Example 6 The absolute value function

Graph the equation $y = |x|$ and state the domain and range. Determine whether the relation is a function.

Solution

Make a table of ordered pairs that satisfy $y = |x|$:

x is any real number

x	0	1	−1	2	−2	3	−3
$y = \|x\|$	0	1	1	2	2	3	3

$y \geq 0$

These ordered pairs suggest the V-shaped graph of Fig. 1.77. Because no vertical line can cross this graph more than once, $y = |x|$ is a function. The domain is $(-\infty, \infty)$ and the range is $[0, \infty)$.

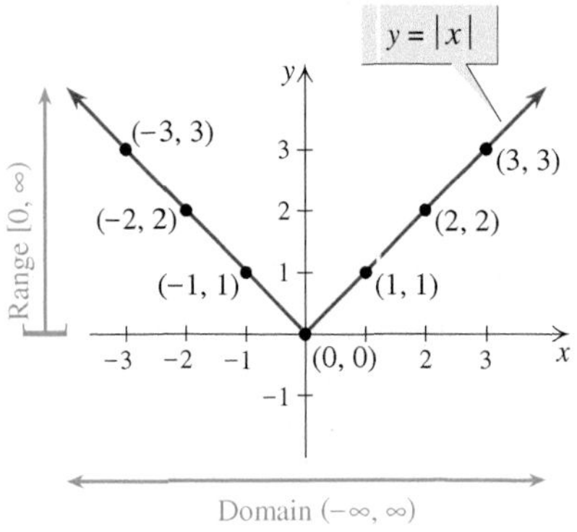

Figure 1.77

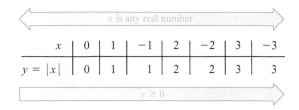

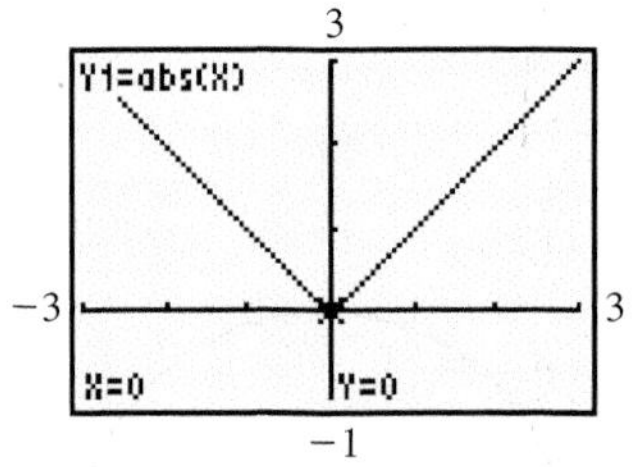

Figure 1.78

To support these conclusions with a graphing calculator, graph $y_1 = \text{abs}(x)$ as shown in Fig. 1.78. ■

In the next example we graph two more piecewise functions.

Example 7 Graphing a piecewise function

Sketch the graph of each function and state the domain and range.

a. $f(x) = \begin{cases} 1 & \text{for } x < 0 \\ -1 & \text{for } x \geq 0 \end{cases}$ **b.** $f(x) = \begin{cases} x^2 - 4 & \text{for } -2 \leq x \leq 2 \\ x - 2 & \text{for } x > 2 \end{cases}$

Solution

a. For $x < 0$ the graph is the horizontal line $y = 1$. For $x \geq 0$ the graph is the horizontal line $y = -1$. Note that $(0, -1)$ is on the graph shown in Fig. 1.79 but

(0, 1) is not, because when $x = 0$ we have $y = -1$. The domain is the interval $(-\infty, \infty)$ and the range consists of only two numbers, -1 and 1. The range is not an interval. It is written in set notation as $\{-1, 1\}$.

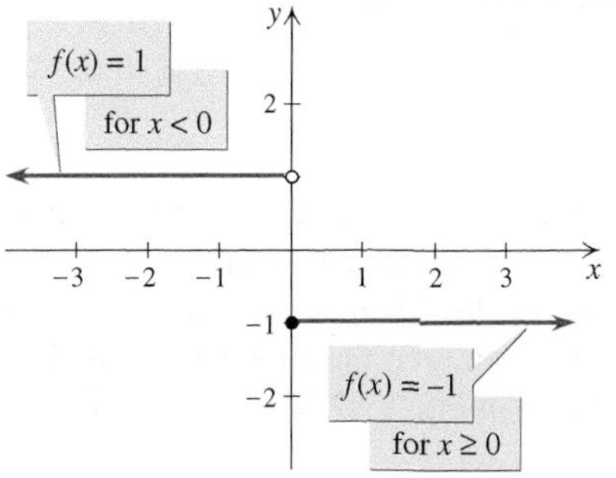

Figure 1.79

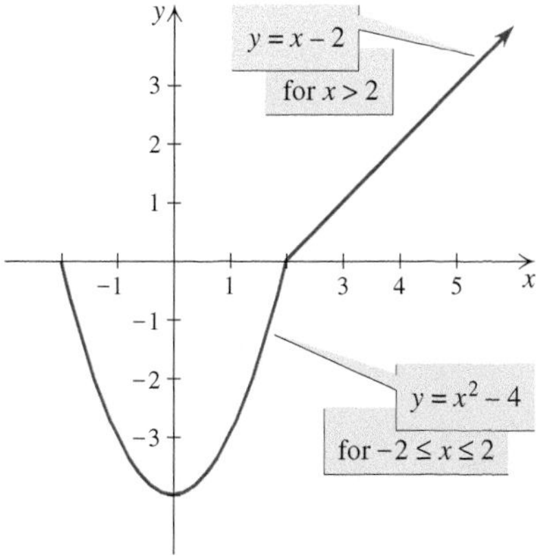

Figure 1.80

b. Make a table of ordered pairs using $y = x^2 - 4$ for x between -2 and 2 and $y = x - 2$ for $x > 2$.

x	-2	-1	0	1	2
$y = x^2 - 4$	0	-3	-4	-3	0

x	2.1	3	4	5
$y = x - 2$	0.1	1	2	3

For x in the interval $[-2, 2]$ the graph is a portion of a parabola as shown in Fig. 1.80. For $x > 2$, the graph is a portion of a straight line through (3, 1), (4, 2), and (5, 3). The domain is $[-2, \infty)$, and the range is $[-4, \infty)$.

Figure 1.81(a) shows how to use the inequality symbols from the TEST menu to enter a piecewise function on a calculator. The inequality $x \geq -2$ is not treated as a normal inequality, but instead the calculator gives it a value of 1 when it is satisfied and 0 when it is not satisfied. So, dividing $x^2 - 4$ by the inequalities $x \geq -2$ and $x \leq 2$ will cause $x^2 - 4$ to be graphed only when they are both satisfied and not graphed when they are not both satisfied. The calculator graph in Fig. 1.81(b) is consistent with the conclusions that we have made.

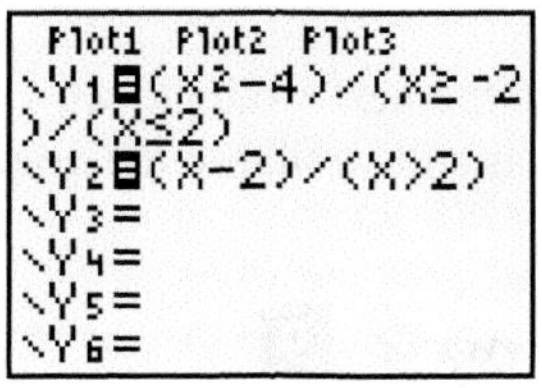

(a)

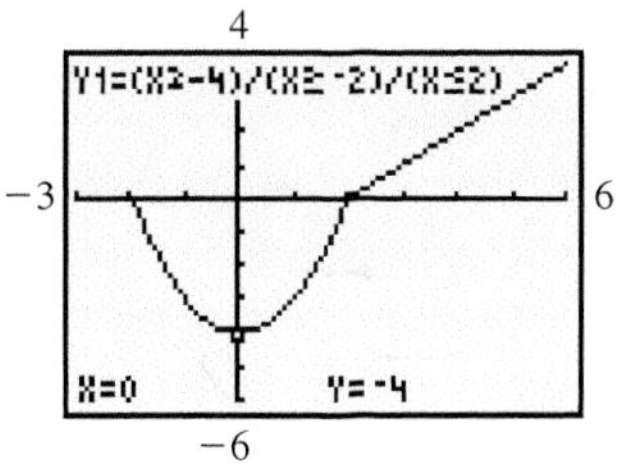

(b)

Figure 1.81

Piecewise functions are often found in shipping charges. For example, if the weight in pounds of an order is in the interval (0, 1], the shipping and handling charge is \$3. If the weight is in the interval (1, 2], the shipping and handling charge is \$4, and so on. The next example is a function that is similar to a shipping and handling charge. This function is referred to as the **greatest integer function** and is written $f(x) = [\![x]\!]$ or $f(x) = \text{int}(x)$. The symbol $[\![x]\!]$ is defined to be the largest integer that is less than or equal to x. For example, $[\![5.01]\!] = 5$, because the greatest integer less than or equal to 5.01 is 5. Likewise, $[\![3.2]\!] = 3$, $[\![-2.2]\!] = -3$, and $[\![7]\!] = 7$.

Example 8 Graphing the greatest integer function

Sketch the graph of $f(x) = [\![x]\!]$ and state the domain and range.

Solution

For any x in the interval $[0, 1)$ the greatest integer less than or equal to x is 0. For any x in $[1, 2)$ the greatest integer less than or equal to x is 1. For any x in $[-1, 0)$ the greatest integer less than or equal to x is -1. The definition of $[\![x]\!]$ causes the function to be constant between the integers and to "jump" at each integer. The graph of $f(x) = [\![x]\!]$ is shown in Fig. 1.82. The domain is $(-\infty, \infty)$, and the range is the set of integers.

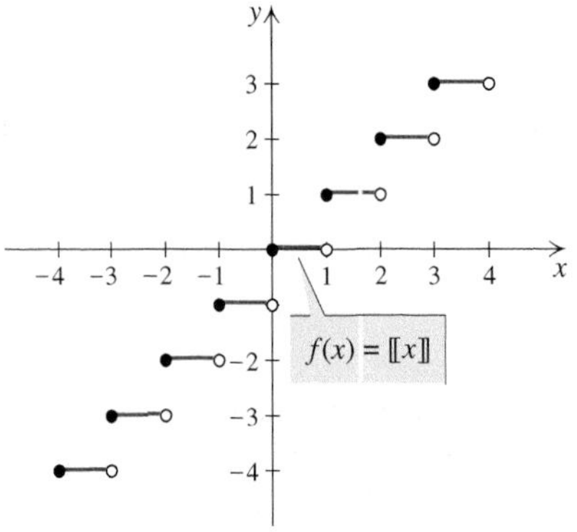

Figure 1.82

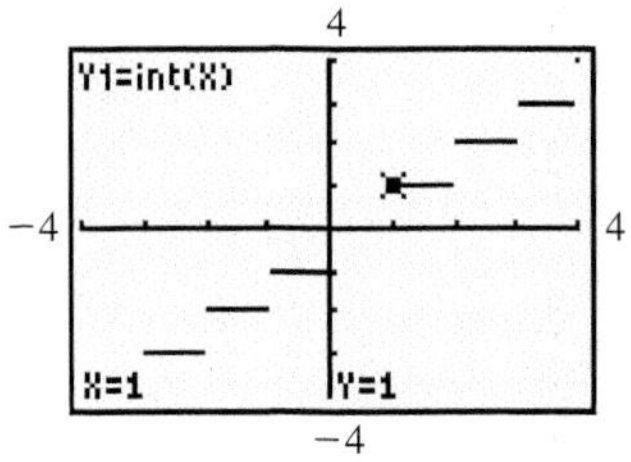

Figure 1.83

The calculator graph of $y_1 = \text{int}(x)$ looks best in dot mode as in Fig. 1.83, because in connected mode the calculator connects the disjoint pieces of the graph. The calculator graph in Fig. 1.82 supports our conclusion that the graph of this function looks like the one drawn in Fig. 1.82. Note that the calculator is incapable of showing whether the endpoints of the line segments are included. ■

In the next example we vary the form of the greatest integer function, but the graph is still similar to the graph in Fig. 1.82.

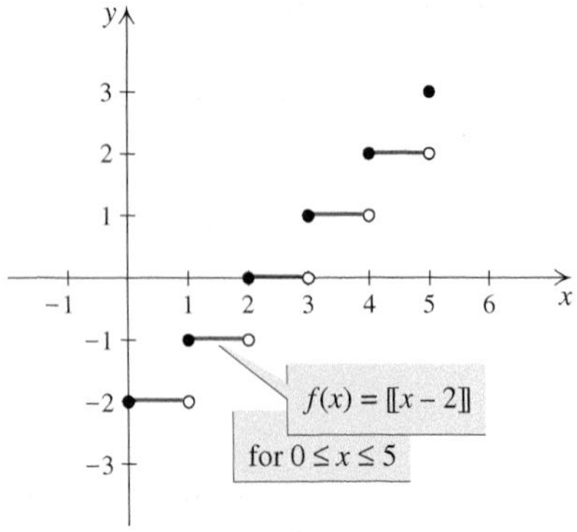

Figure 1.84

Example 9 A variation of the greatest integer function

Sketch the graph of $f(x) = [\![x - 2]\!]$ for $0 \le x \le 5$.

Solution

If $x = 0$, $f(0) = [\![-2]\!] = -2$. If $x = 0.5$, $f(0.5) = [\![-1.5]\!] = -2$. In fact, $f(x) = -2$ for any x in the interval $[0, 1)$. Similarly, $f(x) = -1$ for any x in the interval $[1, 2)$. This pattern continues with $f(x) = 2$ for any x in the interval $[4, 5)$, and $f(x) = 3$ for $x = 5$. The graph of $f(x) = [\![x - 2]\!]$ is shown in Fig. 1.84. ■

Increasing, Decreasing, and Constant

Imagine a point moving from left to right along the graph of a function. If the y-coordinate of the point is getting larger, getting smaller, or staying the same, then the function is said to be **increasing, decreasing,** or **constant,** respectively.

Example 10 Increasing, decreasing, or constant functions

Determine whether each function is increasing, decreasing, or constant by examining its graph.

a.

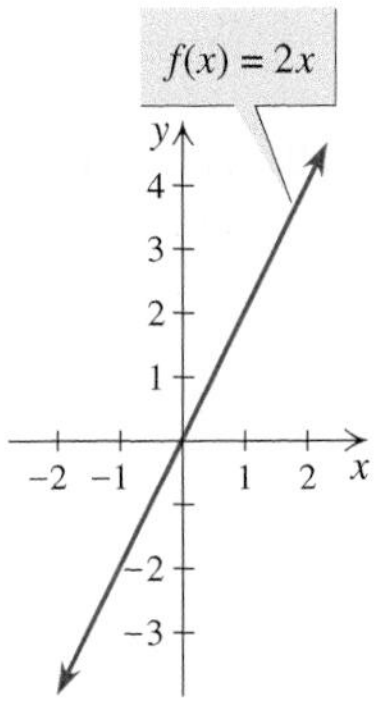

b.

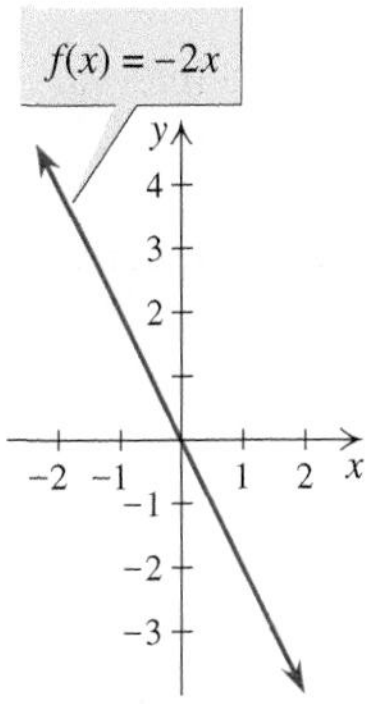

c.

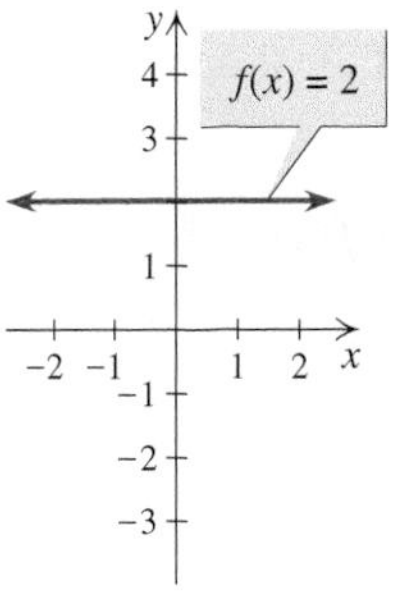

■ Foreshadowing Calculus

Whether a function is increasing, decreasing, or constant is determined analytically in calculus. Here the determination is made graphically.

Solution

If a point is moving left to right along the graph of $f(x) = 2x$, then its y-coordinate is increasing. So $f(x) = 2x$ is an increasing function. If a point is moving left to right along the graph of $f(x) = -2x$, then its y-coordinate is decreasing. So $f(x) = -2x$ is a decreasing function. The function $f(x) = 2$ has a constant y-coordinate and it is a constant function. ■

If the y-coordinates are getting larger, getting smaller, or staying the same when x is in an open interval, then the function is said to be increasing, decreasing, or constant, respectively, on that interval.

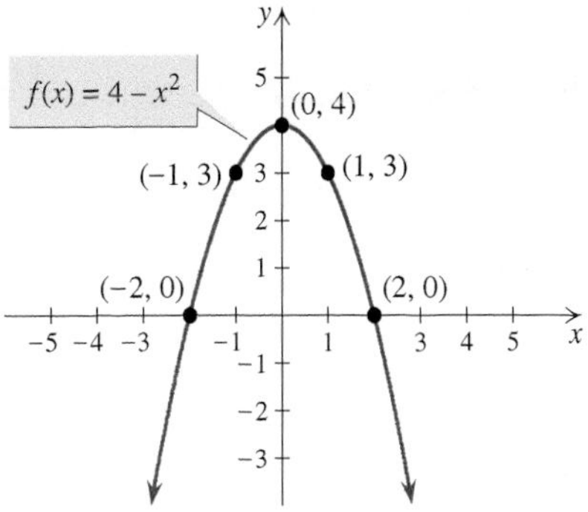

Figure 1.85

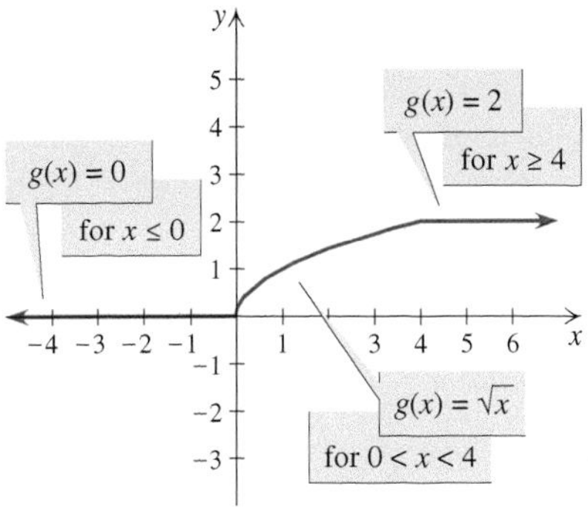

Figure 1.86

Example 11 Increasing, decreasing, or constant on an interval

Sketch the graph of each function and identify any open intervals on which the function is increasing, decreasing, or constant.

a. $f(x) = 4 - x^2$ **b.** $g(x) = \begin{cases} 0 & \text{for} \quad x \le 0 \\ \sqrt{x} & \text{for} \quad 0 < x < 4 \\ 2 & \text{for} \quad x \ge 4 \end{cases}$

Solution

a. The graph of $f(x) = 4 - x^2$ includes the points $(-2, 0)$, $(-1, 3)$, $(0, 4)$, $(1, 3)$, and $(2, 0)$. The graph is shown in Fig. 1.85. The function is increasing on the interval $(-\infty, 0)$ and decreasing on $(0, \infty)$.

b. The graph of g is shown in Fig. 1.86. The function g is constant on the intervals $(-\infty, 0)$ and $(4, \infty)$, and increasing on $(0, 4)$. ■

For Thought

True or False? Explain.

1. The range of $y = -x^2$ is $(-\infty, 0]$.
2. The function $y = -\sqrt{x}$ is increasing on $(0, \infty)$.
3. The function $f(x) = \sqrt[3]{x}$ is increasing on $(-\infty, \infty)$.
4. If $f(x) = [\![x + 3]\!]$, then $f(-4.5) = -2$.
5. The range of the function $f(x) = \frac{|x|}{x}$ is the interval $(-1, 1)$.
6. The range of $f(x) = [\![x - 1]\!]$ is the set of integers.
7. The only ordered pair that satisfies $(x - 5)^2 + (y + 6)^2 = 0$ is $(5, -6)$.
8. The domain of the function $y = \sqrt{4 - x^2}$ is the interval $[-2, 2]$.
9. The range of the function $y = \sqrt{16 - x^2}$ is the interval $[0, \infty)$.
10. The function $y = \sqrt{4 - x^2}$ is increasing on $(-2, 0)$ and decreasing on $(0, 2)$.

1.6 Exercises

Make a table listing ordered pairs that satisfy each equation. Then graph the equation. Determine the domain and range, and whether y is a function of x.

1. $y = 2x$
2. $x = 2y$
3. $x - y = 0$
4. $x - y = 2$
5. $y = 5$
6. $x = 3$
7. $y = 2x^2$
8. $y = x^2 - 1$
9. $y = 1 - x^2$
10. $y = -1 - x^2$
11. $y = 1 + \sqrt{x}$
12. $y = 2 - \sqrt{x}$
13. $x = y^2 + 1$
14. $x = 1 - y^2$
15. $x = \sqrt{y}$
16. $x - 1 = \sqrt{y}$
17. $y = \sqrt[3]{x} + 1$
18. $y = \sqrt[3]{x} - 2$
19. $x = \sqrt[3]{y}$
20. $x = \sqrt[3]{y - 1}$
21. $y^2 = 1 - x^2$
22. $x^2 + y^2 = 4$
23. $y = \sqrt{1 - x^2}$
24. $y = -\sqrt{25 - x^2}$
25. $y = x^3 + 1$
26. $y = -x^3$
27. $y = 2|x|$
28. $y = |x - 1|$
29. $y = -|x|$
30. $y = -|x + 1|$
31. $x = |y|$
32. $x = |y| + 1$

Make a table listing ordered pairs for each function. Then sketch the graph and state the domain and range.

33. $f(x) = \begin{cases} 2 & \text{for } x < -1 \\ -2 & \text{for } x \geq -1 \end{cases}$

34. $f(x) = \begin{cases} 3 & \text{for } x < 2 \\ 1 & \text{for } x \geq 2 \end{cases}$

35. $f(x) = \begin{cases} x + 1 & \text{for } x > 1 \\ x - 3 & \text{for } x \leq 1 \end{cases}$

36. $f(x) = \begin{cases} 5 - x & \text{for } x \leq 2 \\ x + 1 & \text{for } x > 2 \end{cases}$

37. $f(x) = \begin{cases} \sqrt{x + 2} & \text{for } -2 \leq x \leq 2 \\ 4 - x & \text{for } x > 2 \end{cases}$

38. $f(x) = \begin{cases} \sqrt{x} & \text{for } x \geq 1 \\ -x & \text{for } x < 1 \end{cases}$

39. $f(x) = \begin{cases} \sqrt{-x} & \text{for } x < 0 \\ \sqrt{x} & \text{for } x \geq 0 \end{cases}$

40. $f(x) = \begin{cases} 3 & \text{for } x < 0 \\ 3 + \sqrt{x} & \text{for } x \geq 0 \end{cases}$

41. $f(x) = \begin{cases} x^2 & \text{for } x < -1 \\ -x & \text{for } x \geq -1 \end{cases}$

42. $f(x) = \begin{cases} 4 - x^2 & \text{for } -2 \leq x \leq 2 \\ x - 2 & \text{for } x > 2 \end{cases}$

43. $f(x) = [\![x + 1]\!]$

44. $f(x) = 2[\![x]\!]$

45. $f(x) = [\![x]\!] + 2$ for $0 \leq x < 4$

46. $f(x) = [\![x - 3]\!]$ for $0 < x \leq 5$

From the graph of each function in Exercises 47–54, state the domain, the range, and the intervals on which the function is increasing, decreasing, or constant.

47. a.

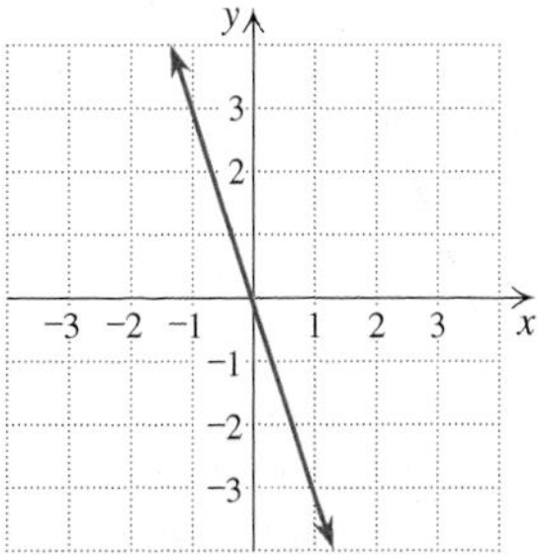

b.

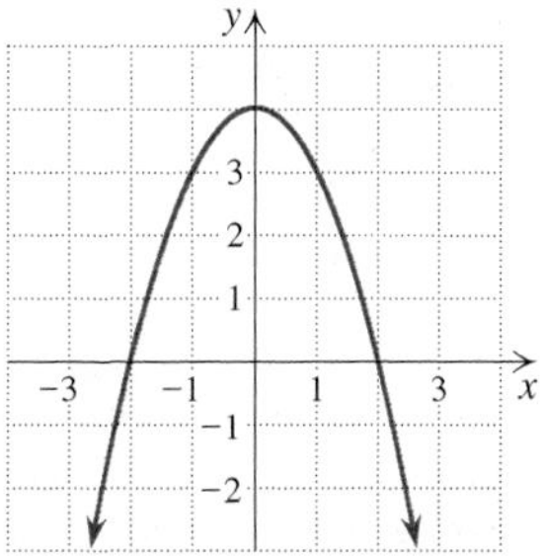

48. a.

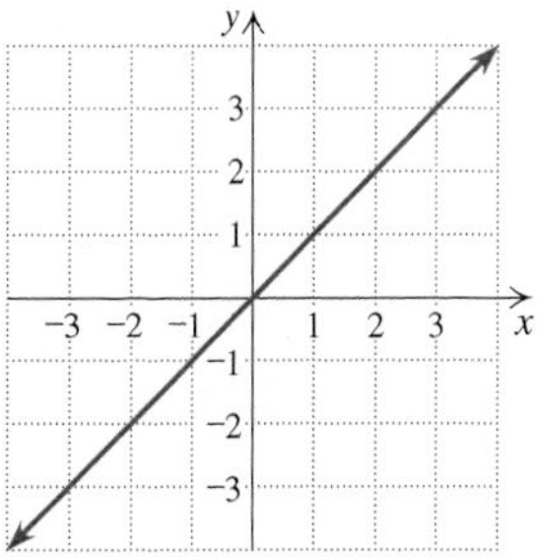

b.

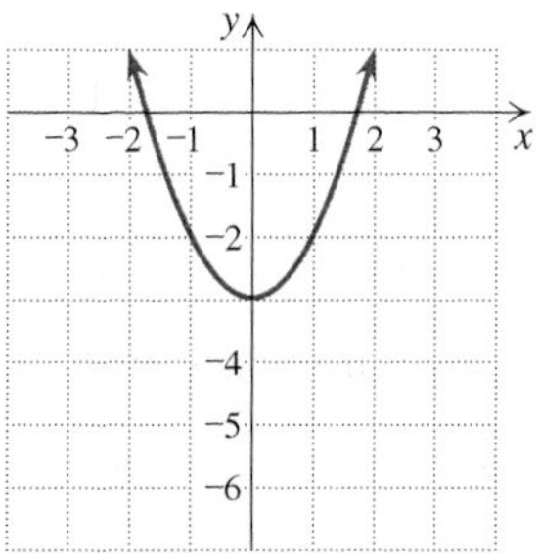

49. a.

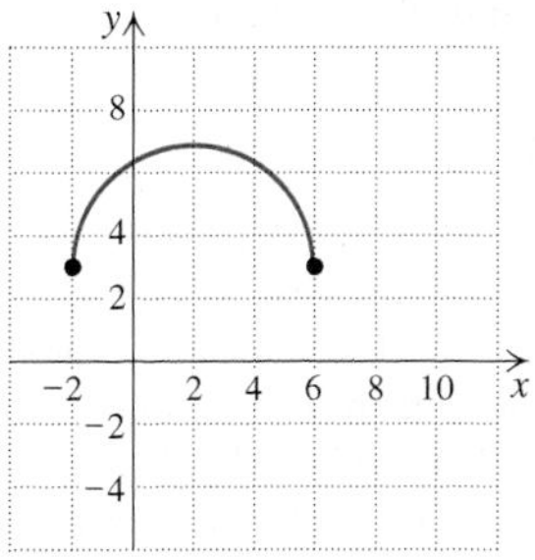

b.

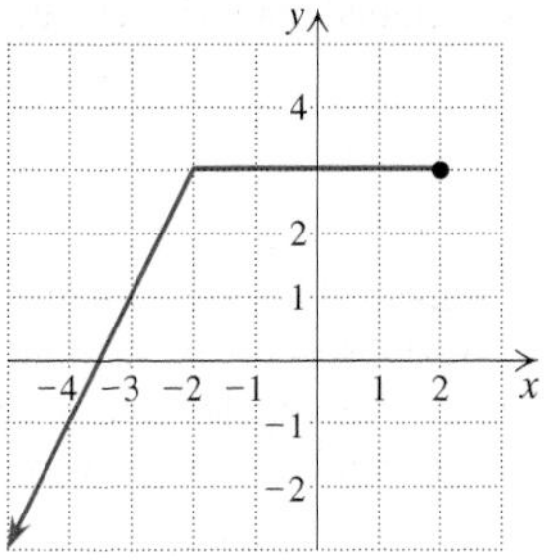

50. a.

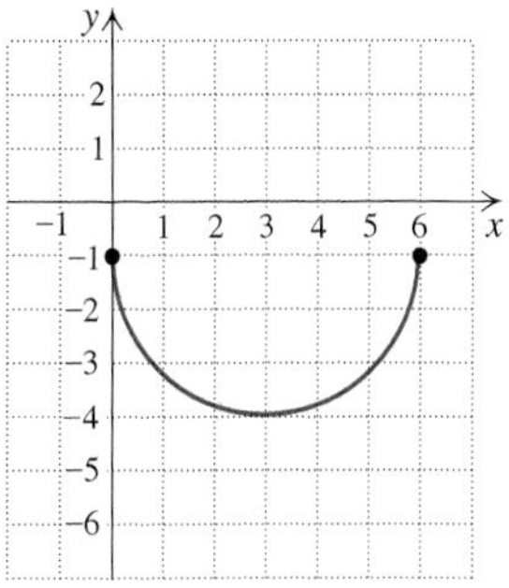

b.

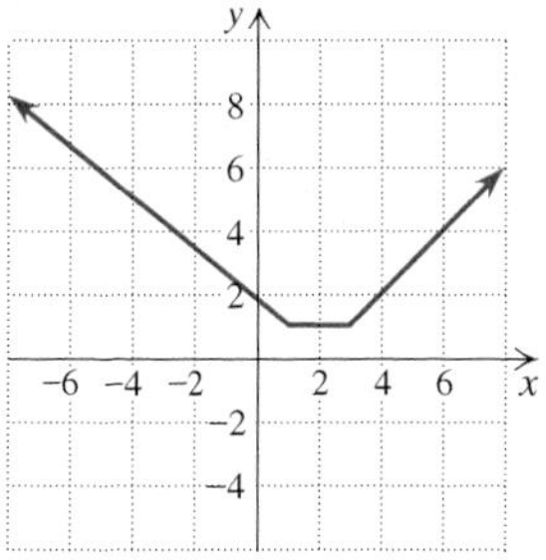

51. a.

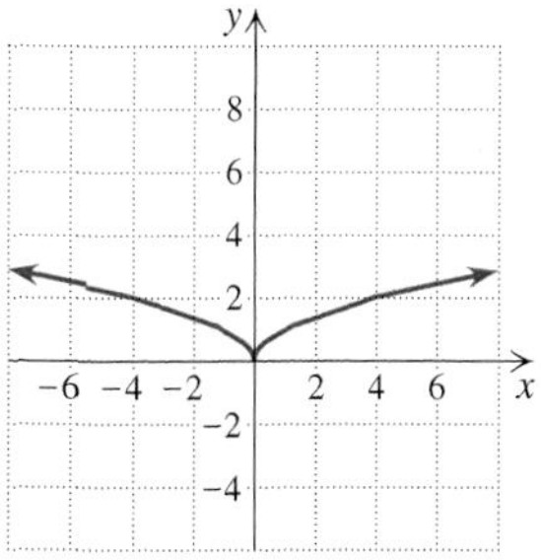

b.

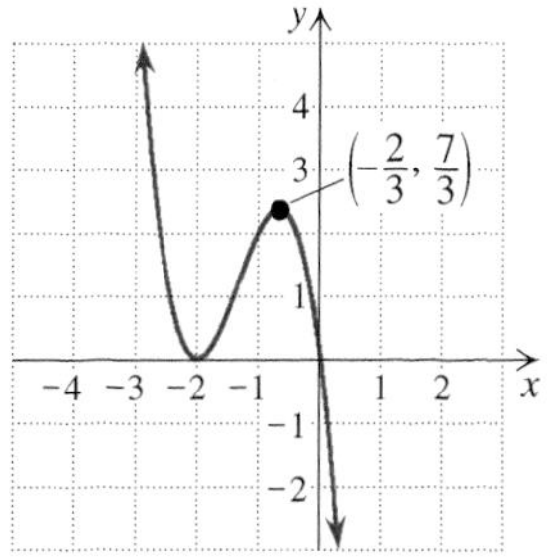

52. a.

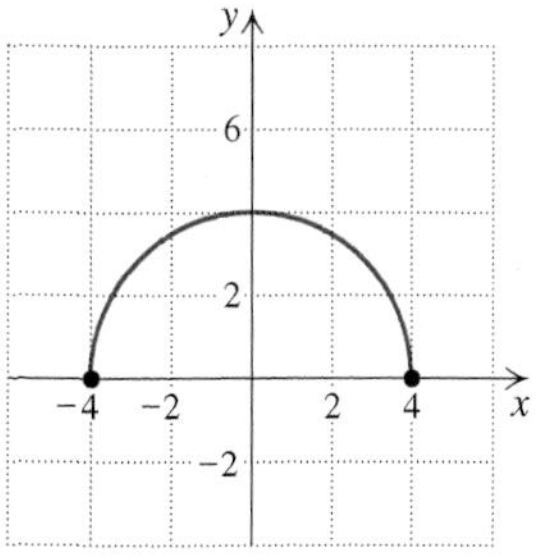

b.

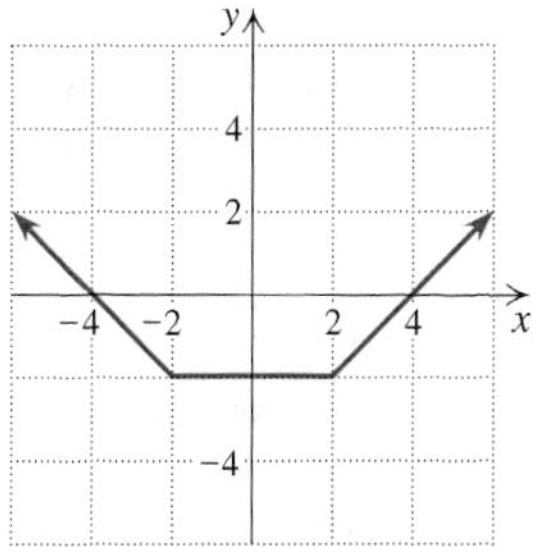

53. a.

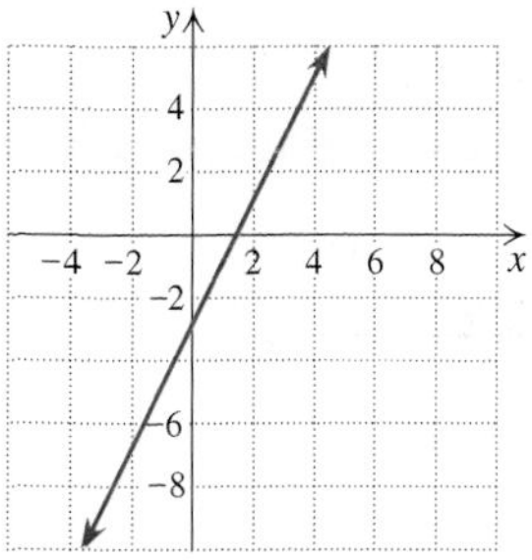

b.

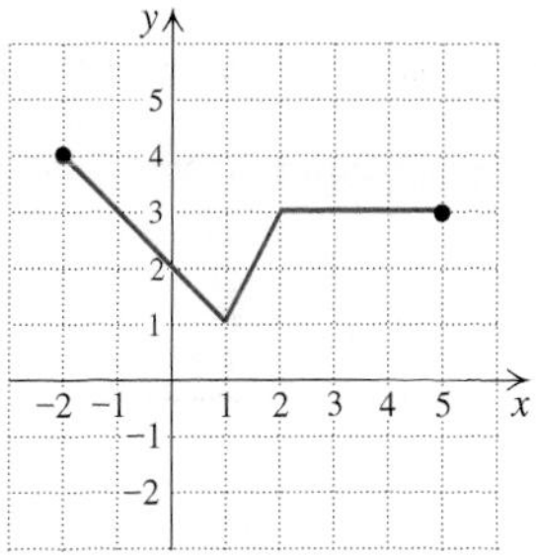

54. a.

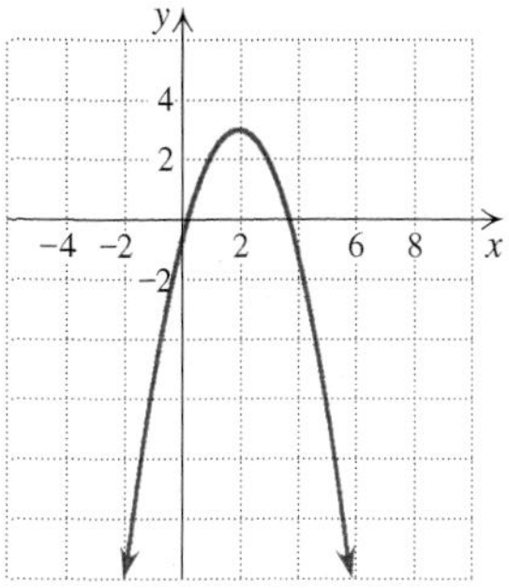

b.

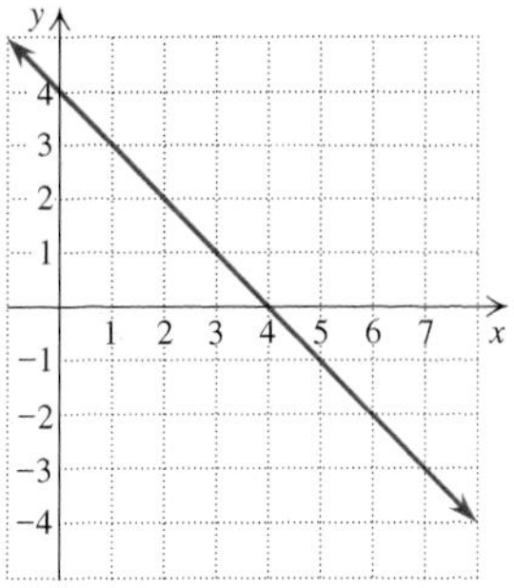

Make a table listing ordered pairs for each function. Then sketch the graph and state the domain and range. Identify any intervals on which f is increasing, decreasing, or constant.

55. $f(x) = 2x + 1$

56. $f(x) = -3x$

57. $f(x) = |x - 1|$

58. $f(x) = |x| + 1$

59. $f(x) = \dfrac{|x|}{x}$

60. $f(x) = \dfrac{2x}{|x|}$

61. $f(x) = \sqrt{9 - x^2}$

62. $f(x) = -\sqrt{1 - x^2}$

63. $f(x) = \begin{cases} x + 1 & \text{for } x \geq 3 \\ x + 2 & \text{for } x < 3 \end{cases}$

64. $f(x) = \begin{cases} \sqrt{-x} & \text{for } x < 0 \\ -\sqrt{x} & \text{for } x \geq 0 \end{cases}$

65. $f(x) = \begin{cases} x + 3 & \text{for } x \leq -2 \\ \sqrt{4 - x^2} & \text{for } -2 < x < 2 \\ -x + 3 & \text{for } x \geq 2 \end{cases}$

66. $f(x) = \begin{cases} 8 + 2x & \text{for } x \leq -2 \\ x^2 & \text{for } -2 < x < 2 \\ 8 - 2x & \text{for } x \geq 2 \end{cases}$

Write a piecewise function for each given graph.

67.

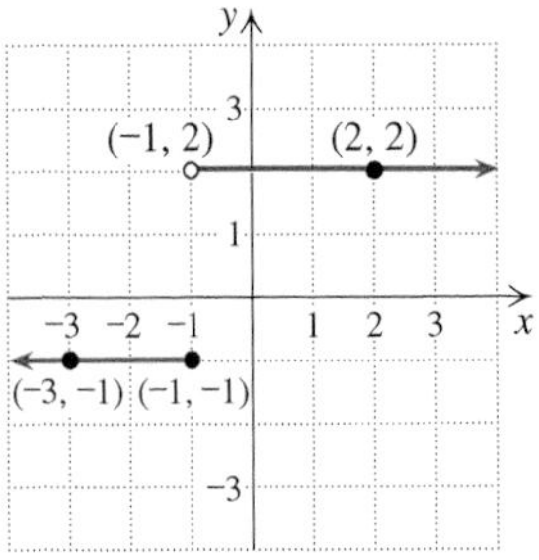

68.

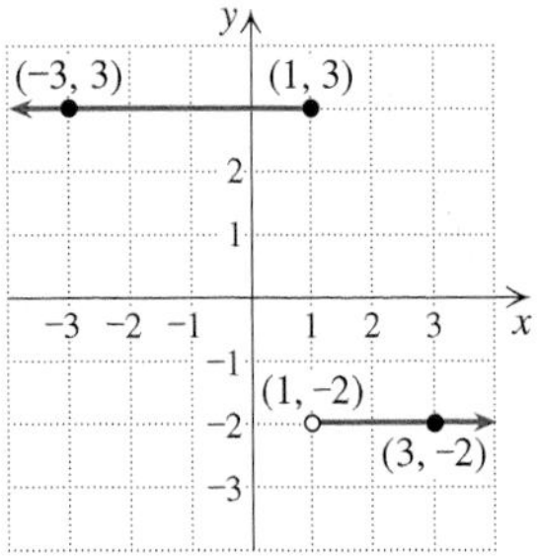

69.

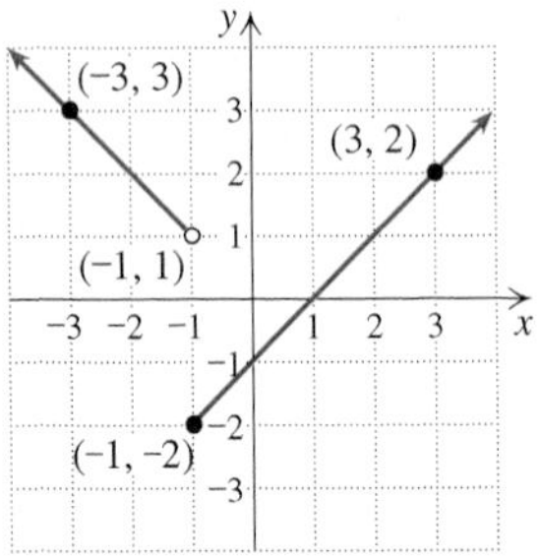

70.

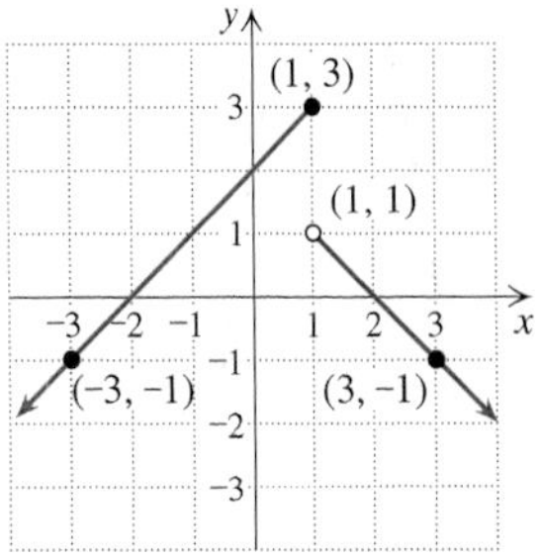

71.

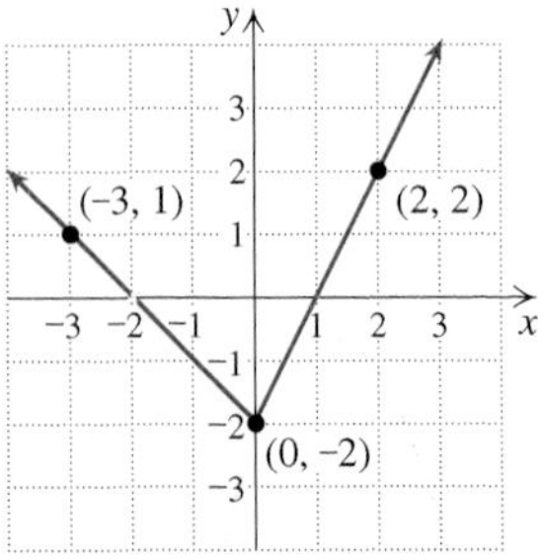

72.

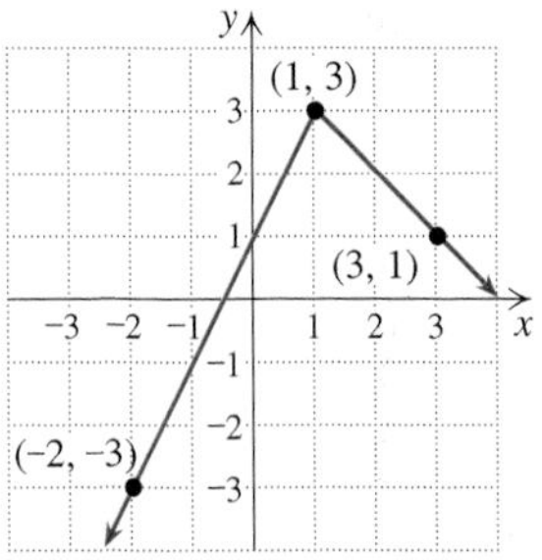

Use the minimum and maximum features of a graphing calculator to find the intervals on which each function is increasing or decreasing. Round approximate answers to two decimal places.

73. $y = 3x^2 - 5x - 4$

74. $y = -6x^2 + 2x - 9$

75. $y = x^3 - 3x$

76. $y = x^4 - 11x^2 + 18$

77. $y = 2x^4 - 12x^2 + 25$

78. $y = x^5 - 13x^3 + 36x$

79. $y = |20 - |x - 50||$

80. $y = x + |x + 30| - |x + 50|$

Solve each problem.

81. *Motor Vehicle Ownership* World motor vehicle ownership in developed countries can be modeled by the function

$$M(t) = \begin{cases} 17.5t + 250 & 0 \leq t \leq 20 \\ 10t + 400 & 20 < t \leq 40 \end{cases}$$

where t is the number of years since 1970 and $M(t)$ is the number of motor vehicles in millions in the year $1970 + t$ (World Resources Institute, www.wri.org). See the accompanying figure. How many vehicles were there in developed countries in 1988? How many will there be in 2010? What was the average rate of change of motor vehicle ownership from 1984 to 1994?

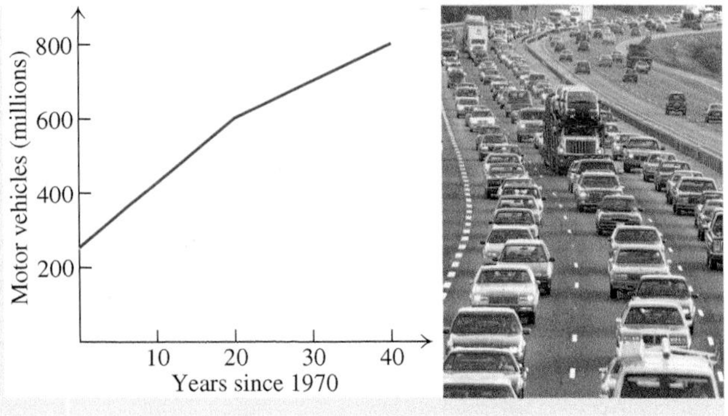

Figure for Exercise 81

82. *Motor Vehicle Ownership* World motor vehicle ownership in developing countries and Eastern Europe can be modeled by the function

$$M(t) = 6.25t + 50$$

where t is the number of years since 1970 and $M(t)$ is in millions of vehicles (World Resources Institute, www.wri.org). Graph this function. What is the expected average rate of change of motor vehicle ownership from 1990 through 2010? Is motor vehicle ownership expected to grow faster in developed or developing countries in the period 1990 through 2010? (See the previous exercise.)

83. *Filing a Tax Return* An accountant determines the charge for filing a tax return by using the function $C = 50 + 40[\![t]\!]$ for $t > 0$, where C is in dollars and t is in hours. Sketch the graph of this function. For what values of t is the charge over \$235?

84. *Shipping Machinery* The cost in dollars of shipping a machine is given by the function $C = 200 + 37[\![w/100]\!]$ for $w > 0$, where w is the weight of the machine in pounds. For which values of w is the cost less than \$862?

Thinking Outside the Box VI

Best Fitting Pipe A work crew is digging a pipeline through a frozen wilderness in Alaska. The cross section of the trench is in the shape of the parabola $y = x^2$. The pipe has a circular cross section. If the pipe is too large, then the pipe will not lay on the bottom of the trench.

a. What is the radius of the largest pipe that will lay on the bottom of the trench?

b. If the radius of the pipe is 3 and the trench is in the shape of $y = ax^2$, then what is the largest value of a for which the pipe will lay in the bottom of the trench?

1.6 Pop Quiz

1. Find the domain and range for $y = 1 - \sqrt{x}$.

2. Find the domain and range for $y = \sqrt{9 - x^2}$.

3. Find the range for

$$f(x) = \begin{cases} 2x & \text{for} \quad x \geq 1 \\ 3 - x & \text{for} \quad x < 1 \end{cases}.$$

4. On what interval is $y = x^2$ increasing?

5. On what interval is $y = |x - 3|$ decreasing?

1.7 Families of Functions, Transformations, and Symmetry

If a, h, and k are real numbers with $a \neq 0$, then the graph of $y = af(x - h) + k$ is a **transformation** of the graph of $y = f(x)$. All of the transformations of a function form a **family of functions.** For example, any function of the form $y = a\sqrt{x - h} + k$ is in the square-root family because it is a transformation of $y = \sqrt{x}$. If a transformation changes the shape of a graph then it is a **nonrigid** transformation. Otherwise, it is **rigid.** We will study two types of rigid transformations—*translating* and *reflecting,* and two types of nonrigid transformations—*stretching* and *shrinking*. We start with translating.

Translation

The idea of translation is to move a graph either vertically or horizontally without changing its shape.

Definition: Translation Upward or Downward

If $k > 0$, then the graph of $y = f(x) + k$ is a **translation of k units upward** of the graph of $y = f(x)$. If $k < 0$, then the graph of $y = f(x) + k$ is a **translation of $|k|$ units downward** of the graph of $y = f(x)$.

Example 1 Translations upward or downward

Graph the three given functions on the same coordinate plane.

a. $f(x) = \sqrt{x}$, $g(x) = \sqrt{x} + 3$, $h(x) = \sqrt{x} - 5$
b. $f(x) = x^2$, $g(x) = x^2 + 2$, $h(x) = x^2 - 3$

Solution

a. First sketch $f(x) = \sqrt{x}$ through (0, 0), (1, 1), and (4, 2) as shown in Fig. 1.87. Since $g(x) = \sqrt{x} + 3$ we can add 3 to the y-coordinate of each point to get (0, 3), (1, 4), and (4, 5). Sketch g through these points. Every point on f can be moved up 3 units to obtain a corresponding point on g. We now subtract 5 from the y-coordinates on f to obtain points on h. So h goes through $(0, -5)$, $(1, -4)$, and $(4, -3)$.

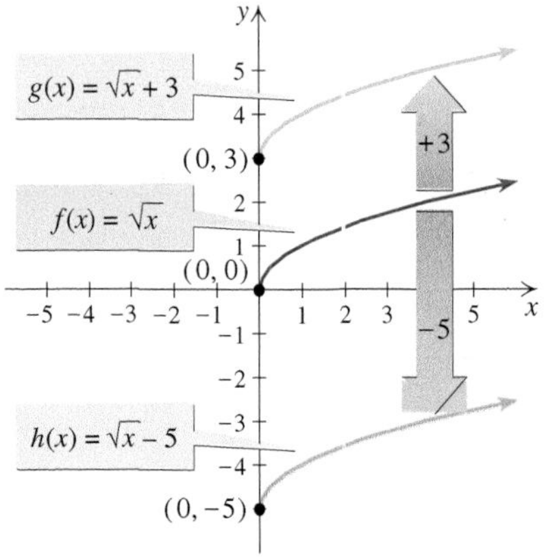

Figure 1.87

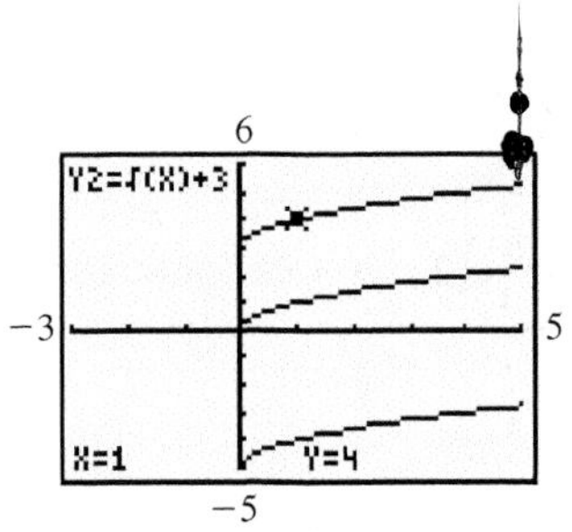

Figure 1.88

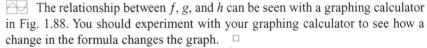

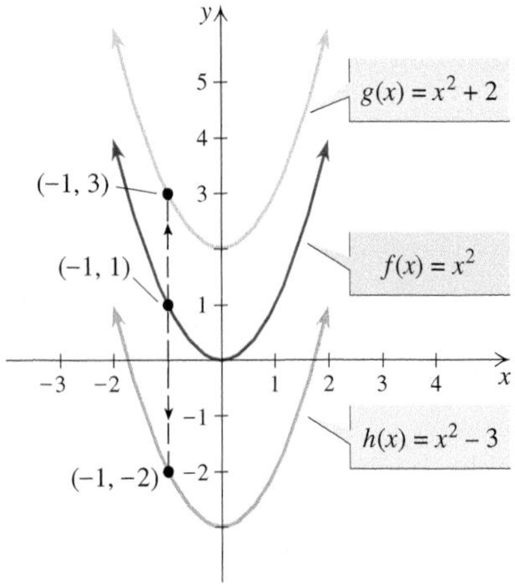

Figure 1.89

The relationship between f, g, and h can be seen with a graphing calculator in Fig. 1.88. You should experiment with your graphing calculator to see how a change in the formula changes the graph. □

b. First sketch the familiar graph of $f(x) = x^2$ through $(\pm 2, 4)$, $(\pm 1, 1)$, and (0, 0) as shown in Fig. 1.89. Since $g(x) = f(x) + 2$, the graph of g can be obtained by translating the graph of f upward two units. Since $h(x) = f(x) - 3$, the graph of h can be obtained by translating the graph of f downward three units. For example, the point $(-1, 1)$ on the graph of f moves up to $(-1, 3)$ on the graph of g and down to $(-1, -2)$ on the graph of h as shown in Fig. 1.89. ■

Any function of the form $y = a(x - h)^2 + k$ is in the **square family** because it is a transformation of $y = x^2$. The graph of any function in the square family is called a **parabola.**

The graph of $y = f(x) + k$ for $k > 0$ is an upward translation of $y = f(x)$ because the last operation performed is addition of k. To make a graph move horizontally, the first operation performed must be addition or subtraction.

Definition: Translation to the Right or Left

If $h > 0$, then the graph of $y = f(x - h)$ is a **translation of h units to the right** of the graph of $y = f(x)$. If $h < 0$, then the graph of $y = f(x - h)$ is a **translation of $|h|$ units to the left** of the graph of $y = f(x)$.

Example 2 Translations to the right or left

Graph $f(x) = \sqrt{x}$, $g(x) = \sqrt{x - 3}$, and $h(x) = \sqrt{x + 5}$ on the same coordinate plane.

Solution

First sketch $f(x) = \sqrt{x}$ through (0, 0), (1, 1), and (4, 2) as shown in Fig. 1.90. Since the first operation of g is to subtract 3, we get the corresponding points by adding 3 to each x-coordinate. So g goes through (3, 0), (4, 1), and (7, 2). Since the first operation of h is to add 5, we get corresponding points by subtracting 5 from the x-coordinates. So h goes through (−5, 0), (−4, 1), and (−1, 2).

The calculator graphs of f, g, and h are shown in Fig. 1.91. Be sure to note the difference between $y = \sqrt{\ }(x) - 3$ and $y = \sqrt{\ }(x - 3)$ on a calculator.

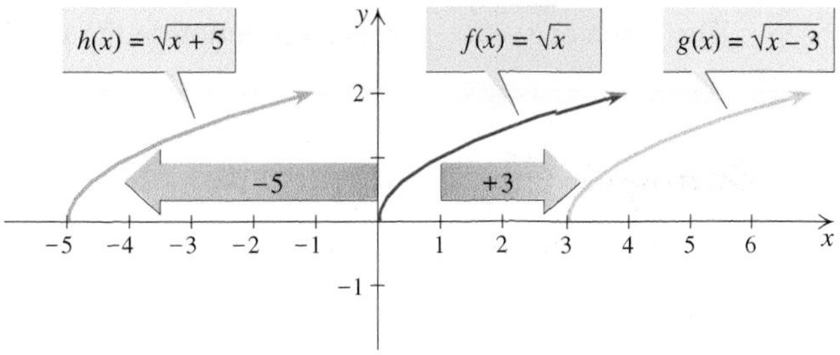

Figure 1.90

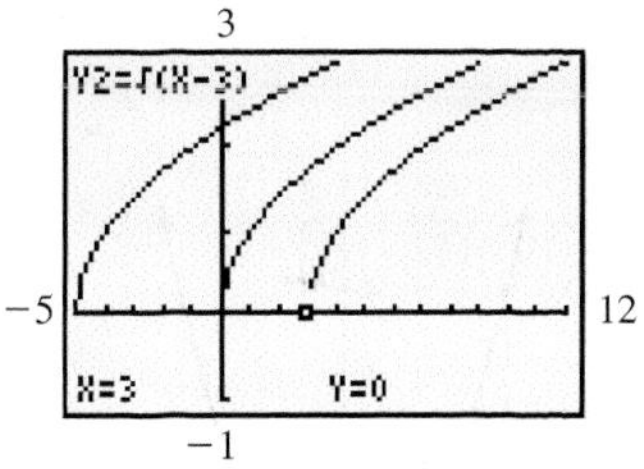

Figure 1.91

Notice that $y = \sqrt{x - 3}$ lies 3 units to the *right* and $y = \sqrt{x + 5}$ lies 5 units to the *left* of $y = \sqrt{x}$. The next example shows two more horizontal translations.

Example 3 Horizontal translations

Sketch the graph of each function.

a. $f(x) = |x - 1|$ **b.** $f(x) = (x + 3)^2$

Solution

a. The function $f(x) = |x - 1|$ is in the absolute value family and its graph is a translation one unit to the right of $g(x) = |x|$. Calculate a few ordered pairs to get an accurate graph. The points (0, 1), (1, 0), and (2, 1) are on the graph of $f(x) = |x - 1|$ shown in Fig. 1.92 on the next page.

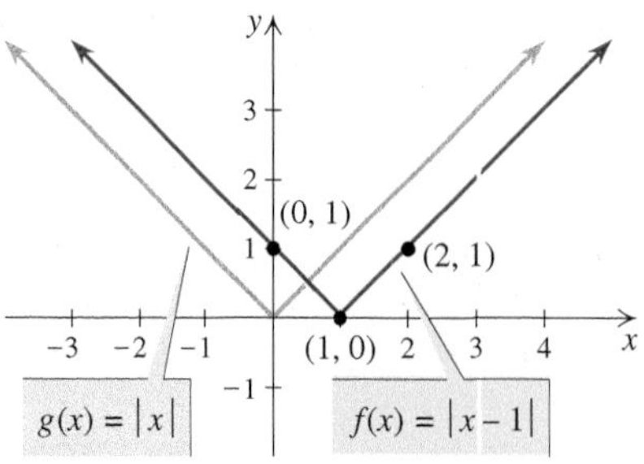

Figure 1.92

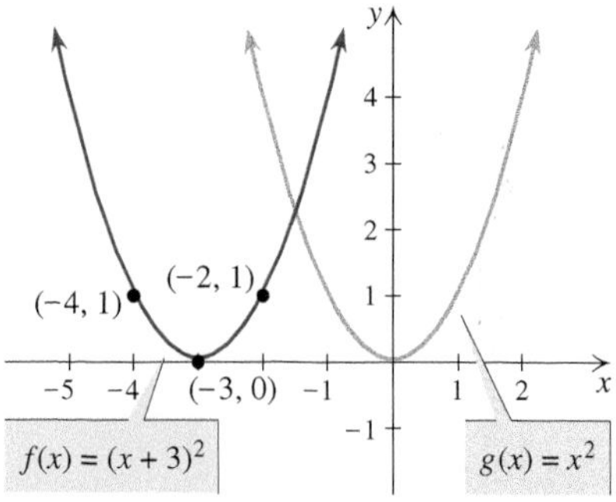

Figure 1.93

b. The function $f(x) = (x + 3)^2$ is in the square family and its graph is a translation three units to the left of the graph of $g(x) = x^2$. Calculate a few ordered pairs to get an accurate graph. The points $(-3, 0)$, $(-2, 1)$, and $(-4, 1)$ are on the graph shown in Fig. 1.93. ■

Reflection

The idea in *reflection* is to get a graph that is a mirror image of another graph, where the mirror is placed on the x-axis. To find the mirror image of a point, we simply change the sign of its y-coordinate.

Definition: Reflection

The graph of $y = -f(x)$ is a **reflection** in the x-axis of the graph of $y = f(x)$.

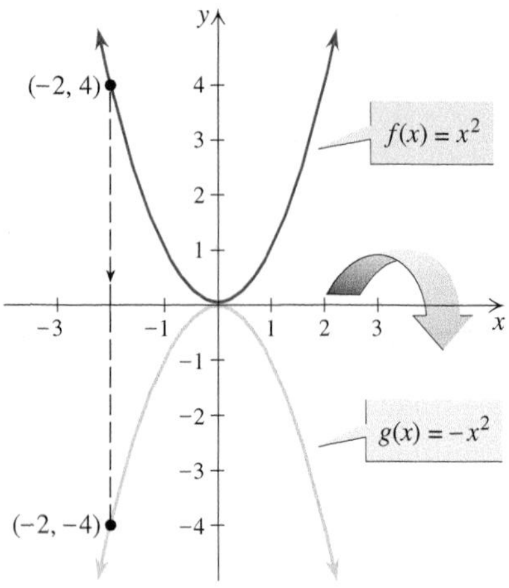

Figure 1.94

Example 4 Graphing using reflection

Graph each pair of functions on the same coordinate plane.

a. $f(x) = x^2$, $g(x) = -x^2$
b. $f(x) = x^3$, $g(x) = -x^3$
c. $f(x) = |x|$, $g(x) = -|x|$

Solution

a. The graph of $f(x) = x^2$ goes through $(0, 0)$, $(\pm 1, 1)$, and $(\pm 2, 4)$. The graph of $g(x) = -x^2$ goes through $(0, 0)$, $(\pm 1, -1)$, and $(\pm 2, -4)$ as shown in Fig. 1.94.
b. Make a table of ordered pairs for f as follows:

x	-2	-1	0	1	2
$f(x) = x^3$	-8	-1	0	1	8

Sketch the graph of f through these ordered pairs as shown in Fig. 1.95. Since $g(x) = -f(x)$, the graph of g can be obtained by reflecting the graph of f in the x-axis. Each point on the graph of f corresponds to a point on the graph of g with the opposite y-coordinate. For example, $(2, 8)$ on the graph of f corresponds to $(2, -8)$ on the graph of g. Both graphs are shown in Fig. 1.95.

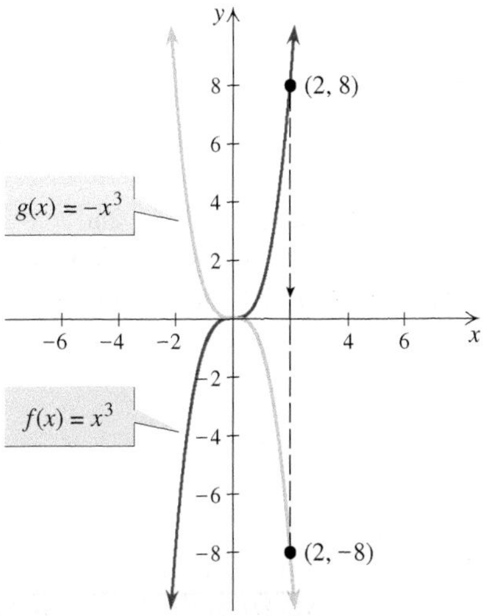

Figure 1.95

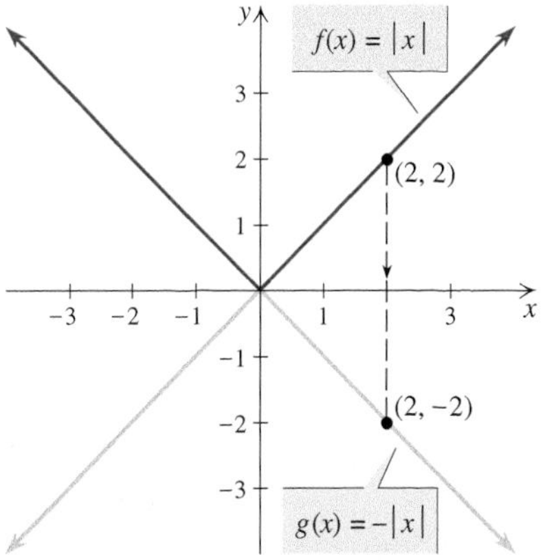

Figure 1.96

c. The graph of f is the familiar V-shaped graph of the absolute value function as shown in Fig. 1.96. Since $g(x) = -f(x)$, the graph of g can be obtained by reflecting the graph of f in the x-axis. Each point on the graph of f corresponds to a point on the graph of g with the opposite y-coordinate. For example, (2, 2) on f corresponds to $(2, -2)$ on g. Both graphs are shown in Fig. 1.96. ■

Note that if $y = x^2$ is reflected in the x-axis and then translated one unit upward, the equation for the graph in the final position is $y = -x^2 + 1$. If $y = x^2$ is translated one unit upward and then reflected in the x-axis, the equation for the graph in the final position is $y = -(x^2 + 1)$ or $y = -x^2 - 1$. The order in which the transformations are done can make the final functions different.

Stretching and Shrinking

To *stretch* a graph we multiply the y-coordinates by a number larger than 1. To *shrink* a graph we multiply the y-coordinates by a number between 0 and 1.

Definitions: Stretching and Shrinking

The graph of $y = af(x)$ is obtained from the graph of $y = f(x)$ by

1. **stretching** the graph of $y = f(x)$ by a when $a > 1$, or
2. **shrinking** the graph of $y = f(x)$ by a when $0 < a < 1$.

Example 5 Graphing using stretching and shrinking

In each case graph the three functions on the same coordinate plane.

a. $f(x) = \sqrt{x},\ g(x) = 2\sqrt{x},\ h(x) = \dfrac{1}{2}\sqrt{x}$

b. $f(x) = x^2,\ g(x) = 2x^2,\ h(x) = \dfrac{1}{2}x^2$

Solution

a. The graph of $f(x) = \sqrt{x}$ goes through (0, 0), (1, 1), and (4, 2) as shown in Fig. 1.97. The graph of g is obtained by stretching the graph of f by a factor of 2. So g goes through (0, 0), (1, 2), and (4, 4). The graph of h is obtained by shrinking the graph of f by a factor of $\frac{1}{2}$. So h goes through (0, 0), $\left(1, \frac{1}{2}\right)$, and (4, 1).

The functions f, g, and h are shown on a graphing calculator in Fig. 1.98. Note how the viewing window affects the shape of the graph. They do not appear as separated on the calculator as they do in Fig. 1.97. □

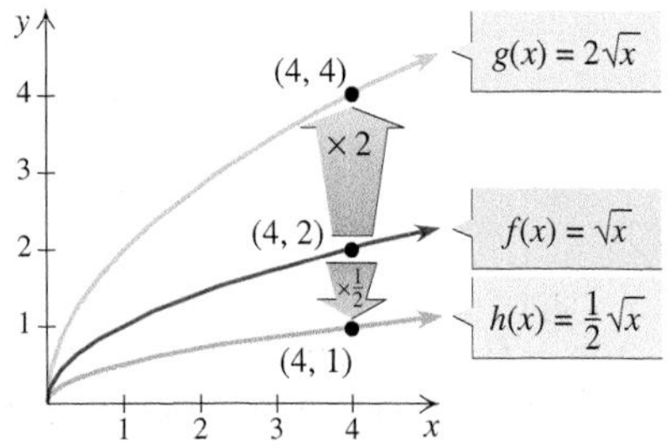

Figure 1.97

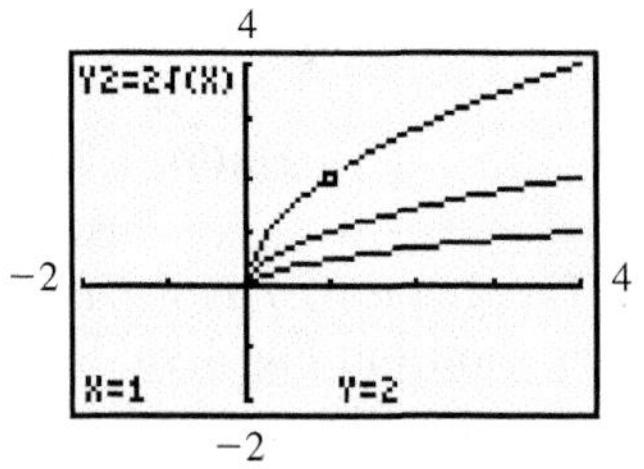

Figure 1.98

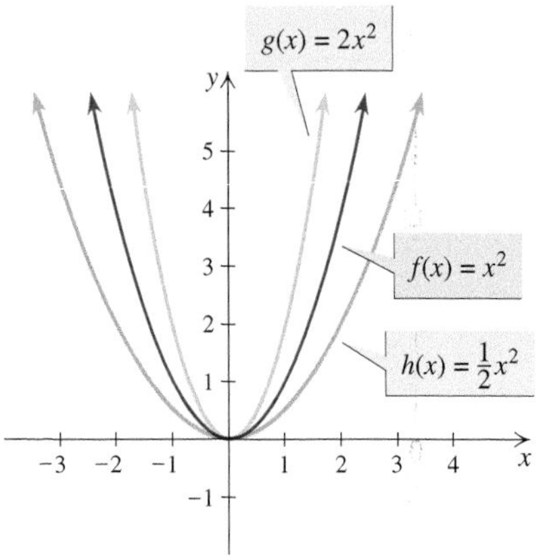

Figure 1.99

b. The graph of $f(x) = x^2$ is the familiar parabola shown in Fig. 1.99. We stretch it by a factor of 2 to get the graph of g and shrink it by a factor of $\frac{1}{2}$ to get the graph of h. ■

A function involving more than one transformation may be graphed using the following procedure.

PROCEDURE **Multiple Transformations**

Graph a function involving more than one transformation in the following order:

1. Horizontal translation
2. Stretching or shrinking
3. Reflecting
4. Vertical translation

The function in the next example involves all four of the above transformations.

Example 6 Graphing using several transformations

Graph the function $y = 4 - 2\sqrt{x + 1}$.

Solution

First recognize that this function is in the square root family. So its graph is a transformation of the graph of $y = \sqrt{x}$. The graph of $y = \sqrt{x + 1}$ is a *horizontal* translation one unit to the left of the graph of $y = \sqrt{x}$. The graph of $y = 2\sqrt{x + 1}$ is obtained from $y = \sqrt{x + 1}$ by *stretching* it by a factor of 2.

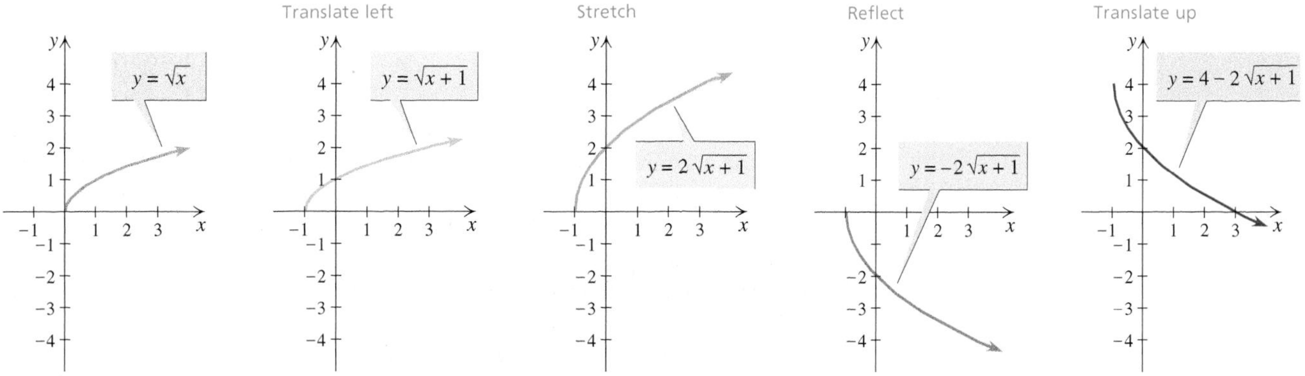

Figure 1.100

Reflect $y = 2\sqrt{x+1}$ in the x-axis to obtain the graph of $y = -2\sqrt{x+1}$. Finally, the graph of $y = 4 - 2\sqrt{x+1}$ is a *vertical* translation of $y = -2\sqrt{x+1}$, four units upward. All of these graphs are shown in Fig. 1.100. ■

The Linear Family of Functions

The function $f(x) = x$ is called the **identity function** because the coordinates in each ordered pair are identical. Its graph is a line through (0, 0) with slope 1. A member of the **linear family,** a **linear function,** is a transformation of the identity function: $f(x) = a(x - h) + k$ where $a \neq 0$. Since a, h, and k are real numbers, we can rewrite this form as a multiple of x plus a constant. So a linear function has the form $f(x) = mx + b$, with $m \neq 0$ (the slope-intercept form). If $m = 0$, then the function has the form $f(x) = b$ and it is a **constant function.**

Example 7 Graphing linear functions using transformations

Sketch the graphs of $y = x$, $y = 2x$, $y = -2x$, and $y = -2x - 3$.

Solution

The graph of $y = x$ is a line through (0, 0), (1, 1), and (2, 2). Stretch the graph of $y = x$ by a factor of 2 to get the graph of $y = 2x$. Reflect in the x-axis to get the graph of $y = -2x$. Translate downward three units to get the graph of $y = -2x - 3$. See Fig. 1.101.

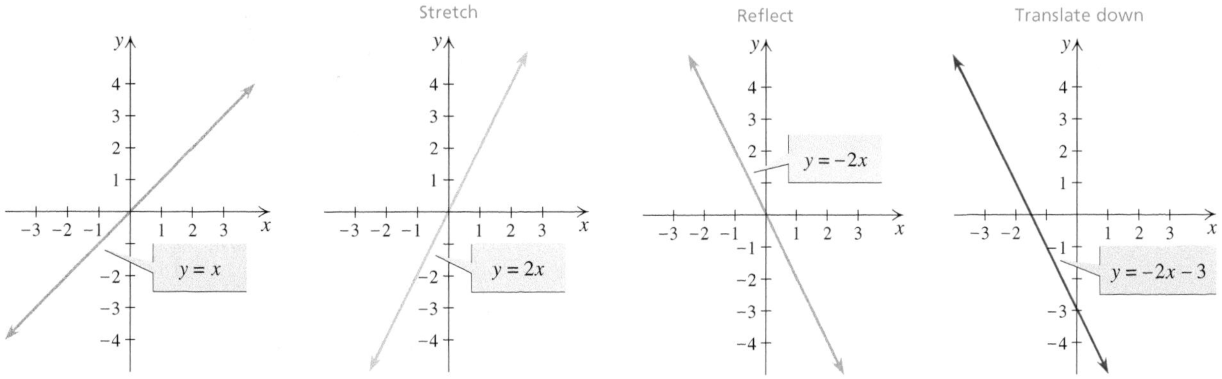

Figure 1.101 ■

Symmetry

The graph of $g(x) = -x^2$ is a reflection in the x-axis of the graph of $f(x) = x^2$. If the paper were folded along the x-axis, the graphs would coincide. See Fig. 1.102. The symmetry that we call reflection occurs between two functions, but the graph of $f(x) = x^2$ has a symmetry within itself. Points such as (2, 4) and $(-2, 4)$ are on the graph and are equidistant from the y-axis. Folding the paper along the y-axis brings all such pairs of points together. See Fig. 1.103. The reason for this symmetry about the y-axis is the fact that $f(-x) = f(x)$ for every value of x. We get the same y-coordinate whether we evaluate the function at a number or at its opposite.

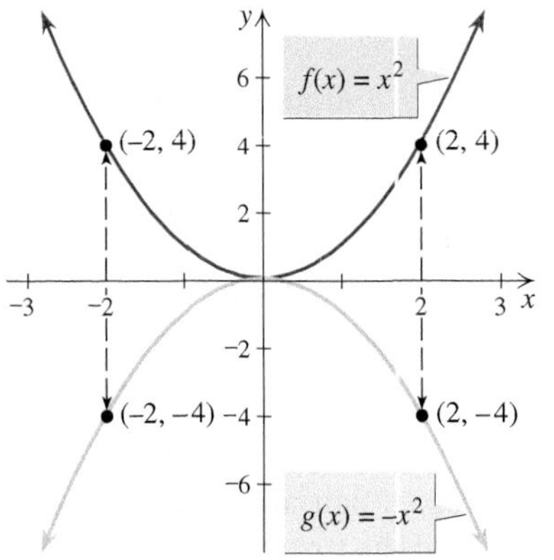

Figure 1.102

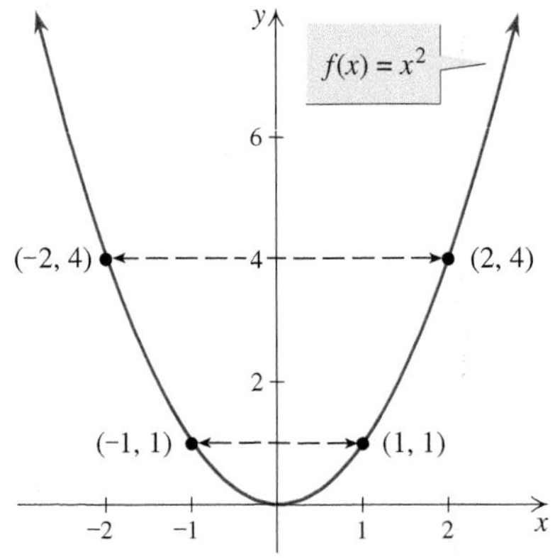

Figure 1.103

Definition: Symmetric about the y-Axis

If $f(-x) = f(x)$ for every value of x in the domain of the function f, then f is called an **even function** and its graph is **symmetric about the y-axis.**

Consider the graph of $f(x) = x^3$ shown in Fig. 1.104. On the graph of $f(x) = x^3$ we find pairs of points such as (2, 8) and $(-2, -8)$. The odd exponent in x^3 causes the second coordinate to be negative when the sign of the first coordinate is changed. These points are equidistant from the origin and on opposite sides of the origin. So the symmetry of this graph is about the origin. In this case $f(x)$ and $f(-x)$ are not equal, but $f(-x) = -f(x)$.

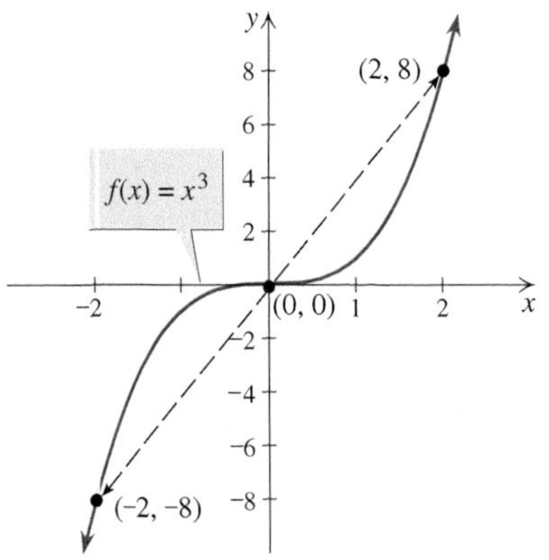

Figure 1.104

Definition: Symmetric about the Origin

If $f(-x) = -f(x)$ for every value of x in the domain of the function f, then f is called an **odd function** and its graph is **symmetric about the origin.**

A graph might look like it is symmetric about the y-axis or the origin, but the only way to be sure is to use the definitions of these terms as shown in the following example. Note that an odd power of a negative number is negative and an even power of a negative number is positive. So for any real number x we have $(-x)^n = -x^n$ if n is odd and $(-x)^n = x^n$ if n is even.

Example 8 Determining symmetry in a graph

Discuss the symmetry of the graph of each function.

a. $f(x) = 5x^3 - x$ **b.** $f(x) = |x| + 3$ **c.** $f(x) = x^2 - 3x + 6$

Solution

a. Replace x by $-x$ in the formula for $f(x)$ and simplify:

$$f(-x) = 5(-x)^3 - (-x) = -5x^3 + x$$

Is $f(-x)$ equal to $f(x)$ or the opposite of $f(x)$? Since $-f(x) = -5x^3 + x$, we have $f(-x) = -f(x)$. So f is an odd function and the graph is symmetric about the origin.

b. Since $|-x| = |x|$ for any x, we have $f(-x) = |-x| + 3 = |x| + 3$. Because $f(-x) = f(x)$, the function is even and the graph is symmetric about the y-axis.

c. In this case, $f(-x) = (-x)^2 - 3(-x) + 6 = x^2 + 3x + 6$. So $f(-x) \neq f(x)$, and $f(-x) \neq -f(x)$. This function is neither odd nor even and its graph has neither type of symmetry. ■

Do you see why functions symmetric about the y-axis are called *even* and functions symmetric about the origin are called *odd?* In general, a function defined by a polynomial with even exponents only, such as $f(x) = x^2$ or $f(x) = x^6 - 5x^4 + 2x^2 + 3$, is symmetric about the y-axis. (The constant term 3 has even degree because $3 = 3x^0$.) A function with only odd exponents such as $f(x) = x^3$ or $f(x) = x^5 - 6x^3 + 4x$ is symmetric about the origin. A function containing both even and odd powered terms such as $f(x) = x^2 + 3x$ has neither symmetry. For other types of functions (such as absolute value) you must examine the function more carefully to determine symmetry.

Note that functions cannot have x-axis symmetry. A graph that is symmetric about the x-axis fails the vertical line test. For example, the graph of $x = y^2$ is symmetric about the x-axis, but the graph fails the vertical line test and y is not a function of x.

Reading Graphs to Solve Inequalities

The solution to an inequality in one variable can be read from a graph of an equation in two variables. Now that we have some experience with graphing, we will solve some inequalities by reading graphs.

Example 9 Using a graph to solve an inequality

Solve the inequality $(x - 1)^2 - 2 < 0$ by graphing.

Solution

The graph of $y = (x - 1)^2 - 2$ is obtained by translating the graph of $y = x^2$ one unit to the right and two units downward. See Fig. 1.105. To find the x-intercepts we solve $(x - 1)^2 - 2 = 0$:

$$(x - 1)^2 = 2$$
$$x - 1 = \pm\sqrt{2}$$
$$x = 1 \pm \sqrt{2}$$

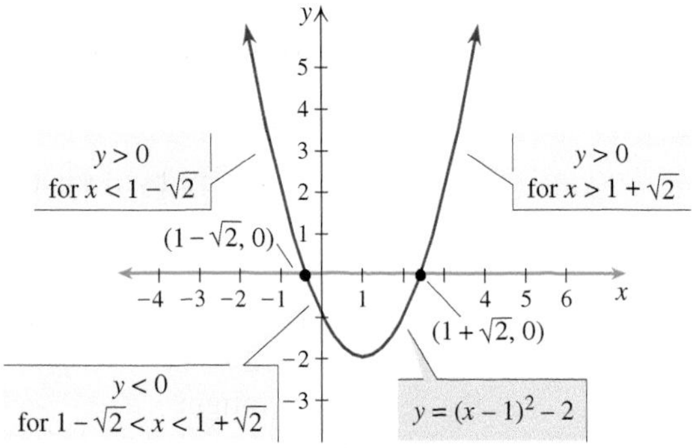

Figure 1.105

The x-intercepts are $(1 - \sqrt{2}, 0)$ and $(1 + \sqrt{2}, 0)$. If the y-coordinate of a point on the graph is negative, then the x-coordinate satisfies $(x - 1)^2 - 2 < 0$. So the solution set to $(x - 1)^2 - 2 < 0$ is the open interval $(1 - \sqrt{2}, 1 + \sqrt{2})$.

Although a graphing calculator will not find the exact solution to this inequality, you can use TRACE to support the answer and see that y is negative between the x-intercepts. See Fig. 1.106.

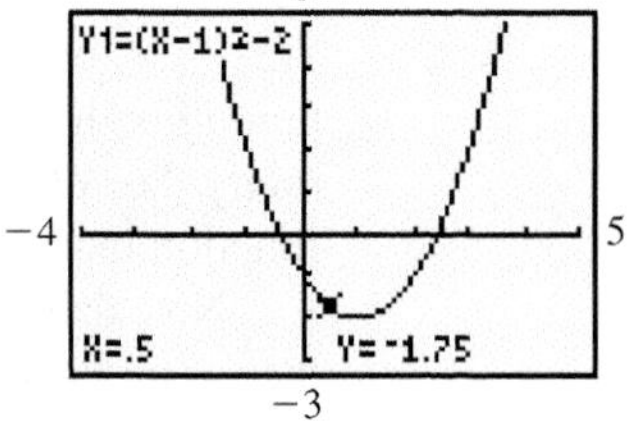

Figure 1.106

■

Note that the solution set to $(x - 1)^2 - 2 \geq 0$ can also be obtained from the graph in Fig. 1.105. If the y-coordinate of a point on the graph is positive or zero, then the x-coordinate satisfies $(x - 1)^2 - 2 \geq 0$. So the solution set to $(x - 1)^2 - 2 \geq 0$ is $(-\infty, 1 - \sqrt{2}] \cup [1 + \sqrt{2}, \infty)$.

Function Gallery: Some Basic Functions and Their Properties

Constant Function

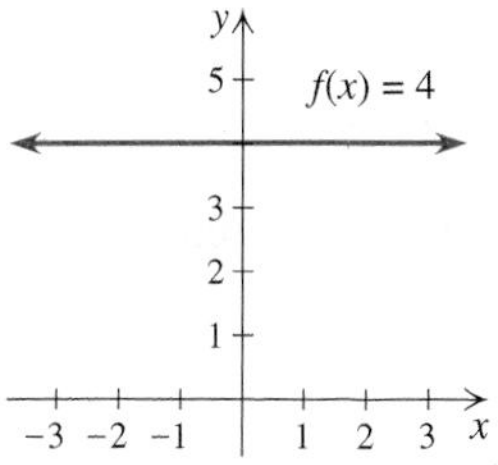

Domain $(-\infty, \infty)$
Range $\{4\}$
Constant on $(-\infty, \infty)$
Symmetric about y-axis

Identity Function

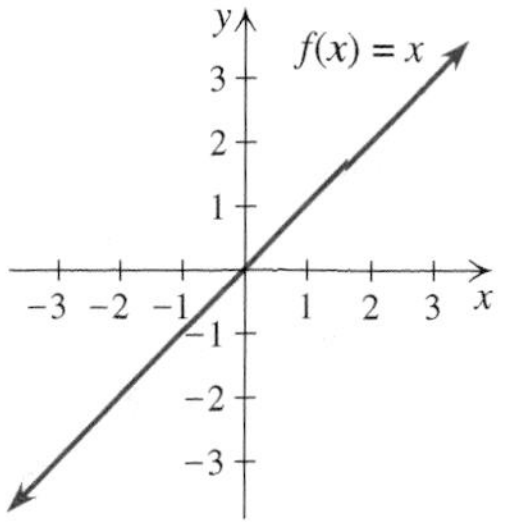

Domain $(-\infty, \infty)$
Range $(-\infty, \infty)$
Increasing on $(-\infty, \infty)$
Symmetric about origin

Linear Function

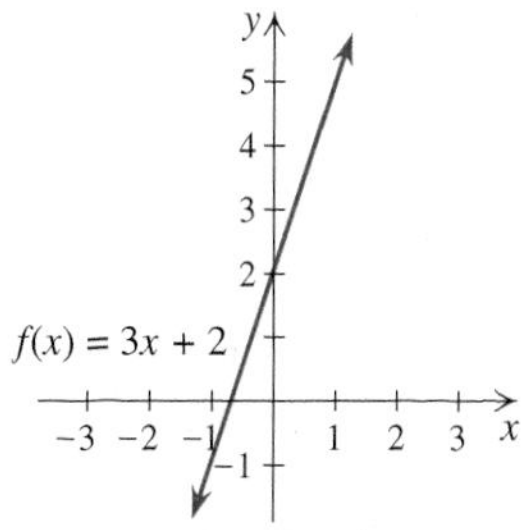

Domain $(-\infty, \infty)$
Range $(-\infty, \infty)$
Increasing on $(-\infty, \infty)$

Absolute-Value Function

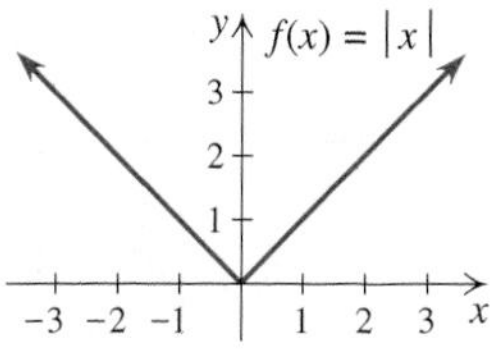

Domain $(-\infty, \infty)$
Range $(0, \infty)$
Increasing on $(0, \infty)$
Decreasing on $(-\infty, 0)$
Symmetric about y-axis

Square Function

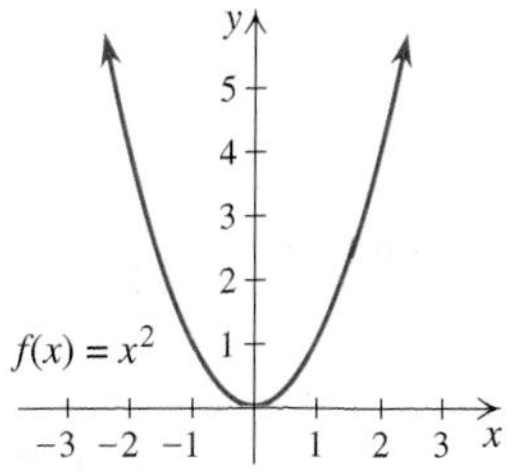

Domain $(-\infty, \infty)$
Range $[0, \infty)$
Increasing on $(0, \infty)$
Decreasing on $(-\infty, 0)$
Symmetric about y-axis

Square-Root Function

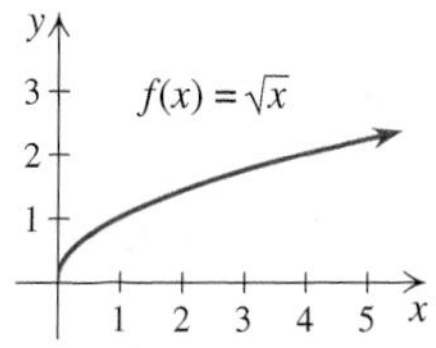

Domain $[0, \infty)$
Range $[0, \infty)$
Increasing on $(0, \infty)$

Cube Function

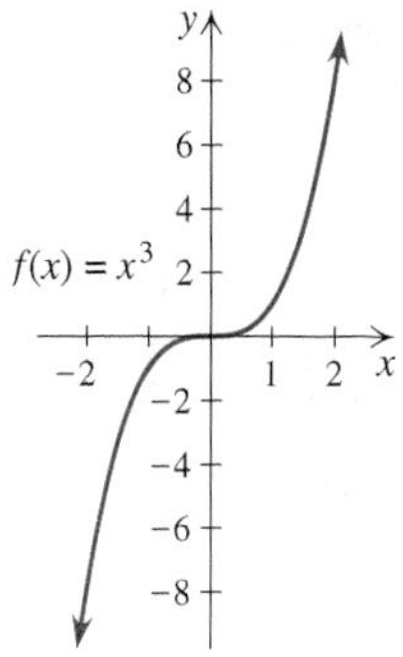

Domain $(-\infty, \infty)$
Range $(-\infty, \infty)$
Increasing on $(-\infty, \infty)$
Symmetric about origin

Cube-Root Function

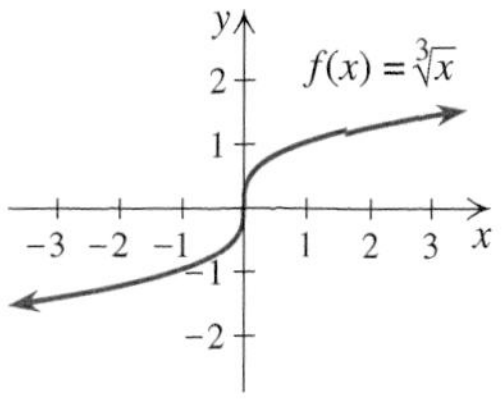

Domain $(-\infty, \infty)$
Range $(-\infty, \infty)$
Increasing on $(-\infty, \infty)$
Symmetric about origin

Greatest Integer Function

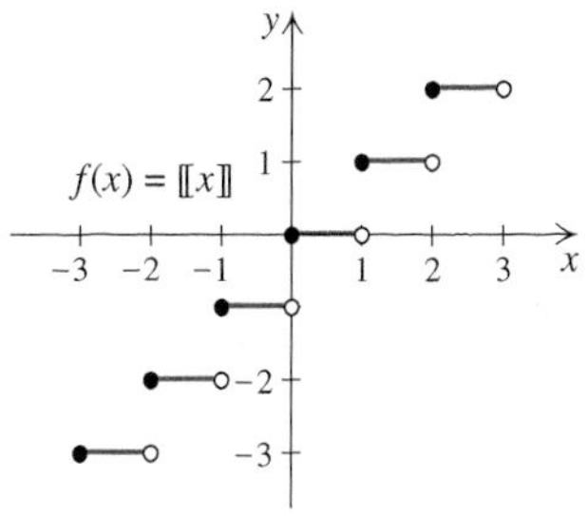

Domain $(-\infty, \infty)$
Range $\{n | n \text{ is an integer}\}$
Constant on $[n, n + 1)$
for every integer n

For Thought

True or False? Explain.

1. The graph of $f(x) = (-x)^4$ is a reflection in the x-axis of the graph of $g(x) = x^4$.
2. The graph of $f(x) = x - 4$ lies four units to the right of the graph of $f(x) = x$.
3. The graph of $y = |x + 2| + 3$ is a translation two units to the right and three units upward of the graph of $y = |x|$.
4. The graph of $f(x) = -3$ is a reflection in the x-axis of the graph of $g(x) = 3$.
5. The functions $y = x^2 + 4x + 1$ and $y = (x + 2)^2 - 3$ have the same graph.
6. The graph of $y = -(x - 3)^2 - 4$ can be obtained by moving $y = x^2$ three units to the right and down four units, and then reflecting in the x-axis.
7. If $f(x) = -x^3 + 2x^2 - 3x + 5$, then $f(-x) = x^3 + 2x^2 + 3x + 5$.
8. The graphs of $f(x) = -\sqrt{x}$ and $g(x) = \sqrt{-x}$ are identical.
9. If $f(x) = x^3 - x$, then $f(-x) = -f(x)$.
10. The solution set to $|x| - 1 \leq 0$ is $[-1, 1]$.

1.7 Exercises

Sketch the graphs of each pair of functions on the same coordinate plane.

1. $f(x) = |x|, g(x) = |x| - 4$
2. $f(x) = \sqrt{x}, g(x) = \sqrt{x} + 3$
3. $f(x) = x, g(x) = x + 3$
4. $f(x) = x^2, g(x) = x^2 - 5$
5. $y = x^2, y = (x - 3)^2$
6. $y = |x|, y = |x + 2|$
7. $y = \sqrt{x}, y = \sqrt{x + 9}$
8. $y = x^2, y = (x - 1)^2$
9. $f(x) = \sqrt{x}, g(x) = -\sqrt{x}$
10. $f(x) = x, g(x) = -x$
11. $y = \sqrt{x}, y = 3\sqrt{x}$
12. $y = \sqrt{1 - x^2}, y = 4\sqrt{1 - x^2}$
13. $y = x^2, y = \frac{1}{4}x^2$
14. $y = |x|, y = \frac{1}{3}|x|$
15. $y = \sqrt{4 - x^2}, y = -\sqrt{4 - x^2}$
16. $f(x) = x^2 + 1, g(x) = -(x^2 + 1)$

Match each function in Exercises 17–24 with its graph (a)–(h). See the procedure for multiple transformations on page 74.

17. $y = x^2$
18. $y = (x - 4)^2 + 2$
19. $y = (x + 4)^2 - 2$
20. $y = -2(x - 2)^2$
21. $y = -2(x + 2)^2$
22. $y = -\frac{1}{2}x^2 - 4$
23. $y = \frac{1}{2}(x + 4)^2 + 2$
24. $y = -2(x - 4)^2 - 2$

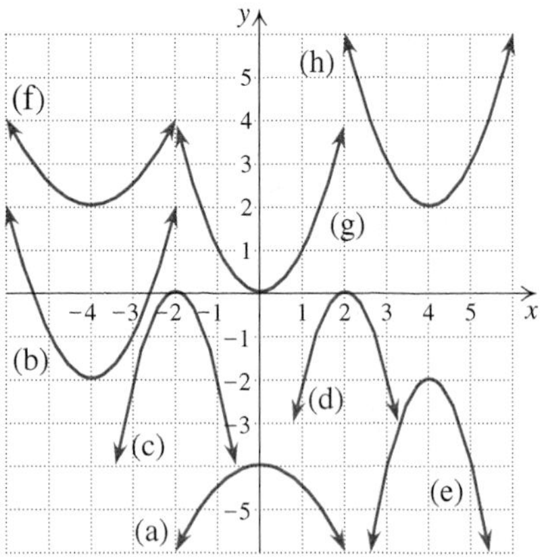

Figure for Exercises 17 to 24

Write the equation of each graph after the indicated transformation(s).

25. The graph of $y = \sqrt{x}$ is translated two units upward.
26. The graph of $y = \sqrt{x}$ is translated three units downward.
27. The graph of $y = x^2$ is translated five units to the right.

28. The graph of $y = x^2$ is translated seven units to the left.

29. The graph of $y = x^2$ is translated ten units to the right and four units upward.

30. The graph of $y = \sqrt{x}$ is translated five units to the left and twelve units downward.

31. The graph of $y = \sqrt{x}$ is stretched by a factor of 3, translated five units upward, then reflected in the x-axis.

32. The graph of $y = x^2$ is translated thirteen units to the right and six units downward, then reflected in the x-axis.

33. The graph of $y = |x|$ is reflected in the x-axis, stretched by a factor of 3, then translated seven units to the right and nine units upward.

34. The graph of $y = x$ is stretched by a factor of 2, reflected in the x-axis, then translated eight units downward and six units to the left.

Use transformations to graph each function and state the domain and range.

35. $y = (x - 1)^2 + 2$

36. $y = (x + 5)^2 - 4$

37. $y = |x - 1| + 3$

38. $y = |x + 3| - 4$

39. $y = 3x - 40$

40. $y = -4x + 200$

41. $y = \frac{1}{2}x - 20$

42. $y = -\frac{1}{2}x + 40$

43. $y = -\frac{1}{2}|x| + 40$

44. $y = 3|x| - 200$

45. $y = -\frac{1}{2}|x + 4|$

46. $y = 3|x - 2|$

47. $y = -\sqrt{x - 3} + 1$

48. $y = -\sqrt{x + 2} - 4$

49. $y = -2\sqrt{x + 3} + 2$

50. $y = -\frac{1}{2}\sqrt{x + 2} + 4$

Determine algebraically whether the function is even, odd, or neither. Discuss the symmetry of each function.

51. $f(x) = x^4$

52. $f(x) = x^4 - 2x^2$

53. $f(x) = x^4 - x^3$

54. $f(x) = x^3 - x$

55. $f(x) = (x + 3)^2$

56. $f(x) = (x - 1)^2$

57. $f(x) = |x - 2|$

58. $f(x) = |x| - 9$

59. $f(x) = x$

60. $f(x) = -x$

61. $f(x) = 3x + 2$

62. $f(x) = x - 3$

63. $f(x) = x^3 - 5x + 1$

64. $f(x) = x^6 - x^4 + x^2$

65. $f(x) = 1 + \frac{1}{x^2}$

66. $f(x) = (x^2 - 2)^3$

Match each function with its graph (a)–(h).

67. $y = 2 + \sqrt{x}$

68. $y = \sqrt{2 + x}$

69. $y = \sqrt{x^2}$

70. $y = \sqrt{\frac{x}{2}}$

71. $y = \frac{1}{2}\sqrt{x}$

72. $y = 2 - \sqrt{x - 2}$

73. $y = -2\sqrt{x}$

74. $y = -\sqrt{-x}$

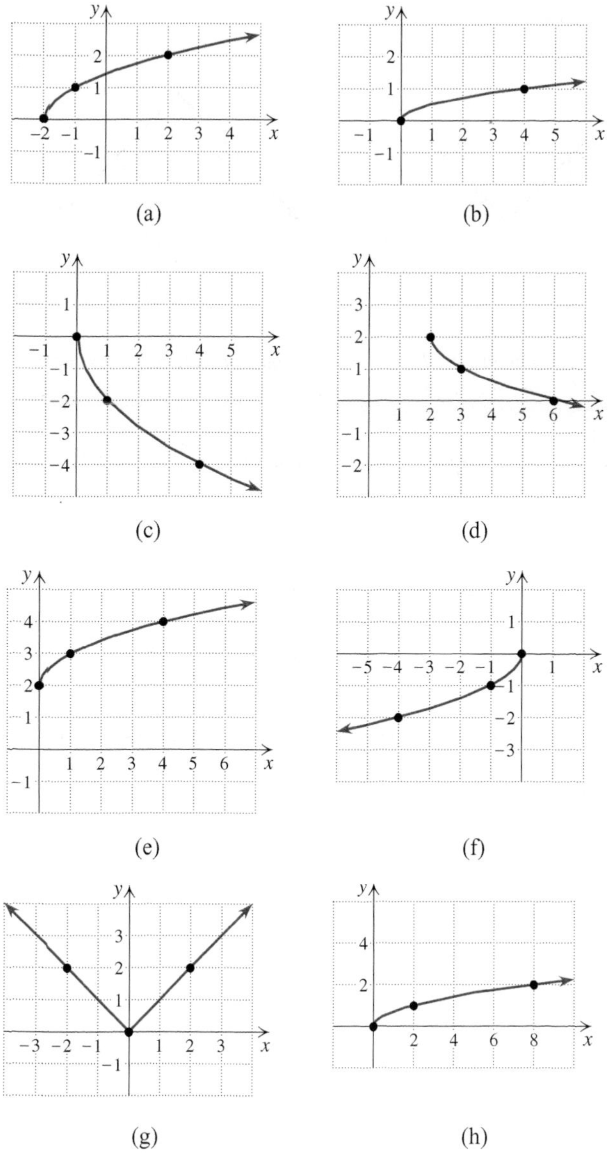

Figure for Exercises 67 to 74

Solve each inequality by reading the corresponding graph.

75. $x^2 - 1 \ge 0$

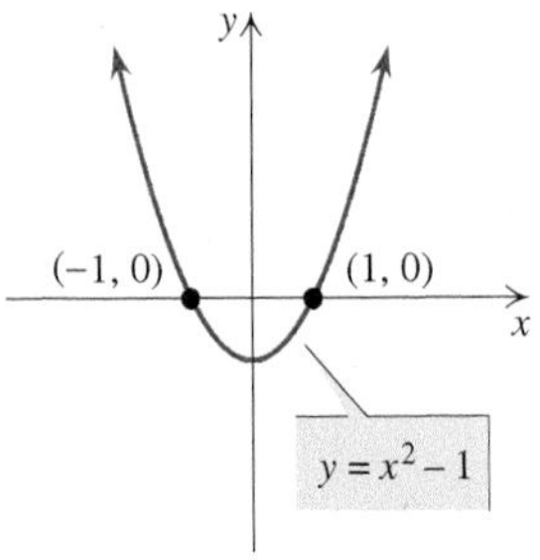

76. $2x^2 - 3 < 0$

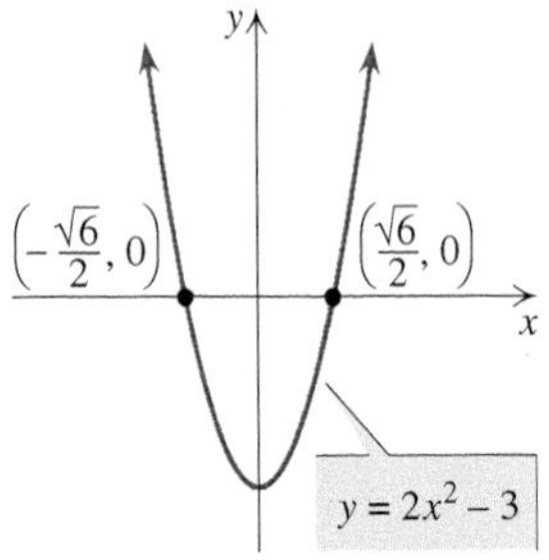

77. $|x - 2| - 3 > 0$

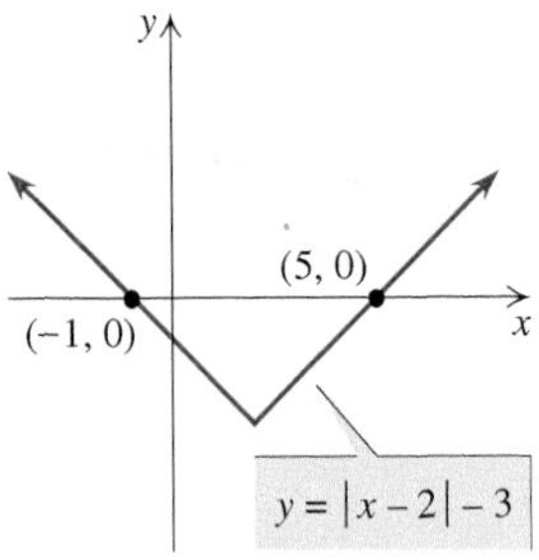

78. $2 - |x + 1| \ge 0$

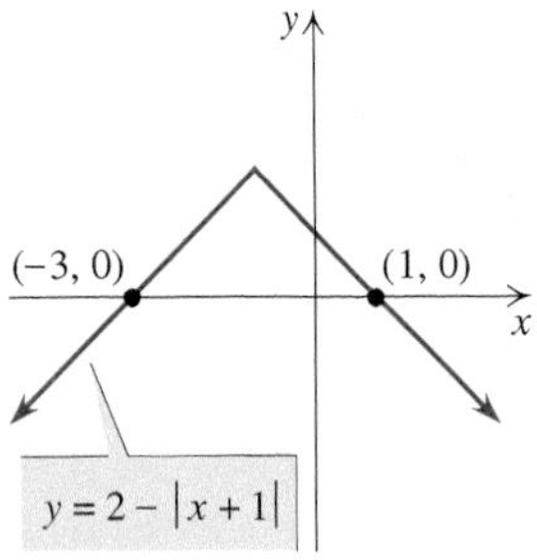

Solve each inequality by graphing an appropriate function. State the solution set using interval notation.

79. $(x - 1)^2 - 9 < 0$

80. $\left(x - \frac{1}{2}\right)^2 - \frac{9}{4} \ge 0$

81. $5 - \sqrt{x} \ge 0$

82. $\sqrt{x + 3} - 2 \ge 0$

83. $(x - 2)^2 > 3$

84. $(x - 1)^2 < 4$

85. $\sqrt{25 - x^2} > 0$

86. $\sqrt{4 - x^2} \ge 0$

Use a graphing calculator to find an approximate solution to each inequality by reading the graph of an appropriate function. Round to two decimal places.

87. $\sqrt{3}x^2 + \pi x - 9 < 0$

88. $x^3 - 5x^2 + 6x - 1 > 0$

Graph each of the following functions by transforming the given graph of $y = f(x)$.

89. **a.** $y = 2f(x)$

b. $y = -f(x)$

c. $y = f(x + 1)$

d. $y = f(x - 3)$

e. $y = -3f(x)$

f. $y = f(x + 2) - 1$

g. $y = f(x - 1) + 3$

h. $y = 3f(x - 2) + 1$

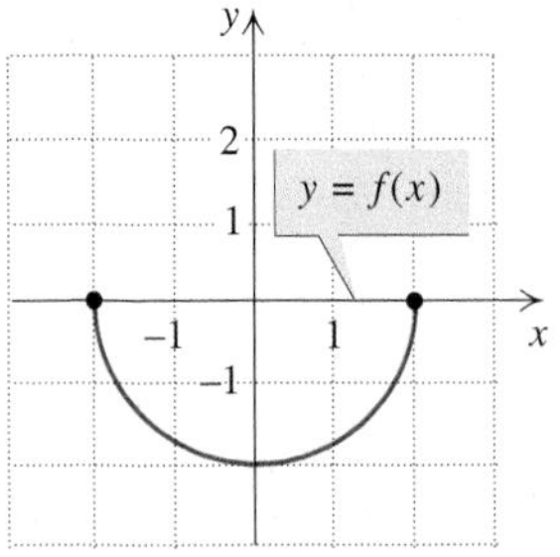

Figure for Exercise 89

90. **a.** $y = -f(x)$

b. $y = 2f(x)$

c. $y = -3f(x)$

d. $y = f(x + 2)$

e. $y = f(x - 1)$

f. $y = f(x - 2) + 1$

g. $y = -2f(x + 4)$

h. $y = 2f(x - 3) + 1$

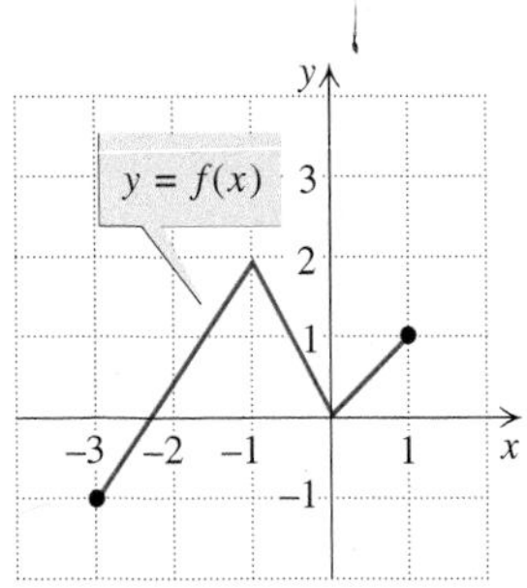

Figure for Exercise 90

Solve each problem.

91. *Across-the-Board Raise* Each teacher at C. F. Gauss Elementary School is given an across-the-board raise of \$2000. Write a function that *transforms* each old salary x into a new salary $N(x)$.

92. *Cost-of-Living Raise* Each registered nurse at Blue Hills Memorial Hospital is first given a 5% cost-of-living raise and then a \$3000 merit raise. Write a function that *transforms* each old salary x into a new salary $N(x)$. Does the order in which these raises are given make any difference? Explain.

Thinking Outside the Box VII

Lucky Lucy Ms. Willis asked Lucy to come to the board to find the mean of a pair of one-digit positive integers. Lucy slowly wrote the numbers on the board. While trying to think of what to do next, she rested the chalk between the numbers to make a mark that looked like a decimal point to Ms. Willis. Ms. Willis said "correct" and asked her to find the mean for a pair of two-digit positive integers. Being a quick learner, Lucy again wrote the numbers on the board, rested the chalk between the numbers, and again Ms. Willis said "correct." Lucy had to demonstrate her ability to find the mean for a pair of three-digit and a pair of four-digit positive integers before Ms. Willis was satisfied that she understood the concept. What four pairs of integers did Ms. Willis give to Lucy? Explain why Lucy's method will not work for any other pairs of one-, two-, three-, or four-digit positive integers.

1.7 Pop Quiz

1. What is the equation of the curve $y = \sqrt{x}$ after it is translated 8 units upward?

2. What is the equation of the curve $y = x^2$ after it is translated 9 units to the right?

3. What is the equation of the curve $y = x^3$ after it is reflected in the x-axis?

4. Find the domain and range for $y = -2\sqrt{x - 1} + 5$.

5. If the curve $y = x^2$ is translated 6 units to the right, stretched by a factor of 3, reflected in the x-axis, and translated 4 units upward, then what is the equation of the curve in its final position?

6. Is $y = \sqrt{4 - x^2}$ even, odd, or neither?

1.8 Operations with Functions

In Sections 1.6 and 1.7 we studied the graphs of functions to see the relationships between types of functions and their graphs. In this section we will study various ways in which two or more functions can be combined to make new functions. The emphasis here will be on formulas that define functions.

Basic Operations with Functions

A college student is hired to deliver new telephone books and collect the old ones for recycling. She is paid \$6 per hour plus \$0.30 for each old phone book she collects. Her salary for a 40-hour week is a function of the number of phone books collected. If x represents the number of phone books collected in one week, then the function $S(x) = 0.30x + 240$ gives her salary in dollars. However, she must use her own car for this job. She figures that her car expenses average \$0.20 per phone book collected plus a fixed cost of \$20 per week for insurance. We can write her expenses as a function of the number of phone books collected, $E(x) = 0.20x + 20$. Her profit for one week is her salary minus her expenses:

$$\begin{aligned} P(x) &= S(x) - E(x) \\ &= 0.30x + 240 - (0.20x + 20) \\ &= 0.10x + 220 \end{aligned}$$

By subtracting, we get $P(x) = 0.10x + 220$. Her weekly profit is written as a function of the number of phone books collected. In this example we obtained a new function by subtracting two functions. In general, there are four basic arithmetic operations defined for functions.

Definition: Sum, Difference, Product, and Quotient Functions

For two functions f and g, the **sum, difference, product,** and **quotient functions,** functions $f + g$, $f - g$, $f \cdot g$, and f/g, respectively, are defined as follows:

$$\begin{aligned} (f + g)(x) &= f(x) + g(x) \\ (f - g)(x) &= f(x) - g(x) \\ (f \cdot g)(x) &= f(x) \cdot g(x) \\ (f/g)(x) &= f(x)/g(x) \qquad \text{provided that } g(x) \neq 0. \end{aligned}$$

Example 1 Evaluating functions

Let $f(x) = 3\sqrt{x} - 2$ and $g(x) = x^2 + 5$. Find and simplify each expression.

a. $(f + g)(4)$ **b.** $(f - g)(x)$ **c.** $(f \cdot g)(0)$ **d.** $\left(\frac{f}{g}\right)(9)$

Solution

a. $(f + g)(4) = f(4) + g(4) = 3\sqrt{4} - 2 + 4^2 + 5 = 25$

b. $(f - g)(x) = f(x) - g(x) = 3\sqrt{x} - 2 - (x^2 + 5) = 3\sqrt{x} - x^2 - 7$

c. $(f \cdot g)(0) = f(0) \cdot g(0) = (3\sqrt{0} - 2)(0^2 + 5) = (-2)(5) = -10$

d. $\left(\frac{f}{g}\right)(9) = \frac{f(9)}{g(9)} = \frac{3\sqrt{9} - 2}{9^2 + 5} = \frac{7}{86}$

Parts (a), (c), and (d) can be checked with a graphing calculator as shown in Fig. 1.107(a) and (b).

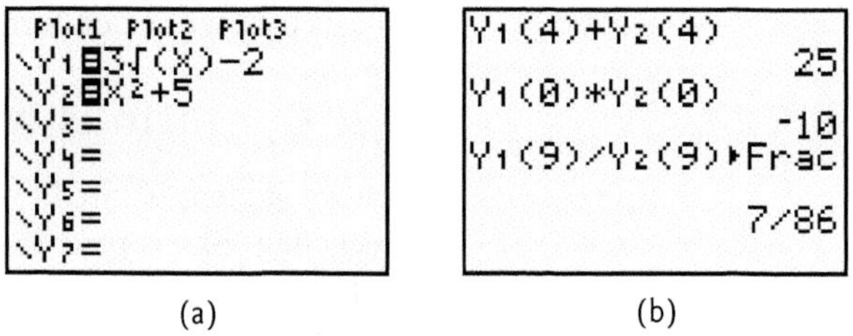

Figure 1.107

Think of $f + g$, $f - g$, $f \cdot g$, and f/g as generic names for the sum, difference, product, and quotient of the functions f and g. If any of these functions has a particular meaning, as in the phone book example, we can use a new letter to identify it. The domain of $f + g$, $f - g$, $f \cdot g$, or f/g is the intersection of the domain of f with the domain of g. Of course, we exclude from the domain of f/g any number for which $g(x) = 0$.

Example 2 The sum, product, and quotient functions

Let $f = \{(1, 3), (2, 8), (3, 6), (5, 9)\}$ and $g = \{(1, 6), (2, 11), (3, 0), (4, 1)\}$. Find $f + g$, $f \cdot g$, and f/g. State the domain of each function.

Solution

The domain of $f + g$ and $f \cdot g$ is $\{1, 2, 3\}$ because that is the intersection of the domains of f and g. The ordered pair (1, 9) belongs to $f + g$ because

$$(f + g)(1) = f(1) + g(1) = 3 + 6 = 9.$$

The ordered pair (2, 19) belongs to $f + g$ because $(f + g)(2) = 19$. The pair (3, 6) also belongs to $f + g$. So

$$f + g = \{(1, 9), (2, 19), (3, 6)\}.$$

Since $(f \cdot g)(1) = f(1) \cdot g(1) = 3 \cdot 6 = 18$, the pair $(1, 18)$ belongs to $f \cdot g$. Likewise, $(2, 88)$ and $(3, 0)$ also belong to $f \cdot g$. So

$$f \cdot g = \{(1, 18), (2, 88), (3, 0)\}.$$

The domain of f/g is $\{1, 2\}$ because $g(3) = 0$. So

$$\frac{f}{g} = \left\{\left(1, \frac{1}{2}\right), \left(2, \frac{8}{11}\right)\right\}.$$

■

In Example 2 the functions are given as sets of ordered pairs, and the results of performing operations with these functions are sets of ordered pairs. In the next example the sets of ordered pairs are defined by means of equations, so the result of performing operations with these functions will be new equations that determine the ordered pairs of the function.

Example 3 The sum, quotient, product, and difference functions

Let $f(x) = \sqrt{x}$, $g(x) = 3x + 1$, and $h(x) = x - 1$. Find each function and state its domain.

a. $f + g$ **b.** $\dfrac{g}{f}$ **c.** $g \cdot h$ **d.** $g - h$

Solution

a. Since the domain of f is $[0, \infty)$ and the domain of g is $(-\infty, \infty)$, the domain of $f + g$ is $[0, \infty)$. Since $(f + g)(x) = f(x) + g(x) = \sqrt{x} + 3x + 1$, the equation defining the function $f + g$ is

$$(f + g)(x) = \sqrt{x} + 3x + 1.$$

b. The number 0 is not in the domain of g/f because $f(0) = 0$. So the domain of g/f is $(0, \infty)$. The equation defining g/f is

$$\left(\frac{g}{f}\right)(x) = \frac{3x + 1}{\sqrt{x}}.$$

c. The domain of both g and h is $(-\infty, \infty)$. So the domain of $g \cdot h$ is $(-\infty, \infty)$. Since $(3x + 1)(x - 1) = 3x^2 - 2x - 1$, the equation defining the function $g \cdot h$ is

$$(g \cdot h)(x) = 3x^2 - 2x - 1.$$

d. The domain of both g and h is $(-\infty, \infty)$. So the domain of $g - h$ is $(-\infty, \infty)$. Since $(3x + 1) - (x - 1) = 2x + 2$, the equation defining $g - h$ is

$$(g - h)(x) = 2x + 2.$$

■

Composition of Functions

It is often the case that the output of one function is the input for another function. For example, the number of hamburgers purchased at \$1.49 each determines the subtotal. The subtotal is then used to determine the total (including sales tax). So the number of hamburgers actually determines the total and that function is called the *composition* of the other two functions. The composition of functions is defined using function notation as follows.

Definition: Composition of Functions

If f and g are two functions, the **composition** of f and g, written $f \circ g$, is defined by the equation

$$(f \circ g)(x) = f(g(x)),$$

provided that $g(x)$ is in the domain of f. The composition of g and f, written $g \circ f$, is defined by

$$(g \circ f)(x) = g(f(x)),$$

provided that $f(x)$ is in the domain of g.

Note that $f \circ g$ is not the same function as $f \cdot g$, the product of f and g.

For the composition $f \circ g$ to be defined at x, $g(x)$ must be in the domain of f. So the domain of $f \circ g$ is the set of all values of x in the domain of g for which $g(x)$ is in the domain of f. The diagram shown in Fig. 1.108 will help you to understand the composition of functions.

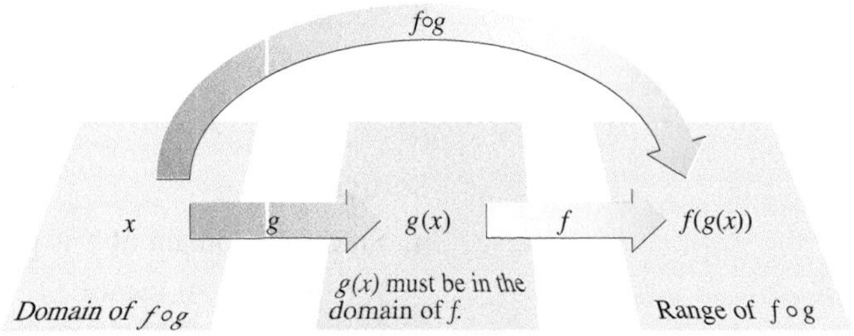

Figure 1.108

Example 4 Composition of functions defined by sets

Let $g = \{(1, 4), (2, 5), (3, 6)\}$ and $f = \{(3, 8), (4, 9), (5, 10)\}$. Find $f \circ g$.

Solution

Since $g(1) = 4$ and $f(4) = 9$, $(f \circ g)(1) = 9$. So the ordered pair $(1, 9)$ is in $f \circ g$. Since $g(2) = 5$ and $f(5) = 10$, $(f \circ g)(2) = 10$. So $(2, 10)$ is in $f \circ g$. Now $g(3) = 6$, but 6 is not in the domain of f. So there are only two ordered pairs in $f \circ g$:

$$f \circ g = \{(1, 9), (2, 10)\}$$ ■

In the next example we find specific values of compositions that are defined by equations.

Example 5 Evaluating compositions defined by equations

Let $f(x) = \sqrt{x}$, $g(x) = 2x - 1$, and $h(x) = x^2$. Find the value of each expression.

a. $(f \circ g)(5)$ **b.** $(g \circ f)(5)$ **c.** $(h \circ g \circ f)(9)$

Solution

a. $(f \circ g)(5) = f(g(5))$ Definition of composition

$= f(9)$ $g(5) = 2 \cdot 5 - 1 = 9$

$= \sqrt{9}$

$= 3$

b. $(g \circ f)(5) = g(f(5)) = g(\sqrt{5}) = 2\sqrt{5} - 1$

c. $(h \circ g \circ f)(9) = h(g(f(9))) = h(g(3)) = h(5) = 5^2 = 25$

You can check these answers with a graphing calculator as shown in Fig. 1.109(a) and (b). Enter the functions using the Y = key, then go back to the home screen to evaluate. The symbols Y_1, Y_2, and Y_3 are found in the variables menu (VARS) on a TI-83.

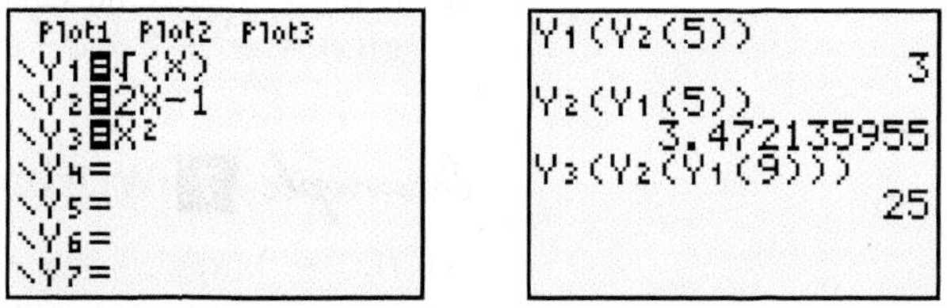

(a) (b)

Figure 1.109 ■

In Example 4, the domain of g is $\{1, 2, 3\}$ while the domain of $f \circ g$ is $\{1, 2\}$. To find the domain of $f \circ g$, we remove from the domain of g any number x such that $g(x)$ is not in the domain of f. In the next example we construct compositions of functions defined by equations and determine their domains.

Example 6 Composition of functions defined by equations

Let $f(x) = \sqrt{x}$, $g(x) = 2x - 1$, and $h(x) = x^2$. Find each composition function and state its domain.

a. $f \circ g$ **b.** $g \circ f$ **c.** $h \circ g$

Solution

a. In the composition $f \circ g$, $g(x)$ must be in the domain of f. The domain of f is $[0, \infty)$. If $g(x)$ is in $[0, \infty)$, then $2x - 1 \geq 0$, or $x \geq \frac{1}{2}$. So the domain of $f \circ g$ is $\left[\frac{1}{2}, \infty\right)$. Since

$$(f \circ g)(x) = f(g(x)) = f(2x - 1) = \sqrt{2x - 1},$$

the function $f \circ g$ is defined by the equation $(f \circ g)(x) = \sqrt{2x - 1}$, for $x \geq \frac{1}{2}$.

b. Since the domain of g is $(-\infty, \infty)$, $f(x)$ is certainly in the domain of g. So the domain of $g \circ f$ is the same as the domain of f, $[0, \infty)$. Since

$$(g \circ f)(x) = g(f(x)) = g(\sqrt{x}) = 2\sqrt{x} - 1,$$

the function $g \circ f$ is defined by the equation $(g \circ f)(x) = 2\sqrt{x} - 1$. Note that $g \circ f$ is generally not equal to $f \circ g$, but in Section 1.9 we will study special types of functions for which they are equal.

c. Since the domain of h is $(-\infty, \infty)$, $g(x)$ is certainly in the domain of h. So the domain of $h \circ g$ is the same as the domain of g, $(-\infty, \infty)$. Since

$$(h \circ g)(x) = h(g(x)) = h(2x - 1) = (2x - 1)^2 = 4x^2 - 4x + 1,$$

the function $h \circ g$ is defined by $(h \circ g)(x) = 4x^2 - 4x + 1$. ■

Some complicated functions can be thought of as a composition of simpler functions. For example, if $H(x) = (x + 3)^2$, we start with x, add 3 to x, then square the result. These two operations can be accomplished by composition, using $f(x) = x + 3$ followed by $g(x) = x^2$:

$$(g \circ f)(x) = g(f(x)) = g(x + 3) = (x + 3)^2$$

So the function H is the same as the composition of g and f, $H = g \circ f$. Notice that $(f \circ g)(x) = x^2 + 3$ and it is not the same as $H(x)$.

Example 7 Writing a function as a composition

Let $f(x) = \sqrt{x}$, $g(x) = x - 3$, and $h(x) = 2x$. Write each given function as a composition of appropriate functions chosen from f, g, and h.

a. $F(x) = \sqrt{x - 3}$ **b.** $G(x) = x - 6$ **c.** $H(x) = 2\sqrt{x} - 3$

Solution

a. The function F consists of subtracting 3 from x and finding the square root of that result. These two operations can be accomplished by composition, using g followed by f. So $F = f \circ g$. Check this answer as follows:

$$(f \circ g)(x) = f(g(x)) = f(x - 3) = \sqrt{x - 3} = F(x)$$

b. Subtracting 6 from x can be accomplished by subtracting 3 from x and then subtracting 3 from that result, so $G = g \circ g$. Check as follows:

$$(g \circ g)(x) = g(g(x)) = g(x - 3) = (x - 3) - 3 = x - 6 = G(x)$$

c. For the function H, find the square root of x, then multiply by 2, and finally subtract 3. These three operations can be accomplished by composition, using f, then h, and then g. So $H = g \circ h \circ f$. Check as follows:

$$(g \circ h \circ f)(x) = g(h(f(x))) = g(h(\sqrt{x})) = g(2\sqrt{x}) = 2\sqrt{x} - 3 = H(x)$$ ■

■ **Foreshadowing Calculus**

One of the big topics in calculus is the instantaneous rate of change of a function. To find the instantaneous rate of change, we often view a complicated function as a composition of simpler functions as is done in Example 7.

Applications

In applied situations, functions are often defined with formulas rather than function notation. In this case, composition can be simply a matter of substitution.

Example 8 Composition with formulas

The radius of a circle is a function of the diameter ($r = d/2$) and the area is a function of the radius ($A = \pi r^2$). Construct a formula that expresses the area as a function of the diameter.

Solution

The formula for A as a function of d is obtained by substituting $d/2$ for r:

$$A = \pi r^2 = \pi\left(\frac{d}{2}\right)^2 = \pi\frac{d^2}{4}$$

The function $A = \pi d^2/4$ is the composition of $r = d/2$ and $A = \pi r^2$. ■

In the next example we find a composition using function notation for the salary of the phone book collector mentioned at the beginning of this section.

Example 9 Composition with function notation

A student's salary (in dollars) for collecting x phone books is given by $S(x) = 0.30x + 240$. The amount of withholding (for taxes) is given by $W(x) = 0.20x$, where x is the salary. Express the withholding as a function of the number of phone books collected.

Solution

Note that x represents the number of phone books in $S(x) = 0.30x + 240$ and x represents salary in $W(x) = 0.20x$. So we can replace the salary x in $W(x)$ with $S(x)$ or $0.30x + 240$, which also represents salary:

$$W(S(x)) = W(0.30x + 240) = 0.20(0.30x + 240) = 0.06x + 48$$

Use a new letter to name this function, say T. Then $T(x) = 0.06x + 48$ gives the amount of withholding (for taxes) as a function of x, where x is the number of phone books. ■

For Thought

True or False? Explain.

1. If $f = \{(2, 4)\}$ and $g = \{(1, 5)\}$, then $f + g = \{(3, 9)\}$.

2. If $f = \{(1, 6), (9, 5)\}$ and $g = \{(1, 3), (9, 0)\}$, then $f/g = \{(1, 2)\}$.

3. If $f = \{(1, 6), (9, 5)\}$ and $g = \{(1, 3), (9, 0)\}$, then $f \cdot g = \{(1, 18), (9, 0)\}$.

4. If $f(x) = x + 2$ and $g(x) = x - 3$, then $(f \cdot g)(5) = 14$.

5. If $s = P/4$ and $A = s^2$, then A is a function of P.

6. If $f(3) = 19$ and $g(19) = 99$, then $(g \circ f)(3) = 99$.

7. If $f(x) = \sqrt{x}$ and $g(x) = x - 2$, then $(f \circ g)(x) = \sqrt{x} - 2$.

8. If $f(x) = 5x$ and $g(x) = x/5$, then $(f \circ g)(x) = (g \circ f)(x) = x$.

9. If $F(x) = (x - 9)^2$, $g(x) = x^2$, and $h(x) = x - 9$, then $F = h \circ g$.

10. If $f(x) = \sqrt{x}$ and $g(x) = x - 2$, then the domain of $f \circ g$ is $[2, \infty)$.

1.8 Exercises

Let $f(x) = x - 3$ and $g(x) = x^2 - x$. Find and simplify each expression.

1. $(f + g)(2)$ **2.** $(g + f)(3)$ **3.** $(f - g)(-2)$

4. $(g - f)(-6)$ **5.** $(f \cdot g)(-1)$ **6.** $(g \cdot f)(0)$

7. $(f/g)(4)$ **8.** $(g/f)(4)$ **9.** $(f + g)(a)$

10. $(f - g)(b)$ **11.** $(f \cdot g)(a)$ **12.** $(f/g)(b)$

Let $f = \{(-3, 1), (0, 4), (2, 0)\}$, $g = \{(-3, 2), (1, 2), (2, 6), (4, 0)\}$, and $h = \{(2, 4), (1, 0)\}$. Find each function and state the domain of each function.

13. $f + g$ **14.** $f + h$ **15.** $f - g$ **16.** $f - h$

17. $f \cdot g$ **18.** $f \cdot h$ **19.** g/f **20.** f/g

Let $f(x) = \sqrt{x}$, $g(x) = x - 4$, and $h(x) = \frac{1}{x-2}$. Find an equation defining each function and state the domain of the function.

21. $f + g$ **22.** $f + h$ **23.** $f - h$ **24.** $h - g$

25. $g \cdot h$ **26.** $f \cdot h$ **27.** g/f **28.** f/g

Let $f = \{(-3, 1), (0, 4), (2, 0)\}$, $g = \{(-3, 2), (1, 2), (2, 6), (4, 0)\}$, and $h = \{(2, 4), (1, 0)\}$. Find each function.

29. $f \circ g$ **30.** $g \circ f$ **31.** $f \circ h$

32. $h \circ f$ **33.** $h \circ g$ **34.** $g \circ h$

Let $f(x) = 3x - 1$, $g(x) = x^2 + 1$, and $h(x) = \frac{x+1}{3}$. Evaluate each expression. Round approximate answers to three decimal places.

35. $f(g(-1))$ **36.** $g(f(-1))$ **37.** $(f \circ h)(5)$

38. $(h \circ f)(-7)$ **39.** $(f \circ g)(4.39)$ **40.** $(g \circ h)(-9.87)$

41. $(g \circ h \circ f)(2)$ **42.** $(h \circ f \circ g)(3)$ **43.** $(f \circ g \circ h)(2)$

44. $(h \circ g \circ f)(0)$ **45.** $(f \circ h)(a)$ **46.** $(h \circ f)(w)$

47. $(f \circ g)(t)$ **48.** $(g \circ f)(m)$

Let $f(x) = x - 2$, $g(x) = \sqrt{x}$, and $h(x) = \frac{1}{x}$. Find an equation defining each function and state the domain of the function.

49. $f \circ g$ **50.** $g \circ f$ **51.** $f \circ h$

52. $h \circ f$ **53.** $h \circ g$ **54.** $g \circ h$

55. $f \circ f$ **56.** $g \circ g$ **57.** $h \circ g \circ f$

58. $f \circ g \circ h$ **59.** $h \circ f \circ g$ **60.** $g \circ h \circ f$

Let $f(x) = |x|$, $g(x) = x - 7$, and $h(x) = x^2$. Write each of the following functions as a composition of functions chosen from f, g, and h.

61. $F(x) = x^2 - 7$ **62.** $G(x) = |x| - 7$

63. $H(x) = (x - 7)^2$ **64.** $M(x) = |x - 7|$

65. $N(x) = (|x| - 7)^2$ **66.** $R(x) = |x^2 - 7|$

67. $P(x) = |x - 7| - 7$ **68.** $Q(x) = (x^2 - 7)^2$

69. $S(x) = x - 14$ **70.** $T(x) = x^4$

Use the two given functions to write y as a function of x.

71. $y = 2a - 3, a = 3x + 1$

72. $y = -4d - 1, d = -3x - 2$

73. $y = w^2 - 2, w = x + 3$

74. $y = 3t^2 - 3, t = x - 1$

75. $y = 3m - 1, m = \frac{x+1}{3}$ **76.** $y = 2z + 5, z = \frac{1}{2}x - \frac{5}{2}$

Define $y_1 = \sqrt{x+1}$ and $y_2 = 3x - 4$ on your graphing calculator. For each function y_3, defined in terms of y_1 and y_2, determine the domain and range of y_3 from its graph on your calculator and explain what each graph illustrates.

77. $y_3 = y_1 + y_2$ **78.** $y_3 = 3y_1 - 4$

79. $y_3 = \sqrt{y_2 + 1}$ **80.** $y_3 = \sqrt{y_1 + 1}$

Define $y_1 = \sqrt[3]{x}$, $y_2 = \sqrt{x}$, and $y_3 = x + 4$. For each function y_4, determine the domain and range of y_4 from its graph on your calculator and explain what each graph illustrates.

81. $y_4 = y_1 + y_2 + y_3$ **82.** $y_4 = \sqrt{y_1 + 4}$

Solve each problem.

83. *Profitable Business* Charles buys factory reconditioned hedge trimmers for \$40 each and sells them on Ebay for \$68 each. He has a fixed cost of \$200 per month. If x is the number of hedge trimmers he sells per month, then his revenue and cost (in dollars) are given by $R(x) = 68x$ and $C(x) = 40x + 200$. Find a formula for the function $P(x) = R(x) - C(x)$. For what values of x is his profit positive?

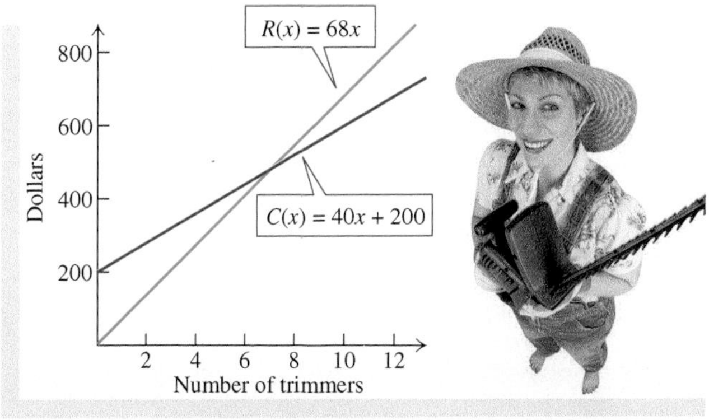

Figure for Exercise 83

84. *Profit* The revenue in dollars that a company receives for installing x alarm systems per month is given by $R(x) = 3000x - 20x^2$, while the cost in dollars is given by $C(x) = 600x + 4000$. The function $P(x) = R(x) - C(x)$ gives the profit for installing x alarm systems per month. Find $P(x)$ and simplify it.

85. Write the area A of a square with a side of length s as a function of its diagonal d.

86. Write the perimeter of a square P as a function of the area A.

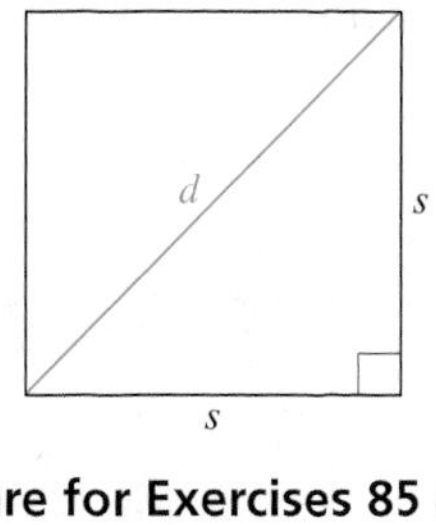

Figure for Exercises 85 and 86

87. *Hamburgers* If hamburgers are \$1.20 each, then $C(x) = 1.20x$ gives the pre-tax cost in dollars for x hamburgers. If sales tax is 5%, then $T(x) = 1.05x$ gives the total cost when the pre-tax cost is x dollars. Write the total cost as a function of the number of hamburgers.

88. *Laying Sod* Southern Sod will deliver and install 20 pallets of St. Augustine sod for \$2200 or 30 pallets for \$3200 not including tax.

a. Write the cost (not including tax) as a linear function of x, where x is the number of pallets.

b. Write a function that gives the total cost (including tax at 9%) as a function of x, where x is the cost (not including tax).

c. Find the function that gives the total cost as a function of x, where x is the number of pallets.

89. *Displacement-Length Ratio* The displacement-length ratio D indicates whether a sailboat is relatively heavy or relatively light:

$$D = (d \div 2240) \div x$$

where d is the displacement in pounds and

$$x = (L \div 100)^3$$

where L is the length at the waterline in feet (*Sailing*, www.sailing.com). Assuming that the displacement is 26,000 pounds, write D as a function of L and simplify it.

90. *Sail Area-Displacement Ratio* The sail area-displacement ratio S measures the sail power available to drive a sailboat:

$$S = A \div y$$

where A is the sail area in square feet and

$$y = (d \div 64)^{2/3}$$

where d is the displacement in pounds. Assuming that the sail area is 6500 square feet, write S as a function of d and simplify it.

91. *Area of a Window* A window is in the shape of a square with a side of length s, with a semicircle of diameter s adjoining the top of the square. Write the total area of the window W as a function of s.

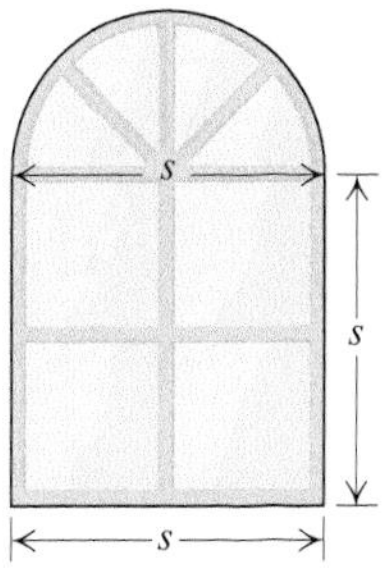

Figure for Exercises 91 and 92

92. *Area of a Window* Using the window of Exercise 91, write the area of the square A as a function of the area of the semicircle S.

Thinking Outside the Box VIII

Whole Number Expression What is the largest whole number N that cannot be expressed as $N = 3x + 11y$ where x and y are whole numbers?

1.8 Pop Quiz

1. Write the area of a circle as a function of its diameter.

Let $f(x) = x^2$ and $g(x) = x - 2$. Find and simplify.

2. $(f + g)(3)$
3. $(f \cdot g)(4)$
4. $(f \circ g)(5)$

Let $m = \{(1, 3), (4, 8)\}$ and $n = \{(3, 5), (4, 9)\}$. Find each function.

5. $m + n$
6. $n \circ m$

Let $h(x) = x^2$ and $j(x) = \sqrt{x + 2}$. Find the domain of each function.

7. $h + j$
8. $h \circ j$
9. $j \circ h$

1.9 Inverse Functions

It is possible for one function to undo what another function does. For example, squaring undoes the operation of taking a square root. The composition of two such functions is the identity function. In this section we explore this idea in detail.

One-to-One Functions

Consider a medium pizza that costs \$5 plus \$2 per topping. Table 1.2 shows the ordered pairs of the function that determines the cost. Note that for every number of toppings there is a unique cost and for every cost there is a unique number of toppings. There is a **one-to-one correspondence** between the domain and range of this function and the function is a *one-to-one function.* For a function that is not one-to-one, consider a Wendy's menu. Every item corresponds to a unique price, but the price \$0.99 corresponds to many different items.

Table 1.2

Toppings x	Cost y
0	\$ 5
1	7
2	9
3	11
4	13

Definition: One-to-One Function

If a function has no two ordered pairs with different first coordinates and the same second coordinate, then the function is called **one-to-one.**

Example 1 One-to-one with ordered pairs

Determine whether each function is one-to-one.

a. $\{(1, 3), (2, 5), (3, 4), (4, 9), (5, 0)\}$
b. $\{(4, 16), (-4, 16), (2, 4), (-2, 4), (5, 25)\}$
c. $\{(3, 0.99), (5, 1.99), (7, 2.99), (8, 3.99), (9, 0.99)\}$

Solution

a. This function is one-to-one because no two ordered pairs have different first coordinates and the same second coordinate.

b. This function is not one-to-one because the ordered pairs (4, 16) and (−4, 16) have different first coordinates and the same second coordinate.

c. This function is not one-to-one because the ordered pairs (3, 0.99) and (9, 0.99) have different first coordinates and the same second coordinate. ■

If a function is given as a short list of ordered pairs, then it is easy to determine whether the function is one-to-one. A graph of a function can also be used to determine whether a function is one-to-one using the **horizontal line test.**

Horizontal Line Test

If each horizontal line crosses the graph of a function at no more than one point, then the function is one-to-one.

The graph of a one-to-one function never has the same y-coordinate for two different x-coordinates on the graph. So if it is possible to draw a horizontal line that crosses the graph of a function two or more times, then the function is not one-to-one.

Example 2 The horizontal line test

Use the horizontal line test to determine whether the functions shown in Fig. 1.110 are one-to-one.

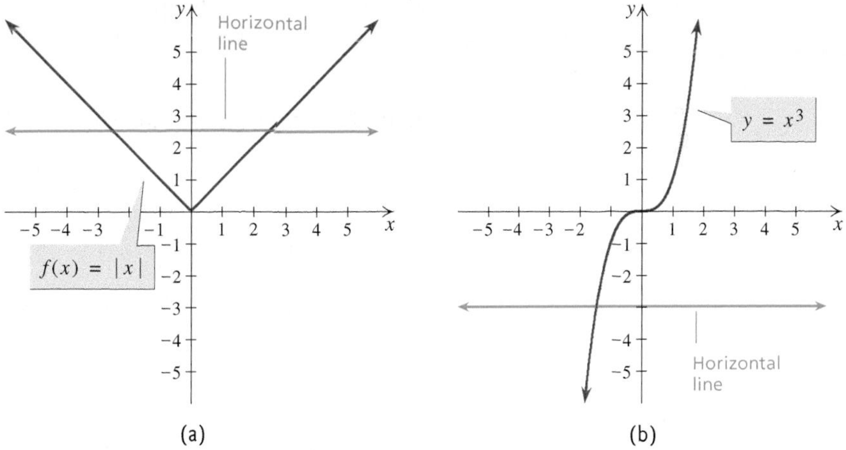

Figure 1.110

Solution

The function $f(x) = |x|$ is not one-to-one because it is possible to draw a horizontal line that crosses the graph twice as shown in Fig. 1.110(a). The function $y = x^3$ in Fig. 1.110(b) is one-to-one because it appears to be impossible to draw a horizontal line that crosses the graph more than once. ■

The horizontal line test explains the visual difference between the graph of a one-to-one function and the graph of a function that is not one-to-one. Because no graph of a function is perfectly accurate, conclusions made from a graph alone may not be correct. For example, from the graph of $y = x^3 - 0.01x$ shown in Fig. 1.111(a) we would conclude that the function is one-to-one. However, another view of the same function in Fig. 1.111(b) shows that the function is not one-to-one.

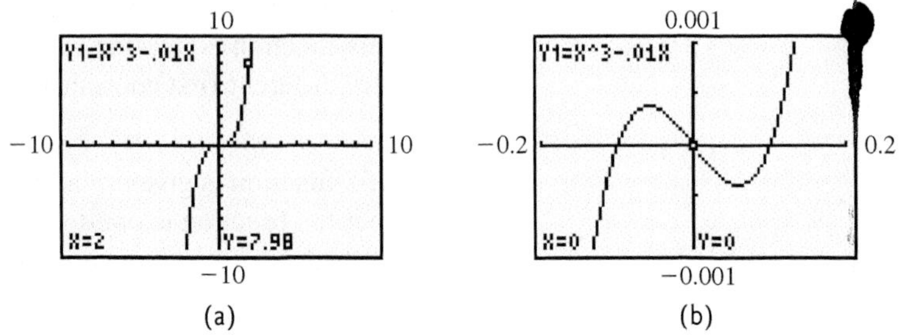

Figure 1.111

Using the equation for a function we can often determine conclusively whether the function is one-to-one. A function f is not one-to-one if it is possible to find two different numbers x_1 and x_2 such that $f(x_1) = f(x_2)$. For example, for the function $f(x) = x^2$, it is possible to find two different numbers, 2 and -2, such that $f(2) = f(-2)$. So $f(x) = x^2$ is not one-to-one. To prove that a function f is one-to-one, we must show that $f(x_1) = f(x_2)$ implies that $x_1 = x_2$.

Example 3 Using the definition of one-to-one

Determine whether each function is one-to-one.

a. $f(x) = \dfrac{2x + 1}{x - 3}$ **b.** $g(x) = |x|$

Solution

a. If $f(x_1) = f(x_2)$, then we have the following equation:

$$\frac{2x_1 + 1}{x_1 - 3} = \frac{2x_2 + 1}{x_2 - 3}$$

$$(2x_1 + 1)(x_2 - 3) = (2x_2 + 1)(x_1 - 3) \quad \text{Multiply by the LCD.}$$

$$2x_1x_2 + x_2 - 6x_1 - 3 = 2x_2x_1 + x_1 - 6x_2 - 3$$

$$7x_2 = 7x_1$$

$$x_2 = x_1$$

Since $f(x_1) = f(x_2)$ implies that $x_1 = x_2$, $f(x)$ is a one-to-one function.

b. If $g(x_1) = g(x_2)$, then $|x_1| = |x_2|$. But this does not imply that $x_1 = x_2$, because two different numbers can have the same absolute value. For example $|3| = |-3|$ but $3 \neq -3$. So g is not one-to-one. ■

Inverse Functions

Consider again the function given in Table 1.2, which determines the cost of a pizza from the number of toppings. Because that function is one-to-one we can make a table in which the number of toppings is determined from the cost as shown in Table 1.3. Of course we could just read Table 1.2 backwards, but we make a new table to emphasize that there is a new function under discussion. Table 1.3 is the *inverse function* for the function in Table 1.2.

Table 1.3

Cost x	Toppings y
\$ 5	0
7	1
9	2
11	3
13	4

A function is a set of ordered pairs in which no two ordered pairs have the same first coordinates and different second coordinates. If we interchange the x- and y-coordinates in each ordered pair of a function, as in Tables 1.2 and 1.3, the resulting set of ordered pairs might or might not be a function. If the original function is one-to-one, then the set obtained by interchanging the coordinates in each ordered pair is a function, the inverse function. If a function is one-to-one, then it has an inverse function or it is **invertible.**

Definition: Inverse Function

The **inverse** of a one-to-one function f is the function f^{-1} (read "f inverse"), where the ordered pairs of f^{-1} are obtained by interchanging the coordinates in each ordered pair of f.

In this notation, the number -1 in f^{-1} does not represent a negative exponent. It is merely a symbol for denoting the inverse function.

Example 4 Finding an inverse function

For each function, determine whether it is invertible. If it is invertible, then find the inverse.

a. $f = \{(-2, 3), (4, 5), (2, 3)\}$ **b.** $g = \{(3, 1), (5, 2), (7, 4), (9, 8)\}$

Solution

a. This function f is *not* one-to-one because of the ordered pairs $(-2, 3)$ and $(2, 3)$. So f is not invertible.

b. The function g is one-to-one, and so g is invertible. The inverse of g is the function $g^{-1} = \{(1, 3), (2, 5), (4, 7), (8, 9)\}$. ■

Example 5 Using inverse function notation

Let $f = \{(1, 3), (2, 4), (5, 7)\}$. Find f^{-1}, $f^{-1}(3)$, and $(f^{-1} \circ f)(1)$.

Solution

Interchange the x- and y-coordinates of each ordered pair of f to find f^{-1}:

$$f^{-1} = \{(3, 1), (4, 2), (7, 5)\}$$

To find the value of $f^{-1}(3)$, notice that $f^{-1}(3)$ is the second coordinate when the first coordinate is 3 in the function f^{-1}. So $f^{-1}(3) = 1$. To find the composition, use the definition of composition of functions:

$$(f^{-1} \circ f)(1) = f^{-1}(f(1)) = f^{-1}(3) = 1$$ ■

Since the coordinates in the ordered pairs are interchanged, the domain of f^{-1} is the range of f, and the range of f^{-1} is the domain of f. If f^{-1} is the inverse function of f, then certainly f is the inverse of f^{-1}. The functions f and f^{-1} are inverses of each other.

Inverse Functions Using Function Notation

The function $f(x) = 2x + 5$ gives the cost of a pizza where \$5 is the basic cost and x is the number of toppings at \$2 each. If we assume that x could be any real number, this function defines the set

$$f = \{(x, y) \mid y = 2x + 5\}.$$

Since the coordinates of each ordered pair are interchanged for f^{-1}, the ordered pairs of f^{-1} must satisfy $x = 2y + 5$:

$$f^{-1} = \{(x, y) \mid x = 2y + 5\}.$$

Since $x = 2y + 5$ is equivalent to $y = \frac{x - 5}{2}$,

$$f^{-1} = \left\{(x, y) \mid y = \frac{x - 5}{2}\right\}.$$

The function f^{-1} is described in function notation as $f^{-1}(x) = \frac{x - 5}{2}$. The function f^{-1} gives the number of toppings as a function of cost.

A one-to-one function f pairs members of the domain of f with members of the range of f, and its inverse function f^{-1} exactly reverses those pairings as shown in Fig. 1.112. The above example suggests the following steps for finding an inverse function using function notation.

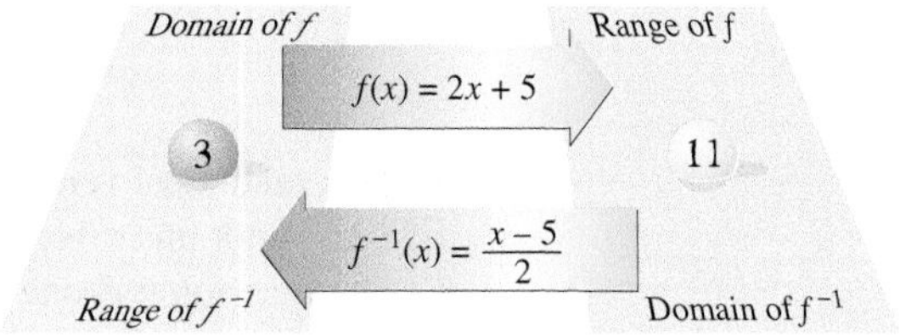

Figure 1.112

PROCEDURE

Finding $f^{-1}(x)$ by the Switch-and-Solve Method

To find the inverse of a one-to-one function given in function notation:

1. Replace $f(x)$ by y.
2. Interchange x and y.
3. Solve the equation for y.
4. Replace y by $f^{-1}(x)$.
5. Check that the domain of f is the range of f^{-1} and the range of f is the domain of f^{-1}.

Example 6 The switch-and-solve method

Find the inverse of each function.

a. $f(x) = 4x - 1$ **b.** $f(x) = \dfrac{2x + 1}{x - 3}$

Solution

a. The graph of $f(x) = 4x - 1$ is a line with slope 4. By the horizontal line test the function is one-to-one and invertible. Replace $f(x)$ with y to get $y = 4x - 1$. Next, interchange x and y to get $x = 4y - 1$. Now solve for y:

$$x = 4y - 1$$
$$x + 1 = 4y$$
$$\frac{x + 1}{4} = y$$

Replace y by $f^{-1}(x)$ to get $f^{-1}(x) = \frac{x + 1}{4}$. The domain of f is $(-\infty, \infty)$ and that is the range of f^{-1}. The range of f is $(-\infty, \infty)$ and that is the domain of f^{-1}.

b. In Example 3(a) we showed that f is a one-to-one function. So we can find f^{-1} by interchanging x and y and solving for y:

$$y = \frac{2x + 1}{x - 3} \quad \text{Replace } f(x) \text{ by } y.$$
$$x = \frac{2y + 1}{y - 3} \quad \text{Interchange } x \text{ and } y.$$
$$x(y - 3) = 2y + 1 \quad \text{Solve for } y.$$
$$xy - 3x = 2y + 1$$
$$xy - 2y = 3x + 1$$
$$y(x - 2) = 3x + 1$$
$$y = \frac{3x + 1}{x - 2}$$

Replace y by $f^{-1}(x)$ to get $f^{-1}(x) = \frac{3x + 1}{x - 2}$. The domain of f is all real numbers except 3. The range of f^{-1} is the set of all real numbers except 3. We exclude 3 because $\frac{3x + 1}{x - 2} = 3$ has no solution. Check that the range of f is equal to the domain of f^{-1}. ■

If a function f is defined by a short list of ordered pairs, then we simply write all of the pairs in reverse to find f^{-1}. If two functions are defined by formulas, it may not be obvious whether the ordered pairs of one are the reverse of the ordered pairs of the other. However, we can use the compositions of the functions to make the determination as stated in the following theorem.

Theorem: Verifying Whether f and g Are Inverses

The functions f and g are inverses of each other if and only if

1. $g(f(x)) = x$ for every x in the domain of f and
2. $f(g(x)) = x$ for every x in the domain of g.

Example 7 Using composition to verify inverse functions

Determine whether the functions $f(x) = x^3 - 1$ and $g(x) = \sqrt[3]{x + 1}$ are inverse functions.

Solution

Find $f(g(x))$ and $g(f(x))$:

$$f(g(x)) = f\left(\sqrt[3]{x+1}\right) = \left(\sqrt[3]{x+1}\right)^3 - 1 = x + 1 - 1 = x$$

$$g(f(x)) = g(x^3 - 1) = \sqrt[3]{x^3 - 1 + 1} = \sqrt[3]{x^3} = x$$

Since $f(g(x)) = x$ is true for any real number (the domain of g) and $g(f(x)) = x$ is true for any real number (the domain of f), the functions f and g are inverses of each other. ■

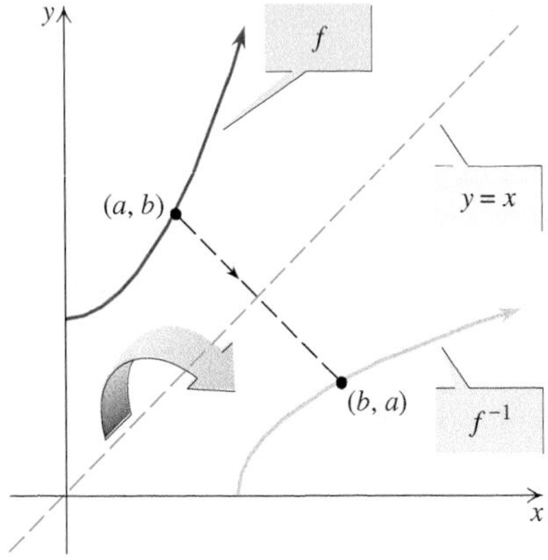

Figure 1.113

Only one-to-one functions are invertible. However, sometimes it is possible to restrict the domain of a function that is not one-to-one so that it is one-to-one on the restricted domain. For example, $f(x) = x^2$ for x in $(-\infty, \infty)$ is not one-to-one and not invertible. But $f(x) = x^2$ for $x \geq 0$ is one-to-one and invertible. The inverse of $f(x) = x^2$ for $x \geq 0$ is the square-root function $f^{-1}(x) = \sqrt{x}$.

Graphs of f and f^{-1}

If a point (a, b) is on the graph of an invertible function f, then (b, a) is on the graph of f^{-1}. See Fig. 1.113. Since the points (a, b) and (b, a) are symmetric with respect to the line $y = x$, the graph of f^{-1} is a reflection of f with respect to the line $y = x$. This reflection property of inverse functions gives us a way to visualize the graphs of inverse functions.

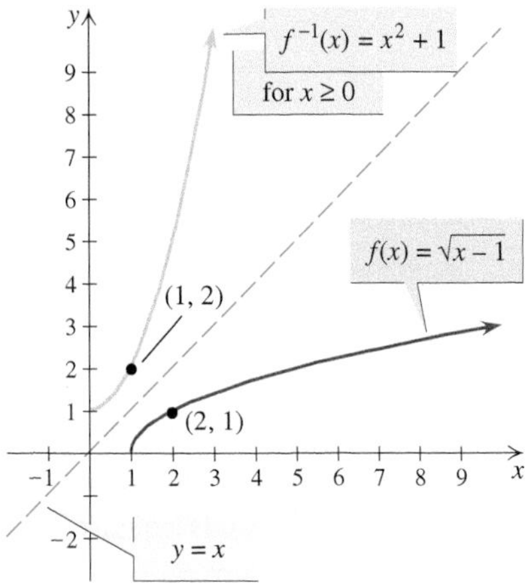

Figure 1.114

Example 8 Graphing a function and its inverse

Find the inverse of the function $f(x) = \sqrt{x - 1}$ and graph both f and f^{-1} on the same coordinate axes.

Solution

If $\sqrt{x_1 - 1} = \sqrt{x_2 - 1}$, then $x_1 = x_2$. So f is one-to-one. Since the range of $f(x) = \sqrt{x - 1}$ is $[0, \infty)$, f^{-1} must be a function with domain $[0, \infty)$. To find a formula for the inverse, interchange x and y in $y = \sqrt{x - 1}$ to get $x = \sqrt{y - 1}$. Solving this equation for y gives $y = x^2 + 1$. So $f^{-1}(x) = x^2 + 1$ for $x \geq 0$. The graph of f is a translation one unit to the right of the graph of $y = \sqrt{x}$, and the graph of f^{-1} is a translation one unit upward of the graph of $y = x^2$ for $x \geq 0$. Both graphs are shown in Fig. 1.114 along with the line $y = x$. Notice that the graph of f^{-1} is a reflection of the graph of f about the line $y = x$, the domain of f is the range of f^{-1}, and the range of f is the domain of f^{-1}. ■

Finding Inverse Functions Mentally

It is no surprise that the inverse of $f(x) = x^2$ for $x \geq 0$ is the function $f^{-1}(x) = \sqrt{x}$. For nonnegative numbers, taking the square root undoes what squaring does. It is also no surprise that the inverse of $f(x) = 3x$ is $f^{-1}(x) = x/3$ or that the inverse of $f(x) = x + 9$ is $f^{-1}(x) = x - 9$. If an invertible function involves a single operation, it is usually easy to write the inverse function because for most operations there is an inverse operation. See Table 1.4. If an invertible function involves more than one operation, we find the inverse function by applying the inverse operations in the opposite order from the order in which they appear in the original function.

Table 1.4

Function	Inverse
$f(x) = 2x$	$f^{-1}(x) = x/2$
$f(x) = x - 5$	$f^{-1}(x) = x + 5$
$f(x) = \sqrt{x}$	$f^{-1}(x) = x^2\ (x \geq 0)$
$f(x) = x^3$	$f^{-1}(x) = \sqrt[3]{x}$
$f(x) = 1/x$	$f^{-1}(x) = 1/x$
$f(x) = -x$	$f^{-1}(x) = -x$

Example 9 Finding inverses mentally

Find the inverse of each function mentally.

a. $f(x) = 2x + 1$ **b.** $g(x) = \dfrac{x^3 + 5}{2}$

Solution

a. The function $f(x) = 2x + 1$ is a composition of multiplying x by 2 and then adding 1. So the inverse function is a composition of subtracting 1 and then dividing by 2: $f^{-1}(x) = (x - 1)/2$. See Fig. 1.115.

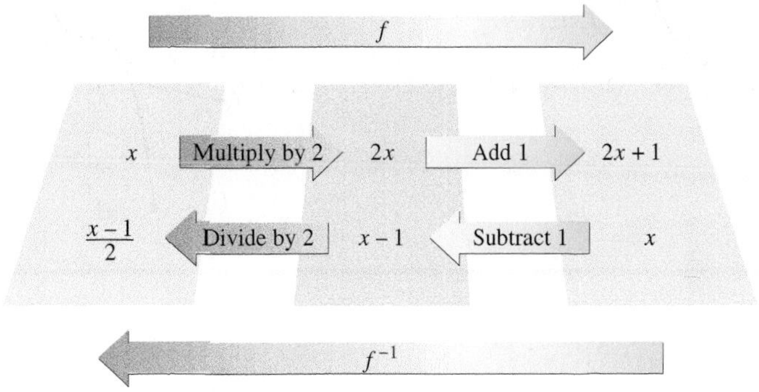

Figure 1.115

b. The function $g(x) = (x^3 + 5)/2$ is a composition of cubing x, adding 5, and dividing by 2. The inverse is a composition of multiplying by 2, subtracting 5, and then taking the cube root: $g^{-1}(x) = \sqrt[3]{2x - 5}$. See Fig. 1.116.

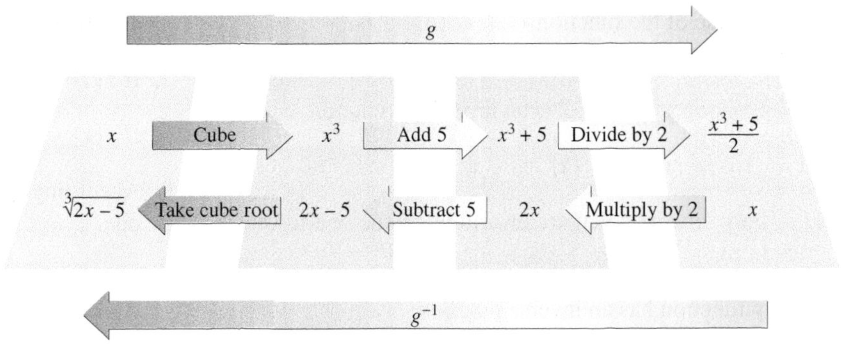

Figure 1.116

■

Function Gallery: Some Inverse Functions

Linear

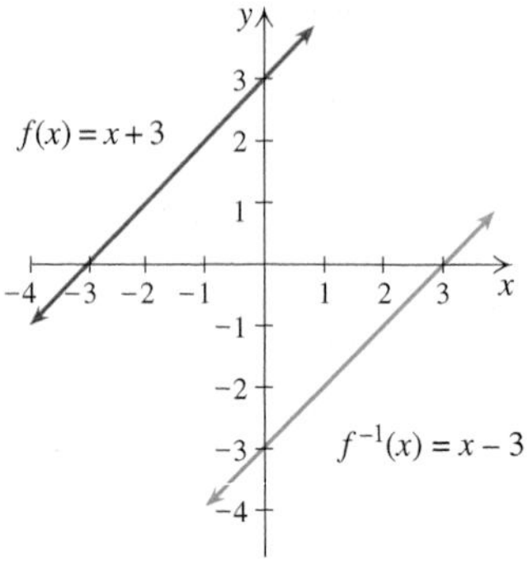

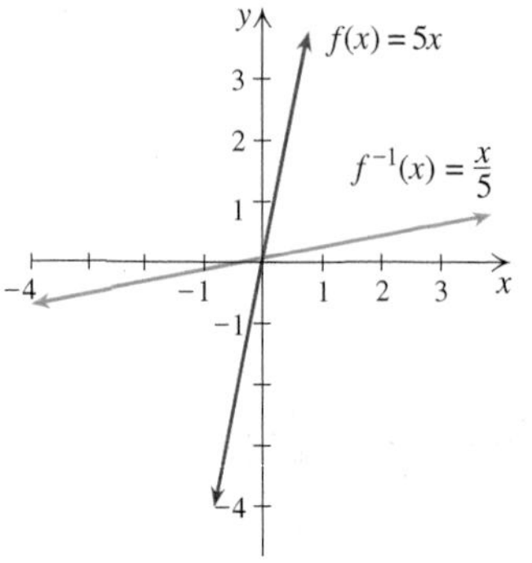

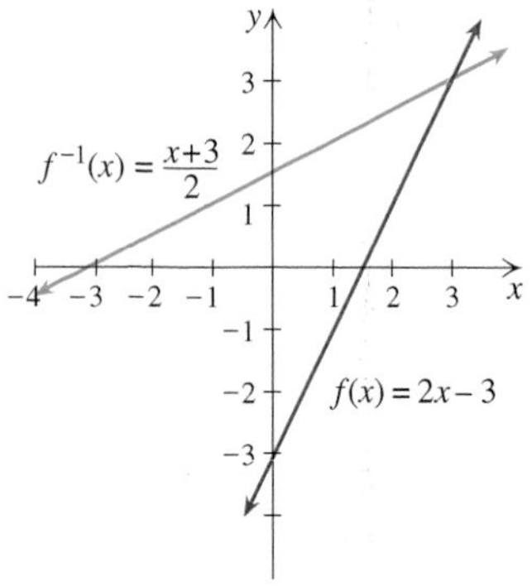

Powers and Roots

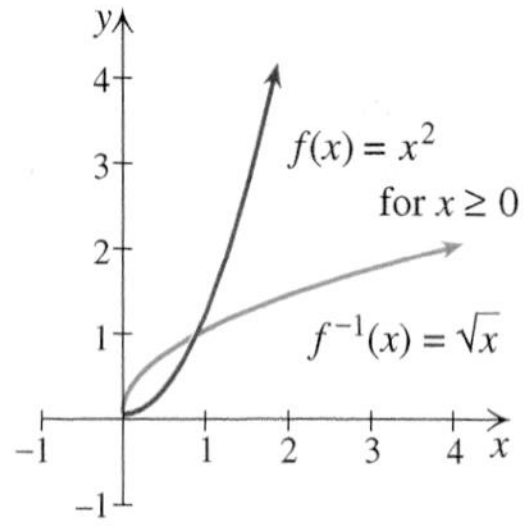

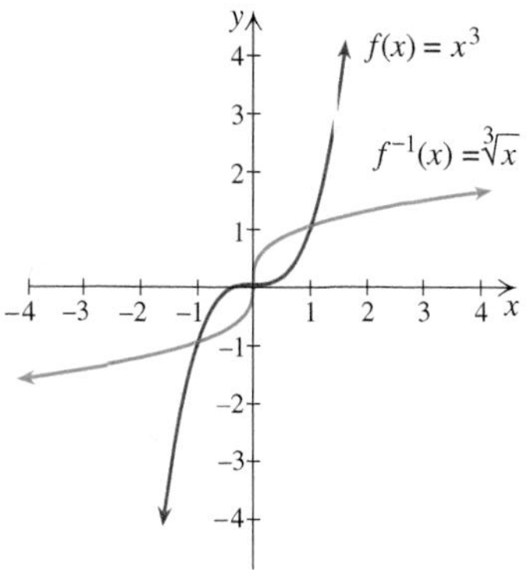

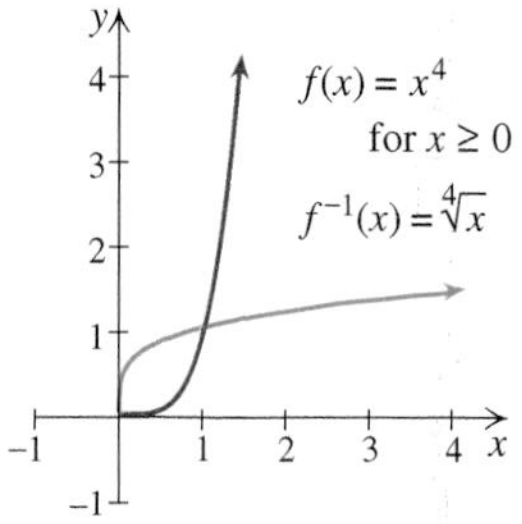

For Thought

True or False? Explain.

1. The inverse of the function $\{(2, 3), (5, 5)\}$ is $\{(5, 2), (5, 3)\}$.
2. The function $f(x) = -2$ is an invertible function.
3. If $g(x) = x^2$, then $g^{-1}(x) = \sqrt{x}$.
4. The only functions that are invertible are the one-to-one functions.
5. Every function has an inverse function.
6. The function $f(x) = x^4$ is invertible.
7. If $f(x) = 3\sqrt{x - 2}$, then $f^{-1}(x) = \frac{(x + 2)^2}{3}$ for $x \geq 0$.
8. If $f(x) = |x - 3|$, then $f^{-1}(x) = |x| + 3$.
9. According to the horizontal line test, $y = |x|$ is one-to-one.
10. The function $g(x) = -x$ is the inverse of the function $f(x) = -x$.

1.9 Exercises

Determine whether each function is one-to-one.

1. $\{(3, 3), (5, 5), (6, 6), (9, 9)\}$

2. $\{(3, 4), (5, 6), (7, 8), (9, 10), (11, 15)\}$

3. $\{(-1, 1), (1, 1), (-2, 4), (2, 4)\}$

4. $\{(3, 2), (5, 2), (7, 2)\}$

5. $\{(1, 99), (2, 98), (3, 97), (4, 96), (5, 99)\}$

6. $\{(-1, 9), (-2, 8), (-3, 7), (1, 9), (2, 8), (3, 7)\}$

Use the horizontal line test to determine whether each function is one-to-one.

7. $f(x) = x^2 - 3x$

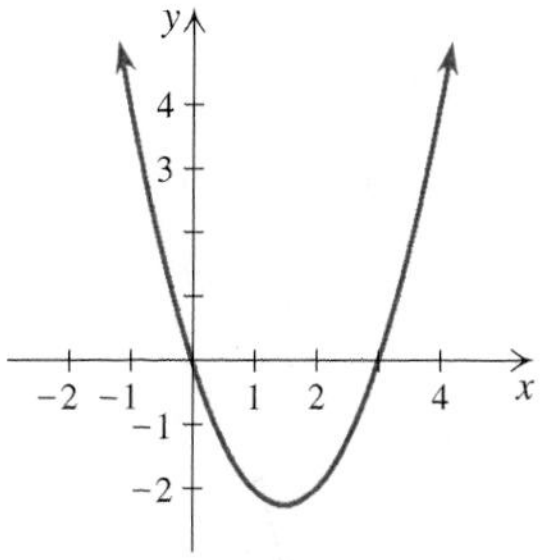

8. $g(x) = |x - 2| + 1$

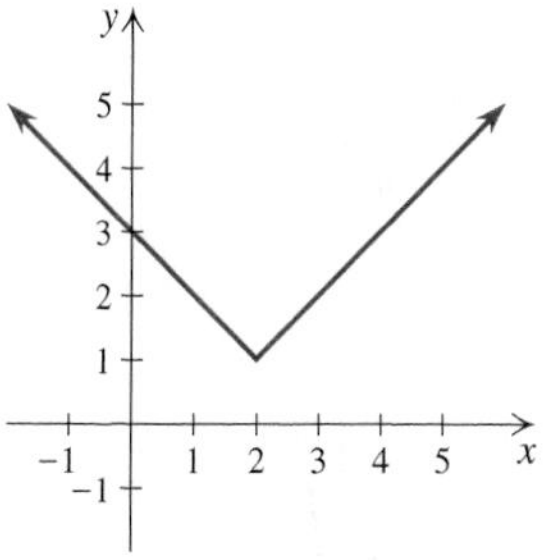

9. $y = \sqrt[3]{x} + 2$

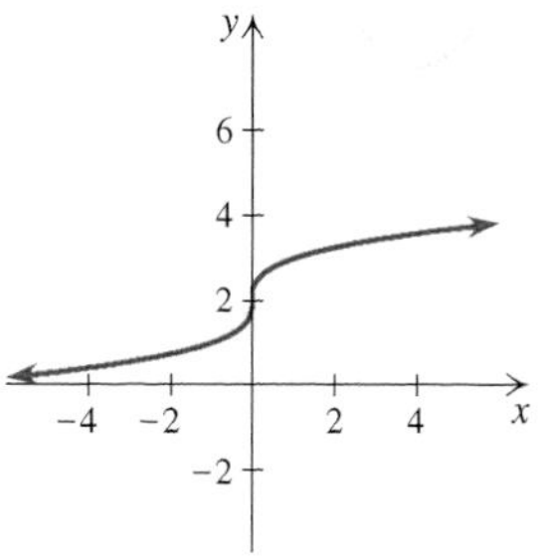

10. $y = (x - 2)^3$

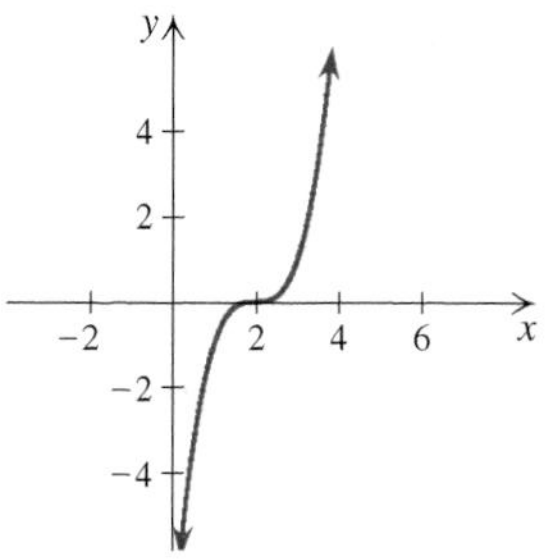

11. $y = x^3 - x$

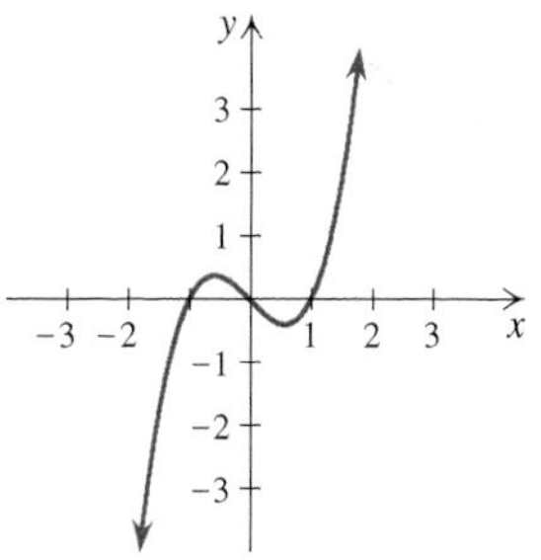

12. $y = \dfrac{1}{x}$

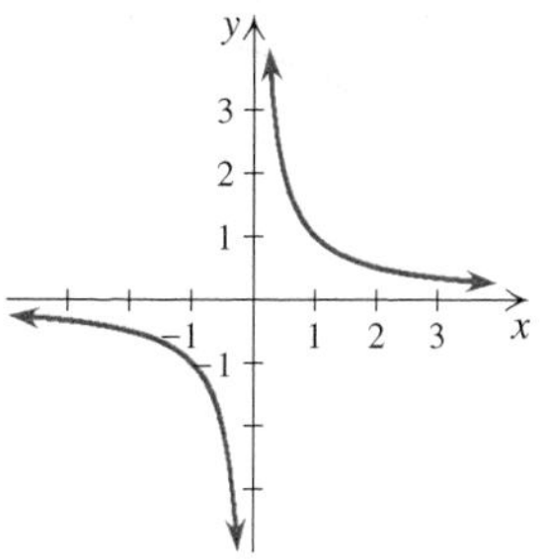

Determine whether each function is one-to-one.

13. $f(x) = 2x - 3$

14. $h(x) = 4x - 9$

15. $q(x) = \dfrac{1 - x}{x - 5}$

16. $g(x) = \dfrac{x + 2}{x - 3}$

17. $p(x) = |x + 1|$

18. $r(x) = 2|x - 1|$

19. $w(x) = x^2 + 3$

20. $v(x) = 2x^2 - 1$

21. $k(x) = \sqrt[3]{x + 9}$

22. $t(x) = \sqrt{x + 3}$

Determine whether each function is invertible. If it is invertible, find the inverse.

23. $\{(9, 3), (2, 2)\}$

24. $\{(4, 5), (5, 6)\}$

25. $\{(-1, 0), (1, 0), (5, 0)\}$

26. $\{(1, 2), (5, 2), (6, 7)\}$

27. $\{(3, 3), (2, 2), (4, 4), (7, 7)\}$

28. $\{(1, 1), (2, 4), (4, 16), (7, 49)\}$

29. $\{(1, 1), (2, 2), (4.5, 2), (5, 5)\}$

30. $\{(0, 2), (2, 0), (1, 0), (4, 6)\}$

Determine whether each function is invertible and explain your answer.

31. The function that pairs the universal product code of an item at Sears with a price.

32. The function that pairs the number of days since your birth with your age in years.

33. The function that pairs the length of a VCR tape in feet with the playing time in minutes.

34. The function that pairs the speed of your car in miles per hour with the speed in kilometers per hour.

35. The function that pairs the number of days of a hotel stay with the total cost for the stay.

36. The function that pairs the number of days that a deposit of \$100 earns interest at 6% compounded daily with the amount of interest.

For each function f, find f^{-1}, $f^{-1}(5)$, and $(f^{-1} \circ f)(2)$.

37. $f = \{(2, 1), (3, 5)\}$

38. $f = \{(-1, 5), (0, 0), (2, 6)\}$

39. $f = \{(-3, -3), (0, 5), (2, -7)\}$

40. $f = \{(3.2, 5), (2, 1.99)\}$

Determine whether each function is invertible by inspecting its graph on a graphing calculator.

41. $f(x) = (x + 0.01)(x + 0.02)(x + 0.03)$

42. $f(x) = x^3 - 0.6x^2 + 0.11x - 0.006$

43. $f(x) = |x - 2| - |5 - x|$

44. $f(x) = \sqrt[3]{0.1x + 3} + \sqrt[3]{-0.1x}$

Find the inverse of each function using the procedure for the switch-and-solve method on page 96.

45. $f(x) = 3x - 7$

46. $f(x) = -2x + 5$

47. $f(x) = 2 + \sqrt{x - 3}$

48. $f(x) = \sqrt{3x - 1}$

49. $f(x) = -x - 9$

50. $f(x) = -x + 3$

51. $f(x) = \dfrac{x + 3}{x - 5}$

52. $f(x) = \dfrac{2x - 1}{x - 6}$

53. $f(x) = -\dfrac{1}{x}$

54. $f(x) = x$

55. $f(x) = \sqrt[3]{x - 9} + 5$

56. $f(x) = \sqrt[3]{\dfrac{x}{2}} + 5$

57. $f(x) = (x - 2)^2$ for $x \geq 2$

58. $f(x) = x^2$ for $x \leq 0$

In each case find $f(g(x))$ and $g(f(x))$. Then determine whether g and f are inverse functions.

59. $f(x) = 4x + 4, g(x) = 0.25x - 1$

60. $f(x) = 20 - 5x, g(x) = -0.2x + 4$

61. $f(x) = x^2 + 1, g(x) = \sqrt{x - 1}$

62. $f(x) = \sqrt[4]{x}, g(x) = x^4$

63. $f(x) = \dfrac{1}{x} + 3, g(x) = \dfrac{1}{x - 3}$

64. $f(x) = 4 - \dfrac{1}{x}, g(x) = \dfrac{1}{4 - x}$

65. $f(x) = \sqrt[3]{\dfrac{x - 2}{5}}, g(x) = 5x^3 + 2$

66. $f(x) = x^3 - 27, g(x) = \sqrt[3]{x} + 3$

For each exercise, graph the three functions on the same screen of a graphing calculator. Enter these functions as shown without simplifying any expressions. Explain what these exercises illustrate.

67. $y_1 = \sqrt[3]{x} - 1, y_2 = (x + 1)^3, y_3 = \left(\sqrt[3]{x} - 1 + 1\right)^3$

68. $y_1 = (2x - 1)^{1/3}, y_2 = (x^3 + 1)/2,$
$y_3 = (2((x^3 + 1)/2) - 1)^{1/3}$

Determine whether each pair of functions f and g are inverses of each other.

69.

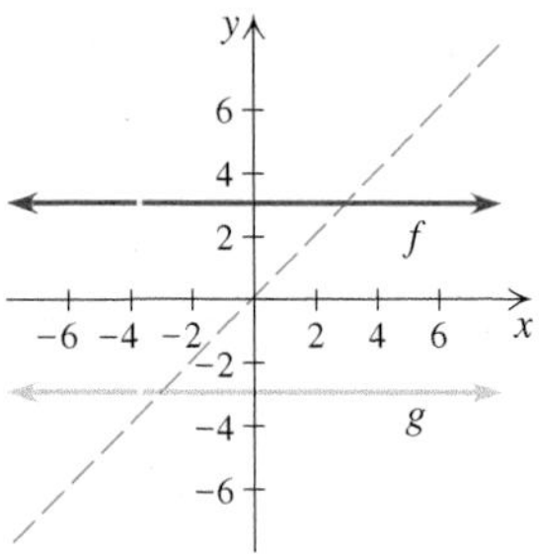

70.

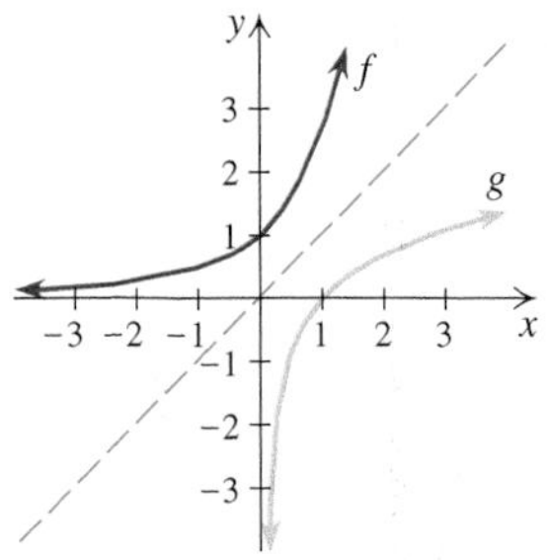

71.

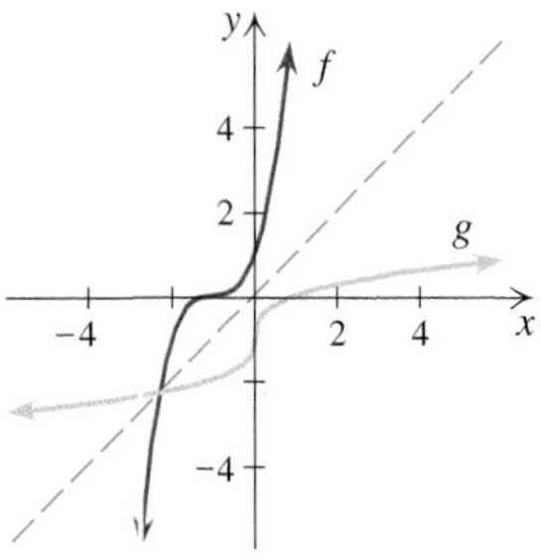

72.

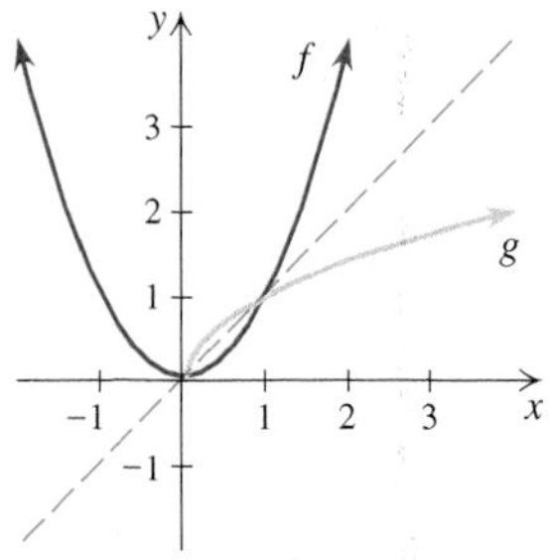

For each function f, sketch the graph of f^{-1}.

73.

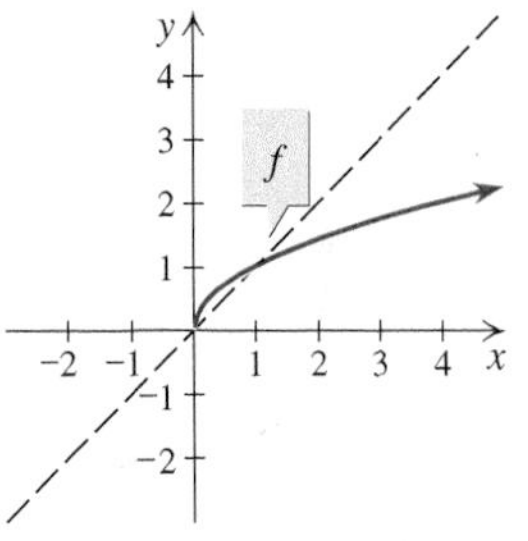

74.

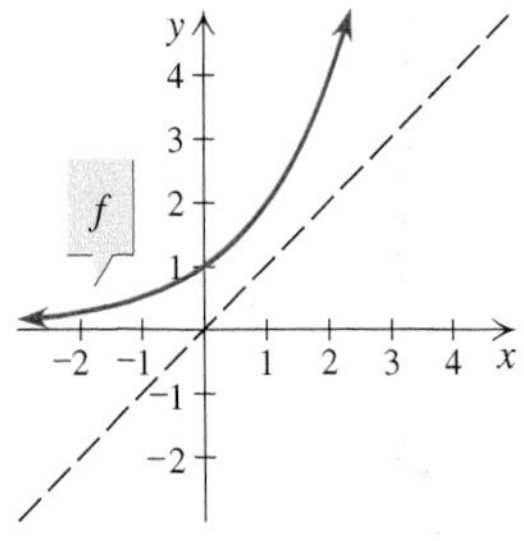

75.

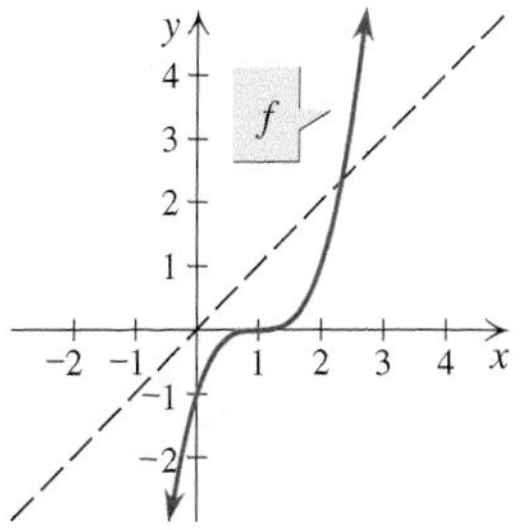

76.

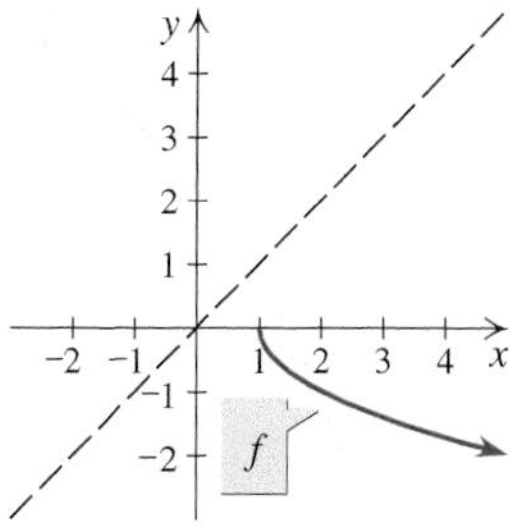

Find the inverse of each function and graph both f and f^{-1} on the same coordinate plane.

77. $f(x) = 3x + 2$

78. $f(x) = -x - 8$

79. $f(x) = x^2 - 4$ for $x \geq 0$

80. $f(x) = 1 - x^2$ for $x \geq 0$

81. $f(x) = x^3$

82. $f(x) = -x^3$

83. $f(x) = \sqrt{x} - 3$

84. $f(x) = \sqrt{x - 3}$

Find the inverse of each function mentally.

85. **a.** $f(x) = 5x$ **b.** $f(x) = x - 88$
c. $f(x) = 3x - 7$ **d.** $f(x) = 4 - 3x$
e. $f(x) = \frac{1}{2}x - 9$ **f.** $f(x) = -x$
g. $f(x) = \sqrt[3]{x} - 9$ **h.** $f(x) = 3x^3 - 7$

86. **a.** $f(x) = \frac{x}{2}$ **b.** $f(x) = x + 99$
c. $f(x) = 5x + 1$ **d.** $f(x) = 5 - 2x$
e. $f(x) = \frac{x}{3} + 6$ **f.** $f(x) = \frac{1}{x}$
g. $f(x) = \sqrt[3]{x - 9}$ **h.** $f(x) = -x^3 + 4$

Solve each problem.

87. *Price of a Car* The tax on a new car is 8% of the purchase price P. Express the total cost C as a function of the purchase price. Express the purchase price P as a function of the total cost C.

88. *Volume of a Cube* Express the volume of a cube $V(x)$ as a function of the length of a side x. Express the length of a side of a cube $S(x)$ as a function of the volume x.

89. *Rowers and Speed* The world record times in the 2000-m race are a function of the number of rowers as shown in the accompanying figure (www.cbs.sportsline.com). If r is the number of rowers and t is the time in minutes, then the formula $t = -0.39r + 7.89$ models this relationship. Is this function invertible? Find the inverse. If the time for a 2000-m race was 5.55 min, then how many rowers were probably in the boat?

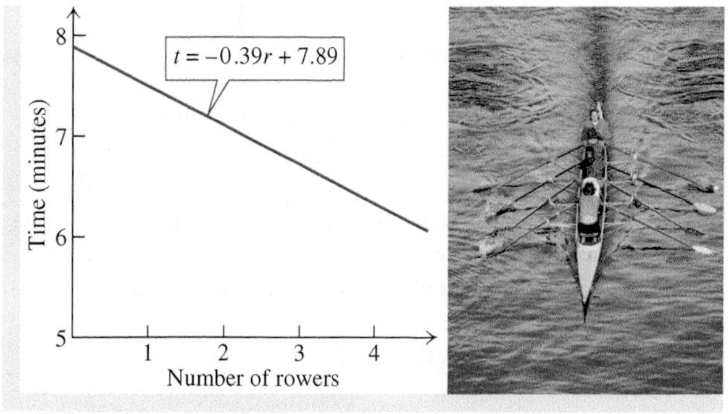

Figure for Exercise 89

90. *Temperature* The function $C = \frac{5}{9}(F - 32)$ expresses the Celsius temperature as a function of the Fahrenheit temperature. Find the inverse function. What is it used for?

91. *Landing Speed* The function $V = \sqrt{1.496w}$ expresses the landing speed V (in feet per second) as a function of the gross weight (in pounds) of the Piper Cheyenne aircraft. Find the inverse function. Use the inverse function to find the gross weight for a Piper Cheyenne for which the proper landing speed is 115 ft/sec.

92. *Poiseuille's Law* Under certain conditions, the velocity V of blood in a vessel at distance r from the center of the vessel is given by $V = 500(5.625 \times 10^{-5} - r^2)$ where $0 \leq r \leq 7.5 \times 10^{-3}$. Write r as a function of V.

93. *Depreciation Rate* The depreciation rate r for a \$50,000 new car is given by the function $r = 1 - \left(\frac{V}{50,000}\right)^{1/5}$, where V is the value of the car when it is five years old.
a. What is the depreciation rate for a \$50,000 BMW that is worth \$28,000 after 5 years?
b. Write V as a function of r.

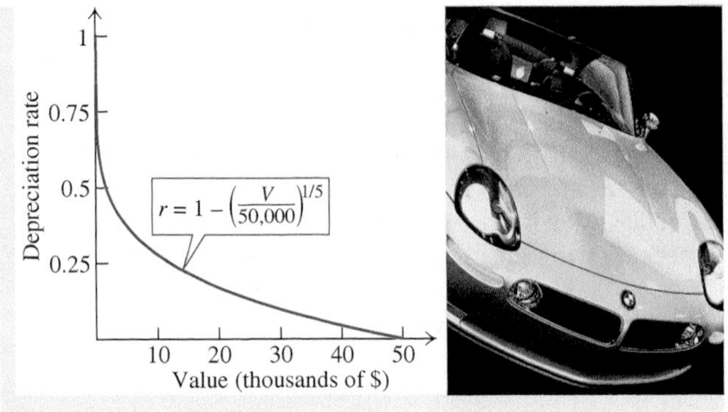

Figure for Exercise 93

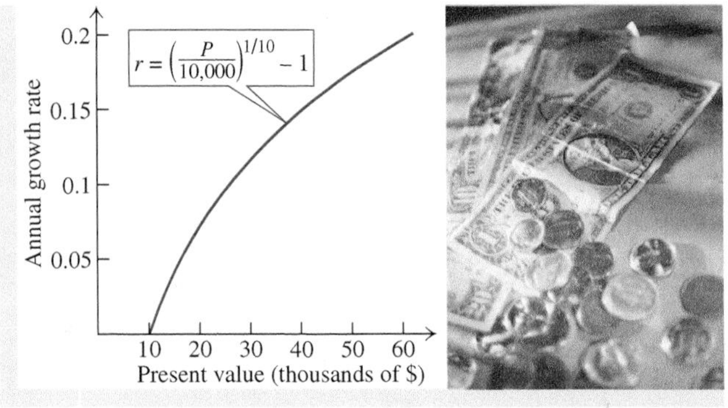

Figure for Exercise 94

94. *Annual Growth Rate* One measurement of the quality of a mutual fund is its average annual growth rate over the last 10 years. The function $r = \left(\frac{P}{10{,}000}\right)^{1/10} - 1$ expresses the average annual growth rate r as a function of the present value P of an investment of \$10,000 made 10 years ago. An investment of \$10,000 in Fidelity's Contrafund in 1995 was worth \$36,555 in 2005 (Fidelity Investments, www.fidelity.com). What was the annual growth rate for that period? Write P as a function of r.

Thinking Outside the Box IX

Costly Computers A school district purchased x computers at y dollars each for a total of \$640,000. Both x and y are whole numbers and neither is a multiple of 10. Find the absolute value of the difference between x and y.

1.9 Pop Quiz

1. Is the function $\{(1, 3), (4, 5), (2, 3)\}$ invertible?

2. If $f = \{(5, 4), (3, 6), (2, 5)\}$, then what is $f^{-1}(5)$?

3. If $f(x) = 2x$, then what is $f^{-1}(8)$?

4. Is $f(x) = x^4$ a one-to-one function?

5. If $f(x) = 2x - 1$, then what is $f^{-1}(x)$?

6. If $g(x) = \sqrt[3]{x + 1} - 4$, then what is $g^{-1}(x)$?

7. Find $(h \circ j)(x)$ if $h(x) = x^3 - 5$ and $j(x) = \sqrt[3]{x + 5}$.

Highlights

1.1 Real Numbers and Their Properties

Rationals and Irrationals	Every real number is either rational (a ratio of integers) or irrational (not a ratio of integers).	Rational: $1, 2/3, -44.7$ Irrational: $\sqrt{2}, \sqrt{7}, \pi$
Commutative Property	Addition: $a + b = b + a$ Multiplication: $ab = ba$	$3 + 4 = 4 + 3$ $5 \cdot 7 = 7 \cdot 5$
Associative Property	Addition: $a + (b + c) = (a + b) + c$ Multiplication: $a(bc) = (ab)c$	$3 + (4 + 5) = (3 + 4) + 5$ $3(4 \cdot 5) = (3 \cdot 4)5$
Distributive	$a(b + c) = ab + ac$	$5(6 + 7) = 5 \cdot 6 + 5 \cdot 7$

Absolute Value	A number's distance from zero on the number line If $a \geq 0$, then $\|a\| = a$. If $a < 0$, then $\|a\| = -a$.	$\|5\| = 5, \|-5\| = 5, \|0\| = 0$
Distance Between Two Real Numbers	The distance between a and b on a number line is $\|a - b\|$.	Distance between -5 and 4 is $\|-5 - 4\|$ or 9.
Absolute Value Equations	If $k > 0$, then $\|x\| = k \Leftrightarrow x = k$ or $x = -k$. If $k < 0$, then $\|x\| = k$ has no solution. If $k = 0$, then $\|x\| = k \Leftrightarrow x = 0$.	$\|x\| = 5 \Leftrightarrow x = \pm 5$ $\|x + 2\| = -1$ has no solution. $\|x - 3\| = 0 \Leftrightarrow x = 3$

1.2 Linear and Absolute Value Inequalities

Linear Inequalities	The inequality symbol is reversed if the inequality is multiplied or divided by a negative number.	$4 - 2x > 10$ $-2x > 6$ $x < -3$
Absolute Value Inequalities	$\|x\| > k \ (k > 0) \Leftrightarrow x > k$ or $x < -k$ $\|x\| < k \ (k > 0) \Leftrightarrow -k < x < k$ $\|x\| \leq 0 \Leftrightarrow x = 0$ $\|x\| \geq 0 \Leftrightarrow x$ is any real number	$\|y\| > 1 \Leftrightarrow y > 1$ or $y < -1$ $\|z\| < 2 \Leftrightarrow -2 < z < 2$ $\|2b - 5\| \leq 0 \Leftrightarrow 2b - 5 = 0$ All real numbers satisfy $\|3s - 7\| \geq 0$.

1.3 Equations and Graphs in Two Variables

Distance Formula	Distance between (x_1, y_1) and (x_2, y_2) is $\sqrt{(x_2 - x_1)^2 + (y_2 - y_1)^2}$.	For $(1, 2)$ and $(4, -2)$, $\sqrt{(4 - 1)^2 + (-2 - 2)^2} = 5$.
Midpoint Formula	The midpoint of the line segment with endpoints (x_1, y_1) and (x_2, y_2) is $\left(\frac{x_1 + x_2}{2}, \frac{y_1 + y_2}{2}\right)$.	For $(0, -4)$ and $(6, 2)$, $\left(\frac{0 + 6}{2}, \frac{-4 + 2}{2}\right) = (3, -1)$.
Equation of a Circle	The graph of $(x - h)^2 + (y - k)^2 = r^2 (r > 0)$ is a circle with center (h, k) and radius r.	Circle: $(x - 1)^2 + (y + 2)^2 = 9$ Center $(1, -2)$, radius 3
Linear Equation: Standard Form	$Ax + By = C$ where A and B are not both zero, $x = h$ is a vertical line, $y = k$ is a horizontal line.	$2x + 3y = 6$ is a line. $x = 5$ is a vertical line. $y = 7$ is a horizontal line.

1.4 Linear Equations in Two Variables

Slope Formula	The slope of a line through (x_1, y_1) and (x_2, y_2) is $(y_2 - y_1)/(x_2 - x_1)$ provided $x_1 \neq x_2$.	$(1, 2), (3, -6)$ slope $\frac{-6 - 2}{3 - 1} = -4$
Slope-Intercept Form	$y = mx + b$, slope m, y-intercept $(0, b)$ y is a linear function of x.	$y = 2x + 5$, slope 2, y-intercept $(0, 5)$
Point-Slope Form	The line through (x_1, y_1) with slope m is $y - y_1 = m(x - x_1)$.	Point $(-3, 2)$, $m = 5$ $y - 2 = 5(x - (-3))$
Parallel Lines	Two nonvertical lines are parallel if and only if their slopes are equal.	$y = 7x - 1$ and $y = 7x + 4$ are parallel.
Perpendicular Lines	Two lines with slopes m_1 and m_2 are perpendicular if and only if $m_1 m_2 = -1$.	$y = \frac{1}{2}x + 4$ and $y = -2x - 3$ are perpendicular.

1.5 Functions

Relation	Any set of ordered pairs	$\{(1, 5), (1, 3), (3, 5)\}$
Function	A relation in which no two ordered pairs have the same first coordinate and different second coordinates	$\{(1, 5), (2, 3), (3, 5)\}$
Vertical Line Test	If no vertical line crosses a graph more than once then the graph is a function.	Function 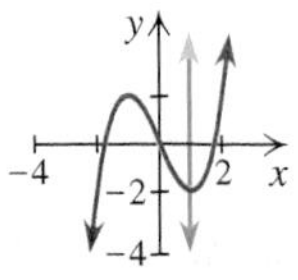 Not function 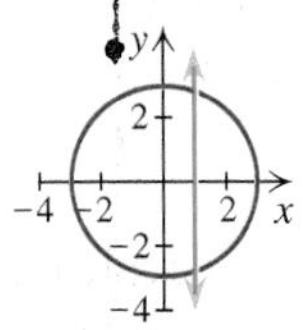
Average Rate of Change	The slope of the line through $(a, f(a))$ and $(b, f(b))$: $\frac{f(b) - f(a)}{b - a}$	Average rate of change of $f(x) = x^2$ on $[2, 9]$ is $\frac{9^2 - 2^2}{9 - 2}$.
Difference Quotient	Average rate of change of f on $[x, x + h]$: $\frac{f(x + h) - f(x)}{h}$	$f(x) = x^2$, difference quotient $= \frac{(x + h)^2 - x^2}{h} = 2x + h$

1.6 Graphs of Relations and Functions

Graph of a Relation	An illustration of all ordered pairs of a relation	Graph of $y = x + 1$ shows all ordered pairs in this function.
Circle	A circle is not the graph of a function	Since $(0, \pm 2)$ satisfies $x^2 + y^2 = 4$, it is not a function.
Increasing, Decreasing, or Constant	When going from left to right, a function is increasing if its graph is rising, decreasing if its graph is falling, constant if it is staying the same.	$y = \lvert x \rvert$ is increasing on $(0, \infty)$ and decreasing on $(-\infty, 0)$ $y = 5$ is constant on $(-\infty, \infty)$

1.7 Families of Functions, Transformations, and Symmetry

Transformations of $y = f(x)$	Horizontal: $y = f(x - h)$ Vertical: $y = f(x) + k$ Stretching: $y = af(x)$ for $a > 1$ Shrinking: $y = af(x)$ for $0 < a < 1$ Reflection: $y = -f(x)$	$y = (x - 4)^2$ $y = x^2 + 9$ $y = 3x^2$ $y = 0.5x^2$ $y = -x^2$
Family of Functions	All functions of the form $f(x) = af(x - h) + k$ $(a \neq 0)$ for a given function $y = f(x)$.	The square root family: $y = a\sqrt{x - h} + k$
Even Function	Graph is symmetric with respect to y-axis. $f(-x) = f(x)$	$f(x) = x^2$, $g(x) = \lvert x \rvert$
Odd Function	Graph is symmetric about the origin. $f(-x) = -f(x)$	$f(x) = x$, $g(x) = x^3$
Inequalities	$f(x) > 0$ is satisfied on all intervals where the graph of $y = f(x)$ is above the x-axis $f(x) < 0$ is satisfied on all intervals where the graph of $y = f(x)$ is below the x-axis	$4 - x^2 > 0$ on $(-2, 2)$ $4 - x^2 < 0$ on $(-\infty, -2) \cup (2, \infty)$

1.8 Operations with Functions

Sum	$(f + g)(x) = f(x) + g(x)$	$f(x) = x^2 - 4, g(x) = x + 2$ $(f + g)(x) = x^2 + x - 2$
Difference	$(f - g)(x) = f(x) - g(x)$	$(f - g)(x) = x^2 - x - 6$
Product	$(f \cdot g)(x) = f(x) \cdot g(x)$	$(f \cdot g)(x) = x^3 + 2x^2 - 4x - 8$
Quotient	$(f/g)(x) = f(x)/g(x)$	$(f/g)(x) = x - 2$
Composition	$(f \circ g)(x) = f(g(x))$	$(f \circ g)(x) = (x + 2)^2 - 4$ $(g \circ f)(x) = x^2 - 2$

1.9 Inverse Functions

One-to-One Function	A function that has no two ordered pairs with different first coordinates and the same second coordinates	$\{(1, 2), (3, 5), (6, 9)\}$ $g(x) = x + 3$ $f(x) = x^2$ is not one-to-one.
Inverse Function	A one-to-one function has an inverse. The inverse function has the same ordered pairs, with the coordinates reversed.	$f = \{(1, 2), (3, 5), (6, 9)\}$ $f^{-1} = \{(2, 1), (5, 3), (9, 6)\}$ $g(x) = x + 3, g^{-1}(x) = x - 3$
Horizontal Line Test	If there is a horizontal line that crosses the graph of f more than once, then f is not invertible.	$y = 4$ crosses $f(x) = x^2$ twice, so f is not invertible.
Graph of f^{-1}	Reflect the graph of f about the line $y = x$ to get the graph of f^{-1}.	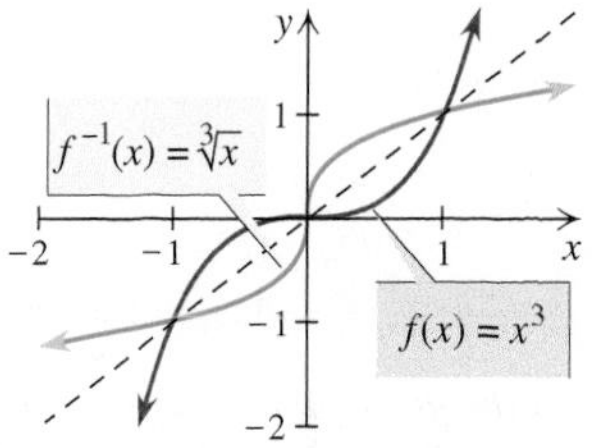

Chapter 1 Review Exercises

Determine whether each statement is true or false and explain your answer.

1. Every real number is a rational number.

2. Zero is neither rational nor irrational.

3. There are no negative integers.

4. Every repeating decimal number is a rational number.

5. The terminating decimal numbers are irrational numbers.

6. The number $\sqrt{289}$ is a rational number.

7. Zero is a natural number.

8. The multiplicative inverse of 8 is 0.125.

9. The reciprocal of 0.333 is 3.

10. The real number π is irrational.

11. The additive inverse of 0.5 is 0.

12. The distributive property is used in adding like terms.

Solve each equation.

13. $|3q - 4| = 2$

14. $|2v - 1| = 3$

15. $|2h - 3| = 0$

16. $4|x - 3| = 0$

17. $|5 - x| = -1$

18. $|3y - 1| = -2$

Solve each inequality. State the solution set using interval notation and graph the solution set.

19. $4x - 1 > 3x + 2$

20. $6(x - 3) < 5(x + 4)$

21. $5 - 2x > -3$

22. $7 - x > -6$

23. $\frac{1}{2}x - \frac{1}{3} > x + 2$

24. $0.06x + 1000 > x + 60$

25. $-2 < \frac{x - 3}{2} \leq 5$

26. $-1 \leq \frac{3 - 2x}{4} < 3$

27. $3 - 4x < 1$ and $5 + 3x < 8$

28. $-3x < 6$ and $2x + 1 > -1$

29. $-2x < 8$ or $3x > -3$

30. $1 - x < 6$ or $-5 + x < 1$

31. $|x - 3| > 2$

32. $|4 - x| \leq 3$

33. $|2x - 7| \leq 0$

34. $|6 - 5x| < 0$

35. $|7 - 3x| > -4$

36. $|4 - 3x| \geq 1$

Sketch the graph of each equation. For the circles, state the center and the radius. For the lines state the intercepts.

37. $x^2 + y^2 = 25$

38. $(x - 2)^2 + y^2 = 1$

39. $x^2 + 4x + y^2 = 0$

40. $x^2 - 6x = 2y - y^2 - 1$

41. $x + y = 25$

42. $2x - y = 40$

43. $y = 3x - 4$

44. $y = -\frac{1}{2}x + 4$

45. $x = 5$

46. $y = 6$

Solve each problem.

47. Find the exact distance between $(-3, 1)$ and $(2, 4)$.

48. Find the midpoint of the line segment with endpoints $(-1, 1)$ and $(1, 0)$.

49. Write in standard form the equation of the circle that has center $(-3, 5)$ and radius $\sqrt{3}$.

50. Find the center and radius for the circle $x^2 + y^2 = x - 2y + 1$.

51. Find the x- and y-intercepts for the graph of $3x - 4y = 12$.

52. What is the y-intercept for the graph of $y = 5$?

53. Find the slope of the line that goes through $(3, -6)$ and $(-1, 2)$.

54. Find the slope of the line $3x - 4y = 9$.

55. Find the equation (in slope-intercept form) for the line through $(-2, 3)$ and $(5, -1)$.

56. Find the equation (in standard form using only integers) for the line through $(-1, -3)$ and $(2, -1)$.

57. Find the equation (in standard form using only integers) for the line through $(2, -4)$ that is perpendicular to $3x + y = -5$.

58. Find the equation (in slope-intercept form) for the line through $(2, -5)$ that is parallel to $2x - 3y = 5$.

Graph each set of ordered pairs. State the domain and range of each relation. Determine whether each set is a function.

59. $\{(0, 0), (1, 1), (-2, -2)\}$

60. $\{(0, -3), (1, -1), (2, 1), (2, 3)\}$

61. $\{(x, y) | y = 3 - x\}$

62. $\{(x, y) | 2x + y = 5\}$

63. $\{(x, y) | x = 2\}$

64. $\{(x, y) | y = 3\}$

65. $\{(x, y) | x^2 + y^2 = 0.01\}$

66. $\{(x, y) | x^2 + y^2 = 2x - 4y\}$

67. $\{(x, y) | x = y^2 + 1\}$

68. $\{(x, y) | y = |x - 2|\}$

69. $\{(x, y) | y = \sqrt{x} - 3\}$

70. $\{(x, y) | x = \sqrt{y}\}$

Let $f(x) = x^2 + 3$ and $g(x) = 2x - 7$. Find and simplify each expression.

71. $f(-3)$

72. $g(3)$

73. $g(12)$

74. $f(-1)$

75. x, if $f(x) = 19$

76. x, if $g(x) = 9$

77. $(g \circ f)(-3)$

78. $(f \circ g)(3)$

79. $(f + g)(2)$

80. $(f - g)(-2)$

81. $(f \cdot g)(-1)$

82. $(f/g)(4)$

83. $f(g(2))$

84. $g(f(-2))$

85. $(f \circ g)(x)$

86. $(g \circ f)(x)$

87. $(f \circ f)(x)$

88. $(g \circ g)(x)$

89. $f(a + 1)$

90. $g(a + 2)$

91. $\dfrac{f(3 + h) - f(3)}{h}$

92. $\dfrac{g(5 + h) - g(5)}{h}$

93. $\dfrac{f(x + h) - f(x)}{h}$

94. $\dfrac{g(x + h) - g(x)}{h}$

95. $g\left(\dfrac{x + 7}{2}\right)$

96. $f\left(\sqrt{x - 3}\right)$

97. $g^{-1}(x)$

98. $g^{-1}(-3)$

Use transformations to graph each pair of functions on the same coordinate plane.

99. $f(x) = \sqrt{x}, g(x) = 2\sqrt{x + 3}$

100. $f(x) = \sqrt{x}, g(x) = -2\sqrt{x} + 3$

101. $f(x) = |x|, g(x) = -2|x + 2| + 4$

102. $f(x) = |x|, g(x) = \dfrac{1}{2}|x - 1| - 3$

103. $f(x) = x^2, g(x) = \dfrac{1}{2}(x - 2)^2 + 1$

104. $f(x) = x^2, g(x) = -2x^2 + 4$

For each exercise, graph the function by transforming the given graph of $y = f(x)$.

105. $y = 2f(x - 2) + 1$

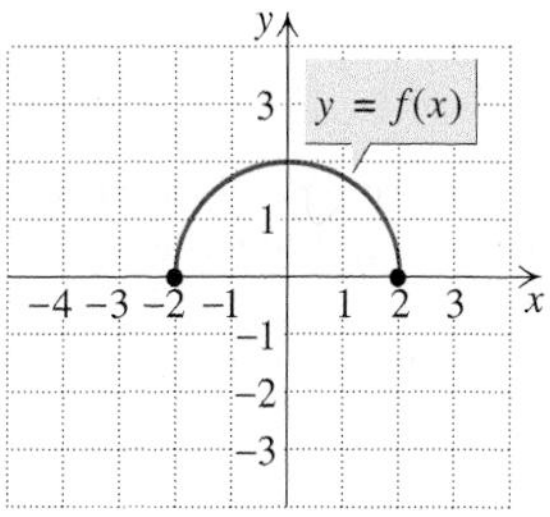

106. $y = 2f(x + 3) - 1$

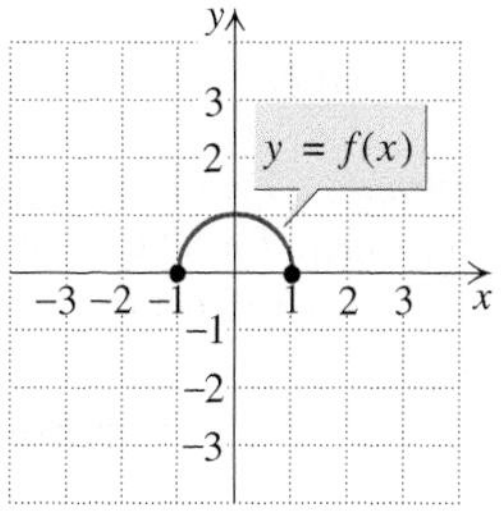

107. $y = -f(x + 1) - 3$

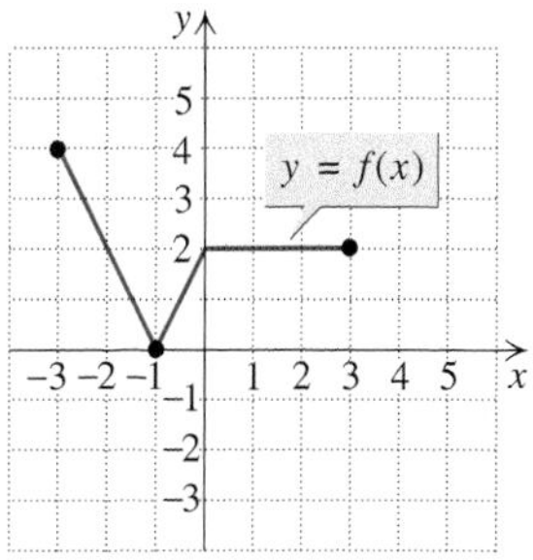

108. $y = -f(x - 1) + 2$

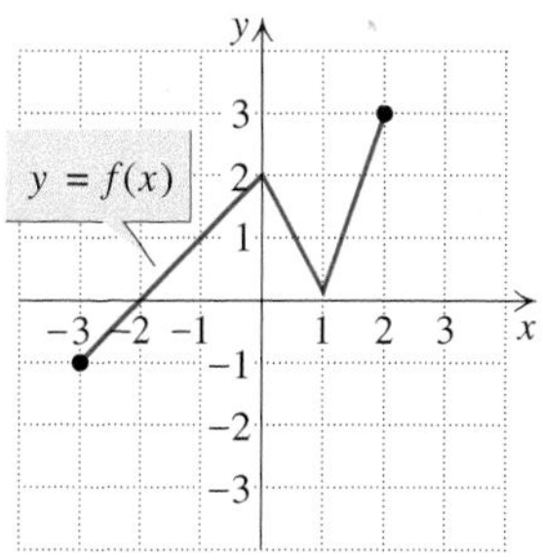

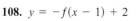

109. $y = -2f(x + 2)$

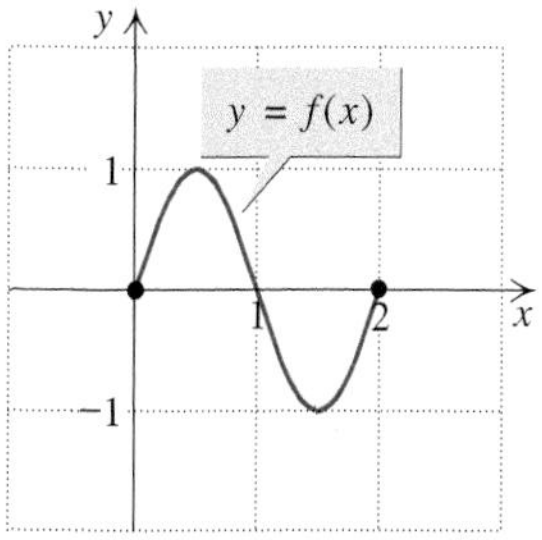

110. $y = -3f(x) + 1$

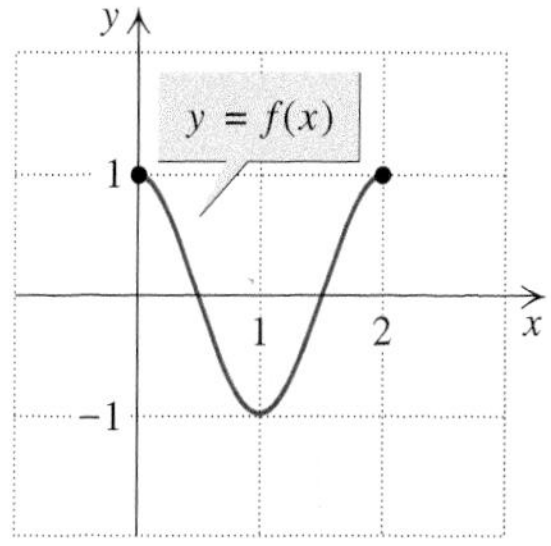

111. $y = -2f(x) + 3$

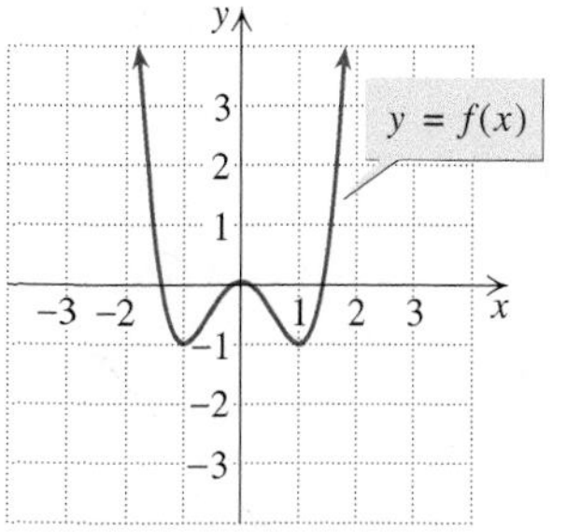

112. $y = 4f(x - 1) + 3$

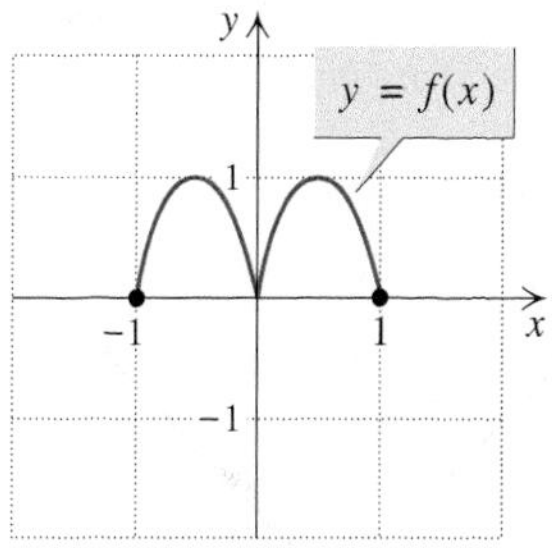

Let $f(x) = \sqrt[3]{x}$, $g(x) = x - 4$, $h(x) = x/3$, and $j(x) = x^2$. Write each function as a composition of the appropriate functions chosen from f, g, h, and j.

113. $F(x) = \sqrt[3]{x - 4}$

114. $G(x) = -4 + \sqrt[3]{x}$

115. $H(x) = \sqrt[3]{\dfrac{x^2 - 4}{3}}$

116. $M(x) = \left(\dfrac{x - 4}{3}\right)^2$

117. $N(x) = \dfrac{1}{3}x^{2/3}$

118. $P(x) = x^2 - 16$

119. $R(x) = \dfrac{x^2}{3} - 4$

120. $Q(x) = x^2 - 8x + 16$

Find the difference quotient for each function and simplify it.

121. $f(x) = -5x + 9$

122. $f(x) = \sqrt{x - 7}$

123. $f(x) = \dfrac{1}{2x}$

124. $f(x) = -5x^2 + x$

Sketch the graph of each function and state its domain and range. Determine the intervals on which the function is increasing, decreasing, or constant.

125. $f(x) = \sqrt{100 - x^2}$

126. $f(x) = -\sqrt{7 - x^2}$

127. $f(x) = \begin{cases} -x^2 & \text{for } x \le 0 \\ x^2 & \text{for } x > 0 \end{cases}$

128. $f(x) = \begin{cases} x^2 & \text{for } x \le 0 \\ x & \text{for } 0 < x \le 4 \end{cases}$

129. $f(x) = \begin{cases} -x - 4 & \text{for } x \le -2 \\ -|x| & \text{for } -2 < x < 2 \\ x - 4 & \text{for } x \ge 2 \end{cases}$

130. $f(x) = \begin{cases} (x + 1)^2 - 1 & \text{for } x \le -1 \\ -1 & \text{for } -1 < x < 1 \\ (x - 1)^2 - 1 & \text{for } x \ge 1 \end{cases}$

Each of the following graphs is from the absolute-value family. Construct a function for each graph and state the domain and range of the function.

131.

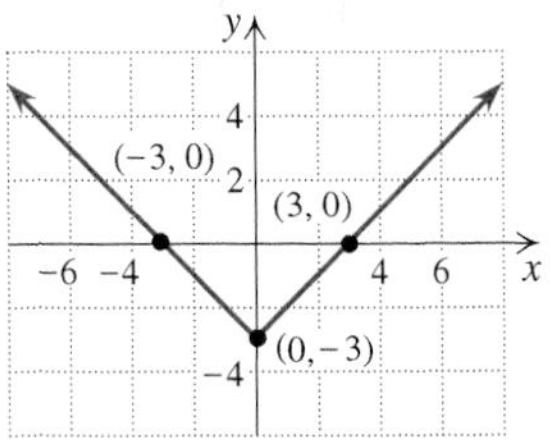

132.

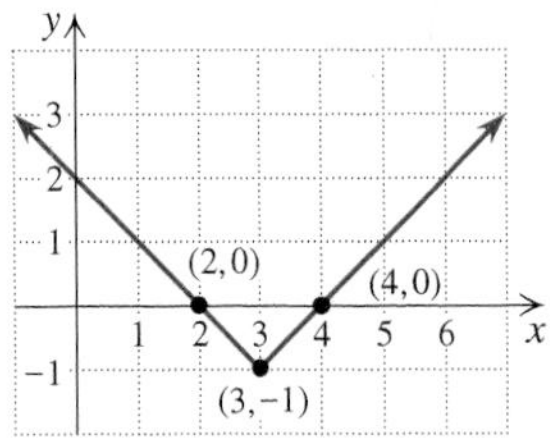

133.

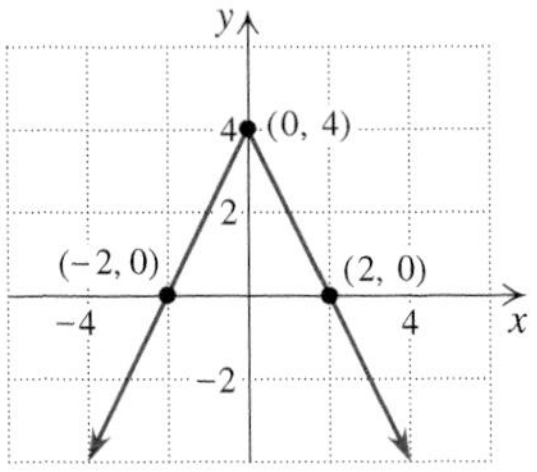

134.

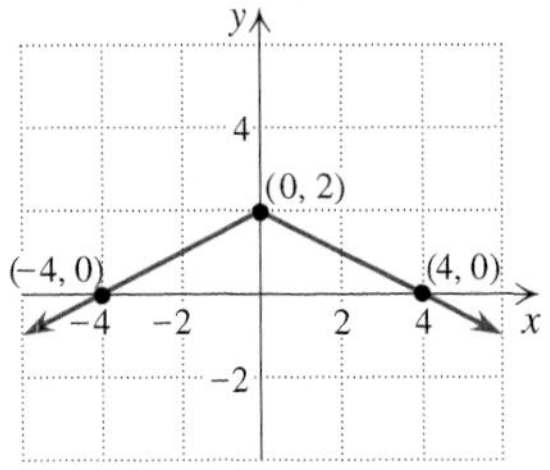

135.

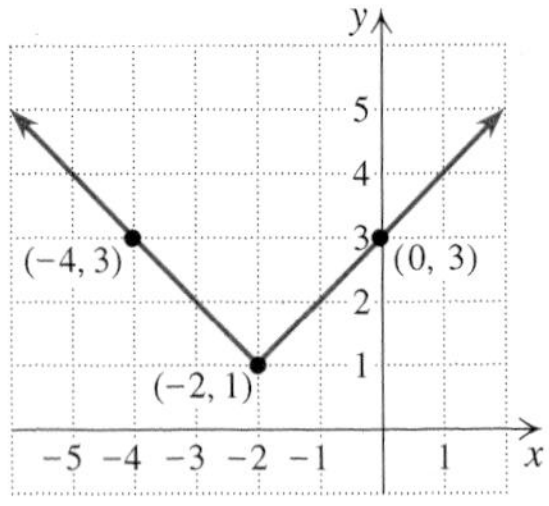

136.

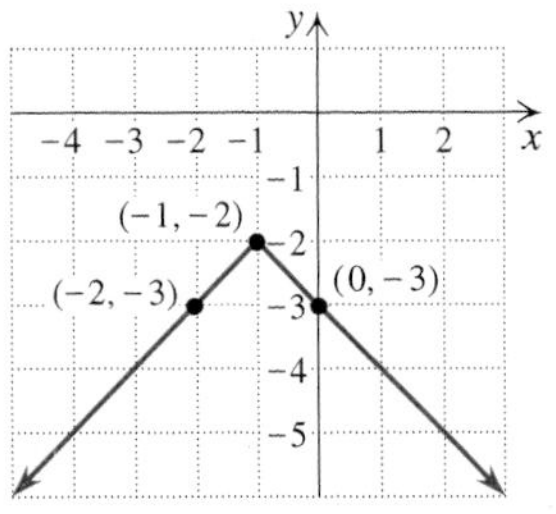

Determine whether the graph of each function is symmetric with respect to the y-axis or the origin.

137. $f(x) = x^4 - 9x^2$

138. $f(x) = |x| - 99$

139. $f(x) = -x^3 - 5x$

140. $f(x) = \dfrac{15}{x}$

141. $f(x) = -x + 1$

142. $f(x) = |x - 1|$

143. $f(x) = \sqrt{x^2}$

144. $f(x) = \sqrt{16 - x^2}$

Graph each pair of functions on the same coordinate plane. What is the relationship between the functions in each pair?

145. $f(x) = \sqrt{x + 3}$, $g(x) = x^2 - 3$ for $x \ge 0$

146. $f(x) = (x - 2)^3$, $g(x) = \sqrt[3]{x} + 2$

147. $f(x) = 2x - 4$, $g(x) = \dfrac{1}{2}x + 2$

148. $f(x) = -\dfrac{1}{2}x + 4$, $g(x) = -2x + 8$

Determine whether each function is invertible. If the function is invertible, then find the inverse function, and state the domain and range of the inverse function.

149. $\{(\pi, 0), (\pi/2, 1), (2\pi/3, 0)\}$

150. $\{(-2, 1/3), (-3, 1/4), (-4, 1/5)\}$

151. $f(x) = 3x - 21$

152. $f(x) = 3|x|$

153. $y = \sqrt{9 - x^2}$

154. $y = 7 - x$

155. $f(x) = \sqrt{x - 9}$

156. $f(x) = \sqrt{x} - 9$

157. $f(x) = \dfrac{x - 7}{x + 5}$

158. $f(x) = \dfrac{2x - 3}{5 - x}$

159. $f(x) = x^2 + 1$ for $x \le 0$

160. $f(x) = (x + 3)^4$ for $x \ge 0$

Solve each problem.

161. *Turning a Profit* Mary Beth buys roses for \$1.20 each and sells them for \$2 each at an outdoor market where she rents space for \$40 per day. She buys and sells x roses per day. Construct her daily cost, revenue, and profit functions. How many roses must she sell to make a profit?

162. *Tin Can* The surface area S and volume V for a can with a top and bottom are given by

$$S = 2\pi r^2 + 2\pi rh \quad \text{and} \quad V = \pi r^2 h,$$

where r is the radius and h is the height. Suppose that a can has a volume of 1 ft^3.

a. Write its height as a function of its radius.

b. Write its radius as a function of its height.

c. Write its surface area as a function of its radius.

163. *Dropping the Ball* A ball is dropped from a height of 64 feet. Its height h (in feet) is a function of time t (in seconds), where $h = -16t^2 + 64$ for t in the interval $[0, 2]$. Find the inverse of this function and state the domain of the inverse function.

164. *Sales Tax Function* If S is the subtotal in dollars of your groceries before a 5% sales tax, then the function $T = 1.05S$ gives the total cost in dollars including tax. Write S as a function of T.

165. Write the diameter of a circle, d, as a function of its area, A.

166. *Circle Inscribed in a Square* A cylindrical pipe with an outer radius r must fit snugly through a square hole in a wall. Write the area of the square as a function of the radius of the pipe.

167. *Load on a Spring* When a load of 5 lb is placed on a spring, its length is 6 in., and when a load of 9 lb is placed on the spring, its length is 8 in. What is the average rate of change of the length of the spring as the load varies from 5 lb to 9 lb?

168. *Changing Speed of a Dragster* Suppose that 2 sec after starting, a dragster is traveling 40 mph, and 5 sec after starting, the dragster is traveling 130 mph. What is the average rate of change of the speed of the dragster over the time interval from 2 sec to 5 sec? What are the units for this measurement?

Thinking Outside the Box X

Nines Nine people applying for credit at the Highway 99 Loan Company listed nine different incomes each containing a different number of digits. Each of the nine incomes was a whole number of dollars and the maximum income was a nine-digit number. The loan officer found that the arithmetic mean of the nine incomes was \$123,456,789. What are the nine incomes?

Concepts of Calculus

Limits

In algebra we can evaluate algebraic expressions for any acceptable value of the variable. The following tables show values of $x^2 + 5$ for certain values of x.

x	2.9	2.99	2.999
$x^2 + 5$	13.41	13.9401	13.994001

x	3.1	3.01	3.001
$x^2 + 5$	14.61	14.0601	14.006001

In calculus we look for trends. What happens to the value of $x^2 + 5$ as x gets closer and closer to 3? From the tables we see that the closer x is to 3, the closer $x^2 + 5$ is to 14. We say that the limit of $x^2 + 5$ as x approaches 3 is 14, and abbreviate this statement as $\lim_{x\to 3}(x^2 + 5) = 14$ or $\lim_{x\to 3} x^2 + 5 = 14$.

Note that we get 14 if we evaluate $3^2 + 5$, but that is not the idea of limits. We are looking for the trend as x approaches but never actually reaches a number. In fact, we often let x approach a number for which the expression cannot be evaluated.

Exercises

1. a. Fill in the second row of each table.

x	1.9	1.99	1.999
$5x - 4$			

x	2.1	2.01	2.001
$5x - 4$			

b. Can you evaluate $5x - 4$ for $x = 2$?

c. What is $\lim_{x\to 2}(5x - 4)$?

2. a. Fill in the second row of each table.

x	0.6	0.66	0.666
$\dfrac{24x^2 - 25x + 6}{3x - 2}$			

x	0.7	0.67	0.667
$\dfrac{24x^2 - 25x + 6}{3x - 2}$			

b. Can you evaluate $\dfrac{24x^2 - 25x + 6}{3x - 2}$ for $x = 2/3$?

c. What is $\lim_{x\to 2/3} \dfrac{24x^2 - 25x + 6}{3x - 2}$?

3. a. Fill in the second row of each table.

x	0.01	0.0001	0.000001
$(1 + \lvert x\rvert)^{1/\lvert x\rvert}$			

x	-0.01	-0.0001	-0.00001
$(1 + \lvert x\rvert)^{1/\lvert x\rvert}$			

b. Can you evaluate $(1 + |x|)^{1/|x|}$ for $x = 0$?

c. What is $\lim_{x\to 0}(1 + |x|)^{1/|x|}$?

4. a. Use a calculator in radian mode to fill in the second row of each table.

x	0.1	0.001	0.0001
$\dfrac{\sin(x)}{x}$			

x	-0.1	-0.001	-0.0001
$\dfrac{\sin(x)}{x}$			

b. Can you evaluate $\dfrac{\sin(x)}{x}$ for $x = 0$?

c. What is $\lim_{x\to 0} \dfrac{\sin(x)}{x}$?

CHAPTER

2 Polynomial and Rational Functions

The Golden Gate Bridge

Location San Francisco and Sausalito, California

Completion Date 1937

Cost $27 million

Length 8981 feet

Longest Single Span 4200 feet

Engineer Joseph B. Strauss

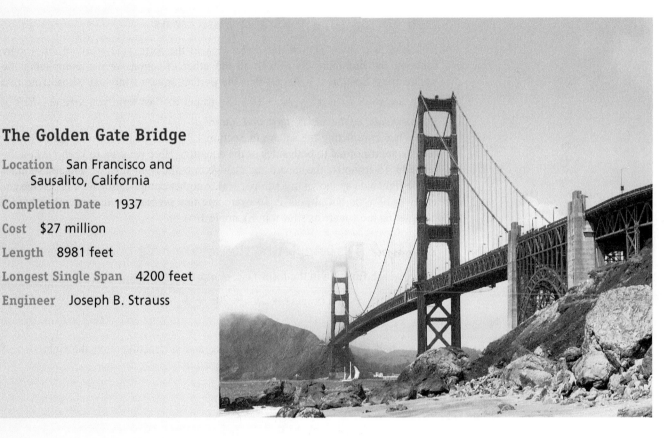

Often called the most spectacular bridge in the world, the Golden Gate Bridge is located less than 8 miles from the epicenter of the most catastrophic earthquake in history. The bridge is also subject to brutal Pacific winds, tide, and fog. When it was first conceived, building the Golden Gate Bridge seemed like an impossible task. But engineer Joseph Strauss was willing to gamble that his bridge could endure all of these destructive forces. Strauss used more than one million tons of concrete to build the massive blocks that grip the bridge's supporting cables. He completed the bridge only five months after the promised date and $1.3 million under budget. For his efforts Strauss received $1 million and a lifetime bridge pass.

2.1 Quadratic Functions and Inequalities

A **polynomial function** is defined by a polynomial. A **quadratic function** is defined by a quadratic or second-degree polynomial. So a quadratic function has the form $f(x) = ax^2 + bx + c$ where $a \neq 0$. We studied functions of the form $f(x) = a(x - h)^2 + k$ in Section 1.7 (though we did not call them quadratic functions there). Once we see that these forms are equivalent, we can use what we learned in Section 1.7 in our study of quadratic functions here.

Two Forms for Quadratic Functions

It is easy to convert $f(x) = a(x - h)^2 + k$ to the form $f(x) = ax^2 + bx + c$ by squaring the binomial. To convert in the other direction we use completing the square from Section 1.3. Recall that the perfect square trinomial whose first two terms are $x^2 + bx$ is $x^2 + bx + \left(\frac{b}{2}\right)^2$. So to get the last term you *take one-half of the coefficient of the middle term and square it.*

When completing the square in Section 1.3, we added the last term of the perfect square trinomial to both sides of the equation. Here we want to keep $f(x)$ on the left side. To complete the square and change only the right side, we add and subtract on the right side as shown in Example 1(a). Another complication here is that the coefficient of x^2 is not always 1. To overcome this problem, you must factor before completing the square as shown in Example 1(b).

Example 1 Completing the square for a quadratic function

Rewrite each function in the form $f(x) = a(x - h)^2 + k$.

a. $f(x) = x^2 + 6x$ **b.** $f(x) = 2x^2 - 20x + 3$

Solution

a. One-half of 6 is 3 and 3^2 is 9. Adding and subtracting 9 on the right side of $f(x) = x^2 + 6x$ does not change the function.

$$\begin{aligned} f(x) &= x^2 + 6x \\ &= x^2 + 6x + 9 - 9 && 9 = \left(\frac{1}{2} \cdot 6\right)^2 \\ &= (x + 3)^2 - 9 && \text{Factor.} \end{aligned}$$

b. First factor 2 out of the first two terms, because the leading coefficient in $(x - h)^2$ is 1.

$$\begin{aligned} f(x) &= 2x^2 - 20x + 3 \\ &= 2(x^2 - 10x) + 3 \\ &= 2(x^2 - 10x + 25 - 25) + 3 && 25 = \left(\frac{1}{2} \cdot 10\right)^2 \\ &= 2(x^2 - 10x + 25) - 50 + 3 && \text{Remove } -25 \text{ from the parentheses.} \\ &= 2(x - 5)^2 - 47 \end{aligned}$$

Because of the 2 preceding the parentheses, the second 25 was doubled when it was removed from the parentheses. ■

In the next example we complete the square and graph a quadratic function.

Example 2 Graphing a quadratic function

Rewrite $f(x) = -2x^2 - 4x + 3$ in the form $f(x) = a(x - h)^2 + k$ and sketch its graph.

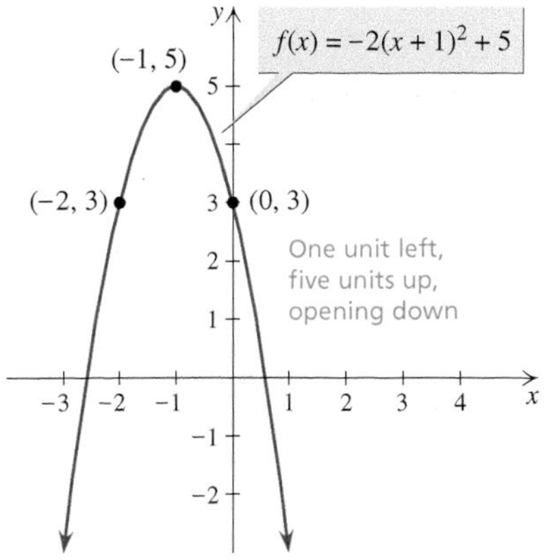

Figure 2.1

Solution

Start by completing the square:

$$
\begin{aligned}
f(x) &= -2(x^2 + 2x) + 3 && \text{Factor out } -2 \text{ from the first two terms.}\\
&= -2(x^2 + 2x + 1 - 1) + 3 && \text{Complete the square for } x^2 + 2x.\\
&= -2(x^2 + 2x + 1) + 2 + 3 && \text{Remove } -1 \text{ from the parentheses.}\\
&= -2(x + 1)^2 + 5
\end{aligned}
$$

The function is now in the form $f(x) = a(x - h)^2 + k$. The number 1 indicates that the graph of $f(x) = x^2$ is translated one unit to the left. Since $a = -2$, the graph is stretched by a factor of 2 and reflected below the x-axis. Finally, the graph is translated five units upward. The graph shown in Fig. 2.1 includes the points (0, 3), (−1, 5), and (−2, 3). ■

We can use completing the square as in Example 2 to prove the following theorem.

Theorem: Quadratic Functions

The graph of any quadratic function is a transformation of the graph of $f(x) = x^2$.

PROOF Since $f(x) = a(x - h)^2 + k$ is a transformation of $f(x) = x^2$, we will show that $f(x) = ax^2 + bx + c$ can be written in that form:

$$
\begin{aligned}
f(x) &= ax^2 + bx + c\\
&= a\left(x^2 + \frac{b}{a}x\right) + c && \text{Factor } a \text{ out of the first two terms.}
\end{aligned}
$$

To complete the square for $x^2 + \frac{b}{a}x$, add and subtract $\frac{b^2}{4a^2}$ inside the parentheses:

$$
\begin{aligned}
f(x) &= a\left(x^2 + \frac{b}{a}x + \frac{b^2}{4a^2} - \frac{b^2}{4a^2}\right) + c\\
&= a\left(x^2 + \frac{b}{a}x + \frac{b^2}{4a^2}\right) - \frac{b^2}{4a} + c && \text{Remove } -\frac{b^2}{4a^2} \text{ from the parentheses.}\\
&= a\left(x + \frac{b}{2a}\right)^2 + \frac{4ac - b^2}{4a} && \text{Factor and get a common denominator.}\\
&= a(x - h)^2 + k. && \text{Let } h = -\frac{b}{2a} \text{ and } k = \frac{4ac - b^2}{4a}.
\end{aligned}
$$

So the graph of any quadratic function is a transformation of $f(x) = x^2$. ■

In Section 1.7 we stated that any transformation of $f(x) = x^2$ is called a parabola. Therefore, the graph of any quadratic function is a parabola.

The technique of completing the square that was used in the preceding proof is also used to prove the well-known *quadratic formula.* In fact, if you replace $f(x)$ with 0 and solve

$$0 = a\left(x + \frac{b}{2a}\right)^2 + \frac{4ac - b^2}{4a}$$

for x, you get the quadratic formula. You should complete the details.

Theorem: The Quadratic Formula

The solutions to $ax^2 + bx + c = 0$ for $a \neq 0$ are given by

$$x = \frac{-b \pm \sqrt{b^2 - 4ac}}{2a}.$$

Opening, Vertex, and Axis of Symmetry

If $a > 0$, the graph of $f(x) = a(x - h)^2 + k$ **opens upward;** if $a < 0$, the graph **opens downward** as shown in Fig. 2.2. Notice that h determines the amount of horizontal translation and k determines the amount of vertical translation of the graph of $f(x) = x^2$. Because of the translations, the point (0, 0) on the graph of $f(x) = x^2$ moves to the point (h, k) on the graph of $f(x) = a(x - h)^2 + k$. Since (0, 0) is the lowest point on the graph of $f(x) = x^2$, the lowest point on any parabola that opens upward is (h, k). Since (0, 0) is the highest point on the graph of $f(x) = -x^2$, the highest point on any parabola that opens downward is (h, k). The point (h, k) is called the **vertex** of the parabola.

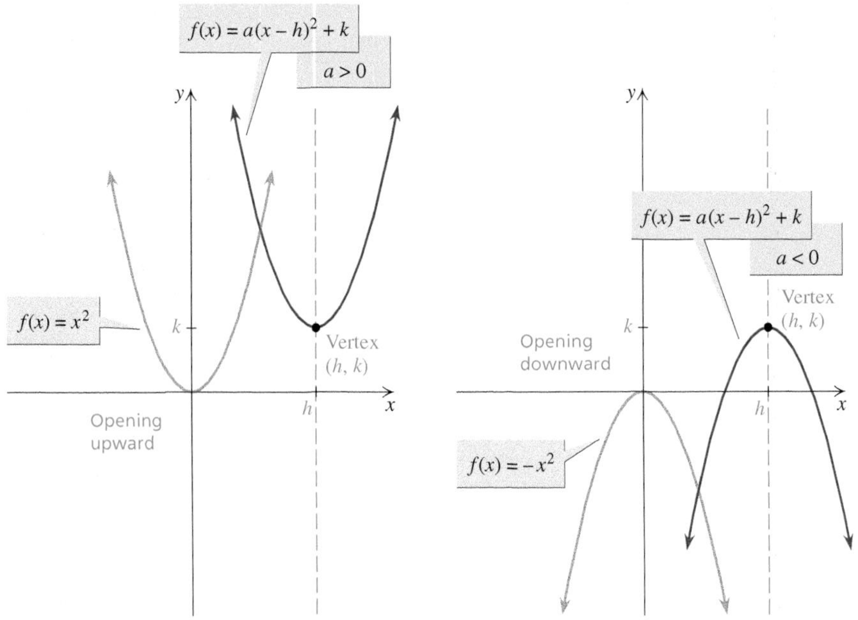

Figure 2.2

You can use a graphing calculator to experiment with different values for a, h, and k. Two possibilities are shown in Fig. 2.3(a) and (b). The graphing calculator allows you to see results quickly and to use values that you would not use otherwise. □

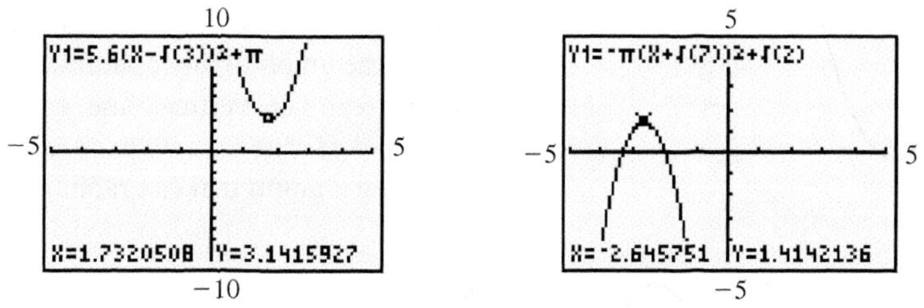

(a) (b)

Figure 2.3

We can also find the vertex of the parabola when the function is written in the form $f(x) = ax^2 + bx + c$. The x-coordinate of the vertex is $-b/(2a)$ because we used $h = -b/(2a)$ when we obtained $y = a(x - h)^2 + k$ from $y = ax^2 + bx + c$. The y-coordinate is found by substitution.

SUMMARY

Vertex of a Parabola

1. For a quadratic function in the form $f(x) = a(x - h)^2 + k$ the vertex of the parabola is (h, k).
2. For the form $f(x) = ax^2 + bx + c$, the x-coordinate of the vertex is $\frac{-b}{2a}$. The y-coordinate is $f\left(\frac{-b}{2a}\right)$.

Example 3 Finding the vertex

Find the vertex of the graph of $f(x) = -2x^2 - 4x + 3$.

Solution

Use $x = -b/(2a)$ to find the x-coordinate of the vertex:

$$x = \frac{-b}{2a} = \frac{-(-4)}{2(-2)} = -1$$

Now find $f(-1)$:

$$f(-1) = -2(-1)^2 - 4(-1) + 3 = 5$$

The vertex is $(-1, 5)$. In Example 2, $f(x) = -2x^2 - 4x + 3$ was rewritten as $f(x) = -2(x + 1)^2 + 5$. In this form we see immediately that the vertex is $(-1, 5)$. The graph in Fig. 2.4 supports these conclusions. ■

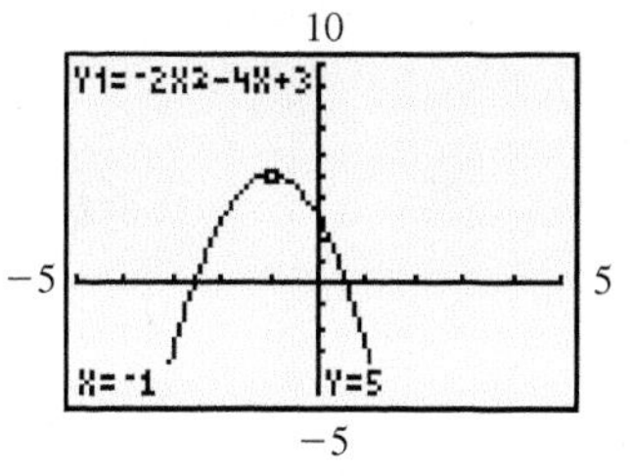

Figure 2.4

The domain of every quadratic function $f(x) = a(x - h)^2 + k$ is the set of real numbers, $(-\infty, \infty)$. The range of a quadratic function is determined from the second

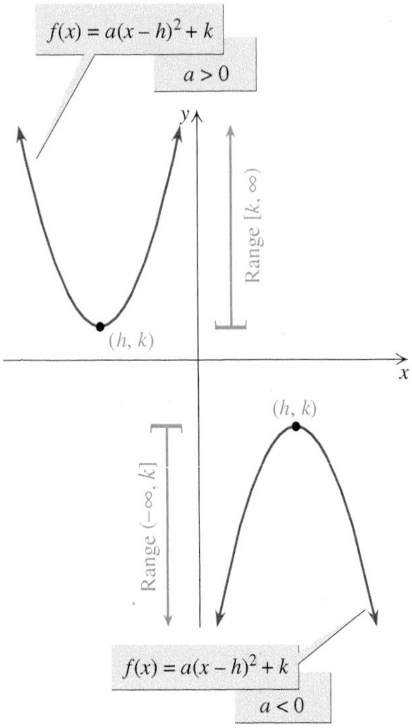

Figure 2.5

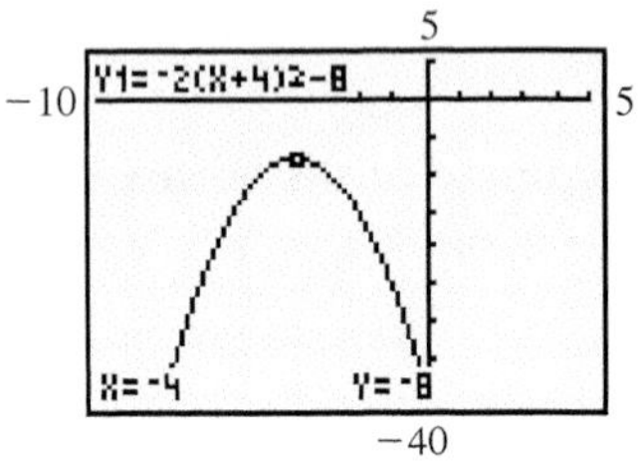

Figure 2.6

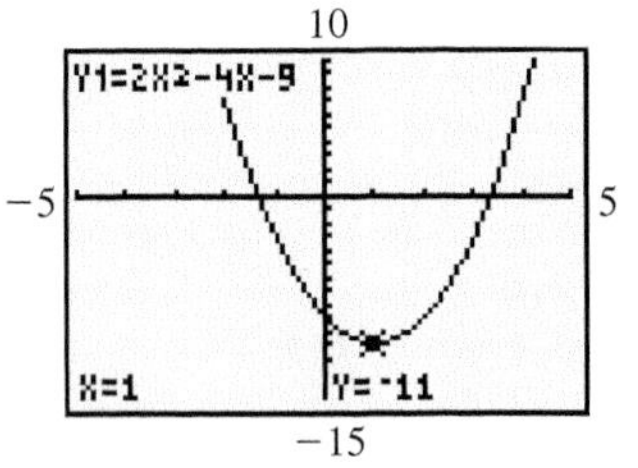

Figure 2.7

coordinate of the vertex. If $a > 0$, the range is $[k, \infty)$ and k is called the **minimum value of the function.** The function is decreasing on $(-\infty, h)$ and increasing on (h, ∞). See Fig. 2.5. If $a < 0$, the range is $(-\infty, k]$ and k is called the **maximum value of the function.** The function is increasing on $(-\infty, h)$ and decreasing on (h, ∞).

The graph of $f(x) = x^2$ is symmetric about the y-axis, which runs vertically through the vertex of the parabola. Since this symmetry is preserved in transformations, the graph of any quadratic function is symmetric about the vertical line through its vertex. The vertical line $x = -b/(2a)$ is called the **axis of symmetry** for the graph of $f(x) = ax^2 + bx + c$. Identifying these characteristics of a parabola before drawing a graph makes graphing easier and more accurate.

Example 4 Identifying the characteristics of a parabola

For each parabola, determine whether the parabola opens upward or downward, and find the vertex, axis of symmetry, and range of the function. Find the maximum or minimum value of the function and the intervals on which the function is increasing or decreasing.

a. $y = -2(x + 4)^2 - 8$ **b.** $y = 2x^2 - 4x - 9$

Solution

a. Since $a = -2$, the parabola opens downward. In $y = a(x - h)^2 + k$, the vertex is (h, k). So the vertex is $(-4, -8)$. The axis of symmetry is the vertical line through the vertex, $x = -4$. Since the parabola opens downward from $(-4, -8)$, the range of the function is $(-\infty, -8]$. The maximum value of the function is -8, and the function is increasing on $(-\infty, -4)$ and decreasing on $(-4, \infty)$.

The graph in Fig. 2.6 supports these results. □

b. Since $a = 2$, the parabola opens upward. In the form $y = ax^2 + bx + c$, the x-coordinate of the vertex is $x = -b/(2a)$. In this case,

$$x = \frac{-b}{2a} = \frac{-(-4)}{2(2)} = 1.$$

Use $x = 1$ to find $y = 2(1)^2 - 4(1) - 9 = -11$. So the vertex is $(1, -11)$, and the axis of symmetry is the vertical line $x = 1$. Since the parabola opens upward, the vertex is the lowest point and the range is $[-11, \infty)$. The function is decreasing on $(-\infty, 1)$ and increasing on $(1, \infty)$. The minimum value of the function is -11.

The graph in Fig. 2.7 supports these results. ■

Intercepts

The x-intercepts and the y-intercept are important points on the graph of a parabola. The x-intercepts are used in solving quadratic inequalities and the y-intercept is the starting point on the graph of a function whose domain is the nonnegative real numbers. The y-intercept is easily found by letting $x = 0$. The x-intercepts are found by letting $y = 0$ and solving the resulting quadratic equation.

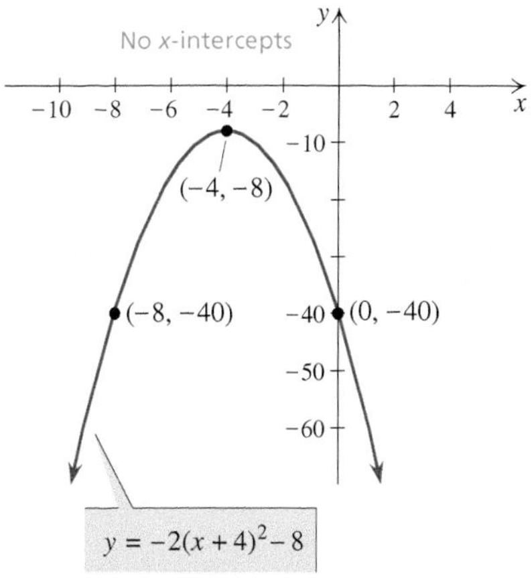

Figure 2.8

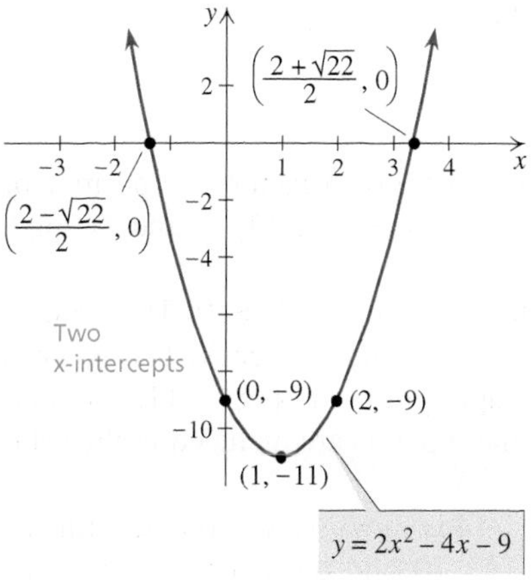

Figure 2.9

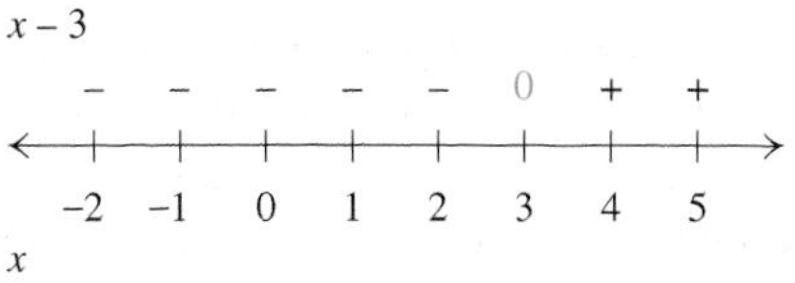

Figure 2.10

Example 5 Finding the intercepts

Find the y-intercept and the x-intercepts for each parabola and sketch the graph of each parabola.

a. $y = -2(x + 4)^2 - 8$ **b.** $y = 2x^2 - 4x - 9$

Solution

a. If $x = 0, y = -2(0 + 4)^2 - 8 = -40$. The y-intercept is $(0, -40)$. Because the graph is symmetric about the line $x = -4$, the point $(-8, -40)$ is also on the graph. Since the parabola opens downward from $(-4, -8)$, which is below the x-axis, there are no x-intercepts. If we try to solve $-2(x + 4)^2 - 8 = 0$ to find the x-intercepts, we get $(x + 4)^2 = -4$, which has no real solution. The graph is shown in Fig. 2.8.

b. If $x = 0, y = 2(0)^2 - 4(0) - 9 = -9$. The y-intercept is $(0, -9)$. From Example 4(b), the vertex is $(1, -11)$. Because the graph is symmetric about the line $x = 1$, the point $(2, -9)$ is also on the graph. The x-intercepts are found by solving $2x^2 - 4x - 9 = 0$:

$$x = \frac{4 \pm \sqrt{(-4)^2 - 4(2)(-9)}}{2(2)} = \frac{4 \pm \sqrt{88}}{4} = \frac{2 \pm \sqrt{22}}{2}$$

The x-intercepts are $\left(\frac{2 + \sqrt{22}}{2}, 0\right)$ and $\left(\frac{2 - \sqrt{22}}{2}, 0\right)$. See Fig. 2.9. ■

Note that if $y = ax^2 + bx + c$ has x-intercepts, they can always be found by using the quadratic formula. The x-coordinates of the x-intercepts are

$$x = \frac{-b \pm \sqrt{b^2 - 4ac}}{2a} = \frac{-b}{2a} \pm \frac{\sqrt{b^2 - 4ac}}{2a}.$$

Note how the axis of symmetry, $x = -b/(2a)$, appears in this formula. The x-intercepts are on opposite sides of the graph and are equidistant from the axis of symmetry.

Quadratic Inequalities

A **sign graph** is a number line that shows where the value of an expression is positive, negative, or zero. For example, the expression $x - 3$ has a positive value if $x > 3$ and a negative value if $x < 3$. If $x = 3$, then the value of $x - 3$ is zero. This information is shown on the sign graph in Fig. 2.10. We can use sign graphs and the rules for multiplying signed numbers to solve **quadratic inequalities**—inequalities that involve quadratic polynomials.

Example 6 Solving a quadratic inequality using a sign graph of the factors

Solve each inequality. Write the solution set in interval notation and graph it.

a. $x^2 - x > 6$ **b.** $x^2 - x \leq 6$

Solution

a. Write the inequality as $x^2 - x - 6 > 0$ and factor to get

$$(x - 3)(x + 2) > 0.$$

Note that $x + 2 > 0$ if $x > -2$ and $x + 2 < 0$ if $x < -2$. If $x = -2$, then $x + 2 = 0$. Combine this information with the sign graph for $x - 3$ in Fig. 2.10 to get Fig. 2.11, which shows the signs of both factors.

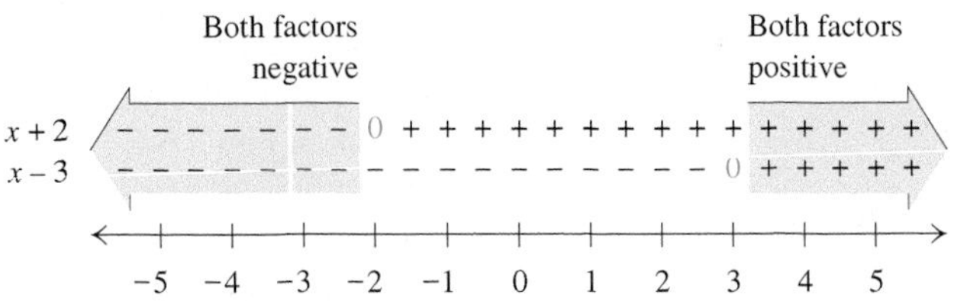

Figure 2.11

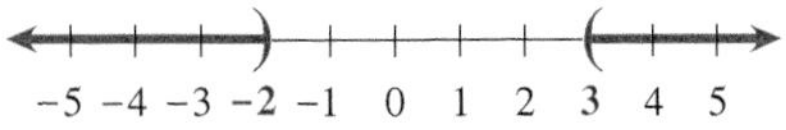

Figure 2.12

The product $(x - 3)(x + 2)$ is positive only where both factors are positive or both factors are negative. So the solution set is $(-\infty, -2) \cup (3, \infty)$ and its graph is in Fig. 2.12.

b. The inequality $x^2 - x \leq 6$ is equivalent to $(x - 3)(x + 2) \leq 0$. The product $(x - 3)(x + 2)$ is negative when x is between -2 and 3, because that is when the factors have opposite signs on the sign graph in Fig. 2.11. Because $(x - 3)(x + 2) = 0$ if $x = 3$ or $x = -2$, these points are included in the solution set $[-2, 3]$. The graph is shown in Fig. 2.13.

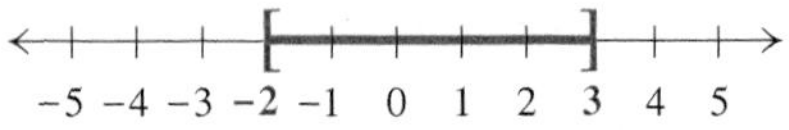

Figure 2.13

The graph of $y = x^2 - x - 6$ in Fig. 2.14 is above the x-axis (y-coordinate greater than 0) when x is in $(-\infty, -2) \cup (3, \infty)$ and on or below the x-axis (y-coordinate less than or equal to 0) when x is in $[-2, 3]$. ■

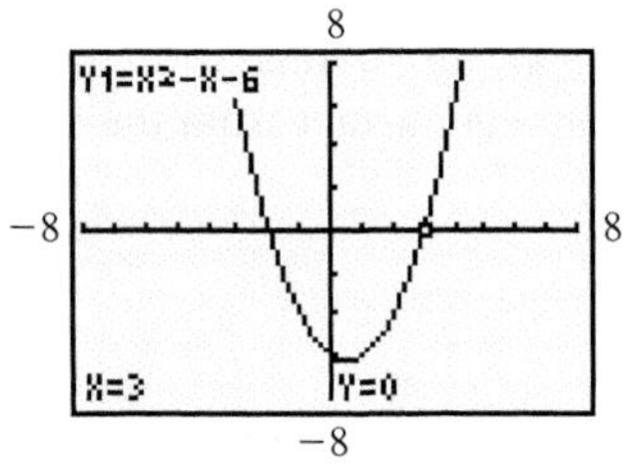

Figure 2.14

Making a sign graph of the factors as in Example 6 shows how the signs of the linear factors determine the solution to a quadratic inequality. Of course, that method works only if you can factor the quadratic polynomial. The **test-point method** works on all quadratic polynomials. For this method, we find the roots of the quadratic polynomial (using the quadratic formula if necessary) and then make a sign graph for the quadratic polynomial itself, not the factors. The signs of the quadratic polynomial are determined by testing numbers in the intervals determined by the roots.

Example 7 Solving a quadratic inequality using the test-point method

Solve $2x^2 - 4x - 9 < 0$. Write the solution set in interval notation.

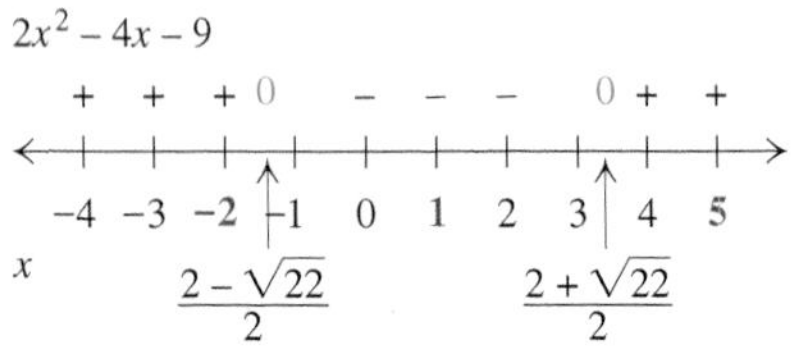

Figure 2.15

Solution

The roots to $2x^2 - 4x - 9 = 0$ were found to be $\frac{2 \pm \sqrt{22}}{2}$ in Example 5(b). Since $\frac{2 - \sqrt{22}}{2} \approx -1.3$ and $\frac{2 + \sqrt{22}}{2} \approx 3.3$, we make the number line as in Fig. 2.15. Select a convenient test point in each of the three intervals determined by the roots.

Our selections −2, 1, and 5 are shown in red on the number line. Now evaluate $2x^2 - 4x - 9$ for each test point:

$$2(-2)^2 - 4(-2) - 9 = 7 \quad \text{Positive}$$
$$2(1)^2 - 4(1) - 9 = -11 \quad \text{Negative}$$
$$2(5)^2 - 4(5) - 9 = 21 \quad \text{Positive}$$

The signs of these results are shown on the number line in Fig. 2.15. Since $2x^2 - 4x - 9 < 0$ between the roots, the solution set is

$$\left(\frac{2 - \sqrt{22}}{2}, \frac{2 + \sqrt{22}}{2}\right).$$

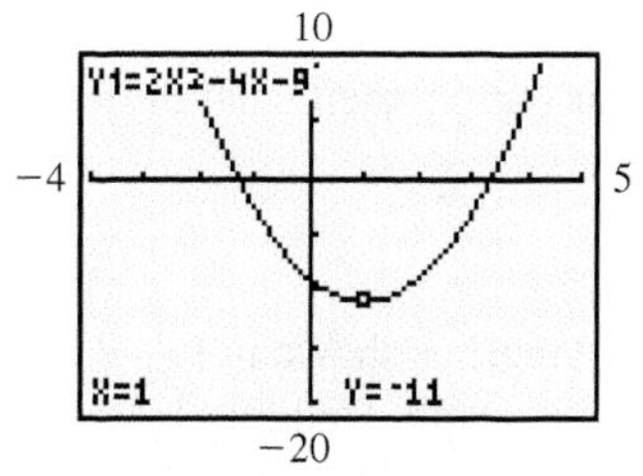

Figure 2.16

The graph of $y = 2x^2 - 4x - 9$ in Fig. 2.16 is below the x-axis between the x-intercepts and supports our conclusion. Note that every point that appears on the graph can be viewed as a test point. ■

If there are no real solutions to the quadratic equation that corresponds to a quadratic inequality, then the solution set to the inequality is either the empty set or all real numbers. For example, $x^2 + 4 = 0$ has no real solutions. Use any number as a test point to find that the solution set to $x^2 + 4 > 0$ is $(-\infty, \infty)$ and the solution set to $x^2 + 4 < 0$ is the empty set $\emptyset$.

Applications of Maximum and Minimum

If one variable is a quadratic function of another, then the maximum or minimum value of the dependent variable occurs at the vertex of the graph of the quadratic function. A nice application of this idea occurs in modeling projectile motion. The formula $h(t) = -16t^2 + v_0t + h_0$ is used to find the height in feet at time t in seconds for a projectile that is launched in a vertical direction with initial velocity of v_0 feet per second from an initial height of h_0 feet. Since the height is a quadratic function of time, the maximum height occurs at the vertex of the parabola.

■ Foreshadowing Calculus

In algebra we can maximize or minimize a quadratic function because we can easily find the vertex of a parabola. However, max/min problems involving other functions are usually solved using techniques of calculus.

Example 8 Finding maximum height of a projectile

A ball is tossed straight upward with an initial velocity of 80 feet per second from a rooftop that is 12 feet above ground level. The height of the ball in feet at time t in seconds is given by $h(t) = -16t^2 + 80t + 12$. Find the maximum height above ground level for the ball.

Solution

Since the height is a quadratic function of t with a negative leading coefficient, the height has a maximum value at the vertex of the parabola. Use $-b/(2a)$ to find the t-coordinate of the vertex. Since $a = -16$ and $b = 80$

$$\frac{-b}{2a} = \frac{-80}{2(-16)} = 2.5.$$

So the ball reaches its maximum height at time $t = 2.5$ seconds. Now

$$h(2.5) = -16(2.5)^2 + 80(2.5) + 12 = 112.$$

So the maximum height of the ball is 112 feet above the ground. ■

In Example 8, the quadratic function was given. In the next example we need to write the quadratic function and then find its maximum value.

Example 9 Maximizing area of a rectangle

If 100 m of fencing will be used to fence a rectangular region, then what dimensions for the rectangle will maximize the area of the region?

Solution

Since the 100 m of fencing forms the perimeter of a rectangle as shown in Fig. 2.17, we have $2L + 2W = 100$, where W is its width and L is its length. Dividing by 2 we get $L + W = 50$ or $W = 50 - L$. Since $A = LW$ for a rectangle, by substituting we get

$$A = LW = L(50 - L) = -L^2 + 50L.$$

So the area is a quadratic function of the length. The graph of this function is the parabola in Fig. 2.18. Since the parabola opens downward, the maximum value of A occurs when

$$L = \frac{-b}{2a} = \frac{-50}{2(-1)} = 25.$$

If $L = 25$ then $W = 25$ also, since $W = 50 - L$. So the length should be 25 meters and the width 25 meters to get the maximum area. The rectangle that gives the maximum area is actually a square with an area of 625 m^2. ■

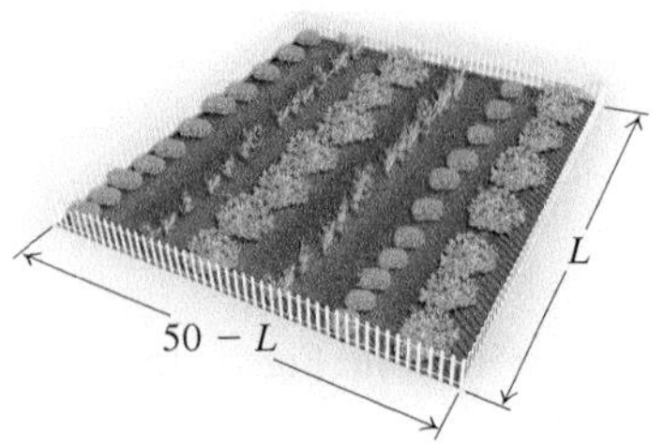

Figure 2.17

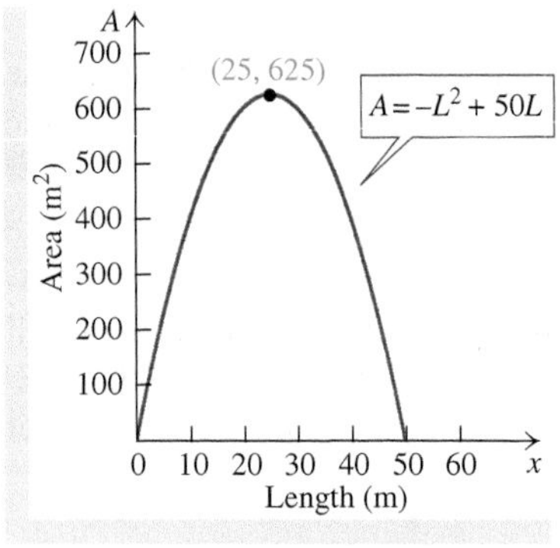

Figure 2.18

For Thought

True or False? Explain.

1. The domain and range of a quadratic function are $(-\infty, \infty)$.

2. The vertex of the graph of $y = 2(x - 3)^2 - 1$ is $(3, 1)$.

3. The graph of $y = -3(x + 2)^2 - 9$ has no x-intercepts.

4. The maximum value of y in the function $y = -4(x - 1)^2 + 9$ is 9.

5. For $y = 3x^2 - 6x + 7$, the value of y is at its minimum when $x = 1$.

6. The graph of $f(x) = 9x^2 + 12x + 4$ has one x-intercept and one y-intercept.

7. The graph of every quadratic function has exactly one y-intercept.

8. The inequality $\pi(x - \sqrt{3})^2 + \pi/2 \leq 0$ has no solution.

9. The maximum area of a rectangle with fixed perimeter p is $p^2/16$.

10. The function $f(x) = (x - 3)^2$ is increasing on the interval $[-3, \infty)$.

2.1 Exercises

Write each quadratic function in the form $y = a(x - h)^2 + k$ and sketch its graph.

1. $y = x^2 + 4x$

2. $y = x^2 - 6x$

3. $y = x^2 - 3x$

4. $y = x^2 + 5x$

5. $y = 2x^2 - 12x + 22$

6. $y = 3x^2 - 12x + 1$

7. $y = -3x^2 + 6x - 3$

8. $y = -2x^2 - 4x + 8$

9. $y = x^2 + 3x + \frac{5}{2}$

10. $y = x^2 - x + 1$

11. $y = -2x^2 + 3x - 1$

12. $y = 3x^2 + 4x + 2$

Find the vertex of the graph of each quadratic function. See the summary on finding the vertex on page 117.

13. $f(x) = 3x^2 - 12x + 1$

14. $f(x) = -2x^2 - 8x + 9$

15. $f(x) = -3(x - 4)^2 + 1$

16. $f(x) = \frac{1}{2}(x + 6)^2 - \frac{1}{4}$

17. $y = -\frac{1}{2}x^2 - \frac{1}{3}x$

18. $y = \frac{1}{4}x^2 + \frac{1}{2}x - 1$

From the graph of each parabola, determine whether the parabola opens upward or downward, and find the vertex, axis of symmetry, and range of the function. Find the maximum or minimum value of the function and the intervals on which the function is increasing or decreasing.

19.

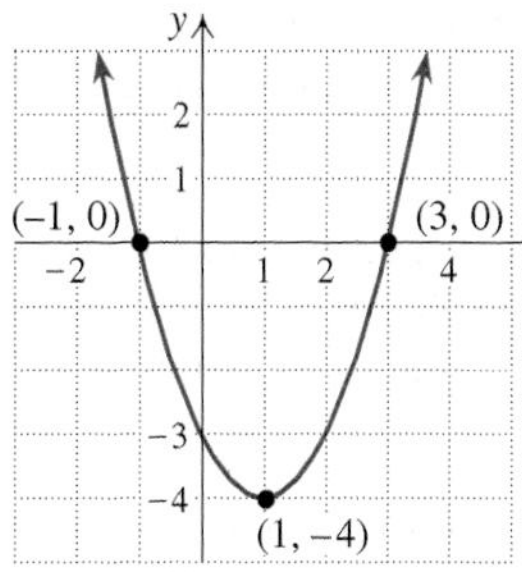

20.

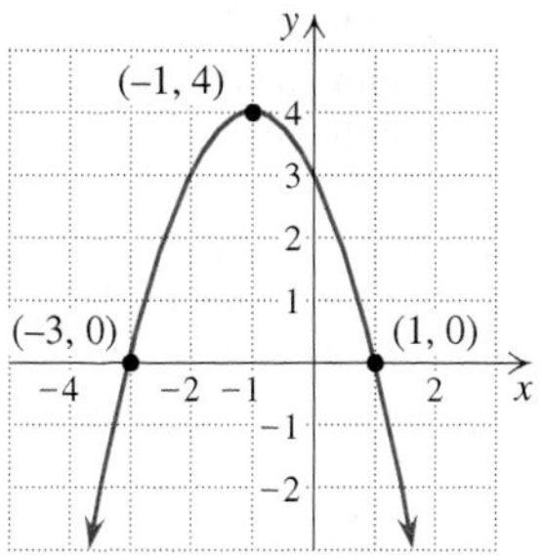

Find the range of each quadratic function and the maximum or minimum value of the function. Identify the intervals on which each function is increasing or decreasing.

21. $f(x) = 3 - x^2$

22. $f(x) = 5 - x^2$

23. $y = (x - 1)^2 - 1$

24. $y = (x + 3)^2 + 4$

25. $y = x^2 + 8x - 2$

26. $y = x^2 - 2x - 3$

27. $y = \frac{1}{2}(x - 3)^2 + 4$

28. $y = -\frac{1}{3}(x + 6)^2 + 37$

29. $f(x) = -2x^2 + 6x + 9$

30. $f(x) = -3x^2 - 9x + 4$

31. $y = -\frac{3}{4}\left(x - \frac{1}{2}\right)^2 + 9$

32. $y = \frac{3}{2}\left(x - \frac{1}{3}\right)^2 - 6$

Identify the vertex, axis of symmetry, y-intercept, x-intercepts, and opening of each parabola, then sketch the graph.

33. $y = x^2 - 3$

34. $y = 8 - x^2$

35. $y = x^2 - x$

36. $y = 2x - x^2$

37. $f(x) = x^2 + 6x + 9$

38. $f(x) = x^2 - 6x$

39. $f(x) = (x - 3)^2 - 4$

40. $f(x) = (x + 1)^2 - 9$

41. $y = -3(x - 2)^2 + 12$

42. $y = -2(x + 3)^2 + 8$

43. $y = -2x^2 + 4x + 1$

44. $y = -x^2 + 2x - 6$

Solve each inequality by making a sign graph of the factors. State the solution set in interval notation and graph it.

45. $2x^2 - x - 3 < 0$

46. $3x^2 - 4x - 4 \le 0$

47. $2x + 15 < x^2$

48. $5x - x^2 < 4$

49. $w^2 - 4w - 12 \ge 0$

50. $y^2 + 8y + 15 \le 0$

51. $t^2 \le 16$

52. $36 \le h^2$

53. $a^2 + 6a + 9 \le 0$

54. $c^2 + 4 \le 4c$

55. $4z^2 - 12z + 9 > 0$

56. $9s^2 + 6s + 1 \ge 0$

Solve each inequality by using the test-point method. State the solution set in interval notation and graph it.

57. $x^2 - 4x + 2 < 0$

58. $x^2 - 4x + 1 \le 0$

59. $x^2 - 9 > 1$

60. $6 < x^2 - 1$

61. $y^2 + 18 > 10y$

62. $y^2 + 3 \ge 6y$

63. $p^2 + 9 > 0$

64. $-5 - s^2 < 0$

65. $a^2 + 20 \le 8a$

66. $6t \le t^2 + 25$

67. $-2w^2 + 5w < 6$

68. $-3z^2 - 5 > 2z$

Identify the solution set to each quadratic inequality by inspecting the graphs of $y = x^2 - 2x - 3$ *and* $y = -x^2 - 2x + 3$ *as shown.*

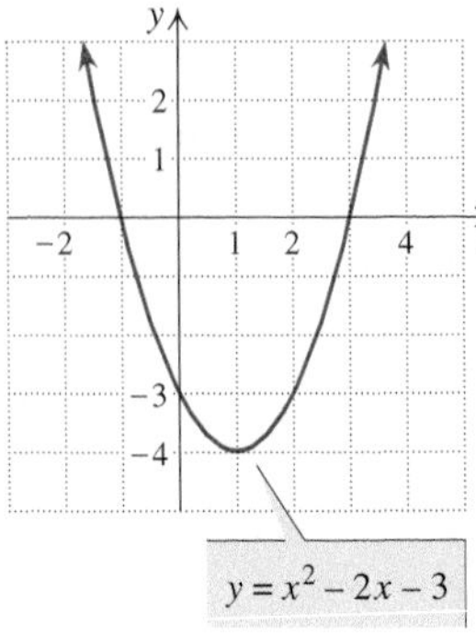

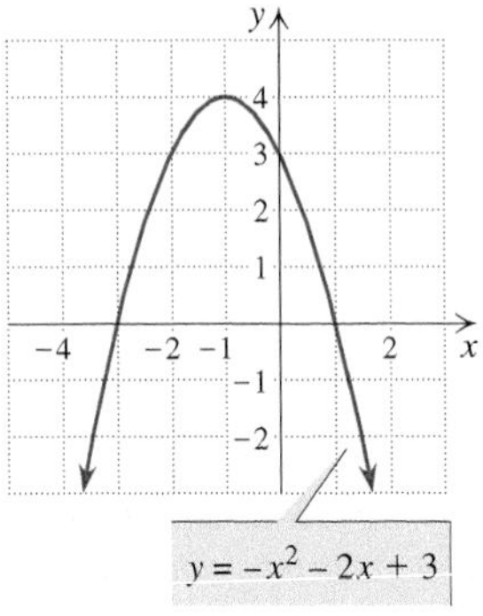

69. $x^2 - 2x - 3 \geq 0$

70. $x^2 - 2x - 3 < 0$

71. $-x^2 - 2x + 3 > 0$

72. $-x^2 - 2x + 3 \leq 0$

73. $x^2 + 2x \leq 3$

74. $x^2 \leq 2x + 3$

The next two exercises incorporate many concepts of quadratics.

75. Let $f(x) = x^2 - 3x - 10$.
a. Solve $f(x) = 0$. **b.** Solve $f(x) = -10$.

c. Solve $f(x) > 0$. **d.** Solve $f(x) \leq 0$.

e. Write f in the form $f(x) = a(x - h)^2 + k$ and describe the graph of f as a transformation of the graph of $y = x^2$.

f. Graph f and state the domain, range, and the maximum or minimum y-coordinate on the graph.

g. What is the relationship between the graph of f and the answers to parts (c) and (d)?

h. Find the intercepts, axis of symmetry, vertex, opening, and intervals on which f is increasing or decreasing.

76. Repeat parts (a) through (h) from the previous exercise for $f(x) = -x^2 + 2x + 1$.

Solve each problem.

77. *Maximum Height of a Football* If a football is kicked straight up with an initial velocity of 128 ft/sec from a height of 5 ft, then its height above the earth is a function of time given by $h(t) = -16t^2 + 128t + 5$. What is the maximum height reached by this ball?

78. *Maximum Height of a Ball* If a juggler can toss a ball into the air at a velocity of 64 ft/sec from a height of 6 ft, then what is the maximum height reached by the ball?

79. *Shooting an Arrow* If an archer shoots an arrow straight upward with an initial velocity of 160 ft/sec from a height of 8 ft, then its height above the ground in feet at time t in seconds is given by the function

$$h(t) = -16t^2 + 160t + 8.$$

a. What is the maximum height reached by the arrow?

b. How long does it take for the arrow to reach the ground?

80. *Rocket Propelled Grenade* If a soldier in basic training fires a rocket propelled grenade (RPG) straight up from ground level with an initial velocity of 256 ft/sec, then its height above the ground in feet at time t in seconds is given by the function

$$h(t) = -16t^2 + 256t.$$

a. What is the maximum height reached by the RPG?

b. How long does it take for the RPG to reach the ground?

81. *Maximum Area* Shondra wants to enclose a rectangular garden with 200 yards of fencing. What dimensions for the garden will maximize its area.

82. *Mirror Mirror* Chantel wants to make a rectangular frame for a mirror using 10 feet of frame molding. What dimensions will maximize the area of the mirror assuming that there is no waste?

83. *Twin Kennels* Martin plans to construct a rectangular kennel for two dogs using 120 feet of chain-link fencing. He plans to fence all four sides and down the middle to keep the dogs separate. What overall dimensions will maximize the total area fenced?

84. *Cross Fenced* Kim wants to construct rectangular pens for four animals with 400 feet of fencing. To get four separate pens she will fence a large rectangle and then fence through the middle of the rectangle parallel to the length and parallel to the width. What overall dimensions will maximize the total area of the pens?

85. *Big Barn* Mike wants to enclose a rectangular area for his rabbits alongside his large barn using 30 feet of fencing. What dimensions will maximize the area fenced if the barn is used for one side of the rectangle?

86. *Maximum Area* Kevin wants to enclose a rectangular garden using 14 eight-ft railroad ties, which he cannot cut. What are the dimensions of the rectangle that maximize the area enclosed?

87. *Maximizing Revenue* Mona Kalini gives a walking tour of Honolulu to one person for $49. To increase her business, she advertised at the National Orthodontist Convention that she would lower the price by $1 per person for each additional person, up to 49 people.

a. Write the price per person p as a function of the number of people n.

b. Write her revenue as a function of the number of people on the tour.

c. What is the maximum revenue for her tour?

88. *Concert Tickets* At $10 per ticket, Willie Williams and the Wranglers will fill all 8000 seats in the Assembly Center. The manager knows that for every $1 increase in the price, 500 tickets will go unsold.
   a. Write the number of tickets sold n as a function of ticket price p.
   b. Write the total revenue as a function of the ticket price.
   c. What ticket price will maximize the revenue?

Thinking Outside the Box XI

Overlapping Region A right triangle with sides of length 3, 4, and 5 is drawn so that the endpoints of the side of length 5 are (0, 0) and (5, 0). A square with sides of length 1 is drawn so that its center is the vertex of the right angle and its sides are parallel to the x- and y-axes. What is the area of the region where the square and the triangle overlap?

2.1 Pop Quiz

1. Write $y = 2x^2 + 16x - 1$ in the form $y = a(x - h)^2 + k$.
2. Find the vertex of the graph of $y = 3(x + 4)^2 + 8$.
3. Find the range of $f(x) = -x^2 - 4x + 9$.
4. Find the minimum y-value for $y = x^2 - 3x$.
5. Find the x-intercepts and axis of symmetry for $y = x^2 - 2x - 8$.
6. Solve the inequality $x^2 + 4x < 0$.

2.2 Complex Numbers

Our system of numbers developed as the need arose. Numbers were first used for counting. As society advanced, the rational numbers were formed to express fractional parts and ratios. Negative numbers were invented to express losses or debts. When it was discovered that the exact size of some very real objects could not be expressed with rational numbers, the irrational numbers were added to the system, forming the set of real numbers. Later still, there was a need for another expansion to the number system. In this section we study that expansion, the set of complex numbers.

Definitions

There are no even roots of negative numbers in the set of real numbers. So, the real numbers are inadequate or incomplete in this regard. The imaginary numbers were invented to complete the set of real numbers. Using real and imaginary numbers, every nonzero real number has *two* square roots, *three* cube roots, *four* fourth roots, and so on. (Actually finding all of the roots of any real number is done in trigonometry.)

The imaginary numbers are based on the solution of the equation $x^2 = -1$. Since no real number solves this equation, a solution is called an *imaginary number*. The number i is defined to be a solution to this equation: i is a number whose square is -1.

Definition: The Number i

> The number i is defined by
> $$i^2 = -1.$$
> We may also write $i = \sqrt{-1}$.

A complex number is formed as a real number plus a real multiple of i.

Definition: Complex Numbers

> The set of **complex numbers** is the set of all numbers of the form $a + bi$, where a and b are real numbers.

In $a + bi$, a is called the **real part** and b is called the **imaginary part.** Two complex numbers $a + bi$ and $c + di$ are **equal** if and only if their real parts are equal ($a = c$) and their imaginary parts are equal ($b = d$). If $b = 0$, then $a + bi$ is a **real number.** If $b \neq 0$, then $a + bi$ is an **imaginary number.**

The form $a + bi$ is the **standard form** of a complex number, but for convenience we use a few variations of that form. If either the real or imaginary part of a complex number is 0, then that part is omitted. For example,

$$0 + 3i = 3i, \qquad 2 + 0i = 2, \qquad \text{and} \qquad 0 + 0i = 0.$$

If b is a radical, then i is usually written before b. For example, we write $2 + i\sqrt{3}$ rather than $2 + \sqrt{3}i$, which could be confused with $2 + \sqrt{3i}$. If b is negative, a subtraction symbol can be used to separate the real and imaginary parts as in $3 + (-2)i = 3 - 2i$. A complex number with fractions, such as $\frac{1}{3} - \frac{2}{3}i$, may be written as $\frac{1 - 2i}{3}$.

Example 1 Standard form of a complex number

Determine whether each complex number is real or imaginary and write it in the standard form $a + bi$.

a. $3i$ **b.** 87 **c.** $4 - 5i$ **d.** 0 **e.** $\dfrac{1 + \pi i}{2}$

Solution

a. The complex number $3i$ is imaginary, and $3i = 0 + 3i$.
b. The complex number 87 is a real number, and $87 = 87 + 0i$.
c. The complex number $4 - 5i$ is imaginary, and $4 - 5i = 4 + (-5)i$.
d. The complex number 0 is real, and $0 = 0 + 0i$.
e. The complex number $\frac{1 + \pi i}{2}$ is imaginary, and $\frac{1 + \pi i}{2} = \frac{1}{2} + \frac{\pi}{2}i$. ■

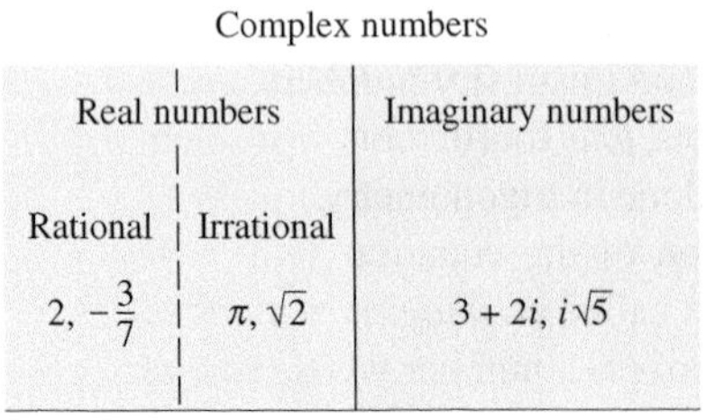

Figure 2.19

The real numbers can be classified as rational or irrational. The complex numbers can be classified as real or imaginary. The relationship between these sets of numbers is shown in Fig. 2.19.

Addition, Subtraction, and Multiplication

Now that we have defined complex numbers, we define the operations of arithmetic with them.

Definition: Addition, Subtraction, and Multiplication

If $a + bi$ and $c + di$ are complex numbers, we define their sum, difference, and product as follows.

$$(a + bi) + (c + di) = (a + c) + (b + d)i$$

$$(a + bi) - (c + di) = (a - c) + (b - d)i$$

$$(a + bi)(c + di) = (ac - bd) + (bc + ad)i$$

It is not necessary to memorize these definitions, because the results can be obtained by performing the operations as if the complex numbers were binomials with i being a variable, replacing i^2 with -1 wherever it occurs.

Example 2 Operations with complex numbers

Perform the indicated operations with the complex numbers.

a. $(-2 + 3i) + (-4 - 9i)$ **b.** $(-1 - 5i) - (3 - 2i)$ **c.** $2i(3 + i)$
d. $(3i)^2$ **e.** $(-3i)^2$ **f.** $(5 - 2i)(5 + 2i)$

Solution

a. $(-2 + 3i) + (-4 - 9i) = -6 - 6i$
b. $(-1 - 5i) - (3 - 2i) = -1 - 5i - 3 + 2i = -4 - 3i$
c. $2i(3 + i) = 6i + 2i^2 = 6i + 2(-1) = -2 + 6i$
d. $(3i)^2 = 3^2i^2 = 9(-1) = -9$
e. $(-3i)^2 = (-3)^2i^2 = 9(-1) = -9$
f. $(5 - 2i)(5 + 2i) = 25 - 4i^2 = 25 - 4(-1) = 29$

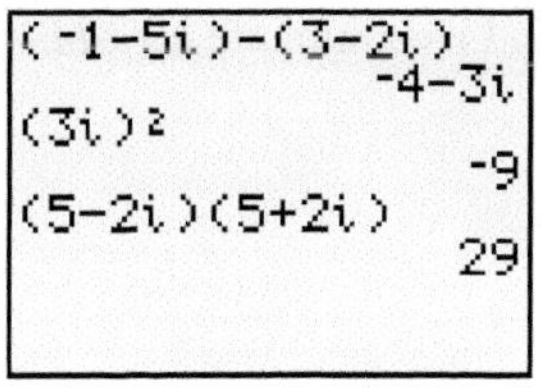

Figure 2.20

Check these results with a calculator that handles complex numbers, as in Fig. 2.20. ■

We can find whole-number powers of i by using the definition of multiplication. Since $i^1 = i$ and $i^2 = -1$, we have

$$i^3 = i^1 \cdot i^2 = i(-1) = -i \quad \text{and} \quad i^4 = i^1 \cdot i^3 = i(-i) = -i^2 = 1.$$

The first eight powers of i are listed here.

$$i^1 = i \quad i^2 = -1 \quad i^3 = -i \quad i^4 = 1$$

$$i^5 = i \quad i^6 = -1 \quad i^7 = -i \quad i^8 = 1$$

This list could be continued in this pattern, but any other whole-number power of i can be obtained from knowing the first four powers. We can simplify a power of i by using the fact that $i^4 = 1$ and $(i^4)^n = 1$ for any integer n.

Example 3 Simplifying a power of i

Simplify.

a. i^{83} **b.** i^{-46}

Solution

a. Divide 83 by 4 and write $83 = 4 \cdot 20 + 3$. So

$$i^{83} = (i^4)^{20} \cdot i^3 = 1^{20} \cdot i^3 = 1 \cdot i^3 = -i.$$

b. Since $-46 = 4(-12) + 2$, we have

$$i^{-46} = (i^4)^{-12} \cdot i^2 = 1^{-12} \cdot i^2 = 1(-1) = -1.$$

Division of Complex Numbers

The complex numbers $a + bi$ and $a - bi$ are called **complex conjugates** of each other.

Example 4 Complex conjugates

Find the product of the given complex number and its conjugate.

a. $3 - i$ **b.** $4 + 2i$ **c.** $-i$

Solution

a. The conjugate of $3 - i$ is $3 + i$, and $(3 - i)(3 + i) = 9 - i^2 = 10$.
b. The conjugate of $4 + 2i$ is $4 - 2i$, and $(4 + 2i)(4 - 2i) = 16 - 4i^2 = 20$.
c. The conjugate of $-i$ is i, and $-i \cdot i = -i^2 = 1$.

In general we have the following theorem about complex conjugates.

Theorem: Complex Conjugates

If a and b are real numbers, then the product of $a + bi$ and its conjugate $a - bi$ is the real number $a^2 + b^2$. In symbols,

$$(a + bi)(a - bi) = a^2 + b^2.$$

We use the theorem about complex conjugates to divide imaginary numbers, in a process that is similar to rationalizing a denominator.

Example 5 Dividing imaginary numbers

Write each quotient in the form $a + bi$.

a. $\dfrac{8 - i}{2 + i}$ **b.** $\dfrac{1}{5 - 4i}$ **c.** $\dfrac{3 - 2i}{i}$

Solution

a. Multiply the numerator and denominator by $2 - i$, the conjugate of $2 + i$:

$$\frac{8 - i}{2 + i} = \frac{(8 - i)(2 - i)}{(2 + i)(2 - i)} = \frac{16 - 10i + i^2}{4 - i^2} = \frac{15 - 10i}{5} = 3 - 2i$$

Check division using multiplication: $(3 - 2i)(2 + i) = 8 - i$.

b. $$\frac{1}{5 - 4i} = \frac{1(5 + 4i)}{(5 - 4i)(5 + 4i)} = \frac{5 + 4i}{25 + 16} = \frac{5 + 4i}{41} = \frac{5}{41} + \frac{4}{41}i$$

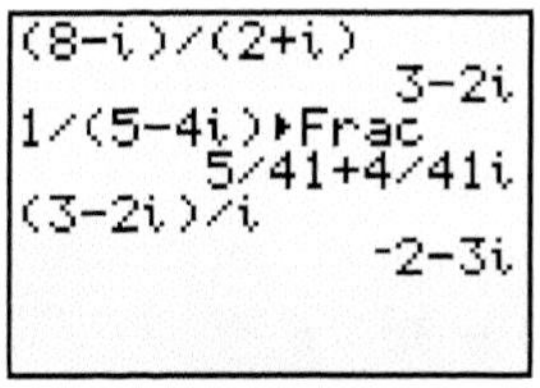

Figure 2.21

Check: $\left(\frac{5}{41}+\frac{4}{41}i\right)(5-4i)=\frac{25}{41}+\frac{20}{41}i-\frac{20}{41}i-\frac{16}{41}i^2$

$$=\frac{25}{41}+\frac{16}{41}=1.$$

You can also check with a calculator that handles complex numbers as in Fig. 2.21. □

c. $\frac{3-2i}{i}=\frac{(3-2i)(-i)}{i(-i)}=\frac{-3i+2i^2}{-i^2}=\frac{-2-3i}{1}=-2-3i$

Check: $(-2-3i)(i)=-3i^2-2i=3-2i.$ ■

Roots of Negative Numbers

In Examples 2(d) and 2(e), we saw that both $(3i)^2=-9$ and $(-3i)^2=-9$. This means that in the complex number system there are two square roots of -9, $3i$ and $-3i$. For any positive real number b, we have $(i\sqrt{b})^2=-b$ and $(-i\sqrt{b})^2=-b$. So there are two square roots of $-b$, $i\sqrt{b}$ and $-i\sqrt{b}$. We call $i\sqrt{b}$ the **principal square root** of $-b$ and make the following definition.

Definition: Square Root of a Negative Number

For any positive real number b, $\sqrt{-b}=i\sqrt{b}$.

In the real number system, $\sqrt{-2}$ and $\sqrt{-8}$ are undefined, but in the complex number system they are defined as $\sqrt{-2}=i\sqrt{2}$ and $\sqrt{-8}=i\sqrt{8}$. Even though we now have meaning for a symbol such as $\sqrt{-2}$, *all operations with complex numbers must be performed after converting to the $a+bi$ form.* If we perform operations with roots of negative numbers using properties of the real numbers, we can get contradictory results:

$$\sqrt{-2}\cdot\sqrt{-8}=\sqrt{(-2)(-8)}=\sqrt{16}=4 \quad \text{Incorrect.}$$
$$i\sqrt{2}\cdot i\sqrt{8}=i^2\cdot\sqrt{16}=-4 \quad \text{Correct.}$$

The product rule $\sqrt{a}\cdot\sqrt{b}=\sqrt{ab}$ is used *only* for nonnegative numbers a and b.

Example 6 Square roots of negative numbers

Write each expression in the form $a+bi$, where a and b are real numbers.

a. $\sqrt{-8}+\sqrt{-18}$ **b.** $\frac{-4+\sqrt{-50}}{4}$ **c.** $\sqrt{-27}\left(\sqrt{9}-\sqrt{-2}\right)$

Solution

The first step in each case is to replace the square roots of negative numbers by expressions with i.

a. $\sqrt{-8}+\sqrt{-18}=i\sqrt{8}+i\sqrt{18}=2i\sqrt{2}+3i\sqrt{2}$

$$=5i\sqrt{2}$$

b. $\dfrac{-4 + \sqrt{-50}}{4} = \dfrac{-4 + i\sqrt{50}}{4} = \dfrac{-4 + 5i\sqrt{2}}{4}$

$$= -1 + \frac{5}{4}i\sqrt{2}$$

c. $\sqrt{-27}\left(\sqrt{9} - \sqrt{-2}\right) = 3i\sqrt{3}\left(3 - i\sqrt{2}\right) = 9i\sqrt{3} - 3i^2\sqrt{6}$

$$= 3\sqrt{6} + 9i\sqrt{3}$$

■

Imaginary Solutions to Quadratic Equations

The quadratic formula $x = \dfrac{-b \pm \sqrt{b^2 - 4ac}}{2a}$ is used to solve the quadratic equation $ax^2 + bx + c = 0$. If the discriminant $b^2 - 4ac$ is negative, then there are no real solutions to the equation. However, square roots of negative numbers exist in the complex number system. So if $b^2 - 4ac < 0$, the equation has two imaginary solutions.

Example 7 Imaginary solutions to a quadratic equation

Find the imaginary solutions to $x^2 - 6x + 11 = 0$.

Solution

Use $a = 1$, $b = -6$, and $c = 11$ in the quadratic formula:

$$x = \frac{-(-6) \pm \sqrt{(-6)^2 - 4(1)(11)}}{2(1)}$$

$$= \frac{6 \pm \sqrt{-8}}{2} = \frac{6 \pm 2i\sqrt{2}}{2} = 3 \pm i\sqrt{2}$$

Check by evaluating $x^2 - 6x + 11$ with $x = 3 + i\sqrt{2}$ as follows:

$$(3 + i\sqrt{2})^2 - 6(3 + i\sqrt{2}) + 11 = 9 + 6i\sqrt{2} + (i\sqrt{2})^2 - 18 - 6i\sqrt{2} + 11$$

$$= 9 + 6i\sqrt{2} - 2 - 18 - 6i\sqrt{2} + 11$$

$$= 0$$

Figure 2.22

The reader should check $3 - i\sqrt{2}$. The imaginary solutions are $3 - i\sqrt{2}$ and $3 + i\sqrt{2}$.

The solutions can be checked with a calculator as in Fig. 2.22. ■

For Thought

True or False? Explain.

1. The multiplicative inverse of i is $-i$.
2. The conjugate of i is $-i$.
3. The set of complex numbers is a subset of the set of real numbers.
4. $\left(\sqrt{3} - i\sqrt{2}\right)\left(\sqrt{3} + i\sqrt{2}\right) = 5$
5. $(2 + 5i)(2 + 5i) = 4 + 25$
6. $5 - \sqrt{-9} = 5 - 9i$

7. If $P(x) = x^2 + 9$, then $P(3i) = 0$.

8. The imaginary number $-3i$ is a root to the equation $x^2 + 9 = 0$.

9. $i^4 = 1$

10. $i^{18} = 1$

2.2 Exercises

Determine whether each complex number is real or imaginary and write it in the standard form a + bi.

1. $6i$

2. $-3i + \sqrt{6}$

3. $\frac{1+i}{3}$

4. -72

5. $\sqrt{7}$

6. $-i\sqrt{5}$

7. $\frac{\pi}{2}$

8. 0

Perform the indicated operations and write your answers in the form a + bi, where a and b are real numbers.

9. $(3 - 3i) + (4 + 5i)$

10. $(-3 + 2i) + (5 - 6i)$

11. $(1 - i) - (3 + 2i)$

12. $(6 - 7i) - (3 - 4i)$

13. $-6i(3 - 2i)$

14. $-3i(5 + 2i)$

15. $(2 - 3i)(4 + 6i)$

16. $(3 - i)(5 - 2i)$

17. $(5 - 2i)(5 + 2i)$

18. $(4 + 3i)(4 - 3i)$

19. $(\sqrt{3} - i)(\sqrt{3} + i)$

20. $(\sqrt{2} + i\sqrt{3})(\sqrt{2} - i\sqrt{3})$

21. $(3 + 4i)^2$

22. $(-6 - 2i)^2$

23. $(\sqrt{5} - 2i)^2$

24. $(\sqrt{6} + i\sqrt{3})^2$

25. i^{17}

26. i^{24}

27. i^{98}

28. i^{19}

29. i^{-4}

30. i^{-13}

31. i^{-1}

32. i^{-27}

Find the product of the given complex number and its conjugate.

33. $3 - 9i$

34. $4 + 3i$

35. $\frac{1}{2} + 2i$

36. $\frac{1}{3} - i$

37. i

38. $-i\sqrt{5}$

39. $3 - i\sqrt{3}$

40. $\frac{5}{2} + i\frac{\sqrt{2}}{2}$

Write each quotient in the form a + bi.

41. $\frac{1}{2 - i}$

42. $\frac{1}{5 + 2i}$

43. $\frac{-3i}{1 - i}$

44. $\frac{3i}{-2 + i}$

45. $\frac{-2 + 6i}{2}$

46. $\frac{-6 - 9i}{-3}$

47. $\frac{-3 + 3i}{i}$

48. $\frac{-2 - 4i}{-i}$

49. $\frac{1 - i}{3 + 2i}$

50. $\frac{4 + 2i}{2 - 3i}$

Write each expression in the form a + bi, where a and b are real numbers.

51. $\sqrt{-4} - \sqrt{-9}$

52. $\sqrt{-16} + \sqrt{-25}$

53. $\sqrt{-4} - \sqrt{16}$

54. $\sqrt{-3} \cdot \sqrt{-3}$

55. $(\sqrt{-6})^2$

56. $(\sqrt{-5})^3$

57. $\sqrt{-2} \cdot \sqrt{-50}$

58. $\frac{-6 + \sqrt{-3}}{3}$

59. $\frac{-2 + \sqrt{-20}}{2}$

60. $\frac{9 - \sqrt{-18}}{-6}$

61. $-3 + \sqrt{3^2 - 4(1)(5)}$

62. $1 - \sqrt{(-1)^2 - 4(1)(1)}$

63. $\sqrt{-8}(\sqrt{-2} + \sqrt{8})$

64. $\sqrt{-6}(\sqrt{2} - \sqrt{-3})$

Evaluate the expression $\frac{-b + \sqrt{b^2 - 4ac}}{2a}$ *for each choice of a, b, and c.*

65. $a = 1, b = 2, c = 5$

66. $a = 5, b = -4, c = 1$

67. $a = 2, b = 4, c = 3$

68. $a = 2, b = -4, c = 5$

Evaluate the expression $\frac{-b - \sqrt{b^2 - 4ac}}{2a}$ *for each choice of a, b, and c.*

69. $a = 1, b = 6, c = 17$

70. $a = 1, b = -12, c = 84$

71. $a = -2, b = 6, c = 6$

72. $a = 3, b = 6, c = 8$

Find the imaginary solutions to each quadratic equation and check your answers.

73. $x^2 + 1 = 0$

74. $x^2 + 9 = 0$

75. $x^2 + 8 = 0$

76. $x^2 + 27 = 0$

77. $2x^2 + 1 = 0$

78. $3x^2 + 2 = 0$

79. $x^2 - 2x + 2 = 0$

80. $x^2 - 4x + 5 = 0$

81. $x^2 - 4x + 13 = 0$

82. $x^2 - 2x + 5 = 0$

83. $x^2 - 2x + 4 = 0$

84. $x^2 - 4x + 9 = 0$

85. $-2x^2 + 2x = 5$

86. $12x - 5 = 9x^2$

87. $4x^2 - 8x + 7 = 0$

88. $9x^2 - 6x + 4 = 0$

Thinking Outside the Box XII

Summing Reciprocals There is only one way to write 1 as a sum of the reciprocals of three different positive integers:

$$\frac{1}{2} + \frac{1}{3} + \frac{1}{6} = 1$$

Find all possible ways to write 1 as a sum of the reciprocals of four different positive integers.

2.2 Pop Quiz

1. Find the sum of $3 + 2i$ and $4 - i$.
2. Find the product of $4 - 3i$ and $2 + i$.
3. Find the product of $2 - 3i$ and its conjugate.
4. Write $\dfrac{5}{2 - 3i}$ in the form $a + bi$.
5. Find i^{27}.
6. What are the two square roots of -16?

2.3 Zeros of Polynomial Functions

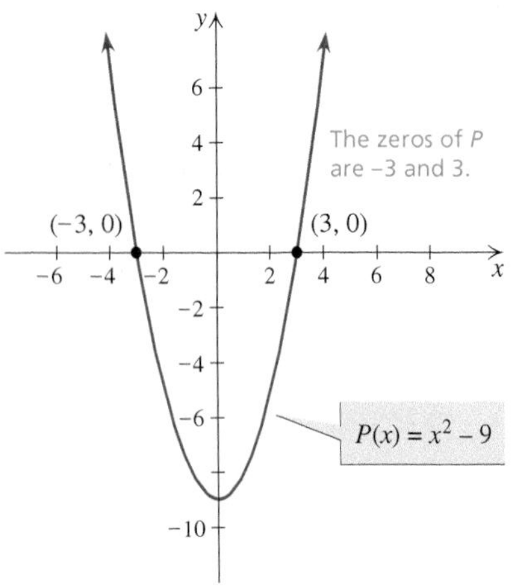

Figure 2.23

We have studied linear and quadratic functions extensively. In this section we will study general polynomial functions.

The Remainder Theorem

If $y = P(x)$ is a polynomial function, then a value of x that satisfies $P(x) = 0$ is called a **zero** of the polynomial function or a zero of the polynomial. For example, 3 and -3 are zeros of the function $P(x) = x^2 - 9$, because $P(3) = 0$ and $P(-3) = 0$. Note that the zeros of $P(x) = x^2 - 9$ are the same as the solutions to the equation $x^2 - 9 = 0$. The real zeros of a polynomial function appear on the graph of the function as the x-coordinates of the x-intercepts. The x-intercepts of the graph of $P(x) = x^2 - 9$ shown in Fig. 2.23 are $(-3, 0)$ and $(3, 0)$.

For polynomial functions of degree 2 or less, the zeros can be found by solving quadratic or linear equations. Our goal in this section is to find all of the zeros of a polynomial function when possible. For polynomials of degree higher than 2, the difficulty of this task ranges from easy to impossible, but we have some theorems to assist us. The remainder theorem relates evaluating a polynomial to division of polynomials.

The Remainder Theorem

> If R is the remainder when a polynomial $P(x)$ is divided by $x - c$, then $R = P(c)$.

PROOF Let $Q(x)$ be the quotient and R be the remainder when $P(x)$ is divided by $x - c$. Since the dividend is equal to the divisor times the quotient plus the remainder, we have

$$P(x) = (x - c)Q(x) + R.$$

This statement is true for any value of x, and so it is also true for $x = c$:

$$\begin{aligned} P(c) &= (c - c)Q(c) + R \\ &= 0 \cdot Q(c) + R \\ &= R \end{aligned}$$

So $P(c)$ is equal to the remainder when $P(x)$ is divided by $x - c$. ■

To illustrate the remainder theorem, we will now use long division to evaluate a polynomial. Long division is discussed in Section A.2 of the Appendix.

Example 1 Using the remainder theorem to evaluate a polynomial

Use the remainder theorem to find $P(3)$ if $P(x) = 2x^3 - 5x^2 + 4x - 6$.

Solution

By the remainder theorem $P(3)$ is the remainder when $P(x)$ is divided by $x - 3$:

$$\begin{array}{r} 2x^2 + x + 7 \\ x - 3 \overline{)\, 2x^3 - 5x^2 + 4x - 6} \\ \underline{2x^3 - 6x^2 } \\ x^2 + 4x \\ \underline{x^2 - 3x } \\ 7x - 6 \\ \underline{7x - 21} \\ 15 \end{array}$$

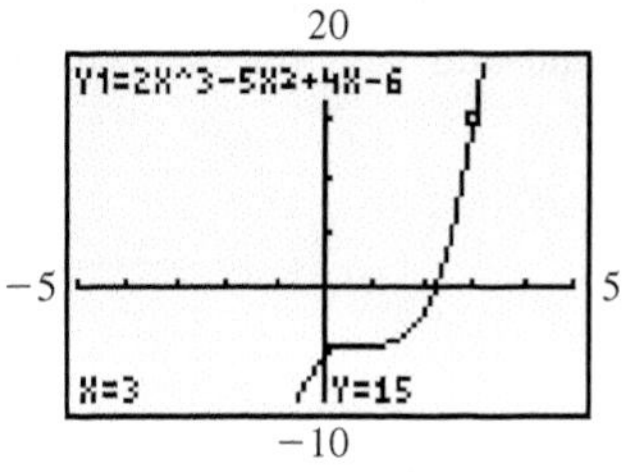

Figure 2.24

The remainder is 15 and therefore $P(3) = 15$. We can check by finding $P(3)$ in the usual manner:

$$P(3) = 2 \cdot 3^3 - 5 \cdot 3^2 + 4 \cdot 3 - 6 = 54 - 45 + 12 - 6 = 15$$

You can check this with a graphing calculator as shown in Fig. 2.24. ■

Synthetic Division

In Example 1 we found $P(3) = 15$ in two different ways. Certainly, evaluating $P(x)$ for $x = 3$ in the usual manner is faster than dividing $P(x)$ by $x - 3$ using the ordinary method of dividing polynomials. However, there is a faster method, called **synthetic division,** for dividing by $x - 3$. Compare the two methods side by side, both showing $2x^3 - 5x^2 + 4x - 6$ divided by $x - 3$:

Ordinary Division of Polynomials

$$
\begin{array}{r l}
 & 2x^2 + x + 7 \quad \leftarrow \text{Quotient} \\
x - 3 & \overline{)2x^3 - 5x^2 + 4x - 6} \\
 & \underline{2x^3 - 6x^2} \\
 & \qquad x^2 + 4x \\
 & \qquad \underline{x^2 - 3x} \\
 & \qquad\qquad 7x - 6 \\
 & \qquad\qquad \underline{7x - 21} \\
 & \qquad\qquad\quad 15 \quad \leftarrow \text{Remainder}
\end{array}
$$

Synthetic Division

$$
\begin{array}{r|rrrr}
3 & 2 & -5 & 4 & -6 \\
 & & 6 & 3 & 21 \\
\hline
 & 2 & 1 & 7 & 15 \leftarrow \text{Remainder}
\end{array}
$$

Quotient (2 1 7)

Synthetic division certainly looks easier than ordinary division, and in general it is faster than evaluating the polynomial by substitution. Synthetic division is used as a quick means of dividing a polynomial by a binomial of the form $x - c$.

In synthetic division we write just the necessary parts of the ordinary division. Instead of writing $2x^3 - 5x^2 + 4x - 6$, write the coefficients 2, -5, 4, and -6. For $x - 3$, write only the 3. The bottom row in synthetic division gives the coefficients of the quotient and the remainder.

To actually perform the synthetic division, start with the following arrangement of coefficients:

$$
\begin{array}{r|rrrr}
3 & 2 & -5 & 4 & -6 \\
 & & & & \\
\hline
\end{array}
$$

Bring down the first coefficient, 2. Multiply 2 by 3 and write the answer beneath -5. Then add:

$$
\begin{array}{r|rrrr}
3 & 2 & -5 & 4 & -6 \\
 & \downarrow & 6 & & \\
\hline
\text{Multiply} \rightarrow & 2 & 1 & & \\
 & & \uparrow \text{Add} & &
\end{array}
$$

Using 3 rather than -3 when dividing by $x - 3$ allows us to multiply and add rather than multiply and subtract as in ordinary division. Now multiply 1 by 3 and write the answer beneath 4. Then add. Repeat the multiply-and-add step for the remaining column:

$$
\begin{array}{r|rrrr}
3 & 2 & -5 & 4 & -6 \\
 & & 6 & 3 & 21 \\
\hline
 & 2 & 1 & 7 & 15
\end{array}
$$

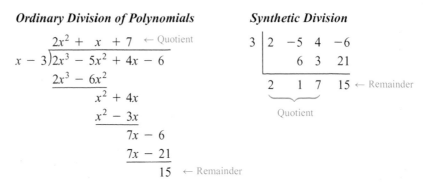

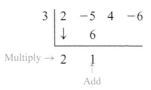

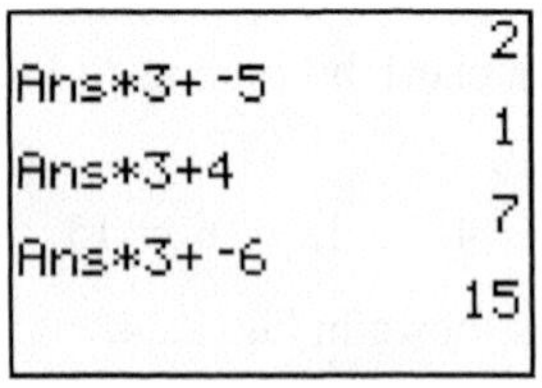

Figure 2.25

To perform this arithmetic on a graphing calculator, start with the leading coefficient 2 as the answer. Then repeatedly multiply the answer by 3 and add the next coefficient as shown in Fig. 2.25. □

The quotient is $2x^2 + x + 7$, and the remainder is 15. Since the divisor in synthetic division is of the form $x - c$, the degree of the quotient is always one less than the degree of the dividend.

Example 2 Synthetic division

Use synthetic division to find the quotient and remainder when $x^4 - 14x^2 + 5x - 9$ is divided by $x + 4$.

Solution

Since $x + 4 = x - (-4)$, we use -4 in the synthetic division. Use 1, 0, -14, 5, and -9 as the coefficients of the polynomial. We use 0 for the coefficient of the missing x^3-term, as we would in ordinary division of polynomials.

$$\begin{array}{r|rrrrr} -4 & 1 & 0 & -14 & 5 & -9 \\ & & -4 & 16 & -8 & 12 \\ \hline \text{Multiply} \rightarrow & 1 & -4 & 2 & -3 & 3 \\ & & \uparrow & & & \\ & & \text{Add} & & & \end{array}$$

The quotient is $x^3 - 4x^2 + 2x - 3$ and the remainder is 3. ■

To find the value of a polynomial $P(x)$ for $x = c$, we can divide $P(x)$ by $x - c$ or we can substitute c for x and compute. Using long division to divide by $x - c$ is not an efficient way to evaluate a polynomial. However, if we use synthetic division to divide by $x - c$ we can actually evaluate some polynomials using fewer arithmetic operations than we use in the substitution method. Note that in part (a) of the next example, synthetic division takes more steps than substitution, but in part (b) synthetic division takes fewer steps.

Example 3 Using synthetic division to evaluate a polynomial

Let $f(x) = x^3$ and $g(x) = x^3 - 3x^2 + 5x - 12$. Use synthetic division to find the following function values.

a. $f(-2)$ **b.** $g(4)$

Solution

a. To find $f(-2)$, divide the polynomial x^3 by $x - (-2)$ or $x + 2$ using synthetic division. Write x^3 as $x^3 + 0x^2 + 0x + 0$, and use 1, 0, 0, and 0 as the coefficients. We use a zero for each power of x below x^3.

$$\begin{array}{r|rrrr} -2 & 1 & 0 & 0 & 0 \\ & & -2 & 4 & -8 \\ \hline & 1 & -2 & 4 & -8 \end{array}$$

The remainder is -8, so $f(-2) = -8$. To check, find $f(-2) = (-2)^3 = -8$.

b. To find $g(4)$, use synthetic division to divide $x^3 - 3x^2 + 5x - 12$ by $x - 4$:

$$\begin{array}{r|rrrr} 4 & 1 & -3 & 5 & -12 \\ & & 4 & 4 & 36 \\ \hline & 1 & 1 & 9 & 24 \end{array}$$

The remainder is 24, so $g(4) = 24$. Check this answer by finding $g(4) = 4^3 - 3(4^2) + 5(4) - 12 = 24$. ■

The Factor Theorem

Consider the polynomial function $P(x) = x^2 - x - 6$. We can find the zeros of the function by solving $x^2 - x - 6 = 0$ by factoring:

$$(x - 3)(x + 2) = 0$$

$$x - 3 = 0 \quad \text{or} \quad x + 2 = 0$$

$$x = 3 \quad \text{or} \quad x = -2$$

Both 3 and -2 are zeros of the function $P(x) = x^2 - x - 6$. Note how each factor of the polynomial corresponds to a zero of the function. This example suggests the following theorem.

The Factor Theorem

The number c is a zero of the polynomial function $y = P(x)$ if and only if $x - c$ is a factor of the polynomial $P(x)$.

PROOF If c is a zero of the polynomial function $y = P(x)$, then $P(c) = 0$. If $P(x)$ is divided by $x - c$, we get a quotient $Q(x)$ and a remainder R such that

$$P(x) = (x - c)Q(x) + R.$$

By the remainder theorem, $R = P(c)$. Since $P(c) = 0$, we have $R = 0$ and $P(x) = (x - c)Q(x)$, which proves that $x - c$ is a factor of $P(x)$.

If $x - c$ is a factor of $P(x)$, then there is a polynomial $Q(x)$ such that $P(x) = (x - c)Q(x)$. Letting $x = c$ yields $P(c) = (c - c)Q(c) = 0$. So c is a zero of $P(x)$. These two arguments establish the truth of the factor theorem. ■

Synthetic division can be used in conjunction with the factor theorem. If the remainder of dividing $P(x)$ by $x - c$ is 0, then $P(c) = 0$ and c is a zero of the polynomial function. By the factor theorem, $x - c$ is a factor of $P(x)$.

Example 4 Using the factor theorem to factor a polynomial

Determine whether $x + 4$ is a factor of the polynomial $P(x) = x^3 - 13x + 12$. If it is a factor, then factor $P(x)$ completely.

Solution

By the factor theorem, $x + 4$ is a factor of $P(x)$ if and only if $P(-4) = 0$. We can find $P(-4)$ using synthetic division:

$$\begin{array}{r|rrrr} -4 & 1 & 0 & -13 & 12 \\ & & -4 & 16 & -12 \\ \hline & 1 & -4 & 3 & 0 \end{array}$$

Since $P(-4)$ is equal to the remainder, $P(-4) = 0$ and -4 is a zero of $P(x)$. By the factor theorem, $x + 4$ is a factor of $P(x)$. Since the other factor is the quotient from the synthetic division, $P(x) = (x + 4)(x^2 - 4x + 3)$. Factor the quadratic polynomial to get $P(x) = (x + 4)(x - 1)(x - 3)$.

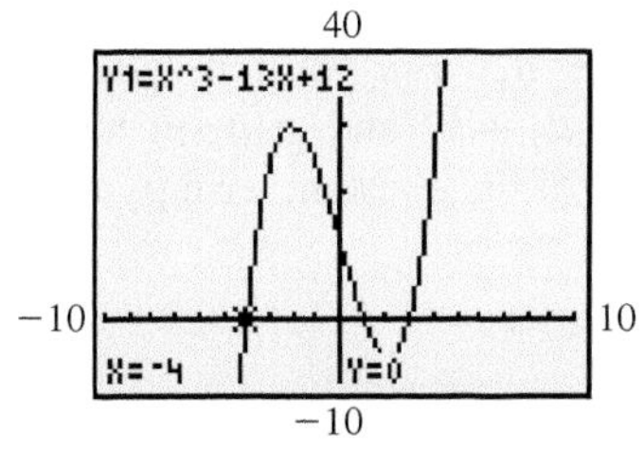

Figure 2.26

You can check this result by examining the calculator graph of $y = x^3 - 13x + 12$ shown in Fig. 2.26. The graph appears to cross the x-axis at -4, 1, and 3, supporting the conclusion that $P(x) = (x + 4)(x - 1)(x - 3)$. ■

The Fundamental Theorem of Algebra

Whether a number is a zero of a polynomial function can be determined by synthetic division. But does every polynomial function have a zero? This question was answered in the affirmative by Carl F. Gauss when he proved the fundamental theorem of algebra in his doctoral thesis in 1799 at the age of 22.

The Fundamental Theorem of Algebra

If $y = P(x)$ is a polynomial function of positive degree, then $y = P(x)$ has at least one zero in the set of complex numbers.

Gauss also proved the n-root theorem of Section 2.4 that says that the number of zeros of a polynomial (or polynomial function) of degree n is at most n. For example, a fifth-degree polynomial function has at least one zero and at most five.

Note that the zeros guaranteed by Gauss are in the set of complex numbers. So the zero might be real or imaginary. The theorem applies only to polynomial functions of degree 1 or more, because a polynomial function of zero degree such as $P(x) = 7$ has no zeros. A polynomial function of degree 1, $f(x) = ax + b$, has exactly one zero which is found by solving $ax + b = 0$. A polynomial function of degree 2, $f(x) = ax^2 + bx + c$, has one or two zeros that can be found by the quadratic formula. For higher degree polynomials the situation is not as simple. The fundamental theorem tells us that a polynomial function has at least one zero but not how to find it. For this purpose we have some other theorems.

Historical Note

Carl Friedrich Gauss (1777–1855) was a German mathematician and scientist of profound genius who contributed significantly to many fields, including number theory, analysis, differential geometry, geodesy, magnetism, astronomy, and optics. Gauss had a remarkable influence in many fields of mathematics and science and is ranked as one of history's most influential mathematicians.

The Rational Zero Theorem

Zeros or roots that are rational numbers, the **rational zeros,** are generally the easiest to find. The polynomial function $f(x) = 6x^2 - x - 35$ has two rational zeros that can be found as follows:

$$6x^2 - x - 35 = 0$$

$$(2x - 5)(3x + 7) = 0 \quad \text{Factor.}$$

$$x = \frac{5}{2} \quad \text{or} \quad x = -\frac{7}{3}$$

Note that in $5/2$, 5 is a factor of -35 (the constant term) and 2 is a factor of 6 (the leading coefficient). For the zero $-7/3$, -7 is a factor of -35 and 3 is a factor of 6. Of course, these observations are not surprising, because we used these facts to factor the quadratic polynomial in the first place. Note that there are a lot of other factors of -35 and 6 for which the ratio is *not* a zero of this function. This example illustrates the rational zero theorem, which is also called the rational root theorem.

The Rational Zero Theorem

If $f(x) = a_n x^n + a_{n-1}x^{n-1} + a_{n-2}x^{n-2} + \cdots + a_1 x + a_0$ is a polynomial function with integral coefficients $(a_n \neq 0$ and $a_0 \neq 0)$ and p/q (in lowest terms) is a rational zero of $f(x)$, then p is a factor of the constant term a_0 and q is a factor of the leading coefficient a_n.

PROOF If p/q is a zero of $f(x)$, then $f(p/q) = 0$:

$$a_n\left(\frac{p}{q}\right)^n + a_{n-1}\left(\frac{p}{q}\right)^{n-1} + a_{n-2}\left(\frac{p}{q}\right)^{n-2} + \cdots + a_1\frac{p}{q} + a_0 = 0$$

Subtract a_0 from each side and multiply by q^n to get the following equation:

$$a_n p^n + a_{n-1}p^{n-1}q + a_{n-2}p^{n-2}q^2 + \cdots + a_1 pq^{n-1} = -a_0 q^n$$

Since the coefficients are integers and p and q are integers, both sides of this equation are integers. Since p is a factor of the left side p must be a factor of the right side, which is the same integer. Since p/q is in lowest terms, p is not a factor of q. So p must be a factor of a_0.

To prove that q is a factor of a_n, rearrange the last equation as follows:

$$a_{n-1}p^{n-1}q + a_{n-2}p^{n-2}q^2 + \cdots + a_1 pq^{n-1} + a_0 q^n = -a_n p^n.$$

Now q is a factor of a_n by the same argument used previously. ■

The rational zero theorem does not identify exactly which rational numbers are zeros of a function; it only gives *possibilities* for the rational zeros.

Example 5 Using the rational zero theorem

Find all possible rational zeros for each polynomial function.

a. $f(x) = 2x^3 - 3x^2 - 11x + 6$ **b.** $g(x) = 3x^3 - 8x^2 - 8x + 8$

Solution

a. If the rational number p/q is a zero of $f(x)$, then p is a factor of 6 and q is a factor of 2. The positive factors of 6 are 1, 2, 3, and 6. The positive factors of 2 are 1 and 2. Take each factor of 6 and divide by 1 to get $1/1$, $2/1$, $3/1$, and $6/1$. Take each factor of 6 and divide by 2 to get $1/2$, $2/2$, $3/2$, and $6/2$. Simplify the ratios, eliminate duplications, and put in the negative factors to get

$$\pm 1, \quad \pm 2, \quad \pm 3, \quad \pm 6, \quad \pm\frac{1}{2}, \quad \text{and} \quad \pm\frac{3}{2}$$

as the possible rational zeros to the function $f(x)$.

b. If the rational number p/q is a zero of $g(x)$, then p is a factor of 8 and q is a factor of 3. The factors of 8 are 1, 2, 4, and 8. The factors of 3 are 1 and 3. If we take all possible ratios of a factor of 8 over a factor of 3, we get

$$\pm 1, \quad \pm 2, \quad \pm 4, \quad \pm 8, \quad \pm\frac{1}{3}, \quad \pm\frac{2}{3}, \quad \pm\frac{4}{3}, \quad \text{and} \quad \pm\frac{8}{3}$$

as the possible rational zeros of the function $g(x)$. ■

Our goal is to find all of the zeros to a polynomial function. The zeros to a polynomial function might be rational, irrational, or imaginary. We can determine the rational zeros by simply evaluating the polynomial function for every number in the list of possible rational zeros. If the list is long, looking at a graph of the function can speed up the process. We will use synthetic division to evaluate the polynomial, because synthetic division gives the quotient polynomial as well as the value of the polynomial.

Example 6 Finding all zeros of a polynomial function

Find all of the real and imaginary zeros for each polynomial function of Example 5.

a. $f(x) = 2x^3 - 3x^2 - 11x + 6$ **b.** $g(x) = 3x^3 - 8x^2 - 8x + 8$

Solution

a. The possible rational zeros of $f(x)$ are listed in Example 5(a). Use synthetic division to check each possible zero to see whether it is actually a zero. Try 1 first.

$$\begin{array}{r|rrrr} 1 & 2 & -3 & -11 & 6 \\ & & 2 & -1 & -12 \\ \hline & 2 & -1 & -12 & -6 \end{array}$$

Since the remainder is -6, 1 is not a zero of the function. Keep on trying numbers from the list of possible rational zeros. To save space, we will not show any more failures. So try $1/2$ next.

$$\begin{array}{r|rrrr} \frac{1}{2} & 2 & -3 & -11 & 6 \\ & & 1 & -1 & -6 \\ \hline & 2 & -2 & -12 & 0 \end{array}$$

Since the remainder in the synthetic division is 0, $1/2$ is a zero of $f(x)$. By the factor theorem, $x - 1/2$ is a factor of the polynomial. The quotient is the other factor.

$$2x^3 - 3x^2 - 11x + 6 = 0$$

$$\left(x - \frac{1}{2}\right)(2x^2 - 2x - 12) = 0 \quad \text{Factor.}$$

$$(2x - 1)(x^2 - x - 6) = 0 \quad \text{Factor 2 out of the second "factor" and distribute it into the first factor.}$$

$$(2x - 1)(x - 3)(x + 2) = 0 \quad \text{Factor completely.}$$

$$2x - 1 = 0 \quad \text{or} \quad x - 3 = 0 \quad \text{or} \quad x + 2 = 0$$

$$x = \frac{1}{2} \quad \text{or} \quad x = 3 \quad \text{or} \quad x = -2$$

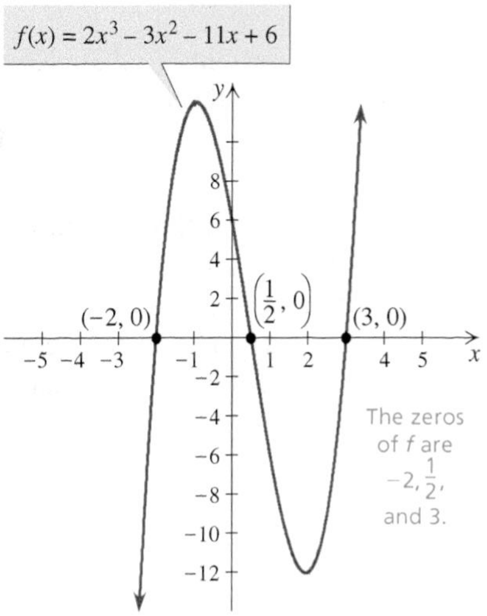

Figure 2.27

The zeros of the function f are $1/2$, 3, and -2. Note that each zero of f corresponds to an x-intercept on the graph of f shown in Fig. 2.27. Because this polynomial had three rational zeros, we could have found them all by using synthetic division or by examining the calculator graph. However, it is good to factor the polynomial to see the correspondence between the three zeros, the three factors, and the three x-intercepts.

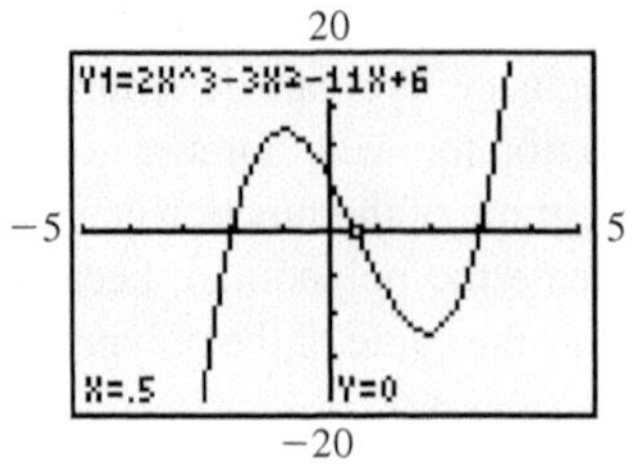

Figure 2.28

You could speed up this process of finding a zero with the calculator graph shown in Fig. 2.28. It is not too hard to discover that $1/2$ is a zero by looking at the graph and the list of possible rational zeros that we listed in Example 5. If you use a graph to find that $1/2$ is a zero, you still need to do synthetic division to factor the polynomial.

b. The possible rational zeros of $g(x)$ are listed in Example 5(b). First check $2/3$ to see whether it produces a remainder of 0.

$$\begin{array}{r|rrrr} \frac{2}{3} & 3 & -8 & -8 & 8 \\ & & 2 & -4 & -8 \\ \hline & 3 & -6 & -12 & 0 \end{array}$$

Since the remainder in the synthetic division is 0, $2/3$ is a zero of $g(x)$. By the factor theorem, $x - 2/3$ is a factor of the polynomial. The quotient is the other factor.

$$3x^3 - 8x^2 - 8x + 8 = 0$$

$$\left(x - \frac{2}{3}\right)(3x^2 - 6x - 12) = 0$$

$$(3x - 2)(x^2 - 2x - 4) = 0$$

$$3x - 2 = 0 \quad \text{or} \quad x^2 - 2x - 4 = 0$$

$$x = \frac{2}{3} \quad \text{or} \quad x = \frac{2 \pm \sqrt{20}}{2}$$

$$x = \frac{2}{3} \quad \text{or} \quad x = 1 \pm \sqrt{5}$$

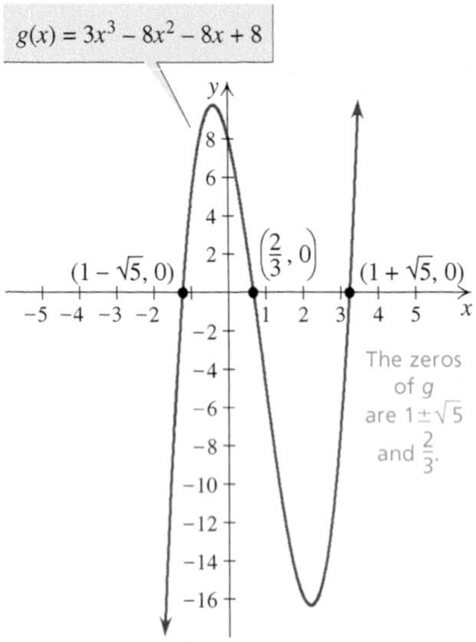

Figure 2.29

There are one rational and two irrational roots to the equation. So the zeros of the function g are $2/3$, $1 + \sqrt{5}$, and $1 - \sqrt{5}$. Each zero corresponds to an x-intercept on the graph of g shown in Fig. 2.29.

You could graph the function with a calculator as shown in Fig. 2.30. Keeping in mind the list of possible rational zeros, it is not hard to discover that $2/3$ is a zero. ■

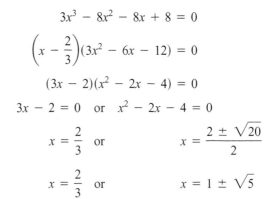

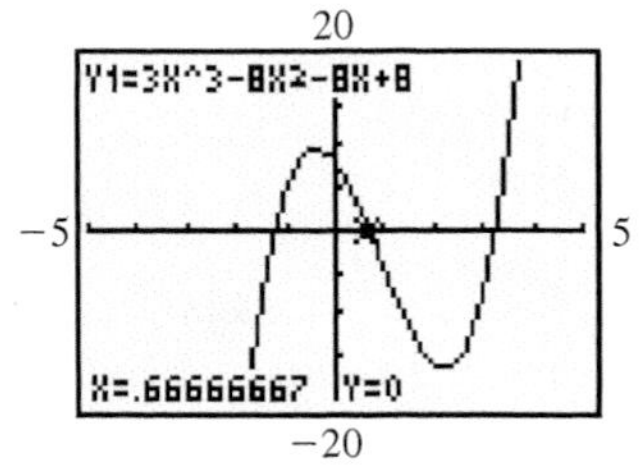

Figure 2.30

Note that in Example 6(a) all of the zeros were rational. All three could have been found by continuing to check the possible rational zeros using synthetic division. In Example 6(b) we would be wasting time if we continued to check the possible rational zeros, because there is only one. When we get to a quadratic polynomial, it is best to either factor the quadratic polynomial or use the quadratic formula to find the remaining zeros.

For Thought

True or False? Explain.

1. The function $f(x) = 1/x$ has at least one zero.

2. If $P(x) = x^4 - 6x^2 - 8$ is divided by $x^2 - 2$, then the remainder is $P(\sqrt{2})$.

3. If $1 - 2i$ and $1 + 2i$ are zeros of $P(x) = x^3 - 5x^2 + 11x - 15$, then $x - 1 - 2i$ and $x - 1 + 2i$ are factors of $P(x)$.

4. If we divide $x^5 - 1$ by $x - 2$, then the remainder is 31.

5. Every polynomial function has at least one zero.

6. If $P(x) = x^3 - x^2 + 4x - 5$ and b is the remainder from division of $P(x)$ by $x - c$, then $b^3 - b^2 + 4b - 5 = c$.

7. If $P(x) = x^3 - 5x^2 + 4x - 15$, then $P(4) = 0$.

8. The equation $\pi^2 x^4 - \frac{1}{\sqrt{2}}x^3 + \frac{1}{\sqrt{7} + \pi} = 0$ has at least one complex solution.

9. The binomial $x - 1$ is a factor of $x^5 + x^4 - x^3 - x^2 - x + 1$.

10. The binomial $x + 3$ is a factor of $3x^4 - 5x^3 + 7x^2 - 9x - 2$.

2.3 Exercises

Use ordinary division of polynomials to find the quotient and remainder when the first polynomial is divided by the second.

1. $x^2 - 5x + 7, x - 2$
2. $x^2 - 3x + 9, x - 4$
3. $-2x^3 + 4x - 9, x + 3$
4. $-4w^3 + 5w^2 - 7, w - 3$
5. $s^4 - 3s^2 + 6, s^2 - 5$
6. $h^4 + 3h^3 + h - 5, h^2 - 3$

Use synthetic division to find the quotient and remainder when the first polynomial is divided by the second.

7. $x^2 + 4x + 1, x - 2$
8. $2x^2 - 3x + 6, x - 5$
9. $-x^3 + x^2 - 4x + 9, x + 3$
10. $-3x^3 + 5x^2 - 6x + 1, x + 1$
11. $4x^3 - 5x + 2, x - \frac{1}{2}$
12. $-6x^3 + 25x^2 - 9, x - \frac{3}{2}$
13. $2a^3 - 3a^2 + 4a + 3, a + \frac{1}{2}$
14. $-3b^3 - b^2 - 3b - 1, b + \frac{1}{3}$
15. $x^4 - 3, x - 1$
16. $x^4 - 16, x - 2$
17. $x^5 - 6x^3 + 4x - 5, x - 2$
18. $2x^5 - 5x^4 - 5x + 7, x - 3$

Let $f(x) = x^5 - 1$, $g(x) = x^3 - 4x^2 + 8$, and $h(x) = 2x^4 + x^3 - x^2 + 3x + 3$. Find the following function values by using synthetic division. Check by using substitution.

19. $f(1)$
20. $f(-1)$
21. $f(-2)$
22. $f(3)$
23. $g(1)$
24. $g(-1)$
25. $g\left(-\frac{1}{2}\right)$
26. $g\left(\frac{1}{2}\right)$
27. $h(-1)$
28. $h(2)$
29. $h(1)$
30. $h(-3)$

Determine whether the given binomial is a factor of the polynomial following it. If it is a factor, then factor the polynomial completely.

31. $x + 3, x^3 + 4x^2 + x - 6$
32. $x + 5, x^3 + 8x^2 + 11x - 20$
33. $x - 4, x^3 + 4x^2 - 17x - 60$
34. $x - 2, x^3 - 12x^2 + 44x - 48$

Determine whether each given number is a zero of the polynomial function following the number.

35. $3, f(x) = 2x^3 - 5x^2 - 4x + 3$
36. $-2, g(x) = 3x^3 - 6x^2 - 3x - 19$
37. $-2, g(d) = d^3 + 2d^2 + 3d + 1$
38. $-1, w(x) = 3x^3 + 2x^2 - 2x - 1$
39. $-1, P(x) = x^4 + 2x^3 + 4x^2 + 6x + 3$
40. $3, G(r) = r^4 + 4r^3 + 5r^2 + 3r + 17$
41. $\frac{1}{2}, H(x) = x^3 + 3x^2 - 5x + 7$
42. $-\frac{1}{2}, T(x) = 2x^3 + 3x^2 - 3x - 2$

Use the rational zero theorem to find all possible rational zeros for each polynomial function.

43. $f(x) = x^3 - 9x^2 + 26x - 24$

44. $g(x) = x^3 - 2x^2 - 5x + 6$

45. $h(x) = x^3 - x^2 - 7x + 15$

46. $m(x) = x^3 + 4x^2 + 4x + 3$

47. $P(x) = 8x^3 - 36x^2 + 46x - 15$

48. $T(x) = 18x^3 - 9x^2 - 5x + 2$

49. $M(x) = 18x^3 - 21x^2 + 10x - 2$

50. $N(x) = 4x^3 - 10x^2 + 4x + 5$

Find all of the real and imaginary zeros for each polynomial function.

51. $f(x) = x^3 - 9x^2 + 26x - 24$

52. $g(x) = x^3 - 2x^2 - 5x + 6$

53. $h(x) = x^3 - x^2 - 7x + 15$

54. $m(x) = x^3 + 4x^2 + 4x + 3$

55. $P(a) = 8a^3 - 36a^2 + 46a - 15$

56. $T(b) = 18b^3 - 9b^2 - 5b + 2$

57. $M(t) = 18t^3 - 21t^2 + 10t - 2$

58. $N(t) = 4t^3 - 10t^2 + 4t + 5$

59. $S(w) = w^4 + w^3 - w^2 + w - 2$

60. $W(v) = 2v^4 + 5v^3 + 3v^2 + 15v - 9$

61. $V(x) = x^4 + 2x^3 - x^2 - 4x - 2$

62. $U(x) = x^4 - 4x^3 + x^2 + 12x - 12$

63. $f(x) = 24x^3 - 26x^2 + 9x - 1$

64. $f(x) = 30x^3 - 47x^2 - x + 6$

65. $y = 16x^3 - 33x^2 + 82x - 5$

66. $y = 15x^3 - 37x^2 + 44x - 14$

67. $f(x) = 21x^4 - 31x^3 - 21x^2 - 31x - 42$

68. $f(x) = 119x^4 - 5x^3 + 214x^2 - 10x - 48$

69. $f(x) = (x^2 + 9)(x^3 + 6x^2 + 3x - 10)$

70. $f(x) = (x^2 - 5)(x^3 - 5x^2 - 12x + 36)$

71. $f(x) = (x^2 - 4x + 1)(x^3 - 9x^2 + 23x - 15)$

72. $f(x) = (x^2 - 4x + 13)(x^3 - 4x^2 - 17x + 60)$

Use division to write each rational expression in the form quotient + remainder/divisor. Use synthetic division when possible.

73. $\dfrac{2x + 1}{x - 2}$

74. $\dfrac{x - 1}{x + 3}$

75. $\dfrac{a^2 - 3a + 5}{a - 3}$

76. $\dfrac{2b^2 - 3b + 1}{b + 2}$

77. $\dfrac{c^2 - 3c - 4}{c^2 - 4}$

78. $\dfrac{2h^2 + h - 2}{h^2 - 1}$

79. $\dfrac{4t - 5}{2t + 1}$

80. $\dfrac{6y - 1}{3y - 1}$

Solve each problem.

81. *Drug Testing* The concentration of a drug (in parts per million) in a patient's bloodstream t hours after administration of the drug is given by the function

$$P(t) = -t^4 + 12t^3 - 58t^2 + 132t.$$

a. Use the formula to determine when the drug will be totally eliminated from the bloodstream.

b. Use the graph to estimate the maximum concentration of the drug.

c. Use the graph to estimate the time at which the maximum concentration occurs.

d. Use the graph to estimate the amount of time for which the concentration is above 80 ppm.

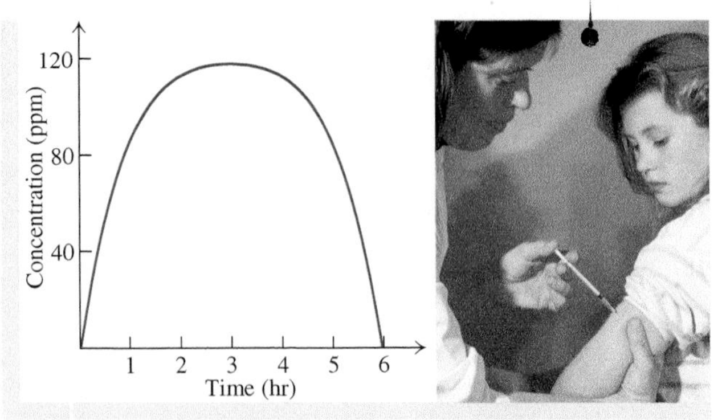

Figure for Exercise 81

82. *Open-Top Box* Joan intends to make an 18-in.^{3} open-top box out of a 6 in. by 7 in. piece of copper by cutting equal squares

(x in. by x in.) from the corners and folding up the sides. Write the difference between the intended volume and the actual volume as a function of x. For what value of x is there no difference between the intended volume and the actual volume?

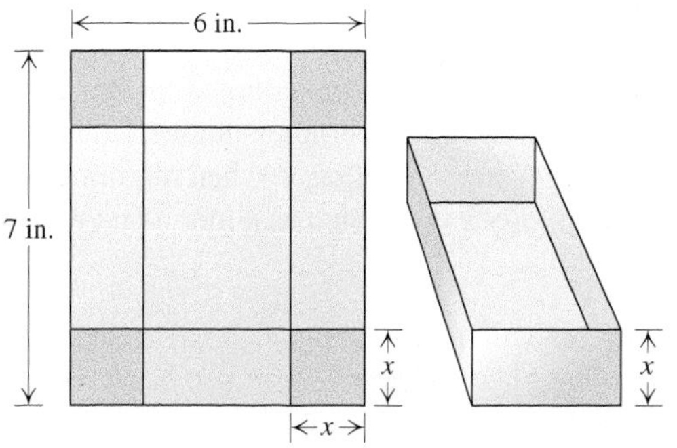

Figure for Exercise 82

83. *Cartridge Box* The height of a box containing an HP Laser Jet III printer cartridge is 4 in. more than the width and the length is 9 in. more than the width. If the volume of the box is 630 in.^{3}, then what are the dimensions of the box?

84. *Computer Case* The width of the case for a 733 megahertz Pentium computer is 4 in. more than twice the height and the depth is 1 in. more than the width. If the volume of the case is 1632 in.^{3}, then what are the dimensions of the case?

Thinking Outside the Box XIII

Moving a Refrigerator A box containing a refrigerator is 3 ft wide, 3 ft deep, and 6 ft high. To move it, Wally lays it on its side, then on its top, then on its other side, and finally stands it upright as shown in the figure. Exactly how far has point A traveled in going from its initial location to its final location?

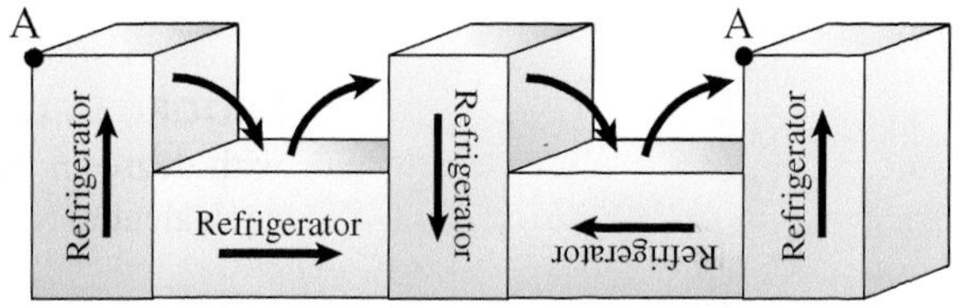

Figure for Thinking Outside the Box XIII

2.3 Pop Quiz

1. Use ordinary division to find the quotient and remainder when $x^3 - 5x + 7$ is divided by $x + 4$.

2. Use synthetic division to find the quotient and remainder when $x^2 - 3x + 9$ is divided by $x - 5$.

3. Use synthetic division to find $f(3)$ if $f(x) = x^3 - 2x^2 + 4x - 1$.

4. List the possible rational zeros for $f(x) = 2x^3 - 3x + 8$.

5. Find all real and imaginary zeros for $f(x) = 2x^3 - x^2 + 18x - 9$.

2.4 The Theory of Equations

One of the main goals in algebra is to keep expanding our knowledge of solving equations. The solutions (roots) of a polynomial equation $P(x) = 0$ are precisely the zeros of a polynomial function $y = P(x)$. Therefore the theorems of Section 2.3 concerning zeros of polynomial functions apply also to the roots of polynomial equations. In this section we study several additional theorems that are useful in solving polynomial equations.

The Number of Roots of a Polynomial Equation

When a polynomial equation is solved by factoring, a factor may occur more than once. For example, $x^2 - 10x + 25 = 0$ is equivalent to $(x - 5)^2 = 0$. Since the factor $x - 5$ occurs twice, we say that 5 is a root of the equation with *multiplicity* 2.

Definition: Multiplicity

If the factor $x - c$ occurs k times in the complete factorization of the polynomial $P(x)$, then c is called a root of $P(x) = 0$ with **multiplicity** k.

If a quadratic equation has a single root, as in $x^2 - 10x + 25 = 0$, then that root has multiplicity 2. If a root with multiplicity 2 is counted as two roots, then every quadratic equation has two roots in the set of complex numbers. This situation is generalized in the following theorem, where the phrase "when multiplicity is considered" means that a root with multiplicity k is counted as k individual roots.

***n*-Root Theorem**

If $P(x) = 0$ is a polynomial equation with real or complex coefficients and positive degree n, then, when multiplicity is considered, $P(x) = 0$ has n roots.

PROOF By the fundamental theorem of algebra, the polynomial equation $P(x) = 0$ with degree n has at least one complex root c_1. By the factor theorem, $P(x) = 0$ is equivalent to

$$(x - c_1)Q_1(x) = 0,$$

where $Q_1(x)$ is a polynomial with degree $n - 1$ (the quotient when $P(x)$ is divided by $x - c_1$). Again, by the fundamental theorem of algebra, there is at least one complex root c_2 of $Q_1(x) = 0$. By the factor theorem, $P(x) = 0$ can be written as

$$(x - c_1)(x - c_2)Q_2(x) = 0,$$

where $Q_2(x)$ is a polynomial with degree $n - 2$. Reasoning in this manner n times, we get a quotient polynomial that has 0 degree, n factors for $P(x)$, and n complex roots, not necessarily all different. ■

Example 1 Finding all roots of a polynomial equation

State the degree of each polynomial equation. Find all real and imaginary roots of each equation, stating multiplicity when it is greater than one.

a. $6x^5 + 24x^3 = 0$ **b.** $(x - 3)^2(x + 14)^5 = 0$

Solution

a. This fifth-degree equation can be solved by factoring:

$$6x^3(x^2 + 4) = 0$$

$$6x^3 = 0 \quad \text{or} \quad x^2 + 4 = 0$$

$$x^3 = 0 \quad \text{or} \quad x^2 = -4$$

$$x = 0 \quad \text{or} \quad x = \pm 2i$$

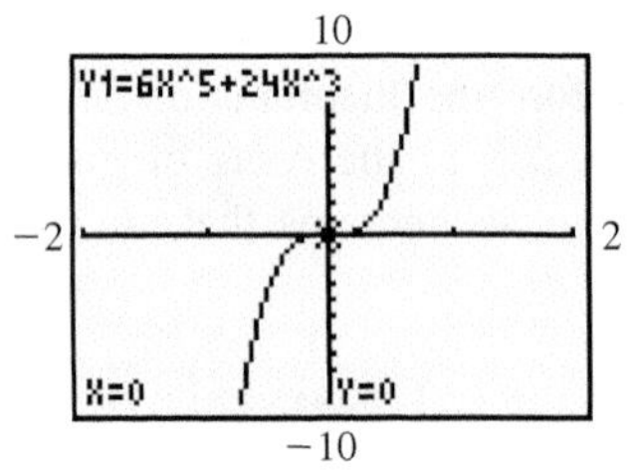

Figure 2.31

The roots are $\pm 2i$ and 0. Since there are two imaginary roots and 0 is a root with multiplicity 3, there are five roots when multiplicity is considered.

Because 0 is the only real root, the graph of $y = 6x^5 + 24x^3$ has only one x-intercept at (0, 0) as shown in Fig. 2.31. □

b. The highest power of x in $(x - 3)^2$ is 2, and in $(x + 14)^5$ is 5. By the product rule for exponents, the highest power of x in this equation is 7. The only roots of

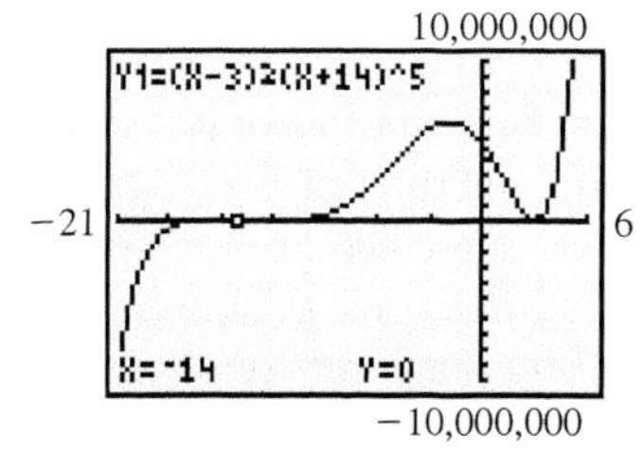

Figure 2.32

this seventh-degree equation are 3 and -14. The root 3 has multiplicity 2, and -14 has multiplicity 5. So there are seven roots when multiplicity is considered. Because the equation has two real solutions, the graph of $y = (x - 3)^2(x + 14)^5$ has two x-intercepts at $(3, 0)$ and $(-14, 0)$ as shown in Fig. 2.32. ■

Note that graphing polynomial functions and solving polynomial equations go hand in hand. The solutions to the equation can help us find an appropriate viewing window for the graph as they did in Example 1, and the graph can help us find solutions to the equation.

The Conjugate Pairs Theorem

For second-degree polynomial equations, the imaginary roots occur in pairs. For example, the roots of $x^2 - 2x + 5 = 0$ are

$$x = \frac{2 \pm \sqrt{(-2)^2 - 4(1)(5)}}{2} = 1 \pm 2i.$$

The roots $1 - 2i$ and $1 + 2i$ are complex conjugates. The $\pm$ symbol in the quadratic formula causes the complex solutions of a quadratic equation with real coefficients to occur in conjugate pairs. The conjugate pairs theorem indicates that this situation occurs also for polynomial equations of higher degree.

Conjugate Pairs Theorem

If $P(x) = 0$ is a polynomial equation with real coefficients and the complex number $a + bi$ $(b \neq 0)$ is a root, then $a - bi$ is also a root.

Example 2 Using the conjugate pairs theorem

Find a polynomial equation with real coefficients that has 2 and $1 - i$ as roots.

Solution

If the polynomial has real coefficients, then its imaginary roots occur in conjugate pairs. So a polynomial with these two roots must actually have at least three roots: 2, $1 - i$, and $1 + i$. Since each root of the equation corresponds to a factor of the polynomial, we can write the following equation.

$$(x - 2)[x - (1 - i)][x - (1 + i)] = 0$$

$$(x - 2)[(x - 1) + i][(x - 1) - i] = 0 \quad \text{Regroup.}$$

$$(x - 2)[(x - 1)^2 - i^2] = 0 \quad (a + b)(a - b) = a^2 - b^2$$

$$(x - 2)[x^2 - 2x + 1 + 1] = 0 \quad i^2 = -1$$

$$(x - 2)(x^2 - 2x + 2) = 0$$

$$x^3 - 4x^2 + 6x - 4 = 0$$

This equation has the required roots and the smallest degree. Any multiple of this equation would also have the required roots but would not be as simple. ■

Historical Note

Évariste Galois (1811–1832) was a French mathematician. While still in his teens, he was able to determine a necessary and sufficient condition for a polynomial equation to be solvable by radicals, thereby solving a longstanding problem. His work laid the fundamental foundations for Galois theory, a major branch of abstract algebra. He died in a duel at the age of twenty.

Descartes's Rule of Signs

None of the theorems in this chapter tells us how to find all of the n roots to a polynomial equation of degree n. However, the theorems and rules presented here add to our knowledge of polynomial equations and help us to predict the type and number of solutions to expect for a particular equation. Descartes's rule of signs is a method for determining the number of positive, negative, and imaginary solutions. For this rule, a solution with multiplicity k is counted as k solutions.

When a polynomial is written in descending order, a **variation of sign** occurs when the signs of consecutive terms change. For example, if

$$P(x) = 3x^5 - 7x^4 - 8x^3 - x^2 + 3x - 9,$$

there are sign changes in going from the first to the second term, from the fourth to the fifth term, and from the fifth to the sixth term. So there are three variations of sign for $P(x)$. This information determines the number of positive real solutions to $P(x) = 0$. Descartes's rule requires that we look at $P(-x)$ and also count the variations of sign after it is simplified:

$$\begin{aligned} P(-x) &= 3(-x)^5 - 7(-x)^4 - 8(-x)^3 - (-x)^2 + 3(-x) - 9 \\ &= -3x^5 - 7x^4 + 8x^3 - x^2 - 3x - 9 \end{aligned}$$

In $P(-x)$ the signs of the terms change from the second to the third term and again from the third to the fourth term. So there are two variations of sign for $P(-x)$. This information determines the number of negative real solutions to $P(x) = 0$.

Descartes's Rule of Signs

Suppose $P(x) = 0$ is a polynomial equation with real coefficients and with terms written in descending order.

- The number of positive real roots of the equation is either equal to the number of variations of sign of $P(x)$ or less than that by an even number.
- The number of negative real roots of the equation is either equal to the number of variations of sign of $P(-x)$ or less than that by an even number.

The proof of Descartes's rule of signs is beyond the scope of this text, but we can apply the rule to polynomial equations. Descartes's rule of signs is especially helpful when the number of variations of sign is 0 or 1.

Example 3 Using Descartes's rule of signs

Discuss the possibilities for the roots to $2x^3 - 5x^2 - 6x + 4 = 0$.

Solution

The number of variations of sign in

$$P(x) = 2x^3 - 5x^2 - 6x + 4$$

is 2. By Descartes's rule, the number of positive real roots is either 2 or 0. Since

$$\begin{aligned} P(-x) &= 2(-x)^3 - 5(-x)^2 - 6(-x) + 4 \\ &= -2x^3 - 5x^2 + 6x + 4, \end{aligned}$$

there is one variation of sign in $P(-x)$. So there is exactly one negative real root.

The equation must have three roots, because it is a third-degree polynomial equation. Since there must be three roots and one is negative, the other two roots must be either both imaginary numbers or both positive real numbers. Table 2.1 summarizes these two possibilities.

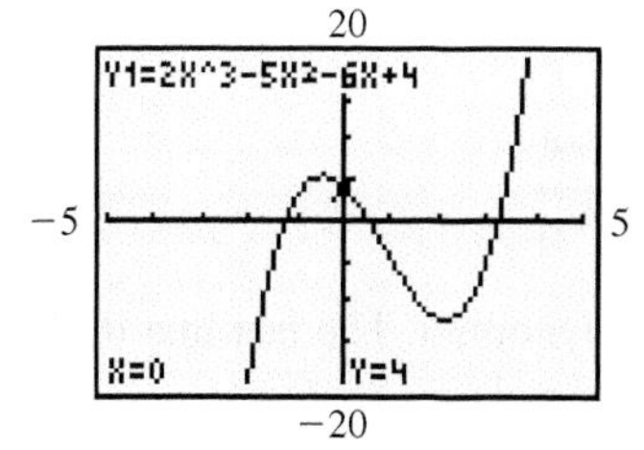

Figure 2.33

Table 2.1 Number of roots

Positive	Negative	Imaginary
2	1	0
0	1	2

The graph of $y = 2x^3 - 5x^2 - 6x + 4$ shown in Fig. 2.33 crosses the positive x-axis twice and the negative x-axis once. So the first case in Table 2.1 is actually correct. ■

Example 4 Using Descartes's rule of signs

Discuss the possibilities for the roots to $3x^4 - 5x^3 - x^2 - 8x + 4 = 0$.

Solution

There are two variations of sign in the polynomial

$$P(x) = 3x^4 - 5x^3 - x^2 - 8x + 4.$$

According to Descartes's rule, there are either two or zero positive real roots to the equation. Since

$$P(-x) = 3(-x)^4 - 5(-x)^3 - (-x)^2 - 8(-x) + 4$$
$$= 3x^4 + 5x^3 - x^2 + 8x + 4,$$

there are two variations of sign in $P(-x)$. So the number of negative real roots is either two or zero. Since the degree of the polynomial is 4, there must be four roots. Each line of Table 2.2 gives a possible distribution of the type of those four roots. Note that the number of imaginary roots is even in each case, as we would expect from the conjugate pairs theorem.

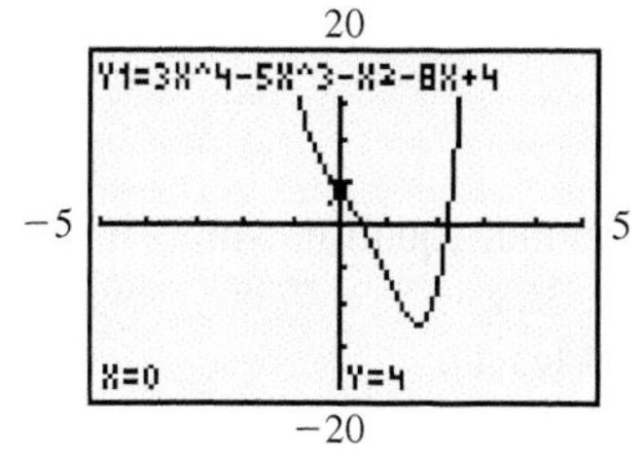

Figure 2.34

Table 2.2 Number of roots

Positive	Negative	Imaginary
2	2	0
2	0	2
0	2	2
0	0	4

The calculator graph of $y = 3x^4 - 5x^3 - x^2 - 8x + 4$ shown in Fig. 2.34 shows two positive intercepts and no negative intercepts. However, we might not have the appropriate viewing window. The negative intercepts might be less than -5. In this case the graph did not allow us to conclude which line in Table 2.2 is correct. ■

Example 5 Using all of the theorems about roots

Find all of the solutions to $2x^3 - 5x^2 - 6x + 4 = 0$.

Solution

In Example 3 we used Descartes's rule of signs on this equation to determine that it has either two positive roots and one negative root or one negative root and two imaginary roots. From the rational zero theorem, the possible rational roots are ± 1, ± 2, ± 4, and $\pm 1/2$. Use synthetic division to start checking the possible rational roots. The only possible rational root that is actually a root is $1/2$:

$$\begin{array}{r|rrrr} \frac{1}{2} & 2 & -5 & -6 & 4 \\ & & 1 & -2 & -4 \\ \hline & 2 & -4 & -8 & 0 \end{array}$$

Since $1/2$ is a root, $x - 1/2$ is a factor of the polynomial. The last line in the synthetic division indicates that the other factor is $2x^2 - 4x - 8$.

$$\left(x - \frac{1}{2}\right)(2x^2 - 4x - 8) = 0$$

$$(2x - 1)(x^2 - 2x - 4) = 0$$

$$2x - 1 = 0 \quad \text{or} \quad x^2 - 2x - 4 = 0$$

$$x = \frac{1}{2} \quad \text{or} \quad x = \frac{2 \pm \sqrt{4 - 4(1)(-4)}}{2} = 1 \pm \sqrt{5}$$

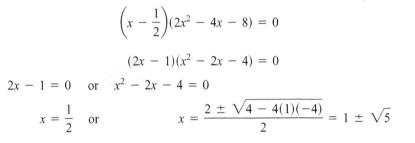

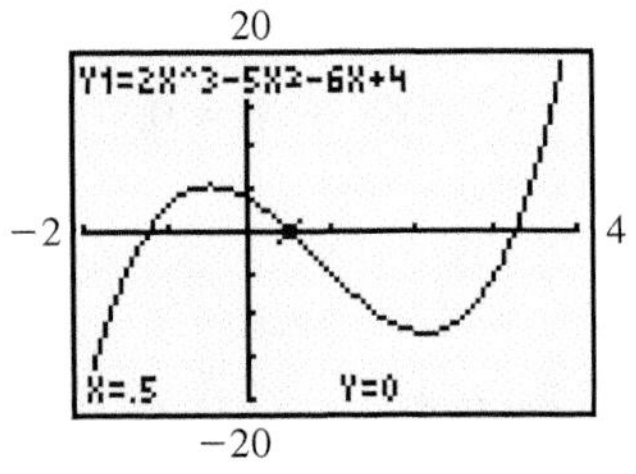

Figure 2.35

There are two positive roots, $1/2$ and $1 + \sqrt{5}$. The negative root is $1 - \sqrt{5}$, which is irrational. The roots guaranteed by Descartes's rule of signs are real numbers but not necessarily rational numbers.

The graph of $y = 2x^3 - 5x^2 - 6x + 4$ in Fig. 2.35 supports these conclusions, because its x-intercepts appear to be $(1 - \sqrt{5}, 0)$, $(1/2, 0)$, and $(1 + \sqrt{5}, 0)$. ■

For Thought

True or False? Explain.

1. The number 1 is a root of $x^3 - 1 = 0$ with multiplicity 3.

2. The equation $x^3 = 125$ has three complex number solutions.

3. For $(x + 1)^3(x^2 - 2x + 1) = 0$, -1 is a root with multiplicity 3.

4. For $(x - 5)^3(x^2 - 3x - 10) = 0$, 5 is a root with multiplicity 3.

5. If $4 - 5i$ is a solution to a polynomial equation with real coefficients, then $5i - 4$ is also a solution to the equation.

6. If $P(x) = 0$ is a polynomial equation with real coefficients and i, $2 - 3i$, and $5 + 7i$ are roots, then the degree of $P(x)$ is at least 6.

7. Both $-3 - i\sqrt{5}$ and $3 - i\sqrt{5}$ are solutions to $5x^3 - 9x^2 + 17x - 23 = 0$.

8. Both $3/2$ and 2 are solutions to $2x^5 - 4x^3 - 6x^2 - 3x - 6 = 0$.

9. The equation $x^3 - 5x^2 + 6x - 1 = 0$ has no negative roots.

10. The equation $5x^3 - 171 = 0$ has two imaginary solutions.

2.4 Exercises

State the degree of each polynomial equation. Find all of the real and imaginary roots of each equation, stating multiplicity when it is greater than one.

1. $x^2 - 10x + 25 = 0$

2. $x^2 - 18x + 81 = 0$

3. $x^5 - 9x^3 = 0$

4. $x^6 + x^4 = 0$

5. $x^4 - 2x^3 + x^2 = 0$

6. $x^5 - 6x^4 + 9x^3 = 0$

7. $(2x - 3)^2(3x + 4)^2 = 0$

8. $(2x^2 + x)^2(3x - 1)^4 = 0$

9. $x^3 - 4x^2 - 6x = 0$

10. $-x^3 + 8x^2 - 14x = 0$

Find each product.

11. $(x - 3i)(x + 3i)$

12. $(x + 6i)(x - 6i)$

13. $\left[x - \left(1 + \sqrt{2}\right)\right]\left[x - \left(1 - \sqrt{2}\right)\right]$

14. $\left[x - \left(3 - \sqrt{5}\right)\right]\left[x - \left(3 + \sqrt{5}\right)\right]$

15. $[x - (3 + 2i)][x - (3 - 2i)]$

16. $[x - (3 - i)][x - (3 + i)]$

17. $(x - 2)[x - (3 + 4i)][x - (3 - 4i)]$

18. $(x + 1)(x - (1 - i))(x - (1 + i))$

Find a polynomial equation with real coefficients that has the given roots.

19. $-3, 5$

20. $6, -1$

21. $-4i, 4i$

22. $-9i, 9i$

23. $3 - i$

24. $4 + i$

25. $-2, i$

26. $4, -i$

27. $0, i\sqrt{3}$

28. $-2, i\sqrt{2}$

29. $3, 1 - i$

30. $5, 4 - 3i$

31. $1, 2, 3$

32. $-1, 2, -3$

33. $1, 2 - 3i$

34. $-1, 4 - 2i$

35. $\frac{1}{2}, \frac{1}{3}, \frac{1}{4}$

36. $-\frac{1}{2}, -\frac{1}{3}, 1$

37. $i, 1 + i$

38. $3i, 3 - i$

Use Descartes's rule of signs to discuss the possibilities for the roots of each equation. Do not solve the equation.

39. $x^3 + 5x^2 + 7x + 1 = 0$

40. $2x^3 - 3x^2 + 5x - 6 = 0$

41. $-x^3 - x^2 + 7x + 6 = 0$

42. $-x^4 - 5x^2 - x + 7 = 0$

43. $y^4 + 5y^2 + 7 = 0$

44. $-3y^4 - 6y^2 + 7 = 0$

45. $t^4 - 3t^3 + 2t^2 - 5t + 7 = 0$

46. $-5r^4 + 4r^3 + 7r - 16 = 0$

47. $x^5 + x^3 + 5x = 0$

48. $x^4 - x^2 + 1 = 0$

Use the rational zero theorem and Descartes's rule of signs to assist you in finding all real and imaginary roots to each equation.

49. $x^3 - 4x^2 - 7x + 10 = 0$

50. $x^3 + 9x^2 + 26x + 24 = 0$

51. $x^3 - 10x - 3 = 0$

52. $2x^3 - 7x^2 - 16 = 0$

53. $x^4 + 2x^3 - 7x^2 + 2x - 8 = 0$

54. $x^4 - 4x^3 + 7x^2 - 16x + 12 = 0$

55. $6x^3 + 25x^2 - 24x + 5 = 0$

56. $6x^3 - 11x^2 - 46x - 24 = 0$

57. $x^4 + 2x^3 - 3x^2 - 4x + 4 = 0$

58. $x^5 + 3x^3 + 2x = 0$

59. $x^4 - 6x^3 + 12x^2 - 8x = 0$

60. $x^4 + 9x^3 + 27x^2 + 27x = 0$

61. $x^6 - x^5 - x^4 + x^3 - 12x^2 + 12x = 0$

62. $2x^7 - 2x^6 + 7x^5 - 7x^4 - 4x^3 + 4x^2 = 0$

63. $8x^5 + 2x^4 - 33x^3 + 4x^2 + 25x - 6 = 0$

64. $6x^5 + x^4 - 28x^3 - 3x^2 + 16x - 4 = 0$

Solve each problem.

65. *Growth Rate for Bacteria* A car's speedometer indicates velocity at every instant in time. The instantaneous growth rate of a population is the rate at which it is growing at every instant in time. The instantaneous growth rate r of a colony of bacteria t hours after the start of an experiment is given by the function

$$r = 0.01t^3 - 0.08t^2 + 0.11t + 0.20$$

for $0 \le t \le 7$. Find the times for which the instantaneous growth rate is zero.

66. *Retail Store Profit* The manager of a retail store has figured that her monthly profit P (in thousands of dollars) is determined by her monthly advertising expense x (in tens of thousands of dollars) according to the formula

$$P = x^3 - 20x^2 + 100x \quad \text{for} \quad 0 \le x \le 4.$$

For what value of x does she get $147,000 in profit?

67. *Designing Fireworks* Marshall is designing a rocket for the Red Rocket Fireworks Company. The rocket will consist of a cardboard circular cylinder with a height that is four times as large as the radius. On top of the cylinder will be a cone with a height of 2 in. and a radius equal to the radius of the base as shown in the figure. If he wants to fill the cone and the cylinder with a total of 114π in.^{3} of powder, then what should be the radius of the cylinder?

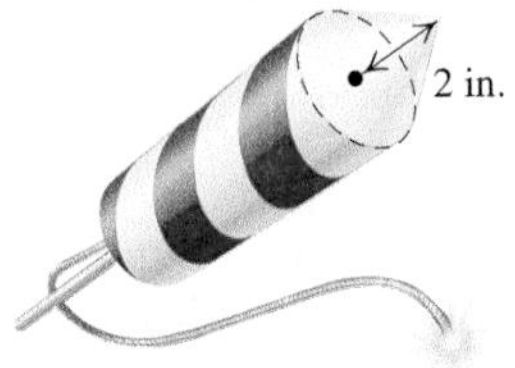

Figure for Exercise 67

68. *Heating and Air* An observatory is built in the shape of a right circular cylinder with a hemispherical roof as shown in the figure. The heating and air contractor has figured the volume of the structure as 3168π ft^3. If the height of the cylindrical walls is 2 ft more than the radius of the building, then what is the radius of the building?

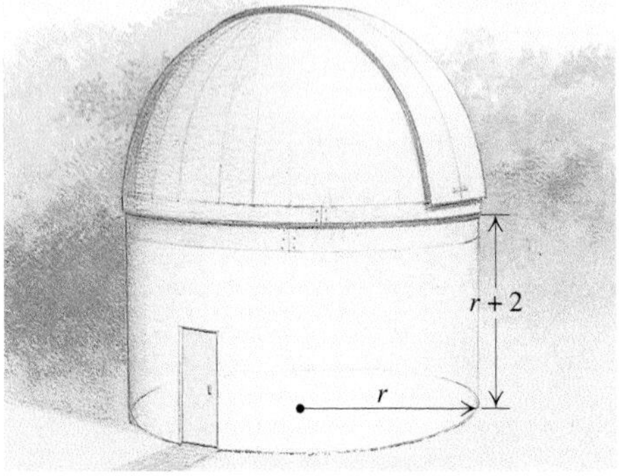

Figure for Exercise 68

Thinking Outside the Box XIV

Packing Billiard Balls There are several ways to tightly pack nine billiard balls each with radius 1 into a rectangular box. Find the volume of the box in each of the following cases and determine which box has the least volume.

a. Four balls are placed so that they just fit into the bottom of the box, then another layer of four, then one ball in the middle tangent to all four in the second layer, as shown in this side view.

b. Four balls are placed so that they just fit into the bottom of the box as in (a), then one is placed in the middle on top of the first four. Finally, four more are placed so that they just fit at the top of the box.

c. The box is packed with layers of four, one, and four as in (b), but the box is required to be cubic. In this case, the four balls in the bottom layer will not touch each other and the four balls in the top layer will not touch each other. The ball in the middle will be tangent to all of the other eight balls.

Figure for Thinking Outside the Box XIV

2.4 Pop Quiz

1. Find all real and imaginary roots to $x^5 - x^3 = 0$, including multiplicities.

2. Find a polynomial equation with real coefficients that has the roots $-4i$ and 5.

3. By Descartes's rule of signs, how many positive roots can $x^4 + x^3 - 3x^2 + 5x + 9 = 0$ have?

4. By Descartes's rule of signs, how many negative roots can $3x^3 + 5x^2 - x + 9 = 0$ have?

5. Find all real and imaginary roots to $x^3 - 3x^2 - 6x + 8 = 0$.

2.5 Miscellaneous Equations

In Section 2.4 we learned that an nth-degree polynomial equation has n roots. However, it is not always obvious how to find them. In this section we will solve polynomial equations using some new techniques and we will solve several other types of equations. Unfortunately, we cannot generally predict the number of roots to nonpolynomial equations.

Factoring Higher-Degree Equations

We usually use factoring to solve quadratic equations. However, since we can also factor many higher-degree polynomials, we can solve many higher-degree equations by factoring. Factoring is often the fastest method for solving an equation.

Example 1 Solving an equation by factoring

Solve $x^3 + 3x^2 + x + 3 = 0$.

Solution

Factor the polynomial on the left-hand side by grouping.

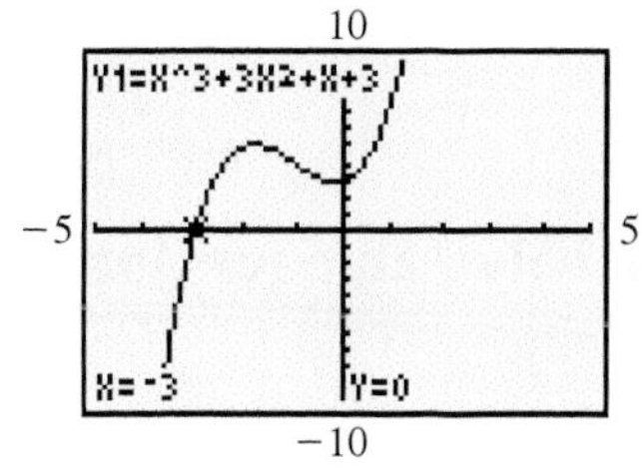

Figure 2.36

$$x^2(x + 3) + 1(x + 3) = 0 \quad \text{Factor by grouping.}$$

$$(x^2 + 1)(x + 3) = 0 \quad \text{Factor out } x + 3.$$

$$x^2 + 1 = 0 \quad \text{or} \quad x + 3 = 0 \quad \text{Zero factor property}$$

$$x^2 = -1 \quad \text{or} \quad x = -3$$

$$x = \pm i \quad \text{or} \quad x = -3$$

The solution set is $\{-3, -i, i\}$.

The graph in Fig. 2.36 supports these solutions. Because there is only one real solution, the graph crosses the x-axis only once. ■

Example 2 Solving an equation by factoring

Solve $2x^5 = 16x^2$.

Solution

Write the equation with 0 on the right-hand side, then factor completely.

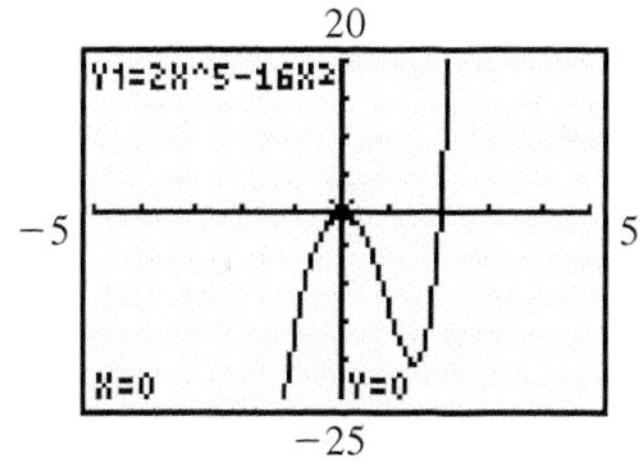

Figure 2.37

$$2x^5 - 16x^2 = 0$$

$$2x^2(x^3 - 8) = 0 \quad \text{Factor out the greatest common factor.}$$

$$2x^2(x - 2)(x^2 + 2x + 4) = 0 \quad \text{Factor the difference of two cubes.}$$

$$2x^2 = 0 \quad \text{or} \quad x - 2 = 0 \quad \text{or} \quad x^2 + 2x + 4 = 0$$

$$x = 0 \quad \text{or} \quad x = 2 \quad \text{or} \quad x = \frac{-2 \pm \sqrt{-12}}{2} = -1 \pm i\sqrt{3}$$

The solution set is $\{0, 2, -1 \pm i\sqrt{3}\}$. Since 0 is a root with multiplicity 2, there are five roots, counting multiplicity, to this fifth-degree equation.

The graph in Fig. 2.37 supports this solution. ■

Note that in Example 2, if we had divided each side by x^2 as our first step, we would have lost the solution $x = 0$. *We do not usually divide each side of an equation by a variable expression.* Instead, bring all expressions to the same side and factor out the common factors.

Equations Involving Square Roots

Recall that $\sqrt{x}$ represents the nonnegative square root of x. To solve $\sqrt{x} = 3$ we can use the definition of square root. Since the nonnegative square root of 9 is 3, the solution to $\sqrt{x} = 3$ is 9. To solve $\sqrt{x} = -3$ we again use the definition of square root. Because $\sqrt{x}$ is nonnegative while -3 is negative, this equation has no solution.

More complicated equations involving square roots are usually solved by squaring both sides. However, squaring both sides does not always lead to an equivalent equation. If we square both sides of $\sqrt{x} = 3$, we get $x = 9$, which is equivalent to $\sqrt{x} = 3$. But if we square both sides of $\sqrt{x} = -3$, we also get $x = 9$, which is not equivalent to $\sqrt{x} = -3$. Because 9 appeared in the attempt to solve $\sqrt{x} = -3$, but does not satisfy the equation, it is called an *extraneous root.* This same situation can occur with an equation involving a fourth root or any other even root. So if you raise each side of an equation to an even power, you must check for extraneous roots.

Example 3 Squaring each side to solve an equation

Solve $\sqrt{x} + 2 = x$.

Solution

Isolate the radical before squaring each side.

$$\sqrt{x} = x - 2$$

$$(\sqrt{x})^2 = (x - 2)^2 \quad \text{Square each side.}$$

$$x = x^2 - 4x + 4 \quad \text{Use the special product } (a - b)^2 = a^2 - 2ab + b^2.$$

$$0 = x^2 - 5x + 4 \quad \text{Write in the form } ax^2 + bx + c = 0.$$

$$0 = (x - 4)(x - 1) \quad \text{Factor the quadratic polynomial.}$$

$$x - 4 = 0 \quad \text{or} \quad x - 1 = 0 \quad \text{Zero factor property}$$

$$x = 4 \quad \text{or} \quad x = 1$$

Checking $x = 4$, we get $\sqrt{4} + 2 = 4$, which is correct. Checking $x = 1$, we get $\sqrt{1} + 2 = 1$, which is incorrect. So 1 is an extraneous root and the solution set is $\{4\}$.

The graph in Fig. 2.38 supports this solution. ■

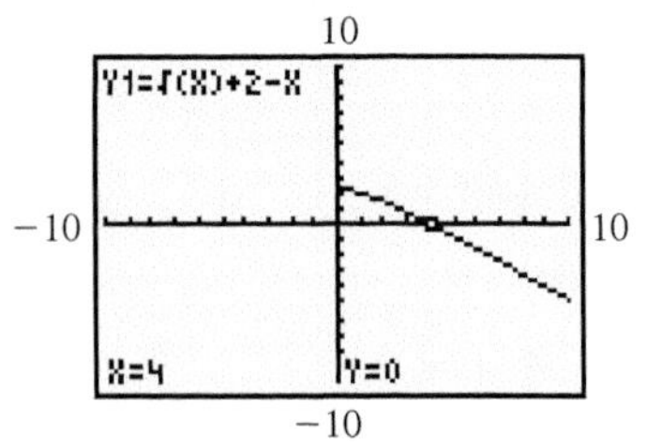

Figure 2.38

The next example involves two radicals. In this example we will isolate the more complicated radical before squaring each side. But not all radicals are eliminated upon squaring each side. So we isolate the remaining radical and square each side again.

Example 4 Squaring each side twice

Solve $\sqrt{2x + 1} - \sqrt{x} = 1$.

Solution

First we write the equation so that the more complicated radical is isolated. Then we square each side. On the left side, when we square $\sqrt{2x + 1}$, we get $2x + 1$. On the right side, when we square $1 + \sqrt{x}$, we use the special product rule $(a + b)^2 = a^2 + 2ab + b^2$.

$$\sqrt{2x + 1} = 1 + \sqrt{x}$$

$$\left(\sqrt{2x + 1}\right)^2 = \left(1 + \sqrt{x}\right)^2 \quad \text{Square each side.}$$

$$2x + 1 = 1 + 2\sqrt{x} + x$$

$$x = 2\sqrt{x} \quad \text{All radicals are not eliminated by the first squaring.}$$

$$x^2 = \left(2\sqrt{x}\right)^2 \quad \text{Square each side a second time.}$$

$$x^2 = 4x$$

$$x^2 - 4x = 0$$

$$x(x - 4) = 0$$

$$x = 0 \quad \text{or} \quad x - 4 = 0$$

$$x = 0 \quad \text{or} \quad x = 4$$

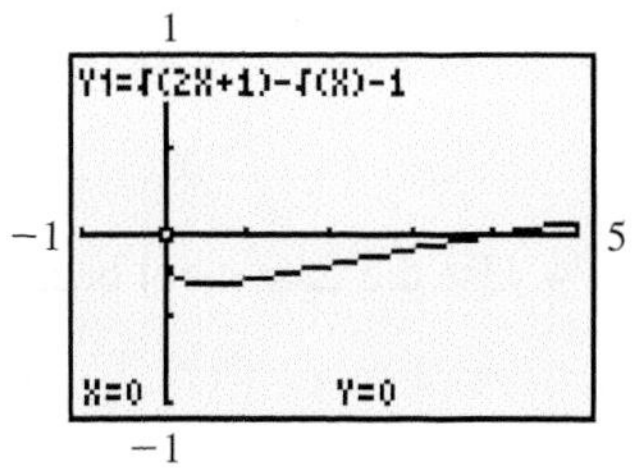

Figure 2.39

Both 0 and 4 satisfy the original equation. So the solution set is $\{0, 4\}$.

The graph in Fig. 2.39 supports this solution. ■

Use the following strategy when solving equations involving square roots.

STRATEGY **Solving Equations Involving Square Roots**

1. Isolate the radical if there is only one. Separate the radicals on opposite sides of the equation if there is more than one.
2. Square both sides and simplify.
3. Isolate or separate any remaining radicals and square again.
4. Check all solutions because squaring can produce extraneous solutions.

Equations with Rational Exponents

To solve equations of the form $x^{m/n} = k$ in which m and n are positive integers and m/n is in lowest terms, we adapt the methods of Examples 3 and 4 of raising each side to a power. Cubing each side of $x^{2/3} = 4$, yields $(x^{2/3})^3 = 4^3$ or $x^2 = 64$. By the square root property, $x = \pm 8$. We can shorten this solution by raising each side of the equation to the power 3/2 (the reciprocal of 2/3) and inserting the $\pm$ symbol to obtain the two square roots.

$$x^{2/3} = 4$$

$$(x^{2/3})^{3/2} = \pm 4^{3/2} \quad \text{Raise each side to the power } 3/2 \text{ and insert } \pm.$$

$$x = \pm 8$$

The equation $x^{2/3} = 4$ has two solutions because the numerator of the exponent $2/3$ is an even number. An equation such as $x^{-3/2} = 1/8$ has only one real solution because the numerator of the exponent $-3/2$ is odd. To solve $x^{-3/2} = 1/8$, raise each side to the power $-2/3$ (the reciprocal of $-3/2$).

$$x^{-3/2} = \frac{1}{8}$$

$$(x^{-3/2})^{2/3} = \left(\frac{1}{8}\right)^{-2/3} \quad \text{Raise each side to the power } -2/3.$$

$$x = 4$$

In the next example we solve two more equations of this type by raising each side to a fractional power. Note that we use the $\pm$ symbol only when the numerator of the original exponent is even.

Example 5 Equations with rational exponents

Solve each equation.

a. $x^{4/3} = 625$ **b.** $(y - 2)^{-5/2} = 32$

Solution

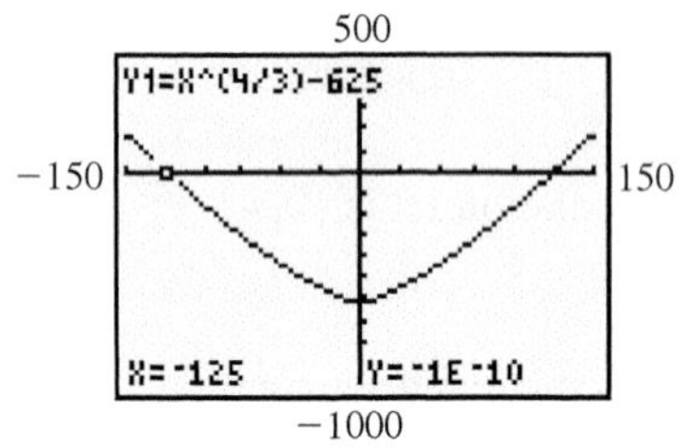

Figure 2.40

a. Raise each side of the equation to the power $3/4$. Use the $\pm$ symbol because the numerator of $4/3$ is even.

$$x^{4/3} = 625$$

$$(x^{4/3})^{3/4} = \pm 625^{3/4}$$

$$x = \pm 125$$

Check in the original equation. The solution set is $\{-125, 125\}$.

The graph in Fig. 2.40 supports this solution. □

b. Raise each side to the power $-2/5$. Because the numerator in $-5/2$ is an odd number, there is only one real solution.

$$(y - 2)^{-5/2} = 32$$

$$((y - 2)^{-5/2})^{-2/5} = 32^{-2/5} \quad \text{Raise each side to the power } -2/5.$$

$$y - 2 = \frac{1}{4}$$

$$y = 2 + \frac{1}{4} = \frac{9}{4}$$

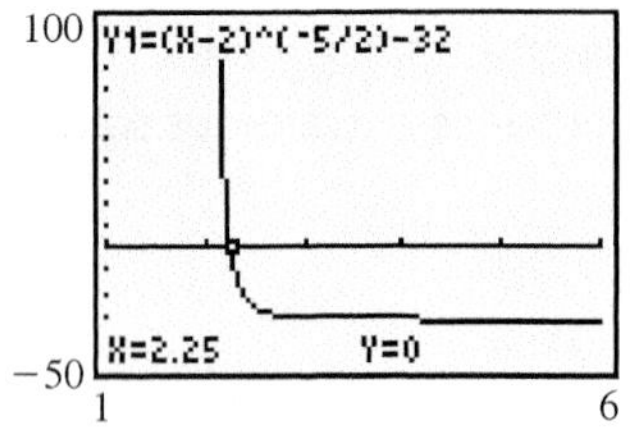

Figure 2.41

Check $9/4$ in the original equation. The solution set is $\left\{\frac{9}{4}\right\}$.

The graph in Fig. 2.41 supports this solution. ■

Equations of Quadratic Type

In some cases, an equation can be converted to a quadratic equation by substituting a single variable for a more complicated expression. Such equations are called **equations of quadratic type.** An equation of quadratic type has the form $au^2 + bu + c = 0$, where $a \neq 0$ and u is an algebraic expression.

In the next example, the expression x^2 in a fourth-degree equation is replaced by u, yielding a quadratic equation. After the quadratic equation is solved, u is replaced by x^2 so that we find values for x that satisfy the original fourth-degree equation.

Example 6 Solving a fourth-degree polynomial equation

Solve $x^4 - 14x^2 + 45 = 0$.

Solution

We let $u = x^2$ so that $u^2 = (x^2)^2 = x^4$.

$$(x^2)^2 - 14x^2 + 45 = 0$$

$$u^2 - 14u + 45 = 0 \quad \text{Replace } x^2 \text{ by } u.$$

$$(u - 9)(u - 5) = 0$$

$$u - 9 = 0 \quad \text{or} \quad u - 5 = 0$$

$$u = 9 \quad \text{or} \quad u = 5$$

$$x^2 = 9 \quad \text{or} \quad x^2 = 5 \quad \text{Replace } u \text{ by } x^2.$$

$$x = \pm 3 \quad \text{or} \quad x = \pm\sqrt{5}$$

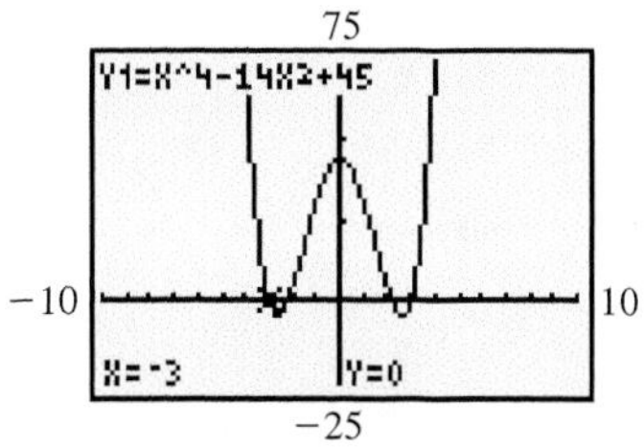

Figure 2.42

Check in the original equation. The solution set is $\{-3, -\sqrt{5}, \sqrt{5}, 3\}$.

The graph in Fig. 2.42 supports this solution. ■

Note that the equation of Example 6 could be solved by factoring without doing substitution, because $x^4 - 14x^2 + 45 = (x^2 - 9)(x^2 - 5)$. Since the next example involves a more complicated algebraic expression, we use substitution to simplify it, although it too could be solved by factoring, without substitution.

Example 7 Another equation of quadratic type

Solve $(x^2 - x)^2 - 18(x^2 - x) + 72 = 0$.

Solution

If we let $u = x^2 - x$, then the equation becomes a quadratic equation.

$$(x^2 - x)^2 - 18(x^2 - x) + 72 = 0$$

$$u^2 - 18u + 72 = 0 \quad \text{Replace } x^2 - x \text{ by } u.$$

$$(u - 6)(u - 12) = 0$$

$$u - 6 = 0 \quad \text{or} \quad u - 12 = 0$$

$$u = 6 \quad \text{or} \quad u = 12$$

$$x^2 - x = 6 \quad \text{or} \quad x^2 - x = 12 \quad \text{Replace } u \text{ by } x^2 - x.$$

$$x^2 - x - 6 = 0 \quad \text{or} \quad x^2 - x - 12 = 0$$

$$(x - 3)(x + 2) = 0 \quad \text{or} \quad (x - 4)(x + 3) = 0$$

$$x = 3 \quad \text{or} \quad x = -2 \quad \text{or} \quad x = 4 \quad \text{or} \quad x = -3$$

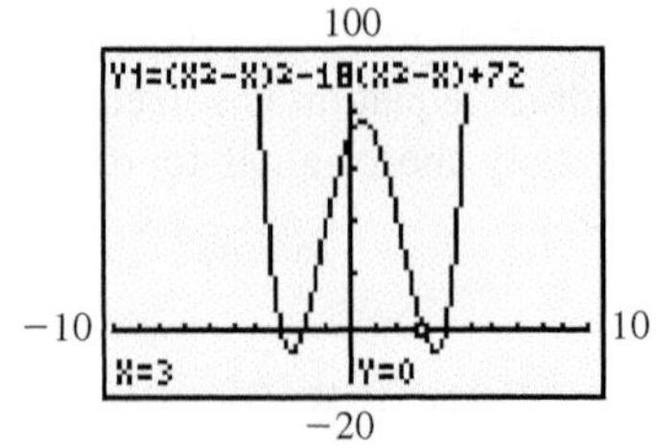

Figure 2.43

Check in the original equation. The solution set is $\{-3, -2, 3, 4\}$.
The graph in Fig. 2.43 supports this solution. ■

The next equations of quadratic type have rational exponents.

Example 8 Quadratic type and rational exponents

Find all real solutions to each equation.

a. $x^{2/3} - 9x^{1/3} + 8 = 0$ **b.** $(11x^2 - 18)^{1/4} = x$

Solution

a. If we let $u = x^{1/3}$, then $u^2 = (x^{1/3})^2 = x^{2/3}$.

$$u^2 - 9u + 8 = 0 \quad \text{Replace } x^{2/3} \text{ by } u^2 \text{ and } x^{1/3} \text{ by } u.$$
$$(u - 8)(u - 1) = 0$$
$$u = 8 \quad \text{or} \quad u = 1$$
$$x^{1/3} = 8 \quad \text{or} \quad x^{1/3} = 1 \quad \text{Replace } u \text{ by } x^{1/3}.$$
$$(x^{1/3})^3 = 8^3 \quad \text{or} \quad (x^{1/3})^3 = 1^3$$
$$x = 512 \quad \text{or} \quad x = 1$$

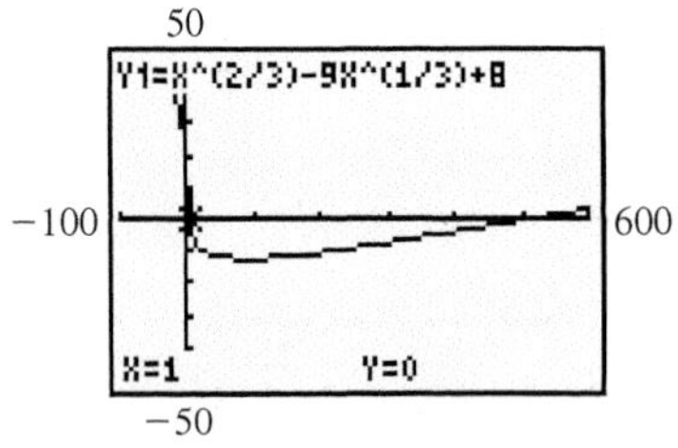

Figure 2.44

Check in the original equation. The solution set is $\{1, 512\}$.
The graph in Fig. 2.44 supports this solution. □

b.
$$(11x^2 - 18)^{1/4} = x$$
$$((11x^2 - 18)^{1/4})^4 = x^4 \quad \text{Raise each side to the power 4.}$$
$$11x^2 - 18 = x^4$$
$$x^4 - 11x^2 + 18 = 0$$
$$(x^2 - 9)(x^2 - 2) = 0$$
$$x^2 = 9 \quad \text{or} \quad x^2 = 2$$
$$x = \pm 3 \quad \text{or} \quad x = \pm\sqrt{2}$$

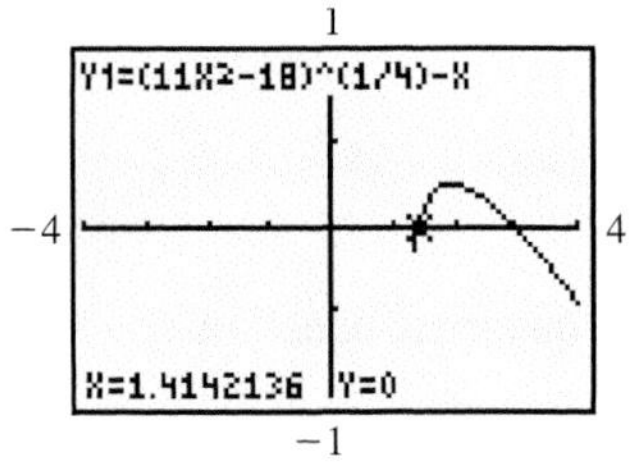

Figure 2.45

Since the exponent $1/4$ means principal fourth root, the right-hand side of the equation cannot be negative. So -3 and $-\sqrt{2}$ are extraneous roots. Since 3 and $\sqrt{2}$ satisfy the original equation, the solution set is $\{\sqrt{2}, 3\}$.
The graph in Fig. 2.45 supports this solution. ■

Equations Involving Absolute Value

We solved basic absolute value equations in Section 1.1. In the next two examples we solve some more complicated absolute value equations.

Example 9 An equation involving absolute value

Solve $|x^2 - 2x - 16| = 8$.

Solution

First write an equivalent statement without using absolute value symbols.

$$\begin{aligned} x^2 - 2x - 16 &= 8 \quad \text{or} \quad x^2 - 2x - 16 = -8 \\ x^2 - 2x - 24 &= 0 \quad \text{or} \quad x^2 - 2x - 8 = 0 \\ (x - 6)(x + 4) &= 0 \quad \text{or} \quad (x - 4)(x + 2) = 0 \\ x = 6 \quad \text{or} \quad x &= -4 \quad \text{or} \quad x = 4 \quad \text{or} \quad x = -2 \end{aligned}$$

The solution set is $\{-4, -2, 4, 6\}$.

The graph in Fig. 2.46 supports this solution. ■

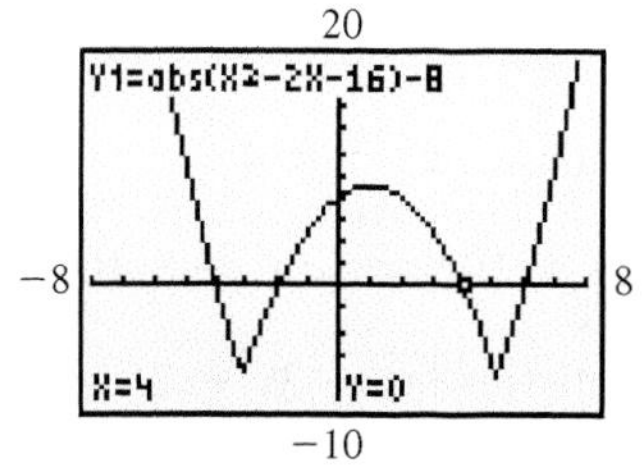

Figure 2.46

In the next example we have an equation in which an absolute value expression is equal to an expression that could be positive or negative and an equation with two absolute value expressions.

Example 10 More equations involving absolute value

Solve each equation.

a. $|x^2 - 6| = 5x$ **b.** $|a - 1| = |2a - 3|$

Solution

a. Since $|x^2 - 6|$ is nonnegative for any value of x, $5x$ must be nonnegative. Write the equivalent statement assuming that $5x$ is nonnegative:

$$\begin{aligned} x^2 - 6 &= 5x \quad \text{or} \quad x^2 - 6 = -5x \\ x^2 - 5x - 6 &= 0 \quad \text{or} \quad x^2 + 5x - 6 = 0 \\ (x - 6)(x + 1) &= 0 \quad \text{or} \quad (x + 6)(x - 1) = 0 \\ x = 6 \quad \text{or} \quad x &= -1 \quad \text{or} \quad x = -6 \quad \text{or} \quad x = 1 \end{aligned}$$

The expression $|x^2 - 6|$ is nonnegative for any real number x. But $5x$ is negative if $x = -1$ or if $x = -6$. So -1 and -6 are extraneous roots. They do not satisfy the original equation. The solution set is $\{1, 6\}$.

The graph in Fig. 2.47 supports this solution. □

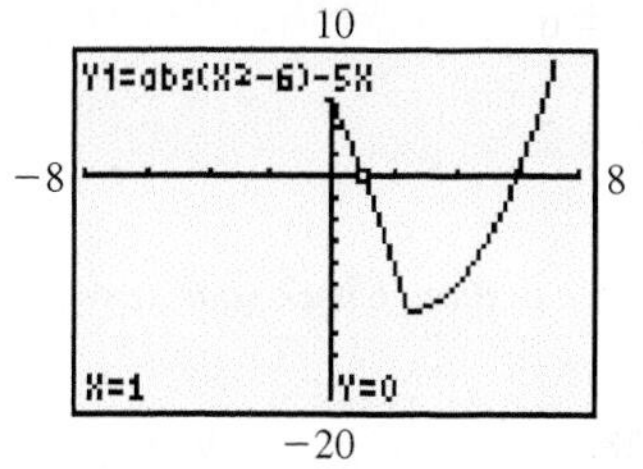

Figure 2.47

b. The equation $|a - 1| = |2a - 3|$ indicates that $a - 1$ and $2a - 3$ have the same absolute value. If two quantities have the same absolute value, they are either equal or opposites. Use this fact to write an equivalent statement without absolute value signs.

$$\begin{aligned} a - 1 &= 2a - 3 \quad \text{or} \quad a - 1 = -(2a - 3) \\ a + 2 &= 2a \quad \text{or} \quad a - 1 = -2a + 3 \\ 2 &= a \quad \text{or} \quad a = \frac{4}{3} \end{aligned}$$

Check that both 2 and $\frac{4}{3}$ satisfy the original absolute value equation. The solution set is $\left\{\frac{4}{3}, 2\right\}$.

The graph in Fig. 2.48 supports this solution. ■

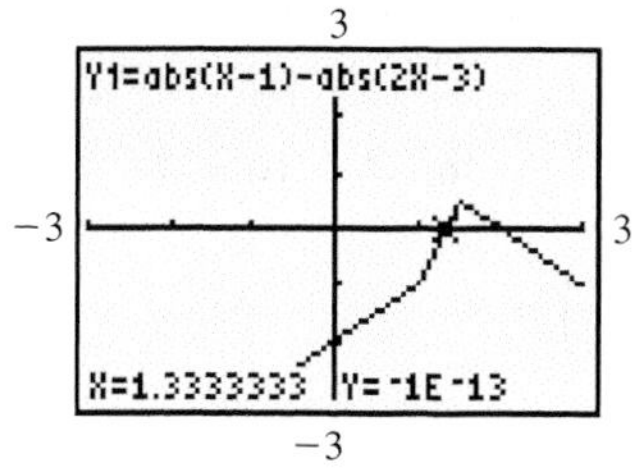

Figure 2.48

For Thought

True or False? Explain.

1. Squaring each side of $\sqrt{x-1} + \sqrt{x} = 6$ yields $x - 1 + x = 36$.
2. The equations $(2x - 1)^2 = 9$ and $2x - 1 = 3$ are equivalent.
3. The equations $x^{2/3} = 9$ and $x = 27$ have the same solution set.
4. To solve $2x^{1/4} - x^{1/2} + 3 = 0$, we let $u = x^{1/2}$ and $u^2 = x^{1/4}$.
5. If $(x - 1)^{-2/3} = 4$, then $x = 1 \pm 4^{-3/2}$.
6. No negative number satisfies $x^{-2/5} = 4$.
7. The solution set to $|2x + 10| = 3x$ is $\{-2, 10\}$.
8. No negative number satisfies $|x^2 - 3x + 2| = 7x$.
9. The equation $|2x + 1| = |x|$ is equivalent to $2x + 1 = x$ or $2x + 1 = -x$.
10. The equation $x^9 - 5x^3 + 6 = 0$ is an equation of quadratic type.

2.5 Exercises

Find all real and imaginary solutions to each equation. Check your answers.

1. $x^3 + 3x^2 - 4x - 12 = 0$
2. $x^3 - x^2 - 5x + 5 = 0$
3. $2x^3 + 1000x^2 - x - 500 = 0$
4. $3x^3 - 1200x^2 - 2x + 800 = 0$
5. $a^3 + 5a = 15a^2$
6. $b^3 + 20b = 9b^2$
7. $3y^4 - 12y^2 = 0$
8. $5m^4 - 10m^3 + 5m^2 = 0$
9. $a^4 - 16 = 0$
10. $w^4 + 8w = 0$

Find all real solutions to each equation. Check your answers.

11. $\sqrt{x+1} = x - 5$
12. $\sqrt{x-1} = x - 7$
13. $\sqrt{x} - 2 = x - 22$
14. $3 + \sqrt{x} = 1 + x$
15. $w = \dfrac{\sqrt{1-3w}}{2}$
16. $t = \dfrac{\sqrt{2-3t}}{3}$
17. $\dfrac{1}{z} = \dfrac{3}{\sqrt{4z+1}}$
18. $\dfrac{1}{p} - \dfrac{2}{\sqrt{9p+1}} = 0$
19. $\sqrt{x^2 - 2x - 15} = 3$
20. $\sqrt{3x^2 + 5x - 3} = x$
21. $\sqrt{x+40} - \sqrt{x} = 4$
22. $\sqrt{x} + \sqrt{x-36} = 2$
23. $\sqrt{n+4} + \sqrt{n-1} = 5$
24. $\sqrt{y+10} - \sqrt{y-2} = 2$
25. $\sqrt{2x+5} + \sqrt{x+6} = 9$
26. $\sqrt{3x-2} - \sqrt{x-2} = 2$

Find all real solutions to each equation. Check your answers.

27. $x^{2/3} = 2$
28. $x^{2/3} = \dfrac{1}{2}$
29. $w^{-4/3} = 16$
30. $w^{-3/2} = 27$
31. $t^{-1/2} = 7$
32. $t^{-1/2} = \dfrac{1}{2}$
33. $(s - 1)^{-1/2} = 2$
34. $(s - 2)^{-1/2} = \dfrac{1}{3}$

Find all real and imaginary solutions to each equation. Check your answers.

35. $x^4 - 12x^2 + 27 = 0$
36. $x^4 + 10 = 7x^2$
37. $\left(\dfrac{2c-3}{5}\right)^2 + 2\left(\dfrac{2c-3}{5}\right) = 8$

38. $\left(\frac{b-5}{6}\right)^2 - \left(\frac{b-5}{6}\right) - 6 = 0$

39. $\frac{1}{(5x-1)^2} + \frac{1}{5x-1} - 12 = 0$

40. $\frac{1}{(x-3)^2} + \frac{2}{x-3} - 24 = 0$

41. $(v^2 - 4v)^2 - 17(v^2 - 4v) + 60 = 0$

42. $(u^2 + 2u)^2 - 2(u^2 + 2u) - 3 = 0$

43. $x - 4\sqrt{x} + 3 = 0$

44. $2x + 3\sqrt{x} - 20 = 0$

45. $q - 7q^{1/2} + 12 = 0$

46. $h + 1 = 2h^{1/2}$

47. $x^{2/3} + 10 = 7x^{1/3}$

48. $x^{1/2} - 3x^{1/4} + 2 = 0$

Solve each absolute value equation.

49. $|w^2 - 4| = 3$

50. $|a^2 - 1| = 1$

51. $|v^2 - 3v| = 5v$

52. $|z^2 - 12| = z$

53. $|x^2 - x - 6| = 6$

54. $|2x^2 - x - 2| = 1$

55. $|x + 5| = |2x + 1|$

56. $|3x - 4| = |x|$

Solve each equation. Find imaginary solutions when possible.

57. $\sqrt{16x + 1} - \sqrt{6x + 13} = -1$

58. $\sqrt{16x + 1} - \sqrt{6x + 13} = 1$

59. $v^6 - 64 = 0$

60. $t^4 - 1 = 0$

61. $(7x^2 - 12)^{1/4} = x$

62. $(10x^2 - 1)^{1/4} = 2x$

63. $\sqrt[3]{2 + x - 2x^2} = x$

64. $\sqrt{48 + \sqrt{x}} - 4 = \sqrt[4]{x}$

65. $\left(\frac{x-2}{3}\right)^2 - 2\left(\frac{x-2}{3}\right) + 10 = 0$

66. $\frac{1}{(x+1)^2} - \frac{2}{x+1} + 2 = 0$

67. $(3u - 1)^{2/5} = 2$

68. $(2u + 1)^{2/3} = 3$

69. $x^2 - 11\sqrt{x^2 + 1} + 31 = 0$

70. $2x^2 - 3\sqrt{2x^2 - 3} - 1 = 0$

71. $|x^2 - 2x| = |3x - 6|$

72. $|x^2 + 5x| = |3 - x^2|$

73. $(3m + 1)^{-3/5} = -\frac{1}{8}$

74. $(1 - 2m)^{-5/3} = -\frac{1}{32}$

75. $|x^2 - 4| = x - 2$

76. $|x^2 + 7x| = x^2 - 4$

Solve each problem.

77. *Maximum Sail Area* According to the International America's Cup Rules, the maximum sail area S for a boat with length L (in meters) and displacement D (in cubic meters) is determined by the equation

$$L + 1.25S^{1/2} - 9.8D^{1/3} = 16.296$$

(America's Cup, www.americascup.org). Find S for a boat with length 21.24 m and displacement 18.34 m^3.

Figure for Exercises 77 and 78

78. *Minimum Displacement for a Yacht* The minimum displacement D for a boat with length 21.52 m and a sail area of 310.64 m^2 is determined by the equation $L + 1.25S^{1/2} - 9.8D^{1/3} = 16.296$. Find this boat's minimum displacement.

79. *Square Roots* Find two numbers that differ by 6 and whose square roots differ by 1.

80. *Right Triangle* One leg of a right triangle is 1 cm longer than the other leg. What is the length of the short leg if the total length of the hypotenuse and the short leg is 10 cm?

81. *Sail Area-Displacement Ratio* The sail area-displacement ratio S is defined as

$$S = A\left(\frac{d}{64}\right)^{-2/3},$$

where A is the sail area in square feet and d is the displacement in pounds. The Oceanis 381 is a 39 ft sailboat with a sail area-displacement ratio of 14.26 and a sail area of 598.9 ft^2. Find the displacement for the Oceanis 381.

82. *Capsize Screening Value* The capsize screening value C is defined as

$$C = b\left(\frac{d}{64}\right)^{-1/3},$$

where b is the beam (or width) in feet and d is the displacement in pounds. The Bahia 46 is a 46 ft catamaran with a capsize screening value of 3.91 and a beam of 26.1 ft. Find the displacement for the Bahia 46.

83. *Radius of a Pipe* A large pipe is placed next to a wall and a 1-foot high block is placed 5 feet from the wall to keep the pipe in place as shown in the accompanying figure. What is the radius of the pipe?

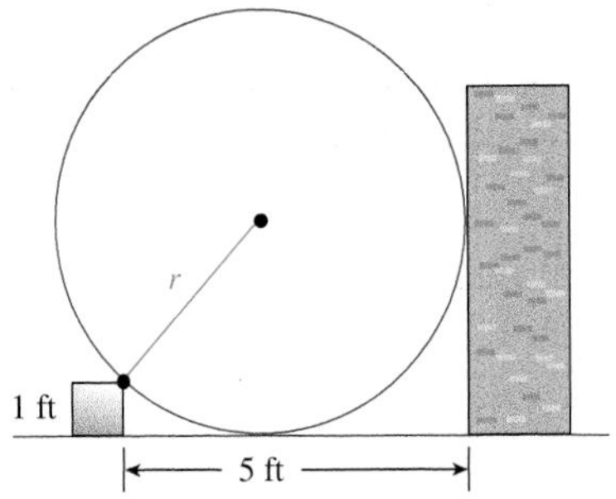

Figure for Exercise 83

84. *Radius of a Pipe* A large pipe is held in place on level ground by using a 1-foot high block on one side and a 2-foot high block on the other side. If the distance between the blocks is 6 feet, then what is the radius of the pipe?

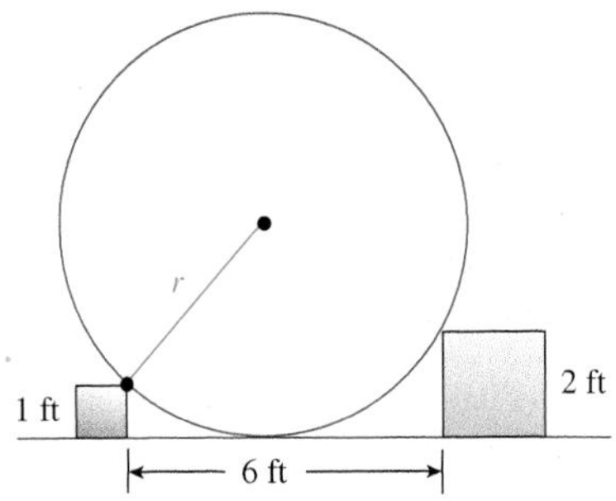

Figure for Exercise 84

Foreshadowing Calculus

The situation in the next exercise is studied also in calculus. However, in calculus we find the route that minimizes the total time for the trip.

85. *Time Swimming and Running* Lauren is competing in her town's cross-country competition. Early in the event, she must race from point A on the Greenbriar River to point B, which is 5 mi downstream and on the opposite bank. The Greenbriar is 1 mi wide. In planning her strategy, Lauren knows she can use any combination of running and swimming. She can run 10 mph and swim 8 mph. How long would it take if she ran 5 mi downstream and then swam across? Find the time it would take if she swam diagonally from A to B. Find x so that she could run x miles along the bank, swim diagonally to B, and complete the race in 36 min. (Ignore the current in the river.)

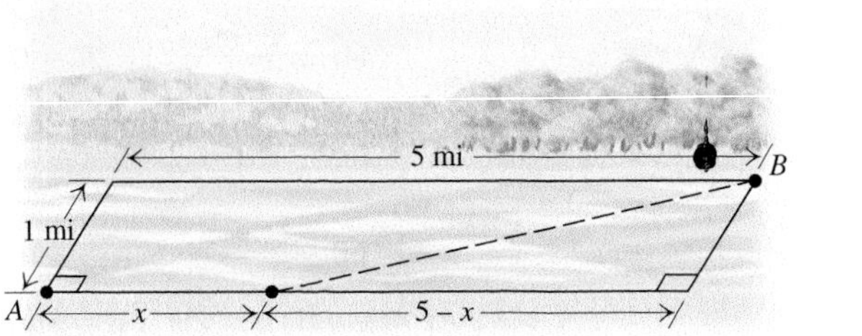

Figure for Exercise 85

86. *Storing Supplies* An army sergeant wants to use a 20-ft by 40-ft piece of canvas to make a two-sided tent for holding supplies as shown in the figure. Write the volume of the tent as a function of b. For what value of b is the volume 1600 ft^3? Use a graphing calculator to find the values for b and h that will maximize the volume of the tent.

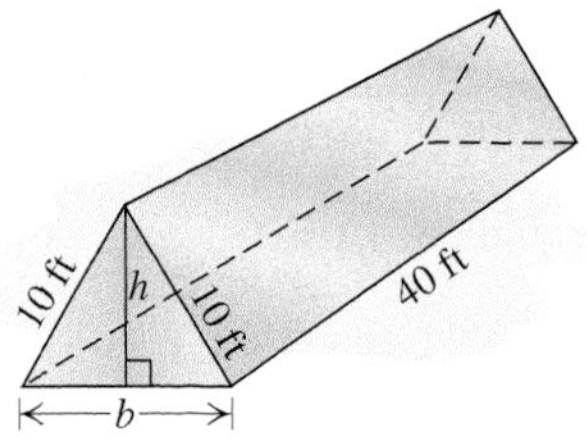

Figure for Exercise 86

Thinking Outside the Box XV

Painting Problem A painter has seven 3-ft by 5-ft rectangular drop cloths. If he lays each drop cloth on the carpet as a 3-ft by 5-ft rectangle, without folding, cutting, or tearing them, then what is the maximum area that he can cover with these drop cloths in an 8-ft by 13-ft room?

2.5 Pop Quiz

Solve each equation. Find imaginary solutions when possible.

1. $x^3 + x^2 + x + 1 = 0$

2. $\sqrt{x + 4} = x - 2$

3. $x^{-2/3} = 4$

4. $x^4 - 3x^2 = 4$

5. $|x + 3| = |2x - 5|$

2.6 Graphs of Polynomial Functions

In Chapter 1 we learned that the graph of a polynomial function of degree 0 or 1 is a straight line. In Section 2.1 we learned that the graph of a second-degree polynomial function is a parabola. In this section we will concentrate on graphs of polynomial functions of degree greater than 2.

Drawing Good Graphs

A graph of an equation is a picture of all of the ordered pairs that satisfy the equation. However, it is impossible to draw a perfect picture of any set of ordered pairs. We usually find a few important features of the graph and make sure that our picture brings out those features. For example, you can make a good graph of a linear function by drawing a line through the intercepts using a ruler and a sharp pencil. A good parabola should look smooth and symmetric and pass through the vertex and intercepts.

A graphing calculator is a tremendous aid in graphing because it can quickly plot many points. However, the calculator does not know if it has drawn a graph that shows the important features. For example, the graph of $y = (x + 30)^2(x - 40)^2$ has x-intercepts at $(-30, 0)$ and $(40, 0)$, but they do not appear on the graph in Fig. 2.49. □

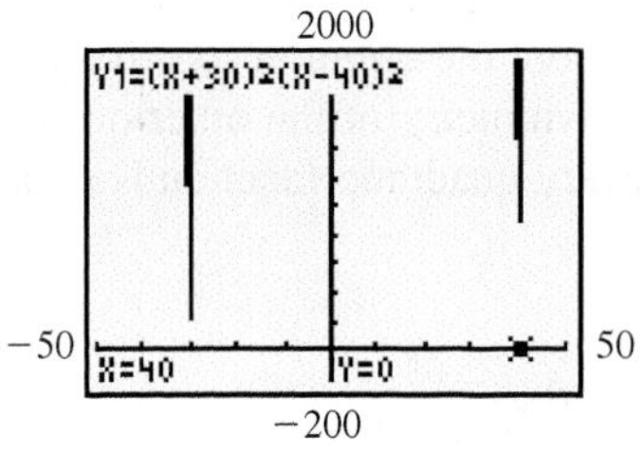

Figure 2.49

An important theorem for understanding the graphs of polynomial functions is the intermediate value theorem (IVT). The IVT says that *a polynomial function takes on every value between any two of its values.* For example, consider $f(x) = x^3$, for which $f(1) = 1$ and $f(2) = 8$. Select any number between 1 and 8, say, 5. By the IVT there is a number c in the interval $(1, 2)$ such that $f(c) = 5$. In this case, c is easy to find: $c = \sqrt[3]{5}$. The IVT allows us to "connect the dots" when drawing a graph. The curve cannot go from $(1, 1)$ to $(2, 8)$ without hitting every y-coordinate between 1 and 8. If one of the values is positive and the other negative, the IVT guarantees that the curve crosses the x-axis on the interval. For example, $f(-2) = -8$ and $f(2) = 8$. By the IVT there is a c in the interval $(-2, 2)$ for which $f(c) = 0$. Of course in this case $c = 0$ and the x-intercept is $(0, 0)$.

Note that the greatest integer function, which is not a polynomial function, does not obey the IVT. The greatest integer function jumps from one integer to the next without taking on any values between the integers.

We will not prove the IVT here. It is proved in calculus. The theorem is stated symbolically as follows.

The Intermediate Value Theorem

Suppose that f is a polynomial function and $[a, b]$ is an interval for which $f(a) \neq f(b)$. If k is a number between $f(a)$ and $f(b)$ then there is a number c in the interval (a, b) such that $f(c) = k$.

Symmetry

Symmetry is a very special property of graphs of some functions but not others. Recognizing that the graph of a function has some symmetry usually cuts in half the work required to obtain the graph and also helps cut down on errors in graphing. So far we have discussed the following types of symmetry.

SUMMARY Types of Symmetry

1. The graph of a function $f(x)$ is *symmetric about the y-axis* and f is an even function if $f(-x) = f(x)$ for any value of x in the domain of the function. (Section 1.7)
2. The graph of a function $f(x)$ is *symmetric about the origin* and f is an odd function if $f(-x) = -f(x)$ for any value of x in the domain of the function. (Section 1.7)
3. The graph of a quadratic function $f(x) = ax^2 + bx + c$ is *symmetric about its axis of symmetry,* $x = -b/(2a)$. (Section 2.1)

The graphs of $f(x) = x^2$ and $f(x) = x^3$ shown in Figs. 2.50 and 2.51 are nice examples of symmetry about the y-axis and symmetry about the origin, respectively. The axis of symmetry of $f(x) = x^2$ is the y-axis. The symmetry of the other quadratic functions comes from the fact that the graph of every quadratic function is a transformation of the graph of $f(x) = x^2$.

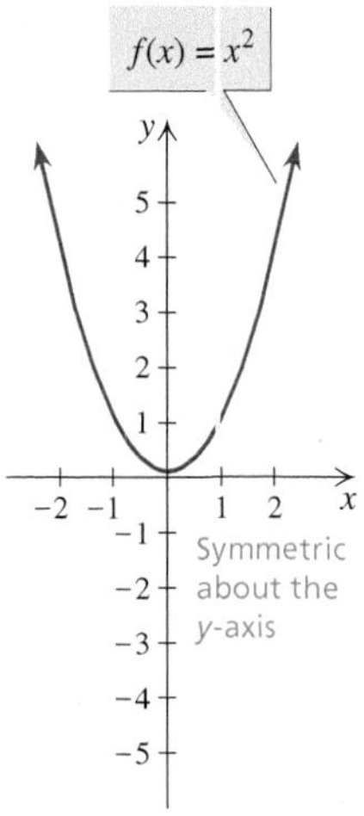

Figure 2.50

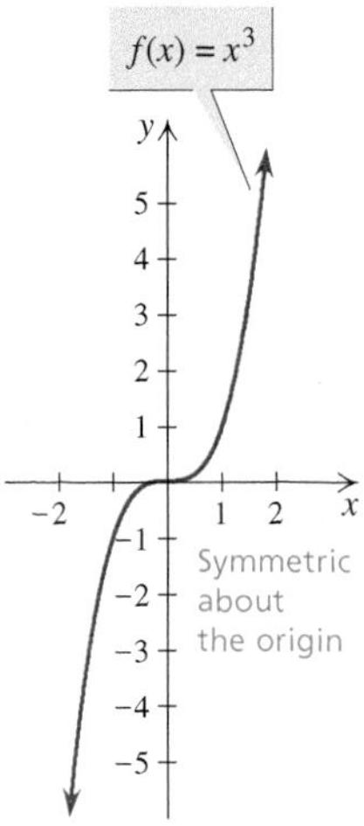

Figure 2.51

Example 1 Determining the symmetry of a graph

Discuss the symmetry of the graph of each polynomial function.

a. $f(x) = 5x^3 - x$ **b.** $g(x) = 2x^4 - 3x^2$ **c.** $h(x) = x^2 - 3x + 6$

d. $j(x) = x^4 - x^3$

Solution

a. Replace x by $-x$ in $f(x) = 5x^3 - x$ and simplify:

$$f(-x) = 5(-x)^3 - (-x)$$
$$= -5x^3 + x$$

Since $f(-x)$ is the opposite of $f(x)$, the graph is symmetric about the origin. Fig. 2.52 supports this conclusion. □

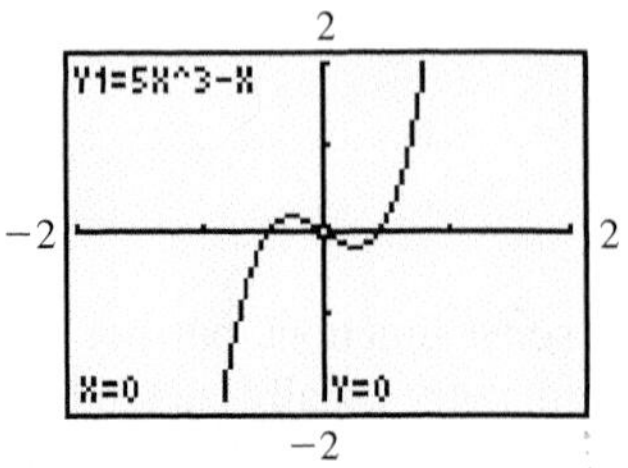

Figure 2.52

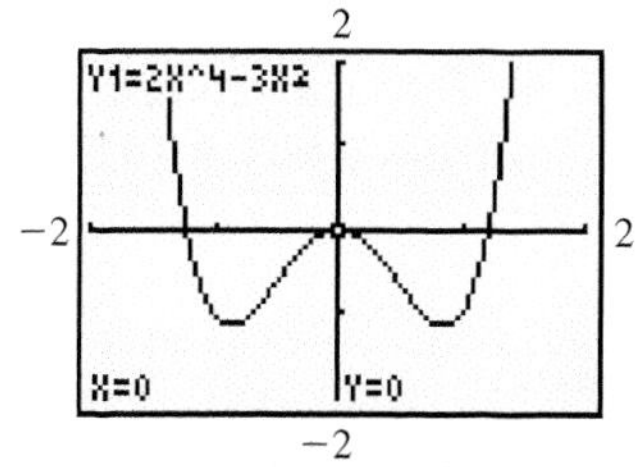

Figure 2.53

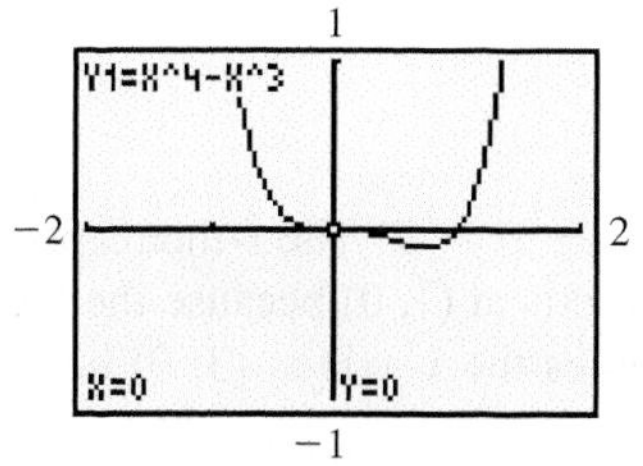

Figure 2.54

b. Replace x by $-x$ in $g(x) = 2x^4 - 3x^2$ and simplify:

$$g(-x) = 2(-x)^4 - 3(-x)^2$$
$$= 2x^4 - 3x^2$$

Since $g(-x) = g(x)$, the graph is symmetric about the y-axis.
Fig. 2.53 supports this conclusion. □

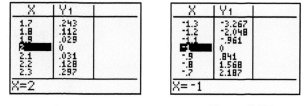

c. Because h is a quadratic function, its graph is symmetric about the line $x = -b/(2a)$, which in this case is the line $x = 3/2$.

d. In this case

$$j(-x) = (-x)^4 - (-x)^3$$
$$= x^4 + x^3.$$

So $j(-x) \neq j(x)$ and $j(-x) \neq -j(x)$. The graph of j is not symmetric about the y-axis and is not symmetric about the origin.
Fig. 2.54 supports this conclusion. ■

Behavior at the x-Intercepts

The x-intercepts are key points for the graph of a polynomial function, as they are for any function. Consider the graph of $y = (x - 2)^2(x + 1)$ in Fig. 2.55. Near 2 the values of y are positive, as shown in Fig. 2.56, and the graph does not cross the x-axis. Near -1 the values of y are negative for $x < -1$ and positive for $x > -1$, as shown in Fig. 2.57, and the graph crosses the x-axis. The reason for this behavior is the exponents in $(x - 2)^2$ and $(x + 1)^1$. Because $(x - 2)^2$ has an even exponent, $(x - 2)^2$ cannot be negative. Because $(x + 1)^1$ has an odd exponent, $(x + 1)^1$ changes sign at -1 but does not change sign at 2. So the product $(x - 2)^2(x + 1)$ does not change sign at 2, but does change sign at -1.

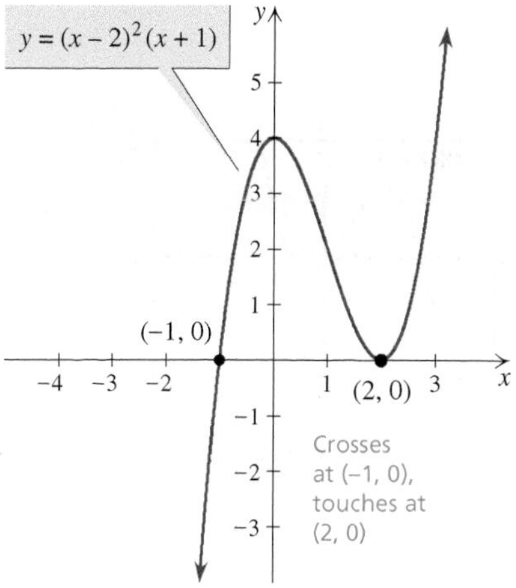

Figure 2.55

X	Y1
1.7	.243
1.8	.112
1.9	.029
2	0
2.1	.031
2.2	.128
2.3	.297

X=2

Figure 2.56

X	Y1
-1.3	-3.267
-1.2	-2.048
-1.1	-.961
-1	0
-.9	.841
-.8	1.568
-.7	2.187

X=-1

Figure 2.57

Every x-intercept corresponds to a factor of the polynomial. Whether that factor occurs an odd or even number of times determines the behavior of the graph at that intercept.

Theorem: Behavior at the x-intercepts

The graph of a polynomial function crosses the x-axis at an x-intercept if the factor corresponding to that intercept is raised to an odd power.
The graph touches but does not cross the x-axis if the factor is raised to an even power.

As another example, consider the graphs of $f(x) = x^2$ and $f(x) = x^3$ shown in Figs. 2.50 and 2.51. Each has only one x-intercept, $(0, 0)$. The factor corresponding to that intercept is x. Note that $f(x) = x^2$ does not cross the x-axis at $(0, 0)$, but $f(x) = x^3$ does cross the x-axis at $(0, 0)$.

Example 2 Crossing at the x-intercepts

Find the x-intercepts and determine whether the graph of the function crosses the x-axis at each x-intercept.

a. $f(x) = (x - 1)^2(x - 3)$ **b.** $f(x) = x^3 + 2x^2 - 3x$

Solution

a. The x-intercepts are found by solving $(x - 1)^2(x - 3) = 0$. The x-intercepts are $(1, 0)$ and $(3, 0)$. The graph does not cross the x-axis at $(1, 0)$ because the factor $x - 1$ occurs to an even power. The graph crosses the x-axis at $(3, 0)$ because $x - 3$ occurs to an odd power.

The graph in Fig. 2.58 supports these conclusions. □

b. The x-intercepts are found by solving $x^3 + 2x^2 - 3x = 0$. By factoring, we get $x(x + 3)(x - 1) = 0$. The x-intercepts are $(0, 0)$, $(-3, 0)$, and $(1, 0)$. Since each factor occurs an odd number of times (once), the graph crosses the x-axis at each of the x-intercepts.

The graph in Fig. 2.59 supports these conclusions.

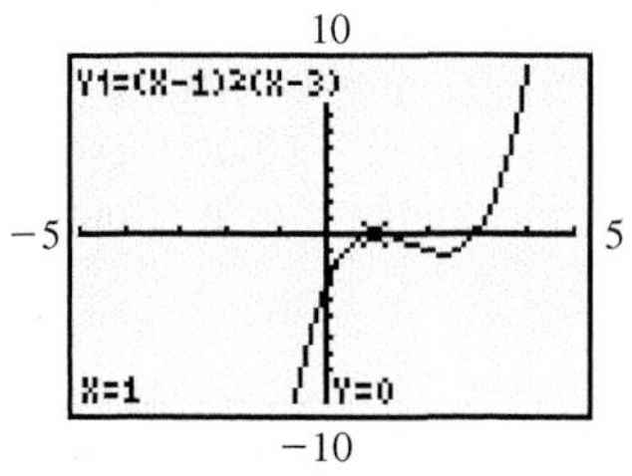

Figure 2.58

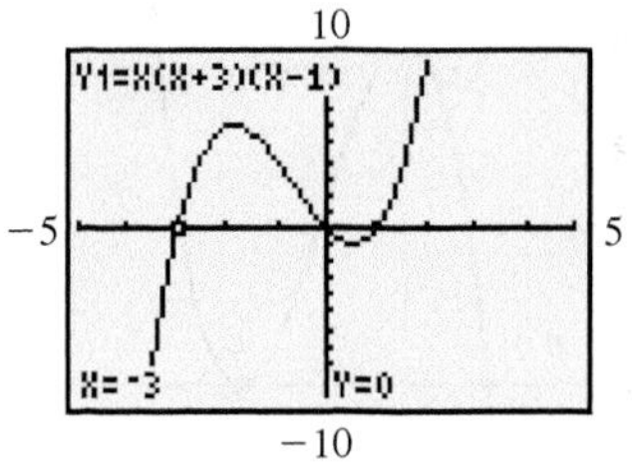

Figure 2.59

The Leading Coefficient Test

We now consider the behavior of a polynomial function as the x-coordinate goes to or approaches infinity or negative infinity. In symbols, $x \to \infty$ or $x \to -\infty$. Since we seek only an intuitive understanding of the ideas presented here, we will not give precise definitions of these terms. Precise definitions are given in a calculus course.

To say that $x \to \infty$ means that x gets larger and larger without bound. For our purposes we can think of x assuming the values 1, 2, 3, and so on, without end. Similarly, $x \to -\infty$ means that x gets smaller and smaller without bound. Think of x assuming the values $-1, -2, -3$, and so on, without end.

As x approaches ∞ the y-coordinates of any polynomial function approach ∞ or $-\infty$. Likewise, when $x \to -\infty$ the y-coordinates approach ∞ or $-\infty$. The direction that y goes is determined by the degree of the polynomial and the sign of the

■ Foreshadowing Calculus

This discussion of the properties of the graph of a function is continued in calculus. Using calculus we can determine precisely where the function is increasing and decreasing, and even describe the direction in which the curve is turning.

leading coefficient. The four possible types of behavior are illustrated in the next example.

Example 3 Behavior as $x \to \infty$ or $x \to -\infty$

Determine the behavior of the graph of each function as $x \to \infty$ or $x \to -\infty$.

a. $y = x^3 - x$ **b.** $y = -x^3 + 1$

c. $y = x^4 - 4x^2$ **d.** $y = -x^4 + 4x^2 + x$

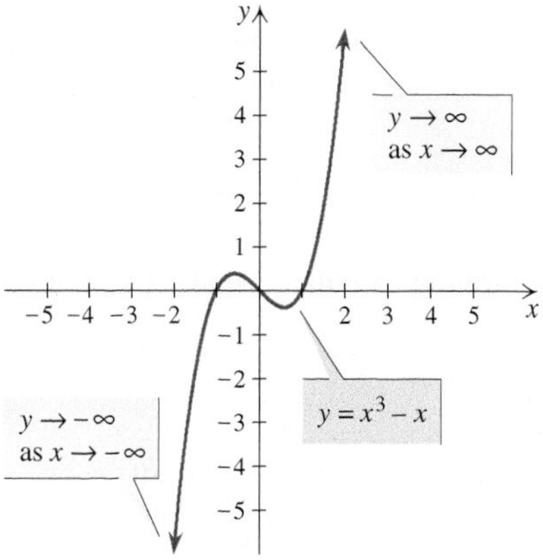

Figure 2.60

Solution

a. Considering the following table. If you have a graphing calculator, make a table like this and scroll through it.

x	−30	−20	−10	0	10	20	30
$y = x^3 - x$	−26,970	−7980	−990	0	990	7980	26,970

$y \to -\infty$ ⟵ ⟶ $y \to \infty$

The graph of $y = x^3 - x$ is shown in Fig. 2.60. As x gets larger and larger $(x \to \infty)$, y increases without bound $(y \to \infty)$. As x gets smaller and smaller $(x \to -\infty)$, y decreases without bound $(y \to -\infty)$. Notice that the degree of the polynomial is odd and the sign of the leading coefficient is positive. The behavior of this function is stated with limit notation as

$$\lim_{x\to\infty} x^3 - x = \infty \qquad \text{and} \qquad \lim_{x\to\infty} x^3 - x = -\infty.$$

The notation $\lim_{x\to\infty} x^3 - x = \infty$ is read as "the limit as x approaches ∞ of $x^3 - x$ is ∞." We could also write $\lim_{x\to\infty} y = \infty$ if it is clear that $y = x^3 - x$. For more information on limits see the Concepts of Calculus at the end of Chapter 1.

b. Consider the following table. If you have a graphing calculator, make a table like this and scroll through it.

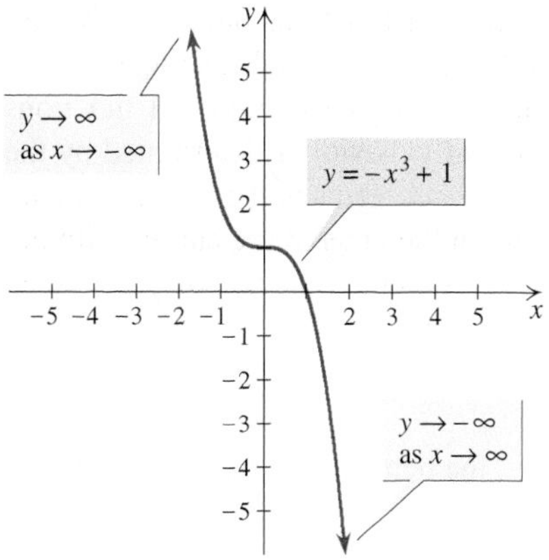

Figure 2.61

x	−30	−20	−10	0	10	20	30
$y = -x^3 + 1$	27,001	8001	1001	1	−999	−7999	−26,999

$y \to \infty$ ⟵ ⟶ $y \to -\infty$

The graph of $y = -x^3 + 1$ is shown in Fig. 2.61. As x gets larger and larger $(x \to \infty)$, y decreases without bound $(y \to -\infty)$. As x gets smaller and smaller $(x \to -\infty)$, y increases without bound $(y \to \infty)$. Notice that the degree of this polynomial is odd and the sign of the leading coefficient is negative. The behavior of this function is stated with limit notation as

$$\lim_{x\to\infty} -x^3 + 1 = -\infty \qquad \text{and} \qquad \lim_{x\to-\infty} -x^3 + 1 = \infty.$$

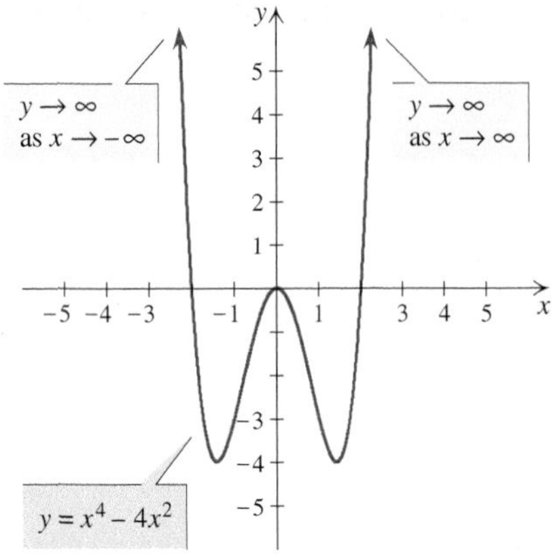

Figure 2.62

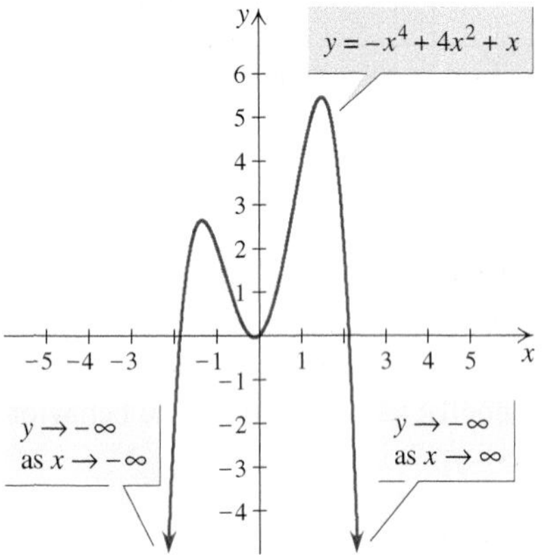

Figure 2.63

c. Consider the following table. If you have a graphing calculator, make a table like this and scroll through it.

x	0	± 10	± 20	± 30	± 40
$y = x^4 - 4x^2$	0	9600	158,400	806,400	2,553,600

$y \to \infty$

The graph of $y = x^4 - 4x^2$ is shown in Fig. 2.62. As $x \to \infty$ or $x \to -\infty$, y increases without bound ($y \to \infty$). Notice that the degree of this polynomial is even and the sign of the leading coefficient is positive. The behavior of this function is stated with limit notation as

$$\lim_{x \to \infty} x^4 - 4x^2 = \infty \quad \text{and} \quad \lim_{x \to -\infty} x^4 - 4x^2 = \infty.$$

d. Consider the following table. If you have a graphing calculator, make a table like this and scroll through it.

x	-20	-10	0	10	20
$y = -x^4 + 4x^2 + x$	$-158{,}420$	-9610	0	-9590	$-158{,}380$

$y \to -\infty$ $\quad$ $y \to -\infty$

The graph of $y = -x^4 + 4x^2 + x$ is shown in Fig. 2.63. As $x \to \infty$ or $x \to -\infty$, y decreases without bound ($y \to -\infty$). Notice that the degree of this polynomial is even and the sign of the leading coefficient is negative. The behavior of this function is stated with limit notation as

$$\lim_{x \to \infty} -x^4 + 4x^2 + x = -\infty \quad \text{and} \quad \lim_{x \to -\infty} -x^4 + 4x^2 + x = -\infty.$$ ■

As $x \to \infty$ or $x \to -\infty$ all first-degree polynomial functions have "end behavior" like the lines $y = x$ or $y = -x$, all second-degree polynomial functions behave like the parabolas $y = x^2$ or $y = -x^2$, and all third-degree polynomial functions behave like $y = x^3$ or $y = -x^3$, and so on. The end behavior is determined by the degree and the sign of the first term. The smaller-degree terms in the polynomial determine the number of "hills" and "valleys" between the ends of the curve. With degree n there are at most $n - 1$ hills and valleys. The end behavior of polynomial functions is summarized in the **leading coefficient test.**

Leading Coefficient Test

If $f(x) = a_n x^n + a_{n-1}x^{n-1} + \cdots + a_1 x + a_0$, the behavior of the graph of f to the left and right is determined as follows:

For n odd and $a_n > 0$,	$\lim_{x \to \infty} f(x) = \infty$	and	$\lim_{x \to -\infty} f(x) = -\infty$.
For n odd and $a_n < 0$,	$\lim_{x \to \infty} f(x) = -\infty$	and	$\lim_{x \to -\infty} f(x) = \infty$.
For n even and $a_n > 0$,	$\lim_{x \to \infty} f(x) = \infty$	and	$\lim_{x \to -\infty} f(x) = \infty$.
For n even and $a_n < 0$,	$\lim_{x \to \infty} f(x) = -\infty$	and	$\lim_{x \to -\infty} f(x) = -\infty$.

The leading coefficient test is shown visually in Fig. 2.64, which shows only the "ends" of the graphs of the polynomial functions.

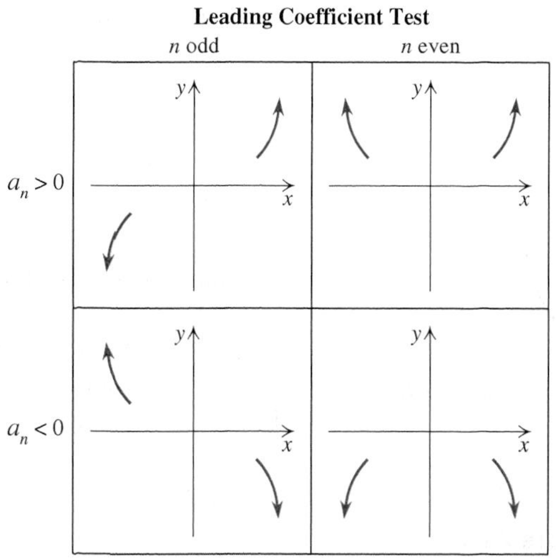

Figure 2.64

Sketching Graphs of Polynomial Functions

A good graph of a polynomial function should include the features that we have been discussing. The following strategy will help you graph polynomial functions.

STRATEGY

Graphing a Polynomial Function

1. Check for symmetry.
2. Find all real zeros of the polynomial function.
3. Determine the behavior at the corresponding x-intercepts.
4. Determine the behavior as $x \to \infty$ and as $x \to -\infty$.
5. Calculate several ordered pairs including the y-intercept to verify your suspicions about the shape of the graph.
6. Draw a smooth curve through the points to make the graph.

Example 4 Graphing polynomial functions

Sketch the graph of each polynomial function.

a. $f(x) = x^3 - 5x^2 + 7x - 3$ **b.** $f(x) = x^4 - 200x^2 + 10{,}000$

Solution

a. First find $f(-x)$ to determine symmetry and the number of negative roots.

$$f(-x) = (-x)^3 - 5(-x)^2 + 7(-x) - 3$$
$$= -x^3 - 5x^2 - 7x - 3$$

From $f(-x)$, we see that the graph has neither type of symmetry. Because $f(-x)$ has no sign changes, $x^3 - 5x^2 + 7x - 3 = 0$ has no negative roots by Descartes's rule of signs. The only possible rational roots are 1 and 3.

$$\begin{array}{r|rrrr} 1 & 1 & -5 & 7 & -3 \\ & & 1 & -4 & 3 \\ \hline & 1 & -4 & 3 & 0 \end{array}$$

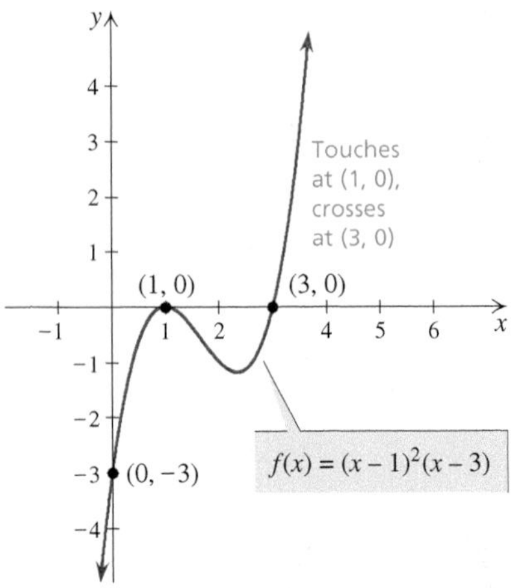

Figure 2.65

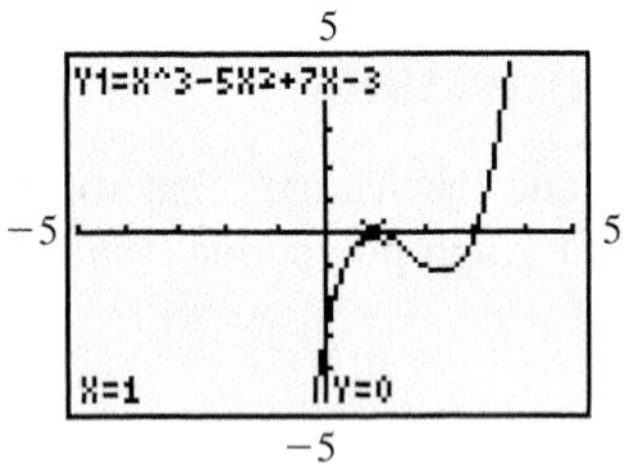

Figure 2.66

From the synthetic division we know that 1 is a root and we can factor $f(x)$:

$$f(x) = (x - 1)(x^2 - 4x + 3)$$
$$= (x - 1)^2(x - 3) \quad \text{Factor completely.}$$

The x-intercepts are $(1, 0)$ and $(3, 0)$. The graph of f does not cross the x-axis at $(1, 0)$ because $x - 1$ occurs to an even power, while the graph crosses at $(3, 0)$ because $x - 3$ occurs to an odd power. The y-intercept is $(0, -3)$. Since the leading coefficient is positive and the degree is odd, $y \to \infty$ as $x \to \infty$ and $y \to -\infty$ as $x \to -\infty$. Calculate two more ordered pairs for accuracy, say $(2, -1)$ and $(4, 9)$. Draw a smooth curve as in Fig. 2.65.

The calculator graph shown in Fig. 2.66 supports these conclusions. □

b. First find $f(-x)$:

$$f(-x) = (-x)^4 - 200(-x)^2 + 10{,}000$$
$$= x^4 - 200x^2 + 10{,}000$$

Since $f(x) = f(-x)$, the graph is symmetric about the y-axis. We can factor the polynomial as follows.

$$f(x) = x^4 - 200x^2 + 10{,}000$$
$$= (x^2 - 100)(x^2 - 100)$$
$$= (x - 10)(x + 10)(x - 10)(x + 10)$$
$$= (x - 10)^2(x + 10)^2$$

The x-intercepts are $(10, 0)$ and $(-10, 0)$. Since each factor for these intercepts has an even power, the graph does not cross the x-axis at the intercepts. The y-intercept is $(0, 10{,}000)$. Since the leading coefficient is positive and the degree is even, $y \to \infty$ as $x \to \infty$ or as $x \to -\infty$. The graph also goes through $(-20, 90{,}000)$ and $(20, 90{,}000)$. Draw a smooth curve through these points and the intercepts as shown in Fig. 2.67.

The calculator graph shown in Fig. 2.68 supports these conclusions. ■

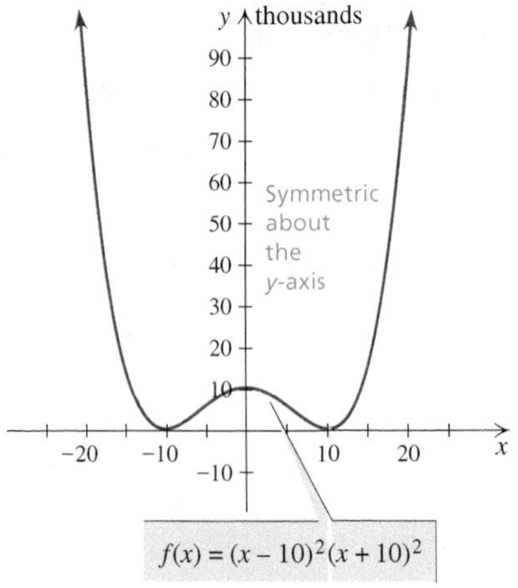

Figure 2.67

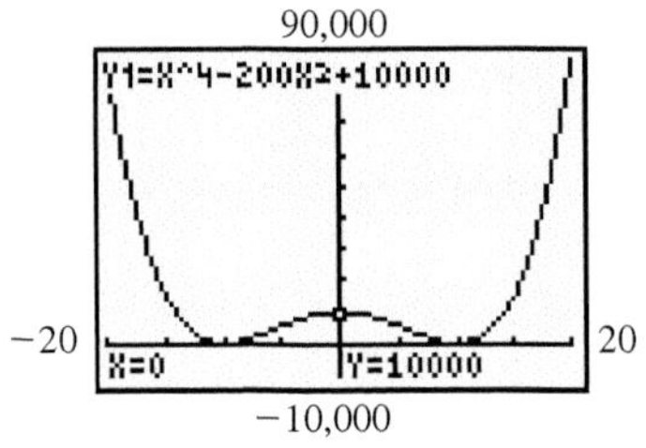

Figure 2.68

Polynomial Inequalities

We can solve polynomial inequalities by the same methods that we used on quadratic inequalities in Section 2.1. The next example illustrates the test-point method. This method depends on the intermediate value theorem. A polynomial function can change sign only at a zero of the function.

Example 5 Solving a polynomial inequality with test points

Solve $x^4 + x^3 - 15x^2 - 3x + 36 < 0$ using the test-point method.

Solution

Use synthetic division to see that 3 and -4 are zeros of the function $f(x) = x^4 + x^3 - 15x^2 - 3x + 36$:

3	1	1	−15	−3	36
		3	12	−9	−36
−4	1	4	−3	−12	0
		−4	0	12	
	1	0	−3	0	

Since $x^4 + x^3 - 15x^2 - 3x + 36 = (x - 3)(x + 4)(x^2 - 3)$, the other two zeros are $\pm\sqrt{3}$. The four zeros determine five intervals on the number line in Fig. 2.69. Select an arbitrary test point in each of these intervals. The selected points -5, -3, 0, 2, and 4 are shown in red in the figure:

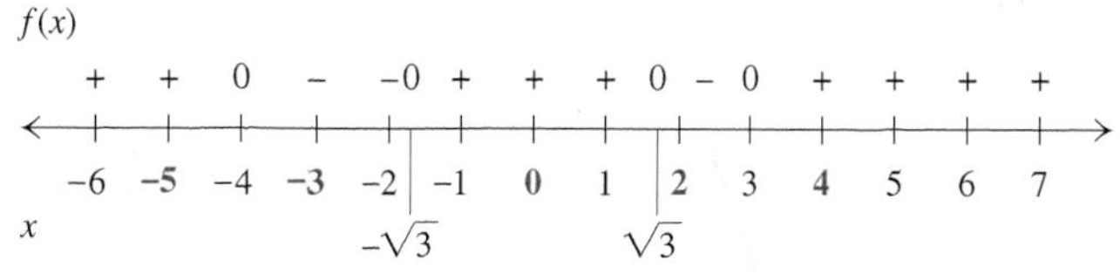

Figure 2.69

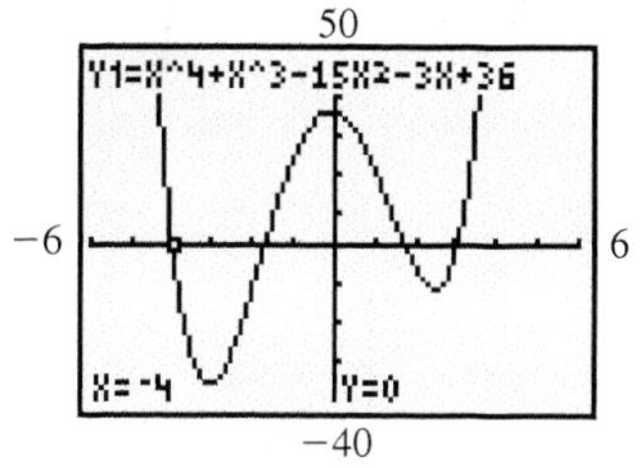

Figure 2.70

Now evaluate $f(x) = x^4 + x^3 - 15x^2 - 3x + 36$ at each test point:

$$f(-5) = 176, \quad f(-3) = -36, \quad f(0) = 36, \quad f(2) = -6, \quad f(4) = 104$$

These values indicate that the signs of the function are $+, -, +, -,$ and $+$ on the intervals shown in Fig. 2.69. The values of x that satisfy the original inequality are the values of x for which $f(x)$ is negative. So the solution set is $(-4, -\sqrt{3}) \cup (\sqrt{3}, 3)$.

The calculator graph of $y = x^4 + x^3 - 15x^2 - 3x + 36$ in Fig. 2.70 confirms that y is negative for x in $(-4, -\sqrt{3}) \cup (\sqrt{3}, 3)$. Since the multiplicity of each zero of the function is one, the graph crosses the x-axis at each intercept and the y-coordinates change sign at each intercept. ■

Function Gallery: Polynomial Functions

Linear: $f(x) = mx + b$

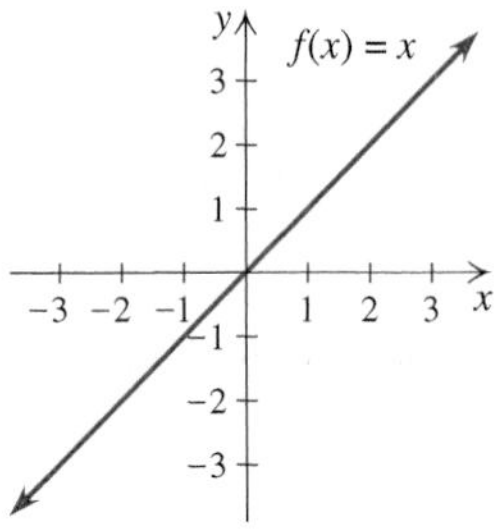

Slope 1, y-intercept (0, 0)

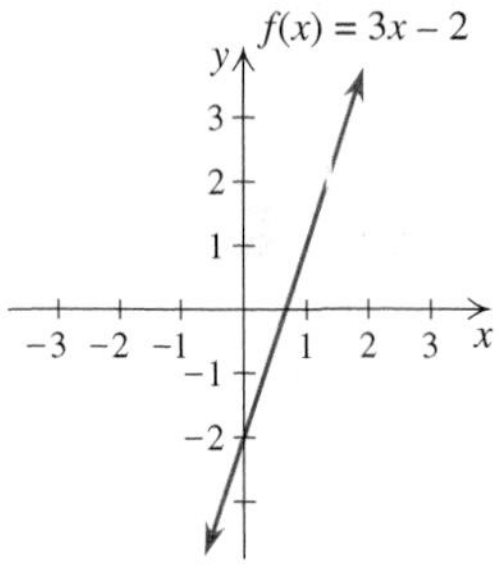

Slope 3, y-intercept (0, −2)

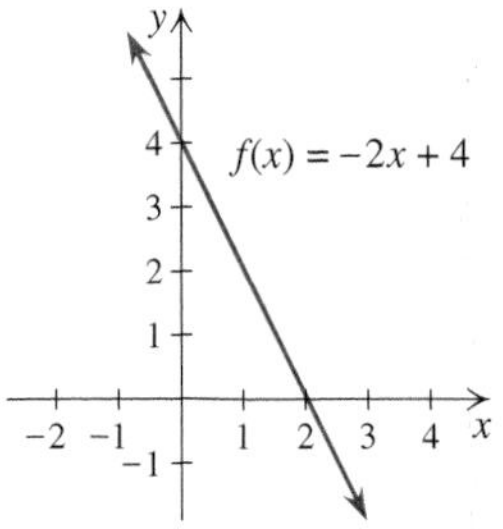

Slope −2, y-intercept (0, 4)

Quadratic: $f(x) = ax^2 + bx + c$ or $f(x) = a(x - h)^2 + k$

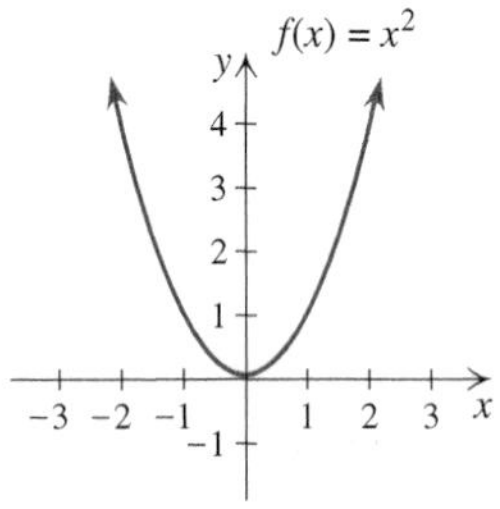

Vertex (0, 0)
Range $[0, \infty)$

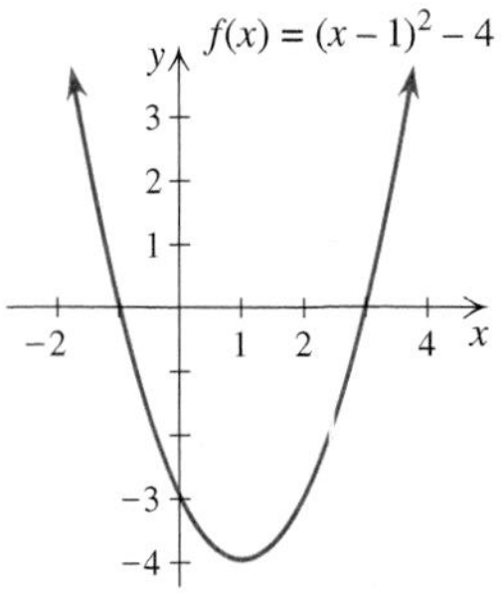

Vertex (1, −4)
Range $[-4, \infty)$

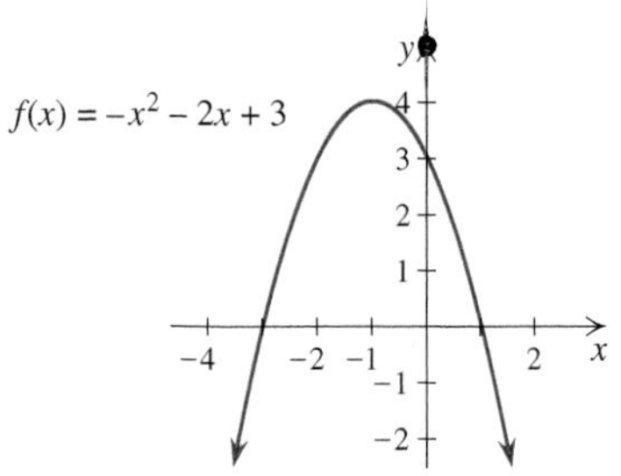

Vertex (−1, 4)
Range $(-\infty, 4]$

Cubic: $f(x) = ax^3 + bx^2 + cx + d$

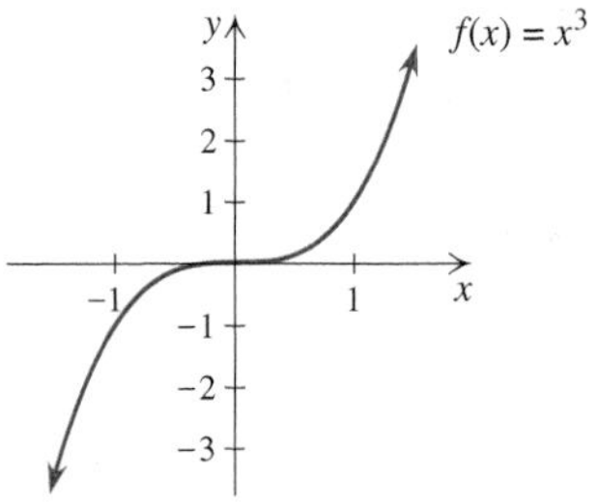

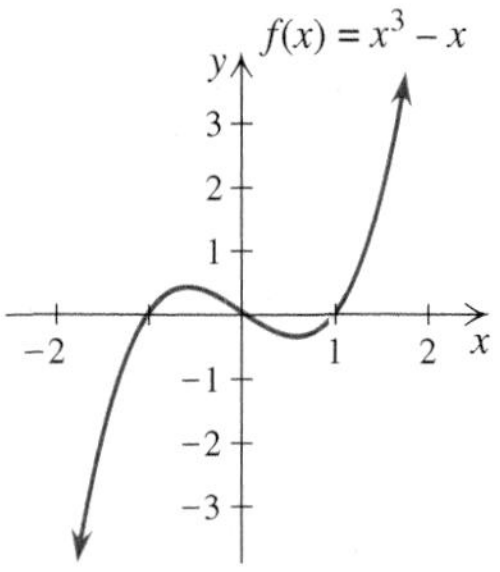

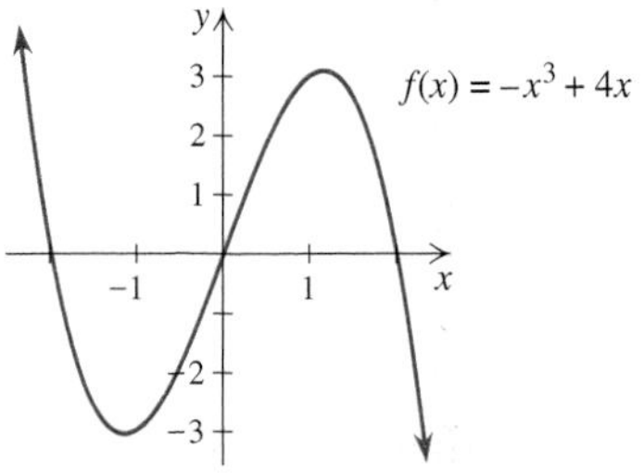

Quartic or Fourth-Degree: $f(x) = ax^4 + bx^3 + cx^2 + dx + e$

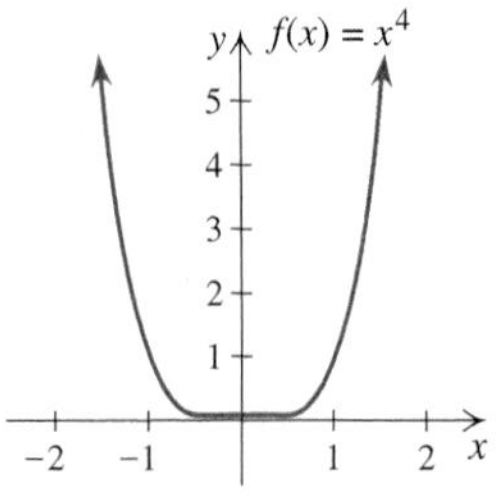

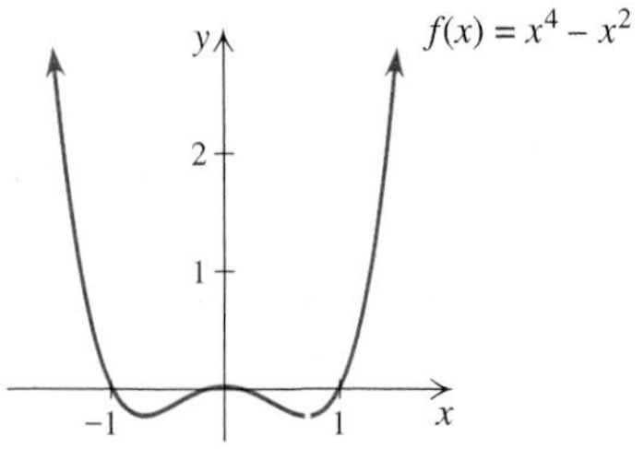

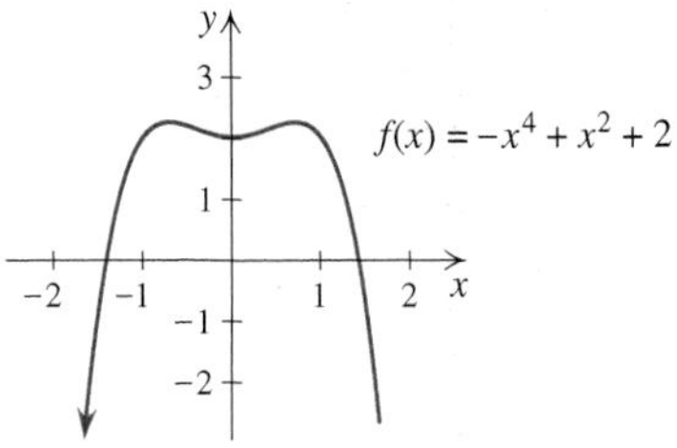

For Thought

True or False? Explain.

1. If P is a function for which $P(2) = 8$ and $P(-2) = -8$, then the graph of P is symmetric about the origin.

2. If $y = -3x^3 + 4x^2 - 6x + 9$, then $y \to -\infty$ as $x \to \infty$.

3. If the graph of $y = P(x)$ is symmetric about the origin and $P(8) = 4$, then $-P(-8) = 4$.

4. If $f(x) = x^3 - 3x$, then $f(x) = f(-x)$ for any value of x.

5. If $f(x) = x^4 - x^3 + x^2 - 6x + 7$, then $f(-x) = x^4 + x^3 + x^2 + 6x + 7$.

6. The graph of $f(x) = x^2 - 6x + 9$ has only one x-intercept.

7. The x-intercepts for $P(x) = (x - 1)^2(x + 1)$ are $(0, 1)$ and $(0, -1)$.

8. The y-intercept for $P(x) = 4(x - 3)^2 + 2$ is $(0, 2)$.

9. The graph of $f(x) = x^2(x + 8)^2$ has no points in quadrants III and IV.

10. The graph of $f(x) = x^3 - 1$ has three x-intercepts.

2.6 Exercises

Discuss the symmetry of the graph of each polynomial function. See the summary of the types of symmetry on page 162.

1. $f(x) = x^6$
2. $f(x) = x^5 - x$
3. $f(x) = x^2 - 3x + 5$
4. $f(x) = 5x^2 + 10x + 1$
5. $f(x) = 3x^6 - 5x^2 + 3x$
6. $f(x) = x^6 - x^4 + x^2 - 8$
7. $f(x) = 4x^3 - x$
8. $f(x) = 7x^3 + x^2$
9. $f(x) = (x - 5)^2$
10. $f(x) = (x^2 - 1)^2$
11. $f(x) = -x$
12. $f(x) = 3x$

Find the x-intercepts and discuss the behavior of the graph of each polynomial function at its x-intercepts.

13. $f(x) = (x - 4)^2$
14. $f(x) = (x - 1)^2(x + 3)^2$
15. $f(x) = (2x - 1)^3$
16. $f(x) = x^6$
17. $f(x) = 4x - 1$
18. $f(x) = x^2 - 5x - 6$
19. $f(x) = x^2 - 3x + 10$
20. $f(x) = x^4 - 16$
21. $f(x) = x^3 - 3x^2$
22. $f(x) = x^3 - x^2 - x + 1$
23. $f(x) = 2x^3 - 5x^2 + 4x - 1$
24. $f(x) = x^3 - 3x^2 + 4$
25. $f(x) = -2x^3 - 8x^2 + 6x + 36$
26. $f(x) = -x^3 + 7x - 6$

For each function use the leading coefficient test to determine whether $y \to \infty$ or $y \to -\infty$ as $x \to \infty$.

27. $y = 2x^3 - x^2 + 9$
28. $y = -3x + 7$
29. $y = -3x^4 + 5$
30. $y = 6x^4 - 5x^2 - 1$
31. $y = x - 3x^3$
32. $y = 5x - 7x^4$

For each function use the leading coefficient test to determine whether $y \to \infty$ or $y \to -\infty$ as $x \to -\infty$.

33. $y = -2x^5 - 3x^2$
34. $y = x^3 + 8x + \sqrt{2}$
35. $y = 3x^6 - 999x^3$
36. $y = -12x^4 - 5x$

For each graph discuss its symmetry, indicate whether the graph crosses the x-axis at each x-intercept, and determine whether $y \to \infty$ or $y \to -\infty$ as $x \to \infty$ and $x \to -\infty$.

37.

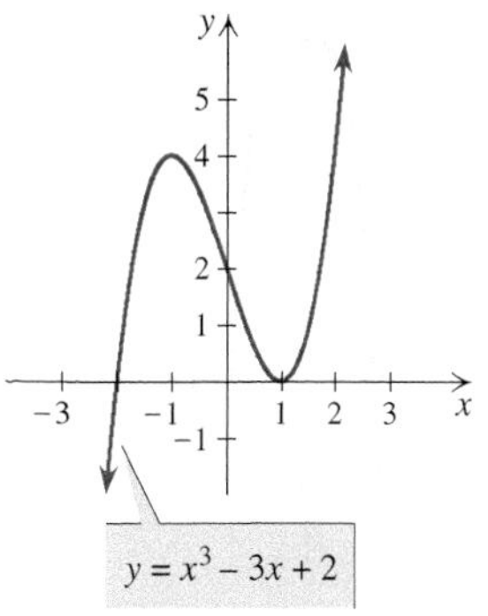

38.

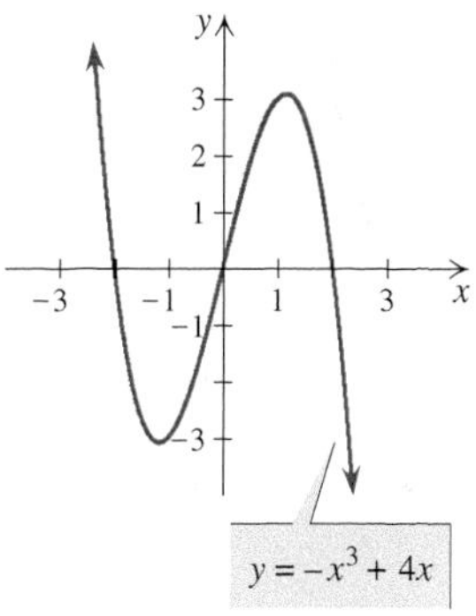

39.

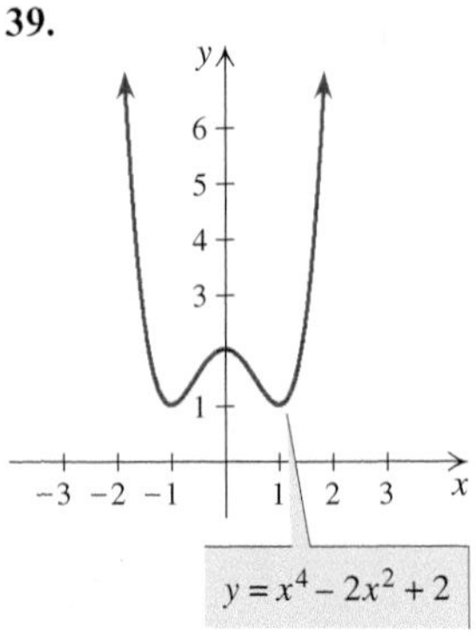

40.

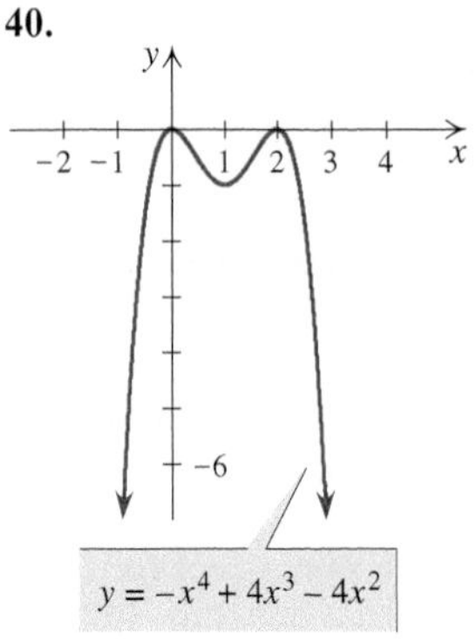

Determine whether each limit is equal to ∞ or $-\infty$.

41. $\lim_{x\to\infty} x^2 - 4$

42. $\lim_{x\to\infty} x^3 + x$

43. $\lim_{x\to\infty} -x^5 - x^2$

44. $\lim_{x\to\infty} -3x^4 + 9x^2$

45. $\lim_{x\to-\infty} -3x$

46. $\lim_{x\to-\infty} x^3 - 5$

47. $\lim_{x\to-\infty} -2x^2 + 1$

48. $\lim_{x\to-\infty} 6x^4 - x$

For each given function make a rough sketch of the graph that shows the behavior at the x-intercepts and the behavior as x approaches ∞ and $-\infty$.

49. $f(x) = (x - 1)^2(x + 3)$

50. $f(x) = (x + 2)^2(x - 5)^2$

51. $f(x) = -2(2x - 1)^2(x + 1)^3$

52. $f(x) = -3(3x - 4)^2(2x + 1)^4$

Match each polynomial function with its graph (a)–(h).

53. $f(x) = -2x + 1$

54. $f(x) = -2x^2 + 1$

55. $f(x) = -2x^3 + 1$

56. $f(x) = -2x^2 + 4x - 1$

57. $f(x) = -2x^4 + 6$

58. $f(x) = -2x^4 + 6x^2$

59. $f(x) = x^3 + 4x^2 - x - 4$

60. $f(x) = (x - 2)^4$

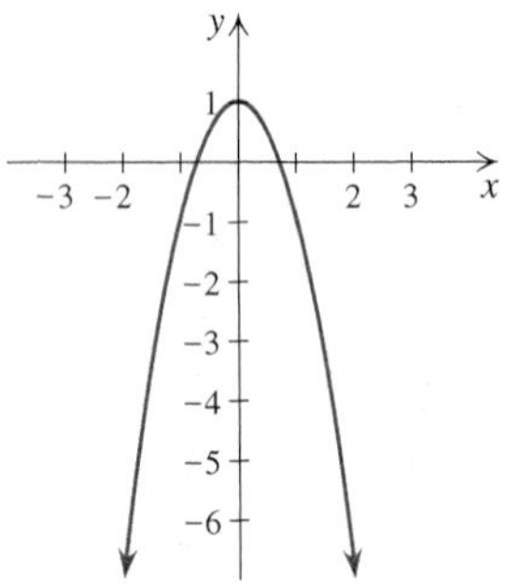

(a)

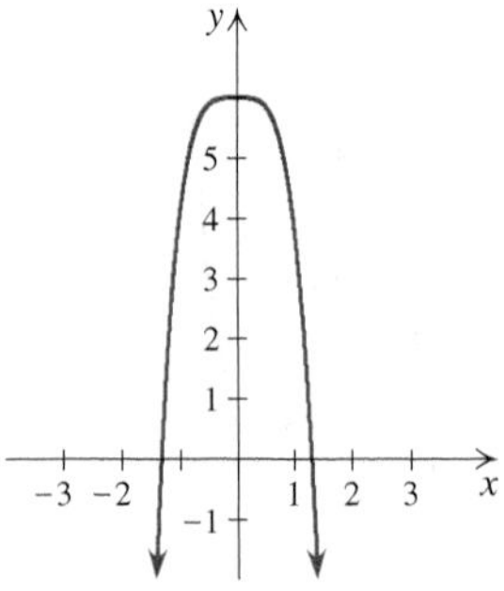

(b)

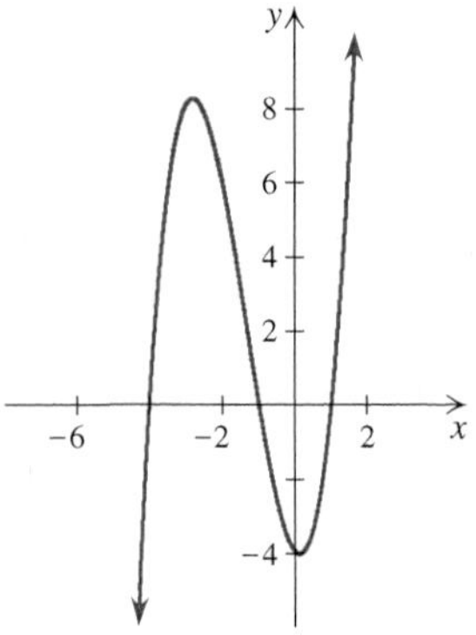

(c)

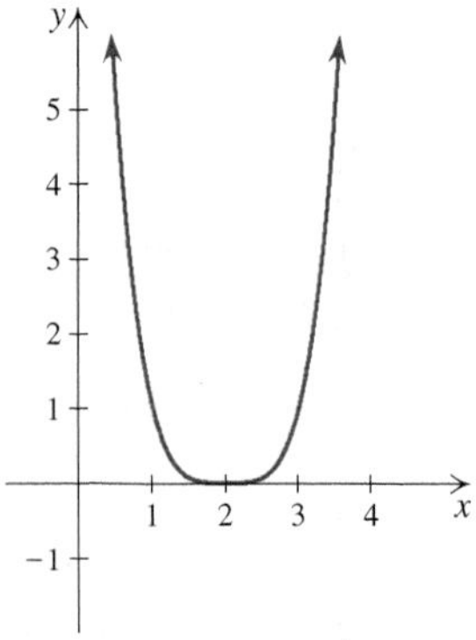

(d)

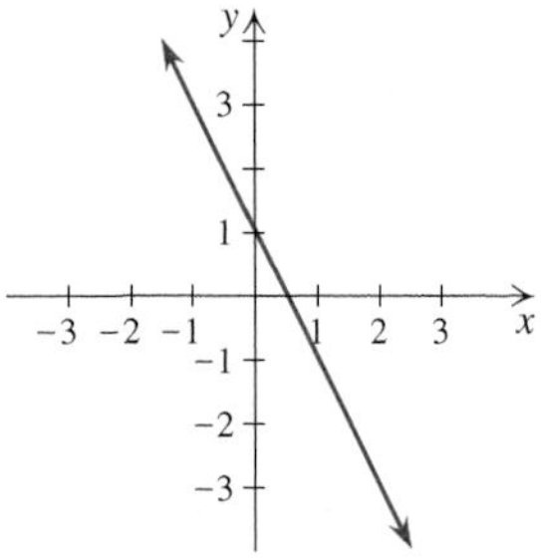

(e)

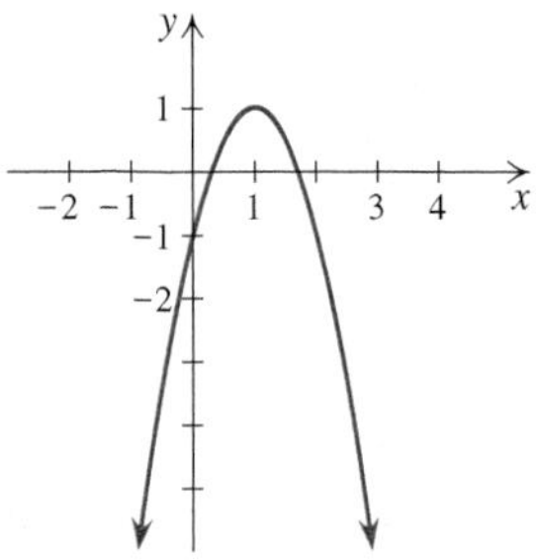

(f)

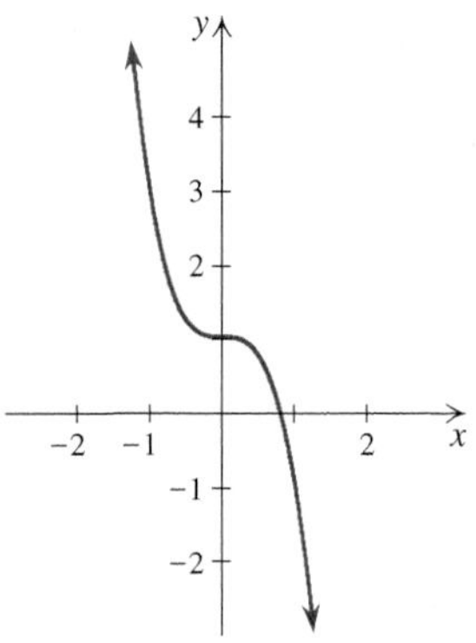

(g)

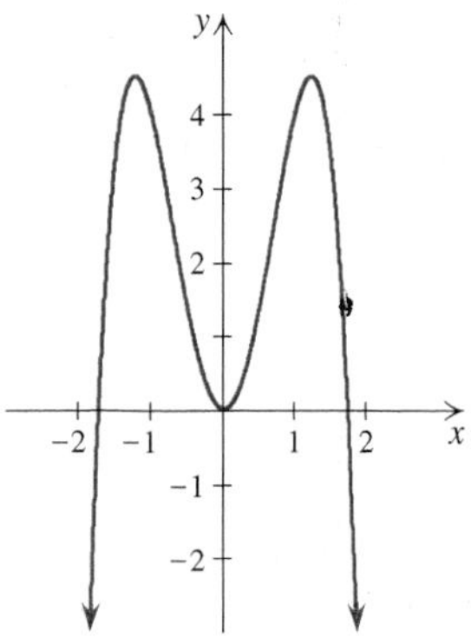

(h)

Sketch the graph of each function. See the strategy for graphing polynomial functions on page 167.

61. $f(x) = x - 30$

62. $f(x) = 40 - x$

63. $f(x) = (x - 30)^2$

64. $f(x) = (40 - x)^2$

65. $f(x) = x^3 - 40x^2$

66. $f(x) = x^3 - 900x$

67. $f(x) = (x - 20)^2(x + 20)^2$

68. $f(x) = (x - 20)^2(x + 12)$

69. $f(x) = -x^3 - x^2 + 5x - 3$

70. $f(x) = -x^4 + 6x^3 - 9x^2$

71. $f(x) = x^3 - 10x^2 - 600x$

72. $f(x) = -x^4 + 24x^3 - 144x^2$

73. $f(x) = x^3 + 18x^2 - 37x + 60$

74. $f(x) = x^3 - 7x^2 - 25x - 50$

75. $f(x) = -x^4 + 196x^2$

76. $f(x) = -x^4 + x^2 + 12$

77. $f(x) = x^3 + 3x^2 + 3x + 1$

78. $f(x) = -x^3 + 3x + 2$

79. $f(x) = (x - 3)^2(x + 5)^2(x + 7)$

80. $f(x) = x(x + 6)^2(x^2 - x - 12)$

Solve each polynomial inequality using the test-point method.

81. $x^3 - 3x > 0$

82. $-x^3 + 3x + 2 < 0$

83. $2x^2 - x^4 \le 0$

84. $-x^4 + x^2 + 12 \ge 0$

85. $x^3 + 4x^2 - x - 4 > 0$

86. $x^3 + 2x^2 - 2x - 4 < 0$

87. $x^3 - 4x^2 - 20x + 48 \ge 0$

88. $x^3 + 7x^2 - 36 \le 0$

89. $x^3 - x^2 + x - 1 < 0$

90. $x^3 + x^2 + 2x - 4 > 0$

91. $x^4 - 19x^2 + 90 \le 0$

92. $x^4 - 5x^3 + 3x^2 + 15x - 18 \ge 0$

Determine which of the given functions is shown in the accompanying graph.

93. a. $f(x) = (x - 3)(x + 2)$ b. $f(x) = (x + 3)(x - 2)$

c. $f(x) = \frac{1}{3}(x - 3)(x + 2)$ d. $f(x) = \frac{1}{3}(x + 3)(x - 2)$

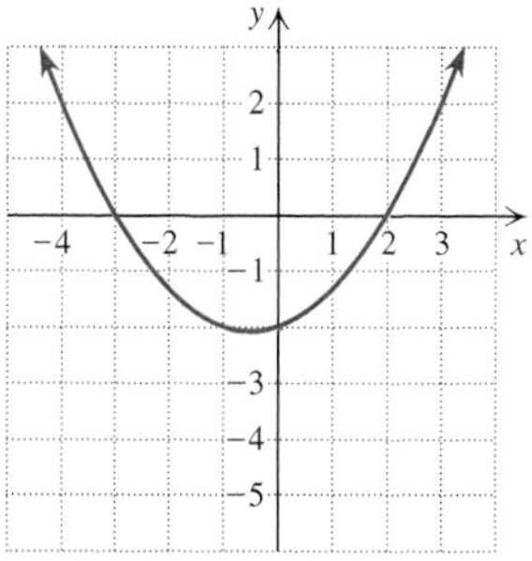

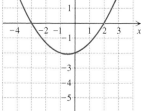

Figure for Exercise 93

94. a. $f(x) = (x + 3)(x + 1)(x - 1)$

b. $f(x) = (x - 3)(x^2 - 1)$

c. $f(x) = \frac{2}{3}(x + 3)(x + 1)(x - 1)$

d. $f(x) = -\frac{2}{3}(x + 3)(x^2 - 1)$

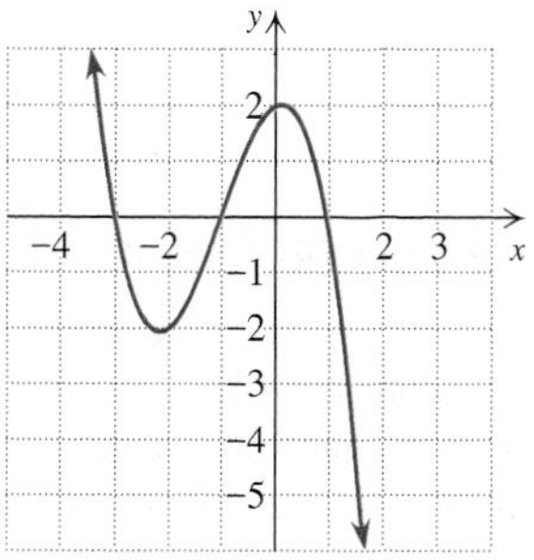

Figure for Exercise 94

Solve each problem.

95. *Maximum Volume* An open-top box is to be made from a 6 in. by 7 in. piece of copper by cutting equal squares (x in. by x in.) from each corner and folding up the sides. Write the volume of the box as a function of x. Use a graphing calculator to find the maximum possible volume to the nearest hundredth of a cubic inch.

Foreshadowing Calculus

Making an open-top box as in Exercise 95 is a classic problem in calculus. However, in calculus we usually find the value of x that maximizes the volume of the box, without using a calculator.

96. *Maximizing Volume* A manufacturer wants to make a metal can with a top and bottom such that its surface area is 3 square feet. (For this right circular cylinder $V = \pi r^2 h$ and $S = 2\pi r^2 + 2\pi rh$.)

a. Write the height of the can as a function of the radius.

b. Write the volume of the can as a function of the radius.

c. Use a calculator graph of the function in part (b) to find the radius and height (to the nearest tenth of a foot) that maximizes the volume of the can.

97. *Packing Cheese* Workers at the Green Bay Cheese Factory are trying to cover a block of cheese with an 8 in. by 12 in. piece of foil paper as shown in the figure on the next page.

The ratio of the length and width of the block must be 4 to 3 to accommodate the label. Find a polynomial function that gives the volume of the block of cheese covered in this manner as a function of the thickness x. Use a graphing calculator to find the dimensions of the block that will maximize the volume.

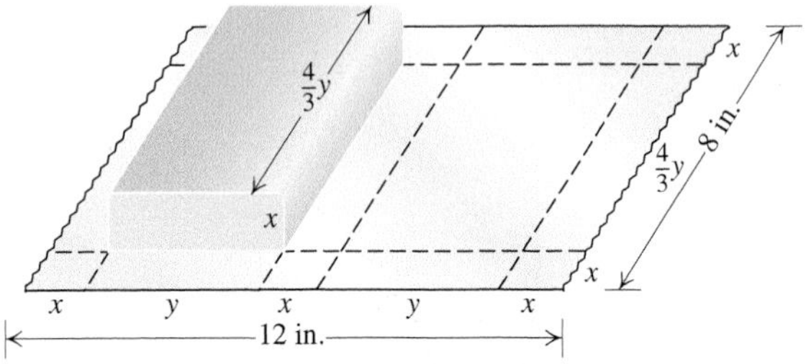

Figure for Exercise 97

98. *Giant Teepee* A casino designer is planning a giant teepee that is 80 ft in diameter and 120 ft high as shown in the figure. Inside the teepee is to be a cylindrical room for slot machines. Write the volume of the cylindrical room as a function of its radius. Use a graphing calculator to find the radius that maximizes the volume of the cylindrical room.

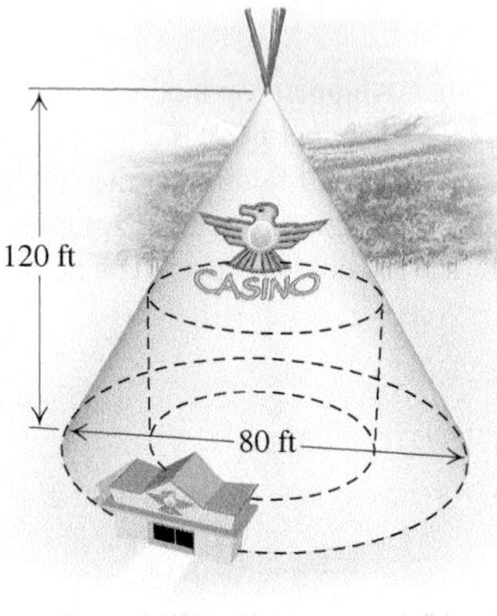

Figure for Exercise 98

Thinking Outside the Box XVI

Leaning Ladder A 7-ft ladder is leaning against a vertical wall. There is a point near the bottom of the ladder that is 1 ft from the ground and 1 ft from the wall. Find the exact or approximate distance from the top of the ladder to the ground.

Figure for Thinking Outside the Box XVI

2.6 Pop Quiz

1. Discuss the symmetry of the graph of $y = x^4 - 3x^2$.

2. Discuss the symmetry of the graph of $y = x^3 - 3x$.

3. Does $f(x) = (x - 4)^3$ cross the x-axis at $(4, 0)$?

4. If $y = x^4 - 3x^3$, does y go to ∞ or $-\infty$ as $x \to \infty$?

5. If $y = -2x^4 + 5x^2$, does y go to ∞ or $-\infty$ as $x \to -\infty$?

6. Solve $(x - 3)^2(x + 1)^3 > 0$.

2.7 Rational Functions and Inequalities

In this section we will use our knowledge of polynomial functions to study functions that are ratios of polynomial functions.

Rational Functions and Their Domains

Functions such as

$$y = \frac{1}{x}, \qquad f(x) = \frac{x - 3}{x - 1}, \qquad \text{and} \qquad g(x) = \frac{2x - 3}{x^2 - 4}$$

are rational functions.

Definition: Rational Function

If $P(x)$ and $Q(x)$ are polynomials, then a function of the form

$$f(x) = \frac{P(x)}{Q(x)}$$

is called a **rational function,** provided that $Q(x)$ is not the zero polynomial.

To simplify discussions of rational functions we will assume that $f(x)$ is in lowest terms ($P(x)$ and $Q(x)$ have no common factors) unless it is stated otherwise.

The domain of a polynomial function is the set of all real numbers, while the domain of a rational function is restricted to real numbers that do not cause the denominator to have a value of 0. The domain of $y = 1/x$ is the set of all real numbers except 0.

Example 1 The domain of a rational function

Find the domain of each rational function.

a. $f(x) = \dfrac{x - 3}{x - 1}$ **b.** $g(x) = \dfrac{2x - 3}{x^2 - 4}$

Solution

a. Since $x - 1 = 0$ only for $x = 1$, the domain of f is the set of all real numbers except 1. The domain is written in interval notation as $(-\infty, 1) \cup (1, \infty)$.

b. Since $x^2 - 4 = 0$ for $x = \pm 2$, any real number except 2 and -2 can be used for x. So the domain of g is $(-\infty, -2) \cup (-2, 2) \cup (2, \infty)$. ■

Horizontal and Vertical Asymptotes

The graph of a rational function such as $f(x) = 1/x$ does not look like the graph of a polynomial function. The domain of $f(x) = 1/x$ is the set of all real numbers except 0. However, 0 is an important number for the graph of this function because of the behavior of the graph when x is close to 0. The following table shows ordered pairs in which x is close to 0.

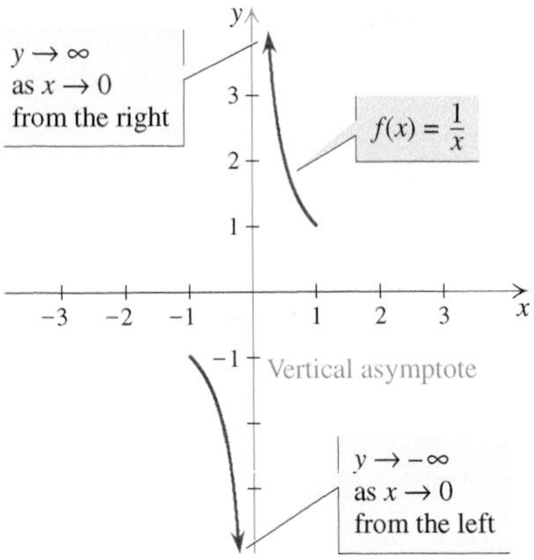

Figure 2.71

	$x \to 0$ from left				$x \to 0$ from right		
x	-0.1	-0.01	-0.001	0	0.001	0.01	0.1
$y = 1/x$	-10	-100	-1000		1000	100	10
	$y \to -\infty$				$y \to \infty$		

Notice that the closer x is to 0, the farther y is from 0. In symbols $y \to \infty$ as $x \to 0$ from the right. Using limit notation we write $\lim_{x \to 0^+} \frac{1}{x} = \infty$, where the plus symbol indicates that x is approaching 0 from above or from the right. If $x \to 0$ from the left, $y \to -\infty$. Using limit notation we write $\lim_{x \to 0^-} \frac{1}{x} = -\infty$, where the negative symbol indicates that x is approaching 0 from below or from the left. Plotting the ordered pairs from the table suggest a curve that gets closer and closer to the vertical line $x = 0$ (the y-axis) but never touches it, as shown in Fig. 2.71. The y-axis is called a *vertical asymptote* for this curve.

The following table shows ordered pairs in which x is far from 0.

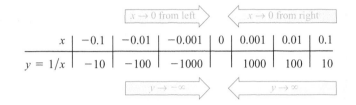

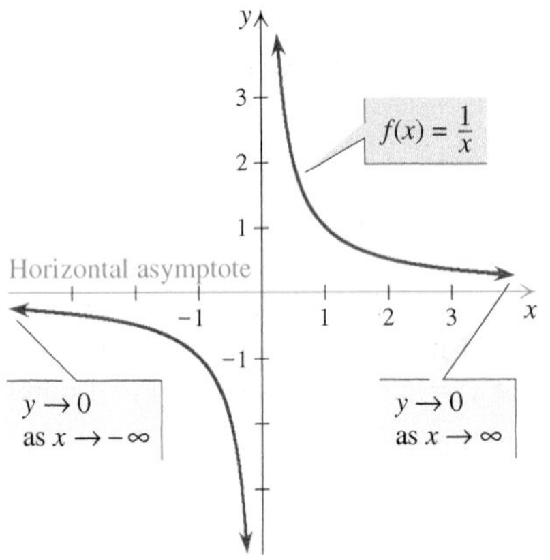

Figure 2.72

	$x \to -\infty$				$x \to \infty$		
x	-1000	-100	-10	0	10	100	1000
$y = 1/x$	-0.001	-0.01	-0.1		0.1	0.01	0.001
	$y \to 0$ from below				$y \to 0$ from above		

Notice that the farther x is from 0, the closer y is to 0. Using limit notation we write $\lim_{x \to \infty} \frac{1}{x} = 0$ and $\lim_{x \to -\infty} \frac{1}{x} = 0$. Plotting the ordered pairs from the table suggests a curve that lies just above the positive x-axis and just below the negative x-axis. The x-axis is called a *horizontal asymptote* for the graph of f. The complete graph of $f(x) = 1/x$ is shown in Fig. 2.72. Since $f(-x) = 1/(-x) = -f(x)$, the graph is symmetric about the origin.

For any rational function expressed in lowest terms, a horizontal asymptote is determined by the value approached by the rational expression as $|x| \to \infty$ ($x \to \infty$ or $x \to -\infty$). A vertical asymptote occurs for every number that causes the denominator of the function to have a value of 0, provided the rational function is in lowest terms. As we will learn shortly, not every rational function has a vertical and a horizontal asymptote. We can give a formal definition of asymptotes as described below.

Definition: Vertical and Horizontal Asymptotes

Let $f(x) = P(x)/Q(x)$ be a rational function written in lowest terms.

If $|f(x)| \to \infty$ as $x \to a$, then the vertical line $x = a$ is a **vertical asymptote.** Using limit notation, $x = a$ is a vertical asymptote if $\lim_{x \to a} |f(x)| = \infty$.

The line $y = a$ is a **horizontal asymptote** if $f(x) \to a$ as $x \to \infty$ or $x \to -\infty$. Using limit notation, $y = a$ is a horizontal asymptote if $\lim_{x \to \infty} f(x) = a$ or $\lim_{x \to -\infty} f(x) = a$.

To find a horizontal asymptote we need to approximate the value of a rational expression when x is arbitrarily large. If x is large, then expressions such as

$$\frac{500}{x}, \quad -\frac{14}{x}, \quad \frac{3}{x^2}, \quad \frac{6}{x^3}, \quad \text{and} \quad \frac{4}{x-5},$$

which consist of a fixed number over a polynomial, are approximately zero. To approximate a ratio of two polynomials that both involve x, such as $\frac{x-2}{2x+3}$, we rewrite the expression by dividing by the highest power of x:

$$\frac{x-2}{2x+3} = \frac{\frac{x}{x} - \frac{2}{x}}{\frac{2x}{x} + \frac{3}{x}} = \frac{1 - \frac{2}{x}}{2 + \frac{3}{x}}$$

Since $2/x$ and $3/x$ are approximately zero when x is large, the approximate value of this expression is $1/2$. We use this idea in the next example.

Example 2 Identifying horizontal and vertical asymptotes

Find the horizontal and vertical asymptotes for each rational function.

a. $f(x) = \frac{3}{x^2 - 1}$ **b.** $g(x) = \frac{x}{x^2 - 4}$ **c.** $h(x) = \frac{2x + 1}{x + 3}$

Solution

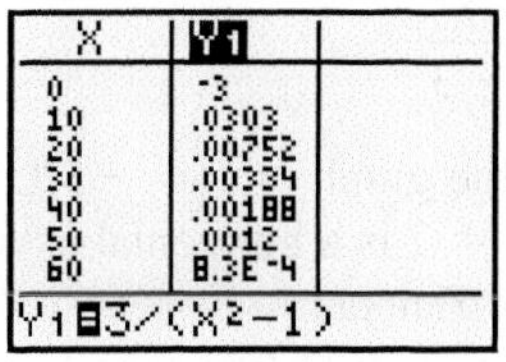

Figure 2.73

a. The denominator $x^2 - 1$ has a value of 0 if $x = \pm 1$. So the lines $x = 1$ and $x = -1$ are vertical asymptotes. As $x \to \infty$ or $x \to -\infty$, $x^2 - 1$ gets larger, making $3/(x^2 - 1)$ the ratio of 3 and a large number. Thus $3/(x^2 - 1) \to 0$ and the x-axis is a horizontal asymptote.

The calculator table shown in Fig. 2.73 supports the conclusion that the x-axis is a horizontal asymptote. □

b. The denominator $x^2 - 4$ has a value of 0 if $x = \pm 2$. So the lines $x = 2$ and $x = -2$ are vertical asymptotes. As $x \to \infty$, $x/(x^2 - 4)$ is a ratio of two large numbers. The approximate value of this ratio is not clear. However, if we divide the numerator and denominator by x^2, the highest power of x, we can get a clearer picture of the value of this ratio:

$$g(x) = \frac{x}{x^2 - 4} = \frac{\frac{x}{x^2}}{\frac{x^2}{x^2} - \frac{4}{x^2}} = \frac{\frac{1}{x}}{1 - \frac{4}{x^2}}$$

As $|x| \to \infty$, the values of $1/x$ and $4/x^2$ go to 0. So

$$g(x) \to \frac{0}{1 - 0} = 0.$$

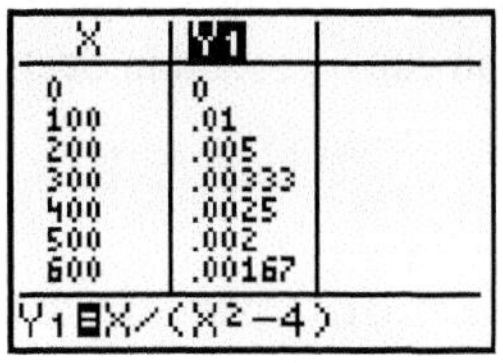

Figure 2.74

So the x-axis is a horizontal asymptote.

The calculator table shown in Fig. 2.74 supports the conclusion that the x-axis is a horizontal asymptote. □

c. The denominator $x + 3$ has a value of 0 if $x = -3$. So the line $x = -3$ is a vertical asymptote. To find any horizontal asymptotes, rewrite the rational expression by dividing the numerator and denominator by the highest power of x:

$$h(x) = \frac{2x + 1}{x + 3} = \frac{\frac{2x}{x} + \frac{1}{x}}{\frac{x}{x} + \frac{3}{x}} = \frac{2 + \frac{1}{x}}{1 + \frac{3}{x}}$$

As $x \to \infty$ or $x \to -\infty$ the values of $1/x$ and $3/x$ approach 0. So

$$h(x) \to \frac{2 + 0}{1 + 0} = 2.$$

So the line $y = 2$ is a horizontal asymptote.

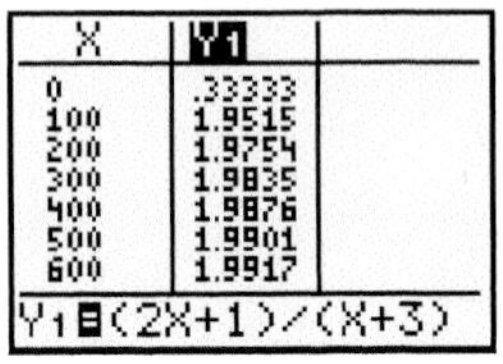

Figure 2.75

The calculator table shown in Fig. 2.75 supports the conclusion that $y = 2$ is a horizontal asymptote. ■

If the degree of the numerator of a rational function is less than the degree of the denominator, as in Example 2(a) and (b), then the x-axis is a horizontal asymptote for the graph of the function. If the degree of the numerator is equal to the degree of the denominator, as in Example 2(c), then the x-axis is not a horizontal asymptote. We can see this clearly if we use division to rewrite the expression as quotient + remainder/divisor. For the function of Example 2(c), we get

$$h(x) = \frac{2x + 1}{x + 3} = 2 + \frac{-5}{x + 3}.$$

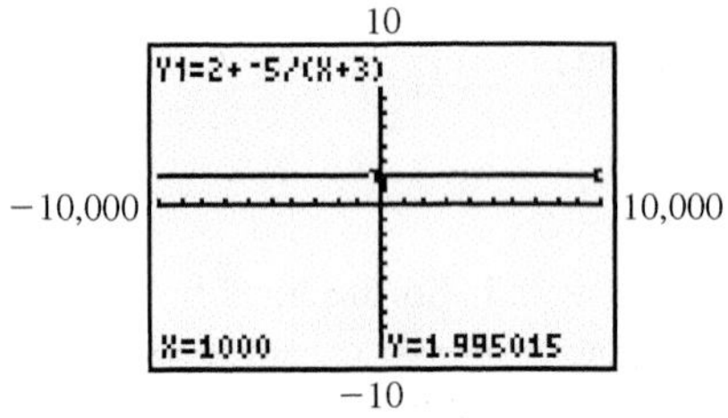

Figure 2.76

The graph of h is a translation two units upward of the graph of $y = -5/(x + 3)$, which has the x-axis as a horizontal asymptote. So $y = 2$ is a horizontal asymptote for h. Note that 2 is simply the ratio of the leading coefficients.

Since the graph of h is very close to $y = 2$, the view of h in Fig. 2.76 looks like $y = 2$. Note how this choice of viewing window causes some of the important features of the graph to disappear. □

Oblique Asymptotes

Each rational function of Example 2 had one horizontal asymptote and had a vertical asymptote for each zero of the polynomial in the denominator. The horizontal asymptote $y = 0$ occurs because the y-coordinate gets closer and closer to 0 as $x \to \infty$ or $x \to -\infty$. Some rational functions have a nonhorizontal line for an asymptote. An asymptote that is neither horizontal nor vertical is called an **oblique asymptote** or **slant asymptote.** Oblique asymptotes are determined by using long division or synthetic division of polynomials. A review of long division can be found in Section A.2 of the Appendix.

■ Foreshadowing Calculus

The asymptotic behavior of functions is studied more extensively in calculus under the topic of *limits*.

Example 3 A rational function with an oblique asymptote

Determine all of the asymptotes for $g(x) = \frac{2x^2 + 3x - 5}{x + 2}$.

Solution

If $x + 2 = 0$, then $x = -2$. So the line $x = -2$ is a vertical asymptote. Because the degree of the numerator is larger than the degree of the denominator, we use long division (or in this case, synthetic division) to rewrite the function as quotient +

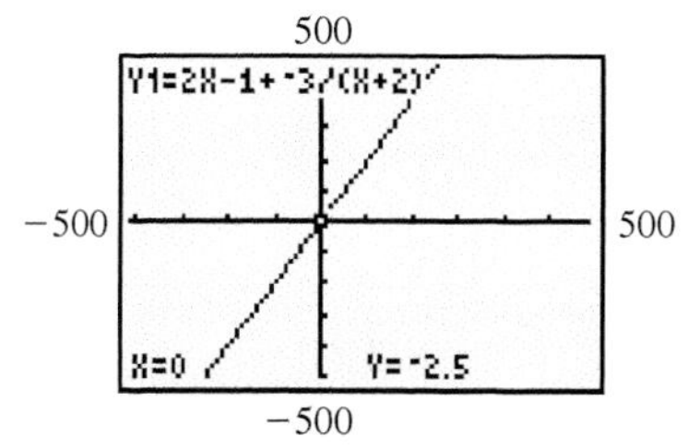

Figure 2.77

remainder/divisor (dividing the numerator and denominator by x^2 will not work in this case):

$$g(x) = \frac{2x^2 + 3x - 5}{x + 2} = 2x - 1 + \frac{-3}{x + 2}$$

If $|x| \to \infty$, then $-3/(x + 2) \to 0$. So the value of $g(x)$ approaches $2x - 1$ as $|x| \to \infty$. The line $y = 2x - 1$ is an oblique asymptote for the graph of g. You may look ahead to Fig. 2.85 to see the graph of this function with its oblique asymptote. Note that the wide view of g in Fig. 2.77 looks like the line $y = 2x - 1$. ■

If the degree of $P(x)$ is 1 greater than the degree of $Q(x)$ and the degree of $Q(x)$ is at least 1, then the rational function has an oblique asymptote. In this case use division to rewrite the function as quotient + remainder/divisor. The graph of the equation formed by setting y equal to the quotient is an oblique asymptote. We conclude this discussion of asymptotes with a summary.

SUMMARY

Finding Asymptotes for a Rational Function

Let $f(x) = P(x)/Q(x)$ be a rational function in lowest terms with the degree of $Q(x)$ at least 1.

1. The graph of f has a vertical asymptote corresponding to each root of $Q(x) = 0$.
2. If the degree of $P(x)$ is less than the degree of $Q(x)$, then the x-axis is a horizontal asymptote.
3. If the degree of $P(x)$ equals the degree of $Q(x)$, then the horizontal asymptote is determined by the ratio of the leading coefficients.
4. If the degree of $P(x)$ is greater than the degree of $Q(x)$, then use division to rewrite the function as quotient + remainder/divisor. The graph of the equation formed by setting y equal to the quotient is an asymptote. This asymptote is an oblique or slant asymptote if the degree of $P(x)$ is 1 larger than the degree of $Q(x)$.

Sketching Graphs of Rational Functions

We now use asymptotes and symmetry to help us sketch the graphs of the rational functions discussed in Examples 2 and 3. Use the following steps to graph a rational function.

PROCEDURE

Graphing a Rational Function

To graph a rational function in lowest terms:

1. Determine the asymptotes and draw them as dashed lines.
2. Check for symmetry.
3. Find any intercepts.
4. Plot several selected points to determine how the graph approaches the asymptotes.
5. Draw curves through the selected points, approaching the asymptotes.

Example 4 Functions with horizontal and vertical asymptotes

Sketch the graph of each rational function.

a. $f(x) = \dfrac{3}{x^2 - 1}$ **b.** $g(x) = \dfrac{x}{x^2 - 4}$ **c.** $h(x) = \dfrac{2x + 1}{x + 3}$

Solution

a. From Example 2(a), $x = 1$ and $x = -1$ are vertical asymptotes, and the x-axis is a horizontal asymptote. Draw the vertical asymptotes using dashed lines. Since all of the powers of x are even, $f(-x) = f(x)$ and the graph is symmetric about the y-axis. The y-intercept is $(0, -3)$. There are no x-intercepts because $f(x) = 0$ has no solution. Evaluate the function at $x = 0.9$ and $x = 1.1$ to see how the curve approaches the asymptote at $x = 1$. Evaluate at $x = 2$ and $x = 3$ to see whether the curve approaches the horizontal asymptote from above or below. We get $(0.9, -15.789)$, $(1.1, 14.286)$, $(2, 1)$, and $(3, 3/8)$. From these points you can see that the curve is going downward toward $x = 1$ from the left and upward toward $x = 1$ from the right. It is approaching its horizontal asymptote from above. Now use the symmetry with respect to the y-axis to draw the curve approaching its asymptotes as shown in Fig. 2.78.

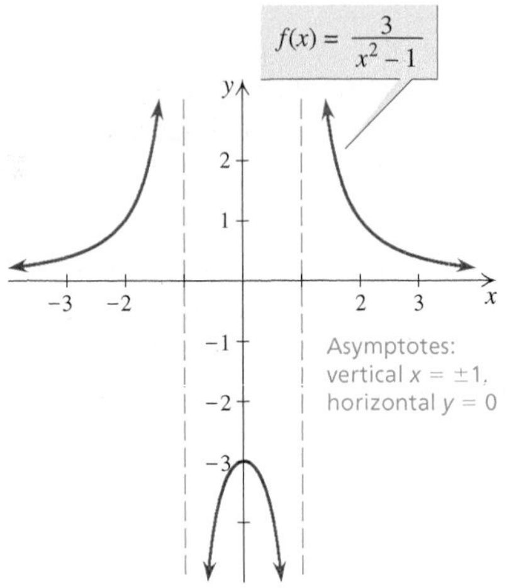

Figure 2.78

The calculator graph in dot mode in Fig. 2.79 supports these conclusions. □

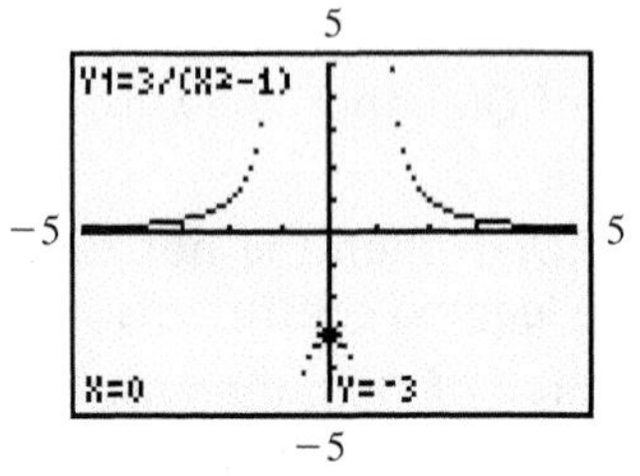

Figure 2.79

b. Draw the vertical asymptotes $x = 2$ and $x = -2$ from Example 2(b) as dashed lines. The x-axis is a horizontal asymptote. Because $f(-x) = -f(x)$, the graph is symmetric about the origin. The x-intercept is $(0, 0)$. Evaluate the function near the vertical asymptote $x = 2$, and for larger values of x to see how the curve approaches the horizontal asymptote. We get $(1.9, -4.872)$, $(2.1, 5.122)$, $(3, 3/5)$, and $(4, 1/3)$. From these points you can see that the curve is going downward toward $x = 2$ from the left and upward toward $x = 2$ from the right. It is approaching its horizontal asymptote from above. Now use the symmetry with respect to the origin to draw the curve approaching its asymptotes as shown in Fig. 2.80.

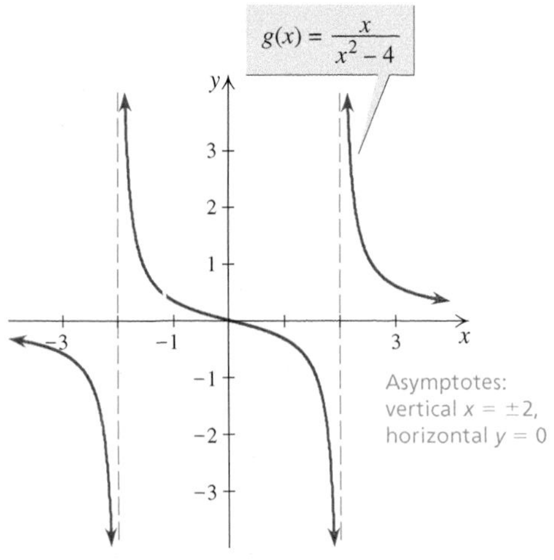

Figure 2.80

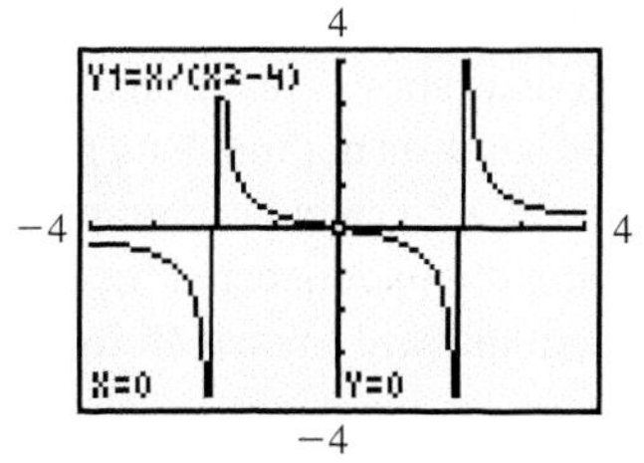

Figure 2.81

The calculator graph in connected mode in Fig. 2.81 confirms these conclusions. Note how the calculator appears to draw the vertical asymptotes as it connects the points that are close to but on opposite sides of the asymptotes. □

c. Draw the vertical asymptote $x = -3$ and the horizontal asymptote $y = 2$ from Example 2(c) as dashed lines. The x-intercept is $(-1/2, 0)$ and the y-intercept is $(0, 1/3)$. The points $(-2, -3)$, $(7, 1.5)$, $(-4, 7)$, and $(-13, 2.5)$ are also on the graph. From these points we can conclude that the curve goes upward toward $x = -3$ from the left and downward toward $x = -3$ from the right. It approaches $y = 2$ from above as x goes to $-\infty$ and from below as x goes to ∞. Draw the graph approaching its asymptotes as shown in Fig. 2.82.

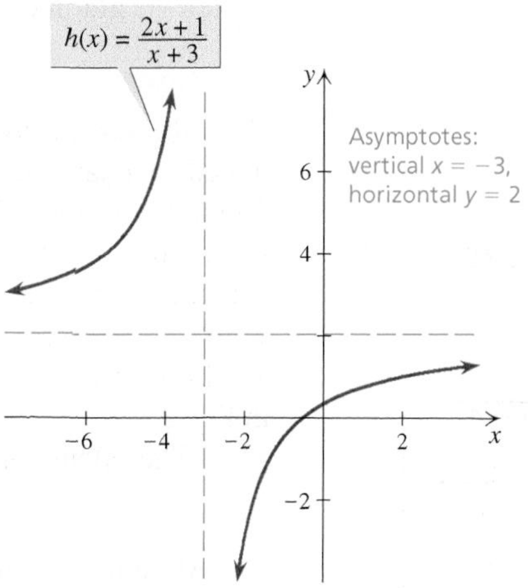

Figure 2.82

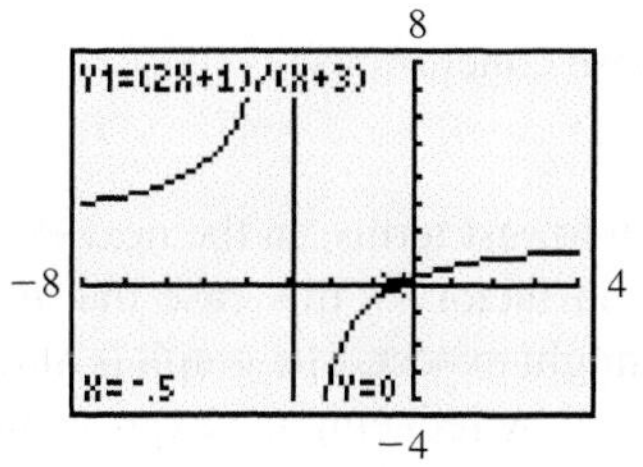

Figure 2.83

The calculator graph in Fig. 2.83 supports these conclusions. ■

The graph of a rational function cannot cross a vertical asymptote, but it can cross a nonvertical asymptote. The graph of a rational function gets closer and closer to a nonvertical asymptote as $|x| \to \infty$, but it can also cross a nonvertical asymptote as illustrated in the next example.

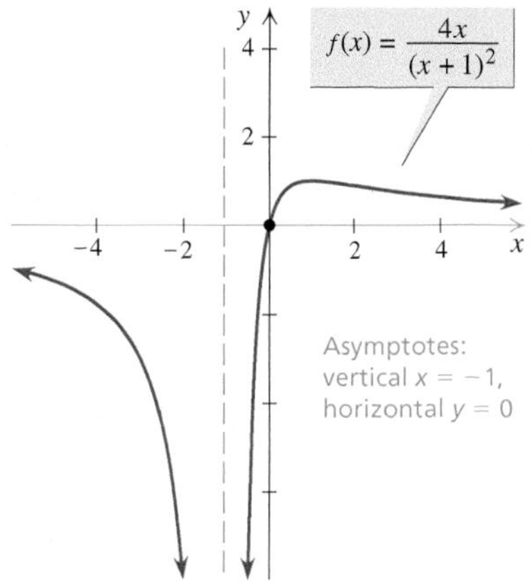

Figure 2.84

Example 5 A rational function that crosses an asymptote

Sketch the graph of $f(x) = \dfrac{4x}{(x + 1)^2}$.

Solution

The graph of f has a vertical asymptote at $x = -1$, and since the degree of the numerator is less than the degree of the denominator, the x-axis is a horizontal asymptote. If $x > 0$ then $f(x) > 0$, and if $x < 0$ then $f(x) < 0$. So the graph approaches the horizontal axis from above for $x > 0$, and from below for $x < 0$. However, the x-intercept is $(0, 0)$. So the graph crosses its horizontal asymptote at $(0, 0)$. The graph shown in Fig. 2.84 goes through $(1, 1)$, $(2, 8/9)$, $(-2, -8)$, and $(-3, -3)$. ■

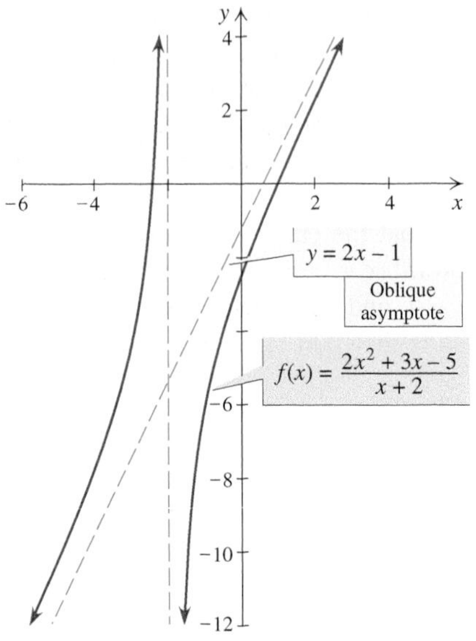

Figure 2.85

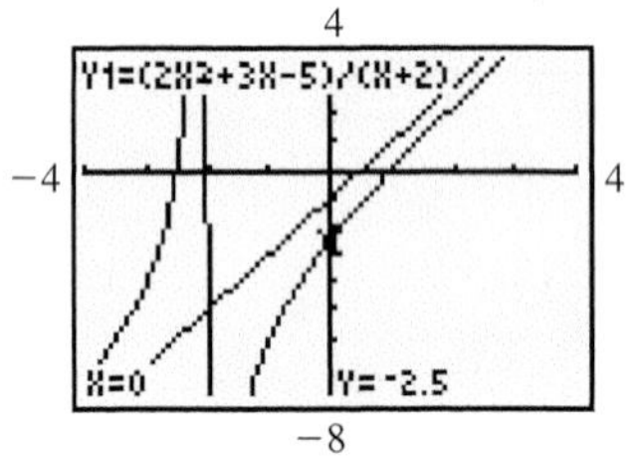

Figure 2.86

The graph of any function should illustrate its most important features. For a rational function that is asymptotic behavior. The graph of a rational function does not cross its vertical asymptotes and the graph approaches but does not touch its nonvertical asymptotes as x approaches ∞ or $-\infty$. So be careful with calculator graphs. On some calculators the graph will cross its vertical asymptote in connected mode and, unless the viewing window is selected carefully, the graph will appear to touch its nonvertical asymptotes.

Example 6 Graphing a function with an oblique asymptote

Sketch the graph of $k(x) = \dfrac{2x^2 + 3x - 5}{x + 2}$.

Solution

Draw the vertical asymptote $x = -2$ and the oblique asymptote $y = 2x - 1$ determined in Example 3 as dashed lines. The x-intercepts, $(1, 0)$ and $(-2.5, 0)$, are found by solving $2x^2 + 3x - 5 = 0$. The y-intercept is $(0, -2.5)$. The points $(-1, -6)$, $(4, 6.5)$, and $(-3, -4)$ are also on the graph. From these points we can conclude that the curve goes upward toward $x = -2$ from the left and downward toward $x = -2$ from the right. It approaches $y = 2x - 1$ from above as x goes to $-\infty$ and from below as x goes to ∞. Draw the graph approaching its asymptotes as shown in Fig. 2.85.

The calculator graph in Fig. 2.86 supports these conclusions. ■

All rational functions so far have been given in lowest terms. In the next example the numerator and denominator have a common factor. In this case the graph does not have as many vertical asymptotes as you might expect. The graph is almost identical to the graph of the rational function obtained by reducing the expression to lowest terms.

Example 7 A graph with a hole in it

Sketch the graph of $f(x) = \dfrac{x - 2}{x^2 - 4}$.

Solution

Since $x^2 - 4 = (x - 2)(x + 2)$, the domain of f is the set of all real numbers except 2 and -2. Since the rational expression can be reduced, the function f could also be defined as

$$f(x) = \frac{1}{x + 2} \quad \text{for } x \neq 2 \text{ and } x \neq -2.$$

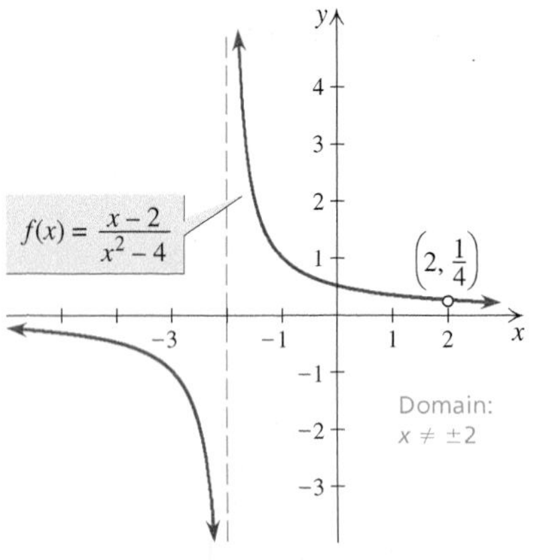

Figure 2.87

Note that the domain is determined before the function is simplified. The graph of $y = 1/(x + 2)$ has only one vertical asymptote $x = -2$. In fact, the graph of $y = 1/(x + 2)$ is a translation two units to the left of $y = 1/x$. Since $f(2)$ is undefined, the point $(2, 1/4)$ that would normally be on the graph of $y = 1/(x + 2)$ is omitted. The missing point is indicated on the graph in Fig. 2.87 as a small open circle. Note that the graph made by a graphing calculator will usually not show the missing point. ■

Rational Inequalities

An inequality that involves a rational expression, such as $\frac{x+3}{x-2} \le 2$, is called a **rational inequality.** Our first thought for solving this inequality might be to clear the denominator by multiplying each side by $x - 2$. But, when we multiply each side of an inequality by a real number, we must know whether the real number is positive or negative. Whether $x - 2$ is positive or negative depends on x. So multiplying by $x - 2$ is not a good idea. *We usually do not multiply a rational inequality by an expression that involves a variable.* However, we can solve rational inequalities using sign graphs as we did with quadratic inequalities in Section 2.1.

Example 8 Solving a rational inequality with a sign graph of the factors

Solve $\frac{x+3}{x-2} \le 2$. State the solution set using interval notation.

Solution

As with quadratic inequalities, we must have 0 on one side. Note that we do not multiply each side by $x - 2$.

$$\frac{x+3}{x-2} \le 2$$

$$\frac{x+3}{x-2} - 2 \le 0$$

$$\frac{x+3}{x-2} - \frac{2(x-2)}{x-2} \le 0 \quad \text{Get a common denominator.}$$

$$\frac{x+3-2(x-2)}{x-2} \le 0 \quad \text{Subtract.}$$

$$\frac{7-x}{x-2} \le 0 \quad \text{Combine like terms.}$$

The sign graph in Fig. 2.88 shows that $7 - x > 0$ if $x < 7$, and $7 - x < 0$ if $x > 7$. If $x > 2$, then $x - 2 > 0$, and if $x < 2$, then $x - 2 < 0$.

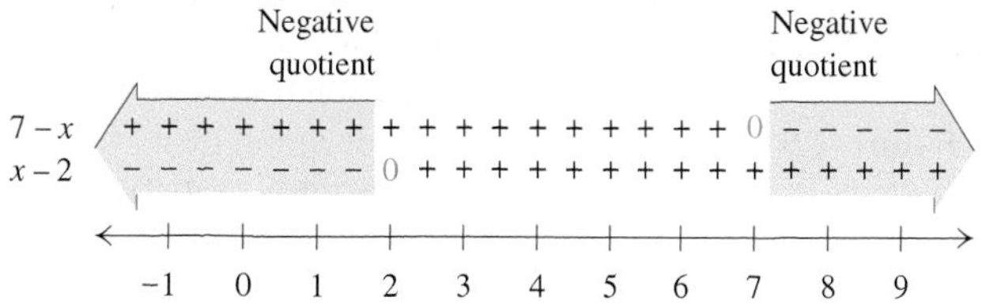

Figure 2.88

The inequality $\frac{7-x}{x-2} \le 0$ is satisfied if the quotient of $7 - x$ and $x - 2$ is negative or 0. Fig. 2.88 indicates that $7 - x$ and $x - 2$ have opposite signs and therefore a negative quotient for $x > 7$ or $x < 2$. If $x = 7$ then $7 - x = 0$ and the quotient is 0. If $x = 2$ then $x - 2 = 0$ and the quotient is undefined. So 7 is in the solution set but 2 is not. The solution set is $(-\infty, 2) \cup [7, \infty)$.

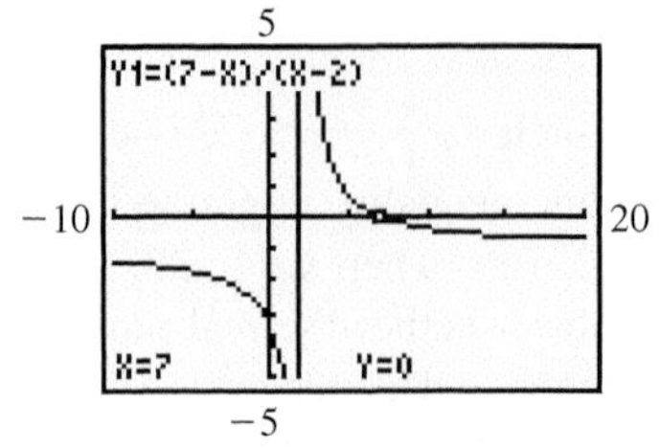

Figure 2.89

The graph of $y = (7 - x)/(x - 2)$ in Fig. 2.89 supports our conclusion that the inequality is satisfied if $x < 2$ or if $x \geq 7$. ■

Making a sign graph of the factors of the numerator and denominator as in Example 8 shows how the signs of the linear factors determine the solution to a rational inequality. Of course that method works only if you can factor the numerator and denominator. The test-point method works on any rational inequality for which we can find all zeros of the numerator and denominator. The test-point method depends on the fact that the graph of a rational function can go from one side of the x-axis to the other only at a vertical asymptote (where the function is undefined) or at an x-intercept (where the value of the function is 0).

Example 9 Solving a rational inequality with the test-point method

Solve $\frac{x + 3}{x^2 - 1} \geq 0$. State the solution set using interval notation.

Solution

Since the denominator can be factored, the inequality is equivalent to

$$\frac{x + 3}{(x - 1)(x + 1)} \geq 0.$$

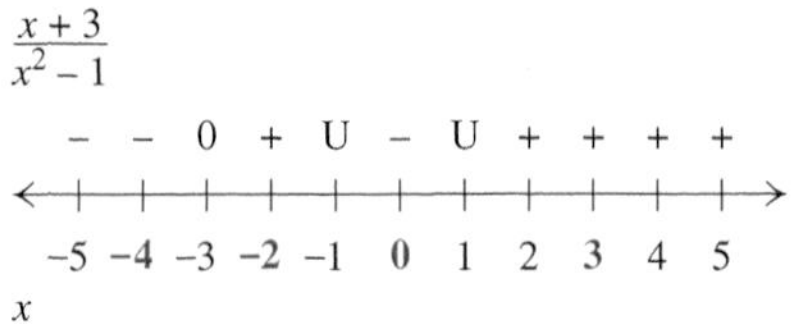

Figure 2.90

The rational expression is undefined if $x = \pm 1$ and has value 0 if $x = -3$. Above each of these numbers on a number line put a 0 or a "U" (for undefined) as shown in Fig. 2.90. Now we select -4, -2, 0, and 3 as test points (shown in red in Fig. 2.90). Let $R(x) = \frac{x + 3}{x^2 - 1}$ and evaluate $R(x)$ at each test point to determine the sign of $R(x)$ in the interval of the test point:

$$R(-4) = -\frac{1}{15}, \quad R(-2) = \frac{1}{3}, \quad R(0) = -3, \quad R(3) = \frac{3}{4}$$

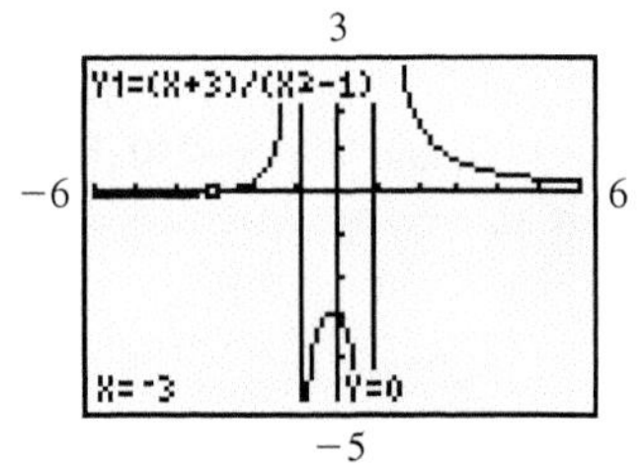

Figure 2.91

So $-$, $+$, $-$, and $+$ are the signs of the rational expression in the four intervals in Fig. 2.90. The inequality is satisfied whenever the rational expression has a positive or 0 value. Since $R(-1)$ and $R(1)$ are undefined, -1 and 1 are not in the solution set. The solution set is $[-3, -1) \cup (1, \infty)$.

The graph of $y = (x + 3)/(x^2 - 1)$ in Fig. 2.91 supports the conclusion that the inequality is satisfied if $-3 \leq x < -1$ or $x > 1$. ■

Applications

Rational functions can occur in many applied situations. A horizontal asymptote might indicate that the average cost of producing a product approaches a fixed value in the long run. A vertical asymptote might show that the cost of a project goes up astronomically as a certain barrier is approached.

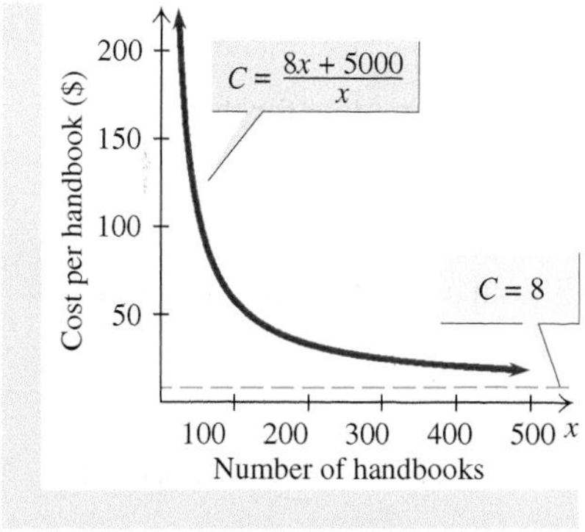

Figure 2.92

Example 10 Average cost of a handbook

Eco Publishing spent \$5000 to produce an environmental handbook and \$8 each for printing. Write a function that gives the average cost to the company per printed handbook. Graph the function for $0 < x \leq 500$. What happens to the average cost if the book becomes very, very popular?

Solution

The total cost of producing and printing x handbooks is $8x + 5000$. To find the average cost per book, divide the total cost by the number of books:

$$C = \frac{8x + 5000}{x}$$

This rational function has a vertical asymptote at $x = 0$ and a horizontal asymptote $C = 8$. The graph is shown in Fig. 2.92. As x gets larger and larger, the \$5000 production cost is spread out over more and more books, and the average cost per book approaches \$8, as shown by the horizontal asymptote. Using limit notation we write $\lim_{x \to \infty} C = 8$. ■

Function Gallery: Some Basic Rational Functions

Horizontal Asymptote x-axis and Vertical Asymptote y-axis

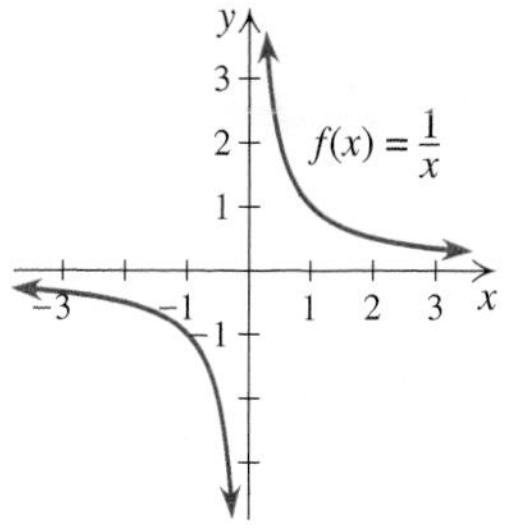

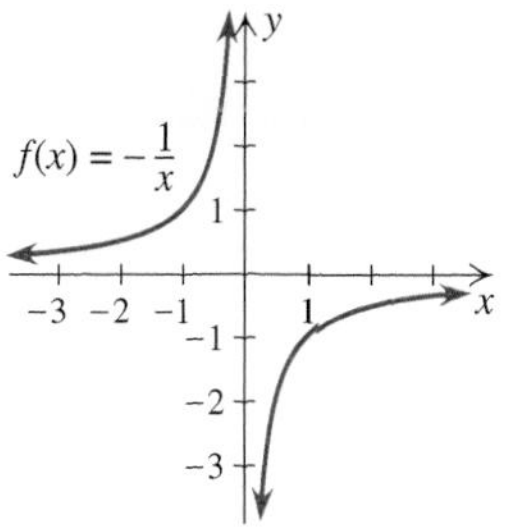

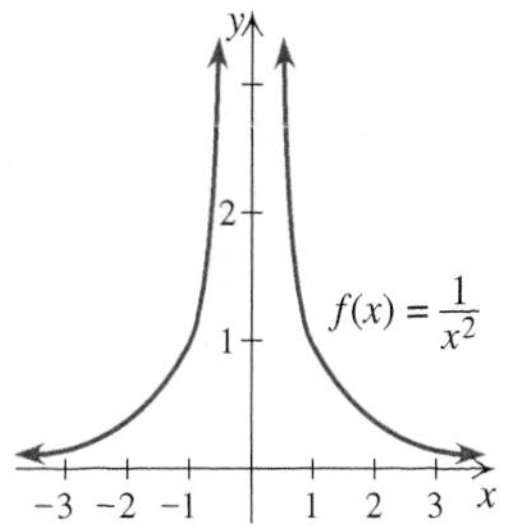

Various Asymptotes

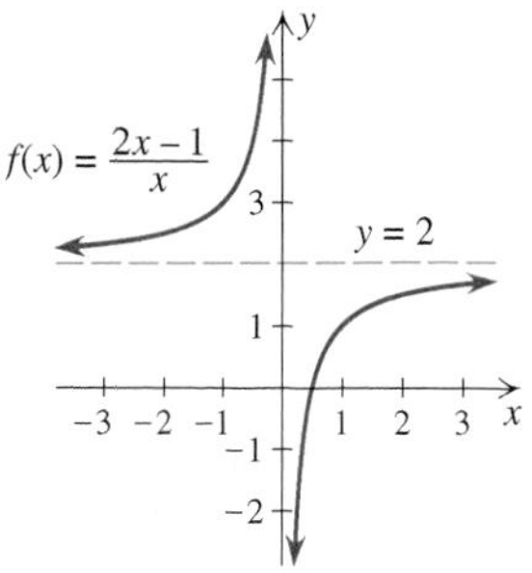

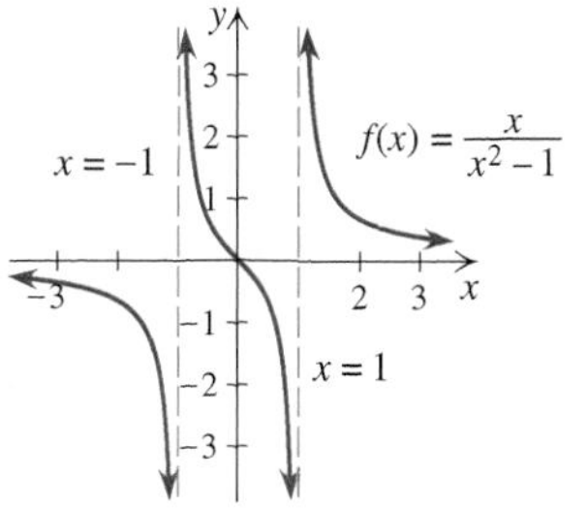

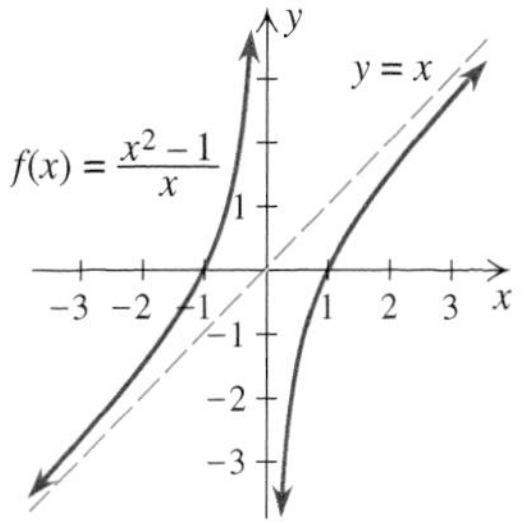

For Thought

True or False? Explain.

1. The function $f(x) = \frac{1}{\sqrt{x} - 3}$ is a rational function.

2. The domain of $f(x) = \frac{x + 2}{x - 2}$ is $(-\infty, -2) \cup (-2, 2) \cup (2, \infty)$.

3. The number of vertical asymptotes for a rational function equals the degree of the denominator.

4. The graph of $f(x) = \frac{1}{x^4 - 4x^2}$ has four vertical asymptotes.

5. The x-axis is a horizontal asymptote for $f(x) = \frac{x^2 - 2x + 7}{x^3 - 4x}$.

6. The x-axis is a horizontal asymptote for the graph of $f(x) = \frac{5x - 1}{x + 2}$.

7. The line $y = x - 3$ is an asymptote for the graph of $f(x) = x - 3 + \frac{1}{x - 1}$.

8. The graph of a rational function cannot intersect its asymptote.

9. The graph of $f(x) = \frac{4}{x^2 - 16}$ is symmetric about the y-axis.

10. The graph of $f(x) = \frac{2x + 6}{x^2 - 9}$ has only one vertical asymptote.

2.7 Exercises

Find the domain of each rational function.

1. $f(x) = \frac{4}{x + 2}$

2. $f(x) = \frac{-1}{x - 2}$

3. $f(x) = \frac{-x}{x^2 - 4}$

4. $f(x) = \frac{2}{x^2 - x - 2}$

5. $f(x) = \frac{2x + 3}{x - 3}$

6. $f(x) = \frac{4 - x}{x + 2}$

7. $f(x) = \frac{x^2 - 2x + 4}{x}$

8. $f(x) = \frac{x^3 + 2}{x^2}$

9. $f(x) = \frac{3x^2 - 1}{x^3 - x}$

10. $f(x) = \frac{x^2 + 1}{8x^3 - 2x}$

11. $f(x) = \frac{-x^2 + x}{x^2 + 5x + 6}$

12. $f(x) = \frac{-x^2 + 2x - 3}{x^2 + x - 12}$

Determine the domain and the equations of the asymptotes for the graph of each rational function.

13.

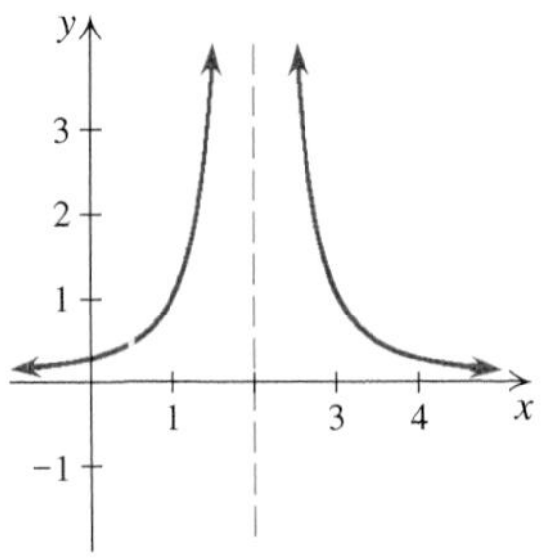

14.

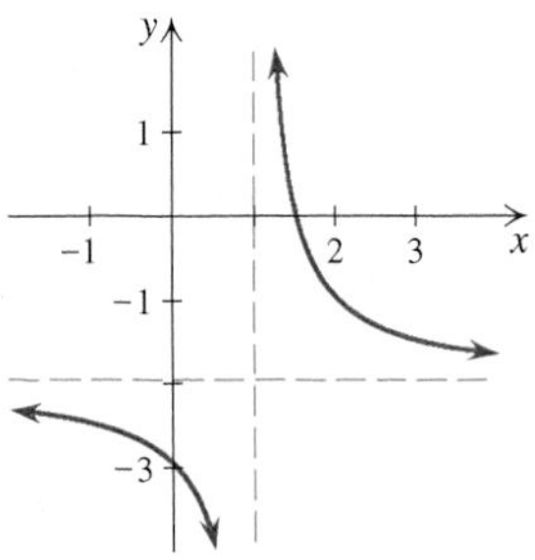

15.

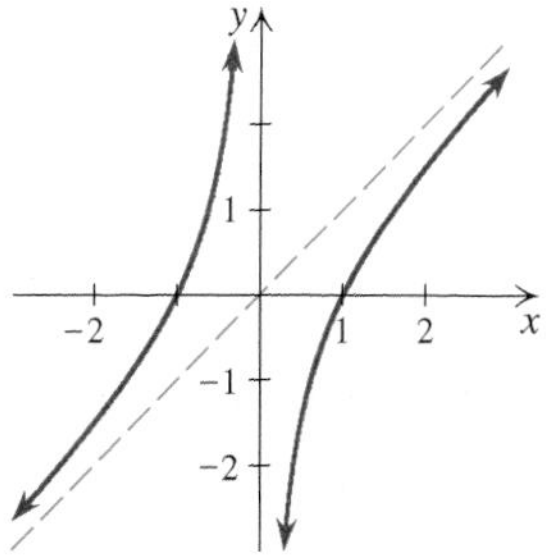

16.

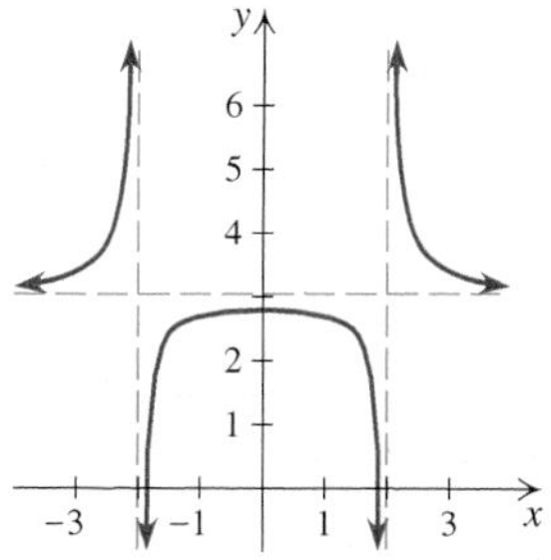

Determine the equations of all asymptotes for the graph of each function. See the summary for finding asymptotes for a rational function on page 179.

17. $f(x) = \dfrac{5}{x - 2}$

18. $f(x) = \dfrac{-1}{x + 12}$

19. $f(x) = \dfrac{-x}{x^2 - 9}$

20. $f(x) = \dfrac{-2}{x^2 - 5x + 6}$

21. $f(x) = \dfrac{2x + 4}{x - 1}$

22. $f(x) = \dfrac{5 - x}{x + 5}$

23. $f(x) = \dfrac{x^2 - 2x + 1}{x}$

24. $f(x) = \dfrac{x^3 - 8}{x^2}$

25. $f(x) = \dfrac{3x^2 + 4}{x + 1}$

26. $f(x) = \dfrac{x^2}{x - 9}$

27. $f(x) = \dfrac{-x^2 + 4x}{x + 2}$

28. $f(x) = \dfrac{-x^2 + 3x - 7}{x - 3}$

Find all asymptotes, x-intercepts, and y-intercepts for the graph of each rational function and sketch the graph of the function. See the procedure for graphing a rational function on page 179.

29. $f(x) = \dfrac{-1}{x}$

30. $f(x) = \dfrac{1}{x^2}$

31. $f(x) = \dfrac{1}{x - 2}$

32. $f(x) = \dfrac{-1}{x + 1}$

33. $f(x) = \dfrac{1}{x^2 - 4}$

34. $f(x) = \dfrac{1}{x^2 - 2x + 1}$

35. $f(x) = \dfrac{-1}{(x + 1)^2}$

36. $f(x) = \dfrac{-2}{x^2 - 9}$

37. $f(x) = \dfrac{2x + 1}{x - 1}$

38. $f(x) = \dfrac{3x - 1}{x + 1}$

39. $f(x) = \dfrac{x - 3}{x + 2}$

40. $f(x) = \dfrac{2 - x}{x + 2}$

41. $f(x) = \dfrac{x}{x^2 - 1}$

42. $f(x) = \dfrac{-x}{x^2 - 9}$

43. $f(x) = \dfrac{4x}{x^2 - 2x + 1}$

44. $f(x) = \dfrac{-2x}{x^2 + 6x + 9}$

45. $f(x) = \dfrac{8 - x^2}{x^2 - 9}$

46. $f(x) = \dfrac{2x^2 + x - 8}{x^2 - 4}$

47. $f(x) = \dfrac{2x^2 + 8x + 2}{x^2 + 2x + 1}$

48. $f(x) = \dfrac{-x^2 + 7x - 9}{x^2 - 6x + 9}$

Use a graph or a table to find each limit.

49. $\lim_{x \to \infty} \dfrac{1}{x^2}$

50. $\lim_{x \to -\infty} \dfrac{1}{x^2}$

51. $\lim_{x \to \infty} \dfrac{2x - 3}{x - 1}$

52. $\lim_{x \to \infty} \dfrac{3x^2 - 1}{x^2 - x}$

53. $\lim_{x \to 0^+} \dfrac{1}{x^2}$

54. $\lim_{x \to 0^-} \dfrac{1}{x^2}$

55. $\lim_{x \to 1^+} \dfrac{2}{x - 1}$

56. $\lim_{x \to 1^-} \dfrac{2}{x - 1}$

Find the oblique asymptote and sketch the graph of each rational function.

57. $f(x) = \dfrac{x^2 + 1}{x}$

58. $f(x) = \dfrac{x^2 - 1}{x}$

59. $f(x) = \dfrac{x^3 - 1}{x^2}$

60. $f(x) = \dfrac{x^3 + 1}{x^2}$

61. $f(x) = \dfrac{x^2}{x + 1}$

62. $f(x) = \dfrac{x^2}{x - 1}$

63. $f(x) = \dfrac{2x^2 - x}{x - 1}$

64. $f(x) = \dfrac{-x^2 + x + 1}{x + 1}$

65. $f(x) = \dfrac{x^3 - x^2 - 4x + 5}{x^2 - 4}$

66. $f(x) = \dfrac{x^3 + 2x^2 + x - 2}{x^2 - 1}$

67. $f(x) = \dfrac{-x^3 + x^2 + 5x - 4}{x^2 + x - 2}$

68. $f(x) = \dfrac{x^3 + x^2 - 16x - 24}{x^2 - 2x - 8}$

Match each rational function with its graph (a)–(h) on the next page, without using a graphing calculator.

69. $f(x) = -\dfrac{3}{x}$

70. $f(x) = \dfrac{1}{3 - x}$

71. $f(x) = \dfrac{x}{x - 3}$

72. $f(x) = \dfrac{x - 3}{x}$

73. $f(x) = \dfrac{1}{x^2 - 3x}$

74. $f(x) = \dfrac{x^2}{x^2 - 9}$

75. $f(x) = \dfrac{x^2 - 3}{x}$

76. $f(x) = \dfrac{-x^3 + 1}{x^2}$

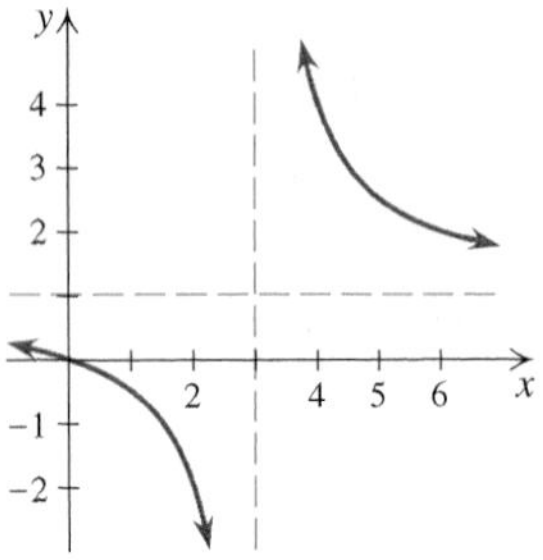

(a)

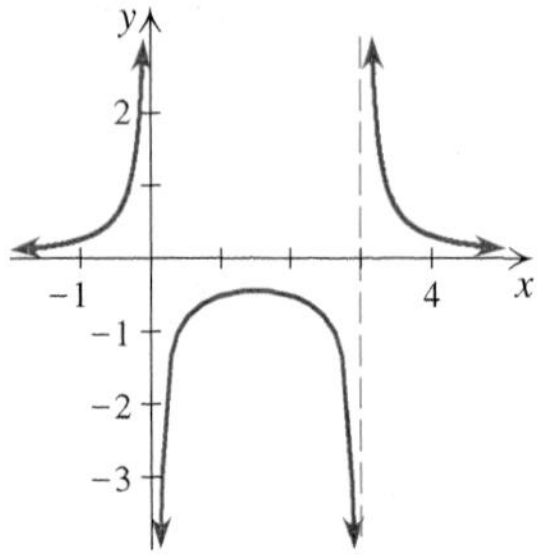

(b)

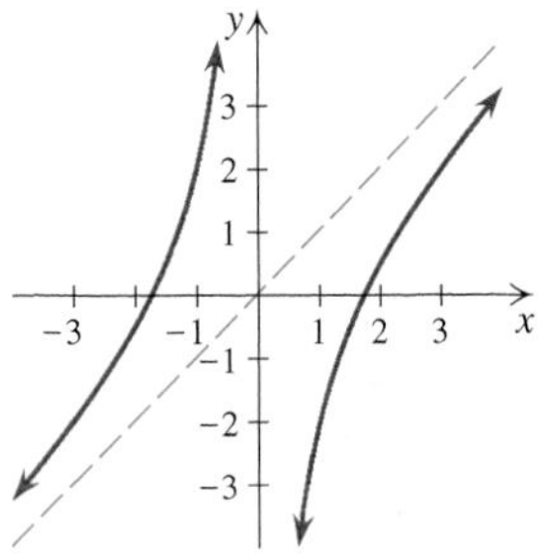

(c)

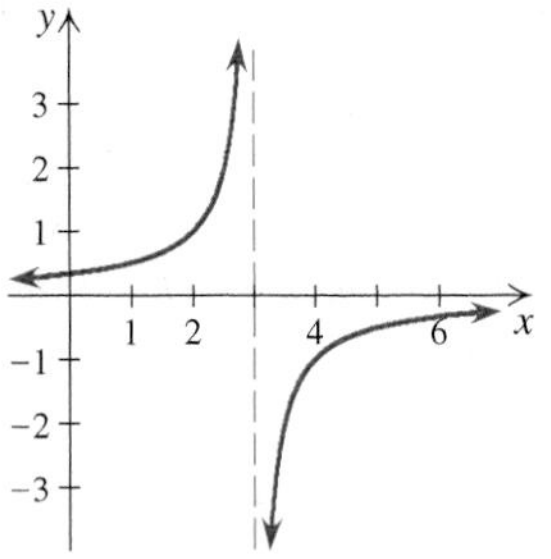

(d)

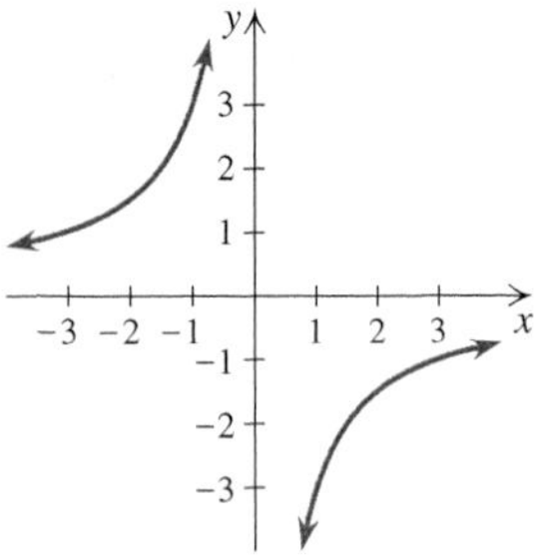

(e)

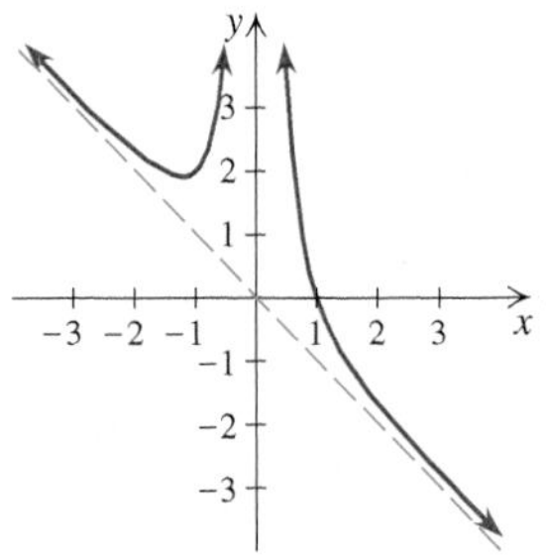

(f)

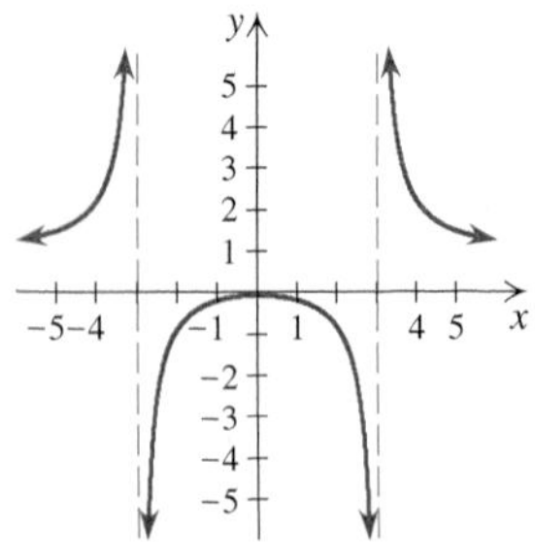

(g)

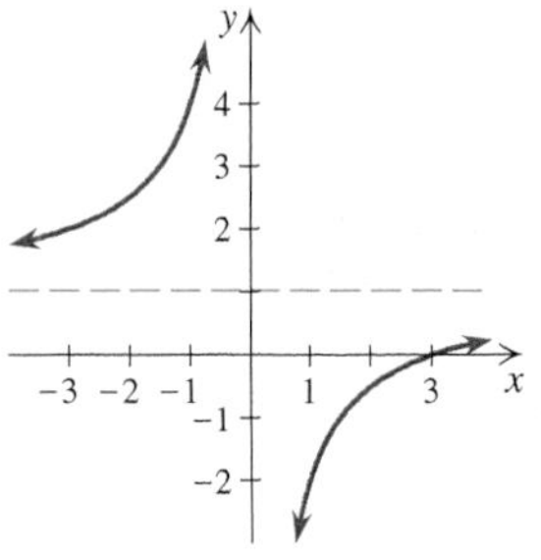

(h)

Sketch the graph of each rational function. Note that the functions are not in lowest terms. Find the domain first.

77. $f(x) = \dfrac{x + 1}{x^2 - 1}$

78. $f(x) = \dfrac{x}{x^2 + 2x}$

79. $f(x) = \dfrac{x^2 - 1}{x - 1}$

80. $f(x) = \dfrac{x^2 - 5x + 6}{x - 2}$

Solve with a sign graph of the factors. State the solution set using interval notation.

81. $\dfrac{x - 4}{x + 2} \le 0$

82. $\dfrac{x + 3}{x + 5} \ge 0$

83. $\dfrac{q - 2}{q + 3} < 2$

84. $\dfrac{p + 1}{2p - 1} \ge 1$

85. $\dfrac{w^2 - w - 6}{w - 6} \ge 0$

86. $\dfrac{z - 5}{z^2 + 2z - 8} \le 0$

87. $\dfrac{1}{x + 2} > \dfrac{1}{x - 3}$

88. $\dfrac{1}{x + 1} > \dfrac{2}{x - 1}$

89. $x < \dfrac{3x - 8}{5 - x}$

90. $\dfrac{2}{x + 3} \ge \dfrac{1}{x - 1}$

Solve with the test-point method. State the solution set using interval notation.

91. $\dfrac{(x - 3)(x + 1)}{x - 5} \ge 0$

92. $\dfrac{(x + 2)(x - 1)}{(x + 4)^2} \le 0$

93. $\dfrac{x^2 - 7}{2 - x^2} \le 0$

94. $\dfrac{x^2 + 1}{5 - x^2} \ge 0$

95. $\dfrac{x^2 + 2x + 1}{x^2 - 2x - 15} \ge 0$

96. $\dfrac{x^2 - 2x - 8}{x^2 + 10x + 25} \le 0$

97. $\dfrac{1}{w} > \dfrac{1}{w^2}$

98. $\dfrac{1}{w} > w^2$

99. $w > \dfrac{w - 5}{w - 3}$

100. $w < \dfrac{w - 2}{w + 1}$

Solve each problem.

101. *Admission to the Zoo* Winona paid \$100 for a lifetime membership to Friends of the Zoo, so that she could gain admittance to the zoo for only \$1 per visit. Write Winona's average cost per visit C as a function of the number of visits when she has visited x times. What is her average cost per visit when she has visited the zoo 100 times? Graph the function for $x > 0$. What happens to her average cost per visit if she starts when she is young and visits the zoo every day?

102. *Renting a Car* The cost of renting a car for one day is \$19 plus 30 cents per mile. Write the average cost per mile C as a function of the number of miles driven in one day x. Graph the function for $x > 0$. What happens to C as the number of miles gets very large?

103. *Average Speed of an Auto Trip* A 200-mi trip by an electric car must be completed in 4 hr. Let x be the number of hours it takes to travel the first half of the distance and write the average speed for the second half of the trip as a function of x. Graph this function for $0 < x < 4$. What is the significance of the vertical asymptote?

104. *Billboard Advertising* An Atlanta marketing agency figures that the monthly cost of a billboard advertising campaign depends on the fraction of the market p that the client wishes to reach. For $0 \le p < 1$ the cost in dollars is determined by the formula $C = (4p - 1200)/(p - 1)$. What is the monthly cost for a campaign intended to reach 95% of the market? Graph this function for $0 \le p < 1$. What happens to the cost for a client who wants to reach 100% of the market?

105. *Balancing the Costs* A furniture maker buys foam rubber x times per year. The delivery charge is \$400 per purchase regardless of the amount purchased. The annual cost of storage is figured as \$10,000/x, because the more frequent the purchase, the less it costs for storage. So the annual cost of delivery and storage is given by

$$C = 400x + \frac{10{,}000}{x}.$$

a. Graph the function with a graphing calculator.

b. Find the number of purchases per year that minimizes the annual cost of delivery and storage.

106. *Making a Gas Tank* An engineer is designing a cylindrical metal tank that is to hold 500 ft^3 of gasoline.

a. The volume of the tank is given by $V = \pi r^2 h$, where r is the radius and h is the height. Write h as a function of r.

b. The surface area of a tank is given by $S = 2\pi r^2 + 2\pi rh$. Use the result of part (a) to write S as a function of r and graph it.

c. Use the minimum feature of a graphing calculator to find the radius to the nearest tenth of a foot that minimizes the surface area. Ignore the thickness of the metal.

d. If the tank costs \$8 per square foot to construct, then what is the minimum cost for making the tank?

Thinking Outside the Box XVII

Filling a Triangle Fiber-optic cables just fit inside a triangular pipe as shown in the figure. The cables have circular cross sections and the cross section of the pipe is an equilateral triangle with sides of length 1. Suppose that there are n cables of the same size in the bottom row, $n - 1$ of that size in the next row, and so on.

a. Write the total cross-sectional area of the cables as a function of n.

b. As n approaches infinity, will the triangular pipe get totally filled with cables? Explain.

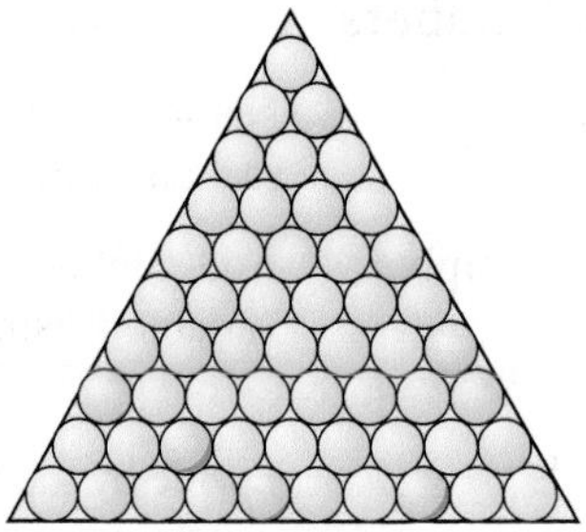

Figure for Thinking Outside the Box XVII

2.7 Pop Quiz

1. What is the domain of $f(x) = \frac{x - 1}{x + 4}$?

2. Find the equations of all asymptotes for the graph of $y = \frac{x - 5}{x + 2}$.

3. Find the x-intercepts and y-intercept for $f(x) = \frac{x^2 - 9}{x^2 - 1}$.

4. What is the horizontal asymptote for $y = \frac{x - 8}{x + 3}$?

5. What is the oblique asymptote for $f(x) = \frac{x^2 - 2x}{x - 3}$?

6. Solve $\frac{x - 1}{x + 4} \ge 0$.

Highlights

2.1 Quadratic Functions and Inequalities

Quadratic Function	$y = ax^2 + bx + c$ where $a \neq 0$ Graph is a parabola opening upward for $a > 0$ and downward for $a < 0$.	$y = 2x^2 + 8x - 1$ Opens upward
Vertex	$x = -b/(2a)$ is the x-coordinate of the vertex. Use $y = ax^2 + bx + c$ to find the y-coordinate.	$x = -8/(2 \cdot 2) = -2$ Vertex: $(-2, -9)$
Maximum Minimum	The y-coordinate of the vertex is the max value of the function if $a < 0$ and the min if $a > 0$.	$y = 2x^2 + 8x - 1$ Min y-value is -9.
Two Forms	By completing the square, $y = ax^2 + bx + c$ can be written as $y = a(x - h)^2 + k$, which has vertex (h, k).	$y = 2x^2 + 8x - 1$ $y = 2(x + 2)^2 - 9$
Inequalities	To solve $ax^2 + bx + c > 0$ find all roots to $ax^2 + bx + c = 0$, then test a point in each interval determined by the roots.	$(x - 2)(x + 3) > 0$ Roots are -3 and 2. Solution set: $(-\infty, -3) \cup (2, \infty)$

2.2 Complex Numbers

Standard Form	Numbers of the form $a + bi$ where a and b are real numbers, $i = \sqrt{-1}$, and $i^2 = -1$	$2 + 3i, -\pi + i\sqrt{2}, 6, 0, \frac{1}{2}i$
Add, Subtract, Multiply	Add, subtract, and multiply like binomials with variable i, using $i^2 = -1$ to simplify.	$(3 - 2i)(4 + 5i)$ $= 12 + 7i - 10i^2$ $= 22 + 7i$
Divide	Divide by multiplying the numerator and denominator by the complex conjugate of the denominator.	$6/(1 + i)$ $= \frac{6(1 - i)}{(1 + i)(1 - i)} = 3 - 3i$
Square Roots of Negative Numbers	Square roots of negative numbers must be converted to standard form using $\sqrt{-b} = i\sqrt{b}$, for $b > 0$, before doing computations.	$\sqrt{-4} \cdot \sqrt{-9} = 2i \cdot 3i = -6$

2.3 Zeros of Polynomial Functions

Remainder Theorem	The remainder when $P(x)$ is divided by $x - c$ is $P(c)$.	$P(x) = x^2 + 3x - 4$ $P(x)$ divided by $x + 1$ has remainder $P(-1)$ or -6.
Synthetic Division	An abbreviated version of long division, used only for dividing a polynomial by $x - c$.	$\begin{array}{r\|rrr} -1 & 1 & 3 & -4 \\ & & -1 & -2 \\ \hline & 1 & 2 & -6 \end{array}$ Dividend: $P(x)$, divisor $x + 1$ quotient $x + 2$, remainder -6
Factor Theorem	c is a zero of $y = P(x)$ if and only if $x - c$ is a factor of $P(x)$.	Since $x - 2$ is a factor of $P(x) = x^2 + x - 6$, $P(2) = 0$.

Fundamental Theorem of Algebra	If $y = P(x)$ is a polynomial function of positive degree, then $y = P(x)$ has at least one zero in the set of complex numbers.	$f(x) = x^7 - x^5 + 3x^2 - 9$ has at least one complex zero and in fact has seven of them.
Rational Zero Theorem	If p/q is a rational zero in lowest terms for $y = P(x)$ with integral coefficients, then p is a factor of the constant term and q is a factor of the leading coefficient.	$P(x) = 6x^2 + x - 15$ $P(3/2) = 0$ 3 is a factor of -15, 2 is a factor of 6

2.4 The Theory of Equations

***n*-Root Theorem**	If $P(x)$ has positive degree and complex coefficients, then $P(x) = 0$ has n roots counting multiplicity.	$(x - 2)^3(x^4 - 9) = 0$ has seven complex solutions counting multiplicity.
Conjugate Pairs Theorem	If $P(x)$ has real coefficients, then the imaginary roots of $P(x) = 0$ occur in conjugate pairs.	$x^2 - 4x + 5 = 0$ $x = 2 \pm i$
Descartes's Rule of Signs	The changes in sign of $P(x)$ determine the number of positive roots and the changes in sign of $P(-x)$ determine the number of negative roots to $P(x) = 0$.	$P(x) = x^5 - x^2$ has 1 positive root, no negative roots

2.5 Miscellaneous Equations

Higher Degree	Solve by factoring.	$x^4 - x^2 - 6 = 0$ $(x^2 - 3)(x^2 + 2) = 0$
Squaring Each Side	Possibly extraneous roots	$\sqrt{x - 3} = -2, x - 3 = 4$ $x = 7$ extraneous root
Rational Exponents	Raise each side to a whole number power and then apply the even or odd root property.	$x^{2/3} = 4, x^2 = 64, x = \pm 8$
Quadratic Type	Make a substitution to get a quadratic equation.	$x^{1/3} + x^{1/6} - 12 = 0$ $a^2 + a - 12 = 0$ if $a = x^{1/6}$
Absolute Value	Write equivalent equations without absolute value.	$\lvert x^2 - 4 \rvert = 2$ $x^2 - 4 = 2$ or $x^2 - 4 = -2$

2.6 Graphs of Polynomial Functions

Axis of Symmetry	The parabola $y = ax^2 + bx + c$ is symmetric about the line $x = -b/(2a)$.	Axis of symmetry for $y = x^2 - 4x$ is $x = 2$.
Behavior at the *x*-Intercepts	A polynomial function crosses the x-axis at $(c, 0)$ if $x - c$ occurs with an odd power or touches the x-axis if $x - c$ occurs with an even power.	$f(x) = (x - 3)^2(x + 1)^3$ crosses at $(-1, 0)$, does not cross at $(3, 0)$
End Behavior	The leading coefficient and the degree of the polynomial determine the behavior as $x \to -\infty$ or $x \to \infty$.	$y = x^3$ $y \to \infty$ as $x \to \infty$ $y \to -\infty$ as $x \to -\infty$
Polynomial Inequality	Locate all zeros and then test a point in each interval determined by the zeros.	$x^3 - 4x > 0$ when x is in $(-2, 0) \cup (2, \infty)$

2.7 Rational Functions and Inequalities

Vertical Asymptote	A rational function in lowest terms has a vertical asymptote wherever the denominator is zero.	$y = x/(x^2 - 4)$ has vertical asymptotes $x = -2$ and $x = 2$.
Horizontal Asymptote	If degree of denominator exceeds degree of numerator, then the x-axis is the horizontal asymptote. If degree of numerator equals degree of denominator, then the ratio of leading coefficients is the horizontal asymptote.	$y = x/(x^2 - 4)$ Horizontal asymptote: $y = 0$ $y = (2x - 1)/(3x - 2)$ Horizontal asymptote: $y = 2/3$
Oblique or Slant Asymptote	If degree of numerator exceeds degree of denominator by 1, then use division to determine the slant asymptote.	$y = \frac{x^2}{x - 1} = x + 1 + \frac{1}{x - 1}$ Slant asymptote: $y = x + 1$
Rational Inequality	Test a point in each interval determined by the zeros and the horizontal asymptotes.	$\frac{x - 2}{x + 3} \le 0$ when x is in the interval $(-3, 2]$.

Chapter 2 Review Exercises

Solve each problem.

1. Write the function $f(x) = 3x^2 - 2x + 1$ in the form $f(x) = a(x - h)^2 + k$.

2. Write the function $f(x) = -4\left(x - \frac{1}{3}\right)^2 - \frac{1}{2}$ in the form $f(x) = ax^2 + bx + c$.

3. Find the vertex, axis of symmetry, x-intercepts, and y-intercept for the parabola $y = 2x^2 - 4x - 1$.

4. Find the maximum value of the function $y = -x^2 + 3x - 5$.

5. Write the equation of a parabola that has x-intercepts $(-1, 0)$ and $(3, 0)$ and y-intercept $(0, 6)$.

6. Write the equation of the parabola that has vertex $(1, 2)$ and y-intercept $(0, 5)$.

Write each expression in the form $a + bi$, where a and b are real numbers.

7. $(3 - 7i) + (-4 + 6i)$

8. $(-6 - 3i) - (3 - 2i)$

9. $(4 - 5i)^2$

10. $7 - i(2 - 3i)^2$

11. $(1 - 3i)(2 + 6i)$

12. $(0.3 + 2i)(0.3 - 2i)$

13. $(2 - 3i) \div i$

14. $(-2 + 4i) \div (-i)$

15. $(1 - i) \div (2 + i)$

16. $(3 + 6i) \div (4 - i)$

17. $\frac{6 + \sqrt{-8}}{2}$

18. $\frac{-2 - \sqrt{-18}}{2}$

19. $i^{34} + i^{19}$

20. $\sqrt{6} + \sqrt{-3}\sqrt{-2}$

Find all the real and imaginary zeros for each polynomial function.

21. $f(x) = 3x - 1$

22. $g(x) = 7$

23. $h(x) = x^2 - 8$

24. $m(x) = x^3 - 8$

25. $n(x) = 8x^3 - 1$

26. $C(x) = 3x^2 - 2$

27. $P(t) = t^4 - 100$

28. $S(t) = 25t^4 - 1$

29. $R(s) = 8s^3 - 4s^2 - 2s + 1$

30. $W(s) = s^3 + s^2 + s + 1$

31. $f(x) = x^3 + 2x^2 - 6x$

32. $f(x) = 2x^3 - 4x^2 + 3x$

For each polynomial, find the indicated value in two different ways.

33. $P(x) = 4x^3 - 3x^2 + x - 1, P(3)$

34. $P(x) = 2x^3 + 5x^2 - 3x - 2, P(-2)$

35. $P(x) = -8x^5 + 2x^3 - 6x + 2, P\left(-\frac{1}{2}\right)$

36. $P(x) = -4x^4 + 3x^2 + 1, P\left(\frac{1}{2}\right)$

Use the rational zero theorem to list all possible rational zeros for each polynomial function.

37. $f(x) = -3x^3 + 6x^2 + 5x - 2$

38. $f(x) = 2x^4 + 9x^2 - 8x - 3$

39. $f(x) = 6x^4 - x^2 - 9x + 3$

40. $f(x) = 4x^3 - 5x^2 - 13x - 8$

Find a polynomial equation with integral coefficients (and lowest degree) that has the given roots.

41. $-\frac{1}{2}, 3$ **42.** $\frac{1}{2}, -5$

43. $3 - 2i$ **44.** $4 + 2i$

45. $2, 1 - 2i$ **46.** $-3, 3 - 4i$

47. $2 - \sqrt{3}$ **48.** $1 + \sqrt{2}$

Use Descartes's rule of signs to discuss the possibilities for the roots to each equation. Do not solve the equation.

49. $x^8 + x^6 + 2x^2 = 0$ **50.** $-x^3 - x - 3 = 0$

51. $4x^3 - 3x^2 + 2x - 9 = 0$

52. $5x^5 + x^3 + 5x = 0$

53. $x^3 + 2x^2 + 2x + 1 = 0$

54. $-x^4 - x^3 + 3x^2 + 5x - 8 = 0$

Find all real and imaginary solutions to each equation, stating multiplicity when it is greater than one.

55. $x^3 - 6x^2 + 11x - 6 = 0$

56. $x^3 + 7x^2 + 16x + 12 = 0$

57. $6x^4 - 5x^3 + 7x^2 - 5x + 1 = 0$

58. $6x^4 + 5x^3 + 25x^2 + 20x + 4 = 0$

59. $x^3 - 9x^2 + 28x - 30 = 0$

60. $x^3 - 4x^2 + 6x - 4 = 0$

61. $x^3 - 4x^2 + 7x - 6 = 0$

62. $2x^3 - 5x^2 + 10x - 4 = 0$

63. $2x^4 - 5x^3 - 2x^2 + 2x = 0$

64. $2x^5 - 15x^4 + 26x^3 - 12x^2 = 0$

Find all real solutions to each equation.

65. $|2v - 1| = 3v$ **66.** $|2h - 3| = |h|$

67. $x^4 + 7x^2 = 18$ **68.** $2x^{-2} + 5x^{-1} = 12$

69. $\sqrt{x + 6} - \sqrt{x - 5} = 1$

70. $\sqrt{2x - 1} = \sqrt{x - 1} + 1$

71. $\sqrt{y} + \sqrt[4]{y} = 6$ **72.** $\sqrt[3]{x^2} + \sqrt[3]{x} = 2$

73. $x^4 - 3x^2 - 4 = 0$

74. $(y - 1)^2 - (y - 1) = 2$

75. $(x - 1)^{2/3} = 4$ **76.** $(2x - 3)^{-1/2} = \frac{1}{2}$

77. $(x + 3)^{-3/4} = -8$ **78.** $\left(\frac{1}{x - 3}\right)^{-1/4} = \frac{1}{2}$

79. $\sqrt[3]{3x - 7} = \sqrt[3]{4 - x}$ **80.** $\sqrt[3]{x + 1} = \sqrt[6]{4x + 9}$

Discuss the symmetry of the graph of each function.

81. $f(x) = 2x^2 - 3x + 9$ **82.** $f(x) = -3x^2 + 12x - 1$

83. $f(x) = -3x^4 - 2$ **84.** $f(x) = \frac{-x^3}{x^2 - 1}$

85. $f(x) = \frac{x}{x^2 + 1}$ **86.** $f(x) = 2x^4 + 3x^2 + 1$

Find the domain of each rational function.

87. $f(x) = \frac{x^2 - 4}{2x + 5}$ **88.** $f(x) = \frac{4x + 1}{x^2 - x - 6}$

89. $f(x) = \frac{1}{x^2 + 1}$ **90.** $f(x) = \frac{x - 9}{x^2 - 1}$

Find the x-intercepts, y-intercept, and asymptotes for the graph of each function and sketch the graph.

91. $f(x) = x^2 - x - 2$ **92.** $f(x) = -2(x - 1)^2 + 6$

93. $f(x) = x^3 - 3x - 2$ **94.** $f(x) = x^3 - 3x^2 + 4$

95. $f(x) = \frac{1}{2}x^3 - \frac{1}{2}x^2 - 2x + 2$

96. $f(x) = \frac{1}{2}x^3 - 3x^2 + 4x$ **97.** $f(x) = \frac{1}{4}x^4 - 2x^2 + 4$

98. $f(x) = \frac{1}{2}x^4 + 2x^3 + 2x^2$

99. $f(x) = \frac{2}{x + 3}$ **100.** $f(x) = \frac{1}{2 - x}$

101. $f(x) = \frac{2x}{x^2 - 4}$ **102.** $f(x) = \frac{2x^2}{x^2 - 4}$

103. $f(x) = \frac{x^2 - 2x + 1}{x - 2}$ **104.** $f(x) = \frac{-x^2 + x + 2}{x - 1}$

105. $f(x) = \frac{2x - 1}{2 - x}$

106. $f(x) = \frac{1 - x}{x + 1}$

107. $f(x) = \frac{x^2 - 4}{x - 2}$

108. $f(x) = \frac{x^3 + x}{x}$

Solve each inequality. State the solution set using interval notation.

109. $8x^2 + 1 < 6x$

110. $x^2 + 2x < 63$

111. $(3 - x)(x + 5) \geq 0$

112. $-x^2 - 2x + 15 < 0$

113. $4x^3 - 400x^2 - x + 100 \geq 0$

114. $x^3 - 49x^2 - 52x + 100 < 0$

115. $\frac{x + 10}{x + 2} < 5$

116. $\frac{x - 6}{2x + 1} \geq 1$

117. $\frac{12 - 7x}{x^2} > -1$

118. $x - \frac{2}{x} \leq -1$

119. $\frac{x^2 - 3x + 2}{x^2 - 7x + 12} \geq 0$

120. $\frac{x^2 + 4x + 3}{x^2 - 2x - 15} \leq 0$

Solve each problem.

121. Find the quotient and remainder when $x^3 - 6x^2 + 9x - 15$ is divided by $x - 3$.

122. Find the quotient and remainder when $3x^3 + 4x^2 + 2x - 4$ is divided by $3x - 2$.

123. *Altitude of a Rocket* If the altitude in feet of a model rocket is given by the equation $S = -16t^2 + 156t$, where t is the time in seconds after ignition, then what is the maximum height attained by the rocket?

124. *Bonus Room* A homeowner wants to put a room in the attic of her house. The house is 48 ft wide and the roof has a 7–12 pitch. (The roof rises 7 ft in a horizontal distance of 12 ft.) Find the dimensions of the room that will maximize the area of the cross section shown in the figure.

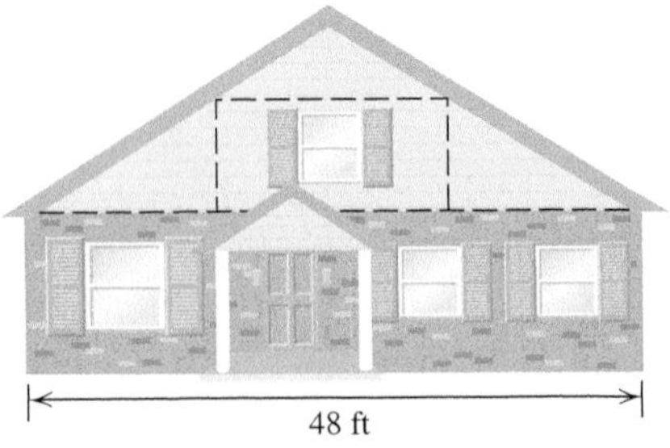

Figure for Exercise 124

125. *Maximizing Area* An isosceles triangle has one vertex at the origin and a horizontal base below the x-axis with its endpoints on the curve $y = x^2 - 16$. See the figure. Let (a, b) be the vertex in the fourth quadrant and write the area of the triangle as a function of a. Use a graphing calculator to find the point (a, b) for which the triangle has the maximum possible area.

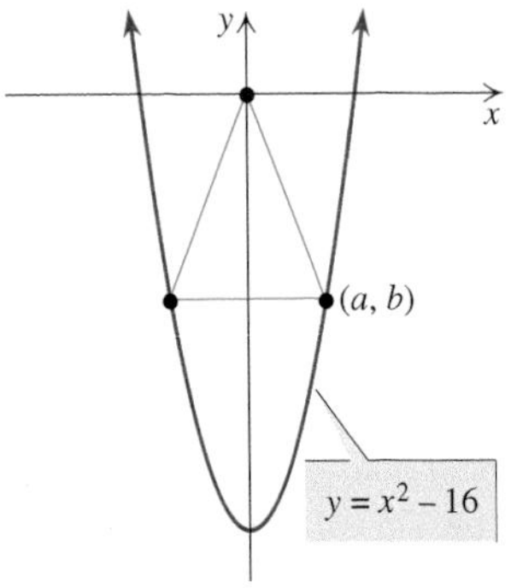

Figure for Exercise 125

126. *Limiting Velocity* As a skydiver falls, his velocity keeps increasing. However, because of air resistance, the rate at which the velocity increases keeps decreasing and there is a limit velocity that the skydiver cannot exceed. To see this behavior, graph

$$V = \frac{1000t}{5t + 8},$$

where V is the velocity in feet per second and t is the time in seconds.

a. What is the velocity at time $t = 10$ sec?

b. What is the horizontal asymptote for this graph?

c. What is the limiting velocity that cannot be exceeded?

Figure for Exercise 126

Thinking Outside the Box XVIII

Polynomial Equation Find a polynomial equation with integral coefficients for which $\sqrt{3} + \sqrt{5}$ is a root.

Concepts of Calculus

Instantaneous rate of change

Suppose that you start at Amarillo and drive west on I-40 for 500 miles. If this trip takes you 10 hours, then the average rate at which your location is changing is 50 miles per hour. At every instant of your trip your speedometer shows the instantaneous rate at which your location is changing. Your instantaneous rate of change might range from 0 miles per hour to 70 miles per hour or more.

We defined the average rate of change of a function $f(x)$ on the interval $[x, x + h]$ as $\dfrac{f(x + h) - f(x)}{h}$. We cannot use a speedometer to find the instantaneous rate of change of a function. We use the idea of limits, which was discussed in the Concepts of Calculus at the end of Chapter 1. For the instantaneous rate of change we shrink the interval to nothing. So we define the instantaneous rate of change of $f(x)$ as $\lim\limits_{h \to 0} \dfrac{f(x + h) - f(x)}{h}$.

Exercises

1. Let $f(x) = x^2$.

a. Find $\dfrac{f(2 + h) - f(2)}{h}$.

b. Find $\lim\limits_{h \to 0} \dfrac{f(2 + h) - f(2)}{h}$.

2. Let $f(x) = x^2 - 2x$.

a. Find $\dfrac{f(x + h) - f(x)}{h}$.

b. Find $\lim\limits_{h \to 0} \dfrac{f(x + h) - f(x)}{h}$.

c. Find the instantaneous rate of change of $f(x) = x^2 - 2x$ when $x = 5$.

3. Let $f(x) = \sqrt{x}$.

a. Find $\dfrac{f(x + h) - f(x)}{h}$ and write your answer with a rational numerator.

b. Find $\lim\limits_{h \to 0} \dfrac{f(x + h) - f(x)}{h}$.

c. Find the instantaneous rate of change of $f(x) = \sqrt{x}$ when $x = 9$.

4. A ball is tossed into the air from ground level at 128 feet per second. The function $f(t) = -16t^2 + 128t$ gives the height above ground (in feet) as a function of time (in seconds).

a. Find $f(0)$ and $f(3)$.

b. How far did the ball travel in the first three seconds of its flight?

c. Find the average rate of change of the height for the time interval $[0, 3]$.

d. Find $\dfrac{f(t + h) - f(t)}{h}$.

e. Find $\lim\limits_{h \to 0} \dfrac{f(t + h) - f(t)}{h}$.

f. Find the instantaneous rate of change of the height (or the *instantaneous velocity*) of the ball at times $t = 0, 2, 4, 6,$ and 8 seconds.

The average rate of change of the function f on the interval $[c, x]$ is $\dfrac{f(x) - f(c)}{x - c}$.

5. Let $f(x) = \dfrac{1}{x}$.

a. Find and simplify $\dfrac{f(x) - f(2)}{x - 2}$.

b. Find $\lim\limits_{x \to 2} \dfrac{f(x) - f(2)}{x - 2}$.

c. Find the instantaneous rate of change of $f(x)$ when $x = 2$.

6. Let $f(x) = x^3$.

a. Find and simplify $\dfrac{f(x) - f(c)}{x - c}$.

b. Find $\lim\limits_{x \to c} \dfrac{f(x) - f(c)}{x - c}$.

c. Find the instantaneous rate of change of $f(x)$ when $x = c$.

CHAPTER

3 Trigonometric Functions

The Verrazano-Narrows Bridge

Location Brooklyn and Staten Island, New York

Completion Date 1964

Cost $325 million

Length 13,700 feet

Longest Single Span 4260 feet

Engineer Othmar H. Ammann

With an overall length of more than 2 miles, the Verrazano-Narrows bridge was the longest suspension bridge in the world in 1964. Today it is only in the top 10. Engineer Othmar Ammann, perhaps the greatest bridge engineer of all time, was also responsible for four other New York City bridges, the Triborough, Bronx-Whitestone, Throgs Neck, and George Washington. Because the bridge's 690 foot towers are so high and far apart, Ammann had to take into account the curvature of the earth when designing the bridge. Like all steel bridges, the Verrazano-Narrows bridge expands and contracts with changes in temperature. The bridge roadway is 12 feet lower in the summer than during the winter.

3.1 Angles and Their Measurements

Trigonometry was first studied by the Greeks, Egyptians, and Babylonians and used in surveying, navigation, and astronomy. Using trigonometry, they had a powerful tool for finding areas of triangular plots of land, as well as lengths of sides and measures of angles, without physically measuring them. We begin our study of trigonometry by studying angles and their measurements.

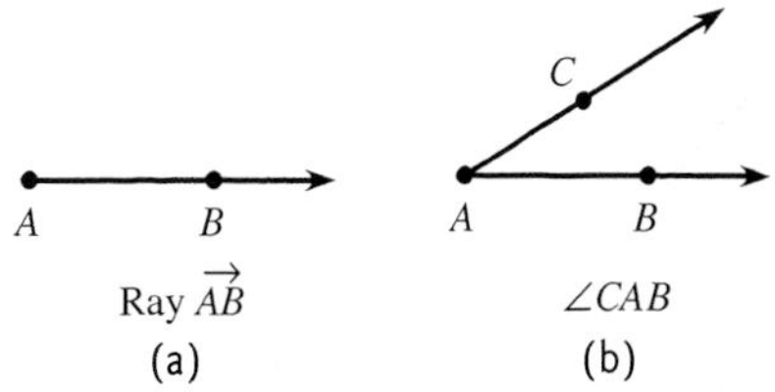

Figure 3.1

Degree Measure of Angles

In geometry a **ray** is defined as a point on a line together with all points of the line on one side of that point. Figure 3.1(a) shows ray $\overrightarrow{AB}$. An **angle** is defined as the union of two rays with a common endpoint, the **vertex.** The angle shown in Fig. 3.1(b) is named $\angle A$, $\angle BAC$, or $\angle CAB$. (Read the symbol $\angle$ as "angle.") Angles are also named using Greek letters such as α (alpha), β (beta), γ (gamma), or θ (theta).

An angle is often thought of as being formed by rotating one ray away from a fixed ray as indicated by angle α and the arrow in Fig. 3.2(a). The fixed ray is the **initial side** and the rotated ray is the **terminal side.** An angle whose vertex is the center of a circle, as shown in Fig. 3.2(b), is a **central angle,** and the arc of the circle through which the terminal side moves is the **intercepted arc.** An angle in **standard position** is located in a rectangular coordinate system with the vertex at the origin and the initial side on the positive x-axis as shown in Fig. 3.2(c).

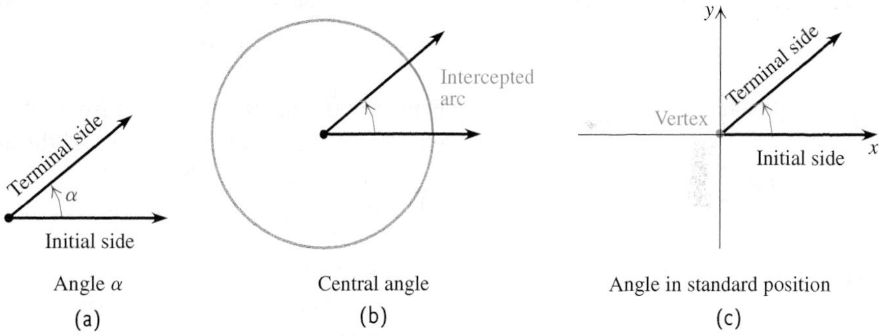

Figure 3.2

The measure $m(\alpha)$, of an angle α indicates the amount of rotation of the terminal side from the initial position. It is found using any circle centered at the vertex. The circle is divided into 360 equal arcs and each arc is one **degree** (1°).

Definition: Degree Measure

The **degree measure of an angle** is the number of degrees in the intercepted arc of a circle centered at the vertex. The degree measure is positive if the rotation is counterclockwise and negative if the rotation is clockwise.

Figure 3.3 on the next page shows the positions of the terminal sides of some angles in standard position with common positive measures between 0° and 360°. An angle with measure between 0° and 90° is an **acute angle.** An angle with measure

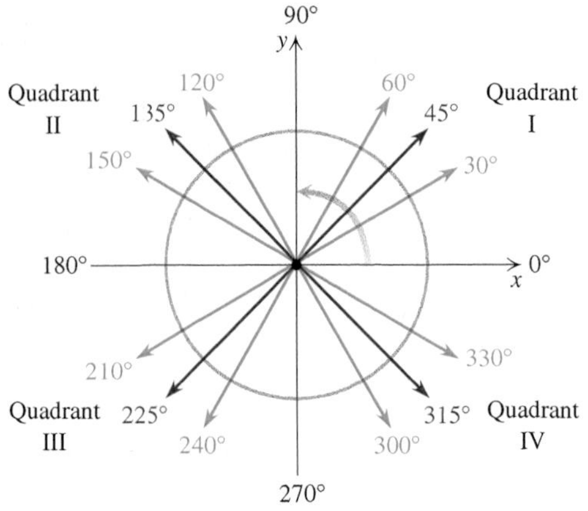

Figure 3.3

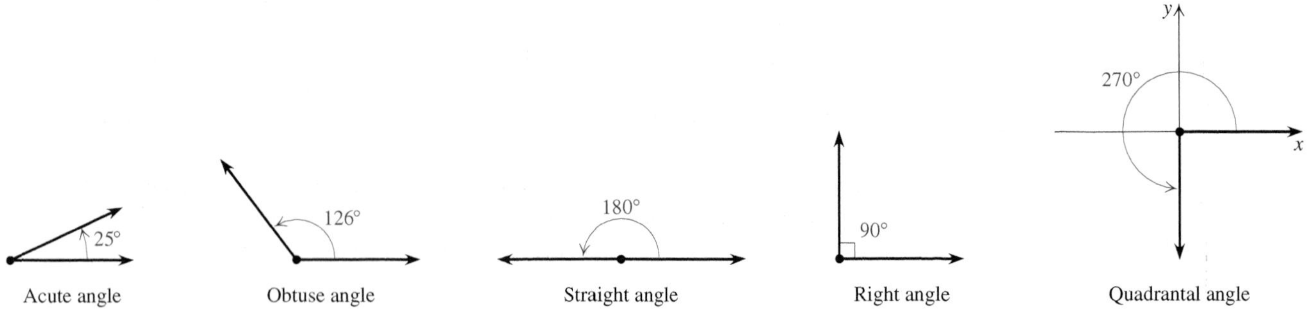

Figure 3.4

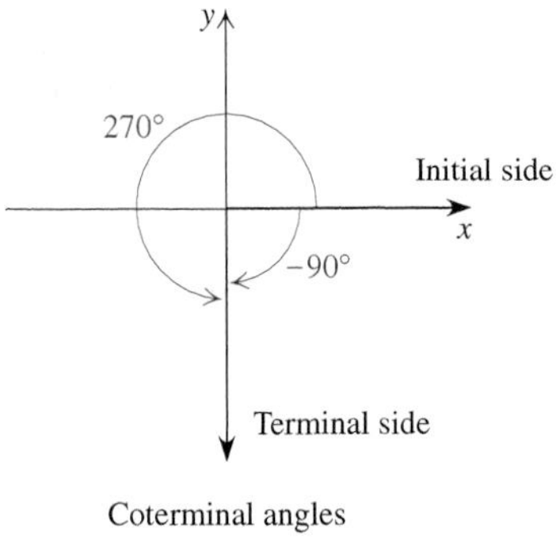

Figure 3.5

between 90° and 180° is an **obtuse angle.** An angle of exactly 180° is a **straight angle.** See Fig. 3.4. A 90° angle is a **right angle.** An angle in standard position is said to lie in the quadrant where its terminal side lies. If the terminal side is on an axis, the angle is a **quadrantal angle.** We often think of the degree measure of an angle as the angle itself. For example, we write $m(\alpha) = 60°$ or $\alpha = 60°$, and we say that 60° is an acute angle.

The initial side of an angle may be rotated in a positive or negative direction to get to the position of the terminal side. For example, if the initial side shown in Fig. 3.5 rotates clockwise for one-quarter of a revolution to get to the terminal position, then the measure of the angle is $-90°$. If the initial side had rotated counterclockwise to get to the position of the terminal side, then the measure of the angle would be 270°. If the initial side had rotated clockwise for one and a quarter revolutions to get to the terminal position, then the angle would be $-450°$. **Coterminal angles** are angles in standard position that have the same initial side and the same terminal side. The angles $-90°$, $-450°$, and 270° are examples of coterminal angles. Any two coterminal angles have degree measures that differ by a multiple of 360° (one complete revolution).

Coterminal Angles

Angles α and β in standard position are coterminal if and only if there is an integer k such that $m(\beta) = m(\alpha) + k360°$.

Note that any angle formed by two rays can be thought of as one angle with infinitely many different measures, or infinitely many different coterminal angles.

Example 1 Finding coterminal angles

Find two positive angles and two negative angles that are coterminal with $-50°$.

Solution

Since any angle of the form $-50° + k360°$ is coterminal with $-50°$, there are infinitely many possible answers. For simplicity, we choose the positive integers 1 and 2 and the negative integers -1 and -2 for k to get the following angles:

$$-50° + 1 \cdot 360° = 310°$$

$$-50° + 2 \cdot 360° = 670°$$

$$-50° + (-1)360° = -410°$$

$$-50° + (-2)360° = -770°$$

The angles $310°$, $670°$, $-410°$, and $-770°$ are coterminal with $-50°$. ■

To determine whether two angles are coterminal we must determine whether they differ by a multiple of $360°$.

Example 2 Determining whether angles are coterminal

Determine whether angles in standard position with the given measures are coterminal.

a. $m(\alpha) = 190°, m(\beta) = -170°$

b. $m(\alpha) = 150°, m(\beta) = 880°$

Solution

a. If there is an integer k such that $190 + 360k = -170$, then α and β are coterminal.

$$190 + 360k = -170$$

$$360k = -360$$

$$k = -1$$

Since the equation has an integral solution, α and β are coterminal.

b. If there is an integer k such that $150 + 360k = 880$, then α and β are coterminal.

$$150 + 360k = 880$$

$$360k = 730$$

$$k = \frac{73}{36}$$

Since there is no integral solution to the equation, α and β are not coterminal. ■

The quadrantal angles, such as $90°$, $180°$, $270°$, and $360°$, have terminal sides on an axis and do not lie in any quadrant. Any angle that is not coterminal with a quadrantal angle lies in one of the four quadrants. To determine the quadrant in which an angle lies, add or subtract multiples of $360°$ (one revolution) to obtain a coterminal angle with a measure between $0°$ and $360°$. A nonquadrantal angle is in the quadrant in which its terminal side lies.

Example 3 Determining in which quadrant an angle lies

Name the quadrant in which each angle lies.

a. $230°$ **b.** $-580°$ **c.** $1380°$

Solution

a. Since $180° < 230° < 270°$, a $230°$ angle lies in quadrant III.

b. We must add $2(360°)$ to $-580°$ to get an angle between $0°$ and $360°$:

$$-580° + 2(360°) = 140°$$

So $140°$ and $-580°$ are coterminal. Since $90° < 140° < 180°$, $140°$ lies in quadrant II and so does a $-580°$ angle.

c. From $1380°$ we must subtract $3(360°)$ to obtain an angle between $0°$ and $360°$:

$$1380° - 3(360°) = 300°$$

So $1380°$ and $300°$ are coterminal. Since $270° < 300° < 360°$, $300°$ lies in quadrant IV and so does $1380°$. ■

Each degree is divided into 60 equal parts called **minutes,** and each minute is divided into 60 equal parts called **seconds.** A minute (min) is $1/60$ of a degree (deg), and a second (sec) is $1/60$ of a minute or $1/3600$ of a degree. An angle with measure $44°12'30''$ is an angle with a measure of 44 degrees, 12 minutes, and 30 seconds. Historically, angles were measured by using degrees-minutes-seconds, but with calculators it is convenient to have the fractional parts of a degree written as a decimal number such as $7.218°$. Some calculators can handle angles in degrees-minutes-seconds and even convert them to decimal degrees.

Example 4 Converting degrees-minutes-seconds to decimal degrees

Convert the measure $44°12'30''$ to decimal degrees.

Solution

Since 1 degree = 60 minutes and 1 degree = 3600 seconds, we get

$$12 \text{ min} = 12 \text{ min} \cdot \frac{1 \text{ deg}}{60 \text{ min}} = \frac{12}{60} \text{ deg} \quad \text{and}$$

$$30 \text{ sec} = 30 \text{ sec} \cdot \frac{1 \text{ deg}}{3600 \text{ sec}} = \frac{30}{3600} \text{ deg}.$$

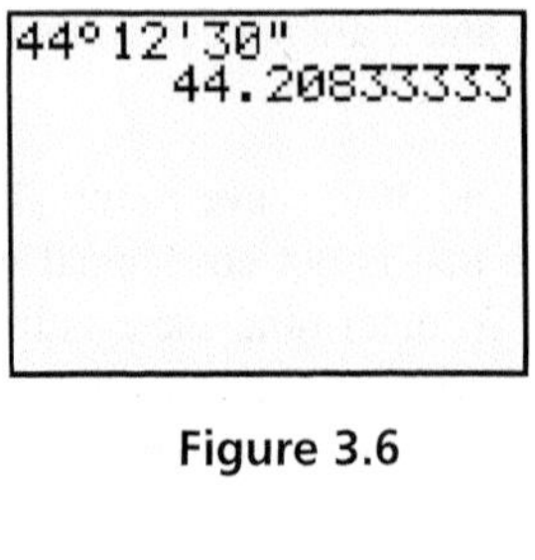

Figure 3.6

So

$$44°12'30'' = \left(44 + \frac{12}{60} + \frac{30}{3600}\right)^{\circ} \approx 44.2083°.$$

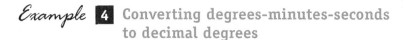

A graphing calculator can convert degrees-minutes-seconds to decimal degrees as shown in Fig. 3.6. ■

Note that the conversion of Example 4 was done by "cancellation of units." Minutes in the numerator canceled with minutes in the denominator to give the result in degrees, and seconds in the numerator canceled with seconds in the denominator to give the result in degrees.

Example 5 Converting decimal degrees to degrees-minutes-seconds

Convert the measure 44.235° to degrees-minutes-seconds.

Solution

First convert 0.235° to minutes. Since 1 degree = 60 minutes,

$$0.235 \text{ deg} = 0.235 \text{ deg} \cdot \frac{60 \text{ min}}{1 \text{ deg}} = 14.1 \text{ min}.$$

So 44.235° = 44°14.1′. Now convert 0.1′ to seconds. Since 1 minute = 60 seconds,

$$0.1 \text{ min} = 0.1 \text{ min} \cdot \frac{60 \text{ sec}}{1 \text{ min}} = 6 \text{ sec}.$$

So 44.235° = 44°14′6″.

A graphing calculator can convert to degrees-minutes-seconds as shown in Fig. 3.7. ■

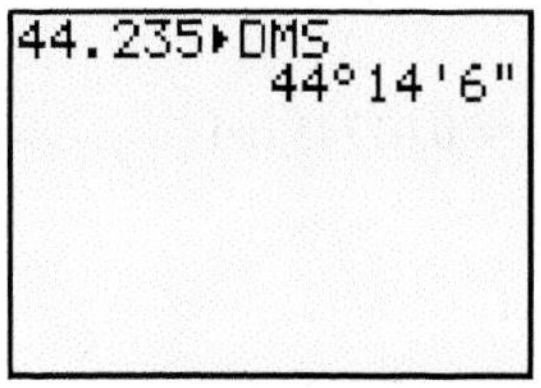

Figure 3.7

Note again how the original units canceled in Example 5, giving the result in the desired units of measurement.

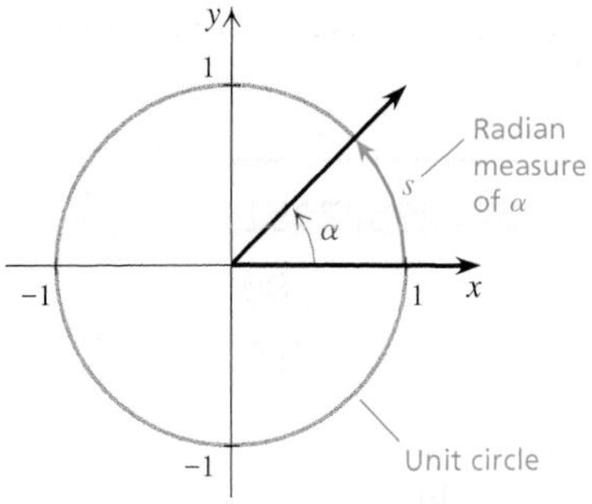

Figure 3.8

Radian Measure of Angles

Degree measure of angles is used mostly in applied areas such as surveying, navigation, and engineering. Radian measure of angles is used more in scientific fields and results in simpler formulas in trigonometry and calculus.

For radian measures of angles we use a **unit circle** (a circle with radius 1) centered at the origin. The radian measure of an angle in standard position is simply the length of the intercepted arc on the unit circle. See Fig. 3.8. Since the radius of the unit circle is the real number 1 without any dimension (such as feet or inches), the length of an intercepted arc is a real number without any dimension and so the radian measure of an angle is also a real number without any dimension. One **radian** (abbreviated 1 rad) is the real number 1.

Definition: Radian Measure

To find the **radian measure** of the angle α in standard position, find the length of the intercepted arc on the unit circle. If the rotation is counterclockwise, the radian measure is the length of the arc. If the rotation is clockwise, the radian measure is the opposite of the length of the arc.

Radian measure is called a **directed length** because it is positive or negative depending on the direction of rotation of the initial side. If s is the length of the intercepted arc on the unit circle for an angle α, as shown in Fig. 3.8, we write $m(\alpha) = s$. To emphasize that s is the length of an arc on a unit circle, we may write $m(\alpha) = s$ radians.

Figure 3.9

Because the circumference of a circle with radius r is $2\pi r$, the circumference of the unit circle is 2π. If the initial side rotates 360° (one complete revolution), then the length of the intercepted arc is 2π. So an angle of 360° has a radian measure of 2π radians. We express this relationship as $360° = 2\pi$ rad or simply $360° = 2\pi$. Dividing each side by 2 yields $180° = \pi$, which is the basic relationship to remember for conversion of one unit of measurement to the other.

Use the MODE key on a graphing calculator to set the calculator to radian or degree mode as shown in Fig. 3.9. □

Degree-Radian Conversion

Conversion from degrees to radians or radians to degrees is based on

$$180 \text{ degrees} = \pi \text{ radians}.$$

To convert degrees to radians or radians to degrees, we use 180 deg $= \pi$ rad and cancellation of units. For example,

$$1 \text{ deg} = 1 \text{ deg} \cdot \frac{\pi \text{ rad}}{180 \text{ deg}} = \frac{\pi}{180} \text{ rad} \approx 0.01745 \text{ rad}$$

and

$$1 \text{ rad} = 1 \text{ rad} \cdot \frac{180 \text{ deg}}{\pi \text{ rad}} = \frac{180}{\pi} \text{ deg} \approx 57.3 \text{ deg}.$$

If your calculator is in radian mode, as in Fig. 3.10(a), pressing ENTER converts degrees to radians. When the calculator is in degree mode, as in Fig. 3.10(b), pressing ENTER converts radians to degrees. □

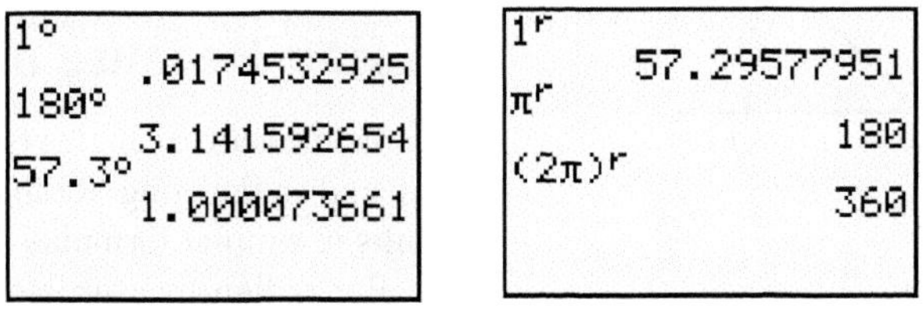

(a) (b)

Figure 3.10

Figure 3.11(a) shows an angle of 1°, and Fig. 3.11(b) shows an angle of 1 radian. An angle of 1 radian intercepts an arc on the unit circle equal in length to the radius of the unit circle.

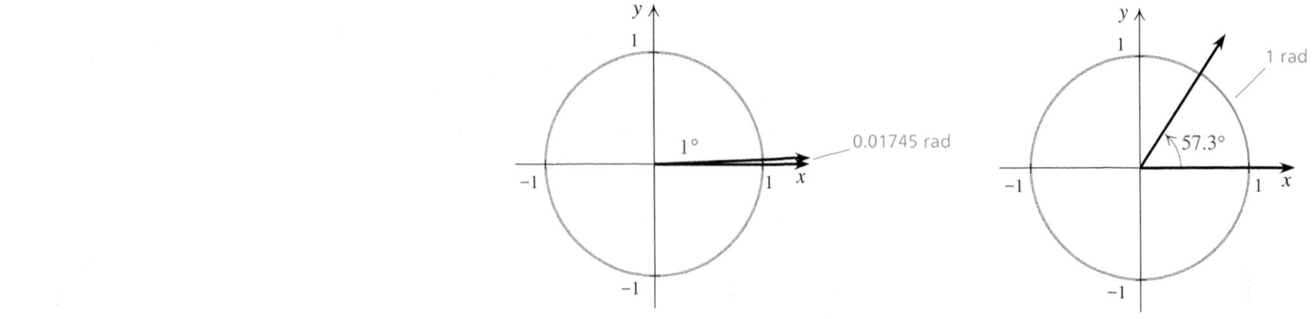

(a) (b)

Figure 3.11

Example 6 Converting from degrees to radians

Convert the degree measures to radians.

a. 270° **b.** −23.6°

Solution

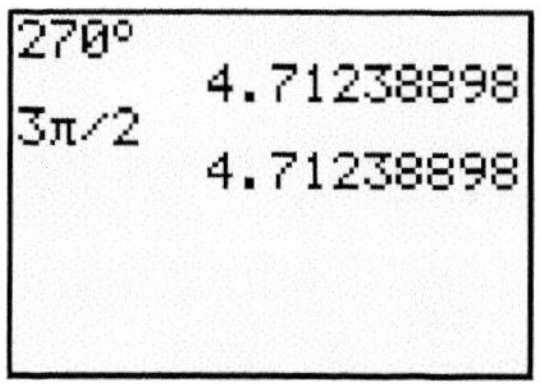

Figure 3.12

a. To convert degrees to radians, multiply the degree measure by π rad/180 deg:

$$270° = 270 \text{ deg} \cdot \frac{\pi \text{ rad}}{180 \text{ deg}} = \frac{3\pi}{2} \text{ rad}$$

The exact value, $3\pi/2$ rad, is approximately 4.71 rad; but when a measure in radians is a simple multiple of π, we usually write the exact value.

Check this result with a calculator in radian mode as shown in Fig. 3.12. □

b. $-23.6° = -23.6 \text{ deg} \cdot \frac{\pi \text{ rad}}{180 \text{ deg}} \approx -0.412 \text{ rad}.$ ■

Example 7 Converting from radians to degrees

Convert the radian measures to degrees.

a. $\frac{7\pi}{6}$ **b.** 12.3

Solution

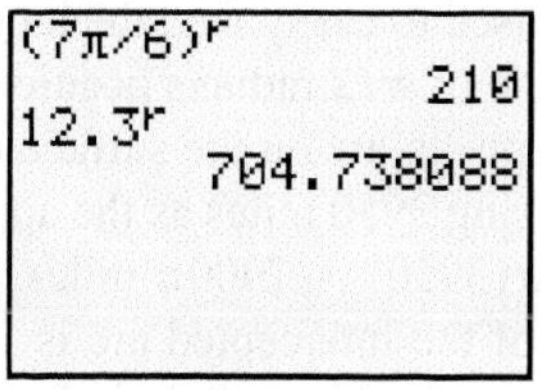

Figure 3.13

Multiply the radian measure by 180 deg/π rad:

a. $\frac{7\pi}{6} = \frac{7\pi}{6} \text{ rad} \cdot \frac{180 \text{ deg}}{\pi \text{ rad}} = 210°$ **b.** $12.3 = 12.3 \text{ rad} \cdot \frac{180 \text{ deg}}{\pi \text{ rad}} \approx 704.7°$

Check these answers in degree mode as shown in Fig. 3.13. ■

Figure 3.14 shows angles with common measures in standard position. Coterminal angles in standard position have radian measures that differ by an integral multiple of 2π (their degree measures differ by an integral multiple of 360°).

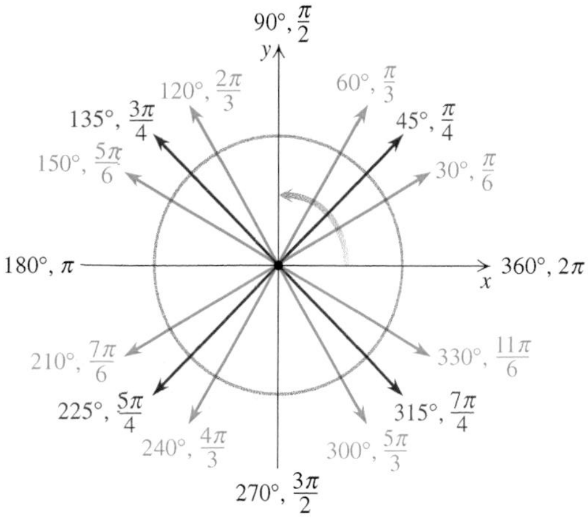

Figure 3.14

Example 8 Finding coterminal angles using radian measure

Find two positive and two negative angles that are coterminal with $\pi/6$.

Solution

All angles coterminal with $\pi/6$ have a radian measure of the form $\pi/6 + k(2\pi)$, where k is an integer.

$$\frac{\pi}{6} + 1(2\pi) = \frac{\pi}{6} + \frac{12\pi}{6} = \frac{13\pi}{6}$$

$$\frac{\pi}{6} + 2(2\pi) = \frac{\pi}{6} + \frac{24\pi}{6} = \frac{25\pi}{6}$$

$$\frac{\pi}{6} + (-1)(2\pi) = \frac{\pi}{6} - \frac{12\pi}{6} = -\frac{11\pi}{6}$$

$$\frac{\pi}{6} + (-2)(2\pi) = \frac{\pi}{6} - \frac{24\pi}{6} = -\frac{23\pi}{6}$$

The angles $13\pi/6$, $25\pi/6$, $-11\pi/6$, and $-23\pi/6$ are coterminal with $\pi/6$. ■

Arc Length

Radian measure of a central angle of a circle can be used to easily find the length of the intercepted arc of the circle. For example, an angle of $\pi/2$ radians positioned at the center of the earth, as shown in Fig. 3.15, intercepts an arc on the surface of the earth that runs from the equator to the North Pole. Using 3950 miles as the approximate radius of the earth yields a circumference of $2\pi(3950) = 7900\pi$ miles. Since $\pi/2$ radians is $1/4$ of a complete circle, the length of the intercepted arc is $1/4$ of the circumference. So the distance from the equator to the North Pole is $7900\pi/4$ miles, or about 6205 miles.

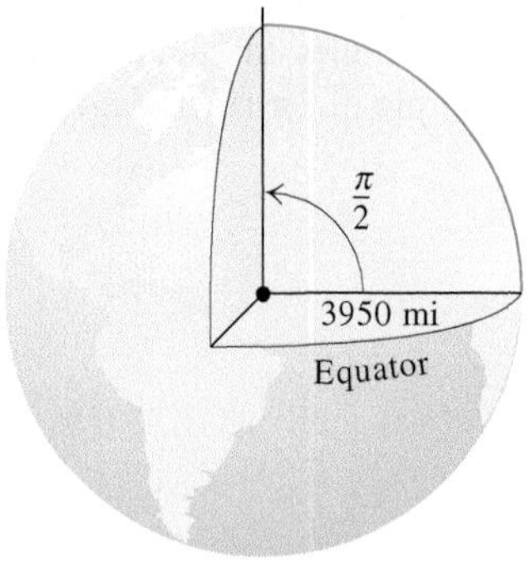

Figure 3.15

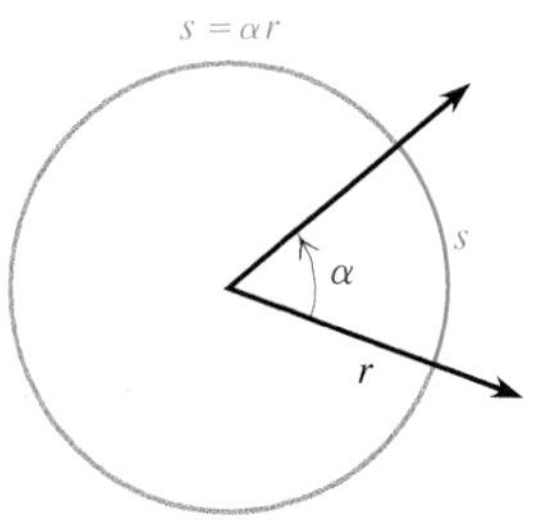

Figure 3.16

In general, a central angle α in a circle of radius r intercepts an arc whose length s is a fraction of the circumference of the circle, as shown in Fig. 3.16. Since a complete revolution is 2π radians, that fraction is $\alpha/(2\pi)$. Since the circumference is $2\pi r$, we get

$$s = \frac{\alpha}{2\pi} \cdot 2\pi r = \alpha r.$$

Theorem: Length of an Arc

The length s of an arc intercepted by a central angle of α *radians* on a circle of radius r is given by

$$s = \alpha r.$$

Historical Note

Eratosthenes (276 B.C.–194 B.C.) was a mathematician, geographer, and astronomer. His contemporaries nicknamed him "Beta" because he was believed to be second in the Mediterranean world in many fields. He is noted for devising a system of latitude and longitude, and for being the first person to calculate the circumference of the earth. Exercise 101 in this section shows how he found the circumference of the earth using the formula for the length of an arc.

If α is negative, the formula $s = \alpha r$ gives a negative number for the length of the arc. So s is a directed length. Note that the formula $s = \alpha r$ applies only if α is in radians.

Example 9 Finding the length of an arc

The wagon wheel shown in Fig. 3.17 has a diameter of 28 inches and an angle of 30° between the spokes. What is the length of the arc s between two adjacent spokes?

Solution

First convert 30° to radians:

$$30° = 30 \text{ deg} \cdot \frac{\pi \text{ rad}}{180 \text{ deg}} = \frac{\pi}{6} \text{ rad}$$

Now use $r = 14$ inches and $\alpha = \pi/6$ in the formula for arc length $s = \alpha r$:

$$s = \frac{\pi}{6} \cdot 14 \text{ in.} = \frac{7\pi}{3} \text{ in.} \approx 7.33 \text{ in.}$$

Since the radian measure of an angle is a dimensionless real number, the product of radians and inches is given in inches.

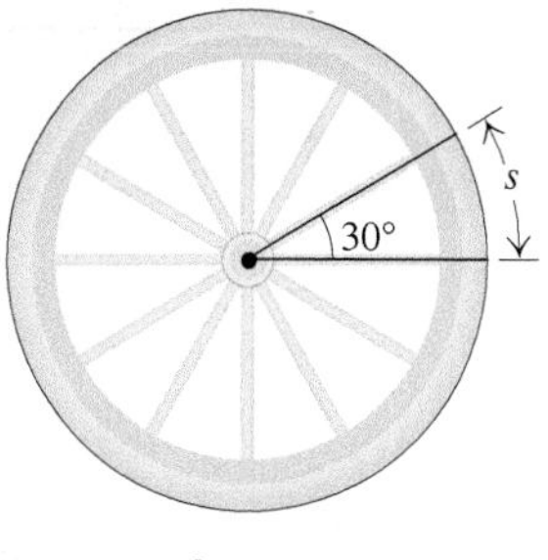

Figure 3.17

For Thought

True or False? Explain.

1. An angle is a union of two rays with a common endpoint.
2. The lengths of the rays of $\angle A$ determine the degree measure of $\angle A$.
3. Angles of 5° and −365° are coterminal.
4. The radian measure of an angle cannot be negative.
5. An angle of $38\pi/4$ radians is a quadrantal angle.
6. If $m(\angle A) = 210°$, then $m(\angle A) = 5\pi/6$ radians.
7. $25°20'40'' = 25.34°$
8. $2\pi + \pi/3 = 7\pi/3$
9. A central angle of $\pi/3$ radians in a circle of radius 3 ft intercepts an arc of length π feet.
10. A central angle of 1 rad in a circle of radius r intercepts an arc of length r.

3.1 Exercises

Find two positive angles and two negative angles that are coterminal with each given angle.

1. $60°$ **2.** $45°$ **3.** $-16°$ **4.** $-90°$

Determine whether the angles in each given pair are coterminal.

5. $123.4°, -236.6°$ **6.** $744°, -336°$

7. $1055°, 155°$ **8.** $0°, 359.9°$

Name the quadrant in which each angle lies.

9. $85°$ **10.** $110°$ **11.** $-125°$ **12.** $-200°$

13. $300°$ **14.** $205°$ **15.** $750°$ **16.** $-980°$

Match each of the following angles with one of the degree measures: $30°, 45°, 60°, 120°, 135°, 150°$.

17.

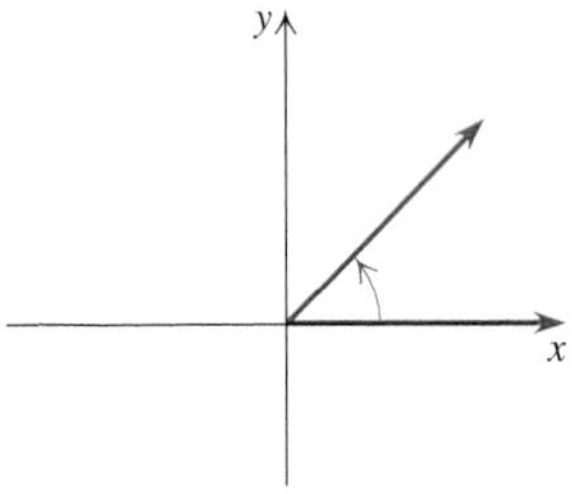

18.

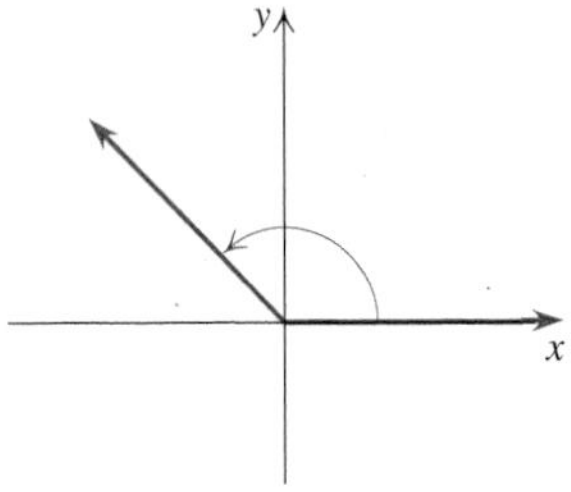

19.

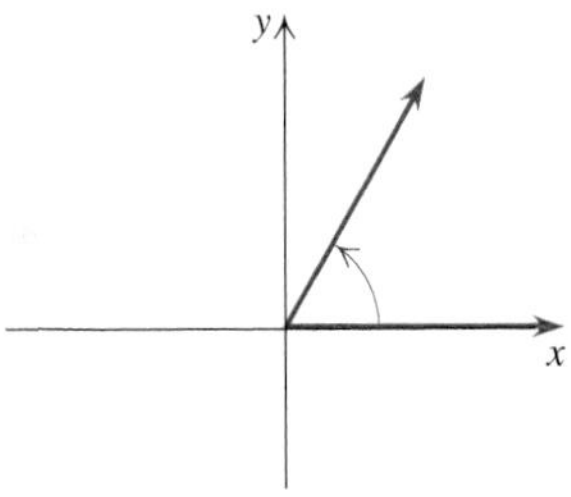

20.

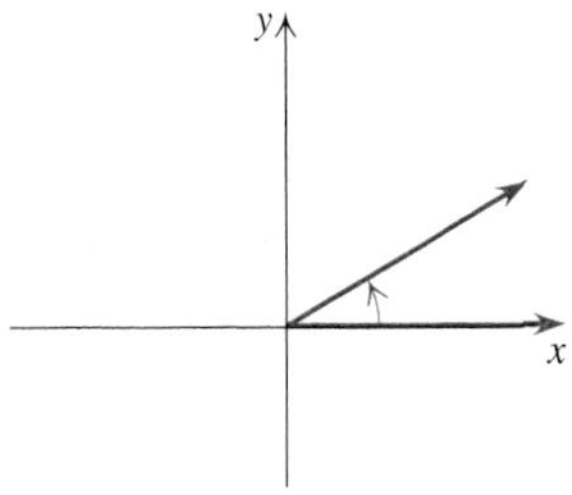

21.

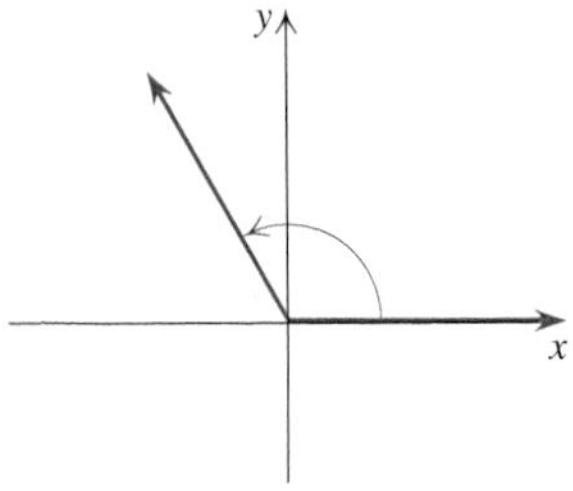

22.

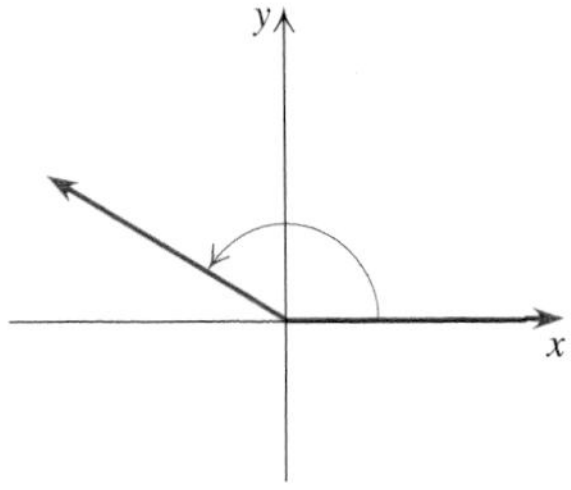

Find the measure in degrees of the least positive angle that is coterminal with each given angle.

23. $400°$ **24.** $540°$ **25.** $-340°$

26. $-180°$ **27.** $-1100°$ **28.** $-840°$

Convert each angle to decimal degrees. When necessary, round to four decimal places.

29. $13°12'$ **30.** $45°6'$ **31.** $-8°30'18''$

32. $-5°45'30''$ **33.** $28°5'9''$ **34.** $44°19'32''$

Convert each angle to degrees-minutes-seconds. Round to the nearest whole number of seconds.

35. $75.5°$ **36.** $39.4°$ **37.** $-17.33°$

38. $-9.12°$ **39.** $18.123°$ **40.** $122.786°$

Convert each degree measure to radian measure. Give exact answers.

41. $30°$ **42.** $45°$

43. $18°$ **44.** $48°$

45. $-67.5°$ **46.** $-105°$

47. $630°$ **48.** $495°$

Convert each degree measure to radian measure. Use the value of π *found on a calculator and round answers to three decimal places.*

49. $37.4°$ **50.** $125.3°$ **51.** $-13°47'$

52. $-99°15'$ **53.** $-53°37'6''$ **54.** $187°49'36''$

Convert each radian measure to degree measure. Use the value of π *found on a calculator and round approximate answers to three decimal places.*

55. $\frac{5\pi}{12}$ **56.** $\frac{17\pi}{12}$ **57.** $\frac{7\pi}{4}$ **58.** $\frac{13\pi}{6}$

59. -6π **60.** -9π **61.** 2.39 **62.** 0.452

Using radian measure, find two positive angles and two negative angles that are coterminal with each given angle.

63. $\frac{\pi}{3}$ **64.** $\frac{\pi}{4}$ **65.** $-\frac{\pi}{6}$ **66.** $-\frac{2\pi}{3}$

Find the measure in radians of the least positive angle that is coterminal with each given angle.

67. 3π **68.** 6π **69.** $\frac{9\pi}{2}$ **70.** $\frac{19\pi}{2}$

71. $-\frac{5\pi}{3}$ **72.** $-\frac{7\pi}{6}$ **73.** $-\frac{13\pi}{3}$ **74.** $-\frac{19\pi}{4}$

75. 8.32 **76.** −23.55

Determine whether the angles in each given pair are coterminal.

77. $\frac{3\pi}{4}, \frac{29\pi}{4}$ **78.** $-\frac{\pi}{3}, \frac{5\pi}{3}$

79. $\frac{7\pi}{6}, -\frac{5\pi}{6}$ **80.** $\frac{3\pi}{2}, -\frac{9\pi}{2}$

Name the quadrant in which each angle lies.

81. $\frac{5\pi}{12}$ **82.** $\frac{13\pi}{12}$ **83.** $-\frac{6\pi}{7}$ **84.** $-\frac{39\pi}{20}$

85. $\frac{13\pi}{8}$ **86.** $-\frac{11\pi}{8}$ **87.** −7.3 **88.** 23.1

Find the missing degree or radian measure for each position of the terminal side shown. For Exercise 89, use degrees between 0° and 360° and radians between 0 and 2π. For Exercise 90, use degrees between −360° and 0° and radians between -2π and 0. Practice these two exercises until you have memorized the degree and radian measures corresponding to these common angles.

89.

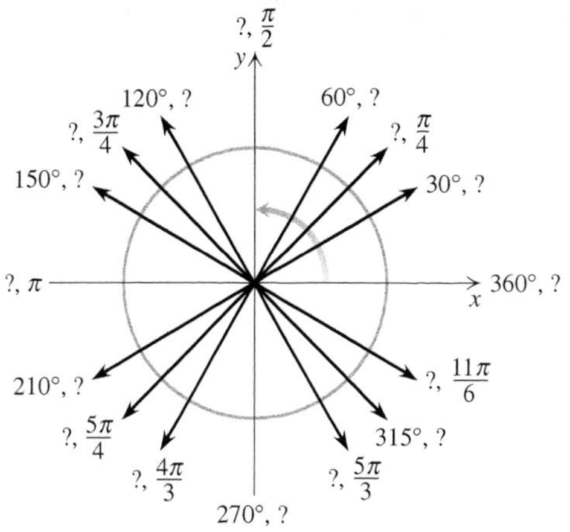

90.

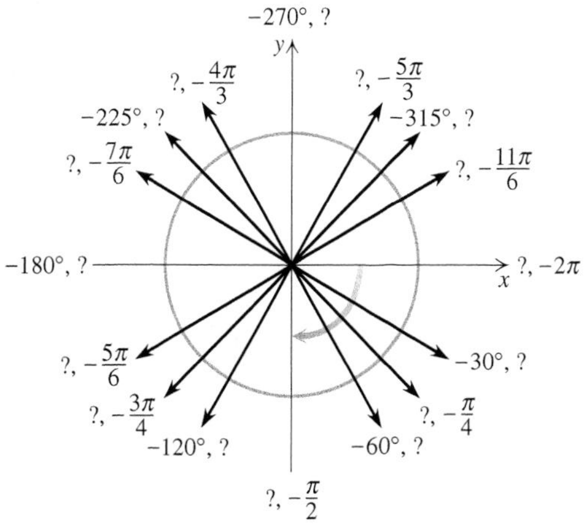

Find the length of the arc intercepted by the given central angle α in a circle of radius r.

91. $\alpha = \frac{\pi}{4}, r = 12$ ft **92.** $\alpha = 1, r = 4$ cm

93. $\alpha = 3°, r = 4000$ mi **94.** $\alpha = 60°, r = 2$ m

Find the radius of the circle in which the given central angle α intercepts an arc of the given length s.

95. $\alpha = 1, s = 1$ mi **96.** $\alpha = 0.004, s = 99$ km

97. $\alpha = 180°, s = 10$ km **98.** $\alpha = 360°, s = 8$ m

Solve each problem.

99. *Distance between Towers* The towers of the Verrazano-Narrows bridge are 693 ft tall and the length of the arc joining the bases of the towers is 4260 ft as shown in the accompanying figure. The radius of the earth is 4000 mi. How much greater in length is the arc joining the tops of the towers than the arc joining the bases?

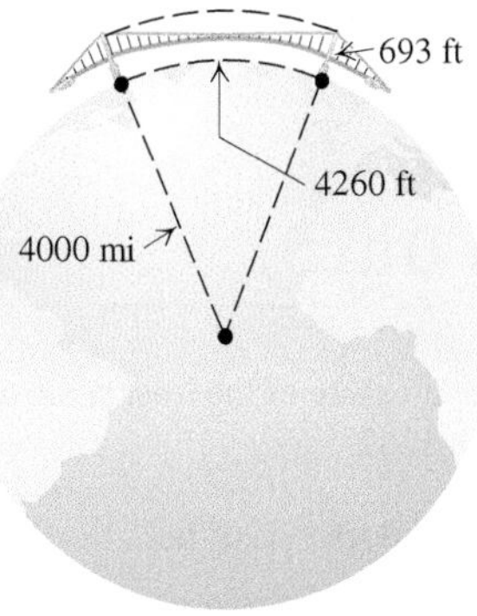

Figure for Exercise 99

100. *Distance to the Helper* A surveyor sights her 6-ft 2-in. helper on a nearby hill as shown in the figure. If the angle of sight between the helper's feet and head is $0°37'$, then approximately how far away is the helper?

Figure for Exercise 100

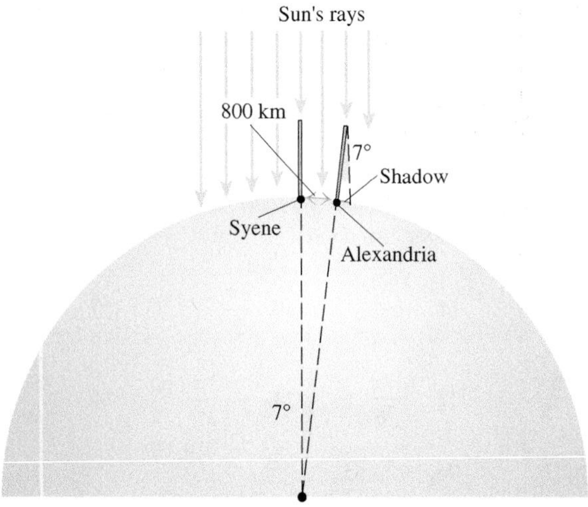

Figure for Exercise 101

101. *Eratosthenes Measures the Earth* Over 2200 years ago Eratosthenes read in the Alexandria library that at noon on June 21 a vertical stick in Syene cast no shadow. So on June 21 at noon Eratosthenes set out a vertical stick in Alexandria and found an angle of 7° in the position shown in the accompanying drawing. Eratosthenes reasoned that since the sun is so far away, sunlight must be arriving at the earth in parallel rays. With this assumption he concluded that the earth is round and the central angle in the drawing must also be 7°. He then paid a man to pace off the distance between Syene and Alexandria and found it to be 800 km. From these facts, calculate the circumference of the earth as Eratosthenes did and compare his answer with the circumference calculated by using the currently accepted radius of 6378 km.

Thinking Outside the Box XIX

Triangles and Circles Each of the five circles in the accompanying diagram has radius r. The four right triangles are congruent and each hypotenuse has length 1. Each line segment that appears to intersect a circle intersects it at exactly one point (a point of tangency). Find r.

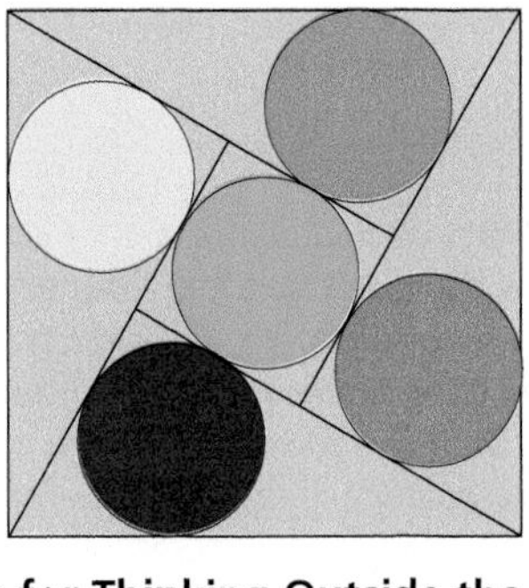

Figure for Thinking Outside the Box XIX

3.1 Pop Quiz

1. Find the degree measure of the least positive angle that is coterminal with 1267°.
2. In which quadrant does $-120°$ lie?
3. Convert $70°30'36''$ to decimal degrees.
4. Convert 270° to radian measure.
5. Convert $7\pi/4$ to degree measure.
6. Are $-3\pi/4$ and $5\pi/4$ coterminal?
7. Find the exact length of the arc intercepted by a central angle of 60° in a circle with radius 30 feet.

3.2 The Sine and Cosine Functions

In Section 3.1 we learned that angles can be measured in degrees or radians. Now we define two trigonometric functions whose domain is the set of all angles (measured in degrees or radians). These two functions are unlike any functions defined in algebra, but they form the foundation of trigonometry.

Definition

If α is an angle in standard position whose terminal side intersects the unit circle at point (x, y), as shown in Fig. 3.18, then **sine of α**—abbreviated $\sin(\alpha)$ or $\sin \alpha$—is the y-coordinate of that point, and **cosine of α**—abbreviated $\cos(\alpha)$ or $\cos \alpha$—is the x-coordinate. Sine and cosine are called **trigonometric functions.**

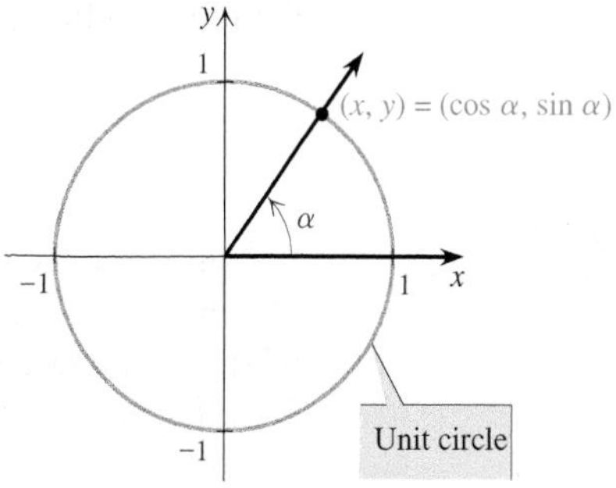

Figure 3.18

Definition: Sine and Cosine

If α is an angle in standard position and (x, y) is the point of intersection of the terminal side and the unit circle, then

$$\sin \alpha = y \quad \text{and} \quad \cos \alpha = x.$$

The domain of the sine function and the cosine function is the set of angles in standard position, but since each angle has a measure in degrees or radians, we generally use the set of degree measures or the set of radian measures as the domain. If (x, y) is on the unit circle, then $-1 \le x \le 1$ and $-1 \le y \le 1$, so the range of each of these functions is the interval $[-1, 1]$.

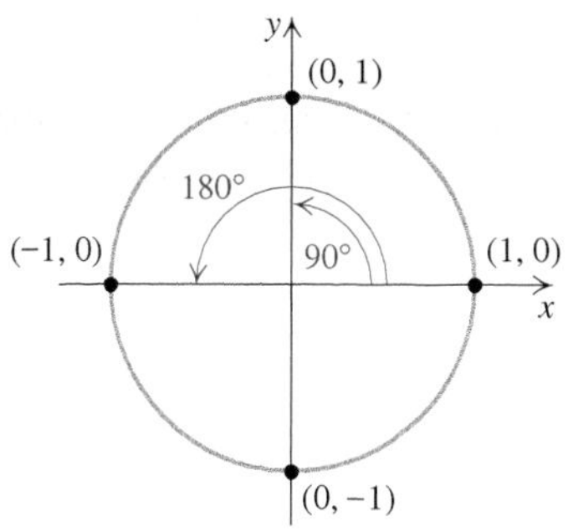

Figure 3.19

Example 1 Evaluating sine and cosine at a multiple of 90°

Find the exact values of the sine and cosine functions for each angle.

a. 90° **b.** $\pi/2$ **c.** 180° **d.** $-5\pi/2$ **e.** $-720°$

Solution

a. Consider the unit circle shown in Fig. 3.19. Since the terminal side of 90° intersects the unit circle at $(0, 1)$, $\sin(90°) = 1$ and $\cos(90°) = 0$.

b. Since $\pi/2$ is coterminal with 90°, we have $\sin(\pi/2) = 1$ and $\cos(\pi/2) = 0$.

c. The terminal side for 180° intersects the unit circle at $(-1, 0)$. So $\sin(180°) = 0$ and $\cos(180°) = -1$.

d. Since $-5\pi/2$ is coterminal with $3\pi/2$, the terminal side of $-5\pi/2$ lies on the negative y-axis and intersects the unit circle at $(0, -1)$. So $\sin(-5\pi/2) = -1$ and $\cos(-5\pi/2) = 0$.

e. Since $-720°$ is coterminal with 0°, the terminal side of $-720°$ lies on the positive x-axis and intersects the unit circle at $(1, 0)$. So $\sin(-720°) = 0$ and $\cos(-720°) = 1$. ■

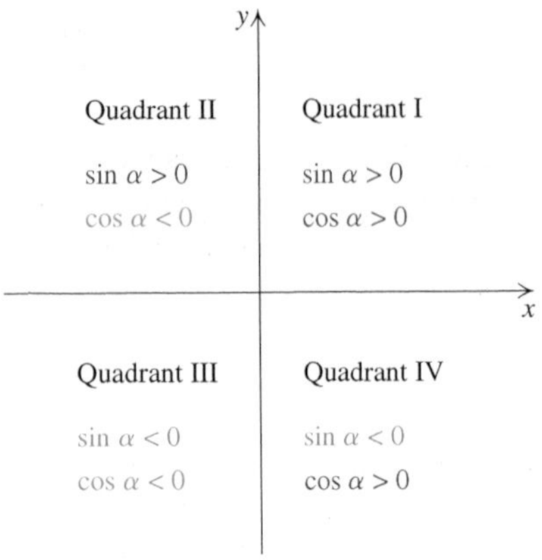

Figure 3.20

The *signs* of the sine and cosine functions depend on the quadrant in which the angle lies. For any point (x, y) on the unit circle in quadrant I, the x- and y-coordinates are positive. So if α is an angle in quadrant I, $\sin\alpha > 0$ and $\cos\alpha > 0$. Since the x-coordinate of any point in quadrant II is negative, the cosine of any angle in quadrant II is negative. Figure 3.20 gives the signs of sine and cosine for each of the four quadrants.

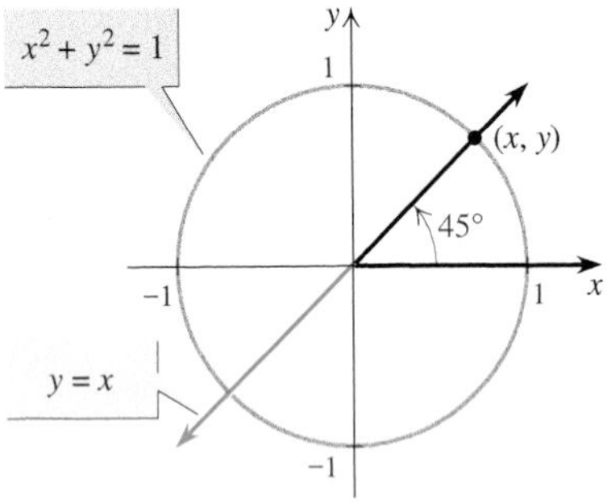

Figure 3.21

Sine and Cosine of a Multiple of 45°

In Example 1, exact values of the sine and cosine functions were found for some angles that were multiples of 90° (quadrantal angles). We can also find the exact values of $\sin(45°)$ and $\cos(45°)$ and then use that information to find the exact values of these functions for any multiple of 45°.

Since the terminal side for 45° lies on the line $y = x$, as shown in Fig. 3.21, the x- and y-coordinates at the point of intersection with the unit circle are equal. From Section 1.3, the equation of the unit circle is $x^2 + y^2 = 1$. Because $y = x$, we can write $x^2 + x^2 = 1$ and solve for x:

$$2x^2 = 1$$

$$x^2 = \frac{1}{2}$$

$$x = \pm\sqrt{\frac{1}{2}} = \pm\frac{\sqrt{2}}{2}$$

For a 45° angle in quadrant I, x and y are both positive numbers. So $\sin(45°) = \cos(45°) = \sqrt{2}/2$.

There are four points where the lines $y = x$ and $y = -x$ intersect the unit circle. The coordinates of these points, shown in Fig. 3.22, can all be found as above or by the symmetry of the unit circle. Figure 3.22 shows the coordinates of the key points for determining the sine and cosine of any angle that is an integral multiple of 45°.

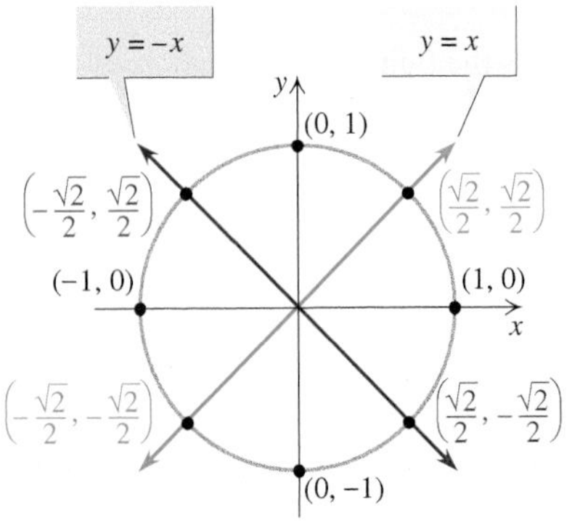

Figure 3.22

Example 2 Evaluating sine and cosine at a multiple of 45°

Find the exact value of each expression.

a. $\sin(135°)$ **b.** $\sin\left(\frac{5\pi}{4}\right)$ **c.** $2\sin\left(-\frac{9\pi}{4}\right)\cos\left(-\frac{9\pi}{4}\right)$

Solution

a. The terminal side for 135° lies in quadrant II, halfway between 90° and 180°. As shown in Fig. 3.22, the point on the unit circle halfway between 90° and 180° is $(-\sqrt{2}/2, \sqrt{2}/2)$. So $\sin(135°) = \sqrt{2}/2$.

b. The terminal side for $5\pi/4$ is in quadrant III, halfway between $4\pi/4$ and $6\pi/4$. From Fig. 3.22, $\sin(5\pi/4)$ is the y-coordinate of $(-\sqrt{2}/2, -\sqrt{2}/2)$. So $\sin(5\pi/4) = -\sqrt{2}/2$.

c. Since $-8\pi/4$ is one clockwise revolution, $-9\pi/4$ is coterminal with $-\pi/4$. From Fig. 3.22, we have $\cos(-9\pi/4) = \cos(-\pi/4) = \sqrt{2}/2$ and $\sin(-9\pi/4) = -\sqrt{2}/2$. So

$$2\sin\left(-\frac{9\pi}{4}\right)\cos\left(-\frac{9\pi}{4}\right) = 2 \cdot \left(-\frac{\sqrt{2}}{2}\right) \cdot \frac{\sqrt{2}}{2} = -1.$$

Sine and Cosine of a Multiple of 30°

Exact values for the sine and cosine of 60° and the sine and cosine of 30° are found with a little help from geometry. The terminal side of a 60° angle intersects the unit circle at a point (x, y), as shown in Fig. 3.23(a), where x and y are the lengths of the legs of a 30-60-90 triangle whose hypotenuse is length 1.

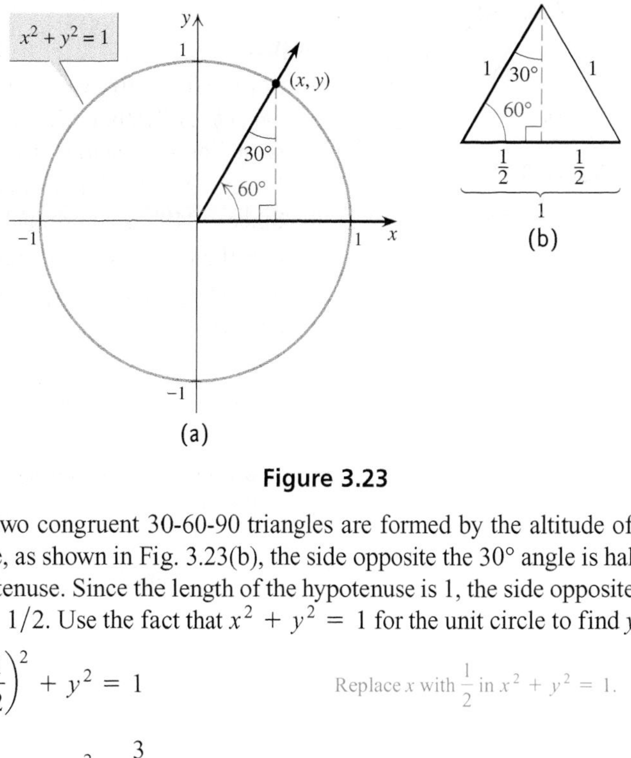

Figure 3.23

Since two congruent 30-60-90 triangles are formed by the altitude of an equilateral triangle, as shown in Fig. 3.23(b), the side opposite the 30° angle is half the length of the hypotenuse. Since the length of the hypotenuse is 1, the side opposite 30° is $1/2$, that is, $x = 1/2$. Use the fact that $x^2 + y^2 = 1$ for the unit circle to find y:

$$\left(\frac{1}{2}\right)^2 + y^2 = 1 \qquad \text{Replace } x \text{ with } \frac{1}{2} \text{ in } x^2 + y^2 = 1.$$

$$y^2 = \frac{3}{4}$$

$$y = \pm\sqrt{\frac{3}{4}} = \pm\frac{\sqrt{3}}{2}$$

Since $y > 0$ (in quadrant I), $\cos(60°) = 1/2$ and $\sin(60°) = \sqrt{3}/2$.

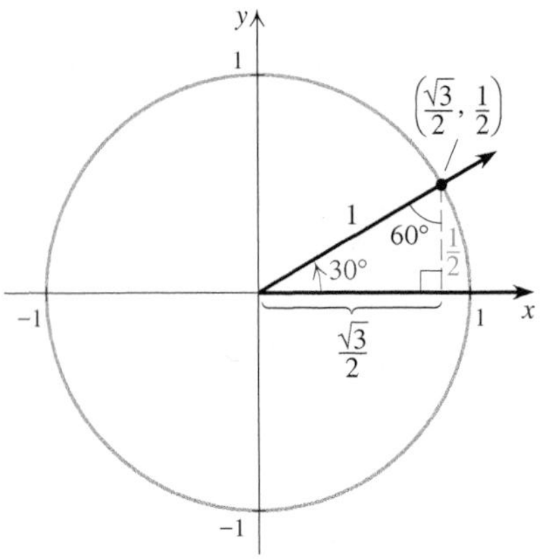

Figure 3.24

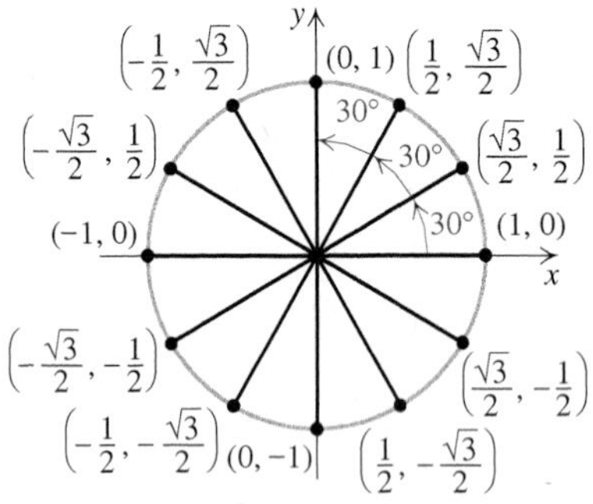

Figure 3.25

The point of intersection of the terminal side for a 30° angle with the unit circle determines a 30-60-90 triangle exactly the same size as the one described above. In this case the longer leg is on the x-axis, as shown in Fig. 3.24, and the point on the unit circle is $\left(\sqrt{3}/2, 1/2\right)$. So $\cos(30°) = \sqrt{3}/2$, and $\sin(30°) = 1/2$.

Using the symmetry of the unit circle and the values just found for the sine and cosine of 30° and 60°, we can label points on the unit circle, as shown in Fig. 3.25. This figure shows the coordinates of every point on the unit circle where the terminal side of a multiple of 30° intersects the unit circle. For example, the terminal side of a 120° angle in standard position intersects the unit circle at $\left(-1/2, \sqrt{3}/2\right)$, because $120° = 4 \cdot 30°$.

In the next example, we use Fig. 3.25 to evaluate expressions involving multiples of 30° ($\pi/6$). Note that the square of $\sin\alpha$ could be written as $(\sin\alpha)^2$, but for simplicity it is written as $\sin^2\alpha$. Likewise, $\cos^2\alpha$ is used for $(\cos\alpha)^2$.

Example 3 Evaluating sine and cosine at a multiple of 30°

Find the exact value of each expression.

a. $\sin\left(\dfrac{7\pi}{6}\right)$ **b.** $\cos^2(-240°) - \sin^2(-240°)$

Solution

a. Since $\pi/6 = 30°$, we have $7\pi/6 = 210°$. To determine the location of the terminal side of $7\pi/6$, notice that $7\pi/6$ is 30° larger than the straight angle 180° and so it lies in quadrant III. From Fig. 3.25, $7\pi/6$ intersects the unit circle at $\left(-\sqrt{3}/2, -1/2\right)$ and $\sin(7\pi/6) = -1/2$.

b. Since −240° is coterminal with 120°, the terminal side for −240° lies in quadrant II and intersects the unit circle at $\left(-1/2, \sqrt{3}/2\right)$, as indicated in Fig. 3.25. So $\cos(-240°) = -1/2$ and $\sin(-240°) = \sqrt{3}/2$. Now use these values in the original expression:

$$\cos^2(-240°) - \sin^2(-240°) = \left(-\frac{1}{2}\right)^2 - \left(\frac{\sqrt{3}}{2}\right)^2 = \frac{1}{4} - \frac{3}{4} = -\frac{1}{2}$$ ■

A good way to remember the sines and cosines for the common angles is to note the following patterns:

$$\sin(30°) = \frac{\sqrt{1}}{2}, \quad \sin(45°) = \frac{\sqrt{2}}{2}, \quad \sin(60°) = \frac{\sqrt{3}}{2}$$

$$\cos(30°) = \frac{\sqrt{3}}{2}, \quad \cos(45°) = \frac{\sqrt{2}}{2}, \quad \cos(60°) = \frac{\sqrt{1}}{2}$$

Sine and Cosine of an Arc

In calculus we study functions such as $f(x) = x^2 + \sin(x)$. For this function to make sense, x must be a real number and not degrees. So in calculus we generally use the set of real numbers or radians as the domain of the trigonometric functions. Since the radian measure of a central angle in the unit circle is the same as the length of the intercepted arc, we also use arcs on the unit circle with initial point (1, 0) and terminal point (x, y) as the domain of the trigonometric functions.

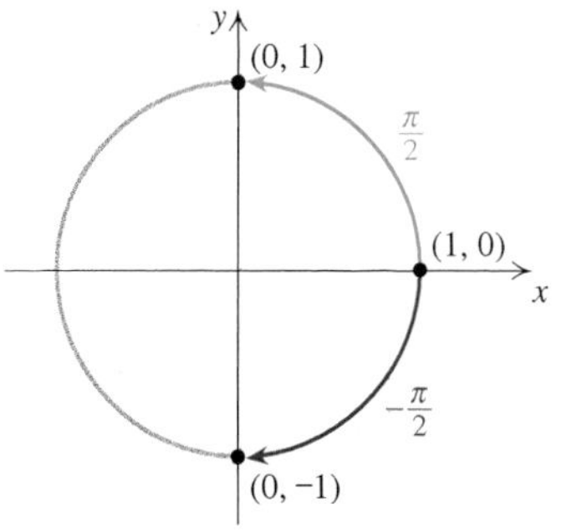

Figure 3.26

Example 4 Sine and cosine of an arc

Find $\sin(\pi/2)$ and $\cos(-\pi/2)$.

Solution

Since the circumference of the unit circle is 2π, an arc of length $\pi/2$ is one-quarter of the circumference. Arcs of length $\pi/2$ and $-\pi/2$ are shown in Fig. 3.26. Since sine is the y-coordinate and cosine is the x-coordinate at the terminal point of an arc, $\sin(\pi/2) = 1$ and $\cos(-\pi/2) = 0$. ■

Approximate Values for Sine and Cosine

The sine and cosine for any angle that is a multiple of 30° or 45° can be found exactly. These angles are so common that it is important to know these exact values. However, for most other angles or real numbers we use approximate values for the sine and cosine, found with the help of a scientific calculator or a graphing calculator. Calculators can evaluate $\sin \alpha$ or $\cos \alpha$ if α is a real number (radian) or α is the degree measure of an angle. Generally, there is a mode key that sets the calculator to degree mode or radian mode. Consult your calculator manual.

Example 5 Evaluating sine and cosine with a calculator

Find each function value rounded to four decimal places.

a. $\sin(4.27)$ **b.** $\cos(-39.46°)$

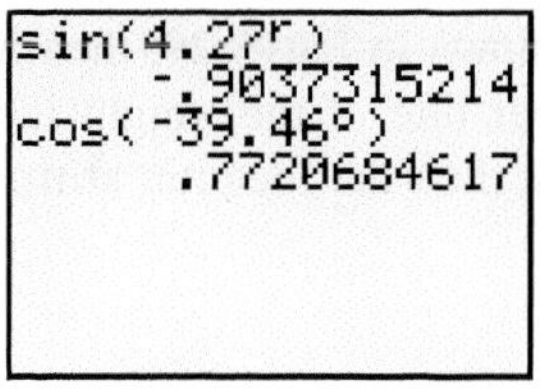

Figure 3.27

Solution

a. With the calculator in radian mode, we get $\sin(4.27) \approx -0.9037$.

b. With the calculator in degree mode, we get $\cos(-39.46°) \approx 0.7721$.

If you use the symbol for radians or degrees, as shown in Fig. 3.27, then it is not necessary to change the mode with a graphing calculator. ■

The Fundamental Identity

An identity is an equation that is satisfied for all values of the variable for which both sides are defined. The most fundamental identity in trigonometry involves the squares of the sine and cosine functions. If α is an angle in standard position, then $\sin \alpha = y$ and $\cos \alpha = x$, where (x, y) is the point of intersection of the terminal side of α and the unit circle. Since every point on the unit circle satisfies the equation $x^2 + y^2 = 1$, we get the following identity.

The Fundamental Identity of Trigonometry

If α is any angle or real number,

$$\sin^2 \alpha + \cos^2 \alpha = 1.$$

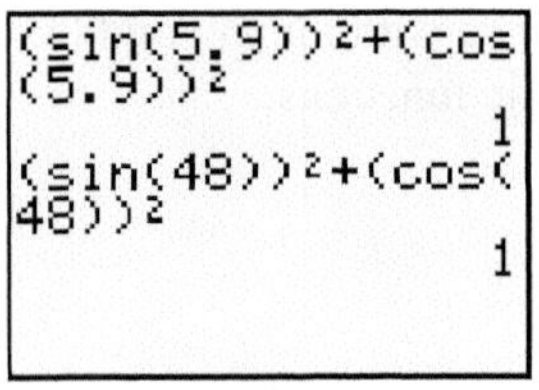

Figure 3.28

The fundamental identity can be illustrated with a graphing calculator as shown in Fig. 3.28. □

If we know the value of the sine or cosine of an angle, then we can use the fundamental identity to find the value of the other function of the angle.

Example 6 Using the fundamental identity

Find $\cos\alpha$, given that $\sin\alpha = 3/5$ and α is an angle in quadrant II.

Solution

Use the fundamental identity $\sin^2\alpha + \cos^2\alpha = 1$ to find $\cos\alpha$:

$$\left(\frac{3}{5}\right)^2 + \cos^2\alpha = 1 \qquad \text{Replace } \sin\alpha \text{ with } 3/5.$$

$$\cos^2\alpha = \frac{16}{25} \qquad 1 - \frac{9}{25} = \frac{16}{25}$$

$$\cos\alpha = \pm\sqrt{\frac{16}{25}} = \pm\frac{4}{5}$$

Since $\cos\alpha < 0$ for any α in quadrant II, we choose the negative sign and get $\cos\alpha = -4/5$. ■

Modeling the Motion of a Spring

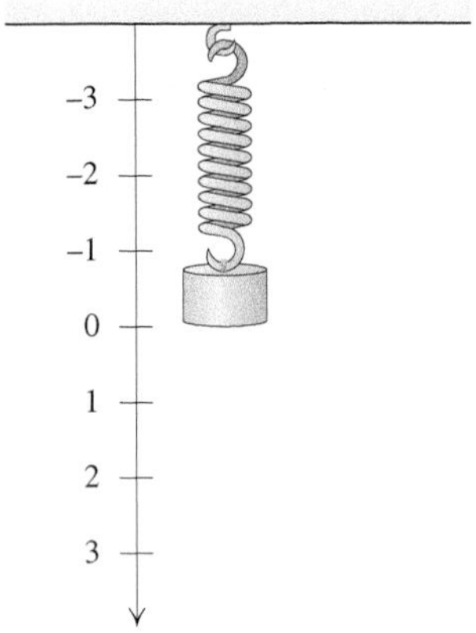

Figure 3.29

The sine and cosine functions are used in modeling the motion of a spring. If a weight is at rest while hanging from a spring, as shown in Fig. 3.29, then it is at the **equilibrium** position, or 0 on a vertical number line. If the weight is set in motion with an initial velocity v_0 from location x_0, then the location at time t is given by

$$x = \frac{v_0}{\omega}\sin(\omega t) + x_0\cos(\omega t).$$

The letter ω (omega) is a constant that depends on the stiffness of the spring and the amount of weight on the spring. For positive values of x the weight is below equilibrium, and for negative values it is above equilibrium. The initial velocity is considered to be positive if it is in the downward direction and negative if it is upward. Note that the domain of the sine and cosine functions in this formula is the nonnegative real numbers, and this application has nothing to do with angles.

Example 7 Motion of a spring

A weight on a certain spring is set in motion with an upward velocity of 3 centimeters per second from a position 2 centimeters below equilibrium. Assume that for this spring and weight combination the constant ω has a value of 1. Write a formula that gives the location of the weight in centimeters as a function of the time t in seconds, and find the location of the weight 2 seconds after the weight is set in motion.

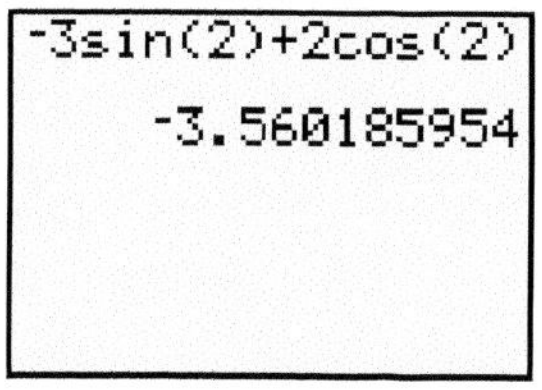

Figure 3.30

Solution

Since upward velocity is negative and locations below equilibrium are positive, use $v_0 = -3$, $x_0 = 2$, and $\omega = 1$ in the formula for the motion of a spring:

$$x = -3\sin t + 2\cos t$$

If $t = 2$ seconds, then $x = -3\sin(2) + 2\cos(2) \approx -3.6$ centimeters, which is 3.6 centimeters above the equilibrium position.

Figure 3.30 shows the calculation for x with a graphing calculator in radian mode. ■

For Thought

True or False? Explain.

1. $\cos(90°) = 1$
2. $\cos(90) = 0$
3. $\sin(45°) = 1/\sqrt{2}$
4. $\sin(-\pi/3) = \sin(\pi/3)$
5. $\cos(-\pi/3) = -\cos(\pi/3)$
6. $\sin(390°) = \sin(30°)$
7. If $\sin(\alpha) < 0$ and $\cos(\alpha) > 0$, then α is an angle in quadrant III.
8. If $\sin^2(\alpha) = 1/4$ and α is in quadrant III, then $\sin(\alpha) = 1/2$.
9. If $\cos^2(\alpha) = 3/4$ and α is an angle in quadrant I, then $\alpha = \pi/6$.
10. For any angle α, $\cos^2(\alpha) = (1 - \sin(\alpha))(1 + \sin(\alpha))$.

3.2 Exercises

Redraw each diagram and label the indicated points with the proper coordinates. Exercise 1 shows the points where the terminal side of every multiple of 45° intersects the unit circle. Exercise 2 shows the points where the terminal side of every multiple of 30° intersects the unit circle. Repeat Exercises 1 and 2 until you can do them from memory.

1.

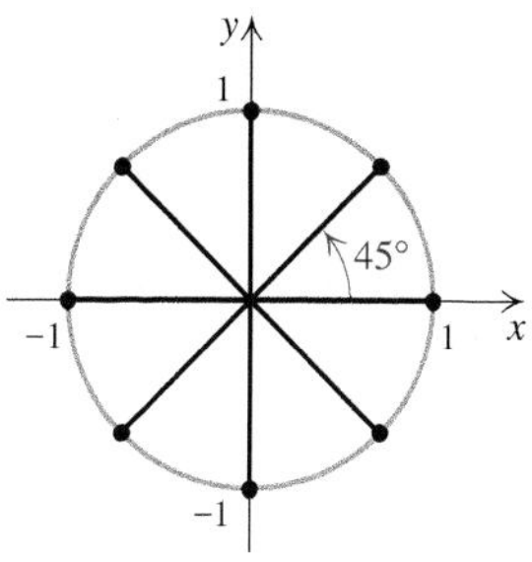

2.

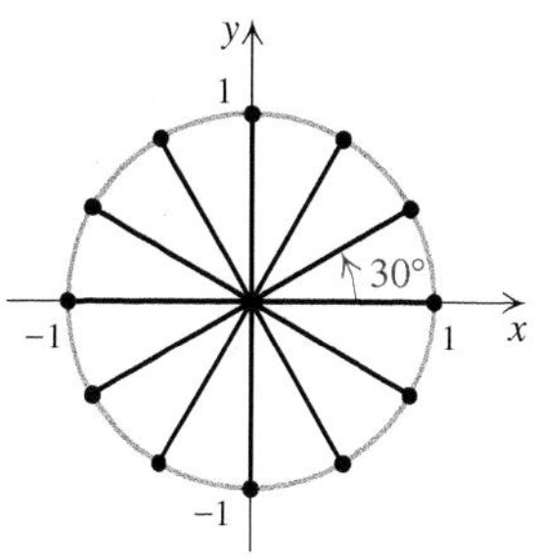

Use the diagrams drawn in Exercises 1 and 2 to help you find the exact value of each function. Do not use a calculator.

3. $\sin(0)$	**4.** $\cos(\pi)$	**5.** $\cos(-90°)$
6. $\sin(0°)$	**7.** $\sin(2\pi)$	**8.** $\cos(-\pi)$
9. $\cos(3\pi/2)$	**10.** $\sin(-5\pi/2)$	**11.** $\sin(135°)$
12. $\cos(-135°)$	**13.** $\sin(-\pi/4)$	**14.** $\sin(3\pi/4)$
15. $\sin(30°)$	**16.** $\sin(120°)$	**17.** $\cos(-60°)$
18. $\cos(-120°)$	**19.** $\cos(7\pi/6)$	**20.** $\cos(-2\pi/3)$
21. $\sin(-4\pi/3)$	**22.** $\sin(5\pi/6)$	**23.** $\sin(390°)$
24. $\sin(765°)$	**25.** $\cos(-420°)$	**26.** $\cos(-450°)$
27. $\cos(13\pi/6)$	**28.** $\cos(-7\pi/3)$	

Evaluate the trigonometric functions for the given arc lengths on the unit circle.

29. $\sin(\pi/4)$ **30.** $\sin(-\pi/4)$ **31.** $\cos(-\pi)$

32. $\cos(\pi)$ **33.** $\sin(\pi/3)$ **34.** $\sin(\pi/6)$

35. $\cos(-\pi/3)$ **36.** $\cos(-\pi/6)$

Find the exact value of each expression without using a calculator. Check your answer with a calculator.

37. $\dfrac{\cos(\pi/3)}{\sin(\pi/3)}$ **38.** $\dfrac{\sin(-5\pi/6)}{\cos(-5\pi/6)}$

39. $\dfrac{\sin(7\pi/4)}{\cos(7\pi/4)}$ **40.** $\dfrac{\sin(-3\pi/4)}{\cos(-3\pi/4)}$

41. $\sin\left(\dfrac{\pi}{3}+\dfrac{\pi}{6}\right)$ **42.** $\cos\left(\dfrac{\pi}{3}-\dfrac{\pi}{6}\right)$

43. $\dfrac{1-\cos(5\pi/6)}{\sin(5\pi/6)}$ **44.** $\dfrac{\sin(5\pi/6)}{1+\cos(5\pi/6)}$

45. $\sin(\pi/4)+\cos(\pi/4)$ **46.** $\sin^2(\pi/6)+\cos^2(\pi/6)$

Determine whether each of the following expressions is positive (+) or negative (−) without using a calculator.

47. $\sin(121°)$ **48.** $\cos(157°)$ **49.** $\cos(359°)$

50. $\sin(213°)$ **51.** $\sin(7\pi/6)$ **52.** $\cos(7\pi/3)$

53. $\cos(-3\pi/4)$ **54.** $\sin(-7\pi/4)$

Use a calculator to find the value of each function. Round answers to four decimal places.

55. $\cos(-359.4°)$ **56.** $\sin(344.1°)$

57. $\sin(23°48')$ **58.** $\cos(49°13')$

59. $\sin(-48°3'12'')$ **60.** $\cos(-9°4'7'')$

61. $\sin(1.57)$ **62.** $\cos(3.14)$

63. $\cos(7\pi/12)$ **64.** $\sin(-13\pi/8)$

Find the exact value of each expression for the given value of θ. Do not use a calculator.

65. $\sin(2\theta)$ if $\theta=\pi/4$

66. $\sin(2\theta)$ if $\theta=\pi/6$

67. $\cos(2\theta)$ if $\theta=\pi/6$

68. $\cos(2\theta)$ if $\theta=\pi/3$

69. $\sin(\theta/2)$ if $\theta=3\pi/2$

70. $\sin(\theta/2)$ if $\theta=2\pi/3$

71. $\cos(\theta/2)$ if $\theta=\pi/3$

72. $\cos(\theta/2)$ if $\theta=\pi/2$

Solve each problem.

73. Find $\cos(\alpha)$, given that $\sin(\alpha)=5/13$ and α is in quadrant II.

74. Find $\sin(\alpha)$, given that $\cos(\alpha)=-4/5$ and α is in quadrant III.

75. Find $\sin(\alpha)$, given that $\cos(\alpha)=3/5$ and α is in quadrant IV.

76. Find $\cos(\alpha)$, given that $\sin(\alpha)=-12/13$ and α is in quadrant IV.

77. Find $\cos(\alpha)$, given that $\sin(\alpha)=1/3$ and $\cos(\alpha)>0$.

78. Find $\sin(\alpha)$, given that $\cos(\alpha)=2/5$ and $\sin(\alpha)<0$.

Solve each problem.

79. *Motion of a Spring* A weight on a vertical spring is given an initial downward velocity of 4 cm/sec from a point 3 cm above equilibrium. Assuming that the constant ω has a value of 1, write the formula for the location of the weight at time t, and find its location 3 sec after it is set in motion.

80. *Motion of a Spring* A weight on a vertical spring is given an initial upward velocity of 3 in./sec from a point 1 in. below equilibrium. Assuming that the constant ω has a value of $\sqrt{3}$, write the formula for the location of the weight at time t, and find its location 2 sec after it is set in motion.

81. *Spacing Between Teeth* The length of an arc intercepted by a central angle of θ radians in a circle of radius r is $r\theta$. The length of the chord, c, joining the endpoints of that arc is given by $c=r\sqrt{2-2\cos\theta}$. Find the actual distance between the tips of two adjacent teeth on a 12-in.-diameter carbide-tipped circular saw blade with 22 equally spaced teeth. Compare your answer with the length of a circular arc joining two adjacent teeth on a circle 12 in. in diameter. Round to three decimal places.

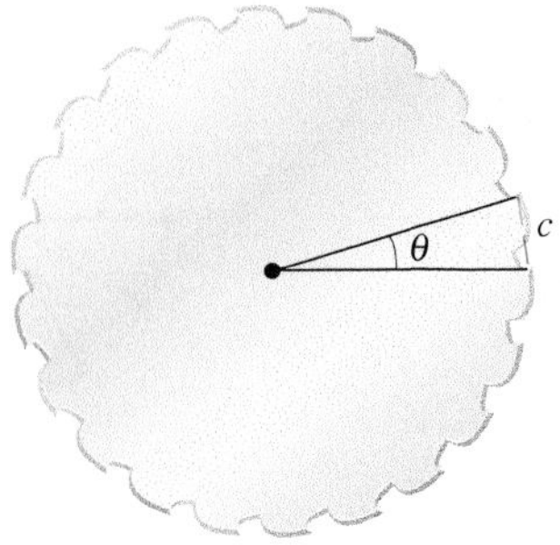

Figure for Exercise 81

82. *Throwing a Javelin* The formula

$$d = \frac{1}{32} v_0^2 \sin(2\theta)$$

gives the distance d in feet that a projectile will travel when its launch angle is θ and its initial velocity is v_0 feet per second. Approximately what initial velocity in miles per hour does it take to throw a javelin 367 feet with launch angle 43°, which is a typical launch angle (www.canthrow.com)?

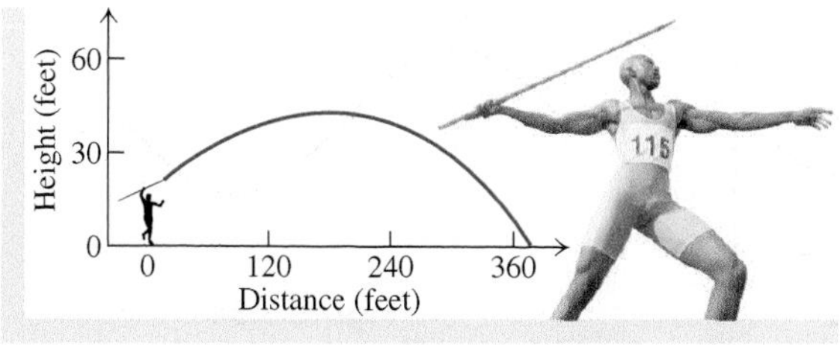

Figure for Exercise 82

Thinking Outside the Box XX

Telling Time At 12 noon the hour hand, minute hand, and second hand of a clock are all pointing straight upward.

a. Find the first time after 12 noon to the nearest tenth of a second at which the angle between the hour hand and minute hand is 120°.

b. Is there a time between 12 noon and 1 P.M. at which the three hands divide the face of the clock into thirds (that is, the angles between the hour hand, minute hand, and second hand are equal and each is 120°)?

c. Does the alignment of the three hands described in part (b) ever occur?

3.2 Pop Quiz

Find the exact value.

1. $\sin(0°)$

2. $\sin(-60°)$

3. $\sin(3\pi/4)$

4. $\cos(90°)$

5. $\cos(-2\pi/3)$

6. $\cos(11\pi/6)$

7. $\sin(\alpha)$, if $\cos(\alpha) = -3/5$ and α is in quadrant III

3.3 The Graphs of the Sine and Cosine Functions

In Section 3.2 we studied the sine and cosine functions. In this section we will study their graphs. The graphs of trigonometric functions are important for understanding their use in modeling physical phenomena such as radio, sound, and light waves, and the motion of a spring or a pendulum.

The Graph of $y = \sin(x)$

Until now, s or α has been used as the independent variable in writing $\sin(s)$ or $\sin(\alpha)$. When graphing functions in an xy-coordinate system, it is customary to use x as the independent variable and y as the dependent variable, as in $y = \sin(x)$. We assume that x is a real number or radian measure unless it is stated that x is the degree measure of an angle. We often omit the parentheses and write $\sin x$ for $\sin(x)$.

Consider some ordered pairs that satisfy $y = \sin x$ for x in $[0, 2\pi]$, as shown in Fig. 3.31. These ordered pairs are best understood by recalling that $\sin x$ is the second coordinate of the terminal point on the unit circle for an arc of length x, as

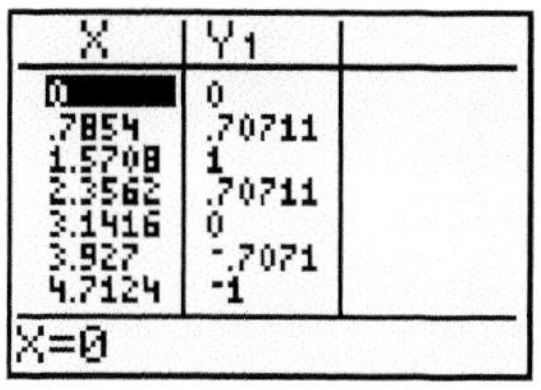

X	Y1
0	0
.7854	.70711
1.5708	1
2.3562	.70711
3.1416	0
3.927	-.7071
4.7124	-1

X=0

Figure 3.31

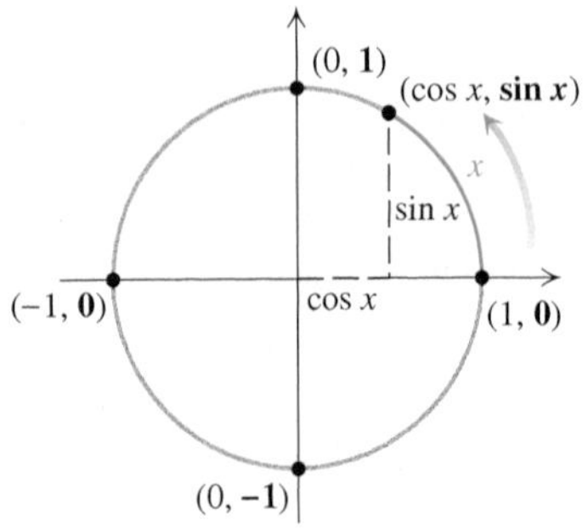

Figure 3.32

shown in Fig. 3.32. As the arc length x increases from length 0 to $\pi/2$, the second coordinate of the endpoint increases to 1. As the length of x increases from $\pi/2$ to π, the second coordinate of the endpoint decreases to 0. As the arc length x increases from π to 2π, the second coordinate decreases to -1 and then increases to 0. The calculator graph in Fig. 3.33 shows 95 accurately plotted points on the graph of $y = \sin(x)$ between 0 and 2π. The actual graph of $y = \sin(x)$ is a smooth curve through those 95 points, as shown in Fig. 3.34.

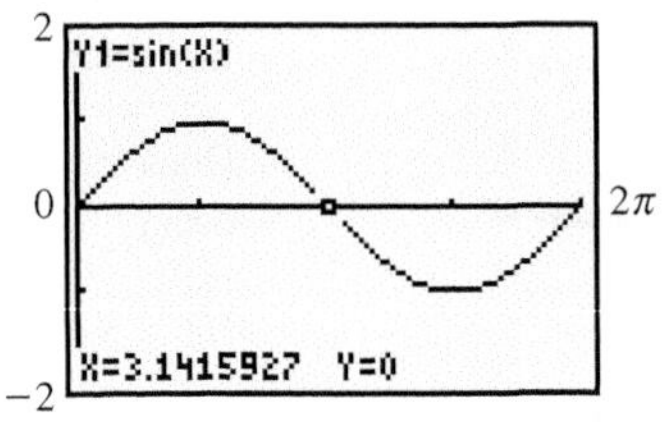

Figure 3.33

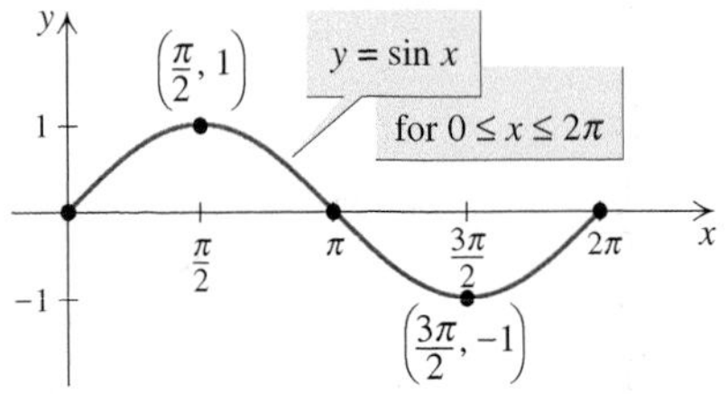

Figure 3.34

Since the x-intercepts and the maximum and minimum values of the function occur at multiples of π, we usually label the x-axis with multiples of π, as in Fig. 3.34. There are five key points on the graph of $y = \sin x$ between 0 and 2π. Their exact coordinates are given in the following table.

x	0	$\pi/2$	π	$3\pi/2$	2π
$y = \sin x$	0	1	0	-1	0

Note that these five points divide the interval $[0, 2\pi]$ into four equal parts.

Since the domain of $y = \sin x$ is the set of all real numbers (or radian measures of angles), we must consider values of x outside the interval $[0, 2\pi]$. As x increases from 2π to 4π, the values of $\sin x$ again increase from 0 to 1, decrease to -1, then increase to 0. Because $\sin(x + 2\pi) = \sin x$, the exact shape that we saw in Fig. 3.34 is repeated for x in intervals such as $[2\pi, 4\pi]$, $[-2\pi, 0]$, $[-4\pi, -2\pi]$, and so on. So the curve shown in Fig. 3.35 continues indefinitely to the left and right. The range of $y = \sin x$ is $[-1, 1]$. The graph $y = \sin x$ or any transformation of $y = \sin x$ is called a **sine wave,** a **sinusoidal wave,** or a **sinusoid.**

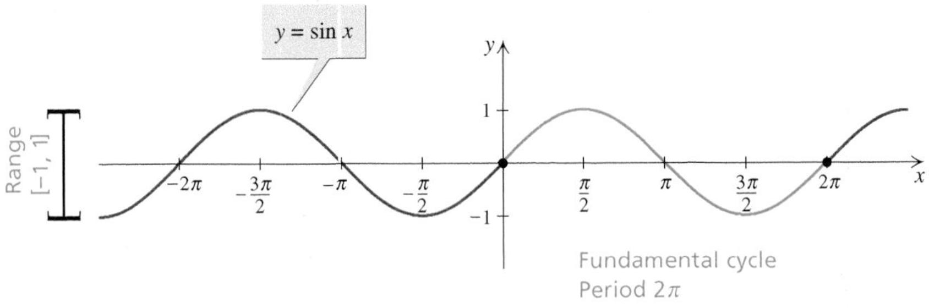

Figure 3.35

Since the shape of $y = \sin x$ for x in $[0, 2\pi]$ is repeated infinitely often, $y = \sin x$ is called a *periodic function.*

Definition: Periodic Function

If $y = f(x)$ is a function and a is a nonzero constant such that $f(x) = f(x + a)$ for every x in the domain of f, then f is called a **periodic function.** The smallest such positive constant a is the **period** of the function.

For the sine function, the smallest value of a such that $\sin x = \sin(x + a)$ is $a = 2\pi$, and so the period of $y = \sin x$ is 2π. To prove that 2π is actually the *smallest* value of a for which $\sin x = \sin(x + a)$ is a bit complicated, and we will omit the proof. The graph of $y = \sin x$ over any interval of length 2π is called a **cycle** of the sine wave. The graph of $y = \sin x$ over $[0, 2\pi]$ is called the **fundamental cycle** of $y = \sin x$.

Example 1 Graphing a periodic function

Sketch the graph of $y = 2\sin x$ for x in the interval $[-2\pi, 2\pi]$.

Solution

We can obtain the graph of $y = 2\sin x$ from the graph of $y = \sin x$ by stretching the graph of $y = \sin x$ by a factor of 2. In other words, double the y-coordinates of the five key points on the graph of $y = \sin x$ to obtain five key points on the graph of $y = 2\sin x$ for the interval $[0, 2\pi]$, as shown in the following table.

x	0	$\pi/2$	π	$3\pi/2$	2π
$y = 2\sin x$	0	2	0	-2	0

The x-intercepts for $y = 2\sin x$ on $[0, 2\pi]$ are $(0, 0)$, $(\pi, 0)$ and $(2\pi, 0)$. Midway between the intercepts are found the highest point $(\pi/2, 2)$ and the lowest point $(3\pi/2, -2)$. Draw one cycle of $y = 2\sin x$ through these five points, as shown in Fig. 3.36. Draw another cycle of the sine wave for x in $[-2\pi, 0]$ to complete the graph of $y = 2\sin x$ for x in $[-2\pi, 2\pi]$.

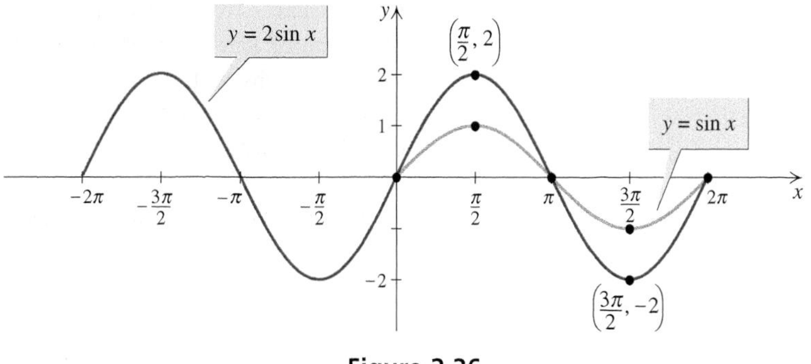

Figure 3.36

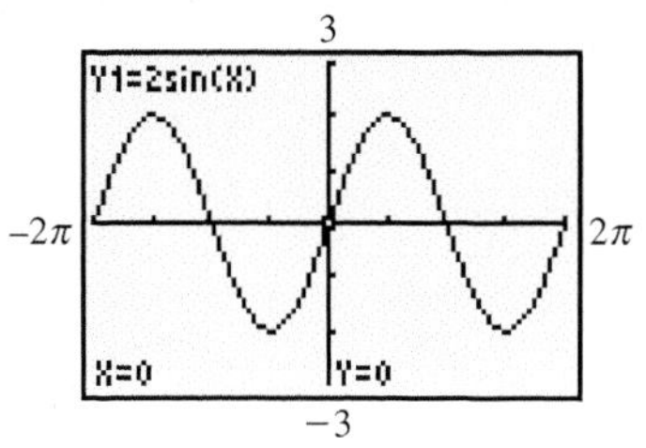

Figure 3.37

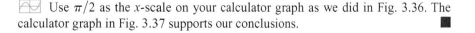

Use $\pi/2$ as the x-scale on your calculator graph as we did in Fig. 3.36. The calculator graph in Fig. 3.37 supports our conclusions. ■

The amplitude of a sine wave is a measure of the "height" of the wave. When an oscilloscope is used to get a picture of the sine wave corresponding to a sound, the amplitude of the sine wave corresponds to the intensity or loudness of the sound.

Definition: Amplitude

The **amplitude** of a sine wave, or the amplitude of the function, is the absolute value of half the difference between the maximum and minimum y-coordinates on the wave.

Example 2 Finding amplitude

Find the amplitude of the functions $y = \sin x$ and $y = 2 \sin x$.

Solution

For $y = \sin x$, the maximum y-coordinate is 1 and the minimum is -1. So the amplitude is

$$\left|\frac{1}{2}[1 - (-1)]\right| = 1.$$

For $y = 2 \sin x$, the maximum y-coordinate is 2 and the minimum is -2. So the amplitude is

$$\left|\frac{1}{2}[2 - (-2)]\right| = 2.$$

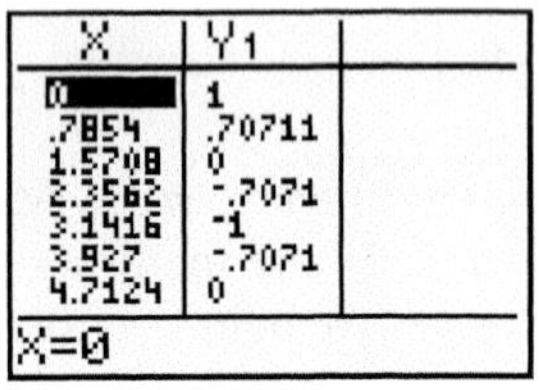

X	Y1
0	1
.7854	.70711
1.5708	0
2.3562	-.7071
3.1416	-1
3.927	-.7071
4.7124	0

X=0

Figure 3.38

The Graph of $y = \cos(x)$

The graph of $y = \cos x$ is best understood by recalling that $\cos x$ is the first coordinate of the terminal point on the unit circle for an arc of length x, as shown in Fig. 3.32. As the arc length x increases from length 0 to $\pi/2$, the first coordinate of the endpoint decreases from 1 to 0. Some ordered pairs that satisfy $y = \cos x$ are shown in Fig. 3.38. As the length of x increases from $\pi/2$ to π, the first coordinate decreases from 0 to -1. As the length increases from π to 2π, the first coordinate increases from -1 to 1. The graph of $y = \cos x$ has exactly the same shape as the graph of $y = \sin x$. If the graph of $y = \sin x$ is shifted a distance of $\pi/2$ to the left, the graphs would coincide. For this reason the graph of $y = \cos x$ is also called a sine wave with amplitude 1 and period 2π. The graph of $y = \cos x$ over $[0, 2\pi]$ is called the **fundamental cycle** of $y = \cos x$. Since $\cos x = \cos(x + 2\pi)$, the fundamental cycle of $y = \cos x$ is repeated on $[2\pi, 4\pi]$, $[-2\pi, 0]$, and so on. The graph of $y = \cos x$ is shown in Fig. 3.39.

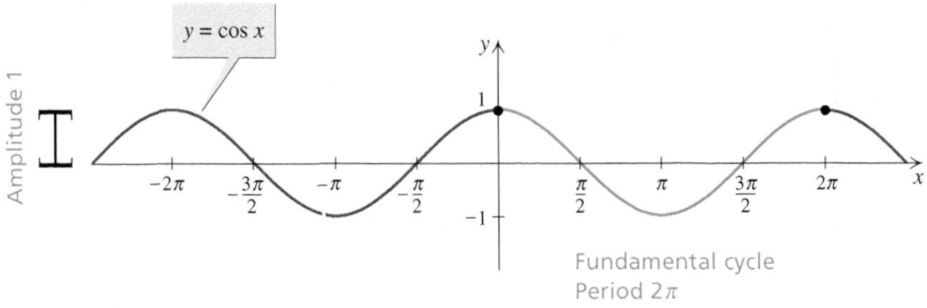

Figure 3.39

Note that there are five key points on the graph of $y = \cos x$ between 0 and 2π. These points give us the highest and lowest points in the cycle as well as the x-intercepts. The exact coordinates are given in the following table.

x	0	$\pi/2$	π	$3\pi/2$	2π
$y = \cos x$	1	0	-1	0	1

These five points divide the fundamental cycle into four equal parts.

Example 3 Graphing another periodic function

Sketch the graph of $y = -3\cos x$ for x in the interval $[-2\pi, 2\pi]$ and find its amplitude.

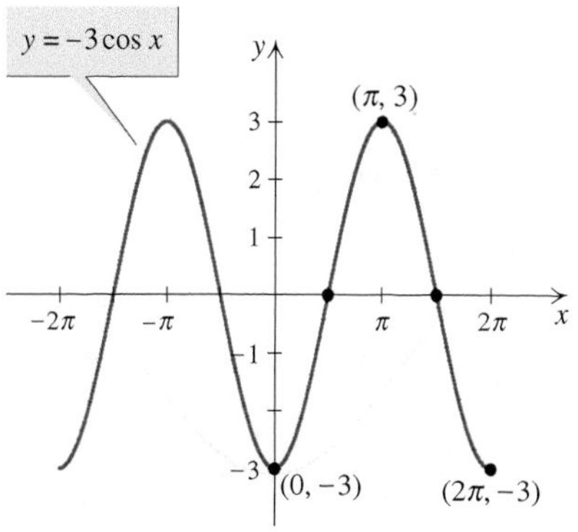

Figure 3.40

Solution

Make a table of ordered pairs for x in $[0, 2\pi]$ to get one cycle of the graph. Note that the five x-coordinates in the table divide the interval $[0, 2\pi]$ into four equal parts. Multiply the y-coordinates of $y = \cos x$ by -3 to obtain the y-coordinates for $y = -3\cos x$.

x	0	$\pi/2$	π	$3\pi/2$	2π
$y = -3\cos x$	-3	0	3	0	-3

Draw one cycle of $y = -3\cos x$ through these five points, as shown in Fig. 3.40. Repeat the same shape for x in the interval $[-2\pi, 0]$ to get the graph of $y = -3\cos x$ for x in $[-2\pi, 2\pi]$. The amplitude is $|0.5(3 - (-3))|$ or 3. ■

Transformations of Sine and Cosine

In Section 1.7 we discussed how various changes in a formula affect the graph of the function. We know the changes that cause horizontal or vertical translations, reflections, and stretching or shrinking. The graph of $y = 2\sin x$ from Example 1 can be obtained by stretching the graph of $y = \sin x$. The graph of $y = -3\cos x$ in Example 3 can be obtained by stretching and reflecting the graph of $y = \cos x$. The amplitude of $y = 2\sin x$ is 2 and the amplitude of $y = -3\sin x$ is 3. In general, the amplitude is determined by the coefficient of the sine or cosine function.

Theorem: Amplitude

The amplitude of $y = A\sin x$ or $y = A\cos x$ is $|A|$.

In Section 1.7 we saw that the graph of $y = f(x - C)$ is a horizontal translation of the graph of $y = f(x)$, to the right if $C > 0$ and to the left if $C < 0$. So the graphs of $y = \sin(x - C)$ and $y = \cos(x - C)$ are horizontal translations of $y = \sin x$ and $y = \cos x$, respectively, to the right if $C > 0$ and to the left if $C < 0$.

Definition: Phase Shift

The **phase shift** of the graph of $y = \sin(x - C)$ or $y = \cos(x - C)$ is C.

Example 4 Horizontal translation

Graph two cycles of $y = \sin(x + \pi/6)$, and determine the phase shift of the graph.

Solution

Since $x + \pi/6 = x - (-\pi/6)$ and $C < 0$, the graph of $y = \sin(x + \pi/6)$ is obtained by moving $y = \sin x$ a distance of $\pi/6$ to the left. Since the phase shift is $-\pi/6$, label the x-axis with multiples of $\pi/6$, as shown in Fig. 3.41. Concentrate on moving the fundamental cycle of $y = \sin x$. The three x-intercepts $(0, 0)$, $(\pi, 0)$, and $(2\pi, 0)$ move to $(-\pi/6, 0)$, $(5\pi/6, 0)$ and $(11\pi/6, 0)$. The high and low points, $(\pi/2, 1)$ and $(3\pi/2, -1)$, move to $(\pi/3, 1)$ and $(4\pi/3, -1)$. Draw one cycle through these five points and continue the pattern for another cycle, as shown in Fig. 3.41. The second cycle could be drawn to the right or left of the first cycle.

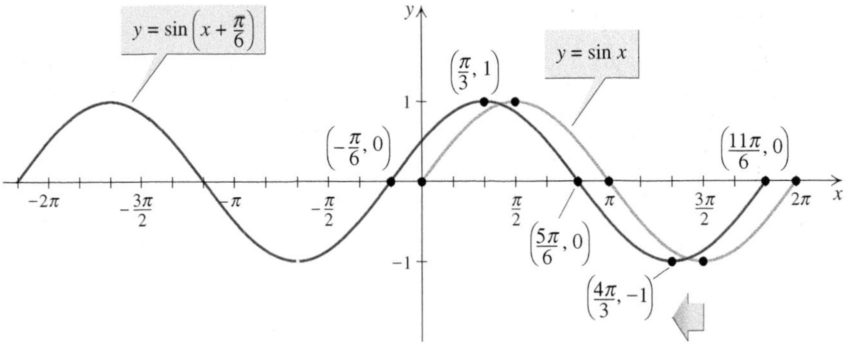

Figure 3.41

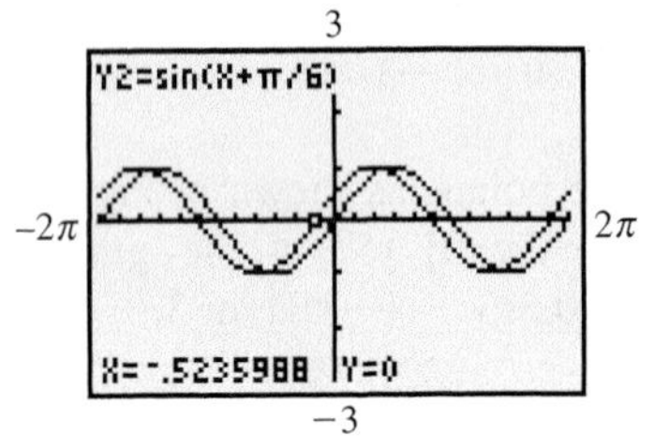

Figure 3.42

Use $\pi/6$ as the x-scale on your calculator graph as we did in Fig. 3.41. The calculator graph in Fig. 3.42 supports the conclusion that $y_2 = \sin(x + \pi/6)$ has shifted $\pi/6$ to the left of $y_1 = \sin(x)$. ■

The graphs of $y = \sin(x) + D$ and $y = \cos(x) + D$ are vertical translations of $y = \sin x$ and $y = \cos x$, respectively. The translation is upward for $D > 0$ and downward for $D < 0$. The next example combines a phase shift and a vertical translation. Note how we follow the five basic points of the fundamental cycle to see where they go in the transformation.

Example 5 Horizontal and vertical translation

Graph two cycles of $y = \cos(x - \pi/4) + 2$, and determine the phase shift of the graph.

Solution

The graph of $y = \cos(x - \pi/4) + 2$ is obtained by moving $y = \cos x$ a distance of $\pi/4$ to the right and two units upward. Since the phase shift is $\pi/4$, label the x-axis with multiples of $\pi/4$, as shown in Fig. 3.43. Concentrate on moving the fundamental cycle of $y = \cos x$. The points $(0, 1)$, $(\pi, -1)$, and $(2\pi, 1)$ move to $(\pi/4, 3)$, $(5\pi/4, 1)$, and $(9\pi/4, 3)$. The x-intercepts $(\pi/2, 0)$ and $(3\pi/2, 0)$ move to $(3\pi/4, 2)$ and $(7\pi/4, 2)$. Draw one cycle through these five points and continue the pattern for another cycle, as shown in Fig. 3.43.

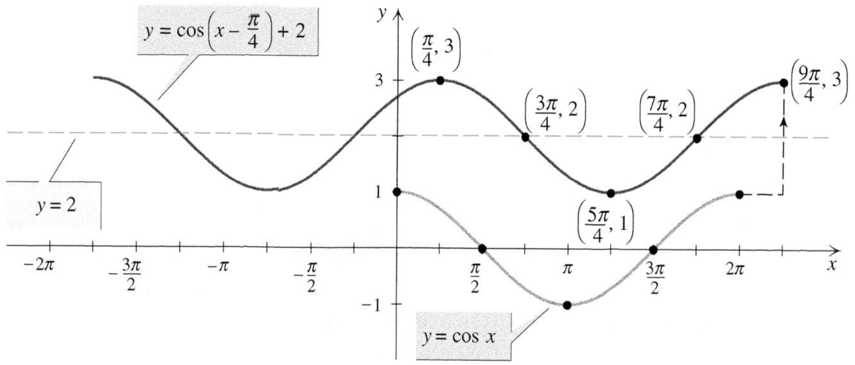

Figure 3.43

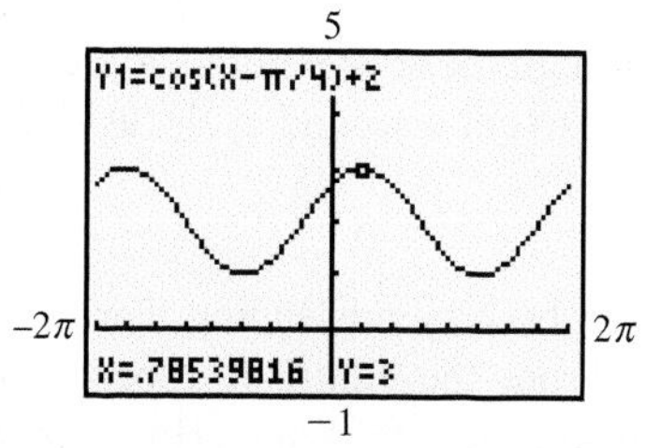

Figure 3.44

Use $\pi/4$ as the x-scale on your calculator graph as we did in Fig. 3.43. The calculator graph in Fig. 3.44 supports the conclusion that the shift is $\pi/4$ to the right and two units upward. ■

Changing the Period

We can alter the sine and cosine functions in a way that we did not alter the functions of algebra in Chapter 1. The period of a periodic function can be changed by replacing x by a multiple of x.

Example 6 Changing the period

Graph two cycles of $y = \sin(2x)$ and determine the period of the function.

Solution

The graph of $y = \sin x$ completes its fundamental cycle for $0 \le x \le 2\pi$. So $y = \sin(2x)$ completes one cycle for $0 \le 2x \le 2\pi$, or $0 \le x \le \pi$. So the period is π. For $0 \le x \le \pi$, the x-intercepts are $(0, 0)$, $(\pi/2, 0)$, and $(\pi, 0)$. Midway between 0 and $\pi/2$, at $x = \pi/4$, the function reaches a maximum value of 1, and the function attains its minimum value of -1 at $x = 3\pi/4$. Draw one cycle of the graph through the x-intercepts and through $(\pi/4, 1)$ and $(3\pi/4, -1)$. Then graph another cycle of $y = \sin(2x)$ as shown in Fig. 3.45. ■

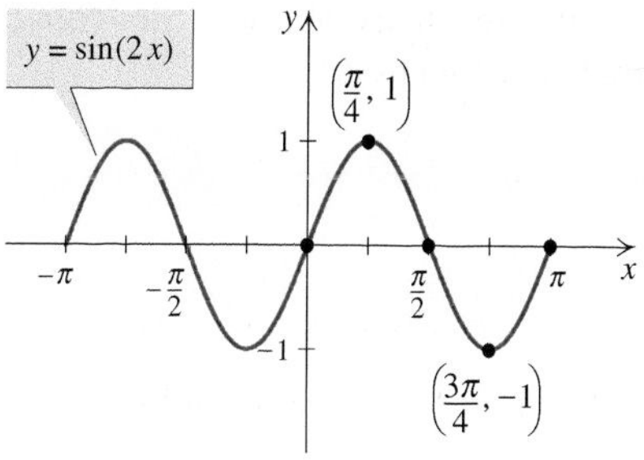

Figure 3.45

Note that in Example 6 the period of $y = \sin(2x)$ is the period of $y = \sin x$ divided by 2. In general, one complete cycle of $y = \sin(Bx)$ or $y = \cos(Bx)$ for $B > 0$ occurs for $0 \le Bx \le 2\pi$, or $0 \le x \le 2\pi/B$.

Theorem: Period of $y = \sin(Bx)$ and $y = \cos(Bx)$

The period P of $y = \sin(Bx)$ and $y = \cos(Bx)$ is given by

$$P = \frac{2\pi}{B}.$$

Note that the period is a natural number (that is, not a multiple of π) when B is a multiple of π.

Example 7 A period that is not a multiple of π

Determine the period of $y = \cos\left(\frac{\pi}{2}x\right)$ and graph two cycles of the function.

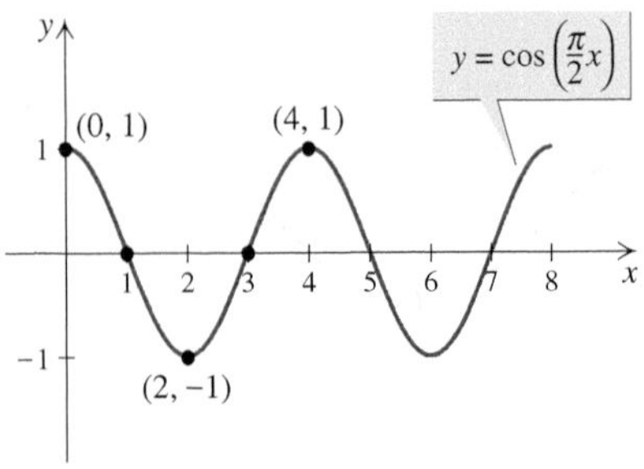

Figure 3.46

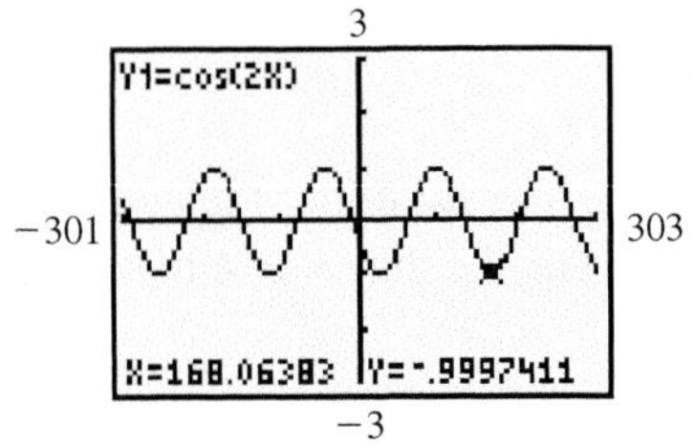

Figure 3.47

Solution

For this function, $B = \pi/2$. To find the period, use $P = 2\pi/B$:

$$P = \frac{2\pi}{\pi/2} = 4$$

So one cycle of $y = \cos\left(\frac{\pi}{2}x\right)$ is completed for $0 \le x \le 4$. The cycle starts at (0, 1) and ends at (4, 1). A minimum point occurs halfway in between, at (2, −1). The x-intercepts are (1, 0) and (3, 0). Draw a curve through these five points to get one cycle of the graph. Continue this pattern from 4 to 8 to get a second cycle, as shown in Fig. 3.46. ■

A calculator graph for a periodic function can be very misleading. For example, consider $y = \cos(2x)$, shown in Fig. 3.47. From the figure it appears that $y = \cos(2x)$ has a period of about 150 and is a left shift of $y = \cos(x)$. However, we know that the period is π and that there is no shift. What we see in Fig. 3.47 is the pattern formed by choosing 95 equally spaced points on the graph of $y = \cos(2x)$. Equally spaced points on the graph of a periodic function will usually have some kind of pattern, but the pattern may not be a good graph of the function. Because x ranges from −301 to 303 in Fig. 3.47, the spaces between these points are approximately 6 units each, which is enough for about two cycles of $y = \cos(2x)$. So the viewing window is much too large to show the relatively small features of $y = \cos(2x)$. □

The General Sine Wave

We can use any combination of translating, reflecting, phase shifting, stretching, shrinking, or period changing in a single trigonometric function.

The General Sine Wave

The graph of

$$y = A\sin[B(x - C)] + D \qquad \text{or} \qquad y = A\cos[B(x - C)] + D$$

is a sine wave with an amplitude $|A|$, period $2\pi/B$ $(B > 0)$, phase shift C, and vertical translation D.

We assume that $B > 0$, because any general sine or cosine function can be rewritten with $B > 0$ using identities from Section 3.7. Notice that A and B affect the shape of the curve, while C and D determine its location.

PROCEDURE

Graphing a Sine Wave

To graph $y = A\sin[B(x - C)] + D$ or $y = A\cos[B(x - C)] + D$:

1. Sketch one cycle of $y = \sin Bx$ or $y = \cos Bx$ on $[0, 2\pi/B]$.
2. Change the amplitude of the cycle according to the value of A.
3. If $A < 0$, reflect the curve in the x-axis.
4. Translate the cycle $|C|$ units to the right if $C > 0$ or to the left if $C < 0$.
5. Translate the cycle $|D|$ units upward if $D > 0$ or downward if $D < 0$.

Example 8 A transformation of $y = \sin(x)$

Determine amplitude, period, and phase shift, and sketch two cycles of $y = 2\sin(3x + \pi) + 1$.

Solution

First we rewrite the function in the form $y = A\sin[B(x - C)] + D$ by factoring 3 out of $3x + \pi$:

$$y = 2\sin\left[3\left(x + \frac{\pi}{3}\right)\right] + 1$$

From this equation we get $A = 2$, $B = 3$, and $C = -\pi/3$. So the amplitude is 2, the period is $2\pi/3$, and the phase shift is $-\pi/3$. The period change causes the fundamental cycle of $y = \sin x$ on $[0, 2\pi]$ to shrink to the interval $[0, 2\pi/3]$. Now draw one cycle of $y = \sin 3x$ on $[0, 2\pi/3]$, as shown in Fig. 3.48. Stretch the cycle vertically so that it has an amplitude of 2. The numbers $\pi/3$ and 1 shift the cycle a distance of $\pi/3$ to the left and up one unit. So one cycle of the function occurs on $[-\pi/3, \pi/3]$. Check by evaluating the function at the endpoints and midpoint of the interval $[-\pi/3, \pi/3]$ to get $(-\pi/3, 1)$, $(0, 1)$, and $(\pi/3, 1)$. Since the graph is shifted one unit upward, these points are the points where the curve intersects the line $y = 1$. Evaluate the function midway between these points to get $(-\pi/6, 3)$ and $(\pi/6, -1)$, the highest and lowest points of this cycle. One cycle is drawn through these five points and continued for another cycle, as shown in Fig. 3.48.

The calculator graph in Fig. 3.49 supports our conclusions about amplitude, period, and phase shift. Note that it is easier to obtain the amplitude, period, and phase shift from the equation than from the calculator graph.

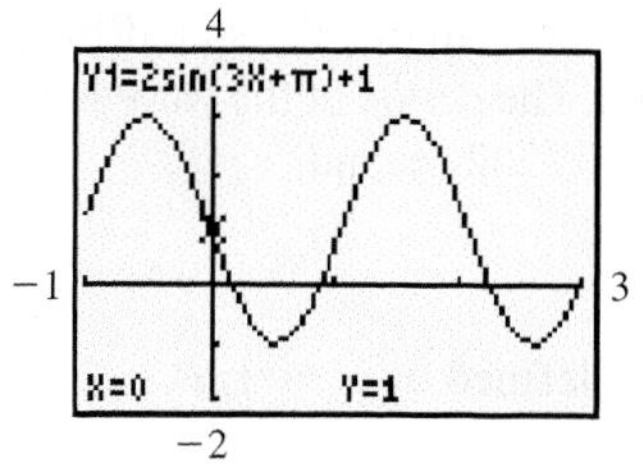

Figure 3.49

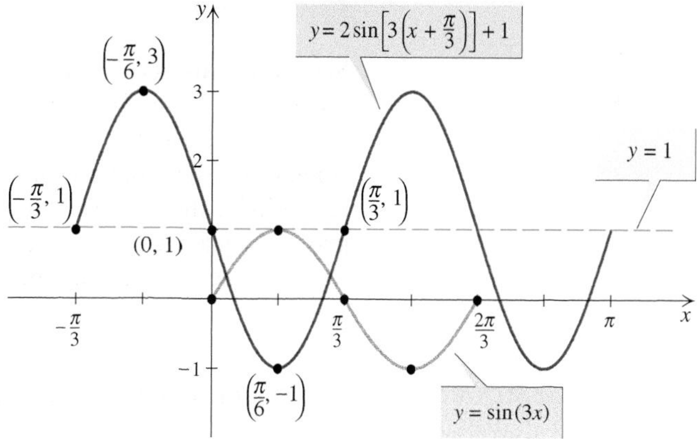

Figure 3.48

Example 9 A transformation of $y = \cos(x)$

Determine amplitude, period, and phase shift, and sketch one cycle of $y = -3\cos(2x - \pi) - 1$.

Solution

Rewrite the function in the general form as

$$y = -3\cos[2(x - \pi/2)] - 1.$$

The amplitude is 3. Since the period is $2\pi/B$, the period is $2\pi/2$ or π. The fundamental cycle is shrunk to the interval $[0, \pi]$. Sketch one cycle of $y = \cos 2x$ on $[0, \pi]$, as shown in Fig. 3.50. This cycle is reflected in the x-axis and stretched by a factor of 3. A shift of $\pi/2$ to the right means that one cycle of the original function occurs for $\pi/2 \le x \le 3\pi/2$. Evaluate the function at the endpoints and midpoint of the interval $[\pi/2, 3\pi/2]$ to get $(\pi/2, -4)$, $(\pi, 2)$, and $(3\pi/2, -4)$ for the endpoints and midpoint of this cycle. Since the graph is translated downward one unit, midway between these maximum and minimum points we get points where the graph intersects the line $y = -1$. These points are $(3\pi/4, -1)$ and $(5\pi/4, -1)$. Draw one cycle of the graph through these five points, as shown in Fig. 3.50.

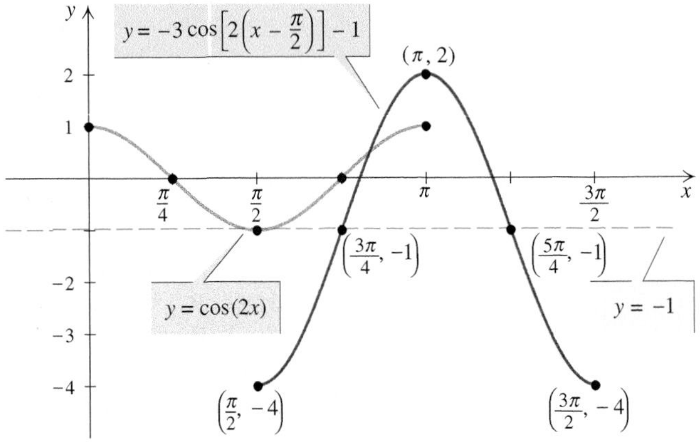

Figure 3.50

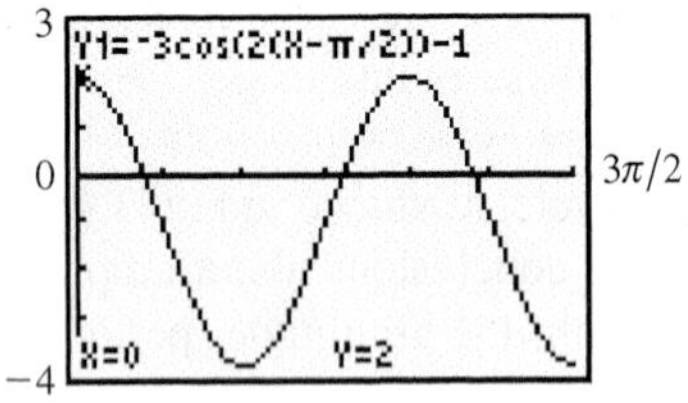

Figure 3.51

The calculator graph in Fig. 3.51 supports our conclusions. ■

Frequency

Sine waves are used to model physical phenomena such as radio, sound, or light waves. A high-frequency radio wave is a wave that has a large number of cycles per second. If we think of the x-axis as a time axis, then the period of a sine wave is the amount of time required for the wave to complete one cycle, and the reciprocal of the period is the number of cycles per unit of time. For example, the sound wave for middle C on a piano completes 262 cycles per second. The period of the wave is $1/262$ second, which means that one cycle is completed in $1/262$ second.

Definition: Frequency

The **frequency** F of a sine wave with period P is defined by $F = 1/P$.

Example 10 Frequency of a sine wave

Find the frequency of the sine wave given by $y = \sin(524\pi x)$.

Solution

First find the period:

$$P = \frac{2\pi}{524\pi} = \frac{1}{262} \approx 0.004$$

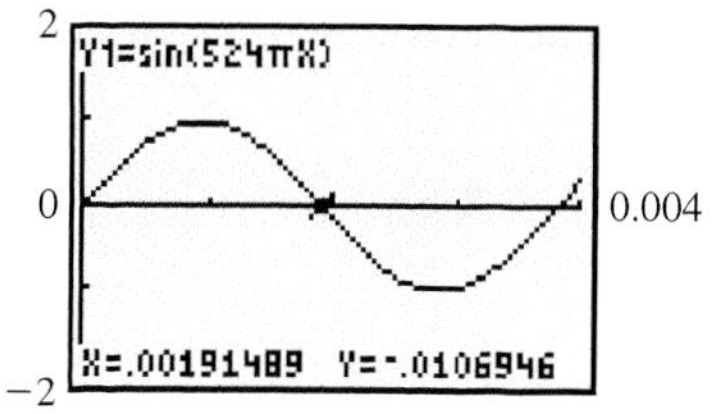

Figure 3.52

Since $F = 1/P$, the frequency is 262. A sine wave with this frequency completes 262 cycles for x in $[0, 1]$ or approximately one cycle in $[0, 0.004]$.

We cannot draw a graph showing 262 cycles in an interval of length one, but we can see the cycle that occurs in the interval $[0, 0.004]$ by looking at Fig. 3.52. ■

Note that if B is a large positive number in $y = \sin(Bx)$ or $y = \cos(Bx)$, then the period is short and the frequency is high.

Function Gallery: The Sine and Cosine Functions

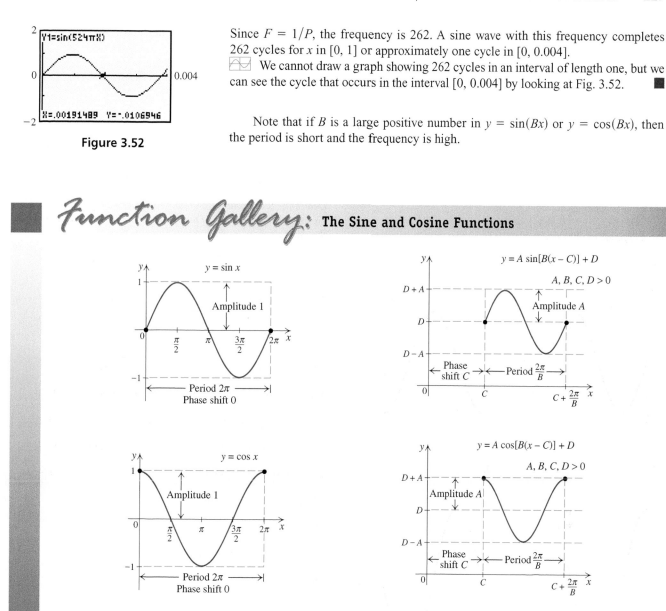

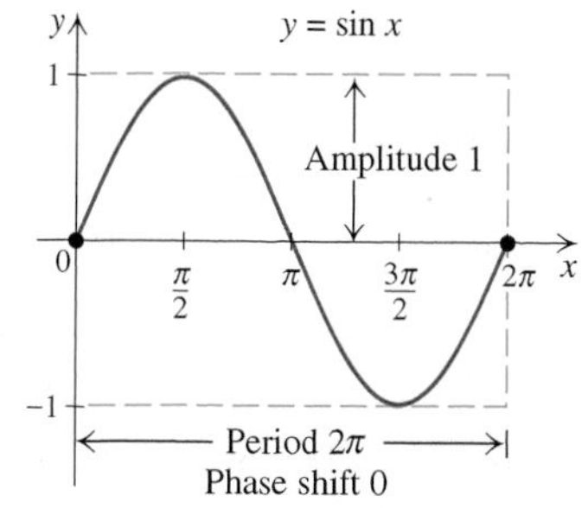

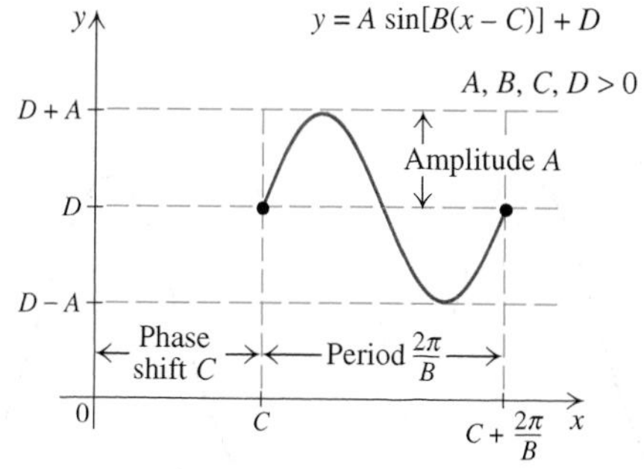

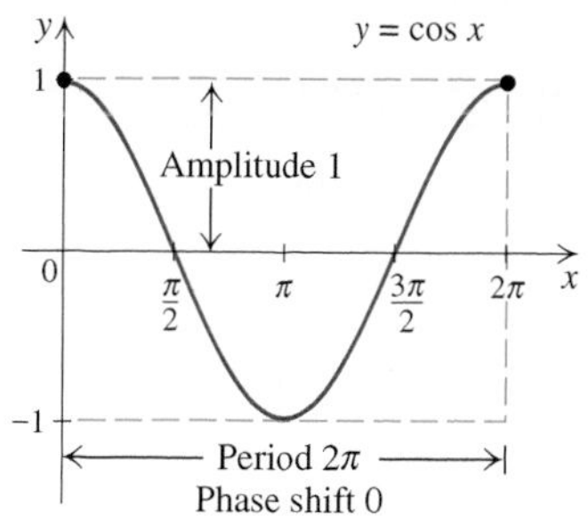

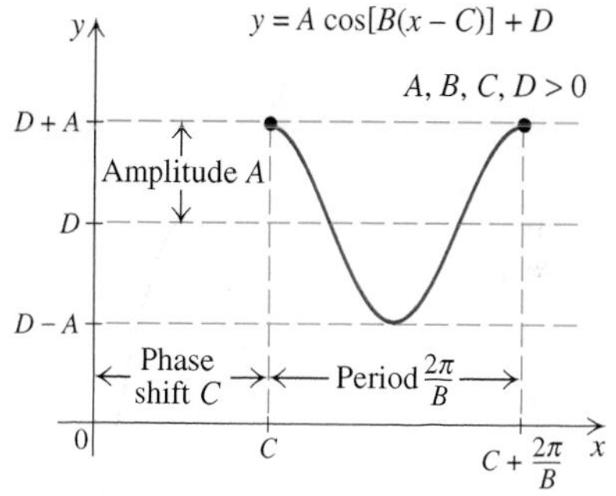

For Thought

True or False? Explain.

1. The period of $y = \cos(2\pi x)$ is π.
2. The range of $y = 4\sin(x) + 3$ is $[-4, 4]$.
3. The graph of $y = \sin(2x + \pi/6)$ has a period of π and a phase shift $\pi/6$.
4. The points $(5\pi/6, 0)$ and $(11\pi/6, 0)$ are on the graph of $y = \cos(x - \pi/3)$.
5. The frequency of the sine wave $y = \sin x$ is $1/(2\pi)$.
6. The period for $y = \sin(0.1\pi x)$ is 20.

7. The graphs of $y = \sin x$ and $y = \cos(x + \pi/2)$ are identical.

8. The period of $y = \cos(4x)$ is $\pi/2$.

9. The maximum value of the function $y = -2\cos(3x) + 4$ is 6.

10. The range of the function $y = 3\sin(5x - \pi) + 2$ is $[-1, 5]$.

3.3 Exercises

Match each graph with one of the functions $y = 3\sin(x)$, $y = 3\cos(x)$, $y = -2\sin(x)$, and $y = -2\cos(x)$. Determine the amplitude of each function.

1.

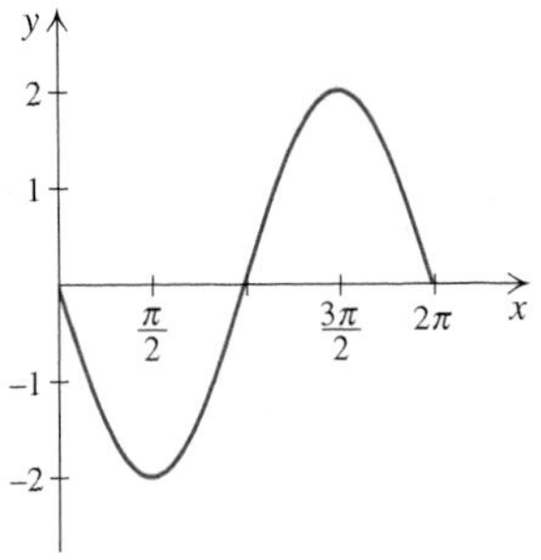

2.

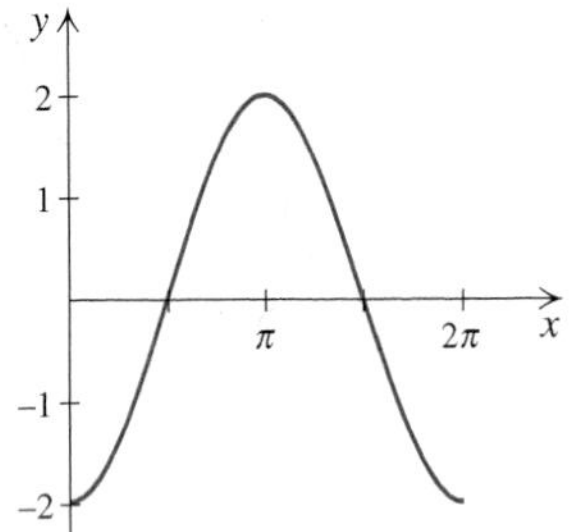

3.

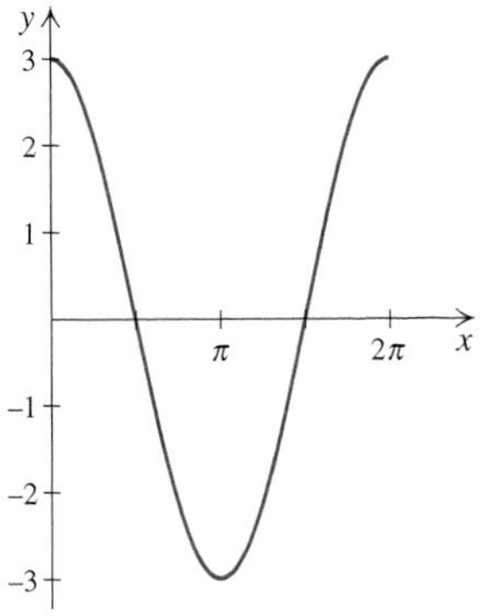

4.

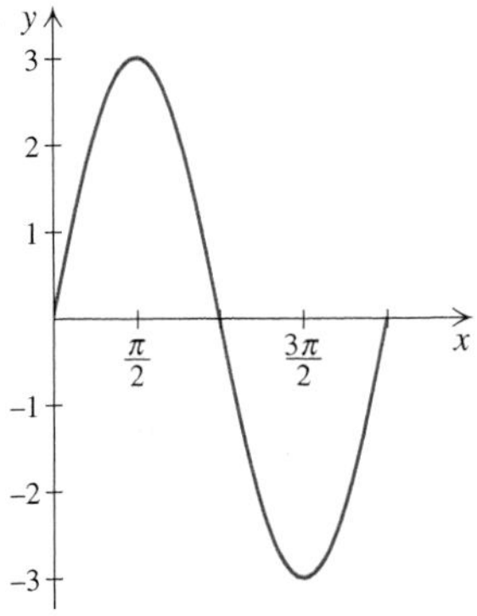

Determine the amplitude, period, and phase shift for each function.

5. $y = -2\cos x$

6. $y = -4\cos x$

7. $f(x) = \cos(x - \pi/2)$

8. $f(x) = \sin(x + \pi/2)$

9. $y = -2\sin(x + \pi/3)$

10. $y = -3\sin(x - \pi/6)$

Determine the amplitude and phase shift for each function, and sketch at least one cycle of the graph. Label five points as done in the examples.

11. $y = -\sin x$

12. $y = -\cos x$

13. $y = -3\sin x$

14. $y = 4\sin x$

15. $y = \dfrac{1}{2}\cos x$

16. $y = \dfrac{1}{3}\cos x$

17. $y = \sin(x + \pi)$

18. $y = \cos(x - \pi)$

19. $y = \cos(x - \pi/3)$

20. $y = \cos(x + \pi/4)$

21. $f(x) = \cos(x) + 2$

22. $f(x) = \cos(x) - 3$

23. $y = -\sin(x) - 1$

24. $y = -\sin(x) + 2$

25. $y = \sin(x + \pi/4) + 2$

26. $y = \sin(x - \pi/2) - 2$

27. $y = 2\cos(x + \pi/6) + 1$

28. $y = 3\cos(x + 2\pi/3) - 2$

29. $f(x) = -2\sin(x - \pi/3) + 1$

30. $f(x) = -3\cos(x + \pi/3) - 1$

Determine the amplitude, period, and phase shift for each function.

31. $y = 3\sin(4x)$

32. $y = -2\cos(3x)$

33. $y = -\cos\left(\dfrac{x}{2}\right) + 3$

34. $y = \sin\left(\dfrac{x}{3}\right) - 5$

35. $y = 2\sin(x - \pi) + 3$

36. $y = -5\cos(x + 4) + \pi$

37. $y = -2\cos\left(2x + \dfrac{\pi}{2}\right) - 1$

38. $y = 4\cos\left(3x - \dfrac{\pi}{4}\right)$

39. $y = -2\cos\left(\frac{\pi}{2}x + \pi\right)$

40. $y = 8\sin\left(\frac{\pi}{3}x - \frac{\pi}{2}\right)$

Find a function of the form $y = A\sin[B(x - C)] + D$ with the given period, phase shift, and range. Answers may vary.

41. $\pi, -\pi/2, [3, 7]$

42. $\pi/2, \pi, [-2, 4]$

43. $2, 2, [-1, 9]$

44. $4, 7, [5, 25]$

45. $\frac{1}{2}, -\pi, [-9, 3]$

46. $\frac{1}{3}, 2\pi, [-6, 2]$

Find the equation for each curve in its final position.

47. The graph of $y = \sin(x)$ is shifted a distance of $\pi/4$ to the right, reflected in the x-axis, then translated one unit upward.

48. The graph of $y = \cos(x)$ is shifted a distance of $\pi/6$ to the left, reflected in the x-axis, then translated two units downward.

49. The graph of $y = \cos(x)$ is stretched by a factor of 3, shifted a distance of π to the right, translated two units downward, then reflected in the x-axis.

50. The graph of $y = \sin(x)$ is shifted a distance of $\pi/2$ to the left, translated one unit upward, stretched by a factor of 4, then reflected in the x-axis.

Sketch at least one cycle of the graph of each function. Determine the period, phase shift, and range of the function. Label five points on the graph as done in the examples. See the procedure for graphing a sine wave on page 224.

51. $y = \sin(3x)$

52. $y = \cos(x/3)$

53. $y = -\sin(2x)$

54. $y = -\cos(3x)$

55. $y = \cos(4x) + 2$

56. $y = \sin(3x) - 1$

57. $y = 2 - \sin(x/4)$

58. $y = 3 - \cos(x/5)$

59. $y = \sin\left(\frac{\pi}{3}x\right)$

60. $y = \sin\left(\frac{\pi}{4}x\right)$

61. $f(x) = \sin\left[2\left(x - \frac{\pi}{2}\right)\right]$

62. $f(x) = \sin\left[3\left(x + \frac{\pi}{3}\right)\right]$

63. $f(x) = \sin\left(\frac{\pi}{2}x + \frac{3\pi}{2}\right)$

64. $f(x) = \cos\left(\frac{\pi}{3}x - \frac{\pi}{3}\right)$

65. $y = 2\cos\left[2\left(x + \frac{\pi}{6}\right)\right] + 1$

66. $y = 3\cos\left[4\left(x - \frac{\pi}{2}\right)\right] - 1$

67. $y = -\frac{1}{2}\sin\left[3\left(x - \frac{\pi}{6}\right)\right] - 1$

68. $y = -\frac{1}{2}\sin\left[4\left(x + \frac{\pi}{4}\right)\right] + 1$

Write an equation of the form $y = A\sin[B(x - C)] + D$ whose graph is the given sine wave.

69.

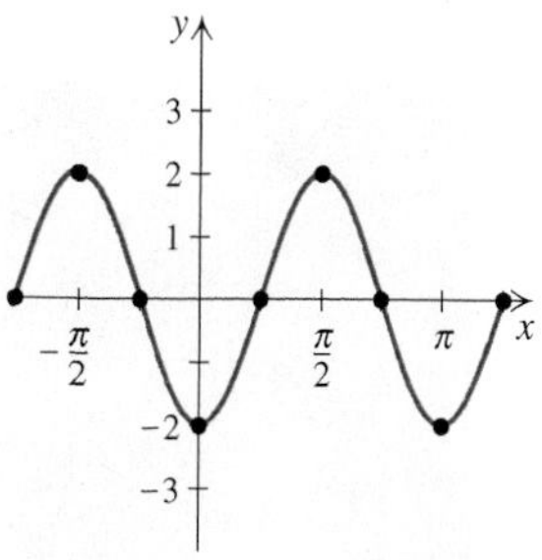

70.

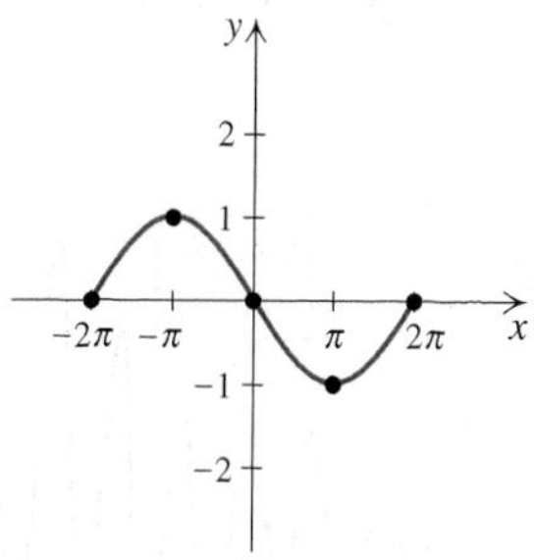

71.

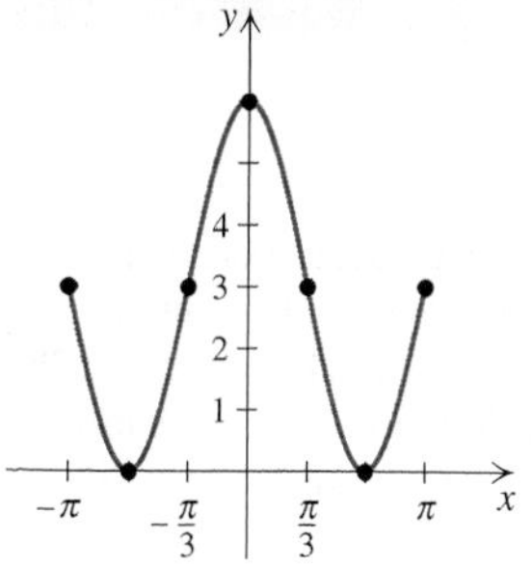

72.

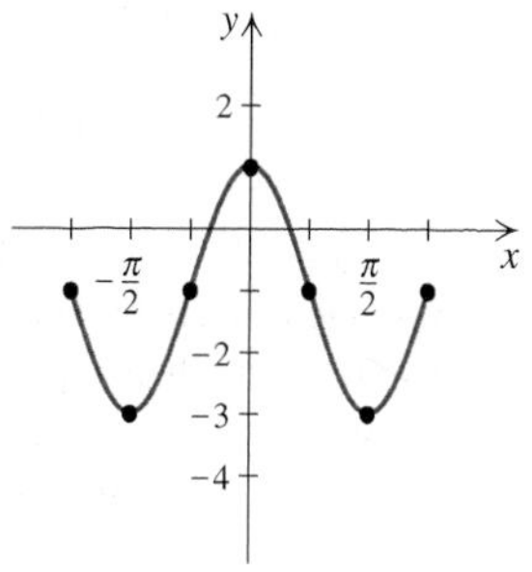

Solve each problem.

73. What is the frequency of the sine wave determined by $y = \sin(200\pi x)$, where x is time in seconds?

74. What is the frequency of the sine wave determined by $y = \cos(0.001\pi x)$, where x is time in seconds?

75. If the period of a sine wave is 0.025 hr, then what is the frequency?

76. If the frequency of a sine wave is 40,000 cycles per second, then what is the period?

77. *Motion of a Spring* A weight hanging on a vertical spring is set in motion with a downward velocity of 6 cm/sec from its equilibrium position. Assume that the constant ω for this particular spring and weight combination is 2. Write the formula that gives the location of the weight in centimeters as a function of the time t in seconds. Find the amplitude and period of the function and sketch its graph for t in the interval $[0, 2\pi]$. (See Section 3.2 for the general formula that describes the motion of a spring.)

78. *Motion of a Spring* A weight hanging on a vertical spring is set in motion with an upward velocity of 4 cm/sec from its equilibrium position. Assume that the constant ω for this particular spring and weight combination is π. Write the formula that gives the location of the weight in centimeters as a function of the time t in seconds. Find the period of the function and sketch its graph for t in the interval $[0, 4]$.

79. *Sun Spots* Astronomers have been recording sunspot activity for over 130 years. The number of sunspots per year varies like a periodic function over time, as shown in the graph. What is the approximate period of this function?

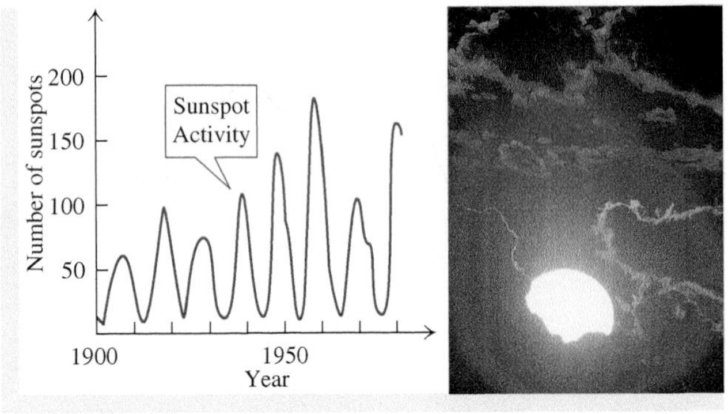

Figure for Exercise 79

80. *First Pulsar* In 1967, Jocelyn Bell, a graduate student at Cambridge University, England, found the peculiar pattern shown in the graph on a paper chart from a radio telescope. She had made the first discovery of a pulsar, a very small neutron star that emits beams of radiation as it rotates as fast as 1000 times per second. From the graph shown here, estimate the period of the first discovered pulsar, now known as CP 1919.

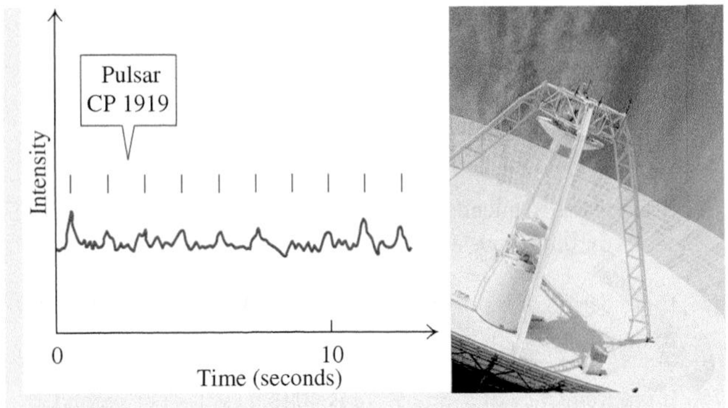

Figure for Exercise 80

81. *Lung Capacity* The volume of air v in cubic centimeters in the lungs of a certain distance runner is modeled by the equation $v = 400 \sin(60\pi t) + 900$, where t is time in minutes.

a. What are the maximum and minimum volumes of air in the runner's lungs at any time?

b. How many breaths does the runner take per minute?

82. *Blood Velocity* The velocity v of blood at a valve in the heart of a certain rodent is modeled by the equation $v = -4 \cos(6\pi t) + 4$, where v is in centimeters per second and t is time in seconds.

a. What are the maximum and minimum velocities of the blood at this valve?

b. What is the rodent's heart rate in beats per minute?

83. *Periodic Revenue* For the past three years, the manager of The Toggery Shop has observed that revenue reaches a high of about \$40,000 in December and a low of about \$10,000 in June, and that a graph of the revenue looks like a sinusoid. If the months are numbered 1 through 36 with 1 corresponding to January, then what are the period, amplitude, and phase shift for this sinusoid? What is the vertical translation? Write a formula for the curve and find the approximate revenue for April.

84. *Periodic Cost* For the past three years, the manager of The Toggery Shop has observed that the utility bill reaches a high of about \$500 in January and a low of about \$200 in July, and the graph of the utility bill looks like a sinusoid. If the months are numbered 1 through 36 with 1 corresponding to January, then what are the period, amplitude, and phase shift for this sinusoid? What is the vertical translation? Write a formula for the curve and find the approximate utility bill for November.

85. *Ocean Waves* Scientists use the same types of terms to describe ocean waves that we use to describe sine waves. The *wave period* is the time between crests and the *wavelength* is the distance between crests. The wave *height* is the vertical distance from the trough to the crest. The accompanying figure shows a *swell* in a coordinate system. Write an equation for the swell, assuming that its shape is that of a sinusoid.

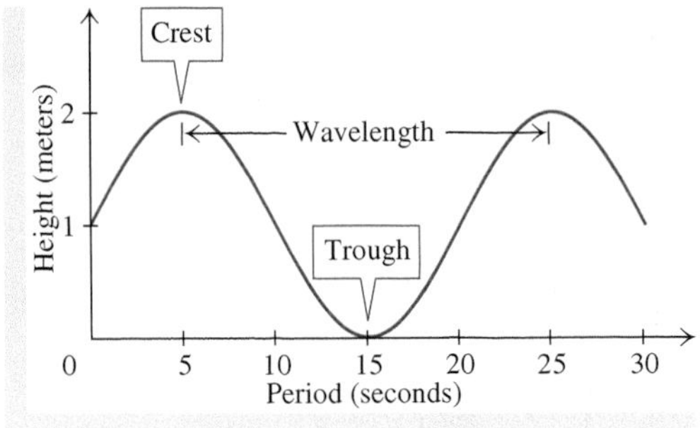

Figure for Exercise 85

86. *Large Ocean Waves* A *tsunami* is a series of large waves caused by an earthquake. The wavelength for a tsunami can be as long as several hundred kilometers. The accompanying figure shows a tsunami in a coordinate system. Write an equation for the tsunami, assuming that its shape is that of a sinusoid.

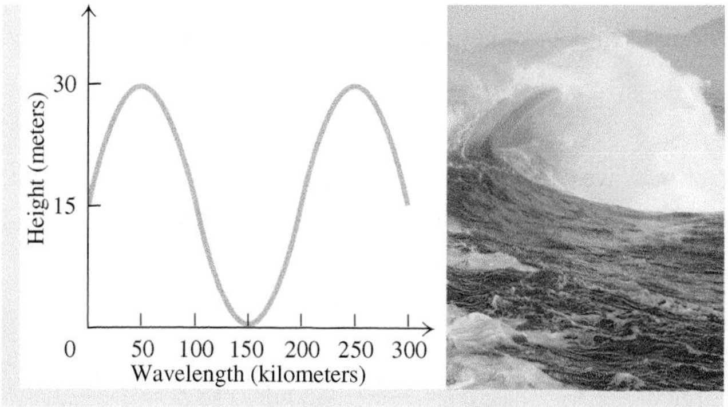

Figure for Exercise 86

Thinking Outside the Box XXI

The Survivor There are 13 contestants on a reality television show. They are instructed to each take a seat at a circular table containing 13 chairs that are numbered consecutively with the numbers 1 through 13. The producer then starts at number 1 and tells that contestant that he is a survivor. That contestant then leaves the table. The producer skips a contestant and tells the contestant in chair number 3 that he is a survivor. That contestant then leaves the table. The producer continues around the table skipping a contestant and telling the next contestant that he is a survivor. Each survivor leaves the table. The last person left at the table is *not* a survivor and must leave the show.

a. For $n = 13$ find the unlucky number k, for which the person sitting in chair k must leave the show.

b. Find k for $n = 8$, 16, and 41.

c. Find a formula for k.

3.3 Pop Quiz

1. Determine the amplitude, period, and phase shift for $y = -5\sin(2x + 2\pi/3)$.

2. List the coordinates for the five key points for one cycle of $y = 3\sin(2x)$.

3. If $y = \cos(x)$ is shifted $\pi/2$ to the right, reflected in the x-axis, and shifted 3 units upward, then what is the equation of the curve in its final position?

4. What is the range of $f(x) = -4\sin(x - 3) + 2$?

5. What is the frequency of the sine wave determined by $y = \sin(500\pi x)$, where x is time in minutes?

3.4 The Other Trigonometric Functions and Their Graphs

So far we have studied two of the six trigonometric functions. In this section we will define the remaining four functions.

Definitions

The tangent, cotangent, secant, and cosecant functions are all defined in terms of the unit circle. We use the abbreviation tan for tangent, cot for cotangent, sec for secant, and csc for cosecant. As usual, we may think of α as an angle, the measure of an angle in degrees, the measure of an angle in radians, or a real number.

Definition: Tangent, Cotangent, Secant, and Cosecant Functions

If α is an angle in standard position and (x, y) is the point of intersection of the terminal side and the unit circle, we define the **tangent, cotangent, secant,** and **cosecant** functions as

$$\tan \alpha = \frac{y}{x}, \quad \cot \alpha = \frac{x}{y}, \quad \sec \alpha = \frac{1}{x}, \quad \text{and} \quad \csc \alpha = \frac{1}{y}.$$

We exclude from the domain of each function any value of α for which the denominator is 0.

Since $\sin \alpha = y$ and $\cos \alpha = x$, we can rewrite the definitions of tangent, cotangent, secant, and cosecant to get the following identities for these four functions.

Identities from the Definitions

If α is any angle or real number

$$\tan \alpha = \frac{\sin \alpha}{\cos \alpha}, \quad \cot \alpha = \frac{\cos \alpha}{\sin \alpha}, \quad \sec \alpha = \frac{1}{\cos \alpha}, \quad \text{and} \quad \csc \alpha = \frac{1}{\sin \alpha},$$

provided no denominator is zero.

■ Foreshadowing Calculus

In trigonometry we see that all of the trigonometric functions are related to each other. These relationships are important in calculus when we study rates of change of the trigonometric functions.

The domain of the tangent and secant functions is the set of angles except those for which $\cos \alpha = 0$. The only points on the unit circle where the first coordinate is 0 are $(0, 1)$ and $(0, -1)$. Angles such as $\pi/2$, $3\pi/2$, $5\pi/2$, and so on, have terminal sides through either $(0, 1)$ or $(0, -1)$. These angles are of the form $\pi/2 + k\pi$, where k is any integer. So the domain of tangent and secant is

$$\left\{\alpha \,\middle|\, \alpha \neq \frac{\pi}{2} + k\pi, \text{ where } k \text{ is an integer}\right\}.$$

The only points on the unit circle where the second coordinate is 0 are $(1, 0)$ and $(-1, 0)$. Angles that are multiples of π, such as 0, π, 2π, and so on, have terminal sides that go through one of these points. Any angle of the form $k\pi$, where k is any integer, has a terminal side that goes through either $(1, 0)$ or $(-1, 0)$. So $\sin(k\pi) = 0$ for any integer k. By definition, the zeros of the sine function are excluded from the domain of cotangent and cosecant; thus the domain of cotangent and cosecant is

$$\{\alpha \,|\, \alpha \neq k\pi, \text{ where } k \text{ is an integer}\}.$$

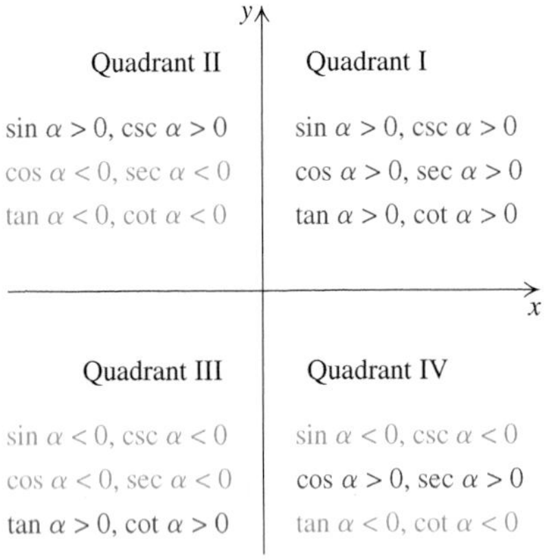

Figure 3.53

To find the values of the six trigonometric functions for an angle α, first find $\sin \alpha$ and $\cos \alpha$. Then use the identities from the definitions to find values of the other four functions. Of course, $\cot \alpha$ can be found also by using $1/\tan \alpha$, but not if $\tan \alpha$ is undefined like it is for $\alpha = \pm\pi/2$. If $\tan \alpha$ is undefined, then $\cot \alpha = 0$, and if $\tan \alpha = 0$, then $\cot \alpha$ is undefined.

The signs of the six trigonometric functions for angles in each quadrant are shown in Fig. 3.53. It is not necessary to memorize these signs, because they can be easily obtained by knowing the signs of the sine and cosine functions in each quadrant.

Example 1 Evaluating the trigonometric functions

Find the values of all six trigonometric functions for each angle.

a. $\pi/4$ **b.** $150°$

Solution

a. Use $\sin(\pi/4) = \sqrt{2}/2$ and $\cos(\pi/4) = \sqrt{2}/2$ to find the other values:

$$\tan(\pi/4) = \frac{\sin(\pi/4)}{\cos(\pi/4)} = \frac{\sqrt{2}/2}{\sqrt{2}/2} = 1 \quad \cot(\pi/4) = \frac{\cos(\pi/4)}{\sin(\pi/4)} = 1$$

$$\sec(\pi/4) = \frac{1}{\cos(\pi/4)} = \frac{2}{\sqrt{2}} = \sqrt{2} \quad \csc(\pi/4) = \frac{1}{\sin(\pi/4)} = \frac{2}{\sqrt{2}} = \sqrt{2}$$

b. The reference angle for 150° is 30°. So $\sin(150°) = \sin(30°) = 1/2$ and $\cos(150°) = -\cos(30°) = -\sqrt{3}/2$. Use these values to find the other four values:

$$\tan(150°) = \frac{1/2}{-\sqrt{3}/2} = -\frac{1}{\sqrt{3}} = -\frac{\sqrt{3}}{3} \qquad \cot(150°) = -\frac{3}{\sqrt{3}} = -\sqrt{3}$$

$$\sec(150°) = \frac{1}{\cos(150°)} = -\frac{2}{\sqrt{3}} = -\frac{2\sqrt{3}}{3} \qquad \csc(150°) = \frac{1}{\sin(150°)} = 2 \quad ■$$

Most scientific calculators have keys for the sine, cosine, and tangent functions only. To find values for the other three functions, we use the definitions. Keys labeled $\sin^{-1}$, $\cos^{-1}$, and $\tan^{-1}$ on a calculator are for the inverse trigonometric functions, which we will study in the next section. These keys do *not* give the values of $1/\sin x$, $1/\cos x$, or $1/\tan x$.

Example 2 Evaluating with a calculator

Use a calculator to find approximate values rounded to four decimal places.

a. $\sec(\pi/12)$ **b.** $\csc(123°)$ **c.** $\cot(-12.4)$

Solution

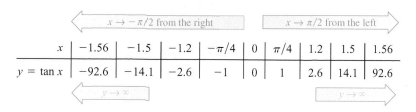

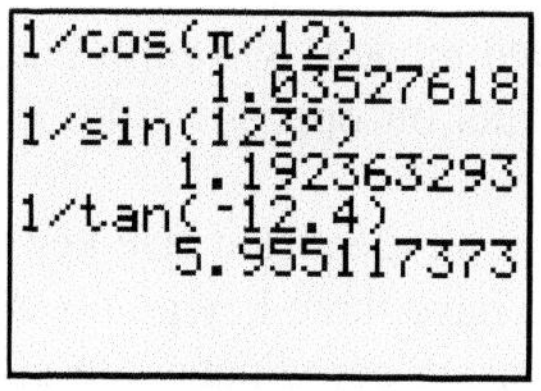

Figure 3.54

a. $\sec(\pi/12) = \dfrac{1}{\cos(\pi/12)} \approx 1.0353$

b. $\csc(123°) = \dfrac{1}{\sin(123°)} \approx 1.1924$

c. $\cot(-12.4) = \dfrac{1}{\tan(-12.4)} \approx 5.9551$

These expressions are evaluated with a graphing calculator in radian mode as shown in Fig. 3.54. Note that in radian mode the degree symbol is used for part (b). ■

Graph of $y = \tan(x)$

Consider some ordered pairs that satisfy $y = \tan x$ for x in $(-\pi/2, \pi/2)$. Note that $-\pi/2$ and $\pi/2$ are not in the domain of $y = \tan x$, but x can be chosen close to $\pm\pi/2$.

$x \to -\pi/2$ from the right | $x \to \pi/2$ from the left

x	-1.56	-1.5	-1.2	$-\pi/4$	0	$\pi/4$	1.2	1.5	1.56
$y = \tan x$	-92.6	-14.1	-2.6	-1	0	1	2.6	14.1	92.6

$y \to -\infty$ | $y \to \infty$

The graph of $y = \tan x$ includes the points $(-\pi/4, -1)$, $(0, 0)$, and $(\pi/4, 1)$. Since $\tan x = \sin x/\cos x$, the graph of $y = \tan x$ has a vertical asymptote for every zero of the cosine function. So the vertical lines $x = \pi/2 + k\pi$ for any integer k are the **vertical asymptotes.** The behavior of $y = \tan x$ near the asymptotes $x = \pm\pi/2$ can be seen from the table of ordered pairs. As x approaches $\pi/2$ (approximately 1.57) from the left, $\tan x \to \infty$. Using limit notation, $\lim_{x\to\pi/2^-} \tan(x) = \infty$. As x approaches $-\pi/2$ from the right, $\tan x \to -\infty$ Using limit notation, $\lim_{x\to-\pi/2^+} \tan(x) = -\infty$. In the interval $(-\pi/2, \pi/2)$, the function is increasing. The graph of $y = \tan x$ is shown in Fig. 3.55. The shape of the tangent curve betwen $-\pi/2$ and $\pi/2$ is repeated between each pair of consecutive asymptotes, as shown in the figure. The period of $y = \tan x$ is π, and the fundamental cycle is the portion of the graph between $-\pi/2$ and $\pi/2$. Since the range of $y = \tan x$ is $(-\infty, \infty)$, the concept of amplitude is not defined for this function.

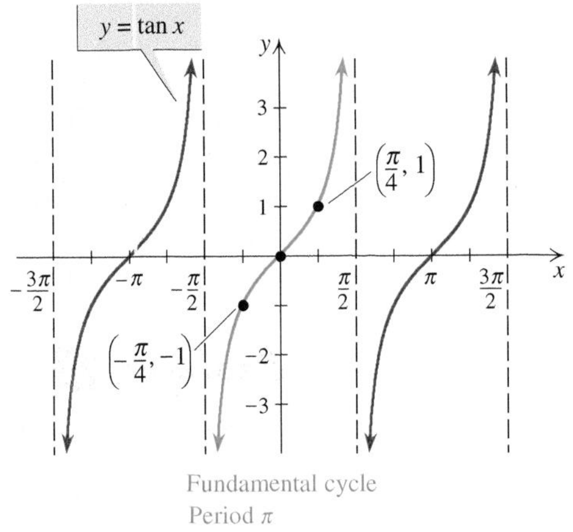

Figure 3.55

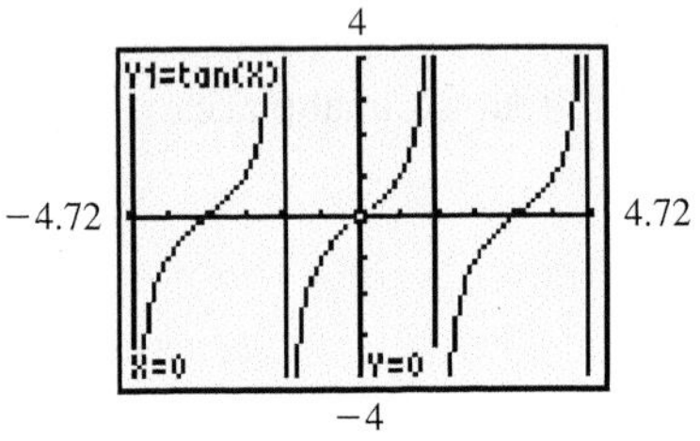

Figure 3.56

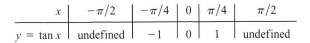

The calculator graph of $y = \tan(x)$ in connected mode is shown in Fig. 3.56. In connected mode the calculator connects two points on opposite sides of each asymptote and appears to draw the vertical asymptotes. □

To help us understand the sine and cosine curve, we identified five key points on the fundamental cycle. For the tangent curve, we have three key points and the asymptotes (where the function is undefined). The exact coordinates are given in the following table.

x	$-\pi/2$	$-\pi/4$	0	$\pi/4$	$\pi/2$
$y = \tan x$	undefined	-1	0	1	undefined

We can transform the graph of the tangent function by using the same techniques that we used for the sine and cosine functions.

Example 3 A tangent function with a transformation

Sketch two cycles of the function $y = \tan(2x)$ and determine the period.

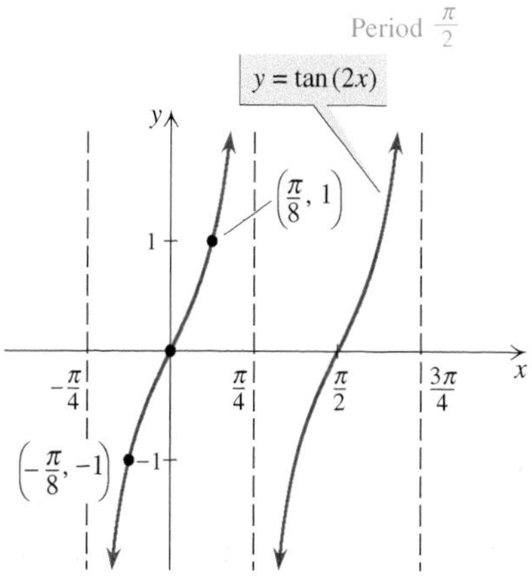

Figure 3.57

Solution

The graph of $y = \tan x$ completes one cycle for $-\pi/2 < x < \pi/2$. So the graph of $y = \tan(2x)$ completes one cycle for $-\pi/2 < 2x < \pi/2$, or $-\pi/4 < x < \pi/4$. The graph includes the points $(-\pi/8, -1)$, $(0, 0)$, and $(\pi/8, 1)$. The graph is similar to the graph of $y = \tan x$, but the asymptotes are $x = \pi/4 + k\pi/2$ for any integer k, and the period of $y = \tan(2x)$ is $\pi/2$. Two cycles of the graph are shown in Fig. 3.57. ■

By understanding what happens to the fundamental cycles of the sine, cosine, and tangent functions when the period changes, we can easily determine the location of the new function and sketch its graph quickly. We start with the fundamental cycles of $y = \sin x$, $y = \cos x$, and $y = \tan x$, which occur over the intervals $[0, 2\pi]$, $[0, 2\pi]$, and $[-\pi/2, \pi/2]$, respectively. For $y = \sin Bx$, $y = \cos Bx$, and $y = \tan Bx$ (for $B > 0$) these fundamental cycles move to the intervals $[0, 2\pi/B]$, $[0, 2\pi/B]$, and $[-\pi/(2B), \pi/(2B)]$, respectively. In every case, divide the old period by B to get the new period. Note that only the nonzero endpoints of the intervals are changed. The following Function Gallery summarizes the period change for the sine, cosine, and tangent functions with $B > 1$.

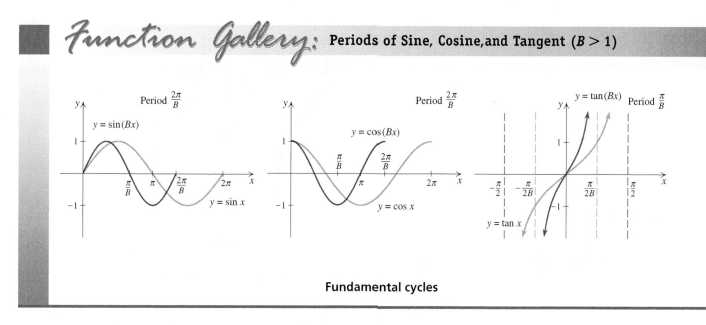

Function Gallery: Periods of Sine, Cosine, and Tangent ($B > 1$)

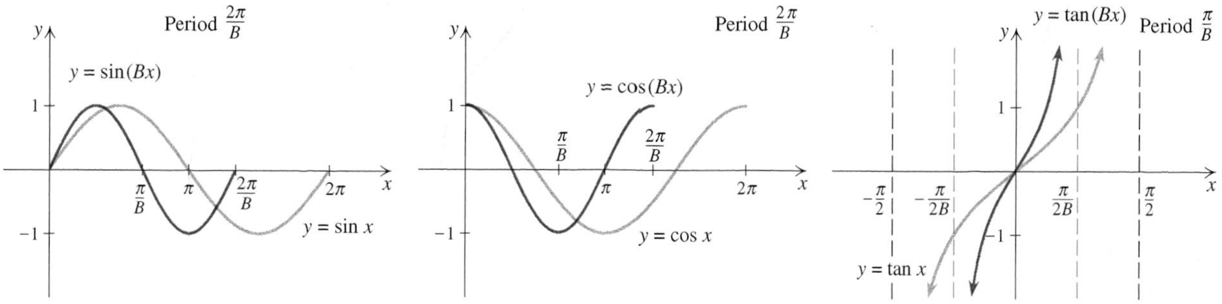

Fundamental cycles

Graph of $y = \cot(x)$

We know that $\cot x = 1/\tan x$, provided $\tan x$ is defined and not 0. So we can use $y = \tan x$ to graph $y = \cot x$. Since $\tan x = 0$ for $x = k\pi$, where k is any integer, the vertical lines $x = k\pi$ for an integer k are the vertical asymptotes of $y = \cot x$.

Consider some ordered pairs that satisfy $y = \cot x$ between the asymptotes $x = 0$ and $x = \pi$:

$x \to 0$ from the right | $x \to \pi$ from the left

x	0.01	0.02	$\pi/4$	$\pi/2$	$3\pi/4$	3.1	3.14
$y = \cot x$	100.00	49.99	1	0	-1	-24.0	-627.9

$y \to \infty$ | $y \to -\infty$

As $x \to 0$ from the right, $\cot x \to \infty$. Using limit notation, $\lim_{x \to 0^+} \cot(x) = \infty$. As $x \to \pi$ from the left, $\cot x \to -\infty$. Using limit notation, $\lim_{x \to \pi^-} \cot(x) = -\infty$. In the interval $(0, \pi)$, the function is decreasing. The graph of $y = \cot x$ is shown in Fig. 3.58. The shape of the curve between 0 and π is repeated between each pair of consecutive asymptotes, as shown in the figure. The period of $y = \cot x$ is π, and the fundamental cycle is the portion of the graph between 0 and π. The range of $y = \cot x$ is $(-\infty, \infty)$.

Because $\cot x = 1/\tan x$, $\cot x$ is large when $\tan x$ is small, and vice versa. The graph of $y = \cot x$ has an x-intercept wherever $y = \tan x$ has a vertical asymptote, and a vertical asymptote wherever $y = \tan x$ has an x-intercept. So for every integer k, $(\pi/2 + k\pi, 0)$ is an x-intercept of $y = \cot x$, and the vertical line $x = k\pi$ is an asymptote, as shown in Fig. 3.58.

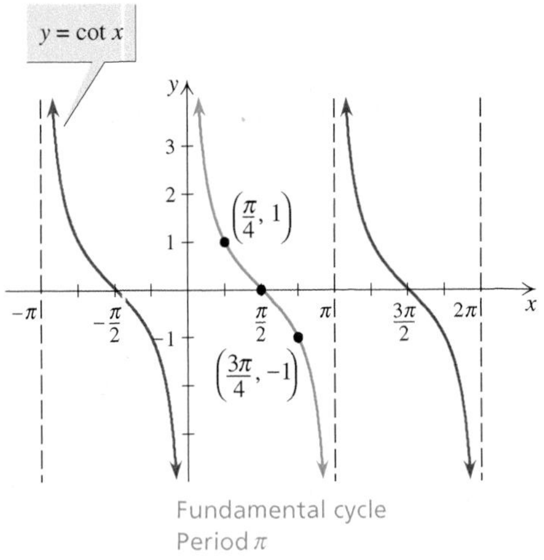

Figure 3.58

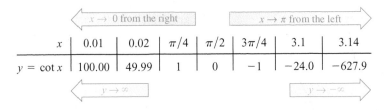

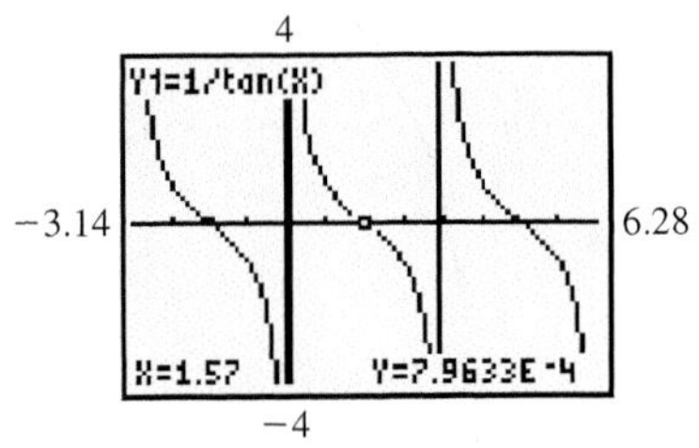

Figure 3.59

To see the graph of $y = \cot(x)$ on a graphing calculator, you can graph $y = 1/\tan(x)$, as shown in Fig. 3.59. □

For the cotangent curve, note the three key points and the asymptotes (where the function is undefined). The exact coordinates are given in the following table.

x	0	$\pi/4$	$\pi/2$	$3\pi/4$	π
$y = \cot x$	undefined	1	0	-1	undefined

When we graph a transformation of the cotangent function, as in the next example, we must determine what happens to these five features.

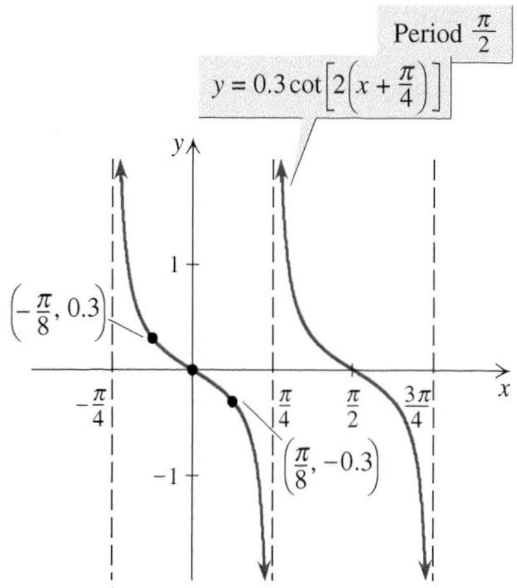

Figure 3.60

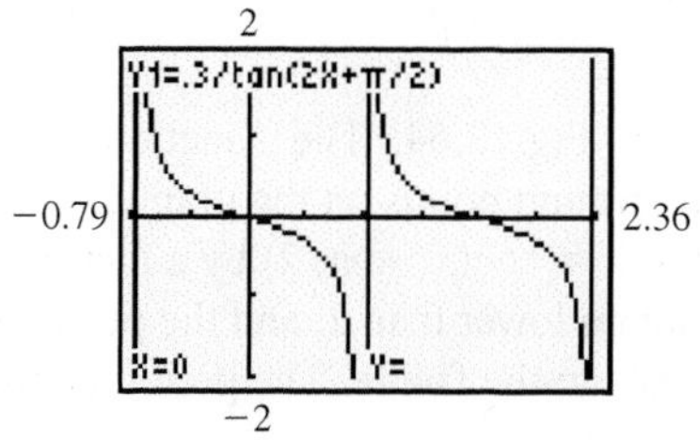

Figure 3.61

Example 4 A cotangent function with a transformation

Sketch two cycles of the function $y = 0.3\cot(2x + \pi/2)$, and determine the period.

Solution

Factor out 2 to write the function as

$$y = 0.3\cot\left[2\left(x + \frac{\pi}{4}\right)\right].$$

Since $y = \cot x$ completes one cycle for $0 < x < \pi$, the graph of $y = 0.3\cot[2(x + \pi/4)]$ completes one cycle for

$$0 < 2\left(x + \frac{\pi}{4}\right) < \pi, \quad \text{or} \quad 0 < x + \frac{\pi}{4} < \frac{\pi}{2}, \quad \text{or} \quad -\frac{\pi}{4} < x < \frac{\pi}{4}.$$

The interval $(-\pi/4, \pi/4)$ for the fundamental cycle can also be obtained by dividing the period π of $y = \cot x$ by 2 to get $\pi/2$ as the period, and then shifting the interval $(0, \pi/2)$ a distance of $\pi/4$ to the left. The factor 0.3 shrinks the y-coordinates. The graph goes through $(-\pi/8, 0.3)$, $(0, 0)$, and $(\pi/8, -0.3)$ as it approaches its vertical asymptotes $x = \pm\pi/4$. The graph for two cycles is shown in Fig. 3.60.

The calculator graph in Fig. 3.61 supports these conclusions. ■

Since the period for $y = \cot x$ is π, the period for $y = \cot(Bx)$ with $B > 0$ is π/B and $y = \cot(Bx)$ completes one cycle on the interval $(0, \pi/B)$. The left-hand asymptote for the fundamental cycle of $y = \cot x$ remains fixed at $x = 0$, while the right-hand asymptote changes to $x = \pi/B$.

Graph of $y = \sec(x)$

Since $\sec x = 1/\cos x$, the values of $\sec x$ are large when the values of $\cos x$ are small. For any x such that $\cos x$ is 0, $\sec x$ is undefined and the graph of $y = \sec x$ has a vertical asymptote. Because of the reciprocal relationship between $\sec x$ and $\cos x$, we first draw the graph of $y = \cos x$ for reference when graphing $y = \sec x$. At every x-intercept of $y = \cos x$, we draw a vertical asymptote, as shown in Fig. 3.62. If $\cos x = \pm 1$, then $\sec x = \pm 1$. So every maximum or minimum point on the

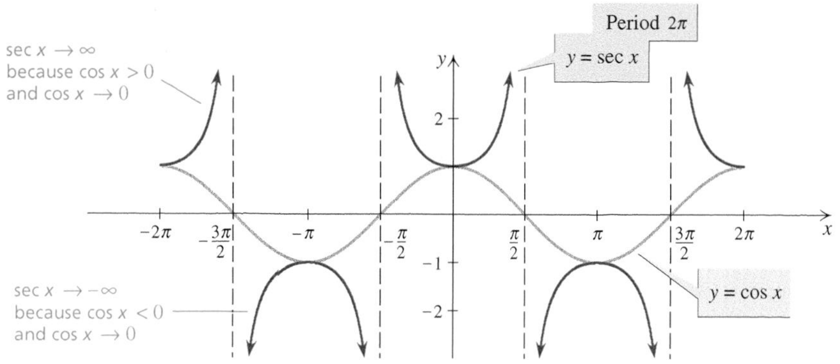

Figure 3.62

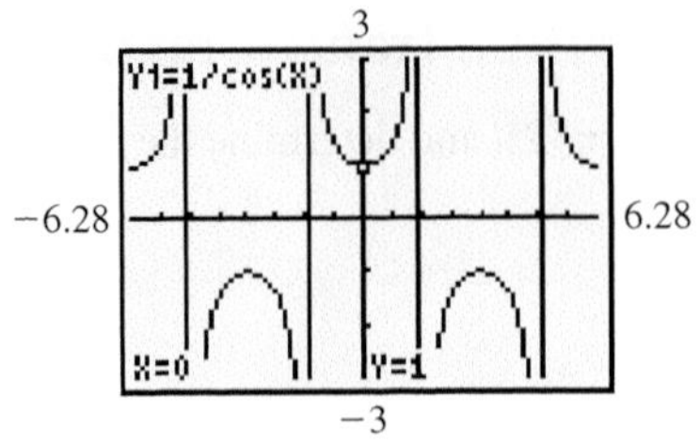

Figure 3.63

graph of $y = \cos x$ is also on the graph of $y = \sec x$. If $\cos x > 0$ and $\cos x \to 0$, then $\sec x \to \infty$. If $\cos x < 0$ and $\cos x \to 0$, then $\sec x \to -\infty$. These two facts cause the graph of $y = \sec x$ to approach its asymptotes in the manner shown in Fig. 3.62. The period of $y = \sec x$ is 2π, the same as the period for $y = \cos x$. The range of $y = \sec x$ is $(-\infty, -1] \cup [1, \infty)$.

The calculator graph in Fig. 3.63 supports these conclusions. □

Example 5 A secant function with a transformation

Sketch two cycles of the function $y = 2\sec(x - \pi/2)$, and determine the period and the range of the function.

Solution

Since

$$y = 2\sec\left(x - \frac{\pi}{2}\right) = \frac{2}{\cos(x - \pi/2)},$$

we first graph $y = \cos(x - \pi/2)$, as shown in Fig. 3.64. The function $y = \sec(x - \pi/2)$ goes through the maximum and minimum points on the graph of $y = \cos(x - \pi/2)$, but $y = 2\sec(x - \pi/2)$ stretches $y = \sec(x - \pi/2)$ by a factor of 2. So the portions of the curve that open up do not go lower than 2, and the portions that open down do not go higher than −2, as shown in the figure. The period is 2π, and the range is $(-\infty, -2] \cup [2, \infty)$.

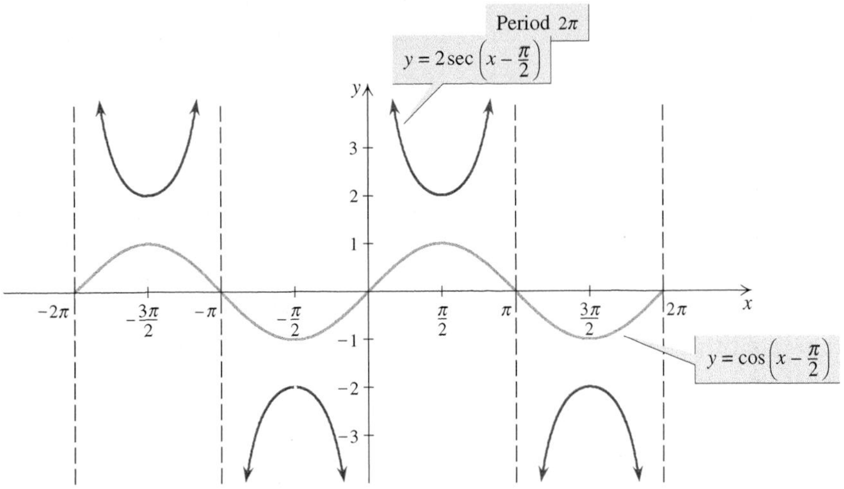

Figure 3.64 ■

Graph of $y = \csc(x)$

Since $\csc x = 1/\sin x$, the graph of $y = \csc x$ is related to the graph of $y = \sin x$ in the same way that the graphs of $y = \sec x$ and $y = \cos x$ are related. To graph $y = \csc x$, first draw the graph of $y = \sin x$ and a vertical asymptote at each x-intercept. Since the graph of $y = \sin x$ can be obtained by shifting $y = \cos x$ a distance of $\pi/2$ to the right, the graph of $y = \csc x$ is obtained from $y = \sec x$ by shifting a distance of $\pi/2$ to the right, as shown in Fig. 3.65. The period of $y = \csc x$ is 2π, the same as the period for $y = \sin x$.

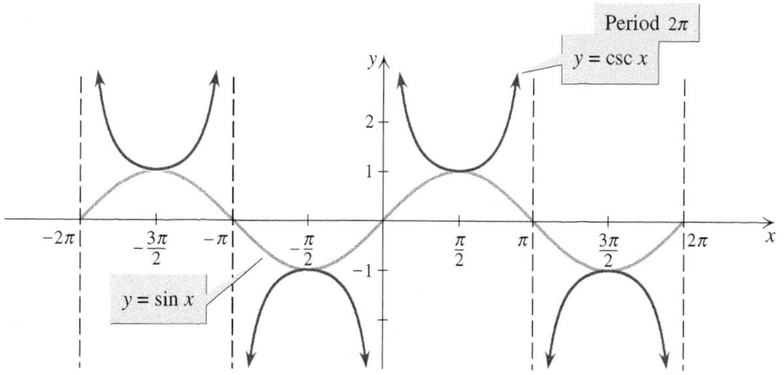

Figure 3.65

Example 6 A cosecant function with a transformation

Sketch two cycles of the graph of $y = \csc(2x - 2\pi/3)$ and determine the period and the range of the function.

Solution

Since

$$y = \csc(2x - 2\pi/3)$$
$$= \frac{1}{\sin[2(x - \pi/3)]}$$

we first graph $y = \sin[2(x - \pi/3)]$. The period for $y = \sin[2(x - \pi/3)]$ is π with phase shift of $\pi/3$. So the fundamental cycle of $y = \sin x$ is transformed to occur on the interval $[\pi/3, 4\pi/3]$. Draw at least two cycles of $y = \sin[2(x - \pi/3)]$ with a vertical asymptote (for the cosecant function) at every x-intercept, as shown in Fig. 3.66.

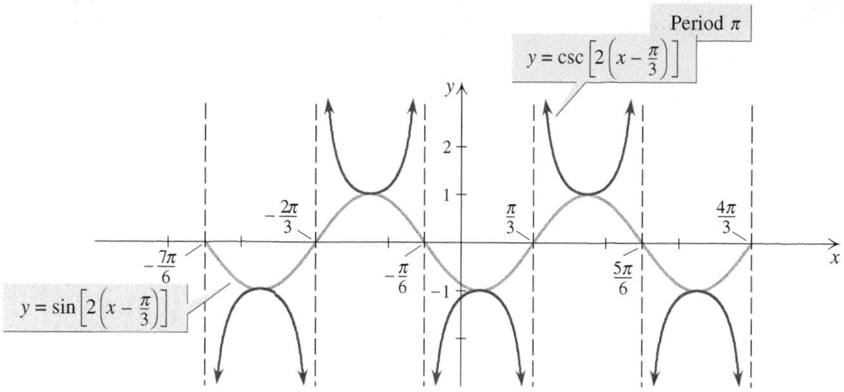

Figure 3.66

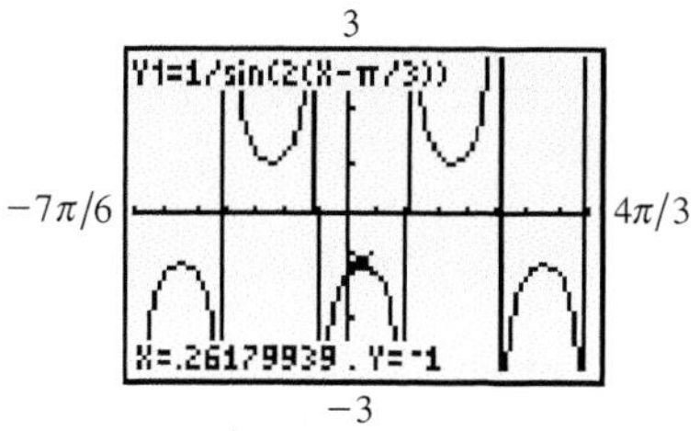

Figure 3.67

Each portion of $y = \csc[2(x - \pi/3)]$ that opens up has a minimum value of 1, and each portion that opens down has a maximum value of -1. The period of the function is π, and the range is $(-\infty, -1] \cup [1, \infty)$.

The calculator graph in Fig. 3.67 supports these conclusions. ■

The Function Gallery summarizes some of the facts that we have learned about the six trigonometric functions. Also, one cycle of the graph of each trigonometric function is shown.

Function Gallery: Trigonometric Functions

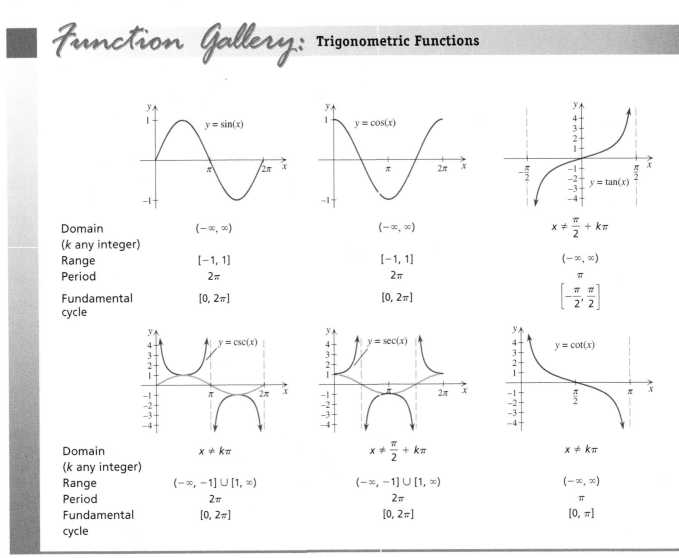

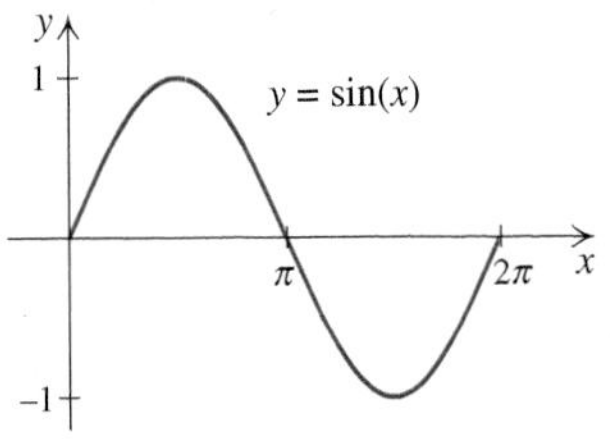

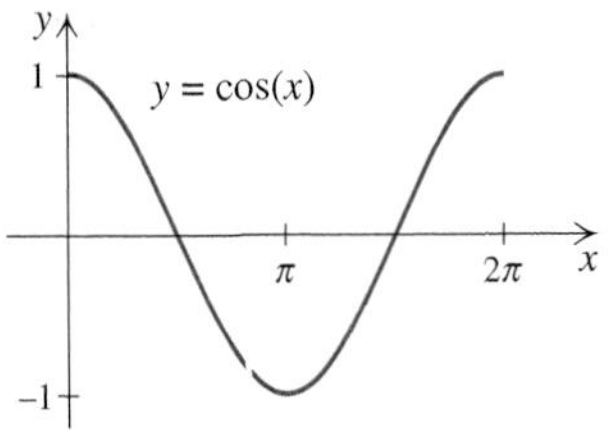

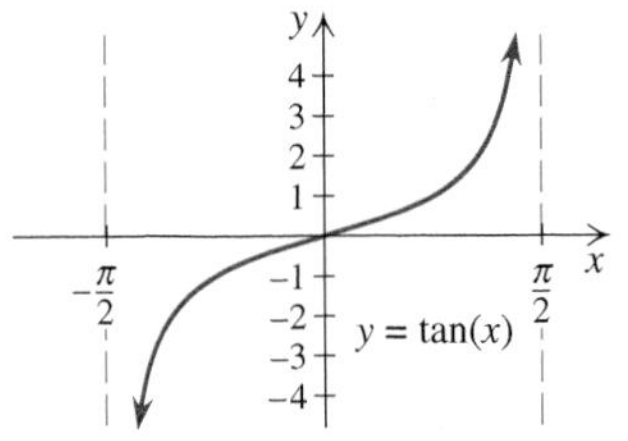

Domain (*k* any integer)	$(-\infty, \infty)$	$(-\infty, \infty)$	$x \neq \frac{\pi}{2} + k\pi$
Range	$[-1, 1]$	$[-1, 1]$	$(-\infty, \infty)$
Period	2π	2π	π
Fundamental cycle	$[0, 2\pi]$	$[0, 2\pi]$	$\left[-\frac{\pi}{2}, \frac{\pi}{2}\right]$

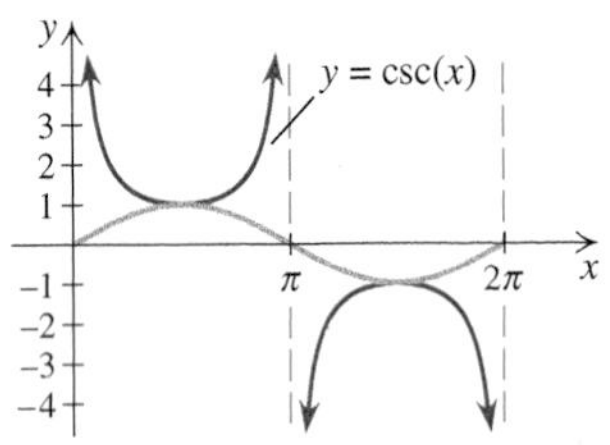

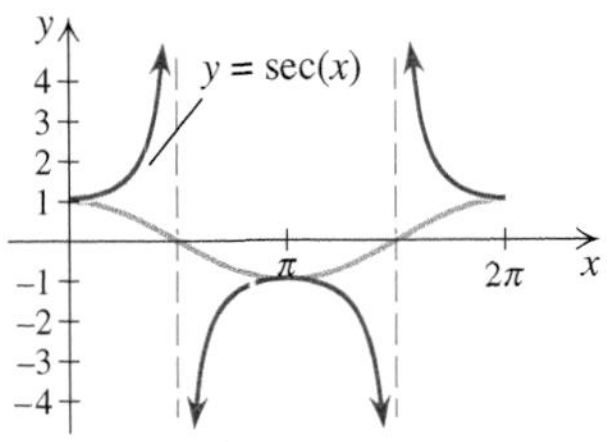

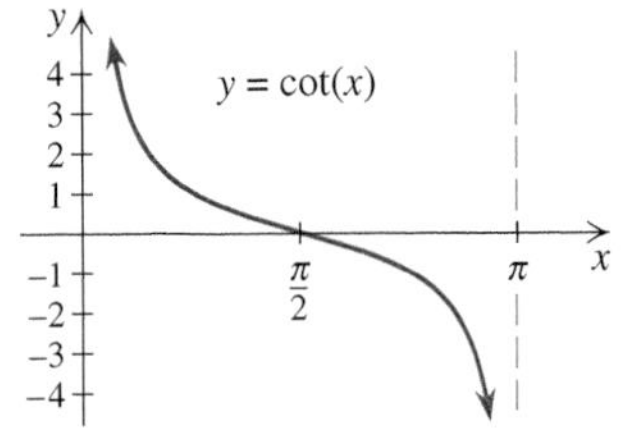

Domain (*k* any integer)	$x \neq k\pi$	$x \neq \frac{\pi}{2} + k\pi$	$x \neq k\pi$
Range	$(-\infty, -1] \cup [1, \infty)$	$(-\infty, -1] \cup [1, \infty)$	$(-\infty, \infty)$
Period	2π	2π	π
Fundamental cycle	$[0, 2\pi]$	$[0, 2\pi]$	$[0, \pi]$

For Thought

True or False? Explain.

1. $\sec(\pi/4) = 1/\sin(\pi/4)$
2. $\cot(\pi/2) = 1/\tan(\pi/2)$
3. $\csc(60°) = 2\sqrt{3}/3$
4. $\tan(5\pi/2) = 0$
5. $\sec(95°) = \sqrt{5}$
6. $\csc(120°) = 2/\sqrt{3}$
7. The graphs of $y = 2 \csc x$ and $y = 1/(2 \sin x)$ are identical.
8. The range of $y = 0.5 \csc(13x - 5\pi)$ is $(-\infty, -0.5] \cup [0.5, \infty)$.
9. The graph of $y = \tan(3x)$ has vertical asymptotes at $x = \pm\pi/6$.
10. The graph of $y = \cot(4x)$ has vertical asymptotes at $x = \pm\pi/4$.

3.4 Exercises

Redraw each unit circle and label each indicated point with the proper value of the tangent function. The points in Exercise 1 are the terminal points for arcs with lengths that are multiples of $\pi/4$. The points in Exercise 2 are the terminal points for arcs with lengths that are multiples of $\pi/6$. Repeat Exercises 1 and 2 until you can do them from memory.

1.

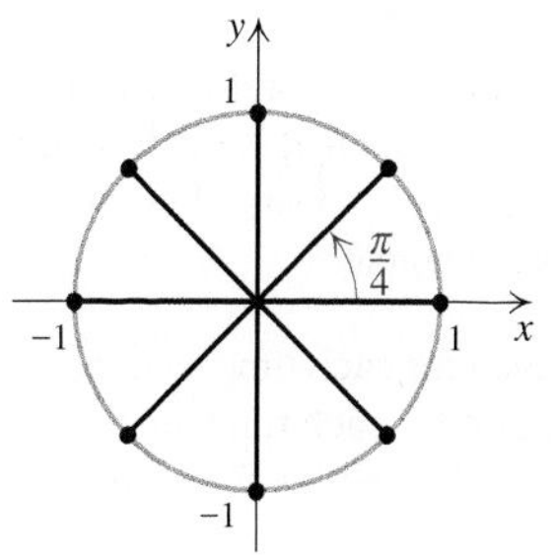

2.

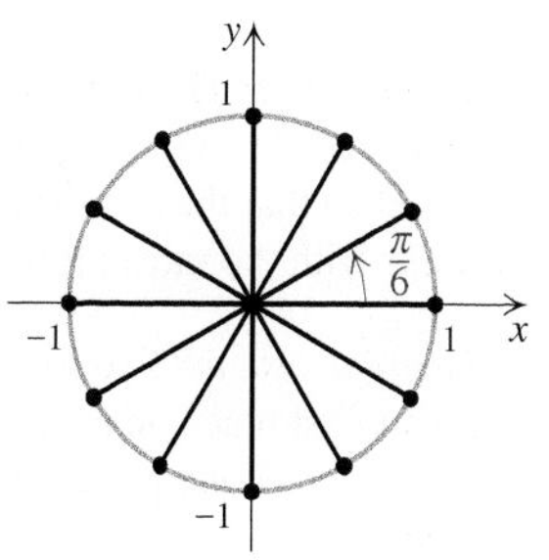

Find the exact value of each of the following expressions without using a calculator.

3. $\tan(\pi/3)$ **4.** $\tan(\pi/4)$

5. $\tan(-\pi/4)$ **6.** $\tan(\pi/6)$

7. $\cot(\pi/2)$ **8.** $\cot(2\pi/3)$

9. $\cot(-\pi/3)$ **10.** $\cot(0)$

11. $\sec(\pi/6)$ **12.** $\sec(\pi/3)$

13. $\sec(\pi/2)$ **14.** $\sec(\pi)$

15. $\csc(-\pi)$ **16.** $\csc(\pi/6)$

17. $\csc(3\pi/4)$ **18.** $\csc(-\pi/3)$

19. $\tan(135°)$ **20.** $\tan(270°)$

21. $\cot(210°)$ **22.** $\cot(120°)$

23. $\sec(-120°)$ **24.** $\sec(-90°)$

25. $\csc(315°)$ **26.** $\csc(240°)$

27. $\cot(-90°)$ **28.** $\cot(270°)$

Find the approximate value of each expression. Round to four decimal places.

29. $\tan(1.55)$ **30.** $\tan(1.6)$

31. $\cot(-3.48)$ **32.** $\cot(22.4)$

33. $\csc(0.002)$ **34.** $\csc(1.54)$

35. $\sec(\pi/12)$ **36.** $\sec(-\pi/8)$

37. $\cot(0.09°)$ **38.** $\cot(179.4°)$

39. $\csc(-44.3°)$ **40.** $\csc(-124.5°)$

41. $\sec(89.2°)$ **42.** $\sec(-0.024°)$

43. $\tan(-44.6°)$ **44.** $\tan(138°)$

Find the exact value of each expression for the given value of θ. Do not use a calculator.

45. $\sec^2(2\theta)$ if $\theta = \pi/6$ **46.** $\csc^2(2\theta)$ if $\theta = \pi/8$

47. $\tan(\theta/2)$ if $\theta = \pi/3$ **48.** $\csc(\theta/2)$ if $\theta = \pi/2$

49. $\sec(\theta/2)$ if $\theta = 3\pi/2$ **50.** $\cot(\theta/2)$ if $\theta = 2\pi/3$

Determine the period and sketch at least one cycle of the graph of each function.

51. $y = \tan(3x)$ **52.** $y = \tan(4x)$

53. $y = \cot(x + \pi/4)$ **54.** $y = \cot(x - \pi/6)$

55. $y = \cot(x/2)$ **56.** $y = \cot(x/3)$

57. $y = \tan(\pi x)$ **58.** $y = \tan(\pi x/2)$

59. $y = -2\tan x$ **60.** $y = -\tan(x - \pi/2)$

61. $y = -\cot(x + \pi/2)$ **62.** $y = 2 + \cot x$

63. $y = \cot(2x - \pi/2)$ **64.** $y = \cot(3x + \pi)$

65. $y = \tan\left(\frac{\pi}{2}x - \frac{\pi}{2}\right)$ **66.** $y = \tan\left(\frac{\pi}{4}x + \frac{3\pi}{4}\right)$

Determine the period and sketch at least one cycle of the graph of each function. State the range of each function.

67. $y = \sec(2x)$ **68.** $y = \sec(3x)$

69. $y = \csc(x - \pi/2)$ **70.** $y = \csc(x + \pi/4)$

71. $y = \csc(x/2)$ **72.** $y = \csc(x/4)$

73. $y = \sec(\pi x/2)$ **74.** $y = \sec(\pi x)$

75. $y = 2\sec x$ **76.** $y = \frac{1}{2}\sec x$

77. $y = \csc(2x - \pi/2)$

78. $y = \csc(3x + \pi)$

79. $y = -\csc\left(\frac{\pi}{2}x + \frac{\pi}{2}\right)$

80. $y = -2\csc(\pi x - \pi)$

81. $y = 2 + 2\sec(2x)$

82. $y = 2 - 2\sec\left(\frac{x}{2}\right)$

Determine the period and range of each function.

83. $y = \tan(2x - \pi) + 3$

84. $y = 2\cot(3x + \pi) - 8$

85. $y = 2\sec(x/2 - 1) - 1$

86. $y = -2\sec(x/3 - 6) + 3$

87. $y = -3\csc(2x - \pi) - 4$

88. $y = 4\csc(3x - \pi) + 5$

Write the equation of each curve in its final position.

89. The graph of $y = \tan(x)$ is shifted $\pi/4$ units to the right, stretched by a factor of 3, then translated 2 units upward.

90. The graph of $y = \cot(x)$ is shifted $\pi/2$ units to the left, reflected in the x-axis, then translated 1 unit upward.

91. The graph of $y = \sec(x)$ is shifted π units to the left, reflected in the x-axis, then shifted 2 units upward.

92. The graph of $y = \csc(x)$ is shifted 2 units to the right, translated 3 units downward, then reflected in the x-axis.

Thinking Outside the Box XXII

Counting Votes Fifteen experts are voting to determine the best convertible of the year. The choices are a Porsche Carrera, a Chrysler Crossfire, and a Nissan Roadster. The experts will rank the three cars 1st, 2nd, and 3rd. There are three common ways to determine the winner.

1. *Plurality:* The car with the most first place votes (preferences) is the winner.

2. *Instant runoff:* The car with the least number of preferences is eliminated. Then the ballots where the eliminated car is first are revised so that the second place car is moved to first. Finally, the car with the most preferences is the winner.

3. *The point system:* Two points are given for each time a car occurs in first place on a ballot, one point for each time the car appears in second place on a ballot, and no points for third place.

When the ballots were cast, the Porsche won when plurality was used, the Chrysler won when instant runoff was used, and the Nissan won when the point system was used. Determine 15 actual votes for which this result would occur.

3.4 Pop Quiz

1. What is the period for $y = \tan(3x)$?

2. Find the equations of all asymptotes for $y = \cot(2x)$.

3. Find the equations of all asymptotes for $y = \sec(2x)$.

4. What is the range of $y = 3\csc(2x)$?

Find the exact value.

5. $\tan(\pi/4)$

6. $\tan(120°)$

7. $\cot(-\pi/3)$

8. $\sec(60°)$

9. $\csc(-3\pi/4)$

3.5 The Inverse Trigonometric Functions

We have learned how to find the values of the trigonometric functions for angles or real numbers, but to make the trigonometric functions really useful we must be able to reverse this process. In this section we define the inverses of the trigonometric functions.

The Inverse of the Sine Function

In Chapter 1 we learned that only one-to-one functions are invertible. Since $y = \sin x$ with domain $(-\infty, \infty)$ is a periodic function, it is certainly not one-to-one.

However, if we restrict the domain to the interval $[-\pi/2, \pi/2]$, then the restricted function is one-to-one and invertible. Other intervals could be used, but this interval is chosen to keep the inverse function as simple as possible.

The graph of the sine function with domain $[-\pi/2, \pi/2]$ is shown in Fig. 3.68(a). Its range is $[-1, 1]$. We now define the inverse sine function and denote it as $f^{-1}(x) = \sin^{-1}x$ (read "inverse sine of x") or $f^{-1}(x) = \arcsin x$ (read "arc sine of x").

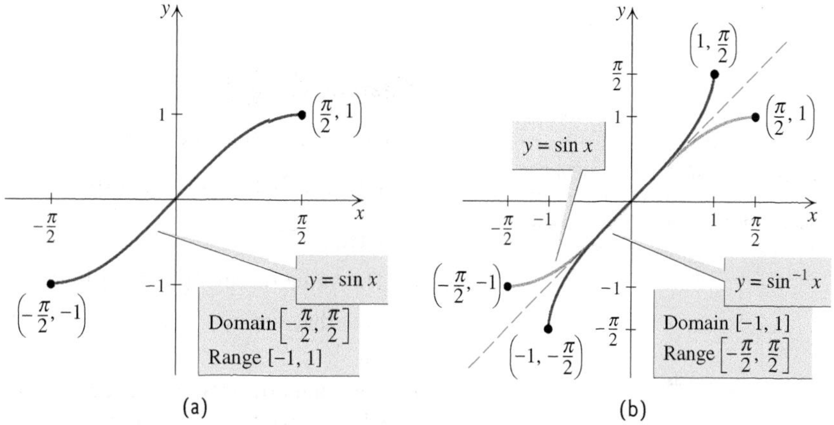

Figure 3.68

Definition: The Inverse Sine Function

The function $\mathbf{y = \sin^{-1}x}$ or $\mathbf{y = \arcsin x}$ is the inverse of the function $y = \sin x$ restricted to $[-\pi/2, \pi/2]$. The domain of $y = \sin^{-1}x$ is $[-1, 1]$ and its range is $[-\pi/2, \pi/2]$.

The graph of $y = \sin^{-1}x$ is a reflection about the line $y = x$ of the graph of $y = \sin x$ on $[-\pi/2, \pi/2]$, as shown in Fig. 3.68(b).

If $y = \sin^{-1}x$, then y is the real number such that $-\pi/2 \le y \le \pi/2$ and $\sin y = x$. Depending on the context, $\sin^{-1}x$ might also be an angle, a measure of an angle in degrees or radians, or the length of an arc of the unit circle. The expression $\sin^{-1}x$ can be read as "the angle whose sine is x" or "the arc length whose sine is x." The notation $y = \arcsin x$ reminds us that y is the arc length whose sine is x. For example, $\arcsin(1)$ is the arc length in $[-\pi/2, \pi/2]$ whose sine is 1. Since we know that $\sin(\pi/2) = 1$, we have $\arcsin(1) = \pi/2$. We will assume that $\sin^{-1}x$ is a real number unless indicated otherwise.

Note that the nth power of the sine function is usually written as $\sin^n(x)$ as a shorthand notation for $(\sin x)^n$, provided $n \ne -1$. The -1 used in $\sin^{-1}x$ indicates the inverse function and does *not* mean reciprocal. To write $1/\sin x$ using exponents, we must write $(\sin x)^{-1}$.

Example 1 Evaluating the inverse sine function

Find the exact value of each expression without using a table or a calculator.

a. $\sin^{-1}(1/2)$ **b.** $\arcsin(-\sqrt{3}/2)$

Solution

a. The value of $\sin^{-1}(1/2)$ is the number α in the interval $[-\pi/2, \pi/2]$ such that $\sin(\alpha) = 1/2$. We recall that $\sin(\pi/6) = 1/2$, and so $\sin^{-1}(1/2) = \pi/6$. Note that $\pi/6$ is the only value of α in $[-\pi/2, \pi/2]$ for which $\sin(\alpha) = 1/2$.

b. The value of $\arcsin(-\sqrt{3}/2)$ is the number α in $[-\pi/2, \pi/2]$ such that $\sin(\alpha) = -\sqrt{3}/2$. Since $\sin(-\pi/3) = -\sqrt{3}/2$, we have $\arcsin(-\sqrt{3}/2) = -\pi/3$. Note that $-\pi/3$ is the only value of α in $[-\pi/2, \pi/2]$ for which $\sin(\alpha) = -\sqrt{3}/2$. ■

■ Foreshadowing Calculus

In calculus we discover some interesting relationships between functions. The rates of change of the trigonometric functions are other trigonometric functions, but the rates of change of the inverse trigonometric functions are algebraic functions.

Example 2 Evaluating the inverse sine function

Find the exact value of each expression in degrees without using a table or a calculator.

a. $\sin^{-1}(\sqrt{2}/2)$ **b.** $\arcsin(0)$

Solution

a. The value of $\sin^{-1}(\sqrt{2}/2)$ in degrees is the angle α in the interval $[-90°, 90°]$ such that $\sin(\alpha) = \sqrt{2}/2$. We recall that $\sin(45°) = \sqrt{2}/2$, and so $\sin^{-1}(\sqrt{2}/2) = 45°$.

b. The value of $\arcsin(0)$ in degrees is the angle α in the interval $[-90°, 90°]$ for which $\sin(\alpha) = 0$. Since $\sin(0°) = 0$, we have $\arcsin(0) = 0°$. ■

In the next example, we use a calculator to find the degree measure of an angle whose sine is given. To obtain degree measure, make sure the calculator is in degree mode. Scientific calculators usually have a key labeled $\sin^{-1}$ that gives values for the inverse sine function.

Example 3 Finding an angle given its sine

Let α be an angle such that $-90° < \alpha < 90°$. In each case, find α to the nearest tenth of a degree.

a. $\sin\alpha = 0.88$ **b.** $\sin\alpha = -0.27$

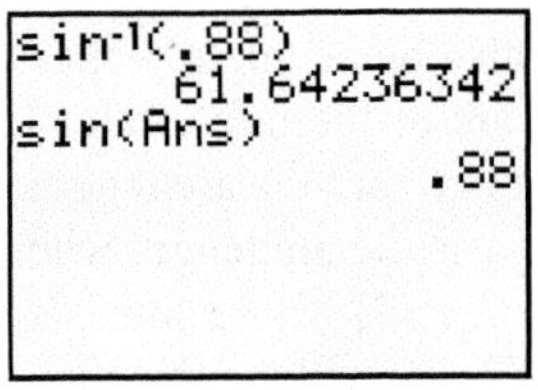

Figure 3.69

Solution

a. The value of $\sin^{-1}(0.88)$ is the only angle in $[-90°, 90°]$ with a sine of 0.88. Use a calculator in degree mode to get $\alpha = \sin^{-1}(0.88) \approx 61.6°$.

b. Use a calculator to get $\alpha = \sin^{-1}(-0.27) \approx -15.7°$.

Figure 3.69 shows how to find the angle in part (a) on a graphing calculator and how to check. Make sure that the mode is degrees. ■

The Inverse Cosine Function

Since the cosine function is not one-to-one on $(-\infty, \infty)$, we restrict the domain to $[0, \pi]$, where the cosine function is one-to-one and invertible. The graph of the cosine function with this restricted domain is shown in Fig. 3.70(a). Note that the range of the restricted function is $[-1, 1]$. We now define the inverse of $f(x) = \cos x$ for x in $[0, \pi]$ and denote it as $f^{-1}(x) = \cos^{-1} x$ or $f^{-1}(x) = \arccos x$.

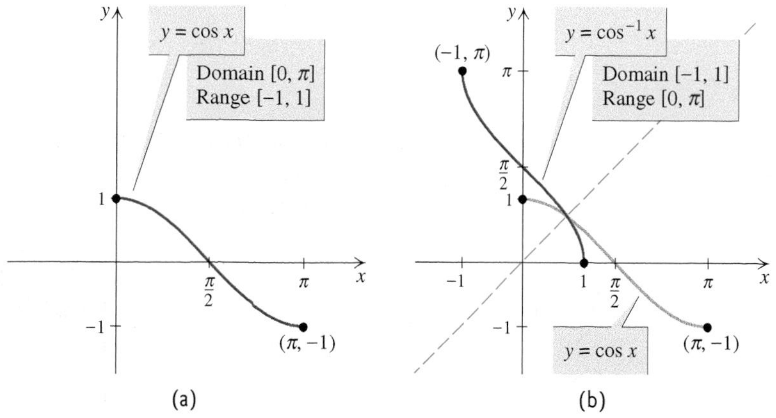

Figure 3.70

Definition: The Inverse Cosine Function

The function $\mathbf{y = \cos^{-1} x}$ or $\mathbf{y = \arccos x}$ is the inverse of the function $y = \cos x$ restricted to $[0, \pi]$. The domain of $y = \cos^{-1} x$ is $[-1, 1]$ and its range is $[0, \pi]$.

If $y = \cos^{-1} x$, then y is the real number in $[0, \pi]$ such that $\cos y = x$. The expression $\cos^{-1} x$ can be read as "the angle whose cosine is x" or "the arc length whose cosine is x." The graph of $y = \cos^{-1} x$, shown in Fig. 3.70(b), is obtained by reflecting the graph of $y = \cos x$ (restricted to $[0, \pi]$) about the line $y = x$. We will assume that $\cos^{-1} x$ is a real number unless indicated otherwise.

Example 4 Evaluating the inverse cosine function

Find the exact value of each expression without using a table or a calculator.

a. $\cos^{-1}(-1)$ **b.** $\arccos(-1/2)$ **c.** $\cos^{-1}(\sqrt{2}/2)$

Solution

a. The value of $\cos^{-1}(-1)$ is the number α in $[0, \pi]$ such that $\cos(\alpha) = -1$. We recall that $\cos(\pi) = -1$, and so $\cos^{-1}(-1) = \pi$.

b. The value of $\arccos(-1/2)$ is the number α in $[0, \pi]$ such that $\cos(\alpha) = -1/2$. We recall that $\cos(2\pi/3) = -1/2$, and so $\arccos(-1/2) = 2\pi/3$.

c. Since $\cos(\pi/4) = \sqrt{2}/2$, we have $\cos^{-1}(\sqrt{2}/2) = \pi/4$. ■

In the next example, we use a calculator to find the degree measure of an angle whose cosine is given. Most scientific calculators have a key labeled $\cos^{-1}$ that gives values for the inverse cosine function. To get the degree measure, make sure the calculator is in degree mode.

Example 5 Finding an angle given its cosine

In each case find the angle α to the nearest tenth of a degree, given that $0° < \alpha < 180°$.

a. $\cos\alpha = 0.23$ **b.** $\cos\alpha = -0.82$

Solution

a. Since $\cos^{-1}(0.23)$ is the unique angle in $[0°, 180°]$ with a cosine of 0.23, $\alpha = \cos^{-1}(0.23) \approx 76.7°$.

b. Use a calculator to get $\alpha = \cos^{-1}(-0.82) \approx 145.1°$.

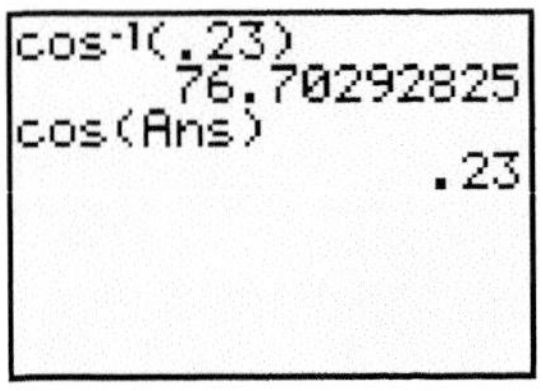

Figure 3.71

Figure 3.71 shows how to find $\cos^{-1}(0.23)$ on a graphing calculator and how to check. Make sure that the mode is degrees. ■

Inverses of Tangent, Cotangent, Secant, and Cosecant

Since all of the trigonometric functions are periodic, they must all be restricted to a domain where they are one-to-one before the inverse functions can be defined. There is more than one way to choose a domain to get a one-to-one function, but we will use the most common restrictions. The restricted domain for $y = \tan x$ is $(-\pi/2, \pi/2)$, for $y = \csc x$ it is $[-\pi/2, 0) \cup (0, \pi/2]$, for $y = \sec x$ it is $[0, \pi/2) \cup (\pi/2, \pi]$, and for $y = \cot x$ it is $(0, \pi)$. The functions $\tan^{-1}$, $\cot^{-1}$, $\sec^{-1}$, and $\csc^{-1}$ are defined to be the inverses of these restricted functions. The notations arctan, arccot, arcsec, and arccsc are also used for these inverse functions. The graphs of all six inverse functions, with their domains and ranges, are shown in the accompanying Function Gallery.

When studying inverse trigonometric functions, you should first learn to evaluate $\sin^{-1}$, $\cos^{-1}$, and $\tan^{-1}$. Then use the identities

$$\csc\alpha = \frac{1}{\sin\alpha}, \qquad \sec\alpha = \frac{1}{\cos\alpha}, \qquad \text{and} \qquad \cot\alpha = \frac{1}{\tan\alpha}$$

to evaluate $\csc^{-1}$, $\sec^{-1}$, and $\cot^{-1}$. For example, $\sin(\pi/6) = 1/2$ and $\csc(\pi/6) = 2$. So the angle whose cosecant is 2 is the same as the angle whose sine is $1/2$. In symbols,

$$\csc^{-1}(2) = \sin^{-1}\left(\frac{1}{2}\right) = \frac{\pi}{6}.$$

In general, $\csc^{-1}x = \sin^{-1}(1/x)$. Likewise, $\sec^{-1}x = \cos^{-1}(1/x)$. For the inverse cotangent, $\cot^{-1}x = \tan^{-1}(1/x)$ only for $x > 0$, because of the choice of $(0, \pi)$ as the range of the inverse cotangent. We have $\cot^{-1}(0) = \pi/2$ and, if $x < 0$, $\cot^{-1}(x) = \tan^{-1}(1/x) + \pi$.

Function Gallery: Inverse Trigonometric Functions

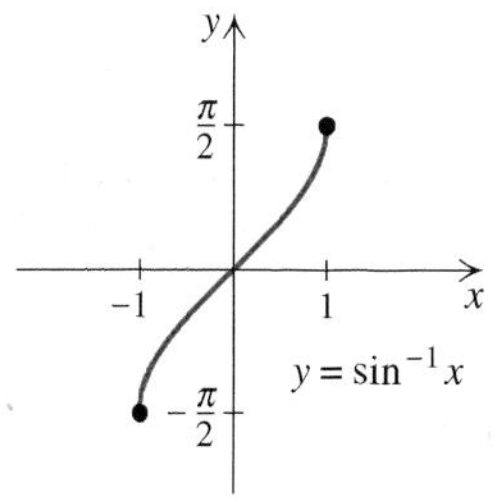

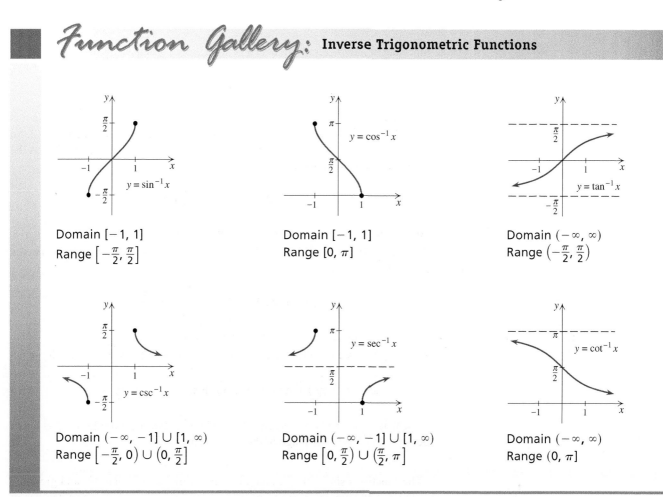

Domain $[-1, 1]$
Range $\left[-\frac{\pi}{2}, \frac{\pi}{2}\right]$

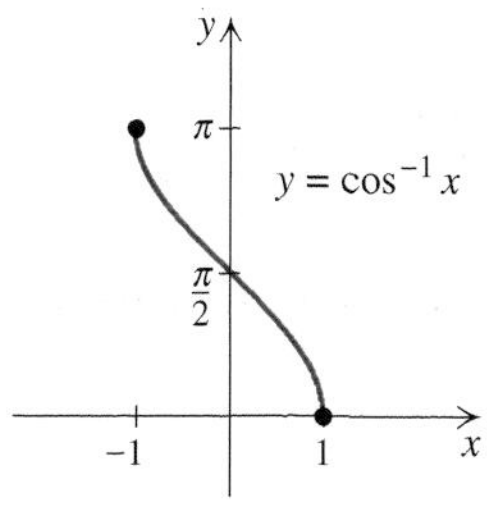

Domain $[-1, 1]$
Range $[0, \pi]$

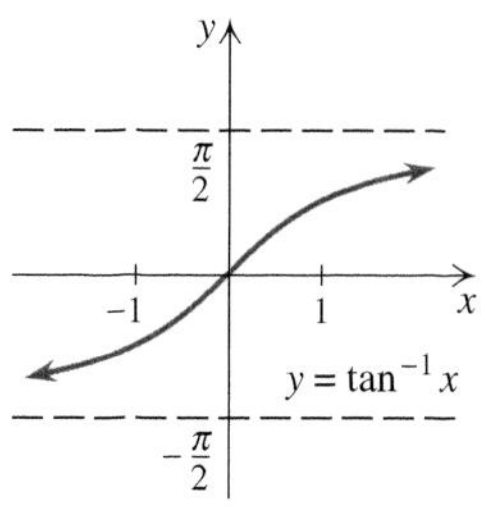

Domain $(-\infty, \infty)$
Range $\left(-\frac{\pi}{2}, \frac{\pi}{2}\right)$

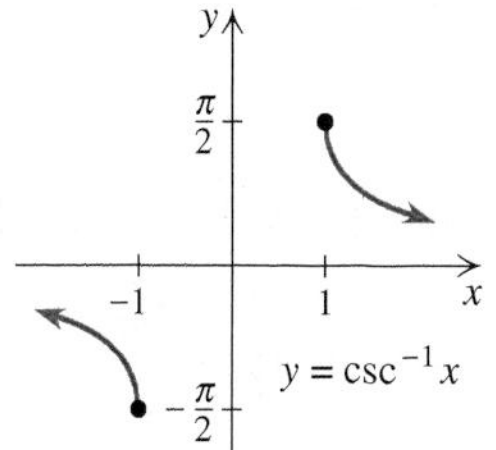

Domain $(-\infty, -1] \cup [1, \infty)$
Range $\left[-\frac{\pi}{2}, 0\right) \cup \left(0, \frac{\pi}{2}\right]$

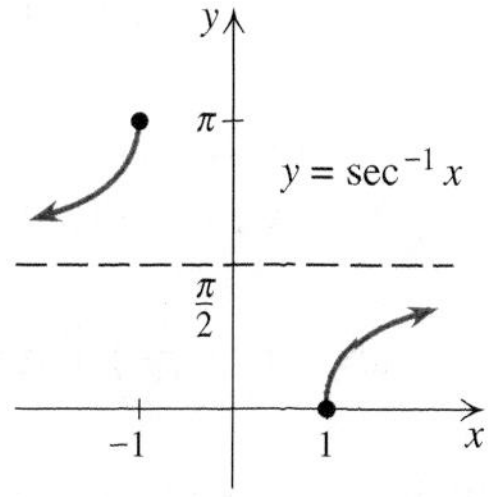

Domain $(-\infty, -1] \cup [1, \infty)$
Range $\left[0, \frac{\pi}{2}\right) \cup \left(\frac{\pi}{2}, \pi\right]$

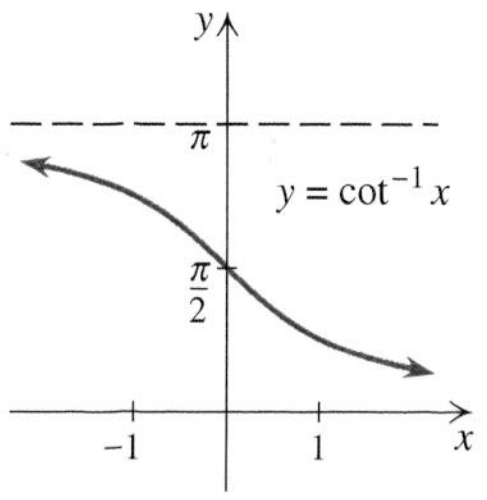

Domain $(-\infty, \infty)$
Range $(0, \pi]$

We can see another relationship between $\cot^{-1}$ and $\tan^{-1}$ from their graphs in the Function Gallery. Notice that the graph of $y = \cot^{-1}(x)$ can be obtained by reflecting the graph of $y = \tan^{-1}(x)$ about the x-axis and then translating $\pi/2$ units upward. So $\cot^{-1}(x) = -\tan^{-1}(x) + \pi/2$ or $\cot^{-1}(x) = \pi/2 - \tan^{-1}(x)$.

Identities for the Inverse Functions

$$\csc^{-1}(x) = \sin^{-1}(1/x) \text{ for } |x| \geq 1$$

$$\sec^{-1}(x) = \cos^{-1}(1/x) \text{ for } |x| \geq 1$$

$$\cot^{-1}(x) = \begin{cases} \tan^{-1}(1/x) & \text{for } x > 0 \\ \tan^{-1}(1/x) + \pi & \text{for } x < 0 \\ \pi/2 & \text{for } x = 0 \end{cases}$$

$$\cot^{-1}(x) = \pi/2 - \tan^{-1}(x)$$

Example 6 Evaluating the inverse functions

Find the exact value of each expression without using a table or a calculator.

a. $\tan^{-1}(1)$ **b.** $\operatorname{arcsec}(-2)$ **c.** $\csc^{-1}(\sqrt{2})$ **d.** $\operatorname{arccot}(-1/\sqrt{3})$

Solution

a. Since $\tan(\pi/4) = 1$ and since $\pi/4$ is in the range of $\tan^{-1}$, we have

$$\tan^{-1}(1) = \frac{\pi}{4}.$$

b. To evaluate the inverse secant, we use the identity $\sec^{-1}(x) = \cos^{-1}(1/x)$. In this case, the arc whose secant is -2 is the same as the arc whose cosine is $-1/2$. So we must find $\cos^{-1}(-1/2)$. Since $\cos(2\pi/3) = -1/2$ and since $2\pi/3$ is in the range of arccos, we have

$$\text{arcsec}(-2) = \arccos\left(-\frac{1}{2}\right) = \frac{2\pi}{3}.$$

c. To evaluate $\csc^{-1}(\sqrt{2})$, we use the identity $\csc^{-1}(x) = \sin^{-1}(1/x)$ with $x = \sqrt{2}$. So we must find $\sin^{-1}(1/\sqrt{2})$. Since $\sin(\pi/4) = 1/\sqrt{2}$ and since $\pi/4$ is in the range of $\csc^{-1}$,

$$\csc^{-1}(\sqrt{2}) = \sin^{-1}\left(\frac{1}{\sqrt{2}}\right) = \frac{\pi}{4}.$$

d. If x is negative, we use the identity $\cot^{-1}(x) = \tan^{-1}(1/x) + \pi$. Since $x = -1/\sqrt{3}$, we must find $\tan^{-1}(-\sqrt{3})$. Since $\tan^{-1}(-\sqrt{3}) = -\pi/3$, we get

$$\text{arccot}\left(\frac{-1}{\sqrt{3}}\right) = \tan^{-1}(-\sqrt{3}) + \pi = -\frac{\pi}{3} + \pi = \frac{2\pi}{3}.$$

Note that $\cot(-\pi/3) = \cot(2\pi/3) = -1/\sqrt{3}$, but $\text{arccot}(-1/\sqrt{3}) = 2\pi/3$ because $2\pi/3$ is in the range of the function arccot. ■

The functions $\sin^{-1}$, $\cos^{-1}$, and $\tan^{-1}$ are available on scientific and graphing calculators. The calculator values of the inverse functions are given in degrees or radians, depending on the mode setting. We will assume that the values of the inverse functions are to be in radians unless indicated otherwise. Calculators use the domains and ranges of these functions defined here. The functions $\sec^{-1}$, $\csc^{-1}$, and $\cot^{-1}$ are generally not available on a calculator, and expressions involving these functions must be written in terms of $\sin^{-1}$, $\cos^{-1}$, and $\tan^{-1}$ by using the identities.

Example 7 Evaluating the inverse functions with a calculator

Find the approximate value of each expression rounded to four decimal places.

a. $\sin^{-1}(0.88)$ **b.** $\text{arccot}(2.4)$ **c.** $\csc^{-1}(4)$ **d.** $\cot^{-1}(0)$

Solution

a. Use the inverse sine function in radian mode to get $\sin^{-1}(0.88) \approx 1.0759$.
b. Use the identity $\cot^{-1}(x) = \tan^{-1}(1/x)$ because $2.4 > 0$:

$$\text{arccot}(2.4) = \tan^{-1}\left(\frac{1}{2.4}\right) \approx 0.3948$$

c. $\csc^{-1}(4) = \sin^{-1}(0.25) \approx 0.2527$

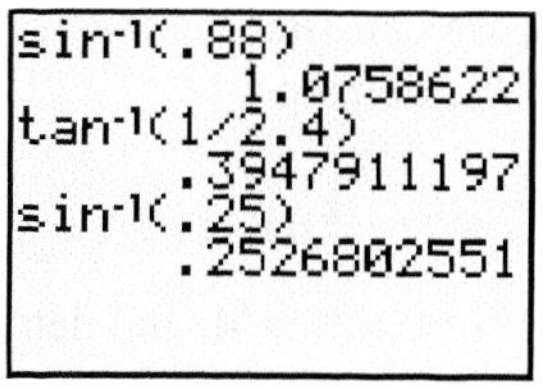

Figure 3.72

d. The value of $\cot^{-1}(0)$ cannot be found on a calculator. But we know that $\cot(\pi/2) = 0$ and $\pi/2$ is in the range $(0, \pi)$ for $\cot^{-1}$, so we have $\cot^{-1}(0) = \pi/2$.

The expressions in parts (a), (b), and (c) are shown on a graphing calculator in Fig. 3.72. ■

Compositions of Functions

One trigonometric function can be followed by another to form a composition of functions. We can evaluate an expression such as $\sin(\sin(\alpha))$ because the sine of the real number $\sin(\alpha)$ is defined. However, it is more common to have a composition of a trigonometric function and an inverse trigonometric function. For example, $\tan^{-1}(\alpha)$ is the angle whose tangent is α, and so $\sin(\tan^{-1}(\alpha))$ is the sine of the angle whose tangent is α.

Example 8 Evaluating compositions of functions

Find the exact value of each composition without using a table or a calculator.

a. $\sin(\tan^{-1}(0))$ **b.** $\arcsin(\cos(\pi/6))$ **c.** $\tan\left(\sec^{-1}\left(\sqrt{2}\right)\right)$

Solution

a. Since $\tan(0) = 0$, $\tan^{-1}(0) = 0$. Therefore,

$$\sin(\tan^{-1}(0)) = \sin(0) = 0.$$

b. Since $\cos(\pi/6) = \sqrt{3}/2$, we have

$$\arcsin\left(\cos\left(\frac{\pi}{6}\right)\right) = \arcsin\left(\frac{\sqrt{3}}{2}\right) = \frac{\pi}{3}.$$

c. To find $\sec^{-1}\left(\sqrt{2}\right)$, we use the identity $\sec^{-1}(x) = \cos^{-1}(1/x)$. Since $\cos(\pi/4) = 1/\sqrt{2}$, we have $\cos^{-1}\left(1/\sqrt{2}\right) = \pi/4$ and $\sec^{-1}\left(\sqrt{2}\right) = \pi/4$. Therefore,

$$\tan\left(\sec^{-1}\left(\sqrt{2}\right)\right) = \tan\left(\frac{\pi}{4}\right) = 1.$$

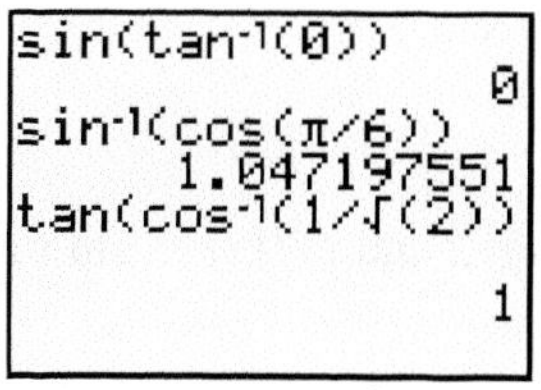

Figure 3.73

You can check parts (a), (b), and (c) with a graphing calculator, as shown in Fig. 3.73. Note that $\pi/3 \approx 1.047$. ■

The composition of $y = \sin x$ restricted to $[-\pi/2, \pi/2]$ and $y = \sin^{-1} x$ is the identity function, because they are inverse functions of each other. So

$$\sin^{-1}(\sin x) = x \quad \text{for } x \text{ in } [-\pi/2, \pi/2]$$

and

$$\sin(\sin^{-1} x) = x \quad \text{for } x \text{ in } [-1, 1].$$

Note that if x is not in $[-\pi/2, \pi/2]$, then the sine function followed by the inverse sine function is not the identity function. For example, $\sin^{-1}(\sin(2\pi/3)) = \pi/3$.

The general sine function $f(x) = A\sin[B(x - C)] + D$ is a composition of a trigonometric function and several algebraic functions. Since the sine function has an inverse and the algebraic functions have inverses, we can find the inverse for a general sine function provided it is restricted to a suitable domain.

Example 9 The inverse of a general sine function

Find the inverse of $f(x) = 3\sin(2x) + 5$, where $-\pi/4 \leq x \leq \pi/4$, and determine the domain of f^{-1}.

Solution

Interchange x and y in $y = 3\sin(2x) + 5$, and then solve for y:

$$x = 3\sin(2y) + 5 \quad \text{Switch } x \text{ and } y.$$

$$\frac{x-5}{3} = \sin(2y)$$

$$2y = \sin^{-1}\left(\frac{x-5}{3}\right) \quad \text{Definition of } \sin^{-1}$$

$$y = \frac{1}{2}\sin^{-1}\left(\frac{x-5}{3}\right)$$

$$f^{-1}(x) = \frac{1}{2}\sin^{-1}\left(\frac{x-5}{3}\right)$$

Since $\sin(2x)$ is between -1 and 1, the range of f is [2, 8] and the domain of f^{-1} is [2, 8]. ■

For Thought

True or False? Explain.

1. $\sin^{-1}(0) = \sin(0)$
2. $\sin(3\pi/4) = 1/\sqrt{2}$
3. $\cos^{-1}(0) = 1$
4. $\sin^{-1}(\sqrt{2}/2) = 135°$
5. $\cot^{-1}(5) = \dfrac{1}{\tan^{-1}(5)}$
6. $\sec^{-1}(5) = \cos^{-1}(0.2)$
7. $\sin(\cos^{-1}(\sqrt{2}/2)) = 1/\sqrt{2}$
8. $\sec(\sec^{-1}(2)) = 2$
9. The functions $f(x) = \sin^{-1} x$ and $f^{-1}(x) = \sin x$ are inverse functions.
10. The secant and cosecant functions are inverses of each other.

3.5 Exercises

Find the exact value of each expression without using a calculator or table.

1. $\sin^{-1}(-1/2)$
2. $\sin^{-1}(0)$
3. $\arcsin(1/2)$
4. $\arcsin(\sqrt{3}/2)$
5. $\arcsin(\sqrt{2}/2)$
6. $\arcsin(1)$

Find the exact value of each expression in degrees without using a calculator or table.

7. $\sin^{-1}(-1/\sqrt{2})$
8. $\sin^{-1}(\sqrt{3}/2)$
9. $\arcsin(1/2)$
10. $\arcsin(-1)$
11. $\sin^{-1}(0)$
12. $\sin^{-1}(\sqrt{2}/2)$

In each case find α to the nearest tenth of a degree, where $-90° \le \alpha \le 90°$.

13. $\sin\alpha = -1/3$

14. $\sin\alpha = 0.4138$

15. $\sin\alpha = 0.5682$

16. $\sin\alpha = -0.34$

Find the exact value of each expression without using a calculator or table.

17. $\cos^{-1}(-\sqrt{2}/2)$

18. $\cos^{-1}(1)$

19. $\arccos(1/2)$

20. $\arccos(-\sqrt{3}/2)$

21. $\arccos(-1)$

22. $\arccos(0)$

Find the exact value of each expression in degrees without using a calculator or table.

23. $\cos^{-1}(-\sqrt{2}/2)$

24. $\cos^{-1}(\sqrt{3}/2)$

25. $\arccos(-1)$

26. $\arccos(0)$

27. $\cos^{-1}(-1/2)$

28. $\cos^{-1}(1)$

In each case find α to the nearest tenth of a degree, where $0° \le \alpha \le 180°$.

29. $\cos\alpha = -0.993$

30. $\cos\alpha = 0.7392$

31. $\cos\alpha = 0.001$

32. $\cos\alpha = -0.499$

Find the exact value of each expression without using a calculator or table.

33. $\tan^{-1}(-1)$

34. $\cot^{-1}(1/\sqrt{3})$

35. $\sec^{-1}(2)$

36. $\csc^{-1}(2/\sqrt{3})$

37. $\text{arcsec}(\sqrt{2})$

38. $\arctan(-1/\sqrt{3})$

39. $\text{arccsc}(-2)$

40. $\text{arccot}(-\sqrt{3})$

41. $\tan^{-1}(0)$

42. $\sec^{-1}(1)$

43. $\csc^{-1}(1)$

44. $\csc^{-1}(-1)$

45. $\cot^{-1}(-1)$

46. $\cot^{-1}(0)$

47. $\cot^{-1}(-\sqrt{3}/3)$

48. $\cot^{-1}(1)$

Find the approximate value of each expression with a calculator. Round answers to two decimal places.

49. $\arcsin(0.5682)$

50. $\sin^{-1}(-0.4138)$

51. $\cos^{-1}(-0.993)$

52. $\cos^{-1}(0.7392)$

53. $\tan^{-1}(-0.1396)$

54. $\cot^{-1}(4.32)$

55. $\sec^{-1}(-3.44)$

56. $\csc^{-1}(6.8212)$

57. $\text{arcsec}(\sqrt{6})$

58. $\arctan(-2\sqrt{7})$

59. $\text{arccsc}(-2\sqrt{2})$

60. $\text{arccot}(-\sqrt{5})$

61. $\text{arccot}(-12)$

62. $\text{arccot}(0.001)$

63. $\cot^{-1}(15.6)$

64. $\cot^{-1}(-1.01)$

Find the exact value of each composition without using a calculator or table.

65. $\tan(\arccos(1/2))$

66. $\sec(\arcsin(1/\sqrt{2}))$

67. $\sin^{-1}(\cos(2\pi/3))$

68. $\tan^{-1}(\sin(\pi/2))$

69. $\cot^{-1}(\cot(\pi/6))$

70. $\sec^{-1}(\sec(\pi/3))$

71. $\arcsin(\sin(3\pi/4))$

72. $\arccos(\cos(-\pi/3))$

73. $\tan(\arctan(1))$

74. $\cot(\text{arccot}(0))$

75. $\cos^{-1}(\cos(3\pi/2))$

76. $\sin(\csc^{-1}(-2))$

77. $\cos(2\sin^{-1}(\sqrt{2}/2))$

78. $\tan(2\cos^{-1}(1/2))$

79. $\sin^{-1}(2\sin(\pi/6))$

80. $\cos^{-1}(0.5\tan(\pi/4))$

Find the inverse of each function and state its domain.

81. $f(x) = \sin(2x)$ for $-\frac{\pi}{4} \le x \le \frac{\pi}{4}$

82. $f(x) = \cos(3x)$ for $0 \le x \le \frac{\pi}{3}$

83. $f(x) = 3 + \tan(\pi x)$ for $-\frac{1}{2} < x < \frac{1}{2}$

84. $f(x) = 2 - \sin(\pi x - \pi)$ for $\frac{1}{2} \le x \le \frac{3}{2}$

85. $f(x) = \sin^{-1}(x/2) + 3$ for $-2 \le x \le 2$

86. $f(x) = 2\cos^{-1}(5x) + 3$ for $-\frac{1}{5} \le x \le \frac{1}{5}$

In a circle with radius r, a central angle θ intercepts a chord of length c, where $\theta = \cos^{-1}\left(1 - \frac{c^2}{2r^2}\right)$. Use this formula for Exercises 87 and 88.

87. An airplane at 2000 feet flies directly over a gun that has a range of 2400 feet, as shown in the figure on the next page. What is the measure in degrees of the angle for which the airplane is within range of the gun?

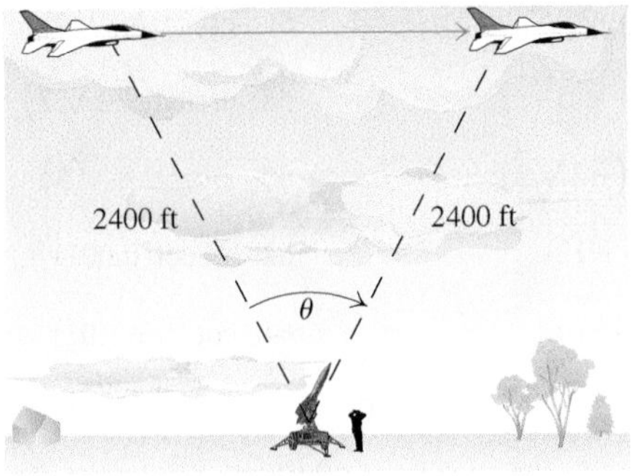

Figure for Exercise 87

88. A triangle has two sides that are both 5.2 meters long and one side with a length of 1.3 meters. Find the measure in degrees for the smallest angle of the triangle.

Thinking Outside the Box XXIII

Clear Sailing A sailor plans to install a windshield wiper on a porthole that has radius 1 foot. The wiper blade of length x feet is to be attached to the edge of the porthole as shown in the figure. The area cleaned by the blade is a sector of a circle centered at the point of attachment.

a. Write the area cleaned by the blade as a function of x.

b. If the blade cleans half of the window, then what is the exact length of the blade?

c. Use a graphing calculator to find the length for the blade that would maximize the area cleaned?

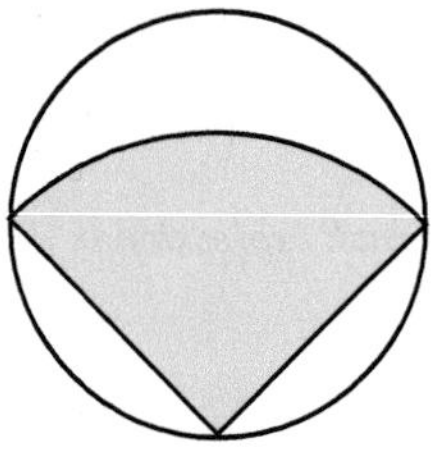

Figure for Thinking Outside the Box XXIII

3.5 Pop Quiz

1. Find $f^{-1}(x)$ if $f(x) = \cos(2x)$ for $0 \leq x \leq \pi/2$.

Find the exact value.

2. $\sin^{-1}(-1)$

3. $\sin^{-1}(1/2)$

4. $\arccos(-1)$

5. $\arctan(-1)$

6. $\tan(\arcsin(1/2))$

7. $\sin^{-1}(\sin(3\pi/4))$

3.6 Right Triangle Trigonometry

One reason trigonometry was invented was to determine the measures of sides and angles of geometric figures without actually measuring them. In this section we study right triangles (triangles that have a 90° angle) and see what information is needed to determine the measures of all unknown sides and angles of a right triangle.

Trigonometric Ratios

We defined the sine and cosine functions for an angle in standard position in terms of the point at which the terminal side intersects the unit circle. However, it is often the case that we do not know that point, but we do know a different point on the terminal side. When this situation occurs, we can find the values for the sine and cosine of the angle using trigonometric ratios.

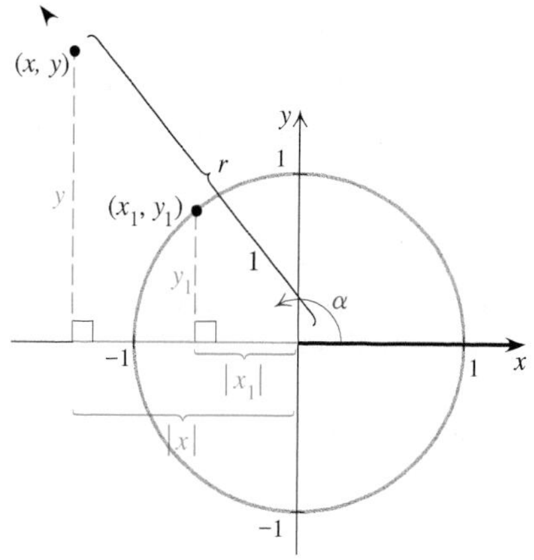

Figure 3.74

Figure 3.74 shows an angle α in quadrant II with the terminal side passing through the point (x, y) and intersecting the unit circle at (x_1, y_1). If we draw vertical line segments down to the x-axis, we form two similar right triangles, as shown in Fig. 3.74. If r is the distance from (x, y) to the origin, then $r = \sqrt{x^2 + y^2}$. The lengths of the legs in the larger triangle are y and $|x|$, and its hypotenuse is r. The lengths of the legs in the smaller triangle are y_1 and $|x_1|$, and its hypotenuse is 1. Since ratios of the lengths of corresponding sides of similar triangles are equal, we have

$$\frac{y_1}{y} = \frac{1}{r} \quad \text{and} \quad \frac{|x_1|}{|x|} = \frac{1}{r}.$$

The first equation can be written as $y_1 = y/r$ and the second as $x_1 = x/r$. (Since x_1 and x are both negative in this case, the absolute value symbols can be omitted.) Since $y_1 = \sin\alpha$ and $x_1 = \cos\alpha$, we get

$$\sin\alpha = \frac{y}{r} \quad \text{and} \quad \cos\alpha = \frac{x}{r}.$$

This argument can be repeated in each quadrant with (x, y) chosen inside, outside, or on the unit circle. These ratios also give the correct sine or cosine if α is a quadrantal angle. Since all other trigonometric functions are related to the sine and cosine, their values can also be obtained from x, y, and r.

Theorem: Trigonometric Ratios

If (x, y) is any point other than the origin on the terminal side of an angle α in standard position and $r = \sqrt{x^2 + y^2}$, then

$$\sin\alpha = \frac{y}{r}, \quad \cos\alpha = \frac{x}{r}, \quad \text{and} \quad \tan\alpha = \frac{y}{x}\ (x \neq 0).$$

Example 1 Trigonometric ratios

Find the values of the six trigonometric functions of the angle α in standard position whose terminal side passes through $(4, -2)$.

Solution

Use $x = 4$, $y = -2$, and $r = \sqrt{4^2 + (-2)^2} = \sqrt{20} = 2\sqrt{5}$ to get

$$\sin\alpha = \frac{-2}{2\sqrt{5}} = -\frac{\sqrt{5}}{5}, \quad \cos\alpha = \frac{4}{2\sqrt{5}} = \frac{2\sqrt{5}}{5}, \quad \text{and}$$

$$\tan\alpha = \frac{-2}{4} = -\frac{1}{2}.$$

Since cosecant, secant, and cotangent are the reciprocals of sine, cosine, and tangent,

$$\csc\alpha = \frac{1}{\sin\alpha} = -\frac{5}{\sqrt{5}} = -\sqrt{5}, \quad \sec\alpha = \frac{1}{\cos\alpha} = \frac{5}{2\sqrt{5}} = \frac{\sqrt{5}}{2}, \quad \text{and}$$

$$\cot\alpha = \frac{1}{\tan\alpha} = -2.$$

■

Right Triangles

So far the trigonometric functions have been tied to a coordinate system and an angle in standard position. Trigonometric ratios can also be used to evaluate the trigonometric functions for an acute angle of a right triangle without having the angle or the triangle located in a coordinate system.

Consider a right triangle with acute angle α, legs of length x and y, and hypotenuse r, as shown in Fig. 3.75(a). If this triangle is positioned in a coordinate system, as in Fig. 3.75(b), then (x, y) is a point on the terminal side of α and

$$\sin(\alpha) = \frac{y}{r}, \qquad \cos(\alpha) = \frac{x}{r}, \qquad \text{and} \qquad \tan(\alpha) = \frac{y}{x}.$$

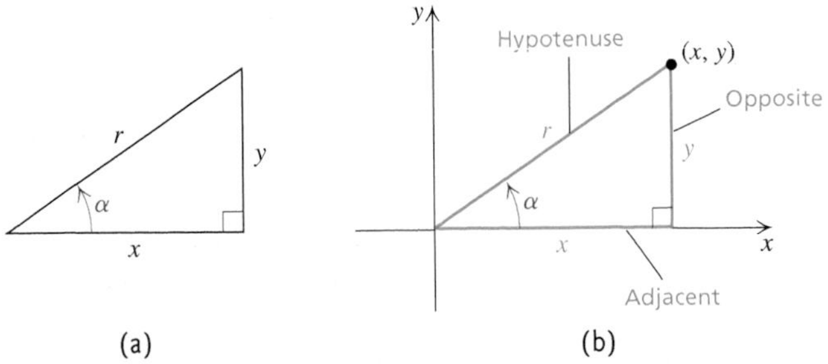

Figure 3.75

However, the values of the trigonometric functions are simply ratios of the lengths of the sides of the right triangle and it is not necessary to move the triangle to a coordinate system to find them. Notice that y is the length of the side **opposite** the angle α, x is the length of the side **adjacent** to α, and r is the length of the **hypotenuse.** We use the abbreviations opp, adj, and hyp to represent the lengths of these sides in the following theorem.

Theorem: Trigonometric Functions of an Acute Angle of a Right Triangle

If α is an acute angle of a right triangle, then

$$\sin \alpha = \frac{\text{opp}}{\text{hyp}}, \qquad \cos \alpha = \frac{\text{adj}}{\text{hyp}}, \qquad \text{and} \qquad \tan \alpha = \frac{\text{opp}}{\text{adj}}.$$

Since the cosecant, secant, and cotangent are the reciprocals of the sine, cosine, and tangent, respectively, the values of all six trigonometric functions can be found for an acute angle of a right triangle.

Example 2 Trigonometric functions in a right triangle

Find the values of all six trigonometric functions for the angle α of the right triangle with legs of length 1 and 4, as shown in Fig. 3.76.

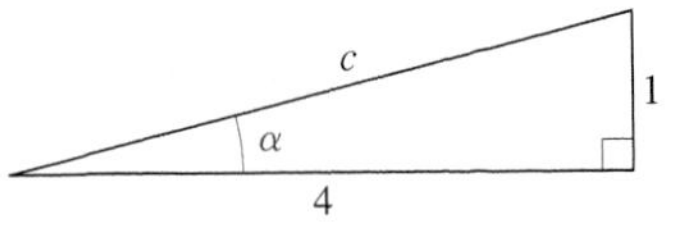

Figure 3.76

Solution

The length of the hypotenuse is $c = \sqrt{4^2 + 1^2} = \sqrt{17}$. Since the length of the side opposite α is 1 and the length of the adjacent side is 4, we have

$$\sin \alpha = \frac{\text{opp}}{\text{hyp}} = \frac{1}{\sqrt{17}} = \frac{\sqrt{17}}{17}, \qquad \cos \alpha = \frac{\text{adj}}{\text{hyp}} = \frac{4}{\sqrt{17}} = \frac{4\sqrt{17}}{17},$$

$$\tan \alpha = \frac{\text{opp}}{\text{adj}} = \frac{1}{4}, \qquad \csc \alpha = \frac{1}{\sin \alpha} = \sqrt{17},$$

$$\sec \alpha = \frac{1}{\cos \alpha} = \frac{\sqrt{17}}{4}, \qquad \cot \alpha = \frac{1}{\tan \alpha} = 4.$$

■

Solving a Right Triangle

The values of the trigonometric functions for an acute angle of a right triangle are determined by ratios of lengths of sides of the triangle. We can use those ratios along with the inverse trigonometric functions to find missing parts of a right triangle in which some of the measures of angles or lengths of sides are known. Finding all of the unknown lengths of sides or measures of angles is called **solving the triangle.** A triangle can be solved only if enough information is given to determine a unique triangle. For example, the lengths of the sides in a 30-60-90 triangle cannot be found because there are infinitely many such triangles of different sizes. However, the lengths of the missing sides in a 30-60-90 triangle with a hypotenuse of 6 will be found in Example 3.

In solving right triangles, we usually name the acute angles α and β and the lengths of the sides opposite those angles a and b. The 90° angle is γ, and the length of the side opposite γ is c.

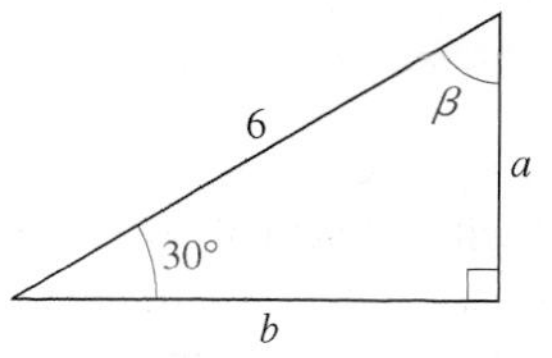

Figure 3.77

Example 3 Solving a right triangle

Solve the right triangle in which $\alpha = 30°$ and $c = 6$.

Solution

The triangle is shown in Fig. 3.77. Since $\alpha = 30°$, $\gamma = 90°$, and the sum of the measures of the angles of any triangle is 180°, we have $\beta = 60°$. Since $\sin \alpha = \text{opp}/\text{hyp}$, we get $\sin 30° = a/6$ and

$$a = 6 \cdot \sin 30° = 6 \cdot \frac{1}{2} = 3.$$

Since $\cos \alpha = \text{adj}/\text{hyp}$, we get $\cos 30° = b/6$ and

$$b = 6 \cdot \cos 30° = 6 \cdot \frac{\sqrt{3}}{2} = 3\sqrt{3}.$$

The angles of the right triangle are 30°, 60°, and 90°, and the sides opposite those angles are 3, $3\sqrt{3}$, and 6, respectively. ■

Example 4 Solving a right triangle

Solve the right triangle in which $a = 4$ and $b = 6$. Find the acute angles to the nearest tenth of a degree.

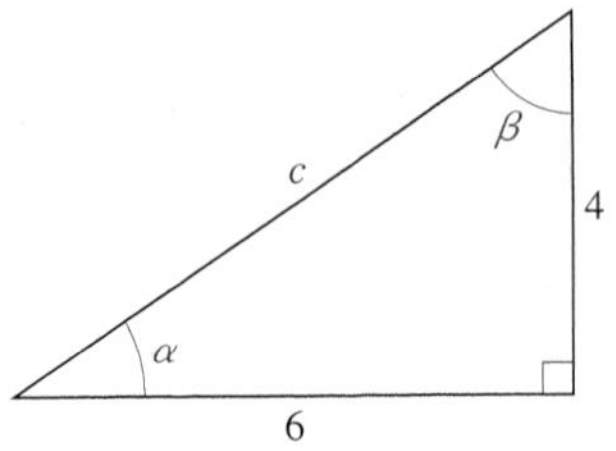

Figure 3.78

Solution

The triangle is shown in Fig. 3.78. By the Pythagorean theorem, $c^2 = 4^2 + 6^2$, or $c = \sqrt{52} = 2\sqrt{13}$. To find α, first find $\sin \alpha$:

$$\sin \alpha = \frac{\text{opp}}{\text{hyp}} = \frac{4}{2\sqrt{13}} = \frac{2}{\sqrt{13}}$$

Now, α is the angle whose sine is $2/\sqrt{13}$:

$$\alpha = \sin^{-1}\left(\frac{2}{\sqrt{13}}\right) \approx 33.7°$$

Since $\alpha + \beta = 90°$, $\beta = 90° - 33.7° = 56.3°$. The angles of the triangle are $33.7°$, $56.3°$, and $90°$, and the sides opposite those angles are 4, 6, and $2\sqrt{13}$, respectively. ■

In Example 4 we could have found α by using $\alpha = \tan^{-1}(4/6) \approx 33.7°$. We could then have found c by using $\cos(33.7°) = 6/c$, or $c = 6/\cos(33.7°) \approx 7.2$. There are many ways to solve a right triangle, but the basic strategy is always the same.

STRATEGY **Solving a Right Triangle**

1. Use the Pythagorean theorem to find the length of a third side when the lengths of two sides are known.
2. Use the trigonometric ratios to find missing sides or angles.
3. Use the fact that the sum of the measures of the angles of a triangle is 180° to determine a third angle when two are known.

Applications

Using trigonometry, we can find the size of an object without actually measuring the object but by measuring an angle. Two common terms used in this regard are **angle of elevation** and **angle of depression.** The angle of elevation α for a point above a horizontal line is the angle formed by the horizontal line and the observer's line of sight through the point, as shown in Fig. 3.79. The angle of depression β for a point below a horizontal line is the angle formed by the horizontal line and the observer's line of sight through the point, as shown in Fig. 3.79. We use these angles and our skills in solving triangles to find the sizes of objects that would be inconvenient to measure.

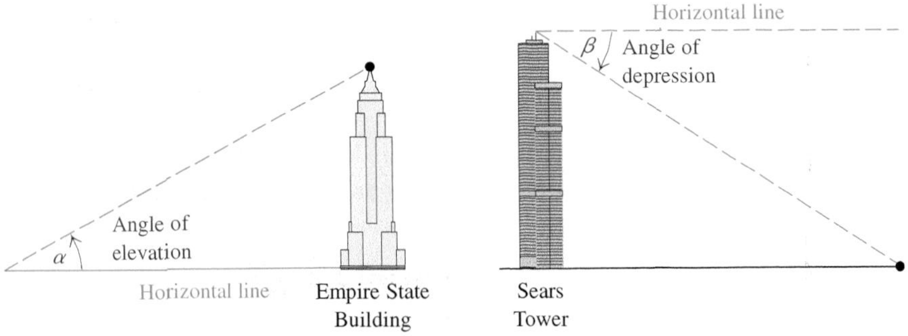

Figure 3.79

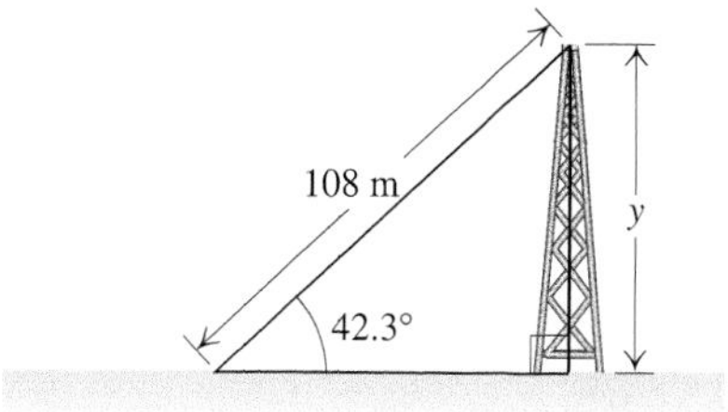

Figure 3.80

Example 5 Finding the height of an object

A guy wire of length 108 meters runs from the top of an antenna to the ground. If the angle of elevation of the top of the antenna, sighting along the guy wire, is 42.3°, then what is the height of the antenna?

Solution

Let y represent the height of the antenna, as shown in Fig. 3.80. Since $\sin(42.3°) = y/108$,

$$y = 108 \cdot \sin(42.3°) \approx 72.7 \text{ meters.}$$ ■

In Example 5 we knew the distance to the top of the antenna, and we found the height of the antenna. If we knew the distance on the ground to the base of the antenna and the angle of elevation of the guy wire, we could still have found the height of the antenna. Both cases involve knowing the distance to the antenna either on the ground or through the air. However, one of the biggest triumphs of trigonometry is being able to find the size of an object or the distance to an object (such as the moon) without going to the object. The next example shows one way to find the height of an object without actually going to it. In Section 3.9, Example 8, we will show another (slightly simpler) solution to the same problem using the law of sines.

Example 6 Finding the height of an object from a distance

The angle of elevation of the top of a water tower from point A on the ground is 19.9°. From point B, 50.0 feet closer to the tower, the angle of elevation is 21.8°. What is the height of the tower?

Solution

Let y represent the height of the tower and x represent the distance from point B to the base of the tower, as shown in Fig. 3.81.

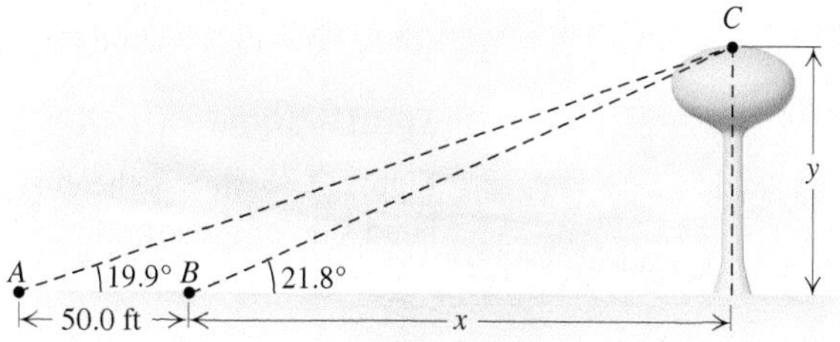

Figure 3.81

At point B, $\tan 21.8° = y/x$ or

$$x = \frac{y}{\tan 21.8°}.$$

Since the distance to the base of the tower from point A is $x + 50$,

$$\tan 19.9° = \frac{y}{x + 50}$$

or

$$y = (x + 50) \tan 19.9°.$$

To find the value of y we must write an equation that involves only y. Since $x = y/\tan 21.8°$, we can substitute $y/\tan 21.8°$ for x in the last equation:

$$y = \left(\frac{y}{\tan 21.8°} + 50\right) \tan 19.9°$$

$$y = \frac{y \cdot \tan 19.9°}{\tan 21.8°} + 50 \tan 19.9° \quad \text{Distributive property}$$

$$y - \frac{y \cdot \tan 19.9°}{\tan 21.8°} = 50 \tan 19.9°$$

$$y\left(1 - \frac{\tan 19.9°}{\tan 21.8°}\right) = 50 \tan 19.9° \quad \text{Factor out } y.$$

$$y = \frac{50 \tan 19.9°}{1 - \frac{\tan 19.9°}{\tan 21.8°}} \approx 191 \text{ feet}$$

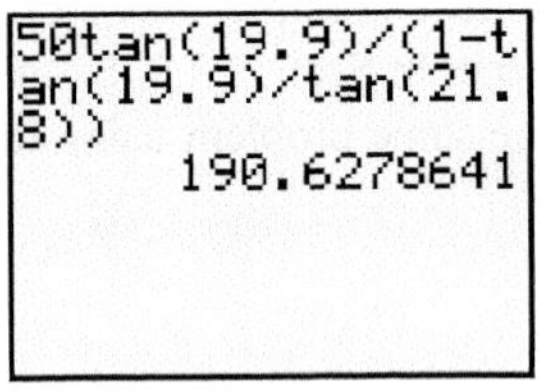

Figure 3.82

This computation is shown on a graphing calculator in Fig. 3.82. ■

In the next example we combine the solution of a right triangle with the arc length of a circle from Section 3.1 to solve a problem of aerial photography.

Example 7 Photography from a spy plane

In the late 1950s, the Soviets labored to develop a missile that could stop the U-2 spy plane. On May 1, 1960, Nikita S. Khrushchev announced to the world that the Soviets had shot down Francis Gary Powers while Powers was photographing the Soviet Union from a U-2 at an altitude of 14 miles. How wide a path on the earth's surface could Powers see from that altitude? (Use 3950 miles as the earth's radius.)

Solution

Figure 3.83 shows the line of sight to the horizon on the left-hand side and right-hand side of the airplane while flying at the altitude of 14 miles.

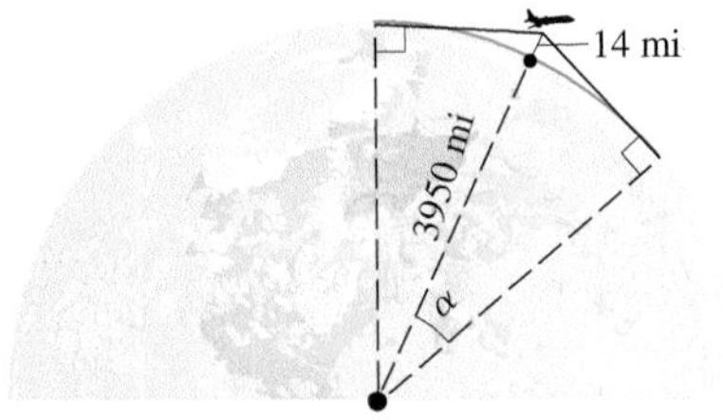

Figure 3.83

Since a line tangent to a circle (the line of sight) is perpendicular to the radius at the point of tangency, the angle α at the center of the earth in Fig. 3.83 is an acute angle of a right triangle with hypotenuse 3950 + 14 or 3964. So we have

$$\cos \alpha = \frac{3950}{3964}$$

$$\alpha = \cos^{-1}\left(\frac{3950}{3964}\right) \approx 4.8°.$$

The width of the path seen by Powers is the length of the arc intercepted by the central angle 2α or 9.6°. Using the formula $s = \alpha r$ from Section 3.1, where α is in radians, we get

$$s = 9.6 \text{ deg} \cdot \frac{\pi \text{ rad}}{180 \text{ deg}} \cdot 3950 \text{ miles} \approx 661.8 \text{ miles}.$$

From an altitude of 14 miles, Powers could see a path that was 661.8 miles wide. Actually, he photographed a path that was somewhat narrower, because parts of the photographs near the horizon were not usable. ■

For Thought

True or False? Explain. For Exercises 1–4, α is an angle in standard position.

1. If the terminal side of α goes through $(5, -10)$, then $\sin \alpha = 10/\sqrt{125}$.
2. If the terminal side of α goes through $(-1, 2)$, then $\sec \alpha = -\sqrt{5}$.
3. If the terminal side of α goes through $(-2, 3)$, then $\alpha = \sin^{-1}(3/\sqrt{13})$.
4. If the terminal side of α goes through $(3, 1)$, then $\alpha = \cos^{-1}(3/\sqrt{10})$.
5. In a right triangle, $\sin \alpha = \cos \beta$, $\sec \alpha = \csc \beta$, and $\tan \alpha = \cot \beta$.
6. If $a = 4$ and $b = 2$ in a right triangle, then $c = \sqrt{6}$.
7. If $a = 6$ and $b = 2$ in a right triangle, then $\beta = \tan^{-1}(3)$.
8. If $a = 8$ and $\alpha = 55°$ in a right triangle, then $b = 8/\tan(55°)$.
9. In a right triangle with sides of length 3, 4, and 5, the smallest angle is $\cos^{-1}(0.8)$.
10. In a right triangle, $\sin(90°) = \text{hyp}/\text{adj}$.

3.6 Exercises

Assume that α is an angle in standard position whose terminal side contains the given point. Find the exact values of $\sin \alpha$, $\cos \alpha$, $\tan \alpha$, $\csc \alpha$, $\sec \alpha$, *and* $\cot \alpha$.

1. $(3, 4)$
2. $(4, 4)$
3. $(-2, 6)$
4. $(-3, 6)$
5. $(-2, -\sqrt{2})$
6. $(-1, -\sqrt{3})$
7. $(\sqrt{6}, -\sqrt{2})$
8. $(2\sqrt{3}, -2)$

For Exercises 9–14 find exact values of $\sin\alpha$, $\cos\alpha$, $\tan\alpha$, $\sin\beta$, $\cos\beta$, *and* $\tan\beta$ *for the given right triangle.*

9.

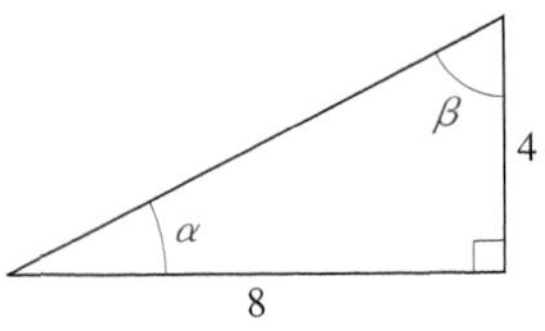

10.

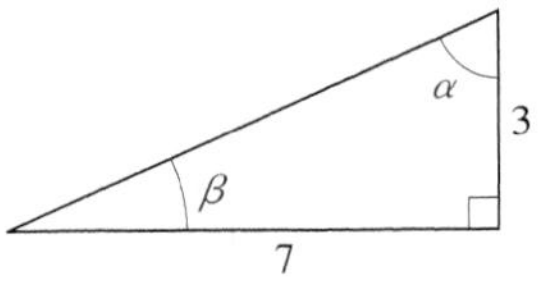

11.

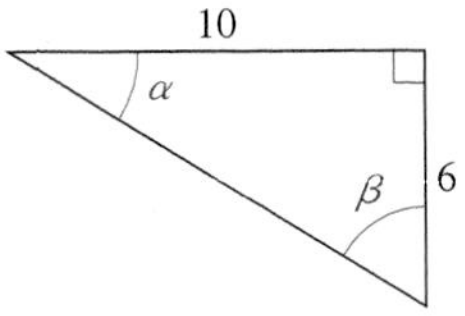

12.

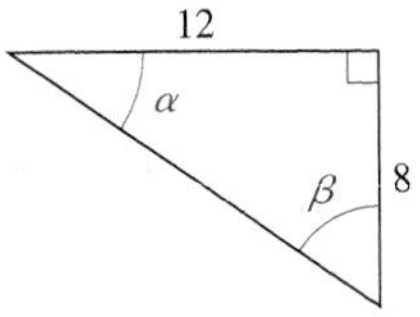

13.

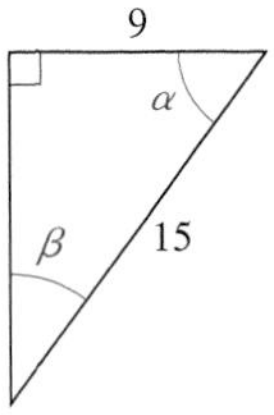

14.

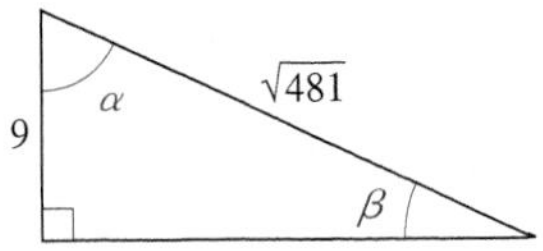

Assume that α *is an angle in standard position whose terminal side contains the given point and that* $0° < \alpha < 90°$. *Find the degree measure of* α *to the nearest tenth of a degree.*

15. $(1.5, 9)$

16. $(4, 5)$

17. $(\sqrt{2}, \sqrt{6})$

18. $(4.3, 6.9)$

Assume that α *is an angle in standard position whose terminal side contains the given point and that* $0 < \alpha < \pi/2$. *Find the radian measure of* α *to the nearest tenth of a radian.*

19. $(4, 6.3)$

20. $(1/3, 1/2)$

21. $(\sqrt{5}, 1)$

22. $(\sqrt{7}, \sqrt{3})$

Solve each right triangle with the given sides and angles. In each case, make a sketch. Note that, α *is the acute angle opposite leg* a *and* β *is the acute angle opposite leg* b. *The hypotenuse is* c. *See the strategy for solving a right triangle on page 256.*

23. $\alpha = 60°, c = 20$

24. $\beta = 45°, c = 10$

25. $a = 6, b = 8$

26. $a = 10, c = 12$

27. $b = 6, c = 8.3$

28. $\alpha = 32.4°, b = 10$

29. $\alpha = 16°, c = 20$

30. $\beta = 47°, a = 3$

31. $\alpha = 39°9', a = 9$

32. $\beta = 19°12', b = 60$

33. *Aerial Photography* An aerial photograph from a U-2 spy plane is taken of a building suspected of housing nuclear warheads. The photograph is made when the angle of elevation of the sun is 32°. By comparing the shadow cast by the building to objects of known size in the illustration, analysts determine that the shadow is 80 ft long. How tall is the building?

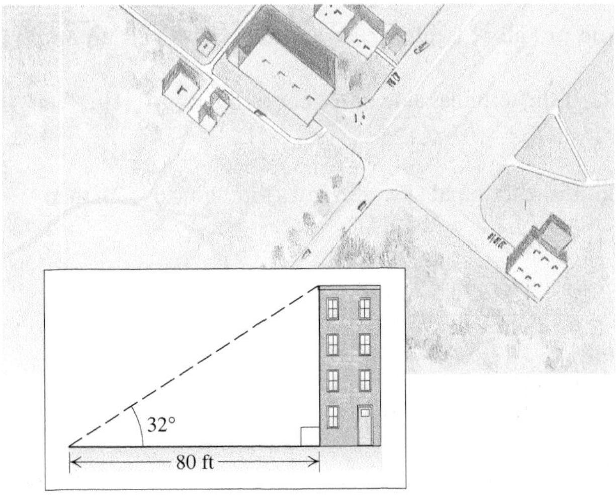

Figure for Exercise 33

34. *Giant Redwood* A hiker stands 80 feet from a giant redwood tree and sights the top with an angle of elevation of 75°. How tall is the tree to the nearest foot?

35. *Avoiding a Swamp* Muriel was hiking directly toward a long, straight road when she encountered a swamp. She turned 65° to the right and hiked 4 mi in that direction to reach the road. How far was she from the road when she encountered the swamp?

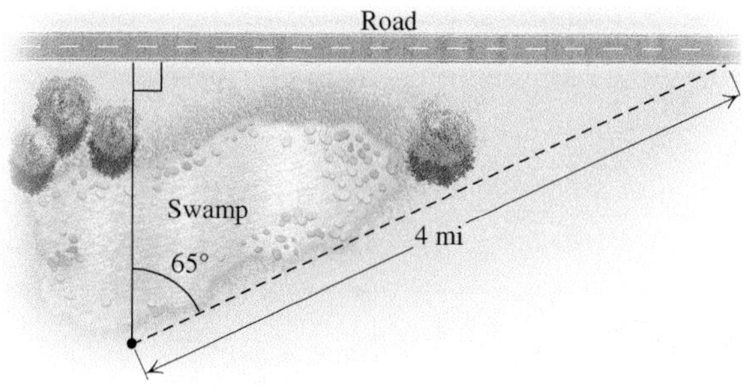

Figure for Exercise 35

36. *Tall Antenna* A 100 foot guy wire is attached to the top of an antenna. The angle between the guy wire and the ground is 62°. How tall is the antenna to the nearest foot?

37. *Angle of Depression* From a highway overpass, 14.3 m above the road, the angle of depression of an oncoming car is measured at 18.3°. How far is the car from a point on the highway directly below the observer?

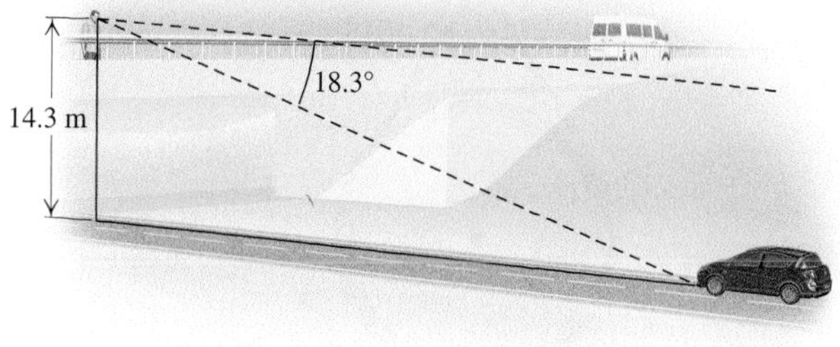

Figure for Exercise 37

38. *Length of a Tunnel* A tunnel under a river is 196.8 ft below the surface at its lowest point, as shown in the drawing. If the angle of depression of the tunnel is 4.962°, then how far apart on the surface are the entrances to the tunnel? How long is the tunnel?

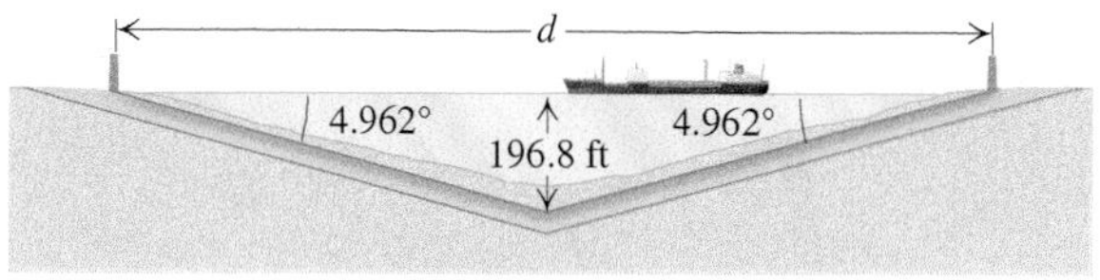

Figure for Exercise 38

39. *Height of a Crosswalk* The angle of elevation of a pedestrian crosswalk over a busy highway is 8.34°, as shown in the drawing. If the distance between the ends of the crosswalk measured on the ground is 342 ft, then what is the height h of the crosswalk at the center?

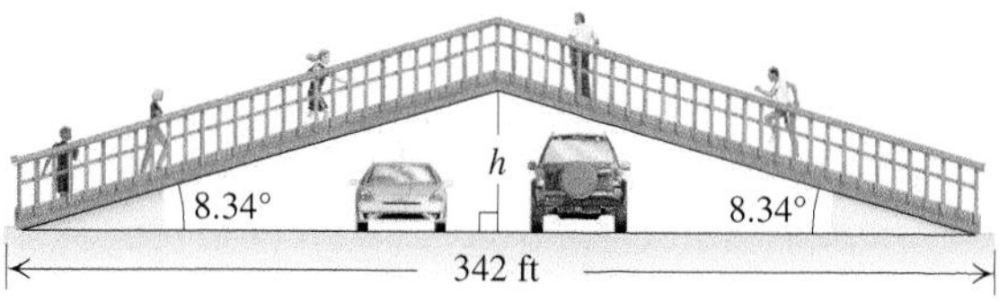

Figure for Exercise 39

40. *Shortcut to Snyder* To get from Muleshoe to Snyder, Harry drives 50 mph for 178 mi south on route 214 to Seminole, then goes east on route 180 to Snyder. Harriet leaves Muleshoe one hour later at 55 mph, but takes US 84, which goes straight from Muleshoe to Snyder through Lubbock. If US 84 intersects route 180 at a 50° angle, then how many more miles does Harry drive?

41. *Installing a Guy Wire* A 41-m guy wire is attached to the top of a 34.6-m antenna and to a point on the ground. How far is the point on the ground from the base of the antenna, and what angle does the guy wire make with the ground?

42. *Robin and Marian* Robin Hood plans to use a 30-ft ladder to reach the castle window of Maid Marian. Little John, who made the ladder, advised Robin that the angle of elevation of the ladder must be between 55° and 70° for safety. What are the minimum and maximum heights that can safely be reached by the top of the ladder when it is placed against the 50-ft castle wall?

43. *Height of a Rock* Inscription Rock rises almost straight upward from the valley floor. From one point the angle of elevation of the top of the rock is 16.7°. From a point 168 m closer to the rock, the angle of elevation of the top of the rock is 24.1°. How high is Inscription Rock?

44. *Height of a Balloon* A hot air balloon is between two spotters who are 1.2 mi apart. One spotter reports that the angle of elevation of the balloon is 76°, and the other reports that it is 68°. What is the altitude of the balloon in miles?

45. *Passing in the Night* A boat sailing north sights a lighthouse to the east at an angle of 32° from the north, as shown in the drawing on the next page. After the boat travels one more kilometer, the angle of the lighthouse from the north is 36°. If the boat continues to sail north, then how close will the boat come to the lighthouse?

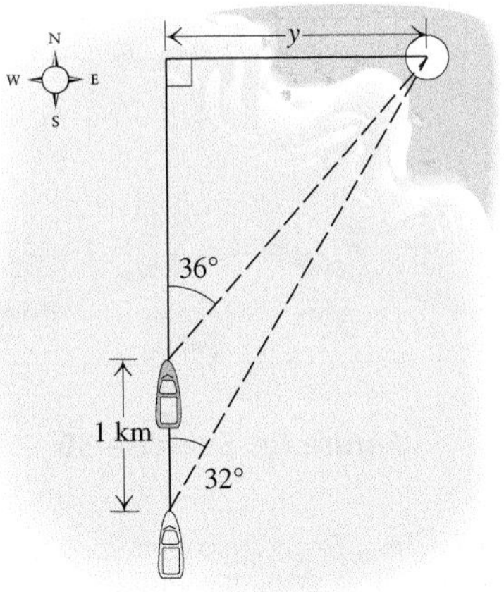

Figure for Exercise 45

46. *Height of a Skyscraper* For years the Woolworth skyscraper in New York held the record for the world's tallest office building. If the length of the shadow of the Woolworth building increases by 17.4 m as the angle of elevation of the sun changes from 44° to 42°, then how tall is the building?

47. *View from Landsat* The satellite Landsat orbits the earth at an altitude of 700 mi, as shown in the figure. What is the width of the path on the surface of the earth that can be seen by the cameras of Landsat? Use 3950 mi for the radius of the earth.

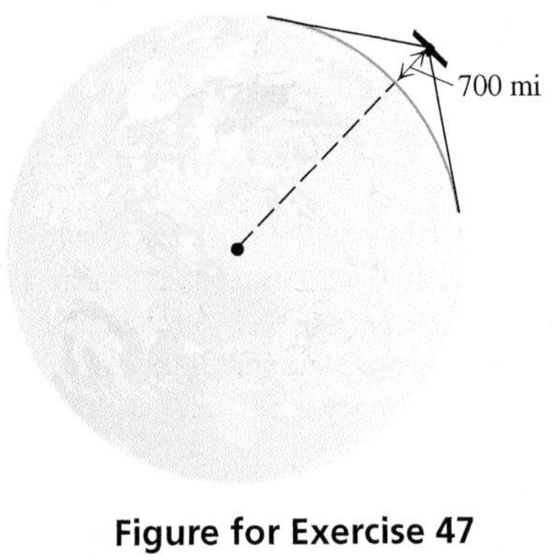

Figure for Exercise 47

48. *Communicating Via Satellite* A communication satellite is usually put into a synchronous orbit with the earth, which means that it stays above a fixed point on the surface of the earth at all times. The radius of the orbit of such a satellite is 6.5 times the radius of the earth (3950 mi). The satellite is used to relay a signal from one point on the earth to another point on the earth. The sender and receiver of a signal must be in a line of sight with the satellite, as shown in the figure. What is the maximum distance on the surface of the earth between the sender and receiver for this type of satellite?

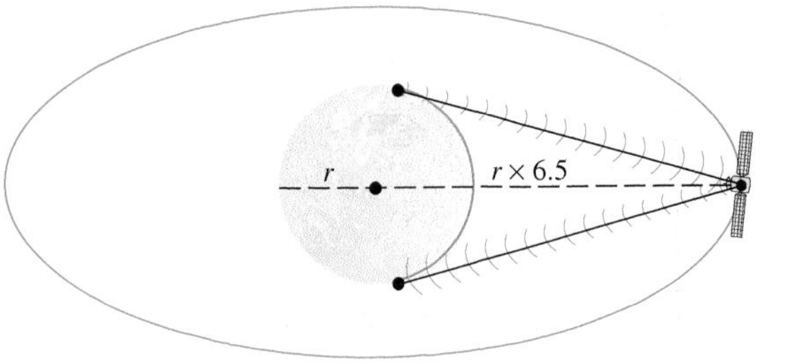

Figure for Exercise 48

49. *Hanging a Pipe* A contractor wants to pick up a 10-ft diameter pipe with a chain of length 40 ft. The chain encircles the pipe and is attached to a hook on a crane. What is the distance between the hook and the pipe? (This is an actual problem that an engineer was asked to solve on the job.)

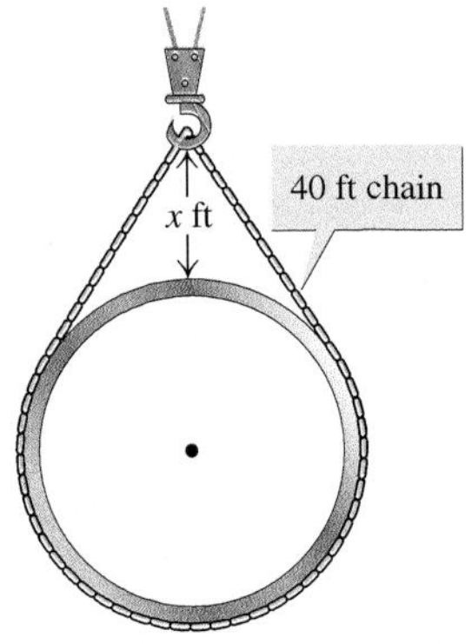

Figure for Exercise 49

50. *Blocking a Pipe* A large pipe is held in place by using a 1-ft high block on one side and a 2-ft high block on the other side. If the length of the arc between the points where the pipe touches the blocks is 6 ft, then what is the radius of the pipe? Ignore the thickness of the pipe.

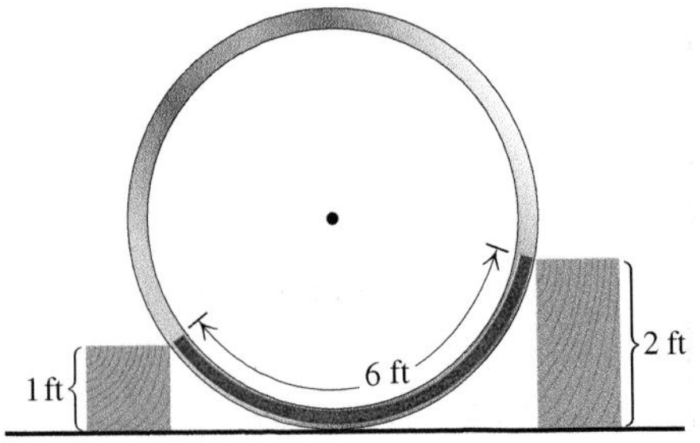

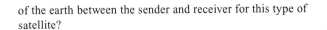

Figure for Exercise 50

Thinking Outside the Box XXIV

Kicking a Field Goal In professional football the ball must be placed between the left and right hash mark when a field goal is to be kicked. The hash marks are 9.25 ft from the center line of the field. The goal post is 30 ft past the goal line. Suppose that θ is the angle between the lines of sight from the ball to the left and right uprights as shown in the figure. The larger the value of θ the easier it is to kick the ball between the uprights. What is the difference (to the nearest thousandth of a degree) between the values of θ at the right hash mark and the value of θ at the center of the field when the ball is 60 ft from the goal line? The two vertical bars on the goal are 18.5 ft apart and the horizontal bar is 10 ft above the ground.

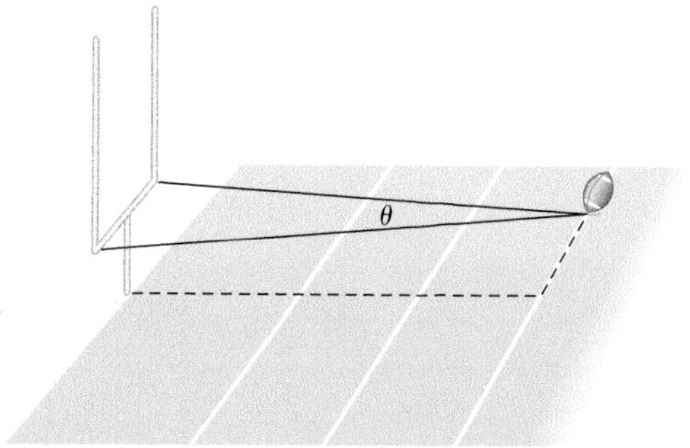

Figure for Thinking Outside the Box XXIV

3.6 Pop Quiz

1. Find $\sin\alpha$, $\cos\alpha$, and $\tan\alpha$ if the terminal side of α in standard position goes through $(-3, 4)$.

2. A right triangle has legs with lengths 3 and 6, and α is the acute angle opposite the smallest leg. Find exact values for $\sin\alpha$, $\cos\alpha$, and $\tan\alpha$.

3. At a distance of 1000 feet from a building the angle of elevation to the top of the building is 36°. Find the height of the building to the nearest foot.

3.7 Identities

An identity is an equation that is satisfied by *every* number for which both sides are defined. In calculus identities are used to simplify expressions and determine whether expressions are equivalent. In this section we review the identities used in calculus, omitting most of the proofs. The proofs can be found in any standard trigonometry text.

Pythagorean Identities

In Section 3.2 we proved the fundamental identity $\sin^2\alpha + \cos^2\alpha = 1$. Dividing each side by $\sin^2\alpha$ yields a new identity:

$$\frac{\sin^2\alpha}{\sin^2\alpha} + \frac{\cos^2\alpha}{\sin^2\alpha} = \frac{1}{\sin^2\alpha}$$

$$1 + \left(\frac{\cos\alpha}{\sin\alpha}\right)^2 = \left(\frac{1}{\sin\alpha}\right)^2$$

$$1 + \cot^2\alpha = \csc^2\alpha$$

■ Foreshadowing Calculus

Trigonometric identities are used extensively in calculus. We often use identities to change the form or simplify a function when solving calculus problems involving trigonometric functions.

Now divide each side of the fundamental identity by $\cos^2 \alpha$:

$$\frac{\sin^2 \alpha}{\cos^2 \alpha} + \frac{\cos^2 \alpha}{\cos^2 \alpha} = \frac{1}{\cos^2 \alpha}$$

$$\tan^2 \alpha + 1 = \sec^2 \alpha$$

These identities are based on the equation of the unit circle $x^2 + y^2 = 1$, which comes from the Pythagorean theorem. They are called the **Pythagorean identities.**

Pythagorean Identities

$\sin^2 \alpha + \cos^2 \alpha = 1 \qquad 1 + \cot^2 \alpha = \csc^2 \alpha \qquad \tan^2 \alpha + 1 = \sec^2 \alpha$

Example 1 Using identities

Simplify $\sin x \cot x \cos x$.

Solution

$$\begin{aligned}
\sin x + \cot x \cos x &= \sin x + \frac{\cos x}{\sin x} \cdot \cos x && \text{Rewrite using sines and cosines.}\\
&= \sin x + \frac{\cos^2 x}{\sin x} &&\\
&= \frac{\sin^2 x}{\sin x} + \frac{\cos^2 x}{\sin x} && \text{Multiply } \sin x \text{ by } \frac{\sin x}{\sin x}.\\
&= \frac{\sin^2 x + \cos^2 x}{\sin x} && \text{Add the fractions.}\\
&= \frac{1}{\sin x} && \text{Since } \sin^2 x + \cos^2 x = 1\\
&= \csc x && \text{Definition of cosecant}
\end{aligned}$$

Odd and Even Identities

An *odd function* is one for which $f(-x) = -f(x)$. An *even function* is one for which $f(-x) = f(x)$. Each of the six trigonometric functions is either odd or even.

Odd and Even Identities

Odd: $\sin(-x) = -\sin(x) \qquad \csc(-x) = -\csc(x)$
$\tan(-x) = -\tan(x) \qquad \cot(-x) = -\cot(x)$

Even: $\cos(-x) = \cos(x) \qquad \sec(-x) = \sec(x)$

Example 2 Using odd and even identities

Simplify $\dfrac{1}{1 + \cos(-x)} + \dfrac{1}{1 - \cos x}$.

Solution

First note that $\cos(-x) = \cos(x)$. Then find a common denominator and add the expressions.

$$\frac{1}{1+\cos(-x)} + \frac{1}{1-\cos x} = \frac{1}{1+\cos x} + \frac{1}{1-\cos x}$$

$$= \frac{1(1-\cos x)}{(1+\cos x)(1-\cos x)} + \frac{1(1+\cos x)}{(1-\cos x)(1+\cos x)}$$

$$= \frac{1-\cos x}{1-\cos^2 x} + \frac{1+\cos x}{1-\cos^2 x} \quad \text{Product of a sum and difference}$$

$$= \frac{1-\cos x}{\sin^2 x} + \frac{1+\cos x}{\sin^2 x} \quad \text{Pythagorean identity}$$

$$= \frac{1-\cos x + 1 + \cos x}{\sin^2 x} \quad \text{Add the fractions.}$$

$$= \frac{2}{\sin^2 x}$$

$$= 2 \cdot \frac{1}{\sin^2 x}$$

$$= 2\csc^2 x \quad \csc x = 1/\sin$$

■

Sum and Difference Identities

The sum and difference identities are used to write a trigonometric function of a sum or difference of angles in terms of trigonometric functions of the angles. Note that each equation in the following box represents two identities. For the first identity we use the top operation in the symbol $\pm$ or $\mp$ and for the second identity we use the bottom operation.

Sum and Difference Identities

$$\cos(\alpha \pm \beta) = \cos\alpha\cos\beta \mp \sin\alpha\sin\beta$$

$$\sin(\alpha \pm \beta) = \sin\alpha\cos\beta \pm \cos\alpha\sin\beta$$

$$\tan(\alpha \pm \beta) = \frac{\tan\alpha \pm \tan\beta}{1 \mp \tan\alpha\tan\beta}$$

Example 3 The cosine of a sum

Find the exact value of cos (75°).

Solution

Use $75° = 30° + 45°$ and the identity for the cosine of a sum.

$$\cos 75° = \cos(30° + 45°)$$

$$= \cos(30°)\cos(45°) - \sin(30°)\sin(45°)$$

$$= \frac{\sqrt{3}}{2} \cdot \frac{\sqrt{2}}{2} - \frac{1}{2} \cdot \frac{\sqrt{2}}{2}$$

$$= \frac{\sqrt{6} - \sqrt{2}}{4}$$

To check, evaluate cos 75° and $(\sqrt{6} - \sqrt{2})/4$ using a calculator. ■

Cofunction Identities

Using $\pi/2$ for one of the angles in the difference identities yields the following cofunction identities.

Cofunction Identities

$$\sin\left(\frac{\pi}{2} - u\right) = \cos u \qquad \cos\left(\frac{\pi}{2} - u\right) = \sin u$$

$$\tan\left(\frac{\pi}{2} - u\right) = \cot u \qquad \cot\left(\frac{\pi}{2} - u\right) = \tan u$$

$$\sec\left(\frac{\pi}{2} - u\right) = \csc u \qquad \csc\left(\frac{\pi}{2} - u\right) = \sec u$$

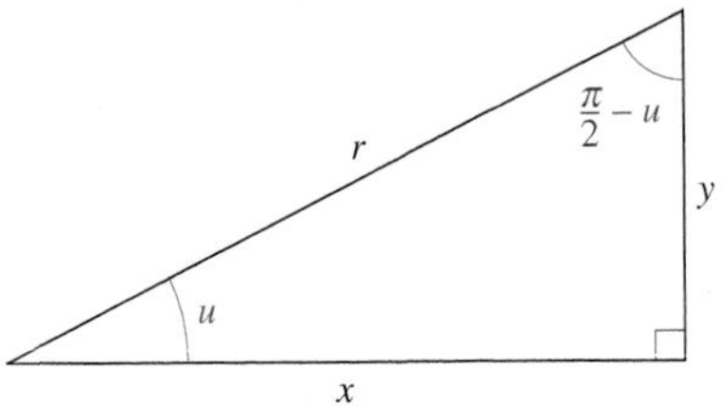

Figure 3.84

If $0 < u < \pi/2$, then u and $\pi/2 - u$ are the measures of the acute angles of a right triangle as shown in Fig. 3.84. The term *cofunction* comes from the fact that these angles are complementary. The cofunction identities indicate that the value of a trigonometric function of one acute angle of a right triangle is equal to the value of the cofunction of the other acute angle. For example, $\sin(20°) = \cos(70°)$ and $\cot(89°) = \tan(1°)$.

Example 4 Using the odd/even and cofunction identities

Verify that $\cos(x - \pi/2) = \sin(x)$ is an identity.

Solution

$$\cos\left(x - \frac{\pi}{2}\right) = \cos\left(-\left(\frac{\pi}{2} - x\right)\right) \qquad \text{Because } x - \frac{\pi}{2} = -\left(\frac{\pi}{2} - x\right)$$

$$= \cos\left(\frac{\pi}{2} - x\right) \qquad \text{Cosine is an even function } (\cos(-\alpha) = \cos(\alpha)).$$

$$= \sin(x) \qquad \text{Cofunction identity}$$

■

Double-Angle and Half-Angle Identities

To get an identity for $\sin 2x$, replace both α and β by x in the identity for $\sin(\alpha + \beta)$:

$$\sin 2x = \sin(x + x) = \sin x \cos x + \cos x \sin x = 2 \sin x \cos x$$

We can repeat this procedure using the identities for the cosine of a sum and the tangent of a sum to get the following **double-angle identities.**

Double-Angle Identities

$$\sin 2x = 2 \sin x \cos x \qquad \tan 2x = \frac{2 \tan x}{1 - \tan^2 x}$$

$$\cos 2x = \cos^2 x - \sin^2 x$$

$$\cos 2x = 2 \cos^2 x - 1$$

$$\cos 2x = 1 - 2 \sin^2 x$$

Be careful to learn the double-angle identities exactly as they are written. A "nice-looking" equation such as $\cos 2x = 2 \cos x$ could be mistaken for an identity if you are not careful. Since $\cos(\pi/2) \neq 2\cos(\pi/4)$, the "nice-looking" equation is not an identity. Remember that an equation is not an identity if at least one permissible value of the variable fails to satisfy the equation.

Example 5 Using the double-angle identities

Find sin(120°), cos(120°), and tan(120°) using double-angle identities.

Solution

Note that $120° = 2 \cdot 60°$ and use the values $\sin(60°) = \sqrt{3}/2$, $\cos(60°) = 1/2$, and $\tan(60°) = \sqrt{3}$ in the appropriate identities:

$$\sin(120°) = 2\sin(60°)\cos(60°) = 2 \cdot \frac{\sqrt{3}}{2} \cdot \frac{1}{2} = \frac{\sqrt{3}}{2}$$

$$\cos(120°) = \cos^2(60°) - \sin^2(60°) = \left(\frac{1}{2}\right)^2 - \left(\frac{\sqrt{3}}{2}\right)^2 = -\frac{1}{2}$$

$$\tan(120°) = \frac{2\tan(60°)}{1 - \tan^2(60°)} = \frac{2 \cdot \sqrt{3}}{1 - (\sqrt{3})^2} = \frac{2\sqrt{3}}{-2} = -\sqrt{3}$$

These results are the well-known values of sin(120°), cos(120°), and tan(120°). ■

The **half-angle identities** are derived from the double-angle identities.

Half-Angle Identities

$$\sin\frac{x}{2} = \pm\sqrt{\frac{1 - \cos x}{2}} \qquad \cos\frac{x}{2} = \pm\sqrt{\frac{1 + \cos x}{2}}$$

$$\tan\frac{x}{2} = \pm\sqrt{\frac{1 - \cos x}{1 + \cos x}} \qquad \tan\frac{x}{2} = \frac{\sin x}{1 + \cos x} \qquad \tan\frac{x}{2} = \frac{1 - \cos x}{\sin x}$$

Example 6 Using half-angle identities

Use the half-angle identity to find the exact value of tan(−15°).

Solution

Use $x = -30°$ in the half-angle identity $\tan\frac{x}{2} = \frac{\sin x}{1 + \cos x}$.

$$\begin{aligned}
\tan(-15°) &= \tan\left(\frac{-30°}{2}\right) \\
&= \frac{\sin(-30°)}{1 + \cos(-30°)} \\
&= \frac{-\frac{1}{2}}{1 + \frac{\sqrt{3}}{2}} \\
&= \frac{-1}{2 + \sqrt{3}} \\
&= \frac{-1(2 - \sqrt{3})}{(2 + \sqrt{3})(2 - \sqrt{3})} = -2 + \sqrt{3}
\end{aligned}$$

■

Example 7 Using the identities

Find $\sin(\alpha/2)$ if $\sin \alpha = 3/5$ and $\pi/2 < \alpha < \pi$.

Solution

Use the identity $\sin^2\alpha + \cos^2\alpha = 1$ to find $\cos \alpha$:

$$\left(\frac{3}{5}\right)^2 + \cos^2 \alpha = 1$$

$$\cos^2 \alpha = \frac{16}{25}$$

$$\cos \alpha = \pm\frac{4}{5}$$

For $\pi/2 < \alpha < \pi$, we have $\cos \alpha < 0$. So $\cos \alpha = -4/5$. Now use the half-angle identity for sine:

$$\sin\frac{\alpha}{2} = \pm\sqrt{\frac{1 - \cos \alpha}{2}} = \pm\sqrt{\frac{1 + \frac{4}{5}}{2}}$$

$$= \pm\sqrt{\frac{9}{10}} = \pm\frac{\sqrt{90}}{10} = \pm\frac{3\sqrt{10}}{10}$$

If $\pi/2 < \alpha < \pi$, then $\pi/4 < \alpha/2 < \pi/2$. So $\sin(\alpha/2) > 0$ and $\sin(\alpha/2) = 3\sqrt{10}/10$. ■

Product and Sum Identities

The sum and difference identities for sines and cosines can be used to derive the **product-to-sum identities.** These identities are not used as often as other identities. It is not necessary to memorize these identities. Just remember them by name and look them up as necessary.

Product-to-Sum Identities

$$\sin A \cos B = \frac{1}{2}[\sin(A + B) + \sin(A - B)]$$

$$\sin A \sin B = \frac{1}{2}[\cos(A - B) - \cos(A + B)]$$

$$\cos A \sin B = \frac{1}{2}[\sin(A + B) - \sin(A - B)]$$

$$\cos A \cos B = \frac{1}{2}[\cos(A - B) + \cos(A + B)]$$

Example 8 Expressing a product as a sum

Use the product-to-sum identities to rewrite each expression.

a. $\sin 12° \cos 9°$ **b.** $\sin(\pi/12) \sin(\pi/8)$

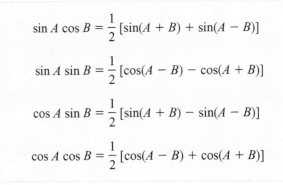

Solution

a. Use the product-to-sum identity for $\sin A \cos B$:

$$\sin 12° \cos 9° = \frac{1}{2}[\sin(12° + 9°) + \sin(12° - 9°)]$$
$$= \frac{1}{2}[\sin 21° + \sin 3°]$$

b. Use the product-to-sum identity for $\sin A \sin B$:

$$\sin\left(\frac{\pi}{12}\right)\sin\left(\frac{\pi}{8}\right) = \frac{1}{2}\left[\cos\left(\frac{\pi}{12} - \frac{\pi}{8}\right) - \cos\left(\frac{\pi}{12} + \frac{\pi}{8}\right)\right]$$
$$= \frac{1}{2}\left[\cos\left(-\frac{\pi}{24}\right) - \cos\left(\frac{5\pi}{24}\right)\right]$$
$$= \frac{1}{2}\left[\cos\frac{\pi}{24} - \cos\frac{5\pi}{24}\right]$$

Figure 3.85

Use a calculator to check as in Fig. 3.85. ■

The **sum-to-product identities** are used to write a sum of two trigonometric functions as a product.

Sum-to-Product Identities

$$\sin x + \sin y = 2\sin\left(\frac{x+y}{2}\right)\cos\left(\frac{x-y}{2}\right)$$
$$\sin x - \sin y = 2\cos\left(\frac{x+y}{2}\right)\sin\left(\frac{x-y}{2}\right)$$
$$\cos x + \cos y = 2\cos\left(\frac{x+y}{2}\right)\cos\left(\frac{x-y}{2}\right)$$
$$\cos x - \cos y = -2\sin\left(\frac{x+y}{2}\right)\sin\left(\frac{x-y}{2}\right)$$

Example 9 Expressing a sum or difference as a product

Use the sum-to-product identities to rewrite each expression.

a. $\cos(\pi/5) - \cos(\pi/8)$ **b.** $\sin(6t) - \sin(4t)$

Solution

a. Use the sum-to-product identity for $\cos x - \cos y$:

$$\cos\left(\frac{\pi}{5}\right) - \cos\left(\frac{\pi}{8}\right) = -2\sin\left(\frac{\pi/5 + \pi/8}{2}\right)\sin\left(\frac{\pi/5 - \pi/8}{2}\right)$$
$$= -2\sin\left(\frac{13\pi}{80}\right)\sin\left(\frac{3\pi}{80}\right)$$

b. Use the sum-to-product identity for $\sin x - \sin y$:

$$\sin 6t - \sin 4t = 2\cos\left(\frac{6t + 4t}{2}\right)\sin\left(\frac{6t - 4t}{2}\right)$$
$$= 2\cos 5t \sin t$$

■

The Function $y = a \sin x + b \cos x$

Functions of the form $y = a \sin x + b \cos x$ occur in applications such as the position of a weight in motion due to the force of a spring, the position of a swinging pendulum, and the current in an electrical circuit. The **reduction formula** is used to express this function in terms of a single trigonometric function from which amplitude, period, and phase shift can be determined.

Theorem: Reduction Formula

If α is an angle in standard position whose terminal side contains (a, b), then

$$a \sin x + b \cos x = \sqrt{a^2 + b^2}\sin(x + \alpha)$$

for any real number x.

To rewrite an expression of the form $a \sin x + b \cos x$ using the reduction formula, we need to find α so that the terminal side of α goes through (a, b). By using trigonometric ratios, we have

$$\sin \alpha = \frac{b}{\sqrt{a^2 + b^2}}, \qquad \cos \alpha = \frac{a}{\sqrt{a^2 + b^2}}, \qquad \tan \alpha = \frac{b}{a}.$$

Since we know a and b, we can find $\sin \alpha$, $\cos \alpha$, or $\tan \alpha$, and then use an inverse trigonometric function to find α. However, because of the ranges of the inverse functions, the angle obtained from an inverse function might not have its terminal side through (a, b) as required. We will address this problem in the next example.

Example 10 Using the reduction formula

Use the reduction formula to rewrite $-3 \sin x - 3 \cos x$ in the form $A \sin(x + C)$.

Solution

Because $a = -3$ and $b = -3$, we have

$$\sqrt{a^2 + b^2} = \sqrt{18}$$
$$= 3\sqrt{2}.$$

Since the terminal side of α must go through $(-3, -3)$, we have

$$\cos \alpha = \frac{-3}{3\sqrt{2}} = -\frac{\sqrt{2}}{2}.$$

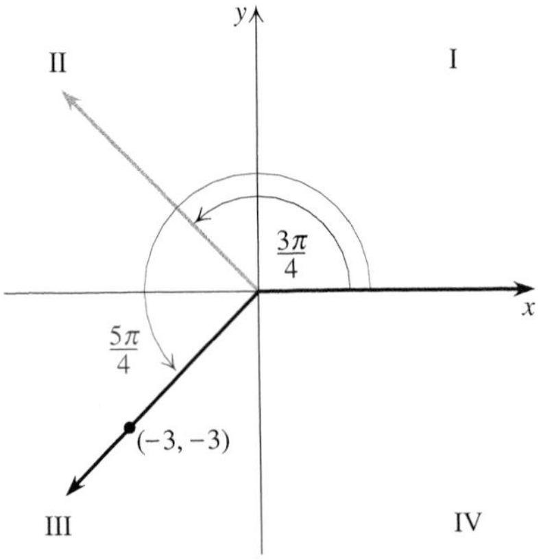

Figure 3.86

Now $\cos^{-1}\left(-\sqrt{2}/2\right) = 3\pi/4$, but the terminal side of $3\pi/4$ is in quadrant II, as shown in Fig. 3.86. However, we also have $\cos(5\pi/4) = -\sqrt{2}/2$ and the terminal

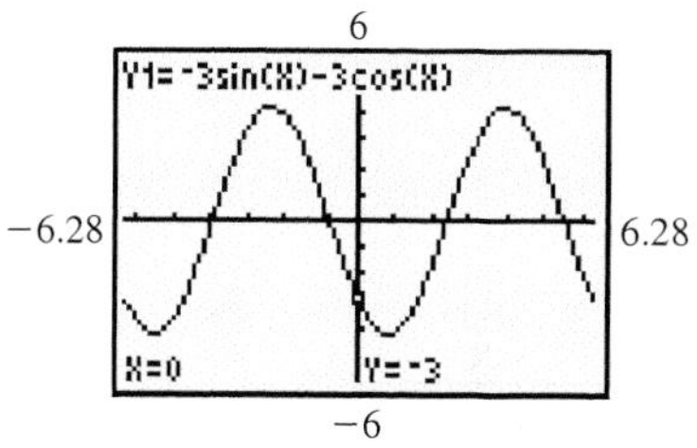

Figure 3.87

side for $5\pi/4$ does pass through $(-3, -3)$ in quadrant III. So $\alpha = 5\pi/4$. By the reduction formula

$$-3\sin x - 3\cos x = 3\sqrt{2}\sin\left(x + \frac{5\pi}{4}\right).$$

The reduction formula explains why the calculator graph of $y = -3\sin x - 3\cos x$ in Fig. 3.87 is a sine wave with amplitude $3\sqrt{2}$. ■

For Thought

True or False? Explain.

1. The equation $(\tan x)(\cot x) = 1$ is an identity.
2. The equation $(\sin x + \cos x)^2 = \sin^2 x + \cos^2 x$ is an identity.
3. $\tan 1 = \sqrt{1 - \sec^2 1}$
4. $\sin^2(-6) = -\sin^2(6)$
5. $\frac{\pi}{4} - \frac{\pi}{3} = \frac{\pi}{12}$
6. $\cos(4)\cos(5) + \sin(4)\sin(5) = \cos(-1)$
7. $\cos(\pi/2 - 5) = \sin(5)$
8. $\sin(7\pi/12) = \sin(\pi/3)\cos(\pi/4) + \cos(\pi/3)\sin(\pi/4)$
9. $\sin 150° = \sqrt{\frac{1 - \cos 75°}{2}}$
10. $\cos 4 + \cos 12 = 2\cos 8\cos 4$

3.7 Exercises

Use identities to simplify each expression. Do not use a calculator.

1. $\frac{1}{\sin^2 x} - \frac{1}{\tan^2 x}$
2. $\frac{1 + \cos\alpha\tan\alpha\csc\alpha}{\csc\alpha}$
3. $\frac{\sin^4 x - \sin^2 x}{\sec x}$
4. $\frac{-\tan^2 t - 1}{\sec^2 t}$
5. $\frac{\cos w\sin^2 w + \cos^3 w}{\sec w}$
6. $\frac{\tan^3 x - \sec^2 x\tan x}{\cot(-x)}$
7. $\sin x + \frac{\cos^2 x}{\sin x}$
8. $\frac{1}{\sin^3 x} - \frac{\cot^2 x}{\sin x}$
9. $\sin(-x)\cot(-x)$
10. $\sec(-x) - \sec(x)$
11. $\frac{\sin(x)}{\cos(-x)} + \frac{\sin(-x)}{\cos(x)}$
12. $\frac{\cos(-x)}{\sin(-x)} - \frac{\cos(-x)}{\sin(x)}$
13. $\cos(5)\cos(6) - \sin(5)\sin(6)$
14. $\cos(7.1)\cos(1.4) - \sin(7.1)\sin(1.4)$
15. $\cos 2k\cos k + \sin 2k\sin k$
16. $\cos 3y\cos y - \sin 3y\sin y$
17. $\sin(23°)\cos(67°) + \cos(23°)\sin(67°)$
18. $\sin(2°)\cos(7°) - \cos(2°)\sin(7°)$
19. $\sin(-\pi/2)\cos(\pi/5) + \cos(\pi/2)\sin(-\pi/5)$
20. $\sin(-\pi/6)\cos(-\pi/3) + \cos(-\pi/6)\sin(-\pi/3)$
21. $\frac{\tan(\pi/9) + \tan(\pi/6)}{1 - \tan(\pi/9)\tan(\pi/6)}$
22. $\frac{\tan(\pi/3) - \tan(\pi/5)}{1 + \tan(\pi/3)\tan(\pi/5)}$
23. $\cos(-3k)\cos(-k) - \cos(\pi/2 - 3k)\sin(-k)$
24. $\cos(y - \pi/2)\cos(y) + \sin(\pi/2 - y)\sin(-y)$
25. $2\sin 13°\cos 13°$

26. $\sin^2\left(\frac{\pi}{5}\right) - \cos^2\left(\frac{\pi}{5}\right)$

27. $\dfrac{\tan 15°}{1 - \tan^2(15°)}$

28. $\dfrac{2}{\cot 5(1 - \tan^2 5)}$

29. $2 \sin\left(\frac{\pi}{9} - \frac{\pi}{2}\right) \cos\left(\frac{\pi}{2} - \frac{\pi}{9}\right)$

30. $2 \cos^2\left(\frac{\pi}{5} - \frac{\pi}{2}\right) - 1$

In each exercise, use identities to find the exact values at α for the remaining five trigonometric functions.

31. $\tan \alpha = 1/2$ and $0 < \alpha < \pi/2$

32. $\sin \alpha = 3/4$ and $\pi/2 < \alpha < \pi$

33. $\cos \alpha = -\sqrt{3}/5$ and α is in quadrant III

34. $\sec \alpha = -4\sqrt{5}/5$ and α is in quadrant II

In each case, find $\sin \alpha$, $\cos \alpha$, $\tan \alpha$, $\csc \alpha$, $\sec \alpha$, *and* $\cot \alpha$.

35. $\cos 2\alpha = 3/5$ and $0° < 2\alpha < 90°$

36. $\cos 2\alpha = 1/3$ and $360° < 2\alpha < 450°$

37. $\cos(\alpha/2) = -1/4$ and $\pi/2 < \alpha/2 < 3\pi/4$

38. $\sin(\alpha/2) = -1/3$ and $7\pi/4 < \alpha/2 < 2\pi$

Use appropriate identities to find the exact value of each expression.

39. $\sin(15°)$

40. $\sin(75°)$

41. $\cos(5\pi/12)$

42. $\cos(7\pi/12)$

43. $\cos(-\pi/12)$

44. $\cos(-5\pi/12)$

45. $\tan(75°)$

46. $\tan(-15°)$

Prove that each of the following equations is an identity.

47. $\tan x \cos x + \csc x \sin^2 x = 2\sin x$

48. $\cot x \sin x - \cos^2 x \sec x = 0$

49. $2 - \csc \beta \sin \beta = \sin^2 \beta + \cos^2 \beta$

50. $(1 - \sin^2 \beta)(1 + \sin^2 \beta) = 2 \cos^2 \beta - \cos^4 \beta$

51. $\dfrac{\sec x}{\tan x} - \dfrac{\tan x}{\sec x} = \cos x \cot x$

52. $\dfrac{1 - \sin^2 x}{1 - \sin x} = \dfrac{\csc x + 1}{\csc x}$

53. $1 + \csc x \sec x = \dfrac{\cos(-x) - \csc(-x)}{\cos(x)}$

54. $\tan^2(-x) - \dfrac{\sin(-x)}{\sin x} = \sec^2 x$

55. $\dfrac{\csc y + 1}{\csc y - 1} = \dfrac{1 + \sin y}{1 - \sin y}$

56. $\dfrac{1 - 2\cos^2 y}{1 - 2\cos y \sin y} = \dfrac{\sin y + \cos y}{\sin y - \cos y}$

57. $\dfrac{1 - \sin^2(-x)}{1 - \sin(-x)} = 1 - \sin x$

58. $\dfrac{1 - \sin^2 x \csc^2 x + \sin^2 x}{\cos^2 x} = \tan^2 x$

59. $\cos(x - \pi/2) = \cos x \tan x$

60. $\dfrac{\cos(x + y)}{\cos x \cos y} = 1 - \tan x \tan y$

61. $\dfrac{\cos(\alpha + \beta)}{\cos \alpha + \sin \beta} = \dfrac{\cos \alpha - \sin \beta}{\cos(\beta - \alpha)}$

62. $\sec(v + t) = \dfrac{\cos v \cos t + \sin v \sin t}{\cos^2 v - \sin^2 t}$

63. $\sin(180° - \alpha) = \dfrac{1 - \cos^2 \alpha}{\sin \alpha}$

64. $\dfrac{\sin(x + y)}{\sin x \cos y} = 1 + \cot x \tan y$

65. $\dfrac{\cos(\alpha + \beta)}{\sin(\alpha - \beta)} = \dfrac{1 - \tan \alpha \tan \beta}{\tan \alpha - \tan \beta}$

66. $\dfrac{\cos(\alpha - \beta)}{\sin(\alpha + \beta)} = \dfrac{1 + \tan \alpha \tan \beta}{\tan \alpha + \tan \beta}$

67. $\cos^4 s - \sin^4 s = \cos 2s$

68. $\sin 2s = -2 \sin s \sin(s - \pi/2)$

69. $\dfrac{\cos 2x + \cos 2y}{\sin x + \cos y} = 2\cos y - 2\sin x$

70. $(\sin \alpha - \cos \alpha)^2 = 1 - \sin 2\alpha$

71. $2\sin^2\left(\frac{u}{2}\right) = \frac{\sin^2 u}{1 + \cos u}$

72. $\cos 2y = \frac{1 - \tan^2 y}{1 + \tan^2 y}$

73. $\frac{1 - \sin^2\left(\frac{x}{2}\right)}{1 + \sin^2\left(\frac{x}{2}\right)} = \frac{1 + \cos x}{3 - \cos x}$

74. $\frac{1 - \cos^2\left(\frac{x}{2}\right)}{1 - \sin^2\left(\frac{x}{2}\right)} = \frac{1 - \cos x}{1 + \cos x}$

75. $\frac{\cos x - \cos 3x}{\cos x + \cos 3x} = \tan 2x \tan x$

76. $\frac{\cos 5y + \cos 3y}{\cos 5y - \cos 3y} = -\cot 4y \cot y$

Use the product-to-sum identities to rewrite each expression.

77. $\sin 13° \sin 9°$

78. $\cos 34° \cos 39°$

79. $\cos\left(\frac{\pi}{6}\right)\cos\left(\frac{\pi}{5}\right)$

80. $\sin\left(\frac{2\pi}{9}\right)\sin\left(\frac{3\pi}{4}\right)$

Find the exact value of each product.

81. $\sin(52.5°)\sin(7.5°)$

82. $\cos(105°)\cos(75°)$

83. $\sin\left(\frac{13\pi}{24}\right)\cos\left(\frac{5\pi}{24}\right)$

84. $\cos\left(\frac{5\pi}{24}\right)\sin\left(-\frac{\pi}{24}\right)$

Use the sum-to-product identities to rewrite each expression.

85. $\sin 12° - \sin 8°$

86. $\sin 7° + \sin 11°$

87. $\cos\left(\frac{\pi}{3}\right) - \cos\left(\frac{\pi}{5}\right)$

88. $\cos\left(\frac{1}{2}\right) + \cos\left(\frac{2}{3}\right)$

Find the exact value of each sum.

89. $\sin(75°) + \sin(15°)$

90. $\sin(285°) - \sin(15°)$

91. $\cos\left(-\frac{\pi}{24}\right) - \cos\left(\frac{7\pi}{24}\right)$

92. $\cos\left(\frac{5\pi}{24}\right) + \cos\left(\frac{\pi}{24}\right)$

Rewrite each expression in the form $A\sin(x + C)$.

93. $\sin x - \cos x$

94. $2\sin x + 2\cos x$

95. $-\frac{1}{2}\sin x + \frac{\sqrt{3}}{2}\cos x$

96. $\frac{\sqrt{2}}{2}\sin x - \frac{\sqrt{2}}{2}\cos x$

97. $\frac{\sqrt{3}}{2}\sin x - \frac{1}{2}\cos x$

98. $-\frac{\sqrt{3}}{2}\sin x - \frac{1}{2}\cos x$

Solve each problem.

99. *Viewing Area* Find a formula for the viewing area of a television screen in terms of its diagonal and the angle α shown in the figure. Rewrite the formula using a single trigonometric function.

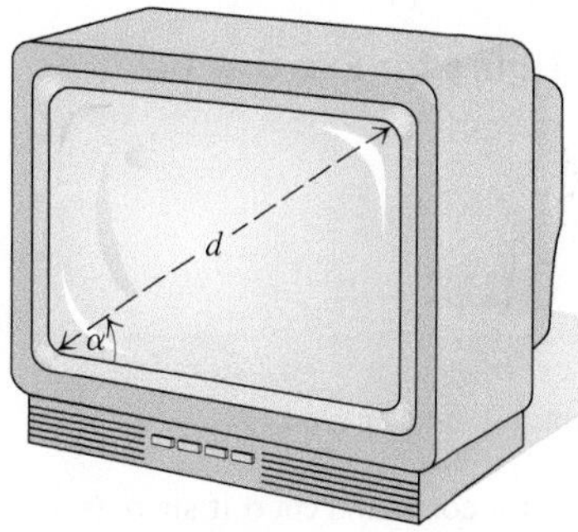

Figure for Exercises 99 and 100

100. Use the formula from the previous exercise to find the viewing area for a 32 in. diagonal television for which $\alpha = 37.2°$.

101. *Motion of a Spring* A block is attached to a spring, as shown in the figure, so that its resting position is the origin of the number line. If the block is set in motion, then it will oscillate about the origin. Suppose that the location of the block at time t in seconds is given in meters by $x = \sqrt{3}\sin t + \cos t$. Use the reduction formula to rewrite this function and find the maximum distance reached by the block from the resting position.

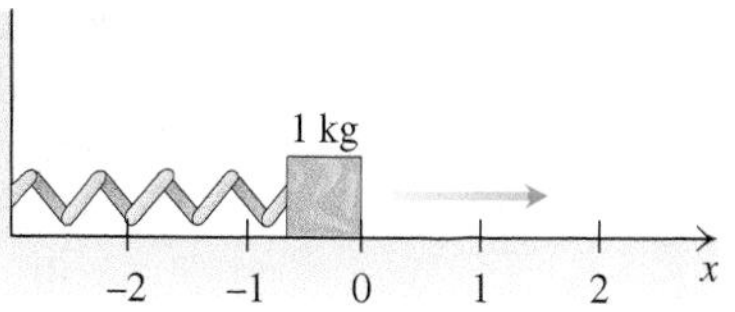

Figure for Exercise 101

102. *Motion of a Spring* A block hanging from a spring, as shown in the figure, oscillates about the origin on a vertical number line. If the block is given an upward velocity of

0.3 m/sec from a point 0.5 m below its resting position, then its position at time t in seconds is given in meters by $x = -0.3 \sin t + 0.5 \cos t$. Use the reduction formula to find the maximum distance that the block travels from the resting position.

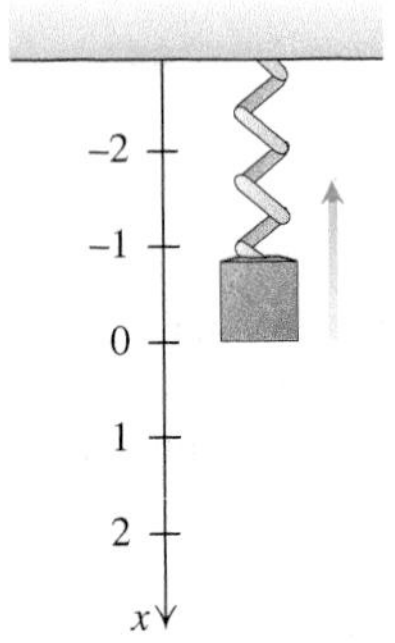

Figure for Exercise 102

Thinking Outside the Box XXV

Tangent Circles The three large circles in the accompanying diagram are tangent to each other and each has radius 1. The small circle in the middle is tangent to each of the three large circles. Find its radius.

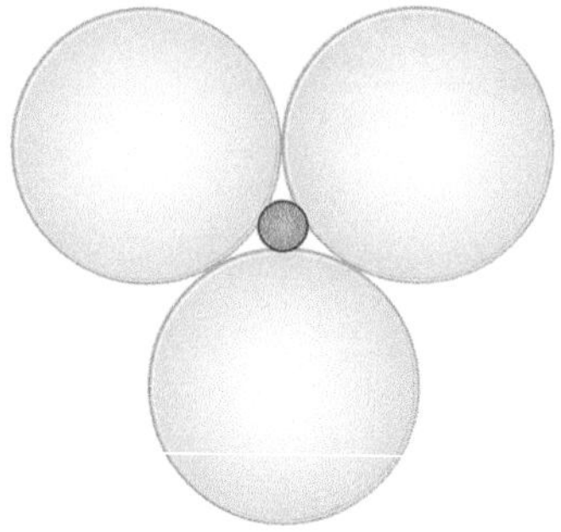

Figure for Thinking Outside the Box XXV

3.7 Pop Quiz

1. Simplify the expression $\cot x \sec x$.
2. Find exact values for $\cos \alpha$ and $\cot \alpha$ if $\sin \alpha = 1/3$ and $0 < \alpha < \pi/2$.
3. Is $f(x) = \cos(3x)$ even or odd?
4. Simplify $\sin(2x)\cos(x) + \cos(2x)\sin(x)$.
5. Simplify $\dfrac{2}{\sec^2 \alpha} + \dfrac{2}{\csc^2 \alpha}$.
6. Prove that $\sin^4 x - \cos^4 x = -\cos(2x)$

3.8 Conditional Trigonometric Equations

An identity is satisfied by *all* values of the variable for which both sides are defined. In this section we investigate **conditional equations,** those equations that are not identities but that have *at least one* solution. For example, the equation $\sin x = 0$ is a conditional equation. Because the trigonometric functions are periodic, conditional equations involving trigonometric functions usually have infinitely many solutions. The equation $\sin x = 0$ is satisfied by $x = 0, \pm\pi, \pm 2\pi, \pm 3\pi$, and so on. All of these solutions are of the form $k\pi$, where k is an integer. In this section we will solve conditional equations and see that identities play a fundamental role in their solution.

Cosine Equations

The most basic conditional equation involving cosine is of the form $\cos x = a$, where a is a number in the interval $[-1, 1]$. If a is not in $[-1, 1]$, $\cos x = a$ has no solution. For a in $[-1, 1]$, the equation $x = \cos^{-1} a$ provides one solution in the interval $[0, \pi]$. From this single solution we can determine all of the solutions because of the periodic nature of the cosine function. We must remember also that the cosine of an arc is the x-coordinate of its terminal point on the unit circle. So arcs that terminate at opposite ends of a vertical chord in the unit circle have the same cosine.

Example 1 Solving a cosine equation

Find all real numbers that satisfy each equation.

a. $\cos x = 1$ **b.** $\cos x = 0$ **c.** $\cos x = -1/2$

Solution

a. One solution to $\cos x = 1$ is

$$x = \cos^{-1}(1) = 0.$$

Since the period of cosine is 2π, any integral multiple of 2π can be added to this solution to get additional solutions. So the equation is satisfied by $0, \pm 2\pi, \pm 4\pi$, and so on. Now $\cos x = 1$ is satisifed only if the arc of length x on the unit circle has terminal point $(1, 0)$, as shown in Fig. 3.88. So there are no more solutions. The solution set is written as

$$\{x \mid x = 2k\pi\},$$

where k is any integer.

b. One solution to $\cos x = 0$ is

$$x = \cos^{-1}(0) = \frac{\pi}{2}.$$

The terminal point for the arc of length $\pi/2$ is $(0, 1)$. So any arc length of the form $\pi/2 + 2k\pi$ is a solution to $\cos x = 0$. However, an arc of length x that terminates at $(0, -1)$ also satisfies $\cos x = 0$, as shown in Fig. 3.89, and these arcs are not included in the form $\pi/2 + 2k\pi$. Since the distance between $(0, 1)$ and $(0, -1)$ on the unit circle is π, all arcs that terminate at these points are of the form $\pi/2 + k\pi$. So the solution set is

$$\left\{x \mid x = \frac{\pi}{2} + k\pi\right\},$$

where k is any integer.

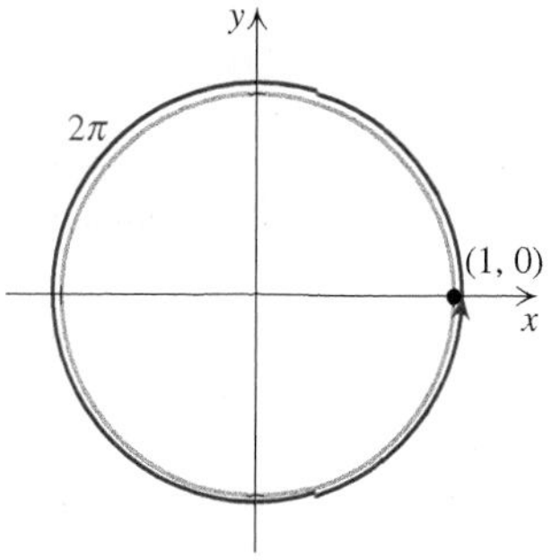

Figure 3.88

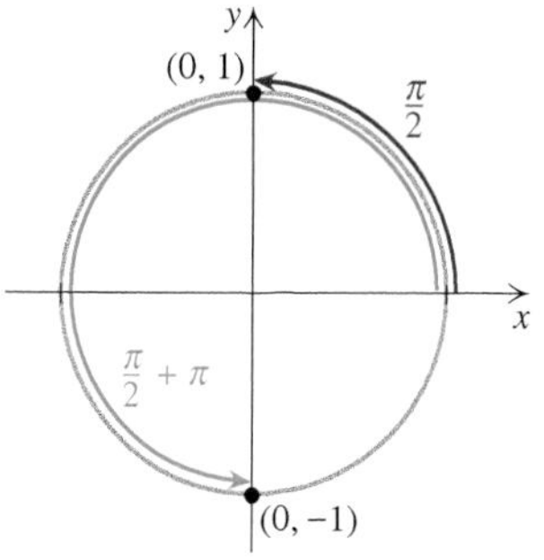

Figure 3.89

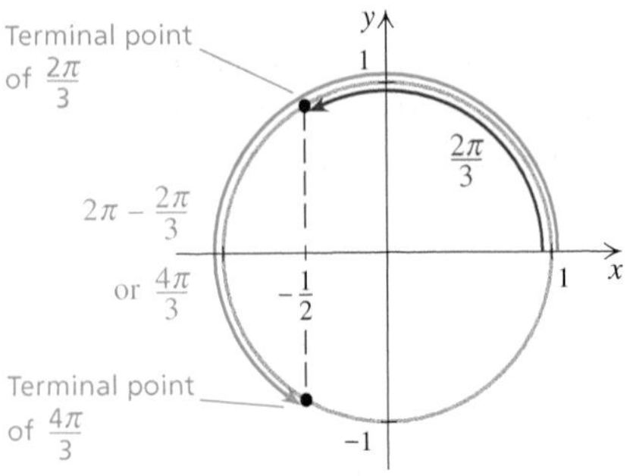

Figure 3.90

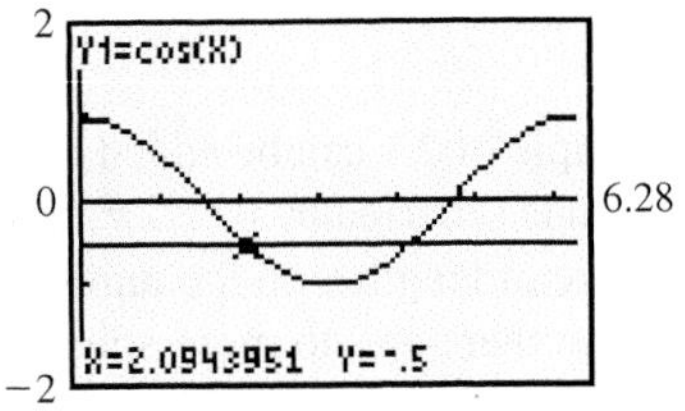

Figure 3.91

c. One solution to the equation $\cos x = -1/2$ is

$$x = \cos^{-1}\left(-\frac{1}{2}\right) = \frac{2\pi}{3}.$$

Since the period of cosine is 2π, all arcs of length $2\pi/3 + 2k\pi$ (where k is any integer) satisfy the equation. The arc of length $4\pi/3$ also terminates at a point with x-coordinate $-1/2$, as shown in Fig. 3.90. So $4\pi/3$ is also a solution to $\cos x = -1/2$, but it is not included in the form $2\pi/3 + 2k\pi$. So the solution set to $\cos x = -1/2$ is

$$\left\{x \middle| x = \frac{2\pi}{3} + 2k\pi \quad \text{or} \quad x = \frac{4\pi}{3} + 2k\pi\right\},$$

where k is any integer. Note that the arcs of length $2\pi/3$ and $4\pi/3$ terminate at opposite ends of a vertical chord in the unit circle.

Note also that the calculator graph of $y_1 = \cos x$ in Fig. 3.91 crosses the horizontal line $y_2 = -1/2$ twice in the interval $[0, 2\pi]$, at $2\pi/3$ and $4\pi/3$. ■

The procedure used in Example 1(c) can be used to solve $\cos x = a$ for any nonzero a between -1 and 1. First find two values of x between 0 and 2π that satisfy the equation. (In general, $s = \cos^{-1}(a)$ and $2\pi - s$ are the values.) Next write all solutions by adding $2k\pi$ to the first two solutions. The solution sets for $a = -1, 0,$ and 1 are easier to find and remember. All of the cases for solving $\cos x = a$ are summarized next. The letter k is used to represent any integer. You should not simply memorize this summary, but you should be able to solve $\cos x = a$ for any real number a with the help of a unit circle.

SUMMARY **Solving $\cos x = a$**

1. If $-1 < a < 1$ and $a \neq 0$, then the solution set to $\cos x = a$ is $\{x | x = s + 2k\pi \text{ or } x = 2\pi - s + 2k\pi\}$, where $s = \cos^{-1} a$.
2. The solution set to $\cos x = 1$ is $\{x | x = 2k\pi\}$.
3. The solution set to $\cos x = 0$ is $\{x | x = \pi/2 + k\pi\}$.
4. The solution set to $\cos x = -1$ is $\{x | x = \pi + 2k\pi\}$.
5. If $|a| > 1$, then $\cos x = a$ has no solution.

Sine Equations

To solve $\sin x = a$, we use the same strategy that we used to solve $\cos x = a$. We look for the smallest nonegative solution and then build on it to obtain all solutions. However, the "first" solution obtained from $s = \sin^{-1} a$ might be negative because the range for the function $\sin^{-1}$ is $[-\pi/2, \pi/2]$. In this case $s + 2\pi$ is positive and we build on it to find all solutions. Remember that the sine of an arc on the unit circle is the y-coordinate of the terminal point of the arc. So arcs that terminate at opposite ends of a horizontal chord in the unit circle have the same y-coordinate for the terminal point and the same sine. This fact is the key to finding all solutions of a sine equation.

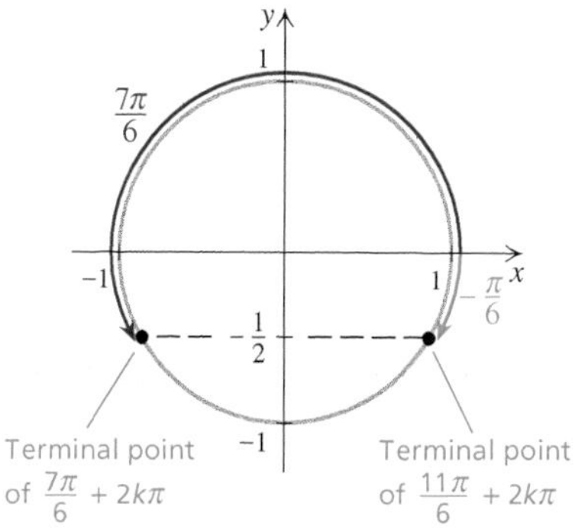

Figure 3.92

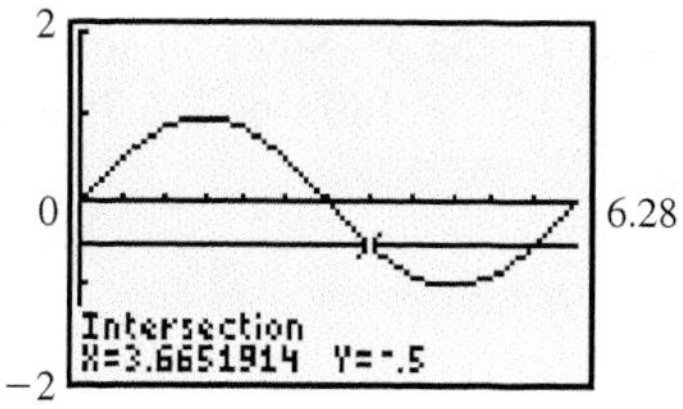

Figure 3.93

Example 2 Solving a sine equation

Find all real numbers that satisfy $\sin x = -1/2$.

Solution

One solution to $\sin x = -1/2$ is

$$x = \sin^{-1}\left(-\frac{1}{2}\right) = -\frac{\pi}{6}.$$

See Fig. 3.92. The smallest positive arc with the same terminal point as $-\pi/6$ is $-\pi/6 + 2\pi = 11\pi/6$. Since the period of the sine function is 2π, all arcs of the form $11\pi/6 + 2k\pi$ have the same terminal point and satisfy $\sin x = -1/2$. The smallest positive arc that terminates at the other end of the horizontal chord shown in Fig. 3.92 is $\pi - (-\pi/6)$ or $7\pi/6$. So $7\pi/6$ also satisfies the equation, but it is not included in the form $11\pi/6 + 2k\pi$. So the solution set is

$$\left\{x \,\middle|\, x = \frac{7\pi}{6} + 2k\pi \quad \text{or} \quad x = \frac{11\pi}{6} + 2k\pi\right\},$$

where k is any integer.

Note that the calculator graph of $y_1 = \sin x$ in Fig. 3.93 crosses the horizontal line $y_2 = -1/2$ twice in the interval $[0, 2\pi]$, at $7\pi/6$ and $11\pi/6$. ■

The procedure used in Example 2 can be used to solve $\sin x = a$ for any nonzero a between -1 and 1. First find two values between 0 and 2π that satisfy the equation. (In general, $s = \sin^{-1} a$ and $\pi - s$ work when s is positive; $s + 2\pi$ and $\pi - s$ work when s is negative.) Next write all solutions by adding $2k\pi$ to the first two solutions. The equations $\sin x = 0$, $\sin x = 1$, and $\sin x = -1$ have solutions that are similar to the corresponding cosine equations. We can summarize the different solution sets to $\sin x = a$ as follows. You should not simply memorize this summary, but you should be able to solve $\sin x = a$ for any real number a with the help of a unit circle.

SUMMARY **Solving sin x = a**

1. If $-1 < a < 1$, $a \neq 0$, and $s = \sin^{-1} a$, then the solution set to $\sin x = a$ is
$$\{x \mid x = s + 2k\pi \text{ or } x = \pi - s + 2k\pi\} \text{ for } s > 0,$$
$$\{x \mid x = s + 2\pi + 2k\pi \text{ or } x = \pi - s + 2k\pi\} \text{ for } s < 0.$$
2. The solution set to $\sin x = 1$ is $\{x \mid x = \pi/2 + 2k\pi\}$.
3. The solution set to $\sin x = 0$ is $\{x \mid x = k\pi\}$.
4. The solution set to $\sin x = -1$ is $\{x \mid x = 3\pi/2 + 2k\pi\}$.
5. If $|a| > 1$, then $\sin x = a$ has no solution.

Tangent Equations

Tangent equations are a little simpler than sine and cosine equations, because the tangent function is one-to-one in its fundamental cycle, while sine and cosine are not one-to-one in their fundamental cycles. In the next example, we see that the solution set to $\tan x = a$ consists of any single solution plus multiples of π.

Example 3 Solving a tangent equation

Find all solutions, in degrees.

a. $\tan\alpha = 1$ **b.** $\tan\alpha = -1.34$

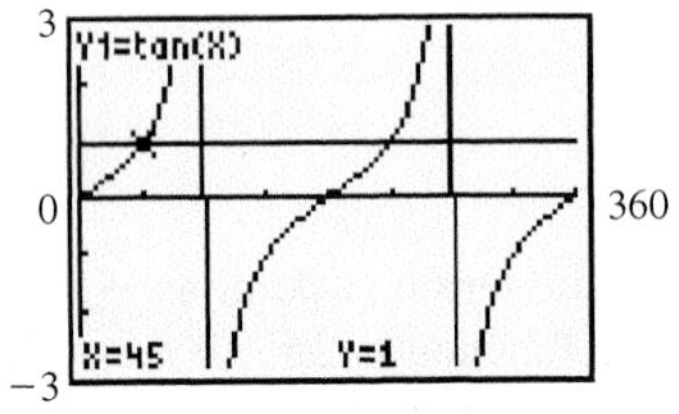

Figure 3.94

Solution

a. Since $\tan^{-1}(1) = 45°$ and the period of tangent is $180°$, all angles of the form $45° + k180°$ satisfy the equation. There are no additional angles that satisfy the equation. The solution set to $\tan\alpha = 1$ is

$$\{\alpha \mid \alpha = 45° + k180°\}.$$

The calculator graphs of $y_1 = \tan x$ and $y_2 = 1$ in Fig. 3.94 support the conclusion that the solutions to $\tan x = 1$ are $180°$ apart. □

b. Since $\tan^{-1}(-1.34) = -53.3°$, one solution is $\alpha = -53.3°$. Since all solutions to $\tan\alpha = -1.34$ differ by a multiple of $180°$, $-53.3° + 180°$, or $126.7°$ is the smallest positive solution. So the solution set is

$$\{\alpha \mid \alpha = 126.7° + k180°\}.$$ ■

To solve $\tan x = a$ for any real number a, we first find the smallest nonnegative solution. (In general, $s = \tan^{-1} a$ works if $s > 0$, and $s + \pi$ works if $s < 0$.) Next, add on all integral multiples of π. The solution to the equation $\tan x = a$ is summarized as follows.

SUMMARY **Solving $\tan x = a$**

If a is any real number and $s = \tan^{-1} a$, then the solution set to $\tan x = a$ is $\{x \mid x = s + k\pi\}$ for $s \geq 0$, and $\{x \mid x = s + \pi + k\pi\}$ for $s < 0$.

In the summaries for solving sine, cosine, and tangent equations, the domain of x is the set of real numbers. Similar summaries can be made if the domain of x is the set of degree measures. Start by finding $\sin^{-1} a$, $\cos^{-1} a$, or $\tan^{-1} a$ in degrees, then write the solution set in terms of multiples of $180°$ or $360°$.

Equations Involving Multiple Angles

Equations can involve expressions such as $\sin 2x$, $\cos 3\alpha$, or $\tan(s/2)$. These expressions involve a multiple of the variable rather than a single variable such as x, α, or s. In this case we solve for the multiple just as we would solve for a single variable and then find the value of the single variable in the last step of the solution.

Example 4 A sine equation involving a double angle

Find all solutions in degrees to $\sin 2\alpha = 1/\sqrt{2}$.

Solution

The only values for 2α between $0°$ and $360°$ that satisfy the equation are $45°$ and $135°$. (Note that $\sin^{-1}(1/\sqrt{2}) = 45°$ and $135° = 180° - 45°$.) See Fig. 3.95. So proceed as follows:

$$\sin 2\alpha = \frac{1}{\sqrt{2}}$$

$$2\alpha = 45° + k360° \quad \text{or} \quad 2\alpha = 135° + k360°$$

$$\alpha = 22.5° + k180° \quad \text{or} \quad \alpha = 67.5° + k180° \qquad \text{Divide each side by 2.}$$

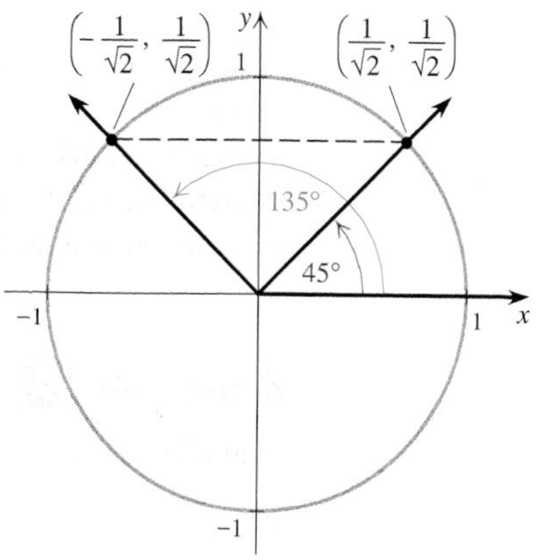

Figure 3.95

The solution set is $\{\alpha \mid \alpha = 22.5° + k180° \text{ or } \alpha = 67.5° + k180°\}$, where k is any integer. ■

Note that in Example 4, all possible values for 2α are found and *then* divided by 2 to get all possible values for α. Finding $\alpha = 22.5°$ and then adding on multiples of $360°$ will not produce the same solutions. Observe the same procedure in the next example, where we wait until the final step to divide each side by 3.

Example 5 A tangent equation involving angle multiples

Find all solutions to $\tan 3x = -\sqrt{3}$ in the interval $(0, 2\pi)$.

Solution

First find the smallest positive value for $3x$ that satisfies the equation. Then form all of the solutions by adding on multiples of π. Since $\tan^{-1}(-\sqrt{3}) = -\pi/3$, the smallest positive value for $3x$ that satisfies the equation is $-\pi/3 + \pi$, or $2\pi/3$. So proceed as follows:

$$\tan 3x = -\sqrt{3}$$

$$3x = \frac{2\pi}{3} + k\pi$$

$$x = \frac{2\pi}{9} + \frac{k\pi}{3} \qquad \text{Divide each side by 3.}$$

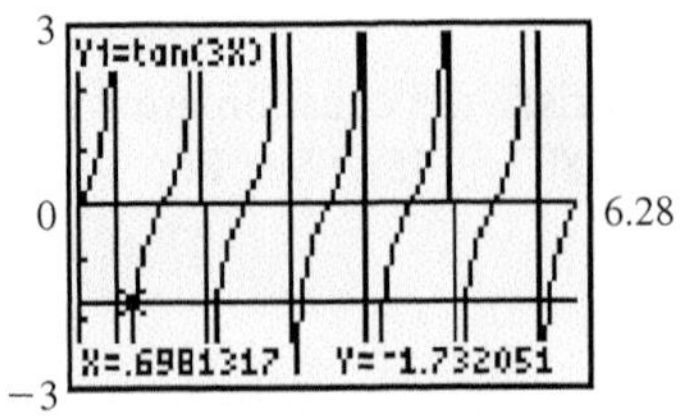

Figure 3.96

The solutions between 0 and 2π occur if $k = 0, 1, 2, 3, 4,$ and 5. If $k = 6$, then x is greater than 2π. So the solution set is

$$\left\{\frac{2\pi}{9}, \frac{5\pi}{9}, \frac{8\pi}{9}, \frac{11\pi}{9}, \frac{14\pi}{9}, \frac{17\pi}{9}\right\}.$$

The graphs of $y_1 = \tan(3x)$ and $y_2 = -\sqrt{3}$ in Fig. 3.96 show the six solutions in the interval $(0, 2\pi)$. ■

More Complicated Equations

More complicated equations involving trigonometric functions are solved by first solving for $\sin x$, $\cos x$, or $\tan x$, and then solving for x. In solving for the trigonometric functions, we may use trigonometric identities or properties of algebra, such as factoring or the quadratic formula. In stating formulas for solutions to equations, we will continue to use the letter k to represent any integer.

Example 6 An equation solved by factoring

Find all solutions in the interval $[0, 2\pi)$ to the equation

$$\sin 2x = \sin x.$$

Solution

First we use the identity $\sin 2x = 2 \sin x \cos x$ to get all of the trigonometric functions written in terms of the variable x alone. Then we rearrange and factor:

$$\sin 2x = \sin x$$

$$2 \sin x \cos x = \sin x \quad \text{By the double-angle identity}$$

$$2 \sin x \cos x - \sin x = 0 \quad \text{Subtract } \sin x \text{ from each side.}$$

$$\sin x(2 \cos x - 1) = 0 \quad \text{Factor.}$$

$$\sin x = 0 \quad \text{or} \quad 2 \cos x - 1 = 0 \quad \text{Set each factor equal to 0.}$$

$$x = k\pi \quad \text{or} \quad 2 \cos x = 1$$

$$\cos x = \frac{1}{2}$$

$$x = \frac{\pi}{3} + 2k\pi \quad \text{or} \quad x = \frac{5\pi}{3} + 2k\pi$$

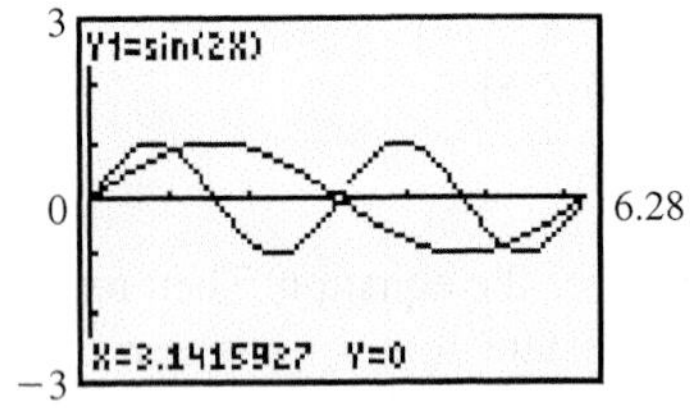

Figure 3.97

The only solutions in the interval $[0, 2\pi)$ are 0, $\pi/3$, π, and $5\pi/3$.

The graphs of $y_1 = \sin(2x)$ and $y_2 = \sin(x)$ in Fig. 3.97 show the four solutions to $\sin 2x = \sin x$ in the interval $[0, 2\pi)$. ■

In algebraic equations, we generally do not divide each side by any expression that involves a variable, and the same rule holds for trigonometric equations. In Example 6, we did not divide by $\sin x$ when it appeared on opposite sides of the equation. If we had, the solutions 0 and π would have been lost.

In the next example, an equation of quadratic type is solved by factoring.

Example 7 An equation of quadratic type

Find all solutions to the equation

$$6\cos^2\left(\frac{x}{2}\right) - 7\cos\left(\frac{x}{2}\right) + 2 = 0$$

in the interval $[0, 2\pi)$. Round approximate answers to four decimal places.

Solution

Let $y = \cos(x/2)$ to get a quadratic equation:

$$6y^2 - 7y + 2 = 0$$

$$(2y - 1)(3y - 2) = 0 \quad \text{Factor.}$$

$$2y - 1 = 0 \quad \text{or} \quad 3y - 2 = 0$$

$$y = \frac{1}{2} \quad \text{or} \quad y = \frac{2}{3}$$

$$\cos\frac{x}{2} = \frac{1}{2} \quad \text{or} \quad \cos\frac{x}{2} = \frac{2}{3} \quad \text{Replace } y \text{ by } \cos(x/2).$$

$$\frac{x}{2} = \frac{\pi}{3} + 2k\pi \text{ or } \frac{5\pi}{3} + 2k\pi \quad \text{or} \quad \frac{x}{2} \approx 0.8411 + 2k\pi \text{ or } 5.4421 + 2k\pi$$

Now multiply by 2 to solve for x:

$$x = \frac{2\pi}{3} + 4k\pi \text{ or } \frac{10\pi}{3} + 4k\pi \quad \text{or} \quad x \approx 1.6821 + 4k\pi \text{ or } 10.8842 + 4k\pi$$

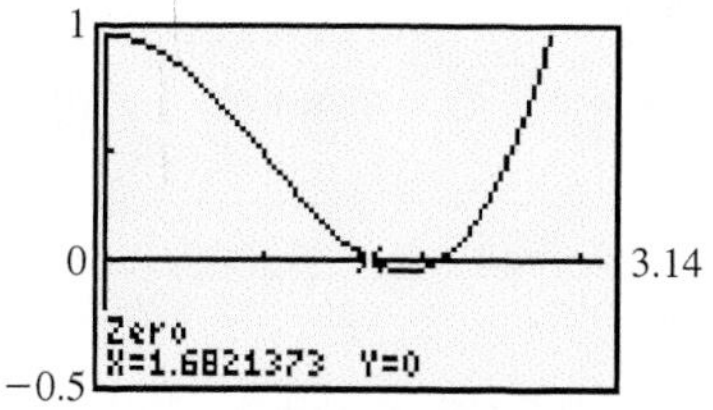

Figure 3.98

For all k, $10\pi/3 + 4k\pi$ and $10.8842 + 4k\pi$ are outside the interval $[0, 2\pi)$. The solutions in the interval $[0, 2\pi)$ are $2\pi/3$ and 1.6821.

The graph of $y = 6(\cos(x/2))^2 - 7\cos(x/2) + 2$ in Fig. 3.98 appears to cross the x-axis at $2\pi/3$ and 1.6821. ■

For a trigonometric equation to be of quadratic type, it must be written in terms of a trigonometric function and the square of that function. In the next example, an identity is used to convert an equation involving sine and cosine to one with only sine. This equation is of quadratic type like Example 7, but it does not factor.

Example 8 An equation solved by the quadratic formula

Find all solutions to the equation

$$\cos^2\alpha - 0.2\sin\alpha = 0.9$$

in the interval $[0°, 360°)$. Round answers to the nearest tenth of a degree.

Solution

$$\cos^2\alpha - 0.2\sin\alpha = 0.9$$

$$1 - \sin^2\alpha - 0.2\sin\alpha = 0.9 \quad \text{Replace } \cos^2\alpha \text{ with } 1 - \sin^2\alpha.$$

$$\sin^2\alpha + 0.2\sin\alpha - 0.1 = 0 \quad \text{An equation of quadratic type}$$

$$\sin\alpha = \frac{-0.2 \pm \sqrt{(0.2)^2 - 4(1)(-0.1)}}{2} \quad \text{Use } a = 1, b = 0.2, \text{ and } c = -0.1 \text{ in the quadratic formula.}$$

$$\sin\alpha \approx 0.2317 \quad \text{or} \quad \sin\alpha \approx -0.4317$$

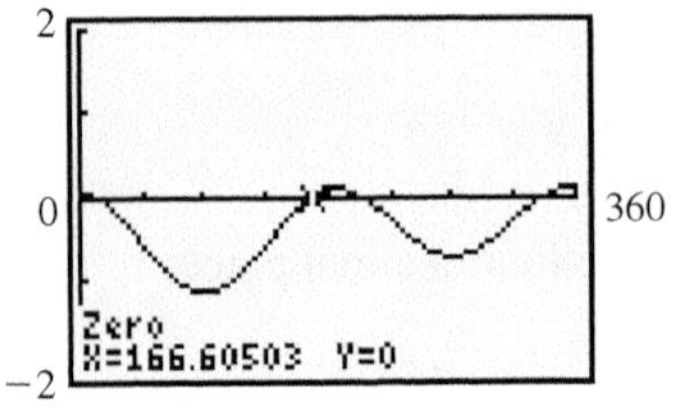

Figure 3.99

Find two positive solutions to $\sin\alpha = 0.2317$ in $[0, 360°)$ by using a calculator to get $\alpha = \sin^{-1}(0.2317) \approx 13.4°$ and $180° - \alpha \approx 166.6°$. Now find two positive solutions to $\sin\alpha = -0.4317$ in $[0, 360°)$. Using a calculator, we get $\alpha = \sin^{-1}(-0.4317) \approx -25.6°$ and $180° - \alpha \approx 205.6°$. Since $-25.6°$ is negative, we use $-25.6° + 360°$ or $334.4°$ along with $205.6°$ as the two solutions. We list all possible solutions as

$$\alpha \approx 13.4°, 166.6°, 205.6°, \quad \text{or} \quad 334.4° \quad (+k360° \text{ in each case}).$$

The solutions in $[0°, 360°)$ are $13.4°$, $166.6°$, $205.6°$, and $334.4°$.

The graph of $y = \cos^2 x - 0.2 \sin x - 0.9$ in Fig. 3.99 appears to cross the x-axis four times in the interval $[0°, 360°)$. ■

The Pythagorean identities $\sin^2 x = 1 - \cos^2 x$, $\csc^2 x = 1 + \cot^2 x$, and $\sec^2 x = 1 + \tan^2 x$ are frequently used to replace one function by the other. If an equation involves sine and cosine, cosecant and cotangent, or secant and tangent, we might be able to square each side and then use these identities.

Example 9 Square each side of the equation

Find all values of y in the interval $[0, 360°)$ that satisfy the equation

$$\tan 3y + 1 = \sqrt{2} \sec 3y.$$

Solution

$$(\tan 3y + 1)^2 = (\sqrt{2}\sec 3y)^2 \quad \text{Square each side.}$$
$$\tan^2 3y + 2\tan 3y + 1 = 2\sec^2 3y$$
$$\tan^2 3y + 2\tan 3y + 1 = 2(\tan^2 3y + 1) \quad \text{Since } \sec^2 x = \tan^2 x + 1$$
$$-\tan^2 3y + 2\tan 3y - 1 = 0 \quad \text{Subtract } 2\tan^2 3y + 2 \text{ from both sides.}$$
$$\tan^2 3y - 2\tan 3y + 1 = 0$$
$$(\tan 3y - 1)^2 = 0$$
$$\tan 3y - 1 = 0$$
$$\tan 3y = 1$$
$$3y = 45° + k180°$$

Because we squared each side, we must check for extraneous roots. First check $3y = 45°$. If $3y = 45°$, then $\tan 3y = 1$ and $\sec 3y = \sqrt{2}$. Substituting these values into $\tan 3y + 1 = \sqrt{2}\sec 3y$ gives us

$$1 + 1 = \sqrt{2} \cdot \sqrt{2}. \quad \text{Correct.}$$

If we add any *even* multiple of 180°, or any multiple of 360°, to 45°, we get the same values for $\tan 3y$ and $\sec 3y$. So for any k, $3y = 45° + k360°$ satisfies the original equation. Now check 45° plus *odd* multiples of 180°. If $3y = 225°$ $(k = 1)$, then

$$\tan 3y = 1 \quad \text{and} \quad \sec 3y = -\sqrt{2}.$$

These values do not satisfy the original equation. Since $\tan 3y$ and $\sec 3y$ have these same values for $3y = 45° + k180°$ for any odd k, the only solutions are of the form

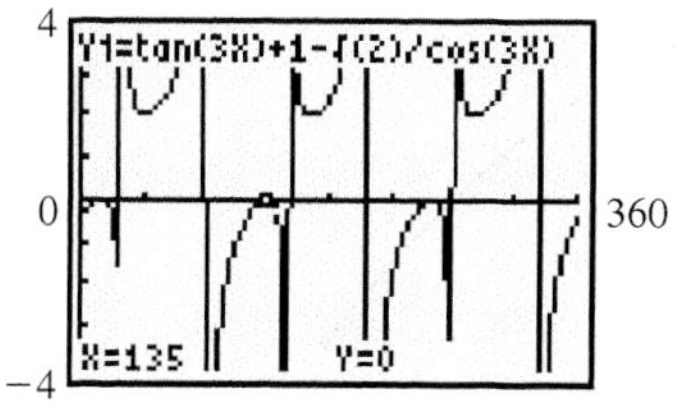

Figure 3.100

$3y = 45° + k360°$, or $y = 15° + k120°$. The solutions in the interval $[0°, 360°)$ are 15°, 135°, and 255°.

The graph of $y = \tan(3x) + 1 - \sqrt{2}/\cos(3x)$ in Fig. 3.100 appears to touch the x-axis at these three locations. ■

There is no single method that applies to all trigonometric equations, but the following strategy will help you to solve them.

STRATEGY **Solving Trigonometric Equations**

1. Know the solutions to $\sin x = a$, $\cos x = a$, and $\tan x = a$.
2. Solve an equation involving only multiple angles as if the equation had a single variable.
3. Simplify complicated equations by using identities. Try to get an equation involving only one trigonometric function.
4. If possible, factor to get different trigonometric functions into separate factors.
5. For equations of quadratic type, solve by factoring or the quadratic formula.
6. Square each side of the equation, if necessary, so that identities involving squares can be applied. (Check for extraneous roots.)

Modeling Projectile Motion

The distance d (in feet) traveled by a projectile fired from the ground with an angle of elevation θ is related to the initial velocity v_0 (in feet per second) by the equation $v_0^2 \sin 2\theta = 32d$. If the projectile is pictured as being fired from the origin into the first quadrant, then the x- and y-coordinates (in feet) of the projectile at time t (in seconds) are given by $x = v_0 t \cos \theta$ and $y = -16t^2 + v_0 t \sin \theta$.

Example 10 The path of a projectile

A catapult is placed 100 feet from the castle wall, which is 35 feet high. The soldier wants the burning bale of hay to clear the top of the wall and land 50 feet inside the castle wall. If the initial velocity of the bale is 70 feet per second, then at what angle should the bale of hay be launched so that it will travel 150 feet and pass over the castle wall?

Solution

Use the equation $v_0^2 \sin 2\theta = 32d$ with $v_0 = 70$ feet per second and $d = 150$ feet to find θ:

$$70^2 \sin 2\theta = 32(150)$$

$$\sin 2\theta = \frac{32(150)}{70^2} \approx 0.97959$$

The launch angle θ must be in the interval $(0°, 90°)$, so we look for values of 2θ in the interval $(0°, 180°)$. Since $\sin^{-1}(0.97959) \approx 78.4°$, both $78.4°$ and $180° - 78.4° = 101.6°$ are possible values for 2θ. So possible values for θ are 39.2° and 50.8°. See Fig. 3.101 on the next page.

Foreshadowing Calculus

A standard calculus problem is to show that a projectile's maximum distance for a given velocity is achieved at 45°. As illustrated in Example 11, there are two angles that can be used to achieve a distance less than the maximum, one less than 45° and one greater than 45°.

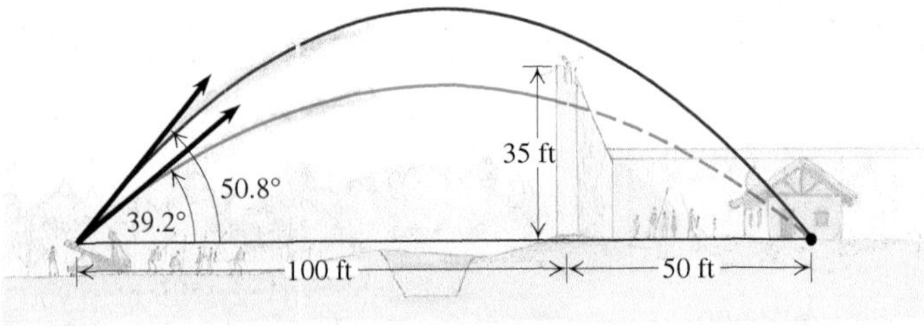

Figure 3.101

Use the equation $x = v_0 t \cos\theta$ to find the time at which the bale is 100 feet from the catapult (measured horizontally) by using each of the possible values for θ:

$$100 = 70t\cos(39.2°) \qquad\qquad 100 = 70t\cos(50.8°)$$

$$t = \frac{100}{70\cos(39.2°)} \approx 1.84 \text{ seconds} \qquad t = \frac{100}{70\cos(50.8°)} \approx 2.26 \text{ seconds}$$

Use the equation $y = -16t^2 + v_0 t \sin\theta$ to find the altitude of the bale at time $t = 1.84$ seconds and $t = 2.26$ seconds:

$$y = -16(1.84)^2 + 70(1.84)\sin 39.2° \qquad y = -16(2.26)^2 + 70(2.26)\sin 50.8°$$

$$\approx 27.2 \text{ feet} \qquad\qquad \approx 40.9 \text{ feet}$$

If the burning bale is launched on a trajectory with an angle of 39.2°, then it will have an altitude of only 27.2 feet when it reaches the castle wall. If it is launched with an angle of 50.8°, then it will have an altitude of 40.9 feet when it reaches the castle wall. Since the castle wall is 35 feet tall, the 50.8° angle must be used for the bale to reach its intended target. ■

As illustrated in Example 10 there are two launch angles, one less than 45° and one greater than 45°, that can be used to propel a projectile a given distance with a given initial velocity. When you throw a ball you usually choose the smaller launch angle so that the ball reaches its target in less time. A standard calculus problem is to show that a projectile's maximum distance for a given initial velocity is achieved at a launch angle of 45°. If you want to throw a ball a fixed distance with a minimum of effort, then what launch angle would you use?

For Thought

True or False? Explain.

1. The only solutions to $\cos\alpha = 1/\sqrt{2}$ in $[0°, 360°)$ are 45° and 135°.

2. The only solution to $\sin x = -0.55$ in $[0, \pi)$ is $\sin^{-1}(-0.55)$.

3. $\{x \mid x = -29° + k360°\} = \{x \mid x = 331° + k360°\}$, where k is any integer.

4. The solution set to $\tan x = -1$ is $\left\{x \mid x = \frac{7\pi}{4} + k\pi\right\}$, where k is any integer.

5. $2\cos^2 x + \cos x - 1 = (2\cos x - 1)(\cos x + 1)$ is an identity.

6. The equation $\sin^2 x = \sin x \cos x$ is equivalent to $\sin x = \cos x$.

7. One solution to $\sec x = 2$ is $\dfrac{1}{\cos^{-1}(2)}$.

8. The solution set to $\cot x = 3$ for x in $[0, \pi)$ is $\{\tan^{-1}(1/3)\}$.

9. The equation $\sin x = \cos x$ is equivalent to $\sin^2 x = \cos^2 x$.

10. $\left\{x \mid 3x = \frac{\pi}{2} + 2k\pi\right\} = \left\{x \mid x = \frac{\pi}{6} + 2k\pi\right\}$, where k is any integer.

3.8 Exercises

Find all real numbers that satisfy each equation. Do not use a calculator. See the summaries for solving $\cos x = a$, $\sin x = a$, *and* $\tan x = a$ *on pages 276, 277, and 278.*

1. $\cos x = -1$

2. $\cos x = 0$

3. $\sin x = 0$

4. $\sin x = 1$

5. $\sin x = -1$

6. $\cos x = 1$

7. $\cos x = 1/2$

8. $\cos x = \sqrt{2}/2$

9. $\sin x = \sqrt{2}/2$

10. $\sin x = \sqrt{3}/2$

11. $\tan x = 1$

12. $\tan x = \sqrt{3}/3$

13. $\cos x = -\sqrt{3}/2$

14. $\cos x = -\sqrt{2}/2$

15. $\sin x = -\sqrt{2}/2$

16. $\sin x = -\sqrt{3}/2$

17. $\tan x = -1$

18. $\tan x = -\sqrt{3}$

Find all angles in degrees that satisfy each equation. Round approximate answers to the nearest tenth of a degree.

19. $\cos\alpha = 0$

20. $\cos\alpha = -1$

21. $\sin\alpha = 1$

22. $\sin\alpha = -1$

23. $\tan\alpha = 0$

24. $\tan\alpha = -1$

25. $\cos\alpha = 0.873$

26. $\cos\alpha = -0.158$

27. $\sin\alpha = -0.244$

28. $\sin\alpha = 0.551$

29. $\tan\alpha = 5.42$

30. $\tan\alpha = -2.31$

Find all real numbers that satisfy each equation.

31. $\cos(x/2) = 1/2$

32. $2\cos 2x = -\sqrt{2}$

33. $\cos 3x = 1$

34. $\cos 2x = 0$

35. $2\sin(x/2) - 1 = 0$

36. $\sin 2x = 0$

37. $2\sin 2x = -\sqrt{2}$

38. $\sin(x/3) + 1 = 0$

39. $\tan 2x = \sqrt{3}$

40. $\sqrt{3}\tan(3x) + 1 = 0$

41. $\tan 4x = 0$

42. $\tan 3x = -1$

43. $\sin(\pi x) = 1/2$

44. $\tan(\pi x/4) = 1$

45. $\cos(2\pi x) = 0$

46. $\sin(3\pi x) = 1$

Find all values of α *in* $[0°, 360°)$ *that satisfy each equation.*

47. $2\sin\alpha = -\sqrt{3}$

48. $\tan\alpha = -\sqrt{3}$

49. $\sqrt{2}\cos 2\alpha - 1 = 0$

50. $\sin 6\alpha = 1$

51. $\sec 3\alpha = -\sqrt{2}$

52. $\csc(5\alpha) + 2 = 0$

53. $\cot(\alpha/2) = \sqrt{3}$

54. $\sec(\alpha/2) = \sqrt{2}$

Find all values of α *in degrees that satisfy each equation. Round approximate answers to the nearest tenth of a degree.*

55. $\sin 3\alpha = 0.34$

56. $\cos 2\alpha = -0.22$

57. $\sin 3\alpha = -0.6$

58. $\tan 4\alpha = -3.2$

59. $\sec 2\alpha = 4.5$

60. $\csc 3\alpha = -1.4$

61. $\csc(\alpha/2) = -2.3$

62. $\cot(\alpha/2) = 4.7$

Find all real numbers in the interval $[0, 2\pi)$ *that satisfy each equation. Round approximate answers to the nearest tenth. See the strategy for solving trigonometric equations on page 283.*

63. $3\sin^2 x = \sin x$

64. $2\tan^2 x = \tan x$

65. $2\cos^2 x + 3\cos x = -1$

66. $2\sin^2 x + \sin x = 1$

67. $5\sin^2 x - 2\sin x = \cos^2 x$

68. $\sin^2 x - \cos^2 x = 0$

69. $\tan x = \sec x - \sqrt{3}$

70. $\csc x - \sqrt{3} = \cot x$

71. $\sin x + \sqrt{3} = 3\sqrt{3}\cos x$

72. $6\sin^2 x - 2\cos x = 5$

73. $\tan x \sin 2x = 0$

74. $3\sec^2 x \tan x = 4\tan x$

75. $\sin 2x - \sin x \cos x = \cos x$

76. $2\cos^2 2x - 8\sin^2 x\cos^2 x = -1$

77. $\sin x\cos(\pi/4) + \cos x \sin(\pi/4) = 1/2$

78. $\sin(\pi/6)\cos x - \cos(\pi/6)\sin x = -1/2$

79. $\sin 2x \cos x - \cos 2x \sin x = -1/2$

80. $\cos 2x \cos x - \sin 2x \sin x = 1/2$

Find all values of θ in the interval $[0°, 360°)$ *that satisfy each equation. Round approximate answers to the nearest tenth of a degree.*

81. $\cos^2\left(\frac{\theta}{2}\right) = \sec\theta$

82. $2\sin^2\left(\frac{\theta}{2}\right) = \cos\theta$

83. $2\sin\theta = \cos\theta$

84. $3\sin 2\theta = \cos 2\theta$

85. $\sin 3\theta = \csc 3\theta$

86. $\tan^2\theta - \cot^2\theta = 0$

87. $\tan^2\theta - 2\tan\theta - 1 = 0$

88. $\cot^2\theta - 4\cot\theta + 2 = 0$

89. $9\sin^2\theta + 12\sin\theta + 4 = 0$

90. $12\cos^2\theta + \cos\theta - 6 = 0$

91. $\dfrac{\tan 3\theta - \tan\theta}{1 + \tan 3\theta \tan\theta} = \sqrt{3}$

92. $\dfrac{\tan 3\theta + \tan 2\theta}{1 - \tan 3\theta \tan 2\theta} = 1$

93. $8\cos^4\theta - 10\cos^2\theta + 3 = 0$

94. $4\sin^4\theta - 5\sin^2\theta + 1 = 0$

95. $\sec^4\theta - 5\sec^2\theta + 4 = 0$

96. $\cot^4\theta - 4\cot^2\theta + 3 = 0$

Solve each problem.

97. *Motion of a Spring* A block is attached to a spring and set in motion on a frictionless plane. Its location on the surface at any time t in seconds is given in meters by

$$x = \sqrt{3}\sin 2t + \cos 2t.$$

For what values of t is the block at its resting position $x = 0$?

98. *Motion of a Spring* A block is set in motion hanging from a spring and oscillates about its resting position $x = 0$ according to the function $x = -0.3\sin 3t + 0.5\cos 3t$. For what values of t is the block at its resting position $x = 0$?

99. *Firing an M-16* A soldier is accused of breaking a window 3300 ft away during target practice. If the muzzle velocity for an M-16 is 325 ft/sec, then at what angle would it have to be aimed for the bullet to travel 3300 ft? The distance d (in feet) traveled by a projectile fired at an angle θ is related to the initial velocity v_0 (in feet per second) by the equation $v_0^2 \sin 2\theta = 32d$.

100. *Firing an M-16* If you were accused of firing an M-16 into the air and breaking a window 4000 ft away, what would be your defense?

101. *Choosing the Right Angle* Cincinnati Reds centerfielder Ken Griffey, Jr., fields a ground ball and attempts to make a 230-ft throw to home plate. Given that Griffey commonly makes long throws at 90 mph, find the two possible angles at which he can throw the ball to home plate. Find the time saved by choosing the smaller angle.

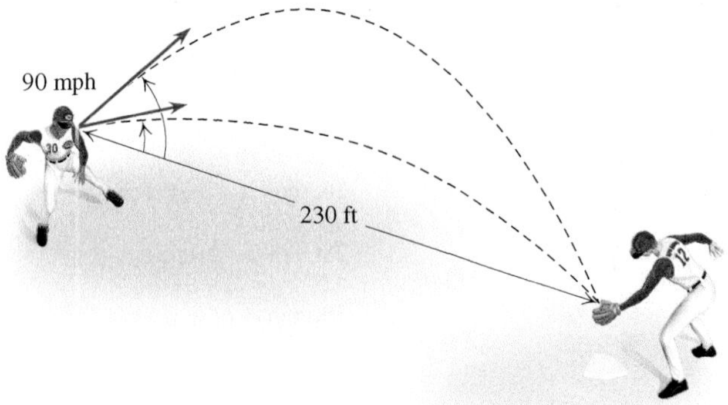

Figure for Exercise 101

102. *Muzzle Velocity* The 8-in. (diameter) howitzer on the U.S. Army's M-110 can propel a projectile a distance of 18,500 yd. If the angle of elevation of the barrel is 45°, then what muzzle velocity (in feet per second) is required to achieve this distance?

Thinking Outside the Box XXVI

Two Common Triangles An equilateral triangle with sides of length 1 and an isosceles right triangle with legs of length 1 are positioned as shown in the accompanying diagram. Find the exact area of the shaded triangle.

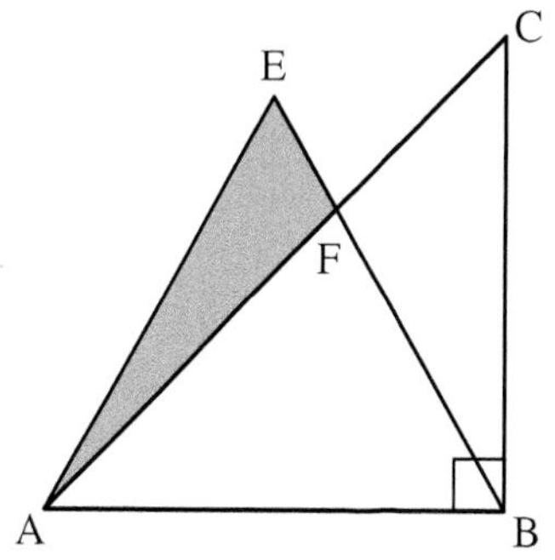

Figure for Thinking Outside the Box XXVI

3.8 Pop Quiz

Find all angles α in degrees that satisfy each equation.

1. $\sin \alpha = \sqrt{2}/2$

2. $\cos \alpha = 1/2$

3. $\tan \alpha = -1$

Find all real numbers in $[0, 2\pi]$ that satisfy each equation.

4. $\sin(x/2) = 1/2$

5. $\cos(x) = 1$

6. $\tan(2x) = 1$

3.9 The Law of Sines and the Law of Cosines

In Section 3.6 we used trigonometry to solve right triangles. In this section and the next we will learn to solve any triangle for which we have enough information to determine the shape of the triangle.

Oblique Triangles

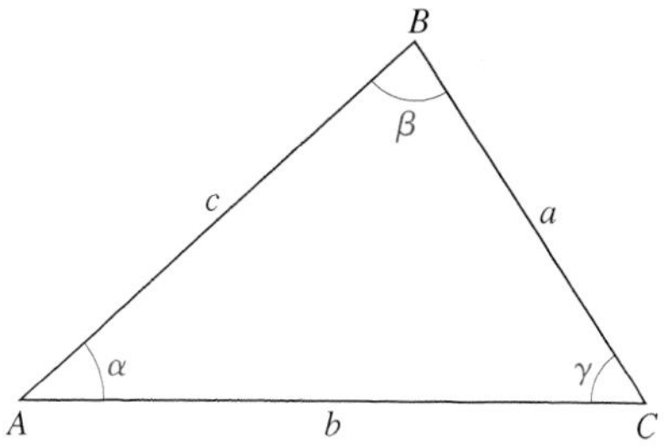

Figure 3.102

Any triangle without a right angle is called an **oblique triangle.** As usual, we use α, β, and γ for the angles of a triangle and a, b, and c, respectively, for the lengths of the sides opposite those angles, as shown in Fig. 3.102. The vertices at angles α, β, and γ are labeled A, B, and C, respectively. To solve an oblique triangle, we must know at least three parts of the triangle, at least one of which must be the length of a side. We can classify the different cases for the three known parts as follows:

1. One side and any two angles (ASA or AAS)
2. Two sides and a nonincluded angle (SSA)
3. Two sides and an included angle (SAS)
4. Three sides (SSS)

We can actually solve all of these cases by dividing the triangles into right triangles and using right triangle trigonometry. Since that method is quite tedious, we develop the *law of sines* and the *law of cosines*. The first two cases can be handled with the law of sines. We will discuss the last two cases when we develop the law of cosines.

The Law of Sines

The **law of sines** says that *the ratio of the sine of an angle and the length of the side opposite the angle is the same for each angle of a triangle.*

Theorem: The Law of Sines

In any triangle,

$$\frac{\sin \alpha}{a} = \frac{\sin \beta}{b} = \frac{\sin \gamma}{c}.$$

PROOF Either the triangle is an acute triangle (all acute angles) or it is an obtuse triangle (one obtuse angle). We consider the case of the obtuse triangle here. The case of the acute triangle is proved similarly. Triangle ABC is shown in Fig. 3.103 with an altitude of length h_1 drawn from point C to the opposite side and an altitude of length h_2 drawn from point B to the extension of the opposite side.

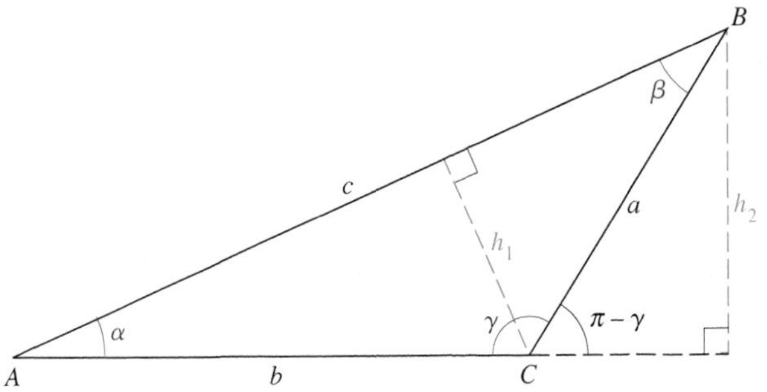

Figure 3.103

Since α and β are now in right triangles, we have

$$\sin \alpha = \frac{h_1}{b} \quad \text{or} \quad h_1 = b \sin \alpha$$

and

$$\sin \beta = \frac{h_1}{a} \quad \text{or} \quad h_1 = a \sin \beta.$$

Replace h_1 by $b \sin \alpha$ in the equation $h_1 = a \sin \beta$ to get

$$b \sin \alpha = a \sin \beta.$$

Dividing each side of the last equation by ab yields

$$\frac{\sin \alpha}{a} = \frac{\sin \beta}{b}.$$

Using the largest right triangle in Fig. 3.103, we have

$$\sin\alpha = \frac{h_2}{c} \quad \text{or} \quad h_2 = c\sin\alpha.$$

Using the identity for the sine of a difference we have

$$\begin{aligned}\sin(\pi - \gamma) &= \sin\pi\cos\gamma - \cos\pi\sin\gamma \\ &= \sin\gamma.\end{aligned}$$

Since $\pi - \gamma$ is an angle of a right triangle in Fig. 3.103, we have

$$\sin\gamma = \sin(\pi - \gamma) = \frac{h_2}{a} \quad \text{or} \quad h_2 = a\sin\gamma.$$

From $h_2 = c\sin\alpha$ and $h_2 = a\sin\gamma$ we get $c\sin\alpha = a\sin\gamma$ or

$$\frac{\sin\alpha}{a} = \frac{\sin\gamma}{c}$$

and we have proved the law of sines. ■

The law of sines can also be written in the form

$$\frac{a}{\sin\alpha} = \frac{b}{\sin\beta} = \frac{c}{\sin\gamma}.$$

In solving triangles, it is usually simplest to use the form in which the unknown quantity appears in the numerator.

In our first example we use the law of sines to solve a triangle for which we are given two angles and an included side.

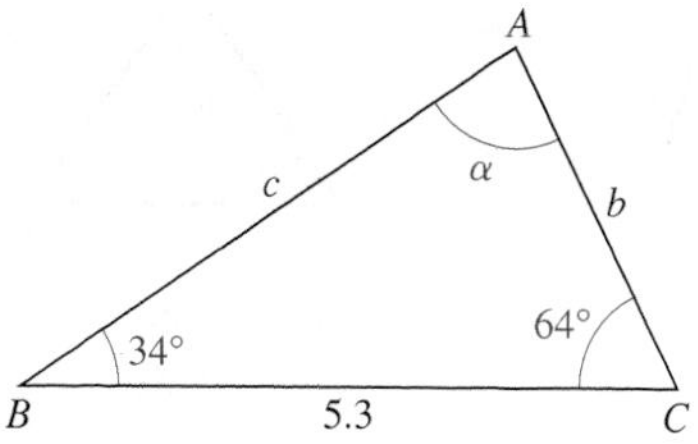

Figure 3.104

Example 1 Given two angles and an included side (ASA)

Given $\beta = 34°$, $\gamma = 64°$, and $a = 5.3$, solve the triangle.

Solution

To sketch the triangle, first draw side a, then draw angles of approximately 34° and 64° on opposite ends of a. Label all parts (see Fig. 3.104). Since the sum of the three angles of a triangle is 180°, the third angle α is 82°. By the law of sines,

$$\frac{5.3}{\sin 82°} = \frac{b}{\sin 34°}$$

$$b = \frac{5.3\sin 34°}{\sin 82°} \approx 3.0.$$

Again, by the law of sines,

$$\frac{c}{\sin 64°} = \frac{5.3}{\sin 82°}$$

$$c = \frac{5.3\sin 64°}{\sin 82°} \approx 4.8.$$

So $\alpha = 82°$, $b \approx 3.0$, and $c \approx 4.8$ solves the triangle. ■

The AAS case is similar to the ASA case. If two angles are known, then the third can be found by using the fact that the sum of all angles is 180°. If we know all angles and any side, then we can proceed to find the remaining sides with the law of sines as in Example 1.

The Ambiguous Case (SSA)

In the AAS and ASA cases we are given any two angles with positive measures and the length of any side. If the total measure of the two angles is less than 180°, then a unique triangle is determined. However, for two sides and a *nonincluded* angle (SSA), there are several possibilities. So the SSA case is called the **ambiguous case.** Drawing the diagram in the proper order will help you in understanding the ambiguous case.

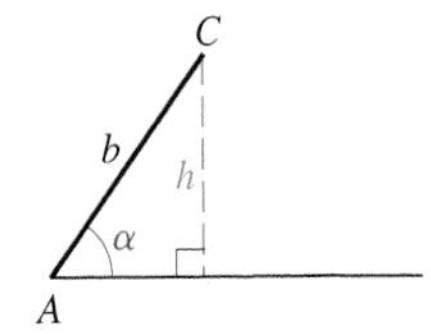

Draw α and b: find h

Figure 3.105

Suppose we are given an acute angle α $(0° < \alpha < 90°)$ and sides a and b. Side a is opposite the angle α, and side b is adjacent to it. Draw an angle of approximate size α in standard position with terminal side of length b, as shown in Fig. 3.105. Don't draw in side a yet. Let h be the distance from C to the initial side of α. Since $\sin \alpha = h/b$, we have $h = b \sin \alpha$. Now we are ready to draw in side a, but there are four possibilities for its location.

1. If $a < h$, then no triangle can be formed, because a cannot reach from point C to the initial side of α. This situation is shown in Fig. 3.106(a) .
2. If $a = h$, then exactly one right triangle is formed, as in Fig. 3.106(b).
3. If $h < a < b$, then exactly two triangles are formed, because a reaches to the initial side in two places, as in Fig. 3.106(c).
4. If $a \geq b$, then only one triangle is formed, as in Fig. 3.106(d).

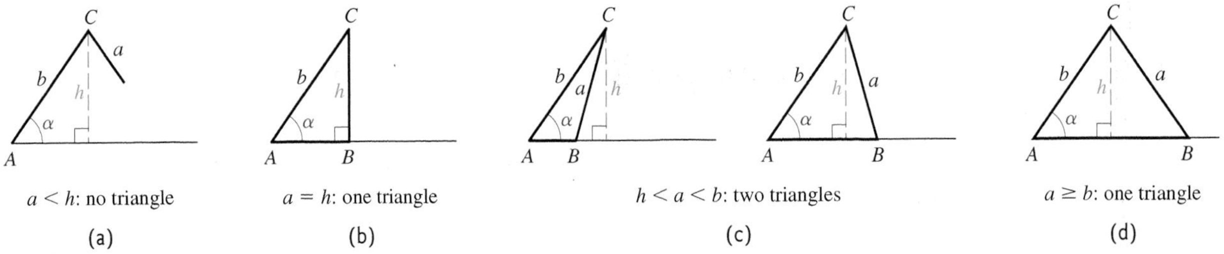

$a < h$: no triangle
(a)
$a = h$: one triangle
(b)
$h < a < b$: two triangles
(c)
$a \geq b$: one triangle
(d)

Figure 3.106

If we start with α, a, and b, where $90° \leq \alpha < 180°$, then there are only two possibilities for the number of triangles determined. If $a \leq b$, then no triangle is formed, as in Fig. 3.107(a). If $a > b$, one triangle is formed, as in Fig. 3.107(b).

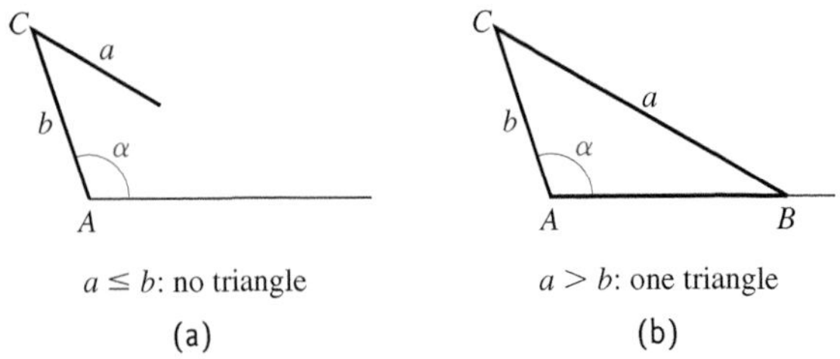

$a \leq b$: no triangle
(a)
$a > b$: one triangle
(b)

Figure 3.107

It is not necessary to memorize all of the SSA cases shown in Figs. 3.106 and 3.107. If you draw the triangle for a given problem in the order suggested, then it will be clear how many triangles are possible with the given parts. We must decide how many triangles are possible, before we can solve the triangle(s).

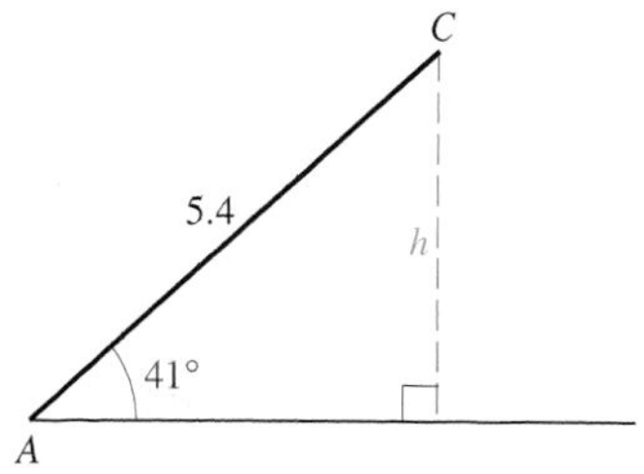

Figure 3.108

Example 2 SSA with no triangle

Given $\alpha = 41°$, $a = 3.3$, and $b = 5.4$, solve the triangle.

Solution

Draw the 41° angle and label its terminal side 5.4, as shown in Fig. 3.108. Side a must go opposite α, but do not put it in yet. Find the length of the altitude h from C. Using a trigonometric ratio, we get $\sin 41° = h/5.4$, or $h = 5.4 \sin 41° \approx 3.5$. Since $a = 3.3$, a is *shorter* than the altitude h, and side a will not reach from point C to the initial side of α. So there is no triangle with the given parts. ■

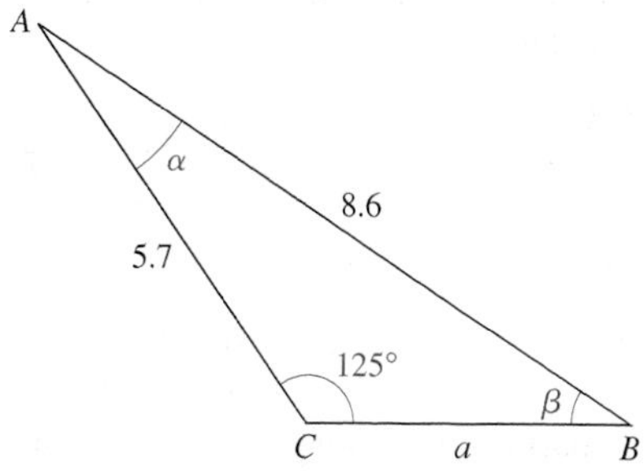

Figure 3.109

Example 3 SSA with one triangle

Given $\gamma = 125°$, $b = 5.7$, and $c = 8.6$, solve the triangle.

Solution

Draw the 125° angle and label its terminal side 5.7. Since $8.6 > 5.7$, side c will reach from point A to the initial side of γ, as shown in Fig. 3.109, and form a single triangle. To solve this triangle, we use the law of sines:

$$\frac{\sin 125°}{8.6} = \frac{\sin \beta}{5.7}$$

$$\sin \beta = \frac{5.7 \sin 125°}{8.6}$$

$$\beta = \sin^{-1}\left(\frac{5.7 \sin 125°}{8.6}\right) \approx 32.9°$$

Since the sum of α, β, and γ is 180°, $\alpha = 22.1°$. Now use α and the law of sines to find a:

$$\frac{a}{\sin 22.1°} = \frac{8.6}{\sin 125°}$$

$$a = \frac{8.6 \sin 22.1°}{\sin 125°} \approx 3.9$$ ■

Example 4 SSA with two triangles

Given $\beta = 56.3°$, $a = 8.3$, and $b = 7.6$, solve the triangle.

Solution

Draw an angle of approximately 56.3°, and label its terminal side 8.3. Side b must go opposite β, but do not put it in yet. Find the length of the altitude h from point C to the initial side of β, as shown in Fig. 3.110(a) on the next page. Since $\sin 56.3° = h/8.3$, we get $h = 8.3 \sin 56.3° \approx 6.9$. Because b is longer than h but

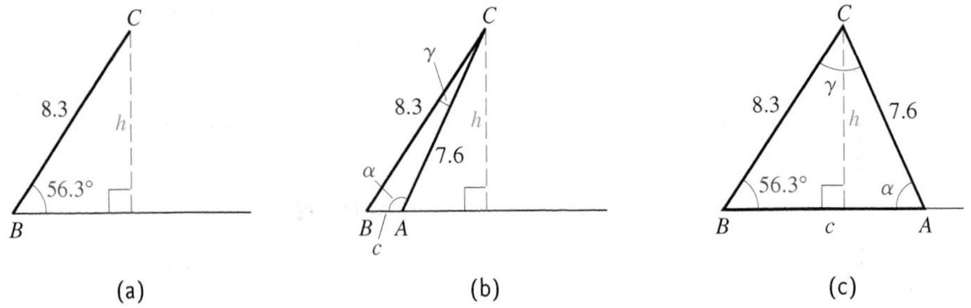

Figure 3.110

shorter than a, there are two triangles that satisfy the given conditions, as shown in parts (b) and (c) of Fig. 3.110. In either triangle we have

$$\frac{\sin \alpha}{8.3} = \frac{\sin 56.3°}{7.6}$$

$$\sin \alpha = 0.9086.$$

This equation has two solutions in $[0°, 180°]$. For part (c) we get $\alpha = \sin^{-1}(0.9086) = 65.3°$, and for part (b) we get $\alpha = 180° - 65.3° = 114.7°$. Using the law of sines, we get $\gamma = 9.0°$ and $c = 1.4$ for part (b), and we get $\gamma = 58.4°$ and $c = 7.8$ for part (c). ■

The Law of Cosines

The **law of cosines** gives a formula for the square of any side of an oblique triangle in terms of the other two sides and their included angle.

Theorem: Law of Cosines

If triangle ABC is an oblique triangle with sides a, b, and c and angles α, β, and γ, then

$$a^2 = b^2 + c^2 - 2bc \cos \alpha,$$

$$b^2 = a^2 + c^2 - 2ac \cos \beta,$$

$$c^2 = a^2 + b^2 - 2ab \cos \gamma.$$

PROOF Given triangle ABC, position the triangle as shown in Fig. 3.111. The vertex C is in the first quadrant if α is acute and in the second if α is obtuse. Both cases are shown in Fig. 3.111.

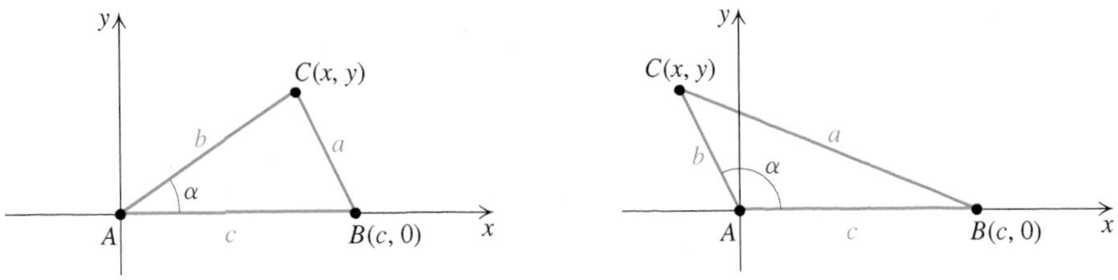

Figure 3.111

In either case, the x-coordinate of C is $x = b \cos \alpha$, and the y-coordinate of C is $y = b \sin \alpha$. The distance from C to B is a, but we can also find that distance by using the distance formula:

$$\begin{aligned} a &= \sqrt{(b \cos \alpha - c)^2 + (b \sin \alpha - 0)^2} \\ a^2 &= (b \cos \alpha - c)^2 + (b \sin \alpha)^2 \\ &= b^2 \cos^2 \alpha - 2bc \cos \alpha + c^2 + b^2 \sin^2 \alpha \\ &= b^2(\cos^2 \alpha + \sin^2 \alpha) + c^2 - 2bc \cos \alpha \end{aligned}$$

Using $\cos^2 x + \sin^2 x = 1$, we get the first equation of the theorem:

$$a^2 = b^2 + c^2 - 2bc \cos \alpha$$

Similar arguments with B and C at $(0, 0)$ produce the other two equations. ■

In any triangle with unequal sides, the largest angle is opposite the largest side, and the smallest angle is opposite the smallest side. We need this fact in the first example.

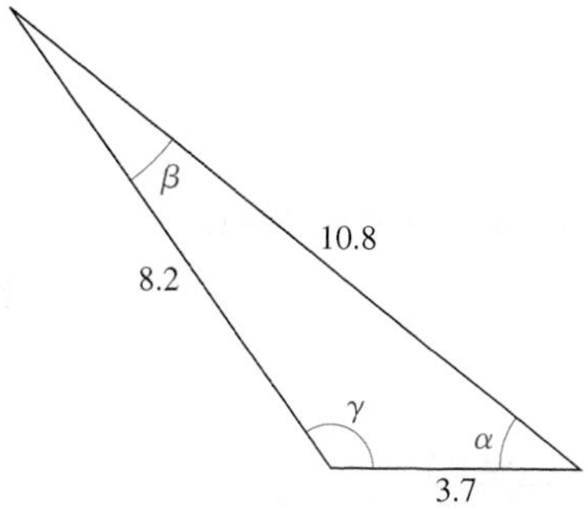

Figure 3.112

Example 5 Given three sides of a triangle (SSS)

Given $a = 8.2$, $b = 3.7$, and $c = 10.8$, solve the triangle.

Solution

Draw the triangle and label it as in Fig. 3.112. Since c is the longest side, use

$$c^2 = a^2 + b^2 - 2ab \cos \gamma$$

to find the largest angle γ:

$$\begin{aligned} -2ab \cos \gamma &= c^2 - a^2 - b^2 \\ \cos \gamma &= \frac{c^2 - a^2 - b^2}{-2ab} = \frac{(10.8)^2 - (8.2)^2 - (3.7)^2}{-2(8.2)(3.7)} \approx -0.5885 \\ \gamma &= \cos^{-1}(-0.5885) \approx 126.1^\circ \end{aligned}$$

We could finish with the law of cosines, but in this case it is simpler to use the law of sines, which involves fewer computations:

$$\begin{aligned} \frac{\sin \beta}{b} &= \frac{\sin \gamma}{c} \\ \frac{\sin \beta}{3.7} &= \frac{\sin 126.1^\circ}{10.8} \\ \sin \beta &\approx 0.2768 \end{aligned}$$

There are two solutions to $\sin \beta = 0.2768$ in $[0^\circ, 180^\circ]$. However, β must be less than 90°, because γ is 126.1°. So $\beta = \sin^{-1}(0.2768) \approx 16.1^\circ$. Finally, $\alpha = 180^\circ - 126.1^\circ - 16.1^\circ = 37.8^\circ$. ■

In solving the SSS case, we always *find the largest angle first,* using the law of cosines. The remaining two angles must be acute angles. So when using the law of sines to find another angle, we need only find an acute solution to the equation.

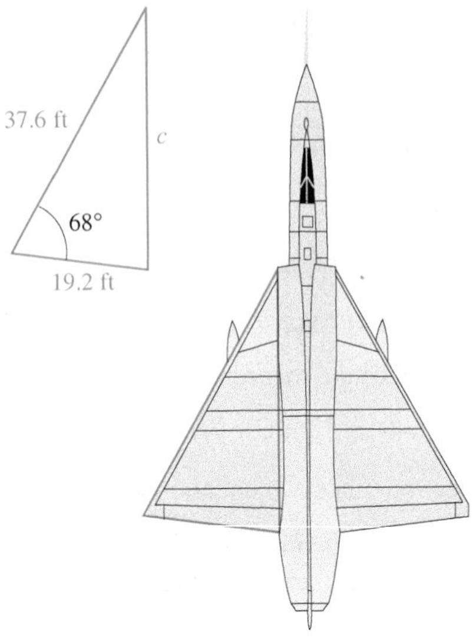

Figure 3.113

We have seen that two adjacent sides and a nonincluded angle (SSA) might not determine a triangle. To determine a triangle with three given sides (SSS), the sum of the lengths of any two must be greater than the length of the third side. This fact is called the **triangle inequality.** To understand the triangle inequality, try to draw a triangle with sides of lengths 1 in., 2 in., and 5 in. Two sides and the included angle (SAS) will determine a triangle provided the angle is between 0° and 180°.

Example 6 Given two sides and an included angle (SAS)

The wing of the F-106 Delta Dart is triangular in shape, with the dimensions given in Fig. 3.113. Find the length of the side labeled c in Fig. 3.113.

Solution

Using the law of cosines, we find c as follows:

$$c^2 = (19.2)^2 + (37.6)^2 - 2(19.2)(37.6)\cos 68° \approx 1241.5$$

$$c \approx \sqrt{1241.5} \approx 35.2 \text{ feet}$$

■

PROCEDURE Solving Triangles (In all cases draw pictures.)

ASA (For example α, c, β)

1. Find γ using $\gamma = 180° - \alpha - \beta$.
2. Find a and c using the law of sines.

SSA (For example a, b, α)

1. Find $h = b \sin \alpha$. If $h > a$, then there is no triangle.
2. If $h = a$, then there is one right triangle ($\beta = 90°$ and b is the hypotenuse). Solve it using right triangle trigonometry.
3. If $h < a < b$ there are two triangles, one with β acute and one with β obtuse. Find the acute β using the law of sines. Subtract it from 180° to get the obtuse β. In each of the two triangles, find γ using $\gamma = 180° - \alpha - \beta$ and c using the law of sines.
4. If $a \geq b$ there is only one triangle and β is acute (α or γ might be obtuse). Find β using the law of sines. Then find γ using $\gamma = 180° - \alpha - \beta$. Find c using the law of sines.

SSS (For example a, b, c)

1. Find the largest angle using the law of cosines. The largest angle is opposite the largest side.
2. Find another angle using the law of sines.
3. Find the third angle by subtracting the first two from 180°.

SAS (For example b, α, c)

1. Find a using the law of cosines.
2. Use the law of sines to find β if $b < c$ or γ if $c < b$. If $b = c$, then find either β or γ.
3. Find the last angle by subtracting the first two from 180°.

Applications

When you reach for a light switch, your brain controls the angles at your elbow and your shoulder that put your hand at the location of the switch. An arm on a robot works in much the same manner. In the next example we see how the law of sines and the law of cosines are used to determine the proper angles at the joints so that a robot's hand can be moved to a position given in the coordinates of the workspace.

Example 7 Positioning a robotic arm

A robotic arm with a 0.5-meter segment and a 0.3-meter segment is attached at the origin, as shown in Fig. 3.114. The computer-controlled arm is positioned by rotating each segment through angles θ_1 and θ_2, as shown in Fig. 3.114. Given that we want to have the end of the arm at the point (0.7, 0.2), find θ_1 and θ_2 to the nearest tenth of a degree.

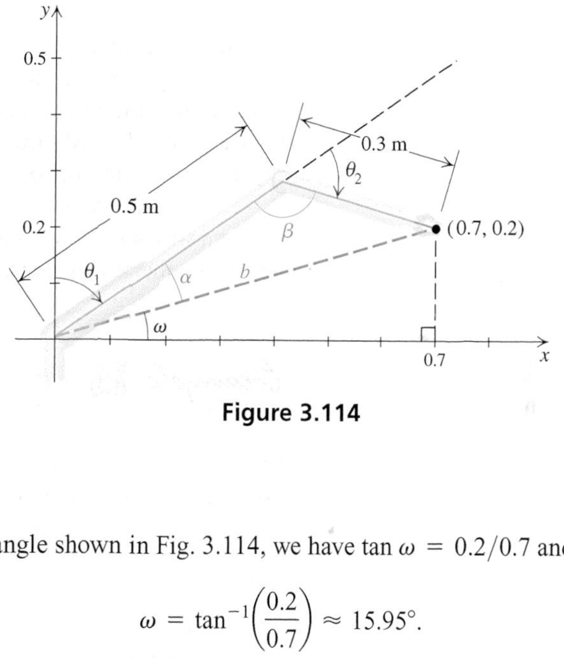

Figure 3.114

Historical Note

Archimedes of Syracuse (287 B.C.–212 B.C.) was a Greek mathematician, physicist, engineer, astronomer, and philosopher. Many consider him one of the greatest mathematicians in antiquity. Archimedes seems to have carried out the first theoretical calculation of π, concluding that $223/71 < \pi < 22/7$. He used a limiting process very similar to what you will do if you try the Concepts of Calculus at the end of this chapter.

Solution

In the right triangle shown in Fig. 3.114, we have $\tan\omega = 0.2/0.7$ and

$$\omega = \tan^{-1}\left(\frac{0.2}{0.7}\right) \approx 15.95°.$$

To get the angles to the nearest tenth, we use more accuracy along the way and round to the nearest tenth only on the final answer. Find b using the Pythagorean theorem:

$$b = \sqrt{0.7^2 + 0.2^2} \approx 0.73$$

Find β using the law of cosines:

$$(0.73)^2 = 0.5^2 + 0.3^2 - 2(0.5)(0.3)\cos\beta$$

$$\cos\beta = \frac{0.73^2 - 0.5^2 - 0.3^2}{-2(0.5)(0.3)} = -0.643$$

$$\beta = \cos^{-1}(-0.643) \approx 130.02°$$

Find α using the law of sines:

$$\frac{\sin \alpha}{0.3} = \frac{\sin 130.02^\circ}{0.73}$$

$$\sin \alpha = \frac{0.3 \cdot \sin 130.02^\circ}{0.73} = 0.3147$$

$$\alpha = \sin^{-1}(0.3147) \approx 18.34^\circ$$

Since $\theta_1 = 90^\circ - \alpha - \omega$,

$$\theta_1 = 90^\circ - 18.34^\circ - 15.95^\circ = 55.71^\circ.$$

Since β and θ_2 are supplementary,

$$\theta_2 = 180^\circ - 130.02^\circ = 49.98^\circ.$$

So the longer segment of the arm is rotated about 55.7° and the shorter segment is rotated about 50.0°. ■

Since the angles in Example 7 describe a clockwise rotation, the angles could be given negative signs to indicate the direction of rotation. In robotics, the direction of rotation is important, because there may be more than one way to position a robotic arm at a desired location. In fact, Example 7 has infinitely many solutions. See if you can find another one.

In the next example we find the height of an object from a distance. This same problem was solved in Section 3.6, Example 6. Note how much easier the solution is here using the law of sines.

Example 8 Finding the height of an object from a distance

The angle of elevation of the top of a water tower from point A on the ground is 19.9°. From point B, 50.0 feet closer to the tower, the angle of elevation is 21.8°. What is the height of the tower?

Solution

Let y represent the height of the tower. All angles of triangle ABC can be determined as shown in Fig. 3.115.

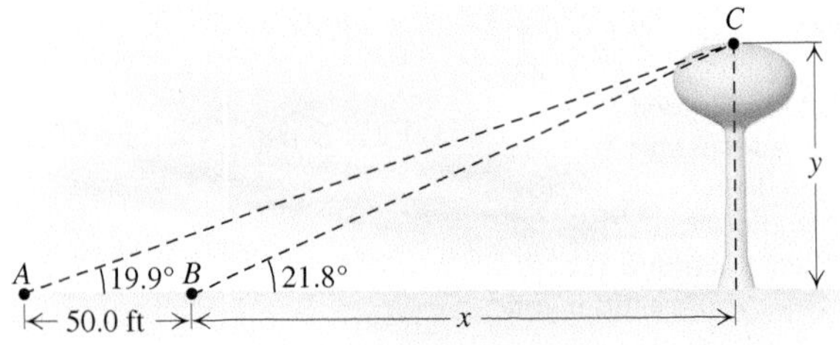

Figure 3.115

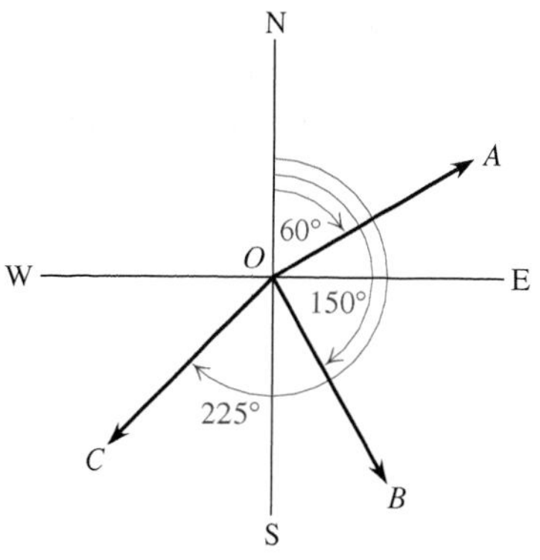

Figure 3.116

Apply the law of sines in triangle ABC:

$$\frac{a}{\sin 19.9°} = \frac{50}{\sin 1.9°}$$

$$a = \frac{50 \sin 19.9°}{\sin 1.9°} \approx 513.3 \text{ feet}$$

Now, using the smaller right triangle, we have $\sin 21.8° = y/513.3$ or $y = 513.3 \sin 21.8° \approx 191$. So the height of the tower is 191 feet. ■

The measure of an angle that describes the direction of a ray is called the **bearing** of the ray. In air navigation, bearing is given as a nonnegative angle less than 360° measured in a clockwise direction from a ray pointing due north. So in Fig. 3.116 the bearing of ray $\overrightarrow{OA}$ is 60°, the bearing of ray $\overrightarrow{OB}$ is 150°, and the bearing of $\overrightarrow{OC}$ is 225°.

Example 9 Using bearing in solving triangles

A bush pilot left the Fairbanks Airport in a light plane and flew 100 miles toward Fort Yukon in still air on a course with a bearing of 18°. She then flew due east (bearing 90°) for some time to drop supplies to a snowbound family. After the drop, her course to return to Fairbanks had a bearing of 225°. What was her maximum distance from Fairbanks?

Solution

Figure 3.117 shows the course of her flight. To change course from bearing 18° to bearing 90° at point B, the pilot must add 72° to the bearing. So $\angle ABC$ is 108°. A bearing of 225° at point C means that $\angle BCA$ is 45°. Finally, we obtain $\angle BAC = 27°$ by subtracting 18° and 45° from 90°.

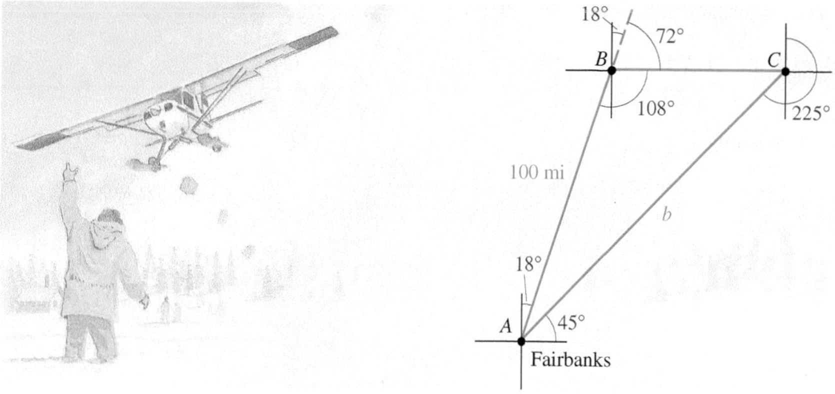

Figure 3.117

We can find the length of $\overline{AC}$ (the maximum distance from Fairbanks) by using the law of sines:

$$\frac{b}{\sin 108°} = \frac{100}{\sin 45°}$$

$$b = \frac{100 \cdot \sin 108°}{\sin 45°} \approx 134.5$$

So the pilot's maximum distance from Fairbanks was 134.5 miles. ■

In marine navigation and surveying, the bearing of a ray is the acute angle the ray makes with a ray pointing due north or due south. Along with the acute angle, directions are given that indicate in which quadrant the ray lies. For example, in Fig. 3.116, $\overrightarrow{OA}$ has a bearing 60° east of north (N60°E), $\overrightarrow{OB}$ has a bearing 30° east of south (S30°E), and $\overrightarrow{OC}$ has a bearing 45° west of south (S45°W).

For Thought

True or False? Explain.

1. If we know the measures of two angles of a triangle, then the measure of the third angle is determined.

2. If $\frac{\sin 9°}{a} = \frac{\sin 17°}{88}$, then $a = \frac{\sin 17°}{88 \sin 9°}$.

3. The equation $\frac{\sin \alpha}{5} = \frac{\sin 44°}{18}$ has exactly one solution in $[0, 180°]$.

4. One solution to $\frac{\sin \beta}{2.3} = \frac{\sin 39°}{1.6}$ is $\beta = \sin^{-1}\left(\frac{2.3 \sin 39°}{1.6}\right)$.

5. $\frac{\sin 60°}{\sqrt{3}} = \frac{\sin 30°}{1}$

6. No triangle exists with $\alpha = 60°$, $b = 10$ feet, and $a = 500$ feet.

7. If $\gamma = 90°$ in triangle ABC, then $c^2 = a^2 + b^2$.

8. If a, b, and c are the sides of a triangle, then $a = \sqrt{c^2 + b^2 - 2bc \cos \gamma}$.

9. If a, b, and c are the sides of any triangle, then $c^2 = a^2 + b^2$.

10. The smallest angle of a triangle lies opposite the shortest side.

3.9 Exercises

Solve each triangle.

1.

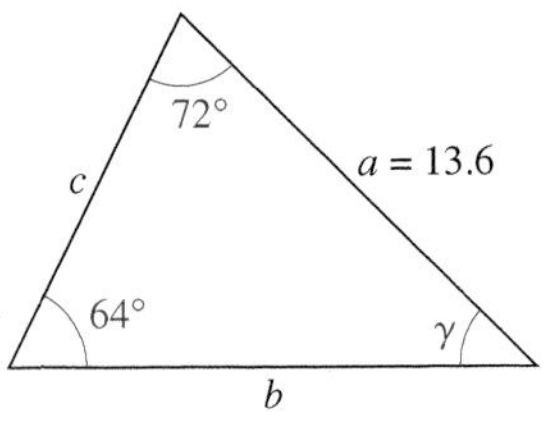

2.

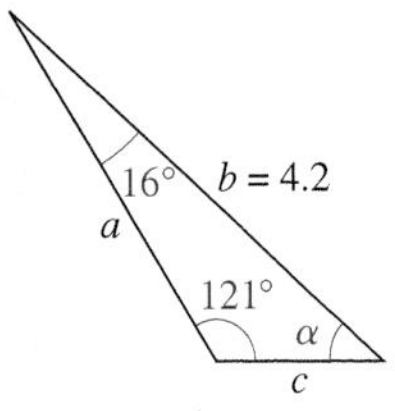

3.

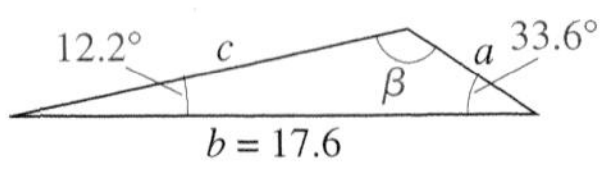

4.

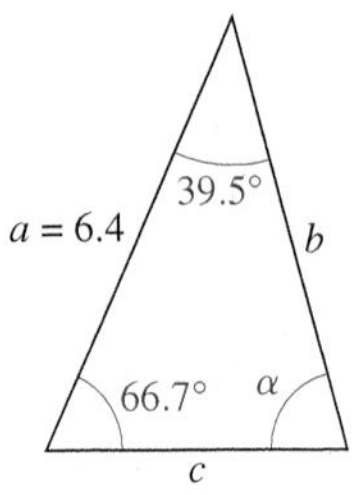

Solve each triangle with the given parts.

5. $\alpha = 10.3°$, $\gamma = 143.7°$, $c = 48.3$

6. $\beta = 94.7°$, $\alpha = 30.6°$, $b = 3.9$

7. $\beta = 120.7°$, $\gamma = 13.6°$, $a = 489.3$

8. $\alpha = 39.7°$, $\gamma = 91.6°$, $b = 16.4$

Determine the number of triangles with the given parts and solve each triangle.

9. $\alpha = 39.6°$, $c = 18.4$, $a = 3.7$

10. $\beta = 28.6°$, $a = 40.7$, $b = 52.5$

11. $\gamma = 60°$, $b = 20$, $c = 10\sqrt{3}$

12. $\alpha = 41.2°$, $a = 8.1$, $b = 10.6$

13. $\beta = 138.1°$, $c = 6.3$, $b = 15.6$

14. $\gamma = 128.6°, a = 9.6, c = 8.2$

15. $\beta = 32.7°, a = 37.5, b = 28.6$

16. $\alpha = 30°, c = 40, a = 20$

17. $\gamma = 99.6°, b = 10.3, c = 12.4$

18. $\alpha = 75.3, a = 12.4, b = 9.8$

Solve each triangle.

19.

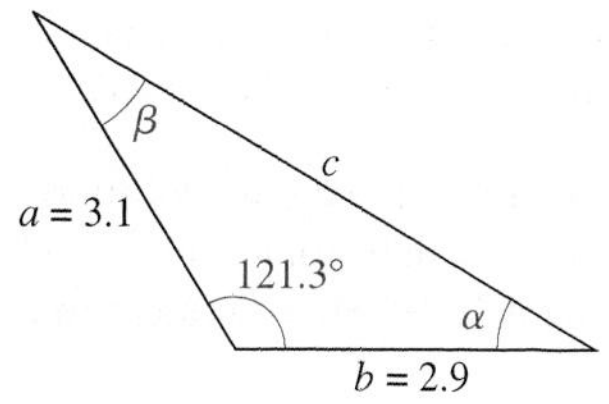

20.

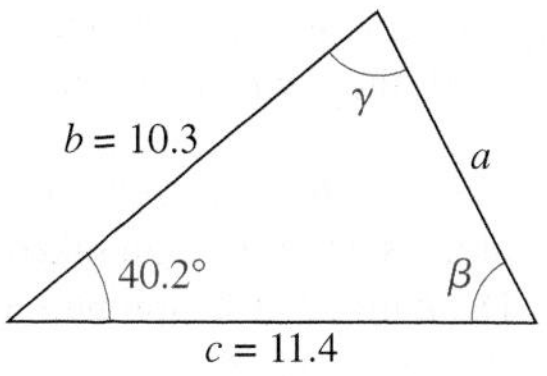

21.

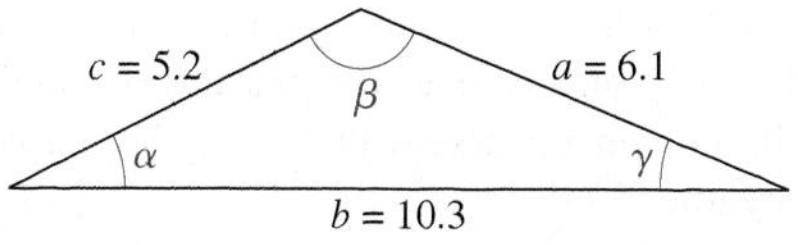

22.

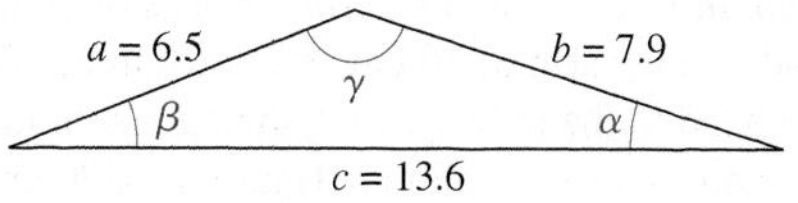

Solve each triangle with the given information. See the procedure for solving triangles on page 294.

23. $a = 6.8, c = 2.4, \beta = 10.5°$

24. $a = 1.3, b = 14.9, \gamma = 9.8°$

25. $a = 18.5, b = 12.2, c = 8.1$

26. $a = 30.4, b = 28.9, c = 31.6$

27. $b = 9.3, c = 12.2, \alpha = 30°$

28. $a = 10.3, c = 8.4, \beta = 88°$

29. $a = 6.3, b = 7.1, c = 6.8$

30. $a = 4.1, b = 9.8, c = 6.2$

31. $a = 7.2, \beta = 25°, \gamma = 35°$

32. $b = 12.3, \alpha = 20°, \gamma = 120°$

Determine the number of triangles with the given parts.

33. $a = 3, b = 4, c = 7$

34. $a = 2, b = 9, c = 5$

35. $a = 10, b = 5, c = 8$

36. $a = 3, b = 15, c = 16$

37. $c = 10, \alpha = 40°, \beta = 60°, \gamma = 90°$

38. $b = 6, \alpha = 62°, \gamma = 120°$

39. $b = 10, c = 1, \alpha = 179°$

40. $a = 10, c = 4, \beta = 2°$

41. $b = 8, c = 2, \gamma = 45°$

42. $a = \sqrt{3}/2, b = 1, \alpha = 60°$

Solve each problem.

43. *Observing Traffic* A traffic report helicopter left the WKPR studios on a course with a bearing of 210°. After flying 12 mi to reach interstate highway 20, the helicopter flew due east along I-20 for some time. The helicopter headed back to WKPR on a course with a bearing of 310° and reported no accidents along I-20. For how many miles did the helicopter fly along I-20?

44. *Course of a Fighter Plane* During an important NATO exercise, an F-14 Tomcat left the carrier Nimitz on a course with a bearing of 34° and flew 400 mi. Then the F-14 flew for some distance on a course with a bearing of 162°. Finally, the plane flew back to its starting point on a course with a bearing of 308°. What distance did the plane fly on the final leg of the journey?

45. *Cellular One* The angle of elevation of the top of a cellular telephone tower from point A on the ground is 18.1°. From point B, 32.5 ft closer to the tower, the angle of elevation is 19.3°. What is the height of the tower?

46. *Moving Back* A surveyor determines that the angle of elevation of the top of a building from a point on the ground is 30.4°. He then moves back 55.4 ft and determines that the angle of elevation is 23.2°. What is the height of the building?

47. *Designing an Addition* A 40-ft-wide house has a roof with a 6-12 pitch (the roof rises 6 ft for a run of 12 ft). The owner plans a 14-ft-wide addition that will have a 3-12 pitch to its roof. Find the lengths of $\overline{AB}$ and $\overline{BC}$ in the accompanying figure on the next page.

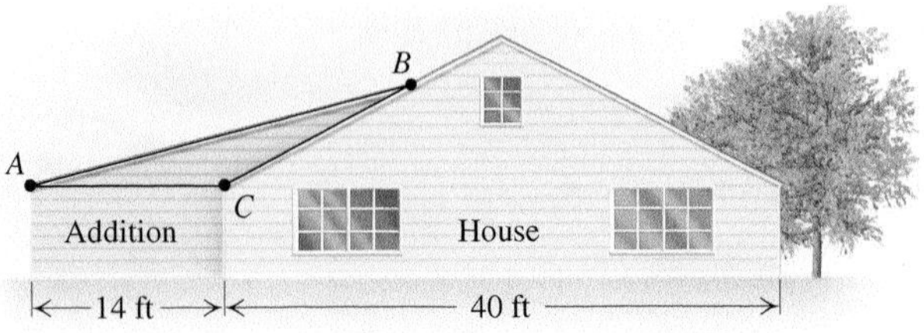

Figure for Exercise 47

48. *Shot Down* A cruise missile is traveling straight across the desert at 548 mph at an altitude of 1 mile, as shown in the figure. A gunner spots the missile coming in his direction and fires a projectile at the missile when the angle of elevation of the missile is 35°. If the speed of the projectile is 688 mph, then for what angle of elevation of the gun will the projectile hit the missile?

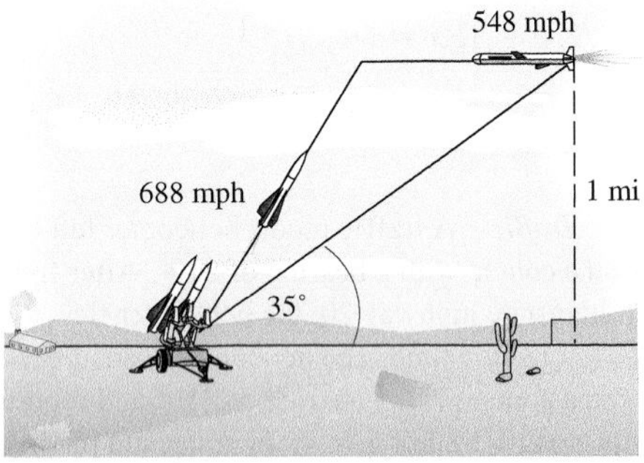

Figure for Exercise 48

49. *Length of a Chord* What is the length of the chord intercepted by a central angle of 19° in a circle of radius 30 ft?

50. *Boating* The boat shown in the accompanying figure is 3 mi from both lighthouses and the angle between the line of sight to the lighthouses is 20°. Find the distance between the lighthouses.

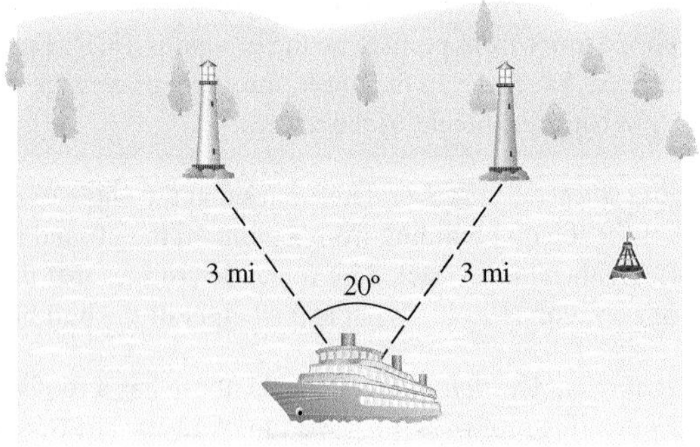

Figure for Exercise 50

51. *The Pentagon* The Pentagon in Washington, D.C. is 921 ft on each side, as shown in the accompanying figure. What is the distance from a vertex to the center of the Pentagon?

Figure for Exercise 51

52. *A Hexagon* If the length of each side of a regular hexagon is 10 ft, then what is the distance from a vertex to the center?

53. *Hiking* Jan and Dean started hiking from the same location at the same time. Jan hiked at 4 mph with bearing N12°E, and Dean hiked at 5 mph with bearing N31°W. How far apart were they after 6 hr?

54. *Flying* Andrea and Carlos left the airport at the same time. Andrea flew at 180 mph on a course with bearing 80°, and Carlos flew at 240 mph on a course with bearing 210°. How far apart were they after 3 hr?

55. *Positioning a Human Arm* A human arm consists of an upper arm of 30 cm and a lower arm of 30 cm, as shown in the figure. To move the hand to the point (36, 8), the human brain chooses angle θ_1 and θ_2, as shown in the figure. Find θ_1 and θ_2 to the nearest tenth of a degree.

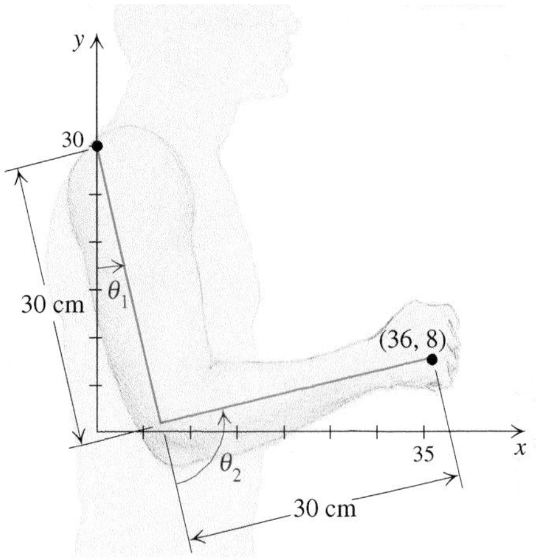

Figure for Exercise 55

56. *Attack of the Grizzly* A forest ranger is 150 ft above the ground in a fire tower when she spots an angry grizzly bear east of the tower with an angle of depression of 10°, as shown in the figure. Southeast of the tower she spots a hiker with an angle of depression of 15°. Find the distance between the hiker and the angry bear.

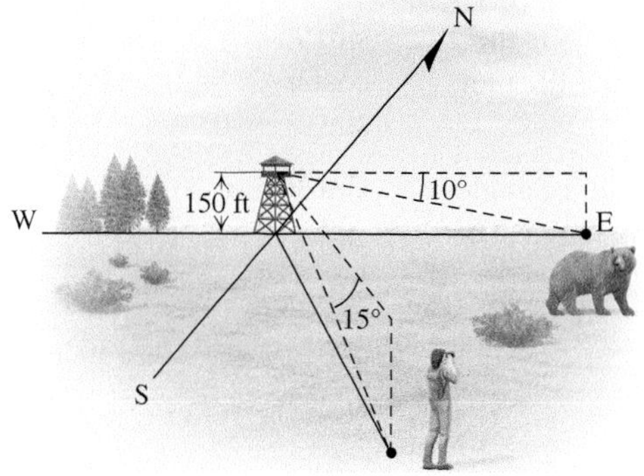

Figure for Exercise 56

Thinking Outside the Box XXVII

Watering the Lawn Josie places her lawn sprinklers at the vertices of a triangle that has sides of 9 m, 10 m, and 11 m. The sprinklers water in circular patterns with radii of 4, 5, and 6 m. No area is watered by more than one sprinkler. What amount of area inside the triangle is not watered by any of the three sprinklers? Give your answer to the nearest thousandth of a square meter.

3.9 Pop Quiz

1. If $\alpha = 80°$, $\beta = 121°$, and $c = 12$, then what is γ?

2. If $\alpha = 20.4°$, $\beta = 27.3°$, and $c = 38.5$, then what is a?

3. If $\alpha = 33.5°$, $a = 7.4$, and $b = 10.6$, then what is β?

4. If $\alpha = 12.3°$, $b = 10.4$, and $c = 8.1$, then what is a?

5. If $a = 6$, $b = 7$, and $c = 12$, then what is γ?

Highlights

3.1 Angles and Their Measurements

Degree Measure	Divide the circumference of a circle into 360 equal arcs. The degree measure is the number of degrees through which the initial side of an angle is rotated to get to the terminal side (positive for counterclockwise, negative for clockwise).	90° is 1/4 of a circle. 180° is 1/2 of a circle.
Radian Measure	The length of the arc on the unit circle through which the initial side rotates to get to the terminal side	$\pi/2$ is 1/4 of the unit circle. π is 1/2 of the unit circle.
Converting	Use π radians $= 180°$ and cancellation of units.	$90° \cdot \frac{\pi \text{ rad}}{180°} = \frac{\pi}{2}$ rad
Arc Length	$s = \alpha r$ where s is the arc intercepted by a central angle of α radians on a circle of radius r	$\alpha = 90°$, $r = 10$ ft $s = \alpha r = \frac{\pi}{2} \cdot 10 \text{ ft} = 5\pi$ ft

3.2 The Sine and Cosine Functions

Sine and Cosine Functions	If α is an angle in standard position and (x, y) is the point of intersection of the terminal side and the unit circle, then $\sin \alpha = y$ and $\cos \alpha = x$.	$\sin(90°) = 1$ $\cos(\pi/2) = 0$ $\sin(0) = 0$
Domain	The domain for sine or cosine can be the set of angles in standard position, the measures of those angles, or the set of real numbers.	$\sin(30°) = 1/2$ $\sin(\pi/4) = \sqrt{2}/2$ $\sin(72.6) \approx -0.3367$
Fundamental Identity	For any angle α (or real number α), $\sin^2(\alpha) + \cos^2(\alpha) = 1$.	$\sin^2(30°) + \cos^2(30°) = 1$ $\sin^2(\sqrt[3]{2}) + \cos^2(\sqrt[3]{2}) = 1$

3.3 The Graphs of the Sine and Cosine Functions

Graphs	The graphs of $y = \sin x$ and $y = \cos x$ are sine waves, each with period 2π.	
General Sine and Cosine Functions	The graph of $y = A \sin[B(x - C)] + D$ or $y = A \cos[B(x - C)] + D$ is a sine wave with amplitude $\|A\|$, period $2\pi/\|B\|$, phase shift C, and vertical translation D.	$y = -3 \sin(2(x - \pi)) + 1$ amplitude 3, period π, phase shift π, vertical translation 1
Graphing a General Sine Function	Start with the five key points on $y = \sin x$: $(0, 0), \left(\frac{\pi}{2}, 1\right), (\pi, 0), \left(\frac{3\pi}{2}, -1\right), (2\pi, 0)$ Divide each x-coordinate by B and add C. Multiply each y-coordinate by A and add D. Sketch one cycle of the general function through the five new points. Graph a general cosine function in the same manner.	$y = 3 \sin\left(2\left(x - \frac{\pi}{2}\right)\right) + 1$ Five new points: $\left(\frac{\pi}{2}, 1\right), \left(\frac{3\pi}{4}, 4\right), (\pi, 1), \left(\frac{5\pi}{4}, -2\right), \left(\frac{3\pi}{2}, 1\right)$ Draw one cycle through these points.
Frequency	$F = 1/P$, P is the period and F is the frequency.	$y = \sin(24\pi x)$, $F = 12$

3.4 The Other Trigonometric Functions and Their Graphs

Tangent, Cotangent, Secant, and Cosecant	If (x, y) is the point of intersection of the unit circle and the terminal side of α, then $\tan \alpha = y/x$, $\cot \alpha = x/y$, $\sec \alpha = 1/x$, and $\csc \alpha = 1/y$. If 0 occurs in a denominator the function is undefined.	$\tan(\pi/4) = 1$ $\cot(\pi/2) = 0$ $\sec(30°) = 2/\sqrt{3}$ $\csc(0)$ is undefined.
Identities	$\tan \alpha = \frac{\sin \alpha}{\cos \alpha}$, $\cot \alpha = \frac{\cos \alpha}{\sin \alpha}$, $\sec \alpha = \frac{1}{\cos \alpha}$, $\csc \alpha = \frac{1}{\sin \alpha}$	
Tangent	Period π, fundamental cycle on $(-\pi/2, \pi/2)$, vertical asymptotes $x = \pi/2 + k\pi$	
Cotangent	Period π, fundamental cycle on $(0, \pi)$, vertical asymptotes $x = k\pi$	
Secant	Period 2π, vertical asymptotes $x = \pi/2 + k\pi$	
Cosecant	Period 2π, vertical asymptotes $x = k\pi$	

3.5 The Inverse Trigonometric Functions

Inverse Sine

If $y = \sin^{-1} x$ for x in $[-1, 1]$, then y is the real number in $[-\pi/2, \pi/2]$ such that $\sin y = x$.

$\sin^{-1}(1) = \pi/2$
$\sin^{-1}(-1/2) = -\pi/6$

Inverse Cosine

If $y = \cos^{-1} x$ for x in $[-1, 1]$, then y is the real number in $[0, \pi]$ such that $\cos y = x$.

$\cos^{-1}(-1) = \pi$
$\cos^{-1}(-1/2) = 2\pi/3$

Inverse Tangent

If $y = \tan^{-1} x$ for x in $(-\infty, \infty)$, then y is the real number in $(-\pi/2, \pi/2)$ such that $\tan y = x$.

$\tan^{-1}(1) = \pi/4$
$\tan^{-1}(-1) = -\pi/4$

3.6 Right Triangle Trigonometry

Trigonometric Ratios

If (x, y) is any point other than $(0, 0)$ on the terminal side of α is standard position and $r = \sqrt{x^2 + y^2}$, then $\sin \alpha = y/r$, $\cos \alpha = x/r$, and $\tan \alpha = y/x$ $(x \neq 0)$.

Terminal side of α through $(3, 4)$, gives $r = 5$ and $\sin \alpha = 4/5$, $\cos \alpha = 3/5$, and $\tan \alpha = 4/3$.

Trigonometric Functions in a Right Triangle

If α is an acute angle of a right triangle, then $\sin \alpha = \text{opp}/\text{hyp}$, $\cos \alpha = \text{adj}/\text{hyp}$, and $\tan \alpha = \text{opp}/\text{adj}$.

$\sin \alpha = 5/13$, $\cos \alpha = 12/13$, $\tan \alpha = 5/12$

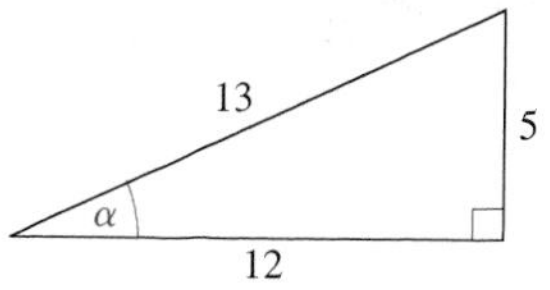

3.7 Identities

Identity

An equation that is satisfied by every number for which both sides are defined.

$\sin^2 x + \cos^2 x = 1$

Disproving an Identity

To show that an equation is not an identity, find a value for the variable that does not satisfy the equation.

$\sin(2x) = 2\sin(x)$ is not an identity because $\sin(2 \cdot \pi/2) \neq 2\sin(\pi/2)$.

Proving an Identity

To verify or prove an identity, start with the expression on one side and use known identities and properties of algebra to convert it into the expression on the other side.

$$\frac{\sin x + \cos x}{\cos x} = \frac{\sin x}{\cos x} + \frac{\cos x}{\cos x}$$
$$= \tan x + 1$$

Reduction Formula

If α is an angle in standard position whose terminal side contains (a, b) and x is a real number, then $a \sin x + b \cos x = \sqrt{a^2 + b^2}\sin(x + \alpha)$.

$\alpha = \tan^{-1}(4/3)$
$3 \sin x + 4 \cos x$
$= 5 \sin(x + \tan^{-1}(4/3))$

3.8 Conditional Trigonometric Equations

Solving $\cos x = a$

If $|a| \leq 1$, find all solutions in $[0, 2\pi]$, then add all multiples of 2π to them and simplify. If $|a| > 1$ there are no solutions.

$$\cos x = 0, x = \frac{\pi}{2} + k\pi$$

$$\cos x = \frac{1}{2}, x = \frac{\pi}{3} + 2k\pi$$

$$\text{or } x = \frac{5\pi}{3} + 2k\pi$$

Solving $\sin x = a$	If $\lvert a \rvert \le 1$, find all solutions in $[0, 2\pi]$, then add all multiples of 2π to them and simplify. If $\lvert a \rvert > 1$ there are no solutions.	$\sin x = 0, x = k\pi$ $\sin x = \frac{1}{2}, x = \frac{\pi}{6} + 2k\pi$ or $x = \frac{5\pi}{6} + 2k\pi$
Solving $\tan x = a$	If a is a real number, find all solutions in $[-\pi/2, \pi/2]$, then add multiples of π to them and simplify.	$\tan x = 1, x = \frac{\pi}{4} + k\pi$

3.9 The Law of Sines and The Law of Cosines

Law of Sines	In any triangle $\frac{\sin\alpha}{a} = \frac{\sin\beta}{b} = \frac{\sin\gamma}{c}$.	$a = \sqrt{3}, b = 1, c = 2$ $\alpha = \pi/3, \beta = \pi/6, \gamma = \pi/2$ $\frac{\sin\left(\frac{\pi}{3}\right)}{\sqrt{3}} = \frac{\sin\left(\frac{\pi}{6}\right)}{1} = \frac{\sin\left(\frac{\pi}{2}\right)}{2}$
Law of Cosines	If a is the side opposite angle α in any triangle then $a^2 = b^2 + c^2 - 2bc\cos\alpha$.	$a = 4, b = 5, c = 6$ $4^2 = 5^2 + 6^2 - 60\cos\alpha$

Function Gallery: Some Basic Functions of Trigonometry

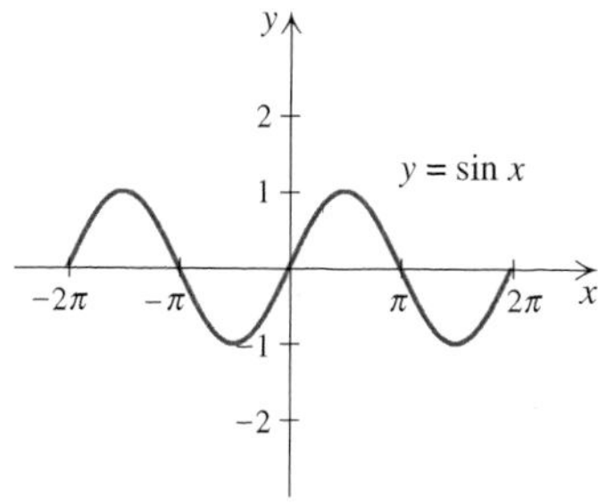

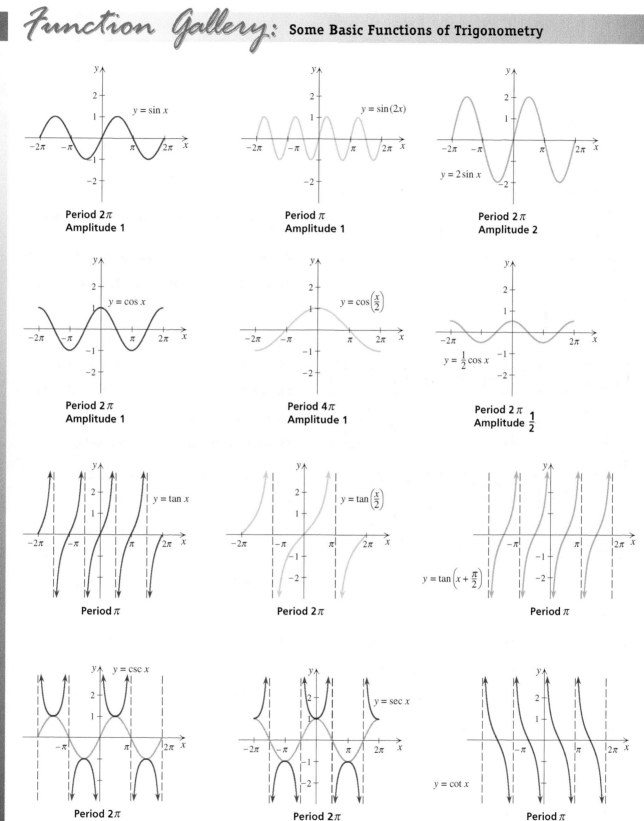

Period 2π
Amplitude 1

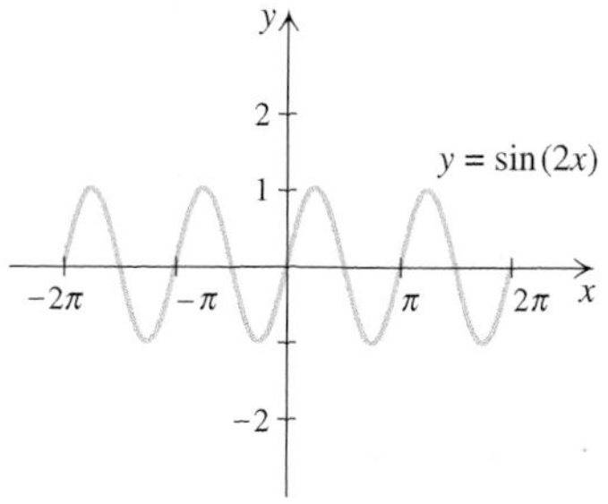

Period π
Amplitude 1

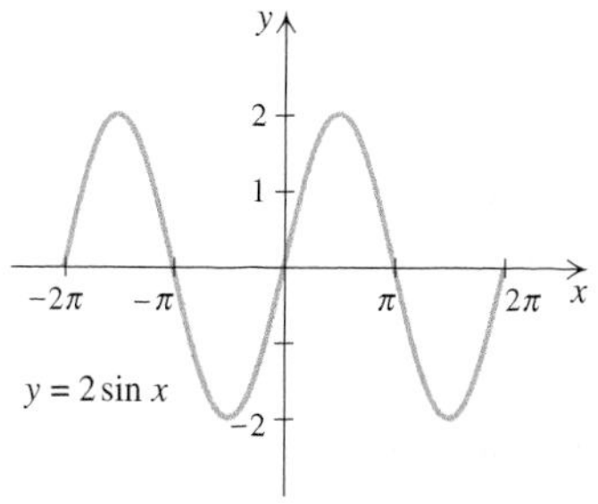

Period 2π
Amplitude 2

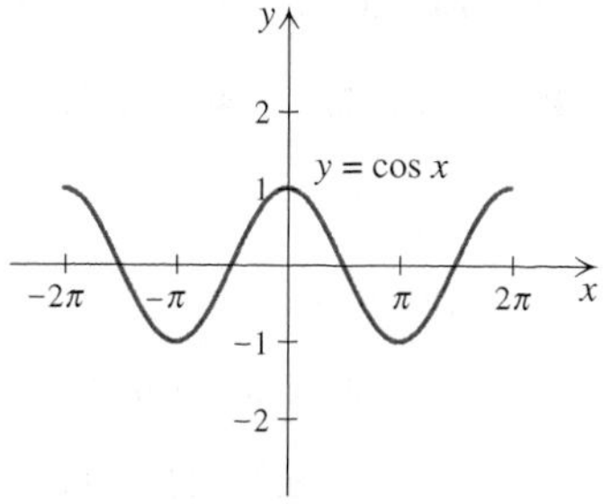

Period 2π
Amplitude 1

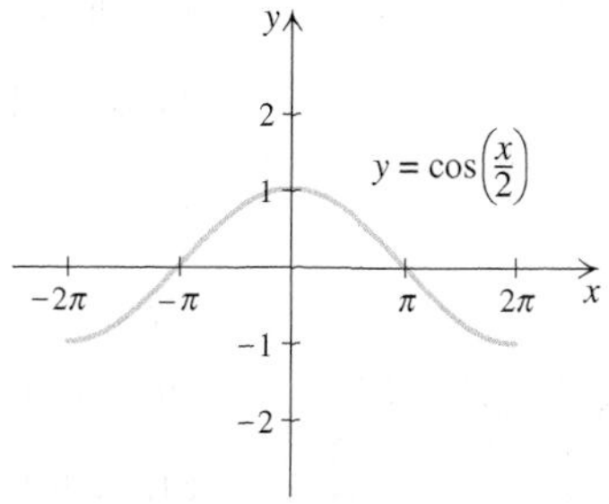

Period 4π
Amplitude 1

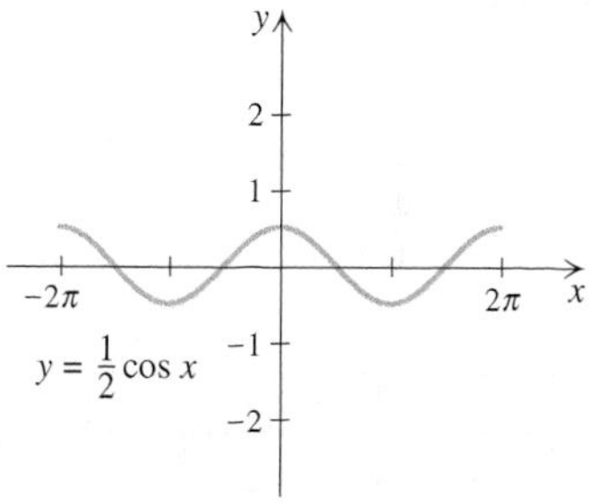

Period 2π
Amplitude $\frac{1}{2}$

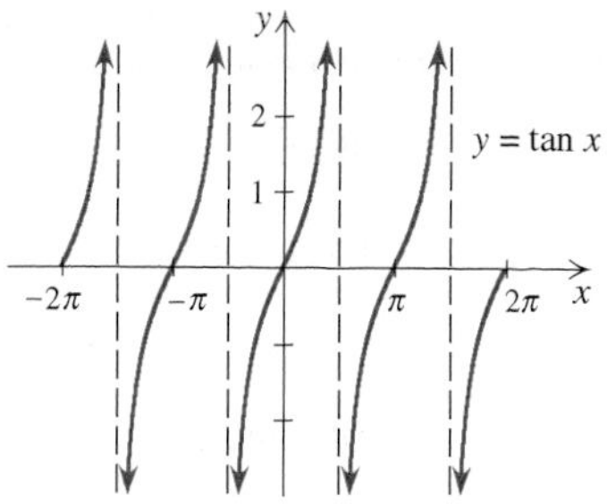

Period π

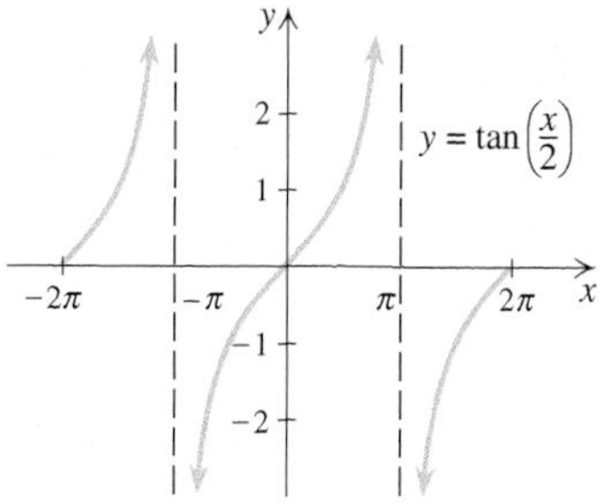

Period 2π

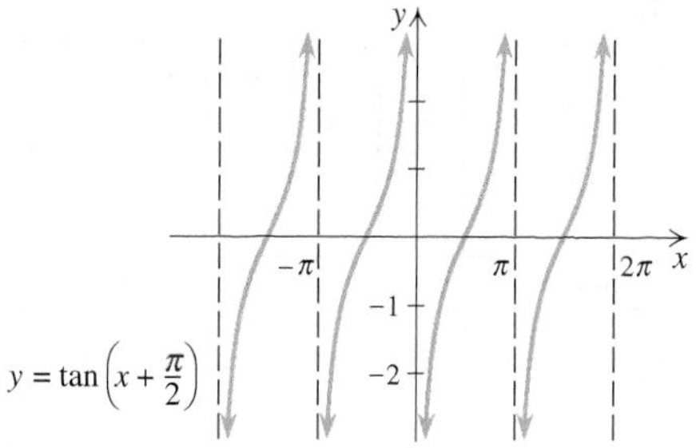

Period π

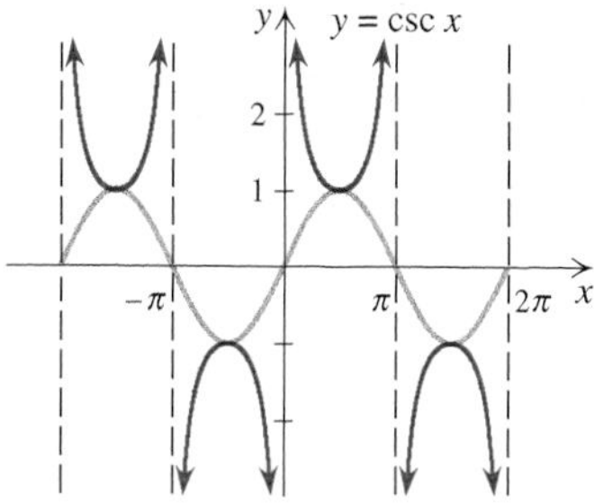

Period 2π

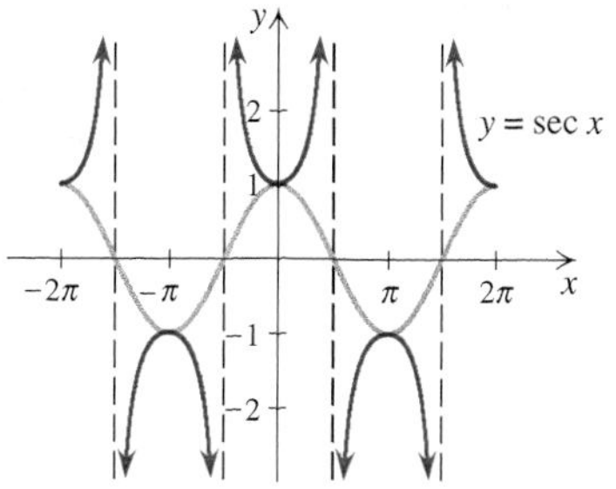

Period 2π

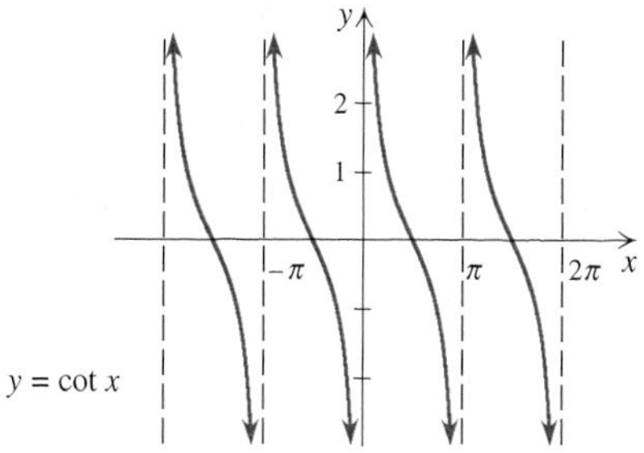

Period π

Chapter 3 Review Exercises

Find the measure in degrees of the least positive angle that is coterminal with each given angle.

1. $388°$ **2.** $-840°$ **3.** $-153°14'27''$

4. $455°39'24''$ **5.** $-\pi$ **6.** $-35\pi/6$

7. $13\pi/5$ **8.** $29\pi/12$

Convert each radian measure to degree measure. Do not use a calculator.

9. $5\pi/3$ **10.** $-3\pi/4$ **11.** $3\pi/2$ **12.** $5\pi/6$

Convert each degree measure to radian measure. Do not use a calculator.

13. $330°$ **14.** $405°$ **15.** $-300°$ **16.** $-210°$

Fill in the tables. Do not use a calculator.

17.

θ deg	0	30	45	60	90	120	135	150	180
θ rad									
$\sin\theta$									
$\cos\theta$									
$\tan\theta$									

18.

θ rad	0	$\frac{\pi}{6}$	$\frac{\pi}{4}$	$\frac{\pi}{3}$	$\frac{\pi}{2}$	$\frac{2\pi}{3}$	$\frac{3\pi}{4}$	$\frac{5\pi}{6}$	π
θ deg									
$\sin\theta$									
$\cos\theta$									
$\tan\theta$									

Give the exact values of each of the following expressions. Do not use a calculator.

19. $\sin(-\pi/4)$ **20.** $\cos(-2\pi/3)$ **21.** $\tan(\pi/3)$

22. $\sec(\pi/6)$ **23.** $\csc(-120°)$ **24.** $\cot(135°)$

25. $\sin(180°)$ **26.** $\tan(0°)$ **27.** $\cos(3\pi/2)$

28. $\csc(5\pi/6)$ **29.** $\sec(-\pi)$ **30.** $\cot(-4\pi/3)$

31. $\cot(420°)$ **32.** $\sin(390°)$ **33.** $\cos(-135°)$

34. $\tan(225°)$ **35.** $\sec(2\pi/3)$ **36.** $\csc(-3\pi/4)$

37. $\tan(5\pi/6)$ **38.** $\sin(7\pi/6)$

For each triangle shown below, find the exact values of $\sin\alpha$, $\cos\alpha$, $\tan\alpha$, $\csc\alpha$, $\sec\alpha$, *and* $\cot\alpha$.

39.

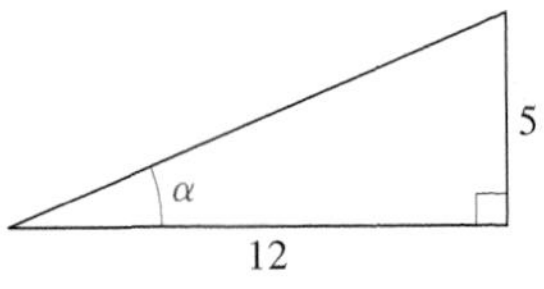

40.

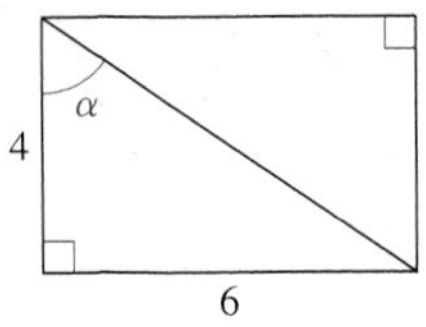

Find an approximate value for each expression. Round to four decimal places.

41. $\sin(44°)$ **42.** $\cos(-205°)$ **43.** $\cos(4.62)$

44. $\sin(3.14)$ **45.** $\tan(\pi/17)$ **46.** $\sec(2.33)$

47. $\csc(105°4')$ **48.** $\cot(55°3'12'')$

Find the exact value of each expression.

49. $\sin^{-1}(-0.5)$ **50.** $\cos^{-1}(-0.5)$

51. $\arctan(-1)$ **52.** $\operatorname{arccot}(1/\sqrt{3})$

53. $\sec^{-1}(\sqrt{2})$ **54.** $\csc^{-1}(\sec(\pi/3))$

55. $\sin^{-1}(\sin(5\pi/6))$ **56.** $\cos(\cos^{-1}(-\sqrt{3}/2))$

Find the exact value of each expression in degrees.

57. $\sin^{-1}(1)$ **58.** $\tan^{-1}(1)$

59. $\arccos(-1/\sqrt{2})$ **60.** $\operatorname{arcsec}(2)$

61. $\cot^{-1}(\sqrt{3})$ **62.** $\cot^{-1}(-\sqrt{3})$

63. $\operatorname{arccot}(0)$ **64.** $\operatorname{arccot}(-\sqrt{3}/3)$

Solve each right triangle with the given parts.

65. $a = 2, b = 3$ **66.** $a = 3, c = 7$

67. $a = 3.2, \alpha = 21.3°$ **68.** $\alpha = 34.6°, c = 9.4$

Sketch at least one cycle of the graph of each function and determine the period and range.

69. $f(x) = 2\sin(3x)$ **70.** $f(x) = 1 + \cos(x + \pi/4)$

71. $y = \tan(2x + \pi)$ **72.** $y = \cot(x - \pi/4)$

73. $y = \sec\left(\frac{1}{2}x\right)$ **74.** $y = \csc\left(\frac{\pi}{2}x\right)$

75. $y = \frac{1}{2}\cos(2x)$

76. $y = 1 - \sin(x - \pi/3)$

77. $y = \cot(2x + \pi/3)$

78. $y = 2\tan(x + \pi/4)$

79. $y = \frac{1}{3}\csc(2x + \pi)$

80. $y = 1 + 2\sec(x - \pi/4)$

For each of the following sine curves find an equation of the form $y = A\sin[B(x - C)] + D$.

81.

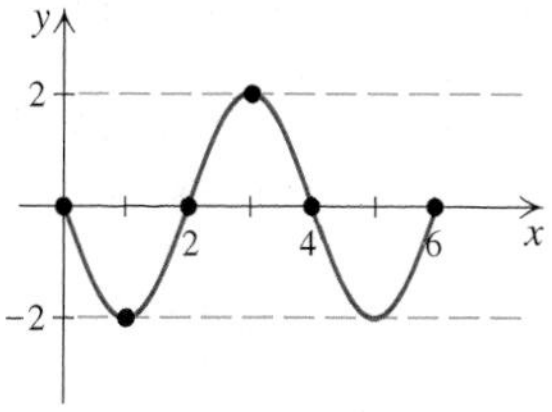

82.

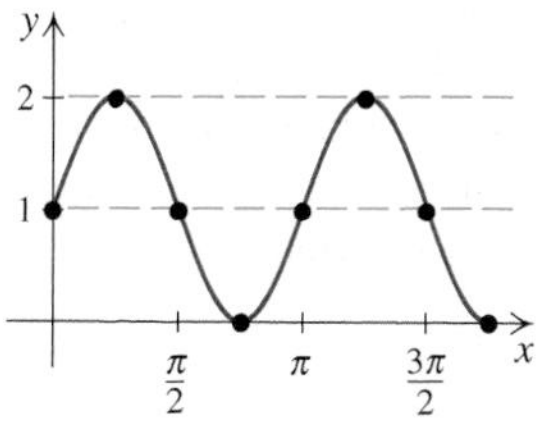

83.

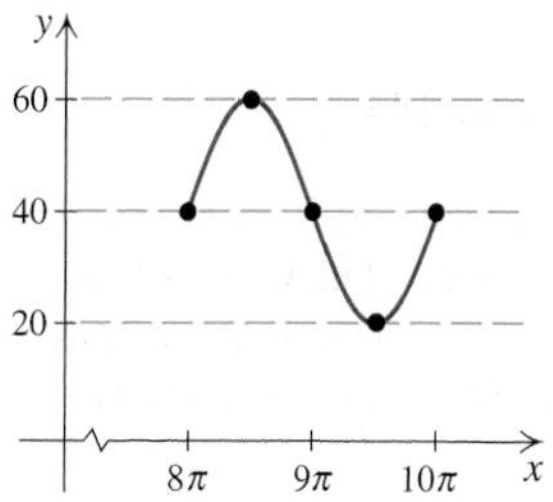

84.

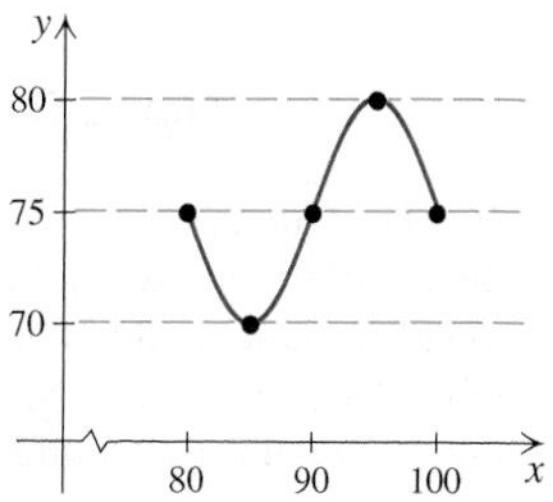

Solve each problem.

85. Find α if α is the angle between 90° and 180° whose sine is $1/2$.

86. Find β if β is the angle between 180° and 270° whose cosine is $-\sqrt{3}/2$.

87. Find $\sin\alpha$, given that $\cos\alpha = 1/5$ and α is in quadrant IV.

88. Find $\tan\alpha$, given that $\sin\alpha = 1/3$ and α is in quadrant II.

89. Find x if x is the length of the shortest side of a right triangle that has a 16° angle and a hypotenuse of 24 ft.

90. Find x if x is the length of the hypotenuse of a right triangle that has a 22° angle and a shortest side of length 12 m.

91. Find α if α is the largest acute angle of a right triangle that has legs with lengths 6 cm and 8 cm.

92. Find β if β is the largest acute angle of a right triangle that has a hypotenuse with length 19 yd and a leg with length 8 yd.

Simplify each expression.

93. $(1 - \sin\alpha)(1 + \sin\alpha)$

94. $\csc x \tan x + \sec(-x)$

95. $(1 - \csc x)(1 - \csc(-x))$

96. $\dfrac{\cos^2 x - \sin^2 x}{\sin 2x}$

97. $\dfrac{1}{1 + \sin\alpha} - \dfrac{\sin(-\alpha)}{\cos^2\alpha}$

98. $2\sin\left(\dfrac{\pi}{2} - \alpha\right)\cos\left(\dfrac{\pi}{2} - \alpha\right)$

99. $\dfrac{2\tan 2s}{1 - \tan^2 2s}$

100. $\dfrac{\tan 2w - \tan 4w}{1 + \tan 2w \tan 4w}$

101. $\sin 3\theta \cos 6\theta - \cos 3\theta \sin 6\theta$

102. $\dfrac{\sin 2y}{1 + \cos 2y}$

103. $\dfrac{1 - \cos 2z}{\sin 2z}$

104. $\cos^2\left(\dfrac{x}{2}\right) - \sin^2\left(\dfrac{x}{2}\right)$

Prove that each of the following equations is an identity.

105. $\sec 2\theta = \dfrac{1 + \tan^2\theta}{1 - \tan^2\theta}$

106. $\tan^2\theta = \dfrac{1 - \cos 2\theta}{1 + \cos 2\theta}$

107. $\sin^2\left(\dfrac{x}{2}\right) = \dfrac{\csc^2 x - \cot^2 x}{2\csc^2 x + 2\csc x \cot x}$

108. $\cot(-x) = \dfrac{1 - \sin^2 x}{\cos(-x)\sin(-x)}$

109. $\cot(\alpha - 45°) = \dfrac{1 + \tan\alpha}{\tan\alpha - 1}$

110. $\cos(\alpha + 45°) = \dfrac{\cos\alpha - \sin\alpha}{\sqrt{2}}$

111. $\dfrac{\sin 2\beta}{2\csc\beta} = \sin^2\beta\cos\beta$

112. $\sin(45° - \beta) = \dfrac{\cos 2\beta}{\sqrt{2}(\cos\beta + \sin\beta)}$

113. $\dfrac{\cot^3 y - \tan^3 y}{\sec^2 y + \cot^2 y} = 2\cot 2y$

114. $\dfrac{\sin^3 y - \cos^3 y}{\sin y - \cos y} = \dfrac{2 + \sin 2y}{2}$

Find all real numbers that satisfy each equation.

115. $2\cos 2x + 1 = 0$

116. $2\sin 2x + \sqrt{3} = 0$

117. $\left(\sqrt{3}\csc x - 2\right)(\csc x - 2) = 0$

118. $\left(\sec x - \sqrt{2}\right)\left(\sqrt{3}\sec x + 2\right) = 0$

119. $2 \sin^2 x + 1 = 3 \sin x$

120. $4 \sin^2 x = \sin x + 3$

121. $-8\sqrt{3} \sin \frac{x}{2} = -12$

122. $-\cos \frac{x}{2} = \sqrt{2} + \cos \frac{x}{2}$

123. $\cos \frac{x}{2} - \sin x = 0$

124. $\sin 2x = \tan x$

125. $\cos 2x + \sin^2 x = 0$

126. $\tan \frac{x}{2} = \sin x$

Solve each triangle that exists with the given parts. If there is more than one triangle with the given parts, then solve each one.

127. $\gamma = 48°, a = 3.4, b = 2.6$

128. $a = 6, b = 8, c = 10$

129. $\alpha = 13°, \beta = 64°, c = 20$

130. $\alpha = 50°, a = 3.2, b = 8.4$

131. $a = 3.6, b = 10.2, c = 5.9$

132. $\beta = 36.2°, \gamma = 48.1°, a = 10.6$

133. $a = 30.6, b = 12.9, c = 24.1$

134. $\alpha = 30°, a = \sqrt{3}, b = 2\sqrt{3}$

135. $\beta = 22°, c = 4.9, b = 2.5$

136. $\beta = 121°, a = 5.2, c = 7.1$

Solve each problem.

137. *Broadcasting the Oldies* If radio station Q92 is broadcasting its oldies at 92.3 FM, then it is broadcasting at a frequency of 92.3 megahertz, or 92.3×10^6 cycles per second. What is the period of a wave with this frequency? (FM stands for frequency modulation.)

138. *AM Radio* If WLS in Chicago is broadcasting at 890 AM (amplitude modulation), then its signal has a frequency of 890 kilohertz, or 890×10^3 cycles per second. What is the period of a wave with this frequency?

139. *Crooked Man* A man is standing 1000 ft from a surveyor. The surveyor measures an angle of 0.4° sighting from the man's feet to his head. Assume that the man can be represented by the arc intercepted by a central angle of 0.4° in a circle of radius 1000 ft. Find the height of the man.

140. *Straight Man* Assume that the man of Exercise 139 can be represented by the side a of a right triangle with angle $\alpha = 0.4°$ and $b = 1000$ ft. Find the height of the man, and compare your answer with the answer of the previous exercise.

141. *Oscillating Depth* The depth of water in a tank oscillates between 12 ft and 16 ft. It takes 10 min for the depth to go from 12 to 16 and 10 min for the depth to go from 16 to 12 ft. Express the depth as a function of time in the form $y = A \sin[B(x - C)] + D$, where the depth is 16 ft at time 0. Graph one cycle of the function.

142. *Oscillating Temperature* The temperature of the water in a tank oscillates between 100°F and 120°F. It takes 30 min for the temperature to go from 100° to 120° and 30 min for the temperature to go from 120° to 100°. Express the temperature as a function of time in the form $y = A \sin[B(x - C)] + D$, where the temperature is 100° at time 20 min. Graph one cycle of the function.

143. *Shooting a Target* Judy is standing 200 ft from a circular target with a radius of 3 in. To hit the center of the circle, she must hold the gun perfectly level, as shown in the figure. Will she hit the target if her aim is off by one-tenth of a degree in any direction?

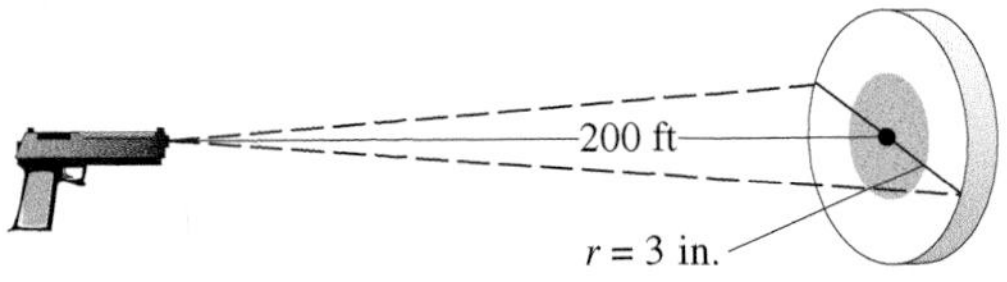

Figure for Exercise 143

144. *Height of Buildings* Two buildings are 300 ft apart. From the top of the shorter building, the angle of elevation of the top of the taller building is 23°, and the angle of depression of the base of the taller building is 36°, as shown in the figure. How tall is each building?

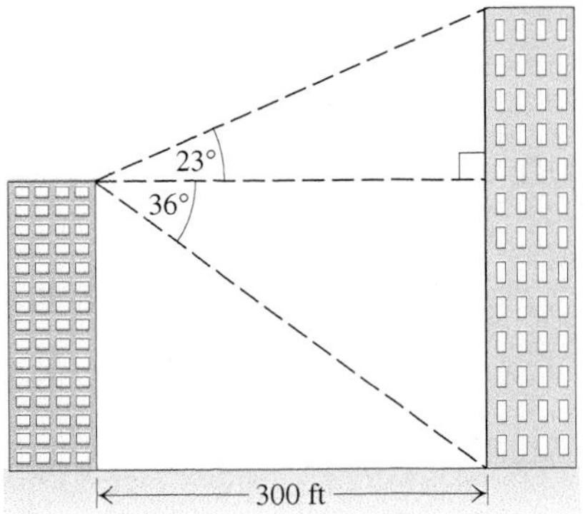

Figure for Exercise 144

145. *John Hancock* From a point on the street the angle of elevation of the top of the John Hancock Building is 65.7°. From a point on the street that is 100 ft closer to the building the angle of elevation is 70.1°. Find the height of the building.

146. *Cloud Height* Visual Flight Rules require that the height of the clouds be more than 1000 ft for a pilot to fly without instrumentation. At night, cloud height can be determined from the ground by using a searchlight and an observer, as shown in the figure. If the beam of light is aimed straight upward and the observer 500 ft away sights the cloud with an angle of elevation of 55°, then what is the height of the cloud cover?

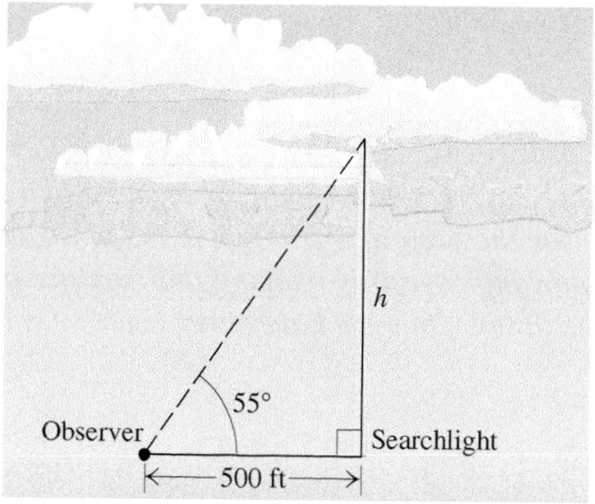

Figure for Exercise 146

147. *Radar Range* The radar antenna on a cargo ship is located 90 feet above the water, as shown in the accompanying figure. Find the distance to the horrizon from that height. Use 3950 miles as the radius of the earth.

148. *Increasing Visibility* To increase its radar visibility, a sailboat has a radar reflector mounted on the mast, 25 feet above the water. Find the distance to the horizon from that height. Assuming that radar waves travel in a straight line, at what distance can the cargo ship of the previous exercise get a radar image of the sailboat?

Figure for Exercises 147 and 148

Thinking Outside the Box XXVIII

Buckling Bridge A 100 ft bridge expands 1 in. during the heat of the day. Since the ends of the bridge are embedded in rock, the bridge buckles upward and forms an arc of a circle for which the original bridge is a chord. What is the approximate distance moved by the center of the bridge?

Concepts of Calculus

Area of a circle and π

The idea of a limiting value to a process was used long before it was formalized in calculus. Ancient mathematicians discovered the formula for the area of a circle and the value of π using the formula for the area of a triangle $A = \frac{1}{2}bh$, trigonometry, and the idea of limits. For the following exercises imagine that you are an ancient mathematician (with a modern calculator), but you have never heard of π or the formula $A = \pi r^2$.

Exercises

1. A regular pentagon is inscribed in a circle of radius r as shown in the following figure.

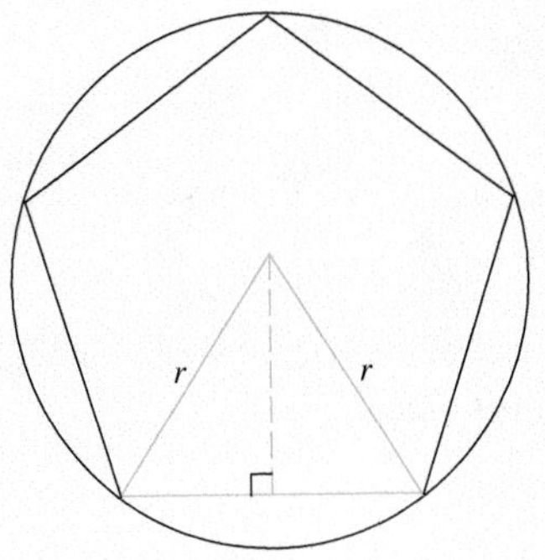

The pentagon is made up of five isosceles triangles. Show that the area of the pentagon is $\frac{5\sin(72°)}{2}r^2$.

2. A regular polygon of n sides is inscribed in a circle of radius r. Write the area of the n-gon in terms of r and n.

3. The area of a regular n-gon inscribed in a circle of radius r is a constant multiple of r^2. Find the constant for a decagon, kilogon, and megagon.

4. What happens to the shape of the inscribed n-gon as n increases?

5. What would you use as a formula for the area of a circle of radius r? (You have never heard of π.)

6. Find a formula for the perimeter of an n-gon inscribed in a circle of radius r.

7. Find a formula for the circumference of a circle of radius r. (You have never heard of π.)

8. Suppose that the π-key on your calculator is broken. What expression could you use to calculate π accurate to nine decimal places?

ANSWERS TO SELECTED EXERCISES

Chapter 1

Section 1.1

For Thought: **1.** F **2.** F **3.** T **4.** F **5.** F **6.** F **7.** F **8.** F **9.** T **10.** T

Exercises: **1.** e, true **3.** h, true **5.** g, true **7.** c, true **9.** All **11.** $\{-\sqrt{2}, \sqrt{3}, \pi, 5.090090009\ldots\}$ **13.** $\{0, 1\}$ **15.** $x + 7$ **17.** $5x + 15$ **19.** $5(x + 1)$ **21.** $(-13 + 4) + x$ **23.** 8 **25.** $\sqrt{3}$ **27.** $y^2 - x^2$ **29.** 7.2 **31.** $\sqrt{5}$ **33.** 5 **35.** 22 **37.** 12 **39.** 3/4 **41.** $|x - 7| = 3$, $\{4, 10\}$ **43.** $|-1 - x| = 3$, $\{-4, 2\}$ **45.** $|x - (-9)| = 4$, $\{-13, -5\}$ **47.** $\{-9, 9\}$ **49.** $\{4/5\}$ **51.** $\{-2, 5\}$ **53.** $\{-10, 0\}$ **55.** $\{2/3\}$ **57.** $\varnothing$

59. Smallest to largest: $-\frac{1}{2}, -\frac{5}{12}, -\frac{1}{3}, 0, \frac{1}{3}, \frac{5}{12}, \frac{1}{2}$

Section 1.2

For Thought: **1.** T **2.** F **3.** F **4.** T **5.** F **6.** F **7.** F **8.** F **9.** F **10.** T

Exercises: **1.** $x < 12$ **3.** $x \geq -7$

5. $[-8, \infty)$ **7.** $(-\infty, \pi/2)$

9. $(5, \infty)$

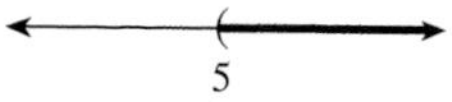

11. $[2, \infty)$

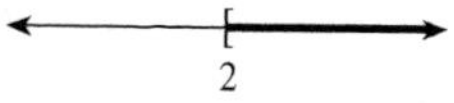

13. $(-\infty, 54)$

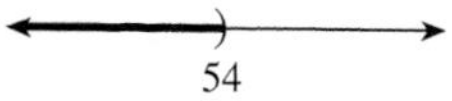

15. $(-\infty, 13/3]$

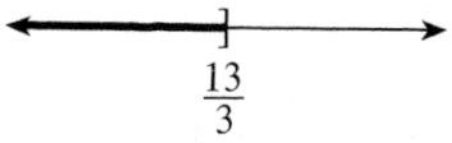

17. $(-\infty, 3/2]$

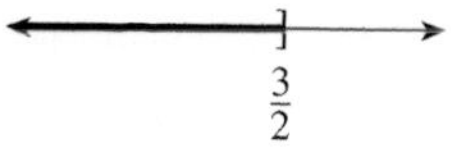

19. $(-\infty, 0]$

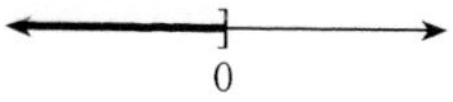

21. $(-3, \infty)$ **23.** $(-3, \infty)$ **25.** $(-5, -2)$ **27.** $\varnothing$ **29.** $(-\infty, 5]$

31. $(3, 6)$

33. $(1/2, \infty)$

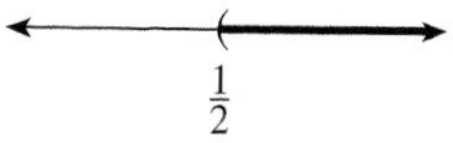

35. $(-3, \infty)$

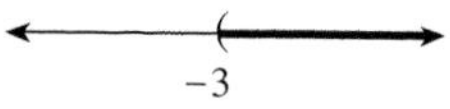

37. $(-\infty, \infty)$

39. $\varnothing$

41. $(2, 4)$

43. $(-3, 1]$

45. $(-1/3, 1)$

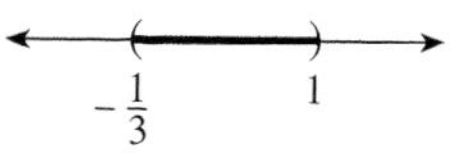

47. $[1, 3/2]$

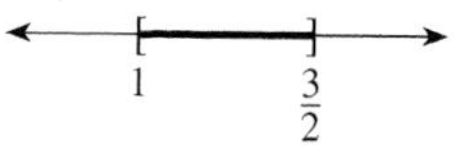

49. $[-1, 9]$

51. $\varnothing$

53. $\varnothing$

55. $(-\infty, 1) \cup (3, \infty)$

57. $(-\infty, 1) \cup (5, \infty)$

59. $|x| < 5$ **61.** $|x| > 3$ **63.** $|x - 6| < 2$ **65.** $|x - 4| > 1$ **67.** $|x| \geq 9$ **69.** $|x - 7| \leq 4$ **71.** $|x - 5| > 2$ **73.** $(93, 115)$ **75.** $(86, 102.5)$ **77.** [\$0, \$7000] **79.** 96, 79, 68, 56, 47, yes **81.** $|x - 74{,}595| > 25{,}000$, $x > 99{,}595$ or $x < 49{,}595$

83. $\dfrac{|x - 35|}{35} < 0.01$, $(34.65°, 35.35°)$ **85.** [2.26 cm, 2.32 cm]

Section 1.3

For Thought: **1.** F **2.** F **3.** F **4.** F **5.** T **6.** F **7.** T **8.** T **9.** T **10.** F

Exercises: **1.** (4, 1), I **3.** (1, 0), x-axis **5.** (5, −1), IV **7.** (−4, −2), III **9.** (−2, 4), II **11.** 5, (2.5, 5)

13. $2\sqrt{2}$, $(0, -1)$ **15.** 6, $\left(\dfrac{-2 + 3\sqrt{3}}{2}, \dfrac{5}{2}\right)$

17. $\sqrt{74}$, $(-1.3, 1.3)$ **19.** $|a - b|$, $\left(\dfrac{a + b}{2}, 0\right)$

21. $\dfrac{\sqrt{\pi^2 + 4}}{2}$, $\left(\dfrac{3\pi}{4}, \dfrac{1}{2}\right)$

23. (0, 0), 4

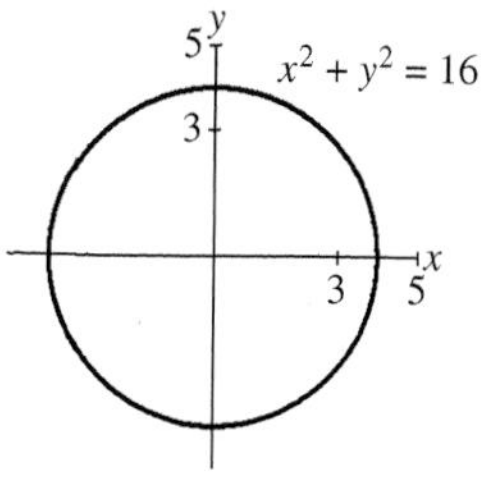

25. (−6, 0), 6

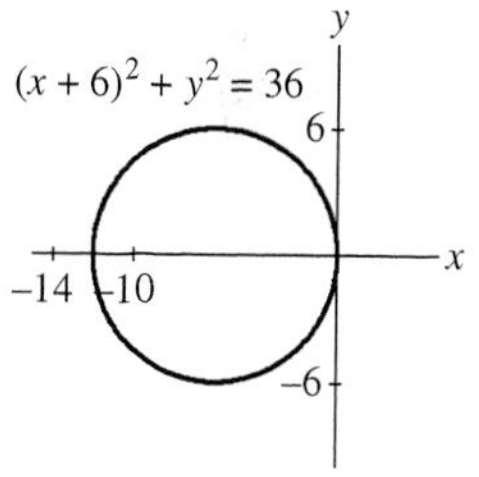

27. (−1, 0), 5

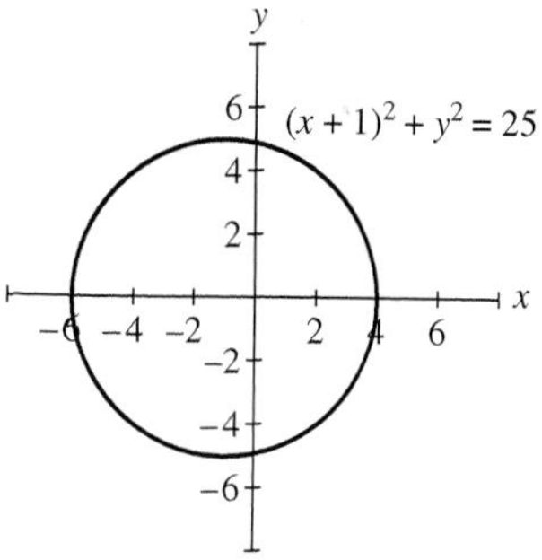

29. $(2, -2)$, $2\sqrt{2}$

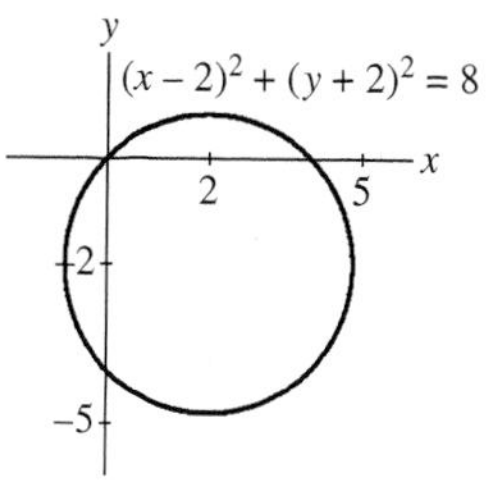

31. $x^2 + y^2 = 49$ **33.** $(x + 2)^2 + (y - 5)^2 = 1/4$ **35.** $(x - 3)^2 + (y - 5)^2 = 34$ **37.** $(x - 5)^2 + (y + 1)^2 = 32$

39. (0, 0), 3

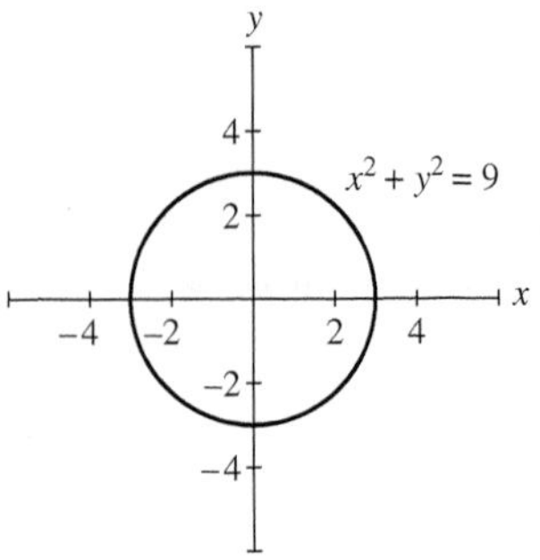

41. (0, −3), 3

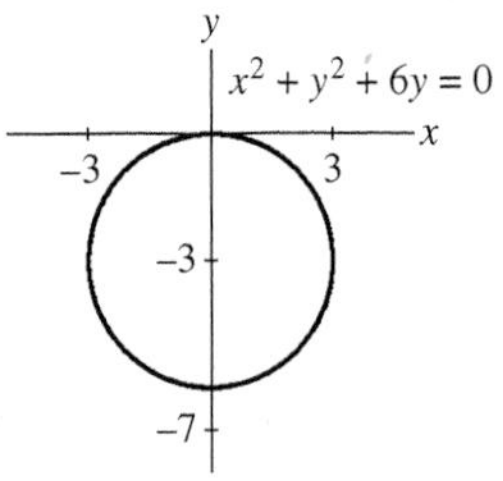

43. (3, 4), 5

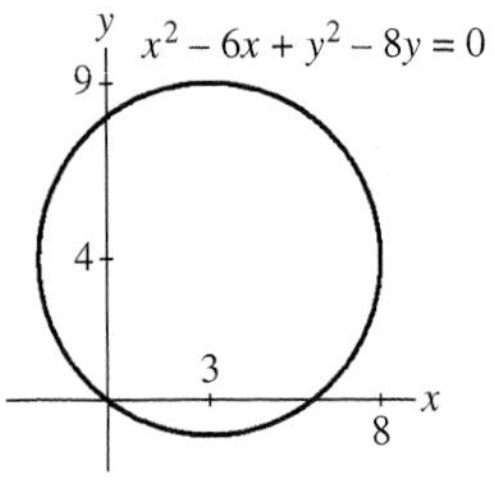

45. (2, 3/2), 5/2

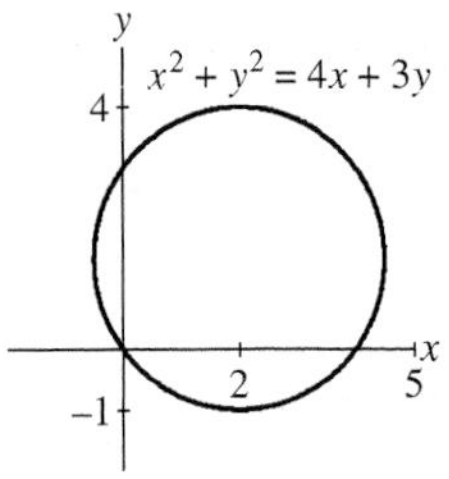

47. (1/4, −1/6), 1/6

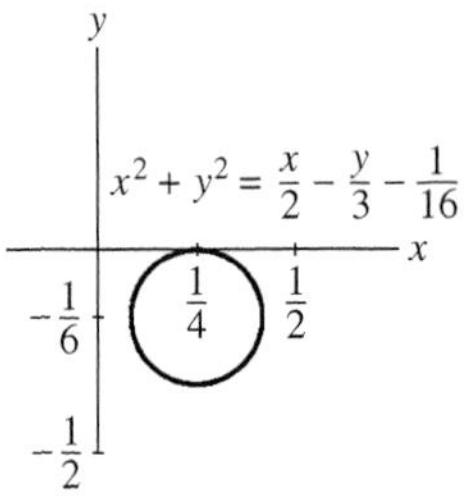

49. **a.** $x^2 + y^2 = 49$ **b.** $(x - 1)^2 + y^2 = 20$
c. $(x - 1)^2 + (y - 2)^2 = 13$

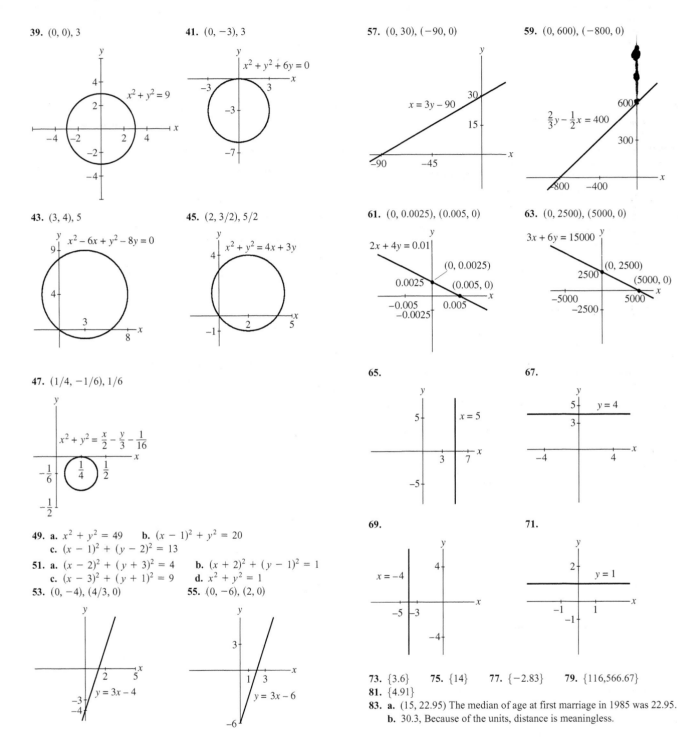

51. **a.** $(x - 2)^2 + (y + 3)^2 = 4$ **b.** $(x + 2)^2 + (y - 1)^2 = 1$
c. $(x - 3)^2 + (y + 1)^2 = 9$ **d.** $x^2 + y^2 = 1$

53. (0, −4), (4/3, 0)

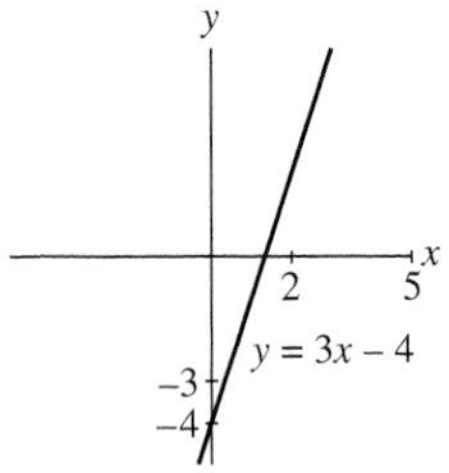

55. (0, −6), (2, 0)

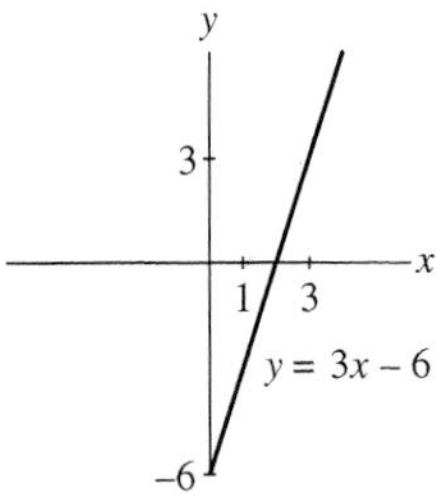

57. (0, 30), (−90, 0)

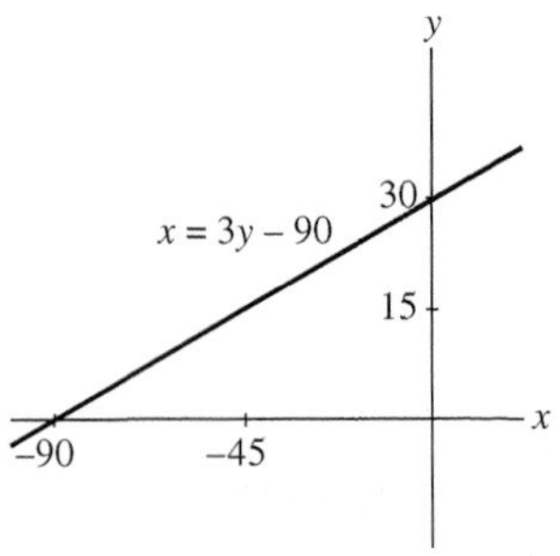

59. (0, 600), (−800, 0)

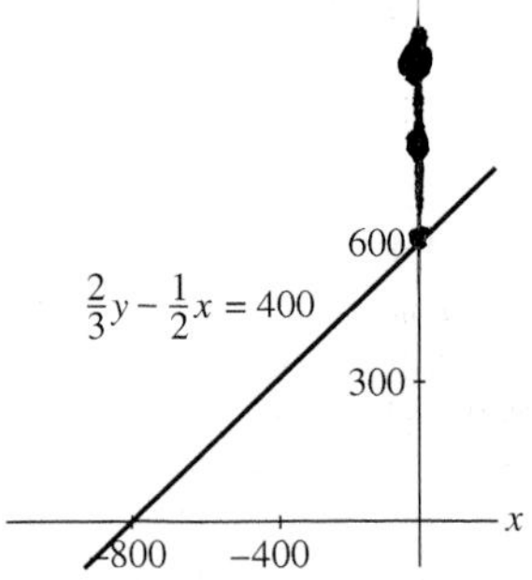

61. (0, 0.0025), (0.005, 0)

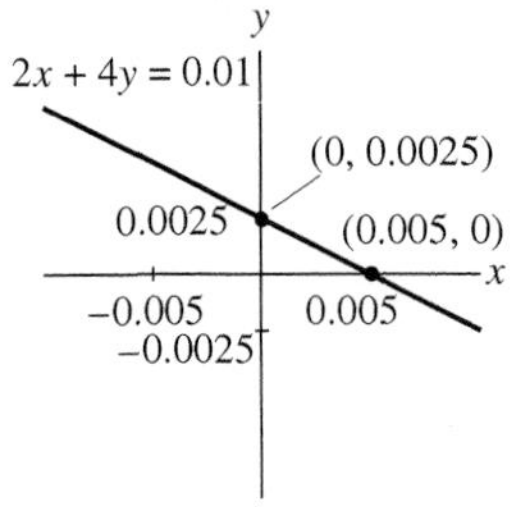

63. (0, 2500), (5000, 0)

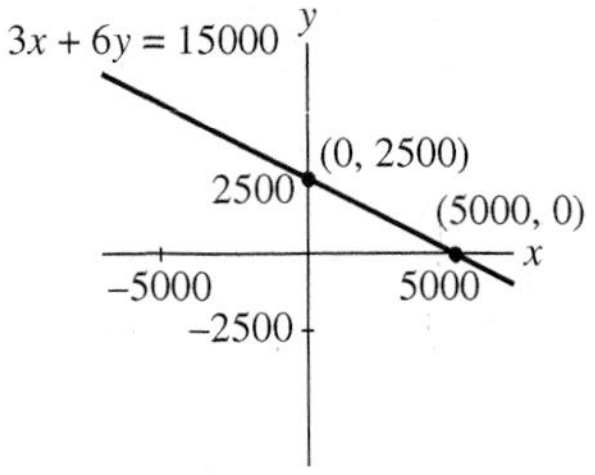

65.

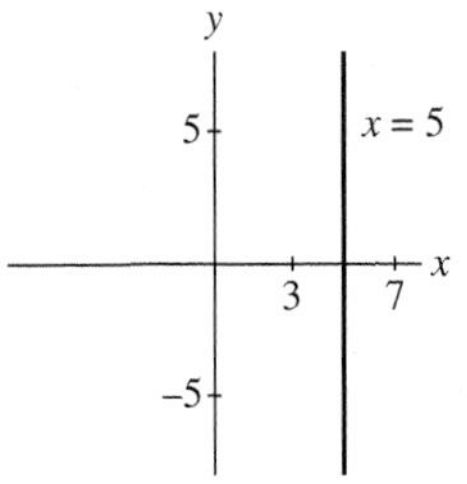

67.

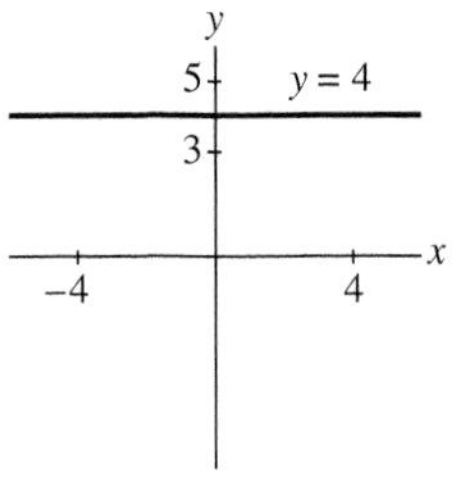

69.

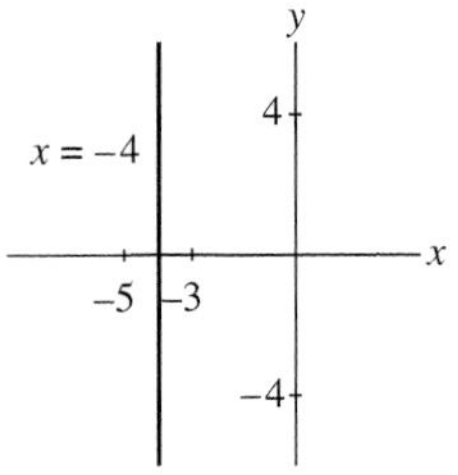

71.

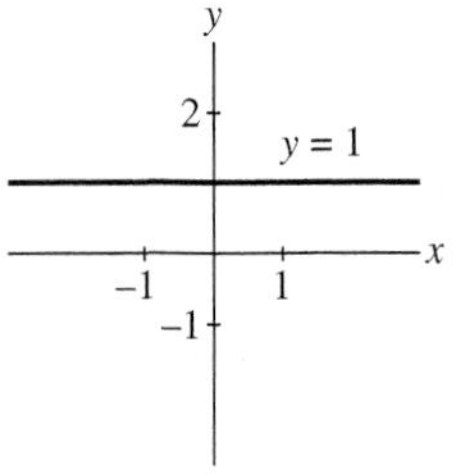

73. {3.6} **75.** {14} **77.** {−2.83} **79.** {116,566.67}
81. {4.91}
83. **a.** (15, 22.95) The median of age at first marriage in 1985 was 22.95.
b. 30.3, Because of the units, distance is meaningless.

85. $C = 1.8$

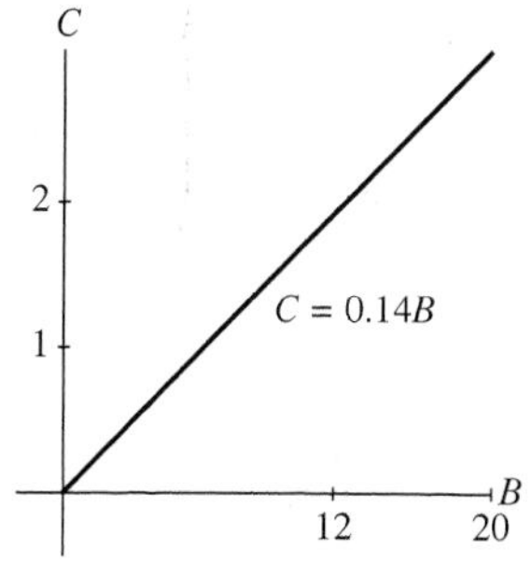

Section 1.4

For Thought: **1.** F **2.** F **3.** F **4.** F **5.** T **6.** F **7.** F **8.** T **9.** F **10.** T

Exercises: **1.** $\frac{1}{3}$ **3.** -4 **5.** 0 **7.** 2 **9.** No slope **11.** $y = \frac{5}{4}x + \frac{1}{4}$ **13.** $y = -\frac{7}{6}x + \frac{11}{3}$ **15.** $y = 5$ **17.** $x = 4$ **19.** $y = \frac{2}{3}x - 1$ **21.** $y = \frac{5}{2}x + \frac{3}{2}$ **23.** $y = -2x + 4$ **25.** $y = \frac{3}{2}x + \frac{5}{2}$ **27.** $y = \frac{3}{5}x - 2, \frac{3}{5}, (0, -2)$ **29.** $y = 2x - 5, 2, (0, -5)$ **31.** $y = \frac{1}{2}x + \frac{1}{2}, \frac{1}{2}, \left(0, \frac{1}{2}\right)$ **33.** $y = 4, 0, (0, 4)$ **35.** $y = 0.03x - 2.6, 0.03, (0, -2.6)$

37.

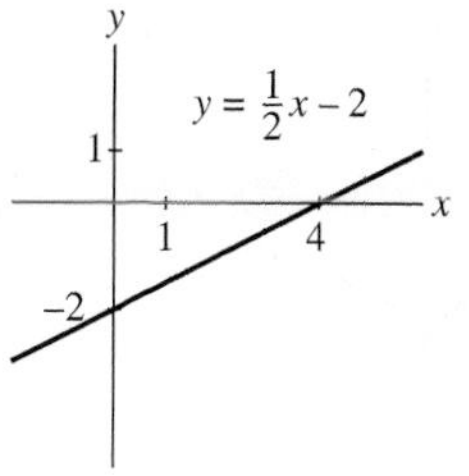

39.

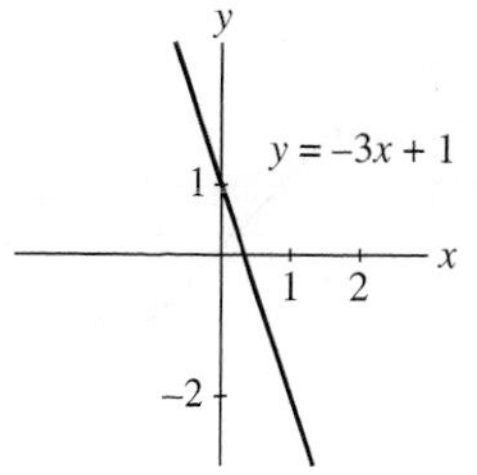

41.

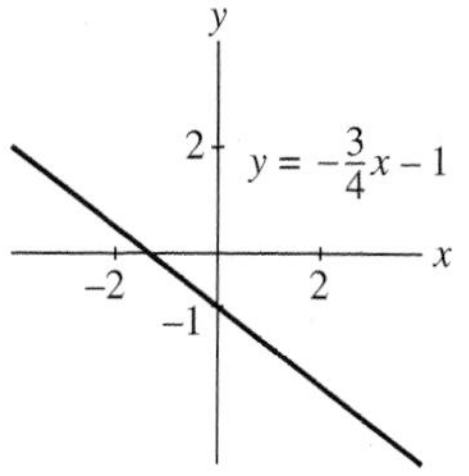

43.

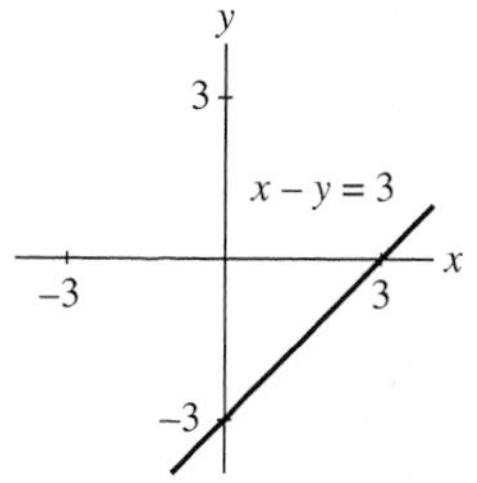

45.

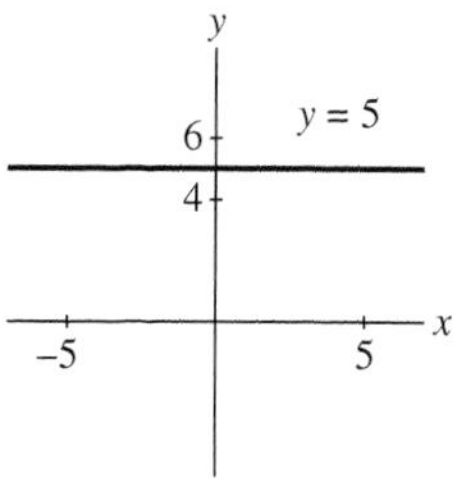

47. $4x - 3y = 12$ **49.** $4x - 5y = -7$ **51.** $x = -4$ **53.** 0.5 **55.** -1 **57.** 0 **59.** $2x - y = 4$ **61.** $3x + y = 7$ **63.** $2x + y = -5$ **65.** $y = 5$ **67.** $F = \frac{9}{5}C + 32$, 302°F **69.** $c = 50 - n$, \$400 **71.** $c = -\frac{3}{4}p + 30, -\frac{3}{4}$, If p increases by 4 then c decreases by 3.

Section 1.5

For Thought: **1.** F **2.** F **3.** T **4.** F **5.** F **6.** F **7.** T **8.** T **9.** T **10.** F

Exercises: **1.** Both **3.** a is a function of b **5.** b is a function of a **7.** Neither **9.** Both **11.** No **13.** Yes **15.** Yes **17.** Yes **19.** No **21.** No **23.** Yes **25.** Yes **27.** Yes **29.** No **31.** Yes **33.** Yes **35.** No **37.** $\{-3, 4, 5\}, \{1, 2, 6\}$ **39.** $(-\infty, \infty), \{4\}$ **41.** $(-\infty, \infty), [5, \infty)$ **43.** $[-3, \infty), (-\infty, \infty)$ **45.** $[4, \infty), [0, \infty)$ **47.** $(-\infty, 0], (-\infty, \infty)$ **49.** 6 **51.** 11 **53.** 3 **55.** 7 **57.** 22 **59.** $3a^2 - a$ **61.** $4a + 6$ **63.** $3x^2 + 5x + 2$ **65.** $4x + 4h - 2$ **67.** $6xh + 3h^2 - h$ **69.** $-\$2{,}400$ per yr **71.** $-32, -48, -62.4, -63.84$, and -63.984 ft/sec **73.** 4 **75.** 3 **77.** $2x + h + 1$ **79.** $-2x - h + 1$ **81.** $\frac{3}{\sqrt{x + h} + \sqrt{x}}$ **83.** $\frac{1}{\sqrt{x + h + 2} + \sqrt{x + 2}}$ **85.** $\frac{-1}{x(x + h)}$ **87.** $\frac{-3}{(x + 2)(x + h + 2)}$

89. a. $A = s^2$ **b.** $s = \sqrt{A}$ **c.** $s = \frac{d\sqrt{2}}{2}$ **d.** $d = s\sqrt{2}$ **e.** $P = 4s$ **f.** $s = P/4$ **g.** $A = \frac{P^2}{16}$ **h.** $d = \sqrt{2A}$

91. a. 4 atm **b.** 130 ft **93.** $h = \left(2\sqrt{3} + 2\right)a$

Section 1.6

For Thought: **1.** T **2.** F **3.** T **4.** T **5.** F **6.** T **7.** T **8.** T **9.** F **10.** T

Exercises:

1. $(-\infty, \infty), (-\infty, \infty)$, yes

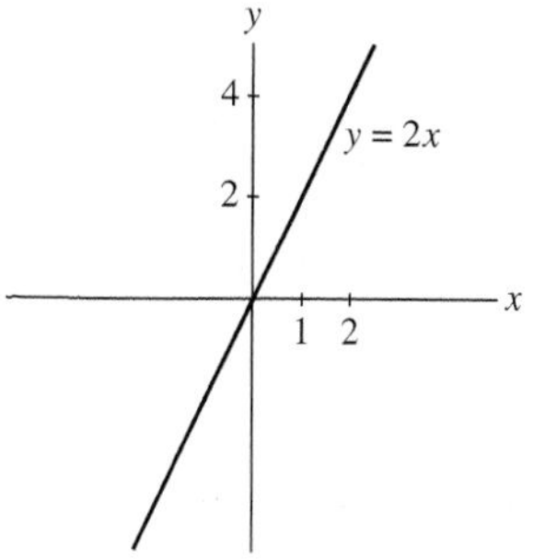

3. $(-\infty, \infty), (-\infty, \infty)$, yes

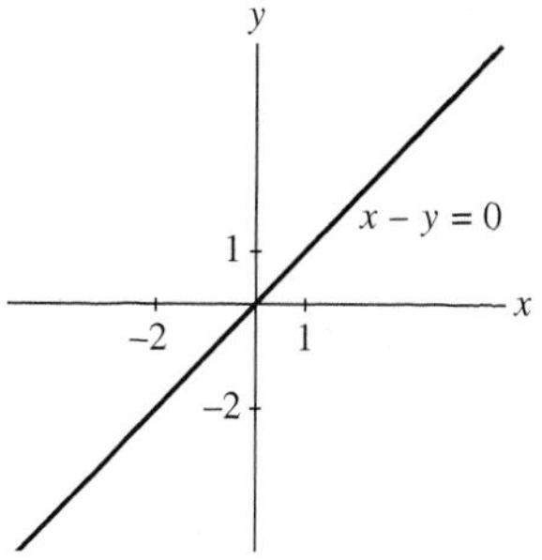

5. $(-\infty, \infty), \{5\}$, yes

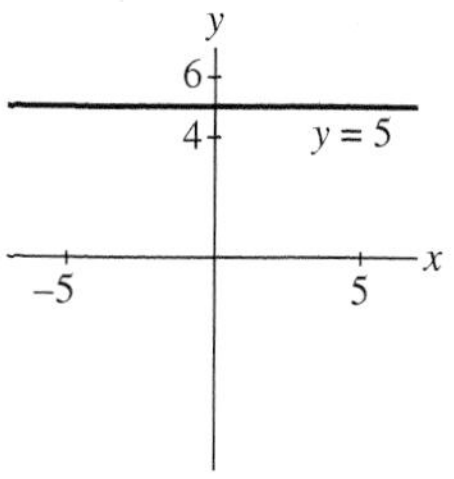

7. $(-\infty, \infty), [0, \infty)$, yes

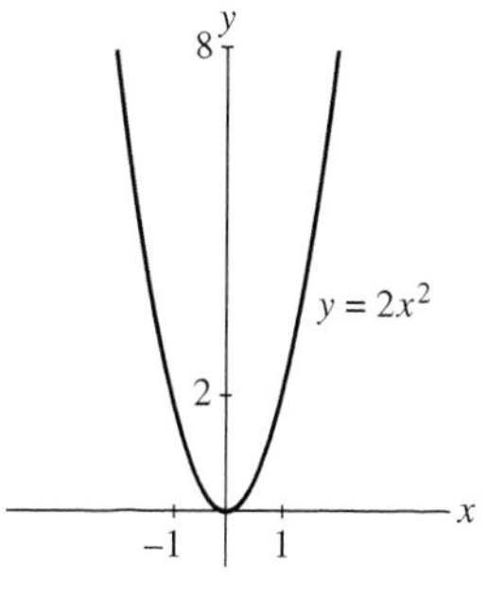

9. $(-\infty, \infty)$, $(-\infty, 1]$, yes

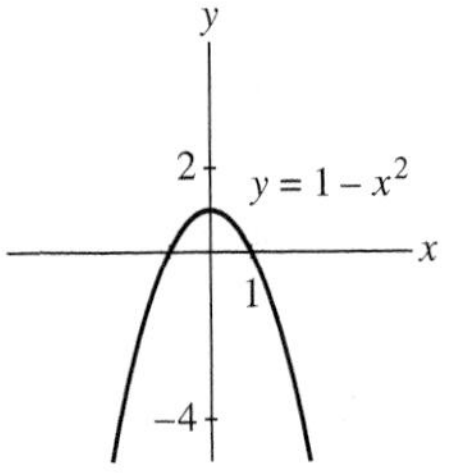

11. $[0, \infty)$, $[1, \infty)$, yes

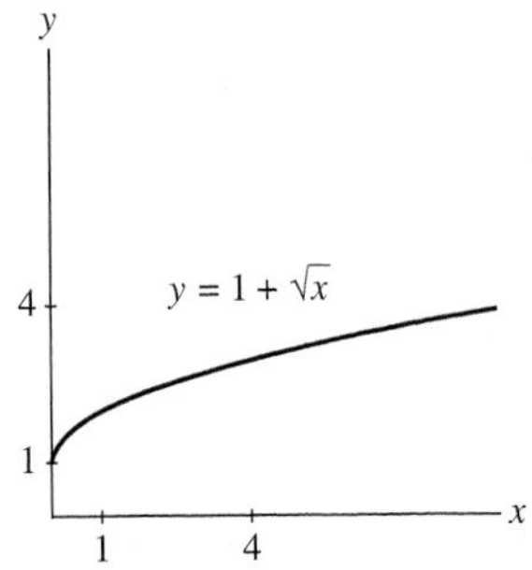

13. $[1, \infty)$, $(-\infty, \infty)$, no

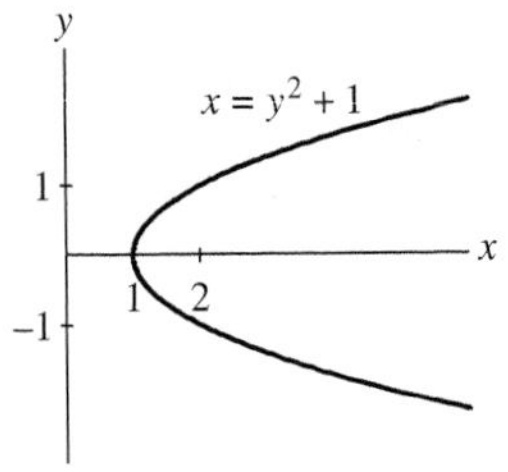

15. $[0, \infty)$, $[0, \infty)$, yes

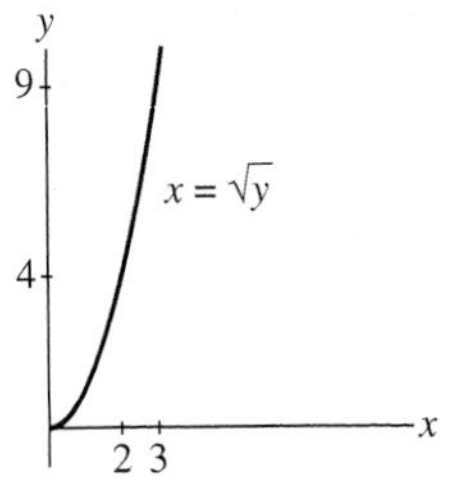

17. $(-\infty, \infty)$, $(-\infty, \infty)$, yes

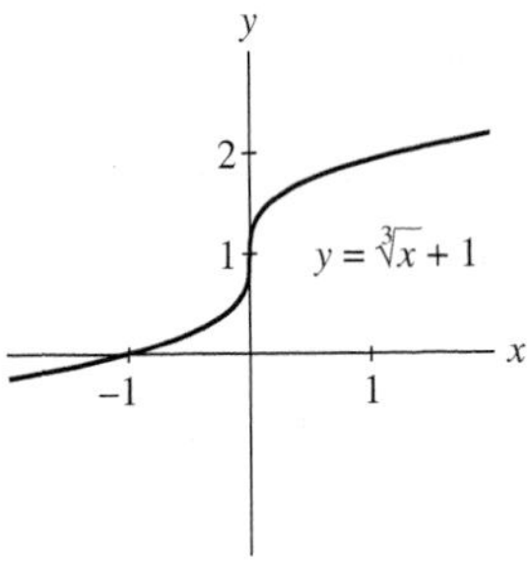

19. $(-\infty, \infty)$, $(-\infty, \infty)$, yes

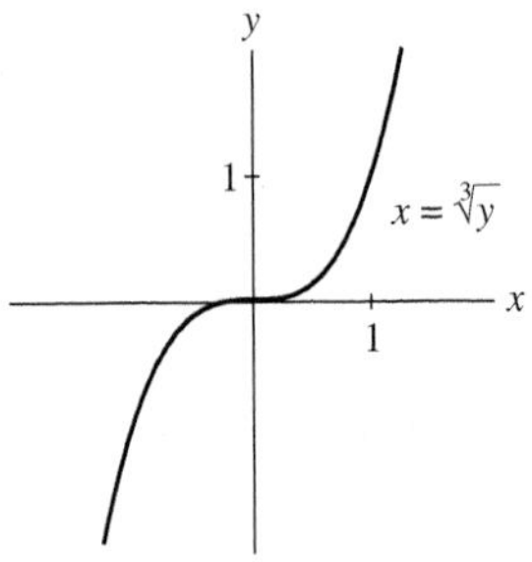

21. $[-1, 1]$, $[-1, 1]$, no

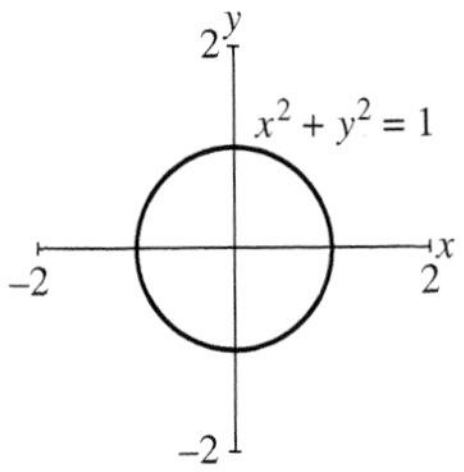

23. $[-1, 1]$, $[0, 1]$, yes

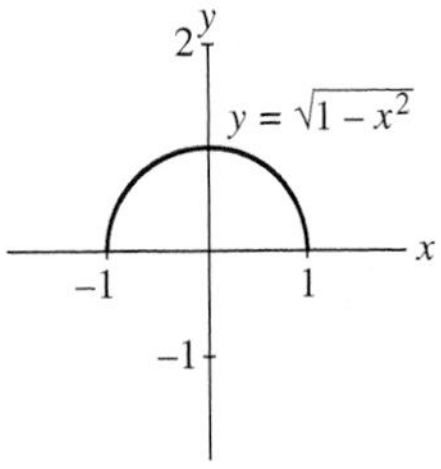

25. $(-\infty, \infty)$, $(-\infty, \infty)$, yes

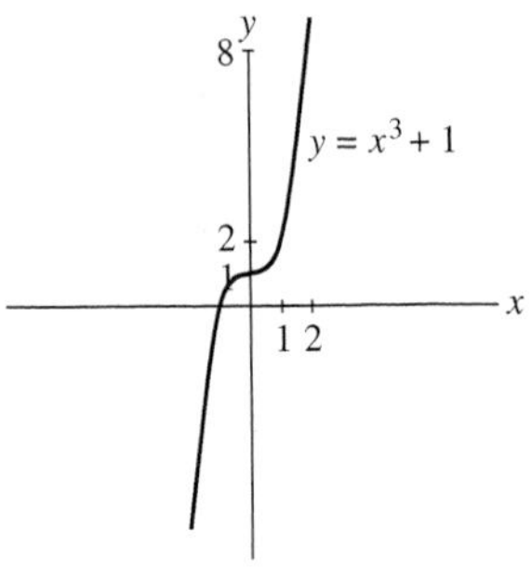

27. $(-\infty, \infty)$, $[0, \infty)$, yes

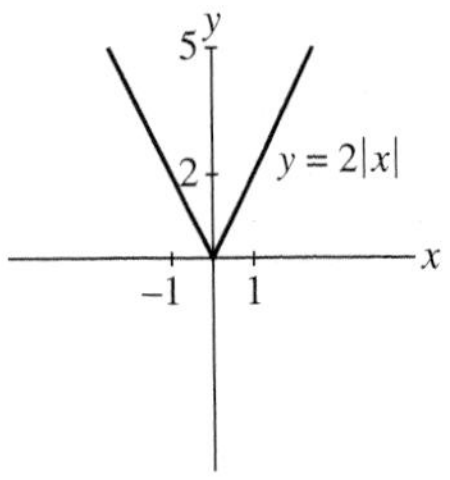

29. $(-\infty, \infty)$, $(-\infty, 0]$, yes

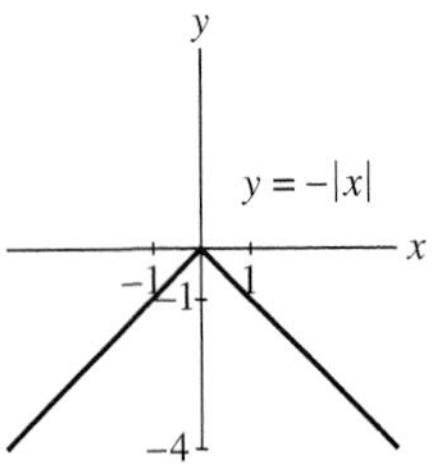

31. $[0, \infty)$, $(-\infty, \infty)$, no

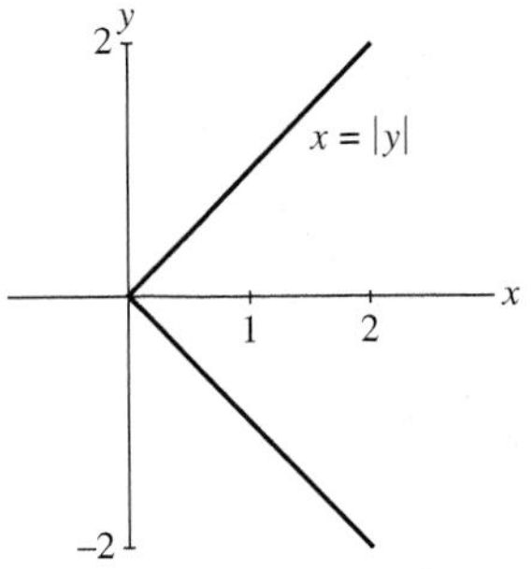

33. $(-\infty, \infty)$, $\{-2, 2\}$

$$f(x) = \begin{cases} 2 & x < -1 \\ -2 & x \geq -1 \end{cases}$$

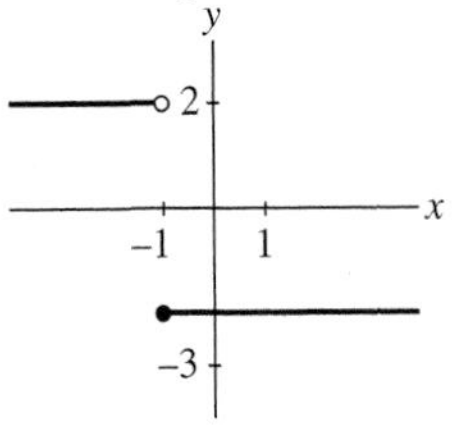

35. $(-\infty, \infty)$, $(-\infty, -2] \cup (2, \infty)$

$$f(x) = \begin{cases} x + 1 & x > 1 \\ x - 3 & x \leq 1 \end{cases}$$

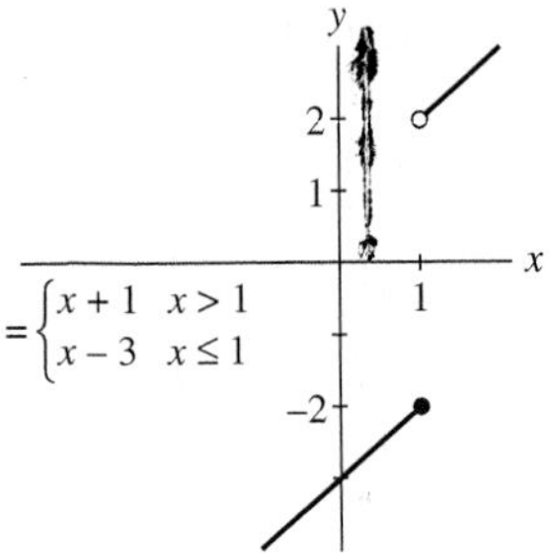

37. $[-2, \infty)$, $(-\infty, 2]$

$$f(x) = \begin{cases} \sqrt{x + 2} & -2 \leq x \leq 2 \\ 4 - x & x > 2 \end{cases}$$

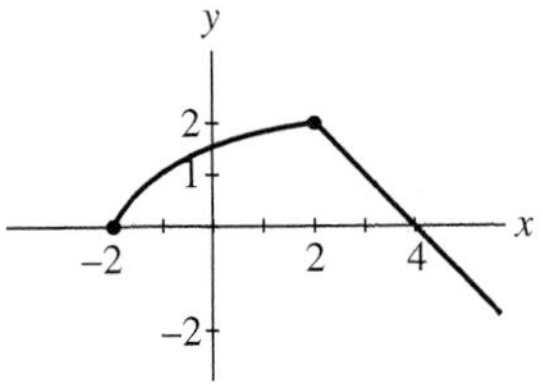

39. $(-\infty, \infty)$, $[0, \infty)$

$$f(x) = \begin{cases} \sqrt{-x} & x < 0 \\ \sqrt{x} & x \geq 0 \end{cases}$$

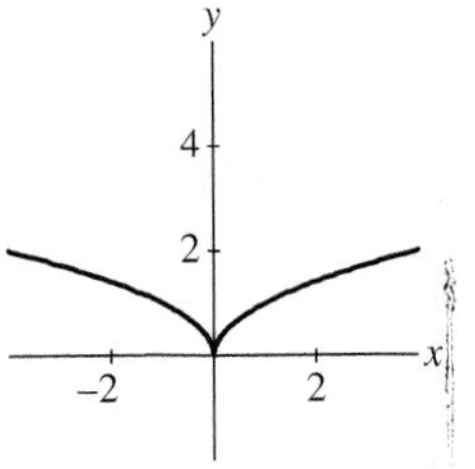

41. $(-\infty, \infty)$, $(-\infty, \infty)$

$$f(x) = \begin{cases} x^2 & x < -1 \\ -x & x \geq -1 \end{cases}$$

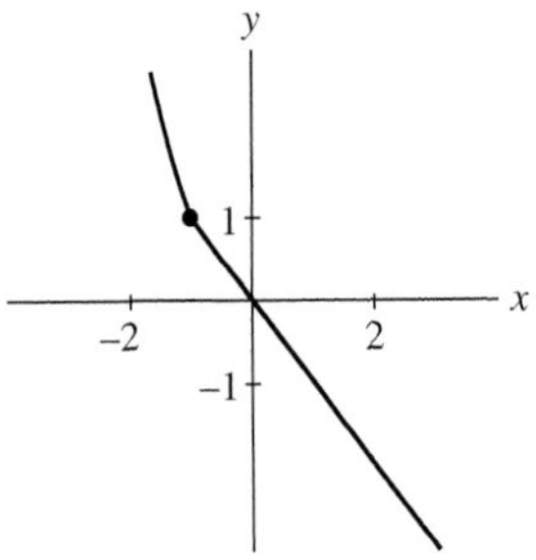

43. $(-\infty, \infty)$, integers

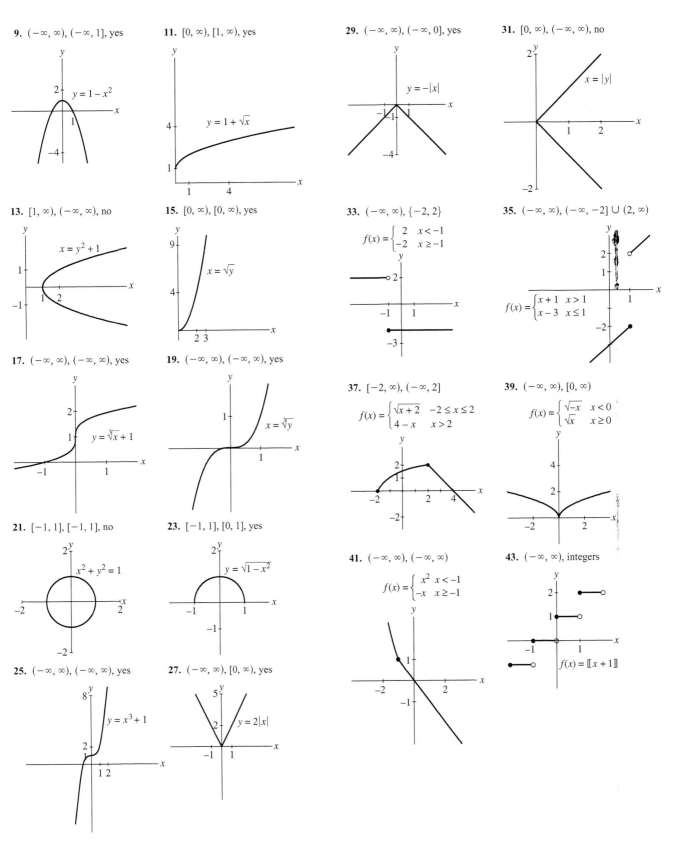

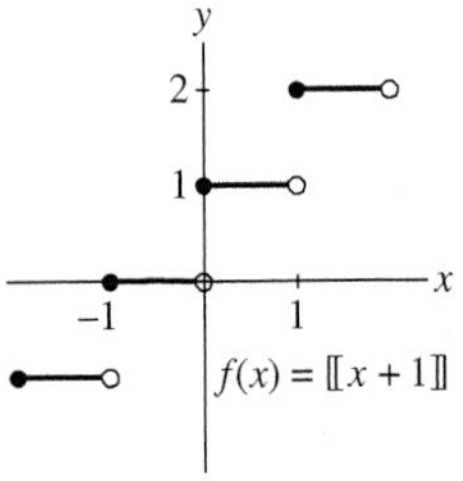

45. $[0, 4), \{2, 3, 4, 5\}$

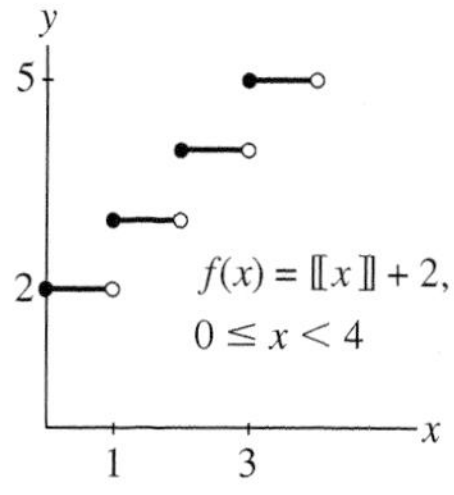

47. a. $D(-\infty, \infty), R(-\infty, \infty)$, dec $(-\infty, \infty)$
b. $D(-\infty, \infty), R(-\infty, 4]$, inc $(-\infty, 0)$, dec $(0, \infty)$

49. a. $D[-2, 6], R[3, 7]$, inc $(-2, 2)$, dec $(2, 6)$
b. $D(-\infty, 2], R(-\infty, 3]$, inc $(-\infty, -2)$, constant $(-2, 2)$

51. a. $D(-\infty, \infty), R[0, \infty)$, dec $(-\infty, 0)$, inc $(0, \infty)$
b. $D(-\infty, \infty), R(-\infty, \infty)$, dec $(-\infty, -2)$ and $(-2/3, \infty)$, inc $(-2, -2/3)$

53. a. $D(-\infty, \infty), R(-\infty, \infty)$, inc $(-\infty, \infty)$
b. $D[-2, 5], R[1, 4]$, dec $(-2, 1)$, inc $(1, 2)$, constant $(2, 5)$

55. $(-\infty, \infty), (-\infty, \infty)$, inc $(-\infty, \infty)$

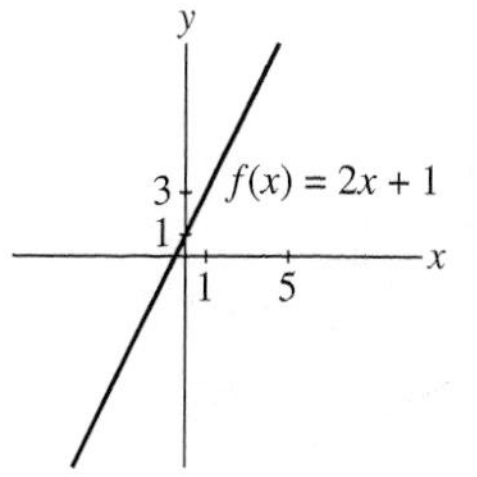

57. $(-\infty, \infty), [0, \infty)$, dec $(-\infty, 1)$, inc $(1, \infty)$

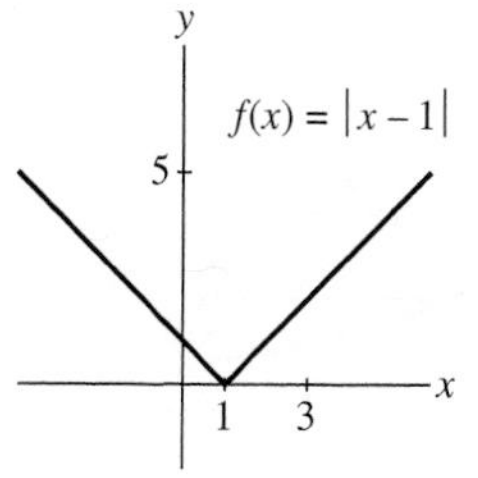

59. $(-\infty, 0) \cup (0, \infty), \{-1, 1\}$, constant $(-\infty, 0), (0, \infty)$

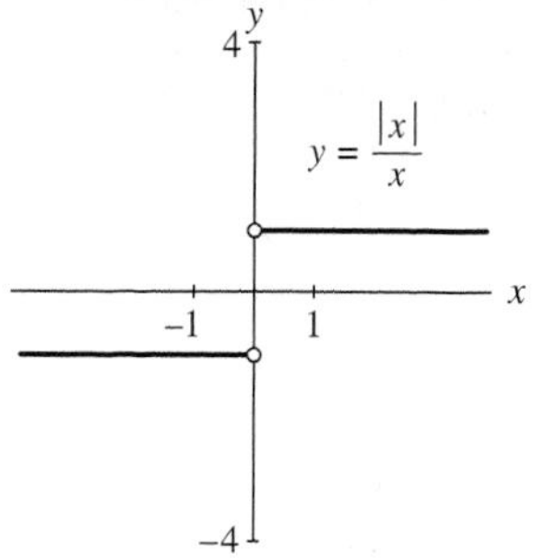

61. $[-3, 3], [0, 3]$, inc $(-3, 0)$, dec $(0, 3)$

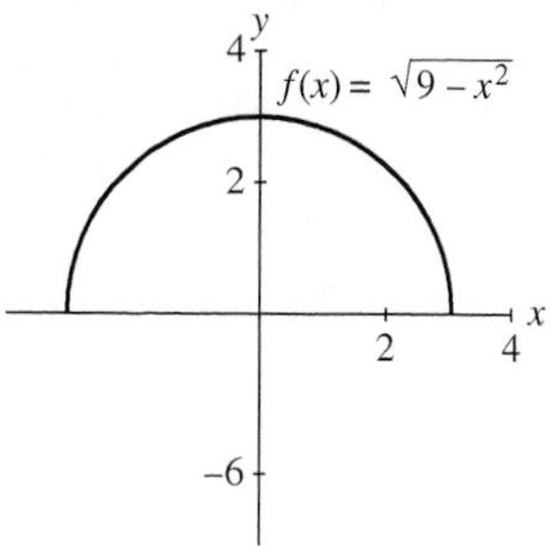

63. $(-\infty, \infty), (-\infty, \infty)$, inc $(-\infty, 3), (3, \infty)$

$$f(x) = \begin{cases} x + 1 & x \ge 3 \\ x + 2 & x < 3 \end{cases}$$

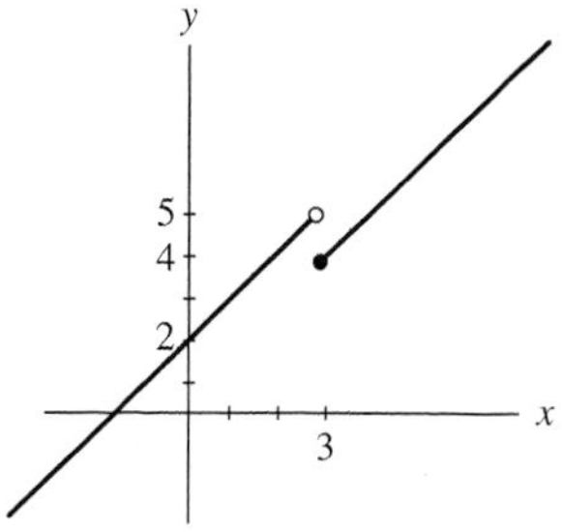

65. $(-\infty, \infty), (-\infty, 2]$, inc $(-\infty, -2), (-2, 0)$ dec $(0, 2), (2, \infty)$

$$f(x) = \begin{cases} x + 3 & x \le -2 \\ \sqrt{4 - x^2} & -2 < x < 2 \\ -x + 3 & x \ge 2 \end{cases}$$

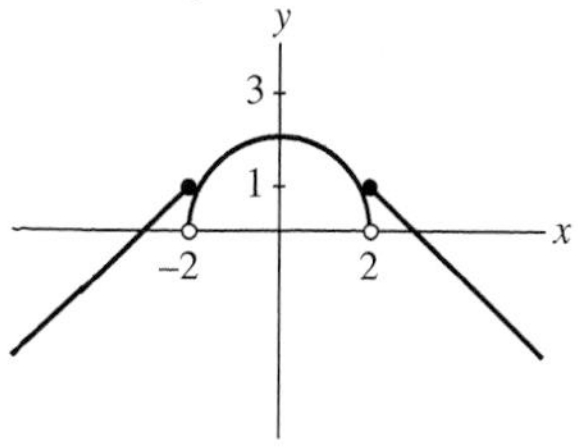

67. $f(x) = \begin{cases} 2 & \text{for } x > -1 \\ -1 & \text{for } x \le -1 \end{cases}$

69. $f(x) = \begin{cases} x - 1 & \text{for } x \ge -1 \\ -x & \text{for } x < -1 \end{cases}$

71. $f(x) = \begin{cases} 2x - 2 & \text{for } x \ge 0 \\ -x - 2 & \text{for } x < 0 \end{cases}$

73. Dec $(-\infty, 0.83)$, inc $(0.83, \infty)$

75. Inc $(-\infty, -1), (1, \infty)$, dec $(-1, 1)$

77. Dec $(-\infty, -1.73), (0, 1.73)$, inc $(-1.73, 0), (1.73, \infty)$

79. Inc $(30, 50), (70, \infty)$, dec $(-\infty, 30), (50, 70)$

81. 565 million, 800 million, 14.5 million/yr

83. $[5, \infty)$

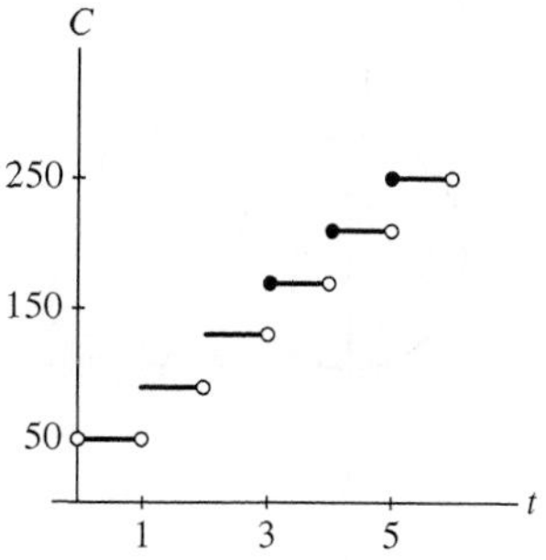

Section 1.7

For Thought: **1.** F **2.** T **3.** F **4.** T **5.** T **6.** F **7.** T **8.** F **9.** T **10.** T

Exercises:

1.

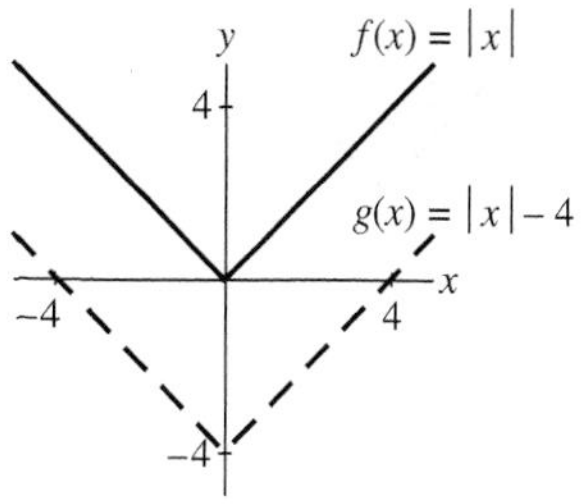

3.

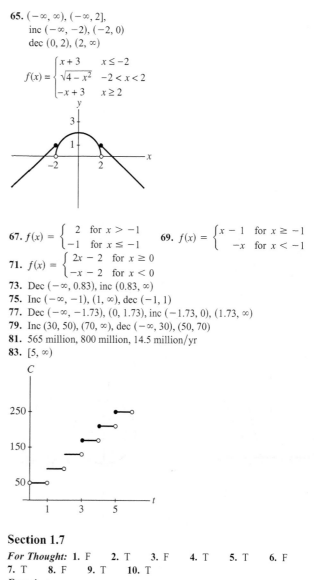

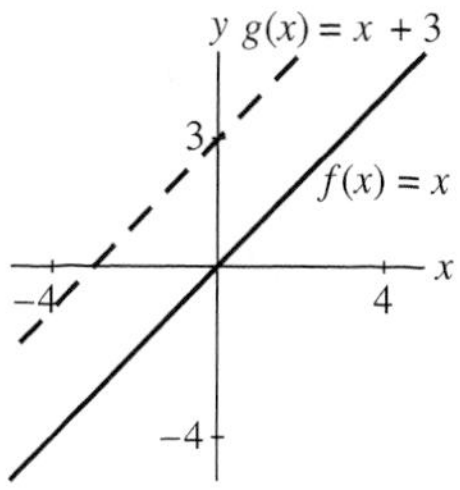

5.

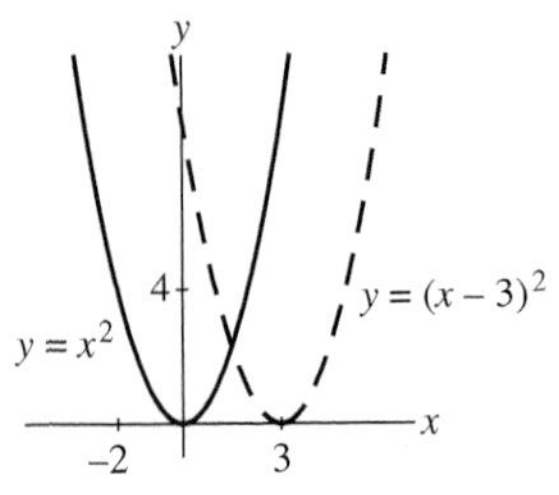

7.

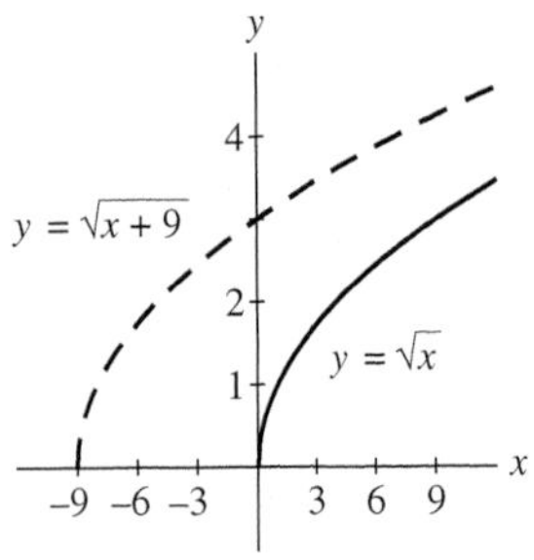

9.

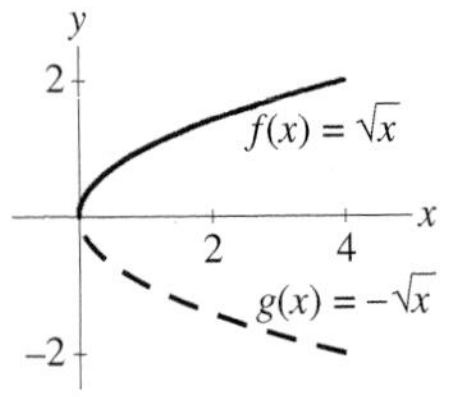

11.

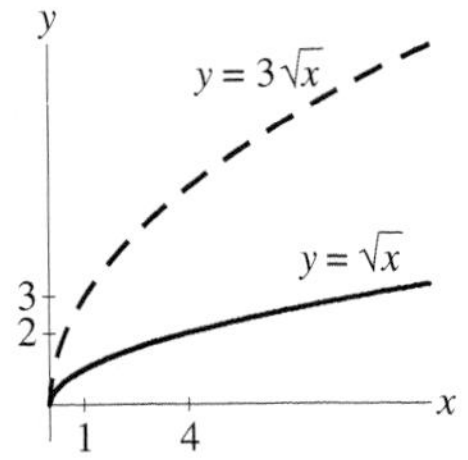

13.

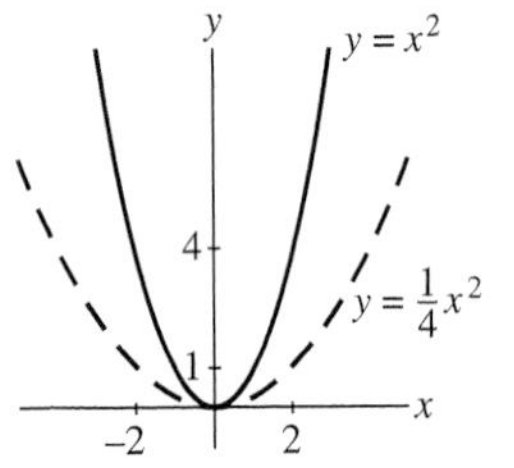

15.

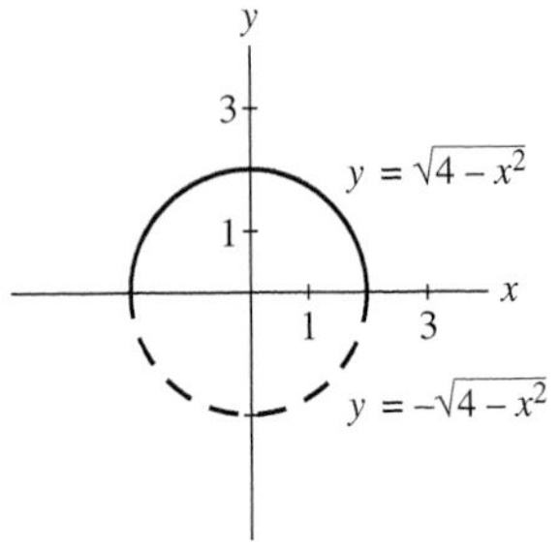

17. g **19.** b **21.** c **23.** f **25.** $y = \sqrt{x} + 2$
27. $y = (x-5)^2$ **29.** $y = (x-10)^2 + 4$
31. $y = -3\sqrt{x} - 5$ **33.** $y = -3|x-7| + 9$
35. $(-\infty, \infty), [2, \infty)$

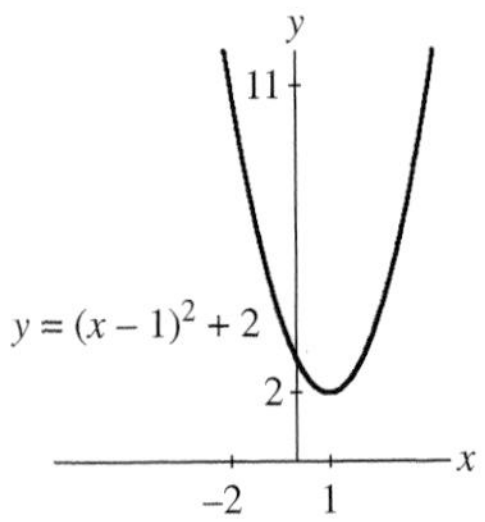

37. $(-\infty, \infty), [3, \infty)$

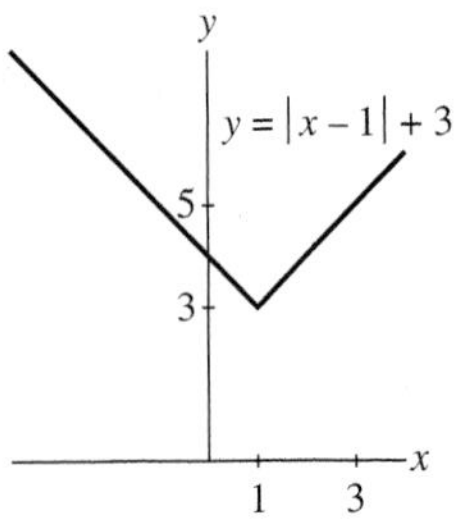

39. $(-\infty, \infty), (-\infty, \infty)$

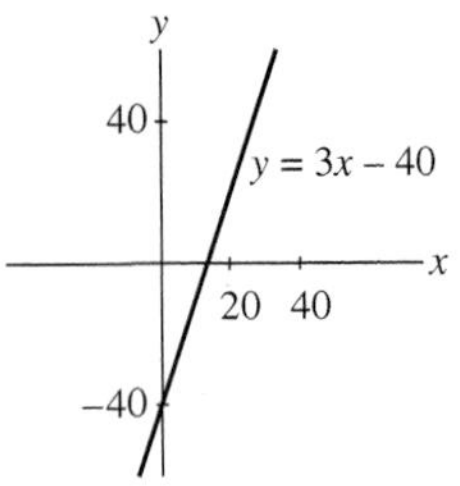

41. $(-\infty, \infty), (-\infty, \infty)$

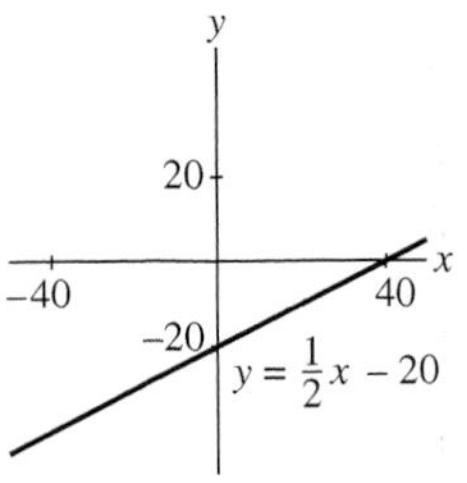

43. $(-\infty, \infty), (-\infty, 40]$

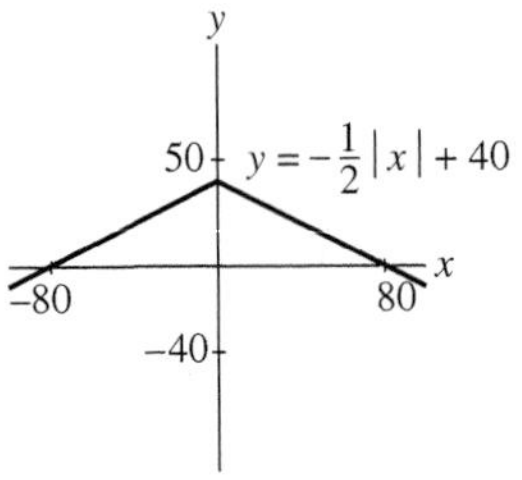

45. $(-\infty, \infty), (-\infty, 0]$

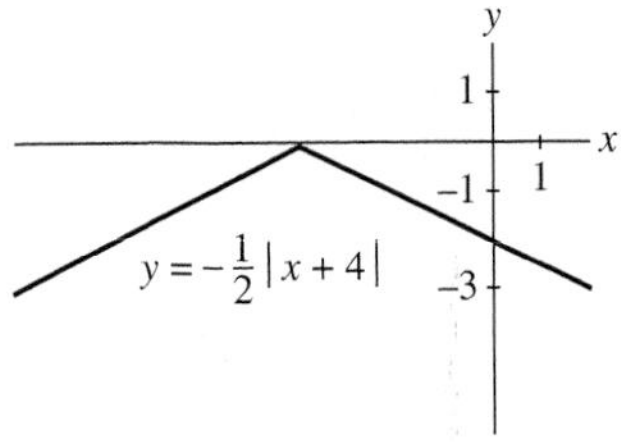

47. $[3, \infty), (-\infty, 1]$

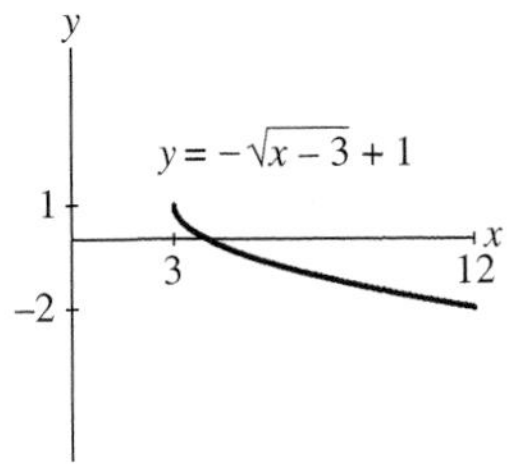

49. $[-3, \infty), (-\infty, 2]$

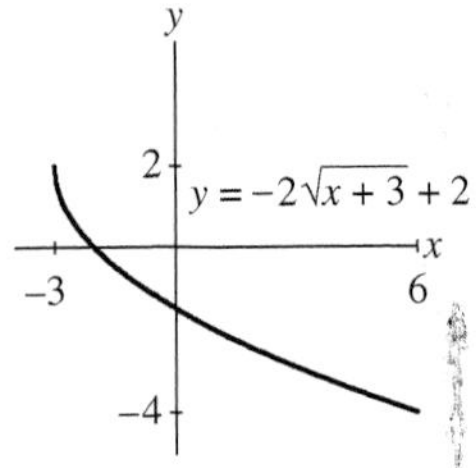

51. y-axis, even **53.** No symmetry, neither
55. $x = -3$, neither **57.** $x = 2$, neither **59.** Origin, odd
61. No symmetry, neither **63.** No symmetry, neither
65. y-axis, even **67.** e **69.** g **71.** b **73.** c
75. $(-\infty, -1] \cup [1, \infty)$ **77.** $(-\infty, -1) \cup (5, \infty)$
79. $(-2, 4)$ **81.** $[0, 25]$ **83.** $(-\infty, 2 - \sqrt{3}) \cup (2 + \sqrt{3}, \infty)$
85. $(-5, 5)$ **87.** $(-3.36, 1.55)$
89. a.

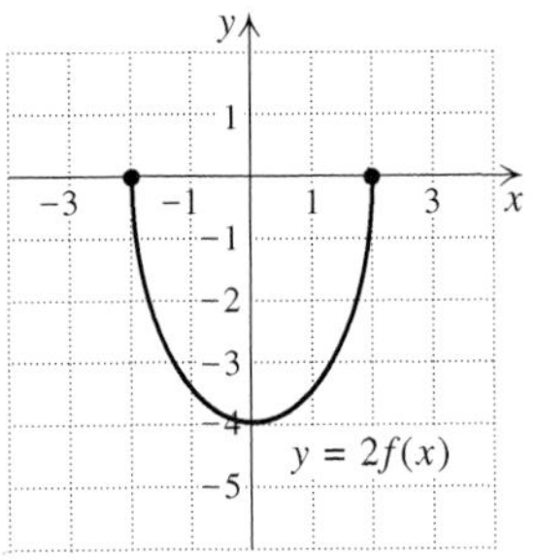

b.

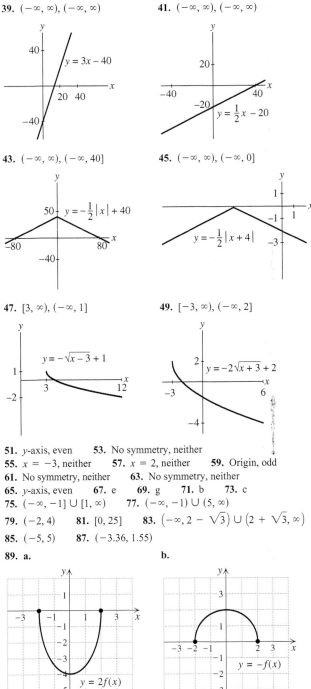

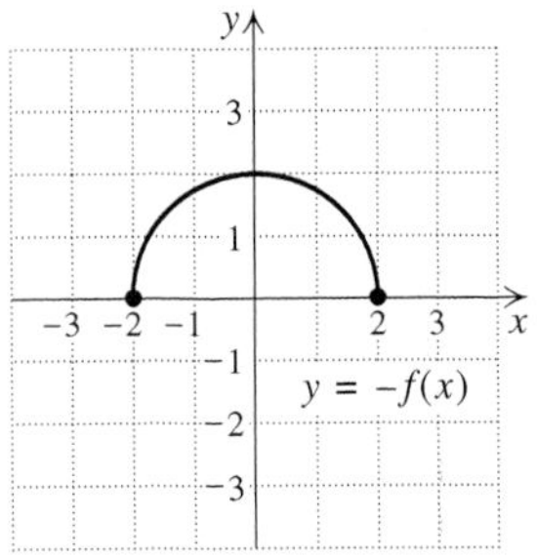

c.

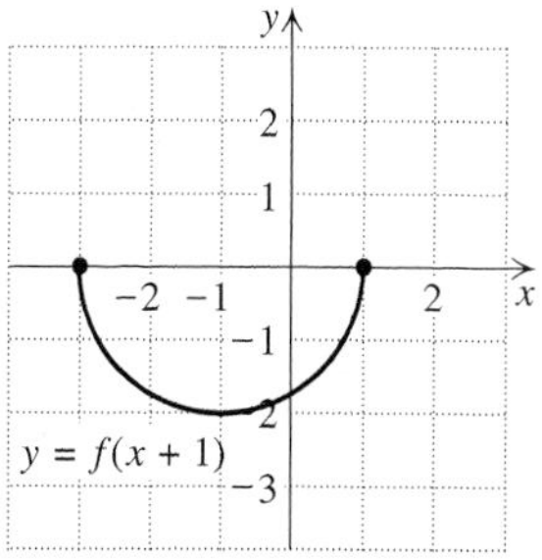

d.

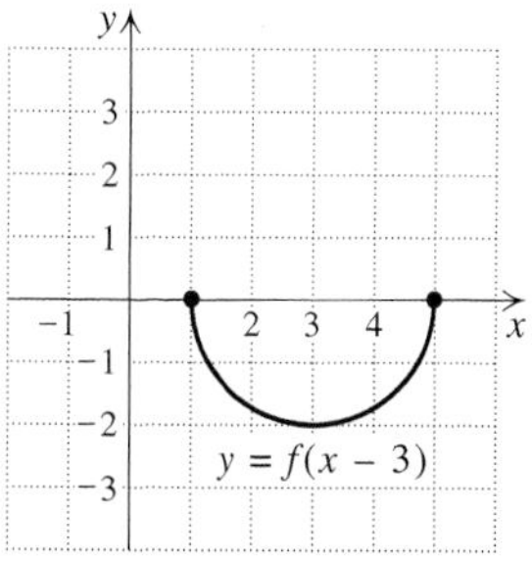

e.

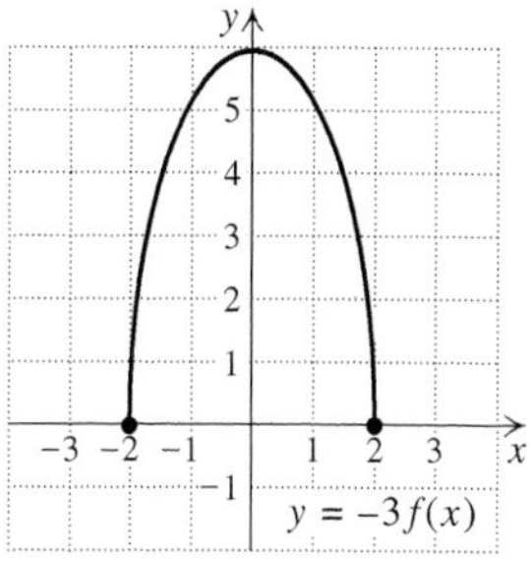

f.

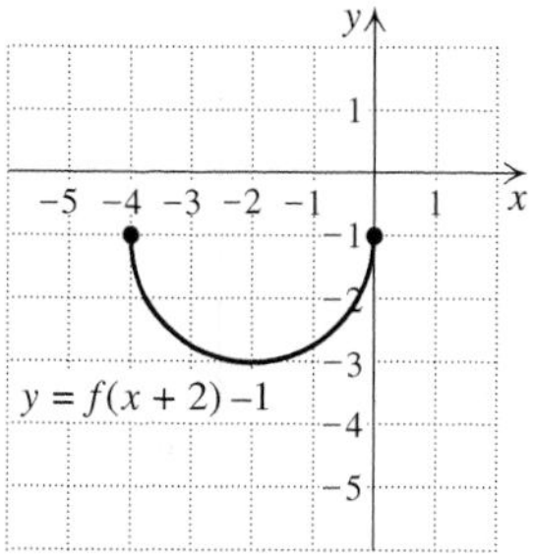

g.

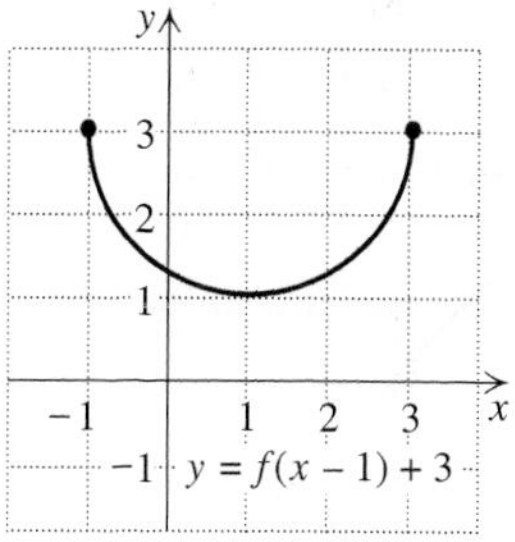

h.

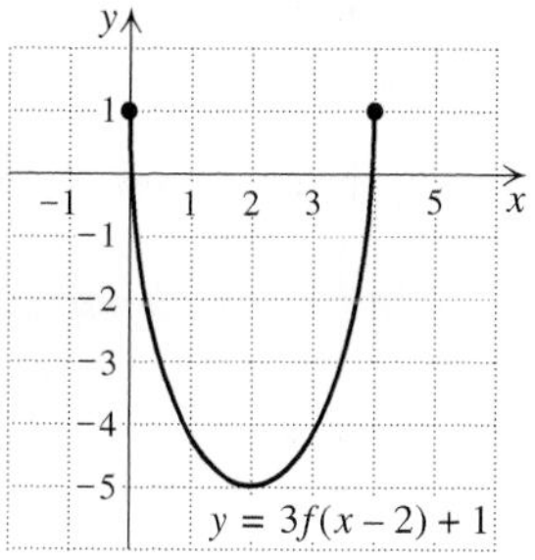

91. $N(x) = x + 2000$

Section 1.8

For Thought: **1.** F **2.** T **3.** T **4.** T **5.** T **6.** T **7.** F **8.** T **9.** F **10.** T

Exercises: **1.** 1 **3.** −11 **5.** −8 **7.** 1/12 **9.** $a^2 - 3$
11. $a^3 - 4a^2 + 3a$ **13.** $\{(-3, 3), (2, 6)\}, \{-3, 2\}$
15. $\{(-3, -1), (2, -6)\}, \{-3, 2\}$ **17.** $\{(-3, 2), (2, 0)\}, \{-3, 2\}$
19. $\{(-3, 2)\}, \{-3\}$ **21.** $(f + g)(x) = \sqrt{x} + x - 4, [0, \infty)$
23. $(f - h)(x) = \sqrt{x} - \dfrac{1}{x - 2}, [0, 2) \cup (2, \infty)$
25. $(g \cdot h)(x) = \dfrac{x - 4}{x - 2}, (-\infty, 2) \cup (2, \infty)$
27. $(g/f)(x) = \dfrac{x - 4}{\sqrt{x}}, (0, \infty)$ **29.** $\{(-3, 0), (1, 0), (4, 4)\}$
31. $\{(1, 4)\}$ **33.** $\{(-3, 4), (1, 4)\}$ **35.** 5 **37.** 5
39. 59.816 **41.** 5 **43.** 5 **45.** a **47.** $3t^2 + 2$
49. $(f \circ g)(x) = \sqrt{x} - 2, [0, \infty)$
51. $(f \circ h)(x) = \dfrac{1}{x} - 2, (-\infty, 0) \cup (0, \infty)$
53. $(h \circ g)(x) = \dfrac{1}{\sqrt{x}}, (0, \infty)$ **55.** $(f \circ f)(x) = x - 4, (-\infty, \infty)$
57. $(h \circ g \circ f)(x) = \dfrac{1}{\sqrt{x - 2}}, (2, \infty)$
59. $(h \circ f \circ g)(x) = \dfrac{1}{\sqrt{x} - 2}, (0, 4) \cup (4, \infty)$
61. $F = g \circ h$ **63.** $H = h \circ g$ **65.** $N = h \circ g \circ f$
67. $P = g \circ f \circ g$ **69.** $S = g \circ g$ **71.** $y = 6x - 1$
73. $y = x^2 + 6x + 7$ **75.** $y = x$ **77.** $[-1, \infty), [-7, \infty)$
79. $[1, \infty), [0, \infty)$ **81.** $[0, \infty), [4, \infty)$
83. $P(x) = 28x - 200, x \geq 8$ **85.** $A = d^2/2$ **87.** $T(x) = 1.26x$
89. $D = \dfrac{1.16 \times 10^7}{L^3}$ **91.** $W = \dfrac{(8 + \pi)s^2}{8}$

Section 1.9

For Thought: **1.** F **2.** F **3.** F **4.** T **5.** F **6.** F **7.** F **8.** F **9.** F **10.** T

Exercises: **1.** Yes **3.** No **5.** No **7.** Not one-to-one
9. One-to-one **11.** Not one-to-one **13.** One-to-one
15. One-to-one **17.** Not one-to-one **19.** Not one-to-one
21. One-to-one **23.** Invertible, $\{(3, 9), (2, 2)\}$
25. Not invertible **27.** Invertible, $\{(3, 3), (2, 2), (4, 4), (7, 7)\}$
29. Not invertible **31.** Not invertible **33.** Invertible
35. Invertible **37.** $\{(1, 2), (5, 3)\}, 3, 2$
39. $\{(-3, -3), (5, 0), (-7, 2)\}, 0, 2$ **41.** Not invertible
43. Not invertible **45.** $f^{-1}(x) = \dfrac{x + 7}{3}$
47. $f^{-1}(x) = (x - 2)^2 + 3$ for $x \geq 2$ **49.** $f^{-1}(x) = -x - 9$
51. $f^{-1}(x) = \dfrac{5x + 3}{x - 1}$ **53.** $f^{-1}(x) = -\dfrac{1}{x}$
55. $f^{-1}(x) = (x - 5)^3 + 9$ **57.** $f^{-1}(x) = \sqrt{x + 2}$
59. $f(g(x)) = x, g(f(x)) = x$, yes **61.** $f(g(x)) = x, g(f(x)) = |x|$, no
63. $f(g(x)) = x, g(f(x)) = x$, yes
65. $f(g(x)) = x, g(f(x)) = x$, yes
67. The functions y_1 and y_2 are inverses. **69.** No **71.** Yes

73.

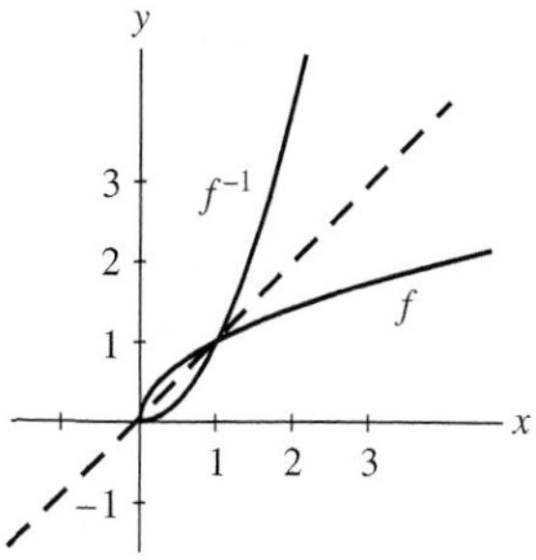

75.

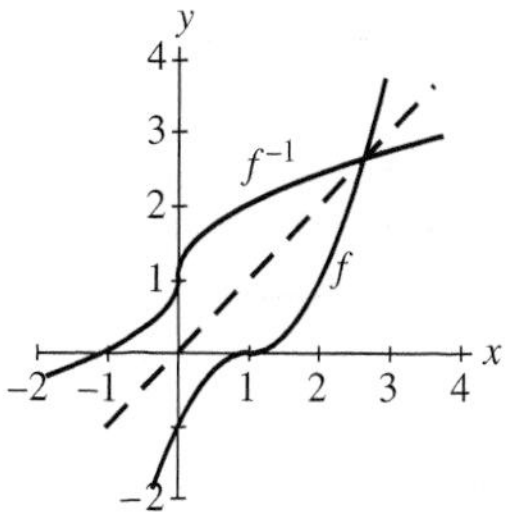

77. $f^{-1}(x) = \dfrac{x - 2}{3}$

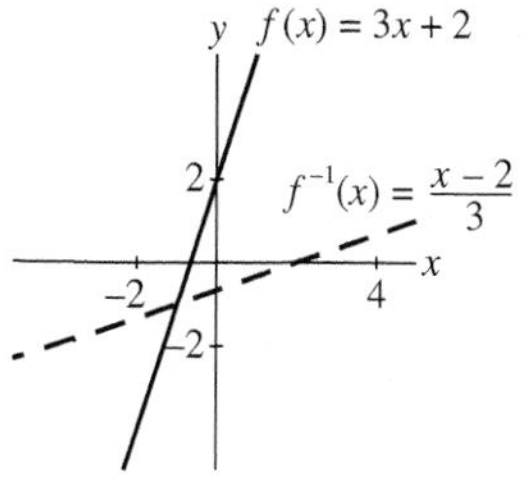

79. $f^{-1}(x) = \sqrt{x + 4}$

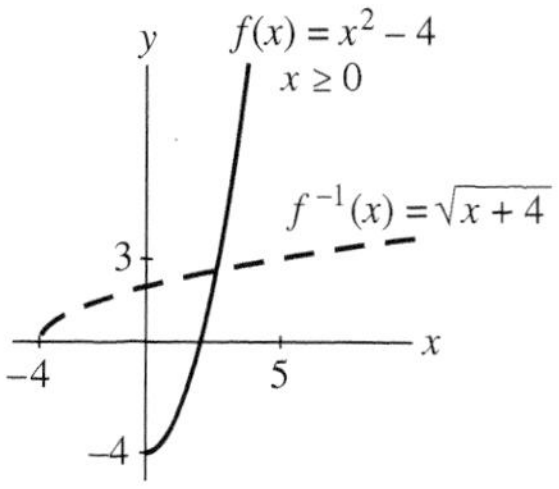

81. $f^{-1}(x) = \sqrt[3]{x}$

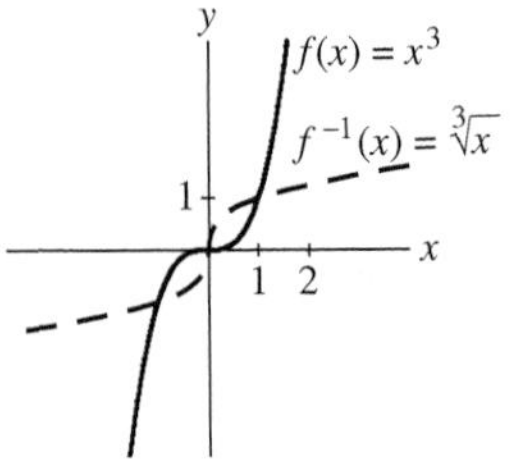

83. $f^{-1}(x) = (x + 3)^2$ for $x \geq -3$

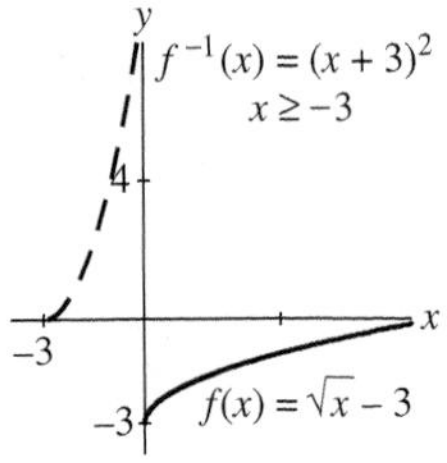

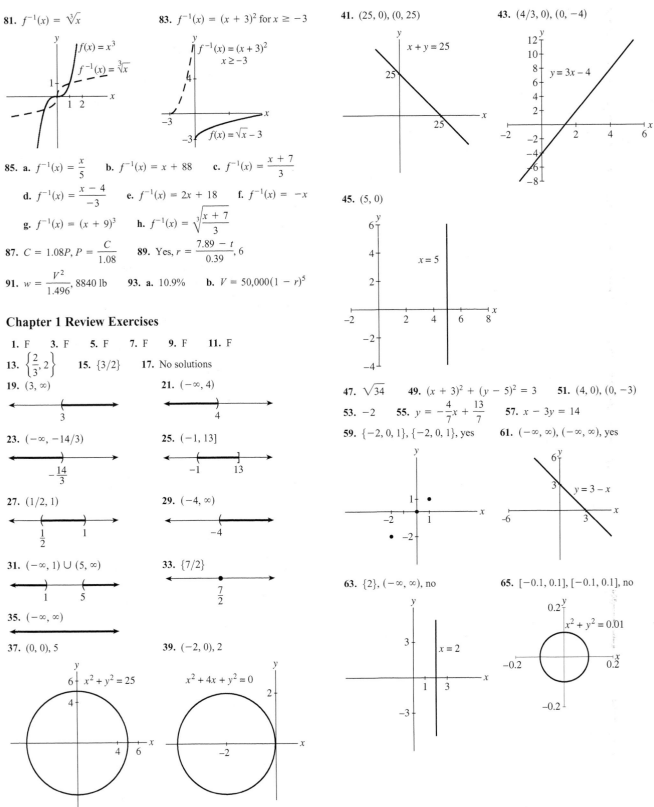

85. **a.** $f^{-1}(x) = \dfrac{x}{5}$ **b.** $f^{-1}(x) = x + 88$ **c.** $f^{-1}(x) = \dfrac{x + 7}{3}$

d. $f^{-1}(x) = \dfrac{x - 4}{-3}$ **e.** $f^{-1}(x) = 2x + 18$ **f.** $f^{-1}(x) = -x$

g. $f^{-1}(x) = (x + 9)^3$ **h.** $f^{-1}(x) = \sqrt[3]{\dfrac{x + 7}{3}}$

87. $C = 1.08P$, $P = \dfrac{C}{1.08}$ **89.** Yes, $r = \dfrac{7.89 - t}{0.39}$, 6

91. $w = \dfrac{V^2}{1.496}$, 8840 lb **93.** **a.** 10.9% **b.** $V = 50{,}000(1 - r)^5$

Chapter 1 Review Exercises

1. F **3.** F **5.** F **7.** F **9.** F **11.** F

13. $\left\{\dfrac{2}{3}, 2\right\}$ **15.** $\{3/2\}$ **17.** No solutions

19. $(3, \infty)$

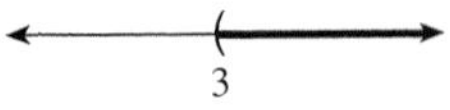

21. $(-\infty, 4)$

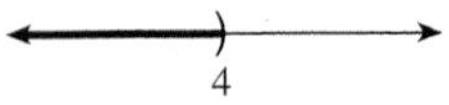

23. $(-\infty, -14/3)$

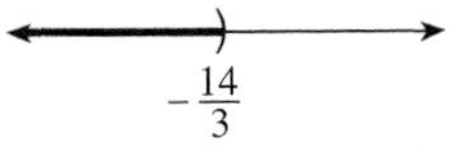

25. $(-1, 13]$

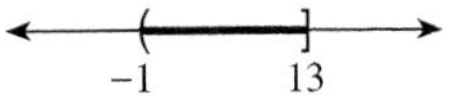

27. $(1/2, 1)$

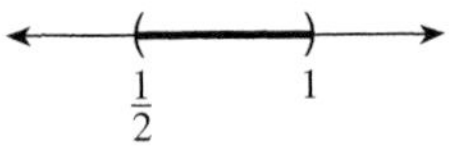

29. $(-4, \infty)$

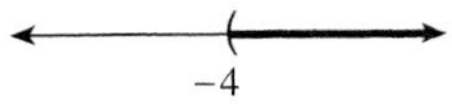

31. $(-\infty, 1) \cup (5, \infty)$

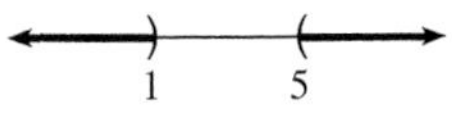

33. $\{7/2\}$

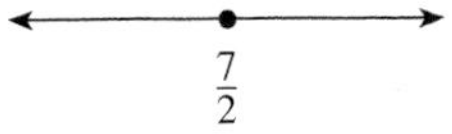

35. $(-\infty, \infty)$

37. (0, 0), 5

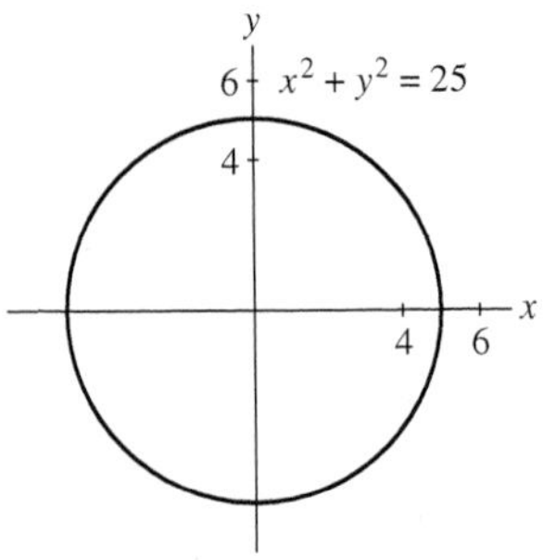

39. (−2, 0), 2

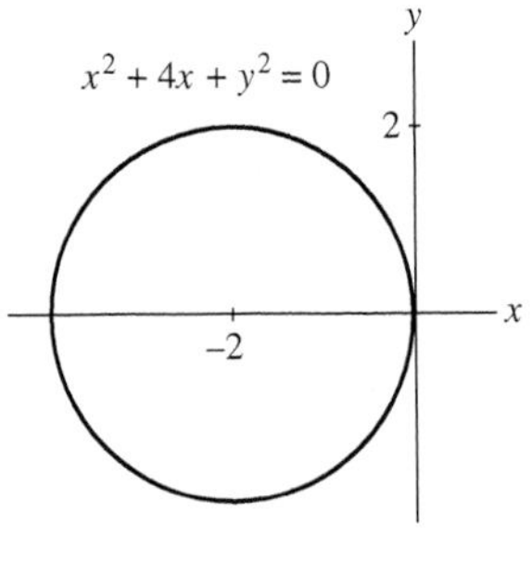

41. (25, 0), (0, 25)

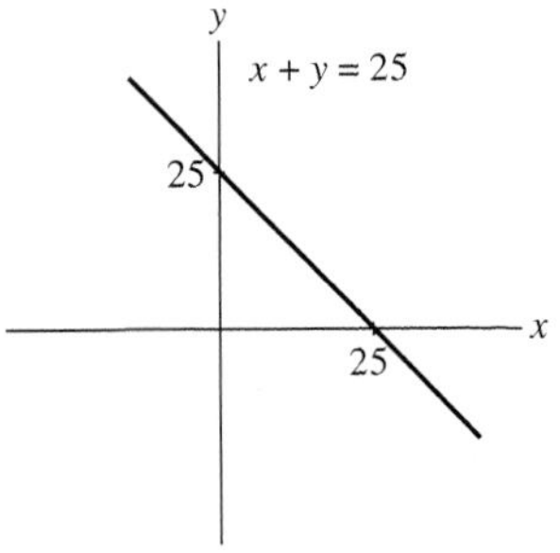

43. (4/3, 0), (0, −4)

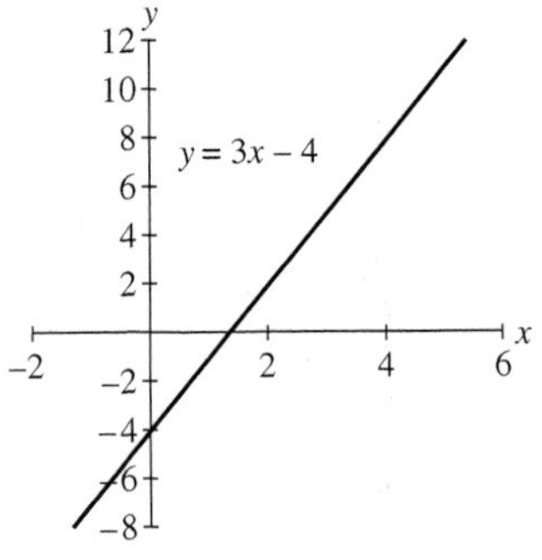

45. (5, 0)

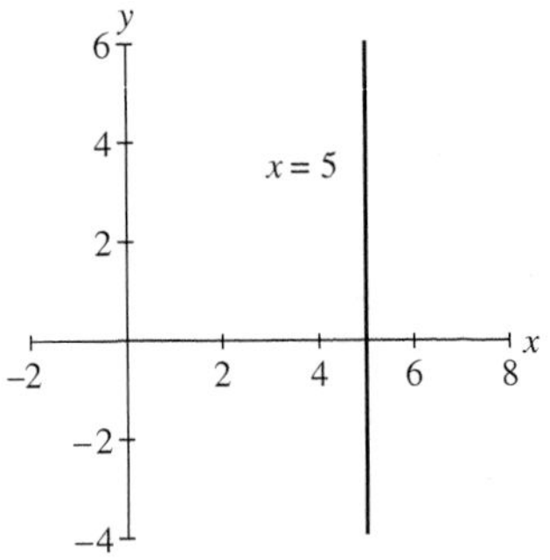

47. $\sqrt{34}$ **49.** $(x + 3)^2 + (y - 5)^2 = 3$ **51.** (4, 0), (0, −3)

53. −2 **55.** $y = -\dfrac{4}{7}x + \dfrac{13}{7}$ **57.** $x - 3y = 14$

59. {−2, 0, 1}, {−2, 0, 1}, yes

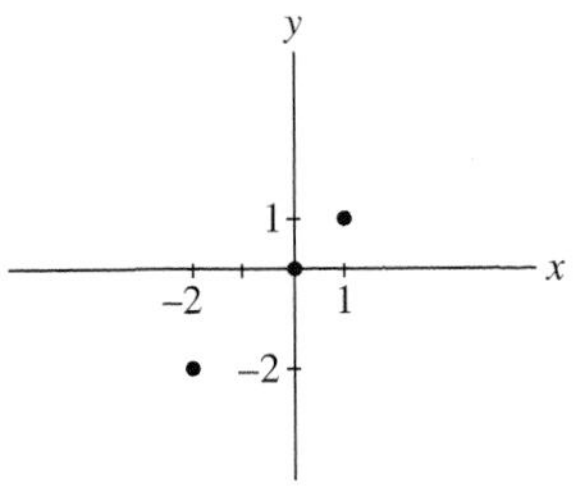

61. $(-\infty, \infty)$, $(-\infty, \infty)$, yes

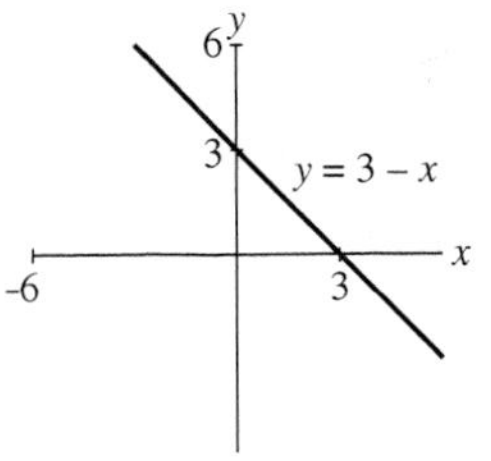

63. {2}, $(-\infty, \infty)$, no

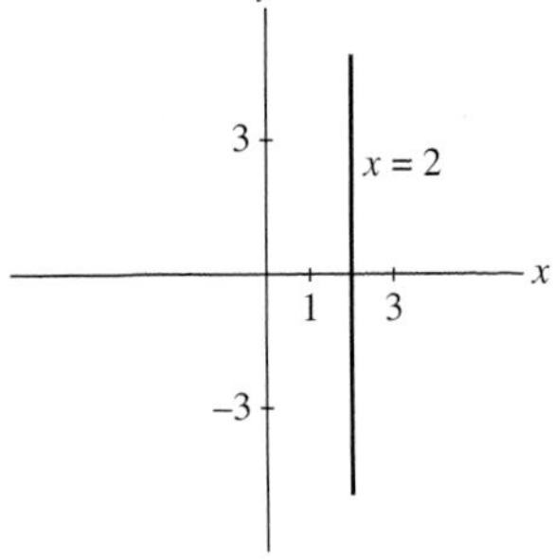

65. [−0.1, 0.1], [−0.1, 0.1], no

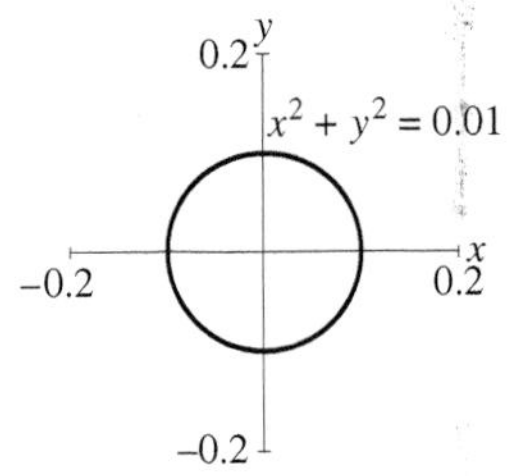

67. $[1, \infty), (-\infty, \infty)$, no

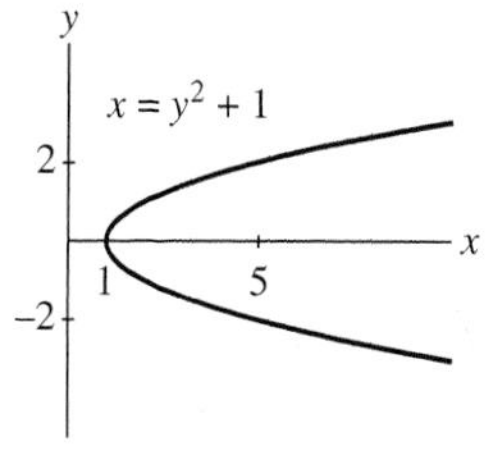

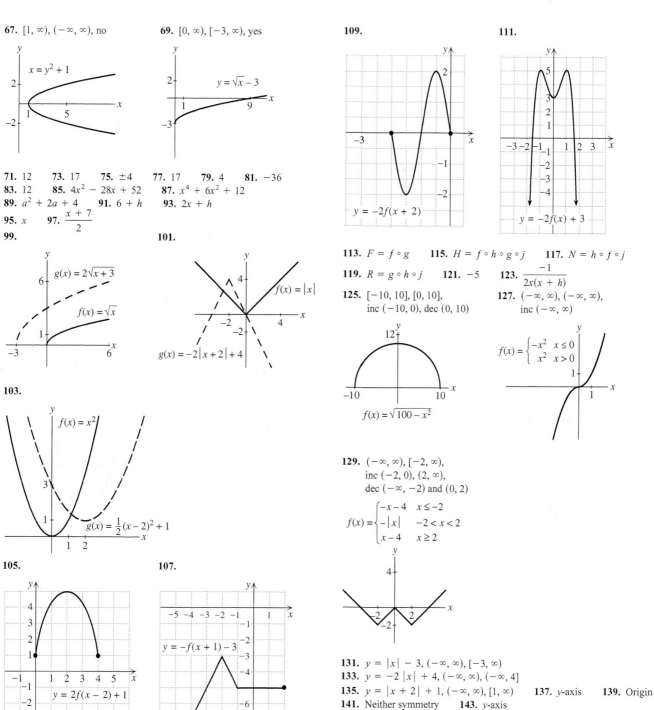

69. $[0, \infty), [-3, \infty)$, yes

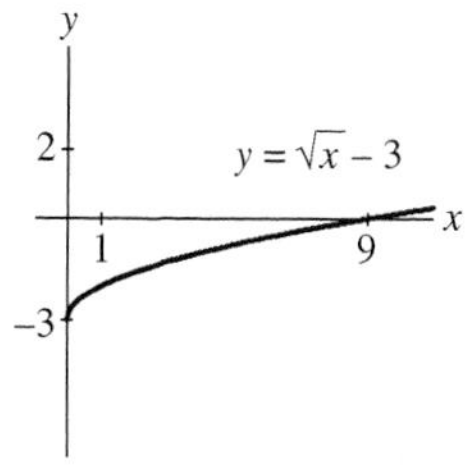

71. 12 **73.** 17 **75.** ± 4 **77.** 17 **79.** 4 **81.** -36
83. 12 **85.** $4x^2 - 28x + 52$ **87.** $x^4 + 6x^2 + 12$
89. $a^2 + 2a + 4$ **91.** $6 + h$ **93.** $2x + h$
95. x **97.** $\dfrac{x + 7}{2}$

99.

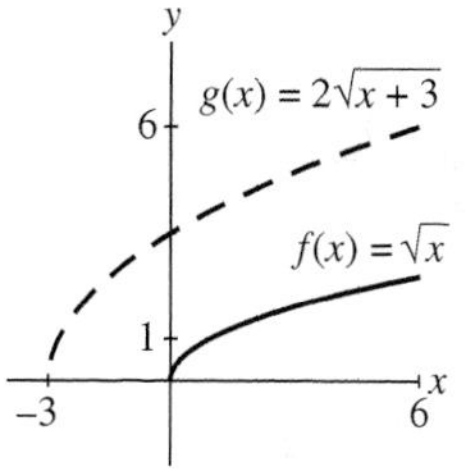

101.

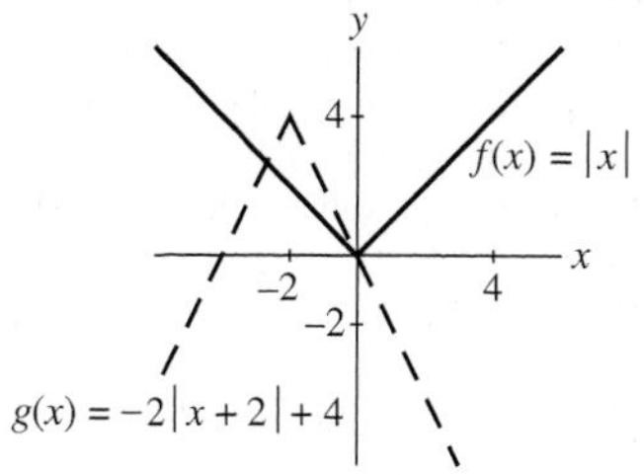

103.

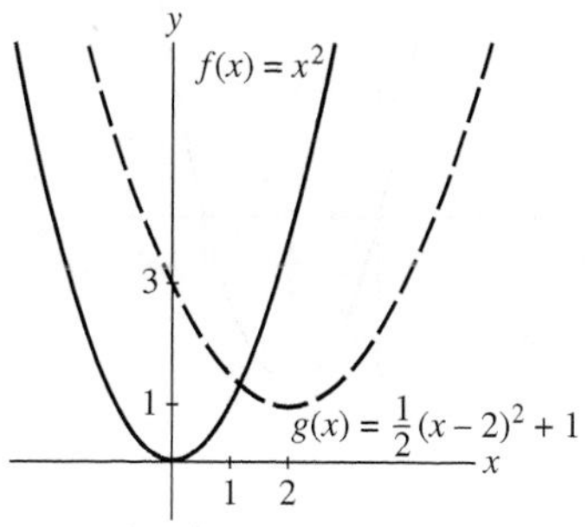

105.

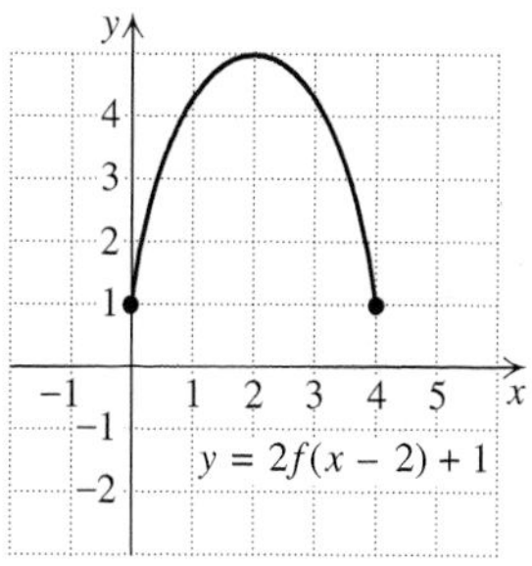

107.

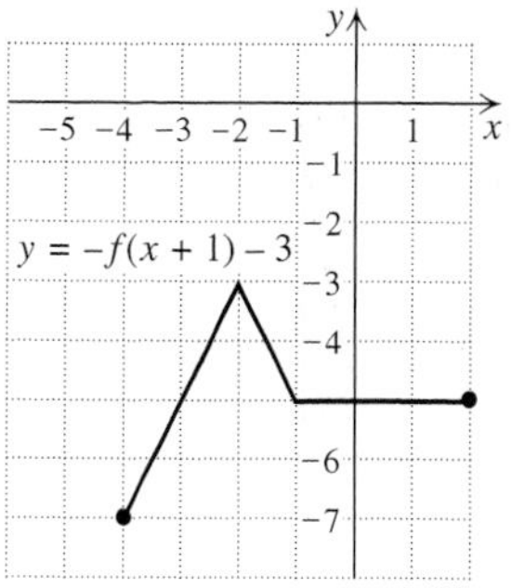

109.

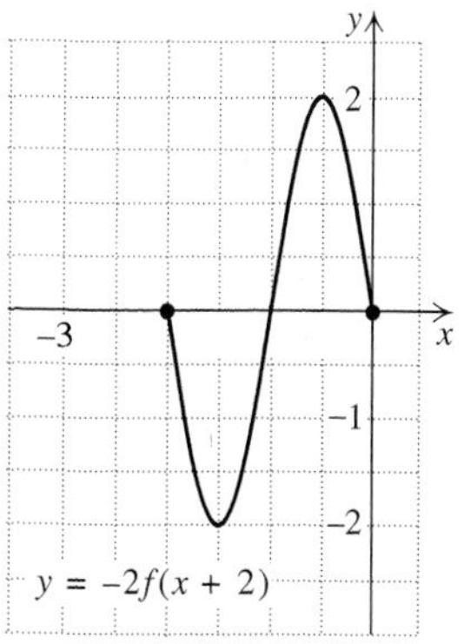

111.

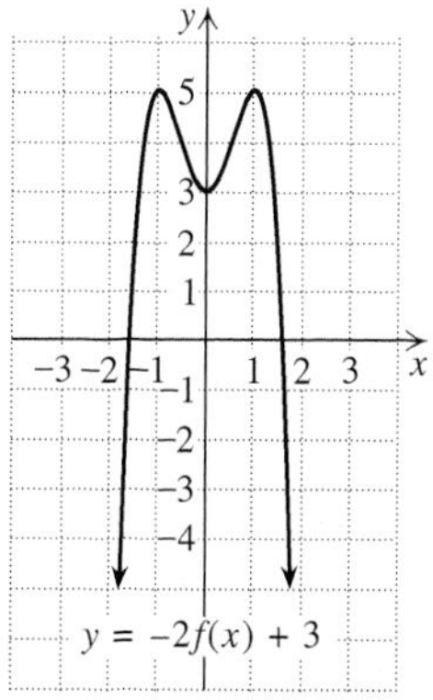

113. $F = f \circ g$ **115.** $H = f \circ h \circ g \circ j$ **117.** $N = h \circ f \circ j$

119. $R = g \circ h \circ j$ **121.** -5 **123.** $\dfrac{-1}{2x(x + h)}$

125. $[-10, 10], [0, 10]$,
inc $(-10, 0)$, dec $(0, 10)$

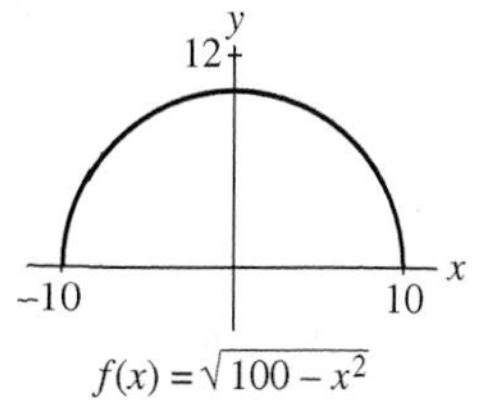

127. $(-\infty, \infty), (-\infty, \infty)$,
inc $(-\infty, \infty)$

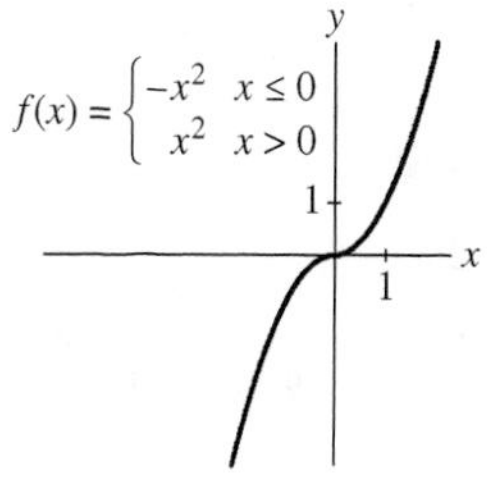

129. $(-\infty, \infty), [-2, \infty)$,
inc $(-2, 0), (2, \infty)$,
dec $(-\infty, -2)$ and $(0, 2)$

$$f(x) = \begin{cases} -x - 4 & x \le -2 \\ -|x| & -2 < x < 2 \\ x - 4 & x \ge 2 \end{cases}$$

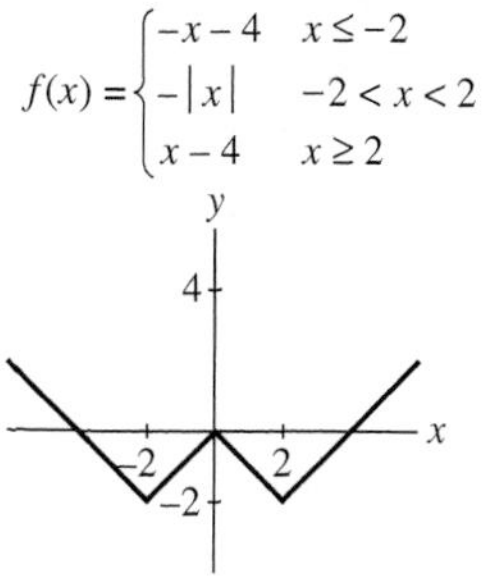

131. $y = |x| - 3, (-\infty, \infty), [-3, \infty)$
133. $y = -2|x| + 4, (-\infty, \infty), (-\infty, 4]$
135. $y = |x + 2| + 1, (-\infty, \infty), [1, \infty)$ **137.** y-axis **139.** Origin
141. Neither symmetry **143.** y-axis

145. Inverse functions

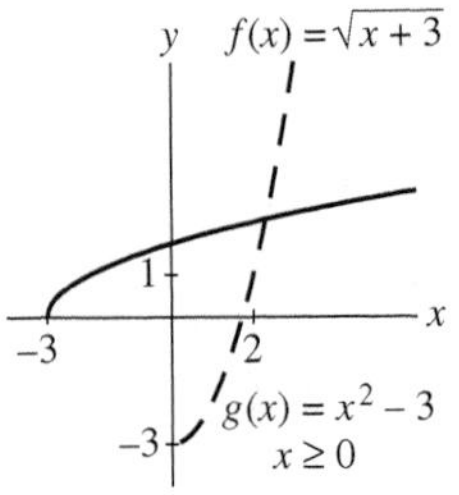

147. Inverse functions

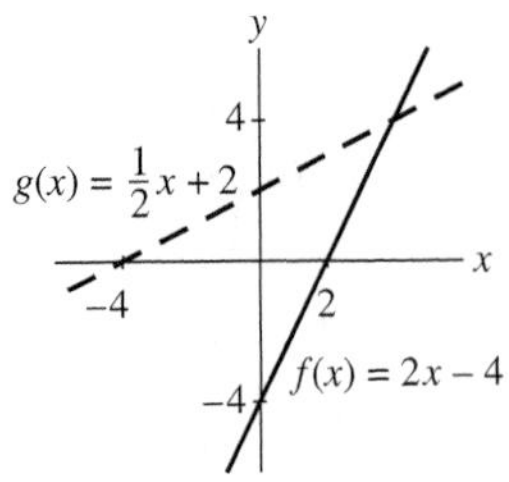

149. Not invertible **151.** $f^{-1}(x) = \dfrac{x + 21}{3}$, $(-\infty, \infty)$, $(-\infty, \infty)$

153. Not invertible **155.** $f^{-1}(x) = x^2 + 9$ for $x \geq 0$, $[0, \infty)$, $[9, \infty)$

157. $f^{-1}(x) = \dfrac{5x + 7}{1 - x}$, $(-\infty, 1) \cup (1, \infty)$, $(-\infty, -5) \cup (-5, \infty)$

159. $f^{-1}(x) = -\sqrt{x - 1}$, $[1, \infty)$, $(-\infty, 0]$

161. $C(x) = 1.20x + 40$, $R(x) = 2x$, $P(x) = 0.80x - 40$ where x is the number of roses, 51 or more roses

163. $t = \dfrac{\sqrt{64 - h}}{4}$, domain $[0, 64]$ **165.** $d = 2\sqrt{A/\pi}$

167. 0.5 in./lb

Chapter 2

Section 2.1

For Thought: **1.** F **2.** F **3.** T **4.** T **5.** T **6.** T **7.** T **8.** T **9.** T **10.** F

Exercises:

1. $y = (x + 2)^2 - 4$

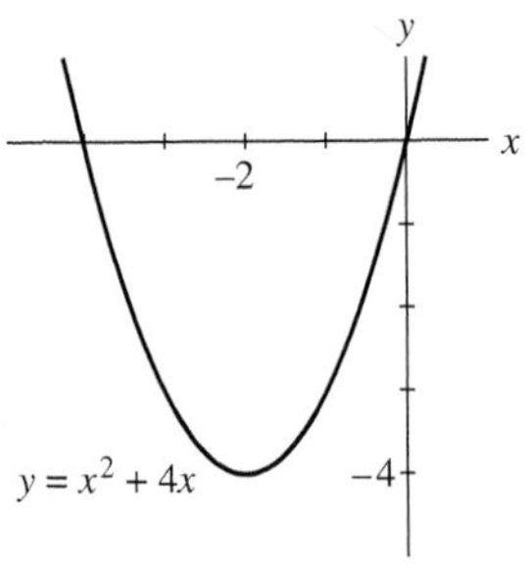

3. $y = \left(x - \dfrac{3}{2}\right)^2 - \dfrac{9}{4}$

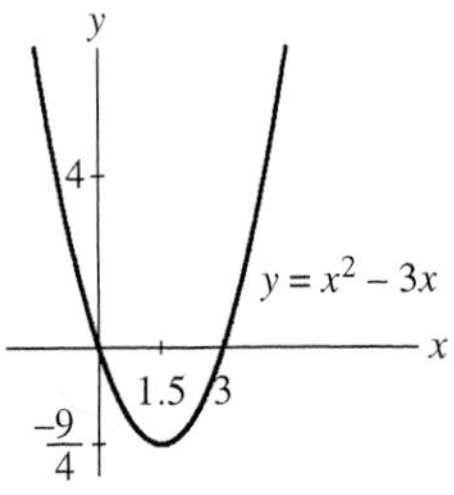

5. $y = 2(x - 3)^2 + 4$

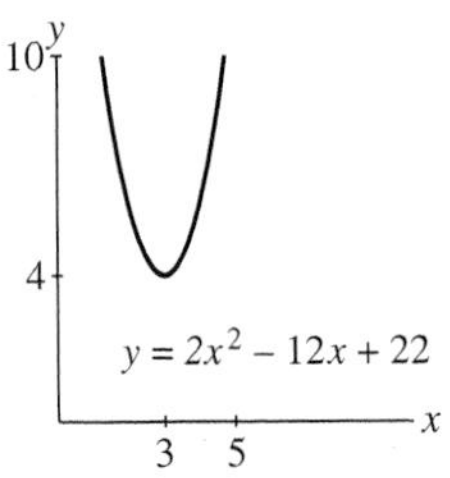

7. $y = -3(x - 1)^2$

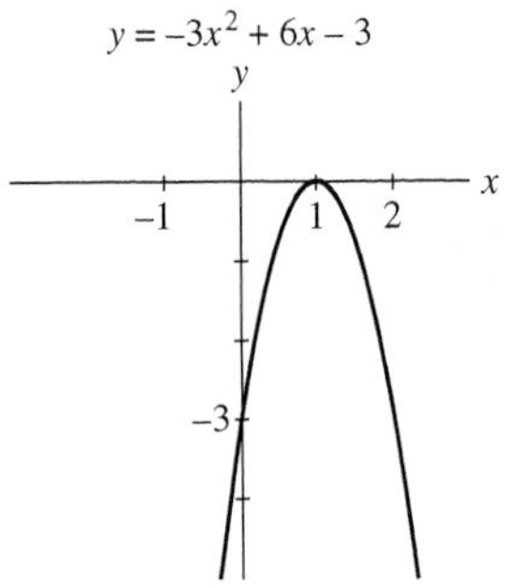

9. $y = \left(x + \dfrac{3}{2}\right)^2 + \dfrac{1}{4}$

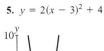

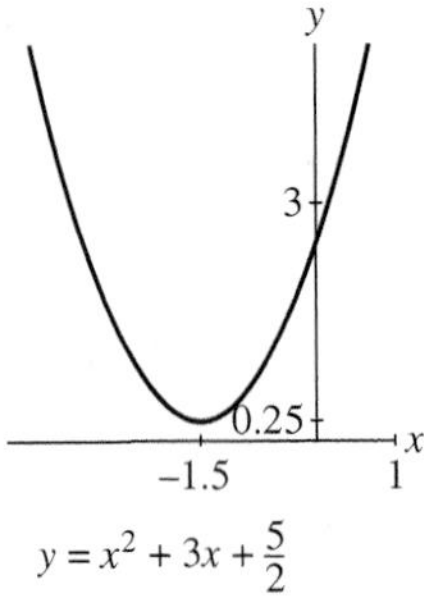

11. $y = -2\left(x - \dfrac{3}{4}\right)^2 + \dfrac{1}{8}$

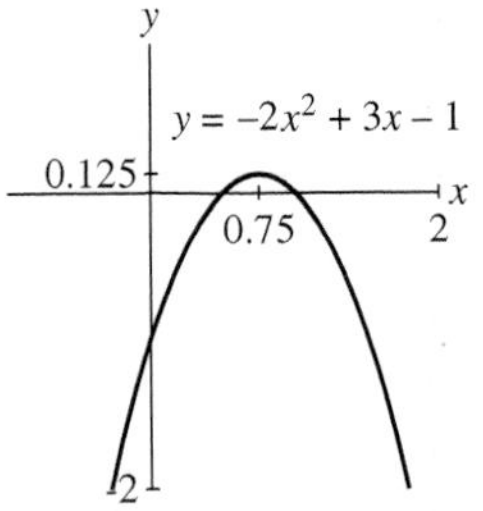

13. $(2, -11)$ **15.** $(4, 1)$ **17.** $(-1/3, 1/18)$

19. Up, $(1, -4)$, $x = 1$, $[-4, \infty)$, min -4, dec $(-\infty, 1)$, inc $(1, \infty)$

21. $(-\infty, 3]$, max 3, inc $(-\infty, 0)$, dec $(0, \infty)$

23. $[-1, \infty)$, min -1, dec $(-\infty, 1)$, inc $(1, \infty)$

25. $[-18, \infty)$, min value -18, dec $(-\infty, -4)$, inc $(-4, \infty)$

27. $[4, \infty)$, min value 4, dec $(-\infty, 3)$, inc $(3, \infty)$

29. $(-\infty, 27/2]$, max $27/2$, inc $(-\infty, 3/2)$, dec $(3/2, \infty)$

31. $(-\infty, 9]$, max 9, inc $(-\infty, 1/2)$, dec $(1/2, \infty)$

33. $(0, -3)$, $x = 0$, $(0, -3)$, $(\pm\sqrt{3}, 0)$, up

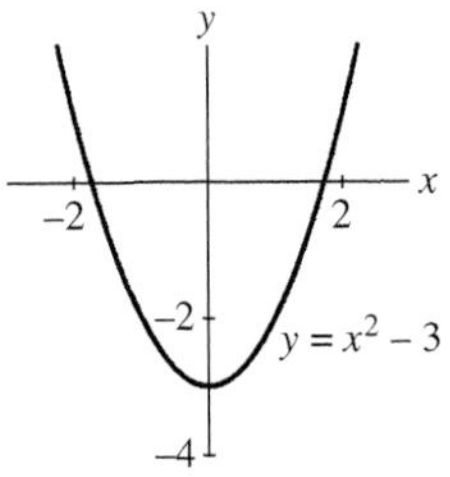

35. $\left(\dfrac{1}{2}, -\dfrac{1}{4}\right)$, $x = \dfrac{1}{2}$, $(0, 0)$, $(1, 0)$, up

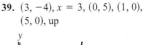

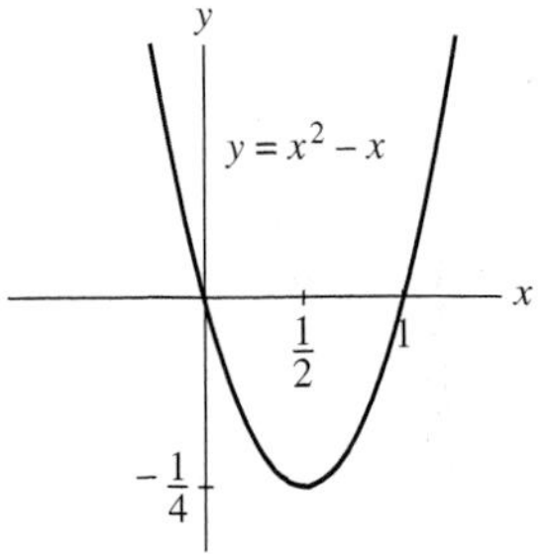

37. $(-3, 0)$, $x = -3$, $(0, 9)$, $(-3, 0)$, up

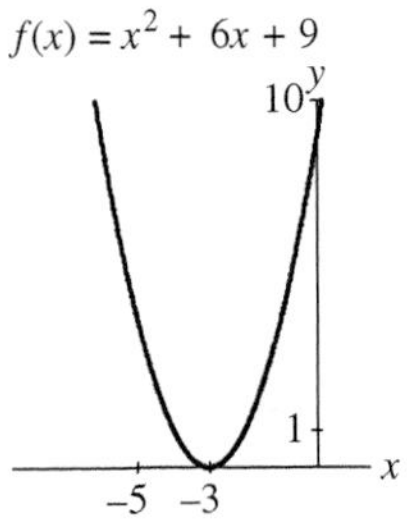

39. $(3, -4)$, $x = 3$, $(0, 5)$, $(1, 0)$, $(5, 0)$, up

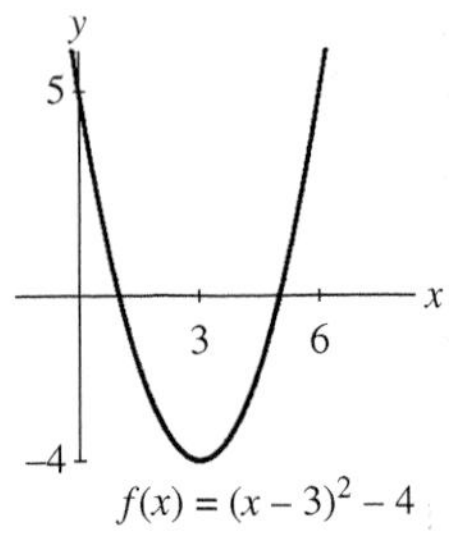

41. $(2, 12), x = 2, (0, 0), (4, 0)$, down

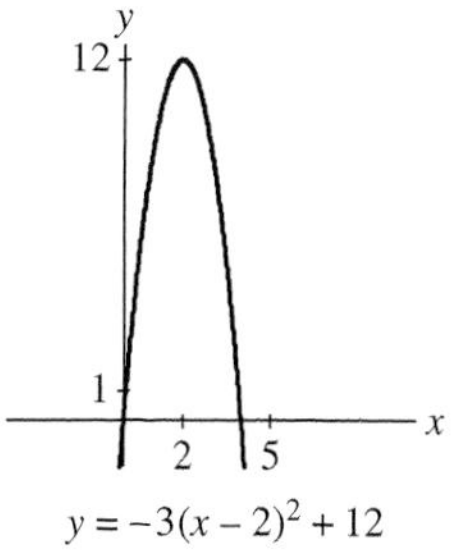

43. $(1, 3), x = 1, (0, 1), \left(1 \pm \frac{\sqrt{6}}{2}, 0\right)$, down

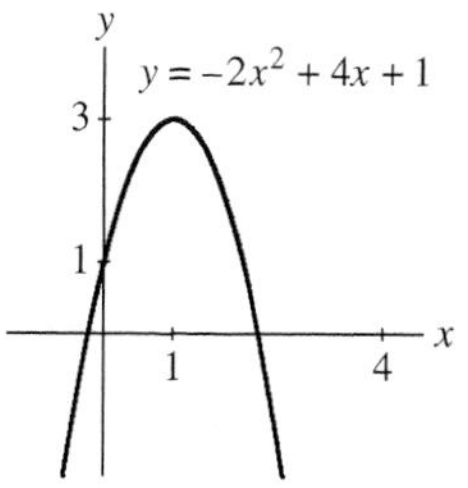

45. $(-1, 3/2)$

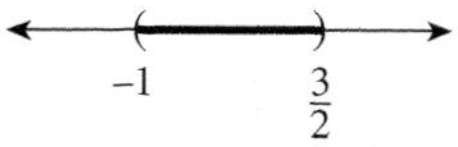

47. $(-\infty, -3) \cup (5, \infty)$

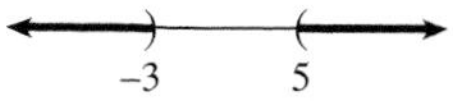

49. $(-\infty, -2] \cup [6, \infty)$

51. $[-4, 4]$

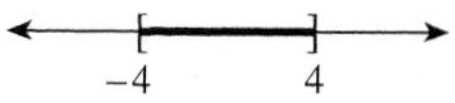

53. $\{-3\}$

55. $(-\infty, 3/2) \cup (3/2, \infty)$

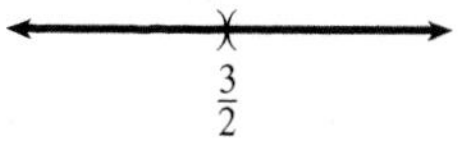

57. $(2 - \sqrt{2}, 2 + \sqrt{2})$

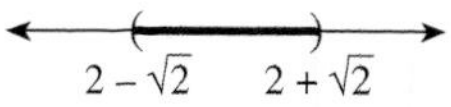

59. $(-\infty, -\sqrt{10}) \cup (\sqrt{10}, \infty)$

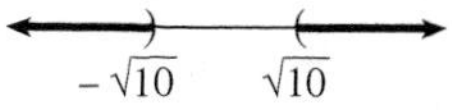

61. $(-\infty, 5 - \sqrt{7}) \cup (5 + \sqrt{7}, \infty)$

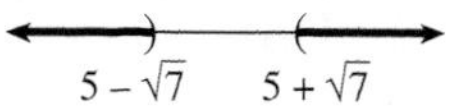

63. $(-\infty, \infty)$

65. No solution

67. $(-\infty, \infty)$

69. $(-\infty, -1] \cup [3, \infty)$ **71.** $(-3, 1)$ **73.** $[-3, 1]$

75. a. $\{-2, 5\}$ **b.** $\{0, 3\}$ **c.** $(-\infty, -2) \cup (5, \infty)$ **d.** $[-2, 5]$

e. $f(x) = \left(x - \frac{3}{2}\right)^2 - \frac{49}{4}$, Move $y = x^2$ to the right $\frac{3}{2}$ and down $\frac{49}{4}$ to obtain f.

f. $(-\infty, \infty), \left[-\frac{49}{4}, \infty\right)$, minimum $-\frac{49}{4}$

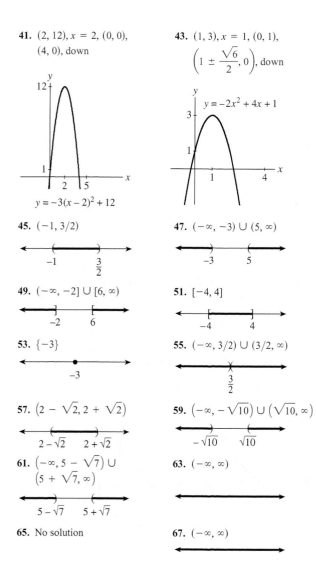

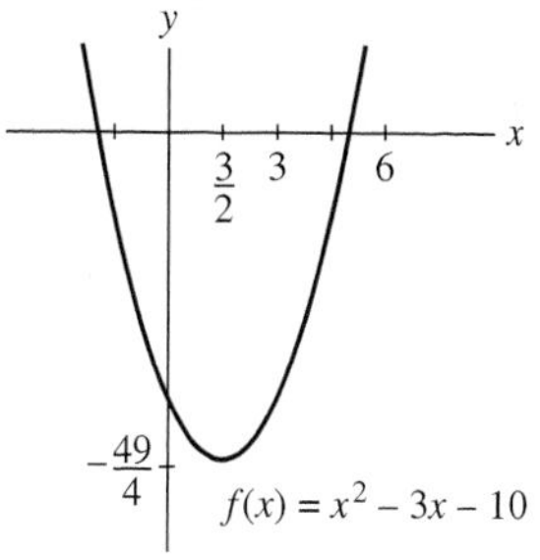

g. The graph of f is above the x-axis when x is in $(-\infty, -2) \cup (5, \infty)$ and on or below the x-axis when x is in $[-2, 5]$.

h. $(-2, 0), (5, 0), (0, -10), x = \frac{3}{2}, \left(\frac{3}{2}, -\frac{49}{4}\right)$, opens upward, dec on $\left(-\infty, \frac{3}{2}\right)$ and inc on $\left(\frac{3}{2}, \infty\right)$

77. 261 ft **79. a.** 408 ft **b.** $(10 + \sqrt{102})/2 \approx 10.05$ sec
81. 50 yd by 50 yd **83.** 20 ft by 30 ft **85.** 7.5 ft by 15 ft
87. a. $p = 50 - n$ **b.** $R = 50n - n^2$ **c.** \$625

Section 2.2

For Thought: **1.** T **2.** T **3.** F **4.** T **5.** F **6.** F **7.** T **8.** T **9.** T **10.** F

Exercises: **1.** Imaginary, $0 + 6i$ **3.** Imaginary, $\frac{1}{3} + \frac{1}{3}i$
5. Real, $\sqrt{7} + 0i$ **7.** Real, $\frac{\pi}{2} + 0i$ **9.** $7 + 2i$ **11.** $-2 - 3i$
13. $-12 - 18i$ **15.** 26 **17.** 29 **19.** 4 **21.** $-7 + 24i$
23. $1 - 4i\sqrt{5}$ **25.** i **27.** -1 **29.** 1 **31.** $-i$ **33.** 90
35. $17/4$ **37.** 1 **39.** 12 **41.** $\frac{2}{5} + \frac{1}{5}i$ **43.** $\frac{3}{2} - \frac{3}{2}i$
45. $-1 + 3i$ **47.** $3 + 3i$ **49.** $\frac{1}{13} - \frac{5}{13}i$ **51.** $-i$
53. $-4 + 2i$ **55.** -6 **57.** -10 **59.** $-1 + i\sqrt{5}$
61. $-3 + i\sqrt{11}$ **63.** $-4 + 8i$ **65.** $-1 + 2i$
67. $\frac{-2 + i\sqrt{2}}{2}$ **69.** $-3 - 2i\sqrt{2}$ **71.** $\frac{3 + \sqrt{21}}{2}$ **73.** $\{\pm i\}$
75. $\{\pm 2i\sqrt{2}\}$ **77.** $\left\{\pm\frac{i\sqrt{2}}{2}\right\}$ **79.** $\{1 \pm i\}$ **81.** $\{2 \pm 3i\}$
83. $\{1 \pm i\sqrt{3}\}$ **85.** $\left\{\frac{1}{2} \pm \frac{3}{2}i\right\}$ **87.** $\left\{1 \pm \frac{\sqrt{3}}{2}i\right\}$

Section 2.3

For Thought: **1.** F **2.** T **3.** T **4.** T **5.** F **6.** F **7.** F **8.** T **9.** T **10.** F

Exercises: **1.** $x - 3, 1$ **3.** $-2x^2 + 6x - 14, 33$ **5.** $s^2 + 2, 16$
7. $x + 6, 13$ **9.** $-x^2 + 4x - 16, 57$ **11.** $4x^2 + 2x - 4, 0$
13. $2a^2 - 4a + 6, 0$ **15.** $x^3 + x^2 + x + 1, -2$
17. $x^4 + 2x^3 - 2x^2 - 4x - 4, -13$ **19.** 0 **21.** -33
23. 5 **25.** $\frac{55}{8}$ **27.** 0 **29.** 8 **31.** $(x + 3)(x + 2)(x - 1)$
33. $(x - 4)(x + 3)(x + 5)$ **35.** Yes **37.** No **39.** Yes
41. No **43.** $\pm(1, 2, 3, 4, 6, 8, 12, 24)$ **45.** $\pm(1, 3, 5, 15)$
47. $\pm\left(1, 3, 5, 15, \frac{1}{2}, \frac{1}{4}, \frac{1}{8}, \frac{3}{2}, \frac{3}{4}, \frac{3}{8}, \frac{5}{2}, \frac{5}{4}, \frac{5}{8}, \frac{15}{2}, \frac{15}{4}, \frac{15}{8}\right)$
49. $\pm\left(1, 2, \frac{1}{2}, \frac{1}{3}, \frac{2}{3}, \frac{1}{6}, \frac{1}{9}, \frac{2}{9}, \frac{1}{18}\right)$ **51.** 2, 3, 4
53. $-3, 2 \pm i$ **55.** $\frac{1}{2}, \frac{3}{2}, \frac{5}{2}$ **57.** $\frac{1}{2}, \frac{1 \pm i}{3}$ **59.** $\pm i, 1, -2$
61. $-1, \pm\sqrt{2}$ **63.** $\frac{1}{4}, \frac{1}{3}, \frac{1}{2}$ **65.** $\frac{1}{16}, 1 \pm 2i$ **67.** $-\frac{6}{7}, \frac{7}{3}, \pm i$
69. $-5, -2, 1, \pm 3i$ **71.** $1, 3, 5, 2 \pm \sqrt{3}$ **73.** $2 + \frac{5}{x - 2}$
75. $a + \frac{5}{a - 3}$ **77.** $1 + \frac{-3c}{c^2 - 4}$ **79.** $2 + \frac{-7}{2t + 1}$
81. a. 6 hr **b.** $\approx$120 ppm **c.** $\approx$3 hr **d.** $\approx$4 hr
83. 5 in. by 9 in. by 14 in.

Section 2.4

For Thought: **1.** F **2.** T **3.** T **4.** F **5.** F **6.** T **7.** F **8.** F **9.** T **10.** T

Exercises: **1.** Degree 2, 5 with multiplicity 2 **3.** Degree 5, ± 3, 0 with multiplicity 3 **5.** Degree 4, 0, 1 each with multiplicity 2 **7.** Degree 4, $-\frac{4}{3}, \frac{3}{2}$ each with multiplicity 2 **9.** Degree 3, 0, $2 \pm \sqrt{10}$ **11.** $x^2 + 9$ **13.** $x^2 - 2x - 1$ **15.** $x^2 - 6x + 13$ **17.** $x^3 - 8x^2 + 37x - 50$ **19.** $x^2 - 2x - 15 = 0$ **21.** $x^2 + 16 = 0$ **23.** $x^2 - 6x + 10 = 0$ **25.** $x^3 + 2x^2 + x + 2 = 0$ **27.** $x^3 + 3x = 0$ **29.** $x^3 - 5x^2 + 8x - 6 = 0$ **31.** $x^3 - 6x^2 + 11x - 6 = 0$ **33.** $x^3 - 5x^2 + 17x - 13 = 0$ **35.** $24x^3 - 26x^2 + 9x - 1 = 0$ **37.** $x^4 - 2x^3 + 3x^2 - 2x + 2 = 0$ **39.** 3 neg; 1 neg, 2 imag **41.** 1 pos, 2 neg; 1 pos, 2 imag **43.** 4 imag **45.** 4 pos; 2 pos, 2 imag; 4 imag **47.** 4 imag and 0 **49.** $-2, 1, 5$ **51.** $-3, \frac{3 \pm \sqrt{13}}{2}$ **53.** $\pm i, 2, -4$ **55.** $-5, \frac{1}{3}, \frac{1}{2}$ **57.** 1, -2 each with multiplicity 2 **59.** 0, 2 with multiplicity 3 **61.** $0, 1, \pm 2, \pm i\sqrt{3}$ **63.** $-2, -1, 1/4, 1, 3/2$ **65.** 4 hr and 5 hr **67.** 3 in.

Section 2.5

For Thought: **1.** F **2.** F **3.** F **4.** F **5.** T **6.** F **7.** F **8.** T **9.** T **10.** F

Exercises: **1.** $\{\pm 2, -3\}$ **3.** $\left\{-500, \pm\frac{\sqrt{2}}{2}\right\}$ **5.** $\left\{0, \frac{15 \pm \sqrt{205}}{2}\right\}$ **7.** $\{0, \pm 2\}$ **9.** $\{\pm 2, \pm 2i\}$ **11.** $\{8\}$ **13.** $\{25\}$ **15.** $\left\{\frac{1}{4}\right\}$ **17.** $\left\{\frac{2 + \sqrt{13}}{9}\right\}$ **19.** $\{-4, 6\}$ **21.** $\{9\}$ **23.** $\{5\}$ **25.** $\{10\}$ **27.** $\{\pm 2\sqrt{2}\}$ **29.** $\left\{\pm\frac{1}{8}\right\}$ **31.** $\left\{\frac{1}{49}\right\}$ **33.** $\left\{\frac{5}{4}\right\}$ **35.** $\{\pm 3, \pm\sqrt{3}\}$ **37.** $\left\{-\frac{17}{2}, \frac{13}{2}\right\}$ **39.** $\left\{\frac{3}{20}, \frac{4}{15}\right\}$ **41.** $\{-2, -1, 5, 6\}$ **43.** $\{1, 9\}$ **45.** $\{9, 16\}$ **47.** $\{8, 125\}$ **49.** $\{\pm\sqrt{7}, \pm 1\}$ **51.** $\{0, 8\}$ **53.** $\{-3, 0, 1, 4\}$ **55.** $\{-2, 4\}$ **57.** $\left\{\frac{1}{2}\right\}$ **59.** $\{\pm 2, -1 \pm i\sqrt{3}, 1 \pm i\sqrt{3}\}$ **61.** $\{\sqrt{3}, 2\}$ **63.** $\{-2, \pm 1\}$ **65.** $\{5 \pm 9i\}$ **67.** $\left\{\frac{1 \pm 4\sqrt{2}}{3}\right\}$ **69.** $\{\pm 2\sqrt{6}, \pm\sqrt{35}\}$ **71.** $\{\pm 3, 2\}$ **73.** $\{-11\}$ **75.** $\{2\}$ **77.** 279.56 m^2 **79.** $\frac{25}{4}$ and $\frac{49}{4}$ **81.** 17,419.3 lbs **83.** $6 - \sqrt{10}$ ft **85.** 37.5 min, 38.2 min, 1.75 mi or 4.69 mi

Section 2.6

For Thought: **1.** F **2.** T **3.** T **4.** F **5.** T **6.** T **7.** F **8.** F **9.** T **10.** F

Exercises: **1.** Symmetric about y-axis **3.** Symmetric about $x = 3/2$ **5.** Neither symmetry **7.** Symmetric about origin **9.** Symmetric about $x = 5$ **11.** Symmetric about origin **13.** Does not cross at (4, 0) **15.** Crosses at (1/2, 0) **17.** Crosses at (1/4, 0) **19.** No x-intercepts **21.** Does not cross at (0, 0), crosses at (3, 0) **23.** Crosses at (1/2, 0), does not cross at (1, 0) **25.** Does not cross at $(-3, 0)$, crosses at (2, 0) **27.** $y \to \infty$ **29.** $y \to -\infty$ **31.** $y \to -\infty$ **33.** $y \to \infty$ **35.** $y \to \infty$ **37.** Neither symmetry; crosses at $(-2, 0)$; does not cross at (1, 0); $y \to \infty$ as $x \to \infty$; $y \to -\infty$ as $x \to -\infty$ **39.** Symmetric about y-axis; no x-intercepts; $y \to \infty$ as $x \to \infty$; $y \to \infty$ as $x \to -\infty$ **41.** ∞ **43.** $-\infty$ **45.** ∞ **47.** $-\infty$

49.

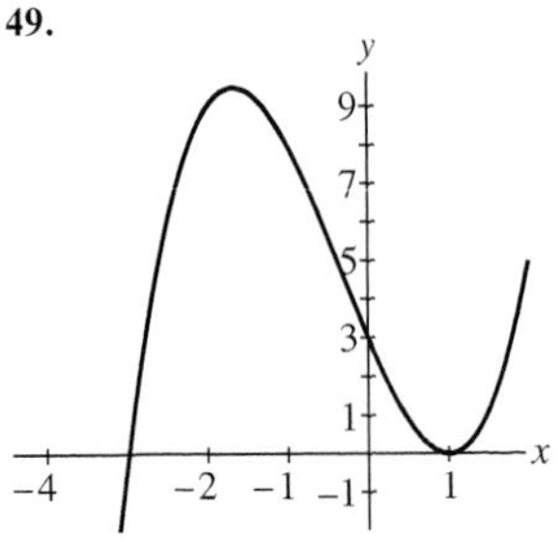

$f(x) = (x - 1)^2(x + 3)$

51.

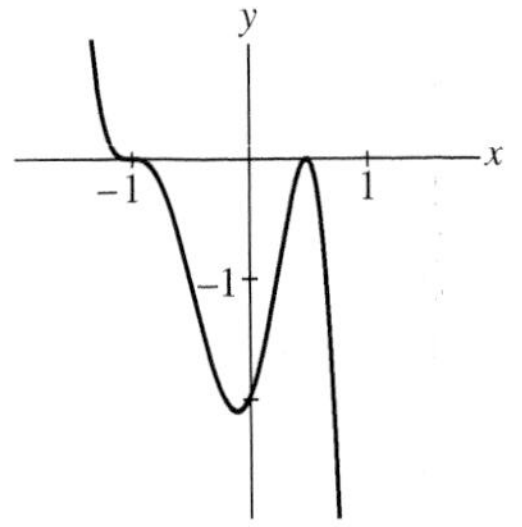

$f(x) = -2(2x - 1)^2(x + 1)^3$

53. (e) **55.** (g) **57.** (b) **59.** (c)

61.

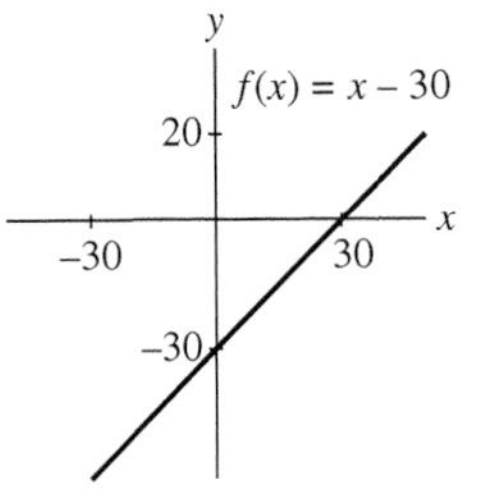

63.

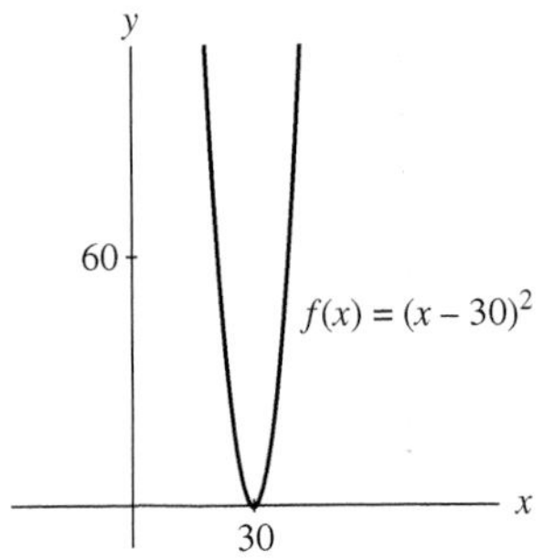

65.

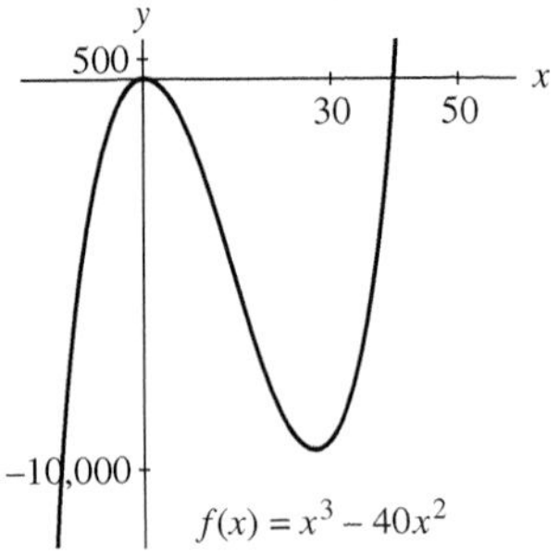

67.

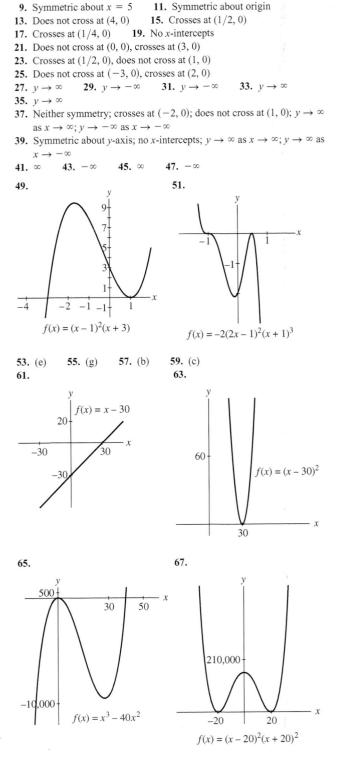

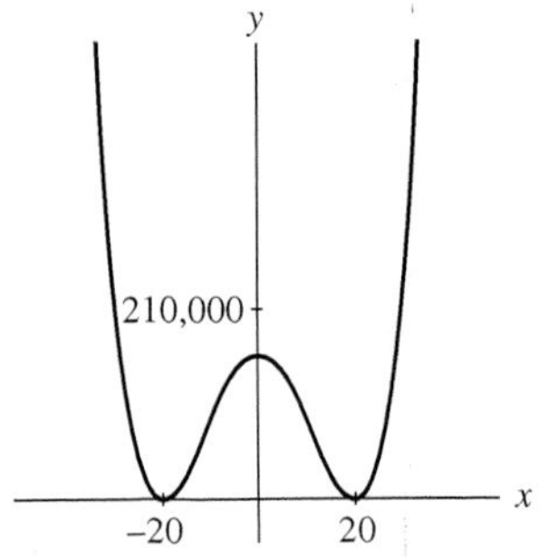

$f(x) = (x - 20)^2(x + 20)^2$

69.

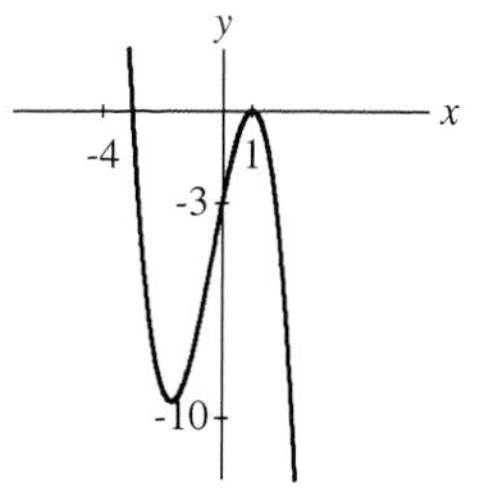

$f(x) = -x^3 - x^2 + 5x - 3$

71.

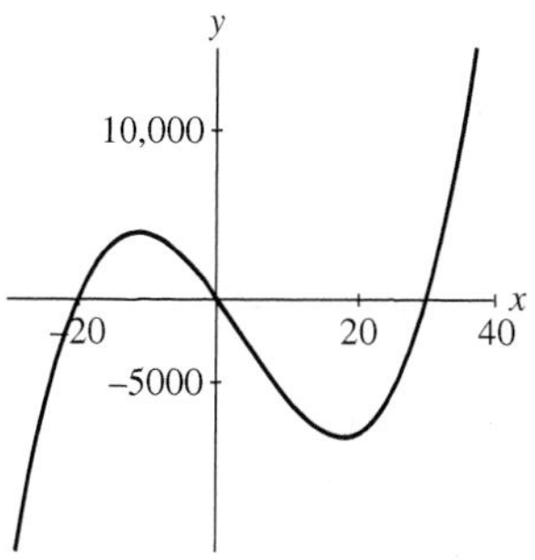

$f(x) = x^3 - 10x^2 - 600x$

73.

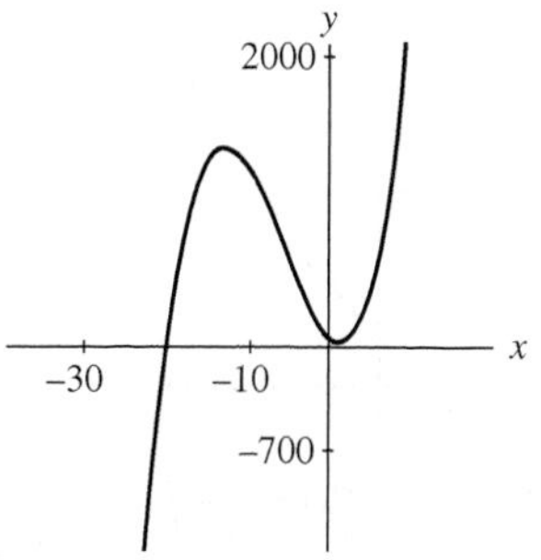

$f(x) = x^3 + 18x^2 - 37x + 60$

75.

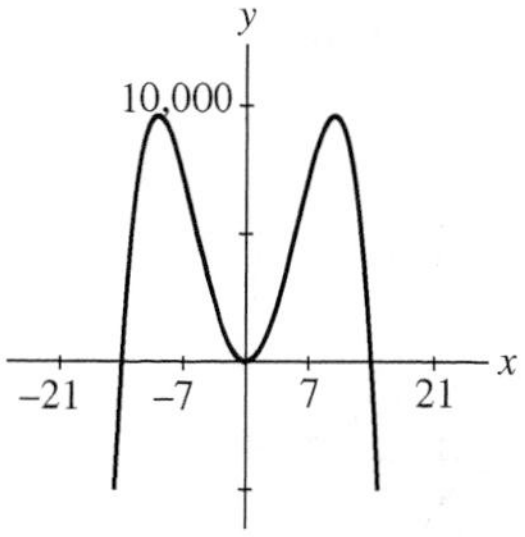

$f(x) = -x^4 + 196x^2$

77.

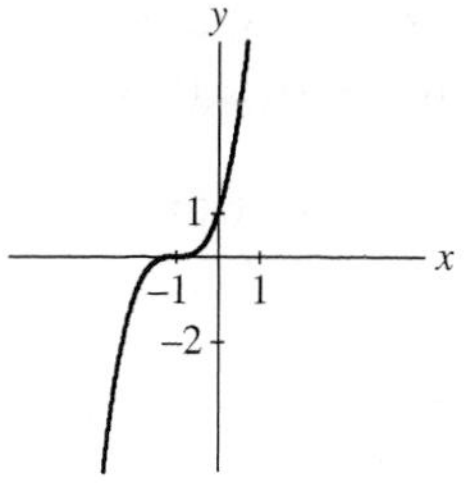

$f(x) = x^3 + 3x^2 + 3x + 1$

79.

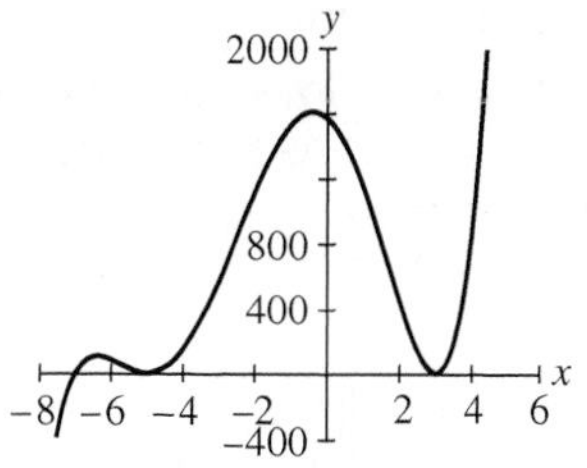

$f(x) = (x - 3)^2 (x + 5)^2 (x + 7)$

81. $(-\sqrt{3}, 0) \cup (\sqrt{3}, \infty)$ **83.** $(-\infty, -\sqrt{2}] \cup \{0\} \cup [\sqrt{2}, \infty)$
85. $(-4, -1) \cup (1, \infty)$ **87.** $[-4, 2] \cup [6, \infty)$ **89.** $(-\infty, 1)$
91. $[-\sqrt{10}, -3] \cup [3, \sqrt{10}]$ **93.** d
95. 20.07 in.^{3} **97.** $V = 3x^3 - 24x^2 + 48x$, 4/3 in. by 4 in. by 16/3 in.

Section 2.7

For Thought: **1.** F **2.** F **3.** F **4.** F **5.** T **6.** F **7.** T **8.** F **9.** T **10.** T

Exercises: **1.** $(-\infty, -2) \cup (-2, \infty)$
3. $(-\infty, -2) \cup (-2, 2) \cup (2, \infty)$ **5.** $(-\infty, 3) \cup (3, \infty)$
7. $(-\infty, 0) \cup (0, \infty)$ **9.** $(-\infty, -1) \cup (-1, 0) \cup (0, 1) \cup (1, \infty)$
11. $(-\infty, -3) \cup (-3, -2) \cup (-2, \infty)$
13. $(-\infty, 2) \cup (2, \infty)$, $y = 0$, $x = 2$
15. $(-\infty, 0) \cup (0, \infty)$, $y = x$, $x = 0$ **17.** $x = 2$, $y = 0$
19. $x = \pm 3$, $y = 0$ **21.** $x = 1$, $y = 2$ **23.** $x = 0$, $y = x - 2$
25. $x = -1$, $y = 3x - 3$ **27.** $x = -2$, $y = -x + 6$
29. $x = 0$, $y = 0$ **31.** $x = 2$, $y = 0$, $(0, -1/2)$

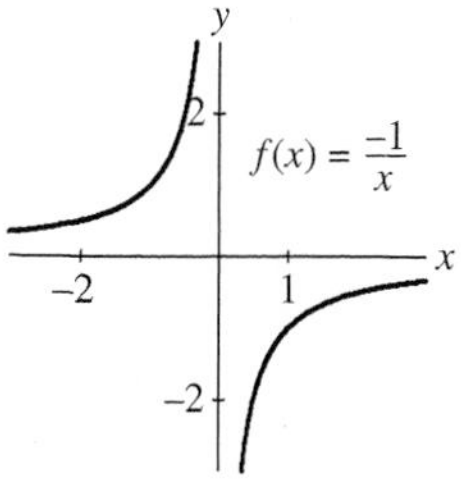

$f(x) = \frac{-1}{x}$

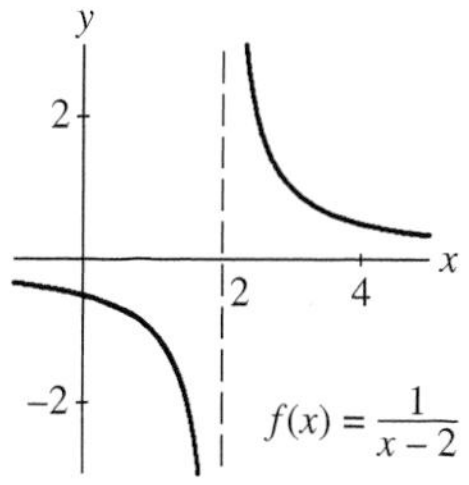

$f(x) = \frac{1}{x - 2}$

33. $x = \pm 2$, $y = 0$, $(0, -1/4)$

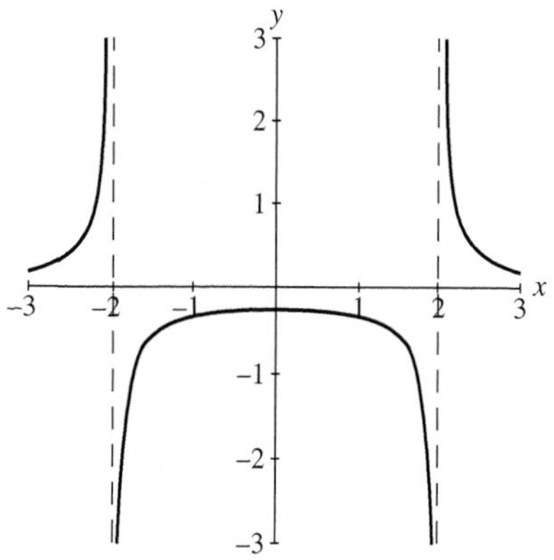

$y = \frac{1}{x^2 - 4}$

35. $x = -1$, $y = 0$, $(0, -1)$ **37.** $x = 1$, $y = 2$, $(0, -1)$, $(-1/2, 0)$

$f(x) = \frac{-1}{(x + 1)^2}$

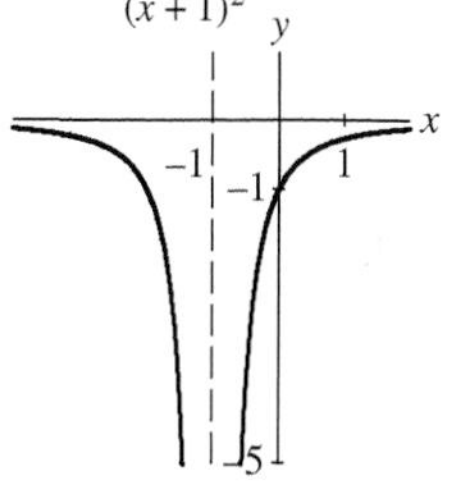

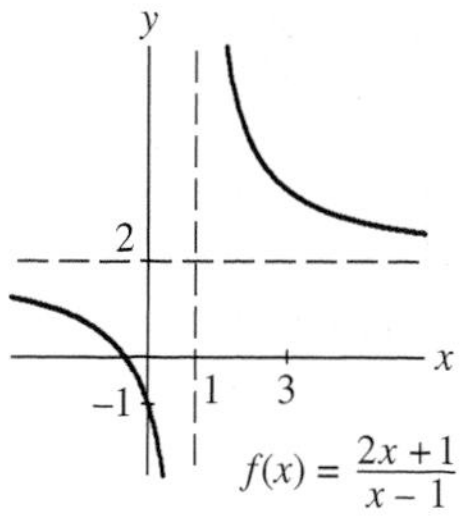

$f(x) = \frac{2x + 1}{x - 1}$

39. $x = -2$, $y = 1$, $(3, 0)$, $(0, -3/2)$ **41.** $x = \pm 1$, $y = 0$, $(0, 0)$

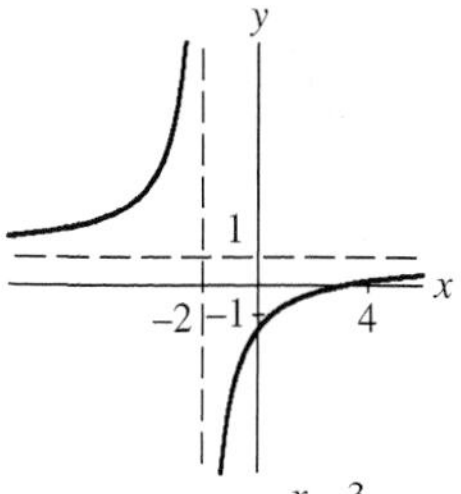

$f(x) = \frac{x - 3}{x + 2}$

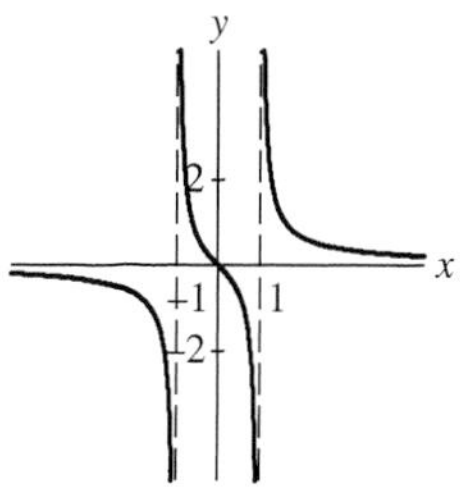

$f(x) = \frac{x}{x^2 - 1}$

43. $x = 1, y = 0, (0, 0)$

$$f(x) = \frac{4x}{x^2 - 2x + 1}$$

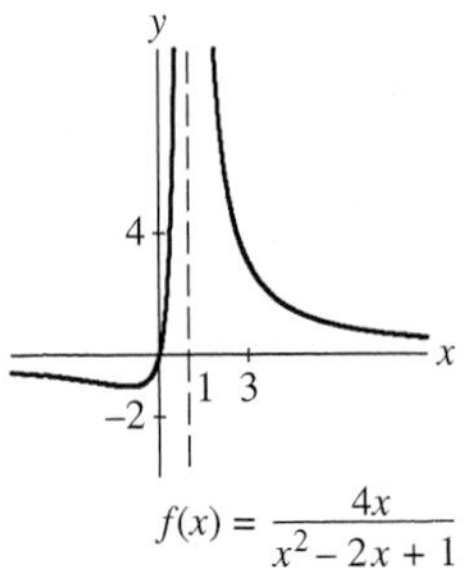

45. $x = \pm 3, y = -1, (0, -8/9),$
$$\left(\pm\sqrt{8}, 0\right)$$

$$f(x) = \frac{8 - x^2}{x^2 - 9}$$

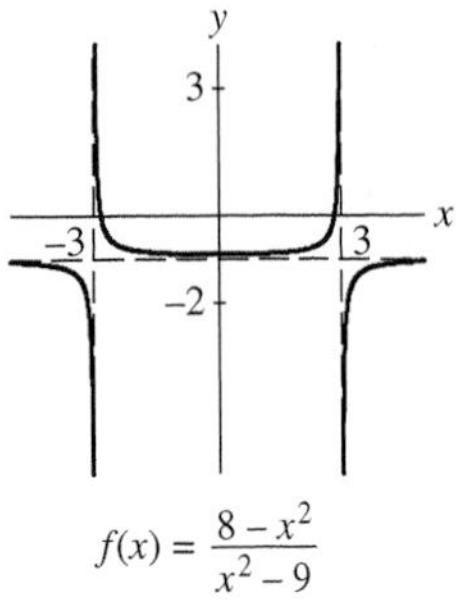

47. $x = -1, y = 2, (0, 2),$
$$\left(-2 \pm \sqrt{3}, 0\right)$$

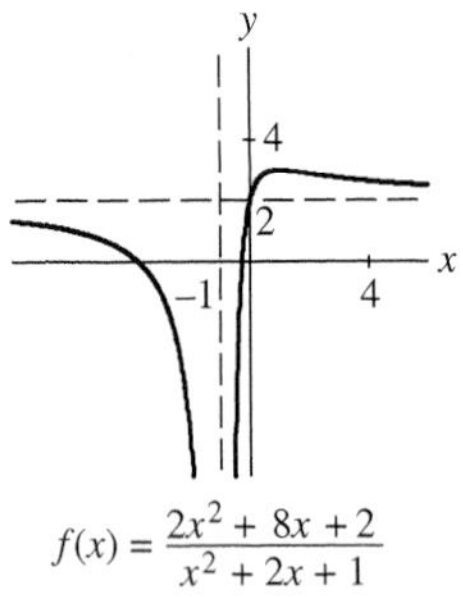

$$f(x) = \frac{2x^2 + 8x + 2}{x^2 + 2x + 1}$$

49. 0 **51.** 2 **53.** ∞ **55.** ∞

57. $y = x$

$$f(x) = \frac{x^2 + 1}{x}$$

59. $y = x$

$$f(x) = \frac{x^3 - 1}{x^2}$$

61. $y = x - 1$

$$f(x) = \frac{x^2}{x + 1}$$

63. $y = 2x + 1$

$$f(x) = \frac{2x^2 - x}{x - 1}$$

65. $y = x - 1$

$$f(x) = \frac{x^3 - x^2 - 4x + 5}{x^2 - 4}$$

67. $y = -x + 2$

$$f(x) = \frac{-x^3 + x^2 + 5x - 4}{x^2 + x - 2}$$

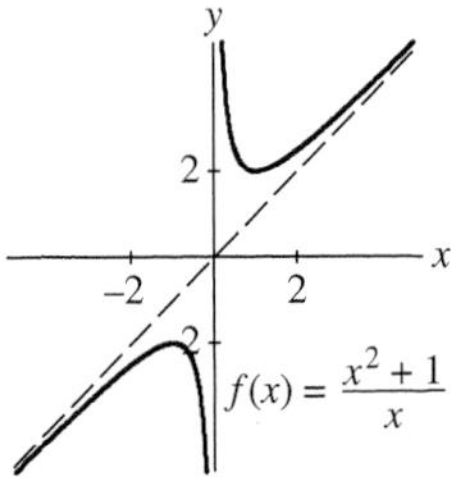

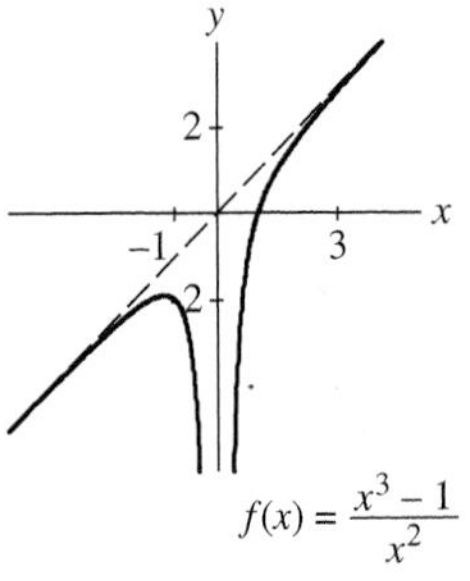

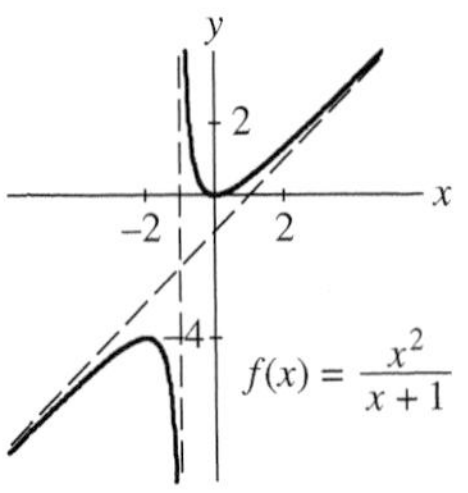

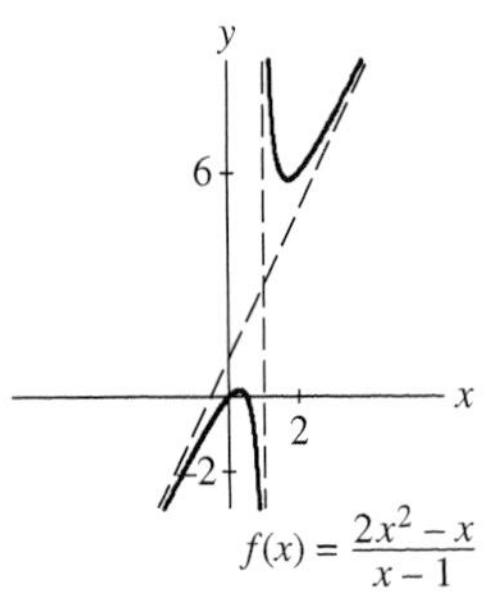

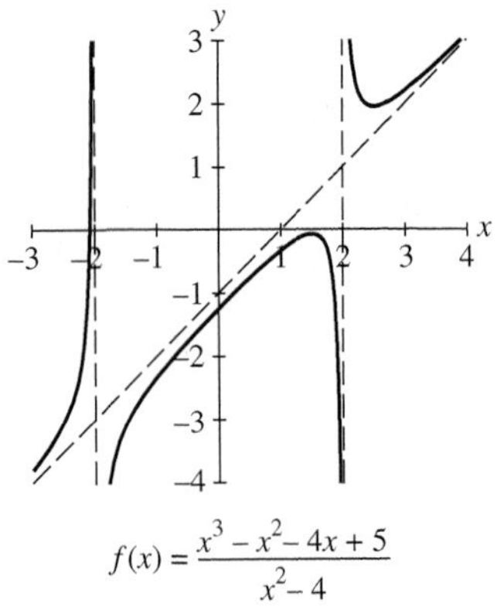

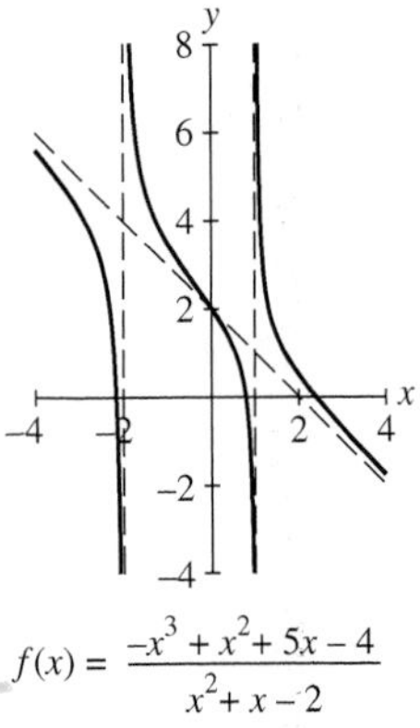

69. (e) **71.** (a) **73.** (b) **75.** (c)
77. $x \neq \pm 1$ **79.** $x \neq 1$

$$f(x) = \frac{x + 1}{x^2 - 1}$$

$$f(x) = \frac{x^2 - 1}{x - 1}$$

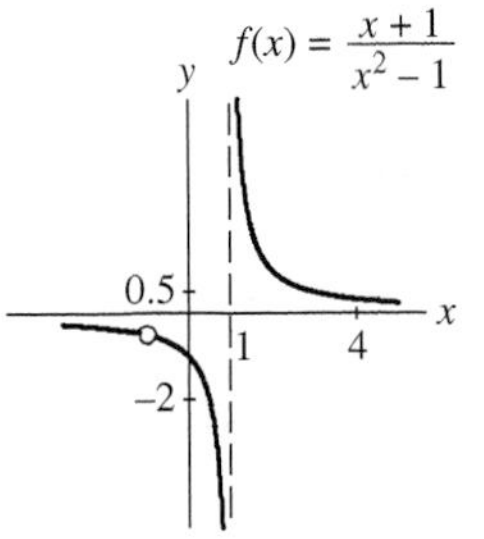

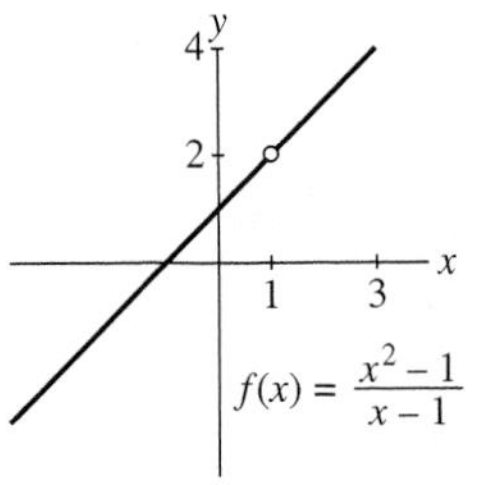

81. $(-2, 4]$ **83.** $(-\infty, -8) \cup (-3, \infty)$ **85.** $[-2, 3] \cup (6, \infty)$
87. $(-2, 3)$ **89.** $(-\infty, -2) \cup (4, 5)$ **91.** $[-1, 3] \cup (5, \infty)$
93. $\left(-\infty, -\sqrt{7}\right] \cup \left(-\sqrt{2}, \sqrt{2}\right) \cup \left[\sqrt{7}, \infty\right)$
95. $(-\infty, -3) \cup \{-1\} \cup (5, \infty)$ **97.** $(1, \infty)$ **99.** $(3, \infty)$
101. $C = \dfrac{100 + x}{x}$, $2, C \to \$1$ **103.** $S = \dfrac{100}{4 - x}$, $S \to \infty$ as $x \to 4$

105. a.

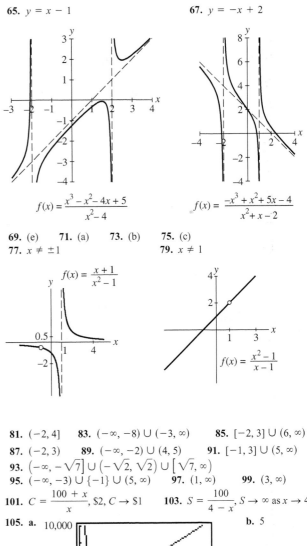

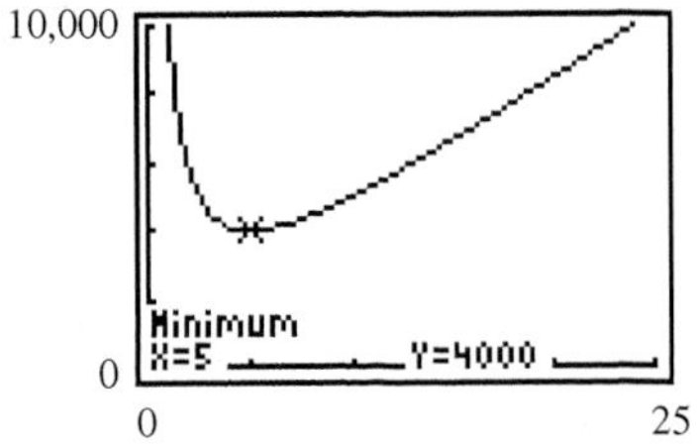

b. 5

Chapter 2 Review Exercises

1. $f(x) = 3\left(x - \dfrac{1}{3}\right)^2 + \dfrac{2}{3}$

3. $(1, -3), x = 1, \left(\dfrac{2 \pm \sqrt{6}}{2}, 0\right), (0, -1)$

5. $y = -2x^2 + 4x + 6$ **7.** $-1 - i$ **9.** $-9 - 40i$

11. 20 **13.** $-3 - 2i$ **15.** $\dfrac{1}{5} - \dfrac{3}{5}i$ **17.** $3 + i\sqrt{2}$

19. $-1 - i$ **21.** $1/3$ **23.** $\pm 2\sqrt{2}$ **25.** $\dfrac{1}{2}, \dfrac{-1 \pm i\sqrt{3}}{4}$

27. $\pm\sqrt{10}, \pm i\sqrt{10}$ **29.** $-\frac{1}{2}, \frac{1}{2}$ with multiplicity 2
31. $0, -1 \pm \sqrt{7}$ **33.** 83 **35.** 5 **37.** $\pm\left(1, 2, \frac{1}{3}, \frac{2}{3}\right)$
39. $\pm\left(1, 3, \frac{1}{2}, \frac{1}{3}, \frac{1}{6}, \frac{3}{2}\right)$ **41.** $2x^2 - 5x - 3 = 0$
43. $x^2 - 6x + 13 = 0$ **45.** $x^3 - 4x^2 + 9x - 10 = 0$
47. $x^2 - 4x + 1 = 0$ **49.** 0 with multiplicity 2, 6 imag
51. 1 pos, 2 imag; 3 pos **53.** 3 neg; 1 neg, 2 imag **55.** 1, 2, 3
57. $\frac{1}{2}, \frac{1}{3}, \pm i$ **59.** $3, 3 \pm i$ **61.** $2, 1 \pm i\sqrt{2}$
63. $0, \frac{1}{2}, 1 \pm \sqrt{3}$ **65.** $\{1/5\}$ **67.** $\{\pm\sqrt{2}\}$ **69.** $\{30\}$
71. $\{16\}$ **73.** $\{\pm 2\}$ **75.** $\{-7, 9\}$ **77.** No solution
79. $\{11/4\}$ **81.** $x = 3/4$ **83.** y-axis **85.** Origin
87. $(-\infty, -2.5) \cup (-2.5, \infty)$
89. $(-\infty, \infty)$
91. $(-1, 0), (2, 0), (0, -2)$

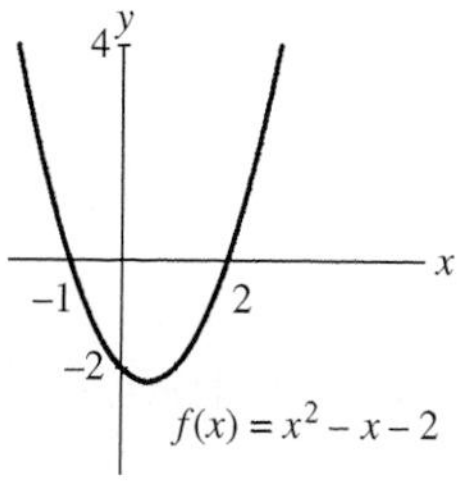

$f(x) = x^2 - x - 2$

93. $(-1, 0), (2, 0), (0, -2)$

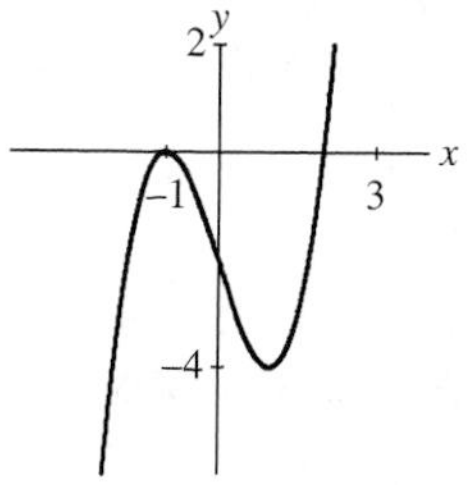

$f(x) = x^3 - 3x - 2$

95. $(\pm 2, 0), (1, 0), (0, 2)$

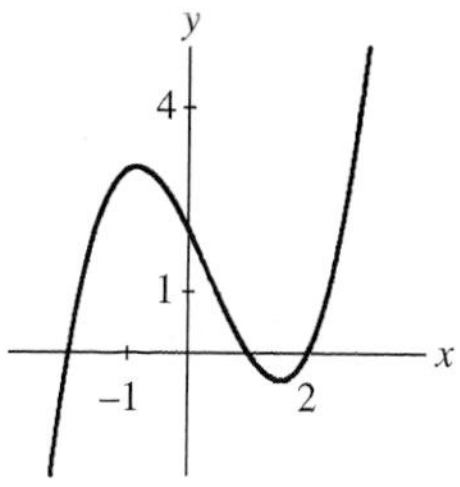

$f(x) = \frac{1}{2}x^3 - \frac{1}{2}x^2 - 2x + 2$

97. $(\pm 2, 0), (0, 4)$

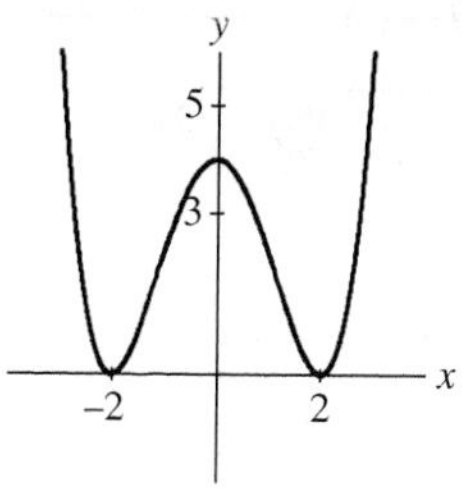

$f(x) = \frac{1}{4}x^4 - 2x^2 + 4$

99. $(0, 2/3), x = -3, y = 0$

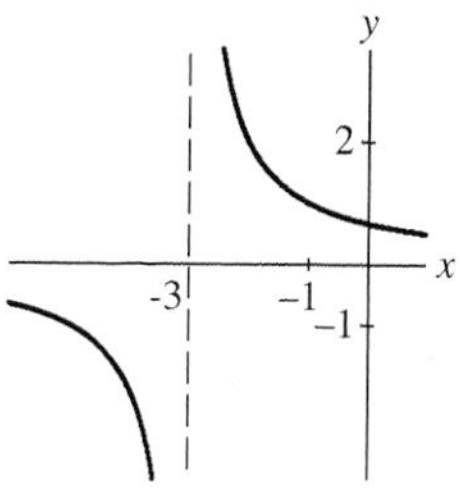

$f(x) = \frac{2}{x+3}$

101. $(0, 0), x = \pm 2, y = 0$

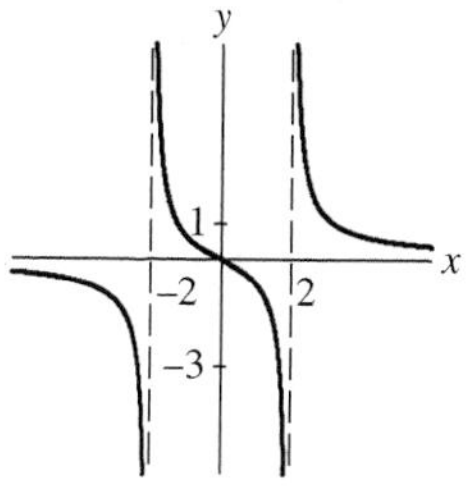

$f(x) = \frac{2x}{x^2 - 4}$

103. $(1, 0), \left(0, -\frac{1}{2}\right), x = 2, y = x$

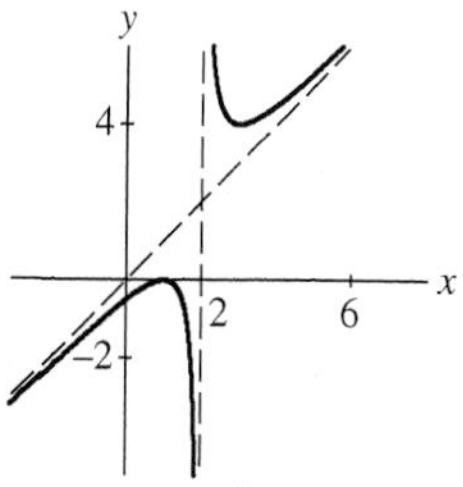

$f(x) = \frac{x^2 - 2x + 1}{x - 2}$

105. $\left(\frac{1}{2}, 0\right), \left(0, -\frac{1}{2}\right), x = 2, y = -2$

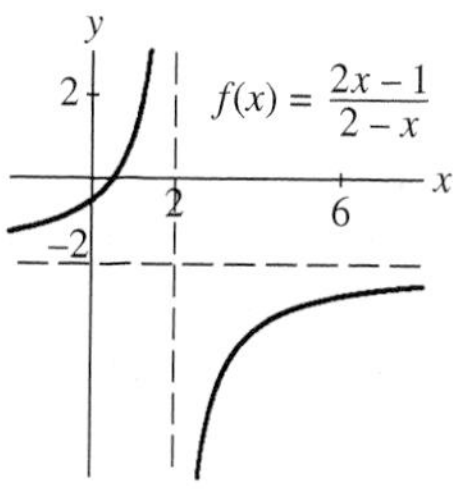

107. $(-2, 0), (0, 2)$

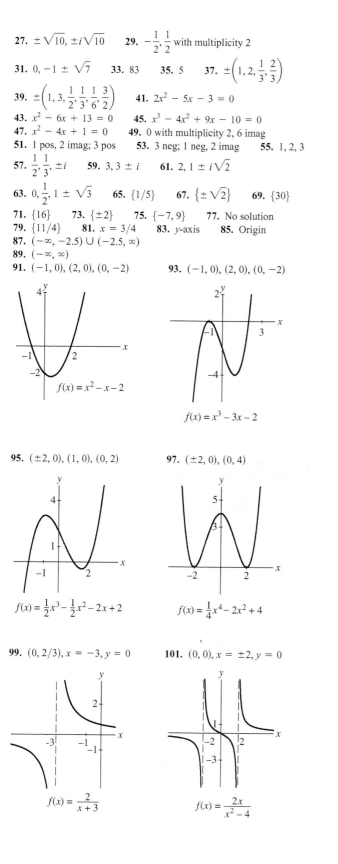

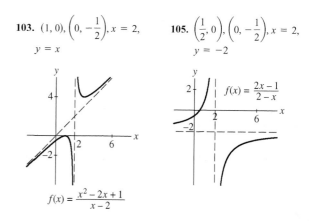

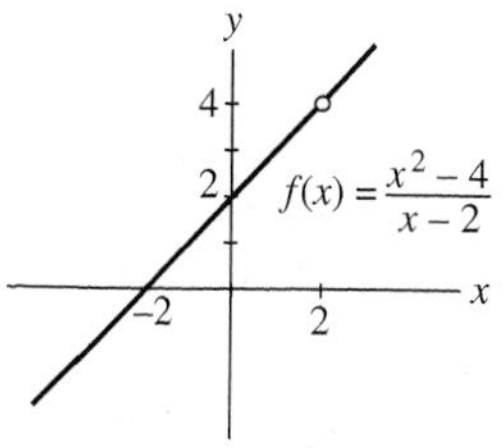

109. $(1/4, 1/2)$ **111.** $[-5, 3]$ **113.** $[-1/2, 1/2] \cup [100, \infty)$
115. $(-\infty, -2) \cup (0, \infty)$ **117.** $(-\infty, 0) \cup (0, 3) \cup (4, \infty)$
119. $(-\infty, 1] \cup [2, 3) \cup (4, \infty)$ **121.** $x^2 - 3x, -15$
123. 380.25 ft **125.** $A = -a^3 + 16a$, (2.3, −10.7)

Chapter 3

Section 3.1

For Thought: **1.** T **2.** F **3.** F **4.** F **5.** T **6.** F **7.** F **8.** T **9.** T **10.** T
Exercises: **1.** 420°, 780°, −300°, −660°
3. 344°, 704°, −376°, −736° **5.** Yes **7.** No **9.** I
11. III **13.** IV **15.** I **17.** 45° **19.** 60° **21.** 120°
23. 40° **25.** 20° **27.** 340° **29.** 13.2° **31.** −8.505°
33. 28.0858° **35.** 75°30′ **37.** −17°19′48″ **39.** 18°7′23″
41. $\pi/6$ **43.** $\pi/10$ **45.** $-3\pi/8$ **47.** $7\pi/2$ **49.** 0.653
51. −0.241 **53.** −0.936 **55.** 75° **57.** 315° **59.** −1080°
61. 136.937° **63.** $7\pi/3, 13\pi/3, -5\pi/3, -11\pi/3$
65. $11\pi/6, 23\pi/6, -13\pi/6, -25\pi/6$ **67.** π **69.** $\pi/2$
71. $\pi/3$ **73.** $5\pi/3$ **75.** 2.04 **77.** No **79.** Yes **81.** I
83. III **85.** IV **87.** IV
89. $30° = \pi/6, 45° = \pi/4, 60° = \pi/3, 90° = \pi/2, 120° = 2\pi/3, 135° = 3\pi/4, 150° = 5\pi/6, 180° = \pi, 210° = 7\pi/6, 225° = 5\pi/4, 240° = 4\pi/3, 270° = 3\pi/2, 300° = 5\pi/3, 315° = 7\pi/4, 330° = 11\pi/6, 360° = 2\pi$
91. 3π ft **93.** 209.4 mi **95.** 1 mi **97.** 3.18 km
99. 1.68 m. **101.** 41,143 km, 40,074 km

Section 3.2

For Thought: **1.** F **2.** F **3.** T **4.** F **5.** F **6.** T **7.** F **8.** F **9.** F **10.** T

Exercises: **1.** $(1, 0), (\sqrt{2}/2, \sqrt{2}/2), (0, 1), (-\sqrt{2}/2, \sqrt{2}/2), (-1, 0), (-\sqrt{2}/2, -\sqrt{2}/2), (0, -1), (\sqrt{2}/2, -\sqrt{2}/2)$
3. 0 **5.** 0 **7.** 0 **9.** 0 **11.** $\sqrt{2}/2$ **13.** $-\sqrt{2}/2$
15. 1/2 **17.** 1/2 **19.** $-\sqrt{3}/2$ **21.** $\sqrt{3}/2$ **23.** 1/2
25. 1/2 **27.** $\sqrt{3}/2$ **29.** $\sqrt{2}/2$ **31.** -1 **33.** $\sqrt{3}/2$
35. 1/2 **37.** $\sqrt{3}/3$ **39.** -1 **41.** 1 **43.** $2 + \sqrt{3}$
45. $\sqrt{2}$ **47.** + **49.** + **51.** − **53.** − **55.** 0.9999
57. 0.4035 **59.** −0.7438 **61.** 1.0000 **63.** −0.2588 **65.** 1
67. 1/2 **69.** $\sqrt{2}/2$ **71.** $\sqrt{3}/2$ **73.** −12/13 **75.** −4/5
77. $2\sqrt{2}/3$ **79.** $x = 4 \sin t - 3 \cos t$, 3.53
81. 1.708 in., 1.714 in.

Section 3.3

For Thought: **1.** F **2.** F **3.** F **4.** T **5.** T **6.** T **7.** F **8.** T **9.** T **10.** T

Exercises: **1.** $y = -2 \sin(x)$, 2
3. $y = 3 \cos(x)$, 3 **5.** $2, 2\pi, 0$
7. $1, 2\pi, \pi/2$ **9.** $2, 2\pi, -\pi/3$

11. $1, 0, (0, 0), (\pi/2, -1), (\pi, 0), (3\pi/2, 1), (2\pi, 0)$

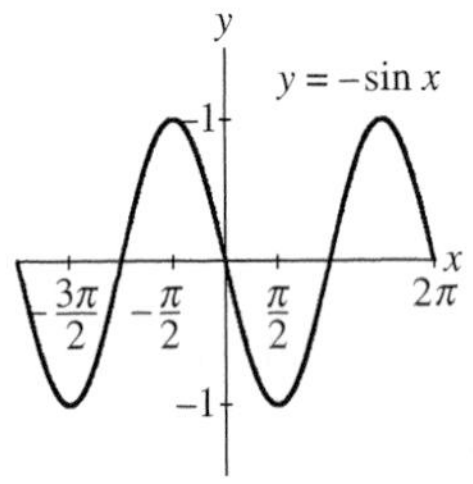

13. $3, 0, (0, 0), (\pi/2, -3), (\pi, 0), (3\pi/2, 3), (2\pi, 0)$

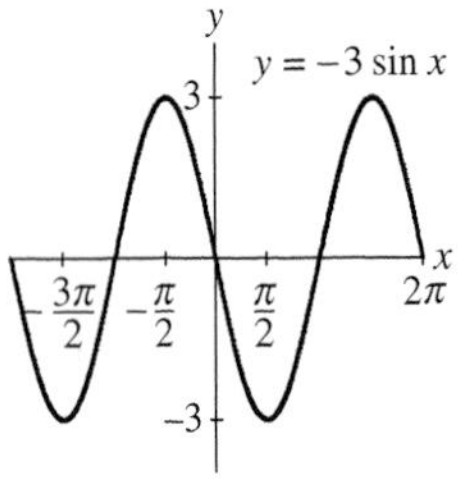

15. $1/2, 0, (0, 1/2), (\pi/2, 0), (\pi, -1/2), (3\pi/2, 0), (2\pi, 1/2)$

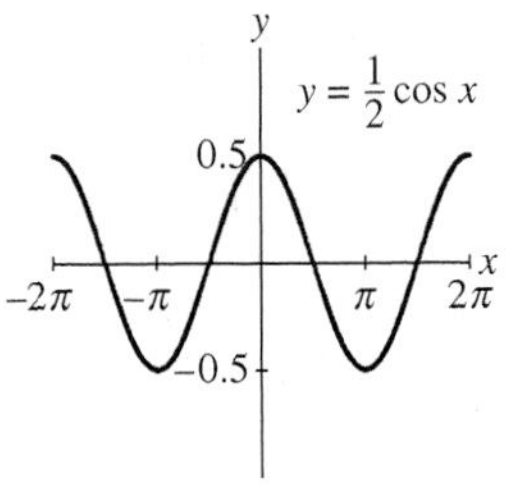

17. $1, -\pi, (0, 0), (\pi/2, -1), (\pi, 0), (3\pi/2, 1), (2\pi, 0)$

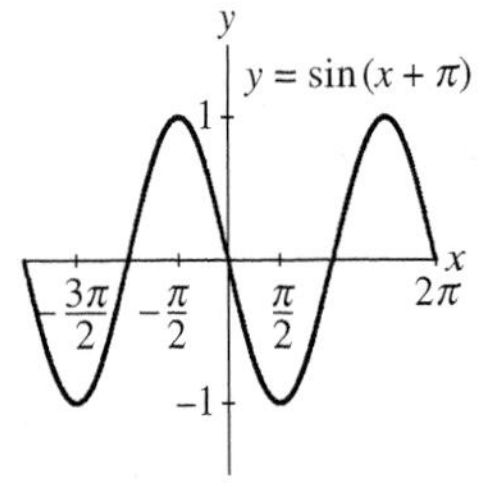

19. $1, \pi/3, (-2\pi/3, -1), (-\pi/6, 0), (\pi/3, 1), (5\pi/6, 0), (4\pi/3, -1)$

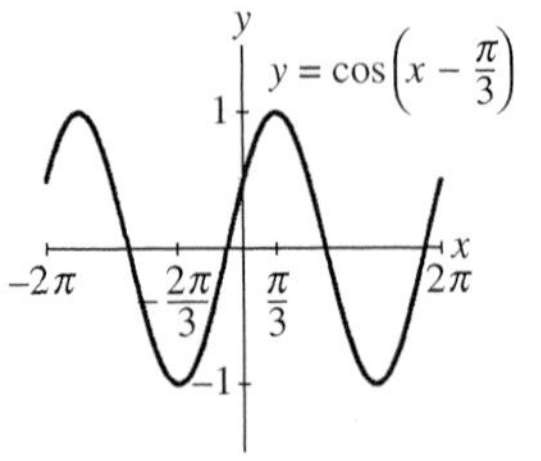

21. $1, 0, (0, 3), (\pi/2, 2), (\pi, 1), (3\pi/2, 2), (2\pi, 3)$

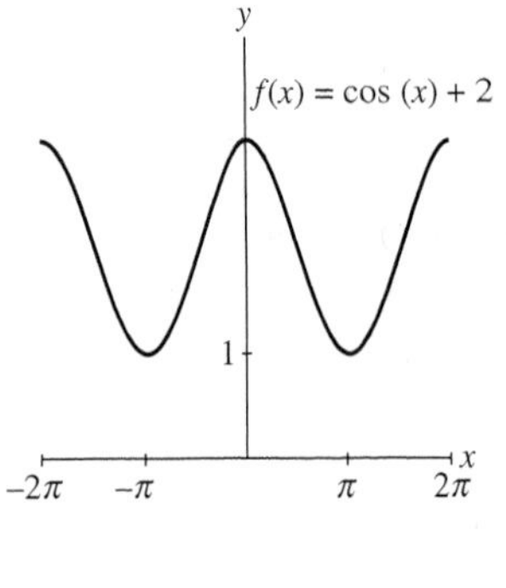

23. $1, 0, (0, -1), (\pi/2, -2), (\pi, -1), (3\pi/2, 0), (2\pi, -1)$

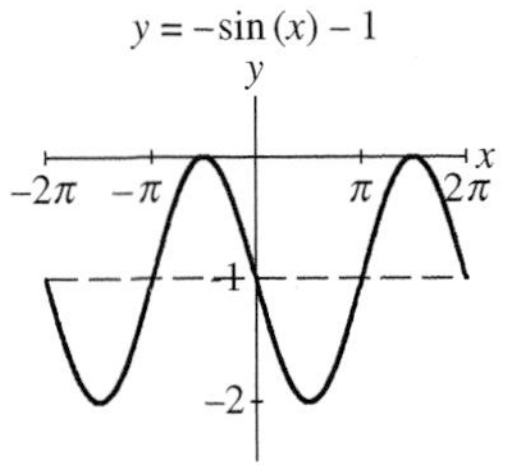

25. $1, -\pi/4, (-\pi/4, 2), (\pi/4, 3), (3\pi/4, 2), (5\pi/4, 1), (7\pi/4, 2)$

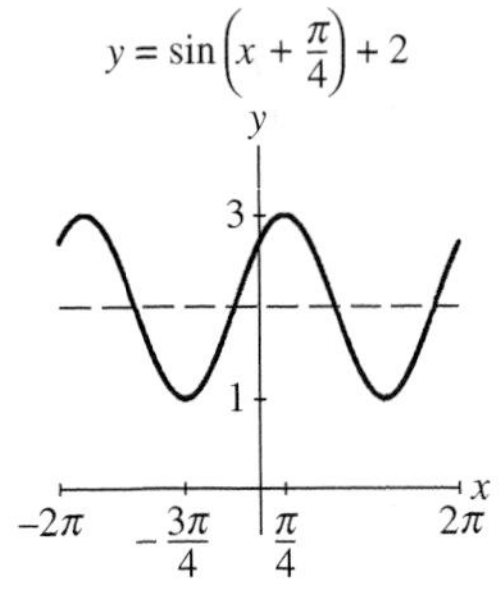

27. $2, -\pi/6, (-\pi/6, 3), (\pi/3, 1), (5\pi/6, -1), (4\pi/3, 1), (11\pi/6, 3)$

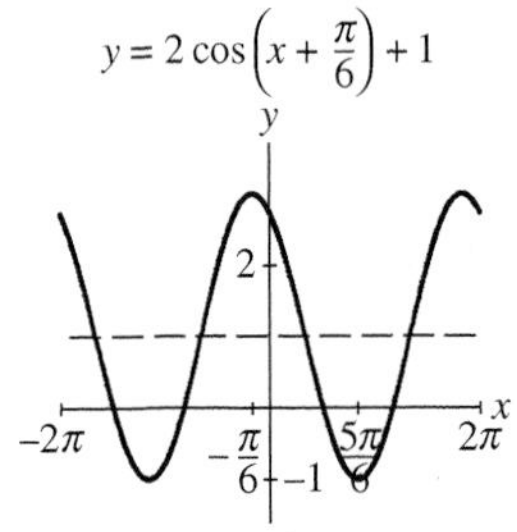

29. $2, \pi/3, (-\pi/6, 3), (\pi/3, 1), (5\pi/6, -1), (4\pi/3, 1), (11\pi/6, 3)$

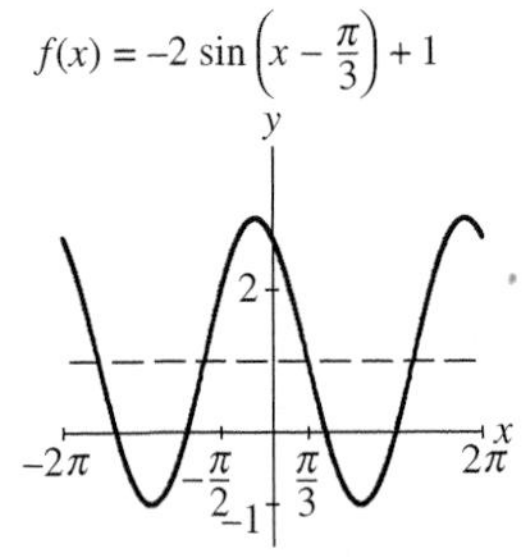

31. $3, \pi/2, 0$ **33.** $1, 4\pi, 0$ **35.** $2, 2\pi, \pi$ **37.** $2, \pi, -\pi/4$
39. $2, 4, -2$ **41.** $y = 2 \sin[2(x + \pi/2)] + 5$
43. $y = 5 \sin[\pi(x - 2)] + 4$ **45.** $y = 6 \sin[4\pi(x + \pi)] - 3$
47. $y = -\sin(x - \pi/4) + 1$ **49.** $y = -3 \cos(x - \pi) + 2$

51. $2\pi/3, 0, [-1, 1], (0, 0), (\pi/6, 1), (\pi/3, 0), (\pi/2, -1), (2\pi/3, 0)$

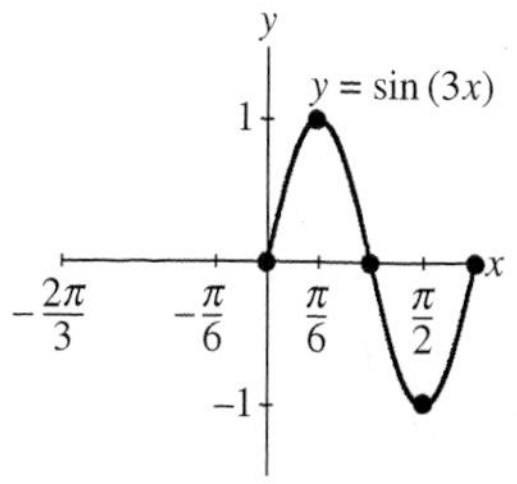

53. $\pi, 0, [-1, 1], (0, 0), (\pi/4, -1), (\pi/2, 0), (3\pi/4, 1), (\pi, 0)$

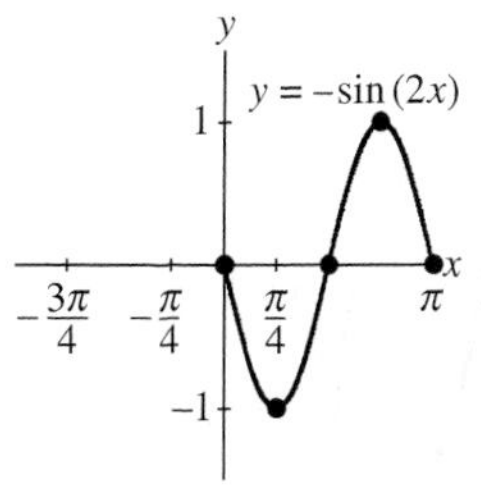

55. $\pi/2, 0, [1, 3], (0, 3), (\pi/8, 2), (\pi/4, 1), (3\pi/8, 2), (\pi/2, 3)$

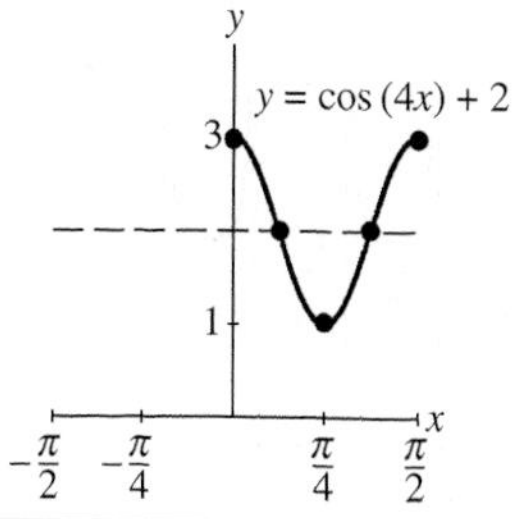

57. $8\pi, 0, [1, 3], (0, 2), (2\pi, 1), (4\pi, 2), (6\pi, 3), (8\pi, 2)$

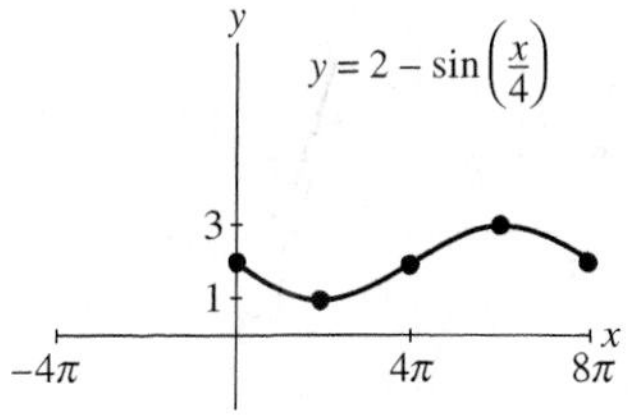

59. $6, 0, [-1, 1], (0, 0), (1.5, 1), (3, 0), (4.5, -1), (6, 0)$

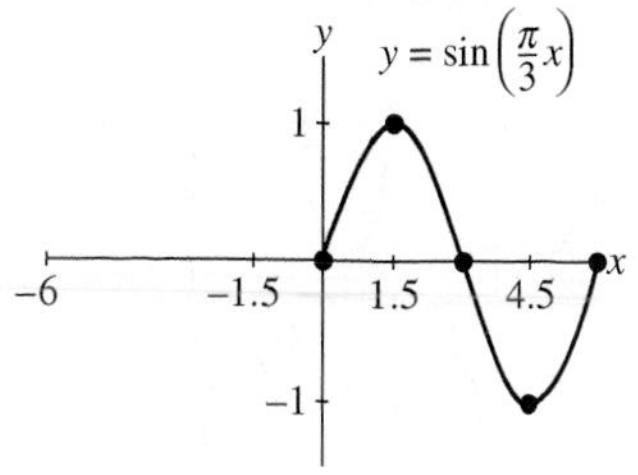

61. $\pi, \pi/2, [-1, 1], (\pi/2, 0), (3\pi/4, 1), (\pi, 0), (5\pi/4, -1), (3\pi/2, 0)$

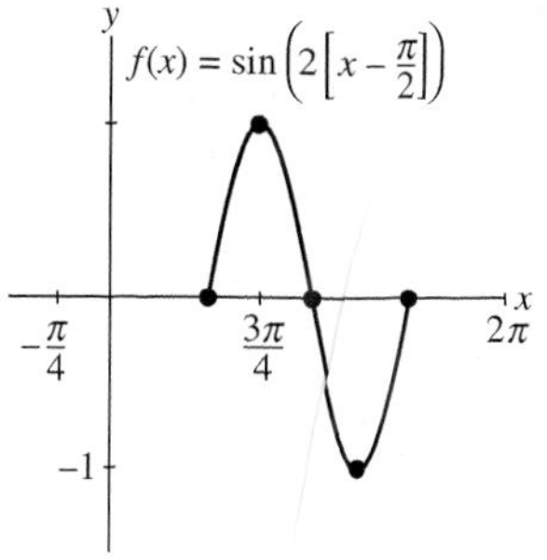

63. $4, -3, [-1, 1], (-3, 0), (-2, 1), (-1, 0), (0, -1), (1, 0)$

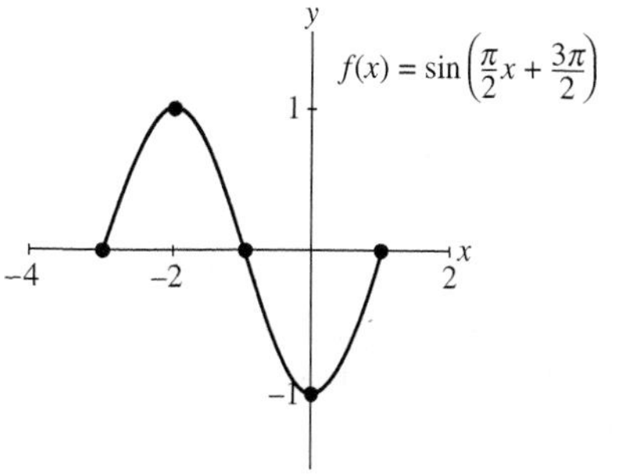

65. $\pi, -\pi/6, [-1, 3], (-\pi/6, 3), (\pi/12, 1), (\pi/3, -1), (7\pi/12, 1), (5\pi/6, 3)$

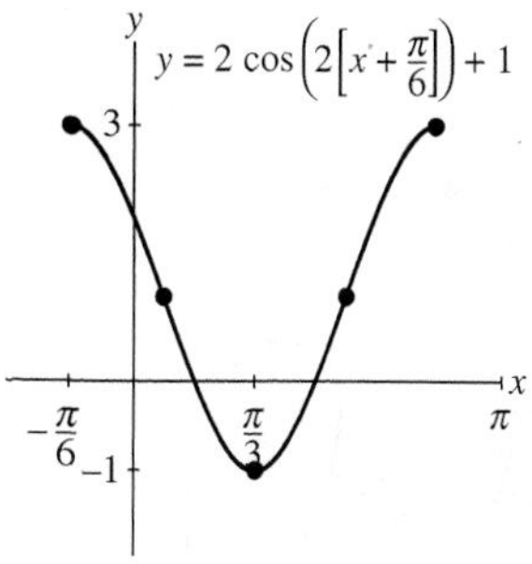

67. $2\pi/3, \pi/6, [-3/2, -1/2], (\pi/6, -1), (\pi/3, -3/2), (\pi/2, -1), (2\pi/3, -1/2), (5\pi/6, -1)$

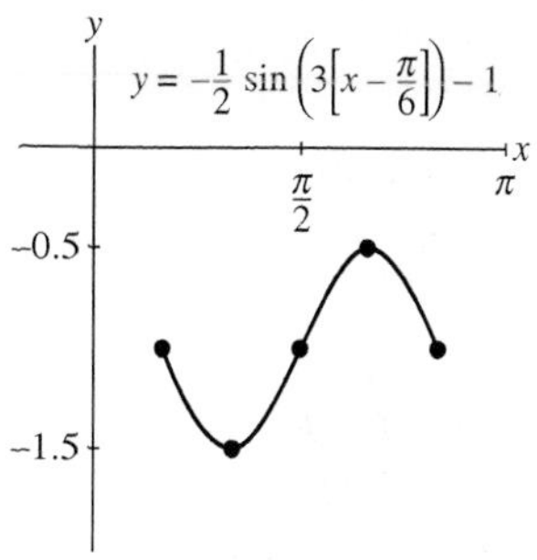

69. $y = 2\sin\left(2\left[x - \frac{\pi}{4}\right]\right)$ **71.** $y = 3\sin\left(\frac{3}{2}\left[x + \frac{\pi}{3}\right]\right) + 3$

73. 100 cycles/sec **75.** 40 cycles/hr

77. $x = 3\sin(2t), 3, \pi$

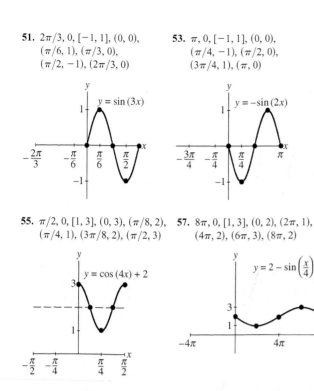

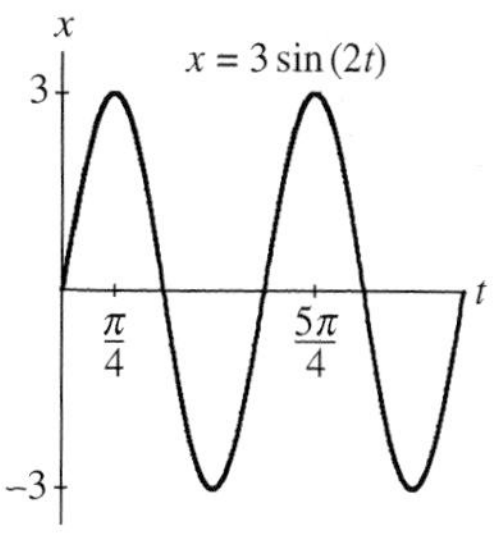

79. 11 yr **81. a.** 1300 cc, 500 cc **b.** 30

83. 12, 15,000, −3, 25,000, $y = 15{,}000 \sin(\pi x/6 + \pi/2) + 25{,}000$, \$17,500

85. $y = \sin(\pi x/10) + 1$

Section 3.4

For Thought: **1.** T **2.** F **3.** T **4.** F **5.** F **6.** T **7.** F **8.** T **9.** T **10.** T

Exercises:

1. $\tan(0) = 0, \tan(\pi/4) = 1, \tan(\pi/2)$ undefined, $\tan(3\pi/4) = -1$, $\tan(\pi) = 0, \tan(5\pi/4) = 1, \tan(3\pi/2)$ undefined, $\tan(7\pi/4) = -1$

3. $\sqrt{3}$ **5.** -1 **7.** 0

9. $-\sqrt{3}/3$ **11.** $2\sqrt{3}/3$

13. Undefined **15.** Undefined **17.** $\sqrt{2}$

19. -1 **21.** $\sqrt{3}$

23. -2 **25.** $-\sqrt{2}$

27. 0 **29.** 48.0785

31. −2.8413 **33.** 500.0003

35. 1.0353 **37.** 636.6192

39. −1.4318 **41.** 71.6221

43. −0.9861 **45.** 4 **47.** $\sqrt{3}/3$ **49.** $-\sqrt{2}$

51. $\pi/3$

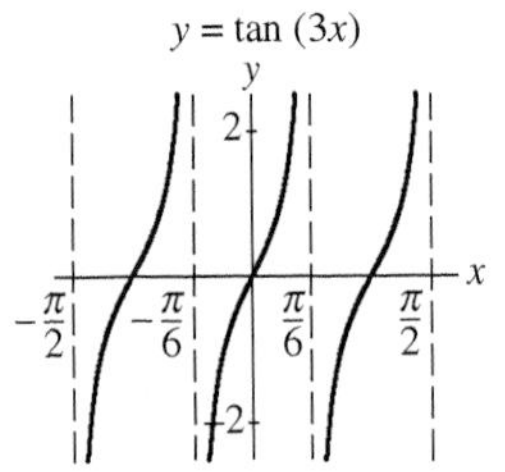

53. π

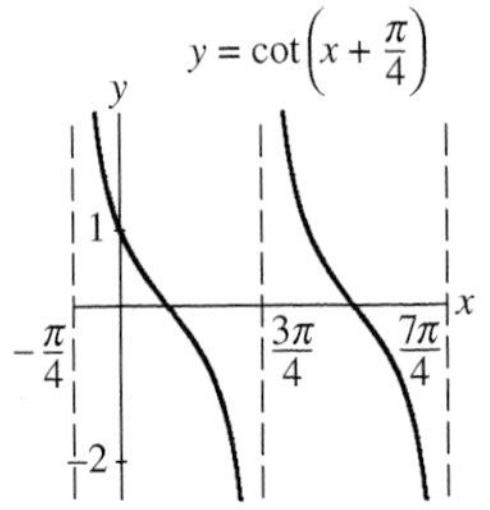

55. 2π

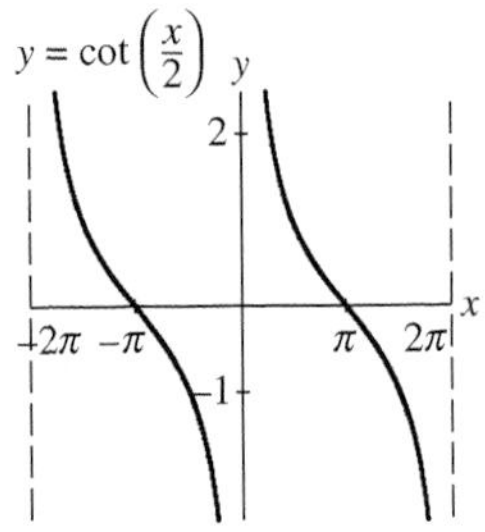

57. 1

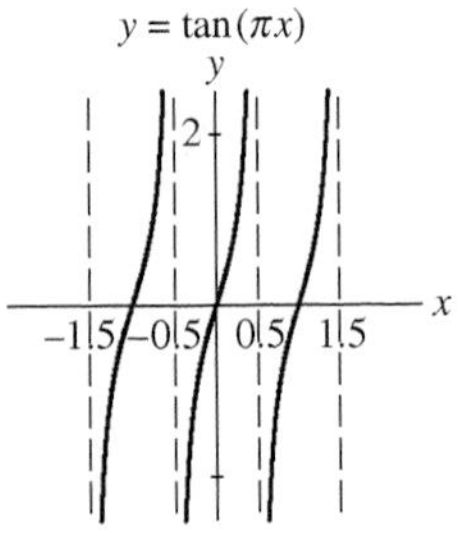

59. π

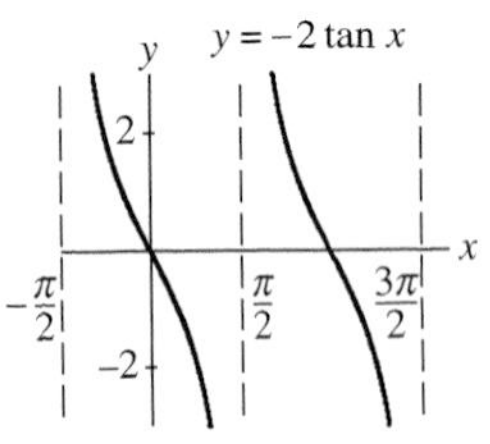

61. π

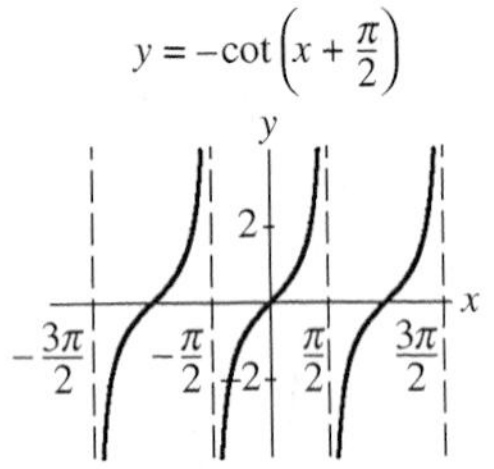

63. $\pi/2$

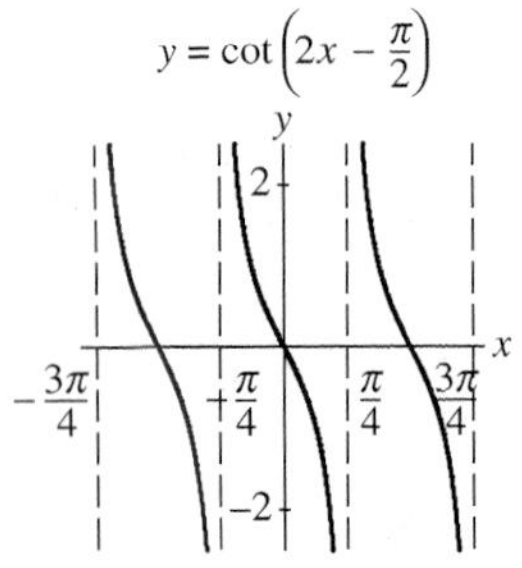

65. 2

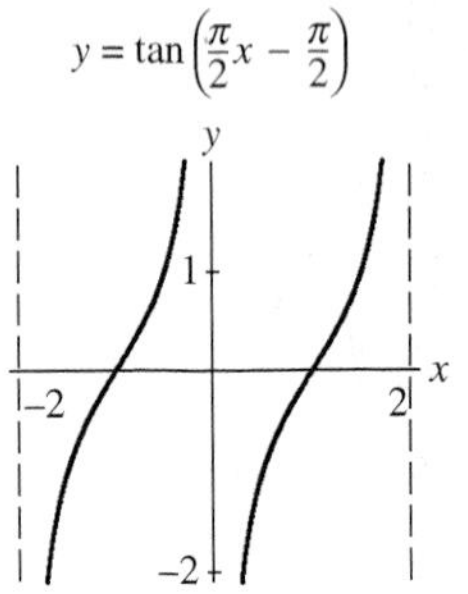

67. π, $(-\infty, -1] \cup [1, \infty)$

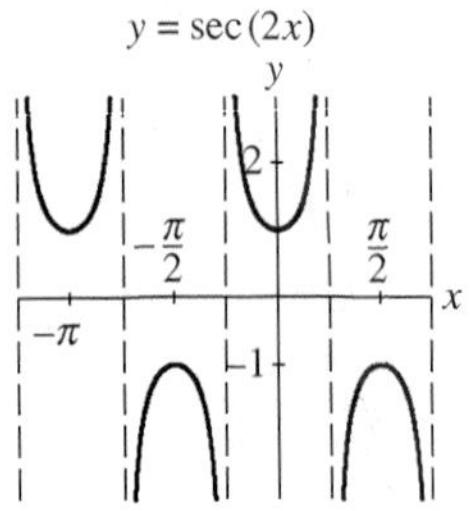

69. 2π, $(-\infty, -1] \cup [1, \infty)$

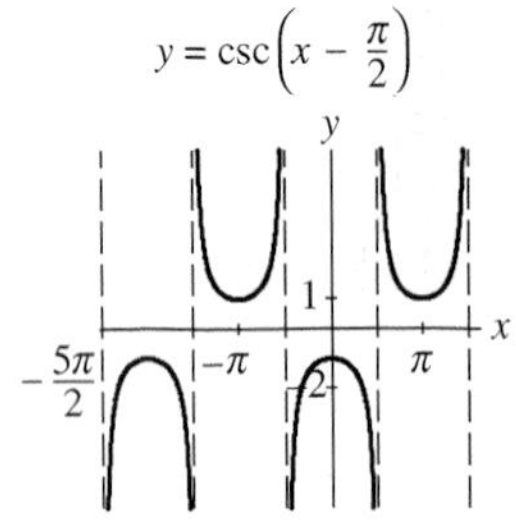

71. 4π, $(-\infty, -1] \cup [1, \infty)$

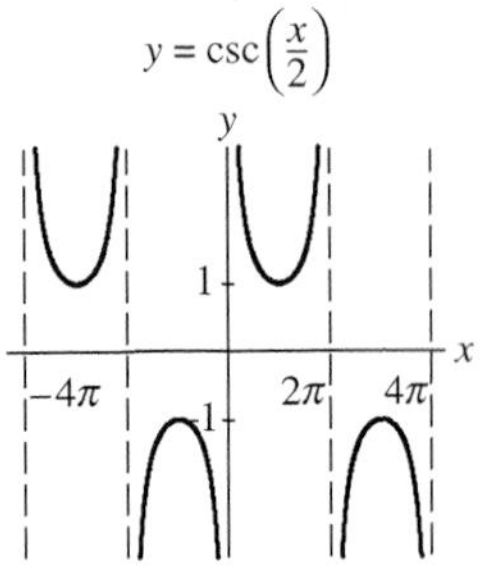

73. 4, $(-\infty, -1] \cup [1, \infty)$

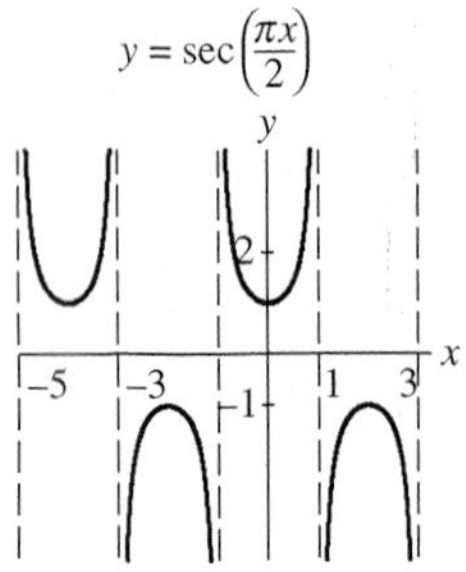

75. 2π, $(-\infty, -2] \cup [2, \infty)$

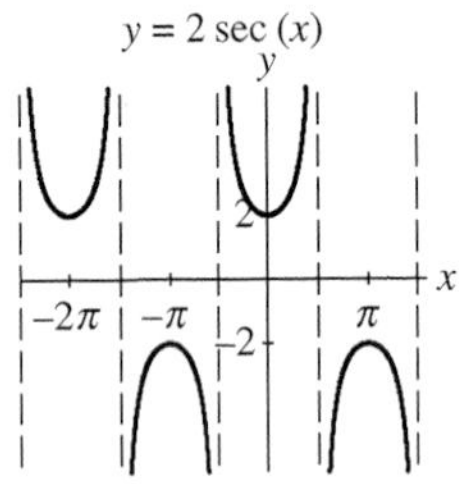

77. π, $(-\infty, -1] \cup [1, \infty)$

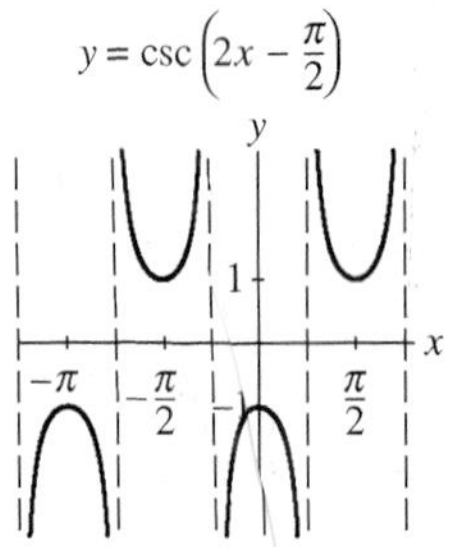

79. 4, $(-\infty, -1] \cup [1, \infty)$

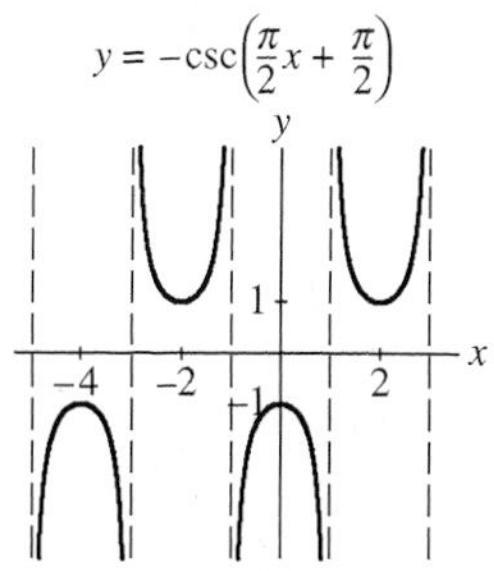

81. π, $(-\infty, 0] \cup [4, \infty)$

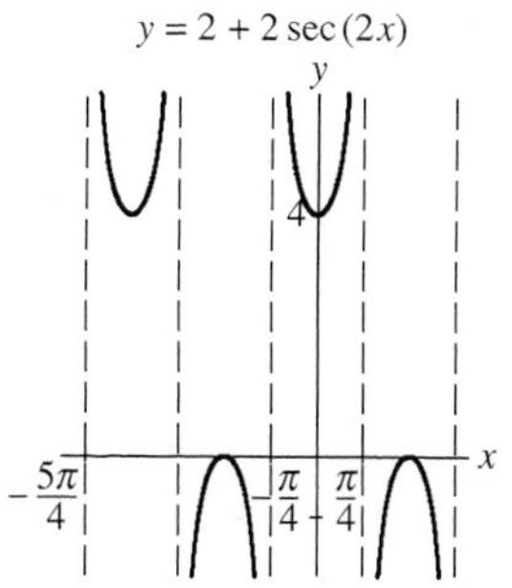

83. $\pi/2$, $(-\infty, \infty)$ **85.** 4π, $(-\infty, -3] \cup [1, \infty)$
87. π, $(-\infty, -7] \cup [-1, \infty)$ **89.** $y = 3\tan(x - \pi/4) + 2$
91. $y = -\sec(x + \pi) + 2$

Section 3.5

For Thought: **1.** T **2.** T **3.** F **4.** F **5.** F **6.** T **7.** T **8.** T **9.** F **10.** F
Exercises: **1.** $-\pi/6$ **3.** $\pi/6$ **5.** $\pi/4$ **7.** $-45°$ **9.** $30°$
11. $0°$ **13.** $-19.5°$ **15.** $34.6°$ **17.** $3\pi/4$ **19.** $\pi/3$
21. π **23.** $135°$ **25.** $180°$ **27.** $120°$ **29.** $173.2°$
31. $89.9°$ **33.** $-\pi/4$ **35.** $\pi/3$ **37.** $\pi/4$ **39.** $-\pi/6$
41. 0 **43.** $\pi/2$ **45.** $3\pi/4$ **47.** $2\pi/3$ **49.** 0.60
51. 3.02 **53.** -0.14 **55.** 1.87 **57.** 1.15 **59.** -0.36
61. 3.06 **63.** 0.06 **65.** $\sqrt{3}$ **67.** $-\pi/6$ **69.** $\pi/6$
71. $\pi/4$ **73.** 1 **75.** $\pi/2$ **77.** 0 **79.** $\pi/2$
81. $f^{-1}(x) = 0.5\sin^{-1}(x)$, $[-1, 1]$
83. $f^{-1}(x) = \frac{1}{\pi}\tan^{-1}(x - 3)$, $(-\infty, \infty)$
85. $f^{-1}(x) = 2\sin(x - 3)$, $[3 - \pi/2, 3 + \pi/2]$ **87.** $67.1°$

Section 3.6

For Thought: **1.** F **2.** T **3.** F **4.** T **5.** T **6.** F **7.** F **8.** T **9.** T **10.** F
Exercises: **1.** $4/5, 3/5, 4/3, 5/4, 5/3, 3/4$
3. $3\sqrt{10}/10, -\sqrt{10}/10, -3, \sqrt{10}/3, -\sqrt{10}, -1/3$
5. $-\sqrt{3}/3, -\sqrt{6}/3, \sqrt{2}/2, -\sqrt{3}, -\sqrt{6}/2, \sqrt{2}$
7. $-1/2, \sqrt{3}/2, -\sqrt{3}/3, -2, 2\sqrt{3}/3, -\sqrt{3}$
9. $\sqrt{5}/5, 2\sqrt{5}/5, 1/2, 2\sqrt{5}/5, \sqrt{5}/5, 2$
11. $3\sqrt{34}/34, 5\sqrt{34}/34, 3/5, 5\sqrt{34}/34, 3\sqrt{34}/34, 5/3$
13. $4/5, 3/5, 4/3, 3/5, 4/5, 3/4$ **15.** $80.5°$ **17.** $60°$ **19.** 1.0
21. 0.4 **23.** $\beta = 30°, a = 10\sqrt{3}, b = 10$
25. $c = 10, \alpha = 36.9°, \beta = 53.1°$
27. $a = 5.7, \alpha = 43.7°, \beta = 46.3°$
29. $\beta = 74°, a = 5.5, b = 19.2$ **31.** $\beta = 50°51', b = 11.1, c = 14.3$
33. 50 ft **35.** 1.7 mi **37.** 43.2 m **39.** 25.1 ft
41. 22 m, $57.6°$ **43.** 153.1 m **45.** 4.5 km **47.** 4391 mi
49. 5.987 ft

Section 3.7

For Thought: **1.** T **2.** F **3.** F **4.** F **5.** F **6.** T **7.** T **8.** T **9.** F **10.** T
Exercises: **1.** 1 **3.** $-\sin^2 x\cos^3 x$ **5.** $\cos^2 w$ **7.** $\csc x$
9. $\cos x$ **11.** 0 **13.** $\cos(11)$ **15.** $\cos(k)$ **17.** 1
19. $-\cos(\pi/5)$ **21.** $\tan(5\pi/18)$ **23.** $\cos(2k)$ **25.** $\sin(26°)$
27. $\sqrt{3}/6$ **29.** $-\sin(2\pi/9)$
31. $\sin\alpha = \sqrt{5}/5, \cos\alpha = 2\sqrt{5}/5, \csc\alpha = \sqrt{5}, \sec\alpha = \sqrt{5}/2, \cot\alpha = 2$
33. $\sin\alpha = -\sqrt{22}/5, \tan\alpha = \sqrt{66}/3, \csc\alpha = -5\sqrt{22}/22, \sec\alpha = -5\sqrt{3}/3, \cot\alpha = \sqrt{66}/22$
35. $\sqrt{5}/5, 2\sqrt{5}/5, 1/2, \sqrt{5}, \sqrt{5}/2, 2$
37. $-\sqrt{15}/8, -7/8, \sqrt{15}/7, -8\sqrt{15}/15, -8/7, 7\sqrt{15}/15$
39. $\frac{\sqrt{2-\sqrt{3}}}{2}$ or $\frac{\sqrt{6}-\sqrt{2}}{4}$ **41.** $\frac{\sqrt{6}-\sqrt{2}}{4}$ **43.** $\frac{\sqrt{2}+\sqrt{6}}{4}$
45. $\frac{1+\sqrt{3}}{\sqrt{3}-1}$ **77.** $0.5(\cos 4° - \cos 22°)$
79. $0.5(\cos(\pi/30) + \cos(11\pi/30))$ **81.** $\frac{\sqrt{2}-1}{4}$
83. $\frac{\sqrt{2}+\sqrt{3}}{4}$ **85.** $2\cos(10°)\sin(2°)$
87. $-2\sin(4\pi/15)\sin(\pi/15)$ **89.** $\sqrt{6}/2$ **91.** $\frac{\sqrt{2-\sqrt{2}}}{2}$
93. $\sqrt{2}\sin(x - \pi/4)$ **95.** $\sin(x + 2\pi/3)$
97. $\sin(x - \pi/6)$ **99.** $A = \frac{d^2}{2}\sin(2\alpha)$
101. $x = 2\sin(t + \pi/6)$, 2 m

Section 3.8

For Thought: **1.** F **2.** F **3.** T **4.** T **5.** T **6.** F **7.** F **8.** T **9.** F **10.** F
Exercises: **1.** $\{x \mid x = \pi + 2k\pi\}$ **3.** $\{x \mid x = k\pi\}$
5. $\left\{x \mid x = \frac{3\pi}{2} + 2k\pi\right\}$
7. $\left\{x \mid x = \frac{\pi}{3} + 2k\pi \text{ or } x = \frac{5\pi}{3} + 2k\pi\right\}$
9. $\left\{x \mid x = \frac{\pi}{4} + 2k\pi \text{ or } x = \frac{3\pi}{4} + 2k\pi\right\}$ **11.** $\left\{x \mid x = \frac{\pi}{4} + k\pi\right\}$
13. $\left\{x \mid x = \frac{5\pi}{6} + 2k\pi \text{ or } x = \frac{7\pi}{6} + 2k\pi\right\}$
15. $\left\{x \mid x = \frac{5\pi}{4} + 2k\pi \text{ or } x = \frac{7\pi}{4} + 2k\pi\right\}$
17. $\left\{x \mid x = \frac{3\pi}{4} + k\pi\right\}$ **19.** $\{x \mid x = 90° + k180°\}$
21. $\{x \mid x = 90° + k360°\}$ **23.** $\{x \mid x = k180°\}$
25. $\{x \mid x = 29.2° + k360° \text{ or } x = 330.8° + k360°\}$
27. $\{x \mid x = 345.9° + k360° \text{ or } x = 194.1° + k360°\}$
29. $\{x \mid x = 79.5° + k180°\}$
31. $\left\{x \mid x = \frac{2\pi}{3} + 4k\pi \text{ or } x = \frac{10\pi}{3} + 4k\pi\right\}$ **33.** $\left\{x \mid x = \frac{2k\pi}{3}\right\}$
35. $\left\{x \mid x = \frac{\pi}{3} + 4k\pi \text{ or } x = \frac{5\pi}{3} + 4k\pi\right\}$
37. $\left\{x \mid x = \frac{5\pi}{8} + k\pi \text{ or } x = \frac{7\pi}{8} + k\pi\right\}$ **39.** $\left\{x \mid x = \frac{\pi}{6} + \frac{k\pi}{2}\right\}$
41. $\left\{x \mid x = \frac{k\pi}{4}\right\}$ **43.** $\left\{x \mid x = \frac{1}{6} + 2k \text{ or } x = \frac{5}{6} + 2k\right\}$
45. $\left\{x \mid x = \frac{1}{4} + \frac{k}{2}\right\}$ **47.** $\{240°, 300°\}$
49. $\{22.5°, 157.5°, 202.5°, 337.5°\}$
51. $\{45°, 75°, 165°, 195°, 285°, 315°\}$ **53.** $\{60°\}$
55. $\{\alpha \mid \alpha = 6.6° + k120° \text{ or } \alpha = 53.4° + k120°\}$

57. $\{\alpha \mid \alpha = 72.3° + k120° \text{ or } \alpha = 107.7° + k120°\}$
59. $\{\alpha \mid \alpha = 38.6° + k180° \text{ or } \alpha = 141.4° + k180°\}$
61. $\{\alpha \mid \alpha = 668.5° + k720° \text{ or } \alpha = 411.5° + k720°\}$
63. $\{0, 0.3, 2.8, \pi\}$ **65.** $\{\pi, 2\pi/3, 4\pi/3\}$
67. $\{0.7, 2.5, 3.4, 6.0\}$ **69.** $\{11\pi/6\}$
71. $\{1.0, 4.9\}$ **73.** $\{0, \pi\}$ **75.** $\{\pi/2, 3\pi/2\}$
77. $\{7\pi/12, 23\pi/12\}$ **79.** $\{7\pi/6, 11\pi/6\}$
81. $\{0°\}$ **83.** $\{26.6°, 206.6°\}$
85. $\{30°, 90°, 150°, 210°, 270°, 330°\}$
87. $\{67.5°, 157.5°, 247.5°, 337.5°\}$ **89.** $\{221.8°, 318.2°\}$
91. $\{120°, 300°\}$ **93.** $\{30°, 45°, 135°, 150°, 210°, 225°, 315°, 330°\}$
95. $\{0°, 60°, 120°, 180°, 240°, 300°\}$
97. $\frac{5\pi}{12} + \frac{k\pi}{2}$ for k a nonnegative integer
99. 44.4° or 45.6° **101.** 12.5° or 77.5°, 6.3 sec

Section 3.9

For Thought: **1.** T **2.** F **3.** F **4.** T **5.** T **6.** F **7.** T **8.** F **9.** F **10.** T

Exercises: **1.** $\gamma = 44°, b = 14.4, c = 10.5$
3. $\beta = 134.2°, a = 5.2, c = 13.6$ **5.** $\beta = 26°, a = 14.6, b = 35.8$
7. $\alpha = 45.7°, b = 587.9, c = 160.8$ **9.** None
11. One: $\alpha = 30°, \beta = 90°, a = 10$
13. One: $\alpha = 26.3°, \gamma = 15.6°, a = 10.3$
15. Two: $\alpha_1 = 134.9°, \gamma_1 = 12.4°, c_1 = 11.4$; or $\alpha_2 = 45.1°, \gamma_2 = 102.2°, c_2 = 51.7$ **17.** One: $\alpha = 25.4°, \beta = 55.0°, a = 5.4$
19. $\alpha = 30.4°, \beta = 28.3°, c = 5.2$
21. $\alpha = 26.4°, \beta = 131.3°, \gamma = 22.3°$
23. $\alpha = 163.9°, \gamma = 5.6°, b = 4.5$
25. $\alpha = 130.3°, \beta = 30.2°, \gamma = 19.5°$
27. $\beta = 48.3°, \gamma = 101.7°, a = 6.2$
29. $\alpha = 53.9°, \beta = 65.5°, \gamma = 60.6°$
31. $\alpha = 120°, b = 3.5, c = 4.8$ **33.** 0 **35.** 1 **37.** 0 **39.** 1
41. 0 **43.** 18.4 mi **45.** 159.4 ft **47.** 28.9 ft, 15.7 ft
49. 9.90 ft^2 **51.** 783.45 ft **53.** 20.6 mi
55. $\theta_1 = 13.3°, \theta_2 = 90.6°$

Chapter 3 Review Exercises

1. 28° **3.** 206°45′33″ **5.** 180° **7.** 108° **9.** 300°
11. 270° **13.** $11\pi/6$ **15.** $-5\pi/3$
17.

θ deg	0	30	45	60	90	120	135	150	180
θ rad	0	$\frac{\pi}{6}$	$\frac{\pi}{4}$	$\frac{\pi}{3}$	$\frac{\pi}{2}$	$\frac{2\pi}{3}$	$\frac{3\pi}{4}$	$\frac{5\pi}{6}$	π
$\sin\theta$	0	$\frac{1}{2}$	$\frac{\sqrt{2}}{2}$	$\frac{\sqrt{3}}{2}$	1	$\frac{\sqrt{3}}{2}$	$\frac{\sqrt{2}}{2}$	$\frac{1}{2}$	0
$\cos\theta$	1	$\frac{\sqrt{3}}{2}$	$\frac{\sqrt{2}}{2}$	$\frac{1}{2}$	0	$-\frac{1}{2}$	$-\frac{\sqrt{2}}{2}$	$-\frac{\sqrt{3}}{2}$	-1
$\tan\theta$	0	$\frac{\sqrt{3}}{3}$	1	$\sqrt{3}$		$-\sqrt{3}$	-1	$-\frac{\sqrt{3}}{3}$	0

19. $-\sqrt{2}/2$ **21.** $\sqrt{3}$ **23.** $-2\sqrt{3}/3$ **25.** 0 **27.** 0
29. -1 **31.** $\sqrt{3}/3$ **33.** $-\sqrt{2}/2$ **35.** -2 **37.** $-\sqrt{3}/3$
39. 5/13, 12/13, 5/12, 13/5, 13/12, 12/5 **41.** 0.6947
43. -0.0923 **45.** 0.1869 **47.** 1.0356 **49.** $-\pi/6$
51. $-\pi/4$ **53.** $\pi/4$ **55.** $\pi/6$ **57.** 90° **59.** 135°
61. 30° **63.** 90° **65.** $c = \sqrt{13}, \alpha = 33.7°, \beta = 56.3°$
67. $\beta = 68.7°, c = 8.8, b = 8.2$
69. $2\pi/3, [-2, 2]$

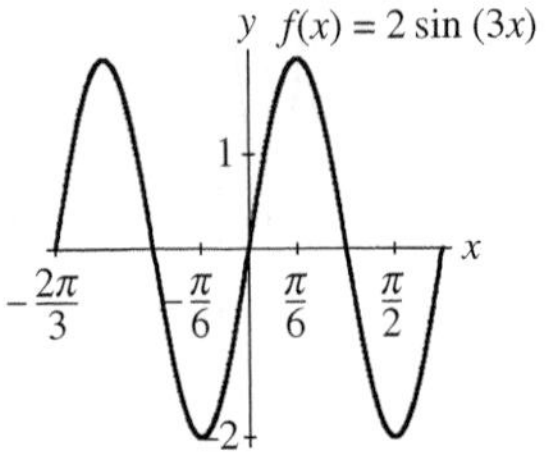

71. $\pi/2, (-\infty, \infty)$

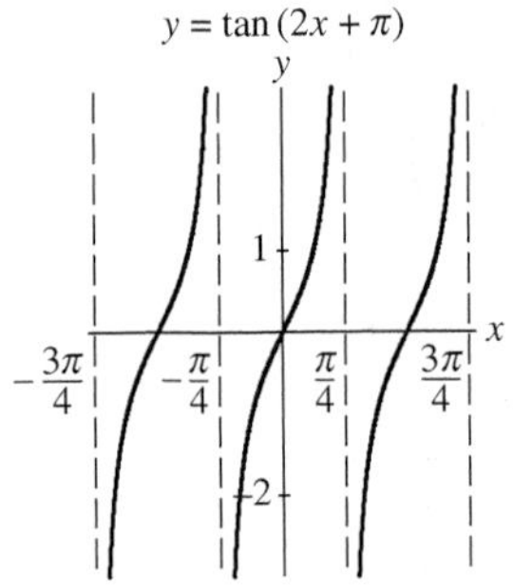

73. $4\pi, (-\infty, -1] \cup [1, \infty)$

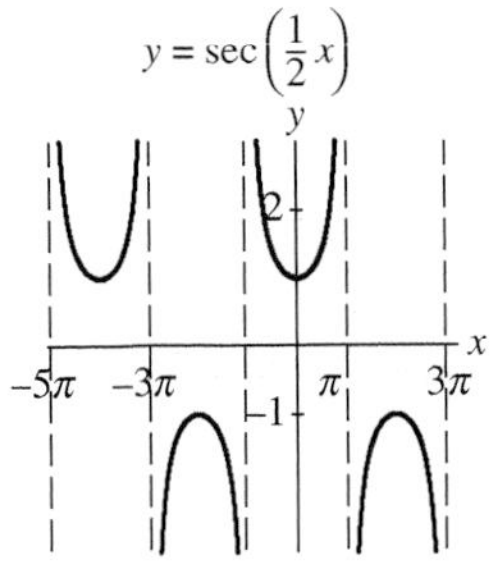

75. $\pi, [-1/2, 1/2]$

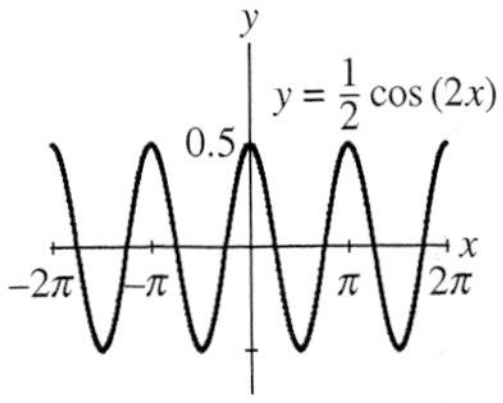

77. $\pi/2, (-\infty, \infty)$

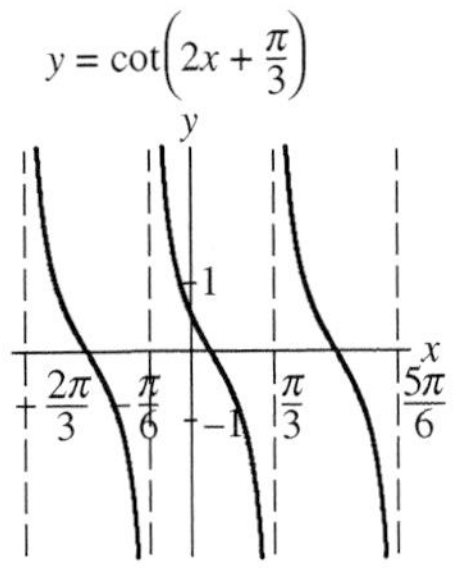

79. $\pi, (-\infty, -1/3] \cup [1/3, \infty)$

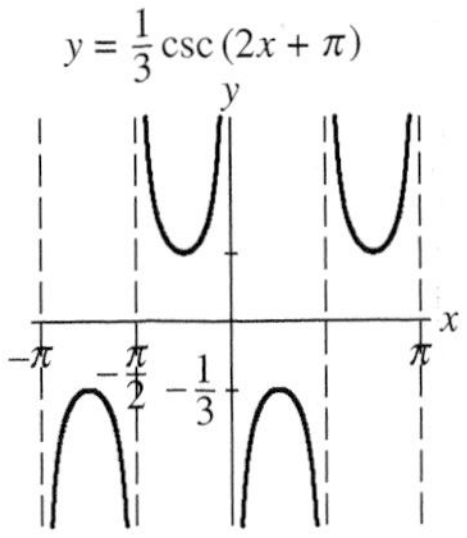

81. $y = 2\sin\left(\frac{\pi}{2}[x - 2]\right)$ **83.** $y = 20\sin(x) + 40$
85. 150° **87.** $-2\sqrt{6}/5$ **89.** 6.6 ft **91.** 53.1°
93. $\cos^2\alpha$ **95.** $-\cot^2 x$ **97.** $\sec^2\alpha$ **99.** $\tan 4s$
101. $-\sin 3\theta$ **103.** $\tan z$
115. $\left\{x \mid x = \frac{\pi}{3} + k\pi \text{ or } x = \frac{2\pi}{3} + k\pi\right\}$
117. $\left\{x \mid x = \frac{\pi}{3} + 2k\pi, \frac{2\pi}{3} + 2k\pi, \frac{\pi}{6} + 2k\pi, \frac{5\pi}{6} + 2k\pi\right\}$
119. $\left\{x \mid x = \frac{\pi}{6} + 2k\pi, \frac{5\pi}{6} + 2k\pi, \frac{\pi}{2} + 2k\pi\right\}$
121. $\left\{x \mid x = \frac{2\pi}{3} + 4k\pi \text{ or } x = \frac{4\pi}{3} + 4k\pi\right\}$
123. $\left\{x \mid x = \pi + 2k\pi, \frac{\pi}{3} + 4k\pi, \frac{5\pi}{3} + 4k\pi\right\}$
125. $\left\{x \mid x = \frac{\pi}{2} + k\pi\right\}$ **127.** $\alpha = 82.7°, \beta = 49.3°, c = 2.5$
129. $\gamma = 103°, a = 4.6, b = 18.4$ **131.** No triangle
133. $\alpha = 107.7°, \beta = 23.7°, \gamma = 48.6°$

135. $\alpha_1 = 110.8°$, $\gamma_1 = 47.2°$, $a_1 = 6.2$; $\alpha_2 = 25.2°$, $\gamma_2 = 132.8°$, $a_2 = 2.8$
137. 1.08×10^{-8} sec **139.** 6.9813 ft
141.

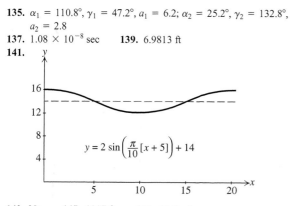

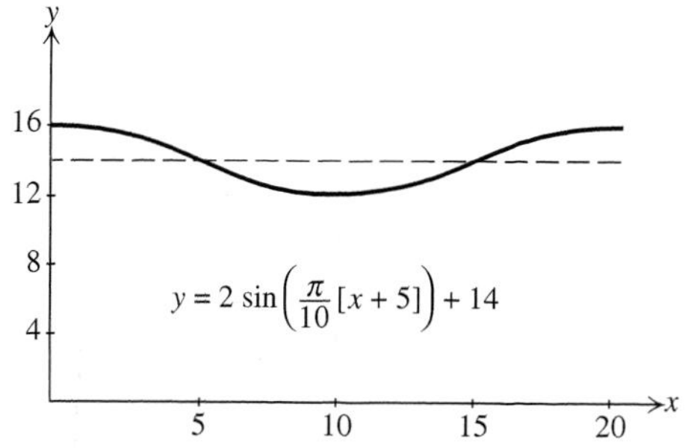

143. No **145.** 1117 ft **147.** 11.6 mi

INDEX

D

E

F

G

Q

R

U

V

X

Y

Z

LIMITS

General Laws

If L, M, c, and k are real numbers and

$$\lim_{x\to c} f(x) = L \quad \text{and} \quad \lim_{x\to c} g(x) = M, \quad \text{then}$$

Sum Rule: $\lim_{x\to c}(f(x) + g(x)) = L + M$

Difference Rule: $\lim_{x\to c}(f(x) - g(x)) = L - M$

Product Rule: $\lim_{x\to c}(f(x) \cdot g(x)) = L \cdot M$

Constant Multiple Rule: $\lim_{x\to c}(k \cdot f(x)) = k \cdot L$

Quotient Rule: $\lim_{x\to c} \frac{f(x)}{g(x)} = \frac{L}{M}, \quad M \neq 0$

The Sandwich Theorem

If $g(x) \leq f(x) \leq h(x)$ in an open interval containing c, except possibly at $x = c$, and if

$$\lim_{x\to c} g(x) = \lim_{x\to c} h(x) = L,$$

then $\lim_{x\to c} f(x) = L$.

Inequalities

If $f(x) \leq g(x)$ in an open interval containing c, except possibly at $x = c$, and both limits exist, then

$$\lim_{x\to c} f(x) \leq \lim_{x\to c} g(x).$$

Continuity

If g is continuous at L and $\lim_{x\to c} f(x) = L$, then

$$\lim_{x\to c} g(f(x)) = g(L).$$

Specific Formulas

If $P(x) = a_n x^n + a_{n-1}x^{n-1} + \cdots + a_0$, then

$$\lim_{x\to c} P(x) = P(c) = a_n c^n + a_{n-1}c^{n-1} + \cdots + a_0.$$

If $P(x)$ and $Q(x)$ are polynomials and $Q(c) \neq 0$, then

$$\lim_{x\to c} \frac{P(x)}{Q(x)} = \frac{P(c)}{Q(c)}.$$

If $f(x)$ is continuous at $x = c$, then

$$\lim_{x\to c} f(x) = f(c).$$

$$\lim_{x\to 0} \frac{\sin x}{x} = 1 \quad \text{and} \quad \lim_{x\to 0} \frac{1 - \cos x}{x} = 0$$

L'Hôpital's Rule

If $f(a) = g(a) = 0$, both f' and g' exist in an open interval I containing a, and $g'(x) \neq 0$ on I if $x \neq a$, then

$$\lim_{x\to a} \frac{f(x)}{g(x)} = \lim_{x\to a} \frac{f'(x)}{g'(x)},$$

assuming the limit on the right side exists.

Limits was taken from *University Calculus: Early Transcendentals,* Second Edition by Joel Hass, Maurice D. Weir, and George B. Thomas, Jr.

DIFFERENTIATION RULES

General Formulas

Assume u and v are differentiable functions of x.

Constant: $\frac{d}{dx}(c) = 0$

Sum: $\frac{d}{dx}(u + v) = \frac{du}{dx} + \frac{dv}{dx}$

Difference: $\frac{d}{dx}(u - v) = \frac{du}{dx} - \frac{dv}{dx}$

Constant Multiple: $\frac{d}{dx}(cu) = c\frac{du}{dx}$

Product: $\frac{d}{dx}(uv) = u\frac{dv}{dx} + v\frac{du}{dx}$

Quotient: $\frac{d}{dx}\left(\frac{u}{v}\right) = \frac{v\frac{du}{dx} - u\frac{dv}{dx}}{v^2}$

Power: $\frac{d}{dx}x^n = nx^{n-1}$

Chain Rule: $\frac{d}{dx}(f(g(x)) = f'(g(x)) \cdot g'(x)$

Trigonometric Functions

$\frac{d}{dx}(\sin x) = \cos x$ $\qquad$ $\frac{d}{dx}(\cos x) = -\sin x$

$\frac{d}{dx}(\tan x) = \sec^2 x$ $\qquad$ $\frac{d}{dx}(\sec x) = \sec x \tan x$

$\frac{d}{dx}(\cot x) = -\csc^2 x$ $\qquad$ $\frac{d}{dx}(\csc x) = -\csc x \cot x$

Exponential and Logarithmic Functions

$\frac{d}{dx}e^x = e^x$ $\qquad$ $\frac{d}{dx}\ln x = \frac{1}{x}$

$\frac{d}{dx}a^x = a^x \ln a$ $\qquad$ $\frac{d}{dx}(\log_a x) = \frac{1}{x \ln a}$

Inverse Trigonometric Functions

$\frac{d}{dx}(\sin^{-1} x) = \frac{1}{\sqrt{1 - x^2}}$ $\qquad$ $\frac{d}{dx}(\cos^{-1} x) = -\frac{1}{\sqrt{1 - x^2}}$

$\frac{d}{dx}(\tan^{-1} x) = \frac{1}{1 + x^2}$ $\qquad$ $\frac{d}{dx}(\sec^{-1} x) = \frac{1}{|x|\sqrt{x^2 - 1}}$

$\frac{d}{dx}(\cot^{-1} x) = -\frac{1}{1 + x^2}$ $\qquad$ $\frac{d}{dx}(\csc^{-1} x) = -\frac{1}{|x|\sqrt{x^2 - 1}}$

Hyperbolic Functions

$\frac{d}{dx}(\sinh x) = \cosh x$ $\qquad$ $\frac{d}{dx}(\cosh x) = \sinh x$

$\frac{d}{dx}(\tanh x) = \operatorname{sech}^2 x$ $\qquad$ $\frac{d}{dx}(\operatorname{sech} x) = -\operatorname{sech} x \tanh x$

$\frac{d}{dx}(\coth x) = -\operatorname{csch}^2 x$ $\qquad$ $\frac{d}{dx}(\operatorname{csch} x) = -\operatorname{csch} x \coth x$

Inverse Hyperbolic Functions

$\frac{d}{dx}(\sinh^{-1} x) = \frac{1}{\sqrt{1 + x^2}}$ $\qquad$ $\frac{d}{dx}(\cosh^{-1} x) = \frac{1}{\sqrt{x^2 - 1}}$

$\frac{d}{dx}(\tanh^{-1} x) = \frac{1}{1 - x^2}$ $\qquad$ $\frac{d}{dx}(\operatorname{sech}^{-1} x) = -\frac{1}{x\sqrt{1 - x^2}}$

$\frac{d}{dx}(\coth^{-1} x) = \frac{1}{1 - x^2}$ $\qquad$ $\frac{d}{dx}(\operatorname{csch}^{-1} x) = -\frac{1}{|x|\sqrt{1 + x^2}}$

Parametric Equations

If $x = f(t)$ and $y = g(t)$ are differentiable, then

$$y' = \frac{dy}{dx} = \frac{dy/dt}{dx/dt} \quad \text{and} \quad \frac{d^2y}{dx^2} = \frac{dy'/dt}{dx/dt}.$$

Differentiation Rules was taken from *University Calculus: Early Transcendentals,* Second Edition by Joel Hass, Maurice D. Weir, and George B. Thomas, Jr.

INTEGRATION RULES

General Formulas

Zero: $\int_a^a f(x)\,dx = 0$

Order of Integration: $\int_b^a f(x)\,dx = -\int_a^b f(x)\,dx$

Constant Multiples: $\int_a^b kf(x)\,dx = k\int_a^b f(x)\,dx$ (Any number k)

$\int_a^b -f(x)\,dx = -\int_a^b f(x)\,dx$ $(k = -1)$

Sums and Differences: $\int_a^b (f(x) \pm g(x))\,dx = \int_a^b f(x)\,dx \pm \int_a^b g(x)\,dx$

Additivity: $\int_a^b f(x)\,dx + \int_b^c f(x)\,dx = \int_a^c f(x)\,dx$

Max-Min Inequality: If $\max f$ and $\min f$ are the maximum and minimum values of f on $[a, b]$, then

$$\min f \cdot (b - a) \le \int_a^b f(x)\,dx \le \max f \cdot (b - a).$$

Domination: $f(x) \ge g(x)$ on $[a, b]$ implies $\int_a^b f(x)\,dx \ge \int_a^b g(x)\,dx$

$f(x) \ge 0$ on $[a, b]$ implies $\int_a^b f(x)\,dx \ge 0$

The Fundamental Theorem of Calculus

Part 1 If f is continuous on $[a, b]$, then $F(x) = \int_a^x f(t)\,dt$ is continuous on $[a, b]$ and differentiable on (a, b) and its derivative is $f(x)$;

$$F'(x) = \frac{d}{dx}\int_a^x f(t)\,dt = f(x).$$

Part 2 If f is continuous at every point of $[a, b]$ and F is any antiderivative of f on $[a, b]$, then

$$\int_a^b f(x)\,dx = F(b) - F(a).$$

Substitution in Definite Integrals

$$\int_a^b f(g(x)) \cdot g'(x)\,dx = \int_{g(a)}^{g(b)} f(u)\,du$$

Integration by Parts

$$\int_a^b f(x)g'(x)\,dx = f(x)g(x)\Big]_a^b - \int_a^b f'(x)g(x)\,dx$$

Integration Rules was taken from *University Calculus: Early Transcendentals,* Second Edition by Joel Hass, Maurice D. Weir, and George B. Thomas, Jr.

A Brief Table of Integrals

Basic Forms

1. $\int k\,dx = kx + C \quad$ (any number k)

2. $\int x^n\,dx = \frac{x^{n+1}}{n+1} + C \quad (n \neq -1)$

3. $\int \frac{dx}{x} = \ln|x| + C$

4. $\int e^x\,dx = e^x + C$

5. $\int a^x\,dx = \frac{a^x}{\ln a} + C \quad (a > 0, a \neq 1)$

6. $\int \sin x\,dx = -\cos x + C$

7. $\int \cos x\,dx = \sin x + C$

8. $\int \sec^2 x\,dx = \tan x + C$

9. $\int \csc^2 x\,dx = -\cot x + C$

10. $\int \sec x \tan x\,dx = \sec x + C$

11. $\int \csc x \cot x\,dx = -\csc x + C$

12. $\int \tan x\,dx = \ln|\sec x| + C$

13. $\int \cot x\,dx = \ln|\sin x| + C$

14. $\int \sinh x\,dx = \cosh x + C$

15. $\int \cosh x\,dx = \sinh x + C$

16. $\int \frac{dx}{\sqrt{a^2 - x^2}} = \sin^{-1}\frac{x}{a} + C$

17. $\int \frac{dx}{a^2 + x^2} = \frac{1}{a}\tan^{-1}\frac{x}{a} + C$

18. $\int \frac{dx}{x\sqrt{x^2 - a^2}} = \frac{1}{a}\sec^{-1}\left|\frac{x}{a}\right| + C$

19. $\int \frac{dx}{\sqrt{a^2 + x^2}} = \sinh^{-1}\frac{x}{a} + C \quad (a > 0)$

20. $\int \frac{dx}{\sqrt{x^2 - a^2}} = \cosh^{-1}\frac{x}{a} + C \quad (x > a > 0)$

Forms Involving $ax + b$

21. $\int (ax+b)^n\,dx = \frac{(ax+b)^{n+1}}{a(n+1)} + C, \quad n \neq -1$

22. $\int x(ax+b)^n\,dx = \frac{(ax+b)^{n+1}}{a^2}\left[\frac{ax+b}{n+2} - \frac{b}{n+1}\right] + C, \quad n \neq -1, -2$

23. $\int (ax+b)^{-1}\,dx = \frac{1}{a}\ln|ax+b| + C$

24. $\int x(ax+b)^{-1}\,dx = \frac{x}{a} - \frac{b}{a^2}\ln|ax+b| + C$

25. $\int x(ax+b)^{-2}\,dx = \frac{1}{a^2}\left[\ln|ax+b| + \frac{b}{ax+b}\right] + C$

26. $\int \frac{dx}{x(ax+b)} = \frac{1}{b}\ln\left|\frac{x}{ax+b}\right| + C$

27. $\int \left(\sqrt{ax+b}\right)^n dx = \frac{2}{a}\frac{\left(\sqrt{ax+b}\right)^{n+2}}{n+2} + C, \quad n \neq -2$

28. $\int \frac{\sqrt{ax+b}}{x}\,dx = 2\sqrt{ax+b} + b\int \frac{dx}{x\sqrt{ax+b}}$

A Brief Table of Integrals was taken from *University Calculus: Early Transcendentals*, Second Edition by Joel Hass, Maurice D. Weir, and George B. Thomas, Jr.

29. (a) $\int \frac{dx}{x\sqrt{ax+b}} = \frac{1}{\sqrt{b}} \ln \left| \frac{\sqrt{ax+b}-\sqrt{b}}{\sqrt{ax+b}+\sqrt{b}} \right| + C$ (b) $\int \frac{dx}{x\sqrt{ax-b}} = \frac{2}{\sqrt{b}} \tan^{-1}\sqrt{\frac{ax-b}{b}} + C$

30. $\int \frac{\sqrt{ax+b}}{x^2}\,dx = -\frac{\sqrt{ax+b}}{x} + \frac{a}{2}\int \frac{dx}{x\sqrt{ax+b}} + C$

31. $\int \frac{dx}{x^2\sqrt{ax+b}} = -\frac{\sqrt{ax+b}}{bx} - \frac{a}{2b}\int \frac{dx}{x\sqrt{ax+b}} + C$

Forms Involving $a^2 + x^2$

32. $\int \frac{dx}{a^2+x^2} = \frac{1}{a}\tan^{-1}\frac{x}{a} + C$

33. $\int \frac{dx}{(a^2+x^2)^2} = \frac{x}{2a^2(a^2+x^2)} + \frac{1}{2a^3}\tan^{-1}\frac{x}{a} + C$

34. $\int \frac{dx}{\sqrt{a^2+x^2}} = \sinh^{-1}\frac{x}{a} + C = \ln\left(x+\sqrt{a^2+x^2}\right) + C$

35. $\int \sqrt{a^2+x^2}\,dx = \frac{x}{2}\sqrt{a^2+x^2} + \frac{a^2}{2}\ln\left(x+\sqrt{a^2+x^2}\right) + C$

36. $\int x^2\sqrt{a^2+x^2}\,dx = \frac{x}{8}(a^2+2x^2)\sqrt{a^2+x^2} - \frac{a^4}{8}\ln\left(x+\sqrt{a^2+x^2}\right) + C$

37. $\int \frac{\sqrt{a^2+x^2}}{x}\,dx = \sqrt{a^2+x^2} - a\ln\left|\frac{a+\sqrt{a^2+x^2}}{x}\right| + C$

38. $\int \frac{\sqrt{a^2+x^2}}{x^2}\,dx = \ln\left(x+\sqrt{a^2+x^2}\right) - \frac{\sqrt{a^2+x^2}}{x} + C$

39. $\int \frac{x^2}{\sqrt{a^2+x^2}}\,dx = -\frac{a^2}{2}\ln\left(x+\sqrt{a^2+x^2}\right) + \frac{x\sqrt{a^2+x^2}}{2} + C$

40. $\int \frac{dx}{x\sqrt{a^2+x^2}} = -\frac{1}{a}\ln\left|\frac{a+\sqrt{a^2+x^2}}{x}\right| + C$

41. $\int \frac{dx}{x^2\sqrt{a^2+x^2}} = -\frac{\sqrt{a^2+x^2}}{a^2x} + C$

Forms Involving $a^2 - x^2$

42. $\int \frac{dx}{a^2-x^2} = \frac{1}{2a}\ln\left|\frac{x+a}{x-a}\right| + C$

43. $\int \frac{dx}{(a^2-x^2)^2} = \frac{x}{2a^2(a^2-x^2)} + \frac{1}{4a^3}\ln\left|\frac{x+a}{x-a}\right| + C$

44. $\int \frac{dx}{\sqrt{a^2-x^2}} = \sin^{-1}\frac{x}{a} + C$

45. $\int \sqrt{a^2-x^2}\,dx = \frac{x}{2}\sqrt{a^2-x^2} + \frac{a^2}{2}\sin^{-1}\frac{x}{a} + C$

46. $\int x^2\sqrt{a^2-x^2}\,dx = \frac{a^4}{8}\sin^{-1}\frac{x}{a} - \frac{1}{8}x\sqrt{a^2-x^2}\,(a^2-2x^2) + C$

47. $\int \frac{\sqrt{a^2-x^2}}{x}\,dx = \sqrt{a^2-x^2} - a\ln\left|\frac{a+\sqrt{a^2-x^2}}{x}\right| + C$

48. $\int \frac{\sqrt{a^2-x^2}}{x^2}\,dx = -\sin^{-1}\frac{x}{a} - \frac{\sqrt{a^2-x^2}}{x} + C$

49. $\int \frac{x^2}{\sqrt{a^2-x^2}}\,dx = \frac{a^2}{2}\sin^{-1}\frac{x}{a} - \frac{1}{2}x\sqrt{a^2-x^2} + C$

50. $\int \frac{dx}{x\sqrt{a^2-x^2}} = -\frac{1}{a}\ln\left|\frac{a+\sqrt{a^2-x^2}}{x}\right| + C$

51. $\int \frac{dx}{x^2\sqrt{a^2-x^2}} = -\frac{\sqrt{a^2-x^2}}{a^2x} + C$

Forms Involving $x^2 - a^2$

52. $\int \frac{dx}{\sqrt{x^2-a^2}} = \ln\left|x+\sqrt{x^2-a^2}\right| + C$

53. $\int \sqrt{x^2-a^2}\,dx = \frac{x}{2}\sqrt{x^2-a^2} - \frac{a^2}{2}\ln\left|x+\sqrt{x^2-a^2}\right| + C$

54. $\int \left(\sqrt{x^2 - a^2}\right)^n dx = \frac{x\left(\sqrt{x^2 - a^2}\right)^n}{n+1} - \frac{na^2}{n+1}\int \left(\sqrt{x^2 - a^2}\right)^{n-2} dx, \quad n \neq -1$

55. $\int \frac{dx}{\left(\sqrt{x^2 - a^2}\right)^n} = \frac{x\left(\sqrt{x^2 - a^2}\right)^{2-n}}{(2-n)a^2} - \frac{n-3}{(n-2)a^2}\int \frac{dx}{\left(\sqrt{x^2 - a^2}\right)^{n-2}}, \quad n \neq 2$

56. $\int x\left(\sqrt{x^2 - a^2}\right)^n dx = \frac{\left(\sqrt{x^2 - a^2}\right)^{n+2}}{n+2} + C, \quad n \neq -2$

57. $\int x^2\sqrt{x^2 - a^2}\, dx = \frac{x}{8}(2x^2 - a^2)\sqrt{x^2 - a^2} - \frac{a^4}{8}\ln\left|x + \sqrt{x^2 - a^2}\right| + C$

58. $\int \frac{\sqrt{x^2 - a^2}}{x} dx = \sqrt{x^2 - a^2} - a\sec^{-1}\left|\frac{x}{a}\right| + C$

59. $\int \frac{\sqrt{x^2 - a^2}}{x^2} dx = \ln\left|x + \sqrt{x^2 - a^2}\right| - \frac{\sqrt{x^2 - a^2}}{x} + C$

60. $\int \frac{x^2}{\sqrt{x^2 - a^2}} dx = \frac{a^2}{2}\ln\left|x + \sqrt{x^2 - a^2}\right| + \frac{x}{2}\sqrt{x^2 - a^2} + C$

61. $\int \frac{dx}{x\sqrt{x^2 - a^2}} = \frac{1}{a}\sec^{-1}\left|\frac{x}{a}\right| + C = \frac{1}{a}\cos^{-1}\left|\frac{a}{x}\right| + C$

62. $\int \frac{dx}{x^2\sqrt{x^2 - a^2}} = \frac{\sqrt{x^2 - a^2}}{a^2x} + C$

Trigonometric Forms

63. $\int \sin ax\, dx = -\frac{1}{a}\cos ax + C$

64. $\int \cos ax\, dx = \frac{1}{a}\sin ax + C$

65. $\int \sin^2 ax\, dx = \frac{x}{2} - \frac{\sin 2ax}{4a} + C$

66. $\int \cos^2 ax\, dx = \frac{x}{2} + \frac{\sin 2ax}{4a} + C$

67. $\int \sin^n ax\, dx = -\frac{\sin^{n-1} ax \cos ax}{na} + \frac{n-1}{n}\int \sin^{n-2} ax\, dx$

68. $\int \cos^n ax\, dx = \frac{\cos^{n-1} ax \sin ax}{na} + \frac{n-1}{n}\int \cos^{n-2} ax\, dx$

69. (a) $\int \sin ax \cos bx\, dx = -\frac{\cos(a+b)x}{2(a+b)} - \frac{\cos(a-b)x}{2(a-b)} + C, \quad a^2 \neq b^2$

(b) $\int \sin ax \sin bx\, dx = \frac{\sin(a-b)x}{2(a-b)} - \frac{\sin(a+b)x}{2(a+b)} + C, \quad a^2 \neq b^2$

(c) $\int \cos ax \cos bx\, dx = \frac{\sin(a-b)x}{2(a-b)} + \frac{\sin(a+b)x}{2(a+b)} + C, \quad a^2 \neq b^2$

70. $\int \sin ax \cos ax\, dx = -\frac{\cos 2ax}{4a} + C$

71. $\int \sin^n ax \cos ax\, dx = \frac{\sin^{n+1} ax}{(n+1)a} + C, \quad n \neq -1$

72. $\int \frac{\cos ax}{\sin ax} dx = \frac{1}{a}\ln|\sin ax| + C$

73. $\int \cos^n ax \sin ax\, dx = -\frac{\cos^{n+1} ax}{(n+1)a} + C, \quad n \neq -1$

74. $\int \frac{\sin ax}{\cos ax} dx = -\frac{1}{a}\ln|\cos ax| + C$

75. $\int \sin^n ax \cos^m ax\, dx = -\frac{\sin^{n-1} ax \cos^{m+1} ax}{a(m+n)} + \frac{n-1}{m+n}\int \sin^{n-2} ax \cos^m ax\, dx, \quad n \neq -m \quad (\text{reduces } \sin^n ax)$

76. $\int \sin^n ax \cos^m ax\, dx = \frac{\sin^{n+1} ax \cos^{m-1} ax}{a(m+n)} + \frac{m-1}{m+n}\int \sin^n ax \cos^{m-2} ax\, dx, \quad m \neq -n \quad (\text{reduces } \cos^m ax)$

77. $$\int \frac{dx}{b + c\sin ax} = \frac{-2}{a\sqrt{b^2 - c^2}} \tan^{-1}\left[\sqrt{\frac{b-c}{b+c}} \tan\left(\frac{\pi}{4} - \frac{ax}{2}\right)\right] + C, \quad b^2 > c^2$$

78. $$\int \frac{dx}{b + c\sin ax} = \frac{-1}{a\sqrt{c^2 - b^2}} \ln\left|\frac{c + b\sin ax + \sqrt{c^2 - b^2}\cos ax}{b + c\sin ax}\right| + C, \quad b^2 < c^2$$

79. $$\int \frac{dx}{1 + \sin ax} = -\frac{1}{a}\tan\left(\frac{\pi}{4} - \frac{ax}{2}\right) + C$$

80. $$\int \frac{dx}{1 - \sin ax} = \frac{1}{a}\tan\left(\frac{\pi}{4} + \frac{ax}{2}\right) + C$$

81. $$\int \frac{dx}{b + c\cos ax} = \frac{2}{a\sqrt{b^2 - c^2}} \tan^{-1}\left[\sqrt{\frac{b-c}{b+c}} \tan\frac{ax}{2}\right] + C, \quad b^2 > c^2$$

82. $$\int \frac{dx}{b + c\cos ax} = \frac{1}{a\sqrt{c^2 - b^2}} \ln\left|\frac{c + b\cos ax + \sqrt{c^2 - b^2}\sin ax}{b + c\cos ax}\right| + C, \quad b^2 < c^2$$

83. $$\int \frac{dx}{1 + \cos ax} = \frac{1}{a}\tan\frac{ax}{2} + C$$

84. $$\int \frac{dx}{1 - \cos ax} = -\frac{1}{a}\cot\frac{ax}{2} + C$$

85. $$\int x\sin ax\,dx = \frac{1}{a^2}\sin ax - \frac{x}{a}\cos ax + C$$

86. $$\int x\cos ax\,dx = \frac{1}{a^2}\cos ax + \frac{x}{a}\sin ax + C$$

87. $$\int x^n \sin ax\,dx = -\frac{x^n}{a}\cos ax + \frac{n}{a}\int x^{n-1}\cos ax\,dx$$

88. $$\int x^n \cos ax\,dx = \frac{x^n}{a}\sin ax - \frac{n}{a}\int x^{n-1}\sin ax\,dx$$

89. $$\int \tan ax\,dx = \frac{1}{a}\ln|\sec ax| + C$$

90. $$\int \cot ax\,dx = \frac{1}{a}\ln|\sin ax| + C$$

91. $$\int \tan^2 ax\,dx = \frac{1}{a}\tan ax - x + C$$

92. $$\int \cot^2 ax\,dx = -\frac{1}{a}\cot ax - x + C$$

93. $$\int \tan^n ax\,dx = \frac{\tan^{n-1} ax}{a(n-1)} - \int \tan^{n-2} ax\,dx, \quad n \neq 1$$

94. $$\int \cot^n ax\,dx = -\frac{\cot^{n-1} ax}{a(n-1)} - \int \cot^{n-2} ax\,dx, \quad n \neq 1$$

95. $$\int \sec ax\,dx = \frac{1}{a}\ln|\sec ax + \tan ax| + C$$

96. $$\int \csc ax\,dx = -\frac{1}{a}\ln|\csc ax + \cot ax| + C$$

97. $$\int \sec^2 ax\,dx = \frac{1}{a}\tan ax + C$$

98. $$\int \csc^2 ax\,dx = -\frac{1}{a}\cot ax + C$$

99. $$\int \sec^n ax\,dx = \frac{\sec^{n-2} ax\tan ax}{a(n-1)} + \frac{n-2}{n-1}\int \sec^{n-2} ax\,dx, \quad n \neq 1$$

100. $$\int \csc^n ax\,dx = -\frac{\csc^{n-2} ax\cot ax}{a(n-1)} + \frac{n-2}{n-1}\int \csc^{n-2} ax\,dx, \quad n \neq 1$$

101. $$\int \sec^n ax\tan ax\,dx = \frac{\sec^n ax}{na} + C, \quad n \neq 0$$

102. $$\int \csc^n ax\cot ax\,dx = -\frac{\csc^n ax}{na} + C, \quad n \neq 0$$

Inverse Trigonometric Forms

103. $$\int \sin^{-1} ax\,dx = x\sin^{-1} ax + \frac{1}{a}\sqrt{1 - a^2x^2} + C$$

104. $$\int \cos^{-1} ax\,dx = x\cos^{-1} ax - \frac{1}{a}\sqrt{1 - a^2x^2} + C$$

105. $$\int \tan^{-1} ax\,dx = x\tan^{-1} ax - \frac{1}{2a}\ln(1 + a^2x^2) + C$$

106. $$\int x^n\sin^{-1} ax\,dx = \frac{x^{n+1}}{n+1}\sin^{-1} ax - \frac{a}{n+1}\int \frac{x^{n+1}\,dx}{\sqrt{1 - a^2x^2}}, \quad n \neq -1$$

107. $$\int x^n\cos^{-1} ax\,dx = \frac{x^{n+1}}{n+1}\cos^{-1} ax + \frac{a}{n+1}\int \frac{x^{n+1}\,dx}{\sqrt{1 - a^2x^2}}, \quad n \neq -1$$

108. $$\int x^n\tan^{-1} ax\,dx = \frac{x^{n+1}}{n+1}\tan^{-1} ax - \frac{a}{n+1}\int \frac{x^{n+1}\,dx}{1 + a^2x^2}, \quad n \neq -1$$

SERIES

Tests for Convergence of Infinite Series

1. **The nth-Term Test:** Unless $a_n \to 0$, the series diverges.
2. **Geometric series:** $\sum ar^n$ converges if $|r| < 1$; otherwise it diverges.
3. **p-series:** $\sum 1/n^p$ converges if $p > 1$; otherwise it diverges.
4. **Series with nonnegative terms:** Try the Integral Test, Ratio Test, or Root Test. Try comparing to a known series with the Comparison Test or the Limit Comparison Test.
5. **Series with some negative terms:** Does $\sum |a_n|$ converge? If yes, so does $\sum a_n$ since absolute convergence implies convergence.
6. **Alternating series:** $\sum a_n$ converges if the series satisfies the conditions of the Alternating Series Test.

Taylor Series

$$\frac{1}{1-x} = 1 + x + x^2 + \cdots + x^n + \cdots = \sum_{n=0}^{\infty} x^n, \qquad |x| < 1$$

$$\frac{1}{1+x} = 1 - x + x^2 - \cdots + (-x)^n + \cdots = \sum_{n=0}^{\infty} (-1)^n x^n, \qquad |x| < 1$$

$$e^x = 1 + x + \frac{x^2}{2!} + \cdots + \frac{x^n}{n!} + \cdots = \sum_{n=0}^{\infty} \frac{x^n}{n!}, \qquad |x| < \infty$$

$$\sin x = x - \frac{x^3}{3!} + \frac{x^5}{5!} - \cdots + (-1)^n \frac{x^{2n+1}}{(2n+1)!} + \cdots = \sum_{n=0}^{\infty} \frac{(-1)^n x^{2n+1}}{(2n+1)!}, \qquad |x| < \infty$$

$$\cos x = 1 - \frac{x^2}{2!} + \frac{x^4}{4!} - \cdots + (-1)^n \frac{x^{2n}}{(2n)!} + \cdots = \sum_{n=0}^{\infty} \frac{(-1)^n x^{2n}}{(2n)!}, \qquad |x| < \infty$$

$$\ln(1+x) = x - \frac{x^2}{2} + \frac{x^3}{3} - \cdots + (-1)^{n-1} \frac{x^n}{n} + \cdots = \sum_{n=1}^{\infty} \frac{(-1)^{n-1} x^n}{n}, \qquad -1 < x \le 1$$

$$\ln \frac{1+x}{1-x} = 2 \tanh^{-1} x = 2\left(x + \frac{x^3}{3} + \frac{x^5}{5} + \cdots + \frac{x^{2n+1}}{2n+1} + \cdots\right) = 2\sum_{n=0}^{\infty} \frac{x^{2n+1}}{2n+1}, \qquad |x| < 1$$

$$\tan^{-1} x = x - \frac{x^3}{3} + \frac{x^5}{5} - \cdots + (-1)^n \frac{x^{2n+1}}{2n+1} + \cdots = \sum_{n=0}^{\infty} \frac{(-1)^n x^{2n+1}}{2n+1}, \qquad |x| \le 1$$

Binomial Series

$$(1+x)^m = 1 + mx + \frac{m(m-1)x^2}{2!} + \frac{m(m-1)(m-2)x^3}{3!} + \cdots + \frac{m(m-1)(m-2)\cdots(m-k+1)x^k}{k!} + \cdots$$

$$= 1 + \sum_{k=1}^{\infty} \binom{m}{k} x^k, \qquad |x| < 1,$$

where

$$\binom{m}{1} = m, \qquad \binom{m}{2} = \frac{m(m-1)}{2!}, \qquad \binom{m}{k} = \frac{m(m-1)\cdots(m-k+1)}{k!} \qquad \text{for } k \ge 3.$$

Series was taken from *University Calculus: Early Transcendentals,* Second Edition by Joel Hass, Maurice D. Weir, and George B. Thomas, Jr.

Functions in Polar Coordinates

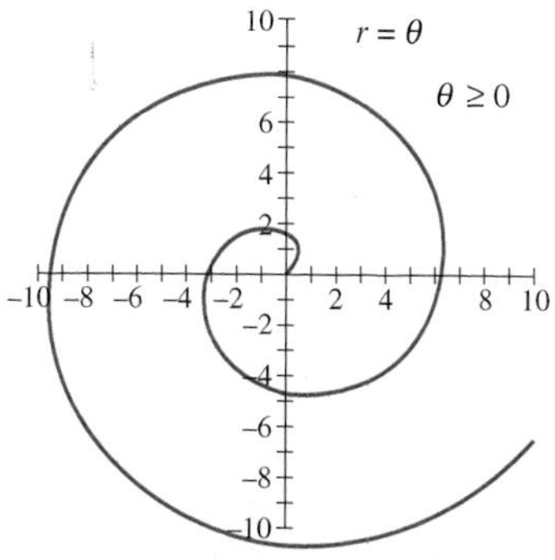

Spiral

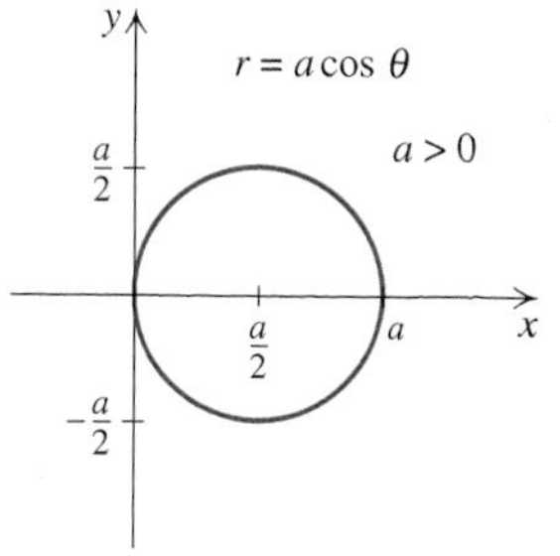

$r = \theta$

$\theta \geq 0$

Circle

$r = a\cos\theta$

$a > 0$

Circle

$r = a\sin\theta$

$a > 0$

Three-Leaf Rose

$r = a\cos 3\theta$

$a > 0$

Four-Leaf Rose

$r = a\cos 2\theta$

$a > 0$

Lemniscate

$r^2 = a\cos 2\theta$

$a > 0$

Cardioid

$r = a(1 - \cos\theta)$

$a > 0$

Limaçon

$r = a - b\cos\theta$

$a > b > 0$

Limaçon

$r = a - b\cos\theta$

$b > a > 0$

Functions in Polar Coordinates was taken from *Fundamentals of Precalculus*, Second Edition by Mark Dugopolski.

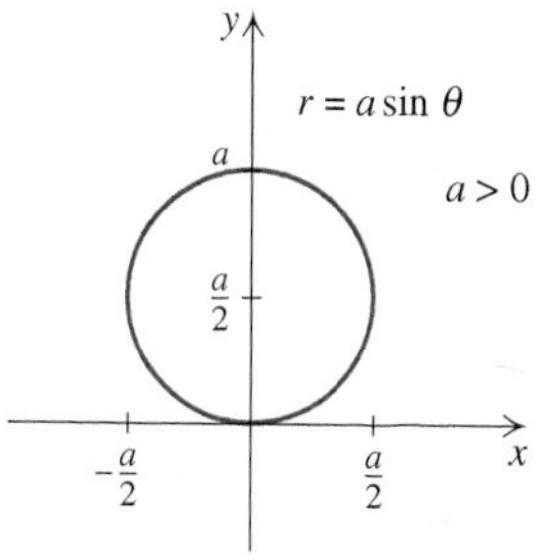

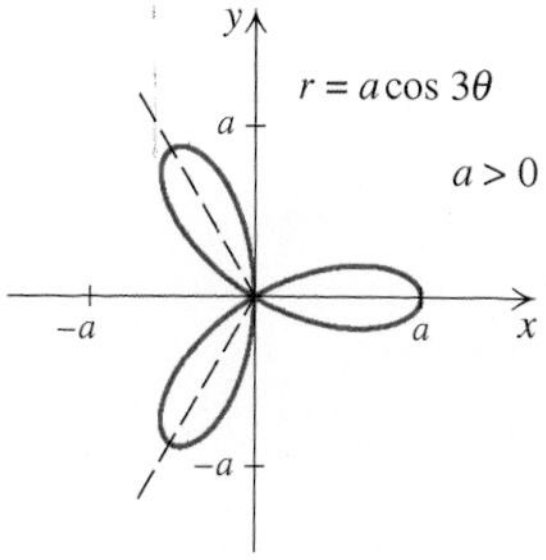

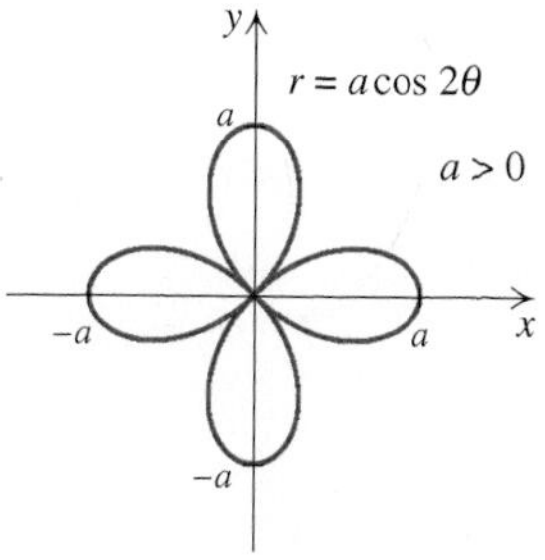

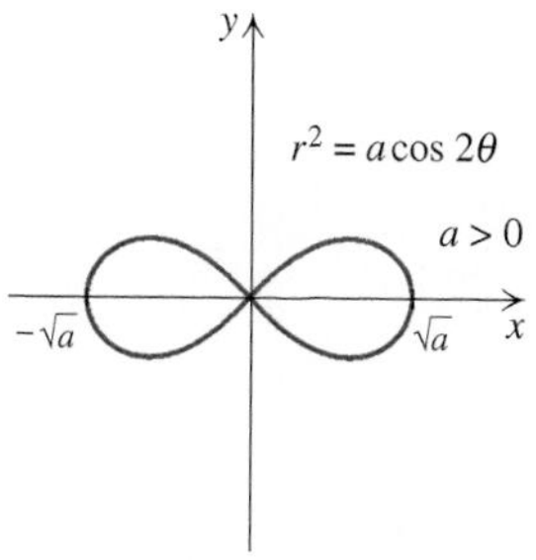

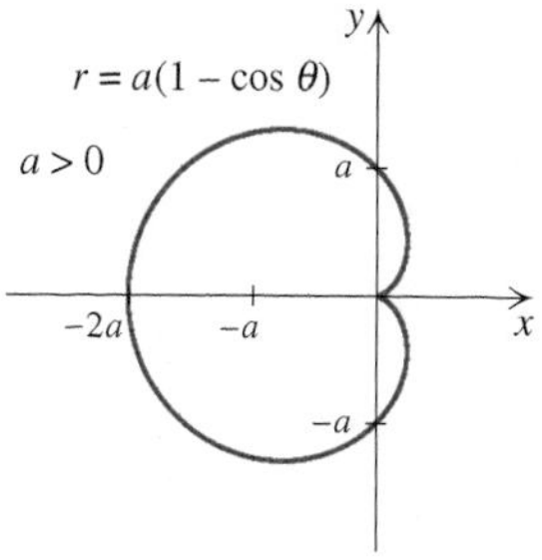

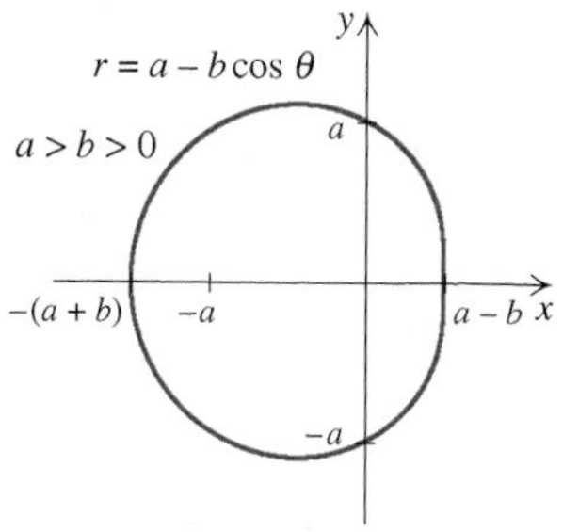

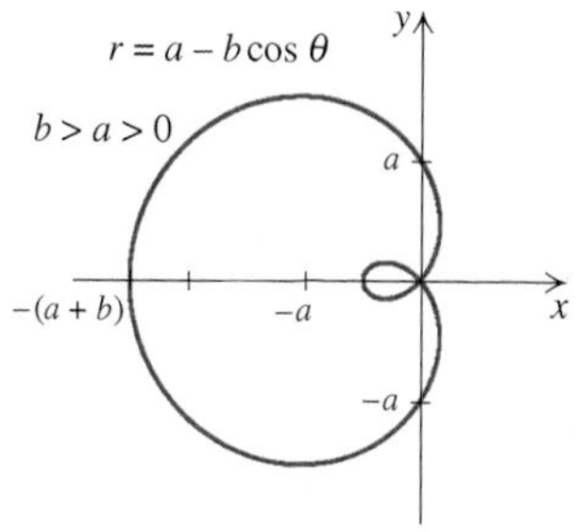